D0913073

EX LIBRIS
NEW YORK INSTITUTE
OF TECHNOLOGY
NEW YORK INSTITUTE
SCIENCE
TECHNOLOGY
HUMANITIES
OF TECHNOLOGY

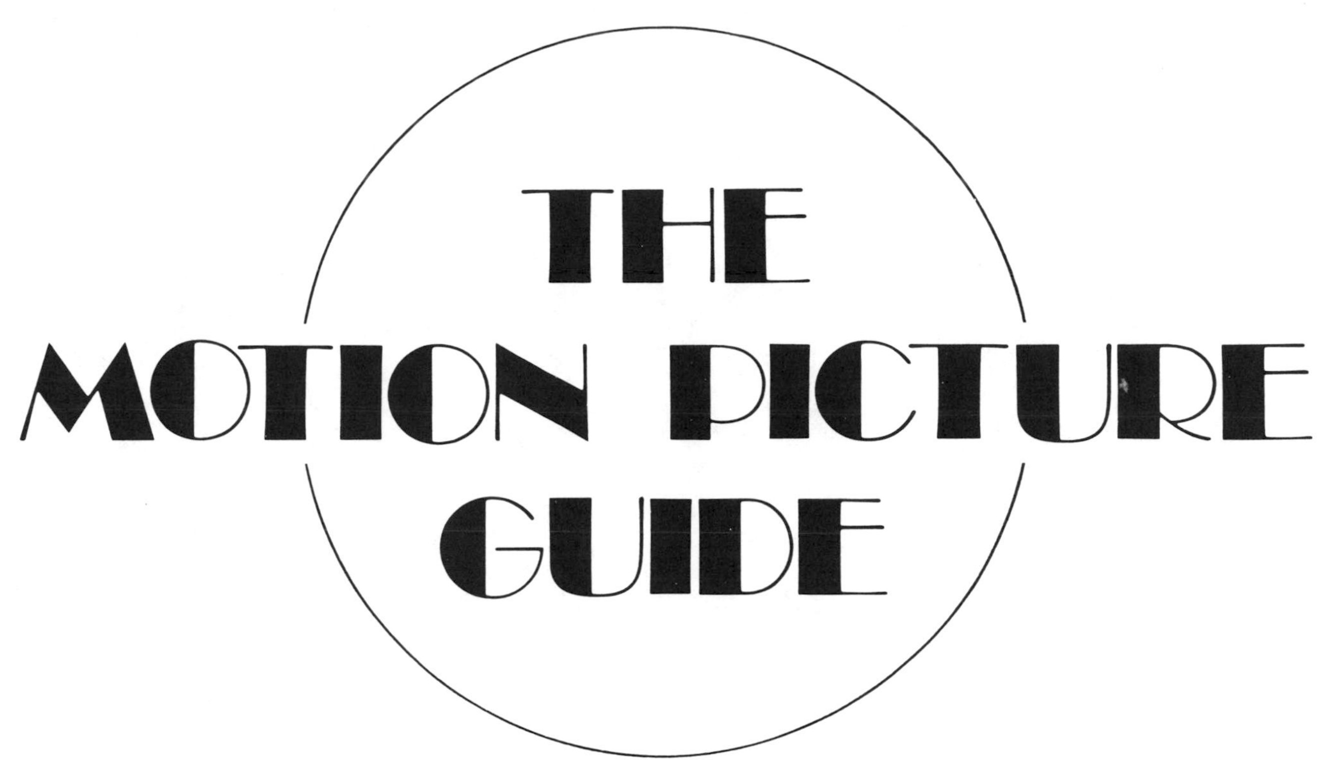
THE
MOTION PICTURE
GUIDE

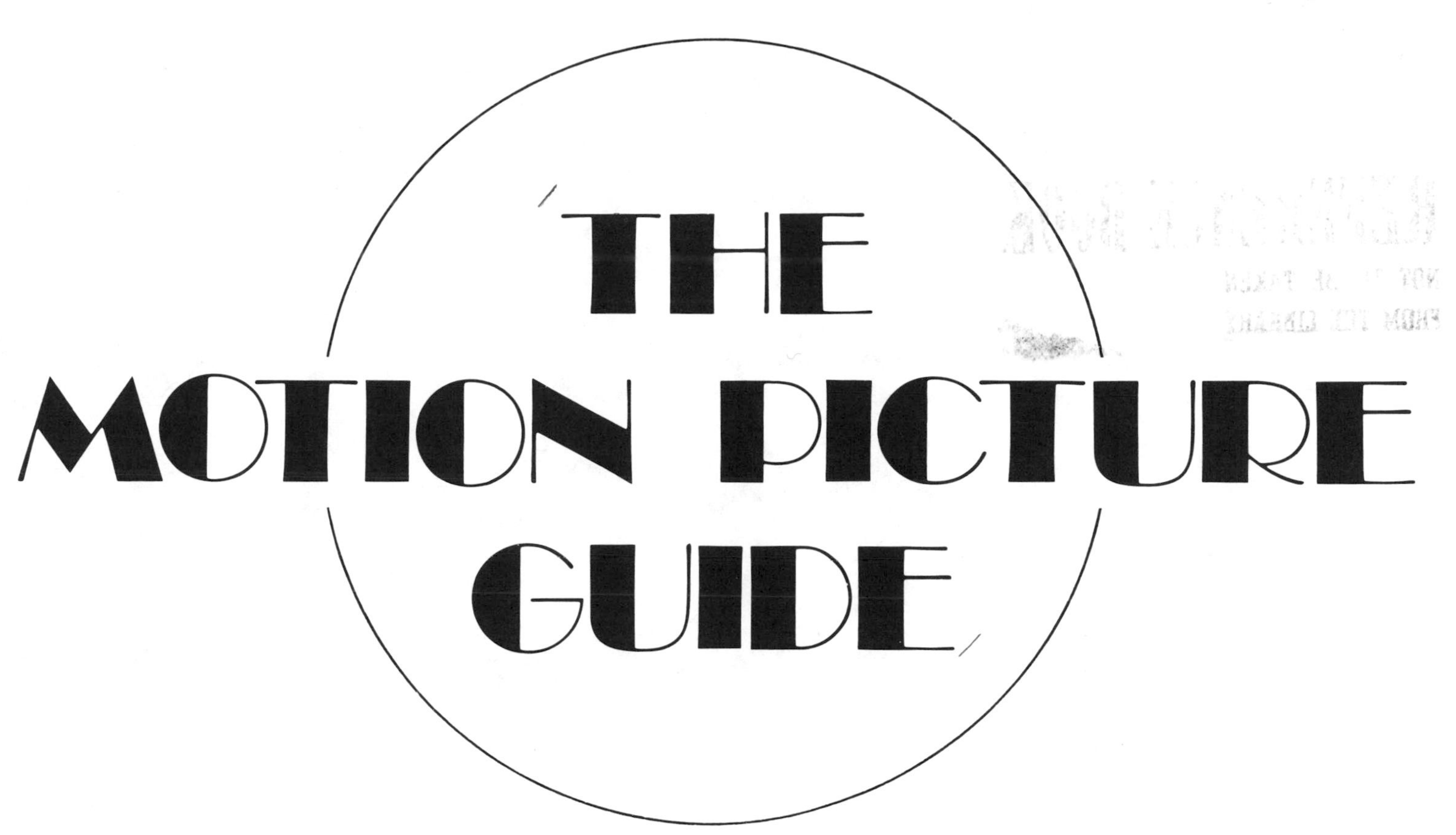

H-K

1927-1983

Jay Robert Nash
Stanley Ralph Ross

CINEBOOKS, INC.
Chicago, 1986
Publishers of THE COMPLETE FILM RESOURCE CENTER

Publishers: Jay Robert Nash, Stanley Ralph Ross; **Editor-in-Chief:** Jay Robert Nash; **Executive Editor:** Stanley Ralph Ross; **Associate Publisher and Director of Development:** Kenneth H. Petchenik; **Senior Editor-in-Charge:** Jim McCormick; **Senior Editors:** David Tardy, Robert B. Connelly; **Production Editor:** William Leahy; **Associate Editors:** Oksana Lydia Dominguez, Jeffrey H. Wallenfeldt, Edie McCormick, Michaela Tuohy, Jeannette Hori, Tom Legge; **Contributing Editors:** James J. Mulay (Chief Contributing Editor), Daniel Curran, Michael Theobald, Arnie Bernstein, Phil Pantone, Brian Brock; **Assistant Editors:** Marla Dorfman, Kim O. Morgan, Susan Doll, Marla Antelis, Debra Schwieder, Susan Fisher, Donna Roth, Marla Kruglik, Kristina Marcy, Sarah von Fremd, Wendy Anderson; **Art Production and Book Design:** Cathy Anetsberger; **Research Staff:** Shelby Payne (Associate Editor and Chief Researcher), William C. Clogston, Tobi Elliott, Carol Pappas, Rosalyn Mathis, Millicent Mathis, Andrea Nash; **Business/Legal:** Judy Anetsberger.

Associate Publishers: Howard Grafman, Lynn Christian, James and Monica Vrettos, Antoinette Mailliard, Brent H. Nettle, Michael Callie, Constance Shea, Barbara Browne Cramer.

Editorial and Sales Offices: CINEBOOKS, 6135 N. Sheridan Road, Chicago, Illinois 60660.

Library of Congress Catalog Card Number: 85-071145
ISBN: 0-933997-00-0 THE MOTION PICTURE GUIDE (10 Vols.)
0-933997-04-3 THE MOTION PICTURE GUIDE, Vol IV (H-K)

Printed in the United States
First Edition
This volume contains 3,205 entries.

1 2 3 4 5 6 7 8 9 10

THIS VOLUME IS DEDICATED TO
FRED ASTAIRE
AND
GINGER ROGERS

HOW TO USE INFORMATION IN THIS GUIDE

ALPHABETICAL ORDER

All entries have been arranged alphabetically throughout this and all subsequent volumes. In establishing alphabetical order, all articles (A, An, The) appear after the main title (AFFAIR TO REMEMBER, AN). In the case of foreign films the article precedes the main title (LES MISERABLES appears in the letter L) which makes, we feel, for easier access and uniformity. Contractions are grouped together and these will be followed by non-apostrophized words of the same letters. B.F.'s DAUGHTER is at the beginning of the letter B, not under BF.

TITLES

It is important to know what title you are seeking; use the *complete* title of the film. The film ADVENTURES OF ROBIN HOOD, THE, cannot be found under merely ROBIN HOOD. Many films are known under different titles and we have taken great pains to cross-reference these titles. (AKA, also known as) as well as alternate titles used in Great Britain (GB). In addition to the cross-reference title only entries, AKAs and alternate titles in Great Britain can be found in the title line for each entry. An alphabetically arranged comprehensive list of title changes appears in the Index volume (Vol. X).

RATINGS

We have rated each and every film at critical levels that include acting, directing, script, and technical achievement (or the sad lack of it). We have a *five-star* rating, unlike all other rating systems, to signify a film superbly made on every level, in short, a masterpiece. At the lowest end of the scale is *zero* and we mean it. The ratings are as follows: *zero* (not worth a glance), * (poor), ** (fair), *** (good), **** (excellent), ***** (masterpiece, and these are few and far between). Half-marks mean almost there but not quite.

YEAR OF RELEASE

We have used in all applicable instances the year of United States release. This sometimes means that a film released abroad may have a different date elsewhere than in these volumes but this is generally the date released in foreign countries, not in the U.S.

FOREIGN COUNTRY PRODUCTION

When possible, we have listed abbreviated names of the foreign countries originating the production of a film. This information will be found within the parenthesis containing the year of release. If no country is listed in this space, it is a U.S. production.

RUNNING TIME

A hotly debated category, we have opted to list the running time a film ran at the time of its initial U.S. release but we will usually mention in the text if the film was drastically cut and give the reasons why. We have attempted to be as accurate as possible by consulting the most reliable sources.

PRODUCING AND DISTRIBUTING COMPANIES

The producing and/or distributing company of every film is listed in abbreviated entries next to the running time in the title line (see abbreviations; for all those firms not abbreviated, the entire firm's name will be present).

COLOR OR BLACK-AND-WHITE

The use of color or black-and-white availability appears as c or bw following the producing/releasing company entry.

CASTS

Whenever possible, we give *the complete cast and the roles played* for each film and this is the case in 95% of all entries, the only encyclopedia to ever offer such comprehensive information in covering the entire field. The names of actors and actresses are in Roman lettering, the names of the roles each played in Italic inside parentheses.

SYNOPSIS

The in-depth synopsis for each entry (when such applies) offers the plot of each film, critical evaluation, anecdotal information on the production and its personnel, awards won when applicable and additional information dealing with the production's impact upon the public, its success or failure at the box office, its social significance, if any. Acting methods, technical innovations, script originality are detailed. We also cite other productions involving an entry's personnel for critical comparisons and to establish the style or genre of expertise of directors, writers, actors and technical people.

REMAKES AND SEQUELS

Information regarding films that have sequels, sequels themselves or direct remakes of films can be found at the very end of each synopsis.

DUBBING AND SUBTITLES

We will generally point out in the synopsis when a foreign film is dubbed in English, mostly when the dubbing is poor. When voices are dubbed, particularly when singers render vocals on songs mimed by stars, we generally point out these facts either in the cast/role listing or inside the synopsis. If a film is in a foreign language and subtitled, we signify the fact in a parenthetical statement at the end of each entry (In Italian, English subtitles).

CREDITS

The credits for the creative and technical personnel of a film are extensive and they include: p (producer, often executive producer); d (director); w (screenwriter, followed by adaptation, if any, and creator of original story, if any, and other sources such as authors for plays, articles, short stories, novels and non-fiction books); ph (cinematographer, followed by camera system and color process when applicable, i.e., Panavision, Technicolor); m (composer of musical score); ed (film editor); md (music director); art d (art director); set d (set decoration); cos (costumes); spec eff (special effects); ch (choreography); m/l (music and lyrics); stunts, makeup, and other credits when merited. When someone receives two or more credits in a single film the credits may be combined (p&d, John Ford) or the last name repeated in subsequent credits shared with another (d, John Ford; w, Ford, Dudley Nichols).

GENRES/SUBJECT

Each film is categorized for easy identification as to genre and/or subject and themes at the left-hand bottom of each entry. (Western, Prison Drama, Spy Drama, Romance, Musical, Comedy, War, Horror, Science-Fiction, Adventure, Biography, Historical Drama, Children's Film, Animated Feature, etc.) More specific subject and theme breakdowns will be found in the Index (Vol. X).

PR AND MPAA RATINGS

The Parental Recommendation provides parents having no knowledge of the style and content of each film with a guide; if a film has excessive violence, sex, strong language, it is so indicated. Otherwise, films specifically designed for young children are also indicated. The Parental Recommendation (**PR**) is to be found at the right-hand bottom of each entry, followed, when applicable, by the **MPAA** rating. The PR ratings are as follows: **AAA** (must for children); **AA** (good for children); **A** (acceptable for children); **C** (cautionary, some objectionable scenes); **O** (completely objectionable for children).

KEY TO ABBREVIATIONS

Foreign Countries:

Arg.	Argentina
Aus.	Australia
Aust.	Austria
Bel.	Belgium
Braz.	Brazil
Brit.	Great Britain (GB when used for alternate title)
Can.	Canada
Chi.	China
Czech.	Czechoslovakia
Den.	Denmark
E. Ger.	East Germany
Fin.	Finland
Fr.	France
Ger.	Germany (includes W. Germany)
Gr.	Greece
Hung.	Hungary
Ital.	Italy
Jap.	Japan
Mex.	Mexico
Neth.	Netherlands
Phil.	Philippines
Pol.	Poland
Rum.	Rumania
S.K.	South Korea
Span.	Spain
Swed.	Sweden

Key to Abbreviations (continued)

Switz.	Switzerland
Thai.	Thailand
USSR	Union of Soviet Socialist Republics
Yugo.	Yugoslavia

Production Companies, Studios and Distributors (U.S. and British)

AA	ALLIED ARTISTS
ABF	Associated British Films
AE	Avco Embassy
AEX	Associated Exhibitors
AH	Anglo-Hollandia
AIP	American International Pictures
AM	American
ANCH	Anchor Film Distributors
ANE	American National Enterprises
AP	Associated Producers
AP&D	Associated Producers & Distributors
ARC	Associated Releasing Corp.
Argosy	Argosy Productions
Arrow	Arrow Films
ART	Artcraft
Astra	Astra Films
AY	Aywon
BA	British Actors
B&C	British and Colonial Kinematograph Co.
BAN	Banner Films
BI	British Instructional
BIFD	B.I.F.D. Films
BIP	British International Pictures
BJP	Buck Jones Productions
BL	British Lion
Blackpool	Blackpool Productions
BLUE	Bluebird
BN	British National
BNF	British and Foreign Film
Boulting	Boulting Brothers (Brit.)
BP	British Photoplay Production
BPP	B.P. Productions
BRIT	Britannia Films
BRO	Broadwest
Bryanston	Bryantston Films (Brit.)
BS	Blue Streak
BUS	Bushey (Brit.)
BUT	Butchers Film Service
BV	Buena Vista (Walt Disney)
CAP	Capital Films
CC	Christie Comedy
CD	Continental Distributing
CHAD	Chadwick Pictures Corporation
CHES	Chesterfield
Cineguild	Cineguild
CL	Clarendon
CLIN	Clinton
COL	COLUMBIA
Colony	Colony Pictures
COM	Commonwealth
COMM	Commodore Pictures
COS	Cosmopolitan (Hearst)
DE	Dependable Exchange
DGP	Dorothy Gish Productions
Disney	Walt Disney Productions
DIST	Distinctive
DM	DeMille Productions
DOUB	Doubleday
EAL	Ealing Studios (Brit.)
ECF	East Coast Films
ECL	Eclectic
ED	Eldorado
EF	Eagle Films
EFF & EFF	E.F.F. & E.F.F. Comedy
EFI	English Films Inc.
EIFC	Export and Import Film Corp.
EL	Eagle-Lion
EM	Embassy Pictures Corp.
EMI	EMI Productions
EP	Enterprise Pictures
EPC	Equity Pictures Corp.
EQ	Equitable
EXCEL	Excellent
FA	Fine Arts
FC	Film Classics
FD	First Division
FN	First National
FOX	20TH CENTURY FOX (and Fox Productions)
FP	Famous Players (and Famous Players Lasky)
FRP	Frontroom Productions
Gainsborough	Gainsborough Productions
GAU	Gaumont (Brit.)
GEN	General
GFD	General Films Distributors
Goldwyn	Samuel Goldwyn Productions
GN	Grand National
GOTH	Gotham
Grafton	Grafton Films (Brit.)
H	Harma
HAE	Harma Associated Distributors
Hammer	Hammer Films (Brit.)
HD	Hagen and Double
HM	Hi Mark
HR	Hal Roach
IA	International Artists
ID	Ideal
IF	Independent Film Distributors (Brit.)
Imperator	Imperator Films (Brit.)
IP	Independent Pictures Corp.
IN	Invincible Films
INSP	Inspirational Pictures (Richard Barthelmess)
IV	Ivan Film
Javelin	Javelin Film Productions (Brit.)
JUR	Jury
KC	Kinema Club
KCB	Kay C. Booking
Knightsbridge	Knightsbridge Productions (Brit.)
Korda	Alexander Korda Productions (Brit.)
Ladd	Ladd Company Productions
LAS	Lasky Productions (Jesse L. Lasky)
LFP	London Films
LIP	London Independent Producers
Lorimar	Lorimar Productions
LUM	Lumis
Majestic	Majestic Films
Mascot	Mascot Films
Mayflowers	Mayflowers Productions (Brit.)
Metro	Metro
MFC	Mission Film Corporation
MG	Metro-Goldwyn
MGM	METRO-GOLDWYN-MAYER
MON	Monogram
MOR	Morante
MS	Mack Sennett
MUT	Mutual
N	National
NG	National General
NGP	National General Pictures (Alexander Korda, Brit.)
NW	New World
Orion	Orion Productions
Ortus	Ortus Productions (Brit.)
PAR	PARAMOUNT
Pascal	Gabriel Pascal Productions (Brit.)
PDC	Producers Distributors Corp.

Key to Abbreviations (continued)

PEER	Peerless
PWN	Peninsula Studios
PFC	Pacific Film Company
PG	Playgoers
PI	Pacific International
PIO	Pioneer Film Corp.
PM	Pall Mall
PP	Pro Patria
PRC	Producers Releasing Corporation
PRE	Preferred
QDC	Quality Distributing Corp.
RAY	Rayart
RAD	Radio Pictures
RANK	J. Arthur Rank (Brit.)
RBP	Rex Beach Pictures
REA	Real Art
REG	Regional Films
REN	Renown
REP	Republic
RF	Regal Films
RFD	R.F.D. Productions (Brit.)
RKO	RKO RADIO PICTURES
Rogell	Rogell
Romulus	Romulus Films (Brit.)
Royal	Royal
SB	Samuel Bronston
SCHUL	B.P. Schulberg Productions
SEL	Select
SELZ	Selznick International (David O. Selznick)
SF	Selznick Films
SL	Sol Lesser
SONO	Sonofilms
SP	Seven Pines Productions (Brit.)
SRP	St. Regis Pictures
STER	Sterling
STOLL	Stoll
SUN	Sunset
SYN	Syndicate Releasing Co.
SZ	Sam Zimbalist
TC	Two Cities (Brit.)
T/C	Trem-Carr
THI	Thomas H. Ince
TIF	Tiffany
TRA	Transatlantic Pictures
TRU	Truart
TS	Tiffany/Stahl
UA	UNITED ARTISTS
UNIV	UNIVERSAL (AND UNIVERSAL INTERNATIONAL)
Venture	Venture Distributors
VIT	Vitagraph
WAL	Waldorf
WB	WARNER BROTHERS (AND WARNER BROTHERS-SEVEN ARTS)
WEST	Westminster
WF	Woodfall Productions (Brit.)
WI	Wisteria
WORLD	World
WSHP	William S. Hart Productions
ZUKOR	Adolph Zukor Productions

Foreign

ABSF	AB Svensk Film Industries (Swed.)
Action	Action Films (Fr.)
ADP	Agnes Delahaie Productions (Fr.)
Agata	Agata Films (Span.)
Alter	Alter Films (Fr.)
Arch	Archway Film Distributors
Argos	Argos Films (Fr.)
Argui	Argui Films (Fr.)
Ariane	Les Films Ariane (Fr.)
Athos	Athos Films (Fr.)
Belga	Belga Films (Bel.)
Beta	Beta Films (Ger.)
CA	Cine-Alliance (Fr.)
Caddy	Caddy Films (Fr.)
CCFC	Compagnie Commerciale Francais Einematographique (Fr.)
CDD	Cino Del Duca (Ital.)
CEN	Les Films de Centaur (Fr.)
CFD	Czecheslovak Film Productions
CHAM	Champion (Ital.)
Cinegay	Cinegay Films (Ital.)
Cines	Cines Films (Ital.)
Cineriz	Cinerez Films (Ital.)
Citel	Citel Films (Switz.)
Como	Como Films (Fr.)
CON	Concordia (Fr.)
Corona	Corona Films (Fr.)
D	Documento Films (Ital.)
DD	Dino De Laurentiis (Ital.)
Dear	Dear Films (Ital.)
DIF	Discina International Films (Fr.)
DPR	Films du Palais-Royal (Fr.)
EX	Excelsa Films (Ital.)
FDP	Films du Pantheon (Fr.)
Fono	Fono Roma (Ital.)
FS	Filmsonor Productions (Fr.)
Gala	Fala Films (Ital.)
Galatea	Galatea Productions (Ital.)
Gamma	Gamma Films (Fr.)
Gemma	Gemma Cinematografica (Ital.)
GFD	General Film Distributors, Ltd. (Can.)
GP	General Productions (Fr.)
Gray	(Gray Films (Fr.)
IFD	Intercontinental Film Distributors
Janus	Janus Films (Ger.)
JMR	Macques Mage Releasing (Fr.)
LF	Les Louvre Films (Fr.)
LFM	Les Films Moliere (Fr.)
Lux	Lux Productions (Ital.)
Melville	Melville Productions (Fr.)
Midega	Midega Films (Span.)
NEF	N.E.F. La Nouvelle Edition Francaise (Fr.)
NFD	N.F.D. Productions (Ger.)
ONCIC	Office National pour le Commerce et L'Industrie Cinematographique (Fr.)
Ortus	Ortus Films (Can.)
PAC	Production Artistique Cinematographique (Fr.)
Pagnol	Marcel Pagnol Productions (Fr.)
Parc	Parc Films (Fr.)
Paris	Paris Films (Fr.)
Pathe	Pathe Films (Fr.)
PECF	Productions et Editions Cinematographique Francais (Fr.)
PF	Parafrench Releasing Co. (Fr.)
PIC	Produzione International Cinematografica (Ital.)
Ponti	Carlo Ponti Productions (Ital.)
RAC	Realisation d'Art Cinematographique (Fr.)
Regina	Regina Films (Fr.)
Renn	Renn Productions (Fr.)
SDFS	Societe des Films Sonores Tobis (Fr.)
SEDIF	Societe d'Exploitation ed de Distribution de Films (Fr.)
SFP	Societe Francais de Production (Fr.)
Sigma	Sigma Productions (Fr.)
SNE	Societe Nouvelle des Establishments (Fr.)
Titanus	Titanus Productions (Ital.)
TRC	Transcontinental Films (Fr.)
UDIF	U.D.I.F. Productions (Fr.)
UFA	Deutsche Universum-Film AG (Ger.)
UGC	Union Generale Cinematographique (Fr.)
Union	Union Films (Ger.)
Vera	Vera Productions (Fr.)

H.A.R.M. MACHINE, THE (SEE: AGENT FOR H.A.R.M., 1966)

H.E.A.L.T.H. (SEE: HEALTH, 1980)

H.M. PULHAM, ESQ.*½** (1941) 120m MGM bw

Hedy Lamarr *(Marvin Myles)*, Robert Young *(Harry Pulham)*, Ruth Hussey *(Kay Motford)*, Charles Coburn *(Mr. Pulham, Sr.)*, Van Heflin *(Bill King)*, Fay Holden *(Mrs. Pulham)*, Bonita Granville *(Mary Pulham)*, Douglas Wood *(Mr. Bullard)*, Charles Halton *(Walter Kaufman)*, Leif Erickson *(Rodney "Bo-Jo" Brown)*, Phil Brown *(Joe Bingham)*, David Clyde *(Hugh the Butler)*, Sara Haden *(Miss Rollo)*, Walter Kingsford *(Skipper)*, Bobby Cooper *(Harry as a Boy)*, Earle Dewey *(Chris Evans)*, Byron Foulger *(Curtis Cole)*, Harry Crocker *(Bob Ridge)*, Harry Brown *(Charley Roberts)*, Douglass Newland *(Sam Green)*, Grant Withers *(Sammy Lee the Harvard Coach)*, Connie Gilchrist *(Tillie)*, Frank Faylen *(Sergeant)*, Anne Revere *(Miss Redfern)*, John Raitt *(Soldier)*, Ottola Nesmith *(Mrs. Prindle)*, Ava Gardner *(Girl)*, Arno Frey *(German Officer)*, Syd Saylor *(Preacher)*.

The story is melancholy and bittersweet but it's so well done that this lengthy film flits by in no time, leaving in its wake the definite feeling of having watched a fine movie if not a classic film. Marquand's superb novel of Boston's high society and the forlorn love affair of one of its leading citizens is memorably captured by director Vidor. Young is Pulham, the product of a wealthy, stuffy Bostonian family who thinks back 20 years on a successful but sedate career as he begins to pen his memoirs. The one exciting period of an otherwise dull existence is the time Young has spent in New York where, in the 1920s, he fell in love with the beautiful Lamarr, a copywriter. He is a Brahman from Back Bay Boston and she is an independent Iowa-bred girl who will have nothing to do with living the blueblood life. Coburn, who is a standout as Young's caste-conscious father, declines to give his blessing to a marriage between his illustrious son and a common girl. The Young-Lamarr affair ends with the flame still burning and Young goes on to wed Hussey, who is family approved. Twenty years later, Lamarr, who said she would go on waiting for Young, calls him and the two begin their affair all over again. But they realize that they can't turn back the clock, go home again, or pick up the threads of their severed relationship. Young returns to the waiting arms of the understanding Hussey. Young is very good and Lamarr perfect as the liberated lady, despite her Viennese accent (excused with a line she delivers: "When my folks moved here from Europe they settled in Iowa"). Heflin and Erickson overreach their roles but Hussey is solid as the wife who waits for her husband's illusions to fade. Lamarr got her part in this film quite by accident, attending a dinner and being seated next to Vidor who began talking about the film and the leading part she might play. Lamarr was later to say: "Of all the films I did, most critics agree this was my best part, and I liked it the best."

p&d, King Vidor; w, Vidor, Elizabeth Hill (based on the novel by John P. Marquand); ph, Ray June; m, Bronislau Kaper; ed, Harold F. Kress; md, Lennie Hayton, Gile Steele; art d, Cedric Gibbons, Malcolm Brown; set d, Edwin B. Willis; cos, Kalloch.

Drama **(PR:A MPAA:NR)**

H.M.S. DEFIANT (SEE: DAMN THE DEFIANT, 1962, Brit.)

H-MAN, THE*** (1959, Jap.) 79m Toho/COL c (BIJO TO EKITAINIGEN; UOMINI H)

Yumi Shirakawa *(Girl)*, Kenji Sahara *(Detective)*, Akihiko Hirata *(Scientist)*, Eitaro Ozawa, Koreya Senda, Mitsuru Sato.

The Tokyo sewer system is an oozing mess after a radioactive liquid turns people into slimy blobs that float down the drains following a rainstorm. To add to the havoc, the gelatinous masses then begin to reproduce. There is a subplot involving a narcotics ring which is soon reduced to mush. The blobs are ultimately destroyed in a fire that lights up the city. The special effects in this film are first-rate and eerie to watch. This is probably director Honda's best film after GODZILLA.

p, Tomoyuki Tanaka; d, Inoshiro Honda; w, Takeshi Kimura (based on a story by Hideo Kaijo); ph, Hajime Koizumi (CinemaScope, Eastmancolor); m, Masaru Sato; art d, Takeo Kita; spec eff, Eiji Tsuburaya.

Science Fiction **(PR:O MPAA:NR)**

H.O.T.S.* (1979) 95m Great American Dream Machine/Derio c

Susan Kiger *(Honey)*, Lisa London *(O'Hara)*, Pamela Jean Bryant *(Teri Lynn)*, Kimberly Cameron *(Sam)*, Mary Steelsmith *(Clutz)*, Angela Aamers *(Boom-Boom)*, Lindsay Bloom *(Melody)*, K.C. Winkler *(Cynthia)*, Donald Petrie *(Doug)*, Larry Gilman *(Mad Dog)*, David Gibbs *(Macho Man)*, Danny Bonaduce *(Richie)*, Ken Olfson *(Dean Chase)*, Dick Bakalyan *(Charlie Ingels)*, Louis Guss *(Bugs Benny)*, Sandy Johnson *(Stephanie)*, Marilyn Rubin *(Jackie)*, Dan Reed *(Stormin' Norman)*, Marvin Katzoff *(Big Boy)*, Steve Bond *(John)*, Talmadge Scott *(Hunk)*, Dorothy Meyer *(Ezzetta)*, Scott Ellsworth *(Professor)*, Bunny Summers *(Singer)*.

With the success of ANIMAL HOUSE in 1978, a slew of cheap imitations quickly followed, of which H.O.T.S. is a remnant. The story revolves around two rivalling university sororities that play a series of nasty practical jokes on one another. The thin plot line is really just an excuse for some bathroom humor and a generous amount of skin displayed. The acting is equal to the plot. You may notice the familiar face of Bonaduce, a refugee from TV's "The Partridge Family." H.O.T.S. is ultimately a waste and demeaning to women.

p, W. Terry Davis, Don Schain, Gerald Sindell; d, Sindell; w, Cheri Caffaro, Joan Buchanan; ph, Harvey Genkins (DeLuxe Color); m, David Davis; ed, Barbara Pokras; art d, Eric Butler.

Comedy **Cas.** **(PR:O MPAA:R)**

HADAKA NO SHIMA (SEE: ISLAND, THE, 1962, Jap.)

HADAKA NO TAISHO (SEE: NAKED GENERAL, THE, 1964, Jap.)

HAGBARD AND SIGNE*** (1968, Den./Iceland/Swed.) 92m ASA-Movie Art of Europe-Edda/Steve Prentoulis c (DEN RODE KAPPE, RAUTHA SKIKKJAN, DEN RODA KAPPAN, AKA: THE RED MANTLE)

Gitte Haenning *(Signe)*, Oleg Vidov *(Hagbard)*, Gunnar Bjornstrand *(King Sigvor)*, Eva Dahlbeck *(The Queen)*, Lisbeth Movin *(Bengerd)*, Johannes Meyer *(Bilvis)*, Hakan Jahnberg *(Bolvis)*, Henning Palmer *(Hake)*, Birgitte Federspiel *(King Hamund's Widow)*, Manfred Reddeman *(Hildegisl)*, Gisli Alfredsson *(Sigvald)*, Folmer Ruhbaek *(Helvin)*, Borgar Gartharsson *(Alf)*, Jorgen Lantz *(Hamund)*, Fredrik Tharaldsen *(Alger)*, Sisse Reingaard *(Rigmor)*, Niels Hinrichsen, Else Hojgaard, Poul Reichhardt, Jakob Nielsen.

This medieval period piece from Scandinavia stars Vidov as the son of a king killed in battle by a rival clan whose kingdom is headed by Bjornstrand. Vidov and his two brothers seek revenge on Bjornstrand's sons. The opposing forces clash on a neutral beach and a powerful battle ensues, but the evenly matched sides are unable to subdue one another. Bjornstrand declares a truce and invites the rival tribe to his castle, where Vidov meets his enemy's lovely daughter, Haenning, and the couple fall in love, much to the dismay of Haenning's jealous suitor Reddemann, who secretly incites the three Bjornstrand sons into breaking the truce. Shortly thereafter, Vidov's brothers are murdered and he flees. But unable to bear the separation from his beloved, Vidov disguises himself as a woman and sneaks into Haenning's room, where their love is consummated. The couple is discovered by a maid, and Vidov is captured and sentenced to death by hanging. The lovers form a suicide pact; Haenning sets fire to her room and burns to death, while Vidov, awaiting his fate at the gallows, kicks the stool out from under him and hangs, thus joining his beloved in eternity.

p, Bent Christensen, Johan Bonnier; d&w, Gabriel Axel (based on a Scandinavian legend); ph, Henning Bendsten (CinemaScope, Eastmancolor); m, Per Norgaard; ed, Lars Brydesen; art d, P.A. Lundgren, Walther Dannerfjord, Niels Wangberg; cos, Ulla Britt Soderlund; spec eff, Josef Moller.

Drama **(PR:C-O MPAA:NR)**

HAIL** (1973) 85m Cine-Globe/Hail c (AKA: HAIL TO THE CHIEF; WASHINGTON B.C.)

Dan Resin *(President)*, Richard B. Shull *(Secretary of Health)*, Dick O'Neill *(Attorney General)*, Joseph Sirola *(Rev. Williams)*, Patricia Ripley *(First Lady)*, Gary Sandy *(Tom)*, Williard Waterman *(Vice President)*, K. Callan *(Burd)*, Constance Forslund *(Sara)*, Phil Foster *(Michael)*, Lee Meredith *(Mrs. Maloney)*, Robert King *(Reporter)*, Douglas Rutherford *(Ellinson)*, Mary Louise Weller *(Mrs. Ellinson)*, Peggy Pope *(Sister Veronica)*, Ron Carroll *(Professor)*, Brandon Maggert *(Sgt. National Guard)*, Doyle Newberry *(Speech Writer)*, Toni Reid *(Doctor)*, Ted Gewant *(Chief Justice)*, Jim Nurtaugh *(Sgt. Johnson)*, Madison Arnold *(Sgt. Mazzola)*.

A paranoid President decides the only way to deal with rebellious youth is have them arrested and put in concentration camps. HAIL doesn't quite hit its target as effectively as it could have, but it's still a nifty little satire. There's some nice reflections on the turmoil the country went through in the late 1960s though things do get a bit repetitive. The different levels of satire and parody are nicely handled by the director, and Resin is terrific as the sinister President-cum-dictator. An interesting historical note: HAIL was viewed at the Cannes Film Festival a little more than three weeks before the Watergate break-in.

p, Roy L. Townsend, Paul Leaf; d, Fred Levinson; w, Larry Spiegel, Phil Dusenberry; ph, William Storz (Metrocolor) m, Trade Martin; ed, Robert DeRise.

Satire **Cas.** **(PR:O MPAA:PG)**

HAIL AND FAREWELL½** (1936, Brit.) 73m WB/FN bw

Claude Hulbert *(Bert)*, Reginald Purdell *(Nobby)*, Nicholas Hannen *(Col. Harvey)*, Joyce Kennedy *(Mrs. Harvey)*, Moira Reed *(Annie Turner)*, Bruce Lister *(Peter Dove)*, Ivan Samson *(Col. Oldham)*, Wally Patch *(Sgt.-Maj.)*, Henry Caine *(Joe Perkins)*, Marie Wright *(Mrs. Perkins)*, Joyce Kirby *(Ruby)*, Helen Goss, Eve Lyntett.

Highly entertaining film that follows the trail of several British sailors during their six-hour leave in the port of Southampton. Their intertwined adventures prove that plenty can take place in a short amount of time, given the right combination of events, as this movie certainly does.

p, Paul Merzbach; d, Ralph Ince; w, Reginald Purdell, John Dighton, Brock Williams (based on the story by Merzbach); ph, Basil Emmott.

Comedy/Drama **(PR:A MPAA:NR)**

HAIL, HERO!½** (1969) 97m Cinema Center/NGP c

Michael Douglas *(Carl Dixon)*, Arthur Kennedy *(Albert Dixon)*, Teresa Wright *(Santha Dixon)*, John Larch *(Mr. Conklin)*, Charles Drake *(Sen. Murchiston)*, Mercer Harris *(Jimmy)*, Deborah Winters *(Becky)*, Peter Strauss *(Frank Dixon)*, Mario Alcalde *(Cong. Arcado)*, Amy Stuart *(Rhetha)*, Rene Tetro *(Tinky)*, Louise Latham *(Miss Mirabel)*, John Qualen *(Billy Hurd)*, Carmen Zapata *(Juana)*, Virginia Christine *(Eleanor Murchiston)*, Heather Menzies *(Molly Adams)*, Dorothy Newman, Marjorie Eaton *(Carl's Aunts)*, James Nusser, Charles Wagenheim, James Griffith, Burt Mustin, Walter Baldwin, Peter Brocco, Lucas White.

Our story finds Douglas returning to his parents' home to inform them of his decision to quit college and enlist in the army. This comes as a surprise to Kennedy and Wright, since their son had been arrested for failing to register for the draft. Douglas explains that he is still a pacifist and intends to go to Viet Nam and "love the enemy" in an effort to work out his own feelings. Though a little heavy-handed and a bit dated, HAIL, HERO! is an intriguing film. Douglas, in his screen debut, handles his role with ease. Kennedy and Wright are effective and believable as the parents unable to communicate with their black sheep son. Strauss, also in his film debut, is fine as the younger brother who was crippled in a childhood accident blamed on Douglas, and who finally comes around to his brother's viewpoint. This is an engaging document on the times and feelings of 1960s America.

p, Harold D. Cohen; d, David Miller; w, David Manber (based on a novel by John Weston); ph, Robert Hauser (Technicolor); m, Jerome Moross; ed, Jack McSweeney; art d, Albert Heschong; set d, Ray Molyneaux; cos, Don MacDonald, Dorothy Rodgers; m/l, Gordon Lightfoot (sung by Lightfoot); makeup, Richard Cobos.

Drama **(PR:C MPAA:M)**

HAIL MAFIA½** (1965, Fr./Ital.) 89m ITTAC-Filmstudio-P.E.C.F./ Goldstone bw (JE VOUS SALUE MAFIA; DA NEW YORK: MAFIA UCCIDE)

Henry Silva *(Schaft)*, Jack Klugman *(Phil)*, Eddie Constantine *(Rudy)*, Elsa Martinelli *(Sylvia)*, Micheline Presle *(Daisy)*, Michel Lonsdale *(Secretary)*, Karl Studer *(Ruidosa)*, Ricky Cooper *(Ben)*, Tener Riggs Eckleberry *(Hyman)*, Marcel Pagliero, Danielle Couprayen, Jean-Marc Allegre.

Constantine is an American hiding out in France while two gangsters, Silva and Klugman, are in deadly pursuit of him, each for his own reasons. Silva has been hired by a big construction company that wants him killed before he can give incriminating testimony against them. Klugman has a personal vendetta against Constantine, and he and Silva team up in Paris to hunt him down. When the construction company is cleared of the charges against them, Silva's orders change, and he now becomes intent on protecting Constantine from Klugman. In a final gun battle, all three men are killed. Klugman and Silva both give standout performances.

p,d,&w, Raoul J. Levy (based on a book by Pierre Viel-Lescu); ph, Raoul Coutard; m, Hubert Rostaing, Pierre Goumy; ed, Victoria Mercanton; art d, Jean Andre.

Crime **(PR:O MPAA:NR)**

HAIL THE CONQUERING HERO**** (1944) 101m PAR bw

Eddie Bracken *(Woodrow Lafayette Pershing Truesmith)*, Ella Raines *(Libby)*, Bill Edwards *(Forrest Noble)*, Raymond Walburn *(Mayor Noble)*, William Demarest *(Sergeant)*, Jimmie Dundee *(Corporal)*, Georgia Caine *(Mrs. Truesmith)*, Alan Bridge *(Political Boss)*, James Damore *(Jonesy)*, Freddie Steele *(Bugsy)*, Stephen Gregory *(Bill)*, Len Hendry *(Juke)*, Esther Howard *(Mrs. Noble)*, Elizabeth Patterson *(Libby's Aunt)*, Jimmy Conlin *(Judge Dennis)*, Arthur Hoyt *(Rev. Upperman)*, Harry Hayden *(Doc Bissell)*, Franklin Pangborn *(Committee Chairman)*, Victor Potel *(Progressive Bandleader)*, Torben Meyer *(Mr. Schultz)*, Jack Norton *(Regular Bandleader)*, Merrill Rodin *(Alfie, Jr., Bandleader)*, Johnny Sinclair *(American Legion Bandleader)*, Robert Warwick *(Marine Colonel)*, Chester Conklin *(Western Union Man)*, George Melford *(Sheriff)*, Frank Moran *(Town Painter)*, Tom McGuire, Philo McCullough, Franklyn Farnum, Kenneth Gibson *(Town Councilmen)*, Paul Porcasi *(Manager of Cafe)*, George Anderson *(Bartender)*, Julie Gibson *(Singer)*, Mildred Harris *(Marine Colonel's Wife)*, Dot Farley *(Mamie's Mother)*, Marjean Neville *(Mamie)*, Maxine Fife *(Colonel's Daughter)*, Pauline Drake *(Telephone Operator)*, Dewey Robinson *(Conductor)*, Charles Moore *(Porter)*, Miriam Franklin *(Dancer)*.

In this warm and zany comedy Sturges satirizes home front America during WW II and the results prove a terrific spoof where everyone can laugh at themselves. Bracken is unbeatable as the woebegone hero who isn't, the little guy who gets involved with a lie that inflates faster than a balloon blown up in a wind tunnel. The sickly Bracken is the son of a WW I Marine who heroically sacrificed his life at Belleau Wood and he enlists to carry on the family honor at the outbreak of WW II. But Bracken's own body is his undoing. He is released from service as unfit, having chronic hay fever. So ashamed is he, Bracken refuses to go home to the little town of Oakridge. Instead, he takes a job in a shipyard and, through his friends in the Marine Corps, sends letters to his mother, Caine, and his sweetheart, Raines, from the Pacific. To avoid telling the truth, Bracken breaks off with Raines through the mail, saying he's fallen in love with another girl. Some actual Marine heroes, returning from battles at Guadalcanal find him drowning his sorrows in a saloon and Steele, who is shell-shocked and holds motherhood above all else, calls Bracken's mother, Caine, and tells her that Bracken is back, that he is a wartime hero and will see her soon. To complete the charade, Demarest and others convince Bracken to put on his uniform, slip into Oakridge, and make his mother happy. He can then put his uniform in the closet and resume his miserable life. Bracken agrees and takes a train back home with his Marine friends. To their surprise the entire town has turned out with two brass bands to greet the conquering hero. The Mayor showers him with awards, the mortgage on his mother's house is destroyed, and a groundswell for Bracken to become mayor begins. "I'm no hero," Bracken insists, but his remarks are interpreted as modesty. Bracken tries desperately to flee town but his Marine buddies foil every attempt. Raines is at his side once again but the fraud nags meek Bracken to no end. He is finally about to be exposed by Walburn, the local mayor, but he beats the politician to the punch by nobly confessing the deceit at a town meeting. "If I could reach as high as my father's shoestrings my whole life would be justified," Bracken confesses to all. "And I would stand before you proudly, instead of as the thief and coward that I am. A coward because I postponed until now what I should have told you a year ago when I was discharged from the Marine Corps for medical unfitness. A coward because I didn't want my mother to know it . . . A thief because I stole your admiration. I stole the ribbons I've worn. I stole this nomination [for mayor]." Instead of being lynched, Bracken is hailed as an even greater person for having told the truth. There is no way this little buffoon can lose, and he doesn't. By the time his Marine pals leave town he is well on the way to becoming its greatest citizen. The iconoclastic Sturges produced a hilarious comedy in this film, which he wrote and directed, once again proving the genius he displayed in THE GREAT McGINTY (1940), THE LADY EVE (1941), and MIRACLE OF MORGAN'S CREEK (1944). Supporting the very funny Bracken is a cast which is composed mostly of Sturges' stock people—Demarest, Pangborn, Walburn, and others—all of them outstanding. The episodic narrative of the film is directed at a dizzying pace with Sturges employing large crowds and capturing down-home humor by understated lensing techniques such as static positioning of cameras. The brilliant director ran afoul of Paramount boss Buddy De Sylva, who insisted on personally editing the film. This caused a battle royal which forever soured the Sturges and Paramount association. Following this film, Sturges was offered fabulous amounts of money from many studios to write and direct his own films at will, but he made the mistake of opting to go with Howard Hughes, an association that came to nothing. By the 1950s the great Preston Sturges was unwanted by the studios and couldn't sell a story to the worst poverty row production company.

p,d&w, Preston Sturges; ph, John F. Seitz; m, Werner Heymann; ed, Stuart Gilmore; md, Sigmund Krumgold; art d, Hans Dreier; set d, Stephen Seymour; m/l, "Home to the Arms of Mother," Sturges; makeup, Wally Westmore.

Comedy **(PR:A MPAA:NR)**

HAIL TO THE CHIEF (SEE: HAIL, 1972)

HAIL TO THE RANGERS*½ (1943) 58m COL bw

Charles Starrett *(Steve McKay)*, Arthur Hunnicutt *(Arkansas)*, Robert Owen Atcher *(Bob Atcher)*, Leota Atcher *(Bonnie Montgomery)*, Norman Willis *(Monte Kerlin)*, Lloyd Bridges *(Dave Kerlin)*, Ted Adams *(Schuyler)*, Ernie Adams *(Latham)*, Tom London *(Jessup)*, Davison Clark *(Maj. Montgomery)*, Jack Kirk *(Sheriff Ward)*, Edmund Cobb, Budd Buster, Art Mix, Eddie Laughton, Dick Botiller.

In a reverse cliche, phoney homesteaders plant themselves on the ranch of an ex-ranger. He's driven off and an unscrupulous newspaper publisher, along with a gambler, plan to take over the ranch. But good guy Starrett rallies to his old friend's aid and, with the help of other rangers, drives off the evil homesteaders, while the newsman and gambler end up shooting each other. The pace is too slow to keep this at anything but minimal interest, though there are a couple of nice cowboy songs, and Bridges makes one of his early film appearances.

p, Jack Fier; d, William Berke; w, Gerald Geraghty; ph, Benjamin Kline; ed, William Claxton; art d, Lionel Banks.

Western **(PR:A MPAA:NR)**

HAIR**** (1979) 118m UA c

John Savage *(Claude)*, Treat Williams *(Berger)*, Beverly D'Angelo *(Sheila)*, Annie Golden *(Jeannie)*, Dorsey Wright *(Hud)*, Don Dacus *(Woof)*, Cheryl Barnes *(Hud's Fiancee)*, Richard Bright *(Fenton)*, Nicholas Ray *(The General)*, Charlotte Rae *(Party Guest)*, Miles Chapin *(Steve)*, Fern Tailer *(Sheila's Mother)*, Charles Deney *(Sheila's Father)*, Herman Meckler *(Sheila's Uncle)*, Agness Breen *(Sheila's Aunt)*, Antonia Rey *(Berger's Mother)*, George Manos *(Berger's Father)*, Linda Surh *(Vietnamese Girl)*, Joe Acord *(Claude's Father)*, Michael Jeter *(Sheldon)*, Janet York *(Prison Psychiatrist)*, Rahsaan Curry *(Lafayette, Jr.)*, Harry Gittleson *(The Judge)*, Donald Alsdurf *(The M.P.)*, Steve Massicotte *(Barracks Officer)*, Mario Nelson *(Barracks Officer)*, Ben Wood *("Aquarius" Soloist)*, Jane Booke, Suki Love *(Debutantes)*, Ren Woods, Toney Watkins, Carl Hall, Howard Porter, Nell Carter, Kurt Yahjian, Leata Galloway, Cyrena Lomba, Ron Young, Laurie Beechman, Debi Dye, Ellen Foley, John Maestro, Fred Ferrara, Jim Rosica, Charlaine Woodard, Trudy Perkins, Chuck Patterson, H. Douglas Berring, Russell Costen, Kenny Brawner, Lee Wells, Melba Moore, Ronnie Dyson, Rose Marie Wright, Tom Rawe, Jennifer Way, Shelley Washington, Christine Uchida, Raymond Kurshals, Richard Colton, Anthony Ferro, Sara Rudner, Pat Benoye, Cameron Burke, Richard Caceres, Tony Constantine, Ron Dunham, Leonard Feiner, Ken Gildin, Kate Glasner, Christian Holder, Chris Komar, Nancy Lefkowith, Joseph Lennon, Robert Levithan, France Mayotte, Hector Mercado, Sharon Miripolsky, Marta Renzi, Donna Ritchie, Ellen Saltonstall, Radha Sukhu, Byron Utley, Earlise Vails, Ronald Weeks, Kimmary Williams, Deborah Zalkind.

Milos Forman had already proven that his talent knows no boundaries with his helming of TAKING OFF and the multiple Oscar-winning ONE FLEW OVER THE CUCKOO'S NEXT, but when this foreign director was chosen for this very American film, some people wondered about the combination. Their fears should have been assuaged by the 1967 success of the long-running (almost 1800 performances) Broadway play. The musical was a pastiche of sketches and tunes, and it took Forman and scenarist Weller to synthesize all the goings-on into a cinematic story that audiences could understand. Unfortunately, the movie was not a hit. Perhaps it was the film itself or the fact that HAIR was made almost 12 years after the play opened and had become outdated by the time of its release in 1979. Savage plays a square Oklahoma Viet Nam draftee adopted by a group of New York "flower children," who take him on a series of adventures which include getting him high on marijuana, and pushing him on a slightly batty debutante (D'Angelo). Along the way, we are treated to many excellent songs and some of the most inventive choreography ever seen, including a "horse ballet" by mounted police in Central Park where they have been assigned to keep their eyes on what used to be called a "be-in." It was too soon to be nostalgic and too late to be contemporary, so HAIR fell somewhere between the stools and no one could get a handle on it. There is a lot to recommend in this film, most notably the lenswork by cinematographer Ondricek, as well as the sheer energy that pours off the screen in every frame. If you look quickly, you'll catch a glimpse of Nell Carter and Melba Moore. The technical credits, as in all of Forman's pictures, including RAGTIME, are first rate. Songs include: "Let The Sunshine In." "(The Age Of) Aquarius," "Colored Spade," "Ain't Got No," "Hair," "Don't Put It Down," "Somebody To Love," "Good Morning Starshine," "What A Piece Of Work Is Man," "Manchester," "Abie Baby," "Electric Blues," "Black Boys/White Boys," "Old-Fashioned Melody," "3-5-0-0," "The Flesh Failures," "Somebody To Hold," "Sodomy," "Donna," "Hashish," "Where Do I Go?" "Easy To Be Hard," "Walking In Space," "Fourscore," "I'm Black," "Party Music," "My Conviction,"

"LBJ," "I Got Life," "Hare Krishna," "Air," (Gerome Ragni, James Rado, Galt MacDermot).

p, Lester Persky, Michael Butler; d, Milos Forman; w, Michael Weller (based on the musical play by Gerome Ragni, James Rado, Galt MacDermot); ph, Miroslav Ondricek (Panavision, Technicolor); m, MacDermot; ed, Lynzee Klingman; prod d, Stuart Wurtzel; set d, George De Titta; cos, Ann Roth; spec eff, Al Griswold; ch, Twyla Tharp.

Musical **Cas.** **(PR:C-O MPAA:PG)**

HAIR OF THE DOG*½ (1962, Brit.) 66m Parroch/RFD bw

Reginald Beckwith *(Fred Tickle)*, Dorinda Stevens *(Ann Tickle)*, John Le Mesurier *(Sir Mortimer Gallant)*, Brian Oulton *(Gregory Willett)*, Alison Bayley *(Violet Tickle)*, Harold Goodwin *(Percy)*, Barbara Windsor *(Elsie Grumble)*, Stanley Morgan *(Jim Lester)*, Stanley Unwin *(Vicar)*, Keith Smith *(Interviewer)*, Tony Hawes *(Mr. Rembrandt)*.

Lame excuse for a premise rests on a commissionaire who doesn't like to shave, thus instigating a strike at a place where shaving is of extreme importance—a razor manufacturing company. To make matters worse, having a beard is not even trendy during this period.

p, C. Jack Parsons; d, Terry Bishop; w, Tony Hawes (based on a story by John O'Gorman).

Comedy **(PR:A MPAA:NR)**

HAIRY APE, THE*** (1944) 90m UA bw

William Bendix *(Hank Smith)*, Susan Hayword *(Mildred Douglas)*, John Loder *(2nd Engineer Tony Lazar)*, Dorothy Comingore *(Helen Parker)*, Roman Bohnen *(Paddy)*, Tom Fadden *(Long)*, Alan Napier *(MacDougald)*, Charles Cane *(Gantry)*, Raphael Storm *(Aldo)*, Charles La Torre *(Portuguese Proprietor)*, Don Zolaya *(Concertina Player)*, Mary Zavian *(Waitress)*, George Sorrel *(Police Captain)*, Paul Weigel *(Doctor)*, Egon Brecher *(Musician)*, Gesela Werbsek *(Refugee Wife)*, Carmen Rachel *(Young Girl)*, Jonathan Lee *(Water Tender)*, Dick Baldwin *(3rd Engineer)*, Ralph Dunn *(Head Guard)*, William Halligan *(Lieutenant)*, Tommy Hughes *(Doorman)*, Bob Perry *(Bartender)*.

Hayward plays the vixen to the hilt in this offbeat O'Neill drama. She is a spoiled, wealthy socialite returning to America on a tramp steamer carrying refugees. First, to amuse herself, Hayward toys with the ship's second engineer, Loder, then falls in love with him. She convinces him to take her to the boiler room where the stokers feed the roaring furnaces with coal, even though this area is off limits to passengers. There, wearing an impeccable white ensemble, Hayward inspects the greasy, soot-stained burly men, largest and fiercest among them being Bendix. He is a simple-minded, almost cretinous worker who is childishly proud of his brawn; he loves his job and the ship he works on, feeling responsible for the steam which powers it. The filthy, sweaty brute takes one look at Hayward and dumbly approaches this beautiful dream woman. She recoils in horror, screaming "You hairy ape!" With that he makes a threatening move and she flees to deckside. Neither forgets the incident. Hayward has nightmares about beast Bendix and he hates her for labeling him a jungle creature. When Bendix later goes to the swanky building where Hayward lives, he is ejected by the doorman and a cop. At a circus, Bendix watches a gorilla crushing a rubber tire and envisions himself as the ape, but crushing the life out of Hayward. He sneaks into her apartment and almost frightens her to death, but does not harm her, seeing that he has already scarred her memory. He returns to his ship, steals a whistle from Loder, the symbol of authority, and happily goes back to stoking the blazing furnaces. Though Bendix does a commendable job as the man-beast, receiving top billing, a rare occurrence, Hayward steals the film and received rave reviews which helped her climb to star status, even though she was labeled by one critic as being "Hollywood's ablest bitch-player." Comingore, who had starred in the classic CITIZEN KANE (1941), makes a brief appearance as a refugee aboard the ship.

p, Jules Levey; d, Alfred Santell; w, Robert D. Andrews, Decla Dunning (based on the play by Eugene O'Neill); ph, Lucien Andriot; m, Michael E. Michlet; ed, William Ziegler; md, Edward Paul; art d, James Sullivan; spec eff, Harry Redmond.

Drama **(PR:A MPAA:NR)**

HAKUCHI (SEE: IDIOT, THE, 1963, Jap.)

HAKUJA DEN (SEE: PANDA AND MAGIC SERPENT, 1961, Jap.)

HALCON Y LA PRESA, EL (SEE: BIG GUNDOWN, THE, 1968, Ital./Span.)

HALF A HERO½** (1953) 71m MGM bw

Red Skelton *(Ben Dobson)*, Jean Hagen *(Martha Dobson)*, Charles Dingle *(Mr. Bascomb)*, Willard Waterman *(Mr. McEstway)*, Mary Wickes *(Mrs. Watts)*, Frank Cady *(Mr. Watts)*, Hugh Corcoran *(Pete Dobson)*, Dorothy Patrick *(Edna Radwell)*, King Donovan *(Sam Radwell)*, Billie Bird *(Ernestine)*, Dabbs Greer *(George Payson)*, Kathleen Freeman *(Welcomer)*, Polly Bergen *(Guest Appearance)*.

Unlike the usual zany slapstick Skelton is noted for, HALF A HERO finds him in a subdued role in this domestic comedy of a hen-pecked husband and his wife, Hagen, who live in a suburban housing development. When assigned by his boss to write an article about the terrible life in suburbia, Skelton complies, seeing this as a chance to move back to the city. But before he finishes the article, he is a changed man who stands up to his grouchy boss and even gets a raise. Rather than the big laughs he usually plays for, Skelton's comedy here is low-keyed and from the heart. It works well in an unusual departure for the great comic. The supporting cast is good, and young Corcoran is a pint-sized Skelton look-alike.

p, Matthew Rapf; d, Don Weis; w, Max Shulman; ph, Paul Vogel; m, Paul Sawtell; ed, Newell P. Kimlin.

Comedy **(PR:AA MPAA:NR)**

HALF A SINNER** (1934) 70m UNIV bw

Sallie Blane *(Phyllis)*, Joel McCrea *(John Adams)*, Berton Churchill *(Deacon)*, Alexandria Carlisle *(Mrs. Clark)*, Gay Seabrook *(Louella)*, Mickey Rooney *(Willie)*, Spencer Charters *(Jim Cunningham)*, Russell Hopton *(Slim Sullivan)*, Guinn Williams *(Bull Moran)*, Theresa Maxwell Conover *(Mrs. Gregory)*, Reginald Barlow *(Sheriff)*, Bert Roach *(Rumplemeyer)*, Walter Brennan *(Radio Announcer)*.

Churchill stars as an amiable card shark disguised as a church deacon, who uses his skills to hoodwink only those who really deserve it. The far-fetched plot is hampered by some bad editing decisions that erase character motivations and leave gaping holes in the story. Still Churchill gives a nice performance, a role he also played on stage. Some good supporting roles, although minor, come through by Rooney, Hopton, and Williams.

d, Kurt Neumann; w, Earle Snell, Clarence Marks (based on the play "Alias The Deacon" by John B. Hymer and LeRoy Clemens); ph, George Robinson; ed, Gilbert Kurland.

Comedy **(PR:A MPAA:NR)**

HALF A SINNER*½ (1940) 59m UNIV bw

Heather Angel *(Anne Gladden)*, John King *(Larry Cameron)*, Constance Collier *(Mrs. Breckenridge)*, Walter Catlett *(Station Attendant)*, Tom Dugan *(Red)*, Robert Elliot *(Officer Kelly)*, Clem Bevans *(Snuffy)*, Emma Dunn *(Granny Gladden)*, Henry Brandon *(Handsome)*, William H. Davidson *(Slick)*, Fern Emmett *(Margaret Reed)*, Sonny Bupp *(Willy)*, Wilbur Mack *(Mason)*, Joe Devlin *(Steve)*, Fred Kohler, Jr. *(Garage Owner)*.

Angel plays an innocent teacher in trouble. She has stolen the wealthy King's car to avoid the overtures of an admirer. Unknown to her, a dead gangster is a back-seat passenger. King comes to the aide of the helpless young lady by posing as a mobster. Though the directing and technical aspects of the film are of good quality, the acting is mediocre at best. Not one of the actors seems to have any interest in what his or her role is. Collier tries to pump some life into her part, but the role is too minor to make a difference in this film.

p&d, Al Christie; w, Frederick Jackson (based on the story "Lady Takes A Chance" by Dalton Trumbo); ph, Charles Van Enger.

Crime **(PR:A MPAA:NR)**

HALF A SIXPENCE*** (1967, Brit.) 148m Ameran/PAR c

Tommy Steele *(Arthur Kipps)*, Julia Foster *(Ann)*, Penelope Horner *(Helen Walsingham)*, Cyril Ritchard *(Harry Chitterlow)*, Grover Dale *(Pearce)* Elaine Taylor *(Kate)*, Julia Sutton *(Flo)*, Sheila Falconer *(Victoria)*, Leslie Meadows *(Buggins)*, Christopher Sandford *(Sid)*, Pamela Brown *(Mrs. Walsingham)*, James Villiers *(Hubert Walsingham)*, Gerald Campion *(Fat Boy)*, Jeffrey Chandler *(Young Kipps)*, Barry Sinclair *(Woodrow)*, Hilton Edwards *(Shalford)*, Jean Anderson *(Lady Botting)*, Allan Cuthbertson *(Wilkins)*, Aleta Morrison *(Laura)*, Deborah Permenter *(Young Ann)*, Bartlett Mullins, Harry Locke, Julian Orchard, James Bolam, Carole Walker, Humphrey Kent, Norman Mitchell, Bridget Armstrong, Frank Crawshaw, Alistair Hunter, Reginald Hearne, Apple Brook, Helen Goss, George Moon, Queenie Watts, Harry Haythorne, Pat Ashton, Jackie Rochelle, Golda Casimir, Sonny Farrar, Sydney Bromley, Joyce Graeme, Des Graham, Don Vernon, Pamela Cundell, Iris Sadler, Roy Evans, Carolyn Archer, Joyanne Delancey, Suzanne France, Ann Frost, Sally Gilpin, Caroline Haig, Sarah Hardenburg, Michele Hardy, Gillian Hough, Lesley Judd, Jane Kells, Caryl Little, Patricia Lovett, Dawn McDonald, Sheila O'Neill, Louanne Richards, Delia Sainsbury, Tessa Steel, Maureen Willsher, Ivan Baptie, Donald Barclay, David Boswell, Jan Colet, Ray Davis, Neil Fitzwilliam, Louis Godfrey, Bill Harvey, David Hepburn, Bob Howe, Leon Lestocq-Prayne, John MacDonald, Paddy McIntyre, Tom Merrifield, Harry Naughton, Albin Pahernik, Barrie Young.

Steele offers a tour-de-force as an apprentice draper who inherits a fortune and goes wild spending it on the high life he had dreamed of. It's a routine story line, but it's not in the least a routine film. Steele lives up to his name, stealing the entire production with his gleefully outstanding performance. Originally a rock singer, he has no trouble adapting to this musical. The stereotyped roles of the wealthy socialites are performed with seasoned satire. Ritchard is particularly good as a slightly eccentric actor-playwright. Foster is terrific as Steele's long-suffering sweetheart, who puts up with his teeter-tottering between "society" ladies and herself. The memorable title song and the punchy "Flash, Bang, Wallop!" are show-stopping numbers. The other musical numbers and their singers include: "All In The Cause Of Economy," "I'm Not Talking To You" (Steele and Apprentices); "Money To Burn," "The Race Is On" (Steele and Chorus); "I Don't Believe A Word Of It" (Foster and Friends), "A Proper Gentleman" (Chorus); "She's Too Far Above Me," "This Is My World" (Steele); "If The Rain's Got To Fall" (Steele, Children, and Chorus); "Entr'acte" (Orchestra); "I Know What I Am" (Foster).

p, Charles H. Schneer, George Sidney; d, Sidney; w, Beverley Cross (based on the novel *Kipps* by H.G. Wells); ph, Geoffrey Unsworth (Panavision, Technicolor); ed, Bill Lewthwaite, Frank Santillo; prod d, Ted Haworth; art d, Peter Murton; cos, Elizabeth Haffenden, Joan Bridge; ch, Gillian Lynn; m/l, David Heneker.

Musical **(PR:A MPAA:NR)**

HALF ANGEL** (1936) 65m FOX bw

Frances Dee *(Allison Lang)*, Brian Donlevy *(Duffy Giles)*, Charles Butterworth *(Felix)*, Helen Westley *(Mrs. Hargraves)*, Henry Stephenson *(Prof. Jerome Hargraves)*, Sara Haden *(Henrietta Hargraves)*, Etienne Girardot *(Dr. Cotton)*, Paul Stanton *(District Attorney)*, Gavin Muir *(Dr. Barth)*, Julius Tannen *(City Editor)*, Nigel de Brulier *(Dr. Hall)*, Hilda Vaughn *(Bertha)*, Philip Sleeman *(Carl)*, William Ingersoll *(Judge)*, Paul McVey, Bruce Mitchell.

Dee has barely recovered from being acquitted on charges of poisoning her father when another poisoning takes place and she is again suspected. Donlevy portrays a brash reporter trying to force Dee into confessing, but ends up falling in love with her. After being fired by his city editor, Donlevy sets out to prove his sweetheart's innocence. Of course he manages to find the real murderers in the end and Dee's reputation is cleared. Fine performances, but what could have been a really funny murder-mystery is hampered by poor writing, a surprise from the team of Fowler and Meredyth, whose work is known for its style and wit.

p, Darryl F. Zanuck; d, Sidney Lanfield; w, Bess Meredyth, Gene Fowler, Allen Rivkin (based on a story by F. Tennyson Jesse); ph, Bert Glennon; ed, Herbert Levy; md, Louis Silvers.

Comedy/Mystery **(PR:C MPAA:NR)**

HALF ANGEL½** (1951) 77m FOX c

Loretta Young *(Nora)*, Joseph Cotten *(John Raymond)*, Cecil Kellaway *(Mr. Gilpin)*, Basil Ruysdael *(Dr. Jackson)*, Jim Backus *(Michael Hogan)*, Irene Ryan *(Kay)*, John Ridgely *(Tim)*, Therese Lyon *(Mrs. McCarey)*, Mary George *(Receptionist)*, Mary Tarcai *(Head Nurse)*, Gayle Pace *(Orderly)*, Steve Pritko *(Intern)*, Edwin Max *(Max)*, Art Smith *(Dan)*, Jack Davidson *(Best Man)*, Roger Laswell *(Furniture Salesman)*, William Johnstone *(Minister)*, Harris Brown *(Justice of the Peace)*, Herbert Vigran *(Thompson)*, Freeman Lusk *(Judge)*, Lou Nova, Luther Crockett, Junius Matthews.

Young is a lady with a problem. During her waking hours she is a prim and proper nurse engaged to stuffy Ridgely. But at night she sleepwalks as an entirely different personality. On one of her nocturnal strolls, she meets up with old flame Cotten and once more falls for him. Of course neither personality is aware of the other's existence which leads to a comedy of errors. Finally on the night before her wedding to Ridgely, her night-time half runs off with Cotten, to her bewilderment the next morning. Of course her psychological problem is discovered in time and all ends on a happy note. Although the cast is not the best combination (Young is terrific while Cotten is dull), the direction is excellent.

p, Julian Blaustein; d, Richard Sale; w, Robert Riskin (based on a story by George Carleton Brown); ph, Milton Krasner (Technicolor); m, Cyril J. Mockridge; ed, Robert Fritch; md, Alfred Newman; art d, Lyle Wheeler, John DeCuir; m/l, "My Castle In The Sand," Newman, Ralph Blane.

Comedy **(PR:A MPAA:NR)**

HALF-BREED, THE** (1952) 81m RKO c

Robert Young (Dan Craig), Janis Carter *(Helen)*, Jack Buetel *(Charlie Wolf)*, Barton MacLane *(Marshal)*, Reed Hadley *(Crawford)*, Porter Hall *(Kraemer)*, Connie Gilchrist *(Ma Higgins)*, Sammy White *(Willy Wayne)*, Damian O'Flynn *(Capt. Jackson)*, Frank Wilcox *(Sands)*, Judy Walsh *(Nah-Lin)*, Tom Monroe *(Russell)*, Lee MacGregor *(Lt. Monroe)*, Charles Delaney *(Sergeant)*, Caleen Calder, Marietta Elliott, Jeane Cochran, Betty Leonard, Shirley Whitney, Mary Menzies, Shelah Hackett.

A half-breed Apache played by Buetel tries to make peace between his people and the white men, while Hadley, who thinks there's gold on the Indian reservation, tries to start trouble and get them to move. Young, who portrays a gambler, joins Buetel and lawman MacLane to stop Hadley's evil plan from hatching. There's a good deal wrong with this picture from the start. The script is overlong and predictable. There is heavy stereotyping among the Indian characters, with Buetel's dialog being reduced to a few "Ughs." Hadley is simply not cut out to play a villain, and Young, despite a bushy, black moustache, is not believable. The camera work is adequate, though the Technicolor use was not as effective as it could have been.

p, Herman Schlom; d, Stuart Gilmore; w, Harold Shumate, Richard Wormser (based on a story by Robert Hardy Andrews); ph, William V. Skall (Technicolor); m, Paul Sawtell; ed, Samuel E. Beetley; md, C. Bakaleinikoff; art d, Albert S. D'Agostino, Ralph Berger; m/l, Lew Pollack, Harry Harris, Harry Revel, Mort Greene.

Western **(PR:A MPAA:NR)**

HALF HUMAN*½ (1955, Jap.) 70m Toho/DCA bw (JUJIN YUKIOTOKO)

Akira Takarada *(Iijima)*, Kenji Kasahara *(Takeno)*, Momoko Kochi *(Shinsuke Takeno)*, Nubuo Nakamura *(Shigeki Koijumi)*, Akemi Negishi, John Carradine *(Dr. John Raybourn)*, Russell Thorsen *(Prof. Philip Osborne)*, Robert Karnes *(Prof. Alan Templeton)*, Morris Ankrum *(Dr. Carl Jordan)*.

In between the successful GODZILLA and RODAN, director Honda made this dull film that is lacking the inventiveness that made the other two features so enjoyable. This time it's a giant apeman that has some resemblance to the abominable snowman and causes hysterics among the people of northern Japan. When released in the U.S., Carradine and Morris were added to new scenes, but the results made little improvement.

p, Tomoyuki Tanaka; d, Inoshiro Honda, Kenneth G. Crane; w, Takeo Murata.

Horror/Fantasy **(PR:C-O MPAA:NR)**

HALF-MARRIAGE** (1929) 68m RKO bw

Olive Borden *(Judy Page)*, Morgan Farley *(Dick Carroll)*, Ken Murray *(Charles Turner)*, Ann Greenway *(Ann Turner)*, Sally Blane *(Sally)*, Richard Tucker *(George Page)*, Hedda Hopper *(Mrs. Page)*, Anderson Lawlor, James Bradbury, Jr., Jack Trent, James Eagle, G. Pat Collins.

A silly romance that sees Borden as a society girl who disappoints her parents, Tucker and future gossip columnist Hopper, by eloping with young architect Farley. What her parents don't know is that Borden and Farley have secretly been married for some time now. The truth is revealed when Lawlor, a rival for Borden's affections, decides he can't live without her and jumps to his death from her apartment. All is resolved in the end as the parents finally accept their daughter's marriage. Despite the macabre note thrown into this film by the suicide, there is good, light comedy sprinkled throughout. Borden has made the dialog her own in this script, and comes off completely natural. There's also some nice vaudeville comedy bits by noted mime Murray.

p, William LeBaron; d, William J. Cowen; w, Jane Murfin (based on a story by George Kibbe Turner), ed, Archie Marshek; m/l, "After The Clouds Roll By," "You're Marvelous," Sidney Clare, Oscar Levant.

Comedy **(PR:A MPAA:NR)**

HALF-NAKED TRUTH, THE*** (1932) 75m RKO bw

Lupe Velez *(Teresita)*, Lee Tracy *(Bates)*, Eugene Pallette *(Achilles)*, Frank Morgan *(Farrell)*, Robert McKenzie *(Col. Munday)*, Shirley Chambers *(Gladys)*, Charles Dow Clark *(Sheriff)*, James Donlon.

A fast-moving and funny film that follows the career of Tracy from carnival barker to top show biz agent. Part of his success is due to the fiery Velez, a carnival coochie dancer whom he turns into an overnight celebrity. There's a great scene with Tracy blackmailing Morgan (better known as the title character from THE WIZARD OF OZ) with an uncompromising photograph of Velez and Morgan. The action is fast-paced and furious. The story is a little far-fetched but the effect is plenty of good fun.

d, Gregory LaCava; w, Bartlett McCormack, Corey Ford, LaCava (based on a story by Ben Markson, H.N. Swanson, from the book *Phantom Fame* by Harry Reichenbach); ph, Bert Glennon; ed, C.K. Kimball.

Comedy **(PR:A MPAA:NR)**

HALF PAST MIDNIGHT** (1948) 69m FOX bw

Kent Taylor *(Wade Hamilton)*, Peggy Knudsen *(Sally Parker)*, Joe Sawyer *(Joe Nash)*, Walter Sande *(Mac)*, Gil Stratton, Jr. *(Chick Patrick)*, Martin Kosleck *(Cortez)*, Mabel Paige *(Hester Thornwall)*, Jean Wong *(Blossom)*, Jane Everett *(Carlotta)*, Damien O'Flynn *(Murphy Evans)*, Richard Lee *(Lee Gow)*, Tom Dugan *(Barker)*, Jean De Briac, Willie Best, Victor Sen Yung, Mettlepuss Lewis.

Routine mystery finds Taylor as a detective who meets up with Knudsen in a nightclub where she's being blackmailed by a dancer. That same night the dancer is murdered and Knudsen becomes a prime suspect. She and Taylor take off to find the real killer, with the police close on their tail. Knudsen is cleared in the end as the young detective manages to find the culprit. This already weak mystery is further hampered by divulging the killer's identity too soon. It is also filled with all the standard B-movie crime motifs which follow one another a little too quickly for the movie's own good.

p, Sol M. Wurtzel; d, William F. Claxton; w, Arnold Belgard; ph, Benjamin Kline; m, Darrell Calker; ed, Frank Baldridge; md, David Chudnow; art d, George Van Marter.

Murder Mystery **(PR:A MPAA:NR)**

HALF PINT, THE** (1960) 73m STER bw

Pat Goldin *(The Tramp)*, Tommy Blackman *(The Half Pint)*, Ray Cordell *(Grandpa)*, Douglas Lockwood *(Sandy)*, Dinke *(Tinker the Chimp)*.

This light-hearted family film revolves around the adventures of a hobo, a runaway chimpanzee, and a six-year-old everyone thinks is lost. The boy, played by Blackman, is trying to find Dinke, his chimp, who's chasing a tramp, played in a Chaplinesque manner by Goldin. Grandpa Cordell, presuming that Blackman has been kidnaped, soon has the police involved in the merry chase. Our happy ending sees Cordell, young Blackman, and the chimp all reunited at the police station. Director Jourdan has a talent for searching out geometric angles and patterns which have been creatively integrated into the film.

p,d&w, Erven Jourdan; ed, Carl Mahakian.

Family Comedy **(PR:AAA MPAA:NR)**

HALF SHOT AT SUNRISE*** (1930) 75m RKO bw

Bert Wheeler *(Tommy)*, Robert Woolsey *(Gilbert)*, John Rutherford *(M.P. Sergeant)*, George MacFarlane *(Col. Marshall)*, Roberta Robinson *(Eileen)*, Leni Stengel *(Olga)*, Dorothy Lee *(Annette)*, Hugh Trevor *(Lt. Jim Reed)*, Edna May Oliver *(Mrs. Marshall)*, Eddie de Lange *(Military Policeman)*, E.H. Calvert *(Gen. Hale)*, Alan Roscoe *(Capt. Jones)*, The Tiller Sunshine Girls.

The Broadway and vaudeville comedy team of Wheeler and Woolsey attack the big screen with lots of heart, and the result is good fun. They portray two enlisted men who go AWOL in Paris and disguise themselves as officers to elude the M.P.'s. Their colonel is also in Paris, along with his two lovely daughters, one of whom is Lee, and before long she and Wheeler become romantically entangled. Plenty of comic complications arise as the film builds up to a final battle scene. As usual, the Wheeler-Woolsey team is terrific, carrying the story with their own unique brand of slapstick. Lee is wonderful opposite Wheeler and went on to play his sweetheart in the four other films made by this comedy team. Steiner received his first credit as music director in this film. All in all, HALF SHOT AT SUNRISE is a wonderful, freewheeling affair from a very talented and unfortunately forgotten pair.

d, Paul Sloane; w, James Ashman Creelman, Anne Caldwell, Ralph Spence (based on a story by Creelman); ph, Nick Musuraca; ed, Arthur Roberts; md, Max Steiner; ch, Mary Read; m/l, "Nothing But Love," Caldwell, Harry Tierney.

Comedy **Cas.** **(PR:A MPAA:NR)**

HALF-WAY HOUSE, THE*** (1945, Brit.) 78m EAL/A.F.E.

Francoise Rosay *(Alice Meadows)*, Tom Walls *(Capt. Harry Meadows)*, Mervyn Johns *(Rhys)*, Glynis Johns *(Gwyneth)*, Alfred Drayton *(Oakley)*, Esmond Knight *(David Davies)*, Richard Bird *(Sub-Lt. Richard French)*, Philippa Hiatt *(Margaret)*, Sally Ann Howes *(Joanna French)*, Guy Middleton *(Fortescue)*, Valerie White *(Jill French)*, Pat McGrath *(Terence)*, C.V. France *(Solicitor)*, John Boxer, Joss Ambler, Eliot Makeham, Jack Jones, Rachel Thomas, Roland Pertwee, Moses Jones.

This eerie mystery has a group of characters meeting at a country inn for the weekend. Among the guests are an infirm symphony conductor, an army officer, a black-market operator, a fallen sea captain and his spiritualist wife, a couple about to get married and another about to get divorced. They notice a strange atmosphere about the inn from the start and the innkeeper and his daughter, played by the two Johns, are very unusual, to say the least. Each of the guests has his or her own set of problems, and things get even more confusing for them when they notice that newspaper and radio broadcasts are a year old. As the bizarre plot unfolds, it is discovered that the Johns are actually ghosts, killed when the inn was bombed a year before. The ghosts' purpose is to teach the guests a few lessons before they leave by lecturing them on their individual vices. Once the ghosts are convinced that the guests have resolved their problems, they send them on their way and the inn once again goes up in a sudden flash of flames. The film is a bit slow in parts, but the acting is excellent, with French actress Rosay handling her first English-speaking role wonderfully. The camera captures the atmosphere of this film well and offers some lovely shots of the English countryside.

p, Michael Balcon; d, Basil Deardeu; w, Angus MacPhail, Diana Morgan (based on the play "The Peaceful Inn" by Denis Ogden); ph, Wilkie Cooper; m, Lord Berners; ed, Charles Haase.

Mystery/Fantasy **(PR:C MPAA:NR)**

HALF WAY TO HEAVEN*½ (1929) 66m PAR bw

Charles "Buddy" Rogers *(Ned Lee)*, Jean Arthur *(Greta Nelson)*, Paul Lukas *(Nick)*, Helen Ware *(Mme. Elsie)*, Oscar Apfel *(Manager)*, Edna West *(Mrs. Lee)*, Nestor Aber *(Eric)*.

The story opens in a carnival lot after Arthur's boy friend is fatally "missed" by jealous Lukas during a trapeze act. Arthur knows it was really murder and escapes from the carnival by hopping a train. There she runs into Rogers and the two become quick friends. What Arthur doesn't know is that Rogers is also a trapeze artist and is on his way to the same carnival troupe to fill in the empty slot. Arthur returns with her new friend and the two eventually expose Lukas as the murderer. The plot and characterizations in HALF WAY TO HEAVEN are all standard, leaving the movie somewhat lifeless.

d&w, George Abbott (based on "Here Comes The Band Wagon" by H.L. Gates); ph, Alfred Gilks; ed, William Shea.

Drama **(PR:A MPAA:NR)**

HALF WAY TO SHANGHAI*½ (1942) 61m UNIV bw

Kent Taylor *(Alexander Barton)*, Irene Hervey *(Vicky Neilson)*, Henry Stephenson *(Col. Blympton)*, J. Edward Bromberg *(Yinpore)*, George Zucco *(Karl Zerta)*, Charles Wagenheim *(Jonathan Peale)*, Alexander Granach *(Nikolas)*, Lionel Royce *(Otto Van Shact)*, Willie Fung *(Mr. Wu)*, Oscar O'Shea *(Mr. McIntyre)*, Charlotte Wynters *(Caroline Wrallins)*, Mary Gordon *(Mrs. McIntyre)*, Fay Helm *(Marion Mills)*, Frank Lackteen *(Conductor)*.

This entire movie takes place aboard a Shanghai-bound train filled with the expected mixture of strange and unusual characters, including Nazi spies trying to get their hands on some secret maps revealing the Chinese defenses and munitions hiding places. The end sees the spies all rounded up. The script is wholly unoriginal with some noticeable holes in the plot. The characterizations lack clarity.

p, Paul Malvern; d, John Rawlins; w, Stuart Palmer; ph, John W. Boyle; ed, Edward Curtiss; md, H.J. Salter; art d, Jack Otterson.

Mystery **(PR:C MPAA:NR)**

HALLELUJAH**** (1929) 100m MGM bw

Daniel L. Haynes *(Zeke)*, Nina Mae McKinney *(Chick)*, William Fontaine *(Hot Shot)*, Harry Gray *(Parson)*, Fannie Belle DeKnight *(Mammy)*, Everett McGarrity *(Spunk)*, Victoria Spivey *(Missy Rose)*, Milton Dickerson, Robert Couch, Walter Tait *(Johnson Kids)*, Dixie Jubilee Singers *(Themselves)*.

This was the first all-black feature film and one of the boldest pictures ever made, especially in view of the fact that MGM knew it would not get much of a release in the deep South. Using many amateurs (Gray had been a janitor at a Harlem newspaper, and McKinney had never been in front of a camera), Vidor proves his genius by eliciting performances from the melange as good as anything you might see in a seasoned troupe. Even today, more than half a century later, this film is not dated. Vidor was a man vitally interested in social issues, as witnessed by his work on THE BIG PARADE and THE CROWD, and he wanted to show the rest of America what the black man was going through. Shot on location in Tennessee, every frame is redolent with authenticity. McKinney is the female lead, a vibrant beauty living among the lowlifes. Haynes is an innocent young man who is very close to his mother, DeKnight, and brother, McGarrity. Later, McGarrity is accidentally shot to death by Haynes who then turns to religion. Some of it gets overly melodramatic, with holy roller meetings, a wake, cabarets and various scenes on the plantation; but it is filled with humanity and a true understanding of the way it was back then. It's a huge film, and no expense was spared to recreate various eras. The love scenes were matter of fact and quite believable. Tunes include "At The End Of The Road," "Swanee Shuffle" (Irving Berlin), and almost every traditional spiritual ever done. Spivey, oddly, didn't have a song to do in the picture, and she is one of the few actors who had any sort of reputation as a singer. Irving Thalberg, the tiny, very young chief of production at MGM, will always be remembered as a man of integrity, and nowhere did he show it more than when he gave Vidor the green light to make HALLELUJAH. This was Vidor's first talkie but was shot as a silent with sound added in post-production. This also may have been the first time a director's name appeared above the title on the credits, something the Writers Guild of America has been fighting ever since.

p&d, King Vidor; w, Wanda Tuchock, Ransom Rideout (based on a story by Vidor); ph, Gordon Avil; m, Irving Berlin; ed, Hugh Wynn, Anson Stevenson; art d, Cedric Gibbons.

Black Drama **(PR:A MPAA:NR)**

HALLELUJAH, I'M A BUM*** (1933) 83m UA bw (GB: HALLELUJAH, I'M A TRAMP; AKA, NEW YORK; THE HEART OF NEW YORK; HAPPY GO LUCKY; THE OPTIMIST; LAZY BONES)

Al Jolson *(Bumper)*, Madge Evans *(June Marcher)*, Frank Morgan *(Mayor Hastings)*, Harry Langdon *(Egghead)*, Chester Conklin *(Sunday)*, Tyler Brooke *(Mayor's Secretary)*, Tammany Young *(Orlando)*, Bert Roach *(John)*, Edgar Connor *(Acorn)*, Dorothea Wolbert *(Apple Mary)*, Louise Carver *(Ma Sunday)*, Richard Rodgers, Lorenz Hart *(Bank Tellers)*, Harold Goodwin, Burr McIntosh.

They renamed this HALLELUJAH, I'M A TRAMP in Great Britain because the word "bum" means something very different and would have been unacceptable to genteel folk. Behrman's screenplay of Hecht's original story is done in rhyming couplets (with help from Lorenz Hart), and that may disturb some ears but their wit is evident in every line. Jolson is a happy tramp who lives in New York's Central Park, and happens to be friends with the mayor of New York, played by Morgan (who replaced Roland Young when he fell ill a few reels into the film). One day Morgan has an argument with his mistress, Evans, and she attempts suicide by jumping in a lake. Jolson rescues her, but she is suddenly stricken with amnesia from the experience. The tramp is now a hero in her eyes and she falls madly in love with him. Jolson too has amorous feelings toward Evans and decides to make a home for her and lead the straight life. He soon gets a job and they are ecstatically happy with their new life, until Morgan tells Jolson of his dire need for his former flame. Out of a sense of honor toward his old friend, Jolson brings the two together in a meeting which causes Evans to snap out of her amnesia and forget ever having known Jolson. In fact, when she looks around at the shabby rooming-house and then at Jolson, she is taken aback with disdain and quickly exits with Morgan. A saddened Jolson returns to being a bum but, of course, will never be the same again. This was a bold film for Jolson who, until then, had contented himself with playing himself. Here, he's sort of a benevolent Mac The Knife, with overtones of Chaplin's Little Fella. The integration of the tunes by Rodgers and Hart (who appear briefly in the film as bankers) was perfectly handled by Milestone and the songs do flow well from the rhymed dialog. Some of them include: "You Are Too Beautiful," "I'll Do It Again," "I've Got To Get Back To New York," "What Do You Want With Money?" "Hallelujah, I'm A Bum" (which had to be re-recorded for the British market). An attempt at this kind of rhyming screenplay was made years later in THE PIED PIPER OF HAMELIN, a TV movie starring Van Johnson that was later released as a feature. Neither was successful as audiences must have felt that rhymed dialog seemed too stilted for their tastes.

p&d, Lewis Milestone; w, S.N. Behrman (based on a story by Ben Hecht); ph, Lucien Adriot; md, Alfred Newman; art d, Richard Day; m/l, Richard Rodgers, Lorenz Hart.

Musical/Comedy **(PR:A MPAA:NR)**

HALLELUJAH THE HILLS½** (1963) 88m Vermont bw

Peter H. Beard *(Jack)*, Martin Greenbaum *(Leo)*, Sheila Finn *(Jack's Vera-Winter)*, Peggy Steffans *(Leo's Vera-Summer)*, Jerome Raphel *(Father)*, Blanche Dee *(Mother)*, Jerome Hill *(1st Convict)*, Taylor Mead *(2nd Convict)*, Emsh *(Gideon)*.

Right out of the early 1960s independent underground film movement comes this fine comedy. The thin story line has to do with a pair of young men, Beard and Greenbaum, pursuing the same young lady at different times of the year. Thus she is played by two actresses; one for winter (Finn) and one for summer (Steffans). The girl's parents are also featured: a wise-cracking father and a no-nonsense mother. Ultimately the two would-be suitors each end up losing the girl to the same bearded stranger. The film plays around with time, space, and character, giving a remarkable freshness to it, and hints of influence by French *nouvelle vague* film making. The Mekas brothers had made a name for themselves on the underground film circuit with their original approaches to film making. Here Adolfas Mekas shows a remarkable flair for visuals, using his forest settings well. The film is packed full of gags and silliness, having a good time with itself and movie cliches. The ending juxtaposes HALLELUJAH THE HILLS' characters with the actual ending from Griffith's classic silent WAY DOWN EAST with Lillian Gish and Richard Barthelmess. HALLELUJAH THE HILLS is a personable and fun bit of film making.

p, David C. Stone; d&w, Adolfas Mekas; ph, Ed Emshviller; m, Meyer Kupferman; ed, Mekas; set d, Shizen; cos, Bathsheba.

Comedy **(PR:C MPAA:NR)**

HALLELUJAH TRAIL, THE½** (1965) 152m Kappa-Mirisch/UA c

Burt Lancaster *(Col. Thadeus Gearhart)*, Lee Remick *(Cora Templeton Massingale)*, Jim Hutton *(Capt. Paul Slater)*, Pamela Tiffin *(Louise Gearhart)*, Donald Pleasence *(Oracle Jones)*, Brian Keith *(Frank Wallingham)*, Martin Landau *(Chief Walks-Stooped-Over)*, John Anderson *(Sgt. Buell)*, Tom Stern *(Kevin O'Flaherty)*, Robert J. Wilke *(Chief Five Barrels)*, Jerry Gatlin *(1st Brother-in-Law)*, Larry Duran *(2nd Brother-in-Law)*, Jim Burk *(Elks-Runner)*, Dub Taylor *(Clayton Howell)*, John McKee *(Rafe Pike)*, Helen Kleeb *(Henrietta)*, Noam Pitlik *(Interpreter)*, Carl Pitti *(Phillips)*, Bill Williams *(Brady)*, Marshall Reed *(Carter)*, Caroll Adams *(Simmons)*, Ted Markland *(Bandmaster)*, Bing Russell *(Horner)*, Billy Benedict *(Simpson)*, Karla Most *(Mary Ann)*, Elaine Martone *(Loretta)*, Hope Summers *(Mrs. Hasselrad)*, Carroll Henry *("A" Company Sgt.)*, Whit Bissell *(Hobbs)*, Val Avery *(Denver Bartender)*, John Dehner *(Narrator)*.

This is a farce about the Old West and the western films. The humor that gets the film started has Denver about to face the winter of 1887 without a drop of whiskey to gladden the tidings. This sets up situations for a whole range of characters and resulting ways they handle the crisis. Remick is leader of the local temperance union-whiskey guardians. They are traveling to Denver under the hopefully safe guard of the cavalry, led by Lancaster. Of course no one can touch a drop of the precious liquid, save for Remick who uses it "for medicinal purposes." Landau hysterically portrays the deadpan leader of a whiskey-craving band of Sioux. Basically it's all a one-joke plot with a few vignettes and gags strung on along the way. The whole thing is held together by an understated narration, which itself is fairly clever. Though directed with the appropriate mix of tongue-in-cheek and out-and-out slapstick, the film runs too long at more than two hours.

p&d, John Sturges; w, John Gay (based on the novel by Bill Gulick); ph, Robert Surtees (Ultra Panavision, Technicolor); m, Elmer Bernstein; ed, Ferris Webster; art d, Cary Odell; set d, Hoyle Barrett; cos, Edith Head; spec eff, A. Paul Pollard; m/l, "Hallelujah Trail," "March To Denver," "We Will Save," Ernie Sheldon.

Comedy/Western Cas. (PR:A MPAA:NR)

HALLIDAY BRAND, THE*** (1957) 79m UA bw

Joseph Cotten *(Daniel)*, Viveca Lindfors *(Aleta)*, Betsy Blair *(Martha)*, Ward Bond *(Big Dan)*, Bill Williams *(Clay)*, Jay C. Flippen *(Chad Burris)*, Christopher Dark *(Jivaro)*, Jeanette Nolan *(Nante)*, Glenn Strange, John Dierkes, I. Stanford Jolley, John Ayres, Robin Short, Jay Lawrence, George Lynn, John Halloran, Michael Hinn.

An intense western drama finds Cotten as the son of all-ruling patriarch and sheriff Bond, who is involved in a series of injustices which disgust his son. Cotten leaves but again returns home, only to be outraged once more when his father refuses to stop a lynch mob from killing the half-breed lover of his sister. When Cotten rebels, he is branded an outlaw by his father. The film climaxes with Cotten facing his father, who is lying on his death bed. Bond points a gun at Cotten, and cocks it—only to die before he can pull the trigger. Told in flashback the film reveals an enormous sense of emotion within each character: the father's loyalty to the family name (from whence comes the film's title); the son's desire for justice; Blair as Bond's daughter, who disapproves but is blindly loyal to her father. Wilson's musical score adds to the first-rate acting and directing.

p, Collier Young; d, Joseph H. Lewis; w, George W. George, George S. Slavin; ph, Ray Rennahan; m, Stanley Wilson; ed, Stuart O'Brien; cos, Irving Leavitt, Patty Page.

Western/Drama (PR:C MPAA:NR)

HALLOWEEN**** (1978) 93m Falcon/Compass c

Donald Pleasence *(Loomis)*, Jamie Lee Curtis *(Laurie)*, Nancy Loomis *(Annie)*, P.J. Soles *(Lynda)*, Charles Cyphers *(Brackett)*, Kyle Richards *(Lindsey)*, Brian Andrews *(Tommy)*, John Michael Graham *(Bob)*, Nancy Stephens *(Marion)*, Arthur Malet *(Graveyard Keeper)*, Mickey Yablans *(Richie)*, Brent LePage *(Lonnie)*, Adam Hollander *(Keith)*, Robert Phalen *(Dr. Wynn)*, Tony Moran *(Michael at 23)*, Will Sandin *(Michael at 6)*, Sandy Johnson *(Judith)*, David Kyle *(Boyfriend)*, Peter Griffith *(Laurie's Father)*, Jim Windburn *(Stunt)*, Nick Castle *(The Shape)*.

Nothing short of a modern classic, HALLOWEEN is a brilliant example of cinematic style. The story is pretty straightforward: on Halloween night, 1963, a 6-year-old boy stabs his sister and her boy friend to death while they are making love. He's put away in a mental institution but exactly 15 years later, he escapes and returns to his small Illinois town to once more wreak Halloween havoc. It's a basic plot made into something special by director Carpenter. The film opens with a point of view shot—a long take seen from beneath a Halloween mask. We see the entire set up through the killer's eyes, and only after the brutal slashing do we discover we have just watched a six-year-old's insane vision. Every shot is compelling and helps us realize what movies are all about. One of the best aspects of HALLOWEEN is not only what we see but what we do not see. There is very little blood in the murder scenes; rather that is left to the viewer's mind. The intensity of the film is sustained from start to finish with plenty of surprises you don't want to see but look at anyway. Even a group of girls playing a joke by peering around a bush is harrowing: is he there or isn't he? The ending is equally frightening as Curtis fends off the maniac and seemingly kills him time after time, only to have him rise again. We see the killer's face only once and that is as the little boy. The adult is always in mask and frighteningly silent. Some critics complained that the only girls killed in HALLOWEEN were the ones that fooled around, while virgin Curtis survived. While this may be a legitimate complaint, it unfortunately is one of the staples on the teen horror market that Carpenter had to work with. A low-budget film, HALLOWEEN has grossed well over $50 million, thus making it the single most successful independent feature of all time. It was the surprise hit of the 1978 Chicago Film Festival. Critics were all full of praise, comparing it with Hitchcock's classic PSYCHO (which starred Curtis' mother, Janet Leigh). HALLOWEEN has the double-dubious honor of spawning a video game and inspiring far too many inferior imitation films. Two sequels, both produced by Carpenter, were dull compared to the original.

p, Debra Hill; d, John Carpenter; w, Hill, Carpenter; ph, Dean Cundey (Panavision, Metrocolor); m, Carpenter; ed, Tommy Lee Wallace, Charles Burnstein; prod d, Wallace; set d, Craig Stearns.

Horror Cas. (PR:O MPAA:R)

HALLOWEEN II*½ (1981) 92m DD/UNIV c

Jamie Lee Curtis *(Laurie)*, Donald Pleasence *(Sam Loomis)*, Charles Cyphers *(Leigh)*, Jeffrey Kramer *(Graham)*, Lance Guest *(Jimmy)*, Pamela Susan Shoop *(Karen)*, Hunter Von Leer *(Gary)*, Dick Warlock *(The Shape)*, Leo Rossi *(Budd)*, Gloria Gifford *(Mrs. Alves)*, Tawny Moyer *(Jill)*, Ana Alicia *(Janet)*, Ford Rainey *(Dr. Mixter)*, Cliff Emmich *(Garrett)*, Nancy Stephens *(Marion)*, John Zenda *(Marshall)*, Catherine Bergstrom *(Producer)*, Alan Haufrect *(Announcer)*, Lucille Bensen *(Mrs. Elrod)*, Bill Warlock *(Craig)*, Jonathan Prince *(Randy)*, Leigh French, Ty Mitchell, Nancy Loomis, Pamela McMyler, Dennis Holahan, Nichole Drucker, Ken Smolka, Adam Gunn, Roger Hampton, Robin Coleman, Jack Verbois, Tony Moran, Kyle Richards, Brian Andrews, Anne Bruner.

A totally unnecessary and extremely poor sequel to the original HALLOWEEN, with Hill and Carpenter once again producing. You'd never think they were capable of the original classic by what goes on in HALLOWEEN II. The cinematic style and sparing use of violence are replaced with plenty of blood and gore that is more repulsive than frightening. However, the plot line (crazed killer on the loose) is the same, as are the surviving cast members of the first film. But the director is now Rosenthal, and the differences are obvious. Rosenthal claimed that Carpenter came in at the end of the shooting and personally directed some gore sequences, though crew members claim this was done to salvage the mess Rosenthal had created. Carpenter himself kept mum on the entire subject. Watch for a thrown-in clip from NIGHT OF THE LIVING DEAD.

p, Debra Hill, John Carpenter; d, Rick Rosenthal; w, Carpenter, Hill; ph, Dean Cundey (Panavision, Metrocolor) m, Carpenter, Alan Howarth; ed, Mark Goldblatt, Skip Schoolnik; prod d, Michael Riva.

Horror Cas. (PR:O MPAA:R)

HALLOWEEN III: SEASON OF THE WITCH** (1982) 96m UNIV c

Tom Atkins *(Dr. Challis)*, Stacey Nelkia *(Ellie)*, Dan O'Herlihy *(Conal)*, Ralph Strait *(Buddy)*, Michael Currie *(Rafferty)*, Jadeen Barbor *(Betty)*, Bradley Schachter *(Little Buddy)*, Garn Stephens *(Marge)*, Nancy Kyes *(Linda)*, Jon Terry *(Starker)*, Patrick Pankurst *(Technician)*, Al Berry *(Harry)*, Wendy Wessberg *(Teddy)*, Dick Warlock *(Assassin)*, Norman Merrill *(Red)*, Michelle Walker *(Bella)*, Joshua Miller *(Willie)*, Essex Smith *(Jones)*, Martin Cassidy *(Watcher)*, Maidie Norman *(Nurse)*, John MacBride *(Sheriff)*, Loyd Catlett *(Charlie)*, Paddie Edwards *(Secretary)*, Jeffrey D. Henry, Michael W. Green *(Technicians)*.

Though the name's the same (as are some of the production credits) this film has nothing to do with its predecessors. The mad slasher has been replaced by O'Herlihy, a mad scientist/mask maker who wants to destroy all the world's children. You can guess what night he picks to do this on. This film can't really make up its mind: does it want to be a "fun" little science fiction piece (at times it's quite funny) or does it want to go the usual blood and gore route. Noted science fiction writer Nigel Kneale wrote the original screenplay but had his name removed from the final production, with writing credits going to director Wallace. A fairly routine shocker.

p, John Carpenter, Debra Hill; d&w, Tommy Lee Wallace; ph, Dean Cundey (Panavision, Technicolor); m, Carpenter, Alan Howarth; ed, Millie Moore; prod d, Peter Jamison; spec eff, Jon G. Belyeu; make-up, Tom Burman.

Science Fiction/Horror Cas. (PR:O MPAA:R)

HALLS OF ANGER*** (1970) 100m UA c

Calvin Lockhart *(Quincy Davis)*, Janet MacLachlan *(Lorraine Nash)*, James A. Watson, Jr. *(J.T. Watson)*, Jeff Bridges *(Douglas)*, Rob Reiner *(Leaky Couloris)*, Dewayne Jesse *(Lerone Johnson)*, Patricia Stich *(Sherry Vaughn)*, Roy Jenseon *(Harry Greco)*, John McLiam *(Lloyd Wilkerson)*, Edward Asner *(McKay)*, Lou Frizzell *(Stewart)*, Helen Kleeb *(Rita)*, Luther Whitsett *(Fowler)*, Florence St. Peter *(Miss Rowland)*, Maye Henderson *(Mrs. Taylor)*, Barry Brown, Alex Clark, Paris Earl, Randy Fredericks, Arline Hamlin, Chris Joy, Richard Levin, Kim Manners, Linda Smith, Linda Thomas, Ta-Tanisha, Gary Tigerman, Cal Wilson.

Timely social piece features Lockhart as an ex-basketball star now teaching English in an all-white suburban school. When an integration program starts up, he is reassigned as a vice-principal to the ghetto school where many of his former students are now being bused. There he confronts McLiam, a no-nonsense principal who simply wants to get on the school board and has no sympathy or understanding of the ghetto children at his school. The sudden invasion of white students causes scenes of reverse-racism shown as black confronts white. Lockhart works with a young illiterate by getting him to read *Lady Chatterly's Lover* and thus making remedial reading a popular course. Though he almost ends up quitting in disgust, Lockhart sticks it out to the film's hopeful ending. HALLS OF ANGER was one of the few honest films about the integration programs and their inherent problems. The scenes of the black students harrassing the white students are honest and show prejudice out in the open. This was an issue few "liberal" filmmakers wanted to confront. The social issues and cultural differences are realistically portrayed. Acting is uniformly excellent. Lockhart is fine as the teacher caught up in a volatile situation, and Jesse is naturally engaging as the young illiterate. The camera work is gritty and realistic, using the Los Angeles locations to their fullest extent. The direction is excellent.

p, Herbert Hirschman; d, Paul Bogart; w, John Shaner, Al Ramrus; ph, Burnett Guffey (DeLuxe Color); m, Dave Grusin; ed, Bud Molin; art d, Addison Hehr; m/l, "Reachin' Out To You," Grusin, Norman Gimbel (sung by Maurice Miller).

Drama (PR:O MPAA:GP)

HALLS OF MONTEZUMA*½** (1951) 113m FOX c

Richard Widmark *(Lt. Anderson)*, Walter [Jack] Palance *(Pigeon Lane)*, Reginald Gardiner *(Sgt. Johnson)*, Robert Wagner *(Coffman)*, Karl Malden *(Doc)*, Richard Hylton *(Cpl. Conroy)*, Richard Boone *(Lt. Col. Gilfilan)*, Skip Homeier *(Pretty Boy)*, Don Hicks *(Lt. Butterfield)*, Jack Webb *(Correspondent Dickerman)*, Bert Freed *(Slattery)*, Neville Brand *(Sgt. Zelenko)*, Martin Milner *(Pvt. Whitney)*, Philip Ahn *(Nomura)*, Howard Chuman *(Capt. Makino)*, Frank Kumagai *(Romeo)*, Fred Coby *(Capt. McCreavy)*, Paul Lees *(Capt. Seaman)*, Jack Lee *(Courier)*, Fred Dale *(Pharmacist's Mate)*, Chris Drake *(Frank)*, George Conrad *(Corpsman)*, Harry McKim *(Radioman)*, Bob McLean *(Marine Guard)*, William Hawes *(Paskowicz)*, Roger McGee *(Davis)*, Clarke Stevens *(Recruit)*, Helen Hatch *(Aunt Emma)*, Michael Road *(Ship's Captain)*, Rollin Moriyama *(Fukado)*, Ralph Nagai *(Willie)*, Marion Marshall *(Nurse)*, Harry Carter *(Bos'n Mate)*, Richard Allan *(Pvt. Stewart)*.

Solid WW II action drama has Widmark as a tough but compassionate Marine officer leading his men through one battle after another across the Pacific. Most of the story takes place when Widmark takes a small patrol through enemy-infested territory to take prisoners who will reveal the location of a Japanese rocket site that is impeding the advance of thousands of American troops. With him go young recruits Wagner and Homeier, one-time boxer Palance, tough old pros Freed, Brand, and Webb, along with an eccentric interpreter, Gardiner. They undergo myriad perils and encounter an insidious enemy that whittles their numbers down considerably. They do take a few prisoners who provide the necessary information to destroy the rockets and allow the Marines to advance. Widmark is full of authority and is convincing as the introspective officer. Palance gives the usual neurotic portrayal, this time as a punch-drunk pug, and Homeier is frightening as the kid who goes berserk at being attacked by Japanese and winds up being killed by one of his own men when he attempts to murder prisoners. Milestone, an old hand at war films, again excels with a top-notch production full of fight, taut drama, and telling characterizations.

p, Robert Bassler; d, Lewis Milestone; w, Michael Blankfort; ph, Winton C. Hoch, Harry Jackson (Technicolor); m, Sol Kaplan; ed, William Reynolds; md, Lionel Newman; art d, Lyle Wheeler, Albert Hogstett; cos, Charles Lemaire.

War Drama **(PR:C MPAA:NR)**

HALLUCINATORS, THE (SEE: NAKED ZOO, THE, 1970)

HALLUCINATION GENERATION*½ (1966) 90m SRS/Trans American bw/c

George Montgomery *(Eric)*, Danny Stone *(Bill Williams)*, Renate Kasche *(Lise)*, Tom Baker *(Denny)*, Marianne Kanter *(Carol)*, Steve Rowland *(Stan)*, Claude Gersene *(Eric's Boy)*.

Montgomery portrays a Timothy Leary inspired LSD guru with a band of dropped-out, turned-on American followers on a Spanish resort island. Stone is a good boy who doesn't join in the LSD parties until his mother cuts off his allowance. He then joins the others in a crime spree that culminates in the murder of an antique dealer, causing Stone to flee to a monastery. The drug is used as a marquee draw and as an excuse for much unmotivated action. The psychedelic drug trips are in color, while the real world is filmed in black and white.

p, Nigel Cox; d&w, Edward A. Mann; ph, Francisco Sempere; m, Bernardo Segall; ed, Fima Noveck; spec eff, Mann, Manuel Sayans.

Drama **Cas.** **(PR:C MPAA:NR)**

HAMILE* (1965, Ghana) 120m Ghana Film Industry bw

Joe Akonor *(King/Claudius)*, Kofi Middleton-Mends *(Hamile/Hamlet)*, Ernest Abbeyquaye *(Ibrahim/Polonius)*, Martin Owusu *(Karim/Horatio)*, Kofi Yirenkyi *(Laitu/Laertes)*, Gad Gadugan *(Abdulai/Rosencrantz and Guildenstern)*, Fred Akuffo-Lartey *(Osuru/Osric)*, Jacob Gharbin *(Musa/Marcellus)*, Franklin Akrofi *(Banda/Bernardo)*, Kwame Adunuo *(Mahama/Francisco)*, Samuel Adumuah *(Awudu/Reynaldo)*, Frances Sey *(Queen/Gertrude)*, Mary Yirenkyi *(Habiba/Ophelia)*, Auhofe Okuampa *(1st Gravedigger)*, Shanco Bruce *(2nd Gravedigger)*, Sandy Arkhurst *(Ghost)*.

This version of Shakespeare's "Hamlet" has the novelty factor, but little else to recommend. It's a filmed version of the University of Ghana's production of the play, in the original English. It undoubtedly did not go over well with the natives of Tongo (where the action was transplanted from Denmark), and the cinematic version is not any better. It is much too stagy a presentation to work as a film, and the production itself is clearly a college, rather than professional, ensemble.

p, Joe de Graft; d, Terry Bishop; w, William Shakespeare; ph, R. O. Fenuku; ed, Egbert Adieso.

Drama **(PR:C MPAA:NR)**

HAMLET**** (1948, Brit.) 155m Rank-TC/GFD bw

Laurence Olivier *(Hamlet)*, Eileen Herlie *(Queen Gertrude)*, Basil Sydney *(King Claudius)*, Jean Simmons *(Ophelia)*, Norman Wooland *(Horatio)*, Felix Aylmer *(Polonius)*, Terence Morgan *(Laertes)*, Stanley Holloway *(Gravedigger)*, John Laurie *(Francisco)*, Edmond Knight *(Bernardo)*, Anthony Quayle *(Marcellus)*, Niall McGinnis *(Captain)*, Harcourt Williams *(Player)*, Peter Cushing *(Osric)*, Russell Thorndike *(Priest)*, Patrick Troughton *(Player King)*, Tony Tarver *(Player Queen)*, Christopher Lee, Anthony Bushell *(Bits)*, Sir John Gielgud *(Voice of Hamlet's Ghost)*.

Oscars for the Best Picture, Olivier (Best Actor), Best Costume Design, Best Set Decoration and Best Art Direction (the latter three designated for black and white films), were awarded to this version of HAMLET. Changes were made from the play, including the jettisoning of Rosencrantz and Guildenstern, as well as some other famous sequences and, at 155 minutes, it was deeply cut from the over four-hour stage version. Basically a story of vengeance, Hamlet swears to his father's ghost that he will wreak revenge for the man's murder by taking the life of Claudius, who is now married to Hamlet's mother, Gertrude. Everyone who has ever played Hamlet has given it his (or her) own interpretation. Olivier was 41 when he made this film—perhaps a bit too lengthy for him as it stood. By cutting the text, he has fashioned a tighter, albeitly *Reader's Digest* abridged version, of the famed play. Olivier had a history of attempting Shakespeare for the screen. In 1936, he was Orlando in AS YOU LIKE IT, then played HENRY V in 1944. After HAMLET, he went on to do RICHARD III, OTHELLO, and even narrated ROMEO AND JULIET in the mid-1960s. It was expensive for 1948 (more than $2 million, which was twice what Rank had originally committed to the project), and was not a success as a major release. It was finally relegated to the art houses where it can still be seen from time-to-time. One of the flaws is that Olivier in directing, should have concentrated more on acting. He had apparently fallen in love with the camera and used many amateur tricks instead of sticking to the immortal words of the immortal Bard. But Olivier has always felt that each different Hamlet is an essay, subject to the individual's interpretation. HENRY V had been done in color and many wondered why Olivier chose black and white for HAMLET, but his reasons were sound and in keeping with the mood of the piece, as well as for various technical problems that arose while doing deep-focus photography. Olivier dyed his hair blonde so no one would feel that it was him playing the melancholy Dane. Rather, he wanted them to feel that what they were seeing was Hamlet himself. Jean Simmons goes properly mad as Ophelia and a very youthful Quayle makes his film debut.

p&d, Laurence Olivier w, Alan Dent (based on the play by William Shakespeare); ph, Desmond Dickinson; m, William Walton; ed, Helga Cranston; prod d, Roger Furse; md, John Hollingsworth, Muir Mathieson; art d, Carmen Dillon; set d, Roger Ramsdell; cos, Elizabeth Hennings; spec eff, Paul Sheriff, Henry Harris, Jack Whitehead; makeup Tony Sforzini.

Drama **Cas.** **(PR:A MPAA:NR)**

HAMLET*½** (1962, Ger.) 130m Dmytryk-Weiler/Bavaria Atelier Gesellschaft bw

Maximillian Schell *(Hamlet)*, Hans Caninberg *(Claudius)*, Wanda Roth *(Gertrude)*, Dunja Movar *(Ophelia)*, Franz Schafheitlin *(Polonius)*, Dieter Kirchlechner *(Laertes)*, Karl Michael Vogler *(Horatio)*, Eckard Dux *(Rosencrantz)*, Herbert Botticher *(Guildenstern)*, Karl Lieffen *(Osric)*, Rolf Boysen *(Bernardo)*, Michael Paryla *(Francisco)*, Alezander Engel *(The Ghost)*, Adolf Gerstung *(First Player)*, Paul Verhoeven *(Gravedigger)*.

Schell takes a shot at the best part in all theatre and comes away pretty well in this originally made-for-German-TV film. There are some nice directorial touches, but on the whole this film is hurt by the difficulties in translating Shakespeare's Elizabethan prose into German—then dubbing the German actors back into English.

p, Hans Gottschalk; d&w, Franz Peter Wirth (based on a translation by A.W. von Schlegel of the play by William Shakespeare); ph, Kurt Gewissen, Hermann Gruber, Rudolf H. Jakob, Boris Geriup; m, Rolf Unkel.

Drama **(PR:A MPAA:NR)**

HAMLET**** (1964) 199m Electronovision-Theatrofilm/WB bw

Frederick Young *(Bernardo)*, Michael Ebert *(Francisco)*, Barnard Hughes *(Marcellus)*, Robert Milli *(Horatio)*, Alfred Drake *(Claudius)*, Philip Coolidge *(Voltimand)*, Hugh Alexander *(Cornelius)*, John Cullum *(Laertes)*, Hume Cronyn *(Polonius)*, Richard Burton *(Hamlet)*, Eileen Herlie *(Gertrude)*, John Gielgud *(Voice of Ghost)*, Dillon Evans *(Reynaldo)*, Clement Fowler *(Rosencrantz)*, William Redfield *(Guildenstern)*, George Voskovec *(Player King)*, John Hetherington *(Player Prologue)*, Christopher Culkin *(Player Queen)*, Geoff Garland *(Lucianus)*, Michael Ebert *(Fortinbras)*, Alex Giannini *(Messenger)*, Richard Sterne *(Gentleman)*, George Rose *(1st Gravedigger)*, Hugh Alexander *(2nd Gravedigger)*, Barnard Hughes *(Priest)*, Dillon Evans *(Osric)*, Hugh Alexander *(English Ambassador)*, Alex Giannini, Frederick Young, Claude Harz, John Hetherington, Gerome Ragni, Linda Seff, Carol Teitel *(Lords, Ladies, and Attendants)*.

This version of Shakespeare's play "Hamlet" was filmed in some murky, mysterious process known as Electronovision with no less than 15 cameras simultaneously recording a single live performance directed for the Broadway stage by John Gielgud and starring an energetic Richard Burton as the Prince of Denmark. At 199 minutes, it is probably the only film of Shakespeare's masterwork not to cut out vast sections of the text, and the cast is superb. Originally this film was intended to be released for two days only, on a reserved seat basis.

p, William S. Sargent, Jr., Alfred W. Crown; d&ph, Bill Colleran (Electronovision); ed, Bruce Pierce; cos, Jane Greenwood; makeup, Bob Philippe.

Drama **(PR:A MPAA:NR)**

HAMLET** (1966, USSR) 148m Lenfilm/Lopert bw (GAMLET)

Innokenti Smoktunovsky *(Hamlet)*, Mikhail Nazvanov *(King)*, Elsa Radzin *(Queen)*, Yuri Tolubeyev *(Polonius)*, Anastasia Vertinskaya *(Ophelia)*, V. Erenberg *(Horatio)*, C. Olesenko *(Laertes)*, V. Medvedev *(Guildenstern)*, I. Dmitriev *(Rosencrantz)*, A. Krevalid *(Fortinbras)*, V. Chekoerski, V. Kolpakov *(Gravediggers)*, A. Chekayevskiy *(The First Player)*, R. Aren *(The Second Player)*, Yu Berkum *(The Third Player)*, A. Lauter *(Priest)*, B. Ilyasov, P. Kilgas, N. Kuzmin, B. Moreno, Andrey Popov, F. Fedorovskiy, V. Shchennikov.

Fairly straightforward screen adaptation of Shakespeare's play performed by the Russians in medieval costume.

d&w, Grigoriy Kozintsev; ph, Ionas Gritsyus (Sovscope); m, Dmitriy Dmitriyevich Shostakovich; ed, Ye. Makhankova; md, N. Rabinovich; art d, Yevgeniy Yeney, G. Kropachyov; cos, Solomon Virsaladze; spec eff, A. Zavyalov, G. Senotov, B. Mikhaylov.

Drama **(PR:C MPAA:NR)**

HAMLET*½** (1969, Brit.) 119m Woodfall-Filmways/COL c

Nicol Williamson *(Hamlet)*, Gordon Jackson *(Horatio)*, Anthony Hopkins *(Claudius)*, Judy Parfitt *(Gertrude)*, Mark Dignam *(Polonius)*, Michael Pennington *(Laertes)*, Marianne Faithfull *(Ophelia)*, Ben Aris *(Rosencrantz)*, Clive Graham *(Guildenstern)*, Peter Gale *(Osric)*, John Carney *(Player King)*, Richard Everett *(Player Queen)*, Roger Livesey *(Lucianus/Gravedigger)*, Robin Chadwick *(Francisco)*, Ian Collier *(Priest)*, Michael Elphick *(Captain)*, Mark Griffith *(Messenger)*, Anjelica Huston *(Court Lady)*, Bill Jarvis *(Courtier)*, Roger Lloyd-Pack *(Reynaldo)*, John Railton *(First Sailor)*, John Trenaman *(Bernardo)*, Jennifer Tudor *(Court Lady)*.

In medieval Denmark, Williamson, portraying Hamlet, arrives home from school to find his father murdered by his uncle, who then marries his widowed mother. The ghost of his father comes to Williamson to tell him to kill the uncle, played by Hopkins. He feigns madness in order to gain the opportunity to slay Hopkins, but he is torn between the desire to avenge his father and his reluctance to shed blood. The end finds most all of them dead. Constantly murky and frequently unintelligible, it's still pure Shakespeare, which makes up for everything else.

p, Neil Hartley; d, Tony Richardson; w, William Shakespeare; ph, Gerry Fisher (Technicolor); m, Patrick Gowers; ed, Charles Rees; prod d, Jocelyn Herbert.

Drama **(PR:A MPAA:G)**

HAMLET** (1976, Brit.) 65m Royal College of Art c

Anthony Meyer, David Meyer, Helen Mirren, Quentin Crisp, Barry Stanton, Vladek Sheybal.

The latest trends in Freudian analysis of literature are staged in this oddity, giving us such spectacles as a schizophrenic Hamlet, played by the two Meyers (who happen to be twins), incest between Meyer and his mother, and many homosexual overtones. If you've seen all the other HAMLETs, you might as well see this surrealistic version for comparison's sake. It was shot on a micro budget of under $5,000.

p,d,&w, Celestino Coronado (based on the play by William Shakespeare); ph, Robina Rose, Dick Perrin, A. Humphreys; m, Carlos Miranda; ed, Richard Melling, Derek Wallbank; set d, Coronado, Anthony Meyer, students of North London Polytechnic; cos, Mircea Marosin, Natasha Korniloff.

Drama **(PR:O MPAA:NR)**

HAMMER** (1972) 92m Essaness/UA c

Fred Williamson *(B.J. Hammer)*, Bernie Hamilton *(Davis)*, Vonetta McGee *(Lois)*, William Smith *(Brenner)*, Charles Lampkin *(Big Sid)*, Elizabeth Harding *(Rhoda)*, Mel Stewart *(Professor)*, D'Urville Martin *(Sonny)*, Stack Pierce *(Roughhouse)*, Jamal Moore *(Henry Jones)*, Nawana Davis *(Mary)*, John Quade *(Riley)*, Johnny Silver *(Tiny)*, John de Carlos *(Bruiser)*, Perrie Lott *(Nagi)*, Leon Isaac *(Bobby Williams)*, Phillip Jackson *(Landlord)*, Al Richardson *(Black Militant)*, Tracy Ann King *("The Black Magic Woman")*, George Wilber *(Irish Joe Brady)*, Gene le Bell *(Referee)*, Jimmy Lennon *(Ring Announcer)*.

Williamson portrays a brawling dock worker, moving up the heavyweight boxing rankings backed by black crime lord Lampkin. Lampkin, in turn, is controlled by the syndicate, and there are typical complications involving dope smuggling and fight fixing. The climax sees Williamson forced to choose between the woman he loves and the title bout. Not quite a classic of black cinema, but HAMMER holds enough action to satisfy. Williamson was a former professional football player who gave himself the nickname "The Hammer."

p, Al Adamson; d, Bruce Clark; w, Charles Johnson; ph, Bob Steadman; m, Solomon Burke; ed, George Folsey, Jr.; art d, Skip Troutman.

Crime **(PR:O MPAA:R)**

HAMMER THE TOFF** (1952, Brit.) 71m Nettlefold/Butchers bw

John Bentley *(Honorable Richard Rollison)*, Patricia Dainton *(Susan Lancaster)*, Valentine Dyall *(Inspector Grice)*, John Robinson *(Linnett)*, Wally Patch *(Bert Ebbutt)*, Katherine Blake *(Janet Lord)*, Roddy Hughes *(Jolly)*, Basil Dignam *(Superintendent)*, Lockwood West *(Kennedy)*, Charles Hawtrey *(Cashier)*, John Powe, Andrea Malandrinos, Ben Williams, Patricia Page, Monte di Lyle, John Mansi, Max Brent, Vivienne Burgess, Michael Mulcaster, Gordon Craig, Ian Fleming, Vi Stevens.

Routine detective yarn in which the suave sleuth Bentley puts his wits to use in assisting Dainton in solving the murder of her uncle. The man originally accused later turns out to be innocent—news that is greeted with enthusiasm as he was a Robin Hood-type thief loved by the poor. Could have been better had the director of the film (based on a novel by John Creasey) put a little bit of creativity into his handling.

p, Ernest G. Roy; d, Maclean Rogers; ph, Geoffrey Faithfull.

Crime **(PR:A MPAA:NR)**

HAMMERHEAD** (1968) 99m COL c

Vince Edwards *(Charles Hood)*, Judy Geeson *(Sue Trenton)*, Peter Vaughan *(Hammerhead)*, Diana Dors *(Kit)*, Michael Bates *(Andreas/Sir Richard)*, Beverly Adams *(Ivory)*, Patrick Cargill *(Condor)*, Patrick Holt *(Huntzinger)*, William Mervyn *(Perrin)*, Douglas Wilmer *(Vendriani)*, Tracy Reed *(Miss Hull)*, Kathleen Byron *(Lady Calvert)*, Jack Woolgar *(Tookey Tate)*, Joseph Furst *(Count Ortega)*, David Prowse *(George)*, Earl Younger *(Brian)*, Romo Gorrara *(Marcel)*, Maggie Wright *(Roselle)*, Veronica Carlson *(Ulla)*, Penny Brahms *(Frieda)*.

Dull spy yarn features Edwards as a US agent trying to infiltrate the lair of villainous-archcriminal, intent on world domination, Vaughan, by pretending to deliver a shipment of vintage pornography. The plot is slow-moving and confusing at times.

p, Irving Allen; d, David Miller; w, William Bast, Herbert Baker (based on a novel by James Mayo); ph, Kenneth Talbot, Wilkie Cooper (Technicolor); m, David Whitaker; ed, Geoffrey Foot; art d, John Howell; cos, Brian Cox; ch, Ralph Tobert.

Spy Drama **(PR:C MPAA:R)**

HAMMERSMITH IS OUT*½ (1972) 108m Cinerama c

Elizabeth Taylor *(Jimmie Jean Jackson)*, Richard Burton *(Hammersmith)*, Peter Ustinov *(Doctor)*, Beau Bridges *(Billy Breedlove)*, Leon Ames *(Gen. Sam Pembroke)*, Leon Askin *(Dr. Krodt)*, John Schuck *(Henry Joe)*, George Raft *(Guido Scartucci)*, Marjorie Eaton *(Princess)*, Lisa Jak *(Kiddo)*, Linda Gaye Scott *(Miss Quim)*, Mel Berger *(Fat Man)*, Anthony Holland *(Oldham)*, Brook Williams *(Peter Rutter)*, Carl Donn *(Cleopatra)*, Jose Espinosa *(Duke)*, Stan Ross *(Patient)*.

Inept Taylor-Burton vehicle is one more variation on the Faust legend with Burton as a lunatic consigned to Ustinov's asylum. There he promises wealth and power to nose-picking male nurse, Bridges, in return for help in escaping. Along with greasy-spoon waitress Taylor, they set out on a string of antisocial, money-making schemes. Before long Bridges has the power and wealth promised him, but Burton and Taylor conspire together to cut him out of the picture. This bloated, uninspired production features Burton staring blankly throughout (director Ustinov told him "Never close your eyes"), but Taylor's screeching, drawling, truck-stop waitress portrayal is not to be missed.

p, Alex Lucas, d, Peter Ustinov; w, Stanford Whitmore; ph, Richard H. Kline; m, Dominic Frontiere; ed, David Blewitt; set d, Robert Benton; cos, Edith Head; m/l, "For Openers," "Requiem," "When Your Dreams Were Worth Remembering," Sally Stevens; makeup, Ron Berkeley.

Drama/Comedy **(PR:C MPAA:R)**

HAMMETT*½** (1982) 100m Orion/WB c

Frederic Forrest *(Hammett)*, Peter Boyle *(Jimmy Ryan)*, Marilu Henner *(Kit Conger/Sue Alabama)*, Roy Kinnear *(English Eddie Hagedorn)*, Elisha Cook *(Eli the Taxi Driver)*, Lydia Lei *(Crystal Ling)*, R.G. Armstrong *(Lt. O'Mara)*, Richard Bradford *(Detective Bradford)*, Michael Chow *(Fong)*, David Patrick Kelly *(Punk)*, Sylvia Sidney *(Donaldina Cameron)*, Jack Nance *(Gary Salt)*, Elmer L. Kline *(Doc Fallon)*, Royal Dano *(Pops)*, Samuel Fuller *(Old Man in Pool Hall)*, Lloyd Kino *(Barber)*, Fox Harris *(News Vendor)*, Rose Wond *(Laundress)*, Liz Roberson *(Lady in Library)*, Jean Francois Ferreol *(Sailor)*, Alison Hong, Patricia Kong *(Young Girls)*, Lisa Lu *(Donaldina's Assistant)*, Andrew Winner *(Guard)*, Kenji Shibuya *(Bouncer)*, James Quinn *(Guard)*.

A highly atmospheric fictional slice of detective writer Dashiell Hammett's life has Forrest in the lead, playing a role he obviously relishes and one where he excels. The locale is San Francisco back in the 1920s when Hammett was quitting the Pinkertons where he had been employed as a detective and was beginning to write his "Continental Op" stories. His old Pinkerton boss, Boyle, upon whose exploits Forrest is basing his stories, shows up and asks Forrest to help him out on a particularly tough case, one dealing with a beautiful Chinese prostitute. She has disappeared and Boyle wants to find her. He and Forrest survive attacks, shootings, druggings, and muggings in San Francisco's fog-bound byways only to discover that the Chinese girl has been blackmailing the city's most influential men, threatening to reveal pornographic photos of them with her unless she receives $1 million. She is thought to be killed but later turns up on a Frisco wharf and Forrest delivers the money to her only to be interrupted by Boyle, who tries to grab it and is shot by Lei for his greedy efforts. She, however, winds up dead in the water, too. Forrest returns to his typewriter to bat out the tale. The lensing is terrific in this moody thriller and it is well directed by Wenders, but the story is a pastiche of many Hammett tales and is sometimes so splintered as to be confusing. Forrest is very effective as the hard-boiled private eye turned writer of hard-boiled detective fiction.

p, Fred Roos, Ronald Colby, Don Guest; d, Wim Wenders; w, Ross Thomas, Dennis O'Flaherty, Thomas Pope (based on the book by Joe Gores); ph, Philip Lathrop, Joseph Biroc (Technicolor); m, John Barry; ed, Barry Malkin, Marc Laub, Robert Q. Lovett, Randy Roberts; prod d, Dean Tavoularis, Eugene Lee; art d, Angelo Graham, Leon Erickson; set d, James Murakami, Bob Goldstein, George R. Nelson, Steve Potter; cos, Ruth Morley.

Crime Drama **Cas.** **(PR:C MPAA:PG)**

HAMNSTED (SEE: PORT OF CALL, 1963 Swed.)

HAMP (SEE: KING AND COUNTRY, 1966, Brit.)

HAMPSTER OF HAPPINESS (SEE: SECOND-HAND HEARTS, 1980)

HANA TO NAMIDA TO HONOO (SEE: PERFORMERS, THE, 1970, Jap.)

HAND, THE** (1960, Brit.) 61m Butcher/AIP bw

Derek Bond *(Roberts and Roger Crawshaw)*, Ronald Leigh Hunt *(Munyard)*, Reed De Rouen *(Michael Brodie)*, Ray Cooney *(Pollitt)*, Bryan Coleman *(Adams)*, Walter Randall *(Japanese Commander)*, Tony Hilton *(Foster)*, Harold Scott *(Charlie Taplow)*, Gwenda Ewen *(Nurse Johns)*, Michael Moore *(Dr. Metcalfe)*, Ronald Wilson *(Doctor)*, Garard Green *(Simon Crawshaw)*, Jean Dallas *(Nurse Geiber)*, David Blake Kelly *(Marshall)*, Reginald Hearne *(Noel Brodie)*, Madeleine Burgess *(Mrs. Brodie)*, Frances Bennett *(Mother)*, Susan Reid *(Little Girl)*, Pat Hicks *(Mrs. Adams)*, John Norman *(Peter Adams)*.

Bizarre crime film that begins during WW II in Burma where a British captain portrayed by Bond, and two of his men, De Rouen and Coleman, are captured and tortured for information. Because of their refusal to talk, De Rouen and Coleman have their right hands severed by their captors. Bond, however, gives in and retains his hand. Years later, a rash of amputation murders spring up in London and the detectives eventually trace the killings to Bond. The police give chase and as Bond flees across some train tracks, he trips and—you guessed it—has his hand severed by an oncoming train.

p, Bill Luckwell; d, Henry Cass; w, Ray Cooney, Tony Hilton; ph, James Harvey; ed, Robert Hill; md, Wilfred Burns; art d, John Earl; makeup, Jimmy Evans.

Crime/Horror **(PR:C MPAA:NR)**

HAND, THE** (1981) 104m Orion/WB c

Michael Caine *(Jon Lansdale)*, Andrea Marcovicci *(Anne Lansdale)*, Annie McEnroe *(Stella Roche)*, Bruce McGill *(Brian Ferguson)*, Viveca Lindfors *(Doctress)*, Rosemary Murphy *(Karen Wagner)*, Mara Hobel *(Lizzie Lansdale)*, Pat Corley *(Sheriff)*, Nicholas Hormann *(Bill Richman)*, Ed Marshall *(Doctor)*, Charles Fleischer *(David Maddow)*, John Stinson *(Therapist)*, Richard Altman *(Hammond)*, Sparky Watt *(Sergeant)*, Tracey Walter *(Cop)*, Brian Kenneth Hume *(Boy in Classroom)*, Lora Pearson *(Girl in Classroom)*, Oliver Stone *(Bum)*, Jack Evans, Scott Evans, Randy Evans, Patrick Evans *(Country Bumpkins)*.

Newspaper cartoonist Caine's career and marriage go out the window when an auto accident claims his right hand. Soon, though, the hand is back, ready to assist Caine to avenge those who did him wrong. Film tries to be grim and relentless, but the basic absurdity of a severed hand scurrying about the floor killing people is a bit too much to take. (Loose remake of THE BEAST WITH FIVE FINGERS.)

p, Edward R. Pressman; d&w, Oliver Stone (based on the book *The Lizard's Tail* by Marc Brandel); ph, King Baggott (Technicolor); m, James Horner; ed, Richard Marks; prod d, John Michael Riva; art d, Richard Sawyer; cos, Ernest Misko; spec eff, Carlo Rambaldi.

Horror **Cas.** **(PR:O MPAA:R)**

HAND IN HAND*** (1960, Brit.) 78m COL bw

Loretta Parry *(Rachel Mathias)*, Philip Needs *(Michael O'Malley)*, John Gregson *(Father Timothy)*, Sybil Thorndike *(Lady Caroline)*, Finlay Currie *(Mr. Pritchard)*, Derek Sydney *(Rabbi Benjamin)*, Miriam Karlin *(Mrs. Mathias)*, Arnold Diamond *(Mr. Mathias)*, Kathleen Byron *(Mrs. O'Malley)*, Barry Keegan *(Mr. O'Malley)*, Martin Lawrence *(The Cantor)*, Barbara Hicks *(Miss Roberts)*, Dennis Gilmore *(Tom)*, Peter Pike *(Harry)*, Susan Reid *(Priscilla)*, Donald Tandy *(George)*, Madge Ryan *(George's Wife)*, Eric Francis, Stratford Johns.

Seven-year old Jewish girl Parry and seven-year old Catholic boy Needs become friends. Their respective parents object and try to keep the two apart, but they resist the bigotry and manage to continue their close bond. Each attends the religious services of the other and is frightened by the strange rituals observed. Intelligent, sympathetic children's film makes a gentle plea for tolerance and love.

p, Helen Winston; d, Philip Leacock; w, Diana Morgan (based on a story by Sidney Harmon); ph, F.A. Young; m, Stanley Black; ed, Peter Tanner; art d, Ivan King.

Drama **(PR:AA MPAA:NR)**

HAND IN THE TRAP, THE½** (1963, Arg./Span.) 90m Angel-Uninci/Angel bw (LA MANO EN LA TRAMPA)

Elsa Daniel *(Laura Lavigne)*, Francisco Rabal *(Cristobal Achaval)*, Leonardo Favio *(Miguel)*, Maria Rosa Gallo *(Ines Lavigne)*, Berta Ortegosa *(Laura's Mother)*, Hilda Suarez *(Laura's Aunt)*, Enrique Vilches *(Postman)*, Maria Puchol, Maria del Pilar Armesto, Mirtha Dubner, Hugo Caprera, Mirko Alvarez.

Haunting drama starring Daniel as a young woman on vacation from boarding school who discovers her aunt (Gallo) cloistered in the attic. Gallo explains to Daniel that she has chosen to stay secluded and alone ever since she was jilted at the altar by her life-long love, the wealthy and handsome Rabal. Daniel decides to reunite Gallo with her lover and sets out to find him. When Daniel locates Rabal she too falls under his spell, but nonetheless lures him into the attic. Upon seeing her former love, Gallo is overwhelmed and dies. After the funeral, Daniel becomes Rabal's mistress and it is only a matter of time until she realizes that she too is left alone—a prisoner of Rabal's love.

p, Nestor R. Gaffet; d, Leopoldo Torre-Nilsson; w, Beatriz Guido, Torre-Nilsson, Ricardo Luna, Ricardo Munoz Suay (based on a story by Guido); ph, Alberto Etchebehere, Juan Julio Baena; m, Atilio Stampone, Cristobal Halffter; ed, Jorge Garate, Pablo Gonzalez del Amo, Jacinto Cascales; art d, Oscar Lagomarsino.

Drama **(PR:C MPAA:NR)**

HAND OF DEATH*½ (1962) 60m AP/FOX bw (AKA: FIVE FINGERS OF DEATH)

John Agar *(Alex Marsh)*, Paula Raymond *(Carol Wilson)*, Steve Dunne *(Tom Holland)*, Roy Gordon *(Dr. Ramsey)*, John Alonzo *(Carlos)*, Jack Younger, Joe Besser, Butch Patrick, Norman Burton, Fred Krone, Kevin Enright, Jack Donner, Chuck Niles, Ruth Terry, Bob Whitney.

Agar plays a research chemist who mistakenly unleashes a poisonous gas that turns him into a bloated, dark monster with a cracked face. He soon discovers that his touch causes instant death. After accidentally killing half a dozen people, Agar realizes he is loosing his mind and nobly walks off into the ocean to drown himself.

p, Eugene Ling; d, Gene Nelson; w, Ling; ph, Floyd Crosby (CinemaScope); m, Sonny Burke; ed, Carl Pierson; md, Burke; set d, Harry Reif; cos, John Intlekofer; makeup, Bob Mark.

Science Fiction **(PR:C MPAA:NR)**

HAND OF NIGHT, THE½** (1968, Brit.) 88m Associated British-Pathe/Schoenfeld c (AKA: BEAST OF MOROCCO)

William Sylvester *(Paul Carver)*, Diane Clare *(Chantal)*, Alizia Gur *(Marisa)*, Edward Underdown *(Gunther)*, Terence De Marney *(Omar)*, William Dexter *(Leclerc)*, Sylvia Marriott *(Mrs. Petty)*, Avril Sadler *(Mrs. Carver)*, Angela Lovell *(Air Hostess)*, Maria Hallowi *(Nurse)*, Boscoe Holder Dancers.

Sylvester plays a man obsessed with guilt over the deaths of his wife and children who were killed in a car wreck. He agrees to accompany Underdown, an archaeologist, to Morocco on a dig. There the crew finds an ancient tomb and Sylvester meets and is seduced by Gur, a mysterious woman who takes him to a Moorish castle. The next morning Underdown and his step-daughter Clare find Sylvester unconscious at the site of a ruin haunted by a vampire, who turns out to be Gur. Clare attempts to break Gur's influence over Sylvester, but she is kidnaped by one of the vampire's servants and left in the desert to die. Eventually Sylvester regains his senses, drives a stake through Gur's evil heart and rescues Clare. Filmed on location in North Africa.

p, Harry Field; d, Fredric Goode; w, Bruce Stewart; ph, William Jordan (Technicolor); m, John Shakespeare, Joan Shakespeare; ed, Fredrick Ives; art d, Peter Moll; spec eff, Biographic Cartoon Films; ch, Boscoe Holder; makeup, Cliff Sharpe.

Horror **(PR:C MPAA:NR)**

HANDCUFFED** (1929) 60m T/C/RAY bw

Virginia Brown Faire *(Gloria Randall)*, Wheeler Oakman *(Tom Bennett)*, Dean Jagger *(Gerald Morely)*, James Harrison *(Billy Hatton)*, Broderick O'Farrell *(John Randall)*, George Chesebro *(Detective)*, Frank Clarke, Charles West.

Jagger's father kills himself after O'Farrell dupes him in a stock swindle. O'Farrell is then murdered by Oakman, who has his butler plant the murder weapon on Jagger. Oakman then makes a play for Faire, who has fallen for Jagger. But the young man is arrested and convicted of murder, leaving the damsel with Oakman. Jagger manages to escape on their wedding night and arrives just as Faire admits her love for him. Oakman, who has had a bit too much to drink, confesses to the crime and dies in a fall. His accomplice in the crime clears Jagger and the two lovebirds are free to marry at last. Though not a bad drama in itself, the script by Hoerl varies little from most of the films he wrote for the studio. The direction also moves this picture a little too slowly, making it just an average film.

d, Duke Worne; w, Arthur Hoerl; ph, Hap Depew; ed, John S. Harrington.

Drama **(PR:A MPAA:NR)**

HANDCUFFS, LONDON** (1955, Brit.) 76m Trinity/Eros bw

Alexander Gauge *(Bardwill)*, Bruce Seton *(Superintendent Fabian)*, Robert Raglan, Noel Howlett, Ursula Howells, Kathleen Byron, Isabel Dean, Maurice Kaufmann, Dorinda Stevens, C. Denier Warren, Michael Craig, Gladys Boot, Derek Aylward.

Seton obtains a rare stamp and goes to art expert Gauge for an appraisal. The stamp proves to be fake, so Seton goes on a hunt for the forger. He must go through three cases before Gauge is revealed to be the man behind the fraud. A fairly unthrilling cops and robbers chase, this film was intended as a three-part television drama before it was reedited for theatrical release.

p, John Larkin; d, Bernard Knowles; w, Brock Williams; ph, Brendan Stafford.

Crime **(PR:A MPAA:NR)**

HANDGUN (SEE: DEEP IN THE HEART, 1983)

HANDLE WITH CARE*½ (1932) 77m FOX bw

James Dunn *(Bill Gordon)*, Boots Mallory *(Helen Barlow)*, El Brendel *(Carl Lundstrom)*, Buster Phelps *(Tommy)*, George Ernest *(Charlie)*, Victor Jory *(1st Public Enemy)*, Pat Hartigan *(Callahan)*, Arthur Vinton *(2nd Public Enemy)*, Frank O'Connor *(Police Lieutenant)*.

Lackluster comedy has Mallory caring for her dead sister's two rambunctious children. Into her life comes the amorous attentions of assistant district attorney Dunn, but the youngsters resent him and drive him away. When they go to his apartment to apologize, they are captured by a couple of hit men who have come to kill Dunn. One of them escapes and warns the police. The climax sees neighborhood children gang up on the thugs and overpower them.

d, David Butler; w, Frank Craven, Sam Mintz (based on a story by Butler); ph, John Schmitz; m, Richard A. Whiting; m/l, Leo Robin (sung by Mallory).

Drama **(PR:A MPAA:NR)**

HANDLE WITH CARE* (1935, Brit.) 55m EM/RKO bw

Molly Lamont *(Patricia)*, Jack Hobbs *(Jack)*, James Finlayson *(Jimmy)*, Henry Victor *(Count Paul)*, Vera Bogetti *(Fifi)*, Margaret Yarde *(Mrs. Tunbody)*, Tonie Edgar Bruce *(Lady Deeping)*, Stafford Hilliard *(Prof. Deeping)*.

A mish-mash of a film about a couple of ex-cons who match their wits with a gang of spies, depending upon a strength pill to achieve their goal. Inane conception that has virtually not a moment of wit or anything else resembling humor.

p, George King, Randall Faye; d, Redd Davis; w, Faye; ph, Geoffrey Faithfull.

Comedy **(PR:A MPAA:NR)**

HANDLE WITH CARE** (1958) 82m MGM bw

Dean Jones *(Zachary Davis)*, Joan O'Brien *(Mary Judson)*, Thomas Mitchell *(Mayor Dick Williston)*, John Smith *(Bill Reeves)*, Walter Abel *(Prof. Bowdin)*, Burt Douglas *(Ray Crowder)*, Anne Seymour *(Matilda Iler)*, Royal Dano *(Al Lees)*, Ted De Corsia *(Sam Lawrence)*, Peter Miller *(Carter)*.

Jones got his first lead in this earnest, unremarkable drama. He's a law student engaged in a class project uncovering evidence of corruption in city hall. After much outrage, it is later revealed that the mayor had issued phony tax receipts to aid economically depressed and drought-stricken families. Overly serious and largely boring.

p, Morton Fine; d, David Friedkin; w, Fine, Friedkin (based on the teleplay "Mock Trial" by Samuel and Edith Grafton); ph, Harold J. Marzorati; m, Alexander Courage; ed, Ben Lewis; art d, William A. Horning, Paul Groesse.

Drama **(PR:A MPAA:NR)**

HANDLE WITH CARE** (1964) 86m Sonac/Cinema Video International c

Georgia Carr *(Melody)*, Otis Greene *(Lonesome)*, Eddie Beale *(Himself)*, Leroy "Sloppy" Daniels *(Swami)*, Ernest "Skillet" Mayhand *(Weary O'Leary)*, Dave Anderson, Cathey Cooper, Carol "Lynne" Stewart.

An all-black musical comedy starring Daniels as an employee of the Brass Rail, a nightclub owned by "Second Rate Kate." One night Daniels loses several hundred dollars in club receipts to a hold-up man and decides to get Mayhand, another club employee, to help him regain the cash. The pair focus their efforts on a young Texan Greene, who is new in town and whom they mistake for a millionaire. Greene, actually an aspiring jazz musician who is dirt poor, gets himself drunk at the club and falls in love with Carr, a singer who can't stand musicians. In the meantime, the money is recovered by Daniels and Mayhand when they spot a drunk carrying a suspicious bag. Greene wakes up in the deserted club and is inspired to play the piano. When Kate hears him she offers him a job. Songs include: "Handle With Care," "Too Little Too Late," and "Sad Dreams and Bitter Teardrops."

p,d,&w, John K. McCarthy; ph, William Troiano (DeLuxe Color); md, Jaime Mendoza-Nava.

Musical Comedy **(PR:A MPAA:NR)**

HANDLE WITH CARE (SEE: CITIZENS BAND, 1977)

HANDS ACROSS THE BORDER½** (1943) 72m REP bw

Roy Rogers *(Roy)*, Ruth Terry *(Kim Adams)*, Guinn "Big Boy" Williams *(Teddy Bear)*, Onslow Stevens *(Brock Danvers)*, Mary Treen *(Sophie Lawrence)*, Joseph

Crehan *(Jeff Adams)*, Duncan Renaldo *(Juan Morales)*, Frederick Burton *(Col. Ames)*, Leroy Mason *(Mac Marclay)*, Larry Steers *(Col. Carter)*, Julian Rivero *(Senor Morales)*, Janet Martin *(Rosita Morales)*, The Wiere Brothers *(Themselves)*, Betty Marion, Chiquita *(Dancers)*, Bob Nolan and the Sons of the Pioneers, "Trigger."

Full-blown, largely plotless Roy Rogers musical extravaganza has Roy helping Terry find the killer of her rancher father. There are two production numbers and a number of songs with a Latin rhythm. (See ROY ROGERS series, Index.)

p, Harry Grey; d, Joseph Kane; w, Bradford Ropes, J. Benton Cheney; ph, Reggie Lanning; ed, Tony Martinelli; md, Morton Scott; art d, Fred Ritter; ch, Dave Gould; m/l, Hoagy Carmichael, Ned Washington, Phil Ohman.

Western **(PR:A MPAA:NR)**

HANDS ACROSS THE TABLE*½** (1935) 81m PAR bw

Carole Lombard *(Regi Allen)*, Fred MacMurray *(Theodore Drew III)*, Ralph Bellamy *(Allen Macklyn)*, Astrid Allwyn *(Vivian Snowden)*, Ruth Donnelly *(Laura)*, Marie Prevost *(Nona)*, Joseph Tozer *(Peter)*, William Demarest *(Matty)*, Edward Gargan *(Pinky Kelly)*, Ferdinand Munier *(Miles, the Butler)*, Harold Minjir *(Couturier at Valentine's)*, Marcelle Corday *(Celeste, the French Maid)*, Bess Flowers *(Diner)*, Harold Miller *(Barber Customer)*, Nell Craig *(Saleslady)*, Jerry Mandy *(Headwaiter)*, Phil Kramer *(Supper Club Waiter)*, Murray Alper *(Cab Driver)*, Nelson McDowell *(Man in Nightshirt)*, Sam Ash *(Maitre D'Hotel)*, Edward Peil, Sr., Jerry Storm, Francis Sayles, Chauncey M. Drake, S.H. Young, Rafael Gavilan, Harry Williams, Sterling Campbell *(Barbers)*, Mary MacLaren *(Chambermaid)*, Rod Wilson *(Piano Player)*, Albert Conti *(Maitre d'Hotel in Speakeasy)*, John Buettner *(Shoe Clerk)*, Pat Sweeney *(Manicurist)*, Alla Mentone *(Saleslady)*, Fred "Snowflake" Toones *(Porter)*, James Adamson *(Porter)*, Peter Allen *(Jewelry Clerk)*, Ira Reed, Dutch Hendrian *(Taxi Drivers)*.

Charming, stylish and light-hearted comedy/romance with snappy badinage and captivating performances from all concerned. Lombard is a manicurist who has been hurt so many times in love that she has become somewhat hardened about amour and is now only interested in marrying for security. She meets Bellamy, who is confined to a wheelchair (a role he was to play again many years later when he did Roosevelt). He is rich, madly in love with her, and has serious matrimonial intentions. MacMurray is a poor playboy from a once-wealthy and prominent family. He is about to marry Allwyn, for the same reasons Lombard may marry Bellamy. When MacMurray comes into Lombard's shop one day, she thinks he is wealthy. While they trade bon mots over his manicure, he invites her to dinner and she accepts. Allwyn had given MacMurray some money for a Bermuda vacation and he blows it on Lombard that evening. By night's end, he is so drunk that he can't make the trip home, so he spends the night at her tiny apartment. When Lombard returns from work the following day, MacMurray does the decent thing and admits that his family's pocketbook is flatter than Kansas. They fall in love and she sheds her previous misgivings about love, then flips a coin to decide which man she will marry. Need we tell you that it's MacMurray she chooses? They decide to get married as soon as he can find a job, thus leaving Allwyn and Bellamy to fend for themselves. Excellent dialog by the trio of screenwriters. A good love story with strong characterizations and believable twists.

p, E. Lloyd Sheldon; d, Mitchell Leisen; w, Norman Krasna, Vincent Lawrence, Herbert Fields (based on the story "Bracelets" by Vina Delmar); ph, Ted Tetzlaff; ed, William Shea; cos, Travis Banton; m/l, Sam Coslow, Mitchell Parish, Jean Delettre, Frederick Hollander.

Comedy **(PR:A MPAA:NR)**

HANDS OF A STRANGER½** (1962) 95m AA bw

Paul Lukather *(Dr. Gil Harding)*, Joan Harvey *(Dina Paris)*, James Stapleton *(Vernon Paris)*, Ted Otis *(Dr. Russ Compton)*, Michael duPont *(Dr. Ken Fry)*, Larry Haddon *(Police Lt. Syms)*, Michael Rye *(George Britton)*, Elaine Martone *(Eileen Hunter)*, George Sawaya *(Cab Driver)*, Barry Gordon *(Skeet)*, David Kramer *(Carnival Barker)*, Sally Kellerman *(Sue)*, Irish McCalla *(Holly)*.

Severed hands are killing again, this time they're from an unidentified murder victim and they've been grafted onto the accident-shortened arms of pianist Stapleton. The victims include the doctors who performed the operation and the now-blind cabbie who caused the accident.

p, Newton Arnold, Michael Du Pont; d&w, Arnold; ph, Henry Cronjager; m, Richard LaSalle; ed, Bert Honey; art d, Theodore Holsopple.

Horror **(PR:C MPAA:NR)**

HANDS OF DESTINY*½ (1954, Brit.) 61m Grosvenor/Adelphi bw

Dr. Josef Ranald, Hilda Fenemore, Terence Alexander, Benedicta Leigh, Asta Bredigand, Richard Burrell.

The work of a palm reader is traced in documentary fashion in this dull, stretched-out feature. First the palmist convinces a suicidal woman her hand foretells great happiness. Next he helps a woman find her long-missing son. The results are tedious and of interest only to those who would fall for such foolishness.

p&d, Tony Young; w, Dr. Josef Ranald; ph, Phil Grindrof.

Drama **(PR:A MPAA:NR)**

HANDS OF ORLAC, THE** (1964, Brit./Fr.) 87m Rivieria-Pendennis/CD bw (LES MAINS D'ORLAC; AKA: HANDS OF A STRANGLER)

Mel Ferrer *(Steven Orlac)*, Christopher Lee *(Nero)*, Dany Carrel *(Li-Lang)*, Felix Aylmer *(Dr. Cochrane)*, Basil Sydney *(Siedelman)*, Lucile Saint-Simon *(Louise Cochrane)*, Donald Wolfit, Antoine Balpetre *(Professor Volcheff)*, Anita Sharp Bolster *(Volcheff's Assistant)*, Mirielle Perrey *(Madame Aliberti, the Landlady)*, Donald Pleasance *(Coates)*, Campbell Singer *(Inspector Henderson)*, Peter Reynolds *(Felix)*, Yanilou *(Emilie)*, Edouard Hemme *(Ange)*, Manning Wilson *(Jagger)*, Arnold Diamond *(Dresser)*, David Peel *(Pilot)*, Walter Randall *(Waiter)*, Franca Bel, Anne Clune, Vicki Woolf *(Cell Whores)*, Katya Wyeth, Beulah Hughes, Tallulah Miller *(Pub Whores)*, Peter Hunt *(Pleasants)*, Philip Ryan *(Police Constable)*, Molly Weir *(Maid)*, Charles Lamb *(Guard)*, Ann Way *(Seamstress)*.

Ferrer plays a concert pianist whose hands are ruined in a plane crash. Wolfit, a surgeon famous for his bone-grafting operations, grafts the hands of a condemned murderer onto Ferrer. The pianist soon becomes obsessed with his murderer's hands and believes they are only capable of destruction. In Marseilles, he meets Lee, a seedy magician who overhears Ferrer's worries that he may have murdered someone. Lee, along with his reluctant assistant Carrel, blackmail Ferrer. Ferrer returns to London, his obsession reaching the breaking point, and attempts to strangle his wife. Before he can finish her off, the cops arrive to tell the pianist that they have discovered that the condemned man was actually innocent and that his hands are not those of a murderer. Finally snapping out of his insanity, Ferrer helps the cops track down Lee, who has killed Carrel to keep her mouth shut. A lackluster version of this material which was filmed simultaneously in two different languages, French and English. A superior version of this story was made in 1935 as MAD LOVE starring Peter Lorre.

p, Steven Pallos, Donald Taylor; d, Edmond T. Greville; w, John Baines, Taylor, Greville; ph, Desmond Dickinson; m, Claude Bolling; ed, Oswald Hafenrichter; art d, John Blezard; md, Ilona Kabos, Stanford Robinson; ch, Hazel Gee.

Horror **(PR:A MPAA:NR)**

HANDS OF THE RIPPER*** (1971, Brit.) 85m Hammer/UNIV c

Eric Porter *(Dr. John Pritchard)*, Angharad Rees *(Anna)*, Jane Merrow *(Laura)*, Keith Bell *(Michael Pritchard)*, Derek Godfrey *(Dysart)*, Dora Bryan *(Mrs. Golding)*, Lynda Baron *(Long Liz)*, Marjorie Lawrence *(Dolly)*, Marjorie Rhodes *(Mrs. Bryant)*, Norman Bird *(Police Inspector)*, Margaret Rawlings *(Mme. Bullard)*, Elizabeth MacLennan *(Mrs. Wilson)*, Barry Lowe *(Mr. Wilson)*, A.J. Brown *(Rev. Anderson)*, April Wilding *(Catherine)*, Anne Clune, Vicki Woolf *(Cell Whores)*, Katya Wyeth, Beulah Hughes, Tallulah Miller *(Pub Whores)*, Peter Munt *(Pleasants)*, Philip Ryan *(Police Officer)*, Molly Weir *(Maid)*, Charles Lamb *(Guard)*.

Hammer luridness again, this time centering on Rees as the daughter of Jack the Ripper. She seeks psychiatric help as she believes she is being driven by her father to commit a particularly lurid series of slayings. Surprisingly good.

p, Aida Young; d, Peter Sasdy; w, L.W. Davidson (based on a story by Edward Spencer Shew); ph, Kenneth Talbot (Technicolor); m, Christopher Gunning; art d, Roy Stanard; spec eff, Cliff Culley; makeup Bunty Phillips.

Horror **Cas.** **(PR:O MPAA:R)**

HANDS OF THE STRANGLER (SEE: HANDS OF ORLAC, 1964, Fr./Brit.)

HANDSOME SERGE (SEE: LE BEAU SERGE, 1959, Fr.)

HANDY ANDY½** (1934) 81m FOX bw

Will Rogers *(Andrew Yates)*, Peggy Wood *(Ernestine Yates)*, Conchita Montenegro *(Fleurette)*, Mary Carlisle *(Janice Yates)*, Roger Imhof *(Doc Burmeister)*, Robert Taylor *(Lloyd Burmeister)*, Paul Harvey *(Charlie Norcross)*, Grace Goodall *(Mattie Norcross)*, Gregory Gaye *(Pierre Martel)*, Frank Melton *(Howard Norcross)*, Jessie Pringle *(Jennie)*, Adrian Rosley, Gregory Gaye, Richard Tucker, Helen Flint.

Rogers plays another small town, homespun type here—this time a druggist whose wife (Wood) has aspirations to high society. She convinces him to sell his store to a chain, and while she makes a fool of herself in the social swirl, he tries to occupy himself with hobbies. They vacation in New Orleans and Rogers determines that gigolo Gaye is paying entirely too much attention to his wife. Rogers dresses in a Tarzan suit, gets thrown in jail, and finally ends up back home with his store back and his wife in her place. Good Rogers vehicle, Taylor's film debut.

d, David Butler; w, William Counselman, Henry Johnson, Kubec Glason, (based on the play "Merry Andrew" by Lewis Beach); ph, Arthur Miller; m, Richard Whiting.

Comedy **(PR:A MPAA:NR)**

HANG 'EM HIGH½** (1968) 114m Malpaso/UA c

Clint Eastwood *(Jed Cooper)*, Inger Stevens *(Rachel)*, Ed Begley *(Cap'n Wilson)*, Pat Hingle *(Judge Adam Fenton)*, Arlene Golonka *(Jennifer)*, James MacArthur *(Preacher)*, Ruth White *(Madam Peaches Sophie)*, Bruce Dern *(Miller)*, Alan Hale, Jr. *(Stone)*, James Westerfield *(Prisoner)*, Dennis Hopper *(The Prophet)*, Ben Johnson *(Sheriff Dave Bliss)*, Bob Steele *(Jenkins)*, Jack Ging *(Marshall Hayes)*, L.Q. Jones *(Loomis)*, Bert Freed *(Schmidt the Hangman)*, Michael O'Sullivan *(Francis Duffy)*, Herb Ellis *(Swede)*, Russell Thorson *(Mr. Maddow)*, Todd Andrews *(Defense Attorney)*, Rick Gates *(Ben)*, Bruce Scott *(Billy Joe)*, Paul Sorenson *(Reno)*, Roy Glenn *(Guard)*, Jonathan Lippe, Barry Cahill, Tony Di Milo, Joseph Sirola, Ned Romero, Richard Guizon, Mark Lenard, Richard Angarola, Larry Blake, Ted Thorpe, Robert Jones, John Wesley, Dennis Dengate, William Zuckert, Hal England, Robert B. Williams.

A minor, though interesting American version of a spaghetti western. After completing Sergio Leone's "Dollars" trilogy (A FISTFUL OF A DOLLARS, FOR A FEW DOLLARS MORE and THE GOOD, THE BAD AND THE UGLY), Eastwood returned to America a major world star and appeared in this derivative, but nonetheless intelligent western directed by the underrated Ted Post (whom Eastwood had worked with and liked in his "Rawhide" television days). Eastwood plays an innocent rancher hung by an angry lynch-mob who mistake him for a rustler and murderer. Saved from death at the last minute by passing marshal Johnson, Eastwood is taken to the notorious "hanging judge" Hingle, who deputizes him and encourages him to track down the men who had tried to hang him, provided that he brings them back to town for trial. Eastwood, of course, ignores Hingle's ground rules and kills the men one-by-one, until their leader, Begley, catches the vigilante lawman off guard and shoots him. Once again Eastwood survivies (thanks to Stevens, a female shopkeeper in love with him who tends his wounds) and goes after Begley who has retreated to his ranch. After a lengthy gun battle in which all of the rancher's henchmen are killed, Eastwood corners Begley, only to find that he has (ironically) hung himself. Though the material is nothing special and relies on the "avenging angel" mystique that had been established for Eastwood in the Leone films, director Post squeezes out some fine and memorable moments in the film. Look for Bob Steele as the dungeon prisoner.

p, Leonard Freeman; d, Ted Post; w, Freeman, Mel Goldberg; ph, Leonard South, Richard Kline (DeLuxe Color); m, Dominic Frontiere; ed, Gene Fowler, Jr.; md, John Capter, Jr.; art d, John B. Goodman; set d, Arthur Krams; cos, Gene Murray, Glen Wright; spec eff, George Swartz.

Western Cas. (PR:C MPAA:R)

HANG YOUR HAT ON THE WIND½** (1969) 48m BV c

Ric Natoli *(Goyo, Indian Boy)*, Judson Pratt *(Father O'Flaherty)*, Angel Tompkins *(Fran Harper)*, Edward Faulkner *(Pilot)*, Pete Logan *(Truck Driver)*, Bill Cornford *(Guide)*, Monica Ramirez *(Tina)*, Carlos Rivas *(Tall Bandit)*, Alex Tinne *(Short Bandit)*.

Natoli stars as a young Indian boy who discovers an abandoned horse in the desert. The boy saves the horse from drowning in a mudhole, saddles it and names it Tom-Tom. The boy and his horse are inseparable until the beast's true owner, Tompkins, arrives to reclaim her prize-winning thoroughbred. The boy reluctantly parts with the horse, but soon spots two bandits kidnaping it. He alerts the authorities and helps them catch the robbers and the horse. Grateful for his help, Tomkins gives the boy a pony.

p&d, Larry Lansburgh; w, Paul West (based on a story by Lansburgh); ph, Edward P. Hughes (Technicolor); m, Billy Liebert; ed, Lloyd L. Richardson; m/l, Randy Sparks.

Drama (PR:AA MPAA:G)

HANGAR 18* (1980) 97m Sunn Classic c (AKA: INVASION FORCE)

Darren McGavin *(Forbes)*, Robert Vaughn *(Gordon)*, Gary Collins *(Steve)*, James Hampton *(Lew)*, Phillip Abbott *(Frank)*, Pamela Bellwood *(Sarah)*, Tom Hallick *(Phil)*, Steven Keats *(Paul)*, William Shallert *(Mills)*, Cliff Osmond *(Sheriff)*, Andrew Bloch *(Neal)*, Stuart Pankin *(Sam)*, Betty Ann Carr *(Flo)*, H.M. Wynant, Bill Zuckert, Jesse Bennett, Robert Bristol, Ed E. Carroll, J.R. Clark, Craig Clyde, John William Galt, Anne Galvan, Ken Hapner, Michael Irving, Bruce Katzman, Peter Liakakis, Debra MacFarlane, Chet Norris, H.E.D. Redford, Max Robinson, Ocie Robinson, Michael Ruud, Joseph Campanella.

Yes, the folks that presented the awful big-screen documentaries IN SEARCH OF NOAH'S ARK and IN SEARCH OF HISTORIC JESUS, Sunn Classic Pictures, attempted to present a straightforward, dramatic science-fiction film with predictable results. McGavin stars as the leader of a group of scientists studying a flying saucer that is being kept hidden in a hangar by the U.S. Government. Vaughn plays the slimy, paranoid politician who keeps the lid on this discovery at any cost. The scientists decode alien plans to invade the Earth and the nearly psychotic White House decides to literally bomb the hangar to destroy the evidence. Not much interest here.

p, Charles E. Sellier, Jr.; d, James L. Conway; w, Steven Thornley, Tom Chapman, Conway (based on a novel by Robert Weverka, Sellier); ph, Paul Hipp; m, John Cacavas; ed, Michael Spence; prod d, Paul Staheli; art d, Chip Radaelli; cos, Julie Staheli.

Science Fiction Cas. (PR:A MPAA:PG)

HANGING TREE, THE*** (1959) 106m Baroda/WB c

Gary Cooper *(Doc Joe Frail)*, Maria Schell *(Elizabeth Mahler)*, Karl Malden *(Frenchy Plante)*, Ben Piazza *(Rune)*, George C. Scott *(Dr. George Grubb)*, Karl Swenson *(Tom Flaunce)*, Virginia Gregg *(Edna Flaunce)*, John Dierkes *(Society Red)*, King Donovan *(Wonder)*, Slim Talbot *(Stage Driver)*, Guy Wilkerson *(Home Owner)*, Bud Osborne *(Horseman)*, Annette Claudier *(Dance Hall Girl)*, Clarence Straight *(Dealer)*.

Cooper is an old West doctor with a past who comes into a small town to start again. He rescues thief Piazza from a lynch mob and reforms him, then helps temporarily blinded Swiss girl Schell. He gives her money to buy into a gold mine with Piazza and heavy Malden and when they strike it rich Malden attacks Schell. Cooper arrives in time and shoots him. An angry mob takes Cooper to the hanging tree to string him up, but Schell buys them off with her gold. She and Piazza cut Cooper down. This carefully paced formalist western is oddly effective despite flaws in the script. Good performances by all, including George C. Scott in his first film.

p, Martin Jurow, Richard Shepherd; d, Delmer Daves; w, Wendell Mayes, Halsted Welles (from a novelette by Dorothy M. Johnson); ph, Ted McCord (Technicolor); m Max Steiner; ed, Owen Marks; art d, Daniel B. Cathcart; set d, Frank Miller; cos, Marjorie Best, Orry-Kelly; m/l "The Hanging Tree," Mack David, Jerry Livingston (sung by Mary Robbins); makeup Gordon Bau.

Western (PR:C MPAA:NR)

HANGMAN, THE*** (1959) 87m PAR bw

Robert Taylor *(Mackenzie Bovard)*, Tina Louise *(Selah Jennison)*, Fess Parker *(Sheriff Buck Weston)*, Jack Lord *(Johnny Bishop)*, Gene Evans *(Big Murph)*, Mickey Shaughnessy *(Al Cruse)*, Shirley Harmer *(Kitty Bishop)*, James Westerfield *(Herb Loftus)*, Mabel Albertson, Lucille Curtis.

Taylor is a deputy marshal (famed for always getting his man) who rides into town to arrest Lord for a crime committed years before. He faces a conspiracy of townfolk trying to shield Lord, who has reformed and become a reputable citizen. Sheriff Parker finally convinces Taylor to leave Lord alone, and the lawman retires to California with Louise, Lord's ex-girl friend from outlaw days. Panned as unmotivated and dull in 1959, the film seems to be improving with age. Taylor is excellent.

p, Frank Freeman, Jr., d, Michael Curtiz; w, Dudley Nichols (based on a story by Luke Short); ph, Loyal Griggs; m, Harry Sukman; ed, Terry Morse, art d, Henry Bumstead, Hal Pereira.

Western (PR:A MPAA:NR)

HANGMAN WAITS, THE** (1947, Brit.) 63m Five Star/BUT bw

John Turnbull *(Inspector)*, Anthony Baird *(Sinclair)*, Beatrice Cambell *(Usherette)*, David Mowbray, Kenneth Warrington, Michel Bazalgette, Edwin Ellis, Leonard Sharp, Robert Wyndham, Hylton Allen, Bessie Courtney, Vi Kayley, Arthur Mack, Stanley Jay, Jeanette Green.

Realistically detailed account of the pursuit of a sadistic killer, an organist in a theater of all things, guilty of a grueling murder in which he cut up the body of one of the theater's usherettes. Turnbull (a famous British character actor given his one and only lead) plays the inspector who trails the killer to the country and back to the city before bringing him to justice.

p, A. Barr-Smith, Roger Proudlock; d&w, Barr-Smith; ph, Denys Coop, Fred Langdon; m, Albert Ferber; ed, Bunch Dixon-Spain; set d, Eric Smith, Janet Green.

Crime (PR:C MPAA:NR)

HANGMAN'S KNOT*** (1952) 80m COL/Scott-Brown c

Randolph Scott *(Matt Stewart)*, Donna Reed *(Molly Hull)*, Claude Jarman, Jr. *(Jamie Groves)*, Frank Faylen *(Cass Browne)*, Glenn Langan *(Capt. Peterson)*, Richard Denning *(Lee Kemper)*, Lee Marvin *(Rolph Bainter)*, Jeanette Nolan *(Mrs. Harris)*, Clem Bevans *(Plunkett)*, Ray Teal *(Quincey)*, Guinn "Big Boy" Williams *(Smitty)*, Monte Blue *(Maxwell)*, John Call *(Egan Walsh)*, Reed Howes *(Hank Fletcher)*, Edward Earle, Post Park, Frank Hagney, Frank Yaconelli.

Scott commands a raiding party of Confederate cavalry at the end of the Civil War. After robbing a Yankee gold shipment in Nevada, they are told by a dying Union soldier that the war has been over for a month. Now facing criminal prosecution for acts committed while they thought the war was on, they take shelter in a stagecoach stop and are soon besieged by bandits. A tense, well-done western with a number of touches of wry humor.

p, Harry Joe Brown; d&w, Roy Huggins; ph, Charles Lawton, Jr. (Technicolor); ed, Gene Havlick; md, Mischa Bakaleinikoff; set d, Frank Tuttle.

Western (PR:C MPAA:NR)

HANGMAN'S WHARF*½ (1950, Brit.) 73m DUK Films bw

John Witty *(Dr. David Galloway)*, Genine Graham *(Alison Maxwell)*, Patience Rentoul *(Mrs. Williams)*, Gerald Nodin *(Sir Brian Roderick)*, Campbell Singer *(Inspector Prebble)*, Max Brimmell *(Krim)*, Patricia Laffan *(Rosa Warren)*, Molly Looe, Tom Masson, Frederick Allen, Barry Faber, John Walker, Harry Hearn, R.C. Huggins, Maureen Williamson.

Routine crime yarn in which a doctor answering an emergency plea for help finds himself the accused in a murder case that occurred at the place where he had been working. Luckily for this man, Graham has taken an interest in the case and is able to prove that the doctor is innocent. This film has a few interesting moments but nothing to lift it above the mundane.

p,d,w&ph, Cecil H. Williamson (based on the radio serial by John Belden).

Crime (PR:A MPAA:NR)

HANGMEN ALSO DIE*½** (1943) 131m UA bw (AKA: LEST WE FORGET)

Brian Donlevy *(Dr. Franz Svoboda)*, Walter Brennan *(Prof. Novotny)*, Anna Lee *(Mascha Novotny)*, Gene Lockhart *(Emil Czaka)*, Dennis O'Keefe *(Jan Horek)*, Alexander Granach *(Alois Gruber)*, Margaret Wycherly *(Aunt Ludmilla Novotny)*, Nana Bryant *(Mrs. Novotny)*, Billy Roy *(Beda Novotny)*, Hans von Twardowski *(Reinhard Heydrich)*, Tonio Selwart *(Haas, Gestapo Chief)*, Jonathan Hale *(Dedic)*, Lionel Stander *(Gabby)*, Byron Foulger *(Bartos)*, Virginia Farmer *(Landlady)*, Louis Donath *(Schirmer)*, Sarah Padden *(Mrs. Dvorak)*, Edmund MacDonald *(Dr. Pilar)*, George Irving *(Necval the Poet)*, James Bush *(Worker)*, Arno Frey *(Itnut, Camp Officer)*, Lester Sharpe *(Rudy, a Hostage)*, Arthur Loft *(Gen. Votruba Bertruba)*, William Farnum *(Viktorin)*, Reinhold Scheunzel *(Inspector Ritter)*, Otto Reichow *(Gestapo)*, Eddy Waller *(Cab Driver)*, Phil Van Zandt *(Officer)*, Erville Alderson *(Liberal Official)*, Ralph Dunn *(Policeman)*, Emmett Lynn, Emmett Vogan, Billy Benedict *(Hostages)*, Charles Middleton, William Haade *(Patriots)*, Philip Merivale.

Deputy Reich Protector Reinhard Heydrich (von Twardowski), Nazi-appointed "governor" of Prague, gathers together the most prominent citizens of the community and voices his displeasure regarding the insidious acts of sabotage occurring in the factories. Not only are the Czech acts of defiance holding up vital production for the Third Reich, but they are also endangering the lives of the civic leaders assembled. Unless production increases, heads will roll. Upon leaving this meeting, Heydrich is assassinated by a member of the Czech resistance, Donlevy (this takes place off screen). On the run, Donlevy is given shelter by a kindly professor, Brennan, and his daughter, Lee. Though Heydrich's death becomes a hopeful symbol for the Czechoslovakian people and improves their morale, the Nazis demand revenge and the Gestapo begin to round up hundreds of innocent Czech citizens suspected of subversion and complicity, and kill them off one by one until the killer is handed over. The Gestapo is aided by Lockhart, and ambitious and greedy Czech who has become an informer for the Nazis. When Brennan is carted off by the Gestapo, Donlevy decides to give himself up. Fearing the effect his execution would have on the Czech people, the leader of the underground, Hale, convinces him to remain in hiding. While the Gestapo suspects Donlevy as the assassin, their efforts to prove it are frustrated. Meanwhile, Hale and his organization have learned that Lockhart is a traitor to the Czech people. Seeking to solve two problems at once, the underground sets into motion a plan to frame Lockhart for the assassination of Heydrich. The plan goes into effect and seems to work until a clever Gestapo investigator, Granach, corners Donlevy and forces a confession. Luckily, Granach is killed by Donlevy and the underground before he can report his findings to his superiors. To put the final nail in Lockhart's coffin, the underground plants Granach's corpse in the traitor's house. Lockhart attempts to flee, but is killed by the Nazis who declare him the assassin, though they know he did not commit the crime. Desperate to end the whole unpleasant affair without any further embarrassment, the Nazis release the surviving hostages. Unfortunately, Brennan isn't among them, as he was one of the last to be murdered by the Gestapo. While HANGMEN ALSO DIE is a much better than average American WW II propaganda film, it is a bit of a disappointment in the impressive career of master director Fritz Lang. Beyond a precious few scenes containing some stunning Lang visuals (Heydrich suspended in his hospital bed, his spine bowed alarmingly is the single most memorable), the film is overlong, the characters haphazardly developed, and several impassioned patriotic speeches are not written or performed particularly well, which tends to grind the film to a halt. Perhaps the most interesting aspect of HANGMEN ALSO DIE is the participation of fellow German expatriate Bertolt Brecht in the writing of the screenplay. When Brecht arrived in America, Lang desperately tried to find a place for him in Hollywood. Inspired by a newspaper account of the assassination of Heydrich on May 27, 1942, the men set about fabricating a fictional account of the events that took place in Prague (years later it was revealed that the actual assassination was planned in Britain and performed by a group of military commandos). Forced to collaborate with bilingual screenwriter John Wexley because he spoke no English, Brecht soon became unhappy with the lack of creative freedom he was allowed. Wexley and Brecht seemed to be working at cross purposes at times, with Lang making his own additions upon receiving their pages. Upon completion of the script (it came in at 280 pages and was eventually cut down to around 190), Brecht demanded equal screen credit with Wexley, but the Guild ruled against him because he had made public his intention to return to Germany after the war, thus the individual credit was more important to the advancement of Wexley's career in Hollywood than Brecht's. In the end, there seems to be little evidence of Brecht's influence on the material, though his exact contributions are practically impossible to determine, though Brecht himself claimed that his only surviving scene was the opening confrontation between Heydrich and the Czech nobility.

p&d, Fritz Lang; w, John Wexley (based on a story by Lang, Bertolt Brecht); ph, James Wong Howe; m, Hans Eisler; ed, Gene Fowler, Jr.; md, Arthur Guttman; art d, William Darling; cos, Julie Heron; m/l, "No Surrender," Eisler, Sam Coslow.

War Drama **(PR:C-O MPAA:NR)**

HANGOVER (SEE: FEMALE JUNGLE, 1956)

HANGOVER SQUARE*** (1945) 77m FOX bw

Laird Cregar *(George Harvey Bone)*, Linda Darnell *(Netta Longdon)*, George Sanders *(Dr. Allan Middleton)*, Glenn Langan *(Carstairs)*, Faye Marlowe *(Barbara Chapman)*, Alan Napier *(Sir Henry Chapman)*, Frederic Worlock *(Supt. Clay)*, J.W. Austin *(Det. Insp. King)*, Leyland Hodgson *(Det. Sgt. Lewis)*, Clifford Brooke *(Watchman)*, John Goldsworthy *(Butler)*, Michael Dyne *(Mickey)*, Ann Codee *(Yvette)*, Francis Ford *(Ogillo)*, Charles Irwin *(Manager)*, Frank Hanson *(Newsman)*, Connie Leon *(Maid)*, Robert Hale *(Costermonger)*, Leslie Denison *(English Policeman)*, Jimmy Aubrey *(Drunk)*, Lea Sketchley *(Doorman)*, J. Farrell MacDonald *(Man)*.

A chilling thriller set in 1903 gaslit London has the fascinating character actor Cregar in the lead role as a sort of Dr. Jekyll and Mr. Hyde. He is a sensitive composer who becomes a maniac when hearing discordant noises, roaming the fog-bound London streets for victims upon which to vent his considerable spleen. When an antique dealer tries to cheat him, Cregar summarily strangles the man. A well-to-do woman hires him to compose a piece, then rejects the work and causes him to kill her. His romance with singer Darnell comes to nothing after he discovers she has been two-timing him. Cregar's vengeance is terrible; he burns her body in a street fire set to celebrate Guy Fawkes Day. Sanders, a Scotland Yard psychologist, penetrates Cregar's malady and brings him to justice in the end. Cregar was only 28 years old when completing this, his first starring vehicle, but he never lived to see it. He became obsessed with maintaining a leading man status once he was given this star billing and immediately launched a crash diet which would reduce his great girth; he literally starved himself to death and Hollywood lost one of its most promising actors. The memorable score for HANGOVER SQUARE was composed by Herrmann, who had done the score for CITIZEN KANE. The composer later adapted the final sequences into a one-movement concerto which was performed to great success.

p, Robert Bassler; d, John Brahm; w, Barre Lyndon (based on a novel by Patrick Hamilton); ph, Joseph La Shelle; m, Bernard Herrmann; ed, Harry Reynolds; art d, Lyle Wheeler, Maurice Ransford; spec eff, Fred Sersen.

Crime Drama **(PR:C MPAA:NR)**

HANGUP* (1974) 94m Brut/WB c (AKA: SUPERDUDE)

William Elliott *(Ken)*, Marki Bey *(Julie)*, Cliff Potts *(Lou)*, Michael Lerner *(Richards)*, Wally Taylor *(Sgt. Becker)*, Timothy Blake *(Gwen)*, Fredd Wayne *(Felder)*, Midori *(Sally)*, David A. Renard *(Bud)*, Pepe Serna *(Enrique)*, Rafael Campos *(Longnose)*, Lynn Hamilton *(Mrs. Ramsey)*, William Bramley *(Simpson)*, Bob Delegall *(Jennings)*, Barbara Baldavin *(Beverly)*, Morris Buchanan *(Dave)*, Danny "Big" Black *(Jim Jim)*, Herbert Jefferson, Jr. *(Ben)*, Jerry Ayres *(Jerry)*, Joe Renteria *(Paul)*, Sy Prescott *(Morton)*, George Murdock *(Capt. Gorney)*.

A disappointing ending to a fine directorial career, HANGUP represents a classic Hollywood example of how studios ignore talented filmmakers. Hathaway was a veteran of 1940s westerns and helmed John Wayne in the marvelous TRUE GRIT. But for his last feature Hathaway was assigned this nonsense black-exploitation film about some drug racketeers. For what this is, it's not bad (Bey gives a nice performance as an ill-fated hooker) but the genre didn't demand much talent from the director.

p, T.W. Sewell; d, Henry Hathaway; w, John B. Sherry, Lee Lazich (based on the novel *The Face of Night* by Bernard Brunner); ph, Robert Houser (Technicolor); m, Tony Camillo; ed, Chris Kaselau; art d, Jim Halsey; m/l, "Hangup," George Barrie.

Drama **(PR:O MPAA:R)**

HANK WILLIAMS STORY, THE (SEE: YOUR CHEATIN' HEART, 1964)

HANK WILLIAMS: THE SHOW HE NEVER GAVE*½** (1982, Can.) 86m Film Consortium of Canada/Simcon c

Sneezy Waters *(Hank Williams)*, Sean McCann *(Betty Anne)*, Sean Hewitt *(Doctor)*, Jackie Washington *(Janitor)*, George Essery *(Musical Director)*, Keith Glass *(Guitar)*, Joel Zifkin *(Fiddle)*, Ron Dann *(Pedal Steel)*, David Harvey *(Bass)*, Peter Beaudoin *(Drums)*.

Adapted from a Canadian cabaret show and shot on 16mm, this film tells of Williams (Waters) riding from a New Year's concert and fantasizing about playing a small saloon. Between songs he is tormented by self-doubt and alcoholism. Includes twenty-plus Williams songs, among which are "Your Cheatin' Heart," "Hey Good Looking," and "Why Don't You Love Me?"

p, William Marshall, Henk Van Der Kolk; d, David Acomba; w, Maynard Collins (based on his play); ph Albert Dunk; ed, Sally Patterson; md, Bill Garrett; art d, Ted Watkins.

Drama **(PR:C MPAA:NR)**

HANKY-PANKY* (1982) 105m COL c

Gene Wilder *(Michael Jordon)*, Gilda Radner *(Kate Hellman)*, Kathleen Quinlan *(Janet Dunn)*, Richard Widmark *(Ransom)*, Robert Prosky *(Hiram Calder)*, Josef Sommer *(Adrian Pruitt)*, Johnny Sekka *(Lacey)*, Jay O. Sanders *(Pilot)*, Sam Gray *(Dr. John Wolf)*, Johnny Brown *(Bus Driver)*, Larry Bryggman *(Stacy)*, Pat Corley *(Pilot)*, Bill Beutel *(Anchorman)*, Madison Arnold *(Cop at Subway)*, Nat Habib *(Cab Driver)*, James Tolkan *(Conferee)*, James Greene *(Doorman)*, Jay Garner *(Buck)*, Stephen D. Newman *(Calder Aide)*, Bill Moor *(Terrance Martin)*, Peter Boyden *(Mailman)*, Doris Belack *(Building Manager)*, Don Plumley, Anthony McKay *(Club Members)*, Floyd Ennis *(Bartender in Club)*, David Snell *(Clerk in Club)*, Donald Symington *(Manager in Club)*, John Wylie *(Waiter in Club)*, Brad English, Richard Southern, Donna Fowler, David Froman, Edmond Genest, Peter Iacangelo, Arthur French, John Blood, Beau Starr, Frankie Faison, Larry Pine, Edwin McDonough, Brian Carney, Richard Russell Ramos, Bill Sadler, Victor Argo, Robert Buka, Craig Vandenburgh, Libi Staiger, Mildred Brion, John Greenwood, Gary Combs, Frank Ferrara.

A mess from the start, HANKY-PANKY is tepid, silly and very unsatisfying when one considers the alleged talents of those involved. A suspense comedy with the same star, director and studio as STIR CRAZY, they must have seen something in this to have lavished so much money on such a minor affair. A patent rip-off of a Hitchcock-type plot (so patent, in fact, one would have thought Colin Higgins had done it), it's the story of an innocent Wilder who is suspected of a murder. He must endure a chase, beatings, and several attempts to kill him. He is teamed with Radner, sister of a man who unexplainedly commits suicide in the first reel. Quinlan is the only pretty face in a picture full of ugly people in various bad taste situations. An example of the humor level must be a lengthy belching scene by pilot Corley, which ends in his death—none too soon for us. A formula movie with Radner mugging worse than she ever did on TV and Wilder resorting, once again, to the acting tricks everyone thought were so cute the first five times we saw them. It was around this time that Wilder and Radner fell in love and got married. Soon after, Wilder, who keeps trying to be a writer-director and star, wore too many hats in another derivative farce, THE WOMAN IN RED. This picture was an embarrassment for everyone connected with it. Dumb.

p, Martin Ransohoff; d, Sidney Poitier; w, Henry Rosenbaum, David Taylor; ph, Arthur Ornitz (Metrocolor); m, Tom Scott; ed, Harry Keller; prod d, Ben Edwards; art d, Christopher Nowack; set d, Fred Weiler; cos, Bernard Johnson.

Comedy **Cas.** **(PR:A-C MPAA:PG)**

HANNAH K.** (1983, Fr.) 108m K.G.-GAU/UNIV c

Jill Clayburgh *(Hannah Kaufman)*, Jean Yanne *(Victor Bonnet)*, Gabriel Byrne *(Josue Herzog)*, Mohamed Bakri *(Selim Bakri)*, David Clennon *(Amnon)*, Shimon Finkel *(Prof. Leventhal)*, Oded Kotler *(The Stranger)*, Michael Bat-Adam *(Russian Woman)*, Dafna Levy *(Dafna)*, Dan Muggia *(Capt. Allenby Bridge)*, Robert Sommer *(Court President)*, Ronald Guttman *(Judge)*, Bruno Corazzari *(Court President)*, Amnon Kapeliouk *(Judge)*, Dalik Wolinitz *(Sergeant)*, Luca Barbareschi *(Young Lawyer)*, Gideon Amir *(Court Lawyer)*, William Berger *(German Journalist)*, Murray Gronwall *(Jail Interpreter)*, Cyrus Elias *(Guard in Jail Parlor)*, Izviad Arad *(Tourist Guide)*, Jacques Cohen *(Ex-Soldier at Airport)*, Uri Gavriel *(Barman at Airport)*, Manuel Cauchi *(Barman at Beach)*, Sinay Peter *(Airport Control)*, Edward Betz *(Huisser)*, Sarit Shatsky *(Ludmilla)*, Tal Ron *(Village Captain)*, Zinedine Soualem *(Village Sergeant)*, Esther Zewko *(TWA Hostess)*.

Frustrating film from Costa-Gravas starring Clayburgh as a lady lawyer who defends a young Palestinian, Bakri, who sues Israel for the right to live on his ancestral homeland. Also involved is a brash, arrogant young Israeli attorney, Byrne, who represents Israel in the case. Both men are romantically involved with Clayburgh, and any attempt at political insight in the film is clouded by the ridiculous romantic flip-flops done by the script. Clayburgh's character is wholly unsympathetic and uninvolving. The Israeli, Byrne, is played as such an obnoxious, vindictive snot that viewer identification with him is nullified, and the Arab, Bakri, is insufferably noble. The film is so manipulative that any hope for a balanced examination of the Middle East problems is dashed. A disappointment.

p, Michele Ray-Gavras; d, Constantine Costa-Gavras; w, Costa-Gavras, Franco Solinas; ph, Ricardo Aronovich (Panavision, Fujicolor); m, Gabriel Yared; ed,

Francoise Bonnot; art d, Pierre Guffroy; cos, Edith Vesperini; m/l, traditional Yiddish songs (performed by Talila and the Kol Aviv ensemble).

Drama **Cas.** **(PR:C MPAA:R)**

HANNAH LEE½** (1953) 78m Broder c (AKA: OUTLAW TERRITORY)

Macdonald Carey *(Bus Crow)*, Joanne Dru *(Hallie)*, John Ireland *(Rochelle)*, Don Haggerty *(Crashaw)*, Peter Ireland *(Willie Stiver)*, Stuart Randall *(Montgomery)*, Frank Ferguson *(Britton)*, Ralph Dumke *(Alesworth)*, Tom Powers *(Sheriff)*, Tris Coffin *(Paulson)*, Alex Pope *(Gare Silver)*, Harold Kennedy *(Bainbridge)*, Kay Riehl *(Mrs. Bainbridge)*, Ruth Whitney *(Mrs. Stiver)*, Dean Cromer *(Beven)*, Norman Leavitt *(Miller)*, Paul Keast *(1st Villager)*, Robin Morse *(2nd Villager)*, Joe McGuinn *(3rd Villager)*, Bill Hale *(1st Cowboy)*, Dick Fortune *(2nd Cowboy)*, Alex Frazer *(Old Man)*, Mort Mills *(Deputy)*, Ferris Taylor *(Station Master)*, Helen Servis *(2nd Woman)*, Ann Loos *(Sheriff's Wife)*, Crane Whitley *(Loafer)*, Charles Keane *(2nd Loafer)*.

Carey is a hired gunman paid $800 for each family of homesteaders he can rid the range of. Dru is a saloon owner who falls in love with him despite her suspicions about his work. Ireland is the marshal who tracks down Carey. The men fight, but before Carey can finish off Ireland, Dru, who has followed the men, drops him. Even though shot in 3-D, it's still only routine.

p&d, John Ireland, Lee Garmes; w, MacKinlay Kantor, Rip Von Ronkle (based on the novel *Wicked Waster* by Kantor); ph, Lee Garmes (3-D, Pathe Color); ed, Chester Schaeffer, Edward Sampson.

Western **(PR:A MPAA:NR)**

HANNIBAL* (1960, Ital.) 103m WB c

Victor Mature *(Hannibal)*, Rita Gam *(Sylvia)*, Gabriele Ferzetti *(Fabius Maximus)*, Milly Vitale *(Danila)*, Rik Battaglia *(Hasdrubal)*, Franco Silva *(Maharbal)*, Mario Girotti *(Quintilius)*, Mirko Ellis *(Mago)*, Andrea Aureli *(Varro)*.

Mature shows off his chest again: this time in a cheesy Italian spectacle as Hannibal, leading the war elephants of Carthage over the Alps to do battle with Rome. Some big battle scenes, but mostly dull.

p, Ottavio Poggi; d, Edgar G. Ulmer, Ludovico Bragaglia (uncredited); w, Mortimer Braus (based on an idea by Allesandro Continenza and a story from Poggi); ph, R. Masciocchi (SuperCineScope, Technicolor); m, Carlo Rustichelli; ed, R. Cinquini; md, Franco Ferrara; art d, E. Kromberg; set d, G. Gentill; cos. Bartolini-Salimbeni.

Historical Epic/War **(PR:A MPAA:NR)**

HANNIBAL BROOKS½** (1969, Brit.) 101m Scimitar/UA c

Oliver Reed *(Hannibal Brooks)*, Michael J. Pollard *(Packy)*, Wolfgang Preiss *(Col. Von Haller)*, Helmut Lohner *(Willi)*, Karin Baal *(Vronia)*, Peter Karsten *(Kurt)*, Ralf Wolter *(Dr. Mendel)*, John Alderton *(Bernard)*, Jurgen Draeger *(Sami)*, Maria Brockerhoff *(Anna)*, Ernst Fritz Furbringer *(Elephant Keeper Kellerman)*, Fred Haltiner *(Josef)*, Eric Jelde *(Zoo Director Stern)*, Til Kiwe *(Von Haller's Sergeant)*, John Porter Davison *(Geordie)*, Terence Seward *(Twilight)*, James Donald *(Padre)*, Peter Bohlke *(Old German Captain)*, Tei de Maal *(Zoo Keeper)*, Aida *(Lucy, the Elephant)*.

World War II is a barrel of laughs as pacifist POW Reed teams with Pollard to escape Germany for Switzerland with an elephant. As idiotic as it sounds.

p&d, Michael Winner; w, Dick Clement, Ian La Frenais (based on a story by Winner and Tom Wright); ph, Robert Paynter, Hans Jura (DeLuxe Color); m, Francis Lai; ed, Lionel Selwyn; prod d, John Stoll; art d, Jurgen Kiebach; set d, Josie MacAvin; spec eff, Erwin Lange; stunts, David Newman; makeup, Richard Mills.

War Comedy **(PR:C MPAA:M)**

HANNIE CALDER** (1971, Brit.) 85m Tigon British-Curtwel/PAR c

Raquel Welch *(Hannie Calder)*, Robert Culp *(Thomas Luther Price)*, Ernest Borgnine *(Emmett Clemens)*, Strother Martin *(Rufus Clemens)*, Jack Elam *(Frank Clemens)*, Christopher Lee *(Bailey)*, Diana Dors *(Madame)*, Stephen Boyd [uncredited] *(The Preacher)*.

Welch hires Culp to help her find and kill the saddle-scum who raped her and killed her husband. Tries to be a fresh, funny look at the genre, but ends up just another addition to it. Predictable and dull, though sleazy brothers Borgnine, Martin, and Elam are terrific.

p, Patrick Curtis; d, Burt Kennedy; w, Z.X. Jones [Kennedy, David Haft] (based on a story by Peter Cooper from characters created by Ian Quicke, Bob Richards); ph, Edward Scaife (Panavision, Eastmancolor); m, Ken Thorne; ed, Jim Connock; art d, Jose Alguero; cos, Ray Aghayan; m/l, theme song, Thorne, Jack Fishman (sung by Bobby Hanna); makeup, John O'Gorman, Ricardo Vasquez Sese.

Western **(PR:O MPAA:R)**

HANOI HANNA—QUEEN OF CHINA (SEE: CHELSEA GIRLS, THE, 1966)

HANOVER STREET½** (1979, Brit.) 109m COL c

Harrison Ford *(David Halloran)*, Lesley-Anne Down *(Margaret Sellinger)*, Christopher Plummer *(Paul Sellinger)*, Alec McCowen *(Maj. Trumbo)*, Richard Masur *(2nd Lt. Jerry Cimino)*, Michael Sacks *(2nd Lt. Martin Hyer)*, Patsy Kensit *(Sarah Sellinger)*, Max Wall *(Harry Pike)*, Shane Rimmer *(Col. Ronald Bart)*, Keith Buckley *(Lt. Wells)*, Sherrie Hewson *(Phyllis)*, Cindy O'Callaghan *(Paula)*, Di Trevis *(Elizabeth)*, Suzanne Bertish *(French Girl)*, Keith Alexander *(Soldier in Barn)*, Jay Benedict *(Cpl. Daniel Giler)*, John Ratzenberger *(Sgt. John Lucas)*, Eric Stine *(Farrell)*, Hugh Fraser *(Capt. Harold Lester)*, William Hootkins *(Beef)*, Kristine Howarth, Shaun Scott, Ronald Letham, Lesley Ward, Eugene Lipinski, Gary Waldhorn, John Rees, Seymour Matthews, Tony Sibbald, George Pravda, Harry Brooks, Jr., Eddie Kidd.

Ford plays an American bomber pilot stationed in England during WW II who meets and falls in love with a young married Englishwoman, Down, whom he is trapped with during an air raid. In the best tradition of melodramatic wartime romances, Ford finds himself having to team up with Down's husband, Plummer, a British secret service agent, on a dangerous espionage mission that will take them behind enemy lines. Director Hyams (CAPRICORN ONE, OUTLAND) tries desperately to evoke the feel of the best of the 1940s wartime romantic dramas, but the material is a bit predictable and trite, leaving the audience little to look forward to. Ford, Downs, and Plummer turn in solid, likable performances, but the production is sloppy at times with the set design looking a bit too calculated an evocation of wartime England and some of Down's coiffures and gowns seem out of place for the period. While the effort to resurrect the simple, wistfully sweet melodramas of the 1940s is admirable, the film just doesn't manage to become more than a thin imitation of better works.

p, Paul N. Lazarus III; d&w, Peter Hyams; ph, David Watkin (Panavision, Technicolor); m, John Barry; ed, James Mitchell; prod d, Philip Harrison; art d, Malcolm Middleton, Robert Cartwright; cos, Joan Bridge; spec eff, Martin Gutteridge.

Romance/War Drama **Cas.** **(PR:C MPAA:PG)**

HANS CHRISTIAN ANDERSEN*** (1952) 120m RKO c

Danny Kaye *(Hans Christian Andersen)*, Farley Granger *(Niels)*, [Renee] Jeanmaire *(Doro)*, Joey [Joseph] Walsh *(Peter)*, Philip Tonge *(Otto)*, Erik Bruhn *(The Hussar)*, Roland Petit *(The Prince)*, John Brown *(Schoolmaster)*, John Qualen *(Burgomaster)*, Jeanne Lafayette *(Celine)*, Robert Malcolm *(Stage Doorman)*, George Chandler *(Farmer)*, Fred Kelsey *(1st Gendarme)*, Gil Perkins *(2nd Gendarme)*, Peter Votrian *(Lars)*, Betty Uitti *(The Princess)*, Jack Klaus *(Sea Witch)*.

A delightful children's film starring Kaye as the beloved Danish author whose rise to literary prominence is detailed here in an admittedly fanciful manner (producer Goldwyn inserted a disclaimer at the beginning stating that the film is not intended to be a biography). The film opens as Kaye, an Odense cobbler, is asked to leave the community because he persists in telling fairy tales to the local children who would prefer to listen to him rather than go to school. Accompanied by his young apprentice, Walsh, Kaye moves to Copenhagen and continues his work as a cobbler. Unfortunately, Kaye unknowingly violates a town ordinance and lands in jail. Walsh escapes the police and, while hiding in the Royal Theater, he overhears the prima ballerina, Jeanmaire, bemoan the fact that she needs a cobbler. Overcoming his fear, Walsh steps out of his hiding place and tells of Kaye's predicament. Jeanmaire secures Kaye's release from jail and commissions him to make her a pair of slippers. Soon the hopelessly romantic cobbler is deeply in love with the ballet dancer, unaware that her marriage to the director of the ballet is quite stable, despite the fact that she and her husband openly quarrel. After being ejected from rehearsals because he dared to intercede during one of these frequent squabbles, Kaye writes Jeanmaire a love letter hidden within a fairy tale of his invention entitled "The Little Mermaid." Upon reading the story, Jeanmaire misunderstands Kaye's intentions and decides to use it as the theme for her next ballet. Before Kaye can openly declare his love to Jeanmaire, she is off on tour with the ballet. Waiting for the ballerina's return, Kaye continues making shoes and telling wonderful stories to the local children. When one of his tales, "The Ugly Duckling," gets printed in the newspaper, Kaye suddenly finds himself famous. Soon after, Jeanmaire returns to Copenhagen to perform the premiere of "The Little Mermaid." Having angered Jeanmaire's husband while backstage, Kaye is locked in a closet by the ballet director and misses the performance. By just listening to the music, however, Kaye imagines what the ballet must be like. Eventually Kaye is released, finally able to declare his devotion to Jeanmaire. The ballerina is quite touched by Kaye's love for her, but she gently explains that she is in love with her husband and that she would never leave him. Dejectedly, Kaye leaves Copenhagen and returns to Odense. Much to his surprise he is greeted as a local hero because of his writing and he continues to weave marvelous tales of fancy for children throughout the world. HANS CHRISTIAN ANDERSEN was something of an obsession with producer Goldwyn. For nearly fifteen years he had been announcing production of the project only to have it once again delayed (Gary Cooper had been chosen for the lead at one point). After paying a king's ransom for sixteen different screenplays, Goldwyn finally found one he liked and offered Kaye $175,000 to star. The deal was accepted and production began. For the role of the ballerina, Goldwyn wanted British dancer Moira Shearer, who had recently starred in Michael Powell's THE RED SHOES (1948) which had been adapted from a Hans Christian Andersen story. This deal was also accepted, but when Shearer became pregnant, she was forced to leave the production and a French ballerina, Renee Jeanmaire, was chosen as her replacement. When it was over, more than $4,000,000 was spent on the film, including $400,000 for a single ballet sequence which takes up 17 minutes of screen time. Luckily, Goldwyn's dream paid off big at the box office with HANS CHRISTIAN ANDERSEN grossing $6,000,000, eventually coming in third behind THE BEST YEARS OF OUR LIVES (1946) and GUYS AND DOLLS (1955) as Goldwyn's biggest moneymaker. Not only was the film popular with the public, the Motion Picture Academy nominated the film six times, for Best Cinematography, Best Score of a Musical Film, Best Song ("Thumbelina"), Best Art/Set Design for a Color Film, Best Costume Design, and Best Sound Recording, but none of the nominations garnered any awards. Goldwyn slowed down his prodigious output of films after HANS CHRISTIAN ANDERSEN, and was to complete only two more (GUYS AND DOLLS [1955], PORGY AND BESS [1959]) before retiring. Songs include "I'm Hans Christian Andersen," "No Two People," "The Ugly Duckling," "Inchworm," "Thumbelina," "Wonderful Wonderful Copenhagen," "Anywhere I Wander," and "The King's New Clothes" (Frank Loesser).

p, Samuel Goldwyn; d, Charles Vidor; w, Moss Hart (based on a story by Myles Connolly); ph, Harry Stradling (Technicolor); m, Frank Loesser; ed, Daniel

Mandell; md, Walter Scharf; art d, Richard Day, Antoni Clave; set d, Howard Bristol; cos, Clave, Mary Wills, Mme. Karinska; ch, Roland Petit; m/l, Loesser.

Children's Film (PR: AAA MPAA:NR)

HANSEL AND GRETEL** (1954) 75m RKO c

Voices: Anna Russell *(Rosina Rubylips, the Witch)*, Mildred Dunnock *(Mother)*, Frank Rogier *(Father)*, Delbert Anderson *(Sandman)*, Helen Boatwright *(Dew Fairy)*, Apollo Boy's Choir *(Angels and Children)*, Constance Brigham *(Hansel and Gretel)*.

The popular opera by Engelbert Humperdinck (the original, not the pop singer) is staged here by a bunch of electronically controlled puppets called Kinemins. It seems like a fine, charming idea for a while, but after about 20 minutes it becomes dull and finally irritating. Kids may enjoy it.

p, Michael Myerberg; d, John Paul; w, Padraic Colum (based on a play be Adelheid Wette from the fairy tale by the Bros. Grimm); ph, Martin Munkasci (Technicolor); m, Engelbert Humperdinck; ed, James F. Barclay; set d, Evalds Dajevskis; cos, Ida Vendicktow; head animator, Joseph Horstmann; animators, Inez Anderson, Daniel Diamond, Ralph Emory, Hobert Rosen, Ted Shepard, Nathalie Schulz; characters designed by James Summers.

Fantasy/Children Cas. (PR:AA MPAA:NR)

HANSEL AND GRETEL½** (1965, Ger.) 52m Schongerfilm/ Childhood Productions c (HANSEL UND GRETEL)

Paul Tripp *(Narrator)*, Jurgen Miksch, Mara Inken Bielenberg, Jochen Diestelmann, Ellen Frank, Barbara Gallauner, Wolfgang Eichberger.

Straightforward film version of the classic Brothers Grimm fairy tale. Originally released in West Germany in 1954.

p, Hubert Schonger; d, Walter Janssen; w, Gerhard F. Hummel (based on *Hansel and Gretel* by Jakob and Wilhelm Grimm, English adaptation by Christopher Cruise); ph, Wolf Schwan (Eastmancolor); m, Guiseppe Becce; art d, Gunther Strupp; m/l, Anne and Milton Delugg.

Fantasy/Children (PR:AA MPAA:NR)

HA' PENNY BREEZE** (1950, Brit.) 72m Storytellers/ Associated British Pathe bw

Don Sharp *(Johnny Craig)*, Edwin Richfield *(David King)*, Gwyneth Vaughan *(Joan King)*, Terry Everett *(Brian King)*, Eva Rowland *(Mrs. King)*, Roger Maxwell *(Mr. Simmonds)*, John Powe *(Barney)*, Darcy Conyers *(Richard Martin)*, Natalie Raine, Frank Hawkins Arthur Goullet, Bartlett Mullins, Owen Reynolds, Chris Halward, Michael Gough.

Richfield plays a soldier who returns to his village to discover it a far cry from the comforting place he grew up. Aided by pal Sharp, the two men start their own little boating company, using a yachting race as a ploy to attract some attention. This inventive way to rejuvenate the failing town, also makes for a likable film that makes the patron feel good.

p, Darcy Conyers, Don Sharp; d, Frank Worth; w, Worth, Sharp; ph, George Stretton, Gordon Lang.

Drama (PR:A MPAA:NR)

HAPPENING, THE½** (1967) 101m Horizon/COL c

Anthony Quinn *(Roc Delmonico)*, George Maharis *(Taurus)*, Michael Parks *(Sureshot)*, Robert Walker Jr. *(Herby)*, Martha Hyer *(Monica Delmonico)*, Faye Dunaway *(Sandy)*, Milton Berle *(Fred)*, Oscar Homolka *(Sam the Tailor)*, Jack Kruschen *(Inspector)*, Clifton James *(O'Reilly)*, James Randolph Kuhl *(Arnold)*, Eugene Roche, Luke Askew *(Motorcycle Officers)*.

Four debauched Miami beach bums looking for a thrill wind up kidnaping Mafioso Quinn. When they try to ransom him off nobody wants to pay to get him back. Quinn angrily seizes the gun and takes over his own kidnaping. He makes a few threatening calls and the ransom soars from $200,000 to $3,000,000. The kidnapers manage to pick up the cash without the FBI spotting them, but the bills are marked. Quinn burns the money and walks out. There might have been a good movie here, but between Quinn's nonperformance and a script lurching from slapstick to pathos to action, it's lost. Faye Dunaway's first film.

p, Jud Kinberg; d, Elliot Silverstein; w, Frank R. Pierson, James D. Buchanan, Ronald Austin (based on a story by Buchanan, Austin); ph, Philip Lathrop; m, De Vol; ed, Philip Anderson; prod d, Richard Day; art d, Albert Brenner; set d, Don Ivey; cos, Eugene Coffin, Jason Silverstein; spec eff, Willis Cook; m/l, "The Happening," De Vol, Eddie Holland, Lamont Dozier, Brian Holland (sung by the Supremes), "Early in the Morning," De Vol, William Roy.

Comedy (PR:C MPAA:NR)

HAPPIDROME* (1943, Brit.) 87m Aldwych/MGM bw

Harry Korris *(Mr. Lovejoy)*, Robbie Vincent *(Enoch)*, Cecil Frederick *(Ramsbottom)*, Bunty Meadows *(Bunty Mossup)*, Lisa Lee *(Tanya/Josephine)*, Jeannie Gregson *(Mrs. Bane)*, Joss Ambler *(Mr. Mossup)*, Valentine Dunn *(Mrs. Mossup)*, Leslie "Hutch" Hutchinson, The Cairoli Brothers, Muriel Zillah, Connie Creighton, Marie Lawson, Olga Stevenson, Arthur Hambling, Bombardier Billy Wells.

This ridiculous name for a film should warn the wary to stay away from the theater, and rightfully so, as whatever potential was lurking behind the idea (one used to a bit better success in Mel Brooks' THE PRODUCERS) was never brought to the screen. Yarn centers around a wealthy man's desire to fulfill the dream of his daughter, which is to become a great dramatic star. He produces a play for her which becomes a tremendous success, not because of its great dramatic rendition, but for its perverseness, which comes off as great comedy. Unfortunately this picture did not produce the laughter that was supposedly created by the play.

p, Harold Boxall, Jack Buchanan, Tom Arnold; d, Phil Brandon; w, Arnold, James Seymour (based on the radio series by Harry Korris); ph, Geoffrey Faithfull.

Comedy (PR:A MPAA:NR)

HAPPIEST DAYS OF YOUR LIFE*½** (1950, Brit.) 81m Individual/BL bw

Alastair Sim *(Wetherby Pond)*, Margaret Rutherford *(Miss Muriel Whitchurch)*, Joyce Grenfell *(Miss Gossage)*, Edward Rigby *(Rainbow)*, Guy Middleton *(Victor Hyde-Brown)*, John Bentley *(Richard Tassell)*, Bernadette O'Farrell *(Miss Harper)*, Muriel Aked *(Miss Jezzard)*, John Turnbull *(Conrad Matthews)*, Richard Wattis *(Arnold Billings)*, Arthur Howard *(Anthony Ramsden)*, Millicent Wolf *(Miss Curtis)*, Myrette Morven *(Miss Chapell)*, Russell Waters *(Mr. West)*, Gladys Henson *(Mrs. Hampstead)*, Kenneth Downey *(Sir Angus McNally)*, Laurence Naismith *(Dr. Collett)*, Stringer Davis *(Reverend Birch)*, Patricia Owens *(Angela Parry)*, Angela Glynne *(Barbara Colhoun)*, Percy Walsh *(M. Jove)*, John Boxer, Harold Goodwin, Patience Rentoul, Alan Broadhurst, Vivienne Wood, Stanley Lemin, Olwen Brookes, Nan Munro, Beryl Ede, George Benson, Margaret Anderson, Betty Blackler, Fred Marshall, John Rhodes, Jim Davies, Keith Faulkner, William Symons, Lilian Stanley.

During the Blitz of London, a girls' school is evacuated to the country and billeted with a boys' school due to a bureaucratic snafu. It's an excuse for a lot of laughs as the students hit if off and headmaster Sim clashes with headmistress Rutherford. Exceptional comedy, inspired casting.

p, Frank Launder, Sidney Gilliat; d, Launder; w, Launder, John Dighton (based on a play by Dighton); ph, Stan Pavey; m, Mischa Spoliansky; ed, Oswald Hafenrichter; prod d, Joseph Bato.

Comedy (PR:A MPAA:NR)

HAPPIEST MILLIONAIRE, THE* (1967) 164m Disney/BV c

Fred McMurray *(Anthony J. Drexel Biddle)*, Tommy Steele *(John Lawless)*, Greer Garson *(Mrs. Cordelia Biddle)*, Geraldine Page *(Mrs. Duke)*, Gladys Cooper *(Aunt Mary Drexel)*, Hermione Baddeley *(Mrs. Worth)*, Lesley Ann Warren *(Cordy Biddle)*, John Davidson *(Angie Dule)*, Paul Peterson *(Tony Biddle)*, Eddie Hodges *(Livingston Biddle)*, Joyce Bulifant *(Rosemary)*, Sean McClory *(Sgt. Flanagan)*, Aron Kincaid *(Walter Blakely)*, Larry Merrill *(Charlie Taylor)*, Frances Robinson *(Aunt Gladys)*, Jim McMullan *(Lt. Powell)*, William Wellman, Jr. *(Lt. Grayson)*, Norman Grabowski *(Joe Turner)*, Jim Gurley *(Marine Lieutenant)*, Joan Marshall *(Maid)*, George *(An Alligator)*.

Overlong, frightfully dull musical has MacMurray as an eccentric millionaire living in Philadelphia with wife Garson, daughter Warren, and a number of pet alligators. This was the last film Walt Disney had anything to do with. Tradeshown at 164 minutes, later cut to 141 before release. Songs include: "What's Wrong With That?" "Watch Your Footwork," "Valentine Candy," "Strengthen the Dwelling," "I'll Always Be Irish," "Bye-Yum Pum Pum," "I Believe in This Country," "Detroit," "There Are Those," "When a Man Has a Daughter," "Let's Have a Drink On It," "Are We Dancing?" "La Belle Fille D'amour," "It Won't Be Long 'til Christmas," "Fortuosity" (Richard B. and Robert M. Sherman).

p, Walt Disney, Bill Anderson; d, Norman Tokar; w, A.J. Carothers (based on the play by Kyle Chrichton, from the book *My Philadelphia Father* by Chrichton, Cordelia Drexel Biddle); ph, Edward Colman (Technicolor); m, Richard M. and Robert B. Sherman; ed, Cotton Warburton; md, Jack Elliott; art d, Carroll Clark, John B. Mansbridge; set d, Emile Kuri, Frank R. McKelvey; cos, Bill Thomas; spec eff, Eustace Lycett, Peter Ellenshaw; ch, Marc Breaux, Dee Dee Wood.

Musical Cas. (PR:AA MPAA:NR)

HAPPILY EVER AFTER (SEE: MORE THAN A MIRACLE, 1967, Fr./Ital.)

HAPPINESS (SEE: LE BONHEUR, 1966, Fr.)

HAPPINESS AHEAD*** (1934) 80m FN/WB bw

Dick Powell *(Bob Lane)*, Josephine Hutchinson *(Jean Bradford)*, John Halliday *(Henry Bradford)*, Dorothy Dare *(Josie)*, Frank McHugh *(Tom Bradley)*, Allen Jenkins *(Chuck)*, Ruth Donnelly *(Anna)*, Marjorie Gateson *(Mrs. Bradford)*, Russell Hicks *(Meehan)*, Mary Louise Treen *(Comedienne)*, J.M. Kerrigan *(Boss of Window Washers)*, Mary Russell *(Girl)*, Gavin Gordon *(Travis)*, Mary Forbes *(Mrs. Travis)*, Jane Darwell.

Pleasant musical comedy features Hutchinson in her screen debut as a bored heiress who decides to join the proletariat by becoming a window washer. Falling in love with fellow washer Powell comes next, of course. There's nothing special in the script or the performances, but LeRoy's impeccable direction makes it work. Songs include: "Beauty Must Be Loved" (Irving Kahal, Sammy Fain), "There Must Be Happiness Ahead," "Pop Goes Your Heart," "All on Account of a Strawberry Sundae" (Mort Dixon, Allie Wrubel), and "Massaging Window Panes" (Bert Kalmar, Harry Ruby).

d, Mervyn LeRoy; w, Harry Sauber, Brian Marlow (based on a story by Sauber); ph, Tony Gaudio; ed, William Clemens; art d, John J. Hughes; cos, Orry-Kelly.

Musical/Comedy (PR:A MPAA:NR)

HAPPINESS C.O.D.** (1935) 70m CHES bw

Maude Eburne *(Aunt Addie)*, Donald Meek *(Thomas Sherridan)*, Irene Ware *(Carroll Sherridan)*, William Bakewell *(Ken Sherridan)*, Polly Ann Young *(Eleanor)*, Lona Andre *(Beatrice Manning)*, Frank "Junior" Coghlan, Jr. *(Larry Sherridan)*, Malcolm MacGregor *(Jim Martin)*, Edwin Maxwell *(Lester Walsh)*, Robert Mackenzie *(Sam Townsend)*, Fred Sumner *(Mr. Manning)*, Richard Carlyle *(Rev. Huxley)*, John Dilson *(Snyder)*, Richard Krammer, Jack Shutta.

Meek is an engineer whose three children put quite a strain on his finances. But when the bank threatens to foreclose on the mortgage, the kids (Ware, Bakewell, and Coghlan) pull together to help. Eburne plays Meek's sister and housekeeper and dominates every scene she's in. Pleasant, but nothing more.

p, George R. Batcheller; d, Charles Lamont; w, Robert Ellis, Helen Logan; ph, M.A. Andersen; ed, Roland Reed.

Comedy **(PR:A MPAA:NR)**

HAPPINESS CAGE, THE** (1972) 94m International Film Ventures/ Cinerama c (AKA: THE MIND SNATCHERS)

Christopher Walken *(Pvt. James Reese)*, Joss Ackland *(Dr. Frederick)*, Ralph Meeker *(The Major)*, Ronny Cox *(Miles)*, Marco St. John *(Orderly)*, Tom Aldredge *(Medic)*, Bette Henritze *(Anna Kraus)*, Susan Travers *(Nurse Schroeder)*, Birthe Newmann *(Lisa)*, Claus Nissen *(Psychiatrist)*.

Strange, pseudo-intellectual drama about Army mind-control experiments. Confusing at best, though Walken is good as a rebellious victim.

p, George Goodman; d, Bernard Girard; w, Ron Whyte (based on the play by Dennis Reardon); ph, Manny Wynn (Movielab Color); m, Phil Ramone, Chris Dedrick; ed, Sidney Katz; art d, William Molyneaux.

Drama **(PR:C MPAA:PG)**

HAPPINESS OF THREE WOMEN, THE½** (1954, Brit.) 79m Advance/Adelphi bw

Brenda de Banzie *(Jane Price)*, Petula Clark *(Delith)*, Donald Houston *(John)*, Patricia Cutts *(Irene)*, Eynon Evans *(Amos)*, Patricia Burke *(Ann)*, Bill O'Connor *(Peter)*, Gladys Hay *(Amelia)*, Glyn Houston *(Morgan)*, Emyra Leyshon *(David)*, Hugh Pryse *(Minister)*, Jessie Evans *(Blodwen)*, John Lewis *(Bus Driver)*, Mary Jones *(Mary Lewis)*, Julie Milton *(Nancy)*, Eira Griffiths *(Hannah)*, Ronnie Harris *(Ben)*.

Three women staying at a remote Welsh inn toss coins in a well wishing for help in their miserable lives. Along comes postman Evans (who also wrote the original play and collaborated on the screenplay) to help them out and set them straight. Nice, but nothing special.

p, David Dent; d, Maurice Elvey; w, Eynon Evans, Maufy Davis (based on the play "The Wishing Well" by Evans); ph, Stan Pavey; m, Ted Astley; ed, Robert Jordan Hill.

Drama **(PR:A MPAA:NR)**

HAPPINESS OF US ALONE½** (1962, Jap.) 114m Tokyo Eiga/ Toho bw (NAMONAKU MAZUSHIKU UTSUKUSHIKU)

Hideko Takamine *(Akiko Katayama)*, Keiju Kobayashi *(Michio Katayama)*, Izumi Hara *(Akiko's Mother)*, Yoichi Numata *(Akiko's Brother)*, Mitsuko Kusabue *(Akiko's Sister)*, Yuzo Kayama *(Akira)*, Kamatari Fujiwara, Chieko Nakakita, Jun Tatara, Takeshi Kato.

Melodramatic but sensitively told tale of Takamine, a deafmute woman, who returns to her mother's home after the death of her husband in WW II. There she meets Kobayashi, a deafmute man, and they fall in love. Kobayashi convinces the wary Takamine that together they can overcome their handicaps and build a successful life. Takamine overcomes her fears and marries Kobayashi, but their life is indeed unhappy. Their first child dies in infancy. Takamine's evil brother sells his mother's house, forcing the old woman to live with the deafmute couple. A second child is born and Takamine's mother gives the couple a gold ring to sell in order to buy a sewing machine with which to start a business. Things begin to look up for the pair until the brother returns and sells the sewing machine. Having come to her breaking point, Takamine goes off to commit suicide, but Kobayashi talks her out of it. When spring arrives the couple's hopes are raised by the announcement that their son has graduated with honors from elementary school. That same day, Takamine is visited by an orphan whose life she had saved during the war. Takamine finally realizes that despite her handicap, she has been a valued member of society.

p, Sanezumi Fujimoto, Ken-ichiro Tsunoda; d&w, Zenzo Matsuyama; ph, Masao Tamai; m, Hikaru Hayashi; ed, Y. Sabura; art d, Satoru Nakakao, Takeshi Kano.

Drama **(PR:A MPAA:NR)**

HAPPY** (1934, Brit.) 80m British International/Wardour bw

Stanley Lupino *(Frank Brown)*, Laddie Cliff *(George)*, Will Fyffe *(Simmy)*, Dorothy Hyson *(Lillian)*, Harry Tate *(Dupont)*, Renee Gadd *(Pauline)*, Gus McNaughton *(Waller)*, Jimmy Godden *(Brummelberg)*, Bertha Belmore *(Mrs. Brummelberg)*, Hal Gordon *(Conjuror)*, Elizabeth Vaughan, Norma Varden.

Pleasant musical comedy about Lupino, a starving, garret-dwelling musician who invents an anti-car theft device, sells it to an insurance company for millions, and marries the daughter of the boss of the company. A thin story, but Lupino, Cliff, and Fyffe are talented comic performers and pull it off.

p&d, Fred Zelnik; w, Austin Melford, Frank Launder, Arthur Woods, Stanley Lupino (based on the musical play "Es War Einmal Ein Musikus" by Jacques Bachrach, Alfred Hahm, Karl Notl); ph, Claude Friese-Greene, Ronald Neame, Bryan Langley.

Musical/Comedy **(PR:A MPAA:NR)**

HAPPY ALEXANDER (SEE: VERY HAPPY ALEXANDER, 1969, Fr.)

HAPPY ANNIVERSARY*** (1959) 83m Fields/UA bw

David Niven *(Chris Walters)*, Mitzi Gaynor *(Alice Walters)*, Carl Reiner *(Bud)*, Loring Smith *(Mr. Gans)*, Monique Van Vooren *(Jeanette)*, Phyllis Povah *(Mrs. Gans)*, Elizabeth Wilson *(Millie)*, Patty Duke *(Debbie Walters)*, Kevin Coughlin *(Okkie Walters)*.

On the thirteenth anniversary of his marriage to Gaynor, a slightly drunk Niven confides to her parents that he and Gaynor had shared a bed a full year prior to taking their vows. He is overheard by daughter Duke, who, believing her parents on the verge of divorce, goes on a children's panel TV show and tells the whole story to the nation. Further complications lead to a reconciliation and happy ending. Good adult comedy with Niven particularly enjoyable as he kicks in TV screen after TV screen.

p, Ralph Fields; d, David Miller; w, Joseph Fields and Jerome Chodorov (based on their play "Anniversary Waltz"); ph, Lee Garmes; m, Robert Allen, Sol Kaplan; ed, Richard Meyer; prod d, Paul Heller; md, Allen; m/l, "I Don't Regret a Thing," "Happy Anniversary," Allen, Al Stillman; makeup, Herman Buchman.

Comedy **(PR:C MPAA:NR)**

HAPPY AS THE GRASS WAS GREEN* (1973) 105m Martin c

Geraldine Page *(Anna Witmer)*, Pat Hingle *(Eli)*, Graham Beckel *(Eric)*, Rachel Thomas *(Hazel)*, Steve Weaver *(Jim Witmer)*, Elvin Byler *(Rufus)*, Noreen Huber *(Sarah)*, John Miller *(Ben)*, Luke Sickles *(Menno Witmer)*.

Beckel is a hippie who travels to Pennsylvania's Mennonite country with college friend Weaver to bury the latter's brother. At first he is bewildered by what he sees, but before long he undergoes a religious conversion, becoming a Mennonite. Most of the cast is made up of real Mennonites, but the film is lacking in something . . . perhaps it's a coherent idea of what it's supposed to be. In any event, this is a very dull movie.

p, Burt Martin; d&w, Charles Davis (based on a novel by Merle Good); ph, Stan Martin (CFI Color); m, Gordon Zahler; ed, Erwin Dumbrille.

Drama **(PR:A MPAA:PG)**

HAPPY BIRTHDAY, DAVY zero (1970) 90m Zenith c (AKA: I AM CURIOUS GAY)

Chuck Roy *(Bob Cassidy)*, Larry Neilsen *(Davy)*, Dick Fontaine *(Mr. Balsam)*, Judy Curtis *(Sis)*, Carl Williams *(Butch)*, Jack Reed *(Dick)*, Robin Roberts *(Nick)*, Joe Bell *(Joe)*. Mary Fordas, Tim Bartlett, Jerry Murray.

On his 21st birthday, Neilsen wanders into a gay bar and meets the man of his dreams. He has some trouble telling his sister about it later, but she is understanding. Awful gay melodrama: too, too sincere. A 16-mm movie to keep in the closet. Originally titled I AM CURIOUS GAY.

p, Richard Fontaine, Chuck Roy; d, Fontaine; w, Roy; ph, Robert Miser; m, Lou Hanagan; ed, Richard Charles; art d, George Lewis.

Drama **(PR:O MPAA:NR)**

HAPPY BIRTHDAY, GEMINI*½ (1980) 107m UA c

Madeline Kahn *(Bunny Weinberger)*, Rita Moreno *(Lucille Pompi)*, Robert Viharo *(Nick Geminiani)*, Alan Rosenberg *(Francis Geminiani)*, Sarah Holcomb *(Judith Hastings)*, David Marshall Grant *(Randy Hastings)*, Timothy Jenkins *(Herschel Weinberger)*, David McIllwraith *(Sam Weinberger)*, Maura Swanson *(Mary O'Donnel)*, Richert Easley *(Judge)*, John William Kennedy *(O'Donnel)*, Michael Donaghue *(Father McBride)*, Alberto de Rosa *(Dominique)*, Michael Holton *(Court Clerk)*, A. Frank Ruffo *(Jerry)*, Dwayne McLean *(Eddie)*, Jeff Wincott *(Taxi Driver)*.

On his 21st birthday, Italian-bred, Harvard-educated Viharo is plagued by concerns over his sexual identity. A fairly good stage production with some bite is reduced to platitudinous pulp in the screenplay as Viharo struggles toward a resolution no audience by then can care much about.

p, Rupert Hitzig, Bruce Calnan; d&w, Richard Benner (based on the play "Gemini" by Albert Innaurato); ph, James B. Kelly; m, Rich Look, Cathy Chamberlain; ed, Stephan Fanfara; prod d, Ted Watkins; cos, D. Lynne MacKay.

Drama **(PR:O MPAA:R)**

HAPPY BIRTHDAY TO ME*½ (1981) 108m COL c

Melissa Sue Anderson *(Virginia)*, Glenn Ford *(Dr. Faraday)*, Tracy Bregman *(Ann)*, Jack Blum *(Alfred)*, Matt Craven *(Steve)*, Lenore Zann *(Maggie)*, David Eisner *(Rudi)*, Lisa Langlois *(Amelia)*, Lawrence Dane *(Hal)*, Frances Hyland *(Mrs. Patterson)*, Sharon Acker *(Estelle)*, Michel Rene LaBelle *(Etienne)*, Richard Rabiere *(Greg)*, Lesleh Donaldson *(Bernadette)*, Earl Pennington *(Lt. Tracy)*, Murray Westgate *(Gatekeeper)*, Jerome Tiberghein *(Prof. Heregard)*, Maurice Pedbrey *(Dr. Feinblum)*, Vlasta Vrana *(Bartender)*, Griffith Brewer *(Verger)*, Alan Katz *(Ann's Date)*, Ron Lea *(Amelia's Date)*, Terry Haig *(Feinblum's Assistant)*, Karen Stephen *(Miss Calhoun)*, Louis Del Grande *(Surgeon)*, Nick Kilvertus *(Anesthestist)*, Aamir Andrei *(Junior Surgeon)*, Gina Dick *(Waitress)*, Stephanie Miller *(Nurse)*, Steven Mayoff *(Police)*, Aram Barkev, Alan Barnett, Paul Board, Marc Degagne, Bruce Gooding, Victor Knight, Rollie Nicheri, Keith Sutherland, Herbert Vool, Len Watt, Joe Wertheimer, Walter Massey *(Conventioneers)*, Nancy Allan, Karen Hynes, Tracy-Marie Langdon, Debbit McGellin, Kathy Reid, Cori Timmons, Debbie Tull, Lynn Wilson *(Cheerleaders)*.

When her friends start dying a series of lurid deaths, Anderson thinks she herself might be the killer. Glenn Ford is her psychiatrist. Not as much blood as most of this sort, but with compensating plot twists for the story-hungry. Otherwise, for viewers without any discrimination at all.

p, John Dunning, Andre Link; d, J. Lee Thompson; w, John Saxton, Peter Jobin, Timothy Bond (based on a story by Saxton); ph, Miklos Lente (Metrocolor); m, Bo Harwood, Lance Rubin; ed, Debra Karen; prod d, Earl Preston; cos, Hugette Gagne.

Horror **Cas.** **(PR:O MPAA:R)**

HAPPY BIRTHDAY, WANDA JUNE*½** (1971) 105m Filmmakers Group-Sourdough-Red Lion/COL c

Rod Steiger *(Harold Ryan)*, Susannah York *(Penelope Ryan)*, George Grizzard *(Dr. Norbert Woodley)*, Don Murray *(Herb Shuttle)*, William Hickey *(Looseleaf Harper)*, Steven Paul *(Paul Ryan)*, Pamelyn Ferdin *(Wanda June)*, Pamela Saunders *(Mildred Ryan)*, Louis Turenne *(Maj. Von Kiningswald)*, C.C. Whitney *(Mrs. Kestenbaum)*, Lester M. Goldsmith *(Mr. Kestenbaum)*.

Lost in the Amazonian jungle for eight years, Steiger returns home to find his once dimwitted carhop wife (York) educated and liberated. Fine comedy full of humor, morbidity, and bite. Good cast with Steiger's macho swaggering adventurer a standout, along with York. The high point comes fairly early as Ferdin explains from Heaven why she is happy that she was run over by an ice cream truck on her birthday.

p, Lester M. Goldsmith; d, Mark Robson; w, Kurt Vonnegut, Jr. (based on his play); ph, Fred Koenekamp; ed, Dorothy Spencer; prod d, Boris Leven; set d, Ruby Levitt; cos, Michael Woulfe; makeup, Ben Lane.

Comedy **(PR:C MPAA:R)**

HAPPY DAYS*** (1930) 86m FOX bw

Charles E. Evans *(Col. Billy Batcher)*, Marjorie White *(Margie)*, Richard Keene *(Dick)*, Stuart Erwin *(Jig)*, Martha Lee Sparks *(Nancy Lee)*, Clifford Dempsey *(Sheriff Benton)*, James J. Corbett, George MacFarlane *(Interlocutors)*, Janet Gaynor, Charles Farrell, Victor McLaglen, El Brendel, William Collier, Sr., Tom Patricola, George Jessel, Dixie Lee, Nick Stuart, Rex Bell, Frank Albertson, Sharon Lynn, Whispering Jack Smith, Lew Brice, J. Farrell MacDonald, Will Rogers, Edmund Lowe, Walter Catlett, Frank Richardson, Ann Pennington, David Rollins, Warner Baxter, J. Harold Murray, Paul Page, The Slate Brothers, Flo Bert, George Olsen and his Orchestra, Helen Mann, Mary Lansing, Beverly Royed, Joan Navarro, Catherine Navarro, John Christensen, Dorothy McNames, Vee Maule, Hazel Sperling, Bo Peep Karlin, Georgia Pembleton, Marbeth Wright, Miriam Hellman, Margaret La Marr, Consuelo De Los Angeles, Lee Auburn, Betty Halsey, Joyce Lorme, Myra Mason, Eileen Bannon, Theresa Allen, Pear La Velle, Barbara La Velle, Gertrude Friedly, Dorothy Krister, Doris Baker, Milissa Ten Eyck, Kay Gordon, Betty Gordon, Jean De Parva, Joan Gaylord, Charlotte Hamill, Alice Goodsell, Gwen Keate, Virginia Joyce, LaVerne Leonard, Betty Grable, Marjorie Levoe, Pat Hanne, Estella Essex *(Chorus Women)*, Jack Frost, John Westerfelt, Douglas Steade, Peter Custulovich, John Lockhart, Randall Reynolds, Carter Sexton, Leo Hanley, George Scheller, Kenneth Nordyke, Marius Langan, Ralph Demaree, Glen Alden, Frank McKee, Bob McKee, Joe Holland, Ed Rockwell, Clarence Brown, Jr., Roy Rockwood, Enrico Cucinelli, Harry Lauder, Ted Waters, Thomas Vartian, J. Harold Reeves, Phil Kolar, Frank Heller, William Hargraves, Ted Smith *(Chorus Men)*.

A thin plot about a Mississippi showboat owned by Evans saved from bankruptcy by a charity show is just the excuse Fox needed to troop out just about every star on the lot for a brief turn in front of the camera. Among the numbers, Gaynor and Farrell sing "We'll Build a Little World of Our Own," (James Hanley, James Brockman) Whispering Jack Smith whispers "Happy Days," and Sharon Lynn sings "Snake Hips" (Con Conrad, Sidney Mitchell, Archie Gottler) as Ann Pennington shows how it's done. Other numbers include "Mona," "Crazy Feet" (Conrad, Mitchell, Gottler), "Minstrel Memories," "I'm On a Diet of Love" (L. Wolfe Gilbert, Abel Baer), "A Toast To the Girl I Love," "Dream On a Piece of Wedding Cake" (Hanley, Brockman), "Vic and Eddie" (Harry Stoddard, Marcy Klauber). Filmed in a 70mm-wide screen process known as "Grandeur." A thoroughly enjoyable piece of entertainment.

d, Benjamin Stoloff; w, Edwin Burke, Sidney Lanfield; ph, Lucien Andriot, John Schmitz (Grandeur camera, J.O. Taylor); ed, Clyde Carruth; art d, Jack Schulze; ch, Earl Lindsay; cos, Sophie Wachner.

Musical **(PR:A MPAA:NR)**

HAPPY DAYS ARE HERE AGAIN*½ (1936, Brit.) 87m Argyle/AP&D bw (AKA: HAPPY DAYS REVUE)

Renee Houston *(Kitty Seymour)*, Billie Houston *(Mickey Seymour)*, Shirley Houston *(Nita)*, Harry Milton *(Chris)*, Billy Watts *(Reg Jarvis)*, George Harris *(Brainwave)*, Viola Compton *(Lil Grayson)*, Sally McBride *(Ella)*, Mark Stone *(Alf)*, Ida Barr *(Girlie)*, Marie Kendall, Bert and Michael Kidd, Syd Seymour and His Mad Hatters, Herbert Cameron, Billie Dix, Tony Smythe.

Contrived musical drama centering around the successes and failures of a three-sister act as they struggle to gain fame, only to meet with the hard-luck blues every would-be star must learn to contend with. The three do achieve a moderate amount of recognition, but not nearly enough to support the type of egos each has developed. So it's back to the basement and another attempt at climbing the steep stairs to success. Only this time their path is made easier by the presence of a helpful agent. Too bad he couldn't do something about aiding the plight of this movie, which despite its poor quality was reissued two years later.

p, John Argyle; d, Norman Lee; w, Dan Birt, F.H. Bickerton, Alan Rennie (based on the story by Renee Houston).

Musical/Drama **(PR:A MPAA:NR)**

HAPPY DEATHDAY*½ (1969, Brit.) 89m Westminster/MRA c

Cyril Luckham *(Josiah Swineyard)*, Harry Biard *(Dr. John Sylvester)*, Clement McCallin *(Prof. Esteban Zoltan)*, Yvonne Antrobus *(Jetta Zoltan)*, Bryan Coleman *(Dr. Oliver Tarquin)*, Harriette Johns *(Rebecca Zoltan)*, John Comer *(Briggs)*.

British weeper in which a man too enmeshed in his scientific work to care about the emotional state of his family, gets a shock when death steps into his life. This comes in the form of a daughter who commits suicide when she becomes pregnant. This jolt apparently has enough force to make him pay some attention to people, especially his aging father who has a short time left to live.

p, Louis Fleming, Donald Loughman; d&w, Henry Cass (based on a play by Peter Howard).

Drama **(PR:C MPAA:NR)**

HAPPY END** (1968, Czech.) 73m Barrandov/CD bw (STASTNY KONEC)

Vladimir Mensik *(Bedrich)*, Jaroslava Obermayerova *(Julie)*, Josef Abrham *(Lothario)*, Bohus Zahorsky *(Father-In-Law)*, Stella Zazvorkova *(Mother-In-Law)*, Helena Ruzickova *(Brunette)*, Josef Hlinomaz *(Policeman)*.

Bizarre Czech film wherein all physical and narrative action occur in reverse motion. The film opens as the severed head of Mensik is returned to his body (he had just been guillotined). He walks back into the prison, and soon walks out the front entrance. He discovers a suitcase on the sidewalk and brings it home. There he finds the dismembered pieces of a dead woman, which he reassembles. He falls in love with the woman and takes her to a seaside resort. There he suspects that his woman is flirting with another man, so he takes his rival into the ocean and drowns him. Dissatisfied with his woman, Mensik decides to "unmarry" her despite her protest. A priest conducts the ceremony, but the woman will not leave Mensik alone. He throws the woman into a burning building and goes off to another romance. An interesting experiment that would have been more successful if it were shorter, by a Czech director of comedies best known for his Wild West satires.

d, Oldrich Lipsky; w, Milos Macourek, Lipsky (based on a story by Macourek); ph, Vladimir Novotny; m, Vlastimil Hala.

Comedy/Drama **(PR:C-O MPAA:NR)**

HAPPY ENDING, THE* (1931, Brit.) 70m GAU bw

Anne Grey *(Mildred Craddock)*, Benita Hume *(Yvonne)*, George Barraud *(Dennis Craddock)*, Alf Goddard *(Alf)*, Cyril Raymond *(Anthony Fenwick)*, Daphne Courtenay *(Mollie Craddock)*, Alfred Drayton *(Life of the Party)*, Irene Russell *(Wife)*.

A woman leads her daughter to believe that her father died in an act of bravery many years previous. The father, who was actually leading a free and easy life while globetrotting, returns, disrupts the woman's lifestyle, and dies. The tricky title is assurance that the daughter never learns the truth about her father.

p, L'Estrange Fawcett; d, Millard Webb; w, H. Fowler Mear, Sidney Gilliat [uncredited] (based on the play by Ian Hay); ph, Percy Strong.

Drama **(PR:A MPAA:NR)**

HAPPY ENDING, THE** (1969) 117m UA c

Jean Simmons *(Mary Wilson)*, John Forsythe *(Fred Wilson)*, Lloyd Bridges *(Sam)*, Teresa Wright *(Mrs. Spencer)*, Dick Shawn *(Harry Bricker)*, Nanette Fabray *(Agnes)*, Robert Darin *(Franco)*, Tina Louise *(Helen Bricker)*, Kathy Fields *(Marge Wilson)*, Gail Hensley *(Betty)*, Shirley Jones *(Flo)*, Eve Brent *(Ethel)*, William O'Connell *(Minister)*, Barry Cahill *(Handsome Man)*, Miriam Blake *(Cindy)*.

Simmons decides that she's not happy with her 16-year marriage to Forsythe, so she walks out in search of herself. The search runs the gamut of booze, affairs, and drugs as her dreary life unfolds to nobody's edification and to a resolution that is half-hearted at best.

p,d&w, Richard Brooks; ph, Conrad Hall (Panavision, Technicolor); m, Michel Legrand; ed, George Grenville; cos, Rita Riggs; spec eff, Geza Gaspar; m/l, "What Are You Doing the Rest of Your Life?" Legrand, Alan Bergman (sung by Michael Dees); makeup, Fred Blau.

Drama **(PR:C MPAA:M)**

HAPPY EVER AFTER½** (1932, Ger./Brit.) 86m UFA/W&F bw (EIN BLONDER TRAUM)

Lilian Harvey *(Jou-Jou)*, Jack Hulbert *(Willie)*, Cicely Courtneidge *(Illustrated Ida)*, Sonnie Hale *(Willie)*, Edward Chapman *(Colonel)*, Clifford Heatherley *(Commissionaire)*, Charles Redgie *(Secretary)*, Percy Parsons *(Merriman)*.

A peppy little musical shot in both German and English with Harvey starring in both as a delicate artist who is conned out of her meager savings by a cheat. Window washers Hulbert and Hale (both known in the film as "Willie") save the girl from a downfall and in the process fall in love with her. With their scheming, Harvey goes on to become a phenomenal songstress. Co-penned by Billy Wilder and Walter Reisch, who both fled their Nazi-infested country soon afterwards, as did producer Pommer.

p, Erich Pommer; d, Paul Martin, Robert Stevenson; w, Jack Hulbert, Douglas Furber (based on a story by Billy Wilder, Walter Reisch); ph, Gunther Rittau, Otto Baecker, Konstantin Tschet; m/l, Werner Richard Heyman, "Somewhere In The World Is a Little Bit of Happiness," "One Day Everybody's Turn Comes."

Musical/Comedy **(PR:A MPAA:NR)**

HAPPY EVER AFTER (SEE: TONIGHT'S THE NIGHT, 1954)

HAPPY FAMILY, THE* (1936, Brit.) 67m BL bw

Hugh Williams *(Victor Hutt)*, Leonora Corbett *(Barbara Hutt)*, Dick Francis *(Mr. Hutt)*, Eve Gray *(Nina Harrison)*, Maidie Hope *(Mrs. Hutt)*, Ellen Pollock *(Leo Hutt)*, Glennis Lorimer *(Robina Hutt)*, Max Adrian *(Noel Hutt)*, D.A. Clarke-Smith *(Mr. Harrison)*, Muriel George *(Housekeeper)*.

Francis, the businessman head of the "happy family," becomes disgusted with the lazy attitude of his brood and cons them into believing that he's gone bankrupt. "Thrift" becomes the key word around the house, especially when Francis really does go bankrupt. Luckily for him, however, daughter Corbett shows some foresight and saves the family with money she has earned.

p, Herbert Smith; d, Maclean Rogers; w, Rogers, Kathleen Butler (based on the play "French Salad" by Max Cotto); ph, George Stretton.

Comedy **(PR:A MPAA:NR)**

HAPPY FAMILY, THE (SEE: MR. LORD SAYS NO, 1952)

HAPPY GO LOVELY*** (1951, Brit.) 97m N.P. Rathvon/RKO c

David Niven *(B.G. Bruno)*, Vera-Ellen *(Janet Jones)*, Cesar Romero *(John Frost)*, Bobby Howes *(Charlie)*, Diana Hart *(Mae)*, Sandra Dorne *(Betty)*, Gordon Jackson *(Paul Tracey)*, Barbara Couper *(Mme. Amanda)*, Henry Hewitt *(Dodds)*, Gladys Henson *(Mrs. Urquhart)*, Hugh Dempster *(Bates)*, Joyce Carey *(Secretary)*, Lohn Laurie *(Jonskill)*, Wylie Watson *(Stage-Doorman)*, Kay Kendall *(Secretary)*, Joan

Heal *(Phylis Gardiner)*, Hector Ross *(Harold)*, Ambrosine Phillpots *(Lady Martin)*, Molly Urquhart *(Mme. Amanda's Assistant)*, David Lober, Jonathon Lucas, Jack Billings, Douglas Scott and his Debonair Boys *(Principal Dancers)*, Rolf Alexander, Ian Stuart, Leon Biedryski.

Dancer Vera-Ellen hitches a ride in a limousine and rumors fly when she is seen exiting it. She is linked to the mysterious millionaire who owns the car and since the show she's in is going under, producer Romero decides to give her the lead in hopes of attracting some of his money. Niven shows up and is thought to be a reporter and Vera-Ellen falls in love with him. He turns out to be the millionaire. Better than it sounds, thanks to excellent performances and a light directorial touch. Songs include: "One-Two-Three" (Mischa Spoliansky); "Would You-Could You" (Spoliansky, Jack Fishman); "London Town."

p, Marcel Hellman; d, Bruce Humberstone; w, Val Guest, Arthur Macrae (based on a story by F. Dammann, H. Rosenfeld); ph, Erwin Hillier (Technicolor); m, Mischa Spoliansky; ed, Bert Bates; md, Louis Levy; art d, John Howell; ch, Jack Billings, Pauline Grant.

Musical **Cas.** **(PR:A MPAA:NR)**

HAPPY-GO-LUCKY½** (1937) 69m REP bw

Phil Regan *("Hap" Cole/Bill Lyons)*, Evelyn Venable *(Mary Gorham)*, Jed Prouty *(Charles Gorham)*, William Newell *(Charlie Davis)*, Jonathan Hale *(Bennett)*, Harlan Briggs *(U.S. Consul Brown)*, Stanley Andrews *(Matzdorf)*, Claude King *(Col. Wallis)*, Carleton Young *(Al)*, Karl Hackett *(Porozzi)*, Guy Kingsford *(Joe)*, Howard Hickman *(Doctor)*, Willie Fung *(Coolie)*.

After her husband, a Marine aviator, vanishes, Venable goes to Shanghai and spots dancer Regan in a show. Since he is a dead ringer for her husband, she decides that it must be him, stricken with amnesia. There's murder, kidnaping, gangsters, and a few songs to fill out the running time. Routine programmer. Songs include: "Right or Wrong" (Ted Koehler, Sammy Stept), "A Treat For the Eyes" (Stept, Cliff Friend), and "Happy-Go-Lucky" (all sung by Regan).

p, Nat Levine; d, Aubrey Scotto; w, Raymond Schrock, Olive Cooper (based on a story by Eric Taylor, Wellyn Totman, Endre Bohem); ph, Ernest Miller; ed, Henry Weber; md, Harry Grey.

Action/Musical **(PR:A MPAA:NR)**

HAPPY GO LUCKY** (1943) 79m PAR c

Mary Martin *(Marjory Stuart)*, Dick Powell *(Pete Hamilton)*, Betty Hutton *(Bubbles Hennessy)*, Eddie Bracken *(Wally Case)*, Rudy Vallee *(Alfred Monroe)*, Mabel Paige *(Mrs. Smith)*, Eric Blore *(Mr. Vespers)*, Clem Bevans *(Mr. Smith)*, Rita Christiani *(Specialty Dancer)*, Sir Lancelot *(Singer)*, Ben Carter *(Joe Brown)*, Lillian Randolph *(Tessie)*, Paul McVey *(Assistant Manager)*, Frederick Clarke *(Doorman)*, William B. Davidson *(Husband)*, Almira Sessions *(Overstuffed Matronly Woman)*, Tom Dugan *(Meek Little Man)*, Sarah Edwards *(Spinster)*, Hillary Brooke *(Young Society Girl)*, Napoleon Simpson *(Tessie's Husband)*, Leyland Hodgson *(Reporter in Lobby)*, Irving Bacon, Arthur Loft *(Reporters)*, Donald Kerr *(Photographer)*, Gene Cole *(Dancer)*, Olaf Hytten *(Jeweler)*, Kay Linaker *(Suzanne)*, Jean Fenwick *(Agnes)*, Harry Barris *(M.C.)*, Edgar Norton *(Captain of Waiters)*, Charles R. Moore *(Pandro)*, Lyle Latell *(Man in Kissing Routine)*.

A formula wartime musical that never acknowledged that the war was going on. Martin is a New York hatcheck/cigarette girl who has saved up her small bankroll and come to what looks like the island of Trinidad in order to snare a rich husband. (It could have been any one of several Caribbean isles and we only surmise Trinidad because of the calypso singers who seem to float in and out every time there's a dull spot in the action, which is a great deal more than somewhat.) She arrives on the same boat with Hutton (who stole the show), a singer who is coming to meet her lover, Bracken, who is a resident of the island. Bracken's best pal is beach comber Powell and once they learn that Martin, who is masquerading as a wealthy type, is not rich at all, the three conspire to help her land Vallee, playing the same kind of snobbish role he did in PALM BEACH STORY and continued for many years up to and including his work in HOW TO SUCCEED IN BUSINESS WITHOUT REALLY TRYING. In the course of events, Martin and Powell fall in love and marry. Although there were some fine songs, Vallee didn't get to sing any of them but Hutton had more than her share and her rendition of "Murder He Says" was a highlight. The legendary "Sir Lancelot" also had a good turn doing the traditional calypso "Never Make A Pretty Woman Your Wife." Other songs by Loesser and McHugh included "Let's Get Lost," "Fuddy Duddy Watchmaker," "Sing A Tropical Song," "Happy Go Lucky," and "Ta-Ra-Ra-Boom-De-Ay" by Sayers, with special lyrics by Loesser. Screenwriters Panama and Frank worked together for many years with great success and whenever a duo break up, producers wonder "which is the strong one?" That question was answered in the subsequent careers of the two. Frank went on to do A TOUCH OF CLASS among many others. Panama almost disappeared after his disastrous THE MALTESE BIPPY and I WILL I WILL . . . FOR NOW.

p, Harold Wilson; d, Curtis Bernhardt; w, Walter DeLeon, Norman Panama, Melvin Frank (adaptation by John Jacoby from a story by Michael Uris); ph, Karl Struss, Wilfrid Cline (Technicolor); ed, Ellsworth Hoagland; md, Robert Emmett Dolan; art d, Hans Dreier, Raoul Rene DuBois; ch, Paul Oscard; m/l, Frank Loesser, Jimmy McHugh, Henry J. Sayers.

Musical/Comedy **(PR:AA MPAA:NR)**

HAPPY GYPSIES (SEE: I EVEN MET HAPPY GYPSIES, 1967, Yugo.)

HAPPY HOOKER, THE* (1975) 96m Cannon c

Lynn Redgrave *(Xaviera Hollander)*, Jean Pierre Aumont *(Yves St. Jacques)*, Lovelady Powell *(Madelaine)*, Nicholas Pryor *(Carl Gordon)*, Elizabeth Wilson *(Mrs. Gordon)*, Tom Poston *(J. Arthur Conrad)*, Conrad Janis *(Fred)*, Richard Lynch *(Cop)*, Owen Hollander *(Lt. Taggert)*, Inga Bunsch *(Finch)*, Stefan Schnabel *(Elderly Gentleman)*, Lee Wallace *(Mr. Knowlton)*, Gwynda Donhowe *(Mrs. Knowlton)*, George Dzunda *(Chet)*, Kenneth Tigar *(Steve)*, Dorothy Fox *(Rosita)*, Barton Heyman *(Dirty Harry)*, Mathew Cowles *(Albert)*, Murray Moston *(Customs Officer)*, Allan Rich *(Desk Sergeant)*, William Duell *(Meek Man)*, Vincent Schiavelli *(Geru)*, Florence Tarlow *(Petulia)*, Dan Resin *(Under-Secretary)*, Guillermo Irizarry *(Carlos)*, Pat Henry *(Aurora)*, Sharon Laughlin *(Nadine)*, Anita Morris *(Linda Jo or May)*, Darlene Parks *(April)*, Trish Hawkins *(Chris)*, Donna Mitchell *(Lucille)*, Denise Galik *(Cynthia)*, Rochelle Oliver *(Norma)*, Mary Olga *(Rosie)*.

Xaviera Hollander's sexy memoirs are watered down and fictionalized to such a point that sex hardly plays a part. Redgrave is the Dutch secretary who leaves her dull office job for success and fame as a high-class prostitute. Not sexy, not funny, not good.

p, Fred Caruso; d, Nicholas Sgarro; w, William Richert (based on the book by Xaviera Hollander, Robin Moore, and Yvonne Dunleavy); ph, Dick Kratina; m, Don Elliott; ed, Jerry Greenberg; prod d, Gene Callahan; cos, Ann Roth; ch, Donald Saddler.

Comedy **Cas.** **(PR:O MPAA:R)**

HAPPY HOOKER GOES TO HOLLYWOOD, THE zero (1980) 85m Cannon c

Martine Beswicke, Adam West, Phil Silvers, Richard Deacon, Edie Adams, Chris Lemmon.

Beswicke is a high-class hooker doing her thing in movieland. This looks like the last of the three-film Happy Hooker series and that is reason for hope, if nothing else.

p, Menahem Golan, Yoram Globus; d, Alan Roberts; w, Devi Goldenberg; ph, Stephen Gray.

Comedy **Cas.** **(PR:O MPAA:R)**

HAPPY HOOKER GOES TO WASHINGTON, THE* (1977) 89m Movie Machine/Cannon c

Joey Heatherton *(Xaviera Hollander)*, George Hamilton *(Ward Thompson)*, Ray Walston *(Sen. Sturges)*, Jack Carter *(Sen. Caruso)*, Phil Foster *(Sen. Krause)*, David White *(Sen. Rawlings)*.

The centerpiece of the Happy Hooker trilogy has Heatherton as the Dutch prostitute and author this time. She is summoned to testify to a Senate committee as to whether sex is ruining the country. She relates a series of liaisons and tells how each had a serious purpose and wasn't just mindless sex. During a recess, CIA agent Billy Barty recruits her to use her charms on an Arab oil shiek. Heatherton gives her all for the country, hidden under a sheet. Writer Bob Kaufman scored with his next film LOVE AT FIRST BITE.

p&d, William A. Levey; w, Robert Kaufman; ph, Robert Caramico (Movielab Color); ed, Lawrence Marinelli; art d, Robin Royce, B.B. Neel; cos, John David Ridge, Gail Viola.

Comedy **Cas.** **(PR:O MPAA:R)**

HAPPY IS THE BRIDE** (1958, Brit.) 84m Panther/Kassler bw

Ian Carmichael *(David Chaytor)*, Janette Scott *(Janet Royd)*, Cecil Parker *(Arthur Royd)*, Terry-Thomas *(Policeman)*, Joyce Grenfell *(Aunt Florence)*, Eric Barker *(Vicar)*, Edith Sharpe *(Mildred Royd)*, Elvi Hale *(Petula)*, John Le Mesurier *(Chaytor)*, Nicholas Parsons *(John Royd)*, Virginia Maskell *(Marcia)*, Thorley Walters *(Jim)*, Irene Handl *(Mme. Edna)*, Sarah Drury *(Miranda Royd)*, Miles Malleson *(1st Magistrate)*, Athene Seyler *(Aunt Harriet)*, Cardew Robinson *(George the Verger)*, Victor Maddern *(Shop Steward)*, Sam Kydd *(Foreman)*, Brian Oulton *(2nd Magistrate)*, Rolf Lefebvre *(Court Clerk)*, Pauline Winters *(Ethel)*, Joan Hickson *(Mrs. Bowels)*, Ian Wilson *(Umpire)*, Margaret Lacey *(Miss Dacres)*, Enid Hewitt *(Lady Yeldham)*, Olive Milbourne *(Miss Illingsworth)*, Peggy Ann Clifford *(Bella)*.

Comedy stars Carmichael and Scott as a couple about to marry but driven to argue by their relatives. They decide to disappear until the day of the wedding, but on that day they are thrown into jail for a driving violation. However, a police car takes them to the wedding in time, and the hectic chuckles at least subside. This is a remake of QUIET WEDDING, 1940.

p, Paul Soskin; d, Roy Boulting; w, Boulting, Jeffrey Dell (based on the play "Quiet Wedding" by Esther McCracken); ph, Ted Scaife; m, Benjamin Frankel; ed, Anthony Harvey; md, Frankel, art d, Albert Witherick.

Comedy **(PR:A MPAA:NR)**

HAPPY LAND*** (1943) 75m FOX bw

Don Ameche *(Lew Marsh)*, Frances Dee *(Agnes)*, Harry Carey *(Gramp)*, Ann Rutherford *(Lenore Prentiss)*, Cara Williams *(Gretchen Barry)*, Richard Crane *(Rusty)*, Henry Morgan *(Tony Cavrek)*, Minor Watson *(Judge Colvin)*, Dickie Moore *(Peter Orcutt)*, William Weber *(Bill Beecher)*, Oscar O'Shea *(Father Case)*, Adeline Reynolds *(Mrs. Schneider)*, Roseanne Murray *(Velma)*, James West *(Rusty Age 12-16)*, Larry Olsen *(Rusty Age 5)*, Bernard Thomas *(Sam Kendall)*, Terry Masengale *(Arch)*, Edwin Mills *(Bud)*, James J. Smith *(Everett Moore)*, Mary Wickes *(Emmy)*, Walter Baldwin *(Jake Hibbs)*, Tom Stevenson *(Mr. MacMurray)*, Eileen Pringle *(Mrs. Prentiss)*, Matt Moore *(Mr. Prentiss)*, Darla Hood *(Lenore Prentiss Age 12)*, Richard Abbott *(Rev. Wood)*, Lillian Bronson *(Mattie Dyer)*, Ferris Taylor *(Mayor)*, Larry Thompson *(Andy)*, Paul Weigel *(Pop Schmidt)*, Ned Dobson, Jr. *(Jackie)*, Jackie Averill *(Ted)*, Joe Bernard *(Clerk)*, Housely Stevenson *(Sam Watson)*, Elvin Field *(Joe)*, Juanita Quigley *(Sally Pierce)*, Milton Kibbee *(Shep Wayne)*, John Dilson *(Charles Clayton)*, Leigh Whipper *(Old Ben)*, Robert Dudley *(Old Man Bowers)*, Pass Le Nori *(Dr. Hammond)*.

Ameche is the proprietor of an Iowa drugstore made bitter by the death of his son (Crane) in a naval battle. Carey turns up as the ghost of his father to show him that Crane had enjoyed his life, brief as it was, and that he, Ameche, has also had a pretty good life, with a loving wife (Dee), and a respectable position in the community. Extensive flashbacks make up the bulk of the film, which sometimes sinks in its own sentimentality and warmth. It usually works, though, and it's well worth checking out if for no other reason than to look for 5-year-old Natalie Wood making her film debut somewhere way back in the support.

p, Kenneth Macgowan; d, Irving Pichel; w, Kathryn Scola, Julien Josephson (based on a novel by MacKinlay Kantor); ph, Joseph La Shelle; m, Cyril J. Mockridge; ed, Dorothy Spencer; md, Emil Newman; art d, James Basevi, Russell Spencer; spec eff, Fred Sersen.

Drama **(PR:A MPAA:NR)**

HAPPY LANDING** (1934) 60m MON bw

Ray Walker *(Nick Terris)*, Jacqueline Wells *(Janet)*, William Farnum *(Colonel)*, Hyram Hoover *(Peter Taylor)*, Morgan Conway *(Harland)*, Warner Richmond *(Powell)*, Noah Beery *(Capt. Terris)*, Donald Reed, Billy Erwin, Ruth Romaine, Edward Fetherstone, Gertrude Simpson.

Minor but enjoyable programmer has thieves in a seaplane threatening to blow up a ship unless they give the loot to an accomplice on board, then stop to let him board the seaplane. Border Patrol agent Walker foils their scheme, of course.

d, R.N. Bradbury; w, Stuart Anthony; ph, Archie Stout.

Crime **(PR:A MPAA:NR)**

HAPPY LANDING½** (1938) 102m FOX bw

Sonja Henie *(Trudy Erickson)*, Don Ameche *(Jimmy Hall)*, Jean Hersholt *(Herr Ericksen)*, Ethel Merman *(Flo Kelly)*, Cesar Romero *(Duke Sargent)*, Billy Gilbert *(Counter Man)*, Wally Vernon *(Al Mahoney)*, El Brendel *(Yonnie)*, Marcelle Corday *(Gypsy)*, Joseph Crehan *(Agent)*, Eddie Conrad *(Waiter)*, Ben Welden *(Manager Madison Square Garden)*, Leah Ray *(Orchestra Vocalist)*, Alex Novinsky *(Count)*, Robert Lowery, Lon Chaney, Jr. *(Reporters)*, Raymond Scott and His Quintet, Peters Sisters, Condos Bros.

Bandleader Romero and manager Ameche travel to Norway, there meeting Henie. Romero woos her, and when he returns to the U.S., she follows. Ameche builds her into a skating star and she falls in love with him (he having loved her all along). Lots of good music and dance and who cares if Henie can't act? Songs include: "Hot and Happy," "Yonny and his Oompah," "You Are The Music to the Words in my Heart," "A Gypsy Told Me" (Jack Yellen, Samuel Pokrass), "You Appeal to Me" (Walter Bullock, Harold Spina).

p, Darryl F. Zanuck; d, Roy Del Ruth; w, Milton Sperling, Boris Ingster; ph, John Mescal; ed, Louis Loeffler; md, Louis Silvers; ch, Harry Losee.

Musical **(PR:A MPAA:NR)**

HAPPY MOTHER'S DAY . . . LOVE, GEORGE** (1973) 90m Cinema 5 c (AKA: RUN, STRANGER, RUN)

Patricia Neal *(Cara)*, Cloris Leachman *(Ronda)*, Bobby Darin *(Eddie)*, Tessa Dahl *(Celia)*, Ron Howard *(Johnny)*, Kathie Browne *(Crystal)*, Joe Mascolo *(Piccolo)*, Simon Oakland *(Ron Howard)*, Thayer David *(Minister Pollard)*, Gale Garnett *(Yolanda)*, Roy Applegate *(Porgie)*, Jan Chamberlain *(Florence)*, Gerald E. Forbes *(Bomber)*, Clarence Greene Jeans *(Mr. Mears)*, Orest Ulan *(Preacher)*.

Muddled tale of bastard Howard, his cafe-owner mother (Leachman), and his strange aunt (Neal). Howard wanders through his Nova Scotia village trying to uncover its dark secrets, and a series of gruesome murders are mixed in for good measure. An excellent cast is lost in this mess, probably an indication of the original film being cut to ribbons before release. Bobby Darin's last movie before his death the same year after open-heart surgery.

p&d, Darren McGavin; w, Robert Clouse; ph, Walter Lassally; m, Don Vincent; ed, George Grenville; cos, Robert Anson, Anne Klein, Pierre Cardin.

Mystery/Horror **(PR:C MPAA:PG)**

HAPPY ROAD, THE*** (1957) 99m MGM bw

Gene Kelly *(Mike Andrews)*, Barbara Laage *(Suzanne Duval)*, Michael Redgrave *(Gen. Medworth)*, Bobby Clark *(Danny Andrews)*, Brigitte Fossey *(Janine Duval)*, Roger Treville *(Dr. Solaise)*, Colette Dereal *(Helene)*, Jess Hahn *(Morgan)*, Maryse Martin *(Mme. Fallere)*, Roger Saget *(Verbier)*, Van Doude *(French Motorcycle Officer)*, Claire Gerard *(Patronne Hotel)*, Colin Mann *(Armbruster)*, Alexandre Rignault *(Bucheron)*, T. Bartlett *(Earl of Boardingham)*, J. Dufilo *(Bicycle Rider)*.

American boy Clark runs away from his Swiss boarding school, trying to reach father Kelly in Paris and prove to him that he is self-sufficient enough to live with him. Fossey, from the same school and harboring a crush on him, goes along to act as interpreter. Kelly and Laage, Fossey's mother, meet at the school and take an instant dislike to each other. They are, however, stuck and so they take to the road in search of their kids. The children, meanwhile, are having a series of adventures, eluding police and NATO patrols, getting help from a group of sympathetic students, and riding into Paris with some bicycle racers. Kelly and Laage give up their search and return to Paris and find the children asleep in Kelly's bed. Their children safe, the hostility melts away and before the close things are looking distinctly matrimonial. Charming film, worth seeking out. Maurice Chevalier sings the title song and is, of course, a joy.

p&d, Gene Kelly; w, Arthur Julien, Joseph Morhaim, Harry Kurnitz (based on a story by Julien and Kurnitz); ph, Robert Juillard; m, George Van Parys; ed, Borys Lewin; art d, Alexandre Traunes.

Comedy/Drama **(PR:A MPAA:NR)**

HAPPY THIEVES, THE½** (1962) 88m Hillworth/UA bw (AKA: ONCE A THIEF)

Rex Harrison *(Jim Bourne)*, Rita Hayworth *(Eve Lewis)*, Joseph Wiseman *(Jean Marie Calbert)*, Gregoire Aslan *(Dr. Munoz)*, Alida Valli *(Duchess Blanca)*, Virgilio Texera *(Cayetano)*, Peter Illing *(Mr. Pickett)*, Brita Ekman [Britt Ekland] *(Mrs. Pickett)*, Julio Pena *(Senor Elek)*, Gerard Tichy *(Antonio)*, Lou Weber, Antonio Fuentes *(Guards)*, George Rigaud *(Inspector)*, Barta Barri *(Chern)*, Karl-Heinz Schwerdtfeger *(Police Official)*, Princess Yasmin Khan *(Girl)*.

This middling muddled comedy/crime drama is a hodge-podge of splintered episodes without a strong connecting theme but it boasts the once-considerable talents of Harrison, Hayworth, and Valli. Harrison is a dapper art thief who enraptures Valli, a wealthy duchess, and then steals a priceless painting by Velazquez from her estate. Hayworth, who is Harrison's paramour and aide-in-crime, smuggles the painting to Paris but here it falls into the hands of Aslan, a berserk art dealer who intends to possess the world's greatest paintings by hook and, mostly, by crook. All of it is too much for Hayworth, who decides she will quit the art theft racket, but Harrison keeps her in the fold by walking her to the altar. Once back in Madrid, they are approached by Aslan, who shows them photos of Harrison stealing the Velazquez and threatens to expose them unless he steals a Goya for him from the Prado. Harrison succumbs to the blackmail and agrees. Wiseman, a master art forger in league with Harrison, then paints a duplicate of the Goya Aslan has selected and the thieves make the switch during a bullfight. To further confuse the police, Aslan ruthlessly kills a matador while he performs in the ring. When Harrison, Wiseman, and Hayworth take Aslan the painting they find him murdered, killed by Valli, who has been hunting for her Velazquez. Police are hot on their heels and arrest the lot. When it appears that Wiseman will be sent to prison for ten years, Harrison takes the blame and goes off to prison, mostly to win Hayworth's favor. Of course, she will wait for him . . . and wait . . . and wait. It's too bad that the producers didn't wait for a better script; this one goes in too many directions at the same time, attempting to be funny via the zany antics of its crooked characters in the mode of THE LAVENDER HILL MOB, but is has one foot in THE ASPHALT JUNGLE's heavy drama. It's confusing and too many incidents are disconnected; Valli's avenging angel image at the end is simply mystifying as she appears out of nowhere. It's sad to see the two once-beauteous stars Hayworth and Valli so unglamorous, unkind age hardening faces that used to soften male hearts around the world. Shot on location in and around Madrid, Spain. This was both the first and the last production of the short-lived Hillworth company, a collaboration between Hayworth and her fifth husband, James Hill (formerly of Hecht-Hill-Lancaster). A second picture had been planned, and extensively publicized, but Hill and Hayworth were divorced before the release of THE HAPPY THIEVES and the follow-up film was cancelled on a day's notice. Hayworth's daughter by Pakistani playboy Prince Aly Khan plays a bit role.

p, James Hill, Rita Hayworth; d, George Marshall; w, John Gay (based on the novel *The Oldest Confession* by Richard Condon); ph, Paul Beeson; m, Mario Nascimbene; ed, Oswald Hafenrichter; art d, Ramiro Gomez; cos, Pedro Rodrigues, Pierre Balmain.

Comedy/Drama **(PR:C MPAA:NR)**

HAPPY TIME, THE*½** (1952) 94m Kramer/COL bw

Charles Boyer *(Jacques Bonnard)*, Louis Jourdan *(Uncle Desmonde)*, Marsha Hunt *(Susan Bonnard)*, Kurt Kasznar *(Uncle Louis)*, Linda Christian *(Mignonette Chappuis)*, Bobby Driscoll *(Bibi)*, Marcel Dalio *(Grandpere Bonnard)*, Jeanette Nolan *(Felice)*, Jack Raine *(Mr. Frye)*, Richard Erdman *(Alfred Grattin)*, Marlene Cameron *(Peggy O'Hare)*, Gene Collins *(Jimmy Bishop)*, Ann Faber *(Yvonne)*, Kathryn Sheldon *(Miss Tate)*, Maurice Marsac *(The Great Gaspari)*, Will Wright *(Dr. Marchaud)*, Eugene Borden *(Monsieur Lafayette)*.

A delightful film version of a stage hit which sees the world opening before the eyes of an innocent, beguiling 12-year-old boy, Driscoll, who lives in Ottawa with his warm, fun-loving largely French-Canadian family. Boyer is the romantically inclined father who gently sees his son through his first crisis when Driscoll is seized with a sudden attraction to the female species. His Scotch-born mother, Hunt, provides balance to a family that is more carefree than responsible, more capricious than realistic. Jourdan, of course, she considers a less-than-solid influence upon Driscoll as the younger uncle with a penchant for chasing skirts and collecting garters from reigning burlesque queens. Kasznar, a wine-loving rather slap-happy older uncle, tells his naive nephew to live for love. Even Dalio, as the infirm grandfather, is ruled by a passionate heart and can't resist springing from his so-called death bed to chase after attractive matrons. Surrounded by such an amorous lot, Driscoll goes a little overboard and falls hopelessly in love with the family maid who has just been hired, a curvy young former showgirl, Christian, who also attracts the appreciating eye of Jourdan. Driscoll eventually deserts the shapely lass, with Boyer's patient guidance toward a healthy outlook on sex and love. The boy becomes the dedicated sweetheart of Cameron, the little girl next door. The dialog is charming and witty and everyone, particularly Boyer, plays out their roles with splendid aplomb. This was Boyer's last starring role and it remained one of his favorite films. Driscoll, who was one of the most versatile child actors in Hollywood, having appeared in such fine films as THE SULLIVANS (1944) and THE WINDOW (1949), is terrific as the young boy suddenly jolted by emotions he never knew existed. He would tragically die of a heart attack from a drug overdose at age thirty. Fleischer directs with elan and provides a zippy pace. A rare film with plenty of vitality that never misses a beat, except for a few in Driscoll's fluttering heart.

p, Stanley Kramer; d, Richard Fleischer; w, Earl Felton (based on the play by Samuel A. Taylor and book by Robert Fontaine); ph, Charles Lawton, Jr.; m, Dmitri Tiomkin; ed, William A. Lyon; art d, Carl Anderson; set d, James Crowe; m/l, Tiomkin, Ned Washington.

Comedy **(PR:AAA MPAA:NR)**

HAPPY YEARS, THE½** (1950) 109m MGM c

Dean Stockwell *(John Humperdink Stover)*, Darryl Hickman *(Tough McCarthy)*, Scotty Beckett *(Tennessee Shad)*, Leon Ames *(Samuel H. Stover, Sr.)*, Margalo Gillmore *(Mrs. Stover)*, Leo G. Carroll *(The Old Roman)*, Donn Gift *(The Big Man)*, Peter Thompson *(Sambo)*, Jerry Mickelsen *(Cheyenne Baxter)*, Alan Dinehart III *(Coffee-Colored Angel)*, David Bair *(White Mountain Canary)*, Danny Mummert *(Butsey White)*, Eddie LeRoy *(Poler Beekstein)*, George Chandler *(Johnny)*, Claudia Barrett *(Miss Dolly Travers)*.

Stockwell is the tiny terror of Lawrenceville school in this plotless, meandering comedy based on a popular series of magazine stories. A pleasant walk down memory lane.

p, Carey Wilson; d, William A. Wellman; w, Harry Ruskin (based on "The Lawrenceville School Stories" by Owen Johnson); ph, Paul C. Vogel (Technicolor); m, Leigh Harline; ed, John Dunning; art d, Cedric Gibbons, Daniel B. Cathcart.

Comedy **(PR:A MPAA:NR)**

HAR HAR DU DITT LIV (SEE: HERE'S YOUR LIFE, 1966, Swed.)

HARAKIRI*** (1963, Jap.) 135m Shochiku-Toho bw (SEPPUKU)

Tatsuya Nakadai *(Hanshiro Tsugumo)*, Shima Iwashita *(Miho Tsugumo)*, Akira Ishihama *(Motome Chijiiwa)*, Yoshio Inaba *(Jinai Chijiiwa)*, Rentaro Mikuni *(Kageyu Saito)*, Masao Mishima *(Tango Inaba)*, Tetsuro Tamba *(Hikokuro Omodaka)*, Ichiro Nakaya *(Hayato Yazaki)*, Yoshio Aoki *(Umenosuke Kawabe)*, Jo Azumi *(Ichiro Shimmen)*, Hisashi Igawa, Shoji Kobayashi, Ryo Takeuchi *(Young Samurai)*, Shichisaburo Amatsu *(Page)*, Kei Sato *(Masakazu Fukushima)*.

After the centralization of political power in Japan in the 17th century, the samurai have been displaced and left to wander the countryside asking estate owners' permission to commit hara-kiri in hopes that the wealthy landowners will take pity and give them work. Nakadai, an aging samurai, wanders into an estate and makes his request. He is told by the estate's chief retainer, Mikuni, of a young samurai, Ishihama, who had arrived earlier asking the same thing. To keep the samurai code pure, Ishihama was forced to commit hara-kiri with a bamboo sword (he had sold his real sword to provide for his family). Undaunted, Nakadai asks each of the estate's three principal swordsmen to serve as his second in the ritual. When the time for the ritual comes and none of the swordsmen show up, Nakadai reveals himself as the father-in-law of the dead Ishihama. To revenge the dead samurai, Nakadai cuts off the top knots of the three swordsmen, thus dishonoring them. Mikuni orders his men to kill Nakadai and in the ensuing battle many are killed by the old samurai, until he, too, falls. Mikuni then orders his three swordsmen to commit hara-kiri and declares that the whole incident must be kept a secret.

p, Tatsuo Hosoya; d, Masaki Kobayashi; w, Shinobu Hashimoto; ph, Toshio Miyajima; m, Toru Takemitsu; ed, Hisashi Sagara; art d, Jun-ichi Ozumi, Shigemasa Toda; fencing master, Seiji Iho.

Drama **(PR:O MPAA:NR)**

HARASSED HERO, THE*½ (1954, Brit.) 61m Corsair/AB-Pathe bw

Guy Middleton *(Murray Selwyn)*, Joan Winmill *(Nurse Brooks)*, Elwyn Brook-Jones *(Logan)*, Mary Mackenzie *(Estelle Logan)*, Harold Goodwin *(Twigg)*, Joss Ambler *(Dr. Grice)*, Clive Morton *(Archer)*, Hugh Moxey *(Willis)*, Gabrielle Brune, Gaylord Cavallaro, Alfred Maron, Stafford Byrne, Simone Lovell, Harold Malin, Alan Rolfe.

Silly comedy routines abound in this patented British farce which casts Middleton as an affluent hypochondriac bachelor who uncovers a plot by a gang of counterfeiters. When he comes into possession of some printing plates the gang wants, they turn on the pressure. Winmill, Middleton's nurse, is kidnaped, but manages to help the bumbling hero snare the culprits.

p, Clive Nicholas; d, Maurice Elvey; w, Brock Williams (based on a novel by Ernest Dudley); ph, Hone Glendinning.

Comedy/Crime **(PR:A MPAA:NR)**

HARBOR LIGHT YOKOHAMA** (1970, Jap.) 91m Shochiku c (KIRI NI MUSEBU YORU)

Asahi Kurizuka *(Akira Taki)*, Yuki Jono *(Reiko Machida)*, Hiroshi Yamanami *(Joli)*, Ken Kuroki *(Ken)*, Ryohei Uchida *(Shuhei Isshiki)*, Ichiro Sugai *(Otaguro)*, Toru Abe *(Ichizo Uchiyama)*, Eriko Sono *(Naomi)*, Michiko Yajima *(Mina)*, Nakajiro Tomita, Hiroshi Wada, Kuniko Ogata, Akiko Nakamura, Ken Yamanouchi.

Japanese gangster film starring Kurizuka as a young man who takes the blame on a murder rap for his girl friend's brother (who had really committed the crime) and flees from Japan. Five years later he returns to learn that his girl, Jono, has married a much older, rich financier (Sugai). Looking for work, Kurizuka is hired by a narcotics dealer to kill Sugai who is trying to block one of the mobster's drug deals. Kurizuka learns that Jono has married Sugai for money with which to support her brother who had promised to give up his life of crime. Her brother, however, has taken the money to improve his standing in the mob. Kurizuka decides to wipe out Jono's brother's mob, but is killed before he can see her one last time. Nicely written mob story with strong American influences.

d, Meijiro Umezu; w, Isao Mori, Hisashi Aku; ph, Kazumi Hamazaki; m, Jun Suzuki; ed, Teruo Nakajima.

Crime **(PR:C-O MPAA:NR)**

HARBOR LIGHTS** (1963) 68m FOX bw

Kent Taylor *(Dan Crown)*, Jeff Morrow *(Cardinal)*, Miriam Colon *(Gina Rosario)*, Antonio Torres Martino *(Capt. Acosta)*, Art Bedard *(Capt. Aristarchus)*, Braulio Castillo *(Manolo)*, Jose de San Anton *(Father Riva)*, Luis Antonio Martinez *(Vallejo)*, Jose Manuel Caicoya *(Mortician)*, Roberto Rivera Negron *(Storekeeper)*, Allan Sague *(Hotel Clerk)*, Victor Mojica, Alfredo Perez, Tino Garcia *(Cardinal's Men)*, Ralph Rodriguez *(Alex Crown)*.

Taylor plays an American gambler who arrives in Puerto Rico to visit his brother. He finds him murdered and learns that his involvement with a stolen diamond caused his death. Taylor decides to get to the bottom of the mystery and finds himself hounded by a police detective, Martino, and a gang leader, Morrow (who thinks Taylor has the gem). Taylor locates the killers and the diamond, and turns them over to the police.

p&d, Maury Dexter; w, Henry Cross; ph, John Nickolaus, Jr.; m, Paul Sawtell, Bert Shefter; ed, Jodie Copelan.

Crime **(PR:A MPAA:NR)**

HARBOR OF MISSING MEN½** (1950) 60m REP bw

Richard Denning *(Brooklyn)*, Barbara Fuller *(Mae Leggett)*, Steven Geray *(Capt. Corcoris)*, Aline Towne *(Angelike)*, Percy Helton *("Rummy" Davis)*, George Zucco *(H.G. Danziger)*, Paul Marion *(Philip Corcoris)*, Ray Teal *(Frank)*, Robert Osterloh *(Johnny)*, Fernanda Eliscu *(Mama Corcoris)*, Gregory Gay *(Capt. Koretsky)*, Jimmie Kelly *(Carl)*, Barbara Stanley *(Leodora)*, Neyle Morrow *(Christopher)*, Charles LaTorre *(John)*.

Fishing boat owner Denning augments his income by using his boat for smuggling, but before he can deliver the money to boss Zucco he is robbed. Zucco thinks Denning stole the money and puts a couple of hit men on his trail. While hiding out, Denning falls in love and decides to go straight. He proves his innocence to Zucco and fingers the robbers, one of whom is soon dead, along with Zucco. Denning faces society ready to pay for his crimes. Good programmer really keeps moving.

p, Sidney Picker; d, R.G. Springsteen; w, John K. Butler; ph, John MacBurnie; m, Stanley Wilson; ed, Arthur Roberts; art d, Frank Arrigo.

Crime **(PR:A MPAA:NR)**

HARD-BOILED CANARY (SEE: THERE'S MAGIC IN MUSIC, 1941)

HARD BOILED MAHONEY** (1947) 63m MON bw

Leo Gorcey *(Slip)*, Huntz Hall *(Sach)*, Bobby Jordan *(Bobby)*, Billy Benedict *(Whitey)*, David Gorcey *(Chuck)*, Gabriel Dell *(Gabe)*, Teala Loring *(Eleanor)*, Dan Seymour *(Armand)*, Bernard Gorcey *(Louie)*, Patti Brill *(Alice)*, Betty Compson *(Selena Webster)*, Danny Beck *(Lennie the Meatball)*, Pierre Watkin *(Dr. Carter)*, Noble Johnson *(Hasson)*, Byron Foulger *(Prof. Quizard)*, Teddy Pavelec *(Thug)*, Pat O'Malley *(Police Lieutenant)*, Jack Cheatham *(Police Sergeant)*, William Ruhl, Tom Faust.

Inspired by the success of films like THE MALTESE FALCON, Monogram stuck the Bowery Boys in this mystery which sees Gorcey and Hall mistaken for detectives by mysterious woman Compson, who hires the boys to find a missing woman. Gorcey finds the woman, Loring, but realizes that she has absolutely no connection with Compson. Loring mentions a man, Seymour, but doesn't elaborate. Gorcey finds the man and discovers that he is a fortune-telling mobster. It is learned that Seymour uses the fortune-telling as a ruse to get private information about people and then blackmail them. Needless to say, the boys trap the crook and bring him to justice. The last Bowery Boys film for Jordan after his career was ended when cables snapped in a New York elevator he was riding in, falling six floors and maiming Jordan in the right knee. (See BOWERY BOYS series, Index.)

p, Jan Grippo; d, William Beaudine; w, Cyril Enfield; ph, Jim Brown; ed, William Austin; md, Edward J. Kay; art d, Dave Milton; set d, George Milo; spec eff, Augie Lohman.

Comedy/Mystery **(PR:A MPAA:NR)**

HARD BUNCH, THE (SEE: HARD TRAIL, 1969)

HARD CONTRACT*** (1969) 106m FOX c

James Coburn *(John Cunningham)*, Lee Remick *(Sheila)*, Lilli Palmer *(Adrianne)*, Burgess Meredith *(Ramsey)*, Patrick Magee *(Alexi)*, Sterling Hayden *(Michael Carlson)*, Claude Dauphin *(Maurice)*, Helen Cherry *(Evelyn Carlson)*, Karen Black *(Ellen)*, Sabine Sun *(Belgian Prostitute)*.

Cold-blooded professional assassin Coburn accepts a contract to murder three people in Europe for his mysterious client, Meredith. Arriving in Spain, Coburn meets a group of rich travelers led by twice-divorced socialite Remick, whose main purpose in life is to amuse herself. Among her party are Palmer, Magee, and Dauphin, each representing a different aspect of complacent, pathetic bourgeois society. Captivated by this strangely distant and furtive man, Remick pursues him. This proves difficult because Coburn, in keeping with his unemotional and detached demeanor, satisfies his sexual needs only in the company of prostitutes. Remick overcomes this obstacle and begins an affair with the killer that softens both of these basically callous people. Meanwhile, Coburn has eliminated the first victim on his hit list and, after another tryst with Remick in Tangiers, he travels to Brussels to fulfill the second part of his contract. Things change, however, when he finds that killing isn't as easy for him as it used to be. With shaking hands he eliminates the victim, but for the first time in his life has second thoughts about his career. Finally, Coburn learns the identity of this third victim and is disturbed to discover that the doomed man is Hayden, a fellow assassin who has retired to live with his family in Madrid. Depressed and in need of companionship, Coburn sends for Remick to meet him in Spain. While waiting in the hotel lobby Coburn is shocked to see Hayden, who senses who Coburn is and why he has come. Shaken, Coburn doubts that he can complete his job. Realizing that he's losing his assassin, Meredith arrives in Spain to ensure that the hit will be completed. Countering this move, Hayden invites all concerned to his home where, during a conversation with Coburn, he says he has become fed up with killing and could never pull the trigger again. Sympathetic to Hayden, allowing himself to love Remick, but still professionally and honorably tied to Meredith, Coburn desperately tries to resurrect his cold killer's instinct by driving them all off a cliff. At the last moment his new sense of judgment overcomes the killer in him and he abandons his plan. Coburn takes Remick and disappears, well aware that someday another assassin will come for him. While the moralistic message in HARD CONTRACT may lack subtlety at times the film is saved by the performances. Coburn is convincing as the killer undergoing an emotional revitalization and he brings a tragic but hopeful air to his character. Remick is fine as the bored socialite, Meredith's portrayal is memorable, and Hayden is as solid as ever. The European locations are used to the best advantage, providing a stunning backdrop to the action, but they are never allowed to overpower the narrative by becoming travelog footage.

p, Marvin Schwartz; d&w, S. Lee Pogostin; ph, Jack Hildyard (Panavision, DeLuxe Color); m, Alex North; ed, Harry Gerstad; art d, Ed Graves; set d, James W. Payne, Fernando Gonzalez; cos, Gladys de Segonzac; spec eff, L.B. Abbott, Art Cruickshank; makeup, Giuliano Laurenti.

Crime/Drama (PR:C MPAA:PG)

HARD COUNTRY*** (1981) 104m Associated Film/UNIV c

Jan-Michael Vincent *(Kyle Richardson)*, Kim Basinger *(Jodie Lynn Palmer)*, Michael Parks *(Royce Richardson)*, Gailard Sartain *(Johnny Bob)*, Tanya Tucker *(Caroline Peters)*, Sierra Pecheur *(Mama Palmer)*, John Chappell *(Daddy Palmer)*, Daryl Hannah *(Loretta Palmer)*, Lewis Van Bergen *(Ransom Winthrop)*, Ted Neely *(Wesley)*, Curtis Credel *(Dale)*, Scotch Byerley *(Aaron)*, Richard Lineback *(Larry)*, Elise Caitlin, Danone Camden, Holly Haber *(Cowgirls)*, Richard Moll *(Top Gun)*, Ron Spivey *(Shitkicker)*, Cisse Cameron *(Royce's Wife)*, Terri Foster Brooks *(Waitress)*, Jack Rader *(Foreman)*, Laura Madison *(Tracy)*, Delana Michaels *(Telephone Operator)*, David Haney *(Bartender)*, Garrie Kelly *(Interviewer)*, A'Leisha Brevard *(Snoopy Lady)*, Jay Kerr *(Deputy)*, Cheryl Carter, Henry G. Sanders *(Customers)*, Tina Menard *(Maid)*, Jane Abbott *(Woman at Airport)*, Delores Aguirre *(Security Guard)*, Stephen C. Bradbury *(Airport Clerk)*, West Buchanan *(Airport Agent)*, Kirby Buchanan, Mitch Carter *(Police at Airport)*.

Surprisingly good rural drama was overshadowed by URBAN COWBOY. Vincent is a small town boy in Texas, working at the chain link fence factory by day and carousing with his friends at a saloon at night. His girl friend, Basinger, is torn between marrying Vincent and settling down, or getting out of town and heading out to California. Her friend Tucker did just that and has become a major C&W star trying to attract Basinger out. It's all done intelligently and is worth seeing.

p, David Greene, Mack Bing; d, David Greene; w, Michael Kane (based on a story by Kane, Michael Martin Murphey); ph, Dennis Dalzell (CFI Color); m, Jimmie Haskell; ed, John A. Martinelli; prod d, Edward Richardson; set d, Mark L. Babus; cos, Dianne Anthony.

Drama Cas. (PR:O MPAA:PG)

HARD DAY'S NIGHT, A**** (1964, Brit.) 83m UA bw

John Lennon *(John)*, Paul McCartney *(Paul)*, George Harrison *(George)*, Ringo Starr *(Ringo)*, Wilfrid Brambell *(Grandfather)*, Norman Rossington *(Norm)*, Victor Spinetti *(TV Director)*, John Junkin *(Shake)*, Deryck Guyler *(Police Inspector)*, Anna Quayle *(Millie)*, Kenneth Haigh *(Simon)*, Richard Vernon *(Man on Train)*, Eddie Malin *(Hotel Waiter)*, Robin Ray *(TV Floor Manager)*, Lionel Blair *(TV Choreographer)*, Alison Seebohm *(Secretary)*, Marianne Stone *(Society Reporter)*, David Langton *(Actor)*, David Jaxon *(Joung Boy)*, Clare Kelly *(Barmaid)*, Michael Trubshawe *(Casino Manager)*, Roger Avon, John Bluthal, Pattie Boyd, Margaret Nolan, Terry Hooper, Derek Nimmo, Bridget Armstrong, Rosemarie Frankland.

Refreshing, innovative, and immensely funny, A HARD DAY'S NIGHT purportedly tells the story of 36 hours in the lives of The Fab Four in a quirky, offbeat fashion that had everyone laughing from the first moment. It was released at the same time as AIP was making the BEACH PARTY pictures and made those trifles seem even more trifling by comparison. Director Lester, an American who went to England and made a name for himself in commercials as well as having directed two minor efforts, IT'S TRAD, DAD! and MOUSE ON THE MOON (a sequel to THE MOUSE THAT ROARED for the same producer, Shenson), thought they would rush this into production and take advantage of the Beatles' instant popularity and hit the theaters before their celebrity waned. How wrong they were. The Beatles only made three pictures (plus cartoons as well as a few films in which they individually appeared) and this was the first, and the best. John, Paul, George, and Ringo are besieged by their frenzied fans as they board a train bound for London where they are to do a live TV appearance. They are accompanied by Rossington, their manager (a parody of Brian Epstein, the man who discovered them and was known as "The Fifth Beatle" before his early death), his aide, Junkin (who also played in Lester's HOW I WON THE WAR which costarrred Lennon) and Brambell, Paul's grandfather who is satirically described in the film as being "a clean old man." Brambell had been the popular star of Britain's "Steptoe And Son" TV show which Norman Lear adapted as "Sanford And Son." Brambell is a mischievous old coot with an eye for pleasure. They arrive in London, visit a night spot, then learn that Brambell has departed to go out gambling. They locate him at the casino as he is chatting up a buxom bird under the annoyed eye of casino manager Trubshawe. Despite his angry protests, the boys snare Brambell and drag him almost kicking and screaming to their hotel. Next day, at the TV studio, production delays cause the boys to spend their time getting involved in a series of sight gags which culminates when Brambell nastily convinces innocent Ringo that he is too good for the group and should go out on his own. Ringo disappears and the others search until he is found at a police station. They get to the studio just in time for the final sequence, a long performance that ends as Brambell comes up through the stage on an elevator. In a Fellini touch, they board a helicopter and take off over the crowd for their next gig. Made in just seven weeks at the miniscule cost of just over a half million dollars, A HARD DAY'S NIGHT returned many times its cost. The sequel, HELP, cost almost three times as much, wasn't as good, and probably won't be remembered as long as this anarchistic, near Marx Brothers film. There is no particular style to the picture; rather, Lester uses every style that every other director ever used plus several that he may have intented himself. Hand-held documentary, surrealistic imagery, neo-realism all combine to give us one of the most inventive pictures of the era and it cemented The Beatles' reputations as musical nihilists. Several fresh jokes in the Owen screenplay make this a constant surprise and we never know where it will go. (There are those who say that the production staff didn't know where it would go, either, and just shot what they could and hoped that Jympson's editing could save it, but the truth is that nothing this good could have possibly been done without a plan—script—to make it work.) It was a musical in the truest meaning of the word in that all of the tunes made sense in the overall story. For sheer spectacle, Busby Berkeley would have approved. It received no Oscars for anything, a tribute to the short-sightedness of the Motion Picture Academy, who felt that The Beatles were a passing fancy. Many youngsters today do not even know the Beatles existed and, when told of the quartet by his parents, a 12-year-old was heard to remark, "You mean Paul McCartney was in *another* group before 'Wings?" [Sic transit gloria mundi.) A wonderful satire that will live long after some of the Oscar winners of 1964 have been forgotten. Songs included "A Hard Day's Night," "Tell me Why," "I Should Have Known Better," "She Loves You," "I'm Happy Just To Dance With You," "If I Fell," "And I Love Her," "This Boy," "Can't Buy Me Love," "I Wanna Be Your Man," and "All My Loving."

p, Walter Shenson; d, Richard Lester; w, Alun Owen; ph, Gilbert Taylor; m, John Lennon, Paul McCartney; ed, John Jympson; md, George Martin; art d, Ray Simm; cos, Dougie Millings & Son (Beatles), Julie Harris.

Musical Comedy Cas. (PR:A MPAA:G)

HARD DRIVER (SEE: LAST AMERICAN HERO, THE, 1973)

HARD, FAST, AND BEAUTIFUL½** (1951) 76m Filmakers/RKO bw

Claire Trevor *(Milly Farley)*, Sally Forrest *(Florence Farley)*, Carleton G. Young *(Fletcher Locke)*, Robert Clarke *(Gordon McKay)*, Kenneth Patterson *(Will Farley)*, Marcella Cisney *(Miss Martin)*, Joseph Kearns *(J.R. Carpenter)*, William Hudson *(Interne)*, George Fisher *(Announcer)*, Arthur Little, Jr. *(Commentator)*, Bert Whitley *(Young Official)*, Edwin Reimers *(Announcer)*, Don Kent, William Irving *(Umpires)*, Barbara Brier, Marilyn Mercer *(Girls)*.

Trevor pushes daughter Forrest up the professional tennis rankings so that she can live easy on the money. To keep her control over the girl, she forbids her to carry on her affair with Clarke. Forrest finally realizes what her mother is doing and walks out on her. Trevor is excellent as the grasping mom, and the tennis court footage adds a dimension that may interest many.

p, Collier Young; d, Ida Lupino; w, Martha Wilkerson (based on a novel by John R. Tunis); ph, Archie Stout; m, Roy Webb; ed, William Ziegler; md, Constantin Bakaleinikoff; art d, Albert D'Agostino, Jack Okey.

Drama (PR:A MPAA:NR)

HARD GUY** (1941) 67m PRC bw

Jack LaRue *(Vic)*, Mary Healy *(Julie)*, Kane Richmond *(Steve)*, Iris Adrian *(Goldie)*, Gayle Mellott *(Doris)*, Jack Mulhall *(Cassidy)*, Howard Banks *(Anthony)*, Ben Taggart *(Sherwood)*, Montague Shaw *(Tremaine, Sr.)*, Inna Gest *(Mona)*, Arthur Gardner *(Dick)*.

LaRue is a suave nightclub owner turning a buck on the side by marrying off his showgirls to rich young playboys and then collecting money from the playboys' fathers for a quick anullment. When one girl refuses to go through with this scheme, LaRue shoots her. Her sister comes from Kansas and, along with Oklahoma-raised, ex-governor's son Richmond, they see that justice finds LaRue. A shootout in the club leaves the villain dead, and Healy and Richmond end up in each other's arms. Okay programmer.

p, George Merrick, Arthur Alexander; d, Elmer Clifton; w, Oliver Drake; ph, Eddie Linden; m, Eddie Durant and his Rhumba band; ed, Charles Henkel.

Crime (PR:A MPAA:NR)

HARD HOMBRE*** (1931) 65m Allied Pictures bw

Hoot Gibson, Lina Basquette, Mathilde Comont, Jesse Arnold, Glenn Strange, Robert Burns, Raymond Nye, Christian Frank, Jack Byron, "Skeeter Bill" Robbins, Rosa Gore, Tiny Sanford, Fernando Galvez, Frank Winklemann.

Gibson is a mild-mannered mama's boy who bears an unfortunate but striking resemblance to a brawling cowpoke. He becomes foreman of a ranch, but the real Gibson turns up and there's a brawl. Easy-going Gibson vehicle with a number of nice comic turns by the star. One of Hoot's best.

p, M.H. Hoffman, Jr.; d, Otto Brower; w, Jack Natteford; ph, Harry Neumann; ed, Mildred Johnston.

Western Cas. (PR:A MPAA:NR)

HARD KNOCKS*½** (1980, Aus.) 85m Andromeda c

Tracey Mann *(Sam)*, John Arnold *(Wally)*, Bill Hunter *(Brady)*, Max Cullen *(Newman)*, Tony Barry *(Barry)*, Hilton Bonner *(Frank)*, Kirsty Grant *(Debbie)*.

Excellent Australian drama about punk-rocking juvenile delinquent Mann trying to straighten out her life after a jail term, but old friends and bad cops won't let her. Gritty, grim picture is held together by the force of Mann's performance (one for which she won the Australian Film Institute Best Actress Award).

p, Don McLennan, Hilton Bonner; d, McLennan; w, McLennan, Bonner; ph&ed, Zbigniew Friedrich; cos, Julie Cutler, Penelope Hester.

Drama (PR:O MPAA:NR)

HARD MAN, THE** (1957) 80m COL/Romson c

Guy Madison *(Steve Burden)*, Valerie French *(Fern Martin)*, Lorne Greene *(Rice Martin)*, Barry Atwater *(George Dennison)*, Robert Burton *(Sim Hacker)*, Rudy Bond *(John Rodman)*, Trevor Bardette *(Mitch Willis)*, Renata Vanni *(Juanita)*, Rickie Sorenson *(Larry Thompson)*, Frank Richards *(Vince Kane)*, Myron Healey *(Ray Hendry)*, Robert B. Williams *(Herb Thompson)*.

Madison is a Texas Ranger who resigns after he gets a reputation for bringing them back dead. He takes a job as deputy sheriff and quickly becomes embroiled in a range war against Greene, a rancher intent on taking over the whole range. He also begins an affair with French, Greene's wife, who wants Madison to kill her husband for her. She ends up doing the job herself. This western seems caught between the old-fashioned oaters of the 1930s and 1940s and the modern westerns of the 1950s and 1960s. The result is only mediocre.

p, Helen Ainsworth; d, George Sherman; w, Leo Katcher (based on his novel); ph, Henry Freulich (Technicolor); m, Mischa Bakaleinikoff; ed, William Lyon; art d, Carl Anderson.

Western **(PR: A MPAA:NR)**

HARD ON THE TRAIL (SEE: HARD TRAIL, 1969)

HARD PART BEGINS, THE*** (1973, Can.) 90m Odyssey c

Donnelly Rhodes *(King)*, Nancy Belle Fuller *(Jenny)*, Paul Bradley *(Duane)*, Linda Sorenson *(Alice)*, Robert Hawkins *(Roxon)*, Doug McGrath *(Al Dawson)*, Les Carlson *(Mechanic)*, Neil Vipond, Vinette Strombergs, Marie Fleming, Cliff Carroll, Hugh Curry, David Daniels.

Rhodes is an aging, small-time country and western singer whose longtime duet partner (Fuller) dumps him to pursue a big-time solo career. On top of that, he is beat up, hounded by his ex-wife, and has to go visit his son in jail. Well done, low-budget look at a man facing middle age and mediocrity. Recommended.

p, John Clifton Hunter, Garrett G. Lee; d, Paul Lynch; w, Hunter; ph, Robert Saad (Kodak Color); m, Ian Guenther; ed, William Gray.

Drama **(PR:C MPAA:NR)**

HARD RIDE, THE½** (1971) 98m AIP c

Robert Fuller *(Phil)*, Sherry Bain *(Sheryl)*, Tony Russell *(Big Red)*, William Bonner *(Grady)*, Marshall Reed *(Father Tom)*, Mikel Angel *(Ralls)*, Biff Elliot *(Mike)*, Al Cole *(Mooch)*, Phyllis Selznick *(Rita)*, R.L. Armstrong *(Jason)*, Robert Swan *(Ted)*, Larry Eisley *(Rice)*, Frank Charolla *(Meyers)*, Herman Rudin *(Little Horse)*, Alfonso Williams *(Lenny)*, Ford Lile *(Floyd)*, John Cestare *(Al)*, Del Russel *(Nico)*, Rachel English, John Lomma, Robert Tessier, Gus Peters, Ron Stokes, Joe Folino, Tony Haig, Tony de Costa, Doug Matheson, David Bradley.

Fuller brings the body of his black buddy back from Vietnam and finds the bike club he used to belong to. He attempts to persuade Bain, the dead man's white girl friend, to attend the funeral as he tries to understand the biker life. Above average for a biker movie, with an excellent soundtrack. Songs "Swing Low Sweet Chariot" (sung by Bill Medley), "Falling In Love With Baby" (sung by Junction), "Be Nobody's Fool," "Shannon's Hook Shop," "Let the Music Play," "Another Kind of War" (sung by Paul Wibier), "Grady's Bunch" (sung by the Arrows), "Where Am I Going Today?" (sung by Bob Moline), "Carry Me Home," "I Came Along to be With You" (sung by Thelma Camacho).

p, Charles Hanawalt; d&w, Burt Topper; ph, Robert Sparks (Movielab Color); m, Harley Hatcher; ed, Kenneth Crane; md, Hatcher.

Biker **(PR:C MPAA:GP)**

HARD ROAD, THE* (1970) 85m Four Star-Excelsior c

Connie Nelson *(Pamela Banner)*, John Alderman *(Jimmy Devlin)*, Catherine Howard *(Jeannie)*, Gary Kent *(Leo)*, Ray Merritt *(Mr. Banner)*, Liz Renay *(Mrs. Banner)*, William Bonner *(Chad)*, Bruce Kimball *(Guard)*, John Parker *(Max)*, Karen Lind *(Mrs. Levin)*, Issa Arnal *(Social Worker)*, Jay Fineberg *(Landlord)*, Chuck Hutchinson *(Transvestite)*, Jeff Graver *(Man in Alley)*, Joe Pepi, Joe Colgan *(Narcotics Agents)*, Alex Eliot *(Bartender)*, Mike Stringer *(Muffin)*, Jean Clark *(Prisoner)*, Mike Weldon *(Man in Motel)*, Fern Holbrook *(Police Worker)*, Roger Everett *(Steve Christopher)*, Jack Valle, Lewis Teague, Greg Corarito.

Nelson is a middle-class girl forced to quit school when she becomes pregnant. From there, it's an inevitable slide through marijuana, LSD, prostitution, to death. Film doesn't seem sure if it is an educational, moralizing movie or a trashy exploitation picture. Whichever, it's another depressant.

p, Ed De Priest; d, Gary Graver; w, Richard Stetson; ph&ed, Graver (Movielab Color); m, Jaime Mendoza-Nava.

Drama **(PR:O MPAA:R)**

HARD ROCK HARRIGAN½** (1935) 60m FOX bw

George O'Brien *("Hard Rock" Harrigan)*, Irene Hervey *("Andy" Anderson)*, Fred Kohler *(Black Jack Riley)*, Dean Benton *(Michael McGinnis)*, Frank Rice, Victor Botel, Olin Francis, William Gould, George Humbert, David Clyde, Ed Keene, Lee Shumway.

O'Brien is the foreman of a crew of laborers digging a tunnel, and Kohler is his assistant and rival. Tension builds between the two, but when a cave-in threatens Kohler's life, O'Brien risks his neck to save him. Strictly program filler.

p, Sol Lesser; d, David Howard; w, Raymond L. Schrock, Dan Jarrett (based on a story by Charles Furthman); ph, Frank G. Good; ed, Donald Barratt.

Drama **(PR:A MPAA:NR)**

HARD STEEL*½ (1941, Brit.) 86m GHW/GFD bw (AKA: WHAT SHALL IT PROFIT)

Wilfrid Lawson *(Walter Haddon)*, Betty Stockfield *(Freda Haddon)*, John Stuart *(Alan Saunders)*, George Carney *(Bert Mortimer)*, Joan Kemp-Welch *(Janet Mortimer)*, James Harcourt *(Jim Calver)*, Frank Atkinson *(Dick Sefton)*, Arthur Hambling *(Lamport)*, John Turnbull *(Rowlandson)*, Hay Petrie *(Kissack)*, Clifton Boyne *(Carter)*, Angela Glynne *(Bunty Phillips)*, Mignon O'Doherty, Philip Godfrey, Cameron Hall, Charles Rolfe, Kenneth Griffith, Harry Riley, Victor Weske, Charles Groves, D.J. Williams, Len Sharp, Roberta Read, Roddy Hughes, Arthur Seaton, Dane Gordon, David Crickett.

An innocuous drama about a likable steel worker, Lawson, who turns vicious when he is promoted to foreman. His unrelenting callousness to his workers is also directed to his wife, Stockfield. When one of the workers dies due to Lawson, his men rise up and his wife leaves. Only with the help of preacher-friend Carney does Lawson see the error of his ways.

p, James B. Sloan; d, Norman Walker; w, Lydia Hayward (based on the novel *Steel Saraband* by Roger Dataller); ph, Claude Friese-Greene.

Drama **(PR:A MPAA:NR)**

HARD TIMES*** (1975) 92m COL c (AKA: THE STREETFIGHTER)

Charles Bronson *(Chaney)*, James Coburn *(Spencer "Speed" Weed)*, Jill Ireland *(Luby Simpson)*, Strother Martin *(Poe)*, Maggie Blye *(Gayleen Schoonover)*, Michael McGuire *(Gandil)*, Robert Tessier *(Jim Henry)*, Nick Dimitri *(Street)*, Felice Orlandi *(Le Beau)*, Bruce Glover *(Doty)*, Edward Walsh *(Pettibon)*, Frank McRae *(Hammerman)*, Maurice Kowalewski *(Caesare)*, Naomi Stevens *(Madam)*, Robert Castleberry *(Counterman)*, Becky Allen *(Poe's Date)*, Joan Kleven *(Carol)*, Anne Welsch *(Secretary)*, Lyla Hay Owen *(Diner Waitress)*, Jim Nickerson *(Barge Fighter)*, John Creamer *(Apartment Manager)*, Fred Lerner *(Caesare's Hitter)*, Chuck Hicks *(Speed's Hitter)*, Walter Scott, Max Kleven *(Poolplayers)*, Valerian Smith *(Handler)*, Bob Minor *(Zack)*, Larry Martindale *(Driver)*, Charles W. Schaeffer, Jr., Leslie Bonano *(Card Players)*, Ronnie Philips *(Cajun Fighter)*, and the Greater Liberty Baptist Church Choir and Congregation.

One of Bronson's best pictures, HARD TIMES is a different kind of boxing yarn that may, or may not, have been based on Jack Dempsey's early years. Bronson is a bare-knuckle streetfighter in the 1930s, a man who makes his living beating the brains out of the foolhardies who think they can take him. (Clint Eastwood also played this kind of part in EVERY WHICH WAY BUT LOOSE and ANY WHICH WAY YOU CAN.) Coburn is the New Orleans promoter who arranges the bouts and Ireland (Bronson's real-life wife, after having been married to TV star David McCallum for many years) is a sweet young thing who has a brief fling with Bronson. Hill made his directorial debut on this and established himself as an "action" director, which he proved again with his work on THE DRIVER and THE WARRIORS, a flawed but interesting look at a Coney Island gang. Bronson was 54 when he made this but in excellent condition and the wrinkles on his face and the gray in his short-cropped hair may have been what inspired his opponents to think they could beat him in a fair fight. Made with tax shelter money, it may have returned its investment to the financiers after a brief stay in the theaters and a fair run on TV. Bronson was low-key and convincing, but the script lacked a driving force and it tumbled into being episodic. Yet it was fun to watch and the settings are painstakingly accurate. There is more action than violence in the film and lots less blood than in any of Sylvester Stallone's boxing features. Director Hill did enough of a rewrite to merit a shared credit by the Writers Guild.

p, Lawrence Gordon; d, Walter Hill; w, Bryan Gindorff, Bruce Henstell, Hill (based on a story by Gindorff, Henstell); ph, Philip Lathrop (Panavision, Metrocolor); m, Barry DeVorzon; ed, Roger Spottiswoode; art d, Trevor Williams; set d, Dennis Peeples; stunts, Max Kleven.

Sports Drama **Cas.** **(PR:A-C MPAA:PG)**

HARD TO GET½** (1929) 80m FN/WB bw

Dorothy Mackaill *(Bobby Martin)*, Jimmie Finlayson *(Pa Martin)*, Louise Fazenda *(Ma Martin)*, Jack Oakie *(Marty Martin)*, Edmund Burns *(Dexter Courtland)*, Clarissa Selwynne *(Mrs. Courtland)*, Charles Delaney *(Jerry Dillon)*.

Mackaill is a working girl who gives up a chance to marry millionaire Burns so that she can marry mechanic Delaney, who will take her as she is and whom she will never have to impress. Pleasantly hypnotic for its scenes of old-fashioned residential New York City.

d, William Beaudine; w, Richard Weil, James Gruen (based on the story "Classified" by Edna Ferber); m/l, "The Things We Want Most Are Hard to Get," Al Bryan, George W. Meyer.

Comedy **(PR:A MPAA:NR)**

HARD TO GET½** (1938) 78m WB bw

Dick Powell *(Bill Davis)*, Olivia de Havilland *(Margaret Richards)*, Charles Winninger *(Big Ben Richards)*, Allen Jenkins *(Roscoe)*, Bonita Granville *(Connie Richards)*, Melville Cooper *(Case)*, Isabel Jeans *(Henrietta Richards)*, John Atwater *(Thurston Hall)*, Hattie *(Penny Singleton)*, Grady Sutton *(Stanley Potter)*, John Ridgely *(Schaff)*, Jack Mower *(Burke)*, Granville Bates *(Judge Harkness)*, Nella Walker *(Mrs. Atwater)*, Sidney Bracey *(Butler)*, Lottie Williams *(Maid)*, Herbert Evans *(Chauffeur)*, Dick Rich *(Truck Driver)*, Edgar Dearing *(Eddie the Motorcycle Cop)*, Arthur Housman *(Drunk)*, Arthur Hoyt *(Man at Flower Convention)*, Vera Lewis *(Mrs. Petewyle)*, Jimmy Conlin *(Dour Diner)*, Herbert Ashley *(Waiter)*, Irving Bacon *(Attendant at Gas Station)*, Cliff Saum, Ben Hendricks *(Rivet Throwers)*, Herbert Rawlinson *(Mr. Jones)*, George Kirby *(Servant)*.

Almost, but not quite, a musical, HARD TO GET came about as the result of Powell's wanting to get out of the mold he'd been placed in by the Brothers Warner (silly stories that were just there so Powell could sing). He wanted to show that he could also act, something he proved many years later in a series of hard-boiled roles for various studios. Here, Powell is an architect who has been reduced to managing a gasoline station. De Havilland (his co-star in A MIDSUMMER NIGHT'S DREAM), a wealthy heiress, drives her spiffy Mercury convertible into the gas station-motel, fills it up, and then, like so many rich folk, realizes she doesn't have a penny with her. (Why is it that the rich never know how much money they have on their persons and the poor *always* do?) Her diffident behavior toward him (before she discovered she was penniless) so infuriates Powell that he forces her to pay the gasoline bill by doing maid service in the motel's cabins. De Havilland is determined to get even with Powell, who has spent quite some time designing a motel complex for a proposed chain of Howard Johnson-type inns across America. He needs money and one of the nabobs he'd like to meet is Winninger, a physical-fitness nut who loves twitting his valet, Cooper. De Havilland doesn't let Powell know that Winninger is her father and says she will work it out that Powell gets an introduction to the wacky old man. She knows her father well and also knows that the man abhors aggressive young men and will, no doubt, toss Powell out within seconds. She's right, and Powell is sent packing after the interview. Not content with that, she masquerades as a maid in her own home and asks Powell to come by. The same result. Next, Powell poses as a maintenance man, a female janitor, and a Western Union boy in order to get close to Winninger, but all his efforts result in getting booted out. Winninger is about to throw a huge party at the estate so Powell dresses up as a musician in blackface. When he overhears De Havilland telling one of her blue-nose pals about what she did to Powell, he is hurt and leaves, but not before he drops his plans for the auto courts. Winninger finds them, takes a gander, and declares them to be terrific. They are exactly what he's been wanting to do for some time but who is the brilliant designer? Once Powell is determined to be that person, De Havilland comes to the realization that she adores him and that she would like to marry him. The best scenes in the picture are between Winninger and Cooper as the two men fence, box, wrestle, and compete on several levels with Cooper always winding up the loser. Two songs are heard, "There's A Sunny Side To Every Situation" and the great Harry Warren-Johnny Mercer standard, "You Must Have Been A Beautiful Baby." Not a hit with 1938 audiences who may have wanted more singing from Powell.

p, Hal B. Wallis; d, Ray Enright; w, Jerry Wald, Maurice Lee, Richard Macauley (based on a screen story by Wally Klein, Joseph Schrank, based on the story "Classified" by Stephen Morehouse Avery); ph, Charles Rosher; ed, Thomas Richards; md, Leo F. Forbstein; art d, Anton Grot; m/l, Harry Warren, Johnny Mercer.

Comedy **(PR:A MPAA:NR)**

HARD TO HANDLE*** (1933) 71m WB/Vitaphone bw

James Cagney *(Lefty Merrill)*, Mary Brian *(Ruth Waters)*, Ruth Donnelly *(Lil Waters)*, Allen Jenkins *(Radio Announcer)*, Claire Dodd *(Marlene Reeves)*, Gavin Gordon *(John Hayden)*, Emma Dunn *(Mrs. Hawks the Landlady)*, Robert McWade *(Charles Reeves)*, John Sheehan *(Ed McGrath)*, Matt McHugh *(Joe Goetz)*, Louise Mackintosh *(Mrs. Weston Parks)*, William H. Strauss *(Antique Dealer)*, Bess Flowers *(Merrill's Secretary)*, Lew Kelly *(Hash Slinger)*, Berton Churchill *(Col. Wells)*, Harry Holman *(Colonel's Associate)*, Grace Hayle *(Fat Lady with Vanishing Cream)*, George Pat Collins *(Dance Judge)*, Douglas Dumbrille *(District Attorney)*, Sterling Holloway *(Andy)*, Charles Wilson *(Jailer)*, Jack Crawford, Stanley Smith, Walter Walker, Mary Doran.

A breakneck pace and Cagney's rat-a-tat performance are what elevate this minor trifle to heights it shouldn't have achieved. Twenty-eight years later, Cagney was to prove he hadn't run out of steam when he played an equally frenetic role in ONE, TWO, THREE for Billy Wilder. Cagney is a quick-witted hustler who promotes various items from fad diets to reducing lotions to marathon dances, a female college, a treasure hunt, and a grapefruit association (no doubt this was an inside joke for it was Cagney who electrified audiences when he smashed a grapefruit in Mae Clarke's face in 1931's PUBLIC ENEMY). Donnelly's daughter, Brian, is in a marathon dance contest and when her feet give out, Donnelly attempts to masquerade as her own daughter and continue the dancing in order to win the big money prize. The only problem is that when Cagney's partner turns out with the money, Donnelly prevails on the promoter to marry the daughter. Which he does. The screenplay was silly and LeRoy's frantic direction just a tad too spirited. It was Cagney all the way in a rip-roaring role that barely allowed audiences to breathe before the next punch line tumbled from his lips. This was the first of five films he made in 1933 (the others were PICTURE SNATCHER, THE MAYOR OF HELL, FOOTLIGHT PARADE, and LADY KILLER), a far cry from the greedy stars of today who make one film every couple of years and take down millions. Cagney was like many British actors who feel that their work is what counts, not how much money they take in. That's why one can still go to London and see some of the greatest actors on the stage, at low prices, just so they can continue to perfect their artistry.

p, Ray Griffith; d, Mervyn LeRoy; w, Wilson Mizner, Robert Lord (based on a story by Houston Branch); ph, Barney "Chick" McGill; ed, William Holmes; md, Leo F. Forbstein; art d, Robert Haas; cos, Orry-Kelly; makeup, Perc Westmore.

Comedy **(PR:A MPAA:NR)**

HARD TRAIL zero (1969) 78m Brentwood International c (AKA: HARD ON THE TRAIL)

Lash LaRue *(Slade)*, Donna Bradley *(Sue)*, Bob Romero *(Rafael)*, Bruce Kemp *(Ox)*, Robert Dalton *(Bixby)*, Arne Dhean *(Jaime)*, Mary Donahue *(Kathy)*, Adam Stan *(Jim Nesson)*, Greg Corarito *(Starret)*, Phil Hoover, Scott Wells, John Bloom, Ron Wade, Jim Feazell, Randy Starr, Mike Armstrong, Monica Gayle, Mal Hutton, Dru Hoy, Victoria Tobian.

Bloody, violent western with much footage devoted to rape and torture. LaRue plays a sadistic gang leader who orders the murders of Stan and his family to obtain the secret location of Stan's gold mine. The killers torture and rape Stan's daughters, Bradley and Donahue, to get the information, but Donahue's fiance, Corarito (who also wrote and directed this trash), arrives in time to kill the scum. Unfortunately, Donahue is also killed in the gun battle, leaving Bradley and Corarito to get revenge on LaRue. After singlehandedly wiping out an army of Mexican bandits, making love to Bradley, and killing LaRue's men with dynamite, Corarito confronts the evil LaRue in his office and accidentally sets off a booby-trap, killing everyone. LaRue, the black-garbed western hero boys once idolized, lived to regret the two days he spent making this film, which marked his brief return to Hollywood after almost 19 years. HARD TRAIL was made in two versions, a triple-X rated one (HARD ON THE TRAIL), and the soft-core HARD TRAIL. Of his part in it, LaRue, who had been touring the South as a bible-thumping evangelist, said, "I wasn't connected with the shooting of the dirty stuff. They spliced that in around me. . . . It was an honest mistake on my part. I was duped."

p, Maurice Smity; d&w, Greg Corarito; ph, Gary Graver; ed, Vic Davis, Ken Stewart.

Western **(PR:O MPAA:NR)**

HARD WAY, THE*½** (1942) 108m WB bw

Ida Lupino *(Helen Chernen)*, Dennis Morgan *(Paul Collins)*, Joan Leslie *(Katherine Chernen)*, Jack Carson *(Albert Runkel)*, Gladys George *(Lily Emery)*, Faye Emerson *(Blonde Waitress)*, Paul Cavanagh *(John Shagrue)*, Leona Maricle *(Laura Bithorn)*, Roman Bohnen *(Sam Chernen)*, Ray Montgomery *(Johnny Gilpin)*, Julie Bishop *(Chorine)*, Nester Paiva *(Max Wade)*, Joan Woodbury *(Maria)*, Ann Doran *(Dorschka)*, Thurston Hall *(Film Executive)*, Lou Lubin *(Frenchy)*, Jody Gilbert *(Anderson)*, Charles Judels *(Flores)*.

Lupino took the Best Actress Award from the New York Film Critics for her role in THE HARD WAY and she should have been nominated for an Oscar. The part was originally offered to Bette Davis (who declined) and Lupino has always felt she was "the poor man's Bette Davis" (her own quote). Lupino plays a woman in the small, industrial town of Greenhill, who is married to a lummox, Bohnen, and living on the edge of poverty. She will not allow that to happen to her young, pretty sister, Leslie, who has just a bit of ability as a singer-dancer. Determined to keep her sister out of the trap of early marriage, pregnancy, and a wasted life, Lupino pushes Leslie into performing. When Morgan and Carson, a couple of song-and-dance men, come to Greenhill to perform in the local vaudeville house, Carson is attracted to Leslie and Lupino maneuvers this into marriage between the two. Now that the duo is a trio, Morgan soon finds himself extraneous and is asked to quit the act. After a while, Lupino feels that Leslie can now cut Carson out of her life and conspires to make Leslie into a single. Leslie leaves Carson and begins a new career, then is stunned to learn that Carson's reaction was to commit suicide. Leslie goes on to become a star and when Lupino once again attempts to lead her sister, Leslie rebels and tosses Lupino out. Lupino is now left with nothing to live for. A depressing and bitter drama, it served to introduce Morgan and Carson as a team, something they repeated in several more films. Carson was a wonderful actor and this may have been his best work as a hale and hearty guy with a sensitive soul beneath all the bravura. Good work in all the small roles and a sharp, though sometimes overplayed, screenplay by Viertel (Deborah Kerr's long-time husband) and Fuchs. Mistakenly regarded as a "woman's" picture, it transcends sexual gender and stands on its own as a fine piece of craftsmanship of a universal theme: living a vicarious life when your own is so drab that you can barely stand it. Tunes include "Was I Blue?" "Goodnight, My Darling," "I Love To Dance."

p, Jerry Wald, d, Vincent Sherman; w, Peter Viertel, Daniel Fuchs (based on a story by Wald); ph, James Wong Howe; m, Heinz Roemheld; ed, Thomas Pratt; spec eff, Willard Van Enger; ch, LeRoy Prinz; m/l, M.K. Jerome, Jack Scholl.

Drama **(PR:A-C MPAA:NR)**

HARDBOILED ROSE*½ (1929) 62m WB bw

Myrna Loy *(Rose Duhamel)*, William Collier, Jr. *(Edward Malo)*, John Miljan *(Steve Wallace)*, Gladys Brockwell *(Julie Malo)*, Joey Beaumont *(Grandmama Duhamel)*, Ralph Emerson *(John Trask)*, Edward Martindel *(Jefferson Duhamel)*, Floyd Schackelford *(Butler)*.

Loy stars in what is really a silent film with a few sound sequences that were hurriedly added just before its release. The result is a boring, uneven film that sees Loy as a refined Southern belle, forced by the suicide of her father, who suffered financial ruin, to work in a gambling house in an effort to pay off the old man's debts. Of course there is a dashing male lead played by Collier who takes her away from it all.

d, F. Harmon Wright; w, Robert Lord (based on a story by Melville Crossman); ph, William Rees; ed, William Holmes.

Drama **(PR:A MPAA:NR)**

HARDCORE zero (1979) 105m COL c (GB: THE HARDCORE LIFE)

George C. Scott *(Jake Van Dorn)*, Peter Boyle *(Andy Mast)*, Season Hubley *(Niki)*, Dick Sargent *(Wes DeJong)*, Leonard Gaines *(Ramada)*, David Nichols *(Kurt)*, Gary Rand Graham *(Tod)*, Larry Block *(Detective Burrows)*, Marc Alaimo *(Ratan)*, Leslie Ackerman *(Felice)*, Charlotte McGinnis *(Beatrice)*, Ilah Davis *(Kristen Van Dorn)*, Paul Marin *(Joe Van Dorn)*, Will Walker *(Jism Jim)*, Hal Williams *(Big Dick Blaque)*, Michael Allan Helie, Tim Dial *(Studs)*, Roy London *(Jim Rucker)*, Bibi Besch *(Mary)*, Tracey Walter *(Male Teller)*, Bobby Kosser *(Film Director)*, Stephen P. Dunn *(Cameraman)*, Jean Allison *(Mrs. Steensma)*, Reb Brown *(Manager)*, James Helder *(John Van Dorn)*, Dave Thompson *(Willem)*, John Otte *(Grandfather Van Dorn)*, Janet Simpson, Karen Kruer, Henry Vandenbroek, Linda Smith, Mary McFerren, Judith Ransdell, Linda Morell, Gigi Vorgan, Michael Hatch, David Hockenberry, Joseph Prus, Jean Reed Bahle, Reinder Vantil, Dee Ann Johnston, Janice Carroll, Mark Natuzzi, Al Cingolani, Cherilyn Parsons, Tracey Ratley, Antonio Esparza, Linda Cremeans, Ed Begley, Jr., Stewart Steinberg.

One of the most self-indulgent, offensive films ever made, HARDCORE is a slow slimy wade through the sewers of pornographic society. Scott, who lowered himself into these stinking depths with a less than enthusiastic performance (proving that even the most brilliant of thespians have little sense of their own destiny, let alone the ability to select roles of value), is an incensed father trying to track down his daughter Davis who has become a sex film star. Scott goes through one pornographic session after another in search of his elusive girl, after seeing her in a sex film, interviewing whores, pimps, the most disgusting and vile creatures dredged up on film. He sits through endless porno films, visits voyeur and massage parlors where girls performed lewd acts behind soiled glass panes for drooling, cretinous customers who endlessly feed coins to keep shields from closing on the naked women cavorting before them. He watches supposed "snuff" films where naked women are actually murdered. He even goes so far as to advertise that he is producing porno films and interviews one repulsive stud after another, all to find a daughter who is best forgotten. He finally plucks her out of the trash heap when locating a sleazy felon she has taken up with, a male porno star who actually kills women in "snuff" films, attacking and capturing this man for police and returning his mindless daughter to human society. There is absolutely nothing redeeming in this overlong garbage production. Not a line of dialog offers an insight into this stinking outhouse world which has none anyway. Scott's presence commanded some attention to the film when it first appeared and the more pretentious and less discerning critics, cowed at his reputation, cringing under his former achievements, attempted to read meaning into an otherwise meaningless celluloid waste dropping, all to their everlasting cowardice and utter lack of taste. Schrader, who is wholly responsible for this insult to any audience, also offered up to the world the equally repugnant TAXI DRIVER, another con job fronted off by talent lacking judgment. Davis' rebellion against her religious upbringing as manifested in her headlong dive into a cesspool is the so-called intellectual excuse for making this moronic movie. What is supposedly indicted here is really promoted, extolled as a social world worthy of expensive attention, peopled by creatures we are asked to understand, perceive, and even accept, at least on the miserable levels of their existence. Schrader is a hopeless, groping, talentless amateur whose only blatant commercial device is to shock without reason, pelt without apology, distort any and all value without compassion. His is the gas-passing cynicism of an uneducated 10 year old who opts for obscenity instead of literature because, like Everest, "it's there." HARDCORE is as inhuman as those films taken of Hitler's death camps showing tons of bodies being bulldozed into graves, except that people actually put up money to make this awful offal. Where Hitler attempted to hide his hideous crimes, this film seeks to exploit and showcase the degraded, the degenerated, the perverted, all in the abused name of "artistic expression," while providing a bivalvic interpretation of social conditions. Well, those running the Spanish Inquisition problably felt they, too, were doing a service to humanity, that inhuman torture purged evil. But here it's odious torture for torture's sake with the viewer as the victim while Schrader and company contemptuously turn the screws of the rack inflicting pain with the dedication of savage sadists. Not fit for children, man, or beast.

p, Buzz Feitshans; d&w, Paul Schrader; ph, Michael Chapman (Metrocolor); m, Jack Nitzsche; ed, Tom Rolf; prod d, Paul Sylbert; art d, Ed O'Donovan; set d, Bruce Weintraub.

Drama Cas. (PR:O MPAA:R)

HARDER THEY COME, THE*** (1973, Jamaica) 98m International Films/New World c

Jimmy Cliff *(Ivan)*, Carl Bradshaw *(Jose)*, Janet Bartley *(Elsa)*, Ras Daniel Hartman *(Pedro)*, Basil Keane *(Preacher)*, Bobby Charlton *(Hilton)*, Winston Stona *(Detective)*.

An outstanding first feature film from Jamaica that has become a major cult hit in the U.S. and done much to popularize reggae with its fabulous musical score. Reggae star Cliff plays a young Jamaican from the country who arrives in Kingston where he hopes to become a star. Work is hard to come by, and after having a rude awakening on the city streets, Cliff becomes a handyman for a local preacher and lives out of an abandoned car. He runs into trouble when he begins an affair with the preacher's ward Bartley. In an argument over a bicycle, Cliff slashes another handyman with a knife and is sent to jail. After his release he moves in with Bartley and pursues the island's biggest record producer, Charlton, who allows him to record his song "The Harder They Come." When Charlton offers him $20 for all rights to it, Cliff balks at the sum and Charlton gets him back by releasing it without giving it a promotion. Penniless, Cliff gets involved in the ganja (marijuana) trade with his friend Bradshaw, but is dissatisfied with the way the business is being run and resents having to pay a middleman. Cliff soon builds a reputation as a troublemaker with the other drug runners and the police, who tolerate the drug trade as long as they get their cut. When Cliff kills several policemen he develops a heroic reputation on the streets and is surprised to find that his record has suddenly become a hit, catapulting him to folk-hero status. Eventually the police track him down and in a violent gun battle Cliff is killed. THE HARDER THEY COME is a gritty, realistic view of urban Jamaica that concentrates on the squalor of the shanty towns the tourists never see. Cliff is superb as the obscure young man who rises to cult status. Much of the film's popularity stems from its outstanding musical score, a veritable cross-section of reggae music, including: "You Can Get It If You Really Want It," "The Harder They Come," "Many Rivers to Cross," "Sitting In Limbo" (written and sung by Jimmy Cliff); "Draw Your Breaks" (Derrick Harriot, D. Scott, sung by Scotty); "Rivers Of Babylon" (B. Dowe, F. McNaughton, sung by The Melodians); "Sweet and Dandy," "Pressure Drop" (F. Hibbert, sung by The Maytals); "Johnny Too Bad" (written and sung by The Slickers); and "Shanty Town" (written and sung by Desmond Dekker).

p&d, Perry Henzell; w, Henzell, Trevor D. Rhone; ph, Peter Jassop, David McDonald (Metrocolor); m, Jimmy Cliff, Desmond Dekker, The Slickers; ed, John Victor Smith, Seicland Anderson, Richard White.

Drama Cas. (PR:C MPAA:R)

HARDER THEY FALL, THE**** (1956) 109m COL bw

Humphrey Bogart *(Eddie Willis)*, Rod Steiger *(Nick Benko)*, Jan Sterling *(Beth Willis)*, Mike Lane *(Toro Moreno)*, Max Baer *(Buddy Brannen)*, Jersey Joe Walcott *(George)*, Edward Andrews *(Jim Weyerhause)*, Harold J. Stone *(Art Leavitt)*, Carlos Montalban *(Luis Agrandi)*, Nehemiah Persoff *(Leo)*, Felice Orlandi *(Vince Fawcett)*, Herbie Faye *(Max)*, Rusty Lane *(Danny McKeogh)*, Jack Albertson *(Pop)*, Val Avery *(Frank)*, Tommy Herman *(Tommy)*, Vinnie DeCarlo *(Joey)*, Pat Comiskey *(Gus Dundee)*, Matt Murphy *(Sailor Rigazzo)*, Abel Fernandez *(Chief Firebird)*, Marion Carr *(Alice)*, J. Lewis Smith *(Brannen's Manager)*, Everett Glass *(Minister)*, William Roerick *(Lawyer)*, Lilian Carver *(Mrs. Harding)*, Jack Daly, Richard Norris, Don Kohler, Ralph Bamble, Charles Tannen, Mark Scott, Russ Whiteman, Mort Mills, Stafford Repp, Sandy Sanders, Emily Belser *(Reporters)*, Paul Frees *(Priest)*, Joe Herrera, Frank Hagney *(Referees)*, Diane Mumby, Elaine Edwards *(Vince's Girl Friends)*, Tina Carver *(Mrs. Benko)*, Anthony Blankley, Penny Carpenter *(Nick's Children)*, Pan Dane *(Shirley)*, Joe Greb.

A rugged, almost merciless profile of the brutal "sport" of boxing, this stark drama has Bogart as a once scrupulous sports writer who has fallen on hard times. To earn a buck he accepts a job from Steiger as a fight promoter, even though he knows his new boss is mob-connected. Wife Sterling cautions hubby Bogart to seek gainful employment elsewhere but the money is big and he goes to work publicizing Steiger's new find, a giant Argentinian fighter, Lane. The towering boxer appears unbeatable but Bogart knows he has a "powder puff punch and a glass jaw." Steiger and his goons arrange for one fixed fight after another, with opponents diving to the canvas under the airy onslaught of the wildly swinging giant who comes to think that he is invincible. Bogart grits his teeth and bears it, even using up favors from one-time media pals like Stone who know it's a horribly fraudulent campaign to build up the fighter (and the odds) for mobdom's own end. The 7-foot simpleton is finally promoted into contender status as Steiger arranges for Lane to have a championship shot. First, he must fight Comiskey, one-time champion who has been badly beaten by present champ Baer. In fact, Comiskey has a clot on the brain and has been warned by doctors not to fight again or risk death. This is kept secret from Lane; Bogart, stifling his conscience, helps promote this fight. Lane meets Comiskey in the ring but even his creampuff punches are lethal to his ill opponent. Comiskey collapses in the ring and Lane is decreed the winner. Comiskey has died of a brain hemorrhage, really from the result of Baer's beating in the earlier match but Lane, convinced of his incredible power, blames himself for killing Comiskey. He refuses to fight again and Steiger pressures Bogart to persuade Lane to meet Baer in a championship bout. Bogart is all Lane has left, the only person he now believes in; Steiger has sent his Argentinian manager Montalban back to his native country. Bogart's conscience dictates that he must save Lane. The huge fighter has to be convinced that he has no punch so Bogart has trainer Walcott take his best punch and counter with a blow that sends Lane reeling. The lesson is counterproductive. Lane now feels he must fight Baer out of honor. He enters the ring where the savage Baer beats him to a pulp. All Lane now wishes to do is return to his small village in the Argentine and retire. He begs Bogart to get his money from Steiger, but when the promoter confronts the mob boss, he is told that Lane only has $49.07 coming. Persoff, the mob bookkeeper, rattles off a phony list of expenses which have apparently eaten up all of the fighter's earnings which Bogart calls bogus. Steiger tells him that Lane will get $49.07, period, then hands him his $26,000 share of the profits and warns Bogie not to interfere with his plans. He has just sold Lane to sleazy fight manager Andrews. Now it will be a slow ride downward in a series of fights where Lane will be heralded as a freak to be beaten into senselessness. Bogart won't stand for it and gives his money to Lane, then puts him on a plane going to Argentina to keep him out of the mob's clutches. Steiger visits Bogart and Sterling, telling the promoter that he intends to take revenge for what he has done. Bogart tells Steiger that he intends to write a series of articles that will expose him and the whole rotten fight racket, vowing to work for the banning of boxing in the U.S. "if it takes an act of Congress to do it." When one of Steiger's thugs makes a move toward Bogart, the mob boss stops him, then sneers at Bogie, telling him: "Who reads, who cares?" Upon his departure, Bogart sits down at a typewriter and begins his series of articles. THE HARDER THEY FALL is one of the most scathing indictments of boxing in film history, ranking with such relentless films as BODY AND SOUL, CHAMPION, REQUIEM FOR A HEAVYWEIGHT, and RAGING BULL. Nothing about it is pretty or charming, with director Robson moving the story along at a frenetic pace and Guffey's stark black and white phtography lending a grim feel to the movie. Moreover, it's all based on fact, author Schulberg rooting his story to the mob-controlled career of one-time heavyweight champion Primo Carnera, a giant with no punch who was promoted into his title, only to lose it to Max Baer in 1934; ironically, Baer does a reprise here of his victory, but is portrayed as a vicious, sadistic fighter who is angered that he actually killed Comiskey by giving him the beating which created the clot that led to his death in the ring with Lane. He is so miffed that Lane is credited with Comiskey's death that he vows to ravage the tall fighter. The punishment he administers is probably the most brutal in film history, captured by Guffey's cameras in the same realistic manner the cinematographer displayed when photographing FROM HERE TO ETERNITY. Director Robson knew well what he wanted to depict, having already helmed the powerful film CHAMPION with Kirk Douglas. Adding further authenticity to the film is Baer and the great Jersey Joe Walcott, both heavyweight champions who do not play themselves, and punch-drunk ex-slugger Joe Greb who does, appearing on camera to slobber incoherence in an unrehearsed interview conducted by Stone. The film is as faithful to Schulberg's story as it can be, a literary loyalty maintained by Robson and producer Yordan who also wrote the telling script where no glamour is attached to a dehumanizing gladiatorial sport, one run by cynics and men of heartless ambitions as tyified by Andrews who sneers at one point: "Fighters ain't human!" This film was first proposed by producer Jerry Wald who, after reading the book, wanted Columbia's nasty mogul Harry Cohn to produce it. Wald asked Schulberg to adapt the novel for the screen but the author was disinclined to work on the Columbia lot, hating Cohn for abusing his father, B.P. Schulberg, one-time co-leader (with Adolph Zukor) of Paramount. When the elder Schulberg's fortunes fell, he went to work for Cohn as a producer and Cohn insulted and degraded the fallen mogul at every turn, emotional abuse Schulberg's son Budd would never forget nor forgive. The author told Wald he would consider writing the film script from his novel but only on the proviso that he did not have to see or deal with Columbia's Harry Cohn, or "White Fang," as he was aptly nicknamed by those who disliked Cohn. In fact, Schulberg insisted that he work at home and never have to step foot on Columbia's lot. Wald agreed but when Cohn heard of these arrangements he exploded, telling the producer (according to Bob Thomas, writing in *King Cohn*): "Goddamnit, I want my writers on the lot. They are to check in at nine, take an hour for lunch, and work until six, just like anyone else." Wald told Schulberg and Schulberg told Wald to get another screenwriter. Yordan was later brought in to replace both Wald and

Schulberg and he did a great job maintaining the story and losing none of its impact. All of the cast give fine performances, even the giant Lane (who had made several brief appearances as monsters and freaks up to this time, including a portrayal of the creature in FRANKENSTEIN 1970). Sterling's performance as the righteous wife is a bit leaden but she is given little to do and appears only briefly. Steiger is terrific as the manipulating mob boss, but he sometimes overreaches in his attempt to take scenes away from Bogart, which proved an impossibility. During the production Bogart took a great dislike to Steiger's Method Acting style, complaining of the new actors employing this method to his friend Wald (from Alan Frank's *Humphrey Bogart*): "Why the hell don't they learn to speak properly? Words are important. This scratch-your-ass-and-mumble school of acting doesn't please me. You have to do something." Bogart down played his role in every frame with Steiger, making the younger actor appear frantic, manic, and even hammy, so that he appeared to be overreacting. The great Bogie registered his part effortlessly and made this one of his most memorable roles, perhaps knowing this would be his last film. He was already dying of cancer and the shooting schedule exhausted him. According to Richard Gehman, writing in *Bogart*, he returned home to wife Lauren Bacall each day from the studio to state: "I feel tired all the time. I don't know what's the matter with me. I don't seem to have any pep at all any more. Old age is catching up with me, I guess." After seeing doctors, Bogart discovered he had cancer of the esophagus. Operations didn't help and his condition worsened daily, although he refused to quit smoking and drinking. Friends visited him at home, having a drink and a laugh, a long line of them, almost as if Bogart were conducting final audiences. Columbia's Harry Cohn showed a rare concern for the actor toward the end. He called Bogie every week, telling him that he planned on filming C. S. Forester's *The Good Shepherd*. "The part's great for you, Bogie," Cohn piped to him one day, "better than THE CAINE MUTINY [which Cohn's Columbia had also produced]. Now I want you to get your ass over to the studio as soon as you can, so we can talk about the script. We want to start rolling as soon as you are okay." Bogart was genuinely moved by Cohn's calls which proved to be encouraging. "Now you know that tough old bastard wouldn't call if he thought I wasn't going to make it," he once remarked. Bogart and Bacall also made plans to star in the film version of John P. Marquand's novel, *Melville Goodwin, U.S.A.* (later filmed as TOP SECRET AFFAIR with Kirk Douglas and Susan Hayward). But it all came to nothing. Bogart died in his California home at 2:10 a.m. on January 14, 1957, nine days short of his 58th birthday. He left this film and many others of equal significance as his heritage.

p, Philip Yordan; d, Mark Robson; w, Yordan (based on the novel by Budd Schulberg); ph, Burnett Guffey; m, Hugo Friedhofer; ed, Jerome Thoms; md, Lionel Newman; art d, William Flannery; set d, William Kiernan; makeup, Clay Campbell.

Sports Drama **Cas.** **(PR:O MPAA:NR)**

HARDLY WORKING* (1981) 91m FOX c

Jerry Lewis *(Bo Hooper)*, Susan Oliver *(Claire Trent)*, Roger C. Carmel *(Robert Trent)*, Deanna Lund *(Millie)*, Harold J. Stone *(Frank Loucazi)*, Steve Franken *(Steve Torres)*, Buddy Lester *(Claude Reed)*, Leonard Stone *(Ted Mitchell)*, Jerry Lester *(Slats)*, Billy Barty *(Sammy)*, Alex Hentelhoff *(Balling)*, Britt Leach *(Gas Station Owner)*, Peggy Mondo *(Woman in Restaurant)*, Amy Krug *(Michele)*, Stephen Baccus *(Peter)*, Tommy Zibelli II *(Bobby)*, Buffy Dee *(C.B.)*, Lou Marsh, Tony Adams, Bob May *(Clowns)*, Angela Bomford *(Curio Lady)*, Jack McDermott *(Banker)*, Cary Hoffman *(Waiter)*, Rick O'Feldman *(Chuck)*, Jack Wakefield *(Disco Manager)*, Woody Woodbury, Charles Pitts, Ed Blessington *(Policemen)*, Jordana Wester *(Lady in House)*, John Disanti, Bobby Kosser *(Newsman)*, Erica Huddy *(Newswoman)*, John Rice, Greg Rice *(Midget Clowns)*.

Lewis makes a comeback after 10 years away from the screen in this bad film, performing his unchanging juvenile antics without a variation to show for the decade-long hiatus. He is an unemployed clown who lives with his sister, Oliver. She gets him a series of jobs, all of which he fumbles, then inexplicably he gets seriously intellectual and discusses the foibles of mankind. A tired, contrived script overmugged by the star, all add up to weary entertainment.

p, James J. McNamara, Igo Kantor; d, Jerry Lewis; w, Michael Janover, Lewis (based on a story by Janover); ph, James Pergola (DeLuxe Color); m, Morton Stevens; ed, Michael Luciano; art d, Don Ivey; set d, Tom Coll.

Comedy **Cas.** **(PR: A MPAA:PG)**

HARDYS RIDE HIGH, THE*** (1939) 80m MGM bw

Mickey Rooney *(Andy Hardy)*, Lewis Stone *(Judge Hardy)*, Cecilia Parker *(Marian Hardy)*, Fay Holden *(Mrs. Hardy)*, Ann Rutherford *(Polly Benedict)*, Sara Haden *(Aunt Milly)*, Don Castle *(Dennis Hunt)*, John King *(Phillip Westcott)*, Virginia Grey *(Consuela McNish)*, Minor Watson *(Terry B. Archer)*, Halliwell Hobbes *(Dobbs)*, George Irving *(Jonas)*, Aileen Pringle *(Miss Booth)*, Marsha Hunt *(Susan Bowen)*, Donald Briggs *(Caleb Bowen)*, William Orr *(Dick Bannersly)*, Truman Bradley *(Clerk)*, John T. Murray *(Don Davis)*.

Everyone's favorite family leaves their small town haunts for the bright lights of Detroit and a $2,000,000 inheritance. They live high off the hog for a while, and Rooney falls for a gold digging chorus girl. After a heartfelt chat with the Judge, though, everything is set straight. The inheritance turns out not to have been theirs after all, and the Hardys return home to await the next film.

d, George B. Seitz; w, Kay Van Riper, Agnes C. Johnson, William Ludwig (based on characters created by Aurania Rouverol); ph, John Seitz; m, David Snell; ed, Ben Lewis.

Comedy **(PR:AAA MPAA:NR)**

HAREM BUNCH; OR WAR AND PIECE, THE*½ (1969) 80m PI/Republic Amusement c
(AKA: THE HAREM BUNCH; OR WAR AND PEACE; DESERT ODYSSEY)

Monica Gayle *(Shwartz)*, Mitch Evans *(Irving)*, Frank Cuva *(Ali)*, Sherrie Land *(Toblosky)*, Albert James *(Customer)*, Warren Ball *(Acaba)*, Leonard Goodman *(Habib)*, Barbara Caron *(Kaplan)*, Tom Counter *(Kalan)*, Bill Kersh *(Beggar)*, Ron Glen *(Shamir)*, Paul Bruce *(Col. Seigal)*, Sanford Mitchell *(Messenger)*, Vick Thorne *(Hagoub)*, Leslie De Larenzo *(Hagoub's Sister)*, Pam Maloney *(Secretary)*, Jane Tsentas, Val Couret, Jane Dabon, Bridget Wienst Raume, Joseph Rip, Tony Oritz.

An oddity in its own right, this farce makes fun of the continual feuding between the Arabs and Jews in the Middle East. Beginning with two opposing armies in a cease-fire, the Jewish leader gets antsy to get back to his favorite pastime of fighting and develops a plan to get the Arabs to start attacking again. This requires sending three beautiful spies into enemy territory, have them get captured, and make the Arabs think that something is up. His plan works perfectly until Cuva decides to seduce the three women into disclosing their mission. After a night of carrying on with Cuva the girls reveal the plan, the fighting stops, and Cuva and the Jewish leader become the best of friends, even opening up a tailor shop together. Film is a bit far-fetched, but can at least be praised for exposing a lighter side to a very serious subject.

p, R.W. Cresse; d, Paul Hunt; w, Cresse; ph, Ron Garcia (Eastmancolor); m, Toufic Barham Players; ed, Abraham Posnic; set d, Garcia; cos, Arnie Weiss; makeup, Dennis Marsh.

Comedy **(PR:C-O MPAA:NR)**

HAREM GIRL** (1952) 70m COL bw

Joan Davis *(Susie Perkins)*, Peggie Castle *(Princess Shareen)*, Arthur Blake *(Abdul Nassib)*, Paul Marion *(Majeed)*, Donald Randolph *(Jamal)*, Henry Brandon *(Hassan)*, Minerva Urecal *(Aniseh)*, Peter Mamoks *(Sarab)*, John Dehner *(Khalil)*, Peter Brocco *(Ameen)*, Russ Conklin *(Sami)*, Wilson Miller *(Habib)*, Ric Roman *(Hamad)*, Nick Thompson *(Ben Ahmed)*, Alan Foster *(Suleman)*, Robert Tafur *(Captain LeBlanc)*, Shepard Menken *(Major Blanchard)*, Guy Teague *(Messenger)*, Peter Virgo *(Maleen)*, George Khoury *(Ben Gali)*, Pat Walter, Vivian Mason, Helen Reichman *(Harem Girls)*.

Evil sheik Randolph is trying to kill Princess Castle in order to take over the oil supply of the mythical kingdom in which HAREM GIRL is set. Davis, as Castle's secretary, does her best to stop it, running around the palace hiding the keys to the armory and such. Not what you'd call a comedy classic, though Davis does a decent job with the poorly written script.

p, Wallace MacDonald; d, Edward Bernds; w, Bernds, Elwood Ullman (based on a story by Bernds); ph, Lester White; ed, Richard Fantl; md, Mischa Bakaleinikoff; art d, Paul Palmentola.

Comedy **(PR:A MPAA:NR)**

HAREM HOLIDAY (SEE: HARUM SCARUM, 1965)

HARLEM GLOBETROTTERS, THE½** (1951) 75m COL bw

Thomas Gomez *(Abe Saperstein)*, Dorothy Dandridge *(Ann Carpenter)*, Bill Walker *(Prof. Turner)*, Angela Clarke *(Sylvia Saperstein)*, Peter Thompson *(Martin)*, Steve Roberts *(Eddie)*, Peter Virgo *(Rocky)*, Ray Walker *(Jack Davis)*, Al Eben *(Charlie Peters)*, Ann E. Allen *(Sara)*, William Forrest *(Prof. Lindley)*, Tom Greenway *(Dave Barrett)*, The Harlem Globetrotters: Billy Brown, Roscoe Cumberland, William "Pop" Gates, Marques Haynes, Louis "Babe" Pressley, Ermer Robinson, Ted Strong, Reese "Goose" Tatum, Frank Washington, Clarence Wilson, Inman Jackson.

College student Brown drops out to go after fame—and particularly fortune—with the title basketball team. After a few setbacks and some sage advice from his girl friend Dandridge, Brown sets himself straight. The story is just an excuse to film the Globetrotters in action, and it is their antics on the court that make this one worth seeing.

p, Buddy Adler; d, Phil Brown (basketball sequences by Will Jason); w, Alfred Palca; ph, Phillip Tannura; m, Arthur Morton; ed, James Sweeney; md, Morris Stoloff; art d, Cary Odell.

Sports Drama **(PR:A MPAA:NR)**

HARLEM IS HEAVEN*** (1932) 60m Lincoln bw

Bill Robinson *(Bill)*, John Mason *(Spider)*, Putney Dandridge *(Stage Manager)*, Jimmy Baskette *(Money Johnson)*, Anise Boyer *(Jean Stratton)*, Henri Wessell *(Chummy Walker)*, Alma Smith *(Gret Rae)*, Bob Sawyer *(Knobs Moran)*, Eubie Blake and His Orchestra.

The lead in this all-black cast, Bill "Bojangles" Robinson, is the director/star of a Harlem theater, uniting lovers Boyer and Wessell, even though he has been secretly in love with Boyer for years. Though famous as a dancer (and he does get to dance here), Robinson makes an impressive showing as an actor and sings one song, "Is You Or Is You Ain't." Eubie Blake and his orchestra are superb.

p, Jack Goldberg; d&w, Irwin R. Franklin; m, Porter Grainger, Joe Jordan, Shelton Brooks, Edgar Dorwell.

Drama **(PR:A MPAA:NR)**

HARLEM ON THE PRAIRIE* (1938) 54m Associated bw
(AKA: BAD MAN OF HARLEM)

Herbert Jeffries, Flourney E. Miller, Manton Moreland, Connie Harris, Maceo B. Sheffield; William Spencer, Jr., George Randall, Nathan Curry, Edward Brandon, James Davis, The Four Tones, The Four Blackbirds.

Jeffries, heroically mounted on a white horse, helps Harris find the gold her father had hidden years before, defeating villain Sheffield in the bargain. It's just like a thousand B westerns of the period, only this one was the first with an all-black cast. The acting and technical standards of the film are poor. There is one comedy routine done by an established black team of the 1930s, Miller and Manton. Jeffries, who was once a vocalist with the Duke Ellington Orchestra, croons two tunes: "Harlem On The Prairie" and "Romance In The Rain."

p, Jed Buell; d, Sam Newfield; w, Fred Myton; ph, William Hyer; ed, Robert Jahns; md, Lew Porter; m/l, Mary Schneffer, Porter, Lyle Womack, Stryker and Lange, Don Swander, Ira Hardin, June Hershey.

Western/Musical **(PR:A MPAA:NR)**

HARLEM RIDES THE RANGE*½ (1939) 58m Hollywood Pictures bw

Herbert Jeffrey [Jeffries], Lucius Brooks, Artie Young, F.E. Miller, Spencer Williams, Clarence Brooks, Tom Southern, John Thomas, Wade Dumas, The Four Tunes, Leonard Christmas.

The second of a trio of all-black westerns produced by Kahn (THE BRONZE BUCKAROO; THE TWO GUN MAN FROM HARLEM) is still a lackluster oater despite its curiosity. Jeffrey is the hero who stops the evil Brooks from stealing a radium mine from the unsuspecting Young. Despite the fact that this film was written by blacks, it was obviously produced for the white audience as it depicts little from the black standpoint.

p&d, Richard C. Kahn; w, Spencer Williams, Jr.; F.E. Miller; ph, Roland Price, Clark Ramsey; m, Lew Porter; art d, Vin Taylor.

Western **Cas.** **(PR:A MPAA:NR)**

HARLEQUIN½** (1980, Aus.) 95m Hemdale/New Image c

Robert Powell *(Gregory Wolfe)*, David Hemmings *(Sen. Rast)*, Carmen Duncan *(Sandra)*, Broderick Crawford *(Doc Wheelan)*.

Powell plays the title character, a modern Rasputin, who cures the leukemia-stricken child of powerful senator Hemmings and seduces the politician's wife Duncan. Seeing the potentially dangerous Powell rising in the nation's power structure, Crawford sets out to ruin the mysterious healer. Another interesting film from down under.

p, Tony Ginnane; d, Simon Powell; w, Everett DeRoche; m, Brian May.

Drama **(PR:C-O MPAA:NR)**

HARLOW* (1965) 107m Electronovision/Magna c

Carol Lynley *(Jean Harlow)*, Efrem Zimbalist, Jr., *(William Mansfield)*, Ginger Rogers *(Mama Jean)*, Barry Sullivan *(Marino Bello)*, Hurd Hatfield *(Paul Bern)*, Lloyd Bochner *(Marc Peters)*, Hermione Baddeley *(Marie Dressler)*, Audrey Totter *(Marilyn)*, John Williams *(Jonathan Martin)*, Audrey Christie *(Thelma)*, Michael Dante *(Ed)*, Jack Kruschen *(Louis B. Mayer)*, Celia Lovsky *(Maria Ouspenskaya)*, Robert Strauss *(Hank)*, Sonny Liston *(1st Fighter)*, James Dobson *(Counterman)*, Cliff Norton *(Billy)*, Paulle Clark *(Waitress)*, Jim Plunkett *(Stan Laurel)*, John "Red" Fox *(Oliver Hardy)*, Joel Marston *(Press Agent)*, Miss Christopher West *(Bern's Secretary)*, Fred Conte *(Photographer)*, Catherine Ross *(Wardrobe Woman)*, Buddy Lewis *(Al Jolson)*, Danny Francis *(Casino Manager)*, Frank Scannell *(Doctor)*, Maureene Gaffney *(Miss Larsen)*, Nick Demitri *(2nd Fighter)*, Ron Kennedy *(Assistant Director)*, Harry Holcombe *(Minister)*, Lola Fisher *(Nurse)*, Fred Klein *(Himself)*.

A rancid screen biography of the 1930s Hollywood sex goddess which tried to capitalize on renewed interest in the star created by a sensationalized best-selling biography. Lynley is horribly miscast as a starlet discovered by an up-and-coming actor played by Bochner, who spotted her as an extra in a Laurel and Hardy comedy (presumably DOUBLE WHOOPEE, 1928). Bochner arranges for Lynley to have a screen test for director Williams (apparently doubling for Howard Hughes), who is thrilled by what he sees and stars her in his next film (in reality, HELL'S ANGELS, 1930). This, of course, catapults her to stardom. Taking full advantage of Lynley's new fame are her mother, Rogers (wasted in a role she should have left to an actress with less of an image to tarnish) and her stepfather, Sullivan, who have quickly grown used to large amounts of disposable cash. Unsatisfied by her stardom, Lynley cannot take her feelings of loneliness and despair. She soon falls in love with producer Paul Bern (Hatfield), and the couple are married. Though deeply in love with Lynley, Hatfield cannot overcome his impotence and the marriage is never consummated. Feeling betrayed by her husband (who knew of his impotence before the marriage, but chose not to tell his future wife), Lynley goes on a spree of affairs which causes Hatfield to commit suicide. Plagued by deep guilt feelings due to the suicide, Lynley attempts another marriage, but that, too, fails. Seeking to change her life, Lynley moves East to get away from Hollywood and to study acting. Upon hearing that her mother has fallen ill, Lynley returns to Los Angeles and, much to her surprise, is welcomed with open arms by Louis B. Mayer (Kruschen) who wants her to star in his next big project. Her confidence and enthusiasm renewed, Lynley launches headlong into her work, and a new romance with popular male star Zimbalist, Jr. (a strange conglomeration of William Powell and Clark Gable, men who played important roles in Harlow's last years). Just as everything seems to be looking up for Lynley, she contracts a fatal illness and dies. Every aspect of HARLOW is cheap and smarmy. In a rush to get their movie out before Paramount's version of the same material, the producers shot the film in a mind-boggling eight days and used a hideous video-to-film process dubbed "Electronovision" (Richard Burton's HAMLET and the rock-n-roll concert documentary THE T.A.M.I. SHOW were previously filmed with the process with the same results) which sapped the life out of the visuals because extremely flat lighting had to be used for the video cameras. From the production approach alone one can see that the people involved in the making of this debacle had no interest in the tragic life of Jean Harlow other than to exploit it for profit.

p, Bill Sargant, Lee Savin; d, Alex Segal; w, Karl Tunberg; ph, Jim Kilgore; m, Al Ham, Nelson Riddle; art d, Duncan Cramer; set d, Harry Gordon; cos, Nolan Miller; makeup, Michael Westmore.

Drama **(PR:C MPAA:NR)**

HARLOW*½ (1965) 125m PAR c

Carroll Baker *(Jean Harlow)*, Martin Balsam *(Everett Redman)*, Red Buttons *(Arthur Landau)*, Michael Connors *(Jack Harrison)*, Angela Lansbury *(Mama Jean Bello)*, Peter Lawford *(Paul Bern)*, Raf Vallone *(Marion Bello)*, Leslie Nielsen *(Richard Manley)*, Mary Murphy *(Studio Secretary)*, Hanna Landy *(Mrs. Arthur Landau)*, Peter Hansen *(Assistant Director)*, Kipp Hamilton *(Girl at Pool)*, Peter Leeds *(Director of '30s)*.

Released only one month after the first version of HARLOW starring Carol Lynley, this screen biography of the popular female star of the 1930s benefits from better production values and a more talented lead actress (Baker). Unfortunately, the script is no better than the first version's, this one attributed to the best-selling biography of Harlow written by Irving Shulman and Arthur Landau (the starlet's former agent). HARLOW treads the same basic ground as its predecessor, though an inordinate amount of screentime is devoted to small-time agent Landau (Buttons), the reasons for which may be related to who wrote the book the film was based on. As Baker's conniving mother and stepfather, Lansbury and Vallone turn in competent performances, but Lawford as the doomed Paul Bern is an incongruous piece of casting. Baker is a much better Harlow than the competition's vapid Lynley, and she conveys a complexity and compassion to a role that could have been a stunner given a better, less sensationalized, script. As far as the HARLOW war at the box-office went, this version broke with Hollywood tradition and made more money than the previous effort, probably due to the costuming and impressive sets. In the end, HARLOW suffers from the same shallowness found in every screen treatment of Hollywood personalities from THE BUSTER KEATON STORY (1957) to FRANCES (1982). Perhaps Hollywood is incapable of the self-analysis needed to honestly portray the frequently tragic circumstances that can consume the talented, sensitive, and somewhat naive people who want their faces to live forever on the silver screen.

p, Joseph E. Levine; d, Gordon Douglas; w, John Michael Hayes; (based on the book *An Intimate Biography* by Irving Shulman, Arthur Landau); ph, Joseph Ruttenberg (Panavision, Technicolor); m, Neal Hefti; ed, Frank Bracht, Archie Marshek; art d, Hal Pereira, Roland Anderson; set d, James Payne; cos, Ruth Stella, Robert Magahay; m/l, "Lonely Girl," Jay Livingston, Ray Evans (sung by Bobby Vinton); makeup, William Reynolds.

Drama **(PR:C MPAA:NR)**

HARMON OF MICHIGAN** (1941) 65m COL bw

Tom Harmon *(Himself)*, Anita Louise *(Peggy Adams)*, Forest Evashevski *(Himself)*, Oscar O'Shea *("Pop" Branch)*, Warren Ashe *(Bill Dorgan)*, Stanley Crown *(Freddy Davis)*, Ken Christy *(Joe Scudder)*, Tim Ryan *(Flash Regan)*, William Hall *(Jimmy Wayburn)*, Lloyd Bridges *(Ozzie)*, Chester Conklin *(Gasoline Chuck)*, Larry Parks *(Harvey)*, Bill Henry, Sam Balter, Wendell Niles, Tom Hanlon, Ken Niles.

College football star Harmon stars in this film loosely based on his life. Starting out with newsreel footage of the 1939-40 season, the film follows him as he drifts in and out of the pros, marries sweetheart Louise, takes a series of coaching jobs and finally ends up as assistant to his old coach, O'Shea, at Michigan. Harmon is illogically characterized here, using an illegal flying wedge formation to defeat his old team; but he does seem comfortable in front of the camera. Football lovers will enjoy this relic.

p, Wallace MacDonald; d, Charles Barton; w, Howard J. Green (based on a story by Richard Goldstone, Stanley Rauh, Fredric Frank); ph, John Stumar; ed, Arthur Seld; md, M.W. Stoloff; art d, Lionel Banks.

Sports Drama/Biography **(PR:A MPAA:NR)**

HARMONY AT HOME*½ (1930) 69m FOX bw

William Collier, Sr., Marguerite Churchill, Charlotte Henry, Charles Eaton, Rex Bell, Dixie Lee, Elizabeth Patterson, Dot Farley.

Another harmless but dull comedy with family man Collier suddenly finding himself running a sweatshop. Meanwhile, Mama Churchill is scaring away all her daughter's suitors by talking marriage as soon as they walk through the door. Nothing special in spite of the fact that six writers worked on the project, originally itself taken from a play.

d, Hamilton MacFadden; w, Claire Kummer, Seton I. Miller, William Collier, Sr., Charles J. McGuirk, Edwin Burke, Elliott Lester (based on the play "The Family Upstairs" by Harry Delf); ph, Dan Clark; ed, Irene Morra.

Comedy **(PR:A MPAA:NR)**

HARMONY HEAVEN* (1930, Brit.) 61m BIP/Wardour c

Polly Ward *(Billie Breeze)*, Stuart Hall *(Bob Farrell)*, Trilby Clark *(Lady Violet Mistley)*, Jack Raine *(Stuart)*, Philip Hewland *(Beasley Cutting)*, Percy Standing *(Producer)*, Gus Sharland *(Stage Manager)*, Aubrey Fitzgerald *(Suggs)*, Edna Prince *(Singer)*.

This poorly-made musical is the story of an ambitious composer, Hall, who jilts the girl who loves him, Ward, and woos Clark instead. When Ward proves her love by gaining Hall some notoriety, the big-headed composer returns to earth and his true sweetheart. Included is the unmemorable tune "Raggedy Romp." Notable only for being an early color film, HARMONY HEAVEN offers nothing more than some flashy reds and greens.

d, Thomas Bentley; w, Arthur Wimperis, Randall Faye, Frank Launder; ph, Theodore Sparkuhl.

Musical **(PR:A MPAA:NR)**

HARMONY LANE*** (1935) 85m Mascot/REP bw

Douglass Montgomery *(Stephen Foster)*, Evelyn Venable *(Susan Pentland)*, Adrienne Ames *(Jane McDowell)*, Joseph Cawthorn *(Kleber)*, William Frawley *(Christy)*, Clarence Muse *(Old Joe)*, Gilbert Emery *(Mr. Foster)*, Florence Roberts *(Mrs. Foster)*, James Bush *(Morrison Foster)*, David Torrence *(Mr. Pentland)*, Victor DeCamp *(William Foster, Jr.)*, Edith Craig *(Henrietta Foster)*, Cora Sue Collins

(Marion), Lloyd Hughes *(Andrew Robinson)*, Ferdinand Munier *(Mr. Pond)*, Mildred Gover *(Delia)*, James B. Carson *(Proprietor)*, Rodney Hildebrand *(Mr. Wade)*, Mary McLaren *(Mrs. Wade)*, Al Herman *(Tambo)*, Earl Hodgins *(Mr. Bones)*, Smiley Burnette *(Singer)*, Hattie McDaniel *(Cook)*.

Probably the best of the films based on Steven Foster's sad life, mainly because it's the most accurate. Montgomery leaves a career as a minister to become a songwriter, marries a woman he doesn't love, while the woman he does love jilts him for another. He winds up a penniless drunk in New York. All the familiar Foster songs are here including: "Oh Susanna," "My Old Kentucky Home," "Old Black Joe," "Weep No More My Lady," and "Swanee River."

p, Nat Levine; d, Joseph Santley; w, Santley, Elizabeth Meehan (based on a story by Milton Krims); ph, Ernest Miller, Jack Marta; ed, Joseph Lewis, Ray Curtis; md, Arthur Kay.

Biography (PR:A MPAA:NR)

HARMONY ROW*½ (1933, Aus.) 80m Efftee bw

George Wallace, Marshall Crossby.

This one was aimed strictly at the Australian audiences who could appreciate Wallace's peculiar type of brazen comedy. The entire film is aimed at Wallace as he undertakes to join the Melbourne police department, with Crossby as the only other prominent member of the cast taking part mainly to provide Wallace a sounding board. Direction is sloppy and haphazard, but serves the purpose of the picture.

d, F.W. Thring; w, George Wallace; ph, Arthur Higgins.

Comedy (PR:A MPAA:NR)

HARMONY TRAIL (SEE: WHITE STALLION, 1944)

HAROLD AND MAUDE*½** (1971) 90m PAR c

Ruth Gordon *(Maude)*, Bud Cort *(Harold)*, Vivian Pickles *(Mrs. Chasen)*, Cyril Cusack *(Sculptor)*, Charles Tyner *(Uncle Victor)*, Ellen Geer *(Sunshine)*, Eric Christmas *(Priest)*, G. Wood *(Psychiatrist)*, Judy Engles *(Candy Gulf)*, Shari Summers *(Edith Fern)*, M. Borman *(Motorcycle Cop)*, Ray Goman, Gordon Devol *(Police Officers)*, Harvey Brumfield *(Cop)*, Henry Dieckoff *(Butler)*, Philip Schultz *(Doctor)*, Sonia Sorrell *(Head Nurse)*, Margot Jones *(Student Nurse)*, Barry Higgins *(Intern)*, Pam Bebermeyer, Joe Hooker *(Stunt Doubles)*, William Lucking *(Motorcycle Policeman)*, Susan Madigan, Jerry Randall.

HAROLD AND MAUDE was soundly trounced by many critics when it was first released, but there is much in this oddball story to recommend. Cort is the son of Pickles, a wealthy woman who pays little attention to him. His frequent depressions and lack of friends cause him to erect more and more elaborate pranks (fake suicides by hanging, self-immolation, etc.), none of which impress his mother who is involved with everyone and everything else. Fascinated by funerals, Cort has an old hearse which he drives to various cemeteries. At two successive services, he meets Gordon, a 79-year-old woman who shares his penchant for death. She is a memorable character with a great passion for life, no guilt, and more than a few aphorisms. Cort and Gordon become great pals and she instills in him a desire to live, to spread his wings, to enjoy his brief time on earth. As time passes, they share several adventures, including stealing a car, crashing through toll gates, stealing a tree and replanting it in a forest where it can grow among friends. They are very happy with each other, except for the moments when concentration camp survivor Gordon speaks of her late husband and becomes teary. Pickles thinks that Cort should be married and has three women, chosen by computer, come to the estate. Cort frightens off the three—Geer, Engles, and Summers—and shows no interest in any other woman besides his octogenarian buddy. Pickles enlists her military uncle, Tyner, to get Cort into the service but the plan is foiled with Gordon's help as Cort pretends to be so sadistic that even Tyner finds it unpalatable. Cort and Gordon make love and he plans to marry her despite the protests of Pickles, Tyner, Christmas, the priest, and Wood, the psychiatrist. Gordon, true to her free-spirit philosophy, celebrates her 80th birthday by happily saying goodbye to her friends, and then taking a fatal dose of sleeping pills. Cort is so stunned that he drives his hearse toward a cliff. But before leaping he takes Gordon's advice to heart, picks up his banjo and dances up a hill in the final scene. It is interesting to note that this creative film was originally a 20-minute script written as a graduate thesis by UCLA student Higgins. He later showed it to his landlady, Lewis, who was the wife of a film producer, and the two collaborated to form their own production company. They made a deal with Paramount in which Howard Jaffe was originally slated to produce the film, but he was soon replaced by Higgins and Mulvehill, while Lewis' status was that of executive producer. HAROLD AND MAUDE doesn't resemble anything else and has survived the bad notices to become a cult classic that keeps cropping up.

p, Charles B. Mulvehill, Colin Higgins; d, Hal Ashby; w, Higgins; ph, John Alonzo (Technicolor); m, Cat Stevens; ed, William A. Sawyer, Edward Warschilka; prod d, Michael Haller; art d, Haller; set d, James Cane; cos, Bill Theiss; spec eff, A.D. Flowers; m/l, "If You Want To Sing" (sung by Stevens).

Comedy Cas. (PR:A-C MPAA:GP)

HAROLD ROBBINS' THE BETSY (SEE: BETSY, THE, 1978)

HAROLD TEEN** (1934) 67m WB bw (GB: THE DANCING FOOL)

Hal LeRoy *(Harold)*, Rochelle Hudson *(Lillums)*, Patricia Ellis *(Mimi)*, Guy Kibbee *(Pa Lovewell)*, Hugh Herbert *(Rathburn)*, Hobart Cavanaugh *(Pop)*, Chic Chandler *(Lilacs)*, Eddie Tamblyn *(Shadow)*, Douglas Dumbrille *(Snatcher)*, Clara Blandick *(Ma Lovewell)*, Mayo Methot, Richard Carle, Charles Wilson.

Dumb small-town journalist LeRoy falls in love with Hudson, who is being forced out of her home by a banker who is threatening to foreclose. There are some pointless complications that make hash of the plot, but LeRoy dances well and often. Musical numbers include: "How Do You Know It's Sunday?" "Simple and Sweet," "Two Little Flies on a Lump of Sugar," and "Collegiate Wedding." This movie was a remake of a 1928 silent version.

d, Murray Roth; w, Paul G. Smith, Al Cohn (based on a comic strip by Carl Ed), ph, Arthur Todd; ed, Terry Morse; md, Leo F. Forbstein; art d, John Hughes; m/l, Irving Kahal, Sammy Fain.

Comedy (PR:A MPAA:NR)

HARP OF BURMA*½** (1967, Jap.) 120m Nikkatsu/Brandon bw (BIRUMANO TATEGOTO; AKA: THE BURMESE HARP)

Shoji Yasui *(Private Mizushima)*, Rentaro Mikuni *(Captain Inouye)*, Taniye Kitabayashi *(Old Woman)*, Tatsuya Mihashi *(Defense Commander)*, Yunosuke Ito.

A chilling antiwar statement set during the final days of WW II as Japanese soldier Yasui is separated from his squadron. The remaining soldiers are taken to a prison camp in Burma, while harp-playing Yasui travels to the island dressed as a Buddhist monk. In addition to finding his comrades, he finds bones and corpses strewn across the island and decides to devote himself to burying them. When his unit attempts to convince him to return home to Japan, Yasui chooses to remain in Burma, burying the dead. An exceptionally photographed film which, despite its slow pace, sensitively portrays the life of a man devoted to his country and his countrymen. Released in 1956, HARP OF BURMA walked away from the Venice Film Fest as a much-heralded prize-winner.

p, Masayuki Takagi; d, Kon Ichekawa; w, Natto Wada (based on the novel by Michio Takeyama); ph, Minoru Yokoyama; m, Akira Ifukube; ed, Masanori Tsujii.

War Drama (PR:C-O MPAA:NR)

HARPER½** (1966) 121m WB c (GB: THE MOVING TARGET)

Paul Newman *(Harper)*, Lauren Bacall *(Mrs. Sampson)*, Julie Harris *(Betty Fraley)*, Arthur Hill *(Albert Graves)*, Janet Leigh *(Susan Harper)*, Pamela Tiffin *(Miranda Sampson)*, Robert Wagner *(Alan Traggert)*, Robert Webber *(Dwight Troy)*, Shelley Winters *(Fay Estabrook)*, Harold Gould *(Sheriff Spanner)*, Strother Martin *(Claude)*, Roy Jensen *(Puddler)*, Martin West *(Deputy)*, Jacqueline de Wit *(Mrs. Kronberg)*, Eugene Iglesias *(Felix)*, Richard Carlyle *(Fred Platt)*.

HARPER did better business than it deserved to do. Perhaps it was because this was Newman's first venture into the tough world of private eyedom or maybe the timing was right; whatever the reason, it was enough of a success to cause a number of other films in the genre to be made in the following few months. Newman is a bust-out private detective who lives in a tiny apartment and drives an old Porsche that he can't afford to have repainted. (He played almost the same type as a lawyer in THE VERDICT). Hill, an old attorney pal, gets him an assignment to investigate the disappearance of Bacall's husband. Bacall is confined to a wheelchair and is an embittered, though fabulously wealthy, woman. At her mansion, Newman encounters Bacall's nubile stepdaughter, Tiffin, and Wagner, the family's private pilot. Newman begins snooping and finds a photo of a once-beautiful movie actress, Winters. When he gets to her, he finds an aging, fat alcoholic. Through Winters he meets drug-addicted nightclub singer, Harris. Further investigation (and a few beatings later), Newman visits a mountaintop retreat for religious zealots that Bacall's husband gave to Martin, leader of the group. Bacall gets a kidnaper's note, agrees to pay the ransom for what she thought was her dead husband, and gives Newman the money to deliver. He does this but the cash is purloined by Harris in a double-cross. Harper suspects Wagner is behind the plot and has planned it with Harris. Wagner pulls a gun but is shot by Hill, who conveniently appears, and just happens to have a gun on him. Harper rushes to Harris' residence and is manhandled by Webber, Winters' husband, who is partnered with Martin in an illegal smuggling operation. Harper kills Webber, and Harris takes him to where Bacall's husband is being kept, an abandoned oil tanker. With Hill at his side, they find the man already dead. Harris, who tries to flee, dies when her car goes over an embankment. On the way back to Bacall's home, Hill admits that he killed the rich man because he hated him for standing in the way of his love for Tiffin. Hill pulls a gun on Newman but cannot bring himself to shoot his old pal. HARPER is overly complex and better had it been left as a novel. Leigh was good as Newman's ex-wife and Martin was perfectly cast as the religious leader. Tiffin is little more than a pretty face and has seldom been heard from since. Too many twists, turns and not enough deep characterizations make this a minor-league effort, despite all of the big names involved. The sequel also starred Newman in THE DROWNING POOL.

p, Elliot Kastner, Jerry Gershwin; d, Jack Smight; w, William Goldman (based on the novel *The Moving Target* by Ross MacDonald); ph, Conrad Hall (Panavision, Technicolor); m, Johnny Mandel; ed, Stefan Arnsten; art d, Alfred Sweeney; set d, Claude Carpenter; cos, Sally Edwards, William Smith; m/l, "Livin' Alone" Andre and Dory Previn (sung by Julie Harris).

Detective Drama Cas. (PR:C MPAA:NR)

HARPER VALLEY, P.T.A. zero (1978) 93m April Fools Production c

Barbara Eden *(Stella Johnson)*, Ronny Cox *(Willis Newton)*, Nannette Fabray *(Alice Finely)*, Susan Swift *(Dee Johnson)*, Louis Nye *(Kirby Baker)*, Pat Paulsen *(Otis Harper, Jr.)*, John Fiedler *(Bobby Taylor)*, Audrey Christie *(Flora Simpson Reilly)*, DeVera Marcus *(Holly Taylor)*, Irene Yah Ling Sun *(Myrna Wong)*, Louise Foley *(Mavis Schroeder)*, Clint Howard *(Corley)*, Jan Teige, Laura Teige *(Reilly Twins)*, Pitt Hervert *(Henry Reilly)*, Faye Dewitt *(Willa Mae Jones)*, Molly Dodd *(Olive Glover)*, Ron Masak *(Herbie Maddox)*, Amzie Strickland *(Shirley Thompson)*, Brian Cook *(Carlyle Ridley)*, Tobias Anderson *(Barney)*, Bob Hastings *(Skeeter)*, Arlene Stuart *(Bertha)*, J.J. Barry *(Nolan)*, Royce D. Applegate *(Dutch)*, Whitey Hughes *(Stunt Man)*.

This is a little joke that wears thin after 20 minutes. Sexy Eden, addicted to short skirts, tight pants, and revealing garb, is thought to be the town hussy by local P.T.A. board members and they intend to make life rough on her teenage daughter Swift at Harper Valley High School until Eden packs up and departs.

She fights back with the help of Fabray, taking photos of skirt-chasing board members, and even manages to produce some pink elephants to drive town drunk Paulsen looney. None of it works, the laughs are purely slapstick, and Eden blatantly bumps and grinds about like some cheap little stripper out of her element. It's embarrassing to watch this middle-age woman jumping about like a female half her age. The script is forced and feeble, the direction prostrate.

p, George Edwards; d, Richard Bennett; w, Edwards (based on the song by Tom T. Hall); ph, Willy Kurant (Deluxe Color); m, Nelson Riddle; ed, Michael Economu; art d, Tom Rasmussen; set d, Bob Breen; cos, Rasmussen; m/l, "Harper Valley P.T.A." Hall (sung by Jeannie C. Riley).

Comedy **Cas.** **(PR:C MPAA:PG)**

HARPOON** (1948) 83m Danches/Screen Guild bw

John Bromfield *(Michael Shand)*, Alyce Louis *(Kitty Canon)*, James Cardwell *(Red Dorsett)*, Patricia Garrison *(Christine McFee)*, Jack George *(Rev. McFee)*, Edgar Hinton *(Kirk Shand)*, Frank Hagney *(Red Dorsett, Sr.)*, Hollis Bane *(Kodiak)*, Ruth Castle *(Patsy)*, Grant Means *(Swede)*, Sally Davis *(Sally)*, James Martin *(Fuzzy)*, Willard Jillson *(Lockerby)*, Gary Garrett *(Prisoner)*, Lee Elson *(Whaler)*, Alex Sharp *(Whaler)*, Lee Roberts *(Whaler)*.

Interesting story of the hatred between two men and their sons who carry it on after their deaths. Hinton is shanghaied aboard Hagney's whaler and after several years of physical abuse he manages to escape. The men continue to hate each other and their children are trained to carry on the fight. As adults, Bromfield finally manages to kill Cardwell and wins Louis and the money. Good location shots filmed entirely in Alaska.

d, Ewing Scott; w, Girard Smith, Scott; ph, Frederick Gately; ed, Robert O. Crandall.

Drama **(PR:A MPAA:NR)**

HARRAD EXPERIMENT, THE*½ (1973) 98m Cinerama c

James Whitmore *(Philip)*, Tippi Hedren *(Margaret)*, Don Johnson *(Stanley)*, B. Kirby, Jr. *(Harry)*, Laurie Walters *(Sheila)*, Victoria Thompson *(Beth)*, Elliot Street *(Wilson)*, Sharon Taggart *(Barbara)*, Robert Middleton *(Sidney)*, Billy Sands *(Jack)*, Melody Patterson *(Jeannie)*, Maggie Wellman *(Cynthia)*, Michael Greene *(Yoga Instructor)*, Ron Kolman *(Evan)*, Eric Server, Robert C. Ross *(Workmen)*, The Ace Trucking Company.

Whitmore and Hedren run an experimental college where for a month they pair off their students for sexual and emotional study. The plot seems to alternate between soap opera and sex exploitation. But usually it's just dull. An equally boring sequel, HARRAD SUMMER, was released in 1974.

p, Dennis F. Stevens; d, Ted Post; w, Ted Cassedy, Michael Werner (based on a novel by Robert H. Rimmer); ph, Richard H. Kline (Eastmancolor); m, Artie Butler; ed, Bill Brame; m/l, "I Hope To Have Your Love Along the Way," "Go Gently," Charles Fox, Norman Gimbel (sung by Lori Lieberman), "It's Not Over," Butler, Mark Lindsay (sung by Don Johnson).

Drama **Cas.** **(PR:O MPAA:R)**

HARRAD SUMMER, THE* (1974) 105m Cinema Arts/Cinerama c

Robert Reiser *(Stanley Kolasukas)*, Laurie Walters *(Sheila Grove)*, Richard Doran *(Harry Schacht)*, Victoria Thompson *(Beth Hillyer)*, Emmaline Henry *(Margaret Tonhausen)*, Bill Dana *(Jack Schacht)*, Jodean Russo *(Paula Schacht)*, Angela Clarke *(Mrs. Kolasukas)*, Tito Vandis *(Mr. Kolasukas)*, Walter Brooke *(Sam Grove)*, Mimi Saffian *(Diane Schacht)*, Lisa Moore *(Annie)*, James Beach *(Brad)*, Pearl Shear *(Fritzi)*, Jane Lambert *(Florence)*, Marty Allen *(Bert Franklin)*, Sylvia Walden, Chuckie Bradley *(Group)*, Lili Valenti *(Great Grandma Oliver)*, Sherry Miles *(Dee)*, Patrice Rohmer *(Marcia)*.

Veterans of the sexual revolution at a small college leave their academic environment for summer vacation and a chance to put what they've learned into practice. A dull sequel (HARRAD EXPERIMENT) to a dull movie.

p, Dennis F. Stevens; d, Steven Hillard Stern; w, Morth Thaw, Steven Zacharias; ph, Richard Kline; m, Pat Williams; ed, Bill Brame.

Drama **Cas.** **(PR:O) MPAA:R)**

HARRIET CRAIG*½** (1950) 94m COL bw

Joan Crawford *(Harriet Craig)*, Wendell Corey *(Walter Craig)*, Lucile Watson *(Celia Fenwick)*, Allyn Joslyn *(Billy Birkmire)*, William Bishop *(Wes Miller)*, K.T. Stevens *(Clare Raymond)*, Raymond Greenleaf *(Henry Fenwick)*, Ellen Corby *(Lottie)*, Fiona O'Shiel *(Mrs. Frazier)*, Patric Mitchell *(Danny Frazier)*, Virginia Brissac *(Harriet's Mother)*, Douglas Wood *(Mr. Norwood)*, Kathryn Card *(Mrs. Norwood)*, Mira McKinney *(Mrs. Winston)*, Al Murphy *(Bartender)*, Susanne Rosser *(Nurse)*.

A disturbing, yet sinfully engrossing third film adaptation (previously made in 1928 and 1936) of the 1925 Pulitzer Prize winning play "Craig's Wife," which is enhanced by modern-day viewer insight into the real-life exploits of its star, Crawford. Crawford was born to play the insufferable, totally domineering housewife whose only concern in life is to completely control the running, upkeep, and maintenance of her lush home. Trapped in her shrewish grip is Corey, her hard-working and unaffected husband, who slowly realizes his wife's true nature. As Crawford's compulsive neuroses get further beyond anyone's, control, Corey begins to resent her domination of his life. Every little detail from the clothes he wears to the decisions he makes at work are incessantly guided by Crawford, who will not accept interference with her authority. While professing undying love and devotion to Corey, Crawford really resents his very existence. (Her hatred of men started at an early age when her father left the family to fend for itself.) As time passes Crawford's domination borders on the psychotic when she sabotages a promotion Corey had been waiting for because it would bring too many changes to her life. Crawford also ruins her young cousin Stevens' romance with Bishop, and her husband's long and close relationship with Joslyn, his best friend. Eventually, Corey comes out of his fog and sees Crawford for what she is. Grabbing her favorite vase, Corey smashes it on the floor and walks out the door, leaving Crawford alone in her big, precisely decorated mausoleum. Crawford is superb in this film, and it is her performance that saves it from being just another filmed stage play. The role is an extremely difficult one to portray properly because Harriet is so selfish and unsympathetic the viewer almost wants to leave the theater rather than witness the hellish machinations of this deeply disturbed woman. Crawford, however (and Rosalind Russell before her), is able to bring a subtle sympathy to her portrayal, which draws the viewer in with a perverse fascination. It is a wonder that HARRIET CRAIG has not attained a strong cult following among the legion of MOMMIE DEAREST (1981) aficionados because the character here is not that far from the one portrayed in daughter Christine Crawford's intepretation of reality.

p, William Dozier; d, Vincent Sherman; w, Anne Froelick, James Gunn (based on the play "Craig's Wife" by George Kelly); ph, Joseph Walker; m, George Duning; ed, Viola Lawrence; md, Morris W. Stoloff; art d, Walter Holscher; cos, Sheila O'Brien.

Drama **(PR:A-C MPAA:NR)**

HARRIGAN'S KID** (1943) 80m MGM bw

Bobby Readick *(Benny McNeil)*, Frank Craven *(Mr. Garnet)*, William Gargan *(Tom Harrigan)*, Jay Ward *(McNamara)*, J. Carroll Naish *(Jed Jerrett)*, Douglas Croft *("Skip")*, Bill Cartledge *(Joe)*, Irving Lee *(Dink)*, Selmer Jackson *(Mr. Ranley)*, Allen Wood *(Atley)*, Jim Toney *(Sam)*, Mickey Martin *(Jockey)*, Russell Hicks *(Col. Lowry)*.

Youngster Readick is taken under the wing of unsilked, unsportsmanlike ex-jockey Gargan. He teaches the boy the skills of racing, and also coaches him on the art of dirty sportsmanship. Of course the man learns his lesson by the end, and has Readick give up the cheating life right before the climactic big race. Gargan isn't all that believable, and Readick has a real propensity for overacting, but all in all this is an acceptable outing.

p, Irving Starr; d, Charles F. Reisner; w, Alan Friedman, Martin Berkeley, Henry Blankfort (based on a story by Borden Chase); ph, Walter Lundin; m, Daniele Amfitheatrof; ed, Ferris Webster; art d, Cedric Gibbons.

Sports Drama **(PR:A MPAA:NR)**

HARRY AND TONTO*** (1974) 115m FOX c

Art Carney *(Harry Coombs)*, Ellen Burstyn *(Shirley)*, Chief Dan George *(Sam Two Feathers)*, Geraldine Fitzgerald *(Jessie)*, Larry Hagman *(Eddie)*, Arthur Hunnicutt *(Wade)*, Phil Burns *(Burt)*, Joshua Mostel *(Norman)*, Melanie Mayron *(Ginger)*, Dolly Jonah *(Elaine)*, Herbert Berghof *(Rivetowski)*, Avon Long *(Leroy)*, Barbara Rhoades *(Happy Hooker)*, Cliff DeYoung *(Burt, Jr.)*, Lou Guss *(Dominic)*, Mike Nussbaum *(Old Age Home Clerk)*, Rene Enriquez *(Grocery Clerk)*, Michael McClery *(Mugger)*, Rashel Novikoff *(Mrs. Rothman)*, Sybil Bowan *(Old Landlady)*, Michael Butler *(Hitchhiker)*.

When his comfortable New York City apartment building is torn down, 72 year-old widower and retired college professor Carney temporarily moves in with his eldest son, but finds his daughter-in-law less than enthusiastic. Perhaps inspired by his grandson, Mostel (son of Zero), currently embroiled in the pursuit of Zen philosophy, Carney decides to postpone a search for new lodgings and instead fulfill a lifelong ambition to travel across the country. With his cat, Tonto, Carney sets out on his trip to California with plans to stop and visit his other children, Burstyn, a daughter who lives in Chicago, and his youngest son, Hagman, who lives on the West Coast. During his journey Carney encounters several situations that give him a new look at the meaning of life. He meets a 15-year-old girl hitchhiker who is eventually swept off to California by Mostel who had joined his grandfather for a spell, leaving Carney once again alone with Tonto. At one point Carney stops to visit an old flame, Fitzgerald, who once danced with Isadora Duncan. Now senile and in a retirement home, she mistakes him for another man, and, allowing the delusion to continue, Carney dances a waltz with her. In Chicago, his visit with Burstyn is less than he had hoped for, so he continues on. On reaching the West Coast, Tonto dies, leaving Carney alone to face his youngest son in Los Angeles. What Carney finds is that is son is a broken man, a failure who is currently drowning himself in alcohol. With only advice and a little money to offer, Carney leaves Hagman, hoping for the best. Wandering toward the beach, Carney spots a cat that looks like Tonto, so he gives chase, trying to capture it. He stops pursuit when he sees a small child building a sandcastle with the Pacific Ocean as a magnificent backdrop. The sight is a revelation to Carney, who, after so much pain and disappointment from his own children, still retains hope for the future. HARRY AND TONTO is a sweet, sentimental movie that garners force and relevance from Carney's touching and detailed performance that won him a Best Actor Oscar (he beat nominees Al Pacino for THE GODFATHER PART II, Dustin Hoffman for LENNY, and Jack Nicholson for CHINATOWN). Incredibly, after nearly 25 years on television this was the experienced actor's first major feature film role. In HARRY AND TONTO director Mazursky shows the innocence of youth and the disappointment of middle-age, but offers solace in old age if one is only willing to rediscover what it was that gave him the energy and ambition to hope that better things will come.

p&d, Paul Mazursky; w, Mazursky, Josh Greenfield; ph, Michael Butler (DeLuxe Color); m, Bill Conti; ed, Richard Halsey; prod d, Ted Haworth; set d, John Godfrey; cos, Albert Wolsky.

Drama **Cas.** **(PR:C MPAA:R)**

HARRY AND WALTER GO TO NEW YORK** (1976) 120m COL c

James Caan *(Harry Dighby)*, Elliott Gould *(Walter Hill)*, Michael Caine *(Adam Worth)*, Diane Keaton *(Lissa Chestnut)*, Charles Durning *(Rufus T. Crisp)*, Lesley Ann Warren *(Gloria Fontaine)*, Val Avery *(Chatsworth)*, Jack Gilford *(Mischa)*, Dennis Dugan *(Lewis)*, Carol Kane *(Florence)*, Kathryn Grody *(Barbara)*, David Proval *(Ben)*, Michael Conrad *(Billy Gallagher)*, Burt Young *(Warden Durgom)*, Bert

Remsen *(Guard O'Meara)*, Ted Cassidy *(Leary)*, Michael Greene *(Dan)*, James DeCloss *(Barney)*, Nicky Blair *(Charlie Bullard)*, George Greif *(Dutch Herman)*, John Hackett *(Ike Marsh)*, Phil Kenneally *(Officer O'Reilly)*, Jack Brodsky, Karlene Gallegly, Colin Hamilton, Roger Til, Tom Lawrence, Ben Davidson, Victor Romito, Alex Rodine, Selma Archerd, Elizabeth Summers, Louise DeCarlo, Michelle Breeze, Carmel Lougene, Suzanne Covington, Sig Frohlich, Christopher Rydell, Maureen Arthur, David Shire, Anthony Columbia, Danny Rees, Brion James, Read Morgan, Kim Lankeford, Yolanda Mayer, George Gaynes, Robert Miller Driscoll, Geraldine Decker, Ginny Gagnon, Walter Willison, Harry Naughton, Carmine Coppola, Jay Thompson, Warren Berlinger, Jimmy Nickerson, Alex Sharpe, Eddy Donno, Seamon Glass, Charlie Murray, Don Ames, Ellen Blake, Lee Wolfberg, Sherry Moore, Emmett Brown, Evelyn Rydell, Ernie Mishko, Ellen Janes, Dee Hoty, Karen Powell.

Gould and Caan are a couple of talentless vaudeville performers thrown into jail on a petty theft charge. There they meet master thief Caine, and are soon involved in a scheme with him to pull off a major bank robbery. An impressive cast and crew all go out for naught here, as this is a singularly boring and unfunny comedy. The recreation of 1890s New York is nice, though.

p, Don Devlin, Harry Gittes; d, Mark Rydell; w, John Byrum, Robert Kaufman (based on a story by Byrum, Kaufman); ph, Laszlo Kovacs (Panavision, Metrocolor); m, David Shire; ed, David Bretherton, Don Guidice; prod d, Harry Horner; art d, Richard Berger; set d, Ruby Levitt; cos, Theoni V. Aldredge; m/l, Alan and Marilyn Bergman.

Comedy Cas. (PR:C MPAA:PG)

HARRY BLACK AND THE TIGER*** (1958, Brit.) 117m FOX c (GB: HARRY BLACK)

Stewart Granger *(Harry Black)*, Barbara Rush *(Christian Tanner)*, Anthony Steel *(Desmond Tanner)*, I.S. Johar *(Bapu)*, Martin Stephens *(Michael Tanner)*, Frank Olegario *(Dr. Chowdhury)*, Kamala Devi *(Nurse Somola)*, John Helier *(German Sergeant)*, Tom Bowman, Allan McLelland, Harold Siddons, Norman Johns *(British Officers)*, Gladys Boot *(Mrs. Tanner)*, George Curzon *(Mr. Philip Tanner)*, Archie Duncan *(Woolsey)*, John Rae *(Fisherman)*, Jan Conrad *(Tower Guard)*, Michael Seaver, Andre Maranne *(Frenchmen)*.

Granger is a one-legged great white hunter in India on the trail of a man-eating tiger. He meets up with Steel, whose moment of cowardice in a German POW camp cost Granger his leg. When they face a tiger, Steel again loses his nerve, and Granger is badly mauled. Nursed back to health by Steel's wife (Rush) he finds himself falling in love with her. He takes solace in drinking until Steel's son is lost in the jungle and Granger goes out to kill the tiger before it finds the boy. The climax sees Granger follow the wounded, trapped animal into a dark cave to finish it off. Good adventure yarn, with the jungle sequences done very well.

p, John Brabourne; d, Hugo Fregonese; w, Sidney Boehm (based on the book *Harry Black* by David Walker); ph, John Wilcox (CinemaScope, DeLuxe Color); m, Clifton Parker; ed, Reginald Beck; md, Muir Mathieson; art d, Arthur Lawson.

Adventure Cas. (PR:C MPAA:NR)

HARRY FRIGG (SEE: SECRET WAR OF HARRY FRIGG, THE, 1968

HARRY IN YOUR POCKET** (1973) 102m UA c

James Coburn *(Harry)*, Michael Sarrazin *(Ray)*, Trish Van Devere *(Sandy)*, Walter Pidgeon *(Casey)*, Michael C. Gwynne *(Fence)*, Tony Giorgio *(1st Detective)*, Michael Sterns *(2nd Detective)*, Sue Mullen *(Francine)*, Duane Bennett *(Salesman)*, Stanley Bolt *(Mr. Bates)*, Barry Grimshaw *(Bellboy)*.

Sarrazin and Van Devere join up with professional pickpockets, Coburn and Pidgeon, to learn the profession. Some interesting tricks of the trade to be seen, but mostly dull and predictable.

p&d, Bruce Geller; w, Ron Austin, James David Buchanan; ph, Fred Koenekamp (DeLuxe Color), m, Lalo Schifrin; ed, Arthur L. Hilton; art d & set d, William Bates; m/l, Schifrin, Geller.

Crime (PR:C MPAA:PG)

HARRY TRACY—DESPERADO** (1982, Can.) 111m Guardian Trust/Quartet c (AKA: HARRY TRACY)

Bruce Dern *(Harry Tracy)*, Helen Shaver *(Catherine)*, Michael C. Gwynne *(Dave)*, Gordon Lightfoot *(Morrie)*.

Interesting but disappointing feature film from director Graham whose made-for-TV films THE AMAZING HOWARD HUGHES and THE GUYANA TRAGEDY showed promise. Dern stars as a likable bank robber who risks romance with a judge's daughter played by Shaver. Gwynne is the failed artist who hangs around Dern in order to record the outlaw way of life. He eventually betrays Dern and they are both killed in a gun battle with the sheriff, Lightfoot (in his movie debut). The film has many good moments, but director Graham can't seem to find the right niche between tragedy and comedy. The problem was that the script writers misrepresented Tracy who was one of the worst, mean-minded killers of Butch Cassidy's old Wild Bunch. When escaping from McNeil's Island Prison, Tracy ordered a ferry captain to sail past the prison's walls so he could "pick off a few of the guards," which he did. There was no honor or loyalty in Tracy who murdered his own partner when he suspected the man of informing on him in the past. Trapped by a posse outside of Davenport, Washington on August 4, 1902, Tracy cursed his pursuers, then blew off his own head rather than surrender.

p, Ronald I. Cohen; d, William A. Graham; w, David Lee Henry; ph, Allen Daviau; m, Mickey Erbe, Maribeth Solomon; ed, Ron Wisman; prod d, Karen Bromley.

Drama Cas. (PR:C MPAA:PG)

HARRY'S WAR½** (1981) 98m Taft International c

Edward Herrmann *(Harry)*, Geraldine Page *(Beverly)*, Karen Grassle *(Kathy)*, David Ogden Stiers *(Ernie)*, Salome Jens *(Wilda)*, Elisha Cook *(Sgt. Billy)*, James Ray *(Commissioner)*, Douglas Dirkson *(Draper)*, Jerrold Ziman *(Attorney)*, Jim McKrell *(Newsman)*, Noble Willingham *(Maj. Andrews)*, Prentiss Rowe *(Sheriff)*, Vernon Weddle *(Ponde)*, Max Lewis *(Judge)*, Alan Cherry, Bruce Robinson, Rex Cutter *(Agents)*, Kamee Aliessa *(Shawn)*, Kieri Valee *(Shelly)*, Scott Wilkinson, Robert Daugherty *(Mailmen)*, David Mason Daniels *(Aide)*, Spencer McMullin *(Hammel)*, Jean Stringham *(Receptionist)*, Leslie Perry *(Relief Girl)*, Oscar Rowland *(Wino)*, Marc Raymond *(Rodney)*, David Sterago *(Reporter)*, Terry Afton Lee *(Soldier)*, Charles Chagnon *(Indigent)*, Dolly Big Soldier *(Indian Mother)*, Paul Anderson *(Banker)*, Larry Roupe *(Supervisor)*, Jack Reddish *(Confused Man)*, Leola Green *(Duchess)*, Star Roman *(Hooker)*, Mickey Wodrich *(Elderly Lady)*, Jay Bernard *(Lumberman)*.

When the IRS tries to take away Page's antique store-soup kitchen, nephew Herrmann comes to her rescue. After she drops dead of a heart attack during a subsequent court appearance, he removes several war souvenirs—including a real tank—from the store and declares his own war on the IRS. Although satisfying in spots, the film as a whole lacks cohesion.

p, Jack N. Reddish, Keith Merrill; d&w, Merrill; ph, Reed Smoot (Deluxe Color); m, Merrill B. Jenson; ed, B. Lovitt, Peter L. McCrea; prod d, Douglas G. Johnson.

Comedy (PR:C MPAA:PG)

HARUM SCARUM* (1965) 95m MGM c (GB: HAREM HOLIDAY)

Elvis Presley *(Johnny Tyronne)*, Mary Ann Mobley *(Princess Shalimar)*, Fran Jeffries *(Aishah)*, Michael Ansara *(Prince Dragna)*, Jay Novello *(Zacha)*, Philip Reed *(King Toranshah)*, Theo Marcuse *(Sinan)*, Billy Barty *(Baba)*, Dirk Harvey *(Mokar)*, Jack Costanza *(Julna)*, Larry Chance *(Capt. Herat)*, Barbara Werle *(Leilah)*, Brenda Benet *(Emerald)*, Gail Gilmore *(Sapphire)*, Wilda Taylor *(Amethyst)*, Vicki Malkin *(Sari)*, Ryck Rydon *(Mustapha)*, Joey Russo *(Yussef)*, Richard Reeves *(Scarred Bedouin)*.

Presley is at his worst here. This time he's a movie star who is kidnaped and taken to an Arab palace, where he is embroiled in a plot to kill the king. There are lots of pretty girls for him to sing to, and he does so in no less than 11 songs, including: "Harum Scarum" (Peter Andreoli, Vince Poncia, Jr., Jimmie Crane), "Golden Coins," "Go East, Young Man," "Shake That Tamborine," "Animal Instinct," "Wisdom Of The Ages," and "Mirage" (Bill Giant, Bernie Baum, Florence Kaye), "Hey Little Girl," "So Close, Yet So Far (From Paradise)" (Joy Byers), "My Desert Serenade" (Stanley Jay Gelber), and "Kismet" (Sid Tepper and Roy C. Bennett). Despite its patent absurdity and incompetent execution, the film made piles of money for Presley and MGM.

p, Sam Katzman; d, Gene Nelson; w, Gerald Drayson Adams; ph, Fred H. Jackman (Metrocolor); m, Fred Karger; ed, Ben Lewis; art d, George W. Davis, H. McClure Capps; set d, Henry Grace, Don Greenwood, Jr.; cos, Beau Vandenecker, Gene Ostler, Margo Weintz; ch, Earl Barton; makeup, William Tuttle, Don Cash.

Comedy Cas. (PR:A MPAA:NR)

HARVARD, HERE I COME** (1942) 64m COL bw

Maxie Rosenbloom *(Himself)*, Arline Judge *(Francie Callahan)*, Stanley Brown *(Harrison Carey)*, Don Beddoe *(Hypo McGonigle)*, Marie Wilson *(Zella Phipps)*, Virginia Sale *(Miss Frisbie)*, Byron Foulger *(Prof. Alvin)*, Boyd Davis *(Prof. Hayworth)*, Julius Tannen *(Prof. Anthony)*, Walter Baldwin *(Prof. MacSquigley)*, Tom Herbert *(Prof. Teeter)*, Larry Parks *(Eddie Spellman)*, George McKay *(Blinky)*, John Tyrrell *(Slug)*, Mary Ainslee *(Phyllis)*, Lloyd Bridges *(Larry)*, Al Hill *(Doorman)*, Yvonne De Carlo *(Bathing Girl)*, Ed Emerson *(Mr. Plunkett)*, Bobby Watson *(Horace)*, Marion Murray *(Oomphie)*, Dan Tobey *(Master of Ceremonies)*, Tommy Seidel *(Boy)*, Charles Ray, Jack Mulhall *(Reporters)*, Harry Bailey *(Guest)*.

Goofy nightclub owner Rosenbloom returns to college where a couple of professors decide he is the missing link in their project. He is given a room, an allowance, and a chance to wander all about the ivy-covered halls and destroy whatever he can. Don't look for any sophisticated humor here.

p, Wallace MacDonald; d, Lew Landers; w, Albert Duffy (based on a story by Karl Brown); ph, Franz Planer; ed, William Lyon; md, Morris Stoloff; art d, Lionel Banks.

Comedy (PR:A MPAA:NR)

HARVEST*½** (1939, Fr.) 77m French Cinema bw (AKA: REGAIN)

Gabriel Gabrio *(Panturle)*, Edouard Delmont *(Gaubert)*, Fernandel *(Gedemus)*, Orane Demazis *(Arsule)*, Le Vigan *(Sergeant)*, Rollan *(Gendarme)*, Henri Poupon *(L'Amoureux)*, Odette Roger *(Alphonsine)*, Paul Dullac *(Grain Dealer)*.

As the crops of a French village are harvested by Gabrio, the final inhabitant of the town, he falls in love with Demazis, who has been raped by a gang of woodsmen. Gabrio soon finds out that she is the property of the lowly Ferdinand who wants, at least, a donkey in return for his woman. Based on a novel by Jean Giorno, this Pagnol film is divided into three seasonal sections, winter, spring, and summer. Initially banned by New York state censors, apparently for its treatment of women, the decision was later over-turned by the state regents. (In French: English subtitles.)

p,d&w, Marcel Pagnol (based on the novel by Jean Giono); ph, Willy Ledru, Roger Ledru; m, Arthur Honneger.

Drama Cas. (PR:O MPAA:NR)

HARVEST MELODY** (1943) 70m PRC bw

Rosemary Lane *(Gilda Parker)*, Johnny Downs *(Tommy)*, Sheldon Leonard *(Chuck)*, Charlotte Wynters *(Nancy)*, Luis Alberni *(Cafe Manager)*, Claire Rochelle *(Daisy)*, Syd Saylor *(Spot)*, Marjorie Manners *(Jane)*, Sunny Fox *(Sunny Fox)*, Henry Hall *(Pa Nelson)*, Billy Nelson *(Canvas)*, Frances Gladwin *(Cigarette Girl)*, The Radio Rogues, The Vigilantes, Eddie LeBaron Orchestra.

Dull musical about fading star Lane traveling to the countryside for some publicity pictures to perk up her career. When a new film contract is offered, Lane opts to settle down to the simple, wholesome country life. Songs include: "You Could Have Knocked Me Over With A Feather," "Put It In Reverse," "Let's Drive Out To The Drive-In," and "Tenderly."

p, Walter Colmes; d, Sam Newfield; w, Allan Gale (based on a story by Martin Mooney, Andre Lamb); ph, James Brown; ed, Holbrook N. Todd; md, David Chudnow; art d, Frank Sylos; m/l, Harry Akst, Leo Shuken, Walter Colmes, Benny Davis.

Musical **(PR:A MPAA:NR)**

HARVESTER, THE* (1936) 72m REP bw

Alice Brady *(Mrs. Biddle)*, Russell Hardie *(David Langston)*, Ann Rutherford *(Ruth Jameson)*, Frank Craven *(Mr. Biddle)*, Cora Sue Collins *(Naomi Jameson)*, Emma Dunn *(Granny Moreland)*, Eddie Nugent *(Bert Munroe)*, Joyce Compton *(Thelma Biddle)*, Roy Atwell *(Jake Eben)*, Spencer Charters *(Stubby Pratt)*, Russell Simpson *(Abner Prewett)*, Phyllis Fraser, Fern Emmett, Burr Caruth, Lucille Ward, Harry Bowen, Grace Hale.

Indiana farm mother Brady tries to marry dull daughter Compton off to dimwitted farmer Hardie. Astoundingly boring.

p, Nat Levine; d, Joseph Santley; w, Gertrude Orr, Homer Croy, Robert Lee Johnson, Elizabeth Meehan (based on a novel by Gene Stratton-Porter); ph, Edward Snyder, Reggie Lanning; ed, Murray Seldeen.

Drama **(PR:A MPAA:NR)**

HARVEY**** (1950) 104m, UNIV bw

James Stewart *(Elwood P. Dowd)*, Josephine Hull *(Veta Louise Simmons)*, Peggy Dow *(Miss Kelly)*, Charles Drake *(Dr. Sanderson)*, Cecil Kellaway *(Dr. Chumley)*, Victoria Horne *(Myrtle Mae)*, Jesse White *(Wilson)*, William Lynn *(Judge Gaffney)*, Wallace Ford *(Lofgren)*, Nana Bryant *(Mrs. Chumley)*, Grace Mills *(Mrs. Chauvenet)*, Clem Bevans *(Herman)*, Ida Moore *(Mrs. McGiff)*, Richard Wessel *(Cracker)*, Pat Flaherty *(Policeman)*, Norman Leavitt *(Cab Driver)*, Maudie Prickett *(Elvira)*, Ed Max *(Salesman)*, Minerva Urecal *(Nurse Dunphy)*, Almira Sessions *(Mrs. Halsey)*, Anna O'Neal *(Nurse)*, Sally Corner *(Mrs. Cummings)*, Sam Wolfe *(Minninger)*, Polly Bailey *(Mrs. Krausmeyer)*, Grace Hampton *(Mrs. Strickleberger)*, Ruth Elma Stevens *(Miss LaFay)*, Eula Guy *(Mrs. Johnson)*, William Val *(Chauffeur)*, Gino Corrado *(Eccentric Man)*, Don Brodie *(Mailman)*, Harry Hines *(Meegels)*, Aileen Carlyle *(Mrs. Tewksbury)*.

This large slice of delightful fluff worked well on Broadway in a long run. Playwright Chase adapted the story for the film to keep it faithful to the original. Stewart is the whimsical inebriate whose kindness spills over into the lives of all about him as he tries to help those in need. As the gentle Elwood P. Dowd, tipsy philosopher of down-home thought, Stewart lurches home one night to see a six-foot rabbit named Harvey leaning against a lamppost. This invisible pooka becomes his friend and follows him everywhere. Stewart's socially prominent sister Hull becomes more disturbed at her brother's eccentric ways and fears to have Stewart about, believing he is a hindrance to getting her daughter Horne married off. On one occasion Stewart returns home while Hull is having a tea with all the society matrons in attendance. Havoc breaks out when Stewart insists upon introducing one flustered spinster after another to a towering rabbit they cannot see. This is the last straw; Hull decides Stewart must be sent to an insane asylum run by Dr. Chumley (Kellaway). He is studied at the asylum by Kellaway and Drake while nurse Dow takes a genuine liking to the colorful Stewart. After Hull is interviewed by Kellaway where she admits that she, too, is beginning to see the vexing Harvey, Stewart is let go and Hull ordered locked up. She is carried to a padded cell by strongarm hospital aide White. When Hull is released, Stewart is searched for by White who visits Horne and strikes up a romance with her. Back at the hospital, Kellaway goes into seclusion, having borrowed Harvey from Stewart for study; he, too, sees the rabbit and they become close friends while Stewart goes about his whimsical business, his strange actions sanctioned by Hull who now realizes that she doesn't want her brother to be normal but to remain the gentle, sweet soul she knows and loves. Stewart plays Stewart here, with his traditional awkward gestures, groping speech, and amiable personality, perfectly suited to a part that Frank Fay made famous on Broadway. Hull is a delight as the frustrated sister, and Kellaway scores well as the capricious psychiatrist. White is a panic as the dimwitted hospital aide, at one point reading from an encyclopedia about pookas and the forms they take, and how they "appear here and there, now and then . . . and how are you, Mr. Wilson?" He slams the book in shock and yells: "Who at the Encyclopedia Britannica wants to know!" Koster's direction is sharp and inventive. This is a happy movie and leaves a long, lingering warm glow.

p, John Beck; d, Henry Koster; w, Mary Chase, Oscar Brodney (based on a play by Chase); ph, William Daniels; m, Frank Skinner; ed, Ralph Dawson; art d, Bernard Herzbrun, Nathan Juran; cos, Orry-Kelly.

Comedy **(PR:A MPAA:NR)**

HARVEY GIRLS, THE*** (1946) 101m MGM c

Judy Garland *(Susan Bradley)*, John Hodiak *(Ned Trent)*, Ray Bolger *(Chris Maule)*, Preston Foster *(Judge Sam Purvis)*, Virginia O'Brien *(Alma)*, Angela Lansbury *(Em)*, Marjorie Main *(Sonora Cassidy)*, Chill Wills *(H. H. Hartsey)*, Kenny Baker *(Terry O'Halloran)*, Selena Royle *(Miss Bliss)*, Cyd Charisse *(Deborah)*, Ruth Brady *(Ethel)*, Catherine McLeod *(Louise)*, Jack Lambert *(Marty Peters)*, Edward Earle *(Jed Adams)*, Virginia Hunter *(Jane)*, William "Bill" Phillips, Norman Leavitt *(Cowboys)*, Morris Ankrum *(Rev. Claggett)*, Ben Carter *(John Henry)*, Mitchell Lewis *(Sandy)*, Stephen McNally *(Goldust McClean)*, Bill Hall *(Big Joe)*, Ray Teal, Robert Emmett O'Connor *(Conductors)*, Vernon Dent *(Engineer)*, Jim Toney *(Mule Skinner)*, Ruth Brady, Dorothy Gilmore, Lucille Casey, Mary Jo Ellis, Mary Jean French, Joan Thorson, Jacqueline White, Daphne Moore, Dorothy Tuttle, Gloria Hope *(Harvey Girls)*, Vera Lee, Dorothy Van Nuys, Eve Whitney, Jane Hall, Bunny Waters, Hazel Brooks, Erin O'Kelly, Peggy Maley, Kay English, Dallas Worth *(Dance Hall Girls)*, Byron Harvey, Jr.

THE HARVEY GIRLS is a lightweight musical comedy with some terrific tunes by Warren and Mercer, including the Oscar-winning "On The Atchison, Topeka And The Santa Fe." It's almost a full-length plug for the Fred Harvey chain of restaurants and although based on reality, it takes great liberties with what actually happened. Garland is a mail-order bride who comes west to meet her husband-to-be, Wills, the town drunk. Hodiak owns the local saloon and his girl friend is Lansbury, a Mae West type who runs a bawdy house in the small New Mexico town. THE HARVEY GIRLS has a little of everything: songs, action, love, dance and the triumph of virtue and chastity over the forces of saloondom. Hodiak is suave and sophisticated as the gambler, and Garland was never more vibrant and buoyant as the female lead. It earned more than $5 million the first time around, and no one expected it to be that successful. It's a fairly familiar plot but several interesting sidelights make THE HARVEY GIRLS somewhat of a landmark. Charisse had her biggest role to date, after first appearing in MISSION TO MOSCOW and SOMETHING TO SHOUT ABOUT. Born Tulla Finklea, she began her career with the name of Lily Norwood before marrying dancer Nico Charisse and changing her name; Stephen McNally was still using his birth name of Horace when he did this film. He changed it two years later for his role in JOHNNY BELINDA. Some excellent supporting work by Bolger, Main and O'Brien. Lansbury was only 21, but already playing roles far older than her real age, something she has continued to do. Charisse's singing voice was dubbed by Betty Russell but everyone else did their own warbling. Tunes include: "Oh You Kid," "It's A Great Big World," "Swing Your Partner 'Round And 'Round," "In The Valley," "Wait And See," "The Train Must Be Fed," "Honky Tonk," and "The Wild Wild West." Lenny Hayton got an Oscar nomination for his musical direction but that was about it in the awards department. The music for "Judy's Rage" was written by orchestrator Salinger and the "Training Sequence" was by associate producer Edens. Although Kay Van Riper gets solo credit for additional dialogue, she was aided by playwright Guy Bolton and Hagar Wilde, thus making a total of eight names associated with the script. Three other songs were written for the film but deleted before final inclusion: "My Intuition," "Hayride," and "March Of The Dogies."

p, Arthur Freed; d, George Sidney; w, Edmund Beloin, Nathaniel Curtis, Harry Crane, James O'Hanlon, Samson Raphaelson (based on a story by Eleanore Griffin, William Rankin, from the novel by Samuel Hopkins Adams); ph, George Folsey (Technicolor); ed, Albert Akst; md, Lennie Hayton; art d, Cedric Gibbons, William Ferrari; set d, Edwin B. Willis, Mildred Griffiths; cos, Helen Rose, Valles; spec eff, Warren Newcombe; ch, Robert Alton; m/l, Harry Warren, Johnny Mercer, Rogers Edens, Kay Thompson.

Musical Comedy **(PR:AAA MPAA:NR)**

HARVEY MIDDLEMAN, FIREMAN** (1965) 76m COL c

Gene Troobnick *(Harvey Middleman)*, Hermione Gingold *(Mrs. Koogleman)*, Patricia Harty *(Lois)*, Arlene Golonka *(Harriet)*, Will MacKenzie *(Dinny)*, Ruth Jaroslow *(The Mother)*, Charles Durning *(Dooley)*, Peter Carew *(Barratta)*, Stanley Myron Handelman *(Mookey)*, Trudy Bordoff *(Cindy)*, Neil Rouda *(Richie)*, Gigi Chevalier *(Comet Receptionist)*, Stacy Graham *(Librarian)*, Maurice Shrog *(Mr. Koogleman)*.

Vaguely experimental, slightly interesting but flawed drama about an ordinary guy, Troobnick, who lives a very ordinary life with his wife and children. Then one day he rescues Harty from a burning building and falls in love with her. His life is endlessly complicated by this attachment and he seeks help from psychiatrist Gingold. Worth seeing.

p, Robert L. Lawrence; d&w, Ernest Pintoff; ph, Karl Malkames (Eastmancolor); m, Pintoff; ed, Hugh A. Robertson, David Donovan; prod d, Gene Callahan; md, Bernard Green; cos, Anna Hill Johnstone.

Drama **(PR:C MPAA:NR)**

HAS ANYBODY SEEN MY GAL?*** (1952) 88m UNIV c

Piper Laurie *(Millicent)*, Rock Hudson *(Dan)*, Charles Coburn *(Samuel Fulton)*, Gigi Perreau *(Roberta)*, Lynn Bari *(Harriet Blaisdell)*, Larry Gates *(Charles Blaisdell)*, William Reynolds *(Howard)*, Skip Homeier *(Carl Pennock)*, Paul Harvey *(Judge Wilkins)*, Frank Ferguson *(Mr. Norton)*, Forrest Lewis *(Martin Quinn)*, Gloria Holden *(Mrs. Pennock)*, Fred Nurney *(Fredericks)*, Sally Creighton *(Arline Benson)*, Helen Wallace *(Shirley White)*, Willard Waterman *(Dr. Wallace)*, Fritz Feld *(Alvarez)*, James Dean *(Youth)*, Emory Parnell *(Clancy)*, Charles Flynn *(Joe)*, Barney Phillips *(Workman)*, William Fawcett *(Caretaker)*, Edna Holland *(Seamstress)*, Leon Tyler *(Personality Boy)*, Charles Williams *(Reporter)*, Paul Bryar *(Man)*, Joey Ray, Sam Pierce *(Gamblers)*, Harmon Stevens *(Real Estate Agent)*, Lyn Wilde *(Charleston Dancer)*, Donna Leary *(Charleston Dancer)*, Spec O'Donnell *(Candy Vendor)*, Larry Carr *(Man)*, Earl Spainard, Eric Alden *(Bits)*.

It's the 1920s and aging millionaire Coburn wants to leave his fortune to the family of a woman who once turned down his proposal of marriage. To see if they are worthy, he pretends to be an eccentric artist who rents a room from them then anonymously gives them $100,000 to see what happens. Bari, the mother, decides that the family should move into a mansion and she sets about trying to marry daughter Laurie off to a rich young snob instead of poor but loving soda jerk, Hudson. Once everybody has learned a lesson, Coburn determines it is all right to leave them the rest of his fortune. Charming, well-done period comedy. Dean makes his film debut and Sirk works with color for the first time. Songs include: "Gimme a Little Kiss, Will Ya, Huh?" (Roy Smith, Roy Turk, Maceo Pinkard, sung by Piper Laurie), "It Ain't Gonna Rain No More" (Wendell Hall, sung by Charles Coburn and Group), "Tiger Rag" (Jelly Roll Morton), "Five Foot Two, Eyes of Blue" (sung by College Boys and Girls), "When the Red, Red Robin Comes Bob-Bob-Bobbin' Along" (Harry Woods, sung by Coburn, Gigi Perreau, Lynn Bari).

p, Ted Richmond; d, Douglas Sirk; w, Joseph Hoffman (based on a story by Eleanor H. Porter); ph, Clifford Stine (Technicolor); m, Joseph Gershenson; ed,

Russell Schoengarth; md, Gershenson; art d, Bernard Herzbrun, Hilyard Brown; set d, Russell A. Gausman, John Austin; cos, Rosemary Odell; ch, Harold Belfer.

Comedy **Cas.** **(PR:A MPAA:NR)**

HASSAN, TERRORIST**½ (1968, Algerian) 90m Office Des Actualities Algeriennes bw (HASSAN TERRO)

Rouiched *(Hassan)*, Keltoum *(Wife)*, Larbi Zekkal *(Terrorist)*.

During the Algerian revolt against France, Rouiched just wants to keep out of it. But one night the rebels force him to shelter a wanted killer and almost immediately he is arrested by French paratroopers and charged with being a terrorist. He denies it, but under torture he tells them anything they want to hear. An honest and thought-provoking film.

d&w, Mohamed Lekhdar Hamina (based on a play by Rouiched).

Drama **(PR:O MPAA:NR)**

HASTY HEART, THE**** (1949) 99m WB bw

Ronald Reagan *(The Yank)*, Patricia Neal *(Sister Margaret)*, Richard Todd *(The Scot)*, Anthony Nicholls *(Col Dunn)*, Howard Crawford *(The Tommy)*, Ralph Michael *(The New Zealander)*, John Sherman *(The Aussie)*, Alfie Bass *(Orderly)*, Orlando Martins *(Blossom)*.

This is one of Reagan's finest films where he turns in a terrific performance as a compassionate but forceful American soldier recuperating from wounds in a military hospital in Burma. The principal actor here, however, is Todd, who is wonderful as the hard-headed, truculent Scottish soldier who is cold and standoffish with the other patients. Neal is a firm but gentle nurse who, along with chief doctor Nicholls, asks Reagan and other patients to go easy with Todd since he is dying of a terminal illness and does not know it. But it's a difficult task; the stubborn Scotsman rejects the friendship of Reagan and the others, and, more or less, tells the other soldiers to mind their own business when they try to strike up conversations or do little favors for him. At his 21st birthday, Todd is given a complete new Scottish uniform, including kilt and bagpipe, as a gift from the patients. This softens his heart toward them and he explains in his own halting manner how he has never before been so touched. He befriends his fellow patients but when Nicholls finally tells him he is dying, Todd again closes up like a clam, this time bitterly lashing out at Reagan and the others because he now sees their actions as being made out of pity. In a forceful confrontation, Reagan tells Todd off when he learns that the Scotsman intends on leaving the hospital and returning to a land where he is alone and friendless. Reagan points out that it is better to die with friends than alone without anyone caring about him. Todd relents and agrees to stay on at the hospital, resolved to spend his last days on earth with the only friends he has. This is poignant drama at its best, well acted on every level, and directed with fluidity by the versatile Sherman; in fact this is one of Sherman's best films, one which used a permanent set, the small hospital and surrounding area, but, through his inventive setups and staging, does not seem claustrophobic nor stagey. The 30-year-old Todd had made only one earlier film (FOR THEM THAT TRESPASS) before completing THE HASTY HEART, even though he had had stage background. He was a standout discovery in this film and undoubtedly drew upon his experience as a paratrooper during WW II for his role, which won him an Academy Award nomination for Best Actor (he would lose out to Broderick Crawford for ALL THE KING'S MEN). The decision by Warner Bros. to make this film at the Elstree Studios in England was simply financial. Following WW II, Britain had frozen part of studio assets, decreeing that a portion of the money producers made in England must remain in that country, so Warners, along with all the major Hollywood studios, quickly began to use up those British bank accounts with overseas productions such as THE HASTY HEART. Reagan was also unhappy about this production. Even though the setting was Burma, the studio sound stage which housed the set was often cold from the gusting winter winds while the actors were compelled to work in light tropical garb. The pace was too leisurely for Reagan, punctured by lengthy "tea breaks," and rigid union schedules. The film was four months in production and, by the time Reagan returned to the U.S., he discovered that his studio—he had been at Warners since 1937—was unhappy about his recent films, NIGHT UNTO NIGHT and THAT HAGEN GIRL, telling him that they had been weak box office outings. Moreover, the lengthy production for THE HASTY HEART had lost Reagan the starring role in a substantial western entitled GHOST MOUNTAIN, later retitled ROCKY MOUNTAIN and starring Errol Flynn. Through clever maneuvering, Reagan's agent, Lew Wasserman, arranged for the actor to go on half salary, making one film a year in the remaining three years of his contract with Warners and allowing him to make films elsewhere. He quickly signed up with Universal for a five-picture deal.

p, Howard Lindsay, Russell Crouse; d, Vincent Sherman; w, Ranald MacDougall (based on the play by John Patrick); ph, Wilkie Cooper; m, Jack Beaver; ed, E.B. Jarvis; md, Louis Levy; art d, Terence Verity; cos, Peggy Henderson.

Drama **(PR:A MPAA:NR)**

HAT CHECK GIRL**½ (1932) 63m FOX bw

Sally Eilers *(Gerry Marsh)*, Ben Lyon *(Buster Collins)*, Ginger Rogers *(Jessie King)*, Monroe Owsley *(Tod Reese)*, Arthur Pierson *(Felix Cornwall)*, Noel Madison *(Dan McCoy)*, Dewey Robinson *(Tony Carlucci)*, Harold Goodwin *(Walter Marsh)*, Eulalie Jensen *(Mrs. Marsh)*, Purnell Pratt *(Collins)*, Lee Moran *(Man on Subway)*, Iris Meredith *(Saleslady)*, Eddie "Rochester" Anderson *(Waiter)*, Fred "Snowflake" Toones *(Bellman)*, Henry Armetta *(Water Wagon Driver)*, Betty Elliott, Bert Roach, Astrid Allwyn, Greta Granstedt, Arthur Housman, Joyce Compton *(Party Guests)*, Richard Carle *(Professor)*, Richard Tucker *(Mr. Reynolds)*, Manya Roberti *(Dancer)*, Ed Brady *(Traffic Cop)*, Hooper Atchley *("Detective" Monahan)*, Lee Moran *(Subway Rider)*, Harry Schultz *(Hotel Waiter)*, Sherry Hall *(Bartender)*, Harvey Clark *(Colonel)*.

Eilers stars as a hat check girl at a nightclub frequented by gangsters like Owsley. She falls in love with millionaire playboy Pratt, who is briefly suspected of murder but is later cleared. Rogers, in her first part as a Fox contract player, is Eilers' worldy, wisecracking partner at the hat check station in this above-average comedy.

d, Sidney Lanfield; w, Philip Klein, Barry Connors (based on a novel by Rian James); ph, Glenn MacWilliams; m, Arthur Lange; ed, Paul Weatherwax; md, George Lipschulta; art d & set d, Gordon Wiles; cos, Rita Kaufman.

Comedy **(PR:C MPAA:NR)**

HAT CHECK HONEY*½ (1944) 66m UNIV bw

Grace McDonald *(Susan Brent)*, Richard Davis *(Dan Briggs, Jr.)*, Leon Errol *(Happy Dan Briggs)*, Walter Catlett *(Tim Martel)*, Ramsay Ames *(Mona Mallory)*, Milburn Stone *(David Courtland)*, Lee Bennett *(Alan Dane)*, Russell Hicks *(Mr. Washington)*, Chester Clute *(Uniformed Officer)*, Mary Gordon *(Jennie)*, Emmett Vogan *(Lynn)*, Jack Rice *(C.B.)*, Minna Phillips *(Flossie)*, Eddie Acuff *(Cameraman)*, Ray Walker *(Gabby Post)*, Eddie Dunn *(Louis)*, Clair Whitney *(Mrs. Worthington)*, Donald Kerr *(Waiter)*, Marie Harmon *(Hat Check Girl)*, Freddie Slack and his Orchestra, Harry Owens and his Royal Hawaiians, Ted Weems and his Orchestra, Jimmy Cash.

Errol is a vaudeville performer who kicks son Davis out of his act so that the boy can go on to better things. Davis quickly lands a job as the singer in a band, thanks to his sweetheart, hat-check girl McDonald. There are some predictable complications until the happy ending is finally reached. Nothing special. Songs include: "Slightly Sentimental," "Nice To Know You," "A Dream Ago," "Rockin' With You," "A Small Batch O'Nod," "Loose Wig," "Drumola," "Rhythm Of The Islands," and "It Happened In Kaloha."

p, Will Cowan; d, Edward F. Cline; w, Maurice Leo, Stanley Davis (based on a story by Al Martin); ph, Milton Krasner; ed, Saul Goodkind; art d, John Goodman; m/l, Milton Rosen, Everett Carter.

Musical **(PR:A MPAA:NR)**

HAT, COAT AND GLOVE** (1934) 64m RKO bw

Ricardo Cortez *(Robert Mitchell)*, Barbara Robbins *(Dorothea Mitchell)*, John Beal *(Jerry Hutchins)*, Margaret Hamilton *(Madame DuBarry)*, Sara Haden *(Mitchell's Secretary)*, Samuel Hinds *(John Walters)*, Murray Kinnell *(The Judge)*, Dorothy Burgess *(Ann)*, Louise Beavers *(Imogene)*, Irving Bacon, Wilbur Higby, Marcelle Corday, Paul Hervey, Edith Van Cleve, Joseph Anthony, Tom Brown, David Durand.

Cortez is a lawyer who witnesses the suicide of a woman at the home of an artist with whom his wife, Robbins, is having an affair. The artist, Beal, is accused of murder and Cortez agrees to defend him only on the condition that his wife come back to him. The courtroom scenes drag on and none of it is worth the effort. Originally intended as a vehicle for John Barrymore who stepped down due to bad health.

d, Worthington Miner; w, Francis Faragoh (based on a play by Wilhelm Speyer); ph, J. Roy Hunt; ed, Ralph Dietrich.

Drama **(PR:A MPAA:NR)**

HATARI!**½ (1962) 159m Malabar/PAR c (AKA: THE AFRICAN STORY

John Wayne *(Sean Mercer)*, Elsa Martinelli *(Dallas)*, Hardy Kruger *(Kurt)*, Gerard Blain *(Chips)*, Red Buttons *(Pockets)*, Michele Girardon *(Brandy)*, Bruce Cabot *(Indian)*, Valentin de Vargas *(Luis)*, Eduard Franz *(Dr. Sanderson)*, Eric Rungren *(Stan)*, Queenie Leonard *(Nurse)*, Jon Chevron *(Joseph)*, Henry Scott *(Sikh Clerk)*, Major Sam Harris *(Man in the Store)*, Jack Williams *(Man/Masai Warrior/Native Boy)*.

Wayne heads a group of men who make their living by capturing wild animals for zoos throughout the world. Into this male-dominated circle enters sensous, man-eating Martinelli, and the group is never the same—especially Wayne who ends up marrying her. The story is nothing more than a poor excuse for what Hawks really seems to be interested in presenting—big game chases over the Kenyan veldt. These sequences are so well done that they are what really saves this otherwise tepid film, which even an outstanding cast could not inflame.

p&d, Howard Hawks; w, Leigh Brackett (based on a story by Harry Kurnitz); ph, Russell Harlan, Joseph Brun (Technicolor); m, Henry Mancini; ed, Stuart Gilmore; art d, Hal Pereira, Carl Anderson; set d, Sam Comer, Claude Carpenter; cos, Edith Head; spec eff, John P. Fulton, Dick Parker; m/l, "Just For Tonight" Johnny Mercer, Hoagy Carmichael; stunts, Carey Loftin.

Drama **Cas.** **(PR:A MPAA:NR)**

HATCHET FOR A HONEYMOON* (1969, Span./Ital.) 83m G.G.P. c (UNA HACKA PARA LA LUNA DE MIEL; IL ROSO SEGMO DELLA POLLIAS; AKA: BLOOD BRIDES)

Stephen Forsyth, Dagmar Lassander, Laura Betti, Gerard Tichy, Alan Collins, Luciano Pigozzi, Jesus Puente, Antonia Mas, Femi Benussi.

A typically sick horror coproduction from Bava. In this one, Forsyth loses touch with reality when his wife gives up the ghost—then returns as one. To fulfill some sort of demented fantasy, Forsyth dresses lovely young women in bridal gowns, then starts swinging a hatchet. He doesn't *really* go off the deep end until later in the picture when he dons the wedding dress himself.

p, Manuel Cano Sanciriaco; d, Mario Bava; w, Bava, Santiago Moncada; m, Sante Romitelli; ed, Soledad Lopez.

Horror **(PR:O MPAA:R)**

HATCHET MAN, THE**½ (1932) 74m FN/WB bw (GB: THE HONORABLE MR. WONG)

Edward G. Robinson *(Wong Low Get)*, Loretta Young *(Toya San)*, Dudley Digges *(Nag Hong Fah)*, Leslie Fenton *(Harry En Hai)*, Edmund Breese *(Yu Chang)*, Tully

Marshall *(Long Sen Yat)*, Noel N. Madison *(Charley Kee)*, Blanche Frederici *(Madame Si-Si)*, J. Carroll Naish *(Sun Yat Sen)*, Toshia Mori *(Miss Ling)*, Charles Middleton *(Li Hop Fat)*, Ralph Ince *(Malone)*, Otto Yamaoko *(Chung Ho)*, Evelyn Selbie *(Wah Li)*, E. Allyn Warren *(Soo Lat)*, Eddie Piel *(Foo Ming)*, Willie Fung *(Fung Loo)*, Gladys Lloyd *(Fan Yi)*, Anna Chang *(Sing Girl)*, James Leong *(Tong Member)*.

A disturbing, brutal film where Robinson is fearsome as a Chinese assassin who is told he must execute a childhood friend, Naish. Understanding that he is acting honorably, Naish wills Robinson all of his assets and makes him promise to marry his daughter, Young, when she grows up. Years after the killing takes place, Robinson is seen as an Americanized member of the Chinese community, wed to Young. She, however, gives her love to the crooked Fenton. Robinson learns of her unfaithfulness and sends her and her lover away. In a strange turn of events, he sells all the property he has accumulated and becomes a farmer. It's not long before he hears news that Fenton and Young have ended up in China selling drugs. Dutifully, Robinson heads east and finds his wife enslaved. He buries his vengeful hatchet in Fenton, and takes his wife home. Robinson's struggles are engrossing for the majority of the film, if one can get used to seeing him dressed in silk robes.

d, William Wellman; w, J.G. Alexander (based on a play "The Honorable Mr. Wong" by Achmed Abdullah, David Belasco); ph, Sid Hickox; ed, Owen Marks.

Drama **(PR:C-O MPAA:NR)**

HATE FOR HATE** (1967, Ital.) 79m West Film bw (ODIO PER ODIO)

Antonio Sabato, John Ireland, Fernando Sancho, Nadia Marconi, Mirko Ellis, Gloria Milland.

An interesting, but flawed, spaghetti western starring Ireland as a bank robber who befriends Sabato after returning the money that Sabato has just deposited in the bank he robbed. However, when Ireland finds that his wife has been murdered, he suspects Sabato and rides off seeking vengeance. Later, it is obvious Sabato has done nothing of the kind, and the two unite and search for Ellis, the true killer of Ireland's wife and one-time partner of Sabato. Critic-turned-director Paolella (who has made films in nearly every genre) attempts to combine the Italian and U.S. variety of westerns and comes up with an uneasy blend.

p, Italo Zingarelli; d, Domenico Paolella; w, Paolella, Bruno Corbucci, Fernando di Leo; ph, Alejandro Ulloa.

Western **(PR:C MPAA:NR)**

HATE IN PARADISE*½ (1938, Brit.) 62m CHES/British Screen Services bw (GB: TEA LEAVES IN THE WIND)

Nils Asther *(Tony Drake)*, Eve Shelley *(Margot Hastings)*, Gibson Gowland *(David Webster)*, Cyril Chadwick, Needham Clarge, Robert Anthony.

Only the splendid cinematography and fine sets keep this lame story from being a failure. Set in Ceylon, Shelley plays a woman who pays her plantation-owning uncle a visit in time to keep him from meeting with financial disaster via the hands of crooks. The uncle is too drunk most of the time to notice what's going on, while his niece falls in love with Asther, giving a sappy finish to the already poor story.

p, Neville Clarke, A. Barr-Smith; d, Ward Wing; w, Lona Bara.

Drama **(PR:A MPAA:NR)**

HATE SHIP, THE*½ (1930, Brit.) 90m British International/FN-Pathe bw

Jameson Thomas *(Vernon Wolfe)*, Jean Colin *(Sylvia Paget)*, Henry Victor *(Count Boris Ivanoff)*, Jack Raine *(Roger Peel)*, Randle Ayrton *(Capt. MacDarrell)*, Edna Davies *(Lisette)*, Carl Harbord *(Arthur Wardell)*, Allan Jeayes *(Dr. Saunders)*, Maria Minetti *(Countess Olga)*, Charles Dormer *(Nigel Menzies)*, Syd Crossley *(Rigby)*, Ivo Dawson *(Col. Paget)*, Charley Emerald.

A far-fetched plot which has Thomas behind a phony oil well scam, and a plan to get a Russian count's yacht. This standard mystery fare is supposedly set on the high seas, though barely a drop of water is shown. A unique murder plot features a concealed gun which fires when the piano player strikes a particular chord.

d, Norman Walker; w, Monckton Hoffe, Eloit Stannard (based on a novel by Bruce Graeme); ph, Rene Guissant.

Mystery **(PR:A MPAA:NR)**

HATE WITHIN (SEE: STARK FEAR, 1963)

HATFUL OF RAIN, A*** (1957) 109m FOX bw

Eva Marie Saint *(Celia Pope)*, Don Murray *(Johnny Pope)*, Anthony Franciosa *(Polo)*, Lloyd Nolan *(John Pope, Sr.)*, Henry Silva *(Mother)*, Gerald O'Loughlin *(Chuck)*, William Hickey *(Apples)*.

The story of drug-addict Murray benefits greatly from its concentration on family relations. Saint is the loving and pregnant wife who is initially kept in the dark about her husband's habit. The chief catalyst is Murray's brother, Franciosa, who repeats his role from the stage version. Nolan is the father who, after placing his sons in an orphanage, returns to give his help, but never really understands the complexity of the situation. MacDonald's fine use of black and white CinemaScope gives an oddly effective documentary quality to it. Herrmann's score provides a perfect atmosphere.

p, Buddy Adler; d, Fred Zinnemann; w, Michael V. Gazzo, Alfred Hayes (based on a play by Gazzo); ph, Joe MacDonald (CinemaScope); m, Bernard Herrmann; ed, Dorothy Spencer; art d, Lyle R. Wheeler, Leland Fuller; cos, Mary Wills.

Drama **Cas.** **(PR:C MPAA:NR)**

HATRED½** (1941, Fr.) 67m World bw

Harry Baur *(Capt. Mollenard)*, Gabrielle Dorziat *(Mme. Mollenard)*, Pierre Renoir *(Bonnerot)*, Albert Prejean *(Kerrotret)*, Robert Lynen *(Jean Mollenard)*.

Baur and Dorziat are a husband and wife who share a passionate dislike for each other, in a film which is more interested in characters than plot. Dorziat raises her children to be as equally unreceptive as she to Baur, especially after he is accused of smuggling arms. Brother of director Jean Renoir has a supporting part here. (In French; English subtitles.)

p, Edward Corniglion-Molinier; d, Robert Siodmak; w, Charles Spaak (based on the novel by O.P. Gilbert); ph, Shuftan.

Drama **(PR:A MPAA:NR)**

HATS OFF* (1937) 65m GN bw

Mae Clarke *(Jo Allen)*, John Payne *(Jimmy Maxwell)*, Helen Lynd *(Ginger Connolly)*, Luis Alberni *(Rosero)*, Skeets Gallagher *(Buzz Morton)*, Franklyn Pangborn *(Churchill)*, Robert Middlemass *(Tex Connelly)*, George Irving *(J.D. Murdock)*, Clarence Wilson *(C.D. Pottingham)*, Val Stanton, Ernie Stanton *(The Two Stooges)*, Jimmy Hollywood, R.D. Bartell, Henry Taylor *(The Three Radio Rogues)*.

The highlight of this tedious musical was a finale with white-robed girls on a cloud-covered merry-go-round. Payne and Clarke are a pair of opposing press agents who surround themselves in romance. Co-scripted by director-to-be Fuller, in a style far-removed from his own. Songs include: "Where Have You Been All My Life?" Little Old Rhythm," "Twinkle, Twinkle, Little Star," "Let's Have Another," "Zilch's Hats," and "Hats Off" (Herb Magidson, Ben Oakland).

p&d, Boris Petroff; w, Sam Fuller, Edmund Joseph; ph, Harry Newman; md, Paul Mertz; ch, Arthur Dreifuss, Victor Petroff.

Musical **(PR:A MPAA:NR)**

HATS OFF TO RHYTHM (SEE: EARL CARROLL SKETCHBOOK, 1946)

HATTER'S CASTLE*½** (1948, Brit.) 101m PAR (British) bw

Robert Newton *(James Brodie)*, Deborah Kerr *(Mary Brodie)*, Beatrice Varley *(Mrs. Brodie)*, James Mason *(Dr. Renwick)*, Emlyn Williams *(Dennis)*, Henry Oscar *(Grierson)*, Enid Stamp-Taylor *(Nancy)*, Anthony Bateman *(Angus Brodie)*, June Holden *(Janet)*, Brefni O'Rorke *(Foyle)*, George Merritt *(Gibson)*, Lawrence Hanray *(Dr. Lawrie)*, Roddy Hughes *(Gordon)*, Claude Bailey *(Paxton)*, Stuart Lindsell *(Lord Winton)*, Mary Hinton *(Lady Winton)*, Ian Fleming *(Sir John Latta)*, David Keir *(Perry)*, Aubrey Mallalieu *(Clergyman)*.

Newton is a vicious Scottish hatmaker who has become very successful with his business tactics. He lives with his wife, Varley, and their daughter, Kerr, in a huge mansion which he calls Hatter's Castle. Varley is ill and fearful of his lightning temper but he shows a softer side to his mistress, Stamp-Taylor, a bar waitress at a local pub. Her one-time amour is Williams and she prevails on Newton to give the man a job at the hat factory. Williams meets Kerr and thinks he can woo her and thereby gain her vast legacy. But she is in love with Mason, a doctor in the area. Williams sees that he must foil that affair so he tells Newton who banishes her from Hatter's Castle. She boards the late train to Glasgow and Williams, insidious as any of the characters he later wrote about (NIGHT MUST FALL, among others), tells her that since Newton has gone bankrupt, he will have nothing to do with her. Kerr jumps off the train which later crashes and several people are killed. It is assumed that she is one of them, and that her body has been mangled beyond identification. Varley doesn't have much time to live as she is suffering from terminal cancer. Just before her death, she tells Mason that she received a letter from Kerr but can't find it. Mason wonders if it's true or just the ramblings of a dying mother. When Varley dies, Stamp-Taylor decides to end her affair with Newton. The result is that he goes mad (is that where the expression 'mad as a hatter' came from?). He now throws all of his dreams and desires on the back of his son, Bateman, and hopes the young lad can win a scholarship. But when Bateman is discovered to have cribbed the answers on his exam, he commits suicide, rather than face the confrontation with his father. Newton now understands that it was his own doing that has caused all of his woes and he blames it on the mansion, so he sets fire to the place and dies among the burning ruins, next to the body of his late son. Kerr hears about the deaths and comes back to the small town to attend the funerals. The local townspeople send her to Coventry (no one will speak to her) but she is reunited with Mason at the village church and they exit together in the hopes of finding happiness as a couple. A flawless cast with superb acting and fine attention to period detail in all the sets and costumes. Fleming is briefly seen as Sir John Latta and the always delightful Mallalieu is the clergyman—one of the rare times when Miles Malleson didn't do the part. Though not credited, we are informed that Paul Merzbach and Rudolph Bernauer also contributed to the script.

p, Isadore Goldsmith; d, Lance Comfort; w, Rodney Ackland (based on the novel by A.J. Cronin); ph, Max Green; m, Horace Shepherd; ed, Douglas Robertson; art d, James Carter.

Historical Drama **(PR:C MPAA:NR)**

HATTER'S GHOST, THE½** (1982, Fr.) 120m Horizons-Films A 2-SFPC/GAU c (LES FANTOMES DU CHAPELIER).

Michel Serrault *(Leon Labbe)*, Charles Aznavour *(Kachoudas)*, Monique Chaumette *(Madam Labbe)*, Aurore Clement *(Berthe)*, Christine Paolini *(Louise)*.

Another Chabrol film which neither fails nor lives up to his previous successes (LES BICHES, among others). Again he pays homage to the world of Hitchcock with a psychopath, Serrault, who first murders his wife, then her 6 elderly friends. When he readies himself to kill her seventh friend, she dies unexpectedly of natural causes and he instead murders a prostitute whom he frequents, which lead the police to his doorstep. Serrault is obsessively right for the part, especially when we see the manner in which he lives with his wife, whom he keeps in the cellar (yet another Hitchcock homage).

p, Philippe Grumbach; d&w, Claude Chabrol (based on the novel by Georges Simenon); ph, Jean Rabier; m, Mathieu Chabrol; ed, Monique Fardoulis; art d, Jean-Louis Poveda.

Crime Drama **(PR:C MPAA:NR)**

HAUNTED* (1976) 81m Northgate Communications c (AKA: THE HAUNTED)

Virginia Mayo, Aldo Ray, Ann Michelle, Jim Negele.

In 1865, an Indian woman was accused of witchcraft and sent to die in the heat of the Arizona desert. Years later, the area is plagued by a series of mysterious deaths. Michelle is believed to be the woman's reincarnated ghost. Ray tries to stop the deaths by putting an end to Michelle's life, but he dies after receiving a mysterious phone call. This makes every attempt to be a serious film, complete with literate dialog and attempts at Bunuel-type surrealism. The results don't work, and the film plods along with often confusing moments. Some sections are unintended camp, but unfortunately not enough.

p,d,&w, Michael De Gaetano; ph, W.E. Hines; m, Lor Crane; art d, R. Wingo; m/l, Crane, Freya Crane.

Horror **Cas.** **(PR:O MPAA:NR)**

HAUNTED AND THE HUNTED (SEE: DEMENTIA 13, 1963)

HAUNTED GOLD** (1932) 57m WB bw

John Wayne *(John Mason)*, Sheila Terry *(Janet Carter)*, Erville Anderson *(Benedict)*, Harry Woods *(Joe Ryan)*, Otto Hoffman *(Simon)*, Martha Mattox *(Mrs. Herman)*, Edgar "Blue" Washington *(Clarence)*, Slim Whitaker, Jim Corey.

An abandoned mine shaft, complete with secret passages, is the setting for this remake of THE PHANTOM CITY. John Wayne in his first western for Warners, is up against a gang of bandits and a mysterious cloaked phantom. The bandits are trying to stake claim to the mine's gold, while the phantom is trying to give them a scare. Wayne, with the aid of Terry, soon discovers that the phantom is Terry's dad who is trying to protect his fortune. This was just one of the 37 B-westerns Wayne made between his 1930 screen debut in THE BIG TRAIL and his elevation to star status in 1939's STAGECOACH. Terry changed her name to the perhaps more recognizable Sheila Bromley several years later.

p, Leon Schlesinger; d, Mack Wright; w, Adele Buffington; ph, Nick Musuraca; ed, William Clemens.

Western **Cas.** **(PR:A: MAAA:NR)**

HAUNTED HONEYMOON (SEE: BUSMAN'S HONEYMOON, 1940, Brit.)

HAUNTED HOUSE, THE*½ (1928) 65m FN bw

Chester Conklin *(Mr. Rackham)*, Flora Finch *(Mrs. Rackham)*, Edmund Breese *(Uncle Herbert)*, Larry Kent *(Billy)*, Barbara Bedford *(Nancy)*, Thelma Todd *(Nurse)*, William V. Mong *(Caretaker)*, Montague Love *(Mad Doctor)*, Eve Southern *(Somnambulist)*, Sidney Bracey *(Tully)*, Johnnie Gough *(Chauffeur)*.

Sliding panels and secret passages are the most intriguing part of this haunted house, which suffers mainly from weak direction. Conklin and Finch are the easily frightened pair adapted to the screen from the 1924 Broadway play of the same name, though here amended considerably. This picture features no dialog, just post-synched sounds and songs. The sleepwalking Southern delivers a pair of ditties in which she seems to be mouthing a different song than what we hear.

p, Richard A. Rowland; d, Benjamin Christenson (based on the Broadway play by Owen Davis).

Comedy **(PR:A MPAA:NR)**

HAUNTED HOUSE, THE** (1940) 70m MON bw

Jackie Moran *(Jimmie)*, Marcia Mae Jones *(Mildred)*, George Cleveland *(Henshaw)*, Henry Hall *(Cy Burton)*, John St. Polis *(Simkins)*, Jessie Arnold *(Mrs. Henshaw)*, Henry Roquemore *(Rufus Tyler)*, Marcelle Ray *(Lucy)*, Buddy Swan *(Junior)*.

Moran is a teenage newsboy and Jones, the publisher's niece that he has his eye on. Together they start snooping around the title locale in search of a killer. They follow the clues, catch their man, and prove the innocence of their wrongly accused friend.

p, William T. Lackey; d, Robert McGowan; w, Dorothy Reid (based on a story by Jack Leonard, Monty Collins); ph, Harry Neumann; ed, Russell Schoengarth.

Mystery **(PR:A MPAA:NR)**

HAUNTED HOUSE OF HORROR (SEE: HORROR HOUSE, 1970)

HAUNTED PALACE, THE½** (1963) 85m Alta Vista/AIP c

Vincent Price *(Charles Dexter Ward/Joseph Curwen)*, Debra Paget *(Ann Ward)*, Lon Chaney, Jr. *(Simon Orne)*, Frank Maxwell *(Dr. Marinus Willet)*, Leo Gordon *(Edgar Weeden)*, Elisha Cook *(Peter Smith)*, John Dierkes *(Jacob West)*, Milton Parsons *(Jabez Hutchinson)*, Cathy Merchant *(Hester Tillinghast)*, Guy Wilkerson *(Leach)*, Harry Ellerby *(Minister)*, I. Stanford Jolley *(Boat Captain)*, Darlene Lucht *(Young Woman Victim)*, Barboura Morris *(Mrs. Weeden)*, Bruno Ve Sota *(Bartender)*.

Price stars once again in another Corman-Poe tale, this time as a warlock who is burned at the stake in 1765 by the villagers of the town of Arkham. Before he dies, the warlock vows vengeance on the townsfolk. One hundred years later the warlock's great-great grandson (also Price) arrives in Arkham with his bride Paget to move into his grandfather's mansion. In the village he finds mutated townspeople who haunt the castle grounds—obviously results of the warlock's curse. Slowly Price becomes obsessed with his grandfather's spirit until he *becomes* the warlock, once again wreaking havoc on the populace with the help of his hulking assistant Chaney and fellow warlock Parsons. Price also brings his former lover and witch, Merchant, back from the dead. The villagers mobilize once again to deal with the mad warlock and storm the castle with torches in hand, interrupting Price's sacrifice of Paget. When they set fire to the castle it burns down, freeing Price from his grandfather's spell. Not bad.

p&d, Roger Corman; w, Charles Beaumont (based on "The Case Of Charles Dexter Ward" by H.P. Lovecraft, with the title taken from a poem by Edgar Allan Poe); ph, Floyd Crosby (Panavision, Pathe Color); m, Ronald Stein; ed, Ronald Sinclair; art d, Daniel Haller; set d, Harry Reif; cos, Marjorie Corso; makeup, Ted Coodley.

Horror **(PR:C-O MPAA:NR)**

HAUNTED RANCH, THE** (1943) 57m MON bw

John King, David Sharpe, Max Terhune, Rex Lease, Julie Duncan, Bud Osborne, Budd Buster, Steve Clark, Glenn Strange, Tex Palmer, Charles King, Fred Toones, Carl Mathews, Jimmy Aubrey, Hank Bell, Augie Gomez, Jim Corey.

An entry in the Monogram "Range Busters" series finds the gang out to solve a mystery. The title tells it all as the cowpokes try to find out what's up at a haunted ranch. (See RANGE BUSTERS Series, Index.)

p, George W. Weeks; d, Robert Tansey; w, Elizabeth Beecher (based on a story by Arthur Hoerl).

Western **Cas.** **(PR:A MPAA:NR)**

HAUNTED STRANGLER, THE*** (1958, Brit.) 81m Anglo-Amalgamated/MGM bw (GB: GRIP OF THE STRANGLER)

Boris Karloff *(James Rankin)*, Jean Kent *(Cora Seth)*, Elizabeth Allan *(Barbara Rankin)*, Anthony Dawson *(Supt. Burk)*, Vera Day *(Pearl)*, Tim Turner *(Kenneth McColl)*, Diane Aubrey *(Lily)*, Dorothy Gordon *(Hannah)*, Peggy Ann Clifford *(Kate)*, Leslie Perrins *(Prison Governor)*, Michael Atkinson *(Styles)*, Desmond Roberts *(Dr. Johnson)*, Jessie Cairns *(Maid)*, Roy Russell *(Medical Supt.)*, Derek Birch *(Supt.)*, George Hirste *(Lost Property Man)*, John G. Heller *(Male Nurse)*, George Spence *(Hangman)*, Joan Elvin *(Can-Can Girl)*.

Karloff is a disturbed novelist who is fascinated with the 20-year-old case of the "Haymarket Strangler." He discovers that Styles, the man executed for the crimes, was really innocent, and that the blame actually belongs to the doctor who performed the murder autopsy. Karloff has Styles' grave unearthed and finds the doctor's missing scalpel, the murder weapon. When he picks it up, however, he becomes possessed with the murderous thoughts of the doctor. Karloff soon learns from his wife that he actually is the doctor, but a wave of amnesia has blotted out the last twenty years from his memory. He goes on an uncontrollable spree of bloodshed, picking up where he left off. He is finally shot down by the police as he is burying the scalpel in Styles' grave.

p, John Croydon; d, Robert Day; w, Jan Read, John C. Cooper (based on a story by Read); ph, Lionel Banes; m, Buxton Orr; ed, Peter Mayhew; md, Frederick Lewis; art d, John Elphick; spec eff, Les Bowie.

Horror **Cas.** **(PR:O MPAA:NR)**

HAUNTING, THE*½** (1963) 112m Argyle/MGM bw

Julie Harris *(Eleanor Vance)*, Claire Bloom *(Theodora)*, Richard Johnson *(Dr. John Markway)*, Russ Tamblyn *(Luke Sanderson)*, Lois Maxwell *(Grace Markway)*, Fay Compton *(Mrs. Sanderson)*, Valentine Dyall *(Mr. Dudley)*, Rosalie Crutchley *(Mrs. Dudley)*, Diane Clare *(Carrie Fredericks)*, Ronald Adam *(Eldridge Harper)*, Freda Knorr *(2nd Mrs. Crain)*, Janet Mansell *(Abigail at 6)*, Pamela Buckley *(1st Mrs. Crain)*, Howard Lang *(Hugh Crain)*, Mavis Villiers *(Landlady)*, Verina Greenlaw *(Dora)*, Paul Maxwell *(Bud)*, Claud Jones *(Fat Man)*, Susan Richards *(Nurse)*, Amy Dalby *(Abigail at 80)*, Rosemary Dorken *(Companion)*.

A truly frightening movie that owes its terror to director Wise's tasteful handling. Although heads never roll and blood is not splattered, the suspense is constant and hearts will beat faster as the master movie maker relentlessly lets the horror creep into each frame. Johnson is a professor of anthropology who is experimenting with ESP and other forms of psychic phenomena. He arrives at Hill House, a New England mansion that is reputed to be crammed with demons and ghosts and is the personification of everything evil. Along with Johnson is Harris, a slim spinster who, until recently, has spent her life caring for her aged mother, and Bloom, a lesbian. Both women have experienced extra-sensory occurrences, and Johnson has enlisted their aid in his quest for knowledge on the subject. Tamblyn, who is the heir to the house and who hopes to sell it at a great profit, goes along for a ride he will regret. Once inside, the quartet are besieged by terror, the sort of frightening things that happened to the family in THE AMITYVILLE HORROR, but here they are more implicit than explicit. Noises, yowls, and eerie events pour off the screen until Harris is convinced that Hill House is alive and wants her to stay there. Maxwell, Johnson's non-believing spouse, arrives and attempts to get him out of there before something dreadful happens. But Harris, a lonely woman consumed by guilt from her mother's death, has fallen in love with Johnson. She leaves the realm of sanity, and the others fear for her existence as her behavior is no longer rational so they convince her to leave. Harris gets into her car and, as she drives away, feels a palpable force wrestle her hands away from the steering wheel. Maxwell suddenly walks into the road and Harris tries to avoid killing her. She grabs the wheel and pulls it with all the might of her 100-pound body, careens off the road, and smashes into a tree where she dies. We then learn it was under that tree that the first woman of Hill House expired. Filmed in England (it must have looked more like New England than New England did to the producers), this chilling film was far more supernatural than many other movies that lay it all out and don't allow the audience to use their imaginations. A true chiller.

p&d, Robert Wise; w, Nelson Gidding (based on the novel *The Haunting Of Hill House* by Shirley Jackson); ph, Davis Boulton (Panavision); m, Humphrey Searle; ed, Ernest Walter; prod d, Elliot Scott; md, Searle; set d, John Jarvis; cos, Mary Quant, Maude Churchill; spec eff, Tom Howard.

Horror/Drama **(PR:C-O MPAA:NR)**

HAUNTING OF CASTLE MONTEGO (SEE: CASTLE OF EVIL, 1967)

HAUNTING OF JULIA, THE*** (1981, Brit./Can.) 96m Discovery c (AKA: FULL CIRCLE)

Mia Farrow *(Julia)*, Keir Dullea *(Magnus)*, Tom Conti *(Mark)*, Jill Bennett *(Lily)*, Robin Gammell *(Swift)*, Cathleen Nesbitt *(Mrs. Rudge)*, Anna Wing *(Mrs. Flood)*, Pauline Jameson *(Mrs. Branscombe)*, Peter Sallis *(Branscombe)*, Sophie Ward *(Kate)*, Samantha Gates *(Olivia)*.

After the death of her young daughter, Farrow is overcome with guilt. With her husband Dullea, she takes up residence in an old house to forget it all, and things really start getting strange. Another unusual story of the supernatural from popular ghost novelist Straub.

p, Peter Fetterman, Alfred Pariser; d, Richard Loncraine; w, Dave Humphries, Harry Bromley Davenport (based on the novel *Julia* by Peter Straub); ph, (Panavision); m, Colin Towns; ed, Ron Wisman.

Horror Cas. (PR:O MPAA:R)

HAUNTING OF M, THE*** (1979) 98m Nu-Image c

Sheelagh Gilbey *(Marianna)*, Nini Pitt *(Halina)*, Evie Garratt *(Daria)*, Alan Hay *(Karol)*, Jo Scott Matthews *(Aunt Teresa)*, William Bryan *(Marion)*, Peter Austin *(Stefan)*, Ernest Bale *(Stahu)*, Isolde Cazelet *(Yola)*, Varvara Pepper *(Irka)*, Peter Stenson *(Doctor)*, Jenny Greenaway *(Gypsy)*, Gwen Williams *(Cousin Julia)*, Ruby Melvin *(Cousin Maria)*, William Payne *(Priest)*, Stephan Hartford *(Fisherman)*, Ina Menzies *(Housekeeper)*, Jack MacPherson *(Fire-eater)*, Austin Brothers Circus.

An engrossing retelling of a gothic haunting. The "M" of the title stands for Marianna, an old spinster played by Gilbey, who is spooked by a gaunt, young spirit. Pitt is M's sister, an actress who does some sleuthing and puts a stop to the mysterious goings-on. An impressive directorial debut from Thomas, which met with enthusiam at the Chicago Film Fest and was called back for a second showing.

p,d&w, Anna Thomas; ph, Gregory Nava; m, Leos Janacek, Gustav Mahler, Frederick Chopin, Colin Wyllie; ed, Michael Bockman, Trevor Black, Thomas.

Horror (PR:C MPAA:R)

HAUNTS* (1977) 98m Intercontinental c (AKA: THE VEIL)

May Britt *(Ingred)*, Aldo Ray *(Sheriff)*, Cameron Mitchell *(Carl)*, William Gray Espy *(Frankie)*, Susan Nohr *(Nel)*, Ben Hammer *(Vicar)*, E.J. Andre *(Doc)*, Kendall Jackson *(Loretta)*.

HAUNTS is a hodge-podge of horror devices which finds Britt a complete mess in her remote farmhouse. She has the nutty idea that her uncle, Mitchell, is around the house even though he is miles away. This film is overflowing with tastelessness (Britt thinks she has been raped by a goat, and hungover sheriff Ray is seen hugging the toilet most of the time). There is an occasional scary moment when the killer scissor-attacks Britt in the dark house.

p, Herb Freed, Bert Weisbourd; d, Freed; w, Freed, Anne Marisse; ph, Larry Secrist (Eastmancolor)

Horror Cas. (PR:O MPAA:PG)

HAVANA ROSE*½ (1951) 77m REP bw

Estelita Rodriguez *(Estelita DeMarco)*, Bill Williams *(Tex Thompson)*, Hugh Herbert *(Filbert Fillmore)*, Florence Bates *(Mrs. Fillmore)*, Fortunio Bonanova *(Ambassador DeMarco)*, Leon Belasco *(Renaldi)*, Nacho Galindo *(Carlo)*, Martin Garralaga *(Philip)*, Rosa Turich *(Maria)*, Tom Kennedy *(Hotel Detective)*, Manuel Paris *(Rudolph)*, Bob Easton *(Hotel Clerk)*, Felix and His Martiniques.

Rodriguez is an ambassador's daughter who consistently messes up her father's attempts to secure a $5 million loan for his country, Lower Salamia. She is sent home but manages to get away and run off to Reno with Texas rancher Williams. Tunes include: "Babalu," "Noche De Ronda" (sung by Rodriguez), "Repiquetea Timbalero" (played by Felix and His Martiniques).

p, Sidney Picker; d, William Beaudine; w, Charles E. Roberts, Jack Townley; ph, Ellis W. Carter; m, Stanley Wilson; ed, Tony Martinelli; art d, Frank Hotaling.

Musical/Comedy (PR:A MPAA:NR)

HAVANA WIDOWS** (1933) 68m FN-WB bw

Joan Blondell *(Mae Knight)*, Glenda Farrell *(Sadie Appleby)*, Guy Kibbee *(Deacon Jones)*, Lyle Talbot *(Bob Jones)*, Allen Jenkins *(Herman Brody)*, Frank McHugh *(Duffy)*, Ruth Donnelly *(Mrs. Jones)*, Hobart Cavanaugh *(Mr. Otis)*, Ralph Ince *(Butch O'Neill)*, Maude Eburne *(Mrs. Ryan)*, George Cooper *(Mullins)*, Charles Wilson *(Timberg)*, Gary Owen *(Wheelman)*.

Broadway chorus girls Blondell and Farrell gets suspended from their jobs and take off for Havana with some borrowed cash from their gangster friend Jenkins. The pair intends to search out a millionaire and soon set their sights on Kibbee. It all builds to a comical climax involving Jenkins, the mob boss, and Havana's police and fire department.

p, Robert Lord; d, Ray Enright; w, Earl Baldwin; ph, George Barnes; ed, Clarence Kolster; art d, Esdras Hartley; cos, Orry-Kelly.

Comedy (PR:A MPAA:NR)

HAVE A HEART*½ (1934) 75m MGM bw

Jean Parker *(Sally)*, James Dunn *(Jimmie)*, Una Merkel *(Joan)*, Stuart Erwin *(Gus)*, Willard Robertson *(Schauber)*, Samuel S. Hinds *(Dr. Spear)*, Paul Page *(Joe)*, Muriel Evans *(Helen)*, Pepi Sinoff, Kate Price.

This movie goes out of its way for tears, and the effect is overdone. On the night before her wedding, dance instructor Parker takes a tumble and is permanently crippled. When her worthless beau finds out, he walks out on her. The understanding Dunn steps in and soon the pair are caught up in romance, but in a confusing plot twist, he too dumps her.

p, John Considine, Jr.; d, David Butler; w, Florence Ryerson, Edgar Allan Woolf (based on a story by Butler, B.G. DeSylva); ph, James Wong Howe; ed, Ben Lewis.

Drama (PR:A MPAA:NR)

HAVE A NICE WEEKEND*½ (1975) 82m Weekend c

M.B. Miller *(Paul)*, Peter Dompe *(Donald)*, Valerie Shepherd *(Joan)*, Nikki Counselman *(Laura)*, Colette Bablon *(Ellen)*, Pat Joyce *(Muffy)*.

This moderately suspenseful slasher picture takes place almost completely on a small New England island where a young man, recently back from the war, asks that the entire family come meet him there. With everybody having their own problems, including one sister with an unstable mind, and some tag-along friends, their numbers start to diminish one-by-one, one of their group being the culprit. The small island offers the appropriate enclosed environment to emphasize an air of impending doom, but the director did not have enough experience to capture all the potential inside the story. Far too frequently he slips into relying upon cliched psychological motivation.

d, Michael Walters; w, Walters, John Byrum, Marsha Sheiness; ph, Robert Ipcar (Eastmancolor); m, Charles Gross; ed, Irwin Krechaf.

Horror (PR:O MPAA:NR)

HAVE ROCKET, WILL TRAVEL** (1959) 76m COL bw

Moe Howard *(Moe)*, Larry Fine *(Larry)*, Joe De Rita *(Curley Joe)*, Jerome Cowan *(J.P. Morse)*, Anna-Lisa *(Dr. Ingrid Naarveg)*, Bob Colbert *(Dr. Ted Benson)*, Don Lamond *(Narrator)*.

It's always been a love-hate relationship with the Three Stooges, and this film is no exception. Moe, Larry, and new Stooge De Rita hop in a rocket and are launched into orbit. They end up on Venus where they discover a talking unicorn and are hailed as heroes. This was De Rita's first appearance as a Stooge, replacing Joe Besser, who replaced Shemp Howard on his death in 1955. Made on a shoestring this pic became phenomenally successful, meaning that it did exactly what it was supposed to do—five more Stooge films were to follow, which saved the break-up of this comedy team at a time when Columbia had decided not to renew their contract.

p, Harry Romm; d, David Lowell Rich; w, Raphael Hayes; ph, Ray Cory; m, Mischa Bakaleinikoff; ed, Danny B. Landres; md, Bakaleinikoff; art d, John T. McCormick; set d, Darrell Silvera; m/l, "Have Rocket, Will Travel," George Duning, Stanley Styne.

Comedy/Science-Fiction (PR:A MPAA:NR)

HAVING A WILD WEEKEND*** (1965, Brit.) 91m WB bw (GB: CATCH US IF YOU CAN)

Dave Clark *(Steve)*, Lenny Davidson *(Lenny)*, Rick Huxley *(Rick)*, Mike Smith *(Mike)*, Denis Payton *(Denis)*, Barbara Ferris *(Dinah)*, David Lodge *(Louis)*, Robin Bailey *(Guy)*, David De Kayser *(Zissell)*, Yootha Joyce *(Nan)*, Robert Lang *(Whiting)*, Clive Swift *(Duffle)*, Ronald Lacey *(Beatnik)*, Hugh Walters *(Grey)*, Michael Gwynn *(Hardingford)*, Marianne Stone *(Mrs. Stone)*, Michael Blakemore *(Officer)*, Julian Holloway *(Assistant Director)*, Susan Hanson *(Laraine)*, David Lodge *(Louis)*, Andrew Tyrrell *(Louis' Son)*, Peter Nichols *(Photographer)*, Edgar Harrison *(Barman)*, John Jones *(Drinker)*, Sheila Fearn *(Shirley)*, Alan Lake *(Cameraman)*, Ronald Cunliffe *(Clapper Boy)*, Anthony Gardner *(Director)*, Peter Eyre *(Art Director)*, Donald Morley *(Barker)*, Ronald Arblaster.

1960s pop group The Dave Clark Five tried jumping on the bandwagon that was headed by The Beatles' film A HARD DAY'S NIGHT. Rock 'n' roller Clark plays a London stunt man who wants to get away from the swinging-set and find some of that proverbial peace and quiet. He and the remaining four-fifths head for a remote island, bringing along actress Ferris. They have anything but a serene time, running into missiles, monsters and general mayhem. While no Richard Lester, first-time director John Boorman (DELIVERANCE, POINT BLANK) displays the taut directorial hold seen in his later work.

p, David Deutsch; d, John Boorman; w, Peter Nichols; ph, Manny Wynn; ed, Gordon Pilkington; prod d, Tony Woollard; md, Dave Clark; cos, Sally Jacobs; m/l, "Catch Us If You Can," "Sweet Memories," "Time," "When," "I Can't Stand It," Clark, Lenny Davidson, "On the Move," "Move On," "Ol Sol," Clark, Denis Payton, "Having A Wild Weekend," Clark, Mike Smith (all songs performed by The Dave Clark Five).

HAVING WONDERFUL CRIME*** (1945) 70m RKO bw

Pat O'Brien *(Michael J. Malone)*, George Murphy *(Jake Justus)*, Carole Landis *(Helene)*, Lenore Aubert *(Gilda)*, George Zucco *(King)*, Anje Berens [Gloria Holden] *(Phyllis)*, Richard Martin *(Lance)*, Charles D. Brown *(Winslow)*, William "Wee Willie" Davis *(Zacharias)*, Blanche Ring *(Elizabeth Lenhart)*, Josephine Whittell *(Myra)*, Edward Fielding *(Dr. Newcomb)*, Jimmy Jordan *(Usher)*, Frank Mayo *(Cop)*, Virginia Belmont, Harry Clay, Tom Burton, Lee Trent, Elaine Riley, Margie Stewart, Nancy Marlow, Chili Williams *(Guests)*, Alex Pollard *(Waiter)*, Cyril Ring *(Hotel Clerk)*, Don Barclay *(Bartender)*, Lorraine Clark, Kerry Vaughn, Evalene Bankston, Sheryle Starr, Mary Starr, Marlyn Gladstone, Ellen Hall, Virginia Cruzon, Shelby Payne, Mary Jane Dolan, Shirley Johnson, Karen Haven *(Bathing Beauties)*, Emory Parnell *(Sergeant)*, Larry Wheat *(Butler)*.

A comedy thriller, HAVING WONDERFUL CRIME is one of those zany, offbeat films RKO specialized in for years and it comes off well, even though the plot is strictly mad-hatter and the characters are as eccentric as the story. O'Brien is a criminal lawyer whose newly married friends Landis and Murphy are forever getting him into crime-solving dilemmas. When magician Zucco vanishes, the couple drag O'Brien into a frantic search for him. The trio wind up at a mountain resort where they combine sleuthing and, for Murphy and Landis, a honeymoon. The body is found and lost many times in an oft-disappearing trunk but O'Brien, Landis, and Murphy set things right and nab the culprit in the end, although the plot leaves even O'Brien a bit befuddled at the finale. Director Sutherland moves the production along at whip-cracking speed and the dialog sparkles with wisecracks and wit.

p, Robert Fellows; d, A. Edward [Eddie] Sutherland; w, Howard J. Green, Stewart Sterling, Parke Levy (based on a story by Craig Rice); ph, Frank Redman; m, Leigh Harline; ed, Gene Milford; md, C. Bakaleinikoff; art d, Albert S. D'Agostino, Al Herman; set d, Darrell Silvera, Claude Carpenter; spec eff, Vernon L. Walker.

Comedy/Crime Drama (PR:A MPAA:NR)

HAVING WONDERFUL TIME*** (1938) 70m RKO-Radio bw

Ginger Rogers *(Teddy Shaw)*, Douglas Fairbanks, Jr. *(Chick Kirkland)*, Peggy Conklin *(Fay Coleman)*, Lucille Ball *(Miriam)*, Lee Bowman *(Buzzy Armbuster)*, Eve Arden *(Henrietta)*, Dorothea Kent *(Maxine)*, Richard "Red" Skelton *(Itchy Faulkner)*, Donald Meek *(P.U. Rogers)*, Jack Carson *(Emil Beatty)*, Clarence H. Wilson *(Mr. G)*, Allan "Rocky" Lane *(Mac)*, Grady Sutton *(Gus)*, Shimen Ruskin *(Shrimpo)*, Dorothy Tree *(Frances)*, Leona Roberts *(Mrs. Shaw)*, Harlan Briggs *(Mr. Shaw)*, Inez Courtney *(Emma)*, Juanita Quigley *(Mabel)*, Kirk Windsor *(Henry)*, Betty Rhodes *(Singer)*, George Meeker *(Subway Masher)*, Elise Cavanna *(Office Supervisor)*, Ann Miller *(Vivian)*, Hooper Atchley, Ronnie Rondell *(Subway Riders)*, Dean Jagger *(Charlie)*, Mary Bovard, Frances Gifford, Peggy Montgomery, Marie Osborne, Mary Jane Irving, Wesley Barry, Dorothy Moore, Stanley Brown, Etienne Girardot, Margaret Seddon, Kay Sutton, Dorothy Day, Lynn Bailey, Tommy Watkins, Cynthia Hobard Fellows, Steve Putnam, Bill Corson, Bob Thatcher, Ben Carter, Russell Gleason, Florence Lake, Vera Gordon, Margaret McWade.

Ginger Rogers proves that she can act, too, playing a city gal who heads for a little rest-and-relaxation in the country. Instead of relaxing, she takes up romancing when she meets Douglas Fairbanks, Jr. Based on his Yiddish play, it was adapted by Arthur Kober who, because of the Hays Code, was told to tame the Jewish references, for fear of offending the audience. The alterations included changing character names to something that sounded more Gentile—Terry Stern became Teddy Shaw and Chick Kessler was now Chick Kirkland. However, they decided to retain the Jewish idiom in the title. This film was the first screen appearance for young comic Richard "Red" Skelton in his soon-to-be-patented role. Ann Miller, who was billed fairly high originally, is barely visible after having the majority of her scenes cut.

p, Pandro S. Berman; d, Alfred Santell; w, Arthur Kober (based on his play); ph, Robert de Grasse; ed, William Hamilton; md, Roy Webb; art d, Van Nest Polglase, Perry Ferguson; set d, Darrell Silvera; cos, Renie; spec eff, Vernon L. Walker; m/l "Nighty Night," "My First Impression Of You," Charles Tobias, Sammy Stept (sung by Betty Rhodes).

Romance Cas. (PR:A MPAA:NR)

HAWAII*** (1966) 186m Mirisch/UA c

Julie Andrews *(Jerusha Bromley)*, Max Von Sydow *(Abner Hale)*, Richard Harris *(Rafer Hoxworth)*, Carroll O'Connor *(Charles Bromley)*, Elizabeth Cole *(Abigail Bromley)*, Diane Sherry *(Charity Bromley)*, Heather Menzies *(Mercy Bromley)*, Torin Thatcher *(Rev. Thorn)*, Gene Hackman *(John Whipple)*, John Cullum *(Rev. Immanuel Quigley)*, Lou Antonio *(Rev. Abraham Hewlett)*, Jocelyne La Garde *(Queen Malama)*, Manu Tupou *(Keoki)*, Ted Nobriga *(Kelolo)*, Elizabeth Logue *(Noelani)*, Lokelani S. Chicarell *(Iliki)*, Malcolm Atterbury *(Gideon Hale)*, Dorothy Jeakins *(Hepzibah Hale)*, George Rose *(Capt. Janders)*, Michael Constantine *(Mason)*, John Harding *(Collins)*, Robert Crawford, Jr. *(Cridland)*, Robert Oakley *(Micah at 4)*, Henrik Von Sydow *(Micah at 7)*, Clas S. Von Sydow *(Micah at 12)*, Bertil Werjefelt *(Micah at 18)*, Bette Midler *(Passenger)*.

Filmed in Hawaii, Norway, Tahiti and New England, Fred Zinnemann nurtured this film for several years and then stepped out before the shooting began. Hill came in, then was briefly replaced by Arthur Hiller as director, and eventually returned to finish what must be one of the most complex jobs of directing ever attempted. It's 1820 and Von Sydow is a recent Yale Divinity School graduate who agrees to take the word of God to the Hawaiian nonbelievers. Von Sydow thinks he would be better off with a wife so he shyly proposes marriage to Andrews, who is in love with Harris, a raffish sea captain with whom she has been corresponding, although he hasn't answered a letter in more than three years. Lacking a better offer, she decides to marry Von Sydow and they set sail for Hawaii and are tempest-tossed as they come around dangerous Cape Horn. Once in Hawaii, they are welcomed royally by the queen, La Garde. The Hawaiians are like children to Andrews and Von Sydow: they love to make love, they enjoy the temperate climate and resist any alterations in their relaxed life style. Andrews soon makes friends with them and realizes that their customs and mores suit their way of life, but Von Sydow is stiff-necked and wants to stamp the Hawaiians with his own beliefs and see them dispose of their paganistic rites and rituals—one of which is the practice of incest between brother and sister. La Garde tells the Hawaiians to listen to Von Sydow and tries unsuccessfully to restrain her passion for her brother, Nobriga. Suddenly, Harris arrives at the port and Andrews must contend with her deep love for him versus the duty she feels as Von Sydow's wife. She spurns Harris and decides to stay with Von Sydow who has forbidden any of the native girls to fraternize with the sailors aboard the many ships that now lie in the harbor. The sailors are outraged and when they learn who is doing this, they burn down Von Sydow's house of worship. Andrews, Von Sydow and the islanders successfully douse the blaze and drive away the tars. A brief period of tranquility is followed by the visit of more and more "civilized" sailors and businessmen who begin to permeate the life of the Hawaiians and commercialize the area. It's not long before this process wreaks disease and unhappiness on the once-serene islanders. La Garde is dying so she asks to be converted into a Christian by Von Sydow. To do this she sends Nobriga into the jungle. Once she is dead and buried in consecrated ground, Nobriga returns and takes her body for a traditional Hawaiian burial. The visit of the white men has brought an epidemic of measles and hundreds of the islanders die, including one of Von Sydow's closest friends, Tupou, a native Hawaiian with whom he had studied at Yale. Tupou had been married to his sister, Logue, and when Von Sydow wants to pray for Tupou's eternal soul, Logue rejects him and says that she wants nothing to do with his God—a cruel and angry manifestation who seems to want nothing for his people but shame and guilt, death and destruction. Andrews gives birth to three sons and never stops attempting to cause Von Sydow to relent from his rigid position and admit that his presence has caused pain to the Hawaiians. Years go by and Harris returns to Hawaii with a pre-fabricated New England home that he wants to give to the natives so they can see how others live. Upon arriving, Harris discovers that Andrews has died. His response is to thrash Von Sydow who keeps turning the other cheek, thus emulating the source of his beliefs. Later Harris attempts to get help for Von Sydow. More time goes by and Von Sydow is told by his superiors thst he must relinquish his post. He sends his sons off to England for proper schooling and remains in Hawaii where he thinks he can continue to do God's will and bring these poor, misguided people God's word. Based on James Michener's novel, this film only told part of the story and the rest of it was filmed four years later as THE HAWAIIANS. O'Connor and Cole are Andrews's parents and don't have much to do. Jeakins (when she wasn't designing the terrific costumes) plays Von Sydow's mother and impresses mightily, giving us an opportunity to understand why Von Sydow is the stiff he is. All of the secondary acting is excellent, particularly Hackman as a doctor-missionary and Michael Constantine as a tough sailor who sees the light. Von Sydow's real-life sons are briefly seen playing two of the four ages of Micah. Terrific technical work by all but, at more than three hours, this didn't hold the interest that some other spectacular movies did. It cost more than fifteen million dollars and every penny is on the screen. Look for Bette Midler as a passenger on the ship bound for Hawaii.

p, Walter Mirisch; d, George Roy Hill; w, Dalton Trumbo, Daniel Taradash (based on the novel by James Michener); ph, Russell Harlan (Panavision, DeLuxe Color); m, Elmer Bernstein; ed, Stuart Gilmore; prod d, Cary Odell; art d, James Sullivan; set d, Edwin G. Boyle, Raymond G. Boltz; cos, Dorothy Jeakins; spec eff, Linwood G. Dunn, James B. Gordon, Marshall M. Borden, Paul Byrd; m/l, "My Wishing Doll," Bernstein, Mack David.

Historical Drama Cas. (PR:C MPAA:NR)

HAWAII BEACH BOY (SEE: BLUE HAWAII, 1961)

HAWAII CALLS** (1938) 72m Principal/RKO bw

Bobby Breen *(Billy Coulter)*, Ned Sparks *(Strings)*, Irvin S. Cobb *(Capt. O'Hare)*, Warren Hull *(Comdr. Milburn)*, Gloria Holden *(Mrs. Milburn)*, Juanita Quigley *(Doris Milburn)*, Mamo Clark *(Hina)*, Pua Lani *(Pua)*, Raymond Paige *(Himself)*, Herbert Rawlinson *(Harlow)*, Dora Clement *(Mrs. Harlow)*, Philip Ahn *(Julius)*, Donald Kirke *(Regon)*, William Abbey *(Lonzo)*, Ward Bond *(Muller)*, Birdie De Bolt *(Aunty Pinau)*, Laurence Duran *(Banana)*, William Harrigan *(Blake)*, Ruben Maldonado *(Solly)*, Aggie Auld, Uilani Silva *(Hula Dancers)*, Jerry Mandy *(Taxi Driver)*, Cy Kendall *(Hawaiian Policeman)*, Ruben Duran *(Ka-ne)*.

10-year-old Breen and buddy Pua are stowaways on a Hawaii-bound liner. They are caught by Sparks, who is the guitarist with the ship's orchestra (which is led by Paige). When the young soprano delivers a tune the kind-hearted captain allows the pair to continue on to the islands. The moppet duo soon become detectives on the trail of a gang which has stolen some naval documents. Pretty hammy for the most part, but tolerable. Tunes include: "That's The Hawaiian In Me" (Johnny Noble); "Hawaii Calls," "Down Where The Trade Winds Blow" (Harry Owens); "Macushia" (Dermot McMurrough, Josephine Rowe); "Aloha Oe" (Queen Liluokalani of Hawaii).

p, Sol Lesser; d, Edward F. Cline; w, Wanda Tuchock (based on the novel *Stowaways In Paradise* by Don Blanding); ph, Jack McKenzie; m, Hugo Riesenfeld; ed, Arthur Hilton; md, Abe Meyer; art d, Lewis Rachmil; ch, Aggie Auld.

Musical/Drama (PR:A MPAA:NR)

HAWAIIAN BUCKAROO** (1938) 62m Principal/FOX bw

Smith Ballew *(Jeff Howard)*, Evalyn Knapp *(Paula Harrington)*, Benny Burt *(Mike)*, Harry Woods *(M'Tigue)*, Pat O'Brien *(Stephen Wainwright)*, George Regas *(Regas)*, Laura Treadwell *(Julia Fraser)*, Carl Stockdale *(Brady)*, Fred "Snowflake" Toones *(Flash)*.

Ballew and Burt take their cowboy know-how to the tropics of Hawaii and open a pineapple plantation. Before they can say "aloha" they are involved in a fight to save Knapp's ranch from a shady foreman. A word of warning for Pat O'Brien fans: the one in this film is an imposter!

p, Sol Lesser; d, Ray Taylor; w, Dan Jarrett (based on his story); ph, Allen Thompson; ed, Albert A. Jordan; md, Abe Meyer; m/l, "Riding To The Memories Of The Roundup," "Hawaiian Memories," "I Left Her On The Beach At Waikiki," Albert von Tilzer, Eddie Grant, Harry McPherson.

Western (PR:A MPAA:NR)

HAWAIIAN NIGHTS, 1934 (SEE: DOWN TO THEIR LAST YACHT, 1934)

HAWAIIAN NIGHTS** (1939) 65m UNIV bw

Johnny Downs *(Ted Hartley)*, Mary Carlisle *(Millie)*, Constance Moore *(Lonnie Lane)*, Eddie Quillan *(Ray Peters)*, Thurston Hall *(T.C. Hartley)*, Etienne Giradot *(Alonzo Dilman)*, Robert Emmett Keane *(Fothering)*, Willie Fung *(Murphy)*, Princess Luana *(Luana)*, Samuel S. Hinds *(Frank Lane)*.

Downs is the energetic son of hotel giant Hall who pressures his son into staying in the family business. Downs has different ideas, however, and heads for Hawaii to become a big-band conductor. Nothing new here, just some more light, tropical entertainment. Songs include: "Hey, Good Lookin'," "I Found My Love," "Hawaii Sang Me To Sleep," "Then I Wrote A Minuet In G" (Frank Loesser, Matt Malneck).

p, Max H. Golden; d, Albert S. Rogell; w, Lee Loeb, Charles Grayson (based on a story by John Grey); ph, Stanley Cortez; ed, Otto Ludwig; md, Charles Previn.

Musical **(PR:A MPAA:NR)**

HAWAIIANS, THE** (1970) 134m Mirisch/UA c (GB: MASTER OF THE ISLANDS)

Charlton Heston *(Whip Hoxworth)*, Geraldine Chaplin *(Purity Hoxworth)*, John Phillip Law *(Noel Hoxworth)*, Tina Chen *(Nyuk Tsin)*, Alec McCowen *(Micah Hale)*, Mako *(Mun Ki)*, Don Knight *(Milton Overpeck)*, Miko Mayama *(Fumiko)*, Virginia Ann Lee *(Me Li)*, Naomi Stevens *(Queen Liluokalani)*, Harry Townes *(American Minister)*, Khigh Dhiegh *(Kai Chung)*, Keye Luke *(Foo Sen)*, James Gregory *(Dr. Whipple, Sr.)*, Lyle Bettger *(Janders)*, Winston Char *(Europe at 17)*, Eric Lin Moon Chu *(Europe)*, Michael Leon *(Africa at 18)*, Eddie Pang *(Africa)*, Randy Kim *(Asia at 19)*, Wayne Chow *(Asia)*, Victor Young *(America at 16)*, Jeffrey Chang *(America)*, Bill Fong *(Australia at 14)*, Steve Choy *(Australia)*, Jules Martin *(Noel at 6)*, George Paulsin *(Noel at 15)*, Tanya Chang *(Me Li at 8)*, Soo Yong *(Mrs. Ching)*, James Hong *(Ti Chong)*, Elizabeth Smith *(Apikela)*, Chris Robinson *(Young Dr. Whipple)*, Mark LeBuse *(Kilauea Captain)*, Mathew Fitzgerald *(Symes)*, Bruce Wilson *(Morris)*, Mary Munday *(Malama)*, Mailie McCauley *(Iliki)*, Alan Nahuai *(Kimo)*, Forrest Wood *(Hewlett)*, Murray Staff *(A. Whipple)*, Harry Holcombe *(Fredericks)*, Daniel Kaleikini, Jr. *(Lt. Keholo)*, Galen Kam *(Jim Wu)*, Herman Wedemeyer *(Fire Chief)*, Victor Sen Yung *(Chun Fat)*.

A duller sequel to a fairly tame movie (HAWAII), this one continues with James Michener's story but has the disadvantage of a supremely wooden Heston. Heston is the grandson of the character portrayed by Richard Harris in HAWAII. He comes to Hawaii and brings with him a shipful of Chinese slaves who have been—almost, but not quite—shanghaied to work the fields. Upon arriving he learns that his grandfather's fortune was left to his cousin McCowen (played by four actors in HAWAII, two of whom were Max Von Sydow's sons), a middle-aged man. Heston refuses to work for McCowen and starts his own rival ranch using the Asians, two of whom are Chen and Mako. With the help of engineer Knight, Heston drills for water, strikes H2O and can now farm the once-dry land. With Chen at his side, he establishes a successful pineapple plantation. Heston is married to Chaplin, a Hawaiian woman, who does not like the white man's ways, so she takes their son (played by Martin, Paulsin, and Law as he ages from six to young manhood) away to raise him in her tradition. Meanwhile, Chen's husband has contracted leprosy so she goes with him to Molokai, the leper colony. Many years pass and Chen comes back to the main island to learn that Heston has taken a Japanese mistress (Mayama). Stevens is the Hawaiian queen attempting to regain control, but Heston, by now a very powerful landowner, makes sure she doesn't succeed. McCowen is named the president of Hawaii but is hard-pressed to handle the woes that beset the new republic. A plague causes the Chinese ghetto to be burned to the ground. Heston helps rebuild the scorched area and also wants to aid Chen, who is now ruined financially. In the end Heston's son and Chen's daughter Lee, are married, thus uniting the two families. They took this story from the final pages of Michener's book and managed to make it last more than two hours. It's historically well-designed but the acting and the script are all of one note—B flat. The highlight performance is by Chen who must age from a young girl to a woman in her middle-years (in the book she went to one hundred years of age). Most of the actors are Asian, including Wedemeyer, the one-time football star who went on to many happy years with Jack Lord on "Hawaii Five-O." Heston's acting ranges from icy to steely as he plays the founder of an Hawaiian dynasty with little warmth, a role he has done to death over the years. Mako, who starred in SAND PEBBLES with Steve McQueen, is better than the script. He and Chen are the only two actors most people remember in THE HAWAIIANS. One of Gries' assistants was Newt Arnold, perhaps the best-known assistant director in the movies for over thirty years.

p, Walter Mirisch; d, Tom Gries; w, James R. Webb (based on the novel *Hawaii* by James Michener); ph, Lucien Ballard, Philip Lathrop (Panavision, DeLuxe Color); m, Henry Mancini; ed, Ralph Winters, Byron Brandt; prod d, Cary O'Dell; art d, George Chan; set d, James Berkey, Daniel McCauley; cos, Bill Thomas; spec eff, Sass Bedig; stunts, Fred Zendar, Chuck Roberson.

Historical Drama **(PR:C MPAA:GP)**

HAWK OF POWDER RIVER, THE* (1948) 54m EL-PRC bw

Eddie Dean *(Eddie)*, Roscoe Ates *(Soapy)*, Jennifer Holt *(Vivian)*, June Carlson *(Carole)*, Eddie Parker *(Cochrane)*, Terry Frost *(Mitchell)*, Lane Bradford *(Cooper)*, Carl Mathews, Ted French *(Heavies)*, Steve Clark *(Bill)*, Tex Palmer *(Stage Driver)*, Charles King, Marshall Reed, Andy Parker and The Plainsmen, White Cloud the Horse.

Holt is cast as the female leader of an outlaw gang who has had her uncle killed and intends the same fate for her cousin. Dean steps in and puts a stopper on her murderous ways. A large portion of this film is lifted from earlier Dean oaters, as are all the tunes. Just a way to make a quick buck.

p, Jerry Thomas; d, Ray Taylor; w, George Smith; ph, Ernest Miller; ed, Joe Gluck; m/l, Eddie Dean, Hal Blair, Pete Gates.

Western **(PR:A MPAA:NR)**

HAWK OF WILD RIVER, THE½** (1952) 53m COL bw

Charles Starrett *(Steve Martin/Durango Kid)*, Smiley Burnette *(Himself)*, Jack "Jock" Mahoney *(Himself)*, Clayton Moore *(The Hawk)*, Edwin Parker *(Skeeter)*, Jim Diehl *(Al Travis)*, Lane Chandler *(George the Storekeeper)*, Syd Saylor *(Yank-em-out Kennedy)*, John Cason *(Duke)*, Leroy Johnson *(Smoky)*, Jack Carry *(Pete)*, Sam Flint *(Clark Mahoney)*, Donna Hall *(Girl)*.

Again cast as the Durango Kid, Charles Starrett pits his six-gun against the bow-and-arrow of the evil Hawk, played by Clayton Moore. Rounding out this fine cast is Smiley Burnett and Jack Mahoney (TV's Range Rider). (See *DURANGO KID* Series, Index.)

p, Colbert Clark; d, Fred F. Sears; w, Howard J. Green; ph, Fayte Browne; m, Mischa Bakaleinikoff; ed, Paul Borofsky; art d, Charles Clague.

Western **(PR:A MPAA:NR)**

HAWK THE SLAYER** (1980, Brit.) 93m Chips/ITC c

John Terry *(Hawk)*, Jack Palance *(Voltan)*, Bernard Bresslaw *(Gort)*, Ray Charleston *(Crow)*, Peter O'Farrell *(Baldin)*, Morgan Sheppard *(Ranulf)*, Cheryl Campbell *(Sister Monica)*, Annette Crosbie *(Abbess)*, Catriona MacColl *(Eliane)*, Shane Briant *(Drogo)*, Harry Andrews *(High Abbot)*, Christopher Benjamin *(Fitzwalter)*, Roy Kinnear *(Innkeeper)*, Ferdy Mayne *(Old Man)*, Graham Stark *(Sparrow)*, Warren Clarke *(Scar)*, Deelan Mulholland *(Sped)*, Derrick O'Connor *(Ralf)*, Peter Benson *(Black Wizard)*, Patrick Magee.

Terry is good guy Hawk, and Palance his evil brother Voltan, both of whom want control of "The Power," a magical flying sword. Comic-bookish sword-and-sorcery gibberish is dragged down by its excess of slow-motion battle scenes. Palance makes for an enjoyable villain.

p, Harry Robertson; d, Terry Marcel; w, Robertson, Marcel; ph, Paul Beeson; m, Robertson; ed, Eric Boyd Perkins; art d, Michael Pickwood; spec eff, Effects Associates; stunts, Eddie Stacey.

Fantasy **Cas.** **(PR:A MPAA:NR)**

HAWKS AND THE SPARROWS, THE*** (1967, Ital.) 91m Arco/Brandon bw (UCCELLACCI E UCCELLINI)

Toto *(Innocenti Toto/Brother Ciccillo)*, Ninetto Davoli *(Innocenti Ninetto/Brother Ninetto)*, Femi Benussi *(Luna)*, Rosanna Di Rocco *(Friend of Ninetto)*, Lena Lin Solaro *(Urganda La Sconosciuta)*, Rosina Moroni *(Peasant Woman)*, Renato Capogna, Pietro Davoli *(Medieval Louts)*, Gabriele Baldini *(Dante's Dentist)*, Riccardo Redi *(Civil Engineer)*, Francesco Leonetti *(Crow's Voice)*, Umberto Bevilacqua, Alfredo Leggi, Renato Montalbano, Flaminia Siciliano, Giovanni Tarallo, Vittorio Vittori, Cesare Gelli, Vittorio La Paglia, Mario Pennisi, Fides Stagni.

Fairly accessible Pasolini film about a man, Toto, and his son Davoli, as they stroll through life under the watchful eye of a talking crow who asks them the question, "Where are you going?" While the bird squawks on and on about political and social philosophy the man and his son become monks in the year 1200 and are commissioned by St. Francis of Assisi to decipher the language of birds so that they can convert the birds to God's message of love. Unfortunately, just as the man and his son have succeeded in winning over the birds, a hawk comes along and kills a sparrow. The film then shifts to modern times where Toto and Davoli find themselves embroiled in a land dispute in which they are forced to play both the roles of the landlord and the debtor. Soon after, they witness the birth of a child and the funeral procession of Palmiro Togliatti, head of the Italian Communist Party until 1963. Eventually the father and son begin to get hungry. Tired of listening to the incessant crow harp about philosophy, Toto and Davoli grab the bird, kill him, eat him and continue down the road of life. Many critics surmised that in HAWKS AND SPARROWS Pasolini was rejecting and burying the Italian neo-realist movement, the films of Fellini, and Marxism, but they failed to see the inherent humor in the film (though Pasolini himself doubted that the film turned out to be very funny, even though he intended it to be), especially in Pasolini's casting of Toto, a very popular Italian comedian, in the lead. The allegorical messages of the film are made quite clear, and HAWKS AND SPARROWS does not suffer from the overbearing self conscious pretension that renders Pasolini's work inaccessible to most movie-goers.

p, Alfredo Bini; d&w, Pier Paolo Pasolini; ph, Mario Bernardo, Tonino delli Colli; m, Ennio Morricone; ed, Nino Baragli; art d, Luigi Scaccianoce; set d, Vittorio Biseo; cos, Danilo Donati; m/l, Amedo Cassola.

Comedy **(PR:C MPAA:NR)**

HAWLEY'S OF HIGH STREET** (1933, Brit.) 67m British International/Wardour bw

Leslie Fuller *(Bill Hawley)*, Judy Kelly *(Millie Hawley)*, Francis Lister *(Lord Roxton)*, Amy Veness *(Mrs. Hawley)*, Moore Marriott *(Mr. Busworth)*, Hal Gordon *(Nichols)*, Wylie Watson *(Rev. Potter)*, Faith Bennett *(Edith Busworth)*, Elizabeth Vaughan *(Lady Evelyn)*, Jimmy Godden *(Mayor)*, Mabel Twemlow *(Mrs. Busworth)*, Syd Courtenay, John Schofield, Leo Shefield.

Fuller delivers his dopey comic routine as a draper who takes on butcher Marriott in the local council election.

p, Walter C. Mycroft; d, Thomas Bentley; w, Charles Bennett, Syd Courtenay, Frank Launder (based on the play by Walter Ellis); ph, John J. Cox.

Comedy **(PR:A MPAA:NR)**

HAWMPS!*½ (1976) 126m Mulberry Square c

James Hampton *(Howard Clemmons)*, Christopher Connelly *(Uriah Tibbs)*, Slim Pickens *(Naman Tucker)*, Denver Pyle *(Col. Seymour Hawkins)*, Gene Conforti *(Hi Jolly)*, Mimi Maynard *(Jennifer Hawkins)*, Jack Elam *(Bad Jack Cutter)*, Lee de Broux *(Fitzgerald)*, Herb Vigran *(Smitty)*, Jesse Davis *(Mariachi Singer)*, Frank Inn *(Cook)*, Larry Swartz *(Cpl. LeRoy)*, Mike Travis *(Logan)*, Tiny Wells *(Higgins)*, Dick Drake *(Drake)*, Henry Kendrick *(Col. Zachary)*, Don Starr, Cynthia Smith, Roy Gunzburg, Rex Janssen, Catherine Hearne, Larry Strawbridge, James Weir, Alvin Wright, Lee Tiplitsky, Joey Camp, Perry Martin, Richard Lundin, Charles Starkey.

Based on a true incident in which Jefferson Davis in pre-Civil War times tried to set up a camel corps in Texas, this picture never moves past dull, sitcom humor. BENJI director Joe Camp, tries his hand at presenting humpbacks this time, and finds them considerably less responsive to his cutesy methods. Hampton is a dimwitted soldier who is assigned the task of replacing horses with camels, as well as holding the audience's attention for the overlong 126 minutes—a chore for any adult and most children. Jack Elam turns in the best performance as a black hat out to sabotage a horse-versus-camel race.

p&d, Joe Camp; w, William Bickley, Michael Warren (based on a story by Bickley, Warren, Camp); ph, Don Reddy (CFI Color); m, Euel Box; ed, Leon Seith; prod d, Harland Wright; art d, Ned Parsons; stunts, George Fisher.

Comedy **Cas.** **(PR:A MPAA:G)**

HAY FOOT** (1942) 48m UA-HR bw

William Tracy, Joe Sawyer, James Gleason, Noah Beery, Jr., Elyse Knox, Douglas Fowley, Harold Goodwin.

Problems arise for a man with a photographic memory. He just can't forget anything, but in the end this gift helps out more people than it harms.

p&d, Fred Guiol; ph, Robert Pittack; m, Edward Ward; ed, Richard Currier; art d, Charles Hall.

Comedy **(PR:A MPAA:NR)**

HAZARD** (1948) 94m PAR bw

Paulette Goddard *(Ellen Crane)*, Macdonald Carey *(J.D. Storm)*, Fred Clark *(Lonnie Burns)*, Stanley Clements *(Joe the Bellhop)*, Maxie Rosenbloom *(Truck Driver)*, James Millican *(Houseman)*, Percy Helton *(Beady)*, Charles McGraw *(Chick)*, Frank Faylen *(Oscar)*, Mary Adams *(Matron)*, Walter Baldwin *(Superintendent)*, Isabel Randolph *(Woman in Hotel)*, Taylor Holmes *(Mr. Meeler)*, Jimmy Conlin *(Mr. Tilson)*, Ann Doran *(Nurse)*, Howard Mitchell, Frank Henry, Ralph Montgomery, Dudley James, Sam Ash *(Poker Players)*, Ed Randolph, Ralf Harolde, Ralph Peters *(Taxi Drivers)*, Babe London, Betty Danko *(Matrons)*, Jack Searl *(Public Defender)*, Charles B. Williams *(Little Man)*, Earle Hodgins *(Doctor)*, Benson Fong *(Chinese House Boy)*, Frank Fenton *(Sheriff)*, Philip Barnes *(Dealer)*, George Douglas *(Bettor)*.

Carey is a private eye hired to track down beautiful gambler Goddard. In a cross-country search he catches up to her and the pair eventually fall in love.

p, Mel Epstein; d, George Marshall; w, Arthur Sheekman, Roy Chanslor (based on a story by Chanslor); ph, Daniel L. Fapp; m, Frank Skinner; ed, Arthur Schmidt; art d, Hans Dreier, Robert Clatworthy; m/l, Ray Evans, Jay Livingston, Troy Sanders.

Comedy **(PR:A MPAA:NR)**

HAZEL'S PEOPLE zero (1978) 105m A People's Place c

Geraldine Page *(Anna Witmer)*, Pat Hingle *(Eli)*, Graham Beckel *(Eric)*, Rachel Thomas *(Hazel)*, Steve Weaver *(Jim Witmer)*, Elvin Byler *(Rufus)*, Noreen Huber *(Sarah)*, John Miller *(Ben)*, Luke Sickle *(Menno Witmer)*.

The only excuse for this horrible thing on celluloid was to allow director-writer Davis a chance to indulge in some of his trite philosophical meanderings. Even by 1978, these ideals seemed old-fashioned and not worth wasting the energy or time for consideration. The plot concerns a New York hippy's excursion among the Mennonites in Pennsylvania, where he undergoes monumental changes while living with these people of different ideals. The Christians undergo vast changes as well, but all too blandly predictable. It's hard to imagine what attracted Page to this project. Her talents are wasted, as are those of the rest of the performers, in roles so shallow they hardly represent human beings at all.

p, Burt Martin; d&w, Charles Davis (based on the novel *Happy as the Grass Was Green* by Merle Good); ph, Stan Martin; ed, Erwin Dumbrille; cos, Phyllis Good; m/l, Bill Loose, Robert Fillies.

Drama **Cas.** **(PR:C MPAA:PG)**

HAZING, THE** (1978) 90m Miraleste c

Jeff East *(Craig Lewis)*, Brad David *(Rod)*, David Hayward *(Carl)*, Charlie Martin Smith *(Barney)*, Sandra Vacey *(Dworsky)*, Kelly Moran *(Wendy)*, Jim Boelsen *(Phil)*.

Another in the rash of frat house initiation-gone-wrong films. The only thing that separates this directorial debut of Doug Curtis from the rest is the appearance of Charlie Martin Smith.

p, Douglas Curtis, Bruce Shelly; d, Curtis; w, Shelly, David Ketchum (based on an idea by Shelly); m, Ian Freebairn-Smith.

Drama **(PR:C MPAA:PG)**

HE COULDN'T SAY NO*½ (1938) 57m WB bw

Frank McHugh *(Lambert Hunkins)*, Jane Wyman *(Violet Coney)*, Cora Witherspoon *(Mrs. Coney)*, Diana Lewis *(Iris Mabby)*, Berton Churchill *(Sen. Mabby)*, Ferris Taylor *(Oxnard O. Parsons)*, William Haade *(Slug)*, Tom Kennedy *(Dimples)*, Raymond Hatton *(Hymie)*, John Ridgely *(The Man-On-The-Street)*, Chester Clute *(Musgrave)*, Cliff Clark *(Auctioneer)*, Rita Gould *(Julia Becker)*.

A surprisingly enjoyable comedy with McHugh cast as a wimpy office clerk who is being forced into a marriage with Wyman by her domineering mother, Witherspoon. When he buys a racy statue of a woman at an auction, mother and daughter respond to McHugh's desires by packing their bags. He soon learns that the model for the sculpture is the daughter of a powerful senator. A gang of blackmailers tries to nab the statue but McHugh outwits them, and by doing so, wins the heart of the model.

p, Bryan Foy; d, Lew Seiler; w, Robertson White, Joseph Schrank, Ben Grauman Kohn (based on the story "Larger Than Life" by Norman Matson); ph, Arthur Todd; ed, Frank Dewar.

Comedy **(PR:A MPAA:NR)**

HE COULDN'T TAKE IT* (1934) 63m MON bw

Ray Walker *(Jimmy Case)*, Virginia Cherrill *(Eleanor Rogers)*, George E. Stone *(Sammy Kohn)*, Stanley Fields *(Sweet Sue)*, Dorothy Granger *(Grace Clarice)*, Jane Darwell *(Mrs. Case)*, Paul Porcasi *(Nick)*, Donald Douglas *(Oakley)*, Astrid Allwyn *(Blonde)*, Franklin Parker *(Radio Announcer)*, Jack Kennedy *(Driscoll)*.

A poor excuse for unrelenting action which surrounds itself in the underworld activities of a mobster named Sweet Sue.

d, William Nigh; w, Dore Schary, George Waggoner; ph, George McKenzie.

Crime **(PR:A MPAA:NR)**

HE FOUND A STAR** (1941, Brit.) 89m GFD bw

Vic Oliver *(Lucky Lyndon)*, Sarah Churchill *(Ruth Cavour)*, Evelyn Dall *(Suzanne)*, Gabrielle Brune *(Diane)*, J.H. Roberts *(Mr. Cavour)*, Barbara Everest *(Mrs. Cavour)*, Joan Greenwood *(Babe Cavour)*, David Evans *(Jimmy Cavour)*, Robert Sansom *(Dick Hargreaves)*, Jonathan Field *(Bob Oliphant)*, Mignon O'Doherty *(Mrs. Mahoney)*, Robert Atkins *(Frank Forrester)*, George Merritt *(Max Nagel)*, The Kellaways *(Elsie and Jack)*, Uriel Porter *(George Washington Brown)*, Raymond Lovell *(Maurier)*, Peter Saunders *(Raymond)*, Charles Victor *(Ben Marsh)*, Peggy Novak.

A theatrical agent puts on a show with a bunch of minor talents. His secretary makes good when she turns singer to cover for the problematic nightclub songstress. Tunes include: "Waitin' " (Manning Sherwin), "Salome" (Sarah Churchill).

p, John Corfield; d, John Paddy Carstairs; w, Austin Melford, Bridget Boland (based on the novel *Ring O' Roses* by Monica Ewer); ph, Ernest Palmer.

Musical **(PR:A MPAA:NR)**

HE HIRED THE BOSS** (1943) 72m FOX bw

Stuart Erwin *(Hubert Wilkins)*, Evelyn Venable *(Emily Conway)*, Thurston Hall *(Mr. Bates)*, Vivian Blaine *(Sally Conway)*, William T. Orr *(Don Bates)*, Bennie Bartlett *(Jimmy)*, James Bush *(Clark)*, Chick Chandler *(Fuller)*, Hugh Beaumont *(Jordan)*, Ken Christy *(Stokes)*, Robert Emmett Keane *(Mason)*, Harold Goodwin *(Hank)*, Eddie Acuff *(Driver)*, Syd Saylor *(Mailman)*, Charles Coleman *(Butler)*, Emmett Vogan *(Perry)*, Ralph Dunn *(Carter)*.

Erwin, a spineless bookkeeper, buys some properties after his girl friend Venable starts getting pushy. He's holding out for a $10 raise from boss Hall, so he'll have enough cash to marry the gal. His investments pay off, however, netting him enough dough to buy the company—which he does. His first task is to fire Hall, though he soon hires him back on the condition that Hall gives him that $10 raise.

p, Sol M. Wurtzel; d, Thomas Z. Loring; w, Ben Markson, Irving Cummings, Jr. (based on a story by Peter B. Kyne); ph, Glen MacWilliams; ed, Louis Loeffler; md, Cyril J. Mockridge; art d, Richard Day, Maurice Ransford.

Comedy **(PR:A MPAA:NR)**

HE KNEW WOMEN*½ (1930) 86m RKO bw

Lowell Sherman *(Geoffrey Clarke)*, Alice Joyce *(Mrs. Alice Frayne)*, David Manners *(Austin Love)*, Frances Dade *(Monica Grey)*.

A pair of romances fill this better-than-average look at love. Sherman is the unadmirable novelist who plays leech to widow Joyce's fortunes, leaving behind loving gal, Dade. Manners comes along, gives Sherman his two-cents, and wins over the endearing Dade. An intelligently scripted and alertly directed adaptation of S.N. Behrman's play "The Second Man."

p, Myles Connolly; d, Hugh Herbert; w, Herbert, William Jutte (based on the play "The Second Man" by S.N. Behrman); ph, Edward Cronjager; ed, Ann McKnight, George Marsh.

Romance **(PR:A MPAA:NR)**

HE KNOWS YOU'RE ALONE* (1980) 92m Lansbury-Beruh/MGM-UA c

Don Scardino *(Marvin)*, Caitlin O'Heaney *(Amy)*, Elizabeth Kemp *(Nancy)*, Tom Rolfing *(Killer)*, Lewis Arlt *(Gamble)*, Patsy Pease *(Joyce)*, James Rebhorn *(Professor)*, Tom Hanks *(Elliot)*, Dana Barron *(Diana)*, Joseph Leon *(Ralph The Tailor)*, Paul Gleason *(Daley)*, James Carroll *(Phil)*, Brian Byers *(Bernie)*, Curtis Hostetter *(Tommy)*, Robin Lamont *(Ruthie)*, Robin Tilghman *(Marie)*, Peter Gumeny *(Thompson)*, John Bottoms *(Father McKenna)*, Debbie Novak, Russell Todd, Dorian Lopinto, Jamie Haskins, Barbara Quinn, Laurie Faso, Anthony Shaw, Ron Englehardt, Michael Fiorillo, Steve W. James.

There's nothing memorable in this addition to the slice-and-dice genre. A knife-wielding killer attacks a wedding party and sets his sights on the bride-to-be. They didn't even have enough imagination to come up with a neat name for the killer. Director Armand Mastroianni is Marcello's American-born cousin.

p, George Manasse, Robert Di Milia, Nan Pearlman; d, Armand Mastroianni; w, Scott Parker; ph, Gerald Feil (Metrocolor); m, Alexander Peskanov, Mark Peskanov; ed, George T. Norris; art d, Susan Kaufman.

Horror **Cas.** **(PR:O MPAA:R)**

HE LAUGHED LAST*½ (1956) 76m COL c

Frankie Laine *(Gino Lupo)*, Lucy Marlow *(Rosemary Lebeau)*, Anthony Dexter *(Dominic)*, Dick Long *(Jimmy Murphy)*, Alan Reed *(Big Dan Hennessy)*, Jesse White *(Max Lassiter)*, Florenz Ames *(George Eagle)*, Henry Slate *(Ziggy)*, Paul Dubov *(Billy Boy Barnes)*, Peter Brocco *(Al Fusary)*, Joe Forte *(Dave Hoffman)*, Robin Morse *(Two-Gun Tommy)*, Dale Van Sickel *(Harry)*, Mara McAfee *(Nurse Rafferty)*, David Tomack, John Truax, John Cason, Richard Benedict *(Hoods)*.

The second film written and directed by Edwards is a cliche-filled spoof of 1920s gangster life which is told in a long flashback. Marlow is a song-and-dance girl who inherits a large fortune from a mob boss, and much to the chagrin of her boy friend, begins to live a life of luxury. There are some funny moments but the picture is irreparably harmed by its weak structure.

p, Jonie Taps; d&w, Blake Edwards (based on a story by Edwards, Richard Quine); ph, Henry Freulich (Technicolor); m, Arthur Morton; ed, Jack W. Ogilvie; md, Fred Karger; art d, Walter Holscher; ch, Miriam Nelson; m/l, "Strike Me Pink," Morton, "Save Your Sorrows," Morton (sung by Frankie Laine).

Comedy **(PR:A MPAA:NR)**

HE LEARNED ABOUT WOMEN*½ (1933) 68m PAR bw

Stuart Erwin, Susan Fleming, Alison Skipworth, Gordon Westcott, Grant Mitchell, Sidney Toler, Tom Ricketts, Claude King, Gertrude Norman, Gertrude Messinger, Geneva Mitchell, Dorothy Granger, Irving Bacon.

Naive, bumbling Erwin, ever youthfully befuddled, inherits millions and secures the services of a sophisticated valet, whose attempts to educate his employer in the ways of the wealthy form the substance of this entertaining entry. Forty-eight years later, the same basic tale was screened with Dudley Moore in the Erwin role (ARTHUR, 1981).

d, Lloyd Corrigan; w, Harlan Thompson, Ray Harris (based on a story by Corrigan); ph, Charles Lang.

HE LOVED AN ACTRESS** (1938, Brit.) 69m Morgan/BL (GB: MAD ABOUT MONEY; STARDUST)

Lupe Velez *(Carla de Huleva)*, Wallace Ford *(Peter Jackson)*, Ben Lyon *(Roy Harley)*, Jean Colin *(Diana West)*, Harry Langdon *(Otto)*, Cyril Raymond *(Jerry Sears)*, Mary Cole *(Peggy)*, Ronald Ward *(Eric Williams, Manager)*, Olive Sloane *(Floria Dane)*, Arthur Finn *(J. D. Meyers)*, Peggy Novak *(Secretary)*, Philip Pearman, Andrea Malandrinos, John Stobart, Ronald Hill, Albert Whelan, Alan Shires.

Lupe Velez is a struggling showgirl who pretends to be a cattle heiress in order to star in a film by Ford and Lyon. It's silent star Langdon, who made his money from a beer company, who comes to Velez's aid. Songs include: "Oh So Beautiful," "Perpetual Motion," "Little Lost Tune," "Dustin' The Stars" (James Dyrenforth, Kenneth Leslie-Smith).

p, William Rowland; d, Melville Brown; w, John Meehan, Jr. (based on a story by John F. Harding); ph, Jack Marta, John Stumar; ed, William Morgan; ch, Larry Ceballos.

Musical **(PR:A MPAA:NR)**

HE MARRIED HIS WIFE½** (1940) 82m FOX bw

Joel McCrea *(T. H. Randall)*, Nancy Kelly *(Valerie)*, Roland Young *(Bill Carter)*, Mary Boland *(Ethel)*, Cesar Romero *(Freddie)*, Mary Healy *(Doris)*, Lyle Talbot *(Paul Hunter)*, Elisha Cook, Jr. *(Dicky Brown)*, Barnett Parker *(Huggins)*, Harry Hayden *(Prisoner)*, Charles Wilson *(Warden)*, Charles D. Brown *(Detective)*, Spencer Charters *(Mayor)*, Leyland Hodgson, William Edmunds *(Waiters)*.

A far-fetched screwball comedy which has Joel McCrea and wife Kelly get a divorce, even though they're still in love. The cause is his devotion to the race track. He soon gets tossed in the slammer for defaulting on his alimony payments, and concocts a plan to marry her off to his friend Talbot. When she takes a fancy to the Romeo Romero, McCrea decides to remarry her.

p, Raymond Griffith; d, Roy Del Ruth; w, Sam Hellman, Darrell Ware, Lynn Starling, John O'Hara (based on the story by Erna Lazarus, Scott Darling); ph, Ernest Palmer; ed, James B. Clark; md, David Buttolph; art d, Richard Day, Joseph C. Wright.

Comedy **(PR:A MPAA:NR)**

HE RAN ALL THE WAY*½** (1951) 77m UA bw

John Garfield *(Nick)*, Shelley Winters *(Peg)*, Wallace Ford *(Mr. Dobbs)*, Selena Royle *(Mrs. Dobbs)*, Gladys George *(Mrs. Robey)*, Norman Lloyd *(Al Molin)*, Bobby Hyatt *(Tommy Dobbs)*, Clancy Cooper *(Stan)*, Keith Hetherington *(Captain of Detectives)*, Renny McEvoy *(Attendant)*, Dale Van Sickel *(Policeman)*, Cameron Grant *(Fat Man)*, James Magill *(Workman)*, Robert Davis *(Delivery Boy)*, Vici Raaf *(Marge)*, John Morgan *(Police Doctor)*, Ralph Brooks *(Detective Lieutenant)*, Jimmy Ames *(Clerk)*, Robert Karnes *(Detective)*, Mark Lowell *(Boy)*, Lucille Sewall *(Mrs. Marsden)*.

Garfield is at the top of his acting prowess in this uncompromising crime drama, sadly his last movie performance before dying prematurely at age thirty-nine. He is a tough, not-too-bright thug who becomes involved with a payroll robbery planned by Lloyd. The scheming Lloyd knows Garfield acts impetuously and tells him: "You think slow, Nick. You move fast but you think slow." During the robbery, Garfield and Lloyd panic and a guard is wounded as is Lloyd. Garfield flees with the money and takes refuge at a swimming pool where he meets and befriends Winters, returning home with her. When her family—Royle, Ford, and Hyatt—go to a movie, Garfield lingers with Winters. The family returns to find him still there and, in another moment of panic, he pulls a gun on them, telling them he will leave in the morning. He orders Ford to arrange for a car so that he and Winters can leave together but the father plans to shoot Garfield before he can run away with his daughter, especially after he learns the guard has died and Garfield is now wanted for murder. The next morning, after Garfield has alternately tried to terrorize and befriend the family, the thief steps from the seedy apartment with Winters. But once on the street where Ford waits to shoot Garfield, it is Winters who chooses between father and lover, and shoots Garfield down in the gutter. The dynamic Garfield is riveting in his performance as the hunted thief and Winters is solid as his confused girl friend, a lonely young woman reaching out for love in her small hopeless world. Ford is outstanding as the protective father and Royle is wonderful as the mother who struggles to keep her family alive. Hyatt, as the young boy who first admires, then hates interloper Garfield, gives a startling, intense performance. Director Berry makes much of an inexpensive production which utilizes the captive family theme done so well in THE DESPERATE HOURS (1955). Garfield's role can be compared with the part of the hooligan enacted by Sterling Hayden in THE ASPHALT JUNGLE (1950). It is one that was ironically similar to the life of Garfield himself, a man alone and estranged from both the Hollywood that made him famous and the Group Theatre in New York where he learned his craft. He was a man with feet in two worlds, uncomfortable in both.

p, Bob Roberts, d, John Berry; w, Guy Endore, Hugo Butler (based on the novel by Sam Ross); ph, James Wong Howe; m, Franz Waxman; ed, Francis D. Lyon; art d, Harry Horner.

Crime Drama **(PR:C MPAA:NR)**

HE RIDES TALL** (1964) 84m UNIV bw

Tony Young *(Marshal Morg Rocklin)*, Dan Duryea *(Bart Thorne)*, Jo Morrow *(Kate McCloud)*, Madlyn Rhue *(Ellie Daniels)*, R. G. Armstrong *(Josh McCloud)*, Joel Fluellen *(Dr. Sam)*, Carl Reindel *(Gil)*, Mickey Simpson *(Onie)*, George Murdock *(Burt)*, Michael Carr *(Lefty)*, George Petrie *(Crowley)*, Myron Healey *(2nd Sheriff)*.

A standard oater which offers nothing more than the promised entertainment. Young is a heroic marshal who gets on the bad side of his foster-father's ranch foreman.

p, Gordon Kay; d, R. G. Springsteen; w, Charles W. Irwin, Robert Creighton Williams (based on a story by Irwin); ph, Ellis W. Carter; m, Irving Getz, ed, Russell Schoengarth; art d, Paul Sylos; set d, Ray Boltz; cos, Seth Banks.

Western **(PR:A MPAA:NR)**

HE, SHE OR IT! (SEE: DOLL, THE, 1963, Fr.)

HE SNOOPS TO CONQUER*½ (1944, Brit.) 103m PC/COL British

George Formby *(George Gribble)*, Robertson Hare *(Sir Timothy Strawbridge)*, Elizabeth Allan *(Jane Strawbridge)*, Claude Bailey *(Councillor Oxbold)*, James Harcourt *(Councillor Hopkins)*, Aubrey Mallalieu *(Councillor Stubbins)*, George McLeod *(Angus McGluee)*, Vincent Holman *(Butler)*, William Rodwell, James Page, Robert Clive, Frank Atkinson, Hugh Dempster, Ian Fleming, Richard Harrison, Charles Paton, John Coyle, Katie Johnson, Jack Vyvyan, John Rae, Arthur Hambling, Jack Williams, Ted Venables, Frank Raymond, Gerald Moore.

In the town hall of the small English town of Tangleton Formby works as an all-around handyman. A pair of reporters from London come to investigate possible corruption in the town's post-war plans and are helped out by the unwitting handyman. Later Formby is ordered to destroy some important housing forms to cover up the political scheming but an accident sends these forms flying in the wind. Finally with the help of crackpot inventor Hare, Formby is able to oust the dishonest government and all is well. Not very good outing for Formby and unlike the formula that made his other comedies much better.

p, Ben Henry, Marcel Varnel; d, Varnel; w, Stephen Black, Howard Irving Young, Norman Lee, Michael Vaughan, Langford Reed; ph, Roy Fogwell.

Comedy **(PR:A MPAA:NR)**

HE STAYED FOR BREAKFAST** (1940) 86m COL bw

Loretta Young *(Marianne Duval)*, Melvyn Douglas *(Paul Beliot)*, Alan Marshal *(Andre Dorlay)*, Eugene Pallette *(Maurice Duval)*, Una O'Connor *(Doreta)*, Curt Bois *(Comrade Tronavich)*, Leonid Kinskey *(Comrade Nicky)*, Trevor Bardette *(Police Lt.)*, Grady Sutton *(Salesman)*, Frank Sully *(Butcher)*, Evelyn Young, Ethelreda Leopold *(Secretaries)*, William Castle *(Policeman)*, Henry Hale *(Police Lt.)*, Ernie Adams *(Workman)*, Jack Rice *(Marianne's Chauffeur)*, Harry Semels *(Comrade)*, Jack Douglas, Nestor Paiva *(Gendarmes)*, Ferdinand Munier *(Cafe Proprietor)*, Guy Repp *(Headwaiter)*, Charles Wagenheim *(Timid Waiter)*, Vernon Dent *(Chef)*, Fredrick Worlock *(Communist President)*, Leonard Mudie *(Communist Secretary)*, George Burr McAnnan *(Communist Vice-President)*, Jack Lowe, Art Miles, Jack Raymond, Bob St. Angelo *(Communists)*, George Andre Beranger *(Maitre d'Hotel)*, Joseph Kamaryt, Bill Newell *(Waiters)*, Eddie Colebrook *(Bus Boy)*, Walter Merrill *(Guard)*.

Given the choice between communism and capitalism, Melvyn Douglas chooses the former. Cast as a red in Paris, he takes a shot at a banker and is pursued by the police. He ducks into the apartment of Young, who lets him use her place as a shelter. She soon reveals that she is the banker's ex-wife. She becomes more and more fascinated with the Commie and begins to show him the benefits of Western civilization—croissants and capitalism. Of course Douglas renounces his Commie ways and opts for the city on the Seine.

p, B. P. Schulberg; d, Alexander Hall; w, P. J. Wolfson, Michael Fessier, Ernest Vajda (based on the play "Liberte Provisoire" by Michel Duran, adaptation Sidney Howard); ph, Joseph Walker; m, Werner R. Heyman; ed, Viola Lawrence; md, M. W. Stoloff; art d, Lionel Banks; cos, Irene Kallosch; m/l, Milton Drake.

Comedy **(PR:A MPAA:NR)**

HE WALKED BY NIGHT**** (1948) 79m Bryan Foy/EL bw

Richard Basehart *(Davis Morgan)*, Scott Brady *(Sgt. Marty Brennan)*, Roy Roberts *(Capt. Breen)*, Whit Bissell *(Reeves)*, Jimmy Cardwell *(Chuck Jones)*, Jack Webb *(Lee)*, Bob Bice *(Detective Steno)*, Reed Hadley *(Narrator)*, Chief Bradley *(Himself)*, John McGuire *(Rawlins)*, Lyle Latell *(Sergeant)*, Jack Bailey *(Pajama Top)*, Mike Dugan, Garret Craig *(Patrolmen)*, Bert Moorhouse, Gaylord Pendleton, Kenneth Tobey, Robert Williams, Doyle Manor, Jim Nolan, Rory Mallinson *(Detectives)*, Bernie Suss *(Business Suspect)*, George Chan *(Chinese Suspect)*, George Goodman *(Fighter Suspect)*, Carlotta Monti *(Woman)*, Louise Kane *(Mrs. Rawlins)*, Kay Garrett *(Doctor)*, Florence Stephens *(Receptionist)*, Tom Browne Henry *(Dunning)*, Harry Harvey *(Detective Prouty)*, Virginia Hunter *(Miss Smith)*, Ruth Robinson *(Mrs. Rapport)*, John Parrish *(Vitale)*, Earl Spainard *(Kelly)*, Alma Beltran *(Miss Montalvo)*, Anthony Jochim *(Thompson)*, Paul Fierro *(Mexican Detective)*, Jane Adams *(Nurse Scanlon)*, John Dehner *(Asst. Chief)*, Byron Foulger *(Avery)*, Felice Ingersoll *(Record Clerk)*, Wally Vernon *(Postman)*, Dorothy Adams *(Housewife)*, Dick Mason, Donald Kerr *(Mailmen)*, Charles Lang *(Policeman)*, Mary Ware *(Dolores)*, Ann Doran *(Woman Dispatcher)*, Harlan Warde *(C.B. Officer)*, Frank Cady *(Suspect)*, Paul Scardon *(Father)*, Charles Meredith *(Desk Sergeant)*, Tim Graham *(Uniformed Sergeant)*, Bill Mauch, John Perri, Tom Kelly, Rex Downing *(Young Men)*, Stan Johnson *(Artist)*.

This is a smashing *film noir* entry with Basehart as a brilliant, cold-hearted thief with underlying psychopathic tendencies that chill the viewer to the bone. Basehart is an electronics wizard who robs electronics stores and warehouses to obtain equipment which he modifies and then rents out to Bissell. The Los Angeles police are in a quandary about this successful burglar since Basehart listens in on their radio network, knowing where they are looking for him. He cleverly alters his *modus operandi* so that his work appears to be that of another burglar, and he is also a master of disguises. But cops Brady and Roberts manage to trap him at Bissell's factory. He shoots his way to freedom, killing a cop, and escaping into the vast sewer system beneath Los Angeles. Basehart is then tracked down to the little bungalow where he lives alone with a dog, his only companion. A gun battle ensues and he again escapes to the drainage system but this time he is cornered and shot. Werker and Mann, the latter uncredited, do a bang-up job by maintaining a hectic pace and Basehart is gripping as the lone, loveless thief who even sacrifices his dog when the going gets tough. His role is based upon thief and cop-killer Erwin Walker, a WW II hero turned burglar who terrorized L.A. in 1946. This film marked the first time the huge drainage system canals in Los Angeles were employed in a film; they would later be put to heavy use in THEM! (1954) and in GREASE (1978), to name a few productions. Jack Webb drew the inspiration for his long-running documentary-style TV series "Dragnet" from this film in which he played a featured role.

p, Robert Kane; d, Alfred Werker, [uncredited] Anthony Mann; w, John C. Higgins, Crane Wilbur, Harry Essex, [uncredited] Beck Murray (based on a story by Wilbur); ph, John Alton; m, Leonid Raab; ed, Alfred De Gaetano; md, Irving Friedman; art d, Edward Ilou; set d, Armor Marlowe, Clarence Steenson; spec eff, George J. Teague, Jack R. Rabin; makeup, Ern Westmore, Joe Stinton.

Crime Drama Cas. (PR:C MPAA:NR)

HE WAS HER MAN½** (1934) 70m WB bw

James Cagney *(Flicker Hayes)*, Joan Blondell *(Rose Lawrence)*, Victor Jory *(Nick Gardella)*, Frank Craven *(Pop Sims)*, Harold Huber *(J.C. Ward)*, Russell Hopton *(Monk)*, Ralf Harolde *(Red Deering)*, Sarah Padden *(Mrs. Gardella)*, J.M. "John" Qualen *(Dutch)*, Bradley Page *(Dan Curly)*, Samuel S. Hinds *(Gassy)*, James Eagles *(Whitey)*, Gino Corrado *(Fisherman)*, Willard Robertson *(Police Captain)*, Sidney Bracey, George Chandler *(Waiters)*, Lee Shumway *(Detective)*, Billy West *(Chick)*, Dennis O'Keefe *(Reporter)*.

Recently released from a prison term he was forced to serve after being set up by his partners, Page and Harolde, safecracker Cagney is determined to pay them back. Pretending that there are no hard feelings, he again teams up with the dishonorable thieves on another job. The robbery is a success, and when Cagney gets his hands on the money, he squeals to the police on Page and Harolde. Page escapes but Harolde is captured and executed. Cagney flees to San Francisco, but, unknown to him, Page is hot on his trail. In San Francisco Cagney meets Blondell, a reformed prostitute who is engaged to Jory, a fisherman. Cagney follows the girl to Jory's fishing village and tries to woo her. His romantic overtures are successful and Blondell falls for him, but before anything can develop between them, he leaves her and is confronted by goons loyal to Page. While trying to escape, Cagney inadvertently involves Blondell and the assassins want her dead as well. Cagney convinces the killers that Blondell knows nothing, and they allow her to live. Cagney however, is taken away by the hoods and presumably murdered, leaving Blondell to renew her relationship with fisherman Jory. HE WAS HER MAN is a disappointing Cagney vehicle hampered by a basically weak and unimaginative script, unaided by helmsman Bacon's direction. Cagney, as usual, struggles mightily to bring more to his role than existed on paper, but even his enthusiastic effort fails to bring this film out of the doldrums. This was the seventh, and last, teaming of Cagney and Blondell. The popular partnership began in 1929 when both were unknowns working on Broadway in the musical "Penny Arcade" which was turned into a film entitled SINNERS HOLIDAY in 1930. Luckily they were asked to recreate their stage roles for the movies, a medium that would soon propel them to stardom.

d, Lloyd Bacon; w, Tom Buckingham, Niven Busch (based on a story by Robert Lord); ph, George Barnes; ed, George Amy; md, Leo F. Forbstein; art d, Anton Grot; cos, Orry-Kelly; m/l, "My Only Romance," Sidney Mitchell, Lew Pollack.

Crime (PR:A-C MPAA:NR)

HE WHO RIDES A TIGER½** (1966, Brit.) 103m BL/Sigma III bw

Tom Bell *(Peter Rayston)*, Judi Dench *(Joanne)*, Paul Rogers *(Supt. Taylor)*, Kay Walsh *(Mrs. Woodley)*, Ray McAnally *(Orphanage Superintendent)*, Jeremy Spenser *(The Panda)*, Peter Madden *(Peepers Woodley)*, Inigo Jackson *(Detective Sgt. Scott)*, Annette Andre *(Julie)*, Edina Ronay *(Anna)*, Nicolette Pendrell *(Ellen)*, Ralph Michael *(Carter)*, Fredrick Piper *(Mr. Steed)*, Rita Webb *(Flower Seller)*, Robin Hughes *(Detective Sgt. Crowley)*, Jimmy Gardner *(Waiter)*, Howard Lang *(Prison Governor)*, Naomi Chance *(Lady Cleveland)*, Pat Shakesby *(Policewoman)*, Grant Lovatt *(Dan)*, The Rapiers *(Themselves)*, Harry Baird *(Stan)*, Margaret Bull *(Mrs. Hutton)*, Frank Sieman *(Prison Officer)*.

Bell is a schizoid cat burglar who is sometimes nice to children but on occasion is violent and hot-tempered. He falls in love with a woman who works in an orphanage, ignorant of his "other side." When he tells her of his nighttime activities she leaves him. Before long she returns, but he turns his back on her, again assuming the criminal life. At times too sentimental, at other times annoying, but consistently well-acted.

p, David Newman; d, Charles Crichton; w, Trevor Peacock; ph, John Von Kotze; m, Alexander Faris; ed, Jack Harris, John S. Smith; md, Faris; art d, Richard Harrison, Seamus Flannery; m/l, "He Who Rides a Tiger," Trevor Peacock.

Crime (PR:A MPAA:NR)

HE WHO SHOOTS FIRST*½ (1966, Ital.) 95m Fida Cinematografica c (DJANGO SPARA PER PRIMO)

Glenn Saxon *(Django)*, Fernando Sancho *(Doc)*, Evelyn Stewart [Ida Galli], Nando Gazzolo, Lee Burton [Guido Lollobrigida], Erika Blanc.

Another in the Django series of spaghetti westerns here played by Saxon. This one is a simple revenge tale which sees Saxon out to revenge the murder of his father. With the help of Sancho, Saxon tracks down the killer, Gazzolo, and gets his revenge.

p, Edmondo Amati; d, Alberto De Martino; w, Sandro Continenza, Massimiliano Capriccioli, Florenzo Carpi, Vincenzo Flamini, Alberto De Martino; ph, Riccardo Pallottini.

Western (PR:C MPAA:NR)

HEAD, THE* (1961, Ger.) 95m Rapid/Trans-Lux bw (DIE NACKTE UND DER SATAN; AKA: A HEAD FOR THE DEVIL, THE SCREAMING HEAD)

Horst Frank *(Dr. Ood)*, Michel Simon *(Prof. Abel)*, Paul Dahlke *(Crime Commissioner)*, Karin Kernke *(Irene)*, Helmut Schmid *(Bert)*, Christiane Maybach *(Lilly)*, Dieter Eppler *(Paul)*, Kurt Muller-Graf *(Dr. Burke)*, Maria Stadler *(Mrs. Schneider)*, Otto Storr *(Bartender)*, Barbara Valentin, Herb Beschanner.

Simon is a noble scientist who has invented a serum that can keep the severed head of a dog alive. His crazed colleague, Frank, performs a heart transplant operation on the unsuspecting scientist and then keeps Simon's severed head in glass with electrodes hooked to it. He then grafts the head of his hunchbacked nurse to the body of a sexy stripper he's had his eye on, thus creating his version of the perfect woman. Simon-the-head's pleas for a humane death are finally answered and the lab burns down. Bizarre and laughable, but interesting for the participation of Hermann Warm, one of the set designers of the silent German masterpiece, THE CABINET OF DR. CALIGARI (1919).

p, Wolfgang Hartwig; d&w, Victor Trivas (based on a story by Trivas, Jacques Mage); ph, Georg Krause; m, Willy Mattes, Jacques Lasry; ed, Friedl Buckow-Schier; md, Erwin Lehn; art d, Hermann Warm, Bruno Monden; spec eff, Theo Nishwitz.

Horror (PR:O MPAA:NR)

HEAD*** (1968) 85m Raybert/COL c

Peter Tork, David Jones, Micky Dolenz, Michael Nesmith *(Monkees)*, Annette Funicello *(Minnie)*, Timothy Carey *(Lord High 'n' Low)*, Logan Ramsey *(Officer Faye Lapid)*, Abraham Sofaer *(Swami)*, Vito Scotti *(I. Vitteloni)*, Charles Macaulay *(Inspector Shrink)*, T.C. Jones *(Mr. and Mrs. Ace)*, Charles Irving *(Mayor Feedback)*, William Bagdad *(Black Sheik)*, Percy Helton *(Heraldic Messenger)*, Sonny Liston *(Extra)*, Ray Nitschke *(Private One)*, Carol Doda *(Sally Silicone)*, Frank Zappa *(The Critic)*, June Fairchild *(The Jumper)*, Terry Garr *(Testy True)*, I.J. Jefferson *(Lady Pleasure)*, Victor Mature *(Big Victor)*.

After the demise of their TV show, the musical group The Monkees took to the screen. The result was a visually daring but redundant film "game" from Bob Rafelson and Jack Nicholson. There is no story line and the film is better off because of it. It is as interesting as anything done by the 1960s underground, though ignored because of its connection with a major producer and its commercial appeal—two avant-guard "no-nos." A number of guest stars appear, including Funicello, Zappa, Liston, Mature, and the then unknown Garr (TOOTSIE). A fun collection of old movie clips are included featuring Ronald Reagan, Bela Lugosi, Charles Laughton, Ann Miller, and Rita Hayworth. The Monkees deliver the songs, "Circle Sky" (Michael Nesmith), "Can You Dig It," "Long Title: Do I Have To Do This All Over Again" (Peter Tork), "Daddy's Song" (Nilsson), "As We Go Along" (Carole King, Toni Stern), "The Porpoise Song" (Carole King, Gerry Goffin).

p, Bob Rafelson, Jack Nicholson; d, Rafelson; w, Rafelson, Nicholson; ph, Michel Hugo (Technicolor); m, Ken Thorne; ed, Mike Pozen; art d, Sidney Z. Litwack; set d, Ned Parsons; cos, Gene Ashman; ch, Toni Basil; spec eff, Butler-Glouner, Chuck Gaspar, Burton Gershfield, Bruce Lane.

Musical/Comedy (PR:A MPAA:G)

HEAD FOR THE DEVIL (SEE: HEAD, THE, 1961)

HEAD FOR THE HILLS (SEE: SOD SISTERS, 1969)

HEAD OF A TYRANT½** (1960, Fr./Ital.) 94m Vic Films-C.E.C. Films/UNIV c (GUIDETTA E OLOFERNE; AKA: JUDITH AND HOLOPHERNES)

Massimo Girotti *(Holophernes)*, Isabelle Corey *(Judith)*, Renato Baldini *(Arbar)*, Yvette Masson *(Rispa)*, Gianni Rizzo *(Ozia)*, Camillo Pilotto *(Belial)*, Lucia Banti *(Servant Girl)*, Riccardo Valle *(Isaac)*, Leonardo Botta *(Gabriele)*, Franco Balducci *(Galaad)*, Luigi Tosi *(Iras)*, Gabriele Antonini *(Brother)*, Daniela Rocca *(Naomi)*, Enzo Doria *(Daniel)*.

When Girotti and his army take over Asia Minor they replace the true god with one of their idols. This causes unrest and an underground network plots Girotti's assassination. This is botched and he orders the schemers to turn themselves in lest he take out his wrath on the population. When the beautiful Corey finds out her brother and fiance are among the plotters, she decides to join the group and finish the assassination herself. But this goes awry when the would-be killer and victim fall in love after she performs a dance. However, Girotti realizes he must destroy the town to look good before his troops. Corey must save her people and ends up decapitating her lover. As Girotti's army flees the city in fear, Corey holds up the severed head and lightning destroys the phony idol. The English dubbing hurts the story somewhat but overall this is good for what it is.

d, Fernando Cerchio; w, Cerchio, Damiano Damiani, Gian Paola Callegari, Guido Malatesta; ph, (Totalscope, Technicolor); m, Carlo Savio.
Biblical Epic **(PR:C MPAA:NR)**

HEAD OF THE FAMILY** (1933, Brit.) 66m FN/WB bw

Irene Vanbrugh *(Mrs. Powis-Porter)*, Arthur Maude *(Mr. Powis-Porter)*, John Stuart *(Bill Stanmore)*, Pat Paterson *(Geraldine Powis-Porter)*, D.A. Clarke-Smith *(Welsh)*, Alexander Field *(Bill Higgins)*, Roland Culver *(Manny)*, Glen Alyn *(Maisie)*, Annie Esmond *(Mrs. Slade)*.

After Maude goes bankrupt he becomes night watchman for the firm that drove him out of business. When he catches his own son attempting a break-in, Maude turns the boy in, proving his integrity. He ends up marrying his new boss' daughter and combines his old company with Stuart's. Unbelievable hokum and too much talk make this a lesser drama.

p, Irving Asher; d, John Daumery; w, Brock Williams.
Drama **(PR:A MPAA:NR)**

HEAD OF THE FAMILY*** (1967, Ital./Fr.) 115m Ultra Film-MN-C.F.C.-Marianne/PAR c

Nino Manfredi *(Marco)*, Leslie Caron *(Paola)*, Ugo Tognazzi *(Romeo)*, Claudine Auger *(Adriana)*, Evi Maltagliati *(Luisa)*, Sergio Tofano *(General)*, Mario Carotenuto *(Gabriele)*, Elsa Vazzoler *(Carla)*, Antonella Della Porta, Adolfo Celi.

A fine marital comedy which takes a bittersweet look at the effects youngsters make on a marriage. Manfredi and Caron's once happy bond goes through some shaky times as their family grows in number.

p, Turi Vasile; d, Nanni Loy; w, Loy, Ruggero Maccari (based on a story by Loy, Giorgio Arlorio, Maccari); ph, Armando Nannuzzi (Eastmancolor); m, Carlo Rustichelli; ed, Franco Fraticelli; md, Bruno Nicolai; art d, Carlo Egidi; set d, Bruno Cesari; cos, Marcel Escoffier.
Comedy **Cas.** **(PR:C MPAA:GP)**

HEAD OFFICE** (1936, Brit.) 90m WB/FN bw

Owen Nares *(Henry Crossman)*, Nancy O'Neil *(Margaret)*, Arthur Margetson *(Dixon)*, Eileen Peel *(Sheila)*, Alexis France *(Janie Clutterbuck)*, Philip Ray *(Gerrard)*, Ronald Simpson *(Knott)*, Charles Carson *(Armstrong)*, Hilda Bayley *(Mrs. Braham)*, Bruce Lister *(Halliday)*, H. F. Maltby *(Blenkinsop)*, Wilfrid Caithness, Stan Paskin.

Nares and Margetson both get post-war jobs through the father of a friend killed in action. Nares discovers his friend stealing company funds but Margetson threatens to reveal the truth about their late friend's cowardly death if Nares exposes him. The truth comes out anyway through unusual circumstances and Margetson ends up going to jail. Though this gives a nice portrait of office life, there's really not much more to this heavy-handed, over-talky drama.

p, Irving Asher; d, Melville Brown; w, Hugh Preston (based on his novel); ph, William Luff.
Drama **(PR:A MPAA:NR)**

HEAD ON* (1971) 91m Leon c

Michael Witney *(Steve)*, Michael Conrad *(Mike)*, Lori Saunders *(Millie)*, Art Lund *(Roger)*, Kathleen Freeman *(Nadine)*, Mickey Morton *(Fred)*.

An embarrassing mess with Witney and Conrad cast as ex-soldiers who take to the road. Along the way there is an array of bloody macho antics, culminating with a rape. Eventually they get hired by a lumberjack who, to no one's disappointment, kills Conrad.

p, Michael Donovan O'Donnell; d&w, Edward Lakso; ph, William Davies (Movielab Color); m, William G. St. Pierre; ed, Bill Waters.
Drama **(PR:O MPAA:GP)**

HEAD ON½** (1981, Can.) 98m Grant c

Sally Kellerman *(Michelle Keys)*, Stephen Lack *(Peter Hill)*, John Huston *(Clarke Hill)*, Lawrence Dane *(Frank Keys)*, John Peter Linton *(Gad Bernstein)*, Mina E. Mina *(Karim)*, Hadley Kay *(Stanley)*, Robert Silverman *(Michelle's Analyst)*, Maxwell Moffett *(Henry)*.

A bizarre sexual drama which begins with a head-on crash. The drivers, Kellerman and Lack, emerge safely and become lovers. As a peace offering, each gives the other a new Mercedes. Eventually they decide to marry, but it turns out to be just another of Lack's cruel games. The movie ends as it began, in a head-on car crash. An impressive but sadistic love story which in the end is only partly successful.

p, Michael Grant, Alan Simmonds; d, Grant; w, James Sanderson, Paul Illidge; ph, Anthony Richmond; m, Peter Mann; ed, Gary Oppenheimer; prod d, Antonin Dimitrov.
Drama **(PR:O MPAA:NR)**

HEAD OVER HEELS (SEE: CHILLY SCENES OF WINTER, 1979)

HEAD OVER HEELS IN LOVE** (1937, Brit.) 84m GAU bw (GB: HEAD OVER HEELS)

Jessie Matthews *(Jeanne)*, Robert Flemyng *(Pierre)*, Louis Borell *(Marcel)*, Romney Brent *(Matty)*, Helen Whitney Bourne *(Norma)*, Paul Leyssac *(Max)*, Eliot Makeham *(Martin)*, Fred Duprez *(Norma's Manager)*, Buddy Bradley *(Instructor)*, Edward Cooper *(Charles)*.

A musical set in Paris which has gangsters Flemyng and Borell falling for Bourne, an American screen star. Matthews, who is cast as a rising song-and-dance girl, was in real life married to director Sonnie Hale. Songs include: "May I Have The Next Romance With You?," "Head Over Heels In Love," "Lookin' Around Corners For You," "There's That Look In Your Eyes Again," "Don't Give A Good Gosh Darn," "Through The Courtesy Of Love" (Mack Gordon, Harry Revel).

p, S. C. Balcon; d, Sonnie Hale; w, Fred Thompson, Dwight Taylor, Marjorie Gaffney (based on the play "Pierre Ou Jac" by Francois de Crosset); ph, Glen MacWilliams; ed, Al Barnes; md, Louis Levy; ch, Buddy Bradley.
Musical **(PR:A MPAA:NR)**

HEAD THAT WOULDN'T DIE (SEE: BRAIN THAT WOULDN'T DIE, THE, 1959)

HEADIN' EAST** (1937) 63m COL bw

Buck Jones *(Benson)*, Ruth Coleman *(Helen)*, Shemp Howard *(Windy)*, Donald Douglas *(Eric)*, Elaine Arden *(Penny)*, Earle Hodgins *(Calhoun)*, John Elliott *(M.H. Benson)*, Stan Blystone *(Lohman)*, Harry Lash *(Joe)*, Dick Rich *(Clipper)*, Al Herman *(Maxie)*.

Interesting Jones oater sees the cowboy discard his chaps and saddle for a suit and tie when he travels to the big city to investigate a produce racket that has been ruining his father's lettuce shipments. There, he meets and falls for produce middleman Hodgins' daughter Coleman and together with Howard (of Three Stooges fame) along for laughs they smash the crooks' operation.

p, L.G. Leonard; d, Ewing Scott; w, Ethel La Blance, Paul Franklin (based on a story by Joseph Hoffman, Monroe Shaff); ph, Allen Thompson; ed, Robert Crandall.
Western/Crime **(PR:A MPAA:NR)**

HEADIN' FOR BROADWAY zero (1980) 89m FOX c

Rex Smith, Terri Treas, Vivian Reed, Paul Carafotes, Gene Foote, Gary Glendell.

Hopeless nonsense from the man who gave cinema the sap-filled YOU LIGHT UP MY LIFE. This time out, Brooks oversteps his bounds (and lack of any real talent) in this portrait of the music world in which he supposedly is a veteran. Smith, a rock star who later played in "The Pirates of Penzance" on Broadway, leads a group of young hopefuls who are just dying to make it on the Great White Way. It's amazing they got as far as this film. Everything about it reeks of incompetence. The filmmaking is amateurish, and shows every sign of emergency-room editing to save what little material there is. Mickey Rooney and Judy Garland these kids aren't.

p&d, Joseph Brooks; w, Brooks, Hilary Henkin, Larry Gross; m, Brooks.
Drama **(PR:C MPAA:PG)**

HEADIN' FOR GOD'S COUNTRY** (1943) 78m REP bw

William Lundigan *(Michael Ranyan)*, Virginia Dale *(Laurie Lane)*, Harry Davenport *(Clem Adams)*, Harry Shannon *(Albert Ness)*, Addison Richards *(District Commissioner)*, J. Frank Hamilton *(Hilary Higgins)*, Eddie Acuff *(Hugo Higgins)*, Wade Crosby *(Jim Talbot)*, Skelton Knaggs *(Jeff)*, John Belfer *(Nickolai)*, Charlie Lung *(Willie Sobs)*, Ernie Adams *(Chuck)*, Eddie Lee *(Gim Lung)*, James B. Leong *(Japanese Officer)*, Anna Q. Nilsson *(Mrs. Nilsson)*, Eddy Waller *(Hank)*.

A strong WW II anti-Japanese film in which the enemy is obliterated as they attack "God's country," the tag name for Alaska. Lundigan is a stranger who visits an isolated town and plants a story that the U.S. is about to be overtaken by a superpower. The climax comes when the story turns out to be true with Pearl Harbor, and the town defeats a real Japanese raiding party.

p, Armand Schaefer; d, William Morgan; w, Elizabeth Meehan, Houston Branch (based on a story by Branch); ph, Bud Thackery; ed, Arthur Roberts; md, Morton Scott; art d, Russell Kimball.
Drama **(PR:A MPAA:NR)**

HEADIN' FOR THE RIO GRANDE½** (1937) 61m GN bw

Tex Ritter *(Tex)*, Eleanor Stewart *(Laura)*, Sid Saylor *(Chile)*, Warner Richmond *(Travis)*, Charles King *(Tick)*, Earl Dwire *(Rand)*, Forrest Taylor *(Saunders)*, William Desmond *(Mack)*, Charles French *(Pop Hart)*, Snub Pollard *(Cookie)*, Budd Buster *(Senator)*, Bud Osborne *(Cactus)*, Tex Palmer, Jack C. Smith, Sherry Tansey, James Mason, Bill Woods, White Flash the Horse.

Tex Ritter in his screen debut is doing just what the title says, and not a whole lot more. His goal is to check into a gang of protectionists. Tex sang: "Campfire Love Song," "Jailhouse Lament," "Night Herding Song," and "Headin' For The Rio Grande" (Ritter, Jack Smith, Stanley Davis).

p, Edward F. Finney; d, Robert N. Bradbury; w, Lindsley Parsons, Robert Emmet.
Western **(PR:A MPAA:NR)**

HEADIN' FOR TROUBLE* (1931) 65m Big 4 bw

Bob Custer, Betty Mack, Andy Shuford, Robert Walker, Jack Harvey, John Ince, Duke Lee.

Trouble is exactly what they were heading for with this lame and forgettable oater, which comes complete with singing cowboys, cowgirls, and cowkids. Even handsome, rugged Custer failed to bring it to box office respectability.

d, J.P. McGowan; w, George Morgan; ph, Edward Kull; ed, Fred Bain.
Western **(PR:A MPAA:NR)**

HEADIN' NORTH** (1930) 57m TIF bw

Bob Steele, Barbara Luddy, Perry Murdock, Walter Shumway, Eddie Dunn, Fred Burns, Gordon DeMain, Harry Allen, Gunner Davis, S.S. Simon, James Welsh, Jack Henderson.

Another in the endless variations on the theme of a man wrongly accused who sets out, with his girl, of course, to prove his innocence. Good guy Steele and his buddy Murdock disguise themselves as members of an English dance hall team and finally corner the culprit, who confesses, freeing Steele of the accusations and the audience from watching any more of this silliness.

p, Trem Carr; d&w, J.P. McCarthy; ph, Archie Stout; ed, Fred Allen.
Western **(PR:A MPAA:NR)**

HEADING FOR HEAVEN** (1947) 65m EL bw

Stu Erwin *(Henry)*, Glenda Farrell *(Nora)*, Russ Vincent *(Swami)*, Irene Ryan *(Molly)*, Milburn Stone *(Harding)*, George O'Hanlon *(Alvin)*, Janice Wilson *(Janie)*, Ralph Hodges *(Danny)*, Dick Elliott *(Wingate)*, Charles Williams *(Eddie)*, Selmer Jackson *(Doctor)*, Harry Tyler *(Professor)*, Ben Welden *(Sam)*, Betty West *(Lila)*, Jack Del Rio.

Erwin is an extremely nervous realtor who wants to create a new housing development. When he receives an incorrect doctor's report giving him only three months to live, he is convinced his life is over. When some of his clothing is taken from a creek, his family and friends assume he's committed suicide rather than face the consequences of his condition. A swami (Vincent) is consulted to reach Erwin's spirit, but Erwin surprises everyone by showing up at the seance in person. Minor fun with fast-paced direction and fine performances for the fare.

p, George Moskov, Jack Schwartz; d, Lewis D. Collins; w, Collins, Oscar Mugge (based on the play by Charles Webb, Daniel Brown); ph, George Robinson; m, Hal Borne; ed, Marty Cohn; art d, Frank Sylos.

Comedy **(PR:A MPAA:NR)**

HEADLESS GHOST, THE** (1959, Brit.) 61m AIP bw

Richard Lyon *(Bill)*, Liliane Sottane *(Ingrid)*, David Rose *(Ronnie)*, Clive Revill *(Fourth Earl)*, Jack Ellen *(Earl of Ambrose)*, Alexander Archdale *(Randolph)*, Carl Bernard *(Sgt. Grayson)*, Josephine Blake *(Dancer)*, John Stacy *(Parker)*, Donald Bissett *(Guide)*, Mary Barclay *(Lady Ambrose)*, Patrick Connor *(Constable)*, Trevor Barnett *(Strong Man)*.

Three young American exchange students decide to check out an English castle. Local legends say the place is haunted, but they've got to find out for themselves. Once the sun goes down, Revill leaps down from a portrait and asks Lyon, Sottane, and Rose if they will help him with another ghost. Seems spirit No. 2 is missing his head and wants it back. The plucky Americans help out despite some trouble raised by a mischeivous third ghost. Strange and not particularly entertaining, this was designed for younger audiences, though even kids will be numbed by this nonsense.

p, Herman Cohen; d, Peter Graham Scott; w, Cohen, Kenneth Langtry; ph, John Wiles.

Comedy/Fantasy **(PR:A MPAA:NR)**

HEADLEYS AT HOME, THE** (1939) 69m Standard bw

Evelyn Venable *(Pamela Headley)*, Grant Mitchell *(Ernest Headley)*, Robert Whitney *(Bide Murphy)*, Betty Roadman *(Louisa Headley)*, Vince Barnett *(Vince Bergson)*, Benny Rubin *(Dr. McLevy)*, Alicia Adams *(Alicia Headley)*, Louise Beavers *(Hyacinth)*, Kenneth Harlan *("Smooth" Adair)*, Edward Earle *(Van Wyck Schuyler)*, Jack Hatfield *(Rowland Perkins)*, Ethel Clark *(Mrs. Brown)*.

When ambitious small-town wife Venable learns that a big-shot banker is in town, she orders her husband, Mitchell, to invite him to dinner, even though Mitchell does not know the man. He arranges for an actor to appear at dinner instead, and the actor turns out to be the culprit who robbed the bank the day of the dinner. He is recognized from his scarred hands by Mitchell, who turns him in to the cops and ends this tiresome feature.

p, B.W. Richards; d, Chris Beute; w, Carrington North, Nicholas Bella (based on a story by North, William Miles); ph, Harry Forbes; ed, Holbrook Todd.

Comedy **(PR:A MPAA:NR)**

HEADLINE** (1943, Brit.) 75m EAL bw

David Farrar *(Brookie)*, Anne Crawford *(Anne)*, John Stuart *(L.B. Ellington)*, Antoinette Cellier *(Mrs. Ellington)*, Billy Hartnell *(Dell)*, Anthony Hawtrey *(Grayson)*, Richard Goolden *(Jones)*, Lorna Tarbat *(Betty)*, Merle Tottenham *(Mrs. Deans)*, Joss Ambler *(sub-editor)*, Nancy O'Neil *(Betty)*, Ian MacLean.

Farrar divides his screen time between playing heartthrob and playing detective in this average newspaper melodrama. He's a crime reporter who pushes his editor to the limits, and then starts snooping around when the boss' wife, a murder witness, disappears. Implausible yarn where the story's twists tangle rather than unravel things.

p, John Corfield; d, John Harlow; w, Maisie Sharman, Ralph Gilbert Bettison (based on the novel *The Reporter* by Ken Attiwill); ph, Geoffrey Faithfull.

Crime **(PR:A MPAA:NR)**

HEADLINE CRASHER* (1937) 58m Guaranteed bw

Frankie Darro *(Jimmy Tallant)*, Kane Richmond *(Larry Deering)*, Muriel Evans *(Edith Arlen)*, John Merton *(Scarlotti)*, Richard Tucker *(Sen. Tallant)*, Edward Earle *(Atwood)*, Jack Ingram *(Al)*, Charles King *(Blake)*, Dick Curtis *(Joe)*, Eddie Kaye *(Bill)*, Eleanor Stewart *(Helen)*, Harry Harvey *(City Editor)*, John Ward *(Campaign Manager)*, Walter Clinton *(Steward)*, Henry Hall *(Powers)*, Wayne Bumpus *(News Photographer)*, Bunny Bronson *(Blondey)*, Ray Martin *(Martin)*.

A senator running for re-election becomes the subject of a flurry of attacks from a group of yellow journalists. Nothing here is up to par—the script and direction are awkward and the casting could have been done better by an amateur.

p, Maurice Conn; d, Les Goodwins; w, Harry O. Hoyt, Sherman Lowe (based on a story by Peter B. Kyne); ph, Gilbert Warrenton; ed, Martin C. Cohn.

Drama **(PR:A MPAA:NR)**

HEADLINE HUNTERS** (1955) 70m REP bw

Rod Cameron, Julie Bishop, Ben Cooper, Raymond Greenleaf, Chubby Johnson, John Warburton, Nacho Galindo, Virginia Carroll, Howard Wright, Stuart Randall, Edward Colmans, Joe Besser.

A cub reporter takes on his assignments with zeal. This leads him to trouble when he gets involved with some racketeers in the big city. Typical Republic fare, reminiscent of its earlier films. Look for an appearance by Besser, one of the latter day Three Stooges. This is a remake of BEHIND THE NEWS, 1940.

p, William J. O'Sullivan; d, William Witney; w, Frederic Louis Fox, John K. Butler; ph, John L. Russell, Jr.; m, R. Dale Butts; ed, Arthur E. Roberts; art d, Carroll Clark; cos, Adele Palmer.

Drama **(PR:A MPAA:NR)**

HEADLINE HUNTERS** (1968, Brit.) 60m Ansus c

Leonard Brockwell *(Terry Hunter)*, Susan Payne *(Joan Hunter)*, Stephen Garlick *(Peter Hunter)*, Jeffrey Chandler *(Alec)*, Bill Owen *(Henry)*, Reginald Marsh *(Bagshot)*, Keith Smith *(Fustwick)*, Glyn Houston *(Gresham)*, David Lodge *(Harry)*, Dermot Kelly *(Ernie)*.

After their father falls ill, a group of children decide to run his newspaper. They pull it off, as only plucky kids in these sort of plots do, until he recuperates. Definitely for the younger viewer.

p, Frank Godwin; d, Jonathan Ingrams; w, Ingrams, C. M. Pennington Richards (based on a story by Geoffrey Bond).

Children's Drama **(PR:AAA MPAA:NR)**

HEADLINE SHOOTER*** (1933) 60m RKO bw (GB: EVIDENCE IN CAMERA)

William Gargan *(Bill Allen)*, Frances Dee *(Jane Mallory)*, Ralph Bellamy *(Hal Caldwell)*, Jack LaRue *(Ricci)*, Gregory Ratoff *(Gottlieb)*, Wallace Ford *(Mike)*, Hobart Cavanaugh *(Happy)*, June Brewster *(Betty Kane)*, Robert Benchley *(Radio Announcer)*, Betty Furness *(Secretary)*, Dorothy Burgess *(Gangster's Moll)*, Purnell Pratt *(City Editor)*, Henry B. Walthall *(Judge Beacon)*, Franklin Pangborn *(Crocker)*, Bill Hudson *(Ed)*, Mary MacLaren *(Murderess)*.

Gargan is a newsreel photographer who devotes more time to capturing reality than to the woman who loves him, Dee. She turns to the more dependable Bellamy, and soon is with them both when they are trapped by a flood. There's also a confrontation with a gang of mobsters, during which Dee decides that the adventurous newsreeler is her man. By incorporating some exciting newsreels of actual fires, earthquakes, and floods, the final product becomes as interesting as those events Gargan documents.

d, Otto Brower; w, Agnes Christine Johnson, Allen Rivkin, Arthur Kober (based on the story "Muddy Waters" by Wallace West); ph Nick Musuraca; ed, Fred Knudtson.

Drama **(PR:A MPAA:NR)**

HEADLINE WOMAN, THE**½ (1935) 74m Mascot bw

Heather Angel *(Myrna Van Buren)*, Roger Pryor *(Bob Grayson)*, Jack LaRue *(Zarias)*, Ford Sterling *(Hugo Meyer)*, Conway Tearle *(Desmond)*, Franklin Pangborn *(Hamilton)*, Jack Mulhall *(Blair)*, Morgan Wallace *(Clarkey)*, Russell Hopton *(Craig)*, Syd Saylor *(Murphy)*, Theodore Von Eltz *(Johnny Corinti)*, George Lewis *(O'Shay)*, Ward Bond *(Johnson)*, Harry Bowen *(Ernie)*, Wade Boteler *(Flanagan)*, Wheeler Oakman *(Fielding)*, Warner Richmond *(Bradley)*.

Pryor is the star reporter trying to get a story while the heat rises between his editor and the police commissioner. He learns that Angel, the publisher's daughter, has some information on the murder of a gambler. To get the scoop, Pryor kidnaps the girl and then has to struggle to keep her name out of the headlines. Neat cast makes this wornout newspaper story viewable.

p, Victor Zobel; d, William Nigh; w, Jack Natteford, Claire Church; ph, Ernest Miller, William Nobles; ed, Joseph Lewis.

Drama **(PR:A MPAA:NR)**

HEADS UP** (1930) 76m PAR bw

Charles "Buddy" Rogers *(Jack Mason)*, Helen Kane *(Betty Trumbull)*, Victor Moore *("Skippy" Dugan)*, Margaret Breen *(Mary Trumbull)*, Gene Gowing *(Rex Cutting)*, Helen Carrington *(Mr. Trumbull)*, Billy Taylor *(Georgie Martin)*, Harry Shannon *(Capt. Denny)*, John Hamilton *(Capt. Whitney)*.

A boyish Rogers stars as a Coast Guard ensign assigned to a yacht which is suspected of rum running. On board, he falls for the lovely Breen, against her mother's wishes. Rogers, as expected, discovers who's behind the illegal boozing and points the finger at mom's hoped-for son-in-law. Songs include: "My Man Is On The Make," "A Ship Without A Sail" (Richard Rodgers, Lorenz Hart), "If I Knew You Better" (Victor Schertzinger).

d, Victor Schertzinger; w, John McGowan, Lewis Stevens, Jack Kirkland (based on the Broadway play by McGowan, Paul Gerard Smith, Richard Rodgers, Lorenz Hart); ph, William Steiner; ch, Georgie Hale.

Musical **(PR:A MPAA:NR)**

HEADS WE GO (SEE: CHARMING DECEIVER, THE, 1933, Brit.)

HEALER, THE*½ (1935) 76m MON bw (AKA: LITTLE PAL)

Ralph Bellamy, Karen Morley, Mickey Rooney, Judith Allen, Robert McWade, Bruce Warren, J. Farrell MacDonald, Vessie Farrell.

Doctor Bellamy forgets his ideals to become successful, but crippled little Rooney shows him where his real obligations lie. Not much of interest save Rooney before he became a star.

d, Reginald Barker; w, James Knox Millen, John Goodrich, George Waggner (based on a story by Robert Herrick); ph, Harry Neumann; ed, Jack Ogilvie.

Drama **(PR:A MPAA:NR)**

HEALTH* (1980) 102m Lion's Gate/FOX c (AKA: H.E.A.L.T.H.)

Glenda Jackson, Carol Burnett, James Garner, Lauren Bacall, Dick Cavett, Paul Dooley, Henry Gibson, Donald Moffat, Alfre Woodard.

Altman's failed attempt to satirize politics, HEALTH is set in Florida during a convention of health food devotees who are on hand to elect a new president of their organization. The leading contenders are Bacall, who plays a remarkably young-looking 83-year-old health authority, and Jackson, who's given to long-winded, rambling diatribes. Bacall claims her youthful vigor is due to her diet and the fact that she has remained a virgin all her life. Burnett is a White House health advisor who becomes sexually aroused only at times of danger, and Garner is her ex-husband, now Bacall's public relations agent. Cavett plays himself, covering the convention for his TV show. The political overtones are more than a little overstated, and the film is filled with wildly overdrawn caricatures. Altman's gift for underscoring the humor inherent in a situation clearly deserted him in HEALTH, a movie that deservedly got only limited distribution.

d, Robert Altman; w, Frank Barhydt, Paul Dooley, Altman; ph, Edmond Koons; ed, Dennis M. Hill.

Satire **(PR:C-O MPAA:PG)**

HEAR ME GOOD*½ (1957) 80m PAR bw

Hal March *(Marty Holland)*, Joe E. Ross *(Max Crane)*, Merry Anders *(Ruth Collins)*, Jean Willes *(Rita Hall)*, Milton Frome *(Mr. Ross)*, Joey Faye *(Charlie Cooper)*, Richard Bakalyan *(Hermie)*, Tom Duggan *(TV Director)*.

Quizmaster of TV's once famous "$64,000 Question" show, Hal March stars in this looney tale of a Manhattan man who tries to fix a beauty pageant. The woman he wants to emerge victorious belongs to a mobster who is rarely seen in public. Along the way, inspired by another beauty, March changes his tune and renounces his evil ways.

p,d&w, Don McGuire; ph, Haskell Boggs (VistaVision); ed, George Tomasini; art d, Hal Pereira, Joseph MacMillan Johnson; cos, Edith Head; spec eff, John P. Fulton.

Comedy **(PR:A MPAA:NR)**

HEARSE, THE*½ (1980) 95m Marimark/Crown c

Trish Van Devere *(Jane Hardy)*, Joseph Cotten *(Walter Pritchard)*, David Gautreaux *(Tom Sullivan)*, Donald Hotton *(Rev. Winston)*, Med Flory *(Sheriff)*, Donald Petrie *(Luke)*, Christopher McDonald *(Peter)*, Perry Lang *(Paul)*, Frederic Franklyn *(Gordon)*, Olive Dunbar *(Mrs. Gordon)*, Al Hansen *(Bo)*, Dominic Barto *(Driver)*, Nicholas Shields *(Dr. Greenwalt)*, Chuck Mitchell *(Counterman)*, Allison Balson *(Alice)*, Jimmy Gatherum *(Boy)*, Victoria Eubank *(Lois)*, Tanya Bowers *(Schoolgirl)*.

Van Devere inherits a mansion from her late aunt and decides to leave San Francisco and move into it. She doesn't understand why the townsfolk are treating her so coldly until she notices that she looks just like the aunt, who was believed to be possessed by Satan. She is continually hounded by an old hearse which keeps showing up in front of her house, and by the crotchety real estate man, Cotten. A weak horror picture which only occasionally delivers a chill.

p, Mark Tenser, Charles Russell; d, George Bowers; w, Bill Bleich (based on an idea by Tenser); ph, Mori Kawa (Metrocolor); m, Webster Lewis; ed, George Berndt; art d, Keith Michl.

Horror **Cas.** **(PR:A MPAA:PG)**

HEART AND SOUL*½** (1950, Ital.) 91m Crest bw

Vittorio De Sica *(Maestro Perboni)*, Maria Mercader *(Clotilde)*, Giorgio De Lullo *(Lt. Gardena)*, Gino Leurini *(Garrone)*, Carlo Ogliotti *(Enrico)*, Luciano De Ambrosis *(Precossi)*, Vito Chiari *(Coretti)*, Carlo Delle Piane *(Garoffi)*, Amerigo Martufi *(Il Muratorino)*, Gualtiero Tomiselli *(Crossi)*, Massimo Randisi *(Nobis)*, Francesco Lengo *(Nelli)*, Rino Moretti *(Stardi)*, Geiogio Guglielmo *(Votini)*, Nerio Bernardi, Arturo Gragaglia, Fiore Davanzati, Augusto Mastrantoni, Armando Migliari, Ave Ninchi *(School Boys)*, Sergio Serardi *(Franti)*.

De Sica proves that he is as invaluable in front of the camera as he is behind it. In Italy's answer to GOODBYE MR. CHIPS, he portrays a devoted and philosophical teacher at a boys' school. Teaching alongside Mercader, he encounters a variety of obstacles including a suspension stemming from his political beliefs. Both De Sica and the children give wonderfully natural portrayals in this idealistic view of humankind. (In Italian; English subtitles.)

p, D. Forges Devanzati; d, Duilio Coletti; w, Oreste Biancoli (based on the novel by Edmondo De Amicis); ph, Mario Montuori; ed, Ivo Batteli; English titles, Charles Clement.

Drama **(PR:A MPAA:NR)**

HEART BEAT** (1979) 109m Orion/WB c

Nick Nolte *(Neal Cassady)*, Sissy Spacek *(Carolyn Cassady)*, John Heard *(Jack Kerouac)*, Ray Sharkey *(Ira)*, Anne Dusenberry *(Stevie)*, Margaret Fairchild *(Mrs. Kerouac)*, Tony Bill *(Dick)*, Mary Margaret Amato *(Waitress)*, Kent Williams *(Ogden)*, Susan Niven *(Ogden's Secretary)*, Marcia Nasatir, Mickey Kelly *(Receptionists)*, Luis Contreras *(Mexican Junkie)*, Sharon Lee *(Blonde in Car)*, Stephen Davies *(Bob Bendix)*, Jenny O'Hara *(Betty Bendix)*, Don Brodie *(Dispatcher)*, Tom Runyon *(Seaman)*, Juliana Tutak *(Cathy)*, Candy Brown *(Claudia)*, Steve Allen *(Himself)*, John Larroquette *(TV Talk Show Host)*, Ray Vitte *(Undercover Agent)*, John Hostetter, Billy Cross, Terry Winkless, Gary Baxley, Lloyd "Sunshine" Parker, Garth Eliassen.

Silly buddy picture allegedly based on the three-way relationship between Beat writers Jack Kerouac, Neal Cassady, and Cassady's wife (from whose book the film takes its title, if not much more). Nolte and Heard wander through the post-WW II American landscape before Nolte settles in San Francisco and marries Spacek. Heard drifts in and out of the couple's life for a number of years after that, occasionally sleeping with Spacek, until *On The Road* is published and he becomes a celebrity and pop icon. From there his rapid decline is slightly illustrated but not at all explained, until his death, two years after Nolte's. The actors try, but the script is one of the worst ever foisted on a talented group of players, filled with banal lines and pseudo-significant moments. For those unfamiliar with Kerouac and Cassady, the film does nothing to explain their impact on American culture, and comes off as little more than a watered-down version of JULES AND JIM; for those who know and appreciate these two figures, the film will only annoy.

p, Alan Greisman, Michael Shamberg; d&w, John Byrum (suggested by the memoir by Carolyn Cassady); ph, Laszlo Kovacs (Panavision, Technicolor); m, Jack Nitzsche; ed, Eric Jenkins; prod d, Jack Fisk; set d, Peter Samish; cos, Patricia Norris.

Drama **Cas.** **(PR:O MPAA:R)**

HEART IS A LONELY HUNTER, THE½** (1968) 124m WB/Seven Arts c

Alan Arkin *(John Singer)*, Laurinda Barrett *(Mrs. Kelly)*, Stacy Keach, Jr. *(Blount)*, Chuck McCann *(Antonapoulos)*, Biff McGuire *(Mr. Kelly)*, Sondra Locke *(Mick Kelly)*, Percy Rodriguez *(Dr. Copeland)*, Cicely Tyson *(Portia)*, Jackie Marlowe *(Bubber Kelly)*, Johnny Popwell *(Willie)*, Wayne Smith *(Harry)*, Peter Mamakos *(Spiramonedes)*, John O'Leary *(Beaudine)*, Hubert Harper *(Brannon)*, Anna Lee Carroll *(Nurse Bradford)*, Ronald A. Riner *(Deputy Sheriff Ivor)*.

The touching McCullers novel is here capsulized in a less than rewarding film where Arkin plays a deaf mute who earns his living as a silversmith engraver. When his closest friend, McCann, another mute who is also retarded, is placed in a distant institution, Arkin moves to a small town to be near him. He rents a room in the home of McGuire and Barrett who need money since McGuire is unemployed and is recuperating with a broken hip. Locke, the family's teenage daughter, resents being moved from her room to make a space for Arkin. He later wins her over by interesting her in classical music. Getting a job in the area, Arkin also befriends Keach, an alcoholic who later develops a kidney infection, and Rodriguez, a segregationist black physician whose only ambition in life is to have his daughter Tyson better her life; she is a domestic servant and is married to an illiterate field hand, Popwell. Moreover, Rodriguez is dying of cancer, a secret he tells Arkin to keep from Tyson. Popwell is later jailed after a run-in with white bigots and he loses a leg after being chained up, following a jailbreak attempt. Locke, meanwhile, has a sexual affair with Smith and loses her virginity, which confuses and angers her. When she learns that her father McGuire will be a permanent cripple and she must work to support the family, she turns against Arkin, making his life miserable. Then Arkin goes to visit his pal Keach only to learn he has been dead for a number of weeks. The world has turned black as well as silent for Arkin; he returns to his lonely room and kills himself. Feeling guilty, Locke visits Arkin's grave and meets Rodriguez. They talk about Arkin and their problems and Locke admits that Arkin in his quiet way has helped her through her crisis. The film does not work well despite Arkin's fine effort. Unlike the novel which details human nuances and the subtleties of racism and hatred for the deformed, the film attempts to encompass too much and misses much, presenting disjointed character development. The direction by Miller is choppy and flat and the entire production is a poor pasteup of the story. Other than Arkin, the cast, including Keach in a stereotyped, predictable role, is unconvincing. Locke is over her head and plays the spoiled brat with no energy at all, just a carping posture and a vocal delivery guaranteed to annoy.

p, Thomas C. Ryan, Marc Merson; d, Robert Ellis Miller; w, Ryan (based on the novel by Carson McCullers); ph, James Wong Howe (Technicolor); m, Dave Grusin; ed, John F. Burnett; art d, LeRoy Deane; cos, Albert Wolsky; makeup, Al Greenway.

Drama **Cas.** **(PR:O MPAA:G)**

HEART LIKE A WHEEL½** (1983) 113m Aurora/FOX c

Bonnie Bedelia *(Shirley Muldowney)*, Beau Bridges *(Connie Kalitta)*, Leo Rossi *(Jack Muldowney)*, Hoyt Axton *(Tex Roque)*, Bill McKinney *("Big Daddy" Don Garlits)*, Anthony Edwards *(John Muldowney Age 15-23)*, Dean Paul Martin *(Sonny Rigotti)*, Paul Bartel *(Chef Paul)*, Missy Basile *(Angela)*, Michael Cavanaugh *(NHRA Boss)*, Ellen Geer *(Mrs. Marianne Kalitta)*, Nora Heflin *(Nurse North)*, Byron Thames *(John Age 10-13)*, Tiny Wells *(Tiny)*, Brandon Brent Williams *(John Age 5-8)*, Jesse Aragon *(Carlos)*, Bruce Barloe *(Bass Player)*, Catherine Paolone *(Mrs. Good Joe)*, Michel Barrere *(NHRA Guard)*, Creed Bratton *(Photographer)*, Tiffany Brissette *(Little Shirley)*, Paul Bryar *(Matt)*, James Burton *(Guitar Player)*, Jill Carroll *(John's Girl Friend)*, Martin Casella, Paul Linke *(Reporters)*, Sandy Chanley *(Fan)*, Diane Delano *(Shirley's Sister)*, Leonard Termo *(Good Joe)*, Terence Knox *(Jack's Friend)*, Sam Posey *(Himself)*, Tom Duffield, Chris Fontana, Marvin Graham, Tim Kimber, Steve Evans, Mitzi Hoag, Dick Miller.

An insightful biography of auto racing champ Shirley "ChaCha" Muldowney. Beginning with the foreshadowing image of little Shirley driving dad Axton's sedan, it leads up to her first race in 1966. Met with the usual sexism, she surprises all by breaking the track record on her qualifying run. It's all the way up from there, at least career-wise. Her marriage to mechanic Rossi ends in divorce when he realizes that he can't handle his wife's success. She then turns to banned driver Bridges for support and love as she goes on to win the National Hot Rod Association World Championship three times. Bedelia in her role as the racing lady is good, carrying her role beyond the tough broad image.

p, Charles Roven; d, Jonathan Kaplan; w, Ken Friedman; ph, Tak Fujimoto (DeLuxe Color); m, Laurence Rosenthal; ed, O. Nicholas Brown; prod d, James William Newport; set d, Tom Duffield; cos, William Ware Theiss; m/l, "Born to Win," Tom Snow (sung by Jill Michaels).

Biography **Cas.** **(PR:C MPAA:PG)**

HEART OF A CHILD*½ (1958, Brit.) 76m Beaconsfield/RANK bw

Jean Anderson *(Maria Heiss)*, Donald Pleasence *(Speil)*, Richard Williams *(Karl Speil)*, Maureen Pryor *(Frau Speil)*, John Glynn Jones *(Priest)*, Andrew Keir *(Constable)*, Norman MacOwan *(Heiss)*, Carla Challoner *(Elsa)*, Willoughby Goddard *(Sott)*, John Boxer.

Pleasence is a cruel man who beats up his young son (Williams) and threatens to sell the boy's beloved St. Bernard dog to the local butcher. Williams sells his dog to an amiable veterinarian, but when Pleasence finds out, he beats the boy again. The dog, with the help of spinster Anderson, rescue Williams after he is trapped in a snowstorm. Anderson marries the vet and Pleasence finally gives in to the boy, allowing him to keep the dog. A heavy-handed drama and not particularly entertaining.

p, Alfred Shaughnessy; d, Clive Donner; w, Leigh Vance (based on the novel by Phyllis Bottome); ph, Peter Hennessy.

Drama **(PR:C MPAA:NR)**

HEART OF A MAN, THE** (1959, Brit.) 92m RANK bw

Frankie Vaughan *(Frankie)*, Anne Heywood *(Julie)*, Tony Britton *(Tony)*, Peter Sinclair *(Bud)*, Michael Medwin *(Sid)*, Anthony Newley *(Johnny)*, Harry Fowler *(Razor)*, George Rose *(Charlie)*, Harold Kasket *(Oscar)*, Vanda *(Cha Cha)*, Leslie Mitchell, Kent Walton, Hogan "Kid" Bassey.

Vaughan stars as a navy man who turns vocalist and shoots to the top with a record contract. The catalysts are an inspirational meeting with a bum, a girl singer and the nightclub where he works. Anthony Newley is successful in providing the support for this mediocre musical. Tunes include: "The Heart Of A Man," "Sometime, Somewhere," and "Walking Tall," all three sung by Vaughan.

p, Anna Neagle; d, Herbert Wilcox; w, Jack Trevor Story, Pamela Bower (based on a story by Rex North); ph, Reginald Wyer; m, Wally Stott; ed, Basil Warren.

Musical **(PR:A MPAA:NR)**

HEART OF A NATION, THE*** (1943, Fr.) 111m TRC bw (UNTEL PERE ET FILS)

Louis Jouvet *(Pierre Froment/Felix)*, Raimu *(Jules Froment)*, Suzy Prim *(Estelle)*, Michele Morgan *(Marie)*, Jean Mercanton *(Alain)*, Renee Devilliers *(Gabrielle)*, Harry Krimer *(Robert Leonard)*, Pierre Jordan *(Christian)*, Lucien Nat *(Bernard)*, Charles Boyer *(Commentator)*, Robert Le Vigan, Biscot, Colette Darfeuil.

The story of occupied France is told in this biography of a Montmarte family from the Franco-Prussian war in 1871 to the Nazi occupation in 1940. Events include Nat's wedding, Raimu's visit to the Moulin Rouge, Morgan losing her arm in WW I, and the arrival of the Nazi troops. Real life began to parallel this picture when the Germans ordered the negative and all prints destroyed after viewing it. But the "cinema resistance" saved the film. A copy was smuggled out and buried by a man alongside a road, a common practice during the Occupation. Henri Langlois and Georges Franju at the Cinematheque Francaise saved literally thousands of films from destruction. This, however, was not done without the cooperation of German officer Frank Hensel, himself a noted film devotee. Eventually, a reel at a time, the film made its way to unoccupied France, and then the U.S. where Duvivier completed it in 1943, though it was shot three years earlier. (In French; English subtitles.)

p, Paul Graetz; d, Julien Duvivier; w, Duvivier, Charles Spaak, Marcel Achard; ph, Jules Kruger; ed, George Freedland; md, Jean Weiner; art d, Guy de Gastyne; cos, Rosine Delamare.

Drama **(PR:A MPAA:NR)**

HEART OF ARIZONA½** (1938) 68m PAR bw

William Boyd *(Hopalong Cassidy)*, George "Gabby" Hayes *(Windy)*, Russell Hayden *(Lucky)*, John Elliott *(Buck Peters)*, Billy King *(Artie)*, Natalie Moorhead *(Belle Starr)*, Dorothy Short *(Jacqueline Starr)*, [Stephen] Alden Chase *(Dan Ringo)*, John Beach *(Sheriff Hawley)*, Lane Chandler *(Trimmer Windler)*, Leo MacMahon *(Twister)*.

Boyd as usual helps out a wronged rancher. This time it's Moorhead who, after some time in prison, returns to the homestead only to wander into the path of blazing bullets, and is saved by Boyd, in an unbelievable rescue. Up to par with the rest of the series, with plenty of gunplay and action. (See HOPALONG CASSIDY series, Index)

p, Harry Sherman; d, Lesley Selander; w, Norman Houston (based on a story by Clarence E. Mulford); ph, Russell Harlan; ed, Sherman Rose.

Western **(PR:A MPAA:NR)**

HEART OF NEW YORK** (1932) 65m WB bw

George Sidney, Joe Smith, Charlie Dale, Aline MacMahon, Anna Appel, Marion Byron, Oscar Apfel, Donald Cook, Ann Brody, Ruth Hall, Harold Waldridge, George MacFarlane, Charles Coleman.

Set on New York's Hester Street, this Mervyn LeRoy helmed picture concerns the saga of a Jewish plumber who invents the washing machine. He becomes a millionaire and finds that a string of domestic problems accompany his new-found luxury. Far too talkative.

d, Mervyn LeRoy; w, Arthur Caesar, Houston Branch (based on the story "Mendel Marantz" by David Freedman); ph, James Van Trees; ed, Perry Morse.

Comedy **(PR:A MPAA:NR)**

HEART OF PARIS*** (1939, Fr.) 85m Tri-National bw (GRIBOUILLE)

Raimu *(Camille)*, Jeanne Provost *(Louise)*, Michele Morgan *(Natalie)*, Gilbert Gil *(Claude)*, Jean Worms *(Presiding Judge)*, Carette *(Lurette)*, Marcel Andre *(Prosecutor)*, Jacques Gretillat *(Counsel for the Defense)*, Jacques Baumer *(Mariner)*, Rene Bergeron *(Kuhlmann)*, Simeon *(Guerin)*, Nicholas Rimsky *(Taxi Driver)*.

Director Allegret again cast Morgan, after her debut in ORAGE, as an outcast girl acquitted of the murder of her boy friend. Raimu is an elderly juror who befriends her and lets her stay in his bourgeois home. This upsets the family's balance and causes his son to take extreme measures. Raimu, who gained fame in Maurice Pagnol's triology (MARIUS, FANNY, CESAR) is exceptional, and the same goes for Morgan who can be remembered in THE FALLEN IDOL. (In French; English subtitles.)

p, Andre Daven; d, Marc Allegret; w, Marcel Achard, H.G. Lustig (based on a story by Achard); ph, G. Benoit, A. Thirard, M. Kelber; ed, Yvonne Beauge.

Drama **(PR:A MPAA:NR)**

HEART OF THE GOLDEN WEST½** (1942) 65m REP bw

Roy Rogers *(Roy)*, Smiley Burnette *(Smiley)*, George "Gabby" Hayes *(Gabby)*, Bob Nolan and The Sons of the Pioneers *(Themselves)*, Ruth Terry *(Mary Lou Popen)*, Walter Catlett *(Col. Silas Popen)*, Paul Harvey *(James Barrabee)*, Edmund MacDonald *(Ross Lambert)*, Leigh Whipper *(Rango)*, William Haade *(Cully Bronson)*, The Hall Johnson Choir, Hal Taliaferro, Cactus Mack, Hank Bell, Fred Burns, Carl Mathews, Horace B. Carpenter, Frank McCarroll, Art Dillard, "Trigger."

The old West gets a shot in the arm from the modern age of transportation when a trucking company and a steamboat vie for the opportunity to haul cattle. With Gene Autry entering the Army, Roy Rogers was given the top singing cowboy spot at Republic. Here he's blessed with a pair of sidekicks, Hayes and Burnette, the latter Autry's former pal. Together with the ever-dependable Trigger the trio foils the trucker's sneaky attempt to get the cattle contract. The Hall Johnson Choir delivers "Carry Me Back To Old Virginny." (See ROY ROGERS series, Index.)

p&d, Joseph Kane; w, Earl Felton; ph, Jack Marta; ed, Richard Van Enger; md, Morton Scott; art d, Russell Kimball.

Western **Cas.** **(PR:A MPAA:NR)**

HEART OF THE MATTER, THE½** (1954, Brit.) 105m London Films/Associated Artists bw

Trevor Howard *(Harry Scobie)*, Elizabeth Allan *(Louise Scobie)*, Maria Schell *(Helen Rolt)*, Denholm Elliott *(Wilson)*, Peter Finch *(Father Rank)*, Gerard Oury *(Yusef)*, George Coulouris *(Portuguese Captain)*, Earl Cameron *(Ali)*, Michael Hordern *(Commissioner)*, Colin Gordon *(Colonial Secretary)*, Cyril Raymond *(Carter)*, Orlando Martins *(Rev. Clay)*, Evelyn Roberts *(Col. Wright)*, Gillian Lind *(Mrs. Carter)*, John Rae *(Loder)*, Peter Burton *(Perrot)*, Eileen Thorndike *(Mrs. Bowles)*, Anthony Snell *(Doctor)*, Jane Henderson *(Miss Malcott)*, Stanley Lunin *(Forbes)*, Eugene Leahy *(Newall)*, Chris Rhodes *(French Officer)*, Judith Furse *(Dr. Sykes)*, Ewan Roberts *(Druce)*, Jack Allen *(RNVR Lieutenant)*, John Akar *(Negro Servant)*, John Glyn-Jones *(Harris)*, Assany Kamara Wilson *(African Sergeant)*, Saidu Fofana, Errol John *(African Policemen)*.

Howard is the very religious police commissioner in Sierra Leone circa 1942. He and Allan have a marriage in name only and when she goes off on vacation, he falls for refugee Schell, a survivor of a boat which had been torpedoed by a Nazi sub. The resultant guilt that Howard suffers becomes the heart of the matter. It's essentially a quadrangle between Howard, Allan, Schell, and religion. Much of what Greene writes takes place in the minds of the protagonists and this is no exception, so there is not as much dramatic revelation as one would desire from a screenplay. Howard cannot conceive of divorce and remarriage and the only alternative is suicide, an even greater sin in the eyes of the church (portrayed nicely by Finch as the local priest). The emotional travails experienced by Howard are what cause him to eventually give up and take his own life. A lot of talk, most of which is quite sophisticated and replete with wise badinage, is what highlights the movie but it never grips the viewer in the way that the novel did.

p, Ian Dalrymple; d, George More O'Ferrall; w, Dalrymple, Lesley Storm (based on the novel by Graham Greene); ph, Jack Hildyard; m, Edric Connor; ed, Sidney Stone; prod d, Joseph Bato; cos, Julia Squire.

Drama **(PR:A-C MPAA:NR)**

HEART OF THE NORTH*** (1938) 74m WB c

Dick Foran *(Sgt. Alan Baker)*, Gloria Dickson *(Joyce McMillan)*, Gale Page *(Elizabeth Spaulding)*, Allen Jenkins *(Bill Hardsock)*, Patric Knowles *(Jim Montgomery)*, Janet Chapman *(Judy Montgomery)*, James Stephenson *(Inspector Stephen Gore)*, Anthony Averill *(Whipple)*, Joe Sawyer *(Red Crocker)*, Joseph King *(Mac Drummond)*, Russell Simpson *(Dave MacMillan)*, Arthur Gardner *(Larry Young)*, Pedro de Cordoba *(Father Claverly)*, Alec Hartford *(Lunnon Dick)*, Robert Homans *(Capt. Ashmun)*, Anderson Lawler *(Burgoon)*, Bruce Carruthers *(Pedeault)*, Garry Owen *(Tom Ryan)*.

Foran and the Northwest Mounted Police pursue a gang of thieves who stole a shipment of gold and furs from an Edmonton-bound freighter. When an innocent trapper is accused of aiding the crooks, Foran saves him by arriving before the angry lynch mob does him in. Photographed in Technicolor, Warners made the best of the picturesque scenery found in the Great Northwest, highlighted by an array of chase scenes—in canoes, boats, and planes—as well as a cliff-top skirmish.

p, Bryan Foy; d, Lewis Seiler; w, Lee Katz, Vincent Sherman (based on a novel by William Byron Mowery); ph, L. William O'Connell, Wilfrid M. Cline (Technicolor); ed, Louis Hesse.

Adventure **(PR:A MPAA:NR)**

HEART OF THE RIO GRANDE*½ (1942) 68m REP bw

Gene Autry *(Himself)*, Smiley Burnette *(Frog)*, Fay McKenzie *(Alice Bennett)*, Edith Fellows *(Connie Lane)*, Pierre Watkin *(Mr. Lane)*, Joe Strauch, Jr. *(Tadpole)*, William Haade *(Hap Callahan)*, Sarah Padden *(Mrs. Forbes)*, Jean Porter *(Pudge)*, The Jimmy Wakely Trio, Milton Kibbee, Edmund Cobb, Budd Buster, Frank Mills, Howard Mitchell, Allan Wood, Nora Lane, Mady Lawrence, Buck Woods, Harry Depp, George Porter, Frankie Marvin, Jeannie Hebers, Kay Frye, Jane Graham, Patsy Fay Northup, Jan Lester, Gloria and Gladys Gardner, "Champion."

One of the least successful Autry westerns has the star and sidekick Burnette lending a hand to a prim and proper gal who tries her luck at running a ranch.

Taking lessons from the singing cowboy and Mother Nature, she soon becomes a seasoned rancher. (See GENE AUTRY series, Index.)

p, Harry Grey; d, William Morgan; w, Lillie Hayward, Winston Miller (based on a story by Newlin B. Wildes); ph, Harry Neumann; ed, Lester Orlebeck; md, Raoul Kraushaar.

Western **Cas.** **(PR:A MPAA:NR)**

HEART OF THE ROCKIES** (1937) 58m REP bw

Robert Livingston *(Stony Brook)*, Ray Corrigan *(Tucson Smith)*, Max Terhune *(Lullaby Joslin)*, Lynne Roberts *(Lorna)*, Sammy McKim *(Davey)*, J.P. McGowan *(Dawson)*, Yakima Canutt *(Enoch)*, Hal Taliaferro [Wally Wales] *(Charlie)*, Georgia Simmons *(Ma Dawson)*, Maston Williams, Guy Wilkerson, Ranny Weeks, George Pierce, Nelson McDowell, Herman's Mountaineers.

Mesquiteers Livingston, Corrigan, and Terhune are wrongly accused of shooting a bear which is dipping into their stock. The park rangers come down on the trio, only to discover that a gang of cattle rustlers are to blame. This was the first of the series to be directed by Joseph Kane, ace low-budget film director for Republic. (See THREE MESQUITEERS series, Index.)

p, Sol C. Siegel; d, Joseph Kane; w, Jack Natteford, Oliver Drake (based on a story by Bernard McConville); ph, Jack Marta; ed, Lester Orlebeck.

Western **Cas.** **(PR:A MPAA:NR)**

HEART OF THE ROCKIES½** (1951) 67m REP bw

Roy Rogers *(Himself)*, Penny Edwards *(June)*, Gordon Jones *(Splinters)*, Ralph Morgan *(Andrew Willard)*, Fred Graham *(Devery)*, Mira McKinney *(Mrs. Edsel)*, Robert "Buzz" Henry *(Dave Braddock)*, William Gould *(Warden Parker)*, Pepe Hern *(Rocky)*, Rand Brooks *(Corley)*, Foy Willing and the Riders of the Purple Sage, "Trigger."

Roy, with faithful horse Trigger and dog Bullet in tow, is put in charge of a highway construction project. The road runs across the land of rancher Morgan who fears that the authorities are going to discover the unscrupulous manner in which he acquired his property. He sends his henchmen out to halt Rogers' progress, but the attempts are thwarted by our hero. Republic had enough foresight to realize that the genre would soon come to an end if it did not modernize its plots, which is exactly what happened. This time Edwards was Rogers' gal, replacing Dale Evans who retired a year earlier. (See ROY ROGERS series, Index.)

p, Edward J. White; d, William Witney; w, Eric Taylor; ph, Reggie Lanning; m, R. Dale Butts; ed, Tony Martinelli; art d, Frank Hotaling; m/l, Foy Willing, Geri Gallian, Jack Elliott.

Western **(PR:A MPAA:NR)**

HEART OF THE WEST½** (1937) 63m PAR bw

William Boyd *(Hopalong Cassidy)*, Jimmy Ellison *(Johnny Nelson)*, George "Gabby" Hayes *(Windy)*, Lynn Gabriel *(Sally Jordan)*, Sidney Blackmer *(Big John Trumbull)*, Charles Martin *(Jim Jordan)*, John Rutherford *(Tom Paterson)*, Warner Richmond *(Johnson)*, Walter Miller *(Whitey)*, Ted Adams *(Saxon)*, Fred Kohler *(Barton)*, Robet McKenzie *(Tim Grady)*, John Elliott.

Boyd and Ellison lend a hand to ranch owner Gabriel, who is involved in a fence war with neighboring rancher Blackmer. The highlight is a cattle stampede brought under control by Boyd's careful use of dynamite charges. (See HOPALONG CASSIDY series, Index.)

p, Harry Sherman; d, Howard Bretherton; w, Doris Schroeder (based on the story by Clarence E. Mulford); ph, Archie Stout; ed, Edward Schroeder; m/l, Sam Coslow, Victor Young.

Western **(PR:A MPAA:NR)**

HEART OF VIRGINIA** (1948) 60m REP bw

Janet Martin *(Virginia Galtry)*, Robert Lowery *(Dan Lockwood)*, Frankie Darro *(Jimmy Easter)*, Paul Hurst *(Whit Galtry)*, Sam McDaniel *("Sunflower" Jones)*, Tom Chatterton *(Dr. Purdy)*, Bennie Bartlett *(Breezy Brent)*, Glen Vernon *(Bud Landeen)*, Edmund Cobb *(Gas Station Attendant)*.

Darro is a jockey who is shaken after he causes the death of a fellow rider during a race. He's put on the right track, however, when the daughter of his ex-boss puts her faith in him.

p, Sidney Picker; d, R.G. Springsteen; w, Jerry Sackheim, John K. Butler; ph, John MacBurnie; ed, Irving M. Schoenberg; md, Morton Scott.

Drama **(PR:A MPAA:NR)**

HEART PUNCH** (1932) 62m Mayfair bw

Lloyd Hughes, Marion Schilling, George Lewis, Wheeler Oakman, Mae Busch, Walter Miller, Gordon De Main, James Leong.

Boxer Hughes kills his opponent with a punch to the heart. He then falls in love with the dead man's sister in this well-photographed though routine boxing picture.

d, Breezy Eason; w, J.T. Neville (based on the story by Frank Howard Clark); ph, George Meehan; ed, Jeanne Spencer; art d, Paul Palmentola.

Sports Drama **(PR:A MPAA:NR)**

HEART SONG** (1933, Brit.) 81m PC-UFA/FOX bw (GB: THE ONLY GIRL)

Lilian Harvey *(Juliette)*, Charles Boyer *(Duke)*, Mady Christians *(Empress)*, Ernest Thesiger *(Chamberlain)*, Maurice Evans *(Didier)*, Friedel Schuster *(Annabel)*, Julius Falkenstein *(Offenbach)*, Huntley Wright *(Doctor)*, Ruth Maitland *(Marianne)*, O.B. Clarence *(Etienne)*, Reginald Smith.

Boyer hears a beautiful singing voice and immediately falls in love with its source. Little does this German duke realize that the voice belongs not to an empress but to hairdresser Harvey. This film is notable as being another unsuccessful attempt to broaden the popularity of Harvey outside of England. It was a British production made at the famed UFA studio in pre-Hitler Germany with a mostly English cast.

p, Erich Pommer; d, Friedrich Hollaender; w, Robert Stevenson, John Heygate (based on a story by Robert Liebman, Walter Reisch, Felix Salten); ph, F. Behn-Grund.

Drama **(PR:A MPAA:NR)**

HEART WITHIN, THE½** (1957, Brit.) 61m Rank bw

James Hayter *(Grandfather Willard)*, Earl Cameron *(Victor Conway)*, David Hemmings *(Danny Willard)*, Clifford Evans *(Matthew Johnson)*, Betty Cooper *(Miss Trevor)*, Dan Jackson *(Joe Martell)*, Jack Stewart *(Inspector Matheson)*, Frank Singineau *(Bobo)*, Gloria Simpson *(Violet)*, Janice Hughes *(Dilli)*, Paula Henriques *(Ella)*, Denton De Gray *(Gow)*, Wally Thomas *(Police Sergeant)*, Brian Tyler *(1st Boy)*, Dawson France *(2nd Boy)*, Frank Pettitt *(1st Constable)*, Glyn Edwards *(2nd Constable)*, Ivor Salter *(3rd Constable)*, Kings of The Caribbean Steel Band.

Well-enacted realization of a man being accused of a murder due to the color of his skin. Cameron is the man from the West Indies under suspicion, aided in his attempt to escape the law by Hemmings. Their friendship develops to the point where Cameron saves the boy's life when he falls into the grips of the actual murderer. Intriguing effort given power mainly through the handling of the theme of prejudice.

p, Jon Penington; d, David Eady; w, Geoffrey Orme (based on the story by John Baxter); ph, Ernest Palmer.

Crime/Drama **(PR:A MPAA:NR)**

HEARTACHES** (1947) 71m PRC bw

Sheila Ryan *(Toni Wentworth)*, Edward Norris *(Jimmy McDonald)*, Chill Wills *(Hoagey Mann)*, Ken Farrell *(Vic Mortan)*, James Seay *(Lt. Armstrong)*, Frank Orth *(Mike Connelly)*, Chili Williams *(Sally)*, Charles Mitchell *(Pete Schilling)*, Al LaRue *(DeLong)*, Phyllis Planchard *(Lila)*, Ann Staunton *(Anne Connelly)*.

Norris is a reporter investigating a pair of killings surrounding the career of screen singer Farrell. When news leaks out that Wills actually does Farrell's crooning, Norris begins to piece together this whodunit.

p, Ben Stoloff, Marvin D. Stahl; d, Basil Wrangell; w, George Bricker (based on a story by Monty F. Collins, Julian I. Peyser); ph, Jack Greenhalgh; ed, Charles Gross, Jr.; md, Irving Freedman; art d, Edward C. Jewell; m/l, Kim Gannon, Walter Kent, John Klenner, Al Hoffman.

Mystery **(PR:A MPAA:NR)**

HEARTACHES*** (1981, Can.) 93m Rising Star c

Margot Kidder *(Rita Harris)*, Annie Potts *(Bonnie Howard)*, Robert Carradine *(Stanley Howard)*, Winston Rekert *(Marcello Di Stassi)*, George Touliatos *(Mario Di Stassi)*, Guy Sanvido *(Aldo)*, Arnie Achtman *(Alvin)*, Michael Zeiniker *(Andy)*, Peggy Feury *(Doctor)*, Jefferson Mappin *(Willy)*, Maureen Fitzgerald *(Anna)*, Albert Bernardo *(Stefane)*.

One of the better tax-shelter pictures to come out of Canada. Potts is the well-meaning wife of Carradine, a drunk who wastes his time racing cars. She leaves him rather than tell him she's carrying another man's child. On her way to the big city she meets the always brassy Kidder, a tough loudmouth, and reluctantly travels with her. The unlikely pair end up working in a factory where Kidder falls for the owner's Italian nephew. Potts is left to deal with Carradine, who tracks her down and tries to win her back. Kidder, as well as the rest of the cast, delivers a strong, if obnoxious, performance.

p, Peter Kroonenburg, David J. Patterson, Jerry Raibourn; d, Donald Shebib; w, Terence Heffernan; ph, Vic Sarin; m, Simon Michael Martin; ed, Gerry Hambling, Peter Boita.

Comedy **Cas.** **(PR:O MPAA:R)**

HEARTBEAT½** (1946) 100m RKO bw

Ginger Rogers *(Arlette)*, Jean Pierre Aumont *(Pierre)*, Adolphe Menjou *(Ambassador)*, Basil Rathbone *(Prof. Aristide)*, Melville Cooper *(Roland Medeville)*, Mikhail Rasumny *(Yves Cadubert)*, Mona Maris *(Ambassador's Wife)*, Henry Stephenson *(Minister)*, Eduardo Ciannelli *(Baron Dvorak)*, Eddie Hayden *(Fat Thief)*.

Ginger Rogers enrolls in Basil Rathbone's pickpocket school in Paris and emerges the star pupil. She takes her newly learned skills to an embassy ball where she tries to make Aumont her first victim. Instead, she falls in love with him. Rogers again was coupled with Sam Wood, the director who brought her the Oscar winning role in KITTY FOYLE. Unfortunately, much of Wood's wit and style had by now begun to diminish. Rogers delivers only one melody, "Can You Guess" penned by Paul Misraki and Ervin Drake. Strong performances by a stellar cast make up for Wood's weaknesses.

p, Robert Hakim, Raymond Hakim; d, Sam Wood; w, Morrie Ryskind, Roland Leigh (based on the French screenplay "Battlement de Coeur" by Hans Wilhelm, Max Kolpe, Michel Duran); ph, Joseph Valentine; m, Paul Misraki; ed, Roland Gross; md, C. Bakaleinikoff; art d, Lionel Banks; set d, George Sawley; cos, Howard Greer; makeup, Mel Burns.

Comedy/Romance **Cas.** **(PR:A MPAA:NR)**

HEARTBEEPS** (1981) 88m UNIV c

Andy Kaufman *(Val)*, Bernadette Peters *(Aqua)*, Randy Quaid *(Charlie)*, Kenneth McMillan *(Max)*, Melanie Mayron *(Susan)*, Christopher Guest *(Calvin)*, Richard B. Shull *(Factory Boss)*, Dick Miller *(Watchman)*, Kathleen Freeman *(Helicopter Pilot)*, Mary Woronov *(Party House Owner)*, Paul Bartel, Anne Wharton *(Guests)*, Barry Diamond, Stephanie Faulkner *(Firing Range Technicians)*, Jeffrey Kramer *(Butler Robot)*, Irene Forrest, Karsen Lee Gould *(Maid Robots)*, David Gene Lebell *(Fork-lift Drive Robot)*.

A flop when first released, HEARTBEEPS is not bad. It's a likable, sentimental film starring Kaufman and Peters as two household robots who, in the year 1995, fall in love and set out on their own. They assemble a smaller "child" robot out of spare parts and even acquire a robot "uncle," a discarded comedian android, thus building themselves a family. The film does have some major problems (John Williams' overbearing musical score being among them), but HEARTBEEPS does have some moments of inescapable charm. Directed by Allan Arkush (ROCK 'N' ROLL HIGH SCHOOL, GET CRAZY).

p, Michael Phillips; d, Alan Arkush; w, John Hill; ph, Charles Rosher (Panavision, Technicolor); m, John Williams; ed, Tina Hirsch; prod d, John W. Corso; cos, Madeline Graneto, Theadora Van Runkle; spec eff, Stan Winston, Albert Whitlock.

Science Fiction/Comedy Cas. (PR:A MPAA:PG)

HEARTBREAK** (1931) 63m FOX bw

Charles Farrell *(John Merrick)*, Madge Evans *(Countess Vima Walden)*, Hardie Albright *(Count Carl Walden)*, Paul Cavanagh *(Capt. Wolke)*, John Arledge *(Jerry Sommers)*, Claude King *(Count Walden)*, John St. Polis *(U.S. Ambassador)*, Capt. Albert Conti *(Liaison Officer)*.

A film set in Vienna in 1916 assures lots of waltzing, and this one delivers. Farrell is berated by his commanding officers when he travels over enemy lines to visit his girl. He brings her the unfortunate news that he killed her brother in an aerial battle, and tells her how sorry he is. She tosses him out, but changes her mind and calls him back—after all, he did risk his life to see her.

d, Alfred Werker; w, Leon Gordon, William Conselman (based on a story by Llewellyn Hughes); ph, Joseph August; ed, Margaret Clancy.

War/Romance (PR:A MPAA:NR)

HEARTBREAK KID, THE** (1972) 104m Palomar/FOX c

Charles Grodin *(Lenny Cantrow)*, Jeannie Berlin *(Lila Kolodny)*, Cybill Shepherd *(Kelly Corcoran)*, Eddie Albert *(Mr. Corcoran)*, Audra Lindley *(Mrs. Corcoran)*, William Prince *(Colorado Man)*, Mitchell Jason *(Cousin Ralph)*, Augusta Dabney *(Colorado Woman)*, Art Metrano *(Entertainer)*, Marilyn Putnam *(Mrs. Kolodny)*, Jack Hausman *(Mr. Kolodny)*, Erik Lee Preminger *(Pecan Pie Waiter)*, Tim Browne *(Kelly's Boy Friend)*, Jean Scoppa *(Flower Girl)*, Greg Pecque *(Young Boy)*, Doris Roberts *(Mrs. Cantrow)*.

Grodin and Berlin are a pair of whiny newlyweds on their way to a Florida vacation, when Grodin finds himself perturbed by Berlin's idiosyncrasies. He turns his affections to the cool blonde Shepherd, whom he meets on the beach, quickly forgetting his matrimonial bond. Elaine May directed from Neil Simon's script which is admittedly less cardboard than usual, but still disturbing. One humiliating scene has Berlin (May's real-life daughter) deliver her lines with egg salad smeared on her face. It is entirely devoid of humor and only brings a cringe to the viewer.

p, Edgar J. Scherick; d, Elaine May; w, Neil Simon (based on a story by Bruce Jay Friedman); ph, Owen Roizman (DeLuxe Color); m, Garry Sherman; ed, John Carter; art d, Richard Sylbert; cos, Anthea Sylbert; m/l, "The Heartbreak Kid," Cy Coleman, Sheldon Harnick.

Comedy Cas. (PR:C-O MPAA:PG)

HEARTBREAKER**½ (1983) 90m Emerson/Monorex c

Fernando Allende *(Beto)*, Dawn Dunlap *(Kim)*, Peter Gonzales Falcon *(Hector)*, Miguel Ferrar *(Angel)*, Michael D. Roberts *(Hopper)*, Robert Dryer *(Wings)*, Pepe Serna *(Loco)*, Rafael Campos *(Alfonso)*, Carmen Martinez *(Minnie)*, Carlo Allen *(Gato)*.

A harmless romance about a Chicano who falls in love with the new girl in town—the blonde Dunlap. The relationship brings the usual hostilities, occasionally rising above the cliche level. If one is searching for cultural insights, this isn't the place to look.

p, Chris P. Nebe, Chris Anders; d, Frank Zuniga; w, Vincente Gutierrez; ph, Michael Lonzo (Eastmancolor); m, Rob Walsh; ed, Larry Bock; art d, Pamela Warner, Mario Torero.

Romance/Drama (PR:C MPAA:R)

HEARTLAND**** (1980) 96m Wilderness Women Production/Filmhaus c

Rip Torn *(Clyde)*, Conchata Ferrell *(Elinore)*, Barry Primus *(Jack)*, Lilia Skala *(Grandma)*, Megan Folson *(Jerrine)*, Amy Wright *(Clara)*, Jerry Hardin *(Cattle Buyer)*, Mary Boyland *(Ma Gillis)*, Jeff Boschee, Robert Overholzer *(Land Office Agents)*, Bob Sirucek *(Dan)*, Marvin Berg *(Justice of Peace)*, Gary Voldseth, Mike Robertson, Doug Johnson *(Cowboys)*.

This authentic frontier story that touches the human heart has Ferrell as a rugged widow determined to make a good life for her 10-year-old daughter, Folson. To that end she answers an ad and travels to Wyoming to be the housekeeper for taciturn, skinflinty Torn, a hard-as-nails Scottish farmer who thinks only of his land and animals. Ferrell scrimps and saves from her meager salary, while slaving night and day for Torn. Slowly his barklike exterior begins to soften and he takes a liking to Ferrell, helping her to get some land of her own from a wealthy old eccentric female rancher, Skala. The harsh winter all but does Ferrell and her child in but Torn comes to their rescue and he marries Ferrell. She becomes pregnant and heroically delivers her child without medical help, but the infant later dies. Undaunted, the little family struggles on to survive, encouraged by the birth of a calf in the middle of savage elements that have decimated their small herd. Ferrell is nothing less than magnificent as the hearty mother who bears all burdens without complaint and looks to the future with inspired optimism. Torn is also superb as the farmer transformed from a bitter recluse to a loving and understanding life partner. This was the debut of director Pearce, a maker of documentaries, and it is sterling. His visual approach is rich and realistic and his restless cameras painstakingly record the hardscrabble existence of iron-willed pioneers attempting to tame the frontier just before the beginning of WW I. The script is sparse and telling and the performances understated and correct in every frame. A wonderful portrait drawn with care and conscience. The marvel of this production is that it was made for about $600,000 but has all the appearances of a major feature with expensive mounting. The moving story is based on the real-life experiences of Elinore Stewart, who described her frontier life in a series of beautifully written letters.

p, Michael Hausman, Beth Ferris; d, Richard Pearce; w, Ferris (based on the books and papers of Elinore Randall Stewart); ph, Fred Murphy (Panavision); m, Charles Gross; ed, Bill Yahraus; art d, Carl Copeland; cos, Hilary Rosenfeld.

Western/Drama Cas. (PR:A MPAA:NR)

HEART'S DESIRE** (1937, Brit.) 80m British International/Wardour bw

Richard Tauber *(Joseph Steidler)*, Leonora Corbett *(Frances Wilson)*, Kathleen Kelly *(Anna)*, Paul Graetz *(Florian)*, Carl Harbord *(Oliver Desmond)*, George Graves *(Granville Wilson)*, Diana Napier *(Diana Sheraton)*, Frank Vosper *(Van Straaten)*, Viola Tree *(Lady Bennington)*, C. Denier Warren *(Ted Mayer)*.

Tauber takes his tenor duties from Vienna's beer gardens to London's opera stage. While there, he falls in love with a Brit socialite, but is rejected and returns home to his Austrian sweetheart. Released in Britain in 1935.

p, Walter C. Mycroft; d, Paul Stein; w, Bruno Frank, L. Du Garde Peach, Roger Burford, Jack Davies, Jr., Clifford Grey (based on a story by Lioni Pickard); ph, John C. Cox; ed, Leslie Norman; md, G.H. Clutsam; art d, Clarence Elder; set d, Cedric Dawe; m/l, Richard Tauber.

Musical Cas. (PR:A MPAA:NR)

HEARTS DIVIDED*½ (1936) 70m COS/FN-WB bw

Marion Davies *(Betsy Patterson)*, Dick Powell *(Capt. Jerome Bonaparte)*, Charles Ruggles *(Henry)*, Claude Rains *(Napoleon)*, Edward Everett Horton *(John)*, Arthur Treacher *(Sir Harry)*, Henry Stephenson *(Charles Patterson)*, Clara Blandick *(Aunt Ellen)*, John Larkin *(Isham)*, Walter Kingsford *(Pichon)*, Etienne Girardot *(Du Fresne)*, Halliwell Hobbes *(Cambaceres)*, Hobart Cavanaugh *(Innkeeper)*, George Irving *(Thomas Jefferson)*, Hattie McDaniel *(Mammy)*, Sam McDaniel *(Servant)*, Freddie Archibald *(Gabriel)*, Beulah Bondi *(Madame Letizia)*, Phillip [Lucky] Hurlic *(Pippin)*, The Hall Johnson Choir.

Unfortunately for Dick Powell he was requested for this role by Marion Davies who wanted no one else for the part. She plays a Baltimore girl who gets romantically involved with Napoleon's brother, Powell. Claude Rains does his best as the French leader, coming across more believably than the rest. Beulah Bondi also appears in a bit. It's all very strained and supplies proof that wigs should not be worn by men, especially Powell. Produced by Cosmopolitan, the company owned by Davies' creator, newspaper mogul William Randolph Hearst. A remake of GLORIOUS BETSY (1928).

p, Harry Joe Brown; d, Frank Borzage; w, Laird Doyle, Casey Robinson (based on the play "Glorious Betsy" by Rida Johnson Young); ph, George Folsey; ed, William Holmes.

Romance (PR:A MPAA:NR)

HEARTS IN BONDAGE** (1936) 72m REP bw

James Dunn *(Kenneth)*, Mae Clarke *(Constance)*, David Manners *(Raymond)*, Charlotte Henry *(Julie)*, Henry B. Walthall *(Buchanan)*, Fritz Leiber *(Ericsson)*, George Irving *(Commodore Jordan)*, Irving Pichel *(Secretary Welles)*, J.M. Kerrigan *(Paddy)*, Frank McGlynn, Sr. *(President Lincoln)*, Ben Alexander *(Eggleston)*, Oscar Apfel *(Cap. Gillman)*, Clay Clement *(Worden)*, Edward Gargan *(McPherson)*, Russell Hicks *(Pillsbury)*, George Hayes *(Ezra)*, Douglas Wood *(Farragut)*, Bodil Rosing *(Mrs. Adams)*, Erville Alderson *(Jefferson Davies)*, John Hyams *(Bushnell)*, Etta McDaniels *(Mammy)*, Warner Richmond *(Bucko)*, Lloyd Ingraham *(Timekeeper)*, Lane Chandler, Hooper Atchley, Smiley Burnette, Eugene Jackson, Earl Aby, Henry Roquemore, Frankie Marvin, Arthur Wanzer, Helen Seaman, Cecil Watson, Maurice Brierre, Clinton Rosemond, Pat Flaherty.

The Civil War battle between the ships Monitor and Merrimac serves as the backdrop for a standard soap opera plot. The familiar romantic angle is taken, this time between naval hero Dunn and the sweet Clarke. This was the first of Lew Ayres' infrequent directing efforts.

p, Nat Levine; d, Lew Ayres; w, Bernard Schubert, Olive Cooper, Karl Brown (based on the story by Wallace McDonald); ph, Ernest Miller, Jack Marta; m, Hugo Riesenfeld; ed, Ralph Dixon; md, Harry Grey.

Drama/War (PR:A MPAA:NR)

HEARTS IN DIXIE**½ (1929) 71m FOX bw

Clarence Muse *(Nappus)*, Stepin Fetchit *(Gummy)*, Eugene Jackson *(Chinquapin)*, Bernice Pilot *(Chloe)*, Clifford Ingram *(Rammey)*, Mildred Washington *(Trallia)*, Zach Williams *(Deacon)*, Gertrude Howard *(Emmy)*, Dorothy Morrison *(Melia)*, Vivian Smith *(Violet)*, A.C.H. Billbrew *(Voodoo Woman)*, Richard Carlysle *(White Doctor)*, Robert Brooks, The Billbrew Chorus.

Unfortunately viewed only in the novelty sense as an "all-Negro film," this Civil War drama is good enough to stand on its own merits. Muse plays Grandpap Nappus who decides that his grandson should be educated in the North. Because of the death of his granddaughter, he must battle to convince the boy's stubborn father who vehemently disagrees. Stepin Fetchit takes on a major role and turns in one of his finest performances. Much of it is a stereotyped view of the black way of life, but this picture is no worse an offender than many other Hollywood products. Originally released with a sympathy-raising speech that opened the film.

p&d, Paul Sloane; w, Walter Weems; ph, Glen MacWilliams; m, Howard Jackson; ch, Fanchon and Marco; m/l, title song, Jackson.

Drama (PR:A MPAA:NR)

HEARTS IN EXILE** (1929) 82m WB bw

Dolores Costello *(Vera Zvanova)*, Grant Withers *(Paul Pavloff)*, James R. Kirkwood *(Baron Serge Palma)*, George Fawcett *(Dmitri Ivanova)*, David Torrence *(Governor)*, Olive Tell *(Anna Rascova)*, William Irving *(Rat Catcher)*, Tom Dugan *(Soldier)*, Rose Dione *(Maid)*, Carrie Daumery.

A weak love story set in Russia which centers on Costello, a fisherman's daughter. After her true love, Withers, refuses to marry her, she weds a baron, Kirkwood. Years later the two men meet, exiled to Siberia. When Withers is given a chance to return home he switches places with the other man, so that he may be reunited with Costello. However, she has journeyed to Siberia where the passion of older flames is rekindled. To prove himself a martyr, the baron commits suicide, thereby sealing the original lovers' future together. At this point director Michael Curtiz lost sight of his aims and filmed two different endings. Depending on which audience you were in you either saw them live happily ever after in freedom, or not so happily in captivity. Either way they spent the remainder of their existence together.

d, Michael Curtiz; w, Harvey Gates (based on a play by John Oxenham); ph, Bill Rees; ed, Thomas Pratt; m/l, "Like a Breath of Springtime," Joe Burke, Al Dubin.

Romance (PR:A MPAA:NR)

HEARTS OF HUMANITY** (1932) 56m Majestic bw

Jean Hersholt, Jackie Searl, J. Farrell MacDonald, Claudia Dell, Charles Delaney, Lucille LaVerne, Dick Wallace, George Humbert, Betty Jane Graham, John Vosberg, Tom McGuire.

A sappy little drama with Hersholt cast as a Jewish antique dealer, and Searl, the son of an Irish cop. When the kid is accidentally shot Hersholt comes up with the idea of adopting him. This all makes for some cute paling around between the pair.

p, John Clein; d, Cristy Cabanne; w, Edward T. Lowe (based on a story by Olga Printzlau); ph, Charles Stumar; m, Brown and Spencer; ed, Don Lindberg; art d, Jack Schultz.

Drama (PR:A MPAA:NR)

HEARTS OF HUMANITY** (1936, Brit.) 75m UK/AP&D bw (AKA: THE CRYPT)

Bransby Williams *(Mike)*, Wilfrid Walter *(Rev. John Maitland)*, Cathleen Nesbitt *(Mrs. Bamford)*, Pamela Randall *(Ann Bamford)*, Eric Portman *(Jack Clinton)*, Hay Petrie *(Alf)*, J. Fisher White *(Dad)*, Fred Duprez *(Manager)*, Stanelli, Mark Daly, Ray Raymond, Patric Curwen, Edgar Driver, Leonard Morris, David Keir, Robert English, Ian Fleming, J. Hubert Leslie, Howard Douglas, Freddy Watts, Stanley Kirby, John Turnbull, Bill Percy, Teddy Joyce and His Band, Romilly Choir, Teddy Reilly.

When clergyman Walter finds that the people under his religious guidance are more concerned with digging up dirt than in practicing more humble versions of their devotion, his life becomes practically unbearable. Forced to flee from the gossipmongers, Walter pursues his work with the less fortunate, namely drunks and bums headed for skid row. The various caricatures make this picture quite a joy, although the pace could definitely be snapped up a bit.

p&d, John Baxter; w, Herbert Ayres.

Drama (PR:A MPAA:NR)

HEARTS OF THE WEST*½** (1975) 102m MGM/UA c (AKA: HOLLYWOOD COWBOY)

Jeff Bridges *(Lewis Tater)*, Andy Griffith *(Howard Pike)*, Donald Pleasence *(A.J. Nietz)*, Blythe Danner *(Miss Trout)*, Alan Arkin *(Kessler)*, Richard B. Shull *(Stout Crook)*, Herbert Edelman *(Polo)*, Alex Rocco *(Earl, Assistant Director)*, Frank Cady *(Pa Tater)*, Anthony James *(Lean Crook)*, Burton Gilliam *(Lester)*, Matt Clark *(Jackson)*, Candy Azzara *(Waitress)*, Thayer David *(Bank Manager)*, Wayne Storm *(Lyle, Film Star)*, Marie Windsor *(Woman in Nevada)*, Dub Taylor *(Nevada Ticket Agent)*.

An homage to the B westerns of the 1930s and 1940s which stars Jeff Bridges as an aspiring young pulp writer after the fashion of Zane Grey. He heads for Hollywood, first making a stop in Nevada where he discovers that his correspondence school is a crooked operation. He accidentally takes the swindled cash and retreats to the desert. Under the hot sun he is rescued by a film crew led by Arkin. He joins up with the bunch as they head back to the studio, falling in love with Arkin's secretary Danner, and becoming pals with elder stunt man Griffith. The crooks pursue but are stopped when Griffith, convincingly dressed as an oater star, outwits them with a prop gun. A charming film which is able to take the conventions and simplicity of early western serials and treat them in a careful and artistic manner. It is also a fine film about filmmaking, which probably explains its box office failure. In keeping with tradition, the old black-and-white Metro lion logo opens the film, delivering his famous three roars.

p, Tony Bill; d, Howard Zieff; w, Rob Thompson; ph, Mario Tosi (Metrocolor); m, Ken Lauber; ed, Edward Warschilka; art d, Robert Luthardt; set d, Charles R. Pierce.

Western Cas. (PR:A MPAA:PG)

HEAT*½ (1970, Arg.) 85m SIFA/Unistar/Haven International/Marvin bw (. . . Y EL DEMONICO CREO A LOS HOMBRES)

Isabel Sarli *(Magda)*, Armando Bo *(Juan)*, Horace [Horacio] Priani *(Fernando)*, Mario Casado *(Marco)*, Anibal Pardeiro, Brenda Trillo, Marusa [Maria Esther] Coran, Paul Moret [Pablo Moret], Maruja Roig, Miguel Paparelli, Alex Castillo, Helene Chanel, Ana Moreno, Coco Martinel.

Overwrought drama starring Sarli as a woman whose boat has capsized and left her stranded on a rocky island. She is reached by three seal hunters who are all seduced by her beauty and compete for her favors. This leads to a fight in which one of the hunters is killed in a stampede of seals. Not wanting anyone else to die because of her, Sarli attempts suicide but she is stopped by Bo (who also produced, wrote and directed), one of the hunters, who convinces her that his love is genuine and she chooses to remain on the island.

p,d&w, Armando Bo [U.S. Version—d, Jack Curtis; w, Paulette Rubenstein Curtis]; ph, Julio Lavera; m, Alfredo Andres; ed, Rosa Canterbet [Rosalino Caterbetti].

Drama (PR:O MPAA:NR)

HEAT AND DUST*** (1983, Brit.) 133m Merchant-Ivory/Curzon-UNIV c

Julie Christie *(Anne)*, Greta Scacchi *(Olivia)*, Christopher Cazenove *(Douglas Rivers)*, Julian Glover *(Crawford)*, Susan Fleetwood *(Mrs. Crawford)*, Shashi Kapoor *(The Nawab)*, Madhur Jaffrey *(The Begum, His Mother)*, Nickolas Grace *(Harry)*, Zakir Hussain *(Inder Lal)*, Barry Foster *(Maj. Minnies)*, Amanda Walker *(Lady Mackleworth)*, Patrick Godfrey *(Dr. Saunders)*, Jennifer Kendal *(Mrs. Saunders)*, Sudha Chopra *(Chief Princess)*, Ratna Pathak *(Rita, Lal's Wife)*, Tarla Mehta *(Mother, Inder Lal's)*, Charles McCaughan *(Chid)*, Jayut Kripilani *(Dr. Gopal)*, Sajik Khan *(Dacoit Chief)*, Leelabhai *(Leelavati)*, Parveen Paul *(Maji)*.

Julie Christie is cast as the grandniece of Scacchi, an Englishwoman living in India 60 years earlier. Christie follows in Scacchi's footsteps in an attempt to discover why her great aunt was the subject of a scandal in the 1920s. The stories of both women are intercut, weaving the different time periods in and out of each other. Scacchi traveled to India, married a man from the country and became pregnant by him. Feelings of objection were aroused in the population, especially after she decided to abort the child—a Western custom. Christie's direction begins to parallel that of her aunt's up to the point of the child. Christie, in a time when abortion is more acceptable, decides to keep the child. An exceedingly interesting exploration of the mystical and seductive atmosphere of India, the film goes much deeper than GANDHI in presenting the nation's culture. However, as one would expect from a British-Indian combination the picture is very proper and sometimes tedious. One cannot overlook the possibility that this may be the intention of the filmmaker.

p, Ismail Merchant; d, James Ivory; w, Ruth Prawer Jhabvala (based on her novel); ph, Walter Lassally; m, Richard Robbins; ed, Humphrey Dixon; prod d, Wilfred Shingleton; art d, Maurice Fowler, Ram Yadekar; cos, Barbara Lane.

Drama Cas. (PR:C MPAA:R)

HEAT LIGHTNING** (1934) 64m WB bw

Aline MacMahon *(Olga)*, Ann Dvorak *(Myra)*, Preston Foster *(George)*, Lyle Talbot *(Jeff)*, Glenda Farrell *(Mrs. Tifton)*, Frank McHugh *(Frank the Chauffeur)*, Ruth Donnelly *(Mrs. Ashton-Ashley)*, Theodore Newton *(Steve)*, Willard Robertson *(Everett)*, Harry C. Bradley *(The Man)*, James Durkin *(The Sheriff)*, Jane Darwell *(The Wife)*, Edgar Kennedy *(The Husband)*, Muriel Evans *(The Blonde)*, Jill Bennett *(Black Bangs)*, James Durkin *(Sheriff)*, Chris-Pin Martin *(Mexican)*, Margareta Montez *(Wife)*, Eddie Shubert *(Man)*.

Gas station attendant MacMahon has a run-in with a pair of killers, Talbot and Foster, the latter of whom was once her lover. Only of interest for its dusty-highway view of the Southwest, putting the filling station in perspective as a piece of Americana. Remade as HIGHWAY WEST (1941).

p, Sam Bischoff; d, Mervyn LeRoy; w, Brown Holmes, Warren Duff (based on a play by Leon Adams, George Abbott); ph, Sid Hickox; ed, Howard Bretherton; md, Leo Forbstein; art d, Jack Okey; cos, Orry-Kelly.

Drama (PR:A MPAA:NR)

HEAT OF MIDNIGHT* (1966, Fr.) 67m Les Films du Griffon/Olympic International bw (ESPIONS A L'AFFUT; AKA: HEAT AT MIDNIGHT)

Claudine Coster *(Fabienne)*, Jean Claudio *(Max Savelan)*, Jean Vinci *(Fred Langlois)*, Anna Gael *(Sybil)*, Robert Lombard *(Henri)*, Dominique Santarelli, Michael Vocoret, Jean-Claude Dague.

This thin crime story has Claudio as the macho detective who is able to get Vinci out of a jam with the mob for stealing from them. For a reward he gets Gael, Vinci's ex-wife's roommate and lover, until Claudio appears. The attempt to insert a lesbian affair into the proceedings only takes away from the general flow of the story, which isn't all that smooth to begin with.

p&d, Max Pecas; w, Maurice Cury, Pecas; ph, Robert Lefebvre; m, Louiguy; ed, Nicole Cayatte.

Crime/Drama (PR:O MPAA:NR)

HEAT OF THE SUMMER** (1961, Fr.) 94m K.L.F./Ajay bw (CHALEURS D ETE)

Patricia Karim *(Lina)*, Yane Barry *(Magali)*, Michel Bardinet *(Robert)*, Claude Sainlouis *(Paul)*, Janine Massina *(Germaine)*.

Dull romance starring Bardinet as a young Parisian writer who visits the countryside to inspect the vineyard he has inherited. There he meets Barry, the pretty maid of the estate, who teaches him what he needs to know to run a vineyard. Though they do develop a friendly relationship, it is purely platonic. Bardinet spends much of his time with Karim, a neighboring farmer's daughter who wishes for him to abandon his vineyard and take her back to Paris with him. One day a jealous fight ensues between Barry and Karim and Bardinet finally realizes that it is Barry and the vineyard he truly loves.

p, Lola Kohn; d, Louis Felix; w, Paule Delsol, Gilles Siry; ph, Marcel Combes, Arthur Raimondo; m, Fernand Clare; ed, Linette Nicolas.

Romance (PR:A MPAA:NR)

HEAT WAVE** (1935, Brit.) 75m Gainsborough/GAU bw

Albert Burdon *(Albert Speed)*, Cyril Maude *(President Allison)*, Les Allen *(Tom Brown)*, Anna Lee *(Jane Allison)*, Vera Pearce *(Gloria Spania)*, Bernard Nedell *(Gen. De Costa)*, C. Denier Warren *(Col. d'Alverez)*, Bruce Winston *(Lenane)*, Edmund Willard *(Hoffman)*, Grace Poggi, Lecuona Cuban Boys.

Potatoes, onions and cabbage take on new meanings in this story of a grocer who is mistakenly identified as a gunrunner, nearly causing a revolution. The names of vegetables are used as code words for various sorts of ammo. When the real thing arrives instead of weapons the rebels have an overabundance of groceries. A pleasantly silly picture, which surprisingly has not been remade on Hollywood's rehash machine.

p, Jerome Jackson; d, Maurice Elvey; w, Austin Melford, Leslie Arliss, Jackson (based on a story by Melford); ph, Glen MacWilliams.

Musical/Comedy (PR:A MPAA:NR)

HEAT'S ON, THE½** (1943) 80m COL bw (GB: TROPICANA)

Mae West *(Fay Lawrence)*, Victor Moore *(Hubert Bainbridge)*, William Gaxton *(Tony Ferris)*, Lester Allen *(Mouse Beller)*, Mary Roche *(Janey Bainbridge)*, Almira Sessions *(Hannah Bainbridge)*, Hazel Scott *(Herself)*, Alan Dinehart *(Forrest Stanton)*, Lloyd Bridges *(Andy Walker)*, Sam Ash *(Frank)*, Lina Romay *(Lina)*, Xavier Cugat and His Orchestra *(Themselves)*, Leonard Sues, Jack Owen, Joan Thorsen, Roy Engel, Harry O. Tyler, Harry Shannon, Leon Balasco, Edward Earle, Harry Harvey.

Gaxton is a Broadway show producer with a dog of a musical on his hands. His star, West, complains to him that the show is awful and is going to ruin her reputation among the critics and public alike. Desperate to attract an audience, Gaxton concocts a plan to generate sensational publicity for his show. Knowing that Moore, the weak-willed brother of snooty society matron Sessions, who runs a public morals watchdog group known as The Foundation, is somewhat star-struck by the stage, Gaxton urges him to pressure Sessions into trying to close the "immoral" Broadway musical. Moore agrees and soon the police raid the show and close it down. Unfortunately, the censure remains permanent and West moves on to star in a new show called "Tropicana," produced by Gaxton's rival, Dinehart. Jealous, Gaxton once again uses Moore and gets him to phone Dinehart to inform the producer that because of the scandal surrounding the banned Gaxton production, West has been added to The Foundation's blacklist. Worried that a thumbs down from The Foundation will ruin him, Dinehart hurriedly sells the show to Gaxton. More clever this time around, Gaxton offers to give Sessions and Moore's young niece, Roche, a part, thus ensuring Foundation approval and financing. Suspecting a confidence job, West seduces Moore into confessing to the scam. She then notifies Sessions of the plot, and the angry matron yanks her niece, her wandering brother, and her money out of show business. Ruined, Gaxton feigns a nervous breakdown to get back in West's good graces. West is no fool, but she is touched by his effort and agrees to resurrect the show. West then has a meeting with Sessions where she gets the persnickety woman to refinance the show by threatening to expose her brother's less than wholesome activities. A giant production number from "Tropicana" concludes the movie. THE HEAT'S ON was West's first screen appearance since MY LITTLE CHICKADEE in 1940. Approached by producer-director Ratoff who proposed what sounded like a good idea for a movie, West agreed to return to the screen and signed a contract without ever seeing a script. When a script was written and West saw it, she was outraged. Claiming the character she was to play could ruin her career (as written, Fay is dumb, gullible, and easily manipulated by men), West wanted out. Ratoff pleaded with her to stay because production had already started (several musical numbers had been shot at this point) and if she walked out he would wind up bankrupt. Not wanting the ruination of a friend on her head, West agreed to stay if she could write her own scenes. The end result of all this patchwork is an alarmingly uneven film with musical numbers that seem to pop up out of nowhere. The plot line plays in a disjointed manner, and with the constant musical interludes it is at times difficult to follow. As far as West was concerned, the whole experience was a total disaster and she didn't make another film for 27 years. Unfortunately that film was MYRA BRECKINRIDGE (1970) and it turned out to be an even bigger disaster than THE HEAT'S ON. Musical numbers include: "Just A Stranger In Town," "Hello, Mi Amigo," "The White Keys and the Black Keys," "There Goes That Guitar" (Henry Meyers, Edward Eliscu, Jay Gorney), "Antonio" (Leo Huntley, John Blackburn, Fabian Andre), "The Caissons Go Rolling Along" (Edmund L. Gruber), "There Goes My Heart" (Benny Davis, Abner Silver).

p&d, Gregory Ratoff; w, Fitzroy Davis, George S. George, Fred Schiller (based on a story by Boris Ingster, Lou Breslow); ph, Franz E. Planer; m, John Leipold; ed, Otto Meyer; md, Yasha Bunchuk; prod d, Nicolai Remisoff; art d, Lionel Banks, Walter Holscher; set d, Joseph Kish; cos, Walter Plunkett; ch, David Lichine.

Musical/Comedy (PR:A-C MPAA:NR)

HEATWAVE** (1954, Brit.) 69m Hammer/ABP-Lippert bw (GB: THE HOUSE ACROSS THE LAKE)

Alex Nicol *(Mark Kendrick)*, Hilary Brooke *(Carol Forrest)*, Sidney James *(Beverly Forrest)*, Susan Stephen *(Andrea Forrest)*, Paul Carpenter *(Vincent Gordon)*, Alan Wheatley *(Inspector MacLennan)*, Cleo Rose *(Abigail)*, Peter Illing *(Harry Stevens)*, Hugh Dempster *(Frank)*, Joan Hickson, Harry Brunnings, John Sharpe, Peter Evans, Angela Glynne, Christine Adrian, Monti de Lyle.

"Femme fatale" Brooke finds a willing new lover in the form of writer Nicol, a lakeside neighbor. When her wealthy husband James is hurt in an accident, the witch tries to get him out of the way by letting him drown in the lake. Nicol won't put up with her shenanigans of making a game out of love. Now just another discarded lover, he is happy to report James' murder to the law. This classic tale of an unscrupulous woman who knows no bounds in attaining her own desires, is given a fitting depiction by Brooke.

p, Anthony Hinds,; d&w, Ken Hughes (based on the novel *High Wray* by Hughes); ph, Jimmy Harvey; m, Ivor Slaney.

Crime (PR:A MPAA:NR)

HEATWAVE** (1983, Aus.) 92m Heatwave-Mainline/New Line c

Judy David *(Kate)*, Richard Moir *(Steven)*, Chris Haywood *(Peter)*, Bill Hunter *(Robert)*, John Gregg *(Phillip)*, Anna Jemison *(Victoria)*, John Meillon *(Freddy)*, Dennis Miller *(Mick)*, Peter Hehir *(Bodyguard)*, Carole Skinner *(Mary)*, Gillian Jones *(Barbie Lee)*, Frank Gallacher *(Dick)*, Tui Bow *(Annie)*, Don Crosby *(Jim)*, Lynette Curran *(Evonne)*.

Fairly intriguing yarn revolving around the efforts of Davis to stop a redevelopment project. Her biggest gripe is that an entire neighborhood would be destroyed in order to line the pockets of some shady characters. Her involvement digs up some interesting coincidences, as well as sparking a slight romance with the architect of the project. The emphasis on atmosphere and an incredible soundtrack only gloss over the script's failure to provide a convincing plot or characters.

p, Hilary Linstead; d, Phillip Noyce; w, Noyce, Marc Rosenberg, Mark Stiles, Tim Gooding; ph, Vincent Monton (Eastmancolor); m, Cameron Allan; ed, John Scott; prod d, Ross Major.

Crime/Drama Cas. (PR:O MPAA:R)

HEAVEN CAN WAIT*½** (1943) 112m FOX c

Gene Tierney *(Martha)*, Don Ameche *(Henry Van Cleve)*, Charles Coburn *(Hugo Van Cleve)*, Marjorie Main *(Mrs. Strabel)*, Laird Cregar *(His Excellency)*, Spring Byington *(Bertha Van Cleve)*, Allyn Joslyn *(Albert Van Cleve)*, Eugene Pallette *(Mr. Strabel)*, Signe Hasso *(Mademoiselle)*, Louis Calhern *(Randolph Van Cleve)*, Helen Reynolds *(Peggy Nash)*, Aubrey Mather *(James)*, Tod Andrews *(Jack Van Cleve)*, Leonard Carey *(Flogdell)*, Clarence Muse *(Jaspe)*, Dickie Moore *(Henry at Age 15)*, Dickie Jones *(Albert at Age 15)*, Trudy Marshall *(Jane)*, Florence Bates *(Mrs. Craig)*, Clara Blandick *(Grandmother)*, Anita Bolster *(Mrs. Cooper-Cooper)*, Alfred Hall *(Albert's Father)*, Grayce Hampton Smith *(Grace's Mother)*, Nino Pipitone, Jr. *(Jack as a Child)*, Claire DuBrey *(Miss Ralston)*, Charles Halton *(Clerk in Britano's)*, James Flavin *(Policeman)*, Michael McLean *(Henry at Age 15 Months)*, Scotty Beckett *(Henry at Age 9)*, Doris Merrick *(Nurse)*, Marlene Mains *(Mary)*, Edwin Maxwell *(Doctor)*, Maureen Rodin-Ryan *(Nurse)*.

A charming, warm, and well-produced film that is stamped with the famous "Lubitsch touch." This movie has Ameche as a rake, shown from infancy to his death at age 70. The film opens with a deceased Ameche standing before the Devil, Cregar, requesting his passport to Hell. Cregar studies his newest applicant and then reviews Ameche's carefree and often careless life. The film follows Ameche through childhood as he entices local girls with his beetle collection then, while pretending to be sophisticated at age 15, gets accidentally drunk while awkwardly trying to impress the family's attractive maid. As a young swain Ameche steals ravishing Tierney away from his stuffed-shirt cousin, Joslyn, and visits his eccentric in-laws, beef tycoons in Kansas, played by Pallette and Main, who have a huge statue of a prize cow named Mabel on their front lawn. Calhern and Byington, Ameche's parents, are outstanding in their flighty roles, as is Coburn, the grandfather who loves romance in any era and sanctions his grandson's amorous adventures in Gay Nineties New York, where Ameche and Tierney finally settle down. Ameche, at film's end, is turned away toward Heaven as being basically good. Ameche is at his comedic best and Tierney is stunning in her beauty. Lubitsch's direction is top drawer and he makes much more out of this delightful fluff than what's really there, aided by a witty and humorous script by his favorite screenwriter, Raphaelson. This was Lubitsch's first color film and it is rich and bright.

p&d, Ernst Lubitsch; w, Samson Raphaelson (based on the play "Birthdays" by Lazlo Bus-Fekete); ph, Edward Cronjager (Technicolor); m, Alfred Newman; ed, Dorothy Spencer; art d, James Basevi, Leland Fuller, Thomas Little, Walter M. Scott; cos, Rene Hubert.

Comedy Cas. (PR:A MPAA:NR)

HEAVEN CAN WAIT*** (1978) 101m PAR c

Warren Beatty *(Joe Pendleton)*, Julie Christie *(Betty Logan)*, James Mason *(Mr. Jordan)*, Dyan Cannon *(Julia Farnsworth)*, Charles Grodin *(Tony Abbott)*, Jack Warden *(Max Corkle)*, Buck Henry *(The Escort)*, Vincent Gardenia *(Lt. Krim)*, Joseph Maher *(Sisk)*, Hamilton Camp *(Bentley)*, Arthur Malet *(Everett)*, Stephanie Faracy *(Corinne)*, Jeannie Linero *(Lavinia)*, Harry D. K. Wong *(Gardener)*, George J. Manos *(Security Guard)*, Larry Block *(Peters)*, Frank Campanella *(Conway)*, Bill Sorrells *(Tomarken)*, Dick Enberg *(TV Interviewer)*, Dolph Sweet *(Head Coach)*, R.G. Armstrong *(General Manager)*, Ed V. Peck *(Trainer)*, John Randolph *(Former Owner)*, Richard O'Brien *(Former Owner's Adviser)*, Joseph F. Makel *(Haitian Ambassador)*, Will Hare *(Team Doctor)*, Lee Weaver *(Way Station Attendant)*, Roger Bowen *(Newspaperman)*, Keene Curtis *(Oppenheim)*, William Larsen *(Renfield)*, Morgan Farley *(Middleton)*, William Bogert *(Lawson)*, Robert E. Leonard, Joel Marston, Earl Montgomery, Robert C. Stevens *(Board Members)*, Bernie Massa *(Coliseum Security Guard)*, Peter Tomarken, Lisa Blake Richards *(Reporters)*, William Sylvester *(Nuclear Reporter)*, Charlie Charles *(High-Wire Performer)*, Nick Outin *(Chauffeur)*, Jerry Scanlan *(Hodges)*, Jim Boeke *(Kowalsky)*, Marvin Fleming *(Gudnitz)*, Deacon Jones *(Gorman)*, Les Josephson *(Owens)*, Jack T. Snow *(Cassidy)*, Charlie Cowan, Joe Corolla *(Football Players)*, Bryant Gumbel, Jim Healy *(TV Sportscasters)*, Curt Gowdy *(TV Commentator)*, Al DeRogatis *(TV Color Analyst)*, Elliott Reid, Bryon Webster *(Waiters)*, Garrett Craig *(Swimmer)*, Paul D'Amato *(Swimmer's Friend)*, Robert Fortier *(Wealthy Man in Restaurant)*.

A remake of HERE COMES MR. JORDAN (and a film having nothing to do with the Lubitsch film of 1943), Beatty is the whole show as a football star who is prematurely taken to Heaven after an accident by a bumbling celestial messenger, Henry. He is temporarily given a new body by Mason, an on-high authority, before a permanent new body can be located. He occupies the body of a wealthy industrialist killed by his sluttish wife Cannon and nitwit secretary Grodin, surviving to astonish the would-be murderers, then falling in love with Christie and buying his old football team with the help of Warden, the coach, who is convinced of the reincarnation and equally confused by it. Beatty is finally killed by Cannon and Grodin, but Mason manages to plant him in another body, this time for keeps. He still keeps Christie, and trots out onto the gridiron to star for Warden's team. It's all a lot of fun but this one doesn't match up to the original film with Robert Montgomery, mostly due to its patchy direction and stuttering delivery on the part of Beatty and Christie. Cannon overacts to the point where one might think she's confused about exactly what film she's playing in. Though enjoyable, the script is too cute and the humor often forced and obvious. Warden is the best thing in the film and he's not used enough. Widely popular, the film grossed about $50 million to the present time, a commercial fact used by some Beatty defenders to answer Katharine Hepburn's charge that the actor, appearing in such dogs as SHAMPOO, was not making wholesome films.

p, Warren Beatty; d, Beatty, Buck Henry; w, Beatty, Elaine May (based on the play by Harry Segall); ph, William A. Fraker (Panavision, Movielab Color); m, Dave Grusin; ed, Robert C. Jones, Don Zimmerman; prod d, Paul Sylbert; art d, Edwin O'Donovan; set d, George Gaines; cos, Theodora Van Runkle, Richard Bruno; spec eff, Robert MacDonald; makeup, Lee Harmon.

Comedy/Fantasy **Cas.** **(PR:C MPAA:PG)**

HEAVEN IS ROUND THE CORNER* (1944, Brit.) 103m BN/Anglo bw

Will Fyffe *(Dougal)*, Leni Lynn *(Joan Sedley)*, Leslie Perrins *(Robert Sedley)*, Magda Kun *(Musette)*, Peter Glenville *(Donald McKay)*, Barbara Couper *(Mrs. Trevor)*, Toni Edgar Bruce *(Mrs. Harcourt)*, Barbara Waring *(Dorothy Trevor)*, Hugh Dempster *(Capt. Crowe)*, Paul Bonifas, Jan van Loewen, Rosamund Greenwood, Elsa Tee, Neville Brook, Louis Lord, Suzy Marquis, Christine Silver, Hal Gordon, Marcel de Haes.

A dry combination of farmhands and opera singers set in and around the British Embassy in Paris. Includes the tune "Heaven Is Round The Corner" (sung by Lynn).

p, Fred Zelnik; d, Maclean Rogers; w, Austin Melford (based on a story by A. Hilarius, Paul Knepler); ph, James Wilson, Arthur Grant; m/l, Desmond O'Connor, Kennedy Russell.

Musical **(PR:A MPAA:NR)**

HEAVEN KNOWS, MR. ALLISON*** (1957) 107m FOX c

Deborah Kerr *(Sister Angela)*, Robert Mitchum *(Mr. Allison)*.

Mitchum is a Marine and Kerr a Roman Catholic nun who has yet to take her final vows and both are trapped on a South Pacific island controlled by Japanese troops. Hiding in a cave by day, the two forage for food by night and Mitchum, though respectful, attempts to get Kerr to tell him her background. Slowly their lives are revealed to each other while they are constantly endangered by the enemy. Mitchum then conducts a wholesale night raid on the Japanese food supplies and is almost detected. He returns with a storehouse of goods, plus a bottle of sake, and proceeds to get drunk. In his cups, the Marine blubbers his affection for Kerr but she sidesteps his awkward advances. After running from him through a rain-soaked jungle, she becomes ill and he nurses her back to health. When more Japanese troops arrive, Mitchum kills one of the enemy and makes away with much-needed blankets. He and Kerr are almost discovered in their cave before U.S. troops invade the island and once more Mitchum goes out, this time to blow up some heavy enemy artillery pieces to prevent them from firing upon American ships. He is seriously wounded in the process but survives. He and Kerr say farewell at the end, Mitchum having more than respect for her and she feeling deeply about him but intending to take her final vows. Although this is an absorbing film, fraught with danger and suspense, director Huston doesn't develop his characters well enough. Mitchum is good as the uneducated but sensitive, understanding Marine with a heart and Kerr is human beneath the habit, but that's it. Visually, the production is top notch. Filmed in Tobago, British West Indies.

p, Buddy Adler, Eugene Frenke; d, John Huston; w, John Lee Mahin, Huston (based on the novel by Charles Shaw); ph, Oswald Morris (CinemaScope, DeLuxe Color); m, Georges Auric; ed, Russell Lloyd; md, Lambert Williamson; art d, Stephen Grimes; cos, Elizabeth Haffenden.

War Drama **Cas.** **(PR:A MPAA:NR)**

HEAVEN ON EARTH** (1931) 78m UNIV bw

Lew Ayres *(States)*, Anita Louise *(Towhead)*, Harry Beresford *(Capt. Lilly)*, Elizabeth Patterson *(Vergie)*, Slim Summerville *(Merchant)*, Harlan Knight *(Preacher Daniel)*, Jack Duffy *(Dr. Boax)*, Peter Richmond [John Carradine] *(Capt. Sam)*, Alf P. James *(Butter Eye)*, Robert Burns *(Marty)*, Lew Kelly *(Andy)*, Jules Cowles *(Buffalo)*, Louise Emmons *(Maggie)*, Mme. Sul-te-wan *(Voodoo Sue)*.

Set on a riverboat on the "mighty Mississippi" this one has Ayres discovering that the man he thought was his father is actually his father's murderer. It's all treated very matter-of-factly, and everyone is living happily at the finale.

d, Russell Mack; w, Ray Doyle (based on Ben Lucien Burman's novel *Mississippi*); ph, Charles Stumar; ed, Milton Carruth.

Drama **(PR:A MPAA:NR)**

HEAVEN ON EARTH*½ (1960, Ital./U.S.) 82m JB Film Enterprises c

Barbara Florian *(Caroline Brent)*, Charles Fawcett *(Henry Brent)*, Gabriele Tinti *(Antonio Verbano)*, Arnoldo Foa *(Count Verbano)*.

For all those folks that couldn't afford a trip to Rome, this picture brings all your favorite Italian tourist traps to you in the convenience of your own theater—no passport, no crowds, no luggage. Essentially a travelog, this film follows an American girl as she visits her dad in Rome. Her guide to all the famous sights is an amiable Italian lad, and soon the spell of amore is upon them. She delivers a tune called "At Seventeen," and Lydia Aldini and the Sistine Chapel Choir sing a fine version of "Ave Maria."

p, Dominick Franco, Fulvio Lucisano; d&w, Robert Spafford (based on a story by Murray Hill Topman); ph, Rino Filippini (Eastmancolor); m, Alberto Vitalini.

Romance **(PR:A MPAA:NR)**

HEAVEN ONLY KNOWS*** (1947) 97m UA bw (AKA: MONTANA MIKE)

Robert Cummings *(Mike)*, Brian Donlevy *(Duke)*, Marjorie Reynolds *(Ginger)*, Jorja Cartwright *(Drusilla)*, Bill Goodwin *(Plumber)*, Stuart Erwin *(Sheriff)*, John Litel *(Reverend)*, Peter Miles *(Speck O'Donnell)*, Edgar Kennedy *(Jud)*, Gerald Mohr *(Treason)*, Lurene Tuttle *(Mrs. O'Donnell)*, Ray Bennett *(Freel)*, Will Orleans.

A pleasant western which enters the realm of fantasy when an angel is sent to Montana. The winged-visitor, Cummings, is on a mission to fix a screwup which occurred in Heaven. It seems that Donlevy, a bar owner and ruthless killer, arrived on earth without having a soul. This is where Cummings comes in—he unites body with soul and Donlevy becomes a decent fellow. Light and breezy entertainment.

p, Seymour Nebenzal; d, Albert S. Rogell; w, Art Arthur, Ernest Haycox, Rowland Leigh (based on a story by Aubrey Wisberg); ph, Karl Struss; m, Heinz Roemheld; ed, Edward Mann; md, David Chudnow; art d, Martin Obzina; spec eff, Ray Binger.

Western/Fantasy **(PR:A MPAA:NR)**

HEAVEN SENT (SEE: THANK HEAVEN FOR SMALL FAVORS, 1965)

HEAVEN WITH A BARBED WIRE FENCE** (1939) 62m FOX bw

Jean Rogers *(Anita))*, Raymond Walburn *(Professor)*, Marjorie Rambeau *(Mamie)*, Glenn Ford *(Joe)*, Nicholas Conte *(Tony)*, Eddie Collins *(Bill)*, Ward Bond *(Hunk)*, Irving Bacon *(Sheriff)*, Kay Linaker *(Nurse)*.

Ford is a New York department store clerk who buys land in Arizona. He hitchhikes out West and on the way he picks up Conte, a young runaway; Walburn, a college professor who has opted for a hobo life; and Rogers, an illegal alien. Rogers has left Spain after that nation's civil war, worked a transatlantic crossing, and jumped ship in New York. To prevent her deportation, Ford marries Rogers when they arrive in Arizona.

p, Sol M. Wurtzel; d, Ricardo Cortez; w, Dalton Trumbo, Leonard Hoffman, Ben Grauman Kohn (based on a story by Trumbo); ph, Edward Cronjager; m, Samuel Kaylin; ed, Norman Colbert.

Drama **(PR:A MPAA:NR)**

HEAVEN WITH A GUN** (1969) 101m King Bros./MGM c

Glenn Ford *(Jim Killian)*, Carolyn Jones *(Madge McCloud)*, Barbara Hershey *(Leloopa)*, John Anderson *(Asa Beck)*, David Carradine *(Coke Beck)*, J.D. Cannon *(Mace)*, Noah Beery *(Garvey)*, Harry Townes *(Gus Sampson)*, William Bryant *(Bart Patterson)*, Virginia Gregg *(Mrs. Patterson)*, James Griffith *(Abraham Murdock)*, Roger Perry *(Ned Hunter)*, Claude Woolman *(Gilcher)*, Ed Bakey *(Scotty Andrews)*, Barbara Babcock *(Mrs. Andrews)*, James Chandler *(Doc Foster)*, Angelique Pettyjohn *(Emily)*, Jessica James *(Jan)*, Bee Tompkins *(Bar Girl)*, Bill Catching *(Willy)*, Al Wyatt *(Indian)*, Ed McCready *(Charlie)*, Eddie Crispell, Barbara Dombre *(Townspeople)*.

Ford, a gunfighter-turned-preacher in a small western town, becomes caught up in a battle between cattlemen and sheep herders. An Indian sheep herder is lynched by Carradine, whose father is cattle baron Anderson. The preacher gets the town together to try to work out a peaceable solution. Cannon, an ex-con who shared a cell with Ford, exposes his true identity at the meeting. The townspeople still stand behind Ford, and together they stop the bloodshed. A bland western.

p, Frank King, Maurice King; d, Lee H. Katzin; w, Richard Carr; ph, Fred Koenekamp (Panavision, Metrocolor); m, Johnny Mandel; ed, Dan Cahn; art d, George W. Davis and Frank Sylos; set d, Henry Grace, Don Greenwood, Jr.; m/l "A Lonely Place," Paul Francis Webster, Mandel.

Western **(PR:C MPAA:M)**

HEAVENLY BODY, THE½** (1943) 95m MGM bw

William Powell *(William B. Whitley)*, Hedy Lamarr *(Vicky Whitley)*, James Craig *(Lloyd X. Hunter)*, Fay Bainter *(Margaret Sibyll)*, Henry O'Neill *(Prof. Stone)*, Spring Byington *(Nancy Potter)*, Robert Sully *(Strand)*, Morris Ankrum *(Dr. Green)*, Franco Corsaro *(Sebastian Melas)*, Connie Gilchrist *(Beulah Murphy)*, Max Willenz *(Dr. Gurtchakoff)*, Earl Schenck *(Forbes)*, Arthur Space *(Pierson)*, Helen Freeman *(Stella)*, Phyllis Kennedy *(Ethel)*, Marietta Canty *(Pearl Harrison)*, Nicodemus *(Willie)*, Howard Mitchell *(Nicholas)*, Dan B. Sheffield *(Frank)*, Gertrude W. Hoffman *(Mrs. Potter's Mother)*, Alex Melesh *(Vladimir)*, James Basquette *(Porter)*, Jac George *(Accompanist)*, Elspeth Dudgeon *(Lady)*, Bertram Marburgh *(Old Man)*, Wheaton Chambers *(Old Gentleman)*, Evelyn Dockson *(Maid)*, Jacqueline Miller *(W.U. Girl)*, Ralph Sanford, John Sheehan *(Cops)*, Lloyd Ford *(Ethel's Husband)*, Buddy Gorman *(Newsboy)*, Cliff Nazarro *(Milkman)*, William Sabbot *(Knife Thrower)*, Andre Charlot *(Dr. Burns)*, John Elliott *(Prof. Collier)*, Howard Hickman, Henry Sylvester, Gus Glassmire *(Scientists)*, Bobby Watson *(Hitler—Photo Insert)*, Rex Evans *(Goering—Photo Insert)*.

Having discovered a new comet in the heavens and had it named after him, Mt. Jefferson Observatory astronomer Powell becomes so absorbed in tracing what he projects will be its path to a moon collision that he ignores his beautiful bride, Lamarr. Feeling lonely and unloved, Lamarr visits an astrologer who tells her that soon, on a specific day, she will meet a man who has traveled extensively and she will fall in love with him. To make him jealous, Lamarr informs Powell of this prediction. Outraged that his wife could believe in such a silly pseudo-science as astrology, Powell leaves her for a few days and goes to his observatory. Lamarr decides to sit and wait for her mystery man to appear. The big day comes, but nothing happens. That evening she phones Powell and apologizes. He agrees to come home. At the stroke of midnight there is a knock on the door. On the porch is an air raid warden, Craig, who informs Lamarr that she has disobeyed a blackout ordinance. After a brief conversation, Lamarr is shocked to learn that Craig has traveled throughout the world. Her man has arrived. After a bit of mild flirtation, Craig goes to leave and bumps into Powell, who has just arrived home. Suspecting something, Powell requests that air raid warden Craig be transferred to another district. Now having fallen in love with Lamarr, Craig refuses the transfer and, despite Powell's attempts to interfere, Lamarr and the air raid warden continue to cross paths. Afraid he is losing his wife to another man, Powell visits the astrologist who started all the trouble and demands she write a bogus horoscope that predicts his demise. Powell then fakes a terminal illness to gain sympathy, but Lamarr learns the truth. Frustrated and lonely, Powell leaves and returns to his observatory. Realizing that her husband really does love her, Lamarr dumps Craig and renews her marriage to Powell. Basically just a silly situation comedy, THE HEAVENLY BODY is merely an hour and a half of mild amusement. All the principals have been better elsewhere, and the script offers little in the way of clever dialog or screwball situations. In fact, Lamarr was given this inferior project after turning down a chance to star in an adaptation of Pearl S. Buck's *Dragon Seed*, a role which finally went to Katharine Hepburn.

p, Arthur Hornblow, Jr.; d, Alexander Hall; w, Michael Arlen, Walter Reisch, Harry Kurnitz (based on a story by Jacques Thery); ph, Robert Planck; m, Bronislau Kaper; ed, Blanche Sewell; art d, Cedric Gibbons, William Ferrari; set d, Edwin B. Willis, McLean Nesbit; cos, Irene; spec eff, Arnold Gillespie.

Comedy **(PR:A MPAA:NR)**

HEAVENLY DAYS** (1944) 72m RKO bw

Jim Jordan *(Fibber McGee)*, Marian Jordan *(Molly McGee)*, Eugene Pallette *(Sen. Bigbee)*, Gordon Oliver *(Dick)*, Raymond Walburn *(Mr. Popham)*, Barbara Hale *(Angie)*, Don Douglas *(Dr. Gallup)*, Frieda Inescort *(Mrs. Clark)*, Irving Bacon *(Butler)*, Charles Trowbridge *(Alvin Clark)*, Chester Carlisle, Bert Moorhouse *(Sergeants-at-Arms)*, J.M. Sullivan *(Detective)*, Henry Hall, Ed Peil, James Farley, Lloyd Ingraham, Fred Fox, Brandon Beach, James Carlisle, J.O. Fowler, Lou Payne, Henry Herbert, Ed Mortimer, Wilbur Mack, Joseph Girard, Dick Rush, John Ince *(Senators)*, Ed Stanley *(Vice-President Wallace)*, Harry Humphrey *(Southern Senator)*, George Reed *(Servant)*, Norman Mayes *(Waiter)*, Helena Benda *(Czech Lady)*, Bertha Feducah *(French Lady)*, William Yip *(Chinese Man)*, Esther Zeitlan *(Russian Lady)*, John Duncan *(Boy)*, Clinton Rosemond *(Black Servant)*, Eva McKenzie *(Clerk)*, Teddy Infuhr *(Czech Boy)*, Oleg Balaeff *(Russian Boy)*, Pat Prest *(Dutch Girl)*, Maurice Tauzin *(French Boy)*, Dena Penn *(Belgian Girl)*, Walter Soo Hoo *(Chinese Boy)*, Yvette Dugay *(Greek Girl)*, Joel Davis *(English Boy)*, Eddie Clark *(Scout)*, Larry Wheat *(Butler)*, Bryant Washburn *(Airport Official)*, Lane Chandler *(Minute Man)*, Gil Perkins *(Confederate Soldier)*, Ken Ferrel *(Union Soldier)*, Selmer Jackson *(Sunday Editor)*, Rosemary La Planche, Margie Stewart *(Bits)*, Sheldon Jett *(Big Fat Man)*, Richard Thorne *(WW I Soldier)*, Erville Alderson *(Farmer)*, Glen Stephens, John Benson *(Military Police)*, Ronald Gaye, Erwin Kaiser *(Drum Boys)*, John Elliott, Charles Griffin, Elmer Jerome *(Men)*, Virginia Sale, Elaine Riley *(Secretaries)*, Molio Sheron *(Russian)*, The King's Men *(Themselves)*, Emory Parnell *(Detective)*.

Radio stars Fibber McGee and Molly came to the screen in this RKO ripoff of Frank Capra's MR. SMITH GOES TO WASHINGTON. McGee is asked to come to Washington by his politician relative, and he tries to tell Congress what must be done for the country. McGee is laughed at until he is named Mr. Average Man by the Gallup Poll. The film did quite poorly at the box office.

p, Robert Fellows; d, Howard Estabrook; w, Estabrook, Don Quinn (based on a story by Estabrook); ph, Roy Hunt; m, Leigh Harline; ed, Robert Swink; md, Constantin Bakaleinikoff; art d, Albert S. D'Agostino, Ralph Berger; set d, Darrell Silvera, William Stevens; spec eff, Vernon L. Walker.

Comedy **(PR:A MPAA:NR)**

HEAVENS ABOVE!**** (1963, Brit.) 118m Charter/BL-Romulus-Janus bw

Peter Sellers *(Rev. John Smallwood)*, Cecil Parker *(Archdeacon Aspinall)*, Isabel Jeans *(Lady Despard)*, Eric Sykes *(Harry Smith)*, Bernard Miles *(Simpson)*, Brock Peters *(Matthew)*, Ian Carmichael *(The Other Smallwood)*, Irene Handl *(Rene Smith)*, Miriam Karlin *(Winnie Smith)*, Joan Miller *(Mrs. Smith-Gould)*, Eric Barker *(Bank Manager)*, Roy Kinnear *(Fred Smith)*, Kenneth Griffith *(Rev. Owen Smith)*, Miles Malleson *(Rockerby)*, William Hartnell *(Maj. Fowler)*, Joan Hickson *(Garrulous Housewife)*, Harry Locke *(Shop Steward)*, Nicholas Phipps *(Director General)*, Thorley Walters *(Tranquilax Executive)*, George Woodbridge *(Bishop)*, Basil Dignam *(Prisoner Governor)*, Colin Gordon *(Prime Minister)*, Joan Heal *(Disgruntled Housewife)*, Malcolm Muggeridge *(Cleric)*, Conrad Phillips *(P.R.O.)*, Cardew Robinson *(Tramp)*, Billy Milton *(Fellowes)*, Howard Pays *(Astronaut)*, Mark Eden *(Sir Geoffrey Despard)*, John Comer *(Butcher)*, Franklyn Engelmann, Tim Brinton *(TV Commentators)*, Ludovic Kennedy *(Ludovic Kennedy)*, Geoffrey Hibbert *(Council Official)*, Marjie Lawrence, Olive Sloane *(Quarreling Housewives)*, Henry Longhurst *(Deaf Gentleman)*, Elsie Wagstaff *(Lady on Parish Church Council)*, Ian Wilson *(Salvation Army Major)*, Josephine Woodford *(Doris Smith)*, Drewe Henley *(Doris' Boy Friend)*, John Harvey.

Released in 1963 and rereleased by Cinema V two years later, HEAVENS ABOVE! could stand another release in the 1980s, as the story is timeless and the humor is rampant. Sellers is a religious prison chaplain who is appointed in error to the post of a wealthy church in an English industrial city. The real reverend that they'd meant to get for this plum parish is Carmichael, a fawning toady who would be quite content to mirror all the desires of the rich parishioners. What they get is Sellers, a man with convictions and the courage to carry those convictions out. The first thing Sellers does is name Peters, a black West Indian, to the post of church warden. Peters had been a trashman prior to his appointment, which shocks the blue-noses who seldom come to church services anyhow. This is too much for their staid mentalities. Then Sellers invites a gypsy troupe to live with him at the parish manse, another act that causes a brouhaha as the gypsies—Sykes, Handl, Karlin and Kinnear—had previously been squatting on land owned by the largest employer in the area, the Tranquilax Company, a firm that manufactures a triple-strength cure-all that is, at once, a laxative, stimulant and sedative. Tranquilax is owned by Jeans, a peeress of the realm, and Sellers' appeal to her to heed the words of The Good Book causes her to begin to give away her fortune to those less fortunate. Now that the local people have free food, the merchants of the town are up in arms. Jeans begins to sell her Tranquilax shares and the market value descends, thus bringing the threat of joblessness to the area. Eventually Jeans realizes the folly of her ways and Sellers' work is decried by the very townspeople he'd sought to help. They flee the church and riots commence. Sellers quits the area, and gets reassigned to a nuclear missile base on a small island. Once there he begins counseling an astronaut who twits him on his deep beliefs. Sellers can take any kind of taunting except that regarding his faith so he ties up the astronaut, gets into the rocket and takes off for the moon, thus becoming "the bishop of outer space." HEAVENS ABOVE! is one of those 1950s and 1960s British comedies that gently made its satirical points without belaboring the issue. Sellers is totally believable as the simple, guileless man who only wants the best for his flock. Just about every supporting role is perfectly cast with special kudos to Malleson as a deranged psychiatrist and Parker as an archdeacon. The film's message seems to be that charity, no matter how Christian, is difficult to bestow and even more difficult to accept in the twentieth century.

p, Roy Boulting; d, John Boulting; w, Frank Harvey, John Boulting (based on an idea by Malcolm Muggeridge); ph, Max Greene; m, Richard Rodney Bennett; ed, Teddy Darvas; md, John Hollingsworth; art d, Albert Witherick; cos, David Ffolkes; makeup, Stuart Freeborn, Gerry Fletcher.

Comedy **Cas.** **(PR:AA MPAA:NR)**

HEAVEN'S GATE* (1980) 205m UA c

Kris Kristofferson *(Marshal James Averill)*, Christopher Walken *(Nathan D. Champion)*, John Hurt *(Billy Irvine)*, Isabelle Huppert *(Ella Watson)*, Sam Waterston *(Frank Canton)*, Jeff Bridges *(John H. Bridges)*, Joseph Cotten *("The Reverend Doctor")*, Roseanne Vela *(Beautiful Girl)*, Ronnie Hawkins *(Wolcott)*, Geoffrey Lewis *(Trapper)*, Paul Koslo *(Mayor)*, Richard Masur *(Cully)*, Mary C. Wright *(Nell)*, Nicholas Woodeson *(Small Man)*, Stefan Shcherby *(Large Man)*, Waldemar Kalinowski *(Photographer)*, Terry O'Quinn *(Capt. Minardi)*, John Conley *(Morrison)*, Margaret Benczak *(Mrs. Eggleston)*, Tom Noonan *(Jake)*, James Knobeloch *(Kopestonsky)*, Erika Petersen *(Mrs. Kopestonsky)*, Robin Bartlett *(Mrs. Lezak)*, Marat Yusim, Aivars Smits, Gordana Rashovich, Jarlath Conroy, Allen Keller, Caroline Kava, Mady Kaplan, Anna Levine, Pat Hodges, Mickey Rourke, Kevin McClarnon, Kai Wulff, Steve Majstorovic, Gabriel Walsh, Norton Buffalo, Jack Blessing, Jerry Sullivan.

One of the most overblown epic westerns of any decade, director Cimino proved to be wildly extravagant with a free-hand budget and produced a film of incredible nonsense, historical inaccuracy, and a flagrant self-indulgence that clutches every scene. The story allegedly relates the events of the bloody 1892 Johnson County wars in Wyoming between cattlemen and the immigrants. Kristofferson, the son of wealthy people, becomes sheriff and must hold the two hating sides in check, a battle which he ultimately loses. Walken is a gunfighter who hires out to the ranchers, then turns on them. Both Walken and Kristofferson share the sexual favors of Huppert, who plays a notorious prostitute. Through various slices of life, shot hodge-podge and without a unifying thread, Cimino tries to depict the lifestyles of both the ranchers and the settlers, placing emphasis on the whorehouse activities of Huppert and the ambush killings between the feuding factions. All of it culminates with a huge battle between the settlers and cattlemen, a wholesale slaughter that turns the sod red with blood. None of the film is based on fact or even remotely deals with a fascinating real life history that certainly would have made a fine film had it not been ignored by the arrogant Cimino. "One uses history in a very free way," Cimino told reporters questioning his distortion of the facts. Averill (Kristofferson) and Ella (Huppert) (better known in the West as "Cattle Kate Watson") were hanged by vigilantes for rustling cattle long before the events depicted in this film occurred. Champion, played by Walken, is shown being shot to death in the film when he lived beyond the county battles. The horror stories of Cimino's financial excesses were legion—that he rebuilt trains to the style of the period for only short sequences, had period costumes made with infinite care for 1,000 extras, that he planted miles of sod in an area he intended to blow up in the big battle scenes. Cimino spent years writing and rewriting the script for this film and finally succeeded in convincing United Artists to produce it, mainly on the strength of his fine film, THE DEER HUNTER which had won the Best Picture Oscar for 1978. But each week during production the budget expanded until it reached more than $35 million by film's end (some reported $50 million). The public reaction to this miserable mess was instant rejection. During the premiere at Grauman's Chinese Theater in Hollywood, pickets paraded before the box office protesting the cruelty to animals as depicted in the film. Inside the audience hooted and jeered at the finish. One woman reportedly ran out to the lobby to tell a man pacing there that this was "the most disgusting, degrading, and horrible film I've ever seen!" She was talking to Cimino, and she was right. Kristofferson is awful, Walken is only a little better, and none in the cast is distinguished in this historic splatter film. Of course it was all Cimino's fault and, worse, his actions caused producers to close the doors for a long period on young and talented directors being entrusted with substantial budgets for major filmmaking. Cimino's career went into a sharp decline thereafter.

p, Joann Carelli; d&w, Michael Cimino; ph, Vilmos Zsigmond (Panavision, Technicolor); m, David Mansfield; ed, Tom Rolf, William Reynolds, Lisa Fruchtman, Gerald Greenberg; art d, Tambi Larsen, Spencer Deverill, Maurice Fowler; cos, Allen Highfill; ch, Eleanor Fazan.

Western **Cas.** **(PR:O MPAA:R)**

HEAVY METAL* (1981, Can.) 91m COL c

The voices of: Roger Bumpass, Jackie Burroughs, John Candy, Joe Flaherty, Don Francks, Martin Lavut, Eugene Levy, Marilyn Lightstone, Alice Playten, Harold Ramis, Susan Roman, Richard Romanos, August Schellenberg, John Vernon, Zal Yanovsky.

The concept for this animated film is derived from the adult fantasy magazine "Heavy Metal," but it sinks far below the adult theme to attract the teenage crowd. HEAVY METAL is broken down into episodes strung together by a sinister jewel called the Lock-Nar. This green, glowing stone catapults the characters into different confrontations. There is a futuristic New York City cab driver who gets involved with a sexy but greedy woman who is being chased by criminals who want to take the Lock-Nar from her. A bookworm boy is transformed into a brawny, heroic stud. He is wanted by all the women of this other-world and saves a maiden from being sacrificed to the jewel. John Candy does the voice for the boy, awe-stricken by his new strength and his sexual encounters. The other pieces don't have the satirical edge of these two episodes, so the film drags toward the end. The music was done by different rock bands and for the most part is obtrusive. Musical performers include Blue Oyster Cult, Black Sabbath, Cheap Trick, Devo, Stevie Nicks, Riggs, Nazareth, Donald Fagen, Don Felder, Grand Funk Railroad, Sammy Hager, and Trust.

p, Ivan Reitman; d, Gerald Potterton; w, Dan Goldberg and Len Blum (based on work and stories by Richard Corben, Angus McKie, Dan O'Bannon, Thomas Warkentin, Berni Wrightson); ph, (Metrocolor); m, Elmer Bernstein; ed Janice Brown; prod d, Michael Gross; animation design, Warkentin, McKie, O'Bannon, Corben, Juan Gimenez, Lee Mishkin.

Animation/Fantasy (PR:O MPAA:R)

HEDDA*** (1975, Brit.) 104m Bowden/Brut c

Glenda Jackson *(Hedda)*, Timothy West *(Tesman)*, Peter Eyre *(Brach)*, Jennie Linden *(Mrs. Elvsted)*, Patrick Stewart *(Lovborg)*, Constance Chapman *(Julie)*, Pam St. Clement *(Bertha)*.

An excellent Royal Shakespeare Company production took to the soundstage for this film version of Ibsen's brooding classic. Jackson is the scheming wife of professor West (a man she has never loved), who will stop at nothing to ensure her husband's promotion. Boredom, fear of social stagnation, and her dark soul drive Jackson as she takes advantage of old friends, steals a manuscript from West's rival for advancement (Stewart), and then urges his suicide. Jackson, West, and Stewart turn in mesmerizing performances, freed by the camera to trade in nuances of character prohibited by the demands of the stage.

p, Robert Enders; d&w, Trevor Nunn (based on the play "Hedda Gabler" by Henrik Ibsen); ph, Douglas Slocombe (Technicolor); m, Laurie Johnson; ed, Peter Tanner; art d, Ted Tester.

Drama Cas. (PR:A-C MPAA:PG)

HEIDI*½** (1937) 87m Darryl F. Zanuck/FOX bw

Shirley Temple *(Heidi)*, Jean Hersholt *(Adolph Kramer)*, Arthur Treacher *(Andrews)*, Helen Westley *(Blind Anna)*, Pauline Moore *(Elsa)*, Thomas Beck *(Pastor Schultz)*, Mary Nash *(Fraulein Rottenmeier)*, Sidney Blackmer *(Herr Sesemann)*, Mady Christians *(Aunt Dete)*, Sig Rumann *(Police Captain)*, Marcia Mae Jones *(Klara Sesemann)*, Delmar Watson *(Peter the Goat Boy)*, Egon Brecher *(Innkeeper)*, Christian Rub *(Baker)*, George Humbert *(Organ Grinder)*.

Johanna Spyri's novel is an excellent vehicle for the young Temple, and Fox chose her because of fan mail demanding her for the title role. She's an orphan who is sent to live with her recluse grandfather, a bitter man because his son had left him, but Temple quickly breaks the old man's cold exterior. Temple is then taken away by an evil aunt, who sells her as a servant girl. She works at Blackmer's home, a wealthy man with an invalid daughter. Temple brightens up their lives while the grandfather struggles to find her. In the end Temple and her grandfather are reunited.

p, Raymond Griffith; d, Allan Dwan; w, Walter Ferris, Julien Josephson (based on a novel by Johanna Spyri); ph, Arthur Miller; ed, Allen McNeil; md, Louis Silvers; art d, Hans Peters; m/l, "In Our Little Wooden Shoes," Lew Pollack, Sidney D. Mitchell (sung by Shirley Temple).

Drama Cas. (PR:AAA MPAA:NR)

HEIDI½** (1954, Switz.) 98m UA bw

Elsbeth Sigmund *(Heidi)*, Heinrich Gretler *(Grandfather)*, Thomas Klameth *(Peter)*, Elsie Attenhofer *(Aunt Dete)*, Margrit Rainer *(Peter's Mother)*, Fred Tanner *(Pastor)*, Isa Gunther *(Klara)*, Willy Birgel *(Herr Sesemann)*, Anita Mey *(Miss Rottenmeyer)*, Karl Wery *(Dr. Classen)*, Theo Lingen *(Sebastian)*.

One of the better renditions of the classic children's tale about the young girl living with her grumpy and hard-to-get-along-with grandfather. His love for the child forces him to lighten up some, thus ensuring that the girl will have a chance to go to school with the rest of the villagers.

p, Lazar Wechsler; d, Luigi Comencini; w, Wilhelm M. Treichlinger, Richard Schweizer (based on the book by Johanna Spyri); ph, Emil Berna; m, Robert Blum.

Drama (PR:AAA MPAA:NR)

HEIDI*½** (1968, Aust.) 94m Sascha/WB-7 Arts c

Eva Maria Singhammer *(Heidi)*, Gertraud Mittermayr *(Klara Sesemann)*, Gustav Knuth *(Grandfather)*, Lotte Ledi *(Aunt Dete)*, Ernst Schroeder *(Herr Sesemann)*, Margot Trooger *(Miss Rottenmeier)*, Rolf Moebius *(Dr. Klassen)*, Rudolf Vogel *(Sebastian)*, Jan Koester *(Peter)*, Rudolf Prack.

This German production of the classic Spyri novel is updated and still retains the warmth and enjoyment of the book. Schweizer's screenplay and Jacobs' direction makes this a film that can be enjoyed by children and adults. Singhammer is the orphaned German girl living with her grandfather and abducted by her aunt to work as a servant for a rich family. Knuth searches for and is finally reunited with his granddaughter. Photography of the Alpine settings is a standout thanks to Angst, who is among a trio of German cameramen noted for their "mountain" films.

p, Richard Deitsch; d, Werner Jacobs; w, Richard Schweizer (adapted by Michael Haller from Johanna Spyri's novel); ph, Gunther Kopf, Richard Angst (Eastmancolor); m, Franz Grothe; ed, Arnd Heyne; art d, Fritz Juptner-Jonstorff, Hans Zehetner, Hans-Gunther Malyjurek; cos, Barbara Langbein; m/l, "Heidi," Grothe (English lyrics by Stanley Styne), "Echo Mountain Song," Moose Charlap (English lyrics by Styne).

Drama Cas. (PR:AAA MPAA:NR)

HEIDI AND PETER** (1955, Switz.) 89m Praesens/UA c

Heinrich Gretler *(Grandfather)*, Elsbeth Sigmund *(Heidi)*, Thomas Klameth *(Peter)*, Emil Hegetschweiler *(Teacher)*, Willy Birgel *(Herr Sesemann)*, Traute Carlsen *(Grandmother Sesemann)*, Anita Mey *(Miss Rottenmeier)*, Thio Lingen *(Sebastian)*, Isa Guenther *(Clara Sesemann)*, Carl Wery *(Dr. Classen)*, Margrit Rainer *(Peter's Mother)*, Fred Tanner *(The Parson)*.

Sequel to HEIDI is a bit too heavy in terms of sentiment to allow the charm of the story, characters, and setting to shine through, but it is still a well-made effort that will keep any tot entranced at the further adventures of the little Swiss girl. This time the problems that erupt as a result of a visit from Sigmund's crippled friend are made secondary in the wake of a gigantic flood.

p, Lazar Wechsler, Peter Riethof; d, Franz Schnyder; w, Richard Schwiezer, Max Weinberg (based on the novel *Heidi Makes Use Of What She Has Learned* by Johanna Spyri); ph, Emil Berna (Technicolor); m, Robert Blum; ed, Herman Haller.

Drama (PR:AAA MPAA:NR)

HEIDI'S SONG** (1982) 94m Hanna-Barbera PAR c

Voices of: Lorne Greene *(Grandfather)*, Sammy Davis, Jr. *(Head Ratte)*, Margery Gray *(Heidi)*, Peter Cullen *(Gruffle)*, Roger DeWitt *(Peter)*, Richard Erdman *(Herr Sessmann)*, Fritz Feld *(Sebastian)*, Pamelyn Ferdin *(Klara)*, Joan Gerber *(Fraulein Rottenmeier)*, Michael Bell *(Willie)*, Virginia Gregg *(Aunt Dete)*, Janet Waldo *(Tinette)*, Frank Walker *(Schnoddle/Hootie)*, Mike Winslow *(Mountain)*.

An animated version of the classic novel finds the story still the same, but now with the added touch of songs written by Sammy Cahn and Burton Lane. The music is no standout and neither is the animation. Enjoyable only for the toddler set.

p, Joseph Barbera, William Hanna; d, Robert Taylor; w, Barbera, Taylor, Jameson Brewer (based on a novel by Johanna Spyri); m, Hoyt S. Curten; ed, Gregory V. Watson, Jr.; art d, Paul Julian; animation, Hal Ambro, Charlie Downs.

Animation Cas. (PR:AA MPAA:G)

HEIGHTS OF DANGER*½ (1962, Brit.) 60m ABF-Children's Film Foundations/CD bw

Basil Appleby *(Mr. Burton)*, Freda Bamford *(Mrs. Burton)*, Wilfred Downing *(Wilfred Burton)*, Annette Cabot *(Annette Burton)*, Christopher Cabot *(Christopher Burton)*, Richard Goolden *(Mr. Henderson)*, Jack Melford *(Mr. Croudson)*, Roger Snowdon *(Wolfing)*, Sebastian Cabot *(Jakes)*.

Routine family drama starring Appleby as the financially strapped owner of a garage who is tempted to sell out to unscrupulous businessman Melford. There is hope, however, in the guise of rich and kind Goolden, who offers to pay Appleby to compete in an Alpine auto race. Despite the frequent attempts at sabotage by Melfords' henchmen, Appleby wins the race and saves his garage. (Released in England in 1953.)

p, Howard Thomas; d, Peter Bradford; w, Betty Davies; ph, Reg W. Cavender; m, Doreen Carwithen; ed, Alex Milner-Gardner; set d, Scott MacGregor.

Drama (PR:A MPAA:NR)

HEINZELMANNCHEN (SEE: SHOEMAKER AND THE ELVES, THE, 1967)

HEIR TO TROUBLE** (1936) 59m COL bw

Ken Maynard *(Ken Armstrong)*, Joan Perry *(Jane Parker)*, Harry Woods *(John Motley)*, Martin Faust *(Ike)*, Harry Bowen *(Hank)*, Wally Wales *(Spurs)*, Dorothy Wolbert *(Tillie)*, Fern Emmett *(Amanda)*, Pat O'Malley *(Dwyer)*, Art Mix, Frank Yaconelli, Frank LaRue, Hal Price, Jim Corey, Lafe McKee, Jack Rockwell, Slim Whitaker, Roy Bucko, Jack Ward, Bud McClure, Artie Ortego, Tarzan the Horse.

Maynard inherits a mine and a baby when a friend dies. The bad guys who have their sights on the mine try to implicate Maynard as the killer of his friend. The real hero and scene stealer is Maynard's horse, Tarzan, which saves the baby when the mine explodes, and also plays nursemaid to it.

p, Larry Darmour; d, Spencer Gordon Bennet; w, Nate Gatzert (based on a story by Ken Maynard); ph, Herbert Kirkpatrick; ed, Dwight Caldwell.

Western (PR:A MPAA:NR)

HEIRESS, THE***** (1949) 115m PAR bw

Olivia de Havilland *(Catherine Sloper)*, Montgomery Clift *(Morris Townsend)*, Ralph Richardson *(Dr. Austin Sloper)*, Miriam Hopkins *(Lavinia Penniman)*, Vanessa Brown *(Maria)*, Mona Freeman *(Marian Almond)*, Ray Collins *(Jefferson Almond)*, Betty Linley *(Mrs. Montgomery)*, Selena Royle *(Elizabeth Almond)*, Paul Lees *(Arthur Townsend)*, Harry Antrim *(Mr. Abeel)*, Russ Conway *(Quintus)*, David Thursby *(Geier)*.

This powerful and compelling drama, based on Henry James' 1881 novel *Washington Square* and the successful Broadway play of 1946-47 by Ruth and Augustus Goetz, owes its triumph to the deft hand of director Wyler and the awesome performance by de Havilland in the lead role, for which she won her second Oscar.

De Havilland is the plain looking daughter of wealthy Richardson, a widowed doctor; they reside at 16 Washington Square about 1850 and life is uneventful, mostly dull. Richardson is a tyrant at home, dictating his daughter's every move, hurtful when telling de Havilland that she unfortunately bears no resemblance to his dear departed wife, a beautiful and charming woman. Suitors shun de Havilland, whose gestures are awkward, conversation uninspired and witless, and manners without grace or charm. She attends a ball where only Clift pays attention to her, flattering her and asking if he may call on her. When Richardson hears of this apprentice suitor, he scoffs at the idea, telling his daughter that the young man is merely a fortune hunter. De Havilland refuses to believe this and meets with Clift. He is exactly what Richardson has described, a youth who has squandered away his own small fortune in Europe and is now looking for a large meal ticket. Richardson insults Clift but the suitor is persistent. The father tells de Havilland he will take her on a European tour if she will forget Clift, but she rejects this notion, saying she will elope with Clift soon. Richardson then tells her that she may have her $10,000-a-year dowry from her mother's estate, but that he will cut off his own $20,000-a-year to her, her substantial inheritance, if she weds cad Clift. When Clift hears this, he begins to back off and, on the night de Havilland waits for him to come for her, disappears. Though devastated, de Havilland stands up to her dictatorial father, saying she might run off with the next fellow who looks in her direction. Again, Richardson threatens to disinherit her and she thrusts pen and paper at him, telling him to do so. He says no, he cannot do such a thing to his only child, then moans that he has no idea what she might do next. "That's right, father, you'll never know—will you?" Richardson dies a short time later of a lung illness, leaving his vast fortune to de Havilland. She does not squander her wealth but lives as a near-recluse in the great mansion. Seven years drag by; then her aunt, Hopkins, brings word that Clift has returned to the city and is anxious to see her. De Havilland is at first reserved, then agrees to see the man who deserted her. Clift arrives world-weary, mustachioed, and full of apologies, explaining that he vanished rather than see her lose her fortune, that what he did was for her benefit and that he has been in agony ever since. Boldly, Clift proposes once more to her, suggesting they now elope as they had planned years ealier. Appearing to be touched, de Havilland agrees, but when Clift returns to the mansion later that night he finds the door bolted. De Havilland stands on the other side, listening, taking great pleasure in her revenge, as Clift frantically bangs on the door, pleading for her to come away with him, banging and banging, as de Havilland turns and slowly climbs the staircase to her room, holding a flickering lamp on high, disappearing into the darkness of her own lonely world. Earlier she had told her aunt: "Yes, I can be very cruel. I have been taught by masters . . . He came twice —I shall see to it he never comes a third time." She does, and with such devastating finality that the viewer perceives not merely a wounded woman taking revenge but a tragically hurt female purging herself of her own misguided beliefs and emotions. This was one of de Havilland's greatest roles and her transformation from docile emotional victim to that of a rational, resolved adult is a masterpiece of acting. Richardson, too, is equal to her performance, essaying a difficult role with majestic presence, rendering a thoroughly hateful portrait of a man who is really so fearful for his daughter's future that he will incur her permanent loathing to protect that future. Hopkins is special as the one eternally bright spot in de Havilland's life, but Clift is unsuited to the role of the manipulating rake. His appearance is too boyish, his delivery too concentrated to make one think him rotten through and through. The actor, hired for $100,000 to perform the role, felt awkward in the part, that he did not have the right handle on playing a young man in mid-19th century New York. He walked with a slouch, almost a stoop, and Wyler tried repeatedly to correct his posture. At one point, when the director asked Clift to assume an erect stance, the actor said: "Please don't bawl me out in front of the crew." Replied the quiet Wyler: "I don't bawl out actors. I might correct something." Clift took to hiding out in his dressing room and would only emerge when called for his scenes. He talked to none of the cast and refused to give interviews to the press. Hopkins, he later complained, tried to steal scenes from him, as did Richardson, and he said de Havilland was so mechanical he could not react to her lines properly. She, on the other hand, felt he was playing his role for his own benefit and was later quoted as saying: "Monty was painstaking and I liked that about him but I had a sense that Monty was thinking almost entirely of himself and leaving me out of the scene. It was difficult for me to adapt to playing that way." Wyler really changed the role Clift played as it was done on Broadway. In the play, the suitor arrives at the mansion and begins inquiring about the expensive paintings and vases, telegraphing to the audience his fortune-hunting nature. None of that was shown by Wyler, who asked the Goetz's to restructure the character so that the audience would think Clift sincere and be genuinely surprised when he did not appear on the night scheduled for the elopement. Wyler worked hard to produce this masterpiece, wanting cameraman Gregg Toland and getting Leo Tover. When Wyler asked for a setup calling for deep focus, Tover took a half day to make preparations where Toland would have achieved the setup in an hour. Moreover, Richardson, who had acted the role of the tyrannical father in England and owned the part, played every one of his scenes to the hilt, trying to take every second of film from de Havilland (she later termed him an "evil" man). Though he acted the role to perfection, Richardson would consciously ask Wyler at the beginning of each scene: "How would you like me to play this one?" The director once asked if there were several ways to hang up a frock coat or lay down a cane or a pair of gloves. Richardson then gave a half dozen interpretations to each question, acting out scenes with aplomb without the cameras rolling. "He gave me a display, laying out his merchandise," remembered the director later. "He entered the set as if he had lived there 20 years. I suspect that all the time he knew which way he wanted to do it. That's an actor for you!" Richardson also employed little tricks to take the scene from de Havilland. He would tap his cane or slap his gloves against his hand, a table, a bannister while she was talking, anything to rivet eyes on him. Wyler was too clever for him, instructing cinematographer Tover to shoot the scene cropped so that only Richardson's head and shoulders would be seen. The sad and tragic story of THE HEIRESS is based on real people researched by author James in London. While interviewing Frances Anne Kemble at the Haymarket Theatre in 1879, the British actress told James about how her impoverished gentleman brother had wooed and won the affections of a rich but plain-looking woman whose father refused to sanction the marriage, threatening to disinherit his daughter if she ran off with the young blackguard. Kemble vanished when he heard of the impending disinheritance but returned 10 years later, when the father was dead, to awkwardly attempt a reconciliation with the spinster who then spurned him. The Goetz adaptation of the James story was a solid stage hit with Basil Rathbone as the father, Wendy Hiller as the daughter (both considered for the film, then dropped as being "too weak"), and Peter Cookson as the fortune-hunter. At the same time the play was mounted in London by John Gielgud with Richardson as the father and Peggy Ashcroft as the daughter (later Hiller took over the role in London). Wyler wanted the play for Paramount as soon as he saw it and took the first draft of the script to de Havilland, who made it her own special project. The director also scored another coup by having Copland do the score, a telling and complimenting piece of haunting music. Copland had scored such films as OF MICE AND MEN and OUR TOWN in 1940 and NORTH STAR in 1943, all outstanding achievements but for the latter he was labeled as "red tinted" during the political witchhunts of the late 1940s and Wyler had to argue heavily with Paramount executives to allow Copland to write the music for THE HEIRESS. Wyler was more than justified in his choice in that Copland won an Oscar for Best Score. Also winning Oscars for THE HEIRESS were set designers Meehan and Horner and costumers Head and Steele. De Havilland picked up her second Oscar (she had previously won for TO EACH HIS OWN) with a prepared short statement: "Your Award for TO EACH HIS OWN I took as an incentive to venture forward. Thank you for this very generous assurance that I have not failed to do so." After the ceremonies at the Pantages Theater the actress told reporters: "When I won the first Award in 1946, I was terribly thrilled. But this time I felt solemn, very serious and . . . shocked. Yes, shocked! It's a great responsibility to win the Award twice."

p&d, William Wyler; w, Ruth and Augustus Goetz (based on their play and the novel *Washington Square* by Henry James); ph, Leo Tover; m, Aaron Copland; ed, William Hornbeck; art d, John Meehan, Harry Horner; set d, Emile Kuri; cos, Edith Head, Gile Steele; spec eff, Gordon Jennings; m/l, "My Love Loves Me," Ray Evans, Jay Livingston; makeup, Wally Westmore, Hal Lierly, Bill Woods.

Drama **Cas.** **(PR:A MPAA:NR)**

HEIRLOOM MYSTERY, THE** (1936, Brit.) 72m GS Enterprises/RKO bw

Edward Rigby *(Charles Marriott)*, Mary Glynne *(Lady Benton)*, Gus McNaughton *(Alfred Fisher)*, Marjorie Taylor *(Mary)*, John Robinson *(Dick Marriott)*, Martin Lewis *(Sir Arthur Benton)*, Kathleen Gibson *(Doris)*, Louanne Shaw *(Millie)*, Bruce Lister *(Alf Dene)*, H.F. Maltby *(Mr. Lewis)*, Basil Langton, Michael Ripper.

The heirloom in question is an antique chest copied by a furniture maker several years ago, but brought out into the open when the actual owner discovers the forgery. The problem was that the owner's husband was in desperate need of cash, so he had cabinetmaker Rigby make a duplicate. The wife finds out, and even after all these years she points the finger at innocent Rigby, leaving his son with the job of figuring out a solution, which he does. Lightweight, but effective.

p, A. George Smith; d, Maclean Rogers; w, Kathleen Butler (based on the story by G.H. Moresby-White); ph, Geoffrey Faithfull.

Drama **(PR:A MPAA:NR)**

HEIST, THE* (1979, Ital.) 85m First American Films c

Robert Hossein, Charles Aznavour, Virna Lisi, Europe's Top Stunt Drivers.

Somewhere in this confusing melange of hot exhaust pipes and daring stunt drivers a cops and robbers story lies waiting, but finding it will take effort. A great cast has little to do as the cameras focus on nothing but cars as they perform thrilling feats along streets and highways. Pretty racy stuff for something that pretends to be a crime and adventure film.

p, Ralph Baum; d&w, Sergio Goffi; ph, Dan Dist; m, George Gararentz.

Crime/Adventure **(PR:A MPAA:NR)**

HELD FOR RANSOM* (1938) 59m GN bw

Blanche Mehaffey *(Betty Mason)*, Grant Withers *(Scott)*, Bruce Warren *(Dan)*, Jack Mulhall *(Morrison)*, Kenneth Harlan *(McBride)*, Harry Harvey *(Mike)*, Edward Foster *(Joe)*, Walter McGrail *(Donnelly)*, George Moore *(Halliday)*, Robert McKenzie *(Storekeeper)*, Richard Lancaster, John McCallum, Joseph Girard.

A weak and confusing crime film with Mehaffey as an FBI agent going after the kidnapers of a wealthy man. The kidnapers have more problems then just a female G-man when the ransom money is picked up by an innocent bystander who tries to return it to its rightful owners. He's killed and the good and bad guys try to find where he hid it.

d, Clarence Bricker; w, Barry Barringer; ph, Arthur Reed, Roland Price; ed, George Halligan.

Crime **(PR:A MPAA:NR)**

HELD IN TRUST*½ (1949, Brit.) 58m Productions Number 1/Do-U-Know Film Productions bw

Ian Proctor *(Charles Ross)*, Dorothy Shaw *(Bess Lovell)*, Guy Verney *(Gang Leader)*.

Tired drama in which Proctor plays a crook turned artist, who sticks to his guns of staying straight and pursuing honest goals despite the efforts of old buddies to entice him to perform one more job. Proctor proves that the handling of his paint brush hasn't interfered with his ability to shoot straight as he kills the gang leader and thwarts a theft of art treasures.

p,d,w,&ph, Cecil H. Williamson.

Crime **(PR:A MPAA:NR)**

HELDEN (SEE: ARMS AND THE MAN, 1962, Ger.)

HELDEN—HIMMEL UND HOLLE (SEE: CAVERN, THE, 1965, Ger.)

HELDINNEN** (1962, Ger.) 97m H.R. Sokal-UFA/Casino c

Marianne Koch *(Minna von Barnhelm)*, Johanna von Koczian *(Franziska)*, Paul Hubschmid *(Maj. von Tellheim)*, Walter Giller *(Just)*, Gunter Pfitzmann *(Werner)*, Willy Trenk-Trebitsch *(Ricaut)*, Alfred Balthoff *(Innkeeper)*, Ursula Diestel, Ilse Kiewiet, Ingeborg Wellmann, Inge Wolffberg.

Hubschmid is a young soldier who returns from the Seven Years War in disgrace due to financial misconduct. He is consoled by his fiancee Koch, but her efforts are spurned due to his code of honor which denies him a continuation of their engagement while he is in disgrace. Seeking to boost his shattered ego, Koch announces that she has been ostracized by her family for loving him, which sparks a confession of love from Hubschmid. Miraculously, Hubschmid's name is cleared by the army soon after. "Minna von Barnhelm," on which the film is based, was one of the three best dramatic works written by "the father" of German drama, Gotthold Lessing. It opened in Hamburg in September, 1767.

p, H.R. Sokal; d, Dietrich Haugk; w, Charlotte Kerr (based on the musical comedy "Minna von Barnhelm oder Das Soldatengluck" by Gotthold Ephraim Lessing); ph, Werner Krien; m, Franz Grothe; ed, Claus von Boro; art d, Hanns Kuhnert; m/l, Willy Dehmel, Kerr; ch, Lilo Herbeth.

Musical/Comedy **(PR:A MPAA:NR)**

HELDORADO (SEE: HELLDORADO, 1946)

HELEN MORGAN STORY, THE*** (1959) 118m WB bw (GB: BOTH ENDS OF THE CANDLE)

Ann Blyth *(Helen Morgan)*, Paul Newman *(Larry)*, Richard Carlson *(Wade)*, Gene Evans *(Whitey Krause)*, Alan King *(Ben)*, Cara Williams *(Dolly)*, Virginia Vincent *(Sue)*, Walter Woolf King *(Ziegfeld)*, Dorothy Green *(Mrs. Wade)*, Ed Platt *(Haggerty)*, Warren Douglas *(Hellinger)*, Sammy White *(Sammy)*, Peggy De Castro, Cheri De Castro, Babette De Castro *(Singers)*, Jimmy McHugh, Rudy Vallee, Walter Winchell *(Themselves)*.

Helen Morgan and the Roaring Twenties were synonymous. In the days of flappers, bootleg hooch, bathtub gin, and blatant gangsters, Morgan was the greatest torch singer of the day, a petite brunette who sat atop pianos and plaintively warbled sad songs about the men who mistreated and deserted her. More of a profile of those songs than a detailed exposition of her life, this film gives only a slice of a fabulous and unforgettable career, a glimpse of a great entertainer that winks out too early to really show the lady and her nightclub-era life. Blyth as Morgan is shown in her Chicago days singing and dancing the hula in sideshows and how she meets smooth operator Newman, an apprentice tough guy. He promotes her into a beauty contest in Canada which she wins, then loses when the authorities learn that she is not a native. He then gets her a few singing jobs in New York while he busies himself with peddling bootleg hooch. When the owner of the club where Blyth is singing refuses to buy his rotgut booze, the unscrupulous Newman calls the cops and has the joint raided, which causes Blyth to be thrown into jail. There she languishes until new-found friend and lawyer Carlson bails her out. Carlson then proceeds to woo Blyth while her star rises and she makes a name for herself along Broadway. Newman, who has left Blyth to warble her way to loneliness, returns to pad his own pockets with her fame. He persuades Carlson to put up the money for the House of Morgan, a nightclub which he, Newman, will manage. He also cuts himself in for a share of Blyth's profits from her appearance in Ziegfeld's production of "Showboat." When Blyth learns that Carlson put up the money for her club and not Newman, she rejects him. Both of their careers take a nosedive. Blyth begins drinking herself into stupors and hits the gutter. Newman is severely wounded in a warehouse robbery with his pal King and sent to prison. When Blyth falls desperately ill and begins to recover from acute alcoholism, Newman visits her in the hospital to cheer her up; he is then returned to prison, unknown to her. When Blyth is released from the hospital, however, Newman is waiting. He takes her to her old boarded up club and, to her surprise, Blyth finds it packed with old friends gathered to wish her well. Blyth once more sits atop the piano and belts out her old songs as the applause showers down upon her and the curtain closes. Of course, most of the wobbly plot is fictional, which is unfortunate since Morgan's true story was much more spectacular and, had it been followed, would have provided a finer film. Blyth is nevertheless effective as the fragile torch singer and Newman is terrific as the leather-hided hood who shows that tiny soft spot at the end. Carlson as the rich man is a prop, but King is good as the uneducated, goony sidekick. The script is predictable, overripe, and maudlin. This was not one of Curtiz's better efforts but he did his best with a worn out backstage story. The best of the film is when Blyth sings, or rather Gogi Grant's voice is dubbed for her vocals, with songs that include "Bill" (Jerome Kern, P.G. Wodehouse), "Don't Ever Leave Me," "Can't Help Lovin' Dat Man," "Why Was I Born?" (Kern, Oscar Hammerstein II), "I Can't Give You Anything but Love" (Dorothy Fields, Jimmy McHugh), "If You Were the Only Girl in the World" (Clifford Grey, Nat D. Ayer), "The Love Nest" (Otto Harbach, Louis A. Hirsch), "I'll Get By" (Roy Turk, Fred Ahlert), "Body and Soul" (Edward Heyman, Robert Sour, Frank Eyton, John Green), "Avalon" (Vincent Rose, Al Jolson), "Breezin' Along with the Breeze" (Haven Gillespie, Seymour Simons, Richard Whiting), "Someone to Watch Over Me," "Do Do Do," "I've Got a Crush on You" (George and Ira Gershwin).

p, Martin Rackin; d, Michael Curtiz; w, Oscar Saul, Dean Reisner, Stephen Longstreet, Nelson Gidding; ph, Ted McCord (CinemaScope); m, Larry Prinz; ed, Frank Bracht; art d, John Beckman; cos, Howard Shoup; ch, LeRoy Prinz.

Biography/Musical **(PR:A MPAA:NR)**

HELEN OF TROY* (1956, Ital) 118m WB c

Rossanna Podesta *(Helen)*, Jack Sernas *(Paris)*, Sir Cedric Hardwicke *(Priam)*, Stanley Baker *(Achilles)*, Niall MacGinnis *(Menelaus)*, Nora Swinburne *(Hecuba)*, Robert Douglas *(Agamemnon)*, Torin Thatcher *(Ulysses)*, Harry Andrews *(Hector)*, Janette Scott *(Cassandra)*, Ronald Lewis *(Aeneas)*, Brigitte Bardot *(Andraste)*, Eduardo Ciannelli *(Andros)*, Marc Lawrence *(Diomedes)*, Maxwell Reed *(Ajax)*, Robert Brown *(Polydorus)*, Barbara Cavan *(Cora)*, Terence Longdon *(Patroclus)*, Patricia Marmount *(Andromache)*, Guido Notari *(Nestor)*, Tonio Selwart *(Adelphous)*, George Zoritch *(Dancer)*, Edmond Knight *(High Priest)*

An overblown production that should have concentrated more on story development than how many extras could be squeezed in. Podesta plays "The Face That Launched a Thousand Ships," and helped Warner Bros. lose $4 million. A comic book script and Wise's careless direction sinks this story from the land of warriors who used to hurl spears and shoot balls of fire at their enemies.

d, Robert Wise; w, John Twist, Hugh Gray, N. Richard Nash (based on Homeric legends); ph, Harry Stradling (CinemaScope, Warner Color); m, Max Steiner; ed, Thomas Reilly; art d, Edward Carrere; cos, Roger Furse; ch, Madi Obolensky.

Drama **(PR:A MPAA:NR)**

HELICOPTER SPIES, THE*½ (1968) 88m MGM c

Robert Vaughan, David McCallum, Carol Lynley, Bradford Dillman, Lola Albright, Julie London, John Carradine, Sid Haig, Leo G. Carroll.

A television series, "The Man From Uncle," was so popular the makers resorted to putting segments together and releasing them theatrically to keep the many fans of the international crime fighters happy. Here Vaughan and McCallum journey to Greece to make sure a new weapon is not put into use by the crazy dabblers in the supernatural who are its holders. Strictly for die-hard fans.

p, Anthony Spinner; d, Boris Segal; w, Dean Hargrove.

Spy **(PR:A MPAA:NR)**

HELL AND HIGH WATER zero (1933) 68m PAR bw

Richard Arlen *(Capt. Jericho)*, Judith Allen *(Sally Driggs)*, Charlie Grapewin *(Peck Wealin)*, Sir Guy Standing *(Rear Admiral)*, Robert Knettles *(Barney)*, Gertrude Hoffman *(Mom Wealin)*, S. Matsui *(Joe Satsanuki)*, William Frawley *(Milton J. Bunsey)*, Esther Muir *(Barney's Mother)*, Selmer Jackson, Mike Morita, Franklin Parker, Barton MacLane, John Marston, Iris Yamoaka.

Arlen is a seafront garbage collector who doesn't like women. One day on his garbage collecting boat he picks up Allen who is trying to drown herself. He also gets the baby a woman left at his doorstep and a story that goes no place. The garbage collector gets into many unbelievable situations and all the characters are improbable.

d, Grover Jones, William Slavens McNutt; w, Agnes Brand Leahy, Jones, McNutt (based on a story by Max Miller); ph, Al Gilks.

Drama **(PR:A MPAA:NR)**

HELL AND HIGH WATER*** (1954) 103m FOX c

Richard Widmark *(Adam Jones)*, Bella Darvi *(Denise)*, Victor Francen *(Prof. Montel)*, Cameron Mitchell *("Ski" Brodski)*, Gene Evans *(Chief Holter)*, David Wayne *(Dugboat Walker)*, Stephen Bekassy *(Neuman)*, Richard Loo *(Fujimori)*, Peter Scott *(Happy Mosk)*, Henry Kulky *(Gunner McCrossin)*, Wong Artarne *(Chin Lee)*, Harry Carter *(Quartermaster)*, Robert Adler *(Welles)*, Don Orlando *(Carpino)*, Rollin Moriyama *(Joto)*, John Gifford *(Torpedo)*, William Yip *(Ho-Sin)*, Tommy Walker *(Crew Member)*, Leslie Bradley *(Mr. Aylesworth)*, John Wengraf *(Col. Schuman)*, Harry Denny *(McAuliff)*, Edo Mita *(Taxi Driver)*, Ramsey Williams *(Lieutenant)*, Robert B. Williams *(Reporter)*, Harlan Warde *(Photographer)*, Neyle Morrow.

Director Fuller used a White House announcement of a nuclear bomb of foreign origin that had been exploded outside the U.S. as the basis for this film. An announcer comes on at the beginning of the film saying that the movie is the story behind the mysterious explosion. Francen is the leader of a group of scientists worried about the government's inability to handle the threat of nuclear war, and they hire Widmark to command a submarine to search for communist atomic arsenals in the North Pacific. Arriving at their destination, the crew and scientists find that the Reds plan to drop an A-bomb from an American B-29 on North Korea and lay the blame on the U.S. Widmark and his men shoot down the plane, causing the bomb to explode. An implausible story that becomes plausible through Fuller's direction.

p, Raymond A. Klune; d, Samuel Fuller; w, Jesse L. Lasky, Jr., Fuller (based on a story by David Hempstead); ph, Joe MacDonald (CinemaScope, Technicolor); m, Alfred Newman; ed, James B. Clark; md, Edward B. Powell; art d, Lyle Wheeler, Leland Fuller; set d, Walter M. Scott, Stuart Reiss; cos, Charles LeMaire, Travilla; spec eff, Ray Kellogg.

Drama **(PR:A MPAA:NR)**

HELL BELOW*** (1933) 105m MGM bw

Robert Montgomery *(Lt. Thomas Knowlton)*, Walter Huston *(Lt.-Comdr. Toler)*, Madge Evans *(Joan)*, Jimmy Durante *(Ptomaine)*, Eugene Pallette *(MacDougal)*, Robert Young *(Lt. Brick Walters)*, Edwin Styles *(Herbert Standish)*, John Lee Mahin *(Lt. Nelson)*, David Newell *(Lt. Radford)*, Sterling Holloway *(Seaman Jenks)*, Charles Irwin *(Buck Teeth Sergeant)*, Henry Kolker *(Admiral)*, Sid Saylor *(Chief Engineer Hendrickson)*, Maude Eburne *(Admiral's Wife)*, Paul Porcasi *(Italian)*.

A rousing submarine drama, Huston is the whole show in HELL BELOW, playing the part of a rugged, disciplined sub captain during WW I. After performing a dangerous secret mission, the submarine is caught by pursuing German destroyers and submerges to escape, leaving Young to be wounded while drifting on the open sea in a lifeboat. Montgomery, who is Young's bosom buddy, disobeys Huston's orders to play it safe and fires a spread of four torpedoes into the destroyers, exploding two of them. The other two destroyers attack the sub, dropping depth charges which explode next to the ship, causing severe leaks and releasing deadly chlorine gas which causes eight of the crew members to die before Huston's eyes. He keeps his nerve and manages to maneuver his vessel to safety but he has such a bad time with Montgomery that he orders him locked up for insubordination. Montgomery, who has acted out of compassion to save Young's life, preserving him for Evans, the girl he and Young both love, is later cashiered out of the service. His sacrifice is the thrust of a very weak plot. Huston, however, manages to surface this somewhat soggy craft with his energetic acting ability. Conway's direction, particularly the action scenes when the submarine is under attack, are exceptional.

d, Jack Conway; w, Laird Doyle, Raymond Schrock, John Lee Mahin, John Meehan (based on the novel *Pigboats* by Comdr. Edward Ellsberg); ph, Harold Rosson; ed, Hal C. Kern; tech adv, Lt.-Comdr. Morris D. Gilmore, U.S.N.

War Drama **(PR:A MPAA:NR)**

HELL BELOW ZERO*** (1954, Brit.) 90m Warwick COL c

Alan Ladd *(Duncan Craig)*, Joan Tetzel *(Judie Nordahl)*, Basil Sydney *(Bland)*, Stanley Baker *(Erik Bland)*, Joseph Tomelty *(Capt. McPhee)*, Niall MacGinnis *(Dr. Howe)*, Jill Bennett *(Gerda Peterson)*, Peter Dyneley *(Miller)*, Susan Rayne *(Kathleen)*, Philo Hauser *(Sandeborg)*, Ivan Craig *(Larsen)*, Paddy Ryan *(Manders)*, Cyril Chamberlain, Paul Homer, Edward Hardwicke, John Witty, Brandon Toomey, Genine Graham, Basil Cunard, Fred Griffiths, John Warren, Philip Ray, Paul Connell, Glyn Houston.

Ladd is on an airplane bound for Capetown, South Africa, to find out what happened to the $10,000 he invested in a mine. On the trip he becomes attracted to Tetzel, who is on her way to search for her missing whaler father and wants nothing to do with Ladd. When he finds that he can't get his money back from his crooked partner, Ladd signs up as first mate on the boat Tetzel is using to hunt for her father. As the ship sets out, Tetzel gets word that her father is dead and his partner Sydney thinks it was a suicide. Ladd finds out from MacGinnis, the ship's drunken doctor, that Sydney and Tetzel are engaged. But he finds out from Tetzel that that was old news; she had recently broken up with her father's partner. The whaling boat joins up with the factory ship (where the whales are processed) and Sydney is on it. Ladd tries to get more information on Tetzel's father's death but a school of whales changes everything. He's assigned to another boat which is rammed by Tetzel's boat when caught in an ice jam. Both ships are abandoned and the crews make camp on the ice floe. It becomes obvious to Ladd and Tetzel that Sydney was the one who killed her father, and a violent fight between the two men breaks out. Sydney is killed when he falls into the freezing water, and with her father's death solved, Tetzel now has time for Ladd. An action-filled story with unusual locale in the Antarctic.

p, Albert R. Broccoli, Irving Allen, George W. Willoughby; d, Mark Robson; w, Alec Coppel, Max Trell, Richard Maibaum (based on Hammond Innes' novel *The White South*); ph, John Wilcox (Technicolor); m, Clifton Parker; ed, John Guthridge.

Adventure **(PR:A MPAA:NR)**

HELL BENT FOR 'FRISCO* (1931) 60m Sono-Art Wide World bw

Charles Delaney, Vera Reynolds, Carroll Nye, Wesley Barry, William Desmond.

A low-budget production with an outdated and melodramatic storyline. Delaney is a newspaper reporter who sets out to prove that Nye murdered the heroine's brother. The story moves like a stone with moldy dialog, and even an editor crying "Hold the presses!"

d, Stuart Paton; w, Arthur Hoerl; ph, Jules Cronjager.

Drama **(PR:A MPAA:NR)**

HELL BENT FOR GLORY (SEE: LAFAYETTE ESCADRILLE, 1957)

HELL BENT FOR LEATHER*½ (1960) 82m UNIV c

Audie Murphy *(Clay)*, Felicia Farr *(Janet)*, Stephen McNally *(Deckett)*, Robert Middleton *(Ambrose)*, Rad Fulton *(Moon)*, Jan Merlin *(Travers)*, Herbert Rudley *(Perrick)*, Malcolm Atterbury *(Gambie)*, Joseph Ruskin *(Shad)*, Allan Lane *(Kelsey)*, John Qualen *(Old Ben)*, Eddie Little Sky *(William)*, Steve Gravers *(Grover)*, Beau Gentry *(Stone)*, Bob Steele *(Jared)*.

Murphy, a horse trader, is wrongly accused of murder and goes on the run. Marshal McNally heads the posse and knows Murphy is innocent, but plans to kill him anyway to get credit for his capture. The innocent cowboy kidnaps Farr and convinces her that Merlin is the real murderer. An uninspired production leaning too much on Murphy to carry the story.

p, Gordon Kay; d, George Sherman; w, Christopher Knopf (based on a novel by Ray Hogan); ph, Clifford Stine (CinemaScope, Eastmancolor); m, William Lava, Irving Gertz; ed, Milton Carruth.

Western **(PR:A MPAA:NR)**

HELL BENT FOR LOVE** (1934) 65m COL bw

Tim McCoy *(Tim Daley)*, Lillian Bond *(Millie)*, Bradley Page *(Trigger Talano)*, Vincent Sherman *(Johnny Frank)*, Lafe McKee *(Dad Daley)*, Harry C. Bradley *(Professor)*, Wedgewood Newell *(Kelly Drake)*, Gloria Warner *(Maid)*, Max Wagner, Guy Usher, Ed LeSaint, Eddie Sturgis, Ernie Adams, Hal Price.

McCoy is a state trooper who is in love with night club singer Bond. The owner of the club, Page, is a crooked man running a dozen rackets through his club. He has McCoy beaten up and the trooper gets together a group of ex-cons he had sent up to help nail Page. They break Page's rackets, and McCoy and Bond get on with their relationship.

d, D. Ross Lederman; w, Harold Shumate; ph, Benjamin Kline; ed, Otto Meyer.

Crime **(PR:A MPAA:NR)**

HELL BOATS** (1970, Brit.) 95m Oakmont/UA c

James Franciscus *(Lt. Comdr. Tom Jeffords)*, Elizabeth Shepherd *(Alison Ashurst)*, Ronald Allen *(Comdr. Roger Ashurst)*, Reuven Bar-Yotam *(Yacov)*, Inigo Jackson *(Stanhope)*, Mark Hawkins *(Barlow)*, Drewe Henley *(Johnson)*, Magda Konopka *(Lucianna)*, Takis Emmanuel *(Salvatore)*, Philip Madoc *(E-Boat Commander)*, Sean Barrett *(Henderson)*, Andreas Malandrinos *(Benny)*.

Average WW II film starring Franciscus as an American commander serving under the British Royal Navy in 1942. He is assigned to blockade the island of Malta and told to formulate a plan to destroy the Nazi arsenal in Sicily. To do this he hits upon the idea of using a captured German "E-Boat" to sneak through the enemy lines and blow up the arsenal. Though they have personal differences, crew member Allen volunteers to pilot the small torpedo boat and complete the mission, which they do after the usual but always exciting acts of heroism. Interesting views of the island fortress in the Mediterranean, Malta.

p, Lewis J. Rachmil; d, Paul Wendkos; w, Anthony Spinner, Donald Ford, Derek Ford (based on a story by S.S. Schweitzer); ph, Paul Beeson (Technicolor); m, Frank Cordell; ed, John S. Smith; art d, Tony Pratt; spec eff, Ron Ballanger; cos, Duncan MacPhee; makeup, Jill Carpenter, Eileen Fletcher; tech adv, Ian Cox (Lt. Comdr. Royal Navy Ret.).

War **(PR:A MPAA:GP)**

HELL BOUND* (1931) 67m TIF bw

Leo Carrillo *(Nick Cotrelli)*, Lola Lane *(Platinum Reed)*, Lloyd Hughes *(Dr. Robert Sanford)*, Helene Chadwick *(Sanford's Sister)*, Richard Tucker *(Gilbert)*, Gertrude Astor *(Rosie)*, Harry Strang *(Gaspipe)*, William Lawrence *(Ham)*, Marty Faust *(Omalm)*, Jack Grey *(Rat)*, Bill O'Brien *(Bilmey)*.

Carrillo is a top mobster who is too nice of a guy to be a gangster, and his wife, Lane, had gotten mixed up with him through mistaken identities. She said too much about a murder and the gangster married her so she couldn't testify against him. She is really in love with doctor Hughes, who got her through a bout with pneumonia. At the end, Carrillo, with the doctor and Lane in the house, goes outside to be shot by a rival gang so as not to have bullets disturb the two lovebirds playing chess. Most of the story's situations are taken from other gangster films and the ones that aren't are unrealistic. Purely of historical interest, if that.

p, James Cruze; d, Walter Lang; w, Julian Josephson, Edward Dean Sullivan, Adele Comandini (based on a story by Sullivan, Comandini); ph, Charles E. Schoenbaum.

Crime **(PR:A MPAA:NR)**

HELL BOUND** (1957) 69m Bel-Air/UA bw

John Russell *(Jordan)*, June Blair *(Paula)*, Stuart Whitman *(Eddie Mason)*, Margo Woode *(Jan)*, George Mather *(Stanley Thomas)*, Stanley Adams *(Herbert Fay, Jr.)*, Gene O'Donnell *(Purser)*, Frank Fenton *(Harry Quantro)*, Virginia De Lee *(Stripteaser)*, Dehl Berti *(Daddy)*, Sammee Tong *(Murdered Seaman)*, Charles Webster *(Ship Captain)*, Edward DeRoo *(Squad Officer)*, Marge Evans, Ann Daro *(Nurses)*, Frank McGrath *(Detective)*, Kay Garrett, Bob Strong, George Mayon, Red Morgan *(Quantro's Men)*, Dick Standish, *(Accomplice A&B—16mm film)*, William Flaherty *(Purser—16mm film)*, George H. Whiteman *(Ship Captain—16mm film)*, Richard Martin *(Dock Worker)*, Jerry Frank *(Police Officer at Auto Accident)*, Larry Thor *(Doctor)*, Scott Peters *(Aide)*.

A drug exploitation film with gangsters stealing a shipment of narcotics. Russell is the mastermind of a scheme to steal war surplus drugs from a ship in Los Angeles harbor. He tries to get backers for the crime by showing a 16mm film presenting his plan to get the $2 million in narcotics. Fenton is the gangster who takes the film around to backers with Blair, who is sent to keep an eye on Russell's investment. She falls for ambulance driver Whitman, who unwittingly becomes involved in the crime. Russell is killed in the attempted heist, the shipment of drugs stays on the ship, and Blair and Whitman walk away hand in hand.

p, Howard W. Koch; d, William J. Hole, Jr.; w, Richard Landau (based on a story by Landau, Arthur Orloff); ph, Carl E. Guthrie; m, Les Baxter; ed, John A. Bushelman; prod d, Jack T. Collis; spec eff, Jack Rabin, Louis DeWitt.

Crime **(PR:A MPAA:NR)**

HELL CANYON OUTLAWS** (1957) 72m ZUKOR/REP bw

Dale Robertson, Brian Keith, Rossana Rory, Dick Kallman, Don Megowan, Mike Lane, Buddy Baer, Charles Fredericks, Alexander Lockwood, James Nusser, James Maloney, William Pullen, George Ross, George Pembroke, Vincent Padula, Tom Hubbard.

Decent oater centering on the efforts of a sheriff to gain vengeance against the outlaws who have been instrumental in seeing him lose his job. The ex-sheriff sees to it that justice is properly carried out, and the town is rid of the crooks who thought they had it by the throat.

p, T. Frank Woods; d, Paul Landres; w, Allan Kaufman, Max Glandbard; ph, Floyd Crosby; m, Irving Gertz; ed, Elmo Williams; md, Gertz; art d, Dave Milton; m/l, Dick Kallman (sung by Kallman).

Western **(PR:A MPAA:NR)**

HELL CAT, THE* (1934) 70m COL bw

Robert Armstrong *(Dan Collins)*, Ann Sothern *(Geraldine)*, Benny Baker *(Snapper Dugan)*, Minna Gombell *(Pauline McCoy)*, Purnell Pratt *(Butler)*, Charles Wilson *(Graham)*, J. Carrol Naish *(Joe Morgan)*, Irving Bacon, Henry Kolker, Guy Usher, Joseph Crehan, Huey White, Nick Copeland, Richard Heming, A. R. Haysel.

A ridiculous film about a team of newspaper reporters that scares everybody, even gangsters, and Armstrong is the toughest of them all. At a social event, Sothern hits the reporter, so naturally he socks her. She decides to teach him a lesson and gets a job on his paper. He covers a dangerous racketeer and discovers that Sothern's father's yacht is being used to smuggle Chinese into the country. This is all being done unknowingly to Sothern and her father. Together, Armstrong and Sothern break the ring and she gets the byline for the story.

d, Albert Rogell; w, Fred Niblo, Jr. (based on a story by Adele Buffington); ph, Benjamin Kline; ed, John Rawlins.

Drama **(PR:A MPAA:NR)**

HELL DIVERS**½ (1932) 100m MGM bw

Wallace Beery *(Windy)*, Clark Gable *(Steve)*, Conrad Nagel *(Duke)*, Dorothy Jordan *(Ann)*, Marjorie Rambeau *(Mame Kelsey)*, Marie Prevost *(Lulu)*, Cliff Edwards *(Baldy)*, John Miljan *(Griffin)*, Landers Stevens *(Admiral)*, Reed Howes *(Lt. Fisher)*, Alan Roscoe *(Captain)*, Frank Conroy *(Chaplain)*, Robert Young *(Young Officer)*, Jack Pennick *(Trainee)*, John Kelly *(Sailor)*, Virginia Bruce *(Girl)*.

A loose remake of WHAT PRICE GLORY?, this action-jammed film sees Gable and Beery as two tough petty officers in the Navy air arm who are constantly squabbling but have genuine affection for each other. Both get drunk in a bar and begin to beat each other's heads in, with Gable winning after a giant struggle which sees the saloon wrecked. Beery sulks about the drubbing and later gets even with Gable by ruining his romance with Jordan. During war games, Gable's plane folds up and he parachutes to a small rocky atoll. Pal Beery, along with pilot Nagel, flies through a raging sea storm to crash-land on the tiny dot but they, too, wind up marooned. Beery manages to fix up his plane and take off, flying to the mainland, but the craft crashes and he is dragged from the burning wreckage dying. Just before going out, Beery tells Navy rescuers where Gable and Nagel are stranded, and they are finally brought back alive, thanks to Beery's brave sacrifice. Gable, in a final salute, buries Beery's body at sea. Hill's direction is top drawer with superb aerial sequences that provide plenty of thrills. This was Gable's eighth film for MGM in 1931; he had started as a bit player that year and finished as a star with this film. Critics panned the film but the public loved it. Gable, though he never cared for the film (and not much more for Beery), researched his role thoroughly by palling about with some Navy men and learned that they never took a twist with their gin, but had a slice of lemon on the side, biting on the lemon between gulps, a habit Gable was to retain for years when drinking. This film was made with the cooperation of the U.S. Navy, shot on location in and around North Island, Panama, on board the U.S. aircraft carrier *Saratoga*, and during Navy maneuvers.

d, George Hill; w, Harvey Gates, Malcolm Stuart Boylan, J. K. McGuinness, Ralph Graves (based on a story by Lt. Comdr. Frank Wead); ph&aerial ph, Harold Wenstrom; ed, Blanche Sewell.

Aviation Drama **(PR:A MPAA:NR)**

HELL DRIVERS*** (1958, Brit.) 108m Rank bw

Stanley Baker *(Tom Yately)*, Herbert Lom *(Gino)*, Peggy Cummins *(Lucy)*, Patrick McGoohan *(Red)*, William Hartnell *(Cartley)*, Wilfrid Lawson *(Ed)*, Sidney James *(Dusty)*, Jill Ireland *(Jill)*, Alfie Bass *(Tinker)*, Gordon Jackson *(Scottie)*, David McCallum *(Jimmy Yately)*, Sean Connery *(Johnny)*, Wensley Pithey *(Pop)*, George Murcell *(Tub)*, Marjorie Rhodes *(Ma West)*, Vera Day *(Blonde)*, Beatrice Varley *(Mother)*, Robin Bailey *(Assistant Manager)*, Jean St. Clair *(Spinster)*, Jerry Stovin *(Chick)*, John Horsley *(Doctor)*, Marianne Stone *(Nurse)*, Ronald Clarke *(Barber Joe)*.

Baker is a ex-con who gets a job as a truck driver and discovers a racket run by top driver McGoohan and manager Hartnell. They are carrying five more drivers on the payroll than there really are and Hartnell has the other drivers make runs for the phantom drivers and splits their pay with McGoohan. After Baker's Italian friend is killed by the two, he sets out to put an end to the scam. McGoohan and Hartnell are killed when their truck goes over the edge of the quarry during the chase. A worthwhile thriller.

p, S. Benjamin Fisz; d, C. Raker Endfield; w, John Kruse, Endfield; ph, Geoffrey Unsworth; m, Hubert Clifford; ed, John D. Guthridge; art d, Ernest Archer.

Drama **(PR:A MPAA:NR)**

HELL FIRE AUSTIN** (1932) 70m TIF bw

Ken Maynard, Ivy Merton, Nat Pendleton, Alan Roscoe, Jack Perrin, William Robyns, Lafe McKee, Fargo Bussey, Charles LeMayne, Jack Rockwell, Jack Ward, Bud McClure, Lew Meehan, Ben Corbett, Tarzan the Horse.

Maynard's last film for Tiffany Studios before it went bankrupt. Maynard is discharged from the Army and goes out west with LeMayne. They meet Merton who owns a ranch and a horse she wants to enter in a $25,000 sweepstakes to get rid of a loan shark. Maynard races the horse and wins the sweepstakes, making a happy ending for everyone except loan shark Pendleton. Unusual amount of comedy for a western, and most of it good.

p, Phil Goldstone; d, Forrest Sheldon; w, Betty Burbridge, Sheldon (based on a story by Sheldon); ph, Ted McCord, Joe Novak.

Western **Cas.** **(PR:A MPAA:NR)**

HELL HARBOR** (1930) 90m Inspiration/UA bw

Lupe Velez *(Anita Morgan)*, Jean Hersholt *(Joseph Horngold)*, John Holland *(Bob Wade)*, Gibson Gowland *(Harry Morgan)*, Al St. John *(Bunion)*, Paul E. Burns *(Blinky)*, Harry Allen *(Peg-Leg)*, George Book-Asta *(Spootty)*, Rondo Hatton *(Dance Hall Proprietor)*, Habanera Sextette.

A descendent of Morgan the Pirate surfaces in the Caribbean and proves to be the father of a headstrong daughter. Her hellfire adventures make up the bulk of this early talky, which seems to have been made to test the parameters of sound (the sound of squeaking shoes, etc.). Exterior shots were made mostly on the west coast of Florida, and the Tampa area in the 1930s is something beautiful to see.

d, Henry King; w, Clark Silvernail, Fred De Gresac, N. Brewster Morse (based on the story "Out of the Night" by Rida Johnson Young); ph, John Fulton, Mack Stengler; ed, Lloyd Nosler; art d, Robert M. Haas.

Adventure **(PR:A MPAA:NR)**

HELL, HEAVEN OR HOBOKEN*** (1958, Brit.) 100m ABF/National Trade Association bw (GB: I WAS MONTY'S DOUBLE)

John Mills *(Maj. Harvey)*, Cecil Parker *(Col. Logan)*, Patrick Allen *(Col. Matthers)*, Patrick Holt *(Col. Dawson)*, Leslie Phillips *(Maj. Tennant)*, Michael Hordern *(Governor of Malta)*, Marius Goring *(Neilson)*, Barbara Hicks *(Hester)*, Duncan Lamont *(Bates)*, Anthony Sagar *(Guard Sergeant)*, Max Butterfield, Michael Oliver *(Guards)*, John Gale *(Osborne)*, Kenneth Warren *(Davies)*, James Hayter *(Sgt. Adams)*, Sidney James *(Porter, YMCA)*, Michael Bird *(Publican)*, Diana Beaumont *(Barmaid)*, Brian Weske *(Dispatch Rider)*, Bill Nagy *(American Captain)*, Victor Maddern *(Orderly Sergeant)*, Alfie Bass *(Small Man)*, Ronald Wilson *(American Driver)*, David Browning *(Sergeant Driver)*, John Le Mesurier *(Adjutant R.A.P.C.)*, Walter Gottell *(German Colonel)*, Macdonald Parke *(American General)*, Marne Maitland *(Arab Proprietor)*, Vera Day *(Angela)*, Maureen Connell *(Peggy)*, Sam Kydd *(Go-Between)*, Allan Cuthbertson *(Guards Officer)*, M.E. Clifton James *(Himself/Gen. Montgomery)*, Geoffrey Hibbert, Ian Whitaker, Alfred Maron, Patrick Connor, Harry Fowler, Martin Shaban, Bill Nagy, Edward Judd, Eric Francis, Derek Briggs, Desmond Roberts, Bryan Forbes, Victor Beaumont, Max Faulkner, George Eugeniou, John Heller, Frederick Jaeger, David Davies, David Lodge, Ernst Walder, Michael Bell, Douglas Blackwell, Otto Friese, Fred Nichols, Freddy Clark, John Dunbar, Gordon Harris, Donald Price, Ronnie Stevens, R. Bryan.

Small-time stock actor M.E. Clifton James plays himself in this true story of a junior British army officer who bears an uncanny resemblance to Gen. Montgomery. He is trained by Mills and studies every minute detail of the general's personality. This army intelligence plan sends James on a tour of North Africa, causing the Nazis to divert their forces, which in turn helps the British invading troops. The climax comes to a head when James, kidnaped by the Germans, is rescued and returned to safety (and a future in film).

p, Maxwell Setton; d, John Guillermin; w, Bryan Forbes (based on a book by M.E. Clifton James); ph, Basil Emmott; m, John Addison; ed, Max Benedict, md, Addison; art d, W.E. Hutchinson.

War **(PR:A MPAA:NR)**

HELL IN KOREA***½ (1956, Brit.) 81m Wessex-Dalrymple/BL bw (GB: A HILL IN KOREA)

George Baker *(Lt. Butler)*, Harry Andrews *(Sgt. Payne)*, Stanley Baker *(Cpl. Ryker)*, Michael Medwin *(Pvt. Docker)*, Ronald Lewis *(Pvt. Wyatt)*, Stephen Boyd *(Pvt. Sims)*, Victor Maddern *(Pvt. Lindop)*, Harry Landis *(Pvt. Rabin)*, Robert Brown *(Pvt. O'Brien)*, Barry Lowe *(Pvt. Neill)*, Robert Shaw *(Lance-Cpl. Hodge)*, Charles Laurence *(Pvt. Kim)*, Eric Corrie *(Pvt. Matthews)*, David Morrell *(Pvt. Henson)*, Michael Caine *(Pvt. Lockyer)*, Percy Herbert *(Pvt. Moon)*.

Well-done war drama set in Korea which details the efforts of a small British Army patrol to find a village infested with enemy soldiers. Much of the action takes place at night as the soldiers slowly make their way to the village, while being careful not to alert the enemy of their presence. Look for Shaw and Caine in small roles, Caine returning to the land where he had served with the British army during the Korean conflict.

p, Anthony Squire; d, Julian Amyes; w, Ian Dalrymple, Squire (based on a novel by Max Catto); ph, Freddie Francis; m, Malcolm Arnold; ed, Peter Hunt.

War **(PR:C MPAA:NR)**

HELL IN THE CITY (SEE: AND THE WILD, WILD WOMEN, 1961, Ital.)

HELL IN THE HEAVENS* (1934) 79m FOX bw

Warner Baxter *(Lt. Steve Warner)*, Conchita Montenegro *(Aimee)*, Russell Hardie *(2nd Lt. Hartley)*, Andy Devine *(Sgt. "Ham" Davis)*, William Stelling *(Cpl. Teddy May)*, Ralph Morgan *(Lt. "Pop" Roget)*, Vince Barnett *(Ace McGurk)*, William Stack *(Capt. Andre DeLaage)*, J. Carroll Naish *(Sgt. Chevalier)*, Johnny Arthur *(Clarence Perkins)*, Arno Frey *(Baron Kurt von Hagen)*, Rudolph Armendt, Vincent Carato.

A WW I dogfight movie with Warner Baxter as an American pilot gunning for ace German pilot Frey. The story never gets off the ground and the climactic capture of Frey is no payoff. Montenegro is a French farm girl chasing after Baxter, who wins his heart in the final moments. Spads and Fokkers again in ancient dogfights.

d, John Blystone; w, Jack Yellen, Byron Morgan, Ted Parsons (based on the play "The Ace" by Herman Rossman); ph, Bert Glennon.

War **(PR:A MPAA:NR)**

HELL IN THE PACIFIC** (1968) 103m Selmur Pictures/Cinerama c

Lee Marvin *(American Soldier)*, Toshiro Mifune *(Japanese Soldier)*.

A brutal and uncompromising film that pits American Marine pilot Marvin against Japanese Navy officer Mifune after both are left alone on an island. They stalk each other in the jungle until finally Mifune captures and hogties Marvin. The American manages to escape and then he captures Mifune and ties him up. Marvin later releases his hostage and both men declare a truce, surviving in the jungle without each other's help. Mifune begins to build a raft and Marvin laughs derisively at him but then helps him complete the little craft and together they sail to another island where they find a deserted camp. They bathe, don fresh uniforms, and then get drunk on sake, ostensibly becoming friends. Mifune finds a *Life* magazine and goes berserk when he sees a photo story showing photos critical of Japanese troops. He attacks Marvin and they both go at it again, finally going off alone, each of them again bloodied. In another version a mine goes off and the viewer is led to believe that both men are killed. Neither version is satisfactory in a story that tries too hard to get the simple message across that war is hell and those who fight wars mostly die without reason. The acting is acceptable but is as extravagant as the script and Boorman's direction is repetitive and ponderous, beating that single anti-war theme to death long before the adversaries do. The violence in the film is broad, explicit, and ugly, certainly not for young viewers.

p, Reuben Bercovitch; d, John Boorman; w, Alexander Jacobs, Eric Bercovici (based on a story by Bercovitch); ph, Conrad Hall (Panavision, Technicolor); m, Lalo Schifrin; ed, Thomas Stanford; art d, Tony Pratt, Masao Yamazaki; set d, Makoto Kikuchi; spec eff, Joe Zomar, Kunishige Tanaka; makeup, Shigeo Kobayashi.

War Drama **Cas.** **(PR:O MPAA:G)**

HELL IS A CITY½** (1960, Brit.) 98m Hammer/COL bw

Stanley Baker *(Inspector Martineau)*, John Crawford *(Don Starling)*, Donald Pleasence *(Gus Hawkins)*, Maxine Audley *(Julia Martineau)*, Billie Whitelaw *(Chloe Hawkins)*, Joseph Tomelty *(Furnisher Steele)*, George A. Cooper *(Doug Savage)*, Geoffrey Frederick *(Devery)*, Vanda Godsell *(Lucky Lusk)*, Charles Houston *(Clogger Roach)*, Joby Blanshard *(Tawny Jakes)*, Charles Morgan *(Laurie Lovett)*, Peter Madden *(Bert Darwin)*, Dickie Owen *(Bragg)*, Lois Daine *(Cecily)*, Warren Mitchell *(Traveller)*, Sarah Branch *(Silver Steele)*, Alister Williamson *(Sam)*, Russell L. Napier *(Superintendent)*.

Baker is a British detective tracking down a dangerous escaped convict, Crawford. He thinks the convict will come back to Manchester where the stolen jewels he was sent up for are stashed. A female clerk of a bookie is killed and robbed while on her way to the bank, and Baker starts to collect clues that point to the convict and a small group of criminals. He arrests everyone but Crawford, who is finally tracked down in an explosive ending. A satisfying British crime drama with a realistic performance from Baker and a script that keeps the action building.

p, Michael Carreras; d&w, Val Guest (based on a novel by Maurice Proctor); ph, Arthur Grant; m, Stanley Black; ed, John Dunsford.

Crime **(PR:A MPAA:NR)**

HELL IS EMPTY*½ (1967, Brit./Ital) 109m Dominion/Rank c

Martine Carol *(Martine Grant)*, Anthony Steel *(Maj. Morton)*, James Robertson Justice *(Angus McGee)*, Shirley Anne Field *(Shirley McGee)*, Isa Miranda *(Isa Grant)*, Carl Mohner *(Carl Schultz)*, Jess Conrad *(Jess Shepherd)*, Anthony Dawson *(Paul Grant)*, Catherine von Schell *(Catherine Grant)*, Irene von Meyendorff *(Helen McGee)*, Patricia Viterbo *(Patricia)*, Anna Gael *(Anna)*, Eugene Deckers *(Counsel)*, Sheila Burrell *(Judge)*.

The last film for the once prominent French screen idol Carol (Max Ophuls' LOLA MONTES) was an uneventful finale for a career which had had its ups and downs. Carol would die soon after production from a heart attack. She was only 45. In this weary film she stars as one member of a group of thieves trying to evade the law by hanging out on a deserted island, with only a mansion to provide them with shelter. (Released in both English and Italian.)

p, Michael Eland; d, John Ainsworth, Bernard Knowles; w, Ainsworth, Knowles, John Fowler (based on the novel by J.F. Straker).

Crime/Drama **(PR:C MPAA:NR)**

HELL IS FOR HEROES*½** (1962) 90m PAR bw

Steve McQueen *(Reese)*, Bobby Darin *(Pvt. Corby)*, Fess Parker *(Sgt. Pike)*, Harry Guardino *(Sgt. Larkin)*, James Coburn *(Cpl. Henshaw)*, Mike Kellin *(Pvt. Kolinsky)*, Joseph Hoover *(Capt. Loomis)*, Bill Mullikin *(Pvt. Cumberly)*, L.Q. Jones *(Sgt. Frazer)*, Michele Montau *(Monique)*, Don Haggerty *(Capt. Mace)*, Nick Adams *(Homer)*, Bob Newhart *(Pvt. Driscoll)*.

An exhausted and depleted combat infantry squad is pulled from a rear area from which they had expected to be sent home and ordered to hold a lengthy section of line facing a huge German pillbox at the Siegfried Line. Among the men is McQueen, formerly the squad sergeant but now busted for drunkenness and sent back to his unit, apparently a familiar routine for this soldier. He is clearly the best soldier in the squad, a natural leader who soon begins advising nominal squad leader Guardino on various ruses to make the Germans think he has a much larger force. They are successful until a German patrol discovers how weak they are, and McQueen realizes the only way to continue to fool the Germans is to attack. Usurping command of the squad, he leads a small force against the pillbox, but runs into a pillbox in front of the fortification. Coburn, carrying a flamethrower, touches a mine and explodes into a human torch, illuminating the others, who barely make it back to their own positions. There platoon sergeant Parker is waiting, enraged at McQueen's action and threatening court martial. Before anything like that can happen, though, McQueen makes his way to the firing slit of the pillbox and throws in a satchel charge, then falls back, shot in the chest. Dying, he looks over and sees the Germans throw the explosive back out. With a last effort, he picks up the charge and rolls into the pillbox with it. The explosion knocks out the pillbox and the American attack moves ahead unhindered. A taut little movie with a fascinating central performance by McQueen as a hardbitten misfit unable to accept authority (even his own, as seen in his string of battlefield promotions and rear area demotions), but possessed of a singular talent for infantry combat. He takes on the suicidal destruction of the pillbox when it becomes obvious to him that he is never going to see battle again. Siegel keeps the action moving along quickly and on line to its inevitable climax. Only Newhart's patented telephone bit, here done for the benefit of Germans listening on a microphone discovered hidden in the American position, detracts from the story by adding a note that would fit better in a Catskill resort than a trench facing the Siegfried Line. A film with uncomfortable things to say about the nature of heroism, and one to see for that reason.

p, Henry Blanke; d, Don Siegel; w, Robert Pirosh, Richard Carr (based on a story by Pirosh); ph, Harold Lipstein; m, Leonard Rosenman; ed, Howard Smith; art d, Hal Pereira, Howard Richmond; set d, Sam Comer, Robert R. Benton; cos, Wally Harton; spec eff, Dick Webb; makeup, William Morley, Bob Hickman.

War **(PR:C MPAA:NR)**

HELL IS SOLD OUT½** (1951, Brit.) 84m Zelstro/Eros bw

Richard Attenborough *(Pierre Bonnet)*, Mai Zetterling *(Valerie Martin)*, Herbert Lom *(Dominic Danges)*, Kathleen Byron *(Arlette de Balzamann)*, Hermione Baddeley *(Mme. Menstrier)*, Zena Marshall *(Honeychild)*, Nicholas Hannen *(Francois)*, Joan Hickson *(Hortense)*, Eric Pohlmann *(Louis)*, Laurence Naismith *(Dr. Monceau)*, Joan Young *(Gertrude Cole)*, Olaf Pooley, Hal Osmond, Aletha Orr, Virginia Bedard, George Margo, Ronald Adam, Joan Elan.

Despite the title this is a farce, and a good one at that, which has Zetterling as a mysterious novelist using the name of Lom, a popular writer thought to have died. But Lom proves to be very much alive and curious about how this new book hit the market when he didn't write it. One thing leading to another, Zetterling and Lom take to the altar, but not before the man has a time of it playing his little game of not letting on to his true identity.

p, Raymond Stross; d, Michael Anderson; w, Guy Morgan, Moie Charles (based on the novel by Maurice Dekobra); ph, Jack Asher.

Comedy **(PR:A MPAA:NR)**

HELL NIGHT zero (1981) 101m Compass International c

Linda Blair *(Marti)*, Vincent Van Patten *(Seth)*, Peter Barton *(Jeff)*, Kevin Brophy *(Peter)*, Jenny Neumann *(May)*, Suki Goodwin *(Denise)*, Jimmy Sturtevant *(Scott)*, Hal Ralston, Cary Fox, Ronald Gans, Gloria Hellman.

Blair is one of four fraternity and sorority members who stay the night at a mansion where a mass murder had been committed. Frat members set out to scare the foursome and the retarded son that had killed his family comes back and kills most of the kids. Another slasher film that isn't worth talking about.

p, Irwin Yablans, Bruce Cohn Curtis; d, Tom DeSimone; w, Randolph Feldman; ph, Mac Ahlberg (Metrocolor); m, Dan Wyman; ed, Tony Di Marco; art d, Steven G. Legler; makeup, Ken Horn, Tom Schwartz.

Horror **Cas.** **(PR:O MPAA:R)**

HELL ON DEVIL'S ISLAND** (1957) 73m FOX bw

Helmut Dantine *(Paul Rigaud)*, William Talman *(Bayard)*, Donna Martell *(Giselle Renault)*, Jean Willes *(Suzanne)*, Rex Ingram *(Lulu)*, Robert Cornthwaite *(Gov. Renault)*, Jay Adler *(Toto)*, Peter Adams *(Jacques Boucher)*, Edward Colmans *(Jean Robert)*, Mel Welles *(Felix Molyneaux)*, Charles Bohbot *(Marcel)*, Alan Lee *(Leon Philippe)*, Henry Rowland *(Guard No. 1)*, Edward Coch *(Gendarme)*, Paul Brinegar *(Arneaux)*, Allen Pinson *(Bruiser No. 2)*, Roy Jenson *(Bruiser No. 1)*, Elena Da Vinci *(Gina)*, Edwin Nelson *(Guard No. 2)*, Paul MacWilliams *(Chauvin)*.

Dantine is a French journalist unjustly sent to Devil's Island for writing against French collaborators during WW II. When he is released the island's governor seeks his aid in stopping a plantation owner from using ex-cons as virtual slaves. Dantine discovers that the prison overseer, Talman, is working with the plantation owner in operating a gold mine and smuggling the gold off the island. Dantine puts the two crooks out of business and wins the governor's daughter, Martell.

p, Leon Chooluck, Laurence Stewart; d, Christian Nyby; w, Steven Ritch (based on a story by Arndt Giusti, Ethel Giusti); ph, Ernest Haller (RegalScope); m, Irving Gertz; ed, Warren Adams; md, Gertz; art d, Frank Sylos.

Drama **(PR:A MPAA:NR)**

HELL ON EARTH½** (1934, Ger.) 64m Rescofilm/Aeolian bw (NIEMANDSLAND; AKA: NO MAN'S LAND)

Georges Peclet *(The Frenchman)*, Hugh Douglas *(The Englishman)*, Wladimir Sokoloff *(The Jew)*, Ernest Busch *(The German)*, Louis Douglas *(The Negro)*, Rose Mal *(Frenchman's Sweetheart)*, Zoe Frank *(Englishman's Wife)*, Elizabeth Lennard *(Jewish Bride)*, Renee Stobrawa *(German Soldier's Wife)*.

Five soldiers of different backgrounds and countries are caught in a bombardment during WW I and take shelter in a dugout in no-man's land. The film presents each man's life during peacetime and then their sudden involvement in the war. There is an Englishman, a Frenchman, a German, a German Jew, and a black man in the dugout, and they voice their opinions and feelings on the war. An anti-war film which is extremely dated today. (Mixed Languages.)

d, Victor Trivas; w, Leonhard Frank; ph, Alexander Lagorio, Georg Stillanudis; m, Hanns Eisler.

War **(PR:A MPAA:NR)**

HELL ON FRISCO BAY*** (1956) 98m Jaguar/WB c (AKA: THE DARKEST HOUR)

Alan Ladd *(Steve Rollins)*, Edward G. Robinson *(Victor Amato)*, Joanne Dru *(Marcia Rollins)*, William Demarest *(Dan Bianco)*, Paul Stewart *(Joe Lye)*, Perry Lopez *(Mario Amato)*, Fay Wray *(Kay Stanley)*, Renata Vanni *(Anna Amato)*, Nestor Paiva *(Lou Fiaschetti)*, Stanley Adams *(Hammy)*, Willis Bouchey *(Lt. Neville)*, Peter Hanson *(Det. Connors)*, Anthony Caruso *(Sebastian Pasmonick)*, George J. Lewis *(Father LaRocca)*, Tina Carver *(Bessie)*, Rodney [Rod] Taylor *(Brodie Evans)*, Peter Votrian *(George Pasmonick)*, Jayne Mansfield *(Blonde)*, Mae Marsh *(Landlady)*.

Not the best of Ladd's tough crime dramas but not bad after all, especially with the electric Robinson present. Ladd is an ex-cop who has just gotten out out of prison, framed for a crime he did not commit. When he returns to San Francisco, he shuns his empathic wife Dru, hurtfully blaming her for seeing other men in his absence, although he knows this is not true. It's a device to make sure she stays clear of him while he plays the dangerous game of tracking down the real murderer of the man he was convicted (for manslaughter) of killing. Moreover, Ladd wants the man behind the killing, the waterfront Mafia rackets czar Robinson, as vicious a brute as ever overlorded a mob of cutthroats. Robinson enjoys bossing about his chief henchman, Stewart, the man who killed the witness in an earlier crime, a killing for which Ladd was sentenced. Whenever Stewart is in the dominating Robinson's presence he begins to stammer, but he ruthlessly carries out the boss' orders, murdering more witnesses when Ladd's one-man investigation begins to reveal the truth. Though married, Robinson has no reservations about propositioning other women, even Stewart's aging mistress Wray. Stewart takes that insult, too, but later tells Robinson that he has completed his last killing for the boss as a gang stooge. He knows much and his silence is worth something, an equal partnership, an equal sharing of the loot. Robinson squashes this turning worm, killing Stewart for daring to step up from his class. Robinson's wife, Vanni, informs on her husband when she learns that he had earlier ordered Stewart to murder her nephew Lopez to keep him from talking. Robinson prepares to flee south of the border and escapes in a speedboat. But Ladd is right behind him in another motor launch. They race across San Francisco Bay in a wild shootout and fight that finishes mobster Robinson. Ladd emerges victorious with wife Dru at his side. The film is somewhat leaden in spots and Ladd's lust for justice becomes desire for revenge. He was ill, having recently recovered from a bout with chicken pox, and his weakened state shows in the movie as he moves and talks without enthusiasm. Robinson, that wonderful and venerable actor, does a reprise of all his early gangster roles, particularly LITTLE CAESAR (1930), and steals every scene with flamboyance and the kind of energy found in a man half his age. Dru is a prop here and when she does appear she is unconvincing and overacts. Stewart, who died in 1986, is simply superb as the much-picked-upon henchman. This was Ladd's production all the way and he picked a lot of old talent that had been with him at Paramount when his star shone brightly there, hiring Tuttle to direct, the same man who had helmed his first big hit, THIS GUN FOR HIRE (1942). Ladd's loyalty extended to hiring cameraman Seitz who, though aged and almost enfeebled, managed to record an exciting tale. Busty star-to-be-Mansfield appears as a blonde floozy in a bit part.

p, George C. Bertholon; d, Frank Tuttle; w, Sydney Boehm, Martin Rackin (based on the *Collier's* magazine serial "The Darkest Hour" by William P. McGivern); ph, John Seitz (CinemaScope, Warner Color); m, Max Steiner; ed, Folmar Blangsted; art d, John Beckman; cos, Moss Mabry.

Crime Drama Cas. (PR:C MPAA:NR)

HELL ON WHEELS*½ (1967) 97m Crown-International bw

Marty Robbins *(Marty)*, John Ashley *(Del)*, Gigi Perreau *(Sue)*, Robert Dornan *(Steve)*, Connie Smith *(Herself)*, The Stonemans *(Themselves)*, Robert Foulk, Frank Gerstle *(Moonshiners)*, Christine Tabbott, Chris Eland, Eddie Crandall, Marvin Miller.

Ashley is a stock car mechanic who is tired of working for his driver brother Robbins and goes out on his own. He sets up a speed shop and becomes a driver himself. He gets involved with a moonshine ring which makes him a good amount of money, but when he tries to get out, the moonshiners take him and his brother hostage. Third brother Doran, a revenue agent, tries to save his brothers, but Ashley is killed during a high-speed chase in the mountains. Robbins sings "Fly Butterfly" and "No Tears, Milady."

p, Robert Patrick; d, Will Zens; w, Wesley Cox; ph, Leif Rise (Technicolor).

Drama (PR:A MPAA:G)

HELL RAIDERS* (1968) 80m AIP c

John Agar, Richard Webb, Joan Huntington.

Routine WW II heroics as the intrepid Agar leads a crack demolition team behind the German lines in Italy to blow up a recently captured American headquarters filled with secret documents. Nothing here audiences haven't seen dozens of times before.

d, Larry Buchanan.

War (PR:A-C MPAA:NR)

HELL RAIDERS OF THE DEEP** (1954, Ital.) 93m Valentia-Ponti-Laurentis/I.F.E. bw

Eleonora Rossi Drago *(Marion)*, Pierre Cressoy *(Silvani)*, Girolamo Manisco, Giovanni Tadini, Luigi Ferraro, Giovanni De Fazio, Giovanni Magello, Giorgio Spaccarelli, Colombo Pamolli, Paul Muller, Riccardo Gallone, Carlo Bellini, Tino Carraro.

Detailed depiction of the efforts of secretly trained frogmen to blow up a British freighter. Cressoy is the officer in charge of the dangerous mission, placing prime importance on the meticulous points in achieving this goal. Several survivors from the real mission took part in this filming venture. When sticking to the details of the mission only, the picture is intriguing, but the addition of other dramatics, such as Drago's sexy/earthy spy antics, do little to enhance it.

p, Enzo Cossa, Luigi De Laurentis; d, Duilio Coletti; w, A. Bragadin, E. De Concini, Coletti; m, Nino Rota.

War Cas. (PR:A MPAA:NR)

HELL-SHIP MORGAN*½ (1936) 64m COL bw

George Bancroft *(Morgan)*, Ann Sothern *(Mary)*, Victor Jory *(Jim)*, George Regas *(Covanci)*, Howard Hickman *(Cabot)*, Ralph Byrd *(Dale)*, Rollo Lloyd *(Hawkins)*, Snowflake *(Pittsburgh)*.

Bancroft is a fish boat captain who has a "love 'em and leave 'em" attitude toward women until he meets, falls in love with and marries Sothern. When they go on a honeymoon on his boat, however, Sothern becomes interested in the first mate, Jory, who's a cleaner, more respectable type than Bancroft. Knowing what is going on, Bancroft still saves Jory during a hurricane and is maimed in the process. The noble captain throws himself overboard to let the romance develop between Sothern and Jory.

p, Irving Briskin; d, D. Ross Lederman; w, Harold Schumate; ph, Henry Freulich; ed, Otto Meyer.

Adventure/Romance (PR:A MPAA:NR)

HELL SHIP MUTINY* (1957) 66m Lovina/REP bw

Jon Hall *(Capt. Knight)*, John Carradine *(Malone)*, Peter Lorre *(Lamouet)*, Roberta Haynes *(Mareva)*, Mike Mazurki *(Ross)*, Charles Mauu *(Tula)*, Stanley Adams *(Roxy)*, Danny Richards, Jr. *(Tatoa)*, Felix Locher *(Parea)*, Peter Coe *(Terahi)*, Michael Barrett *(Pinky)*, Salvador Bagues *(Kuala)*, Salty the Chimp.

Hall is a noble sea captain who helps lovely South Sea island princess Haynes rid her domain of two murderous smugglers, Carradine and Mazurki, who have been forcing the natives to dive for pearls against their will. Enter corrupt French judge Lorre, who orders Carradine and Mazurki to be put on his private yacht. Lorre then brings the duo to a sunken ship containing valuable treasure and offers them their freedom and a cut of the spoils if they will assist in its recovery. The pair agree and, once free, they turn the tables on Lorre by locking him up. Eventually Hall catches up to the murderers and kills them both. Back on the island he is welcomed as a hero and liberator by the natives and their princess. A good cast totally wasted. Associate producer Hall cast his father in the film, as the island chief Parea, thus allowing him to make his film debut at age 75.

p, George Bilson; d, Lee Sholem, Elmo Williams; w, De Vallon Scott, Wells Root; ph, Sam Leavitt (underwater ph, Robert H. Cummings, Bill Judd); m, Paul Sawtell, Bert Shefter; ed, Williams; art d, Ernst Fegte.

Adventure (PR:A MPAA:NR)

HELL SQUAD*½ (1958) 64m AIP bw

Wally Campo *(Russo)*, Brandon Carroll *(German Officer)*, Fred Galvin *(Clemens)*, Greg Stuart *(Nelson)*, Cecil Addis *(Lippy)*, Leon Schrier *(Roth)*, Don Chambers *(American Captain)*, Larry Shuttleworth, Jerry Bob Weston, Gordon Edwards, Jack Sewards, Jim Hamilton, Ben Bigelow, Jow Hearne, Jack N. Kramer, Dick Walsh, Curtis Lozer, Bob Williams.

Five American soldiers are lost in Tunisia during WW II. They can't use their radio because the Nazis are monitoring. The five make their way through the desert and find themselves in skirmishes with enemy patrols and aircraft, leaving Campo the only survivor. He comes upon a mine field and a thirsty German lieutenant with a map of mine placements. Campo gives him water in exchange for the map, but the Nazi tries to doublecross him. If it were double-featured, this one would be the picture on the lower bill.

p,d&w, Burt Topper; ph, Erik Daarstad, John Morrill; m, James Richardson; ed, Marvin Wallowitz.

War (PR:A MPAA:NR)

HELL TO ETERNITY** (1960) 132m Atlantic/AA bw

Jeffrey Hunter *(Guy Gabaldon)*, David Janssen *(Bill)*, Vic Damone *(Pete)*, Patricia Owens *(Sheila)*, Richard Eyer *(Guy as a Boy)*, John Larch *(Capt. Schwabe)*, Miiko Taka *(Ester)*, Sessue Hayakawa *(Gen. Matsui)*, Bill Williams *(Leonard)*, Tsuru Aoki Hayakawa *(Mother Une)*, Michi Kobi *(Sono)*, George Shibata *(Kaz)*, Reiko Sato *(Famika)*, Richard Gardner *(Sullivan)*, Bob Okazaki *(Papa Une)*, George Matsui *(George as a Boy)*, Nickey Blair *(Semperi)*, George Takai *(George)*.

Based on the experiences of Marine war hero Guy Gabaldon, the film begins as young Guy (Eyer) is adopted by a Japanese family, and shows the effects on the West Coast Japanese community he lives in when Pearl Harbor is attacked. Hunter, playing the older Gabaldon, joins the Marines and becomes buddies with Janssen and Damone. In the invasion of Saipan, because he speaks Japanese, Gabaldon is able to get 800 beaten Japanese soldiers to surrender.

p, Irving H. Levin; d, Phil Karlson; w, Ted Sherdeman, Walter Roeber Schmidt (based on a story by Gil Doud); ph, Burnett Guffey; m, Leith Stevens; ed, George White, Roy V. Livingston; ch, Roland Dupree.

War Cas. (PR:A MPAA:NR)

HELL TO MACAO (SEE: CORRUPT ONES, THE, 1967, Fr./Ital./Ger.)

HELL UP IN HARLEM zero (1973) 96m AIP c

Fred Williamson *(Tommy Gibbs)*, Julius W. Harris *(Papa Gibbs)*, Gloria Hendry *(Helen Bradley)*, Margaret Avery *(Sister Jennifer)*, D'Urville Martin *(Reverend Rufus)*, Tony King *(Zach)*, Gerald Gordon *(Mr. DiAngelo)*.

A sequel to BLACK CAESAR with Williamson starring again as the underworld king of Harlem. The film was written, directed, and produced by Larry Cohen (IT'S ALIVE, Q), a B-movie director of questionable talents. His screenplay depicts the streets of New York as a place where one can go around brandishing machineguns in broad daylight, with a district attorney who has a list of criminals he calls when he needs someone killed, and other characters who couldn't exist in the real world. Production qualities are very poor and the acting worse. No doubt hell was raised by audiences that saw this mess.

p,d&w, Larry Cohen; ph, Fenton Hamilton (Movielab Color); m, Fonce Mizell, Freddie Perrin; ed, Peter Honess, Franco Guerri; prod d, Larry Lurin.

Crime (PR:O MPAA:R)

HELL WITH HEROES, THE* (1968) 102m UNIV c

Rod Taylor *(Brynie MacKay)*, Claudia Cardinale *(Elena)*, Harry Guardino *(Lee Harris)*, Kevin McCarthy *(Col. Wilson)*, Peter Deuel *(Mike Brewer)*, William Marshall *(Al Poland)*, Don Knight *(Pepper)*, Michael Shillo *(Pol Guilbert)*, Robert Yuro *(Willoughby)*, Lew Brown *(Sgt. Shaeffer)*, Wilhelm von Homburg *(Hans)*, Tania Lemani *(Jamila)*, Mae Mercer *(Chanteuse)*, Emile Genest *(Inspector Bouchard)*, Louis de Farra *(Pierre)*, Jacqueline Bertrand *(French Girl)*, Sid Haig *(Crespin)*, Jim Creech *(First M.P.)*, Pedro Regas *(Old Arab)*, David Kurzon *(The Lookout)*, Naji Gabbay *(Magid)*, Ric Notoli, Tony Nassour, Ricky Namay, George Samaan, David Sindaha *(Urchins)*.

Taylor and Deuel are former Air Force pilots smuggling black market goods into Africa after WW II. They deliver their air cargos to gangster Guardino, whose mistress is Cardinale. She falls in love with Taylor. When the two airmen try to get out of Guardino's clutches, Deuel is killed. Taylor avenges his buddy's death and goes off with Cardinale, while U.S. agent McCarthy wonders—along with the audience—why they got involved.

p, Stanley Chase; d, Joseph Sargent; w, Halsted Welles, Harold Livingston (based on a story by Livingston); ph, Bud Thackery (Techniscope, Technicolor); m, Quincy Jones; ed, Howard Epstein; art d, Alexander Golitzen, John J. Lloyd; set d, John McCarthy, George Milo; cos, Jean Louis; m/l, "Where There Is Love," Jones, Dorothy Fields (sung by Sue Raney); makeup, Bud Westmore.

Drama **(PR:C MPAA:NR)**

HELLBENDERS, THE** (1967, U.S./Ital./Span.) 92m Alba Cinematografica-TECISA/EM c (I CRUDELI; LOS DESPIADADOS)

Joseph Cotten *(Jonas)*, Norma Bengell *(Claire)*, Julian Mateos *(Ben)*, Gino Pernice *(Jeff)*, Angel Aranda *(Nat)*, Maria Martin *(Kitty)*, Al Mulock *(The Beggar)*, Aldo Sambrell *(Pedro)*, Enio Girolami *(Commander of Fort Brent)*, Jose Nieto *(Sheriff)*, Claudio Gora *(Reverend Pierce)*, Julio Pena *(Sgt. Tolt)*, Benito Stefanelli *(Slim)*, Claudio Scarchilli *(Indian Chief)*, Alvaro de Luna, Rafael Vaquero, Ivan Scratuglia, Simon Arriaga, Jose Canalejas.

A poorly directed Italian western with Cotten giving an equally lame performance. As a renegade one-time Confederate officer, Cotten continues the former war on the North with his three sons. They ambush a Union convoy and get close to $1,000,000. They are chased across the desert by a posse after hiding the money in a coffin which, they explain, contains one of the sons. This gets Cotten and sons through most of the 92 minutes until the anomalous climax.

p, Albert Band; d, Sergio Corbucci; w, Band, Ugo Liberatore, Jose G. Maesso (U.S., Louis Garfinkle) (based on a story by Virgil C. Gerlach); ph, Enzo Barboni (Eastmancolor); m, Leo Nichols [Ennio Morricone]; ed, Nino Baragli, Alberto Gallitti; art d, Jaime Perez Cubero; makeup, Piero Mecacci, Francisco Puyol.

Western **(PR:A MPAA:NR)**

HELLCATS, THE zero (1968) 90m Gemini American/Crown International c

Ross Hagen *(Monte Chapman)*, Dee Duffy *(Linda)*, Sharyn Kinzie *(Sheila)*, Sonny West *(Snake)*, Bob Slatzer *(Mr. Adrian)*, Eric Lidberg *(Hiney)*, Shannon Summers *(Rita)*, Bro Beck *(David Chapman)*, Diane Ryder *(Candy Cave)*, Nick Raymond *(Pepper)*, Dick Merrifield *(Dean)*, Hildegard Wendt *(Hildy)*, Tony Cardoza *(Artist)*, Elena Engstrom *(Model)*, Irene Martin *(Dee)*, Frederic Downs *(Moonfire)*, Noble "Kid" Chissell *(Sheriff)*, Robert Strong *(Deputy)*, Ed Sarquist *(Zombie)*, Gus Trikonis *(Scorpio)*, Lydia Goya *(Betty)*, Tom Hanson *(Moongoose)*, Ray Cantrell *(Scab)*, Joe Coffey *(Pete)*, Eric Tomlin *(Policeman)*, Warren Hammack *(Attorney)*, Jack Denton *(Detective)*, Walt Swanner *(1st Senator)*, Bill Reese *(2nd Senator)*.

This cheaply made girl-gang thriller with a no-name cast has the title gang of bounteous bikers motoring to Mexico to obtain narcotics, which they secret in their headlights during the return trips. Hagen's detective brother was murdered while hot on the trail of the dope-dealing damsels—headed by a mysterious male, played by director Slatzer—so Hagen vows revenge and picks up the pursuit. Aided by his slain sibling's girl Duffy, he infiltrates the group, only to be caught, along with Duffy and head Harley-hog femme Kinzie. The latter escapes as her fellow captives are being dragged to the docks to meet a watery grave. The police arrive in the nick of time. Hagen and Duffy get together as the girl gang roars off to once again rape, loot, and pillage. Songs include "I Can't Take a Chance," "Hellcats," "Mass Confusion," sung by Davy Jones and the Dolphins; "I'm Up," "Marionettes," sung by Somebody's Children.

p, Anthony Cardoza, Herman Tomlin; d, Robert F. Slatzer; w, Tony Houston, Slatzer (based on a story by James Gordon White, John Zila, Jr.); ph, Gil Hubbs; ed, Bud Hoffman; art d, Karen Teichman; cos, Misty Maring.

Crime **(PR:O MPAA:R)**

HELLCATS OF THE NAVY** (1957) 81m Morningside/COL bw

Ronald Reagan *(Cmdr. Casey Abbott)*, Nancy Davis *(Helen Blair)*, Arthur Franz *(Lt. Cmdr. Don Landon)*, Robert Arthur *(Freddy Warren)*, William Leslie *(Lt. Paul Prentice)*, William Phillips *(Carroll)*, Harry Lauter *(Wes Barton)*, Joseph Turkel *(Chick)*, Michael Garth *(Charlie)*, Don Keefer *(Jug)*, Selmer Jackson *(Admiral Nimitz)*, Maurice Manson *(Admiral Lockwood)*.

Reagan is a submarine commander during WW II, and is sent out to retrieve a Japanese mine so Navy experts can find the reason they aren't detectable by sonar. During the operation an enemy ship bears down on Reagan and crew and Ron is forced to leave a frogman behind to save the rest of the crew. Officer Franz thinks his commander left the man behind because the frogman had been chasing after Davis, Reagan's girl friend. Reagan proves through his own acts of sacrifice and heroism that Franz's allegations were unfounded and goes on to marry Davis.

p, Charles H. Schneer; d, Nathan Juran [Nathan Hertz]; w, David Lang, Raymond Marcus (based on the book by Charles A. Lockwood and Hans Christian Adamson); ph, Irving Lippman; m, Mischa Bakaleinikoff; ed, Jerome Thoms; art d, Rudi Feld.

War **Cas.** **(PR:A MPAA:NR)**

HELLDORADO** (1935) 75m FOX bw

Richard Arlen *(Art Ryan)*, Madge Evans *(Glenda Wynant)*, Ralph Bellamy *(J.F. Van Avery)*, James Gleason *(Sam Barnes)*, Henry B. Walthall *(Abner Meadows)*, Helen Jerome Eddy *(Miss Fife)*, Gertrude Short *(Mae)*, Patricia Farr *(Flo)*, Stanley Fields *(Truck Driver)*, Lucky Hurlic *(Sam Ed)*, Stepin Fetchit *(Ulysses)*.

Arlen is a penniless drifter with big dreams. In a raging storm, he leads a group of people to shelter which turns out to be a ghost town. The only person left in the town is old man Walthall, who has lived well in the decaying town. It's soon discovered that the old man knew Arlen's grandfather and they own a gold mine which Walthall can't remember where to find. Arlen finds the mine and marries the snooty millionairess in the stranded group.

p, Jesse L. Lasky; d, James Cruze; w, Frances Hyland, Rex Taylor (based on a story by Frank Mitchell Dazey); ph, John Seitz; ed, Harold Schuster.

Drama **(PR:A MPAA:NR)**

HELLDORADO*½** (1946) 70m REP bw (AKA: HELDORADO)

Roy Rogers *(Himself)*, George "Gabby" Hayes *(Gabby Whittaker)*, Dale Evans *(Carol Randall)*, Paul Harvey *(W.W. Driscoll)*, Barry Mitchell *(Alex Baxter)*, John Bagni *(Johnny)*, John Phillips *(Sheriff)*, James Taggert *(Bellboy)*, Rex Lease *(Charlie)*, Steve Darrell *(Mitch)*, Doye O'Dell *(Tickettaker)*, Leroy Mason *(Ranger)*, Charlie Williams *(Judge)*, Eddie Acuff *(Shooting Gallery Attendant)*, Bob Nolan, The Sons Of The Pioneers, Trigger the Horse.

Las Vegas' Helldorado parade and rodeo is the backdrop for this Rogers western. Roy is out to break up a syndicate of racketeers led by Harvey, which is trying to filter their black market profits through Vegas gambling houses. Rich girl Evans keeps Roy's time split between getting the crooks and keeping her out of trouble. Another enjoyable Rogers western packed with action and singing. (See ROY ROGERS series, Index.)

p, Edward J. White; d, William Witney; w, Gerald Geraghty, Julian Zimet; ph, William Bradford; m, Dale Butts; ed, Lester Orlebeck; md, Morton Scott; art d, Gano Chittenden; spec eff, Howard and Theodore Lydecker; m/l, "Good Neighbor," Jack Elliott (sung by Dale Evans, Roy Rogers), "Helldorado," "My Saddle Pals and I," Rogers, "Silver Stars, Purple Sage, Eyes of Blue," Denver Darling (sung by Rogers).

Western **Cas.** **(PR:A MPAA:NR)**

HELLER IN PINK TIGHTS** (1960) 100m PAR c

Sophia Loren *(Angela Rossini)*, Anthony Quinn *(Tom Healy)*, Margaret O'Brien *(Della Southby)*, Steve Forrest *(Clint Mabry)*, Eileen Heckart *(Lorna Hathaway)*, Edmund Lowe *(Manfred "Doc" Montague)*, Ramon Novarro *(De Leon)*, George Mathews *(Sam Pierce)*, Frank Cordell *(Theodore)*, Cactus McPeters *(William)*, Edward Binns *(Sheriff McClain)*, Warren Wade *(Hodges)*, Frank Silvera *(Santis)*, Cal Bolder *(Goober)*, Robert Palmer *(McAllister)*, Howard McNear *(Photographer)*, Taggert Casey *(1st Gunslinger)*, Leo V. Matranga *(2nd Gunslinger)*, Geraldine Wall *(Madam)*, Amanda Randolph *(Maid)*, David Armstrong *(Achilles)*, Alfred Tonkel *(Calchas)*, Robert Darin *(Servant)*, Bryn Davis *(Venus)*, Cathy Cox *(Juno)*, Iron Eyes Cody, Eddie Little Sky, Rodd Redwing, Chief Yowlachie *(Indians)*, Bernard Nedell *(Acting Double for Edmund Lowe)*.

An offbeat western that wanders about as aimlessly as its script, this Loren vehicle just doesn't travel too far. Quinn is a sleazy manager of a seedy vaudeville troupe, circa 1880, constantly fending off creditors while trying to keep his threadbare show going. When he and his actors hit Cheyenne to play in Mathews' theater, he quickly learns that the wild town demands more than sophisticated comedy; it's raw and raucous entertainment that the cowboys and drunks want and Quinn quickly adapts a version of "Mazeppa," with the buxom and beefy Loren playing the boy strapped to a galloping horse that races through the theater and across the stage; she is strapped back downward so her body jiggles in all the right places for the gawking westerners. Loren has taken a liking to local gunslinger Forrest, though she knows Quinn covets her. Quinn is tolerant of her dallying ways, playing the waiting game. Loren next collects the much-needed troupe's salary from Mathews, only to lose it and herself in a poker game where she and the money become the stakes. Now she has been won by Forrest, but the always forgiving Quinn does not upbraid her; instead the entire troupe sneaks out of town, hotly pursued by Forrest who intends to collect his spoils, meaning voluptuous Loren. Just as he catches up with the struggling troupe, Indians attack and Quinn loses his wagons and costumes. The actors survive, however, thanks to Forrest who takes them to a remote trading post. Forrest discovers that Novarro, an old nemesis, is planning his death to escape paying a huge debt. Loren, persuaded by Forrest, goes to town and cons Novarro into paying off, but instead of returning the money to Forrest, she purchases a new theater for Quinn and the troupe. Forrest is enraged and plans to kill the lot of them, but when he arrives Novarro's gunslingers trap him. Quinn saves his life and gets him out of town, telling him that he will pay him off when the theater is a success. With Forrest gone, Quinn turns his attentions to sexy Loren and proposes. They go on with the show and their lives. Though this film is directed by a top helmsman, Cukor, known for his sophisticated comedies and "Women's" films, it is not a success, having a jumbled, fragmentary look to it, as if scenes were merely tacked on as afterthought. Loren's accent is so thick as to make her words unintelligible and she's about as alluring as a side of beef hanging in a meatpacking factory. Her facial expression is the same throughout—surly, swollen lips curling down into a permanent pout. She's a blonde here but her swarthy Italian complexion and heavy dark eyebrows make her appear garish. Quinn mumbles and stumbles through his role like a spastic with a speech impediment. Only Lowe and Heckart are believable as the down-and-out troupers scrambling for meager applause. One-time child actress O'Brien, here 21, is surprisingly good as the ingenue. Amfitheatrof contributes a fine score and Lipstein's lensing is above average, especially in capturing the splendid countryside outside Tucson, Arizona. The film and the L'Amour novel are based upon the flamboyant theatrical career of Adah Isaacs Menken, whose perennial equestrienne role in "Mazeppa" became legendary in the 19th century. Quinn rightly felt the film was a disaster; he was an action actor and Cukor was all drawing room for the ladies. "All I know," Quinn later remarked, "is that we both [he and Loren] seemed terribly lost in the picture." Loren blamed it all on Hollywood wanting to change her image and she packed up and left for Italy with husband Ponti who backed the movie and lost money on it.

p, Carlo Ponti, Marcello Girosi; d, George Cukor; w, Walter Bernstein, Dudley Nichols (based on the novel *Heller with a Gun* by Louis L'Amour); ph, Harold

Lipstein (Technicolor); m, Daniele Amfitheatrof; ed, Howard Smith; art d, Hal Pereira, Eugene Allen; cos, Edith Head; ch, Val Raset.

Western/Drama **(PR:C MPAA:NR)**

HELLFIGHTERS** (1968) 121m UNIV c

John Wayne *(Chance Buckman)*, Katherine Ross *(Tish Buckman)*, Jim Hutton *(Greg Parker)*, Vera Miles *(Madelyn Buckman)*, Jay C. Flippen *(Jack Lomax)*, Bruce Cabot *(Joe Horn)*, Edward Faulkner *(George Harris)*, Barbara Stuart *(Irene Foster)*, Edmund Hashim *(Colonel Valdez)*, Valentin De Vargas *(Amal Bokru)*, Frances Fong *(Madame Loo)*, Alberto Morin *(General Lopez)*, Alan Caillou *(Harry York)*, Laraine Stephens *(Helen Meadows)*, John Alderson *(Jim Hatch)*, Lal Chand Mehra *(Dr. Songla)*, Rudy Diaz *(Zamora)*, Bebe Louie *(Gumdrop)*, Pedro Gonzales Gonzales *(Hernando)*, Edward Colmans *(Sr. Caldez)*, Chuck Roberson *(Firefighter in Airplane)*, Cactus Pryor, Chris Chandler, Howard Finch, Elizabeth Germaine, William Hardy, Big John Hamilton.

The Duke is an oil-fire fighter running around the world putting out blazes. Miles plays Wayne's ex-wife, who is still in love with him, but can't take Wayne's dangerous profession. Their daughter, Ross, marries Wayne's right-hand man, Hutton, and family feuding erupts. The film was based on the life of fire-fighter "Red" Adair. Great oil-well fire effects.

p, Robert Arthur; Andrew V. McLaglen; w, Clair Huffaker; ph, William H. Clothier (Panavision, Technicolor); m, Leonard Roseman; ed, Folmar Blangsted; art d, Alexander Golitzen, Frank Arrigo; set d, John McCarthy, James S. Redd; cos, Edith Head; spec eff, Fred Knoth, Whitey McMahon, Herman Townsley; stunts, Hal Needham; tech adv, "Red" Adair, "Boots" Hansen, "Coots" Matthews.

Adventure **Cas.** **(PR:A MPAA:G)**

HELLFIRE** (1949) 90m Elliott-McGowan/REP c

William "Bill" Elliott *(Zeb Smith)*, Marie Windsor *(Doll Brown)*, Forrest Tucker *(Bucky McLean)*, Jim Davis *(Gyp Stoner)*, H.B. Warner *(Brother Joseph)*, Paul Fix *(Dusty Stoner)*, Grant Withers *(Sheriff Martin)*, Emory Parnell *(Sheriff Duffy)*, Esther Howard *(Birdie)*, Jody Gilbert *(Full Moon)*, Louis R. Faust *(Red Stoner)*, Harry Woods *(Lew Stoner)*, Denver Pyle *(Rex)*, Trevor Bardette *(Wilson)*, Dewey Robinson, Harry Tyler *(Bartenders)*, Roy Barcroft, Hank Worden, Ken MacDonald, Paula Hill, Eva Novak, Dick Alexander, Edward Keane, Elizabeth Marshall, Keenan Elliott.

Elliott is a gambler who turns to preaching when a minister saves his life. In attempting to build a church, Elliott tries to convince female outlaw Windsor to give herself up so he can collect the $5,000 reward on her. She'll have nothing to do with that even after Elliott saves her life twice. Windsor trades her guns in for the cabaret stage, but that is short lived when her brother-in-law comes hunting for her. In a bloody climax Windsor is wounded and finally repents her sins to Elliott. The McGowans, who scripted this strange sagebrush saga, owe a debt to W. Somerset Maugham; the film is basically Sadie Thompson gone West, played as much for laughs as for any other emotive quality.

p, William J. O'Sullivan; d, R.G. Springsteen; w, Dorrell Stuart, Stuart McGowan; ph, Jack Marta (Trucolor); m, Dale Butts; ed, Tony Martinelli; art d, James Sullivan; m/l, K. Shaw, G.A. Minor.

Western **Cas.** **(PR:A MPAA:NR)**

HELLFIRE CLUB, THE** (1963, Brit.) 88m New World/EM bw/c

Keith Michell *(Jason)*, Kai Fisher *(Yvonne)*, Adrienne Corri *(Lady Isobel)*, Peter Arne *(Thomas)*, David Lodge *(Timothy)*, Bill Owen *(Martin)*, Peter Cushing *(Merryweather)*, Francis Matthews *(Sir Hugh)*, Desmond Walter Ellis *(Lord Chorley)*, Denis Shaw *(Sir Richard)*, Tutte Lemkow *(Higgins)*, Peter Howell *(Earl of Chatham)*, Bernard Hunter *(Marquis de Beauville)*, Michael Balfour *(John the Juggler)*, Miles Malleson *(Judge)*, Jean Lodge *(Lady Netherden)*, Andrew Faulds *(Lord Netherden)*, Martin Stephens *(Jason as a Boy)*, Rupert Osborne *(Thomas as a Boy)*, Skip Martin *(Joey the Dwarf)*.

Eighteenth-century drama featuring Michell as the young son of Faulds, an infamous lecher, leader of the notorious Hellfire Club. When the boy is whipped because he accidentally walks in on an orgy being held by his father, his mother, finally fed up with Faulds' debauchery, flees with her son. Soon after, she is killed in a coach accident. The boy is raised by family retainer Lodge. Years later, with the help of his attorney, Cushing, Michell (who has become a circus acrobat) returns to the estate of his father to reclaim it, only to be fought violently by his cousin, Arne, who has carried on the seedy traditions of his uncle. The cousin kidnaps Michell's childhood sweetheart, Fisher, forcing Michell to pursue and mortally wound him in a duel, thus regaining his estate and his love. For some reason the prints released in America were struck on black-and-white stock.

p&d, Robert S. Baker, Monty Berman; w, Leon Griffiths, Jimmy Sangster (based on a story by Sangster); ph, Baker, Berman (Dyaliscope, black-and-white or Eastmancolor); m, Clifton Parker; ed, Frederick Wilson; md, Muir Mathieson; art d, Ray Simm; set d, Leonard Townsend; cos, Laura Nightingale, Ron Beck; makeup, Jill Carpenter.

Adventure/Historical Drama **(PR:C MPAA:NR)**

HELLGATE** (1952) 87m Commander/Lippert c

Sterling Hayden *(Gil Hanley)*, Joan Leslie *(Ellen Hanley)*, Ward Bond *(Lt. Tod Vorhees)*, Jim [James] Arness *(George Redfield)*, Marshall Bradford *(Doctor Pelham)*, Peter Coe *(Jumper Hall)*, Richard Paxton *(George Nye)*, John Pickard *(Gundy Boyd)*, Pat Coleman *(Hunchy)*, Bob Wilke *(Sgt. Maj. Kearn)*, Sheb Wooley *(Neill Price)*, Richard Emory *(Dan Mott)*, Kyle James *(Vern Brechene)*, Rory Mallinson *(Banta)*, Ed Hinton *(Ault)*, Timothy Carey *(Wyand)*, William Hamel *(Lt. Col. Woods)*, Stanley Price *(Col. Telsen)*, Rod Redwing *(Pima)*.

Hayden is wrongfully accused of being part of a guerrilla gang during the Civil War, and is sent to New Mexico's Hellgate prison. Bond, the warden, holds a grudge against guerrillas because his family was wiped out by a band of them. He puts Hayden through numerous cruelties to force him to attempt an escape. The warden wants to kill the alleged guerrilla legitimately. Hayden does escape, isn't killed but is recaptured, and then helps stop an epidemic from spreading through the prison. This changes Bond's feelings and he helps Hayden get a pardon.

p, John C. Champion; d&w, Charles Marquis Warren (based on a story by Champion and Warren); ph, Ernest W. Miller; m, Paul Dunlap; ed, Elmo Williams.

Western **(PR:A MPAA:NR)**

HELLIONS, THE** (1962, Brit.) 80m Irving Allen-Jamie Uys/COL c

Richard Todd *(Sam Hargis)*, Anne Aubrey *(Priss Dobbs)*, Jamie Uys *(Ernie Dobbs)*, Marty Wilde *(John Billings)*, Lionel Jeffries *(Luke Billings)*, James Booth *(Jubal Billings)*, Al Mulock *(Mark Billings)*, Colin Blakely *(Matthew Billings)*, Ronnie Fraser *(Frank)*, Zena Walker *(Julie Hargis)*, George Moore *(Malachi)*, Bill Brewer *(Mike)*, Jan Bruyns *(Jan Pretorius)*, Lorna Cowell *(Martha Pretorius)*, Ricky Arden *(Bert)*, Freddie Prozesky *(Billy Dobbs)*, Patrick Mynhardt *(Telegraph Operator)*, James Norval *(Store Proprietor)*, Hugh Rouse *(Pastor)*, Leigh Crutchley *(Hotel Clerk)*, Gert Van den Bergh *(Dr. Weiser)*, Al Willox *(Commercial Traveler)*, Gabriel Bayman *(Stationmaster)*, Anna Cloete *(Mrs. Archer)*, Willie Herbst *(Engine Driver)*, Hendrik Van Der Merwe *(Citizen)*.

A violent western-type film set in South Africa in the late 1900s. Todd is a local police sergeant with "The Hellions," a father and his four sons, out to kill him. The townspeople won't back him up as the gang harasses him and his wife. Todd won't take his wife's advice that he quit his job, but finally the storekeeper is pushed into helping him and the rest of the town follows suit. Sort of a Boer version of HIGH NOON.

p, Harold Huth; d, Ken Annakin; w, Harold Swanton, Patrick Kirwan, Huth (based on a story by Swanton); ph, Ted Moore (Technirama, Technicolor); m, Larry Adler; ed, Bert Rule; md, Muir Mathieson; art d, William Constable; m/l, "The Hellions," Adler, Herbert Kretzmer (sung by Mary Wilde).

Adventure **(PR:O MPAA:NR)**

HELLO ANNAPOLIS* (1942) 62m COL bw

Tom Brown, Jean Parker, Larry Parks, Phil Brown, Joseph Crehan, Thurston Hall, Ferris Taylor, Herbert Rawlinson, Mae Busch, Robert Stevens, Stanley Brown, William Blees, Georgia Caine.

Brown and Parks carry their high-school rivalry for Parker into the Naval Academy with them. Negligible romantic comedy of little interest.

p, Wallace MacDonald; d, Charles Barton; w, Donald Davis, Tom Reed (based on a story by Reed); ph, Philip Tannura; ed, Arthur Seid; md, M.W. Stoloff; art d, Lionel Banks.

Comedy **(PR:A MPAA:NR)**

HELLO BEAUTIFUL (SEE: POWERS GIRL, THE, 1942)

HELLO, DOLLY!*** (1969) 129m Chenault/FOX c

Barbra Streisand *(Dolly Levi)*, Walter Matthau *(Horace Vandergelder)*, Michael Crawford *(Cornelius Hackl)*, Louis Armstrong *(Orchestra Leader)*, Marianne McAndrew *(Irene Molloy)*, E.J. Peaker *(Minnie Fay)*, Danny Lockin *(Barnaby Tucker)*, Joyce Ames *(Ermengarde)*, Tommy Tune *(Ambrose Kemper)*, Judy Knaiz *(Gussie Granger)*, David Hurst *(Rudolph Reisenweber)*, Fritz Feld *(Fritz, German Waiter)*, Richard Collier *(Vandergelder's Barber)*, J. Pat O'Malley *(Policeman in Park)*.

HELLO, DOLLY! is a huge galumph of a movie based on Thornton Wilder's play "The Matchmaker" which, in turn, was based on a European play that Otto Preminger swore he saw in Vienna in the early 1920s. Streisand was only 26 when she made this, far too young to convince anyone that she was already a widowed matchmaker earning her living in turn-of-the-century New York as a professional Yenta (Molly Picon was much more convincing in the same role in FIDDLER ON THE ROOF). The story opens with Streisand going to Yonkers, where Matthau is a wealthy grain merchant. She'd like to marry the man, but he is not the least bit interested. He asks her to take his niece, Ames, to the city in order to keep her away from Tune, a poor artist who yearns for her hand (as well as the rest of her). Matthau wants to marry McAndrew, a Big Apple milliner, but Streisand is not about to allow that to occur. She helps Ames and Tune in New York where they enter a dance contest at the Harmonia Gardens, the city's number-one night spot. She then learns that Matthau's two young employees, Crawford and Lockin, are taking a day trip to the city so she asks them to visit McAndrew's shop but to keep mum about why they are there. Once at the store, they pretend to be wealthy men-about-town, and meet McAndrew and her squeaky aide, Peaker. The charade is working well until Matthau and Streisand approach the shop and the boys hide. When Matthau finds them, he can't believe that his own employees are with his intended; all thoughts of a marriage to McAndrew are tossed aside. Streisand is delighted by this turn of events and tells Crawford and Lockin to take McAndrew and Peaker to the Harmonia Gardens. Meanwhile, she tells Matthau that she has a new prospect for him, the fabulously rich heiress, Knaiz, who is, in fact, an actress friend of Streisand's playing a role for her pal. Streisand makes a legendary entrance into the restaurant (the whole reason for the title song as sung by Satchmo Armstrong), and totally entrances Matthau, who now looks at her in a different light. Just as Matthau is about to ask her to be his wife, he espies Tune and Ames on the dance floor and flies into a rage that becomes a ruckus. Crawford and Lockin use the cover of this noisy melee to leave the restaurant without paying their check. Matthau fires the two young stock clerks and, in doing so, incurs Streisand's annoyance. She tells him she will have nothing more to do with him and that he deserves to be a lonely old man in Yonkers. The dawn breaks and Matthau has three changes of heart: he gives his consent to Ames and Tune, rehires Crawford and Lockin and promotes them, and finishes up this remarkable transformation by proposing to Streisand, which is exactly what she wanted from the start. HELLO, DOLLY! was one of three bomb musicals that Fox spent all of its SOUND OF MUSIC profits on. This one cost about $24 million; STAR (with Julie

Andrews) was close to that, with DR. DOLITTLE running third at about $18 million. The biggest winner was David Merrick (he always seems to win), who produced the play. Fox paid Merrick $2 million for the rights and promised they wouldn't make the picture until the play closed on Broadway or on June 20, 1971, whichever date came first. No one thought that the play would run as long as it did; Fox made the picture in 1968 but kept it on the shelf in order to comply with the deal they had with Merrick. But that huge a movie was costing them over a million a year in bank interest, and they realized they had to get it into the theaters before the bank's profits killed them, so they gave Merrick another million for the right to release it prior to the original agreement. Dolly had been played on the stage by such various middle-aged women as Carol Channing, Pearl Bailey, Mary Martin, Betty Grable, and Ginger Rogers, any of whom would have been more believable as the matchmaker. The non-musical film starred Shirley Booth, repeating her stage triumph with Paul Ford as Horace and Tony Perkins (in the Crawford role), with a 22-year-old Robert Morse as one of the stock boys. All of them would have been more suitable than the cast of the musical. The entire entry to Fox studios was transformed into a New York street (at a cost of millions), and the studio managed to amortize it by using the set in various other films (THE GREAT WHITE HOPE among them), but the entire cost of the movie may never be recouped when you multiply it by the usual movie formula of three-to-one to cover prints and advertising. The sure-fire combination Streisand, Matthau, Kelly, and Lehman turned out to be a sputter, despite the tuneful score by Jerry Herman. He wrote two new songs for the feature, replacing "I Put My Hand In" with "Just Leave Everything To Me" and adding "Love Is Only Love" which he'd originally cleffed for the score of "Mame" but cut before it opened. The other stage song that was excised was the delightful "Motherhood." Other tunes in the film include: "Dancing," "Waiter's Gavotte," "It Only Takes A Moment," "Ribbons Down My Back," "Elegance," "It Takes A Woman," "Put On Your Sunday Clothes," "So Long, Dearie," as well as "Before The Parade Passes By" and the title song. Gene Kelly was entrusted with the job of masterminding this musical epic that cost nearly two hundred thousand dollars a day to mount. At a smaller budget, it might have made money and surely wouldn't have suffered from being so overblown. The decision to pull out all stops and spend that incredible sum (since eclipsed by many other turkeys) was a mistake, and yet there is no one who can be given the blame. It's a pleasant movie, but that's about it, and when you spend $24 million, pleasant falls far short of pleasing box office receipts. The same could be said for Coppola's ONE FROM THE HEART, which cost about the same and made even less money. As you might expect, all of the technical credits were wonderful. The play had never been a landmark, and it was mostly Channing's performance and Herman's music that kept the stiles turning. Only one of those elements was present in the picture, and the result was a musical that ranks with DARLING LILI and PENNIES FROM HEAVEN (Steve Martin's version) as a box office bust.

p&w, Ernest Lehman (based on the play "The Matchmaker" by Thornton Wilder); d, Gene Kelly; ph, Harry Stradling, Sr. (Todd-AO, DeLuxe Color); m, Lenny Hayton, Lionel Newman; ed, William Reynolds; md, Hayton, Newman; prod d, John De Cuir; art d, Jack Martin Smith, Herman Blumenthal; set d, Walter M. Scott, George James Hopkins, Raphael Bretton; cos, Irene Sharaff; spec eff, L.B. Abbott, Art Cruickshank, Emil Kosa, Jr.; ch; Michael Kidd; m/l, Jerry Herman; makeup, Dan Striepeke.

Musical/Comedy Cas. (PR:AAA MPAA:G)

HELLO DOWN THERE** (1969) 88m Ivan Tors/PAR c (AKA: SUB-A-DUB-DUB)

Tony Randall *(Fred Miller)*, Janet Leigh *(Vivian Miller)*, Roddy McDowall *(Nate Ashbury)*, Jim Backus *(T.R. Hollister)*, Ken Berry *(Mel Cheever)*, Charlotte Rae *(Myrtle Ruth)*, Kay Cole *(Lorrie Miller)*, Richard Dreyfuss *(Harold Webster)*, Lou Wagner *(Marvin Webster)*, Gary Tigerman *(Tommie Miller)*, Arnold Stang *(Jonah)*, Harvey Lembeck *(Sonarman)*, Merv Griffin *(Himself)*, Lee Meredith *(Dr. Wells)*, Bruce Gordon *(Admiral Sheridan)*, Frank Schuller *(Alan Briggs)*, Henny Backus *(Mrs. Webster)*, Pat Henning *(Reilly)*, Jay Laskay *(Philo)*, Bud Hoey *(Mr. Webster)*, Charles Martin *(Chief Petty Officer)*, Frank Logan *(Captain)*, Andy Jarrell *(Radio Man)*, Lora Kaye *(Secretary)*.

Randall designs an underwater house and, to prove that it works, has his family live in it. They must live there for 30 days and the family has problems adjusting to their new environment. The kids are part of a rock group that is trying to cut a record, and there are plenty of lame generation-gap jokes. A drowned comedy done by the man who directed TARANTULA and THE INCREDIBLE SHRINKING MAN. Richard Dreyfuss is seen in his third film and is wasted, as are the comedy talents of Rae, Stang, and Lembeck. The dolphins and sharks handle their pantomime roles well. Tunes include: "Hello Down There," "I Can Love You," "Glub," "Hey, Little Goldfish," and "Just One More Chance."

p, George Sherman; d, Jack Arnold; w, Frank Telford, John McGreevy (based on a story by Ivan Tors, Art Arthur); ph, Cliff Poland, underwater ph, Lamar Boren, Jordan Klein (Eastmancolor); m, Jeff Barry; ed Erwin Dumbrille; art d, Jack Collis; set d, Don Ivey; m/l, Barry; underwater d, Ricos Browning.

Comedy (PR:A MPAA:G)

HELLO, ELEPHANT*½ (1954, Ital.) Rizzoli-De Sica/Arlan Pictures bw (BVONGIORNO, ELEFANTE! AKA: PARDON MY TRUNK)

Vittorio De Sica *(Mr. Garetti)*, Maria Mereader *(Mrs. Garetti)*, Sabu *(Hindu Ruler)*, Nando Bruno *(The Landlord)*.

Despite a gentle and moving portrayal by De Sica as the head of a family trying to combat poverty, HELLO ELEPHANT, like its title, winds to ridiculousness through the contrived situation of having an elephant pop into the tale. The giant beast is a gift from an Indian ruler to De Sica for the latter's assistance when the ruler visited Italy. Trying to contend with the thing makes for the bulk of the plot, taking away dramatic emphasis for the sake of outdated slapstick. As always, De Sica handles his role with a reserved charm that is a pleasure to watch; unfortunately, it's wasted.

p, Vittorio De Sica; d, Gianni Franciolini; w, Susi Cecchi D'Amico, Cesare Zavattini (based on a story by Zavattini); ph, Aldo Tonti; m, Alessandro Cicognini; prod d, Nino Misiano.

Comedy (PR:A MPAA:NR)

HELLO, EVERYBODY** (1933) 69m PAR bw

Kate Smith *(Kate Smith)*, Randolph Scott *(Hunt Blake)*, Sally Blane *(Lily Smith)*, Julia Swayne Gordon *(Mrs. Smith)*, Jerry Tucker *(Bobby)*, Marguerite Campbell *(Bettina)*, William Davidson *(Mr. Parker)*, George Barbier *(Mr. Blair)*, Paul Kruger *(Mr. Lindle)*, Charles Grapewin *(Jed)*, Fern Emmett *(Ettie)*, Irving Bacon, Ted Collins, Frank Darien, Edwards Davis, Russell Simpson.

A record-setting film starring America's great voiced chanteuse of the airwaves, Smith; the picture cost more than $2 million to make, more than any previous musical film, and it did the worst box-office business of any film up to that time during the first week of its release. This despite the star's popularity with middle America through the media of radio and personal appearances, a situation which led all the major studios to compete for her maiden film, which drove up the cost of production. Tragedy expert Hurst's plot has the booming Smith as a simple rustic who becomes a radio star, while yet preferring domesticity down on the farm. She falls hard for city-slicker Scott, who prefers her sister, Blane—real-life sibling of Loretta Young—whom he ultimately marries. Smith swallows her sorrows and puts on a happy face, consoling herself vicariously with the joys of those she loves, and her good nature propels her to superstardom. Smith was no actress, and the outtake footage weighed more than she did herself. Save for a brief cameo in THIS IS THE ARMY (1943), starring Ronald Reagan (who later, in real life, presented her with a presidential medal), this was both her first and her last picture. Songs include "Shoulda Been for Me," "Moon Song," "Out In the Great Open Spaces," "Queen of Lullabye Land," "Twenty Million People," and the amazing "Pickaninnies' Heaven," which recounts the joys of endless watermelons. The star's real-life Svengali, agent/manager Ted Collins, played—guess what?—Smith's agent in the film, demonstrating rather more acting talent than she herself.

d, William Seiter; w, Dorothy Yost, Lawrence Hazard (based on a story by Fanny Hurst); ph, Gilbert Warrenton; m/l, Arthur Johnson, Sam Coslow.

Musical/Comedy (PR:A MPAA:NR)

HELLO, FRISCO, HELLO*** (1943) 98m FOX c

Alice Faye *(Trudy Evans)*, John Payne *(Johnnie Cornell)*, Jack Oakie *(Dan Daley)*, Lynn Bari *(Bernice Croft)*, Laird Cregar *(Sam Weaver)*, June Havoc *(Beulah Clancy)*, Ward Bond *(Sharkey)*, Aubrey Mather *(Charles Cochran)*, John Archer *(Ned Clark)*, George Barbier *(Col. Weatherby)*, Frank Orth *(Lou)*, George Lloyd *(Proprietor)*, Eddie Dunn *(Foreman)*, Charles Cane *(O'Riley)*, Frank Thomas *(Auctioneer)*, Esther Dale *(Aunt Harriett)*, Frank Darien *(Missionary)*, Harry Hayden *(Burkham)*, Mary Field *(Cockney Maid)*, Fortunio Bonanova, Gino Corrado, Adia Kuznetzoff *(Opera Singers)*, James Sills, Marie Brown *(Roller Skating Specialty)*, Jackie Averill, Jimmie Clemens, Jr. *(Child Danvers)*, Ed Mundy *(Preacher)*, John Sinclair, Jack Stoney *(Drunks)*, James Flavin, Ken Christy *(Headwaiters)*, Edwin Earle *(Stage Manager)*, Kirby Grant *(Specialty Singer)*, Lorraine Elliott, Ruth Gillette *(Singers)*.

A lively and lavish musical in the Fox tradition, this film offers Faye at her attractive best, backed up by a charming Payne who does a commendable job as a San Francisco smoothie (not unlike Clark Gable's role in SAN FRANCISCO). Bond owns the biggest saloon along the Barbary Coast, the Colosseum, where Faye, Payne, Oakie, and Havoc sing as a team. They concoct a number where customers are dragged away from the bar to watch and pay for their inventive act, but Bond fires the lot of them for ruining his drinking business. Payne is undaunted. Not only does he grubstake gold miner Cregar with his last money, but convinces a singing missionary group to play outside of every gin mill in town, ruining business. The owners pay him $500 each to get rid of the psalm-singers but nemesis Bond is compelled to pay $1,000 in this frothy bit of blackmail. With the money Payne opens his own brawling joint, The Grizzly Bear, and Faye becomes his star attraction. All is well until Knob Hill socialite Bari comes into the bar and steals Payne's fickle heart. He prospers as he opens three more emporiums and Faye becomes the rage of San Francisco, but Payne becomes obsessed with the carriage trade and the snobbish Bari. A visiting theatrical impresario, Mather, sees Faye and offers her a grand singing tour of Europe. She refuses, planning to stay with Payne and eventually marry him. Payne, however, has fallen completely for Bari and he marries her to get to the top of Knob Hill Society. Sadly, Faye goes off to Europe to become the toast of the Continent. Bari, meanwhile, through her extravagance, uses up Payne's fortune and finally dumps him. Divorced and broke, all of his showplaces gone, Payne is reduced to being a sideshow barker. Returning rich and famous from Europe, Faye finds him hawking a cooch show and she finances Cregar who, in turn, backs Payne so he can reopen his Grizzly Bear emporium, telling him it's Payne's "share" of the gold mine in which he once invested. Not until the place's grand opening does Payne realize that Faye is behind it all; they reunite on stage while Faye sings their old favorite, "Hello Frisco, Hello" (Louis A. Hirsch, Gene Buck). The film is well done with sumptuous sets and numbers and Faye's winning voice makes for top entertainment. Other songs include: "You'll Never Know" (Mack Gordon, Harry Warren, a brand new song written for this film), "San Francisco" (Bronislau Kaper, Walter Jurmann, Gus Kahn), "Ragtime Cowboy Joe" (Grant Clarke, Maurice Abrahams, Lewis F. Muir), "Sweet Cider Time" (Percy Wenrich, Joesph McCarthy), "Has Anybody Here Seen Kelly" (Will Letters, C.W. Murphy, William J. McKenna), "King Chanticleer" (Nat D. Ayer), "When You Wore a Tulip" (Jack Mahoney, Percy Wenrich), "Strike Up the Band, Here Comes a Sailor" (Andrew B. Sterling, Charles P. Ward), "Why Do They Always Pick On Me? (Harry von Tilzer, Stanley Murphy), "Doin' the Grizzly Bear" (George Botsford, Irving Berlin), "Gee, but It's Great to Meet a Friend from Your Own Home Town" (James McGavish, Fred Fisher, William G. Tracey), "I've Got a Girl in Every Port" (composer unknown), "Bedelia" (Jean Schwartz, William Jerome), "By the Light of the Silvery Moon"

(Gus Edwards, Edward Madden), "It's Tulip Time in Holland" (Richard A. Whiting, Dave Radford).

p, Milton Sperling; d, H. Bruce Humberstone; w, Robert Ellis, Helen Logan, Richard Macauley; ph, Charles Clarke, Allen Davey (Technicolor); ed, Barbara McLean; md, Charles Henderson, Emil Newman; art d, James Basevi, Boris Leven; set d, Thomas Little, Paul S. Fox; cos, Helen Rose; spec eff, Fred Sersen; ch, Val Raset, Hermes Pan.

Musical **(PR:A MPAA:NR)**

HELLO GOD* (1951, U.S./Ital.) 64m Flynn bw

Errol Flynn *(Man on Anzio Beach)*, Sherry Jackson *(Little Italian Girl)*, Joe Muzzuca, Armando Formica, William Marshall *(Narrator)*.

Obscure Flynn film made in Italy quickly by the star as an excuse to get out of his Warner Bros. contract (which stipulated that he must appear in first-class, major studio releases) for his one-time friend William Marshall. HELLO GOD is an antiwar film starring Flynn as an "unknown solider" who tells the stories of four young soldiers who were killed at Anzio Beach during WW II. Flynn tells us the boys' hopes, fears, and desires as they approach heaven and are permitted to enter, though they have left Earth much sooner than God expected. Flynn's ruse against the studio backfired on him. After he renegotiated his contract with Warner Bros., he sued to have the distribution of HELLO GOD halted. Flynn arranged to have the negative of the film literally "kidnaped" at the lab in Hollywood by an associate, but Marshall countered by restructuring the film with outtakes and additional footage shot in California. This led to a falling-out between Flynn and Marshall after Flynn stated that Marshall misrepresented the film and that it was detrimental to the public welfare due to its pacifist nature. The lawsuits were never completely settled, and the revised film was shown only a few times, and only in Europe.

p,d&w, William Marshall; ph, Paul Ivano, Henry Freulich, Leo Barboni.

Drama **(PR:A MPAA:NR)**

HELLO—GOODBYE** (1970) 107m Hakim/FOX c

Michael Crawford *(Harry England)*, Curt Jurgens *(Baron De Choisis)*, Genevieve Gilles *(Dany)*, Ira Furstenberg *(Evelyne Rosson)*, Lon Satton *(Cole)*, Peter Myers *(Bentley)*, Mike Marshall *(Paul)*, Didier Haudepin *(Raymond)*, Vivian Pickles *(Joycie)*, Agathe Natanson *(Monique)*, Georges Bever *(Hotel Porter)*, Denise Grey *(Concierge)*, Jeffry Wickham *(Dickie)*.

A light sex comedy with Crawford as a British car salesman who, on a trip to France, meets Gilles. She appears to be a lonely lady so Crawford puts the make on her and is very successful. He discovers that she is the wife of a baron, Jurgens, who allows her to fool around. The baron hires Crawford to teach his son (from another marriage) all about cars. He finds himself falling deeply in love with Gilles and can't keep his hands off. Jurgens looks the other way because he's bedding down with Furstenberg.

p, Andre Hakim; d, Jean Negulesco; w, Roger Marshall; ph, Henri Decae (DeLuxe Color); m, Francis Lai; ed, Richard Bryan; prod d, John Howell; art d, Auguste Capelier; set d, Pierre Charron, Pamela Cornell; cos, Rosine Delamare; makeup, Georges Bouban; spec eff, Richard Parker.

Comedy **(PR:O MPAA:GP)**

HELLO LONDON zero (1958, Brit.) 78m Kinran/FOX c (AKA: LONDON CALLING)

Sonja Henie, Michael Wilding, Ronnie Graham, Eunice Gayson, Lisa Gastoni, Charles Heslop, Oliver Johnston, Trefor Jones, Stanley Holloway, Dennis Price, Dora Bryan, Robert Coote, Roy Castle, Joan Regan, Oliver Reed *(Themselves.)*.

Wilding and Gayson team up to give Henie a tour of London so extensive that she will miss her plane and have to appear at a charity concert to be given that night. Forgettable songs fill this awful musical. Mercifully, the last film by Henie.

p, George Fowler; d, Sidney Smith; w, Fowler, Herb Sargent, Ken Englund, Guy Elmes; ph, Otto Heller (Eastmancolor); md, Phillip Martell; ch, George Baron, Ted Shuffle; m/l, Michael Carr, Phil Green.

Musical **(PR:A MPAA:NR)**

HELLO SISTER*½ (1930) 70m James Cruze/Sono Art-World Wide bw

Olive Borden *("Vee" Newell)*, Lloyd Hughes *(Marshall Jones)*, George W. Fawcett *(Fraser Newell)*, Bodil Rosing *(Martha Peddie)*, Norman Peck *("Tivvie" Rose)*, Howard Hickman *(John Stanley)*, Raymond Keene *(Randall Carr)*, Wilfred Lucas *(Dr. Saltus)*, James T. Mack *(Horace Peddie)*, Harry MacDonald *(Appleby Sims)*.

Borden is a presumed heiress willed a large fortune by a grandparent. There's a clause to the money stating that Borden must go to church every Sunday for six months. She meets a deacon who's a lawyer, and they fall in love. At first he won't marry her because she's rich, but when it's discovered that the will is a fake they elope.

p, James Cruze; d, Walter Lang; w, Brian Marlow (based on the story "Clipped Wings" by Rita Lambert); ph, Hal Rosen; m, Russell Columbo.

Drama **(PR:A MPAA:NR)**

HELLO SISTER!½** (1933) 55m FOX bw (AKA: WALKING DOWN BROADWAY)

ZaSu Pitts *(Millie)*, Boots Mallory *(Peggy)*, James Dunn *(Jimmy)*, Terrance Ray *(Mac)*, Minna Gombell *(Mona)*, Will Stanton *(Man)*, Henry Kolker *(Bank President)*, Walter Walker *(Man Visiting Bank President)*, Hattie McDaniel *(Black Woman in Partment House)* [in retakes only], Will Stanton *(Drunk)*, Wade boteler *(Fireman)*, Claude King, James Flavin, Astrid Allwyn.

Two small-town girls, Pitts and Mallory, venture to New York and wind up with a pair of city boys, Dunn and Ray. Pitts, a bit on the psychotic side, falls for the shy Dunn, whom she discovers is in love with the more glamorous Mallory. Pitts decides to break them apart by spreading false rumors. The unhappy Pitts thinks that the only way she can get Dunn's attention is to kill herself. She turns on the gas in her house and accidentally causes an explosion. Dunn sees the disaster and rushes into the flames to save his love, but finds only Pitts. After a deathbed confession, the pair end up in each other's bandaged arms, with Pitts dying moments later. Dunn and Mallory, who had tried to leave town, get together at the deathbed. The film described here is actually WALKING DOWN BROADWAY, which was directed by Erich von Stroheim. It was his first (and only) sound film and was also brought in under budget and under schedule—a pleasant surprise from von Stroheim. It was, unfortunately, the last film he was to direct. Caught in a studio war between the sympathetic Winfield Sheehan and the insensitive Sol Wurtzel, von Stroheim's 14,000 feet of film was rewritten, reshot, and recut into this 5800-foot version known as HELLO SISTER! Co-written by Leonard Spigelgass and photographed by James Wong Howe, WALKING DOWN BROADWAY was reportedly void of the spectacular nature so often associated with his work. It was, in fact, a compelling psychological study of a romance clouded with lesbian undertones. Wurtzel is said to have not understood the film, entirely missing the subtle nuances it offered. Although he promised a test screening to let the audience judge for themselves, he arranged only for studio employees to view it. Word was out that Wurtzel hated it, so naturally his spineless yes-men followed suit—forever condemning what most likely would have been a masterpiece. After this injustice, the great director of GREED resorted to a string of unrealized projects, as well as working as a scriptwriter (SAN FRANCISCO, BETWEEN TWO WOMEN) and appearing in numerous films (THE GRAND ILLUSION, SUNSET BOULEVARD). His days as a director were over, however, and the depressing thought still remains—there is no known existing print of WALKING DOWN BROADWAY.

d, Erich von Stroheim; w, von Stroheim, Leonard Spigelgass, Geraldine Nomis, Harry Ruskin, Maurine Watkins (based on an unproduced play, "Walking Down Broadway," by Dawn Powell); ph, James Wong Howe; ed, Frank Hull; art d, William Darling.

Drama **(PR:C-O MPAA:NR)**

HELLO SUCKER zero (1941) 60m UNIV bw

Hugh Herbert *(Hubert)*, Tom Brown *(Bob Wade)*, Peggy Moran *(Rosalie Wilson)*, Lewis Howard *(Walter)*, June Storey *(Trixie)*, Walter Catlett *(Conway)*, Robert Emmett Keane *(Connors)*, Mantan Moreland *(Elevator Boy)*, Elaine Morley *(Receptionist)*, Nell O'Day, Dorothy Darrell *(Girls)*.

Brown and Moran buy a run-down vaudeville agency from a couple of crooks. They pull it back on its feet by having the acts perform in department store windows. Too bad no one could pull the film to its feet. A silly story with cardboard actors and not one funny scene.

p, Ken Goldsmith; d, Edward Cline; w, Maurice Leo, Paul Gerard Smith (based on a story by Arthur T. Horman); ph, Charles Van Enger; ed, Ralph Dixon; md, H.J. Salter; art d, Jack Otterson.

Comedy **(PR:A MPAA:NR)**

HELLO SWEETHEART*½ (1935, Brit.) 70m WB bw

Claude Hulbert *(Henry Pennyfeather)*, Gregory Ratoff *(Joseph Lewis)*, Jane Carr *(Babs Beverley)*, Nancy O'Neil *(Helen Taylor)*, Olive Blakeney *(Daisy Montrose)*, Cyril Smith *(Mac McGuire)*, Morris Harvey *(F.Q. Morse)*, Felix Aylmer *(Peabody)*, Phyllis Stanley, Johnnie Nit, Three Ginx, Marriott Edgar, Carroll Gibbons, Ernest Sefton.

A bunch of shady Americans convince guileless farmer Hulbert to invest his inheritance in their film. When they take off, leaving him with a half-finished film, he turns it into a comedy and it is a success. Watchable comedy, but it could have been much better. The silent version of Kaufman's popular play, released in 1928, was much worse.

p, Irving Asher; d, Monty Banks; w, Brock Williams (based on the play "The Butter And Egg Man" by George S. Kaufman); ph, Basil Emmott.

Comedy **(PR:A MPAA:NR)**

HELLO TROUBLE** (1932) 61m COL bw

Buck Jones, Lina Basquette, Russell Simpson, Otto Hoffman, Wallace MacDonald, Allan Roscoe, Morgan Galloway, Ruth Warren, Frank Rice, Lafe McKee, Ward Bond, Al Smith, Spec O'Donnell, King Baggott, "Silver".

Jones quits the Texas Rangers after killing a boy he once knew. The kid was in a horse-rustling gang, and Jones thought the kid was shooting at him when in reality he was aiming for another member of the gang gunning for Jones. The ex-Ranger goes to work at a ranch owned by one of his father's old friends. The latter is killed when Jones arrives and the niece becomes upset when Jones won't holster his gun again. He does finally pack his gun and goes on the trail of the murderer. The niece, Basquette, chases after him to say she's sorry. (See TEXAS RANGERS series, Index.)

d&w, Lambert Hillyer; ph, Benjamin Kline; ed, Gene Milford.

Western **(PR:A MPAA:NR)**

HELL'S ANGELS*½** (1930) 135m Caddo/UA bw-c

Ben Lyon *(Monte Rutledge)*, James Hall *(Roy Rutledge)*, Jean Harlow *(Helen)*, John Darrow *(Karl Arnstedt)*, Lucien Prival *(Baron von Kranz)*, Frank Clarke *(Lt. von Bruen)*, Roy Wilson *(Baldy)*, Douglas Gilmore *(Capt. Redfield)*, Jane Winton *(Baroness von Kranz)*, Evelyn Hall *(Lady Randolph)*, W. B. Davidson *(Staff Major)*, Wyndham Standing *(Squadron Commander)*, Carl von Haartman *(Zeppelin Commander)*, F. Shumann-Heink *(1st Officer)*, Lena Malena *(Gretchen)*, Stephen Carr *(Elliott)*, Hans Joby *(Von Schleiben)*, Pat Somerset, *(Marryat)*, Marilyn Morgan [Marian Marsh] *(Girl Selling Kisses)*, William von Brinken *(Von Richthofen)*, Harry Semels *(Anarchist)*, Stewart Murphy, Ira Reed, Maurice "Loop the Loop" Murphy, Leo Nomis, Frank Tomick, Al Wilson, Roscoe Turner *(Pilots)*.

The plot isn't much but the aerial photography is sensational and Lyon and Hall do a bang-up job as pilot brothers who leave Oxford to joing the British Royal Flying Corps at the beginning of WW I. Hall falls in love with blonde siren Harlow. Then Lyon meets Harlow, has a quick fling with her, and realizes she will two-time anyone, including his brother. Before leaving on a desperate mission to blow up a German ammunition dump the brothers visit Harlow to find her in the arms of another; moreover she mocks them and tells them she'll love whom she pleases whenever she pleases. The brothers then fly off and accomplish their mission, but they are shot down and captured by the Germans who tell them they will be sent to safety but only if they give the time of the impending British attack. Lyon, who is shell-shocked, cracks and is about to blurt the information when Hall shoots him. Dying in his brother's arms, Lyon forgives Hall. The Germans, incensed over this defeat, execute Hall when he refuses to give them the information they seek. Though much of this film now seems dated, when the movie first appeared it wowed audiences around the world, the Zeppelin raid over London seeming to viewers to be the real thing. Hughes, who launched this film as the first major effort of his own Caddo Productions in 1927, reworked the film so long that sound came into being and he had to redo the entire film which had been made as a silent. Sound effects had to be given to the bombing, the machine-gunning, the roaring of the motors from authentic Sopwith Snipes, German Fokkers, a Gotha bomber, British SE'5s. Both Lyon and Hall had good sound voices but the female lead, Greta Nissen, had a pronounced Norwegian accent, and, though he had paid her handsomely, $2,500-a-week, Hughes scrapped her role completely. He ordered testing of new actresses who could talk convincingly and among the candidates was an 18-year-old blue-eyed girl with albino hair and a voluptuous shape. Hughes saw her test and said no, but her agent, Arthur Landau, talked the millionaire playboy into letting her have the part for $1,500-a-week for six weeks shooting. Harlow was a sex sensation in the film, wearing a dress with hardly any top at all, a neckline that didn't exist and one that caused Hughes endless arguments with the censors. After the film, Hughes inexplicably ignored the new star he had created, though he had had the presence of mind to put her under permanent contract to him. He sold the contract to MGM for a mere $60,000 and she would make millions for that studio as the reigning sex queen of the cinema until her death in 1937. Hughes had originally signed Marshall Neilan to direct but he interferred so much with Neilan that the director quit. Next came Luther Reed, an aviation specialist, but he only lasted two months before he found Hughes' interventions intolerable, one day exploding: "If you know so much, why don't you direct it yourself?" Hughes nodded and took over the assignment. He used up money extravagantly to get each scene just the way he wanted it, and this included the aerial dogfights. Roscoe Turner and other WW I aces were hired to perform incredible stunts and more than 100 mechanics were kept busy on the ground putting the old WW I planes into flying shape. Most of the aerial shots were taken over Mines Field in Inglewood, the present site of Los Angeles International Airport. Hughes could not resist taking up one of the planes himself during a massive dogfight but, when only a few hundred feet in flight, the little plane flopped over and crashed. Hughes was pulled unconscious from the plane, a cheekbone so crushed that he required plastic surgery. There would be many duplications of this scene during the lengthy filming of HELL'S ANGELS, three dead pilots when it was all over. The giant German Gotha bomber used in the film, which is shot down by Allied planes and crashes into burning wreckage, claimed the life of mechanic Phil Jones who apparently did not get the signal to parachute to safety or was trapped and could not get out when the plane was sent into its death spin. Audiences viewing this scene did not realize that it recorded the actual death of one of the crew. After three years of shooting, Hughes had assembled 2.5 million feet of film and this was cut down to 135 minutes and cut many times after that. The cost had been staggering, $3.8 million, the most expensive film ever made up to that time. Hughes was determined to get his money back by the kind of hoopla for which he later became notorious. He had a squadron of planes buzz Grauman's Chinese Theater at the film's premiere while parachutists fell from the sky and landed on Hollywood Boulevard. He tried the same thing in New York by offering the owners of the dirigible *Graf Zeppelin* $100,000 to sail over Broadway and 42nd Street where *two* theaters were premiering the film, advertisements for the film to be painted on the Zeppelin, but they refused. He later hired Grauman's Chinese Theater for a private screening of the film, with himself as the audience; he barred all others. Gossip columnist Louella Parsons slipped inside and Hughes ordered her to leave. "I will not!" she shouted back, and the two of them sat nervously watching the film and each other. Hughes took a bath on the film, losing more than $1.5 million, although, at first, he claimed to have made $2 million. The youthful Hughes, two years later, gave an interview in which he admitted: "Making HELL'S ANGELS by myself was my biggest mistake. It would have been finished sooner and cost less. I had to worry about money, sign checks, hire pilots, get planes, cast everything, direct the whole thing. Trying to do the work of 12 men was just dumbness on my part. I learned by bitter experience that no one man can know everything." Hughes would forget those words quickly enough and repeat the same error over and over again, but he was a man who could afford all of his mistakes, which made him appear to Hollywood a boy genius.

p, Howard Hughes; d, Hughes, Marshall Neilan, Luther Reed; w, Harry Behn, Howard Estabrook, Joseph Moncure March (based on a story by Neilan, March); ph, Gaetano Gaudio, Harry Perry, E. Burton Steene, Elmer Dyer, Zeck and Dewey Wrigley (color scenes in Technicolor); m, Hugo Riesenfeld; ed, Douglas Biggs, Perry Hollingsworth, Frank Lawrence; art d, Julian Boone Fleming, Carroll Clark.

War Drama **Cas.** **(PR:C MPAA:NR)**

HELL'S ANGELS ON WHEELS zero (1967) 95m Fanfare/U.S. Films c

Adam Roarke *(Buddy)*, Jack Nicholson *(Poet)*, Sabrina Scharf *(Shill)*, Jana Taylor *(Abigale)*, John Garwood *(Jock)*, Richard Anders *(Bull)*, Mimi Machu *(Pearl)*, James Oliver *(Gypsy)*, Jack Starrett *(Bingham)*, Gary Littlejohn *(Moley)*, Bruno Ve Sota *(Justice of the Peace)*, Robert Kelljan *(Artist)*, Kathryn Harrow *(Lori)*, Sonny Barger *(Himself)*.

Even Nicholson's presence can't lift this trash to a one-star listing. Nicholson plays a gas-station attendant who is tired of his boring life style and joins up with the Hell's Angels. Talk about an exciting life style, killing a sailor and old men, trading girl friends and partying as often as possible, real fun and great film entertainment. Nicholson tries to steal Roarke's, the leader's, girl friend. The two duel it out in the biker tradition with Roarke on a motorcycle and Nicholson trying not to get run over. Conveniently, the gang leader drives into a fire and burns, but Jack doesn't even get the girl for all his trouble. Real-life Hell's Angel Barger was both actor and technical advisor for the film, which has other Richmond Hell's Angels and Sacramento's Nomads in distant group long shots.

p, Joe Solomon; d, Richard Rush; w, R. Wright Campbell; ph, Leslie Kovacs (Eastmancolor); m, Stu Phillips; ed, William Martin; m/l, "Study In Motion No. 1," Chuck Sedacca, Phillips (sung by The Poor).

Action **Cas.** **(PR:O MPAA:NR)**

HELL'S ANGELS '69 zero (1969) 97m AIP c

Tom Stern *(Chuck)*, Jeremy Slate *(Wes)*, Conny Van Dyke *(Betsy)*, Steve Sandor *(Apache)*, J.D. Spradlin *(Detective)*, Sonny Barger *(Sonny)*, Terry the Tramp *(Terry)*, Bobby Hall, Ray Renard, Michael Michaelian, Bud Ekins, Joe Hooker, Bob Harris, Ric Henry, Danielle Corn, Jerry Randall, Ed Mulder, Members of the Oakland Hell's Angels.

Another flat-tire biker film that even has the real Oakland chapter of the Hell's Angels in featured roles. Stern and Slate are two East Coast rich kids who come to Las Vegas to rob Caesar's Palace. They trick Barger and his Angels into being their diversion and the job goes perfectly. The Angels are mad because they were fooled and didn't get a cut of the money, so they chase Stern, Slate, and gang defector Van Dyke across the desert and give them their just desserts.

p, Tom Stern; d, Lee Madden; w, Don Tait (based on a story by Stern, Jeremy Slate); ph, Paul Loman (Berkey Pathe Color); m, Tony Bruno; ed, Gene Ruggiero; md, John D'Andrea.

Action **Cas.** **(PR:O MPAA:M)**

HELL'S BELLES*½ (1969) 95m AIP c (AKA: GIRL IN THE LEATHER SUIT)

Jeremy Slate *(Dan)*, Adam Roarke *(Tampa)*, Jocelyn Lane *(Cathy)*, Angelique Pettyjohn *(Cherry)*, Michael Walker *(Tony)*, Astrid Warner *(Piper)*, William Lucking *(Gippo)*, Eddie Hice *(Red Beard)*, Dick Bullock *(Meatball)*, Jerry Randall *(Crazy John)*, Jerry Brutsche *(Rabbit)*, Kristian Van Buren *(Zelda)*, Elaine Gefner *(Big Sal)*, Fred Krone *(Burr)*, Ronnie Dayton *(Barney)*, Henry Kendrick *(Gas Station Attendant)*, Frank Kennedy *(Store Owner)*, James Owens *(Leo)*, Larry H. Lane *(Charlie)*, Jackie Hummer *(Girl Friend)*, Bill Thompson *(L. G.)*, Michael Jones *(Donny)*.

Slate has the $2,000 bike he won stolen by Roarke and his gang, and they leave Lane as a trade-off. Slate and the girl become friends and chase the gang across the Arizona desert. The pair kills off the bikers with boulders, booby traps, and a snake pit. In the climactic battle, Slate and Roarke get on their bikes and beat each other with chains.

p&d, Maury Dexter; w, James Gordon White, Robert McMullen; ph, Kenneth Peach (Berkey Pathe Color); m, Lex Baxter; ed, John Schreyer; set d, Harry Reif; cos, Sharon Thober, Richard Bruno; spec eff, Roger Geroge; makeup, Paul Malcolm.

Action **(PR:O MPAA:M)**

HELL'S BLOODY DEVILS* (1970) 92m East-West-Four Crown/Independent-International c (AKA: OPERATION M; THE FAKERS; SMASHING THE CRIME SYNDICATE)

Broderick Crawford *(Brand)*, Scott Brady *(FBI Agent)*, Kent Taylor *(Count von Delberg)*, Keith Andes *(Bremonte)*, John Carradine *(Shop Owner)*, John Gabriel *(Mark Adams)*, Robert Dix *(Cunk)*, Erin O'Donnell *(von Delberg's Daughter)*, Vicki Volante *(Carol Bechtol)*, Anne Randall *(Amanda)*, Jack Starrett *(Rocky)*, Emily Banks *(FBI Agent)*, Dan Kemp *(Henchman)*, William Bonner, Jerry Mills *("Bloody Devils")*, Bambi Allen, Jill Woelfel *(Pick-Up Girls)*, California's Hessians *(Bike Riders)*, Carol Brewster, Leslie McRae, Gene Shane, Arland Shubert, Alyce Andrace, Rhae Andrace, Alice Wong, Jane Wald, Richard Brander, Brand Bell, Greydon Clark, Gary Kent, Sid Lawrence, John Cardos, Kent Osborne, Sheldon Lee, Philip Difermian, Col. Harlan Sanders, The California "Hessians".

Really awful actioner starring Taylor as a crazed Nazi war criminal living in the U.S. and trying to revitalize the neo-nazi movement. To do this Taylor and his equally vile daughter have united with the Las Vegas Mafia and a band of savage motorcyclists known as the Bloody Devils. To combat this evil insurgence the FBI sends Gabriel to infiltrate the gang and destroy it from within. Aided by Israeli agent Volante (whose parents were killed by Taylor), who has also infiltrated the gang as Taylor's mistress, Gabriel attempts to smash the giant crime wave. After much violence and death, and a plug for Kentucky Fried Chicken, good triumphs. Very strange. Songs, sung by Debbie Stuart, are "Faker" (Nelson Riddle, John Gabriel) and "When Did the Sun Come Out?" (Don McGinnis, David MacKechnie).

p&d, Al Adamson; w, Jerry Evans; ph, Laszlo Kovacs, Frank Ruttencutter, Gary Graver (DeLuxe Color); m, Nelson Riddle, Don McGinnis; ed, John Winfield.

Crime **(PR:O MPAA:GP)**

HELL'S CARGO** (1935, Brit.) 58m BIP/Wardour bw (GB: McGLUSKY THE SEA ROVER)

Jack Doyle *(McGlusky)*, Tamara Desni *(Flame)*, Henry Mollison *(Mazarin)*, Cecil Ramage *(Auda)*, Frank Cochrane *(Abu)*, Hugh Miller *(Karim)*, Jackie Short *(Govan)*.

Boxer Doyle makes his screen debut in this mediocre action programmer. He plays a stowaway aboard a ship running guns to Arabs. After he befriends Capt. Mollison, they break over their mutual infatuation with lovely Arab girl Desni. She rejects them both and they go into a profitable partnership.

p, Walter C. Mycroft; d&w, Walter Summers (based on a novel by A. G. Hales).

Adventure **(PR:A MPAA:NR)**

HELL'S CARGO, 1939 (SEE: DANGEROUS CARGO, 1939)

HELL'S CHOSEN FEW zero (1968) 92m Borealis/Thunderbird International c

Jody Daniels *(Joe)*, Kelly Ross *(Sharon)*, Gary Kent *(Willie)*, Joe Follino *(Sheriff)*, William Bonner, Vic McGee, Mick Mehas, Titus Moody, Shirley Cash, Megan Timothy.

Wretched biker film starring Daniels as a returned Viet Nam vet who joins his brother's biker gang after his sibling is jailed for the murder of the sheriff's daughter's boy friend. Taking charge of the gang, Daniels decides to find out what really happened. Aiding him is the sheriff's daughter and his brother's ex-girl friend. Eventually, Daniels discovers that it was actually the sheriff himself who committed the murder; the latter is killed by his own gun in the ensuing fight. Upon his release, the thankless brother rapes his own ex-girl friend, forcing Daniels to kill his own flesh and blood. Really sick stuff.

p&d, David L. Hewitt; w, John K. McCarthy, David Prentiss; ph, Ewing Brown (Eastmancolor); m, Charles Walden.

Crime **(PR:O MPAA:NR)**

HELL'S CROSSROADS*½ (1957) 73m REP c

Stephen McNally *(Vic Rodell)*, Peggie Castle *(Paula Collins)*, Robert Vaughn *(Bob Ford)*, Barton MacLane *(Clyde O'Connell)*, Harry Shannon *(Clay Ford)*, Henry Brandon *(Jesse James)*, Douglas Kennedy *(Frank James)*, Grant Withers *(Sheriff Steve Oliver)*, Myron Healey *(Cole Younger)*, Frank Wilcox *(Governor Crittenden)*, Jean Howell *(Mrs. Jesse James)*, Morris Ankrum *(Wheeler)*.

Vaughn is Bob Ford, the man who killed Jesse James. Vaughn, along with McNally, wants to leave the James gang after the film's opening holdup. McNally wants to give up being an outlaw to marry Vaughn's sister, Castle. Since both are still wanted by the law, Castle makes a deal with the governor, who will pardon both of them if Jesse is brought in dead or alive. Vaughn is the one who finds Jesse and shoots him in the back, which is close to historical fact. McNally is then able to marry Castle and live in peace. The first big screen role for TV star Vaughn, master of the mildly neurotic characterization.

p, Rudy Ralston; d, Franklin Adreon; w, John K. Butler, Barry Shipman (based on a story by Butler); ph, John L. Russell Jr. (Naturama); m, Gerald Roberts; ed, Tony Martinelli; art d, Frank Arrigo.

Western **(PR:A MPAA:NR)**

HELL'S FIVE HOURS** (1958) 73m AA bw

Stephen McNally *(Mike)*, Coleen Gray *(Nancy)*, Vic Morrow *(Nash)*, Maurice Manson *(Dr. Culver)*, Robert Foulk *(Fife)*, Dan Sheridan *(Ken)*, Will J. White *(Al)*, Robert Christopher *(Bill)*, Charles J. Conrad *(George)*, Ray Ferrell *(Eric)*.

Morrow is a disgruntled employee of a rocket fuel factory who threatens to blow himself, the plant, and the surrounding area sky high. McNally, the manager of the plant, keeps Morrow occupied until the fuel is removed and there no longer is danger to the plant or the surrounding residential area. An average thriller that keeps you wondering about the outcome, but slows to a snail's pace in the middle.

p,d&w, Jack L. Copeland; ph, Ernest Haller; m, Nicholas Carras; ed, Walter A. Hannemann; md, Carras; art d, David Milton; cos, Bert Henrikson.

Thriller **(PR:A MPAA:NR)**

HELL'S HALF ACRE*½ (1954) 90m REP bw

Wendell Corey *(Chet Chester)*, Evelyn Keyes *(Dona Williams)*, Elsa Lanchester *(Lida O'Reilly)*, Marie Windsor *(Rose)*, Nancy Gates *(Sally Lee)*, Leonard Strong *(Ippy)*, Jesse White *(Tubby Otis)*, Keye Luke *(Chief Dan)*, Philip Ahn *(Roger Kong)*, Robert Shield *(Frank)*, Clair Widenaar *(Jamison)*, Robert Costa *(Slim Novak)*.

A contrived murder mystery that has only one original thought to it, and that is the Hawaiian backdrop. Corey is a gangster gone straight whose girl friend, Gates, kills one of his ex-partners because the latter was blackmailing Corey. Corey takes the rap, thinking he can beat it. Keyes arrives, trying to find out if Corey is the husband she lost at Pearl Harbor. Gates is mysteriously murdered; Corey escapes from jail to find the killer. Things become very confused and muddled at this point, with the ex-gangster letting killer Ahn take his life so Keyes will be free to start a new life, and their son will still believe his dad died at Pearl Harbor, a hero.

p&d, John H. Auer; w, Steve Fisher; ph, John L. Russell, Jr.; m, R. Dale Butts; ed, Fred Allen; m/l, "Polynesian Rhapsody," Steve Fisher, Jack Pitman, "Lani," Pitman.

Crime/Drama **(PR:A MPAA:NR)**

HELL'S HEADQUARTERS* (1932) 59m Weeks/Mayfair bw

Jack Mulhall, Barbara Weeks, Frank Mayo, Phillips Smalley, Fred Parker, Everett Brown.

Mayo is an African adventurer who kills a man for his secret cache of ivory. He gets his ex-fiancee, Weeks, to pay for an expedition to find the ivory. Mulhall, who was the dead man's partner, also goes after the tusks and Mayo. The hero reaches the ivory first, Mayo is killed by lions and Mulhall shares the ivory with Weeks.

p, Armand Schaeffer; d, Andrew L. Stone; w, Morton S. Parker; ph, Jules Cronjager; ed, Frank Atkinson.

Action/ Adventure **(PR:A MPAA:NR)**

HELL'S HEROES**** (1930) 65m UNIV bw

Charles Bickford *(Bob Sangster)*, Raymond Hatton *(Barbwire Gibbons)*, Fred Kohler *(Wild Bill Kearney)*, Fritzi Ridgeway *(Mother)*, Maria Alba *(Carmelita)*, Jose De LaCruz *(Jose)*, Buck Connors *(Parson Jones)*, Walter James *(Sheriff)*.

Adapted from Peter B. Kyne's novel *The Three Godfathers* which had been done twice in the silent era (in 1916 and again in 1920 by John Ford as MARKED MEN). This was the first sound version, and it would be done again by Ford with John Wayne starring. Wyler's version is a stark, realistic film shot on location in the Mojave Desert and the Panamint Valley near Death Valley. It was the director's first all-talkie and Universal's first on-location talkie. The story is about three outlaws, Bickford, Hatton, and Kohler, who find a woman in a wagon about to give birth. They promise the dying mother that they will be the child's godfathers and take the baby back to its father in New Jerusalem, the town where they just robbed the bank. They head back; one of the outlaws dies from the wounds he received from the robbery. Another dies from thirst; the last drinks from a poisoned spring to gain enough strength to get the baby to the town's church during Christmas services. Overshadowed by Ford's sound version, HELL'S HEROES is an excellent western drama that deserves more critical attention.

p, Carl Laemmle; d, William Wyler; w, Tom Reed (based on Peter B. Kyne's novel *The Three Godfathers*); ph, George Robinson; ed, Harry Marker.

Western **(PR:A MPAA:NR)**

HELL'S HIGHWAY*½** (1932) 62m RKO bw

Richard Dix *(Frank "Duke" Ellis)*, Tom Brown *(Johnny Ellis)*, Louise Carter *(Mrs. Ellis)*, Rochelle Hudson *(Mary Ellen)*, C. Henry Gordon *(Blacksnake Skinner)*, Warner Richmond *(Pop-Eye Jackson)*, Sandy Roth *(Blind Maxie)*, Charles Middleton *(Matthew, the Hermit)*, Clarence Muse *(Rascal)*, Stanley Fields *(Whiteside)*, Jed Kiley *(Romeo Schultz)*, Fuzzy Knight *(Society Red)*, Bert Starkey *(Hype)*, Bob Perry *(Spike)*, Harry Smith *(Buzzard)*, Edward Hart, John Lester Johnson.

Dix is a convict at a brutal prison camp in a Southern state. The prisoners build a new road and are pushed relentlessly. Men are whipped, kept in sweatboxes (a small metal box that absorbs the sun's burning heat) and live in unsanitary conditions. Dix plans his escape when his brother is sent to the camp, and ends up sacrificing his life to prevent his sibling from being killed. Released shortly before Warner Bros. I AM A FUGITIVE FROM A CHAIN GANG. This one established many of the situations and personalities used in later, similar films, including implied inmate homosexuality (here used for comic relief).

p, David Selznick; d, Rowland Brown; w, Samuel Ornitz, Robert Tasker, Brown; ph, Edward Cronjager; ed, William Hamilton; art d, Carroll Clark.

Drama **(PR:A MPAA:NR)**

HELL'S HORIZON*½ (1955) 78m COL bw

John Ireland, Marla English, Bill Williams, Hugh Beaumont, Larry Pennell, Chet Baker, William Schallert, Jerry Paris, Paul Levitt, John Murphy, Wray Davis, Mark Scott, Kenne Duncan, Don Burnett, Stanley Adams.

Ireland is a bomber pilot during the Korean war who goes on a mission with Williams to bomb a bridge over the Yalu River. They plan to use the bad weather for cover, but it clears up and the North Korean fighter planes zero in. Unsurprisingly, the bomber makes it back to base after completing the mission.

p, Wray Davis; d&w, Tom Gries; ph, Floyd Crosby; m, Heinz Roemheld; ed, Aaron Stell; md, Roemheld; art d, Al Goodman.

War **(PR:A MPAA:NR)**

HELL'S HOUSE** (1932) 80m Capital Films Exchange bw

Junior Durkin *(Jimmy Mason)*, Pat O'Brien *(Kelly)*, Bette Davis *(Peggy Gardner)*, Junior Coghlan *(Shorty)*, Charley Grapewin *(Uncle Henry)*, Emma Dunn *(Aunt Emma)*, Morgan Wallace *(Frank Gebhardt)*, Hooper Atchley *(Captain of the Guards)*, Wallis Clark *(Judge Robinson)*, James Marcus *(Superintendent Thompson)*, Mary Alden *(Mrs. Mason)*.

O'Brien is a small-time racketeer who gives teenager Mason a job answering the phone at his bootlegging hideout as a means of getting to his girl friend, Davis. When the police raid the hideout Mason is the only one in the place and he won't talk. He's sent to a reform school where the kids are brutalized by the guards. A crusading newspaper publisher, Wallace, tries to expose the conditions of the school, but the staff learns about the coming inspection. When Mason finds out that O'Brien is seeing his girl friend he escapes to her apartment. Davis tells him she was seeing the racketeer to convince him to help get Mason out of the reform school. The police track down Mason, but O'Brien confesses to the crime and Mason is free.

p, Benjamin F. Zeidman; d, Howard Higgin; w, Paul Gangelin, B. Harrison Orkow (based on a story by Higgin); ph, Allen S. Siegel; ed, Edward Schroeder.

Crime **Cas.** **(PR:A MPAA:NR)**

HELL'S ISLAND** (1930) 77m COL bw

Jack Holt *(Mac)*, Ralph Graves *(Griff)*, Dorothy Sebastian *(Marie)*, Richard Cramer *(Sgt. Klotz)*, Harry Allen *(Bert the Cockney)*, Lionel Belmore *(Mons. Dupont)*, Otto Lang *(German Legionnaire)*, Carl Stockdale *(Colonel)*.

Holt and Graves are two Americans in the French Foreign Legion who love the same girl, Sebastian. Graves informs Holt that he's going to marry her but Holt believes he's the better man and the two argue back and forth. During a military battle, Holt is wounded and he believes that Graves shot him. It was actually their sergeant who shot him and when he refuses to help carry Holt to the ambulance Graves punches him out. For this Graves is sent to Devil's Island and Sebastian, wanting to be with him, convinces Holt to marry her and become a guard at the island prison. There Holt discovers that his friend was not the one who shot him and helps Holt escape with Sebastian.

p, Harry Cohn; d, Edward Sloman; w, Jo Swerling (based on a story by Tom Buckingham); ph, Ted Tetzlaff; ed, Swerling.

Adventure **(PR:A MPAA:NR)**

HELL'S ISLAND** (1955) 83m Pine-Thomas/PAR c (AKA: THE RUBY VIRGIN; LOVE IS A WEAPON; SOUTH SEAS FURY)

John Payne *(Mike Cormack)*, Mary Murphy *(Janet Martin)*, Francis L. Sullivan *(Barzland)*, Eduardo Noriega *(Inspector Pena)*, Arnold Moss *(Paul Armand)*, Walter Reed *(Lawrence)*, Pepe Hern *(Lalo)*, Robert Cabal *(Miguel)*, Sandor Szabo *(Torbig)*, Paul Picerni *(Eduardo Martin)*, Mario Siletti *(Surgeon)*, Matty Fain *(Pitt Boss)*, Ralph Dumke, Lillian Molieri, Paul Marion, Guillermo Barreto, Victor Bartell, Edward Koch, Marguerita Martin, Don Orlando, Julia Montoya, Paul Regas, Carlos Rivero, Argentia Brunetti, David Garcia, Nacho Galindo, Jose G. Gonzales, Ben Frommer, Romiro Jaloma, Delmar Costello, Alex Montoya, Henry Escalante, Manuel Lopez, Jose Oliveira, Joseph Heredia, Tom Bernard.

Payne loses his job as a district attorney because of a drinking problem and takes a job as a bouncer at a Las Vegas casino. Sullivan offers him $5,000 to find a missing ruby which might have been lost in a plane crash in the Caribbean. He soon learns the reason he is given the job is because his ex-fiancee is married to the man who is suspected of sabotaging the plane. His ex, Murphy, asks for help to clear her husband's name, but she is abducted and taken to Hell's Island. Payne tries to rescue her and learns that she was the one who actually caused the plane to crash. After he kills Sullivan and his henchmen, Payne turns Murphy over to the police.

p, William H. Pine, William C. Thomas; d, Phil Karlson; w, Maxwell Shane (based on a story by Jack Leonard, Martin M. Goldsmith); ph, Lionel Lindon (VistaVision, Technicolor); ed, Archie Marshek; art d, Hal Pereira, Al Y. Roelofs; cos, Edith Head.

Crime **(PR:A MPAA:NR)**

HELL'S KITCHEN** (1939) 82m WB bw

Billy Halop *(Tony)*, Bobby Jordan *(Joey)*, Leo Gorcey *(Gyp)*, Huntz Hall *(Ace)*, Gabriel Dell *(Bingo)*, Bernard Punsley *(Ouch)*, Frankie Burke *(Soap)*, Margaret Lindsay *(Beth)*, Ronald Reagan *(Jim)*, Stanley Fields *(Buck)*, Grant Mitchell *(Crispin)*, Fred Tozere *(Steve Garvy)*, Arthur Loft *(Jed Crispin)*, Vera Lewis *(Sarah Crispin)*, Robert Homans *(Hardy)*, Charles Foy *(Flugue)*, Robert Strange *(Callahan)*, Raymond Bailey *(Whitey)*, Clem Bevans *(Mr. Quill)*, George Irving *(Judge Chandler)*, Lee Phelps *(Bailiff)*, Ila Rhodes *(Maizie)*, Don Turner *(Chick)*, Joe Devlin *(Nails)*, Jimmie Lucas *(Roll Mop)*, Jack Kenney *(Pants)*, Sol Gorss *(Sweet Al)*, Cliff Saum *(Guard)*, Reid Kilpatrick *(Announcer)*, George O'Hanlon *(Usher)*, Charles Sullivan, Jack Gardner *(Henchmen)*, Max Hoffman, Jr., Dick Rich, Tom Wilson *(Guards)*, Ruth Robinson *(Mrs. Chandler)*, George Offerman *(Jury Foreman)*.

Another Dead End Kids melodrama with the gang getting out of reform school only to become the victims of Mitchell, the tough superintendent at the Hell's Kitchen Shelter. Fields plays a paroled racketeer who wants to make a new life and tries to straighten out the crooked home. His humanitarian efforts backfire, he gets sent back to prison, but not before seeing Mitchell taken into custody by the authorities. HELL'S KITCHEN is one of two films in which our 40th President of the U.S., Ronald Reagan, was cast with the Dead End Kids. An interesting story has it that the Dead End Kids were actually tough little pranksters in real life, and Reagan is quoted as saying after filming this movie: "You never knew when a canvas chair would go up in smoke or be blown apart by the giant firecrackers they were never without. Having heard lurid tales from other actors, I approached my first picture with them in something of a sweat." (See BOWERY BOYS series, Index.)

p, Mark Hellinger, Brian Foy; d, Lewis Seiler, E. A. Dupont; w, Crane Wilbur, Fred Niblo (based on a story by Wilbur); ph, Charles Rosher; ed, Clarence Kolster; art d, Hugo Reticker; cos, Milo Anderson.

Drama **(PR:A MPAA:NR)**

HELL'S OUTPOST** (1955) 89m REP bw

Rod Cameron *(Tully Gibbs)*, Joan Leslie *(Sarah Moffit)*, John Russell *(Ben Hodes)*, Chill Wills *(Kevin Russel)*, Jim Davis *(Sam Horne)*, Kristine Miller *(Beth Hodes)*, Ben Cooper *(Alec Bacchione)*, Taylor Holmes *(Timothey Byers)*, Barton MacLane *(Sheriff Olson)*, Ruth Lee *(Mrs. Moffit)*, Arthur Q. Bryan *(Harry Bogue)*, Oliver Blake *(Hotel Clerk)*, Harry Woods, Buzz Henry, John Dierkes, Sue England, Almira Sessions, Lizz Slifer, Don Kennedy, Paul Stader, George Dockstader, Don Brodie, Alan Bridge, Edward Clark, Gil Harman, James Lilburn, Ruth Brennan.

Cameron is a Korean War vet who snakes himself into part-ownership of Wills' mine. He convinces the old man that he was friends with his son who was killed in the war. A liar but a hard worker, Cameron tries to rebuild the mine despite opposition from Russell who is trying to get the ownership papers for himself. The film includes one song, "Packin' In The Mail" (composed and sung by Wills).

p&d, Joe Kane; w, Kenneth Gamet (based on Luke Short's novel *Silver Rock*); ph, Jack Marta; m, R. Dale Butts; ed, Richard L. Van Enger; md, Butts; art d, Frank Arrigo.

Drama **(PR:A MPAA:NR)**

HELL'S PLAYGROUND* (1967) Commercial Enterprises c (AKA: RIOT AT LAUDERDALE)

Skip Everett, Jane Ashley, The Surftones, The Pebbles.

The kids are off their college campuses and causing havoc on the beaches of Ft. Lauderdale during their annual spring break. The fun-making gets a bit out of hand, forcing the police to resort to stricter methods to keep things under control. But these hearty party-goers are not so willing to buckle under. These films were made by the dozens during a time when popular culture was sobering because of the Vietnam War so it's hard to pinpoint what exactly these "filmmakers" were aiming at.

p, John Baron; d, Jesse Clark; w, M. O'Neil.

Drama **(PR:A MPAA:NR)**

HELLZAPOPPIN'*** (1941) 84m UNIV bw

Ole Olsen *(Ole)*, Chic Johnson *(Chic)*, Robert Paige *(Jeff Hunter)*, Jane Frazee *(Kitty Rand)*, Lewis Howard *(Woody Tyler)*, Martha Raye *(Betty Johnson)*, Clarence Kolb *(Mr. Rand)*, Nella Walker *(Mrs. Rand)*, Mischa Auer *(Pepi)*, Richard Lane *(Director)*, Elisha Cook, Jr. *(Assistant Director)*, Hugh Herbert *(Detective Quimby)*, Olive Hatch, Harlem Congeroo Dancers *(Specialties)*, Shemp Howard *(Louie)*, Jody Gilbert *(Blonde)*, Andrew Tombes *(Producer)*, George Davis *(Butler)*, Hal K. Dawson, Frank Darien *(Photographers)*, Eddie Acuff *(Drafted Devil)*, Billy Curtis *(Taxi Driver)*, Harry Monti *(Midget)*, Don Brodie *(Theater Manager)*, Gil Perkins *(Butler in Pool)*, Dale Van Sickel *(Man who falls into pool)*, Gus Schilling *(Orchestra Leader)*, Sig Arno *(Cellist)*, Bert Roach *(Man in Audience)*, The Six Hits, Slim and Sam *(Specialties)*, George Chandler *(Man)*.

This is screwball comedy all the way, loaded with sight gags that sometimes work and sometimes fall as flat as a burned pancake. The story begins in Purgatory (or Hell, take your pick), with Olsen and Johnson jumping in and out of a story that's barely there, basically a little romance tale of poor boy meets rich girl and wins her heart after putting on the traditional show. O. and J. constantly argue with the film's director and cameraman on camera about the restraints put upon them while mindless mayhem ensues—someone constantly yelling "Jones!" for no good reason, Auer, a rich count, chasing Martha Raye about madly, and vice versa. At one point a film director, Laine, tells the madcaps Olson and Johnson: "This is Hollywood, we change everything here. We've *got* to!" Songs include: "Watch the Birdie" (Don Raye, Gene De Paul), "Waiting for the Robert E. Lee" (L. Wolfe Gilbert, Lewis F. Muir), "What Kind Of Love is This?" "Hellzapoppin'," "You Were There," "Heaven for Two," "Conga Beso," "Congeroo," "Putting on the Dog" (Ray, De Paul).

p, Jules Levy; d, H.C. Potter; w, Nat Perrin, Warren Wilson (based on the play by Perrin); ph, Woody Bredell; ed, Milton Carruth; cos, Vera West; spec eff, John Fulton; ch, Nick Castle, Edward Prinz.

Comedy **(PR:A MPAA:NR)**

HELP!½** (1965, Brit.) 92m Walter Shenson-Subafilms/UA c

John Lennon *(John)*, Paul McCartney *(Paul)*, Ringo Starr *(Ringo)*, George Harrison *(George)*, Leo McKern *(Clang)*, Eleanor Bron *(Ahme)*, Victor Spinetti *(Foot)*, Roy Kinnear *(Algernon)*, John Bluthal *(Bhuta)*, Patrick Cargill *(Superintendent)*, Ronnie Brody, Bob Godfrey, Louis Mansi, Rupert Evans *(Priests/Thugs)*, Andreas Malandrinos *(Austrian Waiter)*, Golda Casimir *(Cleaner in Temple)*, Deborah du'Lacey, Gai Wright, Zorenah Osborne, Eve Eden, Zienia Merton, Marie-Lise *(High Priestesses)*, Bruce Lacey *(Lawn Mower)*, Warren Mitchell *(Abdul)*, Durra *(Belly Dancer)*, Alfie Bass *(Doorman)*, Danny Almond, Edith Savile, Vera Cook, Joe Gibbons, Sue Reid, Stewart Guidotti, Wally Shufflebottom, Blake Butler, Ian Wilson, Jenny Till, Mary Ford, Jenny Landry, Glenda Warrington, Alex Macintosh, Pat Roberts, Thomas Baptiste, Dandy Nichols, Jeremy Lloyd, Gretchen Franklin.

Even so-so Beatles films are better than most of the comedies one sees these days and HELP! was only that—so-so. The magic of A HARD DAY'S NIGHT has been tossed aside for a somewhat belabored story, color photography and several location shots in the Bahamas, Austria and in the Salisbury Plain. McKern and Bron are religious nuts who are about to make a sacrifice to their idol, Kaili, but they cannot go about it because the sacrificial ring that must be used in the rite has been purloined. In London, Starr has been given the ring by a fan and his life is now in jeopardy as McKern and Bron conspire to get the ring back. Starr can't get the darn thing off his finger so he must die. McKern and his henchman Bluthal attempt to kill him but fail, and Starr, who doesn't care about the ring nearly as much as he cares about his existence, visits Spinetti, a scientist, and Kinnear, his faithful aide. Spinetti thinks that if he owns the ring he can take over the world, so he and Kinnear join in pursuing Starr. Bron gets friendly with Starr and she and the other three Beatles go away with him on an Alpine holiday. They are quickly discovered and a mountainous chase ensues. The Beatles return to London, enlist the help of Scotland Yard (Cargill is the befuddled "Yard" man), and go on to Salisbury where, ringed by what appears to be the entire British Army, they are safe as they record their music. After a near-battle takes place between the army and McKern's crazed hordes, the Beatles fly to the Bahamas but are still not safe. Starr is captured and about to be killed when he manages to slip the ring off his finger and all ends for the best. It's silly at worst and brilliant at best. The working title of the movie was EIGHT ARMS TO HOLD YOU but that was soon abandoned in favor of HELP! Lester repeats his chores as director but the simple insouciance of A HARD DAY'S NIGHT is missing and a heavy attempt at slapstick is what replaces most of the wit and irreverence of the first film. Honors to McKern, Bron, Kinnear and Spinetti for their fine comedy timing, but this film would have benefitted by more of the Beatles and less of the extraneous locations and secondary characterizations. Tunes include: "Help!," "You're Gonna Lose That Girl," "You've Got To Hide Your Love Away," "The Night Before," "Another Girl," "Ticket To Ride" (John Lennon, Paul McCartney), and "I Need You" (George Harrison).

p, Walter Shenson; d, Richard Lester; w, Marc Behm, Charles Wood (based on an original story by Behm); ph, David Watkin (Eastmancolor); m, Ken Thorne; ed, John Victor Smith; md, Thorne; art d, Ray Simm; cos, Julie Harris, Dinah Greet, Arthur Newman; spec eff, Cliff Richardson, Roy Whybrow.

Musical/Comedy **Cas.** **(PR:A MPAA:G)**

HELP I'M INVISIBLE* (1952, Ger.) 88m Junge Film Union bw (HILFE ICHE BIN UNSICHTBAR; AKA: ALAS I'M INVISIBLE)

Theo Lingen, Inge Landgut, Fita Benkhoff, Grethe Weiser, Margarethe Haagen, Kaete Pontow, Arno Aszmann.

There's nothing more painful than to sit through a film that tries desperately to be funny but just isn't. Such is the case with HELP I'M INVISIBLE, a 1950s German attempt at comedy. Businessman Lingen is the head of a family who spends most of his free time playing about in his makeshift lab conducting strange experiments. He just happens to be successful with one of these, and invents a machine that makes him invisible—creating a disaster for the rest of the family. The real disaster came when this thing hit the theaters.

p, Karl Junge; d, E.W. Emo; w, Herbert Tjadens, Erwin Kreker, Kurt Werner; ph, Hans Schneeberger.

Fantasy/Drama **(PR:A MPAA:NR)**

HELP YOURSELF*½ (1932, Brit.) 74m FN/WB bw

Benita Hume *(Mary Lamb)*, Martin Walker *(George Quinnock)*, D.A. Clarke-Smith *(Maj. Fred Harris)*, Carol Coombe *(Dodie)*, Kenneth Kove *(Peter Ball)*, Clifford Heatherley *(Fox-Cardington)*, D. Hay Petrie *(Sam Short)*, Helen Ferrers *(Lady Hermione Quinnock)*, Marie Wright *(Sparrow)*, Hal Gordon *(Bobby Vane)*, Frederick Ross.

Another British farce that relies upon the most ridiculous and contrived scenes in which to force laughter. Centering around a large Christmas party, a safe is broken into and a supposedly valuable necklace taken. The man who threw the party—at his aunt's home without her knowledge—goes to extremes to get the thing back. But the prized jewels that have caused so much of a huff turn out to be phonies. Sound funny? It's not.

p, Irving Asher; d, John Daumery; w, Roland Pertwee, John Hastings Turner (based on the novel *Sinners All* by Jerome Kingston).

Comedy **(PR:A MPAA:NR)**

HELTER SKELTER* (1949, Brit.) 84m Gainsborough/GFD bw

Carol Marsh *(Susan Graham)*, David Tomlinson *(Nick Martin)*, Mervyn Johns *(Ernest Bennett)*, Peter Hammond *(Spencer Stone)*, Richard Hearne *(Prof. Pastry)*, Peter Haddon *(Maj. Basil Beagle)*, Geoffrey Sumner *(Humphrey Beagle)*, Henry Kendall *(Lord Bruce Carlton)*, John Pertwee *(Headwaiter/Charles II)*, Zena Marshall *(Giselle)*, Terry-Thomas *(Announcer)*, Jimmy Edwards *(Dr. James Edwards)*, Patricia Raine *(Amber)*, Colin Gordon *(Chadbeater Longwick)*, Judith Furse *(Mrs. Martin)*, Wilfrid Hyde-White *(Dr. B. Jekyll/Mr. Hyde)*, Harry Secombe *(Alf)*, Robert Lamouret, Shirl Conway, Glynis Johns, Valentine Dyall, Dennis Price, Anthony Steel, George Benson.

A really bad picture about a bunch of people going to the utmost extremes to try and cure Marsh of a case of hiccups. Everything from shock treatment to laughter tactics are tried but nothing seems to work until a ghost shows up and scares the wits out of her. She is cured, but only temporarily, as a marriage proposal shocks her into another bout. It was pretty silly to try and pull out a one-joke idea for such a long film, but someone thought it might be funny and was willing to pay a lot of top actors good money to do this ridiculous picture.

p, Anthony Darnborough; d, Ralph Thomas; w, Patrick Campbell, Jan Read, Gerard Bryant (based on a story by Campbell); ph, Jack Asher.

Comedy **(PR:A MPAA:NR)**

HEMINGWAY'S ADVENTURES OF A YOUNG MAN (SEE: ADVENTURES OF A YOUNG MAN, 1962)

HENNESSY½** (1975, Brit.) 103m AIP c

Rod Steiger *(Hennessy)*, Lee Remick *(Kate)*, Richard Johnson *(Inspector Hollis)*, Trevor Howard *(Cmdr. Rice)*, Peter Egan *(Williams)*, Eric Porter *(Tobin)*, Ian Hogg *(Gerry)*, Stanley Lebor *(Hawk)*, John Hallam *(Boyle)*, Patrick Stewart *(Tilney)*, David Collings *(Covey)*, John Shrapnel *(Tipaldi)*, Hugh Moxey *(Burgess M.P.)*, Margery Mason *(Housekeeper)*, Paul Brennan *(Maguire)*, Oliver Maguire *(Mick)*.

Steiger is an Irishman out for revenge when his wife and child are killed in Belfast. They were caught in a gunfight between the British Army and the IRA, and Steiger now plans to blow up the British Parliament when the Royal Family is in attendance. Johnson heads the Scotland Yard hunt for Steiger while IRA leader Porter hunts for him too, knowing if the bomb does go off there will just be more soldiers in his country. The tension is built well as the story intercuts between the two manhunts.

p, Peter Snell; d, Don Sharp; w, John Gay (based on a story by Richard Johnson); ph, Ernest Steward (Movielab Color); m, John Scott; ed, Eric Boyd-Perkins; prod d, Ray Simm; art d, Bert Davey; set d, Simon Wakefield; stunts, Gerry Crampton.

Drama **Cas.** **(PR:C MPAA:PG)**

HENRIETTE'S HOLIDAY** (1953, Fr.) 105m Regina-FS/Cinedis bw (LA FETE A HENRIETTE)

Dany Robin *(Henriette)*, Hildegarde Neff *(Rita)*, Michel Auclair *(Michel)*, Michel Roux *(Robert)*, Carette *(Ficard)*, Daniel Ivernel *(Adrien)*, Henri Grenieux *(1st Writer)*, Louis Seignier *(2nd Writer)*, Micheline Francey *(Nicole)*.

Two screenwriters can't get their scenario past the censors so they go to a summer resort to write a new storyline. They bring a secretary and their girl friends along and finally come up with a story of a teenage girl who can't wait for a holiday festival when she thinks her boy friend will ask her to marry him. A lot of visual jokes but the comedy becomes redundant.

d, Julien Duvivier; w, Henri Jeanson, Duvivier; ph, Roger Hubert; m, Georges Auric; ed, Martha Poncin.

Comedy **(PR:C MPAA:NR)**

HENRY ALDRICH, BOY SCOUT** (1944) 66m PAR bw

Jimmy Lydon *(Henry Aldrich)*, Charley Smith *(Dizzy Stevens)*, John Litel *(Sam Aldrich)*, Olive Blakeney *(Mrs. Aldrich)*, Joan Mortimer *(Elise)*, Minor Watson *(Ramsey Kent)*, Darryl Hickman *(Peter)*, David Holt *(Irwin Barrett)*, Richard Haydel *(Beany)*.

Lydon is a senior patrol scout leader having a lot of trouble with one particular Boy Scout, Hickman. The boy is the son of a friend so Lydon takes all the blame for Hickman's mischief. After a scout contest that has one misadventure after another, Hickman is promoted to junior assistant scoutmaster. The story is about as exciting as a campfire sing-a-long. Paramount brought the Aldrich series out to compete with Andy Hardy at MGM. (See HENRY ALDRICH series, Index.)

p, Michel Kraike; d, Hugh Bennett; w, Muriel Roy Bolton (based on a story by Agnes Christine Johnston); ph, Daniel Fapp; ed, Everett Douglas; md, Irvin Talbot; art d, Hans Dreier, Walter Tyler.

Comedy **(PR:A MPAA:NR)**

HENRY ALDRICH, EDITOR* (1942) 73m PAR bw

Jimmy Lydon *(Henry Aldrich)*, Charles Smith *(Dizzy Stevens)*, Rita Quigley *(Martha Daley)*, John Litel *(Mr. Aldrich)*, Olive Blakeney *(Mrs. Aldrich)*, Charles Halton *(Ellas Noonan)*, Vaughn Glaser *(Mr. Bradley)*, Maude Eburne *(Mrs. Norris)*, Francis Pierlot *(Nero Smith)*, Cliff Clark *(Fire Chief)*, Oscar O'Shea *(Judge Saunders)*, Edgar Dearing *(McLean)*, Billy Wayne *(Stranger)*, Walter Fenner *(Mr. Johnson)*.

Lydon is the editor of his high school paper—a publication run better than the town newspaper. When Lydon covers a string of fires the police suspect him of being an arsonist. A nit-wit comedy with everyone portrayed as bumbling idiots. (See HENRY ALDRICH series, Index.)

p, Sol C. Siegel; d, Hugh Bennett; w, Muriel Roy Bolton, Val Burton (based on the character created by Clifford Goldsmith); ph, Henry Sharp; ed, Everett Douglas; art d, Hans Dreier, Franz Bachelin.

Comedy **(PR:A MPAA:NR)**

HENRY ALDRICH FOR PRESIDENT½** (1941) 73m PAR bw

James Lydon *(Henry Aldrich)*, Charles Smith *(Dizzy Stevens)*, June Preisser *(Geraldine Adams)*, Mary Anderson *(Phyllis Michael)*, Martha O'Driscoll *(Mary Aldrich)*, Dorothy Peterson *(Mrs. Aldrich)*, John Litel *(Mr. Aldrich)*, Rod Cameron *(Ed Calkins)*, Frank Coghlan, Jr. *(Marvin Bagshaw)*, Lucien Littlefield *(Mr. Crosley)*, Kenneth Howell *(Irwin Barrett)*, Buddy Pepper *(Johnny Beal)*, Vaughan Glaser *(Mr. Bradley)*, Dick Paxton *(Red MacGowan)*, Paul Matthews *(Tubby Gibbons)*, Bob Pittard *(Elmer Pringle)*, Bud McCollister, Carmen Johnson, Helen Westcott, Rosita Butler, Georgia Lee Settle *(Students)*.

Lydon runs for high school class president in one of the better films out of the Aldrich series. Lydon is nominated by a conniving rich kid whose intention is to split the votes and insure a victory for himself. Things backfire when the female candidate Anderson, falls for Lydon and drops from the race. A series of complications arise: Lydon is accused of stealing his opponent's speech, and someone tries to stuff the ballot boxes; but with the help of Smith and Anderson, Lydon finally wins. Lydon became so typecast in the Henry Aldrich role that when he appeared in films other than the series about the bumbling youth, members of the audience would shout: "There's Henry Aldrich." He began the series with this feature but later begged Paramount chief Y. Frank Freeman to give him other roles. Snorted Freeman: "You're getting paid—go do your work!" (See HENRY ALDRICH series, Index.)

p, Sol C. Siegel; d, Hugh Bennett; w, Val Burton (based on the character by Clifford Goldsmith); ph, John Mescall; ed, Thomas Neff; art d, Hans Dreier, Franz Bachelin.

Comedy **(PR:A MPAA:NR)**

HENRY ALDRICH GETS GLAMOUR*** (1942) 72m PAR bw

Jimmy Lydon *(Henry Aldrich)*, Charlie Smith *(Dizzy Stevens)*, John Litel *(Mr. Sam Aldrich)*, Olive Blakeney *(Mrs. Aldrich)*, Diana Lynn *(Phyllis Michael)*, Frances Gifford *(Hilary Dane)*, Gail Russell *(Virginia Lowry)*, Vaughan Glaser *(Mr. Bradley)*, Anne Rooney *(Evelyn)*, William Blees *(Irwin Barrett)*, Janet Beecher *(Mrs. Lowry)*, Bill Goodwin *(Steve)*, Betty Farrington *(Miss Goodhue)*, Lucien Littlefield *(Mr. Quid)*, Harry Hayden *(Mr. Jennifer)*, Walter Fenner *(Mr. Vance)*, Harry Bradley *(Mr. Japes)*, Ann O'Neal *(Mrs. Ikeley)*, Joe Brown, Jr. *(George)*, Shirley Mills *(Hortense)*, Patti Brilhante *(Ida)*, Marilynn Harris *(Gwendolyn)*, Johnny Arthur *(Hotchkiss)*, Isabel Randolph *(Mrs. Stacey)*, Billy Wayne *(Albert-Waiter)*, Arthur Loft *(Jackson)*, Dick Elliott *(McCluskey)*, Nell Craig *(Teddy's Mother)*, Dick Chandlee, Dick Baron *(Droops)*, Buddy Messinger *(Soda Clerk)*, Walter "Spec" O'Donnell *(Bell Boy)*, Keith Richards *(Assistant Director)*, Syd Saylor *(Bus Driver)*, Oscar Smith *(Bootblack)*, Beverly Pratt *(Girl)*.

This is the best in the Aldrich series with a well-written and funny—though implausible—script. Lydon has all the girls in his high school chasing him after he returns from a Hollywood trip where he had a misleading photo taken with a young starlet. A scandal erupts when he becomes involved with the school superintendent's daughter, almost wrecking his father's chances of being elected to a public office. Lydon's big surprise comes when the starlet, in town on a USO tour, accepts his invitation to attend a country club dance. (See HENRY ALDRICH series, Index.)

p, Walter MacEwen; d, Hugh Bennett; w, Edwin Blum, Aleen Leslie (based on a story by Leslie); ph, Daniel Fapp; m, Robert Emmett Dolan; ed, Arthur Schmidt; art d, Hans Dreier, Earl Hedrick.

Comedy **(PR:A MPAA:NR)**

HENRY ALDRICH HAUNTS A HOUSE½** (1943) 73m PAR bw

Jimmy Lydon *(Henry Aldrich)*, Charles Smith *(Dizzy Stevens)*, John Litel *(Mr. Aldrich)*, Olive Blakeney *(Mrs. Aldrich)*, Joan Mortimer *(Elise Towers)*, Vaughan Glaser *(Mr. Bradley)*, Jackie Moran *(Whit Bidecker)*, Lucien Littlefield *(Mr. Quid)*,

George Anderson *(Olin Bidecker)*, Mike Mazurki *(Shadow)*, Edgar Dearing *(Chief of Police Reedy)*, Charles Cane *(Clannahan)*, Jack Gardner *(Charlie)*, Kernan Cripps *(Clannahan's Assistant)*, William Inman *(Kid)*, Ferris Taylor *(The Mayor)*, Anita Bolster *(Mrs. Norris)*, George M. Carleton *(Dr. Danford)*, Dick Rush *(Police Officer)*, Ray Walker *(Beamish)*, George Sherwood *(Mr. Wright)*, Paul McVey *(Mr. Bellows)*, Paul Phillips *(Sykes)*.

Lydon sneaks into a spooky, old mansion where he accidentally drinks a chemical believed to greatly increase a human's strength. Lydon later thinks he is responsible for murdering his school principal while under the influence of the drug. Turns out the principal isn't really dead, and what Lydon drank wasn't really a drug. Funny in spots. (See HENRY ALDRICH series, Index.)

p, Michel Kraike; d, Hugh Bennett; w, Val Burton, Muriel Roy Bolton; ph, Daniel L. Fapp; m, Gerard Carbonara; ed, Everett Douglas; art d, Hans Dreier, Haldane Douglas.

Comedy **(PR:A MPAA:NR)**

HENRY ALDRICH PLAYS CUPID** (1944) 65m PAR bw

Jimmy Lydon *(Henry Aldrich)*, Charles Smith *(Dizzy Stevens)*, John Litel *(Mr. Aldrich)*, Olive Blakeney *(Mrs. Aldrich)*, Diana Lynn *(Phyllis Michael)*, Vaughn Glaser *(Mr. Bradley)*, Vera Vague *(Blue Eyes)*, Paul Harvey *(Sen. Caldicott)*, Harry Bradley *(Male Teacher)*, Betty Farrington *(Female Teacher)*, Gladden James *(Male Teacher)*, Shirley Coates *(Western Union Girl)*, Arthur Loft *(Clancy)*, Walter Fenner *(Stewart)*, Barbara Pepper *(Wild Rose)*, Richard Elliot *(Matthews)*, Harry Hayden *(Anderson)*, Mikhail Rasumny *(Konrad)*, Luis Alberni *(Tony)*, Sarah Edwards *(Mrs. Bradley)*, Gladden James *(Teacher)*, Maude Eburne *(Homely Woman)*, Ronnie Rondell *(Reporter)*, Oscar Smith *(Porter)*, George Anderson *(Mr. Benton)*, Nell Craig *(Miss Lewis)*, Sue Moore *(Mrs. Olson)*, Armand "Curley" Wright *(Guiseppe)*, Bobby Barber *(Waiter)*, Mary Field *(Anxious)*, Ferris Taylor *(Mayor)*.

Lydon is willed $5,000 from a deceased uncle so he can go on to Princeton. The hitch is he must graduate from high school with honors. He is doing well in all his classes except biology, so Lydon sets up a dating service for his grumpy, bachelor teacher, hoping this will help his grade. As usual, things go awry and Lydon has a variety of new problems to work out. (See HENRY ALDRICH series, Index.)

d, Hugh Bennett; w, Muriel Roy Bolton, Val Burton (based on a story by Aleen Leslie); ph, Daniel Fapp; ed, Everett Douglas; md, Irvin Talbot; art d, Hans Dreier, Franz Bachelin.

Comedy **(PR:A MPAA:NR)**

HENRY ALDRICH SWINGS IT** (1943) 64m PAR bw

Jimmy Lydon *(Henry Aldrich)*, Charlie Smith *(Dizzy Stevens)*, John Litel *(Mr. Aldrich)*, Olive Blakeney *(Mrs. Aldrich)*, Mimi Chandler *(Mimi Gray)*, Vaughan Glaser *(Mr. Bradley)*, Marion Hall *(Louise Elliott)*, Beverly Hudson *(Margie)*, Fritz Feld *(Josef Altman)*, Charles Arnt *(Boyle)*.

Lydon gets a crush on his music teacher and joins the school's band as a violinist. A visiting concert violinist gets his priceless violin switched with Lydon's who then loses it. The rest of the film is a mad chase to get the violin back from some music-loving thieves. (See HENRY ALDRICH series, Index.)

p, Walter MacEwen; d, Hugh Bennett; w, Val Burton, Muriel Roy Bolton; ph, Daniel Fapp; ed, Archie Marshek; md, Troy Sanders; art d, Hans Dreier, Frank Bachelin; m/l, "Ding Dong, Sing a Song," Jule Styne, Kim Gannon.

Comedy **(PR:A MPAA:NR)**

HENRY ALDRICH'S LITTLE SECRET** (1944) 75m PAR bw

Jimmy Lydon *(Henry Aldrich)*, Charles Smith *(Dizzy Stevens)*, Joan Mortimer *(Elise Towers)*, John Litel *(Mr. Aldrich)*, Olive Blakeney *(Mrs. Aldrich)*, Ann Doran *(Helen Martin)*, John David Robb *(Ricky Martin)*, Tina Thayer *(Jennifer Dale)*, Sarah Edwards *(Mrs. Winnibegar)*, Harry Bradley *(Mr. Tottle)*, Lucille Ward *(Mrs. O'Hara)*, Almira Sessions *(Aunt Maude)*, Tom Fadden *(Mr. Luther)*, George Carleton *(Judge Hyde)*, Byron Foulger *(Bill Collector)*, Fern Emmet *(Miss Swithen)*, Dorothy Vaughn *(Mrs. Olsen)*, Eddie Dunn *(Policeman)*, Hal K. Dawson *(Photographer)*, Noel Neill *(Daisy)*.

Unconvincing plot sees Lydon act as a lawyer for a woman that his father has accused of being an unfit mother. When the mother leaves town to help prove her husband innocent of a crime he's been convicted of, Lydon holds a filibuster to stall his father's legal proceedings. Lydon's tactics work and he pulls a victory over Dad. (See HENRY ALDRICH series, Index.)

p, Walter MacEwen; d, Hugh Bennett; w, Val Burton, Aleen Leslie (based on a story by Leslie); ph, Daniel L. Fapp; ed, Everett Douglas; md, Irvin Talbot; art d, Hans Dreier, Franz Bachelin.

Comedy **(PR:A MPAA:NR)**

HENRY AND DIZZY* (1942) 68m PAR bw

Jimmy Lydon *(Henry Aldrich)*, Mary Anderson *(Phyllis Michael)*, Charles Smith *(Dizzy Stevens)*, John Litel *(Mr. Aldrich)*, Olive Blakeney *(Mrs. Aldrich)*, Maude Eburne *(Mrs. Bradley)*, Vaughan Glaser *(Mr. Bradley)*, Shirley Coates *(Jennie Kilmer)*, Olin Howland *(Mr. Stevens)*, Minerva Urecal *(Mrs. Kilmer)*, Trevor Bardette *(Mr. Weeks)*, Carl "Alfalfa" Switzer *(Billy Weeks)*, Warren Hymer *(Tramp)*, Noel Neill *(Jean)*, Jane Cowan *(Pamela Rogers)*.

When Lydon and his friend Smith wreck an outboard motor and try to raise $120 to fix it, they nearly demolish the town in the process. An outlandish story that even the kids won't find funny. (See HENRY ALDRICH series, Index.)

p, Sol C. Siegel; d, Hugh Bennett; w, Val Burton (based on characters created by Clifford Goldsmith); ph, Dan Fapp; ed, Everett Douglas; art d, Hans Dreier, Haldane Douglas.

Comedy **(PR:A MPAA:NR)**

HENRY VIII (SEE: PRIVATE LIFE OF HENRY VIII, THE, 1933, Brit.)

HENRY VIII AND HIS SIX WIVES*** (1972, Brit.) 125m Anglo-EMI/MGM-EMI c

Keith Michell *(King Henry VIII)*, Donald Pleasence *(Thomas Cromwell)*, Charlotte Rampling *(Anne Boleyn)*, Jane Asher *(Jane Seymour)*, Frances Cuka *(Katherine of Aragon)*, Lynne Frederick *(Catherine Howard)*, Jenny Bos *(Anne of Cleves)*, Barbara Leigh-Hunt *(Catherine Parr)*, Michael Gough *(Norfolk)*, Brian Blessed *(Suffolk)*, Michael Goodliffe *(Thomas More)*, Bernard Hepton *(Cranmer)*, Garfield Morgan *(Cardiner)*, John Bryans *(Wolsey)*, John Bennett *(Wriothesley)*, Peter Madden *(Fisher)*, Sarah Long *(Mary)*, Richard Warner *(Warham)*, Michael Godfrey *(Sir Ralph Ellerker)*, Michael Byrne *(Edward Seymour)*, Peter Clay *(Thomas Seymour)*, Robin Sachs *(Thomas Culpepper)*, Nicholas Amer *(Chapuys)*, Basil Clarke *(Abbot)*, Alan Rowe *(French Ambassador)*, Clive Merrison *(Weston)*, David Baillie *(Norris)*, Mark York *(Brereton)*, Margaret Ward *(Lady Rochford)*, Colin Rix *(Bowes)*, Damien Thomas *(Smeaton)*, Imogen Claire *(Maria de Salinas)*.

Michell plays the famed English king who can't hold on to one wife. The story is told by flashback as Henry VIII is dying, and covers his relationship with each of his wives. What is going on historically is shoved to the side to make more room for the bedroom romances of the king. A well executed costume drama with good performances from Michell, Rampling, and Pleasence.

p, Roy Baird; d, Waris Hussein; w, Ian Thorne; ph, Peter Suschitzky (Technicolor); m, David Munrow; ed, John Bloom; prod d, Roy Stannard; cos, John Bloomfield; ch, Terry Gilbert.

Drama **(PR:A MPAA:PG)**

HENRY V***** (1946, Brit.) 127m TC/UA c

Laurence Olivier *(King Henry V)*, Robert Newton *(Ancient Pistol)*, Leslie Banks *(Chorus)*, Renee Asherson *(Princess Katherine)*, Esmond Knight *(Fluellen)*, Leo Genn *(Constable of France)*, Felix Aylmer *(Archbishop of Canterbury)*, Ralph Truman *(Mountjoy)*, Harcourt Williams *(King Charles VI of France)*, Ivy St. Helier *(Alice, Lady in Waiting)*, Ernest Thesiger *(Duke of Berri)*, Max Adrian *(The Dauphin)*, Francis Lister *(Duke of Orleans)*, Valentine Dyall *(Duke of Burgundy)*, Russell Thorndike *(Duke of Bourbon)*, Michael Shepley *(Capt. Gower)*, Morland Graham *(Sir Thomas Erpingham)*, Gerald Case *(Earl of Westmoreland)*, Janet Burnell *(Queen Isabel of France)*, Nicholas Hannen *(Duke of Exeter)*, Robert Helpmann *(Bishop of Ely)*, Freda Jackson *(Mistress Quickly)*, Jimmy Hanley *(Williams)*, John Laurie *(Capt. Jamie)*, Niall MacGinnis *(Capt. MacMorris)*, George Robey *(Sir John Falstaff)*, Roy Emerton *(Lt. Bardolph)*, Griffith Jones *(Earl of Salisbury)*, Arthur Hambling *(Bates)*, Frederick Cooper *(Cpl. Nym)*, Michael Warre *(Duke of Gloucester)*, Brian Nissen *(Court)*, Frank Tickle *(Governor of Harfleur)*, George Cole *(Boy)*, Jonathan Field *(French Messenger)*, Vernon Greeves *(English Herald)*, Ernest Hare *(Priest)*.

A dazzling adaptation of Shakespeare's classic by anyone's taste, but all the more amazing because it was made at the height of the German blitz of England, and many sacrifices had to be offered in order to get it done. The brainchild of Italian immigrant lawyer, Del Giudice, who was briefly imprisoned on the Isle of Man at the start of the war because he was suspected of being a spy. The truth was that he fled Mussolini's rule and had to spend a while incarcerated before he could convince the authorities that he was legitimate. Before doing this film, Del Giudice had also been the power behind IN WHICH WE SERVE (Noel Coward's famed paean of praise to the English Navy). HENRY V was always thought to be an impossible project for the screen. Olivier had already done one Shakespeare play for the cinema in 1936 when he played Orlando in AS YOU LIKE IT, but the complex story of Henry seemed out of the realm of plausibility. Olivier was convinced it could be done and was mustered out of the service in order to make the film. He'd been a junior officer in the navy's air department but kept cracking up planes during his training, so they made him an instructor. Twice before, he'd been released in order to make THE INVADERS (GB: 49TH PARALLEL) and Del Giudice's THE DEMI PARADISE, and this time he stayed out. HENRY V was a remarkable melding of one man's talents in that Olivier starred, directed, and co-adapted the script, as well as co-produced it with Del Giudice. His helper on the adaptation (which took the Falstaff scene from Henry IV and added it to this) was film critic Dent, and his old pal Beck sat in the director's chair while Olivier was emoting. Beck also edited the film and was, no doubt, helped in that job by having assumed the directing chores whenever Olivier went before the camera. It's a unique blending of styles as the picture begins with a series of miniatures, circa 1600, and the camera roams over London until it finds the Globe Theater, near the Thames. (Note: American actor Sam Wanamaker, a long-time resident of England since the McCarthy witch-hunt days, has spent many years attempting to rebuild the Globe on the same site it occupied at that time. The Globe had an open roof and patrons stood as they watched Shakespeare's plays, braving heat, rain, and the bitter British cold. Wanamaker wants to build the new Globe in exactly the same way, with open roof. We shall see if 20th century audiences will stand still for that.) The camera dips into the theater and we think we are about to see a filmed version of the play and the backstage lives of the players. We are wrong. The play commences and subtly becomes a movie. The stage miraculously expands, and the rest of the film is an amalgam of reality, fantasy, and a mixture of stage sets, painted drops, and huge battle scenes with hundreds of horses and men and authentic costumes. At the conclusion, Olivier book-ends the movie by returning to the small Globe stage. Until that time, HENRY V had been England's most expensive picture but much more was at stake than money. England was under constant bombardment by the Luftwaffe as well as the V-2 rockets. Now, here was that country's greatest actor in the work of its greatest writer, using the play to rally the people into a united force. Churchill was doing his best with his speeches but more was needed, and HENRY V filled that gap, thus making it, not only a work of art, but an important propaganda piece as well. Olivier is a 28-year-old playboy Prince of Wales with little more in mind than pleasures of the flesh. The country is disorganized in the year of our Lord 1415, and he is advised to lead his men in battle in order to unify them. He sails from Portsmouth to fight the French. There's no real reason for this incursion, just a desire to get everyone behind him. France had always been the enemy and was a perfect scapegoat. With an army of 30,000 (8,000 archers), he lays siege to northern France for 60 days and roars across it, with no little body count of his own men. At Agincourt on October 25th, he had already lost 18,000 of his charges and must now mix it up with France's army of 60,000. With tactics that foreshadowed the guerrilla warfare of 6 centuries later, his unmailed archers wreak havoc on the French cavalry who are weighted down by their armor and cannot move with the alacrity of the lightly-clad Britons. The French forces capitulate, after suffering casualties that were 10 to 1 against them, and a peace treaty is signed at Rouen. Henry goes on to woo Asherson, the French princess, and the royal families of two great countries are united. Shakespearean language has long been a muddle to many in America. The convoluted phrases, the vague references, etc., never before have they been made clearer than in this film. We sometimes forget that Willie was a playwright of the people, offering action, lust, blood, and gore to his audiences. The plays have withstood time because they deal in honest emotions that know no century. Such is the case with HENRY V. Despite all the production woes they had so little color film that every shot had to count and they wound up using nearly three-quarters of each exposed foot (as opposed to the 10 to 1 ratio by many directors, who cover their behinds by shooting every possible angle of every scene and hope to "save it in the editing"); the more than one thousand costumes that were stitched together from odds and ends; the weapons all made of wood, then painted to look like metal; the wool that was sprayed with aluminum paint to appear as chain mail; inexpensive blankets re-dyed to appear as jackets for the many steeds; and all of the tiaras and crowns of papier-mache. Little did anyone know that the same sort of foraging, pleading, and ingenuity was being used on the French film LES ENFANTS DU PARADIS at much the same time. To save lives, Olivier moved the cast up to Ireland in order to shoot the battle scenes. Ireland would not be subject to air raids and he used the estate of Lord Powerscourt at Enniskerry with a cast of extras that included hundreds of men from the Irish Home Guard. Olivier was never more swashbuckling than in the role of HENRY V. His derring-do and swordplay were more reminiscent of silent star Douglas Fairbanks than anything anyone had ever seen him do before. The music of Walton, played by the London Symphony Orchestra, was a landmark in film scoring as was the art direction by Sheriff. Henry V took nominations for Olivier (as actor), best picture and Walton's music in 1946 (although made in 1944, it wasn't released in the USA until after the war). They lost out to March, THE BEST YEARS OF OUR LIVES and Hugo Friedhofer for the aforementioned Goldwyn classic. Any other year, they might have swept up the awards. Olivier had wanted his wife, Vivian Leigh, to play Catherine, the French princess. Although a small role, it was the female lead in the picture, but David O. Selznick owned her contract and refused to allow his Scarlett O'Hara to appear in the film, so Olivier settled for Asherson, who did an excellent job. He had also preferred William Wyler to direct but when that was impossible, he sought both Carol Reed and Terence Young. Neither could do the job for one reason or another, and Olivier was forced to assume the directing mantle, as well as his other tasks. Each of the other three directors mentioned would have brought their own interpretations to the work, but we doubt if any of them could have been more memorable. HENRY V will last as long as people watch movies.

p, Laurence Olivier, Filippo Del Giudice; d, Olivier, Reginald Beck; w, Alan Dent, Olivier (based on the play by William Shakespeare); ph, Robert Krasker, Jack Hildyard (Technicolor); m, William Walton; ed, Beck; md, Muir Mathieson; art d, Paul Sheriff; cos, Roger Furse.

Drama **Cas.** **(PR:A MPAA:NR)**

HENRY GOES ARIZONA** (1939) 66m MGM bw

Frank Morgan *(Henry Conroy)*, Virginia Weidler *(Molly)*, Guy Kibbee *(Judge)*, Slim Summerville *(Sheriff)*, Douglas Fowley *(Ricky)*, Owen Davis, Jr. *(Regan)*, Porter Hall, Mitchell Lewis, Jim Thorpe, Gordon Jones.

Morgan is a vaudevillian who takes over a ranch in Arizona on which his half brother was murdered. Fearful of guns and loud noises, the jumpy Morgan isn't too happy about his acquisition. A banker, Hall, and his two wranglers, Fowley and Jones, want the ranch and make it tough on him. Weidler, who was befriended by the dead brother, helps cowardly Morgan and turns him accidentally into a hero.

d, Edwin L. Marin; w, Florence Ryerson, Milton Merlin (based on a story by W.C. Tuttle); ph, Sidney Wagner, Lester White; m, David Snell; ed, Conrad A. Nervig.

Western/Comedy **(PR:A MPAA:NR)**

HENRY LIMPET (SEE: INCREDIBLE MR. LIMPET, THE, 1964)

HENRY STEPS OUT* (1940, Brit.) 52m Clive/AIP bw

George Turner *(Henry Smith)*, Margaret Yarde *(Cynthia Smith)*, Wally Patch *(Wally)*.

Turner becomes a hero when he discovers a bundle of cash missing from a recent bank heist. Instead of collecting his reward, Turner allows his domineering wife to talk him into joining the army. His high hopes of glory in the service are quickly reduced when he is placed on bathroom duty. His wife, however, gets him out of the mess before he can enjoy the company of some overly-friendly ladies. His previous life is restored along with his well-deserved reward.

p&d, Widgey R. Newman.

Comedy **(PR:A MPAA:NR)**

HENRY, THE RAINMAKER** (1949) 64m Mayfair/MON bw

Raymond Walburn *(Henry Latham)*, Walter Catlett *(Mayor Colton)*, William Tracy *(Charlie Richards)*, Mary Stuart *(Barbara Latham)*, Barbara Brown *(Mrs. Latham)*, Gary Gray *(David Latham)*, Addison Richards *(Steve Richards)*, Lois Austin *(Mrs. Richards)*, George Nokes *(Georgie Colton)*, Mary Field *(Mrs. Sweeney)*, Robert E. Keane *(Seton)*, Ruth Lee *(School Teacher)*, Patty King *(Marilyn Loper)*, Edna Holland *(Mrs. Parker)*, Earle Hodgins *(Mr. Peabody)*, Barton Yarborough *(Rev. Bascom)*, Lennie Bremen *(Bum)*.

Average citizen Walburn runs for mayor when the city's garbagemen go on strike. He gives the incumbent a race for the money causing the present mayor to get moving on the smelly situation. Walburn then turns his attention to correcting a threatening drought. He brings in a rainmaker and nearly causes a flood.

p, Peter Scully; d, Jean Yarbrough; w, Lane Beauchamp (based on a story by D.D. Beauchamp); ph, William Sickner; ed, Scully; art d, Dave Milton.

Comedy **(PR:A MPAA:NR)**

HENTAI** (1966, Jap.) 71m Olympic International bw (AKA: ABNORMAL)

Sayuri Sakurari, Masayonshi Nagami.

Grim Japanese crime film about two detectives searching for the missing daughter of a rich industrialist. The trail leads to a strange crime ring that kidnaps, drugs, and rapes young girls, and forces them to work as prostitutes. Eventually the detectives learn that the industrialist's daughter has suffered the same fate. When they have the Tokyo police round up the leaders of the gang, the industrialist himself is exposed as the mastermind. To his eternal shame and horror he learns that his organization had prostituted his own daughter.

p, Nidemaru Washio, Felix Lomax; d, Takashi Shiga.

Crime **(PR:O MPAA:NR)**

HER ADVENTUROUS NIGHT*½ (1946) 75m UNIV bw

Dennis O'Keefe *(Bill)*, Helen Walker *(Constance)*, Tom Powers *(Carter)*, Fuzzy Knight *(Cudgeons)*, Charles Judels *(Petrucie)*, Scotty Beckett *(Junior)*, Bennie Bartlett *(Horace)*, Milburn Stone *(1st Cop)*, Betty Compson *(Miss Spencer)*, Herbert Vigran *(2nd Cop)*, Lee Phelps *(3rd Cop)*, Joe Granby *(Mr. Gittler)*, John Wald *(Radio Announcer)*, Peggy Webber *(Miss Howard)*, George Eldredge *(Police Radio Announcer)*, Jack Kirk *(1st Neighbor)*, Ralph Brooks *(2nd Neighbor)*, Harry Brown *(Neighbor)*.

Beckett is a teenager who tells some very tall tales. When he's found with a pistol in his possession he tells a wild one that lands his parents and the school principal in jail. The kid straightens out by solving a 15-year-old murder case.

p, Charles F. Haas; d, John Rawlins; w, Jerry Warner; ph, Ernest Miller; ed, Edward Curtiss; md, Hans J. Salter; art d, Jack Otterson, Harold MacArthur.

Action/Comedy **(PR:A MPAA:NR)**

HER BODYGUARD*½ (1933) 71m Schulberg/PAR bw

Edmund Lowe *(Casey McCarthy)*, Wynn Gibson *(Margot Brienne)*, Edward Arnold *(Orson Bitzer)*, Johnny Hines *(Ballyhoo)*, Marjorie White *(Lita)*, Alan Dinehart *(Lester Cunningham)*, Fuzzy Knight *(Danny Dare)*, Zoila Cana, Louise Beavers, Arthur Houseman.

Lowe is a bodyguard with designs to be an actor, who is hired by a wealthy man to protect his blonde actress girl friend from a certain producer who wants to make her his. In the all too predictable ending, Lowe ends up with the girl.

p, B.P. Schulberg; d, William Beaudine; w, Ralph Spence, Walter DeLeon, Frank Partos, Frances Martin (based on a story by Corey Ford); ed, Jane Loring; ph, Leon Shamroy, Harry Fischbeck; m/l, Arthur Johnson, Sam Coslow.

Drama **(PR:A MPAA:NR)**

HER CARDBOARD LOVER½** (1942) 93m MGM bw

Norma Shearer *(Consuelo Croyden)*, Robert Taylor *(Terry Trindale)*, George Sanders *(Tony Barling)*, Frank McHugh *(Chappie Champagne)*, Elizabeth Patterson *(Eva)*, Chill Wills *(Judge)*.

An ancient and overused farcical comedy, this story is handled with as much aplomb as can be expected from Shearer, Taylor, and Sanders, and even with Cukor as director it still falls apart quickly. Shearer is a young, not-too-gay divorcee whose ex-husband is now her ambiguous playboy suitor, Sanders. Shearer hires down-and-out gambler Taylor to pretend to be her gigolo in order to draw Sanders to her but Taylor falls in love with Shearer and the two wind up together after some confused situations. There's not much to it all, even though this chestnut had been filmed as a silent with Marion Davies in 1928. Jeanne Eagles and later Tallulah Bankhead starred successfully in stage versions and Buster Keaton borrowed the thin plot for his 1932 comedy film THE PASSIONATE PLUMBER. This was Shearer's last film, the end of a six-picture contract she signed with the one and only studio she ever worked for after the death of her husband, one-time MGM mogul Irving Thalberg. She herself picked this moldering story out of the MGM vaults for reasons only Shearer would know. It was a sad swan song to an otherwise illustrious career.

p, J. Walter Rubin; d, George Cukor; w, John Collier, Anthony Veiller, William H. Wright, Jacques Deval (based on the play by Deval); ph, Harry Stradling, Robert Planck; m, Franz Waxman; ed, Robert J. Kern; art d, Cedric Gibbons; m/l, "I Dare You," Burton Lane, Ralph Freed.

Romance **(PR:A MPAA:NR)**

HER ENLISTED MAN (SEE: RED SALUTE, 1935)

HER FAVORITE HUSBAND (SEE: TAMING OF DOROTHY, 1950, Brit.)

HER FIRST AFFAIR*** (1947, Fr.) 90m Distinguished bw (PREMIER RENDEZVOUS)

Danielle Darrieux *(Micheline)*, Jacqueline Desmarets *(Henriette)*, Rosine Luguet *(Angele)*, Gabrielle Dorziat *(The Directress)*, Suzanne Dehelly *(Christophine)*, Eliza Rule *(Marie)*, Fernand Ledoux *(Nicolas)*, Jean Tissier *(Rollan)*, Georges Mauloy *(The Director)*, Louis Jourdan *(Pierre)*, Georges Marchal *(De Vaugelas)*.

Darrieux is an orphan who answers a lonely hearts ad, then sneaks out from the orphanage to meet her prince, who turns out to be a college professor. He tells her he is fronting for the real writer of the ad, then takes her to his all-boys' school so she doesn't get in trouble for returning late to the orphanage. The fun begins when the professor attempts to hide Darrieux's presence from the boys, one of whom he later introduces to her as the authentic writer of the ad. But when Darrieux and the young man fall in love, it is revealed that the professor actually wrote the ad, and is himself in love with the girl. The end sees the students raise enough money to get Darrieux out of the orphanage. She leaves with her youthful boy friend and the professor gives the couple his blessing. (In French; English subtitles.)

p,d&w, Henri Decoin.

Comedy **(PR:A MPAA:NR)**

HER FIRST AFFAIRE*½ (1932, Brit.) 75m St. George-STER bw

Ida Lupino *(Anne)*, George Curzon *(Carey Merton)*, Diana Napier *(Mrs. Merton)*, Harry Tate *(Maj. Gore)*, Muriel Aked *(Agatha Brent)*, Arnold Riches *(Brian)*, Kenneth Kove *(Prof. Hotspur)*, Helen Haye *(Lady Bragden)*, Roland Culver *(Drunk)*, Melville Gideon *(Himself)*.

This was Lupino's first leading role at age 18 and has her playing a flapper who wants to have some fun before getting married and settling down. She tries having an affair with Curzin, a writer, and his wife, Napier, helps her out.

p, Frank Richardson; d, Allan Dwan; w, Dion Titheradge, Brock Williams (based on a play by Frederick Jackson, Merrill Rogers).

Drama **(PR:A MPAA:NR)**

HER FIRST BEAU** (1941) 76m COL bw

Jackie Cooper *(Chuck Harris)*, Jane Withers *(Penny Wood)*, Edith Fellows *(Milly Lou)*, Josephine Hutchinson *(Mrs. Wood)*, William Tracy *(Mervyn Roberts)*, Martha O'Driscoll *(Julie Harris)*, Edgar Buchanan *(Elmer Tuttle)*, Una O'Conner *(Effie)*, Jonathan Hale *(Mr. Harris)*, Kenneth Howell *(Roger Van Vleck)*, Addison Richards *(Dr. Wood)*.

Withers and Cooper are childhood sweethearts, but Cooper spends far too much time working on his latest project, a sail-plane. When Withers' uncle brings home a flirtatious, older friend, she begins dating him, but finds that his real intentions are not as innocent as those of Cooper and returns to her industrious beau.

p, B.B. Kahane; d, Theodore Reed; w, Gladys Lehman, Karen DeWolf (based on a story by Florence Ryerson, Colin Clements); ph, George Meehan; ed, Charles Nelson.

Drama **(PR:A MPAA:NR)**

HER FIRST MATE** (1933) 64m UNIV bw

Slim Summerville *(John Horner)*, ZaSu Pitts *(Mary Horner)*, Una Merkel *(Hattie)*, Warren Hymer *(Percy)*, Berton Churchill *(Davis)*, George Marion *(Sam)*, Henry Armetta *(Socrates)*, Jocelyn Lee.

Pitts uses her life savings to buy a ferry boat so she and husband, Summerville, can start their own business. But he trades the boat for a sloop and takes off to explore the world—without his wife. He makes it around the world after doing battle with a U.S. destroyer and swaps the boat back for the ferry. This makes for a happy ending for Pitts and her wanderlust husband.

d, William Wyler; w, Earl Snell, H.M. Walker, Clarence Marks (based on the play "Salt Water" by Dan Jarrett, Frank Craven, John Golden); ph, George Robinson.

Comedy **(PR:A MPAA:NR)**

HER FIRST ROMANCE½** (1940) 77m MON bw (AKA: THE RIGHT MAN)

Edith Fellows, Wilbur Evans, Jacqueline Wells [Julie Bishop], Alan Ladd, Judith Linden, Roger Daniel, Marion Kirby, Marla Dwyer, Ottola Nesmith, Ray Hirsch, Alexander Moreland, Julie Sheldon, John Adamson.

Fellows and Wells are sisters, the former plain looking and the latter a beautiful schemer. Linden is their cousin, a good looking woman herself who has an off-and-on engagement with Ladd. Both sisters fall for Evans and use Ladd in their plots to win his heart. Ladd mistakenly believes Evans is going for his girl and knocks the man down. By the film's end, though, everything is straightened out as Ladd marries Linden and Evans goes for Fellows. This is an enjoyable little comedy made on an unusually large budget for the programmer factory at Monogram. Fellows was a former child star and showed some fine adult talent in this musical comedy. Watching Ladd cavort in such material is a real curiosity considering his later work but he's not bad at all. After he achieved fame with his work in the 1940s, HER FIRST ROMANCE was rereleased as THE RIGHT MAN, now bearing Ladd's name above the title.

p, I.E. Chadwick; d, Edward Dmytryk; w, Adele Comandini (based on the story "Her Father's Daughter" by Gene Stratton Porter); ph, John Mescall; ed, William Ziegler; md, Gregory Stone.

Musical/Comedy **(PR:A MPAA:NR)**

HER FIRST ROMANCE*½ (1951) 72m COL bw

Margaret O'Brien *(Betty Foster)*, Allen Martin, Jr. *(Bobby Evans)*, Jimmy Hunt *(Herbie)*, Sharyn Moffett *(Leona Dean)*, Ann Doran *(Mrs. Foster)*, Lloyd Corrigan *(Mr. Gauss)*, Elinor Donahue *(Lucille Stewart)*, Susan Stevens *(Clara)*, Marissa O'Brien *(Tillie)*, Arthur Space *(Mr. Foster)*, Otto Hulett *(Mr. Evans)*, Lois Pace *(Violet)*, Harlan Warde *(Paul Powers)*, Maudie Prickett *(Miss Pond)*.

O'Brien tricks her parents into sending her to summer camp so she can be close to Martin, on whom she has a wild crush. When he needs money to build a camp project, O'Brien skips into town that night and steals $25 from her father's safe. Unknowingly, she also took the ownership papers of her father's business. The papers finally get returned after a lot of frantic running around, and O'Brien even gets a slap on the wrist and goes on to win the heart of Martin.

d, Seymour Friedman; w, Albert Mannheimer (based on a story by Herman Wouk); ph, Charles Lawton; ed, Jerome Thoms; md, Morris Stoloff; art d, Ross Bellah.

Teen Romance **(PR:A MPAA:NR)**

HER FORGOTTEN PAST* (1933) 55m Golden Arrow/Mayfair bw

Henry B. Walthall, Eddie Phillips, William V. Mong, Dewey Robinson, Monte Blue, Barbara Kent.

A woman is happily married to a district attorney when her supposedly dead husband appears to complicate her life. She had been married to her chauffeur (a past she'd like to forget) when he was allegedly killed. Turns out it was a case of mistaken identity and he's come back to give her a hard time. When the first husband really does get killed, she becomes a strong suspect. The climax sees her father reveal the true facts of the case to save his daughter.

d, Wesley Ford; w, George Morgan (based on a story by Morgan); ph, James S. Brown, Jr.; ed, Fred Bain.

Drama **(PR:A MPAA:NR)**

HER HIGHNESS AND THE BELLBOY** (1945) 108m MGM bw

Hedy Lamarr *(Princess Veronica)*, Robert Walker *(Jimmy Dobson)*, June Allyson *(Leslie Odell)*, Carl Esmond *(Baron Zoltan Faludi)*, Agnes Moorehead *(Countess Zoe)*, "Rags" Ragland *(Albert Weever)*, Ludwig Stossel *(Mr. Pufi)*, George Cleveland *(Dr. Elfson)*, Warner Anderson *(Paul MacMillan)*, Konstantin Shayne *(Yanos von Lankofitz)*, Tom Trout *(Hack)*, Ben Lessy *(Himself)*, Patty Moore *(Fae)*, Edward Gargan *(1st Policeman)*, Ann Codee *(Countess Tradiska)*, Ferdinand Munier *(Mr. Fabler)*, Emil Rameau *(Mr. Korb)*, Gladys Blake *(Pearl)*, Olga Fabian *(Mrs. Korb)*, Jack Norton *(Mr. Pook)*, Audrey Totter *(Mildred)*, Grayce Hampton *(Mrs. Chuduster)*, William Halligan *(Police Capt. Perie)*, Virginia Sale *(Aunt Gertrude Odell)*, Bess Flowers *(Woman)*, Betty Blythe *(Diplomat's Wife)*.

A hit and miss love story with good performances by Lamarr, in one of her rare comedy roles, Allyson, as a sweet young thing, and Walker, playing the ingenuous, charming young man he practically owned a patent on. Lamarr is the princess of a mythical country who has come to New York to see Anderson, a newspaperman she'd met a while ago on her turf. While ensconced at her hotel, Walker, a bellboy, thinks she's a maid (in one of those Hollywood turn of events that no one believes but everyone accepts) and she is faintly amused by his error, so she asks the hotel to assign him to be her personal aide. Lamarr meets with Anderson, who feels that they are of two different worlds and that it would be impossible for them to make a couple. Not that he is temporarily out of ardor, it's just that he can't handle the schism. Lamarr is very sweet to Walker, who thinks that her affection is something more than that. Allyson is an invalid who adores Walker and who lives for his visits to her. Lamarr requests that Walker squire her to a bar where Anderson hangs out and writes his material. The place is raided and Lamarr is tossed into the clink, then bailed out by Anderson. Once free, she learns that her father has died and she is now the queen. She gets ready to depart and tells Walker that he can come with her if he likes. He thinks this is a marriage proposal and tells Allyson that he is going to Europe where he will be a prince consort to Queen Lamarr. But when he sees Allyson, he realizes that he truly loves her. With a mixture of elation and sadness, he tells Lamarr that he must decline her offer of marriage. Lamarr understands what love is from Walker's "rejection" and decides that she would rather be Anderson's wife than queen, so she abdicates and will spend the rest of her life as the mate of a newspaperman. Anyone who has ever been the wife of a newspaperman will know that her decision was 100 percent wrong. Although bed-bound for most of the picture, Allyson was most believable and did get one chance to strut her stuff in a fantasy dance sequence. Ragland is good as Walker's bellhop pal, but Moorehead, a superb actress for all her life, is wasted as the countess.

p, Joe Pasternak; d, Richard Thorpe; w, Richard Connell, Gladys Lehman; ph, Harry Stradling; m, Georgie Stoll; ed, George Boemler; md, Calvin Jackson; art d, Cedric Gibbons, Urie McCleary; set d, Edwin B. Willis; cos, Marion Herwood Keyes, Valles; spec eff, Warren Newcombe; ch, Charles Walters.

Comedy/Romance **(PR:A MPAA:NR)**

HER HUSBAND LIES** (1937) 74m PAR bw

Gail Patrick *(Natalie Martin)*, Ricardo Cortez *(Spade Martin)*, Akim Tamiroff *(Bullock)*, Tom Brown *(Chick)*, Louis Calhern *(Sordoni)*, June Martel *(Betty)*, Dorothy Peterson *(Dorothy Powell)*, Ralf Harolde *(Steve Burdick)*, Adrian Morris *(Carwig)*, Ray Walker *(Maxie)*, Jack LaRue *(Trigger)*, Bradley Page *(Pug)*.

Cortez is a big-time gambler who wants to go straight. His smart-alec younger brother wants to get into the gambling world and Cortez reluctantly teaches him just so he doesn't get duped by one of his gangster cronies. The youth learns all too well and cleans up in a card game with ace gamblers who are convinced he must have set them up. After deciding that he is now too old to change professions, Cortez comes to his brother's rescue by setting everybody down at the card table and proving his sibling's innocence.

p, B.P. Schulberg; d, Edward Ludwig; w, Wallace Smith, Eve Greene (based on the story "Street of Chance" by Oliver H.P. Garrett); ph, Leon Shamroy; ed, Robert Bischoff; m/l, Burton Lane, Ralph Freed.

Drama **(PR:A MPAA:NR)**

HER HUSBAND'S AFFAIRS*½** (1947) 84m Cornell/COL bw

Lucille Ball *(Margaret Weldon)*, Franchot Tone *(William Weldon)*, Edward Everett Horton *(J.B. Cruikshank)*, Mikhail Rasumny *(Prof. Glinka)*, Gene Lockhart *(Peter Winterbottom)*, Nana Bryant *(Mrs. Winterbottom)*, Jonathan Hale *(Gov. Fox)*, Paul Stanton *(Dr. Frazee)*, Mabel Paige *(Mrs. Josper)*, Frank Mayo *(Vice-President Starrett)*, Pierre Watkin *(Vice-President Beitler)*, Carl Leviness *(Vice-President Brady)*, Dick Gordon *(Vice-President Nicholson)*, Douglas Wood *(Tappel)*, Jack Rice *(Slocum)*, Clancy Cooper *(Window Washer)*, Charles C. Wilson *(Police Captain)*, Charles Trowbridge *(Brewster)*, Selmer Jackson *(Judge)*, Arthur Space *(District*

Attorney), Cliff Clark *(Gus)*, Douglas D. Coppin *(Milkman)*, Virginia Hunter, Doris Colleen *(Secretaries)*, Stanley Blystone *(Ike)*, Fred Miller *(Dan)*, Larry Parks *(Himself)*, Nancy Saunders, Wanda Cantlon, Edythe Elliott *(Nurses)*, Harry Cheshire *(Mayor)*, Gerald Oliver Smith *(Harold)*, Robert Emmett Keane *(Manager)*, Emmett Vogan *(Mr. Miller)*, Fred Sears *(Man at Mayor's Party)*, Bob Cason *(Heckler)*, Tommy Lee, James B. Leong, Hom Wing Gim, Owen Song *(Acrobats)*, George Douglas, Stephen Bennett *(Vice Presidents)*, Fred Howard *(Bailiff)*, Bill Wallace, Charles Hamilton, Russell Whitman *(Policemen)*, Charles Bates, Buz Buckley, Teddy Infuhr, Dwayne Hickman *(Boys)*, Charles Williams *(Clerk)*, William Gould *(Jailer)*, Frank Wilcox *(Floorwalker)*, Susan Simon *(Girl)*, Dan Stowell *(Willowcombe)*, Victor Travers *(Jury Foreman)*, Eric Wilton *(Governor's Butler)*, Buddy Gorman *(Youth)*.

A zany comedy with good laughs in every scene. Tone is an advertising wonder and Ball is his loving wife, who always gets the credit for his work. Tone does the advertising for a crazy inventor who is searching for the perfect embalming fluid. Satirical swipes are taken at the advertising world, sponsors, and public figures of the time. Ball and Tone work well as a comic team and Hecht's and Lederer's madcap script, along with Simon's direction, make this film a laugh riot.

p, Raphael Hakim; d, S. Sylvan Simon; w, Ben Hecht, Charles Lederer; ph, Charles Lawton, Jr.; ed, Al Clark; md, M.W. Stoloff; art d, Stephen Goosson, Carl Anderson.

Comedy **(PR:A MPAA:NR)**

HER HUSBAND'S SECRETARY* (1937) 61m FN-WB bw

Jean Muir *(Carol)*, Beverly Roberts *(Diane)*, Warren Hull *(Bart)*, Joseph Crehan *(Stevenson)*, Clara Blandick *(Agatha Kingdon)*, Addison Richards *(Steven Garron)*, Harry Davenport *(Dan Kingdon)*, Gordon Hart *(Mr. Blake)*, Minerva Urecal *(Miss Baldwin)*, Pauline Garon *(Louise)*, Stuart Holmes *(Stanton)*.

Muir and Roberts battle over who will get wealthy Hull. Muir is married to him but she thinks secretary Roberts is getting all of his attention. Attention should have been spent in writing a better script.

d, Frank McDonald; w, Lillie Hayward (based on a story by Crane Wilbur); ph, Arthur Todd; ed, Clarence Kolster.

Drama **(PR:A MPAA:NR)**

HER IMAGINARY LOVER** (1933, Brit.) 66m FN-WB bw

Laura la Plante *(Celia)*, Percy Marmont *(Lord Michael Ware)*, Lady Tree *(Grandma)*, Bernard Nedell *(Davidson)*, Olive Blakeney *(Polly)*, Emily Fitzroy *(Aunt Lydia Raleigh)*, Roland Culver *(Raleigh Raleigh)*.

A congenial British comedy which has la Plante, on advice from her lovable grandma, pretending to have herself a fiance in order to fend off an excess of admirers. Coming to London from New York City to receive an inheritance, she learns that the promise of great wealth is a surefire way to meet a suitor. Her imaginary lover, Lord Michael of Ware, turns out to really exist. Once he meets la Plante his initial anger subsides and he falls in love with the young lady.

p, Irving Asher; d, George King; w, (based on the novel *Green Stockings* by A.E.W. Mason).

Comedy/Romance **(PR:A MPAA:NR)**

HER JUNGLE LOVE** (1938) 81m PAR c

Dorothy Lamour *(Tura)*, Ray Milland *(Bob Mitchell)*, Lynne Overman *(Jimmy Wallace)*, J. Carroll Naish *(Kuasa)*, Dorothy Howe *(Eleanor Martin)*, Jonathan Hale *(J.C. Martin)*, Archie Twitchell *(Roy Atkins)*, Edward Earle *(Capt. Avery)*, Bill Caldwell *(Steward)*, Sonny Choree *(Guard)*, Tony Urchell *(Guard)*, Jiggs *(Gaga)*, The Tiger Cub *(Meewa)*, Virginia Vale *(Eleanor Martin)*, Richard Denning *(Pilot)*, Phillip Warren *(Co-pilot)*.

A Tarzan rip-off with Lamour the jungle woman left in the wilds by her parents and raised by animals. A pilot crashes his plane in the jungle and Milland and Overman head up a rescue party. On the way they meet the jungle girl whom Milland falls in love with, upsetting Lamour's jungle friends—a chimp and a tiger cub. The group fight off savages and crocodiles on their way to save the stranded pilot.

p, George M. Arthur; d, George Archainbaud; w, Joseph M. March, Lillie Hayward, Eddie Welch (based on a story by Gerald Geraghty, Kurt Siodmak); ph, Ray Rennahan (Technicolor); m, Gregory Stone; ed, Hugh Bennett; art d, Natalie Kalmus, Hans Dreier, Earl Hedrick; cos, Edith Head; m/l, Leo Robin, Ralph Rainger, Ralph Freed, Frederick Hollander.

Adventure **(PR:A MPAA:NR)**

HER KIND OF MAN** (1946) 80m WB bw

Dane Clark *(Don Corwin)*, Janis Paige *(Georgia King)*, Zachary Scott *(Steve Maddux)*, Faye Emerson *(Ruby Marino)*, George Tobias *(Joe Marino)*, Howard Smith *(Bill Fellows)*, Harry Lewis *(Candy)*, Sheldon Leonard *(Bender)*.

Scott turns from bootlegger to gambler when prohibition is axed and meets singer Paige. She falls in love with him while newsman Clark falls in love with her and tries to get Scott out of the picture with his pen. Scott has his fall but it's more due to bullets than to Scott's writing. Paige sings "Something To Remember You By" (Howard Deitz, Arthur Schwartz), "Speak To Me Of Love" (Bruce Siever, Jean Lenoir), and "Body and Soul" (Edward Hayman, Johnny Green).

p, Alex Gottlieb; d, Frederick de Cordova; w, Gordon Kahn, Leopold Atlas (based on the story "Melancholy" by Charles Hoffman, James V. Kern); ph, Carl Guthrie; m, Franz Waxman; ed, Dick Richards; md, Leo F. Forbstein; art d, Ted Smith.

Crime **(PR:A MPAA:NR)**

HER LAST AFFAIRE*½ (1935, Brit.) 70m PDC bw

Hugh Williams *(Alan Heriot)*, Viola Keats *(Lady Avril Weyre)*, Francis L. Sullivan *(Sir Julian Weyre)*, Sophie Stewart *(Judy Weyre)*, Cecil Parker *(Sir Arthur Harding)*, Felix Aylmer *(Lord Carnforth)*, John Laurie *(Cobb)*, Eliot Makeham *(Dr. Rudd)*, Googie Withers *(Effie)*, Gerrard Tyrell *(Martin)*, Shayle Gardner *(Boxall)*, Henry Caine.

Williams, the secretary to prominent English politician Sullivan, is in love with his employer's daughter, Stewart. The politician recently married a woman who sent Williams' father to prison for a crime that she committed. The father and step-mother are against Stewart's plans to wed Williams, and this puts the young man's job in jeopardy. When Williams forces the step-mother to sign a confession that she actually committed the crime, she dies of a heart attack. Williams is sent to trial for murder, but is eventually cleared of all charges and is free to marry his love.

p, Simon and Geoffrey Rowson; d, Michael Powell; w, Ian Dalrymple (based on the play "S.O.S." by Walter Ellis); ph, Harry Gilliam, Leslie Rowson.

Drama **(PR:A MPAA:NR)**

HER LUCKY NIGHT** (1945) 63m UNIV bw

Patty Andrews, Maxine Andrews, LaVerne Andrews *(The Andrews Sisters)*, Martha O'Driscoll *(Connie)*, Noah Beery, Jr. *(Larry)*, George Barbier *(J.L. Wentworth)*, Maurice Cass *(Papa)*, Marie Harmon *(Susie)*, Olin Howlin *(Prince de la Mour)*, Robert Emmett Keane *(Lawson)*, Grady Sutton *(Joe)*, Edgar Dearing *(Casey)*, Eddie Acuff *(Chauffeur)*, Rita Gould *(Fannie)*, Charles Jordan *(Bus Driver)*, Billy Newell *(Proprietor)*, Ida Moore *(Mama)*, Jack Rice *(Percy)*, Buzz Henry *(Kid)*, Virginia Sale *(Umbrella Woman)*, Donald Kerr, Eddie Bruce, Perc Launders *(Onlookers)*, Stuart Holmes *(Headwaiter)*, Warren Jackson *(Bit Man)*, Rena Saunders *(Bit Woman)*, Gladys Blake *(Woman-Garter Gag)*, Charles Hall *(Window Washer)*, Paul Hurst *(Maloney)*, Mary McLeod *(1st Usherette)*, Nan Brinkley *(2nd Usherette)*, Dan Quig *(1st Young Man)*, Buddy Wilkerson *(2nd Young Man)*, Genevieve Bell *(Dowager)*, Kay York *(Bit Girl)*, Leslie Denison *(Man)*.

Lame musical starring O'Driscoll as a man-hungry woman who takes a fortune teller's prediction that she will find her Romeo sitting next to her in a movie theater to heart and buys two movie tickets, throwing one out the window. Really thin, with lackluster musical numbers. Songs include: "Dance With A Dolly With A Hole In Her Stocking" (Terry Shand, Mickey Leader, Jimmy Eaton), "Sing A Tropical Song" (Frank Loesser, Jimmy McHugh), "Is You Is Or Is You Ain't My Baby?" (Billy Austin, Louis Jordan), "Straighten Up and Fly Right" (Nat King Cole, Irving Mills), and "The Polka Polka" (Maxine Manners).

p, Warren Wilson; d, Edward Lilley; w, Clyde Bruckman (based on the story "Stars Over Manhattan" by Wilson); ph, Hal Mohr; ed, Paul Landres; md, Edgar Fairchild; art d, John B. Goodman; ch, Louis Da Pron.

Muscial **(PR:A MPAA:NR)**

HER MAD NIGHT* (1932) 67m Like/Mayfair bw

Irene Rich *(Joan Manners)*, Conway Tearle *(Steven Kennedy)*, Mary Carlisle *(Constance Kennedy)*, Kenneth Thomson *(Schuyler Durkin)*, William B. Davidson *(District Attorney)*.

Mother takes the rap for a murder supposedly committed by her daughter, but which turns out to have really been an accident. The daughter, not knowing what her mother has done, is taking a cruise around the world. When she gets back she finds her mother on death row, but manages to straighten eveything out minutes before execution time.

d, E. Mason Hopper; w, John Thomas Neville; ph, Jules Cronjager; ed, Byron Robinson.

Crime **(PR:A MPAA:NR)**

HER MAJESTY LOVE*½ (1931) 75m WB/FN bw

Marilyn Miller *(Lia Toerrek)*, Ben Lyon *(Fred von Wellingen)*, W.C. Fields *(Lia's Father)*, Ford Sterling *(Otmar)*, Leon Errol *(Baron von Schwarzdorf)*, Chester Conklin *(Emil)*, Harry Stubbs *(Hanneman)*, Maude Eburne *(Aunt Harriette)*, Harry Holman *(Reisenfeld)*, Ruth Hall *(Factory Secretary)*, William Irving *(The "Third" Man)*, Mae Madison *(Fred's Sister, Elli)*, Clarence Wilson, Virginia Sale.

A flat, inept musical comedy that is only memorable for having introduced W.C. Fields' juggling act to celluloid. Set in Berlin (where the original play was located), it tells the story of Miller, a sweet young girl, who falls in love with Lyon, heir to a large fortune. Fields is Miller's father, a coarse type who has spent most of his adult existence juggling in various shows. When he picks up a bunch of items at a dinner party where Lyon and Miller have announced their engagement, all of the gathered Teutons are shocked by his lack of couth. Then he tells the assemblage that his regular work is barbering and that Miller is a bar waitress and jaws drop as well as three plates that Fields has been juggling. Lyon's family would like to put the clamp on this budding love affair and they make him an offer he can't refuse: they will pay him 10 thousand marks per month to manage the family business if he agrees to say "auf weidersehen" to Miller. Along comes Errol, a playboy German baron who offers Miller marriage. She is sad without Lyon and he feels the same without her but she accepts Errol's proposal. The wedding takes place in Berlin while Lyon is vainly attempting to get there to stop it. He arrives late, the deed is done, but she is so happy to see him that the two of them walk out of the church, arm in arm, leaving Errol and the wedding party scratching their heads in bewilderment. Now, if that scene doesn't sound familiar, try to recall the last few minutes of THE GRADUATE and it makes one wonder if there is anything new under the cinematic sun. Sterling and Conklin, two comedy stars of silents, are not in this enough to save it. It's a Sacher torte that falls flat. Tunes include: "You're Baby-Minded Now," "Don't Ever Be Blue," "Though You're Not The First Wine," "Because Of You," and "You Have All My Heart."

d, William Dieterle; w, Robert Lord, Arthur Caesar, Henry Blanke, Joseph Jackson (based on the play by R. Bernauer, R. Oesterreicher); ph, Robert Kurrle; ed, Ralph Dawson; art d, Jack Okey; m/l, Walter Jurmann, Al Dubin.

Musical/Comedy **(PR:A MPAA:NR)**

HER MAN** (1930) 85m Pathe bw

Helen Twelvetrees *(Frankie)*, Marjorie Rambeau *(Annie)*, Ricardo Cortez *(Johnnie)*, Phillips Holmes *(Dan)*, James Gleason *(Steve)*, Franklin Pangborn *(Sport)*, Harry Sweet *(Eddie)*, Stanley Fields *(Al)*, Mathew Betz *(Red)*, Thelma Todd *(Nelly)*, Mike Donlin *(Bartender)*, Sally Ferguson, Blythe Daly, Ruth Hiatt, Edith Rosita, Lola Karnelly, Peggy Howard *(Dance Hall Girls)*.

The "Frankie and Johnnie" theme is set in a Parisian seafront dive. Cortez is a pimp who likes to stab men in the back when they give his girls problems, and Twelvetrees is his No. 1 girl. She likes to give men a sob story, then pick their pockets but she meets her match in a sailor, Holmes, who takes her away from it all.

d, Tay Garnett; w, Tom Buckingham (based on a story by Howard Higgin, Garnett); ph, Ed Snyder; ed, Doane Harrison, Joe Kane.

Drama **(PR:C MPAA:NR)**

HER MAN GILBEY*½** (1949, Brit.) 89m TC/UNIV bw (GB: ENGLISH WITHOUT TEARS)

Michael Wilding *(Tom Gilbey)*, Lilli Palmer *(Brigid Knudsen)*, Penelope Ward *(Joan Heseltine)*, Claude Dauphin *(Jean de Freyeinet)*, Roland Culver *(Sir Cosmo Brandon)*, Peggy Cummins *(Bobby Heseltine)*, Albert Lieven *(Felix Dembowski)*, Margaret Rutherford *(Lady Christabel Beauclerk)*, Martin Miller *(Schmidt)*, Felix Aylmer *(Spagott)*, Beryl Measor *(Miss Foljambe)*, Judith Furse *(Elsie Batter-Jones)*, Guy Middleton, Gerald Heinz, Andre Randall, Louise Lord, Joan Misseldine, Irene Handl, Frederick Richter, Antony Holles, Esma Cannon, David Keir, Ivor Barnard, Beryl Laverick, Primula Rollo, Heather Boys, Vida Hope, Margaret McGrath, J.A. Brimstone, Andrea Malandrinos, Johnnie Schofield, Peggy Carlisle, Brian Nissen, Pat Owens.

Ward is a lovely rich girl who ventures to Geneva with her bird-loving aunt, Rutherford, and butler, Wilding. They plead a case in defense of bird migration and in the process Ward and Wilding fall in love. In keeping with the British class system, Wilding rises in the ranks of the army and sheds his manservant tag.

p, Anatole de Grunwald, Sydney Box, William Sassoon; d, Harold French; w, Terence Rattigan, de Grunwald; ph, Bernard Knowles; m, Nicholas Brodsky; ed, Alan Jaggs; md, Charles Williams; art d, Ward Richards.

Comedy/Romance **(PR:A MPAA:NR)**

HER MASTER'S VOICE** (1936) 75m PAR bw

Edward Everett Horton *(Ned Farrar)*, Peggy Conklin *(Queena Farrar)*, Laura Hope Crews *(Aunt Min)*, Elizabeth Patterson *(Mrs. Martin)*, Grant Mitchell *(Twilling)*, Ruth Warren *(Phoebe)*, Charles Coleman *(Craddock)*, Dick Elliott *(Police Captain)*.

Horton plays a radio celebrity who must masquerade as a handy-man when he stays at the home of his wife's aunt. The aunt likes his work so much that she wants him to stay on for good, and this causes a number of funny situations.

p, Walter Wanger; d, Joseph Santley; w, Dore Schary, Harry Sauber (based on the play by Clare Kummer); ph, James Van Trees; ed, Bob Simpson; m/l, "With All My Heart," James McHugh, Gus Kahn.

Comedy **(PR:A MPAA:NR)**

HER NIGHT OUT*½ (1932, Brit.) FN/WB bw

Dorothy Bartlam *(Kitty Vickery)*, Lester Matthews *(Gerald Vickery)*, Joan Marion *(Goldie)*, Jack Raine *(Jim Hanley)*, Dodo Watts *(Toots)*.

A tedious, predictable comedy which begins with a domestic quarrel between husband and wife, Matthews and Bartlam. She leaves in a fury and hops into the first cab she can find, and finds herself sharing the fare with a bank robber on the lam (what ever happened to getaway cars?). It comes as no surprise that she gets ensnared in his felonious doings and is then rescued by her heroic hubbie.

p, Irving Asher; d, William McGann; w, W. Scott Darling.

Comedy **(PR:A MPAA:NR)**

HER PANELLED DOOR** (1951, Brit.) 84m ABF/Souvaine Selective bw (GB: THE WOMAN WITH NO NAME)

Phyllis Calvert *(Yvonne Winter)*, Edward Underdown *(Luke Winter)*, Helen Cherry *(Sybil)*, Richard Burton *(Nick Chamerd)*, Anthony Nicholls *(Doctor)*, James Hayter *(Capt. Bradshaw)*, Betty Ann Davies *(Beatrice)*, Amy Veness *(Sophie)*, Andrew Osborn *(Paul Hammond)*, Patrick Troughton *(Colin)*, Olive Milbourne, June Bardsley, Will Ambro, Harold Scott, Willoughby Gray, Vi Stevens, David Keir, Kathleen Boutall, Irlin Hall, Leslie Phillips, Terence Alexander, Bill Shine, Richard Pearson, Jean Shepheard.

Calvert loses her memory after Nazis bomb the London hotel she is at. She's brought to a country hospital and there meets the pilot, Burton, who saved her life. They fall in love and plan to marry when he's killed on a mission. Calvert's real husband hires detectives to find her. They locate her at the hospital and bring her home where she learns that in her past she had many affairs with other men. Slowly she pieces together what her life was like and finds herself in a house with an angry husband and a conniving half-sister out to destroy their marriage.

p, John Stafford; d, Ladislas Vajda, George More O'Ferrall; w, Vajda, Guy Morgan (based on Theresa Charles' novel *Happy Now I Go*); ph, Otto Heller; m, Allen Gray; set d, Wilfred Arnold.

Drama **(PR:A MPAA:NR)**

HER PRIMITIVE MAN*½** (1944) 80m UNIV bw

Louise Allbritton *(Sheila Winthrop)*, Robert Paige *(Pete Matthews)*, Robert Benchley *(Martin Osborne)*, Edward Everett Horton *(Orrin Tracy)*, Helen Broderick *(Mrs. Winthrop)*, Stephanie Bachelor *(Marcia Stafford)*, Ernest Truex *(Uncle Hubert)*, Walter Catlett *(Hotel Clerk)*, Louis Jean Heydt *(Gerald Van Horn)*, Nydia Westman *(Aunt Penelope)*, Oscar O'Shea *(Jonathan)*, Sylvia Field *(Aunt Martha)*, Ian Wolfe *(Caleb)*, Irving Bacon *(Mr. Smith)*, Beatrice Roberts *(Maid)*, Herbert Evans *(Butler)*, Sarah Selby *(Woman at Track)*.

Hilarious screwball comedy with Paige as a casino employee who authors a book on headhunters. Allbritton, the head of an anthropological society, sets out to prove the book is a fake. Paige tricks her into going on a headhunting expedition, during which he dresses up as a native and lets the socialite take him back for studies. While parading around as a savage, Paige manages to cut a $10,000 deal to do an expose on the wealthy Allbritton's private life. A subplot involves an heiress on Paige's trail to collect $10,000 he owes her.

p, Michael Fessier, Ernest Pagano; d, Charles Lamont; w, Fessier, Pagano (based on a story by Dick Irving Hyland); ph, Charles Van Enger; ed, Ray Snyder; md, Edward Ward; art d, John B. Goodman, Richard H. Riedel.

Comedy **(PR:A MPAA:NR)**

HER PRIVATE AFFAIR** (1930) 70m PATHE bw

Ann Harding *(Vera Kessler)*, Harry Bannister *(Judge Kessler)*, John Loder *(Carl Weild)*, Kay Hammond *(Julia Sturm)*, Arthur Hoyt *(Michael Sturm)*, William Orlamond *(Dr. Zelgler)*, Lawford Davidson *(Arnold Hartmann)*, Elmer Ballard *(Grimm)*, Frank Reicher *(District Attorney)*.

Harding is married to a judge and after a huge domestic argument she takes off to Italy. There she meets a sweet-talking blackmailer. There is no romance but he follows her back and begins blackmailing her not only for money but for her hand. He forces her to come to his apartment and in a struggle she shoots him with his gun. The blackmailer's valet is arrested, tried, and acquitted. The valet tracks down Harding and makes her confess to her crime.

d, Paul Stein; w, Francis Edward Faragoh, Herman Bernstein (based on the play "The Right To Kill" by Leo Urvantzov); ph, Dave Abel, Norbert Brodine.

Drama **(PR:A MPAA:NR)**

HER PRIVATE LIFE** (1929) 72m FN-WB bw

Billie Dove *(Lady Helen Haden)*, Walter Pidgeon *(Ned Thayer)*, Holmes Herbert *(Rudolph Solomon)*, Montagu Love *(Sir Bruce Haden)*, Thelma Todd *(Mrs. Leslie)*, Roland Young *(Charteris)*, Mary Forbes *(Lady Wildering)*, Brandon Hurst *(Sir Emmett Wildering)*, ZaSu Pitts *(Timmins)*.

Dove is an Englishwoman who falls in love with Pidgeon, a gambler accused of cheating at cards, leading to the couple's breakup. She sells her jewelry and heads for the States, where she meets Herbert. His proposal of marriage is met with hesitancy; Dove chooses instead to wait for Pidgeon. All turns out well by the finish when it is revealed that Pidgeon didn't cheat at cards but took the blame for his sister's sleight of hand. A remake of the 1925 silent DECLASSE.

p, Ned Martin; d, Alexander Korda; w, Forrest Halsey (based on the Zoe Akins play "Declassee"); ph, John Seitz; ed, Harold Young; m/l, "Love Is Like A Rose," Al Bryan, George W. Meyer.

Romance **(PR:A MPAA:NR)**

HER REPUTATION* (1931, Brit.) 67m London Screenplays/PAR bw

Iris Hoey *(Dultitia Sloane)*, Frank Cellier *(Henry Sloane)*, Malcolm Tearle *(George Harding)*, Lilian Hall-Davis *(Carruthers)*, Maurice Braddell *(Eric Sloane)*, Joan Morgan *(Veronica Sloane)*, Dorothy Black *(Georgina Pastell)*, Lawrence Hanray *(Mr. Montgomery)*.

Hoey, tired of her dull and dreary marriage, files for a divorce from Cellier, implicating her husband's best friend Tearle. All goes haywire when Cellier and their son, Braddell, become attracted to court clerk Hall-Davis. None of these developments are very involving and you find yourself not caring a bit about her lousy reputation. Worst of all you find yourself not laughing.

p,d&w, Sidney Morgan (based on the play "Passing Brompton Road" by Jevan Brandon-Thomas).

Comedy **(PR:A MPAA:NR)**

HER RESALE VALUE* (1933) 63m Fanchon Royer/Mayfair bw

Noel Francis, Ralf Harolde, Gladys Hulette, Crauford Kent, Richard Tucker, Franklin Parker, June Clyde, George Lewis.

Clyde is the wife of a young doctor who gets tired of waiting for him to make money. She heads for the city and meets an owner of a dress shop. He wants her to model and she misreads his advances as a marriage proposal. A poorly produced and written tale.

d, Reeves "Breezy" Eason; w, John T. Neville (based on a story by Horace McCoy); ph, Ernest Miller; ed, Jeanne Spencer.

Drama **(PR:A MPAA:NR)**

HER SISTER'S SECRET*** (1946) 86m PRC bw

Nancy Coleman *(Toni)*, Margaret Lindsay *(Renee)*, Phillip Reed *(Dick)*, Felix Bressart *(Pepe)*, Regis Toomey *(Bill)*, Henry Stephenson *(Mr. Dubois)*, Fritz Feld *(Wine Salesman)*, Winston Severn *(Billy)*, George Meeker *(Guy)*, Helene Reigh *(Etts)*, Frances Williams *(Matillon)*, Rudolph Anders *(Birdman)*.

At the New Orleans Mardi Gras during WW II Coleman falls in love with soldier Reed. She discovers that she's pregnant after Reed has been shipped overseas. Unsure whether she should tell him or if he'll ever come back, she lets her sister, Lindsay, raise the baby. The film ends happily with Reed returning to Coleman's arms. Well done low-budget production, thanks to the great B director Edgar G. Ulmer.

p, Henry Brash; d, Edgar G. Ulmer; w, Anne Green (based on the novel *Dark Angel* by Gina Kaus); ph, Frank F. Planer; m, Hans Sommer; ed, Jack W. Oglivie; art d, Edward C. Jewell.

Drama/Romance **(PR:A MPAA:NR)**

HER SPLENDID FOLLY*½ (1933) 60m Progressive bw

Lillian Bond *(Girl)*, Beryl Mercer *(Mother)*, Theodore von Eltz *(Wally)*, Alexander Carr *(Producer)*, J. Frank Glendon *(Director)*, Roberta Gale *(Sally)*, Lloyd Whitlock *(Actor)*, Frances Lee, Louise Beavers, William Todd, Burt Todd, Harry Todd.

Bond impersonates a film star and is convincing enough to make her way inside the Hollywood studios. Mercer is her mother who scrubs the studio's floors to be near to her daughter. This low-budget independent production is poorly photographed and only mildly entertaining.

d, William O'Connor; w, (based on the novel by Beulah Poynter); ph, James Diamond, Jules Cronjager; ed, Roy Luby.

Comedy **(PR:A MPAA:NR)**

HER STRANGE DESIRE** (1931, Brit.) 79m British International/Powers bw (GB: POTIPHAR'S WIFE).

Nora Swinburne *(Lady Diana Bromford)*, Laurence Olivier *(Straker)*, Norman McKinnel *(Lord Bromford)*, Guy Newall *(The Honorable Maurice Worthington)*, Donald Calthrop *(Counsel For Defense)*, Ronald Frankau *(Major Tony Barlow)*, Betty Schuster *(Rosita Worthington)*, Marjorie Brooks *(Sylvia Barlow)*, Walter Armitage *(Geoffrey Hayes)*, Henry Wenman *(Stevens)*, Elsa Lanchester *(Therese)*, Matthew Boulton.

An early screen performance from Olivier makes this otherwise standard romance a memorable entry. He takes the role of a chauffeur for the wealthy and attractive Swinburne, the lady to McKinnel's lord. She tries to seduce the respectable Olivier and when he rejects her she takes steps against him. He is tried for a trumped-up assault charge and acquitted, but not before teaching the lord a thing or two about his promiscuous wife. Elsa Lanchester appears in an unnoticed role, one year before hitting it big with husband Charles Laughton in THE PRIVATE LIFE OF HENRY VIII (1932).

p, John Maxwell; d, Maurice Elvey; w, Edgar C. Middleton (based on his play); ph, James Wilson.

Romance/Drama **(PR:A MPAA:NR)**

HER TWELVE MEN*½ (1954) 90m MGM bw

Greer Garson *(Jan Stewart)*, Robert Ryan *(Joe Hargrave)*, Barry Sullivan *(Richard Y. Oliver, Sr.)*, Richard Haydn *(Dr. Avord Barrett)*, Barbara Lawrence *(Barbara Dunning)*, James Arness *(Ralph Munsey)*, Rex Thompson *(Homer Curtis)*, Tim Considine *(Richard Y. Oliver, Jr.)*, David Stollery *(Jeff Carlin)*, Frances Bergen *(Sylvia Carlin)*, Ian Wolfe *(Roger Frane)*, Ronald MacDonald *(Bobby Lennox)*, Dale Hartleben *(Kevin Clark)*, Ivan Triesault *(Erik Haldeman)*, Stuffy Singer *(Jimmy Travers)*, Peter Votrian *(Alan Saunders)*.

Garson was near the end of her MGM days when she made this trifle. She's a teacher who oversees a class of 13 boys, all of whom are determined to make her life difficult. Based on Louise Baker's story "Miss Baker's Dozen" (which means 13), the producers may have felt that "13" was an unlucky number which had no marquee value so they lowered it one to 12. It didn't help. Under prissy headmaster Haydn, she has to run the gauntlet that her boys erect. Meanwhile, she is chased by Ryan, another teacher at the school, and Sullivan, an oillionaire whose son is one of the students. Need we state that love triumphs over money (only in the movies) and she winds up with Ryan? Not much to recommend this film which seems like a half-hour sit-com that's been expanded. James Arness, before he became Matt Dillon, is the gym teacher, a huge lout with single-syllable speeches. Candy's mother, Bergen, plays one of the parents, and Lawrence has a neat turn as a wealthy vamp trying to nail Ryan. A "B" movie with an "A" cast.

p, John Houseman; d, Robert Z. Leonard; w, Laura Z. Hobson, William Roberts (based on the story "Miss Baker's Dozen" by Louise Baker); ph, Joseph Ruttenberg (Ansco Color); m, Bronislau Kaper; ed, George Boemler.

Comedy **(PR:A MPAA:NR)**

HER WEDDING NIGHT** (1930) 78m PAR bw

Clara Bow *(Norma Martin)*, Ralph Forbes *(Larry Charters)*, Charlie Ruggles *(Bertie Bird)*, Skeets Gallagher *(Bob Talmadge)*, Geneva Mitchell *(Marshall)*, Rosita Moreno *(Lulu)*, Natalie Kingston *(Eva)*, Wilson Bege *(Smithers)*, Lillian Elliott *(Mrs. Marshall)*.

A Feydeau-type bedroom farce based on an Avery Hopwood play, HER WEDDING NIGHT features the "It" girl, Clara Bow, near the end of her career before she married cowboy star Rex Bell, who went on to become lieutenant-governor of Nevada. She was only 25 when she made this, had already been in pictures since 1922, and had a number of mental problems just prior to this picture's release. Forbes is a popular songwriter (not unlike Irving Berlin) who convinces his pal, Gallagher, to masquerade as Forbes in order to get away from all of his fans. Forbes goes to the French Riviera where he mistakenly marries Bow, thinking that they are renting separate rooms at the hotel for the night. The trouble arises because neither speaks Italian and they think that the magistrate is the hotel clerk. Charlie Ruggles is Forbes' dimwitted pal and steals what there is to steal of the movie with his comic timing. The last several minutes have the usual bedroom doors opening and closing with the speed that has come to be the trademark of plays like Hopwood's. It probably worked better on the stage because it hardly worked here at all.

p, E. Lloyd Sheldon; d, Frank Tuttle; w, Henry Myers (based on the play by Avery Hopwood); ph, Harry Fischbeck; ed, Doris Drought.

Comedy **(PR:A MPAA:NR)**

HERBIE GOES BANANAS** (1980) 100m BV c

Cloris Leachman *(Aunt Louise)*, Charles Martin Smith *(D.J.)*, John Vernon *(Prindle)*, Stephan W. Burns *(Pete)*, Elyssa Davalos *(Melissa)*, Joaquin Garay III *(Paco)*, Harvey Korman *(Captain Blythe)*, Richard Jaeckel *(Shepard)*, Alex Rocco *(Quinn)*, Fritz Feld *(Chief Steward)*, Vito Scotti, Jose Gonzalez, Rubin Moreno, Tina Melard, Jorge Moreno, Allan Hunt, Tom Scott, Hector Morales, Iris Adrian, Ceil Cabot, Patricia Van Patten, Jack Perkins, Henry Slate, Ernie Fuentes, Antonio Trevino, Dante D'Andre, Alma Beltran, Dolores Aguirre, Aurora Coria, Alex Tinne, Don Diamond, Warde Donovan, Ray Victor, Bert Santos, Buddy Joe Hooker, Steve Boyum, Keney Endoso, Mario Cisneros, Jeff Ramsey, John C. Meier.

The fourth installment in the Disney Volkswagon series that started with THE LOVE BUG (1969). This time around Smith and Burns take Herbie down to South America to race in a Brazilian road race. The car with a mind of its own stops a plan by Vernon to steal the gold from an Incan city. Along the way Herbie gets into a bullfight and picks up Leachman, Korman, and Feld for comic relief. Strictly for the young ones.

p, Ron Miller; d, Vincent McEveety; w, Don Tait (based on characters created by Gordon Buford); ph, Frank Phillips (Technicolor); m, Frank De Vol; ed, Gordon D. Brenner; art d, John B. Mansbridge, Rodger Maus, Augustin Yuarte; set d, Norman Rockett, Roger M. Shook; spec eff, Art Cruickshank, Danny Lee.

Comedy **Cas.** **(PR:AAA MPAA:G)**

HERBIE GOES TO MONTE CARLO** (1977) 105m BV c

Dean Jones *(Jim Douglas)*, Don Knotts *(Wheely Applegate)*, Julie Sommars *(Diane Darcy)*, Jacques Marin *(Inspector Bouchet)*, Roy Kinnear *(Quincey)*, Bernard Fox *(Max)*, Eric Braeden *(Bruno Von Stickle)*, Xavier Saint Macary *(Detective Fontenoy)*, Francoise Lalande *(Mons. Ribeaux)*, Alan Caillou *(Emile)*, Laurie Main *(Duval)*, Mike Kulcsar *(Claude)*, Stanley Brock *(Taxi Driver)*, Gerard Jugnot *(Waiter)*, Johnny Haymer *(Race Official)*, Jean-Marie Proslier *(Doorman)*, Tom McCorry *(Showroom M.C.)*, Jean-Jacques Moreau *(Truck Driver)*, Yveline Briere *(Girl Friend)*, Raoul Delfosse *(Police Captain)*, Ed Marcus *(Exhibit M.C.)*, Lloyd Nelson *(Mechanic)*, Sebastian Floch *(Tourist)*, Madeleine Damien *(Old Woman)*, Alain Janey *(Man at Cafe)*, Richard Warlock, Kevin Johnston, Carey Loftkin, Bill Erickson, Gerald Brutsche, Bob Harris, Jesse Wayne, Reg Parton *(Drivers)*.

In this film, the third in Disney's Herbie series, the famous car is joined by its original owner from THE LOVE BUG, Dean Jones. McEveety takes over the directing duties from Robert Stevenson, who directed THE LOVE BUG and HERBIE RIDES AGAIN. McEveety can't match Stevenson's sense of comic timing and handling of slapstick humor, but he still manages to make HERBIE GOES TO MONTE CARLO an entertaining children's film. Jones takes Herbie over to France for the Paris-Monte Carlo rally. Herbie falls in love with a Lancia and stops Marin from robbing a museum of the most beautiful diamond in the world.

p, Ron Miller; d, Vincent McEveety; w, Arthur Alsberg, Don Nelson (based on characters created by Gordon Buford); ph, Leonard J. South (Technicolor); m, Frank De Vol; ed, Cotton Warburton; art d, John B. Mansbridge, Perry Ferguson; cos, Chuck Keehne, Emily Sundby; spec eff, Eustace Lycett, Art Cruickshank, Danny Lee.

Comedy **Cas.** **(PR:AAA MPAA:G)**

HERBIE RIDES AGAIN*½** (1974) 88m BV c

Helen Hayes *(Mrs. Steinmetz)*, Ken Berry *(Willoughby Whitfield)*, Stefanie Powers *(Nicole)*, John McIntire *(Mr. Judson)*, Keenan Wynn *(Alonzo Hawk)*, Huntz Hall *(Judge)*, Ivor Barry *(Chauffeur)*, Dan Tobin *(Lawyer)*, Vito Scotti *(Taxi Driver)*, Raymond Bailey *(Lawyer)*, Liam Dunn *(Doctor)*, Elaine Devry *(Secretary)*, Chuck McCann *(Loostgarten)*, Richard X. Slattery *(Traffic Commissioner)*, Hank Jones *(Sir Lancelot)*, Rod McCary *(Red Knight)*.

This sequel to THE LOVE BUG was one of Disney's most successful films of the 1970s. Herbie comes to the rescue of Hayes and Powers who are fighting against McIntire and Wynn's plan to build a skyscraper where their house stands. Berry is Wynn's nephew-lawyer, who also joins with the Volkswagen to stop the building. Herbie enlists the help of all the VWs in San Francisco and they arrive like the cavalry to fight off the imposing bulldozers. The Germans started a Herbie ripoff in 1971 with EIN KAEFER GEHT AUFS GANZE (their VW was called Dudu).

p, Bill Walsh; d, Robert Stevenson; w, Walsh (based on a story by Gordon Buford); ph, Frank Phillips (Technicolor); m, George Burns; ed, Cotton Warburton; art d, John B. Mansbridge, Walter Tyler; set d, Hal Gausman; cos, Chuck Keehne, Emily Sundby; spec eff, Art Cruickshank, Alan Maley, Eustace Lycett, Danny Lee.

Comedy **Cas.** **(PR:AAA MPAA:G)**

HERCULE CONTRE MOLOCH (SEE: CONQUEST OF MYCENE, 1963, FR./ITAL.)

HERCULES** (1959, Ital.) O.S.C.A.R.-Galatea/EM-WB 107m bw (LA TATICHE DE ERCOLE)

Steve Reeves *(Hercules)*, Sylva Koscina *(Iole)*, Fabrizio Mioni *(Jason)*, Ivo Garrani *(Pelias)*, Arturo Dominici *(Eurysteus)*, Mimmo Palmara *(Iphitus)*, Lidia Alfonsi *(The Sybil)*, Gina Rovere *(Amazon)*, Gabriele Antonini *(Ulysses)*, Andrea Fantasia *(Laertes)*, Afro Poli *(Chiron)*, Aldo Fiorelli *(Argos)*, Gino Nattera *(Orpheus)*, G.P. Rosmino *(Esculapius)*, Gianna Maria Canale *(Antea)*.

Thanks mainly to American distributor Joseph E. Levine, HERCULES began an avalanche of Italian costume spectaculars with scantily clothed women and armies of musclemen. With HERCULES Levine created saturation booking—distributing the film in as many theaters in the country as possible, with huge TV, radio, and newspaper ad-campaigns. Levine's strategy found a gold mine at the box office and caused an influx of muscleman films and costume dramas from foreign countries. Reeves, a former Mr. Universe from Montana, played the strong man from mythology in this retelling of "Jason and the Golden Fleece." Although it is heavy on sex and violence, HERCULES is lean on aesthetic qualities. Two stars, only because of the film's impact on the motion picture industry.

p, Federico Teti; d, Pietro Francisci; w, Francisci, Ennio De Concini, Gaio Frattini (based on a story by Francisci); ph, Mario Bava (Dyaliscope, Eastmancolor); m, Enzo Masetti; ed, Mario Serandrei; cos, Guilio Coltellacci.

Action/Adventure **Cas.** **(PR:C-O MPAA:NR)**

HERCULES zero (1983) 98m MGM-UA-Cannon c

Lou Ferrigno *(Hercules)*, Mirella D'Angelo *(Circe)*, Sybil Danning *(Arianna)*, Ingrid Anderson *(Cassiopea)*, William Berger *(King Minos)*, Brad Harris *(King Augeius)*, Claudio Cassinelli *(Zeus)*, Rossana Podesta *(Hera)*, Delia Boccardo *(Athena)*, Yehuda Efroni *(Dorcon)*, Gianni Garko *(Valcheus)*, Bobby Rhodes *(King Xenodan)*, Franco Garofolo *(Thief)*, Stellio Candelli *(Tegeus)*, Gabriella Giorgielli *(Chio)*, Allessandro Ardenti *(Young Hercules)*, Raffaele Baldassare *(Sostratus)*, Sergio Bruzzichinini *(Melite)*, Eva Robbins *(Daedalus)*.

When they made this film producers Golan and Globus were looking to cash in on the success of the Conan films, starring bodybuilder Arnold Schwarzenegger. Like Schwarzenegger and earlier Hercules Steve Reeves, Ferrigno's muscles bulge plenty. Coming off the successful TV show "The Incredible Hulk," Ferrigno was the perfect choice for Hercules, but a lame story line and poor special effects deflate the action, most of which takes place on the moon, with Zeus, Hera, and Athena causing problems for the mortals. Ferrigno must save Princess Cassiopea from her kidnapers, so he flies through space and fights mechanical dragons that spit out laser bolts. A strange blend of STAR WARS technology and sword and sorcery that doesn't work at all. Ferrigno's lines were dubbed by another actor.

p, Menahem Golan, Yoram Globus; d&w, Lewis Coates [Luigi Cozzi]; ph, Alberto Spagnoli (Technicolor); m, Pino Donaggio; ed, Sergio Montanari; prod d&art d, Antonello Geleng; cos, Adriana Spadaro; spec eff, Armando Valcauda, Fabio Traversari, Gerard Olivier, Herman Nathan, Jerry Unger, Phil Travers.

Action/Adventure Cas. (PR:A MPAA:PG)

HERCULES AGAINST THE MOON MEN*½ (1965, Fr./Ital.) 90m Nike Cinematografica-Comptoir Francais/Governor c (MACISTE E LA REGINA DI SAMAR; MACISTE CONTRE LES HOMMES DE PIERRE; MACISTE CONTRO GLI UOMINI DELLA LUNA)

Alan Steel [Sergio Ciani] *(Hercules)*, Jany Clair *(Agar)*, Anna Maria Polani *(Selena)*, Nando Tamberlani, Delia D'Alberti, Jean-Pierre Honore, Goffredo Unger.

Steel, who plays Hercules (actually Maciste in Italy), manages to flex all his muscles as he battles moon men attempting to raise their queen from the dead by sacrificing human victims. Throw in a metal-headed giant and a few monsters and you're in for about 90 minutes of mindless entertainment. For fans of this mindless stuff only.

p, Luigi Mondello; d, Giacomo Gentilomo; w, Arpad De Riso, Nino Scolaro (based on a story by De Riso, Scolaro, Gentilomo, Angelo Sangermano); ph, Oberdan Trojani (Cromoscope, Eastmancolor); m, Carlo Franci; art d, Amedeo Mellone; spec eff, Ugo Amadoro.

Fantasy (PR:A MPAA:NR)

HERCULES AGAINST THE SONS OF THE SUN* (1964, Span./Ital.) 91m Screen Gems c (ERCOLE CONTRO I FIGLI DEL SOLE)

Mark Forest *(Hercules)*, Anna Maria Pace, Angela Rhu, Giuliano Gemma, Ricardo Valle, Giulio Donnini, Andrea Scotti.

Forest, as the famed, brawny superhero, helps defeat the contemptible King of the Incas by building unstoppable fighting machines. If you've seen just a couple of minutes of any imported muscleman movie, you should know what to expect with this one.

p,d&w, Osvaldo Civirani.

Adventure (PR:A MPAA:NR)

HERCULES AND THE CAPTIVE WOMEN* (1963, Fr./Ital.) 93m SPA-Comptoir Francais du Film/Woolner Bros. c (ERCOLE ALLA CONQUISTA DI ATLANTIDE; HERCULE A LA CONQUETE DE L'ATLANTIDE; AKA: HERCULES AND THE CONQUEST OF ATLANTIS; HERCULES AND THE HAUNTED WOMEN)

Reg Park *(Hercules)*, Fay Spain *(Antinea)*, Ettore Manni *(Androcles)*, Luciano Marin *(Illus)*, Laura Altan, Mario Petri, Mimmo Palmara, Ivo Garrani, Mario Valdemarin, Enrico Maria Salerno, Salvatore Furnari, Maurizio Caffarelli, Gian Maria Volonte, Luciana Angiolillo, Nicola Sperli, Mino Doro, Allesandro Sperli.

Muscle-bound, dimwit Hercules (Park) goes to Atlantis to rescue his son from the evil clutches of the sadistic Spain who has the power to control all men. Once in Atlantis, Park must overcome several obstacles (yawn) including a small army of identical men and a bizarre looking dragon. Eventually Park gets back his kid and sinks the island (so that's what happened to Atlantis!).

p, Achille Piazzi; d, Vittorio Cottafavi; w, Alessandro Continenza, Vittorio Cottafavi, Duccio Tessari (based on a story by Archibald Zounds Jr.); ph, Carlo Carlini (SuperTechnirama, Technicolor); m, Gino Marinuzzi, Armando Trovajoli (additional music for U.S. version, Gordon Zahler); ed, Maurizio Lucidi (U.S. version, Hugo Grimaldi); art d, Franco Lolli; cos, Vittorio Rossi; ch, Peter Van Der Sloot.

Adventure (PR:A MPAA:NR)

HERCULES IN NEW YORK* (1970) 90m RAF-United c (AKA: HERCULES: THE MOVIE)

Arnold Stang *(Pretzie)*, Arnold Strong [Arnold Schwarzenegger] *(Hercules)*, Deborah Loomis *(Helen)*, James Karen *(The Professor)*, Ernest Graves *(Zeus)*, Tanny McDonald *(Juno)*, Tania Elg *(Nemesis)*, Michael Lipton *(Pluto)*, Howard Blustein *(Rod)*, Merwin Goldsmith *(Maxie)*, George Bartenieff *(Nitro)*, Erica Fitz *(Venus)*, Diane Goble *(Diana)*, Dan Hamilton *(Mercury)*, Tony Carroll *(Monstro)*, Mark Tendler *(Samson)*, Dennis Tinerino *(Atlas)*.

For some reason producer Wisberg decided to revive the long dead Hercules craze, and luckily it didn't take. Schwarzenegger, billed as Arnold Strong, plays Hercules this time. He is sent to modern-day Manhattan where he flexes his muscles by capturing an escaped bear and becoming a professional wrestler (now there's an idea!) He even rides a chariot up Broadway to escape a gang of hoodlums after he is robbed of his mighty strength. This trash was rereleased 13 years later to cash in on the success of Schwarzenegger's CONAN movies.

p&w, Aubrey Wisberg; d, Arthur A. Seidelman; ph, Leo Lebowitz (Eastmancolor); m, John Balamos; ed, Donald P. Finamore.

Adventure (PR:A MPAA:G)

HERCULES IN THE HAUNTED WORLD** (1964, Ital.) 91m SPA Cinematografica/Woolner Bros. c (ERCOLE AL CENTRO DELLA TERRA)

Reg Park *(Hercules)*, Leonora Ruffo *(Deianira)*, Christopher Lee *(Lichas)*, Giorgio Ardisson *(Theseus)*, Franco Giacobini *(Telemachus)*, Marisa Belli, Ely Draco, Mino Doro, Monica Neri, Ida Galli.

Okay fans, this one's about as good as they get. Park as Herc goes to Hell (that's right gang . . . Hell!) to obtain a special plant to cure a dying princess. There he encounters Lee as the evil servant of Pluto, naked maidens in chains (hoo boy!), lots of lava, and more rock men (they look like the moon men in HERCULES AGAINST THE MOON MEN). Eventually our heroic muscleman kills everybody and returns to the surface to marry the princess. Directed with some flair by Bava.

p, Achille Piazzi; d, Mario Bava; w, Alessandro Continenza, Bava, Duccio Tessari, Franco Prosperi; ph, Bava (Totalscope Super/100, Technicolor); m, Armando Trovajoli; ed, Mario Serandrei; art d, Franco Lolli; cos, Mario Giorsi.

Adventure (PR:C MPAA:NR)

HERCULES' PILLS*** (1960, Ital.) 105m Maxima/DD c (LE PILLOLE DE ERCOLE)

Nino Manfredi *(Nino)*, Sylva Koscina *(Silvia)*, Vittorio De Sica *(Col. Cuocolo)*, Jeanne Valerie *(Odette)*.

A light sex comedy that has nothing in common with the standard Hercules films. Unknowing residents of a resort hotel take a Chinese pill that works like an aphrodisiac. This develops most of the situations and humor of the film, which at times is very funny.

d, Luciano Salce; w, Salce, Maccari, Scola, Baratti (based on a play by Maurice Hennequin, Paul Bihaudo); ph, Enrico Menczer; m, Armando Trovajoli; ed, Roberto Cinquini.

Comedy (PR:C MPAA:NR)

HERCULES, SAMSON & ULYSSES* (1964, Ital.) 85m ICD/MGM c (ERCOLE, SFIDA E SANSONE)

Kirk Morris *(Hercules)*, Richard Lloyd *(Samson)*, Liana Orfei *(Delilah)*, Enzo Cerusico *(Ulysses)*, Aldo Giuffre *(Seren)*, Fulvia Franco, Diletta D'Andrea, Nando Angelini, Franco Fantasia, Marco Mariani, Pietro Tordi, Ugo Sasso, Alina Zalewska, Aldo Pini, Fortunato Arena, Willy Colombini, Fulvio Carrara, Stefania Sabatini, Rina Mascetti, Jole Mauro, Mario De Simone, Ettore Zamperini, Marco Wassilli, Gianni Di Benedetto, Cinzia Bruno, Loris Loddi, Walter Grant, Antonio Corevi, Vladimiro Tuilovich, Cyrus Elias.

Three musclemen for the price of one! Morris, Lloyd and Cerusico star as the title baboons, who are thrown together on an island after Morris and Cerusico are shipwrecked while battling a sea monster. On shore, Morris is mistaken for Lloyd when he kills a lion with his bare hands and soon he is made to prove his identity by battling the real Lloyd in a bloody contest. After much grunting and groaning, the match is a draw and the big guys join forces against the sadistic king and his cohorts.

p, Joseph Fryd; d&w, Pietro Francisci; ph, Silvano Ippoliti (Eastmancolor); m, Angelo Francesco Lavagnino; ed, Francisci; art d, Giorgio Giovannini; set d, Franco Loquenzi; cos, Gaia Romanini; ch, Wilbert Bradley.

Adventure (PR:A MPAA:NR)

HERCULES UNCHAINED* (1960, Ital./Fr.) 101m Lux-Galatea-Lux de France/WB-EMC c (ERCOLE E LA REGINA DE LIDIA)

Steve Reeves *(Hercules)*, Sylva Koscina *(Jole)*, Primo Carnera *(Antaeus)*, Sylvia Lopez *(Omphale, Queen of Lydia)*, Carlo D'Angelo *(Creon)*, Patrizia Della Rovere *(Penelope)*, Gabriele Antonini *(Ulysses)*, Sergio Fantoni *(Eteocles)*, Mimmo Palmara *(Polinices)*, Cesare Fantoni *(Oedipus)*, Andrea Fantasia *(Laertes)*.

They should have left him bound and gagged. Reeves returns to the screen in this sequel to the inexplicably successful HERCULES. We see him battle tigers, a giant (ex-boxer Primo Carnera), and evil queen Koscina, who kills and stuffs her lovers (a high price to pay for a little passion!). Reeves is as dull as usual, but from here he would go on to play other mythical heroes. They found 20 other hulks to play Hercules over the next 10 insufferable years.

p, Bruno Vailati; d, Pietro Francisci; w, Ennio De Concini, Francisci (based on a story by Francisci adapted from the legends of Hercules and Omphale); ph, Mario Bava (Dyaliscope, Eastmancolor); m, Enzo Masetti; m/l, "Evening Star," Mitchell Parrish (sung by June Valli).

Adventure Cas. (PR:A MPAA:NR)

HERCULES VS. THE GIANT WARRIORS* (1965 Fr./Ital.) 94m Produzione Cinematografica-Films Jacques Leitienne-Unicite/ John Alexander Film Associates c (IL TRIONFO DI ERCOLE)

Dan Vadis *(Hercules)*, Moria Orfei *(Pasiphae)*, Pierre Cressoy *(Prince Myles)*, Marilu Tolo *(Ate)*, Piero Lulli *(Gordius)*, Enzo Fiermonte *(Eurystheus)*, Renato Rossini *(Hereus)*.

Dull Hercules outing starring the even duller Vadis as the title hero who must do battle against an evil sorceress, Orfei, and 10 bronze giants without his powers, which were taken away by Zeus (they had a spat). Eventually Zeus gives in and Vadis wipes out the baddies.

p, Alberto Chimens; d, Alberto De Martino; w, Roberto Gianviti, Alessandro Ferrau; ph, Pierludovico Pavoni (Eastmancolor); m, Francesco De Masi; ed, Otello Colangeli.

Adventure **(PR:A MPAA:NR)**

HERE COME THE CO-EDS*½** (1945) 88m UNIV bw

Bud Abbott *(Slats)*, Lou Costello *(Oliver Quackenbush)*, Peggy Ryan *(Patty)*, Martha O'Driscoll *(Molly)*, June Vincent *(Diane)*, Lon Chaney, Jr. *(Johnson)*, Donald Cook *(Benson)*, Charles Dingle *(Jonathan Kirkland)*, Richard Lane *(Nearsighted Man)*, Joe Kirk *(Honest Dan)*, Phil Spitalny and His Band, Bill Stern *(Announcer)*, Anthony Warde *(Timekeeper)*, Dorothy Ford *(Bertha)*, Sammy Stein *(Tiger McGurk)*, Carl Knowles *(Basketball Coach)*, Martha Garotto, Naomi Stout, June Cuendet, Muriel Stetson, Marilyn Hoeck, Margaret Eversole, Lorna Peterson *(Amazon Basketball Players)*, Ruth Lee *(Miss Holford)*, Don Costello *(Diamond)*, Rebel Randall *(Woman)*, Maxine Gates *(Woman)*, Dorothy Granger *(Woman)*, Marie Osborn *(Woman in Trailer)*, Milt Bronson *(Ring Announcer)*.

An above-average Abbott and Costello vehicle with the two as caretakers of an all-girls college which is in deep financial trouble, and the comedians help keep it open. Chaney wants the school to close for his own personal gain, and to raise money for the school Bud gets in the wrestling ring with the "Masked Marvel" (Chaney), the funniest bit of the film. The school holds a concert and then a basketball game against an Amazon team to pay off the mortgage. There are a great many hilarious bits in this consistently funny film. At one point Chaney physically spins Lou, who has swallowed some dice, to shoot craps, while using an X-ray machine to determine the throw. There is the silent classic bit (originally developed by Billy Bevan) where Lou is served a bowl of oyster stew with a live oyster in it which squirts his face, bites his fingers, and devours the comedian's necktie when he tries to catch it, yanking Lou's face into the bowl. (This routine appeared three years earlier in a Three Stooges short, "Dutiful But Dumb," with Curly Howard as the victim, and a variation of the gag was employed in THE WISTFUL WIDOW OF WAGON GAP.) Along with the laughs were Ryan's tap-dancing and Phil Spitalny and His All-Girl Orchestra. Songs included, "Hooray For Our Side," "I Don't Care If I Never Dream Again," "Jumping On Saturday Night," "Someday We Will Remember," "Let's Play House" (Edgar Fairchild, Jack Brooks). (See ABBOTT & COSTELLO series, Index.)

p, John Grant; d, Jean Yarbrough; w, Arthur T. Horman, Grant (based on a story by Edmund L. Hartmann); ph, George Robinson; ed, Arthur Hilton; md, Edgar Fairchild; art d, John B. Goodman, Richard H. Riedel; spec eff, John P. Fulton.

Musical/Comedy **(PR:AAA MPAA:NR)**

HERE COME THE GIRLS** (1953) 77m PAR c

Bob Hope *(Stanley Snodgrass)*, Tony Martin *(Allen Trent)*, Arlene Dahl *(Irene Bailey)*, Rosemary Clooney *(Daisy Crockett)*, Millard Mitchell *(Albert Snodgrass)*, William Demarest *(Dennis Logan)*, Fred Clark *(Harry Fraser)*, Robert Strauss *(Jack the Slasher)*, Zamah Cunningham *(Mrs. Snodgrass)*, Frank Orth *(Mr. Hungerford)*, Johnny Downs *(Bob)*, Virginia Lieth, Sheree North, Phyllis Coates *(Chorus Girls)*, Dale Van Sickel *(Policeman)*, Louis Hall *(Belle)*, Nancy Kulp *(Washwoman)*, Alfred T. Williams, Maceo Edward Anderson, Prince C. Spencer, Rufus L. McDonald *(The Four Stepbrothers)*, Hugh Sanders, Inesita, Pepito Perez, Vivian Mason, Alex Jackson, Russ Saunders, Everett Coreill, Loren B. Brown.

Hope is a stage singer fired by producer Clark for incompetence, then rehired when the show's lead, Martin, is stalked by "Jack the Slasher" Strauss. Strauss wants Martin's leading lady, Dahl. The killer chases after Hope, ruining the show. A thinly written comedy that even Hope's talents can't help. Songs and musical numbers: "Girls Are Here to Stay," "Never So Beautiful," "You Got Class," "Desire," "When You Love Someone," "Ali Baba Be My Baby," "Heavenly Days," "See the Circus," "Peace" (Jay Livingston, Ray Evans).

p, Paul Jones; d, Claude Binyon; w, Edmund Hartmann, Hal Kanter (based on a story by Hartmann); ph, Lionel Lindon (Technicolor); m, Lyn Murry; ed, Arthur Schmidt; art d, Hal Pereira, Roland Anderson, ch, Nick Castle.

Musical/Comedy **(PR:A MPAA:NR)**

HERE COME THE HUGGETTS* (1948, Brit.) 93m Gainsborough-Rank/GFD bw

Jack Warner *(Joe Huggett)*, Kathleen Harrison *(Ethel Huggett)*, Jane Hylton *(Jane Huggett)*, Susan Shaw *(Susan Huggett)*, Petula Clark *(Pat Huggett)*, Jimmy Hanley *(Jimmy)*, David Tomlinson *(Harold Hinchley)*, Diana Dors *(Diana Hopkins)*, Peter Hammond *(Peter Hawtrey)*, John Blythe *(Gowan)*, Amy Veness *(Grandma)*, Clive Morton *(Mr. Campbell)*, Maurice Denham *(Mechanic)*.

The first of a British family film series falls way below par. The film revolves around the adventures of the Huggett family, which are boring. The main problem is in the scripting. There is no plot and the dialog is silly and contrived.

p, Betty Box; d, Ken Annakin; w, Mabel and Denis Constanduros, Peter Rogers, Muriel and Sydney Box (based on characters created by Godfrey Winn); ph, Reg Wyer; ed, Gordon Hales.

Comedy **(PR:A MPAA:NR)**

HERE COME THE JETS½** (1959) 72m FOX bw

Steve Brodie *(Logan)*, Lyn Thomas *(Joyce)*, Mark Dana *(Wallack)*, John Doucette *(Randall)*, Jean Carson *(Jean)*, Carleton Young *(Burton)*, Joseph Turkel *(Henley)*, Gloria Moreland *(B-Girl)*, Vikki Dougan *(Blonde)*, I. Stanford Jolley *(Bartender)*, B.B. Hughes *(Stripper)*, W. Maslow *(Joe)*, Tiger Marsh *(Turnkey)*, C. Young.

An entertaining B movie about the production and testing of jet planes. Brodie is an alcoholic Korean War hero given a second chance by aircraft executive Doucette. He believes Brodie is the best man to test a new jet airliner once he's on the wagon. After a couple of setbacks, one being Brodie cracking mentally during a flight simulation, Doucette gets his test pilot in shape to fly his creation.

p, Richard Enfeld; d, Gene Fowler, Jr.; w, Lou Vittes; ph, Karl Struss (CinemaScope); m, Paul Dunlap; ed, Harry Gerstad; art d, Lyle R. Wheeler, John Mansbridge.

Drama **(PR:A MPAA:NR)**

HERE COME THE MARINES** (1952) 66m MON bw (GB: TELL IT TO THE MARINES)

Leo Gorcey *(Slip)*, Huntz Hall *(Sach)*, David Gorcey *(Chuck)*, Bennie Bartlett *(Butch)*, Gil Stratton *(Junior)*, Bernard Gorcey *(Louie)*, Murray Alper *(Cpl. Stacy)*, Hanley Stafford *(Col. Brown)*, Arthur Space *(Capt. Miller)*, Myrna Dell *(Lulu Mae)*, Paul Maxey *(Jolly Joe Johnson)*, Tim Ryan *(Sheriff Benson)*, William Newell *(Desmond)*, Sammy Finn *(Croupier)*, Buck Russel *(Dealer)*.

The Marines were looking for a few good men but they got stuck with the Bowery Boys. Pugnacious Gorcey and cohorts join the Marines by mistake and are hounded by their drill sergeant. Somehow Gorcey becomes a sergeant and the boys break up a gambling ring. The Bowery Boys with their long-running series seem to be running out of gas in this one. (See BOWERY BOYS series, Index.)

p, Jerry Thomas; d, William Beaudine; w, Tim Ryan, Charles R. Marion, Jack Crutcher; ph, Marcel LePicard; m, Edward Kay; ed, William Austin; art d, Martin Obzina.

Comedy/Mystery **(PR:A MPAA:NR)**

HERE COME THE NELSONS½** (1952) 75m UNIV bw (AKA: MEET THE NELSONS)

Ozzie Nelson *(Ozzie)*, Harriet Nelson *(Harriet)*, Ricky Nelson *(Ricky)*, David Nelson *(David)*, Rock Hudson *(Charles Jones)*, Barbara Lawrence *(Barbara)*, Sheldon Leonard *(Duke)*, Jim Backus *(Joe Randolph)*, Paul Harvey *(S.T. Jones)*, Gale Gordon *(H.J. Bellows)*, Ann Doran *(Clara Randolph)*, Chubby Johnson *(Tex)*, Lillian Bronson *(Miss Tompkins)*, Ed Max *(Monk)*, Paul Brinegar *(Thin Cop)*, Maynard Holmes *(Fat Deputy)*, Frank Nelson *(Hastings)*, Arthur Q. Bryan *(Deputy)*, Ed Clark *(Herb)*, William Haade *(Bully)*, Harry Cheshire *(Announcer)*, Milton Kibbee *(Committeeman)*, Lorin Raker *(Man)*, Harold Goodwin, Stuart Wilson *(Men)*, Irwin Jay Berniker, Edna Smith, Forrest Burns.

Ozzie, Harriet and sons bring their 1940s radio and later their TV domestic comedy to the screen with mild success. Ozzie is trying to develop an advertising campaign for a women's garment client with the town's centennial right around the corner. Harriet invites Hudson to stay at their house for the celebration, and Ozzie does the same with Lawrence. This causes a series of misunderstandings with Ozzie out to prove he's still a young man by signing up for the bronco-riding contest in the centennial's rodeo. He backs out at the last minute, but proves himself by capturing the robbers of the rodeo's bank. The bad guys have also taken little Ricky, and Ozzie chases them across mountain roads. He stops them by stringing some of his client's garments across one road and not only gets the robbers but inadvertently gets a winning ad campaign.

p, Aaron Rosenberg; d, Frederick de Cordova; w, Ozzie Nelson, Donald Nelson, William Davenport (based on the radio show "The Adventures of Ozzie and Harriet"); ph, Irving Glassberg; m, Joseph Gershenson; ed, Frank Gross; art d, Bernard Herzbrun, Hilyard Brown.

Comedy **(PR:A MPAA:NR)**

HERE COME THE TIGERS* (1978) 90m AIP c (AKA: MANNY'S ORPHANS)

Richard Lincoln *(Eddie Burke)*, James Zvanut *(Burt Honneger)*, Samantha Grey *(Bette Burke)*, Manny Lieberman *(Felix the Umpire)*, William Caldwell *(Kreeger)*, Fred Lincoln *(Aesop)*, Xavier Rodrigo *(Buster Rivers)*, Kathey Bell *(Patty O'Malley)*, Noel John Cunningham *(Noel Cady)*, Sean P. Griffin *(Art Bullfinch)*, Max McClellan *(Mike "The Bod" Karpel)*, Kevin Moore *("Eaglescout" Terwilliger)*, Lance Norwood *(Ralphy)*, Ted Oyama *(Umeki)*, Michael Pastore *(Fingers)*, Phillip Scuderi *(Danny)*, David Schmalholz *(Bionic Mouth)*, Nancy Willis *(Sharyn)*, Andy Weeks *(Scoop)*, Todd Weeks *(Timmy)*.

A cheap imitation of Michael Ritchie's THE BAD NEWS BEARS trying to cash in on its success. A losing Little League baseball team with a racial mixture wins the championship. Not only a dull movie but a poor imitation, somewhat relieved by passable photography.

p, Sean S. Cunningham, Stephen Miner; d, Cunningham; w, Arch McCoy; ph, Barry Abrams (Movielab Color); m, Harry Manfredini; ed, Miner, art d, Susan E. Cunningham.

Comedy **(PR:C MPAA:PG)**

HERE COME THE WAVES*½** (1944) 99m PAR bw

Bing Crosby *(Johnny Cabot)*, Betty Hutton *(Susan/Rosemary Allison)*, Sonny Tufts *(Windy)*, Ann Doran *(Ruth)*, Gwen Crawford *(Tex)*, Noel Neill *(Dorothy)*, Catherine Craig *(Lieutenant Townsend)*, Marjorie Henshaw *(Isabel)*, Harry Barris *(Bandleader)*, Mae Clarke *(Ensign Kirk)*, Minor Watson *(High Ranking Officer)*, Dorothy Jarnac, Joel Friend, Roberta Jonay, Guy Zanett *(Specialty Dancers)*, Oscar O'Shea *(The Commodore)*, Don Kramer, Eddie Kover, Ruth Miles *(Miles & Kover Trio)*, Mona Freeman *(1st Fainting Girl)*, Carlotta Jelm *(2nd Fainting Girl)*, Jack Norton *(Waiter)*, Jimmy Dundee *(Chief Petty Officer)*, Lillian Bronson *(Cabot Fan)*, Jean Willes *(Girl)*, Alex Havier *(Waiter)*, James Flavin *(Shore Patrolman)*, Weldon Heyburn *(1st Civilian)*, Kit Guard *(Yellow Cab Driver)*, Kay Linaker *(1st Pretty Girl)*, Terry Adams *(2nd Pretty Girl)*, Babe London *(Girl Window Washer)*, Greta Granstedt *(Wave Control Tower Operator)*, Yvonne DeCarlo *(Girl)*, George Turner *(Recruit)*, William Haade *(C.P.O.)*, William Forrest *(Lieutenant Commander)*, Cyril Ring *(Lieutenant Colonel)*, Charles D. Brown *(Capt. Johnson)*.

Bright and breezy war time musical with lots of fun. Crosby is a singing idol whose best friend is Tufts. They meet Hutton, playing two roles as twins, and one of the duo likes der Bingle while the other can't stand him. Only trouble is, Crosby can't tell them apart. He joins the Navy and wants to serve with Tufts aboard a destroyer. Hutton (both) joins as well and Hutton (Susie) gets Crosby assigned to do shows for the sailors. Crosby wants to get into the war, not direct Wave benefits, but he relents when he realizes that he's falling in love with Hutton (Rosemary). Tufts gets jealous and tells Hutton (Rosemary) that Crosby arranged to get the cushy assignment in order to escape the dangers of the war. Hutton (Rosemary) tells Crosby that she never wants to see him again and leaves the ol' groaner scratching his head. Now Crosby learns that Hutton (Susie) made the request for his transfer so he defies orders and boards a ship. Hutton (Susie) tells Hutton (Rosemary) what she did, then races to Crosby to attempt to stop him. But Crosby is adamant about his decision and plans to go on active duty. He puts on a beard and dark glasses to escape his many fans but the minute he steps into the street, Hutton (Susie) blows the whistle and he is soon mobbed by his admirers and can't board the destroyer. On their way back to the base, Crosby learns that Hutton (Rosemary) now knows it was Hutton (Susie) who arranged his transfer and that she forgives him. Tufts and Hutton (Susie) now also find themselves in love and the picture ends with Tufts and Crosby waving ta-ta to Hutton (twice) as they go off to win the war. Lots of satire in the movie including Crosby taking a shot at Frank Sinatra by singing one of the crooner's biggest hits, "That Old Black Magic," in front of a horde of fainting bobby-soxers. Basically a spoof of what people must think an idol's life is like, HERE COME THE WAVES is a cut above many of the genre musicals as it employs Crosby well and features a number of excellent songs including "Accentuate The Positive" (nominated for an Oscar but losing to "Swinging On A Star," from GOING MY WAY, another Crosby vehicle), "I Promise You," "There's A Fellow Waiting In Poughkeepsie," "Let's Take The Long Way Home," "Here Come the Waves," "My Mama Thinks I'm a Star," and "Join the Navy." Yvonne De Carlo and Mona Freeman are seen in tiny bits and Crosby's long-term friend (and co-singer in the old "Rhythm Boys" group) Harry Barris, is seen as the band leader. Vera Marshe was Hutton's double.

p&d, Mark Sandrich; w, Allen Scott, Ken Englund, Zion Myers; ph, Charles Lang; m, Robert Emmett Dolan; ed, Ellsworth Hoagland; art d, Hans Dreier, Roland Anderson; set d, Ray Moyer; spec eff, Gordon Jennings, Paul Lerpae; m/l, Harold Arlen, Johnny Mercer.

Musical/Comedy **(PR:A MPAA:NR)**

HERE COMES CARTER** (1936) 60m FN/WB bw

Ross Alexander *(Kent Carter)*, Glenda Farrell *(Verna Kennedy)*, Anne Nagel *(Linda Warren)*, Craig Reynolds *(Rex Marchbanks)*, George E. Stone *(Boots)*, Hobart Cavanaugh *(Mel Winter)*, John Sheehan *(Slugs Dana)*, Joseph Crehan *(Daniel Bronson)*, Dennis Moore *(Russ McAllen)*, Norman Willis *(Steve Moran)*, John T. Murray *(Ben Rogers)*, Charles Foy, Ed Chandler, Davison Clarke, Wayne Morris, Effie Afton.

Breezy Alexander becomes a radio columnist in Hollywood after being fired from his press agent job. He vents his anger over the airwaves, raking up mud about the actor who got him fired. He tells his listeners that Reynolds' brother is a gangster, and this causes the star's black-balling. Nagel comes along and threatens to leave Alexander if he doesn't tone down his act. He does, and that's the show, folks! Quite nice in some spots, but there are not enough of them.

d, William Clemens; w, Ray Chanslor (based on the story "The Lowdown" by M. Jacoby); ph, Arthur Todd; ed, Louis Hesse; m/l, "You On My Mind," "Through the Courtesy of Love," M.K. Jerome, Jack Scholl.

Drama **(PR:A MPAA:NR)**

HERE COMES COOKIE*** (1935) 65m PAR bw

George Burns *(Himself)*, Gracie Allen *(Herself)*, George Barbier *(Harrison Allen)*, Betty Furness *(Phyllis Allen)*, Andrew Tombes *(Botts)*, Rafael Storm *(Ramon del Ramos)*, James Burke *(Broken-Nose Reilly)*, Lee Kohlmar *(Mr. Dingledorp)*, Mills Davenport *(Mrs. Dingledorp)*, Harry Holman *(Stuffy)*, Frank Darien *(Clyde)*, Jack Powell *(Drummer)*, Irving Bacon *(Thompson)*.

Fast-moving Burns and Allen farce that offers rapid-fire jokes and a host of vaudeville acts ranging from trained seals to acrobats to smart dogs. Gracie is the wealthy daughter of Barbier who temporarily turns over his money to Gracie so as to discourage a gigolo who has eyes for his other daughter, Furness. That's his first and last mistake as Allen turns the Park Avenue mansion into a boarding house (at no charge) for various down-at-the-heels show business types. As Burns hands her straight lines on a silver platter, Allen delivers the punches with her customary technique and the picture ends with a show at the mansion that gives everyone a chance to do their thing. There is hardly any time for plot with the likes of specialty acts like Jack Powell, Cal Norris and Monkey, The Buccaneers, Moro and Yaconelli, Pascale Perry and Partner, The Six Candreva Brothers, Seymour and Corncob, Jester and Mole, Jack Cavanaugh and Partner, Six Olympics and Big Boy Williams (not Guinn "Big Boy" Williams, the character actor). A couple of forgettable tunes including "Vamp Of The Pampas" and "Lazy Moon." Furness went on to a TV career and became a consumer advocate.

p, William Le Baron; d, Norman Z. McLeod; w, Sam Mintz, Don Hartman; ph, Gilbert Warrenton; m/l, Richard Whiting, Leo Robin, Bob Cole, A. Rosamond Johnson.

Comedy **(PR:A MPAA:NR)**

HERE COMES ELMER**½ (1943) 74m REP bw

Al Pearce *(Elmer Blurt/Al Pearce)*, Dale Evans *(Jean Foster)*, Frank Albertson *(Joe Maxwell)*, Gloria Stuart *(Glenda Forbes)*, Wally Vernon *(Himself)*, Nick Cochrane *(Himself)*, Will Wright *(Horace Parrot)*, Thurston Hall *(P.J. Ellis)*, Ben Welden *(Louis Burch)*, Chester Clute *(Postelwaite)*, Luis Alberni *(Dr. Zichy)*, Tom Kennedy *(Johnson)*, Artie Auerbach *("Kitzel")*, William Comstock, "Pinky" Tomlin, Wendell Niles, Arlene Harris, The Sportsmen, The King Cole Trio, Jan Garber and His Band.

Radio star Pearce plays a dual role as himself and a door-to-door salesman. Pearce and friends have a radio show sponsored by Harris' father, and when Pearce decides that Harris isn't right for the show her father pulls out. Searching for a sponsor, Evans finances a trip to a New York City radio station so she can sing with the band. The group lands a gig at a night club in New York which nets them a sponsor and a happy ending. Slight story but plenty of slapdash fun and laughs. Songs: "Straighten Up and Fly Right" (Nat "King" Cole, Irving Mills), "Don't Be Afraid to Tell Your Mother" (Pinky Tomlin, Coy Poe, Jimmie Greer), "You're So Good To Me" (Sammy Cahn, Jule Styne), "Hitch Old Dobbin to the Shag Again" (J.C. Lewis, Jr., Judd Conlon), "Put On Your Old Grey Bonnet" (Stanley Murphy, Percy Wenrich).

p, Armand Schaefer; d, Joseph Stanley; w, Jack Townley, Stanley Davis; ph, Bud Thackery; ed, Richard Van Enger; art d, Russell Kimball.

Musical/Comedy **(PR:A MPAA:NR)**

HERE COMES HAPPINESS** (1941) 56m WB bw

Mildred Coles *(Jessica Vance)*, Edward Norris *(Chet Madden)*, Richard Ainley *(Jelliffe Blaine)*, Russell Hicks *(John Vance)*, Marjorie Gateson *(Emily Vance)*, John Ridgely *(Jim)*, Eddie Acuff *(Bill)*, Lucia Carroll *(Peg)*, Helen Lynd *(Flo)*, Marie Blake *(Clara)*, Edward Gargan *(Joe)*, Vera Lewis *(Mrs. James)*, Joseph Crehan *(Tom Burke)*, Ann Edmonds *(Miss Harnes)*, DeWolf Hopper *(Best Man)*.

Coles is a rich girl who dumps fortune-hunting Ainley, and goes off to live in the Bronx. There she meets Norris, a sandblaster, and they fall in love. Coles' father is pleased and the two get married and live happily in their flat. Pleasant production of an old-hat tale.

p, William Jacobs; d, Noel M. Smith; w, Charles Tedford (based on the story "Gentlemen are Born" by Harry Sauber); ph, James Van Trees; ed, Harold McLernon.

Romance **(PR:A MPAA:NR)**

HERE COMES KELLY**½ (1943) 65m MON bw

Eddie Quillan *(Jimmy Kelly)*, Joan Woodbury *(Margie)*, Maxie Rosenbloom *(Trixie Bell)*, Armida *(Carmencita)*, Sidney Miller *(Sammy Cohn)*, Mary Gordon *(Mrs. Kelly)*, Ian Keith *(L. Herbert Oakley)*, Luis Alberni, Charles Jordan, Emmett Vogan.

Quillan plays a young punk who can't stay away from trouble. His girl friend, Woodbury, helps him get on the right track and he lands a job as a process server. He does a good job and becomes a hero when he serves papers to Rosenbloom. Quillan ends up getting drafted and has to postpone his marriage. Briskly told laugh-getter.

p, William T. Lackey; d, William Beaudine; w, Charles R. Marlon (based on a story by Jeb Aschery); ph, Arthur Martinelli; ed, Carl Pierson.

Comedy **(PR:A MPAA:NR)**

HERE COMES MR. JORDAN**** (1941) 93m COL bw

Robert Montgomery *(Joe Pendleton)*, Evelyn Keyes *(Bette Logan)*, Claude Rains *(Mr. Jordan)*, Rita Johnson *(Julia Farnsworth)*, Edward Everett Horton *(Messenger No. 7013)*, James Gleason *(Max Corkle)*, John Emery *(Tony Abbott)*, Donald MacBride *(Inspector Williams)*, Don Costello *(Lefty)*, Halliwell Hobbes *(Sisk)*, Benny Rubin *(Bugs)*, Bert Young *(Taxi Driver)*, Ken Christy *(Plainclothesman)*, Joseph Crehan *(Doctor)*, Billy Newell *(Handler)*, Abe Roth *(Referee)*, Tom Hanlon *(Announcer)*, Joe Hickey *(Gilbert)*, Warren Ashe *(Charlie)*, Billy Dawson *(Johnny)*, Bobby Larson *(Chips)*, John Kerns *(Sparring Partner)*, Mary Currier *(Secretary)*, William Forrest, Ed Bruce *(Reporters)*, Douglas Wood, Selmer Jackson *(Board Members)*, Joe Conti, Chester Conklin, Gerald Pierce *(Newsboys)*, John Rogers *(Escort)*, Lloyd Bridges *(Co-Pilot)*, Edmund Elton *(Elderly Man)*, Maurice Costello *(Ringsider at Fight)*, John Ince *(Bill Collector)*.

A charming, utterly fascinating fantasy, this film cruises through Heaven and Earth with celestial mirth, thanks to a stellar performance by Montgomery, backed up with the suave Rains and the ever colorful Gleason. Montgomery is an up-and-coming boxer with a quirk for playing the saxophone, and Gleason is his manager. After winning a fight, Montgomery insists upon flying his single engine plane home, much to the dismay of Gleason. En route, the boxer decides to toot out a few notes on his sax and winds up sputtering downward into an unexpected crash. His spirit is plucked from the ruins instantly by Horton, a squeamish Heavenly Messenger, who escorts Montgomery to a celestial level where Rains is checking off newly arrived souls. His eyebrows more than arch when he discovers that Montgomery is not on the list and that Horton, newly appointed to his post, has been too hasty, that he has, indeed, taken Montgomery before his due date. There is nothing left for the chagrined Rains to do but find another body for Montgomery to live inside of and this he proceeds to do, Montgomery at his side, two spirits wandering the world looking for the perfect specimen. Montgomery rejects several candidates until Rains takes him to a huge mansion and tells him that he will be entering the body of a multi-millionaire just as he is murdered in his bath by his scheming wife Johnson and his suave male secretary Emery so the lethal pair can be together and split the loot. To their shock Montgomery emerges from the steam-clouded bathroom very much alive, taking over the myriad business dealings of the deceased who was unscrupulous and little loved. Keyes comes to Montgomery to beg his help; her father is now in jail because of an investment scheme that went haywire and Montgomery, who falls in love with her, cavalierly pays back investors millions so her father will be released. This and many other unpredictable acts cause Johnson and Emery to attempt to get Montgomery certified as insane. Meanwhile, he contacts his former manager Gleason and convinces the befuddled man that he has, indeed, returned to life in another body, insisting that the badly shaken manager try to see the celestial guide, Rains, who is often on hand to guide Montgomery. Gleason never sees Rains, though he tries to carry on half-hearted conversations with the invisible spirit to humor Montgomery. To further encourage those around him to think him crazy, Montgomery fills his mansion with training equipment and has Gleason put him through his paces in anticipation of another big fight, hoping to take the title. Gleason believes that the chances for this flabby millionaire are thin but he goes ahead anyway, persuading himself that he is either daffy or that Montgomery truly is a reincarnated spirit. But before Montgomery can climb back into the ring to get the title bout he so richly desires, Johnson and Emery kill him (again), and this time for keeps. By then Rains has managed to find Montgomery another body, that of a top boxer with honesty and courage, a boxer killed in the ring by crooked fight promoters who want to get rid of him because he will not throw a fight. At the minute the millionaire is successfully murdered, and the fighter is supposedly murdered in the ring, Montgomery's spirit enters the fighter's body. He revives, climbs off the canvas, and wins the fight. But Montgomery can remember nothing. Gleason comes to him, tipped by millionaire Montgomery that this might happen, and tries to get the new Montgomery to remember but he can't. Montgomery does operate on what he thinks is instinct and fires his crooked manager and hires Gleason. Killers Johnson and Emery are trapped by Gleason who has been let in on their plot by Montgomery when he was in the millionaire's body and the parsimonious pair are arrested by police. Keyes, however, is out in the cold. She meets the new Montgomery as he is about to leave the boxing arena, realizing that he is the old Montgomery, remembering what the millionaire had once told her that if anything happened to him, she'd meet a boxer. They go off together to have a cup of coffee and begin their lifetime romance while Gleason glows with the knowledge that Montgomery is not only back but that he will soon have a heavyweight champion. The plot is full of hilarious twists and turns. HERE COMES MR. JORDAN is wonderful all the way, with Montgomery absolutely superb as the disembodied spirit. Rains is wry and wise, Horton a very funny bumbler, and Keyes sweet and trusting, all believable in one of the most unbelievable films ever made. Gleason stands apart as the kind-hearted and utterly confused manager; this is simply one of his greatest roles. Johnson and Emery are evil incarnate or close enough so that you can smell the brimstone. The overall production is top notch and director Hall keeps the story cracking. Columbia mogul Harry Cohn had doubts about doing this film and took some heat from his East Coast financial backers. Buchman conferred with Cohn about the script, which the boss said he liked. The scriptwriter said that the Eastern bankers were "too mechanical" to appreciate the fantasy and Cohn agreed: "All they want is what sold last year. Go ahead with the picture." Cohn borrowed Montgomery from MGM and the actor did his part reluctantly but so well that it brought him an Oscar nomination. Nominations also went to Hall, Walker for cinematography, and Columbia for best picture. None won except Buchman and Miller for Best Screenplay. This beguiling and memorable fantasy inspired a plethora of imitations, some good, like ANGEL ON MY SHOULDER, others not so effective, particularly the remake, HEAVEN CAN WAIT, 1978, and a weak sequel, DOWN TO EARTH with Rita Hayworth.

p, Everett Riskin; d, Alexander Hall; w, Sidney Buchman, Seton I. Miller (based on the play "Heaven Can Wait" by Harry Segall); ph, Joe Walker; m, Morris W. Stoloff; ed, Viola Lawrence; md, Frederick Hollander; art d, Lionel Banks; cos, Edith Head.

Fantasy **Cas.** **(PR:A MPAA:NR)**

HERE COMES THAT NASHVILLE SOUND (SEE: COUNTRY BOY, 1966)

HERE COMES THE BAND*½ (1935) 82m MGM bw

Ted Lewis *(Ted Lowry)*, Virginia Bruce *(Margaret)*, Ted Healy *("Happy")*, Nate Peterson *("Piccolo Pete")*, Harry Stockwell *(Ollie Watts)*, Donald Cook *(Don Trevor)*, Spanky McFarland *(Spanky)*, Addison Richards *(Col. Wallace)*, Robert McWade *(Judge)*, Robert Gleckler *(Simmons)*.

A small musical with Stockwell (father of actor Dean Stockwell) as a songwriter who has one of his songs stolen by music publisher Gleckler. He and his girl friend, Bruce, take the battle to court and, with the aid of Jubilee singers, hillbillies, and cowboys and Indians, prove that he came up with his song by rearranging four folk songs. He's awarded $50,000 and that money should have been used to buy a decent screenplay. There is one hilarious scene with Gilbert trying to sing during a sneezing fit, otherwise the film limps along on a weak story and too little suspense. Songs: "Heading Home" (Ned Washington, Herbert Stothart), "Roll Along Prairie Moon" (Ted Fiorito, Cecil Mack, Albert von Tilzer), "Tender Is the Night" (Harold Adamson, Walter Donaldson), "You're My Thrill" (Washington, Burton Lane), "I'm Bound for Heaven," "The Army Band" (Adamson, Lane).

p, Lucien Hubbard; d, Paul Sloane; w, Sloane, Ralph Spence, Victor Mansfield; ph, Charles Schoenbaum; m, Edward Ward; ed, Frank E. Hill.

Musical **(PR:A MPAA:NR)**

HERE COMES THE GROOM*½ (1934) 66m PAR bw

Jack Haley *(Mike Scanlon)*, Mary Boland *(Mrs. Widden)*, Patricia Ellis *(Patricia Randolph)*, Neil Hamilton *(Jim)*, Isabel Jewell *(Angy)*, Lawrence Gray *(Marvin Hale)*, Sidney Toler *(Detective Weaver)*, E.H. Calvert *(George Randolph)*, James Burtis *(1st Cop)*, Ward Bond *(2nd Cop)*, James Farley *(3rd Cop)*, Fred "Snowflake" Toones *(Porter)*, Arthur Treacher *(Butler)*, Ernest S. Adams *(1st Gunman)*, Edwin Sturgis *(2nd Gunman)*.

Haley is a would-be crook who, believe it or not, must prove his worthiness as a thief to win over Jewell. In doing so, heiress Boland falls in love with him after she is shunned by a masked crooner. A sillier so-called comedy with fewer laughs would be difficult to find.

p, Charles R. Rogers; d, Edward Sedgwick; w, Leonard Praskins, Casey Robinson (based on a story by Richard Flournoy); ph, Henry Sharp.

Comedy **(PR:A MPAA:NR)**

HERE COMES THE GROOM**** (1951) 113m PAR bw

Bing Crosby *(Pete)*, Jane Wyman *(Emmadel Jones)*, Alexis Smith *(Winifred Stanley)*, Franchot Tone *(Wilbur Stanley)*, James Barton *(Pa Jones)*, Robert Keith *(George Degnan)*, Jacques Gencel *(Bobby)*, Beverly Washburn *(Suzi)*, Connie Gilchrist *(Ma Jones)*, Walter Catlett *(McGonigle)*, Alan Reed *(Mr. Godfrey)*, Minna Gombel *(Mrs. Godfrey)*, Howard Freeman *(Governor)*, Maidel Turner *(Aunt Abby)*, H.B. Warner *(Uncle Elihu)*, Nicholas Joy *(Uncle Prentise)*, Ian Wolfe *(Uncle Adam)*, Ellen Corby *(Mrs. McGonigle)*, James Burke *(Policeman)*, Irving Bacon *(Baines)*, Ted Thorpe *(Paul Pippitt)*, Art Baker *(Radio Announcer)*, Anna Maria Alberghetti *(Theresa)*, Laura Elliot *(Maid)*, Dorothy Lamour, Frank Fontaine, Louis Armstrong, Phil Harris, Cass Daley *(Themselves)*, Chris Appel *(Marcel)*, Odette Myrtil *(Gray Lady)*, Charles Halton *(Cusick)*, Rev. Neal Dodd *(Priest)*, Charles Lane *(Burchard)*, Adeline de Walt Reynolds *(Aunt Amy)*, Charles E. Evans *(Mayor)*, Carl Switzer *(Messenger)*, Walter McGrail *(Newsreel Director)*, Howard Joslin *(Newsreel Cameraman)*, J. Farrell MacDonald.

Crosby is a news reporter who comes back from France with two orphans in tow. He must find a wife in five days or lose the kids. He goes to his old flame, Wyman, and finds that she is about to marry millionaire Tone. Crosby uses the two orphans and his singing to recapture Wyman's heart, but it's a hard battle against Tone's $40 million. In a last-ditch effort he gets a phony FBI agent and Smith, who is in love with Tone, to stop the wedding seconds before the ceremony. An excellent comedy with Crosby at his charming best and Capra developing full-bodied characters and situations. A well-structured script and fine performances from Wyman, Tone, and Crosby. Capra owed Paramount two films but production chief Y. Frank Freeman allowed him to take over this property from producer Irving Asher who originally planned to have Richard Haydn direct; this single production would make up for Capra's commitment to the studio. The gifted director brought in Wyman who used her own fine singing voice and showed her long legs in glamour girl costuming. He also brought in Smith, a six-foot actress who had been difficult to cast in the past. She was so tall that she had to stoop or slouch when playing opposite actors such as Humphrey Bogart or Charles Boyer, and stand barefoot in full shots. The always innovative Capra exploited her height by having Crosby crack in the film: "You're the most gorgeous first baseman I ever played against!" The song "In the Cool, Cool, Cool of the Evening" by Johnny Mercer and Hoagy Carmichael won the Oscar for best song of 1951. Other songs include "Caro Nome," "Misto Cristofo," "Bonne Nuit," "Your Own Little House" (Jay Livingston, Ray Evans).

p&d, Frank Capra; w, Virginia Van Upp, Liam O'Brien, Myles Connolly (based on a story by Robert Riskin, O'Brien); ph, George Barnes; ed, Ellsworth Hoagland; md, Joseph J. Lilley; art d, Hal Pereira, Earl Hedrick; set d, Emile Kuri; cos, Edith Head.

Comedy **(PR:A MPAA:NR)**

HERE COMES THE NAVY*** (1934) 86m Vitaphone/WB bw (AKA: HEY SAILOR)

James Cagney *(Chesty O'Connor)*, Pat O'Brien *(Biff Martin)*, Gloria Stuart *(Dorothy Martin)*, Frank McHugh *(Droopy)*, Dorothy Tree *(Gladys)*, Robert Barrat *(Comdr. Denny)*, Willard Robertson *(Lt. Commander)*, Guinn Williams *(Floor Manager)*, Maude Eburne *(Droopy's Ma)*, Martha Merrill *(1st Girl)*, Lorena Layson *(2nd Girl)*, Ida Darling *(Aunt)*, Henry Otho *(Riveter)*, Pauline True *(Hat Check Girl)*, Sam McDaniel *(Porter)*, Frank LaRue *(Foreman)*, Joseph Crehan *(Recruiting Officer)*, James Burtis *(C.P.O.)*, Edward Chandler *(Supply Sergeant)*, Leo White *(Professor)*, Niles Welch *(Officer)*, Fred "Snowflake" Toones *(Sailor)*, Eddie Shubert *(Skipper)*, George Irving *(Admiral)*, Howard Hickman *(Captain)*, Edward Earle *(Navy Chaplain)*, Gordon Elliott *(Officer)*, Nick Copeland *(Workman)*, John Swor *(Attendant)*, Eddie Acuff *(Marine Orderly)*, Chuck Hamilton *(Hood at Dance)*, Eddie Fetherstone *(Sailor)*.

In this fast-moving, wise-cracking sailors-at-sea story Cagney begins as a truculent dance hall lothario whose gal is stolen by Petty Officer O'Brien after a pier six brawl. Cagney later joins the Navy and is assigned to the battleship *Arizona* on which O'Brien is stationed. The two continue their feuding while Cagney breaks all the rules, bringing upon himself one punishment after another. Further, the feisty Cagney woos O'Brien's sister, Stuart, when in port, which aggravates the situation. Cagney's errant ways soon make of him a pariah; no other sailor on board ship will even talk to him, except loyal McHugh. Then Cagney goes AWOL and O'Brien puts him under arrest. At the end, Cagney redeems himself by performing an heroic rescue of a fellow sailor, almost burning to a crisp. He survives, however, to clasp O'Brien's hand in friendship, embrace Stuart, and win Navy honors. This rousing male comedy found a great box office response as the first of eight films Cagney would do with the wonderfully responsive O'Brien, a movie duo that would equal Gable and Tracy. Bacon's energetic, lightning direction, plus a powerhouse cast, caused this film to be nominated for Best Film of 1934. Shot on location at the U.S. Naval Training Station in San Diego, a great deal of footage was also shot on board the great battleship, U.S.S. *Arizona* which was sunk by the Japanese at Pearl Harbor on December 7, 1941, and remains a national shrine, its capsized body still in the harbor with more than 1,000 dead U.S. sailors on board to keep her company. Margaret Lindsay was originally assigned the sister-sweetheart role but required an operation at the last minute and was replaced by Stuart. The action film was not without hazards. In one scene Cagney drops from the gondola of the dirigible *Macon*, also loaned to Warners by the Navy, in an attempt to save O'Brien's life, but he slipped and both fell down the rope, Cagney burning his hands so badly that they "looked like hamburger," as he later remembered.

p, Lou Edelman; d, Lloyd Bacon; w, Ben Markson, Earl Baldwin (based on a story by Markson); ph, Arthur Edeson; ed, George Amy; md, Leo F. Forbstein; art d, Esdras Hartley; cos, Orry-Kelly; makeup, Perc Westmore; tech adv, Com. Herbert A. Jones; m/l, "Hey Sailor," Irving Kahal, Sammy Fain.

Adventure/Comedy **(PR:A MPAA:NR)**

HERE COMES THE SUN** (1945, Brit.) 91m GFD bw

Bud Flanagan *(Corona Flanagan)*, Chesney Allen *(Ches Allen)*, Elsa Tee *(Helen Blare)*, Joss Ambler *(Bradshaw)*, Dick Francis *(Governor)*, John Dodsworth *(Roy Lucas)*, Gus McNaughton *(Barrett)*, Roddy Hughes *(Simpson)*, Horace Kenney *(Gatekeeper)*, Edie Martin *(Mrs. Galloway)*, Peter Barnard *(Barker)*, Harry Terry *(Bill)*, A. A. Harris, "Peter," Ernest Sefton, Walter Roy, Freddie Watts, Vic

Hagen, Jack Buckland, Ian MacLean, Iris Kirkwhite Dancers, Dudley and his Midgets.

Confusing musical has Flanagan and Allen playing a pair of film extras who are re-writing a film script to suit their "social consciousness." Meanwhile, Ambler is re-writing a will for his late partner in a newspaper publishing company. He frames Flanagan who ends up going to jail. Ambler's forged will gets him all of his partner's riches, but Flanagan escapes from jail and, after being arrested once more, exposes Ambler's sham. Some light laughs but not much else.

p&d, John Baxter; w, Geoffrey Orme (based on a story by Bud Flanagan, Reginald Purdell); ph, Stan Pavey.

Musical **(PR:A MPAA:NR)**

HERE COMES TROUBLE*½ (1936) 62m FOX bw

Paul Kelly *(Duke Donovan)*, Arline Judge *(Margie)*, Mona Barrie *(Evelyn Howard)*, Gregory Ratoff *(Ivan Petroff)*, Sammy Cohen *(Grimy)*, Edward Brophy *(Crowley)*, Halliwell Hobbes *(Prof. Howard)*, Andrew Tombes *(Adams)*, Ernie Alexander *(Harry Goodfellow)*, George Chandler *(Purser Brooks)*, Wade Boteler, Stanley Blystone, Frank Hagney, Charles Stevens, Robert Homans, Granville Bates, George Chandler, Ernie Alexander.

A lame comedy with Kelly as an engineer on an ocean liner who is demoted to a job as stoker. He gets involved with a band of jewel thieves when Barrie gives him a cigarette lighter containing stolen gems. She wants him to unknowingly hold on to them because other crooks are after them, too. The film becomes a chase to get the jewels from the innocent Kelly.

p, John Stone; d, Lewis Seiler; w, Robert Ellis, Helen Logan, Barry Trivers (based on a story by John Bright, Robert Tasker); ph, Harry Jackson; ed, Louis Loeffler.

Comedy **(PR:A MPAA:NR)**

HERE COMES TROUBLE*½ (1948) 55m UA c

Bill Tracy *(Dodo)*, Joe Sawyer *(Ames)*, Emory Parnell *(Winfield Blake)*, Betty Compson *(Martha Blake)*, Paul Stanton *(Stafford)*, Beverly Loyd *(Penny Blake)*, Joan Woodbury *(Bubbles LaRue)*, Patti Morgan *(Dexter)*, Thomas Jackson *(McClure)*.

The third of Hal Roach's Laff Time series has Tracy as a cub reporter with a photographic memory. A slapstick comedy with exploding cigars, powder in the face, and a woman falling in a showerbath. The trouble with this film is that there isn't a plot, just a string of silent-film-style gags.

p, Hal Roach, Jr; d, Fred Guiol; w, George Carleton Brown, Edward E. Seabrook; ph, John W. Boyle (Cinecolor); ed, Arthur Seid; md, Heinz Roemheld; art d, Jerome Pycha.

Comedy **Cas.** **(PR:A MPAA:NR)**

HERE I AM A STRANGER****** (1939) 81m FOX bw

Richard Greene *(David)*, Richard Dix *(Duke Allen)*, Brenda Joyce *(Simpson Daniels)*, Roland Young *(Prof. Daniels)*, Gladys George *(Clara)*, Katharine Aldrich *(Lillian Bennett)*, Russell Gleason *(Sortwell)*, George Zucco *(James K. Paulding)*, Edward Norris *(Lester Bennett)*, Henry Kolker *(R.J. Bennett)*, Richard Bond *(Digby)*, Robert Shaw, Robert Kellard *(College Students)*, Charles Wilson *(Managing Editor)*, Jan Duggan *(Landlady)*, Harry Hayden *(Landlord)*, Minor Watson *(Evans)*.

George leaves her alcoholic husband, Dix, takes her son, Greene, and goes to England. There she marries a wealthy Englishman and Greene goes to college in America. He attends the same school his real father did. Dix was an All-American and well-remembered at the college. Greene seeks out his father and their renewed relationship gives Dix strength to get his life on track again. A superb drama with lots of human appeal.

p, Darryl F. Zanuck; d, Roy Del Ruth; w, Milton Sperling, Sam Hellman (based on a story by Gordon Malherbe Hillman); ph, Arthur Miller; m, Louis Silvers; ed, Louis Loeffler; m/l, Mack Gordon, Harry Revel.

Drama **(PR:A MPAA:NR)**

HERE IS A MAN (SEE: DEVIL AND DANIEL WEBSTER, THE, 1941)

HERE IS MY HEART½** (1934) 75m PAR bw

Bing Crosby *(J. Paul Jones)*, Kitty Carlisle *(Princess Alexandra)*, Roland Young *(Prince Nickolas)*, Alison Skipworth *(Countess Rostova)*, Reginald Owen *(Prince Vladimir)*, Cecelia Parker *(Suzette)*, William Frawley *(James Smith)*, Marian Mansfield *(Claire)*, Akim Tamiroff *(Hotel Manager)*, Charles Arnt *(Higgins)*, Arthur Housman *(Waiter)*, Charles Wilson *(Captain)*, Cromwell McKechnie *(Secretary)*.

Crosby is, once again, a crooner. This time he travels to the French Riviera where he meets Carlisle (who became one of the most popular panelists on TV's "What's My Line" after marrying Moss Hart), an ice princess of a mythical country. (This plot was later re-used in THE PRINCE AND THE SHOWGIRL, HER HIGHNESS AND THE BELLHOP, and several other similar ordinary-person-falls-in-love-with-royalty plots.) Crosby masquerades as a waiter to get closer to Carlisle and the result is love. Crosby displays some excellent comedic timing in this film, a forerunner of the many funny roles he was to play later. Lots of songs, not much dancing, and a literate script. Songs include "June In January," "Love Is Just Around The Corner," "With Every Breath I Take," "Here Is My Heart," "You Can't Make A Monkey Of The Moon" (Leo Robin, Ralph Rainger, Lewis Gensler).

p, Louis D. Leighton; d, Frank Tuttle; w, Edwin Justus Mayer, Harlan Thompson (based on the play "The Grand Duchess and the Waiter" by Alfred Savoir); ph, Karl Struss.

Romance/Comedy **(PR:A MPAA:NR)**

HERE WE GO AGAIN½** (1942) 75m RKO bw

Jim Jordan *(Fibber McGee)*, Marian Jordan *(Molly)*, Edgar Bergen *(Himself)*, "Charlie McCarthy" *(Charlie McCarthy)*, Harold Peary *(Great Gildersleeve)*, Ginny Simms *(Jean)*, Bill Thompson *(Wimple)*, Gale Gordon *(Caldwalder)*, Ray Noble *(Himself)*, Isabel Randolph *(Mrs. Uppington)*, "Mortimer Snerd" *(Mortimer Snerd)*.

This was the second in an RKO series starring Edgar Bergen and Fibber McGee and Molly, all big radio stars of the era. McGee and Molly are celebrating their 20th wedding anniversary at the Silver Tip Lodge, and McGee ends up spending all their money. He's conned by Gordon to get Bergen to invest in his synthetic gas. Meanwhile, McCarthy searches for love and Mortimer Snerd plays an inept hunting guide. The synthetic gas doesn't work but Bergen discovers that the gas softens moth cocoons so the threads can be removed. A light, entertaining comedy thanks to Bergen's talent. Songs included "Delicious Delirium" and "Until I Live Again" (Mort Greene, Harry Revel).

p&d, Allan Dwan; w, Paul Gerard Smith, Joe Bigelow (based on a story by Smith and material for "Fibber McGee and Molly" by Don Quinn); ph, Frank Redman; m, C. Bakaleinikoff; ed, Desmond Marquette.

Comedy **Cas.** **(PR:AA MPAA:NR)**

HERE WE GO ROUND THE MULBERRY BUSH*** (1968, Brit.) 94m UA c

Barry Evans *(Jamie McGregor)*, Judy Geeson *(Mary Gloucester)*, Angela Scoular *(Caroline Beauchamp)*, Sheila White *(Paula)*, Adrienne Posta *(Linda)*, Vanessa Howard *(Audrey)*, Diane Keen *(Claire)*, Moyra Fraser *(Mrs. McGregor)*, Michael Bates *(Mr. McGregor)*, Maxine Audley *(Mrs. Beauchamp)*, Denholm Elliott *(Mr. Beauchamp)*, Christopher Timothy *(Spike)*, Nicky Henson *(Craig Foster)*, Allan Warren *(Joe McGregor)*, Roy Holder *(Arthur)*, George Layton *(Gordon)*, Gareth Robinson *(Bruce)*, Oliver Cotton *(Curtis)*, Andrew Hamilton *(Charles Beauchamp)*, Sally Avory *(Cath)*, Erika Raifael *(Ingrid)*, Cavan Kendall *(Michael the Curate)*, Trevor Jones *(Gerald)*, Gillie Austin *(Susan)*, Christopher Mitchell *(Tony)*, Pauline Challoner *(Gloria)*, Mary Griffiths *(1st Woman at Chip Shop)*, Stella Kemble *(2nd Woman at Chip Shop)*, Angela Pleasence *(Scruffy Girl)*, Spencer Davis Group *(Group at Church Dance)*.

An English comedy of Evans' final year at high school when he attempts to lose his virginity. He takes one girl to the church dance but all they do is hold hands in the dark. With another girl he can't unzip her zippers and gets involved in a sexual square dance with her parents. Finally, he spends a weekend with the best looking girl in the school but they end up arguing most of the time. A humorous look at the awkwardness of teenage sexuality without sinking into the gutter. Songs include: "Taking Time Out," "Looking Back," "Every Little Thing," "Virginals Dream," "Picture of Her," "Just Like Me," "Possession" (Spencer Davis Group), "Here We Go 'Round the Mulberry Bush," "Am I What I Was or Was I What I Am" (Stevie Winwood), "Utterly Simple" (Dave Mason), "Waltz for Caroline" (Winwood), "It's Been a Long Time" (Simon Napier-Bell, sung by Andy Ellison).

p&d, Clive Donner; w, Hunter Davies (based on his novel); ph, Alex Thomson (DeLuxe Color); m, Spencer Davis Group, Stevie Winwood, Traffic; ed, Fergus McDonell.

Comedy **(PR:C MPAA:NR)**

HERE'S FLASH CASEY* (1937) 57m GN bw

Eric Linden *(Flash Casey)*, Boots Mallory *(Kay Lanning)*, Cully Richards *(Wade)*, Holmes Herbert *(Maj. Addison)*, Joseph Crehan *(Blaine)*, Howard Lang *(Lawrence)*, Victor Adams *(Ricka)*, Harry Harvey *(Payton)*, Suzanne Kaaren *(Mitzi)*, Matty Kemp *(Rodney)*, Dorothy Vaughn *(Mrs. O'Hara)*, Maynard Holmes *(Joe Gordon)*.

Linden is a photographer who wins a photography award while still in school. When he graduates he gives himself two years to own the world's largest news photography agency. A weak plot that is a sob sister in itself.

p, Max Alexander, Arthur Alexander; d, Lynn Shores; w, John Krafft (based on a story by George Harmon Coxe); ph, Marcel Pickard; ed, Charles Henkel, Jr.

Drama **(PR:A MPAA:NR)**

HERE'S GEORGE½** (1932, Brit.) 64m PDC bw

George Clarke *(George Muffitt)*, Pat Paterson *(Laura Wentworth)*, Ruth Taylor *(Mrs. Wentworth)*, Marriott Edgar *(Mr. Wentworth)*, Syd Crossley *(Commissionaire)*, Alfred Wellesley *(Tenant)*, Merle Tottenham *(Perkins)*, Wally Patch *(Foreman)*, Rene Ray *(Telephonist)*, Victor Fairlie, Jimmie Leslie.

After meeting the girl of his dreams, Clarke borrows a gadget-filled apartment to impress his prospective in-laws. Anything that can go wrong does in this fun comedy. It moves at a swift pace that makes the one joke farce work nicely.

p, Thomas Charles Arnold; d, Redd Davis; w, Marriott Edgar (based on his play "The Service Flat"); ph, Desmond Dickinson.

Comedy **(PR:A MPAA:NR)**

HERE'S THE KNIFE, DEAR: NOW USE IT (SEE: NIGHTMARE, 1964, Brit.)

HERE'S TO ROMANCE* (1935) 82m FOX bw

Nino Martini *(Nino Donelli)*, Genevieve Tobin *(Kathleen Gerard)*, Anita Louise *(Lydia Lubov)*, Maria Gambarelli *(Rosa)*, Mme. Schumann-Heink *(Herself)*, Reginald Denny *(Emery Gerard)*, Vicente Escudero *(Spanish Dancer)*, Pat Somerset *(Fred)*, Albert Conti *(Lefevre)*, Armand Kaliz *(Andriot)*.

This was tenor Martini's screen debut and it was evident that he should have been singing instead of reading his lines. He's struggling to sing at the Metropolitan Opera House and society matron Tobin wants to help him reach his goal. She also would like him to be her beau. This causes problems between Martini and his girl friend, Louise. Martini reaches his goal, but, by that time, the audience is asleep. Songs include, "Midnight In Paris," "Here's To Romance," "I Carry You In My

Pocket" (Herb Magidson, Con Conrad), and operatic excerpts from Pietro Mascagni's "Cavalleria Rusticana," Ruggiero Leoncavallo's "Pagliacci," Giacomo Puccini's "Tosca," and Jules Emile Frederic Massenet's "Manon."

p, Jesse L. Lasky; d, Alfred E. Green; w, Ernest Pascal, Arthur Richman (based on a story by Pascal, Sonya Levien); ph, L.W. O'Connell; m, Louis De Francesco; ed, Irene Morra; ch, Maria Gambarelli.

Musical/Romance (PR:A MPAA:NR)

HERE'S YOUR LIFE½** (1968, Swed.) 110m Svensk Filmindustri/Brandon bw-c (HAR HAR DU DITT LIV)

Eddie Axberg *(Olof)*, Ulla Sjoblom *(Olivia)*, Gunnar Bjornstrand *(Lundgren)*, Per Oscarsson *(Niklas)*, Ulf Palme *(Larsson)*, Signe Stade *(Maria)*, Allan Edwall *(August)*, Anna Maria Blind *(August's Wife)*, Ake Fridell *(Nicke Larsson)*, Holger Lowenadler *(Kristiansson)*, Gudrun Brost *(Olof's Stepmother)*, Goran Lindberg *(Olssen)*, Jan-Erik Lindqvist *(Johansson)*, Max von Sydow *(Smalands-Pelle)*, Stig Tornblom *(Fredrik)*, Ulla Akselson *(Mother)*, Borje Nyberg *(Foreman)*, Katarina Edfeldt *(Maja)*, Ulla Blomstrand *(Elfrisina)*, Bengt Ekerot *(Byberg)*, Bo Wahlstrom *(Older Brother)*, Rick Axberg *(2nd Brother)*, Goran Lindberg *(Olsson)*, Tage Sjogren *(Lund)*, Tage Jonsson *(Linus)*, Birger Lensander *(Manager at Brickworks)*, Friedrich Oshsner *(Smithie)*, Millgard Bjorklund *(Union Member)*, Bertil Linne *(Gustafsson)*.

Hailed as a masterpiece of Swedish cinema on its release, Jan Troell's HERE'S YOUR LIFE remains but an overlong, albeit sensitive look at the rites of passage. The film is a series of vignettes in the life of Axberg as we follow him from the age of 14 in 1914 until he reaches manhood after WW I—his first job, his love of the movies, his nervousness about sex, his burgeoning political awareness, and the pain of emotional relationships.

d, Jan Troell; w, Troell, Bengst Forslund (based on the novel *Romanen om Olof* by Eyvind Johnson); ph, Troell; m, Erik Nordgren; ed, Troell; art d, Rolf Boman.

Drama (PR:C-O MPAA:PG)

HERETIC (SEE: EXORCIST, PART 2, 1977)

HERITAGE** (1935, Aus.) 98m Expeditionary/British Empire bw

Franklyn Bennett, Joe Valli, Margot Rhys, Peggy Maguire, Frank Harvey, Norman French, Victor Gouriet, Ann Wynn.

Very early Australian epic chronicling the rise of the young Aussie nation from an island prison to a world power. Director Chauvel was obviously influenced by the grand-scale sagas of D.W. Griffith in making this useful glimpse into history down under.

d&w, Charles Chauvel (based on his novel; historical research by Raymond Lindsay); ph, Tasman Higgins.

Historical Drama (PR:A MPAA:NR)

HERITAGE OF THE DESERT½** (1933) 63m PAR bw

Randolph Scott *(Jack Hare)*, Sally Blane *(Judy)*, J. Farrell MacDonald *(Adam Nash)*, David Landau *(Judson Holderness)*, Gordon Wescott *(Snap Nash)*, Guinn "Big Boy" Williams *(Lefty)*, Vince Barnett *(Windy)*, Susan Fleming, Charles Stevens, Fred Burns.

This was Paramount's first remake of its silent westerns adapted from Zane Grey stories, as well as Scott's first starring role. Scott is a rancher who saves orphan Blane from Landau and his rustlers. The script is surprisingly poor considering the source, but director Hathaway develops the action and the relationship between Scott and Blane well.

p, Harold Hurley; d, Henry Hathaway; w, Harold Shumate, Frank Partos (based on a story by Zane Grey); ph, Archie Stout.

Western (PR:A MPAA:NR)

HERITAGE OF THE DESERT*** (1939) 74m PAR bw

Donald Woods *(John Abbott)*, Evelyn Venable *(Miriam Naab)*, Russell Hayden *(David Naab)*, Robert Barrat *(Andrew Naab)*, Sidney Toler *(Nosey)*, C. Henry Gordon *(Henry Holderneys)*, Willard Robertson *(Nebraska)*, Paul Guilfoyle *(Snap Thornton)*, Paul Fix *(Chick Chance)*, John Miller *(John Twerk)*, Reginald Barlow *(Judge Stevens)*.

Eastern lawyer Woods heads west to check on his mine holdings and finds that the mine manager, Gordon, has been cheating him over the years. Gordon has one of his henchmen try to kill Woods, but he only wounds him and Barrat comes to the lawyer's aid. Woods falls in love with Barrat's daughter, Venable, and then goes on the trail of Gordon. Thanks to the help of area ranchers, Gordon is brought to justice. This was the third and strongest in Paramount's Zane Grey series with the action building to an explosive ending.

p, Harry Sherman; d, Lesley Selander; w, Norman Houston, Harrison Jacobs (based on a story by Zane Grey); ph, Russell Harlan; m, Victor Young; ed, Sherman Rose; md, Louis R. Lipton; art d, Lewis J. Rachmil; m/l, Victor Young, Frank Loesser.

Western Cas. (PR:A MPAA:NR)

HERKER VON LONDON, DER (SEE: MAD EXECUTIONERS, THE, 1965, Ger.)

HERO, THE (SEE: BLOOMFIELD, 1971)

HERO** (1982, Brit.) 118m Maya-Channel 4 c

Derek McGuire *(Dermid)*, Caroline Kenneil *(Grannia)*, Alastair Kenneil *(Finn)*, Stewart Grant *(O'Shin)*, Steven Hamilton *(Oscar)*.

A British sword-and-fantasy film taking place in medieval Scotland and spoken entirely in Gaelic. McGuire joins the Hero clan after eluding assassins. He sleeps with an old woman and finds the next morning that she has turned into a beautiful young lady. They become lovers, but the leader of the clan desires her and McGuire backs off. The woman disappears, putting a spell on the young man that any woman who looks at him will fall in love with him. The leader's wife falls in love with McGuire and the two escape from the clan by a boat that is hurled into a whirlpool.

p,d&w, Barney Platts Mills (based on a book by J.F. Campbell); ph, Adam Baker-Mill; m, Paul Stern; ed, Robert Hargreaves; art d, Tom Paine; cos, Susan MacLenachan.

Action/Fantasy (PR:C MPAA:NR)

HERO AIN'T NOTHIN' BUT A SANDWICH, A** (1977) 107m NEW WORLD c

Cicely Tyson *(Sweets)*, Paul Winfield *(Butler)*, Larry B. Scott *(Benjie)*, Helen Martin *(Mrs. Bell)*, Glynn Turman *(Nigeria)*, David Groh *(Cohen)*, Kevin Hooks *(Tiger)*, Kenneth Green *(Jimmy Lee)*, Harold Sylvester *(Doctor)*, Erin Blunt *(Carwell)*, Claire Brennen *(Social Worker)*, Arthur French *(Guard)*, Bill Cobbs *(Bartender)*, Sheila Wills *(Admission Clerk)*, Arnold Johnson *(Patient)*, Barbara Alston *(Girl Friend)*, Keny Long *(Male Nurse)*, Hartwell Simms *(Minister)*.

A cityside drug opera with a twist to it, A HERO AIN'T NOTHIN' BUT A SANDWICH tells the story of young Scott, who hates his foster father, Winfield, and takes up with friend Green and neophyte narcotics supplier Blunt. As may well be imagined, Scott cannot escape the seduction of the drugs and is soon addicted as he relies more and more upon Hooks, the head honcho in the area, for his supplies. This causes alienation from Winfield as well as from his grandmother (Martin, in the film's best performance), and the remainder of the picture is Scott's recovery. Brennen does well as a social worker, as does Turman, but Groh, as one of the teachers at Scott's school, is as bland as the script. Producer Radnitz has long prided himself on making sort-of wholesome pictures for family audiences. He even teamed with the Mattel toy company to back this one. In the past, Radnitz has been involved with several "G" or "PG" films that managed to have some excitement about them. Those include ISLAND OF THE BLUE DOLPHINS, SOUNDER (1 and 2), BIRCH INTERVAL, and many others. But until this one, they've all had some sort of internal action to them; not car chases and people yelling "freeze" but a compelling force that drove the picture from start to finish. Unfortunately, that is not the case here and it soon disintegrates into what feels like hours of dialog, philosophy and street cant, with no locomotive to push it across the 107 minutes it takes. Based on Alice Childress' novel and slowly directed by veteran Ralph Nelson (LILLIES OF THE FIELD, CHARLY, many others), this movie takes an intrinsically interesting topic (young city black hooked on drugs and saved from total ruin) and manages to make us yawn. The twist is that, in his attempt to keep from going too far with the subject, Radnitz has gone too far in the other direction.

p, Robert B. Radnitz; d, Ralph Nelson; w, Alice Childress (based on her novel); ph, Frank Stanley (CFI Color); m, Tom McIntosh; ed, Fred Chulack; prod d, Walter Scott Herndon; set d, Cheryal Kearney; cos, Nedra Watt.

Drama Cas. (PR:C-O MPAA:PG)

HERO AT LARGE½** (1980) 98m MGM c

John Ritter *(Steve Nichols)*, Anne Archer *(J. Marsh)*, Bert Convy *(Walter Reeves)*, Kevin McCarthy *(Calvin Donnelly)*, Harry Bellaver *(Eddie)*, Anita Dangler *(Mrs. Havacheck)*, Jane Hallaren *(Gloria Preston)*, Leonard Harris *(Mayor)*, Rick Podell *(Milo)*, Allan Rich *(Marty Fields)*, Kurt Andon *(Fireman)*, Gerry Black, Gerald Castillo *(Heroes at Fire)*, Tony Cacciotti *(Anthony Casselli)*, William Bogert *(TV Moderator)*, Dr. Joyce Brothers *(Herself)*, Kenneth Tobey *(Fire Chief)*, A.J. Carothers *(TV Commentator)*, Natalie Cilona, Tony Crupi, Heidi Gold, Garry Goodrow, Michael Gorrin, Rod Haase, Henrietta Jacobson, Gary Klar, Michael Leon, Andrew Masset, Bryan O'Byrne, James O'Connell, Church Ortiz, William Robertson, Robin Sherwood, Marley Sims, Joseph Stern, Larry Attebery, Kevin Bacon, Vanda Barra, Neill Barry, Chris Borgen, David-James Carroll, Gary Combs, Rita Crafts, Carol Martin, Lionel Pina, Michael Prince, John Roland, Marilyn Salenger, Jack Somack, Rolland Smith, Willy Stern, Nancy Bleier, Robert Carricart, Frank Casey, Tracey Cohn, Kenneth Cory, Penny Crone, Alberto Ferrara, Lenny Geer, Tyler Horn, Peter Iacangelo.

Ritter is an out-of-work actor paying the bills by making public appearances as the comic book hero "Captain Avenger." On his way home after one of these appearances, Ritter foils a holdup at the corner grocery. The city goes wild thinking that there really is a "Captain Avenger" and this prods Ritter back into the streets as the cartoon character. Convy and McCarthy are public relations men for the mayor and they use Ritter to beef up the mayor's image. That backfires, making Ritter look bad, and the public turns on him. Of course he saves face by saving people from a burning building. An interesting concept that uses too many cliches.

p, Stephen Friedman; d, Martin Davidson; w, A.J. Carothers; ph, David M. Walsh; m, Patrick Williams; ed, Sidney Levin, David Garfield; prod d, Albert Brenner; art d, Norman Baron; cos, Sandra Davidson.

Comedy Cas. (PR:A MPAA:PG)

HERO FOR A DAY zero (1939) 65m UNIV bw

Anita Louise *(Sylvia Higgins)*, Dick Foran *("Brainy" Thornton)*, Charley Grapewin *(Frank Higgins)*, Berton Churchill *(Mr. Dow)*, Emma Dunn *("Mom" Higgins)*, David Holt *(Billy)*, Richard Lane *(Abbott)*, Samuel S. Hinds *(Coach Bronson)*, Jerry Marlowe *(Fitz)*, Frances Robinson *(Jean)*, John Gallaudet *(Foreman)*, Paul Barrett *(Ticket Man)*, Cully Richards *(Jesse)*, Eddie Acuff *(Gibbons)*, Russ Powell *(Watchman)*, Bobby Watson *(Stranger)*, Tommy Bupp *(2nd Boy)*, Buster Phelps *(1st Boy)*, Dale Armstrong *(Radio Announcer)*, Kernan Cripps *(Trainer)*, Bobbe Trefts, Frances Robinson, Irene Coleman *(Debutantes)*, Margaret Brayton *(Nurse)*, Marty Faust *(Taxi Driver)*, Eddie Fetherston *(Hotel Clerk)*, Jack Gardner *(2nd*

Reporter), Robert Darrell *(1st Reporter)*, Billy Engle *(Stranger)*, Ben Lewis *(Bus Conductor)*.

Grapewin is a 35-year-old nightwatchman who in his college days was an All-American football player. His alma mater is playing a post-season game and the school thinks it would be great human interest if the old star played in the game. He suits up, helps the team win, and collapses in the closing minutes of the contest. The film collapsed right after the opening titles.

p, Ken Goldsmith; d, Harold Young; w, Harold Buchman (based on the story "Old Grad" by Matt Taylor); ph, John W. Boyle; ed, Charles Maynard.

Drama **(PR:A MPAA:NR)**

HERO OF BABYLON*½ (1963, Ital.) 98m EM-AE c (AKA: BEAST OF BABYLON AGAINST THE SON OF HERCULES)

Gordon Scott, Michael Lane, Moira Orfel, Piero Lulli, Genevieve Grad.

Things aren't coming up roses for the population of Assyria. The evil king is oppressing rights without mercy, in addition to sacrificing people to one of his goddesses. All this third-rate Italian muscle picture needs is a hero to save the day. He arrives in good time, leads the rebellion, and overthrows the evil ruler. This film, like so many others of its ilk, answers that perennial film producer question: how can we recycle the old cliches just one more time?

d, Siro Marcellini.

Adventure **(PR:A MPAA:NR)**

HEROD THE GREAT*½ (1960, Ital.) 93m AA c

Edmund Purdom (Herod), Sylvia Lopez *(Miriam)*, Sandra Milo *(Sarah)*, Alberto Lupo *(Aaron)*, Massimo Girotti *(Octavius)*.

An Italian biblical costume epic heavy on scantily clad women. The film covers the ending of Herod's reign starting with his defeated alliance with Anthony, to his death following his infamous dictate to kill all the newly born males in his kingdom. A lot of sex, glitter, and poor dubbing

p, W. Tourjansky; d, Arnaldo Genoino; w, Damiano Damiani, Federico Zardi, Fernando Cerchio, Tourjansky; ph, Massimo Dallamano (Totalscope, Eastmancolor); m, Carlo Savina; ed, Antoinetta Zitta.

Drama **(PR:C MPAA:NR)**

HEROES*½ (1977) 113m UNIV c

Henry Winkler *(Jack)*, Sally Field *(Carol)*, Harrison Ford *(Ken)*, Val Avery *(Bus Driver)*, Olivia Cole *(Jane)*, Hector Elias *(Dr. Elias)*, Dennis Burkley *(Gus)*, Tony Burton *(Chef)*, Michael Cavanaugh *(Peanuts)*, Helen Craig *(Bus Depot Manager)*, John P. Finnegan *(Munro)*, Betty McGuire *(Mrs. Munro)*, John O'Leary *(Ticket Clerk)*, Rom Rosqui, Ben Fuhrman *(Patrolmen)*, Fred Stuthman *(Nathan)*, Caskey Swain *(Frank)*, Earle Towne *(Leo)*, Kenneth Augustine *(Charles)*, Rick Blanchard *(Andy)*, Louis Carello *(Stokes)*, Robert Kretschmann *(Robert)*, Alex Tinne *(Bridegroom)*, Dick Ziker *(Artie)*, William Ackridge *(Starter)*, Gary Bertz, James W. Gavin *(Pilots)*, Susan Bredhoff *(Nurse)*, Bill Burton, David Ellis *(Bar Patrons)*, Pat Hustis *(Car Driver)*, Bennie Moore *(Adcox)*.

Winkler is a loony Viet Nam War veteran who escapes from a mental hospital to start a worm farm. He hops a bus to California and meets Field. He convinces her to go with him and they hook up with Winkler's war buddy, Ford. A contrived script that fumbles all attempts to make a statement on the problems faced by Viet Nam vets. Winkler exaggerates his mad gambols too broadly to create a real character, but Field displays the strong acting talent that would mature even further in later films.

p, David Foster, Lawrence Turman; d, Jeremy Paul Kagan; w, James Carabatsos; ph, Frank Stanley (Technicolor); m, Jack Nitzsche, Richard Hazard; ed, Patrick Kennedy; prod d, Charles Rosen; set d, James Payne.

Comedy/Drama **Cas.** **(PR:A MPAA:PG)**

HEROES, THE (SEE: INVINCIBLE SIX, 1972, U.S./Iran)

HEROES ARE MADE** (1944, USSR) 76m Artkine bw

V. Periat-Petrenko *(Pavel Korchagin)*, D. Sagal *(Sailor)*, J. Pedotova *(Tonis)*, V. Bubnov *(Artem Korchagin)*, A. Dunsysky *(Ukranian Interpreter)*, A. Khvilla *(Dolinnik)*, B. Runghe *(Seryozha)*, V. Balashov *(Victor Leachinsky)*, V. Krasnovitsky *(German Officer)*.

A 14-year-old kitchen boy working on a railroad buffet is inspired by a partisan sailor to fight against the occupying German army during WW I. The boy sets up a youth underground, but leaves it to save the sailor from the police. He then joins the Red Army to save his underground friends who are to be hanged. (In Russian; English subtitles.)

p,d&w, Mark Donskoy (based on a novel by Nikolai Omtrosky); ph, R. Monsatirsky; m, L. Schwartz; English titles, Charles Clement.

Drama **(PR:C-O MPAA:NR)**

HEROES DIE YOUNG*** (1960) 76m AA bw

Krika Peters *(Nitza)*, Scott Borland *(Manjack)*, Robert Getz *(Hoofer)*, Bill Browne *(Mule)*, James Strother *(Lt. Easton)*, Malcolm Smith *(Sgt. Phelps)*, Donald Joslyn *(Sweitzer)*, Arthur Tennen *(Wilson)*, Chick Bilyeu *(Col. Banners)*, Jack Card *(Sayer)*, Boochie.

Let by American soldier Strother and Rumanian Peters (the daughter of a man killed by the Allies) a group of eight soldiers goes behind enemy lines in WW II. They are to infiltrate the famous Ploesti oil fields and set up bombing flares for an air raid. At first Peters is hostile toward her comrades but gradually she softens up, falling in love with Borland. He is ultimately killed as are several other infiltrators when the Allies finally bomb the oil fields in one of the most devastating attacks the Nazis suffered during the war. Some interesting moments with good direction that maintains the suspense level. Based on a true story of the mighty raid where American fliers, too, died by the hundreds.

p, Frank Russell, Gerald S. Shepard; d&w, Shepard; ph, Glen R. Smith; m, Al Pellegrini.

War Drama/Action **(PR:C MPAA:NR)**

HEROES FOR SALE zero (1933) 71m FN-WB bw

Richard Barthelmess *(Tom)*, Loretta Young *(Ruth)*, Aline MacMahon *(Mary)*, Gordon Westcott *(Roger)*, Robert Barrat *(Max)*, Berton Churchill *(Mr. Winston)*, Grant Mitchell *(George Gibson)*, Robert McWade *(Dr. Briggs)*, Charles Grapewin *(Pa Dennis)*, James Murray *(Blind Man)*, Edwin Maxwell *(President of the Laundry)*, Margaret Seddon *(Mrs. Holmes)*, Arthur Vinton *(Capt. Joyce)*, John Marston *(Judge)*, Douglas Dumbrille *(Chief Engineer)*, Ward Bond *(Red)*, Lee Phelps *(Ed Brady)*, Dewey Robinson *(Arguer)*, Milton Kibbee *(Teller)*, Guy Usher *(Constable)*, George Pat Collins, Robert Elliott, Willard Robertson, Tammany Young, Hans Furberg.

Barthelmess is a WW I veteran who returns home a drug addict. He is shunned by society but then becomes a millionaire through his friendship with Barrat, who has invented a washing machine. Barthelmess becomes his friend's partner and finds himself caught in the middle of a worker's strike. A hokey melodrama that is too far from reality to be enjoyed.

d, William Wellman; w, Robert Lord, Wilson Mizner; ph, James Van Trees.

Drama **(PR:A MPAA:NR)**

HEROES IN BLUE** (1939) 60m MON bw

Dick Purcell *(Terry Murphy)*, Charles Quigley *(Joe Murphy)*, Bernadene Hayes *(Daisy)*, Edward Keane *(Moran)*, Julie Warren *(Kathleen)*, Lillian Elliot *(Mrs. Murphy)*, Frank Sheridan *(Mike Murphy)*.

A B crime film with Purcell and Quigley as brothers who join the police force. One gets involved with gangsters who commit a murder at the race track. Father Sheridan gets in the middle of the mess to help his son. A routine story loaded with action.

p, T.R. Williams; d, William Watson; w, Charles Curran, C.B. Williams; ph, Harry Neumann; ed, Bruce Schoengarth.

Crime **(PR:A MPAA:NR)**

HEROES OF TELEMARK, THE*** (1965, Brit.) 131m Benton-RANK/COL c

Kirk Douglas *(Dr. Rolf Pedersen)*, Richard Harris *(Knut Straud)*, Ulla Jacobsson *(Anna)*, Michael Redgrave *(Uncle)*, David Weston *(Arne)*, Sebastian Breaks *(Gunnar)*, John Golightly *(Freddy)*, Alan Howard *(Oli)*, Patrick Jordan *(Henrik)*, William Marlowe *(Claus)*, Brook Williams *(Elinar)*, Roy Dotrice *(Jensen)*, Anton Diffring *(Maj. Frick)*, Ralph Michael *(Nilssen)*, Eric Porter *(Terboven)*, Wolf Frees *(Knippelberg)*, Karel Stepanek *(Hartmuller)*, Gerard Heinz *(Erhardt)*, Victor Beaumont *(German Sergeant)*, George Murcell *(Sturmfuhrer)*, Mervyn Johns *(Col. Wilkinson)*, Barry Jones *(Prof. Logan)*, Geoffrey Keen *(Gen. Bolt)*, Robert Ayres *(Gen. Courts)*, Jennifer Hilary *(Sigrid)*, Maurice Denham *(Doctor at Hospital)*, David Davies *(Captain of "Galtesund")*, Philo Hauser *(Businessman)*, Faith Brook *(Woman on Bus)*, Elvi Hale *(Mrs. Sandersen)*, Russell Waters *(Mr. Sandersen)*, Jan Conrad *(Watchman in Factory)*, Alf Joint *(German Guard on Ferry)*, Robert Bruce *(Major)*, Brian Jackson *(Norwegian Naval Attache)*, Paul Hansard *(German Official)*, Annette Andre *(Girl Student)*, Pamela Conway *(Girl in Darkroom)*, Grace Arnold, Howard Douglas *("Galtesund" Passengers)*, Jemma Hyde *(Businessman's Girl Friend)*, Terry Plummer, Joe Powell *(Quislings)*.

It is 1942 and Norway is under the thumb of the Nazis. Harris, leader of the Norwegian underground, delivers a microfilmed message from a fellow resistance member working undercover in a Nazi factory to Douglas, a scientist. Upon deciphering the message, Douglas and Harris learn that the Nazis are producing "heavy water" (an essential element in the production of atomic weapons). After sending the message to the British, they are ordered to proceed to the well-guarded factory and prepare for an invasion by British commandos. Unfortunately, the commandos run into a deadly snafu en route, leaving Douglas and Harris to complete the mission on their own. The two men destroy the room where the "heavy water" machinery is kept, but Douglas is wounded and captured. He escapes and catches up with Harris (how Douglas escapes is never explained). The sabotage only causes a minor delay for the Nazis, because new machinery is shipped to the factory and the "heavy water" once again begins to flow. Learning of this setback, the British attempt to bomb the factory, but their efforts end in failure. Meanwhile, the Nazis have grown uncomfortable with all this Allied attention, so the decision is made to remove the "heavy water" and ship it back to Germany. Douglas and Harris discover the route, and manage to sink the ferry and its cargo. After directing some of the best westerns ever made (WINCHESTER '73, 1950, BEND OF THE RIVER, 1952, THE NAKED SPUR, 1953, THE MAN FROM LARAMIE, 1955, and MAN OF THE WEST, 1958), Mann moved to Europe and started making big-budget epics such as EL CID (1961) and THE FALL OF THE ROMAN EMPIRE (1964) with spotty results. THE HEROES OF TELEMARK was Mann's last completed film before his death (he died in 1967 during the production of A DANDY IN ASPIC). Shot on location in Norway, Mann used the impressive landscape to its full advantage, just as he had done in his many rugged westerns. Aided by former members of the Norwegian underground who served as technical advisors during the production, the film has an air of authenticity that would have been difficult to create otherwise. In addition to the former freedom-fighters, Mann also had the assistance of Olympic ski coach Helge Stoylen and his pupils, who helped create some of the stunning sequences in the film (Stoylen held a camera between his legs and shot some impressive footage as he zoomed down the slopes). Even the problems worked to Mann's advantage. His stars, Douglas and Harris, detested each other during the shooting and the set was frequently tense. Luckily the script called for their characters to be at odds through much of the film, so the real tension between the men was effectively translated on screen, much to the betterment of the movie. Despite all these advantages, the film suffers from obvious trimming (one must assume that Mann shot Douglas' escape from the Nazis, but that the scene ended up on the cutting room floor) and some of the supporting characters (especially Redgrave) are left underdeveloped. Fortunately, these problems are minor and THE HEROES OF TELEMARK remains a solid, exciting war film.

p, S. Benjamin Fisz; d, Anthony Mann; w, Ivan Moffat, Ben Barzman; ph, Robert Krasker (Panavision, Eastmancolor); m, Malcolm Arnold; ed, Bert Bates; art d, Tony Masters; set d, Bob Cartwright, Ted Clements; cos, Elsa Fennell; spec eff, John P. Fulton, Ron Ballanger, Syd Pearson, Bill Warrington; stunts, Gerry Crampton; makeup, Neville Smallwood.

War **Cas.** **(PR:C MPAA:NR)**

HEROES OF THE ALAMO zero (1938) 74m COL bw

Lane Chandler *(Davy Crockett)*, Earle Hodgins *(Stephen Austin)*, Ruth Findlay *(Anne Dickinson)*, Rodger Williams *(James)*, Edward Piel *(Sam Houston)*, Rex Lease *(William B. Travis)*, Bruce Warren *(Almerlan Dickinson)*, Julian Rivero *(Gen. Santa Ana)*, Jack C. Smith, Lee Valanios, William Costello, Marlin Hasset, Steve Clark, William McCall, Sherry Tansey, Denver Dixon, Tex Phelps, Jack Evans, Paul Ellis, George Morrell, Tex Cooper, Oscar Gahan, Ben Corbett.

History has never been more boringly represented than in this re-creation of the famous battle at The Alamo. If you manage to stay awake until the battle scene, you may get a laugh out of the unintentionally funny cannon-firing scene. Acting is mediocre at best, but nothing could have saved this poorly written script.

p, Anthony J. Xydias; d, Harry Fraser; w, Roby Wentz; ph, Robert Cline; ed, Arthur A. Brooks; art d, Clarence Bricker.

Western **(PR:A MPAA:NR)**

HEROES OF THE HILLS½** (1938) 55m REP bw

Robert Livingston *(Stony Brooke)*, Ray Corrigan *(Tucson Smith)*, Max Terhune *(Lullaby Joslin)*, Priscilla Lawson *(Madelyn)*, LeRoy Mason *(Red)*, James Eagles *(The Kid)*, Roy Barcroft *(Beaton)*, Barry Hays *(Regan)*, Carleton Young *(Connors)*, Forrest Taylor *(Sheriff)*, John Wade *(Board Chairman)*, Maston Williams *(Nick)*, John Beach *(Crane)*, Jerry Frank *(Slim)*, Roger Williams *(Warden)*, Kit Guard *(Mac)*, Jack Kirk, Curley Dresden.

The Three Mesquiteers decide to turn their ranch into a prison farm because of their belief in prison reform. Barcroft is a contractor whose attempts to have a prison built are put to a halt because of the Mesquiteers' penal efforts. The contractor and his cohorts set out to wreck the ranch, but the Mesquiteers put a quick end to the scheme. An above-average western. (See THREE MESQUITEERS series, Index.)

p, William Berke; d, George Sherman; w, Betty Burbridge, Stanley Roberts (based on a story by Roberts and Jack Natteford); ph, Reggie Lanning; ed, Tony Martinelli; m/l, Eddie Cherkose, Alberto Colombo.

Western **Cas.** **(PR:A MPAA:NR)**

HEROES OF THE RANGE** (1936) 58m COL bw

Ken Maynard *(Ken)*, June Gale *(Joan)*, Harry Woods *(Bull)*, Harry Ernest *(Johnny)*, Robert Kortman *(Slick)*, Bud McClure *(Lem)*, Tom London *(Bud)*, Bud Osborne *(Jame)*, Frank Hagney *(Smith)*, Jack Rockwell *(Sheriff)*, Lafe McKee, Wally Wales, Jay Wilsey, Jerome Ward, Bud Jamison, Bob Reeves, Jack King, Tarzan the Horse.

Maynard is an FBI agent who straps on a gun belt and six-shooter to go after a band of outlaws. The crooks are planning to steal a shipment of gold and they have kidnaped the express clerk so they can get the exact time and date. Maynard poses as one of the outlaws and with no surprises foils the robbery attempt. Action aplenty as usual in a Maynard film.

p, Larry Darmour; d, Spencer G. Bennett; w, Nate Gatzert; ph, James S. Brown, Jr.; ed, Dwight Caldwell.

Western **(PR:A MPAA:NR)**

HEROES OF THE SADDLE*½ (1940) 59m REP bw

Robert Livingston *(Stony Brooke)*, Raymond Hatton *(Rusty Joslin)*, Duncan Renaldo *(Rico)*, Patsy Lee Parsons *(Peggy)*, Loretta Weaver *(Ruth)*, Byron Foulger *(Melloney)*, William Rovis *(Crone)*, Vince Barnett *(Constable)*, Jack Roper *("Killer" McCully)*, Reed Howes *(Wilson)*, Ethel May Halls *(Miss Dobbs)*, Al Taylor *(Hendricks)*, Patsy Carmichael *(Annie)*, Kermit Maynard, Tom Hanlon, Tex Terry, Douglas Deems, Darwood Kaye, Matt McHugh, Harrison Greene.

This Mesquiteer western has the trio trying to adopt the orphaned daughter of an old friend. They are met by miles of red tape and when it starts unraveling they find that the orphans are being used by a corrupt political machine. The Mesquiteers put a quick end to the doings and adopt orphan Parsons. (See THREE MESQUITEERS series, Index.)

p, Harry Grey; d, William Witney; w, Jack Natteford (based on the characters created by William Colt MacDonald); ph, William Nobles; m, Cy Feuer; ed, Lester Orlebeck.

Western **(PR:A MPAA:NR)**

HEROES OF THE SEA** (1941) 80m Odessa/Artkino bw

V.I. Osvetimsky *(Rear Adm. Bellayev)*, S.D. Timokhin *(Division Commissar Lobod)*, S.D. Stolyarov *(Alexander Bellayev, Submarine Commander)*, A.M. Maximova *(1st Lt. Galya Zorina)*, E.G. Yegorova *(Lt. Ivanovskaya)*, S.S. Petrov *(Capt. Choglokov)*, A.A. Arkadev *(Lt. Comdr. Svetlov)*, F.L. Blazhevich *(Fleet Commander)*, N.V. Komissarov *(Admiral)*, G.D. Pluzhnik *(Commander of Battleship)*.

Soviet propaganda on its naval forces that contains an action-packed plot. Osvetimsky is a rear-admiral from a long line of sailors. His son is a submarine commander who is in love with a female naval pilot. The story moves quickly while showing off the latest naval hardware of the time. (In Russian; English subtitles.)

d, Vladimir Braum; w, I. Zeltser, S. Abramovitch-Bleck; ph, Michael Kaplan; m, I.S. Millutin.

Drama **(PR:A MPAA:NR)**

HEROINA** (1965) 105m Royal bw

Kitty de Hoyos *(Laura)*, Jaime Sanchez *(Chico)*, Otto Sirgo *(Marcos)*, Jeddu Mascorieto *(Tito)*, Marta Casanas *(The Mother)*, Jose de San Anton *(The Father)*, Nidia Caro *(Nina)*, Felix Monclova *(Nick)*, Freddie Baez *(Addict)*, Olga Guillot *(Singer)*, Raul Davila *(Judge)*, Kako y Su Combo *(Orchestra)*.

A Spanish language film shot in New York City and starring Sanchez as the son of well-to-do parents who turns to heroin addiction due to an inability to cope with his father. After a six-month jail term, Sanchez comes home to work in his father's business and does well until he meets his old heroin dealer for a drink and a chat. Sanchez's father immediately assumes the boy is back on drugs and kicks him out of the house. With no money and no place to go, Sanchez helps his friend peddle heroin. The temptation proves too much for Sanchez, and he picks up the needle again. Having proved unreliable due to his addiction, the pushers kick him out of the gang. Broke, alone, and desperate, Sanchez returns home, where his father finally realizes his own responsibility for the situation, and he welcomes his son back. (In Spanish; English subtitles.)

p&d, Jeronimo Mitchell Melendez; w, Enrique de la Torre (based on a story by Melendez); ph, Luis A. Maisonet; m, Charlie Palmieri; ed, Gloria A. Pineyro.

Drama **(PR:C MPAA:NR)**

HERO'S ISLAND½** (1962) 94m Daystar-Portland/UA c (AKA: THE LAND WE LOVE)

James Mason *(Jacob Webber)*, Kate Manx *(Devon Mainwaring)*, Neville Brand *(Kingstree)*, Rip Torn *(Nicholas)*, Warren Oates *(Wayte)*, Brendan Dillon *(Thomas Mainwaring)*, Robert Sampson *(Enoch)*, Dean Stanton *(Dixey)*, Morgan Mason *(Cullen)*, Darby Hinton *(Jafar)*, Robert Johnson *(Pound)*, Bill Hart *(Meggett)*, John Hudkins *(Bullock)*.

Dillon, his wife Manx, their three children, and friend Oates make their new home on Bull Island, off the Carolina coast in 1718. They are attacked by fishermen who claim the island is theirs, and Dillon is killed. Castaway Mason is washed ashore and offers his assistance to Manx, but she is a deeply religious woman and doesn't want to resort to violence. Fisherman Torn joins up with the group and Mason reveals that he is Maj. Stede Bonnett, Blackbeard the pirate. The fishermen return with Brand and his two stewards and Mason kills most of them, with his own life saved by Manx.

p, Leslie Stevens, James Mason; d&w, Stevens; ph, Ted McCord (Panavision, Technicolor); m, Dominic Frontiere; ed, Richard Brockway.

Action/Drama **(PR:A MPAA:NR)**

HEROS SANS RETOUR (SEE: COMMANDO, 1964, Belg./Ital./Span./Ger.)

HEROSTRATUS* (1968, Brit.) 140m BFI/BBC c

Michael Gothard *(Max)*, Gabriella Licudi *(Clio)*, Peter Stephens *(Farson)*, Anthony Paul *(Pointer)*, Mona Chin *(Sandy)*, Malcolm Muggeridge *(Himself)*.

A portentous film about a poet who is tired of the "system" and world corruption. He goes to a public relations firm and wants them to publicize his upcoming suicide as a protest against society. Poet Gothard claims that he is from a well-to-do family but the p.r. people find out that he is from a poor family and that he is a bad poet. They decide that they will still publicize his suicide, but when Gothard goes up on a roof to jump he finds another man who tries to stop him. The man ends up falling from the building, and poet is last seen running through the streets. The title refers to the character from Greek mythology who tried to make a name for himself by destroying one of the seven wonders of the world.

p, Don Levy, James Quinn; d&w, Levy (based on a story by Levy and Alan Daiches); ph, Keith Allams (Eastmancolor).

Drama **(PR:C MPAA:NR)**

HERRSCHER OHNE KRONE (SEE: KING IN SHADOW, 1963, Ger.)

HERS TO HOLD½** (1943) 93m UNIV bw

Deanna Durbin *(Penelope Craig)*, Joseph Cotten *(Bill Morley)*, Charles Winninger *(Judson Craig)*, Evelyn Ankers *(Flo Simpson)*, Gus Schilling *(Rosey Blake)*, Nella Walker *(Dorothy Craig)*, Ludwig Stossel *(Binns)*, Samuel S. Hinds *(Dr. Crane)*, Fay Helm *(Hannah Gordon)*, Iris Adrian *(Arlene)*, Murray Alper *(Foreman)*, Douglas Wood *(Mr. Cartwright)*, Minna Phillips *(Mrs. Cartwright)*, Nydia Westman *(Nurse Willing)*, Irving Bacon *(Dr. Bacon)*, Janet Shaw *(Girl at Factory)*, Eddie Acuff, Eddie Dunn *(Reporters)*, Harry Holman *(Doctor)*, Henry Roquemore, Brooks Benedict *(Guests)*, William B. Davidson *(Al, a Guest)*, Billy Nelson *(Aircraft Worker at Inn)*, Billy Wayne *(Joe, Coast Guardsman)*, George O'Hanlon *(Coast Guardsman with Tommy Gun)*, Leon Belasco *(Orchestra Leader)*, Ruth Lee *(Miss Crawford)*, Jody Gilbert *(Babe)*, Eddie Borden *(Guest Eating Sandwich)*, Ernie S. Adams *(Flier's Father)*, George Chandler *(Enlisted Man)*, Alice Talton *(Hazel)*, Marie Harmon *(Ella Mae)*, Virginia Sale *(Personnel Woman)*, James Bush *(Bomber Captain)*, Evelyn Wahle *(Jeanne)*, Spec O'Donnell *(William Morley)*, Teddy Infuhr *(Joey)*, Jennifer Holt *(Girl)*.

Bomber pilot Cotten eyes rich kid Durbin (completing her transition into adulthood), but when she shows interest he backs off. She follows him to an aircraft plant and gets herself hired just to be near him. Things don't end up as the weepy Durbin would like when Cotten takes to the air, leaving her behind. She's not too sad to sing a few tunes, though: "Say A Prayer For The Boys Over There" (Herb Magidson, Jimmy McHugh), "Begin The Beguine" (Cole Porter), "God Bless

America" (Irving Berlin), "Kashmiri Love Song" (Lawrence Hope, Amy Woodforde-Finden), "The Seguidilla" from Bizet's "Carmen."

p, Felix Jackson; d, Frank Ryan; w, Lewis R. Foster (based on a story by John D. Klorer); ph, Elwood Bredell; ed, Ted Kent; md, Charles Previn; art d, John B. Goodman.

Romance (PR:A MPAA:NR)

HE'S A COCKEYED WONDER½** (1950) 76m COL bw

Mickey Rooney *(Freddie Frisby)*, Terry Moore *(Judy Sears)*, William Demarest *(Bob Sears)*, Charles Arnt *(J.B. Caldwell)*, Ross Ford *(Ralph Caldwell)*, Ned Glass *(Sam Phillips)*, Mike Mazurki *("Lunk" Boxwell)*, Douglas Fowley *("Grabs" Freeley)*, William Phillips *("Pick" Reedley)*, Ruth Warren *(Jenny Morrison)*, Eddy Waller *(Pops Dunlap)*, Frank Ferguson *(Sheriff Oliver)*.

Rooney is his blundering self as a lad who inherits a little of his uncle's cash and a lot of his magic props. He spends his free time with his girl, Moore, much to the displeasure of her dad, Demarest. When the pair try out their disappearing act at an orange factory they are accused, instead, of heisting the Sunkists. Rooney is able to turn the tables on the evil-doers and win the approval of Demarest. Rooney does a standout job on his character in the film, and his magic props help keep the movement lively.

p, Rudolph C. Flothow; d, Peter Godfrey; w, John Henley; ph, Lester White; m, Mischa Bakaleinikoff; ed, Richard Fantl; art d, Victor Greene.

Comedy (PR:A MPAA:NR)

HE'S MY GUY** (1943) 64m UNIV bw

Dick Foran *(Van Moore)*, Irene Hervey *(Terry Allen)*, Joan Davis *(Madge Donovan)*, Fuzzy Knight *(Sparks)*, Don Douglas *(Kirk)*, Samuel S. Hinds *(Johnson)*, Bill Halligan *(Elwood)*, Gertrude Niesen *(Singer)*, Mills Brothers *(Themselves)*, Diamond Brothers *(Themselves)*, Beatrice Roberts *(Secretary)*, Louis Da Pron *(Specialty)*, Rex Lease *(Office Manager)*, Lorraine Krueger *(Specialty)*, Eddie Coke *(Counterman)*, Dorothy Ann Jackson, Gene Skinner *(Dorene Sisters)*, Billy Wayne *(Saunders)*, Harry Strang *(Police Officer)*.

Typical Universal programmer designed to help America's WW II war effort. A group of ex-vaudevillians put together a show and take it to the local defense plant to boost morale. Not much, but common for its time.

p, William Cowan; d, Edward F. Cline; w, M. Coates Webster, Grant Garrett (based on a story by Kenneth Higgins); ph, John Boyle; ed, Fred Feitshans; md, Charles Previn; art d, John B. Goodman; ch, Carlos Romeros.

Musical (PR:A MPAA:NR)

HESTER STREET*½** (1975) 90m Midwest bw

Steven Keats *(Jake)*, Carol Kane *(Gitl)*, Mel Howard *(Bernstein)*, Dorrie Kavanaugh *(Mamie)*, Doris Roberts *(Kavarsky)*, Stephen Strimpell *(Joe Peltner)*, Lauren Frost *(Fanny)*, Paul Freedman *(Joey)*, Zvee Scooler *(Rabbi)*, Eda Reiss Merin *(Rabbi's Wife)*.

Keats is a young Jewish immigrant living on the title street while his wife Kane and their child are waiting back in the Old World. While trying to earn the money to bring them to the U.S., he becomes increasingly Americanized. He soon becomes involved with a fast-moving socialite who gives him some cash, which he in turn sends to his wife. Kane arrives but only shames Keats with her old-fashioned ways. They divorce and Keats goes off with his other woman, while Kane falls in love with a family friend. An engagingly simple first feature written and directed by Joan Micklin Silver, which earned an Academy Award nomination for Kane.

p, Raphael D. Stewart; d&w, Joan Micklin Silver (based on the story "Yekl" by Abraham Cahan); ph, Kenneth Van Sickle; m, William Bolcom; ed, Katherine Wenning.

Drama Cas. (PR:C MPAA:PG)

HEX*½ (1973) 92m FOX c

Tina Herazo [Christina Raines] *(Oriole)*, Hilarie Thompson *(Acacia)*, Keith Carradine *(Whizzer)*, Mike Combs *(Golly)*, Scott Glenn *(Jimbang)*, Gary Busey *(Giblets)*, Robert Walker, Jr. *(Chupo)*, Dan Haggerty *(Brother Billy)*, Doria Cook *(China)*, Iggie Wolfington *(Cuzak)*, Patricia Ann Parker *(Elma)*, Tom Jones *(Elston)*, John Carradine *(Old Gunfighter)*.

Offbeat film notable for early screen appearances by Keith Carradine, Busey and Haggerty, and the film debuts of Glenn and Raines (here billed as Tina Herazo). Film is set in 1919 when Keith Carradine leads a wandering group of motorbike riders to the Nebraska farm of two sisters whose Indian father had introduced to witchcraft. Sister Thompson uses her occult powers to cause the deaths of several gang members, but is attracted to Combs. Eventually, Thompson and Combs are left alone to mind the farm while Carradine and Raines head off for California (the two would be paired again two years later in NASHVILLE). After its premiere at the Atlanta Film Festival, Fox decided there was little market for HEX (although Norman Mailer liked it) and never released it.

p, Clark Paylow; d, Leo Garen; w, Garen, Steve Katz (based on a story by Doran William Cannon, Vernon Zimmerman); ph, Charles Rosher, Jr. (DeLuxe Color); m, Charles Bernstein; ed, Robert Belcher, Antranig Mahakian; art d, Gary Weist, Frank Sylos; set d, Walter M. Scott, Ralph Sylos; spec eff, Milt Rice.

Drama (PR:O MPAA:PG)

HEY BOY! HEY GIRL!½** (1959) 83m COL bw

Louis Prima *(Himself)*, Keely Smith *(Dorothy Spencer)*, James Gregory *(Father Burton)*, Henry Slate *(Marty Moran)*, Kim Charney *(Buzz)*, Barbara Heller *(Grace Dawson)*, Asa Maynor *(Shirley)*, Sam Butera and the Witnesses.

A devoted parishioner, Smith, approaches crooner Louis Prima to perform for a church benefit. He agrees and the benefit is a success after he delivers the following tunes: "Oh Marie," "Autumn Leaves" (Joseph Kosma, Jacques Prevert, Johnny Mercer); "Hey Boy, Hey Girl," "Lazy River" (Hoagy Carmichael, Sidney Arodin); "When The Saints Go Marching In," "Fever" (J.R. Davenport, Eddie Cooley); "Nitey Night," "A Banana Split For My Baby," "You Are My Love." A pleasing experience thanks to the likable stars.

p, Harry Romm; d, David Lowell Rich; w, Raphael Hayes, James West; ph, Ray Cory; ed, Al Clark; art d, Ross Bellah.

Musical (PR:A MPAA:NR)

HEY, GOOD LOOKIN'*½ (1982) 76m WB c

Voices: Richard Romanus *(Vinnie)*, David Proval *(Crazy Shapiro)*, Tina Bowman *(Roz)*, Jesse Welles *(Eva)*, Angelo Grisanti *(Solly)*, Danny Wells, Bennie Massa, Gelsa Palao, Paul Roman, Larry Bishop, Tabi Cooper *(Stompers)*, Juno Dawson *(Waitress)*, Shirley Jo Finney *(Chaplin)*, Martin Garner *(Yonkel)*, Terry Haven *(Alice)*, Allen Joseph *(Max)*, Philip M. Thomas *(Chaplin)*, Frank de Kova *(Old Vinnie)*, Candy Candido *(Sal)*, Ed Peck *(Italian Man)*, Lillian Adams, Mary Dean Lauria *(Italian Women)*, Donna Ponterotto *(Gelsa)*, Toni Basil *(The Lockers Staging and Choreography)*.

An animated feature which tries to give a hard-hitting portrait of Brooklyn street gangs in the 1950s. A raw and vulgar effect is attempted, but these characters are cartoons and simply don't intimidate. Begun in 1975, it draws some parallels with Martin Scorsese's MEAN STREETS by using the voices of two of that film's actors, Richard Romanus and David Proval. Surprisingly funny in parts, thanks to its exaggeration and absurdities.

p,d&w, Ralph Bakshi; ph, Ted C. Bemiller (Technicolor); m, John Madara, Ric Sandler; ed, Donald W. Ernst; animators, Brenda Banks, Carl Bell, Bob Carlson, John Gentilella, Steve Gordon, Manny Perez, Virgil Ross, John Sparey, Irven Spence, Tom Tataranowicz, Robert Taylor, John E. Walker, Sr.; background layout, Ira Turek; backgrounds, Johnny Vita.

Animated Drama Cas. (PR:O MPAA:R)

HEY! HEY! U.S.A.*½ (1938, Brit.) 92m GFD bw

Will Hay *(Benjamin Twist)*, Edgar Kennedy *(Bugs Leary)*, David Burns *(Tony Ricardo)*, Eddie Ryan *(Ace Marco)*, Fred Duprez *(Cyrus Schultz)*, Paddy Reynolds *(Mrs. Schultz)*, Tommy Bupp *(Bertie Schultz)*, Arthur Goullet *("Gloves" Johnson)*, Gibb McLaughlin *(Ship's Steward)*, Eddie Pola *(Announcer)*, Peter Gawthorne *(Captain)*.

The English take a look at Chicago gangsters as two rival Windy City gangs fight over a kidnaping aboard an ocean liner. Hay is an ex-school teacher who becomes the ship's porter and runs into the gangs who are after a millionaire's son. They get the boy after some wild, offbeat comic sequences, but funny man Hay manages to outwit them and save the lad.

p, Edward Black; d, Marcel Varnel; w, Marriott Edgar, Val Guest, J.O.C. Orton (based on a story by Jack Swain); ph, Arthur Crabtree.

Comedy (PR:A MPAA:NR)

HEY, LET'S TWIST!** (1961) 80m PAR bw

Joey Dee *(Himself)*, Teddy Randazzo *(Rickey Dee)*, The Starliters *(Themselves)*, Kay Armen *(Angie)*, Zohra Lampert *(Sharon)*, Dino di Luca *(Papa)*, Richard Dickens *(Dore)*, Jo-Ann Campbell *(Piper)*, Alan Arbus *(The Doctor)*, The Peppermint Loungers *(Themselves)*, Hope Hampton.

Brothers Dee and Randazzo turn dad's soda parlor into a twistin' joint in this fictionalized look at N.Y.'s famed Peppermint Lounge. With the arrival of the new dance craze, profits go up in conjunction with its popularity. But instead of being the teen hangout it once was, it becomes a "reservations only" bourgeois haven. Lots of fun as the "reservations only" sign diminishes the business, and Joey returns it to its former hangout for teens and a new success.

p, Harry Romm; d, Greg Garrison; w, Hal Hackady; ph, George Jacobson; m, Henry Glover; ed, Sid Katz; art d, Albert Brenner; cos, Natalie Walker.

Musical (PR:A MPAA:NR)

HEY, ROOKIE** (1944) 71m COL bw

Joe Besser *(Judge Pfeiffer)*, Ann Miller *(Winnie Clark)*, Larry Parks *(Jim Lighter)*, Joe Sawyer *(Sergeant)*, Jimmy Little *(Bert Pfeiffer)*, Selmer Jackson *(Col. Pfeiffer)*, Larry Thompson *(Capt. Jessop)*, Barbara Brown *(Mrs. Clark)*, Charles Trowbridge *(Gen. Willis)*, Charles Wilson *(Sam Jonas)*, Syd Saylor *(Cpl. Trupp)*, Doodles Weaver *(Maxon)*, Hi, Lo, Jack and a Dame, Condos Brothers, The Vagabonds, Jack Gilford, Johnson Brothers, Judy Clark and The Solid Senders, Bob Evans.

War-time comedy about a producer GI assigned to stage a show at an Army base. His problems in getting it done on a budget of $209 charge up the plot and send the film on its way to forced funniness as in so many similar musicals of the time. Songs include: "There Goes Taps," "When the Yardbirds Come to Town," "So What Serenade," "Keep 'em Happy," "He's Got a Wave in His Hair (and a WAC on His Hands)," "Hey, Rookie," "Take a Chance," "You're Good for My Morale," "It's Great To Be In A Uniform," "American Serenade," "Streamlined Sheik," "It's A Swelluva Life In The Army" (Henry Myers, Edward Eliscu, Jay Gorney, Sgt. J.C. Lewis).

p, Irving Briskin; d, Charles Barton; w, Henry Myers, Edward Eliscu, Jay Gorney (based on a play by K.E.B. Culvan, Doris Culvan; ph, L.W. O'Connell; ed, James Sweeney; md, M.W. Stoloff; art d, Lionel Banks; set d, Joseph Kish; ch, Val Raset, Stanley Donen.

Musical (PR:A MPAA:NR)

HEY THERE, IT'S YOGI BEAR** (1964) 89m COL c

Voices: Daws Butler *(Yogi Bear)*, Don Messick *(BooBoo, Ranger Smith)*, Julie Bennett *(Cindy Bear)*, Mel Blanc *(Grifter)*, Hal Smith *(Corn Pone)*, J. Pat O'Malley *(Snively)*, James Darren, Jean Vander Pyl.

A longer version of the TV cartoon which has Yogi, BooBoo, and Cindy up against a circus impresario and his nasty dog, "Mugger." James Darren contributes the tune "Ven-E, Ven-O, Ven-A." The kids will love it.

p&d, William Hanna, Joseph Barbera; w, Hanna, Barbera, Warren Foster; ph, Frank Paiker, Norman Stainback, Roy Wade, Charles Flekal, Frank Parrish, Ted Bemiller, Bill Kotler (Eastmancolor); m, Marty Paich; ed, Greg Watson, Warner Leighton, Tony Milch, Donald A. Douglas, Larry Cowan, Ken Spears; animators, Don Lusk, Irv Spence, George Kreisl, Ray Patterson, Jerry Hathcock, Grant Simmons, Fred Wolf, Don Peterson, Ken Harris, Garry Chiniquy, George Goepper, Edwin Aardal, Ed Parks, Kenneth Muse, Harry Holt; anim d, Charles A. Nichols; m/l, "Hey There, It's Yogi Bear," David Gates; "Ven-E, Ven-O, Ven-A," Ray Gilbert, Doug Goodwin (sung by James Darren); "Like I Like You," "Wet Your Whistle," "St. Louie," "Ash Can Parade," Gilbert, Doug Goodwin.

Animated Feature **(PR:AAA MPAA:G)**

HI BEAUTIFUL** (1944) 64m UNIV bw (GB: PASS TO ROMANCE)

Martha O'Driscoll *(Patty Callahan)*, Noah Beery, Jr. *(Jeff)*, Hattie McDaniel *(Millie)*, Walter Catlett *(Bisbee)*, Tim Ryan *(Babcock)*, Florence Lake *(Mrs. Bisbee)*, Grady Sutton *(Attendant)*, Lou Lubin *(Husband)*, Virginia Sale *(Wife)*, Tom Dugan *(Bus Driver)*, Dick Elliott *(Passenger)*, James [Jimmy] Dodd *(Soldier, Specialty)*, Barbara Perry *(Specialty Dancer)*, Ida Moore *(Landlady)*, Julia Gibson *(Girl)*, Gerald Perreau *(Boy)*, Ruth Lee *(Mother)*, Edna May Wonacott *(Young Girl)*, Gladys Blake *(Operator)*, Arline Harris *(Wacky Woman)*, Beatrice Roberts *(Hostess)*, Jack Rice, Herbert Rawlins, Forbes Murray, John Hamilton *(Board Members)*, Gerald Hamer, Alec Hanford *(Bearded Twins)*, Patty Patterson, Eva Lee Kuney *(Children)*.

After offering soldier Beery lodging in a model home, O'Driscoll falls in love with him. Eventually they win a marital contest for "Happiest G.I. Couple," but they're not even married. A harmless remake of LOVE IN A BUNGALOW. Songs include: "Don't Sweetheart Me," Charles Tobias, Cliff Friend; "Best Of All," Allie Wrubel.

p, Dick Irving Hyland; d, Leslie Goodwins; w, Hyland (from a story by Eleanor Griffin, William Rankin); ph, Paul Ivano; ed, Edward Curtiss; art d, John B. Goodman, Alexander Golitzen.

Romance **(PR:A MPAA:NR)**

HI, BUDDY** (1943) 66m UNIV bw

Dick Foran *(Dave O'Connor)*, Harriet Hilliard *(Gloria Bradley)*, Robert Paige *(Johnny Blake)*, Marjorie Lord *(Mary Parker)*, Bobs Watson *(Tim Martin)*, Tommy Cook *(Spud Winslow)*, Jennifer Holt *(Miss Russell)*, Gus Schilling *(Downbeat Collins)*, Wade Boteler *(Michael O'Shane)*, Drew Roddy *(Pat)*, The King's Men, The Step Brothers, The Four Sweethearts *(Themselves)*, George Chandler *(Oscar)*, Harry Strang *(Recruiting Sergeant)*, Emmett Vogan *(Announcer)*, Lorraine Krueger *(Dance Specialty)*, Dolores Diane *(Specialty)*, Rebel Randall *(Girl)*, Phil Warren *(Jeep Driver)*, Eddie Dew *(Man)*, Ronnie Rondell *(Soldier)*, Marilyn Kay *(Specialty)*, Dick Humphreys *(Specialty)*, Norman Ollstead *(Boy)*, Geraldine Chantlind *(Girl)*.

When an East Side boy's club is in dire financial straits it sets out to find someone to stage a fundraiser. Paige arranges to aid the club, but when his manager dips into the funds, soldier Foran comes to the rescue. The story is only a reason to stage the following tunes: "Hi, Buddy," "We're In The Marines," "Mr. Yankee Doodle" (Everett Carter, Milton Rosen); "We're In The Navy" (Don Ray, Gene DePaul); "Here's To Tomorrow" (Charles Newman, Lew Pollack); "Take Me In Your Arms" (Mitchell Parish, Fritz Rotter, Fred Markush); "Stardust" (Hoagy Carmichael, Parish); "Old Folks At Home," "De Camptown Races" (Stephen Foster).

p, Paul Malvern; d, Harold Young; w, Warren Wilson; ph, John W. Boyle; ed, Charles Maynard; md, Charles Previn; art d, Harold MacArthur.

Musical **(PR:A MPAA:NR)**

HI-DE-HO½** (1947) 72m FP bw

Cab Calloway *(Cab)*, Ida James *(Nettie)*, Jeni Le Gon *(Minnie)*, William Campbell *(Sparks)*, Virginia Garvin *(His Fat Friend)*, George Wiltshire *(Boss Mason)*, James Dunmore *(Mo the Mouse)*, Augustus Smith *(Preacher)*, Edgar Martin *(Owner of Jive Club)*, Leonard Rogers *(Ralph)*, David Bethea *(Owner of Brass Hat)*, Shepard Roberts *(Police Sergeant)*, Frederick Johnson *(Head Waiter)*, Cab Calloway Orchestra, Dusty "Open the Door Richard" Fletcher, The Peters Sisters, Miller Brothers and Lola.

Big band sensation Calloway becomes the interest of two gals' desires—his steady gal Le Gon and his manager James. Jealous of James' maneuvers, Le Gon hires a rival clubowner to do away with Calloway. Guilt takes hold of her, however, and she tries to prevent the killing. Instead, she gets dusted by the thugs, leaving the door open for a Calloway-James wedding. Along with Cab's title tune, are his and Elton Hill's "I Got A Gal Named Nettie." The Peters Sisters also deliver a couple of tunes: "Little Old Lady From Baltimore," "A Rainy Sunday."

p, E.M. Glucksman; d, Josh Binney; w, Hal Seeger; ph, Don Malkames; ed, Louis Hess; m/l, Cab Calloway, Seeger, Jack Palmer, Buster Harding, Elton Hill.

Musical **(PR:A MPAA:NR)**

HI DIDDLE DIDDLE*** (1943) 72m UA bw (AKA: DIAMONDS AND CRIME; TRY AND FIND IT)

Adolphe Menjou *(Col. Hector Phyffe)*, Martha Scott *(Janie Prescott)*, Pola Negri *(Genya Smetana)*, Dennis O'Keefe *(Sonny Phyffe)*, Billie Burke *(Mrs. Prescott)*, June Havoc *(Leslie Quayle)*, Walter Kingsford *(Senator Simpson)*, Barton Hepburn *(Peter Warrington III)*, George Metaxa *(Spinelli)*, Marek Windheim *(Pianist)*, Eddie Marr *(Croupier)*, Paul Porcasi *(Impresario)*, Lorraine Miller *(A Friend)*, Richard Hageman *(Boughton)*, Bert Roach *(Fat Man)*, Chick Chandler *(Chauffeur)*, Ellen Lowe *(Maid)*, Barry McCollum *(Cashier)*, Joe Devlin *(Bartender)*, Hal K. Dawson *(Minister)*, Andrew Tombes *(Doorman)*, Byron Foulger *(Watson)*, Ann Hunter *(Sandra)*.

O'Keefe and Scott are a couple of newlyweds who are only allowed a 48-hour honeymoon because of the sailor-groom's duties. For laughs the pair is continually interrupted by an onslaught of wacky characters. Between the bride's mother, Burke, and the groom's father, Menjou, the newlyweds barely get a chance to be alone. A quick-witted picture which also casts silent screen vamp Pola Negri as Menjou's jealous wife, singing "Evening Star." Other tunes include the honeymooner's lament "Too Little, Too Late," and "Man In the Big Sombrero" both delivered by June Havoc.

p&d, Andrew Stone; w, Frederick Jackson; ph, Charles Schoenbaum; ed, Harvey Manger; md, Phil Boutelje; anim d, Leon Schlesinger; m/l, Boutelje, Foster Carling.

Comedy **(PR:A MPAA:NR)**

HI, GANG!** (1941, Brit.) 100m Gainsborough/GFD bw

Bebe Daniels *(The Victory Girl)*, Ben Lyon *(Her Other Half)*, Vic Oliver *(The Nuisance with the Ideas)*, Moore Marriott *(Uncle Jerry)*, Graham Moffatt *(Albert)*, Felix Aylmer *(Lord Amersham)*, Georgina Mackinnon *(Mrs. Endicott)*, Maurice Rhodes *(Little Ben)*, Percy Parsons *(Hergensheimer)*, Diana Beaumont *(Secretary)*, Jacques Brown *(Botticelli)*, Sam Brown, The Green Sisters, Jay Wilbur and His Band, Mavis Villiers.

Daniels and Lyon are married radio stars who are also on-air rivals. Each gets a British evacuee on his or her respective show. Moffatt, Daniels' guest, is believed to be a missing lord's heir because he resides in a castle. The castle is really just a pub named "Castle," and Lyon discovers the mistake. This leads to an overseas chase and a false alarm announcing an invasion. A little worse for wear and tear, the happy couple returns once more to America and a bit of sanity. Fun on a minor level.

p, Edward Black; d, Marcel Varnel; w, Val Guest, Marriott Edgar, J.O.C. Orton, Howard Irving Young (based on the radio series by Bebe Daniels and Ben Lyon); ph, Jack Cox, Guy Green.

Comedy **(PR:A MPAA:NR)**

HI GAUCHO!* (1936) 59m Radio bw

John Carroll *(Lucio)*, Steffi Duna *(Inez)*, Rod La Rocque *(Escurra)*, Montagu Love *(Hillario)*, Ann Codee *(Dona Vincenta)*, Tom Ricketts *(Don Salvador)*, Paul Porcasi *(Ortegas)*, Enrique DeRosas, Julian Rivero, Frank Mills, Sam Appel, Harold Daniels, Ferike Boros.

In his starring debut Carroll saves the naive Duna from a sleazy bandit who impersonates an even sleazier old Spanish don to whom her hand has been promised in marriage. Set in Argentina, this horse-opry has nothing to offer except overthick accents. Songs include "Little White Rose," "Song Of The Open Road," "Bandit Song," "Panchita" (Albert Hay Malotte).

d, Thomas Atkins; w, Adele Buffington (based on a story by Atkins); ph, Jack MacKenzie.

Western **(PR:A MPAA:NR)**

HI, GOOD-LOOKIN'** (1944) 60m UNIV bw

Harriet Hilliard *(Kelly Clark)*, Eddie Quillan *(Dynamo Carson)*, Kirby Grant *(King Castle)*, Betty Kean *(Peggy)*, Roscoe Karns *(Archie)*, Vivian Austin *(Phyllis)*, Marjorie Gateson *(Mrs. Hardacre)*, Fuzzy Knight *(Joe Smedley)*, Milburn Stone *(Bill Eaton)*, Frank Fenton *(Gib Dickson)*, Robert Emmett Keane *(Homer Hardacre)*, Ozzie Nelson and His Orchestra, Jack Teagarden and His Orchestra, Delta Rhythm Boys, Tip, Tap and Toe *(Themselves)*, Janet Shaw, Jackie Lou Harding *(Information Girls)*, Sidney Miller *(Messenger Boy)*, John Hamilton *(Mr. McGillicuddy)*, Mary O'Brien, Marie Harmon *(Waitresses)*, Emmett Vogan *(Manager)*.

Good looking Hilliard is a vocalist from the Midwest who heads for Hollywood to make it big, and does. Her success doesn't come without the help of Grant, but he remains anonymous at first, then goes public with the new-found sensation. Songs include: "You're Just The Sweetest Thing" (Buzz Adlam, Walter Bishop); "Deacon Jones" (Johnny Lange, Hy Heath, Richard Loring); "Aunt Hagar's Blues" (W.C. Handy); "Just A Stowaway On A Ship Of Dreams" (Vic Knight); "A Slight Case Of Love" (Buzz Adlam); "By Mistake" (Inez James, Sidney Miller); "I Won't Forget The Dawn" (Don Raye, Gene DePaul); "Paper Doll" (Johnny Black).

p, Frank Gross; d, Edward C. Lilley; w, Paul Gerard Smith, Bradford Ropes, Eugene Conrad (based on a story by Smith); ph, Jerome Ash; ed, Edgar Zane; md, Hans J. Salter; art d, John Goodman.

Musical **(PR:A MPAA:NR)**

HI IN THE CELLAR (SEE: UP IN THE CELLAR, 1970)

HI, MOM!** (1970) 87m West End/SIGMA III c/bw

Robert De Niro *(John Rubin)*, Charles Durnham *(Superintendent)*, Allen Garfield *(Joe Banner)*, Abraham Goren *(Pervert in Theater)*, Lara Parker *(Jeannie Mitchell)*, Jennifer Salt *(Judy Bishop)*, Gerrit Graham *(Gerrit Wood)*, Nelson Peltz *(Playboy)*, Peter Maloney *(Pharmacist)*, William Daley *(Co-op Neighbor)*, Floyd L. Peterson *(Newscaster)*, Hector Valentin Lino, Jr., Carole Leverett *(N.I.T. Journal Revolutionaries)*, Ruth Bocour, Bart DePalma, Arthur Bierman *(N.I.T. Journal at Newsstand)*, Buddy Butler, David Conell, Milton Earl Forrest, Carolyn Caraven, Joyce Griffin, Kirk Kirksey *("Be Black, Baby!" Troupe)*, Ruth Alda, Carol Vogel, Beth Bowden, Joe Stillman, Joe Fields, Gene Eldman, Paul Milvy *(Audience)*.

HI, MOM! is one of De Palma's better efforts, before he began to emulate Hitchcock and go too far in his treatment of women. De Niro is a porno filmmaker (8-mm) who leases a ratty apartment in New York, across the street from an expensive co-op down on the lower East Side. In that new building lives Garfield, a high-class producer of high-class pornography, lauded by his compatriots in the adult film business as being the Sam Goldwyn of smut. The best scene in the picture is when a benevolent Garfield takes De Niro under his wing and gives him advice about how to make these sleazy movies. It's sort of like Louis B. Mayer talking to Irving Thalberg. De Niro, now working for Garfield, sets up his camera and begins to film the people in the apartment building. They include Graham, a radical, Peltz, a ne'er-do-well playboy-type, three single girls (led by Salt) and a middle-class family with two kids. De Niro spies Salt and wants to sleep with her (both for his own benefit and the camera's) and he sets up his camera on his window sill, goes across the street, and proceeds to seduce her, but his camera falls and he misses his opportunity to immortalize the encounter on film. De Niro is a Viet Nam veteran who has trouble finding work, so he auditions for an acting job in a revue and gets a small role as a policeman. It's a scathing satire of public television as the crew comes to the theater to film the pretentious show called "Be Black, Baby!" The actors all walk out in whiteface and begin to blacken the faces of the white audience as part of the "Involvement" in the show. All the while, the pseudo-intellectual cameras of NIT (National Intellectual Television) are recording everything. The cast then begins to abuse the liberal audience, both verbally and physically, and the crowd loves it, thinking they are involved in some sort of dramatic breakthrough. Meanwhile, a gang of urban guerrillas, led by Wood, raids the huge apartment building but they are all cut down by machine-gun fire. A young businessman in the high-rise just happens to have a 50 millimeter gun in his apartment. Salt and De Niro marry and she gets pregnant and becomes an instant nag, pestering him forever with her dreams of having a dishwasher. De Niro calmly goes to the building's basement and tosses a huge charge of dynamite into the clothes washer which levels the entire building. Later, De Niro is interviewed by TV reporters and tells them how much he hates violence. De Niro, before he became a huge star, made a fine living playing weird types (MEAN STREETS, TAXI DRIVER, GREETINGS) and his role here is no exception. HI MOM is an original, almost anarchistic picture, that might have been more effective in someone else's hands. De Palma never seems to know when to stop and usually can be found standing at the crossroads of brilliance and bad taste. Unfortunately, he seems always to choose the latter. Three songs: "I'm Looking At You," "Be Black, Baby!" and "Hi, Mom!" Partially filmed in 16mm, black and white.

p, Charles Hirsch; d&w, Brian De Palma (based on a story by De Palma, Hirsch); ph, Robert Elfstrom (Eastmancolor); m, Eric Katz; ed, Paul Hirsch; art d, Peter Bocour; m/l, Katz, John Andreoni.

Comedy **(PR:O MPAA:R)**

HI, NEIGHBOR*½ (1942) 72m REP bw

Jean Parker, John Archer, Janet Beecher, Marilyn Hare, Bill Shirley, Pauline Drake, Fred Sherman, Vera Vague, Don Wilson, Harry "Pappy" Cheshire, Lulubelle and Scotty, Roy Acuff, Lillian Randolph.

A small college is threatened with bankruptcy, so with the help of some "Grand Ole Opry" stars and other radio personalities of the time, it turns into a vacation resort during the summer months. Little noticed when released and little remembered today.

p, Armand Schaefer; d, Charles Lamont; w, Dorrell McGowan, Stuart McGowan; ph, Ernest Miller; ed, Howard O'Neill; md, Cy Feuer; art d, Russell Kimball.

Comedy **(PR:A MPAA:NR)**

HI, NELLIE!** (1934) 75m WB bw

Paul Muni *(Bradshaw)*, Glenda Farrell *(Gerry)*, Douglas Dumbrille *(Harvey Dawes)*, Robert Barrat *(Brownell)*, Ned Sparks *(Shammy)*, Hobart Cavanaugh *(Fullerton)*, Pat Wing *(Sue)*, Edward Ellis *(O'Connell)*, George Meeker *(Sheldon)*, Berton Churchill *(Graham)*, Sidney Miller *(Louie)*, Kathryn Sergava, Paul Kaye, Donald Meek, Dorothy Le Baire, Marjorie Gateson, Harold Huber, Allen Vincent, Pat Wing, Frank Reicher, George Chandler, George Humbert, James Donlan.

This was the second of five times around for this story and Muni's first comedy (it was his sixth picture). United Artists had released a similar picture the year before with Lee Tracy in the lead called ADVICE TO THE LOVELORN. It was remade as LOVE IS ON THE AIR (1937), YOU CAN'T ESCAPE FOREVER (1942) and THE HOUSE ACROSS THE STREET (1949)—and there are probably plans to make it again somewhere. Nathanael West did it best, though, with his novel *Miss Lonelyhearts*, although the movie, starring Montgomery Clift, never realized the potential of the subject. In HI, NELLIE! Muni is the editor of a big city newspaper who has a fight with his publisher and is lowered to the rank of "lonelyhearts" columnist, a job everyone hates and he particularly despises. The result is that Muni begins to make friends with John Barleycorn. He is further miffed when his rival, Dumbrille, is named editor. Farrell had held the lonelyhearts job prior to Muni and she tells him that he can make a go of it if he really tries. Muni decides that his pride is more easily swallowed than he'd thought and he devotes himself to the column until it catches on and becomes widely-read. Some gangsters kidnap and murder a banker and bury him under the name of another person. Muni does a bit of snooping and solves the crime, breaks the story, and gets his old position back. It's a mild comedy, just a few laughs, and Muni struggles through the tepid script with the same doggedness that his character applied to making the lovelorn column work. Not a success at the box office or with the critics, HI, NELLIE! stands as an example of the misuse of a talent.

p, Robert Presnell; d, Mervyn Le Roy; w, Sidney Sutherland, Abem Finkel (based on a story by Roy Chanslor); ph, Sol Polito; art d, Robert Haas.

Crime Comedy **(PR:A MPAA:NR)**

HI-RIDERS* (1978) 90m Dimension c

Mel Ferrer, Stephen McNally, Darby Hinton, Neville Brand, Ralph Meeker, Diane Peterson.

Wretched tale of drag racers and their hangers-on interesting only for a bunch of familiar, if aging, actors who must have been desperate for work.

p, Mike Macfarland; d&w, Greydon Clark; m, Gerald Lee.

Drama **(PR:O MPAA:R)**

HI'YA, CHUM* (1943) 60m UNIV bw (GB: EVERYTHING HAPPENS TO US)

Al Ritz, Jimmy Ritz, Harry Ritz *(Merry Madcaps)*, Jane Frazee *(Sunny)*, Robert Paige *(Tommy Craig)*, June Clyde *(Madge)*, Paul Hurst *(Archie Billings)*, Edmund MacDonald *(Terry Barton)*, Andrew Tombes *(Cook)*, Lou Lubin *(Eddie Gibbs)*, Ray Walker *(Jackson)*, Earl Hodgins *(Man)*, Brooks Benedict, Richard Davies, Ray Miller, Michael Vallon.

The Ritz Brothers hop in a dilapidated Model T with gals Frazee and Clyde, ending up in a California ghost town turned boom town. They open up a diner and soon color it with glamour girls. A no-mentality script can't be saved by the Brothers' stupid antics. Songs include: "You Gotta Have Personality," "He's My Guy," "Two On A Bike," "Doo Dat," "I'm Hitting A High Spot" (Don Raye, Gene DePaul). (See RITZ BROTHERS series, Index.)

p, Howard Benedict; d, Harold Young; w, Edmund L. Hartmann; ph, Charles Van Enger; ed, Maurice Wright; md, H.J. Salter; art d, Jack Otterson.

Comedy **(PR:A MPAA:NR)**

HI' YA, SAILOR** (1943) 61m UNIV bw

Donald Woods *(Bob Jackson)*, Elyse Knox *(Pat Rogers)*, Eddie Quillan *(Corky Mills)*, Frank Jenks *(Deadpan Weaver)*, Phyllis Brooks *(Nanette)*, Jerome Cowan *(Lou Asher)*, Matt Wills *(Bull Rogan)*, Florence Lake *(Secretary)*, Charles Coleman *(Doorman)*, Mantan Moreland *(Sam)*, Jack Mulhall *(Police Lieutenant)*, Martha Vickers *(Bit)*, Ray Eberle and His Orchestra, Wingy Malone and His Orchestra, Delta Rhythm Boys, Leo Diamond Quintet, Mayris Chaney and Her Dance Trio, George Beatty, Hacker Duo, Nilsson Sisters.

After Navyman Woods gets duped by a New York publisher, he heads for the metropolis to find fame and fortune. What he finds is a friendly lady cab driver played by Knox, and a vocalist who covers one of his tunes in Brooks. That's all you're going to find in terms of plot in this big band version of a rock video. The long list of musical numbers includes: "A Dream Ago," "Babies Ball," "Spell Of The Moon," "Hi' Ya, Sailor," "So Goodnight," "Just A Stop Away From Heaven" (Everett Carter, Milt Rosen); "The More I Go Out With Somebody Else" (Billy Post, Don Pierce, Pierre Norman); "Oh Brother" (Maxine Manners, Jean Miller); "One O'Clock Jump" (Count Basie, Harry James).

p&d, Jean Yarbrough; w, Stanley Roberts (based on a story by Fanya Roberts); ph, Jack MacKenzie, Jerome Ash; ed, William Austin; md, H.J. Salter; art d, John Goodman.

Musical **(PR:A MPAA:NR)**

HI-YO SILVER½** (1940) 69m REP bw

Lee Powell *(Allen King/The Lone Ranger)*, Chief Thunder-Cloud *(Tonto)*, Herman Brix [Bruce Bennett] *(Bert Rogers)*, Lynn Roberts *(Joan Blanchard)*, Stanley Andrews *(Jeffries)*, George Cleveland *(Blanchard)*, William Farnum *(Father McKim)*, Hal Taliaferro [Wally Wales] *(Bob Stuart)*, Lane Chandler *(Dick Forrest)*, George Letz *(Jim Clark)*, John Merton *(Kester)*, Sammy McKim *(Sammy)*, Tom London *(Felton)*, Raphael Bennett *(Taggart)*, Maston Williams *(Snead)*, Frank McGlynn, Sr. *(Lincoln)*, Raymond Hatton, Dickie Jones, Silver the horse.

A feature-length version of the 15-chapter 1938 Lone Ranger film serial starring Lee Powell as the masked man. Along with his trusty sidekick Tonto, Powell defeats the marauders who took over in Texas in the days of Reconstruction following the Civil War. Republic added Hatton as a narrator piecing together the reels by telling the story to the young Dickie Jones.

p, Sol C. Siegel; d, William Witney, John English; w, Barry Shipman, George Washington Yates, Franklyn Adreon, Ronald Davidson, Lois Eby (based on the radio serial "The Lone Ranger" by Fran Striker); ph, William Nobles; ed, Helene Turner, Edward Todd; md, Alberto Columbo.

Western **(PR:AA MPAA:NR)**

HIAWATHA** (1952) 79m MON c

Vincent Edwards *(Hiawatha)*, Yvette Dugay *(Minnehaha)*, Keith Larsen *(Pau Puk Keewis)*, Gene Iglesias *(Chibiabos)*, Armando Sylvestre *(Kwasind)*, Michael Tolan *(Neyadji)*, Ian MacDonald *(Megissogwon)*, Katherine Emery *(Nokomis)*, Morris Ankrum *(Igaoo)*, Stephen Chase *(Lakku)*, Stuart Randall *(Mudjekeewis)*, Richard Bartlett *(Chunung)*, Michael Granger *(Ajawac)*, Robert Bice *(Wabeek)*, Gene Peterson *(Hikon)*, Henry Corden *(Ottobang)*.

Edwards is cast as the title character in this family version of the classic Longfellow poem. As a member of the Ojibway (Chippewa) tribe, he heads for the neighboring Dakotah territory to find out if they are planning an attack. He falls in love with Minnehaha and eventually they marry. An entertaining film for kids that masks its theme in a flurry of arrows and romance.

p, Walter Mirisch; d, Kurt Neumann; w, Dan Ullman, Arthur Strawn (based on the poem by Henry Wadsworth Longfellow); ph, Harry Neumann (Cinecolor); m, Marlin Skiles; ed, Walter Hannemann; art d, David Milton.

Drama **(PR:AAA MPAA:NR)**

HICKEY AND BOGGS*** (1972) 111m Film Guarantors/UA c

Bill Cosby *(Al Hickey)*, Robert Culp *(Frank Boggs)*, Rosalind Cash *(Nyona)*, Sheila Sullivan *(Edith Boggs)*, Isabel Sanford *(Nyona's Mother)*, Ta-Ronce Allen *(Nyona's Daughter)*, Lou Frizzell *(Lawyer)*, Nancy Howard *(Apartment Manager's Wife)*, Bernard Nedell *(Used Car Salesman)*, Carmen *(Mary Jane)*, Louis Moreno *(Quemando, Prisoner)*, Ron Henrique *(Quemando, Florist)*, Cary Sanchez *(Mary Jane's Daughter)*, Jason Culp *(Mary Jane's Son)*, Robert Mandan *(Mr. Brill)*, Michael Moriarty *(Ballard)*, Bernie Schwartz *(Bernie)*, Denise Renfro *(Brill's Daughter)*, Vincent Gardenia *(Papadakis)*, Jack Colvin *(Shaw)*, James Woods *(Lt. Wyatt)*, Ed Lauter *(Ted)*, Lester Fletcher *(Rice)*, Gil Stuart *(Perkins)*, Sil Words *(Mr. Leroy)*, Joe Tata *(Coroner's Asst.)*, Jerry Summers *(Bledsoe)*, Dean Smith *(Bagman)*, Bill Hickman *(Monte)*, Matt Bennett *(Fatboy)*, Tommy Signorelli *(Nick)*, Gerald Peters *(Jack)*, Keri Shuttleton, Wanda Spell, Winston Spell *(Playground Kids)*.

Cosby and Culp, who teamed successfully on TV's "I Spy" in the mid-1960s, are private eyes hired to track down a lawyer's missing girl friend who soon find themselves on the trail of $400,000 stolen from a Pittsburgh bank. As it turns out the girl is married to a radical Chicano and is trying to sell the bills by sending out $1,000 samples. They follow her to the LA Coliseum where they break up a meeting with some buyers, saving the girl's life, though she escapes with the cash. After Cosby's wife is brutally murdered by a mob boss, the detective's search becomes vengeful. A perceptive character study of an insignificant pair who must resign themselves to the fact that they can't change the world. *Film noir* with a modern day edge to it, penned by Walter Hill who the same year wrote Sam Peckinpah's THE GETAWAY.

p, Fouad Said; d, Robert Culp; w, Walter Hill; ph, Wilmer Butler (DeLuxe Color); m, Ted Ashford; ed, David Berlatsky; cos, Bill Thiese, Pauline Campbell; spec eff, Joe Lombardi; m/l, title song, George Edwards (sung by Edwards).

Drama **(PR:C MPAA:PG)**

HIDDEN DANGER** (1949) 54m MON bw

Johnny Mack Brown *(Johnny)*, Raymond Hatton *(Banty)*, Max Terhune *(Alibi)*, Christine Larson *(Valerie)*, Myron Healey *(Carson)*, Marshall Reed *(Mason)*, Kenne Duncan *(Benda)*, Edmund Cobb *(Sheriff)*, Steve Clark *(Russell)*, Milburn Morante *(Clerk)*, Carol Henry *(Trigger)*, Bill Hale *(Sanderson)*, Bob Woodward *(Joe)*, Boyd Stockman *(Loop)*, Bill Potter *(Perry)*.

Another Johnny Mack Brown oater in which he cracks Healey's illegit protection of cattle ranchers who are conned into selling their beef to him at a loss. From the "Three Mesquiteer" series, Max Terhune is cast as a ventriloquist.

p, Barney Sarecky; d, Ray Taylor; w, J. Benton Cheney, Eliot Gibbons; ph, Harry Neumann; ed, John C. Fuller; md, Edward Kay.

Western **(PR:A MPAA:NR)**

HIDDEN ENEMY*½ (1940) 63m MON bw

Warren Hull *(Bill)*, Kay Linaker *(Sonia)*, William Von Brinken *(Werner)*, George Cleveland *(McGregor)*, William Costello *(Bowman)*, Fern Emmett *(Aunt Mary)*, Ed Keane *(Editor)*.

When Cleveland invents a metal which is three times lighter than aluminum and stronger than steel, the spies come to his door like lemmings to the sea cliff. Together with his newspaper sleuth son Hull, Cleveland fends off Von Brinken, Costello, and the seemingly naive Linaker. Plenty of problems in the suspense category; building it, that is.

p, T. R. Williams; d, Howard Bretherton; w, C.B. Williams, Marlan Orth (based on the story by Williams); ph, Harry Neumann; ed, Robert Golden.

Crime **(PR:A MPAA:NR)**

HIDDEN EYE, THE*** (1945) 70m MGM bw

Edward Arnold *(Duncan Maclain)*, Frances Rafferty *(Jean Hampton)*, William "Bill" Phillips *(Marty Corbell)*, Ray Collins *(Philip Treadway)*, Paul Langton *(Harry Gifford)*, Thomas Jackson *(Insp. Delaney)*, Morris Ankrum *(Ferris)*, Robert Lewis *(Stormvig)*, Francis Pierlot *(Kossovsky)*, Sondra Rodgers *(Helen Roberts)*, Theodore Newman *(Gibbs)*, Jack Lambert *(Louie)*, Ray Largay *(Arthur Hampton)*, Leigh Whipper *(Alistair)*, Byron Foulger *(Burton Harrison)*, Lee Phelps *(Polasky)*, Eddie Acuff *(Whitey)*, Bob Pepper *(Sgt. Kramer)*, Russell Hicks *(Rodney Hampton)*, Friday the dog.

Blind detective Arnold relies on his remaining senses and his dog Friday to solve a trio of murders and prevent a fourth. He is able to sniff his way to the killer when the common clue turns out to be an Oriental fragrance. The guilty one is a family lawyer who is dipping into his client's funds. Oddly enough, this one is able to hold your attention. A sequel to EYES IN THE NIGHT.

p, Robert Sisk; d, Richard Whorf; w, George Harmon Coxe, Harry Ruskin (based on the characteres created by Baynard Kendrick); ph, Lester White; m, David Snell; ed, George Hively; art d, Cedric Gibbons, Preston Ames.

Crime **(PR:A MPAA:NR)**

HIDDEN FEAR* (1957) 83m UA bw

John Payne *(Mike Brent)*, Alexander Knox *(Hartman)*, Conrad Nagel *(Arthur Miller)*, Natalie Norwick *(Susan Brent)*, Anne Neyland *(Virginia Kelly)*, Kjeld Jacobsen *(Lt. Knudsen)*, Paul Erling *(Gibbs)*, Mogens Brandt *(Lund)*, Marianne Schleiss *(Helga Hartman)*, Knud Rex *(Jacobsen)*, Elsie Albiin *(Inga)*, Buster Larsen *(Hans Ericsen)*, Preben Mahrt *(Slim)*, Kjeld Petersen.

The plot has Payne traveling to Copenhagen to keep a murder rap from being hung on his sister. In the meantime he gets mixed up with Knox's counterfeiting operation. He does some unlikely fist-swinging and puts the gang on ice. Somehow, all this leads to his sister's release. Payne spends most of his time thinking he is a male wonder, frequently eyed by an array of Denmark dames, though he's really quite a bore. Shot on location in Copenhagen.

p, Robert St. Aubrey, Howard E. Kohn II; d, Andre de Toth; w, de Toth, John Ward Hawkins; ph, Wilfred M. Cline; m, Hans Schreiber; ed, David Wages; art d, Erik Aaes; cos, Magasin du Nord.

Crime **(PR:C MPAA:NR)**

HIDDEN FORTRESS, THE**** (1959, Jap.) 137m Toho/Albex bw (KAKUSHI TORIDE NO SAN AKUNIN; AKA: THREE RASCALS IN THE HIDDEN FORTRESS; THREE BAD MEN IN THE HIDDEN FORTRESS)

Toshiro Mifune *(Rokurota)*, Misa Uehara *(Lady Yukihime)*, Minoru Chiaki *(Tahei)*, Kamatari Fujiwara *(Matashichi)*, Susumu Fujita *(The Grateful Soldier)*, Takashi Shimura *(The Old General)*, Eiko Miyoshi *(The Old Woman)*, Toshiko Higuchi *(The Farmer's Daughter)*, Kichijiro Ueda *(Girl-Dealer)*.

Two unlikely-looking soldiers, Chiaki and Fujiwara, flee following the defeat of their army. They stumble across a gold bar hidden in some firewood but before they can take it Mifune, a general in the defeated forces, appears and enlists the two to help him take a wagon load of gold—plus deposed princess Uehara—to safety in the next province. They encounter a series of difficulties, and at one point Mifune has to fight an enemy with lances. One of Kurosawa's best works—with an odd mix of periods, from Medieval to modern—the film is filled with humor and excitement, owing more to Hollywood adventure films than to the Japanese tradition. George Lucas claimed that THE HIDDEN FORTRESS was the chief inspiration for STAR WARS and it is easy to see the resemblance, especially in Chiaki and Fujiwara, who were copied in tin to make R2-D2 and C-3PO. Released in the U.S. in 1959 in an abbreviated 90 minute print, the film quickly disappeared here and was not released in its full-length version until 1983. A classic film by one of the great directors.

d, Akira Kurosawa; w, Ryuzo Kikushima, Hideo Oguni, Shinobu Hashimoto, Kurosawa; ph, Kazuo Yamazaki; m, Masaru Sato.

Adventure **(PR:C MPAA:NR)**

HIDDEN GOLD** (1933) 60m UNIV bw

Tom Mix, Judith Barrie, Raymond Hatton, Eddie Gribbon, Donald Kirke, Willis Clarke, Roy Moore, Tony, Jr., the horse.

A fairly late Mix oater sees the cowboy first as a boxer, then going undercover as a jail inmate to win the confidence of three crooks and locate where they have stashed their golden loot. Climax is a forest fire in which two of the outlaws are killed.

p, Carl Laemmle, Jr.; d, Arthur Rosson; w, Jack Natteford, James Mulhauser; ph, Dan Clark.

Western **(PR:A MPAA:NR)**

HIDDEN GOLD½** (1940) 60m PAR bw

William Boyd *(Hopalong Cassidy)*, Russell Hayden *(Lucky)*, Britt Wood *(Speedy)*, Ruth Rogers *(Jane Colby)*, Roy Barcroft *(Hendricks)*, Minor Watson *(Ed Colby)*, Ethel Wales *(Matilda Purdy)*, Lee Phelps *(Sheriff Cameron)*, George Anderson *(Ward Ackerman)*, Jack Rockwell *(Stage Driver)*, Eddie Dean *(Logan)*, Raphael Bennett *(Fleming)*, Walter Long, Bob Kortman, Merrill McCormack.

All the necessary elements are thrown into this addition to the Hopalong Cassidy series as Boyd and sidekick Hayden stand up to a gang of bandits preying on stagecoaches and gold mines. The big six-gun finale comes at Watson's mine where, once again, our heroes emerge victorious. (See HOPALONG CASSIDY series, Index.)

p, Harry Sherman; d, Lesley Selander; w, Gerald Geraghty, Jack Mersereau (based on the characters created by Clarence E. Mulford); ph, Russell Harlan; ed, Carroll Lewis; md, Irving Talbot; art d, Lewis J. Rachmil.

Western **(PR:A MPAA:NR)**

HIDDEN GUNS*** (1956) 66m REP bw

Bruce Bennett *(Stragg)*, Richard Arlen *(Sheriff Young)*, John Carradine *(Snipe Harding)*, Faron Young *(Faron)*, Lloyd Corrigan *(Judge Wallis)*, Angie Dickinson *(Becky Carter)*, Damian O'Flynn *(Kingsley)*, Irving Bacon *(Doc Carter)*, Tom Hubbard *(Grandy)*, Ron Kennedy *(Burt Miller)*, Bill Ward *(Joe Miller)*, Raymond L. Morgan *(Emmett)*, Edmund Cobb *(Ben Williams)*, Ben Welden *(Peabody)*, Guinn "Big Boy" Williams *(Fiddler)*, Gordon Terry *(Terry)*, Michael Darrin, Charles Heard, Bill Coontz.

Father and son law enforcers Arlen and Young set out to reform a community influenced by gambler Bennett. After Arlen is gunned down, Young tries to bring about Bennett's downfall and is pitted against him in a duel. He notices a hidden sniper, however, but still is able to outshoot the baddies. Carradine is exceptional as Bennett's cold-blooded hired gunman, and country/western music star Young is equally effective. One of the more interesting angles in this film is the use of a choral group as a comment on the action. Erich von Stroheim, Jr., the son of the great director, served as assistant director.

p, Al Gannaway, C.J. Ver Halen, Jr.; d, Gannaway; w, Gannaway, Sam Roeca; ph, Clark Ramsey; m, Ramez Idriss; ed, Leon Barsha; m/l, Gannaway, Hal Levy.

Western **(PR:C MPAA:NR)**

HIDDEN HAND, THE½** (1942) 67m WB bw

Craig Stevens *(Peter Thorne)*, Elisabeth Fraser *(Mary Winfield)*, Julie Bishop *(Rita)*, Willie Best *(Chauffeur)*, Frank Wilcox *(Dr. Lawrence Channing)*, Cecil Cunningham *(Lorinda Channing)*, Ruth Ford *(Estelle)*, Milton Parsons *(John Channing)*, Roland Drew *(Walter Channing)*, Tom Stevenson *(Horace Channing)*, Marian Hall *(Nurse)*, Inez Gary *(Hattie)*, Kam Tong *(Mallo)*, Creighton Hale, Monte Blue.

A confused mystery which has the bug-eyed Parsons cast as an escapee from a mental asylum. He returns home and kills a dozen people before his rage is ended by the heroic Craig Stevens who later became TV's Peter Gunn. At times very creepy, but also, perhaps unintentionally, funny.

p, William Jacobs; d, Ben Stoloff; w, Anthony Coldeway, Raymond Schrock (based on the play "Invitation to a Murder" by Rufus King); ph, Henry Sharp; ed, Harold McLernon; art d, Stanley Fleischer.

Horror **(PR:C MPAA:NR)**

HIDDEN HOMICIDE** (1959, Brit.) 70m RFD/REP bw

Griffith Jones *(Michael Cornforth)*, James Kenney *(Oswald/Mrs. Dodge/Kate)*, Patricia Laffan *(Jean)*, Bruce Seton *(Bill Dodd)*, Maya Koumani *(Marian)*, Robert Raglan *(Ashbury)*, Richard Shaw *(Wright)*, Charles Farrell *(Mungo Peddey)*, Peter Carver *(Wally Gizzard)*, Danny Green *(Darby)*, John Moore *(The Stranger)*, David Chivers *(Chemist)*, Norman Wynne *(Publican)*, Frank Hawkins *(Ben Leacock)*, Jan Wilson *(Porter)*, Joe Wadham *(Marshall)*, John Watson *(Policeman)*.

When a novelist wakes up in his room he finds some unwanted surprises waiting for him. One, there's a gun in his hand. Next, he finds a relative dead. Is he the killer? With the help of a lady hitchhiker, the writer finally discovers that a female impersonator is the true killer. It pays to befriend the needy.

p, Derek Winn; d, Tony Young; w, Young, Bill Luckwell (based on the novel *Murder at Shinglestrand* by Paul Capon); ph, Ernest Palmer; m, Otto Ferrari; ed, John Ferris; md, Ferrari; art d, Wilfred Arnold.

Crime **(PR:C MPAA:NR)**

HIDDEN MENACE, THE** (1940, Brit.) 56m ABF/Alliance bw (GB: STAR OF THE CIRCUS)

Otto Kruger *(Garvin)*, Gertrude Michael *(Yesta)*, John Clements *(Paul Huston)*, Patrick Barr *(Truxa)*, Barbara Blair *(Hilda)*, Gene Sheldon *(Peters)*, John Turnbull *(Tenzler)*, Norah Howard *(Frau Schlipp)*, Alfred Wellesley *(Ackermann)*, Dora Gregory.

Dancer Michael is the object of both Kruger's and Clements' desires. The nasty Kruger, a magician, has invented a light-projecting device which shines at the high-wire, making the one rope appear to be many. Tightrope walker Barr chickens out and hires Clements to do his act while he keeps his feet safely on the sawdust. Set in Vienna, there is an abundance of locale shots, as well as many circus performances.

p, Walter C. Mycroft; d, Albert De Courville; w, Elizabeth Meehan, Hans Zerlett, John Monk Saunders, Dudley Leslie (based on the novel *December With Truxa* by Heinrich Zeiler); ph, Claude Friese-Greene; ed, Lionel Tomlinson.

Drama/Romance **(PR:A MPAA:NR)**

HIDDEN POWER* (1939) 60m COL bw

Jack Holt *(Dr. Garfield)*, Gertrude Michael *(Virginia)*, Dickie Moore *(Steve)*, Marilyn Knowlden *(Imogene)*, Regis Toomey *(Mayton)*, Henry Kolker *(Weston)*, Henry Hayden *(Downey)*, William B. Davidson *(Foster)*, Holmes Herbert *(Dr. Morley)*, Christan Rub.

All about a scientist who spends his every waking hour trying to develop a burn anti-toxin. His wife fails to understand his devotion to research and divorces him, taking son Moore with her. Of course the anti-toxin is used to save Moore's life at the end of the film. Even Dickie Moore, who was close to leaving childhood, can't inject life into this terminal case.

p, Larry Darmour; d, Lewis D. Collins; w, Gordon Rigby; ph, James S. Brown, Jr.; m, Lee Zahler; ed, Dwight Caldwell.

Drama **(PR:A MPAA:NR)**

HIDDEN ROOM, THE*** (1949, Brit.) 98m GFD/EL-RANK bw (GB: OBSESSION)

Robert Newton *(Dr. Clive Riordan)*, Sally Gray *(Storm Riordan)*, Naunton Wayne *(Supt. Finsbury)*, Phil Brown *(Bill Kronin)*, Olga Lindo *(Mrs. Humphreys)*, Ronald Adam *(Clubman)*, James Harcourt *(Aitkin)*, Allan Jeayes *(Clubman)*, Russell Waters *(Detective)*, Betty Cooper, Roddy Hughes, Lyonel Watts, Stanley Baker, Monty *(The Dog)*.

Neat little suspense story has Newton playing a cuckolded doctor. Fed up with his wife's infidelities, he decides to murder her latest lover (Brown.) Newton kidnaps the man and hides him in a cellar while preparing a deadly acid bath. It looks like a grim fate for Brown but the plot is foiled by the wife's pooch who follows the pair and ends up leading the cops to the scene. Some fine moments and good suspense in an interesting story.

p, Nat A. Bronsten; d, Edward Dmytryk; w, Alec Coppel (based on his novel *A Man about a Dog*); ph, C. M. Pennington-Richards; m, Mino Rota; ed, Lito Carruthers; art d, Duncan Sutherland.

Crime/Suspense **(PR:A MPAA:NR)**

HIDDEN ROOM OF 1,000 HORRORS (SEE: TELL-TALE HEART, THE, 1962, Brit.)

HIDDEN VALLEY** (1932) 60m MON bw

Bob Steele, Gertrude Messinger, Francis McDonald, Ray Haller, John Elliott, Arthur Millet, V. L. Barnes, Joe De LaCruz, Dick Dickinson, George Hayes, Capt. Verner L. Smith, Tom London.

An early Steele western finds him riding out in a lonely valley. It seems someone has hidden a treasure there and Steele's out to find the booty.

p, Trem Carr; d, Robert N. Bradbury; w, Wellyn Totman (based on his story).

Western **(PR:A MPAA:NR)**

HIDDEN VALLEY OUTLAWS** (1944) 56m REP bw

Bill Elliott, George Hayes, Anne Jeffreys, Roy Barcroft, Kenne Duncan, John James, Charles Miller, Fred Toones, Budd Buster, Tom London, LeRoy Mason, Earle Hodgins, Yakima Canutt, Jack Kirk, Tom Steele, Bud Geary, Frank McCarroll, Edward Cassidy, Bob Wilke, Charles Morton, Cactus Mack, Forbes Murray, Frank O'Connor.

A gang of landgrabbers decides to take over the Southwest. It's up to Elliott to save the day, a feat he accomplishes nicely.

p, Louis Gray; d, Howard Bretherton; w, John K. Butler, Bob Williams (based on a story by Butler); ph, Reggie Lanning; m, Mort Glickman; ed, Tony Martinelli; art d, Fred Ritter.

Western **(PR:A MPAA:NR)**

HIDE AND SEEK*½ (1964, Brit.) 90m Spectrum/UNIV bw

Ian Carmichael *(David Garrett)*, Janet Munro *(Maggie)*, Curt Jurgens *(Hubert Marek)*, George Pravda *(Frank Melnicker)*, Hugh Griffith *(Wilkins)*, Kieron Moore *(Paul)*, Derek Tansley *(Chambers)*, Judy Parfitt *(Chauffeur)*, Esma Cannon *(Tea Lady)*, John Boxer *(Secretary)*, Cardew Robinson *(Constable)*, Barbara Roscoe *(Bride)*, Tommy Godfrey *(Drunken Songwriter)*, Lance Percival *(Idiot)*, Julian Orchard *(Pompous Man)*, Edward Chapman *(McPherson)*, Kynaston Reeves *(Hunter)*, Frederick Preisley *(Cottrell)*, Charles Lamb *(Porter)*, Ina Venning *(Mrs. Cromer)*, Michael Segal *(Train Guard)*, Brian Alexis *(Groom)*, Robert Moore *(The Father)*, Richard Butler, Maggie London, Mandy Moray, Bill Cartwright, Sydney Vivian, James Houlihan, Leslie Crawford, Barbara Cavan, Lynda Barron, Frank Williams, Piers Keelan, Cyril Cross, Monty Warren, John Millar, Donald Bissett, Tony Quinn, George Spence.

An annoyingly sloppy thriller which symbolically employs not the title game, but a chess match. Carmichael is an astronomy professor working on a missile project who meets a world chess champ from behind the Iron Curtain, an old pal. The professor runs into a variety of shady characters, all of whom are members of a chess team. Jurgens is the head honcho of a sinister group that will do anything for a buck. Carmichael's heroic deeds foil their wickednesses. A bloodless and unexciting pic which is frustrating for chess fans and a chore for those who don't play.

p, Hal E. Chester; d, Cy Endfield; w, David Stone, Robert Foshko (based on a story by Harold Greene); ph, Gilbert Taylor; m, Muir Matheson, Gary Hughes; ed, Thelma Connell; art d, George Provis.

Crime/Action **(PR:A MPAA:NR)**

HIDE IN PLAIN SIGHT*½** (1980) 92m MGM/UA c

James Caan *(Thomas Hacklin, Jr.)*, Jill Eikenberry *(Alisa)*, Robert Viharo *(Jack Scolese)*, Joe Grifasi *(Matty Stanke)*, Barbara Rae *(Ruthie Hacklin)*, Kenneth MacMillan *(Sam)*, Danny Aiello *(Sal)*, Thomas Hill *(Bobby)*, Chuck Hicks *(Frankie Irish)*, Andrew Gordon Fenwick *(Andy)*, Heather Bicknell *(Junie)*, David Margulies *(Det. Reilly)*, David Clennon *(Richard)*, Peter Maloney *(Lee)*, Ken Sylk *(Frantuzzi)*, Leonardo Cimino *(Venucci)*, Nick Corello *(Fiacco)*, Tom Signorelli *(Moriarity)*, Alice Drummond *(Mrs. Novack)*, Beatrice Winde *(Unemployment Clerk)*, Josef Sumner *(Jason)*, Anne Helm, Robert Gerringer, Terrence Currier, Josephine Nichols, Walter Scott, James DeCloss, Danny Costa, Charles Hallahan, Eddy Donno, Gerald Aleck Cantor, Dan Zanghi, H. Jack Jaeger, Nancy Weber, Sidney Ehrenreich, Gary Pace, Carolyn Ferrini, Vinnie DeCarlo, Vincent Cavalleri, Lorena McDonald, John Kiouses, Mina Evans, Jeff Ring, Keith Watts, H.P. Evetts, Ken Bellet, Frederick Seaton, Anne McLeod, Tony Mancini, Ben Gerard, Madonna Young, Sam Ippolito, Joey Giambra, Irv Weinstein.

An impressive directorial debut from James Caan dealing with the U.S. government's witness relocation plan. Without warning, Caan visits the home of his ex-wife to see his two children and finds only an empty house. He discovers that her present husband, Viharo, testified against the mob and, along with his family, was given a new identity and a new home. Desperately, Caan searches for his children. His emotionally charged performance leads the cast in this gripping drama based on a true story.

p, Robert Christiansen, Rick Rosenberg; d, James Caan; w, Spencer Eastman (based on a book by Leslie Waller); ph, Paul Lohmann (Panavision, Metrocolor); m, Leonard Rosenman; ed, Fred Steinkamp, William Steinkamp; prod d, Pato Guzman; set d, Mary Swanson.

Crime/Drama **Cas.** **(PR:C MPAA:PG)**

HIDEAWAY* (1937) 60m RKO bw

Fred Stone *(Frankie)*, Emma Dunn *(Emma)*, Marjorie Lord *(Joan)*, J. Carroll Naish *(Clarke)*, William Corson *(Bill)*, Ray Mayer *(Eddie)*, Bradley Page *(Al)*, Paul Guilfoyle *(Norris)*, Tommy Bond *(Oscar)*, Dudley Clements *(Sheriff)*, Alec Craig *(Nolan)*, Charles Withers *(Yokum)*, Otto Hoffman *(Hank)*, Bob McKenzie *(Mooney)*, Lee Patrick.

Handicapped by poor acting, scripting, and directing, this dull comedy has ne'er-do-well Stone setting his family up in an abandoned house. The former owners return and are revealed to be a gang of crooks led by Naish. A battle ensues between his gang and a rival bunch of thugs, raising quite a ruckus. Stone saves the day, however, and is awarded a medal by his neighbors for his derring-do.

p, Cliff Reid; d, Richard Rosson; w, J. Robert Bren, Edmund L. Hartmann (based on a play by Melvin Levy); ph, Jack McKenzie; m, Henry Berman; art d, Van Nest Polglase.

Comedy **(PR:A MPAA:NR)**

HIDEAWAY GIRL** (1937) 71m PAR bw

Martha Raye *(Helen Flint)*, Shirley Ross *(Toni Ainsworth)*, Robert Cummings *(Michael Winslow)*, Monroe Owsley *(Count de Montaigne)*, Wilma Francis *(Muriel Courtney)*, Elizabeth Russell *(Cellette)*, Louis DaPron *(Tom Flint)*, Ray Walker *(Freddie)*, Robert Middlemass *(Capt. Dixon)*, Edward Brophy *(Buggs)*, James Eagles *(Birdie)*, Bob Murphy *(Capt. McArthur)*, Lee Phelps *(Davis)*, Kenneth Harlan *(Head Steward)*, Jimmie Dundee *(Detective)*, Chill Wills and The Avalon Boys *(Specialty)*, Martin Lamont, Frank Losee, Jr. *(Sailors)*, Pop Byron *(Dock Watchman)*, Chester Gann *(Chinese Cook)*, Harry Jordan *(Chauffeur)*, Allen Pomeroy, James Barton *(Motorcycle Cops)*, Donald Kerr, Bert Moorhouse *(Cameramen)*.

Raye provides only a few laughs as a girl who unknowingly weds a phony count who makes his living by pawning other people's jewels. Tunes include: "Beethoven, Mendelssohn and Liszt" (Sam Coslow); "What Is Love?" (Ralph Rainger, Leo Robin, Victor Young); "Two Birdies Up In A Tree" and "Dancing Into My Heart" (Ralph Freed, Burton Lane).

p, A. M. Botsford; d, George Archainbaud; w, Joseph Moncure March (based on a story by David Garth); ph, George Clemens; ed, Arthur Schmidt; md, Boris Morros.

Musical **(PR:A MPAA:NR)**

HIDEAWAYS, THE (SEE: FROM THE MIXED-UP FILES OF MRS. BASIL E. FRANKWEILER, 1973)

HIDEOUS SUN DEMON, THE*½ (1959) 74m Pacific International bw (AKA: BLOOD ON HIS LIPS; TERROR FROM THE SUN; THE SUN DEMON)

Robert Clarke *(Dr. Gilbert McKenna)*, Patricia Manning *(Ann Russell)*, Nan Peterson *(Trudy Osborne)*, Patrick Whyte *(Dr. Frederick Buckell)*, Fred La Porta *(Dr. Jacob Hoffman)*, Bill Hampton *(Police Lieutenant)*, Donna Conkling *(Mother)*, Xaudra Conkling *(Little Girl)*, Del Courtney *(Radio Announcer)*.

Clarke stars (he also produced and directed) in this sometimes laughable sci-fi film about a physicist who becomes contaminated with radiation at an atomic plant and thereafter regresses into a lizard-like creature with a taste for human flesh whenever he is hit by the rays of the sun (sort of a werewolf in reverse, with scales instead of hair). The physicist tries valiantly to overcome his problem, but can't escape the sun and is eventually killed when he falls from a huge gas tank. Really low-budget stuff, but the costume is great.

p, Robert Clarke; d, Clarke, Thomas Bontross, Gianbatista Cassarino; w, E.S. Seeley, Jr., Doane Hoag (based on the story "Strange Pursuit" by Clarke, Phil Hiner); ph, John Morrill, Vilis Lapenieks, Jr., Stan Follis; m, John Seeley; ed, Bontross.

Science Fiction **Cas.** **(PR:C MPAA:NR)**

HIDE-OUT, THE** (1930) 56m UNIV bw

James Murray *(Jimmy Dorgan)*, Kathryn Crawford *(Dorothy Evans)*, Carl Stockdale *(Dorgan)*, Lee Moran *(Joe Hennessey)*, Edward Hearn *(Coach Latham)*, Robert Elliott *(William Burke)*, Jackie Hanlon *(Jerry)*, George Hackathorne *(Atlas)*, Sarah Padden *(Mrs. Dorgan)*, Jane Keckley *(Mrs. Evans)*, Richard Carlyle *(Dean)*, Dorothy Dwan.

Murray escapes from jail and decides to enter college. Hiding out at Crane U., he joins the rowing team and leads them to victory. Before the big race, however, the investigating detective shows up on campus. He makes Murray a deal—if he throws the race, he can go free; otherwise, it's back to the lock-up. Murray plays it straight and carries the crew across the finish line in first place. The cop then reveals that he was only testing Murray's honesty, and helps him gain his freedom. Songs: "Just You and I" (Sam Perry, Clarence J. Marks), "Wandering Onward."

d, Reginald Barker; w, Arthur Ripley, Lambert Hillyer, Matt Taylor; ph, Gilbert Warrenton; ed, Harry Marker.

Drama **(PR:A MPAA:NR)**

HIDE-OUT** (1934) 80m MGM bw

Robert Montgomery *(Lucky Wilson)*, Maureen O'Sullivan *(Pauline)*, Edward Arnold *(MacCarthy)*, Elizabeth Patterson *(Ma Miller)*, Whitford Kane *(Pa Miller)*, Mickey Rooney *(Willie)*, C. Henry Gordon *(Tony Berrelli)*, Muriel Evans *(Babe)*, Edward Brophy *(Britt)*, Herman Bing *(Jack Lillie)*, Henry Armetta *(Louis Shuman)*, Louise Henry *(Millie)*, Harold Huber *(Dr. Warner)*, Roberta Gale *(Hat Check Girl)*, Arthur Belasco, Billy Arnold, Louis Natheaux *(Henchmen)*, Dick Kipling *(Clerk)*, Frank Leighton *(Headwaiter)*, Lucille Brown, Jeanette Loff, Herta Lind *(Girls)*, Frank Marlowe *(Laundry Driver)*, Bobby Watson *(Emcee)*, Frank O'Connor *(Policeman)*, Douglas Dumbrille *(Nightclub Owner)*.

Montgomery is a fugitive who flees the Big Apple and heads for Connecticut. He falls in love with O'Sullivan, but the law soon catches up with the woosome twosome and drags Montgomery back to serve his time. The ending is upbeat, however, as he hints that he'll return after his prison stint. A very young Mickey Rooney delivers the only noteworthy performance.

d, W. S. Van Dyke II; w, Frances Goodrich, Albert Hackett (based on a story by Mauri Grashin); ph, Ray June, Sidney Wagner; ed, Basil Wrangell.

Crime/Romance **(PR:A MPAA:NR)**

HIDEOUT*** (1948, Brit.) 85m Constellation/BL bw (GB: THE SMALL VOICE)

Valerie Hobson *(Eleanor Byrne)*, James Donald *(Murray Byrne)*, Harold Keel *(Boke)*, David Greene *(Jim)*, Michael Balfour *(Frankie)*, Joan Young *(Potter)*, Angela Foulds *(Jenny)*, Glyn Dearman *(Ken)*, Norman Claridge *(Superintendent)*, Edward Evans *(Inspector)*, Bill Shine, Michael Hordern, Edward Palmer, Lyn Evans, Alan Tilvern, Hugh Owens, Frederic Steger, Godfrey Barrie, Edward Hodge, Barry Wicks, Kathleen Michael, Sidney Benson, Edward Judd, Grace Denbigh-Russell.

Hobson and her husband Donald, a disabled playwright, take in two victims of a car crash. It turns out that the pair are convicts on the run and they take their benefactors hostage. A third man (Keel) joins them, bringing with him two child hostages. Donald begins to play psychological games which force the crooks to spare one of the children who was marked to be killed. This sickly youngster is released and Donald finally is able to kill his captors. The tension is sustained throughout, with some interesting plot twists along the way.

p, Anthony Havelock-Allan; d, Fergus McDonnell; w, Derek Neame, Julian Orde, George Barraud (based on the novel by Robert Westerby); ph, Stan Pavey; m, Stanley Black.

Suspense **(PR:C MPAA:NR)**

HIDEOUT** (1949) 61m REP bw

Adrian Booth *(Hannah Kelly)*, Lloyd Bridges *(George Browning)*, Ray Collins *(Philip J. Fogerty)*, Sheila Ryan *(Edie Hansen)*, Alan Carney *(Evans)*, Jeff Corey *(Beecham)*, Fletcher Chandler *(Joe Bottomly)*, Don Beddoe *(Dr. Hamilton Gibbs)*, Charles Halton *(Gabriel Wotter)*, Emory Parnell *(Arnie Anderson)*, Nana Bryant *(Sybil Elwood Kaymeer)*, Paul E. Burns *(Janitor)*, Douglas Evans *(Radio Announcer)*, Smoki Whitfield *(Pullman Porter)*.

Routine crime plot has an untrustworthy gang member, Collins, giving the slip to his two partners, Carney and Corey. The fugitive crook heads for small-town Iowa while closely pursued by his angry ex-associates. After the pair kill a gem-cutter who gets in their way, attorney Bridges gets on their trail. The finish has Bridges breaking up the entire crime ring.

p, Sidney Picker; d, Philip Ford; w, John K. Butler (based on the novel by William Porter); ph, John MacBurnie; m, Stanley Wilson; ed, Richard L. Van Enger; art d, Frank Hotaling.

Crime **(PR:A MPAA:NR)**

HIDEOUT, THE** (1956, Brit.) 57m Major/Rank bw

Dermot Walsh *(Steve Curry)*, Rona Anderson *(Helen Grant)*, Ronald Howard *(Robert Grant)*, Sam Kydd *(Tim Bowers)*, Howard Lang *(Greeko)*, Edwin Richfield *(Teacher)*, Trevor Reid *(Fraser)*, Frank Hawkins *(Inspector Ryan)*, Richard Shaw, Tommy Clegg, Jessica Cairns, Jack Taylor, Angela Krefeld.

After coming into some banknotes, Walsh finds the money really belongs to Howard. The latter is trying to save his bankrupt fur business by buying anthrax-infected pelts. Howard is murdered and Walsh discovers this is the work of an old friend, Kydd, who is an ex-con. Kydd himself is killed when the truck laden with furs he is driving crashes in a fiery explosion. Confusing—which harms the suspense and results in a rather ordinary and unthrilling thriller.

p, John Temple-Smith, Francis Edge; d, Peter Graham Scott; w, Kenneth R. Hayles; ph, Brendan J. Stafford.

Crime **(PR:C MPAA:NR)**

HIDEOUT IN THE ALPS½** (1938, Brit.) 74m GN bw (GB: DUSTY ERMINE)

June Baxter *(Linda Kent)*, Anthony Bushell *(Inspector Forsyth)*, Ronald Squire *(Jim Kent)*, Margaret Rutherford *(Miss Butterby)*, Davina Craig *(Goldie)*, Athole Stewart *(Mr. Kent)*, Katie Johnson *(Mrs. Kent)*, Hal Gordon *(Sgt. Helmsley)*, Austin Trevor *(Hotel Proprietor)*, Felix Aylmer *(Assistant Commissioner)*, Arthur Macrae *(Gilbert Kent)*.

Though Baxter spends her time hanging around with crooks, she is able to win over Bushell, an understanding cop. Holed up in an Alpine resort with her forger uncle and counterfeiter brother, the gal inevitably gets involved in the gang goings-on. When Baxter and Bushell are trapped by a rival gang, her daring brother climbs down a rope suspended from an aerial tram in order to save the two. An avalanche comes along and does in the whole gang, sparing only the lovers.

p, Julius Hagen; d, Bernard Vorhaus; w, L. du Garde Peach, Michael Hankinson, Arthur Macrea, Paul Hervey Fox, H. Fowler Mear (based on a play by Neil Grant); ph, Curt Courant, Kurt Newbert, Otto Martini.

Crime **(PR:A MPAA:NR)**

HIDING PLACE, THE*** (1975) 150m World Wide c

Julie Harris *(Betsie)*, Eileen Heckart *(Katje)*, Arthur O'Connell *(Papa)*, Jeannette Cliff *(Corrie)*, Robert Rietty *(Willem)*, Pamela Sholto *(Tine)*, Paul Henley *(Peter)*, Richard Wren *(Kik)*, Broes Hartman *(Dutch Policeman)*, Lex Van Delden *(Young German Officer)*, Tom Van Beek *(Dr. Heemstra)*, Nigel Hawthorne *(Pastor De Ruiter)*, David De Keyser *(Eusie)*, Carol Gillies *(The Snake, Camp Matron)*, Lillias Walker *(Chief Nurse)*, Irene Prador *(Wrochek)*, Janette Legge *(Erika)*, John Gabriel *(Prof. Ziener)*.

After the Nazis invade Amsterdam, a Dutch family led by O'Connell devote themselves to saving persecuted Jews. The elderly watchmaker and his daughters spend their time trying to outwit the SS troops that patrol the area, as well as recruiting others to aid in their efforts. They eventually find themselves in a concentration camp, where they all suffer from mental and physical tortures. Based on an autobiographical novel, it is an accurate representation of that period in history which has been placed on film a countless number of times. This version adds nothing new but is as worthwhile as most others, due mainly to the fine performances all around, especially that of Harris.

p, Frank R. Jacobson; d, James F. Collier; w, Allan Sloane, Lawrence Holben (based on the novel by Corrie ten Boom, John Sherill, Elizabeth Sherill); ph, Michael Reed (Metrocolor); ed, Ann Chegwidden; prod d, John Blezard; cos, Klara Kerpin.

War Drama **(PR:C-O MPAA:PG)**

HIGGINS FAMILY, THE** (1938) 65m REP bw

James Gleason *(Joe Higgins)*, Lucile Gleason *(Lillian Higgins)*, Russell Gleason *(Sidney Higgins)*, Lynn Roberts *(Marian Higgins)*, Harry Davenport *(Grandpa)*, William Bakewell *(Eddie Evans)*, Paul Harvey *(Thornwald)*, Wallis Clark *(George)*, Sally Payne *(Lizzie)*, Richard Tucker *(Burgess)*, Doreen McKay *(Miss Keene)*, Gay Seabrook *(Lydia)*, Franklin Parker *(Director)*.

The Gleason clan (James, Lucile, and Russell) head this uncompelling family comedy about a bored husband involved in advertising who has a wife whose radio aspirations put tension on their 25-year marriage. The once-happy couple ends up in divorce court, but it all comes to a still domestic finale. (See HIGGINS FAMILY series, Index.)

p, Sol C. Siegal; d, Gus Meins; w, Paul Gerard Smith, Jack Townley (based on a story by Richard English); ph, Jack Marta; m, Cy Feuer; ed, Ernest Nims.

Comedy **(PR:A MPAA:NR)**

HIGH*½ (1968, Can.) 85m Brenner c

Astri Trorvik *(Vicky)*, Lanny Beckman *(Tom)*, Peter Matthews, Joyce Cay, Denis Payque, Carol Epstein, Doris Cowan, Mortie Golub, Al Mayoff, Melinda McCracken, Janet Amos, Paul Kirby, Jack Epstein, Peter Pyper, Gary Eisencraft, Daphne Kirsten, Sue Kirsten.

A largely improvised look at Canadian teens and their views on sex, drugs, and society. There is only a thread of narrative structure, which climaxes with a murder committed by two of the youths. The film is filled with '60s freakish kids, unrelenting nudity, and infinitely annoying psychedelic special effects. Originally intended for screening at the Montreal Film Fest, it ran into some jury difficulties, and was pulled from the program. The Canadian film underground voiced its sentiments when the Fest's prize money was shared with HIGH's writer, producer, and director, Larry Kent.

p,d&w, Larry Kent; ph, Paul van der Linden; ed, Pierre Savard; m/l, The Side Tracks.

Experimental/Drama **(PR:O MPAA:NR)**

HIGH AND DRY** (1954, Brit.) 92m Rank/UNIV bw (AKA: THE MAGGIE)

Paul Douglas *(Marshall)*, Alex MacKenzie *(Skipper)*, James Copeland *(The Mate)*, Abe Barker *(The Engineer)*, Tommy Kearins *(The Wee Boy)*, Hubert Gregg *(Pusey)*, Geoffrey Keen *(Campbell)*, Dorothy Alison *(Miss Peters)*, Andrew Keir *(The Reporter)*, Meg Buchanan *(Sarah)*, Mark Dingham *(The Laird)*, Jameson Clark *(Dirty Dan)*, Moultrie Kelsall *(C.S.S. Skipper)*, Fiona Clyne *(Sheena)*, Sheila Shand Gibbs *(Barmaid)*, Betty Henderson *(Campbell's Secretary)*, Catherine Fletcher *(Postmistress)*, Herbert C. Cameron *(Gillie)*, Gilbert Stevenson *(Davy MacDougall)*, Russell Waters, Duncan MacIntyre, Roddy McMillan, Jack MacGuire, John Rae, Jack Stewart, Eric Woodburn, Douglas Robin, R.B. Wharrie, David Cameron, William Crichton, Andrew Downie.

British comedy about an American businessman, Douglas, who is conned into sending his cargo to a Scottish island via a rickety old train. A very bumpy ride where Douglas is generally wasted.

p, Michael Truman; d, Alexander Mackendrick; w, William Rose (based on a story by Mackendrick); ph, Gordon Dines; m, John Addison; ed, Peter Tanner.

Comedy **(PR:A MPAA:NR)**

HIGH AND LOW**** (1963, Jap.) 142m Toho/Continental bw/c (TENGOKU TO-JIGOKU)

Toshiro Mifune *(Kingo Gondo)*, Tatsuya Nakadai *(Inspector Tokura)*, Kyoko Kagawa *(Reiko, Gondo's Wife)*, Tatsuya Mihashi *(Kawanishi)*, Yutaka Sada *(Aoki)*, Kenjiro Ishiyama *(Detective Taguchi)*, Tsutomu Yamazaki *(Ginji Takeuchi, the Kidnaper)*, Takashi Shimura *(Director)*, Susumu Fujita *(Commissioner)*, Ko Kimura *(Detective Arai)*, Takeshi Kato *(Detective Nakao)*, Toshio Tsuchiya *(Detective Murata)*, Hiroshi Unayama *(Detective Shimada)*, Koji Mitsui *(Newspaperman)*.

A brilliant Kurosawa film starring Mifune as a rich industrialist who receives word that his son has been kidnaped by a madman who demands an outrageous sum of money that would ruin Mifune financially. Before Mifune can make a decision, his son enters the house and it is discovered that the chauffeur's son, the industrialist's son's playmate, was the child who was kidnaped, by mistake. Mifune is faced with a tough moral decision: is his chauffeur's son worth as much as his own? When the kidnaper calls and admits his mistake, but demands payment anyway, Mifune refuses. Eventually Mifune's conscience dictates that he pay the ransom and, with the help of the police, he arranges payment. The child is returned and Mifune is financially ruined. The police however, work feverishly to find the criminal and retrieve the money, and after an intense man-hunt they succeed and capture Yamazaki, a young intern. In addition to the kidnaping, Yamazaki is also guilty of selling heroin *and* murdering his accomplices in the ransom scheme. Mifune travels to the prison where he confronts the kidnaper through an iron gate. Yamazaki confesses that it was nothing but pure hatred of wealth that drove him to commit his crimes. The reason Mifune was chosen was that his home stands on a hill and Yamazaki would stare at the house every day as if it were in heaven and hate it. During the conversation, Yamazaki proves to be very intelligent, but increasingly insane, until he finally breaks into fitful convulsions of crying and laughter at the thought of his execution. The guards enter and take him away, clanging shut the iron window shade and leaving Mifune sitting alone. In HIGH AND LOW Kurosawa succeeds in developing a highly structural visual style within the wide-screen format. The first half of the film (the opening to the dropping off of the ransom) is located in the living room of Mifune's house and is characterized by static shots which hold for several minutes on a single composition. Time transitions are handled by wipes, creating a very charged, tense atmosphere. This steadiness is suddenly broken by the drop-off on the train scene, which is shot with a normal amount of motion and cutting. Its pace seems frenetic in comparison with the first half of the film. The second half shows the detailed investigation and capture of the kidnaper and is shot on many locations, showing many of the seedier aspects of the community—a direct and stunning contrast with Mifune's life on the hill. In the end, Mifune poses a question to the kidnaper, "Why are you so convinced that it is right that we hate each other?" The question is never answered, for soon after it is posed, the police take Yamazaki away leaving Mifune to ponder it by himself. The literal translation of the title from Japanese to English is HEAVEN AND HELL which has more precise and telling meanings than the title the film now has. (In Japanese; English subtitles.)

p, Tomoyuki Tanaka, Ryuzo Kikushima; d, Akira Kurosawa; w, Kurosawa, Hideo Oguni, Kikushima, Eijiro Hisaita (based on the novel *King's Ransom* by Ed McBain [Evan Hunter]); ph, Choichi Nakai, Takao Saito (Tohoscope); m, Masaru Sato; art d, Yoshiro Muraki; English titles, Herman G. Weinberg.

Crime **(PR:C-O MPAA:NR)**

HIGH AND THE MIGHTY, THE****(1954) 147m Wayne-Fellows/WB c

John Wayne *(Dan Roman)*, Claire Trevor *(May Hoist)*, Laraine Day *(Lydia Rice)*, Robert Stack *(Sullivan)*, Jan Sterling *(Sally McKee)*, Phil Harris *(Ed Joseph)*, Robert Newton *(Gustave Pardee)*, David Brian *(Ken Childs)*, Paul Kelly *(Flaherty)*, Sidney Blackmer *(Humphrey Agnew)*, Karen Sharpe *(Nell Buck)*, John Smith *(Milo Buck)*, Julie Bishop *(Lillian Pardee)*, Gonzalez-Gonzalez *(Gonzalez)*, John Howard *(Howard Rice)*, Wally Brown *(Wilby)*, William Campbell *(Hobie Wheeler)*, Ann Doran *(Mrs. Joseph)*, John Qualen *(Jose Locota)*, Paul Fix *(Frank Briscoe)*, George Chandler *(Ben Sneed)*, Joy Kim *(Dorothy Chen)*, Michael Wellman *(Toby Field)*, Douglas Fowley *(Alsop)*, Regis Toomey *(Garfield)*, Carl Switzer *(Ensign Keim)*, Robert Keys *(Lt. Mowbray)*, William DeWolfe Hopper *(Roy)*, William Schallert *(Dispatcher)*, Julie Mitchum *(Susie)*, Doe Avedon *(Miss Spaulding)*, Robert Easton, Philip Van Zandt.

A stirring and often frightening production, this is a landmark CinemaScope film that takes full advantage of the wide-screen process as well as providing a socko story and wonderful characters that would later become stereotypes when reemployed in the innumerable and far less effective AIRPORT films. The Gann novel about the way in which passengers and crew react to an in-air crisis brought terrific tension to the screen, heightened considerably by one of the most memorable film scores ever by Tiomkin. Wayne is a has-been pilot—"an ancient pelican" according to airline executive Toomey—now co-piloting under the command of cocky Stack. Also on board is an inept navigator, Brown, and an apprentice pilot, Campbell, who constantly derides Wayne, even bringing up a terrible crash occurring years earlier which Wayne survived but one where he lost his wife and young child in the wreck (seen in flashback). Beautiful, statuesque, and cool is stewardess Avedon who makes 22 passengers comfortable as the airliner leaves Honolulu and begins to fly to San Francisco. Early on there is a sign of impending disaster when Wayne discerns a slight trembling in the plane's fuselage. He is an old pro and knows the condition of planes almost by instinct, having been a pioneer aviator. On board is as diversified a lot as ever strapped themselves into seat belts. Day and Howard are unhappy with each other and are about to file for divorce. Sterling, a woman with a shady past, is a mail-order bride on her way to meet her husband-to-be. Newton is a theatrical impressario who believes he is losing his grip, a self-centered creature who has never loved anyone except himself. Trevor is a woman tired of the world and life itself, both having abused her. Brian is a pompous playboy, wealthy and jaded, a man who enjoys stealing other men's wives. Blackmer sits behind Brian, brooding, for he is one of Brian's victims, his wife having had an affair with the playboy. Blackmer is on board for only one reason—he intends to kill Brian. Oblivious to all and wrapped in their own callow world are newlyweds Smith and Sharpe. Kelly, a nuclear scientist, is lost in his own bitter life, one made terrifying and uncertain by his own inventions. Doran and Harris are married and returning from a second honeymoon in Hawaii, eagerly looking forward to seeing their family on the mainland. Unlike most passengers on an airline, almost everyone has a dynamic lifestyle, but this microcosm of humanity obviously serves as a cross-section of people high and low. They are very high when the trouble starts, more trembling and rattling, tremors that increase in velocity until all on board become terrified, including pilot Stack, all except Wayne. The plane is running out of fuel, when one engine quits and, as the craft approaches San Francisco, Stack is convinced that they must set down in the sea. He gives orders for everyone to prepare to swim for it. Wayne estimates the fuel left and the level of descent the plane is forced to follow. He insists that they can make it to San Francisco. Stack panics and begins shouting at him. Wayne slaps him, calls him "yellow," and pilot Stack comes to his senses, asking Wayne to take over. He does, flying the plane almost at tree-top level, skipping over the mountains surrounding San Francisco to make a perfect landing with only a few drops of fuel left. Wellman does a superb job in maintaining the film's suspense and the characters, though drawn only briefly, are deeply etched. One of the most touching scenes is where, faced with the possibility of death, Sterling strips her heavily-coated face of makeup until she appears bland and almost homely, but now honest in the way she will appear for her new husband. Her courageous act jolts Kelly into a more optimistic view of the world. During the crisis Blackmer almost kills Brian but is subdued and quits the idea of taking revenge; Howard and Day are reconciled when facing death. Newton's ego is smashed and he again comes in contact with reality. Wayne's performance as the one fixed and reliable point in a collapsing world was outstanding and the public reacted by voting him the number one box office actor, replacing Gary Cooper. Oddly, Wayne, who co-produced the film, intended to have Spencer Tracy play the pioneer pilot role but when that venerable actor turned down the part Wayne took it over himself. Duke whistles the haunting title song written by Tiomkin (who won an Oscar for the great score), and it became synonymous with Wayne to the point that when this giant died it was the Tiomkin score that was played during his funeral.

p, Robert Fellows, John Wayne; d, William A. Wellman; w, Ernest K. Gann (based on his novel); ph, Archie Stout, William H. Clothier (CinemaScope, Warner Color); m, Dmitri Tiomkin; ed, Ralph Dawson; art d, Al Ybarra; cos, Gwen Wakeling.

Aviation Drama **Cas.** **(PR:A MPAA:NR)**

HIGH ANXIETY*** (1977) 94m FOX c

Mel Brooks *(Richard Thorndyke)*, Madeline Kahn *(Victoria Brisbane)*, Cloris Leachman *(Nurse Diesel)*, Harvey Korman *(Dr. Charles Montague)*, Ron Carey *(Brophy)*, Howard Morris *(Prof. Lilloman)*, Dick Van Patten *(Dr. Wentworth)*, Jack Riley *(Desk Clerk)*, Charlie Callas *(Cocker Spaniel)*, Ron Clark *(Zachary Cartwright)*, Rudy DeLuca *(Killer)*, Barry Levinson *(Bellboy)*, Lee Delano *(Norton)*, Richard Stahl *(Dr. Baxter)*, Darrell Zwerling *(Dr. Eckhardt)*, Murphy Dunne *(Piano Player)*, Al Hopson *(Man Who Is Shot)*, Bob Ridgely *(Flasher)*, Albert J. Whitlock *(Arthur Brisbane).)*,

Mel Brooks deserves a lot of credit, but not as many credits as he took on this film in which he starred, produced, directed, co-wrote and sang the title song (and he has a much better singing voice than you might imagine). Whereas men like Brian De Palma and Colin Higgins will make movies reminiscent of Hitchcock and never offer credit, Brooks is patently spoofing the rotund master with HIGH ANXIETY and even if you don't know the original work, this can stand on its own as a fairly funny picture with more hits than misses. The head of the Institute For The Very Very Nervous is found murdered and Brooks, a man who fears heights so badly that he won't wear elevator shoes, takes over as psychiatrist-in-charge. Korman, the assistant, and nurse Leachman have been spinning a plot to keep the patients captive while bilking them out of their money and they fear that Brooks will put an end to that. Parody is a tricky business, but Brooks pulls it off as he pays his own homage to SPELLBOUND, VERTIGO, PSYCHO, and THE BIRDS with all of the usual middle-cut Hitchcock formulae: innocent man accused of something he didn't do, reluctant heroine (Kahn) who helps, etc. Many familiar scenes out of Hitchcock (shower, lots of camera movement), but played for comedy. The three co-writers all have small roles in the picture and the entire effect is that everyone had a good time shooting it. That feeling must have been felt by audiences who flocked to the theaters and made this a hit. Leachman does go a bit overboard as the sadistic nurse administering bondage to the masochistic Korman. Some interesting sidelights in the casting include famed matte artist Whitlock as Brisbane; successful commercials actors Ridgely and Riley, and co-writer Levinson as the bellboy. Levinson went on to become highly regarded as a director with DINER and THE NATURAL. Howard Morris was for years one of Sid Ceasar's second bananas on TV and now earns his living as a director and sometimes cartoon voice ("The Paw-Paws" for Hanna-Barbera, among others). Callas is a busy nightclub comic and Stahl is one of the best comedy character men in the business. Assistant director Jonathan Sanger stayed with Brooks and eventually became a producer.

p&d, Mel Brooks; w, Brooks, Ron Clark, Rudy DeLuca, Barry Levinson; ph, Paul Lohmann (DeLuxe Color); m, John Morris; ed, John C. Howard; prod d, Peter Wooley; set d, Richard Kent, Anne MacCauley; cos, Patricia Morris; spec eff, Albert J. Whitlock; m/l, Brooks.

Comedy Cas. (PR:C MPAA:PG)

HIGH-BALLIN'* (1978) 100m AIP c

Peter Fonda *(Rane)*, Jerry Reed *(Duke)*, Helen Shaver *(Pickup)*, Chris Wiggins *(King Carroll)*, David Ferry *(Harvey)*, Chris Langevin *(Tanker)*.

Fonda is on the road again, this time shedding his motorcycle for an 18-wheeler in a pic which tries to cash in on the mid-70s trucker craze. Along with Reed and Shaver, he pounds the pavement and blurts out the expected CB lingo. The trio shows their good side by fighting an evil gang that's trying to place more restraints on indie road drivers. It's nothing but the usual gibberish, ranking right down there with SMOKEY AND THE BANDIT.

p, John Slan; d, Peter Carter; w, Paul Edwards (based on a story by Richard Robinson, Stephen Schneck); ph, Rene Verzier (Movielab); m, Paul Hoffert; ed, Eric Wrate; art d, Paul Bonniere; spec eff, Richard Helmer.

Action Cas. (PR:C MPAA:PG)

HIGH BARBAREE* (1947) 91m MGM bw

Van Johnson *(Alec Brooke)*, June Allyson *(Nancy Fraser)*, Thomas Mitchell *(Capt. Thad Vail)*, Marilyn Maxwell *(Diana Case)*, Henry Hull *(Dr. Brooke)*, Claude Jarman, Jr. *(Alec, age 14)*, Cameron Mitchell *(Lt. Moore)*, Geraldine Wall *(Mrs. Brooke)*, Barbara Brown *(Della Parkson)*, Chill Wills *(Lars)*, Paul Harvey *(John Case)*, Charles Evans *(Col. Taylor)*, Joan Wells *(Nancy, age 12)*, Gigi Perreau *(Nancy, age 5)*, James Hunt *(Alec, age 2)*, Stanley Andrews, Jess Cavin *(Farmers)*, Ransom Sherman *(Mr. Fraser)*, Ida Moore *(Old Lady)*, Lee Phelps, Paul Kruger *(Workmen)*, Dick Rush *(Baggage Man)*, Robert Emmett O'Connor *(Stationmaster)*, Sam McDaniel *(Bertram)*, Steve Olsen *(Barker)*, Paul Newlan, Robert Skelton *(Truckmen)*, Tim Ryan *(Ringmaster)*, Florence Stephens *(Mrs. Fraser)*, Florence Howard *(Mrs. Case)*, Lois Austin *(Secretary)*, Lew Smith *(Groundman)*, Mahlon Hamilton *(Ned Flynn)*, Helyn Eby-Rock *(Woman Helper)*, Ruth Brady *(Young Woman Aide)*, George Travell *(Man in Slicker)*, Pietro Sosso *(Old Man)*, Paul Dunn *(Boy)*, Linda Bieber *(Girl)*, Howard Mitchell *(Conductor)*, Phillip Morris *(Baggage Man)*, Saul Martell *(Bernadino)*, Mitchell Rhein, Phil Dunham, Drew Dermorest, Mike Pat Donovan, Bob Rowe, Henry Sylvester, Phil Friedman *(Vendors)*, Don Anderson, Frank Wilcox *(Co-pilots)*, Milton Kibbee *(Waiter)*, Harry Tyler *(Bartender)*, Larry Steers *(Major)*, Bruce Cowling *(Captain)*, Clarke Hardwicke *(Young Man)*, William McKeever Riley *(Office Boy)*, Frank Pharr, Anton Northpole, George Magrill, Harry Wilson *(Vendors)*, William Tannen *(Officer of the Deck)*, Bert Davidson, Robert Dardett *(Naval Officers)*, Jeffrey Sayre *(Night Officer of the Deck)*, Al Kikume *(Tangaros)*, Carl Saxe, Donald S. Lewis *(Marine Sergeants)*.

During WW II Johnson's plane is shot down and lands in the Pacific. He tries to steer the drifting aircraft to the mythical island of the title, having learned of the place through his grandfather's stories. As a means of surviving, he tells his life story to his injured sea mate, Cameron Mitchell. In a flashback we see his growing years, his romance with Allyson, then Maxwell, and then Allyson again, followed by his naval enlistment. We find out that the hopeful Allyson has had her father organize a search party, which eventually locates the nearly-dead Johnson. Unluckily for Mitchell, he dies but not before having had to sit through Johnson's ponderous reminiscences. Everything that occurs in the 91 minutes is totally uncinematic, seeming to be a recitation of the novel the film is based upon. Johnson and Allyson, however, were unduly criticized for performances which, given the unsalvageable script, the most brilliant of thesps couldn't pull off.

p, Everett Riskin; d, Jack Conway; w, Anne Morrison Chapin, Whitfield Cook, Cyril Hume (based on the novel by Charles Nordhoff, James Norman Hall); ph, Sidney Wagner; m, Herbert Stothart; ed, Conrad A. Nervig; art d, Cedric Gibbons, Gabriel Scognamilo; set d, Edwin B. Willis, Ralph S. Hurst; spec eff, A. Arnold Gillespie, Warren Newcombe; tech adv, Lt. John B. Muoio, Jr., USN.

Drama (PR:A MPAA:NR)

HIGH BRIGHT SUN, THE (SEE: MC GUIRE GO HOME, 1965, Brit.)

HIGH COMMAND*½ (1938, Brit.) 59m Fanfare/GN bw

Lionel Atwill *(Maj.-Gen. Sir John Sangye)*, Lucy Mannheim *(Diane)*, Steve Geray *(Martin)*, James Mason *(Heverell)*, Leslie Perrins *(Maj. Carson)*, Allen Jeayes *(H.E. the Governor)*, Kathleen Gibson *(Belinda)*, Tom Gill *(Daunt)*, Philip Strange *(Maj. Challoner)*, Wally Patch *(Crawford)*, Michael Lambart *(Lorne)*, Henry Hewitt *(Defense)*.

Atwill is the commander of a West African garrison which includes Mannheim and Perrins, the latter of which knows that Mannheim is the secret daughter of Atwill. After an inordinate amount of plot-twisting, Mason reveals Atwill's scandalous past, which includes a murder. The tangled script was based on a novel entitled *The General Goes Too Far* which Geray referred to as "The General Has No Legs" because of the many closeups of Atwill in the film. A 90m and a 74m version also were released.

p, Gordon Wong Wellesley; d, Thorold Dickinson; w, Katherine Strueby, Walter Meade, Val Valentine (based on the novel *The General Goes Too Far* by Lewis Robinson); ph, Otto Heller; m, Ernest Irving; ed, Sidney Cole; art d, R. Holmes Paul.

Drama Cas. (PR:A MPAA:NR)

HIGH COMMISSIONER, THE** (1968, U.S./Brit.) 93m Rank-Selmur-Rodlor/Cinerama c (GB: NOBODY RUNS FOREVER)

Rod Taylor *(Scobie Malone)*, Christopher Plummer *(Sir James Quentin)*, Lilli Palmer *(Sheila Quentin)*, Camilla Sparv *(Lisa Pretorius)*, Daliah Lavi *(Madame Cholon)*, Franchot Tone *(Ambassador Townsend)*, Clive Revill *(Joseph)*, Lee Montague *(Denzil)*, Calvin Lockhart *(Jamaica)*, Derren Nesbitt *(Pallain)*, Leo McKern *(Flannery)*, Russell Napier *(Leeds)*, Ken Wayne *(Blundell)*, Burt Kwouk *(Pham Cinh)*, Gerry Crampton *(Rifleman)*, Tony Selby, Keith Bonnard *(Cameramen)*, Paul Grist *(Coburn)*, Charles Tingwell *(Jacaroo)*.

Taylor is an Australian detective sent to London to arrest Plummer, a top-level government negotiator, for the murder of his first wife 25 years before. Plummer is unmoved by the murder charge and asks permission to finish attending a conference before his arrest. Taylor agrees and Plummer even allows the detective to stay in his home, which is occupied by his second wife, Palmer, and his loyal secretary, Sparv. When Plummer goes to the hospital to visit an ailing American diplomat, Taylor saves the ambassador's life from an assassination attempt. That night Taylor meets the sexy Lavi and spends the evening with her only to be severely beaten by thugs on his way home. The next day Taylor again saves Plummer's life when an assassin disguised as a news reporter tries to shoot him. Eventually Palmer confesses to having killed Plummer's first wife, but Plummer refuses to permit her confession. The butler then announces that a bomb has been placed in the living room on the orders of Lavi, who is in reality a foreign agent. Palmer takes the bomb back to Lavi's home and forces her to sit still until the bomb explodes, killing both of them. A good cast ruined by ludicrous scripting.

p, Betty E. Box; d, Ralph Thomas; w, Wilfred Greatorex (based on the novel by Jon Cleary); ph, Ernest Steward (Eastmancolor); m, Georges Delerue; ed, Ernest Hosler; prod d, Tony Woollard; md, Delerue; set d, Peter Young.

Crime/Drama (PR:C-O MPAA:NR)

HIGH CONQUEST½** (1947) 79m MON bw

Anna Lee *(Marie)*, Gilbert Roland *(Hugo Lanier)*, Warren Douglas *(Jeffrey Stevens)*, Beulah Bondi *(Clara Kingsley)*, Sir C. Aubrey Smith *(Col. Hugh Bunning)*, John Qualen *(Peter)*, Helene Thimig *(Mama Oberwalder)*, Alan Napier *(Thomas)*, Eric Feldary *(Jules Koerber)*, Mickey Kuhn *(Young Peter)*, Louis Mercier *(Franz)*, Richard Flato, Geza de Rosner, Al Mathews *(Guides)*, John Good *(Joel)*, John Vosper *(Stefani)*, Wilton Graff *(Douglaston)*, Maurice Cass *(Walter)*, Fritz Leiber *(Pastor)*, Eddie Parks *(Steward)*, Minerva Urecal *(Miss Woodley)*, John Bleifer *(Traveler)*, Douglas Walton *(Young Banning)*, Regina Wallace *(Miss Spencer)*.

Photographed in Switzerland, this film tells the story of a young mountain climber who tries to scale the Matterhorn which took his father's life years earlier. Script and acting are okay, but it's the fine lensing that stands out.

p, Irving Allen; d, Allen; w, Max Troll (based on the novel by James Ramsey Ullman); ph, Jack Greenhalgh, Richard Angst, Tony Braun; m, Lud Gluskin; ed, Charles Craft.

Adventure (PR:A MPAA:NR)

HIGH COST OF LOVING, THE*** (1958) 87m MGM bw

Jose Ferrer *(Jim Fry)*, Gena Rowlands *(Virginia Fry)*, Joanne Gilbert *(Syd Heyward)*, Jim Backus *(Paul Mason)*, Bobby Troup *(Steve Heyward)*, Philip Ober *(Herb Zorn)*, Edward Platt *(Eli Cave)*, Charles Watts *(Boylin)*, Werner Klemperer *(Joseph Jessup)*.

A cute, adult comedy that deserved a better fate than it got at the box office, THE HIGH COST OF LOVING is notable for several reasons, not the least of which is that it debuted Gena Rowlands, hot off her broadway success in the Chayefsky drama "Middle Of The Night" where she played the sweet young thing who falls for the older man, a role she lost to Kim Novak in the film. She was only about 24 when she made this picture so it was hard to envision her as 46 year-old Ferrer's wife, especially after the screenplay established that they had been married and childless for nine years. That aside, the story opens with a smashing ten minutes of silence as Ferrer and Rowlands, in a satire of old married couples, rise from bed, perform their ablutions, dress and eat breakfast bleary-eyed in an accurate depiction of what it's like in many homes. Complications arise when Ferrer paranoically thinks he may be losing his job, since his small company has been bought by a conglomerate, and Rowlands believes that she may finally be expecting. (He was wrong; she was right.) A sharp satire of modern marriage and modern business with Jim Backus scoring as a cliche-mouthing advertising executive and Bobby Troup and Joanne Gilbert—excellent as the wacky wife—as the lead couple's best buddies.

p, Milo Frank, Jr.; d, Jose Ferrer; w, Rip Van Ronkel (based on a story by Van Ronkel, Frank); ph, George J. Folsey; m, Jeff Alexander; ed, Ferris Webster; art d, William Horning, Randall Duell; set d, Henry Grace, Robert Priestley; cos, Helen Rose.

Comedy (PR:A MPAA:NR)

HIGH COUNTRY, THE zero (1981, Can.) 101m Crown c (AKA: THE FIRST HELLO)

Timothy Bottoms *(Jim)*, Linda Purl *(Kathy)*, George Sims *(Larry)*, Jim Lawrence *(Casey)*, Bill Berry *(Carter)*, Walter Mills *(Clem)*, Paul Jolicoeur *(Red)*, Dick Butler *(Herbie)*, Elizabeth Alderton *(Maude)*, Barry Graham *(Rancher)*, John Duthie *(Billy)*, Marsha Stonehouse *(Mary Wilson)*.

A whiny wilderness "adventure" which has escaped convict Bottoms recruiting the semi-handicapped Purl as his guide into the Canadian Rockies. While being pursued by the authorities he finds the energy to fall in love with the dippy gal, who happens to be quite proficient when it comes to climbing mountains and firing guns. The plot simply twists and turns according to the wave of the screenwriter's whim, paying no attention whatsoever to motivation.

p, Bruce Mallen, Ken Gord; d, Harvey Hart; w, Bud Townsend; ph, Robert Ryan (Panavision DeLuxe Color); ed, Ron Wisman; art d, Reuben Freed; cos, Wendy Partridge.

Romance/Adventure Cas. (PR:A MPAA:PG)

HIGH EXPLOSIVE½** (1943) 60m PAR bw

Chester Morris *(Buzz Mitchell)*, Jean Parker *(Connie Baker)*, Barry Sullivan *(Mike Douglas)*, Rand Brooks *(Jimmy Baker)*, Barbara Lynn *(Doris)*, Ralph Sanford *(Squinchy Andrews)*, Dick Purcell *(Dave)*, Vince Barnett *(Man)*, Addison Randall *(Joe)*.

A slightly better than average action melodrama about the high-risk drivers of explosives trucks. Morris is the ace who takes his girl friend's little brother under his wing to teach him the ropes. The kid accidentally gets killed when a runaway nitro truck explodes, but this only makes Morris all the more devoted to his mission. The finale has him taking to the air and flying an emergency shipment through the foggy skies. The same subject was later dealt with in WAGES OF FEAR and again in THE SORCERER.

d, Frank McDonald; w, Maxwell Shane, Howard J. Green (based on a story by Joseph Hoffman); ph, Fred Jackman, Jr.; m, Daniele Amfitheatrof; ed, William Ziegler; art d, F. Paul Sylos.

Action/Adventure (PR:A MPAA:NR)

HIGH FINANCE* (1933, Brit.) 67m WB-FN bw

Gibb McLaughlin *(Sir Grant Rayburn)*, Ida Lupino *(Jill)*, John Batten *(Tom)*, John H. Roberts *(Laddock)*, D.A. Clark-Smith *(Dodman)*, Abraham Sofaer *(Myers)*.

One of Lupino's first screen efforts, a pretty unmemorable venture in which she plays the niece to McLaughlin, a man unwilling to allow her to marry the man of her dreams. But McLaughlin's inability to pay much attention to anyone else's desire eventually lands him in jail when he takes over the chairmanship of a company he had been warned about. This stay in jail forces McLaughlin to put some thought into his poor behavior, and he comes out a new man. Sappy and predictable.

p, Irving Asher; d, George King.

Drama (PR:A MPAA:NR)

HIGH FLIGHT** (1957, Brit.) 95m COL c

Ray Milland *(Wing Cmdr. Rudge)*, Bernard Lee *(Flight Sgt. Harris)*, Kenneth Haigh *(Tony Winchester)*, Anthony Newley *(Roger Endicott)*, Kenneth Fortescue *(John Fletcher)*, Sean Kelly *(Cadet Day)*, Helen Cherry *(Louise)*, Leslie Phillips *(Squadron Leader Blake)*, Duncan Lamont *(Weapons Corporal)*, Kynaston Reeves *(Air Minister)*, John Le Mesurier *(Commandant)*, Jan Brooks *(Diana)*, Frank Atkinson *(Parker)*, Ian Fleming *(Bishop)*, Nancy Nevinson *(Bishop's Wife)*, Grace Arnold *(Commandant's Wife)*, Hal Osmond *(Barman)*, Leslie Weston *(Publican)*, Anne Aubrey *(Susan)*, Jan Holden *(Jackie)*, Bernard Horsfall *(Radar Operator)*, Douglas Gibbon *(Seymour)*, Noel Hood *(Tweedy Lady)*, Andrew Keir *(Valetta Instructor)*, Richard Wattis *(Chauffeur)*, John Downing *(Pringle)*, Richard Bennett *(Phillips)*, Barry Foster *(Wilcox)*, Peter Dixon *(Benson)*, Alan Penn *(Connor)*, William Lucas *(Controller Cranwell)*, Glyn Houston *(Controller Leuchars)*, Alfred Burke *(Controller, Operations Room)*, Owen Holder *(Copilot)*, Frank Atkinson *(Farmer)*, Bill Shine *(Policeman)*, Charles Clay *(Colonel)*, Anne Aubrey *(Susan)*.

Milland is the commanding officer of a flight training school which prepares young Brits for the R.A.F. He comes up against a feisty student in Haigh, who seems to specialize in reckless abandon. Milland has a special disapproval for the youngster's brand of foolishness since he himself was responsible for the death of Haigh's father due to carelessness. Only after Milland saves Haigh during maneuvers, in which the boy gets injured, does Haigh begin to wise up.

p, Irving Allen, Albert R. Broccoli; d, John Gilling; w, Joseph Landon, Kenneth Hughes (based on a story by Jack Davies); ph, Ted Moore; m, Kenneth V. Jones; ed, Jack Slade; md, Muir Mathieson; art d, John Box; spec eff, Cliff Richardson; ch, Tutte Lemkow; m/l, Anthony Newley, Eric Coates.

Action/Aviation Drama (PR:A MPAA:NR)

HIGH FLYERS*½ (1937) 70m RKO bw

Bert Wheeler *(Jerry)*, Robert Woolsey *(Pierre)*, Lupe Velez *(Juanita)*, Marjorie Lord *(Arlene)*, Margaret Dumont *(Mrs. Arlington)*, Jack Carson *(Dave)*, Paul Harvey *(Mr. Arlington)*, Charles Judels *(Mr. Fontaine)*, Lucien Prival *(Mr. Panzer)*, Herbert Evans *(Mr. Hartley)*, Herbert Clifton *(Stone)*, George Irving *(Police Chief)*, Bud Geary *(Bosun's Mate)*, Bruce Sidney *(Ship's Officer)*.

A barely passable Wheeler-Woolsey effort in which the comic pair pose as flyers and find themselves in the center of a jewel smuggling ring. When the gang of thieves takes to the air, they are dimwittedly nabbed by the amateur pilots. You've seen it all before, and for the last time with this comedy team. Woolsey died about a year after this film's release. Tunes include: "I Always Get My Man," "Keep Your Head Above Water," "I'm A Gaucho" (Dave Dreyer, Herman Ruby).

p, Les Marcus; d, Edward Cline; w, Benny Rubin, Bert Granet, Byron Morgan (from a play by Victor Mapes); ph, John MacKenzie; ed, John Lockert; md, Roy Webb; spec eff, Vernon L. Walker.

Comedy (PR:A MPAA:NR)

HIGH FURY** (1947, Brit.) 83m Peak/UA bw (GB: WHITE CRADLE INN)

Madeleine Carroll *(Magda)*, Ian Hunter *(Anton)*, Michael Rennie *(Rudolph)*, Anne Marie Blanc *(Louise)*, Michael McKeag *(Roger)*, Arnold Marle *(Joseph)*, Willy Fueter *(Benny)*, Max Haufler *(Frederick)*, Margarate Hoff *(Maria)*, Gerard Kempinski *(President)*.

In the middle of the Swiss mountains sits the White Cradle Inn, an old and stately manor owned by Carroll's family for many generations. While her husband Rennie is having an affair with one of the Inn's maids, Carroll helps the townspeople by letting some orphans stay in the manor. She becomes attached to McKeag, one of the younger children. Carroll wants to adopt him but the philandering Rennie says no unless she signs the rights of the inn over to him. Because of her love for the boy, she gives in. Later, when the boy and Rennie go mountain climbing, the latter gives his life so McKeag won't die when they are caught in a storm. The chances for a heavy drama here were excellent but the treatment never matches potential. The actors give weak characterizations, never injecting the needed emotion for the story to work. There is some good-looking scenery of the Swiss mountains, but this doesn't compensate for the film's weaknesses.

p, Ivor McLaren; d, Harold French; w, French, Lesley Storm, Elizebeth Everson; ph, Derick Williams, Erwin Hillier; m, Bernard Grun; ed, Bert Bates; md, Grun; art d, Carmen Dillon; cos, Pearl Winther; makeup, Dolly Hamilton, Howard Richmond.

Drama (PR:A MPAA:NR)

HIGH GEAR* (1933) 65m Goldsmith bw

James Murray *(High Gear Sherrod)*, Joan Marsh *(Anne Merritt)*, Jackie Searl *(Jimmy Evans)*, Eddie Lambert *(Jake Cohen)*, Theodore Von Eltz *(Larry Winston)*, Ann Brody *(Mrs. Cohen)*, Mike Donlin *(Ed Evans)*, Lee Moran *(Howard)*, Wesley Girard, Douglas Haig, Gordon DeMain.

Emotions run high at the old auto racing track in this melodramatic programmer starring Murray as a race car driver in love with girl reporter Marsh. Throw into this already hackneyed plotline a crippled boy who was orphaned when his daddy crashed his speeding auto into a retaining wall at the beginning of the movie, and you have the typical Hollywood surrogate family that, of course, will wind up making it all legal by the fade-out.

p&d, Leigh Jason; w, Rex Taylor, Jason, Charles Saxton; ph, Edward Kull.

Drama (PR:A MPAA:NR)

HIGH HAT* (1937) 74m Imperial Pictures bw

Frank Luther *(Suwanee Collier)*, Dorothy Dare *(Elanda Lee)*, Lona Andre *(Carmel Prevost)*, Franklin Pangborn *(Mr. Breton)*, Gavin Gordon *(Gregory Dupont, Jr.)*, Esther Muir *(Dixie Durkin)*, Robert Warwick *(Dupont, Sr.)*, Clarence Muse *(Congo)*, Ferdinand Munier *(Horatio Parker)*, Sonny and Buddy Edwards, Downey Sisters, Don Raymond, Kermit Holven, Ted Dawson Orchestra, Harry Harvey, Bruce Mitchell.

A low-budget musical that tried to beef up its appeal by putting many radio personalities of the day in its cast and failed miserably. A classical singer, Dare, refuses to change her style to swing, and so, although blessed with a beautiful voice, she finds little success until, under the mentorship of Luther, she does change her singing.

p&d, Clifford Sanforth; w, Sherman L. Lowe; ph, Jack Greenhalgh; m, Frank Luther, Clarence Muse; ed, Charles Abbott.

Musical (PR:A MPAA:NR)

HIGH HELL** (1958) 87m Princess/PAR bw

John Derek *(Craig Rhodes)*, Elaine Stewart *(Lenore Davidson)*, Rodney Burke *(Danny Rhodes)*, Patrick Allen *(Luke Fulgham)*, Jerold Wells *(Charlie Spence)*, Al Mulock *(Frank Davidson)*, Colin Croft *(Dell Malverne)*, Nicholas Stuart *(Jed Thomas)*.

Stewart undresses to bathe in a barrel, risking rape by the peeping Allen; the more mendacious miners meet their maker, including Stewart's husband, Mulock. This leaves her free to dally with Derek. This was the first production of the fledgling Princess company headed by Burt Balaban and Arthur L. Mayer, each of whom had influential relatives in the business. Though set in nearby Canada, it was an international production, filmed on location at 12,000 feet of altitude on the Jungfrau in the Swiss Alps, and simultaneously released in England.

p, Arthur Mayer, William N. Boyle; d, Burt Balaban; w, Irve Tunick (based on the novel *High Cage* by Steve Frazee); ph, Jimmy Wilson; m, Phil Cardew; ed, Eric Boyd-Perkins; md, Cardew; art d, Frank White; m/l, "A Man's a Man," Cardew, Sonny Miller (sung by Dick James).

Adventure (PR:C MPAA:NR)

HIGH INFIDELITY** (1965, Fr./Ital.) 120m Documento-Societe Cinematographiques Europeennes/Magna bw (ALTA INFEDELTA; HAUTE INFIDELITE)

The Scandal: Nino Manfredi *(Francesco)*, Fulvia Franco *(Raffaella)*, John Philip Law *(Ronald)*, Eleanor Beaucour, Vittorio La Paglia, Luigi Zerbinati; Sin in the Afternoon: Charles Aznavour *(Giulio)*, Claire Bloom *(Laura)*; The Victim: Monica Vitti *(Gloria)*, Jean-Pierre Cassel *(Tonino)*, Sergio Fantoni *(Paolo)*; Modern People: Ugo Tognazzi *(Cesare)*, Michele Mercier *(Tebaide)*, Bernard Blier *(Reguzzoni)*.

A four-part comedy anthology dealing with the sexual escapades of a number of Italian couples. The Scandal stars Manfredi as a boring and unfeeling husband whose wife, Franco, begins a flirtation with a young man at a vacation resort. After many years of dormancy, Manfredi's jealousy again sparks and he seeks a confrontation with the young man. Sin in the Afternoon stars Aznavour as a movie producer who is dissatisfied with his wife's refusal to touch him. Longing for contact, he picks up a young woman on the street and takes her to a motel. The

Victim stars Vitti as an extremely jealous woman who drives her husband Fantoni out of the house. To get revenge for his desertion she becomes the mistress of his best friend. Modern People stars Tognazzi as a wealthy cheese manufacturer who has run up a considerable gambling debt to Blier. As payment, Blier is willing to accept an evening of sex with Tognazzi's beautiful wife Mercier, leaving a desperate Tognazzi to convince his wife to go along with the plan.

p, Gianni Hecht Lucari; d, The Scandal: Franco Rossi; Sin in the Afternoon: Elio Petri; The Victim: Luciano Salce; Modern People: Mario Monicelli; w, Age and Scarpelli, Ettore Scola, Ruggero Maccari; ph, Ennio Guarnieri, Gianni Di Venanzo; m, Armando Trovajoli.

Comedy/Drama **(PR:O MPAA:NR)**

HIGH JINKS IN SOCIETY** (1949, Brit.) 78m Advance-Adelphi bw

Ben Wrigley *(Ben)*, Barbara Shaw *(Angela)*, Moore Marriott *(Grandpa)*, Basil Appleby *(Hector)*, Netta Westcott *(Lady Barr-Nunn)*, Michael Ward *(Watkins)*, Peter Gawthorne *(Jenkins)*, Ivan Craig, Myrette Morven, Russell Westwood, Jean Lodge, Pamela van Dale, Bill Benny, The Radio Revellers, The Squadronnaires, Otto the Dog.

After her jewels are stolen, a woman must retrieve them from the thieves. Rather than ask the police to help out she hires a window washer to solve the crime. Wouldn't you?

p,d&w, Robert Jordan Hill, John Guillermin.

Comedy **(PR:A MPAA:NR)**

HIGH JUMP*½ (1959, Brit.) 66m Danziger/UA bw

Richard Wyler [Richard Stapley] *(Bill Ryan)*, Lisa Daniely *(Jackie Field)*, Leigh Madison *(Kitty)*, Michael Peake *(Ray Shaw)*, Arnold Bell *(Tom Rowton)*, Nora Gordon *(Mrs. Barlow)*, Tony Doonan *(Frank)*, Robert Raglan *(Inspector)*, Colin Tapley, Stuart Hillier.

Blase attempt to create an exciting crime drama quickly loses much impact in the opening scenes. Wyler plays the trapeze artist unable to ward off the advances of Daniely, who easily wraps the performer around her finger, getting his acrobatic assistance for a jewel heist. But Wyler's moralistic nature takes control; he goes to the police with evidence, motivated by the guilt of two people being killed during the robbery. The addition of a sex angle did absolutely nothing to heighten interest.

p, Edward J. and Harry Danziger; d, Godfrey Grayson; w, Brian Clemens, Eldon Howard; ph, Jimmy Wilson.

Crime **(PR:A MPAA:NR)**

HIGH LONESOME½** (1950) 80m LeMay-Templeton/EL c

John Barrymore, Jr. *(Cooncat)*, Chill Wills *(Boatwhistle)*, John Archer *(Pat Farrell)*, Lois Butler *(Meagan Davis)*, Kristine Miller *(Abbey Davis)*, Basil Ruysdael *(Horse Davis)*, Jack Elam *(Smiling Man)*, Dave Kashner *(Roper)*, Frank Cordell *(Frank)*, Clem Fuller *(Dixie)*, Hugh Aiken *(Art Simms)*, Howard Joslin *(Jim Shell)*.

Set in the cattle country of Texas' Big Bend, HIGH LONESOME stars Barrymore, Jr. as a young drifter whose rootless presence in the area makes him the prime suspect in a series of mysterious murders. He is captured by a rancher and held on his property until it can be established whether or not he is responsible for the deaths. The true killers, brothers Elam and Kashner (who were believed killed in a range war years ago), have returned to the area seeking revenge on the families that had made war on them and it is they who have set up young Barrymore, Jr. to take the fall. Only when Barrymore, Jr. is wounded while defending the ranchers from Elam and Kashner is he proven innocent. This was LeMay's only film direction; he would later be remembered for writing the novel on which John Ford's masterpiece THE SEARCHERS was based.

p, George Templeton; d&w, Alan LeMay; ph, W. Howard Greene (Technicolor); m, Rudolph Schrager; ed, Jack Ogilvie; art d, John Goodman; m/l, "Twenty Miles From Carson," Chill Wills.

Western **(PR:A MPAA:NR)**

HIGH NOON***** (1952) 85m UA bw

Gary Cooper *(Will Kane)*, Grace Kelly *(Amy Kane)*, Thomas Mitchell *(Jonas Henderson)*, Lloyd Bridges *(Harvey Pell)*, Katy Jurado *(Helen Ramirez)*, Otto Kruger *(Percy Mettrick)*, Lon Chaney, Jr. *(Martin Howe)*, Henry Morgan *(William Fuller)*, Ian MacDonald *(Frank Miller)*, Eve McVeagh *(Mildred Fuller)*, Harry Shannon *(Cooper)*, Lee Van Cleef *(Jack Colby)*, Robert Wilke *(James Pierce)*, Sheb Wooley *(Ben Miller)*, Tom London *(Sam)*, Ted Stanhope *(Station Master)*, Larry J. Blake *(Gillis)*, William "Bill" Phillips *(Barber)*, Jeanne Blackford *(Mrs. Henderson)*, James Millican *(Baker)*, Cliff Clark *(Weaver)*, Ralph Reed *(Johnny)*, William Newell *(Drunk)*, Lucien Prival *(Bartender)*, Guy Beach *(Fred)*, Howland Chamberlin *(Hotel Clerk)*, Morgan Farley *(Minister)*, Virginia Christine *(Mrs. Simpson)*, Paul Dubov *(Scott)*, Jack Elam *(Charlie)*, Harry Harvey *(Coy)*, Tim Graham *(Sawyer)*, Nolan Leary *(Lewis)*, Tom Greenway *(Ezra)*, Dick Elliott *(Kibbee)*, John Doucette *(Trumbull)*.

Not a frame is wasted in this taut, superbly directed, masterfully acted western, the first so-called "adult western" to be made, one where the traditional and predictable elements of action, song, and minimal romance gave way to a swift, intense unraveling of a situation and hair-splitting character development. It is also the story of a town, Hadleyville, somewhere in the West, and its sometimes stouthearted citizenry, at the center of which is the stoic, heroic Cooper, a man of the law surrounded by friends and admirers at the start, deserted and doomed at the finish. Cooper has just married beautiful Kelly and is about to leave town forever; he and his blonde Quaker bride intend to put peacemaking behind them and settle down to ranch life. News comes that a fierce killer, MacDonald, is about to arrive and take vengeance against Cooper and the town for sending him to prison years earlier. MacDonald's brother, Wooley, and two gunslingers, Wilke and Van Cleef, are already at the depot, waiting for the train carrying MacDonald, which is due to arrive at high noon. In a moment of panic, and urged on by his friends, Cooper races his buckboard and bride out of town and down the road into the open prairie but he suddenly pulls up. When Kelly asks him why he is stopping, Cooper tells her, "I've got to go back," then adds that even though he is no longer officially the marshal of Hadleyville after that day, it is his duty to return. She argues and he tries to explain that MacDonald will follow them anywhere and he does not want to be caught out on the open prairie. Against Kelly's objections, Cooper returns to town but he finds that all of his friends have scattered, most gone to church services. He calls for his deputies but only Millican shows up, tacks on a badge, and tells him he'll return shortly. Kelly refuses to be a part of what she's sure will be her new husband's death and she buys a ticket on the train leaving town. Cooper's former mistress, Jurado, keeps company with Bridges, Cooper's right-hand deputy. Bridges does not go to Cooper's aid since he wants the marshal's job for himself and he stays clear of Cooper. Jurado, hating Bridges for his devious and seemingly cowardly actions, decides to leave town; MacDonald, also her former lover before Cooper, she knows will kill her, too. She hurriedly sells her interests and packs, heading for the train depot. Cooper goes to the local saloon where he is mocked when asking for men to serve as deputies. His close friend, Kruger, the very judge who married him a few hours earlier, tells Cooper to flee while packing his own judicial books and trappings. He reminds the lawman: "Have you forgotten what he is, how he promised to come back and kill you." Kruger points to a chair in his tiny courtroom. "He sat in that chair and said, 'I'll come back, Will Kane. I'll come back and I'll kill you!' " Cooper ignores Kruger's dire warnings as the judge rides away solemnly. At the local church Cooper appeals to the parishioners. Some are willing to go with him, others argue against putting up a fight, that they should wait for the new marshal to arrive. Town leader Mitchell first champions Cooper, then states that since it's a personal matter between Cooper and MacDonald, it is best settled between them and that the local citizens should stay out of it. Cooper, without a friend, stoically decides to face the four outlaws alone, if need be, turning down offers of aid from a half-blind town drunk and a boy. His good friend Morgan won't even come to the door when Cooper knocks, allowing his wife to lie to the marshal, saying he's not home. Cooper goes to Chaney, a retired old lawman, who also tells him to run, that he would be of no use to him. Chaney holds up claw-like hands, arthritic and ossified. "I'd be no good to you," the old peacemaker tells him, adding that if he did join Cooper he'd worry the marshal so much that he'd cause Cooper to make mistakes and get killed. Cooper goes to a stable and inspects his horse. Bridges suddenly appears and tells him to "put a saddle on him, go ahead, here, let me help you." When Cooper pulls away, saying "I'm tired of people telling me what to do," Bridges strikes him again and again but Cooper fights back, finally knocking Bridges unconscious. By the time he walks back into the street he is bruised and dazed. At the jail he lets another drunk, Elam, out of his cell and when his only deputy, Millican, reappears, Millican deserts him, saying that he and Cooper are not enough to stand up to MacDonald and the others. Alone, Cooper awaits the killers. The train arrives on time and MacDonald gets off, greets his henchmen, straps on a gun, and immediately begins to search for Cooper. Kelly and Jurado get on the train but at the last minute Kelly gets off and runs back into the town. By then Cooper is involved in a running gun battle with the four killers. He kills two but MacDonald and another trap him inside a shop. As MacDonald's pal edges around a corner to get a better shot, he is killed, shot in the back through the window of the sheriff's office by the peace-loving Kelly. MacDonald breaks inside, grabs her, and, using Kelly as a shield, steps into the street, ordering Cooper to come out and he will spare Kelly. "I'll come out," Cooper shouts out. "Let her go!" He steps outside but before MacDonald can get off a shot Kelly spins about and claws MacDonald, momentarily blinding him. He throws her aside and Cooper shoots him to death. Cooper goes to his bride and takes her in his arms as his buckboard is brought to him. The townsfolk appear as if from nowhere, crowding about Cooper who silently and contemptuously scans their midst. He takes off his tin star and drops it into the dust, turns, and climbs into the buckboard and rides off with Kelly. HIGH NOON is a landmark western in every sense, shot with high contrast by Crosby, and much resembling a documentary, an approach endorsed by director Zinnemann that gave amazing authenticity to the film. Crosby had won an Oscar for shooting TABU in 1931, a beautifully filmed documentary of the South Seas. Zinnemann's outstanding economic direction is in full force here as each minute is packed with pertinency and suspense, the film taking almost as much time as Cooper has in the story to prepare for the gun battle. For Cooper, this was a *tour de force*, a film where his mere presence overwhelmed the viewer and carried a story that was only believable through his actions. He utters no long speeches and his dialog is terse at best. Yet his expressions and movements are those of a man resolute in his lonely duty and resigned to his own doom. Everything he does in the town causes him pain and suffering and it shows; in truth, Cooper was in real agony during the production, enduring a bleeding ulcer and an injured hip. He said, after finishing the film: "I'm all acted out." All of his seasoned years before the cameras are evident in this moving, powerful western masterpiece in the pathfinding mold of THE GUNFIGHTER. Cooper was perfect for the role of the taciturn lawman, although Gregory Peck had been offered the part by producer Kramer. He turned it down, saying it was too close to the part he played in THE GUNFIGHTER. Cooper read the script once and jumped at the chance to play the martyr Will Kane. He later stated that he "knew it was a natural for me. My dad used to sit me on his knee and tell me stories about the sheriffs he dealt with in his days on the Montana Supreme Court bench, and all those episodes of the bygone years suddenly came back to me in full blossom right out of HIGH NOON . . . The sheriff I was asked to play was different than any I'd ever known or heard about because Sheriff Kane had to stand alone, literally, against the lawless. It was a challenging role—and I loved it." So did the Academy, voting Cooper his second Oscar; he had received one 11 years earlier for his powerful role of SERGEANT YORK, 1941. Both roles exhausted the actor, he was later to admit: "In HIGH NOON it was a part, like in SERGEANT YORK, that took everything I had—and I gave it everything I had." Though ill during the 31 days shooting, Zinnemann remembered that "it didn't stop him from working very hard and very long hours under some trying conditions . . . He did, in fact, look haggard and drawn, which was exactly what I wanted for the character, even though this was in contrast to the unwritten law, then still in force, that the leading man must always look dashing and romantic." Though Kramer later claimed that the project was entirely his own creation, writer Foreman was quoted as saying "neither Kramer nor anyone around him had any use for the film from the beginning." Kramer did view the first showing with concern. It had a lot of dead spots in his opinion and he quickly ordered a series of closeups showing the anxiety lining Cooper's face and many quick cuts to clocks ticking relentlessly toward the doom of high noon. To further heighten the tension Kramer asked Tiomkin to write a ballad that could be interspersed with the action and, though the composer protested that he only wrote scores, he and Ned Washington produced the wonderful "Do Not Foresake Me, Oh My Darlin'" sung by Tex Ritter, a song that has since become a classic, along with Tiomkin's memorable score, both of which won Oscars. The movie was also nominated for Best Film, and Zinnemann got a nomination for Best Director. Editors Williams and Gerstad won Oscars for Best Film Editing, deservedly so since they had made the film as tight as a drum. The writer of the story, Foreman, reportedly based the role of the much put-upon marshal on his own plight at the time. Foreman, who had written four masterful and socially conscious films for Kramer and was in partnership with the producer (the four being HOME OF THE BRAVE, CHAMPION, CYRANO DE BERGERAC and THE MEN), explained the story to Kramer and others and then someone said that it sounded similar to a story by John W. Cunningham called "The Tin Star," recently published in *The Saturday Evening Post*. The rights were purchased and Cunningham later got story credit. Foreman also wanted to direct this film but Kramer brought in Zinnemann. The writer was having serious problems at the time which was the heyday of the Communist witchhunts; he was called before the House Un-American Activities Committee and proved uncooperative. The political stigma caused Foreman to be blacklisted immediately following the completion of HIGH NOON and he sold off his share of Kramer's production company for a reported $285,000, going to Europe and into what all considered movie limbo. Yet Foreman was not finished. He would write, uncredited, the script for THE BRIDGE ON THE RIVER KWAI which won a Best Picture Oscar in 1958, and he would go on to produce many other brilliant screenplays, including THE GUNS OF NAVARONE. This film is also notable for giving the beautiful Grace Kelly her first major role. For Jurado it was also a first big part. Both would go on to stardom, then fade, one as a princess, the other as a supporting actress. Villain Wooley would gain some oddball distinction as the voice on the novelty record "The Purple People Eater," and another villain in this splendid film, Van Cleef, would plod through one heavy part after another until his career was deemed washed up. Then he went to Italy and starred in spaghetti westerns for Sergio Leone and became an international star.

p, Stanley Kramer; d, Fred Zinnemann; w, Carl Foreman (based on the story "The Tin Star" by John W. Cunningham); ph, Floyd Crosby; m, Dmitri Tiomkin; ed, Elmo Williams, Harry Gerstad; prod d, Rudolph Sternad; art d, Ben Hayne; set d, Emmett Emerson; m/l, "Do Not Forsake Me, Oh My Darlin'," Tiomkin, Ned Washington.

Western Cas. (PR:C MPAA:NR)

HIGH PLAINS DRIFTER*½** (1973) 105m Malpaso/UNIV c

Clint Eastwood *(The Stranger)*, Verna Bloom *(Sarah Belding)*, Mariana Hill *(Callie Travers)*, Mitchell Ryan *(Dave Drake)*, Jack Ging *(Morgan Allen)*, Stefan Gierasch *(Mayor Jason Hobart)*, Ted Hartley *(Lewis Belding)*, Billy Curtis *(Mordecai)*, Geoffrey Lewis *(Stacey Bridges)*, Scott Walker *(Bill Borders)*, Walter Barnes *(Sheriff Sam Shaw)*, Paul Brinegar *(Lutie Naylor)*, Richard Bull *(Asa Goodwin)*, Robert Donner *(Preacher)*, John Hillerman *(Bootmaker)*, Anthony James *(Cole Carlin)*, William O'Connell *(Barber)*, John Quade *(Jake Ross)*, Jane Aull *(Townswoman)*, Dan Vadis *(Dan Carlin)*, Reid Cruickshanks *(Gunsmith)*, James Gosa *(Tommy Morris)*, Jack Kosslyn *(Saddlemaker)*, Russ McCubbin *(Fred Short)*, Belle Mitchell *(Mrs. Lake)*, John Mitchum *(Warden)*, Carl C. Pitti *(Teamster)*, Chuck Waters *(Stableman)*, Buddy Van Horn *(Marshall Jim Duncan)*.

Eastwood directs his first western and it's a knock-out. HIGH PLAINS DRIFTER is a morality tale carved out of the harsh Western desert and directed with a panache that synthesized the styles of Sergio Leone and Don Siegel (two directors who had worked with Eastwood frequently) and came up with one of the best westerns of the Seventies. The story begins as a mysterious stranger (Eastwood) seems to materialize out of the desert heat. He rides into the small town of Lagos, where his presence is considered a threat by the mean and cowardly populace. Before too long, he is attacked by three gunmen, and Eastwood kills them all coolly and efficiently. The stranger then rents a hotel room and the town dwarf, Curtis (who is also disenfranchised in town due to his size), attends to his needs. At night, Eastwood's dreams are plagued by a recurring nightmare of a helpless man being whipped to death in the street by three sadistic criminals while the townsfolk stand by and do nothing to stop it. Meanwhile, the town-council's members debate how to handle the impending threat created by a group of escaped convicts who are out to return to Lagos (where they had committed their crimes) and destroy it. Desperate, the town's leaders cautiously approach Eastwood and plead with him to save their town from the criminals. Eastwood agrees to help them, but then proceeds to turn the town on its head by teaching them self-defense and requesting all sorts of strange things from the townsfolk which eventually leads to having them paint the town red (literally) and rename it "Hell." When the dreaded convicts arrive, Eastwood is nowhere to be found, and the marauders overrun the town with ease, killing, raping, and looting. Soon the buildings are in flames and the convicts are basking in their victory, until suddenly a bull-whip snakes across the neck of one and is snapped, killing him. A second marauder is found hanged, and the third is shot to death. The stranger reappears and the townsfolk have a simultaneous flashback (a device used frequently by Leone) about the night these same criminals savagely bull-whipped their sheriff (whom we now see bears an uncanny resemblance to Eastwood) to death while they all stood and watched. Not quite understanding why Eastwood has stirred these memories in them, one of the townsfolk asks him who he is. He states, "You know who I am," and then rides off into the heat vapors in which he arrived and disappears. An eerie, almost supernatural western that takes the avenging "Man-With-No-Name" character created by Eastwood and Leone to its most logical extreme. Eastwood would later bury the character completely in his own OUTLAW JOSEY WALES only to have him rise like the Phoenix, redefined as a much more human, compassionate, and caring hero who is capable of change, which plays upon the audience's expectations of an Eastwood/western hero and distorts them drastically.

p, Robert Daley; d, Clint Eastwood; w, Ernest Tidyman; ph, Bruce Surtees (Panavision, Technicolor); m, Dee Barton; ed, Ferris Webster; art d, Henry Bumstead; set d, George Milo; stunts, Buddy Van Horn.

Western Cas. (PR:O MPAA:R)

HIGH POWERED*½ (1945) 62m Pine-Thomas/PAR bw

Robert Lowery *(Tim Scott)*, Phyllis Brooks *(Marian Blair)*, Mary Treen *(Cassie McQuade)*, Joe Sawyer *(Spike Kenny)*, Roger Pryor *(Rod Farrell)*, Ralph Sanford *(Sheriff)*, Billy Nelson *(Worker)*, Ed Gargan *(Boss)*, Vince Barnett *(Worker)*.

Lowery is a high-rigger construction worker who loses his nerve for high places after a near-fatal fall. A co-worker blames Lowery for the death of his brother, who was killed in Lowery's accident. Lowery struggles to overcome his fear and regain his confidence. The climax finds Lowery conquering his fear when forced to perform a tricky rescue several stories up.

p, William Pine, William Thomas; d, William Berke; w, Milton Raison, Maxwell Shane (based on an original story by Raison); ph, Fred Jackman, Jr.; m, Alexander Laszlo; ed, Henry Adams; art d, F. Paul Sylos.

Drama (PR:A MPAA:NR)

HIGH-POWERED RIFLE, THE½** (1960) 62m Capri/FOX bw

Willard Parker *(Dancer)*, Allison Hayes *(Sharon Hill)*, Dan Simmons *(Lt. Mac McDonald)*, John Holland *(District Attorney)*, Shirley O'Hara *(Jean Brewster)*, Terrea Lea *(Herself)*, Lennie Geer *(Gus Alpert)*, Clark Howat *(George Markle)*, A.G. Vitanza *(Little Charlie Roos)*.

A slightly better-than-average private-eye action story, THE HIGH-POWERED RIFLE has Parker as a detective who survives a string of attempts on his life by assassins hired by a mysterious killer. His investigation leads him towards several suspects, and into bed with Hayes, the girl friend of his main suspect. All good things come to an end, as it turns out Hayes is the one trying to kill him.

p&d, Maury Dexter; w, Joseph Fritz; ph, Floyd Crosby; ed, Edward Dutko.

Crime/Mystery (PR:A MPAA:NR)

HIGH PRESSURE*** (1932) 72m WB bw

William Powell *(Gar Evans)*, Evelyn Brent *(Francine)*, George Sidney *(Colonel Ginsburg)*, Frank McHugh *(Mike Donoghey)*, Guy Kibbee *(Clifford Gray)*, Evalyn Knapp *(Helen)*, Ben Alexander *(Geoffrey)*, Harry Beresford *(Dr. Rudolph)*, John Wray *(Jimmy Moore)*, Charles Judels *(Salvatore)*, Luis Alberni *(Colombo)*, Lucien Littlefield *(Oscar Brown)*, Charles Middleton *(Banks)*, Alison Skipworth *(Mrs. Miller)*, Harold Waldridge *(Vanderbilt)*, Lilian Bond *(Millie)*, Maurice Black *(Poppolus)*, Bobby Watson *(The Baron)*, Oscar Apfel, Polly Walters.

A fast-paced, well-constructed comedy sporting a charming performance from Powell, who plays a barely-legitimate hustler who sees his ticket to easy street come in the form of an invention that can change sewage to artificial rubber. He sets up a corporation and sells stocks in it to raise some cash and is just about to go into production when he learns that the inventor of the sewage-to-rubber process is a nut case and *he* was the one who got taken. Good casting and direction helped to propel this loony, but well-written, comedy along.

d, Mervyn Le Roy; w, Joseph Jackson (based on the story "Hot Money" by S.J. Peters and the play by Aben Kandel); ph, Robert Kurrle; ed, Ralph Dawson; md, Leo Forbstein.

Comedy (PR:A MPAA:NR)

HIGH RISK*½ (1981) 94m Viacom-Hemdale-City Enterprise/American Cinema c

James Brolin *(Stone)*, Lindsay Wagner *(Olivia)*, Anthony Quinn *(Mariano)*, Cleavon Little *(Rockney)*, Bruce Davison *(Dan)*, Chick Vennera *(Tony)*, James Coburn *(Serrano)*, Ernest Borgnine *(Clint)*, David Young *(Bradley)*, Richard Young *(Mike)*, Stephanie Faulkner *(Charlene)*, Udana Power *(Gail)*, Fernando Palavicini *(Manuel)*, Douglas Sandoval *(Julio)*, Sergio Calderon *(Hueso)*, Eduard Noriega *(General)*, Mario Valdez *(His Assistant)*, Robert Sosa *(Boy)*, Alvaro Carcano, Paco Morayta *(Gays in Jail)*, Tony Rubio *(Bearded Man)*, Sammy Ortiz *(Conductor)*, Polo Salazar Flores *(Waiter)*, Eduardo Paxon *(Mark)*, Samantha Borzaui *(Liz)*, Leonard Smith *(Mike)*, Luz Maria Pena *(Voluptuous Lady)*, Rudolfo de Alexandre *(Skinny Man)*, Xochitl del Rosario *(Fat Whore)*, Gerardo Cepeda *(Policeman)*, Daniel Garcia *(Roberto)*, Rene Barrera *(Guard)*, Angel Aragon, Carlos Romano, Rebecca Johnson *(Pool Players)*, Ana de Sade *(Nude)*, Evelyn Klippian *(Bikini Girl)*, Alejandro Camacho, Juan Vasquez, Nicholas Jasso, Gerardo Zapena, Fernando Palaeicini, Jorge Hernandez Andrew, Daniel Garcia, Josephina Echinova.

A stupid comedy with violent overtones and a wasted cast, HIGH RISK tells the story of some amateur crooks who attempt to make a big sting. Brolin is a documentary filmmaker who discovers the whereabouts of a drug dealer, Coburn, in South America, who has five million dollars waiting to be stolen. Brolin enlists three of his buddies, Little, Davison, and Vennera, to leave their jobs and go on a crime mission. The three buddies are against violence, but Brolin talks them into buying a small arsenal from Borgnine, a gun dealer. Brolin assures them that there will be no violence, and the guns are just for show. The motley crew invades Coburn's hacienda, and makes away with millions while exchanging countless bullets without anyone getting hit. They split up and Little and Vennera are captured by Coburn, while Brolin and Davison run into bandits, led by Quinn. In a slapstick manner, Little and Vennera escape from jail with Wagner and try to find Brolin and Davison so they can let them know that Quinn wants to kill all of them. The humor turns to violence as the four shoot their way out in order to retain the money.

p, Joseph Raffill, Gerald Green; d&w, Stewart Raffill; ph, Alex Phillips, Jr. (Technicolor); m, Mark Snow; ed, Tom Walls, Jr.; prod d, Augustin Ituarte; art d, Ron Foreman.

Comedy/Action **Cas.** **(PR:O MPAA:R)**

HIGH ROAD TO CHINA** (1983) 120m Golden Harvest-Jardan/WB c

Tom Selleck *(O'Malley)*, Bess Armstrong *(Eve)*, Jack Weston *(Struts)*, Wilford Brimley *(Bradley Tozer)*, Robert Morley *(Bentik)*, Brian Blessed *(Suleiman Khan)*, Cassandra Gava *(Alessa)*, Michael Sheard *(Charlie)*, Lynda Marchal *(Lina)*, Timothy Carlton *(Officer)*, Shayur Mehta *(Ahmed)*, Terry Richards *(Ginger)*, Jeremy Child *(Silversmith)*, Peter Williams *(Franjien Khan)*, Dino Shafeek *(Satvinda)*, Robert Lee *(Zura)*, Peggy Sirr *(Alessa's Mother)*, Anthony Chinn *(General Wong)*, Chua Kah Joo *(Wong's Aide)*, Ric Young *(Kim Su Lee)*, Timothy Bateson *(Alec Wedgeworth)*, Wolf Kahler *(Von Hess)*, Marc Boyle *(Henchman)*, Zdenka Hersak *(Countess)*, Domagoj Mukusic *(Chauffeur)*, Sime Jagarinas *(Khan's Nephew)*, Simon Prebble, Daniel Clucas, John Higginson *(British Officers)*.

After Selleck passed up the opportunity to play Indiana Jones in RAIDERS OF THE LOST ARK to star in the highly successful "Magnum P.I." series, he starred in this poor man's RAIDERS. This film, devoid of wit, excitement, or thrilling characters, tells the story of Selleck, a rough and tough boozing biplane pilot who flies in and around China during the 1920's. He is hired by a very annoying Armstrong, who is searching for her missing father, Brimley. She has to find her father before he is declared dead or her inheritance will be stolen. Morley is the man who wants to prevent her from finding Brimley so he may cash in her inheritance. Selleck doesn't want Armstrong around, and for good reason, as she yells and complains the entire time they are together. Romantic sparks never really fly, but they do find her father and foil Morley.

p, Fred Weintraub; d, Brian G. Hutton; w, Sandra Weintraub Roland, S. Lee Pogostin (based on the novel by Jon Cleary); ph, Ronnie Taylor (Technicolor); m, John Barry; ed, John Jympson; prod d, Robert Laing; art d, George Richardson; cos, Betsy Heimann, Franco Antonelli; aerial ph, Peter Allwork.

Adventure **Cas.** **(PR:C MPAA:PG)**

HIGH ROLLING** (1977, Aus.) 89m Hexagon Roadshow c (AKA: HIGH ROLLING IN A HOT CORVETTE)

Joseph Bottoms *(Texas)*, Grigor Taylor *(Alby)*, Judy Davis *(Lynn)*, John Clayton *(Arnold)*, Wendy Hughes *(Barbie)*, Sandy McGregor *(Susie)*, Simon Chilvers *(Sideshow Boss)*, Gus Mercurio *(Ernie)*, Robert Hewitt *(Frank)*, Roger Ward *(Lol)*, Peter Cummins *(Bus Driver)*.

An Australian road picture starring Bottoms and Taylor as two young carnival employees who quit their jobs and hoof it down the highway in search of something better. They soon are picked up by eccentric homosexual Clayton, and it is only a matter of minutes until the gay fixes his sights on Taylor. Clayton, however, is jumped by the guys, who rob him only to discover that he is a drug runner. Overjoyed at their luck, Bottoms and Taylor steal the man's wallet, his dope, and his car. On the road they pick up a rootless girl, Davis, who is wandering the outback in search of a commune to join. Bottoms develops some affection for the girl, but is distracted when Taylor gets hooked up with a couple of disco singers who take him for a sucker. The motley group (Bottoms, Taylor, Davis and the disco singers) decide to stage a badly planned (but amusingly executed) tour bus robbery. From out of their past reappears Clayton, who is out to get his money and dope back, and the film disintegrates into a free-for-all.

p, Tim Burstall; d, Igor Auzins; w, Forest Redlich; ph, Dan Burstall; m, Sherbet; ed, Edward Queen-Mason; art d, Leslie Binns; stunts, Grant Page.

Crime **Cas.** **(PR:O MPAA:PG)**

HIGH SCHOOL** (1940) 74m FOX bw

Jane Withers *(Jane Wallace)*, Joe Brown, Jr. *(Slats Roberts)*, Lloyd Corrigan *(Dr. Henry Wallace)*, Claire Du Brey *(Miss Huggins)*, Lynne Roberts *(Carol Roberts)*, Paul Harvey *(James Wallace)*, Cliff Edwards *(Jeff)*, Lillian Porter *(Cuddles)*, John Kellogg *(Tommy Lee)*, Margaret Brayton *(Miss Witherspoon)*, Marvin Stephens *(Bill)*, Johnnie Pironne *(Terry)*, Mary McCarty *(Mary)*, Emma Dunn *(Mrs. O'Neill)*, The Brian Sisters *(Specialty)*.

This film was an attempt to get child star Withers through her uneasy adolescent years and into an adult film career. The story has Withers as an obnoxious but intelligent teenager who drives all the tutors on her father's Texas ranch crazy. Her father, Harvey, decides to send her to the public high school, run by his brother Corrigan. Once at the school, Withers spites her teachers and schoolmates, causing them to dislike her. Eventually she learns her lessons and gets her act together.

p, Sol M. Wurtzel; d, George Nicholls, Jr.; w, Jack Jungmeyer, Jr., Edith Skouras, Harold Tarshis (based on an idea by Robert Ellis, Helen Logan); ph, Lucien Andriot; ed, Harry Reynolds; md, Samuel Kaylin.

Drama **(PR:A MPAA:NR)**

HIGH SCHOOL BIG SHOT** (1959) 70m Filmgroup-Sparta bw

Tom Pittman *(Marv)*, Virginia Aldridge *(Betty)*, Howard Viet *(Vince)*, Malcolm Atterbury *(Mr. Grant)*, Stanley Adams *(Harry March)*.

"School brain" Pittman's lack of common sense leads to his eventual downfall. Since he is not exactly Mr. Popular at school, a young rendition of a "femme fatale," Aldridge, has no problem coercing him into helping with her homework. Not only does he help, but he does absolutely all the work for her, something that is easily recognizable to the teacher. Fearing his inability to make much of himself in the world of high academia, Pittman turns to crime. The complex job of robbing a shipping office that he cooks up meets with disaster when Aldridge allows her greedy nature to take advantage of Pittman one more time. This film effectively portrays the influences acting upon the youth of America during the late 1950s, but does so with a high degree of compassion for characters, who are the victims of popular culture.

p, Stan Bichman; d&w, Joel Rapp.

Drama/Crime **(PR:C MPAA:NR)**

HIGH SCHOOL CAESAR** (1960) 72m Marathon/Filmgroup bw

John Ashley *(Mat Stevens)*, Gary Vinson *(Bob Williams)*, Lowell Brown *(Kelly Roberts)*, Steve Stevens *(Crickett Davis)*, Judy Nugent *(Wanda Anderson)*, Daria Massey *(Lita Owens)*.

A harsh look at the extent to which an unscrupulous student will go to impress his classmates. Ashley plays the rich kid dying to prove himself to the rest of the students at a small midwestern school. Using gangland-like ethics he creates his own little group of thugs to try and take control of the school. These boys demand protection payments from other students, force unwilling girls to become part of their racket, and drag their hot rods down the strip. Nugent refuses to put up with Ashley's shenanigans, creating the beginning of the end of the punk's brief reign. She and buddy Vinson team up to show just what a jerk Ashley is. The film features believable performances from young actors and an effective use of the rural setting in backwoods Missouri.

p&d, O'Dale Ireland; w, Ethel Mae Page, Robert Slaven; ph, Harry Birch; m, Monty Pearce.

Drama **(PR:C MPAA:NR)**

HIGH SCHOOL CONFIDENTIAL½** (1958) 85m MGM bw (AKA: THE YOUNG HELLIONS)

Russ Tamblyn *(Tony Baker/Mike Wilson)*, Jan Sterling *(Arlene Williams)*, John Drew Barrymore *(J.I. Coleridge)*, Mamie Van Doren *(Gwen Dulaine)*, Diane Jergens *(Joan Staples)*, Jerry Lee Lewis *(Himself)*, Ray Anthony *(Bix)*, Jackie Coogan *(Mr. A.)*, Charles Chaplin, Jr. *(Quinn)*, Burt Douglas *(Jukey Judlow)*, Michael Landon *(Steve Bentley)*, Jody Fair *(Doris)*, Phillipa Fallon *(Poetess)*, Robin Raymond *(Kitty)*, James Todd *(Jack Staples)*, Lyle Talbot *(William Remington Kane)*, William Wellman, Jr. *(Wheeler-Dealer)*, Joe Foster *(Henchman)*, Diana Darrin *(Gloria)*, Carl Thayler *(Petey)*, Irwin Berke *(Morino)*, Kim Chance *(Waitress)*, Della Malzahn *(Woman at Race)*, Gil Perkins *(Police Sergeant)*, Pierre Watkin *(David Wingate)*.

Another typical day at Santo Bello High begins as a pickup truck hauling Jerry Lee Lewis and his piano stops to entertain the teenagers. The "Killer" frantically pounds on the keys and belts out a frenzied rendition of the title song, thus starting HIGH SCHOOL CONFIDENTIAL off with a bang. We then meet Tamblyn, a street tough recently arrived from Chicago, who is living with his over-sexed aunt, Van Doren. Tamblyn ensures his place at the new school by bullying nearly everyone he meets (including the principal), flashing a huge wad of cash, casting a lustful eye at attractive English teacher Sterling, and stealing local gang leader Barrymore's girl friend, Jergens. After this whirlwind entrance, Tamblyn sets out to make a big drug deal. Seeing that Jergens is such a dope fiend that she keeps joints in her bra, Tamblyn cons her into revealing her contact for pot. After weeding his way through a chain of small-time dealers, Tamblyn finally meets the big man himself, Mr. A (played by former child star Jackie Coogan), who works at the local hangout and pounds a piano with an intensity that rivals Lewis. There, Tamblyn sees a girl from his high school, Fair, experiencing painful heroin withdrawal in the back room. Coogan offers to give her a fix, but only if she will agree to become a prostitute. Tamblyn wants to buy some heroin from Coogan, but the ever-suspicious drug dealer wants the kid to prove he needs it by shooting up for him. Tamblyn fakes the injection by shooting the wicked drug into a rubber ball hidden in the crook of his arm. Meanwhile, events occur that indicate tough guy Tamblyn isn't all he seems. At home he is seen to drink milk and he consistently resists the sexual advances of his nymphomaniac aunt. Among his friends he always declines when drugs are offered to him. While waiting for Tamblyn to return home with more marijuana, girl friend Jergens discovers that her beau has tape-recorded his meeting with Coogan. Stopping by to pick up money for the big heroin deal, Tamblyn refuses to explain and asks Sterling to come to his house and keep an eye on Jergens. Soon after he leaves, the home is invaded by Barrymore and his cronies and they discover that Tamblyn is actually a narcotics agent for the FBI. Having been warned by the teenagers that Tamblyn is a narc, Coogan awaits his arrival, gun in hand. When the unsuspecting Tamblyn confronts Coogan, the drug dealer tries to shoot him, but the quick-thinking narco man throws heroin in his face and after a brief struggle the police subdue the criminal and take him away. The film ends with the bad boys in reform school, Jergens kicking her pot habit, Van Doren revealed to actually be no relation to Tamblyn, leaving the FBI man and teacher Sterling vowing to continue their battle against teenage drug abuse. Produced by Zugsmith, a man with an amazingly diverse career (he has been involved in such notable efforts as Orson Welles' TOUCH OF EVIL, 1958, Douglas Sirk's WRITTEN ON THE WIND, 1957, and THE TARNISHED ANGELS, 1958, but then he is also responsible for such vile exploitation films as SEX KITTENS GO TO COLLEGE, 1960, TEACHER WAS A SEXPOT, 1960, and LSD, I HATE YOU! 1967, as well as a host of others), HIGH SCHOOL CONFIDENTIAL was sold to the public as a hard-hitting expose of the tragic drug abuse running rampant in U.S. schools. The teenagers who went to see this film in droves knew better. The film is high camp, tongue-in-cheek fun on a par with the cult classic REEFER MADNESS (1936). The dialog, with its "hip" 1950s jargon, is a delight to hear spoken with such flair, and the rebellious rock-n-roll attitude of the teenagers fits right in among the midnight show crowd. This is not to say that the problems of drug abuse are played for laughs. The film's treatment of these scenes is fairly straightforward and Tamblyn's character is shown to have deep concern for his heroin-addicted classmate. The amusement derives from 20/20 hindsight and the thought that a major studio (MGM) tried to address the horrors of drug abuse in a film that obviously panders to the rebellious attitudes of the very people to whom the "message" is aimed. While certainly not a great film (it's barely even a good one), HIGH SCHOOL CONFIDENTIAL is certainly a curiosity worth looking at. Sequel: COLLEGE CONFIDENTIAL.

p, Albert Zugsmith; d, Jack Arnold; w, Lewis Meltzer, Robert Blees (based on story by Blees); ph, Harold J. Marzorati; ed, Ben Lewis; art d, William A. Horning, Hans Peters; set d, Henry Grace, Arthur Krams; m/l, "High School Confidential" Jerry Lee Lewis, Ron Hargraves; makeup, William Tuttle.

Drama **Cas.** **(PR:O MPAA:NR)**

HIGH SCHOOL GIRL*½ (1935) 55m Foy bw

Helen MacKellar *(Jane Andrews)*, Mahlon Hamilton *(Will Andrews)*, Cecilia Parker *(Beth Andrews)*, Carlyle Moore, Jr. *(Bob Andrews)*, Noel Warwick *(Phil Cudahy)*, Treva Scott *(Peggy Stewart)*, Crane Wilbur *(Bryson)*, Mildred Gover *(Sarah)*, Arthur Wanzer, Eula Gay, Frank LaRue.

A tiresome, preachy, message film about parental neglect and the inability of kids to confide in their parents. The story concerns a young boy (Warwick) and a girl (Parker) who are forced by parental attitudes to sneak around in order to go on dates and to parties. Disaster occurs before the parents realize their mistakes. A biology teacher at the high school, Wilbur (who also directed), tries to help the students cope with their lives and for his efforts is fired. Everyone learns his lesson, and Wilbur gets reinstated at the happy ending.

p, Brian Foy; d, Crane Wilbur; w, Wallace Thurman; ph, William Thompson; ed, Arthur Hilton.

Drama **(PR:A MPAA:NR)**

HIGH SCHOOL HELLCATS* (1958) 69m AIP bw

Yvonne Lime *(Joyce)*, Bret Halsey *(Mike)*, Jana Lund *(Connie)*, Suzanne Sydney *(Dolly)*, Heather Ames *(Meg)*, Nancy Kilgas *(Laurie)*, Rhoda Williams *(Miss Davis)*, Don Shelton *(Martin)*, Viola Harris *(Mrs. Martin)*, Robert Anderson *(Lt. Manners)*, Martin Braddock *(Rip)*, Arthur Marshall *(Mr. Anderson)*.

A great "bad" film about an all-girl gang that rules over the females of a high school like the Gestapo in drag. Transfer student Lime runs up against the gang (led by Lund) on the first day of school. The new girl believes that if she doesn't join them she will never fit in. Lime seeks the advice of a college boy, Halsey, who works at the malt shop, but she ends up in trouble in spite of his good words. The troublemaking fun ends when Lund is killed in an abandoned movie theater, a fate audiences also administered to this film.

p, Charles "Buddy" Rogers, James H. Nicholson, Samuel Z. Arkoff; d, Edward Bernds; w, Mark Lowel, Jan Lowel; ph, Gilbert Warrenton; ed, Edward Sampson; art d, Don Ament; cos, Marjorie Corso.

Crime **(PR:O MPAA:NR)**

HIGH SCHOOL HERO* (1946) 69m MON bw

Freddie Stewart *(Freddie)*, June Preisser *(Dodie)*, Noel Neill *(Betty)*, Ann Rooney *(Addie)*, Jackie Moran *(Jimmy)*, Frankie Darro *(Roy)*, Warren Mills *(Lee)*, Milt Kibbee *(Townley)*, Belle Mitchell *(Miss Hinklefink)*, Isabelita *(Chi-Chi)*, Douglas Fowley *(Coach Carter)*, Edythe Elliott *(Mrs. Rogers)*, Leonard Penn *(Prof. Farrell)*, Pierre Watkin *(Gov. Huffington)*, Dick Elliott *(Mayor Whitehead)*, Freddie Slack *(Himself)*, Joe Derita *(Tiny)*, Freddie Slack Orchestra, Jan Savitt Orchestra Featuring Isabelita.

This dull high school musical concerns the rivalry between two schools and their football teams. The sympathetic team (the one in the white jerseys) has trouble getting the ball up and down the field and it looks as if they'll be pounded into the turf by the bad-guy team (the guys in the black jerseys), who are much better (and bigger). These severe problems are ironed out, with the good guys winning the game *and* putting on a musical show. Songs include: "You're For Me," "Come To My Arms," "Whitney High," "Night Time And You" (Edward J. Kay), "You're Just What I Crave" (Arthur Alexander), "Fairview High" (Phil Grayson), and "Southpaw Serenade" (Freddie Slack).

p, Sam Katzman; d, Arthur Dreifuss; w, Hal Collins, Dreifuss; ph, Ira Morgan; m, Edward Kay; ed, Ace Herman, Richard Currier; ch, Jack Boyle.

Musical **(PR:A MPAA:NR)**

HIGH SCHOOL HONEYMOON (SEE: TOO SOON TO LOVE, 1960)

HIGH SEAS*½ (1929, Brit.) 71m BIP/FN-Pathe bw

Lillian Rich *(Faith Jeffrey)*, John Stuart *(Tiny Bracklethorpe)*, Randle Ayrton *(Capt. Jeffrey)*, Winter Hall *(Lord Bracklethorpe)*, Janet Alexander *(Lady Bracklethorpe)*, James Carew *(Jaeger)*, Daisy Campbell *(Mrs. Jeffery)*.

Originally filmed as a silent, this early British talkie takes place in part on the wide-open ocean where a tyrannical newspaper publisher schemes to make more money from the ships he owns by seeing that the well-insured vessels meet with disastrous ends. This also inadvertently brings ruin to the family of the woman who had planned on marrying his son. The soundtrack was added in 1930 to keep the Britons on or near the cutting edge of the new technology developed in the U.S.

d, Denison Clift; w, Clift, Victor Kendall (based on the story "The Silver Rosary" by Monckton Hoffe); ph, Claude MacDonnell.

Adventure/Drama **(PR:A MPAA:NR)**

HIGH SIERRA**** (1941) 100m WB bw

Humphrey Bogart *(Roy Earle)*, Ida Lupino *(Marie Garson)*, Alan Curtis *(Babe Kozak)*, Arthur Kennedy *(Red Hattery)*, Joan Leslie *(Velma)*, Henry Hull *(Doc Banton)*, Barton MacLane *(Jake Kranmer)*, Henry Travers *(Pa)*, Elisabeth Risdon *(Ma)*, Cornel Wilde *(Louis Mendoza)*, Minna Gombell *(Mrs. Baughman)*, Paul Harvey *(Mr. Baughman)*, Donald MacBride *(Big Mac)*, Jerome Cowan *(Healy)*, John Eldredge *(Lou Preiser)*, Isabel Jewell *(Blonde)*, Willie Best *(Algernon)*, Arthur Aylesworth *(Auto Court Owner)*, Robert Strange *(Art)*, Wade Boteler *(Sheriff)*, Sam Hayes *(Radio Commentator)*, Erville Alderson *(Farmer)*, Spencer Charters *(Ed)*, Cliff Saum *(Shaw)*, Eddy Chandler *(Policeman)*, Richard Clayton *(Bellboy)*, Louis Jean Heydt *(Tourist)*, William Hopper, Robert Emmett Keane *(Men)*, Maris Wrixon *(Another Blonde)*, Lucia Carroll *(Brunette)*, Ralph Sanford *(Fat Man)*, Frank Moran, Lee Phelps *(Officers)*, Frank Cordell *(Marksman)*, Zero the Dog *(Pard the Dog)*, George Lloyd *(Gangster)*, George Meeker *(Pfiffer)*, Charlette Wynters *(Woman)*, Dorothy Appleby *(Margie)*, Gary Owen *(Joe)*, Eddie Acuff *(Bus Driver)*, Harry Hayden *(Druggist)*, Carl Harbaugh *(Fisherman)*.

This was the movie gangster's last stand (other than WHITE HEAT), where Bogart plays a graying criminal whose day is over and whose life is short. He knows it, accepts it, and fatalistically pursues the only goal he understands, the final caper. Released from Mossmoor Prison after serving a long stretch for bank robbery, Bogart is met by a henchman of boss MacBride who has planned a jewel heist at a California resort, one which Bogart must lead. Instead of getting into a car, Bogart goes for a stroll through the park "to see if grass is still green," and watches children playing ball before meeting with MacLane, who is an ex-cop and working for MacBride. MacLane provides Bogart with money and a car and tells him to go to a mountain resort where he will meet two young hoodlums who will help him with the robbery. Bogart shows his dislike for MacLane, who is, in his opinion, "Once a cop, always a cop." On the way West Bogart stops to reminisce at a small Indiana farm his family used to own; he is a gangster with a curious softspot for the past, one with humanity which does not interfere with his ruthless ability to destroy anyone getting in his way. Later Bogart is driving in the desert when he is almost run off the road by an old jalopy being driven by club-footed Leslie, a beautiful young girl. He momentarily befriends her uncle, Travers, then proceeds to the mountain rendezvous with Kennedy and Curtis. The two young toughs are staying in a fishing resort, occupying cabins with Lupino, who is ostensibly Curtis' girl friend. She is immediately attracted to the close-mouthed Bogart, although he shuns her and is disgusted with having to work with two inexperienced hands. Wilde, the contact man inside the resort to be robbed, arrives and is genuinely frightened of the old pro Bogart. With the apprentice hoodlums gathered about him and to make a point to Wilde, whom he suspects of cowardice and being a potential informer, Bogart tells the group about his long dead gangster pal, Lefty Jackson. He relates how, in his old days of bank robbing, he and Jackson confronted a suspected informer in the gang and how Jackson held a machinegun on the man. "He just touched the trigger and the gun went . . ." Bogart taps rapidly on a table to simulate bullets spurting from the machinegun. "And the rat fell out of the chair." Wilde, to whom the story is directed, turns almost white with fear. Curtis later turns on Lupino in Bogart's absence; Bogart has gone to Los Angeles to visit the ailing boss MacBride. En route he again meets Leslie and Travers. They have had an accident and Bogart talks a driver out of prosecuting the hapless, near-penniless Travers. Grateful Travers asks that Bogart come by and see him and Leslie when he can. Bogart finds big boss MacBride bedridden, seriously ill. MacBride complains that "all the A-one guys are gone, dead or in Alcatraz." To Bogart it's a different world than the one he left when going behind bars: "Sometimes I don't know what this is all about anymore" he replies. He pours MacBride and himself a drink, cautioning the boss that the liquor will be his undoing. "I'm gonna die anyway," laughs MacBride. "So are you." He laughs hysterically. "So are we all. To your health, Roy." Old friend Hull, an underworld doctor, arrives to check on MacBride, later telling Bogart that the boss hasn't much time to live. Bogart asks Hull if he can fix a clubfoot, meaning Leslie's deformity, and Hull tells him to have the girl call on him. When Bogart returns to the fishing resort he finds that Curtis has beat up Lupino and, after slugging the upstart, takes Lupino in with him. She later begs to go along with him on the caper and he not only takes her but a mongrel dog he has picked up at the fishing village. "What a sap," he comments, "going on a heist with a girl and a little dog." At the resort Bogart holds rich tourists at bay while Kennedy and Curtis loot the safe deposit vault, taking more than a quarter million in jewels. Lupino, waiting in one of the cars, sees a security guard enter the building and honks the horn to warn Bogart. He shoots the guard and the trio flee to the cars, Wilde running after them, telling them he must be taken along, that he would crack under interrogation. The cars roar away through the desert but the one carrying Kennedy, Curtis, and Wilde takes a wrong turn and goes on to an uncompleted road, turning over and burning. Wilde survives to blab to police as he promised he would. In Los Angeles Bogart finds that Hull has arranged to have Leslie's clubfoot fixed, although she now wants nothing more to do with Bogart. MacBride has died and MacLane, the crooked ex-cop, demands the stolen gems. Bogart refuses and both go for their guns. MacLane is killed and Bogart is wounded. Hull later patches him up; the underworld physician has earlier told Bogart that he would "catch lead at any moment . . . Do you remember what Johnny Dillinger said about guys like you and him? You were just rushing toward death . . . rushing toward death!" Lupino and Bogart are now on their own while Bogart waits to fence the stolen gems. She nags at him and his wound opens up. Lupino mends his wound as they wait in a small cabin in a motor court. The next day Bogart finds the manager calling his dog by name which means he has been spotted. He locks up the manager and goes into a rage over the headlines and his photo on the front page. "Look at the tag they put on me!" he roars. "'Mad Dog Ray Earle'—those newspaper rats!" Bogart flees and then later puts Lupino and the dog on a bus, telling her he'll meet her later. Before she gets on the bus, Lupino apologizes to Bogart for arguing with him. "Aww, I like it," he tells her, "my ma and pa fought like cats and dogs." After she's gone he heads north into the High Sierra range, sticking up a store for pocket money and then picking up police squads and motorcycle cops who pursue him to the foot of Mt. Whitney, the highest mountain in the continental United States. He races upwards, hiding in the rocks, spraying machinegun bullets downward at a growing army of police. "Come on down!" shouts a sheriff. "You haven't got a chance." "Come and get me, copper!" Bogart yells back, "Come on! Whatsamatter? Ya yellow?" He is trapped and the news spreads. Lupino hears about the siege and travels to the spot where scores are on hand to witness the kill. A radio announcer with a remote hookup tells the world that "a farm boy from the flats on Indiana" has come all the way West to meet his doom in the high mountains. Another newsman, Cowan, (who would play Bogart's doomed partner in 1941's THE MALTESE FALCON) spots the dog in Lupino's arms, then identifies her. He brings her to the sheriff who asks her to call out to Bogart to give himself up. "We're gonna get him anyway." She refuses. The sheriff has already sent a sharpshooter to climb the high ridge above Bogart and just as he takes his position, the dog breaks loose and begins running toward Bogart, who realizes Lupino is present. He steps from cover, fully exposed to the sharpshooter's gunsight, shouting her name. He is shot dead and his body rolls down the slope to lie in a mangled heap. The dog whines next to him. Lupino and others run to the spot. Cowan lights a cigarette and says: "Big shot Earle. Look at him lying there. He ain't big any more." The weeping Lupino remembers how Bogart had told her of his prison days and how he was always waiting to "crash out." She looks to Cowan and says: "Mister—what does it mean when you 'crash out'?" Replies Cowan: "Why, it means you're free." "Free," she begins to say as she is led away, the dog in her arms, "free . . ." HIGH SIERRA was a landmark crime film in many ways. It was Bogart's first solid role as a sympathetic lead, playing the good-bad guy out of his element and beyond his time. Bogart's demeanor is nostalgic for the Prohibition era and his physical makeup, like his first gangster role as Duke Mantee in THE PETRIFIED FOREST, is almost wholly based on John Dillinger to whom he bore an amazing resemblance. It is no accident that Dillinger's name is uttered in the film, a mere seven years after that gangster's alleged demise in Chicago. James Cagney, George Raft, and Paul Muni were approached to play the part of the anachronistic gangster but each turned it down, Raft telling Jack Warner that he was sick and tired of playing gangsters and, after reading the script, utterly refused to be killed in the end. Bogart, who was second-billed under Lupino, showed his ability to play sensitive scenes with great depth of character and the public responded enthusiastically. He would never again play second fiddle to Cagney or anyone else. From the point of this film onward, he was a star, top-billed, emerging as one of America's greatest screen personalities. Lupino reportedly disliked the fact that Bogart got the main play of the film. This was also an important film for scriptwriter Huston; his career would take a sharp turn upward following HIGH SIERRA after which he would undertake directing, his first film being made with his good luck actor, Bogart, in the third and best version of THE MALTESE FALCON, 1941. Much of the evocative material in the script stems from veteran *film noir* writer Burnett (LITTE CAESAR, ASPHALT JUNGLE) who co-scripted. Walsh does a superb job in keeping a nonstop action pace, succinctly pausing to give Bogart setups where his character is unraveled and revealed, a masterful balance of movement and study. Walsh, more than any other, was responsible for Bogart's big break in getting the part, suggesting him to Jack Warner when others turned down the role. "How about Bogart, that bit player?" he mused to Warner. "I think I could make him tough enough for the part." Snorted Warner: "He's tough enough already, or thinks he is. He goes around with a big chip on his shoulder, and lately he's been telling people I'm a fairy. But if you want to take a chance, go ahead." Much of Walsh's action takes place around Lone Pine, California, and on the actual slopes of Mount Whitney where cameraman Gaudio was shooting at 11,000 feet. Following the police chase through the desert to the mountains, the longest chase scene Walsh ever directed, Bogart took his stand in the rocks high up on the side of Mount Whitney. Walsh positioned him so that he was exposed to the hot sun and gusting winds, letting him stew for hours until his cameras were set up. Then the director laboriously climbed to Bogart's perch, looked about at the majestic vista, and asked Bogart if he didn't love the great outdoors. Bogart barked an obscenity, then added: "I'll take a parlor, bedroom, and bath any time. When you think what an actor has to do to earn his salary in this goddamn business. That crumby, two-bit hotel last night!" He complained that his breakfast consisted only of a can of stale orange juice. Walsh, who was forever playing practical jokes on his actors, such as the notorious stunts he pulled on George Raft in THE BOWERY, knew Bogart's penchant for the finer things and how he would explode at any discomforts imposed upon him during production. He purposely set up a fake situation where, with Bogart high up on his lonely perch, the actor would be led to believe that he would be lucky if he were fed while on location. While the two stood high in the mountain crags, Walsh waved his hat to a property boy below, a prearranged signal for the boy to shout up: "They forgot to send the lunches!" Bogart was instantly in a rage, yelling: "I'll be an s.o.b. . . . I walk my — off getting up here, then they forget to send the lunches! I'll tell Equity about this!" He raved on for five minutes, then, on cue, the property boy again shouted up to Bogart and Walsh: "The lunch wagon just came! The food is here!" The boy scrambled up the rocks to the sweating, swearing Bogart and handed him a small cardboard box. Bogart held up its contents, first a banana, then a sandwich. "Look at this! And this goddamn sandwich must have been made last year. What's this, a pickle? And here's an olive and a doughnut. I wonder how they can afford it? They feed cons in San Quentin better than this!" Bogart went on ranting against Jack Warner and how that mogul was probably sitting down to a juicy steak lunch in Los Angeles while he starved to death, sweated and burned in the sun atop America's highest mountain. Yet Walsh, who finally had a decent lunch brought to Bogart, was able to get from the actor one of his finest performances. Remade as COLORADO TERRITORY, 1949, and I DIED A THOUSAND TIMES, 1955.

p, Mark Hellinger; d, Raoul Walsh; w, John Huston, W.R. Burnett (based on the novel by Burnett); ph, Tony Gaudio; m, Adolph Deutsch; ed, Jack Killifer; md, Leo F. Forbstein; art d, Ted Smith; cos, Milo Anderson; spec eff, Byron Haskin, H.F. Koenekamp; makeup, Perc Westmore.

Crime Drama Cas. (PR:C MPAA:NR)

HIGH SOCIETY*½ (1932, Brit.) 53m WB-FN bw

Florence Desmond *(Florrie)*, William Austin *(Wilberforce Strangeways)*, Emily Fitzroy *(Mrs. Strangeways)*, Tracy Holmes *(Honorable Tommy Montgomery)*, Joan Wyndham *(Betty Cunningham-Smith)*, Margaret Damer *(Mrs. Cunningham-Smith)*, Leo Sheffield *(Lord Halkirk)*, Syd Crossley *(Simeon)*.

Damer wants daughter Wyndham to marry Austin, but the young woman loves the impoverished Holmes. She enlists her maid (Desmond) to assume her place with Austin while she and Holmes elope. Desmond marries Austin, and Holmes turns out to be in line to inherit a title. A weak comedy built around Desmond, who can't save it.

p, Irving Asher; d, John Rawlins; w, W. Scott Darling, Randall Faye.

Comedy (PR:A MPAA:NR)

HIGH SOCIETY* (1955) 61m AA bw

Leo Gorcey *(Terrence Aloysius "Slip" Mahoney)*, Huntz Hall *(Horace Debussy "Sach" Jones)*, David Condon *(Chuck)*, Bennie Bartlett *(Butch)*, Bernard Gorcey *(Louie Dumbrowski)*, Ronald Keith *(Terwillinger III, Master Twig)*, Dayton Lummis *(H. Stuyvesant Jones)*, Amanda Blake *(Clarissa)*, Gavin Gordon *(Frisbie The Butler)*, Addison Richards *(Attorney Sam Cosgrove)*, Kem Dibbs *(Marten)*, Paul Harvery *(Henry Baldwin)*, Dave Barry *(Palumbo The Pianist)*.

The Bowery Boys, once again led by Gorcey and Hall, get mixed up in high society when rich crook Lummis attempts to steal an inheritance from his nephew, Keith. Lummis hoodwinks Hall and tries to pass him off as the rightful heir to the fortune. Some mildly amusing situations arise as the tough slum kids masquerade as cultured people. Eventually Gorcey exposes the plot and puts the bad guys in the clink. HIGH SOCIETY was accidentally nominated for an Academy Award for best original story due to an oversight in the ballots sent to the Academy voters. This Allied Artist's low-budget programmer was confused with MGM's outstanding musical, HIGH SOCIETY. After a bit of hesitation, writer Bernds notified the Academy of its error; however, he was allowed to keep the nomination plaque. (See BOWERY BOYS series, Index.)

p, Ben Schwalb; d, William Beaudine; w, Bert Lawrence, Jerome S. Gottler (based on a story by Elwood Ullman, Edward Bernds); ph, Harry Neumann; ed, Lester A. Sansom, John C. Fuller; md, Marlin Skiles; art d, David Milton; set d; Joseph Kish; cos, Bert Henrikson; spec eff, Ray Mercer.

Comedy (PR:AA MPAA:NR)

HIGH SOCIETY*** (1956) 107m MGM c

Bing Crosby *(C.K. Dexter-Haven)*, Grace Kelly *(Tracy Lord)*, Frank Sinatra *(Mike Connor)*, Celeste Holm *(Liz Imbrie)*, John Lund *(George Kittredge)*, Louis Calhern *(Uncle Willie)*, Sidney Blackmer *(Seth Lord)*, Louis Armstrong *(Himself)*, Margalo Gillmore *(Mrs. Seth Lord)*, Lydia Reed *(Caroline Lord)*, Gordon Richards *(Dexter-Haven's Butler)*, Richard Garrick *(Lord's Butler)*, Richard Keen *(Mac)*, Ruth Lee, Helen Spring *(Matrons)*, Paul Keast *(Editor)*, Reginald Simpson *(Uncle Willie's Butler)*, Hugh Boswell *(Parson)*.

A musical remake of double Oscar-winning THE PHILADELPHIA STORY, HIGH SOCIETY falls a little flat despite Cole Porter's tuneful score. Veddy rich Kelly (in a role not unlike her own life) lives in Newport and has a trio of men encircling her: her ex-husband, Crosby, with whom she is still on fairly good terms; her fiance, Lund, a professional prig; and Sinatra, a breezy reporter sent to cover the wedding by a *Life* magazine-type periodical. Sinatra's photographer is Holm. Kelly's dad is Blackmer, a run-around type, and her mother is Gillmore, with Calhern as her uncle. Kelly and Sinatra have a drinking bout, get loaded and go for a moonlight swim in the pool where she almost drowns until he saves her. The wedding plans proceed and Kelly has all expectations of marrying Lund, but he is such a stiff that we know from the start that the wedding will never take place. Yet, we wonder if she'll fall for Sinatra or Crosby. In the end, she decides to try it again with Bing and they re marry. High-gloss production and Porter's songs save this from being just another musical remake of a classic straight story, but the bubbling froth of the original is somehow doused here and Sinatra is no match for James Stewart's Oscar-winning performance. Crosby and Sinatra get the chance to be the screen rivals everyone thought they were in real life. The truth is that they admired each other and felt no enmity at all, despite vying for the public's musical attention in the 1940s. Satchmo Armstrong appears as himself, something he did in many films, and is delightful. Oscar nominations to Green, Chaplin and "True Love" (sung by Bing Crosby, Grace Kelly). Besides the aforementioned ditty, other tunes include: "Mind If I Make Love To You?" (sung by Sinatra), "Well, Did You Evah?" (sung by Sinatra, Crosby), "You're Sensational" (sung by Sinatra), "High Society Calypso" (performed by Louis Armstrong and His Band), "Little One" (sung by Crosby), "Now You Has Jazz" (performed by Crosby, Armstrong and His Band), "Who Wants To Be A Millionaire?" (sung by Sinatra, Celeste Holm), "I Love You Samantha" (sung by Crosby). The only song not written for the movie was "Well, Did You Evah?" which was first sung by Betty Grable in Cole Porter's 1939 musical "Dubarry Was A Lady." This was Grace Kelly's last picture before marrying Prince Rainier and becoming Queen of Monaco. Our loss, his gain.

p, Sol C. Siegel; d, Charles Walters; w, John Patrick (based on Philip Barry's play "The Philadelphia Story"); ph, Paul C. Vogel (VistaVision, Technicolor); m, Johnny Green, Saul Chaplin; ed, Ralph E. Winters; md, Green; art d, Cedric Gibbons, Hans Peters; set d, Edwin B. Willis, Richard Pefferle; cos, Helen Rose; spec eff, A. Arnold Gillespie; ch, Walters; m/l, Cole Porter; makeup, William Tuttle.

Musical/Comedy Cas. (PR:A MPAA:NR)

HIGH SOCIETY BLUES** (1930) 98m FOX bw

Janet Gaynor *(Eleanor Divine)*, Charles Farrell *(Eddie Granger)*, William Collier, Sr. *(Horace Divine)*, Hedda Hopper *(Mrs. Divine)*, Louise Fazenda *(Mrs. Granger)*, Lucien Littlefield *(Eli Granger)*, Joyce Compton *(Pearl Granger)*, Brandon Hurst *(Jowles)*, Gregory Gaye *(Count Prunier)*.

This Romeo and Juliet story is set in the swank New York suburb of Scarsdale. The Romeo of the story is Farrell; the Juliet is Gaynor. His family, nouveau riche hicks from Iowa, moves in next to her family, aristocrats with old money. Gaynor is drawn to Farrell because he plays the ukulele and she wants him to teach her to play. Gaynor's parents disapprove of Farrell and his family, and frown upon their romance, particularly since Gaynor is already promised to a French count. The two young lovers elope on the eve of Gaynor's marriage to the count. In the end, the marriage brings a truce between the two families and prosperity to the fathers. Farrell's ukulele and Gaynor's voice are the springboards for several songs, including "I'm In The Market For You," "Eleanor," "High Society Blues," "Just Like in a Story Book," "The Song I Sing in My Dreams," "I Don't Know You Well Enough For That" (Joseph McCarthy, James Hanley).

p, Al Rockett; d, David Butler; w, Howard J. Greene (based on the story "Those High Society Blues" by Dana Burnet); ph, Charles Van Enger; ed, Irene Morra; cos, Sophie Wachner.

Musical **(PR:A MPAA:NR)**

HIGH SPEED*½ (1932) 60m COL bw

Buck Jones, Loretta Sayers, Wallace MacDonald, Mickey McGuire, Ed La Saint, William Walling, Ward Bond, Dick Dickinson, Martin Faust, Joe Bordeaux, Pat O'Malley, Ed Chandler.

Western star Buck Jones was out of the saddle and in the driver's seat in this film about car racing. Jones—a policeman when he is not behind the wheel—brings a mob of crooks to justice, triumphs at the speedway, befriends the son of dead driver, and gets the girl.

d, Ross Lederman; w, Adele Buffington (based on a story by Harold Shumate); ph, Teddy Tetzlaff.

Crime **(PR:A MPAA:NR)**

HIGH STAKES** (1931) 72m RKO bw

Lowell Sherman, Mae Murray, Edward Martindel, Leyland Hodgson, Karen Morely, Charles Coleman, Phillips Smalley, Ethel Levey, Alan Roscoe, Maude Turner Gordon.

Likable, light-hearted comedy in which Murray plays a scheming wench who marries Martindel just for the chance to get into his pockets. Hubby is too blinded by his ego to think that the cute little thing would ever dream of such a thing. It takes his brother, who has spent quite a bit of time dealing with the lower elements of society, to set Martindel straight and free him from this sticky situation.

p, Henry Hobart; d, Lowell Sherman; w, J. Walter Ruben (based on the play by Willard Mack); ph, Roy Hunt.

Comedy **(PR:A MPAA:NR)**

HIGH TENSION*½** (1936) 62m FOX bw

Brian Donlevy *(Steve Reardon)*, Glenda Farrell *(Edith McNeil)*, Norman Foster *(Eddie Mitchell)*, Helen Wood *(Brenda Burke)*, Robert McWade *(Willard Stone)*, Theodore Von Eltz *(Noble Harrison)*, Romaine Callender *(F. Willoughby Tuttle)*, Joseph Sawyer *(Terry Madden)*, Hattie McDaniel *(Hattie)*, Murray Alper *(Chuck)*.

A good comedy about a handsome and rugged deep sea diver, Donlevy, who falls for a tough and independent writer of magazine adventure stories, Farrell. She decides to do a story using him for reference material and romance follows. They constantly fight for dominance in their relationship. He doesn't want to commit to marriage, but he also doesn't want her to go out with other men. After he takes a risky job in Hawaii and realizes just how dangerous his lifestyle is, he decides marriage might be safer. Some good underwater photography for its time.

p, Sol M. Wurtzel; d, Allan Dwan; w, Lou Breslow, Edward Eliscu, John Patrick (based on a story by J. Robert Bren, Norman Houston); ph, Barney McGill; ed, Louis Loeffler; md, Samuel Kaylin.

Comedy **(PR:A MPAA:NR)**

HIGH TERRACE*½** (1957, Brit.) 69m Cipa/RKO-AA bw

Dale Robertson *(Bill Lang)*, Lois Maxwell *(Stephanie Blake)*, Derek Bond *(John Mansfield)*, Eric Pohlmann *(Otto Kellner)*, Mary Laura Wood *(Molly Kellner)*, Lionel Jeffries *(Monkton)*, Jameson Clark *(Detective Inspector MacKay)*, Carl Bernard *(Jock Dunmow)*, Garard Green *(Raymond White)*, Olwen Brookes *(Mother Superior)*, Benita Lydal *(Violet Gage)*, Marianne Stone *(Mansfield's Landlady)*, Frederick Treves *(Constable West)*, Jonathan Field *(Theater Critic)*, Gretchen Franklin *(Mrs. Webb)*, Alan Robinson *(Robert Baines)*, Jack Cunningham *(Priest)*, Arthur Lowe.

This British mystery/thriller is set in the theater world, with most of the action taking place backstage. Maxwell, a beautiful thespian, is the star of a new stage hit produced by Pohlmann, who loves her. Maxwell, however, desires to perform in a new play written by American Robertson, but the jealous (and financially astute) Pohlmann refuses to let her wriggle out of her contract. Soon after, Pohlmann winds up dead in his office with a pair of Maxwell's scissors in his back. Fearing that the actress was set-up, Robertson helps Maxwell move the body. When the crime is discovered the police suspect just about everyone. In the end it appears that Maxwell *indeed* killed Polhmann, but the noble Robertson takes the rap.

p, Robert S. Baker, Monty Berman; d, Henry Cass; w, Alfred Shaughnessy, Norman Hudis, Brock Williams (based on a story by A.T. Weisman); ph, Eric Cross; m, Stanley Black; ed, Henry Richardson; md, Black; art d, Arthur Lawson.

Mystery **(PR:A MPAA:NR)**

HIGH TIDE** (1947) 70m MON bw

Lee Tracy *(Hugh Fresney)*, Don Castle *(Tim Slade)*, Julie Bishop *(Julie Vaughn)*, Anabel Shaw *(Dana Jones)*, Regis Toomey *(Inspector O'Haffey)*, Douglas Walton *(Clinton Vaughn)*, Francis Ford *(Pop Garrow)*, Anthony Warde *(Nick Dyke)*, Wilson Wood *(Cleve Collins)*, Argentina Brunetti *(Mrs. Creaser)*, George H. Ryland *(Interne)*.

An average whodunit set against a newspaper background. Detective Castle is hired by newspaper editor Tracy, who wants protection from some alleged threats on his life. It soon turns out that Tracy is the bad guy of the story. He has killed his publisher, an undercover investigator working for the publisher, and a buddy—all in an effort to gain control of the newspaper. Tracy has hired Castle to throw the blame off himself, but it isn't long before Castle catches on to what's going on and takes care of Tracy.

p, Jack Wrather; d, John Reinhardt; w, Robert Presnell, Sr., Peter Milne (based on the story "Inside Job" by Raoul Whitfield); ph, Henry Sharp; m, Rudy Schrager; ed, Stewart S. Frye, William Ziegler; art d, Lewis H. Creber.

Crime **(PR:A MPAA:NR)**

HIGH TIDE AT NOON*½** (1957, Brit.) 109m Rank bw

Betta St. John *(Joanna MacKenzie)*, William Sylvester *(Alec Douglas)*, Michael Craig *(Nils)*, Flora Robson *(Donna MacKenzie)*, Alexander Knox *(Stephen MacKenzie)*, Peter Arne *(Owen)*, Patrick McGoohan *(Simon Breck)*, Patrick Allen *(Charles MacKenzie)*, Jill Dixon *(Mateel)*, Susan Beaumont *(Kristi)*, John Haywald *(Philip)*, Errol MacKinnon *(Peter Grant)*, Stuart Nichol *(George Breck)*, George Murcell *(Ash Breck)*, Anthony Bate *(Johnny Fernandez)*, Stella Bonheur *(Aunt Mary)*, Bernard Bresslaw *(Tom Robey)*, Victor Chenet *(Mr. Doty)*, Franklin Fox *(Hugo)*, John Stevenson Lang *(Nathan Parr)*, Gerald Lawson *(Marcus Yetton)*, Arthur Massey *(Young Man)*, Bill Nagy *(Sandy McNab)*, Charles Richardson *(Oldish Man)*, Ewan Roberts *(Fred)*, Ryck Rydon *(Milt Tobey)*, Richard Shaw *(Maurice Trudeau)*, Nicholas Stuart *(Jake Trudeau)*, Garry Thorne *(Tim Gray)*, Paul Massie.

Fairly dull travelog-type drama detailing the trials and tribulations of life on a lonely and harsh island off Nova Scotia. Most of the residents are lobster fishermen, and one of them, Sylvester, romances St. John, the daughter of Knox, who owns much of the island. It is not until after they are married that St. John learns of Sylvester's nasty gambling habits, and soon he has lost their nest-egg, leaving them destitute. These developments, combined with a bad economy, eventually force most of the islanders to seek refuge on the mainland.

p, Julian Wintle; d, Philip Leacock; w, Neil Paterson (based on the novel by Elizabeth Ogilvie); ph, Eric Cross; m, John Veale; ed, Sidney Hayers.

Drama **(PR:A MPAA:NR)**

HIGH TIME** (1960) 102m Bing Crosby/FOX c

Bing Crosby *(Harvey Howard)*, Fabian *(Gil Sparrow)*, Tuesday Weld *(Joy Elder)*, Nicole Maurey *(Helene Gauthier)*, Richard Beymer *(Bob Bannerman)*, Yvonne Craig *(Randy Pruitt)*, Patrick Adiarte *(T.J. Padmanagham)*, Jimmy Boyd *(Higgson)*, Kenneth MacKenna *(President Burn)*, Gavin MacLeod *(Thayer)*, Nina Shipman *(Laura)*, Angus Duncan *(Harvey Howard, Jr.)*, Paul Schreiber *(Crump)*, Dick Crockett *(Bones McKinney)*, Frank Scannell *(Tobacco Auctioneer)*.

Fairly dull musical outing that had one saving grace, Cahn and Van Heusen's standard "The Second Time Around." This time, Crosby is a rich Howard Johnson-type restaurateur with a string of eateries across the country. A 51-year-old widower with two grown children, he feels he's missed something by not going to college, so he enrolls in a local university and the film becomes the male musical version of MOTHER IS A FRESHMAN. Once at the school, he has to endure fraternity initiation rites and dress in drag as an aged Scarlett O'Hara to attend a ball. That's the comedic highlight. The rest of HIGH TIME is standard episodic stuff that would have no laugh value at all were it not being played by a man old enough to be the father of the others involved. Fabian, Weld, Craig, Beymer and Adiarte do as well as they can in their small roles as students, and Maurey (and whatever happened to her?) impresses as the French teacher whom Crosby woos and wins. Songs include: "Nobody's Perfect," "The Second Time Around," "I Had A Dream Dear," "Lovely Lady," the traditional "Foggy Foggy Dew," and "It Came Upon A Midnight Clear." Craig went on to co-star in TV's "Batman" as Batgirl. Fabian, who was a better actor than a singer, deserved better parts than he got but his reputation as a teen idol out of Bob Marcucci's Philadelphia song factory did him no good in later life. Fabian's and Frankie Avalon's stories are thinly disguised in the movie THE IDOL MAKER. "Love Boat's" Gavin McLeod manages to eke a few yuks out of his small role as a nutty adviser to the students, but when you consider that the talented Waldman brothers wrote the script and that it was directed by Blake Edwards, this must be reckoned as a feeble attempt at high comedy. Angus Duncan, Crosby's son, is another graduate of Harvey Lembeck's comedy class. Other graduates include Robin Williams, Penny Marshall, John Ritter, Bill Christopher and many more.

p, Charles Brackett; d, Blake Edwards; w, Tom Waldman, Frank Waldman (based on a story by Garson Kanin); ph, Ellsworth Fredericks (CinemaScope, DeLuxe Color); m, Henry Mancini; ed, Robert Simpson; art d, Herman A. Blumenthal, Duncan Cramer; cos, Bill Thomas; ch, Miriam Nelson; m/l, Sammy Cahn, Jimmy Van Heusen.

Musical/Comedy **(PR:A MPAA:NR)**

HIGH TREASON* (1929, Brit.) 95m GAU/TIE bw

Jameson Thomas *(Michael Deane)*, Benita Hume *(Evelyn Seymour)*, Basil Gill *(President Stephen Deane)*, Humberston Wright *(Vicar-General Seymour)*, Henry Vibart *(Lord Sycamore)*, James Carew *(Lord Rowleigh)*, Hayford Hobbs *(Charles Falloway)*, Milton Rosmer *(Ernest Stratton, President of Atlantic States)*, Judd Green *(James Groves)*, Alf Goddard *(Soldier)*, Irene Rooke *(Senator)*, Clifford Heatherley *(Delegate)*, Wally Patch *(Commissionaire)*, Kiyoshi Takase, Rene Ray.

A fairly laughable attempt by the British film industry to outdo Fritz Lang's masterpiece METROPOLIS. Unfortunately for them, HIGH TREASON is badly produced, written, and directed. Set in the then far-flung future of 1940, the film presents the world as a high-tech playground dominated by television, massive skyscrapers, and rooftop airplane taxis. By 1940, the Earth has been split into two rival segments: United Europe (under British rule of course) and United America. This leads to enough tension to start WW II, but a third party, the Peace League (run mainly by women) intervenes and prevents catastrophe by assassinating the leader of United Europe. None of these futuristic forecasts held a candle to METROPOLIS and the naive rendering of the future political situation is a ridiculous example of British wishful thinking.

p, L'Estrange Fawcett; d, Maurice Elvey; w, Fawcett, Noel Pemberton-Billing (based on a play by Pemberton-Billing).

Science Fiction (PR:A MPAA:NR)

HIGH TREASON*½ (1937, Brit.) 73m REAL/RKO-Olympic bw (GB: THE ROCKS OF VALPRE)

John Garrick *(Louis de Monteville)*, Winifred Shotter *(Christine Wyndham)*, Leslie Perrins *(Capt. Rodolphe)*, Michael Shepley *(Trevor Mordaunt)*, Lewis Shaw *(Noel Wyndham)*, Athene Seyler *(Aunt Philippa)*, Agnes Imlay *(Mlle. Gautier)*, Joan Summerfield [Jean Kent].

Sappy drama revolving around Garrick as an officer banished to Devil's Island on the basis of Perrins' perjured testimony. The conniving Perrins then tries to make it with Shotter. Actually a spy, Perrins gets what's coming to him. Garrick gets off the penal colony just in the nick of time to save the lady from a questionable future.

p, Julius Hagen; d, Henry Edwards; w, H. Fowler Mear (based on the novel by Ethel M. Dell); ph, Sidney Blythe; ed, Michael C. Chorlton.

Spy Drama (PR:A MPAA:NR)

HIGH TREASON** (1951, Brit.) 93m Conqueror/GFD-Pacemaker-Mayer-Kingsley bw

Liam Redmond *(Comdr. Robert Brennan)*, Andre Morell *(Superintendent Folland)*, Anthony Bushell *(Major Elliott)*, Kenneth Griffith *(Jimmy Ellis)*, Patric Doonan *(George Ellis)*, Joan Hickson *(Mrs. Ellis)*, Anthony Nichols *(Grant Mansfield)*, Mary Morris *(Anna Braun)*, Geoffrey Keen *(Morgan Williams)*, R. Stuart Lindsell *(Commissioner)*, John Bailey *(Stringer)*, Dora Bryan *(Mrs. Bowers)*, Charles Lloyd Pack *(Percy Ward)*, Laurence Naismith *(Gordon Wells)*, Sam Kydd, Anthony Quinn, Lockwood West, Bruce Seton, Stephen Jack, Helen Harvey, Frank Harvey, Robert Brennan, Harry Fowler, R. Stuart Lindsell, Alfie Bass, Cyril Conway, Mickey Wood.

A less-than-thrilling crime/espionage thriller starring Redmond, Morell, and Bushell as three Scotland Yard investigators out to stop a gang of saboteurs who are running around Europe blowing up arms shipments, munitions, and such. Eventually our heroes track down the insidious traitors, one of whom is a member of Parliament.

p, Paul Soskin; d, Roy Boulting; w, Frank Harvey, Boulting; ph, Gilbert Taylor; m, John Addison; ed, Max Benedict; set d, Alex Vetchinsky.

Crime/Spy Drama (PR:A MPAA:NR)

HIGH VELOCITY** (1977) 106m First Asian Films of California c

Ben Gazzara *(Clifford Baumgartner)*, Britt Ekland *(Mrs. Andersen)*, Paul Winfield *(Watson)*, Keenan Wynn *(Mr. Andersen)*, Alejandro Rey *(Alejandro Martel)*, Victoria Racimo *(Dolores)*.

A good cast has its efforts wasted in this below-par film. The story concerns the head of a large corporation, Wynn, who is kidnaped by a guerrilla force in an unnamed Asian country. Two Viet Nam vets, Gazzara and Winfield, are hired by Wynn's assistant, Rey, and Wynn's wife, Ekland, to rescue the kidnaped industrialist. Gazzara at first doesn't want to do it, but is convinced by the charms of Ekland. At the end of the mission, Gazzara and Winfield are double crossed by Rey, who is Ekland's secret lover.

p, Takashi Ohashi; d, Remi Kramer; w, Michael J. Parsons, Kramer; m, Jerry Goldsmith.

Action/War Drama Cas. (PR:C MPAA:PG)

HIGH VOLTAGE*½ (1929) 95m Pathe bw

William Boyd, Owen Moore, Carole Lombard, Diane Ellis, Billy Bevan, Phillips Smalley.

Tepid drama about a group of bus passengers who find themselves stranded in a lonely cabin during a snowstorm. Among the victims are a deputy sheriff and his blonde prisoner, a bride-to-be, a banker, and the driver. In the cabin they discover a lone man who is also wanted by the police and in the end the prisoner and fugitive declare their love for each other. One of Lombard's early talkie starrers following her independence from her Mack Sennett contract, which had featured her in dozens of two-reelers as foil for Mack Swain, Chester Conklin, and many others. Dialog for this film was penned by the talented James Gleason, an actor from the early 1920s to the late 1950s, both as star and as leading character actor.

d, Howard Higgins; w, Elliott Clawson, James Gleason; ph, John Mescall; ed, Doane Harrison.

Drama Cas. (PR:A MPAA:NR)

HIGH WALL, THE*½** (1947) 100m MGM bw

Robert Taylor *(Steven Kenet)*, Audrey Totter *(Dr. Ann Lorrison)*, Herbert Marshall *(Willard I. Whitcombe)*, Dorothy Patrick *(Helen Kenet)*, H.B. Warner *(Mr. Slocum)*, Warner Anderson *(Dr. George Poward)*, Moroni Olsen *(Dr. Phillip Dunlap)*, John Ridgeley *(David Wallace)*, Morris Ankrum *(Dr. Stanley Griffin)*, Elisabeth Risdon *(Mrs. Kenet)*, Vince Barnett *(Henry Cronner)*, Jonathan Hale *(Emory Garrison)*, Charles Arnt *(Sidney X. Hackle)*, Ray Mayer *(Tom Delaney)*, Bobby Hyatt *(Richard Kenet)*, Dick Wessell *(Jim Hale)*, Robert Emmett O'Connor *(Joe)*, Celia Travers *(Maggie)*, Mary Servoss *(Aunt Martha)*, Eula Guy *(Vera Mercer)*, Jack Davis *(Detective Halloran)*, Tom Quinn *(Detective Schaeffer)*, Frank Jenks *(Drunk)*, Irving Bacon *(Gas Station Proprietor)*, Bernard Gorcey *(Hirsch)*, Bert Hanlon *(Bored Clerk)*, Selmer Jackson *(Inspector Harding)*, John R. Hamilton *(Police Surgeon)*, Lee Phelps *(Telephone Man)*, Matt Willis *(Admittance Clerk)*, Bob Williams, Eddy Dunn *(Deputies)*, Jim Drumm, Paul Kruger, Jack Worth *(Orderlies)*, Lisa Golm *(Dr. Golm)*, Gordon Rhodes *(Dr. Edermann)*, Perry Ivens *(Cackling Patient)*, Dorothy Vaughn *(Harriett)*, Jean Andren *(Nurse)*, Frank Marlowe, John Beck, Henry Sylvester, Phil Dunham, Skeets Noyes, Marta Mitrovich, Kate McKenna, Russell Arms, Al Hill, Erville Alderson, William Fawcett, Guy Beach, Stanley Price, Joel Friedkin *(Patients)*, Helen Eby-Rock *(Josephine)*, Milton Kibbee *(Counterman)*, George Bunny, Bob Wendal, Sammy Shack, Hank Worden *(Customers)*, Georgia Caine *(Miss Twitchell)*, Boyd Davis *(Mrs. Grant)*, Henry Hall *(Rev. Holmsby)*, Howard Michell *(Attendant)*, Frank Darien *(Old Man in the Tub)*, Dorathea Neumann *(Mrs. Miller)*, Ray Teal *(Lieutenant of Police)*, Dan Quigg, Tay Dunn *(Police Clerks)*, Reha Mitchell *(Woman)*, Abe Dinovich *(Cab Driver)*, Jack Chefe, Jack Baxley *(Bartenders)*.

A chilling, eerie psychological thriller, THE HIGH WALL offers a singularly impressive performance from matinee idol Taylor. He is a WW II bomber pilot who returns to a cheating wife following the war. Taylor finds wife Patrick in the apartment of Marshall, a publisher of religious books; it is obvious that she intends to stay the night with paramour Marshall since she has been carrying her overnight bag. Just as Taylor begins to strangle his cuckolding spouse, he blacks out. He is later found unconscious next to his strangled wife in a wrecked car and is arrested for murder. Doctors determine that Taylor's headaches and unexplained loss of consciousness are attributable to a hematoma, a brain injury from his service days, and that he must be operated on. Taylor is no one's fool, realizing that with the injury he will be judged insane until cured but once cured he will be sane enough to be executed for the murder. He refuses the operation and is sent to an asylum for study where psychiatrist Totter examines him and listens to his story. She's as convinced as the police that Taylor is a murderer. Yet Taylor curiously clings to a claim of innocence. Totter gives him drugs and he relates how he followed his wife to Marshall's apartment, began to strangle her, then blacked out. Totter and Taylor then visit Marshall's quarters but are unable to find the traveling case Patrick was carrying on the night of her murder, one not found in the car. Marshall later visits Taylor and tells him that he killed his wife and put the blame on Taylor, a scheme designed to drive Taylor totally mad. Instead Taylor escapes over the asylum's high wall—hence the title—goes to Marshall's apartment where Totter joins him and Taylor struggles with Marshall, knocking him out. Totter injects sodium pentothal into Marshall and he blabbers his guilt just as police arrive to hear the confesssion. Totter and Taylor are now free to enjoy life together; Marshall is on his way to the death house. There are many suspenseful scenes in this taut thriller, not the least of which is one where Marshall realizes that only a lowly elevator operator, Barnett, suspects him of being the real killer; Marshall sees Barnett trying to fix an elevator, its doors open to the gaping shaft while he stands on a stool before it. Almost as a casual afterthought while he strolls by, Marshall stretches out his umbrella, hooking the handle about one of the stool's legs, yanking it and sending Barnett down the shaft to be killed. In this lone, unblinking act Marshall proves himself to be one of the most cold-blooded killers in celluloid history, made further heinous by the fact that he poses to the world as a moralistic publisher of religious books.

p, Robert Lord; d, Curtis Bernhardt; w, Sydney Boehm, Lester Cole (based on the novel and play by Alan R. Clark, Bradbury Foote); ph, Paul Vogel; m, Bronislau Kaper; ed, Conrad A. Nervig; art d, Cedric Gibbons, Leonid Vasian; set d, Edwin B. Willis, Joseph W. Holland; spec eff, Warren Newcombe, A. Arnold Gillespie; makeup, Jack Dawn.

Crime Drama (PR:C MPAA:NR)

HIGH, WIDE AND HANDSOME*½** (1937) 110m PAR bw

Irene Dunne *(Sally Watterson)*, Randolph Scott *(Peter Cortlandt)*, Dorothy Lamour *(Molly Fuller)*, Elizabeth Patterson *(Grandma Cortlandt)*, Raymond Walburn *(Doc Watterson)*, Charles Bickford *(Red Scanlon)*, Akim Tamiroff *(Joe Varese)*, Ben Blue *(Zeke)*, William Frawley *(Mac)*, Alan Hale *(Walt Brennan)*, Irving Pichel *(Mr. Stark)*, Stanley Andrews *(Lem Moulton)*, James Burke *(Stackpole)*, Roger Imhof *(Pop Bowers)*, Lucien Littlefield *(Mr. Lippincott)*, Purnell Pratt *(Colonel Blake)*, Edward Gargan *(Foreman)*, Helen Lowell *(Mrs. Lippincott)*, Jack Clifford *(Wash Miller)*, Russell Hopton *(John Thompson Civil Engineer)*, Ivan Miller *(Marble)*, Raymond Brown *(P.T. Barnum)*, Constance Bergen *(Singer)*, Tommy Bupp *(Boy)*, Billy Bletcher *(Shorty)*, Paul Kruger *(Man)*, Claire McDowell *(Seamstress)*, Fred Warren *(Piano Player)*, Rolfe Sedan *(Photographer)*, Marjorie Cameron *(Blonde Singer)*, John T. Murray *(Mr. Green)*, Sherry Hall *(Piano Player)*, Edward Keane *(Jones)*, Pat West *(Razorback)*, John Maurice Sullivan *(Old Gentleman)*, Ernest Wood *(Hotel Clerk)*, Lew Kelly *(Carpenter)*, Dell Henderson *(Bank President)*, John Marshall *(Teller)*, Philip Morris *(Teamster)*, Harry Semels *(Bartender)*, Frank Sully *(Gabby Johnson)*.

Enthused by the success of their musical SHOW BOAT (1936), Oscar Hammerstein II and Jerome Kern decided to create a new musical which would incorporate the entertainment elements of elaborate production numbers into an exciting western story (albeit with an Eastern setting). The result was HIGH, WIDE AND HANDSOME, and it would reign as the best musical western until "Oklahoma" came along (on stage) six years later. Scott stars as a rugged oil prospector who ventures into the boomtown of Titusville, Pennsylvania and strikes it rich along with a few other once-poor diggers. Unfortunately, the prospectors can't ship their black gold to the refineries because the railroad, led by the evil Bickford, wants to run them off their land and refuses to transport the oil. Scott decides that building a pipeline is the only way around the railroad, so the tiny group of roughnecks begins construction, which means continually fighting off Bickford's goons, who try to stop them. Things look grim for the completion of the project until Scott meets Dunne, the lovely daughter of a medicine-show wagoneer who takes the prospectors' cause as her own and volunteers a circus' elephants to aid in the construction. Director Mamoulian's production is lush and attractive, and he infuses his fine cast with an infectious enthusiasm that successfully pulls off some of the film's more hokey moments. Strangely, the music from HIGH, WIDE AND HANDSOME has all but been forgotten. Songs include: "The Things I Want," "Allegheny Al," "Will You Marry Me Tomorrow, Maria?" "The Folks Who Live on the Hill," and "Can I Forget You?" (Oscar Hammerstein II, Jerome Kern).

p, Arthur Hornblow, Jr.; d, Rouben Mamoulian; w, Oscar Hammerstein II, George O'Neill; ph, Victor Milner, Theodor Sparkuhl; m, Jerome Kern; ed, Archie Marshek; md, Boris Morros; art d, Hans Dreier, John Goodman; set d, A. E. Freudeman; cos, Travis Banton; ch, LeRoy Prinz; spec eff, Gordon Jennings.

Western/Musical (PR:A MPAA:NR)

HIGH WIND IN JAMAICA, A*** (1965) 104m FOX c

Anthony Quinn *(Juan Chavez)*, James Coburn *(Zac)*, Lila Kedrova *(Rosa)*, Gert Frobe *(Dutch Captain)*, Benito Carruthers *(Alberto)*, Viviane Ventura *(Margaret Fernandez)*, Nigel Davenport *(Frederick Thornton)*, Isabel Dean *(Mrs. Thornton)*, Kenneth J. Warren *(Captain Marpole)*, Deborah Baxter *(Emily Thornton)*, Martin Amis *(John Thornton)*, Roberta Tovey *(Rachel Thornton)*, Jeffrey Chandler *(Edward Thornton)*, Karen Flack *(Laura Thornton)*, Henry Beltran *(Harry)*, Brian Phelan *(Curtis)*, Dan Jackson *(The Big One)*, Trader Faulkner *(The Dancer)*, Charles Lawrence *(The Tallyman)*, Charles Hyatt *(Little One)*, Kenji Takaki *(The Cook)*, Danny Williams *(Old Sam)*, Louise Bennett *(Mamie)*, Marion Ward *(Mrs. Fernandez)*, Philip Madoc *(Captain)*, Maude Fuller *(Josephina)*, Elsie Benjamin Barsoe *(Nurse)*, Gordon Richardson *(Judge)*.

Quinn once again strapped on a saber and sailed the seven seas for this swashbuckler which sees him as a soft-hearted Spanish pirate captain who attacks a ship in the Caribbean and winds up baby-sitting a small group of English schoolchildren traveling from Jamaica to England. While his crew loots and burns the ship, the children crawl on board his ship and stowaway in the hold. Once out to sea, the kids are discovered and the crew wants to toss them in the drink because they sense it is a bad omen. Quinn won't allow it and steers the ship to Tampico, where he tries to dump the kids on Kedrova, the madame of a whorehouse. She refuses, and one of the children is killed in an accident, forcing Quinn to bring them back to the ship and set sail again. Another one of the children, Baxter, was also injured and Quinn begins to be more protective of his unwanted charges. The pirates soon spot a Dutch steamer. Quinn orders them to pull alongside to drop the kids off. Coburn, Quinn's first mate, wants to pillage the Dutch ship but Quinn forbids it. This causes a rebellion, and Coburn locks up Quinn, Baxter, and the captain of the Dutch steamer, Frobe, while the pirates loot. Frobe, desperate to be freed, excitedly approaches Baxter with a knife, begging her to cut him free. She misunderstands him, and fearing that he means to kill her, she grabs the knife and stabs him to death. Eventually, the authorities capture the pirates and they are brought to trial for the murder of Frobe *and* the child back in Tampico. While Quinn knows that Baxter is guilty of Frobe's death, he remains quiet while she testifies that it was *he* who killed the Dutch captain. Resigned to his fate, Quinn never refutes her testimony and goes off to the gallows.

p, John Croyden; d, Alexander Mackendrick; w, Stanley Mann, Ronald Harwood, Denis Cannan (based on the novel by Richard Hughes); ph, Douglas Slocombe (CinemaScope, DeLuxe Color); m, Larry Adler; ed, Derek Yorke; art d, John Howell, John Hoesli; cos, John McCorry; spec eff, Bowie Films; makeup, Bill Lodge, Freddie Williamson.

Adventure (PR:A MPAA:NR)

HIGH YELLOW* (1965) 83m Dinero/Thunder bw

Cynthia Hall *(Cindy)*, Warren Hammack *(George)*, Kay Taylor *(Judy)*, Bill McGee *(Joseph)*, Anne MacAdams *(Mrs. Langley)*, Bob Brown *(Mr. Langley)*, Bill Thurman *(Major Bates)*, Jonothan Leford *(Reverend Hatfield)*, Max Anderson *(Officer)*.

A social expose starring Hull as a 17-year-old black servant whose skin is light enough to pass for white. She finds herself trapped in the sordid goings-on at the home of a rich movie producer where she is employed. Brown is the movie producer and MacAdams is his loveless, hypochondriac wife. Taylor plays their daughter, a nymphomaniac, and Hammack their son who was kicked out of West Point because he was accused (falsely) of having homosexual tendencies. The whole clan soon find themselves about to be blackmailed by the handyman and robbed by the black chauffeur. Cynthia is disabused of her ideas about the white gentry. One song, "Going to the Go-Go," is rendered by Jody Daniels.

p, Clyde Knudsen; d, Larry Buchanan; w, (based on *Diary of a Negro Maid* by Erskine Williams).

Drama (PR:C-O MPAA:NR)

HIGHER AND HIGHER** (1943) 90m RKO bw

Michele Morgan *(Millie)*, Jack Haley *(Mike)*, Frank Sinatra *(Frank)*, Leon Errol *(Drake)*, Marcy McGuire *(Mickey)*, Victor Borge *(Fitzroy Wilson)*, Mary Wickes *(Sandy)*, Elizabeth Risdon *(Mrs. Keating)*, Barbara Hale *(Catherine Keating)*, Mel Torme *(Marty)*, Paul Hartman *(Byngham)*, Grace Hartman *(Hilda)*, Dooley Wilson *(Oscar)*, Ivy Scott *(Miss Whiffin)*, Rex Evans *(Mr. Green)*, Stanley Logan *(Hotel Manager)*, Ola Lorraine *(Sarah, Maid)*, King Kennedy *(Mr. Duval)*, Robert Anderson *(Announcer)*, Elaine Riley, Shirley O'Hara, Dorothy Malone, Daun Kennedy *(Bridesmaids)*, Rita Gould *(Woman Assistant)*, Harry Holman *(Banker)*, Warren Jackson *(Contractor)*, Anne Goldthwaite *(Debutante)*, Drake Thorton *(Bellboy)*, Edward Fielding *(Minister)*, Buddy Gorman *(Page Boy)*.

A lackluster musical, notable only as the first big-screen starring role of Frank Sinatra, sees Errol as a bankrupt businessman who, faced with ruination, drafts his servants in a scheme to win back some money. Aided by butler Haley, Errol decides to transform scullery maid Morgan into his beautiful daughter and then marry her off to a rich man. The rich kid next door, Sinatra, is considered a likely candidate (and he's Morgan's personal choice), but then along comes the aristocratic Borge—who fills the bill even better—and the marriage announcements are sent out. Just as Morgan is about to marry Borge, it is revealed that he's nothing but a confidence man. It doesn't really matter because Haley breaks up the ceremony and announces the discovery of a secret wine cellar in the house which contains valuable wines and a golden harpsichord that is worth a fortune. In the end, everyone breaks into song and celebrates. Songs include: "You Belong in a Love Song," "A Most Important Affair," "The Music Stopped," "Today I'm A Debutante," "A Lovely Way To Spend An Evening," "I Couldn't Sleep A Wink Last Night," "You're On Your Own," "I Saw You First" (Jimmy McHugh, Harold Adamson); "Disgustingly Rich" (Richard Rodgers, Lorenz Hart); "Boccherini's Minuet in Boogie."

p&d, Tim Whelan; w, Jay Dratler, Ralph Spence, William Bowers, Howard Harris (based on the play by Gladys Hurlbut and Joshua Logan); ph, Robert De Grasse; m, Roy Webb; ed, Gene Milford; md, Constantin Bakaleinikoff; art d, Albert S. D'Agostino, Jack Okey; set d, Darrell Silvera, Claude Carpenter; cos, Edward Stevenson; ch, Ernst Matray.

Musical Cas. (PR:A MPAA:NR)

HIGHLAND FLING* (1936, Brit.) 68m FOX bw

Charlie Naughton *(Smith)*, Jimmy Gold *(Smythe)*, Eve Foster *(Jean)*, Frederick Bradshaw *(Tony)*, Gibson Gowland *(Delphos)*, Naomi Plaskitt *(Katherine)*, Billy Shine *(Lizards)*, Peter Popp *(Clockmender)*, Winifred Willard, W.S. Percy.

Highly contrived British farce resting upon the conception of having two hapless detectives in search of riches in the north of Scotland. Naughton and Gold are the two chums who ramble through a haunted castle in hopes of finding a will, but not before encountering a number of forced situations ranging from ghosts to missing clocks.

p, John Findlay; d, Manning Haynes; w, Alan d'Egville, Ralph Stock (based on the story by d'Egville); ph, Stanley Grant.

Comedy (PR:A MPAA:NR)

HIGHLY DANGEROUS*½ (1950, Brit.) 88m Two Cities/Lippert bw

Margaret Lockwood *(Frances Gray)*, Dane Clark *(Bill Casey)*, Marius Goring *(Anton Razinski)*, Naunton Wayne *(Hedgerley)*, Wilfrid Hyde-White *(Luke)*, Eugene Deckers *(Alf)*, Olaf Pooley *(Assistant)*, Gladys Henson *(Attendant)*, Paul Hardtmuth *(Priest)*, Michael Hordern *(Rawlings)*, George Benson *(Customer)*, Eric Pohlmann *(Joe)*, Joan Haythorne *(Judy)*, Patric Doonan *(Customs Man)*, Anthony Newley *(Operator)*, Noel Johnson *(Frank Conway, Voice)*, Jill Balcon *(Wardress)*, Ernest Butcher, Lance Secretan, Toni Frost, Michael Ritterman, John Gabriel, John Horsley, Anton Diffring.

A lame little British espionage thriller that takes place in a mythical Balkan country. Lockwood is a female entomologist who is sent by the British general staff to investigate bacteriological warfare tests being done in the little country. She has many problems from her first encounter with the local chief of police, whom she meets on the train, when he sees her microscope and other equipment in her bag. Her contact is killed and the body winds up in her hotel room. As a result, she is given the third degree and truth serum in an effort to discover what she knows of the murder. Eventually she is released and teams up with American press agent, Clark, who helps her to steal some disease-carrying insects. This adventure takes place while she is stoned on truth serum, and she believes herself to be the heroine of a popular English radio serial.

p, Anthony Darnborough; d, Roy Baker; w, Eric Ambler; ph, David Harcourt, Reginald Wyer; ed, Alfred Roome.

Spy/Comedy (PR:A MPAA:NR)

HIGHWAY DRAGNET*½ (1954) 70m AA bw

Richard Conte *(Jim)*, Joan Bennett *(Mrs. Cunningham)*, Wanda Hendrix *(Susan)*, Reed Hadley *(White Eagle)*, Mary Beth Hughes *(Terry)*, Iris Adrian *(Dolly)*, Harry Harvey *(Carson)*, Tom Hubbard *(Ben)*, Frank Jenks *(Marine)*, Murray Alper *(Truck Driver)*, Zon Murray *(Officer)*, House Peters, Jr. *(Cop)*, Joseph Crehan *(2nd Inspector)*, Tony Hughes *(Inspector)*, Bill Hale *(2nd Officer)*, Fred Gabourie *(Al)*.

A poor film that suffers from a one-dimensional plot and characters. Conte is an ex-Marine who is accused of the murder of an ex-Las Vegas model, Hughes. He escapes the police and takes to the road. He hitches a ride with a magazine photographer, Bennett, and her model, Hendrix. By a coincidence we discover that Bennett is the one who killed Hughes because Hughes earlier caused the suicide of her husband. After much cop chasing, Bennett finally confesses, while Conte and Hendrix are left to get together in a romantic embrace. Future AIP "golden boy" Roger Corman earned his first screen credit as a co-writer and associate producer on this film. The title was a blatant rip-off of the highly successful "Dragnet" television series.

p, William F. Broidy, Jack Jungmeyer, Jr.; d, Nathan Juran; w, Herb Meadow, Jerome Odlum, Tom Hubbard, Fred Eggers (based on a story by U. S. Anderson, Roger Corman); ph, John Martin; m, Edward J. Kay; ed, Ace Herman; art d, David Milton.

Crime (PR:A MPAA:NR)

HIGHWAY PATROL*½ (1938) 56m COL bw

Robert Paige *(William Rolph)*, Jacqueline Wells *(Jane Brady)*, Robert Middlemass *(J.W. Brady)*, Arthur Loft *(Walter Brennan)*, Alan Bridge *(Jarvis)*, Eddie Foster *(Carter)*, George McKay *(Martin)*, Eddie Laughton *(Cole)*, Ann Doran *(Estelle)*.

Paige plays a noble cop who helps beseiged oil refinery owner Middlemass thwart his rival's efforts to destroy his business through terrorist tactics such as truck hijacking and bombings. In the end it is revealed that Loft, Middlemass' own general manager, and his security chief have been working for the competition.

d, C.C. Coleman, Jr.; w, Robert E. Kent, Stuart Anthony (based on a story by Lambert Hillyer); ph, Lucien Ballard; ed, James Sweeney.

Crime (PR:A MPAA:NR)

HIGHWAY PICKUP½** (1965, Fr./Ital.) 107m Pans-Interopa/Times bw (CHAIR DE POULE)

Roberto Hossein *(Daniel Boisett)*, Georges Wilson *(Thomas)*, Jean Sorel *(Paul Genest)*, Catherine Rouvel *(Maria)*, Lucien Raimbourg *(Roux)*, Nicole Berger *(Simone)*, Sophie Grimaldi *(Starlet)*, Armand Mestral *(Corenne)*, Jean-Jacques

Delbo *(Joubert)*, Jacques Bertrand *(Marc)*, Robert Dalban *(Brigadier)*, Jean Lefebvre *(Priest)*.

French crime drama starring Hossein and Sorel as accomplices in a safecracking job that goes awry when they are caught by a guard. Sorel kills the man and escapes, but Hossein is left for the police and is eventually convicted for the crime. A year later, Hossein escapes from prison and is befriended by Wilson, who runs a gas station. Wilson is married to Rouvel, an ex-prostitute, who has married him for his money. Rouvel finds out about Hossein's escape from prison and blackmails him into opening her husband's safe. Wilson discovers them and in a struggle is killed by Rouvel. Hossein buries Wilson's body, and then refuses to open the safe. Along comes Hossein's old partner Sorel, and Rouvel tries to seduce *him* into opening the safe, but he too refuses. Later, Rouvel leaves, Sorel attempts to open the safe, but is caught by Rouvel, who wields a shotgun. He kills her, but is killed trying to escape the police. His car crashes into the gas pumps, causing the station to explode into flames. Luckily, Hossein escapes in the nick of time. A stark, tightly woven thriller from one of the "Big Four" French directors, the prolific Duvivier. (In French; English subtitles.)

p, Robert Hakim, Raymond Hakim; d, Julien Duvivier; w, Duvivier, Rene Barjavel (based on the novel *Come Easy—Go Easy* by James Hadley Chase); ph, L.H. Burel; m, Georges Delerue; ed, Suzanne de Troeye; art d, Francois de Lamothe.

Crime **(PR:C MPAA:NR)**

HIGHWAY 13* (1948) 58m Lippert/Screen Guild bw

Robert Lowery *(Hank Wilson)*, Pamela Blake *(Doris)*, Michael Whalen *(Frank Denton)*, Dan Seymour *(Kelleher)*, Clem Bevans *(Pops)*, Maris Wrixon *(Miss Hadley)*, Tom Chatterton *(Morris)*, Mary Gordon *(Aunt Myrt)*, Gaylord Pendleton *(George Montgomery)*, Lyle Talbot *(Detective)*.

A rapidly moving, inoffensive little programmer starring Lowery as a trucker who gets mixed up in a violent trucking-industry war when gangsters Whalen, Bevans, and Wrixon decide to shut down the firm. After many crash-and-burn sequences, Lowery finds out who's responsible and smashes the gang.

p, William Stephens; d, William Berke; w, Maurice Tombragel (based on an original story by John Wilste); ph, Carl Berger; m, David Chudnow; ed, Edward Mann; art d, Martin Obzina.

Crime **(PR:A MPAA:NR)**

HIGHWAY 301** (1950) 83m WB bw

Steve Cochran *(George Legenza)*, Virginia Grey *(Mary Simms)*, Gaby Andre *(Lee Fontaine)*, Edmon Ryan *(Truscott)*, Robert Webber *(Wm. B. Phillips)*, Wally Cassell *(Robert Mais)*, Aline Towne *(Madeline Welton)*, Richard Egan *(Herbie Brooks)*, Edward Norris *(Noyes)*.

A gritty and often violent cops-and-robbers film as seen through the anti-hero eyes of the robbers. The film chronicles the crime spree of the Tri-State Gang, made up of Cochran, Webber, Egan, and Cassell. The film plods through its opening minutes as the governors of Virginia, North Carolina, and Maryland give speeches against crime. The story then moves into the gang's activities as they pull off a successful bank robbery. Accompanied by their molls, Grey, Andre, and Towne, the film follows the group through crimes, chases, gunfights, and violent deaths as the members are killed one by one, proving that crime does not pay.

p, Bryan Foy; d&w, Andrew Stone (based on "The Tri-State Gang," a story by Stone); ph, Carl Guthrie; m, William Lava; ed, Owen Marks; art d, Leo K. Kuter.

Crime **(PR:C MPAA:NR)**

HIGHWAY TO BATTLE** (1961, Brit.) 71m Danziger/PAR bw

Gerard Heinz *(Constantin)*, Margaret Tyzack *(Hilda)*, Ferdy Mayne *(Zeigler)*, Dawn Berrington *(Gerda)*, Peter Reynolds *(Jarvost)*, Vincent Ball *(Ransome)*, George Mikell *(Brauwitz)*, John Gabriel *(Carl)*.

Fairly captivating yarn set prior to WW II when members of Germany's political party were allowed to come and go from England pretty fairly. One of these men has seen the light though, and wishes to stay put in England. However, the Gestapo has different plans for the future of this German. Wishing to show people who have similar plans what type of fate they would meet should they try such a stunt, the Gestapo gives hot pursuit to the defector. Only this man fears being caught so much that he decides to take his own life instead of facing Nazi tortures.

p, Edward J. Danziger, Harry Lee Danziger; d, Ernest Morris; w, Brian Clemens, Eldon Hayward (based on the story by Joseph Pole).

Spy Drama **(PR:A MPAA:NR)**

HIGHWAY WEST*½ (1941) 62m WB bw

Brenda Marshall *(Claire Foster)*, Arthur Kennedy *(George Foster)*, Olympe Bradna *(Myra Abbott)*, William Lundigan *(Dave Warren)*, Slim Summerville *(Gramps)*, Willie Best *(Wellington)*, Frank Wilcox *(Murph)*, John Ridgely *(Alex)*, Dorothy Tree *(Bella)*, Noel Madison *(Salvo)*, Pat Flaherty *(Eddie)*, Victor Zimmerman *(Jake)*, William B. Davidson *(Gorman)*, Dick Rich *(Mike)*, James Westerfield *(Swede)*.

A weak remake of HEAT LIGHTNING (1931) about a criminal, Kennedy, who kills a bank teller in a holdup and goes on the lam with his innocent wife, Marshall, who believes him to be a traveling businessman. He is tracked down and goes to jail, while Marshall returns to her drab existence of running a roadside hotel and gas station with her sister, Bradna. Kennedy makes a jail break three years later and Marshall is forced to give him protection. The tale ends with Kennedy finally getting his just desserts from policeman Summerville.

p, Edmund Grainger; d, William McGann; w, Allen Rivkin, Charles Kenyon, Kenneth Gamet (based on the play "Heat Lightning" by Leon Abrams, George Abbott); ph, Ted McCord; ed, Jack Killifer.

Crime/Drama **(PR:A MPAA:NR)**

HIGHWAYMAN, THE½** (1951) 82m Jack Dietz-AA/MON c

Charles Coburn *(Lord Walters)*, Wanda Hendrix *(Bess)*, Philip Friend *(Jeremy)*, Cecil Kellaway *(Lord Herbert)*, Victor Jory *(Lord Douglas)*, Scott Forbes *(Sergeant)*, Virginia Huston *(Ellen)*, Dan O'Herlihy *(Robin)*, Henry Morgan *(Tim)*, Albert Sharpe *(Forsythe)*, Lowell Gilmore *(Oglethorpe)*, Alan Napier *(Barton)*.

Friend stars as a nobleman who seeks to redistribute the wealth in 18th-century England by posing as a Quaker and going for midnight rides with his gang of cohorts (Hendrix, O'Herlihy, and Kellaway), robbing from the rich to assist the poor. The Robin Hood-type gang gets a change of pace when they discover that villains Coburn and Jory are kidnaping free men and selling them as slaves to the Colonies for a handsome sum, and they seek to put an end to this perversion of free enterprise. In keeping with the poem on which the film was based, a sad finale ensues as Hendrix shoots herself so that the sound of gunfire will warn Friend of an impending ambush. Unfortunately, the warning goes for naught and Friend, too, is killed.

p, Hal E. Chester; d, Lesley Selander; w, Jan Jeffries (based on a poem by Alfred Noyes and a story by Jack DeWitt, Renault Duncan); ph, Harry Neuman (Cinecolor); m, Herschel Burke Gilbert; art d, Martin Obzina.

Adventure **(PR:C MPAA:NR)**

HIGHWAYMAN RIDES, THE (SEE: BILLY THE KID, 1930)

HIGHWAYS BY NIGHT*½ (1942) 62m RKO bw

Richard Carlson *(Tommy Van Steel)*, Jane Randolph *(Peggy Fogarty)*, Jane Darwell *(Grandma)*, Barton MacLane *(Leo Bronson)*, Ray Collins *(Uncle Ben)*, Gordon Jones *(Footsy Fogarty)*, Renee Haal *(Ellen Cromwell)*, George Cleveland *(Judkins)*, Marten Lamont *(Reggie)*, Jack LaRue *(Johnny Lieber)*, John Maguire *(Duke Wellington)*, James Seay *(Westbrook)*, Cliff Clark *(Capt. James)*, Paul Fix *(Gabby)*.

A low-budget film starring Carlson as a naive young millionaire who decides to find out for himself how the "little" people live. Too bad for him: he blunders into a gangland murder and is soon sought by both the cops and the hoodlums. While fleeing, he meets downtrodden maid Randolph and falls in love. Eventually, Carlson is forced to re-surface in the world of the rich, and he uses his considerable financial resources to hire the best lawyers to destroy the mob.

p, Herman Schlom [uncredited]; d, Peter Godfrey; w, Lynn Root, Frank Fenton (based on a serial "Silver Spoon" by Clarence Budington Kelland); ph, Robert de Grasse; m, Roy Webb; ed, Harry Marker; md, C. Bakaleinikoff; art d, Albert D'Agostino, Carroll Clark.

Crime/Drama **(PR:A MPAA:NR)**

HI-JACKED*½ (1950) 66m Lippert bw

Jim Davies *(Joe Harper)*, Marsha Jones *(Jean)*, Sid Melton *(Killer)*, David Bruce *(Matt)*, Paul Cavanagh *(Hagen)*, Ralph Sanford *(Clark)*, Iris Adrian *(Agnes)*, George Eldredge *(Digbey)*.

Hijackings in the trucking industry form the center of interest for this very low-budget film. The story has a parolee, Davis, driving a truck for a freight company. His truck gets hijacked, and suspicion falls on him as he has a criminal record. When Davis gets hijacked a second time, he is fired. He goes out on his own in an effort to track down the culprit and clear his name. Davis discovers that the company dispatcher is behind the hijackings and when he learns of a new robbery being planned, he tips off the police who capture the crooks in the act.

p, Sigmund Neufeld; d, Sam Newfield; w, Fred Myton, Orville Hampton (based on a story by Ray Schrock, Myton); ph, Phil Tannura; m, Paul Dunlap; ed, Edward Mann.

Crime **(PR:A MPAA:NR)**

HI-JACKERS, THE*½ (1963, Brit.) 69m But bw

Anthony Booth *(Terry McKinley)*, Jacqueline Ellis *(Shirley)*, Derek Francis *(Jack Carter)*, Patrick Cargill *(Inspector Grayson)*, Glynn Edwards *(Bluey)*, David Gregory *(Pete)*, Harold Goodwin *(Scouse)*, Anthony Wager *(Smithy)*, Arthur English *(Bert)*.

Road picture with Ellis playing a woman on the run from her husband, hooking up with trucker Booth when he gives her a lift. This ride turns into quite an event when the truck is hijacked, leaving Ellis to aid in detecting the man who is behind this dangerous road play.

p, John I. Phillips; d&w, Jim O'Connolly.

Crime **(PR:A MPAA:NR)**

HIKEN (SEE: YOUNG SWORDSMAN, 1964, Jap.)

HIKEN YABURI½** (1969, Jap.) 90m Daiei c
(AKA: BROKEN SWORDS)

Hiroki Matsukata *(Tenzen Tange)*, Kojiro Hongo *(Yasubei Nakayama)*, Tomomi Iwai *(Chiharu)*, Shigeru Tsuyuguchi *(Ryunoshin Nagao)*, Yoshi Kato, Tatsuo Matsumura.

Matsukata and Hongo are two young men discouraged by the corrupt government that rules their land. They go against the popular trend for collecting art works, instead devoting their lives to samurai training. Hongo's uncle had been killed by 36 men, schooled by Matsukata. He has revenge, killing them all single-handedly, which forces Matsukata to be expelled from the samurai legion for not helping his men. Hongo also is thrown out for the crime of using his skills in a private feud. Two lords are quite impressed with the latter's skill, however, and vie for his services. After meeting Iwai, the sister of one of the lord's retainers, Hongo makes his choice. He learns that she is engaged to his rival, so the brokenhearted samurai retains his honor by choosing the other lord as employer.

d, Kazuo Ikehiro; w, Daisuke Ito (based on a story by Kosuke Gomi); ph, Chishi Makiura (DaieiScope, Fuji Color); m, Takeo Watanabe; art d, Shigenori Shimoishizaka.

Drama/Adventure **(PR:C MPAA:NR)**

HILDA CRANE** (1956) 87m FOX c

Jean Simmons *(Hilda Crane)*, Guy Madison *(Russell Burns)*, Jean Pierre Aumont *(Jacques De Lisle)*, Judith Evelyn *(Mrs. Crane)*, Evelyn Varden *(Mrs. Burns)*, Peggy Knudsen *(Nell Bromley)*, Gregg Palmer *(Dink)*, Richard Garrick *(Dr. Francis)*, Jim Hayward *(Mr. Small)*, Sandee Marriot *(Cab Driver)*, Don Shelton *(Caterer)*, Helen Mayon *(Maid)*, Blossom Rock *(Clara)*, Jay Jostyn *(Minister)*.

A dreary soap opera that had handkerchief salesmen happy, HILDA CRANE tells the story of a disturbed woman with a past who returns to her hometown in an effort to live a "normal" life. Simmons plays the girl who, after two failed marriages and a nowhere professional career, returns home to the arms of Madison, a former boy friend. His spiteful and domineering mother, Varden, disapproves of his marriage to Simmons, and stages a fake heart attack that ends up being the real thing. After Varden's death, the two marry, but Madison is haunted by his mother's death. Lonely and frustrated, Simmons enters into an affair with a French author, Aumont. Madison discovers the two in a hotel room, thus breaking up the affair. Simmons attempts suicide soon after, but things change as Madison gives up his guilty feelings and becomes a better husband.

p, Herbert B. Swope, Jr.; d&w, Philip Dunne (based on a play by Samson Raphaelson); ph, Joe MacDonald (CinemaScope, DeLuxe Color); m, David Raksin; ed, David Bretherton; md, Lionel Newman; art d, Lyle R. Wheeler, Albert Hogsett; cos, Charles Le Maire.

Drama **(PR:A MPAA:NR)**

HILDUR AND THE MAGICIAN*** (1969) 95m Canyon Cinema Cooperative bw

John Graham *(The Magician/Narrator)*, Hildur Mahl *(Hildur)*, Patricia Jordon *(Companion)*, Jim Yensan *(Gnome)*, Jani Novak *(Driad)*, Roy Berger *(Woodcutter)*, Shelby Sache *(His Wife)*, Tres Berger *(Arabelle)*, Sydney Droshin *(Wicked Queen)*, Tito Patri *(Huckster)*, Cook Ruddick *(King)*, Gael Knepfer *(Maid)*, Bunny Kirsch, Gina Batchelder, Sally Berger, Cathy Seitz, Mark Batchelder *(Fairies)*, Joel Andrews, Julie Iger, Avery Faulkner, Paula White *(Musicians)*, Sandra Della Valle.

This is a delightful fairy tale, fine for the kids and with enough good points to interest adults as well. The story, filmed in black-and-white, is about a princess kidnaped by an evil gnome. Mahl, armed with a magic potion, sets out to the rescue. The princess accidentally swallows the potion, making her mortal, but Mahl retains memories of her spritely existence. The story is full of charm, and an interesting, well photographed mise-en-scene. In addition to some excellent animation sequences, the story is played out in mime, with Graham, the film's bumbling wizard, providing a voice-over narration. The cast also served as set constructors and costume makers, giving this independent 16-mm feature a nice group feeling. Its only defect is the running time. An hour and a half is a little long for the material.

p,d&w, Larry Jordan (based on an idea by John Graham, Patricia Jordan); ph, Larry Jordan; m, Joel Andrews, Julie Iger; ed, Larry Jordan; set d, Roy Berger.

Fantasy **(PR:AAA MPAA:NR)**

HILL, THE*** (1965, Brit.) 125m Seven Arts/MGM bw

Sean Connery *(Joe Roberts)*, Harry Andrews *(RSM Bert Wilson)*, Ian Bannen *(Sgt. Charlie Harris)*, Alfred Lynch *(George Stevens)*, Ossie Davis *(Jacko King)*, Roy Kinnear *(Monty Bartlett)*, Jack Watson *(Jock McGrath)*, Ian Hendry *(Sgt. Williams)*, Michael Redgrave *(Medical Officer)*, Norman Bird *(Commandant)*, Neil McCallum *(Sgt. Burton)*, Howard Goorney *(Walters)*, Tony Caunter *(Martin)*.

At a military stockade in North Africa, prisoners are punished by making them run up and down a hill of sand and stone under the hot sun with full equipment. When one drops from exhaustion, busted sergeant major Connery tries to get him medical help, but sadistic sergeant Hendry orders the man to keep marching, and the man soon dies. Connery tries to file a formal complaint but is brutally beaten for his trouble, an act which finally motivates kindly prison doctor Redgrave to step in and put a halt to the cruelty. Before he can act, though, mutiny breaks out and the angry prisoners kill Hendry, losing any chance they ever had for improving their conditions. An intense, if slightly overlong, drama with the social commentary usually found in a Lumet film. The film is well assembled, and the performances are all quite good, especially Connery and Hendry, as evil a character as can be found. One memorable scene has Davis, a West Indian soldier in the brig for stealing and drinking three bottles of Scotch from the officers' mess, resigning from the army by taking off his uniform down to his shorts and parading about, the only light moment in this heavy movie.

p, Kenneth Hyman; d, Sidney Lumet; w, Ray Rigby, R.S. Allen (based on a play by Rigby, Allen), ph, Oswald Morris; m, Art Noel, Don Pelosi; ed, Thelma Connell; art d, Herbert Smith; cos, Elsa Fennell; m/l, "Kiss Me Goodnight, Sergeant Major," Noel, Pelosi; makeup, George Partleton.

Prison Drama **(PR:O MPAA:NR)**

HILL IN KOREA, A (SEE: HELL IN KOREA, 1956, Brit.)

HILL 24 DOESN'T ANSWER*** (1955, Israel) 100m Sikor/CD bw

Edward Mulhare *(James Finnegan)*, Haya Harareet *(Miriam Mizrachi)*, Michael Shillo *(Yehude Berger)*, Michael Wager *(Allan Goodman)*, Margalit Oved *(Ester Hadassi)*, Arich Lavi *(Amiram)*, Zalman Lebiush *(The Rabbi)*, Haim Enav *(Jacob)*, Azaria Rapaport *(Nazi Officer)*, Arie Seidman *(Yitzhak)*, Shoshana Damari *(Druze Woman)*, Yosef Yadin *(Jerusalem Commander)*.

The first feature to be filmed and processed entirely within Israel's borders, the story deals with the 1948 war of attrition between the Jews and the Arabs, with special reference to the attempts of each to gain and hold the Holy Land. This 20th-century Crusade is recounted from the several perspectives of four soldiers, in rather trite cinematic convention, an Irishman, an American, a native of Palestine, and a Yemenite girl, all involved in holding a particular parcel of land on behalf of the new state-to-be. Their stories are told in flashback. Mulhare, the Irishman, was a British policeman enforcing that country's Mandate in the region; underground worker Harareet, once his enemy, turned him from the British cause to that of the Zionist's. Wager, the American, was a tourist; trapped in the street fighting, he found his Jewish roots with the help of rabbi Lebiush. Lavi, the tough, feisty Palestine-born Jew, recounts his triumph over hard-line Nazi Rapaport. The soft, gentle Yemenite girl, Oved, evinces great bravery in support of her cause. These tales are told by corpses; all four have been discovered dead by a United Nations team after the signing of the historic truce which fixed the boundaries of the new land. However, the four *did* hold their hill. An often moving movie, despite its obvious propaganda motives and its cliches. (In English, Hebrew, and other languages; non-English languages subtitled.)

p, Thorold Dickinson, Peter Frye; d, Dickinson; w, Zvi Kolitz, Frye (based on the story by Kolitz); ph, Gerald Gibbs; m, Paul Ben Haim; ed, Joanna Dickinson, Thorold Dickinson; md, Shlomo Riklis; art d, Joseph Carl.

War/Drama **(PR:A MPAA:NR)**

HILLBILLY BLITZKRIEG zero (1942) 63m MON bw (AKA: ENEMY ROUND-UP)

Bud Duncan *(Snuffy Smith)*, Cliff Nazarro *(Barney Google)*, Edgar Kennedy *(Sergeant Gatling)*, Doris Linden *(Julie James)*, Lucien Littlefield *(Professor James)*, Alan Baldwin *(Corporal Bruce)*, Nicolle Andre *(Marlene Zara)*, Jimmie Dodd *(Missouri)*, Teddy Mangean *(Dinky)*, Jerry Jerome *(Boller)*, Jack Carr *(Hertle)*, Frank Austin *(Luke)*, Manart Kipper.

Regretfully, HILLBILLY BLITZKRIEG does not live up to its title (and then again, *what* film could live up to that title!). Alas, it is only the simple, dim-witted tale of popular comic-strip characters Snuffy Smith (Duncan), Barney Google (Nazarro), and their horse Spark Plug, come to life and gone to war. Kennedy plays the Army sergeant sent to a backwoods hideaway in Tennessee in order to guard a top-secret missile site. Duncan is the buck private assigned to assist Kennedy, which gives Kennedy plenty of opportunities to do his "slow burn." Believe it or not, enemy spies have traveled to Tennessee to steal the plans for the rocket, and it is up to Kennedy and Duncan to stop them. All this might have been funny if Monogram had spent more than what seems to be a budget of $20 on the film.

p, Edward Gross; d, Roy Mack; w, Ray S. Harris (based on the comic strip by Billy De Beck); ph, Marcel Le Picard; ed, Ralph Dixon; md, Paul Sawtell.

Comedy **(PR:A MPAA:NR)**

HILLBILLYS IN A HAUNTED HOUSE*½ (1967) 88m Woolner c

Ferlin Husky *(Woody Weatherby)*, Joi Lansing *(Boots Malone)*, Don Bowman *(Jeepers)*, John Carradine *(Dr. Himmil)*, Lon Chaney, Jr. *(Maximillian)*, Basil Rathbone *(Gregor)*, Linda Ho *(Madame Wong)*, George Barrows *(Gorilla)*, Molly Bee, Merle Haggard, Jim Kent, Sonny James, Marcella Wright, Richard Webb, Pat Patterson, Jay Jasin.

The title really says it all. Country music stars Husky and Lansing spend the night in a haunted mansion when they are caught in a storm on the way to the Nashville Jamboree. There they run into the likes of Chaney, Carradine, Rathbone and a gorilla, who are all controlled by the insidious Ho who is out to get an atomic formula. A film that wastes the talents of both the once-major horror film stars and major country-and-western singers who were obviously just trying to make a quick buck. An unfortunate memorial to Rathbone, this being the actor's last film (he was in his seventies, an age that skyrocketed the production's insurance costs), and for director Yarbrough, who began his directorial career with Bela Lugosi in THE DEVIL BAT (1941); this was his final filmic effort as well. Sequel to LAS VEGAS HILLBILLYS.

p, Bernard A. Woolner; d, Jean Yarbrough; w, Duke Yelton; ph, Vaughn Wilkins (Technicolor); m, Hal Borne; ed, Roy Livingston; md, Igo Kantor; art d, Paul Sylos.

Comedy **Cas.** **(PR:A MPAA:NR)**

HILLS HAVE EYES, THE*** (1978) 89m Blood Relations/Vanguard c

Susan Lanier *(Brenda Carter)*, Robert Houston *(Bobby Carter)*, Virginia Vincent *(Ethel Carter)*, Russ Grieve *(Bob Carter)*, Dee Wallace *(Lynne Wood)*, Martin Speer *(Doug Wood)*, Brenda Marinoff *(Katie Wood)*, Flora *(Beauty)*, Stricker *(The Beast)*, James Whitmore *(Jupiter)*, Cordy Clark *(Mama)*, Janus Blythe *(Ruby)*, Michael Berryman *(Pluto)*, Lance Gordon *(Mars)*, Arthur King *(Mercury)*, John Steadman *(Fred)*.

Cult director Wes Craven (whose LAST HOUSE ON THE LEFT has become one of the more infamous films in exploitation history) made one of the best "Horror of the Family" films in recent memory with THE HILLS HAVE EYES. The film opens as a typical suburban family, the Carters, drive through the desert in their wagon and mobile home headed for California. The family consists of Dad (Grieve), a recently retired cop, Mom (Vincent), big sister (Wallace), her husband (Speer), their baby (Marinoff), brother and sister (Houston and Lanier), and the two dogs Beauty and The Beast. Trouble starts when the car's axle breaks and the travelers are left stranded in the desert, miles from help. Slowly, they begin to realize that they have invaded another family's domain. A savage, almost caveman-like family lives in the desert mesas led by Whitworth who, as a baby, was left to die in the wasteland after he was born mutated. His wife, Clark, is a prostitute "no one would miss" whom he kidnaped from a distant town and brought into the desert for companionship. Together the couple had three "children," now full grown. The boys, Berryman, Gordon, and King, all assist their father in protecting their territory (aided by walkie-talkies and guns that somehow found their way into the family's possession) and gathering whatever food they can come across (including, if need be, humans). The daughter, Blythe, has seen civilization (she's the most "human" looking of the family and therefore is sent into town to pick up necessary items provided by her "Grandfather," the man who left Whitworth to die in the desert those long years ago, who runs a lonely gas station and has been waiting for his son to return seeking vengeance) and longs to escape her savage family. Soon the rival families collide, with the desert clan attacking the suburban clan to loot, kill, and eat (horribly, their efforts focus on the baby) them. After many sieges, the "civilized" family has lost all its members except Houston, Lanier, and Speer. With the aid of Blythe (who sees the "normal" family as a way out of the desert) the baby is saved, the more dangerous members of the "savage" family are killed, and the film ends with a freeze frame of Speer, father and husband, savagely killing one of his enemies with a rock. He and his have become just as "uncivilized" as their enemy. THE HILLS HAVE EYES is an extremely intense and disturbing film that tears at taboos viciously and examines them with a keen, unblinking glance, resulting in a grim, horrible, insightful essay on the dark side of the family structure that could only be done in the exploitation horror genre. It is a landmark in a cycle of horror films. Written and intensely executed with intelligence and passion by Wes Craven, it is *definitely not* for children or most viewers,

p, Peter Locke; d&w, Wes Craven; ph, Eric Saarinen; m, Don Peake; ed, Craven; art d, Robert Burns.

Horror **Cas.** **(PR:O MPAA:R)**

HILLS OF DONEGAL, THE* (1947, Brit.) 85m But bw

Dinah Sheridan *(Eileen Hannay)*, James Etherington *(Michael O'Keefe)*, Moore Marriott *(Old Jake)*, John Bentley *(Terry O'Keefe)*, Irene Handl *(Mrs. Mactavish)*, Tamara Desni *(Carole Wells)*, Marie O'Neill *(Hannah)*, Brendan Clegg *(Paddy Hannay)*, Robert [Bob] Arlen *(Daniel)*.

Poorly conceived drama, filled with an obnoxious number of "good ole" Irish tunes, centers around a singing lass' desire to settle down and marry. Bidding her career adieu, she and her new husband flee to the countryside of Ireland, only to discover that the man does not take to this environment very well. This comes mainly in the form of a wench asking for money in exchange for keeping quiet about their past affairs. In trying to do away with his tormentor, he meets his own end. His bride, Sheridan, resumes her singing career with her old partner, Etherington, and romance blossoms. Blarney.

p&d, John Argyle; w, John Dryden; ph, Arthur Grant; ed, Ted Richards; md, Percival Mackey; art d, Charles Gilbert.

Musical/Drama **(PR:A MPAA:NR)**

HILLS OF HOME*** (1948) 97m MGM c (AKA: MASTER OF LASSIE)

Edmund Gwenn *(Dr. William MacLure)*, Donald Crisp *(Drumsheugh)*, Tom Drake *(Tammas Milton)*, Janet Leigh *(Margit Mitchell)*, Rhys Williams *(Mr. Milton)*, Reginald Owen *(Hopps)*, Edmond Breon *(Jaimie Soutar)*, Alan Napier *(Sir George)*, Hugh Green *(Geordie)*, Lumsden Hare *(Lord Kilspindle)*, Eileen Erskine *(Belle Saunders)*, Victor Wood *(David Mitchell)*, David Thursky *(Burnbrae)*, Frederick Worlock *(Dr. Weston)*, Lassie.

One of the better "LASSIE" films to come out in the very successful series. The story has Lassie as the dog of a Scottish doctor, Gwenn. Lassie is suffering from a psychological fear of water and won't go near a stream or pond. Gwenn works with the pooch to rid her of her phobia. In between therapy sessions, Gween busies himself with the medical problems of the area. An accident, which sees Gween badly injured, causes Lassie to overcome her phobia and she swims a raging stream to bring help to her fatally wounded master. A moving deathbed scene and the subsequent burial and cemetery visitations of Lassie to her master's grave, help to bring out the handkerchiefs. Drake plays a young student doctor; Leigh, in one of her early roles, plays his sweetheart, and Crisp plays a rich village friend of Gween. Twenty-five years earlier, Crisp directed a British film based on the same Ian McLaren Story. (See LASSIE series, Index).

p, Robert Sisk; d, Fred Wilcox; w, William Ludwig (suggested by Ian MacLaren's sketches, "Doctor of the Old School"); ph, Charles Schoenbaum (Technicolor); m, Herbert Stothart, Albert Sendrey, Robert Franklyn; ed, Ralph E. Winters; art d, Cederic Gibbons, Eddie Imazu.

Drama **(PR:AAA MPAA:NR)**

HILLS OF OKLAHOMA** (1950) 67m REP bw

Rex Allen *(Himself)*, Elizabeth Fraser *(Sharon Forbes)*, Elizabeth Risdon *(Kate Carney)*, Robert Karnes *(Brock Stevens)*, Fuzzy Knight *(Jigg)*, Roscoe Ates *(Dismal)*, Robert Emmett Keane *(Charles Stevens)*, Trevor Bardette *(Hank)*, Lee Phelps *(Scotty Davis)*, Edmund Cobb *(Johnson)*, Rex Lease *(Joe Brant)*, Ted Adams *(Sam)*, Lane Bradford *(Webb)*, Michael Carr *(Tommy)*, Johnny Downs *(Square Dance Caller)*, Koko.

Allen, a relatively late bloomer in the horse-opera horizon, stars as the leader of a cattlemen's association who decides not to deal with evil meatpacker Keane, so instead he drives his herds through miles of waterless desert in order to divert business to an honest packing company run by the lovely Risdon ("a man's gotta do what a man's gotta do," etc., but did anybody ask the cattle what *they* thought?).

p, Franklin Adreon; d, R.G. Springsteen; w, Olive Cooper, Victor Arthur (based on an original story by Cooper); ph, Ellis W. Carter; m, Stanley Wilson; ed, Arthur Roberts; m/l, "Curtains of Night," Will S. Hays.

Western **Cas.** **(PR:A MPAA:NR)**

HILLS OF OLD WYOMING** (1937) 78m PAR bw

William Boyd *(Hopalong Cassidy)*, George Hayes *(Windy)*, Russell Hayden *(Lucky Jenkins)*, Gail Sheridan *(Alice Hutchins)*, Morris Ankrum *(Andrews)*, Clara Kimball Young *(Ma Hutchins)*, Earle Hodgins *(Thompson)*, Steve Clemente *(Lone Eagle)*, Chief Big Tree *(Chief Big John Tree)*, John Beach *(Saunders)*, George Chesebro *(Peterson)*, Paul Gustine *(Daniels)*, Leo MacMahon *(Steve)*, John Powers *(Smiley, the Cook)*, James Mason *(Deputy-Henchman)*.

Another film in the Hopalong Cassidy series, HILLS OF OLD WYOMING stars Boyd once again in his most popular role. This time Boyd, assisted by his sidekicks Hayes and Hayden (the latter's first stint in the series), is out to stop bad deputy Morris from using Indian half-breeds to rustle cattle. This causes Indian trouble with the cattlemen, but Boyd clears things up and sends the bad guys to the gallows. A good choral group sings the title song and a couple of other tunes. (See HOPALONG CASSIDY series, Index).

p, Harry Sherman; d, Nate Watt; w, Maurice Geraghty (based on the story "The Round-Up" by Clarence E. Mulford); ph, Archie Stout; ed, Robert Warwick; art d, Lewis Rachmil; spec eff, Mel Wolf; m/l, Leo Robin, Ralph Rainger.

Western **(PR:A MPAA:NR)**

HILLS OF UTAH** (1951) 70m COL bw

Gene Autry *(Himself)*, Pat Buttram *(Dusty Cosgrove)*, Elaine Riley *(Karen McQueen)*, Donna Martell *(Nola)*, Onslow Stevens *(Jayde McQueen)*, Denver Pyle *(Bowie French)*, William Fawcett *(Washoe)*, Harry Lauter *(Evan Fox)*, Kenne Duncan *(Ingo Hubbard)*, Harry Harvey *(Marshal Duffield)*, Sandy Sanders *(Rio)*, Tom London *(Mayor Donovan)*, Champion.

New doctor-in-town Autry finds business booming in his small Utah community due to a violent war between copper miners and cattle ranchers (the dredging done by the miners is ruining the water needed by the ranchers' cattle). Pretty soon Autry gets fed up with all the bloodshed and sets out to end the nonsense and reduce his doctoring income. Of course, the usual number of fist-fights, shoot-outs, and songs spring up. Gene sings "Back To Utah" and "Easter Day." (See GENE AUTRY series Index).

p, Armand Schaefer; d, John English; w, Gerald Geraghty (based on a story by Les Savage, Jr.); ph, William Bradford; ed, James Sweeney; md, Mischa Bakaleinikoff; art d, Charles Clague.

Western **Cas.** **(PR:A MPAA:NR)**

HILLS RUN RED, THE** (1967, Ital.) 89m Dino De Laurentiis/UA c (UN FIUME DI DOLLARI; AKA: A RIVER OF DOLLARS)

Thomas Hunter *(Jerry Brewster)*, Henry Silva *(Mendez)*, Dan Duryea *(Getz)*, Nando Gazzolo *(Ken Seagull)*, Nicoletta Machiavelli *(Mary Ann)*, Gianna Serra *(Hattie)*, Loris Loddi *(Tim)*, Geoffrey Copleston *(Horner)*, Paolo Magalotti *(Stayne)*, Tiberio Mitri *(Federal Sergeant)*, Vittorio Bonos *(1st Gambler)*, Mirko Valentin *(Sancho)*, Guglielmo Spoletini *(Pedro)*, Guido Celano *(Burger)*, Mauro Mannatrizio *(Soldier Mitch)*, Gianluigi Crescenzi *(Carson)*.

Former film critic-turned-filmmaker Lizzani tried his hand at Sergio Leone's brand of western and came up with this moderately successful endeavor starring Hunter and Gazzolo as two confederate soldiers who manage to survive the Civil War and steal an army payroll. The pair split up, with Hunter distracting the troops, allowing Gazzolo to escape with the loot. Hunter is captured and spends five years in prison. Upon his release he learns that his former partner is now wealthy and is responsible for the death of Hunter's wife. Knowing that Hunter is loose and seeking revenge, Gazzolo hires crazed gunfighter Silva to kill the ex-convict. Aided by Duryea, Hunter escapes death, manages to infiltrate Gazzolo's fortress, and kills his former partner and his hired gun. Not as good as Leone's films, but it has its moments.

p, Ermanno Donati, Luigi Carpentieri; d, Lee W. Beaver [Carlo Lizzani]; w, Mario Pierotti, Dean Craig; ph, Toni Secchi (Technicolor); m, Leo Nichols [Ennio Morricone]; ed, Ornella Micheli; art d, Aurelio Crugnola; m/l, "Home My Love," "I Know a Girl With Golden Hair," Nichols [Morricone], Audrey Nohra (sung by Gino).

Western **(PR:C MPAA:NR)**

HIM (SEE: EL, 1952, Mex.)

HINDENBURG, THE*½ (1975) 125m UNIV c

George C. Scott *(Col. Ritter)*, Anne Bancroft *(The Countess)*, William Atherton *(Boerth)*, Roy Thinnes *(Martin Vogel)*, Gig Young *(Edward Douglas)*, Burgess Meredith *(Emilio Pajetta)*, Charles Durning *(Capt. Pruss)*, Richard A. Dysart *(Lehmann)*, Robert Clary *(Joe Spah)*, Rene Auberjonois *(Maj. Napier)*, Peter Donat *(Reed Channing)*, Alan Oppenheimer *(Albert Breslau)*, Katherine Helmond *(Mrs. Mildred Breslau)*, Joanna Moore *(Mrs. Channing)*, Stephen Elliott *(Capt. Fellows)*, Joyce Davis *(Eleanore Ritter)*, Jean Rasey *(Valerie Breslau)*, Ted Gehring *(Knorr)*, Lisa Pera *(Freda Halle)*, Joe di Reda *(Schulz)*, Peter Canon *(Ludecke)*, Charles Macaulay *(Kirsch)*, Rex Holman *(Dimmler)*, Jan Merlin *(Speck)*, Betsy Jones-Moreland *(Stewardess Imhoff)*, Colby Chester *(Eliot Howell III)*, Teno Pollick *(Frankel)*, Curt Lowens *(Elevator Man)*, Kip Niven *(Lt. Truscott)*, Michael Richardson *(Rigger)*, Herbert Nelson *(Dr. Eckener)*, Scott Walker *(Gestapo Major)*, Ruth Kobart *(Hattie)*, Greg Mullavey *(Morrison)*, Val Bisoglio *(Lt. Lombardi)*, Simon Scott *(Luftwaffe General)*, William Sylvester *(Luftwaffe Colonel)*, David Mauro *(Goebbels)*, Joseph Turkel *(Detective Moore)*, Sandy Ward *(Detective Grunberger)*, Johnny Lee *(Paul Breslau)*, Stephen Manley *(Peter Breslau)*.

An expensively mounted but basically insipidly boring film, director Wise attempts to make drama from a celebrated disaster, fictionalizing the reasons for the massive dirigible's explosion at Lakehurst, New Jersey, on May 6, 1937. No real explanation for the *Hindenburg's* fiery destruction was ever given, although it's easy to see how the highly flammable aircraft, carrying seven million cubic feet of explosive hydrogen gas, could be touched off. How this incredible disaster, recorded graphically on newsreel footage and its demise narrated by the quavering voice of radio announcer Herbert Morrison (of WLS, Chicago), came to happen is still a matter of debate. Writers Gidding, Levinson, and Link tried to make something of a story out of the puzzle by emphasizing sabotage, but this is pure theory. Scott is a dedicated German security officer put on board as the dirigible sails for America, assisted by Nazi partisan Thinnes. He suspects crew and passengers alike of potential sabotage and his subtle investigations encompass a host of characters, including Bancroft, a reefer-puffing countess, Meredith and Auberjonois, card sharps trying to fleece gullible passengers, and Young, a nervous American ad executive. Also included are several weird-acting crew members, except the stoic cocaptains Durning and Dysart. Throughout the rather uneventful voyage Scott probes and pries but has no answers until the *Hindenburg* is about to dock, finding a bomb at the last minute planted by a crew member who is anti-Nazi and wishes to discredit Hitler's regime. (Thus placing him in the unenviable position of becoming a mass murderer and a freedom fighter at the same time, 36 passengers and crew members actually being killed when the dirigible blew up.) At the landing dock, the craft explodes and director Wise quickly cuts to the original black and white film, covering it with a bloody red tint to conform to color. Passengers and crew jump for their lives or ride the flaming wreckage to earth to either perish or survive. Scott dies trying to diffuse the bomb, and Dysart actually steps from the burning skeletal ruins, ostensibly alive, but he takes a few steps, like the real Capt. Lehmann, and falls dead on his face, his entire back burned out. But none of the characters are even half-heartedly developed and Wise's pace is as ponderously slow as the ship's airborne movements. There's no tension whatsoever and none of the characters are remotely interesting, let alone empathetic. Scott wanders about the floating superstructure like a man foggily looking for a part to play. The lines are dull, the story predictable, and, by the time the explosion occurs, no one is surprised or, even worse, really moved, since the victims have been so poorly drawn. Like most of the drab, uninspired disaster films hacked out by Irwin Allen, this too, enters the same graveyard. The cinematography is superior and is the best thing about this bloated bomb. The worst thing about this dud is Clary's forced humor as the comedy relief; once touted as a brilliant new comic, Clary's mugging downfall is painfully recorded here.

d, Robert Wise; w, Nelson Gidding, Richard A. Levinson, William Link (based on the book by Michael M. Mooney); ph, Robert Surtees (Technicolor); m, David Shire; ed, Donn Cambern; prod d, Edward Carfagno; cos, Dorothy Jeakins.

Disaster Drama Cas. (PR:C MPAA:PG)

HINDLE WAKES** (1931, Brit.) 90m GAU bw

Sybil Thorndike *(Mrs. Hawthorne)*, John Stuart *(Alan Jeffcoate)*, Norman McKinnel *(Nat Jeffcoate)*, Edmund Gwenn *(Chris Hawthorne)*, Belle Chrystal *(Fanny Hawthorne)*, Mary Clare *(Mrs. Jeffcoate)*, Muriel Angelus *(Beatrice Farrar)*, A.G. Poulton *(Sir Timothy)*, Ruth Peterson *(Mary Hollins)*, Lionel Roberts, Bob Johnston.

An early British talking film, one of three re-makes of a better silent version made five years earlier. The story is a simple one, about a Lancashire mill girl, Chrystal, who spends a romantic weekend with the mill-owner's son, but refuses to marry him when he proposes.

p, Michael Balcon; d, Victor Saville; w, Saville, Angus Macphail (based on a play by Stanley Houghton); ph, Mutz Greenbaum.

Drama (PR:A MPAA:NR)

HINDLE WAKES (1952) (SEE: HOLIDAY WEEK, 1952, Brit.)

HINDU, THE½** (1953, Brit.) 89m UA c (AKA: SABAKA)

Boris Karloff *(General Pollegar)*, Nino Marcel *(Gunga Ram)*, Lou Krugman *(Maharajah of Bakore)*, Reginald Denny *(Regent)*, Victor Jory *(Ashok)*, June Foray *(Marku)*, Jay Novello *(Damji)*, Lisa Howard *(Indira)*, Peter Coe *(Taru)*, Paul Marion *(Kumar)*, Vito Scotti *(Rama)*, Lou Merrill *(Koobah)*, Larry Dobkin *(Aide)*, Jeanne Bates *(Durga)*.

Pretty average children's adventure film set in India and starring Marcel as a young animal trainer out to get revenge on a religious cult led by Foray, whose members have accidentally killed his parents in a forest fire that they set. Though his friends the Maharajah (Krugman) and Karloff are sympathetic, they can do nothing to help the boy due to a lack of evidence. Eventually, Marcel discovers the cult's secret hiding place and witnesses strange rituals, but he is captured by the cult and sentenced to be burned alive. Luckily Marcel's two jungle friends, a tiger and an elephant, come to the rescue and destroy Foray's temple. Filmed in India on location, although the few scenes with the always effective Karloff may have been separately shot and later integrated into the whole.

p,d&w, Frank Ferrin; ph, Allen Svensvold, Jack McCoskey (Eastmancolor); m, Daksnamurti; ed, Jack Foley; art d, Ralph Ferrin.

Adventure (PR:AA MPAA:NR)

HINOTORI*** (1980, Jap.) 137m Toho-Hinotori/Toho c

Tomisaburo Wakayama, Masao Kusakari, Kaoru Yumi, Reiko Ohara, Mieko Takamine, Tatsuya Nakadai.

A fine, albeit very bizarre, film from famed Japanese director Ichikawa (THE BURMESE HARP) that combines split screen, slow motion, and animation techniques along with a healthy dose of black humor to create this fable-like essay on the nature of war and life. Set in 180 A.D., the story concerns an extremely bloody war between two rival tribes of warriors who are trying to capture the mythical bird the Phoenix (which is animated) and drink its blood to attain eternal life. Ichikawa piles violence upon violence until it has an almost cartoon-like, numbing effect. HINOTORI was one of the few films directed by Ichikawa in the last ten years because his style had fallen out of favor with the Japanese and he had trouble financing any projects.

d, Kon Ichikawa; w, Shuntaro Tanikawa (based on an original story by Osamu Tezuka); ph, Kiyoshi Hasegawa; m, Michel Legrand, Jun Fukamachi; spec eff, Teruyoshi Nakano; animation, Tezuka Prods.

Action Comedy (PR:O MPAA:NR)

HIPPODROME** (1961, Aust./Ger.) 96m Sascha-Lux/CD c (GELIEBTE BESTIE; MANNER MUSSEN SO SEIN; DAS MADCHEN IM TIGERFELL)

Gerhard Riedmann *(Rudy)*, Margit Nunke *(Beatrice)*, Willy Birgel *(Cameron)*, Mady Rahl *(Marianne)*, Walter Giller *(Dody)*, Massimo Giuliani *(Willi)*, Gustav Knuth *(Carl de Vries)*, Gretl Schorg *(Olga)*, Fred Bertelmann *(John)*, Sigrid Marquardt *(Anita)*, Heinz Moog *(Director Lanzheim)*, Ljuba Welitsch *(Mama Allison)*, Leopold Hainisch *(Riley)*, Emanuel Sackey, Mario Kranz, Karl Kritel, Otto Hejdusek, Hans Kurt, Berta Vitek, Josef Menschik, Charly Baumann's Tiger Group.

Circus melodrama starring Nunke as a beautiful ballerina who is in love from afar with Riedman, a handsome tiger trainer. Her hopes of joining him in his act are shattered, however, when he leaves to join another circus. She is allowed by his replacement to join the act, but she is nearly killed when one of the tigers goes wild. Luckily she is saved by the circus sharpshooter, Birgel, and he asks her to join his act instead. She agrees, but soon after Riedman returns and asks Nunke to join him at the other circus. Jealous, Birgel attempts to ruin Riedman's act by drugging his animals, but his plot is exposed and the sharpshooter kills himself.

p&d, Arthur-Maria Rabenalt; w, Kurt Nachmann, H.F. Kollner (based on *Manner Mussen So Sein* by Heinrich Seiler); ph, Gunther Anders (Afgacolor); m, Bert Grund; ed, Arnd Heyne; art d, Werner Schilichting, Alexander Sawczynski; cos, Charlotte Flemming; ch, Mike De Lutry; m/l, Grund, Walter Brandin; stunts, Theo Nischwitz; makeup, Josef Schober, Leo Umyssa, Hans Nowotny.

Action/Adventure (PR:C-O MPAA:NR)

HIPPOLYT, THE LACKEY** (1932, Hung.) 85m Sohof/Magyar bw

Gyula Csortos, Gyula Kabos, Eva Fenyessy, Mici Erdelyt, Gyula Gozon, Mici Haraszthy, Fino Szenes, Sandor Goth, Maricza Simon, Kalman Zatony, Paul Javor, Lajos Gardonyi, Jeno Herceg, Andor Sarnes; Istvan Barsony, Ferenc Pazmany.

This Hungarian-made film tells the story of a *nouveau riche* family—where the father rose from an expressman to a wealthy entrepreneur. He is a simple man who works hard all day, but his wife wants to be in high society, and to get their daughter to marry well. The daughter, however, is in love with a worker in her father's firm. The wife shakes up the household by hiring a butler, Hippolyt, who has only worked for aristocracy in the past, so he may educate the family in high society living. Hippolyt tells the father that a real gentleman revels in nightlife and should have at least one mistress. He takes the butler's advice and falls for a dancer in a nightclub. The girl follows him home just as his wife is throwing her first society party. A wild mixup ensues that results in the butler's dismissal and the family's return to the simple life.

d, Istvan Szekely; w, Istvan Zigon, Karoly Notl; ph, Istovn Elben; m, Mihaly Eisemann.

Drama (PR:A MPAA:NR)

HIPS, HIPS, HOORAY** (1934) 68m RKO bw

Bert Wheeler *(Andy Williams)*, Robert Woolsey *(Bob Dudley)*, Ruth Etting *(Herself)*, Thelma Todd *(Miss Frisbie)*, Dorothy Lee *(Daisy)*, George Meeker *(Beauchamp)*, James Burtis *(Epstein)*, Matt Briggs *(Sweeney)*, Spencer Charters *(Mr. Clark)*.

An occasionally funny farce starring Wheeler and Woolsey, who were the Abbott and Costello of their day. In this film the two are salesmen, pushing a brand new flavored lipstick. They have romantic forays with Todd, the owner of a glamorous beauty parlor, and Lee, one of the parlor's demonstrators. The boys inadvertently steal some stocks and bonds and have a couple of silly detectives, Burtis and Briggs, on their tails. It all culminates in a cross-country auto race, done in Keystone Kops style. Songs were written by Ruby and Kalmar, who also co-wrote the script. Some of their better efforts were "Tired Of It All," "Keep Romance Alive," and "Keep On Doin' What You're Doin."

p, H.N. Swanson; d, Mark Sandrich; w, Harry Ruby, Bert Kalmar, Edward Kaufman; ph, David Abel; md, Max Steiner; ch, Dave Gould; m/l, Ruby, Kalmar.

Comedy/Musical Cas. (PR:A MPAA:NR)

HIRED GUN, THE½** (1957) 63m Rorvic/MGM bw

Rory Calhoun *(Gil McCord)*, Anne Francis *(Ellen Beldon)*, Vince Edwards *(Kell Beldon)*, John Litel *(Mace Beldon)*, Chuck Connors *(Judd Farrow)*, Robert Burton *(Nathan Conroy)*, Salvadore Baques *(Domingo Ortega)*, Guinn "Big Boy" Williams *(Elby Kirby)*, Regis Parton *(Clint)*.

Rory Calhoun and his agent, Vic Orsatti, produced this offbeat western. The story has Calhoun as a professional gunman hired by a wealthy Texan, Litel, to bring back his dead son's wife, Francis, who is supposed to hang for the murder of his son. A few hours before the hanging, Francis breaks out of jail and escapes into New Mexico, where her father has a ranch. Litel tries to extradite her, but because New Mexico is not yet a state, he is unable to get to her. That is why he resorts to hiring Calhoun to drag her back. Calhoun finds Francis, but while riding back to Texas, she is able to convince him of her innocence. Francis claims her husband's brother, Edwards, is the one responsible for the death. Calhoun proves that Edwards committed the crime and Francis is set free.

p, Rory Calhoun, Victor M. Orsatti; d, Ray Nazarro; w, David Lang, Buckley Angell; ph, Harold J. Marzorati (CinemaScope); m, Albert Glasser; ed, Frank Santillo; art d, William A. Horning, Urie McCleary.

Western (PR:A MPAA:NR)

HIRED GUN (SEE: LAST GUNFIGHTER, THE, 1961, Can.)

HIRED HAND, THE½** (1971) 90m Pando/UNIV c

Peter Fonda *(Harry Collings)*, Warren Oates *(Arch Harris)*, Verna Bloom *(Hannah Collings)*, Robert Pratt *(Dan Griffin)*, Severn Darden *(McVey)*, Ted Markland *(Luke)*, Owen Orr *(Mace)*, Gray Johnson *(Will)*, Rita Rogers *(Mexican Woman)*, Al

Hopson *(Bartender)*, Ann Doran *(Mrs. Sorenson)*, Megan Denver *(Janey Collings)*, Michael McClure *(Plummer)*, Len Marcel.

An occasionally pretentious western that tried to recreate the old west as it really was and was also Fonda's first film as a director. The story is about Fonda, who deserted his wife, Bloom, to drift with Oates. After seven years of drifting, Pratt, a fellow wanderer and friend of the duo is murdered by Darden's men. Fonda and Oates exact revenge on the killers and Fonda decides to go back to his wife, but she is only willing to accept him as a hired hand. Their romance is rekindled, but Fonda is soon off to rescue Oates, who has been captured by the evil Darden. Fonda is killed during the rescue, but Oates goes back to Bloom and takes Fonda's place. Zsigmond's superb photography conveys much of the lyrical quality of the story but the script by Sharp (NIGHT MOVES) falls short by comparison.

p, William Hayward; d, Peter Fonda; w, Alan Sharp; ph, Vilmos Zsigmond (Technicolor); m, Bruce Langhorne; ed, Frank Mazzola; art d, Lawrence G. Paull; set d, Robert De Vestal; cos, Richard Bruno; makeup, Frank Griffin.

Western **(PR:A MPAA:GP)**

HIRED KILLER, THE** (1967, Fr./Ital.) 95m Cinegay-Rome Paris/PAR c (TECNICA DI UN OMICIDIO; TECHNIQUE D'UN MEURTRE)

Robert Webber *(Clint Harris)*, Franco Nero *(Tony Lobello)*, Jeanne Valerie *(Mary)*, Jose Luis de Vilallonga *(Secchy [Goldstein])*, John Hawkwood *(Andrea Ferri)*, Michel Bardinet *(Barry)*, Cec Linder *(Gastel)*, Theodora Bergery *(Lucy)*, Earl Hammond *(Frank)*.

Webber plays a paid assassin who comes out of retirement to kill an ex-gangster who has gone to Europe to have plastic surgery performed to hide his true identity. Aided by Nero, Webber goes to Paris and tracks down his victim with the help of pretty young drug addict Valerie. They kill the man, only to discover that the corpse was an impostor who was set up by the real gangster. Soon, Valerie is killed and so is the gangster. Webber realizes that Nero has been playing both sides against each other all along and is about to murder him. The veteran assassin, however, gets the drop on Nero and kills him first. Strictly routine stuff, but the European locations add some flavor.

p, Felice Testa Gay; d&w, Frank Shannon [Franco Prosperi]; ph, Erico Menczer (Techniscope, Technicolor); m, Robby Poitevin; ed, Mark Sirandrews [Mario Serandrei]; art d, Hugo Naheir.

Crime Drama **(PR:C MPAA:NR)**

HIRED WIFE** (1934) 60m Pinnacle bw

Greta Nissen *(Vivian Mathews)*, Weldon Heyburn *(Kent Johns)*, James Kirkwood *(Philip Marlowe)*, Molly O'Day *(Pat Sullivan)*, Jane Winton *(Dovie Jansen)*, Blanche Taylor *(Mrs. Jansen)*, Carolyn Gales *(Aunt Mancha)*, Evelyn Bennett *(Celesti)*.

HIRED WIFE tells the story of Nissen, who marries Heyburn with an agreement to end the marriage after a year because he needs to be married so he can inherit a large sum of money. Nissen really loves Heyburn, and spends most of the film trying to make him fall in love with her, so that they may be together permanently. Heyburn is at first very indifferent to Nissen, as he still has a desire for a young woman who married another man. Little by little, Nissen works on him until her love is returned.

d, George Melford; w, Alma Sioux Scarberry (based on her novel *The Flat Tire*); ph, Mark Stengler; ed, Helene Turner.

Drama **(PR:A MPAA:NR)**

HIRED WIFE½** (1940) 95m Seiter/UNIV bw

Rosalind Russell *(Kendal Browning)*, Brian Aherne *(Stephen Dexter)*, Virginia Bruce *(Phyllis Walden)*, Robert Benchley *(Van Horn)*, John Carroll *(Jose)*, Hobart Cavanaugh *(William)*, Richard Lane *(McNab)*, Leonard Carey *(Peterson)*, William Davidson *(Mumford)*, Selmer Jackson *(Hudson)*, William Halligan *(Latimer)*, George Humbert *(Chef)*, Virginia Brissac *(Miss Collins)*, Chester Clute *(Peabody)*.

The oft-told tale of the secretary who falls in love with her boss is given another rendering in this romantic comedy. Russell is the extraordinarily efficient secretary of Aherne, a rather dim cement tycoon. She runs his office and wants to run his home also. However, he is infatuated with a beautiful model, Bruce. When Aherne has to get married so he can put his business assets in his wife's name because the IRS is breathing down his neck, Russell immediately volunteers. She vies with Bruce for Aherne's affection, and last name, but when Latin lover Carroll sweeps Bruce off her feet, Russell is left to fill the wife position.

p, Glenn Tryon; d, William A. Seiter; w, Richard Connell, Gladys Lehman (based on a story by George Beck); ph, Milton Krasner; ed, Milton Brown; art d, Jack Otterson.

Comedy **(PR:A MPAA:NR)**

HIRELING, THE*½** (1973, Brit.) 95m World Film Services-Champion/COL-WB c

Robert Shaw *(Leadbetter)*, Sarah Miles *(Lady Franklin)*, Peter Egan *(Cantrip)*, Elizabeth Sellars *(Mother)*, Caroline Mortimer *(Connie)*, Patricia Lawrence *(Mrs. Hansen)*, Petra Markham *(Edith)*, Ian Hogg *(Davis)*, Christine Hargreaves *(Doreen)*, Lyndon Brook, Alison Leggatt.

A fine British drama that is an insightful examination of class barriers in England. Borrowing much from D.H. Lawrence's novel *Lady Chatterley's Lover*, the film is set in 1923 and details the close relationship of a wealthy young widow, Miles, and her hired chauffeur, Shaw. Shaw drives Miles home from a clinic where she has been convalescing from a nervous breakdown. In her state of mind, she starts a love affair with Shaw, and he believes the class barriers are down. However, after she begins to recover her mental stability, the barriers rise up once again. She no longer considers Shaw her equal, and when he confesses his love for her, Miles makes it clear that their relationship is an impossibility. Enraged and frustrated, Shaw attacks her expensive car, which has become the symbol of their doomed romance.

p, Ben Arbeid; d, Alan Bridges; w, Wolf Mankowitz (based on a novel by L.P. Hartley); ph, Michael Reed; m, Marc Wilkinson; ed, Peter Weatherley; prod d, Natasha Kroll; cos, Phyllis Dalton.

Drama **(PR:C MPAA:PG)**

HIROSHIMA, MON AMOUR**** (1959, Fr./Jap.) 88m Argos-Como-Daiei-Pathe/Zenith bw

Emmanuelle Riva *(Elle)*, Eiji Okada *(Lui)*, Stella Dassas *(Mother)*, Pierre Barbaud *(Father)*, Bernard Fresson *(German Lover)*.

A startling, unconventional, and sometimes confounding (to a number of critics) film that was a breakthrough in cinema in that it used many techniques not seen since silent days. It won several awards at Cannes but continues to baffle audiences who are unwilling to give themselves up completely to the film experience and concentrate on what they see. By the time the picture is over, all of the subliminal flash cuts (some only a few seconds in length) make sense and one comes away having understood what director Resnais and writer Duras attempted. Everything happens in slightly more than one day in the lives of the protagonists. A fantasy prologue intercuts documentary footage of Hiroshima after the A-Bomb with quick cuts of nude people, plus a hospital room and a museum. (The newsreel film was part of Sekigawa's 1953 tragic re-enactment, HIROSHIMA.) Now we meet the two naked lovers at four in the morning. Riva is a French actress who is in the process of making a movie on Hiroshima and Okada is a Japanese architect she'd picked up the night before and brought back to her hotel room. They talk briefly and she notices his hand shake for an instant. That throws her memory back to a time when she loved a young German during WW II. Next afternoon, he visits her movie set, then takes her to his home where we learn that both lovers are happily married to other people. They make love again (where his wife is is never explained to anyone's satisfaction but it doesn't matter) and she tells him of her first lover in Nevers, France; the now-dead soldier (Fresson) seen earlier in flashback. She now tells him that she must return to her husband and to her work in Paris. They dine in a cafe near the river and he probes her background. She tells him in random fashion about what happened in Nevers, how Fresson was killed by a sniper, dying in her arms on Liberation Day, the way the partisans shaved her head for fraternizing with a German, and how her embarrassed parents put her in their basement until she suffered a mental breakdown. Her reverie is so deep that Okada must slap her face to return her to reality. Later, she feels terribly alone in her room and walks out, meeting Okada again, who pleads with her to stay in Hiroshima. She cannot make up her mind and walks the streets with him close behind. In the morning, she tells Okada that she must forget him, that this will never work. They hold onto each other as the picture ends, with each referring to the other not by their names, but by the cities they represent: Nevers and Hiroshima. Now, that synopsis doesn't sound so terribly difficult to understand, does it? And yet it has baffled many in their investigation of the spine of this picture. The sparse screenplay feels somewhat Samuel Beckett in that more is left unspoken than stated. There are no dissolves, just fast cuts, thus, we are seldom certain of where we are, so it becomes existential rather than sequential, something else that caused confusion. See it with an open mind and let the picture bathe your senses. You won't be sorry.

p, Samy Halfon; d, Alain Resnais; w, Marguerite Duras; ph, Sacha Vierny, Michio Takahashi; m, Georges Delerue, Giovanni Fusco; ed, Henri Colpi, Jasmine Chasney, Anne Sarraute; prod d, Esaka, Mayo, Petri.

Drama **Cas.** **(PR:C-O MPAA:NR)**

HIS AND HERS** (1961, Brit.) 90m Sabre/Eros bw

Terry-Thomas *(Reggie Blake)*, Janette Scott *(Fran Blake)*, Wilfrid Hyde-White *(Charles Dunton)*, Nicole Maurey *(Simone Rolfe)*, Billy Lambert *(Baby)*, Joan Sims *(Hortense)*, Kenneth Connor *(Harold)*, Kenneth Williams *(Policeman)*, Meier Tzelniker *(Felix McGregor)*, Colin Gordon *(TV Announcer)*, Joan Hickson *(Phoebe)*, Oliver Reed *(Poet)*, Barbara Hicks *(Woman)*, Francesca Annis *(Wanda)*, Dorinda Stevens *(Dora)*, Marie Devereux *(Stunning Wife)*.

A poorly executed comedy about a novelist, Terry-Thomas, who gets lost in the desert. His publisher, Hyde-White, has sold the author's past works on the merit of publicity stunts rather than fine writing. However, just before the release of his latest book, *I Conquered the Desert*, Terry-Thomas really gets lost in the arid wastelands of North Africa, and lives with a group of Bedouins for quite a long time before he is rescued. During this period, he comes to self-realization and adopts all the Bedouin customs and beliefs. He expects his wife, Scott, to do the same. She won't have any of it, and divides the house into two parts, his and hers. She refuses to have anything to do with him, and goes about writing a book entitled, *I Was Conquered By A Middle-Aged Monster*. Terry-Thomas falls for a pretty French girl, Maurey, and is talking divorce when Hyde-White steps in and patches things up.

p, Hal E. Chester, John D. Merriman; d, Brian Desmond Hurst; w, Stanley Mann, Jan and Mark Lowell; ph, Ted Scaife; m, John Addison; ed, Max Benedict.

Comedy **(PR:A MPAA:NR)**

HIS AND HIS (SEE: HONEYMOON HOTEL, 1964)

HIS BROTHER'S GHOST** (1945) 58m PRC bw

Buster Crabbe *(Billy "The Kid" Carson)*, Al "Fuzzy" St. John, Charles King, Ray Brent, Frank McCarroll, Dick Alexander, Bud Osborne, Bob Cason, Karl Hackett, Archie Hall, George Morell.

Fuzzy gets killed early on in this installment in the Billy Carson series, but Crabbe convinces Fuzzy's twin brother to impersonate the fallen sidekick and convince the killers that they are being haunted. Interesting chiefly because it is one of the rare instances of a continuing actor in a series getting killed, even if he is replaced by a look-alike. (See BILLY CARSON series, Index).

p, Sigmund Neufeld; d, Sam Newfield; w, George Milton; ph, Jack Greenhalgh; ed, Holbrook N. Todd.

Western **(PR:A MPAA:NR)**

HIS BROTHER'S KEEPER*½ (1939, Brit.) 70m WB/FN bw

Clifford Evans *(Jack Cornell)*, Tamara Desni *(Olga)*, Una O'Connor *(Eva)*, Peter Glenville *(Hicky Cornell)*, Reginald Purdell *(Bunny Reeves)*, Ronald Frankau *(George Hollis)*, Antoinette Lupino *(Pat)*, Aubrey Dexter *(Sylvester)*, Frederick Burtwell *(Harry)*, Kitty de Legh.

Evans is a trick-shot artist who falls in love with blues singer Desni. When he leaves her, his brother (Glenville) falls for her, though she has set her sights on a rich man. One night, during their act, the distraught Glenville makes a wrong move and is shot by Evans. Wrongly believing his brother dead, Evans turns the gun on Desni, then himself. Lurid melodrama kept afloat by a decent cast.

p, Sam Sax; d, Roy William Neill; w, Neill, Austin Melford, Brock Williams; ph, Basil Emmott.

Drama **(PR:A-C MPAA:NR)**

HIS BROTHER'S WIFE** (1936) 91m MGM bw

Robert Taylor *(Chris)*, Barbara Stanwyck *(Rita Wilson)*, Jean Hersholt *(Professor Fahrenheim)*, Joseph Calleia *(Fish Eye)*, George Eldredge *(Tom)*, Samuel S. Hinds *(Dr. Claybourne)*, Phyllis Clare *(Clara)*, Edith Atwater *(Mary)*, Jed Prouty *(Billy Arnold)*, Rafael Storm [Corio] *(Capt. Tanetz)*, Orrin Burke *(Dr. Claycious)*, Sherry Hall *(Sam)*, William Stack *(Winters)*, Edgar Edwards *(Swede)*, George Davis *(Milkman)*, Syd Saylor *(Gambler)*, Frank Puglia *(Hotel Clerk)*, Leonard Mudie *(Pete)*, Pedro de Cordoba *(Dr. Capolo)*, Inez Palange *(Native Mother)*, Julie Laird, Tommy Beard, Barbara Bedford, Harry Myers, Gertrude Astor, Rosemary Theby, Jean Acker, William Royle, Leonard Moody, Jay Whidden and His Orchestra.

This was Stanwyck's premiere movie for MGM and she got the part, over Jean Harlow, when studio bosses thought it might make a commercial success due to the fact that she and Taylor were dating at the time (They married soon afterwards). Taylor made many films in 1936—SMALL TOWN GIRL, PRIVATE NUMBER, THE GORGEOUS HUSSY—and went on to enormous stardom the following year in CAMILLE. In HIS BROTHER'S WIFE, Taylor is a bright young scientist attempting to find a cure for spotted fever. Stanwyck is a model-cum-gambling shill; they encounter each other at a casino. He has ten days before leaving for South America, and the two have a whirlwind romance that culminates when she asks him to stay. Taylor has another problem; he owes Calleia (who carries the apt name of Fish-Eye) several thousand dollars in gambling debts. He asks his brother, Eldredge, to lend him the money but is refused at first. Finally, Eldredge, a waspish stiff, agrees to hand Taylor the cash if Taylor will leave for South America right away and give up Stanwyck. She is livid at being left in the lurch, gets hold of the IOU from Eldredge, then marries the man, and it's all part of a revenge plot she is cooking up. Later, Taylor returns to New York and sees that Stanwyck and Eldredge's marriage is in name only. She married him for nothing more than pique and Eldredge is rapidly becoming a shambles. He also learns that Stanwyck holds the note. Now Taylor talks Stanwyck into returning to South America with him, an act which causes her to think he still loves her. But when the divorce papers are signed and she feels she can join Taylor in marriage, he brushes her off. While all this is happening, his spotted fever research is going full tilt and he is coming close to a vaccine for the dread disease. Taylor tells Stanwyck that he will have nothing more to do with her; her response is to inject herself with spotted fever germs. Taylor has to save her life and, in the process, falls in love with her once more (did anyone doubt that for an instant?) and they are united. Lots of over-acting on Stanwyck's part but Taylor emits a cool, calm, and controlling style that was to stand him in good stead for the rest of his career. Hersholt again plays a doctor, something he did so well we are surprised that the AMA didn't make him their president.

p, Lawrence Weingarten; d, W. S. Van Dyke; w, Leon Gordon, John Meehan (based on a story by George Auerbach); ph, Oliver T. Marsh; m, Franz Waxman; ed, Conrad A. Nervig; art d, Cedric Gibbons; cos, Dolly Tree.

Drama **(PR:A-C MPAA:NR)**

HIS BUTLER'S SISTER** (1943) 92m UNIV bw

Deanna Durbin *(Ann Carter)*, Pat O'Brien *(Martin Carter)*, Franchot Tone *(Charles Gerard)*, Evelyn Ankers *(Liz Campbell)*, Elsa Janssen *(Severina)*, Walter Catlett *(Mortimer Kalb)*, Akim Tamiroff *(Popoff)*, Alan Mowbray *(Buzz)*, Frank Jenks *(Emmett)*, Sig Arno *(Moreno)*, Franklin Pangborn *(Reeves)*, Andrew Tombes *(Brophy)*, Hans Conreid *(Reeves)*, Florence Bates *(Lady Sloughberry)*, Iris Adrian *(Girl on Train)*, Robin Raymond *(Blonde on Train)*, Stephanie Bachelor *(Pretty Girl)*, Roscoe Karns, Russell Hicks.

Durbin plays a small-town girl from Indiana who goes to New York to embark on a singing career. She plans to visit her half-brother, O'Brien, whom she believes to be a wealthy businessman, but who turns out to be the head butler for a famous composer, Tone. She wants to find work with Tone's help, but O'Brien hires her to do maid work. He fires her after a few days because he believes that Tone may become romantically interested in her. Of course this is exactly what happens, and even after O'Brien tries to split them up the two are still together at the end of the film. Durbin sings quite a variety of songs; an aria from Puccini's "Turandot", a medley of Russian songs, "In The Spirit Of The Moment," (Bernie Grossman and Walter Jurman), "When You're Away" (Victor Herbert, Henry Blossom). Adrian and Raymond also gave voice, dueting "Is It True What They Say About Dixie?" by Irving Caesar, Sammy Lerner, Gerald Marks.

p, Felix Jackson; d, Frank Borzage; w, Samuel Hoffenstein, Betty Reinhardt; ph, Woody Bredell; m, H.J. Salter; ed, Ted Kent; art d, Charles Previn; spec eff, John P. Fulton.

Comedy/Musical **(PR:A MPAA:NR)**

HIS CAPTIVE WOMAN* (1929) 92m FN-WB bw

Milton Sills *(Officer McCarthy)*, Dorothy Mackaill *(Anna Bergen)*, Gladden James *(Alstair de Vries)*, Gertrude Howard *(Lavoris Smythe)*, Marion Byron *(Bobby)*, Frank Reicher *(District Attorney)*, George Fawcett *(Lawyer)*, William Holden *(Judge)*, August Tollaire *(Governor)*, Jed Prouty, Sidney Bracey.

This highly implausible courtroom drama tells the story of Mackaill, a known tramp and golddigger who unabashedly murders a wealthy man who has been supporting her expensive tastes in exchange for her favors. In court, the testimony condemning the girl is told verbally (with sound recording), but the visual representations of the events are shown in silent flashbacks. Several witnesses give airtight testimony that is sure to hang the girl, but just when things look bleak, a police officer, Sills, arrives to make a special plea to the court. He doesn't deny that Mackaill killed the man, but instead essays a long, and apparently unrelated, story concerning the time that they were shipwrecked on a desert island and spent several years together. Sills convinces the judge that if Mackaill would just be allowed to return to the desert island with him, both she and society would be better off. Amazingly, the judge agrees and off they go.

d, George Fitzmaurice; w, Carey Wilson (based on a story by Donn Byrne); ph, Lee Garmes.

Drama **(PR:A MPAA:NR)**

HIS DOUBLE LIFE½** (1933) 63m Dowling-Hopkins/PAR bw

Lillian Gish *(Alice)*, Roland Young *(Priam Farrel)*, Lumsden Hare *(Oxford)*, Lucy Beaumont *(Mrs. Leek)*, Charles Richman *(Witt)*, Oliver Smith, Phillip Tonge *(Leek Twins)*, Montague Love, Audrey Ridgewell, Regina de Valet, Roland Hogue.

A good mixture of light comedy and typical British whimsy make HIS DOUBLE LIFE a humorous film. The story concerns an English painter, Young, whose death is mistakenly reported. His valet is buried in his place and Young is able to attend his own funeral at Westminster Abbey. He is thrown out of the cathedral for sobbing too loudly at the honors his fellow countrymen have heaped upon him. Soon after he marries an attractive, no-nonsense spinster, Gish. Young starts to paint again and when his new works surface, the art world is in a furor and a scandal ensues. In a courtroom sequence, two moles on Young's neck identify the dead painter as still among the living.

p, Ben Jackson; d, Arthur Hopkins; w, Hopkins, Clara Beranger (based on "Buried Alive" and "The Great Adventure" by Arnold Bennett); ph, Arthur Edeson; ed, Arthur Ellis.

Comedy **(PR:A MPAA:NR)**

HIS EXCELLENCY½** (1952, Brit.) 84m Balcon-EAL/Joseph Brenner bw

Eric Portman *(George Harrison)*, Cecil Parker *(Sir James Kirkman)*, Helen Cherry *(Lady Kirkman)*, Susan Stephen *(Peggy Harrison)*, Edward Chapman *(The Admiral)*, Clive Morton *(The G.O.C.)*, Alec Mango *(Jackie)*, Geoffrey Keen *(Morellos)*, John Salew *(Fernando)*, Robin Bailey *(Charles)*, Eric Pohlmann *(Dobrieda)*, Paul Demel *(The Chef)*, Elspeth March *(Fernando's Wife)*, Howard Marion Crawford *(Proprietor)*, Henry Longhurst, Gerard Heinz, Barbara Leake, Barbara Cavan, Basil Dignam, Laurence Naismith, Victor Maddern.

Routine labor drama starring Portman as a former laborer who has risen through strikes, unionization and strife, to the ranks of governor of an industrial island locked in a bitter battle over wages and conditions. Instead of calling in the troops to break the strike, as his predecessors would have, Portman ventures out among the workers and listens to their complaints while stressing that he was once in their shoes. Despite his civilized banter, the violent strike escalates, forcing Portman to send in the dreaded troops. Though the laborers feel betrayed, Portman once again comes to their aid and things are finally settled.

p, Michael Truman; d, Robert Hamer; w, Hamer, W.P. Lipscomb (based on a play by Dorothy and Campbell Christie); ph, Douglas Slocombe; m, Ernest Irving; ed, Seth Holt; md, Irving; art d, Jim Morahan.

Drama **(PR:A MPAA:NR)**

HIS EXCITING NIGHT** (1938) 61m UNIV bw

Charles Ruggles *(Tripp)*, Richard Lane *(Carslake)*, Stepin Fetchit *(Casper)*, Maxie Rosenbloom *(McCoy)*, Marian Martin *(Gypsy)*, Ona Munson *(Anne)*, Frances Robinson *(Margie)*, Regis Toomey *(Bill)*, Georgia Caine *(Aunt Elizabeth)*, Benny Baker *(Taxi Driver)*, Eddie Acuff *(Reporter)*, Raymond Parker *(Bob)*, Stanley Hughes *(McGill)*, Virginia Sale *(Landlady)*, Frank Coghlan, Jr. *(Office Boy)*, Mary Field *(Secretary)*, Frank Sully *(Milk Truck Driver)*.

Ruggles plays a wimpy clerk about to marry socialite Munson, whose aunt, Caine, has a very large account with his company. The owner of the agency, Lane, discovers that after the marriage Munson will withdraw her account from the agency and give it to Ruggles. Lane decides to break up the marriage so he hires the blonde bombshell wife of a vaudevillian friend to pull a practical joke on Ruggles, which nearly causes him to lose his bride-to-be. Munson, however, has complete faith in him and they are wed, despite the weird circumstances.

p, Ken Goldsmith; d, Gus Meins; w, Pat Flick, Edward Eliscu, Morton Grant (based on the play "Adam's Enemy" by Katharine Kavanaugh); ph, Henry Sharp; ed, Phillip Cahn.

Comedy **(PR:A MPAA:NR)**

HIS FAMILY TREE** (1936) 59m RKO bw

James Barton *(Murphy)*, Margaret Callahan *(Elinor Murfree)*, Addison Randall *(Mike Donovan)*, William Harrigan *(Charles Murfree)*, Maureen Delany *(Widow Oulihan)*, Marjorie Gateson *(Margaret Murfree)*, Clifford Jones *(Dudley)*, Ray Mayer *(Terrance Gilligan)*, Herman Bing *(Stonehill)*, Pat Moriarty *(Bat Gilligan)*, Ferdinand Munier *(Mayor)*, Charles Coleman *(Hopkins)*, Orville Caldwell *(Mayor's Henchman)*, William Lemuels *(Brannigan)*.

Barton plays an Irish pubowner who travels to the U.S. to find out why his son, Harrigan, hasn't been writing to him. He discovers his son in the midst of a hot Iowa mayoral election. At the request of his snobby socialite wife, Harrigan changes his last name and denies his Irish heritage. Barton's arrival in town messes up his plans as Harrigan's past becomes public knowledge. All turns out well, however, when the city's Irish votes win him the election.

p, Cliff Reid; d, Charles Vidor; w, Joel Sayre, John Twist (based on the play "Old Man Murphy" by Patrick Kearney, Henry Wagstaff Gribble); ph, Lucien Andriot; md, Alberto Colombo.

Comedy/Drama **(PR:A MPAA:NR)**

HIS FIGHTING BLOOD* (1935) 60m Ambassador bw

Kermit Maynard, Polly Ann Young, Ted Adams, Paul Fix, Joseph Girard, Ben Hendricks, Jr., Frank O'Connor, Charles King, Frank LaRue, Ed Cecil, Theodore Lorch, Jack Cheatham, The Singing Constables [Jack Kirk, Chuck Baldra, Glenn Strange], "Rocky."

Maynard joins the Canadian Mounted Police to fight outlaws in the forests and tundras of Canada. Routine oater, but future Frankenstein monster and "Gunsmoke" bartender Strange does a turn as a singing mountie.

p, Sig Neufeld, Maurice H. Conn; d, John W. English; w, Joseph O'Donnell (based on a story by James Oliver Curwood); ph, Jack Greenhalgh; ed, Richard G. Gray.

Western **Cas.** **(PR:A MPAA:NR)**

HIS FIRST COMMAND*½ (1929) 65m Pathe bw/c

William Boyd *(Terry Culver)*, Dorothy Sebastian *(Judy Gaylord)*, Gavin Gordon *(Lt. Allen)*, Helen Parrish *(Jane)*, Alphonse Ethier *(Col. Gaylord)*, Howard Hickman *(Maj. Hall)*, Paul Hurst *(Sgt. Westbrook)*, Jules Cowles *(Cpl. Jones)*, Rose Tapley *(Mrs. Pike)*, Mabel Van Buren *(Mrs. Sargent)*, Charles Moore *(Homer)*.

Boyd, who was most famous for his Hopalong Cassidy characterizations, is out of the saddle and into an army uniform in this off-beat comedy. Boyd plays a wisecracking young officer who gets his first commission. In real life, anyone acting like him in the army would have found himself in irons. However, Hollywood gave no thought to realism and produced this film about the obnoxious Boyd, who after receiving his commission, marries Sebastian, the daughter of a colonel. There is one color sequence, during a drill of a color guard.

d, Gregory LaCava; w, LaCava, Jack Jungmeyer, James Gleason; ph, J.J. Mescal, Arthur Miller; ed, Doane Harrison.

Comedy **(PR:A MPAA:NR)**

HIS GIRL FRIDAY***** (1940) 92m COL bw

Cary Grant *(Walter Burns)*, Rosalind Russell *(Hildy Johnson)*, Ralph Bellamy *(Bruce Baldwin)*, Gene Lockhart *(Sheriff Hartwell)*, Helen Mack *(Mollie Malloy)*, Porter Hall *(Murphy)*, Ernest Truex *(Roy Bensinger)*, Cliff Edwards *(Endicott)*, Clarence Kolb *(Mayor)*, Roscoe Karns *(McCue)*, Frank Jenks *(Wilson)*, Regis Toomey *(Sanders)*, Abner Biberman *(Diamond Louie)*, Frank Orth *(Duffy)*, John Qualen *(Earl Williams)*, Alma Kruger *(Mrs. Baldwin)*, Billy Gilbert *(Joe Pettibone)*, Pat West *(Warden Cooley)*, Edwin Maxwell *(Dr. Egelhoffer)*, Irving Bacon *(Gus)*, Earl Dwire *(Mr. Davis)*, Ralph Dunn *(Guard)*, Pat Flaherty, Edmund Cobb *(Cops)*, Wade Boteler *(Jail Guard)*, Marian Martin.

This hilarious remake of the brilliant FRONT PAGE by Hecht and MacArthur sees Grant as the scheming editor and, in a switch, the reporter enacted by a savvy Russell. Instead of the editor trying to do all in his power to keep his most brilliant reporter on staff, this remake, one of the few to equal the original, adds the allure of sex and romance. Grant learns that not only is Russell leaving his paper but she intends to marry again, having once been married to the maniacal Grant. Russell is tired of the hectic pace and deadline grind and is opting for the simple life of home, children, and a husband with a predictable job. The intended is Bellamy, at his stuffy best, about as inspiring a groom-to-be as a hollowed out cactus. When radical and accidental killer Qualen escapes his cell and hides in the news room of the jail (inside a rolltop desk), Grant uses the incident to entice Russell back to work. She is to write the scoop of the break, but Grant's deeper motive is to keep Russell near him so he can somehow woo her back. His techniques are unorthodox at best. At one point Grant drives Russell near crazy with his nonstop zany banter, chasing her clockwise, then counter-clockwise, about the newsroom, all the while unleashing a stream of near-hysterical babble. He rightly appeals to her love of the profession, at a one point crying out to her: "This isn't just a newspaper story—it's a career!" And in another scene he declares: "This is war—you can't desert me now." But Russell, who momentarily abandons Bellamy, is tempest-tossed between feminine wants and the newshound in her blood. When Bellamy protests her involvement in the manhunt, she blurts: "Can't you see this is the biggest thing in my life?" But on the other side of the coin are longings to be thought of as a female. "Bruce [Bellamy] treats me like a woman," she tells Grant. "I want to go somewhere and be a woman," she adds. The pressure reduces her to tears which genuinely shock Grant: "You never *cried* before!" But he wants her both as wife and reporter and he somehow manages to keep both, although Grant's tactics are nothing less than the acts of a lunatic. Qualen, the much-sought after felon, is finally caught, his trollop girl friend Mack survives her fall from the newsroom (hurtling herself downward to prove her love for Qualen to the sneering, snide newsmen), and Bellamy is sent packing while Grant gets Russell and also exposes crooked sheriff Lockhart and political cronies for another scoop. It's all hilarious fun with bright dialog written by Lederer, Hecht's friend and sometimes collaborator. Biberman, one of the thugs working for Grant, defends his new girl friend by saying: "She's not an albino; she was born right here in this country!" Russell calling in a report to the city desk: "Shot him right in the classified ads . . . No, 'ads'!" And there are a lot of inside jokes. Grant demeans Bellamy to Russell, saying he "looks like that actor . . . Ralph Bellamy!" Grant again grins as he says: "The last man that said that to me was Archie Leach just a week before he cut his throat." (Archibald or Archie Leach is Grant's real name.) The pace of the film is at whirlwind speed as Hawks instructed his actors to overlap their lines, so much so that, at times, everyone seems to be talking at once. At one point crooked mayor Kolb asks Gilbert, a process server, his name. Gilbert blurts "Pettibone," then inquires, "what's yours?" Kolb wonders about the name out load, "Pettibone," and Gilbert mistakes this for an answer, saying, "not really!" Hawks placed four microphones about the jumbled newsroom set so he could pick up the many newsmen all talking at the same time, and this created havoc for the soundmen who had to make scores of mike switches during takes. One archivist actually timed the hurricane delivery of the actors at 240 words per minute, so fast that the dialog is just discernible, the actors speaking about 130 words per minute above average delivery. Added to this Hawks had his cast members move at twice normal speed so the whole thing was frantic from scene to scene, thus giving urgency to the world of fast-breaking news he was depicting. Walker's cameras, with Hawks hurrying them at every angle, move at jet speed but tell the story beautifully. This overlapping of dialog and speeded up action was actually first devised by Frank Capra for his Depression era film AMERICAN MADNESS, 1932, a landmark film not lost on the ever-watchful Hawks. This film is still distinctly Hawksian, however, bearing his trademark of madcap comedy as so brilliantly shown in BRINGING UP BABY and I WAS A MALE WAR BRIDE, both starring Grant. Hawks loved to remake films, even his own, believing he could always go one better. He remade his own silent film THE ROAD TO GLORY (1927) as a talkie in 1936. BALL OF FIRE (1941) he remade as A SONG IS BORN (1947), and his classic RIO BRAVO (1959) (said to be a response to Fred Zinnemann's HIGH NOON) was remade by Hawks *twice*, as EL DORADO (1967) and as RIO LOBO (1970), the latter being the great director's last film. Grant is in his element here, utterly crazy but in a position of power; instead of the victim, this time he is the aggressor, the persecutor as he cajoles, aggravates, intimidates, argues, upsets, and brings general mayhem to the lives of all around him. It's one of his greatest comedic roles, proving once again the amazing versatility of this fine actor. Russell is almost his equal in their scenes together, demonstrating her own zany comedic talents and bringing to her role a side-splitting dimension that original authors Hecht and MacArthur never envisioned. Actually, Hawks hit upon the happy thought of turning Hildy Johnson into a female when he asked a woman to read the part (while he read that of the editor) at a party and got the idea of making the reporter a woman. He found no objections from Hecht who suggested Lederer write the script since he was busy with other writing chores. Katharine Hepburn, Jean Arthur, Margaret Sullivan, Irene Dunne, Claudette Colbert, and Carole Lombard were offered the role but all turned it down. Russell leapt at the chance to play the screwball role and it turned out to be one of her most effective parts, one for which she is well-remembered. She obviously relished her character, a bawdy, rowdy, cigarette-puffing, wise-cracking female who is no lady but the best reporter in the world. (Unlike Pat O'Brien in the original, she is shown actually working, interviewing, writing, and preparing her copy.) She is dynamic and original in an early-day film that gave women an equal if not shaky footing with men. Russell knew from the start that Hawks was dissatisfied with having her in the role. Columbia mogul Harry Cohn had liked her in CRAIG'S WIFE (1936), done for his studio, and, when other actresses mistakenly turned down the role for HIS GIRL FRIDAY, he again borrowed Russell from MGM. Hawks was pensive in his first meeting with Russell until she said: "You don't want me, do you? But you're stuck with me, so we might as well make the most of it." Her tough manner appealed to the director and he soon realized that she was perfect as the lady reporter who would break any neck to get a story.

p&d, Howard Hawks; w, Charles Lederer (based on the play by Ben Hecht, Charles MacArthur); ph, Joseph Walker; m, Morris W. Stoloff; ed, Gene Havlick; art d, Lionel Banks; cos, Robert Kalloch.

Comedy **Cas.** **(PR:C MPAA:NR)**

HIS GLORIOUS NIGHT** (1929) 86m MGM bw
(GB: BREATH OF SCANDAL)

John Gilbert *(Capt. Kovacs)*, Catherine Dale Owen *(Princess Orsolini)*, Nance O'Neil *(Eugenie)*, Gustav von Seyffertitz *(Krehl)*, Hedda Hopper *(Mrs. Collingsworth Stratton)*, Doris Hill *(Priscilla Stratton)*, Tyrell Davis *(Prince Luigi Caprilli)*, Gerald Barry *(Lord York)*, Madeline Seymour *(Lady York)*, Richard Carle *(Count Albert)*, Eva Dennison *(Countess Lina)*, Youcca Troubetzkoy *(Von Bergman)*, Peter Gawthorn *(Gen. Ettingen)*.

This was John Gilbert's swan song as a movie matinee idol, one most assuredly orchestrated by MGM mogul Louis B. Mayer. A muddled story at best has Gilbert as a swashbuckling captain of royal guards who woos and wins the heart of Owen, a princess betrothed to another. When the queen hears of the liaison she orders her daughter to break off the romance. Gilbert responds by spreading rumors that he is a notorious swindler and this soon brings him before the queen. Gilbert says he has Owen's love letters and will make these torrid missives public unless Owen spends the night with him. Reluctantly, the chaste princess goes to Gilbert but all ends happily as they are subsequently married. This kind of fragile story of troubled royalty and imaginary kingdoms was all right for the silent era where unsophisticated audiences demanded little, but with the birth of talkies the public wanted substantial story content and intelligent dialog. It got neither here, nor a well-made film, one where Lionel Barrymore, veteran character actor turned director, uses a heavy hand with limp material. The dialog was so stilted and the story so corny that audiences first seeing this film threw rotten eggs and tomatoes at the screen. Worse, they laughed at the great John Gilbert whose voice sounded off-key, high, and decidedly unromantic. It was long felt that MGM could have fixed up the sound of Gilbert's voice so that it was acceptable but that Louis B. Mayer, MGM's autocratic boss, hated Gilbert so much that he wanted to ruin his career, spending millions to do it. Gilbert and Mayer had had violent quarrels over the actor's drinking bouts and his attitude toward women, which Mayer interpreted as disrespectful. Some even went so far as to claim that Mayer ordered Gilbert's voice distorted on the sound track of HIS GLORIOUS NIGHT so that it sounded effeminate and weak, an excuse to cancel his contract which had many years to run and was costing the studio millions. Whatever, the great silent star never made a successful transition from silents to talkies and his career soon ended in booze and premature death.

d, Lionel Barrymore; w, Willard Mack (based on the play "Olympia" by Ferenc Molnar); ph, Percy Hilburn; m, Barrymore; ed, William Le Vanway; art d, Cedric Gibbons; cos, David Cox.

HIS GRACE GIVES NOTICE*½ (1933, Brit.) 58m REA/RKO bw

Arthur Margetson *(George Barwick)*, Viola Keats *(Barbara Rannock)*, S. Victor Stanley *(James Roper)*, Barrie Livesey *(Ted Burlington)*, Ben Welden *(Michael Collier)*, Edgar Norfolk *(Capt. Langley)*, Dick Francis *(Mr. Perks)*, Lawrence Hanray *(Mr. Grayling)*, Charles Groves *(Henry Evans)*, O.B. Clarence *(Lord Rannock)*, Gertrude Sterroll *(Lady Rannock)*.

The story has a butler, Margetson, falling in love with his employer's daughter, Keats. She wants nothing to do with a commoner and spurns his love. When Margetson gets word that he has become the Duke of Marlow, he keeps it quiet, as he doesn't want Keats to love him for his title only. Enter a married Chicago gangster who arrives and sweeps Keats off her feet. He persuades Keats to elope to Paris with him, but when they get there, she discovers his intentions are less than noble. Margetson rescues Keats and she responds to him in a much kinder manner. They get married and not until after the ceremony does Margetson reveal that he is a duke.

p, Julius Hagen; d, George A. Cooper; w, H. Fowler Mear (based on a novel by Lady Trowbridge); ph, Ernest Palmer.

Drama **(PR:A MPAA:NR)**

HIS GREATEST GAMBLE* (1934) 70m RKO bw

Richard Dix *(Philip Eden)*, Dorothy Wilson *(Alice, adult)*, Bruce Cabot *(Stephen)*, Erin O'Brien-Moore *(Florence)*, Edith Fellows *(Alice, child)*, Shirley Grey *(Bernice)*, Leonard Carey *(Butler)*, Eily Malyon *(Jenny)*.

An unusual plot for its day, this highly melodramatic film tells the story of a young girl who is victimized by a domineering mother. The story sees the father, Dix, trying to get his young daughter, Fellows, out of the clutches of ex-wife, O'Brien-Moore. However, Dix is serving 15 years in jail after the accidental death of a woman. Dix breaks out of jail when he discovers that his daughter, now played by Wilson, has been turned into a basket-case because of the influence of the ex-wife. He rescues his daughter from O'Brien-Moore's clutches and restores her confidence and vitality. He also helps her into the arms of the man she loves. Dix then turns himself back in to serve out the rest of his sentence.

p, Myles Connolly; d, John Robertson; w, Sidney Buchman, Harry Hervey (based on a story by Salisbury Field); ph, Teddy Tetzlaff; ed, William Hamilton.

Drama **(PR:A MPAA:NR)**

HIS, HERS AND THEIRS (SEE: YOURS, MINE AND OURS, 1968)

HIS KIND OF WOMAN*** (1951) 120m RKO bw

Robert Mitchum *(Dan Milner)*, Jane Russell *(Lenore Brent)*, Vincent Price *(Mark Cardigan)*, Tim Holt *(Bill Lusk)*, Charles McGraw *(Thompson)*, Marjorie Reynolds *(Helen Cardigan)*, Raymond Burr *(Nick Ferraro)*, Leslye Banning *(Jennie Stone)*, Jim Backus *(Myron Winton)*, Philip Van Zandt *(Jose Morro)*, John Mylong *(Martin Krafft)*, Carleton G. Young *(Hobson)*, Erno Verebes *(Estaban)*, Dan White *(Tex Kearns)*, Richard Berggren *(Milton Stone)*, Stacy Harris *(Harry)*, Robert Cornthwaite *(Hernandez)*, Jim Burke *(Barkeep)*, Paul Frees *(Corle)*, Joe Granby *(Arnold)*, Daniel De Laurentis *(Mexican Boy)*, John Sheehan *(Husband)*, Sally Yarnell *(Wife)*, Anthony Caruso *(Tony)*, Robert Rose *(Corle's Servant)*, Tol Avery *(The Fat One)*, Paul Fierro, Mickey Simpson *(Hoodlums)*, Ed Rand, Jerry James *(Cops)*, Joe Fluellen *(Sam)*, Len Hendry *(Customer)*, Joey Ray, Barry Brooks *(Card Players)*, Stuart Holmes, Jim Davies *(Men)*, Marie San Young *(Chinese Waitress)*, Mary Brewer, Jerri Jordan, Joy Windsor, Mamie Van Doren, Barbara Freking *(Girls)*, Marietta Elliott *(Redhead)*, William Justin *(Gyppo)*, Bill Nelson *(Capt. Salazarr)*, Bud Wolf *(Seaman)*, Ralph Gomez *(Mexican Foreman)*, Mike Lally *(Henchman)*, Saul Gorss *(Viscount)*, Gerry Ganzer *(Countess)*.

This Mitchum-Russell vehicle is a delightful crime potboiler with mystery, chases, fights galore, and sex oozing from the pores of the Amazonian leading lady. Sleepy-eyed gambler Mitchum has been given $50,000 to go to a Mexican resort for an unexplained purpose. He walks into a cafe to spot Russell singing in a revealing evening dress which allows broad display of her ample endowments. They immediately hit it off, animal magnetism drawing Mitchum and Russell together. They go on to the resort together, south of Nogales, but as soon as Russell registers at the desk she sees flamboyant Price, an egocentric actor with whom she's been having an affair, and she momentarily departs Mitchum for Price's company. The actor however, is nervous by the mere presence of the voluptuous Russell since he's dodging his wife, Reynolds, who goes into a rampage when seeing Price with any other woman. Mitchum then slowly learns the reason why he has been summoned to this remote spot. His employer turns out to be Burr, a notorious mobster wanted for various crimes, all heinous. Mitchum discovers to his extreme discomfort that Burr has paid him so that a plastic surgeon can change Burr's face to that of Mitchum's, which will allow the mobster to assume a new identity, return to the U.S., and continue to operate free and easy. Moreover, through Russell's help, Mitchum further learns that once the operation is finished, Mitchum will also be finished and be of no more use to Burr. He is slated for murder. Hovering about all these evil doings is Holt, an immigration agent waiting to snatch Burr when he makes a move toward the border (he is later murdered by Burr's henchmen), and McGraw, one of Burr's killers, waiting to bump off Mitchum. Burr cannot wait any longer and has Mitchum dragged on to his yacht where he is beaten, stripped, and then injected with a dangerous drug administered by the plastic surgeon, a one-time Nazi quack who looks upon the operation as a marvelous experiment. Russell, now realizing Mitchum is the true love of her life, enlists the aid of the extravagant Price who organizes a strange group of adventurers and leads a raid against Burr's heavily fortified yacht, freeing Mitchum, who takes care of Burr personally. Mitchum's arms open wide at the finish to embrace his kind of woman, Russell. Everything about this film is crude, rude, sleazy, and coarse, so much so that it has become a camp classic. Price's outrageous performance, an all-time high (or low) in hamminess, is alone worth sitting through the movie for. He is unbelievable, uttering dialog and striking fierce postures that will leave the viewer gaping in wonder. He's so bad that he's wonderful as he chews up the South-of-the-border sets, fellow actors, and the already motheaten script. Mitchum is his usual stoic self, prodded and pummeled like a dyspeptic elephant until finally enraged and let loose to stomp all in his path. Russell's performance can best be described as a towering, walking, jiggling assemblance of pulchritudinous flesh which bursts forth from specially designed skimpy costumes, especially a black bathing suit that is hardly there. She sings three songs in her one-key voice (but what male is really listening?): "Kiss and Run," "Five Little Miles from San Berdoo" (Ben S. Coslow), and "You'll Know" (Jimmy McHugh, Harold Adamson). The dialog is positively out of this world, right from the beginning when Mitchum, who can't pay off a bet, receives Burr's anonymous offer of $50,000 in his cheap hotel room, remarking to his thug visitors: "I was just getting ready to take my tie off . . . wondering whether I should hang myself with it." Price later tells Mitchum that "I've got a little Winchester I'd like you to try. If it feels right to you, I'll let you use it." Price later quotes Shakespeare as he leads the raid against the yacht, between shooting mobsters off of yardarms. Before leaving on the raid he locks Russell in a closet for safekeeping, then tells a crony: "If I'm not here by Wednesday, chop that door down!" To his weird group of raiding volunteers Price shouts: "Survivors will get parts in my next picture!" The classic camp line is delivered by Mitchum when Russell hip-sways into his room to find him pressing wet currency. She asks him what he's doing and he replies: "Whenever I'm bored I always iron my money." Russell's vamping, Mitchum's ridiculous wisecracks, Burr's growling, and Price's outlandish statements make up one of the most spectacular bad movies ever made, naturally a Howard Hughes production. Hughes ballyhooed Russell's bosomy talents once more (his fixation since her debut in THE OUTLAW) with an ad campaign headed by a quote from gossip monger Louella Parsons: "The hottest combination that ever hit the screen!" (You could interpret this to mean Russell and costar Mitchum or just Russell.) Mitchum and Russell teamed up to star in MACAO just after completing HIS KIND OF WOMEN. Though this film was finished in 1950, it was not released until the following year because Howard Hughes was too busy to see it and approve its release. Farrow does a credible job with the poor material and the production values are high. Burr's role, incidentally, is certainly based on the then deported gangster, Charles "Lucky" Luciano, who was scheming a way to reenter the U.S. The violence is excessive, especially where Mitchum is stripped, beaten with a belt buckle, then pistol-whipped and thrown into the boiling hot engine room, awakening to see Burr's gun pressed to his forehead and Burr saying: "Wake up, little boy, I want you to see it coming!"

p, Robert Sparks; d, John Farrow; w, Frank Fenton, Jack Leonard (based on the story "Star Sapphire" by Gerald Drayson Adams); ph, Harry J. Wild; m, Leigh Harline; ed, Eda Warren, Frederic Knudtson; md, Constantin Bakaleinikoff; prod d, J. McMillan Johnson; art d, Albert S. D'Agostino; set d, Darrell Silvera, Ross Dowd; cos, Howard Greer; m/l, Jimmy McHugh, Harold Adamson, Ben S. Coslow; makeup, Mel Burns.

Crime Drama **Cas.** **(PR:C-O MPAA:NR)**

HIS LAST TWELVE HOURS** (1953, Ital.) 98m Cines-Lest Pathe/IFE bw (LE SUE ULTIME 12 ORE)

Jean Gabin *(Carlo Bacchi)*, Mariella Lotti *(His Wife)*, Elena Altieri *(Anna)*, Julien Carette *(Santini)*, Antonella Lualdi *(Maria)*, Maso Lotti *(Nanni)*, Elli Parvo *(Friend)*, Paola Borboni *(Backi)*.

Gabin plays a wealthy businessman who is run over by a truck and killed, but is given 12 more hours on Earth with which to perform good deeds. He is directed to Carette, a porter he once cheated, and told to bring the man some happiness. The industrialist decides that money is the answer and showers Carette with a fortune. But Carette is not content with the money and Gabin realizes that the porter is really an uncaring, greedy grouch who will never be happy. (In Italian; English subtitles.)

p, Carlo Civallero; d, Luigi Zampa; w, Suso Checchi D'Amico, Vitaliano Brancati, Diego Fabbri, Henry Jeason (based on a story by Cesare Zavattini); ph, Carlo Montuori; m, Nino Rota; ed, Eraldo Daroma.

Drama/Comedy **(PR:A MPAA:NR)**

HIS LORDSHIP* (1932, Brit.) 79m WEST/UA bw

Jerry Verno *(Bert Gibbs)*, Janet Megrew *(Ilya Myona)*, Ben Welden *(Washington Lincoln)*, Polly Ward *(Leninia)*, Peter Gawthorne *(Ferguson)*, Michael Hogan *(Comrade Curzon)*, Muriel George *(Mrs. Gibbs)*, V.C. Clinton-Baddeley *(Comrade Howard)*, Patrick Ludlow.

Lame excuse for a musical has Verno, a cockney plumber, suddenly elevated to aristocracy and posing as the fiance of Russian movie star Megrew. Nothing the least bit worthwhile here.

p, Jerome Jackson; d, Michael Powell; w, Ralph Smart (based on the novel *The Right Honourable* by Oliver Heuffer); ph, Geoffrey Faithfull; m/l, Eric Maschwitz, V.C. Clinton-Baddeley.

Musical/Comedy **(PR:A MPAA:NR)**

HIS LORDSHIP, 1936 (SEE: MAN OF AFFAIRS, 1936, Brit.)

HIS LORDSHIP GOES TO PRESS*

(1939, Brit.) 80m Canterbury/RKO bw

June Clyde *(Valerie Lee)*, Hugh Williams *(Lord Bill Wilmer)*, Romney Brent *(Pinkie Butler)*, Louise Hampton *(Mrs. Hodges)*, Leslie Perrins *(Sir Richard Swingleton)*,

H.F. Maltby *(Gen. Tukes)*, Zillah Bateman *(Mrs. Tukes)*, Aubrey Mallalieu *(Hardcastle)*, Michael Ripper, Isobel Scaife.

Snobbish American reporter Clyde is taught a lesson in common courtesy by a Lord, Williams, who pretends to be a poor farmer. The predictable close finds them romantically linked. Not a laugh to be found anywhere.

p, A. George Smith; d, Maclean Rogers; w, Kathleen Butler, H.F. Maltby (based on a story by Margaret McDonnell, Gordon McDonnell).

Comedy **(PR:A MPAA:NR)**

HIS LORDSHIP REGRETS* (1938, Brit.) 78m Canterbury/RKO bw

Claude Hulbert *(Lord Cavender)*, Winifred Shotter *(Mary/Mabel)*, Gina Malo *(Mabel van Morgan)*, Aubrey Mallalieu *(Dawkins)*, Antony Holles *(Guy Reading)*, Eve Gray *(Enid)*, Athole Stewart *(Sir Timothy Kentford)*, Annie Esmond *(Lady Kentford)*, Sally Stewart *(Sally)*, Derek Gorst *(Honorable Percy Hartlock)*, Gerald Rawlinson *(Capt. Arthur Gregson)*, Michael Ripper, Paul Sheridan, Valentine Dunn.

Blah comedy has Hulbert as a down-on-his-luck nobleman who sets about wooing heiress Malo. He soon discovers that his heart belongs to Shotter, who turns out to be a real heiress, while Malo is exposed as a gold-digging crook. Decent cast of familiar British faces doesn't help this one.

p, A. George Smith; d, Maclean Rogers; w, Kathleen Butler, H.F. Maltby (based on the play "Bees and Honey" by Maltby); ph, Geoffrey Faithfull.

Comedy **(PR:A MPAA:NR)**

HIS LUCKY DAY*½ (1929) 59m UNIV bw

Reginald Denny, Otis Harlan, Cissy Fitzgerald, Eddie Phillips, LaRayne DuVal, Tom O'Brien, Harvey Clarke.

Only 30% of this film contains dialog; the rest is silent. The story tells of a dim-witted real estate agent, Denny, who is in love with DuVal. Her father has rented a house from him with the option to renew, but the old man decides to forego a new lease unless Denny can rent the property adjoining his land. Denny ends up renting to a gang of bank robbers whom he believes are legitimate renters looking for a place to stay. This leads to a lot of strange situations before the gang is finally captured.

p, Eddie Cline; w, John B. Clymer, Gladys Lehman; ph, Arthur Todd; m, Joseph Cherniavsky.

Comedy **(PR:A MPAA:NR)**

HIS MAJESTY AND CO*½ (1935, Brit.) 66m FOX bw

John Garrick *(John)*, Barbara Waring *(Princess Sandra)*, Morton Selten *(King of Poldavia)*, Wally Patch *(Bert Hicks)*, Mary Grey *(Queen)*, Jean Gillie *(Nina)*, Desmond Jeans *(Michael)*, H. Saxon-Snell *(Ferguson)*, Howard Douglas *(Sam Bloom)*, Eddie Fitzmaurice, Betty le Brocke, Campbell Russell, Alfredo Campoli and his Tzigane Orchestra.

Garrick falls in love with the daughter of an exiled Ruritanian king and queen. The four of them open a restaurant with the queen, Grey, working as the cook, while the king, Selten, acts as wine steward. Silly, though sporadically charming, musical.

d, Anthony Kimmins; w, Sally Sutherland.

Musical/Comedy **(PR:A MPAA:NR)**

HIS MAJESTY BUNKER BEAN (SEE: BUNKER BEAN, 1936)

HIS MAJESTY, KING BALLYHOO** (1931, Ger.) 87m Sascha bw (MAN BRAUCHT KEIN GELD; WIR BRAUCHEN KEIN GELD; AKA: WE NEED NO MONEY)

Heinz Ruhmann *(Schmidt)*, Hedy Kiesler [Lamarr] *(Kathe Brandt)*, Hans Moser *(Thomas Hoffman)*, Ida Wust *(Frau Brandt)*, Hans Junkermann *(Herr Brandt)*, Kurt Gerron *(Bank President)*, Paul Henckels *(The Mayor)*, Hans Hermann Schaufuss, Albert Florath, Ludwig Stoessel, Hugo Fischer-Koppe, Siegfried Berisch, Wolfgang Von Schwind, Heinrich Schroth, Fritz Odemar, Leopold Von Ledebour, Sigi Hofer, Karl Hannemann, Anna Dammann.

Teutonic comedy starring Moser as an uncle from Chicago who arrives in the small village of Groditzkirchen with only $10 in his pocket and a scheme to get rich on credit. He sets himself up as the village millionaire with lowly bank clerk Ruhmann along for the ride. Though he knows the scheme may go bust, Ruhmann exploits it for all it's worth in order to build a future for himself and his girl Kiesler [Lamarr].

p, Dr. Wilhelm Szekely; d, Karl Boese; w, Karl Noti, Hans Wilhelm (based on a play by F. Altenkirch); ph, Karl Sander, Willy Goldberger; m, Artur Guttmann; ed, G. Pollatschik; md, Artur Guttmann; art d, Julius von Borsody.

Comedy **(PR:A MPAA:NR)**

HIS MAJESTY O'KEEFE*** (1953) 89m WB c

Burt Lancaster *(Capt. David O'Keefe)*, Joan Rice *(Dalabo)*, Andre Morell *(Alfred Tetins)*, Abraham Sofaer *(Fatumak)*, Archie Savage *(Boogulroo)*, Benson Fong *(Mr. Chou)*, Teresa Prendergast *(Kakofel)*, Lloyd Berrell *(Inifel)*, Charles Horvath *(Bully Hayes)*, Philip Ahn *(Sien Tang)*, Guy Doleman *(Weber)*, Grant Taylor *(Lt. Brenner)*, Alexander Archdale *(Harris)*, Harvey Adams *(Friedlander)*, Warwick Ray *(Garcia)*, Paddy Mulelly *(Beldon)*, Jim Crawford *(Rhee)*, Mr. McLardy *(Benson)*, Niranjan Singh *(Singh)*.

Lancaster smiles toothily and laughs his way through this Technicolor swashbuckler based on a real-life American adventurer who traveled to the South Seas to teach the natives the advantages of modern agricultural technology. This wisdom does not come free however, and Lancaster exchanges his expertise for a fortune in Copra (dried coconut meat from which oil can be extracted). This does not disturb the locals, who see him as a god, and even allow him to marry one of their most beautiful maidens, Rice. Lancaster learns to like this lifestyle, and when his reign is threatened by unscrupulous white traders who arrive to get a piece of the action, he bolts into action and waylays the scoundrels.

p, Harold Hecht; d, Byron Haskin; w, Borden Chase, James Hill (based on a novel by Lawrence Klingman, Gerald Green); ph, Otto Heller (Technicolor); m, Dmitri Tiomkin; ed, Manuel Del Campo; md, Tiomkin; ch, Daniel Nagrin; m/l, "Emerald Isle" Tiomkin, Paul Francis Webster.

Adventure **(PR:A MPAA:NR)**

HIS NIGHT OUT** (1935) 74m UNIV bw

Edward Everett Horton *(Homer)*, Irene Hervey *(Peggy)*, Robert McWade *(Davis)*, Jack LaRue *(Ferranza)*, Willard Robertson *(Trent)*, Oscar Apfel *(Dr. Kraft)*, Lola Lane *(Lola)*, Virginia Howell *(Nurse)*, Jack Norton *(Dr. Singer)*, Billy Burrud *(Jimmie)*, Theodore Von Eltz *(Parsons)*, Clara Kimbell Young *(Mrs. Davis)*, Rollo Lloyd, Jack Carnevale, Ward Bond, Dewey Robinson, Arch Robbins, Charles Regan, Jack Kennedy, Eddie Chandler, George Cleveland, Jack Mulhall, Priscilla Lawson, Nan Grey, Diana Gibson.

Horton seemed to specialize in fairly morbid comedies and this one is no exception. Here he plays a timid milquetoast office worker who goes to a quack doctor for a check-up and is informed he has three months to live. Horton decides to finally take some chances with his life and gets involved in situations that he never before allowed himself. When his boss' safe is robbed, the now-daring Horton gives chase to the bandits. Hervey, an equally shy and unassuming co-worker, is attracted to the new Horton and it is she who gives him the drive to commit such daring feats of bravery. In the end, Horton catches the bad guys, wins over Hervey, and learns he will live a long and happy life.

p, Irving Starr; d, William Nigh; w, Doris Malloy, Harry Clork (based on a story by Charles Christensen); ph, Edward J. Snyder; ed, Daniel Mandell.

Comedy **(PR:A MPAA:NR)**

HIS OTHER WOMAN (SEE: DESK SET, 1957)

HIS PRIVATE SECRETARY*½ (1933) 68m Screencraft/Showmen's bw

John Wayne *(Dick Wallace)*, Evalyn Knapp *(Marion Hall)*, Alec B. Francis *(Dr. Hall)*, Reginald Barlow *(Mr. Wallace)*, Natalie Kingston *(Polly)*, Arthur Hoyt *(Little)*, Al St. John *(Garage Owner)*, Hugh Kidder *(Butler)*, Mickey Rentschler *(Boy)*, Patrick Cunning.

An early John Wayne film which sees Wayne dressed in a suit instead of a cowboy outfit. Wayne plays the son of a rich man who enjoys the life of a jet-set playboy. His father wants him to settle down into the family business, but Wayne can't seem to keep his mind off the ladies. He meets Knapp, the granddaughter of a minister, who gets him on the right track and forces Wayne to see his father's point of view.

p, Al Alt; d, Philip H. Whitman; w, John Francis Natteford (based on a screen story by Lew Collins); ph, Abe Schultz; ed, Bobby Ray.

Drama **(PR:A MPAA:NR)**

HIS ROYAL HIGHNESS* (1932, Aus.) 90m Efftee/UNIV bw

George Wallace, Cyril Scott, Mona Barlee, Marshall Crossby, Lou Vernon, Byrl Walkeley.

Nothing special or particularly inspired in this Australian comedy starring burlesque comedian Wallace as a jobless drifter who finally finds work as a stagehand. At his new job, Wallace is struck on the head with a hammer and falls unconscious. While knocked out, he dreams an elaborate musical in which he is made the king of a fanciful nation. Unfortunately, Wallace awakens from his musing and discovers that he is once again out on the street and jobless.

p&d, F.W. Thring; w, C.J. Dennis (based on a story by George Wallace); ph, Arthur Higgins; set d, William Coleman.

Musical/Comedy **(PR:A MPAA:NR)**

HIS WIFE'S MOTHER* (1932, Brit.) 69m BIP/Wardour bw

Gus McNaughton *(Joy)*, Jerry Verno *(Henry)*, Molly Lamont *(Cynthia)*, Jack Hobbs *(Eustace)*, Marion Dawson *(Mrs. Trout)*, Jimmy Godden *(Mr. Trout)*, Renee Gadd *(Tony)*, Hal Gordon *(Munro)*.

Verno pretends to be his own double when his mother-in-law spots him with a showgirl. A dumb comedy, deservedly forgotten.

p, Walter C. Mycroft; d&w, Harry Hughes (based on the play "The Queer Fish" by Will Scott).

Comedy **(PR:A MPAA:NR)**

HIS WOMAN** (1931) 76m PAR bw

Gary Cooper *(Capt. Sam Whalan)*, Claudette Colbert *(Sally Clark)*, Averill Harris *(Mate Gatson)*, Richard Spiro *(Sammy)*, Douglas Dumbrille *(Alisandroe)*, Raquel Davida *(Maria Estella)*, Hamtree Harrington *(Aloysius)*, Sidney Easton *(Mark)*, Joan Blair *(Gertrude)*, Charlotte Wynters *(Flo)*, Herschell Mayall *(Mr. Morrisey)*, Joe Spurin Calleia *(The Agent)*, Lon Haschal *(Captain of Schooner)*, Harry Davenport *(Customs Inspector)*, John T. Doyle *(Doctor)*, Edward Keane *(Boatswain)*, Barton MacLane, Donald McBride, Preston Foster *(Crewmen)*.

Cooper and Colbert were totally wasted in this film. Cooper merely wandered about in his role as a tramp freighter captain. The crew rescues a drifting Navy boat containing a baby. Instead of turning the child in to authorities, Cooper plans to take him back to the states. When he advertises for a sea-going "mother" for the infant, Colbert enters the picture. She has had a shady past as a tramp, but overhears that Cooper is hiring a mother, so she dresses up like a prim and proper woman, tells a fantastic story, and gets the job—as well as a free trip back home. All is well until one of the sailors, Harris, recognizes Colbert and threatens to tell all he knows unless he can have his way with her. Cooper bursts in and throws Harris overboard. Colbert falls in love with Cooper who feels the same about her, but when they dock in New York, Cooper is arrested for attempted murder. To save him, Colbert becomes his witness, but loses his respect and they split up. She becomes a tramp once again and he begins to drink, but the two are reunited when the baby falls ill and a happy ending ensues. This film is a remake of SAL OF SINGAPORE (1929).

d, Edward Sloman; w, Adelaide Heilbron, Melville Baker (based on the novel *The Sentimentalist* by Dale Collins); ph, William Steiner; ed, Arthur Ellis.

Drama **(PR:A MPAA:NR)**

HISTOIRE D'ADELE H (SEE: STORY OF ADELE H, THE, 1975, Fr.)

HISTOIRE D'AIMER (SEE: LOVE IS A FUNNY THING, 1970, Fr./Ital.)

HISTORY IS MADE AT NIGHT**** (1937) 97m UA bw

Charles Boyer *(Paul Dumond)*, Jean Arthur *(Irene Vail)*, Leo Carrillo *(Cesare)*, Colin Clive *(Bruce Vail)*, Ivan Lebedeff *(Michael)*, George Meeker *(Norton)*, Lucien Prival *(Detective Witness)*, Georges Renavent *(Inspector Millard)*, George Davies *(Maestro)*, Adele St. Mauer *(Hotel Maid)*.

In this strange melodrama of spite, revenge, murder, and love, steamship owner Clive is out to frame his wife, Arthur, by planting his chauffeur in her room and bursting in on her with lawyer in tow. Boyer, unaware of all this, happens to climb down her balcony and sees Arthur struggling with the chauffeur. He takes her to safety, then, to give the impression of a robbery, steals some jewels and punches out the chauffeur. Clive, thinking Boyer is Arthur's real lover, bursts into the room and kills the chauffeur, hoping the police will convict Boyer for the crime. Meanwhile, Arthur has fallen in love with Boyer—who never knows he is being sought for murder—and leaves the country with her husband. Boyer follows her and the boat they are on is owned by Clive, who tells the captain to speed through an iceberg zone. The ship crashes into an iceberg and Clive, believing his wife and Boyer are dead, confesses all and commits suicide. Of course, our two lovers are happily alive. Though the plot twists are a bit much tc take at times, the cast is superb and the production nearly flawless.

p, Walter Wanger; d, Frank Borzage; w, Gene Towne, Graham Baker (based on a story by Towne, Graham); ph, Greg Toland; ed, Margaret Clancy.

Drama **Cas.** **(PR:C MPAA:NR)**

HISTORY OF MR. POLLY, THE½** (1949, Brit.) 94m RANK-TC/GFD bw

John Mills *(Alfred Polly)*, Sally Ann Howes *(Cristabel)*, Megs Jenkins *(Plump Woman)*, Finlay Currie *(Uncle Jim)*, Diana Churchill *(Annie)*, Betty Ann Davies *(Miriam)*, Edward Chapman *(Mr. Johnson)*, Shelagh Fraser *(Minnie)*, Moore Marriott *(Uncle Pentstemon)*, Gladys Henson *(Mrs. Larkins)*, Wylie Watson *(Mr. Rusper)*, Miles Malleson *(Old Gentleman)*, Doris Hare *(May Punt)*, Dandy Nichols *(Mrs. Johnson)*, Irene Handl *(Lady on Left)*, Lawrence Baskcomb *(Mr. Rumbold)*, Edie Martin *(Lady on Roof)*, Ernest Jay *(Mr. Hinks)*, Cyril Smith *(Mr. Voules)*, Dennis Arundel *(Clergyman)*, Juliet Mills *(Little Polly)*, David Horne *(Mr. Garvace)*, Wally Patch *(Customer)*, Victor Platt, Michael Ripper, Muriel Russell.

Mills stars as the henpecked dreamer of H.G. Wells' novel who finally undoes the shackles of his domineering wife and goes off in search of a more fulfilling lifestyle. He settles for a handyman job at a small country inn, and it is there that he finds true happiness. Slow-paced, but Mills' performance is engrossing and he pulls the viewer along with him.

p, John Mills; d&w, Anthony Pelissier (based on the novel by H.G. Wells); ph, Desmond Dickinson, Raymond Sturgess; m, William Alwyn; ed, John Seabourne.

Drama **(PR:A MPAA:NR)**

HISTORY OF THE WORLD, PART 1** (1981) 92m Brooksfilm/FOX c

Mel Brooks *(Moses/Comicus/Torquemada/Jacques/King Louis XVI)*, Dom DeLuise *(Emperor Nero)*, Madeline Kahn *(Empress Nympho)*, Harvey Korman *(Count de Monet)*, Cloris Leachman *(Madame de Farge)*, Ron Carey *(Swiftus)*, Gregory Hines *(Josephus)*, Pamela Stephenson *(Mademoiselle Rimbaud)*, Andreas Voutsinas *(Bearnaise)*, Shecky Greene *(Marcus Vindictus)*, Sid Caesar *(Chief Caveman)*, Howard Morris *(Court Spokesman)*, Rudy DeLuca *(Capt. Mucus)*, Mary-Margaret Humes *(Miriam)*, Orson Welles *(Narrator)*, Bea Arthur *(Clerk)*, Charlie Callas *(Soothsayer)*, Dena Dietrich *(Competence)*, Paul Mazursky *(Roman Officer)*, Ron Clark, Jack Riley *(Stoned Soldiers)*, Art Metrano *(Leonardo Da Vinci)*, Diane Day *(Caladonia)*, Henny Youngman *(Chemist)*, Hunter Von Leer *(Lt. Bob)*, Fritz Feld *(Maitre d')*, Hugh Hefner *(Entrepreneur)*, Pat McCormick *(Plumbing Salesman)*, Sid Gould *(Barber)*, Jim Steck *(Gladiator)*, Ronny Graham *(Oedipus)*, John Myhers *(Senate Leader)*, Lee Delano *(Wagon Driver)*, Robert B. Goldberg, Alan U. Schwartz, Jay Burton *(Senators)*, Robert Zappy, Ira Miller, Milt Freedman *(Roman Citizens)*, Johnny Silver *(Small Liar)*, Charles Thomas Murphy *(Auctioneer)*, Rod Haase *(Officer)*, Eileen Saki *(Slave)*, John Hurt *(Jesus)*, Jackie Mason, Ronny Graham *(Jews)*, Phil Leeds *(Chief Monk)*, Jack Carter *(Rat Vendor)*, Jan Murray *(Nothing Vendor)*, Spike Milligan *(M. Rimbaud)*, John Hillerman *(Rich Man)*, Sidney Lassick *(Applecore Vendor)*, Jonathan Cecil *(Poppinjay)*, Andrew Sachs *(Gerard)*, Fiona Richmond *(Queen)*, Nigel Hawthorne *(Official)*, John Gavin *(Marche)*, Rusty Goff *(LeMuff)*, J.J. Barry, Sammy Shore, Michael Champion, Earl Finn, Leigh French, Richard Karron, Susette Carroll, Suzanne Kent, Molly Basler, Christine Dickinson, Deborah Dawes, Lisa Sohm, Michele Drake, Jeana Tomasino, Lisa Welch, Janis Schmitt, Heidi Sorenson, Karen Morton, Kathy Collins, Lori Sutton, Lou Mulford, Henry Kaiser, Zale Kessler, Anthony Messina, Howard Mann, Sandy Helberg, Mitchell Bock, Gilbert Lee, Eddie Heim, David Chavez, John Frayer, Dennon Rawles, Rick Mason, Stan Mazin, Dom Salinaro, Jim Roddy, Ted Sprague, Spencer Henderson, Bill Armstrong, John King, Bella Emberg, Geoffrey Larder, George Lane Cooper, Stephanie Marrian, Royce Mills, Mike Cottrell, Gerald Stadden, Monica Teama, Cleo Rocos, Jilly Johnson, Barry Levinson.

Brooks usually relies on a carload of writers to help him create his oddball comedies. This time, he wrote the picture alone and it suffers for it. An episodic comedy that goes beyond no taste into bad taste, Brooks reaches into his bag of scatological tricks and comes up wanting. Filled with cameos from many superior comics and comic actors, nothing seems to help, and many of the elaborate gags fizzle and sputter as bad as the cowboys did in the famous campfire scene from Brooks' BLAZING SADDLES. There are five major portions of this film: "The Dawn Of Man," "The Stone Age," "The Spanish Inquisition," "The Bible," and "The Future." He even uses some of the hoariest old jokes ever as he portrays a waiter at The Last Supper and asks the diners if they want separate checks. His sequence on The French Revolution seems to go on longer than the revolution did (almost 25 minutes) and doesn't compare to the same material when it was handled in START THE REVOLUTION WITHOUT ME. There doesn't seem to be any group that Brooks leaves unscathed as he takes pot-shots at Christians, Jews, homosexuals, and just about anyone else, in his headlong attempt to cover too many topics. A dishevelment that could have been marvelous had care been attached instead of aiming for low blows. Some of the pals he cast were Mazursky (the director), Burton (the well-known comedy writer), Hefner, McCormick (actor/writer/gourmand), Clark and DeLuca (who co-wrote HIGH ANXIETY with him), comics Greene, Caesar, Gould, Carter, Mason, Graham (who co-wrote TO BE OR NOT TO BE with Brooks) and Gavin, the U.S. Ambassador to Mexico under Ronald Reagan. They should all be ashamed they took the jobs.

p,d&w, Mel Brooks; ph, Woody Omens (Panavision, DeLuxe Color) (French Revolution Sequence, Paul Wilson); m, John Morris; ed, John Howard; prod d, Harold Michelson (French Revolution Sequence, Stuart Craig); art d, Norman Newberry; set d, Daniel Maltese, Gre Pickrell, Robert Goldstein, Robert W. Welch III, Daniel Gluck, Richard McKenzie, Antony Mondello; cos, Patricia Norris; spec eff, Albert J. Whitlock; ch, Alan Johnson; m/l, "The Inquisition," Brooks, Ronny Graham.

Comedy **Cas.** **(PR:C-O MPAA:R)**

HIT** (1973) 134m PAR c

Billy Dee Williams *(Nick Allen)*, Richard Pryor *(Mike Willmer)*, Paul Hampton *(Barry Strong)*, Gwen Welles *(Sherry Nielson)*, Warren Kemmerling *(Dutch Schiller)*, Janet Brandt *(Ida)*, Sid Melton *(Herman)*, David Hall *(Carlin)*, Todd Martin *(Crosby)*, Norman Burton *(The Director)*, Jenny Astruc *(Mme. Frelou)*, Yves Barsacq *(Romain)*, Jean-Claude Bercq *(Jean-Baptiste)*, Henri Cogan *(Bornou)*, Pierre Collet *(Zero)*, Robert Lombard *(Mr. Frelou)*, Paul Mercey *(Jyras)*, Malka Ribovska *(Mme. Orissa)*, Richard Saint-Bris *(Monteca)*, Tina Andrews *(Jeannie Allen)*, Frank Christi *(Judge)*, Mwako Cumbuka *(Boyfriend)*, Lee Duncan *(Pusher)*, Janear Hines *(Esther)*, Jerry Jones *(The Weasel)*.

Williams stars as a federal agent who returns from an assignment only to discover that his daughter has died from a drug overdose. Williams jumps in to find those responsible and learns that a giant, well-organized drug smuggling operation, based in Marseilles, has been shipping huge amounts of illicit materials into the states. Shocked and angered that his own government won't help him smash the dope dealers' operation, Williams organizes his own band of guerrillas to combat the influx of drugs. This of course leads to the action-packed climax of the film, but not before some interesting characterizations from performers like Pryor, Welles, and Brandt are allowed screen time.

p, Harry Korshak; d, Sidney J. Furie; w, Alan R. Trustman, David M. Wolf; ph, John A. Alonzo (Technicolor); m, Lalo Schifrin; ed, Argyle Nelson; art d, George Petitot; set d, Leonard Maizola; spec eff, Joe Lombardi.

Crime **(PR:O MPAA:R)**

HIT AND RUN* (1957) 85m UA bw

Cleo Moore *(Julie)*, Hugo Haas *(Gus)*, Vince Edwards *(Frank)*, Dolores Reed *(Miranda)*, Mari Lea *(Anita)*, Pat Goldin *(Undertaker)*, Carl Militaire *(Lawyer)*, Robert Cassidy *(Sheriff)*, Julie Mitchum *(Undertaker's Wife)*, John Zaremba *(Doctor)*, Steve Mitchel *(Bartender)*, Jan Englund *(Clara)*, Dick Paxton *(Waiter)*.

The story concerns Haas as a rich old man, who owns a combo junkyard-service station. He takes a much younger woman, Moore (this was her seventh Haas film), as his bride. He loses her to his youthful employee, Edwards, who involves Moore in a hit-and-run murder scheme to get Haas out of the way. Moore leaves Haas' estate with the old man's twin brother (also Haas), who was just released from prison. In a twist ending we discover that Haas' convict brother was the one murdered, and Haas himself is still around to scare the truth out of the murderous lovers. Ella Mae Morse sings "What Good'll It Do Me." Another brooding all-Haas production.

p,d&w, Hugo Haas (based on a story by Herbert Q. Phillips); ph, Walter Strenge; m, Frank Steininger; ed, Stefan Arnsten; md, Steininger; art d, Rudi Feld; m/l, Steininger.

Crime **(PR:C MPAA:NR)**

HIT AND RUN** (1982) 94m Movie Making/Comworld c

Paul Perri *(David Marks)*, Claudia Cron *(Diana Douglas)*, Will Lee *(Joseph Kahn)*, Bart Braverman *(Jerry Ramundi)*.

This slowly paced mystery has school teacher and part-time cabbie Perri haunted by a past tragedy. His wife was killed by a hit-and-run driver. Because of this, he is left to raise his two sons alone. Perri is driving a cab in New York to make some extra cash when he picks up a mysterious woman, Cron. He drives her to a house in a small town and after waiting for her, drives her back to New York. He repeats his mysterious trip three times, but the third time Cron doesn't return to the cab. Perri breaks into the house and finds a dead man—whom he recognizes as the hit-and-run driver—but no Cron. It seems Perri has been set up for the crime. He is about to turn himself in when an old amateur sleuth friend, Lee, promises to get to the bottom of it. Perri asks the help of fellow cabbies to find Cron, but Lee eventually solves the mystery in a twist ending.

p&d, Charles Braverman; w, Don Enright (based on novel *80 Dollars To Stamford*); ph, Tony Mitchell; m, Brad Fiedel; prod d, Paul Eads; ed, Dale Beldin.

Crime Cas. (PR:C-O MPAA:NR)

HIT MAN zero (1972) 90m Penelope/MGM c

Bernie Casey *(Tyrone Tackett)*, Pamela Grier *(Gozelda)*, Lisa Moore *(Laural)*, Bhetty Waldron *(Irvelle)*, Sam Laws *(Sherwood)*, Candy All *(Rochelle Tackett)*, Don Diamond *(Theotis)*, Edmund Cambridge *(Zito)*, Bob Harris *(Shag)*, Rudy Challenger *(Julius)*, Tracy Ann-King *(Nita)*, Christopher Joy *(Leon)*, Roger E. Mosley *(Baby Huey)*.

Casey stars as a small-time gangster connected with a porno ring who's out to find the hoods who killed his brother. Casey knows his brother was murdered while seeking revenge for the filmed rape of his young daughter, All. He soon worms his way through the seedy underworld of pornography with his friend Moore, and has a fling with aspiring porno star, Grier. A sleazy remake of GET CARTER.

p, Gene Corman; d&w, George Armitage (based on the novel, *Jack's Return Home* by Ted Lewis); ph, Andrew Davis (Metrocolor); m, H.B. Barnum; ed, Morton Tubor; art d, Lynn Griffin.

Crime/Action (PR:O MPAA:R)

HIT PARADE, THE** (1937) 77m REP bw

Frances Langford *(Ruth Allison)*, Phil Regan *(Pete Garland)*, Louise Henry *(Monica Barrett)*, Pert Kelton *(Eadie White)*, Edward Brophy *(Mulrooney)*, Max Terhune *(Rusty Callahan)*, Inez Courtney *(Tillie)*, Monroe Owsley *(Teddy Leeds)*, Pierre Watkin *(J.B. Hawley)*, Stanley Fields *(Bedtime Story Man)*, Johnny Arthur *(Success Story Teller)*, J. Farrell MacDonald *(Sgt. O'Hara)*, William Demarest *(Parole Officer)*, George Givot *(Herman)*, Sammy White *(Dancer)*, Paul Garner, Sam Wolfe, Richard Hakins *(Gentle Maniacs)*, Yvonne Manoff, Mildred Winston, Barbara Johnston *(Tic Toc Girls)*, Carl Hoff and Band, Duke Ellington and Band, Eddy Duchin and Band, Molasses and January, Pick and Pat, Al Pearce and Gang, Ed Thorgersen, Voice of Experience, Oscar and Elmer.

This was Republic's attempt to come out with a series of musicals similar to Paramount's successful BIG BROADCAST series, but there is little comparison. The thin story has agent Regan trying to sell a new singing sensation, Langford, to spite a rich society girl, Henry. Regan first introduced Henry to radio, and having become a success, she has abandoned him. The search for talent and the radio broadcasts allow the various acts to do their things. Songs include "Sweet Heartache" (Ned Washington, Sammy Stept); "Hail Alma Mater" (Stept); "Last Night I Dreamed Of You," "You'd Like It," "I'll Reach For A Star," "The Lady Wants To Dance," "Was It Rain," "Love Is Good For Anything That Ails You" (Lou Handman, Walter Hirsch); "I've Got To Be A Rug Cutter" (Duke Ellington); "Jungle Rhythm." (See HIT PARADE series, Index.)

p, Nat Levin; d, Gus Meins; w, Bradford Ropes, Samuel Ornitz; ph, Ernest Miller; ed, Ernest Nims, Lester Orlebeck; md, Alberto Colombo; spec eff, John T. Coyle.

Musical (PR:A MPAA:NR)

HIT PARADE OF 1941** (1940) 83m REP bw

Kenny Baker *(David Farraday)*, Frances Langford *(Pat Abbott)*, Hugh Herbert *(Ferdinand Farraday)*, Mary Boland *(Emily Potter)*, Ann Miller *(Annabelle Potter)*, Patsy Kelly *(Judy Abbott)*, Phil Silvers *(Charles Moore)*, Sterling Holloway *(Soda Clerk)*, Donald MacBride *(Harrison)*, Barnett Parker *(Mr. Pasley)*, Franklin Pangborn *(Carter)*, Six Hits and a Miss, Borrah Minevitch and his Harmonica Rascals *(Themselves)*.

Once again Republic attempted to emulate the BIG BROADCAST films and came up short. This time Baker stars as the nephew of thrift shop owner Herbert, who sells his business and buys a rinky-dink radio station with a two-watt frequency. Seeking sponsors, Herbert taps department store owner Boland, who agrees to lend some money to the effort only if her aspiring singer-dancer daughter Miller is allowed to inflict her talents on the listening public. While Miller is great with the tap shoes, she can't carry a tune to save her life, which necessitates hiring songstress Langford to overdub Miller's voice. Langford and Baker soon fall for each other and the usual complications follow. Songs include: "Who Am I?" "Swing Low Sweet Rhythm," "In The Cool Of The Evening," "Make Yourself At Home" (Jule Styne, Walter Bullock); "Dinah" (John Stromberg, Robert B. Smith); "Margie" (Benny Davis, Con Conrad, J. Russell Robinson); "Mary Lou" (Abe Lyman, George Waggner, Robinson), "The Swap Shop Song," "The Trading Post," "Sally," "Ramona," and "Sweet Sue" (Styne, Bullock). (See HIT PARADE series, Index.)

p, Sol C. Siegel; d, John H. Auer; w, Bradford Ropes, F. Hugh Herbert, Maurice Leo (Sid Kuller, Ray Golden); ph, Jack Marta; m, Jule Styne; ed, Murray Seldeen; md, Cy Feuer; art d, John Victor Mackay; ch, Danny Dare.

Musical (PR:A MPAA:NR)

HIT PARADE OF 1943½** (1943) 90m REP bw
(AKA: CHANGE OF HEART)

John Carroll *(Rick Farrell)*, Susan Hayward *(Jill Wright)*, Gail Patrick *(Toni Jarrett)*, Eve Arden *(Belinda Wright)*, Melville Cooper *(Bradley Cole)*, Walter Catlett *(J. MacClellan Davis)*, Mary Treen *(Janie)*, Tom Kennedy *(Westinghouse)*, Astrid Allwyn *(Joyce)*, Tim Ryan *(Brownie)*, Jack Williams, The Harlem Sandman, Dorothy Dandridge, Pops and Louie, Music Maids, 3 Cheers, Chinita, Golden Gate Quartet, Freddy Martin and Orchestra, Count Basie and Orchestra, Ray McKinley and Orchestra.

Republic finally made big box office with this entry in its HIT PARADE series. This film has a fine blend of story and musical numbers and featured the song "A Change of Heart" (Harold Adamson, Jule Styne), which was nominated for an Oscar. The simple tale tells of a washed-up song writer, Carroll, who at first steals a tune written by Hayward. She confronts him with the theft but he begs her to ghost-write for him. She agrees, hoping that when he gets famous with her songs, she will expose his deceit and embarrass him. Instead, they fall in love and sing their way to happiness. Songs include: "Take A Chance," "A Change Of Heart," "Who Took Me Home Last Night," "Tam Boom Bah," "That's How To Write A Song," "Harlem Sandman," "Do These Old Eyes Deceive Me" (Adamson, Styne); "Yankee Doodle Tank" (Andy Razaf, J.C. Johnson), "Nobody's Sweetheart" (Elmer Schoebel, Ernie Erdman, Gus Kahn, Billy Meyers). (See HIT PARADE series, Index.)

p, Albert J. Cohen; d, Albert S. Rogell; w, Frank Gill, Jr.; ph, Jack Marta; m, Marlin Skiles; ed, Thomas Richards; md, Walter Scharf, Jule Styne, Harold Adamson; art d, Russell Kimball; ch, Nick Castle.

Musical (PR:A MPAA:NR)

HIT PARADE OF 1947** (1947) 90m REP bw

Eddie Albert *(Kip Walker)*, Constance Moore *(Ellen Baker)*, Joan Edwards *(Joan)*, Gil Lamb *(Eddie Paige)*, Bill Goodwin *(Rod Huntley)*, William Frawley *(Harry Holmes)*, Richard Lane *(Serial Director)*, Frank Fenton *(Mr. Bonardi)*, Ralph Sanford *(Small)*, Frank Scannell *(Sammy)*, Knox Manning, Del Sharbutt *(Announcers)*, Albert Ruiz *(Specialty Dancer)*, Harland Tucker *(Cooper)*, Chester Clute *(Assistant in Radio Station)*, Woody Herman Orchestra, Roy Rogers and Trigger, Bob Nolan, Sons of the Pioneers.

Another entry in Republic's HIT PARADE series sees Albert and a trio of other performers (Moore, Edwards and Lamb), form a musical nightclub act. Albert, a songwriter, falls in love with Moore. Their act is a hit and they are soon signed to a Hollywood contract. When Moore goes on to a movie career, the rest of the act go their separate ways. Of course, there are the usual song numbers and specialty acts, plus a special appearance by Roy Rogers and Trigger. Songs include, "Chiquita From Santa Anita," "Is There Anyone Here From Texas?" "I Guess I'll Have That Dream Right Away," "Couldn't Be More In Love," "The Customer is Always Wrong," "The Cats Are Going to The Dogs" (Harold Adamson, Jimmy McHugh); "Brooklyn Buckaroos" (Foster Carling); "Out California Way" (Tim Spencer). (See HIT PARADE series, Index.)

p&d, Frank McDonald; w, Mary Loos (based on a story by Parke Levy); ph, John Alton; ed, Tony Martinelli; md, Cy Feuer; art d, Frank Hotaling; ch, Fanchon.

Musical (PR:A MPAA:NR)

HIT PARADE OF 1951** (1950) 85m REP bw

John Carroll *(Joe Blake/Eddie Paul)*, Marie McDonald *(Michele)*, Estelita Rodriguez *(Chicquita)*, Frank Fontaine *(Bingo)*, Grant Withers *(Smokey)*, Mikhail Rasumny *(The Professor)*, Steve Flagg *(Chuck)*, Paul Cavanagh *(Two-to-One Thompson)*, Edward Gargan *(Garrity)*, Gus Schilling *(Studio Guide)*, Rose Rosett *(Rose)*, Wade Crosby *(Jake)*, Duke York *(Cal)*, Al Murphy *(George)*, Firehouse Five Plus Two, Bobby Ramos Band.

Gambler Carroll opens the film by losing $200,000 to fellow card-shark Withers who gives him 48 hours to cough up the money. Desperate, Carroll tumbles across his exact double (also Carroll) who is a crooner for the "Hit Parade" and switches roles with him. Gambler Carroll begins to enjoy the adoration of his double's female fans (something the effeminate Carroll apparently didn't take advantage of), while crooner Carroll begins to rack up lots of chips at the gambling tables. Eventually, after both men have learned more about themselves from the experience, they return to their normal roles. Songs include: "Square Dance Samba," "You're So Nice," "How Would I Know?" "Wishes Come True," "You Don't Know The Other Side Of Me" (Al Rinker, Floyd Huddleston); "Boca Chica" (Sy Miller, Betty Garrett). (See HIT PARADE series, Index.)

p&d, John H. Auer; w, Elizabeth Reinhardt, Aubrey Wisberg, Lawrence Kimble (based on an original story by Wisberg); ph, Reggie Lanning; m, R. Dale Butts; ed, Harry Keller; ch, Val Raset.

Musical (PR:A MPAA:NR)

HIT THE DECK** (1930) 93m RKO bw/c

Jack Oakie *(Bilge)*, Polly Walker *(Looloo)*, Roger Gray *(Mat)*, Frank Woods *(Pat)*, Harry Sweet *(Bunny)*, Marguerita Padula *(Lavinia)*, June Clyde *(Toddy)*, Ethel Clayton *(Mrs. Payne)*, George Ovey, Wallace MacDonald, Nate Slot, Andy Clark, Dell Henderson, Charles Sullivan.

Based on the 1927 Broadway hit that ran 352 consecutive performances, HIT THE DECK, is a lacklustre rendition of the original show. This was RKO's second attempt at a big musical, but they didn't have the success that their first effort, RIO RITA did. Even the 33 percent two-color Technicolor sequences seemed of little help. The meager story concerns a sailor, Oakie, and the owner of a seaside cafe, Walker, who fall in love with him. The small plot seems an excuse to stage many musical numbers. Songs include "Sometimes I'm Happy," "Hallalujah," "Why, Oh Why" (Vincent Youmans, Clifford Grey, Leo Robin); "Keeping Myself For You," (Youmans, Sidney Clare); "More Than You Know," (Youmans, Edward Elisco); "Billy Rose" "I Know That You Know" (Youmans, Anne Caldwell), "Sez You—Sez Me" (Harry Tierney). Remade in 1936 as FOLLOW THE FLEET, with Fred Astaire, and in 1955 under the same title.

d&w, Luther Reed (based on the play by Herbert Fields); ph, Robert Kurrle (color sequence in Technicolor); ch, Pearl Eaton.

Musical (PR:A MPAA:NR)

HIT THE DECK*** (1955) 112m Metro c

Jane Powell *(Susan Smith)*, Tony Martin *(Chief Boatswain's Mate William F. Clark)*, Debbie Reynolds *(Carol Pace)*, Walter Pidgeon *(Rear Adm. Daniel Xavier Smith)*, Vic Damone *(Rico Ferrari)*, Gene Raymond *(Wendell Craig)*, Ann Miller *(Ginger)*, Russ Tamblyn *(Danny Xavier Smith)*, J. Carroll Naish *(Mr. Peroni)*, Kay Armen *(Mrs. Ottavio Ferrari)*, Richard Anderson *(Lt. Jackson)*, Jane Darwell *(Jenny)*, Alan King, Henry Slate *(Shore Patrol)*, Jubalaires *(Themselves)*, Frank Reynolds *(Dancer)*.

The familiar "three sailors on leave" plot line gets a shot in the arm in HIT THE DECK due its outstanding cast, good production numbers, and nice visuals. Martin, Tamblyn and Damone play the three swabbies who venture into San Francisco in search of love. While Tamblyn and Damone must fulfill family obligations (Tamblyn visits his father Pidgeon, an admiral, and Damone goes to see his mother), they all find time to get embroiled in romance. Songs include "Hallelujah," "Lucky Bird," "Leo-Leo," "Join the Navy," "Why Oh Why" (Leo Robin, Clifford Grey, Vincent Youmans); "A Kiss Or Two," "The Lady from the Bayou" (Robin, Youmans); "Sometimes I'm Happy" (Grey, Youmans, Irving Caesar); "I Know That You Know" (Youmans, Anne Caldwell); "More Than You Know" (Youmans, Billy Rose, Edward Eliscu); "Keepin' Myself for You" (Youmans, Sidney Clare); "Ciribiribee" (A. Pestalozza).

p, Joe Pasternak; d, Roy Rowland; w, Sonya Levien, William Ludwig (based on the musical play by Herbert Fields and "Shore Leave" by Hubert Osborne); ph, George Folsey (CinemaScope, Eastmancolor); ed, John McSweeney, Jr.; md, George Stoll; art d, Cedric Gibbon, Paul Groesse; cos, Helen Rose; ch, Hermes Pan.

Musical **(PR:AA MPAA:NR)**

HIT THE HAY*½ (1945) 75m COL bw

Judy Canova *(Judy Stevens)*, Ross Hunter *(Ted Barton)*, Fortunio Bonanova *(Mario Alvini)*, Doris Merrick *(Sally)*, Gloria Holden *(Mimi Valdez)*, Francis Pierlot *(Roger Barton)*, Grady Sutton *(Wilbur Whittlesey)*, Louis Mason *(Frisby)*, Paul Stanton *(J. Bellingham Parks)*, Clyde Pillmore *(Mayor Blackburn)*, Maurice Cass *(Prompter)*, Luis Alberni *(French Professor)*, Cosmo Sardo *(Makeup Man)*, Charles Marsh, Billy Snyder *(Reporters)*, Victor Travers *(Stage Hand)*, Buster Brodie *(Bald Man)*, Jack Frack *(Camera Man)*, William Newell *(Cab Driver)*.

Mindless Canova romp which sees the singing hillbilly sweetheart discovered while milking a cow by an operatic agent, Hunter, who takes her to the big city to perform for the highbrows. Canova doesn't take to the acting requirements of the role however, and Hunter is forced to hire a look-alike actress (also Canova) to perform onstage, while the first Canova belts out the arias in the wings. Tiring of the snooty opera, Canova decides to perform a grass-roots version of Rossini's "William Tell" which she dubs "Tillie Tell" and, of course, it turns out to be a great success. Musical numbers include passages from Flotow's "Martha" and Rossini's "William Tell."

p, Ted Richmond; d, Del Lord; w, Richard Weil, Charles R. Marion; ph, James Van Trees; ed, Viola Lawrence; art d, Perry Smith.

Musical/Comedy **(PR:A MPAA:NR)**

HIT THE ICE*** (1943) 81m UNIV bw (AKA: OH DOCTOR)

Bud Abbott *(Flash Fulton)*, Lou Costello *("Tubby" McCoy)*, Ginny Simms *(Marcia Manning)*, Patric Knowles *(Dr. Bill Elliot)*, Elyse Knox *(Peggy Osborne)*, Joseph Sawyer *(Buster)*, Marc Lawrence *(Phil)*, Sheldon Leonard *("Silky Fellowsby")*, Johnny Long *(Himself)*, Joseph Crehan *(2nd Conductor)*, Edward Gargan *(Cop)*, Pat Flaherty *(Police Lieutenant)*, Eddie Dunn *(Bit Cop)*, Dorothy Vaughn *(Nurse)*, Minerva Urecal *(Wife)*, Mantan Moreland *(Redcap)*, Bobby Barber *(Porter on Train)*, Wade Boteler *(1st Conductor)*, Ken Christy *(Fire Chief)*, Billy Wayne *(Man in Bed)*, Rebel Randall *(Woman in Bed)*, Cordelia Campbell *(Skater)*, Eddie Parker *(Ambulance Driver)*, Helen Young, Gene Williams, The Four Teens, The Fifty Dancing Beauties, Virginia Sale, Harry Strang.

A good Abbott and Costello film that has many laughs and sees the boys in the prime of their career. The story has them as a couple of press photographers who get implicated in a bank robbery. They evade arrest and head west to Sun Valley. Arriving with them is Simms, a singer, and the Johnny Long Orchestra, who have an engagement at a winter resort. The boys get jobs as waiters and try to elude bank robber Leonard and his two thugs who followed them out there. Many humorous episodes occur in the ice and snow, until Abbott and Costello end up capturing the robbers and recouping the money. A very lavish sequence on ice was well done, as were four songs performed by Simms. Songs included, "I'm Like a Fish Out Of Water," "Happiness Bound," "I'd Like to Set You To Music," and "Slap Polka" (Harry Revel, Paul Francis Webster). (See ABBOTT & COSTELLO series, Index.)

p, Alex Gottlieb; d, Charles Lamont; w, Robert Lees, Frederic I. Rinaldo, John Grant (based on a story by True Boardman); ph, Charles Van Enger; ed, Frank Gross; md, Charles Previn; art d, John B. Goodman; ch, Sammy Lee (skating sequence, Harry Losee).

Musical/Comedy **(PR:A MPAA:NR)**

HIT THE ROAD*½ (1941) 61m UNIV bw

Gladys George *(Molly Ryan)*, Barton MacLane *(James J. Ryan, Alias Valentine)*, Billy Halop *(Tom)*, Huntz Hall *(Pig Grogan)*, Gabriel Dell *(String)*, Bernard Punsley *(Ape)*, Bobs Watson *(Pesty)*, Evelyn Ankers *(Patience Ryan)*, Charles Lang *(Paul Revere Smith)*, Walter Kingsford *(Col. Smith)*, Eily Malyon *(Cathy Crookshank)*, Edward Pawley *(Spike)*, John Harmon *(Creeper)*, Jess Lee Brooks *(Rufus)*, Charles Moore *(Martin)*, Shemp Howard *(Dingbat)*, Charles Sullivan *(Sullivan, the Chauffeur)*, Grace Hayle *(Mrs. Hickridge [cut from the film])*, Lee Moore *(2nd Guard)*, Hally Chester *(Trusty)*, Kernan Cripps *(Guard)*, Ernie Stanton *(O'Brien, the First Guard)*.

A lame comedy that sees some of the "Dead End Kids" signing with Universal to form "The Little Tough Guys." This film had very little merit and should have been a good reason to put an end to the often-insipid series, but it would survive another 10 years. The story sees the tough kids once again getting out of a reformatory. A former gangster is trying to straighten them out, but the boys don't seem to pay him much attention. When one of their fathers gets murdered, the boys show their true colors by going undercover in high society to find the murderer. (See BOWERY BOYS series, Index.)

p, Ken Goldsmith; d, Joe May; w, Robert Lee Johnson, Brenda Weisberg (based on a story by Johnson); ph, Jerome Ash; ed, Bernard Burton; md, H. J. Salter; art d, Jack Otterman; set d, R. A. Gausman.

Comedy **(PR:A MPAA:NR)**

HIT THE SADDLE** (1937) 61m REP bw

Robert Livingston *(Stony Brooks)*, Ray Corrigan *(Tucson Smith)*, Max Terhune *(Lullaby Joslin)*, Rita Cansino [Hayworth], *(Rita)*, J. P. McGowan *(Rance McGowan)*, Edward Cassidy *(Sheriff Miller)*, Sammy McKim *(Tim Miller)*, Yakima Canutt *(Buck)*, Harry Tenbrook *(Joe Harvey)*, Robert Smith *(Hank)*, Ed Boland *(Pete)*, George Plues *(Hechman)*, Jack Kirk, Russ Powell, Bob Burns *(Ranchers)*, Volcano *(Stallion)*, Allan Cavan *(Judge)*, George Morrell, Wally West *(Patrons)*, Budd Buster *(Drunk)*, Kernan Cripps *(Bartender)*.

Livingston, Corrigan, and Terhune in yet another of the long-running "Three Mesquiteers" oaters. Nineteen-year-old Rita Hayworth, billed as Rita Cansino, makes an early screen appearance as a saloon songstress and gets to perform an original song, "Winding The Trail," with Livingston. The story tells of a bad cattle rancher, McGowan, who paints his horse to look like a wild stallion in order to rustle wild horses out of a federally protected area. When local sheriff Cassidy investigates, McGowan and his men trample him to death and blame it on a different wild stallion. The three heroes prove that the wild horse is innocent, and McGowan dies under the hooves of his own horse. Famous stuntman Canutt plays one of the rustlers, and does some fine stunt work. It is interesting to note that Livingston and Corrigan had conflicting personalities which caused Livingston to eventually leave the series. He was replaced by a young John Wayne who did five more Mesquiteer films before riding off to better things. (See THREE MESQUITEERS series, Index.)

p, Nat Levine; d, Mack V. Wright; w, Oliver Drake (based on characters created by William Colt MacDonald); ph, Jack Marta; m, Alberto Colombo; ed, Lester Orleback; art d, John Victor Mackay; m/l, Drake, Sam H. Stept.

Western **Cas.** **(PR:A MPAA:NR)**

HITCH HIKE LADY** (1936) 77m REP bw

Alison Skipworth *(Mrs. Amelia Blake)*, Mae Clark *(Judith Martin)*, Arthur Treacher *(Mortimer Wingate)*, Jimmy Ellison *(Jimmy Peyton)*, Warren Hymer *(Chuck Regan)*, Beryl Mercer *(Mrs. Payne)*, J. Farrell MacDonald *(Judge Hale)*, Lionel Belmore *(Green-grocer)*, Otis Harlan *(Mayor)*, Charles C. Wilson *(Mike)*, Wilbur Mack *(Wilbur)*, Clay Clement *(Warden)*, George Hayes *(Miner)*, Dell Henderson *(Williams)*, Harold Waldridge *(Oswald Brown)*, Christian Rub *(Farmer)*.

Plenty of pathos and humor in the story of an elderly English housekeeper, Skipworth, who saves her hard-earned money to go to the U.S. to visit her son whom she believes is doing well. The truth is that he is imprisoned in San Quentin. Skipworth is accompanied on her cross-country journey by a young girl, Clark, a young man who befriends them both, Ellison, a promoter, Treacher, and his tough partner, Hymer. The four know the truth about Skipworth's son and go to extremes to keep it from her. A contest set up by Treacher enables him to give some happiness to the unsuspecting Skipworth.

p, Nat Levine; d, Aubrey Scotto; w, Gordon Rigby, Lester Cole (based on a story by Wallace MacDonald); ph, Ernest Miller, Jack Marta.

Drama **(PR:A MPAA:NR)**

HITCH HIKE TO HEAVEN* (1936) 63m CHES bw

Henrietta Crosman *(Deborah Delaney)*, Herbert Rawlinson *(Melville De La Ney)*, Russell Gleason *(Daniel Delaney)*, Polly Ann Young *(Jerry Daley)*, Al Shean *(Herman Blatz)*, Anita Page *(Claudia Revelle)*, Syd Saylor *(Spud)*, Harry Harvey *(Gabby)*, Harry Holman *(Philmore Tubbs)*, Ethel Sykes *(Kitty O'Brien)*, Lela Bliss *(Nadia De La Ney)*, Crauford Kent *(Edgar)*, John Dilson *(Charlie Reed)*.

A poorly scripted and boring film about a successful actor, Rawlinson, whose career is nearly ruined by a divorce. Young is a film extra who yearns for her big chance at stardom in movies, but becomes innocently named in Rawlinson's wife's divorce action. His mother is portrayed by Crosman, who is the leader of a group of repertory players that Young joins up with. The divorce causes quite a commotion in the film world, and for awhile it looks as if Rawlinson's career is over. All ends on a happy note as his star status is restored, and Young gets her big break.

p, Maury M. Cohen; d, Frank R. Strayer; w, Robert Ellis, Helen Logan; ph, M.A. Andersen; ed, Roland D. Reed.

Drama **(PR:A MPAA:NR)**

HITCH IN TIME, A*** (1978, Brit.) 57m Eyeline/Children's Film c

Michael McVey, Pheona McLellan, Patrick Troughton, Jeff Rawle, Sorcha Cusack, Ronnie Brody.

This okay kiddie film stars Troughton (once a "Dr. Who") as a bumbling scientist who sends youngsters McVey and McLellan back through various periods of time where they meet up with their ancestors. Scripted by Clarke who also gave us the Ealing classics THE LAVENDER HILL MOB and THE TITFIELD THUNDERBOLT.

p, Harold Orton; d, Jan Darnley-Smith; w, T.E.B. Clarke; ph, Tommy Fletcher.

Fantasy/Children **(PR:AA MPAA:NR)**

HITCHHIKE TO HAPPINESS½** (1945) 71m REP bw

Al Pearce *(Kipling "Kippy" Ellis)*, Dale Evans *(Alice Chase)*, Brad Taylor *(Joe Mitchell)*, William Frawley *(Sandy Hill)*, Jerome Cowan *(Tony Riggs)*, Willy Trenk *(Ladislaus Prenska)*, Arlene Harris *(Dolly Ward)*, Joyce Compton *(Joan Randall)*, Maude Eburne *(Mrs. Randall)*, Irving Bacon *(Dennis Colby)*, Lynn Romer, Jeanne Romer *(Romer Twins)*.

Pearce plays a would-be playwright who takes a job as a waiter in a small New York City restaurant frequented by show biz folk in hopes of getting his big break.

Though most of the patrons regard Pearce's ambition as a pipe-dream, he is supported enthusiastically by Taylor, an aspiring songwriter, and Evans, a waitress-turned-singer who has taken a big-time radio job in Hollywood. When Evans stops by in the "Big Apple" to say hello, she and the other patrons decide to pull a fast one on pompous producer Trenk and make him believe that Pearce has written a sure-fire box office hit. Trenk decides to produce the play starring Evans, and to everybody's surprise (except the viewer) the show is a major success. Evans sings: "Hitchhike To Happiness," "For You And Me," "Sentimental," and "My Pushover Heart" (Kim Gannon, Walter Kent).

p, Donald H. Brown; d, Joseph Santley; w, Jack Townley (based on original by Manny Seff, Jerry Horwin); ph, Jack Marta; ed, Fred Allen.

Musical **(PR:A MPAA:NR)**

HITCH-HIKER, THE*** (1953) 71m Filmakers/RKO bw

Edmond O'Brien *(Roy Collins)*, Frank Lovejoy *(Gilbert Bowen)*, William Talman *(Emmett Myers)*, Jose Torvay *(Capt. Alvarado)*, Sam Hayes *(Sam)*, Wendell Niles *(Wendell)*, Jean Del Val *(Inspector General)*, Clark Howat *(Government Agent)*, Natividad Vacio *(Jose)*, Rodney Bell *(William Johnson)*, Nacho Galindo *(Proprietor)*, Martin Garralaga *(Bartender)*, Tony Roux *(Gas Station Owner)*, Jerry Lawrence *(News Broadcaster)*, Felipe Turich, Joe Dominguez *(Men)*, Rose Turich *(Woman)*, Orlando Veltran, George Navarro *(Salesmen)*, June Dinneen *(Waitress)*, Al Ferrara *(Gas Station Attendant)*, Henry Escalante *(Mexican Guard)*, Taylor Flaniken *(Mexican Cop)*, Wade Crosby *(Joe, Bartender)*, Kathy Riggins *(Child)*, Gordon Barnes *(Hendrickson)*, Ed Hinton *(Chief of Police)*, Larry Hudson *(FBI Agent)*.

A perilous and grim *film noir* entry—noted as being the only one of the genre ever directed by a woman, Lupino—THE HITCH-HIKER offers three outstanding performances by victims O'Brien and Lovejoy and killer Talman. O'Brien and Lovejoy leave their families to go on a fishing trip and, en route, make the mistake of picking up hitchhiker Talman who suddenly threatens them with a gun and holds them hostage, forcing the two men to drive him through the southwestern desert and into Mexico. He is a wanted killer and intends to get to Baja, California and leave by boat to points unknown. Talman is no dim-witted slayer—he has already killed a number of people—but a sadistic and utterly cunning psychopathic killer. He toys with the men, first offering them opportunities to overwhelm him, then to escape. At every turn, he second-guesses their desperate moves and is waiting for them with a gun. Slowly, his background is revealed to them. He has been an abused child and early learned to hate humanity. Moreover, Talman has a permanent affliction which strikes permanent terror into O'Brien and Lovejoy; he has an eye which never closes. "So you never know if I'm sleeping or not—pretty scary, isn't it?" When he does appear to fall asleep at a campfire site one night the men try to move in on him but he has been faking and suddenly holds the gun on them, almost killing them both. Just as Talman is about to do the pair in, one of them leaves his wedding ring on the pump of a Mexican gas station, which alerts police who save O'Brien and Lovejoy, and capture Talman. Lupino's direction is superb as she slowly builds the tension, cleverly selecting her setup shots in remote desert areas. She was the only female directing films at the time and she proved her enormous talent with this taut little thriller. Talman's role is based upon the real-life exploits of mass murderer William Cook, who slaughtered six people in 1950-51 before Mexican police captured him; he was executed in San Quentin's gas chamber on December 12, 1951. The story, taken right out of the headlines, was written by Daniel Mainwaring, who had written INVASION OF THE BODY SNATCHERS. He did not receive credit because of his left-leaning politics during the HUAC witchhunts and because Howard Hughes, then running RKO, refused to give "radicals" any credit for film work.

p, Collier Young; d, Ida Lupino; w, Young, Lupino, Robert Joseph (based on a story by Daniel Mainwaring [uncredited]); ph, Nicholas Musuraca; m, Leith Stevens; ed, Douglas Stewart; md, Constantin Bakaleinikoff; art d, Albert S. D'Agostino, Walter E. Keller; spec eff, Harold E. Wellman.

Crime Drama **(PR:C-O MPAA:NR)**

HITCHHIKERS, THE zero (1972) 91m Entertainment Ventures c

Misty Rowe *(Maggie)*, Norman Klar *(Benson)*, Linda Avery *(Diane)*, Tammy Gibbs *(Karen)*, Kathy Stutsman *(Jinx)*, Mary Thatcher *(Brook)*, Denny Nichols *(Truck Driver/Farmer)*, Ted Ziegler *(Church Deacon)*, Efrem Dockter *(Store Manager)*, Lou Jofferd *(Doctor)*, Blue McKenzie *(Reb)*, Lee Morley *(Used Car Salesman)*, Jim Sherwood *(Nemo)*.

This strange independent exploitation film is heavy on nudity, sex, and violence. It tells the story of an "easy" girl, Rowe, who left home because she was pregnant. She finds herself on a hippie ranch led by Klar, who shares his hideout with his "family" of four female lovers—Avery, Gibbs, Stutsman, and Thatcher. The plot centers around the girls hitchhiking on a deserted highway in their underwear in order to attract male drivers and rob them. Rowe and Klar with his femme accomplices romp through the film holding up male drivers, having sex, and goofing off before exiting on an old schoolbus bound for Los Angeles. Don't pick this one up.

p,d&w, Ferd Sebastian, Beverly Sebastian (based on a story by Ann Cawthorne); ph, Ferd Sebastian (Movielab Color); m, Danny Cohen; ed, Jeremy Hoenack.

Crime/Action **Cas.** **(PR:O MPAA:R)**

HITOKIRI (SEE: TENCHU! 1970, Jap.)

HITLER*½ (1962) 107m Three Crown/AA bw (AKA: WOMEN OF NAZI GERMANY)

Richard Basehart *(Adolf Hitler)*, Cordula Trantow *(Geli Raubal)*, Maria Emo *(Eva Braun)*, Martin Kosleck *(Joseph Goebbels)*, John Banner *(Gregor Strasser)*, Martin Brandt *(Gen. Heinz Guderian)*, John Wengraf *(Dr. Morell)*, William Sargent *(Lt. Col. Count von Stauffenberg)*, Narda Onyx *(Gretl Braun)*, Gregory Gay *(Field Marshal Erwin Rommel)*, Theodore Marcuse *(Julius Streicher)*, Berry Kroeger *(Ernst Roehm)*, Rick Traeger *(Heinrich Himmler)*, Lester Fletcher *(Lt. Edmond Heines)*, Celia Lovsky *(Frau Raubal)*, John Mitchum *(Hermann Goering)*, Albert Szabo *(Emil Maurice)*, G. Stanley Jones *(Martin Bormann)*, Walter Kohler *(Gen. Alfred Jodl)*, Carl Esmond *(Field Marshal Wilhelm Keitel)*, Norbert Schiller *(Schoenberg)*, Ted Knight *(Maj. Buch)*, Willy Kaufman *(Wagner)*, Sirry Steffen *(Anna)*, John Siegfried *(Schmidt)*, Otto Reichow *(SS Officer)*.

Basehart (in a dubious piece of casting) stars as you-know-who in this overly Freudian biography of the 20th century's infamous mass-murderer. The film basically concentrates on Hitler's sex life (or the lack thereof), with WW II given subplot status. In the end, the whole sorry character of the dictator is blamed on Basehart's adoration of his mother! An interesting but unintentionally funny film.

p, E. Charles Straus; d, Stuart Heisler; w, Sam Neuman, Straus; ph, Joseph Biroc; m, Hans J. Salter; ed, Walter Hannemann; art d, William Glasgow; set d, Frank Tuttle; spec eff, Daniel W. Hays.

Biography **Cas.** **(PR:C MPAA:NR)**

HITLER—DEAD OR ALIVE** (1942) 72m Charles House bw

Ward Bond *(Steve Maschik)*, Dorothy Tree *(Elsa)*, Warren Hymer *(Hans "Dutch" Havermann)*, Paul Fix *(Joe "The Book" Conway)*, Russell Hicks *(Samuel Thornton)*, Felix Basch *(Col. Hecht)*, Bob Watson *(Hitler)*, Bruce Edwards *(Johnny Stevens)*, Frederick Giermann *(Meyer)*, Kenneth Harlan *(Cutler)*, Faye Wall *(Greta)*, George Sorel *(Capt. Kuhn)*, Myra Marsh *(Miss Grange)*, Eddie Coke *(Jimmy)*, Jack Gardner *(Lou)*.

A story based on a real-offer by an American businessman of $1 million for the capture of Adolf Hitler. Bond, Hymer and Fix play three ex-residents of Alcatraz who attempt to collect the reward offered by Hicks. They hijack a truck, get into the Canadian air force, steal a bomber and fly to Germany. They disguise themselves as musicians sent to play at one of Hitler's parties and nearly pull off the feat. Pretty implausible, but still some fun.

p, Ben Judell; d, Nick Grinde; w, Sam Neumann, Karl Brown (based on a story by Neumann); ph, Paul Ivano.

War/Spy Drama **(PR:A MPAA:NR)**

HITLER, A FILM FROM GERMANY (SEE: OUR HITLER, 1977, Ger.)

HITLER GANG, THE½** (1944) 101m PAR bw

Robert Watson *(Adolf Hitler)*, Roman Bohnen *(Capt. Ernst Roehm)*, Martin Kosleck *(Joseph Goebbels)*, Victor Varconi *(Rudolph Hess)*, Luis Van Rooten *(Heinrich Himmler)*, Alexander Pope *(Hermann Goering)*, Ivan Triesault *(Pastor Niemoeller)*, Poldy Dur *(Geli Raubal)*, Helen Thimig *(Angela Raubal)*, Reinhold Schunzel *(Gen. Ludendorff)*, Sig Rumann *(Gen. Von Hindenburg)*, Alexander Granach *(Julius Streicher)*, Fritz Kortner *(Gregor Strasser)*, Tonio Selwart *(Alfred Rosenberg)*, Richard Ryen *(Adolf Wagner)*, Ray Collins *(Cardinal von Faulhaber)*, Ludwig Donath *(Gustav von Kahr)*, Ernst Verebes *(Anton Drexler)*, Walter Kingsford *(Franz von Papen)*, Fred Nurney *(Gen. von Epp)*, Arthur Loft *(Col. von Reichenau)*, Lionel Royce *(Fritz Thyssen)*.

A fairly accurate recreation of events in the life of Adolf Hitler from the end of WW I to his ascension as Germany's leader in 1934. Watson, who had portrayed the Nazi leader in HITLER—DEAD OR ALIVE (1942), again plays Hitler, beginning in 1918 where he is hospitalized due to shock suffered in WW I. The film then follows him as he founds the National Socialist Party, attracts Himmler, Goering, Hess, Roehm and Goebbles to his cause, and his imprisonment after the Munich beer hall "putsch." In prison, he writes *Mein Kampf* and then continues to campaign for power after his release. At the film's end, he has been appointed Reichchancellor and is ruthlessly attempting to consolidate his power and eliminate his enemies. Reportedly, DeSylva wanted to make this film after seeing a Nazi propaganda film's distorted portrait of the life of Hitler.

p, B.G. DeSylva; d, John Farrow; w, Francis Goodrich, Albert Hackett; ph, Ernest Laszlo; m, David Buttolph; ed, Eda Warren; art d, Hans Dreier, Franz Bachelin.

Biography **(PR:A MPAA:NR)**

HITLER: THE LAST TEN DAYS** (1973, Brit./Ital.) 106m PAR-Tomorrow Entertainment c

Alec Guinness *(Adolf Hitler)*, Simon Ward *(Hauptmann Hoffmann)*, Adolph Celi *(Gen. Krebs)*, Diane Cilento *(Hanna Reitsch)*, Gabriele Ferzetti *(Fieldmarshal Keitel)*, Eric Porter *(Gen. von Greim)*, Doris Kunstmann *(Eva Braun)*, Joss Ackland *(Gen. Burgdorf)*, John Barron *(Dr. Stumpfegger)*, John Bennett *(Josef Goebbels)*, Sheila Gish *(Frau Christian)*, Julian Glover *(Fegelein)*, Michael Goodliffe *(Gen. Weidling)*, John Hallam *(Guensche)*, Barbara Jefford *(Magda Goebbels)*, Mark Kingston *(Martin Bormann)*, Phyllida Law *(Fraulein Manzialy)*, Ann Lynn *(Fraulein Junge)*, Angela Pleasence *(Trude)*, Andrew Sachs *(Walter Wagner)*, Philip Stone *(Gen. Jodi)*, Timothy West *(Prof. Gebhardt)*, William Abney *(Voss)*, Kenneth Colley *(Boldt)*, James Cossins *(German officer)*, Philip Locke *(Hanske)*, Richard Fescud *(Von Below)*, John Savident *(Hewel)*.

Even though Guinness was the finest actor ever to attempt to portray Adolf Hitler, HITLER: THE LAST TEN DAYS is another addition to the long list of failed dramatizations on his personal life. Set almost entirely in Hitler's bunker, the film details the final days of the Third Reich. Unfortunately, nothing much happens in the film, and the claustrophobic atmosphere soon grates on the nerves. Guinness tries hard not to fall into the "raving maniac" portrayal that most actors saddled with his role rely on, but instead goes for a nearly lifeless characterization that makes one wonder where Hitler's famous charisma went.

p, Wolfgang Reinhardt; d, Ennio De Concini; w, De Concini, Marie Pia Fusco, Reinhardt, Ivan Moffat (based on the book, *Last Days of the Chancellery* by Gerhard Boldt); ph, Ennio Guarnieri (Panavision, Technicolor); m, Mischa Spoliansky; ed, Kevin Connor; art d, Roy Walker.

Biography **Cas.** **(PR:C MPAA:PG)**

HITLER'S CHILDREN**½** (1942) 80m RKO bw

Tim Holt *(Karl Bruner)*, Bonita Granville *(Anna Muller)*, Kent Smith *(Prof. Nichols)*, Otto Kruger *(Col. Henkel)*, H. B. Warner *(The Bishop)*, Lloyd Corrigan *(Franz Erhart)*, Erford Gage *(Dr. Schmidt)*, Hans Conreid *(Dr. Graf)*, Nancy Gates *(Brenda)*, Gavin Muir *(Nazi Major)*, Bill Burrud *(Murph)*, Jimmy Zaner *(Irwin)*, Richard Martin *(Gestapo Man)*, Goetz Van Eyck *(Arresting Sergeant)*, John Merton *(Gestapo Officer)*, Max Lucke *(Plane Dispatcher)*, Anna Loos *(N.S.V. Worker)*, Bessie Wade *(Mother)*, Orley Lindgren, Billy Brow, Chris Wren *(Boys)*, Egon Brecher *(Mr. Muller)*, Elsa Janssen *(Mrs. Muller)*, William Forrest *(American Vice Consul)*, Ariel Heath, Rita Corday *(Young Matrons)*, Mary Stuart *(Bit)*, Roland Varno *(Lieutenant S.A.)*, Crane Whitley *(Whipping Sergeant)*, Edward Van Sloan *(Chief Trial Judge)*, Douglas Evans *(Radio Announcer)*, Carla Boehm *(Magda)*, Bruce Cameron *(Storm Trooper)*, Betty Roadman *(1st Matron)*, Kathleen Wilson *(Chief Matron)*, Harry McKim *(Boy)*, John Stockton *(Gestapo Officer)*.

Sensationalistic drama detailing the rise of the Brownshirts and the diabolical lengths the Nazis would go to get more children into the Third Reich. Holt plays a rabid Nazi youth who loves fraulein Granville, despite her nonconformist attitudes. Sadly, Granville is on the list for forced sterilization because of her anti-Nazi stance, but she convinces Holt that the Reich is not all it's cracked up to be, and they are happy in each other's arms long enough to get shot down by the angry Nazis. Incredibly, this cheap propaganda production garnered more profits for RKO than any other film produced to that date, including the hits KING KONG and TOP HAT.

p, Edward A. Golden; d, Edward Dmytryk; w, Emmett Lavery (based on the book *Education for Death* by Gregor Ziemer); ph, Russell Metty; m, Roy Webb; ed, Joseph Noriega; md, C. Bakaleinikoff; art d, Albert S. D'Agostino, Carroll Clark; spec eff, Vernon L. Walker.

Drama **Cas.** **(PR:C MPAA:NR)**

HITLER'S GOLD (SEE: INSIDE OUT, 1975, Brit.)

HITLER'S MADMAN***** (1943) 84m PRC/MGM bw (AKA: HITLER'S HANGMAN)

John Carradine *(Heydrich)*, Patricia Morison *(Jarmila)*, Alan Curtis *(Karel)*, Ralph Morgan *(Hanka)*, Howard Freeman *(Himmler)*, Ludwig Stossel *(Mayor Bauer)*, Edgar Kennedy *(Nepomuk)*, Jimmy Conlon *(Dvorak)*, Blanche Yurka *(Mrs. Hanka)*, Jorja Rollins *(Clara Janek)*, Al Shean *(Priest)*, Elizabeth Russell *(Maria)*, Victor Kilian *(Janek)*, Johanna Hofer *(Mrs. Bauer)*, Wolfgang Zilzer *(Colonel)*, Tully Marshall *(Teacher)*, Ava Gardner *(Katy Chotnik)*, Frances Rafferty *(Eliza Cormak)*, Natalie Draper *(Julia Petschek)*, Betty Jaynes, Celia Travers *(Nurses)*, Lionel Royce *(Capt. Kleist)*, Dennis Moore *(Orderly)*, Lester Dorr *(Sergeant)*, Budd Buster *(Conductor)*, Dick Talmadge *(Chauffeur)*, Chet Brandenburg *(Linesman)*, Ernst Hausman, Sam Waagenaar *(Sentries)*.

German director Douglas Sirk fled to America and with funding from German expatriates independently produced his first American film, which detailed the horrors wrought on the Czechoslovakian town of Lidice after the assassination of Nazi Reinhard Heydrich. Shot in a week, Sirk cast Carradine as the brutal governor of the occupied area of Czechoslovakia who performed his sadistic duties with relish. When Carradine is fatally wounded one day by resistance fighters while driving to his headquarters, the fate of Lidice goes up for grabs. Surprisingly, Carradine denounces Hitler and his ambitions while on his death bed, and rallies the Allies to defeat the madman. Ignoring his comrade's sudden change of heart, Himmler (Freeman) orders the town of Lidice razed and the slaughter begins. The men killed, the women sent to prison camps, and the children taken away, never to be seen again. Upon completion of the film, MGM agreed to distribute it if Sirk would shoot some additional sequences and retakes, which he did. Look in the backgrounds for a very young Ava Gardner as one of the brave Czech women.

p, Seymour Nebenzal; d, Douglas Sirk; w, Peretz Hirshbein, Melvin Levy, Doris Malloy (based on a story by Emil Ludwig, Albrecht Joseph and the story "Hangmen's Village" by Bart Lytton); ph, Jack Greenhalgh, Eugene Shuftan; m, Karl Hajos; ed, Dan Milner; art d, Fred Preble, Edward Willens.

History **(PR:A MPAA:NR)**

HITTIN' THE TRAIL*** (1937) 58m GN bw

Tex Ritter *(Tex Randall)*, Jerry Bergh *(Jean Reed)*, Tommy Bupp *(Billy Reed)*, Earl Dwire *(Clark)*, Jack Smith *(Dad Reed)*, Snub Pollard *(Bartender)*, Archie Ricks *(Tombstone Kid)*, Heber Snow *(Hank)*, Charles King *(Slug)*, Edward Cassidy *(Sheriff Grey)*, Ray Whitley and his Range Ramblers, the Phelps Bros., Tex Ritter's Tornadoes.

Probably one of Ritter's worst saddle operas, this relies on the familiar formula of getting the herd over the border by midnight, the herd in this case being horses instead of cattle. Several numbers are sung by Ritter, which helps to get over the bad taste left by several other range singers.

p, Edward Finney; d, R.N. Bradbury; w, Robert Emmett.

Western **(PR:A MPAA:NR)**

HITTING A NEW HIGH*½** (1937) 80m RKO bw

Lily Pons *(Suzette)*, Jack Oakie *(Corby)*, Eric Blore *(Cosmo)*, Edward Everett Horton *(Blynn)*, John Howard *(Jimmy)*, Eduardo Ciannelli *(Mazzini)*, Luis Alberni *(Marlo)*, Jack Arnold *(Haig)*, Leonard Carey *(Jevons)*.

Pons is a night club singer dreaming of the Met. Her agent, Oakie, hits on the brilliant idea of dressing her as "Ooga-Hunga, the Bird Girl" and sends her chasing opera lover Horton on an African safari. Of course he sees her, and Pons is rewarded with an appearance at the Met. Pons does get to do a few opera numbers. The film lost tons of money and effectively ended Pons' career in the movies. Lasky also left the studio shortly after this bomb's release. Even the normally strong Walsh direction couldn't help it. Songs: "You're Like a Song," "I Hit a New High," "Let's Give Love Another Chance," "This Never Happened Before" (Harold Adamson, Jimmy McHugh). Operatic excerpts: "Lucia Di Lammermoor," (Gaetano Donizetti), "Mignon," "Je Suis Titania" (Ambrose Thomas), "Le Rossignol Et La Rose," (The Nightingale Song) (Charles Camille Saint-Saens' incidental music for Dieulafoy's play "Parysatis").

p, Jesse L. Lasky; d, Raoul Walsh; w, Gertrude Purcell, John Twist (based on a story by Robert Harari and Maxwell Shane); ph, J. Roy Hunt; ed, Desmond Marquette.

Musical **(PR:A MPAA:NR)**

HIYA, CHUM (SEE: HI'YA, CHUM, 1943)

HO*½** (1968, Fr.) 110m Marceau-Cocinor-Filmsonor- Mega/Cocinor c

Jean-Paul Belmondo *(Ho)*, Joanna Shimkus *(Benedite)*, Sidney Chaplin *(Canter)*, Alain Mottet *(Paul)*, Paul Crauchet *(Briand)*.

Belmondo is an ex-race car driver turned getaway wheelman for a bank robber, while dreaming of taking over from his boss. Then the gangster is killed in an accident and Belmondo is up against the other gang members. Along the way he has an affair with a model and kidnaps a reporter to tell his side of the story. But after the girl is killed and a gang war takes place, Belmondo is captured and led away in a flurry of flashbulbs. Belmondo plays his character like a cartoon, not coming close to the brilliant and similar role he had in Jean Luc Godard's BREATHLESS. HO moves jerkily along in poorly connected episodes that have nothing new to say about gangsters or gangster pictures. A minor effort from a period when France was producing some great works.

d, Robert Enrico; w, Pierre Pelegri, Lucienne Hamon, Enrico (based on the book by Jose Giovanni); ph, Jean Boffety (Eastmancolor); ed, Jacqueline Mappiel.

Crime **(PR:O MPAA:NR)**

HOA-BINH***** (1971, Fr.) 93m Madeleine-Parc-Gueville-C.A.P.C./Transvue c

Phi Lan *(Hung)*, Huynh Cazenas *(Xuan)*, Xuan Ha *(Mother)*, Le Quynh *(Father)*, Lan Phuong *(Nam)*, Bui Thi Thanh *(Tran Thi Ha)*, Tran Van Lich *(Political Commissioner)*, Anh Tuan *(Viet Cong Officer)*, Kieu Anh *(Viet Namese Nurse)*, Danielle Delorme *(French Nurse)*.

The famous cinematographer for a number of Truffaut and Godard films undertook the direction of a film himself with HOA-BINH, filming in the midst of the Viet Nam War to create a very powerful and stirring picture. The story follows the plight of an 11-year-old Viet Namese boy after his father leaves to fight with the Viet Cong and his mother is taken to a hospital. Forced to watch over his young sister, he wanders with her to Saigon where the two resort to begging and odd jobs in order to survive. The young girl is eventually brought to an orphanage, leaving the boy alone to scrounge the streets until he is reunited with his father at the film's end. Coutard took a subject that was very near to his heart, having been a photojournalist in Viet Nam prior to working as a cinematographer. Unlike Godard, Coutard avoided making any political comments, allowing the images to speak for themselves. Prior to its U.S. release, HOA-BINH won 1970 awards as Best Picture at the London Film Festival and Best First Film at Cannes, as well as an Oscar nomination for Best Foreign Film.

p, Gilbert De Goldschmidt; d&w, Raoul Coutard (based on the novel *La Colonne De Cendres* by Francoise Lorrain); ph, Georges Liron (Eastmancolor); m, Michel Portal; ed, Victoria Mercanton; m/l "Fire Night," Billy Ellis (sung by Ellis).

War/Drama **(PR:C-O MPAA:PG)**

HOAX, THE**** (1972) 85m All-Scope International c

Bill Ewing *(Cy McCarten)*, Frank Bonner *(Cleta Dempsey)*, Jacques Aubuchon *(Chief Belkins)*, Sharon DeBord *(Gracie)*, Don Dubbins *(Sgt. O'Roherty)*, Harriett Gibson *(Mrs. Petrucci)*.

Post-DOCTOR STRANGELOVE nuclear comedy involving the adventures of Ewing and Bonner as a pair of amateur skin divers who find a hydrogen bomb accidentally dropped from a B-52 bomber into the ocean just off southern California. They decide, jokingly, to order the entire city of Los Angeles to send one dollar per citizen to a Swiss bank account or else they will detonate the bomb. They are caught and pay off the $2 million they collected to smog control in return for leniency by the court. Ewing and Bonner are funny as the two would-be terrorists and carry the premise well to its conclusion. Some scenes drag on longer than necessary.

p&d, Robert Anderson; w, Kevin Davis; ph, John Toll (DeLuxe Color); m, Ray Martin; ed, Frank Urioste.

Comedy **(PR:C MPAA:PG)**

HOBSON'S CHOICE*½** (1931, Brit.) 65m British International/Wardour bw

Viola Lyel *(Maggie Hobson)*, James Harcourt *(Hobson)*, Frank Pettingell *(Will Mossup)*, Belle Chrystal *(Vicky Hobson)*, Jay Laurier *(Tubby Wadlow)*, Joan Maude *(Alice Hobson)*, Amy Veness *(Mrs. Hepworth)*, Reginald Bach *(Albert Prosser)*, Basil Moss *(Freddy Beenstock)*, Herbert Lomas *(Jim Heeler)*, Kathleen Harrison *(Ada Figgins)*.

Harcourt is a bootmaker who chooses a husband for his daughter, Lyel. But she's got a mind of her own and will have nothing to do with a groom handpicked by her father. Based on a successful play, this film is minor at best. It was remade in 1954 with better success by David Lean. A made-for-television version was also done in 1983, featuring Lillian Gish.

p, John Maxwell; d, Thomas Bentley; w, Harold Brighouse (uncredited), Frank Launder (based on the play by Harold Brighouse); ph, Walter Harvey.

Comedy **(PR:A MPAA:NR)**

HOBSON'S CHOICE**** (1954, Brit.) 107m LFP/BL bw

Charles Laughton *(Henry Horatio Hobson)*, John Mills *(Willie Mossop)*, Brenda de Banzie *(Maggie Hobson)*, Daphne Anderson *(Alice Hobson)*, Prunella Scales *(Vicky Hobson)*, Richard Wattis *(Albert Prosser)*, Derek Blomfield *(Freddy Beenstock)*, Helen Haye *(Mrs. Hepworth)*, Joseph Tomelty *(Jim Heeler)*, Julien Mitchell *(Sam Minns)*, Gibb McLaughlin *(Tudsbury)*, Philip Stainton *(Denton)*, Dorothy Gordon *(Ada Figgins)*, Madge Brindley *(Mrs. Figgins)*, John Laurie *(Dr. MacFarlane)*, Raymond Huntley *(Nathaniel Beenstock)*, Jack Howarth *(Tubby Wadlow)*, Herbert C. Walton *(Printer)*.

Laughton is marvelous in this wry comedy as the crusty old curmudgeon who rules his profitable boot shop and his three unmarried daughters with an iron hand. He hypocritically downs his pints of ale at the local pub and cries out against the inhumanity of life at leaving him a widower. His eldest daughter, de Banzie, thirty and, in Laughton's words, "on the shelf"; she finds herself a man in the form of the self-effacing, illiterate, and ambitionless Mills, Laughton's assistant and chief bootmaker for the firm. Mills is a bit dumbfounded when being led to the altar and even more puzzled when de Banzie sets him up in his own bootmaking business after Laughton refuses to award de Banzie a dowry. With de Banzie brainstorming the business, Mills' shop grows and he prospers, so much so that he begins to make inroads into Laughton's once dominant operation. De Banzie, after her father goes on one of his drinking bouts, cleverly entraps him into awarding her spinster sisters their financial settlements. Laughton then falls ill and begs de Banzie to return to his side. She does, but on the proviso that she and Mills not only move into his mansion but that he makes Mills a full partner, which the old grouch reluctantly does at the fade-out. This is a fully developed comedy of human foibles and follies with Laughton rendering a masterful, sly performance, beautifully supported by de Banzie and Mills. Laughton, who played the role on stage years before, was unhappy on the set (although you can't tell by watching the picture). He developed a dislike for de Banzie (who, incredibly, almost upstaged the consummate upstager) and he didn't care for Mills in the role of Willie Mossop, a part he'd wanted Robert Donat to play. Lean's direction is careful and properly mannered as he draws forth one poignant scene after another, some painful, others full of mirth. Arnold's inventive score adds considerable charm to this best of three versions of Harold Brighouse's 1915 stage comedy (filmed in 1920 as a silent with Arthur Pitt and Joan Ritz, again as a talkie in 1931 with James Harcourt and Viola Lyel). This film rightly won the Best British Film award in 1954.

p&d, David Lean; w, Lean, Norman Spencer, Wynyard Browne (based on the play by Harold Brighouse); ph, Jack Hildyard; m, Malcolm Arnold; ed, Peter Taylor; md, Muir Mathieson; prod d, Wilfred Shingleton; cos, John Armstrong.

Comedy **Cas.** **(PR:A MPAA:NR)**

HOEDOWN*½ (1950) 64m COL bw

Eddy Arnold *(Himself)*, Jeff Donnell *(Vera Wright)*, Jock O'Mahoney *(Stoney Rhodes)*, Guinn "Big Boy" Williams *(Small Potatoes Guinn)*, Carolina Cotton *(Herself)*, Fred Sears *(Sam)*, Don Harvey *(Sapper)*, Charles Sullivan *(Tiny)*, Douglas Fowley *(Buttons)*, Ray Walker *(Knoxie)*, Harry Harvey *(Sheriff)*, The Pied Pipers, The Oklahoma Wranglers.

O'Mahoney is a movie cowboy fired by his studio. Along with Donnell, a reporter, he accidentally discovers that the latest residents of Arnold's "singing dude ranch" are really bank robbers. Inspired by love, O'Mahoney saves the day. It's all pretty hokey, starting off as a parody of B westerns but turning into a parody of itself. Arnold made a rare screen appearance, which really was just an excuse for him to sing. His agent at the time was "Colonel" Tom Parker, who would later do an entire series of equally poor films with his number one discovery, Elvis Presley.

p, Colbert Clark; d, Ray Nazzaro; w, Barry Shipman; ph, Fayte Brown; ed, Paul Borofsky; md, Mischa Bakaleinikoff; m/l, Eddy Arnold, Zeke Clements, Steve Nelson, Ed Nelson, Fred Styker, Francis Clark, Bob Hilliard, Bill Hughes.

Musical/Western **(PR:A MPAA:NR)**

HOFFMAN*½ (1970, Brit.) 113m ABF/Levitt-Pickman c

Peter Sellers *(Benjamin Hoffman)*, Sinead Cusack *(Janet Smith)*, Jeremy Bulloch *(Tom Mitchell)*, Ruth Dunning *(Mrs. Mitchell)*, David Lodge *(Foreman)*, Ron Taylor *(Guitarist)*, Kay Hall, Karen Murtagh, Cindy Burrows, Elizabeth Bayley.

A minor comedy Sellers made at a low point in his career tells the story of a lonely middle-aged man desperate for love. After discovering that a secretary's boy friend has been engaging in some illegal activities, Sellers blackmails her by having her stay for a week at his place. He's been mad over her for years and finally sees his chance. When she arrives, he is nothing but a gentleman, taking her to dinner, for walks, and graciously respecting her side of the bed. Originally a television play, HOFFMAN plods on and on with a weak script. Character motivations are contrived and often unbelievable. When the girl finally falls for Sellers it has long been foreseen by the audience. Despite the film's weaknesses, Sellers is not bad, giving the role some signs of life. Cusack is the daughter of Irish character actor Cyril Cusack.

p, Ben Arbeid; d, Alvin Rakoff; w, Ernest Gebler (based on his novel); ph, Gerry Turpin (Technicolor); m, Ron Grainer; ed, Barrie Vince; art d, John Blezard.

Comedy **(PR:A MPAA:GP)**

HOG WILD zero (1980, Can.) 97m Filmplan/AE c

Michael Biehn *(Tim)*, Patti D'Arbanville *(Angie)*, Tony Rosato *(Bull)*, Angelo Rizacos *(Bean)*, Martin Doyle *(Shadow)*, Matt Craven *(Chrome)*, Matt Birman-Feldman *(Lead)*, Claude Philippe *(Indian)*, Thomas C. Kovacs *(Veel)*, Jacoba Knaapan *(Tina)*, Michael Zelniker *(Pete)*, Karen Stephen *(Brenda)*, Jack Blum *(Gil)*, Stephanie Miller *(Sarah)*, Keith Knight *(Vern)*, Mitch Martin *(Polly)*, Robin McCulloch *(Stiff)*.

The Hell's Angels meet a group of high schoolers and it's the audience's choice as to which group is more obnoxious. The episodic story leads to a motorcycle race between the two groups but there's nothing to get excited over between the opening credits and the end titles. What little story there is has such a confusing treatment it is awfully difficult to discern exactly what is going on. This is not helped any by the low-end production values, and the cast's largely limited talents.

p, Claude Heroux; d, Les Rose; w, Andrew Peter Marin (based on an original concept by Victor Solnicki, Stephen Miller); ph, Rene Verzier; ed, Dominique Boisvert; art d, Carol Spier.

Comedy **(PR:O MPAA:PG)**

HOLD BACK THE DAWN**** (1941) 115m PAR bw

Charles Boyer *(Georges Iscovescu)*, Olivia de Havilland *(Emmy Brown)*, Paulette Goddard *(Anita Dixon)*, Victor Francen *(Van Den Luecken)*, Walter Abel *(Inspector Hammock)*, Curt Bois *(Bonbois)*, Rosemary De Camp *(Berta Kurz)*, Eric Feldary *(Josef Kurz)*, Nestor Paiva *(Flores)*, Eva Puig *(Lupita)*, Micheline Cheirel *(Christine)*, Madeleine LeBeau *(Anni)*, Billy Lee *(Tony)*, Mitchell Leisen *(Mr. Saxon)*, Brian Donlevy, Richard Webb, Veronica Lake *(On-the-Set Film Actors)*, Sonny Boy Williams *(Sam)*, Don Douglas *(Joe)*, Gertrude Astor *(Young Woman at Climax Bar)*, Jesus Topete, Tony Roux, Mikhail Rasumny *(Mechanics)*, June Pickrell *(Mrs. Brown)*, Buddy Messinger *(Elevator Boy)*, Ray Mala *(Husky Young Mexican Bridegroom)*, Soledad Jiminez *(Old Peon's Wife)*, Placido Sigueiros *(Old Peon)*, Edward Fielding *(American Consul)*, Chester Clute *(Man)*, Francisco Maran *(Mexican Doctor)*, Carlos Villarias *(Mexican Judge)*, Arthur Loft *(Hollander)*, John Holland *(Mr. MacAdams)*.

A touching and memorable film which is also a great romance story, HOLD BACK THE DAWN offers evocative performances by Boyer and de Havilland. It opens with a typical Wilder twist. Director Leisen is shown actually directing a scene with Brian Donlevy and Veronica Lake on the set of I WANTED WINGS, where he is approached by Rumanian gigolo Boyer, a one-time European dancer and ladies' escort. Boyer wants to sell movie director Leisen a story for $500. He fascinates the director with the following tale shown in flashback: Boyer, stranded in a Mexican border town, lives in a run-down hotel, the Esperanza, which houses all manner of human driftwood from Europe, refugees from Nazi oppression, not the least of whom is Franchen, a Dutch professor who acts as a sort of father confessor to the disenfranchised. One pathetic emigre is Rosemary De Camp, a pregnant refugee who slips across the border to have her child in the United States. Visiting the area with her students is American schoolteacher de Havilland; she becomes Boyer's easy victim in a matrimonial-immigration scam suggested by vixen Goddard. One-time former dance partner to Boyer, Goddard tells him how easy it is to gain U.S. citizenship; simply marry an American citizen. She tells Boyer how she lured a jockey into marrying her and got her citizenship, then quickly divorced the hapless husband. Desperate to escape his plight, Boyer approaches the gullible de Havilland and quickly wins her heart. They are married and take a short touring honeymoon. The warm, trusting de Havilland makes Boyer ashamed of duping her and he fakes a back injury to avoid consummating the marriage. When the couple return to the small Mexican village where they met, troublemaker Goddard tells de Havilland the real motivations behind Boyer's marriage to her. Abel, a tough old U.S. immigration officer, then tells de Havilland that such quickie marriages are typical devices used by migrants to gain access to the U.S. De Havilland confronts Boyer and he confesses that it was all a scheme. The teacher is now totally mortified since she's fibbed about Boyer, having told customs officials at the time of her marriage that she was marrying Boyer out of love and knew all about his background. All of her injured emotions burst when she confronts Boyer: "I live in a small town and we eat at the drugstore but we leave a tip just the same. The lies I told were not too much to pay for one week's happiness. But let me go." In a wild emotional state, de Havilland drives recklessly home and has an accident, seriously injuring herself. Hearing about the accident, Boyer sneaks across the border and visits her, telling her he loves her and respects her and he begs her forgiveness. His declaration gives de Havilland the will to live. Boyer then goes to Paramount Studios and sells Leisen the story, explaining that he needs the $500 to pay for de Havilland's medical expenses. Immigration official Abel is impressed with Boyer's noble actions and he turns the other way when de Havilland and Boyer are reunited at the border and the illegal immigrant enters the U.S. to find happiness. The story is somewhat thin but Leisen's light touch and sensitive direction keep it from becoming maudlin and sloppily sentimental. Boyer and de Havilland give magnificent performances as the cross-purposed lovers. The script by Brackett and Wilder is beautifully written with gentle care and deep understanding of the characters, which were drawn wholly from the life of story writer Frings and her struggle to get her immigrant husband Kurt into the U.S. via Mexico. There is much here that calls to mind ARCH OF TRIUMPH (1948), also starring Boyer, who always felt that HOLD BACK THE DAWN was one of his best films. The film was nominated for Best Picture and it marked the American debut of Franchen, a fascinating character actor. Paramount wanted the 25-year-old de Havilland for the lead role in this film right from the start but played a waiting game with Jack Warner since she was under iron contract to Warner Bros., a studio that never loaned its talent to other studios unless Jack Warner wanted some star from another studio. Warner was planning a movie entitled DIVE BOMBER starring Errol Flynn and he decided that Fred MacMurray should costar, but MacMurray was a Paramount player so Warner called Paramount executives and read off a list of *his* players he would be willing to trade for MacMurray. When Warner mentioned the name of de Havilland, Paramount executives did not respond. They later called back and told Warner that they were *mildly* interested in her and they wound up getting de Havilland, the very star they coveted for HOLD BACK THE DAWN, without having to pay for her services, she and MacMurray being traded evenly for their efforts.

p, Arthur Hornblow, Jr.; d, Mitchell Leisen; w, Charles Brackett, Billy Wilder (based on a story by Ketti Frings); ph, Leo Tover; m, Victor Young; ed, Doane Harrison; art d, Hans Dreier, Robert Usher; cos, Edith Head; m/l, "My Boy, My Boy," Frank Loesser, Jimmy Berg, Fred Speilman, Fred Jacobson.

Romance **(PR:A MPAA:NR)**

HOLD BACK THE NIGHT*** (1956) 80m AA bw

John Payne *(Mackenzie)*, Mona Freeman *(Anne)*, Peter Graves *(Couzens)*, Chuck Connors *(Ekland)*, Audrey Dalton *(Kitty)*, Bob Nichols *(Beany)*, John Wilder *(Tinker)*, Bob Easton *(Ackerman)*, Stanley Cha *(Kato)*, Nicky Blair *(Papiro)*, John Craven *(Maj. MacKay)*, Nelson Leigh *(Lt. Col. Toomey)*.

Payne is a Marine officer fighting in the Korean War. He carries with him a bottle of Scotch, which he also carried during WW II, a gift from his wife, Freeman, who is seen in flashback. The fifth is to be opened upon victory and thus becomes a symbol of hope to the men he leads. A subplot involves flashbacks of Dalton, an Australian woman Payne fell in love with during WW II. Dwan's direction is keen, accurately capturing the look and feeling of field combat. Payne is excellent in his role, as are Connors and Graves as soldiers under his command. The musical score provides a stirring background.

p, Hayes Goetz; d, Allan Dwan; w, John C. Higgins, Walter Doniger (based on a novel by Pat Frank); ph, Ellsworth Fredricks; ed, Robert S. Elsen; art d, Hilyard Brown.

War Drama **(PR:A MPAA:NR)**

HOLD BACK TOMORROW½** (1955) 75m UNIV bw

Cleo Moore *(Dora)*, John Agar *(Joe)*, Frank De Kova *(Priest)*, Dallas Boyd *(Warden)*, Steffi Sidney *(Clara)*, Mel Welles *(1st Guard)*, Harry Guardino *(Detective)*, Mona Knox *(Escort Girl)*, Arlene Harris *(Proprietress)*, Kay Piehl *(Warden's Wife)*, Jan Englund *(Girl)*, Pat Goldin *(Dancing Comedienne)*.

Strange B picture features Agar as a death row inmate who wants female companionship as his last request. The police get him Moore, a suicidal hooker with nothing left to lose. After spending the night together they fall in love and have the prison chaplain marry them. He goes off to the gallows with a sense of satisfaction with life. Before he goes he mentions a dream he has had where the rope breaks at the hanging, the death bell rings, and he is pardoned. As Moore prays for this miracle, the bell rings and the film fades out. Though there's some occasional overacting by the two leads, the film works well in its own quirky way.

p,d&w, Hugo Haas; ph, Paul Ivano; m, Sidney B. Cutner; ed, Henry De Mond; m/l, title song, Franz Steinger, Johnny Rotella.

Drama **(PR:O MPAA:NR)**

HOLD 'EM JAIL** (1932) 65m RKO bw

Bert Wheeler *(Curly Harris)*, Robert Woolsey *(Spider Robbins)*, Edna May Oliver *(Violet Jones)*, Roscoe Ates *(Slippery Sam Brown)*, Edgar Kennedy *(Warden)*, Betty Grable *(Barbara Jones)*, Paul Hurst *(Coach)*, Warren Hymer *(Steel)*, Robert Armstrong *(Sports Announcer)*, John Sheehan *(Mike Maloney)*, Jed Prouty *(Warden Charles Clark)*, Spencer Charters *(Governor)*, Monty Banks *(Timekeeper)*, Lee Phelps *(Spike)*, Ernie Adams, Monte Collins *(Referees)*, Ben Taggart *(Doorman)*.

Prison warden Kennedy is looking for some new blood for the jailhouse football team. Wheeler and Woolsey are a pair of novelty items salesmen who get framed for robbery and are sentenced to Kennedy's detention farm. There is a lot of typical W&W zaniness as everything climaxes at the final "big game." Grable plays the love interest, replacing Dorothy Lee, Wheeler and Woolsey's usual female partner. Though funny, Wheeler and Woolsey were highly predictable in this film and Grable gives no hint whatsoever of what she was to become. Still, Taurog's direction is quickly paced and the film runs smoothly. However, it was a box office bomb, losing over $55,000, no small sum in 1932.

d, Norman Taurog; w, S. J. Perelman, Walter DeLeon, Mark Sandrich, Albert Ray (based on a story by Tim Wheelan, Lou Lipton); ph, Len Smith; m, Max Steiner; ed, Artie Roberts; art d, Carroll Clark.

Comedy **Cas.** **(PR:A MPAA:NR)**

HOLD 'EM NAVY!** (1937) 62m PAR bw

Lew Ayres *(Tommy Gorham)*, Mary Carlisle *(Judy Holland)*, John Howard *(Chuck Baldwin)*, Benny Baker *(Stuffy Miller)*, Elizabeth Patterson *(Grandma Holland)*, Archie Twitchell *(Jerry Abbott)*, Lambert Rogers *(Ritter)*, Les Bennett *(Blake)*, Alston Cockrell *(Carner)*, Tully Marshall *(The "Admiral")*, Billy Daniels *(Steve Crenshaw)*, George Lollier *(Doctor)*, Pat Flaherty *(Coach Hanley)*, Dick French *(Announcer)*, Harold Adams *(Referee)*, Gwen Kenyon *(Caroline)*, Priscilla Moran *(Kitty Hollingsbee)*, Richard Denning *(Jepson)*, Jack Hubbard *(Fruit Vendor)*, Ethel Clayton, Diana Forest, Gloria Williams *(Women)*, Marie Burton, Carol Parker, Virginia Pound, Suzanne Ridgway, Alma Ross, Dorothy White *(Girls)*, Frank Nelson *(Radio Announcer)*, Wade Boteler *(O'Brien, Guard)*, Robert Allen *(Midshipman)*.

Ayres is a freshman plebe at the U.S. Naval academy. He meets and falls for Carlisle, who, unbeknownst to the young man, is the sweetie of upperclassman Howard. There's some bitterness between the two men but all is resolved when they must work together during the last play in the annual Army-Navy football game. Simple fare told straightforwardly.

d, Kurt Neumann; w, Erwin Gelsey, Lloyd Corrigan (based on a story by Albert Shelby LeVino); ph, Henry Sharp; ed, Edward Dmytryk; md, Boris Morros; art d, Hans Dreier, Robert Odell.

Drama **(PR:A MPAA:NR)**

HOLD 'EM YALE½** (1935) 61m PAR bw

Patricia Ellis *(Clarice Van Cleve)*, Cesar Romero *(Gigolo Georgie)*, Larry Crabbe *(Hector Wilmot)*, William Frawley *(Sunshine Joe)*, Andy Devine *(Liverlips)*, George Barbier *(Mr. Van Cleve)*, Warren Hymer *(Sam The Gonoph)*, George E. Stone *(Bennie South Street)*, Hale Hamilton *(Mr. Wilmot)*, Guy Usher *(Coach Jennings)*, Grant Withers *(Cleary)*, Gary Owen, Ethel Griffies, Leonard Carey, Kendall Evans, Theodore Lorch, Oscar Smith, Stanley Andrews, Tony Merlo, Phillips Smalley, Kid Herman, Marshall Ruth, Georgia French, Arthur S. Hull, Arthur Housman, Ruth Clifford, James Farley, Charles McMurphy, Father Dodd, Jack Judge, Edward Gargan, Paul Wing, Fred Anderson.

Frawley, Devine, Hymer, and Stone are ticket scalpers. They "inherit" Ellis from Romero, who has used her for what he could and then cut out. The quartet is assigned by her father to calm her wild ways and find her a nice boy to marry. They find a third-string Yale football player, Crabbe, and convince the coach to let him play in the big game against Harvard. Through a freak accident he wins the game and Ellis' heart as well. The weak plot is more than compensated for by the great Runyon dialog.

p, Charles R. Rogers; d, Sidney Lanfield; w, Paul Gerard Smith, Eddie Welch (based on a story by Damon Runyon); ph, Milton Drasner; ed, Jack Dennis.

Comedy **(PR:A MPAA:NR)**

HOLD EVERYTHING*** (1930) 78m WB c

Joe E. Brown *(Gink Schiner)*, Winnie Lightner *(Toots Breen)*, Georges Carpentier *(Georges LaVerne)*, Sally O'Neill *(Sue Burke)*, Edmund Breese *(Pop O'Keefe)*, Bert Roach *(Nosey Bartlett)*, Dorothy Revier *(Norine Lloyd)*, Jack Curtis, Tony Stabeneau, Lew Harvey, Jimmy Quinn.

Brown is a nickel-and-dime fighter with pretensions for higher glory. Lightner is his girl friend, fed up with his flirting ways. Brown is in a training camp where real-life pro boxer Carpentier is preparing for a heavyweight championship. Carpentier gets involved with Revier, a rich society girl. There is a promoter who is trying to fix a fight, but good guy Brown saves the day. Brown runs away with the film, and his mugging and comic sense are right on target. Songs: "Take It On the Chin," "When Little Red Roses Get the Blues for You," "Sing a Little Theme Song," "Physically Fit," "Girls We Remember," "All Alone Together," "Isn't This a Cockeyed World," "You're the Cream In My Coffee" (Al Dubin, Joe Burke).

d, Roy Del Ruth; w, Robert Lord (based on the play by B.G. DeSylva, John McGowan); ph, Dev Jennings; m, Ray Henderson, Al Dubin, Lew Brown, Joe Burke; ed, William Holmes; ch, Larry Ceballos.

Musical/Comedy **(PR:AA MPAA:NR)**

HOLD ME TIGHT*½ (1933) 69m FOX bw

James Dunn *(Chuck)*, Sally Eilers *(Molly)*, Frank McHugh *(Billy)*, June Clyde *(Dottie)*, Kenneth Thomson *(Dolan)*, Noel Francis *(Trudie)*, Dorothy Peterson *(Mary Shane)*, Clay Clement *(Blair)*.

Dunn is a shipping clerk in a department store and Eilers is his wife, who works in the dress department. When a crooked security agent frames Dunn for robbery, the hapless clerk loses his job, which causes problems within the marriage. All is righted in the end and the two lovebirds reconcile. The dialog is as empty as the plot, though the acting is fine.

d, David Butler; w, Gladys Lehman (based on a story by Gertrude Rigdon); ph, Arthur Miller.

Drama **(PR:A MPAA:NR)**

HOLD MY HAND** (1938, Brit.) 76m ABP bw

Stanley Lupino *(Eddie Marston)*, Fred Emney *(Lord Milchester)*, Barbara Blair *(Jane Howard)*, Sally Gray *(Helen)*, Polly Ward *(Paula Pond)*, Bertha Belmore *(Lady Milchester)*, Jack Melford *(Pop Currie)*, John Wood *(Bob Crane)*, Syd Walker *(Inspector Rogers)*, Arthur Rigby *(Norman Love)*, Gibb McLaughlin *(Bank Manager)*.

Lupino puts up his own money to finance his young ward's newspaper, but she thinks he is embezzling money from the operation. It all gets sorted out in the end, with Lupino marrying his secretary and the ward marrying Lupino's friend. Occasionally amusing farce.

p, Walter C. Mycroft; w, Thornton Freeland; w, Clifford Grey, Bert Lee, William Freshman (based on a play by Stanley Lupino); ph, Otto Kanturek.

Comedy **(PR:A MPAA:NR)**

HOLD ON** (1966) 83m MGM c

Peter Noone, Karl Green, Keith Hopwood, Derek Leckenby, Barry Whitwam *(Herman's Hermits)*, Shelley Fabares *(Louisa)*, Sue Ane Langdon *(Cecilie)*, Herbert Anderson *(Lindquist)*, Bernard Fox *(Dudley)*, Harry Hickox *(Grant)*, Hortense Petra *(Mrs. Page)*, Mickey Deems *(Publicist)*, Ray Kellogg, John Hart *(Detectives)*, Phil Arnold *(Photographer)*.

British pop group Herman's Hermits is featured in this so-so answer to the Beatles' film HELP. In this film the Hermits are touring the U.S. followed by NASA scientist Anderson, who is to determine whether the group is worthy of having a space capsule named after it. Langdon is a starlet dreaming of glory and willing to do what she must to get there, while Fabares is Noone's girl. In the end the boys do a big show at the Rose Bowl and get their moniker on that capsule. Quick, painless, and campy by today's standards. Songs: "Hold On!" "A Must to Avoid," "All the Things I Do For You, Baby," "Where Were You When I Needed You?" (P.F. Sloan, Steve Barri), "Make Me Happy," "The George and Dragon," "Got a Feeling," "We Want You, Herman," "Wild Love," "Gotta Get Away" (Fred Karger, Sid Wayne, Ben Weisman), "Leaning on a Lamp Post" (Noel Gray).

p, Sam Katzman; d, Arthur Lubin; w, James B. Gordon; ph, Paul C. Vogel (Panavision, Metrocolor); m, Fred Karger; ed, Ben Lewis; art d, George W. Davis, Eddie Imazu; set d, Henry Grace, Keogh Gleason; spec eff, J. McMillan Johnson; ch, Wilda Taylor.

Musical Comedy **(PR:A MPAA:NR)**

HOLD THAT BABY!** (1949) 64m MON bw

Leo Gorcey *(Slip Mahoney)*, Huntz Hall *(Sach Debussey Jones)*, Frankie Darro *(Bananas)*, Anabel Shaw *(Laura Andrews)*, Gabriel Dell *(Gabe Moreno)*, John Kellogg *(Cherry Nose Gray)*, Edward Gargan *(Burton)*, Billy Benedict *(Whitey)*, Bennie Bartlett *(Butch)*, David Gorcey *(Chuck)*, Ida Moore *(Hope Andrews)*, Florence Auer *(Faith Andrews)*, Bernard Gorcey *(Louie)*, Pierre Watkin *(John Winston)*, Torben Meyer *(Dr. Hans Heinrich)*, Fred Nurney *(Dr. Hugo Schiller)*,

Frances Irvin *(Cynthia)*, Emmett Vogan *(Dr. Foster)*, Meyer Grace *(Joe the Crooner)*, Max Marx *(Gypsy Moran)*, Dunn Twins Judy and Jody *(Jonathan Andrews III)*, William Ruhl *(1st Policeman)*.

Typical witless Bowery Boys comedy finds the group running an automatic laundry. Shaw is a young mother whose baby is being held hostage so she can't collect an inheritance. Gorcey, Hall, and company come to her aid. Gorcey has some moments impersonating a foreign psychologist with Hall as his idiot patient, but it's limited humor. Lots of low comedy, and little of the melodrama mix the boys are noted for. (See BOWERY BOYS series, Index)

p, Jan Grippo; d, Reginald LeBorg; w, Charles B. Marion, Gerald Schnitzer; ph, William Sickner; ed, William Austin; md, Edward Kay; art d, David Milton; set d, Raymond Boltz, Jr.

Comedy **(PR:A MPAA:NR)**

HOLD THAT BLONDE** (1945) 76m PAR bw

Eddie Bracken *(Ogden Spencer Trulow III)*, Veonica Lake *(Sally Martin)*, Albert Dekker *(Inspector Callahan)*, Frank Fenton *(Mr. Phillips)*, George Zucco *(Pavel Sorasky)*, Donald MacBride *(Mr. Kratz)*, Lewis L. Russell *(Mr. Henry Carteret)*, Norma Varden *(Mrs. Henry Carteret)*, Ralph Peters *(Mr. Reddy)*, Robert Watson *(Edwards the Butler)*, Lyle Latell *(Tony)*, Edmund MacDonald *(Victor)*, Willie Best *(Willie Shelley)*, Jack Norton *(Drunk)*, Lee Shumway *(Detective)*, William Frambes *(Elevator Boy)*, James Flavin *(Laundry Truck Driver)*, Jody Gilbert *(Matron)*, Crane Whitley *(Reporter)*, Boyd Davis *(Mr. Sedgemore)*, Mira McKinney *(Mrs. Sedgemore)*, Olaf Hytten *(Charles)*, Grayce Hampton *(Mrs. Case)*, Ralph Dunn *(Radio Cop)*, Shimen Ruskin *(Russian Waiter)*, Kenneth Hunter *(Mr. Van Gelder)*, Mary Currier *(Mrs. Van Gelder)*, Jim Toney *(Kent)*, Kernan Cripps *(Murphy)*.

Lake is a lady thief involved with a gang trying to steal the Romanoff necklace. Bracken is a rich kleptomaniac who tries to stop her. The gang assumes that Lake is a double-crosser and also tries to rub out Bracken. A weak film that tries, unsuccessfully, to combine the gangster milieu with slapstick, though Bracken, as usual, strives mightily to save the day.

p, Paul Jones; d, George Marshall; w, Walter DeLeon, Earl Baldwin, E. Edwin Moran (based on the play by Paul Armstrong), ph, Daniel L. Fapp; m, Werner Heymann; ed, LeRoy Stone; art d, Hans Dreier, Walter Tyler; spec eff, Gordon Jennings.

Comedy/Crime **(PR:A MPAA:NR)**

HOLD THAT CO-ED** (1938) 80m FOX bw (GB: HOLD THAT GIRL)

John Barrymore *(Governor)*, George Murphy *(Rusty)*, Marjorie Weaver *(Marjorie)*, Joan Davis *(Lizzie)*, Jack Haley *(Wilbur)*, George Barbier *(Breckenridge)*, Ruth Terry *(Edie)*, Donald Meek *(Dean Thatcher)*, Johnny Downs *(Dink)*, Paul Hurst *(Slapsy)*, Guinn Williams *(Mike)*, Frank Sully *(Steve)*, Brewster Twins *(Themselves)*, Billy Benedict *(Sylvester)*, Charles C. Wilson *(Coach Burke)*, Glenn Morris *(Spencer)*, Charles Williams *(McFinch)*, John Elliott *(Tremont)*, Fred Kohler, Jr. *(Daly)*, Doodles Weaver *(Gilks)*, Carroll Nye *(Announcer)*, Stanley Andrews *(Belcher)*, Paul McVey *(Man)*, Dora Clement *(Miss Weatherby)*, Russell Hicks *(President)*.

Barrymore plays a governor seeking a Senate seat. He vests his interests in a small college football team and his rival does the same and the two colleges square off in a big game. Barrymore's team wins the game when tomboy Davis kicks a winning field goal, and he then wins the election. Barrymore is quite good in one of his last film roles, a takeoff on the infamous Huey Long of Louisiana. Songs: "Here I Am Doing It," title song (Mack Gordon, Harry Revel); "Limpy Dimp" (Sidney Clare, Nick Castle, Jule Styne); "Heads High" (Lew Brown, Lew Pollack).

p, Darryl F. Zanuck; d, George Marshall; w, Karl Tunberg, Don Ettinger, Jack Yellen (based on a story by Tunberg, Ettinger); ph, Robert Planck; ed, Louis Loeffler; md, Arthur Lange; art d, Bernard Herzbrun, Hans Peters; ch, Nicholas Castle, Geneva Sawyer.

Musical **(PR:A MPAA:NR)**

HOLD THAT GHOST*** (1941) 85m UNIV bw (AKA: OH, CHARLIE)

Bud Abbott *(Chuck Murray)*, Lou Costello *(Ferdinand Jones)*, Richard Carlson *(Dr. Jackson)*, Evelyn Ankers *(Norma Lind)*, Joan Davis *(Camille Brewster)*, Ted Lewis *(Himself)*, Mischa Auer *(Maitre D')*, Marc Lawrence *(Charlie Smith)*, Milton Parsons *(Harry Hoskins)*, Frank Penny *(Snake-Eyes)*, Edgar Dearing *(Irondome)*, Don Terry *(Strangler)*, Edward Pawley *(High Collar)*, Nestor Paiva *(Glum)*, Russell Hicks *(Lawyer Bannister)*, William H. Davidson *(Moose Matson)*, Paul Fix *(Lefty)*, Howard Hickman *(Judge)*, Harry Hayden *(Jenkins)*, William Forrest *(State Trooper)*, Paul Newlan *(Big Fink)*, Joe LaCava *(Little Fink)*, Bobby Barker *(Waiter)*, Shemp Howard *(Soda Jerk)*, Thurston Hall *(Alderman)*, Janet Shaw *(Alderman's Girl)*, Frank Richards *(Gunman)*, William Ruhl *(Customer)*, Mrs. Gardner Crane *(Mrs. Gitledge)*, The Andrews Sisters, Ted Lewis and his Orchestra.

Abbott and Costello inherit a haunted house after a gangster is murdered. There are all sorts of strange goings on that Costello always sees and Abbott does not. Film opens in a nightclub which was an excuse to have The Andrews Sisters and Lewis do two numbers apiece. Though the music cuts into the pace of the story, it's still great to hear those old tunes done by the masters of 1940s pop. An above-average film for the funny twosome with Lou performing some brilliant pantomime as his terror-wracked body bumbles and bounces about the haunted house. Some funny bits occur while the boys attempt to perform gas station jobs. "Suppose someone comes in and asks for ethyl?" Bud queries Lou. The fat man shrugs and says: "I'd tell 'em it's her day off." The rubber-legged Davis later does a slapstick ballet with Lou that is hilarious. Sight gags run rampant and all over Lou who sees a flickering candle ostensibly held by a ghost floating through his room. He frantically calls for Bud but by the time the sidekick arrives the candle is stationary. Lou tucks himself into bed only to find his room suddenly transformed into a gambling den, his bed converted into a crap table. When he runs for Bud the room changes back to a bedroom. When Bud can't stand it anymore he chides Lou, telling him: "Ah, that ghost is just a rumor." Retorts Lou: "I don't care if he's the landlord!" The routines in this film so impressed madcaps Olsen and Johnson that they used some of them in their own GHOST CATCHERS (1944). Exceptional heavy Lawrence is superb as a sinister gangster. In the original ending of this film, Bud and Lou are running a fat farm for the super rich where Davis is the dietician. Lou, just before the fadeout, yanks a bell cord to ring for his dinner but this triggers the opening of a closet door and Lawrence's body falls out. This scene was cut as Universal opted for a more upbeat, musical finale. This one is low comedy at its belly-laughing best. Songs: "Sleepy Serenade" (Mort Greene, Lou Singer, sung by The Andrews Sisters); "Aurora" (Harold Adamson, Mario Lago, Roberto Roberti, sung by The Andrews Sisters); "When My Baby Smiles at Me" (Harry Von Tilzer, Andrew B. Sterling, sung by Ted Lewis); "Me and My Shadow" (Billy Rose, Al Jolson, Dave Dreyer, sung by Lewis). (See ABBOTT & COSTELLO series, Index.)

p, Alex Gottlieb; d, Arthur Lubin; w, Robert Lees, Frederic I. Rinaldo, John Grant (based on a story by Lees and Rinaldo); ph, Elwood Bredell, Joseph Valentine; ed, Philip Cahn.

Comedy **Cas.** **(PR:AAA MPAA:NR)**

HOLD THAT GIRL½** (1934) 70m FOX bw

James Dunn *(Barney Sullivan)*, Claire Trevor *(Tony Bellamy)*, Alan Edwards *(Tom Mallory)*, Gertrude Michael *(Dorothy Lamont)*, John Davidson *(Ackroyd)*, Robert McWade *(McCloy)*, Effie Ellsler *(Grandmother)*, Jay Ward *(Warren)*.

Trevor is a reporter who goes incognito with a troupe of fan dancers. After their show is raided, the troupe is obliged to appear in court. Dunn, a detective, has a love-hate relationship with Trevor and bribes the magistrate so that Trevor is forced to perform the fan dance before the court. A light comedy with an acceptable plot and good feelings throughout.

d, Hamilton MacFadden; w, Dudley Nichols, Lamar Trotti; ph, George Schneiderman.

Comedy **(PR:A MPAA:NR)**

HOLD THAT HYPNOTIST** (1957) 61m AA bw

Huntz Hall *(Satch)*, Stanley Clements *(Duke)*, Jane Nigh *(Cleo)*, Robert Foulk *(Dr. Noble)*, James Flavin *(Morgan)*, Queenie Smith *(Mrs. Kelly)*, David Condon *(Chuck)*, Jimmy Murphy *(Myron)*, Murray Alper *(Gale)*, Dick Elliott *(Clerk)*, Mel Welles *(Blackbeard)*.

In another Bowery Boys romp, Hall falls in with evil hypnotist Foulk who sends him back in time (through hypnosis) to the days of Blackbeard the pirate to learn the location of some buried treasure. When Hall awakes, the doctor pulls a gun and runs off to dig up the treasure. The boys beat him there, subdue the villain, and learn that the treasure is actually loot that was never recovered from a jewelry store robbery, and they turn it over to the cops. (See BOWERY BOYS series, Index.)

p, Ben Schwalb; d, Austen Jewell; w, Dan Pepper; ph, Harry Neumann; ed, George White; md, Marlin Skiles; art d, David Milton; set d, Joseph Kish.

Comedy **(PR:A MPAA:NR)**

HOLD THAT KISS** (1938) 75m MGM bw

Maureen O'Sullivan (June Evans), Dennis O'Keefe *(Tommy Bradford)*, Mickey Rooney *(Chick Evans)*, George Barbier *(Mr. Peirpont)*, Jessie Ralph *(Aunt Lucy)*, Edward S. Brophy *(Al)*, Fay Holden *(Mrs. Evans)*, Philip Terry *(Ted Evans)*, Ruth Hussey *(Nadine Peirpont)*, Barnett Parker *(Maurice)*, Frank Albertson *(Steve Evans)*.

O'Sullivan and O'Keefe meet at a wedding reception. Both think the other is wealthy and from a good family. Neither is, but they carry on a courtship until the truth is discovered. A minor film with an old plot that had some freshness in its handling. Typical MGM B picture used as a trainer for the growing Rooney.

p, John W. Considine, Jr.; d, Edwin L. Marin; w, Stanley Rauh; ph, George Folsey; m, Edward Ward; ed, Ben Lewis; art d, Cedric Gibbons.

Comedy **(PR:A MPAA:NR)**

HOLD THAT LINE** (1952) 67m MON bw

Leo Gorcey *(Slip)*, Huntz Hall *(Sach)*, Gil Stratton, Jr. *(Junior)*, David Gorcey *(Chuck)*, Bennie Bartlett *(Butch)*, Bernard Gorcey *(Louie)*, Taylor Holmes *(Dean Forrester)*, Francis Pierlot *(Billingsley)*, Pierre Watkin *(Stanhope)*, John Bromfield *(Biff)*, Bob Nichols *(Harold)*, Mona Knox *(Katie Wayne)*, Gloria Winters *(Penny)*, Paul Bryar *(Coach Rowland)*, Bob Peoples *(Assistant Coach)*, Veda Ann Borg *(Candy Calin)*, Byron Foulger *(Prof. Grog)*, Tom Hanlon *(Football Announcer)*, George Lewis *(Mike Donelli)*, Al Eben *(Big Dave)*, Ted Stanhope *(Prof. Wintz)*, Percival Vivian *(Prof. Hovel)*, Tom Kennedy *(Murphy)*, Bert Davidson *(Police Sergeant)*, Marjorie Eaton *(Miss Whitsett)*, Jean Dean *(Girl Student)*, Steve Wayne *(Boy Student)*, Ted Jourdan *(1st Player)*, George Sanders *(2nd Player)*, Marvelle Andre *(Girl)*.

"Pygmalion meets the Bowery Boys" plot has Gorcey and Hall enrolling at an Ivy League school to test whether uncouth and vulgar types can become cultured and refined. The formula series mayhem follows. There's a climactic football game, which director Beaudine handled better than the comedy scenes. (See BOWERY BOYS series, Index).

p, Jerry Thomas; d, William Beaudine; w, Tim Ryan, Charles Marion, Bert Lawrence, ph, Marcel Le Picard; ed, William Austin; md, Edward J. Kay; art d, Martin Obzina.

Comedy **(PR:A MPAA:NR)**

HOLD THAT WOMAN* (1940) 61m PRC bw

James Dunn *(Jimmy Parker)*, Frances Gifford *(Mary Mulvaney)*, George Douglas *(Steve Brady)*, Martin Spellman *(Mike Mulvaney)*, Rita LaRoy *(Lulu Driscoll)*, Eddie Fetherston *(Conroy)*, Guy Usher *(Officer Mulvaney)*, Paul Bryar *(Duke Jurgens)*, William Newell, Ed Miller, John Dilson, Dave O'Brien, Anna Lisa, William Hall, Jack Roper, Marie Rice, Frank Meredith, Alaine Brandeis.

Dunn is a repossession agent for a company called Skip Tracers, Ltd., and he is after a radio on which the installments have not been paid. After recovering the radio, he is pursued by gangsters, and he finally learns that the radio is a receptacle for some stolen jewels. It is all resolved with Dunn bringing about the capture of the crooks, and the lame story hobbles to an end.

p, Sigmund Neufeld; d, Sherman Scott; w, George Bricker (based on a story by William L. Schrock, William Pierce), ph, Jack Greenhalgh; ed, Holbrook Todd.

Crime **(PR:A MPAA:NR)**

HOLD THE PRESS** (1933) 65m COL bw

Tim McCoy *(Tim)*, Shirley Grey *(Edith)*, Henry Wadsworth *(Frankie)*, Oscar Apfel *(Bishop)*, Wheeler Oakman *(Abbott)*, Samuel Hinds *(Taylor)*, Joseph Crehan *(Brennan)*, Bradley Page *(Serrano)*, Julian Rivero *(Gross)*, Ed Le Saint *(Judge)*.

Though he was more at home on a horse, McCoy is good as a reporter in this film. He's the typical hardboiled reporter after a murderer and of course the shootout is there for McCoy's western fans. An interesting career departure for the star.

d, Phil Rosen; w, Horace McCoy; ph, Benjamin Kline; ed, Otto Meyer.

Crime **(PR:C MPAA:NR)**

HOLD-UP A LA MILANAISE (SEE: FIASCO IN MILAN, 1963, Fr.)

HOLD YOUR MAN* (1929) 60m UNIV bw

Laura La Plante, Scott Kolk, Eugene Borden, Mildred Van Dorn, Walter Scott.

Insipid piece about La Plante as an artistic woman bored with businessman husband Kolk. She runs off to Paris to find herself, and meets a man she thinks is royalty but is actually a gangster. Meanwhile, hubby has an affair with Van Dorn. La Plante decides she wants him back and schemes a way to do it. Boring and unbelievable, with poorly handled scenes. La Plante's scene in satin pajamas raised a few eyebrows when she gets her body wiggled by a reducing machine.

d, Emmett J. Flynn; w, Harold Shumate (based on a story by Maxine Alton); ph, Gilbert Warrenton; ed, Jack English.

Drama **(PR:C MPAA:NR)**

HOLD YOUR MAN*** (1933) 88m MGM bw

Jean Harlow *(Ruby Adams)*, Clark Gable *(E. "Eddy" Huntington Hall)*, Stuart Erwin *(Al Simpson)*, Dorothy Burgess *(Gypsy)*, Muriel Kirkland *(Bertha Dillon)*, Garry Owen *(Slim)*, Barbara Barondess *(Sadie Kline)*, Paul Hurst *(Aubrey Mitchell)*, Elizabeth Patterson *(Miss Tuttle)*, Theresa Harris *(Lily Mae Crippen)*, Inez Courtney *(Maizie)*, Blanche Friderici *(Mrs. Wagner)*, Helen Freeman *(Miss Davis)*, George Reed *(Rev. Crippen)*, Louise Beavers *(Maid)*, Jack Cheatham, Frank Hagney *(Cops)*, Jack Randall *(Dance Extra)*, G. Pat Collins *(Phil Dunn)*, Harry Semels *(Neighbor)*, Nora Cecil *(Miss Campbell, the Sewing Instructor)*, Eva McKenzie *(Cooking Teacher)*.

Gable is a heel in this film, but one with a heart, and the girl he falls for is Harlow. After pulling off a caper and running from the police, Gable hides in Harlow's apartment and stays on to develop an affair. She gives up all for him, including sappy boy friend Erwin, but still she's worried about his wandering eye. To make him jealous she tells him that wealthy laundry owner Hurst has big plans for her and this gives Gable the idea of pulling a scam. He and pal Owen corner Hurst but the laundry owner becomes feisty and, in a fight, is accidentally killed. Gable flees and Harlow is blamed for the death, being sent to prison for three years. Through Burgess, a former girl friend of Gable's and a cellmate of Harlow's, Gable learns that Harlow is pregnant with his child. Burgess has just been released from prison and her way has been made easier by good-natured Harlow who has given her some contacts on the outside. She wants to return the favor and Gable asks her to smuggle him into the women's prison. She does, arranging for a black preacher visiting his daughter to marry Gable and Harlow so the child will be legitimate. Police barge in just as the ceremony is completed and Gable is arrested and sent to prison. Harlow is released and is waiting for him with their child for a happy if sloppily sentimental reunion. The improbable story is punctuated with crackling dialog. At one point Gable tells Harlow: "Wait till you see how I'll grow on you." Playing the hooker with a heart (what else?), the wisecracking Harlow replies: "Yeah—like a carbuncle!" Wood's direction drags at times, particularly when he tries to infuse interest in the dull prison work Harlow is compelled to do. But the Gable-Harlow combination, begun with the steamy RED DUST, 1932, still sparkles with their electric personalities. Harlow married Rosson, the cinematographer of this film (he shot four of her films, this being the third), but after their 1935 divorce, MGM prudently gave the blonde bombshell another cameraman, Ray June.

p&d, Sam Wood; w, Anita Loos, Howard Emmett Rogers (based on a story by Loos); ph, Harold G. Rosson; ed, Frank Sullivan; art d, Cedric Gibbons, Merrill Pye; set d, Edwin B. Willis; cos, Adrian; m/l, Arthur Freed, Nacio Herb Brown.

Romance Drama **(PR:C MPAA:NR)**

HOLE IN THE HEAD, A½** (1959) 120m UA c

Frank Sinatra *(Tony Manetta)*, Edward G. Robinson *(Mario Manetta)*, Eddie Hodges *(Ally Manetta)*, Eleanor Parker *(Mrs. Rogers)*, Carolyn Jones *(Shirl)*, Thelma Ritter *(Sophie Manetta)*, Keenan Wynn *(Jerry Marks)*, Joi Lansing *(Dorine)*, George DeWitt *(Mendy)*, Jimmy Komack *(Julius Manetta)*, Dub Taylor *(Fred)*, Connie Sawyer *(Miss Wexler)*, Benny Rubin *(Mr. Diamond)*, Ruby Dandridge *(Sally)*, B.S. Pully *(Hood No. 1)*, Joyce Nizzari *(Alice)*, Pupi Campo *(M.C.)*, Robert B. Williams *(Cabby)*, Emory Parnell *(Sheriff)*, Billy Walker *(Andy)*.

Not one of Capra's best efforts, this family opus has Sinatra as an irresponsible widower with a young son, Hodges. Instead of trying to improve his run-down little Miami Beach hotel, Sinatra flits about with bongo player Jones, trying to promote himself into big time deals. His dream is to establish a giant amusement park in Florida. When he fails to make mortgage payments on his hotel, he is threatened with losing the place. In desperation, the 40-year-old improvident promoter calls his all-business brother, Robinson, a clothing manufacturer in New York. He lies to Robinson, telling him he needs money because his son is sick and this brings Robinson and wife Ritter quickly to Florida where they learn the truth. Sinatra's business is about to collapse because he is an inept dreamer, and, moreover, he has neglected his devoted son, which angers the practical Robinson. He tells Sinatra that if he settles down, takes over a respectable business in the Bronx, and marries Parker, an attractive but penniless widow (with tinted vermillion hair), he will back him financially. Sinatra attacks Robinson for being square. He approaches Wynn, an old friend who has become a big time promoter, and offers him plans for his real estate-amusement park. Wynn toys with him sadistically, then turns him down, saying that Sinatra's plans are fine "for Disney!" Sinatra collapses emotionally and gives up his son to Robinson. Hodges is tearfully taken away from the one man he adores but Robinson can't bring himself to break them up and in the end returns Hodges to Sinatra's waiting arms, finances the hotel, and watches his brother wind up with Jones. The acting here is routine, except for Robinson and Ritter who stand out, he as a crusty and stern patriarch with a soft spot, she with a huge soft spot for Hodges. Too many tears flow from Hodges for him to be believable and Jones waltzes through her prop role delivering forgettable lines in a monotone. Capra's gifts are seen only slightly since the material does not allow him to shine; his characters simply are not appealing, memorable, or worthy of down-home distinction. The play on which the movie is based is far superior to the film. The best thing about the film is the song "High Hopes" (Sammy Cahn, Jimmy Van Heusen). The pair also offered "All My Tomorrows." Filmed in Cypress Gardens, Florida, with main titles bannered on a passing Goodyear blimp.

p&d, Frank Capra; w, Arnold Shulman (based on his play); ph, William H. Daniels (CinemaScope, DeLuxe Color); m, Nelson Riddle; ed, William Hornbeck; art d, Eddie Imazu; cos, Edith Head; m/l, Sammy Cahn, Jimmy Van Heusen.

Comedy **(PR:A MPAA:NR)**

HOLE IN THE WALL½** (1929) 73m PAR bw

Claudette Colbert *(Jean Oliver)*, Edward G. Robinson *(The Fox)*, David Newell *(Gordon Grant)*, Nelly Savage *(Mme. Mystera)*, Donald Meek *(Goffy)*, Alan Brooks *(Jim)*, Louise Closser Hale *(Mrs. Ramsay)*, Katherine Emmet *(Mrs. Carslake)*, Marcia Kagno *(Marcia)*, Barry Macollum *(Dogface)*, George McQuarrie *(Inspector)*, Helen Crane *(Mrs. Lyons)*, Gamby-Hall Girls *(Dancers)*.

Upon release from prison for a crime she didn't commit, Colbert decides to pose as a fortune teller to enact revenge on the woman who set her up, Hale. Disguised as a gypsy, Colbert kidnaps Hale's young granddaughter, Kagno, and plans to raise the child as a thief. She is temporarily distracted from her plan when the town's local gangster, Robinson, and newspaper reporter Newell both fall in love with her. Blinded by her thirst for vengeance, Colbert ignores the men (though she has loved Newell from afar since they were in school) and proceeds with her plot. Desperate for her attention, Robinson kidnaps Kagno from Colbert and agrees to release the child if she will reciprocate his love. While awaiting her response, Robinson has one of his hoods take the child to a nearby railway dock for safekeeping. As the goon ties Kagno to a post, he loses his footing, falls into the harbor, and drowns. Kagno however, remains tied to the post with the tide about to come in. Newell, unaware of Colbert's secret identity, leads the police to the fortune teller's parlor where they arrest her. Realizing that Colbert doesn't love him, Robinson nobly decides to make a deal with the police for her freedom. They agree and the daughter is saved, leaving Colbert and Newell to marry. While HOLE IN THE WALL is nothing more than an overly melodramatic crime story, the film is saved by Robinson's complex and energetic performance—his first as a gangster. Bringing many shades to his characterization, Robinson manages to portray an outwardly intimidating hoodlum, who deep down needs to give and receive love. When his misfired attempt at romance is rebuffed, the frustrated gangster's baser instincts take over and he tries to force Colbert to love him. Eventually Robinson's rational mind returns and after realizing he will never have Colbert, he sacrifices himself so that she may be happy. This is a moment of self-realization and compassion rarely attributed to movie gangsters, especially when the genre was in its infancy, making HOLE IN THE WALL valuable to anyone interested in the genesis of the gangster film.

p, Monta Bell; d, Robert Florey; w, Pierre Collings (based on the play by Fred Jackson); ph, George Folsey; ed, Morton Blumenstock.

Crime **(PR:A-C MPAA:NR)**

HOLIDAY*** (1930) 83m Pathe bw

Ann Harding *(Linda Seton)*, Robert Ames *(John Case)*, Mary Astor *(Julia Seton)*, Edward Everett Horton *(Nick Potter)*, Hedda Hopper *(Susan Potter)*, Monroe Owsley *(Ned Seton)*, William Holden *(Edward Seton)*, Hallam Cooley *(Seton Cram)*, Mable Forrest *(Laura)*, Creighton Hale *(Pete Hedges)*, Mary Elizabeth Forbes *(Mrs. Pritchard Ames)*, Elizabeth Forrester *(Laura)*.

Harding and Astor play two sisters in a wealthy family. Ames is engaged to Astor but ends up with the flippant Harding. A funny and little known film, probably because of the more famous re-make done eight years later with Cary Grant and Katharine Hepburn. The dialog in this earlier version is fresh and crisp, with good acting all around. Watch for an appearance by Hopper, who was to become one of Hollywood's most notorious gossip columnists.

p, E. B. Derr; d, E. H. Griffith; w, Horace Jackson, Philip Barry (based on a story by Barry); ph, Norbert Brodine; m, Josiah Zuro; ed, Daniel Mandell; art d, Carroll Clark; cos, Gwen Wakeling.

Comedy **(PR:A MPAA:NR)**

HOLIDAY*½** (1938) 93m COL bw (GB: FREE TO LIVE; UNCONVENTIONAL LINDA)

Katharine Hepburn *(Linda Seton)*, Cary Grant *(Johnny Case)*, Doris Nolan *(Julia Seton)*, Lew Ayres *(Ned Seton)*, Edward Everett Horton *(Nick Potter)*, Henry Kolker *(Edward Seton)*, Binnie Barnes *(Laura Cram)*, Jean Dixon *(Susan Potter)*, Henry Daniell *(Seton Cram)*, Charles Trowbridge *(Banker)*, George Pauncefort *(Henry)*, Charles Richman *(Thayer)*, Mitchell Harris *(Jennings)*, Neil Fitzgerald *(Edgar)*, Marion Ballou *(Grandmother)*, Howard Hickman *(Man in Church)*, Hilda Plowright *(Woman in Church)*, Henry Allen, Edward Cooper *(Scotchmen)*, Margaret McWade *(Farmer's Wife)*, Frank Shannon *(Farmer)*, Aileen Carlyle *(Farm Girl)*, Matt McHugh *(Taxi Driver)*, Maurice Brierre *(Steward)*, Esther Peck *(Mrs. Jennings)*, Lillian West *(Mrs. Thayer)*, Luke Cosgrave *(Grandfather)*, Bess Flowers *(Countess)*, George Hickman *(Telegraph Boy)*, Maude Hume *(Maid)*.

A delightful comedy with all the sophistication that Cukor could muster, which was plenty, the famous Barry play is enlightened and enhanced with the blinding talents of Hepburn and Grant. She's a rich socialite who wants to experience the newness of life high and low, to taste all the extraordinary pleasures and excel in them. Her sister Nolan is engaged to Grant, an unlikely husband-to-be. Grant is the poor boy from the wrong side of the tracks and Nolan's love for him includes an ambition to have him go into her father's bank and rise through the ranks of ledgers and mortgages. He wants to do anything but spend the rest of his life in the musty confines of a stuffy, unfeeling banking institution. He refuses to conform to Nolan's dictates and, after some zany confrontations, they break it off. But before Grant can vanish forever, Hepburn, who has loved him and his independent ways from afar, declares her undying affection and admiration for his unconquered spirit. Grant is smooth as a marble foyer in a rich man's mansion and Hepburn is spontaneous (or appears to be), bursting with energy, hope, and no little wit, although her flat metallic voice sometimes creates a ringing in the ears, and this is because she must handle some lengthy speeches that are more wistful than forceful. This was Cukor's special kind of light humor film, a casual study of the wealthy so ironically popular in the 1930s when most filmgoers were poor; oddly, the public seemed to clamor to see how it was at the top where the rich were truly idle, even wasteful, and, with no real work to do, struggling heroically to fight off boredom. Nolan is the epitome of this malaise. (The public fascination here was somewhat masochistic, not dissimilar to that of a stoned alcoholic compelling himself to sit through endless anti-saloon lectures.) Ayres, as the dissolute, heavily drinking brother who has condemned his own uppercrust class as worthless and has a fatalistic view of the world and his own future, is outstanding, as is Horton. Wry humor pours from the script as quickly as a dry martini, the kind of quick wit without emotional resolution for which scripter Stewart was famous and Barry celebrated. Yet much of it seems sadly dated today, redeemed only by Grant's down-to-earth stance and Hepburn's incredible ebullience. Grant had nothing but praise for Hepburn after completing this comedy: "As an actress, she's a joy to work with. She's in there trying every minute. There isn't anything passive about her. She 'gives.' And, as a person, she's real. There's no pretense about her. She's the most completely honest woman I've ever met." Hepburn needed the bolstering in 1938. The Independent Theatre Owners Association had recently given her her walking papers, reporting that she was box office poison. This was Columbia's answer, a top flight production to back the actress. Studio boss Harry Cohn had paid RKO in 1936 about $80,000 for HOLIDAY, THE AWFUL TRUTH, and other scripts; RKO had made HOLIDAY in 1930 with Ann Harding, Robert Ames, and Mary Astor, an unsuccessful effort. Cohn originally wanted Irene Dunne to play the lead but when he got Hepburn through Cukor's insistence, he backed her 100 percent. The lascivious mogul first interviewed her and interrupted her nonstop chatter by saying: "Leland Hayward tells me you're a great lay in the hay," a crude ploy meant to disarm Hepburn's poise. She ignored the remark and went on talking. He repeated the sexist comment and she still went on talking. Cohn gave up. The film did not make money (even Hepburn's finest film for RKO, BRINGING UP BABY (1938) lost $365,000) and Cohn refused to put Hepburn into another Columbia film. Stewart, however, became one of the actress' favorite writers and he would go on doing scripts for her, including THE PHILADELPHIA STORY, 1940, KEEPER OF THE FLAME, 1942, and WITHOUT LOVE, 1945.

p, Everett Riskin; d, George Cukor; w, Donald Ogden Stewart, Sidney Buchman (based on the play by Philip Barry); ph, Franz Planer; m, Sidney Cutner; ed, Otto Meyer, Al Clark; md, M. W. Stoloff; art d, Stephen Goosson, Lionel Banks; set d, Babs Johnstone; cos, Robert Kalloch.

Comedy **(PR:A MPAA:NR)**

HOLIDAY AFFAIR½** (1949) 86m RKO bw

Robert Mitchum *(Steve)*, Janet Leigh *(Connie)*, Griff Barnett *(Mr. Ennis)*, Wendell Corey *(Carl)*, Esther Dale *(Mrs. Ennis)*, Henry O'Neill *(Mr. Crowley)*, Henry Morgan *(Police Lieutenant)*, Larry J. Blake *(Plainclothesman)*, Helen Brown *(Emily)*, Gordon Gebert *(Timmy)*, James Griffith *(Floorwalker)*, Frances Morris *(Housekeeper)*, Allen Mathews *(Mr. Gow)*, Frank Johnson *(Santa Claus)*, Al Murphy, Mame Henderson, Pat Hall, Bill Henry, Jim Hawkins, Robert Lyden, Jack Chete, Don Dillaway, Joe Ray, Mary Stewart, Frank Mills, Philip Morris, Chick Chandler.

Sentimental Christmas movie features Leigh as the widowed mother of six year-old charmer Gebert. The young lad wants a set of trains for the holiday and Leigh treks off to the department store to satisfy his wish. There she meets sales clerk Mitchum, who is immediately taken with her. He spends his own money on the train set, winning her heart and incurring the wrath of her fiance, Corey. Mitchum gives a surprisingly strong performance in a character-type he normally steered away from. The picture was a box office disaster and as a result RKO cancelled director Hartman's contract after this, his second film for the studio.

p&d, Don Hartman; w, Isobel Lennart (based on the story "Christmas Gift" by John D. Weaver); ph, Milton Krasner; m, Roy Webb; ed, Harry Marker; md, C. Bakaleinikoff; art d, Albert S. D'Agostino, Carroll Clark.

Romance **(PR:A MPAA:NR)**

HOLIDAY CAMP½** (1947, Brit.) 97m Gainsborough/UNIV bw

Flora Robson *(Esther Harman)*, Dennis Price *(Squad Leader Hardwicke)*, Jack Warner *(Joe Huggett)*, Hazel Court *(Joan Martin)*, Emrys Jones *(Michael Halliday)*, Kathleen Harrison *(Ethel Huggett)*, Yvonne Owen *(Angela Kirby)*, Esmond Knight *(Announcer)*, Jimmy Hanley *(Jimmy Gardner)*, Peter Hammond *(Harry Huggett)*, Dennis Harkin *(Charlie)*, Esma Cannon *(Elsie Dawson)*, John Blythe *(Steve)*, Jeannette Tregarthan *(Valerie Thompson)*, Beatrice Varley *(Aunt)*, Susan Shaw *(Patsy Crawford)*, Maurice Denham *(Doctor)*, Jane Hylton *(Receptionist)*, Jack Raine, John Stone *(Detectives)*, Reginald Purdell, Jack Ellis, Alfie Bass, Phil Fowler *(Red Coats)*, Patricia Roc *(Herself)*, Cheerful Charlie Chester *(Himself)*, Gerry Wilmot *(Herself)*, Pamela Bramah *(Beauty Queen)*.

A variety of people with different stories and backgrounds are on vacation at the same summer holiday camp. Just about every type is represented: a bus driver with his family; a jilted seaman; a homely maid; a young couple out on a fling; a refined old spinster; and a supposed RAF pilot who really is a killer. The film is told episodically with the search for the killer woven through the different stories. The performances are fine and the direction lets the story naturally unfold.

p, Sydney Box; d, Ken Annakin; w, Box, Muriel Box, Peter Rogers, Mabel Constanduros, Denis Constanduros, Ted Willis (based on a story by Godfrey Winn); ph, Jack Cox; m, Bob Busby; ed, Alfred Roome; md, Louis Levy.

Comedy/Drama **(PR:C MPAA:NR)**

HOLIDAY FOR HENRIETTA**** (1955, Fr.) 118m Regina-Filmsonor/Ardee bw (LA FETE A HENRIETTE)

Dany Robin *(Henriette)*, Hildegarde Neff *(Rita Solar)*, Michel Auclair *(Maurice/Marcel)*, Michel Roux *(Robert)*, Louis Seigner, Henri Cremieux *(Script Writers)*, Daniel Ivernel *(Detective)*, Micheline Francey *(Script Girl)*, Saturnin Fabre *(Man in Cafe)*, Paulette Dubost *(Mother)*, Alexandre Rignault *(Father)*, Odette Laure *(Valentine)*, Jeanette Batti *(Gisele)*, Julien Carette *(Arthur)*.

Charming comedy that was remade nine years later into a slapdash film called PARIS WHEN IT SIZZLES. Seigner and Cremieux are two script writers who are crushed when their newest work is snipped to bits by censors. They begin to improvise a story about Robin, a dressmaker in Paris, with two very different versions being dreamed up by each as one of them favors *noir* and the other *rose*. Cremieux concocts a sleazy melodrama while Seigner thinks up a story of love, naivete, and warmth. Both their ideas are seen by the audience and the film gets written with an hysterical culmination on Bastille Day. Then their balloon is burst when Auclair, an actor, informs them that someone else has already written that story. A whimsical satire of movies with Duvivier employing many cinematic techniques to make his point. It's intelligent, clever, and eye-catching, and one wishes it had been released widely in the U.S. before the dull remake. Robin began her show business career as a ballerina with the Paris Opera and only had a few credits in English-speaking films—WALTZ OF THE TOREADORS, FOLLOW THE BOYS, TOPAZ, and THE BEST HOUSE IN LONDON being the most prominent. Co-star Neff (born Knef in Ulm, Germany, same town as Albert Einstein) is well-spoken in several languages and made films in France, Germany, England, and the U.S. before appearing on Broadway in Cole Porter's "Silk Stockings" and then becoming a writer. Her two most famous books were *The Gift Horse*, her autobiography, and *The Verdict*, a highly personal account of her cancer surgeries. Auclair was born Vladimir Vujovic in Germany, son of a Serbian father and a French mother. He has mainly appeared in French films with but one English-speaking credit in FUNNY FACE. Director/co-writer Duvivier achieved great fame with his work on THE LITTLE WORLD OF DON CAMILLO as well as ANNA KARENINA, PEPE LE MOKO, FLESH AND FANTASY and many more in a career that lasted almost half a century.

d, Julien Duvivier; w, Henri Jeanson, Duvivier; ph, Roger Hubert; m, George Auric; ed, Marthe Poncin.

Comedy **(PR:A MPAA:NR)**

HOLIDAY FOR LOVERS** (1959) 103m FOX c

Clifton Webb *(Robert Dean)*, Jane Wyman *(Mary Dean)*, Jill St. John *(Meg Dean)*, Carol Lynley *(Betsy Dean)*, Paul Henreid *(Eduardo Barroso)*, Gary Crosby *(Paul Gattling)*, Nico Minardos *(Carlos)*, Wally Brown *(Joe)*, Henny Backus *(Connie)*, Nora O'Mahoney *(Mrs. Murphy)*, Buck Class *(Staff Sergeant)*, Al Austin *(Technical Sergeant)*, Jose Greco, Nestor Amaral and his Orchestra.

Webb is a Boston psychiatrist on holiday in South America, along with his spouse, Wyman, and daughters, St. John and Lynley. He finds himself spending most of his time trying to keep his girls away from men. He is angry when St. John falls for architect Henreid and becomes more enraged when it is discovered that St. John really is after Henreid's beatnik son, Minardos. Meanwhile, Lynley, the younger daughter, has amorous designs on Air Force sergeant Crosby. Eventually Webb comes to terms with his children and their respective love lives. Some marvelous footage of Rio de Janeiro and Lima, Peru, and exciting bullfighting scenes as well.

p, David Weisbart; d, Henry Levin; w, Luther Davis (based on the play by Ronald Alexander); ph, Charles G. Clarke (CinemaScope, DeLuxe Color); m, Leigh Harline; ed, Stuart Gilmore; md, Alfred Newman; art d, Lyle R. Wheeler, Herman A. Blumenthal; spec eff, L.B. Abbott; m/l, title song, Sammy Cahn, James Van Heusen.

Romance/Comedy **(PR:A MPAA:NR)**

HOLIDAY FOR SINNERS** (1952) 72m MGM bw

Gig Young *(Jason Kent)*, Keenan Wynn *(Joe Piavi)*, Janice Rule *(Susan Corvier)*, William Campbell *(Danny Farber)*, Richard Anderson *(Father Victor)*, Michael Chekhov *(Dr. Konndorff)*, Sandro Giglio *(Nick Muto)*, Edith Barrett *(Mrs. Corvier)*, Porter Hall *(Louie)*, Ralph Dumke *(Mike Hennighan)*, Frank DeKova *(The Wiry Man)*, Will Wright *(Man with Cigar)*, Jack Raine *(Dr. Surtees)*.

Grim film with the New Orleans Mardi Gras celebration serving as a backdrop. Doctor Young, ex-fighter Wynn, and priest Anderson are three friends who grew up together in a poor New Orleans neighborhood. Young is in love with Rule and is also fighting his ungrateful patients, poor people inherited from his father's practice. Wynn is in trouble after killing a crooked fight promoter who owed him some money, and eventually he, too, is killed by the promoter's thugs. The individual episodes don't quite work as a whole and placing all of this unhappiness against the gaiety of the Mardi Gras doesn't come off as well as it should.

p, John Houseman; d, Gerald Mayer; w, A.I. Bezzerides (based on the novel by Hamilton Basso); ph, Paul Vogel; ed, Frederick Y. Smith; md, Alberto Colombo; art d, Cedric Gibbons, Arthur Longergan.

Drama **(PR:C MPAA:NR)**

HOLIDAY IN HAVANA½** (1949) 70m COL bw

Desi Arnaz *(Carlos Estrada)*, Mary Hatcher *(Lolita Valdez)*, Ann Doran *(Marge Henley)*, Steven Geray *(Lopez)*, Minerva Urecal *(Mama Valdez)*, Sig Arno *(Pepe)*, Ray Walker *(Sam Keegan)*, Nacho Galindo *(Police Sergeant)*, Tito Renaldo *(Juan)*, Argentina Brunetti *(Mrs. Estrada)*, Martin Garralaga *(Mr. Estrada)*, Elsa Zepeda *(Marin Estrada)*, Lillian Molieri *(Felicia)*, Leon Belasco *(Luis Amantado)*, Cecelia Callejo *(Pepita)*, Fred Godoy *(Head Waiter)*.

Arnaz is a Cuban bandleader in love with Hatcher, a dancer at the club where he performs. Through a misunderstanding they break up, only to reunite at an important Havana music festival. There they find their lost love once more, as well as fame. Light fare at best, but enjoyable. Songs: "Holiday in Havana," "The Arnaz Jam" (Arnaz); "Straw Hat Song" (Fred Karger, Allan Roberts); "Rhumba Rumbero" (Albert Gamse, Miguelito Valdez); "Copacobana" (Doris Fisher, Allan Roberts); "Made for Each Other" (Ervin Drake, Jimmy Shirl, Rene Touzet); "I'll Take Romance" (Oscar Hammerstein II, Ben Oakland).

p, Ted Richmond; d, Jean Yarbrough; w, Robert Lees, Frederic I. Rinaldo, Karen DeWolf (based on a story by Morton Grant); ph, Vincent Farrar; ed, Henry Batista; md, Paul Mertz; art d, Robert Peterson.

Musical **(PR:A MPAA:NR)**

HOLIDAY IN MEXICO** (1946) 127m MGM c

Walter Pidgeon *(Jeffrey Evans)*, Jose Iturbi *(Himself)*, Roddy McDowall *(Stanley Owen)*, Ilona Massey *(Toni Karpathy)*, Xavier Cugat *(Himself)*, Jane Powell *(Christine Evans)*, Hugo Haas *(Angus)*, Mikhail Rasumny *(Baranga)*, Helene Stanley *(Yvette Baranga)*, William "Bill" Philips *(Sam)*, Amparo Iturbi *(Herself)*, Tonia Hero *(Herself)*, Teresa Hero *(Herself)*, Marina Koshetz *(Mme. Baranga)*, Linda Christian *(Angel)*, Ann Codee *(Margaret)*, Paul Stanton *(Sir Edward Owen)*, Doris Lloyd *(Cady Millicent Owen)*, Rosia Marstini *(Maria)*, Fidel Castro.

Pidgeon is the U.S. Ambassador to Mexico. His daughter Powell thinks she is in love with the much older Iturbi. McDowall is her jealous boy friend, with Massey as the love interest for Pidgeon. A simplistic story that's really just an excuse for lavish song-and-dance numbers. Lots of color, big sets, and all-out production numbers, Cugat and his orchestra perform a few Latin tunes, while Iturbi takes on Rachmaninoff and Chopin. There are also some arrangements of Wagner thrown in with the Latin numbers. Of historical interest is the fact that Cuban premier Fidel Castro appeared in HOLIDAY IN MEXICO as a teenager. According to Cugat, Castro appeared in several crowd scenes in several South American-theme movies because he was a "typical Latin American boy." Songs: "I Think of You" (Jack Elliott, Don Marcotte—based on the 2nd theme of the 1st movement of Sergei Vassilievich Rachmaninoff's Piano Concerto No. 2); "Walter Winchell Rhumba" (Carl Sigman, Noro Morales); "Yo Te Amo Mucho—And That's That" (Sammy Stept, Ervin Drake, Cugat, Morales); "You, So It's You" (Earl Brent, Nacio Herb Brown); "And Dreams Remain" (Ralph Freed, Raoul Soler); "Holiday in Mexico" (Freed, Sammy Fain); Ave Maria" (Franz Peter Schubert); "Les Filles de Cadiz" (Leo Delibes, Alfred De Musset); "Italian Street Song" (Victor Herbert, Rida Johnson Young); "Polonaise in A Flat Major" (Frederic Francois Chopin), "Goodnight Sweetheart" (Ray Noble, James Campbell, Reg Connelly); "Three Blind Mice" (arranged by Andre Previn); "The Music Goes 'Round and Around" (Red Hodgson, Ed Farley, Mike Riley); "Liebestod" (from "Tristan and Isolde" by Richard Wagner); "Someone to Love."

p, Joe Pasternak; d, George Sidney; w, Isobel Lennart (based on a story by William Kozlenko); ph, Harry Stradling (Technicolor); m, Georgie Stoll; ed, Adrienne Fazan; art d, Cedric Gibbons, Jack Martin Smith; spec eff, Warren Newcombe; ch, Stanley Donen.

Musical **(PR:A MPAA:NR)**

HOLIDAY IN SPAIN (SEE: SCENT OF MYSTERY, 1960)

HOLIDAY INN**** (1942) 100m PAR bw

Bing Crosby *(Jim Hardy)*, Fred Astaire *(Ted Hanover)*, Marjorie Reynolds *(Linda Mason)*, Virginia Dale *(Lila Dixon)*, Walter Abel *(Danny Reid)*, Louise Beavers *(Mamie)*, John Gallaudet *(Parker)*, James Bell *(Dunbar)*, Irving Bacon *(Gus)*, Shelby Bacon *(Vanderbilt)*, Leon Belasco *(Flower Shop Owner)*, Harry Barris *(Bandleader)*, Judith Gibson *(Cigarette Girl)*, Katharine Booth *(Hat-check Girl)*, Joan Arnold *(Daphne)*.

Which came first, the movie or the chain of hotels? Well, if you guessed that the hotels were the reason for this film, you're wrong. They, in fact, took their name from the movie. Based on an idea by Irving Berlin, it's a small musical about two song-and-dance men who plan to retire. Crosby wants to relax on his New England farm after a life of traveling on the road and maintaining a breakneck pace. It doesn't take long before he realizes that the bucolic life is far more strenuous than his former career in show business and he has to go to a rest home to recover from the rigors of running his farm. He still loves performing so he decides to convert his huge house into a very special hostelry, a hotel that will only open on national holidays. That way, he can work as a farmer and an entertainer. He revamps the house and throws open the doors on New Year's Eve. It's instantly crowded and Crosby sees that he has a huge hit on his hands. Astaire enters wearing a face miles long. He'd like to find someone to dance with as his girl friend, Dale, has just announced she is seeking greener pastures and is now going to marry a Texas millionaire. Crosby likes Reynolds and is less than happy when Astaire finds her on the floor and proceeds to trip the light fantastic with her. Sometime later, Astaire tells Crosby that a pair of movie producers wants to make a film about the inn and use Reynolds and Astaire as the leads. Crosby wishes they'd all go away but relents when Reynolds accuses him of putting a damper on her chance for fame and fortune. Still later, Crosby is stunned to learn that Astaire and Reynolds are not only a smash in the movies, they are preparing to make their duet legal. Crosby doesn't know what to do so he seeks the advice of Beavers, his maid-factotum, and she says that the only way to a woman's heart is to tell her how much you love her. No red-blooded American woman can resist that direct approach. Crosby travels to California and learns that Reynolds is very unhappy and sees how empty success can be. She often muses about the quiet times she spent at the Holiday Inn with Crosby and wishes that somehow she had that serenity again. After she and Crosby reunite, she walks out on her contract with the studio and returns to New England. It's now Astaire's turn to be devastated but devastation seldom lasts long in musicals and he is back on top when Dale decides that her oil man was a little too oily and she comes back to Astaire's arms. Berlin wrote a ton of songs for the film and the music never stops. Astaire dances six times and that should be enough for even the most dedicated Fredophile. Many of the songs had to do with holidays and that's where one of the greatest standards of all emerged, "White Christmas." Among others, Berlin also wrote "Be Careful, It's My Heart" (for Valentine's Day), "Plenty To Be Thankful For" (for Thanksgiving), "Abraham, Abraham" (for Lincoln's Birthday), "Let's Say It With Firecrackers" (for July 4th), "I Gotta Say I Love You Cause I Can't Tell A Lie" (for Washington's Birthday), "Let's Start The New Year Right," "Happy Holidays," "Song Of Freedom," "Lazy," "Holiday Inn," "I'll Capture Your Heart," "Easter Parade" (of course), "Any Bonds Today," "You're So Easy To Dance With." Lots of production numbers including a whopping July 4th sequence with boats, planes, Gen. Douglas MacArthur, and the flag. The only drawback to this magnificent film is that it would have been twice as good in color. Berlin makes a mistake in his introduction to "White Christmas" where he refers to Beverly Hills being in Los Angeles. The truth is that Beverly Hills is the only major American city that is surrounded on all four sides by the same city, Los Angeles. (Remake: WHITE CHRISTMAS.)

p&d, Mark Sandrich; w, Claude Binyon, Elmer Rice (based on an idea by Irving Berlin); ph, David Abel; ed, Ellsworth Hoagland; md, Robert Emmett Dolan; art d, Hans Dreier, Roland Anderson; cos, Edith Head; ch, Danny Dare.

Musical/Comedy **Cas.** **(PR:A MPAA:NR)**

HOLIDAY RHYTHM** (1950) 60m Lippert bw

Mary Beth Hughes *(Alice)*, David Street *(Larry)*, Wally Vernon *(Klaxon)*, Donald McBride *(Earl E. Byrd)*, Alan Harris *(Mr. Superdyne)*, Ike Carpenter Orchestra, Glenn Turnbull, Nappy Lamare Dixieland Band, Vera Lee and Tom Ladd, Unger and Martell Twins, George Arnold "Rhythm on Ice" Show, Tom Noonan and Peter Marshall, Bill Burns and Birds, Cass County Boys, Gloria Grey, Tex Ritter, Four Moroccans, Moana, Freddie Letull, Regina Day, Bobby Chang, Sid Melton, Lynn Davis, Richard Farmer and Jack Reitzen, Chuy Reyes and his Mambo Orchestra.

Street wants to produce a variety show but is turned down by a television sponsor. Determined, he takes Hughes and Vernon around the world to find acts. It's silly nonsense disguised as plot, and all the excuse necessary to showcase a variety of performers in one hour. There are an ice show, Chinese jugglers, Apache dancers, Irish jigs, and numerous other variety acts. It's fun, but a little campy today.

p, Jack Leewood; d, Jack Scholl; w, Lee Wainer; ph, Benjamin Kline; m, Bert Shefter; ed, Lou Hegge; m/l, "Holiday Rhythm," Wainer, "Lost In a Dream," Paul Herrick, Shefter, "I'll Think It Over," Scholl, M.K. Jerome (all sung by David Street and Mary Beth Hughes), "Old Chisholm Trail" (sung by Tex Ritter), "Pass the Biscuits, Mirandy" (performed by Cass County Boys), "Concussion Mambo" (played by Chuy Reyes Orchestra).

Musical **(PR:A MPAA:NR)**

HOLIDAY WEEK*½ (1952, Brit.) 82m Monarch bw (GB: HINDLE WAKES)

Lisa Daniely *(Jenny Hawthorne)*, Leslie Dwyer *(Chris Hawthorne)*, Brian Worth *(Alan Jeffcoate)*, Sandra Dorne *(Mary Hollins)*, Ronald Adam *(Nat Jeffcoate)*, Joan Hickson *(Mrs. Hawthorne)*, Michael Medwin *(George Ramsbottom)*, Mary Clare *(Mrs. Jeffcoate)*, Bill Travers *(Bob)*, Tim Turner *(Tommy Dykes)*, Lloyd Pearson *(Tim Farrar)*, Diana Hope *(Betty Farrar)*, Beatrice Varley, Rita Webb, Ian Wilson, Cyril Smith, Alistair Hunter, Lionel Grose.

Daniely is a lowly millworker falling for the son of the owner of the mill during a vacation. Wishing to keep her affair secret from her demanding parents, she gets her pal Dorne to say that the two girls spent the whole time together. However, trouble erupts when Dorne loses her life in an automobile accident, with Daniely's parents sticking their noses into their daughter's business. Old-fashioned type of romance is a bit hard to swallow, but does have a certain amount of charm.

p, William J. Gell, Phil Brandon; d, Arthur Crabtree; w, John Baines (based on the play by Stanley Houghton); ph, Geoffrey Faithfull.

Drama **(PR:A MPAA:NR)**

HOLIDAY'S END** (1937, Brit.) 70m B&D/PAR bw

Sally Stewart *(Betty Sulgrave)*, Wally Patch *(Sgt. Yerbury)*, Rosalyn Boulter *(Joyce Deane)*, Aubrey Mallalieu *(Bellamy)*, Kenneth Buckley *(Arthur Marsh)*, Henry Victor *(Maj. Zwanenberg)*, Leslie Bradley *(Peter Hurst)*, Robert Field *(Des Voeux)*, Bruce Moir, Denis Cowles.

Mystery and mayhem in a boys' school as suspicion shifts from teacher to teacher when one of their ranks is killed at the same time a boy-king comes to the school to be tutored. All the fuss turns out to be a waste of time as the real murderer is a man scheming to get the little king out of the way. Carstairs did his best to overcome the trying material, but his effort fails.

p, Anthony Havelock-Allan; d, John Paddy Carstairs; w, Gerald Elliott; ph, Desmond Dickinson.

Mystery **(PR:A MPAA:NR)**

HOLIDAYS WITH PAY* (1948, Brit.) 115m Mancunian bw

Frank Randle *(Jack Rogers)*, Tessie O'Shea *(Pansy Rogers)*, Dan Young *(Phil Rogers)*, Josef Locke *(Himself)*, Sally Barnes *(Pamela Rogers)*, Joyanne Bracewell *(Joyannne Rogers)*, Sonny Burke *(Michael Sandford)*, Bert Tracy *(Ephraim)*, Pat Heywood and Her Troupe, Peter Lily, Effi McIntosh.

Another mixing bowl of a plot for a British farce revolves around the strange encounters of a vacationing family. Prime among these are the attempts of a friend of the daughter's to deal with a maniacal cousin who wants him dead. A dreadful length of nearly two hours makes this haphazard production excrutiating to watch.

p&d, John E. Blakely; w, Harry Jackson, Frank Randle (based on a story by Anthony Toner); ph, Ben Hart; art d, Joseph Gomersall.

Comedy **(PR:A MPAA:NR)**

HOLLOW TRIUMPH*½** (1948) 83m EL bw (AKA: THE SCAR)

Paul Henreid *(John Muller/Dr. Bartok)*, Joan Bennett *(Evelyn Nash)*, Eduard Franz *(Frederick Muller)*, Leslie Brooks *(Virginia Taylor)*, John Qualen *(Swangron)*, Mabel Paige *(Charwoman)*, Herbert Rudley *(Marcy)*, Paul Burns *(Clerk)*, Charles Trowbridge *(Deputy)*, Ann Staunton *(Blonde)*, Mack Williams *(Cashier)*, Franklyn Farnum *(Big Winner)*, Morgan Farley *(Howard Anderson)*, Joel Friedkin *(Williams)*, Rennie McEvoy *(Clerk)*, Phillip Morris *(Doorman)*, Tom Stevenson *(Lester)*, Benny Rubin *(Cabbie)*, Charles Arnt *(Coblenz)*, Sid Tomack *(Artell the Manager)*, George Chandler *(Aubrey the Assistant)*, Alvin Hammer *(Jerry)*, Jerry Marlowe *(Hiker)*, Cliff Clark, Eddie Dunn *(Men)*, Constance Purdy *(Mrs. Neyhmer)*, Cay Forester *(Nurse)*, Carmencita Johnson *(Elevator Operator)*, Lucien Littlefield *(Davis)*, Norma Varden *(Mrs. Gerry)*, Catherine Doucet *(Mrs. Nielsen)*, Victor Jones *(Bellboy)*, Babe London *(Lady with Orchid)*, Flo Wix, Lulu Mae Bohrman *(Guests)*, Cy Ring *(Croupier)*, Sam Finn *(Patron)*, Joaquin Elizando *(Houseman)*, Felice Ingersoll, Vera Marshe, Jeanne Blackford, Dulcy Day *(Women)*, Ray Bennett *(Official)*, Steve Carruthers, Sayre Dearing *(Men)*, Bob Bice, Dave Shilling *(Thugs)*, Nolan Leary *(Newcomer)*, Tony Horton *(Patron)*, Robert Ben Ali *(Rosie)*, Bud Wolfe *(Al)*, Henry Brandon *(Big Boy)*, Tom Henry *(Stansyck)*, Jack Webb *(Bullseye)*, Dick Wessell *(Sidekick)*.

Henreid served as producer and played a dual role in this *film noir* piece. He is an ex-medical student involved in various confidence games, thefts, and illegal gambling. After a bungled robbery from which only he and Rudley escape, Henreid takes back his old job at a medical supply firm. Nearby works a psychiatrist who is his exact look-alike, with the exception of a scar on the doctor's cheek. Henreid sees a chance to get a new start on life and devises a scheme. First he woos the doctor's secretary (Bennett) and uses her to learn about the practice as well as get a copy of the psychiatrist's signature. He then becomes a parking attendant at the garage where Henreid the doctor parks his car. Using an enlarged photograph, the younger man makes an incision on his own cheek so the duplicate look will be complete. He then kills the doctor and takes over the practice. But to his horror, Henreid discovers that the photograph was printed in reverse and his scar is on the wrong cheek. Bennett discovers what's going on. She wants to leave town but Henreid insists on going with her, booking a passage for two to Hawaii. On the way to the ship, Henreid is stopped by two thugs who believe he is the doctor. It seems the psychiatrist was deeply in debt to a professional gambler. Henreid tries to explain his identity, but to no avail. He tries to escape but is shot by the thugs. The film ends with Henreid crawling toward the ship, people uncaringly passing by as he dies.

p, Paul Henreid; d, Steve Sekely; w, Daniel Fuchs (based on the novel by Murray Forbes); ph, John Alton; m, Sol Kaplan; ed, Fred Allen; md, Irving Friedman; art d, Edward Ilou, Frank Durlauf; set d, Amor Marlowe, Clarence Steenson; cos, Kay Nelson; spec eff, George J. Teague; make-up, Ern Westmore, Frank Westmore.

Crime **(PR:A MPAA:NR)**

HOLLY AND THE IVY, THE*½** (1954, Brit.) 80m LFP/Pacemaker bw

Ralph Richardson *(Rev. Martin Gregory)*, Celia Johnson *(Jenny Gregory)*, Margaret Leighton *(Margaret Gregory)*, Denholm Elliott *(Michael "Mick" Gregory)*, John Gregson *(David Patterson)*, Hugh Williams *(Richard Wyndham)*, Margaret Halstan *(Aunt Lydia)*, Maureen Delany *(Aunt Bridget)*, William Hartnell *(Company Sergeant-Major)*, Robert Flemyng *(Major)*, Roland Culver *(Lord B)*, John Barry *(Clubman)*, Dandy Nichols *(Neighbor)*.

A Christmas story that combines comedy with drama, sentiment with wit, THE HOLLY AND THE IVY was based on a successful London play that ran in the late 1940s and was beautifully adapted for the screen by de Grunwald, who assembled a near-perfect cast to speak his words. The stage-bound origins are clearly indicated as the action takes place in a little more than one day in the lives of the principals. Richardson is a widower reverend who gathers his family to his bosom at Christmas in the vicarage. Many characters descend on the normally quiet manse for the holiday, including his sister, Delany, his sister-in-law Halstan, and his late wife's cousin, Williams. Two of his children also appear—his son, Elliott, a soldier home for Christmas, and his devil-may-care youngest daughter, Leighton, a pixilated London newspaperwoman. His eldest daughter is Johnson, a woman so devoted to her father's welfare that she can't leave him and marry her long-time fiance, Gregson, a civil engineer who is about to depart with a five-year contract overseas and wants to take her with him. Elliott loves his father but has never been able to take the stuffy life in the country. Leighton hides the fact that she'd had a baby out of wedlock by a man who died during the war. That child's death is what turned her to taking solace from a bottle. She admits this to Elliott and Johnson on the eve of Christmas and is then prevailed upon by her two aged aunts to return to the vicarage to take care of Richardson so Johnson can marry Gregson. Leighton refuses to consider that and she and Elliott decide to go to the movies. Before entering the theater, they change their minds and opt for getting very drunk at the local pub. Next morning, Richardson wonders why his son and daughter had to get so inebriated. Elliott betrays Leighton by telling Richardson of her dead child. Richardson confronts Leighton and they play a wonderfully written, poignant scene that brings father and daughter closer. By the time the film is over, Leighton has agreed to take Johnson's place at home and Richardson, who had spent his life counseling people and offering his spiritual aid, has learned that he didn't see the forest for the trees and that some of the neediest parishioners in his flock were his own flesh and blood. Halstan and Delany repeated their stage roles in the film and the other members of the cast were equal to the two aunt's studied performances. The worst part of the movie is that it wasn't filmed well. By that we mean that it felt claustrophobic and could have used some "air" between the interior scenes. The best part of the movie was everything else. Don't wait for Christmas to see this. It's a story that stirs the emotions on any given day of the year.

p, Anatole de Grunwald; d, George More O'Ferrall; w, de Grunwald (based on the play by Wynyard Browne); ph, Ted Scaife; m, Malcolm Arnold; ed, Bert Bates, md, Muir Mathieson; set d, Vincent Korda, Frederick Pusey; cos, Ivy Baker.

Drama **(PR:A MPAA:NR)**

HOLLYWOOD AND VINE½** (1945) 59m PRC bw

James Ellison *(Larry)*, Wanda McKay *(Martha)*, June Clyde *(Gloria)*, Ralph Morgan *(B.B. Benton)*, Franklyn Pangborn *(Reggie)*, Leon Belasco *(Cedric)*, Emmett Lynn *(Pop)*, Vera Lewis *(Fanny)*, Karin Lang *(Ann)*, Robert Greig *(Jenkins)*, Charlie Williams *(Chick)*, Ray Whitley *(Tex)*, Dewey Robinson *(Mug)*, Cy Ring *(Attorney Hudson)*, Grandin Rhodes *(Attorney Wilson)*, Billy Benedict *(Joe the Newsboy)*, Donald Kerr *(Assistant Director)*, Lillian Bronson *(Abigail)*, John Elliott *(Judge)*, Jack Raymond *(Gateman)*, Charles Jordan *(Cop)*, Lou Crocker *(Doctor)*, Hal Taggert *(Casting Director)*.

A big-time movie producer, with a good percentage of his family under his command, decides to do a blockbuster film guaranteed to make a new star of the film's lead, a dog. Ellison is a bewildered writer, taken from the New York streets to Holywood. There is the girl with dreams of stardom who comes from a small town to Dreamland (McKay). Best is Lynn who, through a series of happenstances, climbs from hamburger stand proprietor to powerful landlord of studio property. A funny parody of life in the movie industry.

p, Leon Fromkess; d, Alexis Thurn-Taxis; w, Edith Watkins, Charles Williams (based on a story by Watkins, Williams, Robert Wilmot); ph, Ira Morgan; m, Lee Zahler; ed, Don Hayes; art d, George Van Marter.

Comedy **(PR:AA MPAA:NR)**

HOLLYWOOD BARN DANCE*½ (1947) 73m Screen Guild bw

Ernest Tubb *(Ernie)*, Lori Talbott *(Helen)*, Helen Boyce *(Ezzy)*, Earle Hodgins *(Cartwright)*, Frank McGlynn *(Pa Tubb)*, Phil Arnold *(Toppitt)*, Larry Reed *(Pete Dixon)*, Red Herron *(Jack)*, Anne Kundi *(Ma Tubb)*, Betty Mudge *(Ma Perkins)*, Cy Ring *(Theater Manager)*, Frank Bristow *(Hotel Clerk)*, Albin Robeling *(Croupier)*, Dotti Hackett *(Roper)*, Pat Combe *(Young Ernie)*, Jack Guthrie *(Specialty Act)*, The Philharmonic Trio.

Limp attempt to capitalize on a popular radio program of the same title. Tubb and his trio seek fame and fortune, and Hodgins, in the only real performance the film offers, is a theatrical agent who takes them into his fold. They want to leave home to make enough money to replace the local church they somehow accidentally burned while practicing. How's that for motivation? Tubb has six solos among the 18 tunes scattered within the film, including "Walking the Floor Over You" and "You Nearly Lose Your Mind." Among the other songs are: "Oakie Boogie" (sung by Jack Guthrie), "Two Wrongs Don't Make a Right," "If It's a Dream," "Only Teasing Me."

p, Jack Schwarz; d, B.B. Ray; w, Dorothea Knox Martin (based on a story by Ray); ph, Jack Greenhalgh; m, Walter Greene; ed, Robert Crandell; m/l, Ernest Tubb, Zeb Turner, Henry Stewart, T. Texas Tyler, Sam Neuman, Michael Breen, Jimmie Short, Leon Short, Willis Brothers, Al Clauser, Tex Hoepner, Bob Nolan, Johnnie Tyler, Helen Boice.

Musical **(PR:A MPAA:NR)**

HOLLYWOOD BOULEVARD** (1936) 75m PAR bw

John Halliday *(John Blakeford)*, Marsha Hunt *(Patricia Blakeford)*, Robert Cummings *(Jay Wallace)*, C. Henry Gordon *(Jordan Winslow)*, Frieda Inescort *(Alice Winslow)*, Esther Ralston *(Flora)*, Esther Dale *(Martha)*, Betty Compson *(Betty)*, Albert Conti *(Sanford)*, Richard Powell *(Moran)*, Rita La Roy *(Nella)*, Oscar Apfel *(Dr. Inslow)*, Purnell Pratt *(Mr. Steinman)*, Irving Bacon *(Gus The Bartender)*, Lois Kent *(Little Girl)*, Gregory Gay *(Russian Writer)*, Eleanore Whitney *(Herself)*, Tom Kennedy *(Bouncer)*, Gertrude Simpson *(Gossip)*, Francis X. Bushman *(Director)*, Maurice Costello *(Director)*, Mae Marsh *(Carlotta Blakeford)*, Charles Ray *(Assistant Director)*, Herbert Rawlinson *(Theater Manager)*, Jane Novak *(Mrs. Steinman)*, Kathryn "Kitty" McHugh *(Secretary)*, Bryant Washburn *(Robert Martin)*, William Desmond *(Guest)*, Jack Mulhall *(Man At Bar)*, Roy D'Arcy *(Sheik)*, Creighton Hale *(Man At Bar)*, Mabel Forrest *(Mother)*, Bert Roach *(Screenwriter)*, Gary Cooper *(Man At Bar)*, Harry Myers, Jack Mower, Frank Mayo, Pat O'Malley *(Themselves)*, Hyman Fink, Thomas Jackson, Ed Cecil, Phil Tead, Eddie Dunn, Monty Vandegrift, Frances Morris, Ruth Clifford, Joanne Dudley.

If you read the cast list before this synopsis then you'll recognize many silent screen names in the smaller bits and that should give you a clue as to the subject matter of the film. It's a cameo-filled drama that was somewhat of a forerunner to Nathanael West's DAY OF THE LOCUST in that it shows much of the dark side of Tinsel Town. A somewhat predictable drama that is only interesting by virtue of the many "do you remember that actor?" roles in the piece, HOLLYWOOD BOULEVARD tells the lurid story of Halliday, a washed-up and broken-down actor who has seen his day in Hollywood and now must swallow his pride and accept just about anything to keep his aged body and indomitable soul together. Gordon is a sleazy magazine publisher (sort of an ancestor to the people who publish the rags one finds today at the checkout counter at most supermarkets) who offers Halliday $25,000 if the man will tell all and name names in his memoirs. Desperate, Halliday accepts. The first installment comes out and is, as you might imagine, a sensation. Halliday's family is appalled and want to have nothing to do with him as he has brought filth to an otherwise fine family reputation. Halliday's daughter, Hunt, begs him to stop the serialization of his book in the magazine but he says that he's signed a contract and there's no way out. She then pleads with Gordon but he refuses. Then Gordon tells Halliday that he had better complete those memoirs or he's going to make sure the man never works again. Further, Halliday is in line to perform in a new movie and Gordon will make sure the job goes away. Gordon and Halliday have an argument that erupts into a fight and culminates when Gordon shoots Halliday to death. Police suspect that Hunt killed her own father, but that is quickly disproven when Cummings, Hunt's boyish fiance, exhibits his cleverness and realizes that the dictaphone machine in Gordon's office had been on. When he plays back the recording, Hunt is cleared of Halliday's death and Gordon is arrested. Without the cameos by Bushman, Marsh, Cooper, et al, this would have had little interest as it really wasn't a story of the Hollywood mentality as much as it was just a blackmail tale. But it gave a lot of the old-timers some work at a time when the silent stars of old were probably having the same kind of financial trouble as Halliday's character was having in the story. Of special interest are actual shots profiling real life Hollywood hot spots of the era—Cinegrill, Sardi's, Vendome. Many of the silent screen personalities are shown briefly enacting or directing movie scenes on studio lots and inside sound stages at Paramount, a device later used in SUNSET BOULEVARD by the same studio.

p, A.M. Botsford; d, Robert Florey; w, Marguerite Roberts (based on a story by Faith Thomas); ph, George Clemens, Karl Struss, m, Gregory Stone; ed, Harvey Johnston; art d, Hans Dreier, Earl Hedrick.

Crime/Drama **(PR:A MPAA:NR)**

HOLLYWOOD BOULEVARD*** (1976) 83m New World Pictures c

Candice Rialson *(Candy Wednesday)*, Mary Woronov *(Mary McQueen)*, Rita George *(Bobbi Quackenbush)*, Jeffrey Kramer *(Patrick Hobby)*, Dick Miller *(Walter Paisley)*, Richard Doran *(Producer)*, Tara Strohmeier *(Jill McBain)*, Paul Bartel *(Erich Von Leppe)*, John Kramer *(Duke Mantee)*, Jonathan Kaplan *(Scotty)*, George Wagner *(Cameraman)*, W.L. Luckey *(Rico Bandello)*, David Boyle *(Obnoxious Kid)*, Glen Shimada *(Filipino)*, Joe McBride *(Drive-In Rapist)*, Barbara Pieters *(Drive-In Mother)*, Sean Pieters *(Drive-In Kid)*, Sue Veneer *(Dyke)*, Charles B. Griffith *(Mark Dentine)*, Miller Drake *(Mutant)*, Godzina *(Herself)*, Roberta Dean, Milt Kahn *(Reporters)*, Todd McCarthy *(Author)*, Commander Cody and the Lost Planet Airmen *(Themselves)*.

An affectionate self-parody of the movie business and Corman's B-factory New World Pictures. Rialson is a would-be actress who wants stardom. Her agent, Miller, sends her to Miracle Pictures where she lands a role in the studio's latest epic, MACHETE MAIDENS OF MARATAU. But actress Woronov doesn't like competition and suddenly a series of murders begins. The film ends with a shootout atop the famous Hollywood sign. HOLLYWOOD BOULEVARD is that rarest of creatures: a parody of a parody that actually is funny and works well. Not to be missed by camp fans.

p, Jon Davison; d, Joe Dante, Allan Arkush; w, Patrick Hobby; ph, Jamie Anderson (Metrocolor); m, Andrew Stein; ed, Amy Jones, Arkush, Dante; art d, Jack DeWolfe; set d, Jeff Bernini; cos, Jane Rum; spec eff, Roger George; stunts, C.D. Smith.

Comedy **Cas.** **(PR:O MPAA:R)**

HOLLYWOOD CANTEEN**** (1944) 124m WB bw

Robert Hutton *(Slim)*, Dane Clark *(Sergeant)*, Janis Paige *(Angela)*, Jonathan Hale *(Mr. Brodel)*, Barbara Brown *(Mrs. Brodel)*, Steve Richards, Dick Erdman *(Soldiers on Deck)*, James Flavin *(Marine Sergeant)*, Eddie Marr *(Dance Director)*, Theodore von Eltz *(Director)*, Ray Teal *(Captain)*, Rudolph Friml, Jr. *(Orchestra Leader)*, George Turner *(Tough Marine)*, As Themselves: Joan Leslie, Andrews Sisters, Jack Benny, Joe E. Brown, Eddie Cantor, Kitty Carlisle, Jack Carson, Joan Crawford, Helmut Dantine, Bette Davis, Faye Emerson, Victor Francen, John Garfield, Sydney Greenstreet, Alan Hale, Sr., Paul Henreid, Andrea King, Peter Lorre, Ida Lupino, Irene Manning, Nora Martin, Joan McCracken, Dolores Moran, Dennis Morgan, Eleanor Parker, William Prince, Joyce Reynolds, John Ridgely, Roy Rogers and Trigger, S.Z. Sakall, Alexis Smith, Zachary Scott, Barbara Stanwyck, Craig Stevens, Joseph Szigeti, Donald Woods, Jane Wyman, Jimmy Dorsey and his Band, Carmen Cavallaro and his Orchestra, Golden Gate Quartet, Rosario and Antonio, Sons of the Pioneers, Virginia Patton, Lynne Shayne, Johnny Mitchell, John Sheridan, Colleen Townsend, Angela Green, Paul Brooke, Marianne O'Brien, Dorothy Malone, Bill Kennedy, Mary Gordon, Chef Joseph Milani, Betty Brodel.

Just one glance at the cast list and you know what this picture is about. Delmer Daves had a smash with STAGE DOOR CANTEEN and followed it quickly with this one, which was even better in many ways. The actors read like a roll call of everyone who didn't go overseas in 1944 to either fight the good fight or entertain the troops. Hutton is a young soldier recovering from war wounds in a New Guinea hospital when he sees a Joan Leslie movie, an actress he dreams of meeting but he despairs of ever having that chance. He returns to the U.S. on leave and goes to the Hollywood Canteen with his best pal, Clark. The Canteen is tended by John Garfield, Bette Davis, and a host of other stars playing themselves, and when they learn of Hutton's crush on Leslie, Brown, Wyman, Carson, and Garfield arrange a phony raffle that makes Hutton the one millionth serviceman to enter the canteen. His prize is a night in Hollywood with any actress he wants and is there any doubt who that can be? Now Hutton has to travel to San Francisco to be reassigned and he plans to meet Leslie for one final dance at the Canteen. All of his pals are with him and think that it must have been some huge scam as she doesn't show up. Hutton is crushed and leaves Leslie a note saying that his night with her is one he'll always remember. At Union Station, the troop train is just about to depart when Leslie rushes up to it. She'd run out of gas and that's why she didn't make the appointment at the Canteen. With all his pals watching, she runs alongside the train and tells Hutton that she loves him and will be waiting for him at war's end. An MP lifts the sweet, slim young actress and she kisses Hutton goodbye as the train pulls out. Not much of a plot but so what? This movie had enough talent in it for 10 films and the list of songs is almost as long as the cast. Nominated for three Oscars; sound recording (Nathan Levinson), Best Song ("Sweet Dreams, Sweetheart") and Ray Heindorf's scoring. All of the actors agreed to take part in the picture for a minimum fee after the Screen Actors Guild hassled with Warner Bros. over payments. The Guild didn't want pressure applied on other actors to appear in cameo roles "for patriotic reasons" and feared studios would use that guilt bludgeon. No one did, however, and this picture was a smash the moment it came out. Songs include "Don't Fence Me In" (Cole Porter, sung by Rogers); "Sweet Dreams, Sweetheart" (Ted Kohler, M. K. Jerome, sung by Carlisle); "You Can Always Tell A Yank" (E. Y. Harburg, Burton Lane, sung by Morgan and Brown); "We're Having A Baby" (Harold Adamson, Vernon Duke, sung by Cantor and Martin); "What Are You Doin' The Rest of Your Life" (Kohler, Lane, sung by Wyman and Carson); "The General Jumped at Dawn" (Larry Neal, Jimmy Monday, sung by Golden Gate Quartet); "Gettin' Corns For My Country" (Jean Barry, Leah Worth, Dick Charles, sung by The Andrews Sisters); "Voodoo Moon" (Obdulio Morales, Julio Blanco, Marion Sunshine, played by the Cavallaro orchestra); "Tumblin' Tumbleweeds" (sung by the Sons of the Pioneers); "Ballet In Jive" (danced by Joan McCracken); "The Bee" (violin duet by Szigeti, Benny); "Once To Every Heart" (sung by Carlisle).

p, Alex Gottlieb; d&w, Delmer Daves; ph, Bert Glennon; m, Ray Heindorf; ed, Christian Nyby; md, Leo F. Forbstein; art d, Leo Kuter; set d, Casey Roberts; cos, Milo Anderson; ch, LeRoy Prinz.

Musical/Comedy **(PR:A MPAA:NR)**

HOLLYWOOD CAVALCADE*** (1939) 100m FOX c

Alice Faye *(Molly Adair)*, Don Ameche *(Michael Linnett Connors)*, J. Edward Bromberg *(Dave Spingold)*, Alan Curtis *(Nicky Hayden)*, Stuart Erwin *(Pete Tinney)*, Jed Prouty *(Chief of Police)*, Buster Keaton *(Himself)*, Donald Meek *(Lyle P. Stout)*, George Givot *(Claude)*, Eddie Collins, Hank Mann, Heinie Conklin, James Finlayson, Snub Pollard *(Keystone Kops)*, Chick Chandler *(Chick, Assistant Director)*, Russell Hicks *(Roberts)*, Willie Fung *(Willie)*, Ben Turpin *(Bartender in Western)*, Chester Conklin *(Sheriff in Western)*, Robert Lowery, Ben Welden, Paul Stanton, Mary Forbes, Irving Bacon, Marjorie Beebe, Victor Potel, Lee Duncan, Mack Sennett, Al Jolson, Lynn Bari.

Hollywood seems to like nothing better than making movies about Hollywood and this is a terrific example of how well it knows its own business. In Technicolor, it screamed to have music with it but there was none at all, despite the presence of the fine musical voices of Faye and Ameche. Later, it was discovered that three tunes were written for the movie (when it was still called "Shooting Stars"), but they were cut from the final print. One was the hit "Whispering." It's a story that is so close to the real-life drama of Mack Sennett and Mabel Normand that it might have occasioned a lawsuit were it not for the fact that Sennett appeared as himself in the picture, so his permission was implicit. This same story was told in Jerry Herman's failed Broadway musical "Mack and Mabel." Ameche, playing a well-known silent screen director, and Bromberg, his affable pal, visit New York in 1913 and attend a Broadway play. The star gets sick in the middle of the show and her understudy, Faye, comes forward and knocks the crowd on its ear with her acting abilities. (Something like this really did happen when young Shirley MacLaine took over for Carol Haney in "Pajama Game," after Haney had broken her leg. Hal B. Wallis happened to be in the audience that night, signed MacLaine to a film deal, and the rest is, as they say, history.) Ameche visits Faye's dressing room after the show and offers her a movie deal but her heart is on the stage, so she declines. Next day he sweetens the offer to the princessly sum of $100 per week and she accepts. In California, Ameche directs Faye in her debut, a wacky comedy that stars Buster Keaton and features pie-throwing, sight gags, etc. The picture is a smash and Faye is an immediate star, thus making studio chief Meek a little happier, as he had balked at the enormous amount of money Ameche promised the untested young actress. Time goes by and Ameche is the king of directors with Faye the queen of comic actresses. Bromberg is left a bundle by a dead relative, comes West, and finances Ameche in his own studio with Faye as their No. 1 star. Curtis joins the band of zanies and exhibits immediate interest in Faye who dearly loves Ameche but he is so wrapped up in making movies that he pays little attention to her. Faye marries Curtis in a pique while they are in the midst of making a film. Once it's over, Ameche angrily fires them both and they go abroad on a honeymoon. When they come back, they sign with MGM and watch their careers continue spiraling upward as Ameche's pictures start to fail. It's now the "Roaring Twenties" and Faye and Curtis are the No. 1 couple in movies. At the famous Coconut Grove nightclub, she sees Ameche, now a despondent man, and tells Bromberg (who has taken over as her agent), to get Ameche to direct her latest movie. While shooting the film, Curtis and Faye are involved in an auto accident which kills him and hospitalizes her. At the same time, Jolson (who makes an appearance as himself in the film and sings the Hebrew "Kol Nidre" in the sequence regarding the sound breakthrough of THE JAZZ SINGER) makes film history. Ameche is told to finish the movie, using a double for Curtis, and rush it out as soon as possible. Since the movie is a silent, the advent of sound will make it unsalable if they don't get it to the theaters immediately. Ameche won't hear of it. He purloins the negative and waits until Faye recovers enough to finish the shooting. He adds a few talking sequences, the picture is released, and it is a hit. In the final scene, Faye, Ameche, and Bromberg reminisce about the old days and talk about the future and how they are going to continue their association in talking movies. The best part of the film was the comedy effort (directed by veteran Malcolm St. Clair and supervised by Sennett) that utilized Keaton, Conklin, Collins, Finlayson, Turpin, and all the rest of the Sennettmen who made America laugh so hard.

p, Darryl F. Zanuck; d, Irving Cummings (silent sequences directed by Malcolm St. Clair, supervised by Mack Sennett); w, Irving Pascal (based on a story by Hilary Lynn, Brown Holmes, from an idea by Lou Breslow); ph, Ernest Palmer, Allen M. Davey (Technicolor); ed, Walter Thompson; md, Louis Silvers; art d, Richard Day, Wiard B. Ihnen; set d, Thomas Little; cos, Herschel; tech cons, Natalie Kalmus, Henry Jaffa.

Drama/Comedy **(PR:A MPAA:NR)**

HOLLYWOOD COWBOY*** (1937) 60m RKO bw (AKA: WINGS OVER WYOMING)

George O'Brien *(Jeffery Carson)*, Cecilia Parker *(Joyce Butler)*, Maude Eburne *(Violet Butler)*, Joe Caits *(G. Gadsby Holmes)*, Frank Milan *(Westbrook Courtney)*, Charles Middleton *(Doc Kramer)*, Lee Shumway *(Benson)*, Walter De Palma *(Rolfe Metzger)*, Al Hill *(Camby)*, William Royle *(Klinker)*, Al Herman *(Steger)*, Frank Hagney *(Gillie)*, Dan Wolheim *(Morey)*, Slim Balch *(Slim)*, Sid Jordan *(Morgan)*, Lester Dorr *(Joe Garvey)*, Harold Daniels *(Hotel Clerk)*.

City gangsters move West in hopes of expanding their operations. They put muscle on the area ranchers but who should come along but vacationing movie cowboy O'Brien. He finds his vacation is no vacation as he must play real-life cowboy now to save the ranchers. What could have been corny and hackneyed is saved by a sense of humor and a wonderful performance by O'Brien. O'Brien, who became a superstar western hero in John Ford's silent classic THE IRON HORSE, had been a boxing champion in the Navy and was a rugged outdoorsman who rode a horse and used a lariat with the best of them. He signed with RKO only a year before HOLLYWOOD COWBOY was released, a film which typified his career but an oater with unusual applications in that airplanes are used to stampede cattle and Chicago gangsters invade the West to establish a protection racket for cattlemen, cutting themselves in on livestock profits. O'Brien would do twenty westerns for RKO within four years, this being his third for that studio.

p, George A. Hirliman; d, Ewing Scott; w, Scott, Dan Jarrett; ph, Frank B. Good; ed, Robert Crandall; md, Abe Meyer; art d, F. Paul Sylos.

Western/Comedy **(PR:A MPAA:NR)**

HOLLYWOOD COWBOY, 1975 (SEE: HEARTS OF THE WEST, 1975)

HOLLYWOOD HIGH zero (1977) 81m PPP c

Marcy Albrecht *(Bebe)*, Sherry Hardin *(Candy)*, Rae Sperling *(Monica)*, Susanne *(Jan)*, Kevin Mead *(The Fenz)*, John Young *(Mike)*, Joseph Butcher *(Buzz)*, Richard Hynes *(Sam)*, Marla Winters *(June East)*, Kress Hytes *(Ms. Crotch)*, Hy Camp *(Mr. Flowers)*, Phil J. Macias *(Surfer)*, Mark Lawhead *(Big-Dick)*, Lori Bump *(Carhop)*, Dan Howard *(Rocky)*, Scott Gale *(Waiter)*, Tino Dominguez *(Cook)*, Dale Caldwell, Jon Page *(Students)*.

This feature, like so many of its ilk, is aimed straight at the heart of horny adolescents who think base stereotypes are what the movies are all about. The story, for what it's worth, tells of four California high school girls who spend more time outside of the classroom than in it. They meet an ex-movie queen and ask her for acting lessons to gain access to the many bedrooms of her mansion. You can pretty well guess what happens next. Every predictable scene is in place, including mad sexual encounters; stupid, domineering high school teachers; and the obligatory food fight. The results are pretty wretched, with a filmmaking style and acting to match the amateur plot. A stereotyped gay history teacher is played by one Hy Camp. Someone once observed that funny character names only work for Groucho Marx, and the examples here (a midget named Big-Dick, get it?) are living proof of that axiom.

p, Peter Perry; d, Patrick Wright; ph, Jonathan Silveira (Eastmancolor); m, Scott Gale; ed, Marco Perri; cos, Fay Gates.

Comedy **Cas.** **(PR:O MPAA:R)**

HOLLYWOOD HOODLUM (SEE: HOLLYWOOD MYSTERY, 1934)

HOLLYWOOD HOTEL*½** (1937) 100m WB/FN bw

Dick Powell *(Henry Bowers)*, Rosemary Lane *(Virginia Stanton)*, Lola Lane *(Mona Marshall)*, Hugh Herbert *(Chester Marshall)*, Ted Healy *(Fuzzy)*, Glenda Farrell *(Jonesey)*, Johnny "Scat" Davis *(Georgia)*, Frances Langford *(Alice)*, Alan Mowbray *(Alexander Dupre)*, Mabel Todd *(Dot Marshall)*, Allyn Joslyn *(Bernie Walton)*, Grant Mitchell *(B.L. Faulken)*, Edgar Kennedy *(Callaghan)*, Fritz Feld *(The Russian)*, Curt Bois *(Dress Designer)*, Eddie Acuff *(Cameraman)*, Sarah Edwards *(Mrs. Marshall)*, William B. Davidson *(Director Kelton)*, Wally Maher *(Assistant Director Drew)*, Paul Irving *(Bragwell)*, Libby Taylor *(Cleo)*, Joseph Romantini *(Headwaiter)*, Jerry Fletcher *(Bellboy)*, Benny Goodman and His Orchestra, Louella Parsons, Ken Niles, Jerry Cooper, Duane Thompson, Raymond Paige and His Orchestra *(Themselves)*, Jeffrey Sayre *(Copilot)*, Jack Mower *(Airport Guard)*, John Ridgely *(Desk Clerk)*, Jean Maddox *(Hotel Maid)*, David Newell, Frances Morris, Sidney Perlman, Patsy Kane *(Casting Assistants)*, Carole Landis *(Hat Check Girl)*, Betty Farrington *(Woman Onlooker)*, Jean Perry *(Restaurant Manager)*, Robert Homans *(Hollywood Bowl Watchman)*, Janet Shaw *(Girl)*, Don Barclay *(Friend)*, Susan Hayward *(Starlet at Table)*, Ronald Reagan *(Radio Announcer)*.

HOLLYWOOD HOTEL is a delightful spoof of the hand that feeds them and it has many interesting sidelights that'll cause you to want to see it. Ronald Reagan does an unbilled bit, Susan Hayward is seen briefly, as is Carole Landis, and Louella Parsons plays herself. This was the last big musical that Warner Bros. made at that time. The cycle had begun with 42ND STREET and ended here with Busby Berkeley once again at the helm. As America suffered the Depression, people flocked to see the escapist movies, but the country was recovering by 1937 and new types of movies were beginning to sway audiences. Warners smelled the trend and ended their successful (and expensive) musical movies with this. Based on the title of a successful CBS radio show, HOLLYWOOD HOTEL has a featherweight plot but heavyweight talents. Powell is a saxophonist with the Benny Goodman band. He wins a talent contest that brings him to Hollywood where he thinks he is going to squire movie star Rosemary Lane but, instead, winds up with her stand-in, Lola Lane (Rosemary's real-life sister and also the sister of Priscilla Lane). Powell goes on Parsons' radio show (the announcer was Reagan) and is a hit. Not really much more than that in the plot but the sidebar satires are often hysterical and poke good fun at the industry (a film studio called "Miracle Pictures" has an ironic sign above the entrance that reads: "If It's A Good Picture, It's A Miracle." Some terrific tunes by Whiting and Mercer including the motion picture business' national anthem "Hooray For Hollywood" (sung wonderfully by "Scat" Davis), which has some of Mercer's best lyrics. Other songs include: "Let That Be A Lesson To You," "Sing, You Son Of A Gun," "I'm Like A Fish Out Of Water," "I've Hitched My Wagon To A Star," "Silhouetted In The Moonlight," "Can't Teach My Heart New Tricks" and "I'm A Ding Dong Daddy From Dumas" by Phil Baxter, as well as "Blue Moon," by Rodgers and Hart.

p, Hal B. Wallis; d, Busby Berkeley; w, Jerry Wald, Maurice Leo, Richard Macauley; ph, Charles Rosher, George Barnes; ed, George Amy; md, Leo F. Forbstein; art d, Robert Haas; m/l, Richard W. Whiting, Johnny Mercer, Richard Rodgers, Lorenz Hart, Phil Baxter.

Musical Comedy **Cas.** **(PR:AA MPAA:NR)**

HOLLYWOOD KNIGHTS, THE zero (1980) 91m Poly-Gram COL c

Fran Drescher *(Sally)*, Leigh French *(Jacqueline Freedman)*, Randy Gornel *(Wheatly)*, Gary Graham *(Jimmy Shine)*, Sandy Helberg *(Officer Clark)*, James Jeter *(Smitty)*, Stuart Pankin *(Dudley Laywicker)*, P. R. Paul *(Simpson)*, Michelle Pfeiffer *(Suzi Q.)*, Gailard Sartain *(Rimbeau)*, Richard Schaal *(Nevans)*, Robert Wuhl *(Newbomb Turk)*, Tony Danza *(Duke)*.

Cheap, worthless imitation of the classic AMERICAN GRAFFITI. On Halloween night, 1965, a group of teenagers decides to get back at the grown-ups for closing down the main drag street in Beverly Hills. Their antics include urination gags, obscenities, and racism along with other gross features. Ripoffs from GRAFFITI include sabatoging a police car and a disc jockey playing tunes all night long. Not for children or the civilized.

p, Richard Lederer; d, Floyd Mutrux; w, Mutrux (based on a story by Mutrux, Lederer, William Tennant); ph, William A. Fraker (Metrocolor); ed, Danford B. Greene, Stan Allen, Scott Conrad; art d, Lee Fischer; set d, Bruce Kay; cos, Darryl Levine.

Comedy **(PR:O MPAA:R)**

HOLLYWOOD MYSTERY*½ (1934) 53m RF bw (AKA: HOLLYWOOD HOODLUM)

June Clyde, Frank Albertson, Jose Crespo, Tenen Holz, John Davidson, Stanley Price, Cyril Ring, Edith Terry Preuss.

Albertson is a publicity agent for a small studio who loses his job just as he is planning a big build-up for his girl friend. The studio tells him he'll be rehired if he can find a way to get a troublesome director off the lot. He succeeds, gets his job back and his girl gets a shot at stardom. Albertson's good performance can't save this confusing and poorly scripted project.

d, Breezy Eason; w, John Thomas Neville (based on a story by William Bloecher); ph, Ernest Miller; ed, Jeanne Spencer.

Drama **(PR:C MPAA:NR)**

HOLLYWOOD OR BUST*½ (1956) 94m PAR c

Dean Martin *(Steve Wiley)*, Jerry Lewis *(Malcolm Smith)*, Anita Ekberg *(Herself)*, Pat Crowley *(Terry)*, Maxie Rosenbloom *(Bookie Benny)*, Willard Waterman *(Manager Neville)*, Jack McElroy *(Stupid Sam)*, Mike Ross *(Guard)*, Frank Wilcox *(Director)*, Wendell Niles *(M.C.)*, Kathryn Card *(Old Lady)*, Richard Karlan *(Sammy Ross)*, Tracey Roberts *(Redhead)*, Ben Welden *(Boss)*, Ross Westlake *(Sheep Woman)*, Gretchen Houser *(Specialty Dancer)*, Sandra White, Adele August.

The last film Martin and Lewis did as a team. Lewis is a movie fan with a big crush on Amazonian Ekberg (the "bust" of the title . . . get it?). After Martin forges some lottery tickets to win a car, he convinces Lewis that the two should travel cross-country so they can meet the girl of Lewis' dreams. This gives way to zaniness by the pair as well as a few songs, including the title song, "Let's be Friendly," and "The Wild and Woolly West" all sung by Martin with Lewis occasionally supplying a shriek or two. There are a few funny bits scattered here and there, but mostly it is unfunny. Other songs were "A Day In the Country," and "It Look Like Love."

p, Hal Wallis; d, Frank Tashlin; w, Erna Lazarus (based on her story "Beginner's Luck"); ph, Daniel Fapp (VistaVision, Technicolor); m, Walter Scharf; ed, Howard Smith; md, Scharf; art d, Hal Pereira, Henry Bumstead; m/l, Charles O'Curran, Sammy Fain and Paul Francis Webster; ch, O'Curran.

Comedy **(PR:A MPAA:NR)**

HOLLYWOOD PARTY** (1934) 68m MGM bw/c

Stan Laurel ((*Himself*), Oliver Hardy *(Himself)*, Jimmy Durante *(Schnarzan the Shouting Conqueror)*, Mrs. Jean Durante *(Herself)*, Lupe Velez *(Herself/Jaguar Woman)*, Ted Healy *(Himself)*, Moe Howard, Curly Howard, Larry Fine *(The Stooges)*, Frances Williams *(Herself)*, Robert Young *(Himself)*, Charles Butterworth *(Harvey Clemp)*, Polly Moran *(Henrietta Clemp)*, Tom Kennedy *(Beavers the Doorman)*, Ben Bard *(Charley)*, Richard Carle, *(Knapp, Schnarzan's Manager)*, George Givot *(Liondora the Rival Star)*, Eddie Quillan *(Bob)*, Jack Pearl *(Baron Munchausen)*, June Clyde *(Linda the Clemps' Niece)*, Leonid Kinskey *(Cabdriver)*, Tom Herbert *(Bartender)*, Tom London *(Paul Revere, in Flashback)*, Jed Prouty *(Theater Manager)*, Arthur Jarrett, Harry Barris, The Shirley Ross Quartet *(Singers)*, Edwin Maxwell *(Buddy Goldfard, Liondora's Manager)*, Richard Cramer, Clarence Wilson, Nora Cecil *(Scientific Pendants)*, Baldwin Cooke *(Holding the*

Door for the Scientific Gentlemen), Bess Flowers *(Opening Scenes Dress Extra)*, Muriel Evans *(Seated at the Table During Bidding)*, Sidney Bracey, Arthur Treacher *(Butlers)*, Irene Hervey *(Show Girl)*, Frank Austin *(Party Guest)*, Ray Cooke *(Theater Patron)*, Ernie Alexander *(Servant at the Party)*, Walt Disney *(Voice of Mickey Mouse)*, Billy Bletcher *(Voice of Big Bad Wolf)*.

Just a showcase (and a poor one) for a number of stars to walk around with little to do. Durante plays a film jungle star whose films are bombing because of his anemic lions. Pearl, reprising his famous radio role, is the explorer getting more lions for Durante, but rival jungle star Givot wants them for himself. Durante throws a party for Pearl that climaxes with the arrival of the lion's owners Laurel and Hardy. There is some color footage when live action is combined with Disney's Mickey Mouse and Big Bad Wolf of THE THREE LITTLE PIGS fame. Eleven songs by Richard Rodgers and Lorenz Hart, including the classic "Blue Moon," were cut before the film's release. Songs remaining were: "Hollywood Party," "Hello," "Reincarnation" (Rodgers, Hart); "I've Had My Moments" (Gus Kahn, Walter Donaldson); "Feeling High" (Donaldson, Howard Dietz); "Hot Chocolate Soldiers" (Arthur Freed, Nacio Herb Brown). British music hall mimic Florence Desmond (born Dawson) had cut a record entitled "Hollywood Party" in 1933 wherein she imitated the voices of Marlene Dietrich, Greta Garbo and Janet Gaynor. When Gaynor heard the popular record she called MGM bosses to suggest Desmond be given a film contract. Desmond was given a two-film contract and was scheduled to appear in MGM's HOLLYWOOD PARTY in 1934 but no room was made for her talents in the script. She appeared in MR. SKITCH (1933) and in I AM SUZANNE (1934) where she imitated Garbo, Dietrich and others as voices of various puppets. After using up Desmond's special talents in poor programmers, MGM sent her packing back to England. (See LAUREL & HARDY series, Index.)

p, Harry Rapf, Howard Dietz; d, Richard Boleslawski, Allan Dwan, (uncredited) Roy Rowland; w, Dietz, Arthur Kober; ph, James Wong Howe; ed, George Boemier; art d, Fredric Hope; set d, Edwin B. Willis, cos, Adrian; ch, Seymour Felix, George Hale, David Gould.

Musical Comedy **(PR:AAA MPAA:NR)**

HOLLYWOOD ROUNDUP*** (1938) 62m COL bw

Buck Jones *(Buck Kennedy)*, Helen Twelvetrees *(Carol Stevens)*, Grant Withers *(Grant Drexel)*, Shemp Howard *(Oscar)*, Dickie Jones *(Dickie Stevens)*, Eddie Kane *(Henry Westcott)*, Monty Collins *(Freddie Foster)*, Warren Jackson *(Perry King)*, Lester Dorr *(Louis Lawson)*, Lee Shumway *(Carl Dunning)*, Edward Keane *(Lew Wallach)*, George A. Beranger *(Hotel Clerk)*.

Jones is a stunt double for the temperamental and fragile cowboy star Withers. When Jones goes for leading lady Twelvetrees, Withers gets angry and attempts to frame the stunt man without success. But Jones gets caught in the middle of a bank robbery and despite his innocence he is jailed. His younger brother Dickie Jones helps him escape and Jones becomes a hero when he captures the real robbers. A neat backstage look at cowboy films, with the tricks behind a lot of the seemingly dangerous stunts shown. The story has a certain charm and Jones is wonderful in his role. Jones was forty-seven when he made HOLLYWOOD ROUNDUP, long past his palmy days as a western matinee hero, having reached stardom as early as 1920. He was, along with Tim McCoy, Ken Maynard, Hoot Gibson and a handful of other western stars, a real rugged man of the saddle who shook his head in disappointment at the appearance in the late 1930s of the new cowboy heroes of the screen, chiefly Gene Autry and Roy Rogers, who sang their ways along the trails, wore spotless stetsons, drew silverplated pistols and never got an ounce of dirt beneath a fingernail. While on a WW II bond tour, Jones would die in the inferno that engulfed Boston's posh Cocoanut Grove nightclub on November 11, 1942 where 491 persons lost their lives. He was a hero to the end, repeatedly going into the flames to rescue several persons before a wall of fire closed over this man of true grit.

p, L.G. Lenard; d, Ewing Scott; w, Joseph Hoffman, Monroe Shaff, Ethel LaBlanche; ph, Allen G. Thompson, ed, Robert Crandall; art d, F. Paul Sylos; md, Morris Stoloff.

Western **(PR:A MPAA:NR)**

HOLLYWOOD SPEAKS** (1932) 71m COL bw

Pat O'Brien *(Jimmie Reed)*, Genevieve Tobin *(Greta Swan)*, Lucien Prival *(Landau)*, Rita LeRoy *(Millie Coreen)*, Leni Stengel *(Mrs. Landau)*, Ralf Harolde *(Carp)*, Anderson Lawlor *(Joe Hammond)*.

Supposed look at the darker side of Hollywood aimed at the heart of the fan magazine reader. O'Brien is a Hollywood columnist exposing the horrors of Tinsel Town—directors using starlets for their own lecherous purposes and mobsters controling what goes on in the picture business. Prival does a bad impersonation of an arrogant foreign director a la von Stroheim; Stengel, Prival's neglected wife, commits suicide, leaving a note which blames Tobin who has been bedding Prival to further her career. Tobin herself, at the film's beginning, was about to take poison in the lobby of Grauman's Chinese Theater over a failed Hollywood career when O'Brien stops her and pushes her into stardom and, unwittingly, the scandal with Prival-Stengel, which is exposed by gangsters when she refuses to pay blackmail to recover Stengel's note. O'Brien again comes to the rescue, marrying Tobin for a smiling finish. Naive in its view of the industry and the audience watching the film.

d, Eddie Buzzell; w, Norman Krasna, Jo Swerling (based on a story by Krasna); ph, Teddy Tetzlaff; ed, Gene Havelick.

Drama **(PR:C-O MPAA:NR)**

HOLLYWOOD STADIUM MYSTERY** (1938) 66m REP bw

Neil Hamilton *(Bill Devons)*, Evelyn Venable *(Polly Ward)*, Jimmy Wallington *(Nick Nichols)*, Barbara Pepper *(Althea Ames)*, Lucien Littlefield *(Watchman)*, Lynn Roberts *(Edna)*, Charles Williams *(Jake)*, James Spottswood *(Slats Keefe)*, Reed Hadley *(Mortimer)*, Robert Homans *(Capt. Filsom)*, William Haade *(Champ)*, Pat Flaherty *(Ace)*, Dan Tobey *(Announcer)*, Smiley Burnette *(Smiley)*, Al Bayne *(Max)*.

Despite a weak plot this mystery holds up thanks to good acting. A fighter is mysteriously killed before his big match with the champ. Hamilton is the D.A. assigned to investigate the case. Wallington is a sports announcer, guilty of the murder. His performance is fine as are the supporting roles of Pepper and Roberts. The direction is slow to start but things finally get going strongly.

p, Armand Schaefer; d, David Howard; w, Stuart Palmer, Dorrell McGowan, Stuart McGowan (based on a story by Palmer), ph, Ernest Miller; ed, Edward Mann.

Mystery **(PR:A MPAA:NR)**

HOLLYWOOD STORY** (1951) 76m UNIV bw

Richard Conte *(Larry O'Brien)*, Julia Adams *(Sally Rousseau)*, Richard Egan *(Lt. Lennox)*, Henry Hull *(Vincent St. Clair)*, Fred Clark *(Sam Collyer)*, Jim Backus *(Mitch Davis)*, Houseley Stevenson *(Mr. Miller)*, Paul Cavanagh *(Roland Paul)*, Katherine Meskill *(Mary)*, Louis Lettieri *(Jimmy)*, Francis X. Bushman, Betty Blythe, William Farnum, Helen Gibson, Joel McCrea.

In the wake of the success of HOLLYWOOD BOULEVARD the previous year, every studio in the city was making its own contribution to the mythology of the screen. One of the lesser efforts was Universal's HOLLYWOOD STORY. Roughly borrowing the unsolved murder case of director William Desmond Taylor in 1922, it tells the story of Conte, an independent producer who comes to Hollywood to make a movie about the murder of a silent film director. He locates Hull, the dead director's scriptwriter, and puts him to work on the screenplay. Eventually it develops that Hull is actually the brother of the dead man, jealous of his brother's talents (which extended to writing, too, using Hull's name as a pseudonym). This could have been a much better film if had more closely followed the actual facts in the case of Taylor. A successful director who had recently testified before federal authorities on narcotics use in the film community, he was apparently shot and killed sometime on the night of Feb. 1, 1922. Witnesses saw a man (or possibly a woman in a man's clothes) leaving the victim's apartment just after they heard a shot. Later investigation found packets of love letters and monogrammed handkerchiefs from silent star Mary Miles Minter, then 20 years of age, and more love letters from actress Mabel Normand, a well-known narcotics user. No charges were ever brought in the case, but Minter's career was ruined. She lived long after as a recluse and eccentric. Universal tried to capitalize on the presence in the film of several silent stars, some of them extras. At the press screening where the old-timers were displayed like museum pieces, a bitter Elmo Lincoln, the screen's first "Tarzan," told a newsman, "Every time they want to exploit something like HOLLYWOOD STORY they call on us. We're not getting any money out of this. . . . All of us who worked in HOLLYWOOD STORY got $15.56 a day, the minimum rate for a day's work. Principals like Helen Gibson and Francis X. Bushman, who had speaking parts, got $55 for their day's work. They paid us for that one day and they've got $15,000 worth of free publicity out of it. If I had the opportunity, I'd stand right there on that stage tonight and say: 'Why don't we get work?. . . The motion picture business is the most unappreciative, selfish business in America today."

p, Leonard Goldstein; d, William Castle; w, Frederick Kohner, Fred Brady; ph, Carl Guthrie; ed, Virgil Vogel; md, Joseph Gershenson; art d, Bernard Herzbrun, Richard H. Riedel.

Mystery **(PR:A MPAA:NR)**

HOLLYWOOD STRANGLER, THE (SEE: DON'T ANSWER THE PHONE, 1980)

HOLLYWOOD THRILLMAKERS (SEE: MOVIE STUNT MEN, 1954)

HOLOCAUST 2000 (SEE: CHOSEN, THE, 1978, Brit., Ital.)

HOLY MATRIMONY*½** (1943) 87m FOX bw

Monty Woolley *(Priam Farli)*, Gracie Fields *(Alice Challice)*, Laird Cregar *(Clive Oxford)*, Una O'Connor *(Mrs. Leek)*, Alan Mowbray *(Mr. Pennington)*, Melville Cooper *(Dr. Caswell)*, Franklin Pangborn *(Duncan Farli)*, Ethel Griffies *(Lady Vale)*, Eric Blore *(Henry Leek)*, Montagu Love *(Judge)*, Richard Fraser *(John Leek)*, Edwin Maxwell *(King Edward VII)*, Ian Wolfe *(Strawley)*, Alec Craig *(Aylmer)*, Milton Parsons *(Clerk)*, Thomas Louden *(Court Clerk)*, Geoffrey Steele *(Matthew Leek)*, Lumsden Hare *(Lady Vale's Footman)*, Whit Bissell *(Harry Leek)*, Leyland Hodgson *(Solicitor)*, Fritz Feld, William Austin *(Critics)*, George Zucco *(Mr. Crepitude)*.

Woolley is a British artist who has been living and painting in seclusion on a Pacific island for 20 years, accompanied only by his valet, Blore. When King Edward VII decides to award Woolley with a knighthood, the painter and servant reluctantly pack up and head back to Britain. By a stroke of fortune, Blore dies along the way and Woolley seizes the opportunity to assume the dead valet's identity. Arriving in an England draped in mourning in his honor, he tries to go to his funeral but is chased away. Before long Fields shows up with a letter from Blore proposing marriage, and Woolley is forced to marry her to maintain his ruse. To his surprise he finds wedded bliss quite pleasing, but then Blore's first wife, O'Connor, shows up at his door with three children and demanding to know where he's been for the last 20 years. In court facing a charge of bigamy, Woolley finally manages to clear the identity problem and ends up with Fields. An excellent, sophisticated comedy tailored by writer-producer Johnson to fit the screen persona that Woolley had established in THE MAN WHO CAME TO DINNER two years before. Superbly played by Woolley and Fields (who would prove such good foils for each other that they would be reteamed two years later in MOLLY AND ME) are at their peaks. The supporting cast is loaded with talent as well, with perpetual butler Blore, Cregar, and everyone's favorite hatchet-faced crone O'Connor making every scene a pleasure.

p, Nunnally Johnson; d, John Stahl; w, Johnson (based on the novel *Buried Alive* by Arnold Bennett); ph, Lucien Ballard; m, Cyril J. Mockridge; ed, James B. Clark; md, Emil Newman; art d, James Basevi, Russell Spencer; set d, Thomas Little, Paul S. Fox; spec eff, Fred Sersen.

Comedy **(PR:A MPAA:NR)**

HOLY MOUNTAIN, THE** (1973, U.S./Mex.) 126m ABKCO Films c

Alexandro Jodorowsky *(Master)*, Horacio Salinas *(Christ Figure)*, Ramona Saunders *(Disciple)*.

This inventive and bizarre adventure involves the search by Jodorowsky (the film's writer and director) for the Holy Mountain, on which dwell nine wise men who know the secret of immortality. Jodorowsky's route is littered with exotic, violently sacriligious images as he gains a group of followers that includes whores, thieves, and a chimpanzee. The *mise-en-scene* is packed with colorful, often shocking images (blood and body wastes are recurring motifs) but orchestrated in a creative delirium. THE HOLY MOUNTAIN quickly attained something of a cult following, as did Jodorowsky's earlier (and better known) EL TOPO. In preparation for the film, Jodorowsky spent a sleep-deprived week with a Japanese Zen master. "Maybe I am a prophet," he claimed during the production. "I really hope one day there will come Confucius, Mohammed, Buddha, and Christ to see *me*. And we will sit at a table taking tea and eating some brownies."

p, Allen Klein; d&w, Alexandro Jodorowsky; ph, Rafael Corkidi (Telchniscope, Technicolor); m, Jodorowsky, Ronald Frangipane, Don Cherry; ed, Frederic Landeros.

Drama **(PR:O MPAA:R)**

HOLY TERROR, A** (1931) 52m FOX bw

George O'Brien *(Tony Hard)*, Sally Eilers *(Jerry Foster)*, Rita La Roy *(Kitty Carroll)*, Humphrey Bogart *(Steve Nash)*, James Kirkwood *(William Drew)*, Stanley Fields *(Butch Morgan)*, Robert Warwick *(Thomas Woodbury)*, Richard Tucker *(Tom Hedges)*, Earl Pingree *(Jim Lawler)*.

O'Brien is a rich easterner who discovers his father murdered after a polo match. After going through his father's papers, he discovers that the family name originally may have been different, and finds evidence that causes him to believe western rancher Kirkwood may know something about the death. He flies out West but loses control of his plane, crashing into Eilers bathroom. She falls in love with him after this unusual meeting, which causes her sweetheart, ranch foreman Bogart, to become jealous. Meanwhile, Kirkwood orders Bogart and Fields to bring in O'Brien unarmed. But O'Brien escapes and meets Kirkwood for a showdown, where he learns that Kirkwood is his real father. He had killed the other man accidentally after going East for a reckoning with the man who stole his wife and son. Probably best viewed as an historical curiosity with Bogart playing a minor part as a cowboy in one of his earliest films.

p, Edmund Grainger; d, Irving Cummings; w, Alfred A. Cohn, Myron Fagan, Ralph Block (based on the novel *Trailin'* by Max Brand); ph, George Schneiderman; ed, Ralph Dixon.

Western **(PR:A MPAA:NR)**

HOLY TERROR, THE½** (1937) 66m FOX bw

Jane Withers *(Corky Wallace)*, Anthony Martin *(Danny Walker)*, Leah Ray *(Marjorie Dean)*, Joan Davis *(Lil)*, El Brendel *("Bugs" Svenson)*, Joe E. Lewis *("Pelican" Beek)*, John Eldredge *(Lt. Wallace)*, Gloria Roy *(Woman Spy)*, Andrew Tombes *(Commander Otis)*, Gavin Muir *(The Badger)*, Fred Kohler, Jr. *(Carson)*, Victor Adams *(Flandro)*, Raymond Brown *(Phelps)*, Louis Bacigalupi, Oscar Rudolf, William Moore, Allen Fox *(Sailors)*, Henry Otho *(Master at Arms)*, Gaylord Pendleton *(Yeoman)*, Ben Hendricks *(Ben)*, Emmett Vogan *(Squadron Commander)*, Clark and Dexter *(Eccentric Dancers)*, Stanley Taylor, Lew Harvey *(Spies)*.

Withers is the daughter of a Navy officer and everyone's sweetie because she stages shows for the men. A spy network fakes a fight in order to close the cafe where the shows are held. The cafe is near a strategic area and the spies need it for their operations. Withers finds out their plan and her Navy friends save the day. This simple story is the excuse for a wide variety of production numbers and comedy acts that dominate the film. Songs: "There I Go Again," "Don't Know Myself Since I Know You," "Don't Sing," "The Call of the Siren," "Everybody Swing" (Sidney Clare, Harry Akst).

p, John Stone; d, James Tinling; w, Lou Breslow, John Patrick; ph, Daniel B. Clark; ed, Nick De Maggio; md, Samuel Kaylin; ch, Jack Haskell.

Musical **(PR:A MPAA:NR)**

HOLY TERROR (SEE: ALICE, SWEET ALICE, 1978)

HOMBRE*** (1967) 110m FOX c

Paul Newman *(John Russell)*, Fredric March *(Favor)*, Richard Boone *(Grimes)*, Diane Cilento *(Jessie)*, Cameron Mitchell *(Braden)*, Barbara Rush *(Audra Favor)*, Peter Lazer *(Billy Lee)*, Margaret Blye *(Doris)*, Martin Balsam *(Mendez)*, Skip Ward *(Steve Early)*, Frank Silvera *(Mexican Bandit)*, David Canary *(Lamar Dean)*, Val Avery *(Delgado)*, Larry Ward *(Soldier)*, Pete Hernandez, Merrill C. Isbell *(Apaches)*, Linda Cordova *(Mrs. Delgado)*.

Newman, a white man raised by Apaches, has come into some property. His one white friend, Balsam, the stage coach driver, urges him to cut his hair and wear "white" clothing in order to avoid any trouble on the coach journey he needs to take. March, one of the passengers, sells dog meat to the Indians, passing it off as beef. Rush is his wife. Other passengers are Lazer and Blye as a young married couple, Boone as a mean character, and Cilento, the woman who manages the boarding house Newman has inherited. Gunmen hold up the stage and take Rush hostage in a robbery staged by Boone. Newman shoots and kills two of them. The stolen goods are recovered and Newman leads the crew to an abandoned mine to hide out. An offer is made by the two remaining badmen to exchange Rush for $12,000. Cilento tries to take the money to Boone and company. Newman catches up with her and sends her back. He goes in her place and a gun battle breaks out. The gunmen are killed, as is Newman, who dies saving the lives of his companions. Noble in intent, the filmmakers took the brave step of making the white man look bad in a western film. A competent and interesting story. This is a sharply violent film which pulls no punches. The prevalent racism of the old West against Indians is blatantly expressed by March who tells Newman that "white people stick together." Newman's perspective is pure Apache—blunt, practical, few words and action based on survival. He does well with his succinct delivery and cold-blooded mannerisms when playing opposite March's florid delivery. (It was rumored, with the spate of Newman films beginning with the letter H, that the actor insisted on doing only those so-designated films for luck—HUD, HARPER, HOMBRE, THE HUSTLER.) Cilento is convincing as the worldly landlady and Boone is chilling as the sadistic bad man who is ready to murder anyone standing in his way, the type of role he specialized in for decades. Rush has classic facial beauty but her overacting is an embarrassment. Here she plays a woman of middleage who employs the gestures and looks of a youthful coquette. She also seems to be swallowing her words which bubble out again in gulping sounds, a habit that has deepened over the years. The harsh realism of this film is memorable but also disturbing, particularly the brutal treatment of Rush who is denied water by Boone until her lips split and her face cracks, then hogtied in the sun to await death. Not for children or those with little tolerance for inhuman behavior.

p, Martin Ritt, Irving Ravetch; d, Ritt; w, Ravetch, Harriet Frank, Jr. (based on the novel by Elmore Leonard); ph, James Wong Howe (Panavision, Deluxe Color); m, David Rose; ed, Frank Bracht; md, Rose; art d, Jack Martin Smith, Robert I. Smith; set d, Walter M. Scott, Raphael Bretton; cos, Don Feld; makeup, Ben Nye.

Western **Cas.** **(PR:C MPAA:NR)**

HOMBRE Y EL MONSTRUO, EL (SEE: MAN AND THE MONSTER, THE, 1958, Mex.)

HOME AND AWAY*½ (1956, Brit.) 81m Guest-Conquest bw

Jack Warner *(George Knowles)*, Kathleen Harrison *(Elsie Harrison)*, Lana Morris *(Mary Knowles)*, Charles Victor *(Ted Groves)*, Thora Hird *(Margie Groves)*, Leslie Henson *(Uncle Tom)*, Valerie White *(Mrs. Jarvis)*, Harry Fowler *(Syd Jarvis)*, Merrie Carroll *(Annie Knowles)*, Margaret St. Barbe West *(Aunt Jean)*, Sam Kydd, Bernard Fox, Ross Pendleton.

A football pool causes problems for two families when the two underage sons turn out to be winners of a cash prize both parents wanted to get their hands on. The mother of one boy devises a method whereby she can get the entire lot. Luckily Warner, father of the other boy, is more honorable, and sees to it that both boys make out all right, even getting them under way in a business venture. A few entertaining moments.

p, George Maynard; d, Vernon Sewell; w, Sewell, R.F. Delderfield (based on the play "Treble Trouble" by Heather McIntyre); ph, Basil Emmott.

Comedy **(PR:A MPAA:NR)**

HOME AT SEVEN (SEE: MURDER ON MONDAY, 1952, Brit.)

HOME BEFORE DARK*** (1958) 137m WB bw

Jean Simmons *(Charlotte Bronn)*, Dan O'Herlihy *(Arnold Bronn)*, Rhonda Fleming *(Joan Carlisle)*, Efrem Zimbalist, Jr. *(Jake Diamond)*, Mabel Albertson *(Inez Winthrop)*, Steve Dunne *(Hamilton Gregory)*, Joan Weldon *(Frances Barrett)*, Joanna Barnes, *(Cathy Bergner)*, Kathryn Card *(Mattie)*, Marjorie Bennett *(Hazel Evans)*, Johnstone White *(Malcolm Southey)*, Eleanor Audley *(Mrs. Hathaway)*.

Simmons gives a superb performance that overcomes the glossy direction of LeRoy. She is returning home to husband O'Herlihy after spending time in a mental institution because of a breakdown. Upon her return she finds her stepmother Albertson and stepsister Fleming. Since the hint of a possible romance between her husband and Fleming triggered the breakdown, Simmons is already on unsteady ground. She befriends Zimbalist, a colleague of her husband at a small New England college. He is the only Jewish faculty member and is disliked by O'Herlihy. Zimbalist and Simmons fall in love and the film ends with hopeful feelings. This is heavy material but LeRoy treats it as little more than soap opera. At the heart of it all is Simmons. There is a marvelous poignancy to her role that is played with even intensity.

p&d, Mervyn LeRoy; w, Eileen Bassing, Robert Bassing (based on the novel by Eileen Bassing); ph, Joseph F. Biroc; m, Franz Waxman, Ray Heindorf; ed, Phillip W. Anderson; md, Heindorf; art d, John Backman; cos, Howard Shoup; m/l, title song, Jimmy McHugh, Sammy Cahn.

Drama **(PR:C MPAA:NR)**

HOME FOR TANYA, A** (1961, USSR) 97m Gorky/Artkino bw (OTCHIY DOM)

Vera Kuznetsova *(Natalya Avdeyevna)*, Lyudmila Marchenko *(Tanya)*, Nikolay Novlyanskiy *(Grandfather Avdey)*, Valentin Zubkov *(Sergey Ivanovich)*, Nonna Mordyukova *(Stepanida)*, Lyudmila Ovchinnikova *(Nyurka)*, P. Kiryutkin *(Mokeich)*, Pytor Aleynikov *(Fyodor)*, Yelena Maksimova *(Markarikha)*, Yu Arkhintsev, V. Vsevolodov, Tatyana Guretskaya, G. Shapovalov, I. Kuzbetsov, Ye. Melnikova.

The usual propagandist drama from the Soviets, this time concerning Marchenko, a young girl who was believed to be orphaned during WW II and was taken in by a well-to-do urban family. One day she receives a letter from her natural mother urging her to come and visit the remote farm where she lives. Marchenko finds it hard to adjust to the simple, industrious life of a farmer (she is used to the unrewarding, soft, urban existence), but inevitably the pull of the land lures her into a great respect and admiration for her mother, who has sacrificed all (including a husband and two sons in the war) for the good of Mother Russia. Inoffensive and fairly well done, but predictable.

d, Lev Kulidzhanov; w, Budimir Metalnikov; ph, P. Katayev; m, Yu. Biryukov; ed, L. Zhuchkova; art d, Mark Gorelik, Sergey Serebrenikov; cos, Ye. Aleksandrova.

Drama **(PR:A MPAA:NR)**

HOME FREE ALL** (1983) 92m P.O.P. c

Allan Nicholls *(Barry Simon)*, Roland Caccavo *(Al)*, Lorry Goldman *(Marvin)*, Mary Ellyn *(Cathy)*, Jose Ramon Rosario *(Custodian)*.

This, the first dramatic feature from documentary filmmaker Bird (THE WOBBLIES, COMING HOME—not the Fonda film) concerns Viet Nam-vet-turned-radical-turned-writer Nicholls, who renews some old friendships after his live-in girl friend has moved out. He meets up with an old buddy, Caccavo, who is now a successful suburbanite and family man. Nicholls also encounters another friend from the past, Goldman, who is a force in the Jewish Mafia. Nicholls works for Goldman for a short while, but eventually backs out when he learns that his girl friend is pregnant. In the end there is a reconciliation at the home of Caccavo around a Thanksgiving turkey. Though pat at times, HOME FREE ALL tells the story of three fairly well-adjusted men who have built lives for themselves after the war.

p, Stewart Bird, Peter Belsito; d&w, Bird; ph, Robert Levi; m, Jay Chattaway; ed, Daniel Loewenthal.

Drama **(PR:A MPAA:NR)**

HOME FROM HOME** (1939, Brit.) 73m BL bw

Sandy Powell *(Sandy)*, Rene Ray *(Gladys Burton)*, Roy Emerton *(Bill Burton)*, Kathleen Harrison *(Mabel)*, Bruce Lister *(Jim)*, Wally Patch *(Banks)*, Norma Varden *(Mrs. Fairweather)*, Peter Gawthorne *(Governor)*, The Five Harmonica Rascals, The Gaillard Brothers, George Horold, Dennis Cowles, Jack Vyvyan.

Decent farce revolving around the efforts of Powell to maintain the peace and quiet of prison life. Try as hard as he might, he just can't remain in the pen, away from the wife who drives him up a wall. Even the crime he commits to insure his incarceration ends with him being rewarded with freedom and more of his nasty wife. Powell is the whole show, a position he fills by supplying an array of laughs.

p&d, Herbert Smith; w, Fenn Sherie, Ingram d'Abbes; ph, George Stretton.

Comedy **(PR:A MPAA:NR)**

HOME FROM THE HILL*** (1960) 150m MGM c

Robert Mitchum *(Capt. Wade Hunnicutt)*, Eleanor Parker *(Hannah Hunnicutt)*, George Peppard *(Rafe Copley)*, George Hamilton *(Theron Hunnicutt)*, Everett Sloane *(Albert Halstead)*, Luana Patten *(Libby Halstead)*, Anne Seymour *(Sarah Halstead)*, Constance Ford *(Opal Bixby)*, Ken Renard *(Chauncey)*, Ray Teal *(Dr. Reuben Carson)*, Hilda Haynes *(Melba)*, Charlie Briggs *(Dick Gibbons)*, Guinn "Big Boy" Williams *(Hugh Macauley)*, Dan Sheridan *(Peyton Stiles)*, Orville Sherman *(Ed Dinwoodie)*, Dub Taylor *(Bob Skaggs)*, Stuart Randall *(Ramsey)*, Tom Gilson *(John Ellis)*, Joe Ed Russell *(Foreman)*, Burt Mustin *(Gas Station Attendant)*, Rev. Duncan Gray, Jr. *(Minister)*.

Mitchum is a rich Texas landowner who cheats on wife Parker. Their grown son, Hamilton, and Mitchum's illegitimate son, Peppard, are about the same age. Both live on Mitchum's ranch. Scarred by his parents' stormy relationship and not wishing to follow in their footsteps, Hamilton hesitates to marry Patten. She has a child by him, but ironically it is Peppard who gives the child a legal father. Though it is a little longer than it need be, HOME FROM THE HILL is a fine film that handles its delicate subject with the utmost sensitivity. The scene where the two brothers confess their common progenitor is a gem. Camera work is fine, and the direction gives the story a natural flow. The ending, however, where Mitchum is shot by Patten's father, who in turn is killed by Hamilton, simply does not work and mars an otherwise fine film.

p, Edmund Grainger; d, Vincente Minelli; w, Harriet Frank, Jr. (based on the novel by William Humphrey); ph, Milton Krasner (CinemaScope, Metrocolor); m, Bronislau Kaper; ed, Harold F. Kress; md, Charles Wolcott; art d, George W. Davis, Preston Ames; cos, Walter Plunkett; spec eff, Robert R. Hogue.

Drama **(PR:O MPAA:NR)**

HOME IN INDIANA*** (1944) 103m FOX c

Walter Brennan *(J.P. "Thunder" Bolt)*, Lon McCallister *(Sparke Thorton)*, Jeanne Crain *(Char)*, June Haver *(Cri-Cri)*, Charlotte Greenwood *(Penny)*, Ward Bond *(Jed Bruce)*, Charles Dingle *(Godaw Boole)*, Robert Condon *(Gordon Bradley)*, Charles Saggau *(Jitterbug)*, Willie Best *(Mo' Bum)*, George H. Reed *(Tuppy)*, Noble "Kid" Chissell *(Fleaflit Dryer)*, Walter Baldwin *(Ed)*, George Cleveland *(Sam)*, Arthur Aylesworth *(Blacksmith)*, Libby Taylor *(Maid)*, Roger Imhof *(Old Timer)*, Matt McHugh *(Dave)*, Eddy Waller *(Bill)*, Billy Mitchell *(Waiter)*, Tom Dugan *(Soft Drink Man)*, Sam McDaniel, Emmett Smith *(Swipes)*, Hobart Condon *(Gordon)*.

Homey story about McCallister, a city kid who goes to live in the country with his aunt and uncle (Greenwood and Brennan). They are semi-retired horse breeders with only one trotter left on their farm. Crain and Haver are two lovelies who show McCallister a different side of country living (swimming holes and jitterbugging are about the extent of it—this is the 1940s). McCallister decides to raise a filly and become a champion sulky racer himself. With help from his uncle and handyman Best, this goal is accomplished. This is a cheerful, upbeat film with some nice location work on the race tracks of Kentucky, Indiana, and Ohio. The sequence wherein the filly is born is sensitively handled and quite effective. The young actors handle their roles well, while the seasoned performers give nice support in their background roles. The direction keeps things rolling along nicely. HOME IN INDIANA is a better-than-average horse flick and fine family fare.

p, Andre Daven; d, Henry Hathaway; w, Winston Miller (based on the novel *The Phantom Filly*, by George Agnew Chamberlain); ph, Edward Cronjager (Technicolor); m, Hugo Freidhofer; ed, Harmon Jones; md, Emil Newman; art d, James Baseri, Chester Gore; ch, Geneva Sawyer.

Family Drama **(PR:AAA MPAA:NR)**

HOME IN OKLAHOMA½** (1946) 72m REP bw

Roy Rogers *(Himself)*, George "Gabby" Hayes *(Gabby Whitaker)*, Dale Evans *(Connie Edwards)*, Carol Hughes *(Jan Holloway)*, George Meeker *(Steve McClory)*, Lanny Rees *(Luke Lowry)*, Ruby Dandridge *(Devoria Lassiter)*, George Lloyd *(Sheriff Barclay)*, Arthur Space *(Judnick)*, Frank Reicher *(Lawyer Cragmyle)*, Bob Nolan and The Sons of the Pioneers, George Carleton, Flying "L" Ranch Quartette, "Trigger."

One of Rogers' better films. An editor of a small-town newspaper, he's hot on the trail of some killers who have murdered a local rancher. Evans is a big-city reporter who helps him on both the investigative and musical ends (they duet on "Miguelito"). There is plenty of two-fisted action and Rogers comes out on top, but that's no surprise. Hayes is fine, as usual, in his supporting role. Trigger has a relatively small part this time out. Enjoyable. (See ROY ROGERS series, Index.)

p, Eddy White; d, William Witney; w, Gerald Geraghty; ph, William Bradford; ed, Les Orlebeck; m, Joseph Dubin; md, Morton Scott; art d, Frank Hotaling; m/l, Jack Elliott, Tim Spencer.

Western Musical **Cas.** **(PR:A MPAA:NR)**

HOME IN WYOMIN'** (1942) 67m REP bw

Gene Autry *(Gene)*, Smiley Burnette *(Frog)*, Fay McKenzie *(Clem Benson)*, Olin Howlin *(Sunrise)*, Chick Chandler *(Hack Hackett)*, Joseph Strauch, Jr. *(Tadpole)*, Forrest Taylor *(Pop)*, James Seay *(Tex Harrison)*, George Douglas *(Crowley)*, Charles Lane *(Editor)*, Hal Price *(Sheriff)*, Bud Geary, Ken Cooper, Jean Porter, James McNamara, Kermit Maynard, Roy Butler, Billy Benedict, Cyril Ring, Spade Cooley, Ted Mapes, Jack Kirk, William Kellogg, Betty Farrington, Rex Lease, Tom Hanlon, Lee Shumway, "Champion."

Sub-par Autry flick with him as a singing radio cowboy. A former employer is having financial problems with his rodeo and Autry goes back to Wyoming to assist his old pal. Autry's performance is listless and his singing is poorly synchronized. Burnette and juvenile Strauch are look-alikes, hence the character nicknames Frog and Tadpole. Actually, the whole film is about that clever. Direction and photography are okay, but the film is a departure from the normally high standards of Autry's work. (See GENE AUTRY series, Index.)

p, Harry Grey; d, William Morgan; w, Robert Tasker, M. Coates Webster; ph, Ernest Miller; ed, Edward Mann; md, Raoul Kraushaar; art d, Russell Kimball.

Western **(PR:A MPAA:NR)**

HOME IS THE HERO*** (1959, Ireland) 80m Emmett Dalton/BL-Showcorporation bw

Walter Macken *(Paddo O'Reilly)*, Eileen Crowe *(Daylia O'Reilly)*, Arthur Kennedy *(Willie O'Reilly)*, Joan O'Hara *(Josie O'Reilly)*, Maire O'Donnell *(Maura Green)*, Harry Brogan *(Dovetail)*, Maire Keane *(Bid)*, Philip O'Flynn *(Trapper)*, Patrick Layde *(Mr. Green)*, Eddie Golden *(Mr. Shannon)*, John Hoey *(Finnegan)*, Michael Hennessy *(Manchester Monaghan)*, Michael O'Briain *(1st Pub Customer)*, Dermot Kelly *(2nd Pub Customer)*, Geoffrey Golden *(O'Conner)*.

Film version of a play that bombed on Broadway five years earlier. Macken (who wrote the play) returns home after five years in prison for killing a man. Both he and his family need to make adjustments; much has changed in his absence. Kennedy is the crippled son who helps the old man readjust to the world. With the exception of Kennedy, the players are from Dublin's Abbey Theater Company, where the play originated with much better success than in its New York run. The acting is consistently good. Macken plays his part well and we watch his growth with sympathy. Kennedy gives a quiet dignity to his character in a sensitive performance. The ensemble creates a magical chemistry, making this a completely believable story. Cook has captured this element well with his direction and the film rarely disappoints.

p, Robert S. Baker, Monty Berman; d, J. Fielder Cook, w, Henry Keating (based on the play by Walter Macken), ph, Stanley Pavey; m, Bruce Montgomery; ed, John Ferris; md, Philip Martell; art d, Allan Harris.

Drama **(PR:C MPAA:NR)**

HOME MOVIES½** (1979) 90m SLC Films/UA c

Kirk Douglas *(Dr. Tuttle, "The Maestro")*, Nancy Allen *(Kristina)*, Keith Gordon *(Denis)*, Gerrit Graham *(James)*, Vincent Gardenia *(Dr. Byrd)*, Mary Davenport *(Mrs. Byrd)*, Captain Haggerty *(Policeman)*, Bunny *(Himself)*.

Douglas is a cult leader who is influenced by movies, to say the least. His group is called Star Therapy and members are encouraged "to put your name above the title." He singles out Gordon, "an extra in his own life," and inspires the young man to become the leading player of his own personal movie. Gordon responds by chasing after his brother's fiancee, exposing his doctor-father's affair with a Swedish nurse, and attempting to film himself in a variety of situations. Graham is the brother, a cult freak devoted to Spartan ideals. Allen (DePalma's real-life wife at the time) is Graham's spacey, though business-minded, girl friend. As for Douglas, he lives his film-cult ideals fully, constantly documenting his life on 16mm film. DePalma made this film with students from his directing class at Sarah Lawrence College. It has a nice, offbeat feel to it, recalling DePalma's early post-film school work (HI MOM and GREETINGS). The masking technique used on Douglas' "documentary" works nicely. Donaggio's music has a comic touch. A highly professional job considering that it was written and produced with a student crew. Though normally considered a suspense and horror director, HOME MOVIES proves DePalma has a comic flair.

p, Brian DePalma, Jack Temchin, Gil Adler; d, DePalma; w, Robert Harders, Gloria Norris, Kim Ambler, Dana Edelman, Stephan LeMay, Charles Loventhal (based on a story by DePalma); ph, James L. Carter; m, Pino Donaggio; ed, Corky Ohara; art d, Tom Surgal, Rachel Feldman.

Comedy **(PR:C MPAA:PG)**

HOME OF THE BRAVE*** (1949) 88m Screen Plays/UA bw

Douglas Dick *(Maj. Robinson)*, Steve Brodie *(T.J.)*, Jeff Corey *(Doctor)*, Lloyd Bridges *(Finch)*, Frank Lovejoy *(Mingo)*, James Edwards *(Moss)*, Cliff Clark *(Colonel)*.

HOME OF THE BRAVE is a provocative film, particularly when viewed from an historical perspective. Edwards is a black soldier who becomes paralyzed from the waist down. He and four white men have been on a reconnaissance mission to a Japanese-held South Pacific island. His slice-of-life comrades include the major in charge of the mission (Dick); a sergeant who has found out his wife has been unfaithful (Lovejoy); Edwards' boyhood friend (Bridges); and a bigoted corporal (Brodie), who delights in baiting Edwards. After a terrible shock, Edwards becomes paralyzed and is sent to a hospital where his story slowly unfolds for psychiatrist Corey. Originally produced on Broadway with a Jew as the minority, HOME OF THE BRAVE's film version took a real risk, showing the plight of blacks during World War II. This was still a time when blacks were largely ignored in both everyday America as well as Hollywood. Typical of Kramer's hard-hitting "message" films to come, this was a revelation in its time. Edwards gives a sensitive performance and Robson's direction never condescends or makes Edwards a figure of bleeding-heart pity.

p, Stanley Kramer; d, Mark Robson; w, Carl Foreman (based on the play by Arthur Laurents); ph, Robert De Grasse; m, Dmitri Tiomkin; ed, Harry Gerstad; md, Tiomkin; art d, Rudolph Sternad; spec eff, J.R. Rabin.

Drama **Cas.** **(PR:C MPAA:NR)**

HOME ON THE PRAIRIE** (1939) 58m REP bw

Gene Autry, Smiley Burnette, June Storey, George Cleveland, Jack Mulhall, Walter Miller, Gordon Hart, Hal Price, Earl Hodgins, Ethan Laidlaw, John Beach, Jack Ingram, Bob Woodward and The Rodeoliers, Sherven Brothers, "Champion."

Average Autry entry with an unintended gimmick: there's more action here than singing, rare for the "B's" Singing Cowboy. Autry is a border inspector whose job is to make sure no diseased animals enter the U.S. Miller and Hart are a pair of cattlemen trying to ship in their hoof-and-mouth infected herd. When Autry quarantines these cattle, the two bad guys try to implicate Storey. Things look bad for her until Autry saves the day. Burnette is involved in a comic sub-plot with an elephant that has escaped from a a traveling medicine show. Storey is the best thing in this otherwise average film. She is natural in her role and really acts, unlike the majority of the western leading ladies. The songs are definite lesser Autry. (See GENE AUTRY series, Index.)

p, Harry Grey; d, Jack Townley; w, Charles Arthur Powell, Paul Franklin; ph, Reggie Lanning; ed, Lester Orlebeck.

Western **(PR:A MPAA:NR)**

HOME ON THE RANGE*½ (1935) 54m PAR bw

Jackie Coogan *(Jack)*, Randolph Scott *(Tom Hatfield)*, Evelyn Brent *(Georgie)*, Dean Jagger *(Thurman)*, Addison Richards *(Beady)*, Fuzzy Knight *("Cracker")*, Ann Sheridan *(Girl Entertainer)*, Ralph Remley, Philip Morris, Frances Sayles, Clarence Sherwood, Allen Wood, Howard Wilson, Albert Hart, Richard Carle, Joe Morrison, C.L. Sherwood, Jack Clark, Alfred Delcambre.

A combination race track-western that really doesn't work. Coogan is Scott's younger brother. They own a stable of horses with one steed (Scott's famous "Midnight') that is a sure winner. But bad guys want to foreclose, coveting not only the ranch but also the horse. In the climactic big race Coogan rides Midnight to victory, beating the bad guys' jockey handily. He wins enough money to save the stable and keep the two brothers together. Midnight stays too. But then, he's earned it. Coogan is not much in his part, still very much the juvenile. Scott, on the other hand, showed progress as a lead. Eventually he went on to do his own series of popular B westerns.

p, Harold Hurley; d, Arthur Jacobson; w, Harold Shumate, Ethel Doherty, Grant Garrett, Charles Logue (based on the novel *Code of the West* by Zane Grey); ph, William Mellor; ed, Jack Dennis.

Western/Sports Drama **(PR:A MPAA:NR)**

HOME ON THE RANGE** (1946) 55m REP c

Monte Hale *(Monte Hale)*, Adrian Booth *(Bonnie Garth)*, Tom Chatterton *(Grizzly Garth)*, Bobby Blake *(Cub Garth)*, LeRoy Mason *(Dan Long)*, Roy Barcroft *(Clint Baker)*, Kenne Duncan *(Slim Wallace)*, Budd Buster *(Sheriff Cutler)*, Jack Kirk *(Benson)*, John Hamilton *(Statesman)*, Bob Nolan and the Sons of the Pioneers.

This western is different from most due to its theme. Rather than stress action, bad guys, and robbery, HOME ON THE RANGE features action, bad guys, and ecology. Hale is a rancher out to preserve the wild creatures on a zoned range. Mason is the black hat who wants the land for his own nefarious purposes. Booth is a lady rancher who sides with Hale, but not before she regards him as some sort of fool. Finally seeing things his way, she teams up with him to fight Mason. Though the motives are certainly different, it's really the same old package: fistfights, hard riding, and some gunplay mixed with some poorly written (and poorly synchronized) songs. The color photography helps a little, but in the end doesn't make much difference. Hale's okay in his first cowboy picture.

p, Louis Gray; d, Robert Springsteen; w, Betty Burbridge (based on a story by Burbridge, Bernard McConville); ph, Marcel LePicard (Magnacolor); m, Dale Butts; ed, Charles Craft; md, Morton Scott; spec eff, Howard Lydecker, Theodore Lydecker; m/l, "Happy-Go-Lucky Cowboy," "Down at the Old Hoe Down," "Over the Rainbow Trail," "Take Your Time," Gordon Forster, Ken Carson, Glen Spencer.

Western **Cas.** **(PR:A MPAA:NR)**

HOME, SWEET HOME** (1933, Brit.) 74m REA/RKO bw

John Stuart *(Richard Pelham)*, Marie Ney *(Constance Pelham)*, Richard Cooper *(Tupman)*, Sydney Fairbrother *(Mrs. Bagshaw)*, Cyril Raymond *(John Falkirk)*, Eve Becke *(Betty Martin)*, Eliot Makeham *(James Merrick)*, Felix Aylmer *(Robert Wilding KC)*, Ben Welden *(Santos)*, Joan Carter, Barbara Everest.

Just before he is to return home to England, Stuart, a mining engineer working in South America, receives a letter from his wife (Ney). Seems she's been unfaithful since he's been gone, and wants to run off with her new beau, Raymond. But in the interim, she changes her mind and drives to the hotel where Raymond is staying. En route she is involved in an accident and is taken to the hotel. Stuart arrives knowing only that his wife wants to run off with another man. He finds the spurned lover and accidentally kills him. Stuart has to stand trial for murder but is given a lighter sentence when Ney testifies that she had been having the affair for a long time. This film is typical of the cheap B quickies coming from the English studios at the time. Production values and acting are okay, though nothing terribly fresh or creative is going on.

p, Julius Hagen; d, George A. Cooper; w, Terence Egan, H. Fowler Mear.

Drama **(PR:A MPAA:NR)**

HOME SWEET HOME*½ (1945, Brit.) 92m Mancunian/But bw

Nicolette Roeg *(Jacqueline Chantry)*, Frank Randle *(Frank)*, Tony Pendrell *(Eric Wright)*, H.F. Maltby *(Col. Wright)*, Hilda Bayley *(Mrs. Wright)*, Cecil Fredericks *(Webster)*, Stan Little *(Young Herbert)*, Bunty Meadows *(Bunty)*, Gerhard Kempinski *(Pagoli)*, George Merritt *(Dr. Handy)*, Howard Douglas, Iris Vandeleur, Esma Lewis, Vincent Holman, Lily Lapidus, Ben Williams, Max Melford, Rawicz & Landauer, Helen Hill, Donovan & Byl, Arnley & Gloria.

A moderately amusing musical comedy which centers on the romance between Roeg, a charming orphan girl, and Pendrell, the son of a colonel and his class-conscious wife. When the colonel's wife refuses to give her approval for the marriage, Roeg packs her bags and becomes a nightclub chanteuse. Pendrell chases after her, but she's already found Randle, a likable chap who leanrs that Roeg is really a wealthy heiress. It passes the time but it's not especially memorable.

p&d, John E. Blakeley; w, Roney Parsons, Anthony Toner, Frank Randle; ph, Geoffrey Faithfull.

Musical/Comedy **(PR:A MPAA:NR)**

HOME SWEET HOME*½ (1981) 85m c

Sallee Elyse, Jake Steinfeld.

A family hopes it will find serenity in an isolated country home. But nobody gets away with that in the movies, and sure enough, the happy clan find themselves being stalked by a schizophrenic killer. Nothing new.

d, Nettie Pena.

Horror **(PR:O MPAA:NR)**

HOME SWEET HOMICIDE*** (1946) 85m FOX bw

Peggy Ann Garner *(Dinah Carstairs)*, Randolph Scott *(Lt. Bill Smith)*, Lynn Bari *(Marian Carstairs)*, Dean Stockwell *(Archie Carstairs)*, Connie Marshall *(April Carstairs)*, James Gleason *(Sgt. O'Hare)*, Anabel Shaw *(Polly Walker)*, Barbara Whiting *(Jo-Ella Holbrook)*, John Shepperd *(Mr. Sanford)*, Stanley Logan *(Mr. Cherrington)*, Olin Howlin *(Luke)*, Marietta Canty *(Housekeeper)*, Pat Flaherty, Phillip Morris *(Policemen)*.

Cute little film features Bari as a mother/mystery novelist with three kids (Garner, Stockwell, Marshall). The precocious youngsters stumble onto a neighborhood murder. They work on confounding the cops so Mom can solve the murder and have a new story. But the kids get in over their heads and danger is afoot until Scott, a handsome policeman and love interest for Bari, saves the day. It's a nice little film with a script based on the true experiences of authoress Rice. The kids are far beyond the typical movie brats, very natural and amusing in their respective roles. Scott, on a break from his cowboy adventures, does a fine job. The direction is quickly paced, keeping a nice mix between the comedy and suspense. A fun film for children.

p, Louis D. Lighton; d, Lloyd Bacon; w, F. Hugh Herbert (based on a novel by Craig Rice); ph, John Seitz; m, David Buttolph; ed, Louis Loeffler; art d, James Basevi, Boris Leven.

Comedy/Suspense **(PR:AAA MPAA:NR)**

HOME TO DANGER*½ (1951, Brit.) 66m New World/Eros bw

Guy Rolfe *(Robert)*, Rona Anderson *(Barbara)*, Francis Lister *(Wainwright)*, Alan Wheatley *(Hughes)*, Bruce Belfrage *(Solicitor)*, Stanley Baker *(Willie Dougan)*, Dennis Harkin *(Jimmy-The-One)*, Peter Jones *(Lips Leonard)*, Christopher Hodge *(Policeman)*, Joe Stern, Glyn Houston, Toni Frost, Frederick Buckland, Amy Dalby, Cyril Conway, Betty Henderson.

Anderson is the chief beneficiary of a will left by her father, who has committed suicide. She is left his entire estate and quickly becomes the target of a crazed killer. She is targeted for death during a shooting party, but survives only to be attacked again later. The murderer turns out to be Wheatley, the proprietor of an orphanage. Baker, the family servant, takes the role of the hero and saves Anderson from an early demise.

p, Lance Comfort; d, Terence Fisher; w, John Temple-Smith, Francis Edge; ph, Reg Wyler.

Crime/Mystery **(PR:A MPAA:NR)**

HOME TOWN STORY*½ (1951) 61m MGM bw

Jeffrey Lynn *(Blake Washburn)*, Donald Crisp *(John MacFarland)*, Marjorie Reynolds *(Janice Hunt)*, Alan Hale, Jr. *(Slim Haskins)*, Marilyn Monroe *(Miss Martin)*, Barbara Brown *(Mrs. Washburn)*, Melinda Plowman *(Katie Washburn)*, Renny McEvoy *(Taxi Driver)*, Griff Barnett *(Uncle Cliff)*, Virginia Campbell *(Phoebe)*, Harry Harvey *(Andy Butterworth)*, Nelson Leigh *(Mr. Johnson)*, Speck Noblitt *(Motorcycle Officer)*, Glenn Tryon, Byron Foulger.).

Lynn is an ex-politico, defeated after two years in office. He is convinced that big business is behind his defeat. After becoming editor of his uncle's newspaper, he tries to expose big business as a massive all-controlling power monster. But when his little sister is buried in a cave-in it's the town's largest company that saves the day. The company president flies the girl to the state capital for life-saving surgery after the firm's machinery digs her out of her predicament. Lynn changes his tune quickly. The film was sponsored and supervised by John K. Ford, head of General Motors film division. The overt theme of big business championing itself over liberals is repeated throughout the film. Try to ignore the lumbering message and watch for an early appearance by Monroe.

p,d&w, Arthur Pierson; ph, Lucien Androit; m, Louis Forbes; ed, William Claxton; art d, Hilyard Brown.

Drama **(PR:C MPAA:NR)**

HOME TOWNERS, THE½** (1928) 94m WB bw

Richard Bennett *(Vic Arnold)*, Doris Kenyon *(Beth Calhoun)*, Robert McWade *(P.H. Bancroft)*, Robert Edeson *(Mr. Calhoun)*, Gladys Brockwell *(Lottie Bancroft)*, John Miljan *(Joe Roberts)*, Vera Lewis *(Mrs. Calhoun)*, Stanley Taylor *(Wally Calhoun)*, James T. Mack *(Casey)*, Patricia Caron *(Maid)*.

Bennett is rapidly approaching fifty and none too happy about it. He meets youngster Kenyon and romance develops. But Bennett's old friend McWade thinks Kenyon is a gold digger after the groom's riches. He tries to cause trouble between the lovers and almost succeeds. McWade is proven wrong in the end and the pair marry with his consent. The film is slow to start and some scenes run a little long, but it does have certain historical value. This film was one of the best technical achievements in the early stages of talkies, using the dialog to carry the story instead of employing it as a money making gimmick. THE HOME TOWNERS is based on a successful play by famed showman Cohan. The early sound recording techniques are fairly obvious. Covered mikes are easy to spot—just listen to the voice levels when the actors turn away from flower pots, and other camouflage. A remake in 1940 was titled LADIES MUST LIVE.

d, Bryan Foy; w, Addison Burkhart, Murray Roth (based on the play by George M. Cohan); ph, Barney McGill.

Comedy **(PR:A MPAA:NR)**

HOMEBODIES½** (1974) 96m Cinema Entertainment/AE c

Peter Brocco *(Blakely)*, Frances Fuller *(Emily)*, William Hansen *(Sandy)*, Ruth McDevitt *(Mrs. Loomis)*, Paula Trueman *(Mattie)*, Ian Wolfe *(Loomis)*, Linda Marsh *(Miss Pollack)*, Douglas Fowley *(Crawford)*, Kenneth Tobey *(Construction Boss)*, Wesley Lau *(Foreman)*, Norman Gottschalk *(Superintendent)*, Irene Webster *(Woman in Floppy Hat)*, Nicholas Lewis, John Craig, Joe De Meo *(Construction Workers)*, Michael Johnson *(Policeman)*, Alma Du Bus *(Super's Wife)*, Eldon Quick *(Insurance Inspector)*, William Benedict *(Watchman)*.

Strange little shocker about a murderous group of geriatrics. Marsh is a social worker with no soul. She evicts a number of elderly people from their apartment building. The building is in the way of a new construction project and simply has to go. Rather than fight City Hall the senior citizens take a more direct approach. The social worker is stabbed to death and construction workers are gruesomely done away with. The six oldsters are portrayed as everyday people fed up with an uncaring system; this makes the fairly graphic violence all the more shocking. It's an excellent example of what can be done with a small budget and a good sense of the macabre. Made in Cincinnati.

p, Marshal Backlar; d, Larry Yust; w, Yust, Howard Kaminsky, Bennett Sims; ph, Isidore Mankofsky; m, Bernardo Segall; ed, Peter Parasheles; art d, John Retsek; set d, Raymond Molyneaux; cos, Lynn Bernay; spec eff, Donald Courtney; m/l, Segall, Jeremy Kronsberg.

Horror **Cas.** **(PR:O MPAA:PG)**

HOMECOMING** (1948) 113m MGM bw

Clark Gable *(Ulysses Delby Johnson)*, Lana Turner *(Lt. Jane "Snapshot" McCall)*, Anne Baxter *(Penny Johnson)*, John Hodiak *(Dr. Robert Sunday)*, Ray Collins *(Lt. Col. Avoy Silver)*, Gladys Cooper *(Mrs. Kirby)*, Cameron Mitchell *(Monkevickz)*, Art Baker *(Williams)*, Lurene Tuttle *(Miss Stoker)*, Jessie Grayson *(Sarah)*, J. Louis Johnson *(Sol)*, Bill Self *(Jr. Lieutenant)*, Jeff Corey *(Cigarette Smoker)*, Thomas E. Breen *(Young Man)*, Wheaton Chambers *(Doctor)*, Phil Dunham *(Elevator Operator)*, Frank Mayo, Roger Moore, Dan Quigg, Broderick O'Farrell, George Sherwood, Charles Miller, Nolan Leary *(Doctors)*, Kay Mansfield *(Mrs. Lovette)*, Peggy Baday *(Miss Simpson)*, William Forrest, Dorothy Christy, Anne Nagel *(Guests)*, James Bush *(Instructor)*, David Clark *(Sergeant)*, Joseph Crehan *(Colonel Morgan C.O.)*, Bert Moorhouse, David Newell *(Surgeons)*, Johnny Albright *(Corpsman)*, Arthur Space *(Col. Norton)*, Wally Cassell *(Patient)*, Frances Pyle *(Red Cross Field Worker)*, Vernon Downing *(British Soldier)*, Danielle Day *(Young French Girl)*, James Taggart, Jerry Jerome *(Lieutenants)*, Alphonse Martel, George Offerman, Jr. *(Clerks)*, Lisa Gold *(Anna)*, Geraldine Wall *(Head Nurse)*, Marshall Thompson *(Sgt. McKeen)*, Frank Arnold *(Maitre d'Hotel)*, Leslie Dennison *(British Colonel)*, Olga Borget *(Newswoman)*, Francine Bordeau, Queenie Leonard, Virginia Keiley, Fern Eggen, Mary Joe Ellis, Mimi Doyle, Eloise Hardt *(Nurses)*, Michael Kirby, Lew Smith *(Corpsmen)*, Edwin Cooper *(Head Surgeon)*, William Tannen *(Attendant)*, Gregg Barton *(Captain)*, Louise Colombet *(Frenchwoman)*, Ralph Montgomery, Robert Skelton *(G.I.'s)*, Gaylord Pendelton *(Orderly)*, Hobart Manning, Jay Norris *(Officers)*, Charles Meredith *(Major)*, Arthur O'Connell *(Driver)*, Alan Hale, Jr. *(M.P.)*, Albert Pollet *(Waiter)*, Jean LaFayette *(Girl)*, Leo Vandervelde *(Page Boy)*.

Gable is a highly successful New York doctor married to socialite Baxter. The doctor is also caught up in the social scene and is too busy to help old colleague Hodiak aid a small, disease-plagued town. After the U.S. enters WW II, Gable is enlisted into the Medical Corps as a major. Hodiak resents Gable's condescending airs and lets his old pal know it. On the transport to Africa Gable meets nurse Turner who is to be his assistant. She too takes a dislike to Gable. In the field the pair are constantly fighting each other, but slowly they fall in love. She leaves and Gable re-examines his life. He sees how selfish he has been and starts to change. On a one week leave in Paris he runs once more into Turner and they enjoy seven idyllic days. But a new offensive cuts short their affair, as they must return to their work. Turner is eventually killed at the Battle of the Bulge. Gable returns to Baxter with plans for a new life with her. This film has some good and bad moments. The cast is excellent. This was Gable and Turner's first film together after a long absence and their chemistry is fine. But the story is pure soap opera and is far below the talents of the leads. The film panders to stereotyping and easy solutions for complex problems. Some critics complained that WW II was still fresh in memory and the attempts here to trivialize and sentimentalize the war were inappropriate. Originally producer Franklin had wanted Turner's character to leave rather than die but Gable objected, wanting feelings and emotions in the film to be honest. Despite Gable winning this argument, the film does not live up to his aspirations. Though it was voted by the New York Critics as one of the ten worst movies of 1948, the public loved it. At the time Baxter was married to Hodiak. She was loaned out from 20th Century Fox to MGM for this film. Gable and Turner recreated their HOMECOMING parts for "Screen Guild Playhouse."

p, Sidney Franklin; d, Mervyn LeRoy; w, Paul Osborn, Jan Lustig (based on the story "The Homecoming of Ulysses" by Sidney Kingsley); ph, Harold Rosson; m, Bronislau Kaper; ed, John Dunning; md, Charles Previn; art d, Cedric Gibbons, Randall Duell; set d, Edwin B. Willis, Henry W. Grace; cos, Helen Rose; spec eff, Warren Newcombe, A. Arnold Gillespie; makeup, Jack Dawn.

War/Romance **(PR:A MPAA:NR)**

HOMECOMING, THE**** (1973) 111m American Film Theatre c

Cyril Cusack *(Sam)*, Ian Holm *(Lenny)*, Michael Jayston *(Teddy)*, Vivien Merchant *(Ruth)*, Terence Rigby *(Joey)*, Paul Rogers *(Max)*.

Excellent adaptation of the Pinter play for the American Film Theater series of the early 1970s. The simple plot features Jayston returning to his childhood home with wife Merchant. There he sees his father (Rogers), uncle (Cusack), and his brothers (Holm and Rigby), who are a pimp and boxer, respectively. The small family is held together by volatile fighting, boredom, and ultimate dependency on one another. Each performance is a gem. The individual quirks of each character are well handled and utterly believable. Hall's direction is sensitive to Pinter's script and to the acting of the ensemble (who all played in the original 1965 stage production). There is a magical chemistry within every aspect of this film. Powerful and unforgettable.

p, Ely A. Landau; d, Peter Hall; w, Harold Pinter (based on his play); ph, David Watkin; ed, Rex Pike; prod d, John Bury; art d, Jack Stevens; cos, Elizabeth Haffenden, Joan Bridge.

Drama **(PR:C MPAA:PG)**

HOMER** (1970) 90m Palomar/NG c

Don Scardino *(Homer Edwards)*, Alex Nicol *(Mr. Edwards)*, Tisa Farrow *(Laurie Grainger)*, Lenka Peterson *(Mrs. Edwards)*, Ralph Endersby *(Hector)*, Trudy Young *(Sally)*, Arch McDonnell *(Mr. Grainger)*, Jan Campbell *(Mrs. Grainger)*, Tim Henry *(Eddie Cochran)*, Murray Westgate *(Mr. Cochran)*, Mona O'Hearn *(Mrs. Cochran)*, Bob Werner *(Sheriff)*, Dennis Pendrith, Mike Ferry, Tom Harvey, Ted Gunn, Allen Doremus, Tony Parr, Frank Aldous, Debbie Turnbull, Hughie Sullivan, Larry Reynolds, Sam Turturici, Chelo Scardino.

Well-meaning though cliche-ridden film about the kids of the 1960s. Pop singer Scardino is the standard misunderstood young man, who also leads a rock group. Nicol and Peterson are his rigid parents; Endersby and Henry are his buddies. Henry is in the army, back home on furlough. Both Scardino and Endersby oppose the Vietnam War. Farrow (Mia's sister and daughter of John and Maureen O'Sullivan) has more or less a walk-on role that requires her to be shy and introverted until she gets into bed with someone. The photography is awkward at moments and the film is riddled with cliched shots of sunsets, silhouetted sex, and dope smoking. The direction is far too simplistic, as is the script. Nicol is surprisingly good in his role, rising well above the material. Set in Wisconsin but shot in Canada. Scardino performs his own rock songs and the soundtrack also features tunes from a number of rock 'n' roll bands, including: "Turn, Turn, Turn," performed by The Byrds, "Bluebird," "Rock 'n' Roll Woman," "For What It's Worth," performed by Buffalo Springfield, "Nashville Cats," performed by The Lovin' Spoonful, "Brave New World," performed by Steve Miller, "How Many More Times?" performed by Led Zeppelin, "Rock 'n' Roll Gypsies," performed by Hearts And Flowers, "Spoonful," performed by Cream.

p, Terence Dene, Steven North; d, John Trent; w, Claude Harz (based on a story by Harz, Matt Clark); ph, Lazlo George (Technicolor); m, Don Scardino; ed, Michael Menne; prod d, Jack McAdams; set d, Keith Barrie.

Drama **(PR:C MPAA:PG)**

HOMESTEADERS, THE** (1953) 62m AA bw

Wild Bill Elliott *(Mace Corbin)*, Robert Lowry *(Clyde Moss)*, Emmett Lynn *(Grimer)*, George Wallace *(Meade)*, Buzz Henry *(Charlie)*, Stanley Price *(Van)*, Rick Vallin *(Slim)*, William Fawcett *(Hector)*, James Seay *(Kroger)*, Tom Monroe *(Jake)*, Barbara Allen *(Jenny)*, Ray Walker *(Col. Peterson)*, Barbara Woodell.

Elliott is a homesteader heading off to a Midwest Army base. There he's to pick up a load of dynamite for clearing land in his home state of Oregon. But land-grabber

Seay hires Lowry, Elliott's partner, to double-cross his comrade on the way home. Before this can happen they must deal with a few standards: a gang of ex-soldiers, a band of Indians, and a few malcontents. After some fighting between the partners, Lowry sees the error of his ways and joins once more with Elliott to stop Seay. Despite many available opportunities, there is relatively little action in this slow-paced western. The script is weak, leaving most plot exposition to the dialog. This gets boring very quickly. Production and acting are standard for the genre.

p, Vincent M. Fennelly; d, Lewis Collins; w, Sid Theil, Milton Raison; ph, Ernest Miller; m, Raoul Kraushaar; ed, Sam Fields; art d, David Milton.

Western (PR:A MPAA:NR)

HOMESTEADERS OF PARADISE VALLEY*½ (1947) 59m REP bw

Allan Lane, Bobby Blake, Martha Wentworth, Ann Todd, Gene Stutenroth, John James, Mauritz Hugo, Emmett Vogan, Milton Kibbee, Tom London, Edythe Elliott, George Chesebro, Edward Cassidy, Jack Kirk, Herman Hack.

Lane stars in this RED RYDER series western, lending a hand to a group of homesteaders who are constructing a dam in the title valley. There's trouble in paradise, however, when a couple of local outlaws act as an obstacle. Lane and little Blake (who made a name for himself the same year in THE TREASURE OF SIERRA MADRE) wipe the valley clean of bandit dirt and make it a pleasant place to live. (See RED RYDER series, Index.)

p, Sidney Picker; d, R.G. Springsteen; w, Earle Snell; ph, Alfred Keller; ed, Charles Craft; md, Mort Glickman; art d, Fred A. Ritter; spec eff, Howard Lydecker, Theodore Lydecker.

Western Cas. (PR:A MPAA:NR)

HOMESTRETCH, THE½** (1947) 99m FOX c

Cornel Wilde *(Jock Wallace)*, Maureen O'Hara *(Leslie Hale)*, Glenn Langan *(Bill Van Dyke)*, Helen Walker *(Kitty Brant)*, James Gleason *(Doc Ellborne)*, Henry Stephenson *(Balcares)*, Margaret Bannerman *(Ellamae Scott)*, Ethel Griffies *(Aunt Martha)*, Tommy Cook *(Pablo)*, Nancy Evans *(Sarah)*, John Vosper *(Cliff)*, Michael Dyne *(Julian Scott)*, Edward Earle *(Mac)*, Charles Stevens *(Mexican Father)*, Nina Campana *(Mexican Mother)*, Rose Mary Lopez *(Mexican Girl)*, Claire Du Brey *(Carl)*, Anne O'Neal *(Maid)*, Harry Cheshire *(Col. Albright)*, George Reed *(Dee Dee)*, Juan Torena *(Hernandez)*, Inez Palange *(Gypsy Woman)*, Edmund Cobb *(Mac's Helper)*, Buddy Roosevelt *(Brakeman)*, Clinton Rosemond *(Black Man)*, Keith Hitchcock *(Bobbie)*.

O'Hara is a Boston society girl who marries gambler Wilde. Together they go to the famous racetracks of the world until he finally runs out of money. He borrows from ex-girl friend Walker and she won't let go of him. O'Hara wonders why she gave up a fiance in the State Department for this sort of life and considers divorce. But Wilde has a change of heart, and, hoping to rebuild his stables, wagers everything on his last horse's Kentucky Derby run. His horse loses by a nose to O'Hara's but Wilde and O'Hara reconcile their differences at the film's happy ending. THE HOMESTRETCH is not a bad movie, but it is hard to care much about a plot that seems so familiar. There is some wonderful footage of world-famous race tracks like Ascot in England, Palermo in South America, as well as Saratoga and Churchill Downs. The technicolor is used well and the final horse race is an exciting sequence.

p, Robert Bassler; d, H. Bruce Humberstone; w, Wanda Tuchock; ph, Arthur Arling (Technicolor); m, David Raksin; ed, Robert Simpson; md, Alfred Newman; art d, James Basevi, Leland Fuller; set d, Thomas Little, Walter M. Scott; spec eff, Fred Sersen.

Drama (PR:A MPAA:NR)

HOMETOWN U.S.A.** (1979) 93m Film Ventures International c

Gary Springer *(Rodney C. "Rodent" Duckworth)*, David Wilson *(Recil Calhoun)*, Brian Kerwin *(T.J. Swackhammer)*, Pat Delaney *(Marilyn)*, Julie Parsons *(Andrea)*, Mitzi Hoag *(Mrs. Duckworth)*, Ned Wertimer *(Mr. Duckworth)*, Bo Kaprall *(Arnold)*, Betty McGuire *(Mrs. Smith)*, Michael Prince *(Mr. Smith)*, Nancy Osborne *(Rhina)*, Cindy Fisher *(Ginger)*, Debi Richter *(Dolly)*, Shirley Anne Broger *(Joanie)*, Jim Bohan *(Childres)*, Virginia Feingold *(Edna)*, Betsee Finlee, Sally Julian, Sally Kirkland, Bradley Lieberman, Kathy Mulrooney, Meliisa O'Bryant, Anne O'Donnell, Lorraine Adele Osborne, Sunshine Parker, Yuliis Ruval, Jesse Vint III, Steve Kavner, Evan Gordon, Larry Cooper, Gene Hartline, Harry Monty, Maida Belove, Jon Cutler, Sherry Marks, Julia Embree, Brenda Smith, Sheri Jason, Susan Kamins, Sandy Serrano.

This harmless little ripoff of AMERICAN GRAFFITI is merely a series of vignettes about a group of kids in the 1950s that drive around in hot rods. The dialog is believable, and there are a few slightly satirical moments. The soundtrack of those great 1950s oldies just can't be beat. This film is probably best remembered for its director Baer, who was desperately trying to shake his image as Jethro, the idiotic hayseed nephew on the 1960s TV series "The Beverly Hillbillies."

p, Roger Camras, Jesse Vint; d, Max Baer; w, Vint; ph, (Panavision, CFI Color); ed, Frank Morris; md, Marshall Leib; art d, Keith Michl; cos, Nancy Frechtling.

Comedy (PR:C MPAA:R)

HOMEWORK zero (1982) 90m Junior/Jensen Farley c

Joan Collins *(Diana)*, Michael Morgan *(Tommy)*, Shell Kepler *(Lisa)*, Lanny Horn *(Ralph)*, Erin Donovan *(Sheila)*, Lee Purcell *(Ms. Jackson)*, Renee Harris *(Cookie)*, Mark Brown *(Mix)*, Steve Gustafson *(John)*, Carrie Snodgress *(Dr. Delingua)*, Wings Hauser *(Red Dog)*, Joy Michael *(Diana, age 16)*, Mel Welles, Beverly Todd, John Romano, Ernestina Jackson, Bill Knight, Newell Alexander, Deedee Downs, Howard Storm, Betty Thomas.

Poor Morgan. He and his buddies are all sex-starved teenagers. While they somehow are making time with substitute French teachers and rock bands he just can't get it together. He pours his heart out to school shrink Snodgress and runs around Sunset Strip desperately trying to find someone to "do it" with. As luck would have it, his good friend Donovan's mom just happens to be the sultry Collins. Like all other older women in these sort of sex epics, she's salivating slavishly for a real man of 16. Originally made in 1979 under the title GROWING PAINS, it was shelved for one major reason: it stinks. But when Collins achieved great success as the bitchy Alexis of TV's "Dynasty," the film was dusted off, given a new title, and released to some success. Thomas was advertised as having a feature role, in response to her fame on the excellent TV series "Hill Street Blues." Actually she's in this film for all of ten seconds. The same production company went on to make a similarly themed film, PRIVATE LESSONS, which was better than HOMEWORK, though that's not saying much.

p&d, James Beshears; w, Maurice Peterson, Don Safran; ph, Paul Goldsmith (Movielab Color); m,Tony Jones, Jim Wetzel; ed, Allen Persselin.

Comedy Cas. (PR:O MPAA:R)

HOMICIDAL½** (1961) 87m COL bw

Glenn Corbett *(Karl)*, Patricia Breslin *(Miriam Webster)*, Jean Arless *(Emily/Warren)*, Eugenie Leontovich *(Helga)*, Alan Bunce *(Dr. Jonas)*, Richard Rust *(Jim Nesbitt)*, James Westerfield *(Mr. Adrims)*, Gilbert Green *(Lt. Miller)*, Wolfe Barzell *(Olie)*, Hope Summers *(Mrs. Adrims)*, Teri Brooks *(Mrs. Forest)*, Ralph Moody *(1st Clerk)*, Joe Forte *(2nd Clerk)*, William Castle *(Narrator)*.

Good, nasty, gleeful fun from horror-maker-deluxe Castle. In this strange-but-true story (based on a 10-year-old Scandanavian case) Arless pays a bellboy to marry her, then murders the justice of the peace who has performed the ceremony. From there she's off to a gloomy old house owned by a paralyzed old woman and her strange young son. (Where have we seen these two characters before?) The half-sister of the young man is nearly murdered by Arless; the older woman is not so lucky. The ending keeps the pseudo-PSYCHO imagery steadfast: Arless is in reality both the wife and husband seen in the marriage ceremony at the film's beginning. It's a little difficult to follow but this wasn't meant to be great art. Five minutes before it's all over, the film is interrupted by a "Fright Break." The audience is given 45 seconds to follow "the yellow streak to the cowards' corner" or, if brave enough, sit it out.

p&d, William Castle; w, Robb White; ph, Burnett Guffey; m, Hugo Friedhofer; ed, Edwin Bryant; art d, Cary Odell; set d, Darrell Silvera.

Horror (PR:O MPAA:NR)

HOMICIDE** (1949) 77m WB bw

Robert Douglas *(Lt. Michael Landers)*, Helen Westcott *(Jo Ann Rice)*, Robert Alda *(Andy)*, Monte Blue *(Sheriff)*, Warren Douglas *(Brad Clifton)*, Richard Benedict *(Nick Foster)*, John Harmon *(Pete Kimmel)*, James Flavin *(Boylan)*, Cliff Clark *(Capt. Mooney)*, Esther Howard *(Mrs. Brucker)*, Sarah Padden *(Mrs. Webb)*.

Warren Douglas is a young hitchhiker who accidentally comes upon a murder. Later he is found dead, having apparently committed suicide, but Robert Douglas, a homicide cop, knows better. He takes time off his regular job to investigate. The trail leads him to the desert hideout of some tough gangsters, led by Alda. It's an intriguing little film up until the investigation begins and then quickly becomes a formula piece. The direction is average, though the fight between the detective Douglas and Alda is nicely handled. The romance between the detective and Westcott is minor and unbelievable.

p, Saul Elkins; d, Felix Jacoves; w, William Sackheim (based on his story "Night Beat"); ph, Peverell Marley; ed, Thomas Reilly; m, William Lava; art d, Hugh Reticker.

Crime/Drama (PR:C MPAA:NR)

HOMICIDE BUREAU* (1939) 56m COL bw

Bruce Cabot *(Jim Logan)*, Rita Hayworth *(J. G. Bliss)*, Marc Lawrence *(Chuck Brown)*, Richard Fiske *(Hank)*, Moroni Olsen *(Captain Raines)*, Norman Willis *(Briggs)*, Gene Morgan *(Blake)*, Robert Paige *(Thurston)*, Lee Prather *(Jamison)*, Eddie Fetherston *(Specks)*, Stanley Andrews *(Police Commissioner)*, John Tyrrell *(Employee in Poolroom)*, Charles Trowbridge *(Henly)*, George Lloyd *(Boat Captain)*, Ann Doran *(Nurse)*, Joseph De Stefani *(Miller)*, Beatrice Curtis *(Stewardess)*, Beatrice Blinn *(Woman)*, Dick Curtis *(Radio Broadcaster)*, Stanley Brown *(Police Photographer)*, George De Normand *(Trigger)*, Harry Bernard *(Joe)*, Nell Craig, Georgia Cooper *(Committeewomen)*, Kit Guard *(Mug)*, Gene Stone *(Man)*, Ky Robinson *(Casey)*, Dick Rush *(Cop)*, Lee Shumway *(Police Switchboard Operator)*, Wedgewood Nowell *(Committee Man)*, Lester Dorr *(Gangster)*.

Cabot's a pre-DIRTY HARRY-style cop who believes in force first, questions later. He's out to stop some gangsters who are preying on junk dealers. The citizens are outraged by Cabot's tactics and protect the ex-convicts he leans on for information. Cabot is demoted by superiors, but this doesn't mean a thing to him. He finally tracks down the crooks just before they are to ship a heap of scrap metal to help an unnamed foreign power's war effort. Cabot's performance is one-dimensional and the production values are not even average for the genre. A mean, nasty little film, a product of "One-Take" Irving Briskin's unit at Columbia, whose habits were such that an existing forensic-laboratory set must have been available within the studio. Hayworth is wasted as a laboratory technician; the romance *motif* is minimal, which gives her little to do.

p, Jack Frier; d, C. C. Coleman, Jr.; w, Earle Snell; ph, Benjamin Kline; ed, James Sweeney; md, Morris Stoloff; art d, Stephen Goosson.

Crime (PR:O MPAA:NR)

HOMICIDE FOR THREE** (1948) 60m REP bw

Audrey Long *(Iris Duluth)*, Warren Douglas *(Lt. Peter Duluth)*, Grant Withers *(Joe Hatch)*, Lloyd Corrigan *(Emmanual Cait)*, Stephanie Bachelor *(Mrs. Rose)*, George Lynn *(Bill Daggett)*, Tala Birell *(Rita Brown)*, Benny Baker *(Timothy)*, Joseph Crehan *(Capt. Webb)*, Sid Tomack *(Cab Driver)*, Dick Elliott *(Doorman)*, Eddie Dunn *(Circus Doorman)*, John Newland *(Desk Clerk)*, Billy Curtis *(Midget)*, Patsy Moran *(Maid)*.

Douglas and Long are newlyweds with a few problems. First, they only have 36 hours together as he's a Navy man on a weekend pass. Next, they need a place to stay. They are offered an apartment by a mysterious stranger on her way to an elopement. Now the problems really begin! It seems the apartment was formerly shared by three show girls who had sent some gangsters to jail. The gangsters are out now and seek revenge. Not much suspense, despite the seemingly gripping plot and title.

p, Stephen Auer; d, George Blair; w, Bradbury Foote, Albert DeMond (based on the novel by Patrick Quentin); ph, John MacBurnie; ed, Harry Keller, Earl Crain, Sr.; md, Morton Scott; art d, Frank Hotaling.

Thriller **(PR:C MPAA:NR)**

HOMICIDE SQUAD** (1931) 63m UNIV bw

Leo Carrillo *(Louie)*, Noah Beery, Sr. *(Capt. Buckley)*, Mary Brian *(Millie)*, Russell Gleason *(Joe Riley)*, George Brent *(Jimmy)*, Walter C. Percival *(Proctor)*, J. Carroll Naish *(Hugo)*, Pat O'Malley *(Man)*.

Carrillo is a gangster looking for his long-lost-son, Gleason. Beery is a police captain on a different kind of quest for his son: his son has been murdered by gangsters and he wants revenge. Gleason is also a gangster. To avoid the murder rap, he helps the cops frame his father. Brian is Gleason's love interest, though this is not really developed. Not a bad movie, but not very original. The film is dedicated to the police forces of America. The opening shows a still of New York City's Police Commissioner Murooney, titled with excerpts of an anti-crime speech he made at Madison Square Garden.

p, Samuel Bischoff; d, George Melford, Edward L. Kahn; w, John Thomas Neville, Tom Reed, Charles Logue (based on the story "The Bob" by Henry La Cossitt); ph, George Robinson; ed, Maurice Pivar, Harry Lieb.

Crime **(PR:A MPAA:NR)**

HONDO*** (1953) 84m WB c

John Wayne *(Hondo Lane)*, Geraldine Page *(Angie)*, Ward Bond *(Buffalo)*, Michael Pate *(Vittoro)*, James Arness *(Lennie)*, Rodolfo Acosta *(Silva)*, Leo Gordon *(Ed Lowe)*, Tom Irish *(Lt. McKay)*, Lee Aaker *(Johnny)*, Paul Fix *(Major Sherry)*, Rayford Barnes *(Pete)*.

While riding on dispatch for the cavalry, Wayne arrives at an isolated ranch run by Page and her young son Aaker. Wayne learns that Page's husband abandoned her during Apache raids. Despite the dangers of remaining on the ranch, she refuses Wayne's offer to take her away. Soon after there is another Apache raid and Aaker fends off the attackers by wounding second-in-command Acosta. His valor impresses Indian chief Pate, who declares the boy a blood brother and vows not to attack again. Meanwhile, Wayne has returned to his fort, and he meets Gordon, Page's husband. They scuffle, and Wayne decides to bring Page and Aaker to safety. En route, he is ambushed by Gordon and a partner. Wayne kills Gordon and, upon examining the dead man's pocket and finding a picture of Aaker, learns who Gordon was. He is soon captured and tortured by a band of Apaches under Pate's command. Pate is impressed by Wayne's pain threshold and decides to release him, but Acosta objects. A knife fight is held between Wayne and Acosta, with Wayne winning, though sparing Acosta's life. Wayne reaches the ranch and tells Page the entire story. Though saddened by her husband's death, she cannot deny her love for Wayne. Woman and boy accompany Wayne to his land in California and they are again attacked by Acosta, who is now chief as Pate has died. Wayne kills Acosta during a clash and the rest of the Apaches flee. Wayne, Page, and Aaker continue on their way to California as the film ends. The film is partly inspired by SHANE, accentuating the close relationship of hero-worshipping youngster to virtuous gunfighter, and its exterior shooting has the look of a John Ford work, but HONDO stands tall on its own. The Indians are given credible three-dimensional treatment, at least by Hollywood standards.

p, John Wayne, Robert Fellows; d, John Farrow; w, James Edward Grant (based on the story "The Gift of Cochise" by Louis L'Amour); ph, Robert Burke, Archie Stout (Warner Color, 3-D); m, Emil Newman and Hugo Friedhofer; ed, Ralph Dawson; art d, Al Ybarra.

Western **(PR:C MPAA:NR)**

HONEY½** (1930) 73m PAR bw

Nancy Carroll *(Olivia Dangerfield)*, Stanley Smith *(Burton Crane)*, Skeets Gallagher *(Charles Dangerfield)*, Lillian Roth *(Cora Falkner)*, Harry Green *(J. William Burnstein)*, Mitzi Green *(Doris)*, ZaSu Pitts *(Mayme)*, Jobyna Howland *(Mrs. Falkner)*, Charles Sellon *(Randolph Weeks)*.

Carroll and Gallagher, a brother and sister down on their luck, are forced to rent the family mansion to Pitts, a wealthy New York woman with a bratty kid, played by Mitzi Green. Comic turns result along with a few musical numbers. It's quite funny in parts but technically inferior. Gallagher was half of the famous vaudeville team of Gallagher and Al Shean. An early screenplay by future director Mankiewicz. Songs: "Sing You Sinners," "Let's Be Domestic," "In My Little Hope Chest," "I Don't Need Atmosphere (to Fall In Love With You)," "What is This Power I Have?" (Sam Coslow, W. Franke Harling).

d, Wesley Ruggles; w, Herman J. Mankiewicz (based on the musical "Come Out of the Kitchen" by Alice Duer Miller and A.E. Thomas); ph, Henry Gerrard; ch, David Bennett.

Musical/Comedy **(PR:A MPAA:NR)**

HONEY POT, THE** (1967, Brit.) 150m UA c (AKA: IT COMES UP MURDER; ANYONE FOR VENICE?; MR. FOX OF VENICE)

Rex Harrison *(Cecil Fox)*, Susan Hayward *(Mrs. Lone-Star Crockett Sheridan)*, Cliff Robertson *(William McFly)*, Capucine *(Princess Dominique)*, Edie Adams *(Merle McGill)*, Maggie Smith *(Sarah Watkins)*, Adolfo Celi *(Inspector Rizzi)*, Herschel Bernardi *(Oscar Ludwig)*, Cy Grant, Frank Latimore *(Revenue Agents)*, Luigi Scavran *(Massimo)*, Mimmo Poli *(Cook)*, Antonio Corevi *(Tailor)*, Carlos Valles *(Assistant Tailor)*, Hugh Nanning *(Volpone)*, David Dodimead *(Mosca)*.

Harrison is an apparent millionaire living in the lap of luxury. After seeing a performance of the famed play "Volpone," he is inspired to seek out three former mistresses and trick them. He hires actor Robertson to be a secretary/servant and invites the three to his home, under the false pretense that he—Harrison—is dying. First comes Adams, a fading-star sex-symbol who had gotten an early boost to her career through Harrison. Next is the dashing princess, Capucine, and finally Texas millionairess Hayward, a hypochondriac who travels with nurse Smith. The latter claims to be entitled to the "dying" man's riches, but that night she is found dead from an overdose of sleeping pills. Nurse Smith suspects Robertson, and the flunky locks her up. But she escapes via a dumbwaiter and discovers Harrison, who is a frustrated ballet dancer, dancing about in his room to Ponchielli's "Dance of the Hours." His scheme is discovered, for he is deeply in debt and killed Hayward for her money. Unable to face a murder charge, Harrison commits suicide by leaping into a Venice canal. Smith and Robertson end up inheriting Hayward's fortune. This was Mankiewicz's first film after a long period of silence, and the results are mixed. At times the plot is too complicated and becomes confusing. There is far too much talk and not enough action, with a two-and-a-half-hour running time. Trimming the film down certainly would have been to advantage. Updating the Volpone story is a clever idea, but just doesn't quite work. No fault lies with the actors, however. Performances are excellent and the cast handles the bizarre plot twists with ease, making it all quite believable. Harrison is clearly enjoying his role. The color photography is lush and opulent.

p, Charles K. Feldman, Joseph L. Mankiewicz; d&w, Mankiewicz (based on the play "Mr. Fox of Venice," adapted from the novel *The Evil of the Day* by Thomas Sterling, which was based on the play "Volpone" by Ben Jonson); ph, Gianni Di Venanzo (Technicolor); m, John Addison; ed, David Bretherton; prod d, John De Cuir; art d, Boris Juraga; cos, Rolf Gerard; ch, Lee Theodore.

Comedy **(PR:A MPAA:NR)**

HONEYBABY, HONEYBABY* (1974) 89m Kelly-Jordan c

Diana Sands *(Laura Lewis)*, Calvin Lockhart *(Liv)*, Seth Allen *(Sam)*, J. Eric Bell *(Skiggy Lewis)*, Brian Phelan *(Harry)*, Bricktop *(Harry's Mother)*, Thomas Baptiste *(General Christian Awani)*, Gay Suilin *(Mme. Chan)*, Nabih Aboul Hoson *(Herb)*, Mr. Sunshine *(Real Makuba)*.

Filmed in Beirut. Sands is an American interpreter who has won a Mideast vacation, but her prize turns into far more than she expected when comic complications develop. Lockhart is an adventurer-for-hire, transporting the body of a deposed African leader. The plot twists are confusing and often inexplicable, leading to a tedious 89 minutes. Watch for American singer Bricktop in a small role.

p, Jack Jordan; d, Michael Schultz; w, Brian Phelan (based on a story by Leonard Kantor); ph, Andreas Bellis; m, Michael Tschudin; ed, Hortense Beveridge; cos, Yvonne Stoney.

Comedy **(PR:C MPAA:PG)**

HONEYCHILE** (1951) 89m REP c

Judy Canova *(Judy)*, Eddie Foy, Jr. *(Eddie Price)*, Alan Hale, Jr. *(Joe Boyd)*, Walter Catlett *(Al Moore)*, Claire Carleton *(Betty Loring)*, Karolyn Grimes *(Effie)*, Brad Morrow *(Larry)*, Roy Barcroft *(Walter Judson)*, Leonid Kinskey *(Chick Lester)*, Gus Schilling *(Window Washer)*, Irving Bacon *(Abner)*, Fuzzy Knight *(Ice Cream Vendor)*, Roscoe Ates *(Bob)*, Ida Moore *(Harriet)*, Sarah Edwards *(Sarah)*, Emory Parnell *(Mayor)*, Dick Elliott *(Sheriff)*, Dick Wessel *(Bartender)*, William Fawcett *(Ben Todd)*, Robin Winans *(Boy)*, Stanley Blystone *(Mr. Olson)*, Donia Bussey *(Mrs. Olson)*, John Crawford *(Martin McKay)*, Cecile Elliott, Cecil Weston *(Women)*.

Canova's a hillbilly songwriter with a great little number, "Honeychile." Foy, Jr. and Catlett are a pair of publishers who desperately want the rights to the song, but Canova won't sell. Hale, Jr. (later to achieve everlasting renown as the Skipper on TV's "Gilligan's Island") is her jealous boy friend. He gets in trouble after some crooks fix a chuckwagon race. In order to free her love, Canova decides to sell her song. For what this film is, it's not too bad. It's certainly Canova's show all the way. She gets to sing a number of ditties including the title piece and an operatic version of the famous "Ragmop" by Johnny Lee Wills and Deacon Anderson, arranged by Jack Elliott. This was her return to corn comedy after a number of years away from the genre (the first of six films in Republic's second Canova series) and she's just fine. It's also her first appearance in color. The production values are smooth and the film has a certain charm to it. Other songs include "Honeychile," Jack Elliott, Harold Spina; "Tutti Frutti," Elliott, Ann Canova; "More Than I Care To Remember," Ted Johnson, Matt Terry.

p, Sidney Picker; d, R.G. Springsteen; w, Jack Townley, Charles E. Roberts, Barry Trivers; ph, Jack Marta (TruColor); m, Victor Young; ed, Richard L. Van Enger; art d, Frank Hotaling; spec eff, Howard Lydecker, Theodore Lydecker.

Comedy/Musical **(PR:A MPAA:NR)**

HONEYMOON½** (1947) 74m RKO bw (GB: TWO MEN AND A GIRL)

Shirley Temple *(Barbara Olmstead)*, Franchot Tone *(David Flanner)*, Guy Madison *(Phil Vaughn)*, Lina Romay *(Raquel Mendoza)*, Gene Lockhart *(Prescott)*, Corinna Mura *(Senora Mendoza)*, Grant Mitchell *(Crenshaw)*, Julio Villareale *(Sr. Mendoza)*, Manuel Arvide *(Registrar)*, Jose R. Goula *(Dr. Diego)*, Carol Forman *(Nurse)*, Charles Trowbridge *(Judge Riberol)*, John Parrish *(Gilhooley)*, Forbes Murray *(American Ambassador)*, Franklin Farnum *(American Diplomat)*, Rodolpho Hoyos, Sr. *(Storekeeper)*, Mario Santos *(Singer)*.

Temple in one of her post-cutie-pie, pre-ambassador films. She's a young woman out to elope with soldier Madison. She follows him south of the border but finds out that he is stuck in Panama's Canal Zone when she is in Mexico City. She tries to get help from the American Consulate. There she meets consul Tone and immediately forgets about what's-his-name. But Tone is already engaged and complications, which of course get solved by the film's end, are the result. Temple gets a chance to sing a few numbers, including "I Love Geraniums" and "Ven Aqui," but they're no "Good Ship Lollipop." Tone is completely miscast and clearly uncomfortable in his slapsticky role. There's a lot of nice Mexican scenery and a couple of decent production numbers, but overall it's a boring formula piece. The story is dragged out, and it isn't all that difficult to figure out what's going to happen along the way. Direction can't make up its mind whether to be comic or romantic. Temple just couldn't repeat the successes she had as a child. The film cost a lot to produce, and it lost a lot at the box office.

p, Warren Duff; d, William Keighley; w, Michael Kanin (based on a story by Vickie Baum); ph, Edward Cronjager; m, Leigh Harline; ed, Ralph Dawson; md, C. Bakaleinikoff; art d, Albert D'Agostino, Ralph Berger; m/l, Leigh Harline, Mort Greene.

Musical Comedy **(PR:A MPAA:NR)**

HONEYMOON ADVENTURE, A
(SEE: FOOTSTEPS IN THE NIGHT, 1932, Brit.)

HONEYMOON AHEAD½** (1945) 60m UNIV bw

Allan Jones *(Orpheus)*, Grace McDonald *(Evelyn)*, Raymond Walburn *(Rollie Mack)*, Vivian Austin *(Rosita)*, Jack Overman *(Knuckles)*, Murray Alper *(Spike)*, Eddie Acuff *(Connors)*, John Abbott *(Welles)*, William Haade *(Trigger)*, Arthur Loft *(Sheriff Weeks)*, Ralph Peters *(George)*, Charles Miller *(Ephraim)*, Sarah Padden *(Mrs. Halett)*, Jack Clifford *(Gus)*, Lee Phelps *(Browning)*, William Newell *(Joe)*, George Eldredge *(Caldwell)*, John Berkes *(Lug)*, Charles Williams *(Dinky)*, Charles Sullivan *(Control Man)*, Harry Semels *(2nd Convict)*, Bobby Barbier *(1st Convict)*, Gary Owen *(Announcer)*, Billy Nelson *(Fingers Morelli)*, Pierre Watkin *(Warden Lawlor)*, Earle Dewey *(Blodgett)*, Davison Clark *(Capt. Lynn)*, Jimmy Conlin *(Grant)*, Al Ferguson *(Guard)*, Joseph Bernard *(Man)*, Jack George *(Orchestra Leader)*, Dee Greene *(Girl with Umbrella)*, Spec O'Donnell *(Boy with Umbrella)*.

Jones is a singing convict released on parole, but his comrades in the prison chorus need his voice so they concoct a plot to involve him in a bank robbery. Trying to keep him on the straight and narrow is McDonald. Enjoyable second feature musical. Songs include: "Time Will Tell," "Now And Always," "Round The Bend," "How Lovely" (Everett Carter, Milton Rosen).

p, Will Cowan; d, Reginald Le Borg; w, Val Burton, Elwood Ullman (based on the story "Romance, Incorporated" by Burton); ph, Paul Ivano; md, Ray Sinatra; art d, John B. Goodman, Abraham Grossman.

Musical/Comedy **(PR:A MPAA:NR)**

HONEYMOON DEFERRED*½ (1940) 59m UNIV bw

Edmund Lowe *(Adam Farradene)*, Margaret Lindsay *(Janet Payne)*, Elisabeth Risdon *(Sarah Frome)*, Joyce Compton *(Kitty Kerry)*, Chick Chandler *("Hap" Maguire)*, Anne Gwynne *(Cecile Blades)*, Jerry Marlowe *(Jimmy Blades)*, Cliff Clark *(Mathews)*, Julie Stevens *(Eve Blades)*, Emmett Vogan, Jimmy Conlin, Joe Sawyer.

Lowe is an insurance investigator about to go on his honeymoon with Lindsay. He's had it with the business and wants a more sedate life. But, as luck would have it, his former employer is murdered. He and his bride forget about their cruise to Bermuda and go after the killer. This is a cheap, ineffective version of THE THIN MAN, though Lowe and Lindsay are good as the leads. The script, however, leaves much to be desired. The killer is revealed early on, so there's really no mystery to speak of. The ending is more confusing than anything. Risdon is good as a villainous auntie. The direction is lackluster and fails to cover the gaping holes in the plot.

p, Ken Goldsmith; d, Lew Landers; w, Roy Chanslor, Elliot Gibbons (based on a story by Chanslor); ph, Elwood Bredell.

Comedy/Mystery **(PR:A MPAA:NR)**

HONEYMOON DEFERRED** (1951, Brit.) 79m Vic Films/BL bw

Sally Ann Howes *(Katherine)*, Griffith Jones *(David)*, Kieron Moore *(Rocco)*, Lea Padovani *(Rosina)*, Anna Dondini *(Mama Pia)*, Moneta *(Grandpa Maggini)*, David Keir *(Professor)*, "Little" Freddie Meloni *(Churchill)*, L. Rivanera, Helen Goss, W.E. Holloway.

A few years after the war, newlyweds Jones and Howes go to Italy for their honeymoon. They visit the small Italian village Jones claims to have "single-handedly" liberated, but find the population to be less than grateful. After a few menacing events, Jones is able to clear his name with the townspeople and continue the honeymoon. The comedy is typical English humor transplanted into an Italian setting. The result isn't very funny, though the production is paced well.

p, John Sutro, Joseph Janni; d, Mario Camerini; w, John Hunter, Franco Brusati, C. Denis Freeman (based on a story by Suso d'Amici, A. Pietrangelli); ph, Geoffrey Faithfull.

Comedy **(PR:A MPAA:NR)**

HONEYMOON FOR THREE½** (1935, Brit.) 81m Gaiety Films/ABF bw

Stanley Lupino *(Jack Denver)*, Aileen Marson *(Yvonne Daumery)*, Jack Melford *(Raymond Dirk)*, Robert English *(Herbert Denver)*, Dennis Hoey *(M. Daumery)*, Arty Ash *(Herbert Jones)*, Roddy Hughes *(Toomes)*, Syd Crossley *(Police Constable Smithers)*, Doris Rogers *(Mme. Daumery)*, Barry Clifton *(Crooner)*, Percival Mackey and his Band.

Lupino (who also served as the film's producer and provided its story) is a devil-may-care playboy who compromises young French lass Marson. Though flat broke, he's forced to marry Marson by her irate banker father. The pair board a ship bound for America, accompanied by Marson's former fiance. The idea is for the newlyweds to obtain a quickie divorce, but along the way plans change when Lupino realizes he does indeed love Marson. Some cute moments in this nice little musical comedy.

p, Stanley Lupino; d, Leo Mittler; w, Frank Miller (based on a story by Lupino); ph, George Dudgeon Stretton.

Comedy/Musical **(PR:A MPAA:NR)**

HONEYMOON FOR THREE*½ (1941) 63m WB bw

Ann Sheridan *(Anne Rogers)*, George Brent *(Kenneth Bixby)*, Charles Ruggles *(Harvey Wilson)*, Osa Massen *(Julie Wilson)*, Jane Wyman *(Elizabeth Clochessy)*, William T. Orr *(Arthur Westlake)*, Lee Patrick *(Mrs. Pettijohn)*, Walter Catlett *(Waiter)*, Herbert Anderson *(Floyd T. Ingram)*, Johnny Downs *(Chester T. Farrington III)*.

Brent's a popular talker, both on the literary circuit and with the ladies. He comes to a Cleveland college and meets his old flame Massen (in her second film). She's now the overbearing wife of Ruggles. Sheridan billed as "the oomph girl," is Brent's secretary-fiancee who saves Brent from making a complete fool of himself. There are a good many problems with this film, the foremost being Brent. He's woefully miscast, with no sense of comedy at all. The script is too farcical to work, and the director seems to have quit trying before he began. A restaurant scene, where Brent tries to handle two dates at the same time, is mildly amusing, but that's about it. Surprisingly, the Epstein writing team scored a major success with their next film: CASABLANCA. You'd never know it came from the same hands after viewing this mess.

p, Henry Blanke; d, Lloyd Bacon; w, Earl Baldwin, Julius J. and Philip G. Epstein (based on the play "Goodbye Again" by Alan Scott and George Haight); ph, Ernest Haller; ed, Rudi Fehr.

Comedy **(PR:A MPAA:NR)**

HONEYMOON HOTEL** (1946, Brit.) 90m Mancunian/But bw (AKA: UNDER NEW MANAGEMENT)

Nat Jackley *(Nat)*, Norman Evans *(Joe Evans)*, Dan Young *(Dan)*, Betty Jumel *(Betty)*, Nicolette Roeg *(Brenda Evans)*, Tony Dalton *(Tony)*, Marianne Lincoln *(Marianne)*, Bunty Meadows *(Bunty)*, Aubrey Mallalieu *(John Marshall)*, G. H. Mulcaster *(William Barclay)*, John Rorke *(Father Flannery)*, Hay Petrie *(Groom)*, Cavan O'Connor, Lynda Ross, Donovan Octette, Mendel's Female Sextette, Percival Mackey, Babs Valerie, Michael Taylor, Lily Lapidus, Gordon McLeod, Joss Ambler, David Keir, Marcel Vallee, Andre Genin, Jacques Varennes, John Allan.

A chimneysweep inherits an old hotel. Things change pretty quickly around the place when he decides to put in his old army buddies as the new hotel staff. Two sharpers attempt to purchase the hotel and grounds for a few pence upon learning that an airport is to be constructed nearby, but the once-sooty sweep, Evans, with the aid of his pals, retains possession. Like some of the guests, this lengthy musical outstays its leave. The reissue of 1948 was trimmed somewhat, to the film's advantage.

p&d, John E. Blakeley; w, Roney Parsons, Anthony Toner; ph, Geoffrey Faithfull.

Comedy/Musical **(PR:A MPAA:NR)**

HONEYMOON HOTEL*½ (1964) 89m MGM c

Robert Goulet *(Ross Kingsley)*, Nancy Kwan *(Lynn Hope)*, Robert Morse *(Jay [Jason] Menlow)*, Jill St. John *(Sherry)*, Keenan Wynn *(Mr. Sampson)*, Anne Helm *(Cynthia)*, Elsa Lanchester *(Chambermaid)*, Bernard Fox *(Room Clerk)*, Elvia Allman *(Mrs. Sampson)*, Sandra Gould *(Mabel)*, David Lewis *(Mr. Hampton)*, Chris Noel *(Nancy Penrose)*, Dale Malone *(Fatso)*, Pauline Myers *(Hogan)*.

One of the American sex farces of the 1960s patterned after a continuing stream of such light trifles from France, this film featured two relative cinema unknowns, Goulet and Morse, who had made significant splashes on the Broadway stage. While Morse had appeared in a few features at this juncture, singer Goulet's only cinematic credential was a voice-over in a cartoon feature, GAY PURR—EE (1962), as a singing tomcat. The silly plot of HONEYMOON HOTEL has Morse, jilted at the alter by Helm, electing to cash in on his tropical-island honeymoon arrangements anyway, substituting his erstwhile best man, Goulet, for his putative bride in the for-honeymooning-couples-only hotel suite. Goulet, supposedly a surrogate for his boss, Wynn, at a business convention, has stolen the time for this vacation. He quickly becomes involved with Kwan, the resort's social director, thereby allaying some of the fears of the hotel's management. Having the time of his life, Goulet exerts every effort to prevent a telephone reconciliation between Morse and the repentant Helm, a call which would surely cut short his pleasurable stay on the island. The gravy of the plot thickens when Wynn arrives in the company of empty-headed floozy St. John, to be shortly joined by his pursuing wife, Allman, followed by the second-thinking Helm. The reciprocal self-protective blackmail that follows results in both Kwan and Helm believing their respective males to be involved with the sanguine St. John. All comes right at the conclusion, with Goulet and Kwan uniting and Morse achieving parity by jilting the horrible Helm in his turn and joining St. John in her stead. Songs, sung by Goulet, include "I've Been Had," "Honeymoon Hotel," "Love Is Oh So Easy," "You're It," by Sammy Kahn and James Van Heusen.

p, Pandro S. Berman; d, Henry Levin; w, R.S. Allen, Harvey Bullock; ph, Harold Lipstein (Panavision, Metrocolor); m, Walter Scharf; ed, Rita Roland; md, Scharf; art d, George W. Davis, Paul Groesse; set d, Henry Grace, George R. Nelson; cos, Bill Thomas; ch, Miriam Nelson; makeup, William Tuttle.

Comedy **(PR:C MPAA:NR)**

HONEYMOON IN BALI½** (1939) 95m PAR bw (AKA: MY LOVE FOR YOURS)

Fred MacMurray *(Bill Burnett)*, Madeleine Carroll *(Gail Allen)*, Allan Jones *(Eric Sinclair)*, Akim Tamiroff *(The Window Washer)*, Helen Broderick *(Miss Lorna Smith)*, Osa Massen *(Noel Van Ness)*, Carolyn Lee *(Rosie)*, Astrid Allwyn *(Fortune Teller)*, Georgia Caine *(Miss Stone)*, John Qualen *(Man)*, Fritzi Brunette *(Secretary)*, William B. Davidson *(Store Detective)*, Bennie Bartlett *(Messenger Boy)*, Wally

Maher *(Elevator Man)*, Monty Woolley *(Publisher)*, Thomas Louden *(Butler)*, Renie Riano *(Head Saleswoman)*, Connie Leon *(Native Housekeeper)*, Edward Van Sloan *(Priest)*, John Bagni *(Salesman)*, Jack Raymond *(Cab Driver)*, Gus Kerner, Hooper Atchley *(Headwaiters)*, Jack Maclennan *(Waiter)*, Jacqueline Dalya *(Hat Check Girl)*, Ethel May Halls *(Maid)*, Johnny Morris *(Office Boy)*, Luana Walters *(Girl Having Her Fortune Told)*, Janet Waldo *(Her Companion)*.

Carroll is a businesswoman determined not to have a man interfere with her career. Enter MacMurray—determined, with a will as strong as Carroll's, to penetrate her icy exterior. They make the rounds together, but she gets cold feet and runs off to Nassau. He returns to his home in Bali, presumably to marry his boss' daughter. Carroll arrives in Bali, but discovers MacMurray's plans and heads back to New York. But MacMurray is stuck on Carroll, and follows her back to the Big Apple. Naturally, they are married at the film's end. It's a cute little comedy, though the title has nothing to do with the film. The direction merrily takes the story on its frenzied pace without getting the least bit ahead or behind. Jones sings an operatic piece. He is Carroll's other man, a star at the Met. Tamiroff is the funniest thing going as a simple window washer giving Carroll advice about clothing, men, and life. This film was Massen's American cinematic debut, after doing two features in Denmark. She appeared to specialize in honeymooning; her second American feature was HONEYMOON FOR THREE. The working title of HONEYMOON IN BALI was the rather more descriptive ARE HUSBANDS NECESSARY? but Paramount executives decided that the working press would have too much fun with the latter, since Carroll was in the midst of a messy divorce at the time of release, so they changed the name. Times also change; at a later date, any studio public relations man worth his salt would have given his left eyetooth to be able to exploit the innuendo inherent in the original title.

p, Jeff Lazarus; d, Edward H. Griffith; w, Virginia Van Upp (based on stories by Grace Sartwell Mason and Katharine Brush); ph, Ted Tetzlaff; ed, Eda Warren.

Comedy **Cas.** **(PR:A MPAA:NR)**

HONEYMOON KILLERS, THE*** (1969) 115m Roxanne/Cinerama bw (AKA: THE LONELY HEARTS KILLERS)

Shirley Stoler *(Martha Beck)*, Tony LoBianco *(Ray Fernandez)*, Mary Jane Higby *(Janet Fay)*, Doris Roberts *(Bunny)*, Kip McArdle *(Delphine Downing)*, Marilyn Chris *(Myrtle Young)*, Dortha Duckworth *(Mrs. Beck)*, Barbara Cason *(Evelyn Long)*, Ann Harris *(Doris)*, Mary Breen *(Rainelle Downing)*, Elsa Raven *(Matron)*, Mary Engel *(Lucy)*, Guy Sorel *(Mr. Dranoff)*, Mike Haley *(Jackson)*, Diane Asselin *(Severns)*, Col. William Adams *(Justice of the Peace)*.

Unusual B movie that doesn't approach the "underground classic" its makers hoped for, but an interesting effort nonetheless. Stoler is a lonely, sexually frustrated 200-pound nurse at a Mobile, Alabama, hospital. She lives alone with her senile mother, which only adds to her frustration. In desperation she joins a lonely-hearts correspondence club and soon begins receiving torrid love letters from LoBianco, a Spanish immigrant in New York. He finally comes to visit Stoler, only to take her money and run. Heartbroken, she rigs a plan to visit him and discovers he is a gigolo who uses the lonely hearts club to find his victims. But rather than lose the only man who has shown her attention, she volunteers to be his partner in crime, posing as his "sister." After her supervisor reads LoBianco's letters, Stoler is fired. She explains that they are secretly married, and then puts her mother in a nursing home. The story takes its next odd twist as LoBianco and Stoler pursue victims. At first he woos the women, and then escapes with the ill-gotten money, but when LoBianco marries Chris to give her baby a father, a jealous Stoler turns to murder. LoBianco then has an affair with another member of the lonely hearts club and Stoler, heartbroken, tries to drown herself. LoBianco saves her and swears to be true. They buy a house together and then meet Higby. At first the sixty-year-old matron is charmed by the younger man's affections, but gradually she becomes suspicious. When she threatens to tell her children of her doubts, Stoler bludgeons her with a hammer, and LoBianco finishes the job by strangulation. They make love, then bury the corpse in the basement. They flee once more, this time to Grand Rapids, Michigan. There they meet McArdle. After she falls for LoBianco, the jealous Stoler feeds her some sleeping pills. LoBianco returns home and is forced to shoot the dazed McArdle. This time it is Stoler who completes the murder, drowning the victim's child, Breen, in a washing machine. Realizing that her love will never be true to her, Stoler goes to the police and confesses all. The two are arrested and the film ends with them both in jail, once more sending letters back and forth. Based on an actual case that got much press in the late forties, THE HONEYMOON KILLERS is a mixed bag of a film. Kastle was an opera composer who co-wrote the film with his friend Steibel. After the original director was fired, Kastle took over the helm. It was his first time behind the camera, and isn't too bad for a debut. The black-and-white photography is stark, shot in documentary style. A fine sense of claustrophobia is achieved by placing characters in closed-in spaces, both physically and psychologically. The music of Mahler is used well to counterpoint the action within scenes, often at loud volume with marvelous trivializing effects. The acting is second to none: the two leads are frighteningly good in their psychotic roles. Supporting characters are also excellent. These are real people with real personal quirks. On the other hand, there's too much shadow in the frame along with some highly visible microphones. Even worse is the choppy editing job, which jumbles the story at times. Still, the straightforwardness of the telling is not totally destroyed, and there's a certain sense of honor on behalf of the filmmakers in not romanticizing the brutality of the crime and criminals. The film seemed destined for the scrap heap until a fairly good *Variety* review. After that, critic after critic heaped praise on THE HONEYMOON KILLERS. Truffaut called it his favorite American film. This may have been a result of some camerawork (long takes, stationary camera, documentary-style shooting) that recalls Truffaut's early work. Surprisingly, *New Yorker* critic Pauline Kael thought it was terrible. She was usually at the forefront of praise for the low-budget artistic shocker. The original working title was DEAR MARTHA, taken from LoBianco's letters to Stoler. Despite its problems, this is one definitely worth taking a look at. LoBianco went on to star in other pictures; Stoler's other major role was as the amazing, brutal Nazi prison camp commandant in Lina Wertmuller's marvelous SEVEN BEAUTIES.

p, Warren Steibel; d&w, Leonard Kastle; ph, Oliver Wood; m, Gustav Mahler; ed, Stan Warnow, Richard Brophy.

Crime/Drama **Cas.** **(PR:O MPAA:R)**

HONEYMOON LANE* (1931) 71m A.V. & D.-Sono-Art/PAR bw

Eddie Dowling *(Tim Dugan)*, June Collyer *(Mary Baggott)*, Raymond Hatton *("Dynamite")*, Ray Dooley *(Gerty Murphy)*, Noah Beery *(Tom Baggott)*, Mary Carr *(Mother Murphy)*, Armand Kaliz *(King of Bulgravia)*, Adolph Milar *(Paulino, His Major Domo)*, Gene Lewis *(Col. Gustave, the King's Aide)*, Lloyd Whitlock *(Arnold Bookstein)*, George Kotsonaros *("Noisy")*, Corliss Palmer *(Betty Royce)*, Ethel Wales *(Mrs. Gotrocks)*.

Stage star Dowling—whose real-life wife and stage partner Dooley is also in the film in a small, strange, apparently created-for-her role—wrote this unfortunate film by taking all the music out of the musical stage play in which he had starred some years previously, and by jazzing up the script with the then-popular gangster theme. Dowling is the simple-minded but helpful runt who assists Carr in the problems she has with her health-resort hotel when it is simultaneously invaded by big-city gambler Whitlock (in a thinly veiled parody of contemporary mobster Arnold Rothstein) and by a Balkan king who wants to be considered just one of the boys. Complications ensue as Dowling attempts to rescue Beery, the father of his intended, Collyer, from the results of his proclivity for gambling. His Majesty, Kaliz, and the heavies are all reformed by the magic of Mother Murphy's (Carr's) marvelous, health-giving cherry pies. Reviewers of the time attested that writer Dowling should have stuck to acting.

d, William James Craft; w, Barney Sarecky, Jack Jevne (based on the musical play by Eddie Dowling and on Dowling's adaptation); ph, Gilbert Warrenton; ed, Doris Drought.

Comedy **(PR:A MPAA:NR)**

HONEYMOON LIMITED* (1936) 73m MON bw

Neil Hamilton *(Dick)*, Irene Hervey *(Judy)*, Lloyd Hughes *(Henry)*, Russell Hicks *(Slug)*, Lorin Raker *(Babe)*, Joy Filmer *(Jack)*, June Filmer *(Jill)*, George Hayes *(Pinkham)*, Henry Kolker.

Hamilton is a down-on-his-luck writer. In order to raise some money, he undertakes a six month New York-to-San Francisco stroll, during which he writes about the experience. A friend bets that Hamilton won't make it, so there's added incentive. During a storm, the plucky adventurer takes refuge in a cabin where he meets runaway Hervey and her two younger sisters, the Filmers. Along comes the cabin's owner, as well as some gangsters after some stolen money. Realizing that the things going on around him are what good stories are made of, Hamilton immediately starts to pen it all down. An overlong piece that suffers from too literary a script. Hamilton seems bored throughout. He went on to fame as Commissioner Gordon on the sixties TV hit "Batman."

p, Mrs. Wallace Reid; d, Arthur Lubin; w, Dorothy Reid, Betty Burbridge (based on a story by Vida Hurst); ph, Milton Krasner; ed, Carl Pierson.

Drama **(PR:A MPAA:NR)**

HONEYMOON LODGE** (1943) 63m UNIV bw

David Bruce *(Bob Sterling)*, Harriet Hilliard *(Lorraine Logan)*, June Vincent *(Carol Sterling)*, Rod Cameron *(Big Boy)*, Franklin Pangborn *(Cathcart)*, Andrew Tombes *(Judge Wilkins)*, Martin Ashe *(George Thomas)*, Joseph Crehan *(Judge)*, Selmer Jackson *(Carol's Lawyer)*, Margaret Seddon *(Elderly Woman)*, Robert Dudley *(Elderly Man)*, Fay Helm *(Mrs. Thomas)*, Mary Eleanor Donahue *(Mary Thomas)*, Clarence Muse *(Porter)*, David Street *(Man)*, Emmett Vogan *(Bob's Lawyer)*, Jack Rice *(Male Character)*, Billy Newell *(Bartender)*, Herbert Heywood *(Conductor)*, Charles Jordan *(Motor Cop)*, Charles Hall *(Workman)*, Alphonse Martell *(Headwaiter)*, John Frazer *(Young Man)*, Francis Sayles *(Bailiff)*, Jack Gardner *(Waiter)*, Hooper Atchley *(Theatrical Man)*, Eddy Polo *(Gas Station Attendant)*, Willie Thomas *(Blaney Lewis)*, Ozzie Nelson and His Orchestra, Veloz and Yolanda, Tip, Tap, and Toe, Bobby Brooks and His Quartet, Hattie Noel, Ray Eberle.

Bruce and Vincent are an unhappy couple trying to give their marriage one more try. They head off to the mountain resort where their love first began. But whom should they meet but their respective old flames, Cameron and Hilliard. Jealousies and confusions result until all is resolved in the end. The simple plot is padded out with musical numbers by Nelson and Orchestra, vocally accompanied by Hilliard. Tip, Tap, and Toe do exactly what their names imply. It's an amusing little film, though nothing special. In real life, Nelson and Hilliard were husband and wife. They went on to become an American popular myth as one of the great 1950s TV couples. Songs include "Do I Worry" (Bobby Worth, Stanley Cowan, sung by high tenor Brooks); "I'm Through With Love" (Gus Kahn, Matt Malneck, Fud Livingston); "Why Don't You Fall In Love With Me?" (Al Lewis, Mabel Wayne); "I Never Knew" (Tom Pitts, Ray Egan, Roy K. Marsh); "Jersey Jive" (Minor Hassell, Ozzie Nelson).

p, Warren Wilson; d, Edward Lilley; w, Clyde Bruckman (based on the story "Second Honeymoon" by Wilson); ph, Paul Ivano; ed, Russell Schoengarth; art d, John Goodman.

Musical/Comedy **(PR:A MPAA:NR)**

HONEYMOON MACHINE, THE½** (1961) 88m MGM c

Steve McQueen *(Lt. Fergie Howard)*, Brigid Bazlen *(Julie Fitch)*, Jim Hutton *(Jason Eldridge)*, Paula Prentiss *(Pam Dunstan)*, Dean Jagger *(Adm. Fitch)*, Jack Weston *(Signalman Burford Taylor)*, Jack Mullaney *(Ens. Beau Gilliam)*, Marcel Hillaire *(Inspector of Casino Games)*, Ben Astar *(Russian Consul)*, William Lanteau *(Tommy Dane)*, Ken Lynch *(Capt. James Angle)*, Simon Scott *(Capt. Harvey Adam)*, Norman Grabowski *("Max's" Operator)*.

McQueen and Mullaney are two naval officers who team with civilian computer expert Hutton in Venice. The trio come up with a scam to use their on-ship computer (known as Max) to figure out the Lido casino roulette wheel. After analyzing the data on computer, they hope to break the bank. Jagger is the admiral who intercepts the heliographed ship-to-shore communications. He has no idea of the real scheme and interprets the signals to mean the ship is about to be attacked. Some craziness develops as he prepares for war, but all is righted in the end, with McQueen landing Jagger's progeny, Bazlen. Based on a fairly successful play, the film works well as light farce. The direction is quickly paced and gets the most laughs it can from the material. Hutton and Prentiss are romantic interests, repeating their on-screen romance from WHERE THE BOYS ARE (and they would do so once more in BACHELOR IN PARADISE). The sets are quite elaborate. The hotel suites are ornate and the computer room is movie technology at its best. A fun little movie, it capitalized on the public's lack of knowledge of computers, a relatively new subject in 1961.

p, Lawrence Weingarten; d, Richard Thorpe; w, George Wells (based on the play "The Golden Fleecing" by Lorenzo Semple, Jr.); ph, Joseph LaShelle (CinemaScope, Metrocolor); m, Leigh Harline; ed, Ben Lewis; art d, George W. Davis, Preston Ames; set d, Henry Grace, Jerry Wunderlich; cos, Helen Rose; spec eff, Robert R. Hoag, Lee LeBlank; makeup, William Tuttle; m/l, "Love is Crazy," Harline, Jack Brooks.

Comedy **(PR:A MPAA:NR)**

HONEYMOON MERRY-GO-ROUND½** (1939, Brit.) 63m London Screenplays-Fanfare/RKO bw (AKA: OLYMPIC HONEYMOON)

Claude Hulbert *(Bob Bennett)*, Monty Banks *(Orban)*, Princess Pearl *(Bunny)*, Sally Gray *(Miss America)*, Tully Comber *(Cosmo)*, Bob Bowman *(Announcer)*, Wembley Lions Ice Hockey Team.

Two newlyweds go to Switzerland for what they hope will be an idyllic honeymoon. However, the two get into a fight and the husband, Hulbert, marches off, only to be mistaken for an ice hockey champion for a visiting English team. The novice skater's pratfalls actually assist the Britons in winning an important victory, as well as assisting him in winning the renewed regard of his bride.

p, Sidney Morgan; d, Alfred Goulding; w, Goulding, Monty Banks, Warren Chetwynd Strode, Joan Morgan (based on the novel *He and Ski* by F. Dawson Gratrix); ph, Ernest Palmer.

Comedy **(PR:AA MPAA:NR)**

HONEYMOON OF HORROR* (1964) 82m Flamingo/Manson c (AKA: THE DEADLY CIRCLE; THE GOLDEN NYMPHS; ORGY OF THE GOLDEN NUDES

Robert Parsons *(Emile Duvre)*, Abbey Heller *(Lilli Duvre)*, Alexander Panas *(Max Duvre)*, Vincent Petti *(Hajmir Dallali)*, Beverly Layne *(Helene Russel)*, Dorothy Farol *(Myra Arnstadt)*, Monroe Myers *(Duane Albright)*, Michael De Beausset *(Socki Van Bridge)*, "Snuffy" Miller *(Toulouse)*, Christy Foushee *(Tutti-Frutti Johnson)*, Reuben Guberman *(Baron von Turko)*, Yanka Mann *(Waitress)*.

Heller plays the new bride of sculptor Parsons, who immediately upon moving into his mansion begins to receive threatening phone calls. Heller also notices a series of potentially life-threatening accidents occurring around her and it is eventually revealed that all of her husband's friends are out to kill her. Filmed entirely in Florida.

p, Herb Meyer; d, Irwin Meyer; w, Alexander Panas; ph, Clifford Poland (Eastmancolor); ed, Tele-Visual Aids Inc.; spec eff, Jack Johnson.

Mystery **(PR:O MPAA:NR)**

HONEYMOON OF TERROR zero (1961) 62m Sonney Amusement/ Associated Film Distributors of California bw (AKA: ECSTASY ON LOVERS ISLAND; ECSTASY OF LOVERS)

Doug Leith *(Frank)*, Dwan Marlow *(Marion)*, Anton Van Stralen *(Fiend)*, Dick Crane *(Garageman)*.

Marlow and Leith star as newlyweds who decide to spend their honeymoon on an island. One day Leith goes to town to gather supplies, leaving his bride to enjoy fun in the sun. Suddenly, a clubfooted maniac appears from nowhere and tries to rape Marlow, but the frisky newlywed is able to escape. In town, Leith hears the story of the "Ridge Runner," a clubfooted maniac who raped and killed women some years ago. Putting two-and-two together, Leith hustles back to the island just as the brute is brutalizing his wife. Leith manages to get himself knocked out in the ensuing struggle, which forces Marlow to stab the crazed clubfoot to death. Real pleasant. In the movies, clubfooted people seem to spend most of their time chasing nubile young women, who seem seldom able to escape their clutches, despite the slow speed of ambulation imposed on them by their unfortunate deformity.

p, Basil Bradbury, Peter Perry; d, Peri.

Drama **(PR:O MPAA:NR)**

HONEYMOON'S OVER, THE** (1939) 70m FOX bw

Stuart Erwin *(Donald)*, Marjorie Weaver *(Betty)*, Patric Knowles *(Pat)*, Russell Hicks *(Walker)*, Jack Carson *(Donroy)*, Hobart Cavanaugh *(Butterfield)*, June Gale *(Peggy)*, E.E. Clive *(Colonel)*, Renie Riano *(Annie)*, Harrison Greene *(Winslow)*, Lelah Tyler *(Mrs. Winslow)*, Harry Hayden *(Burton)*, Nedda Harrigan *(Mrs. Burton)*, Frank McGlynn, Sr. *(Thin Man)*, Chester Clute *(Higginsby)*, Robert Greig *(Kellogg)*, William Davidson *(Crane)*.

Erwin is a young advertising man who marries Weaver, the girl one desk over. The two have a high time with married life, spending all their money, and more, on cars, country clubs, and liquor. Clive, Gale, Knowles, Greene, and Tyler are a pack of social leeches who hang out as long as the liquor keeps flowing. Finding themselves deeply in debt, the young couple quickly switch over from the fast lane to a more conservative life style. Simplistic and highly moralistic, but with enough funny moments to be entertaining. The direction keeps things moving right along at a good rhythm. Carson has a great bit as an obnoxious car salesman.

p, Sol M. Wurtzel; d, Eugene Forde; w, Hamilton MacFadden, Clay Adams, Leonard Hoffman (based on the play "Six Cylinder Love" by William Anthony McGuire); ph, Virgil Miller; ed, Nick DeMaggio; md, Samuel Kaylin.

Comedy **(PR:C MPAA:NR)**

HONEYSUCKLE ROSE*** (1980) 119m WB c (AKA: ON THE ROAD AGAIN)

Willie Nelson *(Buck)*, Dyan Cannon *(Viv)*, Amy Irving *(Lily)*, Slim Pickens *(Garland)*, Joey Floyd *(Jamie)*, Charles Levin *(Sid)*, Priscilla Pointer *(Rosella)*, Mickey Rooney, Jr. *(Cotton)*, Pepe Serna *(Rooster)*, Lane Smith *(Brag)*, Diana Scarwid *(Jeanne)*, Emmylou Harris *(Emmylou)*, Rex Ludwick *(Tex)*, Mickey Raphael *(Kelly)*, Bee Spears *(Bo)*, Chris Ethridge *(Easter)*, Paul English *(Paul)*, Bobby Nelson *(Bonnie)*, Jody Payne *(Jonas)*, Randy Locke *(Poodie)*, T. Snake *(Snake)*, Johnny Gimble, Kenneth Threadgill, Grady Martin, Hank Cochran, Jeannie Seeley, Gene Rader, Frank Stewart, Lubelle Camp, A. L. Camp, Jackie Ezzell, Bernedette Whitehead, Harvey Christiansen, Hackberry Johnson, Kenneth Eric Hamilton, Nelson Fowler, Guy Houston Garrett, Centa Boyd, Cara Kanak, Augie Myers, Robert Gotschall, Emilio Gonzales, Mary Jane Valle, Randy Arlyn Fletcher, Ray Liberto, Sam Allred, Boy Baty, John Meadows, Crody Hubach, Dick Gimble, Maurice Anderson, Ray D. Hollingsworth, Bill Mounce, Kenny Frazier.

Nelson more or less plays himself in this semi-autobiographical picture. He's a married man who deeply loves his wife, Cannon, and son, Floyd. But he's torn between them and his love for performing—as well as for liquor. The family is always happy together, but the shadow of Nelson's impending road trips always looms. Pickens is marvelous as the old-time band partner who retires and is replaced by daughter Irving. She has adored Nelson since childhood, and is unafraid of the consequences when she tries to fulfill her dreams. The film is neatly directed, keeping a good balance between the music and the drama. This was Nelson's first lead role, after a few minor supporting parts, and he's just fine. "On the Road Again," Nelson's theme song in the film, became a big hit. Interestingly enough, this is a re-make (country-western style) of the classic film INTERMEZZO.

p, Gene Taft; d, Jerry Schatzberg; w, Carol Sobieski, William D. Wittliff, John Binder (based on the story "Intermezzo" by Gosta Steven, Gustav Molander); ph, Robby Muller (Panavision, Technicolor); m, Willie Nelson, Richard Baskin; ed, Aram Avakian, Norman Gay, Marc Laub, Evan Lottman; prod d, Joel Schiller; cos, Jo Ynocencio; m/l, Nelson.

Drama **Cas.** **(PR:C MPAA:PG)**

HONG KONG½** (1951) 90m PAR c (AKA: BOMBS OVER CHINA)

Ronald Reagan *(Jeff Williams)*, Rhonda Fleming *(Victoria Evans)*, Nigel Bruce *(Mr. Lighton)*, Lady May Lawford *(Mrs. Lighton)*, Marvin Miller *(Tao Liang)*, Claude Allister *(Hotel Clerk)*, Danny Chang *(Wei Lin)*, Lowell Gilmore *(Bit)*.

Reagan stopped monkeying around with Bonzo and took up with a charming kid in this adventure. He's a crooked (that's right, Reagan crooked!) ex-soldier who hangs out in the Orient after WW II. After failing in some shady deals, he gets caught in a Communist airplane raid in China. As he escapes, he meets Chang, a young Chinese orphan with a valuable antique statue. Reagan wants it, so he takes the kid with him. They meet sexy, flaming-haired Fleming at a Red Cross mission. The trio flees to Hong Kong and scams its way into a hotel room. Slowly, Reagan is wooed by the charms of the woman and the boy, and his hardened core starts to melt. But he still has some crook in him; he goes to art dealer Miller to sell the boy's statue. When he discovers that Miller is involved with gangsters, Reagan's attitude changes completely, but it is too late. The gang kidnaps Chang, and Reagan's bid to save him goes afoul. But everything is righted by the police and Reagan marries Fleming. The happy couple pay regular visits to the boy at an orphanage as the film ends. The color photography nicely captures the hustle and business of Hong Kong. Chang is a natural actor (Reagan had high praise for him). This was the second of what would be three films with the team of Reagan and Fleming, with THE LAST OUTPOST and TROPIC ZONE being first and last respectively. Though Reagan is fine in his role, the film just can't be taken seriously today for obvious reasons. Just try and keep a straight face when the future president gets involved with the commies. If you can get past this, it's really a nice little thriller.

p, William H. Pine, William C. Thomas; d, Lewis R. Foster; w, Winston Miller (based on a story by Foster); ph, Lionel Lindon (Technicolor); m, Lucien Cailliet; ed, Howard Smith; art d, Lewis H. Creber.

Drama **(PR:A MPAA:NR)**

HONG KONG AFFAIR** (1958) 79m Claremont/AA bw

Jack Kelly *(Steve Whalen)*, May Wynn *(Chu Lan)*, Richard Loo *(Li Noon)*, Lo Lita Shek *(Sou May)*, Gerald Young *(Louis Jordon)*, Michael Bulmer *(Inspector Stuart)*, James Hudson *(Jim Long)*.

Though his plantation is making a good deal of money producing Iron Lady Buddha Tea, Kelly has yet to see a dime. He arrives in Hong Kong to see what's up. There he meets Wynn, the Chinese secretary of English attorney Young. After the usual amount of intrigue, the pair discover that Young has been keeping all the profits for himself while smuggling out opium in the tea shipments. Kelly stops his attorney and delivers him to the cops. It's a formula thriller that is greatly helped by nice photography of the city. The direction is good, though it could stand a little tightening up. Kelly is fine in his part, giving a realistic and honest performance. Wynn is the complete opposite, a poor actress with an unbelievably phoney accent.

p, Paul F. Heard, J. Raymond Friedgen; d, Heard; w, Herbert G. Luft, Heard, Friedgen, Helene Turner; ph, S.T. Chow; m, Louis Forbes; ed, Turner; m/l, "Hong Kong Affair," Forbes, Paul Herrick (vocal by Ronnie Deauville).

Crime/Mystery **(PR:A MPAA:NR)**

HONG KONG CONFIDENTIAL½** (1958) 67m UA bw

Gene Barry *(Casey Reed)*, Beverly Tyler *(Fay Wells)*, Allison Hayes *(Elene Martine)*, Noel Drayton *(Owen Howard)*, Edward Kemmer *(Frank Paige)*, Michael Pate *(John Blanchard)*, W. Beal Wong *(Muto)*, Mel Prestige *(Mao)*, King Calder *(Dan Young)*, Bryan Roper *(Brooks)*, Rico Alaniz *(Fernando)*, Philip Ahn *(Chung)*, Walter Woolf King *(Chief)*, Joe Vitale *(Youseff)*, Asa Maynor *(Redhead)*, Owen McGivney *(Inspector)*, Lou Krugman *(Linou)*, Jack Kenny *(Maitre D')*, Bill Saito *(Jen)*.

Barry is a U.S. agent working undercover as a singer in a Hong Kong nightspot. The son of an important Middle East potentate is kidnaped by communists and Barry's got to save him. The commies want to make it look like the whole thing was a U.S. plot to put pressure on the Arabs. Barry heads off an intrigue from Hong Kong to nearby Macao and the eventual denouement. The film is better than most suspense thrillers of the time because of its intimacy within the larger setting. A narration holds all the action together, and characters are not complex, though certainly not simplistic. The photography is fine, making a Hollywood set more than passable as Hong Kong. There's a nice integration of stock footage as well. Direction is snappy, keeping things moving well, and handling the plot twists with ease.

p, Robert E. Kent; d, Edward L. Cahn; w, Orville H. Hampton; ph, Kenneth Peach; m, Paul Sawtell, Bert Shefter; ed, Edward Mann; art d, William Glasgow; cos, Jack Masters.

Thriller **(PR:A MPAA:NR)**

HONG KONG NIGHTS½** (1935) 59m Futter-WAFilms/FD bw

Tom Keene [George Duryea] *(Tom)*, Wera Engels *(Trina)*, Warren Hymer *(Wally)*, Tetsu Komai *(Wong)*, Cornelius Keefe *(Burris)*, Freeman Lang *(Capt. Evans)*, Tom London *(Blake)*.

"Smugglers, bullets, and Chinese knives!" read the ads for this independent thriller. Keene and Hymer are a pair of customs agents on the trail of some gun runners. The trail leads to some expected dangers when they're ordered to stop Keefe, a hustling businessman. Engels is the girl who becomes involved with Keefe, despite the good advice of Keene. Komai (a Japanese gentleman who, thanks to Hollywood prejudices, always played Chinese villains) is in cahoots with Keefe. But by the end he has switched loyalties, killing his former partner and shooting into a clump of oil drums to set off a spectacular fire. For a small film this isn't bad at all. The plot is a little confusing, but the action never lets up. It's all played in a hardy style that's fun to watch. For the oil drum explosion over an acre of land on the Sennett lot was set ablaze. Most of the film was shot at the Mack Sennett Studio, with Los Angeles' Chinatown and Catalina Island substituting for the mysterious Orient. The director was an old hand with the Sennett Studio, having directed a few Mabel Normand comedies. Shooting was interrupted on the third day when a Tong war, complete with gangs brandishing knives and throwing rocks, broke out on the location set. Keene, under the name George Duryea, had been the star of King Vidor's classic OUR DAILY BREAD. That film, made just before this one, proved to be his only memorable role, as the actor faded into obscurity, with countless westerns and a few romantic roles comprising the majority of his career.

p, Walter Futter, Fenn Kimball; d, E. Mason Hopper; w, Norman Houston (based on a story by Roger Allman); ph, Arthur Reed; art d, Charles Gardner.

Adventure **(PR:A MPAA:NR)**

HONKERS, THE½** (1972) 102m UA c

James Coburn *(Lew Lathrop)*, Lois Nettleton *(Linda Lathrop)*, Slim Pickens *(Clete)*, Anne Archer *(Deborah Moon)*, Richard Anderson *(Royce)*, Joan Huntington *(Rita Ferguson)*, Jim Davis *(Mel Potter)*, Ramon Bieri *(Jack Ferguson)*, Ted Eccles *(Bob Lathrop)*, Mitchell Ryan *(Lowell)*, Wayne McLaren *(Everett)*, John Harmon *(Sam Martin)*, Richard O'Brien *(Matt Weber)*, Pitt Herbert *(Hat Store Proprietor)*, Chuck Parkison *(Announcer)*, Larry Mahan *(Himself)*, Ross Dollarhyde *(Travis)*, Jerry Gatlin *(Shorty)*, Bobby Hall *(Dave)*, Bud Walls *(Harve)*, Kitty Sadock *(Waitress)*, Chuck Henson, Larry McKinney, Buzz Henning, Wayne McClellan, Chris Howell.

Disappointing rodeo epic starring Coburn as an unappealing, quick-tempered bronco-buster who seeks to regain the respect of his wife (Nettleton), his son (Eccles) and his best friend (Pickens) while still retaining his freedom. The film is at its best when illustrating rodeo life, but the characters are ill-drawn and weak. Director Ihnat (an actor who helmed his last feature here; he died soon after the film was released) brings some interesting and realistic details to the setting, but he fails when it comes to handling the actors' performances (especially Coburn, who appears too genial a personality to be so mean and thoughtless to his family). Songs are "Easy Made For Lovin," "My Special Day," composed and sung by Bobby Russell, "I'm a Rodeo Cowboy," composed and sung by Slim Pickens. THE HONKERS was one of four rodeo pictures to be released between 1972 and 1973 (the others were JUNIOR BONNER, J.W. COOP, and WHEN LEGENDS DIE) and unfortunately it was the weakest of the bunch.

p, Arthur Gardner, Jules Levy; d, Steve Ihnat; w, Ihnat, Stephen Lodge; ph, James Crabe (DeLuxe Color); m, Jimmie Haskell; ed, Tom Rolf; spec eff, Cliff Wenger; stunts, Jerry Gatlin.

Western **(PR:C MPAA:PG)**

HONKY** (1971) 92m Getty-Fromkess-Stonehenge/Jack H. Harris c

Brenda Sykes *(Shelia Smith)*, John Nielson *(Wayne "Honky" Divine)*, Maia Danziger *(Sharon)*, John Lasell *(Archie Divine)*, William Marshall *(Dr. Craig Smith)*, Amentha Dymally *(Mrs. Smith)*, Marion Ross *(Mrs. Divine)*, John Fiedler, Elliott Street, Matt Clark, Ivor Francis, Lincoln Kilpatrick.

"Socially relevant" at the time, now just an overblown, cliched anachronism, HONKY details an interracial relationship between young white man Nielson and rich black girl Sykes. They meet innocently enough in a Midwestern high school, becoming close friends and then eventually lovers. This causes endless tension between Nielson and his parents, which drives the couple out of their respective homes and into trouble with drug dealers. Eventually, the film leads to a grim climax which sees Nielson beaten to a pulp by brutish whites, who then rape Sykes.

p, Will Chaney, Ron Roth; d, William A. Graham; w, Chaney (based on the novel *Shelia* by Gunard Selberg); ph, Ralph Woolsey (DeLuxe Color); m, Quincy Jones; ed, Jim Benson; art d, Frank Sylos.

Drama **(PR:O MPAA:R)**

HONKY TONK** (1929) 68m WB bw

Sophie Tucker *(Sophie Leonard)*, Lila Lee *(Sophie's Daughter Beth)*, Audrey Ferris *(Jean Gilmore, Beth's Friend)*, George Duryea *(Freddie Gilmore)*, Mahlon Hamilton *(Jim)*, John T. Murray *(Cafe Manager)*, Wilbur Mack.

Tucker stars in her first feature as a nightclub singer who sacrifices everything to send her young daughter abroad to be educated. When the grown daughter (Lee) returns from Europe, she is shocked to discover that her mother is nothing more than a nightclub entertainer singing for drunks (a secret that had been kept from her since childhood), and disowns her. Tucker spends the rest of the film playing the rejected but loving mother while crooning sad songs. The songs (written by Jack Yellen and Milton Ager) include: "I'm The Last Of The Red Hot Mommas"; "I'm Doin' What I'm Doin' For Love"; "He's A Good Man To Have Around"; "I'm Feathering A Nest (For A Little Bluebird)"; and "I Don't Want to Get Thin." "Some Of These Days," Tucker's theme song, was by Shelton Brooks.

d, Lloyd Bacon; w, V.C. Graham Baker, Jack Yellen (based on a story by Leslie S. Barrows); ch, Larry Ceballos.

Musical/Drama **(PR:A MPAA:NR)**

HONKY TONK*** (1941) 105m MGM bw

Clark Gable *(Candy Johnson)*, Lana Turner *(Elizabeth Cotton)*, Frank Morgan *(Judge Cotton)*, Claire Trevor *("Gold Dust" Nelson)*, Marjorie Main *(Rev. Mrs. Varner)*, Albert Dekker *(Brazos Hearn)*, Chill Wills *(The Sniper)*, Henry O'Neill *(Daniel Wells)*, John Maxwell *(Kendall)*, Morgan Wallace *(Adams)*, Douglas Wood *(Gov. Wilson)*, Betty Blythe *(Mrs. Wilson)*, Hooper Atchley *(Sen. Ford)*, Harry Worth *(Harry Gates)*, Veda Ann Borg *(Pearl)*, Dorothy Granger *(Saloon Girl)*, Sheila Darcy *(Louise)*, Cy Kendall *(Man with Tar)*, Erville Alderson *(Man with Rail)*, John Farrell *(Man with Feathers)*, Don Barclay *(Man with Gun)*, Ray Teal *(Poker Player)*, Esther Muir *(Prostitute)*, Francis X. Bushman, Jr. *(Ralph Bushman)*, Art Miles *(Dealer)*, Anne O'Neal *(Nurse)*, Russell Hicks *(Dr. Otis)*, Henry Roquemore *(Butcher)*, Lew Harvey *(Blackie)*, John "Jack" Carr *(Brazos' Henchman)*, Demetrius Alexis *(Tug)*, Art Belasco, Frank Mills, Ralph Peters, Eddie Gribbon, Syd Saylor, Harry Semels *(Pallbearers)*, Fay Holderness *(Bricklayer)*, Eddy Waller *(Train Conductor)*, Will Wright, Alan Bridge, Lee Phelps *(Men in Meeting House)*, Heinie Conklin *(Dental Patient)*, Dick Rush *(Dentist)*, Lew Kelly, Charles McAvoy, Joe Devlin, Malcolm Waite, Earl Gunn, Ted Oliver, Charles Sullivan, Monte Montague, William Haade, Al Hill *(Miners)*, Ed Brady *(Waiter)*, Edward Cassidy, Jack Baxley, Carl Stockdale, Howard Mitchell, William Pagan, Jack C. Smith, John Sheehan, Bill Telaak, Tom Chatterton *(Citizens)*, Gordon O'Malley *(Guests)*, Elliott Sullivan *(Candy's Man)*, Horace Murphy *(Butler)*, Tiny Newlan *(Gentleman)*, Dorothy Ates *(Dance Hall Girl)*.

Gable is a heel and Turner is the beautiful daughter of corrupt judge Morgan in this western soap opera which is routine and mostly predictable. The stars, however, infused the film with an aura of excitement and pounding panache that the script did not originally provide. Con artist Gable arrives in Yellow Creek, Nevada, and slowly ingratiates himself with the townsfolk. He and Wills and their cronies pose as do-gooders, establishing a fire department, schoolhouse, and, of course, their own saloon. Morgan, the venal judge who has been in Gable's pocket all along and has helped him scam the citizenry, suddenly gets religion and tries to prevent Gable's wholesale takeover of the town, suffering a heart attack and dying in the process. By this time Gable has wed pretty Turner, and gotten her pregnant. She now suffers a miscarriage and loses the child, mostly at the distress of losing her father. Jolted by events, Gable penitently exits the town, giving up his miscreant ambitions. But love conquers all adversities and Turner decides she loves her "candy man" after all, and follows after him. The studio hyped this film in trying to create another great love duo, similar to that of Gable and the dead Harlow of the 1930s, inserting into its ad campaign for HONKY TONK such lines as "Clark Gable kisses Lana Turner and it's screen history." In fact, he and Turner kiss 11 times in this steamy production with an equal number of clinches. "Let's be specific, they're terrific," the promoters in the front office hacked out. Carole Lombard, Gable's then wife, did not think MGM's new blonde bombshell was so terrific. She thought of her as a maneater and Turner's reputation at the time supported Lombard's fears. Turner had been dubbed "Queen of the Nightclubs" in the late 1930s, with hundreds of stellar names from the male ranks of Hollywood serving as her escorts. She had tried to marry Howard Hughes, did marry bandleader Artie Shaw, her co-star of DANCING CO-ED (1939), but only briefly. The 33-year-old Lombard feared Turner would vamp her gullible husband and stormed into the posh office of Louis B. Mayer to tell him so. The mogul smiled and let her rave on. Then Lombard began appearing on the set, which disturbed Turner no end. In a *Ladies' Home Journal* article whe was quoted as saying: "We rehearsed our first love scene . . . and suddenly I turned around and froze. There was beloved Carole Lombard, Mrs. Gable! She seldom came on the set but I guess she wanted to see who the new kid was." Turner could not finish the love scene with Lombard looking over her shoulder and quickly retreated to her dressing room. She told director Conway that only after Lombard left the set would she return. Gable convinced his fiery wife to go home and the screen lovers continued to conjure what Turner later termed "a wonderful chemical rapport." She later denied that the lovemaking went on after the cameras stopped rolling: "Ours was a closeness without intimacy. There was a dear loving for him but never an affair. No way." Gable had originally not thought a lot about the fledgling actress who was to become, with Ava Gardner, MGM's top sex goddess of the 1940s and 1950s. She was 17 in 1938 when she made a screen test with Gable. He was called off the set of TOO HOT TO HANDLE to do the test and he thought Turner was simply awful when the two did a scene from the Gable-Harlow smash hit RED DUST. "She couldn't read lines," he later said. "She didn't make them mean anything, it was obvious she was an amateur." But Turner had since paid her MGM dues in a spate of minor films, including LOVE FINDS ANDY HARDY in 1938. She had scored heavily as the consumptive, forlorn showgirl in ZIEGFELD GIRL (1941) and was rising fast by the time of HONKY TONK. Gable had changed his mind about Turner and showed it. When arriving at her dressing room on the first day of the production she found a box of flowers with a note attached that read: "I'm the world's worst talent scout. Clark." A few minutes later the 41-year-old King of Hollywood poked his head inside the dressing room, giving Turner that sheepish grin long since famous and piped: "Baby, you sure have learned a thing or two." Gable publicly endorsed this new perspective by saying that Turner "was so much better an actress. Gone was the amateur." Their bedroom scenes in the film had firecrackers exploding in them and the public made the film an enormous hit, despite its potboiler premise and script. Dekker, playing the heavy Gable must confront and later kill, was outstanding, as was Main as a feisty widow. Trevor, who played "the other woman" in the film, a good-natured slattern (a patented role for her by then), was exceptional in the few scenes MGM editors left in the film. She later remarked: "I had some great scenes in HONKY TONK. At least, I *thought* I had them until I went to the press preview of it. My scenes had been scissored." She went home swearing that she'd never make another film, a hollow vow, of course. Lombard, who was to die tragically in an air crash the following year, feared that MGM would put temptress Turner in another film with her husband. She was right; the studio tried to build another great love team by starring Gable and Turner in SOMEWHERE I'LL FIND YOU the next year and the two would make two more films together, none of them memorable beyond the speculation of what Gable and Turner were doing off-screen together, if anything.

p, Pandro S. Berman; d, Jack Conway; w, Marguerite Roberts, John Sanford; ph, Harold Rosson; m, Franz Waxman; ed, Blanche Sewell; art d, Cedric Gibbons, Eddie Imazu; set d, Edwin B. Willis; cos, Robert Kalloch, Gile Steele; m/l, Jack Yellen, Milton Ager.

Adventure/Romance **(PR:C MPAA:NR)**

HONKY TONK FREEWAY** (1981) 107m EMI/UNIV-AFD c

Beau Bridges *(Duane Hansen)*, Hume Cronyn *(Sherm)*, Beverly D'Angelo *(Carmen Shelby)*, William Devane *(Mayor Calo)*, George Dzundza *(Eugene)*, Teri Garr *(Ericka)*, Joe Grifasi *(Osvaldo)*, Howard Hesseman *(Snapper)*, Paul Jabara *(T.J. Tupus)*, Geraldine Page *(Sister Mary Clarise)*, Jessica Tandy *(Carol)*, Frances Lee McCain *(Claire Calo)*, Deborah Rush *(Sister Mary Magdalen)*, Alice Beardsley *(Betty Boo Radley)*, Daniel Stern, David Rasche, Sandra McCabe, Renny Roker, Celia Weston, Jenn Thompson, Peter Billingsley, Ron Frazier, Jerry Hardin, John Ashton, John C. Becher, Davis Roberts, Loretta Tupper, Francis Bay, Rollin Moriyama, Kimiko Hiroshige, James Staley, Shelley Batt, Jason Keller, Shane Keller, Kelly Lange, Kent Williams, Arnold Johnson, Nancy Parsons, Jessica Rains, Ann Risley, Helen Hanft, Don Morgan, Paul Keenan, Robert Stoneman, Randy Norton, Al Corley, Murphy Dunn, Leo Burmester, Jeffrey Combs, Jack Murdock, Ann Coleman, Gordon Haight, Jack Thibeau, Martha Gehman, George Solomon, Dick Christie, Anita Dangler, Mags Kavanaugh, Gloria Leroy.

A notorious disaster when it was originally released (it cost $25 million, was saddled with an awful ad campaign, and grossed only $500,000), HONKY TONK FREEWAY isn't as bad as it's supposed to be (on the other hand, it's not great, either). Director Schlesinger (MIDNIGHT COWBOY, THE FALCON AND THE SNOWMAN) made the mistake of structuring this slice-of-American-life comedy much the same as Robert Altman's NASHVILLE. The film is filled with dozens of characters and the action is cross-cut among them, creating a hit-or-miss fragmentation of a movie that only occasionally succeeds. The plot (such as it is) circles around the efforts of a small Florida town, Ticlaw, led by crazy mayor Devane, to have a freeway exit ramp go through their dying community. Devane bribes some officials to ensure the ramp's construction, but he is double-crossed and is forced to trick motorists into venturing into his town. Among the hapless travelers who end up in Ticlaw are: D'Angelo, who plays a young woman aimlessly wandering throughout the country with the ashes of her dead mother sitting on the dashboard; Cronyn and Tandy, as a wacky elderly couple; Rush, as a disillusioned nun; Bridges, as the author of a disastrous children's book entitled *Randy The Carnivorous Pony;* and a water-skiing elephant named Bubbles. The film is on occasion very funny, but its length and confusing narrative style sap it of any real chance at hilarity. An interesting failure.

p, Don Boyd, Howard W. Koch, Jr.; d, John Schlesinger; w, Edward Clinton; ph, John Bailey (Technicolor); m, George Martin, Elmer Bernstein; ed, Jim Clark; art d, Edwin O'Donovan; cos, Ann Roth.

Comedy **Cas.** **(PR:C MPAA:R)**

HONKYTONK MAN½** (1982) 122m WB c

Clint Eastwood *(Red Stovall)*, Kyle Eastwood *(Whit)*, John McIntire *(Grandpa)*, Alexa Kenin *(Marlene)*, Verna Bloom *(Emmy)*, Matt Clark *(Virgil)*, Barry Corbin *(Arnspriger)*, Jerry Hardin *(Snuffy)*, Tim Thomerson *(Highway Patrolman)*, Macon McCalman *(Dr. Hines)*, Joe Regalbuto *(Henry Axle)*, Gary Grubbs *(Jim Bob)*, Rebecca Clemons *(Belle)*, John Gimble *(Bob Wells)*, Linda Hopkins *(Flossie)*, Bette Ford *(Lulu)*, Jim Boelsen *(Junior)*, Tracey Walter *(Pooch)*, Susan Peretz *(Miss Maud)*, John Russell *(Jack Wade)*, Charles Cyphers *(Stubbs)*, Marty Robbins *(Smoky)*, Ray Price, Shelly West, David Frizzell *(Singers)*, Porter Wagoner *(Dusty)*, Bob Ferrera, Tracy Shults, R.J. Ganzert, Hugh Warden, Kelsie Blades, Jim Ahart, Steve Autry, Peter Griggs, Julie Hoopman, Rozelle Gayle, Robert V. Barron, DeForest Covan, Lloyd Nelson, George Orrison, Glenn Wright, Frank Reinhard, Roy Jenson, Sherry Allurd, Gordon Terry, Tommy Alsup, Merle Travis, Robert D. Carver, Thomas Powels.

Clint Eastwood, an aspiring country musician trying for his big break in the midst of the Depression, turns up drunk at his sister's lonely farm house. Having become an alcoholic to quell the pain of tuberculosis that is killing him, Clint is taken in by his sister and her family. The drunken would-be musician holds a special fascination for his young nephew (played by Clint's son, Kyle Eastwood), and the two grow close. Determined to make it to Nashville so that he can audition at the Grand Old Opry, the financially strapped musician drafts Kyle in his effort to steal salable chickens. Clint Eastwood is caught and jailed, but the clever Kyle Eastwood breaks his uncle out. With permission from his mother (who wants the boy to keep an eye on her brother), Kyle is allowed to accompany his uncle on the trip to Nashville. The duo is joined by McIntire, Kyle's grandfather, who wishes to return home to Tennessee and is willing to help pay for the trip. Stopping in Tulsa to collect a debt owed him by his former manager, Corbin, Clint stupidly becomes involved in a robbery arranged by Corbin for insurance purposes. The scheme goes awry and the angry Clint instead robs Corbin and his poker buddies. Escaping with Clint is Kenin, Corbin's long-suffering girl friday who also dreams of playing Nashville. Before they go much farther the car breaks down and grandpa decides he'd get to Tennessee quicker by bus. That night Clint gets drunk and winds up in bed with Kenin who claims the next morning she has conceived. Determined that nothing will stop his audition (including his illness which, predictably, is getting worse), Clint hustles off, telling Kyle to lose Kenin before catching up. Kyle obeys and the duo finally get to the Grand Old Opry. The audition goes fairly well until Clint is shaken by a violent coughing fit. The concerned music people recommend to Kyle that Clint be placed in a sanitarium, but when a record company offers Clint a chance to cut a record, the musician leaps at the chance. Despite the knowledge that the long recording sessions will probably end up killing him, Clint seizes the opportunity to finally realize his dreams and dies soon after finishing the record. Kenin (who isn't pregnant after all) finds Kyle and the two leave together. In HONKYTONK MAN Clint Eastwood continues the examination of his screen image and this film, along with the superior BRONCO BILLY (1980), are the most radical departures from the Man With No Name/Dirty Harry personas so popular with the public. Unfortunately, HONKYTONK MAN suffers from a fairly weak script which is plagued with predictable situations and underdeveloped characters. The nagging "Camille" cough, the young-boy-learns-hard-lessons-on-the-road cliche, and the hint that Clint's only record is going to make him some sort of posthumous country-western demigod are all a bit hard to take at times, leaving the intelligent Eastwood fan nothing more than some fairly interesting musings from the actor/director regarding the nature of his screen persona. While it is this aspect of Eastwood's self-directed films that make him such an interesting superstar, these examinations of his publicly perceived character should be presented in a less trite manner such as in the complex and thoughtful OUTLAW JOSEY WALES (1976), the utterly charming BRONCO BILLY, and the gripping, disturbing SUDDEN IMPACT (1983). The public, however, could care less about Eastwood taking chances with his image. BRONCO BILLY and HONKYTONK MAN died at the box office, which may have forced Eastwood to return as Dirty Harry in SUDDEN IMPACT to appease the fans, though he did manage to brilliantly continue his self-appraisal in that monstrous box office smash.

p&d, Clint Eastwood; w, Clancy Carlile (based on his novel); ph, Bruce Surtees (Technicolor); m, Steve Dorff; ed, Ferris Webster, Michael Kelly, Joel Cox; prod d, Edward Carfagno.

Drama **Cas.** **(PR:A-C MPAA:PG)**

HONOLULU½** (1939) 82m MGM bw

Eleanor Powell *(Dorothy March)*, Robert Young *(Brooks Mason/George Smith)*, George Burns *(Joe Duffy)*, Gracie Allen *(Millie de Grasse)*, Rita Johnson *(Cecelia Grayson)*, Clarence Kolb *(Mr. Horace Grayson)*, Jo Ann Sayers *(Nurse)*, Ann Morriss *(Gale Brewster)*, Willie Fung *(Wong)*, Cliff Clark *(First Detective)*, Edward Gargan *(Second Detective)*, Eddie Anderson *(Washington)*, Sig Rumann *(Psychiatrist)*, Ruth Hussey *(Eve)*, Kealoha Holt *(Native Dancing Girl)*, Edgar Dearing *(Jailer)*, Ken Darby and The Kings's Men.

A standard screwball musical starring Young in a dual role as a Hollywood star and a Hawaiian plantation owner who meet in California and decide to switch places for a short time to give their lives a little zest. The star goes to Hawaii for what he thinks will be a quiet vacation and the plantation owner goes to Hollywood to get a taste of fame and adoration. On board the ship to the islands, the actor meets and falls for Powell, but once in Hawaii he finds himself about to marry the real plantation owner's fiancee. Eventually, the farmer returns to the islands in the nick of time, and prevents his girl from marrying the wrong man. Powell provides the dance numbers (including a black-face parody of Bill "Bojangles" Robinson), with Burns and Allen and Eddie "Rochester" Anderson providing the laughs. Songs include: "The Leader Doesn't Like Music" (Harry Warren, Gus Kahn, sung by Allen), "This Night Was Made For Dreaming," "Honolulu" (Warren, Kahn), and "Hymn To The Sun" (P.G. Wodehouse, Armand Vesey).

p, Jack Cummings; d, Edward Buzzell; w, Herbert Fields, Frank Partos; ph, Ray June; m, Franz Waxman; ed, Conrad A. Nervig; md, Georgie Stoll; ch, Bobby Connelly, Sammy Lee.

Musical **(PR:A MPAA:NR)**

HONOLULU LU*½ (1941) 72m COL bw

Lupe Velez *(Consuelo Cordoba)*, Bruce Bennett *(Skelly)*, Leo Carrillo *(Don Estaban Cordoba)*, Marjorie Gateson *(Mrs. Van Derholt)*, Don Beddoe *(Bennie Blanchard)*, Forrest Tucker *(Barney)*, George McKay *(Horseface)*, Helen Dickson *(Mrs. Smythe)*, Nina Campana *(Aloha)*, Curtis Railing *(Mrs. Frobisher)*, Roger Clark *(Bill Van Derholt)*, Romaine Callender *(Hotel Manager)*, John Tyrrell *(Duffy)*, Eileen O'Hearn, Janet Shaw *(Debutantes)*, Joe Bautista *(Bellboy)*, Rudy Robles *(Elevator Boy)*, Lloyd Bridges *(Desk Clerk)*, Ed Mortimer, Elinor Counts, Mary Bovard *(Tourists)*, Harry Bailey *(Deaf Man)*, Charlie Lung *(Cab Driver)*, Dick Jensen, George Barton, Earl Bunn, Charles D. Freeman, Kit Guard, Harry Anderson *(Sailors)*, Ed Mundy *(Magician)*, Hank Mann, Chester Conklin *(Comedians)*, Grace Lenard *(Soubrette)*, Blanche Payson *(Mezzo Soprano)*, Ernie Adams *(Pierre)*, Ray Mala *(Native Cop)*, Sam Appel *(Sergeant)*, Harry Depp *(Dentist)*, Mickey Simpson

(Strong Man), Jack Raymond *(Mr. Astouras)*, Kay Hughes *(Nurse)*, Al Hill *(Detective)*, Jamiel Hasson *(Police Sergeant)*, John Harmon *(Clerk)*, Al Bridge *(Shooting Gallery Proprietor)*.

Varying little from her persona of the "Mexican Spitfire," Velez is up to her usual antics out in Hawaii. Becoming involved with a gang of well-meaning sailors, she goes from a risque nightclub act to becoming a beauty queen.

p, Wallace MacDonald; d, Charles Barton; w, Eliot Gibbons, Paul Yawitz, Ned Dandy (based on a story by Gibbons); ph, Franz F. Planer; m/l, Sammy Cahn, Saul Chaplin.

Musical/Comedy **(PR:A MPAA:NR)**

HONOLULU-TOKYO-HONG KONG*½ (1963, Hong Kong/Jap.) 102m Toho-Cathay/Toho c

Akira Takarada *(Yuichi Okamoto)*, Yu Ming *(Wu Ai-ling)*, Yuzo Kayama *(Jiro Okamoto)*, Yuriko Hoshi *(Teruko)*, Wang Ing *(Cheng Hao)*, Ken Uehara *(Father)*, Haruko Togo *(Mother)*, Choko Iida *(Granny)*, Mitsuko Kusabue.

Ridiculous oriental romance starring Takarada as a young Japanese who flies to Honolulu to visit his younger brother, Kayama, who is studying at the University of Hawaii. That evening, they go to a party honoring a new beauty queen, Ming, who won a contest after Kayama submitted her photo to the judges. The prize is a two-week trip to Tokyo and Hong Kong. Takarada joins her on his way back to Tokyo. Eventually, the pair fall in love, much to the shock of brother Kayama who is also in love with Ming. Luckily, Ming happens to have a long-lost sister (who is also beautiful) and the boys marry the sisters. Basically an excuse to show off the gorgeous Far-East locations.

p, Sanezumi Fujimoto, Lin Yung-tai; d, Yasuki Chiba; w, Zenzo Matsuyama; ph, Rokuro Nishigaki; m, Hachiro Matsui.

Romance **(PR:A MPAA:NR)**

HONOR AMONG LOVERS*** (1931) 75m PAR bw

Claudette Colbert *(Julia Traynor)*, Fredric March *(Jerry Stafford)*, Monroe Owsley *(Philip Craig)*, Charles Ruggles *(Monty Dunn)*, Ginger Rogers *(Doris Blake)*, Avonne Taylor *(Maybelle)*, Pat O'Brien *(Conroy)*, Janet McLeary *(Margaret)*, John Kearney *(Inspector)*, Ralph Morgan *(Riggs)*, Jules Epailly *(Louis)*, Leonard Carey *(Butler)*, Grace Kern, Roberta Beatty, Charles Halton, Granville Bates, Si Wills, Betty Morrissey, Dr. Nathan Rozofsky.

Like other star vehicles of its kind, HONOR AMONG LOVERS was criticized for being a "shopgirl's delight," because it offered little more than the usual dose of woman's magazine romance. HONOR AMONG LOVERS, however, can boast a top-notch cast of Hollywood faces including the rising starlet Claudette Colbert, who was fast becoming one of Paramount's busiest players. Here she stars as an assertive young secretary to March, a well-to-do Wall Street broker. March makes a calculated play for her, only to have her reply with a blunt "No" to his offer of a world cruise. Unknown to March is Colbert's romance with Owsley, a young securities broker. Afraid that she may be won over by March's charm, Colbert quickly accepts Owsley's proposal of marriage. It isn't until after Colbert has already tied the knot that March also makes an offer to marry her. March irrationally fires Colbert and predicts that her matrimonial bliss will sour after six months. He apologizes, however, and offers Colbert her job back. To make further amends, he even offers Owsley an important account. It's not long before March realizes that Owsley is swindling the company and using March's own money for stock speculations. The market crash occurs and Owsley emerges from the rubble without a penny. As a last hope, Colbert offers herself to March in return for some financial support. March nobly refuses her offer but agrees to write out a check for $100,000. When Owsley learns that Colbert went to March for help he becomes enraged and threatens his rival with a gun. A bullet is fired and March is wounded. March decides to protect Owsley by insisting that his wound was self-inflicted. Owsley, however, blames the shooting on Colbert. She is arrested and the police, suspicious of the events, record a conversation she has with Owsley—implicating him as the guilty one. Moved by March's decision not to continue the prosecution, Colbert finally is convinced that she married the wrong man and leaves Owsley. The fantasy-come-true finale has March and Colbert preparing to take that long-awaited world cruise. While a nominal effort for stars Colbert and March, and a respectable showing for Ruggles, O'Brien, and Rogers—all of whom would soon take off to bigger and brighter careers—HONOR AMONG LOVERS did little for the forgotten career of Monroe Owsley. Here he turns in a fine tortured performance, but still was unable to make more than a slight ripple in film history.

d, Dorothy Arzner; w, Austin Parker, Gertrude Purcell (based on a story by Parker); ph, George Folsey; m, Johnny Green; ed, Helene Turner; art d, Charles Kirk, J. Franklin Whitman; cos, Caroline Putnam.

Drama **(PR:A MPAA:NR)**

HONOR OF THE FAMILY*½ (1931) 66m FN-WB bw

Bebe Daniels *(Laura)*, Warren William *(Capt. Boris)*, Alan Mowbray *(Tony Revere)*, Blanche Frederici *(Mme. Boris)*, Frederick Kerr *(Paul Barony)*, Dita Parlo, Allan Lane, Harry Cording, Murray Kinnell, Henry Gordon, Alphonse Ethier, Carl Miller.

Melodramatic tale set in Budapest stars Daniels as a young vamp who becomes doddering old man Kerr's mistress to get at his fortune. With the help of her swordsman lover Mowbray she intimidates the old man's family into accepting her domination of him until Kerr's nephew William returns from the Foreign Legion and kicks the crooks out. This was William's first swashbuckler; he went on to be the Errol Flynn of an earlier time.

d, Lloyd Bacon; w, James Ashmore Creelman, Roland Pertwee (based on a play by Emil Fabre from a story by Honore de Balzac); ph, Ernest Haller.

Drama/Adventure **(PR:A MPAA:NR)**

HONOR OF THE MOUNTED*½ (1932) 57m MON bw

Tom Tyler, Cecilia Ryland, Francis McDonald, Charles King, Tom London, Stanley Blystone, William Dwire, Arthur Millet, Gordon Wood [Gordon DeMain], Ted Lorch.

Mountie Tyler is suspected of murder but escapes capture and chases the real culprit across the border and into the States to get his man. Somewhat preposterous chase sees Tyler knocked out by a fall and left unconscious while the killer paddles off in a canoe. Tyler wakes up much later, leaps into the drink fully clothed, and swims after his quarry, who had been left floating at a standstill when his paddle conveniently snapped.

p, Trem Carr; d&w, Harry Fraser; ph, Archie Stout.

Adventure **(PR:A MPAA:NR)**

HONOR OF THE PRESS*½ (1932) 61m Mayfair bw

Edward J. Nugent, Rita La Roy, Dorothy Gulliver, Reginald Simpson, Franklin Parker, Franklyn Farnum, Vivian Fields, Charles K. French, John Ince, Wheeler Oakman, Reginald Simpson.

Silly newspaper saga starring Nugent as a cub reporter who can't understand why every crime scoop he calls into the paper has already been reported by a rival newshound. Nugent smells a rat when he discovers that the bank hold-up he witnesses has already been reported, and with the help of his girl, he reveals that the paper's publisher and the rival reporter are members of a crime cartel that has been terrorizing the city.

p, Fanchon Royer; d, Reeves "Breezy" Eason; w, John Thomas Neville (based on a story by M.L. Simmons, J.K. Foster); ph, Ernest Miller; ed, Frank Ware; art d, Paul Palmentola.

Crime **(PR:A MPAA:NR)**

HONOR OF THE RANGE** (1934) 60m UNIV bw

Ken Maynard *(Ken/Clem)*, Cecilia Parker *(Mary)*, Fred Kohler *(Rawhide)*, Frank Hagney *(Boots)*, Jack Rockwell *(Rocky)*, James Marcus *(Turner)*, Al Smith *(Smoky)*, Eddie Barnes *(Charlie)*, Franklin Farnum *(Saloonkeeper)*, Al Bridge, Jack Kirk, Art Mix, Charles Whitaker, Fred McKaye, Wally Wales, Hank Bell, Lafe McKee, William Patton, Bud McClure, Nelson McDowell, Ben Corbett, Pascale Perry, Jack Ward, Roy Bucko, Buck Bucko, Fred Burns, Tarzan the Horse.

Maynard plays a dual role in this oater, a sheriff and his evil twin brother. The evil half kidnaps Maynard's true love and takes her to crook Kohler's mountain hideout. Disguised as an English song-and-dance man, Maynard goes undercover and tracks his twin down. The evil Maynard has a change of heart at the last minute and touches off some dynamite that explodes Kohler's mountain, making it possible for his brother and the girl to escape. Pretty bizarre.

p, Ken Maynard; d, Alan James; w, Nate Gatzert; ph, Ted McCord.

Western **(PR:A MPAA:NR)**

HONOR OF THE WEST** (1939) 60m UNIV bw

Bob Baker *(Bob)*, Marjorie Bell [Marge Champion] *(Diane)*, Carleton Young *(Russ)*, Jack Kirk *(Heck)*, Dick Dickenson *(Luke)*, Frank O'Connor *(Butch)*, Reed Howes *(Tom)*, Glenn Strange *(Bat)*, Forrest Taylor *(Walker)*, Murdock McQuarrie.

Baker plays a noble sheriff who helplessly watches as a gang of rustlers entice his friend Young into their evil clutches. Baker quits his job and rides off after the gang in the hopes of reforming his buddy. A three-way gunfight ensues between the gang, new sheriff Strange, and Baker who has convinced Young to be on his side. When the smoke clears the gang leader and Young have been killed and the gang captured. Good exterior location photography and two decent tunes sung by Baker: "The Old Chuck Wagon" and "Pride of the Prairie" help move things along.

p, Trem Carr; d, George Waggner; w, Joseph West; ph, Harry Neumann.

Western **(PR:A MPAA:NR)**

HONOURABLE MURDER, AN* (1959, Brit.) 69m Danzigers/Warner-Pathe bw

Norman Wooland *(Brutus Smith)*, Margaretta Scott *(Claudia Caesar)*, Lisa Daniely *(Paula)*, Douglas Wilmer *(R. Cassius)*, Philip Saville *(Mark Anthony)*, John Longden *(Julian Caesar)*, Marion Mathie *(Portia Smith)*, Colin Tapley *(Casca)*, Kenneth Edwards *(Trebon)*, Arnold Bell *(Ligar)*, Stuart Saunders, Olive Kirby, Elizabeth Saunders, John Brooking, Shirley Cain, Sandra Yelland, Diana Chesney, Vernon Smythe.

Odd and largely unsuccessful attempt to update Shakespeare's "Julius Caesar" in a business world setting. Longden is chairman of the board for a large company. Wilmer and other directors are jealous of his success, and with the help of a somewhat reluctant Wooland, manage to vote Longden out of power. This sets off a fatal heart attack in the man; his old friend Saville later takes over as board chairman. He gets rid of the traitorous members, and Wooland ends up killing himself. Though ambitious in scope, the film is hampered by its pipsqueak budget. The idea isn't well handled, resulting in a ludicrous picture.

p, Edward J. Danziger, Harry Lee Danziger; d, Godfrey Grayson; w, Brian Clemens, Eldon Howard (based on the play "Julius Caesar" by William Shakespeare); ph, Jimmy Wilson.

Drama **(PR:C MPAA:NR)**

HONOURS EASY** (1935, Brit.) 61m British International bw

Greta Nissen *(Ursula)*, Margaret Lockwood *(Ann)*, Chili Bouchier *(Kate)*, Patric Knowles *(Harry Markham)*, Ivan Samson *(William Barton)*, Robert Rendel *(Sir Henry Markham)*, George Graves *(Col. Bagnall)*, W.H. Berry *(Joe Budd)*.

Samson plays a crazed art dealer who wreaks his revenge on the son of the man who ruined his career years ago by framing the kid for the theft of $2,500 stolen from his gallery's safe. Unfortunately, the kid has an easily traceable alibi which leads to Samson's own wife, thus preventing the art dealer from proceeding with his plan because of the public humiliation he would incur from the revelation of his wife's affair with the young man.

p, Walter C. Mycroft; d, Herbert Brenon; w, Norman Watson, Roland Pertwee (based on the play by Pertwee); ph, Bryan Langley, Ronald Neame.

Drama **(PR:A MPAA:NR)**

HOODLUM, THE** (1951) 61m Jack Schwarz/UA bw

Lawrence Tierney, Allene Roberts, Marjorie Riordan, Lisa Golm, Edward Tierney, Stuart Randall, Ann Zika, John De Simone, Tom Hubbard, Eddie Foster, O.Z. Whitehead, Richard Barron, Rudy Rama.

Fair gangster film starring Tierney (famed for his title role in the ridiculous DILLINGER [1945] also directed by Nosseck) as a convict paroled by the state after his mother tearfully pleads for his release. To fulfill the parole obligations, Tierney's brother (played by Tierney's real-life brother, Eddie) hires his sibling to work at his gas station. After five years of behaving himself in prison, Tierney is once again bitten by the crime bug when he sees an armored car pull up in front of the bank across the street from the gas station. Tierney gathers up his old gang and plans an elaborate robbery which, when put into action, ends up getting most of the gang killed, including Tierney. Once again, crime doesn't pay. Neither did this movie.

p, Maurice Kosloff; d, Max Nosseck; w, Sam Neuman, Nat Tanchuck; ph, Clark Ramsey; m, Darrell Calker; ed, Jack Killifer; art d, Fred Preble.

Crime **(PR:C MPAA:NR)**

HOODLUM EMPIRE½** (1952) 98m REP bw

Brian Donlevy *(Sen. Bill Stephens)*, Claire Trevor *(Connie Williams)*, Forrest Tucker *(Charley Pignatalli)*, Vera Ralston *(Marte Dufour)*, Luther Adler *(Nicky Mansani)*, John Russell *(Joe Gray)*, Gene Lockhart *(Sen. Tower)*, Grant Withers *(Rev. Andrews)*, Taylor Holmes *(Benjamin Lawton)*, Roy Barcroft *(Louie Draper)*, William Murphy *(Pete Dailey)*, Richard Jaeckel *(Ted Dawson)*, Don Beddoe *(Sen. Blake)*, Roy Roberts *(Chief Tayls)*, Richard Benedict *(Tanner)*, Phillip Pine *(Louis Barretti)*, Damian O'Flynn *(Foster)*, Pat Flaherty *(Mikkelson)*, Ric Roman *(Fergus)*, Douglas Kennedy *(Brinkley)*, Don Haggerty *(Mark Flynn)*, Francis Pierlot *(Uncle Jean)*, Sarah Spencer *(Mrs. Stephens)*, Thomas Browne Henry *(Comdr. Mermant)*, Jack Pennick *(Tracey)*, Dick Wessel *(Keiller)*, Paul Livermore *(Mike)*, Fred Kohler, Jr. *(German Soldier)*, Tony Dante *(Tommy)*, Tom Monroe *(Rocco)*, Leah Waggner *(Billie)*, Betty Ball *(Pearl)*, William Schallert *(Inquiry Clerk)*, John Phillips *(Radio Commander)*, Joe Bailey *(Eckert of the FBI)*, Lee Shumway *(U.S. Marshal)*, Charles Trowbridge *(Commissioner Garrison)*, Elizabeth Flournoy *(Miss Adams)*, John Halloran *(Inspector Willard)*, John Pickard *(Man)*, Gil Herman *(Officer O'Neil)*, Mervin Williams *(Floyd the Servant)*, Mikel Conrad *(Chunce)*, Richard Reeves *(Rollins)*, Matty Fain *(Eddie Fostie)*, Stanley Waxman *(Lonnie)*, Sydney Mason *(Burns)*, Whit Bissell *(Filby)*, Sid Tomack *(Meyers)*, Eddie Foster *(Doorman)*, Dick Paxton *(Elevator Operator)*, Sam Scar *(Sporty)*, George Volk *(Finter)*, Don Michael Drysdale *(Joe Gray's Boy)*, Andy Brennan *(Taxi Driver)*.

This rather plodding crime melodrama, which takes its impetus from the Kefauver investigations into organized crime in 1950-51, has Donlevy as a crusading senator (a la Sen. Estes Kefauver) out to destroy Adler's criminal empire. The flabby plot begins with Russell, a one-time mobster who has gone off to war, performed heroically, and has undergone a moralistic transformation, refusing to associate with his former associates when returning. He seeks anonymity by opening a gas station, but mobsters find Russell, then use his name in a vast money-laundering scheme which brings him to the attention of Donlevy and law enforcement officers. Russell fights back with his Army friends and a full-scale battle ensues with several murders recorded. Donlevy, meanwhile, outlines the evil doings of Adler's cartel, later exposing and ruining the crime czar. Russell survives to pump more gas. The story is pedestrian and the acting only occasionally above par. George Raft was originally offered the role played by Adler, one which was based upon Raft's one-time underworld friend and syndicate leader, Frank Costello. He declined. Adler is the best part of the film, aptly essaying Costello as a shifty, insidious, and wholly reprehensible criminal. Ralston, wife of Republic boss Herbert J. Yates, has a forgettable supporting role, her nepotistic stardom being in quick decline by the release of this film.

p, Herbert J. Yates; d, Joseph Kane; w, Bruce Manning, Bob Considine; ph, Reggie Lanning; m, Nathan Scott; ed, Richard L. Van Enger; art d, Frank Arrigo; cos, Adele Palmer.

Crime Drama **(PR:A MPAA:NR)**

HOODLUM PRIEST, THE*** (1961) 101m UA bw

Don Murray *(Rev. Charles Dismas Clark, S.J.)*, Larry Gates *(Louis Rosen)*, Cindi Wood *(Ellen Henley)*, Keir Dullea *(Billy Lee Jackson)*, Logan Ramsey *(George Hale)*, Don Joslyn *(Pio Gentile)*, Sam Capuano *(Mario Mazziotti)*, Vincent O'Brien *(Assistant District Attorney)*, Alan Mack *(Judge Garrity)*, Lou Martini *(Angelo Mazziotti)*, Norman MacKaye *(Father Dunne)*, Joseph Cusanelli *(Hector Sterne)*, Bill Atwood *(Weasel)*, Roger Ray *(Detective Shattuck)*, Kelley Stephens *(Genny)*, William Wardord *(District Attorney's Aide)*, Ralph Peterson *(Governor)*, Jack Eigen *(A Prisoner)*, Walter L. Wiedmer *(Father David Michaels)*, Warren Parker *(Warden)*, Joseph Hamilton *(Prison Chaplain)*.

This rather improbable but oft-times likable film stars Murray as the real life Father Clark who became famous for his wonderful work in helping juvenile delinquents in St. Louis, as well as trying mightily to rehabilitate ex-convicts. Dullea is a young thief who gets a job in a produce market through Murray after his release from prison. He falls in love with socialite Henley and they plan to wed. Then the firm's manager accuses Dullea of wrongdoing and summarily fires him, even though he is innocent. Realizing that he has been fired simply because he is an ex-con, Dullea becomes enraged and seeks vengeance by later attempting to rob his former employer. In the process, a company employee is killed and Dullea is sent to prison to await execution. Murray consoles Dullea in his last moments, telling him: "When I walk out of this gas chamber I want you to keep thinking of what I've told you about St. Dismas. Remember, the only person in the Bible who went to heaven right away was a convict just like you." Murray, of course, was referring to St. Dismas, the good thief who was crucified with Christ, Dismas also being the middle name of real-life priest Clark. Murray does a more than credible job as the priest and his overall production, done for less than $400,000, has all the earmarks of a major production, with Wexler's sharp, crisp black and white photography being topflight. Murray's script, done under the nom de plume of Deer, is tight and creative. Dullea, who made his film debut here, is compelling and sympathetic as the victimized "good thief."

p, Don Murray, Walter Wood; d, Irvin Kershner; w, Don Deer [Murray], Joseph Landon; ph, Haskell Wexler; m, Richard Markowitz; ed, Maurice Wright; art d, Jack Poplin; set d, Karl Brainard; cos, Alexis Davidoff; makeup, Ted Coodley.

Crime Drama **(PR:C MPAA:NR)**

HOODLUM SAINT, THE½** (1946) 91m MGM bw

William Powell *(Terry Ellerton O'Neill)*, Esther Williams *(May Lorrison)*, Angela Lansbury *(Dusty Millard)*, James Gleason *(Sharp)*, Lewis Stone *(Father Nolan)*, Rags Ragland *(Fishface)*, Frank McHugh *(Three-Fingers)*, Slim Summerville *(Eel)*, Roman Bohnen *(Father O'Doul)*, Charles Arnt *(Cy Nolan)*, Louis Jean Heydt *(Mike Flaherty)*, Charles Trowbridge *(Uncle Joe Lorrison)*, Henry O'Neill *(Lewis J. Malbery)*, Matt Moore *(Father Duffy)*, Trevor Bardette *(Rabbie Meyerberg)*, Addison Richards *(Reverend Miller)*, Tom Dugan *(Buggsy)*, Emma Dunn *(Maggie)*, Mary Gordon *(Trina)*, Ernest Anderson *(Sam)*, Charles D. Brown *(Ed Collner)*, Paul Langton *(Burton Kinston)*, Al Murphy *(Benny)*, Jack Davis, Garry Owen *(Cops)*, Byron Foulger *(J. Cornwall Travers)*, Will Wright *(Allan Smith)*, Mary Lord *(Mary)*, Sam Finn, William A. Janssen, Harry Tenbrook, Sol Davis, Phil Friedman, John George, Captain Fred Somers, Billy Engle, Al Thompson, Heinie Conklin *(Muggs)*, Aileen Haley, Alice Wallace, Marilyn Kinsley, Beryl McCutcheon, Frances Donelan *(Bridesmaids)*, Jean Thorsen, Lucille Casey, Mary Jane French, Ethel Tobin *(Second Group of Bridesmaids)*, Charles Judel *(Waiter Captain)*, William Newell *(Waiter)*, Connie Weiler, Peggy O'Neill *(Cigarette Girls)*, William B. Davidson *(Annoyed Man)*, Tom Dillon, Chester Conklin *(Cops)*, William Eddritt, Gordon Dumont, Jack Daley, Bob Thom, Charles Griffin, William "Billy" Wayne, James Darrell, Leonard Mellin, Phil Dunham, George Bunny, Jessie Arnold, Lucille Curtis, Rhea Mitchell *(Reporters)*, Nolan Leary, Roger Cole, Hansel Warner, Henry Sylvester, Tom Coleman *(Reporters in Utility Offices)*, George Sherwood *(Well-Dressed Pool Player)*, Stanley Blystone *(Cop at Employment Office)*, Budd Buster *(Jitney Driver)*, Roy Butler, Tom Leffingwell, Walter Bacon *(Board Executives)*, Hope Landin *(Mae, the Spinster)*, Joe Devlin *(Bartender)*, Fred Nurney *(Big Jim Banby)*, Katherine Booth, Tim Murdock *(Bridal Couple)*, Eddie Dunn *(Gateman)*, Miska Egan *(Chef)*, Ruthellen Johnson *(Prize Daughter)*, Robert Emmett O'Connor *(Conductor)*, Fred "Snowflake" Toones *(Pullman Porter)*, George Renavent *(Jeweler)*, John Valentino *(Man Servant)*, Helyn Eby Rock, Margaret Bert *(Secretaries)*, Jack Cheatham *(Jailer)*, Harry Denny *(Elevator Man)*, Jerry Lascoe, Jr. *(Newsboy)*, George Carleton *(Apartment Manager)*, Sarah Edward, Betty Blythe *(Women)*, Frances McInnerney *(Pert Secretary)*, Russell Hicks *(Marty Martindale)*, Frank Orth *(Chronicle Editor)*, Stanley Andrews *(Chronicle Publisher)*, Jack Norton *(Drunk)*, Robert Emmett Keane *(Doctor)*, Dwayne Hickman *(Johnny Ryan)*, Leila McIntyre *(Mrs. Ryan)*, Charles Bates *(Johnny's Brother)*, Charles Wagenheim *(Mr. Cohn)*, Ruth Robinson *(Mrs. Cohn)*, Jill Gervon, Adrienne Trazillo, Charles Polizzi *(Cohn Children)*, Paul E. Burns *(Mr. Smith)*, Harry Hayden *(Mr. Samuels)*, Forbes Murray *(Rich Man)*.

Powell's role here is unusual. Instead of the suave sophisticated type he ordinarily played, he is an out-and-out con man. Powell returns from WW I and finds that his ideals won't make him a dime and he will soon be selling apples on the corner if he doesn't improve his lot. Society girl Williams, in a rare non-aquatic role, falls for Powell but withdraws from him as his nature turns decidedly avaricious. Powell had decided to put scruples in the closet and take in all the money he can. He first shuns his down-and-out Broadway pals by setting them up in a charity operation under the banner of St. Dismas, the good thief crucified with Christ. He then goes into the money-making business with a vengeance, occupying his few off hours with nightclub singer Lansbury (her voice dubbed, she sings "If I Had You" (Ted Shapiro, Jimmy Campbell, Reg Connelly) and "How Am I to Know" (Jack King, Dorothy Parker), the latter song offering the only lyrics Dorothy Parker ever wrote). Powell turns into an utter cad but gets his comeuppance when the stock market collapses in 1929 and his fortune is wiped out. His nature reverts back to good guy as he finds religion with Gleason and pals who have been involved in the St. Dismas charity movement which Powell had earlier tried to turn into a racket. Williams, who sees Powell's transformation to decent guy, returns to him for a happy if improbable ending. Taurog's direction is a bit sloppy and the film lags due to an indecisive story. Powell saves this one, though, through his slick presence. Williams, pretty and statuesque, is bland, and Lansbury is miscast. Solid support comes from Gleason and other venerable character actors McHugh, Ragland, Summerville, and Stone. June's camerawork and Shilkret's score are above average. This film went lame at the box office, mostly because customers wanted Powell as the unforgettable THIN MAN character Nick Charles, not some tin-horn hustler without a conscience. Benny Goodman and His Band contributed "Sweetheart" to the soundtrack.

p, Cliff Reid; d, Norman Taurog; w, Frank Wead, James Hill; ph, Ray June; m, Nathaniel Shilkret; ed, Ferris Webster; art d, Cedric Gibbons, Harry McAfee; set d, Edwin B. Willis; cos, Irene, Herwood Keyes, Valles; spec eff, Warren Newcombe.

Drama **(PR:A MPAA:NR)**

HOODWINK*** (1981, Aus.) 99m C.B./New South Wales c

John Hargreaves *(Martin)*, Judy Davis *(Sarah)*, Dennis Miller *(Ralph)*, Les Foxcroft *(Baldy)*, Wendy Strehlow *(Martin's Sister)*, Wendy Hughes *(Lucy)*, Kim Deacon *(Marian)*, Max Cullen *(Buster)*, Paul Sonkilla *(Lancaster)*.

Well-done crime/prison film based on a true Australian criminal—played by Hargreaves—who faked blindness in order to ease his sentence when sent up for his crimes. The film starts out during the height, going to the downfall of Hargreaves' criminal career, and traces the likable rogue's con-game with the prison officials. Not a masterpiece of the genre by any means, but a surprisingly pleasant entertainment with a top-rate performance by Hargreaves.

p, Pam Oliver, Erroll Sullivan; d, Claud Whatham; w, Ken Quinnell; ph, Dean Semmler; ed, Nick Beauman; prod d, Ross Major; cos, Kate Duffy.

Crime **(PR:C MPAA:NR)**

HOOK, THE** (1962) 98m Perlberg-Seaton/MGM bw

Kirk Douglas *(Sgt. P. J. Briscoe)*, Robert Walker [Jr.] *(Pvt. O. A. Dennison)*, Nick Adams *(Pvt. V. R. Hackett)*, Enrique Magalona *(The Prisoner)*, Nehemiah Persoff *(Capt. Van Ryn)*, Mark Miller *(Lt. D. D. Troy)*, John Bleifer *(Steward)*.

A muddy war drama, THE HOOK is soggy with emotional and pseudo-intellectual diatribes that drag its interest into tedium. Douglas, Walker, and Adams are the lone survivors of a bombing attack in Korea, 1953, just as they have been preparing to destroy equipment and evacuate an area surrounded by enemy troops. They spot a supply ship off the beach and swim to it, picking up a North Korean pilot who has dropped into the water after his plane has been shot down. The supply ship captain, Persoff, orders all four men to stay in one cabin but Douglas, a tough, ruthless, and rootless sergeant, manages to get to the ship-to-shore radio and contact a South Korean major who orders him to kill the wounded North Korean. Adams, a lickspittle who slavishly does anything Douglas orders, mostly because Douglas has suppressed information about an earlier desertion from the Army by Adams, merely shrugs when told they must kill the pilot. Walker, who has pulled the pilot from the water and is basically a decent man, rebels against the order. The debate ensues; Douglas tells Walker that he doesn't like the order any more than Walker does but orders are orders. While the two men struggle with their separate consciences the Armistice is signed. Now killing the enemy pilot is a moot point, but the North Korean, who speaks no English, only knows he is menaced. He frees the bonds holding him to his bunk and escapes to a cargo hold. As Douglas, Walker, and Adams close in on him, trying to tell him that the war is over, the North Korean prepares to defend himself against what he believes is an attack and is accidentally killed. Seaton's direction is too mannered and pensive to sustain continued interest and Douglas looks like he's reaching with material that just isn't dramatic enough for his intensive kind of performance. Walker, as the quiet, conscientious soldier with noble instincts, comes off the best, while Adams is merely repulsive. Walker, the son of the tragic 1940s actor, proves here in his film debut that his talent is more than promising. On the whole, THE HOOK is a mistake, a film that misses every opportunity to develop character and speed up the shallow plot.

p, William Perlberg; d, George Seaton; w, Henry Denker (based on the novel *L'Hamecon* by Vahe Katcha); ph, Joseph Ruttenberg; m, Larry Adler; ed, Robert J. Kern, Jr.; art d, George W. Davis, Hans Peters; set d, Henry Grace, Keogh Gleason; makeup, William Tuttle, David Grayson.

War Drama **(PR:C MPAA:NR)**

HOOK, LINE AND SINKER** (1930) 72m RKO bw

Bert Wheeler *(Wilbur Boswell)*, Robert Woolsey *(Addington Ganzy)*, Dorothy Lee *(Mary Marsh)*, Jobyna Howland *(Mrs. March)*, Ralf Harolde *(John Blackwell)*, Natalie Moorhead *(Duchess Bessie Venessie)*, George F. Marion, Sr. *(Bell Boy)*, Hugh Herbert *(House Detective)*, William B. Davidson, Stanley Fields.

The comedy team of Wheeler and Woolsey star as a pair of bumbling insurance investigators who help young Miss Lee restore a run-down hotel she has inherited. Lee falls in love with Wheeler against her mother's (Howland) wishes (Mom wants her to marry lawyer Harolde), but when Howland herself falls for Woolsey, she is helpless to protest. While the romantic angle works itself out, two rival bands of gangsters show up at the hotel to grab the contents of the safe, and shoot it out in the lobby, practically destroying the place. As it turns out, lawyer Harolde is the mastermind behind the villainous plot, and Woolsey and Wheeler marry Mother and Daughter at the fade-out.

p, Myles Connolly; d, Edward Cline; w, Tim Whelan, Ralph Spence (based on a story by Whelan); ph, Nick Musaraca; ed, Archie Marshek.

Comedy **(PR:A MPAA:NR)**

HOOK, LINE AND SINKER* (1969) 91m COL c

Jerry Lewis *(Peter Ingersoll)*, Peter Lawford *(Scott Carter)*, Anne Francis *(Nancy Ingersoll)*, Pedro Gonzalez Gonzalez *(Perfecto)*, Jimmy Miller *(Jimmy)*, Jennifer Edwards *(Jennifer)*, Eleanor Audley *(Mrs. Durham)*, Henry Corden *(Kenyon Hammercher)*, Sylvia Lewis *(Karlotta Hammercher)*, Phillip Pine *(Head Surgeon)*, Felipe Turich *(Foreign Mortician)*, Kathleen Freeman *(Baby Sitter)*.

Stupid Lewis comedy has the obnoxious comedian told by his family doctor Lawford that he has only a few months left to live due to a severe heart ailment. Lewis' wife Francis takes pity on her husband and tells him to take all his credit cards and to indulge himself in his favorite pastime, fishing, while traveling around the world. Lewis takes his wife's advice and charges over $100,000 on his plastic before Lawford tracks him down in Lisbon and informs him that the electrocardiogram was wrong, he is as healthy as a horse. With financial ruin staring him in the face, Lewis is easily persuaded by Lawford to stage his own "death"—which would allow his wife to collect on his $150,000 life insurance policy—and then lay low for seven years until the statute of limitations runs out so he can return to his family. The whole thing, however, is a plot cooked up by Francis and Lawford to eliminate Lewis and run off together with the dough. Aside from a few amusing Lewis bits at the beginning, the film tries to be a comedy version of a James M. Cain novel, but turns out to be about as funny as a heart attack.

p, Jerry Lewis; d, George Marshall; w, Rod Amateau (based on a story by Amateau, David Davis); ph, W. Wallace Kelley (Technicolor); m, Dick Stabile; ed, Russell Wiles; art d, John Beckman; set d, Frank Tuttle.

Comedy **(PR:A MPAA:G)**

HOOKED GENERATION, THE zero (1969) 92m AA c

Jeremy Slate *(Daisey)*, Steve Alaimo *(Mark)*, John Davis Chandler *(Acid)*, Willie Pastrano *(Dum Dum)*, Cece Stone *(Kelly)*, Socrates Ballis, Walter Philbin, Milton Smith, Lee Warren, William Kerwin, Dete Parson, Stuart Merrill, Marilyn Nordman, Curtis Perdue, Burt Huttinger, Michael De Beausset, Gay Perkins, Terry Smith, Clinton Nye, Emil Deaton, The Bangles.

Wretched drug movie starring Slate as the leader of a gang of pushers. The film opens on the crooks meeting a boat from Cuba carrying heroin for sale in America. The gang gets the Cubans high on pot, kills them, burns their boat, and steals the dope. They spot a Coast Guard cutter in the distance and toss the heroin overboard in water-tight containers, planning to retrieve it later. Unfortunately, innocent young couple Alaimo and Stone, who are out on a moonlight cruise, spot them and inform the Coast Guard. The gang kills the Coast Guard investigators and takes the big-mouthed couple hostage to their hideout in a Seminole Indian camp, where Chandler rapes and kills a native girl. Soon after, he is sent into town to get supplies, but is killed in a shoot-out with police. Now the FBI gets involved and chases the gang into the Everglades where Pastrano is bitten by a water moccasin and dies. Slate is about to make good his escape when Alaimo plunges a hypodermic needle into his neck, killing him. Goreful.

p&d, William Grefe; w, Quinn Morrison, Ray Preston, Grefe; ph, Gregory Sandor (Eastmancolor); m, Chris Martell; ed, Julio C. Chavez; set d, William P. Kelley.

Crime Drama **(PR:O MPAA:R)**

HOOPER* (1978) 99m WB c

Burt Reynolds *(Sonny Hooper)*, Jan-Michael Vincent *(Ski)*, Sally Field *(Gwen)*, Brian Keith *(Jocko)*, John Marley *(Max Berns)*, Robert Klein *(Roger Deal)*, James Best *(Cully)*, Adam West *(Adam)*, Alfie Wise *(Tony)*, Terry Bradshaw *(Sherman)*, Norm Grabowski *(Hammerhead)*, George Furth *(Bidwell)*, Jim Burk *(Jimbo)*, Donald "Red" Barry *(Sheriff)*, Princess O'Mahoney *(Wanda)*, Robert Tessier *(Amtrac)*, Richard Tyler *(Doctor)*, Tara Buckman *(Debbie)*, Hal Floyd *(Cliff)*.

One of the least offensive Needham and Reynolds efforts, but still lousy. This one is supposed to be a tribute to the unheralded group of movie-making employees known as stunt men and it should have been a better film, considering that both director Needham and Reynolds were once stunt men themselves. As is, it's just another mindless exercise in unexciting, unmotivated action sequences punctuated by moments of stupid, redneck, good-ol'-boy humor. Reynolds is an aging king-of-the-stuntmen type whose battle-scarred body is convincing him to retire. Enter young, up-and-coming stuntman Vincent who challenges the "old man" to perform the most difficult and dangerous stunt in his career for a sum of $50,000. The film loses from both angles, with the action scenes lackluster and repetitive and the dramatic scenes maudlin and trite. Needham spent almost $35 million to make this mindless roll-'em and audiences went to see it in droves, paving the way for the even-worse CANNONBALL RUN movies.

p, Hank Moonjean; d, Hal Needham; w, Thomas Rickman, Bill Kerby (based on a story by Walt Green, Walter S. Herndon); ph, Bobby Byrne (Metrocolor); m, Bill Justis; ed, Donn Cambern; set d, Ira Bates; cos, Norman Salling; spec eff, Cliff Wegner, Cliff Wegner Jr.; m/l, "Hooper," Bent Myggen; stunts, Bobby Bass.

Comedy/Action **Cas.** **(PR:A MPAA:PG)**

HOOPLA** (1933) 85m FOX bw

Clara Bow *(Lou)*, Preston Foster *(Nifty)*, Richard Cromwell *(Chris)*, Herbert Mundin *(Hap)*, James Gleason *(Jerry)*, Minna Gombell *(Carrie)*, Florence Roberts *(Ma Benson)*, Roger Imhof *(Col. Gowdy)*.

Another Clara Bow talkie where she seduces a naive 18-year-old and turns him into a man. This time the lucky victim is played by Cromwell and the action is set in a traveling carnival. Climax has the action taking place at the 1933 Chicago World's Fair, which may interest some.

d, Frank Lloyd; w, Bradley King, J.M. March (based on the play "The Barker" by Kenyon Nicholson); ph, Ernest Palmer; m, Louis De Francesco.

Romance **(PR:C MPAA:NR)**

HOORAY FOR LOVE** (1935) 75m RKO bw

Ann Sothern *(Pat)*, Gene Raymond *(Doug)*, Bill Robinson *(Bill)*, Thurston Hall *(Commodore)*, Pert Kelton *(Trixie)*, Georgia Caine *(Duchess)*, Lionel Stander *(Chowsky)*, Etienne Girardot *(Judge)*, Harry Kernell *(Regan)*, Sam Hardy *(Ganz)*, Eddie Kane *(Grady)*, Maria Gambarelli, "Fats" Waller, Jeni LeGon.

Sub-par musical stars Raymond as the never-say-die show producer whose string of bad luck ends with his bankruptcy and a short hitch in the hoosegow. Sothern plays Raymond's faithful singing girlfriend who convinces her starstruck father to marry an ugly old but wealthy woman and bail out the show (and Raymond) in time to turn it into a smash. Lame premise and lackluster musical numbers are almost rescued by Bill "Bojangles" Robinson and "Fats" Waller. Songs: "Hooray for Love," "I'm in Love All Over Again," "I'm Living in a Great Big Way," "You're an Angel," "Palsie Walsie," "Got a Snap in My Fingers" (Dorothy Fields, Jimmy McHugh).

p, Felix Young; d, Walter Lang; w, Lawrence Hazard, Ray Harris (based on a story by Marc Lachmann); ph, Lucien Andriot; ed, George Crone; md, Alberto Colombo; ch, Sammy Lee.

Musical **(PR:A MPAA:NR)**

HOOSIER HOLIDAY** (1943) 72m REP bw

George D. Hay *(Old Judge)*, Dale Evans *(Dale Fairchild)*, Idabel Randolph *(Abigail Fairchild)*, George Byron *(Jim Baker)*, Emma Dunn *(Molly Baker)*, Thurston Hall *(Henry P. Fairchild)*, "Nicodemus" *(Aloysius Lincoln)*, Ferris Taylor *(Gov. Manning)*, Georgia Davis *(Grace Manning)*, "Sleepy" Williams and His Three Shades of Rhythm, The Hoosier Hot Shots, The Music Maids, George "Shug" Fisher, Lillian Randolph.

Farm hokum stars the country novelty band known as The Hoosier Hotshots who play the Baker Boys, a local singing group adored by the community but abhorred by small-town potentate Hall. Normally this wouldn't be a problem for the boys, but they want to enlist in the Air Corps and head of the draft board is Hall, who refuses the boys enlistment out of spite. Enter Hall's five daughters who have just returned from finishing school. The Baker boys decide to pair up with them and make it appear that a five-way marriage is imminent, so that the old coot will ship them off to war pronto. The plan backfires when Hall has a sudden (and ridiculous) change of heart and decides that his daughters should marry the Baker boys after all. Songs include: "Hoosier Holiday" and "Granddaddy Of Boogie Woogie" (Johnny Marvin, Charles Henderson).

p, Armand Schaefer; d, Frank McDonald; w, Dorell & Stuart McGowen (based on an idea by Edward James); ph, Reggie Lanning; ed, Ralph Dixon; md, Morton Scott; art d, Russell Kimball; ch, Josephine Earle.

Musical **(PR:A MPAA:NR)**

HOOSIER SCHOOLBOY** (1937) 62m MON bw

Mickey Rooney *(Shockey)*, Anne Nagel *(Mary Evans)*, Frank Shields *(Jack Matthew)*, Edward Pawley *(Captain)*, William Gould *(John Matthew Sr.)*.

Midwestern melodrama stars Rooney as the boy from the other side of the tracks whose only family is his shell-shocked WWI vet father AKA the town drunkard. Rooney gets into dozens of fights over his old man with the other kids (and scornful teachers who treat him like trash) until a new schoolteacher (Nagel) comes to town and takes an interest in the boy. Soon the father reforms and gets a job driving a milk truck, giving some hope for the future. But then tragedy strikes when Rooney's father is killed by farmers as he tries to break the picket line during a strike. All ends well when the incident spurs the end of the strike and Nagel adopts Rooney. Sappy.

p, Ken Goldsmith; d, William Nigh; w, Robert Lee Johnson (based on the novel by Edward Eggleston); ph, Paul Ivano.

Drama **Cas.** **(PR:A MPAA:NR)**

HOOSIER SCHOOLMASTER** (1935) 71m MON bw

Norman Foster *(Ralph)*, Charlotte Henry *(Hannah)*, Dorothy Libaire *(Martha)*, Sarah Padden *(Sarah)*, Otis Harlan *(Hawkins)*, Russell Simpson *(Doc Small)*, William V. Mong *(Jake)*, Fred Kohler, Jr. *(Bud)*, Wallace Reid Jr. *(Hank)*, George Hayes, Joe E. Bernard, Tommy Bupp.

Post-Civil War drama starring Foster as an ex-Union soldier who travels to a small town in Indiana to settle down as the schoolmaster. Trouble arises when he learns of the crooked town council's plans to juggle federal land grants illegally to benefit their own coffers. Romantic trouble also looms when Foster discovers that the girl he loves, Henry, is also the gal of the school bully whom he has tried to befriend. Climax sees an attempt by the council to frame Foster when they learn he has blown the whistle on their scheme. Do they? Does grass grow on the moon?

p, Trem Carr; d, Lewis D. Collins; w, Charles Logue (based on the novel by Edward Eggleston); ph, Harry Neuman; ed, Carl Pierson.

Drama **(PR:A MPAA:NR)**

HOOTENANNY HOOT** (1963) 91m MGM bw

Peter Breck *(Ted Grover)*, Ruta Lee *(A.G. Bannister)*, Joby Baker *(Steve Laughlin)*, Pam Austin *(Billy-Jo Henley)*, Bobo Lewis *(Claudia Hoffer)*, Loren Gilbert *(Howard Stauton)*, Nick Novarro *(Jed Morse)*, Vikki Dougan *(Vikki)*, The Brothers Four, Sheb Wooley, Johnny Cash, The Gateway Trio, Judy Henske, George Hamilton IV, Joe and Eddie, Cathie Taylor, Chris Crosby *(Guest Stars)*.

1950s horror and exploitation star Breck plays a down-on-his-luck (personally as well as professionally) TV producer who travels the country in search of a new idea. He stumbles across a new "folk" craze in the midwest that will be bigger than rock 'n' roll! He turns the weekly college "hootenanny" into a phenomenally successful TV show and solves all of his problems, including those with his wife, Lee. A silly movie with decent musical appearances from the likes of Johnny Cash and The Brothers Four.

p, Sam Katzman; d, Gene Nelson; w, James B. Gordon; ph, Ellis W. Carter; ed, Al Clark; md, Fred Karger; art d, George W. Davis; set d, Henry Grace, Jerry Wunderlich; m/l, "Hootenanny Hoot," Sheb Wooley, Karger; ch, Hal Belfer.

Musical **(PR:A MPAA:NR)**

HOOTS MON!*½** (1939, Brit.) 77m WB-FN bw

Max Miller *(Harry Hawkins)*, Florence Desmond *(Jenny McTavish)*, Hal Walters *(Chips)*, Davina Craig *(Annie)*, Garry Marsh *(Charlie Thompson)*, Edmund Willard *(Sandy McBride)*, Gordon McLeod *(McDonald)*, Mark Daly *(Campbell)*, Robert Gall.

Miller is England's funniest comic and Desmond is "Scotland's Bluebelle," a top male impersonator. When she dares him to try his material on Scottish audiences, Miller accepts, only to die a wretched on-stage death. His manager tries sending Miller to a smaller club to fix up the material but the audience is even more hostile there. Miller winds up in the hospital, well taken care of by Desmond disguised as a nurse. The story serves as nothing more than a simple line on which to hang the talents of its stars, and the pair's nuttiness in this slight comedy works in an off-beat manner.

p, Sam Sax; d, Roy William Neill; w, Neill, Jack Henley, John Dighton; ph, Basil Emmott.

Comedy **(PR:A MPAA:NR)**

HOPALONG CASSIDY*** (1935) 60m PAR bw
(AKA: HOPALONG CASSIDY ENTERS)

William Boyd *(Bill Cassidy)*, James Ellison *(Johnny Nelson)*, Paula Stone *(Mary Meeker)*, Robert Warwick *(Jim Meeker)*, Charles Middleton *(Buck Peters)*, Frank McGlynn, Jr. *(Red Conners)*, Kenneth Thomson *(Pecos Jack Anthony)*, George Hayes *(Uncle Ben)*, James Mason *(Tom Shaw)*, Frank Campeau *(Frisco)*, Ted Adams *(Hall)*, Willie Fung *(Salem the Cook)*, Franklin Farnum *(Doc Riley)*, John Merton *(Party Guest)*, Wally West.

The first of the HOPALONG CASSIDY oaters that became one of the longest-running series of westerns in the history of movies and made an international star of the nearly washed-up silent actor William Boyd. Boyd, youngster Ellison, and McGlynn, Jr., try to prevent a range war between two cattlemen which is instigated by an evil ranch foreman who plays both sides against the middle and helps an outlaw gang snatch the cattle. The plot succeeds because each side blames the other for the missing stock. Eventually, with Boyd's help, both ranchers wise up and they combine their efforts, sending a small army of cowboys into the gang's mountain hideout where justice eventually triumphs. During the course of the movie, Hayes' old-timer character is killed, but he was brought back to life in subsequent entries of the series. Independent producer Sherman bought the rights to Clarence E. Mulford's series of "Bar 20" western novels which featured a grizzled, tough-talking, hard-drinking, slightly crippled old cowboy named Hopalong Cassidy. When producer Sherman asked Boyd to play the ranch foreman, he refused but agreed to play Cassidy if the character was rewritten to be a clean-living, noble hero (the limp was also abandoned after the first few movies, leaving the name "Hopalong" something of a mystery years later). The result was a seemingly unending string of westerns. After 50 films, Sherman sold out his ownership to Boyd, who saw the series to its eventual conclusion and its 1950s TV craze. (See HOPALONG CASSIDY series, Index.)

p, Harry Sherman; d, Howard Bretherton; w, Doris Schroeder, Harrison Jacob (based on a story by Clarence E. Mulford); ph, Archie Stout; ed, Edward Schroeder; m/l, Sam H. Stept, Dave Franklin.

Western **(PR:A MPAA:NR)**

HOPALONG CASSIDY RETURNS*½** (1936) 71m PAR bw

William Boyd *(Hopalong Cassidy)*, George Hayes *(Windy Halliday)*, Gail Sheridan *(Mary Saunders)*, Evelyn Brent *(Lili Marsh)*, Stephen Morris [Morris Ankrum] *(Blackie)*, William Janney *(Buddy Cassidy)*, Irving Bacon *(Peg Leg Holden)*, Grant Richards *(Bob Claiborne)*, John Beck *(Robert Saunders)*, Ernie Adams *(Benson)*, Al St. John *(Luke)*, Joe Rickson *(Buck)*, Ray Whitley *(Davis)*, Claude Smith *(Dugan)*.

The seventh film in the HOPALONG CASSIDY series, the first to be directed by Watt, and one of the most brutal. Boyd falls for dance hall proprietess Brent, who is in reality the leader of a vicious gang of cutthroats. The film opens sadistically as we see an invalid, who is bound and gagged, thrown off a cliff to his death. The climax is a three-way shoot-out in which Brent's henchman Morris guns her down. Then he is shot twice by Boyd at point-blank range. (See HOPALONG CASSIDY series, Index.)

p, Harry Sherman; d, Nat Watt; w, Harrison Jacobs (based on a story by Clarence E. Mulford); ph, Archie Stout; ed, Robert Warwick.

Western **(PR:C MPAA:NR)**

HOPALONG RIDES AGAIN** (1937) 65m PAR bw

William Boyd *(Hopalong Cassidy)*, George Hayes *(Windy Halliday)*, Russell Hayden *(Lucky Jenkins)*, William Duncan *(Buck Peters)*, Lois Wilde *(Laura Peters)*, Billy King *(Artie Peters)*, Nora Lane *(Nora Blake)*, Harry Worth *(Prof. Hepburn)*, John Rutherford *(Blackie)*, Ernie Adams *(Keno)*, Frank Ellis *(Rider)*, Artie Ortego, Ben Corbett, John Beach, Blackjack Ward.

Decent Boyd vehicle sees the foreman of the Bar 20 ranch heading up a cattle drive through some bad territory accompanied by camp cook Hayes, youngster King, and sidekick Hayden. On the trail they meet an eccentric professor who is searching for the missing link, but is in reality a clever cattle rustler who uses dynamite to scatter the herds and siphon off a good selection of steers in the ensuing confusion. Luckily, Boyd and the Bar 20 boys catch on fast and bring the crook to justice. (See HOPALONG CASSIDY series, Index.)

p, Harry Sherman; d, Les Selander; w, Norman Houston (based on a story by Clarence E. Mulford); ph, Russell Harlan; ed, Robert Warwick.

Western **(PR:A MPAA:NR)**

HOPE OF HIS SIDE** (1935, Brit.) 69m B & D/UA bw
(AKA: WHERE'S GEORGE?)

Sydney Howard *(Alf Scodger)*, Mabel Constanduros *(Mrs. Scodger)*, Leslie Sarony *(Willy Yates)*, Frank Pettingell *(Harry Swan)*, Sam Livesey *(Sir Richard Lancaster)*, Wally Patch *(Ted Sloane)*.

Far-fetched British programmer features Howard as a henpecked blacksmith. From this humble beginning he manages to rise up to become a soccer star. As they say, "Only in the movies . . ."

p, Herbert Wilcox; d, Jack Raymond; w, R. P. Weston, Bert Lee, Jack Marks, John Paddy Carstairs.

Comedy **(PR:A MPAA:NR)**

HOPELESS ONES, THE (SEE: ROUND UP, THE, 1969, Hung.)

HOPPITY GOES TO TOWN (SEE: MR. BUG GOES TO TOWN, 1941)

HOPPY SERVES A WRIT** (1943) 67m UA bw

William Boyd *(Hopalong Cassidy)*, Andy Clyde *(California Carlson)*, Jay Kirby *(Johnny Travers)*, Victor Jory *(Tom Jordan)*, George Reeves *(Steve Jordan)*, Jan Christy *(Jean Hollister)*, Hal Taliaferro *(Greg Jordan)*, Forbes Murray *(Ben Hollister)*, Bob Mitchum *(Rigney)*, Byron Foulger *(Storekeeper Danvers)*, Earle Hodgins *(Jim Belnap, Clerk)*, Roy Barcroft *(Tod Colby)*, Ben Corbett *(Card Player)*.

Boyd plays a Texas sheriff who must figure out a way to lure villain Jory and his outlaw gang (among whose members is a young Robert Mitchum) out of Oklahoma and back to the Lone Star state so he can bring him to justice. This was the last of the HOPALONG CASSIDY oaters to be based on an original story by Clarence Mulford (the author of the books the series was based on). (See HOPALONG CASSIDY series, Index.)

p, Harry Sherman; d, George Archainbaud; w, Gerald Geraghty (based on characters created by Clarence E. Mulford); ph, Russell Harlan; ed, Sherman A. Rose; md, Irwin Talbot; art d, Ralph Berger.

Western **Cas.** **(PR:A MPAA:NR)**

HOPPY'S HOLIDAY*½ (1947) 70m UA bw

William Boyd *(Hopalong Cassidy)*, Andy Clyde *(California Carlson)*, Rand Brooks *(Lucky Jenkins)*, Andrew Tombes *(Mayor Patton)*, Leonard Penn *(Danning)*, Jeff Corey *(Jed)*, Mary Ware *(Gloria)*, Donald Kirke *(Sheriff)*, Hollis Bane *(Ace)*, Gil Patric *(Jay)*, Frank Henry *(Bart)*.

After producer Harry Sherman sold his share of the series to Boyd in 1944, the quality of the HOPALONG CASSIDY films suffered somewhat. This one sees Boyd and his pals, Clyde and Brooks, on vacation. They stumble across a new kind of trouble, bank robbers who drive automobiles, but the Bar 20 boys rise to this challenge and defeat the modern-day crooks using the trusty horses and six-guns of the Old West. (See HOPALONG CASSIDY series, Index.)

p, Lewis J. Rachmil; d, George Archainbaud; w, J. Benton Cheney, Bennett Cohen, Ande Lamb (based on a story by Ellen Corby, Cecile Kramer); ph, Mack Stengler; m, David Chudnow; ed, Fred W. Berger; art d, Harvey T. Gillett.

Western **(PR:A MPAA:NR)**

HOPSCOTCH*½** (1980) 104m AE c

Walter Matthau *(Miles Kendig)*, Glenda Jackson *(Isobel von Schmidt)*, Sam Waterston *(Cutter)*, Ned Beatty *(Myerson)*, Herbert Lom *(Mikhail Yaskov)*, David Matthau *(Ross)*, George Baker *(Westlake)*, Ivor Roberts *(Ludlum)*, Lucy Saroyan *(Carla)*, Severn Darden *(Maddox)*, George Pravda *(Saint Breheret)*, Jacquelyn Hyde *(Realtor)*, Mike Gwilym *(Alfie)*, Allan Cuthbertson *(Chartermain)*, Terry Beaver *(Tobin)*, Ray Charleson *(Clausen)*, Ann Haney *(Mrs. Myerson)*, Christopher Driscoll *(Policeman No. 1)*, Michael Cronin *(Policeman No. 2)*, Roy Sampson *(Police Sergeant)*, Douglas Dirkson *(Follett)*, Shan Wilson *(Spy in Octoberfest)*, Randy Patrick *(Mechanic)*, Joe Dorsey *(Security Guard)*, Candice Howard *(Maddox's Receptionist)*, Susan McShayne *(Cocktail Waitress)*, Yolanda King *(Coffee Shop Manager)*, Antony Carrick *(Salesman in Electric Shop)*, Osman Ragheb *(CIA Telephone Technician)*, Roland Frohlich *(Border Guard)*, Jeremy Young *(Immigration Officer)*, Sally Nesbitt *(Telephone Operator)*, Susan Engels *(Westlake's Receptionist)*, Joanna McCallum *(Bookshop Cashier)*, Laura Whyte *(Myerson's Secretary)*, Larry Larson *(FBI Technician)*, Sean Worthy *(FBI Man)*, Danny Covington *(Bellman)*, Richard Moore *(Seaplane Pilot)*, Philip Voss *(Helicopter Pilot)*, Jesse Wayne *(Stunt Coordinator)*, Roger Creed, Richard Geary *(Stuntmen)*, Debra Hook *(Band Singer)*, The Silversmith Band *(Disco Group)*.

A well-crafted classic comedy about a top drawer CIA agent, Matthau, who is demoted to managing the office files because he refuses to succumb to his boss Beatty's bureaucratic whims and play by the books. He instead shreds his personnel file and leaves without any further word. He takes off to Europe and meets Lom, the top Russian agent and Matthau's old friend. When Lom offhandedly suggests that Matthau write his memoirs, Matthau takes him seriously. He flies off to Salzburg and meets Jackson, a love from his past and a former agent, who now lives comfortably off her dead husband's wealth. The unlikely couple—the perpetually rumpled, beer-drinking Matthau and the prim wine-sipping Jackson—then slip off to the bedroom. The following morning, Matthau sits down at his typewriter and begins to bang out Chapter One of his memoirs, blasting the secrets of world espionage out of the water. He mails the first chapter to agencies all over the world—Washington, Moscow, Paris, and Berlin—enraging and embarrassing everyone involved. In Washington, the flustered Beatty becomes determined to capture Matthau before the Russians catch up to him and force him to reveal more secrets. Beatty enlists Waterston, a young agent trained by Matthau, who has a certain fondness for the old codger. Matthau, however, manages to keep one step ahead of his pursuers, making the top Soviet and U.S. agents look like tenderfoots. He delivers additional chapters while hopping from Salzburg to London to Washington and finally to Georgia, all the time outwitting Beatty, Waterston, and Lom. Meantime, Jackson is being shadowed by Dirkson, a geeky agent who is frightened off by Jackson's Doberman watchdog. Using one of his many aliases, Matthau rents Beatty's summer cottage and finishes the final chapter of his memoirs. The CIA finally traces a Matthau phone call to Beatty's house, infuriating the foolish-looking CIA head even further. Matthau again eludes his pursuers, but not before the Georgia FBI practically destroys Beatty's house. The chase continues to London, where Matthau has struck a deal with a scrupulous publisher. Matthau leaves enough clues to make the chase a little more fun. Beatty, Waterston, and Lom, thinking that they've finally outsmarted Matthau, take a helicopter to a small airfield. Matthau, however, is preparing to put the icing on the cake. He gets into a classic World War I biplane and leads his pursuers in a game of aerial cat-and-mouse. Matthau's plane then suddenly bursts into flames over the sea. While Waterston and Lom lament the loss of their friend, Matthau emerges from a nearby woodshed with a radio control box. He has outsmarted them one final time. He and Jackson then take off for a two-week trip on the French Riviera. Matthau's book is published—aptly named *Hopscotch*—and the pair head off together for a quiet, secluded future, after successfully shaking up world espionage and having some fun in the process. A thoroughly entertaining picture, HOPSCOTCH was originally written as a serious spy novel. The casting of Matthau, however, makes that seem practically unimaginable since the most loveable aspect of HOPSCOTCH is Matthau's playfulness—fighting the bureaucracy by turning the CIA on its head. Contributing further to the odd mix of comedy and espionage is Matthau's love of classical music and opera. Throughout the film he is playing records and tapes of his favorites. In one memorable scene he is singing along to an excerpt of Giacchino Antonio Rossini's "Barber of Seville" ("Largo Al Faciotum" sung by Tito Gobbi) while crossing into Switzerland, utterly confusing the border guard. Other musical selections include: "Non Pul Andrai" (sung by Hermann Prey), "Un Bel Di Vedramo" (from "Madame Butterfly" by Giacomo Puccini), and "Once A Night" (Jackie English, Beverly Bremers). As surprising as it seems, Matthau and Jackson have built an interesting chemistry which dates to their previous film HOUSE CALLS (1978). HOPSCOTCH is not only superior to that film, but also to the majority of comedies in recent memory. If it's a classically-styled throwback to Hollywood espionage films of the 1940s and 1950s that you desire, HOPSCOTCH is it.

p, Edie Landau, Ely Landau; d, Ronald Neame; w, Brian Garfield, Bryan Forbes (based on Garfield's novel); ph, Arthur Ibbetson (Panavision, Movielab Color); m, Ian Fraser, Wolfgang Amadeus Mozart; ed, Carl Kress; prod d, William Creber.

Comedy/Espionage **Cas.** **(PR:C MPAA:R)**

HORIZONS WEST½** (1952) 81m UNIV c

Robert Ryan *(Dan Hammond)*, Julia Adams *(Lorna Hardin)*, Rock Hudson *(Neal Hammond)*, John McIntire *(Ira Hammond)*, Judith Braun *(Sally)*, Raymond Burr *(Cord Hardin)*, James Arness *(Tiny)*, Frances Bavier *(Martha Hammond)*, Dennis Weaver *(Dandy Taylor)*, Tom Powers *(Frank Tarleton)*, Rodolfo Acosta *(General Escobar)*, John Hubbard *(Sam Hunter)*, Douglas Fowley *(Tompkins)*, Walter Reed *(Layton)*, Raymond Greenleaf *(Eli Dodson)*, Tom Monroe *(Jim Clawson)*, Lillian Molieri *(Teresa)*, Dan White *(Dennis)*, Edward Coch, Jr. *(Juan)*, Paulette Turner *(Celeste)*, John Harmon *(Deputy Sheriff Johnson)*, Robert Bice *(Righteous Citizen)*, Dan Poore *(Henchman)*, Frank Chase *(Borden)*, Tom Riste *(Al)*, Mae Clarke *(Mrs. Tarleton)*, Peter Mamakos *(Lt. Salazar)*, Alberto Morin *(M. Auriel)*, Tyler McVey *(Player)*, Edwin Parker *(Northerner)*, Fred Coby *(Irate Citizen)*, Philo McCullough *(Rancher)*, Monte Montague *(Doctor)*, Forbes Murray *(Another Player)*, Buddy Roosevelt *(Bit)*.

Badly scripted Boetticher western redeemed by a great performance from Ryan. Plot has Ryan and Hudson as half-brothers who go their separate ways after the Civil War. Hudson decides to settle down and become a rancher, but Ryan, who has grown accustomed to action and violence, launches a campaign to build a personal empire in the West. Ryan murders Burr, another unscrupulous heavy who tries to cross him, and Burr's widow, Adams, falls for Ryan despite the fact that he killed her husband. Eventually the brothers' paths cross and the inevitable showdown occurs. The film is well directed by Boetticher, but Stevens' implausible script (much weaker than the screenplays Burt Kennedy would later pen for the director), combined with a haphazard performance from a young Hudson, sap the film's vitality.

p, Albert J. Cohen; d, Budd Boetticher; w, Louis Stevens; ph, Charles P. Boyle (Technicolor); ed, Ted J. Kent; md, Joseph Gershenson; art d, Bernard Herzbrun, Robert Clatworthy; set d, Russell A. Gausman, Joe Kish.

Western **(PR:A MPAA:NR)**

HORIZONTAL LIEUTENANT, THE** (1962) 90m MGM c

Jim Hutton *(2nd Lt. Merle Wye)*, Paula Prentiss *(Lt. Molly Blue)*, Jack Carter *(Lt. William Monck)*, Jim Backus *(Cmdr. Jerry Hammerslag)*, Charles McGraw *(Col. Charles Korotny)*, Miyoshi Umeki *(Akiko)*, Yoshido Yoda *(Sgt. Roy Tada)*, Marty Ingels *(Yeoman Buckles)*, Lloyd Kino *(Sgt. Jess Yomuru)*, Yuki Shimoda *(Kobayashi)*, Linda Wong *(Michido)*, Argentina Brunetti.

The fifth teaming of romantic comedy team Hutton and Prentiss comes up a misfire. Hutton is an accident-prone lieutenant given the task of flushing out a harmless Japanese soldier who is hiding in the brush and stealing supplies on a recaptured island in 1944. While Hutton dashes around the island trying to spring traps on the Japanese he also tries to find time to romance Army nurse Prentiss. He eventually traces the wily Japanese soldier to his hiding place, but is knocked unconscious in the scuffle, forcing Prentiss to make the capture. In the end, Hutton gets all the credit for the job, and Prentiss. The tall, gangling Prentiss, married to actor-director Richard Benjamin (who has displayed miserable talents in both categories) has a voice delivery similar to a morning gargle; if she'd only spit it out once in a while, we'd know what she was talking about.

p, Joe Pasternak; d, Richard Thorpe; w, George Wells (based on the novel *The Bottletop Affair* by Gordon Cotler); ph, Robert Broner (CinemaScope, Technicolor); m, George Stoll; ed, Richard Farrell; art d, George W. Davis; set d, Henry Grace, Otto Siegel; m/l, "The Horizontal Lieutenant," Stella Unger, Stoll, "How About You?" Burton Lane, Ralph Freed.

Romance/Comedy **(PR:A MPAA:NR)**

HORLA, THE (SEE: DIARY OF A MADMAN, 1967)

HORN BLOWS AT MIDNIGHT, THE*** (1945) 78m WB bw

Jack Benny *(Athanael)*, Alexis Smith *(Elizabeth)*, Dolores Moran *(Fran)*, Allyn Joslyn *(Osidro)*, Reginald Gardiner *(Archie Dexter)*, Guy Kibbee *(The Chief)*, John Alexander *(Doremus)*, Franklin Pangborn *(Sloan)*, Margaret Dumont *(Miss Rodholder)*, Bobby Blake *(Junior)*, Ethel Griffies *(Lady Stover)*, Paul Harvey *(Thompson)*, Truman Bradley *(Radio Announcer)*, Mike Mazurki *(Humphrey Rafferty)*, John Brown *(Lew)*, Murray Alper *(Tony)*, Pat O'Moore *(Clerk)*, Isobel Elsom,

James Burke, Harry Morgan, Monte Blue, Jack J. Ford, Emma Dunn, Harry Rosenthal.

In a delightful if lightweight screwball comedy, Benny is an inept third-chair trumpet player in a band. He falls asleep and dreams that he is an archangel named Athanael, ordered to go to earth and blow the horn at midnight, which will signal the end of this world and bring about Judgment Day, as decreed by heavenly Chief Kibbee who is fed up with the way humans conduct themselves on earth. Smith, another heavenly type, is enamored of the scatterbrained Benny but knows he's a lost cause. Benny arrives on earth and is about to blast it to eternity when he spots a girl about to jump from the top of a skyscraper and, while saving her, he misses tooting at the appointed moment. He gets mixed up with con man Gardiner and his efforts are further spoiled by two fallen angels, Joslyn and Alexander, who do all in their power to prevent the final trumpeting. They even steal Benny's horn to prevent his second attempt at bringing about Armageddon. Through a lot of forced humor and zany slapstick that doesn't work slip some comedic gems, real side splitting laughs, particularly the smash finale where Benny and a bunch of other lunatics dangle precariously from the top of a skyscraper and Benny falls into a giant cup of coffee. (It was a coffee commercial hyping sleep-inducing java that put Benny to sleep on the bandstand in the first place.) An enormous spoon descends and begins to stir Benny around in the huge coffee cup and, just as he is about to spill from this to his doom, he awakens on the bandstand, plays the few notes given him—ineptly—and the film ends. It's frothy piffle with little sense of direction but mirthful all the same, although director Walsh, a Warner Bros. workhorse of action films, is clearly out of his element here.

p, Mark Hellinger; d, Raoul Walsh; w, Sam Hellman, James V. Kern (based on an idea by Aubrey Wisberg); ph, Sid Hickox; m, Franz Waxman; ed, Irene Morra; md, Leo F. Forbstein; art d, Hugh Reticker, Clarence Steensen; spec eff, Lawrence Butler.

Comedy **(PR:AAA MPAA:NR)**

HORNET'S NEST, THE*½ (1955, Brit.) 64m Kenilworth/GFD-RANK bw

Paul Carpenter *(Bob Bartlett)*, June Thorburn *(Pat)*, Marla Landi *(Terry Savarese)*, Charles Farrell *(Posh Peterson)*, Larry Burns *(Alfie)*, Alexander Gauge *(Mr. Arnold)*, Christine Silver *(Becky Crumb)*, Nora Nicholson *(Rachel Crumb)*, Colin Douglas, Wilfred Fletcher, Gaylord Cavallaro, Jan Holden, Christopher Steele, Ronnie Stevens, Anita Sharp Bolster, Max Brimmell, Trevor Reid, Stuart Nichol.

Farrell is a jewel thief who hides some booty on a deserted barge. When he is tossed in the pokey on assault charges, two young models (Landi and Thorburn) buy the barge, which is then nearly sunk in an accident and the jewels end up being taken by Silver and Nicholson, two semi-sweet little old ladies. The older pair helps the younger claim the reward money in this confusing and decidedly weak comedy.

p, Guido Coen; d, Charles Saunders; w, Allan Mackinnon (based on a story by John Roddick); ph, Harry Waxman.

Comedy/Crime **(PR:A MPAA:NR)**

HORNET'S NEST** (1970) 109m UA c

Rock Hudson *(Capt. Turner)*, Sylva Koscina *(Bianca)*, Sergio Fantoni *(Von Hecht)*, Jacques Sernas *(Maj. Taussig)*, Giacomo Rossi Stuart *(Schwalberg)*, Tom Felleghi *(Col. Jannings)*, Andrea Bosic *(Gen. Von Kleger)*, Bondy Esterhazy *(Gen. Dohrmann)*, Gerard Herter *(Capt. Kruger)*, Hardy Stuart *(Gunther)*, Max Turilli *(Col. Weede)*, Raphael Santos *(Lt. with Taussig)*, Viti Caronia *(Lt. at Village)*, Jacques Stany *(Ehrlich)*, Bruno Marco Gobbi *(Hermann)*, Alain Shammas *(First Sentry)*, Amos Davoli *(Second Sentry)*, Jean Valmont *(Scarpi)*, Alessandro Jogan *(Non-Com)*, Giancarlo Prete *(Giulio)*, Mino Doro *(Italian Doctor)*, Wehrner Hasselmann *(Gen. Lewis)*, Rod Dana *(US Colonel)*, John Lemma *(Jumpmaster)*, Rick Peterson *(Pilot)*, Mark Colleano *(Aldo)*, John Fordyce *(Dino)*, Mauro Gravina *(Carlo)*, Daniel Keller *(Tekko)*, Daniel Dempsey *(Giorgio)*, Joseph Cassuto *(Franco)*, Fabrizio Tempio, Maurizio Tempio *(Mario)*, Vincenzo Danaro *(Silvio)*, Luisa Giancinti, Anna Giancinti *(Maria)*, Amedeo Castracane, Ronald Colomaioni, Giancarlo Colobaioni, Valerio Colobaioni, Gaetano Danaro, Luigi Criscuolo, Giuseppe Coppola, Gaetano Colisano *(Gang Members)*.

Distasteful WW II drama starring Hudson as an American commando who parachutes into Italy with his team of men to blow up an important dam. Unfortunately, the Nazis discover the plan and shoot the Americans as they land, leaving Hudson the sole survivor. Wounded and dazed, Hudson is discovered by a gang of Italian youths led by Colleano who have been working for the resistance. The boys take Hudson to a female German doctor, Koscina, and force her to mend his wounds. After his recovery, Hudson decides to recruit the boys as his "squad" and complete his mission. Koscina, who has been held hostage by the gang, tries to stab Hudson with a pair of scissors, but he slaps her to the floor where he then rapes her. The boys agree to help Hudson only if they are allowed to attack a small Italian town that was once their home, but is now held by the Nazis. Hudson agrees and the boys viciously slaughter the unprepared Nazis, aided, inexplicably, by Koscina, whose feelings about Hudson have changed dramatically since her rape. Eventually Hudson makes his way to the dam and destroys it, sparing Nazi commander Fantoni from the wrath of Colleano who wishes to kill him.

p, Stanley S. Canter; d, Phil Karlson; w, S.S. Schweitzer (based on a story by Schweitzer, Stanley Colbert); ph, Gabor Pogani (DeLuxe Color); m, Ennio Morricone; ed, Terry Williams; md, Morricone; art d, Arrigo Equini; set d, Andrea Fantacci; spec eff, Paul Pollard.

War **(PR:O MPAA:GP)**

HOROSCOPE*½ (1950, Yugo.) 87m Bosna/Trans-National bw (HOROSKOP)

Milena Dravic *(Girl)*, Pavle Vujisic *(Stationmaster)*, Dragan Nikolic *(Vidak)*, Mihajlo Janketic *(Boy)*, Josif Tatic *(Buddy)*, Milos Kandic, Dragan Zaric, Mirko Kraljev, Veljko Mandic.

Tasteless tale about a gang of young hoodlums who terrorize the small province of Herzegovina by harassing tourists and townsfolk and young women. They concentrate their efforts on the new girl in town, Dravic, who sells newspapers. The boys bet against each other over who will make love to the girl first, despite the fact that she has absolutely no interest in them. Eventually this competition leads to her rape by the boys, and their subsequent capture by the police.

d, Boro Draskovic; w, Draskovic, Zuko Dzumhur; ph, Ognjen Milicevic; m, Zoran Hristic.

Drama **(PR:O MPAA:NR)**

HORRIBLE DR. HICHCOCK, THE** (1964, Ital.) 76m Panda/Sigma III c (L'ORRIBILE SEGRETO DEL DR. HICHCOCK)

Robert Flemyng *(Dr. Bernard Hichcock)*, Barbara Steele *(Cynthia)*, Teresa Fitzgerald [Maria Teresa Vianello] *(Margaret)*, Harriet White *(Martha)*, Montgomery Glenn *(Dr. Kurt Lowe)*, Neil Robinson, Spencer Williams *(Hospital Assistants)*, Howard Nelson Rubien *(Laboratory Specialist)*, Al Christianson, Evar Simpson, Nat Harley.

Italian gothic horror film starring Flemyng as the title doc, a demented necrophiliac who subjects his very-much-alive bride to sexual "funeral games" involving a strange drug which simulates her death. One day the doc goes too far and accidentally kills his wife. Twelve years later Flemyng marries another woman, Steele, only to find that wifey No. 1 isn't dead at all and had been buried alive. Though she is old and rotting, Flemyng tries to restore his first wife's beauty by stringing Steele up by the heels and draining her blood. Eventually Steele is rescued, the house burned down, and Flemyng and his wife destroyed. Nevertheless, a sequel, THE GHOST, followed.

p, Louis Mann [Luigi Carpentieri, Ermanno Donati]; d, Robert Hampton [Riccardo Freda]; w, Julyan Perry; ph, Donald Green [Raffaele Masciocchi] (Panoramic, Technicolor); m, Roman Vlad; ed, Donna Christie [Ornella Micheli]; art d, Frank Smokecocks [Franco Fumagalli]; set d, Joseph Goodman; cos, Inoa Starly.

Horror **(PR:O MPAA:NR)**

HORRIBLE HOUSE ON THE HILL, THE

(SEE: DEVIL TIMES FIVE, 1974)

HORRIBLE MILL WOMEN, THE

(SEE: MILL OF THE STONE WOMEN, 1963, Fr./Ital.)

HORROR CASTLE** (1965, Ital.) 83m Zodiac c (LA VERGINE DE NORIMBERGA; AKA: TERROR CASTLE; CASTLE OF TERROR; CASTLE OF THE LIVING DEAD; THE VIRGIN OF NUREMBURG)

Rossana Podesta *(Mary)*, Georges Riviere *(Max Hunter)*, Christopher Lee *(Erich)*, Jim Dolen *(Selby)*, Anny Delli Uberti *(Marta)*, Luigi Severini *(Doctor)*, Luciana Milone *(Trude)*, Lucile Saint-Simon, Patrick Walton, Consalvo Dell'Arti, Peter Hardy, Rex Vidor, James Borden, Bredon Brett, Robert Mayor, Carole Windsor.

Haunted castle shocker starring Lee as the horribly scarred chauffeur/caretaker of a mansion on the Rhine. Enter honeymooning couple Riviere (a German ancestor of the owners of the castle) and his American wife Podesta. Soon after their arrival a series of brutal mutilation murders occur and Podesta begins to suspect that her husband and the ugly Lee are responsible. Eventually it is revealed that the murderer is actually Riviere's father who had been tortured and mutilated by the Nazis after he had attempted to assassinate Hitler. Riviere's dad corners Podesta, and is about to kill her when her husband and Lee come to the rescue as the castle and Riviere's father are consumed in flames.

p, Mario Vicario; d, Antonio Margheriti [Anthony Dawson]; w, Margheriti, Gasted Green, Edmond T. Greville (based on the novel *The Virgin of Nuremberg* by Frank Bogart); ph, Riccardo Pallottini (Anamorphic, Eastmancolor); m, Riz Ortolani; ed, Angel Coly; art d, Riccardo Domenici; set d, Albert Griffiths.

Horror **(PR:O MPAA:NR)**

HORROR CHAMBER OF DR. FAUSTUS, THE*½** (1962, Fr./Ital.) 84m Champs-Elysees-Lux/Lopert bw (LES YEUX SANS VISAGE; OCCHI SENZA VOLTO; AKA; EYES WITHOUT A FACE)

Pierre Brasseur *(Prof. Genessier)*, Alida Valli *(Louise)*, Edith Scob *(Christiane)*, Francois Guerin *(Jacques)*, Juliette Mayniel *(Edna Gruber)*, Beatrice Altariba *(Paulette)*, Alexandre Rignault *(Inspector Parot)*, Rene Genin *(Bereaved Father)*, Claude Brasseur, Michel Etcheverry, Yvette Etievant, Lucien Hubert, Marcel Peres.

A haunting horror film in which Brasseur stars as a famed plastic surgeon who becomes obsessed with reconstructing the face of his daughter, Scob, after she is disfigured in an automobile accident in which he was the driver. He sends his loyal female assistant Valli to Paris where she kidnaps young women who resemble his daughter. She brings them to Brasseur's laboratory where he removes their faces in an attempt to graft the flesh to Scob's scarred visage, which is kept hidden behind a wax mask which reveals only her melancholy eyes. (The skin-grafting scenes are spine-tingling, even compared to the high-tech gore effects so prevalent in the '70s and '80s.) While Brasseur feverishly tries again after every failure (leaving Valli to dispose of the bodies), Scob slowly goes mad until she finally stabs Valli in the throat with a scalpel and unleashes her kennel of dogs to attack and kill her father, ripping his face off. Freed from her prison, Scob removes her mask and wanders down the moonlit streets.

p, Jules Borkon; d, Georges Franju; w, Franju, Jean Redon, Claude Sautet, Pierre Boileau, Thomas Narcejac (based on the novel *Les yeux sans visage* by Jean Redon); ph, Eugene Shuftan; m, Maurice Jarre; ed, Gilbert Natot; art d, Auguste Capelier.

Horror **(PR:O MPAA:NR)**

HORROR CREATURES OF THE PREHISTORIC PLANET (SEE: HORROR OF THE BLOOD MONSTERS, 1970, U.S./Phil.)

HORROR EXPRESS*** (1972, Span./Brit.) 90m Granada/Benmar-Scotia c (PANICO EN EL TRANSIBERIANO; AKA: PANIC ON THE TRANS-SIBERIAN EXPRESS)

Christopher Lee *(Prof. Alex Caxton)*, Peter Cushing *(Dr. Wells)*, Telly Savalas *(Capt. Kazan)*, Alberto de Mendoza *(Inspector)*, Silvia Tortosa, Jorge Rigaud.

Lee, an explorer, is transporting (on the Trans-Siberian Express, c. 1906) the frozen body of an ape-man he has discovered in China. On the train the ape-man defrosts and reveals itself to be an alien come to Earth in prehistoric times to claim the planet. The alien is able to assimilate itself into the bodies of any living being and absorb its intellect. Unfortunately, the process ruins the brain of the host bodies, causing their eyes to turn white and making them walking zombies. Soon the alien is flying around possessing most of the passengers (including a small army of Cossacks led by Savalas) in a desperate attempt to gather enough knowledge to build a spacecraft so it can get home. Eventually Lee and rival doctor Cushing team up to defeat the marauding alien. Producer Gordon decided to make the film because he owned the model train used in NICHOLAS AND ALEXANDRA and could use it in this.

p, Bernard Gordon; d, Eugenio Martin; w, Arnaud D'Usseau, Julian Halvey; ph, Alejandro Ulloa (Eastmancolor); spec eff, Pablo Perez.

Horror **Cas.** **(PR:C MPAA:R)**

HORROR HIGH zero (1974) 85m Crown International c (AKA: TWISTED BRAIN)

Pat Cardi *(Vernon Potts)*, Rosie Holotik *(Girl Friend)*, Joyce Hash *(Miss Grinstaf)*, Austin Stoker *(Lt. Bozeman)*.

Bargain basement gore shot on 16mm starring Cardi as a wimpy high school student who creates a chemical which turns him into a monster, enabling him to get his revenge on all the girls who teased him, his parents who hate him, and even the school janitor who made fun of him. Probably a life-long wish fulfillment on the part of the director.

p, James P. Graham; d, Larry Stouffer; w, Jake Fowler.

Horror **(PR:O MPAA:PG)**

HORROR HOSPITAL*½ (1973, Brit.) 91m Noteworthy/Hallmark c (AKA: COMPUTER KILLERS)

Michael Gough, Robin Askwith, Vanessa Shaw, Ellen Pollock, Skip Martin, Dennis Price.

Barely funny horror spoof about young pop singer Askwith, who visits a hospital to relax from his grueling schedule, only to find it is run by mad doctor Gough (who really hams it up here) and staffed by his hideous creations. Eventually he befriends one of the monsters, Martin, a dwarf, and persuades Martin to free him.

p, Richard Gordon; d, Anthony Balch; w, Balch, Alan Watson; ph, David McDonald (Movielab Color).

Comedy/Horror **Cas.** **(PR:O MPAA:PG)**

HORROR HOTEL½** (1960, Brit.) 76m Vulcan/Trans-Lux bw (GB: THE CITY OF THE DEAD)

Patricia Jessel *(Elizabeth Selwyn/Mrs. Newless)*, Betta St. John *(Patricia Russell)*, Christopher Lee *(Prof. Driscoll)*, Dennis Lotis *(Richard Barlow)*, Venetia Stevenson *(Nan Barlow)*, Valentine Dyall *(Jethrow Keane)*, Norman MacOwan *(Rev. Russell)*, Ann Beach *(Lottie)*, Tom Naylor *(Bill Maitland)*, Fred Johnson *(Elder)*.

Fairly creepy witchcraft film with a twist opening similar to PSYCHO. We follow a young student of the occult, Stevenson, as she visits a run-down village in Massachusetts on the recommendation of her history professor, Lee. She discovers that the inn is run by a witch who was burned at the stake in 1692, but brought back to life by the Devil. Stevenson finds herself the main ingredient in a human sacrifice—presided over by none other than her history professor, Lee. The girl is killed and shortly after her boyfriend, Naylor, and her brother come looking for her. Eventually, after a hair-raising battle with the coven, Naylor is mortally wounded, but manages to destroy the cult by throwing the shadow of a cemetery cross over them while Stevenson's brother escapes.

p, Milton Subotsky [uncredited], Donald Taylor; d, John Moxey; w, George Baxt (based on a story by Subotsky); Desmond Dickinson; m, Douglas Gamley, Ken Jones; ed, John Pomeroy; md, Gamley; art d, John Blezard; spec eff, Cliff Richardson; cos, Freda Gibson; makeup, George Claff.

Horror **(PR:C MPAA:NR)**

HORROR HOTEL, 1976 (SEE: EATEN ALIVE!, 1976)

HORROR HOUSE*½ (1970, Brit.) 79m Tigon/AIP c (GB: THE HAUNTED HOUSE OF HORROR; AKA: THE DARK)

Frankie Avalon *(Chris)*, Jill Haworth *(Sheila)*, Richard O'Sullivan *(Peter)*, Veronica Doran *(Madge)*, Julian Barnes *(Richard)*, Robin Stewart *(Henry)*, Mark Wynter *(Gary)*, Gina Warwick *(Sylvia)*, Carol Dilworth *(Dorothy)*, Dennis Price *(Inspector Wainwright)*, George Sewell *(Kellett)*, Jan Holden *(Peggy)*, Clifford Earl *(Police Sergeant)*, Robert Raglan *(Bradley)*, Freddie Lees *(Dave)*.

Unintentionally funny British horror film starring American beach-party star Frankie Avalon as a London youth who gets wrapped up in an adventure that leads him and his dope-smoking friends into a dangerous haunted house. There the wacky group of wayward youths tries to conjure up dead spirits by holding a seance, but their efforts fail. The group decides to split up and explore the house and before you know it one of their number turns up murdered. Wondering whether a demon did the deed or perhaps even one of their drug-crazed friends, the gang decides to hide the corpse, leave the house, and stay mum about the whole thing. But soon the cops are poking around asking questions and Avalon decides that he and his buddy Barnes should go back to the house and search for clues. Unfortunately for him, Barnes turns out to be the killer and stabs Avalon to death just before the police arrive.

p, Tony Tenser; d, Michael Armstrong; w, Armstrong, Peter Marcus; ph, Jack Atcheler (Movielab Color); m, Reg Tilsley; ed, Peter Pitt; art d, Hayden Pearce; set d, Jack Holden; spec eff, Arthur Beavis.

Horror **(PR:O MPAA:GP)**

HORROR ISLAND zero (1941) 61m UNIV bw

Dick Foran *(Bill)*, Leo Carrillo *(Tobias)*, Peggy Moran *(Wendy)*, Fuzzy Knight *(Stuff)*, John Eldredge *(George)*, Lewis Howard *(Thurman)*, Hobart Cavanaugh *(Jasper)*, Walter Catlett *(McGoon)*, Ralph Harolde *(Rod)*, Iris Adrian *(Arleen)*, Foy Van Dolson *(The Phantom)*, Emmett Vogan *(The Stranger)*.

The bottom of the low-budget barrel was scraped for this one. Foran, Knight, Carrillo and crummy comedy star Catlett were starred among a group of witless explorers who travel to a haunted castle in search of a buried treasure. Unfunny, unterrifying, and uninteresting.

p, Ben Pivar; d, George Waggner; w, Maurice Tombragel, Victor McLeod (based on the story "Terror of the South Seas" by Alex Gottlieb); ph, Elwood Bredell; ed, Otto Ludwig.

Horror/Comedy **(PR:A MPAA:NR)**

HORROR MANIACS
(SEE: GREED OF WILLIAM HART, THE, 1953, Brit.)

HORROR OF DRACULA, THE**** (1958, Brit.) 82m Hammer/UNIV c (GB: DRACULA)

Peter Cushing *(Van Helsing)*, Michael Gough *(Arthur Holmwood)*, Melissa Stribling *(Mina Holmwood)*, Christopher Lee *(Count Dracula)*, Carol Marsh *(Lucy)*, John Van Eyssen *(Jonathan Harker)*, Miles Malleson *(Marx, the Undertaker)*, Valerie Gaunt *(Vampire Woman)*, Charles Lloyd Pack *(Dr. Seward)*, Janina Faye *(Tania)*, Olga Dickie *(Gerda)*, George Woodbridge *(Landlord)*, Barbara Archer *(Inga)*, George Benson *(Frontier Official)*, Guy Mills, George Merritt, William Sherwood, John Mossman, Stedwell Fulcher, Judith Nelmes, Humphrey Kent, Paul Cole, Dick Morgan, Geoffrey Bayldon.

Hammer Studio's horror masterpiece which finally gave the Dracula legend the treatment it deserved. The plot followed Bram Stocker's novel more closely than any previously filmed attempt (excluding, perhaps, the silent German classic NOSFERATU) and begins with Eyssen's trip to Transylvania where he is employed by the mysterious Count Dracula, Lee. Eventually Eyssen learns that his employer is a vampire, a member of the undead who must suck the blood of the living to survive, and he becomes one of Lee's victims. Lee travels to London and tracks down Eyssen's fiancee, Marsh, and transforms her into one of the undead, also. Enter Dr. Van Helsing (played with zest and vigor by Cushing) and the battle lines are drawn. Cushing eventually tracks Lee down at his castle, and in a stunningly choreographed climax, he kills the vampire, using sunlight and two gold candlesticks put together in the shape of the cross. In a fantastic special-effects sequence (which still holds up even when measured against the technological wonders of modern movies), Lee rots away into a pile of dust. This Hammer version of the Dracula legend brought with it many innovative (and, yes, subsequently overdone) approaches to the genre. The film moves quickly and forcefully from one scene to the next, keeping the audience on the very edges of their seats. The sets are lush and magnificent looking, the actors cast perfectly to their roles, and of course, the blood and sex. Blood and sex in vampire films (the essential elements) had been studiously avoided by previous horror film makers, probably due to restrictions imposed on them. Hammer had no such restrictions and freely played up Lee's obvious sensuality (why else would all these beautiful women allow him to get so close and remain his slaves?) to the advantage of the character and plot motivation. (Admittedly, the studio drove this style of horror into the ground and exploited its impact in several other, less finely crafted efforts.) The result is a terrific combination of the intellectual and visceral that continues to work today (though Hammer never managed to duplicate its success). Followed by DRACULA PRINCE OF DARKNESS and five more sequels.

p, Anthony Hinds; d, Terence Fisher; w, Jimmy Sangster (based on the novel *Dracula*, by Bram Stoker); ph, Jack Asher (Eastmancolor); m, James Bernard; art d, Bernard Robinson; ed, Bill Lenny, James Needs; md, John Hollingsworth, cos, Molly Arbuthnot.

Horror **Cas.** **(PR:O MPAA:NR)**

HORROR OF FRANKENSTEIN, THE* (1970, Brit.) 95m Hammer-EMI/American Continental c

Ralph Bates *(Victor Frankenstein)*, Kate O'Mara *(Alys)*, Graham James *(Wilhelm)*, Veronica Carlson *(Elizabeth)*, Bernard Archard *(Elizabeth's Father)*, Dennis Price *(Grave Robber)*, Joan Rice *(Grave Robber's Wife)*, David Prowse *(The Monster)*.

Feeble attempt by Hammer to bring some freshness to their series of Frankenstein films by introducing black humor. The jokes are told in such a straightforward and dry manner, however, that one is never sure whether or not they are supposed to be taken seriously. Bates stars as the son of Count Frankenstein who kills his father in order to take over the castle, including the charms of the comely and buxom housekeeper, O'Mara. Soon he decides to build a monster, Prowse (who would go on to play Darth Vader in the STAR WARS movies), which requires the gory murders of various townsfolk. Bates uses a number system to assemble the various pieces of the monster, practicing by putting together a dead turtle and bringing it back to life first. Sequel: FRANKENSTEIN AND THE MONSTER FROM HELL.

p&d, Jimmy Sangster; w, Sangster, Jeremy Burnham (based on the characters created by Mary Shelley); ph, Moray Grant (Technicolor); m, James Bernard; ed, Chris Barnes; art d, Scott McGregor; makeup, Tom Smith.

Horror/Comedy **Cas.** **(PR:O MPAA:R)**

HORROR OF IT ALL, THE** (1964, Brit.) 75m Lippert/FOX bw

Pat Boone *(Jack Robinson)*, Erica Rogers *(Cynthia)*, Dennis Price *(Cornwallis)*, Andree Melly *(Natalia)*, Valentine Dyall *(Reginal)*, Jack Bligh *(Percival)*, Erick Chitty *(Grandpapa)*, Archie Duncan *(Muldoon)*, Oswald Laurence *(Young Doctor)*.

Boone stars as an American who travels to England to ask permission to marry one of an eccentric British family's daughters, Rogers. While he's there he discovers family member Dyall talks like Bela Lugosi, Melly thinks she's a vampire, Duncan is kept locked in a padded cell, Bligh is excited over his invention of the horseless carriage (about 50 years too late), and Chitty, the grandfather of the clan, reads *Playboy* on his death-bed. (Scripter Russell was Hugh Hefner's first editor a dozen years before.) Strangely, one by one the looney family members are killed off and it's up to Boone to discover which of the clan seeks to be the sole inheritor of the family fortune. Really dumb effort, inexplicably directed by the king of Hammer Studios horror, Terence Fisher.

p, Margia Dean; d, Terence Fisher; w, Ray Russell; ph, Arthur Lavis; m, Douglas Gamley; ed, Robert Winter; md, Philip Martell; art d, Harry White; cos, Jean Fairlie; makeup, Bill Lodge.

Comedy/Mystery (PR:A MPAA:NR)

HORROR OF PARTY BEACH, THE* (1964) 72m Inzom/FOX bw

John Scott *(Hank Green)*, Alice Lyon *(Elaine Gavin)*, Allen Laurel *(Dr. Gavin)*, Eulabelle Moore *(Eulabelle)*, Marilyn Clark *(Tina)*, Augustin Mayer *(Mike)*, Damon Klebroyd *(Lt. Wells)*, Monroe Wade *(Television Announcer)*, Carol Grubman, Dina Harris, Emily Laurel *(Girls in Car)*, Sharon Murphy, Diane Prizio *(Two Girls)*, The Del-Aires *(Vocal Group)*.

An all-time bad movie classic! Radioactive waste at the bottom of the ocean turns human skeletons lying there into mutated sea monsters that surface and ruin a teenage beach party by killing the rock-'n'-rollers for their blood. Lots of silly monster costumes! Lots of bad rock 'n' roll songs! Lots of bad screams from lousy teenage actresses! Lots of phony newspaper headlines explaining what is happening! Eventually an inept scientist stumbles across the solution to the problem by pouring sodium on the beasts. This dissolves them (actually his black maid Eulabelle discovers the secret, but she doesn't get the credit). THE HORROR OF PARTY BEACH was heralded as "the first horror monster musical" and luckily few followed. Really bad and really fun. Songs: "Drag," "You Are Not a Summer Love," "Elaine," "Wigglin' 'n' Wobblin'" and "The Zombie Stomp."

p&d, Del Tenney; w, Richard L. Hilliard, Ronald Gianettino, Lou Binder; ph, Hilliard; ed, Gary Youngman; md, Bill Holmes; art d, Robert Verberkmoss.

Horror (PR:C MPAA:NR)

HORROR OF THE BLOOD MONSTERS zero (1970, U.S./Phil.) 85m TAL/Independent-International c/bw (AKA: CREATURES OF THE PREHISTORIC PLANET; HORROR CREATURES OF THE RED PLANET; FLESH CREATURES OF THE RED PLANET; THE FLESH CREATURES; SPACE MISSION OF THE LOST PLANET; VAMPIRE MEN OF THE LOST PLANET)

John Carradine *(Dr. Rynning)*, Robert Dix *(Col. Manning)*, Vicki Volante *(Valerie)*, Joey Benson *(Willy)*, Jennifer Bishop *(Lian Malian)*, Bruce Powers *(Bryce)*, Fred Meyers *(Capt. Bob Scott)*, Britt Semand *(Linda)*, Theodore [Gottlieb] *(Narrator)*.

Truly awful sci-fi film where most of the special effects sequences were lifted from a different, black & white Filipino movie and given a color tint which was acclaimed as "Spectrum X." Scientists Carradine, Volante, and Dix learn of a vampire invasion from space and quickly build a rocket and shoot to the vampire planet to stop the evil blood-suckers in their tracks. There they do battle with "Claw Creatures," "Snake Men," and "Bat Demons" (all from the other movie), and eventually save Earth. Believe it or not, famed cinematographer Vilmos Zsigmond (DELIVERANCE, CLOSE ENCOUNTERS OF THE THIRD KIND) shot all the original footage.

p, Al Adamson; d, Adamson, George Joseph; w, Sue McNair; ph, William [Vilmos] Zsigmond, William G. Troiano (Movielab Color); m, Mike Velarde; ed, Ewing Brown, Peter Perry; spec eff, David L. Hewitt; makeup, Jean Hewitt.

Science Fiction (PR:O MPAA:GP)

HORROR OF THE STONE WOMEN (SEE: MILL OF THE STONE WOMEN, 1963, Fr./Ital.)

HORROR OF THE ZOMBIES* (1974, Span.) 85m Independent International c (EL BUQUE MALDITO)

Maria Perschy, Jack Taylor, Carlos Lemos, Manuel de Blas, Barbara Rey, Blanca Estrada.

The Spanish zombies return in this sequel to THE BLIND DEAD which takes place almost entirely on a sailing ship inhabited by bikini-wearing fashion models who are attacked by the title creatures. Yet a third zombie film in the series, NIGHT OF THE SEAGULLS, was soon to be released.

p, J.L. Bermuder De Castro; d&w, Armando De Ossorio; ph, Raul Artigot; m, A. Garcia Abril.

Horror Cas. (PR:C MPAA:R)

HORROR ON SNAPE ISLAND (SEE: BEYOND THE FOG, 1981, Brit.)

HORROR PLANET zero (1982, Brit.) 86m Jupiter/Almi c (AKA: INSEMINOID)

Judy Geeson *(Sandy)*, Robin Clarke *(Mark)*, Jennifer Ashley *(Holly)*, Stephanie Beacham *(Kate)*, Steven Girves, Barry Houghton, Rosalind Lloyd, Victoria Tennant; Trevor Thomas, Heather Wright, David Baxt, Dominic Jephcott.

Gory attempt to cash in on the success of ALIEN has a group of space explorers investigating the caves of a distant planet. A bug-eyed little monster attacks crewmember Geeson and impregnates her, and she goes mad and kills off the crew, one by one. (Somehow, due to her condition, she is able to breathe both the ship's oxygen and the planet's atmosphere, acquiring thereby a super-human strength that enables her to survive all attacks.) Eventually she gives a messy birth to a monster kid.

p, Richard Gordon, David Speechley; d, Norman J. Warren; w, Nick Maley, and Gloria Maley; ph, John Metcalfe (Rank Color); m, John Scott; ed, Peter Boyle; prod d, Hayden Pearce; spec eff, Oxford Scientific Films, Camera Effects; stunts, Peter Brayham; makeup, Nick Maley.

Horror Cas. (PR:O MPAA:R)

HORRORS OF SPIDER ISLAND (SEE: IT'S HOT IN PARADISE, 1959, Ger./Yugo.)

HORRORS OF THE BLACK MUSEUM** (1959, U.S./Brit.) 94m Anglo-Amalgamated-AIP c

Michael Gough *(Edmond Bancroft)*, June Cunningham *(Joan Berkley)*, Graham Curnow *(Rick)*, Shirley Ann Field *(Angela)*, Geoffrey Keen *(Superintendent Graham)*, Gerald Anderson *(Dr. Ballan)*, John Warwick *(Inspector Lodge)*, Beatrice Varley *(Aggie)*, Austin Trevor *(Commissioner Wayne)*, Malou Pantera *(Peggy)*, Howard Greene *(Tom Rivers)*, Dorinda Stevens *(Gail)*, Stuart Saunders *(Fun Fair Barker)*, Hilda Barry, Nora Gordon *(Women in Hall)*, Maya Koumani.

Sick little film starring Gough as a frustrated writer of mystery novels. Believing that the public will respond to real-life gore, Gough decides to perpetrate unusual and imaginative killings and then use this fresh, first-hand material to write fiendishly explicit novels. He throws a hypnotic spell over his faithful assistant Curnow, turning him into a lumpy-faced monster that does the writer's evil bidding. The murders are committed with a variety of gadgets including a pair of binoculars that plunge two steel spikes into the victim's eyes; a guillotine hidden above a girl's bed; and ice tongs that impale the victim. An acid vat disposes of the bodies. Eventually Curnow turns on his master and kills Gough in an amusement park. The film was originally released in something called "Hypnovision"; this was a 13-minute lecture on hypnotism shown before the movie.

p, Herman Cohen, Jack Greenwood; d, Arthur Crabtree; w, Cohen, Aben Kandel; ph, Desmond Dickinson (CinemaScope, Eastmancolor); m, Gerard Schurmann; ed, Geoffrey Muller; md, Muir Mathieson; art d, Wilfred Arnold.

Horror (PR:O MPAA:R)

HORRORS OF THE BLACK ZOO (SEE: BLACK ZOO, 1963)

HORSE FEATHERS**** (1932) 70m PAR bw

Groucho Marx *(Professor Wagstaff)*, Harpo Marx *(Harpo)*, Chico Marx *(Chico)*, Zeppo Marx *(Zeppo)*, Thelma Todd *(Connie Bailey)*, David Landau *(Jennings)*, Florine McKinney *(Peggy Carrington)*, James Pierce *(Mullens)*, Nat Pendleton *(McCarthy)*, Reginald Barlow *(President of College)*, Robert Grieg *(Professor Hornsvogel)*.

This is probably the most madcap film the Brothers Marx ever made, and one that has so many literary inside jokes that they're impossible to count, all streaming from the fertile and capricious brain of that wonderful humorist, Perelman. As usual, there's not much to the plot. Groucho is the president of madhouse Huxley College, while Chico provides him and the rest of the campus with plenty of booze, being the resident bootlegger and local iceman, his assistant Harpo providing stunts so looney that even Chico is shocked by his outrageous antics. Zeppo, who nominally plays Groucho's son and is busy wooing beautiful blonde Todd, the campus widow, is again straight man to the bonmots, barbs, and bombast of his older brothers. Gamblers plant some pros on an opposing football team to win the big match and glean the loot. When Groucho learns of this, he goes to a local speakeasy and hires two men he thinks are professional football players to counter the opposition. Naturally and mistakenly, he has hired Chico and Harpo, who win the game through their zany maneuvers. Ruby and Kalmar, who wrote the so-called screenplay, also provided the two songs, one, "I'm Against It" croaked out by Groucho and (sung by Zeppo) "Everyone Says 'I Love You'." The incredible pace of this film is maintained by the hard-working McLeod and he had his hands full in controlling the uncontrollable Marx Brothers. The funniest scenes are bare sight gags. A bum approaches Harpo on the street and begs money for a cup of coffee. Harpo opens his baggy coat and produces a steaming cup of coffee. Moments later cups, saucers, plates, and more sterling silver than Revere ever made waterfalls from the same coat. Another scene, a spoof on Theodore Dreiser's *An American Tragedy*, shows Todd and Groucho in a canoe, sliding across a placid lake; she is trying to worm information from him about the secret plays his football team will employ in the upcoming match. Somehow she falls overboard and screams for him to throw her a lifesaver. He pulls out a tube of the candy, leisurely peels off the wrapper and throws her a piece of the candy. After the scene was over Todd kept flopping wildly about in the lake, continuing to scream for help. Groucho, who didn't know she could not swim, ("I thought she was kidding!") told her to "aww, shut up," and paddled away. Six technicians then dove into the lake and saved the actress from drowning at the last minute. (Todd died on December 15, 1935 under circumstances that led most to believe she was murdered in her car, parked in a garage next to her posh cliffside home which stood above her roadside restaurant in Pacific Palisades. The mystery of her death was never resolved.) Offscreen Groucho kept making a play for Todd but she managed to evade his blunt advances. The production was halted many times while Chico was hunted down and brought onto the set; he could usually be found shooting craps in the prop room with stagehands. Harpo stopped acting in the middle of a take during filming when he noticed the most beautiful little girl he had ever seen. He walked off the set to talk to the little girl's parents, saying he would give them $50,000 if they would let him adopt the child. They told him no and walked away with their tot, a precocious little girl who grew up to be Shirley Temple. The brothers made life impossible for writers Ruby, Kalmar, and especially the witty Perelman, whose carefully chiseled prose they chipped to pieces with unexpected ad-libbing. Said Perelman later of these delightful zanies: "Anybody who ever worked on any picture for the Marx Brothers said he would rather be chained to a galley oar and lashed at ten-minute intervals than ever work for these sons of bitches again . . . [To get them to stay with written scenes and lines] it took drudgery and Homeric quarrels, ambuscades, and intrigues that would have shamed the Borgias . . . As far as temperaments and their personalities were concerned, they were capricious, tricky beyond endurance, and altogether unreliable. They were also megalomaniacs to a degree which is impossible to describe."

d, Norman Z. McLeod; w, Bert Kalmar, Harry Ruby, S. J. Perelman; ph, Ray June; m/l, Kalmar, Ruby.

Comedy **(PR:A MPAA:NR)**

HORSE IN THE GRAY FLANNEL SUIT, THE*½ (1968) 112m Disney/BV c

Dean Jones *(Fred Bolton)*, Diane Baker *(Suzie Clemens)*, Lloyd Bochner *(Archer Madison)*, Fred Clark *(Tom Dugan)*, Ellen Janov *(Helen Bolton)*, Morey Amsterdam *(Charlie Blake)*, Kurt Russell *(Ronnie Gardner)*, Lurene Tuttle *(Aunt Martha)*, Alan Hewitt *(Harry Tomes)*, Federico Pinero *(Lieut. Lorendo)*, Florence MacMichael *(Catherine)*, Joan Marshall *(Mimsey)*, Robin Eccles *(Judy Gardner)*, Adam Williams *(Sgt. Roberts)*, Norman Grabowski *(Truck Driver)*, Nydia Westman *(Lady In Elevator)*, Bill Baldwin, Sr. *(Announcer)*, Albarado *(Aspercel)*, Sir Winston, Could Be *(Stand-ins for Aspercel)*.

Overlong, tedious and badly shot Disney picture starring Jones as a widower ad executive stuck with a lousy campaign for an aspirin called Aspercel and a bill for $900 that was run up by his daughter, Janov, whose hobby is riding horses at an expensive stable run by Baker. Hit with a brain storm to solve both his problems, Jones decides to buy a horse, name it "Aspercel," and have Baker train his daughter to ride the horse at shows as a promotional device. The horse does well at shows but the advertising revenue is disappointing. By accident Jones discovers that the horse is a great runner and jumper and enters the nag in a championship steeplechase jockeyed by Baker. Of course after a torturously long steeplechase scene (clocked at 26 minutes), the horse wins and all problems are solved.

p, Winston Hibler; d, Norman Tokar, Larry Lansburgh; w, Louis Pelletier (based on the book *The Year Of The Horse* by Eric Hatch); ph, William Snyder (Technicolor); m, George Bruns; ed, Robert Stafford; art d, Carroll Clark, John B. Mansbridge; set d, Emile Kuri, Frank R. McKelvy; spec eff, Tim Barr; cos, Bill Thomas; makeup, Otis Malcolm, Walter Schenck.

Drama **(PR:AAA MPAA:G)**

HORSE NAMED COMANCHE, A (SEE: TONKA, 1958)

HORSE OF PRIDE½** (1980, Fr.) 120m Bela/Planfilm c (LE CHEVAL D'ORGEUIL)

Jacques Dufilho, Bernadette Le Sache, Francois Cluzet, Paul Le Person, Pierre Le Rumeur, Michel Rabin, Dominique Lavanant, Georges Wilson *(Narrator)*.

Based on a French best-seller, this picture is a departure from the Chabrol that most people connect with Hitchcock homages. Here the director takes an unpretentious look at peasant life in Brittany from 1908-18, with a concentration on their customs and tradition of oral storytelling. Instead of letting the characters do the talking, however, there is an emphasis on voice-over narration which enhances the already beautiful photography by Jean Rabier. Hilton McConnico's set design (DIVA) is equally dazzling.

p, Georges de Beauregard; d, Claude Chabrol; w, Chabrol, Daniel Boulanger (from the novel *Le Cheval D'Orgeuil* by Pierre-Jakez Helias); ph, Jean Rabier (Eastmancolor); m, Pierre Jansen; ed, Monique Fardoulis; art d, Hilton McConnico; cos, Magali Dray.

Drama **(PR:A MPAA:NR)**

HORSE SOLDIERS, THE**** (1959) 119m Mirisch/UA c

John Wayne *(Col. John Marlowe)*, William Holden *(Maj. Henry Kendall)*, Constance Towers *(Hannah Hunter)*, Althea Gibson *(Lukey)*, Hoot Gibson *(Brown)*, Anna Lee *(Mrs. Buford)*, Russell Simpson *(Sheriff)*, Stan Jones *(Gen. U.S. Grant)*, Carleton Young *(Col. Jonathan Miles)*, Basil Ruysdael *(Boys School Commandant)*, Willis Bouchey *(Col. Phil Secord)*, Ken Curtis *(Wilkie)*, O.Z. Whitehead *("Hoppy" Hopkins)*, Judson Pratt *(Sgt. Maj. Kirby)*, Denver Pyle *(Jagger Jo)*, Strother Martin *(Virgil)*, Hank Worden *(Deacon)*, Walter Reed *(Union Officer)*, Jack Pennick *(Sgt. Maj. Mitchell)*, Fred Graham *(Union Scout)*, Chuck Hayward *(Capt. Woodward)*, Charles Steel *(Newton Station Bartender)*, Stuart Holmes *(Train Passenger)*, Major Sam Harris *(Confederate Major)*, Richard Cutting *(Gen. Sherman)*, Bing Russell *(Dunker)*, William Forrest *(Gen. Steve Hurburt)*, Fred Kennedy *(Cavalryman)*, Bill Henry *(Confederate Lieutenant)*, William Leslie *(Maj. Richard Gray)*, Ron Hagerthy *(Bugler)*, Donald Foster *(Dr. Marvin)*, Cliff Lyons *(Sergeant)*, William Wellman, Jr. *(Bugler)*, Jan Stine *(Dying Man)*, Dan Borzage.

John Ford was not only the master of the modern western film, if not its father (certainly its most important uncle) but also the greatest director of films dealing with the old U.S. Cavalry. His superb trilogy about those long-ago soldiers on horseback (FORT APACHE, 1948, SHE WORE A YELLOW RIBBON, 1949 and RIO GRANDE, 1950) have endured and will continue to endure as great historic film sagas. With the exception of the Civil War segment in HOW THE WEST WAS WON, Ford directed only one complete film about cavalrymen in the Civil War, THE HORSE SOLDIERS (1963) and it is exceptional, a realistic, action-filled and poignant film. It's spring 1863 and the North is faring badly in its titanic struggle with the South. To put pressure on then under seige Vicksburg, Union General Grant (Jones) decides to send a cavalry unit deep into Confederate territory, cutting supply lines and creating havoc, enough to draw Confederate troops away from the defense of Vicksburg so he can take the city. The man selected to lead this daring raid (known as Grierson's Raid in reality, a real event as exciting and harrowing as this film) is tough, no-nonsense Wayne, a citizen soldier. With him goes a bevy of officers with mixed motives, including Bouchey, whose political ambitions following the war dictate his every action, and Holden, a conscientious physician who sees no glory in war, wounds, or death on the battlefield. Dodging Confederate scouting parties, the Union regiment finally encounters southern skirmishers and beats off an attack. Wayne then splits his command, sending fully a third of his troops back to the Union lines to mislead the Confederates into believing that the entire regiment has retreated. Next, he cuts through swamps and penetrates even deeper into southern territory, coming upon the plantation home of Towers, a blonde, beautiful southern belle who lives alone with her faithful black servant, Gibson. She graciously invites Wayne and his officers to dinner, serving them her last chicken and acting the flighty female but then engineers the group into a parlor while she retires to her room to listen through a heating duct to the plans they are making. Suspicious, Holden interrupts Towers and unmasks her real intentions. She curses all the Union officers as Wayne orders her taken into custody; the information she has learned makes her too dangerous to leave behind. The regiment rides off pell-mell to attack Newton Station, a key southern railhead. This they take without a fight, finding only a few wounded Confederate soldiers in the town, southern women showering them with curses and dirt as the Union troops ride through. Holden spots Young, an old friend, now a Confederate officer who has lost an arm. They reminisce and then part while Wayne gives orders for the railroad supplies to be destroyed. Young manages to get to the depot and orders the telegraph operator to send a message. A short time later a train pulls into town loaded with southern troops which Young leads in a desperate charge against Wayne's barricaded position. The Union fire is withering and the southerners are slaughtered; Young is shot down as he stumbles forward with the Confederate banner in his hands. He falls into Holden's arms but later survives. While Wayne's men destroy the depot and railway equipment, rails, and ties, Wayne goes to the local bar and begins drinking, carping about doctors. He hates all physicians, particularly the self-assured Holden. He later explains that his wife died in an operation she did not need to have. To Wayne all doctors are butchers, "croakers." Now Wayne and his men, Towers still in tow, make a mad dash for the Amite River and permanent escape, full Confederate regiments under the command of Nathan Bedford Forrest on his heels. His way is blocked by a stubborn Confederate battery of guns and he prepares to charge them. Meanwhile, at the begging request of the Confederate officer in charge of the artillery, the elderly head of a boys' military academy orders out the youths to attack the interloping Yankees. The Union cavalry charges and overwhelms the Confederate battery but then Wayne sees the neat ranks of the southern cadets advancing upon his troops. They suddenly charge but Wayne will not let his men fire upon these boys and orders a retreat. This rout comes just after Wayne and Holden have been having a fist fight over Wayne's remarks about doctors, a fight that must be postponed as the cavalry runs wildly from the triumphant southern cadets. Further south, when Holden stops to give aid to some ailing blacks, Gibson is shot and killed by a southern sniper. The Union troops are only miles from Union lines but they must first break through a strong southern defense line along the river and on the other side of a bridge they must cross. Wayne leads several charges across the bridge and clears the way but he must leave his wounded behind. Holden insists upon staying with them and Towers, even though he knows it means captivity in a southern prison. Wayne, before bidding Towers farewell, shows his respect for her and especially for the heroic Holden. As he dashes to freedom, Confederate cavalry come upon the scene, a Confederate officer telling Holden that he will have his regimental surgeon help him with the Union wounded. This rousing, historically accurate and colorful film epitomizes the fluid and masterful talents of Ford, America's pantheon director of the sound era. He paints his scenes, as it were, with memorable camerawork, scene by careful scene, from the first moments when the officers meet beneath a huge tree to have their regimental photo taken. Ford, ever the consummate researcher, studied the Civil War photographs of Matthew Brady and others for months before doing his own art panels and planning his scenes. The arrangement of his troop movements, long lines of mounted cavalrymen, Union and Confederate, stretching across ridges seemingly to the horizon, give the awesome image of the war encompassing an entire nation. It is full of thunder, honor, and death without frills, bloody, awful death that war always brings. His leading characters are fully developed—you know *why* Wayne is as hard-bitten as he is, and *why* Holden is as devoted to medicine as he is disrespectful of the military. And always there is that wonderful touch of Fordian humanity, such as Wayne ordering his tough troopers to run in the face of green cadets who could have easily been slaughtered. On another occasion, Wayne comes across two Confederate deserters, brigands really, Martin and Pyle, who are about to hang an elderly sheriff, Simpson, who has been hunting them for theft and mayhem. Wayne slugs both deserters and turns them over to the southern sheriff. And many of Ford's wonderful stock company characters are present, Worden, Pennick, and the great silent and early talkie cowboy star, Hoot Gibson. Every detail, from the number of stripes on a sergeant's sleeve to the regulation Civil War canteen, is correct. Clothier's camera work reflects the always restless vision of Ford and the score is moving and military when necessary, with a theme song entitled "I Left My Love" by Jones, who also plays General Grant. (Also included is a little heard waltz, "Lorena.") The film has all the elements of a superior production, offering viewers excitement, adventure, brisk pace, beautiful color, and romance, mostly for the cavalry itself. Wayne and Holden are perfectly cast in their roles and they bring enthusiasm and energy to their parts. In her film debut, Towers is fine as the southern belle (she would be the feminine lead of Ford's SERGEANT RUTLEDGE) but Gibson, one-time tennis star, always seems to be looking into the air for her lines. Ford's great star creation Wayne was ever under his master's directorial eye and doubly suffered in this rigorous production in that Ford, once a great imbiber, had been ordered to quit drinking or die by his doctors and he imposed his own abstinence upon Wayne, who had no such orders from his physician. Wayne begged producer Rackin to get him away from the on-location area outside of Natchitoches in southern Louisiana and beyond Ford's paternal gaze. Rackin lied to Ford, telling him that Duke's teeth were beginning to show up yellow on the rushes and he had to take the Duke and Holden to New Orleans to get their teeth cleaned. After a roaring night on the town, the three returned to a fuming Ford who knew through his tailing spies exactly how many bars the trio had visited. At the beginning, when the film was being planned, Ford had expressed his misgivings to Rackin, saying to him: "You know where we should make this picture?" Replied Rackin: "No, where?" Ford laughed and said: "Lourdes, because it's going to take a miracle to pull this one off." Yet after painstaking work on the script and scouting the proper locations, Ford felt confident that he would produce a first class film, which he did. It was not inexpensive. Ford himself got $200,000, plus 10 percent of the profits for his services. Wayne and Holden each received $750,000, plus 20 percent of the profits. The entire film cost $3.5 million but it earned that amount back in its first release, plus much more. The film was marked with a personal tragedy for Ford. Fred Kennedy, an old stunt player who had appeared in many of his films, begged the director for a stunt so he could make some extra money; he was broke. Ford pointed out that he was too old for such efforts but finally relented. He then told Towers, as a joke, to run over to Kennedy when he fell from his horse and give him a big kiss. Kennedy took the dangerous spill and the blonde leading lady raced to him, grabbed him in her arms, leaned down to kiss him, and screamed. She then shouted to Ford: "This man is dying!" Ford and crew rushed to Kennedy. The old actor had broken his neck and was dead before he arrived at the nearest hospital. The scene showing Kennedy's fatal fall was kept in the film. Ford was so crushed by Kennedy's death that he closed down the location site and returned to California, finishing the last battle scene in the San Fernando Valley. He hurried completion of the film and then left for Hawaii where he guiltily fell off the wagon.

p, John Lee Mahin, Martin Rackin; d, John Ford; w, Mahin, Rackin (based on the novel by Harold Sinclair); ph, William Clothier (DeLuxe Color); m, David Buttolph; ed, Jack Murray; art d, Frank Hotaling; cos, Frank Bretson, Ann Peck; spec eff, Augie Lohman; makeup, Webb Overlander.

Civil War Drama **Cas.** **(PR:C MPAA:NR)**

HORSEMEN, THE** (1971) 105m Frankenheimer-Lewis/COL c

Omar Sharif *(Uraz)*, Leigh Taylor-Young *(Zereh)*, Jack Palance *(Tursen)*, David De *(Mukhi)*, Peter Jeffrey *(Hayatal)*, Mohammed Shamsi *(Osman Bey)*, George Murcell *(Mizrar)*, Eric Pohlmann *(Merchant Of Kandahar)*, Despo *(Uljan)*, Vernon Dobtcheff *(Zam Hajji)*, Ishaq Bux *(Amjad Kahn)*, Saeed Jaffrey *(District Chief)*, John Ruddock *(Scribe)*, Mark Colleano *(Rahim)*, Sy Temple *(Quadir)*, Aziz Resh *(Bacha to Ghulam)*, Vida St. Romaine *(Gypsy Woman)*, Leon Lissek *(Chikana Proprietor)*, Milton Reid *(Aqqul)*, Salman Peer *(Salih)*, Ricardo Palacios *(Ghulam)*, Jesus Tordesilla *(Little Governor)*, J.L. Chinchilla *(Head Syce)*, P. De Quevedo *(King)*, Carlos Casaravilla *(Messenger)*, Barbara Wain *(Nurse)*.

Beautifully photographed on magnificent locations in Afghanistan and Spain, THE HORSEMEN is ruined by an overly talky (with bad dialog to boot), trite script by Dalton Trumbo. Story concerns the son of an Afghan sheik, Sharif, who enters a deadly game of buzkashi, a brutal version of soccer played with the headless carcass of a calf, to prove his manhood to his father, Palance. During the game Sharif is humiliated and his leg is badly hurt. He is taken home by his untrustworthy servant, De, and a nomadic "untouchable," Taylor-Young, but not before they must stop in an outlying town and amputate the young heir's leg at the knee. Upon his return, Sharif is still determined to prove his manhood to his father and he begins a slow rehabilitation that culminates in a dramatic display of his equestrian skills. Having proved his prowess, Sharif rides off forever in search of himself.

p, Edward Lewis; d, John Frankenheimer; w, Dalton Trumbo (based on the novel by Joseph Kessel); ph, Claude Renoir, Vladimir Ivanov, Andre Domage (Super Panavision); m, Georges Delerue; ed, Harold Kress; prod d, Pierre Thevenet; art d, Gil Parrondo; cos, Jacqueline Moreau; spec eff, Alex Weldon; stunts, Chuck Hayward, Pierre Pakamoff; makeup, Giuliano Laurenti; animal trainer, Corky Randall.

Drama **(PR:C MPAA:GP)**

HORSEMEN OF THE SIERRAS** (1950) 59m COL bw

Charles Starrett *(Steve Saunders/The Durango Kid)*, Smiley Burnette *(Himself)*, Lois Hall *(Patty McGregor)*, Tommy Ivo *(Robin Grant)*, John Dehner *(Duke Webster)*, Jason Robards, Sr. *(Phineas Grant)*, Daniel M. Sheridan *(Morgan Webster)*, Jock O'Mahoney *(Bill Grant)*, George Chesebro *(Ellory Webster)*, T. Texas Tyler *(Himself)*.

Another Starrett oater in the DURANGO KID series sees the cowboy ending a range war started by two "rival" ranchers to scare the surrounding cattlemen off the rest of the land so that they alone can claim the oil-rich territory. O'Mahoney was also Starrett's stunt double. (See DURANGO KID series, Index.)

p, Colbert Clark; d, Fred F. Sears; w, Barry Shipman; ph, Fayte Browne; ed, Paul Borofsky; art d, Charles Clague.

Western **(PR:A MPAA:NR)**

HORSEPLAY*½ (1933) 67m UNIV bw

Slim Summerville *(Slim Perkins)*, Andy Devine *(Andy)*, Leila Hyams *(Angelica Wayne)*, May Beatty *(The Duchess)*, Una O'Connor *(Clementia)*, David Torrence *(Uncle Percy)*, Cornelius Keefe *(Philip Marley)*, Ferdinand Gottschalk *(Oswald)*, Ethel Griffies *(Emily)*, Lucille Lund *(Iris)*.

Dim rural comedy starring Summerville and Devine as a pair of Montana hayseeds who strike it rich when radium is discovered on their ranch. The boys take their new-found financial freedom to England where Summerville's Montana sweetheart was shipped by her daddy to stay with blue-blood relatives to discourage the lowly rancher's attentions. The boys arrive in London and set about stirring up as much trouble as they can until they redeem themselves by exposing a phony aristocrat who is wanted by the police.

d, Edward Sedgwick; w, H.M. Walker, Dale Van Every (based on a story by Ebba Havey, Clarence Marks); ph, George Robinson.

Comedy **(PR:A MPAA:NR)**

HORSE'S MOUTH, THE*½ (1953, Brit.) 84m Group 3/GFD bw (GB: THE ORACLE)

Robert Beatty *(Bob Jefferson)*, Joseph Tomelty *(Terry Roche)*, Mervyn Johns *(Tom Mitchum)*, Michael Medwin *(Timothy Blake)*, Virginia McKenna *(Shelagh)*, Gillian Lind *(Jane Bond)*, Ursula Howells *(Peggy)*, Arthur Macrae *(Alan Digby)*, Louise Hampton *(Miss Turner)*, John Charlesworth *(Denis)*, Maire O'Neill *(Mrs. Lenham)*, Gilbert Harding *(Oracle's Voice)*, Lockwood West, John McBride, Derek Tansley, Patrick McAlinney, Lionel Marson, Jean St. Claire, Jack May.

Silly attempt at satire has Medwin as a reporter who tries to make a story out of the "oracle" he discovers at the bottom of a well while vacationing. His editor thinks it's just whimsy and fires him; then the oracle is discovered to be the real thing. People start to ask too much from the gifted being, however, and it splits to where it came from.

p, John Grierson, Colin Lesslie; d, C. Pennington Richards; w, Patrick Campbell (based on the radio play "To Tell You the Truth" by Robert Barr); ph, Wolfgang Suschitzky.

Fantasy **(PR:A MPAA:NR)**

HORSE'S MOUTH, THE**** (1958, Brit.) 95m UA bw

Alec Guinness *(Gully Jimson)*, Kay Walsh *(Coker)*, Renne Houston *(Sarah)*, Mike Morgan *(Nosey)*, Robert Coote *(Sir William Beeder)*, Arthur Macrae *(Alabaster)*, Veronica Turleigh *(Lady Beeder)*, Reginald Beckwith *(Capt. Jones)*, Michael Gough *(Abel)*, Ernest Thesiger *(Hickson)*, Gillian Vaughn *(Lollie)*, Richard Caldicott *(Butler)*.

This is an hilarious comedy with hardly any plot to it at all, the entire film held together through the side-splitting antics of genius Guinness. He is a completely mad painter who lives like the worst sort of bum but whose talent is brilliant if not orthodox. Released from prison after serving time as a vagrant, Guinness returns to his wife and becomes enraged to find that she has been surviving by selling off his paintings which he considers sacrosanct. He learns that a wealthy collector, Coote, is interested in his work and he goes to see the man but finds that he is out of town. Guinness looks about at the enormous flat with its huge white walls and decides that he will simply move in and affix his latest masterpieces to the walls. At the moment he is obsessed with feet, any kind of human feet, large ones, lean ones, small and fat feet, the feet of Indians, of blacks, of Caucasians, it matters not, women or men, come one, come all. His unsavory friends pose with naked feet for Guinness, then decide to use not only the flat but the entire building for their own ends, cutting a hole in the floor and dropping to the lower level where apprentice sculptor Gough lowers a huge block of granite to begin *his* masterpiece of sculpture. After finishing his incredible mural (actually painted by John Bratby), Guinness departs, leaving the entire building destroyed and ready for the bulldozer. He winds up painting an enormous outside wall, and, by film's end is measuring the side of a huge transatlantic ship for his next madcap mural. Guinness as the wild and unpredictable Gulley Jimson is sublime, his every move measured in fine madness, his every word growled out with a voice strained through sharp gravel. Guinness saw the film in Mexico City where it was being shown at a film festival. It had not been dubbed, had no subtitles, and was presented in English. Even though the audience did not understand the dialog they became uproarious with approval at the end, but factions of the crowd who considered the film an insult to true art caused fighting and a full-scale riot erupted. Guinness and the British Ambassador and his wife escaped unnoticed in the fleeing crowd.

p, John Bryan; d, Ronald Neame; w, Alec Guinness (based on the novel by Joyce Carey); ph, Arthur Ibbetson (Technicolor); m, Kenneth V. Jones; ed, Anne V. Coates; md, Muir Mathieson; set d, Bill Andrews.

Comedy **(PR:A MPAA:NR)**

HOSPITAL, THE*** (1971) 103m Gottfried-Chayefsky/UA c

George C. Scott *(Dr. Herbert Bock)*, Diana Rigg *(Barbara Drummond)*, Barnard Hughes *(Drummond)*, Richard Dysart *(Dr. Welbeck)*, Andrew Duncan *(William Mead)*, Nancy Marchand *(Mrs. Christie, Head Nurse)*, Stephen Elliott *(Sunstrom)*, Donald Harron *(Milton Mead)*, Roberts Blossom *(Guernsey)*, Tresa Hughes *(Mrs. Donovan)*, Lenny Baker *(Dr. Schaefer)*, Robert Walden *(Dr. Brubaker)*, Frances Sternhagen *(Mrs. Cushing)*, Lorrie Davis *(Nurse Divine)*, Nancy McKay *(Sheilah)*, Norman Berns *(Dr. Biegelman)*, David Hooks *(Psychiatrist)*, Arthur Junaluska *(Indian)*, Rehn Scofield *(Dr. Spezio)*, Jordan Charney *(Hitchcock)*, Cynthia Belgrave *(Nurse Reardon)*, Julie Garfield *(Nurse Perez)*, Janet Sarno *(Nurse Rivers)*, Angie Ortega *(Nurse Campanella)*, Charles Bershatsky *(Medical Student Boswell)*, Paul Mace *(Intern Ambler)*, David Hooks *(Dr. Einhorn)*, Kate Harrington *(Nurse Dunne)*, Lou Polan *(Dr. Lagerman)*, Richard Goode *(Dr. Sutcliffe)*, Douglas Owen *(Mallory)*, Reid Cruikshanks *(Chief Engineer)*, Paul Jott *(Administrative Resident)*, Jacqueline Brookes *(Dr. Immelman)*, Ruth Attaway Morrison *(Circulating Nurse)*, Lee Beery *(Mead's Secretary)*, Christopher Guest *(Resident)*, Sabrina Grant *(Nurse X)*, Bette Henritze *(Mrs. Kimball)*, Tom Spratley *(Mitgang)*, Robert Anthony *(Dr. Ives)*, Katherine Helmond *(Marilyn Mead)*, William Perlow, M.D. *(Cardiac Arrest Doctor)*, Alex Colon *(Young Lord)*, Nat Grant *(Black Panther)*, Milton Earl Forrest *(Militant Leader)*, Carolyn Krigbaum *(Gloria Lebow)*, Paul Whaley *(Hospital Spokesman)*.

Scott's great performance as a N.Y. medical center's chief surgeon whose personal life has driven him to the brink of suicide is the only thing that saves this only occasionally successful black comedy written by Paddy Chayefsky. Scott presides over a veritable looney-bin of activity in a hospital that is being torn apart by a string of inexplicable murders of staff members. The laughs are sporadic at best and Chayefsky's heavy-handed message (i.e., hospitals treat their patients badly) eats away at the satire.

p, Howard Gottfried; d, Arthur Hiller; w, Paddy Chayefsky; ph, Victor J. Kemper (DeLuxe Color), m, Morris Surdin; ed, Eric Albertson; prod d, Gene Rudolf; set d, Herb Mulligan; cos, Frank Thompson; makeup, Vincent Callaghan.
Comedy/Drama Cas. (PR:C MPAA:GP)

HOSPITAL MASSACRE zero (1982) 90m Cannon c
(GB: X-RAY; AKA: WARD 13; BE MY VALENTINE, OR ELSE . . .)
Barbi Benton *(Susan)*, Chip Lucia *(Harry)*, Jon Van Ness *(Jack)*, John Warner Williams *(Saxon)*, Gay Austin *(Jacobs)*, Den Surles *(Beam)*, Michael Frost *(Ned)*, Karen Smith *(Kitty)*, Billy Jacoby *(Young Harry)*, Marian Beeler, Elly Wold, Jonathan Moore, Tammy Simpson, Bill Errigo, Lanny Duncan, Thomas McClure, Beverly Hart, Jon Greene, Gloria Morrison.
Following in the glorious tradition of *Playboy* favorites, Hugh Hefner's great friend Benton opted to appear in this vile exploitation vehicle where she is given an opportunity to be terrorized by evil hospital employees, scream at the top of her ample lungs, *and* take off her clothes.
p, Menahem Golan, Yoram Globus; d, Boaz Davidson; w, Marc Behm; ph, Nicholas von Sternberg; m, Arlon Ober; prod d, Jac McAnelly; art d, J.R. Fox; spec eff, Joe Quinlavin; makeup, Allan Apone, Kathy Shorkey.
Horror Cas. (PR:O MPAA:R)

HOSTAGE, THE* (1956, Brit.) 80m Douglas Fairbanks-Westridge/Eros bw
Ron Randell *(Bill Trailer)*, Mary Parker *(Rosa Gonzuelo)*, John Bailey *(Dr. Main)*, Carl Jaffe *(Dr. Pablo Gonzuelo)*, Anne Blake *(Mrs. Steen)*, Cyril Luckham *(Hugh Ferguson)*, Margaret Diamond *(Mme. Gonzuelo)*, Victor Brooks *(Inspector Clifford)*.
Poorly conceived attempt to create a political thriller looks anything but thrilling. In an unnamed country the local revolutionaries get it in their heads to avert the execution of their leader by staging a kidnaping of the president's daughter. Only they don't reckon on pilot Randell to escape their hold and perform some ludicrous heroics. The revolutionary leader is killed and the girl is saved because of Randell's efforts.
p, Thomas Clyde; d, Harold Huth; w, Alfred Shaughnessy; ph, Brendan Stafford.
Thriller (PR:A MPAA:NR)

HOSTAGE, THE½** (1966) 83m Heartland/Crown International c
Don O'Kelly *(Bull)*, Harry Dean Stanton *(Eddie)*, John Carradine *(Otis Lovelace)*, Danny Martins *(Davey Cleaves)*, Ron Hagerthy *(Steve Cleaves)*, Jennifer Lea *(Carol Cleaves)*, Ann Doran *(Miss Mabry)*, Raymond Guth *(Sam)*, Nora Marlowe *(Selma)*, Shirley O'Hara *(Mrs. Primus)*, Mike McCloskey *(Bartender)*, Dick Spry *(Mr. Thomas)*, Leland Brown *(Glenn)*, Pearl Faessler.
Taut low-budget drama starring Martins as a six-year-old boy who finds himself trapped in a moving van filled with his family's belongings (they are moving to another city) which is being driven by two murderers, the brutish O'Kelly and the weak-willed Stanton. After miles on the road, the pair stop in a deserted area to bury the corpse of their victim. Upon discovering the boy, they realize that he is an eyewitness to their crime and he must be silenced. Sensing he is about to be killed, Martins flees to a nearby farm house owned by an elderly couple. When O'Kelly arrives to capture the boy, he is able to convince the couple that he is Martins' father and that the boy has run away. The old folks turn the boy over to O'Kelly. Meanwhile, Martins' parents have launched a massive man-hunt for the missing child and the cops are hot on the killers' trail. Fearing O'Kelly, but sympathetic to Martins' plight, Stanton finally stands up to his evil partner and after a near fatal crash, turns the boy over to the authorities and resigns himself to his fate.
p&d, Russell S. Doughton; w, Robert Laning (based on the novel by Henry Farrell); ph, Ted Mikels (Technicolor); m, Jaime Mendoza-Nava; ed, Gary Kurtz, Ron Honthaner; md, Mendoza-Nava; prod d, Ray Storey; m/l, "The Hostage," Ronald Hanna (sung by Steve Smith).
Crime (PR:A MPAA:G)

HOSTAGES** (1943) 88m PAR bw
Arturo de Cordova *(Paul Breda)*, Luise Rainer *(Milada Pressinger)*, William Bendix *(Janoshik)*, Roland Varno *(Jan Pavel)*, Oscar Homolka *(Lev Pressinger)*, Katina Paxinou *(Maria)*, Paul Lukas *(Rheinhardt)*, Fred Giermann *(Capt. Patzer)*, Felix Basch *(Dr. Wallerstein)*, Michael Visaroff *(Solvik)*, Eric Feldary *(Peter Lovkowitz)*, John Mylong *(Proskosch)*, Mikhail Rasumny *(Joseph)*, Philip Van Zandt *(Lt. Eisner)*, Rex Williams *(Lt. Marschmann)*, Hans Conried *(Lt. Glasenapp)*, Louis Adlon *(Young Nazi Soldier)*, Richard Ryen *(Elderly Nazi Soldier)*, Kurt Neumann *(Sergeant)*.
Typical war-time drama starring Bendix (in a questionable bit of casting) as the leader of the Czech underground who is captured (though they do not know his true identity), along with wealthy Nazi collaborator Homolka and 24 other Czechs, and held hostage pending the outcome of an investigation into the death of a Nazi officer. Eventually the coroner concludes the Nazi's death was a suicide, but the Gestapo attempts to make the death appear to be a murder so that they can confiscate Homolka's fortune. Bendix finally makes good his escape and manages to blow up the Nazi munitions dumps.
p, Sol C. Siegel; d, Frank Tuttle; w, Lester Cole, Frank Butler (based on the novel by Stefan Heym); ph, Victor Milner; m, Victor Young; ed, Archie Marshek; art d, Hans Dreier, Franz Bachelin.
War (PR:A MPAA:NR)

HOSTILE COUNTRY** (1950) 59m Lippert bw
Jimmy Ellison *(Shamrock)*, Russell Hayden *(Lucky)*, Raymond Hatton *(Colonel)*, Fuzzy Knight *(Deacon)*, Betty [Julie] Adams *(Ann)*, Tom Tyler *(Tom)*, George J. Lewis *(Knowlton)*, John Cason *(Ed)*, Stanley Price *(Sheriff)*, Stephen Carr *(Curt)*, Dennis Moore *(Pete)*, George Chesebro *(Oliver)*, Bud Osborne *(Agate)*, Jimmy Martin *(Fred)*, J. Farrell MacDonald *(Mr. Lane)*, I. Stanford Jolley *(Bartender)*, Cliff Taylor *(Dad)*, Judith Webster *(Marie)*, George Sowards, James Van Horn *(Ranchers)*, Ray Jones.
Veteran HOPALONG CASSIDY sidekicks Ellison and Hayden started a series of oaters of their own after the success of the "Hoppy" movies on television. This one sees the partners off to visit their stepfather in another territory, but they find their relative missing and a range war being fought on his land. Eventually the boys find their dad and kick the baddies out of the area.
p, Ron Ormond; d, Thomas Carr; w, Maurice Tombragel, Ormond; ph, Ernest Miller; m, Walter Greene; ed, Hugh Winn; art d, Fred Preble.
Western (PR:A MPAA:NR)

HOSTILE GUNS½** (1967) 91m A.C. Lyles/PAR c
George Montgomery *(Gid McCool)*, Yvonne De Carlo *(Laura Mannon)*, Tab Hunter *(Mike Reno)*, Brian Donlevy *(Marshal Willett)*, John Russell *(Aaron)*, Leo Gordon *(Hank Pleasant)*, Robert Emhardt *(R.C. Crawford)*, Pedro Gonzalez Gonzalez *(Angel)*, James Craig *(Ned Cooper)*, Richard Arlen *(Sheriff Travis)*, Emile Meyer *(Uncle Joe)*, Donald Barry *(Johnson)*, Fuzzy Knight *(Buck)*, William Fawcett *(Jensen)*, Joe Brown *(Bunco)*, Reg Parton *(Chig)*, Read Morgan *(Tubby)*, Eric Cody *(Alfie)*, Roy Jenson, Jack Catron.
Routine oater starring Montgomery as a U.S. marshal given charge of four criminals (Gordon, a child murderer; Emhardt, a corrupt railway executive convicted on graft charges; Gonzalez Gonzalez, a goat-thief who looks forward to learning a trade in prison; and De Carlo, a dance-hall girl who shot her two-timing lover) in a prison wagon journeying across the Texas badlands. Riding shotgun for Montgomery is Hunter, a hot-headed, naive young deputy. During the four-day trek, De Carlo attempts to seduce Hunter into letting her go, and nearly succeeds, until Montgomery throws the gullible kid in with the crooks so that he has no chance of being swayed from his duty. Then the small band is besieged by Emhardt's vicious relatives who have arrived to break him out. Realizing that Montgomery will never be able to fight off the killers alone, De Carlo convinces Hunter that she doesn't really love him and, with this information, Hunter talks Montgomery into letting him help fight off the attack. Together the lawmen rout the gunslingers and complete their mission. Film has some interest due to the cameos of such veteran oater stars as Arlen, Donlevy, Knight, and Barry.
p, A.C. Lyles; d, R.G. Springsteen; w, Steve Fisher, Sloan Nibley (based on a story by Nibley, James Edward Grant); ph, Lothrop Worth (Techniscope, Technicolor); m, Jimmie Haskell; ed, John F. Schreyer; art d, Hal Pereira, Al Roelofs; set d, Robert R. Benton, Budd S. Friend; spec eff, Paul K. Lerpae; makeup, Wally Westmore.
Western (PR:A MPAA:NR)

HOSTILE WITNESS*½ (1968, Brit.) 101m Caralan-Dador/UA c
Ray Milland *(Simon Crawford, Q. C.)*, Sylvia Sims *(Sheila Larkin)*, Felix Aylmer *(Mr. Justice Osborne)*, Raymond Huntley *(John Naylor)*, Geoffrey Lumsden *(Maj. Hugh Maitland)*, Norman Barrs *(Charles Milburn)*, Percy Marmont *(Sir Matthew Gregory)*, Dulcie Bowman *(Lady Gregory)*, Ewan Roberts *(Hamish Gillespie)*, Richard Hurndall *(Inspector Elsy)*, Ronald Leith-Hunt *(Dr. Wimborne)*, Sandra Fehr *(Joanna Crawford)*, Edward Waddy *(Usher)*, Maggie McGrath *(Julia Kelly)*, Ballard Berkeley *(Count Clerk)*.
After a British barrister's daughter is killed by a hit-and-run driver, the grieved father vows revenge. Later his neighbor turns up dead and all evidence points towards the barrister as his killer. He goes on trial for murder and is forced to question his very sanity. This potentially fascinating psychological drama never delivers, hampered as it is by flat direction and performances that belong more on stage than in a film. The complex plot twists only confuse. Milland directed as well as starred.
p, David E. Rose; d, Ray Milland; w, Jack Roffey (based on his play); ph, Gerry Gibbs (DeLuxe Color); ed, Bernard Gribble; art d, George Provis.
Courtroom Drama (PR:A MPAA:NR)

HOT ANGEL, THE*½ (1958) 73m PAR bw
Jackie Loughery *(Mandy Wilson)*, Edward Kemmer *(Chuck Lawson)*, Mason Alan Dinehart *(Joe Wilson)*, Emory Parnell *(Judd Pfeifer)*, Lyle Talbot *(Van Richards)*, Zon Teller *(Mick Pfeifer)*, Heather Ames *(Lynn Conners)*, Steffi Sidney *(Myrna)*, John Nolan *(Ray)*, Richard Stauffer *(Monk)*, Kathi Thornton *(Liz)*, Harold Mallet *(Pilot)*.
Kemmer plays a plane-flying Korean war vet charged with looking after his dead war buddy's younger sister, Loughery, and kid brother, Dinehart. Much to the dismay of his sister, young Dinehart has taken up with a nasty gang of motorcyclists. The clever Kemmer eventually convinces the spunky youngster that it is much more exciting flying observation planes for a uranium prospector (which is what he does) than raising hell on wheels. And Loughery falls in love with Kemmer.
p, Stanley Kallis; d, Joe Parker; w, Kallis; ph, Karl Struss (aerials, Elmer G. Dyer); m, Richard Markowitz; ed, Eda Warren, Leon Selditz; md, Robert Drasnin.
Drama (PR:C MPAA:NR)

HOT BLOOD*** (1956) 85m COL c
Jane Russell *(Annie Caldash)*, Cornel Wilde *(Stephen Torino)*, Luther Adler *(Marco Torino)*, Joseph Calleia *(Papa Theodore)*, Mikhail Rasumny *(Old Johnny)*, Nina Koshetz *(Nita Johnny)*, Helen Westcott *(Velma)*, Jamie Russell *(Xano)*, Wally Russell *(Bimbo)*, Nick Dennis *(Korka)*, Richard Deacon *(Mr. Swift)*, Robert Foulk *(Sgt. McGrossin)*, John Raven *(Joe Randy)*, Joe Merritt *(Skinny Gypsy)*, Faye Nuell *(Gypsy Woman)*, Joan Reynolds *(Girl)*, Ethan Laidlaw *(Bit)*, Peter Brocco *(Doctor)*, Les Baxter, Ross Bagdasarian *(Gas Station Attendants)*, Manuel Paris *(Elder)*.
Strange dramatic musical directed by Nicholas Ray and starring Russell and Wilde as a gypsy couple whose marriage was pre-arranged by their relatives. Though the couple have little interest in each other at first and regard each other with suspicion (especially Wilde, who wants to become a dancer and doesn't have time for a wife), they eventually clinch in the fadeout. Ray milks the comedy element for

all it's worth and the musical numbers are staged surprisingly well by a director mainly known for his gritty dramas. Songs include: "Tsara, Tsara" and "I Could Learn To Love You."

p, Howard Welsch, Harry Tatelman; d, Nicholas Ray; w, Jesse Lasky, Jr. (based on a story by Jean Evans); ph, Ray June (CinemaScope, Technicolor); m, Les Baxter; ed, Otto Ludwig; art d, Robert Peterson; ch, Matt Mattox, Sylvia Lewis; m/l, Baxter, Ross Bagdasarian.

Romance/Musical **(PR:A MPAA:NR)**

HOT BOX, THE½** (1972, U.S./Phil.) 85m New World c

Andrea Cagan *(Bunny)*, Margaret Markov *(Lynn)*, Rickey Richardson *(Ellie)*, Laurie Rose *(Sue)*, Carmen Argenziano *(Flavio)*, Charles Dierkop *(Garcia/Maj. Dubay)*.

This film, produced and written by Demme, was shot in the Philippines, using that country's ambiguous political condition as the means of exploring commitment to a cause. Four American nurses (Cagan, Markov, Richardson and Rose) working for the Peace Corps, are kidnaped by a band of guerrillas in order to give aid to wounded soldiers. The nurses remain politically aloof to the rebels' cause until they begin to understand their dedication. Their final change comes when the foursome has been captured by a sadistic officer of the government. After being taken advantage of sexually by this major, they get their own revenge and then rejoin the rebels.

p, Jonathan Demme; d, Joe Viola; w, Viola, Demme; ph, Felipe Sacdalan (Metrocolor); m, Resti Umali; ed, Ben Barcelon; art d, Ben Otico.

War/Drama **(PR:O MPAA:R)**

HOT CAR GIRL*½ (1958) 71m AA bw

Richard Bakalyan *(Duke)*, June Kenney *(Peg)*, John Brinkley *(Fred)*, Robert Knapp *(Ryan)*, Jana Lund *(Janice)*, Sheila McKay *(Mickey)*, Bruno Ve Sota *(Joe)*, George Albertson *(Mrs. Dale)*, Jack Lambert *(Older Sheriff)*, Ed Nelson *(Young Sheriff)*, Hal Smith *(Dolman)*, Howard Culver *(Desk Sergeant)*, Tyler McVey *(Mr. Wheeler)*.

Violent juvenile delinquent drama starring Bakalyan as a wayward youth who hangs around with a group of troublemakers that steals and resells auto parts to pay for beer and parties. When Bakalyan meets and falls for sweet young thing Kenney, she nearly convinces him to give up his unsocial behavior, but too late. He runs one last game of chicken against tough-gal Lund and she is killed. Rather than face the law, he grabs Kenney and flees, only to be eventually gunned down by the cops (after seeing Kenney to safety). Only then is it revealed that his anti-social behavior was caused by a beating he received from the police as a youth! Roger Corman was the executive producer.

p, Gene Corman; d, Bernard L. Kowalski; w, Leo Gordon; ph, John M. Nickolaus; m, Cal Tjader; ed, Irene Morra; md, Tjader; art d, Dan Haller.

Drama **(PR:O MPAA:NR)**

HOT CARGO** (1946) 57m Pine-Thomas/PAR bw

William Gargan *(Joe Harkness)*, Jean Rogers *(Jerry Walters)*, Philip Reed *(Chris Bigelow)*, Larry Young *(Warren Porter)*, Harry Cording *(Matt Wayne)*, Will Wright *(Tim Chapman)*, Virginia Brissac *(Mrs. Chapman)*, David Holt *(Pete Chapman)*, Dick Elliot *(Frankie)*.

Gargan and Reed play two rough-and-tumble WW II vets who stop off to visit the family of a buddy killed in the war. They find the family in serious financial trouble, so they decide to stick around and help out with the clan's log-trucking business. Rival trucking firms have been trying to force the family out of business and things turn ugly when the family's youngest son is killed by the villains. Gargan and Reed soon settle the score.

p, William Pine, William Thomas; d, Lew Landers; w, Geoffrey Holmes; ph, Fred Jackman, Jr.; ed, Henry Adams; art d, F. Paul Sylos.

Drama **(PR:A MPAA:NR)**

HOT CARS** (1956) 60m Bel-Air/UA bw

John Bromfield *(Nick Dunn)*, Joi Lansing *(Karen Winter)*, Mark Dana *(Smiley Ward)*, Carol Shannon *(Jane Dunn)*, Ralph Clanton *(Arthur Markel)*, Robert Osterloh *(George Hayman)*, Dabbs Greer *(Det. Davenport)*, Charles Keane *(Lt. Jefferson)*, Kurt Katch *(Otto Krantz)*, George Sawaya *(Lt. Holmes)*, John Merrick *(Hutton)*, Joan Sinclair *(Miss Rogers)*, Maurice Marks *(Paul the Bartender)*, Marilee Earle *(Betty Carson)*, Vic Cutrier *(Bret Carson)*, Paula Hill *(Mrs. Davenport)*.

Fast-paced programmer starring Bromfield as a likable car salesman who is forced to sell stolen autos because he needs the cash to pay for the expensive surgery needed by his infant son. He tries to pull out of the racket, but when a nosy cop gets too close to the gangsters, they kill him and pin the murder on Bromfield. The climax sees a well-staged battle between Bromfield and the killer on a zooming roller-coaster at an amusement park. The plot motivation borders on the ludicrous.

p, Howard W. Koch; d, Donald McDougall; w, Don Martin, Richard Landau (based on a novel by H. Haile Chace); ph, William Marguiles; m, Les Baxter; ed, George Gittens; md, Baxter; cos, Wesley V. Jefferies, Angela Alexander.

Crime **(PR:A MPAA:NR)**

HOT CURVES** (1930) 83m Tiffany bw

Marceline [Alice] Day, Benny Rubin, Pert Kelton, Natalie Moorhead, Rex Lease, Mary Carr, John Ince, Paul Hurst, Mike Donlin.

Racial drama starring Rubin as the first Jewish baseball player signed to play ball in the major league. Though the management signs Rubin just to draw Jewish customers, the kid turns out to be a virtuoso on the field and becomes the team's hero.

d, Norman Taurog; w, Earle Snell, Frank Mortimer, Benny Rubin (based on a story by Mortimer, A. P. Younger); ph, Max Dupont; ed, Clarence Kolster.

Drama **(PR:A MPAA:NR)**

HOT ENOUGH FOR JUNE (SEE: AGENT 8 3/4, 1963, Brit.)

HOT FOR PARIS** (1930) 71m FOX bw

Victor McLaglen *(John Patrick Duke)*, Fifi Dorsay *(Fifi Dupre)*, El Brendel *(Axel Olson)*, Polly Moran *(Polly)*, Lennox Pawle *(Mr. Pratt)*, August Tollaire *(Papa Gouset)*, George Fawcett *(Chop Captain)*, Charles Judels *(Charlott Gouset)*, Eddie Dillon *(Ship's Cook)*, Rosita Marstini *(Fifi's Mother)*, Agostino Borgato *(Fifi's Father)*, Yola D'Avril *(Babette Dupre)*, Anita Murray *(Mimi)*, Dave Valles *(Monsieur Furrier)*.

McLaglen stars as a dim-witted sailor adventuring in Paris who has won a million-dollar prize in a horse lottery and doesn't know it. The lottery officials dispatch an agent to give him his prize, but when McLaglen mistakes the man for a detective, he takes it on the lam through the streets of Paris. While staying one step ahead of what he believes to be the law, McLaglen finds time to romance Dorsay, and all turns out well when the fortune is eventually handed over to him. Songs are "Sweet Nothings Of Love," "Look Into My Eyes, Baby," "If You Want to See Paree," sung by Dorsay, and the comedy tune "I'm the Duke of Kakiyak," sung by McLaglen.

d, Raoul Walsh; w, William K. Wells, Charles McGuirk (based on a story by Walsh); ph, Charles Van Enger; art d, David Hall; set d, Ben Carre; m/l, Walter Donaldson, Edgar Leslie.

Musical **(PR:A MPAA:NR)**

HOT FRUSTRATIONS (SEE: FRUSTRATIONS, 1967, Fr./Ital.)

HOT HEIRESS** (1931) 81m FN-WB bw

Ben Lyon *(Hap Harrigan)*, Ona Munson *(Juliette Hunter)*, Walter Pidgeon *(Clay)*, Tom Dugan *(Bill Dugan)*, Holmes Herbert *(Mr. Hunter)*, Inez Courtney *(Margie)*, Thelma Todd *(Lola)*, Nella Walker *(Mrs. Hunter)*, George Irving, Joe Bernard.

Rodgers and Hart musical starring Lyon as a hapless riveter who falls into the life of rich society gal Munson when he invades her penthouse in search of a hot rivet that had gotten away. The bored Munson decides to have some fun with this "common" worker and she sets out to pass him off as a society architect to her friends. The gag soon wears thin and the viewer is left to sort through the surprisingly lackluster tunes which include: "You're the Cats," "Nobody Loves a Riveter," "Like Ordinary People Do," and "Too Good To Be True" (which was cut before the film's original release). Rodgers and Hart were so disappointed with this critical and commercial failure that they withdrew from their next two assignments for First National. Remade in 1934 as HAPPINESS ABROAD and again in 1941.

d, Clarence Badger; w, Herbert Fields, Richard Rodgers, Lorenz Hart; ph, Sol Polito ed, Thomas Pratt; m/l, Rodgers, Hart.

Musical **(PR:A MPAA:NR)**

HOT HORSE (SEE: ONCE UPON A HORSE, 1958)

HOT HOURS½** (1963, Fr.) 90m KLF/Raleigh-Joseph Brenner bw (HEURES CHAUDES)

Liliane Brousse *(Olivia)*, Francoise Deldick *(Lise)*, Claude Sainlouis *(Bruno)*, Michele Philippe *(Clemence)*, Pierre Richard *(Manuel)*, Liliane Sorval *(Claire, Aunt Irma)*, Pierre Mirat, Michel Vocoret.

After being stood-up on her wedding day, Brousse and her younger sister, Deldick, leave their small town to look for better things. They stay with their aunt, Sorval, at her boarding house, and are warned about Sainlouis, the resident womanizer. Deldick is fascinated by the man and tries to seduce him away from his mistress Philippe. But instead he falls for her older sister, leaving Deldick alone as Brousse makes love with Sainlouis.

p, Lola Kohn; d, Louis Felix; w, Gilles Siry, Felix; ph, Arthur Raimondo; m, Daniel White; ed, Linette Nicolas.

Drama **(PR:O MPAA:NR)**

HOT ICE½** (1952, Brit.) 65m Present Day-SWH Piccadilly/Apex bw

John Justin *(Jim Henderson)*, Barbara Murray *(Mary)*, Ivor Barnard *(Edwin Carson)*, John Penrose *(Freddie Usher)*, Michael Balfour *(Jacobson)*, Gabrielle Brune *(Marcella)*, Anthony Pendrell *(Burroughs)*, Bill Shine *(Henry)*, Fred Gray, Dorothy Wheatley, Sam Kydd, Derek Sidney, Archie Duncan, Keith Grieve, Billy Howard, Ida Patlanski, Freddie Tripp, Kendal Chalmers.

Justin is invited for a weekend party to Barnard's plush English estate, where he learns that his host is simply out to steal his guests' valuable jewels. Justin enlists the help of Barnard's adopted daughter, Murray, to foil the plan, but she ends up getting locked away in the jewel room. When Barnard tries to make a quick getaway, he ends up being foiled by his butler Balfour. The servant turns on the ground's electric current, thus electrocuting his employer. Though highly implausible, this comic caper works in a manner only the British can pull off. The direction and script are well thought out, taking some neat twists along the way.

p, Charles Reynolds; d&w, Kenneth Hume (based on the play "A Weekend At Thrackley" by Alan Melville); ph, Ted Lloyd.

Crime/Comedy **(PR:A MPAA:NR)**

HOT IN PARADISE (SEE: IT'S HOT IN PARADISE, 1962, Ger.)

HOT LEAD** (1951) 60m RKO bw (AKA: A TASTE OF HOT LEAD)

Tim Holt *(Tim)*, Joan Dixon *(Gail)*, Ross Elliott *(Dave Collins)*, John Dehner *(Turk Thorne)*, Paul Marion *(Dakota)*, Lee MacGregor *(Bob)*, Stanley Andrews *(Warden)*, Paul E. Burns *(Duke)*, Kenneth MacDonald *(Sheriff)*, Robert Wilke *(Stoney Dawson)*, Richard Martin *(Chito Rafferty)*.

Standard Holt oater which sees the cowboy and his sidekick Martin vowing vengeance on a gang of train robbers who murder one of their friends during a hold-up. Gang member Elliott (who wants to go straight), telegraphs when the next robbery is about to take place and Holt and Martin get their revenge.

p, Herman Schlom; d, Stuart Gilmore; w, William Lively; ph, Nicholas Musuraca; m, C. Bakaleinikoff; ed, Robert Golden; art d, Albert D'Agostino, Feild Gray.

Western **(PR:A MPAA:NR)**

HOT LEAD AND COLD FEET½** (1978) 90m Disney/BV c

Jim Dale *(Eli/Wild Billy/Jasper Bloodshy)*, Karen Valentine *(Jenny)*, Don Knotts *(Denver Kid)*, Jack Elam *(Rattlesnake)*, Darren McGavin *(Mayor Ragsdale)*, John Williams *(Mansfield)*, Warren Vanders *(Boss Snead)*, Debbie Lytton *(Roxanne)*, Michael Sharrett *(Marcus)*, Dave Cass *(Jack)*, Richard Wright *(Pete)*, Don "Red" Barry *(Bartender)*, Jimmy Van Patten *(Jake)*, Gregg Palmer *(Jeff)*, Ed Bakey *(Joshua)*, John Steadman *(Old Codger)*, Eric Server, Paul Lukather, Hap Lawrence, Robert Rothwell, Terry Nicholas, Dallas McKennon, Stanley Clements, Don Brodie, Warde Donovan, Ron Honthaner, Norland Benson, Jim Whitecloud, Brad Weston, Russ Fast, Mike Howden, Art Burke, James Michaelford.

Disappointing Disney western starring British actor Dale in a triple role: a wealthy land-owner who has supposedly died and his sons, one a gunslinger, the other a Bible-reader. Plot concerns the rival brothers' efforts to win the family fortune and take over the town. It is the usual "good vs. evil" morality play which has been handled better by Disney elsewhere. Veteran western star Elam and superb character actor McGavin are totally wasted.

p, Ron Miller; d, Robert Butler; w, Joe McEveety, Arthur Alsberg, Don Nelson (based on a story by Rod Piffath); ph, Frank Phillips (Technicolor); m, Buddy Baker; ed, Ray de Leuw; art d, John Mansbridge, Frank T. Smith; cos, Ron Talsky, spec eff, Eustace Lycett, Art Cruikshank, Danny Lee, Hal Bigger, Billy Lee; stunts, Buddy Joe Hooker.

Western **Cas.** **(PR:AA MPAA:G)**

HOT MILLIONS*½** (1968, Brit.) 106m Milberg-MGM/MGM c

Peter Ustinov *(Marcus Pendleton)*, Maggie Smith *(Patty Terwilliger)*, Karl Malden *(Carlton J. Klemper)*, Bob Newhart *(Willard C. Gnatpole)*, Robert Morley *(Caesar Smith)*, Cesar Romero *(Customs Inspector)*, Melinda May *(Nurse)*, Ann Lancaster *(Landlady)*, Frank Tragear *(Bus Inspector)*, Julie May *(1st Charwoman)*, Margaret Courtenay *(Mrs. Hubbard)*, Elizabeth Counsell *(Miss Glyn)*, Patsy Crowther *(2nd Charwoman)*, Carlos Douglas *(Barber)*, Lynda Baron *(Louise)*, Billy Milton *(Agent)*, Peter Jones *(Prison Governor)*, David Bedard *(Co-Pilot)*, Elizabeth Hughes *(Air Hostess)*, Anne De Vigier *(Secretary/Receptionist)*, Sally Faulkner *(Stewardess on Rio Plane)*, Paul Farrell *(Larry)*, Wilfred Carter *(Theatre Manager)*, Geoffrey Frederick *(Customs Man)*, Betty Duncan *(Nun)*, Frank Singuineau *(Customs Man in Rio)*, Raymond Huntley *(Bayswater)*, William Mervyn *(Sir Charles Wilson)*, Kynaston Reeves *(Quayle)*, Bob Todd *(British Commissionaire)*, Anthony Sharp *(Hollis)*, Paul Dawkins *(Pritchard)*, Hugo De Vernier *(French Bank Official)*, Jimmy Thompson *(Salesman)*, Harold Holness *(Pygny)*, William Burleigh *(Page Boy)*, Victor Platt *(Barman)*, Penelope Jago *(Ticket Girl)*.

Often hysterical comedy that didn't find an audience at the box office but has since been recognized as one of the better comedies of the late 1960s due to many TV showings. Ustinov is an embezzler who has just finished serving time in jail. He'd been caught by one of those infernal computers and that's caused him to study the critters until he becomes as expert at them as the men who discovered his last illegal enterprise. He cons Morley, a renowned computer genius, into leaving the country, then assumes Morley's identity and secures employment at a huge corporation headed by Malden. Once inside the conglomerate, Ustinov uses the computer to issue large checks to fictitious firms in Frankfurt, Paris, and Rome. Then he flies to those cities, picks up the checks and cashes them. Ustinov also falls in love with Smith, his secretary. They marry and she quickly becomes pregnant. They leave for Rio immediately. Soon enough, Malden uncovers the robberies and enlists Newhart, his resident computer maven (in his first major acting role), to help nab Ustinov and Smith. All Malden wants is the money back, and that is taken care of when it is learned that Smith wisely invested the ill-gotten gains in a soaring stock market, made a fortune, and is now able to repay the stolen money. Ustinov now exercises his penchant for classical music and leads a concert orchestra, with Smith playing the flute. In the end, no one is hurt, the money is safe, and the perpetrators of the plot get away with it—something not often seen in those days when there was still some censorship. Made in London, at Borehamwood, the bright script by Wallach and Ustinov must have gone right over the heads of the late 1960s audiences because it surely is funny today.

p, Mildred Freed Alberg; d, Eric Till; w, Ira Wallach, Peter Ustinov; ph, Ken Higgins (Metrocolor); m, Laurie Johnson; ed, Richard Marden; art d, Bill Andrews; cos, Germinal Rangel; m/l, "This Time," Johnson, Don Black (sung by Lulu).

Comedy **(PR:C MPAA:G)**

HOT MONEY*½ (1936) 68m WB bw

Ross Alexander *(Chick Randall)*, Beverly Roberts *(Grace Lane)*, Joseph Cawthorn *(Max Dourfuss)*, Paul Graetz *(Dr. David)*, Andrew Tombes *(Willie)*, Harry Burns *(Pasquale Romenetti)*, Ed Conrad *(Antonio Romenetti)*, Anne Nagel *(Ruth McElniney)*, Frank Orth *(Hank Ford)*, Cy Kendall *(Joe Morgan)*, Andre Beranger *(Ed Biddie)*, Joe Cunningham *(Gus Vanderbilt)*, Addison Richards *(Forbes)*, Charley Foy *(Ratto)*, R. Emmett Keane *(Prof. Kimberly)*, Ed Stanley *(Joe Thomas)*.

Low-budget comedy chronicling the efforts of conniving salesman Alexander to market inventor Graetz's new product, a water-based gasoline. Alexander needs cash fast so that the inventor can complete his research, so he concocts a phony stock promotion and announces that Graetz has already perfected his product. Of course the money pours in from excited investors, and Alexander sets up a fake corporation with a dummy board of directors. It looks like the scheme will work until the inventor is kidnaped, leaving Alexander to solve the crime or face financial ruin and prison.

p, Bryan Foy; d, William McGann, Harry Seymour; w, William Jacobs (based on an idea by Aben Kandel); ph, Arthur Edeson; ed, Clarence Kolster; art d, Esdras Hartley; m/l, "What Can I Do? I Love Him," Ruth Hersher, Louis Herscher.

Comedy **(PR:A MPAA:NR)**

HOT MONEY GIRL** (1962, Brit./Ger.) 81m Beaconsfield-Orbit-Sydney Box-Kurt Ulrich/United Producers bw (RHAPSODIE IN BLEI; GB: THE TREASURE OF SAN TERESA; LONG DISTANCE)

Willy Witte *(General von Hartmann)*, Eddie Constantine *(Larry Brennan)*, Dawn Addams *(Hedi von Hartmann)*, Gaylord Cavallaro *(Mike Jones)*, Marius Goring *(Rudi Siebert)*, Nadine Tallier *(Zizi)*, Walter Gotell *(1st Inspector of Hamburg Police)*, Christopher Lee *(Jaeger)*, Hubert Mittendorf *(Schneider)*, Derek Sydney *(Barman)*, Penelope Horner *(Bar Girl)*, Tsai Chin, Diane Potter *(Bar Girls in Fight)*, Tom Bowman *(Tough)*, Steve Plytas *(Station Sergeant)*, Anna Turner *(Maid at Billie's)*, Marie Devereux *(Girl with the Mink)*, Thomas Gallagher *(Truck Driver)*, Clive Dunn *(Cemetery Keeper)*, Stella Bonheur *(Sister Angelica)*, Margaret Boyd *(Sister Catherine)*, Sheldon Lawrence *(Patrolling Policeman)*, Egon Mohr *(2nd Inspector of Hamburg Police)*, Walter Buhler *(Uniformed Policeman)*, Georgina Cookson *(Billie)*, Hutch *(Piano Player at Billie's)*, Susan Travers *(Girl at Billie's)*.

Fast-paced drama starring Constantine as an American O.S.S. man who hid a fortune in jewels in Czechoslovakia for a Nazi general soon after the war. Though the general kills himself before he can reclaim the gems, Constantine is persuaded by the general's former aide, Goring, to recover the fortune. With the help of the general's daughter, Addams, who is now a prostitute, the trio locate the jewels. But Constantine and Addams are then betrayed by Goring who was working in cahoots with Addams' roommate Tallier. She, then, kills Addams and makes her getaway on the Munich Express. Constantine, however, manages to get aboard the speeding train and is about to reclaim the gems when the box slips and falls into the river below. The police arrive and arrest Tallier, and Constantine decides to build a new life with Addams.

p, John Nasht, Patrick Filmer-Sankey; d, Alvin Rakoff; w, Jack Andrews (based on a story by Jeffrey Dell); ph, Wilkie Cooper; m, Philip Martell, Jeff Davis, Don Banks; ed, Jim Connock; art d, George Provis; cos, Jim Dunlevy, Barbara Gillett; makeup, George Partleton.

Drama **(PR:C MPAA:NR)**

HOT MONTH OF AUGUST, THE* (1969, Gr.) 79m Viktoria/Kapsaskis-Danfilm/J.E.R. bw (HO ZESTOS MENAS AUGOUSTOS)

Petros Fissoun, Betty Arvaniti, Yannis Fertis, Vania Aksar.

Convoluted romantic drama about a young man who becomes seduced into the deadly web of the wife of a dangerous and rich industrialist. The woman becomes both sexual and criminal partners with the private detective that her husband has hired to watch her, and the two secretly plan her husband's murder. The plan backfires, however, when her husband overhears the plot and murders her instead, framing the young man. Eventually the young man is saved by an alibi from his real sweetheart who wants to protect him, and the crooks are brought to justice.

p,d&w, Sokrates Kapsaskis; ph, Demetris Papakonstantis; m, Stavros Xarhakos; ed, Emil Habib.

Drama **(PR:C MPAA:NR)**

HOT NEWS*½ (1936, Brit.) 77m St. George's/COL bw

Lupino Lane *(Jimmy Selby)*, Phyllis Clare *(Betty Mason)*, Wallace Lupino *(Horace Wells)*, Barbara Kilner *(Princess Ina)*, Ben Welden *(Slug Wilson)*, Glen Raynham *(Barbara O'Neill)*, Reginald Long *(Prince Stephen)*, Fred Leslie *(Leslie Fredericks)*, George Pughe *(Slim McGill)*, Edward Pierce, Scott Harold, Geoffrey Clarke, Henry Longhurst, The Dorchester Girls.

British newspaper reporter Lane is chosen to be a guest journalist for a Chicago newspaper and while traveling via ship to his new assignment, mistakes some ordinary travelers for hardened criminals. His problems are further compounded when he thinks an heiress is a cabaret crooner, causing the real singer to be kidnaped by some actual criminals. Lane ends up rescuing the girl, but missing a big scoop. He also misses any chance at comedy in this unfunny bit of fluff.

p, Ian Sutherland; d, W.P. Kellino; w, Reginald Long, Arthur Rigby; ph, Jack Barker.

Comedy **(PR:A MPAA:NR)**

HOT NEWS** (1953) 61m MON/AA bw

Stanley Clements *(Mark Miller)*, Gloria Henry *(Kerry Barker)*, Ted De Corsia *(Rizzo)*, Veda Ann Borg *(Doris Burton)*, Scotty Beckett *(Bill Burton)*, Mario Siletti *(Dominic)*, Carl Milletaire *(Dutch)*, James Flavin *(All Bragg)*, Hal Baylor *(Augie)*, Paul Bryar *(Doc Allen)*, Myron Healy *(Jim O'Hara)*.

Former boxer Clements, goes on a one-man crusade to crush a gambling ring run by the slimy deCorsia and his stooges. Fellow fighter Healy is killed in the ring because of a mismatched fight the gang had arranged, so Clements, now a sports columnist, goes after deCorsia himself, nearly getting killed, but bringing the gambler to justice.

p, Ben Schwalb; d, Edward Bernds; w, Charles R. Marion, Elwood Ullman; ph, Carl Guthrie; ed, Lester A. Sansom; art d, David Milton.

Crime **(PR:A MPAA:NR)**

HOT PEPPER** (1933) 70m FOX bw

Edmund Lowe *(Quirt)*, Victor McLaglen *(Flagg)*, Lupe Velez *(Pepper)*, El Brendel *(Olsen)*, Boothe Howard *(Trigger Thorne)*, Lillian Bond *(Hortense)*, Gloria Roy *(Lily)*, Russ Clark *(Egan)*.

The fourth and weakest pairing of Lowe and McLaglen as the rival WW I buddies, Quirt and Flagg, who had spent the last three movies (WHAT PRICE GLORY?,

THE COCK-EYED WORLD, and WOMEN OF ALL NATIONS) genially trying to outdo each other. This time the boys are civilians, and we see McLaglen as a wealthy bootlegger who has little success against Lowe who swipes $10,000, and Latin bombshell Velez from him. McLaglen doesn't let go that easily and Velez finds herself trapped in a tug-of-war between the two rivals. Eventually the battle is ended when Velez walks out on the two of them and the boys end up as generals in the Chinese Army. The series had pretty much gasped its last breath at this point. Velez sings the title song "Hot Pepper."

d, John Blystone; w, Barry Conners, Philip Klein, Dudley Nichols (based on Laurence Stallings' and Maxwell Anderson's "Capt. Flagg" and "Sgt. Quirt" characters); ph, Charles Clarke; m/l, Val Burton, Will Jason.

Comedy **(PR:A MPAA:NR)**

HOT POTATO*½ (1976) 87m WB c

Jim Kelly *(Jones)*, George Memmoli *(Rhino)*, Geoffrey Binney *(Chicago)*, Irene Tsu *(Pam)*, Judith Brown *(Leslie/June)*, Sam Hiona *(Rangoon)*, Ron Prince *(General)*, Hardy Stockmann *(Krugman)*, Metta Rungrat *(Rhino's Lady)*, Supakorn Songermvorakul *(Boy)*, Somcjai Meekunsut *(Pujo)*, Veerapol Pitavan *(Longkat)*, Punchong Nakaraj *(Hoss)*, Kachain Onching *(Little Joe)*.

Less-than-thrilling karate picture which sees black martial-arts expert, Kelly, sent to China to rescue an American senator's daughter, Brown, from an evil Mandarin warlord, Hiona, who has threatened the lass with man-eating tigers.

p, Fred Weintraub, Paul Heller; d&w, Oscar Williams (based on characters created by Alex Rose, Weintraub); ph, Ronald Garcia (CFI Color); m, Christopher Trussell; ed, Peter Berger; art d, Urai Sirisombat; cos, Sherry Chen.

Martial Arts **(PR:O MPAA:PG)**

HOT RHYTHM** (1944) 79m MON bw

Dona Drake *(Mary)*, Robert Lowery *(Jimmy)*, Tim Ryan *(O'Hara)*, Irene Ryan *(Polly)*, Sidney Miller *(Sammy)*, Jerry Cooper *(Taylor)*, Robert Kent *(Strobach)*, Harry Langdon *(Whiffie)*, Lloyd Ingraham *(Brown)*, Cyril Ring *(Jackson)*, Joan Curtis *(Receptionist)*, Paul Porcasi *(Cafe Owner)*.

Lowery and his sidekick Miller are a pair of radio jingle writers who try to make Lowery's singer-girlfriend, Drake, famous by getting her a gig with a big-name band. Irene Ryan is the comedy standout as an eccentric secretary. Directed by the infamous William "One-Shot" Beaudine. Songs include: "Where Were You?" "Talk Me Into It," "Happiest Girl In Town," "Right Under My Nose," and "Say It With Your Heart" (Edward J. Kay, N. Brown, Virginia Wicks, Lou Herscher).

p, Lindsley Parsons; d, William Beaudine; w, Tim Ryan, Charles Marion; ph, Ira Morgan; ed, Richard Currier; md, Edward Kay; art d, E.R. Hickson.

Musical **(PR:A MPAA:NR)**

HOT ROCK, THE*** (1972) 105m FOX c (GB: HOW TO STEAL A DIAMOND IN FOUR EASY LESSONS)

Robert Redford *(Dortmunder)*, George Segal *(Kelp)*, Ron Leibman *(Murch)*, Paul Sand *(Alan Greenberg)*, Zero Mostel *(Abe Greenberg)*, Moses Gunn *(Dr. Amusa)*, William Redfield *(Lt. Hoover)*, Topo Swope *(Sis)*, Charlotte Rae *(Ma Murch)*, Graham P. Jarvis *(Warden)*, Harry Bellaver *(Bartender Rollo)*, Seth Allen *(Happy Hippie)*, Robert Levine *(Cop at Police Station)*, Lee Wallace *(Dr. Strauss)*, Robert Weil *(Albert)*, Lynne Gordon *(Miasmo)*, Grania O'Malley *(Bird Lady)*, Fred Cook *(Otto)*, Mark Dawson *(Big Museum Guard)*, Gilbert Lewis, George Bartenieff *(Museum Guards)*, Ed Bernard, Charles White, Christopher Guest *(Policemen)*.

Redford is a professional thief just out of prison after a four-year stretch, and he is immediately recruited for a job by his brother-in-law, Segal. They meet with Gunn, the ambassador of an African nation, and he financially backs their attempt to steal a priceless diamond from a museum, a stone he says rightfully belongs to his government. They recruit wheelman Leibman and explosives expert Sand to help in the robbery, but when the caper comes off, guards swoop down on Sand while he is holding the stone and he swallows it. Redford and Segal then go to Mostel, Sand's father, and he helps them launch an assault on the jail to get Sand out. The breakout goes well, but once free Sand tells the robbers that the gem is hidden in the police station. When they go to get it, however, they find it is missing and they immediately realize that Mostel must have gotten to it first. They force him to admit that the stone is in his safety deposit box, but when they try to get Gunn to finance another robbery, he balks, preferring simply to buy the stone from Mostel. Redford goes into the bank on his own and hypnotizes the guard, who lets him into the box. On his way out of the bank, he sees Mostel and Gunn on their way in. An entertaining comic caper film, THE HOT ROCK was a strange choice for Redford, and he seems very out of place. Originally, writer Goldman wrote the script with Segal in mind for the Redford part and George C. Scott in the Segal part (Scott actually did appear in another film based on the same novel by Donald Westlake, THE BANK SHOT, 1974). Director Yates, critically hailed for BULLITT (1968), seems to have little idea what to do with Redford and the slowest parts of the film are the scenes developing his character into someone the audience still doesn't especially care about. The rest of the film, though, is quite enjoyable as the gang commits elaborate caper after elaborate caper, always finding their objective has just eluded them.

p, Hal Landers, Bobby Roberts; d, Peter Yates; w, William Goldman (based on a novel by Donald E. Westlake); ph, Ed Brown (Panavision, DeLuxe Color); m, Quincy Jones; ed, Frank P. Keller, Fred W. Berger; prod d, John Robert Lloyd; art d, Bob Wrightman; set d, Robert Drumheller; cos, Ruth Morley; m/l, "When You Believe," Bill Rinehart; stunts, Carey Loftin; makeup, Irving Buchman.

Comedy **Cas.** **(PR:A-C MPAA:PG)**

HOT ROD*½ (1950) 61m MON bw

James Lydon *(David Langham)*, Art Baker *(Judge Langham)*, Gil Stratton, Jr. *(Swifty Johnson)*, Gloria Winters *(Janie Pitts)*, Myron Healey *(Joe Langham)*, Tommy Bond *(Jack Blodgett)*, Jean Dean *(Gloria)*, Bret Hamilton *(Joe's Partner)*, Marshall Reed *(Roberts)*, Dennis Moore *(Patrolman)*, William Vincent *(Holdup Man)*.

Lydon (star of the HENRY ALDRICH series) plays the hot-rod driving son of stuffy, but kind, judge, Baker, who lands himself in a heap of trouble when it is discovered that his car has been involved in a hit-and-run fatality. All the evidence points to Lydon, and even Dad has suspicions, but the plucky youngster manages to find the real killer thanks to the teenager's skillful driving during a police chase. To reward Lydon and his pals who helped in the capture, the town grants the kids a public race track. The cast includes Winters of the "Sky King" TV series.

p, Jerry Thompson; d, Lewis D. Collins; w, Dan Ullman; ph, Gilbert Warrenton; m, Edward J. Kay; ed, Roy Livingston; art d, Dave Milton.

Drama **(PR:A MPAA:NR)**

HOT ROD GANG½** (1958) 71m AIP bw (AKA: FURY UNLEASHED)

John Ashley *(John Abernathy III)*, Jody Fair *(Lois Cavendish)*, Gene Vincent *(Himself)*, Steve Drexel *(Mark)*, Henry McCann *(Dave)*, Maureen Arthur *(Marley)*, Gloria Grant *(Tammy)*, Dorothy Newman *(Anastasia Abernathy)*, Helen Spring *(Abigail Abernathy)*, Lester Dorr *(Dryden Philpot)*, Doodles Weaver *(Wesley Cavendish)*, Russ Bender *(Bill)*, Claire Dubray *(Agatha)*, Dub Taylor *(Al Berrywhiff)*, Scott Peters *(Jack)*, Robert Whiteside *(Jimmy)*, Simmy Bow *(Johnny Red Eye)*, Earl McDaniels *(Himself)*, Kay Wheeler *(Specialty Dancer)*.

Ashley stars as the frustrated young nephew of a pair of stuffy spinster aunts who force him to live a subdued lifestyle if he wishes to inherit their fortune. Unbeknownst to the aunts, Ashley has formed a hot-rod club which he bankrolls by singing incognito, in a rock 'n roll band led by none other than Vincent. With the money he earns from singing, Ashley is able to enter his hot-rod in a national meet. Silly story is made fun by some great tunes sung by Vincent including: "Dance In The Street," "Dance to the Bop," "Baby Blue," and "Lovely Loretta" (backup by the Bluecaps and Eddie Cochran). A must for fans of early rock 'n roll.

p, Lou Rusoff; d, Lew Landers; w, Rusoff; ph, Floyd Crosby; m, Ronald Stein; ed, Robert S. Elsen; art d, Don Ament.

Musical/Drama **(PR:A MPAA:NR)**

HOT ROD GIRL*½ (1956) 79m Nacirema/AIP bw (AKA: HOT CAR GIRL)

Lori Nelson *(Lisa)*, John Smith *(Jeff)*, Chuck Connors *(Ben)*, Frank J. Gorshin *(Flat-Top)*, Roxanne Arlen *(L.P.)*, Mark Andrews *(Bronc)*, Carolyn Kearney *(Judy)*, Ed Reider *(Two Tanks)*, Del Erickson *(Steve)*, Fred Essler *(Yo-Yo)*, Russ Thorson *(Logan)*, Charles Keane *(Pat)*, Dabbs Greer *(Henry)*.

Connors stars as a concerned police officer who seeks to stem the rising tide of illegal drag racing in his community by organizing a supervised hot-rod racing program with the help of experienced dragster Smith. Disaster strikes when Smith's younger brother is killed in a crash and the devastated Smith quits the project. Soon the streets are back to their dangerous, disorganized, and delinquent ways, leaving Connors frustrated. Much to his surprise Connors learns that Smith has been arrested for the hit-and-run death of a child, and the disbelieving cop chases down the real culprit.

p, Norman Herman; d, Leslie H. Martinson; w, John McGreevey; ph, Sam Leavitt; ed, Leon Barsha.

Action/Drama **(PR:A MPAA:NR)**

HOT ROD HULLABALOO* (1966) 81m Silvercliff/AA bw

John Arnold, Arlen Dean Snyder, Kendra Kerr, Ron Cummins, Val Bisoglio, Marsha Mason, William Hunter, Gene Bua, Robert Paget.

A young student decides to enter an illegal drag race in order to win money to pay his college tuition. He doesn't know that his chief competitor will let nothing stand in the way of victory—even if it means shooting his opponent. The student's best friend learns of this treachery, but before he can inform his buddy the nasty drag racer runs him down. Luckily, the student's girl friend manages to hear the dying boy's last words, and manages to stick a pencil in the barrel of the killer's gun before the big race. When it's obvious that the student is going to win the race, the evil dragster pulls out his pistol but blows his own head off when the jammed gun backfires. Shot on location in Washington, D.C.

p, Martin L. Low, William T. Naud; d, Naud; w, Stanley Schneider; ph, Thomas E. Spalding; m, Elliot Lawrence; ed, Frank Toth; md, Lawrence.

Drama **(PR:C MPAA:NR)**

HOT ROD RUMBLE*½ (1957) 79m Nacirema/AA bw

Leigh Snowden, Richard Hartunian, Brett Halsey, Wright King, Joey Forman, Larry Dolgin, John Brinkley, Chuck Webster, Ned Glass, Phil Adams, Joe Mell.

An innocent hot-rodder is accused of running his girl friend and her friend off the road and into an accident which kills her companion. The young man seeks to clear his name and by the time of a big race it is revealed that a fellow gearhead is the culprit who did the deed to get revenge after having his romantic overtures rebuffed.

p, Norman T. Herman; d, Leslie Martinson; w, Meyer Dolinsky; ph, Lester Shorr; m, Alexander Courage; ed, Richard C. Meyer.

Crime/Drama **(PR:C MPAA:NR)**

HOT RODS TO HELL½** (1967) 89m Four Leaf/MGM c (AKA: 52 MILES TO TERROR; 52 MILES TO MIDNIGHT)

Dana Andrews *(Tom Phillips)*, Jeanne Crain *(Peg Phillips)*, Mimsy Farmer *(Gloria)*, Laurie Mock *(Tina Phillips)*, Paul Bertoya *(Duke)*, Gene Kirkwood *(Ernie)*, Tim Stafford *(Jamie Phillips)*, George Ives *(Lank Dailey)*, Hortense Petra *(Wife at Picnic)*, William Mims *(Man at Picnic)*, Paul Genge *(Policeman)*, Peter Oliphant *(Little Boy)*, Harry Hilcox *(Bill Phillips)*, Charles P. Thompson *(Charley)*, Mickey Rooney, Jr. *(Combo Leader)*.

Unintentionally funny juvenile delinquent picture that has developed something of a cult following in recent years. Andrews and Crain star as husband and wife who set off through the California desert in their sedan with their two children, Mock and Stafford, to begin a new life as owner-operators of a motel. The trip turns into a nightmare when the family is assaulted by teenage rebel Farmer and her repulsive boy friends, Bertoya and Kirkwood. By the time Andrews and his clan arrive at their dream location their nerves are frazzled. To their horror, the motel is run-down, and Andrews learns that the former owner allowed it to be used by unruly teenagers for illicit drinking. Andrews breaks off the deal and sets out to his brother's house which is 52 miles away. On the road the youths attack full-force and Andrews finally snaps. He stops the car, blinds Bertoya with his headlights, causing his hot-rod to crash, then hauls the young hoods out of their car. Andrews forces the youngsters to promise to behave like sensible adults or face a long stretch in jail. The punks opt for reformation, while Andrews decides to return and make a go of running the motel. Originally shot for television, but it was later deemed too severe and MGM decided to release HOT RODS TO HELL in the theaters. Nowadays the film turns up on television regularly with no cuts. Music provided by Mickey Rooney, Jr. and his forgettable combo.

p, Sam Katzman; d, John Brahm, James Havens; w, Robert E. Kent (based on a story by Alex Gaby); ph, Lloyd Ahern (Metrocolor); m, Fred Karger; ed, Ben Lewis; md, Karger; art d, George W. Davis, Merrill Pye; set d, Henry Grace, Keogh Gleason; spec eff, J. McMillan Johnson, Carroll L. Shephird; makeup, William Tuttle; m/l, Karger, Sid Wayne, Ben Weisman.

Drama **(PR:C-O) MPAA:NR)**

HOT SATURDAY** (1932) 72m PAR bw

Cary Grant *(Romer Sheffield)*, Nancy Carroll *(Ruth Brock)*, Randolph Scott *(Bill Fadden)*, Edward Woods *(Conny Billop)*, Lillian Bond *(Eva Randolph)*, William Collier, Sr. *(Harry Brock)*, Jane Darwell *(Mrs. Brock)*, Rita La Roy *(Camille)*, Rose Coghlan II *(Annie Brock)*, Oscar Apfel *(Ed W. Randolph)*, Jessie Arnold *(Aunt Minnie)*, Grady Sutton *(Archie)*, Stanley Smith *(Joe)*, Dave O'Brien *(Guest)*, Marjorie Main, Nora Cecil *(Gossips)*.

Carroll stars in this screwball romp as a society gal who, after an argument with her beau, Scott, decides to get revenge by spending the rest of the day, and most of the night (in a platonic way) with infamous playboy Grant. Her plan backfires when she loses her job due to the gossip incurred by her excursion, and the scandal threatens to ruin her wedding plans with Scott. All ends well when Grant declares Carroll's innocence and later takes her hand in marriage. Familiar Strauss and Rodgers-and-Hart melodies are heard throughout much of the film.

d, William Seiter; w, Seton I. Miller (based on a novel by Harvey Ferguson); ph, Arthur L. Todd.

Romantic Comedy **(PR:A MPAA:NR)**

HOT SHOTS* (1956) 61m AA bw

Huntz Hall *(Sach [Horace DeBussy Jones])*, Stanley Clements *(Duke [Stanislaus Coveleske])*, Joi Lansing *(Connie Forbes)*, Jimmy Murphy *(Myron)*, David Gorcey *(Chuck)*, Queenie Smith *(Mrs. Kelly)*, Philip Phillips *(Joey Munroe)*, Robert Shayne *(P.M. Morley)*, Mark Dana *(George Slater)*, Henry Rowland *(Karl)*, Dennis Moore *(Tony)*, Isabel Randolph *(Mrs. Taylor)*, Frank Marlowe *(Henry [Bartender])*, Joe Kirk *(Bit Man)*, Ray Walker *(Capt. W.K. Wells)*.

Very late entry into the Bowery Boys series sees Hall and Clements getting involved in the budding television industry when they're forced to go after Phillips, a bratty 8-year-old TV star, who has stolen their car. The TV executives are so impressed by the way the Bowery Boys handle the youngster that they are given the job of being the boy's guardians. Trouble arises when Phillips' uncle and manager kidnap him for a big ransom, but Hall and Clements come to the rescue. The laughs are few and far between, and technically the film looks as if it were shot for television. (See BOWERY BOYS series, Index.)

p, Ben Schwalb; d, Jean Yarbrough; w, Jack Townley, Elwood Ullman (based on a story by Townley); ph, Harry Neumann; m, Marlin Skiles; ed, Neil Brunnenkant; md, Skiles; art d, David Milton; set d, Joseph Kish.

Comedy **(PR:A MPAA:NR)**

HOT SPELL** (1958) 87m PAR bw

Shirley Booth *(Alma Duval)*, Anthony Quinn *(Jack Duval)*, Shirley MacLaine *(Virginia Duval)*, Earl Holliman *(Buddy Duval)*, Eileen Heckart *(Fan)*, Clint Kimbrough *(Billy Duval)*, Warren Stevens *(Wyatt)*, Jody Lawrance *(Dora May)*, Harlan Warde *(Harry)*, Valerie Allen *(Ruby)*, Irene Tedrow *(Essie Mae)*, Anthony Jochim *(Preacher)*, Elsie Waller *(Librarian)*, Stafford Repp *(Baggage Man)*, Bill Walker *(Attendant)*, Louise Franklin *(Colored Woman)*, Johnny Lee *(Colored Man)*, Len Hendry, John Indrisano *(Pool Players)*, Watson H. Downs *(Funeral Car Driver)*, William Duray *(Conductor)*, Tony Merrill, Fred Zendar.

Heavy Deep South drama that feels as though it was conceived by Tennessee Williams but written by someone else. We're in New Orleans and the weather outside is frightful; hot, muggy, the kind of climate that sends tempers soaring. Booth is a housewife in a loveless marriage with Quinn. His birthday is coming up and she hopes to reawaken the love they knew years before by buying three birthday gifts for Quinn and giving them to their three children to give to him—anything to put the enraged Quinn in a better mood. She knows that he's been having an affair with Allen, but she's turned her sensibilities away from that (not unlike the role she played with Lancaster in COME BACK, LITTLE SHEBA). At the party, an argument erupts with Holliman, the oldest son, who works for Quinn at his employment agency, because Holliman wants to leave the business and open his own agency. All of this causes youngest son Kimbrough to leave the dinner table. Now Quinn discovers daughter MacLaine mushing it up on the porch with her fella, Stevens. Quinn doesn't like anyone taking liberties with his only daughter so he point-blank asks if Stevens intends to marry MacLaine. Later, Quinn takes Kimbrough to the local pool room in an attempt to get closer to the boy. He tries to explain to him that a grown man must be true to himself, besides being a father and a husband, and that life is short and one must take things as they come. Kimbrough doesn't understand a word of what Quinn is saying until he sees his father drive off with Allen under the guise of having to "see someone on business." At the Quinn house, MacLaine is despondent because Stevens has admitted he has no plans to marry her. Booth thinks she could get her marriage back together if she and Quinn would exit Sodom By The Levee and return to their beginnings in New Paris, a small town where they met, married, and had so many happy years together. Quinn can no longer tolerate Booth's nagging and he leaves for Florida with Allen. On the road, both are killed in an auto accident, and Booth returns Quinn's body to the little town of their childhood where she begins to understand that she cannot change the past and that it's time to live in the present. The acting techniques seen in HOT SPELL were fascinating to note. Booth came from the stage, MacLaine was in the process of still learning how to make movies, and Quinn had been a child of motion pictures from the start. It just didn't blend and the result was an oppressive, sometimes dull, film that never found its way.

p, Hal B. Wallis; d, Daniel Mann; w, James Poe (based on Lonnie Coleman's unproduced play "Next Of Kin"); ph, Loyal Griggs (Vista Vision); m, Alex North; ed, Warren Low; art d, Hal Pereira, Tambi Larsen; spec eff, John P. Fulton.

Drama **(PR:C-O MPAA:NR)**

HOT SPOT (SEE: I WAKE UP SCREAMING, 1941)

HOT SPUR zero(1968) 91m Olympic International/Republic Amusements c (AKA: THE NAKED SPUR; FIERY SPUR; THE LONGEST SPUR)

James Arena *(Jason O'Hare)*, Virginia Gordon *(Susan O'Hare)*, Joseph Mascolo *(Carlo)*, Wes Bishop, Tom McFadden, John Alderman, Paul Frank, Monique Heguy, Angel Carter, Ellen Gaines, Paul Wilmoth, Rod Wilmoth, Sky.

Rancid "western" which is basically an excuse for lots of sick sex and bloody violence. Mascolo plays a young Mexican who must watch helplessly while a gang of demented cowboys, led by Arena, rape his 17-year-old sister, who eventually dies from the horrible experience. Years later, seeking revenge, a much older Mascolo goes to Arena's ranch and gets a job as a stableboy. There he kidnaps Arena's voluptuous wife and rapes her in a cave, leaving clues so that the rancher and his men will find him. The climax sees Mascolo killing all of Arena's henchmen, Arena shooting Mascolo, and then his wife stabbing her husband to death when she mistakes him for her kidnaper.

p, R.W. Cresse; d&w, R.L. Frost (based on a story by Cresse), ph, (Eastmancolor); m, Denny Martin; spec eff, Harry Woolman.

Western **(PR:O MPAA:NR)**

HOT STEEL* (1940) 61m UNIV bw

Richard Arlen *(Frank Stewart)*, Andy Devine *(Matt Morrison)*, Peggy Moran *(Babe Morrison)*, Anne Nagel *(Rita Martin)*, Donald Briggs *(George Barnes)*, Joe Besser *("Siggie")*, Robert Emmett O'Connor *(Police Inspector)*, Wade Boteler *(Joe Farley)*, Edward McWade *(Carlton)*, William Wayne *(Dave Martin)*.

Dull tale starring Arlen as a brilliant metallurgist who arrives in Devine's steel town with a formula for a new high-test steel, only to have the secret stolen and a murder rap placed on his head. Morrison plays Devine's kid sister who has a hankering for the unlucky stranger.

p, Ben Pivar; d, Christy Cabanne; w, Clarence Upson Young (based on a story by Maurice Tombragel); ph, William Sickner.

Crime/Mystery **(PR:A MPAA:NR)**

HOT STUFF*½ (1929) 72m FN-WB bw

Alice White *(Barbara "Babe" Allen)*, Louise Fazenda *(Aunt Kate)*, William Bakewell *(Mack Moran)*, Doris Dawson *(Thelma)*, Ben Hall *(Sandy McNab)*, Charles Sellon *(Wiggam)*, Buddy Meswinger *(Tuffy)*, Andy Devine, Larry Banthim.

Fazenda stars as a fun-loving aunt who uses a $10,000 insurance settlement to send her niece, White, to college. Fazenda tags along as White's chaperone and has her hands full when all the boys peg her niece as the "hottest thing on campus." College playboy Bakewell takes a liking to White and the whole school's abuzz when the pair is found in a compromising situation. But Bakewell defends White's honor by punching out a smart-aleck student and declaring his love for White. Pretty silly stuff with only 30% dialog.

p, Wid Gunning; d, Mervyn LeRoy; w, Louis Stevens (based on a story by Robert S. Carr); ph, Sid Hickox, Alvin Knechter; art d, John Hughes.

Drama **(PR:A MPAA:NR)**

HOT STUFF* (1979) 103m Rastar-Mort Engelberg/COL c

Dom DeLuise *(Ernie Fortunato)*, Suzanne Pleshette *(Louise Webster)*, Jerry Reed *(Doug Van Horne)*, Ossie Davis *(Capt. Geibarger)*, Luis Avalos *(Ramon)*, Marc Lawrence *(Carmine)*, Dick Davalos *(Charles)*, Alfie Wise *(Nick)*, Bill McCutcheon *(Paully)*, Sydney Lassick *(Hymie)*, Barney Martin *(Kiley)*, Pat McCormick *(Cigars)*, Sid Gould *(Sid)*, Carol DeLuise *(Gloria)*, Peter DeLuise, David DeLuise, Michael DeLuise, Mike Falco, Crispin Tyrone Jackson, Raymond George Forchion, Luke Halpin, Joe Ruggiero, Angela Bomford, Mel Pape, Steve Gladstone, Matthew Burch, Peppy Fields, Shirley Galabow, Eduardo Corbe, Jose Bahamonde, John Disanti, Sandy Mielke, Cedar Stump, Artie Lewis, Ginger Scott, Sid Raymond, Al Nessor, Pete Conrad, George Warren, Danny Bardisa, Leonard Haber, Terese Heston, Shirley Cowell, Gigi Carrier, Katy Reaves, Norma Davids, Mike Baches, Louis Silvers, Bobby Self, Diane Johnson, Laurie Stark, Tim Chitwood, Vic Hunter, Victor Helou, Jack White, Tony Coffman, William Fuller, Ed Lupinski, Jim Ridarsick, Beau Gillespie, Don Soffer, Barry Noel, Mimi Julia Keating.

A silly slapstick comedy directed by and starring DeLuise (who seemingly hauled his entire family in front of the camera for this one) about a police undercover task force, Pleshette, Reed, and DeLuise, who decide to capture criminals by opening a fencing operation and entrapping them. The plot seems just an excuse to parade dozens of pointless, eccentric, and silly characters across the screen in desparate hopes that some of them may draw laughs.

p, Mort Engelberg; d, Dom DeLuise; w, Michael Kane, Donald E. Westlake; ph, James Pergola (Panavision, Metrocolor); m, Patrick Williams; ed, Neil Travis; m/l, "Hot Stuff," Jerry Reed.

Comedy **Cas.** **(PR:C MPAA:PG)**

HOT SUMMER NIGHT**** (1957) 85m MGM bw

Leslie Nielsen *(William Joel Partain)*, Colleen Miller *(Irene Partain)*, Edward Andrews *(Lou Follett)*, Jay C. Flippen *(Oren Kobble)*, James Best *(Kermit)*, Paul Richards *(Elly Horn)*, Robert Wilke *(Tom Ellis)*, Claude Akins *(Truckdriver)*, Marianne Stewart *(Ruth Childers)*.

Nielsen stars as a down-on-his-luck reporter who hopes to get a massive crime scoop by getting an exclusive interview with Flippen, the leader of a notorious gang of bank robbers. Obtaining the story becomes an obsession with Nielsen, and his persistence makes Miller, his newlywed bride, a nervous wreck. Foolishly, the reporter gets too close to the murderous gang and winds up getting kidnaped and held hostage. Miller leads the rescue party and Flippen winds up dead, giving Nielson the big scoop he was looking for.

p, Morton S. Fine; d, David Friedkin; w, Fine, Friedkin (based on a story by Edwin P. Hicks); ph, Harold J. Marzorati; m, Andre Previn; ed, Ben Lewis; art d, William A. Horning, Merrill Pye.

Crime/Drama **(PR:A MPAA:NR)**

HOT SUMMER WEEK* (1973, Can.) 80m Fanfare c

Kathleen Cody, Michael Ontkean, Diane Hull, Ralph Waite, John McMurty, Pamela Serpe, Riggs Kennedy.

Two innocent young things join an encounter group run by a former soldier. When some strange murders commence, the girls are forced to kill their host. Before they know it, the real killer turns up and they decide to beat a hasty retreat. Waite, in a featured role, went from this to a much more sedate life style as the father of television's "The Waltons."

p&d, Thomas J. Schmidt; w, Larry Bischof, David Kaufman.

Thriller **(PR:O MPAA:PG)**

HOT TIMES*½ (1974) 82m William Mishkin c

Henry Cory *(Archie)*, Gail Lorber *(Ronnie)*, Amy Farber *(Bette)*, Bob Lesser *(Coach/Guru)*, Steve Curry *(Mughead)*, Clarissa Ainley *(Kate)*, Bonnie Gondel *(Gloria)*, Jack Baran *(Alex Mogulmuph)*, Betty Mur *(La Chochita)*, Irving Horowitz *(Potemkin, the Director)*.

Senseless and unfunny comedy starring Cory as a sex-starved high school student who wanders aimlessly through basketball games, drinking bouts with his buddies, a stag party, and eventually Times Square, in search of carnal fulfillment. Boring, tedious and ultimately distasteful.

p, Lew Mishkin; d&w, Jim McBride; ph, Affonso Beato (Eastmancolor); ed, Jack Baran.

Comedy **Cas.** **(PR:O MPAA:R)**

HOT TIP**½** (1935) 70m RKO bw

ZaSu Pitts *(Belle McGill)*, James Gleason *(Jimmy McGill)*, Margaret Callahan *(Jane McGill)*, Russell Gleason *(Ben)*, Ray Mayer *(Tyler)*, J.M. Kerrigan *(Matt)*, Arthur Stone *(Hooper)*, Donald Kerr *(Spider)*, Kitty McHugh *(Queenie)*.

Okay comedy starring Gleason as a racing enthusiast who handicaps the ponies for his own amusement. Unfortunately, all his friends take his advice and lose big bucks, including his future son-in-law who blows the soon-to-be-newlyweds' nest egg. Gleason's wife Pitts, who loathes gambling, flies into a fury when she hears the news, and Gleason must desperately pull together all his handicapping skills to win back the dough so the kid can marry his daughter. Well-written script is pulled off by a professional cast.

p, William Sistrom; d, Ray McCarey, James Gleason; w, Hugh Cummings, Olive Cooper, Louis Stevens (based on a story by William Slavens McNutt); ph, Jack MacKenzie.

Comedy **(PR:A MPAA:NR)**

HOT TOMORROWS***** (1978) 73m American Film Institute c

Ken Lerner *(Michael)*, Ray Sharkey *(Louis)*, Herve Villechaize *(Alberict)*, Victor Argo *(Tony)*, George Memmoli *(Man in Mortuary)*, Donne Daniels *(Night Embalmer)*, Rose Marshall *(Tante Ethel)*, Paul Schumacher *(Lecturer)*, Marie Elfman, Danny Elfman *(Singers)*, Dennis Madden *(Bartender)*, Sondra Lowell *(Polly)*, Marion Beeler *(Waitress)*, Shelby Leverington *(Hospital Receptionist)*, David Garfield *(Dr. Stern)*, Vice Palmieri *(Man in Car)*, Janet Brandt *(Old Woman in Bus)*, Sonya Berman *(Old Woman Watching Television)*, Esther Cohen *(Old Woman with Postcard)*, Edith Gwinn *(Old Woman in Mortuary)*, Orson Welles *(Voice of Parklawn Mortuary)*.

With the budgets of Hollywood filmmakers rising to prepostorous levels (for some equally prepostorous films) in the late 1970s, it took a young filmmaker to prove quality material could still be made on a budget of just $33,000. For his debut feature, produced in association with the American Film Institute, director Brest depicts a student overwhelmed by his obsession with death. There's a lot of energy in this black comedy, leading up to a fine ending which counterpoints the visuals with appropriate music. Brest uses his cast of professionals (most notably Welles, and Villechaize of television's "Fantasy Island") with good skill, combining footage of an old Laurel and Hardy film in the piece as well. Brest later became a victim of the Hollywood spend syndrome himself, directing the over-budgeted (and overrated) BEVERLY HILLS COP.

p,d&w, Martin Brest; ph, Jacques Haitkin; ed, Brest; ch, Lloyd Gordon.

Comedy **(PR:C MPAA:NR)**

HOT WATER**** (1937) 56m FOX bw

Jed Prouty *(John Jones)*, Shirley Deane *(Bonnie Jones)*, Spring Byington *(Mrs. John Jones)*, Russell Gleason *(Herbert Thompson)*, Kenneth Howell *(Jack Jones)*, George Ernest *(Roger Jones)*, June Carlson *(Lucy Jones)*, Florence Roberts *(Granny Jones)*, Billy Mahan *(Bobby Jones)*, Joan Marsh *(Bebe Montaine)*, Willard Robertson *(Dr. Enfield)*, Robert Gleckler *(Hal Lynch)*, Arthur Hohl *(Walter Whittaker)*, Selmer Jackson *(Maxwell)*, Joseph King *(Mayor Roberts)*, Marjorie Weaver.

In this Jones family saga, Dad (Prouty) runs for mayor. Trouble starts when young son Howell secretly prints a newspaper detailing his dad's negative comments about his opponent in the political race. Prouty gets upset, and his opponent gets some political mileage out of the chaos caused within the family, but in the end the Jones family triumphs. (See JONES FAMILY series, Index).

p, Max Golden; d, Frank R. Strayer; w, Robert Chapin, Karen De Wolf (based on a story by Ron Ferguson, Elenor De Lamater from characters created by Katharine Kavanaugh); ph, Edward Snyder; ed, Nick De Maggio; md, Samuel Kaylin.

Drama **(PR:A MPAA:NR)**

HOTEL***** (1967) 124m WB c

Rod Taylor *(Peter McDermott)*, Catherine Spaak *(Jeanne Rochfort)*, Karl Malden *(Keycase)*, Melvyn Douglas *(Warren Trent)*, Richard Conte *(Dupere)*, Merle Oberon *(The Duchess)*, Michael Rennie *(Duke of Lanbourne)*, Kevin McCarthy *(Curtis O'Keefe)*, Carmen McRae *(Christine)*, Alfred Ryder *(Capt. Yolles)*, Roy Roberts *(Bailey)*, Al Checco *(Herbie)*, Sheila Bromley *(Mrs. Grandin)*, Harry Hickox *(Sam)*, William Lanteau *(Mason)*, Ken Lynch *(Laswell)*, Clinton Sundberg *(Morgan)*, Tol Avery *(Kilbrick)*, Davis Roberts *(Dr. Adams)*, Jack Donner *(Elliott)*, Lester Dorr *(Elevator Operator)*, Dee Carroll *(Mother)*, Judy Norton *(Daughter)*.

The Arthur Hailey novel was vastly improved on by the film, which was a cut above average, but no more. HOTEL is really a variation on the 1930s GRAND HOTEL by Vicki Baum but with a different locale and cast of characters. Here it's the fictitious St. Gregory Hotel in New Orleans, one of the last of the great luxury hotels whose elegance and grace is reflected by the personality of its elderly owner, gentlemanly Douglas. But the hotel is in financial trouble. To help him seek a solution, Douglas relies upon his smart, loyal manager, Taylor. McCarthy, owner of a chain of plastic hotel palaces who wants to buy the St. Gregory and reshape it in his own pedestrian, tasteless taste, arrives with mistress Spaak. She tries to vamp Taylor to help out her boy friend but quickly grows to respect him. Meanwhile Rennie and Oberon, British aristocrats, arrive and are soon in trouble. Rennie, after having one too many, runs over a person but leaves the scene of the accident and hides his car in the hotel garage. Hotel detective Conte discovers this and begins blackmailing the couple. Malden, one of the cleverest hotel thieves around, takes a room and begins looting the wallets of the guests but finds that they all have credit cards and no cash. Shifty McCarthy pays a black couple to try to register at the hotel and they create a scene when turned away, an incident which prevents a union from buying the hotel. Taylor, however, outwits McCarthy in the end and Spaak joins Taylor. Douglas decides that he would rather see his hotel razed then turned into a cheap hostelry. Just as police are closing in on Rennie, he is killed when one of the hotel elevators gives way. Police let Oberon go and, since Rennie is dead, drop their investigation, but Conte gets his comeuppance at the end for his attempted blackmail. Malden is apprehended with some difficulty but displays his incurable larceny to the end. As he is led from the hotel in handcuffs, he can't resist pocketing a hotel ash tray. It's all lightweight fare but the super cast raises this potboiling story above the average, as does Quine's inventive direction. Hailey's story and dialog are sometimes ludicrous and often laughable. Some location shots were taken in New Orleans. Carmen McRae appears as a singer in the hotel lounge and she is really special.

p, Wendell Mayes; d, Richard Quine; w, Mayes (based on the novel by Arthur Hailey); ph, Charles Lang (Technicolor); m, Johnny Keating; ed, Sam O'Steen; art d, Cary Odell; set d, George James Hopkins; cos, Howard Shoup, Edith Head; makeup, Gordon Bau.

Drama **(PR:A MPAA:NR)**

HOTEL BERLIN***** (1945) 98m WB bw

Helmut Dantine *(Martin Richter)*, Andrea King *(Lisa Dorn)*, Raymond Massey *(Arnim Von Dahnwitz)*, Faye Emerson *(Tillie Weiler)*, Peter Lorre *(Johannes Koenig)*, Alan Hale,Sr. *(Hermann Plottke)*, George Coulouris *(Joachim Helm)*, Henry Daniell *(Von Stetten)*, Peter Whitney *(Heinrichs)*, Helene Thimig *(Frau Sarah Baruch)*, Steven Geray *(Kliebert)*, Kurt Krueger *(Maj. Otto Kauders)*, Paul Andor *(Walter)*, Erwin Kalser *(Dr. Dorf)*, Dickie Tyler *(Bellboy No. 6)*, Elsa Heiis *(Woman Telegraph Messenger)*, Frank Reicher *(Fritz)*, Paul Panzer *(Kurt)*, John Mylong *(Von Buelow)*, Ruth Albu *(Gretchen)*, Jay Novello *(Gomez)*, Lotte Stein *(Frau Plottke)*, Torben Meyer *(Franz, Barber)*, Johanna Hofer.

The setting is Berlin 1945, and the Allies are rapidly closing in on what is left of the Third Reich. The once luxurious Hotel Berlin now houses a small group of scared Germans who wait in hiding for the inevitable. Among them: Lorre, a Noble Prize winning scientist who has been virtually destroyed by the Nazis; Dantine, a former student of Lorre's who has escaped from Dachau and taken refuge in the hotel disguised as a waiter; Emerson, the hotel's treacherous hostess who continues her devotion to the Reich; and King, a beautiful actress. King recognizes Dantine from wanted posters that have been put up all over Berlin and strikes a deal with the refugee: if Dantine will help her escape Germany before the Allies arrive, she will remain silent regarding his identity. Unfortunately, Emerson suspects the couple of treason and reports them to an SS captain played by Coulouris. In a violent confrontation, Dantine kills Coulouris by knocking him down the hotel's elevator shaft. Meanwhile, the panic-stricken King double-crosses Dantine and sides with the Gestapo to save her skin. She agrees to tell the Nazis the whereabouts of the secret underground and goes off to set Dantine up while Lorre and the other residents of the hotel decide to join the anti-Nazi forces and take a stand. Dantine discovers King's treachery, and seeing no other alternative, kills her. HOTEL

BERLIN was based on a novel by author Baum who also penned the phenomenally successful GRAND HOTEL (an achievement that would haunt her during her lengthy career). The post-production of the film was done in a great rush because the studio feared that Berlin would actually fall before they could get the movie into the theaters, thus destroying any topicality the publicity department could exploit. Editor Richards was given only five days to cut the film and musical composer Waxman had to work 20 hours a day to complete the score. The hurried result was an entertaining, though sometimes confusing, film that may have been better if a bit more time and care was taken piecing it together.

p, Louis F. Edelman; d, Peter Godfrey, Jack Gage; w, Jo Pagano, Alvah Beassie (based on the novel *Berlin Hotel* by Vicki Baum); ph, Carl Guthrie; m, Franz Waxman; ed, Frederick Richards; art d, John Hughes.

War/Spy Drama **(PR:A MPAA:NR)**

HOTEL CONTINENTAL** (1932) 67m TIF/Sono Art-World Wide bw

Peggy Shannon *(Ruth)*, Theodore Von Eltz *(Bennett)*, Alan Mowbray *(Mr. Underwood)*, J. Farrell MacDonald *(Martin)*, Rockliffe Fellowes *(Tierney)*, Ethel Clayton *(Mrs. Underwood)*, Henry B. Walthall *(Winthrop)*, Bert Roach *(Layton)*, William Scott *(Mills)*, Mary Carlisle *(Alicia)*.

A GRAND HOTEL inspired drama that was slapped together and released just before the more famous (and vastly superior) adaptation of the successful novel. The main storyline circles around Von Eltz as an ex-con jewel thief who arrives at a famed New York City hotel soon before it is to be torn down so that he can uncover the fortune in gems he had stashed in a fireplace years before. Unfortunately, the room in which he stashed the jewels is occupied, forcing him to stay in a room adjoining it. The majority of the film details Von Eltz's attempts to retrieve his stash, until he is finally caught red-handed by the cops who, inexplicably, have been waiting all these years for him to make the attempt.

d, Christy Cabanne; w, Warren B. Duff, F. Hugh Herbert, Paul Perez (based on a story by Herbert and Perez); ph, Ira Morgan; ed, Rose Loweinger.

Drama **(PR:A MPAA:NR)**

HOTEL FOR WOMEN** (1939) 83m FOX bw
(AKA: ELSA MAXWELL'S HOTEL FOR WOMEN)

Ann Sothern *(Eileen Connelly)*, Linda Darnell *(Marcia Bromley)*, James Ellison *(Jeff Buchanan)*, Jean Rogers *(Nancy Prescott)*, Lynn Bari *(Barbara Hunter)*, June Gale *(Joan Mitchell)*, Joyce Compton *(Emeline Thomas)*, Elsa Maxwell *(Mrs. Tilford)*, John Halliday *(John Craig)*, Katharine Aldridge *(Melinda Craig)*, Alan Dinehart *(Stephen Gates)*, Sidney Blackmer *(McNeil)*, Chick Chandler *(Ben Ritchie)*, Gregory Gaye *(Fernando Manfredi)*, Charles Wilson *(Albert)*, Herbert Ashley *(Butch)*, Ivan Lebedeff *(Galdos)*, Helen Ericson *(Miss Collins)*, Dorothy Dearing *(Miss Wilson)*, Barnett Parker *(Photographer)*, Amanda Duff *(Receptionist)*, Kay Linaker *(Jane)*, Hal K. Dawson *(Dave Moore)*, Ruth Terry *(Craig's Receptionist)*, Virginia Brissac *(Woman)*, Edward Earle *(Man)*, Bess Flowers *(Bit)*, Allen Wood *(Taxi Driver)*, Kay Griffith *(Model)*, Arthur Rankin *(Photographer)*, Russell Lee *(Elevator Boy)*, Russel Hicks *(Van Ellis)*.

A 16-year-old Darnell made her movie debut here as a young girl from Syracuse who travels to the "Big Apple" to visit her boy friend Ellison, now a successful architect. Unfortunately, he is no longer interested in the disappointed Darnell. While boarding in a women's hotel, Darnell is encouraged by the other guests to show Ellison what she's made of and make him wish he never left her. She does just that by becoming a famous fashion model. This finally renews Ellison's interest, except now he has to fight to get her back. Famed Gotham gossip monger and party-giver Maxwell penned this one and also appeared before the cameras dispensing her own advice. It was during the making of this film that teenaged Darnell met cameraman Marley, whom she later married.

p, Darryl F. Zanuck; d, Gregory Ratoff; w, Kathryn Scola, Darrell Ware (based on a story by Elsa Maxwell, Scola); ph, Peverell Marley; ed, Louis Loeffler; md, David Buttolph; m/l, Maxwell.

Drama **(PR:A MPAA:NR)**

HOTEL HAYWIRE** (1937) 65m PAR bw

Leo Carrillo *(Dr. Zodiac Z. Zippe)*, Mary Carlisle *(Phyllis Parkhouse)*, Lynne Overman *(Dr. Parkhouse)*, George Barbier *(L. Ketts, Sr.)*, Spring Byington *(Mrs. Parkhouse)*, Benny Baker *(Bertie Sterns)*, Collette Lyons *(Genevieve Sterns)*, John Patterson *(Frank Ketts)*, Porter Hall *(Judge Newhall)*, Josephine Whittell *(Mrs. Newhall)*, Guy Usher, Lucien Littlefield, Howard Mitchell, Mitchell Ingraham, James Donlan, Oscar Rudolph, Frank Rowan, Chester Conklin, Hayden Stevenson, Teddy Hart, Colin Tapley, Nick Lukats, Billy Arnold, Phillips Smalley, Richard Neill, Lowell Drew, Sidney DeGrey, Terry Raye, Wally Maher, Frank Dawson, Don Brodie, Frank Hammond, Helen Dickson, Almeda Fowler, Jack Clark, George Anderson, Harry Semels, Franklin Pangborn.

Inoffensive comedy starring Overman as a smart aleck husband who tries to spring a joke on a buddy at a poker game, but the trick's on him when he returns home with a delicate item of female clothing in his pocket that does not belong to his wife. The rest of the film is devoted to the vengeful will of Overman's wife Byington, along with con-man and fortune teller Carrillo, and a dull juvenile romance thrown in between Carlisle and Patterson for good measure. Not one of writer Sturges' better efforts.

d, George Archainbaud; w, Preston Sturges; ph, Henry Sharp; ed, Arthur Schmidt.

Comedy **(PR:A MPAA:NR)**

HOTEL IMPERIAL*½** (1939) 67m PAR bw

Isa Miranda *(Anna)*, Ray Milland *(Lt. Nemassy)*, Reginald Owen *(Gen. Videnko)*, Gene Lockhart *(Elias)*, J. Carroll Naish *(Krupin)*, Curt Bois *(Anton)*, Henry Victor *(Sultancy)*, Albert Dekker *(Sergeant)*, Don Cossack Chorus *(Themselves)*, Ernst Verebes *(Ivan)*, Robert Middlemass *(Gen. Von Schwartzberg)*, Michel Werboff *(Russian Sergeant)*, Spencer Charters *(Visoff)*, Betty Compson *(Soubrette)*, Bodil Rosing *(Ratty Old Woman)*, Wolfgang Zilzer *(Limping Tenor)*, Bert Roach *(Fat Comic)*, Agostino Borgato *(Old Actor)*, Paul Everton *(Troupe Manager)*, George Magrill *(Austrian Sentry)*, Lee Shumway *(Russian Officer)*, Davison Clark *(Irate Officer)*, Harry Tenbrook, Paul Kruger, Ethan Laidlaw *(Sentries)*, William Bakewell *(Cadet)*, Norman Phillips *(Butcher Boy)*, Robert Frazer *(Austrian Courier)*, Russell Hicks *(Austrian Officer)*, George MacQuarrie *(Frightened Old Man)*, Arnold Cernitz, General Savitsky, Joseph Marievsky, Andre Marsaudon *(Staff Officers)*, Bull Anderson *(Videnko Sentry)*, Marek Windheim *(Feinberger)*, Gustav Von Seyffertitz *(Priest)*, Sheila Darcy, Norah Gale, Paula de Cardo, Judith King, Luana Walters *(Nurses)*, Robert Kortman *(Austrian Sergeant)*, Jack Knoche *(Cossack Soldier)*, Stanley Andrews *(Col. Paloff)*, Harry Holman *(Burgomaster)*.

This truly was a jinxed film, based on a celebrated Hungarian play by Lajos Biro and made as a silent in 1927 with Pola Negri. It was revived as a talkie twice during the 1930s and was finally completed with Italian star Miranda (who would make only two other American films before returning permanently to Europe). She plays a chambermaid in a small hotel in Gallacia which is overrun during WW I by Russians and Austrians who keep taking and retaking the town. Miranda, however, is only impersonating a maid while she seeks the killer of her sister and, after endless intrigues and with the help of Austrian officer Milland, she finally unearths the murderer, Naish, taking her revenge. This was an expensively produced film but it is so muddled by an ambiguous script and is so lamely directed by Florey that it could not help but flop. Then, no one really expected this film to succeed since its history had been pockmarked with disaster. The original silent had been directed by the great Swedish director Mauritz Stiller, who had discovered Greta Garbo and brought her to the U.S. When Garbo rejected Stiller he completed the silent version of HOTEL IMPERIAL and left for Sweden where he reportedly died of "a broken heart" the following year. Negri, the star of the silent film, received word that her so-called lover Rudolph Valentino had fallen ill in New York but she could not fly to his bedside until she finished HOTEL IMPERIAL. By the time she did, Valentino was dead and all pretty Pola could do was rush to New York and drape her body, clad in black mourning dress, across his funeral bier. In 1936 Paramount dug out this story, hired Henry Hathaway to direct it as a talkie, and ordered Marlene Dietrich to go before the cameras to enact the role of the vengeance-seeking lady. Dietrich was then in box-office decline, even though the studio was paying her $200,000 a film, making her—next to Mae West—the highest paid actress in Hollywood. She had been protected and coddled by director Josef von Sternberg, but after breaking with him she relied upon Ernst Lubitsch, then running Paramount, to make sure she received the right vehicles and proper directors who would respect her talents. Hathaway respected only action and males who mistreated ladies in films. He was rough-and-tumble and to him Dietrich was just another prima donna. The film was retitled INVITATION TO HAPPINESS and Dietrich didn't bother to read the script. Hathaway wanted to take the glamor out of the star. In the biography *Marlene* he is quoted as saying: "My idea for HOTEL IMPERIAL was to start with a shot of a long, wide hallway, and a woman scrubbing and mopping the floor. She has dirty hair and dirty clothes; she is wearing old carpet slippers. She's a slob. As she gets the guy and hides him and as she falls in love with him, she gets progressively prettier." At first Dietrich played along, but she never dirtied herself up the way Hathaway wanted. She would appear on the set and look clean, with traces of makeup. "You're not supposed to be pretty until next Thursday," Hathaway would yell. "Can't I be pretty by this Wednesday?" Dietrich would implore. Dietrich finally rejected the script and Hathaway rewrote the original John van Druten script with Grover Jones, retitling the film I LOVED A SOLDIER. Lubitsch, meanwhile, had been ousted from studio control and Dietrich seized upon this to quit the film, pointing out that if Lubitsch was not the line producer of her films, as it appeared in her Paramount contract, she was under no obligation. Dietrich walked off the set after 28 days of shooting, which cost Paramount $900,000. This version of HOTEL IMPERIAL was scrapped. Then the studio decided to make the film once more, this time with Margaret Sullavan. Hathaway thought she would be perfect because "she didn't care how ugly she looked." But Sullavan was capricious. She and supporting actor Stuart Erwin took to tussling off camera. She squirted him with a water gun and he tackled her and both crashed to the floor, Sullavan screaming with pain. She had broken her arm and it would be in a cast for months. When studio bosses insisted she play the role in a sling, director Hathaway threw up his hands and then *he* quit, as had Dietrich. Dietrich then came back to the studio with her faithful director von Sternberg in tow; she said she was ready to resume doing the film, but Hathaway had to go. Only the great Josef von Sternberg could direct her in HOTEL IMPERIAL or whatever the studio decided to call the film. Paramount executives told her no, they would not let her dictate such terms. Miranda was brought into the project two years later. She was Italy's reigning sex star—reputedly Mussolini's mistress, or one of them—the dictator having personally selected the slinky, husky-voiced blonde to star in his super spectacular bomb, SCIPIO AFRICANUS. Her English was atrocious and she had to speak her part phonetically, which made Miranda sound like a mechanical wind-up doll. Milland has a puppet role, one that almost ended his career after he was ordered by Florey to lead a wild cavalry charge and was thrown from his horse, landing head-first on a pile of bricks and suffering a concussion. (It was 48 hours before he came to in Cedars of Lebanon Hospital where nine stitches were required to close a gash in his skull.) Paramount took a loss on the third and final version of this story but clung to one of its unused titles, using it in modification as I LOVE A SOLDIER in 1944 for a Paulette Goddard-Sunny Tufts vehicle.

d, Robert Florey; w, Gilbert Gabriel, Robert Thoeren (based on the play by Lajos Biro); ph, William Mellor; ed, Chandler House; m/l, Frederick Hollander, Ralph Freed.

Historical Drama **(PR:A MPAA:NR)**

HOTEL PARADISO½** (1966, U.S./Brit.) 100m Trianon/MGM c

Alec Guinness *(Benedict Boniface)*, Gina Lollobrigida *(Marcelle Cot)*, Robert Morley *(Henri Cot)*, Peggy Mount *(Angelique Boniface)*, Akim Tamiroff *(Anniello)*, Marie Bell *(La Grande Antoinette)*, Derek Fowldes *(Maxime)*, Douglas Byng *(Mr. Martin)*, Robertson Hare *(Duke)*, Ann Beach *(Victoire)*, Leonard Rossiter *(Inspector)*, David Battley *(George)*, Dario Moreno *(Turk)*, Peter Glenville *(Georges Feydeau)*, Eddra Gale *(Hotel Guest)*, Candy Le Beau, Helen Mathison, Denise Powell, Melody Kaye *(Mr. Martin's Daughters)*.

Guinness fans won't be disappointed with this film but neither will they see their favorite actor in a top-notch production. This is a bedroom farce which had been a successful play in London and New York, both productions starring the versatile Guinness. Tamiroff, as he had in FIVE GRAVES TO CAIRO, presides over the sleazy hotel noted for assignations. Lollobrigida is the sexpot wife of pompous architect Morley who entices the timid Guinness as an answer to her husband's neglect of his sexual duties. Guinness' wife Mount, a dominating shrew, has gone off to visit a sick relative and he's prime for the picking. Morley arrives at the hotel unexpectedly to examine the faulty plumbing and this throws Guinness and Lollobrigida into a panic so that the rendezvous is turned into an elaborate game of hide and seek as the would-be lovers flit from room to room, bed to bed, hiding in closets, chimneys, and bathrooms, donning all manner of disguises to outwit Morley. They barely manage to avoid detection before returning to their respective hearths. The following night Morley and Lollobrigida and Guinness and Mount attend a play written by Feydeau—played by director Glenville—the author of the actual story (sort of a play within a movie of the same subject) where the actors are obviously performing their roles as Lollobrigida and Guinness, despite their heavy makeup, revealing the very assignation which they tried so desperately to keep from their spouses. It's all a bit too cute and the film suffers from repetitive tightspots and predictable situations. Guinness does the best he can and has some precious moments in the many disguises he assumes, one of his theatrical specialties. Busty, sultry Lollobrigida steams earthy sex but her noodle-thick accent so badly mangles the English that it's difficult to understand her words. The 1910 setting, however, is nicely managed and well-staged, although Glenville's direction is a bit too slow and lacks the action to sustain anything more than casual interest.

p&d, Peter Glenville; w, Glenville, Jean-Claude Carriere (based on the play "L'Hotel du Libre Echange" by Georges Feydeau, Maurice Desvallieres); ph, Henri Decae (Panavision, Metrocolor); m, Laurence Rosenthal; ed, Anne V. Coates; md, Rosenthal; prod d, Francois de Lamothe; set d, Robert Christides; cos, Jacques Dupont; makeup, Louis Bonnemaison, Odette Berroyer.

Comedy (PR:C MPAA:NR)

HOTEL RESERVE*** (1946, Brit.) 79m RKO bw

James Mason *(Peter Vadassy)*, Lucie Mannheim *(Madame Suzanne Koche)*, Raymond Lovell *(Monsieur Robert Duclos)*, Julien Mitchell *(Monsieur Beghin)*, Clare Hamilton [Flory Fitzsimmons] *(Miss Mary Skelton)*, Martin Miller *(Herr Walter Vogel)*, Herbert Lom *(Monsieur Andre Roux)*, Frederick Valk *(Herr Emil Schimler)*, Ivor Barnard *(The Chemist)*, Valentine Dyall *(Mr. Warren Skelton)*, Patricia Medina *(Madame Odette Roux)*, David Ward *(Monsieur Henri Asticot)*, Hella Kurty *(Frau Hilda Vogel)*, Anthony Shaw *(Maj. Anthony Clandon-Hartley)*, Lawrence Hanray *(Police Commissaire)*, Patricia Hayes *(Jacqueline)*, Josef Almas *(Albert)*, Ernest Ulman *(Man in Black)*, Mike Johnson *(Old Man)*, Hugo Schuster *(Inspector Fournier)*, Henry T. Russell *(Gendarme)*, John Baker *(Policeman)*.

A solid thriller with a fine cast is set on the Riviera during the summer before WW II exploded in Europe. Mason is an Austrian refugee, a medical student photographing marine life. He leaves a roll of film to be developed at a local shop but is soon contacted by French police who interrogate him, coming close to charging him with espionage. Mason is in shock when officials show him what has been developed from his roll of film—the military installations at Toulon. He protests, saying that the photographs he has taken are all of lizards, his special study. Mason must now unravel the mystery, with police help, to vindicate himself. He begins probing into the lives of the few guests at the small hotel, attempting to find the person who substituted his film for the spy photos; this is the only way in which he can qualify for French citizenship. It's either that or deportation back to Nazi-occupied Austria. Mason goes through a bevy of harrowing experiences, chiefly suspecting German tourist Miller as the spy. On the side, he becomes emotionally involved with Hamilton. Even strange-acting Mannheim, who owns the small resort, becomes a prime suspect, but in the end Mason discovers the agent to be the suave Lom whose seductive wife Medina has been making eyes in Mason's direction, only to further entrap him in a web of guilt. Just as he is about to close in on Lom, Mason is again arrested but escapes, chasing Lom, just as police had planned. The culprit is captured at the last minute in a chilling chase and Mason is exonerated, set free to woo the attractive Hamilton and enjoy French citizenship, a dubious honor in that France would soon fall to Nazi domination. Mason's character here is sympathetic but feckless and, although he performs brilliantly, the actor never cared much for the film. Released in England in 1944, the film did not do well at American box offices when shown in the U.S. two years later.

p, Victor Hanbury; d, Hanbury, Lance Comfort, Max Greene [Mutz Greenbaum]; w, John Davenport (based on the novel *Epitaph For a Spy* by Eric Ambler); ph, Greene; m, Lennox Berkeley; ed, S. Stone; art d, W. C. Andrews.

Spy Drama (PR:A MPAA:NR)

HOTEL SAHARA½** (1951, Brit.) 87m Tower/UA bw

Yvonne De Carlo *(Yasmin Pallas)*, Peter Ustinov *(Emad)*, David Tomlinson *(Capt. Puffin Cheyne)*, Roland Culver *(Maj. Bill Randall)*, Albert Lieven *(Lt. Gunther von Heilicke)*, Bill Owen *(Pvt. Binns)*, Sydney Tafler *(Cpl. Pullar)*, Tom Gill *(Pvt. O'Brien)*, Mireille Perrey *(Mme. Pallas)*, Ferdy Mayne *(Yusef)*, Guido Lorraine *(Capitano Guiseppi)*, A.C.2 Lewis *(Suleiman the Goat)*, Eugene Deckers *(French Spahi Officer)*, Rolf Richards, Henrik Jacobsen, Anton Diffring *(German Soldiers)*, Massimo Caen, Enzo Plazzotta *(Italian Soldiers)*, Bettina Hayes *(American Woman)*, John Salew *(American Husband)*, Harold Kaskett *(Oriental Gentleman)*, Olga Lowe *(Fatima)*.

Competent WW II comedy starring Ustinov as the proprietor of a dusty hotel located in the midst of the war-torn Sahara, and De Carlo as his loyal fiancee who tries to keep the military guests happy. Most of the laughs come from the frantic efforts of the staff to switch the appearance of their loyalties in the war, depending on which occupying force has control of the area. The switches go from Italian to British to German to French, and then back to British and German simultaneously, when both sides invade together. De Carlo is fine as she tries to vamp the soldiers from every nation, and Ustinov is good as the harried hotel owner.

p, George H. Brown; d, Ken Annakin; w, Patrick Kirwan, Brown; ph, David Harcourt; m, Benjamin Frankel; ed, Alfred Roome; art d, Ralph Brinton; set d, Betty Pierce; cos, Julie Harris; spec eff, Bill Warrington; makeup, George Blackler.

Comedy (PR:A MPAA:NR)

HOTEL SPLENDIDE*½ (1932, Brit.) 53m Film Engineering/ID bw

Jerry Verno *(Jerry Mason)*, Vera Sherburne *(Joyce Dacre)*, Antony Holles *(Mrs. leGrange)*, Edgar Norfolk *(Gentleman Charlie)*, Sybil Grove *(Mrs. Harkness)*, Philip Morant *(Mr. Meek)*, Paddy Browne *(Miss Meek)*.

Verno is a publicity manager who inherits a seaside hotel. He moves in, only to discover the property was built on a field used by jewel thieves to bury their loot. He accidentally finds the hidden booty before the crooks and collects a handsome reward. Not much of a comedy; most notable as an early effort for the director of THE RED SHOES.

p, Jerome Jackson; d, Michael Powell; w, Ralph Smart (based on a story by Philip Macdonald); ph, Geoffrey Faithfull.

Comedy (PR:A MPAA:NR)

HOTEL VARIETY*½ (1933) 65m Screencraft/Capital bw

Hal Skelly, Olive Borden, Charlotte Walker, Sally Rand, Glorian Gray, Shannon Day, Martin Burton, Jackie Jordan, Marshall Montgomery, Ned Norworth, Lilya Vallon, Hershell Mayall, Bernard Randall, Alan Brooks.

Another urban hotel drama, this time starring Borden as a speakeasy dancer who witnesses a mob murder. She flees to the Hotel Variety to hide out and there meets aspiring hoofer Skelly and his small son and the couple fall in love. Meanwhile a mob hit-man has tracked Borden down and is searching the halls for her. Things look grim until the gangster is killed in a fall from the hotel's fire escape and a benevolent investor hires Skelly, Borden, and most of the rest of the frustrated performers in the hotel, to be in his next movie.

p, Arthur Hoerl; d, Raymond Cannon; w, Hoerl; ph, Marcel Le Picard, William Bitzer, William Steiner; ed, Bernard Rogan; art d, Al Panci; m/l, Paul Vincent, Lou Hirscher, Al Kopell, Alan Taub, Ben Gordon.

Drama (PR:A MPAA:NR)

HOTHEAD* (1963) 72m Cinema Video International bw

John Delgar *(Frank)*, Robert Glenn *(Tom)*, Barbara Joyce *(Iris)*, Steve Franklin *(Bud)*, Linda Kane *(Suzie)*.

Low-budget drama about a violent, anti-social young man, Delgar, whose problems are traced to his long-missing father. One day Delgar, his buddy, Franklin, and Franklin's girl friend, Joyce, go to the beach and meet up with middle-aged drifter, Glenn. Delgar senses a similarity between his father and Glenn, and after Glenn breaks into a house to use it for drinking and dancing, Delgar is convinced that the stranger *is* his father. When Glenn attempts to force himself on Joyce, Delgar explodes and there is a fight. Franklin breaks it up before anyone gets seriously hurt, and Glenn wanders off down the beach, leaving Delgar wondering if it really was his father.

p, Milton Mann; d, Edward Mann; w, Milton Mann.

Drama (PR:C MPAA:NR)

HOTSPRINGS HOLIDAY½** (1970, Jap.) 90m Geiei/Shochiku Films of America bw (ONSEN GERIRA DAI SHOGEKI; KIGEKI DAI SHOGEKI)

Hiroshi Inuzuka *(Daisuke Yamato)*, Osami Nabe *(Kosuke Yamato)*, Yoshiko Kayama *(Emiko Kano)*, Hajime Hana *(Chief of Police)*, Kingoro Yanagiya *(Yamanouchi Boss)*, Chosuke Ikariya, Chu Arai, Bo Takaki, Koji Nakamoto, Cha Kato, Michiyo Kogure, Etsuko Ikuta, Masumi Harukawa, Kumi Hayase, Norihei Miki, Akiyoshi Kitaura, Yoshijiro Uyeda, Hachiro Misumi, Koree Nakamura, Ryusuke Kita, Mitsuru Ooya, Tosen Hidari, Fukuoka Shogo, Michiko Saga, Tonpei Hidari, Taisuke Kobayashi.

Inuzuka and Nabe are members of two rival gangs that fight for control over a small port town in northern Japan. In addition to the professional rivalry, the men are both attracted to the same woman, the daughter of an inn-keeper, who won't have anything to do with either of them. Eventually the hoodlums become so taken with the beautiful girl that they decide to join her in ridding the town of all gangsters. When she still refuses to get involved with either of them romantically, the former rivals, now friends, leave town in search of adventure.

p, Kunio Sawamura; d, Hirokazu Ichimura; w, Yasuo Tanami, Toshiro Hasebe (based on a story by Tanami); ph, Masao Kosugi; m, Hirooki Ogawa; art d, Chiyoo Umeda.

Crime/Drama (PR:A MPAA:NR)

HOTTENTOT, THE** (1929) 79m WB bw

Edward Everett Horton *(Sam Harrington)*, Patsy Ruth Miller *(Peggy Fairfax)*, Edmund Breese *(Ollie Gilford)*, Edward Earle *(Larry Crawford)*, Stanley Taylor *(Alec Fairfax)*, Douglas Gerrard *(Swift the Butler)*, Maude Turner Gordon *(May Gilford)*, Gladys Brockwell, Otto Hoffman.

Horton stars in this comedy (remade from a First National silent picture released in 1923) as a braggart horse lover who suddenly finds himself as the jockey for the infamous steed "Hottentot" in an important steeplechase race. The lengthy and funny racing scene is hampered somewhat by the rather obvious trick photography.

d, Roy Del Ruth; w, Harvey Thew (based on the play by William Collier, Victor Mapes).

Comedy **(PR:A MPAA:NR)**

HOUDINI*** (1953) 105m PAR c

Tony Curtis *(Houdini)*, Janet Leigh *(Bess)*, Torin Thatcher *(Otto)*, Angela Clark *(Mrs. Weiss)*, Stefan Schnabel *(Prosecuting Attorney)*, Ian Wolfe *(Fante)*, Sig Rumann *(Schultz)*, Michael Pate *(Dooley)*, Connie Gilchrist *(Mrs. Schultz)*, Mary Murphy, Joanne Gilbert *(Girls)*, Mabel Paige *(Medium)*, Malcolm Lee Beggs *(Warden)*, Frank Orth *(White-haired Man)*, Barry Bernard *(Inspector)*, Douglas Spencer *(Sims)*, Peter Baldwin *(Fred)*, Richard Shannon *(Miner)*, Elsie Ames, Nick Arno *(Entertainers)*, Esther Garber *(Esther's Girl Friend)*, Norma Jean Eckart *(Girl in Guillotine Act)*, Lewis Martin *(Editor)*, Lawrence Ryle *(German Judge)*, Jody Gilbert *(Fat Girl)*, Edward Clark *(Doorman)*, Grace Hayle *(Woman Who Screams)*, Fred Essler *(Official Looking Man)*, Arthur Gould Porter *(Alhambra Manager)*, Alex Harford *(Assistant)*, Tudor Owen *(Blacksmith)*, Harry Hines, Oliver Blake, Cliff Clark, Harold Neiman *(Barkers)*, Erno Verebes *(Prof. Allegari)*, Anthony Warde *(M.C.)*, Jody Gilbert *(Fat Girl)*, Frank Jaquet *(Foreman)*, Billy Bletcher *(Italian Basso)*, Lyle Latell *(Calcott)*, Torben Meyer *(Headwaiter)*, Tor Johnson *(Strong Man)*.

The fictitious screen biography of master magician and escape artist Harry Houdini begins when he is 21 years old and trying to make ends meet by performing as a "wild man" in a New York amusement house. There Curtis meets schoolgirl Leigh and after a quick courtship they are married (Curtis and Leigh had been married in real life since 1951). Curtis incorporates Leigh into his magic act, but after seeing her husband treated shabbily by the audience she talks him into hanging up his cape and getting a normal job. While working in a lock and safe factory Curtis learns the inner secrets of the devices, but the job bores him. At a magician's convention Curtis wins a trip to Europe by proving he can free himself from the confines of a straightjacket. The couple travel to London where Curtis wows the audiences by escaping from a variety of supposedly "escape-proof" devices, including a jail. His tricks soon make him a major hit in Europe, but when he returns to New York his arrival is greeted with little enthusiasm. Determined to become a sensation in the U.S., Curtis performs dozens of dangerous stunts in public and soon his dream is fulfilled. At the peak of his career, Curtis' mother dies and the famous magician takes two years off and submerges himself in a desperate effort to contact her spirit in the great beyond. Relying on a variety of spiritualists and mediums, Curtis spends a fortune trying to summon his mother's ghost, to no avail. Eventually the magician learns that the mediums are nothing but con artists, and he exposes their tricks to the police and public alike. Abandoning his obsession, Curtis returns to the stage and is welcomed back warmly. Tragedy strikes, however, when, during a performance in his dangerous and popular Water Torture Cell trick (Curtis is tied in a straightjacket and hung upside down in a tank of water with stocks around his ankles, then the tank was sealed with a variety of padlocks—the trick took at least 20 minutes to perform) his appendix bursts and though his quick-thinking assistants smash the tank and free him, he dies in Leigh's arms. Like the death scene, most of HOUDINI is factual hogwash (Houdini did die of advanced appendicitis, but nowhere near the stage). Historical accuracy notwithstanding, HOUDINI is a very entertaining film that was something of a change of pace for producer George Pal whose forays into the fantastic were usually in the science fiction genre (DESTINATION MOON, 1950, WHEN WORLDS COLLIDE, 1951, THE WAR OF THE WORLDS, 1953). Pal hired magician Dunninger to serve as technical advisor on the film. Upon her death, Mrs. Houdini willed nearly 300 of her late husband's tricks to the young magician, so logic would dictate that Dunninger knew more about Houdini's methods than anyone alive. The film makes no attempt to reveal Houdini's tricks on screen, but just to present an accurate recreation of them. Pal also capitalized on the public's fascination for married Hollywood stars Curtis and Leigh, whose shining faces appeared in hundreds of newspapers and magazines, by casting them in their first film together. HOUDINI moves along at a rapid clip, with dozens of tricks performed for the cameras. While the film may be short on character (Houdini was something of a tyrannical egomanic), the episode detailing the magician's attempts at contacting his dead mother and his subsequent expose of mediums was well founded in fact and quite fascinating. In 1976 a more accurate version of Houdini's life was presented in a fine made-for-TV film starring Paul Michael Glaser entitled THE GREAT HOUDINIS.

p, George Pal; d, George Marshall; w, Philip Yordan (based on the book by Harold Kellock); ph, Ernest Laszlo (Technicolor); m, Roy Webb; ed, George Tomasini; art d, Hal Pereira, Al Nozaki; set d, Sam Comer, Ray Moyer; cos, Edith Head.

Drama **(PR:A MPAA:NR)**

HOUND OF THE BASKERVILLES½** (1932, Brit.) 72m Gainsborough/FD bw

Robert Rendel *(Sherlock Holmes)*, Frederick Lloyd *(Dr. Watson)*, John Stuart *(Sir Henry Baskerville)*, Reginald Bach *(Stapleton)*, Heather Angel *(Beryl)*, Wilfred Shure *(Dr. Mortimer)*, Sam Livesey *(Sir Hugo)*, Elizabeth Vaughn *(Mrs. Laura Lyons)*, Sybil Jane *(Mrs. Barrymore)*, Leonard Hayes *(Cartwright)*, Henry Hallett *(Barrymore)*, Champion Egmund of Send *(The Hound of the Baskervilles)*.

The first sound version of the classic Doyle mystery which was produced by a very young Balcon (he would later go on to produce dozens of fine British films, including Alfred Hitchcock's THE THIRTY-NINE STEPS). The result is a flawed effort, hampered by some questionable casting decisions (Rendel made a husky, imposing Holmes, much different in appearance from the character in Doyle's novels) and a routine, overly melodramatic treatment. One of the positive elements of this version of BASKERVILLES is the script's dialog, which was penned by famed mystery writer Wallace, who lent his flair for snappy, telling exchanges, while retaining Doyle's flavor. The plot itself is a fairly straightforward telling of the story which embroils Holmes and Watson in a search for the mysterious glowing beast that haunts the swamps of Dartmoor and preys on the relatives of the Baskerville clan. This version of THE HOUND OF THE BASKERVILLES was thought to be "lost" for many years (reportedly only a few short sequences remained, and the soundtrack had completely disappeared), but a few prints still exist in private collections. (See SHERLOCK HOLMES series, Index.)

p, Michael Balcon; d, V. Gareth Gundrey; w, Edgar Wallace, Gundrey (based on the novel by Arthur Conan Doyle); ph, Bernard Knowles; ed, Ian Dalrymple.

Mystery **(PR:A MPAA:NR)**

HOUND OF THE BASKERVILLES, THE**** (1939) 80m FOX bw

Richard Greene *(Sir Henry Baskerville)*, Basil Rathbone *(Sherlock Holmes)*, Wendy Barrie *(Beryl Stapleton)*, Nigel Bruce *(Dr. Watson)*, Lionel Atwill *(James Mortimer, M.D.)*, John Carradine *(Barryman)*, Barlowe Borland *(Frankland)*, Beryl Mercer *(Mrs. Jenifer Mortimer)*, Morton Lowry *(John Stapleton)*, Ralph Forbes *(Sir Hugo Baskerville)*, E.E. Clive *(Cabby)*, Eily Malyon *(Mrs. Barryman)*, Nigel de Brulier *(Convict)*, Mary Gordon *(Mrs. Hudson)*, Peter Willes *(Roderick)*, Ivan Simpson *(Shepherd)*, Ian MacLaren *(Sir Charles)*, John Burton *(Bruce)*, Dennis Green *(Jon)*, Evan Thomas *(Edwin)*.

This was the first time that Rathbone and Bruce were cast as Holmes and Watson and their superlative performances demanded and got the delightful series that followed this excellent mystery. In a faithful adaptation of the Doyle novel, the film is set in the 1880s period of gaslit London with all its wet cobblestone streets, billowing fog, and eerie atmosphere. Even more chilling to the bone and mind are the desolate moors of Dartmoor in Devonshire where the camera shows a running man, frightened witless, as the sound of a baying hound is heard. A bearded man appears in the shadows to watch the running man fall. Then a shaft of light appears as a servant of Baskerville Hall opens a door to find the master, Sir Charles Baskerville, dead before her. At a coroner's inquest, Dr. Mortimer, Atwill, wearing thick-lensed glasses, announces that Baskerville has died of a heart attack. A voice erupts in the grumbling crowd, that of Borland, a neighbor of the dead man, to openly state what all are thinking, that the deceased did not die of natural causes, that he was murdered. "There's more than one person in this room knows I speak the truth," he adds. At 221-B Baker Street the great detective Sherlock Holmes, Rathbone, and his erstwhile companion, Dr. Watson, Bruce, occupy their time with homey pursuits as Big Ben chimes. Watson is clipping an article of the London *Times* which reports that Sir Henry Baskerville, Greene, will soon arrive from Canada to assume his role as heir to the Baskerville estate. Rathbone, who has been playing his violin, quickly speculates that the young heir is marked for murder. Gordon, as housekeeper Hudson, a role she was to make her own in the enchanting series, enters to tell Rathbone and Bruce that Atwill has visited them while they were out and has left his walking stick. By merely observing the stick Rathbone, in his usual exercise of "elementary observation," deduces that their visitor is "a doctor with a small practice in the country and the owner of a dog." He is, of course, proven correct, as soon as Atwill appears a short time later. Atwill comes to the point quickly, telling Rathbone that he fears for Greene's life, particularly when the young heir visits London. He goes on to explain that violent death has pursued the Baskerville masters since 1650 when Sir Hugo Baskerville was torn to shreds by an incredible hound which caught him on the moors. Holmes agrees to protect the heir and Greene is brought to him upon his arrival, explaining that someone had thrown a brick through the window of his hansom cab as he was being driven to Rathbone's digs, a note wrapped around the brick warning him to stay away from the moors. He also explains that one of his shoes, left outside his hotel room for the porter to polish, has been stolen. Greene discounts the Baskerville curse: "This story of the hound, it's nonsense, a silly legend." Rathbone explains that important business demands he stay in London but he will send reliable Bruce with Greene to Baskerville Hall. As Greene, Bruce, and Mortimer are later shown riding in a cart toward the mansion, making their way over the evil-looking Dartmouth terrain, boggy moors all about them, Atwill describes the Great Grimpen Mire "as treacherous a morass as exists anywhere . . . Thousands of lives have been sucked down to its bottomless depths." At the manor the threesome is welcomed by the dour butler, Carradine, and his housekeeper wife, Malyon. Later, Bruce finds Carradine at a window, signaling someone on the moors with a lantern. Bruce and Greene run outside to discover a bearded, furtive man hurling a rock at them before racing off into the gloom. The next day Bruce explores the moors and encounters Lowry, a naturalist studying the eerie landscape. Greene, meanwhile, encounters Lowry's beautiful sister Barrie as she rides horseback across the moors and they begin what will become a love affair. Greene later attends a dinner party at Lowry's home. There, Atwill's wife Mercer, an amateur medium, is persuaded to conduct an impromptu seance and she tries to contact the dead Sir Charles Baskerville so he can explain the mystery of the family curse. Just then a bone-chilling howl of a dog is heard and Mercer screams, ending her trance. Barrie grasps Greene's hand, genuinely afraid for him, saying: "I wish you wouldn't have come here." The next day Greene and Barrie explore the ruins of Stonehenge and High Tor, remnants of a civilization dead for 50,000 years. There Greene proposes and Barrie accepts. Watson later meets a grizzled old peddler who turns out to be Rathbone in disguise, one he has assumed so he can watch over Greene without being observed. As they stand on the moors, a wild howling ensues and both look up to see the bearded man seen earlier on the moors. He is suddenly attacked by a huge, fierce mastiff; the monster dog reduces the screaming victim to shreds. The body falls from the ridge and Rathbone soon identifies the victim as an escaped convict. He is wearing Greene's clothes and this leads Rathbone to discover that the suit was given to the victim by butler Carradine. The dead man was a relative of his wife's and he and Malyon have been smuggling food and clothing to him while he hid from police on the moors. Greene feels that the mystery of the Baskervilles is now solved with the death of the convict, the person obviously responsible for the demise of Sir Charles. He is jubilant and plans to wed Barrie and leave for Canada shortly. Rathbone and Bruce make plans to return to London but Rathbone lingers a moment as he studies a portrait on the wall of Sir Hugo Baskerville. On the train going to London Bruce tells Rathbone he still has doubts about recent events. How could the convict be in London to throw the rock and steal Greene's shoe while hiding out on the moors? Rathbone nods knowingly, telling Bruce that the murderer is still on the loose and that he has only pretended to quit the case. The two switch trains at the next stop and hurry back toward Baskerville Hall. Greene dines at Lowry's cottage that night, leaving Barrie and strolling across the moors alone, believing he now has nothing to fear. Then the fierce hound howls and races after Greene who begins to run for his life. Just as the enormous dog jumps into the air to fall upon Greene, Rathbone and Bruce appear and Rathbone fires two shots from his pistol. The dog yelps, then dashes off, mortally wounded. Greene is mauled but intact. Bruce helps him to the mansion while Rathbone pursues the dog. He finds a huge pit with a cover and climbs inside. The cover then slams down on top of him. Lowry is above, locking the detective inside the dog's lair. Lowry goes to Baskerville Hall where he reports that "Now we know for certain this is no legend, no myth. There really is a hound!" Lowry gets Bruce to dash out to the moors to help Rathbone, and orders Malyon to go to the kitchen to boil water for Greene's slight wounds. He then pours the weakened Greene a glass of water and pours some poison into it, telling him to drink it. Just as Greene lifts the glass to his lips, Rathbone suddenly appears and shouts "Sir Henry!" Greene pauses and Rathbone quickly enters the room, then clumsily knocks over the fatal glass of poisoned water as if by accident. He goes to the portrait of Sir Hugo Baskerville. "The most amazing instance of a throwback I've ever seen," Rathbone intones. The camera shows a closeup of the eyes in the painting and that of Lowry's; they are almost identical. Lowry realizes that he is exposed as the killer and draws a pistol, running outside. Rathbone calmly explains that he won't get far, that the escape routes are all blocked by constables and that "the only way is across the Grimpen Mire." Lowry is never to be seen again, presumed sucked to his death in the bottomless mire. Rathbone explains how it was Lowry who threw the brick into Greene's cab, knowing it would challenge the feisty youth into going to Baskerville Hall and that the shoe was stolen so that the fierce hound would be able to pick up Greene's scent. Lowry, of course, was a distant relative of the Baskervilles and, upon Greene's demise, would gain control of the vast estate. Fatigued, Rathbone begs to retire. He begins to go, then turns to Bruce and says: "Quick Watson, the needle!" This last startling statement, delivered with obvious relish by Rathbone, refers to Holmes' addiction to drugs, notably cocaine which, according to the immortal Doyle stories, Holmes mainlined through injection, along with heroin, morphine, and other exotic drugs. (This was the way in which Fox producers got around the censors of the day but the statement is still startling for that guarded era. Reference to Holmes' drug addiction would not again appear overtly until the frivolous but delightful THE SEVEN PERCENT SOLUTION, although there is an intriguing exchange of dialog in SHERLOCK HOLMES AND THE SECRET WEAPON, 1942. Here Atwill, as the malevolent Professor Moriarity, is about to kill Rathbone but the great detective stalls him, challenging him to come up with an inventive demise, stating that he, Rathbone, would certainly devise a more ingenious ending for Atwill if the shoe were on the other foot, then suggests that he would drain off the five pints of blood in the average human body, making death agonizingly slow, a method which Atwill adopts. Atwill smiles at the suggestion, and says: "The needle till the end, eh?" an oblique reference to Holmes' drug addiction.) This version of THE HOUND OF THE BASKERVILLES was an enormous success immediately upon release, and it proved to be the best. Rathbone was the perfect Holmes, his well-modulated voice, his sharply-honed features, his lanky figure all conforming to the public's image of the great detective as Sidney Paget first drew his imagined likeness in the *Strand Magazine* in 1889 when Doyle created the character (the same year in which the notorious Jack the Ripper appeared and proved the police were incapable of capturing him; at least, in that year, Doyle's fictional sleuth was unbeatable, one of the reasons for Holmes' immense popularity). One of the many totemic arbiters of Holmesian work was author Graham Greene who saw the film and extolled Rathbone's virtues, amazed at "that dark knife-blade face and snapping mouth," a face offering "an expression of intense and high-strung energy." He had earned the role and would keep it for life as would Bruce claim the amiable character of Dr. Watson, the two becoming a beloved screen team. Greene, then being groomed for leading man status by Fox, was given top billing but never again would Rathbone as Holmes have to play second fiddle in the credits. Lanfield's direction is solid and careful as he unfolds the sinister tale. Carradine, Lowry, and particularly Atwill, are all superb in their supporting roles. The film was such a great success that Fox quickly put THE ADVENTURES OF SHERLOCK HOLMES into production and that film, too, met with widespread approval. THE HOUND OF THE BASKERVILLES was always Rathbone's favorite film, even though he considered it "a negative from which I merely continued to produce endless positives of the same photograph." Rathbone would go on to appear in 16 films as Sherlock Holmes and more than 200 radio shows dealing with the indefatigable sleuth between 1939 and 1946. The part became so much of Rathbone's life that he literally ran away from Holmes in 1946, refusing to again play the sleuth. He sold his home in California and moved East, determined to appear only on the stage. His decision left Bruce high and dry and caused a deep rift between them. But the image of Holmes, the long shadow that Rathbone himself had provided, fell across the actor's path for the remainder of his life. He would always, from this film forth, be in the minds of moviegoers worldwide as the immortal Sherlock, and it was his svelte voice that would always be identified with the triumphant words "Elementary, my dear Watson."

p, Gene Markey; d, Sidney Lanfield; w, Ernest Pascal (based on the story by Arthur Conan Doyle); ph, Peverell Marley; ed, Robert Simpson; md, Cyril J. Mockridge; art d, Richard Day, Hans Peters; cos, Gwen Wakeley.

Mystery **(PR:A MPAA:NR)**

HOUND OF THE BASKERVILLES, THE*** (1959, Brit.) 88m Hammer/UA c

Peter Cushing *(Sherlock Holmes)*, Andre Morell *(Dr. Watson)*, Christopher Lee *(Sir Henry Baskerville)*, Marla Landi *(Cecile)*, David Oxley *(Sir Hugo Baskerville)*, Miles Malleson *(Bishop Frankland)*, Francis De Wolff *(Dr. Mortimer)*, Ewen Solon *(Stapleton)*, John Le Mesurier *(Barrymore)*, Sam Kydd *(Perkins)*, Judi Moyens *(Servant Girl)*, Helen Goss *(Mrs. Barrymore)*, Dave Birks *(Servant)*, Michael Mulcaster *(Seldon)*, Michael Hawkins *(Lord Caphill)*, Ian Hewitson *(Lord Kingsblood)*, Elizabeth Dott.

After riding the success of a new cycle of horror films that they had nearly single-handedly created, Hammer Studios decided to resurrect a beloved British character by the name of Sherlock Holmes and give him his first full-blown color treatment. Cast as Holmes was Cushing (who aside from the inimitable Basil Rathbone, was perfect for the part) who had built quite a reputation from his portrayals of Dr. Frankenstein and Dr. Van Helsing in the Hammer horror films. Not wanting to break up a good team (they had worked together successfully in nearly every Hammer picture) the studio cast Lee as the Canadian heir to the Baskerville estate. Morell turned in a competent, if unspectacular, performance as Dr. Watson. Hammer lent its usual lush production values to this Holmes effort, filling the regrettably claustrophobic sets (the film was shot in a suburban studio that was actually a large house) with accurate period detail and creating an unforgettably creepy moor. The film begins with a flashback detailing the brutal murder of a young girl who had escaped the lecherous Oxley's orgy. After the murder, there is a terrifying sound and Oxley is found dead, having been killed by a mysterious beast. The story then shifts to modern (for the period) times and we learn that what we have just seen is the legend of the Baskerville curse, as related by De Wolff to Cushing. Eventually Cushing and Morell wind up trying to save Lee from the horrible fate that awaits him. In the end it is revealed that local lovely Landi is behind the murders, seeking revenge on the Baskerville clan because she and her destitute family are the illegitimate descendants of Oxley. After telling a trapped Lee this, she sends her massive Great Dane in for the kill, but Cushing and Morell arrive just in time to save his life. Landi flees, but she is trapped in the moor's quicksand and sinks to her fate. The film is something of a disappointment, but the color and production values add a certain flair to it, as do the performances of Cushing and Lee. (See SHERLOCK HOLMES series, Index.)

p, Anthony Hinds; d, Terence Fisher; w, Peter Bryan (based on the novel by Arthur Conan Doyle); ph, Jack Asher (Technicolor); m, James Bernard; ed, Alfred Cox; md, John Hollingsworth; art d, Bernard Robinson.

Mystery **Cas.** **(PR:C MPAA:NR)**

HOUND OF THE BASKERVILLES, THE* (1980, Brit.) 84m Hemdale International/Atlantic c

Peter Cook *(Sherlock Holmes)*, Dudley Moore *(Dr. Watson/Mrs. Holmes/Mrs. Spiggott)*, Denholm Elliott *(Stapleton)*, Joan Greenwood *(Beryl Stapleton)*, Terry-Thomas *(Dr. Mortimer)*, Max Wall *(Mr. Barrymore)*, Irene Handl *(Mrs. Barrymore)*, Kenneth Williams *(Sir Henry Baskerville)*, Hugh Griffith *(Frankland)*, Dana Gillespie *(Mary)*, Roy Kinnear *(Seldon)*, Prunella Scales *(Glynis)*, Penelope Keith *(Massage Parlor Receptionist)*, Spike Milligan *(Baskerville Police Force)*.

Tasteless spoof of the famous Sherlock Holmes tale stars Cook and Moore as Holmes and Watson in a seemingly endless string of unfunny jokes told at the expense of Doyle's characters. Directed by Andy Warhol favorite Morrissey (FRANKENSTEIN, DRACULA and TRASH) and not released in the U.S. until after Moore's success in Blake Edwards' 10. (See SHERLOCK HOLMES series, Index.)

p, John Goldstone; d, Paul Morrissey; w, Peter Cook, Dudley Moore, Morrissey (based on the novel by Arthur Conan Doyle); ph, Dick Busch, John Wilcox; m, Moore; ed, Richard Marden, Glenn Hyde; prod d, Roy Smith; cos, Charles Knode.

Comedy/Mystery **(PR:C MPAA:NR)**

HOUND OF THE BASKERVILLES, THE**

(1983, Brit.) 100m Mapleton/Weintraub c

Ian Richardson *(Sherlock Holmes)*, Donald Churchill *(Dr. Watson)*, Martin Shaw *(Sir Henry Baskerville)*, Nicholas Clay *(Jack Stapleton)*, Denholm Elliott *(Dr. Mortimer)*, Brian Blessed *(Geoffrey Lyons)*, Ronald Lacy *(Inspector Lestrade)*, Eleanor Bron, Edward Judd, Glynis Barber.

Yet another pointless re-make of the most famous of the Sherlock Holmes tales. This version sees the master sleuth go undercover disguised as a gypsy to see what he can learn of the local surroundings. (See SHERLOCK HOLMES series, Index.)

p, Otto Plaschkes; d, Douglas Hickox; w, Charles Pogue (based on the novel by Arthur Conan Doyle); ph, Ronnie Taylor; m, Michael J. Lewis; ed, Malcolm Cooke; prod d, Michael Stringer; cos, Julie Harris; spec eff, Alan Whibley; makeup, Tom Smith, John Webber.

Mystery **(PR:C MPAA:NR)**

HOUND-DOG MAN*** (1959) 87m FOX c

Fabian *(Clint)*, Carol Lynley *(Dony)*, Stuart Whitman *(Blackie Scantling)*, Arthur O'Connell *(Aaron McKinney)*, Dodie Stevens *(Nita Stringer)*, Betty Field *(Cora)*, Royal Dano *(Fiddling Tom Waller)*, Margo Moore *(Susie Bell)*, Claude Akins *(Hog Peyson)*, Edgar Buchanan *(Doc Cole)*, Jane Darwell *(Grandma Wilson)*, L.Q. Jones *(Dave Wilson)*, Virginia Gregg *(Amy Waller)*, Dennis Holmes *(Spud Kinney)*, Rachel Stephens *(Rachael Wilson)*, Jim Beck *(Terminus Dooley)*, Hope Summers *(Jewell Crouch)*, Harry Carter *(Sol Fikes)*.

Charming tale of a young boy (played by a 16-year-old Fabian in his movie debut) in 1912 who, with his older friend, Whitman, spend an idyllic summer goofing off when they should be home working the farm. In addition to the title tune there are plenty of songs sung by Fabian, including: "What Big Boy?" "Single," "This Friendly World," "Pretty Little Girl," "I'm Giving Up," "Hill-Top Song," "Hay Foot, Straw-Foot" (Ken Darby, Frankie Avalon, Saul Ponti, Robert Marcucci, Pete

De Angelis, Doc Pomus, Mort Shuman). Well directed by Siegel with beautiful rustic location shots.

p, Jerry Wald; d, Don Siegel; w, Fred Gipson, Winston Miller (based on the novel by Gipson); ph, Charles G. Clarke (CinemaScope, DeLuxe Color); m, Cyril Mockbridge; ed, Louis Loeffler; md, Lionel Newman; art d, Lyle R. Wheeler, Walter M. Simonds; cos, Adele Palmer; ch, Josephine Earl.

Musical (PR:A MPAA:NR)

HOUNDS . . . OF NOTRE DAME, THE½** (1980, Can.) 95m Fraser/Pan-Canadian c

Thomas Peacocke *(Father Athol Murray)*, Frances Hyland *(Mother Therese)*, Barry Morse *(Archbishop Williams)*, David Ferry *(Ron Fryer)*, Lawrence Reese *(Tom Howard)*, Lenore Zahn *(Lila Petri)*, Phil Ridley *(Bob Cormack)*, Dale Heibein *(Terry Gladwell)*, Paul Bougie *(Frank Lasuisse)*, Rob MacLean *(Ben McCauley)*, Bill Sorenson *(Stephen Kessler)*, Bill Morton *(Bashinsky)*.

A fairly dull, low-budget Canadian film which details the life and struggles of Murray (Peacocke), the controversial priest who founded the College of Notre Dame in Saskatchewan. Peacocke, described as a drinking, chain-smoking, opinionated man, believed that a combination of tough education and athletics is what the boys of his college needed to succeed in life. The film details the rise of the school from a dilapidated, heatless dump, to a modern, respectable college. Typical material (despite its authenticity) which has been done better elsewhere.

p, Fil Fraser; d, Zale Dalen; w, Ken Mitchell; ph, Ron Orieux; m, Maurice Marshall; ed, Tony Lower; art d, Richard Hudolin.

Biography (PR:A MPAA:NR)

HOUR BEFORE THE DAWN, THE*½ (1944) 74m PAR bw

Franchot Tone *(Jim Hetherton)*, Veronica Lake *(Dora Bruckmann)*, John Sutton *(Roger Hetherton)*, Binnie Barnes *(May Hetherton)*, Henry Stephenson *(Gen. Hetherton)*, Phillip Merivale *(Sir Leslie Buchannan)*, Nils Asther *(Kurt van der Breughel)*, Edmond Breon *(Freddy Merritt)*, David Leland *(Tommy Hetherton)*, Aminta Dyne *(Hertha Parkins)*, Morton Lowry *(Jackson)*, Ivan Simpson *(Magistrate)*, Donald Stuart *(Farmer Searle)*, Harry Allen *(Mr. Saunders)*, Mary Gordon *(Annie)*, Ernest Severn *(Willie)*, Raymond Severn *(Jim as a Boy)*, Leslie Denison *(Capt. Atterley)*, Harry Cording *(Sam)*, Hilda Plowright *(Mrs. Merritt)*, Viola Moore *(Maid)*, David Clyde *(Farmer)*, Tempe Pigott *(Mrs. Saunders)*, Marjean Neville *(Evie)*, Marie deBecker *(Amelia)*, Thomas Louden *(Wilmington)*, Deidre Gale *(Emma)*, Nigel Morton *(Observer Pilot)*, Otto Reichow, Charles H. Faber *(German Pilots)*.

This slow and often tedious film takes place in England during the early part of WW II. The story concerns Tone, a wealthy young man with a strong aversion to killing, who becomes a conscientious objector. Lake is a governess in his mansion and also a German spy. At the outbreak of the war, she marries Tone for protection. Because of his beliefs, he is deferred for farmwork, while Lake does her work for the enemy. After an air blitz, in which the Germans try to knock out a secret air strip in the vicinity of Tone's mansion, Lake is uncovered as a spy. Tone kills her in the end and joins the Royal Air Force.

p, William Dozier; d, Frank Tuttle; w, Michael Hogan, Lester Samuels (based on the novel by W. Somerset Maugham); ph, John F. Seitz; m, Miklos Rozsa; ed, Stuart Gilmore; art d, Hans Dreier, Earl Hedrick; spec eff, Gordon Jennings.

Spy Drama (PR:A MPAA:NR)

HOUR OF DECISION*½ (1957, Brit.) 81m Tempean/Eros bw

Jeff Morrow *(Joe Sanders)*, Hazel Court *(Peggy Sanders)*, Lionel Jeffries *(Elvin Main)*, Anthony Dawson *(Garry Bax)*, Mary Laura Wood *(Olive Bax)*, Carl Bernard *(Inspector Gower)*, Vanda Godsell *(Eileen Chadwick)*, Alan Gifford *(J. Foster Green)*, Gerard Green *(Tony Pendleton)*, Margaret Allworthy *(Denise March)*, Richard Shaw *(Detective Sgt. Dale)*, Marne Maitland *(Waiter)*, Anthony Snell *(Andrew)*, Robert Sansom *(Rees Chadwick)*, Michael Balfour.

When an unscrupulous newspaper columnist is murdered, reporter Morrow is assigned to investigate. The trail leads him to Court, his own wife, as the possible killer. In an effort to prove her innocence, Morrow goes out to find the real murderer. Typical newspaper investigation story without much originality or steam to it.

p, Robert Baker, Monty Berman; d, C. Pennington Richards; w, Norman Hudis; ph, Stan Pavey.

Murder/Mystery (PR:A MPAA:NR)

HOUR OF GLORY½** (1949, Brit.) 108m LFP-Archers/BL bw (GB: THE SMALL BACK ROOM)

David Farrar *(Sammy Rice)*, Kathleen Byron *(Susan)*, Jack Hawkins *(R.B. Waring)*, Leslie Banks *(Col. Holland)*, Cyril Cusack *(Cpl. Taylor)*, Robert Morley *(Minister)*, Emrys Jones *(Joe)*, Renee Asherson *(ATS Corporal)*, Walter Fitzgerald *(Brine)*, Anthony Bushell *(Col. Strang)*, Milton Rosmer *(Prof. Maor)*, Michael Gough *(Capt. Stewart)*, Michael Goodliffe *(Till)*, Henry Caine *(Sgt.-Maj. Rose)*, James Dale *(Brigadier)*, Sam Kydd *(Crowhurst)*, Elwyn Brook-Jones *(Gladwin)*, June Elvin *(Gillian)*, David Hutcheson *(Norval)*, Sidney James *(Knucksie)*, Roderick Lovell *(Pearson)*, James Carney *(Sgt. Graves)*, Roddy Hughes *(Welsh Doctor)*, Geoffrey Keen *(Pinker)*, Bryan Forbes *(Dying Gunner)*, Ted Heath's Kenny Baker Swing Group and Fred Lewis.

Farrar plays a young scientist with a lame foot that gives him a complex other people find hard to understand, thus making him a lonely person. But he is content with his work, finding occasional solace for his loneliness in drinking bouts. When an enemy bomb threatens a number of people's lives, Farrar finally wins some recognition for the confidence he displays when dismantling the bomb. A quiet but unsung hero, which is handled in a convincing manner by Farrar.

p,d&w, Michael Powell, Emeric Pressburger (based on the novel by Nigel Balchin); ph, Christopher Challis; m, Brian Easdale; ed, Clifford Turner; prod d, Hein Heckroth; set d, John Hoesli.

War Drama (PR:A MPAA:NR)

HOUR OF THE GUN*½** (1967) 101m Mirisch-Kappa/UA c

James Garner *(Wyatt Earp)*, Jason Robards, Jr. *(Doc Holliday)*, Robert Ryan *(Ike Clanton)*, Albert Salmi *(Octavius Roy)*, Charles Aidman *(Horace Sullivan)*, Steve Ihnat *(Andy Warshaw)*, Michael Tolan *(Pete Spence)*, Frank Converse *(Virgil Earp)*, Sam Melville *(Morgan Earp)*, Austin Willis *(Anson Safford)*, Richard Bull *(Thomas Fitch)*, Larry Gates *(John P. Clum)*, Karl Swenson *(Dr. Goodfellow)*, Bill Fletcher *(Jimmy Ryan)*, Robert Phillips *(Frank Stilwell)*, William Schallert *(Herman Spicer)*, Jon Voight *(Curly Bill Brocius)*, Lonny Chapman *(Turkey Creek Johnson)*, Monte Markham *(Sherman McMasters)*, William Windom *(Texas Jack Vermillion)*, Edward Anhalt *(Denver Doctor)*, Walter Gregg *(Billy Clanton)*, David Perna *(Frank McLowery)*, Jim Sheppard *(Tom McLowery)*, Jorge Russek *(Latigo)*.

Superb Wyatt Earp saga, more or less a sequel to GUNFIGHT AT THE O.K. CORRAL, has Garner as the legendary lawman. The solemn Sturges western, taut and tight in every scene, begins with the celebrated gunfight and goes on to show how Garner's brothers Converse and Melville are shot from ambush by gunslingers in the employ of rustler Ryan. Garner slowly succumbs to vengeance, losing his high moral principles and disregarding the law. He deputizes his best friend, gunman Robards—essaying the role of famous Doc Holliday—and gathers a small posse to search for his brothers' killers. One by one he hunts them down and kills them himself, including Ryan whom he tracks across the border into Mexico. Robards follows his friend through one state after another, watching and helping him gun down the killers, but gaining a sense of morality where Garner appears to lose his own. An interesting, often absorbing offbeat western with excellent production values. Garner is surprisingly effective as the grim, unswerving lawman and Robards is jocularly right as the savvy but deadly Holliday. Ryan as gang leader Ike Clanton registers high as do Ihnat, Tolan, and Phillips as the gunmen who killed the Earp Brothers. Future star Voight appears in a small role as lethal gunman Curly Bill Brocius. The script is intelligent and witty; its author Anhalt appears in a bit role as a medic who keeps Robards company at the end when the tubercular gunman goes to a Colorado sanitarium to die which, in reality, he did.

p&d, John Sturges; w, Edward Anhalt; ph, Lucien Ballard (Panavision, DeLuxe Color); m, Jerry Goldsmith; ed, Ferris Webster; art d, Alfred Ybarra; set d, Lawrence J. Cuneo, Victor Gangelin; spec eff, Sass Bedig; makeup, Charles Blackman.

Western (PR:C MPAA:NR)

HOUR OF THE WOLF, THE** (1968, Swed.) 88m Svensk Filmindustri/Lopert bw (VARGTIMMEN)

Liv Ullmann *(Alma Borg)*, Max von Sydow *(Johan Borg)*, Erland Josephson *(Baron von Merkens)*, Gertrud Fridh *(Corinne von Merkens)*, Gudrun Brost *(Gamla Fru von Merkens)*, Bertil Anderberg *(Ernst von Merkens)*, Georg Rydeberg *(Arkivarie Lindhorst)*, Ulf Johanson *(Kurator Heerbrand)*, Naima Wifstrand *(Old Lady With Hat)*, Ingrid Thulin *(Veronica Vogler)*, Lenn Hjortzberg *(Kapellmastare Kreisler)*, Agda Helin *(Maidservant)*, Mikael Rundqvist *(Young Boy)*, Mona Seilitz *(Woman in Mortuary)*, Folke Sundquist *(Tamino I. Trollflojten)*.

Another fairly tedious Bergman discourse on the nature of art and artists in relation to their society . . . or something like that. Shrouded in the trappings of gothic horror, THE HOUR OF THE WOLF sees von Sydow as a painter haunted by bad dreams and apparitions, while secluded on an island with his pregnant wife Ullmann for the summer. Von Sydow sees the image of a beautiful boy, a ghost able to walk on walls, and an ancient woman who tears off her face. Soon Ullmann also sees these visions and is instructed by the old woman to read her husband's diary. There she learns of a love affair her husband had with Thulin. This leads to an estrangement and, during a fight, von Sydow shoots and wounds Ullmann. He then rushes to the castle of Josephson and his strange brood where he finds the corpse of his former lover lying naked on a slab. Von Sydow caresses the cadaver and it comes to life, laughing at him. He is chased into the forest by Josephson and his followers where they savagely humiliate him in front of Ullmann. In the end, von Sydow disappears, leaving Ullmann to tell the bizarre tale. If you like Bergman, you'll love sorting out the symbolism and what-nots. (In Swedish; English subtitles.)

d&w, Ingmar Bergman; ph, Sven Nykvist; m, Lars Johan Werle; ed, Ulla Ryghe; art d & set d, Marik Vos-Lundh; cos, Mago; spec eff, Evald Andersson; m/l, "Die Zauberflote," Wolfgang Amadeus Mozart, "Experiment," Johann Sebastian Bach; subtitles, Alan Blair.

Drama (PR:O MPAA:NR)

HOUR OF THIRTEEN, THE*** (1952) 79m MGM bw

Peter Lawford *(Nicholas Revel)*, Dawn Addams *(Jane Frensham)*, Roland Culver *(Connor)*, Derek Bond *(Sir Christopher Lenhurst)*, Leslie Dwyer *(Ernie Perker)*, Michael Hordern *(Sir Herbert Frensham)*, Colin Gordon *(MacStreet)*, Heather Thatcher *(Mrs. Chumley Orr)*, Jack McNaughton *(Ford)*, Campbell Cotts *(Mr. Chumley Orr)*, Fabia Drake *(Lady Elmbridge)*, Michael Goodliffe *(Anderson)*, Moultrie Kelsall *(Magistrate of Court)*, Peter Copley *(Cummings)*, Richard Shaw *(The Terror)*, Sam Kydd.

A well-made thriller set in London of the 1890s sees Lawford as a jewel thief who, along with his accomplices Dwyer and Gordon, steal a valuable emerald at a ritzy party. At the same time, and totally unrelated, is the murder of a bobby by a police killer called the "terror," played by Shaw. The murder complicates the escape of Lawford and company and causes them to come under suspicion of Scotland Yard superintendent, Culver, for both the theft and the killing. Lawford uses his quick wits to keep one step ahead of the law, biding his time until the heat is off and he may dispose of the emerald. But as long as the string of police murders continues, the chase for Lawford doesn't die down. As a result, Lawford comes up with a scheme to capture Shaw which works but sees Lawford sent to prison anyway. A good remake of the 1934 film, THE MYSTERY OF MR. X.

p, Hayes Goetz; d, Harold French; w, Leon Gordon, Howard Emmett Rogers (based on a novel by Philip MacDonald); ph, Guy Green; m, John Addison; ed, Robert Watts, Raymond Poulton; md, Addison; art d, Alfred Judge.

Mystery/Crime **(PR:A MPAA:NR)**

HOURS OF LONELINESS* (1930, Brit.) 65m Carlton/WB bw

Sunday Wilshin *(Cella Stuart)*, Walter Sondes *(John Stuart)*, Carl Harbord *(Michael Turner)*, Marjorie Jennings *(Betty Chase)*, Michael Hogan *(Trimmett)*, Iris Ashley *(Babe Garson)*, Mina Burnett *(Manette)*, Harold Huth *(Gustave)*.

While having an affair with married lady Wilshin, her lover, Harbord, shoots a man breaking into her Riviera home. This leads to a blackmailing plot over the illicit affair, in this bland, poorly handled drama.

p,d&w, G. G. Glavany.

Crime **(PR:C MPAA:NR)**

HOURS OF LOVE, THE½** (1965, Ital.) 89m DD/Cinema V bw (LE ORE DELL'AMORE)

Ugo Tognazzi *(Gianni)*, Emmanuelle Riva *(Maretta)*, Barbara Steele *(Leila)*, Mara Berni *(Jolanda)*, Umberto D'Orsi *(Ottavio)*, Diletta D'Andrea *(Mimma)*, Brunello Rondi *(Cipriani)*, Renato Speziali *(Psychiatrist)*, Fabrizio Moroni *(Roberto)*, Irene D'Aloisi, Luciano Salce.

Charming little romantic comedy starring Tognazzi and Riva as successful lovers who finally decide to get married. They soon discover, however, that marriage is ruining their relationship. With the excitement of courtship gone, they focus on each other's annoying habits until they split up. Finding that living without each other is worse, they return to their original arrangement and resume being lovers.

p, Isidoro Broggi, Renato Libassi; d, Luciano Salce; w, Salce, Franco Castellano, Pipolo, Diego Fabbri (based on a story by Castellano, Pipolo); ph, Erico Menczer (CinemaScope); m, Luiz Bonfa; ed, Roberto Cinquini; art d, Nedo Azzini; set d, Guiseppe Ranieri; cos, Giuliano Papi; makeup, Giannetto De Rossi.

Comedy/Romance **(PR:A MPAA:NR)**

HOUSE ACROSS THE BAY, THE½** (1940) 88m UA bw

George Raft *(Steve Larwitt)*, Joan Bennett *(Brenda "Lucky" Bentley)*, Lloyd Nolan *(Slant Kolma)*, Walter Pidgeon *(Tim Nolan)*, Gladys George *(Mary Bogale)*, William "Billy" Wayne *(Barney the Bartender)*, June Knight *(Babe Davis)*, Peggy Shannon *(Alice)*, Cy Kendall *(Crawley)*, Max Wagner *(Jim the Chauffeur)*, Frank Bruno *(Jerry the Henchman)*, Joseph Sawyer *(Charlie)*, William Halligan, Kenneth Harlan *(Men in Nightclub)*, Mack Gray *(Doorman-Lookout)*, Sam Finn *(Head Waiter)*, Marcelle Corday *(French Maid)*, Sam Ash *(Broker)*, Norman Willis, Eddie Marr *(Taresca's Henchmen)*, Frances Morris *(Secretary to Slant)*, Freeman Wood *(Mr. Hanson)*, Elsa Petersen *(Mrs. Hanson)*, Joseph Crehan, Charles Griffin *(Federal Men)*, Edward Fielding *(Federal Judge)*, Paul Phillips, John Bohn *(Reporters)*, Virginia Brissac *(Landlady)*, Franklyn Farnum, James Farley, Martin Cichy, Al Ferguson, Pat O'Malley *(Prison Guards)*, Dorothy Vaughn, Ruth Warren, Maxine Leslie, Helen Shipman, Kitty McHugh *(Prisoners' Wives on Ferry Boat)*, Etta McDaniel *(Lydia, the Maid)*, Miki Morita *(Tim's Japanese House Boy)*, Peter Camlin *(French Pilot)*, Georges Renevant, Jean Del Val *(French Officials)*, Emmett Vogan *(U.S. Official)*, Armand "Curly" Wright *(Barber)*, Harrison Greene *(Irate Customer)*, Allen Wood *(Newsboy)*, Herbert Ashley *(Man in Park)*, Sam Wren *(Draughtsman)*, Harry Tyler *(Fur Peddler)*, Victoria Vinton, Jean O'Donnell, Edith Haskins, Mitzi Uehlein, Lurline Uller, Kay Gordon, Pearlie Norton *(Chorus Girls)*, Donald Kerr, Max Hoffman, Jr. *(Drivers)*, Harry Harvey, Isabelle Withers *(Club Couple)*, James Craig, Jack Lubell *(Brenda's Boy Friends)*, Kit Guard *(Taresca's Driver)*, Cy Ring *(Dance Extra)*, Dick Rush *(Bailiff)*.

Raft is a suave and wealthy nightclub owner who hires Indiana-bred Bennett to sing in his club. He is so enamored of her that he proposes and for a short time they are happy, even though both Raft's lawyer Nolan and Pidgeon, a rich airplane manufacturer, also have hot eyes for the sultry brunette. When Bennett learns that a rival gambling faction is out to kill Raft she concocts what she thinks to be a clever scheme to protect hubby. She turns him in to the IRS for tax evasion, believing he will be tucked away safely in jail for a short time until the opposition tires of trying to kill him. Nolan, however, purposely conducts a lame-dog defense and Raft gets the book thrown at him, ten years in Alcatraz. Bennett, ever the dutiful wife, takes a swanky apartment in San Francisco, one which gives a clear view of Alcatraz in the Bay and, night after lonely night, she watches the prison searchlights scan the waters. She visits him regularly but Raft has no intention of spending ten years in the clink, especially when he learns that Nolan has doublecrossed him and is now moving in on his wife. He makes a desperate escape, swimming to San Francisco (a feat no con ever performed in real life!), confronts Nolan, and kills the sleazy lawyer in a struggle. He then attempts to return to prison but is killed by police. Bennett winds up in the arms of sedate, safe Pidgeon, who has been waiting to gather up luscious Bennett for his love nest. The plot is fair to the middle of the film, but it then becomes so ludicrous that one cannot suspend disbelief enough to believe in it. Raft hams it up and his snarling style is infectious, leading Nolan to follow suit. Bennett, one of those women whose smile always came close to a sneer (like Jane Russell), walks through the film in one revealing negligee after another and utters lines as mindless as the plot.

p, Walter Wanger; d, Archie Mayo; w, Kathryn Scola (based on a story by Myles Connolly); ph, Merritt Gerstad; m, Werner Janssen; ed, Dorothy Spencer; md, Janssen; art d, Alexander Golitzen, Richard Irvine; set d, Julie Heron; cos, Irene; spec eff, Ray Singer; ch, Sammy Lee; m/l, Jule Styne, Nick Castle, Sidney Clare, Al Siegel, George R. Brown, Irving Actman.

Crime Drama **Cas.** **(PR:A MPAA:NR)**

HOUSE ACROSS THE LAKE, THE (SEE: HEAT WAVE, 1954, Brit.)

HOUSE ACROSS THE STREET, THE*½ (1949) 69m WB bw

Wayne Morris *(Dave Joslin)*, Janis Paige *(Kit Williams)*, Bruce Bennett *(Keever)*, Alan Hale *(Grennell)*, James Mitchell *(Marty Bremer)*, Barbara Bates *(Beth Roberts)*, James Holden *(Carl Schrader)*, Ray Montgomery *(Reporter)*.

An often rehashed tale of a newspaperman-turned-sleuth, Morris, who takes on a big-time racketeer in order to get him behind bars. When the campaign against the syndicate causes too much trouble, the publisher of the paper, Hale, demotes Morris from managing editor to the love-lorn column. While working on the column, Morris finds a very important clue for his campaign against the mobster. With the aid of tough reporter Paige, he gets the proper dirt on the bad guy and all ends well for the former editor.

p, Saul Elkins; d, Richard Bare; w, Russell Hughes (based on the story "Hi Nellie!" by Roy Chanslor); ph, William Snyder; m, William Lava; ed, Frank Magee.

Crime **(PR:A MPAA:NR)**

HOUSE AT THE END OF THE WORLD (SEE: DIE, MONSTER, DIE, 1965)

HOUSE AT THE END OF THE WORLD (SEE: TOMB OF LIGEIA, THE, 1965, Brit.)

HOUSE BROKEN** (1936, Brit.) 74m British and Dominions/PAR British bw

Mary Lawson *(Angela Macgregor)*, Enid Stamp-Taylor *(Peggy Allen)*, Louis Borell *(Charles Delmont)*, Jack Lambert *(Jock Macgregor)*.

When Borell visits his friend Lawson and overstays his welcome, she turns to Stamp-Taylor, a local newspaper advice columnist, for help. The two plot to get rid of her unwanted houseguest in schemes that grow to outrageous proportions. In the end Borell finally leaves, accompanied by Stamp-Taylor who's fallen for the lug. The script has some very clever moments and nice dialog which unfortunately is given a less than deft handling by the cast.

p, Anthony Havelock-Allan; d, Michael Hankinson; w, Vera Allinson (based on a story by Paul Hervey Fox); ph, Francis Carver.

Comedy **(PR:A MPAA:NR)**

HOUSE BY THE LAKE, THE** (1977, Can.) 89m Quadrant-Dal/AIP c (AKA: DEATH WEEKEND)

Brenda Vaccaro *(Diane)*, Don Stroud *(Lep)*, Chuck Shamata *(Harry)*, Richard Ayres *(Runt)*, Kyle Edwards *(Frankie)*, Don Granbery *(Stanley)*, Ed McNamara *(Spragg)*, Michael Kirby *(Ralph)*, Richard Donat *(Policeman)*, Denver Mattson *(Smokey)*, Al Bernardo *(Mr. Doobie)*, Roselle Stone *(Mrs. Doobie)*, Elaine Yarish *(Campground Girl)*.

Vaccaro did little to help the women's movement in this multiple-gore film. The story sees her and playboy Shamata off to spend what she believes to be a weekend with friends at his remote country mansion. Enroute they are harrassed by a carful of drunken troublerousers, who are forced off the road when Vaccaro outdrives them. At Shamata's house, Vaccaro finds she is the only guest, and that her friend has more in mind for the evening than she does. In the meantime, the gang has followed them and breaks into the mansion, terrorizing Vaccaro and murdering Shamata. Vaccaro manages to kill off the men one by one, except for the last one, Stroud, who tries to stop her as she drives away, causing her to run him over.

p, Ivan Reitman; d&w, William Fruet; ph, Robert Saad (Eastmancolor); ed, Jean LaFleur, Debbie Karjala; art d, Roy Forge Smith; cos, Erla Gliserman; spec eff, Tony Parmalee; stunts, Denver Mattson, Jess Wayne, Robert Hannah, Dwayne McLean, John Stoneham.

Horror **(PR:O MPAA:R)**

HOUSE BY THE RIVER½** (1950) 88m Fidelity/REP bw

Louis Hayward *(Stephen Byrne)*, Lee Bowman *(John Byrne)*, Jane Wyatt *(Marjorie Byrne)*, Dorothy Patrick *(Emily Gaunt)*, Ann Shoemaker *(Mrs. Ambrose)*, Jody Gilbert *(Flora Bantam)*, Peter Brocco *(Coroner)*, Howland Chamberlin *(District Attorney)*, Margaret Seddon *(Mrs. Whittaker)*, Sarah Padden *(Mrs. Beach)*, Kathleen Freeman *(Effie Ferguson)*, Will Wright *(Inspector Sarten)*, Leslie Kimmell *(Mr. Gaunt)*, Effie Laird *(Mrs. Gaunt)*.

Hayward stars in this minor Lang effort as a writer who lives with his wife Wyatt in a decaying mansion on the banks of a putrid river. While attempting to seduce his housemaid, Hayward accidentally kills her. Desperate, he convinces his crippled brother Bowman to help him get rid of the body and together they dump the corpse in the river. The tide, however, washes the body ashore and after an investigation, Bowman is blamed for the murder. Hayward panics and tries to pile the evidence against his brother, but Bowman threatens to tell the truth unless Hayward helps him. Meanwhile, Wyatt has figured out what actually happened and joins Bowman against Hayward. Seeing no other way to extricate himself from this dilemma, Hayward decides to kill them both, but is killed himself in the process. In an effort to be taken seriously by the majors, Republic studios hired several "big" directors to make films for them after WW II (Orson Welles, John Ford, Lewis Milestone). Lang was among the directors drafted, but Republic's budgets were still low, and their talent below par (especially writers and actors in this case) for any true block-busters to be produced. While HOUSE BY THE RIVER is, at least, a typically interesting Lang film, it suffers from a weak script and uninspired performances that even the director's moody visuals have trouble saving.

p, Howard Welsch; d, Fritz Lang; w, Mel Dinelli (based on a novel by A.P. Herbert); ph, Edward Cronjager; m, George Antheil; ed, Arthur D. Hilton; art d,

Bert Leven; set d, Charles Thompson, John McCarthy, Jr.; cos, Adele Palmer; spec eff, Howard Lydecker, Theodore Lydecker.

Crime/Drama **(PR:C MPAA:NR)**

HOUSE CALLS½** (1978) 98m UNIV c

Walter Matthau *(Dr. Charley Nichols)*, Glenda Jackson *(Ann Atkinson)*, Art Carney *(Dr. Amos Willoughby)*, Richard Benjamin *(Dr. Norman Solomon)*, Candice Azzara *(Ellen Grady)*, Dick O'Neill *(Irwin Owett)*, Thayer David *(Pogostin)*, Anthony Holland *(TV Moderator)*, Reva Rose *(Mrs. DeVoto)*, Sandra Kerns *(Lani Mason)*, Brad Dexter *(Quinn)*, Jane Connell *(Mrs. Conway)*, Lloyd Gough *(Harry Grady)*, Gordon Jump *(Dr. O'Brien)*, William J. Fiore *(Dr. Sloan)*, Taurean Blacque *(Levi)*, Charlie Matthau *(Michael Atkinson)*, Ken Olfson *(Make-up Man)*, Len Lesser *(Waiter)*, Nancy Hsueh *(Gretchen)*, Lee Weaver *(Anaesthesiologist)*, Susan Batson *(Shirley)*, Alma Beltran *(Gina)*, Pamela Toll *(Sarah)*, Anita Alberts *(Nurse)*, Enzo Gagliardi, Bob Goldstein, Bernie Kuby, Patch Mackenzie, Maurice Marks, Sally K. Marr, Harlee McBride, Judith Brown, David Bond, Walter D. O'Donnell, Kyle Oliver, George Sasaki, Roberto Trujillo, Kedric Wolfe, Michael Mann, David Morick, John Pleshette, Jack Griffin.

A pleasant comedy, but any film starring Matthau and Jackson, and written by such funnymen as Shulman and Epstein (among others), should have been much funnier. Matthau is a doctor whose long-time wife has just passed away. He was totally faithful to her for more than 30 years and is now determined to make up for lost time and becomes a middle-aged lecher. Jackson has just divorced a world-class adulterer, and wants the kind of man Matthau used to be as a new husband. Carney is a dotty chief-of-staff who can't even remember the name of the hospital, and Benjamin is a young doctor whose main role is to take care of the plot points. Jackson and Matthau meet, have some very predictable romantic goings-on, and eventually unite against the screwball background of a medical facility not unlike Chayevsky's horror in HOSPITAL. Although Jackson seemed ill-at-ease in this comedy, she and Matthau must have loved the experience of working together as they teamed again a couple of years later for HOPSCOTCH. HOUSE CALLS made almost $20 million but never did catch comedic fire under commercials-veteran Zeiff's direction. In a small bit, look for Sally Marr, long-time comedy actress and Lenny Bruce's mother.

p, Alex Winitsky, Arlene Sellers; d, Howard Zeiff; w, Max Shulman, Julius J. Epstein, Alan Mandel, Charles Shyer (based on a story by Epstein, Shulman); ph, David M. Walsh (Panavision, Technicolor); m, Henry Mancini; ed, Edward Warschilka; prod d, Henry Bumstead; set d, Mickey S. Michaels; cos, Burton Miller.

Comedy **Cas.** **(PR:C MPAA:PG)**

HOUSE DIVIDED, A½** (1932) 70m UNIV bw

Walter Huston *(Seth Law)*, Kent Douglas *(Matt Law)*, Helen Chandler *(Ruth Evans)*, Vivian Oakland *(Bess)*, Frank Hagney *(Bill)*, Mary Fay *(Mary)*, Lloyd Ingraham *(Doctor)*, Charles Middleton *(Minister)*, Marjorie Main *(Woman)*.

Huston plays a hard-drinking fisherman, who, as the film opens, has just buried his wife. Left alone with his son, Douglas, whom he considers a good-for-nothing weakling, Huston becomes lonely and signs up with a marriage agency to send him a new wife. Enter the young and pretty Chandler and it is soon obvious that Douglas has fallen for her, and she for him. This leads to a climactic fight between father and son which leaves Huston crippled for life and filled with hate. Chandler and Douglas prepare to leave the house when a severe storm blows their way. Chandler is trapped on a boat drifting out to sea until father and son swallow their pride and pull together to save her life. Douglas finally overcomes his cowardice, but Huston's boat capsizes and the old man drowns. Though based on the story "Heart and Hand," this material is obviously inspired by Eugene O'Neill's "Desire Under The Elms," a debt that remains clear despite the last-minute dialog changes by then-screenwriter (and son of Walter) John Huston.

p, Paul Kohner; d, William Wyler; w, John B. Clymer, Dale Van Every, John Huston (based on the story "Heart and Hand" by Olive Edens); ph, Charles Stumar.

Drama **(PR:C MPAA:NR)**

HOUSE IN MARSH ROAD, THE** (1960, Brit.) 70m Eternal/GN bw

Tony Wright *(David Linton)*, Patricia Dainton *(Jean Linton)*, Sandra Dorne *(Valerie Stockley)*, Derek Aylward *(Richard Foster)*, Sam Kydd *(Lumley)*, Llewellyn Rees *(Webster)*, Anita Sharp Bolster *(Mrs. O'Brien)*, Roddy Hughes *(Daniels)*, Olive Sloan *(Mrs. Morris)*.

A book critic and his mistress decide the man's wife stands in the way of their happiness. A murder plot is hatched only to be foiled by a watchful poltergeist.

p, Maurice J. Wilson; d, Montgomery Tully; w, Wilson (based on the novel by Laurence Meynell).

Fantasy **(PR:A MPAA:NR)**

HOUSE IN NIGHTMARE PARK, THE (SEE: NIGHT OF THE LAUGHING DEAD, 1973, Brit.)

HOUSE IN THE SQUARE, THE (SEE: I'LL NEVER FORGET YOU, 1951, Brit.)

HOUSE IN THE WOODS, THE½** (1957, Brit.) 60m Film Workshop/Archway bw

Ronald Howard *(Spencer Rowland)*, Patricia Roc *(Carol Carter)*, Michael Gough *(Geoffrey Carter)*, Andrea Troubridge *(Mrs. Shellaby)*, Bill Shine *(Col. Shellaby)*, Norah Hammond *(Mrs. Bletchley)*, Tim Ellison *(An Elegant Young Man)*, Leigh Crutchley, Geoffrey Goodhart, Tony Doonan.

A writer and his wife (Gough and Roc) decide to rent a small countryside cottage. Gough intends to use this for his work but soon learns that the landlord (Howard), a rather odd painter, is out to kill Roc. Howard was a suspect in his own wife's death and is stopped from murdering Roc just in the nick of time. An interesting and well-handled thriller that never lets up despite some problems with plot holes.

p, Geoffrey Goodhart; d&w, Maxwell Munden (based on the short story "Prelude to Murder" by Walter C. Brown); ph, Cedric Williams.

Thriller **(PR:C MPAA:NR)**

HOUSE IS NOT A HOME, A*½ (1964) 98m EM bw

Shelley Winters *(Polly Adler)*, Robert Taylor *(Frank Costigan)*, Cesar Romero *(Lucky Luciano)*, Ralph Taeger *(Casey Booth)*, Kaye Ballard *(Sidonia)*, Broderick Crawford *(Harrigan)*, Mickey Shaughnessy *(Sgt. John Riordan)*, Lisa Seagram *(Madge)*, Meri Welles *(Lorraine)*, Jesse White *(Rafferty)*, Connie Gilchrist *(Hattie Miller)*, Constance Dane *(Laura)*, Allyson Ames *(Gwen)*, Lewis Charles *(Angelo)*, Steve Peck *(Vince)*, Michael Forest *(Bernie Watson)*, Stanley Adams *(Harry)*, Dick Reeves *(Pete Snyder)*, Roger C. Carmel *(Dixie Keeler)*, J. Pat O'Malley *(Muldoon)*, Alice Reinheart *(Sarah Ludwig)*, Ben Astar *(Max Ludwig)*, Hayden Rorke *(Bill Cameron)*, Benny Rubin *(Happy Charlie)*, Tom D'Andrea *(Gabe)*, Gee Gee Galligan *(Dorothy)*, Alex Gerry *(Doctor)*, Edmon Ryan *(Sam)*, George Casir *(Dr. Saunders)*, Charles E. Fredericks *(Bert)*, Baynes Barron *(Matt)*, Jerry James *(Tim)*, Mike Ross *(Dance Hall Manager)*, Larry Barton *(Baldheaded Man)*, Steve Carruthers *(Ogle-Eyed Man)*, Billy Beck *(Goggle-Eyed Man)*, June Gleason *(Irate Wife)*, Wynne Brown *(Secretary)*, John Indrisano *(Man)*, Max Power *(2nd Man)*, Sandra Scott *(Scarred Girl)*, Roxanne Arlen *(Hattie's Girl)*, Wilda Taylor *(Exotic Dancer)*, Amedee Chabot, Danica D'Hondt, Leona Gage, Sandra Grant, Diane Libby, Patricia Manning, Inga Neilsen, Francine Pyne, Astrid Schultz, Patricia Thomas, Raquel Welch, Edy Williams *(Polly's Girls)*.

Poorly and unimaginatively adapted from the autobiography of Polly Adler, one of the most successful Broadway bordello madams of the 1920s, A HOUSE IS NOT A HOME tells her story. As a young girl Adler (Winters) is seduced and raped by the foreman of the sweat shop where she works. Her uncle, whom she lives with, refuses to believe that it wasn't her fault and throws her out of the house. She moves into an apartment owned by racketeer Taylor, who gets Winters started on her career when he pays her to bring some of her girl friends to a party for some of his gangster chums. She sees that the money is good and starts to work up her own clientele. As she gets more business her addresses change to more fashionable locations. Her house becomes a meeting place for corrupt politicians, racketeers, and businessmen. Winters enters into a love affair with young songwriter Taeger, whose career she helps boost. She keeps her career a secret and finally breaks up with him to keep him from being ruined by her reputation.

p, Clarence Greene; d, Russell Rouse; w, Rouse, Greene (based on the book by Polly Adler); ph, Harold Stine; m, Joseph Weiss; ed, Chester Schaeffer; art d, Hal Pereira, Alexander Roelofs; set d, Sam Comer, James Roach; cos, Edith Head; make-up, Gene Hibbs.

Biography **(PR:O MPAA:NR)**

HOUSE OF A THOUSAND CANDLES, THE** (1936) 68m REP bw

Phillips Holmes *(Tony)*, Mae Clarke *(Carol)*, Irving Pichel *(Sebastian)*, Rosita Moreno *(Raquel)*, Fred Walton *(Alf)*, Hedwiga Reicher *(Marta)*, Lawrence Grant *(Sir Andrew)*, Fredrik Vogeding *(Travers)*, Michael Fitzmaurice *(Barrie)*, Rafael Storm *(Jules)*, Mischa Auer *(Dimitrios)*, Paul Ellis *(Agent)*, Keith Daniels *(Steward)*, Olaf Hytten, Charles De Ravenne, Lal Chand Mehra, Charles Martin, Max Wagner, Count Stepanelli.

An undistinguished espionage yarn tells the story of British courier Holmes, who tries to take an important message from London to Geneva. Holmes is beset by a slew of difficulties due to clever agents who don't want him to reach his goal. Clarke is Holmes' American sweetheart, who—though told to stay behind—always manages to tag along after her beau on his exploits.

p, Nat Levine, Mrs. Wallace Reid; d, Arthur Lubin; w, H.W. Hanemann, Endre Boehm (based on the novel by Meredith Nicholson); ph, Ernest Miller, Jack Marta; ed, Ralph Dixon; md, Arthur Kay; art d, Ralph Oberg; spec eff, Ellis Thackery, Howard Lydecker.

Spy Drama **(PR:A MPAA:NR)**

HOUSE OF BAMBOO*½** (1955) 102m FOX c

Robert Ryan *(Sandy Dawson)*, Robert Stack *(Eddie Kenner/Spanier)*, Shirley Yamaguchi *(Mariko)*, Cameron Mitchell *(Griff)*, Brad Dexter *(Capt. Hanson)*, Sessue Hayakawa *(Inspector Kito)*, Biff Elliot *(Webber)*, Sandro Giglio *(Ceram)*, Elko Hanabusa *(Japanese Screaming Woman)*, Harry Carey, Jr. *(John)*, Peter Gray *(Willy)*, Robert Quarry *(Phil)*, De Forest Kelley *(Charlie)*, John Doucette *(Skipper)*, Teru Shimada *(Nagaya)*, Robert Hosai *(Doctor)*, Jack Maeshiro *(Bartender)*, May Takasugi *(Bath Attendant)*, Robert Okazaki *(Mr. Hommaru)*, Neyle Morrow *(Army Corporal)*, Kazue Ikeda, Clifford Arashiro, Robert Kino *(Policemen)*, Frank Kwanaga *(File Clerk)*, Rollin Moriyama *(Pearl Man)*, Reiko Sato *(Charlie's Girl)*, Sandy "Chikaye" Azeka *(Charlie's Girl at Party)*, Fuji, Frank Jumagai *(Pachinko Managers)*, Harris Matsushige *(Office Clerk)*, Kinuko Ann Ito *(Servant)*, Barbara Uchiyamada *(Japanese Girl)*, Fred Dale *(Man)*, Barry Coe *(Hanson's Deputy)*, Reiko Hayakawa *(Mariko's Girl Friend)*, A Sandy Ozeka *(Sandy's "Kimono Girl")*, Samuel Fuller *(Policeman)*, The Shochiku Troupe from Kokusai Theater.

Hard-hitting postwar crime drama that owes much of its origin to THE STREET WITH NO NAME, except that this is now set in Japan and the addition of the Asian background adds much to the story. Ryan is a gangleader in Japan who has gathered a group of ex-servicemen around him and organized the lucrative pachinko parlors. Ryan appears to be a homosexual sadist who rules his gang with a vicious streak. Stack is sent by the army to get inside the gang in order to solve the murder of a GI. Stack manages to convince Ryan that he is a hoodlum (Ryan does some checking but the intelligence community has arranged a totally fraudulent background for Stack) and joins the mob, which is the Oriental version of the Chicago-type gangs of the 1920s. Stack moves in with Yamaguchi, widow of one of the gang's dead compatriots. There's a robbery and it's evident that the gang has been betrayed by someone inside. Ryan thinks it's Mitchell, kills him, and then elevates Stack to the position of ichi-ban (number one man) in the operation. Eventually, Ryan figures out that Stack is the snake in the grass and tries to have him killed but fails. In an exciting final sequence the two men duel it out on top of a building at an amusement park. Stack emerges the victor and is united with Yamaguchi. Beautifully photographed and well-written, HOUSE OF BAMBOO has many underlying themes. It was one of the rare postwar pictures made in Japan and effectively melded Japanese culture with the American criminal mentality. Stack knows that Ryan is physically attracted to him and uses this to hoist the villain on his own petard, thus making Stack's role somewhat unsympathetic. "Star Trek's" Kelley has a small role and old-time star Hayakawa is very convincing as the police inspector. Filmed in Japan in excellent color. The color consultant was Leonard Doss who moonlighted as a home decorator for movie people.

p, Buddy Adler; d, Samuel Fuller; w, Harry Kleiner, Fuller; ph, Joe MacDonald (CinemaScope, DeLuxe Color); m, Leigh Harline; ed, James B. Clark; md, Lionel Newman; art d, Lyle R. Wheeler, Addison Hehr; set d, Walter M. Scott, Stuart A. Reiss; cos, Charles LeMaire; spec eff, Ray Kellog; m/l, "House of Bamboo," Harline, Jack Brooks; makeup, Ben Nye.

Crime Drama **(PR:C MPAA:NR)**

HOUSE OF BLACKMAIL** (1953, Brit.) 72m ACT/Monarch bw

Mary Germaine *(Carol Blane)*, William Sylvester *(Jimmy)*, Alexander Gauge *(John Markham)*, John Arnatt *(Pete Carter)*, Denis Shaw *(Bassett)*, Ingeborg Wells *(Emma)*, Patricia Owens *(Joan)*, C. Denier Warren *(Jock)*, Barry Wynne, Hugo Schuster.

On her way to a blackmailer a woman picks up a hitchhiker. This proves to be a ride he'll never forget when the blackmailer is later killed by high-tension wires and the rider is accused of the crime. Ordinary but fast paced.

p, Phil Brandon; d, Maurice Elvey; w, Allan Mackinnon; ph, Phil Grindrod.

Crime **(PR:C MPAA:NR)**

HOUSE OF CARDS, 1934 (SEE: DESIGNING WOMEN, 1934, Brit.)

HOUSE OF CARDS*** (1969) 105m Westward/UNIV c

George Peppard *(Reno Davis)*, Inger Stevens *(Anne de Villemont)*, Orson Welles *(Claude Leschenhaut)*, Keith Michell *(Hubert Morillon)*, Ralph Michael *(Claude de Gonde)*, Maxine Audley *(Matilde Vosiers)*, William Job *(Bernard Bourdon)*, Peter Bayliss *(Edmond Vosier)*, Patience Collier *(Gabrielle de Villemont)*, Barnaby Shaw *(Paul de Villemont)*, Ave Ninchi *(Signora Braggi)*, Renzo Palmer *(Monk)*, Francesco Mule *(Trevi Policeman)*, Rosemary Dexter *(Daniella Braggi)*, Raoul Delfosse *(Louis Le Buc)*, Perrette Pradier *(Jeanne-Marie)*, Genevieve Cluny *(Veronique)*, James Mishler *(Jesse Hardee)*, Jean Louis *(Driot)*, Jacques Roux *(Maguy)*, Jean Hebey *(French Conductor)*, Jacques Stany *(Georges)*, Paule Albert *(Sophie)*.

In this very complex and sometimes confusing mystery Peppard plays a boxer-turned-writer drifting in France. He stumbles upon a neofascist group (led by Michell, Welles, and Michael) that is attempting to overthrow France, annex Algeria, and take over Europe. Peppard takes a job in a Paris household as a tutor to Shaw, the 8-year-old son of lovely widow Stevens, whose husband was a general killed in the Algerian war. She believes that Shaw is the object of a kidnaping plot. Peppard discovers that Stevens' family is an important link in the fascist group and they frame him for murder when they think he has learned too much about the family and their plans to kidnap Shaw. Peppard and Stevens go on a chase to find the child, and discover that Stevens' supposedly dead husband is alive and the head of the fascist ring. A lot of gunplay and a thrilling showdown in the Colosseum in Rome ensue, with Peppard, Stevens, and Shaw reunited at the end.

p, Dick Berg; d, John Guillermin; w, Irving Ravetch, Harriet Frank, Jr. (based on the novel by Stanley Ellin); ph, Piero Portalupi, Alberto Pizzi (Technicolor); m, Francis Lai; ed, Terry Williams; art d, Frank Arrigo, Alexander Golitzen, Aurelio Crugnola; set d, John McCarthy, Ferdinando Ruffo; cos, Edith Head; m/l, "House of Cards," Lai, Pierre Barouh; makeup, Bud Westmore, Giuseppe Banchelli, Cesare Gambarelli.

Crime/Mystery **(PR:C MPAA:G)**

HOUSE OF CONNELLY (SEE: CAROLINA, 1934)

HOUSE OF CRAZIES (SEE: ASYLUM, 1972, Brit.)

HOUSE OF DANGER* (1934) 62m Hollywood Film Exchange bw

Onslow Stevens, Janet Chandler, James Bush, Howard Lang, Desmond Roberts.

This cheap attempt to create a thrilling crime-drama looks anything but that, relying too heavily upon the rather inane premise of one man taking on the identity of another. He then sees to it that some killers are brought to justice and that the femme lead is safe to continue in her ways.

d, Charles Hutchinson; w, John Francis Natteford (based on the story by C.C. Cheddon); ed, Fred Bain.

Crime **(PR:A MPAA:NR)**

HOUSE OF DARK SHADOWS½** (1970) 97m MGM c

Jonathan Frid *(Barnabus Collins)*, Joan Bennett *(Elizabeth Collins Stoddard)*, Grayson Hall *(Dr. Julia Hoffman)*, Kathryn Leigh Scott *(Maggie Evans)*, Roger Davis *(Jeff Clark)*, Nancy Barrett *(Carolyn Stoddard)*, John Carlen *(Willie Loomis)*, Thayer David *(Prof. T. Eliot Stokes)*, Louis Edmonds *(Roger Collins)*, Donald Briscoe *(Todd Jennings)*, David Henesy *(David Collins)*, Dennis Patrick *(Sheriff George Patterson)*, Lisa Richards *(Daphne Rudd)*, Jerry Lacy *(Minister)*, Barbara Cason *(Mrs. Johnson)*, Paul Michael *(Old Man)*, Humbert Astredo *(Dr. Forbes)*, Terry Crawford *(Todd's Nurse)*, Michael Stroka *(Pallbearer)*, Philip Larson *(Deputy)*.

The successful television horror soap opera "Dark Shadows" was the basis for this film that features the same television cast aboard for some scary action. Frid is the 150-year-old vampire Barnabus Collins, who is accidentally released from his coffin by the handyman of the Collinswood mansion. Frid introduces himself as a cousin from England and gains access to the mansion and the people who live there. When Frid sucks the blood from Bennett, two doctors, Hall and David, are called in to determine the cause of death. They make a diagnosis of vampirism, and this is confirmed when Bennett returns from the dead. They dispatch her permanently with a stake in the heart, and discover that Frid is the vampire. Hall falls in love with Frid, and tries to find a medical cure for him, but soon both she and David fall prey to his blood lust. Frid loves Scott, the beautiful governess who looks exactly like his long-lost love. He seeks to make her his vampire bride, but Scott's fiance, Davis, kills Frid by shooting a wooden arrow through his heart. The old-age makeup was done by Dick Smith who had performed similar duty on Dustin Hoffman for LITTLE BIG MAN. A sequel was released soon after entitled NIGHT OF DARK SHADOWS, and it was awful.

p&d, Dan Curtis; w, Sam Hall, Gordon Russell (based on the TV series "Dark Shadows"); ph, Arthur J. Ornitz (Metrocolor); m, Robert Cobert; prod d, Trevor Williams; ed, Sidney Katz, Arline Garson; md, Cobert; set d, Ken Fitzpatrick; cos, Ramse Mostoller; stunts, Alex Stevens; makeup, Dick Smith, Robert Layden.

Horror **(PR:C-O MPAA:GP)**

HOUSE OF DARKNESS** (1948, Brit.) 77m International Motion Pictures/BL bw

Lawrence Harvey *(Francis Merivale)*, Lesley Brook *(Lucy)*, John Stuart *(Lawyer)*, George Melachrino *(Himself)*, Lesley Osmond *(Elaine Merivale)*, Henry Oscar *(Film Director)*, Alexander Archdale *(John)*, John Teed *(Noel)*, Grace Arnold *(Tessa)*, Pauline Winter *(Rosie)*, Sydney Monckton *(Doctor)*, Charles Paton *(Clerk)*.

Harvey is a man possessed with a burning desire to take over his stepbrother's Dorset home. Knowing his stepbrother (Archdale) has a bad heart, Harvey smashes a violin, setting off a fatal heart attack in Archdale. After forcing his own wife and remaining step-brother from the home, Harvey begins a descent into madness. He thinks he hears the violin being played and tries to drown out its music by playing the piano. Finally, driven by maddening fear, Harvey crashes on the keyboard he obsessively played, felled by the same heart condition that took Archdale's life. Though the script is just a few cliches strung together, the direction manages to give this tale a good creepy feeling.

p, Harry Reynolds; d, Oswald Mitchell; w, John Gilling, Robin Estridge (based on the play "Duet" by Batty Davies); ph, Cyril Bristow; ed, Robert Johnson; md, George Melachrino; art d, George Haslam; cos, Bert Rooke.

Thriller **(PR:O MPAA:NR)**

HOUSE OF DEATH** (1932, USSR) 73m Mejrabpomfilm/Artkino bw

N.P. Chmelioff *(F.M. Dostoevski)*, N.A. Podgorny *(K.P. Pobedonstzev)*, N.M. Radin *(L.V. Doubelt)*, N.M. Viteftof *(Nicholas I)*, G.P. Kuznetzov *(Soldier of the Guards)*, V.V. Belokourov *(Stammering Announcer)*.

Russian melodrama which details the inspiration of Dostoevski (Chmelioff) when he spots an old man being brutally whipped in the street. Forgetting his aristocratic heritage, Chmelioff registers a strong protest over the man's violent treatment, and soon finds himself on the next train to Siberia. After many months in that frigid hellhole, Chmelioff returns to civilization a broken man, willing to be the pawn of the Czar. Typical Soviet propaganda made watchable by impressive technical expertise and decent performances. (In Russian; English subtitles.)

d, V.F. Federov; w, Victor Schlowski (based on the novel *House of Death* by Feodor Dostoevski); ph, V.M. Pronin; m, V.I. Kriukov.

Biography **(PR:C MPAA:NR)**

HOUSE OF DRACULA½** (1945) 67m UNIV bw

Lon Chaney *(Lawrence Talbot)*, John Carradine *(Count Dracula)*, Martha O'Driscoll *(Miliza Morell)*, Lionel Atwill *(Inspector Holtz)*, Jane Adams *(Nina)*, Onslow Stevens *(Dr. Edelman)*, Ludwig Stossel *(Zeigfried)*, Glenn Strange *(The Monster)*, Skelton Knaggs *(Steinmuhl)*, Joseph E. Bernard *(Brahms)*, Dick Dickinson *(Villager)*, Fred Cordova, Carey Harrison *(Gendarmes)*, Harry Lamont *(Villager)*, Gregory Muradian *(Johannes)*, Beatrice Gray *(Mother)*.

An entertaining if not frightening horror film where Universal revived all its resident monsters. Chaney as The Wolf Man and Carradine as Dracula arrive at Stevens' sprawling laboratory in Visaria (in FRANKENSTEIN MEETS THE WOLF MAN it's Varsaria). Both monsters are fed up with their killing instincts and beg for a cure. Well, Chaney is sincere but Carradine is only shamming; he's really after luscious nurse O'Driscoll, intending to make her one of his brides of darkness. Stevens hospitalizes Chaney while he develops his carefully nurtured spores. He has promised to operate on Adams, his hunch-backed assistant, but she begs him to fix up Chaney with the spores first. Before that happens, Chaney goes berserk and, before completely turning into a wolf by the light of the full moon, hurls himself off a cliff into the sea. He is washed into an underwater cave, however, and Stevens goes after him. By then he is a wolf and attacks the doctor but the spell wears off before he can kill Stevens. The doctor then finds the Frankenstein Monster buried in the cave and drags it to his laboratory where he begins to tinker with it. While zapping the creature with electricity to bring it around, Stevens manages to operate on Chaney and cure him of his lycanthropy once and for all. But Dracula is another matter. While giving him a transfusion to drain off his impure blood, Stevens lapses into a coma and Carradine infuses Stevens with *his* vampire blood, turning him into a monster. Before this happens, Stevens finds Carradine taking O'Driscoll, his chief nurse, off into vampire land but overtakes them, and Carradine is caught and destroyed by the sun's rays at dawn. O'Driscoll and Chaney then clinch but Stevens is far gone with Carradine's tainted blood coursing through his veins. He gives the Monster all the juice he can muster with his electricity machines and the heinous Monster comes to life, bent on the usual annihilation of the human race. (The Monster is played by Strange, reprising the role from THE HOUSE OF FRANKENSTEIN.) The villagers, however, led by Atwill, bring about the destruction of Stevens' laboratory and the mad doctor and Monster are killed. It's all pretty hokey, although Stevens manages to evoke some terror as he transforms from benevolent physician to lunatic killer. The dynamic horror trio bowed out at this point, not to be revived for another three years when they would meet a couple of guys who would terrorize *them*—Abbott and Costello.

p, Paul Malvern; d, Erle C. Kenton; w, Edward T. Lowe; ph, George Robinson, John P. Fulton; m, Edgar Fairchild; ed, Russell Schoengarth; art d, John B. Goodman, Martin Obzina; cos, Vera West.

Horror **(PR:A MPAA:NR)**

HOUSE OF ERRORS*½ (1942) 63m PRC bw

Harry Langdon, Marian Marsh, Ray Walker, Charles Rogers, Betty Blythe, John Holland, Guy Kingsford, Roy Butler, Gwen Gazo, Monte Collings, Vernon Dent, Bob Baron, Lynn Star, Ed Cassidy.

A mishmash of outdated comic routines, this film features such Hollywood silent stars as Langdon and Marsh (the latter in her last screen appearance). A pair of deliverymen pretend to be reporters to keep the bad guys from getting away with a newly developed machinegun. The contrived plot was little more than an excuse for the film's merriment. Langdon was well past his prime by this time, but was unwilling to quit.

p&d, Bernard B. Ray; w, Ewart Adamson, Eddie Davis (based on the story by Harry Langdon); ph, Bob Cline; ed, Dan Milner; md, Lee Zahler; art d, Fred Prebble.

Comedy **(PR:A MPAA:NR)**

HOUSE OF EVIL*½ (1968, U.S./Mex.) 83m Azteca-COL c

Boris Karloff.

This rarely seen work was unfortunately the final movie for one of filmdom's most illustrious horror figures. Karloff is involved with a torture dungeon in this cheap Mexican production, the fourth in a series he did for the studio. Karloff's scenes were shot in Los Angeles. Shortly after completing his work for the picture Karloff passed away, thus ending his career on a most-unhappy note. Directed by Hill, the shock-horror man behind THE TERROR and BLOOD BATH.

p, Enrique Vergara, Jhon Ibanez; d, Vergara, Jack Hill; w, Hill; ph, Austin McKinney; m, Alice Uretta.

Horror **(PR:O MPAA:NR)**

HOUSE OF EXORCISM, THE zero (1976, Ital.) 90m Peppercorn-Wormser c (LA CASA DELL' EXORCISMO; AKA: LISA AND THE DEVIL)

Telly Savalas, Elke Sommer, Robert Alda, Sylva Koscina, Alida Valli, Alessio Orano, Gabriele Tinti, Kathy Leone, Eduardo Fajardo, Carmen Silva, Franz Von Treuberg, Espartaco Santoni.

Savalas is the lollipop-licking butler of the sadistic household in which Sommer finds a possessed mannequin of herself. A totally putrid film—every last frame of it. Could Telly have gotten paid *that* badly for "Kojak"?

p, Alfred Leone; d, Mickey Lion [Mario Bava]; w, Alberto Tintini, Leone; m, Carlo Savina.

Horror **Cas.** **(PR:O MPAA:R)**

HOUSE OF FEAR, 1929 (SEE: LAST WARNING, THE, 1929)

HOUSE OF FEAR, THE*½ (1939) 65m UNIV bw

William Gargan *(Arthur McHugh)*, Irene Hervey *(Alice Tabor)*, Dorothy Arnold *(Gloria DeVere)*, Alan Dinehart *(Joseph Morton)*, Harvey Stephens *(Richard "Dick" Pierce)*, Walter Woolf King *(Carleton)*, Robert "Bobby" Coote *(Robert Morton)*, El Brendel *(Jeff)*, Tom Dugan *(Mike)*, Jan Duggan *(Sarah Henderson)*, Donald Douglas *(John Woodford)*, Harry Hayden *(Coroner)*, Emory Parnell, William Gould *(Policemen)*, Charles E. Wilson *(Police Chief)*, Milton Kibbee *(Telephone Repair Man)*, Ben Lewis, Stanley Hughes, Raymond Parker.

This routine comedy/mystery opens with an actor murdered during a performance of a play. The body disappears and the crime remains unsolved until a year later, when frustrated detective Gargan rents out the same theater and hires the same actors to perform the play again, so that he can sort out some clues. During rehearsals a series of "accidents" occurs, warning all to abandon the project. Gargan doesn't give in, and on opening night the killer is revealed. Made in 1929 as THE LAST WARNING.

p, Edmund Grainger; d, Joe May; w, Peter Milne (based on the story and play "The Last Warning" by Thomas F. Fallon and the novel *Backstage Phantom* by Wadsworth Camp); ph, Milton Krasner; ed, Frank Gross; cos, Vera West.

Mystery **(PR:A MPAA:NR)**

HOUSE OF FEAR, THE½** (1945) 68m UNIV bw

Basil Rathbone *(Sherlock Holmes)*, Nigel Bruce *(Dr. Watson)*, Aubrey Mather *(Alastair)*, Dennis Hoey *(Lestrade)*, Paul Cavanagh *(Simon Merrivale)*, Holmes Herbert *(Alan Cosgrave)*, Harry Cording *(John Simpson)*, Sally Shepherd *(Mrs. Monteith)*, Gavin Muir *(Chalmers)*, Florette Hillier *(Alison MacGregor)*, David Clyde *(Alex MacGregor)*, Doris Lloyd *(Bessie)*, Cyril Delevanti *(Stanley Raeburn)*, Wilson Benge *(Guy Davies)*, Dick Alexander *(Ralph King)*, Leslie Denison *(Sgt. Bleeker)*, Alec Craig *(Angus)*.

Another entry in the highly successful series of Sherlock Holmes films that starred Rathbone as Holmes and Bruce as Watson. After attempting to move Holmes and Watson into the modern WW II era, Universal decided to return the pair to Victorian times for this, one of the better films made at this stage of the series. Rathbone and Bruce are called out to a dreary Scottish mansion where the seven middle-aged members of "the Good Comrades Club" live. It seems that someone is killing off the members one by one. There is a curse on the mansion stating that none of the inhabitants will ever go to the grave whole. The seven members, being bachelors with no families, have bought a large insurance policy naming the other members as beneficiaries. The members, each in turn, receive envelopes containing orange pits (harbingers of death according to one African tribe) and then promptly drop dead. They all die in ways which make it impossible to determine their indentities. But Rathbone discovers that they have faked their deaths (substituting fresh corpses exhumed from a local cemetery) in order that the lone surviving member might collect the large amount of insurance money and split it with the rest of them. (See SHERLOCK HOLMES series, Index.)

p&d, Roy William Neill; w, Roy Chanslor (based on the story "The Adventures Of The Five Orange Pips" by Sir Arthur Conan Doyle); ph, Virgil Miller; ed, Saul Goodkind; md, Paul Sawtell; art d, John B. Goodman, Eugene Lowrie.

Mystery **(PR:A MPAA:NR)**

HOUSE OF FRANKENSTEIN½** (1944) 71m UNIV bw

Boris Karloff *(Dr. Gustav Niemann)*, Lon Chaney, Jr. *(Lawrence Stewart Talbot)*, J. Carroll Naish *(Daniel)*, John Carradine *(Count Dracula)*, Anne Gwynne *(Rita Hussman)*, Peter Coe *(Carl Hussman)*, Lionel Atwill *(Inspector Arnz)*, George Zucco *(Prof. Bruno Lampini)*, Elena Verdugo *(Ilonka)*, Glenn Strange *(The Monster)*, Sig Ruman *(Burgomaster Russman)*, William Edmunds *(Fejos)*, Charles Miller *(Toberman)*, Philip Van Zandt *(Inspector Muller)*, Julius Tannen *(Hertz)*, Hans Herbert *(Meier)*, Dick Dickinson *(Born)*, George Lynn *(Gerlach)*, Michael Mark *(Frederick Strauss)*, Olaf Hytten *(Hoffman)*, Frank Reicher *(Ullman)*, Brandon Hurst *(Dr. Geissler)*.

An all-star cast of creatures from our fondest nightmares people this Universal horror film. This time Karloff does not play the eternal monster but is replaced by Strange so that he can enact a mad doctor. The film opens with Karloff and hunchbacked assistant Naish languishing in a cell. They have been imprisoned for criminal operations, Karloff having been caught transplanting dogs' brains. A storm comes up and lightning strikes the prison, collapsing the floor of the cell housing Karloff and Naish. They fall into an abandoned sewer and make their escape. On the road they encounter Zucco, a traveling professor of horrors. One of his prized possessions is the skeleton of super vampire Count Dracula, now inert, having a stake driven through its heart. At a signal from Karloff, Naish kills Zucco and the two take over the Chamber of Horrors show. They arrive at Reigelburg where the local burgomaister, Ruman, recognizes Karloff as the crackpot doctor he had testified against years earlier. To shut his mouth, Karloff removes the stake from Dracula's coffin and Carradine appears. Karloff, under the threat of replacing the stake, gets Carradine to agree to kill Ruman. He, in turn, will protect Carradine's coffin and sacred soil from Transylvania which preserves his immortal carcass. Carradine does his bidding and sucks the blood out of Ruman. He then goes after newlywed Gwynne, a luscious looking bride, mesmerizing her. He leaves with the stupefied woman but her husband Coe and policeman Atwill are in hot pursuit and they catch Carradine's coach on the road where it is delayed until the sun rises. Carradine tries to get back to his coffin but the sun's rays reach him first and he is reduced to ashes. Karloff and Naish, however, escape, and arrive at the village of Frankenstein. Here Karloff visits the ruins of the castle occupied by Dr. Frankenstein. He not only finds his precious records but discovers the bodies of the Monster and the Wolf Man, and he goes about reviving both. A gypsy girl, Verdugo, whom Naish has saved from a whipping and taken with him, falls in love with Chaney, but when he turns into a wolf as promised he kills her just as she shoots him with a silver bullet. Naish finds her body and takes it to Karloff, begging him to bring her back to life. When Karloff refuses, Naish mangles him. But the Monster has been brought to life by Karloff and it breaks free, grabbing Naish and hurling the hunchback through a skylight. Meanwhile, the ever tardy villagers, bearing torches, arrive to chase the Monster and Karloff, the mad doctor being dragged along by the creature, into a swamp. Karloff tells the monster to stay clear of the quicksand but he is ignored and both sink out of view, waiting for the next sequel, which was THE HOUSE OF DRACULA (1945). Strange learned much from Karloff on how to play the Monster and would go on doing the part in several more films. Karloff was at least grateful to get out from under that flat head.

p, Paul Malvern; d, Erle C. Kenton; w, Edward T. Lowe (based on the story "The Devil's Brood" by Curt Siodmak); ph, George Robinson; ed, Philip Cahn; md, Hans J. Salter; art d, John B. Goodman, Martin Obzina; set d, Russell A. Gausman; cos, Vera West; spec eff, John P. Fulton; makeup, Jack P. Pierce.

Horror **(PR:A MPAA:NR)**

HOUSE OF FREAKS zero (1973, Ital.) 80m Cinerama/Aquarius c (EL CASTELLO DELL' ORRORE; AKA: FRANKENSTEIN'S CASTLE OF FREAKS)

Rossano Brazzi *(Count Frankenstein)*, Michael Dunn, Edmund Purdom, Christiane Royce.

Brazzi, the star of SOUTH PACIFIC, shows no shame and a real desperation for decent roles as he stars in this cheapie horror flick. He's the proprietor of the title dwelling, helped by Dunn (a popular movie midget). Among his denizens are a giant, plenty of naked females (are these sort of films ever complete without them?) and Ook the Neanderthal man. Some enchanted evening!

p, Robert Randall; d, Robert Oliver; w, Mario Francini.

Horror **(PR:O MPAA:PG)**

HOUSE OF FRIGHT** (1961) 80m AIP c (GB: TWO FACES OF DR. JEKYLL; AKA: JEKYLL'S INFERNO)

Paul Massie *(Dr. Henry Jekyll/Mr. Edward Hyde)*, Dawn Addams *(Kitty Jekyll)*, Christopher Lee *(Paul Allen)*, David Kossoff *(Ernest Litauer)*, Francis De Wolff

(Inspector), Norma Marla *(Maria)*, Joy Webster, Magda Miller *(Sphinx Girls)*, William Kendall *(Clubman)*, Helen Goss *(Nannie)*, Pauline Shepherd *(Girl in Gin Shop)*, Percy Cartwright *(Coroner)*, Joe Robinson *(Corinthian)*, Arthur Lovegrove *(Cabby)*.

A weak entry into the Hammer horror stable, HOUSE OF FRIGHT was originally released in England as THE TWO FACES OF DR. JEKYLL and told yet another version of the age-old, done-to-death tale based on Robert Louis Stevenson's superb novel *The Strange Case Of Dr. Jekyll and Mr. Hyde*. Massie stars as an aged and dying Dr. Jekyll who develops a serum that turns him into the young, handsome, and virile Mr. Hyde. In his younger identity, Massie discovers the affair between his wife, Addams, and his best friend, Lee. Massie kills Lee and then rapes his wife. Addams kills herself, and seeking to cover up his crimes, Massie kills a stableboy and sets the corpse aflame. In a bizarre twist, Massie manages to convince the police that all the crimes were committed by the deranged Jekyll, whose charred body lies before them. It seems as if Hyde will get away with murder, but at the coroner's inquest, the formula wears off and Hyde turns back into Jekyll and the truth comes out. Not as lively or gory as the previous Hammer efforts, THE TWO FACES OF DR. JEKYLL had trouble finding an American distributor until AIP agreed to release it and changed its title to HOUSE OF FRIGHT (JEKYLL'S INFERNO was considered and later rejected). (See DR. JEKYLL AND MR. HYDE series, Index.)

p, Michael Carreras; d, Terence Fischer; w, Wolf Mankowitz (based on the novel *The Strange Case of Dr. Jekyll And Mr. Hyde* by Robert Louis Stevenson); ph, Jack Asher (Megascope, Eastmancolor); m, Monty Norman, David Heneker; ed, James Needs, Eric Boyd-Perkins; md, John Hollingsworth; m/l, Norman Heneker.

Horror (PR:C MPAA:NR)

HOUSE OF GREED* (1934, USSR) 70m Soyuzfilm/Artkino bw

Vladimir Gardin *(Profiri Golovleff)*, T. Balach *(Anna)*, N. Latonia *(Lubinka)*, Korchagina-Alexandrovskaya *(Ulita)*, M.N. Tarchanov *(Derunov)*, Taskin *(Petenka)*, Bogdanov *(Kykishev)*.

The story of three generations of a Russian family is told in this adaptation of Shchedrin's classic Russian novel *Gaspadin Golovleff*. The film centers on venal, petty, and ruthless landowner Gardin as he viciously oppresses the peasants and members of his own family in an effort to gain control of all the land in his domain. Eventually he drives himself mad with his unholy activities. (In Russian; English Subtitles.)

d&w, A.V. Ivanovsky; w, K.N. Derjavin (based on the novel *Gaspadin Golovleff* by N. Shchedrin [Mikhail Saltykov]); m, A.F. Paschenko.

Drama (PR:A MPAA:NR)

HOUSE OF HORROR* (1929) 65m FN-WB bw

Louise Fazenda, Chester Conklin, Thelma Todd, William V. Mong, Dale Fuller, T. Holtz, Yola D'Averile [Avril].

Just barely considered a talkie (the film contains about two minutes worth of sound in its first four minutes), HOUSE OF HORROR is a typical sliding panel, secret passageway, things-that-go-bump-in-the-night thriller which stars Fazenda and Conklin as the owners of an antique shop beseiged by crooks after a valuable gem.

d, Benjamin Christensen; w, William Irish; m, Louis Silver.

Comedy/Mystery (PR:A MPAA:NR)

HOUSE OF HORRORS½** (1946) 65m UNIV bw (GB: JOAN MEDFORD IS MISSING)

Robert Lowery *(Steven Morrow)*, Virginia Grey *(Joan Medford)*, Bill Goodwin *(Lt. Larry Brooks)*, Rondo Hatton *("The Creeper")*, Martin Kosleck *(Marcel De Lange)*, Alan Napier *(F. Holmes Harmon)*, Howard Freeman *(Hal Ormiston)*, Joan Fulton [Shawlee] *(Stella McNally)*, Virginia Christine *(Lady of the Streets)*, Janet Shaw *(Beautiful Cab Driver)*, Mary Field *(Nora, the Switchboard Operator)*, Byron Foulger *(Mr. Samuels)*, Syd Saylor *(Morgue Clerk)*.

After saving the hulking lug Hatton (a non-actor afflicted with a grotesque gargoyle face) from drowning, mad Greenwich Village sculptor Kosleck carves a bust of the man, then decides to make use of Hatton's homicidal urges by sending him out after art critics. That's one way to insure good reviews. Off-beat and actually a pretty entertaining bit of horror on its own level. This was Hatton's first leading role and he would spend the next two years playing psychopathic killers before fading off into cinema history.

p, Ben Pivar; d, Jean Yarbrough; w, George Bricker (based on a story by Dwight V. Babcock); ph, Maury Gertsman; ed, Philip Cahn; md, H.J. Salter; art d, John B. Goodman, Abraham Grossman; makeup, Jack P. Pierce.

Crime (PR:C MPAA:NR)

HOUSE OF INTRIGUE, THE** (1959, Ital.) 94m AA c (LONDRA CHIAMA POLO NORD)

Curt Jurgens *(Bernes)*, Dawn Addams *(Mary)*, Folco Lulli *(Kaarden-Gorilla)*, Dario Michaelis *(John)*, Philippe Hersent *(Landers)*, Rene Deltgen *(Hermann)*, Albert Lieven *(Matt)*, Giacomo Rossi Stuart *(Henry)*, Matteo Spinola *(Chris)*, Ludovico Ceriana *(Herbert)*, Adriano Uriani *(Allan)*, Alphonse Mathis *(Mac)*, Chris Hofer *(Felix)*, Edith Jost *(Gerda)*, Stephen Garret *(Wilhelm)*.

A good spy drama based on a real WW II incident. Shot by Italians, this film tells of the deception played by the Germans on the British, when one of their secret operatives is captured in Amsterdam. A high German intelligence officer, Jurgens, discovers that the British agent is supposed to radio information to London every day, so Jurgens sees to it that the broadcasts continue with false information. This leads to the capture of other British agents.

p,d&w, Duilio Coletti; w, Ennio De Concini, Giuseppe Scoponi Massimo Mida (based on the novel *London Calling North Pole* by H.J. Giskes); ph, Gabor Pogany (CinemaScope, Ferraniacolor); m, Nino Rota; ed, Vittoria De Fazio Vigorelli; art d, Franco Lolli.

Spy/Drama (PR:A MPAA:NR)

HOUSE OF LIFE*½ (1953, Ger.) 95m Intl. Film bw (HAUS DES LEBENS)

Gustav Froehlich, Cornell Borchers, Gertrude Kuckelman, Edith Mill.

A German tear-jerker that concerns itself with the events in a large maternity hospital. The story unfolds in GRAND HOTEL style, with stories of several women told in interlocking fashion. There is a woman whose husband neglects her because she has only given him girls, an opera singer whose husband uses her hospital stay to cheat on her, and a deserted mother who later finds love with a gardener. The women are taken care of by Froehlich and his young female assistant. The assistant loves children, but discovers—to her horror—that a childhood accident has left her sterile. However, a happy ending is prescribed for all by Dr. Froehlich.

d&w, Karl Hartl; w, Felix Lutzendorf (based on the novel by Kathe Lambert); ph, Frank Koch, Josef Illig; m, Bernard Eichorn; set d, Franz Bi, Botho Hofer.

Drama (PR:A MPAA:NR)

HOUSE OF LONG SHADOWS, THE** (1983, Brit.) 96m Cannon c

Vincent Price *(Lionel)*, Christopher Lee *(Corrigan)*, Peter Cushing *(Sebastian)*, Desi Arnaz, Jr. *(Kenneth Magee)*, John Carradine *(Lord Grisbane)*, Sheila Keith *(Victoria)*, Julie Peasgood *(Mary Norton)*, Richard Todd *(Sam Allison)*, Louise English *(Diana)*, Richard Hunter *(Andrew)*, Norman Rossington *(Stationmaster)*.

An amusing, old-fashioned haunted house film that is little more than an excuse to reunite the grand old stars of the low-budget Gothic horror films, Price, Lee, Cushing, and Carradine. The film centers on a bizarre family reunion at a decaying Welsh manor house. Young American writer Arnaz, Jr. is using the reunion to shut himself up in the old house to crank out a suspense novel. However, he is unable to write as the ghosties do their thing. Just about every haunted house cliche in the book is used tongue in cheek. *Seven Keys to Baldpate*, the novel on which this film was based, was filmed five times between 1917 and 1947.

p, Menahem Golan; d, Peter Walker; m, Michael Armstrong (based on the novel *Seven Keys to Baldpate* by Earl Derr Biggers); ph, Norman Langley; m, Richard Harvey; ed, Robert Dearberg; art d, Mike Pickwood.

Horror Cas. (PR:O MPAA:NR)

HOUSE OF MORTAL SIN, THE (SEE: CONFESSIONAL, 1977, Brit.)

HOUSE OF MYSTERY** (1934) 62m MON bw

Ed Lowry *(Jack Armstrong)*, Verna Hillie *(Ella Browning)*, John Sheehan *(Harry Smith)*, Brandon Hurst *(Hindu Priest)*, Liya Joy [Joyzelle] *(Chanda)*, Fritzi Ridgeway *(Stella Walters)*, Clay Clement *(John Pren)*, George [Gabby] Hayes *(David Fells)*, Dale Fuller *(Mrs. Carfax)*, Harry C. Bradley *(Prof. Potter)*, Irving Bacon *(Ned Pickens)*, Mary Foy *(Mrs. Potter)*, Samuel Godfrey *(Ellis)*, George Cleveland *(Clancy)*, Bruce Mitchell *(Bartender)*, Dick Botiller *(Hindu)*, James Morton *(Englishman)*.

A group of people are gathered together for a weekend at the eerie mansion of a man who has stolen priceless jewels from a Hindu temple. Their reason is to have a chance at a portion of these gems, but a curse surrounding the killing of a sacred ape creates an atmosphere ripe for murder. Though the mystery angle is overly predictable, it provides for the necessary chills and added laughs. In his only screen appearance, Lowry stars as an insurance investigator, guest to the house. The lack of success for the film prompted him to return to the stage and radio. An odd performance for lovable Hayes has him in the role of one of the menacing heavies.

p, Paul Malvern; d, William Nigh; w, Albert DeMond (based on the play by Adam Hull Shirk); ph, Archie Stout; ed, Carl Pierson; md, Abe Meyer; art d, E.R. Hickson.

Mystery/Comedy (PR:A MPAA:NR)

HOUSE OF MYSTERY** (1941, Brit.) 61m MONO bw (GB: AT THE VILLA ROSE)

Kenneth Kent *(Inspector Hanaud)*, Judy Kelly *(Celia Harland)*, Peter Murray Hill *(Harry Wethermill)*, Walter Rilla *(Mr. Ricardo)*, Ruth Maitland *(Madame Dauvray)*, Antoinette Ceillier *(Adele Rossignol)*, Clifford Evans *(Tace)*, Martita Hunt *(Helen Vaquier)*, Ronald Adam *(Mons. Besnard)*, Arthur Hambling *(Mons. Perrichet)*.

An above average British mystery film, HOUSE OF MYSTERY tells of the attempts by French detective Kent to solve a near-perfect crime. A group of jewel thieves kill a rich widow in order to get her valuable gems. After the woman is dead, the thieves are unable to locate the jewels. The thieves kidnap a fake spiritualist in order to frame her for the murder. Kent has a difficult time piecing together the clues, but his clever sleuthing finally cracks the case.

d, Walter Summers; w, Doreen Montgomery (based on the novel by A.E.W. Mason); ph, Claude Friese-Green.

Mystery/Crime (PR:A MPAA:NR)

HOUSE OF MYSTERY** (1961, Brit.) 56m Independent Artists/AA bw

Jane Hylton *(Stella Lemming)*, Peter Dyneley *(Mark Lemming)*, Nanette Newman *(Joan Trevor)*, Maurice Kaufmann *(Henry Trevor)*, Colin Gordon *(Burdon)*, Molly Urquhart *(Mrs. Bucknall)*, John Merivale *(Clive)*, Colette Wilde *(Wife)*.

Hylton and Dyneley are a newlywed couple who move into an old house. They aren't alone, though, for the place is inhabited by a ghost who informs the couple about the murder of some past tenants.

p, Julian Wintle, Leslie Parkyn; d&w, Vernon Sewell (based on a play by Pierre Mills, C. Vylars).

Fantasy (PR:C MPAA:NR)

HOUSE OF NUMBERS½** (1957) 90m MGM bw

Jack Palance *(Bill Judlow/Arne Judlow)*, Barbara Lang *(Ruth Judlow)*, Harold J. Stone *(Henry Nova)*, Edward Platt *(Warden)*.

Palance plays twin brothers, one good, the other a convict in San Quentin. Good brother breaks into the prison to prepare for the bad brother's escape. It comes off as expected, but is complicated by the fact that good Palance has fallen in love with his sister-in-law, Lang. Good Palance and Lang come to the conclusion that bad Palance is in need of psychiatric help and they inform police where he is hidden, so he may be returned to prison to get professional help.

p, Charles Schnee; d&w, Russell Rouse; w, Don Mankiewicz (based on the novel by Jack Finney); ph, George J. Folsey (CinemaScope); m, Andre Previn; ed, John McSweeney, Jr.

Drama (PR:A MPAA:NR)

HOUSE OF 1,000 DOLLS* (1967, Ger./Span./Brit.) 78m Constantin-P.C. Hispamer/AIP c (HAUS DER TAUSEND FREUDEN)

Vincent Price *(Felix Manderville)*, Marthya Hyer *(Rebecca)*, George Nader *(Stephen Armstrong)*, Anne Smyrner *(Marie)*, Maria Rohm *(Diane)*, Wolfgang Kieling *(Inspector Emil)*, Sancho Gracia *(Fernando)*, Louis Rivera *(Paul)*, Jose Jaspe *(Ahmed)*, Juan Olaguivel *(Salim)*, Herbert Fuchs *(Abdul)*, Yelena Samarina *(Mme. Viera)*, Diane Bond *(Liza)*, Andrea Lascelle, Ursula Janis, Monique Aime, Marisol Anon, Jill Echols, Loli Munoz, Lara Lenti, Sandra Petrelli, Kitty Swan, Karin Skarreso, Carolyn Coon, Francoise Fontages *(Dolls)*.

Price and Hyer are magicians who supply a white-slave ring with young girls by drugging them. Nader puts an end to the operation by killing Price. Nothing special here in this English-dubbed film, unless you're a die-hard Price devotee.

p, Harry Alan Towers; d, Jeremy Summers; w, Peter Welbeck; ph, Manuel Merino (Techniscope, Technicolor); m, Charles Camilleri; ed, Allan Morrison; art d, Santiago Ontanon; m/l, "House of 1,000 Dolls," Don Black, Mark London (sung by Cliff Bennett and the Rebel Rousers).

Drama (PR:O MPAA:NR)

HOUSE OF PLEASURE (SEE: LE PLAISIR, 1952, Fr.)

HOUSE OF PSYCHOTIC WOMEN, THE zero (1973, Span.) 87m Independent International c (LOS OJOS AZULES DE LA MUNECA ROTA)

Paul Naschy, Maria Perschy, Diana Lorys, Eva Leon.

Disgusting, gory work involves a trio of nasty sisters with a taste for blood. There's a sex murderer who dwells outside the snowbound house they live in as well. About the only thing of worth here is the campy title. Not for children or adults.

p, Modesto Perez Redondo; d, Carlos Aured; w, Jacinto Molina.

Horror Cas. (PR:O MPAA:R)

HOUSE OF ROTHSCHILD, THE**** (1934) 94m Twentieth Century bw/c

George Arliss *(Mayer Rothschild/Nathan Rothschild)*, Boris Karloff *(Count Ledrantz)*, Loretta Young *(Julie Rothschild)*, Robert Young *(Capt. Fitzroy)*, C. Aubrey Smith *(Duke of Wellington)*, Arthur Byron *(Baring)*, Helen Westley *(Gudula Rothschild)*, Reginald Owen *(Herries)*, Florence Arliss *(Hannah Rothschild)*, Alan Mowbray *(Metternich)*, Noel Madison *(Carl Rothschild)*, Ivan Simpson *(Amschel Rothschild)*, Holmes Herbert *(Rowerth)*, Paul Harvey *(Solomon Rothschild)*, Georges Renavent *(Talleyrand)*, Murray Kinnell *(James Rothschild)*, Oscar Apfel *(Prussian Officer)*, Lumsden Hare *(Prince Regent)*, Leo McCabe *(Secretary)*, Gilbert Emery *(Prime Minister)*, Charles Evans *(Nesserolde)*, Ethel Griffies *(Woman Guest)*, Lee Kohlmar *(Doctor)*, Reginald Sheffield *(Stock Trader)*, Gerald Pierce, Milton Kahn, George Offerman, Jr., Cullen Johnson, Bobbie La Mache *(Rothschild Children)*, Wilfred Lucas *(Page)*, Leonard Mudie *(Tax Collector in Prussia)*.

An outstanding historical biography of the rise of the Rothschild financial dynasty during the Napoleonic wars, starring one of the greatest early film actors, George Arliss. THE HOUSE OF ROTHSCHILD was the ambitious brainchild of Darryl F. Zanuck who had left Warner Bros. to form Twentieth Century Productions and was soon to complete a merger with Fox, from which would spring 20th Century Fox. Arliss plays a dual role and is first seen as the patriarch of the German/Jewish ghetto family who, on his deathbed, urges his five sons to travel to the five capitols of Europe and establish powerful banking firms. Led by their brother, Arliss, the Rothschilds slowly build the most powerful banking conglomerate in Europe. Threatened by Napoleon, the Rothschild banks secretly lend money to the armies of England, Austria, Italy, and Prussia to defeat him. Once Napoleon is in exile, however, anti-Semitism rears its ugly head in the form of Karloff, a Prussian ambassador to England who refuses Arliss' offer of money to rebuild France. Outraged, Arliss creates financial havoc in the bond markets, but this only results in Karloff launching violent and bloody pogroms in the Jewish districts. Fate intervenes when Napoleon escapes from exile and rises again to threaten Europe. Faced with defeat, the leaders of the five nations, including Karloff, are forced to ask the Rothschilds for more financial aid. On the condition that the pogroms be suspended for good, Arliss releases the money and Napoleon is once again defeated. Arliss is considered a hero and is made a baron by the King of England (this final sequence was shot in early three-strip Technicolor). THE HOUSE OF ROTHSCHILD was nominated for Best Picture of 1934 by the Academy, but it lost to Frank Capra's IT HAPPENED ONE NIGHT.

p, Darryl F. Zanuck; d, Alfred Werker; w, Nunnally Johnson (based on the play by George Humbert Westley); ph, Peverell Marley (Technicolor); m, Alfred Newman; ed, Alan McNeil, Barbara McLean.

Biography/Drama (PR:A MPAA:NR)

HOUSE OF SECRETS* (1929) 60m CHES bw

Marcia Manning *(Margery Gordon)*, Joseph Striker *(Barry Wilding)*, Elmer Grandin *(Dr. Gordon)*, Herbert Warren *(Joe Blake)*, Francis M. Verdi *(Sir Hubert Harcourt)*, Richard Stevenson *(Bill)*, Harry M. Southard *(Wharton)*, Edward Roseman *(Wu Chang)*, Walter Ringham *(Home Secretary Forbes)*.

One of the first independently produced films that contained complete sound recording, HOUSE OF SECRETS is really nothing more than another hokey mystery film. A mad doctor accidentally kills his maid during one of his experiments and is sent to prison. A close friend and fellow scientist breaks him out of his cell and hides him in the home of a friend. The owner of the hideout keeps his mouth shut because he is in love with the scientist's daughter, but trouble erupts when a vicious crook arrives in search of hidden riches that he believes are stashed in the house. Soon the escaped con-doctor and his friend are faced with a dilemma: Call the cops to rid themselves of this menace and risk going back to jail, or let the crook terrorize them.

d, Edmund Lawrence; w, Sidney Hall, Adeline Leitzbach (based on the novel by Sydney Horler); ph, George Webber, Irving Browning, George Peters, Lester Lang; ed, Selma Rosenbloom.

Mystery (PR:O MPAA:NR)

HOUSE OF SECRETS, THE** (1937) 70m CHES bw

Leslie Fenton *(Barry Wilding)*, Muriel Evans *(Julie Fenmore)*, Noel Madison *(Dan Wharton)*, Sidney Blackmer *(Tom Starr)*, Morgan Wallace *(Dr. Kenmore)*, Holmes Herbert *(Sir Bertram Evans)*, Ian MacLaren *(Commissioner Cross)*, Jameson Thomas *(Coventry)*, Matty Fain *(Jumpy)*, Sid Saylor *(Ed)*, George Rosener *(Hector Munson)*, Rita Carlyle *(Mrs. Shippam)*, Tom Ricketts *(Peters)*, Matty Kemp *(Man on Ship)*, David Thursby *(Gregory)*, R. Lancaster *(English Policeman)*, Ramsey Hill *(Police Inspector)*.

Fenton is an American who travels to England to collect on his inheritance of a giant, musty old manor. Standing in his way, however, is Wallace, a doctor living in the mansion who refuses to leave. Fenton is aided by Wallace's daughter, Evans, but further complications arise when two crooks, Madison and Blackmer, show up with half a treasure map (Fenton has the other half), determined to find the loot in the mansion. This, of course, leads to chases, tricks, fist-fights and defeat for the crooks as Fenton finds the treasure and claims the love of Evans. A last gasp for Chesterfield Corp., remaking its 1929 talkie of the same title.

p, George R. Batcheller; d, Roland D. Reed; w, John W. Krafft (from the novel and play by Sydney Horler); ph, M.A. Anderson; ed, Dan Milner; md, Abe Meyer.

Mystery (PR:A MPAA:NR)

HOUSE OF SECRETS, 1956 (SEE: TRIPLE DECEPTION, 1956, Brit.)

HOUSE OF SEVEN CORPSES, THE** (1974) 90m International Amusements c

John Ireland, Faith Domergue, John Carradine, Carole Wells.

A cheapie horror movie with Ireland starring as the director of a cheapie horror movie. Carradine is the proprietor of a haunted house where the crew is shooting, and when a ghoul pops up people start dying left and right. Director Harrison's claim to fame is being the writer of the television series "H.R. Puf'n'Stuf."

p,d&w, Paul Harrison.

Horror Cas. (PR:C-O MPAA:PG)

HOUSE OF SEVEN GABLES (SEE: HOUSE OF THE SEVEN GABLES, 1940)

HOUSE OF SEVEN JOYS (SEE: WRECKING CREW, THE, 1969)

HOUSE OF STRANGE LOVES, THE*½ (1969, Jap.) 83m Nikkatsu c (ONNA UKIYOBURO)

Ryoji Hayama *(Shinzo)*, Jiro Okazaki *(Takichi)*, Toshie Nihonyanagi *(Hatsue)*, Miki Hayashi *(Shun)*, Kaoru Miya *(Toyo)*, Takako Uchida *(Hatsuse)*.

In 18th-century Japan, Hayama is a spy for the government, investigating female-slave trading operations being run from a public bath house. He exposes a government official who is behind the illegal activities—and tries to get a law passed prohibiting mixed bathing.

p, Eisei Koe; d, Tan Ida; w, Iwao Yamazaki; ph, Hidemitsu Iwahashi (Fuji Color); m, Seitaro Omori; art d, Haruyasu Kurosawa.

Spy Drama (PR:C MPAA:NR)

HOUSE OF STRANGERS*** (1949) 101m FOX bw

Edward G. Robinson *(Gino Monetti)*, Susan Hayward *(Irene Bennett)*, Richard Conte *(Max Monetti)*, Luther Adler *(Joe Monetti)*, Paul Valentine, *(Pietro Monetti)*, Efrem Zimbalist, Jr. *(Tony)*, Debra Paget *(Maria Domenico)*, Hope Emerson *(Helena Domenico)*, Esther Minciotti *(Theresa Monetti)*, Diana Douglas *(Elaine Monetti)*, Tito Vuolo *(Lucca)*, Albert Morin *(Victoro)*, Sid Tomack *(Waiter)*, Thomas Henry Brown *(Judge)*, David Wolfe *(Prosecutor)*, John Kellogg *(Danny)*, Ann Morrison *(Woman Juror)*, Dolores Parker *(Nightclub Singer)*, Mario Siletti, Tommy Garland, Maurice Samuels, Frank Jacquet *(Men)*, Charles J. Blynn, Howard Mitchell, Phil Tully *(Guards)*, Joseph Mazzuca *(Bat Boy)*, John Pedrini, Charles McClelland, James Little *(Cops)*, Scott Landers, Fred Hillebrand *(Detectives)*, Argentina Brunetti, Rhoda Williams *(Women)*, Donna La Tour, Maxine Ardell, Sally Yarnell, Jeri Jordan, Marjorie Holliday *(Chorus Dancers)*, Bob Castro, Eddie Saenz *(Preliminary Fighters)*, Herbert Vigran *(Neighbor)*, Mushy Callahan *(Referee)*, George Spaulding *(Doorman)*, John "Red" Kullers *(Taxi Driver)*, Lawrence Tibbett *(Voice on Recording)*.

Robinson, though top-billed here, appears all too briefly in this grim, almost murky crime drama. He is the father of four sons, the favorite being Conte who opens the film by being released from Sing Sing after serving seven years for bribery. He returns to New York's Little Italy and goes to his father's trust company where brothers Adler, Valentine, and Zimbalist greet him affably, offer him money, and are collectively offended when he spurns their friendship and greenbacks. Conte then visits Hayward at her apartment; she tries to convince him to leave New York with her immediately and begin a new life. The embittered Conte rejects this notion; all he can think of is taking vengeance upon his brothers and he soon goes to the family mansion where he stands before a portrait of father Robinson. The memories come flooding back in flashback. It's 1932 and Robinson is shown making loan after loan but at exorbitant interest rates. At home he is an absolute tyrant, lording it over his sons—cunning and self-serving Adler, the oldest; Zimbalist the clothes horse; Valentine a dumb-head who is an amateur boxer; and Conte, the smart, loyal son. Though Conte is engaged to young, pretty Paget, he tumbles for Hayward the minute she enters his office seeking financial advice, and a steamy affair ensues. Robinson, meanwhile, has gotten himself entangled in deep legal problems through his unorthodox lending methods. He is indicted and all his sons save Conte desert him. Conte goes so far as to bribe a juror at Robinson's trial, a fact traitorous Adler points out to police which gets Conte arrested and sent to prison. Robinson is set free through a mistrial but, before he dies, Robinson visits Conte in prison and tells him how his brothers have betrayed them both. The three brothers have taken over the business and are living like kings. Zimbalist has married Paget and Robinson demands that Conte swear vendetta on his siblings. He does, which leads us back to the present. By this time Robinson has died of a broken heart and busted bank account and the brothers know they must get rid of Conte or face financial or even physical extermination. In a confrontation, Valentine is ordered by Adler to kill Conte and he almost breaks his back and throws him off a balcony but Conte survives. He decides to walk away from the entire mess with Hayward, his loyal love. There is little or no humor here, merely a tough, sometimes hard-to-take story. This is Conte's film all the way and his stoic personality bogs down the story considerably, although it is well-directed by Mankiewicz. In the style of the day, the costuming for this film, though mostly set in the 1930s, maintained the late 1940s styles, particularly Hayward's wardrobe. Then, as it would be through the 1960s, revisionist views were in full force so as not to upset current fashions with an eye to lady viewers. Hayward is merely a prop in this, her first film for Fox. Her star contract got her $5,000-a-week, specifying that she not be ordered to cut her hair and would not do so unless she agreed, that she would not be asked to work beyond 6 p.m., and that she had her pick of hairdressers, makeup personnel, and cinematographers.

p, Sol C. Siegel; d, Joseph L. Mankiewicz; w, Philip Yordan (based on the novel *I'll Never Go There Any More* by Jerome Weidman); ph, Milton Krasner; ed, Harmon Jones; md, Daniele Amfitheatrof; art d, Lyle Wheeler, George W. Davis; set d, Thomas Little, Walter M. Scott; cos, Charles Le Maire; spec eff, Fred Sersen; makeup, Ben Nye.

Drama **(PR:C MPAA:NR)**

HOUSE OF THE ARROW, THE½** (1930, Brit.) 76m Twickenham/WB bw

Dennis Neilson-Terry *(Inspector Hanaud)*, Benita Hume *(Betty Harlow)*, Richard Cooper *(Jim Frobisher)*, Stella Freeman *(Ann Upcott)*, Wilfred Fletcher *(Wabersky)*, Toni de Lungo *(Maurice Thevene)*, Barbara Gott *(Mrs. Harlow)*, Betty de Malero *(Francine)*.

A rich woman is poisoned at her French home. Her niece becomes suspect after getting the bulk of the inheritance, so Neilson-Terry is assigned to investigate. Two remakes followed.

p, Julius Hagen, Henry Edwards; d, Leslie Hiscott; w, Cyril Twyford (based on the novel by A. E. W. Mason).

Mystery **(PR:A MPAA:NR)**

HOUSE OF THE ARROW, THE, 1940 (SEE: CASTLE OF CRIMES, Brit., 1940)

HOUSE OF THE ARROW, THE*** (1953, Brit.) 73m Stratford Pictures Corp./ABF-Pathe Film Dist. bw

Oscar Homolka *(Inspector Hanaud)*, Yvonne Furneaux *(Betty Harlowe)*, Robert Urquhart *(Jim Frobisher)*, Anthony Nicholls *(Jeremy Haslett)*, Josephine Griffin *(Ann Upcott)*, Pierre le Fevre *(Thevenet)*, Andrea Lea *(Francine)*, Harold Kasket *(Boris Wabersky)*, Jeanne Pali *(Mme. Harlowe)*, Jacques Cey, Pierre Chaminade, Keith Pyott, Ruth Lodge, Rene Leplat, Colette Wilde, Rene Poirier.

Good version of the oft-filmed story features Homolka as the detective assigned to investigate the murder of a French widow. The woman's adopted niece and heir (Furneaux) is found to be the killer, using a rather unique weapon—a poisoned arrow. The thrills are nicely handled and humor is mixed in, with fine results.

p, Vaughan M. Dean; d, Michael Anderson; w, Edward Dryhurst (based on the novel by A. E. W. Mason); ph, Erwin Hillier.

Mystery **(PR:A MPAA:NR)**

HOUSE OF THE BLACK DEATH** (1965) 89m Medallion-Taurus (AKA: BLOOD OF THE MAN DEVIL; NIGHT OF THE BEAST)

Lon Chaney, Jr. *(Belial Desade)*, John Carradine *(Andre Desade)*, Katherine Victor, Tom Drake, Andrea King.

Strange, obscure horror piece has Chaney and Carradine playing the Desade brothers. Carradine is a good warlock and bedridden to boot. Chaney, complete with devil horns, is a bit more naughty, wreaking havoc as only devils can. Though the two are featured stars there is not a single scene featuring the pair together and it's been suggested that each man had his own director. Look for appearances by Drake and King, two 1940s film vets.

p, William White, Richard Shotwell; d, Harold Daniels, Reginald Le Borge; w, Richard Mahoney.

Horror **(PR:O MPAA:NR)**

HOUSE OF THE DAMNED* (1963) 63m FOX bw

Ron Foster *(Scott Campbell)*, Merry Anders *(Nancy Campbell)*, Richard Crane *(Joseph Schiller)*, Erika Peters *(Loy Schiller)*, Georgia Schmidt *(Priscilla Rochester)*, Dal McKennon *(Mr. Quinby)*, Stacey Winters *(The Nurse)*, Richard Kiel *(The Giant)*, Ayllene Gibbons *(The Fat Woman)*, John Gilmore *(The Legless Man)*, Frieda Pushnik *(The Legless Girl)*.

It seems that any time circus freaks are incorporated into a horror film people will get frightened. Same here, though most of the picture is pretty dull. Foster and wife Peters visit an old mansion on business and something tries to scare them away. Naturally, they stay. Foster gets angry when his wife is found decapitated and decides to get to the bottom of such head-hunting. It turns out that the house is occupied by some relatively harmless circus freaks who simply want their asylum-bound owner to return. Peters, as it happens, was never really beheaded—it was just a circus trick to scare off Foster. Richard Kiel as the giant went on years later to gain fame as "Jaws" in THE SPY WHO LOVED ME.

p&d, Maury Dexter; w, Harry Spaulding; ph, John Nickolaus, Jr.; m, Henry Vars; ed, Jodie Copelan.

Horror **(PR:C MPAA:NR)**

HOUSE OF THE LIVING DEAD* (1973, S. Afr.) 87m Associated Film Producers c (AKA: DOCTOR MANIAC)

Mark Burns, Shirley Ann Field, David Oxley, Margaret Inglis, Dia Sydow, Lynne Maree.

Burns is a maniacal doctor who imprisons the souls of dead animals for his own bizarre studies. Things get out of hand when his experiments begin to include the souls of his own family. With the help of a sensible medical man (Oxley), Burns is stopped, but not without the help of a swarm of escaped souls. This one is as exciting as watching grass grow.

p, Matt Druker; d, Ray Austin; w, Marc Marais; ph, Lionel Friedberg; spec eff, Protea Holdings.

Horror **Cas.** **(PR:C MPAA:PG)**

HOUSE OF THE SEVEN GABLES, THE½** (1940) 89m UNIV bw

George Sanders *(Jaffrey Pyncheon)*, Margaret Lindsay *(Hepzibah Pyncheon)*, Vincent Price *(Clifford Pyncheon)*, Dick Foran *(Matthew Holgrave)*, Nan Grey *(Phoebe Pyncheon)*, Cecil Kellaway *(Philip Barton)*, Alan Napier *(Fuller)*, Gilbert Emery *(Gerald Pyncheon)*, Miles Mander *(Deacon Foster)*, Charles Trowbridge *(Judge)*, Harry Woods *(Wainwright)*, Margaret Fealy, Caroline Cooke, John K. Loofbourrow, Marty Faust, Murdock MacQuarrie *(Town Gossips)*, Charles Trowbridge *(Judge)*, Hugh Sothern *(Rev. Smith)*, Edgar Norton *(Weed)*, Mira McKinney *(Mrs. Reynold)*, Ellia Irving *(Man)*, Harry Stubbs *(Printer)*, Harry Cording *(Blacksmith)*, Kernan Cripps *(Workman)*, Colin Kenny *(Foreman)*, Robert Dudley *(Bailiff)*, Etta McDaniel *(Black Woman)*, Nelson McDowell *(Courtroom Spectator)*, Hal Budlong *(Driver)*, Ed Brady *(Man with Blacksmith)*, Margaret Fenly *(Woman Customer)*, Russ Powell *(Grocer)*, Leigh De Lacy *(Laundress)*, Claire Whitney *(Woman)*.

A plodding adaptation of Nathaniel Hawthorne's classic American novel starring Sanders and Price (in one of his first big roles) as brothers of the cursed house of Pyncheon. The evil Sanders accuses Price of murdering their father and the innocent sibling is sent to prison for 20 years. Sanders, meanwhile, is after the family fortune he believes is buried somewhere on the family estate, which has just been inherited by Lindsay, his cousin and Price's fiancee. Eventually, Price is released from prison and the family curse is shifted to the head of Sanders, who finally meets his doom, leaving Lindsay and Price free to spend the rest of their lives in each other's arms. Luckily the atmospheric photography and fine sets (Universal claimed it built an exact duplicate of the original Salem house) pull the sometimes melodramatic performances through.

p, Burt Kelly; d, Joe May; w, Lester Cole (based on the novel by Nathaniel Hawthorne; adaptation by Harold Greene); ph, Milton Krasner; ed, Frank Gross; art d, Jack Otterson; set d, Russell Gausman.

Drama **(PR:A MPAA:NR)**

HOUSE OF THE SEVEN HAWKS, THE** (1959) 91m MGM bw

Robert Taylor *(John Nordley)*, Nicole Maurey *(Constanta Sluiter)*, Linda Christian *(Elsa)*, Donald Wolfit *(Van Der Stoor)*, David Kossoff *(Wilhelm Dekker)*, Gerard Heinz *(Inspector Sluiter, Anselm)*, Eric Pohlmann *(Capt. Rohner)*, Philo Hauser *(Charlie Ponz)*, Paul Hardmuth *(Beukleman)*, Lily Kahn *(Gerta)*, Richard Shaw *(Straatman)*, Guy Deghy *(Desk Lieutenant)*, Peter Welch *(Gannett)*, Andre Van Gyseghem *(Hotel Clerk)*, Leslie Weston *(Tulper)*.

Crime thriller starring Taylor as the skipper of a small boat that runs off the coast of England. He is hired out by a strange foreigner, Heinz, who pays him a large sum of money to be transported to Holland. Enroute to Holland, the man dies and Taylor discovers an interesting map on his body. Upon arrival in Holland, a woman claiming to be Heinz's daughter, Christian, is caught searching the cabin. She escapes, and soon after Taylor learns that his passenger was in reality an investigator on the trail of valuables stolen by the Nazis and stashed in Holland. Determined to get to the bottom of the mystery, Taylor enlists the aid of Heinz's real daughter, Maurey, and they set sail for the destination on the map. Eventually they find the treasure, a cache of diamonds, but the Nazis, who followed the foolish pair to the loot, have them cornered. Thank goodness, the Dutch police arrive and save the day.

p, David Rose; d, Richard Thorpe; w, Jo Eisinger (based on the novel *The House of the Seven Flies* by Victor Canning); ph, Ted Scaife; m, Clifton Parker; ed, Ernest Walter; cos, Jacques Heim.

Mystery **(PR:A MPAA:NR)**

HOUSE OF THE SPANIARD, THE** (1936, Brit.) 70m Independent Film Producers-Phoenix/ABF bw

Brigitte Horney *(Margarita de Guzman)*, Peter Haddon *(David Grey)*, Jean Galland *(Ignacio)*, Allan Jeayes *(Don Pedro de Guzman)*, Gyles Isham *(John Gilchrist)*, Hay Petrie *(Orlando)*, Ivor Barnard *(Mott)*, David Horne *(Captain)*, Minnie Rayner *(Mrs. Blossom)*, Fred O'Donovan *(McNail)*.

At an old English house, Haddon, who is routinely dismissed as "a silly ass" clerk, accidentally discovers his boss is a Spanish revolutionary and head of a counterfeiting gang. Haddon is kidnaped by the group and spirited away to Spain. There he is assisted in his escape by Horney, the head man's daughter. After regaining his freedom, Haddon returns to rescue Horney as well.

p, Hugh Perceval; d, Reginald Denham; w, Basil Mason (based on the novel by Arthur Behrend).

Crime/Adventure (PR:A MPAA:NR)

HOUSE OF THE THREE GIRLS, THE** (1961, Aust.) 102m Erma-Aspa/Atlantic c (DAS DREIMADERLHAUS)

Karlheinz Boehm *(Franz Schubert)*, Gustav Knuth *(Christian Tschoell)*, Magda Schneider *(Frau Tschoell)*, Ewald Balser *(Beethoven)*, Johanna Matz *(Hanner)*, Helga Neuner *(Heider)*, Gerda Siegl *(Heder)*, Richard Romanowsky *(Diabelli)*, Rudolph Schock *(Franz von Schober)*, Helmuth Lohner *(Moritz von Schwind)*, Erich Kunz *(Johann Mayrhofer)*, Albert Rueprecht *(Leopold Kupelweiser)*, Eberhard Waechter *(J.M. Vogl)*, Else Rambausek *(Mrs. Prametzberger)*, Edith Elmay *(Franzi Seidl)*, Liselotte Bav *(Therese Pichler)*, Lotte Lang *(Kathi)*.

Based in part on the life of composer Franz Schubert, the picture has some interesting moments, but on the whole lacks real drama. Boehm falls in love with Matz and has a young baron sing her a song which he has written. Matz, however, falls in love with the baron, leaving Boehm to his piano. Balser is cast as Beethoven who, by the end of the picture, has gone deaf, inspiring Schubert to leave his Eighth Symphony unfinished out of respect for the great Ludwig.

p, Karl Erlich; d&w, Ernst Marischka (based on the novel *Schwammer* by Rudolf Hans Bartsch and the libretto to *Das Dreimaderlhaus* by A.M. Willner, Hans Reichert, Heinrich Berte); ph, Bruno Mondi (Agfacolor); m, Franz Schubert, Anton Profes.

Biography/Drama (PR:A MPAA:NR)

HOUSE OF TRENT, THE** (1933, Brit.) 74m Ensign/BUT bw

John Stuart *(Dr. Trent/John Trent)*, Anne Grey *(Rosemary Trent)*, Wendy Barrie *(Angela Fairdown)*, Norah Baring *(Barbara)*, Peter Gawthorne *(Lord Fairdown)*, Hope Davy *(Joan)*, Jack Raine *(Peter)*, Moore Marriott *(Ferrier)*, Estelle Winwood *(Charlotte)*, Victor Stanley *(Spriggs)*, Hay Plumb *(Foreman of the Jury)*, Humbertson Wright *(Coachman)*.

After country doctor Stuart saves the life of press lord Gawthorne's young daughter, the important man is grateful. Later the doctor passes away and his son (Stuart in a dual role) begins his own training for a medical career. He meets Barrie, who just happens to be the girl his father saved years earlier. The two fall in love, to Gawthorne's displeasure. He decides to thwart the romance by printing a damaging article about Stuart but stops when he learns who Stuart's father was.

p, W. G. D. Hutchinson; d, Norman Walker; w, Charles Bennett, Billie Bristow; ph, Robert Martin.

Drama (PR:A MPAA:NR)

HOUSE OF UNREST, THE*½ (1931, Brit.) 58m Associated Pictures Productions/PDC bw

Dorothy Boyd *(Diana)*, Malcolm Keen *(Hearne)*, Tom Helmore *(David)*, Leslie Perrins *(Cleaver)*, Hubert Carter *(Ben)*, Mary Mayfren *(Agnes)*.

A tired mystery that lacks the element of surprise, THE HOUSE OF UNREST turns a bleak Scottish island mansion into a deathtrap for those who enter. The inhabitants are terrorized by a mysterious killer who soon reveals himself to be the owner of a precious diamond. His plan to steal an heiress' fortune is botched before it can be carried out.

p, Seymour Hill; d&w, Leslie Howard Gordon (based on his play); ph, Desmond Dickinson.

Mystery (PR:A MPAA:NR)

HOUSE OF USHER*½** (1960) 79m AIP c (AKA: FALL OF THE HOUSE OF USHER)

Vincent Price *(Roderick Usher)*, Mark Damon *(Philip Winthrop)*, Myrna Fahey *(Madeline Usher)*, Harry Ellerbe *(Bristol)*, Bill Borzage, Mike Jordon, Nadajan, Ruth Oklander, George Paul, David Andar, Eleanor LeFaber, Geraldine Paulette, Phil Sylvestre, John Zimeas *(Ghosts)*.

A real first for Roger Corman and AIP, HOUSE OF USHER was the first of their horror films with a decent budget ($350,000), scheduled for shooting longer than ten days (they were allowed 15), shot in color and CinemaScope, and "inspired" by Edgar Allen Poe. The resulting gamble paid off big and the film was a critical and commercial hit which unleashed scads of other Poe films (only two of which are really very good: THE PIT AND THE PENDULUM and the minor masterpiece THE RAVEN). Price stars as the creepy, white-haired owner of the mysterious house of Usher. He, along with his sister, Fahey, live in virtual seclusion in their aging, groaning, and creaking old house. One day Fahey's fiance Damon arrives to visit. Damon and Price immediately loathe one another and Price informs both Damon and Fahey of his disapproval of their union. Price tells Damon that his sister and he are the last of the blood line of Ushers who suffer from a bizarre madness that must not be continued. Damon refuses to leave the spooky house despite this warning, however, and the warnings of the Usher's butler, Ellerbe. Soon strange accidents begin befalling Damon, and he is nearly killed. Meanwhile, Fahey falls ill and soon after, Price informs Damon that she has died of a heart attack. Price places his sister in a coffin and entombs her in the family chapel. The butler, however, informs Damon that his fiancee had suffered from periodic fits and that she could very well have been buried alive. An enraged Damon confronts Price with his discovery and Price merely shrugs off the suggestion, confident that he has done the proper thing. That night Damon finds that Fahey is indeed alive and has clawed her way out of her coffin, seeking revenge. Crazed, she attacks him, but he escapes and tries to bring her to her senses. This doesn't work and Fahey breaks away from Damon and runs off into the house, which is cracking and groaning fitfully due to a violent thunderstorm. Fahey finally catches up with Price, and as the house begins to crumble around them, she strangles him. The house then catches fire and Damon leaves the insane brother and sister, barely escaping with his life. Moody, atmospheric and effective, HOUSE OF USHER actually succeeds in making the house the "monster" (the selling point a desperate Corman tried on skeptical executive producer Sam Arkoff when the boss voiced dismay over the fact that there was no monster in the movie—or so the story goes). With the garish color, musty cobwebs, creaking and groaning sound effects, the *house* in THE HOUSE OF USHER seems to be the cause of all the madness. Price is wonderful as the spooky owner, but the other three players are only competent at best. All in all, a superlative Corman/AIP effort and a great beginning to a fitfully successful (artistically speaking), but always interesting series of horror films.

p&d, Roger Corman; w, Richard Matheson (based on Edgar Allen Poe's story, "The Fall of the House of Usher"); ph, Floyd Crosby; m, Les Baxter; ed, Anthony Carras; prod d, Daniel Haller; spec eff, Pat Dinga; makeup, Fred Phillips.

Horror Cas. (PR:O MPAA:NR)

HOUSE OF WAX*** (1953) 90m WB c-3D

Vincent Price *(Prof. Henry Jarrod)*, Frank Lovejoy *(Lt. Tom Brennan)*, Phyllis Kirk *(Sue Allen)*, Carolyn Jones *(Cathy Gray)*, Paul Picerni *(Scott Andrews)*, Roy Roberts *(Matthew Burke)*, Angela Clarke *(Mrs. Andrews)*, Paul Cavanagh *(Sidney Wallace)*, Dabbs Greer *(Sgt. Jim Shane)*, Charles Buchinsky [Bronson] *(Igor)*, Reggie Rymal *(Barker)*, Philip Tonge *(Bruce Allison)*, Darwin Greenfield, Jack Kenney *(Lodgers)*, Ruth Warren *(Scrubwoman)*, Riza Royce *(Ma Flanagan)*, Richard Benjamin, Jack Mower *(Detectives)*, Grandon Rhodes *(Surgeon)*, Frank Ferguson *(Medical Examiner)*, Eddie Parks *(Morgue Attendant)*, Oliver Blake *(Pompous Man)*, Leo Curley *(Portly Man)*, Mary Lou Holloway *(Millie)*, Joanne Brown *(Girl Friend)*, Lyle Latell *(Waiter)*, Terry Mitchell, Ruth Whitney, Trude Wyler *(Women)*, Merry Townsend *(Ticket Taker)*.

HOUSE OF WAX was not the first 3-D picture released, but it made better use of the process than any of the others. BWANA DEVIL began the craze that forced audiences to buy little plastic glasses for ten cents and spend the rest of the evening gulping aspirin to get rid of their headaches. Next came the black-and-white MAN IN THE DARK, then IT CAME FROM OUTER SPACE and SIGN OF THE PAGAN, the latter featuring wild horses that appeared to charge the people in the theater. A remake of 1933's THE MYSTERY OF THE WAX MUSEUM (which starred Lionel Atwill and was directed by Michael Curtiz), HOUSE OF WAX also employed what they described as "WarnerPhonic Sound," which utilized many speakers to direct the sound at the audience from various directions, a forerunner of stereophonic sound. Price is a wax sculptor in New York at the turn of the century. He is a partner with Roberts in a museum that could use more business, since Price's figures are beautiful but don't bring the customers in. Roberts wants Price to create sculptures that are more sensational, but Price resists. Art critic Cavanagh agrees with Price and will buy out Roberts as soon as he can raise the money. Roberts won't wait and sets fire to the museum in order to get the insurance money, which is a huge sum in those days ($25,000). It is presumed that Price died with his creations but when Roberts is about to get the insurance check and run off with girl friend Jones, Price reappears, now terribly scarred, and strangles Roberts to death. Jones recovers quickly and plans to go out with another man. She tells this to best friend Kirk. Later, Kirk goes to Jones' room in the small boardinghouse where both live and finds Jones dead at the hands of Price, who is still in the room. Price tries to strangle Kirk but she escapes to her boy friend's house (Picerni). Later that evening, Jones' body is stolen from the police morgue as are the bodies of Roberts and one more corpse, that of a dead attorney. Cavanagh backs Price in a new enterprise, a wax museum with a well-equipped laboratory in the cellar. Price is in a wheelchair and his hands have been so burned that he can no longer sculpt so he has two assistants do the work under his supervision. One of them is Young and the other is Buchinsky (who later changed his name to the more commercial Bronson), a mute. (In the original, Young's character was a drug addict. Here, the producers took the safer route and made him a drunk.) When Kirk and Picerni come to the opening of the new museum (which now features more bizarre tableaux), she is shocked to see that the Joan of Arc statue looks just like her dead friend, Jones. Price says that he took the face from a newspaper photo, then offers Picerni a job. Picerni is a starving sculptor, so he takes the employment and Kirk also agrees to pose for Price's next work, Marie Antoinette. Kirk is still not convinced of the story Price told her so she asks detectives Lovejoy and Greer to look deeper into matters. They recognize Price's Edwin Booth character as looking like the late lawyer whose body was stolen the same night Roberts and Jones were taken. When they meet Young, they realize he is a criminal who has broken his parole. After finding the late lawyer's watch on Young, they give him the third degree and he admits that Price has been killing people and using them as the basis for the figures in the museum. Late that night, Price has sent Picerni off to fetch something and Kirk appears at the museum. She examines the Joan of Arc statue more closely and discovers that it is the body of Jones. Now Price appears, out of his wheelchair. He tries to kill her but she struggles mightily and, in doing so, pounds on his face, thereby breaking the wax mask he wears and exposing his scarred face. She recognizes the face as the man who strangled Jones and she faints. Price takes Kirk to the basement where he plans to dip her in wax, but Picerni and the cops arrive. Price falls into the boiling cauldron of hot wax and Kirk is rescued. Even in two dimensions, this film is fun, filled with action, and Price reaches new heights in hamminess, but that's what we like from him so it's just fine. It was actually better than the original, which was also in an early color process. One of the strangest notes about HOUSE OF WAX is that it was directed by a one-eyed man, de Toth, and one might have thought that the absence of an eye might have hurt his ability to create three-dimensional effects. It didn't hurt one bit, and the items kept coming and coming at the viewers, causing many of them to duck. Every few years, somebody makes a film in 3-D (JAWS III, for example) and even Hitchcock did one, DIAL M FOR MURDER, but it has never been realized completely and probably never will be unless it can be watched without those annoying plastic green and red spectacles. Special mention should be given to sound man Charles Lang for having supervised the auditory effects, something that enhanced the experience of HOUSE OF WAX in the theaters but will be lost on anyone watching this on TV. Produced by Bryan Foy, of the Foys' vaudeville act seen in the bio THE SEVEN LITTLE FOYS.

p, Bryan Foy; d, Andre de Toth; w, Crane Wilbur (based on a play by Charles Welden); ph, Bert Glennon, Peverell Marley (Natural Vision 3-D, Warner Color); m, David Buttolph; ed, Rudi Fehr; art d, Stanley Fleischer.

Horror **Cas.** **(PR:C MPAA:GP)**

HOUSE OF WHIPCORD zero (1974, Brit.) 94m AIP c

Barbara Markham *(Mrs. Wakehurst)*, Patrick Barr *(Justice Bailey)*, Penny Irving *(Ann-Marie Di Verney)*, Ray Brooks *(Tony)*, Anne Michelle *(Julia)*, Sheila Keith *(Walker)*, Dorothy Gordon *(Bates)*, Ivor Salter *(Jack)*, Robert Tayman *(Mark E. Desade)*, Judy Robinson *(Claire)*, Karen David *(Karen)*, Jane Hayward *(Estelle)*, Celia Quicke *(Denise)*, Celia Imrie *(Barbara)*, David McGillivray *(Caven)*, Ron Smerczak *(Ted)*, Barry Martin *(Al)*, Tony Sympson *(Henry)*, Rose Hill *(Henry's Wife)*, Dave Butler *(Ticket Collector)*, Denis Tinsley *(Police Sergeant)*, Pete Walker *(Cyclist)*.

A sadomasochistic splatter movie which brims with buckets of blood. The festivities, including the torture of beautiful women, take place in an isolated prison run by a pair of old folks who are upset with the moral standards of today's young ladies.

p&d, David Walker; w, David McGillivray; ph, (Movielab Color).

Horror **(PR:O MPAA:R)**

HOUSE OF WOMEN** (1962) 85m WB bw (AKA: LADIES OF THE MOB)

Shirley Knight *(Erica)*, Andrew Duggan *(Warden Cole)*, Constance Ford *(Sophie Brice)*, Barbara Nichols *(Candy Kane)*, Margaret Hayes *(Zoe Stoughton)*, Jeanne Cooper *(Helen Jennings)*, Virginia Gregg *(Mrs. Hunter)*, Patricia Huston *(Doris)*, Jason Evers *(Doctor)*, Jennifer Howard *(Addie Gates)*, Caroline Richter *(Clemens)*, Gayla Graves *(Jackie)*, Colette Jackson *(Aggie)*, Jacqueline Scott *(Mrs. Stevens)*, Paul Lambert *(Mr. Dunn)*, Carolyn Komant *(Nan)*, Virginia Capers *(Sarah)*, Drew Vigen *(Tommy)*, Laurie Sheridan *(Robin)*.

An inferior remake of the 1950 women's prison classic CAGED, HOUSE OF WOMEN stars Knight as the innocent, very pregnant, woman convicted as an accomplice to armed robbery and sentenced to five years. Once her baby is born, Knight is allowed custody for three years and then the child is put up for adoption unless she can find a legal guardian to care for it until she's paroled. The jail's sadistic and vile warden, Duggan, takes a liking to her and makes her his maid. Because of his love for Knight, Duggan begins to lighten up on the other female inmates of the prison. Soon Knight's three years are up, but it doesn't matter because she has been a perfect prisoner and should be paroled just before she would have to give up her child. Faced with the reality of losing Knight, Duggan stops her parole and denies all prison mothers custody of their babies. This causes a bloody uprising among the inmates. Through her heroism and good sense, Knight ends the revolt and the newspaper coverage gets Duggan fired and Knight released.

p, Bryan Foy; d, Walter Doniger; w, Crane Wilbur; ph, Harold Sline; m, Howard Jackson; ed, Leo H. Shreve; art d, Leo K. Kuter, set d, John P. Austin; cos, Alexis Davidoff, Florence Hackett; makeup, Gordon Bau, Louis La Cava.

Drama **(PR:O MPAA:NR)**

HOUSE ON 56TH STREET, THE½** (1933) 69m WB bw

Kay Francis *(Peggy)*, Ricardo Cortez *(Bill Blaine)*, Gene Raymond *(Monte Van Tyle)*, John Halliday *(Lindon Fiske)*, Margaret Lindsay *(Eleanor Burgess)*, Frank McHugh *(Hunt)*, Sheila Terry *(Dolly)*, William "Stage" Boyd *(Bonelli)*, Hardie Albright *(Henry Burgess)*, Phillip Reed *(Freddy)*, Philip Faversham *(Gordon)*, Henry O'Neill *(Baxter)*, Walter Walker *(Dr. Wyman)*, Nella Walker *(Mrs. Van Tyle)*.

It isn't easy to cram almost 30 years of people's lives into almost 70 minutes but this adaptation of Joseph Santley's novel almost does. Francis is a New York chorus girl in the early 1900s. She is in love with wealthy Raymond, and he with her, but she has also been seeing Halliday, an equally rich but aged stagedoor Johnny. She leaves Halliday for Raymond and he takes her to his home on 56th Street, a gorgeous town house just off Park Avenue. They are married, she has a daughter, and life is wonderful. Halliday comes back into the picture and threatens to commit suicide if she doesn't leave Raymond and her child and return to him. She goes to his apartment to attempt to convince him that she is a happily married woman and when he pulls out his gun to shoot himself, she grabs for it. The result is that he dies and she is sent to prison for manslaughter for two decades. Raymond believed in her innocence all the time but he is killed during The Great War (WW I) in France. She's in her forties when she gets out of jail in 1925 and immediately attempts to see her now-grown daughter, but Raymond's family won't allow it and gives her some money to keep her away. Francis is bewildered by all the alterations in the quality of life in the once-genteel New York she knew. The city is now the center of a maddening whirl of The Roaring Twenties. She takes an ocean voyage and encounters Cortez, a professional card cheater. They team up and are soon bilking rich people around the world. Francis' father had been a cardsharp and she inherited his love for the pasteboards. Cortez tells Francis that he's invested their money in a speakeasy on 56th Street and they have the gambling concession. When she arrives at the street, she sees it is the house where she once lived so happily and that the interior still contains many of the original decorations, including a Florentine medallion on the fireplace that her late husband assured her would be the symbol of their love that would last forever. One night, Lindsay arrives. She is Francis' daughter and must have also inherited a wild streak as she is a fierce gambler. She loses a lot of money and when she can't pay, Cortez threatens to tell her fiance and her family about her gambling. A fight between Lindsay and Cortez ensues and she shoots him. Francis tries to take the blame for the murder but that's seen through immediately by Boyd, who runs the establishment. He says he'll cover up the killing if she will agree to stay at the gambling house and work for him forever. She walks to the fireplace, looks at the medallion and softly says "forever" as the picture ends. This almost seemed like three different stories; the happy love affair between Francis and Raymond; the early fling with Halliday and the final one with Cortez. It was too much story in not enough time and could have used some fleshing out of the characters instead of seeking to keep it so fast-moving that we are seldom able to focus on someone before they are off the screen. But there have been several plays and films about what happens in one house over a long period and this is better than most of them.

p, James Seymour; d, Robert Florey; w, Austin Parker, Sheridan Gibney (based on the novel by Joseph Santley); ph, Ernest Haller; ed, Bud Bretherton; art d, Esdras Hartley; cos, Orry-Kelly.

Historical Drama **(PR:C MPAA:NR)**

HOUSE ON HAUNTED HILL*** (1958) 75m AA bw

Vincent Price *(Frederick Loren)*, Carol Ohmart *(Annabelle Loren)*, Richard Long *(Lance Schroeder)*, Alan Marshal *(Dr. David Trent)*, Carolyn Craig *(Nora Manning)*, Elisha Cook *(Watson Pritchard)*, Julie Mitchum *(Ruth Bridgers)*, Leona Anderson *(Mrs. Slykes)*, Howard Hoffman *(Jonas)*.

Horror producer/director William Castle churned out a series of well-made little creepies that used some fairly outrageous gimmicks to pull folks into the theaters and THE HOUSE ON HAUNTED HILL was no exception. At the precise, terrifying moment, theater owners were supposed to release a full-sized skeleton which would "leap" from the screen and zip over the audience's heads suspended on an invisible wire. It may have worked the first time, but clever movie-goers soon got wise, waited for the skeleton to appear, and then fought back by pelting the bones with concession stand items. The theater owners then stopped with the in-house "special effects" nonsense. Despite the gimmicks, Castle's films are okay. In this one, Price stars as the owner of a supposedly haunted mansion who offers $10,000 to any sucker dumb enough to attempt spending an entire night there. Price is delightfully hammy as he hands the brave guests little coffins that contain handguns the visitors may use to protect themselves. While Price happily tries to scare the wits out of his guests, his wife, Ohmart, along with her lover, Marshal, try to arrange things so that dear Vincent will be shot "accidentally" by one of the visitors. Silly, but good fun.

p&d, William Castle; w, Robb White; ph, Carl E. Guthrie; m, Von Dexter; ed, Roy Livingston; art d, David Milton.

Horror **Cas.** **(PR:C MPAA:NR)**

HOUSE ON 92ND STREET, THE**** (1945) 88m FOX bw

William Eythe *(Bill Dietrich)*, Lloyd Nolan *(Inspector George A. Briggs)*, Signe Hasso *(Elsa Gebhardt)*, Gene Lockhart *(Charles Ogden Roper)*, Leo G. Carroll *(Col Hammersohn)*, Lydia St. Clair *(Johanna Schmedt)*, William Post, Jr. *(Walker)*, Harry Bellaver *(Max Coburg)*, Bruno Wick *(Adolphe Lange)*, Harro Meller *(Conrad Arnulf)*, Charles Wagenheim *(Gus Huzmann)*, Alfred Linder *(Adolph Klaen)*, Renee Carson *(Luise Vadja)*, John McKee *(Dr. Arthur C. Appleton)*, Edwin Jerome *(Major General)*, Elisabeth Neumann *(Freda Kassel)*, George Shelton *(Jackson)*, Alfred Zeisler *(Col. Strassen)*, Reed Hadley *(Narrator)*, Rusty Lane *(Admiral)*, Salo Douday *(Franz Von Wirt)*, Paul Ford *(Sergeant)*, William Adams *(Customs Officer)*, Lew Eckles, Fred Hillebrand *(Policemen)*, Tom Brown *(Intern)*, Bruce Fernald, Jay Wesley *(FBI Agents)*, Benjamin Burroughs *(Aide)*, Douglas Rutherford *(Colonel)*, Frieda Altman, William Beach, Hamilton Benz, Henry Cordy, Mita Cordy, James J. Coyle, Hans Hansen, Kenneth Konopka, Scott Moore, Delmar Nuetzman, John Zak, Gertrude Wottitz, Bernard Lenrow *(Saboteurs)*, George Brandt *(German Man)*, Yoshita Tagawa *(Japanese Man)*, Sheila Bromley *(Customer)*, Elmer Brown, Jack Cherry *(Scientists)*, Victor Sutherland *(Toll Guard)*, Stanley Tackney *(Instructor)*, Robert Culler, Vincent Gardenia, Carl Benson, Frank Richards, Ellsworth Glath, Edward Michaels, Harrison Scott, Anna Marie Hornemann, Sara Strengell, Eugene Stuckmann, Marriott Wilson *(Trainees)*, Frank Kreig *(Travel Agent)*, Antonio J. Pires *(Watchmaker)*, Danny Leone *(Delivery Boy)*, Edward Marshall *(Attendant at Morgue)*, Reed Hadley *(Narrator)*, J. Edgar Hoover, Baron von Genin, Dr. Hans Thomson *(Themselves)*, Edgar Deering *(Cop)*.

Suspense-packed espionage yarn, approached from a documentary angle, has Nolan as a no-nonsense federal investigator who is sought out by German-American Eythe, a brilliant student. He has been contacted by Nazi spies, he tells Nolan, and asked to work with them. Nolan encourages Eythe to accept the offer and work as a double agent, reporting all Nazi activities to the FBI. Slowly, Eythe ingratiates himself to several Nazi agents and is assigned, as a technician, to transmit messages to Germany via short-wave radio. He establishes a remote radio hideout and begins sending messages, really to FBI headquarters, and its operators pass on fake information to Germany. Through this system Eythe is able to learn that Nazi agents are after data concerning the U.S. development of the atomic bomb (referred to here as "Process 97"), pinpointing one of the scientists working on the apparatus, Lockhart, as a Nazi agent. Just as Eythe is unearthed as an undercover American agent, Lockhart and others are picked up and the A-bomb secrets kept secure. Eythe is taken to the notorious house on 92nd Street in New York, where, behind a posh dress shop used as a front, the leader of Nazi espionage in America resides, the mysterious "Mr. Christopher." Before Eythe can be executed, FBI agents close in and a shootout with the spies occurs, with Hasso attempting to escape. She flees into her labyrinthine suite and emerges dressed as a man, the notorious "Mr. Christopher," and is shot while fleeing. Eythe survives as do Amerca's top secrets. Hathaway's direction is fast-clipped and in the newsreel style made famous by producer de Rochemont, who produced the MARCH OF TIME series. The film was shot on location in New York and other points where actual spy cases from FBI files really occurred. The semi-documentary style Hathaway employed gave sharp authenticity to the film and the use of nonprofessional actors (many of whom were FBI agents and technical personnel), along with the stentorian narration provided by Hadley who made a handsome living in films narrating such stories, further convinced viewers that they were watching the real thing. In some instances they were; Hathaway incorporated newsreel shots of real German spies being rounded up at the beginning of WW II, along with telephotos of the German consulate in New York and its real life spies going and coming. The tremendous atmospherics gave birth to a series of films adopting the same semi-documentary approach, notably T-MEN (1947), THE NAKED CITY (1948), and WALK A CROOKED MILE (1948). Nolan is unemotional and almost robot-like in his role of FBI supervisor, and Eythe is too wide-eyed to be wholly believed as a clever double agent. But Hasso is incomparable as the super Nazi agent in this, her most impressive film. Carroll, as the sophisticated Nazi agent Hammersohn, is a marvelous study in understated evil.

p, Louis de Rochemont; d, Henry Hathaway; w, Barre Lyndon, Charles G. Booth, John Monks, Jr. (based on the story by Booth); ph, Norbert Brodine; m, David Buttolph; ed, Harmon Jones; md, Emil Newman; art d, Lyle Wheeler, Lewis Creber; set d, Thomas Little, William Sittel; cos, Bonnie Cashin; spec eff, Fred Sersen.

Spy Drama **(PR:A MPAA:NR)**

HOUSE ON SKULL MOUNTAIN, THE* (1974) 89m FOX c

Victor French *(Andrew Cunningham)*, Janee Michelle *(Lorena Christophe)*, Jean Durand *(Thomas)*, Mike Evans *(Phillippe)*, Xernona Clayton *(Harriet Johnson)*, Lloyd Nelson *(Sheriff)*, Ella Woods *(Louette)*, Mary J. Todd McKenzie *(Pauline)*, Don Devendorf *(Priest)*, Jo Marie *(Doctor)*, Georgia State Senator Leroy Johnson *(Lawyer LeDoux)*.

A dreadfully boring black exploitation horror film produced by a group of black Atlanta businessmen. Let us hope they were looking for a tax deductible business loss, because this stinker probably wouldn't sell to late-night cable stations. Four relatives converge on the spooky mansion of dying old hag McKenzie to hear the reading of her will. Unfortunately, the butler, Durand, practices a little voodoo on the side and begins bumping off the relatives one by one until token white man French (who has learned during the evening that he's got more than a few drops of black blood in him) manages to rescue lovely black girl Michelle, with whom he's fallen in love. Pretty lame, and surprisingly racist—to both blacks and whites.

p, Ray Storey; d, Ron Honthaner; w, Mildred Pares; ph, Monroe Askins (Movielab Color); m, Jerrold Immel; ed, Gerard Wilson; art d, James Newport; set d, Dorothy Crowe; m/l, Ruth Talmadge, Art Freeman, John Susan Welsh, Jaime Mendoza-Nava.

Horror **(PR:C MPAA:PG)**

HOUSE ON SORORITY ROW, THE** (1983) 91m VAE/Film Ventures/ARC c (GB: HOUSE OF EVIL; AKA: SEVEN SISTERS)

Kathryn McNeil *(Katherine)*, Eileen Davidson *(Vicki)*, Janis Zido *(Liz)*, Robin Meloy *(Jeanie)*, Harley Kozak *(Diane)*, Jodi Draigie *(Morgan)*, Ellen Dorsher *(Stevie)*, Lois Kelsa Hunt *(Mrs. Slater)*, Christopher Lawrence *(Dr. Beck)*, Michael Kuhn, Michael Sergio, Ruth Walsh, Larry Singer, Jean Schertler, Ed Heath, Charles Serio, Peter McClung, Brian T. Small, Alan Treadwell, Ken Myers.

Another one of those "You've seen one, you've seen 'em all" slasher films with the word "House" in the title. This one is barely a cut above the rest, with a group of college girls suffering at the hands of their nutty house mother. An excellent argument against sorority houses.

p, Mark Rosman, John G. Clark; d, Rosman; w, Rosman, Bobby Fine; ph, Timothy Suhrstedt (TVC Color); m, Richard H. Band; ed, Jean-Marc Vasseur, Paul Trejo; art d, Vincent Perrania.

Horror **Cas.** **(PR:O MPAA:R)**

HOUSE ON TELEGRAPH HILL*** (1951) 93m FOX bw

Richard Basehart *(Alan Spender)*, Valentina Cortesa *(Victoria Kowelska)*, William Lundigan *(Maj. Marc Anders)*, Fay Baker *(Margaret)*, Gordon Gebert *(Chris)*, Kei Thing Chung *(Houseboy)*, Steve Geray *(Dr. Burkhardt)*, Herbert Butterfield *(Callahan)*, John Burton *(Mr. Whitmore)*, Katherine Meskill *(Mrs. Whitmore)*, Mario Siletti *(Tony)*, Charles Wagenheim *(Man at Accident)*, David Clarke *(Mechanic)*, Tamara Schee *(Maria)*, Natasha Lytess *(Karin)*, Ashmead Scott *(Inspector Hardy)*, Mari Young *(Chinese Girl Singer)*, Tom McDonough *(Farrell)*, Henry Rowland *(Sergeant-Interpreter)*, Les O'Pace *(UNRRA Sergeant)*, Don Kohler *(Chemist)*, Harry Carter *(Detective Ellis)*.

A good spine-tingler, this film offers a sinister, calculating Basehart working to undo Cortesa, a WW II refugee who has assumed another identity. Cortesa, who had been in a Nazi concentration camp, takes the identity of another prisoner who died and this impersonation leads her to San Francisco to see the son of the dead woman, a boy who has lived with his wealthy great-aunt almost since birth. The aunt dies just before Cortesa arrives and she inherits a vast fortune. She meets and falls in love with Basehart, trustee to the fortune, and both go to live in the family mansion atop Telegraph Hill. Here Cortesa looks after the small boy as if he were her own but she begins to notice strange accidents that prove near-fatal to the boy and also to herself. Next she learns that Basehart and the child's governess, Baker, are in love and in league to kill her and the child. They have murdered the aunt to obtain the great fortune and now plan on killing Cortesa and the boy to get their hands on the money. Through a ruse Cortesa gets Basehart to drink a glass of poison he has intended for her and then further dupes Baker into stalling a call to the hospital to aid Basehart so that Baker is later arrested for his murder. She has thus eliminated her two persecutors and can go on living a decent life with a small boy she intends to call her own. It's a muddy mystery but there's plenty of fright and enough clever twists to keep the viewer's attention. Basehart is a standout as the opportunistic fortune-hunter and subtle murderer. This is gothic *film noir* in the style of GASLIGHT and THE SPIRAL STAIRCASE but it lacks a solid script equal to those classics.

p, Robert Bassler; d, Robert Wise; w, Elick Moll, Frank Partos (based on the novel *The Frightened Child* by Dana Lyon); ph. Lucien Ballard; m, Sol Kaplan; ed, Nick De Maggio; md, Alfred Newman; art d, Lyle Wheeler, John DeCuir; set d, Thomas Little, Paul S. Fox; cos, Rennie; makeup, Ben Nye.

Thriller/Mystery **(PR:C MPAA:NR)**

HOUSE ON THE FRONT LINE, THE*** (1963, USSR) 90m Artkino bw (NA SEMI VETRAKH)

Larisa Luzhina *(Svetlana Ivashova)*, Klara Luchko *(Doctor)*, Vyacheslav Tikhonov *(Capt. Susdalev)*, Leonid Bykov *(Postman)*, S. Pilyavskaya, M. Strunova, L. Savchenko, Svetlana Druzhinina, Lea Chursina, Mark Troyanovskiy, V. Nevinnyy, V. Pechnikov, V. Zamanskiy, A. Romashin, A. Ignatyev, B. Vatayev, V. Pavlov, V. Denisov, G. Dunts, V. Markin, M. Zharova, Vladimir Prokofyev, P. Vinnik, S. Korenev, Y. Fomichyov, A. Trusov, S. Kramarov, V. Savchenko, A. Safonov, K. Lipanova, A. Titov, G. Poloskov.

A subtle and minimal picture about Soviet nationalism during the later half of WW II. Luzhina is the faithful fiancee of a postal worker who gets drafted before the lovers can rendezvous at the local post office. Luzhina decides to wait for him there, in the local post office, becoming involved in a variety of duties to help the Soviet troops defeat the Germans. She first helps to publish a newspaper, and later when the post office houses a hospital she works as a nurse. Eventually she earns a medal for her efforts and is reunited with her fiance when he returns from the front. A 105-minute version also exists.

d, Stanislav Rostotskiy; d, Alexandr Galich, Rostotskiy; ph, Vyacheslav Shumskiy; m, K. Molchanov; ed, V. Mironova; art d, Sergey Serebrenikov.

War Drama **(PR:A MPAA:NR)**

HOUSE ON THE SAND*½ (1967) 90m Emerson Film bw

Tony Zarindast, Sandra Evans, Clayton Foster, David Werthriemer.

Cliched treatment of the development and eventual problems that are created when a mulatto woman and Iranian student have an affair. No new insights into racial problems are offered in this look at the prejudice which arises against the couple's relationship.

p,d&w, Tony Zarindast.

Drama **(PR:C MPAA:NR)**

HOUSE ON THE SQUARE, THE (SEE: I'LL NEVER FORGET YOU, 1951)

HOUSE OPPOSITE, THE*½ (1931, Brit.) 66m BIP/Pathe bw

Henry Kendall *(Hobart)*, Frank Stanmore *(Ben)*, Celia Glyn *(Nadine)*, Arthur Macrae *(Randall)*, Wallace Geoffrey *(Clitheroe)*, Rene Macready *(Jessica)*, Abraham Sofaer *(Fahmy)*, Molly Lamont *(Doris)*, Charles Farrell *(Wharton)*.

A male-female detective team battles the destructive plans of a mad Egyptian scientist and his gang of blackmailers. With the help of an amicable bum, the private eyes put a lid on the gang's activities. For the finale, the scientist's title house is reduced to a smoldering mound of ashes.

p,d&w, Walter Summers (based on the play by J. Jefferson Farjeon).

Crime **(PR:A MPAA:NR)**

HOUSE THAT CRIED MURDER, THE (SEE: BRIDE, THE, 1973)

HOUSE THAT DRIPPED BLOOD, THE½** (1971, Brit.) 101m Amicus c

Denholm Elliott *(Charles)*, Joanna Dunham *(Alice)*, Tom Adams *(Dominick)*, Robert Lang *(Psychiatrist)*, Peter Cushing *(Philip)*, Joss Ackland *(Rogers)*, Wolfe Morris *(Waxworks Owner)*, Christopher Lee *(Reid)*, Nyree Dawn Porter *(Ann)*, Chloe Franks *(Jane)*, Jon Pertwee *(Paul)*, Ingrid Pitt *(Carla)*, Geoffrey Bayldon *(Von Hartmann)*, John Bennett *(Holloway)*, John Bryans *(Stoker)*.

Another Amicus horror anthology film, this one is skillfully made with no gore, extracting its horror from suggested action. The four stories take place in a single house in the English countryside which is continually leased by real estate agent Bryans. The temporary tennants all meet bloody deaths. Inspector Bennett is called out to investigate, with the stories being told as part of a police file. The first, "Method For Murder," has murder mystery writer Elliott obsessed with a strangler in one of his books and falling victim to a similar killer. The second, "Waxworks," has Cushing and Ackland lured to a wax museum by a living statue of Salome. The owner, Morris, then axes Cushing and Ackland. The third, "Sweets To The Sweets," has Lee as the victim of his young daughter, who stick pins in a voodoo daddy doll. The last segment "The Cloak," is a humorous tale that stars Pertwee as big-headed actor who, in his quest for authenticity, is given a cloak owned by a real vampire. He in turn thinks he has become a vampire, but falls prey to his intended victim, Pitt.

p, Max Rosenberg, Milton Subotsky; d, Peter Duffell; w, Robert Bloch; ph, Ray Parslow (Eastmancolor); m, Michael Dress; ed, Peter Tanner; art d, Tony Curtis; makeup, Harry Frampton, Peter Frampton.

Horror **(PR:O MPAA:GP)**

HOUSE THAT SCREAMED, THE½** (1970, Span.) 104m Anabel Films/AIP c (LA RESIDENCIA)

Lilli Palmer *(Senora Fourneau)*, Christina Galbo *(Teresa)*, John Moulder Brown *(Luis)*, Mary Maude *(Irene)*, Candida Losada *(Senorita Desprez)*, Tomas Bianco *(Pedro Baldie)*, Maribel Martin *(Isabel)*, Pauline Challenor *(Catalina)*, Teresa Hurtado *(Andrea)*, Conchita Paredes *(Susana)*, Victor Israel *(Brechard)*, Maria Jose Valero *(Elena)*, Ana Maria Pol *(Claudia)*, Blanca Sendino *(Cook)*, Paloma Pages *(Margarita)*, Maria del Carmen Duque *(Julia)*.

Effective tale of repression and murder in a French girls' school. Brown is the headmistress' son, building the perfect girl out of pieces of his mother's pupils. A chilling, well-done shocker.

d, Narciso Ibanez Serrador; w, Luis Penafiel (based on a story by Juan Tebar); ph, Manuel Berenguer (Franscope 70mm, Eastmancolor); m, Waldo de los Rios; ed, Mercedes Olonso.

Horror Cas. (PR:O MPAA:GP)

HOUSE THAT VANISHED, THE* (1974, Brit.) 95m AIP c (AKA: SCREAM AND DIE)

Andrea Allan, Karl Lanchbury, Judy Matheson.

A model sees a murder committed in an old house, but after telling her boy friend about the crime, can't seem to find the house. Her beau's in on the scheme—in fact, he's the murderer. More proof, if more were needed, that most horror pictures with the word "house" in them aren't worth the price of admission.

p, Diana Daubeney; d, Joseph Larraz; w, Derek Ford.

Horror Cas. (PR:O MPAA:R)

HOUSE WHERE EVIL DWELLS, THE*½ (1982) 88m MGM/UA c

Edward Albert *(Ted)*, Susan George *(Laura)*, Doug McClure *(Alex)*, Amy Barrett *(Amy)*, Mako Hattori *(Otami)*, Toshiyuki Sasaki *(Shugoro)*, Toshiya Maruyama *(Masanori)*, Tsuyako Okajima *(Witch)*, Henry Mitowa *(Zen Monk)*.

After directing the humorous and successful MOTEL HELL, Connor came out with this poor effort at a straight haunted house horror film. The film takes place in a Japanese dwelling in which an 1840 Japanese love triangle ended in two murders and a suicide. The adulterous wife, Hattori; her lover, Sasaki; and her husband, Maruyama, are doomed to haunt the house forever. A young American couple, Albert and George, along with daughter Barrett, move into the haunted house. The ghosts take over the Americans bodies, and when diplomat friend McClure comes to visit the triangle is re-enacted. A Zen monk is called in to exorcise the house, but the ghosts get back in, and take over the bodies again. This leads to a karate fight and an eventual slaughter. Not many scary parts in this one, but quite a bit of nudity and unintentional humor.

p, Martin B. Cohen; d, Kevin Connor; w, Robert Suhosky (based on the novel by James Hardiman); ph, Jacques Haitkin (Technicolor); m, Ken Thorne; ed, Barry Peters, art d, Yoshikazu Sano.

Horror Cas. (PR:O MPAA:R)

HOUSE WITH AN ATTIC, THE½** (1964, USSR) 86m Artkino c (DOM S MEZONINOM)

Sergey Yakovlev *(The Artist)*, Ninel Myshkova *(Lidiya)*, Lyudmila Gordeychik *(Misyus)*, Olga Zhizneva *(Yekaterina Pavlovna)*, Y. Leonidov *(Belokurov)*, Vera Altayskaya *(Lyubov Ivanova)*, V. Ananina *(Dasha)*, Sergey Kalinin *(Belokurov's Footman)*, G. Smirnova, N. Oleshchenko, D. Tarasov, A. Pokorskiy.

Yakovlev is a 19th-century landscape painter who notices a young girl (Gordeychik) on a neighboring estate and falls in love with her. Her older sister, however, doesn't agree with his revolutionary views and sends the girl away. Yakovlev arrives at the house one day to propose to the girl and finds that she is gone.

d, Yakov Bazelyan; w, P. Yerofeyev (based on the story by Anton Chekhov); ph, A. Tybin (SovColor); m, Aleksey Muravlev; ed, G. Sadovnikova; art d, B. Komyakov.

Drama (PR:A MPAA:NR)

HOUSEBOAT*** (1958) 110m PAR-Scribe/PAR c

Cary Grant *(Tom Winston)*, Sophia Loren *(Cinzia Zaccardi)*, Martha Hyer *(Caroline Gibson)*, Harry Guardino *(Angelo)*, Eduardo Ciannelli *(Arturo Zaccardi)*, Murray Hamilton *(Alan Wilson)*, Mimi Gibson *(Elizabeth Winston)*, Paul Petersen *(David Winston)*, Charles Herbert *(Robert Winston)*, Madge Kennedy *(Mrs. Farnsworth)*, John Litel *(Mr. Farnsworth)*, Werner Klemperer *(Harold Messner)*, Peggy Connelly *(Elizabeth Wilson)*, Kathleen Freeman, Helen Brown *(Women in Laundromat)*, Julian Rivero *(Spanish Diplomat)*, Mary Forbes *(British Society Woman)*, Wally Walker, Brooks Benedict, Joe McTurk *(Pitchmen)*, Marc Wilder *(Specialty Dancer)*, Pat Moran *(Clown)*, Bill Hickman *(Handsome Man)*, Gilda Oliva *(Pitch Saleswoman)*.

A sophisticated, pleasant comedy sees Grant upset at how his motherless children are farmed out to wealthy Virginia relatives and he gathers them to him, installing them in his Washington, D.C. apartment. Living arrangements are cramped, however, and Grant solves the dilemma by moving the whole brood into a houseboat, including Loren, who has fled her dictatorial father Ciannelli, a famous orchestra conductor. She acts as housemaid and governess to the children while Grant tries to keep order on the floating domicile. Grant and Loren, after several amusing mishaps, find themselves in love and, ignoring the opposition of the children, marry and settle down for keeps. Grant is the whole show here and he does a marvelously funny job of assuming the role of working father, although his children put him through some hilarious paces. Loren is fetching, though her accent makes her lines next to impossible to understand. She is also much too voluptuous, sensuous, and earthy for the youthful ingenue role she played. Just why these spoiled children are drawn to her is never made clear. The children are precocious and create just enough mayhem to keep things moving along. Shavelson does an outstanding job as director, his specialty being comedy; his timing works perfectly with Grant's matchless delivery. Loren, during the filming, was married to Italian film mogul Carlo Ponti by proxy in Mexico. It was reported that the 53-year-old Grant and the 24-year-old Loren became emotionally involved during the production but this ended with the proxy marriage. Shavelson had some difficulty in getting Loren's swarthy complexion lightened with makeup, saying at one point that she looked as if she were doing an "imitation of Al Jolson." She also affected a high-pitched voice, attempting to imitate Grant's sophisticated delivery, and again the director had to correct her. Her stunning dark beauty notwithstanding, Loren was basically inept here and continued to be an inept actress through most of her films where, with a few rare exceptions, her bosom and bottom did most of the acting. She was wholly the product of publicity departments and Ponti's millions, a manufactured star whose off-screen scandals and cheesecake postures continued a career long beyond the point where it should have been thrown out with the old pasta.

p, Jack Rose; d, Melville Shavelson; w, Shavelson, Rose; ph, Ray June (VistaVision, Technicolor); m, George Duning; ed, Frank Fracht; md, Duning; art d, Hal Pereira, John Goodman; set d, Sam Comner, Grace Gregory; cos, Edith Head; spec eff, John P. Fulton; m/l, "Almost In Your Arms," "Bing, Bang, Bong" Jay Livingstone, Ray Evans (sung by Sam Cooke).

Comedy (PR:A MPAA:NR)

HOUSEHOLDER, THE* (1963, US/India) 100m Royal bw (GHARBAR)

Shashi Kapoor *(Prem Sagar)*, Leela Naidu *(Indu)*, Durga Khote *(The Mother)*, Hariendernath Chattopadaya *(Mr. Chadda)*, Pro Sen *(Sohanlal)*, Romesh Thappar *(Mr. Khanna)*, Indu Lele *(Mrs. Khanna)*, Achla Sachdev *(Mrs. Saigal)*, Pincho Kapoor *(Mr. Saigal)*, Prayag Raaj *(Raj)*, Shama Beg *(Mrs. Raj)*, Usha Amin *(1st Lady)*, Praveen Paul *(2nd Lady)*, Pahari Snayal *(The Swami)*, Jabeen Jalil *(Bobo)*, Patsy Dance *(Kitty)*, Walter King *(Professor)*, Ernest Castaldo *(Ernest)*.

Kapoor is a school teacher who relates a story to a friend about the responsibilities of marriage. An affair with an American woman who is searching for spirituality makes the confused Kapoor realize that he needs his wife. He returns home to her, finds that she has left, but he is able to get her to come back. The music recording was supervised by Satyajit Ray.

p, Ismail Merchant; d, James Ivory; w, Ruth Prawer Jhabvala (based on her novel *The Householder*); ph, Subrata Mitra; m, Ustad Ali Akbar Khan, Jyotirendera Moitra; ed, Pran Mehra.

Comedy (PR:A MPAA:NR)

HOUSEKEEPER'S DAUGHTER½** (1939) 81m UA bw

Joan Bennett *(Hilda)*, Adolphe Menjou *(Deakon Maxwell)*, John Hubbard *(Robert Randall)*, William Gargan *(Ed O'Malley)*, George E. Stone *(Benny)*, Peggy Wood *(Olga)*, Donald Meek *(Editor Wilson)*, Marc Lawrence *(Floyd)*, Lilian Bond *(Gladys)*, Victor Mature *(Lefty)*, John Hyams *(Prof. Randall)*, Leila McIntyre *(Mrs. Randall)*, Luis Alberni *(Veroni)*, Rosina Galli *(Mrs. Veroni)*, Tom Dugan *(Floyd's Boy)*, J. Farrell MacDonald *(Captain)*, James Flavin *(Detective)*.

A fairly amusing crime comedy starring Bennett as gangster Lawrence's moll. She gets fed up with the rackets and goes home to mother, Wood, a housekeeper for a wealthy family. Hubbard, one of the children, is an aspiring reporter anxious to land his first big scoop. By accident, the kid begins to unravel some clues leading to a possible murder indictment for Lawrence. Aided by veteran newshound Menjou and his photographer Gargan (who are hanging around the kid just to bump into Bennett), Hubbard pulls the facts together while dodging mobster Lawrence's bullets. The script pulls some implausible gymnastics at times, but Menjou and Gargan keep the laughs coming, making this one worth sitting through. Look for a very young Victor Mature as one of the gangsters in this, his first role.

p&d, Hal Roach; w, Rian James, Gordon Douglas (based on a story by Donald Henderson Clarke); ph, Norbert Brodine; m, Amedeo de Filippi; ed, William Ziegler; md, Lud Gluskin; art d, Charles D. Hall.

Comedy (PR:A MPAA:NR)

HOUSEMASTER½** (1938, Brit.) 95m AB bw

Otto Kruger *(Charles Donkin)*, Diana Churchill *(Rosemary Faringdon)*, Phillips Holmes *(Philip de Courville)*, Joyce Barbour *(Barbara Fane)*, Rene Ray *(Chris Faringdon)*, Kynaston Reeves *(Rev. Edmund Ovington)*, Walter Hudd *(Frank Hastings)*, John Wood *(Flossie Nightingale)*, Cecil Parker *(Sir Berkeley Nightingale)*, Henry Hepworth *(Bimbo Faringdon)*, Michael Shepley *(Victor Beamish)*, Jimmy Hanley *(Travers)*, Rosamund Barnes *(Button Faringdon)*.

A good British comedy about a housemaster in British public (that is, private) school. The housemaster, Kruger, is a kind person with a good understanding of the problems that face his boys. A new headmaster comes to the college, and he is a stern and unmovable man who cannot understand Kruger's techniques or his importance to his boys. The headmaster is constantly on Kruger's back, and when a couple of the boys rebel the headmaster tries to dismiss him. With some fancy footwork by some of Kruger's boys, it is the headmaster who gets transferred, not Kruger.

p, Walter C. Mycroft; d, Herbert Brenon; w, Dudley Leslie, Elizabeth Meehan (based on the play "Bachelor Born" by Ian Hay); ph, Otto Kanturek.

Comedy (PR:A MPAA:NR)

HOUSEWIFE** (1934) 70m WB bw

George Brent *(William Reynolds)*, Ann Dvorak *(Nan Wilson Reynolds)*, Bette Davis *(Patricia Barclay/Ruth Smith)*, John Halliday *(Paul Duprey)*, Robert Barrat *(Sam Blake)*, Hobart Cavanaugh *(George Wilson)*, Ruth Donnelly *(Dora Wilson)*, Joseph Cawthorn *(Kruger)*, Harry Tyler *(Plumber)*, Leila Bennett *(Jennie)*, Ronald Cosbey *(Buddy)*, Willard Robertson *(Judge)*, John Murray *(Salesman)*, Gordon "Bill" Elliott *(Clerk)*, Leo White *(Waiter)*, Eula Guy *(Miss Finch)*, Phil Regan *(Hathaway, the*

Crooner), John Hale *(Doctor)*, Lee Phelps *(Court Clerk)*, Charles Coleman *(Bolton)*.

Bette Davis plays a home-wrecker siren involved in a love triangle. Brent is a successful copywriter who, with the support of his wife, Dvorak, opens his own ad agency. He has a rough time of it, but when Dvorak gets him drunk, he is able to sell himself to the owner of a cosmetics company, Halliday. Davis, who is a fellow copywriter and former lover of Brent, writes a dynamic commercial for him to get his firm off the ground. In return she wants to resume their relationship. Davis' commercial is a success and soon clients are beating down Brent's office door. Flustered by his new-found success, Brent is about to divorce his wife and marry Davis until he overhears some nasty remarks made by Davis concerning Dvorak and realizes that he still loves his wife. Remembering that Dvorak was his inspiration from the start, Brent leaves Davis and returns to his wife.

p, Jack L. Warner; d, Alfred E. Green; w, Manuel Seff, Lillie Hayward (based on a story by Robert Lord, Hayward); ph, William Rees; m, Mort Dixon, Allie Wrubel; ed, James Gibbon; md, Leo F. Forbstein; art d, Robert Haas; m/l, "Cosmetics by Dupree," Mort Dixon, Allie Wrubel.

Drama **(PR:A MPAA:NR)**

HOUSTON STORY, THE½** (1956) 79m Clover/COL bw

Gene Barry *(Frank Duncan)*, Barbara Hale *(Zoe Crane)*, Edward Arnold *(Paul Atlas)*, Paul Richards *(Gordie Shay)*, Jeanne Cooper *(Madge)*, Frank Jenks *(Louie)*, John Zaremba *(Emile Constant)*, Chris Alcaide *(Chris Barker)*, Jack V. Littlefield *(Willie)*, Paul Levitt *(Duke)*, Fred Krone *(Marsh)*, Pete Kellett *(Kalo)*, Leslie Hunt *(Inspector Gregg)*, Claudia Bryar *(Clara)*, Larry W. Fultz *(Talbot)*, Charles Gray *(Stokes)*.

A fine crime film directed by horror king William Castle, starring Barry as an enterprising crook of an oil company employee who devises a way to siphon off oil and gasoline from big companies and then sell it on his own. He stupidly goes to the mob with his discovery and comes under the thumb of gang chieftain Zaremba and his buddy Arnold. Other small-time hoodlums join the bandwagon and soon Barry is in up to his neck. Eventually he fights off his oppressors, but ends up going to the hoosegow when his waitress girl friend, Hale, finks on him.

p, Sam Katzman; d, William Castle; w, James B. Gordon; ph, Henry Freulich; m, Mischa Bakaleinikoff; ed, Edwin Bryant; art d, Paul Palmentola.

Crime **(PR:A MPAA:NR)**

HOVERBUG** (1970, Brit.) 57m Fanfare/CFF c

Jill Riddick *(Jenny Brewster)*, John Trayhorn *(Dick Brewster)*, Francis Attard *(Charlie)*, Gary Cann *(Sydney)*, Arthur Howard *(Mr. Watts)*, Michael Balfour *(Father)*, Peter Myers *(Mr. Brewster)*, Cardew Robinson.

An unimpressive children's film which has a group of kiddies making friends with an eccentric inventor whose super-bonding glue assures victory in a hovercraft race. Most kid viewers would probably enjoy reading the back of a cereal box as much as sitting through this film's 57 minutes of predictable situations.

p, George H. Brown; d, Jan Darnley-Smith; w, Michael Barnes.

Children's Adventure **(PR:AA MPAA:NR)**

HOW ABOUT US? (SEE: EPILOGUE, 1964, Den.)

HOW COME NOBODY'S ON OUR SIDE?* (1975) 84m American Films c

Adam Roarke *(Person)*, Larry Bishop *(Brandy)*, Alexandra Hay *(Brigitte)*, Rob Reiner *(Miguelito)*, Penny Marshall *(Theresa)*, John Garwood *(Border Guard)*, Eldon Quick *(Hal)*, Richard Yniguez *(Juan)*, Robert Rothwell *(Lawyer)*, Betty Hanna *(Receptionist)*, Gil Barreta *(Farmer)*, Bert Madrid *(Store Owner)*, Eddie LoRusso *(Truck Driver)*, Priscilla Garcia *(Pisces Girl)*, Roger La Joie *(Theater Manager)*, Margaret Garcia *(Juan's Mother)*, Woody Lee *(Bartender)*, George Banks *(Second Guard)*, Bill Barney, Bob Tessier *(Bike Riders)*.

A pair of movie stuntmen and some bit players take to the road after becoming disgusted with the self-indulgent Hollywood life style. The search for a better life is standard material, only the characters' occupations present a new angle—one which is hardly convincing. The presence of TV sitcom personalities Reiner ("All in the Family") and Marshall ("Laverne and Shirley") give the film an undesirable made-for-TV feel.

p, Maurice Smith; d, Richard Michaels; w, Lee Chapman; ph, Jack Beckett (Movielab Color); m, Lamont Johnson; ed, Rick Beckmeyer.

Comedy **(PR:A MPAA:PG)**

HOW DO I LOVE THEE?*½ (1970) 110m ABC/CINERAMA c

Jackie Gleason *(Stanley Waltz)*, Maureen O'Hara *(Elsie Waltz)*, Shelley Winters *(Lena Mervin)*, Rosemary Forsyth *(Marion Waltz)*, Rick Lenz *(Tom Waltz)*, Clinton Robinson *(Tom Waltz, age 11)*, James McCallion *(Pete McGurk)*, Don Sebastian *(Art Salerno)*, Jack Nagle *(Dean Bagley)*, Judy Wallace *(Mrs. Bagley)*, Don Beddoe *(Prof. Norman Littlefield)*, J. Edward McKinley *(Hugo Wellington)*, Templeton Fox *(Mrs. Wellington)*, Fritzie Burr *(Mrs. Gromulka)*, Marcia Knight *(Rachel)*, Alex Gerry *(Walter Wetzel)*, Maurice Marsac *(Bishop)*, Olga Vargas *(Mother Superior)*, Dick Sterling *(Dr. Giroux)*, Robertson White *(Old Geezer)*, Harriet Veloshin *(Dean Bagley's Secretary)*, Evelyn Turner *(French Nurse)*, Ed Ross *(French Dentist)*, Soroya Farah *(Belly Dancer)*, Frank Logan *(Frank, the Bartender)*.

When novelist Peter De Vries is funny, he is one of the best. When he tries to be philosophical and sage, he is beyond boredom, and co-producer Freeman and co-writer Tunberg have collaborated with De Vries to bring us one of the dullest attempts at comedy ever attempted. Lenz is a philosophy professor who has long been at odds with his father, Gleason. When he learns that Gleason is at Lourdes, attempting to recover from some unnamed illness, he rushes off to France over the misgivings of his wife, Forsyth, who thinks that Gleason is the reason Lenz is not the man she would like him to be. In a long flashback while he's aboard a plane jetting to Europe, we see Lenz's life unfold in memory. Gleason is then a devout atheist at odds with O'Hara, a born-again woman with equally dogmatic beliefs. Gleason seeks other pastures and has a fling with Winters, a bohemian artist, but that fling never is consummated (in a series of flat comedy scenes where the two behemoths attempt to make love and never can get together). Winters decides she should exit and gifts Gleason with a poem as her farewell present. Lenz becomes a philosophy teacher and marries one of his students, Forsyth, and everything seems hunky (if not dory) with Lenz in line for a promotion. Gleason sends Winters' poem to a poetry contest and wins a huge prize of $10,000, which he intends to donate to his son's department at the college, a selfless motion of love on Gleason's part, as he is only a furniture mover and could use the money himself. Then it is learned that the poem was actually by Elizabeth Barrett Browning, and the money is rescinded, thereby shaming Gleason and causing Lenz to lose his chance for a better position. That goes, instead, to Beddoe, whom Lenz despises, and Lenz must content himself with doing the same old thing for the rest of his life or leave the school and find some other job. Gleason relents on his atheism and goes into a church, where he promises God he'll stay out of Lenz's life if his son can be granted the job he thought was his. That prayer evidently works, as Beddoe dies almost instantly, and Lenz moves up a notch. We flash out of flashback, and when Lenz gets to Gleason's bed, he learns that Gleason feels personally responsible for Beddoe's demise, believing the man would still be alive had he not stumbled into church to make a deal with the Lord. Lenz assures him that's not the case, and that Beddoe had expired *before* Gleason marched into the house of worship. Once Gleason realizes that his prayer had nothing to do with Beddoe's exit, he recovers miraculously. Forsyth, who has come on the next plane, arrives and announces that she is pregnant as the film ends. It takes just under two hours to tell this story, which might have been far more effective if more judiciously edited, but Freeman, who also did THE MALTESE BIPPY, apparently doesn't like to edit his writing. They shot the whole script, thereby causing a lot of dozing in the seats. Even Jackie Gleason isn't funny in this movie, and that takes a lot of doing. A disappointing outing for all concerned, mostly the audience.

p, Everett Freeman, Robert Enders; d, Michael Gordon; w, Freeman, Karl Tunberg (based on Peter De Vries's novel *Let Me Count The Ways*); ph, Russell Metty (Metrocolor); m, Randy Sparks; ed, Ronald Sinclair; md, Tim Helms; art d, Walter M. Simonds; set d, Ned Parsons; cos, Moss Mabry; m/l, "How Do I Love Thee?" Sparks and Freeman; makeup, Allan Snyder (for O'Hara), Guy Del Russo.

Comedy/Drama **(PR:C MPAA:PG)**

HOW DO YOU DO?*½ (1946) 80m PRC bw

As themselves: Bert Gordon, Harry Von Zell, Cheryl Walker, Ella Mae Morse, Claire Windsor, Keye Luke, Thomas Jackson, James Burke, Fred Kelsey, Leslie Denison; Frank Albertson *(Tom Brandon)*, Charles Middleton *(Sheriff)*, Matt McHugh *(Deputy)*, Francis Pierlot *(Proprietor)*, Sidney Marion *(Dr. Kolmar)*.

Another one of those "Gee, lets get a whole bunch of radio performers and parade them in front of the camera!" movies. This one sees a troupe of radio personalities venture to a desert resort. That night, a less-than-loved radio agent is murdered and everybody has a motive. Gordon calls in his movie-detective buddies to solve the crime. In the end, it is discovered that the dead man had been given some powerful drugs by his doctor. Cut to a screening room, where we see all the players watching what has transpired on the big screen. It was all just a movie. They don't like it, either, so it's retake time.

p, Harry Sauber; d, Ralph Murphy; w, Sauber, Joseph Carole (based on a story by Sauber); ph, Benjamin H. Kline; m, Hal Borne, Paul Webster; ed, Thomas Neff; md, Howard Jackson; art d, Edward C. Jewell; m/l, Borne, Webster.

Mystery **(PR:A MPAA:NR)**

HOW GREEN WAS MY VALLEY***** (1941) 118m FOX bw

Walter Pidgeon *(Mr. Gruffydd)*, Maureen O'Hara *(Angharad)*, Donald Crisp *(Mr. Morgan)*, Anna Lee *(Bronwyn)*, Roddy McDowall *(Huw)*, John Loder *(Ianto)*, Sara Allgood *(Mrs. Morgan)*, Barry Fitzgerald *(Cyfartha)*, Patric Knowles *(Ivor)*, Morton Lowry *(Mr. Jonas)*, Arthur Shields *(Parry)*, Ann Todd *(Cienwen)*, Fredric Worlock *(Dr. Richards)*, Richard Fraser *(Davy)*, Rhys Williams *(Dai Bando)*, Clifford Severn *(Mervyn)*, Lionel Pape *(Mr. Evans)*, Ethel Griffies *(Mrs. Nicholas)*, Eve March *(Meillyn Lewis)*, Marten Lamont *(Iestyn Evans)*, Irving Pichel *(Narrator)*, Mary Field *(Eve)*, Evan S. Evans *(Gwinlyn)*, James Monks *(Owen)*, Mary Gordon.

Emotionally majestic, visually awesome, and spiritually uplifting in every scene, this was one of John Ford's undisputed masterpieces, a film that does not fade nor fail after repeated viewings. The mining area in South Wales and its hard-working miners and their families are shown through the juvenile McDowall, the youngest of six children in a family headed by Crisp and Allgood. Set at the turn of the century (shown in flashback with Pichel narrating first person), we see McDowall at age 10, happily living in a valley still green and dwelling in a stone cottage full of love and warmth. His father and five older, grown brothers all work in the colliery, earning good wages and looking to a bright future. The greedy mine owners decide to cut wages and this brings about a union movement involving the brothers, but one which old-fashioned Crisp will not join. In fact, the heated arguments over the union cause the older brothers to move out of the house. Crisp is left with son McDowall, beautiful but unmarried daughter O'Hara, and his wife. He stubbornly refuses to join the union when its members walk out and remain off the job for 22 weeks through a bitter, debilitating winter. Hearing the menacing talk about her husband, Allgood, accompanied by McDowall, attends an outdoor union meeting during a snowstorm and threatens to kill any man who attempts to harm her husband. While attempting to return home she falls into an icy river and is plucked from the waters by her older sons and taken home to recuperate. The sons return home to aid their mother and to encourage McDowall, whose legs have been paralyzed since it was he who held his mother afloat in the icy river until help came. Local preacher Pidgeon, who is in love with O'Hara, visits the boy regularly and, in the spring, carries him to a hill overlooking the mining community and tells him: "You can walk, Huw, if you try." McDowall feebly stands alone, then takes one step after another until falling into Pidgeon's arms. Pidgeon is not so successful with O'Hara. Though they both love each other, Pidgeon will not marry her, refusing to bring her to a life of poverty. She resists this idea but, tired of waiting, finally accepts the proposal of the son of the mine owner and goes to live in the great mansion, later moving abroad. When McDowall regains the use of his legs he goes off to attend school for the first time. Insulted and bullied by a sadistic and repulsive teacher, Lowry, he is miserable, especially when his schoolmates make fun of him and he is later beaten up by a class bully. Crisp, noticing his son's bruises, sends for Rhys Williams, the great boxing champion of the valley. Williams teaches young McDowall how to box and when the bully again picks on him, McDowall administers a beating. Lowry, witnessing this, hauls the boy into his classroom and whips him mercilessly on the back, leaving deep scars. McDowall staggers home to fall into the arms of his towering brothers, Loder, Evans, Fraser, Monks, and Knowles. They are incensed and intend to tear Lowry limb from limb but McDowall asks them not to interfere. His request is ignored, however, by Williams and his erstwhile drinking companion, Fitzgerald, who proceed to give Lowry a lesson in the manly art of boxing, knocking him senseless before the class. Williams is simply magnificent here, taking sweet vengeance on the despicable Lowry, telegraphing his intentions when asking Lowry politely: "What do you think of a man who would take a whip to a child?" He then proceeds to demonstrate the various techniques of boxing and types of punches thrown, all to the insufferable body of Lowry, finally crushing the brutish teacher's jaw with a smashing right cross. When the strike is finally over, McDowall's brothers see wages cut further still and, one by one, they leave the valley, going to America and other distant points, all except Knowles, who marries local girl Lee. Knowles is killed in a mining accident on the very day his wife delivers their child. Instead of going on to school, McDowall nobly goes to live in Lee's house and to work in the cruel colliery to help support her and his brother's child. O'Hara, who has gone to live in South Africa, returns to the owner's mansion and innocently meets with Pidgeon, but they are viciously denounced by the church elders, led by smug, sanctimonious Shields, and accused of adultery. Pidgeon, in disgust, resigns his post as vicar and he, too, plans to leave Wales. Just then part of the mine collapses and word comes that Crisp is trapped far below. Volunteers are called for by Pidgeon: "Who is for Willum Morgan?" he asks. Williams, now completely blind, smiles broadly and steps from the crowd. "I for one," he says, "for he is the blood of my heart!" Pidgeon, Williams, who is led by McDowall, and some others, go below and wade through the mine shaft now filled waist high with water, McDowall calling out his father's name and finally finding the old man buried beneath fallen pilings, barely alive. He is pried loose and taken to the top in the elevator, dead, his body cradled by McDowall. It is the heart-wrenching end of the boy's once wonderful world. He has seen his family and a way of life disintegrate and go to ashes. The last scene, however, is hopeful in memory, showing Crisp and McDowall walking the flower-bursting hills above the mining valley as they once were, happy with spring growing under their feet. Over the scene comes Pichel's mellifluous voice, saying: "Men like my father cannot die. They remain a living truth in my mind . . . They are with me still—real in memory as they were real in flesh—loving and beloved forever. How green was my valley, then." Everything about this film is touching as the master director Ford (he won an Oscar for this film, one of four as Best Director) builds one simple scene upon another without much plot at all, using incidents affecting one family to tell the tale, to show the change and record the tragedies. This was a family history at its theatrical best with Crisp the patriarch, his loyal wife, his strapping sons, beautiful daughter, and little boy captured in one poignant scene after another, simple little scenes such as the one where Crisp and his huge sons return from work at the beginning of the film to bathe in old wooden tubs, scrubbing the grime of the coal mine from their bodies. Or the scene at the dining table where Crisp says grace and carves a roast they have all worked so hard to have. None but Ford could take such a simple tale and make of it masterpiece filmmaking. Beautifully assisted by cameraman Miller, who also won an Oscar, Ford received strong support from Fox chief Zanuck, who personally produced this film. Zanuck originally wanted to film the movie in Rhondda Valley, Wales, but WW II prevented the on-location shooting so he had the entire Welsh village, coal mine, and adjacent buildings constructed on 80 acres in California's San Fernando Valley (which brought forth some minor criticism in Wales that the film did not conform to the topography of the original novel). More than 150 workmen labored for six months to create the marvelous outdoor set. Zanuck, who had produced THE GRAPES OF WRATH, also directed by Ford, a year earlier, was then in a period when he favored adapting significant novels to the screen, even though the compromises were considerable. He was to say: "When I think of what I got away with [in making HOW GREEN WAS MY VALLEY] . . . and won the Academy Award with the picture, it is really astonishing. Not only did we drop five or six characters but we eliminated the most controversial element in the book which was the labor and capital battle in connection with the strike." Yet, like GRAPES OF WRATH, this film was a family in stress film and Ford placed the emphasis where it counted most in front of the camera. Just after completing this film Ford joined the photographic branch of America's super spy service, the OSS (Office of Strategic Services), taking a host of Hollywood talent with him as a private contribution to the war effort, including Gregg Toland, Budd Schulberg, Garson Kanin, Daniel Fuchs, Ray Kellogg and Joseph Walker. In addition to Oscars won by Ford and cameraman Miller, Oscars went to Fox for Best Picture, Day and Juran for Best Art Direction, Little for Best Interior (set) Decoration, and to Donald Crisp for Best Supporting Actor. Crisp, who had begun his long career with film patriarch D.W. Griffith in 1908, stated when accepting that "others, old-timers, should be given a chance, and they, too, could win Awards." When he sat down, Walter Brennan, three-time Oscar winner, kissed Crisp on the top of his head.

p, Darryl F. Zanuck; d, John Ford; w, Philip Dunne (based on the novel by Richard Llewellyn); ph, Arthur Miller; m, Alfred Newman; ed, James B. Clark; art d, Richard Day, Nathan Juran; set d, Thomas Little; cos, Gwen Wakeling; makeup, Guy Pierce.

Drama **(PR:A MPAA:NR)**

HOW I WON THE WAR*½** (1967, Brit.) 109m UA c

Michael Crawford *(Lt. Ernest Goodbody)*, John Lennon *(Gripweed)*, Roy Kinnear *(Clapper)*, Lee Montague *(Sgt. Transom)*, Jack MacGowran *(Juniper)*, Michael Hordern *(Grapple)*, Jack Hedley *(Melancholy Musketeer)*, Karl Michael Vogler *(Odlebog)*, Ronald Lacey *(Spool)*, James Cossins *(Drogue)*, Ewan Hooper *(Dooley)*, Alexander Knox *(American General)*, Robert Hardy *(British General)*, Sheila Hancock *(Mrs. Clapper's Friend)*, Charles Dyer *(Flappy-Trousered Man)*, Bill Dysart *(Paratrooper)*, Paul Daneman *(Skipper)*, Peter Graves *(Staff Officer)*, Jack May *(Toby)*, Richard Pearson *(Old Man at Alamein)*, Pauline Taylor *(Woman In Desert)*, John Ronane *(Operator)*, Norman Chappell *(Soldier at Alamein)*, Bryan Pringle *(Reporter)*, Fanny Carby *(Mrs. Clapper)*, Dandy Nichols, Gretchen Franklin *(Old Ladies)*, John Junkin *(Large Child)*, John Trenaman *(Driver)*, Mick Dillon, Kenneth Colley *(Replacements)*.

Richard Lester, the man who directed the two smash-hit Beatles movies, A HARD DAY'S NIGHT and HELP, makes an anti-war statement in this hard-biting black satire. Lester took John Lennon away from the Beatles and put him in a supporting role. The story is the reminiscence of a middle aged British WW II vet, Crawford, who remembers his triumphs as an officer in His Majesty's army. His career—which is a string of disasters piled one on top of another—is distorted by him into something wonderful. Told almost entirely in flashback, Crawford's career is off to a bad start as his lower-class beginnings and humble education make him one of the worst officers of one of the worst units. The shabby corps is made up of a variety of losers: Kinnear, an overweight draftee, obsessed with his wife's unfaithfulness; Lennon, a cynical laborer; MacGowran, a goof-ball, who dresses up in a burlesque clown outfit to keep up morale; Hedley, a sniveling yellowbelly; and Montague, the only competent military man, who tries in vain to correct the blunders of his superior officer. The troop is first sent to the desert of North Africa to set up an advance cricket field for V.I.P.'s. There are several battles in the film, each one tinted in a different color. When a soldier dies in a certain battle, his ghost remains with the troop, but is colored from head to toe in the color of the battle he died in. When a few of the men are killed in North Africa, they tag along as colored ghosts to the troop's next detail in France. As the troop progresses into Germany, the battles get bloodier and the ghosts get greater in number. Crawford is soon left alone, as all his men but the cowardly Hedley have died. He is cornered by Vogler, a Nazi commandant guarding the last intact bridge across the Rhine who hopes to release it to the Allies, but for a price. Vogler is a satire of the "nice" Nazi, who was just obeying orders. The end sees Crawford throwing a troop reunion with the sole survivor, Hedley. Lennon's billing far exceeds his part.

p&d, Richard Lester; w, Charles Wood (based on the novel by Patrick Ryan); ph, David Watkin (Eastmancolor); m, Ken Thorne; ed, John Victor Smith; art d, Philip Harrison, John Stoll; cos, Dinah Greet; spec eff, Eddie Fowlie.

Comedy/War **Cas.** **(PR:C MPAA:NR)**

HOW LOW CAN YOU FALL? (SEE: TILL MARRIAGE DO US PART, 1979, Ital.)

HOW MANY ROADS (SEE: LOST MAN, THE, 1969)

HOW NOT TO ROB A DEPARTMENT STORE*** (1965, Fr./Ital.) 95m France Cinema-P.C.M./Artixo bw (CENT BRIQUES ET DES TUILES; COLPO GROSSO A PARIGI)

Jean-Claude Brialy *(Marcel)*, Marie Laforet *(Ida)*, Sophie Daumier *(Moune)*, Jean-Pierre Marielle *(Justin)*, Michel Serrault *(Meloune)*, Albert Remy *(Etienne)*, Daniel Ceccaldi *(Leon)*, Roland Blanche *(Curly)*, Pierre Clementi *(Raf)*, Renaud Verlay *(Charles)*, Madeleine Barbulee *(Limonade)*, Robert Manuel *(Palmoni)*, Rene Genin *(Shopkeeper)*, Gabrielle Doulcet *(His Wife)*, Paul Preboist *(The Cousin)*, Dominique Davray *(Poulaine)*, Philippe Brizard *(Zecca)*, J.P. Rambal *(Store Manager)*, Roger Trapp *(Brigadier)*, Bernard Fresson *(Cop)*.

Brialy has just one week to pay back a gambling debt, so with the aid of dim-witted criminal Remy, he decides to rob Paris' *Galeries Lafayette* department store. They make Christmas Eve their big day and Marielle, another of Brialy's little helpers, disguises himself as Santa Claus. They fill up a bag with the stolen money, but it winds up in the hands of Barbulee, who plans to head for Chile. After some more bumbling and chasing Brialy gets the money back in his hands, but it has inadvertently been coated with glue and needs to be washed and dried. For all his efforts, poor Brialy is caught in the end. The picture is filled with favorites of the New Wave directors—Brialy appeared in both Claude Chabrol's and Jacques Rivette's first films (LE BEAU SERGE and PARIS BELONGS TO US, respectively); Remy is a veteran of Truffaut's pictures (THE 400 BLOWS and SHOOT THE PIANO PLAYER) as well as Marcel Carne's CHILDREN OF PARADISE. (In French; English subtitles.)

p&d, Pierre Grimblat; w, Grimblat, Clarence Weff (based on the novel by Weff); ph, Michel Kelber; m, Georges Garvarentz; ed, Robert and Monique Isnardon; art d, Raymond Gabutti.

Crime/Comedy **(PR:A MPAA:NR)**

HOW SWEET IT IS½** (1968) 99m Cherokee NGP/NGP c

James Garner *(Grif Henderson)*, Debbie Reynolds *(Jenny Henderson)*, Maurice Ronet *(Philippe Maspere)*, Terry-Thomas *(Gilbert Tilly)*, Paul Lynde *(The Purser)*, Marcel Dalio *(Louis)*, Gino Conforti *(Agatzi)*, Donald Losby *(Davey Henderson)*, Hilarie Thompson *(Bootsie Wax)*, Alexandra Hay *(Gloria)*, Mary Michael *(Nancy Leigh)*, Walter Brooke *(Haskell Wax)*, Elena Verdugo *(Vera Wax)*, Ann Morgan Guilbert *(Bibi)*, Patty Regan *(Midge)*, Vito Scotti *(Cook)*, Christopher Ross *(Paul)*, Larry Hankin, Jerry Riggio *(Policemen)*, Jack Colvin *(Assistant Chief)*, Leigh

French *(Marie)*, Erin Moran *(Little Girl)*, Robert Homel *(Dubrow)*, Jon Silo *(Hotel Clerk)*, Don Diamond *(Bartender)*, Lenny Kent *(Cabbie)*, Rico Cattani, Nikita Knatz *(Bouncers)*, Bella Bruck *(Woman)*, Ogden Talbot, Michael French, Bert Aretsky *(Customers)*, Johnny Silver *(Zipper Man)*, Penny Marshall, Terri Messina, Patti Braverman, Arlene Parness, Carey Lynn, Erin O'Reilly, Rori Gwynne, Julee Hunter, Peggy Babcock, Mary O'Brien, Susan Meredith, Heather Menzies *(Tour Girls)*, Margot Nelson, Marti Litis, Myrna Ross, Jenie Jackson, Sharon Cintron, Sheila Layton, Shiva Rozier, Barbara E. Fuller, Katherine Darc, Luana Anders, Marjorie Dayne, Margie Duncan, Jenny Fridolfs, Bea Bradley, Eve Bruce, Emese Williams, Marilyn White *(Agatzi's Girls)*.

A very clean-cut family film that has the look of a made for TV movie. This could be explained by the fact that the producer, writers, and director all came from television sitcoms. The story concerns a family going through relationship problems. Mom, Reynolds, discovers that her son, Losby, has a crush on a girl going on a European summer tour. Losby wants to go along because of the girl; Reynolds talks her husband, Garner, into chaperoning and covering the tour for a magazine for which he is a photographer. Reynolds puts a large down payment on a Riviera villa and plans to spend the summer in Europe also. They get to Europe and split up, Garner and Losby with the tour, Reynolds to her villa. She finds, upon arrival, that she was swindled by Terry-Thomas, the real estate agent, because the villa is really owned by a rich French playboy, Ronet. After discovering the mixup, he asks Reynolds to stay with him as a guest. Meanwhile, Garner is getting attention from a pretty tour guide, Michael. Reynolds meets the tour group and Garner in San Remo, and is disturbed by Michael's attraction to her husband and his indifference to the fact that she is living with Ronet in his villa. She angrily returns to the villa, disappointed and frustrated with Garner. When Garner shows up at the villa and sees her parading around in a skimpy bikini, given her by Ronet, Garner gets mad and punches the Frenchman. After a bus chase, and an arrest which sees the prim, demure Reynolds released in the custody of procurer Conforti, accompanying his ladies of the evening to a bordello, the couple reconcile for a rather trite ending.

p, Garry Marshall, Jerry Belson; d, Jerry Paris; w, Marshall, Belson (based on the novel *The Girl in The Turquoise Bikini* by Muriel Resnik); ph, Lucien Ballard (Panavision, Technicolor); m, Pat Williams; ed, Bud Molin; art d, Arthur Lonergan; set d, James Payne, Arthur Krams, Charles S. Thompson; cos, Helen Rose; makeup, William Reynolds; spec eff, Pacific Title; m/l, title song, Jim Webb (sung by Picardi).

Comedy **(PR:C-O MPAA:NR)**

HOW THE WEST WAS WON**** (1962) 165m MGM/Cinerama c

Spencer Tracy *(Narrator)*, Carroll Baker *(Eve Prescott)*, Lee J. Cobb *(Lou Ramsey)*, Henry Fonda *(Jethro Stuart)*, Carolyn Jones *(Julie Rawlings)*, Karl Malden *(Zebulon Prescott)*, Gregory Peck *(Cleve Van Valen)*, George Peppard *(Zeb Rawlings)*, Robert Preston *(Roger Morgan)*, Debbie Reynolds *(Lilith Prescott)*, James Stewart *(Linus Rawlings)*, Eli Wallach *(Charlie Gant)*, John Wayne *(Gen. William T. Sherman)*, Richard Widmark *(Mike King)*, Brigid Bazlen *(Dora Hawkins)*, Walter Brennan *(Col. Hawkins)*, David Brian *(Attorney)*, Andy Devine *(Cpl. Peterson)*, Raymond Massey *(Abraham Lincoln)*, Agnes Moorehead *(Rebecca Prescott)*, Harry Morgan *(Gen. Ulysses S. Grant)*, Thelma Ritter *(Agatha Clegg)*, Mickey Shaughnessy *(Deputy Marshall)*, Russ Tamblyn *(Reb Soldier)*, Tudor Owen *(Scotsman)*, Barry Harvey, Jamie Ross *(His Sons)*, Willis Bouchey *(Surgeon)*, Kim Charney *(Sam Prescott)*, Bryan Russell *(Zeke Prescott)*, Claude Johnson *(Jeremiah Rawlings)*, Jerry Holmes *(Railroad Clerk)*, Rudolfo Acosta *(Desperado)*, Chief Weasel, Red Cloud, Ben Black Elk *(Indians)*, Mark Allen *(Colin)*, Lee Van Cleef *(Marty)*, Charles Briggs *(Barker)*, Jay C. Flippen *(Huggins)*, Clinton Sundberg *(Hylan Seabury)*, James Griffith, Walter Burke *(Gamblers)*, Joe Sawyer *(Ship's Officer)*, John Larch *(Grimes)*, Jack Pennick *(Cpl. Murphy)*, Craig Duncan *(James Marshall)*, Paul Bryar *(Auctioneer's Assistant)*, Ken Curtis *(Ben, Union Corporal)*, Walter Reed, Carleton Young *(Union Soldiers)*, Dean Stanton *(Outlaw)*, Karl Swenson *(Train Conductor)*, Jack Lambert *(Gant Henchman)*, Christopher Dark *(Poker Player)*, Gene Roth *(Riverboat Poker Player)*, Edward J. McKinley *(Auctioneer)*, Bill Henry *(Staff Officer)*, Ken Dibbs *(Blacksmith)*, Red Perkins *(Union Soldier)*, John Damler, Robert Nash *(Lawyers)*, Saul Gorss, Roy Jensen, Victor Romito, Harvey Parry *(Henchmen)*, Beulah Archuletta, Chuck Roberson, Boyd "Red" Morgan.

A great epic, a wonderful western, a thrilling and poignant motion picture by any standard, HOW THE WEST WAS WON is so jampacked with action and stars it's difficult to keep the events and personalities straight. Yet it is forthright picture-making at its best and is one of the few giant episodic adventure tales that holds viewer interest throughout. It's basically a family picture, showing the growth of one family and how its line either survived or collapsed during the momentous events of 19th century America. As such it becomes living, colorful history, the kind that could have been made from many an American family tree. This one is an oak. Three generations of one pioneer family are episodically shown from 1839 to 1889, beginning with "The Rivers." Malden and his sturdy wife, Moorehead, their two daughters, Baker and Reynolds, and two sons, seek a new future in the West and set out with other pioneers along the Erie Canal and then into the Ohio River via raft. They encounter mountain man Stewart who is returning East with rich animal pelts he intends to sell and use the profits from for a roaring drunk. At a river campsite Baker and Stewart dally but she finds him gone in the morning. Stewart paddles upstream where he stops at a supply depot which is situated in a huge cave. Here river pirate Brennan and his brood sell whiskey and sundries to the unwary before robbing and killing them. Stewart begins to live it up, swilling down raw liquor poured generously by Brennan, who extolls the virtues of the United States, an American flag proudly displayed behind his bar. His daughter, Bazlen, a fetching young hussy, entices Stewart to a deep black pit, asking him if he wants to see the fierce "varmint" they keep captive. His natural curiosity compels Stewart to lean over the pit and stare downward with wondrous expectation. Just at that time he is struck from behind, robbed, his pelts stashed in his canoe taken, and he is thrown into the pit, believed to be dead. But he manages to survive and returns to the river, floating away downstream. Malden and his family, joined by Owen and his sons, visit the same place, but when Brennan and his cut-throats attack them the pioneers put up a wild fight and either kill or drive off the pirates, Owen losing one of his sons. Malden puts his family on a raft and goes down the treacherous Ohio River, running into wild rapids that splits the raft apart and sends the family into the river. Malden, Moorehead, and their little son, Charney, perish, but Baker and Reynolds survive. Stewart shows up and helps them bury their dead but he cannot find enough courage to leave Baker whom he loves. In his squirming attempt to escape matrimony, Stewart confesses to Baker that "I'll always be going to see the varmint." But it's no use; he's lost. He forsakes his wanderlust and settles down with her as Reynolds continues west to seek her fortune. In the second segment, "The Plains," Reynolds finds a job singing in a St. Louis saloon where tinhorn gambler Peck sees her. He's in no position, however, to improve Debbie's lot since he's lost heavily to thug gamblers and must pay off by dawn or face annihilation. The next day Reynolds takes her hard-earned money and pools it with Ritter, both women joining a covered wagon caravan heading west and led by rugged Preston who has an eye for Reynolds. Just before they leave Peck appears and begs to be taken along, offering Reynolds and Ritter his manly protection on the dangerous plains. Reynolds rejects the offer but Ritter, flattered by the suave gambler, allows him to come along in their wagon, over the protests of Preston. They later come under Indian attack but Peck manages to save them. He and Reynolds are later married, go to San Francisco, and Peck makes his fortune after gambling setbacks on the Mississippi River steamboats. The third segment is entitled "The Civil War." In the East, the war has broken out and Peppard, the son of Baker and Stewart, goes off to join Union troops at the battle of Shiloh. There one night he witnesses a meeting between generals Sherman (Wayne) and Grant (Morgan). Watching with him is another young soldier, a Confederate, Tamblyn. Both young men have earlier talked about the futility of war and their not knowing exactly why they are fighting each other, and, in the dim light, it is suggested that they do not even know they are on opposite sides. Tamblyn suddenly raises his rifle to shoot Morgan and Peppard jumps him. They struggle and Peppard drives a bayonet into Tamblyn, killing him. Peppard is later shown returning home to find his mother Baker dead (his father, Stewart, has already died in the Civil War) and his younger brother Johnson tending the family farm in Ohio. He tells him the farm is all his, that he's heading west, that the war has changed him, that he intends to seek his future with the U.S. Cavalry. We next see Peppard guarding the train builders in the fourth segment, "The Railroads," battling with railway boss Widmark who ruthlessly orders his road gangs to cut through Indian territory, violating treaties. Peppard warns him that the Indians will not stand for another violation of their lands, but Widmark ignores him. Fonda, an old Indian scout and trapper, one-time friend of Peppard's father, Stewart, has been shooting buffalo to feed the railroad workers but he is disgusted with the brutal way Widmark and other train bosses are mistreating the land and the Indians, and he quits. Peppard's repeated warnings become reality when the Indians drive stampeding herds of buffalo through the railhead camp, destroying buildings, equipment, and trampling scores to death. Peppard, too, has had enough. After the slaughter he confronts Widmark, telling him: "They just sent a bunch of animals" to kill the white men. He then points to the trampled area littered with dead, a small child crying over her mother's body. "You can live with that?" he asks Widmark. The callous railway boss sneers and says, "That? That's just new life going on!" Peppard visits Fonda in the high mountains where the trapper intends to spend the rest of his life, safe from the encroachments of civilization. He asks Peppard to stay with him but the young man decides to move off and make his own life. In San Francisco, Reynolds is now an old woman watching her heirlooms being auctioned off in a mansion no longer hers, consoled by lawyer Brian. Peck is dead and she now decides that she will spend the rest of her days with her nephew Peppard, a rancher and ex-lawman in Arizona. She journeys southeast to appear in the final segment, "The Outlaws," welcomed at the train depot by Peppard, his wife Jones, and their young sons. Also at the station is Wallach and his henchmen, a gang of desperadoes Peppard has earlier dealt with; Peppard, when sheriff, had shot and killed Wallach's brother. Wallach taunts Peppard, who avoids gunplay, instead going to the new sheriff, Cobb. Wallach has done no wrong, explains Cobb, and therefore can't be arrested. Peppard explains that he and his men are present for only one purpose, to rob a large shipment of gold on that day's train. Cobb doesn't believe him but is later persuaded to ride in one of the passenger cars with his deputies and Peppard. Wallach and his gang soon appear, riding after the train and getting on board, but when they enter the mail car carrying the gold they are met by Peppard, Cobb, and the deputies, and a wild gunfight breaks out. All of the outlaws are shot off the train except Wallach and he and Peppard square off on a flat car loaded with giant logs. Some of the chains holding the logs break away and Peppard is swung out with one of them so he momentarily hangs over the side of the racing train. Meanwhile, part of the train carrying Cobb and his deputies has been separated from the flatcar and must back up to save Peppard who is about to be killed. Peppard manages to get back on the flatcar but Wallach takes aim at him. Just before he can shoot Peppard, Cobb fires a fatal bullet into the outlaw. Peppard jumps back onto the front of the train as the rear part is derailed and sends flatcar, caboose, and Wallach smashing into the desert. (This is truly one of the most spectacular action sequences ever filmed.) With the outlaws eliminated, Peppard gathers his family, including rugged Reynolds, and heads for his ranch and tranquility. This marathon, mammoth film, beautifully narrated by Tracy, is directed by three Hollywood stalwarts, all action western directors of the first rank. Hathaway handled the segments entitled "The Rivers," "The Plains," and "The Outlaws." George Marshall directed "The Railroad," and the venerable Ford "The Civil War." Transitional sequences were directed by Richard Thorpe, but he is uncredited. All handle their segments well, with Hathaway carrying most of the directorial burden. Though the story is lengthy it is well-written and properly pithy, with the emphasis correctly on action. Veteran screenwriter Webb, who wrote such notable films as THE BIG COUNTRY (1958), TRAPEZE (1956), and

PORK CHOP HILL (1959), doesn't have the space in presenting such a panoramic tale to fully develop any characters, except that of Reynolds and Peppard who carry most of the "linking" elements of the story, yet he infuses his characters with enough personality to make each distinctive. The Cineramic photography, which loses much on TV and on cassette, was handled beautifully by cinematographers LaShelle, Daniels, Krasner, and Lang as their cameras recorded the vastness of the American frontier. (The location shots alone are worth the viewing; filming was conducted at Battery Rock on the Ohio River in Illinois, in the rolling hills outside of Paducah, Kentucky, Custer State Park, South Dakota, Chimney Rock in the Colorado Rockies, Monument Valley on the Arizona-Utah border, Pinnacles National Monument in California, near Uncompaghre in Colorado, desert locations outside of Tonto, Arizona, and the National Forests near Inyo on the California-Nevada border.) This was the first theatrical release in the Cinerama process created by Fred Waller, a system of three cameras mounted as one with a single shutter; three 27mm lenses on these cameras encompassing a field of 146 degrees wide by 55 degrees high, the approximate scope of the human eye. In projection, the result is a gigantic image that was shown on a wide screen wrapping about theatergoers to completely fill peripheral vision. Immensely popular when first introduced, Cinerama ultimately became a novelty and eventually lost public support. MGM devoted most of its entire studio to this production, involving 38 of its specialized departments, employing more than 400 technicians, and thousands of extras. Scores of cowboys were hired to corral 2,000 buffalo shown in the stampede scene shot in South Dakota at Custer National Park. More than 5,000 costumes were hand-sewn and the same number of period shoes and Indian moccasins were also made for the actors. Great care was taken in assembling thousands of Indians for this epic western. MGM brought together five tribes—the Brules, Oglalas, and Minnecanjous factions of the Sioux, the Cheyennes, the Arapahoes. Among them were such celebrated Indians as Ben Black Elk, son of a medicine man, who became the most photographed Indian in the U.S., Red Cloud, almost 100 years old, who had fought as a young warrior at the Little Big Horn against Custer, and 81-year-old Chief Weasel, who had been part of Buffalo Bill Cody's Wild West Show and had survived the slaughter of the Oglala tribe at Wounded Knee. The more than 600 horses used in the film required 20,000 pounds of hay and 1,000 pounds of grain daily. The cast was enormous with 12,617 bit players and extras employed at one time or another during production. In addition to 630 horses, 150 mules were used, along with 50 head of oxen tended by 203 wranglers. The studio looted its prop departments and that of other studios, coming up with 107 ancient Conestoga and trail wagons for "The Plains" segment. Hundreds of studio vehicles moved the main cast more than a million miles across the roads of America during the year-long production. (The film was released in various lengths, initially at 165m but some segments, such as panoramic helicopter views of America at the end, were later cut and versions were later shown at 162 minutes and as short as 155 minutes and 149 minutes.) The enormous film cost about $15 million to produce (a fourth of what some mammoth flops cost today, but slightly less than what President Thomas Jefferson paid for the entire Louisiana Territory in 1803). The film grossed more than $50 million in theatrical rentals since its first release and continues to pile up revenue. It's a perennial film, one that improves on viewing in that there's just so much more to see each time. The acting is top drawer, even though many of the roles are limited to cameo performances. Super stars Stewart, Fonda, Peck, Wayne, Widmark all do commendable jobs, and Peppard, who appears more consistently than anyone else, is excellent, from brash Civil War recruit to seasoned lawman of a West that has seen the last of the old outlaws. Reynolds is wonderful in the early segments and as a high-kicking saloon hall dancer, but she is woefully unconvincing as an elderly woman, as is Baker when sending off her son Peppard to war. Ritter is terrific as a salty pioneer woman and so is Devine as a jovial mailman, Cobb as a bellowing, belicose lawman, Malden as a hardy pioneer father, Brennan as a sleazy, conniving pirate, Preston as a dogged wagon master, and Wallach as a snarling, murderous outlaw, all shine brilliantly. Unwieldy as it might have been, the film works, chiefly because Hollywood brought its finest technical talent to bear in this most memorable of films. Newman's score, comprising many folk ballads, and the main theme song, developed by Newman, Robert Emmett, Dolan, Darby and Sammy Cahn, "Home In the Meadow," is nothing less than magnificent. Oscars were won by scriptwriter Webb, film editor Kress, and the MGM sound department.

p, Bernard Smith; d, Henry Hathaway, John Ford, George Marshall, (uncredited) Richard Thorpe; w, James R. Webb (based on articles in *Life Magazine*); ph, Joseph LaShelle, Charles Lang, Jr., William Daniels, Milton Krasner, Harold Wellman (Cinerama, Technicolor non-roadshow shown in 35mm CinemaScope); m, Alfred Newman, Ken Darby; ed, Harold F. Kress; art d, George W. Davis, William Ferrari, Addison Hehr; set d, Henry Grace, Don Greenwood, Jr., Jack Mills; cos, Walter Plunkett; spec eff, A. Arnold Gillespie, Robert R. Hoag; m/l, "How the West Was Won," Alfred Newman, Ken Darby, "Raise a Ruckus," "Wait for the Hoedown," "What was Your Name in the States?" lyrics by Johnny Mercer, "Home in the Meadow," folk singing by Dave Guard and the Whiskeyhill Singers; makeup, William Tuttle.

Western Epic (PR:AAA MPAA:NR)

HOW TO BE VERY, VERY, POPULAR**½ (1955) 89m FOX c

Betty Grable *(Stormy)*, Sheree North *(Curly)*, Robert Cummings *(Wedgewood)*, Charles Coburn *(Tweed)*, Tommy Noonan *(Eddie)*, Orson Bean *(Toby)*, Fred Clark *(Mr. Marshall)*, Charlotte Austin *(Midge)*, Alice Pearce *(Miss Syl)*, Rhys Williams *(Flagg)*, Andrew Tombes *(Moon)*, Noel Toy *(Cherry Blossom Wang)*, Emory Parnell *(Chief of Police)*, Harry Carter *(Bus Driver)*, Jesslyn Fax *(Music Teacher)*, Jack Mather *(1st Policeman)*, Michael Lally *(2nd Policeman)*, Milton Parsons *(Mr. X)*, Harry Seymour *(Teacher)*, Hank Mann *(Newsvendor)*, Leslie Parrish *(Girl On Bus)*, Janice Carroll, Jean Holcombe, Iona McKenzie, Howard Petrie, Jean Walters, Stanley Farrar, Willard Waterman, Anthony Redondo.

This silly comedy was Betty Grable's last film. She and North play a couple of strip-tease dancers who witness the murder of a Chinese stripper and flee to a college town to take refuge. The girls are hidden by a group of college boys in their fraternity house until the murderer is caught. Grable falls in love with Cummings, a man who has put off graduating for 17 years, so that his inheritance money will keep coming. North falls for Bean, a dimwitted student who is in college only by the virtue of his father's money. Coburn is hilarious as the college president who will accept anyone with the right amount of cash. North steals the spotlight from Grable with a great number, "Shake, Rattle and Roll." Other songs include "Bristol Bell" (Ken Dardy, Lionel Newman) and "How to Be Very, Very Popular" (Jule Styne, Sammy Cahn). This film was a remake of SHE LOVES ME NOT (1934).

p,d&w, Nunnally Johnson (based on a play by Howard Lindsay from a novel by Edward Hope and a play by Lyford Moore, Harlan Thompson); ph, Milton Krasner (CinemaScope, DeLuxe Color); m, Cyril J. Mockridge; ed, Louis Loeffler; md, Lionel Newman; art d, Lyle R. Wheeler, John De Cuir; cos, Travilla; ch, Paul Godkin, Sonia Shaw.

Comedy/Musical (PR:A MPAA:NR)

HOW TO BEAT THE HIGH COST OF LIVING* (1980) 110m Filmways/AIP c

Susan Saint James *(Jane)*, Jane Curtin *(Elaine)*, Jessica Lange *(Louise)*, Richard Benjamin *(Albert)*, Fred Willard *(Robert)*, Eddie Albert *(Max)*, Dabney Coleman *(Jack Heintzel)*, Art Metrano *(Gas Station Attendant)*, Ronnie Schell *(Bill Pike)*, Garrett Morris *(Power and Light Man)*, Cathryn Damon *(Natalie)*, Sybil Danning *(Charlotte)*, Al Checco *(Tim Lundy)*, Carmen Zapata *(Mama Figueroa)*, Dru Wagner *(Harriet)*, Michael Bell, Susan Tolsky, Byron Morrow, Allan Warnick, David Lunney, Michael K. Daly, James "Izzy" Whetstine, Jack Krupnick, James Aday, Wesley Baldwin, Sarah Leonard, Robin Hickman, Daniel Maves, Tom Morrison, Jonathan Schwartz, Jane Van Boskirk, Jon Dickman, Bill Ritchie, Robert Canaga, Colleen Murff, Stan Boyd, Jerry Zinnamon, Tom Gressler, Philip Miller, Ralph Garrett, Robert W. Talbot, Harvey Lewis, Nanci Westerland, Joan Schumacher, Scott Barkhurst, Linda Hall, Craig Jackson, Larry Woodruff, Wendy Shawn.

A poor story of three middle-class suburbanites who turn to crime when faced with poverty. The skimpy plot deals with Saint James, a divorcee, who needs money for her kids' expenses; Curtin, who has been deserted by her husband and left without an income; and Lange, whose husband, Benjamin, can no longer support her fashionable but profitless antique shop. The three get together and decide to steal a large amount of money from a huge plastic ball displayed in a suburban shopping center. The three would-be crooks make about every goof and blunder in the book, but manage to pull off the heist. While Curtin does a striptease act in the shopping mall to divert attention, Saint James and Lange lose the $1 million in cash. The raft that they are using to escape down a small creek springs a leak and sinks, and the money floats off in garbage bags.

p, Jerome M. Zeitman, Robert Kaufman; d, Robert Scheerer; w, Kaufman (based on a story by Leonora Thuna); ph, James Crabe (Movielab Color); m, Patrick Williams; ed, Bill Butler; prod d, Lawrence G. Paull; set d, Peg Cummings.

Comedy Cas. (PR:A MPAA:PG)

HOW TO COMMIT MARRIAGE**½ (1969) 98m Naho/Cinerama c

Bob Hope *(Frank Benson)*, Jackie Gleason *(Oliver Poe)*, Jane Wyman *(Elaine Benson)*, Maureen Arthur *(Lois Grey)*, Leslie Nielsen *(Phil Fletcher)*, Tina Louise *(LaVerne Baker)*, Paul Stewart *(Attorney)*, Irwin Corey *(The Baba Ziba)*, Joanna Cameron *(Nancy Benson)*, Tim Matthieson *(David Poe)*, The Comfortable Chair *(Themselves)*.

A hopelessly "un-hip" Hope comedy, despite the fact that it tries so hard to be "hip." Hope and Wyman play a husband and wife about to dissolve their marriage after 20 years. At the same time, their daughter, Cameron, announces that she and her college beau, Matthieson, are going to be married. This development pleases her family, but Matthieson's father, Gleason, is outraged and sets out to stop the wedding. Gleason succeeds in ruining the ceremony, but the two youngsters run off to live with a rock 'n' roll band instead. Meanwhile, Hope finds solace in the arms of a well-endowed divorcee, Arthur, while Wyman is seen in the company of divorced man Nielsen. A few months later, Hope and Wyman learn that their daughter is about to have a baby, and that she plans to put it up for adoption, in keeping with the advice of her guru, Corey. Hope and Wyman adopt the child themselves, but no one knows that they are the foster parents. This leads to a series of uninspired comedy situations that sees Hope and Wyman faking a happy marriage for the sake of the adoption agency, and then running off to their lovers when they have a chance. Gleason, however, suspects the truth and goes on a crusade to expose the sham. Hope tries to convince the guru to tell Cameron and Matthieson to reclaim the child, but the latter refuses. Desperate, Hope steals the guru's robes and disguises himself in order to convince the congregation that their children should be with them. The trick works and the young couple get their baby back. The whole experience has brought Hope and Wyman back together and everyone is happy for the fadeout.

p, Bill Lawrence; d, Norman Panama; w, Ben Starr, Michael Kanin; ph, Charles Lang (Technicolor); m, Joseph J. Lilley; ed, Ronald Sinclair; md, Lilley; art d, Edward Engoron; set d, John Lamphear; md, Lilley; cos, Nolan Miller; spec eff, Justus Gibbs; makeup, Mike Moschella, Fred Williams; ch, Jack Baker.

Comedy/Drama (PR:A MPAA:M)

HOW TO FRAME A FIGG** (1971) 103m UNIV c

Don Knotts *(Hollis Figg)*, Joe Flynn *(Kermit Sanderson)*, Edward Andrews *(Mayor Chisolm)*, Elaine Joyce *(Ema Lethakusic)*, Yvonne Craig *(Glorianna)*, Frank Welker *(Prentiss Gates)*, Parker Fennelly *(Old Charley Loring)*, Bill Zuckert *(Commissioner Henderson)*, Pitt Herbert *(Doctor Schmidt)*, Robert P. Lieb *(Commissioner Hayes)*,

Bob Hastings *(Chris Groat)*, Bruce Kirby *(Dale Groat)*, Stuart Nisbet *(Gentry Groat)*, James Millhollin *(Funeral Director)*, Fay De Witt *(Grace)*, Savannah Bentley *(Ethel Purvis)*, Athena Lorde *(Agnes)*, Bill Quinn *(Carmoni)*, John Archer *(Gerard)*, Eddie Quillan *(Old Man)*, Benny Rubin *(Max)*, Billy Sands *(Bowling Alley Manager)*, Clay Tanner *(Officer)*.

Typical Don Knotts vehicle sees him as a bumbling assistant bookkeeper in the city hall of the small town of Dalton. Corrupt city officials Fennelly—who's so decrepit that he must be transported around town in an ambulance—Flynn, and Andrews have been stealing from the public till, so they frame Knotts to take the fall. This leads to the usual spastic Knotts antics, and aided by wholesome girl Joyce, he's able to clear his name. A computer named Leo, which undergoes a funeral and a disinterment, plays a role as important as that of any of the other characters. This was the twitchy Knotts' fifth comedy for producer Montagne.

p, Edward J. Montagne; d, Alan Rafkin; w, George Tibbles (based on a story by Montagne and Don Knotts); ph, William Margulies (Technicolor); m, Vic Mizzy; ed, Sam E. Waxman; art d, Alexander Golitzen, John Lloyd; set d, James M. Walters, Sr.; cos, Helen Colvig; makeup, Bud Westmore.

Comedy **(PR:AA MPAA:G)**

HOW TO MAKE A MONSTER½** (1958) 75m AIP bw/c

Robert H. Harris *(Pete Drummond)*, Paul Brinegar *(Rivero)*, Gary Conway *(Tony Mantell)*, Gary Clarke *(Larry Drake)*, Malcolm Atterbury *(Richards)*, Dennis Cross *(Monahan)*, John Ashley *(Guest Star)*, Morris Ankrum *(Capt. Hancock)*, Walter Reed *(Detective Thompson)*, Paul Maxwell *(Jeff Clayton)*, Eddie Marr *(John Nixon)*, Heather Ames *(Arlen Dow)*, Robert Shayne *(Gary Droz)*, Rod Dana *(Lab Technician)*, Jacqueline Ebeier *(Jane)*, Joan Chandler *(Marilyn)*, Thomas B. Henry *(Martin Brace)*, John Phillips *(Detective Jones)*, Pauline Myers *(Millie the Maid)*.

A classic AIP film which incorporated the popular monsters of the "I WAS A TEENAGE . . ." series, the Frankenstein monster and the Werewolf, into the same film. HOW TO MAKE A MONSTER features Harris as a master makeup artist who specializes in horror effects. Harris is an artist, obsessed with his work, who considers himself a genius (his shop is filled with props and masks from previous AIP releases). When the studio he works for is bought out by an East coast conglomerate that decides horror films are no longer worth producing, Harris goes mad and decides to get his revenge while shooting the studio's final horror film, which happens to star the Frankenstein monster and the Werewolf. The crazed makeup man develops an insidious new application that turns the made-up actor into a mindless zombie who will obey orders. Taking innocent teenage film stars Conway (who also played the Frankenstein monster in I WAS A TEENAGE FRANKENSTEIN) and Clarke (they couldn't get Michael Landon to repeat his role from I WAS A TEENAGE WEREWOLF), Harris applies their "special" makeup and sends them out to kill the ignorant studio executives who sold his artistry down the river. Eventually, justice catches up to him, when Harris stupidly informs his young monsters that he's going to kill them and have them stuffed so all the world can see his greatest achievements. This doesn't set well with the two teenagers, so they go on a rampage and destroy Harris and his shop, which held 25 years of his work, by setting the place on fire (this scene was shot in color). Silly, sort of stupid, but a lot of fun if you love old AIP movies.

p, James H. Nicholson, Samuel Z. Arkoff; d, Herbert L. Strock; w, Kenneth Langtry, Herman Cohen; ph, Maury Gertzman; m, Paul Dunlap; ed, Jerry Young; cos, Oscar Rodriquez; m/l, Paul Dunlap, Skip Redwine.

Horror **(PR:C MPAA:NR)**

HOW TO MAKE IT (SEE: TARGET: HARRY, 1969)

HOW TO MARRY A MILLIONAIRE*** (1953) 95m FOX c

Betty Grable *(Loco)*, Marilyn Monroe *(Pola)*, Lauren Bacall *(Schatze Page)*, David Wayne *(Freddie Denmark)*, Rory Calhoun *(Eben)*, Cameron Mitchell *(Tom Brookman)*, Alex D'Arcy *(J. Stewart Merrill)*, Fred Clark *(Waldo Brewster)*, William Powell *(J.D. Hanley)*, George Dunn *(Mike the Elevator Man)*, Harry Carter *(Elevator Operator)*, Robert Adler *(Cab Driver)*, Tudor Owen *(Mr. Otis)*, Percy Helton *(Benton)*, Maurice Marsac *(Antoine)*, Emmett Vogan *(Man at Bridge)*, Hermone Sterler *(Madame)*, Abney Mott *(Secretary)*, Rankin Mansfield *(Bennett)*, Ralph Reid *(Jewelry Salesman)*, Jan Arvan *(Tony)*, Ivis Goulding *(Maid)*, Dayton Lummis *(Justice)*, Van Des Autels *(Best Man)*, Eric Wilton *(Butler)*, Ivan Triesault *(Captain of Waiters)*, Herbert Deans *(Stewart)*, George Saurel *(Emir)*, Hope Landin *(Mrs. Salem)*, Tom Greenway *(Motorcycle Cop)*, Charlotte Austin, Merry Anders, Ruth Hall, Lida Thomas, Beryl McCutcheon *(Models)*, James Stone, Tom Martin *(Doormen)*, Eve Finnell *(Stewardess)*, Benny Burt *(Reporter)*, Richard Shackleton *(Bellboy)*.

After THE ROBE'S appearance as the first CinemaScope production and the great box office response to that Biblical epic, Fox decided to come back on the popular wide screen process with a modern comedy loaded with sex, chiefly Marilyn Monroe. The story isn't much, just three beautiful, dumb blondes trying to land millionaire husbands. All are models who put their money together to rent a posh penthouse in Manhattan, a swanky lair into which Monroe, Grable, and Bacall plan to lure their male victims. Grable is returning home with bags of groceries when Mitchell helps carry her burden. He meets Bacall and instantly falls for her but she spurns him after concluding that he's poor. In fact, Mitchell is a multimillionaire. Just when the money begins running out, Grable digs up oil tycoon Powell, who is attracted to Bacall. Then Grable agrees to take a trip to a Maine resort with wealthy but married Clark, but once there, comes down with the measles and accidentally meets forest ranger Calhoun, and they tumble for each other. Meanwhile, myopic Monroe is enroute to meet D'Arcy in Atlantic City but her eyesight is so poor (she refuses to wear glasses because she thinks they spoil her looks) that she gets on the wrong plane and winds up sitting next to wealthy Wayne, owner of her penthouse. He is on his way to find an elusive public accountant who has gotten him into trouble with the IRS. Wayne convinces Monroe that she is just as or more attractive when wearing her glasses (disproving the Dorothy Parker adage that "men seldom make passes at girls who wear glasses"). Bacall, almost broke, decides to marry Powell. Just before the wedding Grable shows up with Calhoun and Monroe with Wayne. Mitchell also appears and Powell steps aside for him, realizing that he is the man Bacall really loves. Mitchell and Bacall are reunited and the three couples retire to a diner where all three would-be golddiggers go into a dead faint when Mitchell pulls forth a huge wad of big bills to pay for the check, affirming that he is, indeed, the opulent object of their original goal, a bone fide millionaire. The dialog by veteran scriptwriter Johnson is spritely and humorous, and Negulesco's direction keeps the antics moving at a brisk pace. It's all frothy and fun. Contrary to gossipy predictions the two sex goddesses, Grable and Monroe, got along famously. This was Wayne's fourth and last film with Monroe. The CinemaScope process was well used here, with panoramic shots of Manhattan and Newman's entire orchestra performing his composition "Street Scene" in prolog and epilog shots. Remake of THE GREEKS HAD A WORD FOR IT.

p, Nunnally Johnson; d, Jean Negulesco; w, Johnson (based on the play *The Greeks Had a Word For It* by Zoe Akins and the play *Loco* by Dale Eunson, Katherine Albert); ph, Joe MacDonald (CinemaScope, Technicolor); ed, Louis Loeffler; md, Alfred Newman, Cyril Mockridge; art d, Lyle Wheeler, Leland Fuller.

Comedy **Cas.** **(PR:A MPAA:NR)**

HOW TO MURDER A RICH UNCLE½** (1957, Brit.) 79m COL bw

Nigel Patrick *(Henry)*, Charles Coburn *(Uncle George)*, Wendy Hiller *(Edith)*, Katie Johnson *(Alice)*, Anthony Newley *(Edward)*, Athene Seyler *(Grannie)*, Noel Hood *(Aunt Marjorie)*, Kenneth Fortescue *(Albert)*, Patricia Webster *(Constance)*, Michael Caine *(Gilrony)*, Trevor Reid *(Inspector Harris)*, Cyril Luckham *(Coroner)*, Johnson Bayly *(Radio Officer)*, Martin Boddey *(Police Sergeant)*, Kevin Stoney *(Bar Steward)*, Anthony Shaw *(Colonial Type)*, Ian Wilson *(Postman)*.

A funny satire of British aristocracy and their refusal to enter into honest labor even when poverty stricken. Nobleman Patrick is destitute and plans to kill his rich uncle from Canada, Coburn, to get his inheritance. His murder attempts backfire; his English family is accidentally picked off one by one as each meets the violent death meant for Coburn. Absent-minded Patrick is finally killed by his own trap when he walks back into Coburn's room, which he has rigged up with a shotgun. Coburn is arrested by the police for the murder of Patrick, but is saved when Patrick's elderly aunt, Johnson, steps forward and clears him. Patrick co-directed this film, as well as starring in it.

p, John Paxton; d, Nigel Patrick, Max Varnel (uncredited); w, Paxton (based on the play "Il Faut Tuer Julie," by Didier Daix); ph, Ted Moore (CinemaScope); m, Kenneth V. Jones; ed, Bert Rule.

Comedy **(PR:A MPAA:NR)**

HOW TO MURDER YOUR WIFE*½** (1965) 118m UA c

Jack Lemmon *(Stanley Ford)*, Virna Lisi *(Mrs. Ford)*, Terry-Thomas *(Charles)*, Eddie Mayehoff *(Harold Lampson)*, Claire Trevor *(Edna)*, Sidney Blackmer *(Judge Blackstone)*, Max Showalter *(Tobey Rawlins)*, Jack Albertson *(Dr. Bentley)*, Alan Hewitt *(District Attorney)*, Mary Wickes *(Harold's Secretary)*.

This slaphappy comedy stars Lemmon as a successful cartoonist who loathes the idea of marriage. His widely syndicated cartoon strip about secret agent "Bash Brannigan" has earned him a fortune and a lifestyle the envy of any devout bachelor. His slavishly devoted valet-butler-confidante, Terry-Thomas, makes sure that Lemmon's every wish and whim is fulfilled, down to the exact temperature of his morning shower. Lemmon indulges his imagination by enacting most of the adventures he later infuses into his character Brannigan and his antics about town earn him a likable reputation, especially among male chauvinists. Into Lemmon's well-organized life comes Italian blonde bombshell Lisi, as sexy and sensuous a woman to ever pop out of a stag party cake. In fact, that's when Lemmon sees and falls in love with her. He's drunk, she snakes out of the cake, and he winds up waking the next morning with Lisi beside him. She wears a wedding ring and he realizes to his horror that he's gotten married to someone he doesn't even know. He tries to get rid of her but she's stuck on him and, being an Italian Catholic, divorce is out of the question. His lawyer, goofy Mayehoff, and Mayehoff's manipulating wife, Trevor, tell Lemmon that he should stay married and avoid serious legal problems. He reluctantly settles down, puts valet Terry-Thomas in limbo, and gets bloated eating Lisi's enormous, fattening pasta dishes. His only escape from a clinging wife is his all-men's club where he bemoans his fate with fellow members. But even here, Lemmon is not safe; Lisi barges right into the club to check on him. The comic strip suffers, too, being changed to "The Brannigans," a tepid saga of married life that is resented by Lemmon's legion of action fans. They want "Bash" back and they want him single. To soothe his nagging fans and satisfy his own inner discontent, Lemmon goes through a mock murder of his wife, putting knock-out drops in her drink during a party. She at first goes into a hip-gyrating, sexy dance, giving all the males the come-hither, clawing at her voluptuous body and out-doing Salome until the drug finally knocks her off the top of a piano and onto Lemmon's waiting shoulder. He takes her to his room, plops her in bed, then uses a dummy of his wife as a body, carrying it through a skylight, across rooftops and finally disposing of it in a cement mixer at a construction site. Lemmon then sits down and draws a cartoon strip which outlines the murder of "Bash's" wife and goes to sleep. Lisi comes out of her stupor, sees the strip, and concludes that Lemmon really hates her. She slips into her spiked heels, dons her tight-fitting leather coat, and vanishes. After Lemmon's latest cartoon strip appears and news comes that his real-life wife has disappeared, it is generally concluded that he really did kill his wife, especially when witnesses come forth to say how they saw him carrying the body across rooftops and dumping it into the cement mixer. Lemmon's own quirkish habit of enacting the actions of his cartoon character now serves to indict him on a murder charge. He is put on trial with inept Mayehoff feebly trying to mount a defense. Lemmon thinks the whole thing ludicrous and turns the trial around by having his lawyer testify that if he could eliminate his wife by pressing a single button, he'd do it. So does the all male jury. Lemmon is freed to rousing cheers of the jury and male spectators who carry him from the courtroom on their shoulders, cheering, as female spectators grimace and fume. Lisi returns to settle matters but Lemmon discovers he really does love her and they sink into oodles of noodles and married bliss. This is a delightful frolic and Lemmon's comedic genius shines in every frame. Quine's direction is spontaneous and snappy as is Lemmon's delivery. Mayehoff and Trevor are wonderful as the woebegone couple, and Lisi is a feast for the eyes. Lisi presented great problems in that she could hardly speak any English and what she did utter was phonetically learned and confusing. Moreover, during the scene where she slowly emerges from a cake in a scant bikini, her Italian husband appeared, he being a burly construction company owner who had just flown over from Italy to see what his wife was doing. Upon seeing her gaped and whistled at during the stag party scene, he exploded, almost tearing the set apart. It took a half dozen strong men to keep him from spreading mayhem. Lemmon later walked into the wrong dressing room, Lisi's, and found her "stark naked, standing in front of a full-length mirror fussing with her makeup." Her husband was seated on a couch and no sooner had Lemmon begun to back-pedal out of the dressing room, mouthing apologies, than the husband leaped upward and lunged toward the actor. As he later described the scene in *Lemmon* by Don Widener: "I shot out the door and took off like a bird. I ran right off the lot, past the gate and up the street, and didn't stop or look back until I whipped in the back door of Nickodel's Restaurant . . . I don't know what he [the husband] thought, but I wasn't about to stick around to find out." In one of the many stunts Lemmon did on his own, a pipe on which he was swinging from one floor to the next on an outside fire escape broke and sent him hurling downward to almost certain death. He spied a pipe sticking from the building in his descent and he "threw out my arm and hooked it right at the elbow. It stopped my descent and I just swung there like a pendulum in a grandfather's clock." He then dropped safely to the ground while director Quine and crew took a few deep breaths. He had pulled muscles in his arm and shoulder and chest and the injury would bother the actor for a year after finishing the film.

p&w, George Axelrod; d, Richard Quine; ph, Harry Stradling (Technicolor); m, Neal Hefti; ed, David Wages; prod d, Richard Sylbert; set d, William Kiernan; cos, Moss Mabry; ch, Robert Sidney.

Comedy **(PR:A MPAA:NR)**

HOW TO SAVE A MARRIAGE—AND RUIN YOUR LIFE** (1968) 102m NobHill/COL c (AKA: BAND OF GOLD)

Dean Martin *(David Sloane)*, Stella Stevens *(Carol Corman)*, Eli Wallach *(Harry Hunter)*, Anne Jackson *(Muriel Laszlo)*, Betty Field *(Thelma)*, Jack Albertson *(Mr. Slotkin)*, Katharine Bard *(Mary Hunter)*, Woodrow Parfrey *(Eddie Rankin)*, Alan Oppenheimer *(Everett Bauer)*, Shelley Morrison *(Marcia Borie)*, George Furth *(Roger)*, Monroe Arnold *(Wally Hammond)*, Claude Stroud *(Hall Satler)*.

Martin stars in another fairly lame sex comedy that is neither very funny nor sexy. He plays an unmarried lawyer who takes it upon himself to save the marriage of his best friend, Wallach, by seducing Wallach's mistress and removing her from the picture. Unfortunately, Martin assumes that Wallach's secretary Stevens is the mistress (he's wrong), and he soon has her devoted to him and housed in a lush apartment. When Martin informs Wallach that he's stolen his mistress, Wallach panics, dumps his real mistress, next-door-neighbor Jackson, and tries to save his marriage. Meanwhile, the confused Stevens and Jackson finally figure out what's going on and demand that Martin and Wallach marry them. Martin agrees to marry Stevens, with the provision that she can back out if she feels things aren't working out. This never arises however, because after one night of marital bliss, Stevens decides it's to her liking.

p, Stanley Shapiro; d, Fielder Cook; w, Shapiro, Nate Monaster; ph, Lee Garmes (Panavision, Pathe Color); m, Michel Legrand; ed, Philip Anderson; prod d, Robert Clatworthy; set d, George R. Nelson; cos, Moss Mabry; spec eff, Geza Gaspar; makeup, Steve Lane, Hank Edds, Faye Chaney; m/l, "The Winds of Change," Legrand, Mack David, (sung by Ray Conniff Singers).

Comedy **(PR:A MPAA:NR)**

HOW TO SEDUCE A PLAYBOY* (1968, Aust./Fr./Ital.) 94m Intercontinental-Metheus/Chevron c (BEL AMI 2000 ODER: WIE VERFUHRT MAN EINEN PLAYBOY?; 100 RAGAZZE PER UN PLAYBOY)

Peter Alexander *(Peter Keller)*, Renato Salvatori *(Boy Schock)*, Antonella Lualdi *(Vera)*, Scilla Gabel *(Anita Biondo)*, Joachim Fuchsberger *(Sokker)*, Jocelyn Lane *(Ginette)*, Helga Anders *(Lucy)*, Linda Christian *(Lucy's Mother)*, Elaine d'Almeida *(Coco)*, Christiane Rucker *(Millie)*, Joachim Teege *(Emile)*, Georg Corten *(Director Zwerch)*, Otto Ambros *(Schladitz)*, Carla Calo, Mylene Demongeot, Bernard Blier, Isarco Ravaioli.

Alexander is chosen "playboy of the year" by an international men's magazine after a malfunctioning computer spits out his name. In order to avoid embarrassment, the publishers decide to take the ball and run with it (as they say), making Alexander into the playboy that he's not. They parade him all across Europe, arranging photo sessions with the world's most gorgeous women. Lualdi, an investigative reporter, uncovers the computer error and is about to go public with the news when Alexander becomes the subject of a famous actress' desires. Thinking he really is a playboy, she drops her story. An idea which could be funny but instead is about as exciting as watching paint dry.

p, Karl Spiehs; d, Michael Pfleghar; w, Pfleghar, Klaus Munro (based on a story by Anatol Bratt); ph, Ernst Wild (Eastmancolor); m, Heinz Kiessling; ed, Margot von Schlieffen; art d, Herta Hareiter.

Comedy **(PR:C MPAA:NR)**

HOW TO SEDUCE A WOMAN** (1974) 110m Forward/Cinerama c

Angus Duncan *(Luther Lucas)*, Angel Tompkins *(Pamela Balsam)*, Heidi Bruhl *(Dr. Winifred Sisters)*, Alexandra Hay *(Nell Brinkman)*, Jo Anne Meredith *(Melissa)*, Judith McConnell *(Ramona)*, Vito Scotti *(Bill)*, Marty Ingels *(Jim)*, Janice Carroll *(Estelle)*, Hope Holiday *(Mary)*, Lillian Randolph *(Matilda)*, Kay Peters *(Jane)*, Dita Cobb *(Fanny)*, James Bacon *(Himself)*, Jack Bailey *(Mr. Toklas)*, Fran Ryan *(Mrs. Toklas)*, Joe E. Ross *(Bartender)*, Joe Alfasa *(Guido)*, Jackie Brett *(Sally)*, Dave Barry *(Ticket Seller)*, Eve Brent *(Dr. Sisters' Sister)*, Herb Vigran *(1st Policeman)*, John Craig *(2nd Policeman)*, Billy Curtis *(Toulouse)*, Billy Frick *(Adolf Hitler)*, Jerry Mann *(Rental Agent)*, Marvin Miller *(Race Track Announcer)*, Ilona Wilson *(Girl at Party)*, Maurice Dallimore *(Butler)*, Eileen McDonough *(Little Girl)*, Angus Duncan Mackintosh *(Little Boy)*, Schoneberg *(Himself)*.

A stilted sex comedy starring Duncan as a masterful lover who manages to have women chase after him. In episodic fashion, Duncan beds five different women: McConnell, a bank teller; Meredith, a wealthy trend-setter; Hay, an art museum owner; Bruhl, a sexy psychiatrist; and Tompkins, a secretary determined to wait until her wedding night to lose her virginity (but once she meets Duncan, she changes her mind).

p,d&w, Charles Martin; ph, William H. Cronjager (Eastmancolor); m, Stu Phillips; ed, William A. Sawyer; art d, Jack Senter; ch, Yuri Smaltzoff.

Comedy **(PR:O MPAA:R)**

HOW TO STEAL A MILLION*½** (1966) 127m FOX c

Audrey Hepburn *(Nicole Bonnet)*, Peter O'Toole *(Simon Dermott)*, Eli Wallach *(David Leland)*, Hugh Griffith *(Charles Bonnet)*, Charles Boyer *(De Solnay)*, Fernand Gravey *(Grammont)*, Marcel Dalio *(Senor Paravideo)*, Jacques Marin *(Chief Guard)*, Moustache *(Guard)*, Roger Treville *(Auctioneer)*, Eddie Malin *(Insurance Clerk)*, Bert Bertram *(Marcel)*, Louise Chevalier *(Cleaning Woman in Museum)*, Remy Longa *(Young Man)*, Gil Delamare *(Stunt Double for Audrey Hepburn)*.

A stylish comedy-crime caper that's far too long, but filled with so much fun we can forgive it the extraneous length. Griffith is an old reprobate, the third in a generation of art forgers who have made fine livings by duping those snobs of the art world who seem to live to hear their own words. His scam is that he allows pseudo-experts to appraise the art and pronounce it real; that allows him to sell the forgeries for huge sums. He pulls out something his grandfather did, a phoney Cellini Venus, and gives it to a Paris museum to be exhibited. Hepburn knows that it will soon be recognized as a hoax, and that might put her father in jeopardy, so she enlists the aid of O'Toole to help steal the bogus statue from what is supposed to be an impregnable security system. Hepburn is engaged to American Wallach, an art collector, and she thinks that O'Toole is a burglar. The truth is that he is a detective whose specialty is recovering stolen *objets d'art*. O'Toole is amused and entranced by Hepburn, so he agrees to help her steal the Venus. In an elaborate sequence (of the sort seen many times before in TOPKAPI, RIFIFI, and countless other films), they get into the museum, nab the Venus, and then offer it to Wallach on the condition that he take the statue back to the US, tell no one about it, and that he forget about Hepburn. Wallach is such a nut about art that he reckons there are many pretty girls in the world but only one Cellini Venus, so he takes the statue and leaves Hepburn happily in O'Toole's arms as Griffith is already planning his next caper. A charming, literate script, lovely photography, and the Parisian backgrounds make this a superior piece of fluff. The original title was "How To Steal A Million Dollars And Live Happily Ever After" but they wisely shortened it for the marquees. Good work by several French actors including Boyer and Gravey, who had his name changed to Gravet when he came to America many years before, but changed it back to the original upon his return to France.

p, Fred Kohlmar; d, William Wyler; w, Harry Kurnitz (based on the story "Venus Rising" by George Bradshaw); ph, Charles Lang (Panavision, DeLuxe Color); m, Johnny Williams; ed, Robert Swink; prod d, Alexander Trauner; cos, Hubert de Givenchy; makeup, Alberto De Rossi, Freddie Williamson.

Crime/Comedy **Cas.** **(PR:A MPAA:NR)**

HOW TO STUFF A WILD BIKINI** (1965) 90m AIP c

Annette Funicello *(Dee Dee)*, Dwayne Hickman *(Ricky)*, Brian Donlevy *(B.D.)*, Harvey Lembeck *(Eric Von Zipper)*, Beverly Adams *(Cassandra)*, Jody McCrea *(Bonehead)*, John Ashley *(Johnny)*, Marianne Gaba *(Animal)*, Len Lesser *(North Dakota Pete)*, Irene Tsu *(Native Girl)*, Arthur Julian *(Dr. Melamed)*, Bobbi Shaw *(Khola Koku)*, Frankie Avalon *(Frankie)*, Buster Keaton *(Bwana)*, The Kingsmen *(Themselves)*, Alberta Nelson *(Puss)*, Andy Romano *(J.D.)*, John Macchia, Jerry Brutsche, Bob Harvey, Myrna Ross, Alan Fife *(Rat Pack)*, Alan Frohlich, Tom Quine, Hollis Morrison, Guy Hemric, George Boyce, Charles Reed *(Ad Men)*, Patti Chandler *(Patti)*, Mike Nader *(Mike)*, Luree Holmes, Jo Collins, Mary Hughes, Stephanie Nader, Jeannine White, Janice Levinson *(Beach Girls)*, Ed Garner, John Fain, Mickey Dora, Brian Wilson, Bruce Baker, Ned Wynn, Kerry Berry, Dick Jones, Ray Atkinson, Ronnie Dayton *(Beach Boys)*, Salli Sachse, Linda Bent *(Bookends)*, Marianne Gordon *(Chickie)*, Sheila Stephenson *(Secretary)*, Rosemary Williams *(English Girl)*, Sue Williams *(Peanuts)*, Tonia Van Deter *(Italian Girl)*, Uta Stone *(German Girl)*, Toni Harper *(Barberette)*, Michele Barton *(Manicurist)*, Victoria Carroll *(Shoe Shine Girl)*, Mickey Rooney *(Peachy Keane)*.

A really silly Frankie and Annette beach movie which sees Avalon serving in the Naval Reserve and shipped off to Tahiti where he frets over whether or not Funicello is being faithful to him. Desperate, he seeks out local witch doctor Keaton (in a sad and embarrassing cameo) who creates a flying bikini into which lovely redhead Adams is "stuffed." Adams then wanders over to Hickman and seduces him away from Funicello, with whom he'd been flirting. Lembeck returns as motorcycle gang leader Eric Von Zipper, along with the usual gang of Playmates, singers, and comedians. Brian Wilson of the famed singing group plays one of the beach boys. Among the girls are four *Playboy* Playmates, who look good—as may be expected—in a state of relative undress. The same can *not* be said for one-time Mouseketeer Funicello, who was totally covered, being pregnant at the time. Sequel: GHOST IN THE INVISIBLE BIKINI.

p, James H. Nicholson, Samuel Z. Arkoff; d, William Asher; w, Asher, Leo Townsend; ph, Floyd Crosby (Panavision, Pathe Color); m, Les Baxter; ed, Fred Feitshans, Eve Newman; art d, Howard Campbell; cos, Richard Bruno; ch, Jack Baker; m/l, Guy Hemric, Jerry Styner.

Musical/Comedy **Cas.** **(PR:A MPAA:NR)**

HOW TO SUCCEED IN BUSINESS WITHOUT REALLY TRYING**** (1967) 121m Mirisch/UA c

Robert Morse *(J. Pierpont Finch)*, Michele Lee *(Rosemary Pilkington)*, Rudy Vallee *(J. B. Biggley)*, Anthony Teague *(Bud Frump)*, Maureen Arthur *(Hedy LaRue)*, Murray Matheson *(Benjamin Ovington)*, Kay Reynolds *(Smitty)*, Sammy Smith *(Mr. Twimble/Wally Womper)*, John Myhers *(Bratt)*, Jeff DeBenning *(Gatch)*, Ruth Kobart *(Miss Jones)*, George Fenneman *(TV Announcer)*, Anne Seymour *(Mrs. Biggley)*, Erin O'Brien-Moore *(Mrs. Frump)*, Joey Faye *(Taxi Cab Driver)*, Helen Verbit *(Finch's Landlady)*, Virginia Sale *(Cleaning Woman)*, Al Nessor *(Newspaper Seller)*, Carol Worthington *(Miss Krumholtz)*, Janice Carroll *(Brenda)*, Lory Patrick *(Receptionist)*, Pat O'Moore, Wally Strauss *(Media Men)*, Ivan Volkman *(President of the U.S.)*, David Swift *(Elevator Operator)*, Carl Princi *(Voice of the Book)*, Dan Tobin *(Johnson)*, Robert Q. Lewis *(Tackaberry)*, John Holland *(Matthews)*, Paul Hartman *(Toynbee)*, Justin Smith *(Jenkins)*, Hy Averback *(2nd Executive)*, Bob Sweeney *(3d Executive)*, Paul Bradley *(TV Board Member)*, Tucker Smith *(Junior Executive)*, Sheila Rogers, Don Kroll.

The memorable and clever title of this movie is the only thing about it that is not true, because it's the story of a young man who works very hard indeed to sit atop the corporate ladder in a scathing musical satire. David Swift attempted to wear several hats with this film and, wonder of wonders, he brought it off. He produced, directed, adapted, and even played a small role in HOW TO SUCCEED and didn't fail at any of them. Based on Shepherd Mead's non-fiction comic taunt at business, which was later brought to the stage with the combined talents of Loesser and Burrows (they previously collaborated successfully on the quintessential American musical, GUYS AND DOLLS), who co-wrote the stage book with Gilbert and Weinstock. Morse is an elfin, yet aggressive, window washer who buys a copy of Mead's book on his way to work and decides to put its tenets to work immediately. He walks into the office of World Wide Wickets, a huge conglomerate, and talks Lee, a pretty secretary, into introducing him to the chief of personnel. Once inside, he convinces the man that he is a great pal of Vallee, who heads the company. That bit of trickery gets him as far as the mailroom. It isn't long before he finagles, cajoles, and charms his way into a junior executive position and endears himself to all the women in the company, but incurs the enmity of Teague, Vallee's insidious nephew. Soon after, Morse is made chief of an advertising department where more heads have rolled than in the French Revolution. Teague knows that Vallee absolutely despises TV giveaway shows, so he tells Morse the opposite, thinking that when Morse presents the idea to Vallee, he will be rewarded by a pink slip. But Morse is smarter than Teague and names Vallee's girl friend, the curvaceous and incredibly dumb Arthur, to be the Giveaway Girl. What else can Vallee do but accept? The new show intends to bestow many shares of the company on anyone who can figure out the clue of a huge World Wide Wicket Treasure Hunt, but everything goes awry when Arthur mistakenly tells the TV audience that the shares are hidden in the company's offices. Thousands of greedy TV viewers descend on the building and wreck it as they forage for the stock certificates. Then Vallee's boss, chairman of the board Smith, comes in, and Morse is forced to confess that he doesn't know anything about anything and that he is but a window washer who has parlayed himself into the top ad job. But luck remains with Morse when Smith says that he started in the business as a window washer, too, and that Morse should be proud. And with that, Smith announces that he is going to retire and names Morse as chairman of the board, thus vaulting him over Vallee. Now at the apex of business, Morse can finally admit to Lee that he loves her and she responds that she would love him whatever he did and it doesn't make a bit of difference if he were a mail boy or the President of the United States. In the final scene, Morse is found washing the White House windows. Swift elected to shoot the film in a semi-cartoon, semi-realistic fashion and it worked well, as the characters were bold strokes of caricature, rather than any attempt at mirroring actual people. It's good fun from start to finish and Moreda's choreography keeps the original Fosse feel while widening it for the Panavision screen. Several of the Broadway tunes were cut from the film score, including "Cinderella Darling," "Happy To Keep His Dinner Warm," "Love From A Heart Of Gold," and the "Pirate Ballet," but there were more than enough songs to keep the ear satisfied, such as "I Believe In You" (sung by Morse himself as he looks in the men's room mirror), "The Company Way," "Coffee Break," "The Brotherhood of Man," "A Secretary is Not a Toy," "Grand Old Ivy," "Been a Long Day," "Rosemary," "Finch's Frolic," "Gotta Stop That Man," and the title song. The play won the Pulitzer Prize, but the movie failed to garner any awards from the movie people, the more fools they. Film director and sometime-actor Hy Averback is briefly seen, as is TV producer Bob Sweeney, but most acting kudos must be given to Morse, in a role that must have been written for him, and Lee, a refreshing and attractive actress who went on to great national fame on TV after her divorce from actor James Farentino. Veteran TV panelist Robert Q. Lewis plays a small role as an executive and proves to be a much better actor than anyone realized. Myhers does his usual hammy job, but it isn't out of place here. Producer-director-writer-actor Swift was the man responsible for one of television's most beloved early shows, "Mr. Peepers," and he should be working more.

p,d&w, David Swift (based on the musical book by Abe Burrows, Willie Gilbert, Jack Weinstock, from the book by Shepherd Mead); ph, Burnett Guffey (Panavision, DeLuxe Color); m, Nelson Riddle; ed, Ralph E. Winters, Allan Jacobs; art d, Robert Boyle; set d, Edward G. Boyle; cos, Micheline; ch, Dale Moreda (based on original staging by Bob Fosse); m/l, Frank Loesser; makeup, Robert Schiffer.

Musical/Comedy **(PR:A MPAA:NR)**

HOW WILLINGLY YOU SING½** (1975, Aus.) 90m Inch/Melbourne Cinema Co-op c

Garry Patterson *(Simon Dore)*, Isaac Gerson *(The Astrologer)*, Jim Robertson *(The Cop)*, Jerry Powderly *(The Psychiatrist)*, Morris Gradman *(The Wandering Jew)*, Braham Glass *(The Mother)*, Allan Levy *(The Revolutionary)*.

Obscure but intriguing allegorical feature has Patterson a young man plagued by troubling dreams. Psychiatrist Powderly offers various remedies, but none do the trick. In desperation, he consults an astrologer who teaches him the first half of a chant that can save the world, but only if he can find the Wandering Jew who knows the second half. Shot on a miniscule budget, the film has a thoroughly professional look that belies its underground origins. Not likely to turn up, but worth checking out if it does.

p,d&w, Garry Patterson; ph, Peter Tammer; md, Robert Patterson.

Fantasy **(PR:A-C MPAA:NR)**

HOWARD CASE, THE*½ (1936, Brit.) 62m Sovereign/UNIV bw

Jack Livesey *(Jerry)*, Olive Melville *(Pat)*, Arthur Seaton *(Howard/Phillips)*, Olive Sloane *(Lena Maxwell)*, David Keir *(Barnes)*, Jack Vyvyan *(Sgt. Halliday)*, Ernest Borrand, Vincent Sternroyd, Gladys Mason, Renaud Lockwood.

Seaton, a dishonest lawyer, turns on his partner, Livesey, and embezzles company funds to buy gold shares. He goes into hiding by killing his near-twin, a sanatarium patient, and taking his place. The fugitive life proves to be too much for Seaton and his true identity is revealed, driving him to suicide. The emotions are as distanced and cold as the clinical title implies, avoiding, like most programmers, any sense of drama.

p, Fraser Foulsham; d, Frank Richardson; w, H.F. Maltby (based on the play "Fraud" by Maltby).

Crime **(PR:A MPAA:NR)**

HOWARDS OF VIRGINIA, THE*** (1940) 116m COL bw (GB: TREE OF LIBERTY)

Cary Grant *(Matt Howard)*, Martha Scott *(Jane Peyton Howard)*, Sir Cedric Hardwicke *(Fleetwood Peyton)*, Alan Marshal *(Roger Peyton)*, Richard Carlson *(Thomas Jefferson)*, Paul Kelly *(Captain Jabez Allen)*, Irving Bacon *(Tom Norton)*, Elisabeth Risdon *(Aunt Clarissa)*, Anne Revere *(Mrs. Betsy Norton)*, Tom Drake *(James Howard at Age 16)*, Phil Taylor *(Peyton Howard at Age 18)*, Rita Quigley *(Mary Howard at Age 17)*, Libby Taylor *(Dicey)*, Richard Gaines *(Patrick Henry)*, George Houston *(George Washington)*, Sam McDaniel *(Uncle Robert, the Butler)*, Virginia Sale *(Neighbor)*, Ralph Byrd *(James Howard)*, Dickie Jones *(Matt Howard at Age 12)*, Buster Phelps *(Thomas Jefferson at Age 11)*, Wade Boteler *(Uncle Reuben)*, Mary Field *(Susan Howard)*, R. Wells Gordon *(Colonel Jefferson)*, Charles Francis *(Mr. Douglas)*, Olaf Hytten *(Gentleman)*, Emmett Vogan *(Representative)*, J. Anthony Hughes *(Tidewater Representative)*, Lane Chandler *(Major)*, Brandon Hurst *(Wilton)*, Alan Ladd *(Neighbor)*, Pat Somerset, James Westerfield *(Friends)*.

A good Colonial period drama that failed to catch fire at the box office, THE HOWARDS OF VIRGINIA uses just a portion of Elizabeth Page's gigantic novel *The Tree Of Liberty*, because to have shot the entire book might have made for a six-hour film. Lensed at John D. Rockefeller, Jr.'s recreation of Williamsburg, THE HOWARDS OF VIRGINIA is physically authentic in every way, but it was ill-timed for release, as it took shots at the British who were, in 1940, suffering at the hands of the Nazis. Carlson is Jefferson, who helps Grant get surveying employment with wealthy Hardwicke. Grant meets Hardwicke's daughter, Scott; they fall in love and marry, then return to Grant's home area. Years pass, and Grant enters Colonial politics. When the revolution occurs, Grant sides with the rebels over Scott's disagreement. His two sons join him in the hostilities, and one of them is hurt as the war ends. He returns to Virginia to take up a peaceful life once more with Scott. The family is seen against the background of the Boston Tea Party, Valley Forge, and all of the other famous incidents of the War Of Independence. A lot of money was spent recreating the skirmishes, but much of what we saw on screen had already been drummed into our heads in various classes, and the inclusion of a fictional family was not enough to take this out of the realm of being one huge history lesson. If you don't feel like sitting down and reading a large tome, this is just as good a way as any to acquire a thumbnail sketch of the way it was before these States became United.

p&d, Frank Lloyd; w, Sidney Buchman (based on Elizabeth Page's novel *The Tree Of Liberty*); ph, Bert Glennon; m, Richard Hageman; ed, Paul Weatherwax; art d, John Goodman; set d, Howard Bristol; cos, Irene Saltern (for Scott); spec eff, Slavko Vorkapich; tech adv, Waldo Twitchell.

Historical Drama **(PR:A MPAA:NR)**

HOWLING, THE*½** (1981) 91m AE c

Dee Wallace *(Karen White)*, Patrick Macnee *(Dr. George Waggner)*, Dennis Dugan *(Chris)*, Christopher Stone *(R. William "Bill" Neill)*, Belinda Balaski *(Terry Fisher)*, Kevin McCarthy *(Fred Francis)*, John Carradine *(Erle Kenton)*, Slim Pickens *(Sam Newfield)*, Elisabeth Brooks *(Marsha)*, Robert Picardo *(Eddie)*, Dick Miller *(Walter Paisley)*, Margie Impert *(Donna)*, Noble Willingham, James Murtaugh, Jim McKrell, Kenneth Tobey, Don McLeod, Steve Nevil, Herb Braha, Joe Bratcher, Roger Corman.

A wonderful combination of horror, laughs and state-of-the-art special effects from director and Roger Corman alumnus Joe Dante (PIRANHA, GREMLINS, EXPLORERS), screenwriter (now screenwriter/director) John Sayles (PIRANHA, RETURN OF THE SECAUCUS SEVEN, BROTHER FROM ANOTHER PLANET) and makeup artist Rob Bottin. Wallace plays a TV anchorwoman who, after being severely traumatized while investigating a story, decides to venture to Macnee's ultra-exclusive California transcendental meditation spa accompanied by her husband Stone. Unfortunately, the members of the Macnee's cult are all werewolves. The transformation scenes are incredible—the highlight being when sexy siren Brooks seduces Stone and they make love under the moonlight while turning into werewolves. Dante fills the film with hysterical cameos from Corman, Miller, McCarthy, Carradine, and Pickens, and demonstrates a subtle wit and a flair for horror much more sophisticated than anything John Landis came up with in his subsequent AMERICAN WEREWOLF IN LONDON. A must-see for horror fans, with more than one viewing recommended.

p, Michael Finnell, Jack Conrad; d, Joe Dante; w, John Sayles, Terence H. Winkless (based on the novel by Gary Brandner); ph, John Hora (CFI color); m, Pino Donaggio; ed, Mark Goldblatt, Joe Dante; art d, Robert A. Burns; set d, Steve Legler; spec eff, Roger George; makeup eff, Rob Bottin.

Horror/Comedy **Cas.** **(PR:O MPAA:R)**

HOW'S ABOUT IT?** (1943) 60m UNIV bw

Robert Paige *(George Selby)*, Grace McDonald *(Marion Bliss)*, Shemp Howard *(Alf)*, Walter Catlett *(Whipple)*, Buddy Rich *(Orchestra Leader)*, David Bruce *(Oliver)*, Mary Wickes *(Mike Tracy)*, Bobby Scheerer *(Bobby)*, Dorothy Babb *(Waitress)*, The Andrews Sisters, Guss Glassmire, Louis Da Pron.

The Andrews Sisters star as a trio of elevator operators who are employed in an office building which houses a music publishing business. By working in the building the girls hope to garner some attention and get their big break. Also hoping to make it big is songwriter Paige, who finds himself slapped with a plagiarism charge by the lovely McDonald. Seeking to extricate himself from these legal hassles, Paige hires McDonald to a staff job in his firm and eventually romances her over to his side. Meanwhile, the singing Andrews Sisters are finally discovered (after belting out a few tunes) and everybody's happy. Songs include: "Don't Mind The Rain" (Ned Miller, Chester Cohn), "Take It And Git" (William and Melville Chapman), "East Of The Rockies" (Sid Robin), "Going Up" (Irving Gordon, Allen Roth), "Here Comes The Navy" (Lew Brown, W.A. Timm, J. Vejvoda, Clarence P. Oakes).

p, Ken Goldsmith; d, Erle C. Kenton; w, Mel Ronson, John Grey (based on a story by Jack Goodman, Albert Rice); ph, Woody Bredell; m, Vic Schoen; ed, Charles Maynard; art d, John Goodman; ch, Louis DaPron.

Musical **(PR:A MPAA:NR)**

HOW'S CHANCES (SEE: DIPLOMATIC LOVER, THE, 1934, Brit.)

HOWZER** (1973) 82m URI c

Peter Desiante *(Howard "Howzer" Carsell)*, Melissa Stocking *(Debora)*, Royal Dano *(Nick Murack)*, William Gray *(Albert Murack)*, Virgil Frye *(Joe Day)*, Olive Deering *(Mary Carver)*, Edmund Gilbert *(Edward Carsell)*, Allyn Ann McLerie *(Faye Carsell)*, Elaine Partnow, Wonderful Smith, Steven Vaughan, David Dean, Ed Van Nordic.

A pair of middle-class youngsters—12-year-old Desiante and his 14-year-old friend Stocking—run away from home with Los Angeles as their destination. Along the way they meet hunter Dano and his retarded son Gray, and later are befriended by a pot-smoking hippie couple who run a tavern. The first portion of the picture has a certain innocent quality which is soon reduced to a nauseating, dated collection of rites-of-passage situations. Given the cliches of the script, newcomers Desiante and Stocking perform well under the rookie directing hand of former American Film Institute student Laurence.

p, Philip Clarke Kaufman; d&w, Ken Laurence; ph, Bruce Logan (DeLuxe Color); m, Stephen Scull; ed, Logan.

Drama **(PR:A MPAA:NR)**

HUCKLEBERRY FINN*** (1931) 79m PAR bw

Jackie Coogan *(Tom Sawyer)*, Mitzi Green *(Becky Thatcher)*, James Durkin *(Huckleberry Finn)*, Jackie Searl *(Sid Sawyer)*, Clarence Muse *(Jim)*, Clara Blandick *(Aunt Polly)*, Jane Darwell *(Widow Douglas)*, Eugene Pallette *(Junior)*, Oscar Apfel *(Senior)*, Warner Richmond *(Finn)*, Charlotte V. Henry *(Mary Jane)*, Doris Short, Lillian Harmer, Cecil Weston, Guy Oliver, Aileen Manning, Frank McClynn.

Mark Twain must have lived many of the incidents in his Missouri books, as they smack of so much authenticity it is difficult to believe that he dreamed them up. HUCKLEBERRY FINN has been made countless times and ripped off even more, the latest incarnation being the Broadway musical "Big River," which took all the 1985 Tony Awards, mainly because there was no competition. Even though Coogan is top-lined, it is Durkin who steals the show as the lovable Finn in this sequel to TOM SAWYER, which came out shortly before it. In that film Coogan, Durkin, Searl and Green were co-starred. Here Green and Searl are seen just briefly in the first reel or so, then gone to allow the remainder of the story to progress. Blandick and Darwell take the youth under their wings in the hopes of civilizing him but he rebels. His father, Richmond, arrives and wants some of the money that Durkin had in his name. Durkin flees rather than face the wrath of his 'pap' and goes down the river with Muse, an escaped slave. They run into river rats Pallette and Apfel, and have them climb aboard. Later, both men attempt to pull off a con that doesn't work. When Durkin turns up missing, Muse is accused of having done the boy in, but Durkin later races back to save Muse from a lynching and finally agrees to allow Blandick and Darwell to raise him properly. A good version of the Twain classic but not as effective as the one MGM did eight years later, in which Blandick reprised her role as Aunt Polly. Charlotte Henry was delightful as Mary Jane and it was this performance that probably got her the title role two years hence in Paramount's all-star version of ALICE IN WONDERLAND.

d, Norman Taurog; w, Grover Jones, William Slavens McNutt (based on the novel by Mark Twain); ph, David Abel.

Comedy/Drama **(PR:AAA MPAA:NR)**

HUCKLEBERRY FINN*½** (1939) 88m MGM bw
(AKA: THE ADVENTURES OF HUCKLEBERRY FINN)

Mickey Rooney *(Huckleberry Finn)*, Walter Connolly *(The "King")*, William Frawley *(The "Duke")*, Rex Ingram *(Jim)*, Lynn Carver *(Mary Jane)*, Jo Ann Sayers *(Susan)*, Minor Watson *(Capt. Brandy)*, Elizabeth Risdon *(Widow Douglass)*, Victor Kilian *("Pap" Finn)*, Clara Blandick *(Miss Watson)*.

The second of four (so far) versions of *The Adventures Of Huckleberry Finn* by Mark Twain, this is the best to date. The story is the same one America grew up on but the team of Thorpe, Mankiewicz and Butler managed to infuse more fun into this remake than all the others combined. With Rooney as the irrepressible Huck, the fast-moving story grabs the audience at the start and never ceases to amuse. This time Risdon and Blandick (in the same role she did eight years earlier in the Paramount version) are properly prissy in their determination to raise Rooney to become a gentleman. It was in TOM SAWYER that Huck became a wealthy young man and when his father, the drunken Kilian, enters, Rooney wants no part of the man and flees on a river raft with Ingram, a slave who is running away from the authorities. Poling down the Ol' Miss, Rooney and Ingram encounter Frawley and Connolly, a pair of con artists who live from hand to mouth but still refer to themselves as the "King" and the "Duke." Rooney gets bitten by a rattler and must take a while to recover. It's then that Ingram is captured, and when he won't tell Rooney's whereabouts, he is scheduled to be hung for the boy's murder. All ends well as Rooney gets back to town in time to save Ingram's life, then turns himself over to Blandick and Risdon in order to go back to school, get dressed in (gasp) shoes, and make a Missouri mensch of himself. None of the Sawyer characters appear in this version, as MGM had nothing to do with the TOM SAWYER film and felt it was foolish to attempt to totally duplicate the Paramount picture of 1931.

p, Joseph L. Mankiewicz; d, Richard Thorpe; w, Hugo Butler (based on the novel by Mark Twain); ph, John Seitz; m, Franz Waxman; ed, Frank E. Hull.

Comedy/Drama **(PR:AAA MPAA:NR)**

HUCKLEBERRY FINN (1960) (SEE: ADVENTURES OF HUCKLEBERRY FINN, THE, 1960)

HUCKLEBERRY FINN*½ (1974) 117m UA c

Jeff East *(Huckleberry Finn)*, Paul Winfield *(Jim)*, Harvey Korman *(King)*, David Wayne *(Duke)*, Arthur O'Connell *(Col. Grangerford)*, Gary Merrill *(Pap)*, Natalie Trundy *(Mrs. Loftus)*, Lucille Benson *(Widder Douglas)*, Kim O'Brien *(Maryjane)*, Jean Fay *(Susan)*, Ruby Leftwich *(Miss Watson)*, Odessa Cleveland *(Jim's Wife)*, Joe Boris *(Jason)*, Danny Lantrip *(Kyle)*, Van Bennett *(Wayne)*, Linda Watkins *(Mrs. Grangerford)*, Jean Combs *(Miss Emmeline)*, Frances Fawcett *(Miss Charlotte)*, Suzanne Prystup *(Miss Maryanne)*, H.L. Rowley *(Horatio)*, Doris Owens *(Marybelle)*, Frank Mills *(Buck)*, Sherree Sinquefield *(Miss Sophia)*, Morris Denton *(Boat Captain)*, Hoskins Deterly *(Lot)*, Elliott Trimble *(Uncle Harvey)*, Forrest Colebank *(Abner)*, Charles C. Burns *(Sheriff)*, Orville Meyer *(Tomkins)*, R. Norwood Smith, Jack Millstein, Larry Forney, Albert Schilling, Clayton Starling, Rex Commack, George Prescott, Mrs. James Torrey, Rose Pansano, John Schwartzman, Gray Montgomery, Pat O'Connor, Sam Blackmon, Ron Wright, Louis Wentworth III, Andrew Knight, Ken Wannberg.

After the success of *The Readers Digest* and Arthur P. Jacobs musical adaptation of Mark Twain's *Tom Sawyer* the same group decided to do a film just like it. They adapted *Huckleberry Finn*. The results are terrible, and give family entertainment a bad name. None of the mood or atmosphere from the Mark Twain story comes through, and the songs written by screen writers Richard and Robert Sherman are very forgettable. The story is the classic one of an orphaned boy, East, who takes off with a runaway slave, Winfield, and rides down the Mississippi River on a raft. He gets mixed up with a couple of confidence men, Korman and Wayne, who pose as European royalty. A poor effort all around. The songs include: "Freedom," "Huckleberry Finn," "Someday Honey Darlin," "Cairo, Illinois," "Rose in a Bible," "Royal Nonesuch," "What's Right, What's Wrong," "Rotten Luck" (Richard M. and Robert B. Sherman).

p, Arthur P. Jacobs; d, J. Lee Thompson; w, Robert B. Sherman, Richard M. Sherman (based on the novel by Mark Twain); ph, Laszlo Kovacs (Panavision, DeLuxe Color); ed, Michael Anderson; prod d, Philip Jeffries; md, Fred Werner; set d, Robert De Vestel; cos, Donfeld; ch, Marc Breaux.

Musical **Cas.** **(PR:AAA MPAA:G)**

HUCKSTERS, THE**** (1947) 115m MGM bw

Clark Gable *(Victor Albee Norman)*, Deborah Kerr *(Kay Dorrance)*, Sydney Greenstreet *(Evan Llewellyn Evans)*, Adolphe Menjou *(Mr. Kimberly)*, Ava Gardner *(Jean Ogilvie)*, Keenan Wynn *(Buddy Hare)*, Edward Arnold *(Dave Lash)*, Aubrey Mather *(Valet)*, Richard Gaines *(Cooke)*, Frank Albertson *(Max Herman)*, Clinton Sundberg *(Michael Michaelson)*, Douglas Fowley *(Georgie Gaver)*, Gloria Holden *(Mrs. Kimberly)*, Connie Gilchrist *(Betty)*, Kathryn Card *(Regina Kennedy)*, Lillian Bronson *(Miss Hammer)*, Vera Marshe *(Secretary)*, Ralph Bunker *(Allison)*, Virginia Dale *(Kimberly Receptionist)*, Jimmy Conlin *(Blake)*, George O'Hanlon *(Freddie Callahan)*, Ransom Sherman *(George Rockton)*, Tom Stevenson *(Paul Evans)*, John Hiestand *(Radio Announcer)*, Robert Emmett O'Connor *(Doorman)*, Marie Windsor *(Girl)*, Richard Abbott *(Elevator Starter)*, Anne Nagel *(Teletypist)*, Joan Valerie *(Receptionist)*, Almeda Fowler *(Woman in Elevator)*, Byron Morgan *(Radio Soundman)*, Tiny Jones *(Flower Woman)*, Sammy McKim *(Western Union Messenger)*, Chief Yowlachie *(Indian)*, Edwin Cooper *(Harry Spooner)*, Harry V. Cheshire *(Joe Lorrison)*, Billy Benedict *(Bellboy)*, Mahlon Hamilton *(Businessman)*.

Madison Avenue ad agencies, radio commercials, and bigshot businessmen all got a lashing in this superb drama where Gable is the leading "huckster" and Greenstreet the most tyrannical business mogul in screen history. The world's been at war for five years and Gable with it; by the time he rejoins society, the former radio advertising executive witnesses a whole new breed of "hucksters," and new methods bred at the bottom of the barrel. He takes a position with a top ad agency headed by Menjou, a suave lickspittle to any clients with money, the chief employer being tyrant Greenstreet, owner of a firm making Beautee Soap. Greenstreet has been mercilessly hammering at Menjou to get his product in the limelight. Menjou gives Gable the assignment of rounding up 25 society women to endorse Beautee Soap as part of an advertising campaign. He first visits Kerr, daughter of an English noblewoman and an American general killed in the war. They fall in love and she signs on the dotted line. Then Gable invites her to spend a weekend at a resort but when he arrives at the place, one of his favorite retreats before the war, he finds it has gone to pot and the separate rooms he's asked for are interconnecting. When Kerr arrives she believes she's been lured to an assignation and departs, not wishing to see a man she now thinks of as a bounder. Gable and Menjou are next brought before the impossible Greenstreet who holds a board meeting surrounded by toadies. He gathers up a great strand of spittle and hawks this repulsive deposit down upon the board room table, saying as he wipes it away with his handkerchief: "You've just seen me do a disgusting thing, but it got your attention!" He believes he's made his point. He wants his product to get attention and he doesn't care how Menjou and Gable do it. He tells them that he has heard what he believes to be a splendid radio comedian, Wynn, and he wants Gable to sign him to a contract as talent to be aired on a Beautee Soap radio program. Gable learns that Wynn's agent, Arnold, is taking the train to California and he books a room on the same train, meeting old friend Gardner, a singer on her way to Hollywood. He uses her in a scheme to get Arnold to sign over Wynn's contract to him and, once in Hollywood, enlists writers Fowley and Albertson to provide some comic material for a demonstration record which also contains a few songs by thrush Gardner. He later goes to Arnold who has brought in lawyers to undo the new contract after learning that he has sold Wynn's talents for a pittance when he could have gotten a fortune for his services had he known Greenstreet was going to star him on a radio program. Gable asks that they settle the matter without attorneys and Arnold asks his legal aides to step out of his office. Then Gable practically blackmails Arnold by telling him that his image as a sponsor of youth clubs across the nation could be severely damaged if news got out that Arnold, as a youth, was convicted of theft. He tells him he knows that Arnold has been the soul of virtue since then but that that one black mark, were it known, would destroy Arnold's public image of benefactor. Arnold capitulates and tells him to keep Wynn. At that moment Gable realizes how low he has gotten and apologizes to Arnold, telling him the deal is off. No, Arnold tells him, ending their long friendship, it's on, but Gable is never to contact him again. Gable has an evening date with Gardner who cooks a home-made meal for him but he's unresponsive to her; he has Kerr on his mind and Kerr later appears, having flown from New York just to tell him that she loves him. After finishing his assignment in California, Gable returns East with his demo record which Greenstreet plays. After toying with Menjou and Gable at another board meeting of yea-sayers, he tells Gable the demo record is great and that he's done a wonderful job for Beautee Soap. Gable's response is to tell Greenstreet off, then dump a pitcher of water over his head, adding: "You're all wet!" Gable has had enough of dirty deals. He walks out, leaving a stunned Menjou and an enraged Greenstreet, now thoroughly unemployed. He joins Kerr to tell her that he is out of the advertising business and he must start all over in a new business, from the bottom. She reassures him that it's all right, that they will be together. Gable at first was not interested in doing this film but MGM toned down the hard-hitting best-seller by Wakeman and softened Gable's character to the point where he maintained some scruples at the finish. He approved of both his leading ladies and was particularly fond of Gardner who had facetiously said when first arriving in Hollywood that she intended to marry "the king," meaning Gable. But he was then married to Carole Lombard and she married Mickey Rooney instead, he being the number one box office star of the Andy Hardy series. Both Gable and Gardner palled around together off camera during production. Kerr kept her distance. She had been in films for about six years but this was her first American film and she was feeling her way slowly through Hollywood society. Although she was effective in her role, few thought she would ever reach the superstar status that would come with later films like FROM HERE TO ETERNITY. MGM mogul Louis B. Mayer was convinced Kerr would make it to the top and it was he who suggested a line the studio used in its advertisements for THE HUCKSTERS when listing her name: "Deborah Kerr (rhymes with 'star')." Greenstreet is positively malignant in his role of the perverse soap manufacturer, a part reportedly based on a real-life tobacco tycoon.

p, Arthur Hornblow, Jr.; d, Jack Conway; w, Luther Davis, Edward Chodorov, George Wells (based on the novel by Frederic Wakeman); ph, Harold Rosson; m, Lennie Hayton; ed, Frank Sullivan; art d, Cedric Gibbons, Urie McCleary; set d, Edwin B. Willis, Jack D. Moore; spec eff, Warren Newcombe, A. Arnold Gillespie; m/l, "Don't Tell Me," Buddy Pepper.

Drama **(PR:A MPAA:NR)**

HUD½** (1963) 112m PAR bw

Paul Newman *(Hud Bannon)*, Melvyn Douglas *(Homer Bannon)*, Patricia Neal *(Alma Brown)*, Brandon de Wilde *(Lon Bannon)*, Whit Bissell *(Burris)*, John Ashley *(Hermy)*, Crahan Denton *(Jesse)*, Val Avery *(Jose)*, Sheldon Allman *(Thompson)*, Pitt Herbert *(Larker)*, Peter Brooks *(George)*, Curt Conway *(Truman Peters)*, Yvette Vickers *(Lily Peters)*, George Petrie *(Joe Scanton)*, David Kent *(Donald)*, Frank Killmond *(Dumb Billy)*, N. Candido *(Patron)*, Monty Montana, John Indrisano, John M. Quijada *(Cowboys)*, Sy Prescott *(Man Greased in Pig Sequence)*, Carl Saxe *(Proprietor)*, Robert Hinkle *(Announcer)*, Sharyn Hillyer *(Myra)*.

Newman is awesome as the title character, as rotten a human being as can be found anywhere, especially in Texas. In a downbeat, even dismal story, Newman is an insensitive, crude, amoral, disrespectful, avaricious, disloyal, irresponsible, sexually arrogant poacher of human rights. He's just no good. His father is at the other end of the stick—a moral, decent human being who has long ago rejected Newman, written him off. In between is de Wilde, innocent and full of hero worship for Newman, charmed by his animal magnetism as is tired out hired housekeeper Neal. Newman does as little as possible around the ranch his father owns, ignoring the proud past and concerned only with having a good old time. He takes de Wilde to a small dinner to guzzle beer and comes to his rescue when the boy is upbraided by another good old boy for staring too long at his woman. Drunk, Newman later returns home to make a racket and wake up the old man. Douglas tells him to go to bed but Newman rants against his father, accusing him of not loving him and creating an unloving man. The crybaby act only causes Douglas to sneer and return to bed. Later the drunken Newman enters Neal's small cabin and forces himself on her, shown in a wild rape attempt scene as he tears at her clothes, debasing her, the camera lingering luridly, almost perversely on the drawn-out scene of huffing struggle, with extreme closeups that go blurry in covering the action. Then there is trouble with the cattle, Douglas' herd, including his prized longhorns, coming down with the dreaded hoof-and-mouth disease. Naturally, Newman sees money being lost and immediately proposes selling off the cattle quickly before the news spreads. Noble, right-minded Douglas refuses and does the moral thing, ordering the entire herd destroyed. A huge pit is bulldozed, the herd driven down into it, and then many rifle-aiming cowboys let loose with a murderous fusillade, killing off the entire lot in a slaughter that is relentlessly disturbing, traumatic for anyone with delicate stomachs. "It don't take long to kill things," laments Douglas. "Not like it does to grow." Douglas later shoots his own prized longhorns and then rides across his deserted range, suffering a heart attack and dying. Neal, who was originally attracted to Newman, is now thoroughly disgusted by his brutal, inhuman conduct. She packs her meager belongings and leaves. De Wilde now sees Newman for what he is—a swaggering, despicable creature and he tells him so, then leaves. None of it means anything to Newman. He opens a can of beer then slams the door. End. There is no redeeming virtue to Newman here, his character best summed up by Douglas: "You're an immoral man, Hud. You don't give a damn." The film is considered to be a modern "realistic" western and is often linked with such films as LONELY ARE THE BRAVE, THE MISFITS, THE LUSTY MEN, and JUNIOR BONNER, stressing, as did these films, a passing of the Old West and all of its practiced or imagined ideals. In its place came the Huds who not only ignored the Code of the West but refused to have any kind of code at all. The viewer can have no empathy for this wretch, only contempt, and that is most of the fascination with the film itself by its makers who, in keeping with a superficial pseudo-intellectual cynicism popular in the groping 1960s, dwelled upon villains, not the devout western heroes of the 1930s and 1940s, giving vent to the unimaginative spleen instead of the inspired heart. Of course, this was and is Ritt's viewpoint in most of his films, a rather jaded, limp perspective of humanity, an attitude somewhat similar to making the cretinous Mexican bandit Alfonso Bedoya the hero of THE TREASURE OF THE SIERRA MADRE. Great plaudits were given this film when it first appeared because of its radical departure from traditional westerns and Newman's frightening turnabout as a bad guy, albeit his incredible performance is the best thing about this wholly brutal film (not for youngsters), a brutality not ameliorated by Douglas' presence or de Wilde's innocuous gullibility which can easily be considered a sop to the vicious portrayal of humanity. The film received seven Oscar nominations and won three—Douglas as Best Supporting Actor, Neal as Best Actress, and Howe as Best Cinematographer. Ritt and Newman got nominations but failed to pick up statuettes; even an admiring Academy could not bring itself to give Oscars to the two men most responsible for this cruel film.

p, Martin Ritt, Irving Ravetch; d, Ritt; w, Ravetch, Harriet Frank, Jr. (based on the novel *Horseman, Pass By* by Larry McMurtry); ph, James Wong Howe; m, Elmer Bernstein; ed, Frank Bracht; art d, Hal Pereira, Tambi Larsen; set d, Sam Comer, Robert Benton; cos, Edith Head; spec eff, Paul K. Lerpae; makeup, Wally Westmore.

Drama **Cas.** **(PR:O MPAA:NR)**

HUDDLE*½ (1932) 103m MGM bw (GB: IMPOSSIBLE LOVER)

Ramon Novarro *(Tony)*, Madge Evans *(Rosalie)*, Una Merkel *(Thelma)*, Ralph Graves *(Coach Malcolm)*, John Arledge *(Pidge)*, Frank Albertson *(Larry)*, Kane Richmond *(Tom Stone)*, Martha Sleeper *(Barbara)*, Henry Armetta *(Mr. Amatto)*, Ferike Boros *(Mrs. Armatto)*, Rockliffe Fellows *(Mr. Stone)*, Joe Sauers *(Slater)*.

An extremely long and slow-moving football film that chronicles the college career of Novarro, a tough Italian kid who tries to use his football prowess to make it as the big man on campus. It doesn't work, as he is passed over in the fraternity elections, and shunned by a girl, Evans, whom he tries to romance. It is a hard battle for Novarro, but in his senior year he turns his attitude around and gets the acceptance he desires on and off the football field.

d, Sam Wood; w, Walton Hall Smith, C. Gardner Sullivan, Robert Lee Johnson, Arthur S. Hyman (based on a story by Francis Wallace); ph, Harold Wenstrom; ed, Hugh Wynn.

Sports/Drama **(PR:A MPAA:NR)**

HUDSON'S BAY½** (1940) 95m FOX bw

Paul Muni *(Pierre Radisson)*, Gene Tierney *(Barbara Hall)*, Laird Cregar *(Gooseberry)*, John Sutton *(Lord Edward Crew)*, Virginia Field *(Nell Gwynn)*, Vincent Price *(King Charles)*, Nigel Bruce *(Prince Rupert)*, Montagu Love *(Governor d'Argenson)*, Morton Lowry *(Gerald Hall)*, Robert Greig *(Sir Robert)*, Chief Thundercloud *(Grimha)*, Frederick Warlock *(English Governor)*, Ian Wolfe *(Mayor)*, Chief Big Tree *(Chief)*, Jody Gilbert *(Germaine)*, Jean Del Val *(Captain)*, Eugene Borden, Constant Frank *(Sentries)*, Kilyan Irene *(Maid)*, Keith Hitchcock *(Footman)*, Dorothy Dearing *(Girl)*, John Rogers *(Sailor)*, Reginald Sheffield *(Clerk)*, Robert Cory *(Orderly)*, Denis d'Auburn, Eric Wilton *(Concillors)*, Florence Bates, Lumsden Hare, Lionel Pape.

Muni gives another fascinating character performance in a talky production about the 17th century fur trade in Canada. As Radisson, a flamboyant adventurer in real life, Muni and his sidekick Cregar encounter Sutton, British nobleman who has been sent to Canada as an exile for transgressions at court. He is taught trapping and trading by the colorful frontiersmen who then return with him to the court of King Charles (Price) where Muni proposes establishing the Hudson's Bay Trading

Company. At first Price declines but when he listens to Muni's promise of great riches from such a trading post, he changes his mind and funds the enterprise. Muni returns to Canada in 1667 with Cregar, Sutton, Sutton's fiancee Tierney, and her snobbish brother, Lowry. With the trading post built, the enterprise flourishes but Lowry brings it to a dangerous halt when he gets drunk and kills an Indian. The local chief demands that Lowry be brought to justice and punished or the fort will be leveled and all of its occupants killed. Muni, to save lives, orders Lowry executed and averts a war. Sutton's objection to the execution is ignored; he will not forget Muni's actions. When Muni, Cregar, and Sutton return to report the progress of the trading post to Price, the Canadian trappers are arrested for killing Lowry and thrown into prison. Eloquent-tongued Muni, however, is able to convince Price at the last moment that the lucrative trading post in Canada will collapse without his leadership to keep it going. He and Cregar are freed by the greedy monarch and leave the court, heading back to Hudson's Bay. Pichel's direction is lame, even though Fox put $800,000 behind the production, then a whopping amount, to make it a super epic. But there is very little action, even though the cameras dwell on splendid scenery in the northern wilds of Idaho where much of the on-location shooting was made. Muni, an independent and powerful actor, simply overwhelmed Pichel and, given his head, he overplayed his part lavishly, relishing the long windy speeches that often turn into diatribes. Cregar, who later became hammy in many roles when not curbed by a strong directorial hand, appears here in his second film and is surprisingly effective as he renders the understated role of Muni's sidekick. Sutton and Tierney enact some very syrupy love scenes and Price, too, is allowed to gnaw on the sets as the bewigged King Charles II. Field is good in her brief role as the celebrated mistress Nell Gwyn. On the whole, HUDSON'S BAY is entertaining if not historically accurate.

p, Kenneth Macgowan; d, Irving Pichel; w, Lamar Trotti; ph, Peverell Marley, George Barnes; m, Alfred Newman; ed, Robert Simpson; art d, Richard Day, Wiard B. Ihnen; tech adv, Clifford Wilson.

Adventure **(PR:A MPAA:NR)**

HUE AND CRY** (1950, Brit.) 82m EAL/GFD bw

Alastair Sim *(Felix H. Wilkinson)*, Valerie White *(Rhona)*, Jack Warner *(Jim Nightingale)*, Harry Fowler *(Joe Kirby)*, Frederick Piper *(Mr. Kirby)*, Heather Delaine *(Mrs. Kirby)*, Douglas Barr *(Alec)*, Joan Dowling *(Clarry)*, Alec Flinter *(Detective Sgt. Fothergill)*, Ian Dawson *(Norman)*, Gerald Fox *(Dicky)*, David Simpson *(Arthur)*, Albert Hughes *(Wally)*, John Hudson *(Stan)*, David Knox *(Dusty)*, Jack Lambert *(Inspector Ford)*, Stanley Escane *(Roy)*, Bruce Belfrage *(BBC Announcer)*, Jeffrey Sirett *(Bill)*, James Crabb *(Terry)*, Paul Demel *(Sago)*, Grace Arnold *(Dicky's Mother)*, Arthur Denton *(Vicar)*, Howard Douglas *(Watchman)*, Robin Hughes *(Selwyn Pike)*, Henry John Puvic *(Larry the Bull)*, Joey Carr *(Shorty)*, Blood and Thunder Boys.

This half-hearted British comedy takes place in London's East End. A gang of crooks uses a serialized story in a weekly children's magazine as a means of sending messages. Fowler, a bright Cockney kid, spots the messages and tries to bring them to the attention of his boss and a detective. Both tell him to forget about what he's seen, so he gets his Cockney pals together to capture the crooks.

p, Michael Balcon, Henry Cornelius; d, Charles Crichton; w, T.E.B. Clarke; ph, Douglas Slocombe, J. Seaholme; m, Georges Auric; ed, Charles Hasse; md, Ernest Irving; art d, Norman J. Arnold.

Comedy/Crime **(PR:A MPAA:NR)**

HUGGETTS ABROAD, THE*½ (1949, Brit.) 87m Gainsborough/GFD bw

Jack Warner *(Joe Huggett)*, Kathleen Harrison *(Ethel Huggett)*, Susan Shaw *(Susan Huggett)*, Petula Clark *(Pet Huggett)*, Dinah Sheridan *(Jane Huggett)*, Hugh McDermott *(Bob McCoy)*, Jimmy Hanley *(Jimmy)*, Peter Hammond *(Peter Hawtrey)*, Amy Veness *(Grandma)*, John Blythe *(Gowan)*, Esma Cannon *(Brown Owl)*, Everley Gregg, Brian Oulton, Olaf Pooley, Martin Miller, Meinhart Maur, Philo Hauser, Peter Illing, Frith Banbury, Marcel Poncin, Ferdy Mayne.

Warner drags his clan to Africa when he decides that he's had enough of his humdrum existence. The family soon gets tangled up with a diamond smuggler, McDermott, and winds up imprisoned by French authorities. Light is soon seen at the end of their tunnel full of comic mishaps when Warner gets an offer to return to his job. The Huggett family never returned to the screen, however, ending the short-lived and unmemorable series. (See HUGGETTS FAMILY series, Index.)

p, Betty Box; d, Ken Annakin; w, Mabel Constanduros, Denis Constanduros, Ted Willis, Gerard Bryant; ph, Reginald Wyer.

Comedy **(PR:A MPAA:NR)**

HUGO THE HIPPO***½ (1976, Hung./U.S.) 78m Brut/FOX c

Voices of: Robert Morley, Paul Lynde, Jesse Emmet, Lance Taylor, Sr., Ronnie Cox, Len Maxwell, Percy Rodriguez, Burl Ives, Marie Osmond, Jimmy Osmond.

Well-animated in Hungary, HUGO THE HIPPO is a charming children's film that tells a fable-like tale about a small hippo trying to escape death at the hands of angry Africans who are out to get him. The little hippo has run away from his captors after the Africans have drafted his fellow hippos into service to scare off shark attacks. When the shark menace is gone, the Africans have no use for the hippos, so they let them starve. Hugo flees and with the aid of a young African boy, he manages to call attention to the slaughter of his species and is soon given protection from extinction by a national decree. Marie and Jimmy Osmond and Burl Ives handle the singing chores.

p, Robert Halmi; d, Bill Feigenbaum; w, Tom Baum; m, Burt Keyes; prod d, Graham Percy; m/l, Robert Larimer; anim d; Joszef Gemes.

Animation/Juvenile/Musical **Cas.** **(PR:AAA MPAA:G)**

HUGS AND KISSES**½ (1968, Swed.) 93m Sandrews/Avco Embassy bw (PUSS OCH KRAM)

Agneta Ekmanner *(Eva)*, Sven-Bertil Taube *(Max)*, Hakan Serner *(John)*, Lena Granhagen *(Hickan)*, Rolf Larsson *(Photographer)*, Ingrid Bostrom, Carl Johann Ronn, Peter Cornell.

After Serner's girl friend throws him out, old school pal Taube takes in his forlorn, would-be writer chum. At first Taube's wife, Ekmanner, resents the strange man's presence and habits (he likes to read holding a piece of cat fur to his cheek). Gradually she takes a liking to the eccentric though, and begs him to stay. Serner brings over Granhagen, an obnoxious typing teacher, and the couple gradually take over the small apartment. Taube and Ekmanner plot to get rid of her with the wife attempting to falsely seduce Serner. The plan works, but too well, as Ekmanner realizes she loves Serner. The two make frenzied love, as the cuckold Taube throws on his friend's old undershirt and goes to sleep in the guest room. This is a sweet film, with many moments of genuine whimsy. The dialog is crisp, and realistic, giving this a nice edge. Unfortunately the direction doesn't quite match the plot's eccentricities, resulting in an "almost but not quite" comic menage a trois.

p, Goran Lindgren; d&w, Jonas Cornell; ph, Lars Swanberg; m, Bengt Ernyrd; ed, Ingemar Ejve; art d, Walter Hirsch.

Comedy **(PR:O MPAA:NR)**

HUK*½ (1956) 84m UA c

George Montgomery *(Greg Dickson)*, Mona Freeman *(Cindy Rogers)*, John Baer *(Bart Rogers)*, James Bell *(Steven Rogers)*, Teddy Benivedes *(Maj. Balatbat)*, Mario Barri *(Kalak)*, Ben Perez *(Pinote)*.

A confused post-WW II drama set in the Philippines and starring Montgomery as a young plantation owner who must contend with an uprising staged by Filipino natives, formerly freedom fighters, who have gone on the rampage. Written by future Academy Award winning screenwriter Silliphant (IN THE HEAT OF THE NIGHT) from his own novel. Brutal and explicitly violent.

p, Collier Young; d, John Barnwell; w, Stirling Silliphant (based on a novel by Silliphant); ph, William Snyder (Eastmancolor); m, Albert Glasser; ed, Helene Turner.

War Drama **(PR:O MPAA:NR)**

HULLABALOO**½ (1940) 77m MGM bw

Frank Morgan *(Frank Merriweather)*, Virginia Grey *(Laura Merriweather)*, Dan Dailey, Jr. *(Bob Strong)*, Billie Burke *(Penny Merriweather)*, Nydia Westman *(Lulu Perkins)*, Ann Morriss *(Wilma Norton)*, Donald Meek *(Clyde Perkins)*, Reginald Owen *("Buzz" Foster)*, Charles Holland *(Bellhop)*, Leni Lynn *(Judy Merriweather)*, Virginia O'Brien *(Virginia Ferris)*, Curt Bois *(Armand Francois)*, Sara Haden *(Sue Merriweather)*, Larry Nunn *(Terry Merriweather)*, Barnett Parker *(Stephens)*, George Lessey *(Arthur Jay Norton)*, Cy Kendall *(Wilson)*, Connie Gilchrist *(Arline Merriweather)*.

A bravura performance from Morgan is the only thing that pulls this weak musical comedy off its knees. Morgan plays an old song-and-dance man who sees radio as the only viable money-making medium open to him. While trying to win his big break in radio, he is attacked on all sides by his three ex-wives and their children. Morgan bumbles his first big job by staging a "War of the Worlds" type broadcast that gets him canned because of the panic it creates. He then moves into vocal impressions of famous movie stars (Wallace Beery, Al Jolson, Mickey Rooney, and a three-way Clark Gable, Spencer Tracy, Claudette Colbert exchange from their popular film BOOM TOWN) and is finally a hit. Songs include: "We've Come A Long Way Together" (Ted Koehler, Sammy Stept), "Carry Me Back To Old Virginny" (James Bland), "A Handful Of Stars" (Jack Lawrence, Ted Shapiro), "You Were Meant For Me" (Arthur Freed, Nacio Herb Brown).

p, Louis K. Sidney; d, Edwin L. Marin; w, Nat Perrin (based on an idea by Bradford Ropes and Val Burton); ph, Charles Lawton; ed, Conrad A. Nervig.

Comedy/Musical **(PR:A MPAA:NR)**

HULLABALOO OVER GEORGIE AND BONNIE'S PICTURES** (1979, Brit.) 82m Contemporary c

Peggy Ashcroft *(Lady Gwyneth)*, Victor Bannerjee *(Georgie)*, Larry Pines *(Clark Haven)*, Aparna Sen *(Bonnie)*, Saeed Jaffrey *(Sri Narain)*, Jane Booker *(Lynn)*, Shamsuddin *(Deaf Mute)*, Alladdin Langa *(Servant)*, Jenny Beavan *(Governess)*.

A witty comedy of manners originally made for British television which found its way to American shores. Set in post-colonial India, Bannerjee plays a young maharajah, and Sen his sister, who are besieged with art collectors and buyers from throughout the world when it is discovered that they own a priceless collection of paintings. The paintings are of little concern to Bannerjee, as he keeps them stored haphazardly in a room filled with junk. The kind of art he appreciates is the type Hugh Hefner publishes. Among the art collectors is Ashcroft (who won best supporting actress for A PASSAGE TO INDIA in 1984), a kindly British aristocrat determined that the paintings should be displayed in a British museum, who soon finds herself competing with rich American Pine for possession of the art work.

p, Ismail Merchant; d, James Ivory; w, Ruth Prawer Jhabwala; ph, Walter Lassally; m, Vic Flick; ed, Humphrey Dixon; art d, Bansi Chandragupta.

Comedy **(PR:A MPAA:NR)**

HU-MAN*** (1975, Fr.) 105m Romantique-ORTF

Terence Stamp, Jeanne Moreau, Agnes Stevenin, Frederick Van Pallandt, Franck Schwacke, Gabriella Rysted.

Stamp plays an aging actor named (conveniently) Terence Stamp who takes part in an experiment to travel through time. The project, organized by ex-lover Jeanne Moreau, allows him to venture into the past where he witnesses the death of his wife. He then is sent into the future. He discovers a way to manipulate his time travels without Moreau's assistance and he reunites himself with his wife in the past, where they face death together. A winner of the Trieste Festival of Science Fiction Films which is vaguely similar to both Alain Resnais' JE T'AIME, JE T'AIME and Chris Marker's short LA JETEE.

p, Yves Pauthe, M.F. Mascaro; d, Jerome Laperrousaz; w, Laperrousaz, Guillaume Laperrousaz, Andre Ruellan, Francis Guilbert; ph, Jimmy Glasberg.

Science Fiction/Romance **(PR:C MPAA:NR)**

HUMAN BEAST, THE (SEE: LA BETE HUMAINE, 1938, Fr.)

HUMAN CARGO*½ (1936) 65m FOX bw

Claire Trevor *(Bonnie Brewster)*, Brian Donlevy *(Packy Campbell)*, Alan Dinehart *(Lionel Crocker)*, Ralph Morgan *(District Attorney Cary)*, Helen Troy *(Susie)*, Rita Cansino [Hayworth] *(Carmen Zoro)*, Morgan Wallace *(Gilbert Fender)*, Herman Bing *(Fritz Shulz)*, John McGuire *(Spike Davis)*, Ralf Harolde *(Tony Sculla)*, Wade Boteler *(Bob McSweeney)*, Harry Wood *(Ira Conklin)*, Wilfred Lucas *(Lieutenant)*, Pat Hartigan, Edward Cooper, Tom O'Grady, Stanley Blystone, Ivan "Dusty" Miller *(Detectives)*, Paul McVey *(Ship's Officer)*, Tom Ricketts *(Reporter)*, Harry Semels *(Barreto)*, Edward Cooper *(Butler)*, Fredrik Vogeding *(Captain)*, Lee Phelps, Alonzo Price *(Gangsters)*, Eddie Buzard *(Copy Boy)*, Claudia Coleman *(Sob Sister)*, Hector V. Sarno *(Italian)*, Otto A. Fries *(German Cook)*, Arno Frey, Rosalie Hegedus *(German Couple)*, Hans Fuerberg, Milla Davenport *(Other Germans)*.

Cansino (Rita Hayworth) made her last supporting appearance for Fox in this drama detailing the activities of a smuggling ring that transports illegal aliens across the border (Hayworth among them) and then blackmails them for the rest of their lives. Crusading reporters Donlevy and Trevor go after the gang, and after a few harrowing adventures, succeed in exposing the ringleaders and destroying their operation. HUMAN CARGO inspired the studio to churn out a short series of films featuring "The Roving Reporters."

p, Sol M. Wurtzel; d, Allan Dwan; w, Jefferson Parker, Doris Malloy (based on Kathleen Shepard's novel *I Will Be Faithful*); ph, Daniel B. Clark; ed, Louis Loeffler; md, Sammy Kaylin; art d, Duncan Cramer; cos, Gwen Wakeling; makeup, Ernest Westmore.

Crime **(PR:A MPAA:NR)**

HUMAN COMEDY, THE*½** (1943) 118m MGM bw

Mickey Rooney *(Homer Macauley)*, Frank Morgan *(Willie Grogan)*, James Craig *(Tom Spangler)*, Marsha Hunt *(Diana Steed)*, Fay Bainter *(Mrs. Macauley)*, Ray Collins *(Mr. Macauley)*, Van Johnson *(Marcus Macauley)*, Donna Reed *(Bess Macauley)*, Jackie "Butch" Jenkins *(Ulysses Macauley)*, Dorothy Morris *(Mary Arena)*, John Craven *(Tobey George)*, Ann Ayars *(Mrs. Sandoval)*, Mary Nash *(Miss Hicks)*, Henry O'Neill *(Charles Steed)*, Katherine Alexander *(Mrs. Steed)*, Alan Baxter *(Brad Stickman)*, Darryl Hickman *(Lionel)*, Barry Nelson *(Pat)*, Rita Quigley *(Helen Elliott)*, Clem Bevans *(Henderson)*, Adeline De Walt Reynolds *(Librarian)*. S. Z. Sakall *(Mr. Ara)*, Don DeFore *(Texas)*, Bob Mitchum *(Horse)*, Ernest Whitman *(Black)*, Mark Daniels *(1st Soldier)*, William Roberts *(2nd Soldier)*, David Holt *(Hubert Ackley)*, Connie Gilchrist *(Dolly)*, Howard J. Stevenson *(Mr. Mechano)*, Frank Jenks *(Larry)*, Howard Freeman *(Rev. Holly)*, Jay Ward *(Felix)*, Gibson Gowland *(Leonine Type Man)*, Don Taylor *(Soldier)*, Byron Foulger *(Blenton)*, Wallis Clark *(Principal)*, Mary Servoss *(Mrs. Beaufrere)*, Morris Ankrum *(Mr. Beaufrere)*, Lynne Carver *(Daughter)*, Carl "Alfalfa" Switzer *(Auggie)*, Robert Emmett O'Connor *(Bartender)*, Emory Parnell *(Policeman)*, Wally Cassell *(Flirt)*.

It's sloppily sentimental in spots and brilliantly moving in others, it's true as the blue skies over America in some scenes and in others it's so artificial as to make the viewer squirm with embarrassment, yet overall this is a wonderful film, thanks to Rooney's fine effort and to the little boy that almost stole it all from him on celluloid, the marvelous "Butch" Jenkins. Like Saroyan's own peculiar literary style, the film has an up-and-down quality that somewhat disrupts interest as the simple tale is unfolded. Collins is the narrator of the story, speaking from somewhere in the spirit world since he's been dead for two years when he decides to return to the family homestead in idealized Ithaca, California. He oversees the lives of his family, consisting of wife Bainter, grown son Johnson, a private in the Army, daughter Reed, a college student, teenage son Rooney, a high school junior, and precocious 4-year-old Jenkins. Close to the family is Johnson's childhood sweetheart and the girl next door, Morris, Craig, the operator of the local telegraph office for which lovable drunk Morgan works and Rooney delivers telegrams when not in school. There's also Craven, who has been orphaned and is Johnson's service pal, who is later "adopted" by Collins' warm-hearted family when Johnson is killed in battle. It's a study in everyday life and presents the little joys of childhood, the triumphs of adulthood, and the everyday tragedy that the war brought with telegrams delivered by Rooney, telegrams that meant only one thing, death or wounding of a loved one. The burden of delivering these heart-tearing missives wears so heavily upon Rooney that, at one point, he thinks of leaving home, but his little brother innocently talks him out of the notion. Craig is solid as the supportive telegraph office boss and Morgan's whiskey-laced, down-home philosophy is both quaint and humorous. Rooney is sensational as the human link between families as he makes his rounds via bicycle, touching one life after another and being touched by each person he meets. This was his finest role and it shows in his youthful admiration for big brother Johnson, love for mother and sister, and protective tolerance for kid brother Jenkins. Jenkins himself almost takes every scene from the ebullient Rooney. This was the favorite film of MGM mogul Louis B. Mayer and his favorite scene of all time and of all movies was the opening scene where "Butch" Jenkins is peering in utter rapture at a gopher hole. Mayer's love for anything by Saroyan was inexplicable. From the first moment producer Arthur Freed introduced Saroyan to Mayer, the mogul was taken by the fast-talking, utterly charming Armenian from Fresno, California (the actual setting for THE HUMAN COMEDY). Saroyan's nonstop chatter amused and enlightened Mayer and he later asked Freed to offer the writer a job at MGM. At the time Saroyan was the rage, an *enfant terrible* who bluntly spoke his mind and whose electricity-charged stories captivated the American reading public in the late 1930s. His tempestuous talkathon play, "The Time of Your Life," won the Pulitzer Prize in 1940 and his career shot ever upward. Freed came back to Mayer, telling him that Saroyan didn't want to write for the movies, a stance Mayer could not understand. He told Freed to offer Saroyan $300 a week just to hang around the studio (and basically spend his time amusing Mayer with his Armenian stories which reminded the mogul of Jewish family life that was no more). Saroyan took the job, such as it was, but never showed up at the studio, let alone drop by to pick up his paychecks. Freed tracked the writer down in Fresno and convined him to write a story for the studio. The result was "The Human Comedy" which Mayer had read to him three times weeping deeply at each reading. Mayer wanted to film the story instantly but Saroyan's asking price of $300,000 was astronomical at that time. Mayer met with Saroyan and offered him $50,000. The writer cavalierly produced a coin and said: "I'll tell you what I'll do. I'll toss you for it—one hundred thousand or nothing." Mayer pulled away, saying: "I can't gamble the company's money." He later compromised and paid Saroyan $60,000, plus $1,500 a week for writing the script. Mayer wanted him around, telling his cronies that he would turn Saroyan into another Irving Thalberg, a bright new producer-director. But when it came time to commit himself, Mayer refused to let Saroyan direct THE HUMAN COMEDY, which angered the volatile Armenian. Mayer instead asked the writer to adapt for the screen an ancient play, "The Rosary," but Saroyan turned him down. Mayer let him do whatever he wanted and Saroyan amused himself by having a player piano put into his studio office and producing and directing a short film entitled THE GOOD JOB. The writer spent endless hours watching MGM films he had missed in his youth. After three months of such loafing, Saroyan left for good. He later condemned studio employment in a *Daily Variety* article, stating "I left the joint because sooner or later a man gets bored with bores, finaglers, and jitney politicians." Later he wrote a play called "Get Away Old Man," a vicious little drama that savaged Louis B. Mayer, his one-time admirer and benefactor. Look for quick cameos of Barry Nelson, Don DeFore and Robert Mitchum.

p&d, Clarence Brown; w, Howard Estabrook (based on the novel by William Saroyan); ph, Harry Stradling; m, Herbert Stothart; ed, Conrad A. Nervig; art d, Cedric Gibbons; ch, Ernst Matray.

Comedy **(PR:A MPAA:NR)**

HUMAN CONDITION, THE*** (1959, Jap.) 200m Shochiku Co./Shochiku Films of America bw (NINGEN NO JOKEN; AKA: NO GREATER LOVE)

Tatsuya Nakadai *(Kaji)*, Michiyo Aratama *(Michiko)*, So Yamamura *(Okishima)*, Eitaro Ozawa *(Okazaki)*, Akira Ishihama *(Chen)*, Shinji Nambara *(Kao)*, Ineko Arima *(Yang Chun Lan)*, Chikage Awashima *(Jin Tung Fu)*, Keiji Sada *(Kageyama)*, Toru Abe *(Watai)*, Masao Mishima *(Kuroki)*, Koji Mitsui *(Furya)*, Kyu Sazanka *(Cho Meisan)*, Seiji Miyaguchi *(Wang Heng Li)*, Nobuo Nakamura *(Chief of Head Office)*.

An interesting look at the fate of a pacifist in war-torn Japan of 1943, when the tide of the Pacific battles was beginning to turn against it. Nakadai is the pacifist whose good treatment of some mine workers and, later, some prisoners of war, turns his superiors against him. Through an attempted escape of the prisoners, incited by one of Nakadai's enemies, things come to a head, and a trusted member of his circle is beheaded, an act Nakadai is forced to observe. Finally, after being tortured, charged with conspiracy, and released, the pacifist hero is served with a draft notice. This is the first of a three-part series entitled THE HUMAN CONDITION. The second film, ROAD TO ETERNITY, was released in 1961 and the third in 1970, under the title A SOLDIER'S PRAYER.

p, Shigeru Wakatsuki; d, Masaki Kobayashi; w, Zenzo Matsuyama, Kobayashi; ph, Yoshio Miyajima (Shochiku Grandscope); m, Chuji Kinoshita; ed, Keiichi Uraoka; art d, Kazue Hirataka.

Drama **(PR:O MPAA:R)**

HUMAN DESIRE½** (1954) 90m COL bw

Glenn Ford *(Jeff Warren)*, Gloria Grahame *(Vicki Buckley)*, Broderick Crawford *(Carl Buckley)*, Edgar Buchanan *(Alec Simmons)*, Kathleen Case *(Ellen Simmons)*, Peggy Maley *(Jean)*, Diane DeLaire *(Vera Simmons)*, Grandon Rhodes *(John Owens)*, Dan Seymour *(Bartender)*, John Pickard *(Matt Henley)*, Paul Brinegar *(Brakeman)*, Dan Riss *(Prosecutor Gruber)*, Victor Hugo Greene *(Davidson)*, John Zaremba *(Russell)*, Carl Lee *(John Thurston)*, Olan Soule *(Lewis)*, Dan Riss *(Prosecutor Gruber)*.

Remake of Jean Renoir's LA BETE HUMAINE, based on Zola's novel of the same name, HUMAN DESIRE switches the locale to Oklahoma with the background being the Rock Island Railroad Line. Crawford is a hot-tempered railroad employee in danger of losing his job because there is yet to be a handle he has not flown off. He appeals to his wife, Grahame, because she is pals with his boss, Rhodes. She hates to do it but finally relents and Crawford gets to keep his job. But Crawford is a very jealous man and thinks that Grahame may have used more than just wiles on Rhodes. He arranges for the two of them to be together in a train compartment, then enters and kills Rhodes. She'd been spotted at the scene of the crime by Ford, an engineer, but he lies at the post-mortem and says he saw no one. Soon enough, Grahame and Ford are involved in what Crawford suspected of Grahame and Rhodes. Relations between Crawford and Grahame disintegrate and he begins to drink to excess. He loves her very much and holds an incriminating letter she wrote over her head to keep them together. Eventually, Crawford is fired and now wants to leave town with Grahame, but she has other plans for him and prevails upon Ford to kill Crawford and attempt to make it look accidental. Ford can't bring himself to do that and only succeeds in retrieving the missive. Grahame leaves town with Crawford aboard a train. In the compartment, she tells him all about her plans for his murder as well as her sexual liaison with Ford. Enraged, Crawford kills her. It's a sordid little tale that was not nearly as sensuous or sexual as the French version, nor was it very suspenseful. And the only person we could root for was Ford and even *he* was a man sleeping with a married woman. Lang's moody photography (with Guffey) serves to make this movie look better than it actually is.

p, Lewis J. Rachmil; d, Fritz Lang; w, Alfred Hayes (based on Emile Zola's novel *La Bete Humaine*); ph, Burnett Guffey; m, Daniel Amfitheatrof; ed, William A. Lyon; md, Morris Stoloff; art d, Robert Peterson; set d, William Kiernan.

Crime/Drama **(PR:C MPAA:NR)**

HUMAN DUPLICATORS, THE* (1965) 80m Crest c

George Nader *(Glenn Martin)*, Barbara Nichols *(Gale Wilson)*, George Macready *(Prof. Dornheimer)*, Dolores Faith *(Lisa)*, Richard Kiel *(Kolos)*, Richard Arlen *(National Intelligence Agency Head)*, Hugh Beaumont *(Austin Welles)*, Ted Durant *(Voice from Outer Space)*, Tommy Leonetti, Lonnie Sattin, John Indrisano.

Cheap sci-fi adventure starring the giant Kiel ("Jaws" in the James Bond movies) as an alien sent to Earth to make duplicates of all the world's leaders so that his planet can infiltrate and take over with ease. Luckily, government agents Nader and Nichols sort things out and turn a new laser beam on the bad guy which destroys him and his minions. Pretty sad.

p, Hugo Grimaldi, Arthur C. Pierce; d, Grimaldi; w, Pierce; ph, Monroe Askins (Eastmancolor); ed, Donald Wolfe; md, Gordon Zahler; art d, Paul Sylos; set d, Ray Boltz; cos, Mickey Myers; spec eff, Roger George; makeup, John Chambers, Bob Mark.

Science Fiction **(PR:A MPAA:NR)**

HUMAN EXPERIMENTS*½ (1980) 82m Crown International c (AKA: BEYOND THE GATE)

Linda Haynes *(Rachel Foster)*, Geoffrey Lewis *(Dr. Kline)*, Ellen Travolta, Aldo Ray, Jackie Coogan, Darlene Carviotto.

Haynes stars as a backroads country and western singer who stumbles onto a mass murder and is arrested and quickly imprisoned for the crime. There she is tormented by crazed prison psychologist Lewis who seeks to cure insanity by driving his patients insane, erasing their memories, and then starting over by filling their brains with new memories (i.e., proper upbringing, pleasant childhoods, etc.). From what opened as a fairly promising, well-directed thriller, HUMAN EXPERIMENTS soon degenerated into so much sadism.

p, Summer Brown, Gregory Goodell; d, Goodell; w, Richard Rothstein; ph, Joao Fernandes; m, Marc Bucci.

Horror **Cas.** **(PR:O MPAA:R)**

HUMAN FACTOR, THE* (1975) 95m Bryanston c

George Kennedy *(John Kinsdale)*, John Mills *(Mike McAllister)*, Raf Vallone *(Dr. Lupo)*, Arthur Franz *(Gen. Fuller)*, Rita Tushingham *(Janice)*, Frank Avianca *(Kamal)*, Haydee Politoff *(Pidgeon)*, Tom Hunter *(Taylor)*, Barry Sullivan *(Edmonds)*, Fiamma Verges *(Ann Kinsdale)*, Danny Houston *(Mark Kinsdale)*, Michael Mandeville *(Phillips)*, Ricky Harrison *(Jeffrey Kinsdale)*, Hillary Lief *(Linda Kinsdale)*, Robert Lowell *(Eddy Fonseca)*, Mrs. Robert Lowell *(Agnes Fonseca)*, Shane Rimmer *(Carter, CIA)*, Anne Ferguson *(Mrs. Simpson)*, Lewis Charles *(Mr. Gerardi)*, Corinne Dunne *(Mrs. Gerardi)*, Sharon Kellogg *(Alice Gerardi)*, Eugene Wade *(Rodney Gerardi)*, West Buchanan *(Aldo)*, Conchita Airoldi *(Sandra Pallavicini)*, Joe Jenkins *(CIA Man)*, Vincenzo Crocitti *(Lupo's Driver)*.

Senseless, bloody revenge film starring Kennedy as a NATO war planner stationed in Italy whose family is slaughtered by terrorists led by Avianca (who also produced this mess). Fueled by the great American notion of "might makes right," Kennedy goes out in search of the terrorists to kill them. Director Dmytryk, along with writers Hunter and Powell, ignore any political, social, or emotional aspects of the material and play directly to the blood-lust instincts of the viewer.

p, Frank Avianca; d, Edward Dmytryk; w, Tom Hunter, Peter Powell; ph, Qusama Rawi (Technicolor); m, Ennio Morricone; ed, Alan Strachen.

Action **(PR:O MPAA:R)**

HUMAN FACTOR, THE** (1979, Brit.) 115m MGM/UA c

Richard Attenborough *(Col. Daintry)*, Joop Doderer *(Cornelius Muller)*, John Gielgud *(Brigadier Tomlinson)*, Derek Jacobi *(Davis)*, Robert Morley *(Percival)*, Ann Todd *(Castle's Mother)*, Richard Vernon *(Sir John Hargreaves)*, Nicol Williamson *(Castle)*, Iman *(Sarah)*, Keith Marsh *(Porter)*, Anthony Woodruff *(Dr. Barker)*, Gary Forbes *(Sam)*, Angela Thorne *(Lady Mary Hargreaves)*, Tony Haygarth *(Buffy)*, Paul Curran *(Halliday)*, Cyd Haygarth *(Cynthia)*, Ken Jones *(Messenger)*, Paul Seed *(Shop Assistant)*, Chantal Gray *(Stripper)*, Fiona Fullerton *(Elizabeth)*, Adrienne Corri *(Sylvia)*, Walter Hinds, Philip Chege, Tony Vogel, Norbert Okare, Vicky Udall, Brian Epson, Mike Andrews, Leon Green, Martin Benson, Giles Watling, Marianne Stone, Edward Dentith, Robert Dorning, Patrick O'Connell, Sean Caffrey, Clifford Earl, Tom Chatto, Rawyn Blade, Glenna Forster-Jones, Sylvia Coleridge, Boris Isarov, Dennis Hawthorne, Frank Williams.

Director Preminger was handed his first project in five years, given a great cast and good material (based on a Graham Greene novel), and he came up with this anemic little thriller. Williamson plays a middle-aged British Secret Service employee who betrays his country by passing information to the Soviets in order to aid an old friend in Africa. As a result of his indiscretion, an innocent man is "removed" by the British and Williamson is forced to defect to the USSR, leaving his wife and child behind. While far from a bad film, THE HUMAN FACTOR fails to convey the desperation and stagnation felt by the Williamson character.

p&d, Otto Preminger; w, Tom Stoppard (based on a novel by Graham Greene); ph, Mike Molloy (Technicolor); ed, Richard Trevor; m, Richard Logan, Gary Logan; art d, Ken Ryan; cos, Hope Bryce.

Spy/Drama **(PR:C MPAA:R)**

HUMAN HIGHWAY* (1982) 90m Shakey c

Neil Young *(Lionel Switch)*, Russ Tamblyn *(Fred Kelly)*, Dean Stockwell *(Otto Quartz)*, Dennis Hopper *(Cracker)*, Charlotte Stewart *(Charlotte Goodnight)*, Sally Kirkland *(Katherine)*, Geraldine Baron *(Irene)*, Devo's Nuclear Garbagemen.

Young and Tamblyn play two dimwitted, redneck gas station attendants who work near a new nuclear power plant. Constantly on the brink of nuclear oblivion, the folks of "Cal Neva" are ever-fearful of the big disaster. One day Young gets hit in the head and spins off into a fantasy sequence featuring the "new wave" rock band Devo. Unfortunately, this is the highlight of the movie. A celebrity cast of Young's buddies (Hopper, Stockwell, and Tamblyn) look like they should have spent the four years the film was in the making elsewhere.

p, L. A. Johnson; d, Bernard Shakey, Dean Stockwell; w, Shakey, Jeanne Fields, Stockwell, Russ Tamblyn, James Beshears; ph, David Myers; m, Neil Young, Devo.

Fantasy/Musical **(PR:O MPAA:NR)**

HUMAN JUNGLE, THE*½** (1954) 82m AA bw

Gary Merrill *(Danforth)*, Jan Sterling *(Mary)*, Paula Raymond *(Pat Danforth)*, Emile Meyer *(Rowan)*, Regis Toomey *(Geddes)*, Chuck Connors *(Swados)*, Pat Waltz *(Strauss)*, George Wallace *(O'Neil)*, Chubby Johnson *(Greenie)*, Don Keefer *(Cleary)*, Rankin Mansfield *(Bledsoe)*, Lamont Johnson *(Lannigan)*, Leo Cleary *(Karns)*, Florenz Ames *(Ustick)*, Claude Akins *(Mandy)*, Hugh Boswell *(Lynch)*, James Westerfield *(Capt. Harrison)*.

A good low-budget cop movie starring Merrill as a police captain about to quit the force to become a lawyer, but instead accepts the challenge from his superiors, who want to install him as head of their worst district to clean it up. Merrill is met with stiff opposition from the criminal element, as well as the corrupt members of his own force. Through tough leadership and perseverance, he succeeds in making the district a better place to live.

p, Hayes Goetz; d, Joseph M. Newman; w, William Sackheim, Daniel Fuchs (based on a story by Sackheim); ph, Ellis Carter; m, Hans Salter; ed, Lester Sansom, Samuel Fields; m/l, Max Rich.

Crime Drama **(PR:A MPAA:NR)**

HUMAN MONSTER, THE*** (1940, Brit.) 76m MON bw (GB: DARK EYES OF LONDON)

Bela Lugosi *(Dr. Orloff)*, Hugh Williams *(Inspector Holt)*, Greta Gynt *(Diana Stuart)*, Edmond Ryan *(Lt. O'Reilly)*, Wilfrid Walter *(Jake, Monster)*, Alexander Field *(Grogan)*, Arthur E. Owen *(Dumb Lew)*, Julie Suedo *(Secretary)*, Gerald Pring *(Henry Stuart)*, Bryan Herbert *(Walsh)*, May Hallatt *(Policewoman)*, Charles Penrose *(The Drunk)*.

Creepy British horror film starring Lugosi as an evil doctor treating patients in a home for the blind, who is also posing as the blind owner of the institution. When several inmates sign over their insurance policies to Lugosi and are then found floating in the Thames, the police get suspicious. Aided by Gynt, daughter of one of the victims, the police trace the killings to Lugosi, but the inquisitive gal is kidnaped by the doctor's menacing, blind assistant, Walter. Lugosi is about to kill Gynt, but the girl manages to enrage Walter by informing him that it is Lugosi who has killed the inmates of the institute, helpless blind people like himself. Walter struggles with Lugosi and is shot, but the blind monster manages to throw Lugosi out of the window to his death into the murky Thames before dying from his wounds. Lugosi turns in one of his best performances in THE HUMAN MONSTER, managing to underplay his role(s) (unusual for him) thus balancing the more contrived moments in the script. Walter helped create the effective makeup for his character.

p, John Argyle; d, Walter Summers; w, Patrick Kirwan, Summers, Argyle (based on Edgar Wallace's "Dark Eyes of London"); ph, Bryan Langley; m, Guy Jones; ed, E.G. Richards.

Horror **Cas.** **(PR:O MPAA:NR)**

HUMAN SIDE, THE*** (1934) 60m UNIV bw

Adolphe Menjou *(Gregory Sheldon)*, Doris Kenyon *(Vera Sheldon)*, Charlotte Henry *(Lucille Sheldon)*, Joseph Cawthorn *(Fritz Speigle)*, Reginald Owen *(James Dalton)*, Betty Lawford *(Alma Hastings)*, Dick Winslow *(Phil Sheldon)*, George Ernest *(Tom Sheldon)*, Dickie Moore *(Bobbie Sheldon)*, Ward Bond *(Cop)*, Lois January, Anne Darling *(High School Girls)*, John Sheehan *(Gardy)*, Eddie Kane *(Hagen)*, Richard Powell *(Al)*, Charles Wilson *(Furniture Buyer)*, Jack Mulhall *(Actor)*, Arthur S. Hull, George Kirby, Bernardine Hayes, Leland Hodgson, Ara Haskell, Lew Kelly, Lew Phelps.

Menjou plays a theatrical producer gone broke who is trying to convince his ex-wife Kenyon to marry a wealthy man so that he won't have to pay alimony or child support for his four kids. Menjou's girl friend, Lawford, becomes increasingly jealous of all the undue attention he pays to his ex-wife, a fact not lost on the children who set things into motion which lead to a reconciliation of the parents. Charmingly performed with the children being the real standouts.

d, Edward Buzzell; w, Frank Craven, Ernest Pascal (based on a play by Christine Ames [Margaret Morrison Smith]); ph, Norbert Brodine.

Comedy **(PR:A MPAA:NR)**

HUMAN TARGETS** (1932) 60m Big Four bw

Rin-Tin-Tin, Buzz Barton, Francis X. Bushman, Jr., Tom London, Edmund Cobb, Ted Adams, Leon Kent, Nanci Price, John Ince, Edgar Lewis, Pauline Parker, Helen Gibson, Franklyn Farnum, Fred Toones.

Yet another western boy-and-his-dog shoot 'em up starring Barton and Rin-Tin-Tin. Barton punches the gold-stealing baddies and Rin-Tin-Tin puts the bite on them. The good guys win. The bad guys need medical attention.

p, Burton Kent; d, J. P. McGowan; w, George Morgan; ph, Edward Kull; ed, Fred Bain.

Western (PR:A MPAA:NR)

HUMAN TORNADO, THE*½ (1976) 98m Comedian International/Dimension c

Rudy Ray Moore *(Dolemite)*, Lady Reed *(Queen Bee)*, Glorya De Lani *(Hurricane Annie)*, Jimmy Lynch *(Mr. Motion)*, Lady Java *(Captive)*, Jerry Jones *(Detective Pistol Pete)*, Herb Graham *(Gang Leader)*, Howard Jackson, J. D. Baron.

The flashy, classy , and all-around trashy sequel to DOLEMITE starring standup comedian Rudy Ray Moore (who also produced). The rhyming, criming, two-timing Moore hightails on out of town when the white sheriff discovers him sleeping with his wife. His shuffling feet take him to California where he has a fine time with tough and sexy madam Reed. She and her kung fu fighting girls stand up to the mean local mobster. Moore beats some sense into the thick-headed bad boys, but in his moment of victory is gunned down by the sheriff. Not man nor bullet can bring down The Human Tornado, however, and the jive-talking Moore rises up from the ground to reveal a bulletproof vest. THE HUMAN TORNADO (like DOLEMITE) survives on its wit and ability to laugh at itself. The excess of violence, sex, and female degradation is present, as usual, but somehow approaches an inoffensive level of absurdity rather than a more objectionable anti-women stance. A "brain-battering, mind-splattering" cyclone full of vulgar fun.

p, Rudy Ray Moore; d, Cliff Roquemore; w, Jerry Jones; ph, Bob Wilson, Gene Conde; m, Arthur Wright; m/l, "The Human Tornado," Wright.

Action/Crime (PR:O MPAA:R)

HUMAN VAPOR, THE*½ (1964, Jap.) 79m Toho/Brenco c (GASU NINGEN DAIICHIGO)

Yoshio Tsuchiya *(Mizuno/The Vapor Man)*, Kaoru Yachigusa *(Fujichiyo the Dancer)*, Tatsuya Mihashi *(Okamoto the Detective)*, Keiko Sata *(Kyoko the Reporter)*, Bokuzen Hidari.

Tsuchiya is an ex-con who is blessed (or cursed) with the ability to transform himself into a gas, leaving nothing but a pile of clothes behind him. When a girl he loves is accused of a robbery, he takes the rap, turning into vapor and re-enacting the crime for the coppers. He proceeds to strangle the officers, who futilely fire bullets at the gaseous con. Hoping to get their man, the police enlist the aid of the woman, who in true Dillinger fashion leads the Vapor Man into a theater. They pipe some gas into the movie house and light a match. Poof goes Vapor Man. Directed by Inoshiro Honda (GODZILLA) who discovered that vapors are not as visual as giant flame-throwing lizards. Released in Japan in 1960.

p, Tomoyuki Tanaka; d, Inoshiro Honda; w, Takeshi Kimura; ph, Hajime Koizumi (TohoScope, Eastmancolor); m, Kunio Miyauchi; spec eff, Eiji Tsuburaya.

Science-Fiction/Crime Cas. (PR:A MPAA:NR)

HUMANITY* (1933) 70m FOX bw

Ralph Morgan *(Dr. William MacDonald)*, Boots Mallory *(Nancy Moore)*, Alexander Kirkland *(Bill MacDonald)*, Irene Ware *(Olive Pelton)*, Noel Madison, Wade Boteler, Christian Rub, Betty Jane Graham, Ferike Boros, George Irving, Crauford Kent, Nella Walker.

A soppy melodrama starring Morgan as a widowed New York doctor who has struggled to raise his son, Kirkland, and continues his back-breaking labors to pay for his son's medical training in Europe. Filled with anticipation for the day that his boy will work by his side helping the sick, Morgan is shocked when Kirkland arrives with a wealthy girl friend and announces his desire to practice medicine on Park Avenue. This leaves Morgan gravely disappointed, but when the son tends to a wounded mobster to make extra money, dad takes the fall, is drummed out of medical circles, and dies. Kirkland finally dumps his rich girl friend and picks up his father's practice on the Lower East Side.

d, John Francis Dillon; w, Bradley King (based on the story "The Road to Heaven" by Harry Fried); ph, L.W. O'Connell.

Drama (PR:A MPAA:NR)

HUMANOID, THE** (1979, Ital.) 100m Merope/COL c (L'UMANOIDE)

Richard Kiel *(Golob)*, Corinne Clery, Leonard Mann, Barbara Bach, Arthur Kennedy, Marco Yeh, Ivan Rassimov.

A tolerable STAR WARS attempt from Italy which has Kiel in an expanded version of his "Jaws" character from THE SPY WHO LOVED ME and MOONRAKER. He tries to stop the universal domination of a crazed scientist with the help of Clery, Kennedy, his girl friend Bach, and a little mysterious Tibetan. Rounding out the similarities is a robot dog. The score by Ennio Morricone is, per usual, top-flight.

p, Giorgio Venturini; d, George B. Lewis; w, Adriano Bolzoni, Aldo Lado; ph, Silvano Ippoliti; m, Ennio Morricone; spec eff, Ermanno Biamonte, Anthony M. Dawson [Antonio Margheriti], Armando Valcuada.

Science Fiction (PR:C MPAA:NR)

HUMANOIDS FROM THE DEEP½** (1980) 80m New World c (GB: MONSTER)

Doug McClure *(Jim)*, Ann Turkel *(Dr. Susan Drake)*, Vic Morrow *(Hank Slattery)*, Cindy Weintraub *(Carol Hill)*, Anthony Penya *(Johnny)*, Denise Galik *(Linda)*, Lynn Theel *(Peggy)*, Meegan King *(Jerry)*, Breck Costin *(Tommy)*, Hoke Howell *(Deke)*, Don Maxwell *(Dickie)*, David Strassman *(Billy)*, Greg Travis, Linda Shayne, Lisa Glaser, Bruce Monette, Shawn Erler, Frank Arnold, Amy Barrett, Jo Williams, Henry T. Williams, Lyle Isom, Jonathan Lehan.

Monsters from the ocean floor surface in a seaside community, kill the men, rape the women, and generally wreak havoc. Enter scientist Turkel, who, aided by fisherman McClure, sets out to learn where these creatures come from and why they are doing these horrible things. In the end the horny devils attack a carnival and destroy it. McClure and Turkel find a way to kill the beasties and the world is saved. But wait! One of the raped women gives birth and it looks just like. . . . Obviously relishing the chance to show everything they couldn't back in the early days of exploitation horror, the New World gang goes whole hog and breaks all the monster-movie taboos, while injecting heavy doses of black humor. Surprisingly, the film was directed by a woman. Not for everybody.

p, Martin B. Cohen, A. Hunt Lowry; d, Barbara Peeters; w, Frederick James (based on a story by Frank Arnold, Cohen); ph, Daniel Lacambre (Metrocolor); m, James Horner; ed, Mark Goldblatt; art d, Michael Erler; humanoid design, Rob Bottin.

Horror/Comedy Cas. (PR:O MPAA:R)

HUMONGOUS* (1982, Can.) 91m EM c

Janet Julian *(Sandy Rawlston)*, David Wallace *(Eric Simmonds)*, Janet Baldwin *(Donna Blake)*, John Wildman *(Nick Simmonds)*, Joy Boushel *(Carla Simmonds)*, Layne Coleman *(Burt Defoe)*, Shay Garner *(Ida Parsons)*, Ed McFadyen *(Mr. Parsons)*, Garry Robbins *(Ida's Son)*.

More gory horror trash from Canada which features the perennial group of teenagers out for an illicit weekend on the folks' boat. They wind up marooned on an island and in moments get hacked to bits by the giant, dog-eating madman who lives there. There's the usual nonsense about a legend which explains who this nut is and why he's killing everybody. Not only is this stupid, it's dull.

p, Anthony Kramreither; d, Paul Lynch; w, William Gray; ph, Brian Hebb; m, John Mills Cockwell; ed, Nick Rotundo; art d, Carol Spier; spec eff, Martin Malivoire.

Horror Cas. (PR:O MPAA:R)

HUMORESQUE*½** (1946) 123m WB bw

Joan Crawford *(Helen Wright)*, John Garfield *(Paul Boray)*, Oscar Levant *(Sid Jeffers)*, J. Carroll Naish *(Rudy Boray)*, Joan Chandler *(Gina)*, Tom D'Andrea *(Phil Boray)*, Peggy Knudsen *(Florence)*, Ruth Nelson *(Esther Boray)*, Craig Stevens *(Monte Loeffler)*, Paul Cavanagh *(Victor Wright)*, Richard Gaines *(Bauer)*, John Abbott *(Rozner)*, Bobby Blake *(Paul Boray as a Child)*, Don McGuire *(Eddie)*, Fritz Leiber *(Hagerstrom)*, Tommy Cook *(Phil Boray as a Child)*, Peg LaCentra *(Nightclub singer)*, Richard Walsh *(Teddy)*, Nestor Paiva *(Orchestra Leader)*, Creighton Hale *(Professor)*, Monte Blue *(Furniture Moving Man)*, Patricia Barry *(Fritzie the Telephone Operator)*, Don Turner *(Man with Dog)*, Ann Lawrence *(Florence as a Girl)*, Sylvia Arslan *(Gina as a Girl)*.

While in the midst of shooting HUMORESQUE, Crawford was awarded the Oscar for MILDRED PIERCE and what was a smallish role was suddenly expanded to make it a full-fledged costarring part with Garfield. With her favorite cameraman behind the lenses (Haller), Crawford never looked more ravishing nor was her acting ever any more controlled. This was made long before she decided that the scenery might be suitable for chewing, and her restraint, in what could have been an over-the-top role, was admirable. Adapted from Fannie Hurst's tearjerker (which had already been made as a silent film in 1920), the Odets-Gold screenplay crackles with wit (most of which comes from the mouth of Levant) and irony, thereby taking the onus off the bathetic story. Garfield (in a role not unlike the one he did in BODY AND SOUL) is a tough, temperamental, and highly ambitious violinist who is hired to play a party at the home of Crawford, a wealthy dilettante trapped in a loveless marriage to Cavanagh, who allows her to engage in various sexual forays with many different kinds of men. Crawford is a bored nymphomaniac who uses her wealth to get men to do her bidding, sort of like a QUEEN BEE (a role Crawford did nine years later). She takes Garfield to her attractive bosom but soon learns that he is not buyable and that his music matters more to him than all the trappings she can offer. The more he resists her, the more she falls in love with him and love is something she has seldom, if ever, felt, so she doesn't know how to handle it. She continues to help his career, then, functioning as his impresario, she presents him to the public and he is hailed as a bright star on the classical horizon. Garfield's poor-but-proud family wishes he would get rid of her as they are from two distinctly different universes and the family feels that nothing good can come of it. Crawford goes so far as to visit Naish and Nelson, Garfield's parents, to make herself known to them and to show that she is not just a married slut fiddling with a violinist, but that she truly loves him. Nelson cruelly tells her to keep away from Garfield. Crawford and Garfield can't stay away from each other but they are always quarreling and when she spots him with an old lover, she hits the ceiling and they both realize that this love cannot go anywhere. Crawford understands that her affair with Garfield, while deep and emotional, is but one of many that she's had over the years, all of which ended disastrously. While listening to Garfield perform on the radio, she makes the decision to end it all by walking into the ocean, in a scene reminiscent of A STAR IS BORN. Garfield's playing was so believable in the movie that he was often asked to pick up a violin while tub-thumping the movie. The reason for the requests was a brilliant bit of inventiveness on someone's part; a real violinist's arm was passed through a hole in Garfield's coat so the fingering would be authentic. At the same time, a second violinist hid behind Garfield and took care of the bow work. Then Isaac Stern dubbed all of the violin playing and voila, movie magic! The results were convincing and helped the picture enormously. Levant acts as the comedic counterpoint to the heavy love story and his presence is not only welcome, it's necessary to maintain a balance in the screenplay or this would have collapsed into hankiedom. More than 20 classical pieces also help to raise the level of the movie to auditory heights. Look for Robert Blake, playing Garfield as a young boy and proving already that he can act. Conversely, Cook, who plays Garfield's brother, was proving that he couldn't act, a trait he continued into adulthood.

p, Jerry Wald; d, Jean Negulesco; w, Clifford Odets, Zachary Gold (based on the story by Fannie Hurst); ph, Ernest Haller; m, Franz Waxman; ed, Rudi Fehr; md,

Leo F. Forbstein; art d, Hugh Reticker; set d, Clarence Steenson; spec eff, Roy Davidson; mus adv, Isaac Stern.

Drama **(PR:A-C MPAA:NR)**

HUMPHREY TAKES A CHANCE* (1950) 62m MON bw

Leon Errol *(Knobby)*, Joe Kirkwood *(Joe Palooka)*, Lois Collier *(Anne Howe)*, Robert Coogan *(Humphrey Pennyworth)*, Jack Kirkwood *(Phiffeney)*, Andrew Tombes *(Sheriff Grogan)*, Stanley Prager *(Ward)*, Tim Ryan *(Bentley)*, Almira Sessions *(Mrs. Hardwig)*, Joel Friedkin *(Hootleman)*, Tom Neal *(Gordon Rogers)*, Gil Lamb *(Martin)*, Chester Conklin *(Prentice)*, Hank Mann *(Hiram)*, Clarence Hennecke *(Zeke)*, Chester Clute *(Upperbottom)*, Victoria Horne *(Miss Tucker)*, Mary Happy *(Mary)*, Frank Sully *(Looie)*, Eddie Gribbon *(Canvas)*, Jim Drum *(2nd Heavy)*, Paul Gardini *(Artist)*, Iris Adrian *(Miss Tuttle)*.

Joe Palooka pummels again in another one of his comedy-boxing movies. This time, Kirkwood and his pal Errol must do battle with a shady mayor and a dishonest fight promoter who have fooled punchy boxer Coogan into signing a lousy contract with them. The crooks just want to use the dimwitted Coogan to snare Kirkwood into a contract. Luckily, the boys sort things out and Coogan is installed as the town's new mayor. (See JOE PALOOKA series, Index).

p, Hal E. Chester; d, Jean Yarbrough; w, Henry Blankfort; ph, William Sickner; ed, Otho Lovering; md, Edward J. Kay.

Sports/Comedy **(PR:A MPAA:NR)**

HUNCH, THE** (1967, Brit.) 56m Anvil/CFF c

Alex Norton *(Ian)*, Gordon Robb *(Harry)*, Amanda Jones *(Janet)*, Ross Campbell *(Saul)*, John Bannerman *(Granddad)*, Douglas Murchie *(Skipper)*, Bill McCabe *(Mate)*, Ian Dewar *(Pat McAinch)*.

A children's adventure tale has a group of youngsters off the coast of Scotland helping to salvage a disabled ship. Exciting enough to hold the interest of kiddie viewers but no one else.

p, J. B. Holmes; d&w, Sarah Erukker.

Children's Adventure **(PR:AA MPAA:NR)**

HUNCHBACK OF NOTRE DAME, THE***** (1939) 115m RKO bw

Charles Laughton *(The Hunchback)*, Sir Cedric Hardwicke *(Frollo)*, Thomas Mitchell *(Clopin)*, Maureen O'Hara *(Esmeralda)*, Edmond O'Brien *(Gringoire)*, Alan Marshal *(Proebus)*, Walter Hampden *(Claude)*, Harry Davenport *(Louis XI)*, Katharine Alexander *(Mme. De Lys)*, George Zucco *(Procurator)*, Fritz Leiber *(A Nobleman)*, Etienne Girardot *(The King's Physician)*, Helene Whitney *(Fleur)*, Minna Gombell *(Queen of Beggars)*, Arthur Hohl *(Olivier)*, Rod La Rocque *(Phillipo)*, Spencer Charters *(Court Clerk)*, Rondo Hatton.

It's often box office poison to remake a movie that has already been a great success but this was different because the Lon Chaney version of Hugo's tale was a silent and the addition of sound made it unique enough to warrant another try. Then, when they added the brilliance of Laughton and the comeliness of O'Hara to the Levien script, they had box office history. Unfortunately, this film was released at nearly the same moment as GONE WITH THE WIND and it had to take a back seat to that event. Made in black and white for almost $2 million, THE HUNCHBACK OF NOTRE DAME took great chances with its grotesqueries. Men are boiled alive, the hunchback is flogged, molten lead is poured on the heads of a huge crowd. No one knew if the public would sit still for this kind of realism but it did and made the picture a hit that year and an enduring classic forever. It's a beauty and the beast story with O'Hara as a gorgeous gypsy girl whom Laughton, the deformed hunchback in charge of the bells at Paris' Notre Dame Cathedral, has befriended and mutely loves. We know from the start that Laughton is doomed but after first cringing at his face and form (a marvel of makeup and prosthetics), we begin to get used to it and by the time the movie ends, we are in tears at what the corrupt clergy have done to him. The sets are enormous, well-researched, and almost overpower the story. Hampden is the Notre Dame Archbishop who accedes to the wishes of Hardwicke's insidious King's High Justice. Mitchell is the chief of the beggars, and O'Brien, in his first film, plays the poet (Hugo's character, no doubt) with conviction. (He'd recently arrived from a stint with Orson Welles' Mercury Theatre.) There were actually six films of Hugo's immortal tale (ESMERALDA in 1906, French, NOTRE DAME DE PARIS, 1911, French; THE DARLING OF PARIS, 1917, U.S. with Theda Bara as Esmeralda; and again in 1957 with Anthony Quinn). None of them compared to Laughton in what may have been the greatest role of his career. Oddly enough, this film took no Oscars and only had one nomination to Newman for his magnificent score. But that was not only the year of GONE WITH THE WIND, it was also the year for WUTHERING HEIGHTS, MR. SMITH GOES TO WASHINGTON, BABES IN ARMS, DARK VICTORY, GOODBYE, MR. CHIPS, NINOTCHKA, STAGECOACH, THE WIZARD OF OZ, and WHEN TOMORROW COMES. One of the greatest stories in literature has been made into one of the best adaptations in movies. The co-editor was Robert Wise, who was to distinguish himself as a director not too long after.

p, Pandro S. Berman; d, William S. Dieterle; w, Sonya Levien, Bruno Frank (based on the novel by Victor Hugo); ph, Joseph August; m, Alfred Newman; ed, William Hamilton, Robert Wise; art d, Van Nest Polglase; spec eff, Vernon L. Walker.

Historical Drama **Cas.** **(PR:A-C MPAA:NR)**

HUNCHBACK OF NOTRE DAME, THE** (1957, Fr.) 103m c (NOTRE DAME DE PARIS)

Gina Lollobrigida *(Esmeralda)*, Anthony Quinn *(Quasimodo)*, Jean Danet *(Capt. Phoebus)*, Alain Cuny *(Claude Frollo)*, Philippe Clay *(Clopin Trouillefou)*, Danielle Dumont *(Fleur de Lys)*, Robert Hirsch *(Gringoire)*, Jean Tissier *(Louis XI)*, Valentine Tessier *(Aloyse de Gondelaurier)*, Jacques Hilling *(Charmolue)*, Jacques Dufilho *(Guillaume Rousseau)*, Roger Blin *(Mathias Hungadi)*, Marianne Oswald *(La Falourdel)*, Pieral *(The Dwarf)*, Camille Guerini *(The President)*, Damia *(Beggar Woman)*, Robert Lombard *(Coppenole)*, Albert Remy *(Jupiter)*, Hubert de Lapparent *(Haraucourt)*, Boris Vian *(The Cardinal)*, Paul Bonifas *(Maitre Lecornu)*, Madeleine Barbulee *(Mme. Lecornu)*, Albert Michel *(Night Watchman)*, Daniel Emilfork *(Andry Le Rouse)*, Georges Douking *(Hoodlum)*.

The weakest film version of Victor Hugo's classic novel starring Quinn as the misshapen bellringer hopelessly in love with gypsy girl Lollobrigida. Quinn is passable as Quasimodo (though he doesn't hold a candle to Lon Chaney, Sr., or to Charles Laughton), but the production is slow and ponderous, as are most of the performances, leaving only the Technicolor and widescreen presentation of Paris as points of interest.

p, Robert Hakim, Raymond Hakim; d, Jean Delannoy; w, Jacques Prevert, Jean Aurenche (based on the novel by Victor Hugo); ph, Michel Kelber (CinemaScope, Technicolor); m, Georges Auric; ed, Henri Taverna; art d, Rene Renoux; ch, Leonide Massine; cos, Colosantis and Benda; m/l, Auric, Francisco Lavagnino, Paul Lafargs.

Historical/Drama **(PR:A-C MPAA:NR)**

HUNCHBACK OF ROME, THE½** (1963, Ital.) 84m Orsay/Royal bw (IL GOBBO)

Gerard Blain *(The Hunchback)*, Anna Maria Ferrero *(Ninetta)*, Ivo Garrani *(Moretti)*, Bernard Blier *(The Marshal)*, Pier Paolo Pasolini *(Er Monco)*, Teresa Pellati *(Fiorin Fiorello)*, Luba Bodine *(Nella)*, Enzo Cerusico *(Scheggia)*, Franco Balducci *(Pellaccia)*, Nino Castelnuovo *(Cencio)*, Roy Ciccolini *(Er Bello)*, Liuba Otasevic, Angela Luce, Piero Bugli.

An interesting version of the "Hunchback" legend, which has Blain cast as the title character. Set in Rome in 1944, Blain, a top figure in the Resistance movement, rapes Ferrero, the daughter of a Nazi collaborator. Eventually he falls in love with the girl. The hunchback is wounded by Nazi troops when he tries to steal some weapons from an arsenal and holes up in Ferrero's house. He kills the girl's dad and is caught by Fascist officials and tortured. As time goes by, Ferrero is made pregnant by the Hunchback, loses her child, and becomes a prostitute. Meanwhile, the Hunchback has taken over a Rome suburb with 150 armed rebels. He tries to raise enough cash to allow the town whores to live without prostitution, but is in turn laughed at. He enlists Ferrero's aid in escaping, but is killed in his attempt. A good attempt by director Carlo Lizzani to present a classically heroic character who is confronted with prejudice and social injustice. Director Pier Paolo Pasolini appears in one of his two film roles.

p, Dino De Laurentiis; d, Carlo Lizzani; w, Luciano Vincenzoni, Ugo Pirro, Elio Petri, Tommaso Chiaretti, Vittoriano Petrilli, Mario Socrate, Lizzani; ph, Leonida Barboni, Aldo Tonti; m, Piero Piccioni; ed, Franco Fraticelli; art d, Mario Chiari; set d, Giorgio Herman.

War/Drama **(PR:C MPAA:NR)**

HUNCHBACK OF THE MORGUE, THE zero (1972, Span.) 88m Cinemation c (EL JORBADO DE LA MORGUE)

Paul Naschy, Rossana Yanni, Vic Winner, Alberto Dalves, Maria Perschy.

Out of the bell tower and into the morgue, this hunchback is a perverse and gruesome murderer, played by Naschy. He spends his time snatching bodies for a scientist involved in a demented experiment with a living head. A piece of trash not intended for any living individual.

p, F. Lara Polop; d, Javier Aguirre; w, Aguirre, Jacinto Molina, Albert Insua; ph, Raul Perez Cubero (Eastmancolor); m, Carmelo Bernaola; ed, Petra de Nieva.

Horror **(PR:O MPAA:R)**

HUNDRED HOUR HUNT½** (1953, Brit.) 92m Nettleford/But bw (GB: EMERGENCY CALL)

Jack Warner *(Inspector Lane)*, Anthony Steel *(Dr. Carter)*, Joy Shelton *(Laura Bishop)*, Sidney James *(Danny Marks)*, Freddie Mills *(Tim Mahoney)*, Earl Cameron *(George Robinson)*, John Robinson *(Dr. Braithwaite)*, Thora Hird *(Mrs. Cornelius)*, Eric Pohlmann *(Flash Harry)*, Sydney Tafler *(Brett)*, Vida Hope *(Brenda)*, Geoffrey Hibbert *(Jackson)*, Henry Hewitt *(Mr. Wilberforce)*, Avis Scott *(Marie)*.

A young girl needs a transfusion of a rare blood and only three people can provide it: a black sailor about to depart for the orient, a boxer in trouble for refusing to throw the big fight, and a murderer who has been a fugitive for 12 years. The film follows each of these men as they are persuaded to come in to save the girl's life. Interesting if routine medical drama.

d, Lewis Gilbert; w, Vernon Harris, Gilbert; ph, Wilkie Cooper; m, Wilfred Burns; ed, Charles Hasse; art d, Bernard Robinson.

Drama **(PR:A MPAA:NR)**

HUNDRED POUND WINDOW, THE*½ (1943, Brit.) 90m WB-FN bw

Anne Crawford *(Joan Draper)*, David Farrar *(George Graham)*, Frederick Leister *(Ernest Draper)*, Mary Clare *(Millie Draper)*, Richard Attenborough *(Tommy Draper)*, Niall MacGinnis *(Chick Slater)*, David Hutcheson *(Steve Halligan)*, Francis Lister *(Capt. Johnson)*, Claud Allister *(Hon. Freddie)*, Claude Bailey *(John D. Humphries)*, Peter Gawthorne *(Van Rayden)*, John Slater *(O'Neil)*, David Horne *(Baldwin)*, Anthony Hawtrey *(Evans)*, Ruby Miller *(Mrs. Remington)*, Hazel Bray, C. Denier Warren.

Leister stars as an auditor who, after years of service, suddenly finds himself in a job at the race track where he works as a clerk at the betting windows. He soon becomes involved with gamblers who con him into participating in their crooked schemes, but he wises up and exposes them. Good-natured effort well performed.

d, Brian Desmond Hurst; w, Abem Finkel, Brock Williams, Rodney Ackland (based on a story by Mark Hellinger); m Hans May; m/l, Alan Stranks.

Crime **(PR:A MPAA:NR)**

HUNGER*** (1968, Den./Norway/Swed.) 115m Henning Carlsen-ABC Film-Sandrews-Svensk/Sigma III bw (SULT; SVALT)

Per Oscarsson *(The Writer)*, Gunnel Lindblom *(Ylajali)*, Sigrid Horne-Rasmussen *(Landlady)*, Osvald Helmuth *(Pawnbroker)*, Birgitte Federspiel *(Ylajali's Sister)*, Henki Kolstad *(Editor)*, Sverre Hansen *(Beggar)*, Egil Hjort Jensen *(Man in the Park)*, Per Theodor Haugen *(Shop Assistant)*, Lars Nordrum *("The Count")*, Roy Bjornstad *(Painter)*, Hans W. Petersen, Knud Rex, Wilhelm Lund, Ola B. Johannesen, Wilfred Breistrand, Else Heiberg, Veslemoy Haslund, Pal Skjonberg, Bjarne Andersen, Frimann Falck Clausen, Leif Enger, Lise Fjeldstad, Per Gjersoe, Toralf Sando, Carsten Byhring, Carl Ottosen, Kare Wichlund, Rolf Sand.

Oscarsson plays a writer at the end of the 19th century who is literally starving to death and forced to eat remnants from the garbage and bits of paper in order to stay alive. He is eventually kicked out of his apartment and takes to sleeping on park benches. But all through this ordeal the writer never loses his hope or pride, almost always certain that some money will come his way from his craft. Even when given money by a woman who is attracted to his arty nature, he tosses the gift away out of pride. When Oscarsson finally realizes that his situation has gotten unbearable, he takes a job aboard a ship. Oscarsson won the Best Acting Award at the Cannes Film Festival for his moving performance of a desperate man who never gives up. Though much of this film is depressing, it always carries a slight ray of hope, lifting it out of a dismal abyss.

p, Bertil Ohlsson; d, Henning Carlsen; w, Carlsen, Peter Seeberg (based on the novel *Sult* by Knut Hamsun); ph, Henning Kristiansen; m, Krzysztof Komeda; ed, Anja Breien; art d, Erik Aaes, Walther Dannerfjord; cos, Ada Skolmen.

Drama **(PR:O MPAA:NR)**

HUNGER, THE zero (1983) 99m MGM/UA c

David Bowie *(John)*, Catherine Deneuve *(Miriam)*, Susan Sarandon *(Sarah Roberts)*, Cliff DeYoung *(Tom Haver)*, Beth Ehlers *(Alice Cavender)*, Dan Hedaya *(Lt. Allegrezza)*, Rufus Collins *(Charlie Humphries)*, Suzanne Bertish *(Phyllis)*, James Aubrey *(Ron)*, Ann Magnuson, John Stephen Hill *(Disco Couple)*, Shane Rimmer *(Jelinek)*, Bauhaus *(Disco Group)*, Douglas Lambert *(TV Host)*, Bessie Love *(Lillybelle)*, John Pankow, Willem Dafoe *(Phone Booth Youths)*, Sophie Ward, Philip Sayer *(London House Couple)*, Lise Hilboldt *(Waiting Room Nurse)*, Michael Howe, Edward Wiley *(Interns)*, Richard Robles *(Skater)*, George Camiller *(Eumenes)*, Oke Wambu *(Egyptian Slave)*.

Bowie and Deneuve come on great in their tight leather outfits and dark glasses, intercut with shots of a rabid test monkey and the post-punk band Bauhaus playing "Bela Lugosi Is Dead." After this opening scene, however, the film takes a nose dive into the trashcan, as if the first sequence was directed by someone else. Bowie and Deneuve do what they can with the moronic script about two immortal vampires who must kill to retain their youth. Bowie senses that he is aging by the minute and pays a visit to scientist Sarandon. Dressed in a raincoat and hat, he waits for hours to see Sarandon. In a marvel of editing and makeup, he ages nearly 200 years in minutes. Sarandon pays a visit to Bowie's cryptic house where she encounters Deneuve and they make love. Rarely can one watch a picture and point to the spot where it falls apart, but in THE HUNGER it is easy. After the vampyric Deneuve sinks her teeth into Sarandon's flesh there is an abrupt and unintentionally funny cut to a knife slicing into a red chunk of steak. From this point on, the picture forgets about its tale of eternal love and decides to become a vampire story, which concludes with an awful rising of the dead in Bowie's attic. Director Tony Scott delivers a film so bad we forget about the merits of the first half.

p, Richard A. Shepard; d, Tony Scott; w, Ivan Davis, Michael Thomas (based on the novel by Whitley Strieber); ph, Stephen Goldblatt (Panavision, Metrocolor); m, Michel Rubini, Denny Jaeger; ed, Pamela Power; prod d, Brian Morris; art d, Clinton Cavers, Vicky Paul; cos, Milena Canonero.

Horror **Cas.** **(PR:O MPAA:NR)**

HUNGRY HILL** (1947, Brit.) 100m RANK/GFD bw

Margaret Lockwood *(Fanny Ross)*, Dennis Price *(Greyhound John)*, Cecil Parker *(Copper John)*, Dermot Walsh *(Wild Johnnie)*, Michael Denison *(Henry Brodrick)*, Arthur Sinclair *(Morty Donovan)*, Jean Simmons *(Jane Brodrick)*, Barbara Waring *(Barbara Brodrick)*, Dan O'Herlihy *(Harry Brodrick)*, Eileen Crowe *(Bridget)*, Eileen Herlie *(Katherine)*, Anthony Wager *(Young Johnnie)*, Michael Golden *(Sam Donovan)*, F.J. McCormick *(Old Tim)*, Shamus Locke *(Young Tim)*, Tony Quinn *(Denny Donovan)*, Henry Mollison *(Dr. Armstrong)*, Siobhan McKenna *(Kate Donovan)*, Hector McGregor *(Nicholson)*, Peter Murray *(Lt. Fox)*, Guy Rolf *(Bit)*.

Overworked dramatization of Daphne du Maurier's novel detailing a 50-year family feud that spans three generations of Irishmen. Set in 1840, the tale begins as the patriarch of the Donovan clan starts a rebellion against the Brodrick family which owns the copper mine that used to sit on Donovan property. In the battle the mine is burned down and the oldest Brodrick boy killed. This leaves Price as the head of the Brodrick family, and having little interest in the mining business, he spends much of his time courting local beauty Lockwood. They are soon married, and have four children, the eldest of which, Walsh, is spoiled by Lockwood. Eventually Price dies, leaving the greedy Lockwood and Walsh with control of the mine. Surprisingly, Walsh turns on his mother and she leaves for London, knowing when she's not wanted. Once in the big city, Lockwood turns to gambling and drug addiction for solace. One day Walsh bumps into his aging mother and he guiltily asks her to return to Ireland. She does and arrives just in time to see Walsh killed during a labor dispute with one of the Donovans. Lockwood has one of the clan arrested, but is eventually talked out of prosecuting by an elderly maid who implores her to end the feud. Lockwood does, and ends the film gloomily overlooking the mine.

p, William Sistrom; d, Brian Desmond Hurst; w, Daphne du Maurier, Terence Young (based on du Maurier's novel); ph, Desmond Dickinson; m, John Greenwood; ed, Alan L. Jaggs; md, Muir Mathieson; art d, A. Vetchinsky; cos, Eleanor Abbey.

Drama **(PR:C MPAA:NR)**

HUNGRY WIVES* (1973) 130m Latent Image/Jack H. Harris c (AKA: JACK'S WIFE; SEASON OF THE WITCH)

Jan White *(Joan)*, Ray Laine *(Gregg)*, Anne Muffly *(Shirley)*, Joedda McClain *(Nikki)*, Bill Thunhurst *(Jack)*, Virginia Greenwald *(Marion)*, Neil Fisher *(Dr. Miller)*, Esther Lapidus *(Sylvia)*, Jean Wechsler *(Gloria)*, Shirley Strasser *(Grace)*, Bob Trow *(Detective Mills)*, Dan Mallinger *(Sgt. Frazer)*, Ken Peters *(John Fuller)*, Marvin Lieber *(Jerry)*, Bill Hinzman *(Intruder)*, Daryl Montgomery, Charlotte Carter, Linda Creagan, Paul McCollough, Sue Michaels, Hal Priore, Luis Yuchum, Virginia Greenwald.

With his NIGHT OF THE LIVING DEAD trilogy, and such diverse films as MARTIN and CREEPSHOW, George Romero has emerged as one of America's leading independent filmmakers. But that doesn't necessarily always mean quality work, as is the case with HUNGRY WIVES. The idea is rife with black humor. White is a bored and lonely housewife who picks up a copy of *How to Become a Witch, a Primer*. After reading the advice in this volume, she proceeds to kill her idiotic husband and takes up with a local witch coven. One might expect a delicious satire of modern America with this premise, but surprisingly, HUNGRY WIVES is poorly made and extremely boring. The project looks as if it were thrown together on the smallest of budgets. But Romero has shown he can do great things on the skimpiest of budgets, making this all the more disappointing. Though Romero cultists might want to take a look, others should definitely avoid this low-class effort. Later releases of the film were cut down to 90 minutes, and a 1982 version tried to capitalize on the popularity of Romero's DAWN OF THE DEAD, and the just released HALLOWEEN III: SEASON OF THE WITCH. (A Donovan song on the soundtrack, "Season of the Witch," was all the inspiration needed by the releasing company to use a nearly identical title in an effort to snare unwary consumers.)

p, Nancy M. Romero; d&w, George A. Romero; ph, George Romero, Bill Hinzman; m, Steve Gorn; ed, George Romero.

Horror **(PR:O MPAA:R)**

HUNS, THE* (1962, Fr./Ital.) 85m Comptoir Francais-Film Columbus/Producers International c (LA REINE DES BARBARES; LA REGINA DEI TARTARI)

Chelo Alonso *(Tanya)*, Jacques Sernas *(Malok)*, Folco Lulli *(Igor)*, Philippe Hersent, Ciquita Coffelli, Piero Lulli, Mario Petri, Andrea Scotti, Pietro Tordi.

Set in the 1400s, the fighting between the Tartar hordes, known as the Huns, is the central idea in this picture. Alonso is raised by the Bala tribe after her village is destroyed. Trained as a warrior, she becomes queen and in a clash with a rival tribe emerges victorious and spares the life of Sernas. Together they take over the wealthy town of Kwarizim, and all ends peacefully.

p, Carlo Lombardi; d, Sergio Grieco; w, Marcello Ciorciolini, Rate Furlan (based on a story by Eric Klauss); ph, Alfio Contini (Totalscope, Eastmancolor); m, Bruno Canfora; ed, Enzo Alfonsi; art d, Alberto Boccianti; cos, Mario Giorsi.

Historical Drama/Action **(PR:C MPAA:NR)**

HUNT, THE**** (1967, Span.) 93m Elias Querejeta/Trans-Lux bw (LA CAZA)

Ismael Merlo *(Jose)*, Alfredo Mayo *(Paco)*, Jose Maria Prada *(Luis)*, Emilio Gutierrez Caba *(Enrique)*, Fernando Sanchez Polack *(Juan)*, Violetta Garcia *(Nina)*, Maria Sanchez Arosa.

This is an excellent and brutal moral tale, set against a story dealing with four rabbit hunters. Three Spanish Civil War veterans, along with a teen-ager about to experience his first hunt, return to an old battleground that is now filled with rabbits. Merlo, the outing organizer, hopes to borrow some money from his war buddy Mayo, a rich businessman. The tensions between the two friends, along with Prada, their alcoholic third comrade, build with frightening force. Old angers and rivalries flare up, taken out with frightening brutality on the rabbits. The inevitable conclusion leads to man against man as Mayo is killed by an accidental shot from Merlo's gun. Prada, believing the shot intentional, drives his jeep head on towards Merlo, who shoots the on-coming driver full force in his face. He too is fatally wounded, leaving Caba, Mayo's teen-age brother-in-law, staring numbly at the bloodied corpses. The tensions within the story are well realized by the ensemble. The anger and emotion are genuine, and help further the director's allusions to the Spanish Civil War. In his pitting of friend against friend in senseless slaughter, Saura has created a fine allegory for that terrible conflict. (In Spanish; English subtitles.)

p, Elias Querejeta; d, Carlos Saura; w, Saura, Angelino Fons (based on a story by Saura); ph, Luis Cuadrado; m, Luis de Pablo; ed, Pablo Gonzalez del Amo; art d, Carlos Ochoa.

Drama **(PR:O MPAA:NR)**

HUNT THE MAN DOWN*** (1950) 68m RKO bw

Gig Young *(Paul)*, Lynne Roberts *(Sally)*, Mary Anderson *(Alice McGuire)*, Willard Parker *(Eric Appleby)*, Carla Balenda *(Rolene Wood)*, Gerald Mohr *(Walter Long)*, James Anderson *(Kinkaid)*, John Kellogg *(Kerry McGuire)*, Harry Shannon *(Mr. Bennett)*, Cleo Moore *(Pat Sheldon)*, Christy Palmer *(Joan Brian)*, Paul Frees *(Packy Collins)*, James Scay *(Prosecutor)*.

Young plays a hard-working public defender seeking to clear the name of a fugitive who escaped years ago when found guilty for a murder he didn't commit. The man, James Anderson, had remained underground for 12 years and was only caught when he played hero during a bank robbery and was spotted by authorities. Back in jail, a sympathetic Young listens to his tale. One night, after being taken to a wild party by some new-found friends, Anderson was framed for the murder of one of the guests. Young believes Anderson and sets out to interview the original witnesses. The witnesses, of course, begin to die before Young can see them, convincing the attorney that the real killer is still at large. Meanwhile, at Anderson's new trial, the killer is tricked into blowing his cover when testifying against the innocent man. Well-written, performed, and directed with a sharp economy of style by veteran low-budget helmsman Archainbaud.

p, Lewis J. Rachmil; d, George Archainbaud; w, DeVallon Scott; ph, Nicholas Musuraca; m, Paul Sawtell; ed, Samuel E. Beetley; md, C. Bakaleinikoff; art d, Albert S. D'Agostino, Walter E. Keller.

Crime **Cas.** **(PR:A MPAA:NR)**

HUNT TO KILL (SEE: WHITE BUFFALO, THE, 1977)

HUNTED (SEE: STRANGER IN BETWEEN, THE, 1952, Brit.)

HUNTED, THE*½ (1948) 88m AA bw

Preston Foster *(Saxon)*, Belita *(Laura)*, Pierre Watkin *(Simon Rand)*, Edna Holland *(Miss Turner)*, Russell Hicks *(Meredith)*, Frank Ferguson *(Harrison)*, Joseph Crehan *(Police Captain)*, Larry Blake *(Hollis Smith)*, Cathy Carter *(Sally)*, Thomas Jackson, Charles McGraw, Tristram Coffin *(Detectives)*.

Foster plays a detective forced to send his fiancee to prison when it appears she is deeply involved in a bank robbery. She was framed, of course, but when she's released on parole she is framed again, this time for murder, and Foster has a hard time swallowing her sob story twice. The real killer is found and the surprisingly forgiving fiancee seems pleased as punch to be back in the arms of her detective. Stretches one's suspension of belief to the limits.

p, Scott R. Dunlap; d, Jack Bernhard; w, Steve Fisher; ph, Harry Neumann; m, Edward J. Kay; ed, Richard Heermance.

Mystery **(PR:A MPAA:NR)**

HUNTED, THE (SEE: TOUCH ME NOT, 1976, Brit.)

HUNTED IN HOLLAND** (1961, Brit.) 61m Wessex/CFF c

Sean Scully *(Tim)*, Jacques Verbrugge *(Piet)*, Sandra Spurr *(Aanike)*, Thom Kelling *(Van Kelling)*.

A young British boy, Scully, befriends some Dutch youngsters during a visit to Holland and finds himself in the middle of a diamond theft ring. He and his friends manage to prove themselves to the adults by capturing the crooks.

p, Ian Dalrymple; d, Derek Williams; w, Dalrymple, Williams.

Children's Film **(PR:AA MPAA:NR)**

HUNTED MEN½** (1938) 65m PAR bw (AKA: CRIME GIVES ORDERS)

Lloyd Nolan *(Joe Albany)*, Mary Carlisle *(Jane Harris)*, Lynne Overman *(Peter Harris)*, J. Carroll Naish *(Henry Rice)*, Delmar Watson *(Robert Harris)*, Larry "Buster" Crabbe *(James Flowers)*, Anthony Quinn *(Legs)*, Johnny Downs *(Frank Martin)*, Dorothy Peterson *(Mary Harris)*, Louise Miller *(Virgie)*, Regis Toomey *(Donovan)*, Fern Emmett *(Miss Quinn)*, George Davis *(Waiter)*, Hooper Atchley *(Headwaiter)*, Dick Rich *(Tiny)*, Dick Rush, J.P. McGowan *(Cops)*, John Elliott *(Detective Chief)*, John Hamilton *(Commissioner)*, Mitchell Ingraham *(Homicide Squad Chief)*, Wallis Clark *(Police Chief)*, Ivan Miller *(Police Captain)*, Howard Mitchell *(Doorman)*, Zeffie Tilbury *(Flower Woman)*, Phillip Warren *(Gangster)*, Stanley Price *(Cabbie)*, Scott Groves, Edwin Brian, John Hart *(Party Guests)*, Ruth Rogers, Janet Waldo, Laurie Lane, Mary Parker *(Girls)*.

Nolan is a tough gangster boss forced to go on the lam after murdering double-crossing nightclub owner Crabbe in a money dispute. Picked up by friendly (and drunken) middle-class homeowner Overman, Nolan can't believe his luck when the man mistakes him for an old buddy and invites him to stay in his home. Nolan accepts the invitation and soon grows to like Overman's family (especially daughter Carlisle) and they him. Overman's young son Watson takes a special liking to the stranger and begins a case of hero worship. Nolan's lawyer, Naish, likes the setup and drops by occasionally to update his boss on police progress into the case. Eventually Nolan is forced to reveal his identity to the family, and when the cops close in he can't force himself to hold them hostage. Not wanting to be a hero to Watson, Nolan forces the cops to kill him. A taut little thriller that falls precariously close to being maudlin. For the best rendition of similar material see THE DESPERATE HOURS with Frederic March and Humphrey Bogart.

p, Harold Hurley; d, Louis King; w, William R. Lipman, Horace McCoy (based on a play by Albert Duffy, Marian Grant); ph, Victor Milner; m, Boris Morros; ed, Anne Bauchens; art d, Hans Dreier, Franz Bachelin.

Crime/Drama **(PR:A MPAA:NR)**

HUNTER, THE* (1980) 107m PAR c

Steve McQueen *(Papa Thorson)*, Eli Wallach *(Ritchie Blumenthal)*, Kathryn Harrold *(Dotty)*, LeVar Burton *(Tommy Price)*, Ben Johnson *(Sheriff Strong)*, Richard Venture *(Spota)*, Tracey Walter *(Rocco Mason)*, Tom Rosales *(Bernardo)*, Theodore Wilson *(Winston Blue)*, Ray Bickel *(Luke Branch)*, Bobby Bass *(Matthew Branch)*, Karl Schueneman, Margaret O'Hara, James Spinks, Frank Delfino, Zora Margolis, Murray Rubin, Poppy Lagos, Dea St. La Mount, Lillian Adams, Thor Nielsen, Stan Wojno, Jr., Jodi Moon, Kathy Cunningham, Kelly Learman, Michael D. Roberts, Kevin Hagen, Luis Avalos, Wynn Irwin, Frank Arno, Ric DiAngelo, Ralph Thorson, Matilda Calnan, F. William Parker, Nathaniel Taylor, Tony Burton, Morgan Roberts, Frederick Sistaine, Taurean Blackque.

Steve McQueen became a TV star with a western bounty hunter show called "Wanted, Dead Or Alive." In THE HUNTER, he returns to his bounty-hunting roots but this film was far more dead than alive. Little more than a varied series of shticks, it is supposedly based on a real man's life and they made the mistake of trying to cram just about every incident that ever happened to the bounty hunter into just under two hours. The result is that we are never anywhere long enough to care and characters race in and out of the movie with no introduction and barely any by-play before McQueen's off to hunt the next person. Several attempts at action sequences fall flat and the gag about McQueen being a poor driver and crashing several automobiles only works if you recall that he was supposed to be a whiz behind the wheel in BULLITT. They must have clipped the core out of this movie because so much of what is seen makes no sense whatsoever. Better you should watch reruns of "Wanted, Dead Or Alive" as they had beginnings, middles, and ends. This only has a middle, and a fairly dull one at that. This was McQueen's last film.

p, Mort Engelberg; d, Buzz Kulik; w, Ted Leighton, Peter Hyams (based on the book by Christopher Keane and the life of Ralph Thorson); ph, Fred J. Koenekamp; m, Michel Legrand; ed, Robert Wolfe; prod d, Ron Hobbs; set d, Jim Tocci, George Gaines, Rick Simpson.

Crime Drama **Cas.** **(PR:C MPAA:PG)**

HUNTERS, THE*** (1958) 108m FOX c

Robert Mitchum *(Maj. Cleve Saville)*, Robert Wagner *(Lt. Ed Pell)*, Richard Egan *(Col. "Dutch" Imil)*, May Britt *(Kristina)*, Lee Phillips *(Lt. Carl Abbott)*, John Gabriel *(Lt. Corona)*, Stacy Harris *(Col. "Monkey" Moncavage)*, Victor Sen Yung *(Korean Farmer)*, Candace Lee *(Korean Child)*, Leon Lontoc *(Casey Jones)*, John Doucette *(Sergeant)*, Vinnie De Carlo *(Korean Bartender)*, Larry Thor *(Capt. Owynby)*, Ralph Manza *(Gifford)*, Nobu McCarthy *(Japanese Clerk)*, Nina Shipman *(WAF Lieutenant)*, Alena Murray *(Mrs. Mason)*, Jay Jostyn *(Maj. Dark)*, Robert Reed *(Jackson)*, Jimmy Baya *(Greek Sergeant)*, John Caler, Bob Olen, Mae Maeshire, Frank Kumagai, Chiyoko Tota Baker, Kam Tong, Rachel Stephens, Mary Song, James Yagi, Whamok Kim, Mabel Lim, Frank Tang.

Superb aviation footage is what takes this film out of the ordinary and sends it skyward. Set in Korea in 1952 at the apex of the euphemistically named "Police Action," it's the story of Mitchum, Wagner, and Phillips with a love triangle including Britt tossed in. The American pilots have been assigned to dogfight the Chinese "volunteer" pilots who are in Russian MIGs, but the Americans are not allowed to chase the enemy into North Korea. Mitchum is the leader, a tough coot with absolutely no fear in his heart. His diametrical opposite, Phillips, is so frightened that he begins drinking whenever he is supposed to fly a mission. Mitchum is a veteran of many WW II battles and has seen it all. Britt, who is married to Phillips, asks Mitchum to take a personal interest in the young man and Mitchum promises he will. Meanwhile, Mitchum and Britt have some romantic trysts in Japan (replete with the lovely scenery of famous locations). Phillips is shot down by the enemy and crash-lands behind enemy lines. Since they cannot go there officially, Mitchum and Wagner make an unofficial foray into the area to rescue Phillips. It's on this mission that Wagner, an overly egocentric type, learns the meaning of humility and Phillips finds strength in himself that he didn't know existed. In the end, Britt opts for husband Phillips, and Mitchum remains in Korea to fight the battle to its unconcluded conclusion. Directed by Dick Powell for maximum action effect, THE HUNTERS was an exciting wartime adventure that had just enough ground-level scenes to make the aerial stuff that much more effective.

p&d, Dick Powell; w, Wendell Mayes (based on the novel by James Salter); ph, Charles G. Clarke, Tom Tutwiler (CinemaScope, De Luxe Color); m, Paul Sawtell; art d, Lyle R. Wheeler, Maurice Ransford; ed, Stuart Gilmore, cos, Charles LeMaire; spec eff, Stuart Gilmore.

War Drama **(PR:A-C MPAA:NR)**

HUNTING IN SIBERIA** (1962, USSR) 60m Moscow Popular Science Studio/Artkino c (ZVEROLOVY)

Ivan Savkin *(Yegorov)*, Radner Muratov *(Dudin)*, K. Albanov *(Shirvakhun)*, B. Sitko *(Zharkov)*, Ivan Koval-Samborskiy *(Gloomy Hunter)*, Grigoriy Mikhaylov *(Makarov)*, Konstantin Nemolyayev *(Cherepanov)*, P. Lyubeshkin *(Zotov)*, D. Netrebin *(Trofimov)*, Georgiy Millyar, V. Boriskin, Sh. Tyumenbayev, Y. Dubasov, G. Okhrimenko.

Savkin, a young tiger hunter, is hired to capture one of the animals for a zoo, but kills it out of fear. Eventually he becomes a skillful hunter and familiarizes himself with the ways of the wilderness. The Soviet version is 82 minutes.

d, Gleb Nifontov; w, Serafima Burlyuk, Anatoliy Zhadan; ph, Georgiy Kholnyy (Sovcolor); m, Aleksandr Lokshin, A. Sevastyanov; art d, G. Rozhalin, Y. Benin.

Adventure/Drama **(PR:A MPAA:NR)**

HUNTING PARTY, THE* (1977, Brit.) 108m Levy-Gardner-Laven/UA c

Oliver Reed *(Frank Calder)*, Candice Bergen *(Melissa Ruger)*, Gene Hackman *(Brandt Ruger)*, Simon Oakland *(Matthew Gun)*, Ronald Howard *(Watt Nelson)*, G.D. Spradlin *(Sam Bayard)*, Bernard Kay *(Buford King)*, Eugenio Escudero Garcia *(Mario)*, Mitchell Ryan *(Doc Harrison)*, L.Q. Jones *(Hog Warren)*, William Watson *(Loring)*, Rayford Barnes *(Crimp)*, Dean Selmier *(Collins)*, Ritchie Adams *(Owney Clark)*, Carlos Bravo, Bud Strait *(Cowboys)*, Ralph Brown *(Sheriff)*, Marian Collier *(Teacher)*, Max Slaten *(Telegrapher)*, Rafael Escudero Garcia *(Mexican)*, Emilio Rodriques Guiar *(Priest)*, Sara Atkinson *(Redhead)*, Francisca Tu *(Chinese Girl)*, Lilibeth Solison *(Blonde)*, Marisa Tovar *(Mexican Girl)*, Christine Larroude, Stephanie Pieritz *(Other Girls)*.

A very poor British attempt to imitate an Italian western by shooting it in Spain, and splattering blood all over the country-side. A fine cast is totally wasted in this film. Hackman plays a millionaire rancher who goes away on a hunting trip with some of his friends. While he is gone, Reed and his gang of badmen kidnap Hackman's wife, Bergen, mistaking her for the schoolteacher Reed has planned to coerce into teaching him to read. When Hackman gets back and learns of his wife's abduction, he goes out looking for the kidnapers with his high-powered hunting rifle. Slowly he guns down the gang at long distance, until only Bergen and Reed are left. Bergen has fallen in love with Reed by this point, and Hackman kills the two of them on a desert flat before dying himself of heat exhaustion.

p, Lou Morheim; d, Don Medford; w, William Norton, Gilbert Alexander, Morheim (based on a story by Alexander, Morheim); ph, Cecilio Paniagua (DeLuxe Color); m, Riz Ortolani; ed, Tom Rolf; md, Ortolani; art d, Enrique Alarcon; cos, Tony Pueo; spec eff, Manuel Baquero.

Western **(PR:O MPAA:R)**

HURRICANE* (1929) 60m COL bw

Hobart Bosworth *(Hurricane)*, Johnny Mack Brown, Leila Hyams, Allan Roscoe, Tom O'Brien.

An early Columbia talkie, this film is not an earlier version of the 1937 John Ford classic. The title, HURRICANE, is derived from the name of the main character, played by Bosworth. The main action comes from the attempted mutiny by captain Bosworth and his sea-going henchmen when they are left stranded. Also thrown in is a love angle between Brown and Hyams. The soundtrack has no musical background, just sound effects and dialog, and in scenes where both dialog and sound effects are present the sound effects win.

d, Ralph Ince; w, Norman Houston (based on a story by Norman Springer).

Action **(PR:A MPAA:NR)**

HURRICANE, THE****** (1937) 110m Goldwyn/UA bw

Dorothy Lamour *(Marama)*, Jon Hall *(Terangi)*, Mary Astor *(Madame Germaine De Laage)*, C. Aubrey Smith *(Father Paul)*, Thomas Mitchell *(Dr. Kersaint)*, Raymond Massey *(Governor Eugene De Laage)*, John Carradine *(Jailer)*, Jerome Cowan *(Capt. Nagle)*, Al Kikume *(Chief Mehevi)*, Kuulei DeClercq *(Tita)*, Layne Tom, Jr. *(Mako)*, Mamo Clark *(Hitia)*, Movita Castenada *(Arai)*, Reri *(Reri)*, Francis Kaai *(Tavi)*, Pauline Steele *(Mata)*, Flora Hayes *(Mama Rua)*, Mary Shaw *(Marunga)*, Spencer Charters *(Judge)*, Roger Drake *(Captain of Guards)*, Inez Courtney *(Girl on Ship)*, Paul Stader *(Stuntman)*, William B. Davidson *(Man Who's Injured)*.

This South Seas spectacular proved to be another superlative film from the great John Ford, one of those perennial films the viewer never tires of seeing. Again Ford builds a great film with a simple story as he would later do with STAGECOACH, THE GRAPES OF WRATH, HOW GREEN WAS MY VALLEY, and other unforgettable productions. Lamour and Hall are childhood sweethearts who live on the small but inviting island of Manakoora. Following their marriage, Hall leaves his native surroundings as the strong first mate of a ship captained by Cowan. When the ship docks in Tahiti, Cowan warns Hall to watch his volatile temper while they are in port. Hall and some of the other native crew members go to a saloon and share some innocent fun when Davidson, an overbearing, drunken white man, passes their table. Hearing them laugh he turns and heaps curses at them, picking a fight with Hall who lashes out and, with one mighty blow, breaks the bully's jaw. Hall is thrown into prison where sadistic jailer Carradine beats him. Cowan protests the imprisonment to the governor but he is told that the man who has had his jaw broken is influential and the powerful native must serve some time to satisfy the victim's complaint. Cowan explains that the governor doesn't understand such natives as Hall, that they cannot take captivity and will try to escape at any cost. The governor is adamant; Hall must serve his time. Working under the whip the next day on a hilltop with other convicts, Hall sees Cowan's ship sailing out to sea. He breaks free, jumps a fence, runs down a hill and leaps off a cliff, swimming wildly after the ship as the guards shoot at him. He almost catches up with the vessel but its sails billow full of wind and it quickly outdistances the exhausted Hall who vainly shouts after his friends who are now out of earshot. He turns sadly back to shore where he collapses. Hall is given another lengthy term on top of his initial sentence for attempting to escape. Repeated escape attempts year after year increase Hall's original six-month sentence to fifteen years, an injustice ranted against by Manakoora's hard-drinking physician, Mitchell, who had been present at the wedding of Hall and Lamour. The local priest, Smith, joins with Mitchell in appealing Hall's case to the new island governor, Massey. But Massey is a rules-and-regulations autocrat who intends to enforce the law. He turns a deaf ear to his attractive wife Astor when she too asks that he pardon Hall. Hall finally manages to break out of prison again, this time killing a guard accidentally in the process. He slips into the town, breaks into a supply store, and takes food and water, diving into the water when guards detect his presence and fire at him. Pushing an outrigger canoe away from the docks, Hall manages to get into open water and then begins his perilous 600-mile journey back to Manakoora. He barely survives starvation, thirst, and the savage sea which overturns his craft. Just when he is about to give up hope, he is spotted clinging half conscious to the overturned canoe by Smith and a small boy. The priest takes him into his boat and back to Manakoora, refusing to tell authorities whether Hall has returned or not. Hall meanwhile is reunited with Lamour and sees his young daughter for the first time. Hall, Lamour, and their child load a large boat with supplies as they prepare to leave Manakoora and sail to a distant island to live in peace. The seas suddenly rise and hurricane winds begin to lash the island. The winds grow fiercer as the natives and the few whites take refuge. Massey's governor's house is being torn to shreds and his wife Astor takes refuge in the church with Smith, at the highest point on the island. The hurricane mounts in intensity, shredding buildings, whipping the waves ever higher over the small island, driving half the population into the church where Smith beseeches God to save his parishioners. The wind howls like a pack of starving dogs, drowning out the prayers. Mitchell is outside the church at the ocean's edge, inside a large boat, trying to help a native woman give birth to a child while her family surrounds him. Others take to small boats and tie themselves inside. The blast of wind is now full force, tearing away everything on the island and blowing it into the sea—people, animals, buildings, bending palm trees double, hurtling the living to instant death in the black sky and seas. Hall, Lamour, and their child take refuge in the oldest, strongest tree, lashing themselves to the trunk. When Hall sees the church begin to crumble, he fights through the ever-rising waves to the church with a lifeline, also tied to the tree, and begs the natives, Astor, and Smith to follow him and save themselves. Some leave, including Astor at Smith's insistence, but those remaining quickly die with the priest as the storm peaks and a mountain of water crashes down on the church, tearing it and its occupants away to their doom. Those in the tree take a bitter beating and the tree is finally wrenched away and sent to sea. At dawn, Astor, Hall, Lamour, and the child are safe on a sandbar. A single canoe has washed up on the tiny reef. Cowan's battered ship, its masts ripped away, moving under the power of its small motors, is seen by those on the sandbar. On board the ship is Massey, peering anxiously through a telescope, searching for his wife Astor. He spots her alone on the sandbar and the ship goes to her rescue. Later, gratefully standing at her side, Massey again scans the now tranquil sea and spots the canoe carrying Hall and his family to safety. Astor, fearing that her husband will not bend his iron will and still seek to recapture Hall, even though he has saved her life, implores her husband to see something other than what he really sees. "It's only a floating log, Eugene," Astor says. Massey sees clearly through the telescope that it's Hall, the man he has been searching for, but he turns with a smile to his anxious wife and says: "Yes, you're right—it's only a floating log." THE HURRICANE is not only a rousing first-class adventure but a study of man's inhumanity to man, and, in Massey's case, a portrait of unswerving moral injustice not dissimilar to Charles Laughton's blood-hound character in LES MISERABLES (1935). The scenes of the actual hurricane are terrifyingly spectacular, one of the most brilliant and horrific climaxes ever brought to the screen, done on actual and miniature scales so cleverly edited that it is next to impossible to discern where one leaves off and the other element takes over. The disaster segment, which shows all of Irwin Allen's hokey efforts amateurish by comparison, is spellbinding. Basevi directed the entire 20-minute storm sequence, utilizing a $400,000 budget Goldwyn awarded him for that purpose. Hall and Lamour, two relatively unknown actors, do surprisingly well in their roles of scantily clad natives while Astor is effective as the governor's wife sympathetic to Hall's plight. Lamour, a $75-a-week bit player at Paramount with only four films to her credit, was borrowed by Goldwyn from that studio. Goldwyn originally wanted Howard Hawks to direct this film but they had argued violently over the making of COME AND GET IT (1936) and Goldwyn next turned to John Ford to direct THE HURRICANE. The mogul had also intended Joel McCea to enact the part of the persecuted native Terangi but McCrea convinced Ford that he was not right for the role and Ford came up with Hall, cousin of the co-author of the book, a handsome, virile-looking actor Ford had spotted in a minor production of the Hollywood Playhouse. Hall would have a checkered career after THE HURRICANE, coming to prominence in the early 1940s in a series of adventure and fantasy tales with exotic co-star Maria Montez. Lamour's star would rise even higher, especially after parlaying her sarong to fame—she first wore it in THE JUNGLE PRINCESS, 1936—one she would wear through many a Bob Hope-Bing Crosby road film. Astor's role was more of a supporting part and she was exposed to the full blast of the hurricane shot in the tank and on the back lot where the entire island had been reconstructed. Shots of Tahiti, taken by a second unit as early as 1935 when Goldwyn bought the Nordhoff-Hall novel in galley sheets, were intercut with the set shots. Astor would later remember how "we walked against winds, carefully calculated to blow at near hurricane level. Huge propellers kept us fighting for every step, with sand and water whipping our faces, sometimes leaving little pinpricks of blood on our cheeks from the stinging sand." In the tree shots where the wave machines and wind propellers were concentrated, Astor and others are tied to branches. The branch to which Astor was tied almost tore away, which would have sent her crashing downward to certain serious injury. It partially broke and she swayed to and fro until Ford called "cut!" When Astor looked over to the great director she noticed that the handkerchief he had alternately exchanged with his long-stemmed pipe to chew upon, was in pieces, the storm sequence and possible injuries to his actors having wholly unnerved him. Veteran character actors Mitchell, Smith, and Cowan were exceptional. It amused Ford to see the elderly Smith, playing the role of the kindly priest, insist upon stopping scenes in the afternoon to enjoy "tea time" where tea, rolls, and jam were served to the cast. Massey, as the intransigent governor, does his usual job of overacting but is fascinating to watch as he inexplicably spends his passion and energy in a search for a lowly native, an almost berserk obsession similar to Walter Huston's driving compulsion to eradicate lowly prostitute Joan Crawford in RAIN (1932). The storm was the real star of the film, created by wizard Basevi, who built a 600-foot set which contained the entire island, wharves, church, huts, the governor's house, trees, a beach, and a lagoon which was really a 200-foot tank. To recreate the seismic sea wave that finally engulfs the entire island, Basevi unleashed 2,000 gallons of water from overhead tanks. Accompanying the fierce storm was a sound never before heard by moviegoers—that of the howling, screeching, moaning, sighing hurricane. Studio technicians recorded the sounds for the storm separately and these were later added to the sound track. They achieved the weird noises by rolling marbles around in a box and running sandpaper across steel wire. The sound department would receive an Oscar for its inventiveness. The overall effect was astounding and the disaster sequence ranks with those scenes of natural calamity depicted in THE GOOD EARTH (1937) when the locusts cover the earth and in SAN FRANCISCO (1936) when the earth itself opens to swallow stricken humanity. Even the downpour of rain in the storm segment was enhanced. Since real rain shows only like tiny scratches across the film, milk was added to give it dimension (just as snow does not photograph as snow and so therefore parched cornflakes, soap chips, and plastic snowflakes are substituted to appear more real than the real thing). Ford paid tribute to Basevi's startling creation: "Jim Basevi conceived the hurricane itself and actually did all the mechanics. While he and I were shooting it, I gave Stu Heisler a second camera—you never knew what the hell would happen—and I said, 'If the roof blows off or a sarong blows off or somebody falls down—get it!' And, as a matter of fact, I think he [Heisler] had quite a few shots in the picture." The haunting song, "Moon of Manakoora" (Frank Loesser and Alfred Newman) later became a nationwide record hit.

p, Samuel Goldwyn; d, John Ford, (uncredited) Stuart Heisler; w, Dudley Nichols, Oliver H. P. Garrett (based on the novel by Charles Nordhoff, James Norman

Hall); ph, Bert Glennon; m, Alfred Newman; ed, Lloyd Nosler; art d, Richard Day, Alexander Golitzen; set d, Julia Heron; cos, Omar Kiam; spec eff, James Basevi.

Disaster/Adventure (PR:A MPAA:NR)

HURRICANE, THE 1964

(SEE: VOICE OF THE HURRICANE, 1964)

HURRICANE zero (1979) 119m DD/PAR c (AKA: FORBIDDEN PARADISE)

Jason Robards, Jr. *(Capt. Bruckner)*, Mia Farrow *(Charlotte Bruckner)*, Max von Sydow *(Dr. Bascomb)*, Trevor Howard *(Father Malone)*, Dayton Ka'Ne *(Matangi)*, Timothy Bottoms *(Jack Sanford)*, James Keach *(Sgt. Strang)*, Richard Sarcione *(Lt. Howard)*, Ariirau Tekurarere *(Moana)*, Willie Myers *(Cpl. Morrah)*, Nick Rutgers *(Cmdr. Blair)*, Nancy Hall Rutgers *(Mrs. Blair)*, Manu Tupou *(Samolo)*, Simplet Tefane *(Velaga)*, Piero Bushin *(Running Man)*, Noel Teparii *(Tano)*, John Taea *(Flaeiva)*, Taeve Tetuamia *(Elder)*, Bernadette Sarcione *(Siva)*, Roo *(Fire Dancer)*.

Another wretched Dino De Laurentiis, multi-million dollar (22 million to be exact) flop, this time a remake of John Ford's classic 1937 HURRICANE (well, if not classic, at least darn better than this). Farrow stars as the white-bread daughter of Navy man Robards, traveling to Eastern Samoa to visit her papa. Despite her racial misgivings she soon falls in love with young island prince Ka'Ne, much to her daddy's dismay. After about ninety minutes of soap opera, the giant hurricane hits and the last twenty minutes of the film are spent on tidal waves, high winds and uprooted palm trees. While the effects are fine (supervisor Glen Robinson also headed up the effects for the 1937 version), the story and performances are mindless and the film packs about as much punch as a waterlogged lei.

p, Dino De Laurentiis; d, Jan Troell; w, Lorenzo Semple, Jr. (based on the novel *Hurricane* by Charles Nordhoff, James Norman Hall); ph, Sven Nykvist (Todd AO, Technicolor); m, Nino Rota; ed, Sam O'Steen; prod d, Danilo Donati; art d, Giorgio Postiglione; set d&cos, Donati; spec eff, Glen Robinson, Aldo Puccini, Joe Day; ch, Coco.

Romance Cas. (PR:A MPAA:PG)

HURRICANE HORSEMAN*½ (1931) 59m State Rights bw

Lane Chandler, Marie Quillan, Walter Miller, Lafe McKee, Yakima Canutt, Dick Alexander, Charles "Rube" Shaefer, Robert Smith, Raven the Horse.

A low-budget western that stars Chandler as its gun-toting hero. A gunsmith who travels through the West doing six-shooter repairs, he comes upon a camp of outlaws holding a Spanish woman for ransom. He works out a plan to rescue the woman after doing repair work on the outlaw band's guns. When he rides off with the girl, and the badmen shoot at them, their guns either fizzle out or blow up in their hands. Good fun.

p, Willis Kent; d, Armand Schaefer; w, Oliver Drake (based on a story by Douglas Dawson); ph, William Nobles; ed, Ethel Davey.

Western (PR:A MPAA:NR)

HURRICANE ISLAND** (1951) 71m COL c

Jon Hall *(Capt. Carlos Montalvo)*, Marie Windsor *(Jane Bolton)*, Marc Lawrence *(Angus Macready)*, Romo Vincent *(Jose)*, Edgar Barrier *(Ponce de Leon)*, Karen Randle *(Maria)*, Jo Gilbert *(Okahla)*, Nelson Leigh *(Padre)*, Marshall Reed *(Rolfe)*, Don Harvey *(Valco)*, Rick Vallin *(Coba)*, Rus Conklin *(Owanga)*, Alex P. Montoya *(Alfredo)*, Lyle Talbot *(Physician)*, Rusty Wescoatt *(Crandall)*, Zon Murray *(Lynch)*.

A fanciful account of Ponce de Leon's search for the Fountain of Youth. The central character is Hall, a Spanish captain accompanying Ponce de Leon (Barrier) on his new world explorations. Along with the explorers is a female pirate, Windsor, who hopes to grab the gold they believe will be found at the fountain. When Barrier is injured during a landing in Florida, the group goes out in search of the fountain that will restore him. Their trail leads them to female Indian leader Gilbert, who is also the guardian of the magical spring. She heals Barrier, but dies when the fountain dries up. With her last bit of waning magical energy, Gilbert conjures up a hurricane that just about kills everybody. Windsor reforms at the end and enters into a romance with Hall.

p, Sam Katzman; d, Lew Landers; w, David Mathews; ph, Lester White (Supercinecolor); ed, Richard Fantl; md, Mischa Bakaleinikoff; art d, Paul Palmentola.

Adventure (PR:A MPAA:NR)

HURRICANE SMITH** (1942) 68m REP bw

Ray Middleton *(Hurricane Smith)*, Jane Wyatt *(Joan Wyatt)*, Harry Davenport *(Robert Ingersoll Reed)*, J. Edward Bromberg *(Eggs Bonelli)*, Harry Brandon *(Sam Carson)*, Casey Johnson *(Johnny Smith)*, Charles Trowbridge *(Mark Harris)*, Frank Darien *(Pop Wessell)*, Howard Hickman *(Sen. Bradley)*, Emmett Vogan *(Prosecuting Attorney)*.

Middleton is mistaken for a holdup man and jailed. He breaks out, catches up to the real crooks, and gets the loot away from them. Instead of returning the loot and clearing his name, he marries Wyatt, and they use the money to build a city in the desert. Of course, after establishing themselves as pillars of the community, one of the original crooks, Bromberg, shows up to do some blackmailing. Wyatt ends up killing him, and the nightmare ends.

p, Robert North; d, Bernard Vorhaus; w, Robert Presnell (based on a story by Charles G. Booth); ph, Ernest Miller; ed, Edward Mann.

Western (PR:A MPAA:NR)

HURRICANE SMITH*½ (1952) 90m PAR c

Yvonne De Carlo *(Luana)*, John Ireland *(Hurricane Smith)*, James Craig *(Gorvahlsen)*, Forrest Tucker *(Dan McGuire)*, Lyle Bettger *(Clobb)*, Richard Arlen *(Brundage)*, Mike Kellin *(Dicer)*, Murray Matheson *(Dr. Whitmore)*, Henry Brandon *(Sam)*, Emile Meyer *(Capt. Raikes)*, Stuart Randall *(Matt Ward)*, Ralph Dumke *(Ben Hawkins)*, Kim Spalding *(Brown)*, Don Dunning *(Adams)*, Ethan Laidlaw *(Old Tom)*, Eric Alden, George Barton, Loren B. Brown, James A. Cornell, Clint Dorrington, Al Kikume, Leo J. McMahon, King Mojave, Fred N. Revelala, Jack Trent, Leon Lontoc *(Sailors)*, Leon C. "Buck" Young *(Guard)*, Cliff Clark *(Australian Policeman)*, Anthony Warde *(Bos'n)*, Ted Ryan, Eddie Magill *(Policemen)*, Harvey Parry *(Cook)*, Maiola Kalili *(Malinka)*.

Ireland stars as the leader of a trio of swashbucklers (Tucker and Arlen being his cohorts) who find themselves stranded on a desert isle. One day a ship full of slave traders arrives in search of natives to kidnap and sell, so the trio of pirates steal their ship (including the captain and first mate) and set sail for Australia. Once "down-under" the gang looks for ways to raise enough cash in order to set sail again in search of the loot that Ireland had buried years ago in case of an emergency. Luckily, scientists Craig and Matheson, accompanied by the lovely (and unnecessary) De Carlo, want to hire out the ship for a scientific expedition. Ireland and his cronies jump at the chance, but once out to sea they realize that these "scientists" are actually after their loot. Knowing that his cover is blown, Craig enlists the kidnaped captain and first mate and takes over the ship. Craig and De Carlo have fallen in love and disguise themselves as normal sailors and slip away to find the treasure.

p, Nat Holt; d, Jerry Hopper; w, Frank Gruber (based on the story *Hurricane Williams* by Gordon Ray Young); ph, Ray Rennahan (Technicolor); m, Paul Sawtell; ed, Frank Bracht; art d, Hal Pereira, Walter Tyler; set d, Sam Comer, Bertram Granger.

Adventure (PR:A MPAA:NR)

HURRY, CHARLIE, HURRY** (1941) 65m RKO bw

Leon Errol *(Daniel Boone)*, Mildred Coles *(Beatrice Boone)*, Kenneth Howell *(Jerry Grant)*, Cecil Cunningham *(Mrs. Boone)*, George Watts *(Horace Morris)*, Eddie Conrad *(Wagon Track)*, Noble Johnson *(Poison Arrow)*, Douglas Walton *(Michael Prescott)*, Renee Haal *(Josephine Whitley)*, Georgia Caine *(Mrs. Whitley)*, Lalo Encinas *(Frozen Foot)*.

Errol stars in this sporadically funny little comedy as a henpecked banker of a small town at odds with his snobby wife Cunningham over the future of their daughter Coles. Cunningham wants Coles to marry someone rich, while Errol sees that the girl loves a lowly bakery delivery boy and urges her to marry for love, not money. In the meantime, Errol manages to get out of going to a ritzy mountain resort with his wife by using the excuse that he must travel to Washington for a meeting with the vice president. Errol is actually going to Washington, Oklahoma, on a fishing trip. When he returns, he is surprised to learn that he is now considered an important man due to his impressive (though nonexistent) political connections and the whole town turns out to greet him. This leads to some bizarre situations as Errol scrambles to maintain his credibility by dressing up his buddies as the vice president to fool the townsfolk. Luckily the *real* vice president shows up and vindicates him.

p, Howard Benedict; d, Charles E. Roberts; w, Paul Gerard Smith (based on a story by Luke Short); ph, Nicholas Musuraca; ed, George Hively.

Comedy Cas. (PR:A MPAA:NR)

HURRY SUNDOWN* (1967) 146m Sigma/PAR c

Michael Caine *(Henry Warren)*, Jane Fonda *(Julie Ann Warren)*, Loring Smith *(Thomas Elwell)*, Peter Goff *(Lipscomb)*, George Kennedy *(Sheriff Coombs)*, John Phillip Law *(Rad McDowell)*, Luke Askew *(Dolph Higginson)*, Robert Hooks *(Reeve Scott)*, Beah Richards *(Rose Scott)*, Burgess Meredith *(Judge Purcell)*, Madeleine Sherwood *(Eula Purcell)*, Donna Danton *(Sukie Purcell)*, Frank Converse *(Rev. Clem De Lavery)*, William Elder *(Bishop)*, Steve Sanders *(Charles McDowell)*, Faye Dunaway *(Lou McDowell)*, Dawn Barcelona *(Ruby McDowell)*, David Sanders *(Wyatt McDowell)*, Michael Henry Roth *(Timmy McDowell)*, Gladys Newman *(Mrs. Coombs)*, Joan Parks *(Kissie)*, John Mark *(Colie Warren)*, Diahann Carroll *(Vivian Thurlow)*, Rex Ingram *(Prof. Thurlow)*, Doro Merande *(Ada Hemmings)*, Jim Backus *(Carter Sillens)*, Robert C. Bloodwell *(Ozzie Higginson)*, Charles Keel *(Kenny)*, Kelly Ross *(Dottie)*, Ada Hall Covington *(Clara)*, Robert Reed *(Lars Finchley)*, Gene Rutherford, Bill Hart, Dean Smith *(Hunt Club)*.

Boring, lifeless, and in bad taste, the only reason why this terrible movie rates any mention at all is that it's chock full of stars and one wonders what in the world they saw in the script to make them do it. Preminger always seems to attract heavyweight actors and to place them in lightweight films (SKIDDOO! SUCH GOOD FRIENDS, ROSEBUD, THE HUMAN FACTOR and a host of other bombs). The reviews were universally damning and all correct. Set in the South at the end of WW II, HURRY SUNDOWN depicts Caine as a mean real estate developer buying up all the property he can lay his greedy paws on in the hopes of putting them all together for a huge profit. Two small lots evade him. One is owned by a poor white family and the other by a poor black family. Caine sends his wife, Fonda, to the black family's home to attempt to convince them to sell. She knows the family from before, as the matriarch, Richards, had been Fonda's "nanny" when she was growing up. Fonda appeals to Richards to sell out and Richards responds by having a heart attack and dying in the most ridiculous scene ever shot by Preminger (well, maybe not the *most* ridiculous, but close). With Richards out of the way, Hooks, her son, becomes the leader of the family but carries on Richards' tradition of not selling out. Caine is enraged and attempts to get Hooks into trouble by claiming that Hooks doesn't own the right and proper deed to the land. Bigoted judge Meredith tries to nail Hooks but peace and happiness with justice triumph in the court of law when schoolmarm Carroll arrives with proof of Hooks' ownership. Caine is even angrier now and gathers a lynch mob around him to string up Hooks. But when the posse gets to the Hooks' home, what they see is a happy family eating watermelon, fried chicken and singing spirituals: what almost seems to be a parody of every cliche about black people, except that Preminger is doing this for real! The lynchers look at the lynchees, change their minds and go back home. Caine is so mad he could eat his hat! He then tries to get the property owned by the white family, cousins of his, but they are equally adamant in their refusal to sell. Law and Dunaway are in charge of that family and very much in love, but quite naive. Hooks and Law decide to team up and farm their land together and Caine goes through the ceiling. There's nothing else to do but a violent deed, so he dynamites the dam above the farms and water pours down. Law's son is drowned despite an attempt to save him. Fonda leaves Caine just before this and relinquishes claims to any of the land. They'd had a retarded son but Caine was so busy trying to make the deal for the land (a northern canning company wants it for a factory) that he neglected her and the child. In the end, the black and white families join forces to help rebuild the area. Based on the novel by K.B. Gliden (Katya and Bert Gliden), HURRY SUNDOWN cost about $4 million and never returned its investment. To Preminger's credit, this was the first film shot in the South that had blacks in the leads and that caused many problems. State troopers had to guard the set and the motels where the crew and cast lived, but that didn't stop someone from defacing their cars. Although set in Georgia, Preminger chose St. Francisville, Louisiana, as his location and somebody must have forgotten to tell him that St. Francisville is a hotbed of KKK activities. It would have been a sensation in 1945, but in 1968 it was just a dreadful movie. And the sight of Fonda fondaling (sic) a saxophone in what only could be called a prurient fashion, is enough reason to question the logic of the people who approved this movie for production. Montenegro's score (his first for films) was the only saving grace. Everything else was graceless.

p&d, Otto Preminger; w, Thomas C. Ryan, Horton Foote (based on the novel by K.B. Gliden); ph, Loyal Griggs, Milton Krasner (Panavision, Technicolor); m, Hugo Montenegro; ed, Louis Loeffler, James D. Wells; prod d, Gene Callahan; set d, John Goodman; cos, Estevez; spec eff, Willis Cook; m/l, "Hurry Sundown," Montenegro, Buddy Kaye (sung by Robert Hooks).

Period Drama **(PR:O MPAA:NR)**

HURRY UP OR I'LL BE 30**½ (1973) 88m AE c

John Lefkowitz *(George Trapani)*, Linda De Coff *(Jackie Tice)*, Ronald Anton *(Vince Trapani)*, Maureen Byrnes *(Flo)*, Danny De Vito *(Petey)*, David Kirk *(Mr. Trapani)*, Frank Quinn *(Mark Lossier)*, Selma Rogoff *(Mrs. Trapani)*, George Welbes *(Ken Harris)*, Steve Inwood *(Tony)*, Faith Langford *(Gypsy Girl/Bar Girl)*, Samantha Lynche *(Audition Girl No. 1)*, Susan Peretz *(Miss Walsh)*, Bob O'Connell *(Bartender)*, Bill Nunnery *(Gas Station Attendant)*.

We have never been able to understand why they always seem to cast Jewish actors as Italians and Italians as Jews (Peter Falk as "Colombo," Barry Newman as "Petrocelli," Harvey Keitel in MEAN STREETS, Robert DeNiro as "Noodles" in ONCE UPON A TIME IN AMERICA). That was the case in this simple-minded, but engaging, comedy with Lefkowitz and Rogoff as two people in a patently Italian family. The script is derivative and much of the technical side is poor, but there was a lot of love applied to this story of a paunchy 29-year-old who works at his father's print shop and still lives at home. He wants to make a go of the business but his father and younger brother won't let him. His social life is no better as he has a shallow relationship with waitress Byrnes. It's an update of MARTY in that Lefkowitz is not unlike Chayefsky's memorable butcher and his friends are younger versions of Mantell and the others. Lefkowitz eventually has a fling with actress De Coff, but she leaves him for a producer and he winds up the way he started, a loser. One of the first efforts for De Vito, who went on to television in "Taxi," and has since emerged as a fine comic actor and sometime producer. Lots of cliches, but just as many touching moments.

p&d, Joseph Jacoby; w, David Wiltse, Jacoby (based on a story by Jacoby); ph, Burleigh Wartes; ed, Stan Warnow Hart; m/l, Stephen Lawrence, Bruce Hart (sung by Dennis Cooley).

Comedy **(PR:C MPAA:R)**

HUSBANDS**½ (1970) 154m Faces Music/COL c

Ben Gazzara *(Harry)*, Peter Falk *(Archie)*, John Cassavetes *(Gus)*, Jenny Runacre *(Mary Tynan)*, Jenny Lee Wright *(Pearl Billingham)*, Noelle Kao *(Julie)*, Leola Harlow *(Leola)*, Meta Shaw *(Annie)*, John Kullers *(Red)*, Delores Delmar *(Countess)*, Peggy Lashbrook *(Diana Mallabee)*, Eleanor Zee *(Mrs. Hines)*, Claire Malis *(Stuart's Wife)*, Lorraine McMartin *(Annie's Mother)*, Edgar Franken *(Ed Weintraub)*, Sarah Felcher *(Sarah)*, Antoinette Kray *("Jesus Loves Me")*, Gwen Van Dam *("Jeannie")*, John Armstrong *("Happy Birthday")*, Eleanor Gould *("Normandy")*, Carinthia West *(Susanna)*, Rhonda Parker *(Margaret)*, Joseph Boley *(Minister)*, Judith Lowry *(Stuart's Grandmother)*, Joseph Hardy *("Shanghai Lil")*, K. C. Townsend *(Barmaid)*, Anne O'Donnell, Gena Wheeler *(Nurses)*, David Rowlands *(Stuart Jackson)*, Nick Cassavetes *(Nick)*, Alexandra Cassavetes *(Xan)*, Bill Britton, Arthur Clark, Charles Gaines, Fred Draper.

Not unlike BYE BYE BRAVERMAN (two years earlier), this is the Italian version of that very Jewish film that starred George Segal and was based on Wallace Markfield's superb novel *To An Early Grave*. HUSBANDS was slightly better than the aforementioned, but Cassavetes sometimes falls so in love with his work that he doesn't know how to edit it—which is the exact reverse of Woody Allen who oftens edits too deeply, and we wind up paying full fare for a 72-minute picture. Cassavetes, Gazzara, and Falk (who actually became great friends while making the picture and have stayed close since then) are thunderstruck when their pal, Rowlands, dies suddenly of a heart attack. As three middle-aged husbands with wives and houses in the New York suburbs, they now confront their own mortality, and respond by tossing aside all of their cares and obligations and going on a spree. Cassavetes and Falk both are happy types. Gazzara is the most brooding of the bunch. For the next two days, the trio sleep in the subways, get drunk, play basketball, and try to recreate memories of the way it was when they were young and single. After 48 hours, Falk and Cassavetes are ready to pack it in, but Gazzara has had a monumental fight with his wife and decides to fly to London. He talks the other two into accompanying him, and they arrive in England, change into formal clothing, and lurch around a gambling casino, thinking they all look like Bogart in CASABLANCA. There they meet three women and take them off to their rooms. Cassavetes goes with Runacre, Falk with Kao, and Gazzara with Wright. Gazzara finds the thought of adultery hard to handle but makes an effort to get over his guilt. Next day, Cassavetes and Falk are ready to go back to their Long Island homes, but Gazzara has decided to stay on and has already lined up Lashbrook (who also served as continuity person for the London shooting) and two more women for his pals. They no-thanks him and leave. Once back in New York, the two men load up with gifts of stuffed animals and other folderol for their families and say goodbye to each other. An adventure is over. HUSBANDS might have been one of the best films of 1970 if greater care were given to pruning it. Just when a scene hits its highest apogee, Cassavetes lets it continue and peter out at a nadir. Lots of the words were improvised (or so we're told) and it looks to be the case. A script would have served them in better stead.

p, Al Ruban; d&w, John Cassavetes; ph, Victor Kemper (DeLuxe Color); ed, Peter Tanner; md, Stanley Wilson, Jack Ackerman; art d, Rene D'Auriac; cos, Louis Brown; makeup, Robert Laden, Tommy Manderson.

Drama **(PR:C MPAA:GP)**

HUSBAND'S HOLIDAY*½ (1931) 70m PAR bw

Clive Brook *(George Boyd)*, Charles Ruggles *(Clyde Saunders)*, Vivienne Osborne *(Mary Boyd)*, Juliette Compton *(Christine Kennedy)*, Harry Bannister *(Andrew Trask)*, Dorothy Tree *(Cecily Reid)*, Charles Winninger *(Mr. Reid)*, Elizabeth Patterson *(Mrs. Caroline Reid)*, Leni Stengel *(Molly Saunders)*, Dickie Moore *(Philip)*, Marilyn Knowlden *(Anne)*, Adrienne Ames, Kent Taylor, Burton Churchill, Marjorie Gateson.

Osborne is a passive woman who knows of her husband's long time affair with another woman, Compton, but does nothing about it. She refuses to give her husband, Brook, a divorce even after he leaves and moves in with Compton. Osborne allows Brook to drop in occasionally to visit with the children, but treats him as if he were just another house guest. She believes that Brook will come home eventually, and he does after Compton, frustrated with her mistress status, commits suicide by taking poison.

d, Robert Milton; w, Ernest Pascal, Viola Brothers Shore (based on the stage play "The Marriage Bed" by Ernest Pascal); ph, Charles Rosher.

Drama **(PR:A MPAA:NR)**

HUSH-A-BYE MURDER (SEE: MY LOVER, MY SON, 1970, U.S./Brit.)

HUSH . . . HUSH, SWEET CHARLOTTE***½ (1964) 134m FOX bw

Bette Davis *(Charlotte)*, Olivia de Havilland *(Miriam)*, Joseph Cotten *(Drew)*, Agnes Moorehead *(Velma)*, Cecil Kellaway *(Harry)*, Victor Buono *(Big Sam)*, Mary Astor *(Jewel Mayhew)*, Wesley Addy *(Sheriff)*, William Campbell *(Paul Marchand)*, Bruce Dern *(John Mayhew)*, Frank Ferguson *(Editor)*, George Kennedy *(Foreman)*, David Willock *(Taxi Driver)*, John Megna *(New Boy)*, Percy Helton *(Funeral Director)*, Kelly Flynn *(2nd Boy)*, Michael Petit *(Gang Leader)*, Alida Aldrich *(Young Girl)*, Kelly Aldrich *(3rd Boy)*, William Aldrich *(Boy Dancer)*, Ellen Corby, Marianne Stewart, Helen Kleeb *(Town Gossips)*, Carol De Lay *(Geraldine)*, Mary Henderson, Lillian Randolph, Geraldine West *(Cleaning Women)*, William Walker *(Chauffeur)*, Idell James *(Ginny Mae)*, Teddy Buckner and His All-Stars.

Following the critical and financial success of WHAT EVER HAPPENED TO BABY JANE? (which gave a much needed boost to the falling stars of Bette Davis and Joan Crawford), producer/director Aldrich decided to reunite the actresses in another psychological horror film. Despite the successful on-screen chemistry between the performers, Davis and Crawford really didn't get along with each other on a personal level, and it took some time for Aldrich to come up with a project to please them both. When HUSH . . . HUSH, SWEET CHARLOTTE was ready to go into production, Crawford fell ill and bowed out. Davis suggested her friend de Havilland as a replacement, so Aldrich flew to Europe and convinced her to play the role. Set in a decaying Louisiana mansion, HUSH . . . HUSH, SWEET CHARLOTTE sees Davis as an aging, somewhat demented, spinster who is haunted by the bad memories of her past. Back in 1927, when Davis was a young woman, her married lover, Dern, was killed when a mysterious person chopped off his hand and then decapitated him. Davis always felt that her father, Buono, had committed the crime, but the dismembered body parts were never recovered, and the crime remained unsolved. Thirty-seven years later, with her father dead and only her maid Moorehead around for company, Davis sits and frets that the upcoming demolition of her house (to make way for a proposed highway) will uncover the long missing body parts and prove her father to be a murderer. Desperate, Davis calls upon her cousin, de Havilland, to help her in her fight to stop the highway commission from demolishing her home. De Havilland arrives, accompanied by the family doctor, Cotten, and together they set out to soothe Davis' nerves. That night, Davis is lured into another room when she hears strange harpsichord music and there finds a severed head. This sends her into a state of shock, and Cotten sedates her. Eventually it is revealed that de Havilland and Cotten are working together to drive Davis mad so that they can take the family fortune. Loyal servant Moorehead discovers the truth and informs insurance investigator Kellaway, but she is killed shortly after trying to warn Davis. To push Davis over the brink, de Havilland fakes the death of Cotten and convinces her cousin that it was *she* who murdered him while in a drugged stupor. The panicked Davis helps de Havilland dispose of the body and when they return to the house, there stands Cotten, the man they had just buried, covered with blood and dirt. Davis becomes hysterical and passes out. Upon awakening, she peers out of her balcony and sees de Havilland and Cotten embrace while discussing the success of their scheme. Seeking revenge, Davis pushes a large cement flower pot off the balcony and kills them. The police arrive to take her away and Davis learns that her long-dead lover Dern was actually killed by his jealous wife. She smiles, realizing that she's not crazy after all.

p&d, Robert Aldrich; w, Henry Farrell, Lukas Heller; ph, Joseph Biroc; m, Frank De Vol; ed, Michael Luciano; art d, William Glasgow; set d, Raphael Bretton; cos,

Norma Koch; ch, Alex Ruiz; makeup, Gene Hibbs; m/l, De Vol, Mack David (sung by Al Martino).

Horror Cas. (PR:O MPAA:NR)

HUSH MONEY*½ (1931) 68m FOX bw

Joan Bennett *(Janet Gordon)*, Hardie Albright *(Stuart Elliot)*, Owen Moore *(Steve Pelton)*, Myrna Loy *(Flo Curtis)*, C. Henry Gordon *(Jack Curtis)*, Douglas Cosgrove *(Dan Emmett)*, George Raft *(Maxie)*, Hugh White *(Puggie)*, George Byron, Andre Cheron, Henry Armetta, George Irving, Nella Walker, Joan Castle.

HUSH MONEY misfires from the start and any intended suspense just doesn't happen. Bennett is living in the same house as a group of small-time confidence hustlers. They get involved in a holdup scheme that winds up in a murder, and Bennett is sent to jail for a year. She'd thought that she would marry ringleader Moore and had gone along for the ride, but once out of jail, she meets Cosgrove, a cop, and the big galoot takes a liking to her and will help her start over again. She also meets Albright, the urbane, suave, and essential man-about-town. They soon wed but she never tells him of her past. When Moore gets out of jail, he tries to blackmail Bennett. Cosgrove tells the other members of the gang that it was Moore who finked on them and they soon take him for a ride, thus leaving Bennett to enjoy her life with Albright. Raft is seen briefly as one of the gang in his third movie of 1931, after QUEEN OF THE NIGHT CLUBS and QUICK MILLIONS. Loy is also a gang member, but how could anyone believe sweet Myrna in a part like that?

d, Sidney Lanfield; w, Philip Klein, Courtney Terrett, Lanfield, Dudley Nichols (based on a story by Lanfield, Klein); ph, John Seitz.

Crime Drama (PR:A MPAA:NR)

HUSTLE*½** (1975) 120m PAR c

Burt Reynolds *(Lt. Phil Gaines)*, Catherine Deneuve *(Nicole Britton)*, Ben Johnson *(Marty Hollinger)*, Paul Winfield *(Sgt. Louis Belgrave)*, Eileen Brennan *(Paula Hollinger)*, Eddie Albert *(Leo Sellers)*, Ernest Borgnine *(Santoro)*, Catherine Bach *(Peggy Summers)*, Jack Carter *(Herbie Dalitz)*, James Hampton *(Bus Driver)*, Sharon Kelly *(Gloria Hollinger)*, Chuck Hayward *(Morgue Attendant)*, David Estridge *(Albino)*, Peter Brandon *(Minister)*, David Spielberg *(Jerry Bellamy)*, Naomi Stevens *(Woman Hostage)*, Med Flory *(Albino Beating Cop)*, Steve Shaw, Dino Washington *(Cops in Elevator)*, Anthony Eldridge *(Laugher)*, John Duke Russo *(Man in Phone Booth)*, Don Billett *(Cop in Tee Shirt)*, Hal Baylor *(Police Captain)*, Nancy Bonniwell *(Girl in Airport Bar)*, Don "Red" Barry *(Airport Bartender)*, Karl Lukas *(Charley)*, Gene Chronopoulos *(Bartender)*, Patrice Rohmer *(Linda, a Dancer)*, Alvin Hammer *(Liquor Store Clerk)*, Dave Willock *(Liquor Store Clerk)*, Queenie Smith, Marilyn Moe *(Customers)*, Robert Englund *(Holdup Man)*, George Memoli *(Foot Fetish Man)*, Fred Willard *(Interrogator)*, Thad Geer *(2nd Holdup Man)*, Kelly Wilder *(Nancy Gaines)*, Ben Young *(First Detective)*, Tasso Bravos, Jimmy R. Hampton, Nathan Harding *(Boys on Beach)*, John Furlong *(Waiter)*, Jason Wingreen *(Jim Lang)*, Ron Nyman *(Pan Am Clerk)*, Victoria Carrol *(Guest)*.

A disturbing and grim modern *film noir* directed by Aldrich who was a master of the genre in the early 1950s (KISS ME DEADLY, THE BIG KNIFE, WORLD FOR RANSOM). Reynolds stars as a bitter, cynical cop who lives with his girl friend, Deneuve, a high-class call-girl, who, unbeknownst to Reynolds, is owned by sleazy, but powerful, attorney Albert. One day, while on an outing with Deneuve, Reynolds finds the body of a young girl washed up on the beach and is soon back at police headquarters trying to determine who she is. Identified as a small-time hooker and porno actress, Reynolds calls in the girl's parents, Johnson (in a superb performance), and Brennan, to identify the body. Though the coroner has determined the death a suicide (drug overdose), Johnson demands to know the circumstances forcing Reynolds to investigate the identity of the man in a photograph that was found on the body. The man in the picture is Albert, and when questioned by the detective, he admits knowing the girl, but is ignorant of her death. At the same time, Johnson searches on his own for clues and winds up getting stomped by some hoods for his trouble. Undeterred, Johnson learns of Albert's connection with his daughter and seeks a confrontation. Reynolds and his partner try to stop him, but they arrive too late and discover that the half-crazed Johnson has shot and killed Albert. Knowing Johnson will be tried for murder, Reynolds rearranges the evidence so that it appears the distraught father killed Albert in self-defense. Relieved that the case is over, Reynolds arranges to spend a weekend in San Francisco with Deneuve, but is killed while trying to stop a liquor store robbery that he witnessed on the way to the airport. Director Aldrich offers an unrelentingly diseased portrait of modern society in HUSTLE. Reynolds is trapped in this disgusting, seedy world from the opening of the film when his pleasant day off is intruded upon by the washed-up corpse which forces him back into the underworld. There is no way out. HUSTLE is one of the few examples of *true* modern *film noir*, and along with Arthur Penn's NIGHT MOVES, one of the most disturbing, depressing and powerful.

p&d, Robert Aldrich; w, Steve Shagan; ph, Joseph Biroc (Eastmancolor); m, Frank DeVol; ed, Michael Luciano; art d, Hilyard Brown; set d, Raphael Bretton; cos, Oscar Rodriguez, Betsy Cox; spec eff, Henry Miller; ch, Alex Romero; m/l, "Yesterday When I Was Young," Charles Aznavour, Herbert Kretzmer (sung by Aznavour), "So Rare" Jack Sharpe, Jerry Herst, "A Man And A Woman" Francis Lai, "Mission Impossible" Lalo Schifrin, "Begin The Beguine" Cole Porter.

Crime/Mystery Cas. (PR:O MPAA:R)

HUSTLER, THE***** (1961) 134m FOX bw

Paul Newman *("Fast" Eddie Felson)*, Jackie Gleason *(Minnesota Fats)*, Piper Laurie *(Sarah Packard)*, George C. Scott *(Bert Gordon)*, Myron McCormick *(Charlie Burns)*, Murray Hamilton *(Findlay)*, Michael Constantine *(Big John)*, Stefan Gierasch *(Preacher)*, Jake LaMotta *(Bartender)*, Gordon B. Clarke *(Cashier)*, Alexander Rose *(Scorekeeper)*, Carolyn Coates *(Waitress)*, Carl York *(Young Hustler)*, Vincent Gardenia *(Bartender)*, Gloria Curtis *(Girl with Fur Coat)*, Charles Diercep, Donald Crabtree, Brendan Fay *(Pool Room Hoods)*, Cliff Fellow, Willie Mosconi, Don De Leo, Tom Ahearne.

Paul Newman was a promising and somewhat successful actor until performing the part of the brash, lonely, love-and-reputation seeking poolshark, "Fast" Eddie Felson. This single role turned Newman's career around 180 degrees and made of him an overnight superstar. And he deserved it, along with the Oscar he did not get for one of the most memorable roles ever enacted. Street smart and poolroom wise, Newman, accompanied by elderly sidekick and shill McCormick, plays the come-on game with local shooters. He first allows them to win game after game, making small bets and losing, letting the adversary gloat and inflate his own prowess to the point where the other player suggests raising the stakes. Once the big bets are down Newman goes to work, making enough spectacular shots, seemingly aided by luck, to take the winnings and leave the sucker high and dry. Beginning in California, Newman and McCormick work their way across the country until arriving in New York. They go to Ames, a second-story poolroom, the most prestigious poolhall in the U.S., site of great historic matches and the stomping grounds for the most brilliant pool player alive, Minnesota Fats (Gleason). He hangs around until Gleason shows up and then proposes some big time pool with heavy stakes, thousands of dollars pulled forth by McCormick. Gleason looks over to a sinister-looking man in an expensive business suit, Scott, who nods, Scott being Gleason's backer and the one who gives him the go-ahead. The two begin a Homeric struggle on the green felt table with Newman gaining ground with each game. Hours go by, the games more and more quickly decided by Newman's incredible shots. Deep into the night the two masters of the table play, gathering about their table a host of fascinated pool-knowledgeable spectators. Flush with victory and tens of thousands of dollars ahead, Newman watches in admiration as Gleason, in dapper dress, pauses to wash and tidy up, applying powder to his face and hands, then giving a gopher some money to buy some expensive liquor. "Fats, you're beautiful," gushes Newman. "All pink . . . just like a baby." Newman orders some booze and then Gleason, appearing as fresh as when the monumental battle began, says: "Let's play some pool." When the liquor arrives, the strutting Newman begins to drink heavily, then he starts to miss some shots. Slowly the struggle begins to shift in victories towards Gleason. By dawn the next day Newman is exhausted and has been losing one game after another. His bankroll had dwindled to nothing, as McCormick reports with a sour face. Newman begs the triumphant Gleason for one more game but Gleason, with a sideways glance at the ever-watchful Scott, refuses. It's strictly a cash-and-carry situation. Newman, utterly destroyed, leaves Ames a wreck. He later stops in a cheap restaurant and there meets attractive Laurie, a young hooker so world-weary that her only desire is to drink. Jaded, alcoholic, and afflicted with a crippled leg, she nevertheless goes off with Newman, taking him back to her apartment where they set up housekeeping. McCormick visits them and Newman accuses him of holding out on him, which he admits, turning over a small grub-stake. Newman then tells McCormick to disappear. Newman goes off on his own, frequenting small, out-of-the-way poolhalls and mean bars with pool tables, hustling the suckers. In one bar another hustler so riles Newman that he pulls out all the stops and utterly devastates his opponent. But when he goes to pick up his money, several thugs confront him. One tells him: "Pick up your money, boy. We always pay our debts." Newman reluctantly picks up his money from the pool table. The thugs tell Newman that they don't like hustlers and he responds by saying that his opponent is a hustler. "Yeah, but you're a pool shark, boy," the leader tells Newman. They then take him behind a partition and break both his thumbs, throwing him out of the place and telling him never to come back. He shows up at Laurie's apartment in great pain and she nurses him back to health. While his thumbs are in casts they spend some pleasant time together, even going on a picnic. Here Newman tries to explain how wonderful it is for him when he's shooting pool and making every impossible shot ("then it's really good"). She is amazed and tells him that she has always wanted to feel that deeply about something, anything. Once recovered, Newman tries to regain his status by becoming a contract pool player for sports promoter Scott, a manipulative, sadistic creature who takes him and Laurie to Louisville during Kentucky Derby week, spending lavishly on them, getting them suites in the celebrated Brown's Hotel. Scott pits Newman against wealthy Hamilton who takes them to his private pool room in his mansion, but when he removes the cover from the table, Newman and Scott are shocked to see it's a billiards table. "My house, my game," the smug Hamilton tells him. Scott backsteps, believing that Newman can't beat Hamilton at billiards. Newman begs to play Hamilton, saying he can beat him. After receiving his share of groveling, Scott plays the indulgent boss and allows Newman to play Hamilton at $1,000 a game. After a grueling marathon match, a psychologically wrecked Hamilton cries for mercy and pays Scott, a percentage of these winnings going to Newman. Drunken Laurie later lambasts Newman for becoming Scott's fawning pawn; he leaves and she continues to drink heavily. Scott, whose suite adjoins hers and Newman's, and who is also drinking heavily, entices Laurie into his bedroom. She later emerges, disgusted with herself and life in general, going to a bathroom to write the word "perverted" in lipstick on the bathroom mirror. When Newman returns to the hotel he finds his suite full of police detectives and, in the bathroom, Laurie dead on the bathroom floor, a suicide. Scott, drunk and disheveled, is sitting bleary-eyed, answering questions from cops, when Newman enters his interconnecting suite. He looks up and slobbers; "She come in here, Eddie . . . She come in here . . ." Newman goes berserk and dives at Scott's throat but is prevented from killing the promoter by cops who drag him away. Later Newman shows up at Ames, going to a table and opening the case in which he carries his specially made pool cue, assembling it. He challenges Gleason to another game. Scott nods his approval and Newman proceeds to utterly destroy Gleason in game after game, methodically winning with one brilliant shot after another. He soon pockets an enormous bankroll, his winnings, but Scott yells at him: "You owe me money!" Newman refuses to pay him his percentage, telling Scott that what he has just done, he has done for the memory of the dead Laurie and then indicts himself and Scott for being inhuman and equally responsible for her death. "We killed her, Bert." When some goons make a move to attack

Newman, Scott calls them off, telling Newman to go but he warns him: "Don't ever walk into a big time poolroom again." Newman leaves and so too does Gleason, as the occupants of Ames are caught in a freeze-frame. Rossen, whose personal project this was, offers a grim, dirty world to the viewer here, one where the only bright spot is the top of the pool table, but, in their lowly ways, the leads have their share of pedestrian chivalry. The scenes have no waste and the acting, from Newman to Laurie, from Scott to Gleason, is excellent. Gleason is probably the most empathetic of the lot, a cool, detached technician with style, grace, wit, and charm, all that his world not only lacks but cannot understand, even the envious and ambitious Newman whose only pretense at style is his custom-made pool cue. It is Gleason, with one sad look, who captures a lonely courage in the tawdry poolhall world. Newman's passionate portrayal added a new dimension to his acting ability. Laurie, despite her drunkenness and self-pity, still manages to exude steamy sex and glimmers of school girl hope. This was undoubtedly her finest role. Scott is evil incarnate, a Mephisto in a tailor-made suit whose hatred for humanity oozes through every pore. His is a role that will also be long remembered. Granted, there is a gloom and doom to the film, one which reflects Rossen's indelible stamp, for he always excelled in such tough but sensitive films as his masterful ALL THE KING'S MEN. The great pool player, Willie Mosconi, coached Gleason and Newman in their shots, making those himself that were shot in closeup. Newman practiced pool shooting obsessively; he trained at home every night. He would clear his dining room of furniture and roll in the pool table. He would later admit: "I would spend many happy hours playing with Mosconi. What I called a perfect way to rehearse a part . . ." Rossen, who became seriously ill following the completion of the film (although he would live until 1966), told associates that he could now die in peace, that THE HUSTLER was the best film he had ever made. The film was considered the best film Fox released in 1961 and perhaps the best film the studio produced throughout the 1960s, an era that offered the worst films ever made. Oddly, the film had nothing to do with studio endorsement. It was exclusively Rossen's enterprise and most of the Fox executives predicted the film would suffer a quick box office death. It remains a classic to this day. It also remains one of Newman's favorite films, but then he reportedly has a fixation for any film in which he appeared beginning with the letter "H" and some later claimed that he insisted upon having his films begin with that letter for luck. Given the spate of such films—HUD, HOMBRE, THE HUSTLER, HARPER, all blockbusters—there might be something to the actor's supposed superstition.

p&d, Robert Rossen; w, Sidney Carroll, Rossen (based on the novel by Walter Tevis); ph,, Gene Shufton (CinemaScope); m, Kenyon Hopkins; ed, Dede Allen; prod d, Harry Horner; art d, Albert Brenner, Horner; set d, Gene Callahan; cos, Ruth Morley; makeup, Bob Jiras; tech adv, Willie Mosconi.

Drama (PR:C MPAA:NR)

HUSTLER SQUAD, THE (SEE: DOLL SQUAD, THE, 1974)

HYDE PARK CORNER½**
(1935, Brit.) 85m Grosvenor/Pathe bw

Gordon Harker *(Constable Cheatle)*, Binnie Hale *(Sophie)*, Gibb McLaughlin *(Sir Arthur Gannett)*, Harry Tate *(Taxi Driver)*, Eric Portman *(Edward Chester)*, Robert Holmes *(Concannon)*, Eileen Peel *(Barbara Ainsworth)*, Donald Wolfit *(Howard)*.

A good adaptation of Walter Hackett's stage production which tells of a 1780 duel to the death and how it repeats itself in 1935.

p, Harcourt Templeman; d, Sinclair Hill; w, D.B. Wyndham-Lewis, Selwyn Jepson (based on a play by Walter Hacket); ph, Cyril Bristow.

Comedy (PR:A MPAA:NR)

HYPERBOLOID OF ENGINEER GARIN, THE** (1965, USSR) 96m Gorki bw (GIPERBOLOID INGENERA GARINA; AKA: ENGINEER GARIN'S DEATH RAY)

Yevgeny Yevstigneev, Vsevolod Safanov, Mikhail Astangov, Natalya Klimova.

Set in the mid-1920s, the picture revolves around a death ray which falls into the hands of the crazed Yevstigneev. After stealing the blueprints from his teacher he decides to use the machine for villainous purposes, until the state intervenes.

d, Alexander Gintsburg; w, Gintsburg, Joseph Manevich (based on a novel by Alexei Tolstoy); ph, Alexander Rybin.

Science-Fiction (PR:A MPAA:NR)

HYPNOSIS* (1966, Ger./Sp./Ital.) 86m International Germania-Domiziana-Procusa/United Film Enterprises bw (NUR TOTE ZEUGEN SCHWEIGEN; HIPNOSIS; IPNOSI)

Elenora Rossi-Drago *(Magda Bergen)*, Jean Sorel *(Erik Stein)*, Gotz George *(Chris Kronberger)*, Massimo Serato *(Georg von Cramer)*, Mara Cruz *(Carmen)*, Margot Trooger *(Katharina)*, Heinz Drache *(Inspector Herbert Kaufmann)*, Werner Peters *(Police Commissioner)*, Guido Celano *(Tony)*, Michael Cramer *(Pablo)*, Ana Maria Montaner *(Loren)*, Diana Rabito, Jose Maria Caffarel, Antonio Queipo, Antonio Casas, Hildegard Knef.

Sorel is an assistant in a ventriloquist-hypnotism act which is run by Rossi-Drago and her fiance. Sorel, secretly in love with Rossi-Drago, kills off just about everyone who comes between him and Rossi-Drago, until policeman Cramer gets involved. Sorel is frightened into confessing when he is tormented by the ventriloquist's dummy and tape recordings of the dummy's laughter.

p, Alfons Carcasina; d, Eugenio Martin; w, Giuseppe Mangione, Gabriel Moreno Burgos, Francis Niewal, Gerhard Schmidt, Martin (based on a story by Burgos); ph, Francisco Sempere; m, Francesco De Masi, Angelo Francesco Lavagnino, Roman Vlad; ed, Antonio Gimeno, Edith von Seydewitz; art d, Ramiro Gomez.

Crime/Drama (PR:C-O MPAA:NR)

THE HYPNOTIC EYE*½ (1960) 77m AA bw

Jacques Bergerac *(The Great Desmond)*, Allison Hayes *(Justine)*, Marcia Henderson *(Marcia Blane)*, Merry Anders *(Dodie Wilson)*, Joe Patridge *(Detective Steve Kennedy)*, Guy Prescott *(Dr. Philip Hecht)*, James Lydon *(Emergency Doctor)*, Phyllis Cole *(Mrs. McNear)*, Carol Thurston *(Doris Scott)*, Holly Harris *(Mrs. Stevens)*, Mary Foran *(June Mayes)*, Ferdinand W. "Fred" Demara *(Hospital Doctor)*, Lawrence Lipton *(King of the Beatniks)*, Eric "Big Daddy" Nord *(Bongo Drummer)*, Eva Lynd.

Bergerac is a hypnotist whose female subjects mutilate themselves after being hypnotized. One washes her face with acid, another takes a scalding shower, and a third ignites her hair with a lit burner. Behind the mutilations is Bergerac's assistant and wife, Hayes (the giant in THE ATTACK OF THE 50 FOOT WOMAN), who is disfigured herself and takes out her anger on the innocent women. Patridge is a detective who uses his girl friend to find the perpetrator of the crimes. A gimmick to attract box office for the film had Bergerac hypnotizing the theater audience. During this special segment he would have the audience stamp its feet, lift balloons which were handed out at the door, and clasp their hands. A cult horror classic.

p, Ben Schwalb, Charles B. Bloch; d, George Blair; w, Gitta and William Read Woodfield (based on a story by Bloch); ph, Archie Dalzell; m, Marlin Skiles, Eve Newman; ed, William Austin.

Horror (PR:O MPAA:NR)

HYPNOTIST, THE (SEE: SCOTLAND YARD DRAGNET, 1957, Brit.)

HYPNOTIZED zero (1933) 70m World Wide bw

Charlie Mack *(Egbert Jackson)*, George Moran *(Henry Johnson)*, Ernest Torrence *(Prof. Limberly)*, Charlie Murray *(Charlie O'Brien)*, Wallace Ford *(Bill Bogard)*, Maria Alba *(Princess Mitzi)*, Marjorie Beebe *(Pearl)*, Herman Bing *(Capt. Von Stromberg)*, Alexander Carr *(Abe Shapiro)*, Luis Alberni *(Consul)*, Harry Schultz *(Ludwig)*, Matt McHugh *(Drummer)*, Mitchell Harris *(Ringmaster)*.

A terrible film starring the comedy team of Mack and Moran. No story exists and the film seems more like a string of coming attractions. Avoid at all costs.

d, Mack Sennett; w, Sennett, Arthur Ripley, John Waldon, Earle Rodney, Gene Towne; ph, John W. Boyle, George Unholz; ed, William Hornbeck, Francis Lyon.

Comedy (PR:A MPAA:NR)

HYSTERIA*** (1965, Brit.) 85m Hammer/MGM bw

Robert Webber *("Mr. Smith")*, Anthony Newlands *(Dr. Keller)*, Jennifer Jayne *(Gina)*, Maurice Denham *(Hemmings)*, Leila Goldoni *(Denise)*, Peter Woodthorpe *(Marcus Allan)*, Sandra Boize *(English Girl)*, Sue Lloyd *(French Girl)*, John Arnatt, Marianne Stone, Irene Richmond, Kiwi Kingston.

Webber is an American in England who suffers amnesia after an auto accident. He finds himself in a London hospital and doctor Newlands tells him that an anonymous benefactor is paying his hospital bills and also has an apartment for him to stay at. Released, Webber hires private detective Denham to learn the identity of a woman in a torn photograph in his pocket, and moves into the flat. Horrible visions follow; he learns that the woman in the photo was murdered in her shower. Then he finds the body of a dead woman in his shower, which then disappears. A woman shows up at his door claiming to be the widow of the man responsible for the accident that sent Webber to the hospital. She looks just like the woman in the picture, and with Denham's help he discovers that the doctor and the alleged widow were trying to set him up for the murder of the physician's wife. A taut shocker with chilling psychological undertones.

p, Jimmy Sangster; d, Freddie Francis; w, Sangster; ph, John Wilcox; m, Don Banks; ed, James Needs; prod d, Edward Carrick.

Drama Cas. (PR:O MPAA:NR)

HYSTERICAL zero (1983) 86m H&W Filmworks-Cinema Group Venture/EMB c

William Hudson *(Frederick)*, Mark Hudson *(Paul)*, Brett Hudson *(Fritz)*, Cindy Pickett *(Kate)*, Richard Kiel *(Capt. Howdy)*, Julie Newmar *(Venetia)*, Bud Cort *(Dr. John)*, Robert Donner *(Ralph)*, Murray Hamilton *(Mayor)*, Clint Walker *(Sheriff)*, Franklin Ajaye *(Leroy)*, Charlie Callas *(Dracula)*, Keenan Wynn *(Fisherman)*, Gary Owens *(TV Announcer)*, Helena Makela, John Larroquette, Pat Colbert, Indy Shriner, Amanda H. Bearde, Pamela Bowman, Robert Alan Browne, Sue Casey, Natalie Core, Mary Ellen Flaherty, Annie Willette, Gene Castle, Kathy Cherry, Dick Chudnow, Maurice Sneed.

The Hudson Brothers, who try to pass themselves off as comedians, star in this insipid parody of horror movies, which offers nothing even remotely similar to a laugh. They simply thought that filling this picture with people who have been funny—Bud Cort, Charlie Callas, Keenan Wynn—would get laughs. If there was a way for this one to get a less-than-zero rating it most definitely would.

p, Gene Levy; d, Chris Bearde; w, William Hudson, Mark Hudson, Brett Hudson, Trace Johnston; ph, Donald Morgan (DeLuxe Color); m, Robert Alcivar, Robert O. Ragland; ed, Stanley Frazen; prod d, J. Dennis Washington; spec eff, Henry Millar; makeup, Michael Germain.

Comedy Cas. (PR:O MPAA:PG)

I

I ACCUSE (SEE: J'ACCUSE, 1939, Fr.)

I ACCUSE!* 1/2** (1958, Brit.) 99m MGM bw

Jose Ferrer *(Alfred Dreyfus)*, Anton Walbrook *(Maj. Esterhazy)*, Viveca Lindfors *(Lucie Dreyfus)*, Leo Genn *(Maj. Picquart)*, Emlyn Williams *(Emile Zola)*, David Farrar *(Mathieu Dreyfus)*, Donald Wolfit *(Gen. Mercier)*, Herbert Lom *(Maj. DuPaty de Clam)*, Harry Andrews *(Maj. Henry)*, Felix Aylmer *(Edgar Demange)*, Peter Illing *(Georges Clemenceau)*, George Coulouris *(Col. Sandherr)*, Carl Jaffe *(Col. Von Schwarzkoppen)*, Eric Pohlmann *(Bertillon)*, John Chandos *(Drumont)*, Ernest Clark *(Prosecutor, 1st Dreyfus Trial)*, Anthony Ireland *(Judge)*, Laurence Naismith *(Judge)*, John Phillips *(Prosecutor, Esterhazy Trial)*, Michael Hordern *(Prosecutor, 2nd Dreyfus Trial)*, Keith Pyott *(Judge)*, Ronald Howard *(Capt. Avril)*, Charles Gray *(Capt. Brossard)*, Michael Anthony *(Capt. Leblanc)*, Arthur Howard *(Capt. Lauth)*, Michael Trubshawe *(English Publisher)*, Malcolm Keen *(President of France)*.

Ferrer stars and directs in this screen version of the factual trials of Alfred Dreyfus. Dreyfus, a Jewish staff officer in the French Army, is wrongly accused of treason. He is sentenced to life imprisonment and sent to Devil's Island. Later the real traitor (Walbrook) is exposed but the military turns his trial into a whitewash. Soliciting the aid of some of France's most famous citizens (most notably novelist Emile Zola), Ferrer's friends gain a retrial for him. Again he is found guilty; however, the French president steps in to pardon the noble captain. Ferrer's direction and Vidal's script make this a compelling drama, especially the courtroom scenes.

p, Sam Zimbalist; d, Jose Ferrer; w, Gore Vidal (based on the book *Captain Dreyfus—A Story of Mass Hysteria* by Nicholas Halasz); ph, F.A. Young (CinemaScope); m, William Alwyn; ed, Frank Clarke; md, Muir Mathieson; art d, Elliot Scott; cos, Elizabeth Haffenden.

Drama **(PR:A MPAA:NR)**

I ACCUSE MY PARENTS* (1945) 68m PRC bw

Mary Beth Hughes *(Kitty Reed)*, Robert Lowell *(James Wilson)*, John Miljan *(Dan Wilson)*, Vivienne Osborne *(Mrs. Wilson)*, George Meeker *(Charles Blake)*, Edward Earle *(Judge)*, George Lloyd *(Al Frazier)*, Patricia Knox *(Vera Moore)*, Florence Johnson *(Shirley Clark)*, Richard Bartell *(Joe Holden)*.

In this reflection on juvenile delinquency a high school criminal blames his parents for his crimes. The boy gets involved with a jewel theft ring and ends up murdering the leader. He is acquitted though, because the judge feels the kid's parents have set a bad example with their drinking and gambling.

p, Max Alexander; d, Sam Newfield; w, Harry Fraser, Marjorie Dudley (based on a story by Arthur Caesar); ph, Robert Cline; ed, Charles Henkel, Jr., md, Lee Zahler, art d, Paul Palmentola; m/l, Ray Evans, Jay Livingston.

Crime/Drama **(PR:A MPAA:NR)**

I ADORE YOU** (1933, Brit.) 74m WB/FN bw

Margot Grahame *(Margot Grahame)*, Harold French *(Norman Young)*, Clifford Heatherley *(Louis B. Koenig)*, O.B. Clarence *(Mr. Young)*, Peggy Novak *(Operator)*, Georgie Harris *(Peter Butcher)*, Ernest Sefton *(Pilbeam)*, Gavin Gordon *(Alphonso Bouillabaise)*, Carroll Gibbons and the Savoy Orpheans.

French falls desperately in love with actress Grahame, buying the film company that owns her contract in order that he can marry her. With the company on its last legs, French's purchase makes everyone happy. Musical numbers flesh out the story.

p, Irving Asher; d, George King; w, Paul England (based on the story by W. Scott Darling).

Musical/Comedy **(PR:A MPAA:NR)**

I AIM AT THE STARS 1/2** (1960) 106m Morningside Worldwide/COL bw

Curt Jurgens *(Older Wernher von Braun)*, Victoria Shaw *(Maria)*, Herbert Lom *(Anton Reger)*, Gia Scala *(Elizabeth Beyer)*, James Daly *(Maj. William Taggert)*, Adrian Hoven *(Mischke)*, Gunther Mruwka *(Young Wernher von Braun)*, Arpad Diener *(Horst)*, Hans Schumm *(Baron von Braun)*, Lea Seidl *(Baroness von Braun)*, Gerard Heinz *(Prof. Oberth)*, Karel Stepanek *(Capt. Bornberger)*, Peter Capell *(Dr. Neumann)*, Helmo Kindermann *(Gen. Kulp)*, Eric Zuckmann *(Himmler)*, Austin Willis *(John B. Medaris)*.

Jurgens plays Wernher von Braun, the man who invented the V-2 rocket. The apolitical scientist is forced by the Nazis to create the rocket against his wishes. After the war he surrenders to the Americans and not the Soviets. Daly is an army major who is opposed to allowing Jurgens a new home in America because his family was killed by a V-2 rocket attack on London. Jurgens is allowed to live in the U.S. and becomes an important part of the U.S. space program.

p, Charles H. Schneer; d, J. Lee Thompson; w, Jay Dratler (based on a story by George Froeschel, U. Wolter and H.W. John); ph, Wilkie Cooper; m, Laurie Johnson; ed, Frederick Wilson; art d, Hans Berthel.

Drama **(PR:A MPAA:NR)**

I AM A CAMERA**
(1955, Brit.) 98m Romulus-Remus/Distributors Corporation of America bw

Julie Harris *(Sally Bowles)*, Laurence Harvey *(Christopher Isherwood)*, Shelley Winters *(Natalia Landauer)*, Ron Randell *(Clive)*, Lea Seidl *(Fraulein Schneider)*, Anton Diffring *(Fritz)*, Ina De La Haye *(Herr Landauer)*, Jean Gargoet *(Pierre)*, Stanley Maxted *(American Editor)*, Alexis Bobrinskoy *(Proprietor [Troika])*, Andre Mikhelson *(Head Waiter [Troika])*, Frederick Valk *(Doctor)*, Tutte Lemkow *(Electro-Therapist)*, Patrick McGoohan *(Swede)*, Julia Arnall *(Model)*, Zoe Newton *(Cigarette Girl)*, David Kossoff, Paddy Smith, Bill Brandon, Ann Elsdon, Stanley Morrell, Bill Billington, Anita Douglas, Charles Sayner, Vincent Edwards, Henry Purvis, Geoffrey Dunn, Peter Prowse, Stan Bernard Trio, Harold Siddons.

In the beginning there were Christopher Isherwood's "Berlin Stories." From them came the award-winning play that provided the basis for both I AM A CAMERA and CABARET. Unfortunately this version is little more than a filmed stage play. The action is static and plot development is done mostly through dialog. The comedy deals with the episodic adventures of Harvey, a poor, struggling writer, and Harris, a night club chanteuse: roommates caught up in the swirl of pre-WW II Berlin. Winters is a German girl who begins to experience the anti-Semitic dogma of the Nazi regime.

p, Jack Clayton; d, Henry Cornelius; w, John Collier (based on the play by John Van Druten from the "Berlin Stories" by Christopher Isherwood); ph, Guy Green; m, Malcolm Arnold; ed, Clive Donner; md, Muir Mathieson; art d, William Kellner; m/l, Ralph Maria Siegel, Paul Dehn.

Drama/Comedy **(PR:A MPAA:NR)**

I AM A CRIMINAL** (1939) 74m MON bw

John Carroll *(Brad McArthur)*, Kay Linaker *(Linda)*, Craig Reynolds *(Clint Reynolds)*, Martin Spellman *(Bobby)*, Lester Matthews *(George)*, Mary Kornman *(Alice Martin)*, May Beatty *(Maggie)*, Robert Fiske *(Collins)*, Byron Foulger, Edward Earle, Jack Kennedy, Allen Cavan.

Gangster Carroll uses newsboy Spellman to sway the jury in his upcoming manslaughter trial. The 10-year-old boy greatly admires Carroll and slowly softens the heart of the criminal. Carroll's girl friend, Linaker, plans to rip off her boy friend, but Spellman foils the attempt.

p, E.B. Derr; d, William Nigh; w, John Krafft (based on an original idea by Harrison Jacobs); ph, Paul Ivano; ed, Russell Schoengarth; md, Abe Meyer; art d, Frank Dexter.

Crime Drama **(PR:A MPAA:NR)**

I AM A FUGITIVE FROM A CHAIN GANG*****
(1932) 93m WB bw (GB: I AM A FUGITIVE FROM THE CHAIN GANG)

Paul Muni *(James Allen)*, Glenda Farrell *(Marie Woods)*, Helen Vinson *(Helen)*, Preston Foster *(Pete)*, Allen Jenkins *(Barney Sykes)*, Edward Ellis *(Bomber Wells)*, John Wray *(Nordine)*, Hale Hamilton *(Rev. Robert Clinton Allen)*, Harry Woods *(Guard)*, David Landau *(Warden)*, Edward J. McNamara *(2nd Warden)*, Robert McWade *(Ramsey)*, Willard Robertson *(Prison Commissioner)*, Noel Francis *(Linda)*, Louise Carter *(Mrs. Allen)*, Berton Churchill *(Judge)*, Sheila Terry *(Allen's Secretary)*, Sally Blane *(Alice)*, James Bell *(Red)*, Edward LeSaint *(Chairman, Chamber of Commerce)*, Douglas Dumbrille *(District Attorney)*, Robert Warwick *(Fuller)*, Charles Middleton *(Train Conductor)*, Reginald Barlow *(Parker)*, Jack LaRue *(Ackerman)*, Charles Sellon *(Hot Dog Stand Owner)*, Erville Alderson *(Chief of Police)*, George Pat Collins *(Wilson)*, William Pawley *(Doggy)*, Lew Kelly *(Mike, Proprietor of Diner)*, Everett Brown *(Sebastian T. Yale)*, William LeMaire *(Texas)*, George Cooper *(Vaudevillian)*, Wallis Clark *(Lawyer)*, Walter Long *(Blacksmith)*, Frederick Burton *(Georgia Prison Official)*, Irving Bacon *(Barber Bill)*, Lee Shumway, J. Frank Glendon *(Arresting Officers)*, Dennis O'Keefe *(Dance Extra)*.

Don't look for romance, humor, or a happy ending; this is one of the toughest movies ever made, an uncompromising and frightening film that lays bare the inhuman conditions and treatment of a penal system that crawled out of the Dark Ages and settled in Georgia, U.S.A. Muni is stunning and totally compelling as a victim of that bestial system, a civilized person who learns with excruciating pain that civilization has fled his world, replacing it with his worst nightmares. It is 1919 and Muni returns with tens of thousands of other soldiers from WW I. He has served his country and democracy well, earning medals and the respect of his small community. When at home he is lectured by his parson brother, Wray, to find gainful employment and not mope about like some of the returning veterans. But Muni is restless; he has ambitions to see the country and find work that will challenge him. To edify his mother, Carter, and brother, Muni takes a menial clerk's job in a local firm but he yearns to work at great outdoor projects, having been trained as an engineer. His wanderlust finally gets the better of him and he quits, hitting the road. Jobs are scarce, the country flooded with unemployed veterans. He gets one job and is laid off in a short time and this situation is repeated again and again, until Muni is not much more than a hobo tramping the roads and riding the rails. He goes to a pawn shop and tries to sell his *Croix de Guerre*, a distinguished French medal awarded him during the Great War. The pawnbroker shows him a tray full of the same medals and shrugs, saying: "They're a drug on the market." Again Muni hits the road, this time going into the Deep South. Penniless, starving, he meets a tough-looking big tramp, Foster, who tells him he knows where there is a kindly operator of a lunch wagon where they are sure to get a free hamburger. Muni's mouth waters at the prospect and he accompanies Foster to the diner. Foster asks for another handout and the owner reluctantly flops two hamburgers on the grill, dumping raw onions on top. Muni's eyes gape at the sizzling meat and he does not see Foster withdraw a pistol. Foster then sticks up the place, taking the money from the till and running outside where he bumps into two cops going to dinner. They shoot Foster and then race inside. Muni is on his feet, terrified. The rattled owner points to him as Foster's partner and he dashes out the side door but another cop stops him with a gun to his chest. He is next brought before a hard-as-granite southern judge who ignores his protest of being innocent and throws the book at him, giving Muni 10 years of hard labor on a chain gang. He is then taken to the prison farm where shackles are put about his legs by a blacksmith, a short chain between allowing him to take mincing, painful steps. He will live with these leg irons for the length of his term. He endures hardships undreamed of; he is whipped and flogged for the slightest infraction. When working in the quarry slinging a sledge against mountains of rocks, Muni stops and wipes the sweat from his brow. A guard slams him to the ground with a rifle butt. Grizzled prisoner Ellis, a lifer, tells Muni: "Ya gotta ask permission for everything, even to wipe the sweat away." He demonstrates by stopping, turning to a guard and shouting: "Wiping it off!" A guard shouts back: "Wipe it off!" Ellis runs a bony hand across his forehead and wipes away the bands of sweat. The same applies, Muni learns, when he must relieve himself. The food served him and other convicts is nothing but bug-crawling slop. He is denied sanitary conditions and his human dignity is stripped from him layer by layer by inhuman guards. He watches in rage and registers agony for a prisoner who has been too ill to do a good day's work and is dragged to a back room where his shirt is stripped away and his back flogged raw by a sadistic guard wielding a leather strap. When Muni looks crossways at a guard, he, too, is whipped. There are other devices of medieval-like torture, such as the sweatbox, where prisoners are made to stand rigid for days and nights for the slightest infractions. Muni finds this subhuman existence intolerable and decides to escape. He watches as one prisoner is released, Jenkins, along with another who has died and is being shipped out in a pine box. "That's the only way you get outa here," Ellis says as he and Muni and others peer from a window to see the gates swing open for the wagon carrying the coffin. "Serve your time or die." Jenkins waves goodbye to his friends, then hops on the wagon, sitting atop the coffin, as he rides to freedom. Muni is later working with a road gang repairing a stretch of railroad. He asks a huge, powerful black prisoner swinging a sledge behind him to strike his shackles as he braces them against the side of the rail, just enough to loosen them. The black agrees but asks that Muni not cry out with the pain the blows will bring. The black swings mightily and lands several blows; Muni grits his teeth, keeps working, and is later able to slip out of the shackles. He asks guards the next day for permission to step behind some bushes to relieve himself, slips out of his shackles, and then races off, running through swamps where the inevitable bloodhounds cannot pick up his trail. Muni makes it to a small town where he enters a barbershop and Bacon gives him a shave. While he sits with a hot towel covering his face, a cop comes into the shop and he and Bacon discuss the escaped convict, concluding that he will not get far. Muni next gets up, pays the barber, and heads for the door. Bacon calls out after him and he turns apprehensively. "Was the shave close enough?" the barber asks him. He rubs his face nervously, and before going out says "plenty." Muni, with Jenkins' help, makes his way to Chicago where he gets a job with a construction company, slowly rising through the ranks to earn good money. His landlady, Farrell, is attracted to the reclusive Muni and she more or less browbeats him into marrying her, she, discovering his chain gang history and really blackmailing him to the altar, saying at one point: "I wouldn't tell, if I had a reason to protect you." He soon regrets doing so. Working his way into managerial status, and finally an executive position with the firm, he finds that his wife is nothing more than a crude, brassy embarrassment to him. Moreover, he meets sweet and cultured socialite Vinson and, after leaving his wife, develops a careful relationship with her. At one point, when he seems not to respond to her charms she delivers a line that would never be tolerated today, saying: "I'm free, white, and over twenty-one." Before Muni can make plans to divorce Farrell and marry Vinson, his treacherous estranged spouse turns him in to southern authorities, taking her vengeance upon Muni. The state of Illinois, however, is not so ready to allow one of its leading citizens to be extradited to the south. Expensive lawyers advise Muni to resist extradition but the governor of the southern state sends a message that if Muni cooperates and surrenders voluntarily to southern prison officials and allows himself to be taken back to the chain gang, he will be pardoned. His brother also believes that Muni should surrender and he is convinced that the southern state only wants to save face and will pardon him shortly after he goes back. He does, and is thrown back into the same chain gang where guards who have almost lost their jobs over his escape take their vengeance with merciless beatings and degradations heaped upon Muni. He soon learns that the pardons board has no intention of granting his release, that the governor has lied, and that it was all a ruse to get Muni back to the chain gang. Then he is told that he not only has to serve his original 10 years but another long term for his escape. Muni considers himself one of the living dead and appears to accept his fate, yet lurking inside of him is the thought of another escape. He takes his chance with old man Ellis at the quarry, stealing a truck and driving madly down country roads, carloads of guards following in hot pursuit, firing at the fugitives. Ellis finds some dynamite used for blasting in the truck and hurls a stick at the pursuers, blowing up a bridge, which stops them. One guard, however, gets off a well-aimed shot and kills Ellis who falls from the truck. Later, Muni uses the meshing gears of the dump truck to sever his shackles. He then makes good his escape. In the final scene, one of the most chilling in the history of motion pictures, Vinson is shown driving her car into a garage. As she steps into the alleyway, she hears a noise and there stands Muni, haggard in rags, a gaunt, hollow-eyed creature, appearing half crazed. "It's been a year since you escaped," she cries out to him. "I haven't escaped," he rasps. "They're still after me. They'll always be after me. I hide in rooms all day and travel by night. No friends, no rest, no peace. . .Forgive me, Helen, I had to see you tonight, just to say goodbye." He takes a few steps backward into the shadows. "It was all going to be so different," Vinson says. Muni's voice seems to come from a bottomless pit as he says with rage: "It is different! They've made it different!" There is a sudden noise in the alley and Muni begins to retreat quickly into the darkness. Vinson calls out after him: "Can't you tell me where you're going?" He shakes his head. "Will you write?" Again Muni shakes his head, sinking back into the gloom of night, until only his terrified, wide-eyed face can be seen, the ravaged face of a hunted, hopeless man. "How do you live?" implores Vinson. All is now blackness where Muni has been standing and he is gone, almost, like a ghost, but from the pervasive darkness comes his final, hissing, desperate reply: "I steal!" With this shocking and powerful statement one of the great films of the 1930s comes to an end. Perhaps more than any other film he directed, this film and the reputation of the socially conscious LeRoy are synonymous. Here the director of LITTLE CAESAR (1930) and later THEY WON'T FORGET (1937) which explored the horrors of lynching, pulls no punches in the vehement social protest implanted in every scene of I AM A FUGITIVE FROM A CHAIN GANG. Although he did not feel it necessary to graphically show the floggings and beatings, he did display these horrors by showing the shadows of a prisoner being held and that of a guard lashing him. The brutality is not ignored, nor is the pain. When Muni's shackles are smashed by the black convict, the horrible blows that almost break his ankles are registered on Muni's face, not on his feet. Of course, Muni's enormous talent allowed LeRoy to achieve this effect, where today's director, given the type of talent available, would undoubtedly prefer to show the bloodied feet. The startling end of this film, however, was not specifically a stroke of LeRoy's genius, but he did have the ability to take advantage of a happy accident. When Muni and Vinson appeared in the final scene and the lights grew dim about them as he announced: "I steal" LeRoy was beside himself. The scene called for the scene to suddenly go black but, before that, a klieg light blew a fuse and gradually dimmed the entire scene. Said LeRoy later: "It was an accident but I immediately recognized it as an accident that worked. . . Eventually, after some experimentation, I decided that a sudden blackout wasn't as effective as a gradual dimming of the lights, and that's the way it was done." Much of this film's story and technique would later influence many a prison film, especially those dealing with prison farm systems, which would liberally lift ideas from the LeRoy classic. The escape through the swamps was duplicated by Edward G. Robinson, who eludes chain gang guards in BLACKMAIL (1939). The escape by truck is employed by Paul Newman in COOL HAND LUKE (1967). Muni's totally captivating performance is nothing short of masterpiece acting. This marvelous actor, whose 1930s heyday on the screen established the criteria of acting excellence, stripped away his own identity to assume that of the victim, James Allen. Muni's incredible ability to assume any role he undertook to play meant he really became that person. He proved his adaptability in one marvelous performance after another, from the brutish Tony Camonte in Howard Hawks' ultra-violent portrait of Al Capone and gang warfare in SCARFACE, released the same year as I AM A FUGITIVE FROM A CHAIN GANG, to his role of the simple Chinese peasant in THE GOOD EARTH (1937). He would later appear as stirring and unforgettable historical characters—Benito Juarez, Louis Pasteur, Emile Zola. As with all his roles, Muni proved himself a perfectionist. He would study his subject and do deep research with speech patterns of the person he was to play, studying the habits, mannerisms and personality and then transforming himself into that person's identity. Muni was a recluse off screen and offstage, preferring to appear in live theater than in films. When his roles in the movies became unsatisfactory to him, Muni simply tore up a contract (worth $800,000) and walked away from Hollywood. His wife later described how, with the contract in shreds, "he did somersaults in the living room. . . He jumped up and down yelling, 'No one owns me. I'm a free man!' " Muni, as well as LeRoy, were exceptional talents that were nevertheless unorthodox talents that would not normally have found homes in most Hollywood studios. But Warner Bros. was their logical residence because this was the one studio that took the big risks with social protest films, a studio that took its material right out of the headlines and was surprisingly fearless in presenting vital issues, risking total box office failure if the public failed to respond. But the public did respond, especially to I AM A FUGITIVE FROM A CHAIN GANG. Though the film specifically excluded the name of Georgia from its title (where the book title included it) and never mentioned the state in the entire film, the indictment of that state's cruel chain gang system was clear. A storm of protest arose from the public to the point where the sadistic prison system was finally abolished and reforms instituted, but this was a slow process. Initially, Georgia's political sachems had nothing but sneers and jeers for one and all connected to the film. LeRoy and Jack Warner were both specifically told that if they ever crossed the border and entered Georgia they might be in for a taste of unexpected southern hospitality. The film was banned in the state and Georgia filed a libel suit against the studio. Two prison wardens in Georgia also filed million-dollar suits against Warner Bros. but it all came to nothing. Georgia, however, was relentless in its attempt to recapture the man who had caused the upheaval, the real James Allen, Robert Elliot Burns who, in 1920, to obtain money to eat, burglarized a store of $5.29. He was sent to a Georgia chain gang, escaping two years later. He became a respected Chicago citizen and esteemed $20,000-a-year magazine editor. Then his first wife informed on him and he was inveigled back to Georgia where he slaved on a chain gang until escaping again in 1930, surfacing in New Jersey as a tax expert. He wrote a series of articles later collected into the book *I Am A Fugitive from a Georgia Chain Gang* which caused a national sensation. When LeRoy and Warners decided to make its historic film based on the book, Burns was asked to travel to Hollywood to serve as an advisor on the film. Burns smuggled himself into Los Angeles and on to the Warner Bros. lot, using the name Richard M. Crane. He not only suggested ideas for the script but reportedly helped write dialog. Playwright Sheridan Gibney, who was originally assigned to work on the screenplay, was cloistered with Burns on the lot but the experience was nerve-wracking. Burns was as skittish as a cat in a doghouse, twitching and turning at every noise. A siren went off and Burns grabbed his hat and raced outside, vanishing for hours. What had startled him were the sound effects of a crime film being made in a nearby sound stage. He fled to New Jersey after a few weeks of anonymous work. Georgia kept demanding the state of New Jersey extradite him but three governors of that state refused to do so. Petitions with hundreds of thousands of names on them supported the fugitive. Georgia even sent goon squads to New Jersey to kidnap Burns but he eluded them. As late as 1941, a vengeful Georgia governor, Eugene Talmadge, still tried to get Burns back, but the New Jersey governor refused to cooperate. Then married a second time and having two children, the harassed Burns cried out publicly: "How long will they keep this up? Will I never have peace?" But reform governor Ellis Arnall of Georgia got Burns' sentence commuted to time served in 1945. He would never receive a pardon, dying in 1955. He was, as Muni so convincingly portrayed him, a real life Jean Valjean.

p, Hal Wallis; d, Mervyn LeRoy; w, Howard J. Green, Brown Holmes, Sheridan Gibney (based on the autobiography *I Am a Fugitive from a Georgia Chain Gang* by Robert E. Burns); ph, Sol Polito; m, Leo F. Forbstein; ed, William Holmes; art d, Jack Okey; cos, Orry-Kelly.

Prison Drama Cas. (PR:0 MPAA:NR)

I AM A GROUPIE* (1970, Brit.) 86m Salon/EF c (GB: GROUPIE GIRL)

Esme Johns *(Sally)*, Billy Boyle *(Wes)*, Richard Shaw *(Morrie)*, Neil Hallett *(Detective Sergeant)*, Charles Finch *(Dog Handler)*, Donald Sumpter *(Steve)*, Paul Bacon *(Part Host)*, Lynda Priest *(Dancer)*, Cherokee *(Groupie at Hotel)*, Walter Swash *(Hotel Porter)*, James Beck *(1st Group Manager)*, Jimmie Edwards *(Bob)*, Eliza Terry *(Mooncake)*, The Sweaty Betty, Orange [Opal] Butterfly.

A silly look at the young girls who become hangers-on to popular rock bands. Johns is one such girl. She stows away in a pop group's van, trading her boring small-town life for the excitement of London, but trouble follows. She winds up as the band's sexual plaything, gets entangled with drugs, is involved in a car accident, and ends up being arrested by the police.

p, Barry Jacobs, Stanley Long; d, Derek Ford; w, Ford, Suzanne Mercer; ph, Long (Eastmancolor); m, John Fiddy, Alan Hawkshaw; ed, N.C.S.; m/l, "You're a Groupie Girl," "Gigging Song" (performed by Opal Butterfly), "To Jackie," "Yesterday's Rose," "Love's A World Away" (performed by English Rose), "Now You're Gone," "Love Me," "Give Me A Little" (performed by Virgin Stigma), "True Blue," "Disco 2," "Four Wheel Drive" (performed by Salon Band), "Looking for Love," "I Wonder Did You" (performed by Billy Boyle), and "Groupie Girl" (sung by Peter Lee Stirling).

Drama (PR:O MPAA:NR)

I AM A THIEF** (1935) 64m WB bw

Mary Astor *(Odette Mauclair)*, Ricardo Cortez *(Pierre Londals)*, Dudley Digges *(Col. Jackson)*, Robert Barrat *(Baron Van Kampf)*, Irving Pichel *(Count Trentini)*, Florence Fair *(Mme. Cassiet)*, Hobart Cavanaugh, Arthur Aylesworth, Ferdinand Gottschalk, Frank Reicher, John Wray, Oscar Apfel.

Cortez is carrying the Karenina diamonds on the Paris to Istanbul Express. Astor and other thieves attempt to make the jewels theirs. There is a murder, one of the groups of thieves is arrested, and Astor marries Cortez. A routine crime-on-a-train film.

p, Henry Blanke; d, Robert Florey; w, Ralph Block, Doris Malloy; ph, Sid Hickox; ed, Terry Morse; art d, Jack Okey.

Crime/Mystery (PR:A MPAA:NR)

I AM CURIOUS GAY (SEE: HAPPY BIRTHDAY, DAVY, 1970)

I AM NOT AFRAID*½ (1939) 59m WB bw

Jane Bryan *(Madge Carter)*, Charley Grapewin *(Ulysses Porterfield)*, Henry O'Neill *(Matthew Carter)*, Elizabeth Risdon *(Jessie Carter)*, Jimmy McCallion *(Ralph Carter)*, Dickie Jones *(Bill Carter)*, John Russell *(Ted Carter)*, Fred Tozere *(Stephen Palmer)*, John Gallaudet *(Nick Bartel)*, Don Douglas *(Miller)*, William Royle *(Howard)*, Emmett Vogan *(Stuart McCrary)*, Boyd Irwin *(Arthur Shepherd)*, Grace Stafford *(Mary McCrary)*, George Guhl *(Brown)*, Norman Willis *(Max)*, Alan Davis *(Frank)*, Charles Richman *(Mayor Lawton)*, Millard Vincent *(Mayor's Secretary)*, Elliott Sullivan *(Slug)*, Walter Fenner *(Magistrate)*, Kenneth Harlan *(Dalton)*.

A remake of Warner Brothers' STAR WITNESS (1931). Bryan and family witness a police lieutenant planting a bomb in a neighbor's garage. The family is afraid to testify because of continuing threats by gangsters. Finally, Grapewin comes forward to give the district attorney the testimony needed for the case.

p, Bryan Foy; d, Crane Wilbur; w, Lee Katz (based on the story "Star Witness" by Lucien Hubbard); ph, Arthur Todd; ed, Harold McLernon.

Crime Drama (PR:A MPAA:NR)

I AM SUZANNE** (1934) 99m FOX bw

Lillian Harvey *(Suzanne)*, Gene Raymond *(Tony)*, Leslie Banks *(Baron)*, Georgia Caine *(Mama)*, Geneva Mitchell *(Fifi)*, Halliwell Hobbes *(Dr. Lorenzo)*, Murray Kinnell *(Luigi)*, Edward Keane *(Manager)*, Lionel Belmore *(Satan)*, The Piccoli Marionette Troupe, The Yale Puppeteers, Florence Desmond (voices imitating Greta Garbo, Marlene Dietrich and others).

Dancer Harvey breaks her leg and is taken care of by puppeteer Raymond. They fall in love. This routine story line is boosted by the clever use of puppets which symbolize the relationship between Harvey and Raymond at its various stages. In the film's best sequence Harvey dreams that she is put on trial for attempting to kill the puppet likeness of herself. Both puppets and people perform the production numbers. Songs include "Just A Little Garret," "Oh How I've Sinned," "One Word," "San Moritz," "Wooden Woman," "Oski-O-Lay-Li-O-Mo" (Frederick Hollander).

p, Jesse L. Lasky; d, Rowland V. Lee; w, Lee, Edwin Justus Mayer; ch, Sammy Lee.

Drama (PR:A MPAA:NR)

I AM THE CHEESE* (1983) 100m Almi c

Robert MacNaughton *(Adam)*, Hope Lange *(Betty)*, Don Murray *(David)*, Robert Wagner *(Dr. Brint)*, Cynthia Nixon *(Amy)*, Frank McGurran *(Young Adam)*, Russell Goslant *(Gardener)*, Robert Cormier *(Hertz)*, Dorothea MacNaughton *(Produce Lady)*, Milford Keene *(Harvester)*, Lee Richardson *(Grey)*, Joey Jerome *(Whipper)*, Ronnie Bradbury *(Corn)*, Robert Dutil *(Jed)*, Jeff Rumney *(Counterman)*, David Lange *(Montgomery)*, Christopher Murray *(Eric)*, Sudie Bond *(Edna)*, John Fielder *(Arnold)*, John Bernek *(Store Owner)*, Paul Romero *(Coke)*.

MacNaughton (the older brother in E.T.) plays a disturbed young man who falls into a fantasy world after witnessing the death of his parents. It's a poor psychiatric exercise.

p, David Lange; d, Robert Jiras; w, Lang, Jiras (based on the novel by Robert Cormier); ph, David Quaid; m, Jonathan Tunick; ed, Nicholas Smith.

Drama Cas. (PR:A MPAA:PG)

I AM THE LAW*** (1938) 83m COL bw

Edward G. Robinson *(John Lindsay)*, Barbara O'Neil *(Jerry Lindsay)*, John Beal *(Paul Ferguson)*, Wendy Barrie *(Frankie Ballou)*, Otto Kruger *(Eugene Ferguson)*, Arthur Loft *(Tom Ross)*, Marc Lawrence *(Eddie Girard)*, Douglas Wood *(Berry)*, Robert Middlemass *(Moss Kitchell)*, Ivan Miller *(Inspector Gleason)*, Charles Halton *(Leander)*, Louis Jean Heydt *(J.W. Butler)*, Emory Parnell *(Brophy)*, Joseph Downing *(Cronin)*, Theodore Von Eltz *(Martin)*, Horace McMahon *(Prisoner)*, Frederick Burton *(Governor)*, Lucien Littlefield *(Roberts)*, Ed Keane, Robert Cummings, Sr., Harvey Clark, James Flavin, Harry Bradley, Edward J. LeSaint, Billy Arnold, Frank Mayo, Oliver Eckhardt *(Witnesses)*, Kane Richmond, James Bush, Anthony Nace, Robert McWade, Jr., Will Morgan, James Millican *(Students)*, Ed Fetherston *(Austin)*, Scott Colton, Gaylord "Steve" Pendleton, Marshall Ruth, Philip Grant, Alan Bruce, Nick Lukats *(Graduate Law Students)*, Walter Soderling *(Prof. Perkins)*, Bud Jamison *(Bartender)*, Iris Meredith *(Girard's Girl)*, Mary Brodel *(Hat Check Girl)*, Frank Bruno, Chick Collins, Jack Woody *(Gangsters)*, Joseph De Stefani, George Pearce *(Cigar Store Proprietors)*, Eddie Foster, Jeffrey Sayre *(Thugs)*, George Turner, Charles Hamilton, Bud Wiser, Lane Chandler *(Policemen)*, Phil Smalley *(University Dean)*, William Worthington *(Committee Man)*, Lee Shumway *(Police Sergeant)*, Russell Heustis *(Man)*, Ed Thomas *(Steward)*, Walter Anthony Merrill, Lester Dorr *(Reporters)*, Reginald Simpson, Cyril Ring, Allen Fox, Charles Sherlock, Ernie Alexander *(Photographers)*, J.G. MacMahon *(Waiter)*, Bess Flowers *(Secretary)*, Lloyd Whitlock *(Headwaiter)*, Eugene Anderson, Jr. *(Schoolboy)*, Fay Helm *(Mrs. Butler)*.

Law professor Robinson is named special prosecutor, assigned to put an end to gangster activity in the city. Civic leader Beal, who got Robinson his job, is involved in the rackets and desires to monitor and sway Robinson's investigation. Everyone Robinson's office persuades to testify turns up dead. The district attorney fires Robinson, but he continues his investigation as a private citizen. With the help of his former law students he finds enough evidence on Beal and the rackets to put a dead stop to both. Robinson and the police round up all the criminals involved and herd them into a circus tent where they are shown a filmed electrocution. Robinson also presents a filmed murder committed by Barrie, Beal's assistant. His fate sealed, Beal gets into Robinson's car knowing that a bomb has been planted on the starter.

p, Everett Riskin; d, Alexander Hall; w, Jo Swerling (based on a story by Fred Allhoff); ph, Henry Freulich; ed, Viola Lawrence; md, Morris Stoloff; art d, Stephen Goosson, Lionel Banks; set d, Babs Johnstone; cos, Kalloch.

Crime Drama (PR:A MPAA:NR)

I BECAME A CRIMINAL**

(1947) 78m Shipman-Gloria-Alliance/WB bw (GB: THEY MADE ME A FUGITIVE) (AKA: THEY MADE ME A CRIMINAL)

Sally Gray *(Sally)*, Trevor Howard *(Clem Morgan)*, Griffith Jones *(Narcey)*, Rene Ray *(Cora)*, Mary Merrall *(Aggie)*, Vida Hope *(Mrs. Fenshawe)*, Ballard Berkeley *(Inspector Rockliffe)*, Phyllis Robins *(Olga)*, Eve Ashley *(Ellen)*, Charles Farrell *(Curley)*, Jack McNaughton *(Soapy)*, Cyril Smith, Maurice Denham, Michael Brennan, Bill O'Connor, Lyn Evans.

Howard is an RAF officer who falls from grace, winds up a crook, gets framed by Jones, and is thrown in the pen. He gets out and heads for Soho seeking revenge on Jones and his dope-dealing gang. Luckily the lovely Gray saves Howard from sinking too low.

p, N.A. "Nat" Bronsten, James Carter; d, Alberto Cavalcanti; w, Noel Langley (based on the novel *A Convict Has Escaped* by Jackson Budd); ph, Otto Heller; m, Marius Francois Gaillard; ed, Margery Saunders; md, John Hollingsworth; art d, A. Mazzei.

Crime (PR:A MPAA:NR)

I BELIEVE IN YOU*** (1953, Brit.) 95m EAL/UNIV bw

Celia Johnson *(Matty)*, Cecil Parker *(Henry Phipps)*, Godfrey Tearle *(Mr. Pyke)*, Harry Fowler *(Hooker)*, George Relph *(Mr. Dove)*, Joan Collins *(Norma)*, Laurence Harvey *(Jordie)*, Ernest Jay *(Mr. Quayle)*, Ursula Howells *(Hon. Ursula)*, Sidney James *(Sgt. Brodie)*, Katie Johnson *(Miss Macklin)*, Ada Reeve *(Mrs. Crockett)*, Brenda de Banzie *(Mrs. Hooker)*, Alex McCrindle *(Mr. Haines)*, Laurence Naismith *(Sgt. Braxton)*, Gladys Henson *(Mrs. Stevens)*, Cyril Waites *(Dai)*, Stanley Escane *(Buck)*, John Orchard *(Braxton)*, David Hannaford *(Bit)*, Herbert L. Walton *(Frost)*, Gladys Henson *(Mrs. Stevens)*, Fred Griffiths *(Crump)*, Richard Hart *(Eric Stevens)*, Judith Furse *(Athletics Secretary)*, Gwynne Whitby.

A documentary-style drama about two British probation officers and the slum youths they deal with. Parker and Johnson are the officers; Collins and Fowler are the two youths they try to help. An engaging drama with surprisingly good performances from Collins, Fowler, and Harvey.

p&d, Michael Relph, Basil Dearden; w, Jack Whittingham, Nicholas Phipps, Relph,

Dearden (based on the book *Court Circular* by Sewell Stokes); ph, Gordon Dines; m, Ernest Irving; ed, Peter Tanner; art d, Maurice Carter.

Drama **(PR:A MPAA:NR)**

I BELIEVED IN YOU* (1934) 68m FOX bw

Rosemary Ames *(True Merrill)*, Victor Jory *(Jim Crowl)*, John Boles *(Michael Harrison)*, Gertrude Michael *(Pamela Banks)*, George Meeker *(Saracen Jones)*, Leslie Fenton *(Russell Storm)*, Joyzelle *(Vavara)*, Jed Prouty *(Joe)*, Morgan Wallace *(Oliver)*, Luis Alberni *(Giacomo)*.

Jory, a professional agitator, takes off for New York with struggling writer Ames. Jory gets into trouble with the law in the city; Ames falls in with an arty Greenwich Village crowd. Boles offers to help out Ames and her artist friends, determined to prove that it isn't poverty that is holding them back. Jory is unfaithful to Ames and she contemplates suicide. Deciding against the rash action, she is rewarded with a published book. Boles woos her, but the future of any relationship between them is left unclear at the film's end. A dull melodrama.

d, Irving Cummings; w, William Counselman (based on a story by William Anthony McGuire); ph, Barney McGill; ed, Al De Gaetano.

Drama **(PR:A MPAA:NR)**

I BOMBED PEARL HARBOR**

(1961, Jap.) 100m Toho/Parade c (TAIHEIYO NO ARASHI; AKA: THE STORM OVER THE PACIFIC)

Yosuke Natsuki *(Lt. Koji Kitami)*, Toshiro Mifune *(Adm. Isoroku Yamaguchi [Yamamoto])*, Koji Tsuruta *(Lt. Tomonari)*, Misa Uehara *(Keiko)*, Aiko Mimasu *(Sato)*, Jun Tazaki *(Captain)*, Makoto Sato *(Lt. Matsuura)*, Takashi Shimura *(Tosaku)*, Daisuke Kato, Akira Takarada, Hiroshi Koizumi.

What could have been an interesting look at the Japanese view of WW II is passed over for standard war action and situations. Mifune plays Admiral Isoroku Yamaguchi, commander of the task force that attacked Pearl Harbor, and Natsuki is a flight navigator who returns to Japan after the attack. Uehara is the childhood sweetheart that Natsuki is afraid to marry, fearing that marriage will make him a less competent officer. As the war goes on and the Japanese begin to experience defeat, Natsuki wonders about the purported invincibility of the Japanese fleet. His carrier is sunk by American dive bombers at Midway, and the men go down with the ship, offering a final salute.

p, Tomoyuki Tanaka, Hugo Grimaldi, d, Shue Matsubayashi; w, Shinobu Hashimoto, Takeo Kunihiro, Riley Jackson, Grimaldi; ph, Kazuo Yamada (Tohoscope, Eastmancolor); m, Ikuma Dan, Gordon Zahler, Walter Greene; ed, Grimaldi; spec eff, Eiji Tsuburaya.

War Drama **(PR:A MPAA:NR)**

I BURY THE LIVING** (1958) 76m Maxim/UA bw

Richard Boone *(Robert Kraft)*, Theodore Bikel *(Andy McKee)*, Peggy Maurer *(Ann Craig)*, Herb Anderson *(Jess Jessup)*, Howard Smith *(George Kraft)*, Robert Osterloh *(Lt. Clayborne)*, Russ Bender *(Henry Trowbridge)*, Matt Moore *(Charles Bates, Sr.)*, Ken Drake *(Bill Honegger)*, Glenn Vernon *(Stu Drexel)*, Lynn Bernay *(Beth Drexel)*, Cyril Delevanti *(W. Isham)*.

Boone is the newly appointed chairman of the local cemetery. The cemetery has a map marking plots: black pins indicate that someone is buried in a plot, white ones indicate a plot that is sold but unoccupied. Boone mistakenly mixes up some of the pins. This causes the owners of those plots to die, and Boone begins to wonder if he has some evil power. It turns out that caretaker Bikel is killing these people to drive Boone crazy. The absence of plot complications in the film is filled by engaging photographic tricks and artwork.

p, Albert Band, Louis Garfinkle; d, Band; w, Garfinkle; ph, Frederick Gately; m, Gerald Fried; ed, Frank Sullivan; art d, E. Vorkapich.

Horror/Mystery **(PR:A MPAA:NR)**

I CALL FIRST (SEE: WHO'S THAT KNOCKING AT MY DOOR?, 1968)

I CAN GET IT FOR YOU WHOLESALE*1/2**

(1951) 90m FOX bw (AKA: ONLY THE BEST)

Susan Hayward *(Harriet Boyd)*, Dan Dailey *(Teddy Sherman)*, George Sanders *(Noble)*, Sam Jaffe *(Cooper)*, Randy Stuart *(Marge)*, Marvin Kaplan *(Four Eyes)*, Harry Von Zell *(Savage)*, Barbara Whiting *(Ellie)*, Vicki Cummings *(Hermione Griggs)*, Ross Elliott *(Ray)*, Richard Lane *(Kelley)*, Mary Philips *(Mrs. Boyd)*, Benna Bard *(Fran)*, Steve Geray *(Bettini)*, Charles Lane *(Pulvermacher)*, Jan Kayne *(Ida)*, Marion Marshall *(Terry)*, Jayne Hazard, Aline Towne *(Models)*, Eda Reis Merin *(Miss Marks)*, Marjorie Hoshelle *(Louise)*, Doris Kemper *(Nurse)*, Elizabeth Flournoy *(Secretary)*, Jack P. Carr *(Bartender)*, Tamara Shayne *(Mrs. Cooper)*, Ed Max *(Tiffany Joe)*, David Wolfe *(Speaker)*, Harry Hines *(Elevator Man)*, Diana Mumby, Shirlee Allard, Beverly Thompson *(Blondes)*, Michael Hogan *(Ship's Officer)*, Bess Flowers *(Saleswoman)*.

Smooth but not stellar adaptation of Weidman's novel, which later went to the Broadway stage as a musical and served to introduce Barbra Streisand to a waiting world. In this version Hayward is a model in a dress house on Seventh Avenue in New York. But she has aspirations far beyond the modeling ramp and decides to use her designing abilities to open her own company. To do this, she raids the firm she's with and steals Dailey, their best salesman, and Jaffe, the overseer of manufacturing. They pool their money and begin making clothes. Hayward is all business and tougher than the average Seventh Avenue shark, but Dailey falls in love with her despite that. Sanders runs a Neiman-Marcus type department store and tells Hayward that he can make her a national designer if she will concentrate on creating evening gowns for his store and its exclusive clientele. Dailey is against it and feels they should stay with what they know: dresses for the people, not some high-priced line for Park Avenueites. Hayward attempts to weasel out of the triumvirate but Dailey won't allow that. She then enters into a covert deal with Sanders to make evening gowns, thus allowing her desire for notoriety to blind her in her relationship with Dailey. Afterwards she tells Jaffe and Dailey that if they don't deliver the gowns she's designing, she'll let the company go belly up. Jaffe and Dailey are not impressed by her threats and the small company goes bankrupt. Sanders and Hayward are about to sail to Europe when he comes to the correct conclusion, that she is only traveling with him to hurt Dailey, not because she loves Sanders. He does the uncadlike thing and tells Hayward that she would be better off with Dailey. She returns to the company's offices, rushes into Dailey's arms, and the film ends with the presumption that they can get back into business again, as well as into their former love attitude. I CAN GET IT FOR YOU WHOLESALE is about as accurate an image as one can get of the "Rag Trade" circa 1951. These days, many of the larger firms have been acquired by conglomerates, but there are still enough small manufacturers around who would identify with the problems faced by the characters in this film. It's a boy meets girl story but in a new setting that sustains the viewer's interest. Marvin Kaplan, one of TV's earliest character actors, does his usual fine job as "Four Eyes." Shot on location in New York City, one scene called for Hayward and Dailey to be inside a car; before the cameras rolled, a crowd began to form around the auto, dozens, then hundreds of fans pressing in on the auto which frightened the actors who thought the car might be turned over. Director Gordon saved the day by worming his way through the immense throng and ordering Hayward and Dailey to sign autographs from either window which they did until they were arm-weary. Hayward, by this film, was a Hollywood superstar and enjoyed strolling down Fifth Avenue, wearing dark glasses but being recognized anyway (which is what she hoped for) by her flaming red hair. "It's wonderful being a movie star," she bubbled to a New York *Post* reporter on the set, "being able to go to the best Fifth Avenue shops and buy the toys for your children you never could have."

p, Sol C. Siegel; d, Michael Gordon; w, Abraham Polonsky, Vera Caspary (based on the novel by Jerome Weidman); ph, Milton Krasner; m, Sol Kaplan; ed, Robert Simpson; md, Lionel Newman; art d, Lyle Wheeler, John De Cuir; set d, Thomas Little; cos, Charles LeMaire; spec eff, Fred Sersen; makeup, Ben Nye.

Drama **(PR:A MPAA:NR)**

I CAN'T ESCAPE*1/2 (1934) 60m Beacon/SYN bw

Onslow Stevens *(Steve Nichols/Cummings)*, Lila Lee *(Mae)*, Russell Gleason *(Tom Martin)*, Otis Harlan *(Bonn)*, Hooper Atchley *(Harley)*, Clara Kimball Young *(Mrs. Wilson)*, Nat Carr *(Mr. Watson)*, Eddie Gribbon *(Policeman)*, Kane Richmond *(College Boy)*.

Stevens finds it hard to shake the stigma of serving a jail sentence for a crime he didn't commit. He can't get a job but he does get the girl he loves. He foils a plan to sell phony stocks and finally clears his name.

p, Peter A. Kassler; d, Otto Brower; w, Faith Thomas (based on a story by Jerry Sackheim, Nathan Ash); ph, Jerome Ash; ed, Lou Sackin, Fred Knudtson.

Crime Drama **(PR:A MPAA:NR)**

I CAN'T GIVE YOU ANYTHING BUT LOVE, BABY zero

(1940) 61m UNIV bw

Broderick Crawford *(Sonny McGann)*, Peggy Moran *(Linda Caroll)*, Johnny Downs *(Bob Gunther)*, Warren Hymer *(Big Foot Louie)*, John Sutton *(Boston)*, Gertrude Michael *(Magda Delys)*, Jessie Ralph *(Mama McGann)*, Horace MacMahon *(Bugs)*, Dewey Robinson *(Roundhouse)*, Murray Alper *(Nails)*, Sunshine Sammy *(Joe)*, Jeni LeGon *(Annie)*, Virginia Sale *(Landlady)*.

Crawford, a gangster who fancies himself a lyricist, wants to write a song that will act as a message for his long-lost love Moran. He kidnaps composer Downs to take care of the music, and together they create a song that sends Moran running to the gangster. A ludicrous story without even a single moment of film entertainment. Songs include the hit "I Can't Give You Anything But Love" (Dorothy Fields, Jimmy McHugh), "Sweetheart of School 59," "Day by Day" (Paul Gerard Smith, Frank Skinner).

p, Ken Goldsmith; d, Albert S. Rogell; w, Arthur T. Horman, Paul Gerard Smith (based on the story "Trouble in B Flat" by James Edward Grant); ph, Elwood Bredell; m&md, Charles Previn.

Musical/Comedy **(PR:A MPAA:NR)**

I CAN'T . . . I CAN'T (SEE: WEDDING NIGHT, 1969)

I CHANGED MY SEX (SEE: GLEN OR GLENDA, 1953)

I CHEATED THE LAW*1/2 (1949) 69m Belsam/FOX bw

Tom Conway *(John Campbell)*, Steve Brodie *(Frank Bricolle)*, Robert Osterloh *(Joe Corsi)*, Barbara Billingsley *(Mrs. John Campbell)*, Russell Hicks *(D.A. Randolph)*, James Seay *(Rodd Simpson)*, Chet Huntley *(Himself)*, Tom Noonan *(Sad Sam Carney)*, William Gould *(1st Judge)*, Harry Harvey *(2nd Judge)*, Garry Owen *(Jerry)*, Charles Wagenheim *(Al Markham)*, Louis Mason, Phil Arnold.

Conway is a lawyer who gets gangster Brodie acquitted on murder charges. After the trial, Brodie informs Conway that he tricked him into being his alibi. Conway, unable to bring Brodie to trial again for the murder, goes out to pin something else on him. He gets Brodie back in court on another murder charge and tricks the gangster into confessing to both murders.

p, Sam Baerwitz; d, Edward L. Cahn; w, Richard G. Hubler (based on a story by

Baerwitz); ph, Jackson A. Rose; ed, Arthur Hilton; md, Edward J. Kay; art d, Frank Sylos.

Crime Drama **(PR:A MPAA:NR)**

I COLTELLI DEL VENDICATORE (SEE: KNIVES OF THE AVENGER, 1967, Ital.)

I COMPAGNI (SEE: ORGANIZER, THE, 1964, Fr./Itooal./Yugo.))

I CONFESS*** (1953) 95m WB Alfred Hitchcock-WB/bw

Montgomery Clift *(Father Michael William Logan)*, Anne Baxter *(Ruth Grandfort)*, Karl Malden *(Inspector Larrue)*, Brian Aherne *(Willy Robertson, Attorney)*, O. E. Hasse *(Otto Keller)*, Dolly Haas *(Alma Keller)*, Roger Dann *(Pierre Grandfort)*, Charles Andre *(Father Millais)*, Judson Pratt *(Murphy, a Policeman)*, Ovila Legare *(Vilette, the Lawyer)*, Gilles Pelletier *(Father Benoit)*, Nan Boardman *(Maid)*, Henry Corden *(Farouche)*, Carmen Gingras *(1st French Girl)*, Renee Hudson *(2nd French Girl)*, Albert Goderis *(Nightwatchman)*.

I CONFESS is based on a 1902 play which has the feeling that it might have come from real life. In the years since the movie was released, several true incidents have occurred around the central theme of this movie. Hitchcock had a strict Jesuit upbringing which must have contributed to his desire to make a movie about the vow of confidentiality that priests must take in regard to revealing anything they may hear in the confessional. Filmed in Quebec, Canada, I CONFESS begins as refugee Hasse murders Legare, an attorney, when caught in the act of burglary. Later, Hasse confesses his crime to priest Clift. Hasse has been working as the sexton at the church and knows that Clift will never betray him. Legare had been extracting money from Baxter, who is married to Dann. Baxter had been Clift's lover before he took the vows. Hasse had worn a religious cassock when he committed the foul deed and so the description of the killer (the face was never seen) is that of a cleric. When Clift can't provide an alibi for the time of the killing, he is arrested and tried for the murder. Despite the possibility that he may be convicted of a crime for which he is innocent, Clift will not break his vow. A jury can't find enough evidence to convict and Clift is released, but a lynch mob awaits outside the courtroom. Hasse's wife, Haas (and isn't that a coincidence for two actors playing spouses to have such similar names? Not actually; Robert Taylor and Elizabeth Taylor played husband and wife in CONSPIRATOR) accuses him of being the killer; he responds by shooting her. He then escapes, and is trailed by the police, who wound him. Hasse then receives extreme unction in the arms of Clift, the man he sought to frame. There was little room for Hitchcock's usual humor in I CONFESS, and it suffered from the gloom, without any laughter or even much suspense. Karl Malden is the police inspector in the case, but doesn't get much of a chance to shine. The same goes for Aherne as the prosecutor who is hampered by having to do an abrupt change of allegiance. Less than great, but still intriguing after all these years.

p&d, Alfred Hitchcock; w, George Tabori, William Archibald (based on the play "*Nos Deux Consciences*" "Our Two Consciences" by Paul Anthelme); ph, Robert Burks; m, Dimitri Tiomkin; ed, Rudi Fehr; md, Ray Heindorf; art d & set d, Edward S. Haworth, George James Hopkins; cos, Orry-Kelly; tech adv, Father Paul la Couline; police adv, Inspector Oliver Tangvay.

Drama **Cas.** **(PR:A MPAA:NR)**

I CONQUER THE SEA* (1936) 68m Academy bw

Steffi Duna *(Rosita)*, Stanley Morner [Dennis Morgan] *(Tommy)*, Douglas Walton *(Leonard)*, George Cleveland *(Caleb)*, Johnny Pirrone *(Pedro)*, Fred Warren *(Sebastian)*, Madame Delinsky *(Mrs. Gonzales)*, Olin Francis *(Gabe)*, Fred Peters *(Stubby)*, Jim Hertz *(Tiny)*, Albert Russell *(Josh)*, Charles McMurphy *(Zack)*.

Morner and Walton are brothers in the whaling business who are both in love with Duna. One brother loses his arm during a whaling trip and the other brother then gets the girl. A plodding B melodrama with a plot worn down by over use.

p&d, Victor Halperin; w, Howard Higgins, Rollo Lloyd (based on a story by Richard Carroll); ph, Arthur Martinelli; md, Arthur Kay.

Drama **(PR:A MPAA:NR)**

I COULD GO ON SINGING** (1963) 99m Barbican/UA c

Judy Garland *(Jenny Bowman)*, Dirk Bogarde *(David Donne)*, Jack Klugman *(George Kogan)*, Aline MacMahon *(Ida)*, Gregory Phillips *(Matt)*, Pauline Jameson *(Miss Plimpton)*, Jeremy Burnham *(Young Hospital Doctor)*, Russell Waters *(Reynolds)*, Gerald Sim *(Assistant Manager of Palladium)*, Leon Cortez *(The Busker)*.

Judy Garland's 35th and last film and, sadly, it doesn't compare with her fine performances in other films. She plays a famous singer who goes on tour in England after her second divorce. In London she looks up Bogarde, a doctor with whom she had an affair some years ago. Garland had his child and Bogarde, married at the time, adopted the child with the agreement that Garland would stay out of their lives. Bogarde's wife had conveniently died and Judy quickly fills the void. The son finds out about his true parents and will have nothing to do with Garland. Bogarde drives her to one of her performances, convinces her that singing is what she was meant to do, and not parenting, and departs with their son from Garland's life. Garland sings "By Myself" (Arthur Schwartz, Howard Dietz), "Hello Bluebird" (Cliff Friend), "It Never Was You" (Maxwell Anderson, Kurt Weill), "I Am The Monarch Of The Sea" (W.S. Gilbert, Sir Arthur Sullivan), and the title song (Harold Arlen, E.Y. Harburg).

p, Stuart Millar, Lawrence Turman; d, Ronald Neame; w, Mayo Simon (based on a story by Robert Dozier); ph, Arthur Ibbetson (Panavision, Eastmancolor); m, Mort Lindsey; ed, John Shirley; prod d, Wilfred Shingleton; md, Lindsey; art d, Shingleton; set d, John Hoesli; cos, Edith Head, Beatrice Dawson; makeup, Harold Fletcher.

Musical **(PR:A MPAA:NR)**

I COULD NEVER HAVE SEX WITH ANY MAN WHO HAS SO LITTLE REGARD FOR MY HUSBAND zero FOR MY HUSBAND zero (1973) 86m Cinema 5 c

Carmine Caridi *(Marvin)*, Andrew Duncan *(Stanley)*, Cynthia Harris *(Laura)*, Lynne Lipton *(Mandy)*, Gail and Martin Stayden *(The DeVrooms)*, Dan Greenburg *(Herb)*.

Two hip couples rent a summer house in Martha's Vineyard, and sit around arguing whether they should have affairs. The film tries to come off as a sophisticated sex comedy, but the script contains no insights into relationships and adultery. What we do get is a lot of sight gags, lowbrow humor, and one-dimensional characters. The virgin production of the Stayden team, who, with author Greenburg, cast themselves in this near-home movie. Two good actors, Duncan and Lipton, are wasted here.

p, Gail and Martin Stayden; d, Robert McCarty; w, Dan Greenburg (based on his novel *Chewsday: A Sex Novel*); ph, Jeri Sopanen; m, Joe Liebman; ed, John Carter.

Comedy **(PR:O MPAA:PG)**

I COVER BIG TOWN** (1947) 62m Pine-Thomas/PAR bw (AKA: I COVER THE UNDERWORLD)

Philip Reed *(Steve Wilson)*, Hillary Brooke *(Lorelei Kilbourne)*, Robert Lowery *(Pete Ryan)*, Robert Shayne *(Chief Tom Blake)*, Louis Jean Heydt *(John Moulton)*, Mona Barrie *(Dora Hilton)*, Frank Wilcox *(Harry Hilton)*, Leonard Penn *(Norden Royal)*, Vince Barnett *(Louis Murkil)*.

Based on the radio program "Big Town," this was the second in the screen series. Reed and Brooke are newspaper reporters who help a man who is framed for murder, expose a deal to drive a building firm into bankruptcy, and capture a wanted criminal. It's surprising these journalists have enough time to write their stories. (See BIG TOWN series, Index).

p, William Pine, William Thomas; d, William C. Thomas; w, Whitman Chambers (based on the radio program "Big Town"); ph, Jack Greenhalgh; m, Darrell Calker; ed, Howard Smith; art d, F. Paul Sylos.

Drama **(PR:A MPAA:NR)**

I COVER CHINATOWN* 1/2 (1938) 64m BAN-COMM bw

Norman Foster *(Barton)*, Elaine Shepard *(Gloria)*, Theodore Von Eltz *(Clark)*, Polly Ann Young *(Myra)*, Arthur Lake *(Agent)*, Bruce Mitchell *(Detective)*, Robert Love *(Policeman)*, Eddie Gribbon *(Trucker)*, George Hackathorne *(Head Waiter)*, Vince Barnett *(Puss)*, Edward Emerson *(Victor)*, Cherita Alden Ray *(Woman)*.

Contrary to the misleading title, this film is about a bus driver who gets mixed up with jewel thieves. His sightseeing bus route is in Chinatown. A good amount of action makes up for the shoddy story line. This was Fox contract actor Foster's first directorial chore, one in which he also played the lead. A personable light comedy actor, Foster's career was in a decline during this period; he was losing roles to an up-and-coming Henry Fonda. This film was a portent for his conversion to director; his later tasks included other Oriental motifs, such as the CHARLIE CHAN and MISTER MOTO series.

p, Fenn Kimball; d, Norman Foster; w, Harry Hamilton; ph, Arthur Reed, James V. Murray; ed, Carl Pierson; md, Abe Meyer; art d, Ralph Berger.

Crime **(PR:A MPAA:NR)**

I COVER THE UNDERWORLD (SEE: I COVER BIG TOWN, 1947)

I COVER THE UNDERWORLD** (1955) 70m REP bw

Sean McClory *(John O'Hara)*, Joanne Jordan *(Joan Marlowe)*, Ray Middleton *(Police Chief)*, Jaclynne Greene *(Gilda)*, Lee Van Cleef *(Flash Logan)*, James Griffith *(Smiley Di Angelo)*, Hugh Sanders *(Tim Donovan)*, Roy Roberts *(District Attorney)*, Peter Mamakos *(Charlie Green)*, Robert Crosson *(Danny Marlowe)*, Frank Gerstle *(Dum-Dum Wilson)*, Willis Bouchey *(Warden Lewis L. Johnson)*, Philip Van Zandt *(Jake Freeman)*.

McClory is a divinity student who poses as his jailed gangster brother to help the police break the rackets. He infiltrates the gang and convinces them to team up with other gangs to run better and smoother operations. He also has them keep files on their rackets. McClory's brother—also played by McClory—breaks out of jail, and when it looks like the good McClory is going to be exposed, his bad brother is killed by mistake by one of his own men. Of course, the gangsters are jailed and the rackets busted up. The good McClory's romance with nightclub singer Jordan is subverted by his return to divinity school and, presumably, to holy orders.

p, Herbert J. Yates; d, R.G. Springsteen; w, John K. Butler; ph, Reggie Lanning; m, R. Dale Butts; ed, Tony Martinelli; md, Butts; art d, Walter Keller.

Crime Drama **(PR:A MPAA:NR)**

I COVER THE WAR 1/2** (1937) 69m UNIV bw

John Wayne *(Bob Adams)*, Gwen Gaze *(Pamela)*, Don Barclay *(Elmer Davis)*, Pat Somerset *(Archie)*, Major Sam Harris *(Col. Armitage)*, Charles Brokaw *(El Kader/ Muffadi)*, James Bush *(Don Adams)*, Arthur Aylesworth *(Logan)*, Earl Hodgins *(Blake)*, Jack Mack *(Graham)*, Franklyn Parker *(Parker)*, Frank Lackteen *(Mustapha)*, Olaf Hytten *(Sir Herbert)*, Keith Kenneth *(Sergeant Major)*, Abdulla *(Abdul)*, Richard Tucker *(Man)*.

A fresh and entertaining low-budget Wayne picture with the Duke playing a newsreel cameraman. Wayne and partner Barclay are sent to cover a rebel uprising in the Arab country of Samari. Wayne is out to get the picture of the rebel leader, Brokaw, and in the process encounters gun-runners, spies and Gaze, who becomes Wayne's romantic interest. Wayne gets the rebel leader on film and saves a British regiment from being massacred. The newsreel cameraman theme was popular in the era; the following year saw MGM's enormously successful TOO HOT TO HANDLE with Clark Gable and Myrna Loy, in which Gable was a newsreel ace with his sidekick, Leo Carrillo.

p, Trem Carr; d, Arthur Lubin; w, George Waggner (based on an idea by Bernard McConville); ph, Harry Neumann; ed, Charles Craft; art d, E.R. Hickson.

Action Adventure **(PR:A MPAA:NR)**

I COVER THE WATERFRONT** (1933) 70m UA bw

Claudette Colbert *(Julie Kirk)*, Ben Lyon *(Joseph Miller)*, Ernest Torrence *(Eli Kirk)*, Hobart Cavanaugh *(McCoy)*, Maurice Black *(Ortegus)*, Harry Beresford *(Old Chris)*, Purnell Pratt *(John Phelps)*, George Humbert *(Silva)*, Rosita Marstina *(Mrs. Silva)*, Claudia Coleman *(Mother Morgan)*, Wilfred Lucas *(Randall)*, Lee Phelps *(Reporter)*, Al Hill *(Sailor)*.

Torrence is a ship captain and smuggler and Colbert is his daughter. Lyon is a newspaper reporter who wants to get an expose on Torrence. The reporter starts seeing the unsuspecting Colbert so he can get closer to her father. He discovers that Torrence has been smuggling Chinese into the country inside sharks' hides and that he's falling in love with Colbert. A dilemma arises for Lyon but in the end he gets the girl and his expose. Actor Torrence died before the film's release.

d, James Cruze; w, Wells Root, Jack Jevne (based on the book by Max Miller); ph, Ray June; ed, Grant Whytock; m/l, Edward Heyman, Johnny Green.

Drama **Cas.** **(PR:A MPAA:NR)**

I CROSSED THE COLOR LINE (SEE: BLACK KLANSMAN, THE, 1966)

I DEAL IN DANGER* ½ (1966) 90m Rogo-FOX/FOX c

Robert Goulet *(David March)*, Christine Carere *(Suzanne Duchard)*, Donald Harron *(Spauling)*, Horst Frank *(Luber)*, Werner Peters *(Elm)*, Eva Pflug *(Gretchen Hoffmann)*, Christiane Schmidtmer *(Ericka von Lindendorf)*, John van Dreelen *(von Lindendorf)*, Hans Reiser *(Richter)*, Margit Saad *(Baroness)*, Peter Capell *(Eckhardt)*, Osman Ragheb *(Brunner)*, John Alderson *(Gorleck)*, Dieter Eppler *(Stolnitz)* , Manfred Andrae *(Dr. Zimmer)*, Alexander Allerson *(Kraus)*, Paul Glawton *(Submarine Pilot)*, Dieter Kirchlechner *(Becker)*.

I DEAL WITH DANGER is three episodes from the TV show "Blue Light" strung together for theatrical release. Goulet is an American spy during WW II who convinces the Nazis that he's a traitor to his country, thereby gaining their confidence. His objective is to blow up an underground weapon factory. He is aided by a German scientist, Pflug, and Carere, a French agent and Goulet's love interest. All right as a TV movie, but it doesn't make it as a theatrical film.

p, Buck Houghton; d, Walter Grauman; w, Larry Cohen; ph, Sam Leavitt, Kurt Grigoleit (DeLuxe Color); m, Lalo Schifrin, Joseph Mullendore; ed, Jason Bernie, Dolf Rudeen; art d, Jack Martin Smith, Jack Collis, Rolf Zehetbauer; set d, Walter M. Scott, Lucien Hafley; spec eff, Karl Baumgartner, Erwin Lange; makeup, Ben Nye.

War **(PR:A MPAA:NR)**

I DEMAND PAYMENT* ½ (1938) 55m Imperial bw

Jack LaRue *(Smiles Badolio)*, Betty Burgess *(Judith Avery)*, Matty Kemp *(Toby Locke)*, Guinn (Big Boy) Williams *(Happy Crofton)*, Lloyd Hughes *(Doctor Craig Mitchell)*, Sheila Terry *(Rita Avery)*, Bryant Washburn, Sr. *(Joe Travis)*, Donald Kirke *(Mr. Twitchett)*, Harry Holman *(Justice of Peace)*, Edward Keane *(District Attorney)*, Norma Taylor *(Miss Farnsworth)*.

Kemp is in the loan-shark racket and LaRue and Williams are out to rub him out. The reason they want Kemp dead is because he pocketed some of the gang's money for himself. He hides out with the help of Burgess but the gangsters find him and in the climactic gun battle the gangsters and Kemp are killed.

p&d, Clifford Sanforth; w, Sherman L. Lowe (based on the novel by Rob Eden); ph, Robert Doran; ed, Douglas Biggs.

Crime **(PR:A MPAA:NR)**

I DIDN'T DO IT ½** (1945, Brit.) 97m COL bw

George Formby *(George Trotter)*, Billy Caryll *(Pa Tubbs)*, Hilda Mundy *(Ma Tubbs)*, Gaston Palmer *(Le Grand Gaston)*, Jack Daly *(Terry O'Rourke)*, Carl Jaffe *(Hilary Vance)*, Marjorie Browne *(Jill Dixon)*, Wally Patch *(Sgt. Carp)*, Ian Fleming *(Inspector Twyning)*, Vincent Holman *(Erasmus Montague)*, Dennis Wyndham *(Tom Driscoll)*, Jack Raine *(J.B. Cato)*, The Boswell Twins, Georgina Cookson, Merle Tottenham, Gordon McLeod.

Formby, a Londoner with the urge to get in front of the footlights, is boarding in a hotel with a number of theater personalities. Soon after he unpacks his bags an Australian acrobat is killed. Blame is placed at Formby's doorstep when the corpse is found in the room next to his. The killer makes an attempt on Formby's life, shooting at him in a Hall of Mirrors (3 years before Welles' famous scene in THE LADY FROM SHANGHAI). Formby survives, clears his name, pins the crime on the real culprit, and lands a job on stage. Five screenwriters collaborated on the script, churning out a lively, witty programmer.

p, Marcel Varnel, Ben Henry; d, Varnel; w, Norman Lee, Howard Irving Young, Stephen Black, Peter Fraser, Michael Vaughan; ph, Roy Fogwell.

Comedy **(PR:A MPAA:NR)**

I DIED A THOUSAND TIMES** (1955) 108m WB c

Jack Palance *(Roy Earle)*, Shelley Winters *(Marie Gibson)*, Lori Nelson *(Velma)*, Lee Marvin *(Babe)*, Earl Holliman *(Red)*, Perry Lopez *(Louis Mendoza)*, Pedro Gonzalez Gonzalez *(Chico)*, Lon Chaney, Jr. *(Big Mac)*, Howard St. John *(Doc Banton)*, Ralph Moody *(Pa)*, Olive Carey *(Ma)*, James Millican *(Jack Kranmer)*, Richard Davalos *(Lon Preisser)*, Bill Kennedy *(Sheriff)*, Peggy Maley *(Kranmer's Girl)*, Dub Taylor *(Ed)*, Dick Reeves, Chris Alcaide, Larry Hudson, John Pickard *(Deputies)*, Karolee Kelly *(Cigar Counter Vendor)*, John Stephenson *(Pfeiffer)*, Mae Clarke *(Mabel Baughman)*, Hugh Sanders *(Mr. Baughman)*, Howard Hoffman *(Fisherman)*, Nick Adams, Darren Dublin *(Bellboys)*, Myrna Fahey *(Margie)*, Herb Vigran *(Art)*, Dennis Hopper *(Joe)*, David McMahon *(Owner of Auto Court)*, Paul Brinazar *(Bus Driver)*, Wendell Niles *(Radio Announcer)*, John Daheim, Dennis Moore, Mickey Simpson *(Officers)*, Steve Darrell *(Detective)*, Gil Perkins *(Slim)*, Larry Blake *(Healy)*, Nesdon Booth, Ed Fury, Larve Farlow, Hubie Kerns, Tony Hughes, Mary Benoit, Paul Power, Charles Watts, Don Dillaway, Fay Baker *(People)*, James Seay *(Man in Tropico Lobby)*.

A soggy remake of a classic, I DIED A THOUSAND TIMES was an attempt to do HIGH SIERRA with Palance in the Bogart role. When are studios going to let well enough alone and realize that the inclusion of color and wide screen photography is just not enough to make up for the new casting? The story remains the same (it should; W.R. Burnett wrote the original with John Huston. This time, he penned the screenplay solo). Chaney, Jr. is a dying criminal who wants to go out in a blaze of glory by heisting the Frontier Hotel in Palm Springs. He arranges for Palance to get sprung from prison to aid him in the robbery. Palance gets to the aerie in the mountains where he will be in on the planning with the other members of the gang, Marvin, Holliman, and Lopez. Winters is an ex-taxi dancer who is attached to the mob. She likes Palance, but he finds himself entranced by Nelson, a crippled girl from a poor family. Eventually, he helps Nelson get the operation she needs to be able to function in the world once more. The robbery occurs and, since there is no honor among thieves (at least not in remakes), the criminals have a falling out. The final chase sequence, which was so exciting in the original, is an attempt to recreate the HIGH SIERRA feeling but, even though they use just about the same cuts and set-ups, it fails to sustain any suspense. Palance is tracked down and slain, and what might have been almost a Greek tragedy becomes little more than the average shoot-'em-up in the hands of director Heisler. Palance, who was Walter Jack Palance (in the credits of SHANE), does his best, but he is acting in the shadow of Bogart and that is an impossible task. One of the highlights of HIGH SIERRA was Bogart's relationship with his dog. In this film, the attempt to use the animal to act as a harbinger of death just became too cutesy for words. The only humor in the film comes from Gonzalez, who got his start as a contestant on the Groucho Marx TV show "You Bet Your Life," and provided America with twelve of the funniest minutes ever seen on the tube.

p, Willis Goldbeck; d, Stuart Heisler; w, W.R. Burnett (based on his novel); ph, Ted McCord (CinemaScope, Warner Color); m, David Buttolph; ed, Clarence Kolster; art d, Edward Carrere; set d, William L. Kuehl; cos, Moss Mabry; makeup, Gordon Bau.

Crime Drama **(PR:A-C MPAA:NR)**

I DISMEMBER MAMA zero
(1974) 87m Europix c (AKA: POOR ALBERT AND LITTLE ANNIE)

Zooey Hall *(Albert)*, Geri Reischl *(Annie)*, Joanne Moore Jordan, Marlene Tracy, Greg Mullavey *(Detective)*.

Low-budget horror epic that stars Hall as a psychopath with a mother complex who feels it is his duty to seek out and destroy all "immoral" women. Eventually he meets and falls in love with his "ideal" woman—a nine-year-old girl. Luckily, the cops track him down, and the diseased killer grabs a couple of naked mannequins and leaps out a window to his death. Directed by the same man who wrought upon the public PLEASE DON'T EAT MY MOTHER, this was released on a double bill with the equally distasteful THE BLOOD-SPATTERED BRIDE.

p, Leon Roth; d, Paul Leder; w, William Norton; m, Herschel Burke Gilbert.

Horror **Cas.** **(PR:O MPAA:R)**

I DON'T CARE GIRL, THE** (1952) 78m FOX c

Mitzi Gaynor *(Eva Tanguay)*, David Wayne *(Ed McCoy)*, Oscar Levant *(Bennett)*, Bob Graham *(Larry)*, Craig Hill *(Keene)*, Warren Stevens *(Lawrence)*, Hazel Brooks *(Stella Forrest)*, Marietta Canty *(Maid Dolly)*, Sam Hearn *(Alhambra Theatre Owner)*, Wilton Graff *(Flo Ziegfeld)*, Dwayne Ratliff, Bill Foster, Gwyneth [Gwen] Verdon *(Specialty Dancers)*, Betty Onge, Ruth Hall, Barbara Carroll, George Jessel *(Himself)*.

A sappy biography of an early show business star features producer Jessel (as himself) trying to find out some things about Eva Tanguay so he can make a movie of her life. He interviews those who knew her best, and the episodes are supposed to congeal into one story. They don't. It remains episodic and flat and is little more than a singalong. Several flashbacks and many songs that are done with virtually no justification are what mar good performances by Levant and Wayne. Gaynor is a human dynamo (to this day) and never stops for an instant to allow us to get any feel for the character she is portraying. Jack Cole's production numbers were terribly anachronistic but well done. Sort of like showing Break Dancing in a musical about the French Revolution. Songs include: "I Don't Care" (Jean Lenox, Harry O. Sutton), "The Beale Street Blues" (W.C. Handy), "The Johnson Rag" (Jack Lawrence, Guy H. Hall, Henry Kleinkauf), "This Is My Favorite City" (Mack Gordon, Josef Myrow), "Here Comes Love Again" (Jessel, Eliot Daniel), "On The

Mississippi" (Ballard MacDonald, Harry Carroll, Arthur Fields), "Hello, Frisco, Hello" (Louis A. Hirsch, Gene Buck), "Pretty Baby" (Gus Kahn, Tony Jackson, Egbert Van Alstyne), "Oh, You Beautiful Doll" (Nat D. Ayer, A. Seymour Brown), "Liebestraum" (Franz Liszt), "Piano Concerto Number One" (Liszt), "Little G Minor Fugue" (Johann Sebastian Bach), "Largo Al Factotum" (Giacchino Rossini). Gwen Verdon, while she still used her given name of Gwyneth, does a bit of dancing but goes by very quickly.

p, George Jessel; d, Lloyd Bacon; w, Walter Bullock; ph, Arthur E. Arling (Technicolor); ed, Louis Loeffler; md, Lionel Newman; art d, Lyle Wheeler, Richard Irvine; ch, Jack Cole, Seymour Felix.

Musical/Biography **(PR:A MPAA:NR)**

I DON'T WANT TO BE BORN (SEE: DEVIL WITHIN HER, THE, 1976)

I DOOD IT** (1943) 102m MGM bw (GB: BY HOOK OR BY CROOK)

Red Skelton *(Joseph Rivington Renolds)*, Eleanor Powell *(Constance Shaw)*, Richard Ainley *(Larry West)*, Patricia Dane *(Surelia Brenton)*, Sam Levene *(Ed Jackson)*, Thurston Hall *(Kenneth Lawlor)*, Lena Horne *(Herself)*, Hazel Scott *(Herself)*, John Hodiak *(Roy Hartwood)*, Butterfly McQueen *(Annette)*, Marjorie Gateson *(Mrs. Spelvin)*, Andrew Tombes *(Mr. Spelvin)*, Helen O'Connell, Bob Eberly, Jimmy Dorsey and Orchestra.

A patchwork Red Skelton vehicle adapted from the Buster Keaton silent comedy SPITE MARRIAGE (1929) and directed by Vincente Minnelli after the original helmsman was fired. Only his second film, Minnelli struggled mightily to pull something of value from the mess he had inherited, but the result was a film which saw its star run roughshod over the material in a vain attempt to compensate for the inherent inadequacies of the production. Skelton plays a hapless tailor's assistant who becomes deeply infatuated with a young actress, Powell, who is appearing nearby in a play about the Civil War. To impress Powell, Skelton "borrows" some of his customer's fancy clothes, hoping she will think he is a man of means. Having recently been spurned by her boy friend who ran off with another woman, Powell allows Skelton to court her and eventually agrees to marry the delighted tailor, but only to spite her former sweetheart. Following a series of increasingly unlikely situations, Skelton stumbles across a plot by foreign spies to sabotage America's war effort and bravely finds a way to expose them. Now that Skelton's a hero, Powell finally realizes she loves him and all ends well. Basically I DOOD IT is just an excuse to peddle the popularity of Skelton, Powell, Jimmy Dorsey and His Orchestra, and Lena Horne, and it succeeds on that level. Unfortunately the narrative context that the comedy and musical numbers are presented in is thoughtless, haphazard, and sloppily executed. MGM was only concerned with the number of musical performances that would draw an audience and director Minnelli was forced to incorporate several uninspired dance routines that were shot before he took over production. One of these sequences was the climax of the film, a number based on Cole Porter's "Swinging The Jinx Away," which was lifted almost verbatim from an earlier MGM Eleanor Powell film, BORN TO DANCE (1936). Saddled with unwanted baggage, there was little for Minnelli to do but try to salvage what was left and the results are hardly satisfying. Songs include "Star Eyes" (Don Raye, Gene De Paul), "Hola E Pae" (Johnny Noble), "Taking A Chance On Love" (Vernon Duke, Ted Fetter, John Latouche), "Jericho" (Leo Robin, Richard Myers), "One O'Clock Jump" (Count Basie), "So Long Sarah Jane" (Lew Brown, Sammy Fain).

p, Jack Cummings; d, Vincente Minnelli; w, Sig Herzig, Fred Saidy; ph, Ray June; ed, Robert J. Kern; md, George Stoll; art d, Cedric Gibbons; ch, Bob Connolly; m/l, Don Raye, Gene De Paul, Lew Brown, Ralph Freed, Sammy Fain, Count Basie, Cole Porter, Vernon Duke, John Latouche, Ted Fetter, Leo Robin, Richard Myers.

Musical/Comedy **(PR:A MPAA:NR)**

I DREAM OF JEANIE* (1952) 90m Allan Dwan/REP c

Ray Middleton *(Edwin P. Christy)*, Bill Shirley *(Stephen Foster)*, Muriel Lawrence *(Inez McDowell)*, Eileen Christy *(Jeanie McDowell)*, Lynn Bari *(Mrs. McDowell)*, Richard Simmons *(Dunning Foster)*, Robert Neil *(Milford Wilson)*, Andrew Tombes *(R.E. Howard)*, James Dobson *(Spike)*, Percy Helton *(Mr. Horker)*, Glenn Turnbull *(Specialty Dancer)*, Louise Beavers *(Mammy)*, James Kirkwood *(Doctor)*, Carl Dean Switzer *(Freddie)*, Freddie Moultrie *(Chitlins)*, Rex Allen *(Narrator and Mr. Tambo)*.

The third and worst screen biography of composer Stephen Foster (the other two films being HARMONY LANE, 1935, and SWANEE RIVER, 1939). Shirley plays Foster, a dim-witted bookkeeper who writes the songs that made him famous when he isn't chasing Lawrence. She spurns him and her sister, Christy, grabs him. Christy becomes his inspiration for the title song. It's too bad nobody connected with the film was similarly inspired. Featured are 21 of Foster's familiar ballads, including the title song, "My Old Kentucky Home," "The Old Folks at Home," "Ring, Ring, De Banjo," "Swanee River," "Oh Susanna," "Old Dog Tray," "Camptown Races," "On Wings of Song," "Lo! Hear the Gentle Lark," "A Ribbon In Your Hair," "I See Her Still In My Dreams," "Come Where My Love Lies Dreaming," by Stephen Foster, and "Head Over Heels" by Laura Lee and producer-director Dwan.

p, Herbert J. Yates; d, Allan Dwan; w, Alan LeMay; ph, Reggie Lanning (Trucolor); ed, Fred Allen; md, Robert Armbruster; art d, Frank Hotaling.

Drama **(PR:A MPAA:NR)**

I DREAM TOO MUCH** (1935) 95m RKO bw

Lily Pons *(Annette Monard Street)*, Henry Fonda *(Jonathan Street)*, Eric Blore *(Roger Briggs)*, Osgood Perkins *(Paul Darcy)*, Lucien Littlefield *(Hubert Dilley)*, Esther Dale *(Mrs. Dilley)*, Lucille Ball *(Gwendolyn Dilley)*, Mischa Auer *(Pianist)*, Paul Porcasi *(Tito)*, Scotty Beckett *(Boy on Merry-Go-Round)*, Clarence Wilson *(Detective)*, Oscar Apfel *(Cafe Owner)*, Ferdinand Munier *(Carousel Owner)*, Billy Gilbert *(Cook)*, Esther Dale *(Tourist)*, Richard Carle, Ferdinand Gottschalk *(Snobs)*, Russ Powell *(Merry-Go-Round Operator)*, Al Haskel *(Wagon Driver)*, Kirby Grant *(Violinist-Quartet Singer)*, Elise Cavanna *(Darcy's Secretary)*, June Storey *(Girl in "I Dream Too Much" Number)*.

With Columbia's success in making opera singer Grace Moore a movie star, RKO got the most popular opera star of the time, Pons, to star in I DREAM TOO MUCH. RKO pulled out all the stops for this production in an attempt to outshine Columbia and Moore, but even with Fonda as the leading man the film is just a minor effort. Husband Fonda pushes his wife, Pons, into a singing career. She's reluctant, but tries and becomes a big success. This sours Fonda, a struggling opera composer, and Pons uses her new-found influence to get Fonda's opera turned into a successful musical comedy. Once this is done she slows her singing career to start a family. Songs include, "The Jockey on the Carousel," "I'm the Echo," "I Got Love" and the title song (Jerome Kern and Dorothy Fields), "Bell Song" from the opera *Lakme* by Leo Delibes, with libretto by Gondinet and Gille, and "Caro Nome" from Giuseppe Verdi's opera *Rigoletto*. This film featured up-and-coming Fonda in his first non-bucolic screen role. It also had actress Ball in her second featured-player role; much later, she was to buy the studio.

p, Pandro S. Berman; d, John Cromwell; w, James Gow, Edmund North (based on a story by Elsie Finn, David G. Wittels); ph, David Abel; ed, William Morgan; md, Max Steiner, Andre Kostalanetz; art d, Van Nest Polglase; cos, Bernard Newman; ch, Hermes Pan.

Musical Comedy **Cas.** **(PR:A MPAA:NR)**

I DRINK YOUR BLOOD* (1971) 83m Cinemation c

Bhaskar *(Horace Bones)*, Jadine Wong *(Sue-Lin)*, Ronda Fultz *(Molly)*, Elizabeth Marner-Brooks *(Mildred Nash)*, George Patterson *(Rollo)*, Riley Mills *(Pete)*, Iris Brooks *(Sylvia)*, John Damon *(Roger Davis)*, Richard Bowler *(Doc Banner)*, Tyde Kierney *(Andy)*, Lynn Lowry, Alex Mann, Bruno Damon, Mike Gentry.

I DRINK YOUR BLOOD is a bizarre, violent, black comedy about a traveling band of satan-worshiping hippies who invade a small town and slip some LSD to an old man for laughs. The elderly man's 12-year-old son gets revenge by injecting meat pies with rabid dog blood, which he then sells to the dopers. The hippies, of course, turn rabid and cannibalistic and go on a rampage, killing each other. A few survive, and one of the females seduces a few conservative "America First"-type construction workers; soon they too are infected. Will the disease spread throughout America? You bet. Pretty gross. Initially rated X by the MPAA— believed to be one of the few films ever so rated for violence, rather than explicit sex—but then cut by the producer, and with new footage added to attain its more comfortable R rating.

p, Jerry Gross; d&w, David Durston; ph, Jacques Demarecaux (Widescreen, DeLuxe Color); m&md, Clay Pitts.

Horror **(PR:O MPAA:R)**

I EAT YOUR SKIN zero
(1971) 82m Cinemation bw (AKA: VOODOO BLOOD BATH; ZOMBIE; ZOMBIES)

William Joyce *(Tom Harris)*, Heather Hewitt *(Jeanine Biladeau)*, Betty Hyatt Linton *(Carol Fairchild)*, Dan Stapleton *(Duncan Fairchild)*, Walter Coy *(Charles Bentley)*, Robert Stanton *(Dr. Biladeau)*, Vanore Aikens, Don Strawn's Calypso Band.

Filmed in 1964 as VOODOO BLOOD BATH, this feast of blood and guts wasn't released until 7 years later when producer Jerry Gross picked the film up to round out a double bill with I DRINK YOUR BLOOD. By far the lower half of the pairing, I EAT YOUR SKIN is set on Voodoo Island in the Caribbean. Novelist Harris flies there in search of material for a new book and winds up falling in love with Hewitt, the daughter of a careless scientist whose experiments are transforming the islanders into zombies. Hewitt is abducted and prepared for a sacrifice, only to be saved by her heroic honey. They both narrowly escape the hungry jaws of the zombies, leaving the scientist behind to become lunch. In many cases horror and exploitation films are so bad that they're good. I EAT YOUR SKIN doesn't even rank with the good-bad.

p, d&w, Del Tenney; ph, Francois Farkas; m, Lon Norman; ed, Larry Keating; md, Norman; art d, Robert Verberkmoes.

Horror **(PR:O MPAA:NR)**

I ESCAPED FROM DEVIL'S ISLAND zero (1973) 87m UA c

Jim Brown *(Le Bras)*, Christopher George *(Davert)*, Rick Ely *(Jo-Jo)*, Richard Rust *(Zamorra)*.

A cheap, in all senses of the word, Corman-produced action film with Brown and George as prisoners of the famous island. After they are beaten and abused for half the film, they decide to escape. The action is dull and uninspired and the acting is insufferable. One can fairly assume that the producers Corman located an available prison set and elected to construct a film around it.

p, Roger and Gene Corman; d, William Witney; w, Richard L. Adams; ph, Rosalio Solano (DeLuxe Color); m, Les Baxter; ed, Alan Collins, Tom Walls, Barbara Pokras; art d, Roberto Silva; set d, Jose Gonzalez.

Prison Drama **(PR:O MPAA:R)**

I ESCAPED FROM THE GESTAPO**
(1943) 75m King Brothers/MON bw (AKA: NO ESCAPE)

Mary Brian *(Helen)*, Dean Jagger *(Lane)*, John Carradine *(Martin)*, Bill Henry *(Gordan)*, Sidney Blackmer *(Bergen)*, Anthony Warde *(Lokin)*, William Vine *(One-Arm Sailor)*, Charles Wagenheim *(Haft)*, Billy Marshall *(Lunt)*, Norman Willis *(Rodt)*, Ian Keith *(Gerard)*, Peter Dunne *(Olin)*, Spanky MacFarland *(Billy)*, Edward Keane *(Domack)*, Greta Grandstedt *(Hilda)*.

A misleading title because all action happens in the United States. Jagger is a counterfeiter who is helped to escape from prison by a group of Nazis led by Carradine. When Jagger discovers what they want him to do—forge securities of the U.S. and other countries to help the Axis war effort—he goes to the authorities and puts a stop to the Nazi spies.

p, Maurice King; d, Harold Young; w, Henry Blankfort, Wallace Sullivan (based on a story by Blankfort); ph, Ira H. Morgan; m, W. Franke Harling; ed, S.K. Winston; art d, Dave Milton.

Spy Drama **(PR:A MPAA:NR)**

I EVEN MET HAPPY GYPSIES**
(1968, Yugo.) 90m Avala/Prominent c (SKUPLJACI PERJA; SREO SAM CAK I SRECNE CIGANE)

Bekim Fehmiu *(Bora)*, Gordana Jovanovic *(Tisa)*, Bata Zivojinovic *(Mirta)*, Olivera Vuco *(Lence)*, Mija Aleksic *(Father Pavle)*, Etelka Filipovski *(Bora's Wife)*, Milorad Jovanovic *(Toni)*, Milivoje Djordjevic *(Sandor)*, Rahela Ferari *(Nun)*, Severin Bijelic *(Religious Peasant)*.

A Yugoslavian film starring Fehmiu as a frustrated gypsy merchant who feels pressured and constrained by his family life. One day he meets a beautiful young girl, Jovanovic, who has been sold into a marriage with a 12 year-old boy by her evil stepfather, Zivojinovic. The girl escapes her unwanted situation and is later found by Fehmiu, who takes her home with him. Eventually she finds her way back into the vile clutches of Zivojinovic, and in a rage, Fehmiu kills the latter and disappears. Star Fehmiu made a sufficient impression to be pursued and groomed for Hollywood, appearing as the handsome lead in a number of forgettable English-language features.

d&w, Aleksandar Petrovic; ph, Tomislav Pinter (Eastmancolor); m, Petrovic; ed, Milo Mica; art d, Veljko Despotovic.

Drama **(PR:A MPAA:NR)**

I FOUND STELLA PARISH** (1935) 84m FN-WB bw

Kay Francis *(Stella Parish)*, Ian Hunter *(Keith Lockridge)*, Paul Lukas *(Stephen Norman)*, Sybil Jason *(Gloria Parish)*, Jessie Ralph *(Nana)*, Joseph Sawyer *(Chuck)*, Eddie Acuff *(Dimmy)*, Walter Kingsford *(Reeves)*, Robert Strange *(Jed Duffy)*, Ferdinand Munier *(Andrews)*, Rita Carlyle, Shirley Simpson, Elspeth Dudgeon, Tempe Pigott *(Women)*, Charles Evans *(Old Actor)*, Lotus Liu *(Mabel)*, Olaf Hytten *(Butler)*, Elsa Buchanan *(Maid)*, Vesey O'Davoren *(Deck Steward)*, Lotus Thompson *(Secretary)*, Milton Kibbee *(Costumer)*, John Dilson *(Producer's Assistant)*, Harlan Briggs *(Theatre Manager)*, Alice Keating *(New York Operator)*, Marie Wells *(Hotel Operator)*, Phyllis Coghlan *(London Operator)*, Emmett Vogan, Lew Harvey, Gordon "Bill" Elliott *(Reporters)*, Crauford Kent *(Lord Chamberlain)*, Edward Cooper *(Caligula)*, Hugh Huntley *(Cemellus)*, Ralph Bushman [Francis X. Bushman, Jr.] *(Erik)*, Vernon Downing, Vernon Steele *(Slaves)*, Mary Treen *(Sob Sister)*, Barton MacLane *(Clifton Jeffords)*, Harry Beresford *(James)*.

Kay Francis at the zenith of her uneven career starred in this heart-wrenching tear-jerker as a glamorous actress desperately trying to conceal her unsavory past from her young daughter, Jason. Routine soap-opera stuff which director LeRoy could sometimes save, but not this time.

p, Harry Joe Brown; d, Mervyn LeRoy; w, Casey Robinson (based on a story by John Monk Saunders); ph, Sid Hickox; ed, William Clemens; md, Leo F. Forbstein; art d, Robert M. Haas; cos, Orry-Kelly.

Drama **(PR:A MPAA:NR)**

I GIORNI DELL'IRA (SEE: DAY OF ANGER, 1970, Ital./Ger.)

I GIVE MY HEART
(SEE: LOVES OF MADAME DUBARRY, THE, 1938, Brit.)

I GIVE MY LOVE** (1934) 70m UNIV bw

Paul Lukas *(Paul Vadja)*, Wynne Gibson *(Judy Blair)*, Eric Linden *(Paul, Jr. at 21)*, Anita Louise *(Lorna March)*, John Darrow *(Alex Blair)*, Dorothy Appleby *(Alice Henley)*, Tad Alexander *(Paul, Jr. at 12)*, Sam Hardy *(Pogey)*, Kenneth Howell *(Frank Howard)*, Louise Beavers *(Maid)*.

A good tear-jerker, set partly in Paris, about a woman, Gibson, who murders her husband and spends ten years in prison. She has a child whom she gave up when she went to jail. The son, Lukas, has been told that his mother is dead. We see the son at different ages in his life (played by two other actors). He becomes an artist and when Gibson gets out of jail she works as a model, eventually posing for her own son, who doesn't realize who she is.

d, Karl Freund; w, Doris Anderson, Milton Krims (based on a story by Vicki Baum); ph, George Robinson; ed, Edward Curtis.

Drama **(PR:A MPAA:NR)**

I HAD SEVEN DAUGHTERS
(SEE: MY SEVEN LITTLE SINS, 1956, Fr./Ital.)

I HATE BLONDES**
(1981, Ital.) 89m Clesi Cinematographica/Summit c (ODIO LE BIONDE)

Enrico Montesano *(Emilio Serrantoni)*, Jean Rochefort *(Donald Rose)*, Corinne Clery *(Angelica)*, Marina Langner *(Valeria)*, Paola Tedesco *(Teresa)*, Renato Mori *(Literary Agent)*, Ivan Desny *(Mr. Brown)*, Roberto Della Casa *(Serge)*.

Montesano is a ghost-writer for a successful writer, Rochefort, and crooks begin using his crime plots as blueprints for their crimes. The criminals get the ghost-writer involved in one of their heists. Things are straightened out and Montesano goes on to get his own writing contract.

p, Silvio and Anna Maria Clementelli; d, Giorgio Capitani; w, Laura Toscano, Franco Maratta; ph, Roberto and Silvano Ippoliti; m, Piero Umiliani; ed, Sergio Montanari.

Comedy **Cas.** **(PR:A MPAA:NR)**

I HATE MY BODY* 1/2
(1975, Span./Switz.) 97m Galaxia Films c (ODIO MI CUERPO)

Alexandra Bastedo, Byron Mabe, Narcisco Ibanez Menta, Gemma Cuervo, Manuel Zarzo, Eva Leon, Maria Silva.

A pretty awful science fiction/horror film in which rampant, ignorant sexism resides. The brain of a male engineer is transplanted into the body of a woman and soon he/she is shocked to learn that no one will hire a woman for an engineering position, though he/she held superior jobs when in a male body. Soon the film degenerates into a series of offensive male-trapped-in-a-female-body stereotypes that see our character unable to deal with a female sexuality, so he/she begins to demonstrate lesbian inclinations. From here on in the movie disintegrates into an incomprehensible mish-mosh of sexist attitudes that are fairly disturbing.

p, Juan Ramon Jimenez, Andre Kuhn; d, Leon Klimovsky; w, Klimovsky, Solly Wollodarski; ph, Francisco Sanchez.

Science Fiction/Drama **(PR:A MPAA:NR)**

I HATE YOUR GUTS! (SEE: INTRUDER, THE, 1961)

I HAVE LIVED* (1933) 69m CHES/FD bw

Alan Dinehart *(Thomas Langley)*, Anita Page *(Jean St. Clair)*, Allen Vincent *(Warren White)*, Gertrude Astor *(Harriet Naisson)*, Maude Truax *(Mrs. Reynolds)*, Matthew Betz *(Blackie)*, Eddie Boland *(Sidney Cook)*, Dell Henderson *(J.W.)*, Gladys Blake, Florence Dudley.

A trite and archaic handling of the age-old tale of a brilliant new playwright who discovers a brilliant new actress to star in his brilliant new play. He's met with opposition along the way, but come opening night, the crowd is whipped into a frenzy of applause. Not surprisingly, marriage follows for the pair.

d, Richard Thorpe; w, Winifred Dunn (based on a story by Lou Heifetz); ph, M.A. Anderson.

Drama **(PR:A MPAA:NR)**

I HAVE SEVEN DAUGHTERS
(SEE: MY SEVEN LITTLE SINS, 1954, Fr./Ital.)

I, JANE DOE** (1948) 85m REP bw (GB: DIARY OF A BRIDE)

Ruth Hussey *(Eve Meredith Curtis)*, John Carroll *(Stephen Curtis)*, Vera Ralston *(Annette Dubois, alias Jane Doe)*, Gene Lockhart *(Arnold Matson)*, John Howard *(William Hilton)*, Benay Venuta *(Phyllis Tuttle)*, Adele Mara *(Marga-Jane Hastings)*, Roger Dann *(Julian Aubert)*, James Bell *(Judge Bertrand)*, Leon Belasco *(Duroc)*, John Litel *(Horton)*, Eric Feldary *(Robert Dubois)*, Francis Pierlot *(Father Martin)*, Marta Mitrovich *(Marie)*, John Albright *(Reporter)*, Louis Mercier *(Francois)*, Gene Gary *(Degnan)*, Henry Rowland *(German Lieutenant)*, Walden Boyle *(Court Clerk)*, E.L. Davenport, Roy Darmour *(Reporters)*, Ed Rees *(Court Stenographer)*, Howard Mitchell *(Bailiff)*, Nolan Leary *(Jury Foreman)*, Eva Novak *(Jury Woman)*, Martha Holliday *(Trudy Marsh)*, Myron Healey *(Interne)*, Charles Flynn, Harry Strang, Chuck Hamilton, Stanley Blystone *(Policemen)*, Jack Clifford *(Police Captain)*, Sonia Darrin *(Nurse)*, Frank Reicher, Boyd Irwin *(Doctors)*, Willy Wickerhauser, Frederic Brunn *(Soldiers)*, Cliff Clark *(City Editor)*, Jeff Corey *(Immigration Officer)*, Frances Robinson *(Dorothy Winston)*, Dave Anderson *(Black Man)*, Sammy McKim, Bobby Stone, Ray Hirsch *(Newsboys)*, James Dale *(Assistant Editor)*, Jerry Lynn Myers *(Baby)*.

Ralston is a French girl on trial for murder, and through flashbacks we find out why. During WW II she got involved with Carroll, a well-to-do soldier. They married, but after the war, he disappeared. She comes to the United States and finds that he is married to another woman. He tries to get her deported, and she accidentally kills him. She is found guilty of murder, but when it's discovered that she's pregnant, the widow comes to her defense.

p&d, John H. Auer; w, Lawrence Kimble, Decla Dunning; ph, Reggie Lanning; m, Heinz Roemheld; ed, Richard L. Van Enger; md, Morton Scott; art d, James Sullivan; set d, Charles Thompson; cos, Adele Palmer; makeup, Bob Mark.

Drama **(PR:A MPAA:NR)**

I KILLED EINSTEIN, GENTLEMEN**
(1970, Czech.) 95m Czechoslovensky Film (ZABIL JSEM EINSTEINA, PANOVE)

Jiri Sovak, Jana Brezhova, Iva Janzurova, L. Lipsky.

A broad Czechoslovakian comedy science-fiction film that starts out in the future. The plot tells how after a nuclear holocaust, all the surviving women of the world have become sterile, and the future of the world is threatened. Scientists build a time machine and send a group of people into the past to murder Albert Einstein. The idea being that if Einstein were to be killed before he could come up with his nuclear theories, there would be no atomic bombs, and no future war that will threaten future children from being bred. The film's action comes off as predictable, and some potentially funny ideas are wasted.

d, Oldrich Lipsky; w, Lipsky, Josef Nesvadba, Milos Makourek; ph, Ivan Slapeta.
Comedy/Science Fiction **(PR:A MPAA:NR)**

I KILLED GERONIMO*½ (1950) 62m EL bw

James Ellison *(Capt. Jeff Packard)*, Chief Thunder Cloud *(Geronimo)*, Virginia Herrick *(Julie)*, Smith Ballew *(Lt. Furness)*, Ted Adams *(Walt Anderson)*, Myron Healey *(Frank)*, Wesley Hudman *(Red)*, Dennis Moore *(Luke)*, Hart Wayne *(Gen. Ives)*, Luther Crockett, Jean Andren.

Ellison is an army officer who goes undercover to put an end to the people who are supplying Geronimo and his braves with guns. The officer works his way into the gang of gunrunners lead by Adams and bags both them and Geronimo. A good amount of action that doesn't cover over the weak story line.

p, Jack Schwarz; d, John Hoffman; w, Sam Neuman, Nat Tanchuck.
Western **(PR:A MPAA:NR)**

I KILLED THAT MAN½** (1942) 72m MON bw

Ricardo Cortez *(Phillips)*, Joan Woodbury *(Geri)*, Iris Adrian *(Verne Drake)*, George Pembroke *(King)*, Herbert Rawlinson *(Warden)*, Pat Gleason *(Bates)*, Ralf Harolde *(Nick Ross)*, Jack Mulhall *(Collins)*, Vince Barnett *(Drunk)*, Gavin Gordon *(J. Reed)*, John Hamilton *(District Attorney)*, Harry Holman *(Lanning)*.

A surprisingly good mystery produced by low-budget sleeper experts Maurice and Franklin King as an independent, their second such film distributed through Monogram. Lots of action and a few surprises. Cortez, who had been a Latin lover—the low-cost equivalent of Rudolph Valentino or Ramon Novarro—stars in one of his last tough-guy roles before turning to character parts.

p, Maurice King; d, Phil Rosen; w, Henry Bancroft (based on a story by Leonard Fields, David Silverstein); ph, Harry Neuman; ed, Martin C. Cohen; md, Lew Porter, Johnny Lang; art d, Frank Dexter.
Mystery **(PR:A MPAA:NR)**

I KILLED THE COUNT (SEE: WHO IS GUILTY? 1939, Brit.)

I KILLED WILD BILL HICKOK*½ (1956) 63m Wheeler c

John Forbes [John Carpenter] *(Johnny Rebel)*, Helen Westcott *(Bell Longtree)*, Tom Brown *(Wild Bill Hickok)*, Virginia Gibson *(Ann James)*, Denver Pyle *(Jim Bailey)*, Frank "Red" Carpenter *(Ring Pardo)*, I. Stanford Jolley *(Henry Longtree)*, R.J. Thomas *(Tommy)*, Ray Canada *(Nato)*, Harvey Dunn *(Doc Reid)*, Bill Chaney *(Tex)*, Bron Delar *(Arizona Kid)*, Phil Barton *(Poncho)*, Bill Mims *(Dan)*, Billy Dean *(Bronco)*, Lee Sheldon *(Kate)*.

Tom Brown as the famous legend, though in this case portrayed as a shiftless villain. As the local sheriff, Brown doublecrosses the U.S. Government in a horse deal for the cavalry, with no explanation as to why this western hero figure dirties his integrity. Forbes (pseudonym for John Carpenter, who also wrote and produced this picture) is the former gunman turned horse trader, who meets Brown in an unexciting and non-historical shootout. Directed with little belief in the project or script. Unmatched color stock footage, combined with poor performances and technical work, serves to mar believability.

p, John Carpenter; d, Richard Talmadge; w, Carpenter; ph, Virgil Miller; ed, Marvin Wright.
Western **(PR:A MPAA:NR)**

I KNOW WHERE I'M GOING*** (1947, Brit.) 91m Archers/GFD-UNIV bw

Roger Livesey *(Torquil McNeil)*, Wendy Hiller *(Joan Webster)*, Pamela Brown *(Catriona Potts)*, Nancy Price *(Mrs. Crozier)*, Finlay Currie *(Ruairidh Mur)*, John Laurie *(John Campbell)*, George Carney *(Mr. Webster)*, Walter Hudd *(Hunter)*, Murdo Morrison *(Kenny)*, Margot Fitzsimmons *(Bridie)*, Jean Cadell *(Postmistress)*, Norman Shelley *(Sir Robert Bellinger)*, Petula Clark *(Cheril)*, Catherine Lacey *(Mrs. Robinson)*, Valentine Dyall *(Mr. Robinson)*, Herbert Lomas *(Mr. Campbell)*, Graham Moffatt *(RAF Sergeant)*, Capt. Duncan McKechnie *(Capt. Lochinvar)*, Captain C.W.R. Knight *(Col. Barnstaple)*, Ian Sadler, John Rae, Duncan McIntyre, Ivy Milton, Anthony Eustrel, Alec Faversham, Kitty Kirwan, Boyd Stevens, Maxwell Kennedy, Jean Houston, Arthur Chesney, Donald Strachan.

Northern Scotland is one of the realistic settings for this story of a venal young girl from London. Hiller, on her way to marry an elderly millionaire, is swept off course by a gale and by young naval officer Livesey. Determined to have her way against the wishes of her bank manager father, Carney, Hiller sets out to marry the elderly millionaire boss of a large chemical company, whose only attraction is his great wealth. As she nears the tiny island in the Hebrides which the industrialist has rented, a storm forces her to stay on the mainland with the native Scots. Here she meets and falls in love with the young naval officer, Livesey, on his way to do some hunting on the island. In reality he is a Scottish lord and owner of the small island, who vehemently opposes the money-grubbing ways of the rich businessman. Hiller is at first determined to pursue her goal of marrying the elderly millionaire, but her sentiments change as she grows more attached to Livesey. A climactic ending has her finally tossing away her original plans, as she and Livesey are barely saved from drowning in a last attempt to reach the island. Contributions from the local Scots and the Glasgow Orpheus Choir add a unique Scottish flavor to this picture. In a supporting role, Pamela Brown gives an outstanding performance as an unconventional native. Scottish folk songs play a role in the film, particularly the one from which the title is derived. Running sporadically through the movie, the song carries the theme of the film: "I know where I'm going/And I know who's going with me/I know who I love/But my love knows who I'll marry." Early in the film, as Hiller travels on a train to the Scottish Highlands, she is a participant in a surrealistic dream sequence which might have stemmed from Salvador Dali and Luis Bunuel, one in which heroine Hiller dreams she is marrying, not a man, but a huge industrial empire. This sequence contrasts strangely with the almost documentary flavor of the latter part of the film.

p,d&w, Michael Powell, Emeric Pressburger; ph, Erwin Hiller; m, Allan Gray; ed, John Seabourne; md, Walter Goehr; art d, Alfred Junge.
Romance/Comedy **(PR:A MPAA:NR)**

I LED TWO LIVES (SEE: GLEN OR GLENDA, 1953)

I LIKE IT THAT WAY** (1934) 70m UNIV bw

Gloria Stuart *(Anne Rogers)*, Roger Pryor *(Jack Anderson)*, Marian Marsh *(Joan Anderson)*, Shirley Grey *(Peggy)*, Lucille Gleason *(Mrs. Anderson)*, Noel Madison *(Stuart)*, Gloria Shea *(Trixie)*, Mae Busch *(Elsie)*, Merna Kennedy *(Information Girl)*, Clarence Wilson *(The Professor)*, Eddie Wilson *(A Pupil)*, Mickey Rooney *(Messenger Boy)*, John Darrow *(Harry Rogers)*.

An unmemorable musical from the early thirties has insurance agent Pryor falling head-over-heels for Stuart, but dumping her once he finds that she's a nightclub singer, a touchy matter with his moral principles. Spice is added to the cake when his sister, Marsh, quits her job as a telephone operator to join a chorus line. High production costs, good performances, and some nice musical numbers were wasted in this effort. Songs include: "Blue Sky Avenue" (Con Conrad, Herb Magidson); "Let's Put Two and Two Together," "I Like it That Way," and "Goin to Town" (Sidney Mitchell, Archie Gottler).

d, Harry Lachman; w, Chandler Sprague and Joseph Santley (based on a story by Harry Sauber); ph, Charles Stumar; ed, Milton Carruth; ch, Max Sheck.
Musical **(PR:A MPAA:NR)**

I LIKE MONEY½** (1962, Brit.) 97m FOX c (GB: MR. TOPAZE)

Peter Sellers *(Mr. Topaze)*, Nadia Gray *(Suzy Courtois)*, Herbert Lom *(Castel Benac)*, Leo McKern *(Headmaster Muche)*, Martita Hunt *(Baroness)*, John Neville *(Roger de Berville)*, Billie Whitelaw *(Ernestine)*, Michael Gough *(Tamise)*, Anne Leon *(His Wife)*, Joan Sims *(Colette)*, John Le Mesurier *(Blackmailer)*, Pauline Shepherd *(Lilette)*, Thomas Gallagher *(Policeman)*, Michael Sellers *(Gaston)*.

Sellers plays a dull, honest schoolmaster in a small French town who suddenly finds himself jobless after he flunks the nephew of a local baroness. He soon falls in with a shifty city councilman, Lom, who sees Sellers' mild-mannered, unassuming character as the perfect front for his crooked wheelings and dealings. Lom hires Sellers and sets him up in a fancy Paris office as the managing director of his new company. Eventually, Sellers learns he is being played for a fool, and he experiences a sort of catharsis. Tired of being manipulated, he decides to out-fox them all and become a master confidence man. He succeeds beyond his wildest dreams and eventually takes over Lom's whole operation. A remake of the U.S. film TOPAZE (1933), starring John Barrymore (the film was remade twice in France, in 1935 and 1952).

p, Pierre Rouve, Dimitri de Grunwald; d, Peter Sellers; w, Rouve (based on the play "Topaze" by Marcel Pagnol); ph, John Wilcox (CinemaScope, Eastmancolor); m, Georges Van Parys; ed, Geoffrey Foot; prod d, Don Ashton; md, Leighton Lucas; art d, Peter Murton; set d, Pamela Cornell; cos, Felix Evans, Anthony Mendleson, Pierre Balmain; makeup, Stuart Freeborn; m/l, "I Like Money," George Martin, Herbert Kretzmer (sung by Nadia Gray).
Comedy **(PR:A MPAA:NR)**

I LIKE YOUR NERVE*½ (1931) 70m FN-WB bw

Douglas Fairbanks, Jr. *(Larry O'Brien)*, Loretta Young *(Diane)*, Edmund Breon *(Clive Latimer)*, Henry Kolker *(Pachecho)*, Claud Allister *(Archie Lester)*, Ivan Simpson *(Butler)*, Paul Porcasi *(Patron)*, Andre Cheron *(Franko)*, Boris Karloff *(Luigi)*, Henry Bunston *(Colonel)*.

Predictable turn of events has Fairbanks, Jr. as a mousy bookworm who takes off for Central America on the advice of a fortune teller. He transforms into a dashing hero as he attempts to save Young from being sold in marriage. Her father, Kolker, the Minister of Finance, attempts to save his reputation by selling his daughter to a wealthy man. But Fairbanks spoils these plans as he rescues Young from her father and her fiance, who attempt to kidnap the girl. Fairbanks, Jr. and Young marry in the end. Good performance by Kolker, with a few laughs added by Allister.

d, William McGann; w, Houston Branch, Roland Pertwee (based on a story by Pertwee); ph, Ernest Haller; ed, Peter Fritsch.
Comedy **(PR:A MPAA:NR)**

I LIVE FOR LOVE** (1935) 64m WB bw (GB: I LIVE FOR YOU)

Dolores Del Rio *(Donna Alvares)*, Everett Marshall *(Roger Kerry)*, Guy Kibbee *(George Henderson)*, Allen Jenkins *(Jimmy McNamara)*, Hobart Cavanaugh *(Townsend C. Morgan)*, Berton Churchill *(Howard Fabian)*, Don Alvarado *(Rico Cesaro)*, Sam Shaw, Al Lee, Eddy Conrad *(Street Musicians)*, Mary Treen *(Clementine)*, Miki Morita *(Toya)*, Frank DuFrane, Eddie Morgan *(Actors)*, Gordon "Bill" Elliott *(Friend)*, Emmett Vogan *(Announcer)*, Ernest Van Pelt *(Stage Director)*, Nick Copeland *(Stage Manager)*, Betty Farrington, Bess Flowers, Mary Marsh, Gertrude Astor *(Interviewers)*, Florence Fair *(Dowager)*.

Del Rio plays a fiery South American stage actress who has a passionate affair with street singer Marshall. The lovers must part when their careers and callings force them to separate. Competently directed, given the weak plot and poor script. Del Rio is stunningly photographed, and gives an acceptable performance, but Marshall lacks the charm his role required. Songs, performed by Marshall, were: "Mine Alone," "Silver Wings," "I Wanna Play House," "I Live for Love," "A Man Must Shave," none of exceptional quality.

p, Bryan Foy; d, Busby Berkeley; w, Jerry Wald, Julius J. Epstein, Robert Andrews; ph, George Barnes; ed, Terry Morse; art d, Esdras Hartley; cos, Orry-Kelly; m/l, Allie Wrubel, Mort Dixon.

Musical **(PR:A MPAA:NR)**

I LIVE FOR YOU (SEE: I LIVE FOR LOVE, 1935)

I LIVE IN FEAR*½**
(1967, Jap.) 105m Toho/Brandon bw (IKIMONO NO KIROKU; AKA: RECORD OF A LIVING BEING)

Toshiro Mifune *(Kiichi Nakajima)*, Eiko Miyoshi *(Toyo Nakajima)*, Haruko Togo *(Yoshi)*, Takashi Shimura *(Harada)*, Masao Shimizu *(Takao Yamazaki)*, Kazuo Kato *(Susumu, His Son)*, Yukata Sada *(Ichiro Nakajima)*, Noriko Sengoku *(Kimi Nakajima)*, Minoru Chiaki *(Jiro Nakajima)*, Kyoko Aoyama *(Sue Nakajima)*, Kiyomi Mizunoya *(Kiichi's First Mistress)*, Saoko Yonemura *(Taeko, Her Daughter)*, Akemi Negishi *(Asako Kuribayashi)*, Kichijiro Ueda *(Kuribayashi)*, Yoichi Tachikawa *(Ryoichi Suyama)*, Ken Mitsuda *(Judge Araki)*, Toranosuke Ogawa *(Hori)*, Eijiro Tono *(Old Man From Brazil)*, Kamatari Fujiwara *(Okamoto)*, Nobuo Nakamura *(Psychiatrist)*, Haruko Togo *(Yoshi Yamazaki)*.

One of the first serious efforts by the Japanese to deal with the fear of atomic warfare and radiation, directed masterfully and subtly by Akira Kurosawa with a superb performance from Mifune (the film was released in 1955 in Japan). Mifune plays an elderly industrialist (he owns a foundry) whose increasing fear of atomic war and radiation obsesses him enough to declare his desire to pack up his family and move them to Brazil—an area that, for some reason, he considers safe. His children balk at the suggestion (they fear they would be ruined financially). Mifune's stubborn determination to go ahead with the move forces them to call upon the Family Court to declare him mentally incompetent. Though condemned as mentally unstable, Mifune refuses to give up his quest. Irrationally deciding that if his children *are* ruined financially they will join him in the move to Brazil, Mifune burns down his foundry and unwittingly puts all his employees out of work. Realizing his error, Mifune nonetheless pleads with his workers to join him in his quest for safety. Fearing that he may do even greater damage to himself or others, the Family Court is forced to have Mifune committed to an asylum. Shimura, a Family Court employee who has grown more concerned about the problems of radiation during the case, visits Mifune at the asylum and finds him happily content. The old industrialist believes he is on another planet; he stares at the sun thinking that it is the Earth which has finally been engulfed in a nuclear holocaust, vindicating his prediction. Kurosawa's film is not only about nuclear issues, but about a man's love for his family. Mifune's character is that of a powerful man who could have moved to Brazil himself, with nobody to stop him, but his love for his family (even as worthless as they appear) holds him from deserting them in what he considers their final hours. Visually, the film is striking. Heat and its effects are in every scene, from the sweaty backs of the attorneys in the courtroom scene to the blazing sun that closes the film. Throughout the film people are seen fanning themselves or using rickety electric fans to cool themselves off. The compositions are filled with such heat that the viewer could very well expect Mifune's fears to come true at any moment, and by the time the film ends, we are left wondering just *who* is really insane. I LIVE IN FEAR holds a special place in the heart of Kurosawa, as his close friend and masterful music composer Fumio Hayasaka (who also did the music for RASHOMON and THE SEVEN SAMURAI) died of tuberculosis during the production, an event that shattered the director and sapped his energies during the final months of the film.

p, Sojiro Motoki; d, Akira Kurosawa; w, Shinobu Hashimoto, Hideo Oguni, Kurosawa; ph, Asakazu Nakai; m, Fumio Hayasaka, Masaru Sato; art d, Yoshiro Muraki.

Drama **(PR:A MPAA:NR)**

I LIVE IN GROSVENOR SQUARE
(SEE: YANK IN LONDON, A, 1946, Brit.)

I LIVE MY LIFE*** (1935) 85m MGM bw

Joan Crawford *(Kay)*, Brian Aherne *(Terry)*, Frank Morgan *(Bentley)*, Aline MacMahon *(Betty)*, Eric Blore *(Grove)*, Fred Keating *(Gene)*, Jessie Ralph *(Grandma)*, Arthur Treacher *(Gallup)*, Frank Conroy *(Doctor)*, Etienne Girardot *(Professor)*, Edward Brophy *(Picture Hanger)*, Sterling Holloway *(Mac)*, Hilda Vaughn *(Miss Morrison)*, Vince Barnett *(Clerk)*, Lionel Stander *(Yaffitz)*, Hedda Hopper *(Alvin's Mother)*, Esther Dale *(Brumbaugh)*, Jan Duggan *(Aunt Mathilde)*, Nella Walker *(Ruth's Mother)*, Ronnie Cosbey *(Alvin)*, Tom Dugan *(Guard)*, George Baxter *(Bishop)*, Howard Hickman *(Teacher)*, Adrian Rosley, Blanche Craig, Howard Wilson, Arthur Stuart Hull *(Bits)*, Armand "Curley" Wright *(Greek Merchant)*, Freeman Wood *(Waterbury, Jr.)*, Barbara Worth *(Miss Waterbury)*, Harry Bradley *(Curator)*, Agnes Anderson *(Sheila)*, Harry Tyler *(Photographer)*, Hale Hamilton *(Uncle Carl)*.

Stylish, chic, and often witty, I LIVE MY LIFE is typical of the Crawford pictures of the era as they parade her in several sophisticated outfits, give her some sharp lines to say and let her nibble, but not chew up, the scenery. Crawford is a devil-may-care New York debutante who is mired in ennui. She travels to Greece and meets Aherne, a bright archaeologist with naught but disdain for the society crowd. Crawford finds him somewhat amusing and flirts a bit before making her way back to her life in the big city. Aherne mistakes her flirtations for something more serious and follows her to the States. She introduces him to her hedonistic pals, and he is totally out of place in that milieu. Somewhat of a Socialist, Aherne puts them all down for their various practices. They are not insulted, just tolerant of this slightly-pink intellectual. Ralph, Crawford's grandmother, likes Aherne and thinks he has something on the ball and might be able to lead Crawford out of her dissolute life. Aherne continues his courtship of Crawford and encounters some comedy relief with Morgan, Crawford's blotto Dad, as well as Treacher and Blore doing their patented snobbish butler routines. She finally relents and they are engaged but, just before the wedding, they have a huge row and decide that they are from two different worlds. Aherne agrees to save her any societal embarrassment by showing up at the church and allowing himself to play the jilted swain. Need we tell you that Crawford sees the folly of her ways and shows up at the house of worship? The wedding takes place and the happy couple plan to spend the rest of their lives excavating artifacts in the Middle East. It was not one of Mankiewicz's best scripts, but there was enough brittle humor there to satisfy most people, and Van Dyke's brisk direction took care of the pace.

p, Bernard H. Hyman; d, W.S. Van Dyke, II; w, Joseph Mankiewicz, Gottfried Reinhardt, Ethel B. Borden (based on the short story "Claustrophobia" by A. Carter Goodloe); ph, George Folsey; m, Dimitri Tiomkin; ed, Tom Held; art d &cos, Adrian.

Drama/Comedy **(PR:A MPAA:NR)**

I LIVE ON DANGER½** (1942) 73m PAR bw

Chester Morris *(Jeff Morrell)*, Jean Parker *(Susan Richards)*, Elizabeth Risdon *(Mrs. Morrell)*, Edward Norris *(Eddie Nelson)*, Dick Purcell *(Norm Thompson)*, Roger Pryor *(Bert Jannings)*, Douglas Fowley *(Joey Farr)*, Ralph Sanford *(Angie Moss)*, Edwin Maxwell *(Wingy Keefe)*, Patsy Nash *(Dilly)*, Joe Cunningham *(Inspector Conlon)*, Bernadene Hayes *(Jonesy)*, Billy Nelson *(George "Longshot" Harrison)*, Vicki Lester *(Keefe's Secretary)*, William Bakewell *(Mac)*, Charlotte Henry *(Nurse)*, Anna Q. Nilsson *(Mrs. Sherman)*.

Fast-moving thriller stars Morris as a special-events newscaster who gets involved in saving wrongly accused Norris from a murder charge. Nelson's sister, Parker, is fundamental in sparking Morris' interest in the case. Strong performances by the entire cast and top-notch photography help to smooth over weaknesses in the script. This was the first feature for director Sam White, who had served as a Hollywood writer prior to this.

p, William H. Pine, William C. Thomas; d, Sam White; w, Maxwell Shane, Richard Murphy, Lewis R. Foster (based on a story by Foster, Alex Gottlieb); ph, Fred Jackman, Jr.; ed, William Ziegler; art d, F. Paul Sylos.

Drama **(PR:A MPAA:NR)**

I LIVED WITH YOU½** (1933, Brit.) 100m Twickenham/GAU bw

Ivor Novello *(Prince Felix Lenieff)*, Ursula Jeans *(Gladys Wallis)*, Ida Lupino *(Ada Wallis)*, Minnie Rayner *(Mrs. Wallis)*, Eliot Makeham *(Mr. Wallis)*, Jack Hawkins *(Mort)*, Cicely Oates *(Flossie Williams)*, Davina Craig *(Maggie)*, Douglas Beaumont *(Albert Wallis)*, Molly Fisher, Beryl Harrison.

Exiled Russian prince Novello, downtrodden in London, is brought home by a Cockney shopgirl, creating havoc in the working-class home. Further instability is created when Lupino is kicked out of the home for having an affair with her employer. Originally a play by Novello, who transplanted almost the entire cast for the filmed version, the main exception to the stage cast being Lupino, who gave a strong emotional performance.

p, Julius Hagen; d, Maurice Elvey; w, H. Fowler Mear (based on the play by Novello); ph, Sydney Blythe.

Romance **(PR:A MPAA:NR)**

I LOVE A BANDLEADER** (1945) 70m COL bw

Phil Harris *(Phil Burton)*, Eddie "Rochester" Anderson *(Newton H. Newton)*, Leslie Brooks *(Ann Carter)*, Walter Catlett *(B. Templeton Jones)*, Frank Sully *(Dan Benson)*, James Burke *(Gibley)*, Pierre Watkin *(Dr. Gardener)*, The Four V's *(The Jordan Sisters)*, Robin Short *(Edwin)*, Philip Van Zandt *(Bill)*, Nick Stewart *(Willie Winters)*.

An amusing musical comedy which has Harris in the role of a house-painter stricken with amnesia. He forgets about his talent with paint and a brush and thinks he is really a bandleader. Co-billed is Anderson (Jack Benny's "butler") whose role is unfortunately small but does include a peppy tune called "Eager Beaver" (Sammy Cahn, Jule Styne). "Good, Good, Good" (Allan Roberts, Doris Fisher) is sung by Harris and Brooks.

p, Michel Kraike; d, Del Lord; w, Paul Yawitz (based on a story by John Grey); ph, Franz F. Planer; ed, James Sweeney; md, Mischa Bakaleinikoff, Paul Sawtell; art d, Carl Anderson.

Musical/Comedy **(PR:A MPAA:NR)**

I LOVE A MYSTERY** (1945) 69m COL bw

Jim Bannon *(Jack Packard)*, Nina Foch *(Ellen Monk)*, George Macready *(Jefferson Monk)*, Barton Yarborough *(Doc Long)*, Carole Mathews *(Joan Anderson)*, Lester Mathews *(Justin Reeves)*, Gregory Gay *(Dr. Han)*, Leo Mostovoy *(Vovaritch)*, Frank O'Connor *(Ralph Anderson)*, Isabel Withers *(Miss Osgood)*, Joseph Crebun *(Capt. Quinn)*.

Macready plays a rich playboy, whose wife, Foch, creates a crazy scheme involving Oriental mystics who are to drive her husband to suicide, leaving her with $2 million. Macready is led to believe that a group of Oriental mystics wants his head to replace that of their founder on his tomb. Bannon and Yarborough are the detectives who uncover the plot. Shaky direction and script, but good performances from Bannon and Foch.

p, Wallace MacDonald; d, Henry Levin; w, Charles O'Neal (based on the radio program of same name by Carleton E. Morse); ph, Burnett Guffey; ed, Aaron Stell; art d, George Brooks.

Mystery **(PR:A MPAA:NR)**

I LOVE A SOLDIER** (1944) 106m PAR bw

Paulette Goddard *(Eva Morgan)*, Sonny Tufts *(Dan Gilgore)*, Mary Treen *(Cissy Grant)*, Walter Sande *(Stiff Banks)*, Ann Doran *(Jenny)*, Beulah Bondi *(Etta Lane)* , Marie McDonald *(Gracie)*, Barry Fitzgerald *(Murph)*, James Bell *(Williams)*, Hugh Beaumont *(John)*, Frank Albertson *(Little Soldier)*, Roy Gordon *(Doctor)*, Almira Sessions *(Mrs. Munn)*, James Millican *(Georgie)*, Eddie Hall *(Freddie Rogers)*, Bobby Barber *(Attendant-Fun House)*, Frank Moran *(Hammer Machine Operator)*, Charles Quigley *(Soldier)*, Larry Steers *(Minister)*, Jimmie Dundee, Eddie Dunn *(Passengers)*, Barbara Pepper, Terry Adams *(Blondes)*.

Goddard is a welder during WW II who won't become a war bride. She helps the war effort by working as an evening hostess at USO base. There she meets and becomes romantically involved with soldier Tufts. She leaves him twice: the first time because he's married, though she discovers that he's in the process of getting a divorce; the second time because she feels she'll be on his mind during battle, increasing his chances of being killed.

p&d, Mark Sandrich; w, Allan Scott; ph, Charles Lang; m, Robert Emmett Dolan; ed, Ellsworth Hoagland; art d, Hans Dreier, Earl Hedrick.

Drama **(PR:A MPAA:NR)**

I LOVE IN JERUSALEM (SEE: MY MARGO, 1967, Israel)

I LOVE MELVIN** 1/2** (1953) 76m MGM c

Donald O'Connor *(Melvin Hoover)*, Debbie Reynolds *(Judy LeRoy)*, Una Merkel *(Mom Schneider)*, Richard Anderson *(Harry Flack)*, Allyn Joslyn *(Pop Schneider)*, Les Tremayne *(Mr. Hennenman)*, Noreen Corcoran *(Clarabelle)*, Jim Backus *(Mergo)*, Barbara Ruick *(Studio Guide)*, Robert Taylor, Howard Keel *(Guest Stars)*.

Chorus girl Reynolds dreams of becoming a movie star, and O'Connor, assistant to Backus, a *Look* magazine photographer, promises he'll get her on the cover of the magazine. Pretending that he's a photographer himself, O'Connor takes pictures of Reynolds and has her whole family waiting for their girl to appear on the *Look* cover. O'Connor makes a fake cover, but the ruse boomerangs at first. The magazine's editor, Tremayne, gets a look at Reynolds' picture and decides that she does belong on the cover. Robert Taylor makes a guest appearance in one of Reynolds' dreams of stardom. Songs include, "A Lady Loves," "Saturday Afternoon Before The Game," "I Wanna Wander," "We Have Never Met As Of Yet," "Life Has Its Funny Little Ups And Downs," "Where Did You Learn To Dance?" "And There You Are" (Mack Gordon, Josef Myrow).

p, George Wells; d, Don Weis; w, Wells, Ruth Brooks Flippen (based on a story by Laslo Vadnay); ph, Harold Rosson (Technicolor); m, Skip Martin; ed, Adrienne Fazan; md, Georgie Stoll; art d, Cedric Gibbons, Jack Martin Smith, Eddie Imazu; ch, Alton.

Musical **(PR:A MPAA:NR)**

I LOVE MY WIFE* 1/2 (1970) 95m UNIV c

Elliott Gould *(Dr. Richard Burrows)*, Brenda Vaccaro *(Jody Burrows)*, Angel Tompkins *(Helene Donnelly)*, Dabney Coleman *(Frank Donnelly)*, Joan Tompkins *(Grandma Dennison)*, Leonard Stone *(Dr. Neilson)*, Helen Westcott *(Mrs. Burrows)*, Ivor Francis *(Dr. Korngold)*, Al Checco *(Dr. Meyerberg)*, Joanna Cameron *(Nurse Sharon)*, Veleka Gray *(Stewardess)*, Damian London *(Leslie)*, Tom Toner *(John Bosley)*, Gloria Manion *(Prostitute)*, Frederic Downs *(Minister)*, Todd Baron *(Richard, Age 12)*, Laura Lacey *(Woman Neighbor)*, Peter Stuart *(Andy, Age 7)*, Dawn Lyn *(Stephanie, age 5)*, Heather North *(Betty)*, Nikita Knatz *(Art Teacher)*, Andy Stuart *(Andy, Age 2)*, Janice Pennington *(Nurse Cynthia)*, Robert Kaufman *(Devil)*.

Gould is a medical student married to the pregnant Vaccaro. Because he can't have sex with her, he begins having affairs with nurses. Vaccaro discovers this at a New Year's Eve party and keeps him out of their bedroom. Their relationship is not helped by the birth of a son and is strained even more when Vaccaro's mother moves in. Gould meets model Angel Tompkins, has an affair, and both decide to get divorces. He has a change of heart and tries to patch things up with his wife. He sends her mother packing and Vaccaro to a spa to lose the weight she gained from childbirth. She loses the weight and wants to lose Gould too. He finds that Tompkins doesn't want anything to do with him either and goes back to having affairs with the nurses. A mindless sex comedy with Gould playing a very unsympathetic character.

p, Stan Margulies; d, Mel Stuart; w, Robert Kaufman; ph, Vilis Lapenieks (Technicolor); m, Lalo Schifrin; ed, David Saxon; art d, Alexander Golitzen and George C. Webb; set d, Frank McKelvy; cos, Helen Colvig.

Comedy **(PR:O MPAA:R)**

I LOVE THAT MAN* 1/2 (1933) 73m PAR bw

Edmund Lowe *("Brains" Stanley)*, Nancy Carroll *(Grace Clark)*, Lew Cody *(Labela)*, Robert Armstrong *(Driller)*, Warren Hymer *(Mousey)*, Dorothy Burgess *(Ethel)*, Grant Mitchell *(Dentist)*, Luis Alberni *(Angelo)*, Susan Fleming, Walter Walker, Inez Courtney, Harvey Clark, Belle Mitchell, Lee Kohlmar, Leon Holmes, Esther Muir, Irving Bacon.

Con man Lowe peddles everything from stolen booze to glass caskets. He makes money but gambles it away as quickly as he gets his hands on it. Carroll is his girl friend, determined to put him on the right track. Armstrong and Hymer are two thugs cheated by Lowe. They shoot him, but with his dying breath he marries Carroll.

p, Charles R. Rogers; d, Harry Joe Brown; w, Gene Towne, Graham Baker, Casey Robinson (based on a story by Towne, Baker); ph, Milton Krasner.

Crime **(PR:A MPAA:NR)**

I LOVE TROUBLE** (1947) 93m Cornell/COL bw

Franchot Tone *(Stuart Bailey)*, Janet Blair *(Norma Shannon)*, Janis Carter *(Mrs. Caprillo)*, Adele Jergens *(Boots Nestor)*, Glenda Farrell *(Hazel Bixby)*, Steven Geray *(Keller)*, Tom Powers *(Ralph Johnston)*, Lynn Merrick *(Mrs. Johnston)*, John Ireland *(Reno)*, Donald Curtis *(Martin)*, Eduardo Ciannelli *(John Vega Caprillo)*, Robert H. Barrat *(Lt. Quint)*, Raymond Burr *(Herb)*, Eddie Marr *(Sharpy)*, Arthur Space *(Sgt. Muller)*, Sid Tomack *(Buster Buffin)*.

Tone is a private detective hired by politician Powers to check on his wife's background. The mystery has plenty of unexpected sidelights to hold audience interest through the shallow story. Tone takes a few beatings and finds himself with a couple of sexy women before he finally catches up with Merrick and her past.

p&d, S. Sylvan Simon; w, Roy Huggins (based on his novel *The Double Take*); ph, Charles Lawton, Jr.; ed, Al Clark; art d, Stephen Goosson.

Mystery **(PR:A MPAA:NR)**

I LOVE YOU (SEE: JE T'AIME, 1974, Can.)

I LOVE YOU AGAIN* 1/2** (1940) 97m MGM bw

William Powell *(Larry Wilson/George Carey)*, Myrna Loy *(Kay Wilson)*, Frank McHugh *(Doc Ryan)*, Edmund Lowe *(Duke Sheldon)*, Donald Douglas *(Herbert)*, Nella Walker *(Kay's Mother)*, Pierre Watkin *(Mr. Sims)*, Paul Stanton *(Mr. Littlejohn)*, Morgan Wallace *(Mr. Belenson)*, Charles Arnt *(Billings)*, Harlan Briggs *(Mayor Carver)*, Dix Davis *(Cpl. Belenson)*, Carl "Alfalfa" Switzer *(Harkspur, Jr.)*, Bobby Blake *(Littlejohn, Jr.)*, Winifred Harris *(Mrs. Watkins)*, Mary Currier *(Mrs. Gordon)*, Hazel Keener *(Mrs. Lederer)*, Bea Nigro *(Mrs. Kurnitz)*, Leni Lynn *(Maurine)*, Edward Earle *(Mr. Watkins)*, Harry Hayden *(Mr. Wayne)*, Harry Lash *(Steward)*, William Tannen *(Clerk)*, Ray Teal *(Watchman)*, Barbara Bedford *(Miss Stingecombe)*, George Lloyd *(Police Sgt.)*, Charles Wagenheim *(Fingerprint Man)*, Jack Mulhall, Jason Robards, Sr., John Dilson, Ted Thomson, Hooper Atchley, Warren Rock, Paul Parry, Hal Cooke, Raymond Bailey *(Men)*, Nell Craig *(Maid)*, Arthur Hoyt *(Floorwalker)*, Joe Bernard *(Watchman)*, Jack Daley *(Band Leader)*, Eric Wilton *(Headwaiter)*, George Lollier *(Police Photographer)*, Howard Mitchell *(Ranger Leader)*, Sally Payne, Claire Rochelle, Gladys Blake *(Salesgirls)*, Edward Hearn *(Guard)*.

A very funny screwball comedy with a refreshing idea behind it and equally sparkling performances. Powell and Loy are reunited in a film that has nothing at all to do with their highly successful THIN MAN series. Powell is a dour businessman who is the stick-in-the-mud of all times. She's about to divorce him for being such a sour Babbitt when matters take an unexpected turn. McHugh and Powell are on a pleasure cruise and McHugh falls overboard drunkenly, dragging Powell with him. When they are saved Powell is acknowledged as a hero, but an oar cracks his head and he is jolted out of nine years of amnesia. We now discover (as does Powell) that he is not a conservative businessman at all. It turns out that he was a wild con man who has lived on the edge of legality all his life. He is just as amazed as he can be to learn that he is a respectable citizen. Rather than make that known, he decides to use his criminal tendencies, and his solid citizen image to bilk a bunch of people, then hightail for other parts. When he meets Loy he doesn't recall ever marrying her, but he falls in love with her again. She tries to convince him that they had agreed upon a divorce but he won't hear of it. Now he starts to woo her, but with his new and somewhat rapscallion personality, and she is at first repelled, then attracted. He eventually confesses his background to her and promises to stay on the right side of the law. Suddenly, he is accidentally hit on the head again and we wonder which Powell will come out of the faint. It's the right one and he and Loy begin a new life together. A lot of laughs and some fine direction by Van Dyke make this a sleeper film that shouldn't be missed. Robert Blake and Alfalfa Switzer do well in their brief roles. The mirthful dialog is punctured with such sharp exchanges as Powell saying to Loy "You turn my head," when trying to woo her again and she retorting: "I've often wished I could turn your head—on a spit over a slow fire." A good example of how to make a comedy without wasting one word of script or one foot of film. Excellent editing by Ruggiero keeps this moving at a perfect rhythm.

p, Lawrence Weingarten; d, W.S. Van Dyke II; w, Charles Lederer, George Oppenheimer, Harry Kurnitz (based on a story by Leon Gordon, Maurine Watkins from the novel by Octavus Roy Cohen); ph, Oliver T. Marsh; ed, Gene Ruggiero; md, Franz Waxman; art d, Cedric Gibbons, Daniel B. Cathcart; set d, Edwin Willis.

Comedy **(PR:A MPAA:NR)**

I LOVE YOU, ALICE B. TOKLAS!****
(1968) 92m WB c (AKA: KISS MY BUTTERFLY)

Peter Sellers *(Harold)*, Jo Van Fleet *(Mother)*, Leigh Taylor-Young *(Nancy)*, Joyce Van Patten *(Joyce)*, David Arkin *(Herbie)*, Herbert Edelman *(Murray)*, Salem Ludwig *(Father)*, Louis Gottlieb *(Guru)*, Grady Sutton *(Funeral Director, Mr. Walsh)*, Janet E. Clark *(Mrs. Foley)*, Jorge Moreno *(Mr. Rodriguez)*, Ed Peck *(Man in Dress Shop)*, Jack Margolis *(Big Bear)*, Eddra Gale *(Love Lady)*, Carol O'Leary *(Anita)*, Gary Brown *(Ed Greco)*, Sidney Clute *(Mechanic)*, Roy Glenn *(Gas Station Attendant)*, Joe Dominguez *(Grandfather Rodriguez)*, William Bramley *(1st Patrolman)*, Vince Howard *(2nd Patrolman)*, Robert Miller Driscoll *(Crying Hippie)*, Karen Mickievic *(Crying Hippie's Wife)*.

There was no way to translate the title in Europe so they called it KISS MY BUTTERFLY, which referred to one of the scenes. Any which way it's called, this film ranks as one of the sharpest satires of the hippie culture and remains funny to this day. Sellers is a fortyish attorney from a Jewish family. His mother, Van Fleet (absolutely flawless in the role), and father, Salem Ludwig, wish their son would settle down and marry already. He becomes engaged to Van Patten, a sweet blonde woman who is perfect for him except that she is painfully boring. Sellers has a raft of ailments, including asthma, and he is the picture of neurosis. He agrees to marry Van Patten. The day they are to wed, he has an auto accident (he also specializes in personal injury cases, and when a huge Mexican family comes into his office wearing the ubiquitous neck braces, you could fall down laughing) and borrows a garish station wagon painted in the au courant psychedelic hues. Van Fleet has asked that he attend the funeral of her favorite butcher. But before that he has to pick up his hippie brother, Arkin, who has Taylor-Young with him. She is a flower child who sleeps with everyone and doesn't see anything wrong with that. Her attitude is both refreshing and disturbing to Sellers and he doesn't know how to handle these feelings. At the funeral the hearse drivers are on strike, so the casket is placed on top of the multi-colored wagon for the ride to the cemetery. Later that day Sellers meets Taylor-Young again, and when he learns that she doesn't live anywhere, he allows her to stay at his place. She is so thankful that she bakes him some marijuana brownies, the recipe of which was culled from the real *Alice B. Toklas Cook Book.* (Note: In case you don't know who the woman was, Toklas had been author Gertrude Stein's lifelong companion and lesbian lover.) After Sellers tries the brownies he shouts the title of the film. In a later scene Sellers, Van Patten, and his parents are all stoned by the pastries. Still later Sellers decides that he can no longer stand the straight life, walks out on the wedding, lets his hair grow long, dons beads, and transforms his once-swank apartment into a crash pad for itinerant hippies. He loves the life and thinks that his new existence is the reason why his asthma has fled. He and Taylor-Young have a sexual relationship, but he can't put up with her ability to sleep around, lacking loyalty to him. When the wheezing begins again, he cuts his hair, throws everyone out, and decides to go straight and marry Van Patten. The wedding is planned, the guests assemble, Sellers walks in, and chickens out again, racing into the street shouting happily "I don't know where I'm going!" as the film ends. Mazursky and Tucker came from TV's "Monkees" and set a new standard for hip comedies in the late 1960s. They never spoke down to the audience and it was appreciated, as the picture made tons of money in proportion to the cash invested. The Guru was played by the long-time bass player (and leader) of the folk group "The Limelighters." Edelman, another graduate of Coney Island's remarkable Lincoln High School, is charming in a nervous way. He played another character named Murray in THE ODD COUPLE. Grady Sutton, the butt of so many W.C. Fields jokes, is effective in a small role. To play his role, Jack Margolis took time out from authoring such books as "A Child's Garden of Grass," "The Ins and Outs Of Orgies," and "Cooking For Orgies And Other Large Parties," which should give you an idea of what he's all about.

p, Charles Maguire; d, Hy Averback; w, Paul Mazursky, Larry Tucker; ph, Phillip Lathrop (Technicolor); m, Elmer Bernstein; ed, Robert C. Jones; prod d, Pato Guzman; set d, Audrey Blasdel; cos, Theadora Van Runkle; m/l, "I Love You, Alice B. Toklas," Bernstein, Tucker, Mazursky (performed by Harper's Bizarre).

Comedy **Cas.** **(PR:O MPAA:NR)**

I LOVE YOU, I KILL YOU**
(1972, Ger.) 94m New Yorker c (ICH LIEBE DICH TOETE DICH)

Rolf Becker *(Hunter)*, Hannes Fuchs *(Teacher)*, Helmut Basch *(Mayor)*, Thomas Eckelmann, Nikolaus Dutsch *(Police)*, Marianne Blomquist, Monika Hansen *(Village Girls)*, Wolfgang Ebert, Stefen Moses.

With this film, producer-director-writer Brandner took the very popular German *Heimat* (village) movie (which usually depicted solid, rural, family values) and turned it on its head. Set in the near future, Brandner's village is populated by emotionless citizens, kept in place with pills and pleasures. Once a year the wealthy people arrive to hunt in a nearby area where the villagers are never allowed. One day a new citizen begins hunting illegally, not out of malice, but out of a desire to do something different. A strange, homosexual gamekeeper spots him, and the two begin an affair. They attempt to stage an uprising, but are shot down. A grim, disheartening film: not because the film itself is disturbing, but because the message conveyed—that only anarchy and terrorism as perpetrated by social outcasts can bring an end to the mindless existence of the majority—is short-sighted and scary.

p,d,&w, Uwe Brandner; ph, Andre Debreuil; m, Wolfgang Amadeus Mozart, Brandner, Heinz Hetter, Kid Olanf; ed, Heide Genee.

Drama **(PR:O MPAA:NR)**

I LOVE YOU, I LOVE YOU NOT (SEE: TOGETHER, 1981, Ital.)

I LOVED A WOMAN 1/2** (1933) 90m FN-WB bw

Kay Francis *(Laura McDonald)*, Edward G. Robinson *(John Hayden)*, Genevieve Tobin *(Martha Lane Hayden)*, J. Farrell MacDonald *(Shuster)*, Henry Kolker *(Sanborn)*, Robert Barrat *(Charles Lane)*, George Blackwood *(Henry)*, Murray Kinnell *(Davenport)*, Robert McWade *(Larkin)*, Walter Walker *(Oliver)*, Henry O'Neill *(Farrell)*, Lorena Layson *(Maid)*, Sam Godfrey *(Warren)*, E.J. Ratcliffe *(Theodore Roosevelt)*, Paul Porcasi *(Hotel Proprietor)*, William V. Mong *(Bowen)*.

Robinson, the owner of a Chicago meat packing company, is married to self-centered social climber Tobin. Robinson meets and falls in love with Francis, but his wife won't give him a divorce. He continues his affair with Francis secretly and she begins to make big steps in her singing career. Robinson becomes the head of a meat packing trust that sends embalmed beef to American troops fighting in Cuba. When Theodore Roosevelt becomes president Robinson is indicted, but then cleared of all charges. Francis' career takes off and Robinson tries to duplicate her success. He fails miserably, and with his company going bankrupt he leaves for Greece. When Francis finds this out she takes a boat to be with him. This was the film in which Robinson began to earn a reputation of being tough on writers, insisting they more sharply define characters, especially his own. He bullied Kenyon and Sutherland into tightening his dialog while director Green stood mutely by.

p, Henry Blanke; d, Alfred Green; w, Charles Kenyon, Sidney Sutherland (based on the novel by David Karsner); ph, James Van Trees; ed, Bert Levy.

Drama **(PR:A MPAA:NR)**

I LOVED YOU WEDNESDAY* 1/2 (1933) 77m FOX bw

Warner Baxter *(Phillip Fletcher)*, Elissa Landi *(Vicki Meredith)*, Victor Jory *(Randall Williams)*, Miriam Jordan *(Cynthia Williams)*, Laura Hope Crews *("Doc Mary" Hanson)*.

Baxter and Jory are competing for the same woman, Jory's ex-mistress, Landi. She and Jory's wife, Jordan, are fighting for his affections. Baxter, an engineer, is kept away from Landi by Jory's trickery, but in the end it is Baxter who ends up with Landi. A romantic comedy that is low on humor and cinematic energy.

d, Henry King, William C. Menzies; w, Phillip Klein, Horace Jackson (based on the play by Molly Ricardel and William DuBois); ph, Hal Mohr; ed, Frank Hull; ch, Sammy Lee.

Comedy **(PR:A MPAA:NR)**

I MARRIED A COMMUNIST (SEE: WOMAN ON PIER 13, 1949)

I MARRIED A DOCTOR 1/2** (1936) 83m FN-WB bw

Pat O'Brien *(Dr. William P. Kennicott)*, Josephine Hutchinson *(Carol Kennicott)*, Ross Alexander *(Erik Valborg)*, Guy Kibbee *(Samuel Clark)*, Louise Fazenda *(Bea Sorenson)*, Olin Howland *(Dave Dyer)*, Margaret Irving *(Maude Dyer)*, Alma Lloyd *(Fern Winters)*, Grace Stafford *(Vera Sherwin)*, Ray Mayer *(Miles Bjornstam)*, Robert Barrat *(Nels Valborg)*, Hedwiga Reicher *(Bessie Valborg)*, Edith Elliott *(Mrs. Clark)*, Willard Robertson *(Guy Pollock)*, Thomas Pogue *(Rev. Champ Perry)*, Janet Young *(Dolly Perry)*, Harry Hayden *(Prof. George Edwin Mott)*, Frank Rhodes *(Ezra Stowbody)*, Gaby Fay *(Ella Stowbody)*, Sam Wren *(Chet Sashaway)*, Dora Clement *(Mrs. Jackson Elder)*, John T. Murray *(Nat Hicks)*, Raymond Brown *(Grocer)*, Ralph Remley *(Oleson)*, George Hayes *(Agent)*, Leo White *(Dance Extra)*, Milton Kibbee *(Station Agent)*.

O'Brien is a small town doctor and Hutchinson is his Chicago wife. She finds it hard to adapt to the rural lifestyle, and the townspeople have a hard time accepting her. Not only does she have problems with gossiping neighbors, but her relationship with her husband doesn't go too well either. She heads back to Chicago but finds, as her husband has told her, that every city and town has a main street (a gossip center). The film ends happily with Hutchinson returning to her husband—quite different from the downbeat ending of Sinclair Lewis' book.

p, Harry Joe Brown; d, Archie L. Mayo; w, Casey Robinson, Harriet Ford, Harvey O'Higgins (based on the novel *Main Street* by Sinclair Lewis); ph, Byron Haskin; ed, Owen Marks; md, Leo F. Forbstein.

Drama **(PR:A MPAA:NR)**

I MARRIED A MONSTER FROM OUTER SPACE*** (1958) 78m PAR bw

Tom Tryon *(Bill Farrell)*, Gloria Talbott *(Marge Farrell)*, Peter Baldwin *(Swanson)*, Robert Ivers *(Harry)*, Chuck Wassil *(Ted)*, Valerie Allen *(B Girl)*, Ty Hungerford *(Mac)*, Ken Lynch *(Dr. Wayne)*, John Eldredge *(Collins)*, Alan Dexter *(Sam Benson)*, James Anderson *(Weldon)*, Jean Carson *(Helen Rhodes)*, Jack Orrison *(Schultz)*, Steve London *(Charles Mason)*, Maxie Rosenbloom *(Bartender)*, Mary Treen.

Don't let the exploitation title fool you, this is a fine science fiction film directed by Gene Fowler, who was an editor for Fritz Lang and directed a good horror film with an equally exploitative title, I WAS A TEENAGE WEREWOLF. Similar in many ways to INVASION OF THE BODY SNATCHERS (1955), I MARRIED A MONSTER FROM OUTER SPACE not only gives you the point of view of a normal human, Talbott, but of the alien creatures too. This helps build suspense and tension by showing just how perilous Talbott's situation is. Days before his wedding to Talbott, Tryon is taken over by an alien creature, and during their first year of marriage Talbott slowly realizes that the man she married isn't the man she once knew. Tryon now sees in the dark, kills a puppy even though he is supposed to be an animal lover, is allergic to alcohol, and has no apparent emotions. When Talbott discovers his true identity she also finds that most of the other men in town are also aliens. She goes to her godfather, the sheriff, to tell him her discovery and finds that he's one of the aliens. Talbott tries to contact Washington, but the operator tells her all lines are busy. She tries to send a telegram, but her message is discarded. When she tries to leave town she is stopped by the police, who tell her that the bridge is out. She goes back to her monster-husband and tells him what she knows. He explains that on his planet, Andromenda, women have become extinct, forcing the men to venture earthward to mate with earth women and ultimately take over the world. Talbott goes to Lynch, the town doctor, who believes her story, and together they assemble all the men who haven't been taken over (men who have just become fathers) and go after the aliens. Bullets have no effect on the aliens, but when attack dogs are unleashed they rip the monsters' exposed arteries. When the aliens die, the doctor and the other men board the alien spacecraft, finding more possessed townsmen. But when these men are released they expire in a jellylike heap. Fowler magnifies the film's tension by including scenes of the aliens dealing with each other: Tryon strangling a puppy when it recognizes his true identity; the aliens talking about mating with earth women and how they dislike their human disguises; and the cold-blooded murder that the aliens are capable of. Consequently, we know more than Talbott, creating an even greater fear for her situation. The film's moody quality seems to be influenced by Lang, and Fowler uses what he learned from the German director to create a standout low-budget 1950s science fiction film.

p&d, Gene Fowler, Jr.; w, Louis Vittes; ph, Haskell Boggs; ed, George Tomasini; art d, Hal Pereira, Henry Bumstead; spec eff, John P. Fulton; makeup, Charles Gemora.

Science Fiction/Horror **Cas.** **(PR:O MPAA:NR)**

I MARRIED A NAZI (SEE: MAN I MARRIED, THE, 1940)

I MARRIED A SPY** (1938) 59m IF-Phoenix/GN bw (GB: SECRET LIVES)

Brigitte Horney *(Lena Schmidt)*, Neil Hamilton *(Lt. Pierre de Montmalion)*, Gyles Isham *(Franz Abel)*, Ivor Barnard *(Baldhead)*, Charles Carson *(Henri)*, Raymond Lovell *(German Secret Service Chief)*, Frederick Lloyd *(French Secret Service Chief)*, Ben Field *(Karl Schmidt)*, Hay Petrie *(Robert Pigeon)*, Leslie Perrins *(J 14)*.

Horney is a German-born, French-raised girl who is enlisted into the French Secret Service after her escape from a German concentration camp during WW I. After the war, to avoid deportation, she marries French Soldier Hamilton—falling in love with him only after they have tied the knot.

p, Hugh Perceval; d, Edmond T. Greville; w, Basil Mason, Perceval, Greville (based on the novel *Secret Lives* by Paul de Sainte-Colombe); ph, Otto Heller; m, Walter Goher; ed, Ray Pitt.

Spy Drama **(PR:A MPAA:NR)**

I MARRIED A WITCH*½** (1942) 82m PAR/UA bw

Fredric March *(Wallace Wooley)*, Veronica Lake *(Jennifer)*, Robert Benchley *(Dr. Dudley White)*, Susan Hayward *(Estelle Masterson)*, Cecil Kellaway *(Daniel)*, Elizabeth Patterson *(Margaret)*, Robert Warwick *(J.B. Masterson)*, Eily Malyon *(Tabitha Wooley)*, Nora Cecil *(Harriet)*, Emory Parnell *(Allen)*, Helen St. Rayner *(Vocalist)*, Aldrich Bowker *(Henry, Justice of the Peace)*, Emma Dunn *(Wife of the Justice of the Peace)*, Harry Tyler, Ralph Peters *(Prisoners)*, Charles Moore *(Rufus)*, Ann Carter *(Jennifer, Jr., the Daughter)*, George Guhl *(Fred the Policeman)*, Wade Boteler *(Policeman)*, Eddy Chandler *(Motorcycle Cop)*, Jack Luden *(Ambulance Driver)*, Monte Blue *(Doorman)*. Lee Shumway *(Fireman)*, Billy Bevan *(Puritan Vendor)*, Marie Blake *(Puritan)*, Reed Hadley *(Young Man)*, Florence Gill *(Woman Playing Chess)*, Robert Greig *(Town Crier)*, Viola Moore *(Martha)*, Mary Field *(Nancy Wooley)*, Kathryn Sheldon *(Elderly Wife)*, Charles Bates *(Wooley Son)*, William Haade *(Policeman)*, Ralph Dunn, Alan Bridge *(Prison Guards)*, Frank Mills *(Joe the Cabbie)*, Jack Gardner *(Radio Voice)*, Billy Bletcher *(Photographer)*, Ernie Shields *(Waiter)*, Beverly Andre, Mickey Rentschler *(Young Folks at Country Club)*, Gordon DeMain *(Man with Masterson)*, Georgia Backus *(Older Woman)*. Arthur Stuart Hull *(Guest)*, Chester Conklin *(Bartender)*.

A delightful ghost-witch film which spoofs the genre and still offers a lot of fun. Kellaway and his daughter Lake are branded witches in 1690 by an early Wooley ancestor (also played by March), and condemned to a New England stake. After they are burned, the witches are buried beneath a large oak tree but they pass a curse on the Wooley family, predicting that no male member will ever find happiness. The curse is shown taking effect through the generations by various mishaps befalling Wooley descendants, all played by March, until coming to the then present 1942 and the current Wooley male member, March, a stuffed shirt with a snobbish fiancee, Hayward. He's running for governor of the state and plans to marry Hayward whose filthy rich father, Warwick, an influential publisher, is backing him. A storm comes up and lightning splits the ancient oak under which the capricious spirits of Kellaway and daughter Lake reside. They are suddenly freed, emerging as puffs of smoke that talk to each other, then later taking human form, he a rotund, booze-loving fellow, she a blonde-haired siren. And it's sirens that March hears when his car is stopped on a busy street and he is told that he and his party cannot proceed because the famous local hotel, The Puritan House, has caught fire. March gets out and looks around, crossing police lines when he hears a voice crying out from the blazing hotel, a voice only he hears. He rushes inside to locate Lake whom he can barely see in the thick smoke. Since she is without clothes, he loans her his coat and rescues her. From that point on, Lake does all in her power to make March fall in love with her and take him from the clutches of spoiled and dominating rich girl Hayward. Though using all her witchcraft to win March, including some spectacular wizardry—a taxi driven by her sorcerer father that sails through the air and later crashes at the site of the oak tree being only one incredible piece of spiritual special effects—she cannot thwart Hayward from her marital goal. At the time of the March-Hayward wedding, however, she and Kellaway come up with a pip of a witchcraft stunt. They create a hurricane which blows down the guests and all but destroys the building in which the marriage is to take place. The wedding is called off and a short time later Lake engineers a spellbound March into her arms just as Hayward enters the room. Infuriated, Hayward calls off the ceremonies and Lake makes her supreme effort to marry March. Kellaway is opposed to the match, however, and does everything in his power to prevent his daughter from wedding a hated Wooley, including committing suicide and trying to blame the crime on March. But Lake is too fast for him, forcing him to return to life in front of startled investigators. She next gets booze-loving Kellaway drunk and imprisons him in a bottle so he can do no further harm. On their wedding night, Lake gets pangs of guilt and confesses to March that she is a witch and that he has been responding to her love only because she has a spell on him. He refuses to believe her and she proves her point by manipulating the ballots on election night so that March, who originally had nothing more than a slim chance, wins the election in a record landslide. He is thoroughly disgraced. Moreover, the devilish Kellaway escapes from the bottle and reclaims the witch spirit of his daughter. But love wins out and Lake's mortal being stays on earth to settle down happily with March. At the end, however, the blissful couple are startled to see their daughter, her long blonde hair covering one eye, straddling a broomstick. March brings two decades as a seasoned actor to this sprightly comedy and Lake, who had only been in films for a year, is surprisingly effective. The two did not get along well at the outset of production. March thought Lake an amateur and all but told her so. She called him a "pompous poseur." Director Clair also had a low opinion of Lake and refused to hire her until producer-director Sturges insisted. Clair later told Lake that he was mistaken and that she was a fine comedienne, a rare apology coming from the distinguished French director. Hayward was so effective at playing shrews that she was typecast here and all she could do was look pretty and surly at the same time, no small feat. This film, with its wonderful special effects by Jennings, was in the hilarious tradition of TOPPER and THE GHOST GOES WEST. Clair's direction is swift and sure, producing a much better effort here than his first Hollywood production, THE FLAME OF NEW ORLEANS which fizzled at the box office. The Thorne Smith tale, taken from an incomplete novel, was in the mold of his TOPPER stories and it worked well on screen. The supporting players, particularly Kellaway as the pixie like warlock-witch, shine in their hexed parts. Humorist Benchley, who had turned more and more to acting to make a living at the end of his literary career, is very funny as March's confused political adviser. This film would inspire the popular TV series, "Bewitched."

p, Preston Sturges; d, Rene Clair; w, Robert Pirosh, Marc Connelly, Dalton Trumbo (based on the novel *The Passionate Witch* by Thorne Smith, Norman Matson); ph, Ted Tetzlaff; m, Roy Webb; ed, Eda Warren; art d, Hans Dreier, Ernst Fegte; set d, George Sawley; cos, Edith Head; spec eff, Gordon Jennings; makeup, Wally Westmore.

Fantasy/Comedy **Cas.** **(PR:A MPAA:NR)**

I MARRIED A WOMAN* (1958) 80m RKO/UNIV bw/c

George Gobel *(Marshall "Mickey" Briggs)*, Diana Dors *(Janice Briggs)*, Adolphe Menjou *(Frederick W. Sutton)*, Jessie Royce Landis *(Mother Blake)*, Nita Talbot *(Miss Anderson)*, William Redfield *(Eddie Benson)*, Steve Dunne *(Bob Sanders)*, John McGiver *(Felix Girard)*, Cheerio Meredith *(Mrs. Wilkins)*, Steve Pendleton *(Photographer)*, Stanley Adams *(Cab Driver)*, Kay Buckley *(Camera Girl)*, Angie Dickinson *(Screen Wife)*, John Wayne *(Himself)*.

Gobel, a 1950s TV personality, is an advertising man who comes up with the "Miss Luxemberg Beer Beauty Contest." This makes his boss, Menjou, very happy and Gobel marries the contest winner, Dors. Pressure from his boss to come up with another successful ad campaign puts a strain on his marriage. The rest of this unfunny film pertains to Gobel's struggle to hold on to his wife and job. Though most of the film is in black-and-white, there is a fantasy sequence featuring John Wayne that was shot in color.

p, William Bloom; d, Hal Kanter; w, Goodman Ace; ph, Lucien Ballard; m, Cyril Mockridge; ed, Otto Ludwig, Kenneth Marstella; art d, Albert S. D'Agostino, Walter E. Keller; cos, Howard Shoup.

Comedy **(PR:A MPAA:NR)**

I MARRIED AN ANGEL** (1942) 84m MGM bw

Jeanette MacDonald *(Anna Zador/Brigitta)*, Nelson Eddy *(Count Willie Palaffi)*, Binnie Barnes *(Peggy)*, Edward Everett Horton *(Peter)*, Reginald Owen *(Herman "Whiskers" Rothbart)*, Mona Maris *(Marika)*, Janice [Janis] Carter *(Sufi)*, Inez Cooper *(Iren)*, Douglas Dumbrille *(Baron Szigetti)*, Leonid Kinskey *(Zinski)*, Marion Rosamond *(Dolly)*, Anne Jeffreys *(Polly)*, Marek Windheim *(Marcel)* Georges Renavent *(Pierre)*, Max Willenz *(Assistant Manager)*, Francine Bordeaux *(1st Maid)*, Mildred Shay *(2nd Maid)*, Odette Myrtil *(Modiste)*, Tyler Brooke *(Lucien)*, Jacques Vanaire *(Max)*, Luis Alberni *(Jean Frederique)*, Micheline Cheirel *(Annette)*, Rafaela Ottiano *(Madelon)*, Margaret Moffat *(Mother Zador)*, Vaughan Glaser *(Father Andreas)*, Gino Corrado *(Valet)*, Sid D'Albrook *(Porter)*, Sig Arno *(Waiter)*, Mitchell Lewis *(Porter)*, Jacqueline Dalya *(Olga)*, George Humbert *(Taxi Driver)*, Ben Hall *(Delivery Boy)*, Ferdinand Munier *(Rich Man)*, George Davis *(Pushcart Vendor)*, Jack Vlaskin *(Milk Wagon Driver)*, Veda Ann Borg, Carol Hughes *(Willie's Morning Ladies)*, Ludwig Stossel *(Janitor)*, Robert Grieg *(Major-domo)*, Maxine Leslie, Lillian Eggers *(Willie's Evening Ladies)*, Frederick Vogeding, Charles Judels *(Customs Officers)*, Anthony Blair, Joel Friedkin, Major McNamara, Earle S. Dewey, Bert Roach *(Board Members)*, Maude Eburne *(Juli)*, Suzanne Kaaren *(Simone)*, Lisl Valetti *(2nd Maid)*, Leonard Carey, Guy Bellis *(Servants)*, Esther Dale *(Mrs. Gherkin)*, Grace Hayle *(Mrs. Gabby)*, Gertrude W. Hoffman *(Lady Gimcrack)*, Maude Allen, Eva Dennison *(Women)*, Florence Auer *(Mrs. Roquefort)*, Walter Soderling *(Mr. Kipper)*, Dick Elliott *(Mr. Scallion)*, Oliver B. Prickett [Blake] *(Mr. Gherkin)*, Almira Sessions *(Mrs. Scallion)*, Lon Poff *(Mr. Dodder)*, Charles Brabin *(Mr. Fairmind)*, Otto Hoffman *(Mr. Flit.)*, Beryl Wallace *(Fifi)*, Anita Bolster *(Mrs. Kipper)*, Frank Reicher *(Driver)*, Rafael Storm *(Berti)*, Cecil Cunningham *(Mrs. Fairmind)*, Jack "Tiny" Lipson *(Mr. Roquefort)*, Harry Worth, James B. Carson *(Waiters)*, Alphonse Martell *(Headwaiter)*, Arthur Dulac, Harry Horwitz *(French News Vendors)*, Sam Savitsky *(Doorman)*, Evelyn Atchinson *(Marie Antoinette)*, Charles Bancroft *(Chimney Sweep)*, Muriel Barr *(Mermaid)*, Edwina Coolidge *(Queen Elizabeth)*, Ruth Adler *(Night No. 1)*, Leda Nicova *(Night No. 2)*, Vivian DuBois *(Night No. 3)*, Betty Hayward *(Night No. 4)*, George Ford *(Neptune)*, Guy Gabriel, Dorothy Hans, Aileen Haley *(Infantas)*, Joe Hartman (Marc Anthony), John Marlowe *(Louis XIV)*, Scottish Highlander *(Paul Power)*, Robert Spencer *(Peacock)*.

The highly successful musical team of Jeanette MacDonald and Nelson Eddy made their last appearance on screen together in this shoddily conceived and haphazardly executed fantasy that neither star cared much for. The film is set in Budapest and Eddy stars as a bored, very rich playboy who owns a bank. All the eligible ladies in town arrive at a massive costume party thrown in honor of his birthday to parade before him in the hopes he will chose them for marriage. Seeking to escape the attentions of all these women, Eddy decides to dance with one of his employees, MacDonald , a quiet, shy and unassuming girl whom the rest of the guests look upon with scorn. After an innocuous conversation in which it becomes apparent that the boss knows nothing about his employee, Eddy excuses himself and disappears to his room with a piece of birthday cake. There he falls asleep and dreams that a beautiful angel complete with wings and a halo (who looks just like MacDonald) floats into his room declaring that she has come to marry him. Soon Eddy and his angel are whisked off to a honeymoon and on their first night together MacDonald tries to leave her husband to sleep on a cloud. Eddy insists she stay with him and the next morning MacDonald awakens to discover she has lost her wings. Their idyllic honeymoon is cut short, however, when news arrives that his business associates in Budapest have panicked and there may be a run on his bank. Returning home, Eddy decides to introduce his bride by throwing a large banquet for his investors. Depressed over the loss of her wings, MacDonald vows to become more virtuous, and at the dinner party she shocks the guests by speaking honestly and frankly about her husband's business secrets. The businessmen leave the banquet a bit stunned and the next day there is a run on the bank. Just as suddenly as it began, the dream ends and Eddy awakens relieved that it was all a fantasy. He dashes downstairs and finds MacDonald right where he had left her. Desperately in love with her now, Eddy proposes to the stunned MacDonald and she accepts. Having purchased the rights to I MARRIED AND ANGEL for MacDonald in 1933, MGM decided the portrayal of an angel who loses her virtue to a man was too controversial and shelved the project. In 1938 Lorenz Hart and Richard Rodgers turned the story into a highly successful Broadway musical starring Vera Zorina and MGM finally moved to capitalize on their investment. MGM tried to get Zorina for the lead, but the actress had been signed by Paramount and the studio refused to lend Mayer her services. The studio then settled on MacDonald and Eddy, but both performers had reservations about the project. By the time the film was ready to be shot it was plagued with problems. Screenwriter Antia Loos was juggling three movie projects and one Broadway show at the same time and had little enthusiasm to follow the production closely. Studio hacks then began reshaping her material and cut whatever life there was out of it. Rodgers and Hart refused to participate, forcing the studio to employ Bob Wright and Chet Forrest to "adapt" the original songs, an assignment both men were extremely unhappy with and it led to their resignations. Several sequences where cut, including scenes showing that Eddy and the angel had produced no less than four children, because puritanical religious groups voiced strong protest. After months of cutting, reshaping, and quick reshooting, I MARRIED AN ANGEL was released to angry critics and an apathetic public. Songs include "I Married an Angel," "I'll Tell the Man In the Street," "Spring is Here," "Tira Lira La" (Richard Rodgers, Bob Wright, Chet Forrest), "A Twinkle in Your Eye" (Rodgers, Hart, Wright, Forrest), "Aloha Oe" (Princess Lilivokalani), "Caprice Viennoise" (Fritz Kreisler), "Chanson Boheme" (from Bizet's "Carmen," English lyrics by Wright, Forrest), "Anges Purs" (from Gounod's "Faust"), "Hey Butcher," "There Comes a Time," "To Count Palaffi," "May I Present the Girl," "Now You've Met The Angel," "But What of Truth" (Herbert Stothart, Wright, Forrest).

p, Hunt Stromberg; d, Maj. W.S. Van Dyke II; w, Anita Loos (based on the stage musical by Richard Rodgers, Lorenz Hart from the play by Vaszary Janos); ph, Ray June; m, Rodgers; ed, Conrad A. Nervig; art d, Cedric Gibbons, John S. Detlie, Motley; set d, Edwin B. Willis; cos, Motley, Kalloch; ch, Ernst Matray; spec eff, Arnold Gillespie, Warren Newcombe; makeup, Jack Dawn.

Musical **(PR:A MPAA:NR)**

I MARRIED TOO YOUNG (SEE: MARRIED TOO YOUNG, 1962)

I, MAUREEN* 1/2 (1978, Can.) 85m Jandu-P.W.S./New Cinema bw

Colleen Collins *(Maureen)*, Diane Bigelow *(Diana)*, Donna Preece *(Vinnie)*, Robert Crone *(Charlie)*, Michael Ironside *(Dr. Paul Johnson)*, Brian Damude *(Dennis)*.

An independent first feature that is rooted in a feminist ideology. Collins is the title character who, after having a premonition, packs her bags and leaves the responsibility of her husband and child behind. The cast is moderate to poor, but they all come out looking fine due to Champion's top-notch cinematography.

p, Duane Hanson; d&w, Janine Manatis (based on a short story by Elizabeth Spencer); ph, Marc Champion; m, Hagood Hardy; ed, Kirk Jones; art d, Nadia Salnick.

Drama **(PR:A MPAA:NR)**

I MET A MURDERER 1/2** (1939, Brit.) 79m GN bw

James Mason *(Mark Warrow)*, Pamela Kellino *(Jo)*, Sylvia Coleridge *(Martha Warrow)*, William Devlin *(Warrow)*, Peter Coke *(Horseman)*, Esma Cannon *(Hiker)*, James Harcourt *(Cart Driver)*, Sheila Morgan, Sheppie the Dog.

Mason is a young farmer who is married to Coleridge. She is a nagging bitch and after an argument she kills Mason's dog. Upset, Mason kills her, buries her in the garden, and flees. Coleridge's brother becomes suspicious and contacts the police. Mason hooks up with writer Kellino and they fall in love. Then Mason realizes that she knows who he is and is using him for material for a novel. The police bear down and Mason is forced to flee again. From a high cliff overlooking the sea, Kellino watches helplessly as Mason wades into the water and drowns. A fugitive picture with several novel twists make this one fascinating.

p, Roy Kellino, Pam Kellino, James Mason; d, R. Kellino; w, P. Kellino and Mason (based on a story by P. Kellino); ph, R. Kellino; m, Eric Ansell; ed, Fergus Macdonnell.

Crime Drama **(PR:C-O MPAA:NR)**

I MET HIM IN PARIS*** (1937) 85m PAR bw

Claudette Colbert *(Kay Denham)*, Melvyn Douglas *(George Potter)*, Robert Young *(Gene Anders)*, Lee Bowman *(Berk Sutter)*, Mona Barrie *(Helen Anders)*, George Davis *(Cutter Driver)*, Fritz Feld *(Swiss Hotel Clerk)*, Rudolph [Anders] Amant *(Romantic Waiter)*, Alexander Cross *(John Hadley)*, Louis La Bey, Jacques Lory, Joe Ploski *(Bartenders)*, Egon Brecher *(Emile the Upper Tower Man)*, Hans Joby *(Lower Tower Man)*, Jacques Vanaire *(Frenchman Flirt)*, Gennaro Curci *(Double-Talk Waiter)*, Eugene Borden, Albert Morin *(Headwaiters)*, Capt. Fernando Garcia *(Elevator Operator)*, Albert Pollet *(Conductor)*, Francesco Maran, Yola d'Avril *(French Couple in Apartment)*, Jean De Briac *(Steward)*, Charles Haas, Otto Jehly, Paco Moreno, Roman Novins *(Waiters)*, Alexander Schoenberg *(Porter)*, Gloria Williams, Priscilla Moran *(Women)*, Joe Thoben *(Assistant Bartender)*, George Sorel, Arthur Hurni *(Hotel Clerks)*.

A good comedy with sprightly dialog has Colbert throwing over stick-in-the mud Bowman, a dull fiance, to commit "a one-woman rebellion against everything that's sweet and conventional." She takes a holiday in Paris where she becomes entangled with playwright Douglas and playboy Young who is secretly married. Colbert is initially attracted to Young because he appears sincere but explodes when she finds that he's married. The threesome go to Switzerland and a comedy of enjoyable errors in slapstick follows as they almost break their necks on skates, skis, bobsleds, and snow deeper than the Grand Canyon. The situations are implausible but the leads handle it all deftly, providing consistent laughs. And Colbert does wind up with Douglas, after telling Young: "You're as irresponsible as a two-month-old kitten." The Swiss scenes were shot on location in Sun Valley, Idaho.

p&d, Wesley Ruggles; w, Claude Binyon (based on a story by Helen Meinardi); ph, Leo Tover; ed, Otho Lovering; md, Boris Morros; art d, Hans Dreier, Ernst Fegte; spec eff, Farciot Edouart; m/l, Helen Meinardi, Hoagy Carmichael.

Comedy **(PR:A MPAA:NR)**

I MET MY LOVE AGAIN 1/2** (1938) 77m Wanger/UA bw

Joan Bennett *(Julie)*, Henry Fonda *(Ives)*, Dame May Whitty *(Aunt William)*, Alan Marshal *(Michael)*, Louise Platt *(Brenda)*, Alan Baxter *(Tony)*, Tim Holt *(Budge)*, Dorothy Stickney *(Mrs. Towner)*, Florence Lake *(Carol)*, Gene Hall *(Michael)*, Alice Cavenna *(Agatha)*.

This is what Hollywood producers in the 1930s would term "a woman's film," one that concentrated on romance, lost love, and a last chance for bliss. Studious, shy Fonda and exciting Bennett are a twosome in a small Vermont town until dashing young writer Marshal appears and captures Bennett's heart. It's 1927 and the decade is still roaring. Bennett and Marshal roar off with it to Paris where they settle down, live in a loft, have a child, and he becomes a stone alcoholic, dead a decade later. Bennett returns to the Vermont homestead to find Fonda, a dour biology professor and a dedicated bachelor. With Bennett is her 10-year-old daughter. Fonda pretends he's no longer interested in her and most of the town mistreats the wayward Bennett for spurning the hometown boy. Fonda's life is made more miserable since one of his students, Platt, is continually on the prowl for him. She is a rich, spoiled brat of a young lady who demands that Fonda love her, threatening to commit suicide if he doesn't. Fonda finally escapes Platt's machinations and returns to the warm embrace of Bennett. The pair pick up almost where they left off 10 years earlier and plan a life together, surmounting the wagging tongues of gossips, interference from love-sick sophomores, and a series of mishaps to rekindle a love that has never died. It's pretty gooey in places, but a palatable film nevertheless. Bennett, who was the paramour and wife-to-be of producer Wanger, does a good job as the adventurous lady, and Fonda is properly phlegmatic as the jilted lover, though his lack of enthusiasm for the role is apparent. There's not much to it, and Wanger only selected him because he had appeared in a similar vehicle with Bette Davis, THAT CERTAIN WOMAN, in 1937. The only interest the actor had in this lackluster production was that his old friend Joshua Logan—they had worked together in the University Players in New York—co-directed the film, an assignment Logan did not appreciate, particularly when George Cukor was later brought in to reshoot many of Logan's scenes. Logan would leave Hollywood after this brief stint and not return until he directed PICNIC in 1956, a hiatus of 18 years.

p, Walter Wanger; d, Arthur Ripley, Joshua Logan, George Cukor; w, David Hertz (based on the novel *Summer Lightning* by Allene Corliss); ph, Hal Mohr; m, Heinz Roemheld; ed, Otho Lovering, Edward Mann.

Romance **(PR:A MPAA:NR)**

I MISS YOU, HUGS AND KISSES** (1978, Can.) 90m Paradise/Astral c

Elke Sommer *(Magadalene Kruschen)*, Donald Pilon *(Charles Kruschen)*, Chuck Shamata *(Gershen Isen)*, Cindy Girling *(Pauline Corte)*.

Based on the real-life murder case of Toronto realtor Peter Demeter, who was accused of killing his wife in 1975. This picture puts forth a number of methods by which the crime could have taken place. It also concentrates on the common belief that he hired an outside party to do the deed, a view which guided the jurors to a guilty plea. Violence and sex cloud the interesting narrative approach director Markowitz chose to take.

p, Murray and Charles Markowitz; d&w, Murray Markowitz; ph, Don Wilder; m, Howard Shore; ed, Don Ginsburg.

Crime **(PR:C-O MPAA:NR)**

I MISTERI DELLA GIUNGLA NERA
(SEE: MYSTERY OF THUG ISLAND, THE, 1966, Ital./Ger.)

I, MOBSTER*** (1959) 80m FOX bw

Steve Cochran *(Joe Sante)*, Lita Milan *(Teresa Porter)*, Robert Strauss *(Black Frankie Udino)*, Celia Lovsky *(Mrs. Sante)*, Lili St. Cyr *(Herself)*, John Brinkley *(Ernie Porter)*, Yvette Vickers *(The Blonde)*, Robert Shayne *(Senator)*, Grant Withers *(Joe Moran)*, Frank Gerstle *(District Attorney)*, Wally Cassell *(Cherry-Nose)*, John Mylong *(Mr. Sante)*, Jeri Southern.

Cochran is a gang leader whose story is told through flashbacks as he goes in front of a U.S. Senate subcommittee. He started out when he was just a kid, collecting bets for a small-time racketeer. Then he became a drug dealer, hooked up with Strauss, and then became kingpin of the underworld after he killed the boss, Withers. The syndicate decides that Cochran is of no use to them after his Senate testimony and has Strauss kill him. I, MOBSTER was made to cash in on the success of MACHINE GUN KELLY, which was made the year before.

p, Edward L. Alperson, Gene Corman, Roger Corman; d, Roger Corman; w, Steve Fisher (based on a story by Joseph Hilton Smyth); ph, Floyd Crosby (CinemaScope); m, Gerald Fried, Edward L. Alperson, Jr.; ed, William B. Murphy; art d, Daniel Haller; cos, Marjorie Corso.

Crime **(PR:C-O MPAA:NR)**

I, MONSTER** 1/2 (1971, Brit.) 75m Amicus/Cannon c

Christopher Lee *(Marlowe/Mr. Blake)*, Peter Cushing *(Utterson)*, Mike Raven *(Enfield)*, Richard Hurndall *(Lanyan)*, George Merritt *(Poole)*, Kenneth J. Warren *(Dean)*, Susan Jameson *(Diane)*.

An eerie, stylish retelling of Robert Louis Stevenson's lonely tale of Dr. Jekyll and Mr. Hyde. The names have been changed to Dr. Marlowe and Mr. Blake, but the story remains the same. Lee turns in a fine performance as the doctor with personality problems, and Cushing is a fellow doctor attempting to halt Lee's hideous metamorphosis.

p, Max J. Rosenberg, Milton Subotsky; d, Stephen Weeks; w, Subotsky; ph, Moray Grant.

Horror **(PR:C MPAA:PG)**

I NEVER PROMISED YOU A ROSE GARDEN*** 1/2 (1977) 96m Imorh/New World c

Bibi Andersson *(Dr. Fried)*, Kathleen Quinlan *(Deborah Blake)*, Ben Piazza *(Mr. Blake)*, Lorraine Gary *(Mrs. Blake)*, Darlene Craviotto *(Carla)*, Reni Santoni *(Hobbs)*, Susan Tyrrell *(Lee)*, Signe Hasso *(Helene)*, Norman Alden *(McPherson)*, Martine Bartlett *(Secret Wife of Henry VIII)*, Robert Viharo *(Anterrabae)*, Jeff Conaway *(Lactamaeon)*, Dick Herd *(Dr. Halle)*, Sarah Cunningham *(Mrs. Forbes)*, June C. Ellis *(The Spy)*, Diane Varsi *(Sylvia)*, Mary Carver *(Eugenia)*, Barbara Steele *(Idat)*, Donald Bishop *(Doctor in Ward D)*, Samantha Harper *(Teacher in Ward D)*, Dolores Quentin *(Receptionist)*, Pamela Seaman *(Student Nurse)*, Cynthia Szigetti, Carol Androsky, Elizabeth Dartmoor, Cherry Davis *(Nurses in Ward D)*, Lynn Stewart, Carol Worthington, Margo Burdichevsky, Gertrude Granor, Helen Verbit, Jan Burrell, Irene Roseen, Nancy Parsons, Leigh Curran *(Women in Ward D)*, Patricia Singer *(Kathryn)*, Sylvia Sidney *(Miss Coral)*.

An excellent drama about the terrors of schizophrenia, I NEVER PROMISED YOU A ROSE GARDEN is almost, but not quite, the distaff version of ONE FLEW OVER THE CUCKOO'S NEST. Quinlan is a certified mental case who is taken to what appears to be a new and tranquil hospital by her parents, Gary and Piazza. Where the similarity between this and CUCKOO'S NEST ends is in the fact that most of the patients in that one are only mildly afflicted and the ward becomes a microcosm of society. In ROSE GARDEN, there is no question of the horrors taking place inside the brains of the inmates. Quinlan is counseled by Andersson, her psychiatrist, and the bulk of the film deals with exorcising the various demons inside Quinlan. The film falls short in the simplistic analysis of Quinlan's problem although, thank heaven, we don't see that "instant cure" so popular on television. We never know much about her interaction with her family except for a brief indication of some resentment toward her brother. The byplay between Quinlan and Andersson is what distinguishes this film and puts it into a Bergman mold (without aping the great Swede) and keeps our interest high. Some casting sidelights include 1930s star Sidney as a patient who opts to come back to the hospital after being released; Signe Hasso (who made her name playing what everyone thought was a man in THE HOUSE ON 92ND STREET); horror-film star Steele and Conaway, who was later to become popular on TV's "Taxi." Quinlan's mother is Gary (you saw her in JAWS and JAWS II) who is an excellent actress and who has kept her private life as separate as she could, never using the nepotism aspect. She is married to the chief executive at Universal Studios, Sid Sheinberg, and usually works away from that studio. A good actress and getting better with each film. Before schlockmeister Roger Corman sold New World, he had attempted to upgrade the company by distributing some important foreign pictures and making some good domestic films.

p, Terence F. Deane, Michael Hausman, Daniel H. Blatt; d, Anthony Page; w, Lewis John Carlino, Gavin Lambert (based on the novel by Joanne Greenberg); ph, Bruce Logan (Technicolor); m, Paul Chihara; ed, Garth Craven; prod d, Toby Rafelson; cos, Jane Ruhm.

Drama **Cas.** **(PR:O MPAA:R)**

I NEVER SANG FOR MY FATHER*** 1/2 (1970) 92m COL c

Melvyn Douglas *(Tom Garrison)*, Gene Hackman *(Gene Garrison)*, Dorothy Stickney *(Margaret Garrison)*, Estelle Parsons *(Alice)*, Elizabeth Hubbard *(Peggy)*, Lovelady Powell *(Norma)*, Daniel Keyes *(Dr. Mayberry)*, Conrad Bain *(Rev. Pell)*, Jon Richards *(Marvin Scott)*, Nikki Counselman *(Waitress)*, Carol Peterson *(1st Nurse)*, Sloane Shelton *(2nd Nurse)*, James Karen *(Mr. Tucker, Old Age Home Director)*, Gene Williams *(Dr. Jensen, State Hospital Director)*, Jean Dexter *(Hostess)*, Beverly Penberthy *(Special Nurse)*, Valerie Ogden *(3rd Nurse)*.

This was a frustrating film because what was good about it was memorable and what was bad detracted from what was good. Based on Robert Anderson's stage play (which opened in January, 1968, ran 124 performances, and lost the entire $200,000 investment), it's the familiar tale of estrangement between father and son. Hackman is a fortyish New York professor who tells his aging parents, Douglas and Stickney, that he is planning to change his life by marrying Hubbard, a divorced doctor, then moving cross-country to California. Stickney understands Hackman's need to break away (at his advanced age) but warns him that moving that far away may have a deleterious effect on Douglas. Just before the wedding, Stickney dies of heart failure. Parsons is Hackman's sister and she has been disowned by Douglas for marrying a Jewish man. While at the funeral of their mother, Parsons tells Hackman that he cannot allow himself to be manipulated by the old man and that he must make his life for himself. Hackman introduces Douglas to Hubbard and they both ask him to accompany them to California. Douglas is adamant to the end, tells them he'll have none of that. Hackman shrugs, realizes that the time has come to say goodbye, and exits, leaving Douglas awash in his own bitterness. The film betrays its stage origins but Cates does fairly well in keeping the action moving, though slightly confined. Douglas is excellent as the domineering father who has unrealistic expectations for his son. Douglas, Hackman, and Anderson all received Oscar nominations. It was only a few years later that Bain became a television star and was seen by more people on one show than all of the audiences that went to see I NEVER SANG FOR MY FATHER. The play had been produced on Broadway by Cates and Doris Warner Vidor (now *there* are two famous film names) and directed by Alan Schneider. A very touching movie.

p&d, Gilbert Cates; w, Robert W. Anderson (based on his play); ph, Morris Hartzband, George Stoetzel (Technicolor); m, Barry Mann, Al Gorgoni; ed, Angelo Ross; art d, Hank Aldrich; cos, Theoni V. Aldredge; m/l, "Strangers," Mann, Cynthia Weil (sung by Roy Clark).

Drama **(PR:A-C MPAA:GP)**

I NUOVI MOSTRI (SEE: VIVA ITALIA, 1978, Ital.)

I ONLY ASKED!*** (1958, Brit.) 82m Hammer-Granada/COL bw

Michael Medwin *(Cpl. Springer)*, Bernard Bresslaw *(Popeye Poppiewell)*, Alfie Bass *(Excused Boots Bisley)*, Geoffrey Sumner *(Maj. Upshott-Bagley)*, Charles Hawtrey *(Professor)*, Norman Rossington *(Cupcake Cook)*, David Lodge *(Sgt. Potty Chambers)*, Michael Bentine *(Fred)*, Arthur Howard *(Sir Redvers)*, Francis Matthews *(Mahmoud)*, Marne Maitland *(King Fazim)*, Marie Devereux *(Harem Girl)*, Ewen McDuff *(Ferrers)*, Michael Ripper *(Azim)*, Wolf Morris *(Salaman)*, Martin Boddey.

A bumbling British army squad is sent to a Middle East country to help prevent a revolution. The governor of the country was expecting a crack regiment and gets an officer, a sergant major, a corporal, and four privates. The soldiers hook up with some harem girls and together they stop the revolution and find oil. An enjoyable British slapstick comedy.

p, Anthony Hinds; d, Montgomery Tully; w, Sid Colin, Jack Davies (based on a TV series "The Army Game" by Colin); ph, Lionel Banes; m, Benjamin Frankel; ed, Alfred Cox.

Comedy **(PR:A MPAA:NR)**

I OUGHT TO BE IN PICTURES*** 1/2 (1982) 108m FOX c

Walter Matthau *(Herbert Tucker)*, Ann-Margret *(Stephanie)*, Dinah Manoff *(Libby)*, Lance Guest *(Gordon)*, Lewis Smith *(Soldier)*, Martin Ferrero *(Monte Del Rey)*, Eugene Butler *(Marty)*, Samantha Harper *(Larane)*, Santos Morales *(Mexican Truck Driver)*, David Faustino *(Martin)*, Shelby Balik *(Shelley)*, Bill Cross *(Truck Driver)*, Virginia Wing *(Auto Cashier)*, Larry Barton *(Harry)*, Michael Dudikoff *(Boy on the Bus)*, Gillian Farrell *(Waitress)*, Jose Rabelo, Norberto Kerner *(Groundskeepers)*, Calvin Ander *(Rabbi)*, Muni Zano *(Motel Cashier)*, Allan Graf, Art LaFleur, Nomi Mitty, Charles Parks, Wayne Woodson, Tom Wright *(Baseball Fans)*.

With each successive play, and picture, Neil Simon continues to expand. Not satisfied with a barrage of one-liners, he has begun to examine more serious themes, showing us how to laugh and cry at the same time. Manoff (daughter of playwright Arnold Manoff and Actress Lee Grant) is a 19-year-old Brooklynite who hitches a ride to Los Angeles. It would seem that she's doing it to break into the movies, but the underlying reason is to find her wastrel father, Matthau, who left her, her brother, and her mother 16 years before. Matthau is a failed screenwriter who once had his moment but has now given up the typewriter in favor of gambling and booze. His girl friend is Ann-Margret, in yet another excellent acting job, and while she is pleasant and helpful in the situation between father and daughter, she has her own kids who take up her time. Manoff moves in with Matthau and begins to re-do his life, from his personal appearance to his habits. It is this by-play that forms the crux of the story and while the lines still have Simon's tart wit, there is much more to the film than just gags. After all the insults have been flung, he tugs at your tear ducts for an emotionally satisfying conclusion. Herbert Ross, who also directed the stage play, does well enough with the material, but Simon's films never seem to have the impact they do on stage. Perhaps it's the intimacy of the proscenium that makes them work or the fact that Simon writes for "live audiences" and film directors just can't handle the timing for the screen. Ann-Margret gets better with each film and, after a disastrous early career which included such films as KITTEN WITH A WHIP, THE SWINGER and THE TIGER AND THE PUSSYCAT, she has matured into an excellent actress. Composer Hamlisch also collaborated with Simon on "They're Playing Our Song" for the stage.

p, Herbert Ross, Neil Simon; d, Ross; w, Simon (based on his play); ph, David M. Walsh (DeLuxe Color); m, Marvin Hamlisch; ed, Sidney Levin; prod d, Albert Brenner; cos, Ruth Morley; m/l, Hamlisch, Carole Bayer Sager.

Comedy **Cas.** **(PR:C MPAA:PG)**

I PASSED FOR WHITE** (1960) 91m AA bw

Sonya Wilde *(Bernice Lee/Lila Brownell)*, James Franciscus *(Rick)*, Pat Michon *(Sally)*, Elizabeth Council *(Mrs. Leyton)*, Isabelle Cooley *(Bertha)*, James Lydon *(Jay)*, Thomas Browne Henry *(Dr. Merrett)*, Max Mellinger *(Mr. Gordon)*, Phyllis

Cox *(Nurse)*, Calvin Jackson *(Eddie, in Dance School)*, Temple Hatton *(Eddie, Friend of Bernice)*, Freita Shaw *(Gram)*, Lon Ballantyne *(Chuck)*, Ed Shashe *(Character)*, Ray Kellogg *(Bartender)*, Elizabeth Harrowe *(Woman)*.

A romantic melodrama that raises questions on racial issues, then sweeps them under the rug. Wilde is a black woman whose fair skin enables her to pass for white. She leaves the black community and pretends that she is a white. She discovers that this has a set of problems all its own when she marries Franciscus but doesn't dare tell him her true race. The deception and lies build until Wilde leaves her husband because of the strains put on her and the marriage. A handsome role for Wilde, and she does a top job with it.

p,d&w, Fred M. Wilcox (based on a novel by Mary Hastings Bradley); ph, George Folsey; m, Jerry Irving; ed, George White; ch, Phil Orlando.

Drama **(PR:A MPAA:NR)**

I PROMISE TO PAY**1/2 (1937) 68m COL bw

Chester Morris *(Eddie Lang)*, Leo Carrillo *(Farra)*, Helen Mack *(Mary Lang)*, Thomas Mitchell *(Curtis)*, Thurston Hall *(Hall)*, John Gallaudet *(Al)*, Patsy O'Connor *(Judy)*, Wallis Clark *(Wilson)*, James Flavin *(Seava)*, Edward Keane *(Reardon)*, Harry Woods *(Fats)*, Henry Brandon *(Fancyface)*, Marc Lawrence *(Whitehat)*.

A true Depression-era tearjerker finds Morris wanting to take his wife and children on a vacation—cost, $50. But he only earns $27.50 a week at his office job and has nothing left over to feed the family's wanderlust. So he goes to a loan shark and obtains the money, at an interest rate of 1,000 percent. This is solid mobster juice, of course, so, when he cannot make the payments, thugs go after him and beat him limp. A grand jury hearing finally saves the day, but that's the way it was then, honestly. A nice anti-juice exploitation picture for its time.

p, Myles Connolly; d, D. Ross Lederman; w, Mary McCall, Jr., Lionel Houser; ph, Lucien Ballard; ed, James Sweeney.

Crime Drama **(PR:A MPAA:NR)**

I PROMISE TO PAY, 1962 (SEE: PAYROLL, 1962)

I REMEMBER MAMA**** (1948) 134m RKO bw

Irene Dunne *(Mama)*, Barbara Bel Geddes *(Katrin)*, Oscar Homolka *(Uncle Chris)*, Philip Dorn *(Papa)*, Sir Cedric Hardwicke *(Mr. Hyde)*, Edgar Bergen *(Mr. Thorkelson)*, Rudy Vallee *(Dr. Johnson)*, Barbara O'Neil *(Jessie Brown)*, Florence Bates *(Florence Dana Moorhead)*, Peggy McIntyre *(Christine)*, June Hedin *(Dagmar)*, Steve Brown *(Nels)*, Ellen Corby *(Aunt Trina)*, Hope Landin *(Aunt Jenny)*, Edith Evanson *(Aunt Sigrid)*, Tommy Ivo *(Cousin Arne)*, Lela Bliss, Constance Purdy *(Nurses)*, Stanley Andrews *(Minister)*, Franklyn Farnum *(Man)*, Cleo Ridgley *(Schoolteacher)*, George Atkinson *(Postman)*, Howard Keiser *(Bellboy)*, Ruth Tobey, Alice Kerbert, Peggy McKim, Peggy Kerbert *(Girls)*.

Bel Geddes narrates from her diary the history of her Norwegian family, immigrants living in a large house in San Francisco, shown in flashbacks to record the family's trials, tribulations, and triumphs. At the heartwarming core of the story is central character Dunne, mother and inspiration to all. Dunne is wise and understanding, hardworking but never blind to the emotional needs of her family and boarders. Dorn plays the gentle father and Homolka is the bombastic uncle creating minor havoc by his presence—but he also spreads a humanistic philosophy to family members and the world at large, unsolicited, of course. Dunne is indefatigable as Mamma, keeping the house, setting the standards, and dispensing the meager savings of this turn-of-the-century family, while raising her children—Bel Geddes, Brown, Hedin, and McIntyre, the latter an impish, lovable child who is afflicted by a mastoid condition. A host of colorful characters people the family's episodic adventures, including boarders Hardwicke, an unemployed British actor who reads from his unpublished literary work to amuse the family and whose rent never seems to get paid. Bergen, a neighbor and operator of a funeral parlor, is forever dropping by, as is Vallee, the quirkish doctor treating McIntyre. Regular visitors also include three eccentric aunts, Corby, Landin, and Evanson, who all bring whimsy and unintentional laughter to the high-spirited clan. There is a great deal of appealing warmth and human interest in the film, most of it generated by Dunne in one of the best performances of her career (her Norwegian accent is flawless). Stevens, ever the careful, painstaking helmsman, superbly shows his story in one delicate scene after another. It is all quaint, nostalgic, and certainly magical to watch. Peggy Wood would later appear in the long-running (1946 to 1957) TV series based on this story. The film was expensive, costing more than $3 million to make, and RKO did not initially recoup its investment despite a good box office response. This tender tale began as a series of short autobiographical stories by Kathryn Forbes entitled "Mama's Bank Account." It was later mounted as a major Broadway production by Richard Rodgers and Oscar Hammerstein II, dramatized by John Van Druten. Stevens and Dunne had had many earlier successes at RKO and their return to the studio for this film produced a happy collaboration. The long running time of the film is typical of Stevens' meticulous direction, one where he would linger over each scene, milking out the last drop of wonderful sentiment, as it were.

p, George Stevens, Harriet Parsons; d, Stevens; w, DeWitt Bodeen (based on the play by John Van Druten and novel *Mama's Bank Account* by Kathryn Forbes); ph, Nick Musuraca; m, Roy Webb; ed, Robert Swink, Tholen Gladden; md, C. Bakaleinikoff; art d, Albert S. D'Agostino, Carroll Clark; set d, Darrell Silvera, Emil Kuri; cos, Edward Stevenson, Gile Steele; spec eff, Russell A. Cully, Kenneth Peach; makeup, Gordon Bau.

Drama **Cas.** **(PR:AAA MPAA:NR)**

I RING DOORBELLS*1/2 (1946) 67m PRC bw

Anne Gwynne *(Brooke)*, Robert Shayne *(Dick)*, Roscoe Karns *(Stubby)*, Pierre Watkin *(G.B. Barton)*, Harry Shannon *(Shannon)*, John Eldredge *(Ransome)*, Harry Tyler *(Tippy)*, Doria Caron *(Yvette)*, Jan Wiley *(Helen)*, Joel McGinns *(Clyde)*, Charles Wilson *(The Inspector)*, Hank Patterson *(Mr. Bradley)*, Eugene Stutenroth *(O'Halloran)*, Roy Darmour *(Willie)*.

Shayne is an unsuccessful playwright who goes back to his previous profession, journalism. The publisher sends him on the trail of a gold-digging female out for his son. He flirts with the woman's French maid and gets into the apartment to hide a camera. The woman is murdered and Shayne discovers that he has the crime on film and that the murderer is the paper's drama critic. The obituary page for this newspaper yarn.

p, Martin Mooney; d, Frank Strayer; w, Dick Irving Hyland, Raymond L. Schrock (based on the novel by Russell Birdwell); ph, Benjamin H. Kline; m, Leo Erdody; ed, George McGuire.

Mystery **(PR:A MPAA:NR)**

I SAILED TO TAHITI WITH AN ALL GIRL CREW*

(1969) 95m United National-National Telefilm/WORLD c

Gardner McKay *(Gardner)*, Fred Clark *(Fred)*, Pat Buttram *(Pat)*, Diane McBain *(Liz)*, Richard Denning *(Commodore)*, Edy Williams, Jeanne Ranier, Arlene Charles, Mary O'Brien, Bebe Louie, Duke Kahanamoku International Surfing Champions.

McKay bets sailing pal Clark that with an all-girl crew he can beat him in a race to Tahiti. A purse of $20,000 rides on the outcome, which, due to Clark's sabotage efforts, goes to Clark and his crew. McKay is determined to get even, however, and makes another wager—he'll race him back to the mainland with an all-baboon crew. Clark eagerly accepts, but is humiliated when he learns that the "baboons" are a group of expert Polynesian sailors who double as a musical combo. Pretty corny contretemps on the high seas.

p&d, Richard Bare; w, Bare, Henry Irving (based on a story by Bare, George O'Hanlon); ph, Leonard South, Frederic Gately (DeLuxe Color); m, Philip Springer; ed, John Schreyer; song, "Take Me With You," Kellie Sullivan.

Comedy **(PR:A MPAA:NR)**

I SAW WHAT YOU DID*** (1965) 82m UNIV bw

Joan Crawford *(Amy Nelson)*, John Ireland *(Steve Marak)*, Leif Erickson *(Dave Mannering)*, Sarah Lane *(Kit)*, Andi Garrett *(Libby)*, Sharyl Locke *(Tess)*, Patricia Breslin *(Ellie Mannering)*, John Archer *(John Austin)*, John Crawford *(Trooper)*, Joyce Meadows *(Judith Marak)*, Douglas Evans *(Tom Ward)*, Barbara Wilkins *(Mary Ward)* .

Lane and Garrett are teenage girls who are making prank phone calls one night while baby-sitting. To each caller they say, "I saw what you did. I know who you are." One call is to Ireland, who has just murdered his wife. Ireland's hair goes up; he tries to track down the caller. Crawford, who has a crush on him, drops over and finds his wife's bloody clothing, putting her next in line to die. Sure enough, Ireland tracks down the two girls and Crawford tries to protect them, but goes down with a bread knife in her stomach for her trouble. Ireland rushes over to the girls' house, but they are saved as the police and their parents arrive in time to stop the crazed killer. Pretty thin stuff to hang two murders on, but a menacing atmosphere and Crawford's unique beauty carry it through handily.

p&d, William Castle; w, William P. McGivern (based on the novel *Out of the Dark* by Ursula Curtiss); ph, Joseph Biroc; m, Van Alexander; ed, Edwin H. Bryant; art d, Alexander Golitzen, Walter M. Simonds; set d, John McCarthy, George Milo; dog trainer, Frank Weatherwax.

Suspense **(PR:C-O MPAA:NR)**

I SEE A DARK STRANGER (SEE: ADVENTURESS, THE, 1946)

I SEE ICE**1/2 (1938) 77m ATB/ABF bw

George Formby *(George Bright)*, Kay Walsh *(Judy Gaye)*, Betty Stockfeld *(Mrs. Hunter)*, Cyril Ritchard *(Paul Martine)*, Garry Marsh *(Galloway)*, Frederick Burtwell *(Detective)*, Ernest Sefton *(Outhwaite)*, Gavin Gordon *(Night Club Singer)*, Ernest Jay *(Theater Manager)*, Andreas Malandrinos *(Lotus Club Manager)*, Gordon McLeod *(Lord Feistead)*, Archibald Batty *(Col. Hunter)*, Frank Leighton *(Manager)*, Roddy McDowall, Jack Vyvyan, R. Meadows White, Esma Cannon, Laura Smithson, Dominick Sterlini, Ernest Borrow.

Formby is a property man for an ice ballet troupe who becomes a newspaper photographer through a mixup with a camera he has invented. Wild little comedy with Formby performing uproariously as usual.

p, Basil Dean; d, Anthony Kimmins; w, Kimmins, Austin Melford; ph, Ronald Neame, Gordon Dines.

Comedy **(PR:A MPAA:NR)**

I SELL ANYTHING*1/2 (1934) 70m FN/WB bw

Pat O'Brien *(Spot Cash Cutler)*, Ann Dvorak *(Barbara)*, Claire Dodd *(Millicent Clark)*, Roscoe Karns *(Monk)*, Hobart Cavanaugh *(Stooge)*, Russell Hopton *(Smiley Thompson)*, Robert Barrat *(McPherson)*, Harry Tyler *(2nd Stooge)*, Gus Shy *(3rd Stooge)*, Leonard Carey *(Pertwee)*, Ferdinand Gottschalk *(Barouche)*, Clay Clement *(Peter Van Gruen)*, David Calles *(Half-Witted Customer)*, Milton Kibbee *(Spectator)*, Sherry Hall *(Porter)*, Pudgy White *(Taxi Driver)*, Eddie Schubert *(Truck Driver)*, John Elliott *(Lawyer)*, Herman King *(Dutch Man)*, Arthur Hoyt *(Pedestrian)*.

O'Brien is an auctioneer who is cheated by Dodd who buys an antique for $50.00 that is worth $5,000. Dodd talks O'Brien into working an auction at her boyfriend's home but she pulls another fast one on him by using antiques that are fake. O'Brien sells off an old trunk that Dodd has been keeping her money and goods in. She steals the trunk and takes off with the boyfriend to Europe. O'Brien finally takes his mind off the problem by marrying his faithful gal, Dvorak.

d, Robert Florey; w, Brown Holmes, Sidney Sutherland (based on a story by Albert J. Cohen and Robert T. Shannon); ph, Sid Hickox; ed, Terry Morse; art d, Jack Holden.

Drama **(PR:A MPAA:NR)**

I SENT A LETTER TO MY LOVE*** (1981, Fr.) 112m Atlantic c

Simone Signoret *(Louise)*, Jean Rochefort *(Gilles)*, Delphine Seyrig *(Yvette)*.

A touching performance for Signoret in which she plays an aging woman whose devotion to her brother Rochefort, a paralyzed man requiring almost constant attention, has not allowed her to taste some of the sweeter things in life. A pen pal allows her to express some of these hidden desires, as their correspondence slowly develops into a slight romance. An extremely cunning twist has this unknown and unseen admirer being none other than Signoret's own brother. Slow-moving story is given a poignant and sensitive emphasis through a vivid portrayal of a woman trapped by her loneliness. (In French; English subtitles.)

p, Lise Fayolles, Giorgio Silvagni; d, Moshe Mizrahi; w, Mizrahi, Gerard Brach (based on the novel by Bernice Rubens); ph, Ghislain Cloquet; m, Philippe Sarde; ed, Francoise Bonnot.

Drama **Cas.** **(PR:A MPAA:PG)**

I SHALL RETURN
(SEE: AMERICAN GUERRILLA IN THE PHILIPPINES, AN, 1950)

I SHOT BILLY THE KID*1/2 (1950) 57m Lippert bw

Don Barry *(Billy)*, Robert Lowery *(Garrett)*, Wally Vernon *(Vicenti)*, Tom Neal *(Bowdre)*, Wendy Lee *(Francesca)*, Claude Stroud *(Wallace)*, John Merton *(Ollinger)*, Henry Marco *(Juan)*, Billy Kennedy *(Poe)*, Archie Twitchell *(Grant)*, Jack Perrin *(Man)*, Richard Farmer *(McSween)*, Felice Richmond *(Mrs. McSween)*, Jack Geddes *(Sheriff)*, Tommy Monroe *(Maxwell)*.

Barry plays Billy the Kid, and Lowery the famous lawman on his trail. The Kid tries to follow the straight and narrow path, but killing 21 men in his 22 years makes it a little difficult. He falls in love with Lee, a Mexican girl, but just when the relationship is picking up steam, Lowery shows up and puts a fatal bullet through him.

p&d, William Berke; w, Ford Beebe, Orville Hampton; ph, Ernest Miller; ed, Carl Pierson.

Western **Cas.** **(PR:A MPAA:NR)**

I SHOT JESSE JAMES*** (1949) 81m Lippert/Screen Guild bw

Preston Foster *(John Kelley)*, Barbara Britton *(Cynthy Waters)*, John Ireland *(Bob Ford)*, Reed Hadley *(Jesse James)*, J. Edward Bromberg *(Kane)*, Victor Kilian *(Soapy)*, Barbara Woodell *(Mrs. Zee James)*, Tom Tyler *(Frank James)*, Tom Noonan *(Charles Ford)*, Byron Foulger *(Room Clerk)*, Eddie Dunn *(Bartender)*, Jeni Le Gon *(Maid)*, Robin Short *(Troubadour)*, Phil Pine *(Man in Saloon)*, Gene Collins *(Young Man Who Tries To Kill Bob Ford)*, Margia Dean *(Saloon Singer)*, Chuck Roberson *(Reed Hadley's Double)*.

Fuller's first directorial effort made evident the great talent he possessed as a filmmaker. Ireland plays the man who guns down James, but Fuller avoids the obvious route and concentrates on what compels the man to kill his one-time friend. Ireland has a childhood sweetheart, Britton, whom he hopes to marry by shooting James and obtaining a pardon and reward money. But once Hadley is dead Britton will have nothing to do with Ireland. A stylish western with Fuller using mainly close-ups to tell the story with a script that strips the characters to their emotional base.

p, Carl K. Hittleman; d&w, Samuel Fuller (based on an article by Homer Croy); ph, Ernest Miller; m, Albert Glasser; ed, Paul Landres; art d, Frank Hotaling; set d, John McCarthy, James Redd.

Western **(PR:A MPAA:NR)**

I SPIT ON YOUR GRAVE*
(1962, Fr.) 100m C.T.I.-S.I.P.R.O./Audubon bw (J'IRAL CRACHER SUR VOS TOMBES)

Christian Marquand *(Joe Grant)*, Antonella Lualdi *(Lizabeth Shannon)*, Paul Guers *(Stan Walker)*, Renate Ewert *(Sylvia Shannon)*, Jean Sorel *(Elmer)*, Fernand Ledoux *(Chandley)*, Daniel Cauchy *(Don)*, Marina Petrowa *(Sheila)*, Jean Droze *(Ted)*, Andre Versini, Catherine Fontenay, Lud Germain, Gisele Gallois, Monique Just, Marie-Blanche Vergnes, Claude Berri, Christian Boisseau.

After his brother is lynched for trying to marry a white woman, Marquand, a light-skinned black, moves from Memphis to a small southern town. There he passes for white and gets a job in a bookstore, which he later finds is involved in a blackmail ring. To avenge his brother's death, he seduces Lualdi, a wealthy white girl, and then plans to kill her. Instead the two fall in love, and Lualdi—who discovers Marquand is black—offers to run away with him when the blackmail ring assaults him for not cooperating with them. Her fiance, Guers, organizes a man-hunt for the two, purporting that Marquand intends to rape Lualdi, and the lovers are gunned down by police while attempting to cross the Mason-Dixon Line.

d, Michel Gast; w, Boris Vians, Jacques Dopagne (based on a story by Vians); ph, Marc Fossard, Paul Rodier; m, Alain Goraguer; ed, Eliane Bensdorp; set d, Robert Bouladoux.

Drama **(PR:O MPAA:NR)**

I SPIT ON YOUR GRAVE zero
(1983) 100m Cinemagic Pictures c (AKA: DAY OF THE WOMAN)

Camille Keaton *(Jennifer)*, Eron Tabor *(Johnny)*, Richard Pace *(Matthew)*, Gunter Kleeman *(Andy)*, Alexis Magnotti *(Attendant's Wife)*, Tammy Zarchi, Terry Zarchi *(Children)*, Traci Ferrante *(Waitress)*, Bill Tasgal *(Porter)*, Isac Agami *(Butcher)*, Ronit Haviv *(Supermarket Girl)*.

After being repeatedly raped by the same group of men at a vacation retreat, Keaton goes on a terrifying rampage, systematically killing each one off. The gore and violence has been strong in other films, but never has a film been so irresponsible with handling and presenting it, making it totally repugnant.

p, Joseph Zbeda; d&w, Meir Zarchi; ph, Yuri Haviv (Eastmancolor); ed, Zarchi.

Terror **Cas.** **(PR:O MPAA:R)**

I SPY*1/2 (1933, Brit.) 69m British International/Wardour bw

Sally Eilers *(Thelma Coldwater)*, Ben Lyon *(Wally Sawyer)*, Harry Tate *(George)*, H.F. Maltby *(Herr Doktor)*, Harold Warrender *(NBG)*, Andrews Engelmann *(CO)*, Dennis Hoey *(MNT)*, Henry Victor *(KPO)*, Marcelle Rogez *(Girl)*.

Lyon is an American who mistakenly tells taxi driver Tate the wrong apartment to go to and the apartment's owner mistakes the American for one of his spies. The owner is part of a spy ring trying to overthrow a small monarchy. Lyon is sent to frame a countess by planting papers on her which will cause her execution. The countess turns out to be an American actress, Eilers. There are some twists and double-crosses, with some situations almost slapstick, but finally the two Americans escape to bring a happy ending.

p, Walter Mycroft; d, Allan Dwan; w, Dwan, Arthur Woods (based on a story by Fred Thompson); ph, James Wilson.

Spy Drama **(PR:A MPAA:NR)**

I SPY, YOU SPY (SEE: BANG, BANG, YOU'RE DEAD, 1966, Brit.)

I STAND ACCUSED** (1938) 63m REP bw

Robert Cummings *(Fred)*, Helen Mack *(Alison)*, Lyle Talbot *(Eastman)*, Thomas Beck *(Paul)*, Gordon Jones *(Blackie)*, Robert Paige *(Joe Gilman)*, Leona Roberts *(Mrs. Davis)*, Robert Middlemass *(Mitchell)*, Thomas E. Jackson *(Gilroy)*, John Hamilton *(Brower)*, Howard Hickman *(Gilbert)*, Harry Stubbs *(Mr. Moss)*, Robert Strange *(Ryan)*.

Cummings and Talbot, fresh out of law school, open their own law practice. Cummings wants to become successful by any means, and gets involved with helping a killer who works for the mob. Cummings becomes the gangster's mouthpiece, grows wealthy, and soon separates himself from his wife, family, and partner. In the meantime, Talbot becomes assistant D.A. and is pitted against his former partner. Talbot loses case after case until Cummings comes in his office and gives enough evidence to blow open the rackets.

p&d, John H. Auer; w, Gordon Kahn, Alex Gottlieb; ph, Jack Marta; ed, Ernest Nims; md, Cy Feuer; art d, John Victor Mackay.

Crime Drama **(PR:A MPAA:NR)**

I STAND CONDEMNED**
(1936, Brit.) 76m LFP/UA bw (GB. MOSCOW NIGHTS)

Harry Baur *(Brioukow)*, Laurence Olivier *(Capt. Ignatoff)*, Penelope Dudley Ward *(Natasha)*, Robert Cochran *(Polonsky)*, Morton Selten *(Kovrin)*, Athene Seyler *(Mme. Sabline)*, Kate Cutler *(Mme. Kovrin)*, Walter Hudd *(Doctor)*, C.M. Hallard *(President of Court Martial)*, Edmund Willard *(Prosecution)*, Charles Carson *(Defence)*, Morland Graham *(Servant)*, Hay Petrie *(Spy)*, Richard Webster *(2nd Servant)*.

A Russian soldier, Olivier, falls in love with a nurse, Ward, but she's engaged to war profiteer Baur. The profiteer cleans the soldier out in a game of cards and Olivier gets involved with spies. He's caught and is tried for treason, and the only person who can clear his name is Baur, who hates him. Ward convinces Baur to help by promising to marry him, and the old man takes the stand and prevents Olivier's execution. Remake of the French film NUITS MOSCOVITES made in 1934.

p, Alexander Korda, Alexis Granowsky, Max Schach; d, Anthony Asquith; w, Asquith, Erich Seipmann (based on the novel *Les Nuits De Moscou* by Pierre Benoit); ph, Philip Tannura; ed, Francis Lyon; md, Muir Mathieson; set d, Vincent Korda; cos, John Armstrong.

Drama **Cas.** **(PR:A MPAA:NR)**

I START COUNTING** (1970, Brit.) 105m UA c

Jenny Agutter *(Wynne)*, Bryan Marshall *(George)*, Clare Sutcliffe *(Corinne)*, Simon Ward *(Conductor)*, Gregory Phillips *(Len)*, Lana Morris *(Leonie)*, Billy Russell *(Granddad)*, Madge Ryan *(Mother)*, Fay Compton *(Mrs. Bennett)*, Lally Bowers *(Aunt Rene)*, Michael Feast *(Jim)*, Charles Lloyd Pack *(Priest at School)*, Lewis Fiander *(Priest at Church)*, Gordon Richardson *(Tramp)*.

A forerunner of the teenage slasher pictures of the late 1970s and 1980s has some substance beyond the usual sexual titilation and chiller type aspects. Agutter is the English country girl with an insurmountable crush on Marshall, the brother in the family into which she has been adopted. This never falters, even when the bizarre sex murders which have been plaguing the countryside all point to Marshall as the culprit. A trek to the woods by Agutter and her girl friend, who constantly tries to make off as being a real sexpot, makes them ample prey for the fiendish killer. Agutter eventually proves her brother's innocence, but not before her friend is raped and murdered by the psychopath. Though some of the situations are forced and a bit far fetched, I START COUNTING is pretty provocative in the manner in which it treats a teenager's fascination with sex, and how infatuations are formed.

p, Stanley Jaffe, David Greene; d, Greene; w, Richard Harris (based on the novel by Audrey Erskine Lindop); ph, Alex Thomson (DeLuxe Color); m, Basil Kirchin; ed, Keith Palmer; prod d, Brian Eatwell; art d, Arnold Chapkis; cos, Sandy Moss.

Crime/Drama **(PR:O MPAA:NR)**

I STOLE A MILLION*** (1939) 76m UNIV bw

George Raft *(Joe Laurik/"Harris")*, Claire Trevor *(Laura Benson)*, Dick Foran *(Paul Carver)*, Henry Armetta *(Nick Respino)*, Victor Jory *(Patton)*, Joseph Sawyer *(Billings)*, Robert Elliott *(Paterson)*, Stanley Ridges *(George Downs)*, Irving Bacon *(Simpson)*, Jerry Marlowe *(Photographer)*, Edmund MacDonald, Dick Wessel, Emory Parnell *(Cops)*, Ben Taggart *(Police Captain)*, Tom Fadden *(Verne)*, John Hamilton *(District Attorney Wilson)*, Wallis Clark *(Jenkins)*, Hobart Cavanaugh, Billy Engle *(Bookkeepers)*, Sarah Padden *(Lady in Post Office)*, Arthur Q. Bryan, Henry Roquemore *(Managers)*, Emmett Vogan, Charles Irwin *(Theater Managers)*, Dick Elliott *(Small Town Doctor)*, Harry Tyler *(Kibitzer)*, Harold Minjir *(Jewelry Salesman)*, Hal K. Dawson, J. Anthony Hughes, Mack Gray, Harry B. Stafford, Ed Fliegl *(Men)*, George Chandler *(Clerk in Clothing Store)*, Mira McKinney *(Mrs. Loomis)*, Virginia Brissac, Mary MacLaren *(Nurses)*, Margaret McWade, Dot Farley *(Women)*, Phil Tead *(Charlie)*, John Butler *(Logan, the Cab Manager)*, Eddie Dunn *(Superintendent)*, Al Hill *(Guard)*, John Berkes *(Tramp)*, William Ruhl *(Detective)*, James Farley *(Doorman)*, Malcolm McTaggart, Jack Gardner, Drew Demarest *(Reporters)*, Harry Bradley *(Sexton)*, Betty Roadman, Mary Foy, Claire Whitney *(Matrons)*, Frances Morris *(Prisoner)*, Ernie Adams *(The Mooch)*, Billy Wayne *(Mild Cabby)*, Raymond Bailey, Sammy Finn *(Cabbies)*, Landers Stevens *(Businessman)*, Ralph Dunn *(Bartender)*, Joey Ray *(Clerk)*, Larry McGrath *(Gas Station Attendant)*, Jason Robards *(Bank Teller)*, Russ Powell *(Watchman)*, Charles Sullivan *(Gas Station Helper)*, Jimmy O'Gatty *(Mug)*, Harold Hoff *(Garage Attendant)*, Ed Peil, Sr. *(Doorman)*, Mike Lally *(Croupier)*, Constantine Romanoff *(Wrestler)*, Lee Murray *(Jockey)*, Dave Sharpe *(Cabby/George Raft's Double)*, Tom Steele *(Cop)*, Eddy Chandler *(Baggage Car Guard)*, Frances Robinson *(Elsie, The Movie Cashier)*, Lee Ford *(Usher)*, Art Yeoman *(Telegrapher)*.

Raft is a tough cab driver who has his life savings stolen by a phony finance company. Getting no cooperation from the police, he turns to crime and becomes a wanted man. He flees to California where he meets Trevor who drops her lawyer boy friend, Foran, to marry Raft. She helps him get set up as a legitimate garage owner and when she becomes pregant she talks Raft into clearing his name with the police. He goes along with this but first goes out on a robbing spree so his wife and baby will be provided for while he's in prison. He pulls off a million dollar caper but the money is worthless and he dies in a police shoot-out. This film, to a lesser degree than HIGH SIERRA (1941), indicated where the film criminal hero was heading; the dark corners of film noir.

p, Burt Kelly; d, Frank Tuttle; w, Nathanael West (based on a story by Lester Cole); ph, Milton Krasner; ed, Edward Curtis.

Crime Drama **(PR:A MPAA:NR)**

I SURRENDER DEAR*1/2 (1948) 67m COL bw

Gloria Jean *(Patty Nelson)*, David Street *(Al Tyler)*, Don McGuire *(Tommy Tompkins)*, Alice Tyrrell *(Trudy Clements)*, Robert Emmett Keane *(Russ Nelson)*, Douglas Wood *(R.H. Collins)*, Regina Wallace *(Mrs. Nelson)*, Byron Foulger *(George Rogers)*, Jack Eigen, Dave Garroway, Peter Potter *(Disc Jockeys)*, The Novelites.

Street is a band-leader who decides to become a disc jockey. Jean is his girlfriend and it's her father whom Street bumps for the radio job. The problems this causes make up the thin story line. Songs include, "Amado Mio," "How Can You Tell?", (Allan Roberts, Doris Fisher), "I Surrender Dear" (Harry Barris, Gordon Clifford), "When You are In the Room" (Oscar Hammerstein II, Ben Oakland), "Nobody Else But Elsie" (Allie Wrubel), and the title song.

p, Sam Katzman; d, Arthur Dreifuss; w, M. Coates Webster; ph, Vincent Farrar; ed, Richard Fantl; md, Paul Mertz; art d, Paul Palmentola.

Musical **(PR:A MPAA:NR)**

I TAKE THIS OATH* (1940) 64m PRC bw

Gordon Jones *(Steve Hannigan)*, Joyce Compton *(Betty Casey)*, Craig Reynolds *(Joe Kelly)*, J. Farrell MacDonald *(Inspector Ryan)*, Robert E. Homans *(Mike Hannigan)*, Guy Usher *(Capt. Casey)*, Mary Gordon *(Mrs. Hannigan)*, Sam Flint *(Uncle Jim Kelly)*, Brooks Benedict *(Burly)*, Veda Ann Borg *(Flo)*, Eddie Piel, Sr. *(Riley)*, Budd Buster *(Jones)*.

A dismal crime movie with a story that is rotting from overuse. Jones is a policeman who is told by Reynolds that his uncle is a wanted crime boss. The uncle is also responsible for the death of Jones' partner. In the end Reynolds saves the cop's life and is killed in the process.

p, Sigmund Neufeld; d, Sherman Scott; w, George Bricker (based on a story by William A. Ullman, Jr.); ph, Jack Greenhalgh; ed, Holbrook Todd; md, David Chudnow.

Crime Drama **(PR:A MPAA:NR)**

I TAKE THIS WOMAN** (1931) 74m PAR bw

Gary Cooper *(Tom McNair)*, Carole Lombard *(Kay Dowling)*, Helen Ware *(Aunt Bessie)*, Lester Vail *(Herbert Forrest)*, Charles Trowbridge *(Mr. Dowling)*, Clara Blandick *(Sue Barnes)*, Gerald Fielding *(Bill Wentworth)*, Albert Hart *(Jake Mallory)*, Guy Oliver *(Sid)*, Syd Saylor *(Shorty)*, Mildred Van Dorn *(Clara Hammell)*, Leslie Palmer *(Phillips)*, Ara Haswell *(Nora)*, Frank Darien *(The Station Agent)*, David Landau *(Circus Ross)*, Lew Kelly *(Foreman)*.

This plot was already old in 1931. Lombard (who replaced Fay Wray before shooting began) is a rich, bored heiress from New York who has to leave the city rather than face embarrassment due to what would today be a very innocent incident. Trowbridge, her conservative father, orders her to the family ranch in Wyoming. Once there, she meets cowboy-ranch hand Cooper (a character as obstinate as Glenn Ford in THE SHEEP MAN), who refuses to kowtow to her high-falutin' ways, and the more he backs off, the more she comes on. Eventually, they marry but his heart isn't in it, and she regards Cooper as almost a plaything, rather than a husband. Trowbridge is livid at the union as he wanted her to marry Vail, a dull New Yorker. Lombard and Cooper attempt to make a commercial go of ranching but she eventually leaves him and returns to Trowbridge in New York after a year. Cooper follows her and is astounded to see how wealthy she is. Once he realizes that they are so far apart in backgrounds and culture, he agrees to the divorce she's asked for. Lombard has second thoughts about it now and trails Cooper to his new employment. He's doing a cowboy act (not unlike Clint Eastwood's BRONCO BILLY) in a circus, and when she approaches him, he scorns her, not wanting to be dangled at the end of her fickle string, and fearing being hurt again. When he's thrown from his horse in an accident, she races to his side. He is told that he will never be able to ride again, but it doesn't matter anymore as Lombard is there to comfort him forever. This could have been a lovely comedy in someone else's hands, but it wallows in a morass of melodrama. The most interesting facet is the two very different styles of Cooper and Lombard as they weave in and out of the scenes. Talkies had been invented just four years previously, and the sound on this film left much to be desired.

d, Marion Gering; w, Vincent Lawrence (based on the novel *Lost Ecstasy* by Mary Roberts Rinehart); ph, Victor Milner; cos, Travis Banton.

Drama **(PR:A MPAA:NR)**

I TAKE THIS WOMAN*1/2 (1940) 96m MGM bw

Spencer Tracy *(Karl Decker)*, Hedy Lamarr *(Georgi Gragore)*, Verree Teasdale *(Mme. Maresca)*, Kent Taylor *(Phil Mayberry)*, Mona Barrie *(Sandra Mayberry)*, Paul Cavanagh *(Bill Rodgers)*, Jack Carson *(Joe)*, Louis Calhern *(Dr. Duveen)*, Laraine Day *(Linda Rodgers)*, Reed Hadley *(Bob Hampton)*, Frances Drake *(Lola Estermonte)*, Marjorie Main *(Gertie)*, George E. Stone *(Katz)*, Willie Best *(Sambo)*, Leon Belasco *(Pancho)*, Don Castle *(Ted Fenton)*, Charles Trowbridge *(Dr. Morris)*, Charles D. Brown *(Lieutenant of Police)*, Gayne Whitman *(Dr. Phelps)*, John Shelton, Tom Collins *(Interns)*, Florence Shirley *(Mrs. Bettincourt)*, Rafael Storm *(Raoul Cedro)*, Natalie Moorhead *(Saleslady)*, Syd Saylor *(Taxi Driver)*, David Clyde *(Steward)*, Nell Craig *(Nurse on Boat)*, Lee Phelps *(Policeman)*, Matt McHugh, Polly Bailey, George Humbert, Rosina Galli, Esther Michelson *(People at Clinic)*, Peggy Leon *(Georgi's Maid)*, Edward Keane *(Dr. Harrison)*, Jack Chefe *(Waiter)*, Jean De Briac *(Headwaiter)*, Florence Wix *(Mrs. Winterhalter)*, Jimmie Lucas *(Taxi Driver)*, Charles Sherlock *(Steward)*, William Cartledge *(Newsboy)*, Dalies Frantz *(Joe Barnes)*, Lowden Adams *(Butler)*.

The back-set machinations of this movie were far more exciting than the movie itself. Louis B. Mayer was determined to make Lamarr a huge star in MGM's firmament and he interfered so much with the shooting that two directors left, thousands of feet were thrown out and the joke around town was that it should have been called "I Re-Take This Woman" because of all the extra shooting that transpired. Tracy was irate when he saw that his talents were being used to beef up Lamarr's career, but sat still for it and fumed. The movie changed directions several times as many writers played with the original MacArthur story. Some of the actors who worked on the film, but were left on the cutting room floor, were Walter Pidgeon, Ina Claire and Adrienne Ames. The story, for what it's worth, sees Tracy, a doctor returning to the U.S. after a research stint in Europe, saving Lamarr's life as she attempts to dive off the ocean liner on which both are sailing. The reason is that she is disappointed in love. Her amour, Taylor, had promised to divorce his wife, Barrie, and marry her. When that didn't happen, he went back to the U.S. and she decided to drown her sorrows and herself. Tracy is attracted to her and suggests she forget about her position in the fashion industry and come to work for him in research. This she does and they are soon side by side in a slum clinic. Tracy goes head over heels for Lamarr, proposes marriage, and she accepts. He immediately quits his altruistic calling in order to provide Lamarr with all of life's frills and becomes a physician for the upper crust. Despite all of Tracy's adoration, Lamarr can't get Taylor out of her heart or mind. She makes a surreptitious visit to Taylor and learns, to her amazement and relief, that the thrill is gone and she can return to Tracy, loving him completely. She intends to go on a second honeymoon with him but that's torpedoed when Tracy learns she went to see her old flame. He is hurt and jealous and makes plans to divorce Lamarr. Tracy is later called to the hospital and finds that a young resident has bollixed up a case and his career may be over before it's begun. Tracy is so depressed by what's happened in his domestic life that he claims responsibility for the medical error, thus getting the intern off the hook. Now he arrives at the clinic to say farewell to all his old associates and is surprised to see Lamarr working there. Good news arrives when Tracy hears that the error at the hospital was not nearly as difficult as had been imagined and the whole matter has been taken care of. Tracy realizes that the society life never was right for him so he and Lamarr kiss and decide to remain at the clinic where they both feel they belong. The movie began with von Sternberg at the helm, but he marched out when Mayer kept sticking his nose into matters. Borzage followed for a while, but he left and only a few feet of his work remain. Van Dyke, who always seemed to be able to rescue failing projects, entered and completed the movie, but 18 months had already passed and the production was well over budget and never did recoup the cost.

p, Bernard H. Hyman, Lawrence Weingarten (uncredited); d, W.S. Van Dyke (Josef von Sternberg, Frank Borzage are uncredited); w, James Kevin McGuiness (based on the story by Charles MacArthur); ph, Harold Rosson; m, Bronislau Kaper, Arthur Guttman; ed, George Boemler; art d, Cedric Gibbons, Paul Groesse; cos, Adrian.

Drama **(PR:A MPAA:NR)**

I THANK A FOOL** (1962, Brit.) 100m MGM c

Susan Hayward *(Christine Allison)*, Peter Finch *(Stephen Dane)*, Diane Cilento *(Liane Dane)*, Cyril Cusack *(Capt. Ferris)*, Kieron Moore *(Roscoe)*, Athene Seyler *(Aunt Heather)*, Richard Wattis *(Ebblington)*, Brenda De Banzie *(Nurse Drew)*, Miriam Karlin *(Woman in the Black Maria)*, Laurence Naismith *(O'Grady)*, Clive Morton *(Judge)*, J. G. Devlin *(Coroner)*, Richard Leech *(Irish Doctor)*, Yolande Turner *(Polly)*, Edwin Apps *(Junior Counsel)*, Marguerite Brennan *(Irish Barmaid)*, Judith Furse *(Wardress)*, Grace Arnold *(2nd Wardress)*, Peter Sallis *(Sleazy Doctor)*, Joan Benham *(Restaurant Manageress)*, Joan Hickson *(Landlady)*.

The moral decision of helping a terminally ill person to die has been debated in the courts several times with many different results. In this film, Hayward is a Canadian physician who follows her married lover across the sea to England. He pleads with her to help him die and she injects him with an overdose of morphine. She is immediately arrested and tried by Finch, the prosecuting attorney, who is eager to make a name for himself and thinks that this case will do it. Consequently, he goes after her viciously and secures a manslaughter conviction and a two year prison term for Hayward. When she is released, she is no longer allowed to practice medicine, the only job she's ever had. She's alone and broke when she gets an intriguing proposition: an anonymous person wishes her to come to a house in the country for a position that might be to her advantage. Once there, she learns that her prospective employer is Finch, whose wife, Cilento, has been mentally ill ever since her father was accidentally killed. Finch asks Hayward to tend Cilento. Having no other hope of a job, Hayward accepts. But all is not what it seems and soon Cilento's father, Cusack, shows up very much alive. Hayward realizes there are some sort of shenanigans going on. She is genuinely fond of her ward and takes her to what Cilento has described as a "mansion," the old family estate in Ireland. It turns out to be a ramshackle house in the fishing village of Crookhaven, in County Cork, Ireland (and it really was, for that's where they shot all the locations). Cilento admits that there was a scheme to prove her father dead. Cusack is an old reprobate and conniver and Cilento now has a real mental breakdown. With a doctor to advise her, Hayward administers a mild sedative to Cilento to calm her. Later, Cilento is found dead and Hayward realizes this is one large frame-up, and suspects Finch. At the coroner's inquest, Finch appears to be defending her against coroner Devlin's questions, but Hayward can't trust a man who has already put her in jail once. Then Cusack is questioned and we find that Cilento had taken a pill overdose herself and when her body was found by Cusack, he hid the bottle. After his dramatic confession on the stand, Cusack tries to escape the hearing room, but falls to his death, and none too soon. Finch is now looking at Hayward in a slightly different light. She's innocent and he's free of a blonde millstone who used to hang around his neck. The film ends with just an inkling that perhaps the two may find some common interests and could possibly wind up as a duo. Hayward and director Stevens clashed repeatedly on the script which the actress disliked, thought weak, and generally treated with contempt, although her usual flamboyant posture improves the anemic production. The volatile actress also had little use for Finch whose most dynamic response to her charms was little more than a torporous stare. The whole thing limped into theaters which produced little box office response.

p, Anatole De Grunwald; d, Robert Stevens; w, Karl Tunberg (based on the novel by Audrey Erskine Lindop); ph, Harry Waxman (CinemaScope, Metrocolor); m, Ron Goodwin; ed, Frank Clarke; prod d, Sean Kenny; Md, Goodwin; Kenny; set d, Pamela Cornell; cos, Elizabeth Haffenden; spec eff, Tom Howard.

Drama **(PR:A-C MPAA:NR)**

I THANK YOU** (1941, Brit.) 81m Gainsborough/GFD bw

Arthur Askey *(Arthur)*, Richard Murdoch *(Stinker)*, Lily Morris *(Lady Randall)*, Moore Marriott *(Pop Bennett)*, Graham Moffatt *(Albert)*, Peter Gawthorne *(Dr. Pope)*, Kathleen Harrison *(Cook)*, Felix Aylmer *(Henry Potter)*, Cameron Hall *(Lomas)*, Wally Patch *(Bill)*, Issy Bonn, Forsythe, Seamon and Farrell.

Askey and Murdoch star in this slapstick tale about a pair of performers who try to raise enough money to put on a dazzling stage show. They resort to becoming servants in the home of a society woman who was previously a star performer. After convincing her to be in the show, it is, of course, a smashing success.

p, Edward Black; d, Marcel Varnel; w, Val Guest, Marriott Edgar (based on a story by Howard Irving Young); ph, Jack Cox, Arthur Crabtree; m, Noel Gay, Frank Eyton.

Comedy **(PR:A MPAA:NR)**

I, THE JURY*** (1953) 87m UA bw

Biff Elliot *(Mike Hammer)*, Preston Foster *(Capt. Pat Chambers)*, Peggie Castle *(Charlotte Manning)*, Margaret Sheridan *(Velda)*, Alan Reed *(George Kalecki)*, Frances Osborne *(Myrna)*, Robert Cunnignham *(Hal Kines)*, Elisha Cook, Jr. *(Bobo)*, Paul Dubov *(Marty)*, Mary Anderson *(Eileen Vickers)*, Tani Seitz *(Mary Bellamy)*, Dran Seitz *(Esther Bellamy)*, Robert Swanger *(Jack Williams)*, John Qualen *(Dr. Vickers)*.

The first film adaptation of Mickey Spillane's trashy bestseller, written and directed by Harry Essex, the screenwriter of two of the best science fiction-horror films of the 1950s—IT CAME FROM OUTER SPACE (1953) and CREATURE FROM THE BLACK LAGOON (1954), both originally released in 3D, as was I, THE JURY. As the film opens we hear "Hark the Herald Angels Sing" playing in the background, establishing that it is Christmas time. The yuletide spirit is shattered by a gunman shrouded in darkness as he brutally shoots Swanger, an amputee, several times. Still alive, Swanger painfully crawls towards his gun. The mysterious killer allows the dying man a chance at the weapon and then finishes him off before he can retaliate. Enter Elliot, a private detective and friend of the victim. Swanger had saved Elliot's life during WW II and now the detective is determined to avenge his savior's death. Warned against breaking the law by police detective Foster, Elliot begins to dig for clues. What he finds is a seedy world populated by junkies, nymphomaniacs, and drug dealers. Elliot swaggers through the sleaze and a number of bodies complicate the case. Along the way the private eye meets a woman psychiatrist, Castle, and falls in love with her. During the investigation they decide to marry. Elliot discovers that the man responsible for Swanger's death is Reed, a former boxing promoter turned art collector who also happens to be the kingpin of a vicious drug racket. Elliot kills the man only to discover that Castle, too, is involved in the narcotics ring and has committed several murders in an effort to wrest control from Reed. Elliot grimly confronts his fiance with the facts, and to placate him, Castle begins to disrobe. She embraces Elliot and as they move to kiss a gunshot is heard. The mortally wounded Castle stumbles backward to reveal that she had been reaching for a hidden gun to kill Elliot with. Dying, Castle looks Elliot in the eyes and asks, "How could you?" He looks at her coldly and responds, "It was easy." The opening and closing scenes of I, THE JURY are stunningly brutal and skillfully executed. The murder of the amputee while "Hark The Herald Angels Sing" plays in the background is profoundly chilling, as is Elliot's "It was easy." Unfortunately, the film's center is weak and suffers from Elliot's feeble performance as Spillane's brutish detective. Audiences would have to wait two years for Ralph Meeker to deliver the definitive Mike Hammer performance in director Robert Aldrich's incredible KISS ME DEADLY.

p, Victor Saville; d, Harry Essex; w, Essex (based on the novel by Mickey Spillane); ph, John Alton; m, Franz Waxman; ed, Frederick Y. Smith; art d, Wiard Ihnen.

Crime **(PR:C–O MPAA:NR)**

I, THE JURY* 1/2 (1982) 109m American Cinema-Larco-Solofilm/FOX c

Armand Assante *(Mike Hammer)*, Barbara Carrera *(Charlotte Bennett)*, Laurence Landon *(Velda)*, Alan King *(Charles Kalecki)*, Geoffrey Lewis *(Joe Butler)*, Paul Sorvino *(Pat Chambers)*, Judson Scott *(Kendricks)*, Barry Snider *(Romero)*, Julia Barr *(Norma Childs)*, Jessica James *(Hilda Kendricks)*, Frederick Downs *(Jack Williams)*, Lee Anne Harris *(1st Twin)*, Lynette Harris *(2nd Twin)*, Mary Margaret Amato, F.J. O'Neil, William Schilling, Robert Sevra, Don Pike, Timothy Myers, Gwynn Gillis, Mike Miller, Alex Stevens, Bobbi Burns, M. Sharon Madigan, Richard Russell Ramos, Norm Blankenship, Daniel Faraldo, H. Richard Greene, Felicity Adler, Jodi Douglas, Lee H. Doyle, Cheryl Henry, Michael Fiorello, Herb Peterson, Richard Dahlia, Aaron Barsky, Ernest Harada, Larry Pine, Joe Farago, Alan Dellay, Jack Davidson, Loring Pickering, Corrinne Bohrer.

Spillane's Mike Hammer novels have been difficult to translate to the screen. With the exception of Robert Aldrich's KISS ME DEADLY, all Hammer films have been disappointments, and this second version of I, THE JURY is no exception. Even with graphic violence and nudity—main ingredients of Spillane's novels—there isn't the foreboding, violent, and urgent atmosphere that exists in the books. The handling is of a cartoon-like quality. Cohen, who wrote the screenplay, was to direct but was fired just before production, and it is obvious that Heffron didn't have a handle on Cohen's screenplay or on Spillane's character. The elements of parody that Cohen put into the script have been pushed back, and Heffron tries for a hard-boiled detective movie but doesn't have the style to breathe life into it. The villains have been up-dated—a crazed slasher with an eye for redheads, a former CIA agent, and slinky Carrera as the chief doctor at a sex therapy clinic. Assante, of course, puts bullet holes in all of them. He was the first actor to play Hammer since Spillane portrayed the character himself in THE GIRL HUNTERS. (Remake of the 1953 United Artists' version of I, THE JURY, filmed in 3D).

p, Robert Solo; d, Richard T. Heffron; w, Larry Cohen (based on the novel by Mickey Spillane); ph, Andrew Laszlo (Technicolor); m, Bill Conti; ed, Garth Craven; prod d, Robert Gundlach; cos, Celia Bryant; stunts, Don Pike.

Crime **Cas.** **(PR:O MPAA:R)**

I TITANI (SEE: MY SON, THE HERO, 1963, Ital./Fr.)

I, TOO, AM ONLY A WOMAN* 1/2
(1963, Ger.) 89m Rialto/Gloria c (ICH BIN AUCH NUR EINE FRAU)

Maria Schell *(Lilli Koenig)*, Paul Hubschmid *(Martin Bohlen)*, Hans Nielsen *(Dr. Katz)*, Agnes Windeck *(Housekeeper)*, Anita Hoefer *(Pauline)*, Ingrid van Bergen *(Annabella)*, Hannelore Auer *(Gerda)*, Tilly Lauenstein *(Mrs. Starke)*.

A poorly scripted German sex comedy with Schell as a female psychiatrist with rich women as her clients. Hubschmid is a photographer and ladies man who has his eye set on the doctor. He pretends to have problems and becomes one of her patients. Very early in the film it becomes apparent what the ending will be.

p, Preben Philipsen; d, Alfred Weldenmann; w, Johanna Sibelius, Eberhard Keindorff; ph, Heinz Hoelscher; m, Peter Thomas; ed, Walter Wischniewsky.

Comedy **(PR:C MPAA:NR)**

I TRE VOLTI (SEE: THREE FACES OF A WOMAN, 1965, Ital.)

I TRE VOLTI DELLA PAURA (SEE: BLACK SABBATH, 1963, Ital.)

I VAMPIRI (SEE: DEVIL'S COMMANDMENT, THE, 1956, Ital.)

I VITELLONI (SEE: VITELLONI, 1956, Ital./Fr.)

I WAKE UP SCREAMING*** (1942) 82m FOX bw (GB: HOTSPOT)

Betty Grable *(Jill Lynn)*, Victor Mature *(Frankie Christopher/Botticelli)*, Carole Landis *(Vicky Lynn)*, Laird Cregar *(Ed Cornell)*, William Gargan *(Jerry McDonald)*, Alan Mowbray *(Robin Ray)*, Allyn Joslyn *(Larry Evans)*, Elisha Cook, Jr. *(Harry Williams)*, Chick Chandler *(Reporter)*, Morris Ankrum *(Assistant District Attorney)*, May Beatty *(Mrs. Handel)*, Cyril Ring, Basil Walker, Bob Cornell *(Reporters)*, Charles Lane *(Florist Keating)*, Frank Orth *(Cemetery Caretaker)*, Gregory Gaye *(Headwaiter)*, Stanley Clements, George Hickman *(Newsboys)*, Dick Rich, James Flavin, Stanley Blystone, Tim Ryan, Ralph Dunn, Wade Boteler, Eddie Dunn, Phillip Morris *(Detectives)*, Cecil Weston *(Police Matron)*, Harry Strang, Russ Clark (Policemen), Edward McWade, Paul Weigel *(Old Men)*, Harry Seymour *(Bartender)*, Pat McKee *(Newsman)*, Albert Pollet *(Waiter)*, Dorothy Dearing *(Girl at Table)*, Forbes Murray *(Mr. Handel)*, Brooks Benedict *(Man)*.

Mature is a promoter accused of the murder of an actress he represents. He hides out with Grable, the actress' sister, but is finally tracked down by police detective Cregar. In prison the detective tells Mature that he doesn't think he's guilty although there is enough evidence to put him in "the chair." Mature escapes from jail so he can clear his name and discovers that Cook, the actress' neighbor, has covered his walls with pictures of the dead girl. Cook confesses to her murder and explains how he went to Cregar who told him to keep his mouth shut because he wanted Mature to be executed. Seems Cregar had his eye on the actress and was jealous of her agent. Mature turns Cregar and Cook in and returns to Grable. Remade as Vicki.

p, Milton Sperling; d, H. Bruce Humberstone; w, Dwight Taylor (based on the novel by Steve Fisher); ph, Edward Cronjager; m, Cyril J. Mockridge; ed, Robert Simpson; md, Mockridge; art d, Richard Day, Nathan Juran; set d, Thomas Little; m/1, Harold Barlow, Lewis Harris.

Crime Drama **(PR:A MPAA:NR)**

I WALK ALONE*** (1948) 98m PAR bw

Burt Lancaster *(Frankie Madison)*, Lizabeth Scott *(Kay Lawrence)*, Kirk Douglas *(Noll Turner)*, Wendell Corey *(Dave)*, Kristine Miller *(Mrs. Richardson)*, George Rigaud *(Maurice)*, Marc Lawrence *(Nick Palestro)*, Mike Mazurki *(Dan)*, *Mickey Knox (Skinner)*, Roger Neury *(Felix)*, John Bishop *(Ben the Bartender)*, Bruce Lester *(Charles)*, Jean Del Val *(Henri the Chef)*, Gino Corrado *(George the Assistant Chef)*, Freddie Steele *(Tiger)*, Dewey Robinson *(Heinz)*, Fred G. Somers *(Butcher)*, Charles D. Brown *(Lt. Hollaran)*, Walter Anthony Merrill *(Schreiber)*, Bobby Barber *(Newsboy)*, Jack Perrin *(Policeman)*, Bert Moorehouse *(Toll Gate Policeman)*, Olin Howlin *(Watchman)*, James Davies *(Masseur)*.

This is a top notch moody crime melodrama, the kind so popular in the mid-1940s and, with Lancaster and Douglas in the leads, it packs a wallop. Lancaster and Douglas are rum-running partners during the bootleg era. While driving a load of illegal hootch they find their way blocked by a police barricade. They decide to split up, one running on foot, the other driving the truck, making an on-the-spot agreement that whichever one escapes will keep their nightclub going and put aside half the profits for the other. Lancaster is caught and Douglas remains free. After serving a 14-year prison term, Lancaster, embittered and seeking revenge, is released. He immediately heads for the big city and the posh nightclub owned by Douglas. An affable, wealthy Douglas greets his former partner Lancaster, sweet-talking him into waiting until his accountant, Corey, can determine a cash settlement. Meanwhile, Douglas placates the seething Lancaster by having his girl friend and club singer Scott keep time with Lancaster. They fall in love, which vexes the cool Douglas, but he takes his villainous revenge through his meek-mannered accountant Corey who later explains to a perplexed Lancaster that he has little split coming, that the profits from the old club were eaten up through bonds, mergers, and involved financial investments, and that this labyrinthine corporate structure Douglas now controls will show no profit for Lancaster. Realizing he is an old-fashioned gangster without any understanding of such intricate financial dealings, Lancaster tries to force Douglas to pay him off and gets the beating of his life from goon Mazurki. Through Scott's urging, however, Corey finds the courage to stand up to shrewd Douglas. He is about to expose the fraudulent books to Lancaster when Douglas has Corey murdered. Lancaster then sets up a clever trap where Douglas admits his crimes and is ruined. Lancaster then plans to go into a legitimate business with songbird Scott at his side. The plot is a bit busy but the performances are solid, even though Douglas seems to be doing a reprise of his role in OUT OF THE PAST (1947), as a cruel, unfeeling villain. Songs: "Don't Call It Love" (Ned Washington, Allie Wrubel), "Isn't It Romantic" (Richard Rodgers, Lorenz Hart), "My Ideal" (Leon Robin, Richard A. Whiting, J. Newell Chase), "It's Easy to Remember" (Rodgers, Hart), "Two Sleepy People" (Frank Loesser, Hoagy Carmichael), "Heart and Soul" (Loesser, Carmichael), "I'm Yours" (E.Y. Harburg, Johnny Green), "You Leave Me Breathless" (Fred Hollander, Ralph Freed, performed by the Regency Three).

p, Hal B. Wallis; d, Byron Haskins; w, Charles Schnee, Robert Smith, John Bright (based on the play "Beggars Are Coming to Town" by Theodore Reeves); ph, Leo Tover; m, Victor Young; ed, Arthur Schmidt; art d, Hans Dreier, Franz Bachelin; set d, Sam Comer, Patrick Delany.

Crime Drama **(PR:C MPAA:NR)**

I WALK THE LINE*** (1970) 95m Frankenheimer-Lewis COL c

Gregory Peck *(Sheriff Henry Tawes)*, Tuesday Weld *(Alma McCain)*, Estelle Parsons *(Ellen Haney)*, Ralph Meeker *(Carl McCain)*, Lonny Chapman *(Bascomb)*, Charles Durning *(Hunnicutt)*, Jeff Dalton *(Clay McCain)*, Freddie McCloud *(Buddy McCain)*, Jane Rose *(Elsie)*, J.C. Evans *(Grandpa Tawes)*, Margaret Ann Morris *(Sybil)*, Bill Littleton *(Pollard)*, Leo Yates *(Vogel)*, Dodo Denney *(Darlene Hunnicutt)*.

Peck is a backwoods Tennessee sheriff who falls in love with teenager Weld. Her father, Meeker, is a moonshiner and Peck becomes involved in their operations, making sure his men and federal agents stay clear of the stills. When deputy Durning stumbles upon the still, Meeker kills him and Peck becomes an accomplice to the crime. Peck leaves his wife and plans to flee to California with Weld but when he arrives at her house, he finds that the entire family has packed up and left. He finds them and tries to persuade Weld to come with him. She won't, Peck wounds Meeker, and Weld slashes the sheriff with a baling hook. They drive away, leaving Peck wounded and bleeding on the road. Cash's score fits perfectly with the mood of the story.

p, Harold D. Cohen; d, John Frankenheimer; w, Alvin Sargent (based on the novel *An Exile* by Madison Jones); ph, David M. Walsh (Panavision, Eastmancolor); ed, Henry Berman; md, Robert Johnson; art d, Albert Brenner; cos, Lewis Brown; m/1, "I Walk The Line," "Flesh And Blood," "'Cause I Love You," "This Side Of The Law," "Hungry," "Amazing," Johnny Cash; makeup, Frank Prehoda, Jack Petty.

Drama **(PR:A MPAA:GP)**

I WALKED WITH A ZOMBIE*** (1943) 69m RKO bw

James Ellison *(Wesley Rand)*, Frances Dee *(Betsy)*, Tom Conway *(Paul Holland)*, Edith Barrett *(Mrs. Rand)*, James Bell *(Dr. Maxwell)*, Christine Gordon *(Jessica Holland)*, Teresa Harris *(Alma)*, Sir Lancelot *(Calypso Singer)*, Darby Jones *(Carre Four)*, Jeni LeGon *(Dancer)*, Richard Abrams *(Clement)*, Martin Wilkins *(Houngan)*, Jieno Moxzer *(Sabreur)*, Arthur Walker *(Ti-Joseph)*, Katheleen Hartfield *(Dancer)*, Clinton Rosemond *(Coachman)*, Alan Edmiston *(Mr. Wilkens)*, Norman Mayes *(Bayard)*, Melvin Williams *(Baby)*, Vivian Dandridge *(Melisse)*.

I WALKED WITH A ZOMBIE was the second in the series of thought-provoking, literate horror films produced by Lewton in the 1940s (the first was THE CAT PEOPLE) and it enjoys a well- deserved reputation of excellence. The story idea and title were borrowed from a series of newspaper articles which detailed voodoo and witchcraft in Haiti. Dee stars as a young nurse who is hired by rich American planter Conway and sent to Haiti to take care of his catatonic wife, Gordon. Conway feels that his wife has gone insane, and is guilt-ridden with feelings that he may have caused it. The nearby natives suspect, however, that Gordon has become a zombie—one of the living dead. Dee, who makes little progress with Gordon, meets the other members of Conway's family. His mother, Barrett, is a contradictory woman who is torn between her strong belief in the Christian church *and* voodoo. Conway's brother, Ellison, is slowly drinking himself to death as he watches his brother's mistreatment of Gordon, whom he has always secretly loved. To make matters worse, nurse Dee and her employer begin to fall in love. Their desire to marry is intense, but it is impossible while Gordon lives. Not wanting to lose Conway, nor see him torture himself, Dee attempts to cure Gordon by taking her to a voodoo ceremony, in hopes that the experience will shock her back to "life." The memorable conclusion sees Ellison, in desperation, stabbing Gordon and walking with her into the ocean before the unholy voodoo priest can "take her soul." Lewton's horror was based on the imaginary "monsters" that earmarked horror films in the 1930s and 40s. The terror was presented in a shadowy, low-key atmosphere that allowed the audience to *imagine* and *feel* the unease instead of *showing* it to them, making the chills much more effective. The most outstanding example of this is the lengthy, haunting and elegiac sequence when Dee walks through the sugar cane fields with the silent Gordon to the voodoo ceremony. Visually the scene is filled with gentle, floating movements (Gordon's white gown, the movement of the sugar cane in the wind) that are abruptly stopped by the presence of the massive zombie guard, Jones, whose appearance signals the woman's arrival at their destination. Lewton's films also were among the first to treat black character actors with respect and dignity in horror films. Songs are used throughout the movie, often in a narrative way. They include: "O Marie Congo," "British Grenadiers," "Fort Holland Calypso Song," "O Legba," "Walee Nan Guinan," as well as Chopin's E Minor Etude.

p, Val Lewton; d, Jacques Tourneur; w, Curt Siodmak, Ardel Wray (based on an original story by Inez Wallace); ph, J. Roy Hunt; m, Roy Webb; ed, Mark Robson; md, C. Bakaleinikoff; art d, Albert D'Agostino, Walter Keller; set d, Darrell Silvera, Al Fields.

Horror **Cas.** **(PR:C-O MPAA:NR)**

I WANNA HOLD YOUR HAND*** (1978) 104m UNIV c

Nancy Allen *(Pam Mitchell)*, Bobby DiCicco *(Tony Smerko)*, Marc McClure *(Larry Dubois)*, Susan Kendall Newman *(Janis Goldman)*, Theresa Saldana *(Grace Corrigan)*, Wendie Jo Sperber *(Rosie Petrofsky)*, Eddie Deezen *(Richard "Ringo" Klaus)*, Christian Juttner *(Peter Plimpton)*, Will Jordan *(Ed Sullivan)*, Read Morgan *(Peter's Father)*, Claude Earl Jones *(A1)*, James Houghton *(Eddie)*, Michael Hewitson *(Neil)*, Dick Miller *(Sgt. Bresner)*, Vito Carenzo *(CBS Security Guard)*, Luke Andreas *(Police Officer in Alley)*, Roberta Lee Carroll, Sherry Lynn *(Cafeteria Girls)*, Irene Arranga *(Sheet Girl)*, Carole H. Field *(Club Leader)*, Nancy Osborne *(Amazon)*, Newton Arnold *(Barber)*, Murray the K, Wil Albert *(Goldman)*, Troy Melton *(Guard)*, Nick Pellegrino *(Lou)*, Martin Fiscoe *(Elevator Operator)*, Marilyn Moe *(Woman On Elevator)*, Michael Ross Verona *(Reporter)*, Marilyn Fox *(Interviewee)*, Kristine DeBell *(Cindy)*, Gene LeBell *(Reese)*, Victor Brandt *(Foley)*, Roger Pancake *(Sergeant)*, Kimberly Spengel *(Sheet Girl)*, Bob Maroff *(Bartender)*, Ivy Bethune *(Foreigner)*, Craig Spengel, Frank Verroca *(Protestors)*, Derek Barton *(Driver)*, Edward Call, John Malloy, Larry Pines, Dave Adams, Poppy Lagos, Robyn Petti, Paula Watson, Leslie Hoffman, Chuck Waters, Rick Sawaya, Jim Nickerson, George Sawaya, The Romanos.

An engaging comedy that takes a slapstick look at the effect the Beatles had on the U.S. when they crossed the Atlantic. The setting is February, 1964, and the Beatles are soon to be appearing on the Ed Sullivan Show. Allen is about to get married but wants just a single night with one of the "Fab Four." Saldana is a struggling photographer who knows that exclusive pictures of the band will get her career going. Sperber and Deezen are supreme Beatle groupies, and Newman and DiCicco are Beatle-haters planning to ruin their TV appearance. They all converge on the New York City hotel where the band is staying and then move on to the TV studio. After slowly introducing the characters, the film moves up to an entertaining pace. Directer Zemeckis (USED CARS) handles comedy well. He and close friend Steven Spielberg co-wrote 1941 and Spielberg was executive producer on I WANNA HOLD YOUR HAND. Songs include: "I Want To Hold Your Hand," "Please, Please Me," "I Saw Her Standing There," "Thank You Girl," "Misery," "Love Me Do," "Do You Want To Know A Secret?" "P.S. I Love You," "From Me To You," "There's A Place," "She Loves You" (John Lennon, Paul McCartney), "Boys" (Carl Perkins), "Twist and Shout" (Phil Medley, Bert Berns), "Til There Was You" (Meredith Willson), "Money" (Janie Bradford, Berry Gordy, Jr.), "Please Mr. Postman" (Brian Hollan, Freddy C. Gorman).

p, Tamara Asseyev, Alex Rose; d, Robert Zemeckis; w, Zemeckis, Bob Gale; ph, Donald M. Morgan (Panavision, Technicolor); m, The Beatles; ed, Frank Morriss; art d, Peter Jamison; set d, John Dwyer; spec eff, Curtis Dickson, Albert Whitlock; cos, Roseanna Morton.

Comedy **(PR:A MPAA:PG)**

I WANT A DIVORCE** (1940) 92m PAR bw

Joan Blondell *(Geraldine "Jerry" Brokaw)*, Dick Powell *(Alan MacNally)*, Gloria Dickson *(Wanda Holland)*, Frank Fay *(Jeff Gilman)*, Jessie Ralph *(Grandma Brokaw)*, Harry Davenport *(Grandpa Brokaw)*, Conrad Nagel *(David Holland, Sr.)*, Mickey Kuhn *(David Holland, Jr.)*, Dorothy Burgess *("Peppy" Gilman)*, Sidney Blackmer *(Erskine Brandon)*, Louise Beavers *(Celestine)*, George Huntley *(Michael)*, Brandon Tynan *(Judge)*, Herbert Rawlinson *(Lan Howard)*, Natalie Moorhead *(Mrs. Tyrell)*, George Meader *(Murietta)*, Charles McAvoy *(Captain of Detectives)*, Roscoe Ates *(Process Server)*, Elizabeth Valentine *(Maid)*, Byron Foulger *(Secretary)*, Edward Earle, Ed Stanley *(Ministers)*, Frank Austin *(Taxi Driver)*, Isabel Withers *(Secretary)*, Frank Wayne *(Bailiff)*, Fred "Snowflake" Toones *(Porter)*, Paco Moreno *(Peppy's Father)*, Eva Puig *(Peppy's Mother)*, Archie Twitchell, Frances Morris *(Couple)*, Ruth Cherrington, *(Dowager)*, John Kelly *(Marine)*.

In this dated melodrama about divorce, Powell plays a struggling attorney who marries Blondell. When his buddy Fay talks him into entering the divorce field, Blondell is against it and the couple begin to float apart. Powell then handles the divorce of Dickson and Nagel, whose son is caught in the middle. When Dickson commits suicide, Powell quits as a divorce lawyer and he and Blondell are happily reunited.

p, George Arthur; d, Ralph Murphy; w, Frank Butler (based on a story by Adela Rogers St. John); ph, Ted Tetzlaff; ed, LeRoy Stone; art d, Hans Dreier, Ernst Fegte.

Drama **(PR:A MPAA:NR)**

I WANT HER DEAD (SEE: W, 1974)

I WANT TO LIVE!*** (1958) 120m Figaro/UA bw

Susan Hayward *(Barbara Graham)*, Simon Oakland *(Ed Montgomery)*, Virginia Vincent *(Peg)*, Theodore Bikel *(Carl Palmberg)*, Wesley Lau *(Henry Graham)*, Philip Coolidge *(Emmett Perkins)*, Lou Krugman *(Jack Santo)*, James Philbrook *(Bruce King)*, Bartlett Robinson *(District Attorney)*, Gage Clark *(Richard Tibrow)*, Joe De Santis *(Al Matthews)*, John Marley *(Father Devers)*, Dabbs Greer *(San Quentin Captain)*, Raymond Bailey *(Warden)*, Alice Backes *(Nurse)*, Gertrude Flynn *(Matron)*, Russell Thorson, Stafford Repp *(Sergeants)*, Gavin Macleod *(Lieutenant)*, Peter Breck *(Ben Miranda)*, Marion Marshall *(Rita)*, Olive Blakeney *(Corona Warden)*, Lorna Thayer *(Corona Guard)*, Evelyn Scott *(Personal Effects Clerk)*, Jack Weston *(NCO)*, Leonard Bell *(San Francisco Hood)*, George Putnam *(Himself)*, Bill Stout *(Newsman)*, Jason Johnson *(Bixel)*, Rusty Lane *(Judge)*, S. John Launer *(San Quentin Officer)*, Dan Sheridan *(Police Broadcaster)*, Wendell Holmes *(Detective)*, Gerry Mulligan, Art Farmer, Bud Shank, Frank Rosolino, Pete Jolly, "Red" Mitchell, Shelly Manne *(Musicians)*.

This is a murky, often depressing crime melodrama but the electrifying performance rendered by Hayward makes it a must see by any devotees of *film noir*. She plays the real-life Barbara Graham, whose sensational trial brought her a conviction and death sentence that made her a nation-wide *cause celebre*. The film depicts Hayward, the product of a broken home, as a thoroughly amoral woman: perjurer, prostitute, thief. She arrives in San Francisco and is quickly sent to prison for falsely testifying to help out a friend. When released, she contacts two gamblers at the recommendation of fellow inmates. The gamblers, Coolidge and Krugman, use her as a shill; Hayward steers gullible suckers into their crooked card games and begins to make considerable money. With a bank account, Hayward decides to go straight, but she makes the mistake of marrying corrupt Lau—one of Coolidge's associates—and he introduces her to drugs. By the time she has a baby, she is an addict and her husband takes her last $10 for a fix. She leaves him and goes back to work for Coolidge and Lau. A short time later the three are arrested and charged with murdering a widow whom they have robbed. Hayward, like Graham herself, loudly protests, screaming her innocence. While awaiting trial she confides to a cellmate many of her fears and these confidences are later revealed in court by the cellmate who turns out to be a law enforcement officer. It is this testimony along with circumstantial evidence, and the reluctance of the two other defendants to clear her—that leads to the conviction of all three, who are later sentenced to death in San Quentin's death chamber. Her appeals are denied and she, like Graham, goes to the death chamber on June 5, 1955. What sealed Graham's fate in the movie and in real life was the fact that another defendant, to save himself, turned state's evidence and named her as the actual killer of Mrs. Mabel Monahan. Hayward's performance is so intense that the viewer will be exhausted watching her suffer through one agony after another. Wise directs brilliantly with the perspective that Hayward/Graham was innocent all along, although the film does not offer any real evidence to support this assumption, a stance that brought universal criticism from law enforcement agencies. Hayward had been denied the Oscar for many deserving performances in the past—SMASH-UP, THE STORY OF A WOMAN, 1947; MY FOOLISH HEART, 1949; I'LL CRY TOMORROW, 1955—but this time the Academy could not ignore her bravura performance. Hayward dug deep into Graham's personality, reading her letters, studying her habits, learning that she was a lover of literature and jazz. "I became so fascinated with the woman I simply had to play her," she later stated. Producer Wanger also felt that Hayward had to play the role and no one else. On top of a whopping salary, she received 37.5 percent of the profits of the film, script and cast approval, and sole star billing. When contemplating what she would say when accepting the Oscar, Hayward jokingly stated that she would announce: "There is one person I would like to thank above all—*me!*" But at the awards ceremonies she raced to the stage (timed at a 12-second run), grabbed the statuette and mouthed a few thank-yous to the Academy and Wanger (forgetting director Wise) and went off to party. Wise's direction is relentlessly gloomy and as swift as a bullet, telling Graham's story in adroitly crafted scenes. He undoubtedly strives to prove Graham innocent, even going so far as to show the 32-year-old woman at home with her husband and child on the night of the murder. The film is also a celluloid crusade against capital punishment. Yet no real case is made that will convince anyone seriously studying the Monahan murder that Graham was innocent. The picture received five other Oscar nominations: Best Director, Writing, Cinematography, Sound, and Film Editing. A silly, specious reaction came in 1960 with the release of American International's third-rate WHY MUST I DIE? which predicated Graham's guilt. The film starred Terry Moore, of all people; it received no Oscar nominations.

p, Walter Wanger; d, Robert Wise; w, Nelson Gidding, Don Mankiewicz (based on newspaper articles by Ed Montgomery, letters of Barbara Graham); ph, Lionel Lindon; m, John Mandel; ed, William Hornbeck; md, Mandel; art d, Edward Haworth; set d, Victor Gangelin.

Crime Drama/Biography **(PR:O MPAA:NR)**

I WANT WHAT I WANT** (1972, Brit.) 91m Marayan/Cinerama c

Anne Heywood *(Roy/Wendy)*, Harry Andrews *(Father)*, Jill Bennett *(Margaret Stevenson)*, Paul Rogers *(Mr. Waites)*, Michael Coles *(Frank)*, Sheila Reid *(June)*, Virginia Stride *(Shirley)*, Jill Melford *(Lorna)*, Rachel Gurney *(Mrs. Parkhurst)*, Anthony Sharpe *(Mr. Parkhurst)*, Robin Hawdon *(Tony)*, Philip Bond *(Philip)*, Paul Prescott *(Roger Parkhurst)*, Liza Goddard *(Carole)*, Hilda Fenemore, John Baskcombe, Deborah Grant, Laurie Goode.

Films about transexuality are usually treated as high camp, which makes it hard to take the proceedings very seriously. I WANT WHAT I WANT manages to keep from falling into such a trap by remaining more concerned with the personal anguish the character is going through than with sexual ambiguities. In fact director Dexter tried to stay as clear from sex as possible and still maintain a sense of the problems inherent in a subject like transexualism. Heywood plays the young man who finds satisfaction in dressing up in women's clothing and adopting other feminine characteristics. A confrontation occurs when his father catches him in the act. The elder man being a bull headed brute, Heywood is terrified and flees to a place where he can feel comfortable in his new garb. Parading about full time as a girl, he toys with the idea of having a sex change operation, though not going through with the operation until a neighbor nearly rapes Heywood after having his advances turned down. Discovering the woman's true sex, he beats Heywood, driving the confused and depressed lad to attempt castration with a bit of broken glass. An odd bit of casting has the lead being performed by a woman to capture inner feminine qualities a man would find hard to portray. Heywood accomplishes this task quite well, while maintaing an exterior that mainly consists of her lowering her voice a couple of notches. In any case she is very convincing in a hard role for any actor or actress to undertake.

p, Raymond Stross; d, John Dexter; w, Gillian Freeman, Gavin Lambert (based on the novel by Geoff Brown); ph, Gerry Turpin (Eastmancolor); m, Johnny Harris; ed, Peter Thornton; md, Harris; art d, Bill Andrews; cos, Sue Yelland; makeup, Trevor Crole Rees.

Drama **(PR:O MPAA:R)**

I WANT YOU*** (1951) 102m Goldwyn/RKO bw

Dana Andrews *(Martin Greer)*, Dorothy McGuire *(Nancy Greer)*, Farley Granger *(Jack Greer)*, Peggy Dow *(Carrie Turner)*, Robert Keith *(Thomas Greer)*, Mildred Dunnock *(Sarah Greer)*, Ray Collins *(Judge Jonathan Turner)*, Martin Milner *(George Kress, Jr.)*, Jim Backus *(Harvey Landrum)*, Marjorie Crossland *(Mrs. Celia Turner)*, Walter Baldwin *(George Kress, Sr.)*, Walter Sande *(Ned Iversen)*, Peggy Maley *(Gladys)*, Jerrilyn Flannery *(Anne Greer)*, Erik Nielsen *(Tony Greer)*, Ann Robin *(Gloria)*, Carol Savage *(Caroline Krupka)*, James Adamson *(Train Porter)*, Harry Lauter *(Art Stacey)*, Frank Sully *(Bartender)*, Robert Johnson *(Porter)*, David McMahon *(Taxi Driver)*, Melodi Lowell *(Girl)*, Jimmy Ogg *(Soldier)*, Jean Andren *(Secretary)*, Charles Marsh *(Mr. Jones)*, Don Hayden *(Another Candidate)*, Dee Carroll *(Woman)*, Lee Turnbull *(Fat Boy)*, Ralph Brooks *(Albert)*, Roland Morris *(Sergeant)*, Al Murphy *(Man)*, Paul Smith.

Producer Goldwyn tried to capture the success of his film THE BEST DAYS OF OUR LIVES with this one about the problems faced by people dealing with military service during war time. The war here is the Korean conflict and the effects are felt by men and women, young and old. Andrews is a WW II veteran and a family man who is unsure about his decision to re-enlist. His wife, McGuire, is totally against the idea. Granger is a young man faced with the draft and in love with Dow. Being taken away from his sweetheart builds a growing resentment inside him. Dunnock is Granger's mother who doesn't want to have another son killed in action. She confronts her husband, Keith, about his continuous lectures to their son on the heroics of war. Milner tries to deal with his possessive father, Baldwin. Not as insightful as THE BEST DAYS OF OUR LIVES; it was still a very powerful film with an important message about the effect war has on individuals and families.

p, Samuel Goldwyn; d, Mark Robson; w, Irwin Shaw (based on stories by Edward Newhouse); ph, Harry Stradling; m, Leigh Harline; ed, Daniel Mandell; art d, Richard Day; cos, Mary Wills.

Drama **(PR:A MPAA:NR)**

I WANTED WINGS*** (1941) 131m PAR bw

Ray Milland *(Jeff Young)*, William Holden *(Al Ludlow)*, Wayne Morris *(Tom Cassidy)*, Brian Donlevy *(Capt. Mercer)*, Constance Moore *(Carolyn Bartlett)*, Veronica Lake *(Sally Vaughn)*, Harry Davenport *("Sandbags" Riley)*, Phil Brown *(Jimmy Masters)*, Edward Fielding *(President of the Court)*, Willard Robertson *(Judge Advocate)*, Richard Lane *(Flight Commander)*, Addison Richards *(Flight Surgeon)*, Hobart Cavanaugh *(Mickey)*, Douglas Aylesworth *(Lt. Hopkins)*, John Trent *(Lt. Ronson)*, Archie Twitchell *(Lt. Clankton)*, Richard Webb *(Cadet Captain)*, John Hiestand *(Radio Announcer)*, Harlan Warde *(Montgomery, the Co-Pilot)*, Lane Chandler *(Ranger)*, Jack Chapin, Charles Drake, Alan Hale, Jr., Renny McEvoy *(Cadets)*, Arthur Gardner *(Mechanic)*, Lane Allan *(Corporal Mechanic)*, Jack Shea *(Crew Chief)*, Ed Peil, Sr., Frank O'Connor *(Detectives)*, Michael Gale, James Millican *(Corporals)*, Emory Johnson, Tom Quinn *(Sergeants)*, Russ Clark *(Supply Sergeant)*, George Turner, Hal Brazeale *(Privates)*, Warren Ashe *(Cadet Adjutant)*, Charles A. Hughes *(Meteorology Instructor)*, George Lollier *(Buzzer Class Instructor)*, Hedda Hopper *(Mrs. Young)*, Herbert Rawlinson *(Mr. Young)*, Rod Cameron *(Voice on Loud Speaker)*, Jack Luden, Anthony Nace *(Captains at Court Martial)*, Lee Shumway *(Policeman in Car)*, Phillip Terry *(Radio Operator)*, Lester Dorr *(Evaluating Officer)*, James Farley *(Fire Chief)*, Charles D. Waldron *(Commanding Officer)*, Gladden M. James *(Surgeon)*, Edward Peil, Jr. *(Lieutenant)*, John Sylvester *(Flight Dispatcher)*.

This salute to the Army Air Corps (as the U.S. Air Force was then called) is packed with exciting aerial sequences and special effects as air cadets Milland, Holden and Morris go after their wings. They are from divergent walks of life, Milland a Manhattan playboy (a background undoubtedly awarded because of his subtle British accent), Holden a tough garage mechanic, and Morris, a college athlete. Their ramrod instructor is Donlevy who goes by the book and does everything humanly possible to wash out his nervous trainees. Director Leisen and his film crew arrived at Randolph Field, Texas (shooting was also conducted at Kelly Field in Texas) just as a group of new recruits appeared and the director wisely threw his actors into the same training program, filming their story along with that of the new trainees, and throwing in Moore and Lake—the latter appearing in her film debut—to add the romantic touch. The appearance of the ladies, especially Lake peeking around her long golden hairdo, was later soundly criticized as superfluous. Moore is a lady photographer with her eyes on Milland; Lake is a vamp tramping after Holden. Leisen manages to make the various ground and air training phases interesting and interjects some spine-tingling aerial sequences. In one hedge-hopping scene, the planes almost touch the ground and one finally does, Morris', killing him. Holden eventually washes out but Milland comes through with flying colors and gets his wings. One of the most spectacular scenes shows a huge bomber crash-landing in the desert. The original director of this film was Ted Weeks but he only lasted two weeks, treating officers and enlisted men as if they were Paramount extras. When some planes flew overhead ruining a ground shot he was directing, Weeks screamed at a general: "Get those planes out of the air." Leisen replaced him immediately. It was for this film that producer Hornblow changed Constance Keane's name to Veronica Lake; since her original name was Ockleman it was all the same to Ms. Lake.

p, Arthur Hornblow, Jr.; d, Mitchell Leisen; w, Richard Maibaum, Lt. Beirne Lay, Jr., Sid Herzog (based on a story by Eleanor Griffin, Frank Wead from the book *I Wanted Wings* by Lay); ph, Leo Tover; m, Victor Young; ed, Hugh Bennett; art d, Hans Dreier, Robert Usher; spec eff, Gordon Jennings; m/1, Ned Washington, Young, Capt. William J. Clinch.

Aviation Drama **(PR:A MPAA:NR)**

I WAS A CAPTIVE IN NAZI GERMANY*½ (1936) 72m Malvina bw

Isobel Lillian Steele *(Herself)*.

Poorly acted and produced anti-Nazi propaganda based on the experiences of Isobel Lillian Steele (who also plays the lead), a woman held prisoner by the Nazis in 1934 under the accusation of being a spy. Almost immediately after her release Steele capitalized on her captivity as much as possible, first writing books and articles, and then coming up with this movie. As a whole the picture sheds no insight into Germany at the time, but only seems to be saying that Hitler and his gang were very bad men. Steele also proved to be a bad actress, even though she was only playing herself, remaining incapable of generating any real dimension.

War Drama **(PR:A MPAA:NR)**

I WAS A COMMUNIST FOR THE F.B.I.** (1951) 83m WB bw

Frank Lovejoy *(Matt Cvetic)*, Dorothy Hart *(Eve Merrick)*, Philip Carey *(Mason)*, Dick Webb *(Crowley)*, James Millican *(Jim Blandon)*, Ron Hagerthy *(Dick Cvetic)*, Paul Picerni *(Joe Cvetic)*, Frank Gerstle *(Tom Cvetic)*, Russ Conway *(Frank Cvetic)*, Hope Kramer *(Ruth Cvetic)*, Kasia Orzazekski *(Mrs. Cvetic)*, Eddie Norris *(Harmon)*, Ann Morrison *(Miss Nova)*, Konstantin Shayne *(Gerhardt Eisler)*, Roy Roberts *(Father Novac)*, Paul McGuire *(McIntyre)*, Douglas Evans *(Chief Agent)*, Janet Barrett, Karen Hale *(Secretaries)*, Joseph Smith, Jim O'Gatty *(Goons)*, Frank Marlowe, Barry Sullivan *(Workers)*, Mike Ross *(Foreman)*, Lenita Lane *(Principal)*, Alma Mansfield *(Teacher)*, Ann Kimball, Paula Sowl *(Students)*, Charles Sherlock, George MacGrill *(Men)*, Grace Lenard *(Wife)*, Eric Neilsen *(Jackie)*, Roy Engle *(Jackie's Father)*, Bill Lester *(Brown)*, John Crawford *(McGowan)*, Ernest Anderson, Sugarfoot Anderson *(Black Men)*, Johnny Bradford *(Dobbs)*, Jimmy Gonzales *(Brennan)*, David MacMahon *(Masonvitch)*, Charles Horvath *(Good Leader)*, Phil Tully *(Irish Mick)*, Howard Negley *(Union Chairman)*, Bobby Gilbert, James Adamson *(Pickets)*, Mary Hokanson, Mildred Boyd *(Women)*, Barry Reagan *(Officer)*, Hugh Sanders *(Garson)*, Lyle Latill *(Cahill)*, Chuck Colean *(Brakeman)*, Dick Gordon, William Bailey, Paul Bradley, Buddy Shaw *(Lawyers)*, William Forrest *(Senator Wood)*, Bert Moorhouse *(Senator Gray)*.

Lovejoy, a common Pittsburgh steelworker, is recruited by the F.B.I. to infiltrate his union which, in reality, is a communist organization that has been trying to increase its membership among the disenfranchised laborers. At a big Communist convention Lovejoy is shocked to find the Red leaders gorging themselves on caviar and champagne while boasting that when they take America, everyone will live the good life. The scene reconfirms the evil duplicity of the Communists who spout populist propaganda while living high on the hog off the rank-and-file's union dues. Of course living this double life takes its toll on the noble Lovejoy who cannot even confide in his worried wife lest he blow his cover. Lovejoy's apparently Communist leanings cause tension between him and his all-American brother who thinks his sibling has gone "pinko" and worries that his nephew's young mind will be corrupted. Bigger things are at stake, however, and Lovejoy works hard to save the political consciousness of Hart, a naive schoolteacher who has been seduced by the Communists. Eventually Hart comes to her America-First senses and is saved from the clutches of the Reds after Lovejoy kills one of her recruiters. Having done his job to keep the Red Menace from under the beds of common Americans, Lovejoy can finally reveal his true-blue sympathies to his relieved family. Viewed as a mature social drama I WAS A COMMUNIST FOR THE F.B.I. is a totally repulsive and reprehensible film that portrays labor unions, intellectuals, schoolteachers, and independent-minded people as potentially dangerous Communist dupes who, through their stupidity, could destroy the very fabric of American life. Supposedly based on the memoirs of the real-life Matt Cvetic who spent years undercover for the F.B.I., joining scores of Communist organizations and providing Washington with nearly a thousand names of potentially threatening subversives, I WAS A COMMUNIST FOR THE F.B.I. is totally self-serving, panders to thoughtless paranoia, and was produced by Hollywood to placate Joe McCarthy and the House Committee on Un-American Activities. In fact, Hollywood was so desperate to convince the public of its sincerity that the film was nominated by the Motion Picture Academy for Best *Documentary* of 1951. Thankfully, hindsight has taken the edge off the film and it remains a disturbing curio of an era that has—hopefully—passed.

p, Bryan Foy; d, Gordon Douglas; w, Crane Wilbur (based on the Saturday Evening Post article "I Posed as a Communist for the F.B.I." by Matt Cvetic as told to Pete Martin); ph, Edwin DuPar; ed, Folmar Blangsted; art d, Leo K. Kuter; set d, Lyle B. Reifsnider; makeup, Gordon Bau.

Drama **(PR:C MPAA:NR)**

I WAS A CONVICT*½ (1939) 62m REP bw

Barton MacLane *(Ace King)*, Beverly Roberts *(Judy)*, Clarence Kolb *(J.B. Harrison)*, Janet Beecher *(Mrs. Harrison)*, Horace MacMahon *(Missouri Smith)*, Ben Welden *(Rocks)*, Leon Ames *(Jackson)* Clara Blandick *(Aunt Sarah)*, Russell Hicks *(District Attorney)*, John Harmon *(Matty)*, Chester Clute *(Evans)*.

Millionaire businessman Kolb gets out of jail for income tax fraud and then makes two of his cell mates executives in his company. One of them, MacLane, tries unsuccessfully to get a romance going with Kolb's daughter, Roberts. But once he decides to go straight he gets both Roberts and the family fortune.

p, Herman Schlom; d, Aubrey Scotto; w, Ben Markson, Robert D. Andrews (based on a story by Andrews); ph, Edward Snyder; md, Cy Feuer; ed, Gene Milford.

Drama **(PR:A MPAA:NR)**

I WAS A MALE WAR BRIDE***

(1949) 105m FOX bw (AKA: YOU CAN'T SLEEP HERE)

Cary Grant *(Capt. Henri Rochard)*, Ann Sheridan *(Lt. Catherine Gates)*, William Neff *(Capt. Jack Rumsey)*, Marion Marshall, Randy Stuart *(WACS)*, Eugene Gericke *(Tony Jowitt)*, Ruben Wendorf *(Innkeeper's Assistant)*, John Whitney *(Trumble)*, Ken Tobey *(Seaman)*, Joe Haworth, John Zilly *(Shore Patrol)*, William Pullen, William Self, Bill Murphy *(Sergeants)*, Robert Stevenson, Harry Lauter *(Lieutenants)*, *Barbara Perry (Tall WAC)*, Otto Reichow, William Yetter *(German Policemen)*, David McMahon *(Chaplain)*, Alfred Linder *(Bartender)*, Andre Charlot *(French Minister)*, Lester Sharpe, Alex Gerry *(Waiters)*, Gil Herman *(Naval Officer)*, Ben Pollock *(Officer)*, William McLean *(Expectant GI)*, Russ Conway *(Comdr. Willis)*, Mike Mahoney *(Sailor)*, Kay Young *(Maj. Prendergast)*, Lillie Kann *(Innkeeper's Wife)*, Carl Jaffe *(Jail Officer)*, Martin Miller *(Schindler)*, Paul Hardmuth *(Burgomeister)*, John Serrett *(French Notary)*, Patricia Curts *(Girl in Door)*.

Hawks, one of America's premiere directors, always felt that if a film had one or two exceptional scenes it would be considered above average and the director would have done his job. This film has many good scenes and can be considered one of his better comedies. Hawks certainly did his job here, and so did Grant and Sheridan. Grant is a French officer and Sheridan a WAC lieutenant who are assigned duties together in occupied Europe just after WW II. They are at odds from the beginning, bickering and squabbling over petty problems but, despite this adversarial posture, they fall in love and decide to get married. Now their problems really begin. He and Sheridan decide that they will go to the U.S. to settle down but the only way the couple can get around the mountains of red tape and allow Grant to enter the U.S. is for him to be considered a "war bride" (there being no regulation for "war groom"). As it turns out Grant dons female garments, a WAC uniform no less, and a ridiculous black wig, to conform to U.S. regulations and scoots about in a motorcycle with a sidecar, he in the sidecar, Sheridan driving, trying to get the proper papers signed. The sleeping arrangements present insurmountable problems. No military billet will allow wives bedding down with husbands and vice-versa. Grant's charade continues on board a troopship where the accommodations become impossible and the couple play a game of hide and seek in and out of cabins and hammocks. There is no relief in sight until the couple reach New York and Grant can get out of drag. Hawks keeps the whole farce going at a brisk pace and inserts his usual flair, dwelling upon the absurd to get the necessary laughs. Only the sophisticated Grant could convincingly play such an outlandish part. Oddly, he is a Frenchman thoroughly familiar with American slang but has trouble pronouncing the word "Massachusetts." Filmed on location in Germany and England.

p, Sol C. Siegel; d, Howard Hawks; w, Charles Lederer, Leonard Spigelgass, Hagar Wilde (based on the novel by Henri Rochard); ph, Norbert Brodine, O.H. Borradaile; m, Cyril Mockridge; ed, James B. Clark; md, Lionel Newman; art d, Lyle Wheeler, Albert Hogsett; set d, Thomas Little, Walter M. Scott; spec eff, Fred Sersen.

Comedy **(PR:A MPAA:NR)**

I WAS A PRISONER ON DEVIL'S ISLAND* (1941) 71m COL bw

Sally Eilers *(Claire)*, Donald Woods *(Joel Grant)*, Edward [Eduardo] Ciannelli *(Dr. Martel)*, Victor Kilian *(Guissart)*, Charles Halton *(Commandant)*, Dick Curtis *(Jules)*, John Tyrrell *(Gerault)*, Eddie Laughton *(Brisson)*, Edmund Cobb *(Quarry Guard)*, Robert Warwick *(Governor)*.

Woods is a freighter's first officer and gets in a fight with the captain over wages. He ends up killing the captain and is sent to Devil's Island. Eilers, the woman he met on a French port and fell in love with, is on the Island with her doctor husband, who is selling the prisoner's medical supplies to the mainland black market. When Woods braves a storm to get supplies for sick prisoners, they don't even pardon him. Woods then escapes from the Island and hooks up with Eilers. Smacks strongly of STRANGE CARGO.

p, Wallace MacDonald; d, Lew Landers; w, Karl Brown (based on a story by Otto and Edgar Van Eyss); ph, John Stumar; ed, Richard Fantl.

Drama **(PR:A MPAA:NR)**

I WAS A SHOPLIFTER*½ (1950) 74m UNIV bw

Scott Brady *(Jeff Andrews)*, Mona Freeman *(Faye Burton)*, Andrea King *(Ina Perdue)*, Anthony [Tony] Curtis *(Pepe)*, Charles Drake *(Herb Klaxon)*, Gregg Martell *(The Champ)*, Larry Keating *(Harry Dunson)*, Robert Gist *(Barkie Neff)*, Michael Raffetto *(Sheriff Bascom)*, Rock Hudson *(Store Detective)*, Nana Bryant *(Aunt Clara)*, Harold Goodwin *(San Diego Sheriff)*, Nestor Paiva, Charles Watts *(Detectives)*, Marshall Reed *(L.A. Sheriff)*, Mickey O'Ryan, Conrad Binyon *(Petty Thieves)*, Steve Darrell *(Detective)*, Paul Fierro *(Mechanic)*, Peggy Castle *(Store Operator)*, Charles McGraw *(Man)*.

Freeman is a socialite who is caught shoplifting at a department store. A theft ring headed by King forces her into their ranks and detective Brady is hot on their trail. He rescues Freeman and captures the gang down in Tia Juana. The part of King was originally offered to Alexis Smith who was suspended from the studio for not taking it.

p, Leonard Goldstein; d, Charles Lamont; w, Irwin Gielgud; ph, Irving Glassberg; ed, Otto Ludwig, md, Milton Schwartzwald.

Crime Drama **(PR:A MPAA:NR)**

I WAS A SPY½** (1934, Brit.) 83m GAU-British/FOX bw

Madeleine Carroll *(Martha Cnockhaert)*, Conrad Veidt *(Commandant Oberaertz)*, Herbert Marshall *(Stephan)*, Gerald du Maurier *(Doctor)*, Edmund Gwenn *(Burgomaster)*, Donald Calthrop *(Cnockhaert)*, Anthony Bushell *(Otto)*, Eva Moore *(Canteen Ma)*, Nigel Bruce *(Scotty)*, May Agate *(Mme. Cnockhaert)*, George Merritt *(Reichmann)*, Martita Hunt *(Aunt Lucille)*, Gavin Gordon.

The film is the true story of Martha Cnockhaert McKenna, a Belgian nurse, who becomes a spy during WW I. She easily infiltrates the German high command and passes vital information to the Allied Forces. When she is caught and faced with the firing squad, co-spy Marshall steps forward and reveals his identity. He takes her place on the firing squad and, soon after, the Allies arrive to save her. Above average performances by Carroll and Veidt and Marshall save this one from sinking into sticky melodrama.

p, Michael Balcon; d, Victor Saville; w, W.P. Lipscomb, Ian Hay (based on the book by Marthe Cnockhaert McKenna); ph, William Van Engen.

Spy Drama **(PR:A MPAA:NR)**

I WAS A TEENAGE FRANKENSTEIN*½
(1958) 72m AIP bw/c (GB: TEENAGE FRANKENSTEIN)

Whit Bissell *(Professor Frankenstein)*, Phyllis Coates *(Margaret)*, Robert Burton *(Dr. Karlton)*, Gary Conway *(Teenage Monster)*, George Lynn *(Sgt. Burns)*, John Cliff *(Sgt. McAffee)*, Marshall Bradford *(Dr. Randolph)*, Claudia Bryar *(Arlene's Mother)*, Angela Blake *(Beautiful Girl)*, Russ Whiteman *(Dr. Elwood)*, Charles Seel *(The Jeweler)*, Paul Keast *(Man at Crash)*, Gretchen Thomas *(Woman in the Corridor)*, Joy Stoner *(Arlene)*, Larry Carr *(Young Man)*, Pat Miller *(Police Officer)*.

This was the followup to Cohen's I WAS A TEENAGE WEREWOLF and is far below the first production. Bissell, a descendant of Dr. Frankenstein, has a lab in Los Angeles where he creates his monster from different body parts, including the head of teenager, Conway, whom he kidnaped. With Conway's face grafted on, Bissell plans to go to London to unveil his creation. But as the doctor prepares to disconnect Frankenstein for shipping, the monster kills him, and then is itself electrocuted as police close in. The only thing done well here is the grotesque make-up for the monster. The final minutes of the film are in color.

p, Herman Cohen; d, Herbert L. Strock; w, Kenneth Langtry; ph, Lothrop Worth (Pathe Color); m, Paul Dunlap; ed, Jerry Young; md, Dunlap; art d, Leslie Thomas.

Horror **(PR:C-O MPAA:NR)**

I WAS A TEENAGE WEREWOLF*** (1957) 76m AIP bw

Michael Landon *(Tony)*, Yvonne Lime *(Arlene)*, Whit Bissell *(Dr. Alfred Brandon)*, Tony Marshall *(Jimmy)*, Dawn Richard *(Theresa)*, Barney Phillips *(Detective Donovan)*, Ken Miller *(Vic)*, Cindy Robbins *(Pearl)*, Michael Rougas *(Frank)*, Robert Griffin *(Police Chief Baker)*, Joseph Mell *(Dr. Hugo Wagner)*, Malcolm Atterbury *(Charles)*, Eddie Marr *(Doyle)*, Vladimir Sokoloff *(Pepi)*, Louise Lewis *(Miss Ferguson)*, S. John Launer *(Bill)*, Guy Williams *(Chris Stanley)*, Dorothy Crehan *(Mary)*.

I WAS A TEENAGE WEREWOLF successfully combined the troubled teenager-horror movies, two very popular genres in the 1950s. Young Landon is the troubled teenager who can't control his anger and is always into fights. Detective Phillips, with the help of Landon's girl friend, Lime, convinces the youth to see a psychiatrist, Bissell, who has been dabbling with hypnosis and regression (bringing a person back to their primal roots). Every time Landon is startled he is transformed—not into a werewolf, but a prehistoric primate. This film touched a subject that was explored further in ALTERED STATES (1980). The regression topic is put on the shelf in the last third of the film as Landon goes on the rampage, and this is when the movie becomes just another low-budget horror film. The sequence where Landon is transformed into the beast as he watches a girl practice on the parallel bars is a classic moment in horror film history. Director Fowler (in his first feature) aptly blended horror, science fiction, rock'n'roll, and teen problems smoothly into one entertaining film.

p, Herman Cohen; d, Gene Fowler, Jr.; w, Ralph Thornton; ph, Joseph La Shelle; m, Paul Dunlap; ed, George Gittens; m/l, Jerry Blaine.

Horror **(PR:C-O MPAA:NR)**

I WAS AN ADVENTURESS*** (1940) 80m FOX bw

Vera Zorina *(Countess Tanya Vronsky)*, Richard Greene *(Paul Vernay)*, Erich von Stroheim *(Andre Desormeaux)*, Peter Lorre *(Polo)*, Sig Rumann *(Herr Protz)*, Fritz Feld *(Henri Gautier)*, Cora Witherspoon *(Aunt Cecile)*, Anthony Kemble Cooper *(Cousin Emil)*, Paul Porcasi *(Fisherman)*, Inez Palange *(Fisherman's Wife)*, Egon Brecher *(Jacques Dubois)*, Roger Imhof *(Henrich Von Kongen)*, Rolfe Sedan, Eddie Conrad *(Waiters)*, Fortunio Bonanova *(Orchestra Leader)*.

An entertaining film in which Lorre, von Stroheim, and ballet dancer Zorina are a con-artist team. Lorre is a compulsive pickpocket, and von Stroheim is Zorina's mentor. When Zorina marries Greene, who believes she is a countess, she breaks off from her former associates. Lorre and von Stroheim later blackmail Zorina and then steal the jewelry of her party guests. A chase ensues and, once the stolen jewels are recovered, Zorina reveals her true identity. All ends well and Zorina finishes the film by performing the ballet, "Swan Lake." The material becomes thin at points but there are plenty of great moments to compensate. Lorre and von Stroheim make an odd, but electrifying pair. Ratoff greatly admired von Stroheim whose directing days in the silent era had made him famous. Out of respect, Ratoff allowed von Stroheim to tighten the script and insert some arresting scenes, one of which shows the fascinating Austrian sitting at a boulevard cafe where he studies passersby and describes their personalities by virtue of their feet, an ironic or nostalgic look backward to his smash silent hit THE MERRY WIDOW, in which von Stroheim dwelled upon one character suffering from *locomotor ataxia*, a slow, mind-distorting degenerative syphilitic paralysis, which, in that instance, caused the character to develop a slobbering foot fetish.

p, Darryl F. Zanuck; d, Gregory Ratoff; w, Karl Tunberg, Don Ettlinger, John O'Hara (based on an original production by Gregor Rabinovitch, written by Jacques Companeez, Herbert Juttke, Hans Jacoby, Michael Duran); ph, Leon Shamroy, Edward Cronjager; ed, Francis D. Lyon; md, David Buttolph; art d, Richard Day, Joseph C. Wright; set d, Thomas Little; ch, George Balanchine.

Comedy/Drama **(PR:A MPAA:NR)**

I WAS AN AMERICAN SPY** (1951) 84m MON-AA bw

Ann Dvorak *(Claire Phillips)*, Gene Evans *(Boone)*, Douglas Kennedy *(John Phillips)*, Richard Loo *(Col. Masamoto)*, Leon Lontoc *(Pacio)*, Chabing *(Lolita)*, Philip Ahn *(Capt. Arito)*, Marya Marco *(Fely)*, Nadene Ashdown *(Dian)*, Lisa Ferraday *(Dorothy)*, Howard Chuman *(Kamuri)*, Freddie Revelala *(Zig Zag)*, James Leong *(Ho Sang)*, Leo Abbey *(Torres)*, Escolastico Baucin *(Memerto)*, Toshi Nakaki, Jerry Fujikawa, Weaver Levy *(Japanese Guards)*, Celeste Madamba *(Pressa)*, Andres Lucas *(Siggy)*, Frank Jenks *(Mac)*, Gil Herman *(Lieutenant)*, George Fields *(Harmonica Player)*, Dennis Moore *(Sgt. Borden)*, Kei Thing Chung *(Native Newsboy)*, Richard Bartlett *(American Soldier)*, Riley Hill *(Thompson)*, Lane Nakano *(Advance Guard)*, Bret Hamilton *(G.I.)*, Ed Sojin, Jr., Li Sun *(Japanese Soldiers)*, Wong Artarne, Eddie Lee *(Japanese M.P.'s)*, Remedos Jacobe *(Woman Clerk)*, William Yip *(Gen. Saito)*, William Yakota *(Admiral)*, Frank Iwanaga *(Submarine Officer)*, Harold Fong, Harry Hamada *(Japanese Lieutenants)*, Lane Bradford *(Driver)*, John Damler *(Soldier)*, Jack Reynolds *(U.S. Sergeant)*, Angel Crux *(Mashito)*, William Tannen *(U.S. Army Captain)*.

This film depicts the life of Claire Phillips (Dvorak), a spy during the Japanese occupation of Manila. She marries Kennedy just as Manila falls, but he is killed during the Bataan death march and Dvorak teams up with Evans. They wage guerrilla war fare on the Japanese and she then assumes the identity of a dead woman and opens a nightclub to get valuable information from the Japanese soldiers and officers. This she forwards to Evans who continues the guerrilla fighting.

When Dvorak is caught, Evans and his men save her from the firing squad. An opening narrative is presented by Gen. Mark W. Clark. Songs include: "Because Of You" (sung by Dvorak), and "Tokyo Ondo."

p, David Diamond; d, Lesley Selander; w, Sam Roeca (based on the novel *Manila Espionage* by Claire Phillips, Myron B. Goldsmith); ph, Harry Neumann; m, Edward J. Kay; ed, Phillip Cahn; art d, Dave Milton; m/l, Arthur Hammerstein, Dudley Wilkinson.

War Drama **(PR:A MPAA:NR)**

I WAS FAITHLESS (SEE: CYNARA, 1932)

I WAS FRAMED** (1942) 61m WB bw

Michael Ames *(Ken Marshall)*, Julie Bishop *(Ruth Marshall)*, Regis Toomey *(Bob Leeds)*, Patty Hale *(Penny Marshall)*, John Harmon *(Clubby Blake)*, Aldrich Bowker *(Dr. Phillip Black)*, Roland Drew *(Gordon Locke)*, Oscar O'Shea *(Cal Beamish)*, Wade Boteler *(Ben Belden)*, Howard Hickman *(Stuart Gaines)*, Norman Willis *(Paul Brenner)*, Hobart Bosworth *(D.L. Wallace)*, Guy Usher *(Police Chief Taylor)*, Sam McDaniel *(Kit Carson)*, Joan Winfield.

Ames is a reporter thrown in jail on trumped-up charges by a crook he is about to expose. The reporter escapes from jail and flees with his expectant wife to a small town to start anew. Life is rosy again until five years later, when a cellmate arrives in town. He remembers Ames and attempts to blackmail him. Just in time one of the governor's men steps forth to clear Ames' name by showing he was framed.

d, D. Ross Lederman; w, Robert E. Kent (based on the story "Dust Be My Destiny" by Jerome Odlum); ph, Ted McCord; ed, Frank Magee.

Crime Drama **(PR:A MPAA:NR)**

I WAS HAPPY HERE
(SEE: TIME LOST AND TIME REMEMBERED, 1966, Brit.)

I WAS MONTY'S DOUBLE
(SEE: HELL, HEAVEN OR HOBOKEN, 1958, Brit.)

I WILL . . . I WILL . . . FOR NOW*1/2 (1976) 107m Brut/FOX c

Elliott Gould *(Les Bingham)*, Diane Keaton *(Katie Bingham)*, Paul Sorvino *(Lou Springer)*, Victoria Principal *(Jackie Martin)*, Robert Alda *(Dr. Magnus)*, Madge Sinclair *(Dr. Williams)*, Warren Berlinger *(Steve Martin)*, Candy Clark *(Sally Bingham)*, Carmen Zapata *(Maria)*, George Tyne *(Marriage Counsellor)*.

Gould and Keaton are a hip couple who, displeased with their divorce, decide to give marriage another go. Gould has his lawyer, Sorvino, draw up a marriage contract without realizing that Sorvino has become Keaton's lover. The couple's mid-1970s mentality has them sign into a sex clinic where they both attempt to find themselves. This stock comedy is now commonplace on television sitcoms.

p, George Barrie; d, Norman Panama; w, Panama, Albert E. Lewin; ph, John A. Alonzo (Panavision, DeLuxe Color); m, John Cameron; ed, Robert Lawrence; prod d, Fernando Carrere; set d, Robert Signorelli.

Comedy **Cas.** **(PR:C MPAA:R)**

I WONDER WHO'S KISSING HER NOW1/2** (1947) 105m FOX c

June Haver *(Katie)*, Mark Stevens *(Joe Howard)*, Martha Stewart *(Lulu Madison)*, Reginald Gardiner *(Will Hough)*, Lenore Aubert *(Fritzi Barrington)*, William Frawley *(Jim Mason)*, Gene Nelson *(Tommy Yale)*, Truman Bradley *(Martin Webb)*, George Cleveland *(John McCullem)*, Harry Seymour *(Charley)*, Lewis L. Russell *(T.J. Milford)*, John "Skins" Miller *(Kassel)*, Lew Hearn *(Karl)*, Eve Miller *(Anita)*, Florence O'Brien *(Marie)*, Emmett Vogan *(Harris)*, Charles Judels *(Herman Bartholdy)*, Milton Parsons *(Mr. Fennabeck)*, Dewey Robinson *(King Louis)*, John Merton *(President Theodore Roosevelt)*, Robert Emmett Keane *(Mr. Kurlinger)*, John Sheehan *(Stage Doorman)*, Sam McDaniel *(Chef)*, John Arledge *(Clerk)*, Steve Olsen *(Song Plugger)*, Frank Scannell, Harry Cheshire *(Stage Managers)*, Joe Whitehead *(Bartender)*, Perry Ivins *(Critic)*, Herbert Heywood *(Doorman)*, Claire Richards *(Cigarette Girl)*, Antonio Filauri *(Italian Barber)*, Eddie Dunn, Ralph Dunn *(Stagehands)*, Almira Sessions *(Miss Claybourne)*, Merrill Rodin *("Willie")*, Alice Mock *(Singer)*.

Stevens is cast as vaudeville singer-songwriter Joe Howard, while Haver poses as his kid sister and manages to woo him away from sultry European star Aubert. The backstage sets of turn-of-the- century Broadway are often fascinating. Buddy Clark did the dubbing for all of Stevens' vocals. The songs include: "I Wonder Who's Kissing Her Now" (Joe Howard, Frank Adams, Will Hough, Harold Orlob), "Honeymoon," "What's The Use of Dreaming?" (Howard, Hough), "Hello My Baby" (Howard, Ida Emerson), "Oh, Gee, Be Sweet To Me Kid," "How'd You Like To Be The Umpire?" (Howard, Hough, Adams), "Goodbye My Lady Love" (Howard), with additional songs by Charles Henderson and producer Jessel.

p, George Jessel; d, Lloyd Bacon; w, Lewis R. Foster, Marion Turk; ph, Ernest Palmer (Technicolor); ed, Louis Loeffler; md, Alfred Newman; art d, Richard Day, Boris Leven; set d, Joseph C. Wright; spec eff, Fred Sersen, ch, Hermes Pan.

Musical **(PR:A MPAA:NR)**

I WOULDN'T BE IN YOUR SHOES** (1948) 70m MON bw

Don Castle *(Tom)*, Elyse Knox *(Ann)*, Regis Toomey *(Judd)*, Charles D. Brown *(Inspector Stevens)*, Rory Mallinson, Bill Kennedy *(Detectives)*, Ray Dolciame *(Shoe Shine Boy)*, William Ruhl *(Police Lieutenant)*, Esther Michelson *(Mrs. Finkelstein)*, Steve Darrell *(District Attorney)*, Wally Walker *(Shoe Clerk)*, John Sheehan *(Judge)*, Herman Cantor *(Jury Foreman)*, John H. Elliott *(Lawyer)*, Tito Vuolo *(Grocer)*, Jimmy Aubrey *(Tramp)*, John Shay (Salesman), Donald Kerr *(Vaudevillian)*, Joe Bernard *(Janitor)*, Stanley Blystone *(McGee)*, Dorothy Vaughn *(Mrs. Alvin)*, Robert Lowell *(Kosloff)*, Matty Fain, Dan White, John Doucette, Bill Walker *(Prisoners)*, Ray Teal, Paul Bryar *(Guards)*, Lou Marcelle *(Announcer)*, Walden Boyle *(Priest)*, Hugh Charles *(Counterman)*, Laura Treadwell *(Mrs. Stevens)*, Edwin Parker *(Policeman)*.

Standard whodunit has dancer Castle pinned for murder after his shoe prints are found at the scene of the crime. The real culprit is Toomey, who tries to cover his guilt by posing as a detective in love with Castle's sleuthing wife, Knox. She saves the day by squeezing a confession out of Toomey.

p, Walter Mirisch; d, William Nigh; w, Steve Fisher (based on the novel by Cornell Woolrich), ph, Mack Stengler; m, Edward J. Kay; ed, Roy Livingston; md, Kay: art d, Dave Milton; set d, Raymond Boltz, Jr.

Crime **(PR:A MPAA:NR)**

I'D CLIMB THE HIGHEST MOUNTAIN*** (1951) 87m FOX c

Susan Hayward *(Mary Elizabeth Eden Thompson/Narrator)*, William Lundigan *(William Asbury Thompson)*, Rory Calhoun *(Jack Stark)*, Barbara Bates *(Jenny Brock)*, Gene Lockhart *(Mr. Brock)*, Lynn Bari *(Mrs. Billywith)*, Ruth Donnelly *(Glory White)*, Kathleen Lockhart *(Mrs. Brock)*, Alexander Knox *(Salter)*, Jean Inness *(Mrs. Salter)*, Frank Tweddell *(Dr. Fleming)*, Jerry Vandiver *(George Salter)*, Richard Wilson *(Bill Salter)*, Dorothea Carolyn Sims *(Martha Salter)*, Thomas Syfan, Grady Starnes *(Pike Boys)*, Kay and Fay Fogg *(Martin Twins)*, Claude Stowers *(Station Master)*, Dr. Wallace Roger *(Minister)*, Myrtle Stovall *(Minister's Wife)*, Bobby C. Canup *(Two-Headed Boy)*, Nina G. Brown, Arispah Palmer, Caroline White *(Women)*.

The film is set in Georgia's Blue Ridge Mountains, where country preacher Lundigan and his city wife, Hayward, settle down in a small community. A neighbor, Bates, is stricken with a fever and, in her delirium, calls for her wild, but loving, beau, Calhoun. Against the wishes of the girl's father, Calhoun shows up and is nearly the recipient of an angry fist. It is Lundigan that keeps the peace by taking some children on a picnic. When Knox, the town atheist, finds that his children were taken along, he goes after the preacher. Lundigan's faith is temporarily shaken when Knox drowns in a nearby lake. Later an epidemic strikes and, by preaching the word of the Lord, Lundigan gives the townsfolk the strength to survive. After three years in the community, Lundigan and Hayward pack it up and head for another town. Though saccharine and unrealistic, this sentimental piece of Americana in enjoyable all the same. The tempestuous Hayward liked director King who treated her with kid gloves and was to become her favorite helmsman but she resented being co-starred with Lundigan, a B-film leading man. While on location outside of Dawsonville, Georgia, Hayward got absorbed in taking some snapshots of the breathtaking scenery of Amicolola Falls. She was backing up while taking photographs and didn't notice that she was about to step into space and fall into a 729-foot gorge. Studio chauffeur Will Gray spotted her and, in seconds, darted to her side to catch her at the last second before the actress plummeted to certain death. Fox promoted this film into a big hit, particularly in the South; Georgia Governor Herman Talmadge was given an engraved copy of the script and this led to the state senate voting Hayward "an adopted daughter of Georgia."

p, Lamar Trotti; d, Henry King; w, Trotti (based on the novel by Corra Harris); ph, Edward Cronjager (Technicolor); m, Sol Kaplan; ed, Barbara McLean; md, Lionel Newman; art d, Lyle Wheeler, Maurice Ransford; set d, Thomas Little, Al Orenbach; spec eff, Fred Sersen; makeup, Ben Nye.

Drama **(PR:A MPAA:NR)**

I'D GIVE MY LIFE*1/2 (1936) 82m PAR bw

Sir Guy Standing *(Gov. Bancroft)*, Frances Drake *(Mary Reyburn)*, Tom Brown *(Nickie Elkins)* Janet Beecher *(Mrs. Bancroft)*, Robert Gleckler *(Buck Gordon)*, Helen Lowell *(Mrs. Bancroft, Sr.)*, Paul Hurst *(Conly)*, Charles C. Wilson *(Warden)*, Charles Richman *(Attorney Chase)*, Tom Jackson, Charles Judels, Robert Elliott, William Burress, Corbett Morris, Franklyn Parker, James Eagles.

A spiteful gambler plans on revealing that his reform-schooled son was mothered by the woman who is presently wife to the governor, Standing. The delinquent son decides to take matters into his own hands when he learns of his father's ruinous intentions. Drake delivers the tune, "Someday We'll Meet Again."

p, Richard Rowland; d, Edwin L. Marin; w, George O'Neill, Ben Ryan (based on the play "The Noose" by H.H. Van Loan, Willard Mack); ph, Ira Morgan; ed, Duncan Mansfield; m/l, Con Conrad, Herb Magidson.

Drama **(PR:A MPAA:NR)**

I'D RATHER BE RICH1/2** (1964) 96m UNIV c

Sandra Dee *(Cynthia Dulaine)*, Robert Goulet *(Paul Benton)*, Andy Williams *(Warren Palmer)*, Maurice Chevalier *(Philip Dulaine)*, Charlie Ruggles *(Dr. Crandall)*, Gene Raymond *(Martin Wood)*, Hermione Gingold *(Miss Grimshaw)*, Allen Jenkins *(Fred)*, Rip Taylor *(Airline Clerk)*, Laurie Main *(Harrison)*, Dort Clark *(Albert)*, Hayden Rorke *(MacDougall)*, Alex Gerry *(Cartwright)*, Jill Jackson *(Mrs. MacDougall)*, Milton Frome *(Max)*, George Milan, Dick Ryan *(Directors)*, Ben Lessy *(First Hunter)*, Carol Lawrence *(Herself)*, Jonathan Hole *(Clergyman)*, Dorothy Neumann *(Elderly Maid)*, Edward Holmes *(Second Hunter)*, Ruth Clifford, Georgine Cleveland *(Stockholders' Wives)*, Robert Riordan, Kenneth Patterson, Austin Green, Charles Bell *(Directors)*, Paul Lukather *(Reporter)*, Lucille Fenton *(Housewife)*, Richard Flato *(Maitre D')*, Stuart Wade *(Policeman)*, Jack Orrison *(Husband)*, Paul Micale *(Waiter)*, Richard McGrath, Ray Kellogg, Lincoln Demyan, Bob Duggan *(Reporters)*.

Chevalier is charming as the ailing grandfather anxious to meet daughter Dee's fiance. She invites beau, Williams (in his first film role), to pay a visit, but his plane gets fogged in and he can't make it. Determined to please her grandfather, she asks her friend Goulet (his second film after CAMELOT) to double for the fiance, whom the father has never met. After meeting Dee's dubious love, Chevalier makes a miraculous recovery, and soon learns Goulet's real identity. Having taken a liking to the lad, he feigns illness whenever Goulet readies to leave. When Williams shows up, Chevalier clearly prefers the psuedo-fiance to the real thing, a preference Dee soon begins to share. Songs include: "Almost There" (Jerry Keller, Gloria Shayne), "Where Are You?" (Harold Adamson, Jimmy McHugh), "It Had To Be You" (Gus Kahn, Isham Jones, sung by Andy Williams), "I'd Rather Be Rich" (Richard Maltby, Jr., David Shire, sung by Williams, Robert Goulet). A remake of the 1941 film IT STARTED WITH EVE.

p, Ross Hunter; d, Jack Smight; w, Oscar Brodney, Norman Krasna, Leo Townsend; ph, Russell Metty (Eastmancolor); m, Percy Faith; ed, Milton Carruth; md, Joseph Gershenson; art d, Alexander Golitzen, George Webb; set d, Howard Bristol; ch, Miriam Nelson, Hal Belfer.

Romantic Comedy **(PR:A MPAA:NR)**

I'LL BE SEEING YOU*1/2** (1944) 83m Vanguard/UA bw

Ginger Rogers *(Mary Marshall)*, Joseph Cotten *(Zachary Morgan)*, Shirley Temple *(Barbara Marshall, Mary's Cousin,)* Spring Byington *(Mrs. Marshall)*, Tom Tully *(Mr. Marshall)*, Chill Wills *(Swanson)*, Dane Harris *(Lt. Bruce)*, Kenny Bowers, John Derek *(Sailors on the Train)*, Olin Howlin *(Hawker)*, Dorothy Stone *(Salesgirl)*, John James *(Paratrooper)*, Eddie Hall *(Charlie Hartman)*, Joe Haworth *(Sailor in Coffee Shop)*, Jack Carr *(Counterman)*, Bob Meredith *(Soldier-Father on Train)*, Robert Dudley *(YMCA Hotel Attendant)*, Margaret Bert *(Mother of Boys)*, Mickey Laughlin, Hank Tobias, Gary Gray *(Boys Outside Theater)*, Earl W. Johnson *(Dog Owner)*, Stanley Ridges *(Warden)*, Walter Baldwin *(Vendor)*.

A quietly moving film based on a radio play that starred James Cagney and Gertrude Lawrence, I'LL BE SEEING YOU is a love story with quite a twist. Rogers is on Christmas furlough from the penitentiary where she is serving a term for manslaughter. She had accidentally killed her boss when the man made sexual advances and she had to defend herself. She meets Cotten, a shell-shocked veteran of the war. He is on a brief Christmas holiday away from the hospital where he is being treated in the neuropsychiatric ward. They're thrown together by fate on a train; she's visiting relatives and he has been sent out by his doctors who want to see if he's fit to join the population. He's quite nervous but calms down with Rogers, who invites him to stay at her home for his 10-day vacation. The central portion of the film is the respite that they share, with all the usual Christmas scenes, but done in such excellent taste that they never appear mawkish. Cotten struggles with his memories and Rogers holds back the information about herself being away from the pen for a short spell. When they find that they are both equally attracted, to one another she decides to come clean. That stirs up a hornet's nest but all ends well. Cotten is very believable as a man struggling between normality and a breakdown. Rogers again proves that she doesn't need a pianist or tap shoes to give a compelling performance. Temple was 17 when she played Rogers' sister and didn't seem to be going through an "awkward age" at all. There were those who were eager to jettison her after her phenomenal childhood career began to wane, but she remained a good actress and always turned in a professional job. Dieterle's directorial hand was a trifle heavy at times, but not enough to mar this sleeper that's ripe for a remake.

p, Dore Schary; d, William Dieterle; w, Marion Parsonnet (based on the radio play "Double Furlough" by Charles Martin); ph, Tony Gaudio; m, Daniele Amfitheatrof; ed, William H. Ziegler; art d, Mark-Lee Kirk; set d, Earl B. Wooden, Emile Kuri; m/l, "I'll Be Seeing You," Sammy Fain, Irving Kahal.

Romance **(PR:A MPAA:NR)**

I'LL BE YOUR SWEETHEART*1/2 (1945, Brit.) 104m Gainsborough/GFD bw

Margaret Lockwood *(Edie Storey)*, Vic Oliver *(Sam Kahn)*, Michael Rennie *(Bob Fielding)*, Peter Graves *(Jim Knight)*, Moore Marriott *(George le Brunn)*, Frederick Burtwell *(Pacey)*, Garry Marsh *(Wallace)*, George Merritt *(T.P. O'Connor)*, Muriel George *(Mrs. le Brunn)*, Ella Retford *(Dresser)*, Alf Goddard *(Henchman)*, Eliot Makeham *(John Friar)*, Maudie Edwards *(Mrs. Jones)*, Jonathan Field *(Kelly)*, Barry Lupino, David Crowley, Joss Ambler, Wendy Toye.

Tin Pan Alley is glorified in this story of naive songwriters Oliver, Marriott, and Field and the vile tactics of music pirates. Rennie is a young musician from Yorkshire who benefits from Parliamentary member Merritt's new copyright law. An OK plot which doesn't receive much help from this average treatment. Songs include: "The Honeysuckle And The Bee," "Oh Mr. Porter," "Little Wooden Hut."

p, Louis Levy; d, Val Guest; w, Guest, Val Valentine; ph, Phil Grindrod.

Musical **(PR:A MPAA:NR)**

I'LL BE YOURS1/2** (1947) 93m UNIV bw

Deanna Durbin *(Louise Ginglebusher)*, Tom Drake *(George Prescott)*, William Bendix *(Wechsberg)*, Adolphe Menjou *(J. Conrad Nelson)*, Walter Catlett *(Mr. Buckingham)*, Franklin Pangborn *(Barber)*, William Trenk *(Captain)*, Joan Fulton [Shawlee] *(Blonde)*, Patricia Alphin *(Usherette)*, William Brooks *(Stagedoor Johnny)*, Lorin Raker, Richard Abbott, John Hamilton, Cyril Delevanti, Joseph Granby, Charles Miller, Dudley Dickerson, Willene Luckett.

Durbin stars as a small town youngster who heads for the Big Apple and becomes an usherette at the Buckingham, a fictionalized version of Radio City Music Hall. It is here that she gets involved with Menjou, a pushy millionaire, and Drake, an unsuccessful lawyer. She and the latter eventually fall in love, and she sneakily tries to get her beau a job in Menjou's meat-packing house. Bendix, in a supporting role as a waiter, delivers his usual outstanding performance. Durbin delivers four tunes; "It's Dreamtime," "Cobbleskill School Song" (Jack Brooks, Walter Schumann), "Granada" (Augustin Lara, English lyrics Dorothy Dodd), "Sari Waltz" (C.C.S. Cushman, E.P. Heath, Emmerich Kalman). A remake of the 1935 Margaret Sullavan vehicle THE GOOD FAIRY, which was also penned by this film's writer, Sturges who, unfortunately, added nothing new to this version.

p, Felix Jackson; d, William A. Seiter; w, Preston Sturges (based on the play "The Good Fairy" by Ferenc Molnar, translated and adapted by Jane Hinton); ph, Hal Mohr; m, Frank Skinner; ed, Otto Ludwig; md, Walter Schumann; art d, John B. Goodman; set d, Russell Gausman; cos, Travis Banton; makeup, Jack P. Pierce.

Musical **(PR:A MPAA:NR)**

I'LL CRY TOMORROW**** (1955) 117m MGM bw

Susan Hayward *(Lillian Roth)*, Richard Conte *(Tony Bardeman)*, Eddie Albert *(Burt McGuire)*, Jo Van Fleet *(Katie Roth)*, Don Taylor *(Wallie)*, Ray Danton *(David Tredman)*, Margo *(Selma)*, Virginia Gregg *(Ellen)*, Don Barry *(Jerry)*, David Kasday *(David as a Child)*, Carole Ann Campbell *(Lillian as a Child)*, Peter Leeds *(Richard)*, Tol Avery *(Fat Man)*, Jack Daley *(Cab Driver)*, Ralph Edwards *(Himself)*, Tim Carey *(Derelict)*, Charles Tannen, Harlan Warde *(Stage Managers)*, Ken Patterson, Stanley Farrar *(Directors)*, Voltaire Perkins *(Mr. Byrd)*, George Lloyd *(Messenger)*, Nora Marlowe *(Nurse)*, Peter Brocco *(Doctor)*, Bob Dix *(Henry)*, Anthony Jochim *(Paul, the Butler)*, Kay English *(Dress Designer)*, Eve McVeagh *(Ethel)*, Veda Ann Borg *(Waitress)*, Jack Gargan *(Drug Clerk)*, Robert R. Stephenson, Joe DuVal *(Bartenders)*, Vernon Rich *(Club Manager)*, Cheerio Meredith *(Elderly Lady)*, Gail Ganley *(Lillian at 15)*, Ruth Storey *(Marge Belney)*, James Ogg *(Usher)*, George Pembroke, Mary Bear *(Couple)*, Bernadette Withers, Kathy Garner *(Girls)*, Henry Kulky, Marc Krah, Guy Wilkerson *(Men)*, Robert B. Williams *(Stagehand)*, Bob Hopkins *(M. C.)*, Herbert C. Lytton *(Conductor)*, George Selk *(Switchman)*.

A hard-hitting, intense biography of Lillian Roth, who had it all in the palm of her hand and let it slide through her fingers as she reached for another drink. Campbell is the childhood Roth whose mother, Van Fleet, pushes her unmercifully towards stardom. Before she is a teenager, Campbell is already appearing on Broadway and working regularly. Now Hayward is in the role. She falls in love with Danton but he dies unexpectedly, and she begins a downward spiral with the bottle as her substitute for love. She marries an equally-drunk serviceman, Taylor, but that marriage soon disintegrates. Her next husband is also a drunk, as well as a sadist, Conte, and he beats her during their drinking bouts. She winds up on California's Skid Row. Van Fleet can't understand why her daughter is in such a state and wonders what her role was in making Hayward the way she is. While attempting to commit suicide by jumping from a fleabag hotel window, Hayward is too weak to do even that and faints. She finally realizes that there is only one way out, short of death, and that's through Alcoholics Anonymous. It is at one of the meetings that she meets Albert, Margo, and Barry, who all help bring her back to reality. Eventually, she marries Albert after suffering a series of withdrawal symptoms. She understands that there are many people in the same position as she is who are hiding their affliction and feels she can help them by going public. She is interviewed on "This is Your Life" and the world then knows the story. I'LL CRY TOMORROW does not shrink from the truth of Roth's life one bit, and that was a refreshing change from so many film biographies that swept the truth under the rug. Hayward won the Cannes Film Festival Best Actress Award, as well as an Oscar nomination. Hayward, upon reading Roth's bestselling book, immediately lobbied to play her life, as did a score of other actresses, but Hayward was so aggressive she literally bullied herself into one of her best roles. Personally going to MGM boss Dore Schary, who had been considering June Allyson for the part, Hayward sold herself, stressing that she had provided box office successes in movies dealing with women in crisis, pointing out what hits she had made of WITH A SONG IN MY HEART and SMASH-UP. To make sure of the studio's decision, Hayward contacted Roth and got her blessing. The film also received nominations in the categories of Cinematography, Costumes, and Art and Set Directions. Costumes took the only Oscar for the film. Hayward did her own singing in a light but pleasant voice, and Roth was annoyed because they would not ask her to dub herself. Roth, who served as a technical advisor on the film, made a nightclub comeback in the 1950s, then wrote a sequel, *Beyond My Worth*, which did not sell nearly as well. Hayward was a troubled woman in her early years and, just prior to acting in this film, she took sleeping pills and was hospitalized. Lillian Roth, who had already been through the tortures, came to Hayward's side almost immediately and did her best to help the Brooklyn redhead through her travails. Roth's major disagreement with the film, other than not being able to sing her songs, was that Van Fleet's role was slightly altered. In real life, Roth's aggressive stage-mother spoke with a cultured Boston accent but someone in the studio felt that Van Fleet should be given a Mittel-European manner of speech in order to make the point that they were of Jewish descent. Songs include: "Sing You Sinners" (Sam Coslow, W. Frank Harling), "When The Red Red Robin Comes Bob Bob Bobbin' Along," and "Happiness Is Just A Thing Called Joe" (E.Y. Harburg, Harold Arlen). The "Vagabond King Waltz" was shot but cut before the final release print was issued. I'LL CRY TOMMORROW was a huge success for MGM, which proved again that the public will sit still for quality.

p, Lawrence Weingarten; d, Daniel Mann; w, Helen Deutsch, Jay Richard Kennedy (based on the book by Lillian Roth, Mike Connolly, Gerold Frank); ph, Arthur E. Arling; m, Alex North; ed, Harold F. Kress; md, Charles Henderson; art d, Cedric Gibbons, Malcolm Brown; set d, Edwin B. Willis, Hugh Hunt; cos, Helen Rose; spec eff, Warren Newcombe.

Drama/Musical **(PR:A-C MPAA:NR)**

I'LL FIX IT* (1934) 68m COL bw

Jack Holt *(Bill Grimes)*, Mona Barrie *(Anne Barry)*, Winnie Lightner *(Elizabeth)*, Jimmy Butler *(Bobby)*, Edward Brophy *(Tilly)*, Nedda Harrigan *(Miss Burns)*, Charles Moore *(Nifty)*, Helena Phillips Evans *(Mrs. Murphy)*, Charles Levison, John

Wray, Wallis Clark, Edward Van Sloan, Clarence Wilson, Selmer Jackson, Harry Holman, Robert Gunn, Dorian Johnston, Frank Conroy.

An underhanded effort which sees Holt running a town and getting whatever he wants—legally or not. When his kid brother is refused a spot on his school's ball team, Holt tries to fix things with Barrie, the hard-edged principal. When she won't bend to his pressures, Holt fires her, causing the rest of the teachers to revolt. A newspaper story has him in hot water over a corrupt real estate deal, but he is saved before meeting the judge. The once moralistic Barrie, now seeing things through love-colored glasses, lies in his favor and the accusations are dismissed.

d, Roy William Neill; w, Ethel Hill, Dorothy Howell (based on the story by Leonard Spiegelgass); ph, Benjamin Kline; ed, Richard Cahoon.

Drama **(PR:A MPAA:NR)**

I'LL GET BY½** (1950) 82m FOX c

June Haver *(Liza Martin)*, William Lundigan *(William Spencer)*, Gloria De Haven *(Terry Martin)*, Dennis Day *(Freddy Lee)*, Harry James *(Himself)*, Thelma Ritter *(Miss Murphy)*, Steve Allen *(Peter Pepper)*, Danny Davenport *(Chester Dooley)*, Reginald Gardiner, Jeanne Crain, Dan Dailey, Victor Mature *(Guest Stars)*, Tom Hanlon *(Announcer)*, Peggy O'Connor *(USO Girl)*, Harry Seymour *(Stage Manager)*, Harry Lauter, Don Hicks *(Assistant Directors)*, Charles Tannen *(Director)*, Kathleen Hughes *(Secretary)*, Vincent Renno *(Head Waiter)*, Bob McCord *(Commentator)*, John Butler *(Man by Fireplace)*, Paul Picerni *(Marine Sergeant)*, Dick Winslow *(Cooky Myers)*, Stanley Prager *(Song Plugger)*, Frank Mills *(Fish Market Man)*.

After getting fired from his job, music publisher Lundigan teams up with Dailey and the two become involved with sisters Haver and De Haven. The girls, who earn their keep by singing with the Harry James Band, do their best to get Lundigan and Dailey's tunes plugged. The amorous twosomes get split up after a romantic misunderstanding, but soon team up again in a South Pacific USO show. The plot is enveloped to the point of obscurity by a constant barrage of tunes. Included are: "Deep In The Heart Of Texas" (June Hershey, Don Swander), "You Make Me Feel So Young" (Mack Gordon, Josef Myrow) "I've Got The World On A String" (Ted Koehler, Harold Arlen), "Once In A While" (Bud Green, Michael Edwards), "Yankee Doodle Blues" (Buddy De Sylva, Irving Caeser, George Gershwin), "Fifth Avenue," "There Will Never Be Another You" (Gordon, Harry Warren), "McNamara's Band" (Shamus O'Connor, J.J. Stamford), "It's Been A Long, Long Time" (Sammy Cahn, Jule Styne), "No Love, No Nothin' " (Leo Robin, Warren), Auld Lang Syne (lyrics, Robert Burns). "Taking A Chance On Love" (John Latouche, Ted Fetter, Vernon Duke, sung by De Haven), "I'll Get By" (Roy Turk, Fred Ahlert, sung by De Haven). A remake of TIN PAN ALLEY made in 1940.

p, William Perlberg; d, Richard Sale; w, Sale, Mary Loos (based on the story by Robert Ellis, Helen Logan, Pamela Harris); ph, Charles G. Clarke (Technicolor); ed, J. Watson Webb, Jr.; md, Lionel Newman; art d, Lyle Wheeler, Loos; ch, Larry Ceballos.

Musical **(PR:A MPAA:NR)**

I'LL GET YOU**

(1953, Brit.) 78m Banner-Eros/Lippert bw (GB: ESCAPE ROUTE)

George Raft *(Steve Rossi)*, Sally Gray *(Joan Miller)*, Clifford Evans *(Michael Grand)*, Reginald Tate *(Col. Wilkes)*, Patricia Laffan *(Miss Brooks)*, Frederick Piper *(Inspector Reid)*, Roddy Hughes *(Porter)*, June Ashley *(Girl)*, John Warwick *(Brice)*.

Atomic scientists are disappearing left and right with FBI agent Raft and British Intelligence gal Gray pursuing at a snail's pace. They trace the missing men to an Iron Curtain hideout held by Evans' gang. After what feels like years, the criminals are apprehended at a Thames River wharf.

p, Bernard Luber; d, Seymour Friedman; w, John V. Baines, Nicholas Phipps; ph, Eric Cross; m, Hans May; ed, Tom Simpson.

Spy **(PR:A MPAA:NR)**

I'LL GET YOU FOR THIS (SEE: LUCKY NICK CAIN, 1950, Brit.)

I'LL GIVE A MILLION½** (1938) 70m FOX bw

Warner Baxter *(Tony Newlander)*, Marjorie Weaver *(Jean)*, Peter Lorre *(Louie)*, John Carradine *(Kopelpeck)*, Jean Hersholt *(Victor)*, J. Edward Bromberg *(Editor)*, Lynn Bari *(Cecelia)*, Fritz Feld *(Max Primerose)*, Sig Rumann *(Anatole Primerose)*, Christian Rub *(Corncomaire)*, Paul Harvey *(Corcoran)*, Charles Halton *(Mayor)*, Frank Reicher *(Prefect of Police)*, Frank Dawson *(Albert)*, Harry Hayden *(Gilman)*, Stanley Andrews *(Captain)*, Lillian Porter *(Flower Girl)*, Luis Alberni *(Reporter)*, Rafaela Ottiano *(Proprietress)*, Georges Renavent *(Gendarme)*, Rolfe Sedan *(Telegraph Clerk)*, Eddie Conrad *(Pastry Shop Proprietor)*, Armand Kaliz *(Hotel Manager)*.

A disillusioned millionaire, Baxter, stands aboard his yacht on the verge of suicide when he hears the cries of Lorre, a bum who has just taken a death leap into the water. Baxter saves Lorre's life and proceeds to tell him how everyone is constantly sponging from him. He goes on to proclaim that he will give a million francs to anyone who treats him kindly, without regard to his pocketbook. When the skeptical Lorre awakes the next morning, he finds Baxter gone and his ragged bum clothes missing. In return, the millionaire has left his own wardrobe and a roll of 100 franc notes as compensation. Lorre spreads the tale to anyone who'll listen, and hobos from all over the country wander the area when the townsfolk begin giving the royal treatment to everyone with tattered clothes. The millionaire eventually marries Weaver, a circus performer, and donates the million-franc purse to the entire community. Lorre and Carradine carry the show, delivering wonderful performances as tramps.

p, Darryl F. Zanuck; d, Walter Lang; w, Boris Ingster, Milton Sperling (based on the story "I Shall Give A Million" by Cesare Zavattini, Giaci Mondaini); ph, Lucien Andriot; m, Louis Silvers; ed, Louis Loeffler; md, Silvers; art d, Bernard Herzbrun, David Hall.

Comedy/Drama **(PR:A MPAA:NR)**

I'LL GIVE MY LIFE* (1959) 79m Concordia/Howco bw

John Bryant, Angie Dickinson, Ray Collins, Katherine Warren, Donald Woods, Jon Shepodd, Stuart Randall, Richard Benedict, Milton Woods, Sam Flint, Mimi Gibson.

A slow-moving drama about a father and son with vastly different values. Collins, a construction tycoon, is appalled, when his son, Bryant, graduates with an engineering degree and chooses to become a missionary rather than enter the family business. When Bryant dies of jungle fever, however, Collins feels a deep loss, and organizes a fund-raiser in his son's memory.

p, Sam Hersh; d, William F. Claxton; w, Herbert Moulton.

Drama **(PR:A MPAA:NR)**

I'LL LOVE YOU ALWAYS*½ (1935) 75m COL bw

Nancy Carroll *(Nora Clegg)*, George Murphy *(Carl Brent)* Raymond Walburn *(Charlie)*, Jean Dixon *(Mae Waters)*, Arthur Hohl *(Jergens)*, Paul Harvey *(Sandstone)*, Harry Beresford *(Henry Irving Clegg, Old Actor)*, Robert Allen.

Young engineer, Murphy, and his ex-actress wife, Carroll, find their marriage on shaky ground soon after the honeymoon ends. When Carroll discovers she is pregnant, she keeps the news from her husband. Meanwhile, Murphy spends his time stealing cash and spending it senselessly. He is arrested and sent to prison, but he manages to keep it a secret from Carroll by telling her he is in Russia on business. Predictably, the two are reunited when Murphy is parolled and sees his infant son for the first time.

p, Everett J. Riskin; d, Leo Bulgakov; w, Vera Caspary, Sidney Buchman (based on the story by Lawrence Hazard); ph, Joseph August; ed, Richard Cahoon.

Drama **(PR:A MPAA:NR)**

I'LL NEVER FORGET WHAT'S 'IS NAME**

(1967, Brit.) 97m Scimitar-UNIV/REG c

Orson Welles *(Jonathan Lute)*, Oliver Reed *(Andrew Quint)*, Carol White *(Georgina)*, Harry Andrews *(Gerald Sater)*, Michael Hordern *(Headmaster)*, Wendy Craig *(Louise Quint)*, Marianne Faithfull *(Josie)*, Norman Rodway *(Nicholas)*, Frank Finlay *(Chaplain)*, Harvey Hall *(Maccabee)*, Ann Lynn *(Carla)*, Lyn Ashley *(Susannah)*, Veronica Clifford *(Anna)*, Edward Fox *(Walter)*, Stuart Cooper *(Lewis Force)*, Roland Curran *(Eldrich)*, Peter Graves *(Bankman)*, Mark Burns *(Michael Cornwall)*, Mark Eden *(Kellaway)*, Josephine Rueg *(Marian)* Mona Chong *(Vietnamese Girl)*, Robert Mill *(Galloway)*, Terence Seward *(Pinchin)*, Basil Dignam.

"Nothing Succeeds Like Excess" seems to be the credo adopted by the makers of this film. Had someone exercised a little restraint, it could have been a devastating satire on the British advertising world, as well as the folkways and mores of the 1960s. The tragicomedy begins as Reed, a hot-shot TV commercials director, walks through London and into his office with a huge axe in his hand. He proceeds to smash everything in sight, then resigns from his job. He is disgusted with the meaninglessness of his work and his empty relationship with his wife, Craig, as well as his frequent liaisons with his various mistresses. He returns to the small literary magazine he worked for just after leaving Cambridge, thinking he can at last achieve intellectual freedom and some peace. But the office machinations of this small journal are every bit as distasteful to him as what went on in the advertising world. He has an affair with prim White, the office secretary, and is at constant odds with old pal Finlay, who edits the periodical. Welles, who owns the vast corporation that Reed worked with, wants Reed back so he buys the magazine agency. Reed agrees to make one last commercial, thinking he will have the last laugh. When White is killed in an auto accident, Reed directs the spot—a bitter attack on advertising that uses clips from the Nazi concentration camps, as well as cuts from nuclear devastation films. His plans go awry when the commercial wins the top award at a festival. Welles is top-lined here, but doesn't have that large a part. What he does with it, however, is brilliant. He is the epitome of the "fat cat" both physically and mentally. The film falls apart because Winner, in his mad passion to keep us from being bored, directs the film in such a quirky style that we can never settle back and enjoy the deliciousness of Draper's script. Filmed on location in London and Cambridge, it looks marvelous, but the diffusion of the story causes us to ultimately forget I'LL NEVER FORGET WHAT'S 'IS NAME.

p&d, Michael Winner; w, Peter Draper; ph, Otto Heller (Technicolor); m, Francis Lai; ed, Bernard Gribble; art d, Scamus Flannery; cos, Bibas; makeup, Richard Mills.

Comedy/Drama **(PR:AC MPAA:NR)**

I'LL NEVER FORGET YOU***

(1951) 89m FOX bw/c (GB: THE HOUSE ON THE SQUARE)

Tyrone Power *(Peter Standish)*, Ann Blyth *(Helen Pettigrew/Martha Forsyth)*, Michael Rennie *(Roger Forsyth)*, Dennis Price *(Tom Pettigrew)*, Beatrice Campbell *(Kate Pettigrew)*, Kathleen Byron *(Duchess of Devonshire)*, Raymond Huntley *(Mr. Throstle)*, Irene Browne *(Lady Anne Pettigrew)*, Robert Atkins *(Dr. Samuel Johnson)*, Ronald Adam *(Ronson)*, Gibb McLaughlin *(Jacob)*, Hamlyn Benson *(Magistrate)*, Ronald Simpson *(Sir Joshua Reynolds)*, Felix Aylmer *(Sir William, the Physician)*, Diane Hart *(Dolly)*, Tom Gill *(Macaroni)*, Alexander McCrindle *(James Boswell)*, Jill Clifford *(Maid)*, Peter Drury *(Policeman)*, Victor Maddern *(Geiger Man)*, Alec Finter *(Throstle's Coachman)*, Anthony Pelly *(Footman)*, Catherine

Carlton *(Girl)*, Richard Carrickford *(Bow Street Runner)*, Rose Howlett *(Woman)*, Arthur Denton *(Loonies' Driver)*.

Filmed in black and white *and* Technicolor (for certain sequences), I'LL NEVER FORGET YOU is a remake of the 1933 Leslie Howard feature, BERKELEY SQUARE, which was based on the play by Balderston. It was later made into a musical for Broadway and then the film, ON A CLEAR DAY YOU CAN SEE FOREVER. Power was already in London, having just completed starring in the touring company of "Mr. Roberts," so he walked right into this film the following week. (NOTE: in that same production of "Mr. Roberts" a teenage actor was making one of his first appearances before going on to film acting and eventually directing. That was Ray Danton.) While shooting the film, they couldn't decide on a title, and it was alternately called BEYOND TIME AND SPACE as well as MAN OF TWO WORLDS. In Europe, it was sometimes known as THE HOUSE ON THE SQUARE. Power is a dour American atomic physicist living in a Berkeley Square mansion he's inherited. His mood swings cause him to believe he may be about to have a mental breakdown. Power's best friend is Rennie, who tells him about some documents he's found in the house that speak of an ancestor who also came from the U.S. to live in England. Power believes he can actually change places with his antecedent because, according to his theory, time does not exist and the past, present and future all happen simultaneously (this same theory was used to great advantage in Jack Finney's brilliant book *Time and Again.* It has since been "appropriated" several times, most notably in SOMEWHERE IN TIME [Christopher Reeve], TIME AFTER TIME [Malcolm McDowell, Mary Steenburgen] and BACK TO THE FUTURE [Michael Fox, Christopher Lloyd]). Rennie says pish-tosh to all that and tells Power that what he needs is a month in the country to clear those cobwebs out. Power later strolls through the streets during a thunderstorm and is struck by a lightning bolt. He comes out of his faint and finds that he is now in the 18th century! His fiancée is Campbell, and he is staying at the mansion with her and her family. Since he'd already read all the information about his ancestor, he is able to function in his new role, except for when he meets Campbell's sister, the beauteous Blyth (she took over the role when Constance Smith became ill). She was never mentioned in the old books about the family and is so enchanting that he cannot take his eyes off her. Their mother, Browne, and their brother, Price, are angered when they see Power begin to transfer his affection to Blyth. Power's picture of the tranquil 18th century is shattered when he comes upon conditions that he thought existed only in Dickens' mind. He decides to improve things by setting up a workshop and using his scientific knowledge to create startling inventions. (This is very similar to the situation advanced by Mark Twain in A CONNECTICUT YANKEE IN KING ARTHUR'S COURT). Campbell thinks Power is nuts and wants to have him put away, but Blyth believes in Power and stands by him. During another thunderstorm Power is shot forward to the 20th century where he awakens to find that he's been ill for several weeks. Rennie now introduces his sister, Blyth, to Power. She is the image of the woman he loved so much in the 18th century. Power digs further and learns that the 18th century Blyth died just after his ancestor mysteriously vanished back then. Power and Blyth fall in love immediately and are enabled to carry out the attraction that began 200 years before. It's a terrific story but less than a terrific film. Power is given little opportunity to show any of his humor and the entire mood of the film is lethargic and a bit sombre.

p, Sol C. Siegel; d, Roy Baker; w, Ranald MacDougall (based on the play "Berkeley Square" by John L. Balderston); ph, Georges Perinal (Technicolor); m, William Alwyn; ed, Alan Osbiston; md, Muir Mathieson; art d, C.P. Norman; cos, Margaret Furse.

Drama **(PR:A MPAA:NR)**

I'LL REMEMBER APRIL* 1/2 (1945) 63m UNIV bw

Gloria Jean *(April)*, Kirby Grant *(Dave Ball)*, Milburn Stone *(Winchester)*, Edward S. Brophy *(Shadow)*, Samuel S. Hinds *(Garfield)*, Jacqueline de Wit *(Whisper)*, Hobart Cavanaugh *(Billings)*, Addison Richards *(Police Inspector)*, Pierre Watkin *(Dr. Armitage)* Clyde Fillmore *(J.C. Cartwright)*, Mary Forbes *(Mrs. Barrington)*, Morgan Wallace *(Childs)*, Paul Porcasi *(Popolopolis)*, The Cotton Sisters *(Dancing Specialty)*, Nan Leslie *(Western Union Girl)*, Louise Burnette *(Secretary)*, John Archer, Irene Thomas, Mike Musso, Marion Musso, Venna Archer, Bill Alcorn *(Jitterbugs)*.

Jean is as sugary as possible playing a do-good singer who tries for a radio job in order to keep her bankrupt family afloat. She finds herself in the middle of a feud between radio commentators, which soon leads to a murder mystery. There's not much to remember, especially Jean's vocals on "Hittin' The Beach Tonite" (Marty Roberts, Chic Dornish), and "I'll Remember April" (Don Raye, Gene De Paul, Pat Johnson).

p, Gene Lewis; d, Harold Young; w, M. Coates Webster (based on the story "Mike Goes To A Party" by Gene Lewis and "Amateur Nights" by Bob Dillon); ph, Jerome Ash; ed, Philip Cahn; md, Edgar Fairchild; art d, John B. Goodman, Abraham Grossman.

Crime/Musical **(PR:A MPAA:NR)**

I'LL SAVE MY LOVE (SEE: TWO LOVES, 1961)

I'LL SEE YOU IN MY DREAMS 1/2** (1951) 109m WB bw

Doris Day *(Grace LeBoy Kahn)*, Danny Thomas *(Gus Kahn)*, Frank Lovejoy *(Walter Donaldson)*, Patrice Wymore *(Gloria Knight)*, James Gleason *(Fred)*, Mary Wickes *(Anna)*, Jim Backus *(Sam Harris)*, Julie Oshins *(Johnny)*, Minna Gombell *(Mrs. LeBoy)*, Harry Antrim *(Mr. LeBoy)*, William Forrest *(Florenz Ziegfeld)*, Bunny Lewbel *(Irene, at 6)*, Robert Lyden *(Donald, at 8)*, Mimi Gibson *(Irene, at 3)*, Christy Olson *(Donald, at 4)*, Dick Simmons *(Bert)*, Else Neft *(Mrs. Kahn)*, Jack Williams, Clarence Landry *(Negro Dancers)*, Ray Kellogg *(John McCormack)*, George Neise *(Isham Jones)*, Vince Barnett *(Comic)*, Dan Barton *(Hollywood Producer)*.

An entertaining and heartfelt biography of songwriter Gus Kahn (Thomas), and his wife and inspiration Grace LeBoy (Day). Kahn's life is traced from his Chicago roots to his New York rise with Ziegfeld. His temporary downslide is seen after the 1929 market crash and the departure of his wife. Day, however, returns and stays with him until his death in 1941. The songs, all of whose lyrics are by Kahn, include: "Ain't We Got Fun," "Ukelele Lady" (Richard Whiting, Ray Egan), "The One I Love Belongs To Somebody Else," "I'll See You In My Dreams," "It Had To Be You," "Swingin' Down The Lane" (Isham Jones), "My Buddy," "Makin' Whoopee!," "Yes Sir, That's My Baby," "Carolina In The Morning," "Love Me Or Leave Me" (Walter Donaldson), "I Wish I Had A Girl" (Grace LeBoy Kahn), "Nobody's Sweetheart" (Billy Meyers, Elmer Schoebel, Ernie Erdman), "Pretty Baby" (Egbert Van Alstyne, Tony Jackson), "Memories" (Van Alstyne), "I Never Knew" (Ted Fio Rito), "Toot Toot Tootsie Goodbye" (Al Jolson, Ernie Erdman, Dan Russo), "No No Nora" (Fio Rito, Erdman), "Your Eyes Have Told Me So" (Van Alstyne, Walter Blaufuss), "San Francisco" (Bronislau Kaper), "The Carioca" (Edward Eliscu, Vincent Youmans), "I'm Through With Love" (Fud Livingston, Matt Malneck), "Liza" (George and Ira Gershwin). The only tune not by Kahn was "Shine On Harvest Moon" (Jack Norworth, Nora Bayes).

p, Louis F. Edelman; d, Michael Curtiz; w, Melville Shavelson, Jack Rose (based on a story by Grace Kahn, Edelman); ph, Ted McCord; ed, Owen Marks; md, Ray Heindorf; art d, Douglas Bacon; set d, George James Hopkins; cos, Leah Rhodes, Marjorie Best; ch, LeRoy Prinz.

Musical/Biography **(PR:A MPAA:NR)**

I'LL SELL MY LIFE* 1/2 (1941) 73m Select bw

Rose Hobart, Michael Whalen, Stanley Fields, Joan Woodbury, Roscoe Ates, Richard Bond, Ben Taggart, Robert Regent, Paul Maxey, Munro Brown, Robert Walker.

The bond between brother and sister proves to be the most important thing in a young woman's life as she sacrifices her own life in order to get her brother out of a jam. Mildly thrilling drama.

d, Elmer Clifton; w, George Rosener, Clifton (based on the story by Walter Ripperger).

Drama **(PR:A MPAA:NR)**

I'LL STICK TO YOU* 1/2 (1933, Brit.) 66m BL bw

Jay Laurier *(Adam Tipper)*, Betty Astell *(Pauline Mason)*, Louis Hayward *(Ronnie Matthews)*, Ernest Sefton *(Mortimer Moody)*, Hal Walters *(Wilkins)*, Annie Esmond *(Eve Oglethorpe)*, Mary Gaskell *(Millie Wiggins)*, Charles Childerstone *(Pilgrim)*.

A young lady nearly loses her inheritance when she is told that she must find herself an equally wealthy husband. The boy she loves, however, is far from rich until he invents a super-glue. He is cheated out of his profits by a conniving boss, but the young lovers enact a plan to get the recognition they deserve. A juvenile attempt to pry a few laughs out of the audience.

p, Herbert Smith; d, Leslie Hiscott; w, Michael Barringer.

Comedy **(PR:A MPAA:NR)**

I'LL TAKE ROMANCE 1/2** (1937) 85m COL bw

Grace Moore *(Elsa Terry)*, Melvyn Douglas *(James Guthrie)*, Helen Westley *(Madame Della)*, Stuart Erwin *("Pancho" Brown)*, Margaret Hamilton *(Margot)*, Walter Kingsford *(William Kane)*, Richard Carle *(Rudi)*, Ferdinand Gottschalk *(Girard)*, Esther Muir *(Pamela)*, Frank Forest *(Pinkerton)*, Walter O. Stahl *(Johan)*, Barry Norton *(Juan)*, Lucio Villegas *(Montez)*, Gennaro Curci *(Bondini)*, Marek Windheim *(Henri)*, Franklin Pangborn *(Secretary)*, Greta Meyer *(Opera Singer)*, Albert Conti *(Lepino)*, Adia Kuznetzoff *(Conductor)*, George Andre Beranger *(Male Dressmaker)*, John Gallaudet *(Photographer)*, Ernest Wood *(Hotel Clerk)*, Mareo Vido, Al Hill *(Taxi Drivers)*, Allan Garcia *(Himself)*, Bruce Sidney *(Stage Manager)*, Mildred Gover *(Maid)*, Louis Mercier, Manuel Emanuel, Alex Palasthy, Genaro Spagneli, Manuel Paris *(Men)*, Meeka Aldrich, Mariska Aldrich, Irene Crane *(Women)*, Bruce Wyndham *(Young German)*, Bud Wolfe *(Bartender)*, Carrie Daumery *(Dowager)*, Mary Emery *(Girl)*, George Hickman *(Page Boy)*, Len Davis *(Sailor)*, Bill Lally *(Steward)*.

The thin plot has diva Moore scheduled to open the Buenos Aires opera season, but instead opting to take a better offer in Paris. Douglas takes off from Argentina and sets his sights on kidnaping the singer. He tries to win her over through his charms and eventually gets his way. Selections from various operas are included, such as "La Traviata" (Verdi), "Madame Butterfly" (Puccini), "Manon" (Massenet). Also included is the title tune by Oscar Hammerstein II and Ben Oakland, and "A Frangesa" (Milton Drake, Marie Costa). On the lighter side, the tune "She'll Be Comin' Around The Mountain" found its way into the plot.

p, Everett Riskin; d, Edward H. Griffith; w, George Oppenheimer, Jane Murfin (based on the story by Stephen Morehouse Avery); ph, Lucien Andriot; ed, Otto Meyer, William Lyon; md, M.W. Stoloff, Isaac Van Grove; art d, Stephen Goosson, Lionel Banks; set d, William Von Wymetal, Jr.

Musical **(PR:A MPAA:NR)**

I'LL TAKE SWEDEN 1/2** (1965) 96m Superior/UA c

Bob Hope *(Bob Holcomb)*, Tuesday Weld *(JoJo Holcomb)*, Frankie Avalon *(Kenny Klinger)*, Dina Merrill *(Karin Grandstedt)*, Jeremy Slate *(Erik Carlson)*, Rosemarie Frankland *(Marti)*, Walter Sande *(Bjork)*, John Qualen *(Olaf)*, Peter Bourne *(Ingemar)*, Fay De Witt *(Hilda)*, Alice Frost *(Greta)*, Roy Roberts *(Captain)*, Maudie Prickett *(Spinster)*, Beverly Hills *(Electra)*, Siv Marta Aberg *(Inter)*, The Vulcanes *(Musical Group)*.

Hope is the overprotective father of Weld and determined to rid her of her guitar-twanging, motorcycle-revving beau, Avalon. To break up the young lovers, he gets himself transferred to Sweden by the oil company he works for. Weld soon finds herself with another mate, this time in the form of debonair playboy Slate. Hope also finds romance, falling under the spell of interior decorator Merrill. It is not long, however, before Hope is disgusted with Slate and his idea of a trial honeymoon. Frantically, he tries to get Avalon to come to Sweden and win back Weld. Avalon takes the trip and, upon meeting Slate, promptly knocks him out with his guitar. On the return trip via the Atlantic, Hope and Merrill and Weld and Avalon have the ship's captain perform a double marriage. Songs include "The Bells Keep Ringin'," "Peep Show," "There'll Be Rainbows Again" ("By" Dunham, Bobby Beverly), "Nothing Can Compare With You" (Dunham), "Would Ya' Like My Last Name?" (Kenneth Lampert, Diane Lampert), "Killin' Polka," "Mad Latina," "Take It Off," "Tell Me, Tell Me," "Give It To Me," (Dunham, Jimmie Haskell), "Watusi Joe" (Haskell, Jim Economides).

p, Edward Small; d, Frederick DeCordova; w, Nat Perrin, Bob Fisher, Arthur Marx (based on a story by Perrin); ph, Daniel L. Fapp (Technicolor); m, Jimmie Haskell, "By" Dunham; ed, Grant Whytock; art d, Robert Peterson; set d, Frank Tuttle; cos, Paula Giokaris; ch, Miriam Nelson.

Musical/Comedy **(PR:A MPAA:NR)**

I'LL TELL THE WORLD* (1934) 76m UNIV bw

Lee Tracy *(Stanley Brown)*, Gloria Stuart *(Jane Hamilton)*, Roger Pryor *(William S. Briggs)*, Onslow Stevens *(Prince Michael)*, Alec B. Francis *(Grand Duke Ferdinand)*, Lawrence Grant *(Count Strumsky)*, Willard Robertson *(Hardwick)*, Leon Waycoff [Leon Ames] *(Marshall)*, William Von Brincken *(Joseph)*, Herman Bing *(Adolph)*, Hugh Enfield *(Aviator)*, Dorothy Granger *(Dancing Girl)* Edwin Mordant, Arthur Stone, Edward McWade.

Tracy is a standard newspaper reporter who gets in over his head with a plot to overthrow a mythical government. He is sent to Paris to follow an archduke, and runs into a princess disguised as an American. Of course, he saves the day and ends up with the princess in his arms. Countless unexplained plot points are detrimental to this picture's believability. Remade in 1945 under the same title.

d, Edward Sedgwick; w, Dale Van Every, Ralph Spence (based on a story by Lincoln Quarberg, Frank Wead); ph, Jerome Ash; ed, Daniel Mandell.

Comedy/Drama **(PR:A MPAA:NR)**

I'LL TELL THE WORLD*½ (1945) 61m UNIV bw

Lee Tracy *(Gabriel Patton)*, Brenda Joyce *(Lorna Gray)*, Raymond Walburn *(H.I. Bailey)*, June Preisser *(Marge Bailey)*, Thomas Gomez *(J.B. Kindell)*, Howard Freeman *(Lester Westchester)*, Lorin Raker *(Perkins)*, Janet Shaw *(Switchboard Operator)*, Pierre Watkin *(Dr. Mullins)*, Peter Potter *(Announcer)*, Gene Rodgers *(Piano Specialty)*, Jimmy Dean and His Trail Riders *(Western Specialty)*, Jean Aloise *(Dance Specialty)*, Eddie Small *(Boy)*, Ian Bernard *(Gabby, Sr.)*, John Hamilton *(President)*, Ruth Lee *(Ethel)*, William Haade *(Joe)*, Jim Zaner *(Messenger)*, Harry Tyler *(Announcer)*, Eddie Hart, Max Wagner *(Men)*, Franklin Parker *(Character)*, Ida Moore *(Old Lady)*, Jack Overman *(Butch King)*, Ella Ethridge *(Woman)*, Ferris Taylor, Sam Flint, Edward Earle *(Stockholders)*, George Irving *(Smith)*, John Mylong *(Dr. Johnston)*, Barry Bernard *(Tyron Hayes)*, Tom Daly *(Harry)*, Forrest Lewis *(Joe Sunshine)*, David Peter *(Band Leader)*, Charles Marsh *(Escort)*, Rita Gould *(Prissy Woman)*, Alan Ray, Evelyne Eaton *(Young Couple)*, John Kelly *(Driver)*.

A lonely hearts program helps a nose-diving radio station stay in the air. Tracy plays the station announcer who organizes specialty acts and the following musical numbers: "Slap Polka" (Harry Revel, Paul Francis Webster), "Walk A Little Faster" (Dave Franklin), "Moonlight Fiesta" (Harry Tobias, Al Sherman), "Where The Prairie Meets The Sky" (Everett Carter, Milton Rosen).

p, Frank Gross; d, Leslie Goodwins; w, Henry Blankfort; ph, Paul Ivano; ed, Ray Snyder; md, H.J. Salter; art d, John B. Goodman, Abraham Grossman.

Comedy/Musical **(PR:AA MPAA:NR)**

I'LL TURN TO YOU½** (1946, Brit.) 96m But bw

Terry Randall *(Aileen Meredith)*, Don Stannard *(Roger Meredith)*, Harry Welchman *(Mr. Collins)*, Ann Codrington *(Mrs. Collins)*, George Merritt *(Cecil Joy)*, Irene Handl *(Mrs. Gammon)*, Ellis Irving *(Henry Browning)*, Nicolette Roeg *(Flora Fenton)*, Tony Pendrell *(Dick Fenton)*, Leslie Perrins *(Chigwell)*, John McHugh, Cameron Hall, Aubrey Mallalieu, Jonathan Field, Janet Morrison, Olive Kirby, Michael Gainsborough, Melville Crawfurd, Peter Penn, David Keir, John Allen, Hamilton Keene, Grace Arnold, Hal Gordon, Arthur Denton, Jack Vyvyan, Davina Craig, Evelyn Laye, Albert Sandler & The Palm Court Orchestra, Sylvia Welling, Sandy MacPherson, Choir Of The Welsh Guards, London Symphony Orchestra.

Randall stars in this pleasant musical as the center of two men's affections—Stannard, her loving, former fighter-pilot husband, and Irving, her former flame. Stannard decides to be noble and allow his wife to accept a luxurious life with Irving. Instead of jumping at the chance, Irving becomes equally noble and talks Stannard into staying with his wife. Keenly acted with a score to match, I'LL TURN TO YOU proves to be a lively piece of entertainment.

p, F.W. Baker; d, Geoffrey Faithfull; w, David Evans (based on a story by Kathleen Butler); ph, Arthur Grant.

Musical **(PR:A MPAA:NR)**

I'LL WAIT FOR YOU* (1941) 73m MGM bw

Robert Sterling *("Lucky" Wilson)*, Marsha Hunt *(Pauline Miller)*, Virginia Weidler *(Lizzie Miller)*, Paul Kelly *(Lt. McFarley)*, Fay Holden *(Mrs. Miller)*, Henry Travers *(Mr. Miller)*, Don Costello *(Sgt. Brent)*, Carol Hughes *(Sally Travers)*, Reed Hadley *(Tony Barolli)*, Ben Welden *(Dr. Anderson)*, Theodore Von Eltz *(Cassell)*, Leon Belasco *(Lapagos)*, Mitchell Lewis *(Al)*, Joe Yule *(Butch)*, Eddie Hart *(Joe)*, Jerry Jerome *(Pete)*, Steve Darrell *(Napkin Counter)*, William Tannen *(Driver)*.

Sterling is a hard-edged gangster from the big city who spends some time hiding out in the country and begins to like it. After getting used to all the fresh air, and with some convincing from farm girl Hunt and her rustic relatives, Sterling goes straight. A weak remake of HIDEOUT (1934).

p, Edwin Knopf; d, Robert B. Sinclair; w, Guy Trosper (based on a story by Mauri Grashin); ph, Sidney Wagner; ed, Elmo Veron; m/l, "A Lesson In Latin," Al Siegel, Ralph Freed.

Drama **(PR:A MPAA:NR)**

I'LL WALK BESIDE YOU** (1943, Brit.) 88m But bw

Richard Bird *(John Brent)*, Lesley Brook *(Ann Johnson)*, Percy Marmont *(Vicar)*, Leslie Bradley *(Tom Booth)*, Sylvia Marriott *(Joan Tremayne)*, Hugh Miller *(Dr. Stevenson)*, Beatrice Varley *(Miss McKenzie)*, Irene Handl *(Ma Perkins)*, George Merritt *(Hancock)*, Hilda Bayley *(Mrs. Tremayne)*, John McHugh, St. David's Singers, London Symphony Orchestra.

Sweethearts Bird and Brook plan marriage when Bird returns from his war duty, but their future is altered when he is listed as missing. Brook takes a job as a nurse and falls in love with a doctor. Bird returns suffering from amnesia and regains his memory only upon hearing his favorite romantic tune, restoring his bond with Brook. Another in a seemingly endless supply of movies that revolve around amnesia—a medical condition which could have been created solely for the use of bad melodramas.

p, F. W. Baker; d, Maclean Roberts; w, Kathleen Butler (based on a story by Mabel Constanduros); ph, Geoffrey Faithfull.

Drama **(PR:A MPAA:NR)**

I'M A STRANGER*½ (1952, Brit.) 60m Corsair/Apex bw

Greta Gynt *(Herself)*, James Hayter *(Horatio Flowerdew)*, Hector Ross *(Inspector Craddock)*, Jean Cadell *(Hannah Mackenzie)*, Patric Doonan *(George Westcott)*, Charles Lloyd Pack *(Mr. Cringle)*, Martina Mayne *(Mary)*, Fulton Mackay *(Alastair Campbell)*, Raymond Young, John Kelly.

Norwegian actress Gynt stars as herself in this comic tale of an heir, Doonan, who must battle the disinherited members of his family to receive his grandfather's fortune. He wins the inheritance thanks to the efforts of Gynt, window washer Hayter, and police inspector Ross. Amusing at times but all together unmemorable.

p, Harold Richmond; d&w, Brock Williams; ph, Gordon Lang.

Comedy/Drama **(PR:A MPAA:NR)**

I'M ALL RIGHT, JACK**** (1959, Brit.) 105m Boulting/BL bw

Ian Carmichael *(Stanley Windrush)*, Peter Sellers *(Fred Kite)*, Terry-Thomas *(Maj. Hitchcock)*, Richard Attenborough *(Sidney de Vere Cox)*, Dennis Price *(Bertram Tracepurcel)*, Margaret Rutherford *(Aunt Dolly)*, Irene Handl *(Mrs. Kite)*, Liz Frazer *(Cynthia Kite)*, Miles Malleson *(Windrush, Sr.)*, Marne Maitland *(Mr. Mohammed)*, John Le Mesurier *(Waters)*, Raymond Huntley *(Magistrate)*, Victor Maddern *(Knowles)*, Kenneth Griffith *(Dai)*, Fred Griffiths *(Charlie)*, Donal Donnelly *(Perce Carter)*, Malcolm Muggeridge *(TV Panel Chairman)*, John Glyn-Jones *(Detto Executive)*, Terry Scott *(Crawley)*, Muriel Young *(TV Announcer)*, Basil Dignam *(Minister of Labor)*, Sam Kydd, Cardew Robinson, Bruce Wightman *(Shop Stewards)*, Fred Griffiths *(Charlie)*, Ronnie Stevens *(Hopper)*, Martin Boddey *(Num Yum's Executive)*, Brian Oulton *(Board Examiner)*, Maurice Colbourne *(Missiles Director)*, Michael Ward, Stringer Davis *(Reporters)*, Esma Cannon *(Spencer)*, Terry Scott *(Crawley)*, Wally Patch *(Workman)*, Alun Owen *(TV Producer)*, Frank Phillips *(BBC Announcer)*, David Lodge, Keith Smith, Kenneth J. Warren *(Card Players)*, Harry Locke *(Trade Union Official)*, John Comer, Tony Comer, Billy Rayment, Jeremy White, John Van Eyssen, Michael Bates, Robert Bruce, Robin Hay, Tony Spear, Arthur Skinner, William Leacock, Eynon Evans, Robert Young, Roy Purcell, Marianne Stone, Edie Martin, Marion Shaw, Ian Wilson, Margaret Lacey, George Selway, Alan Wilson, E.V.H. Emmett *(Narrator)*, Alan Wilson.

A hilarious and pointed satirical look at the British trade unions. This is an excellent example of humor used to make points and the unions had always been sacred cows before this movie took them on and gave them what for. Carmichael is an addled but earnest young man who has just finished his army service and now seeks a career in industry. He visits his uncle, Price, who is in cahoots with Attenborough in a most interesting scheme; they would like to arrange a strike at Price's factory so Attenborough's factory can take over the contracts and do the work at inflated prices. They give Carmichael a job as an unskilled laborer and his intelligence soon detects several ways to streamline the factory's operation and reap larger profits. This, of course, angers the union shop steward, Sellers, as pompous a Laborite as ever wiped a lathe. Carmichael figures out a way to load and unload deliveries and suggests that a new schedule be printed so the workers can live up to it instead of taking "tea breaks" every other hour. Sellers is livid and calls a strike, which delights Price. But the laborers at Attenborough's plant go out in sympathy, thus tossing all their plans into a cocked hat. The strike grows and becomes a matter of national importance as the transport and shipping unions also go out in sympathy and the nation is slowing down to a crawl. Carmichael can't see why all this should be happening and continues crossing the picket lines, unmindful of the chaos he has caused. His solitary beliefs turn him into a national hero and he is shocked when Price offers him a large sum of money to quit the job. Sellers and Carmichael are both interviewed on a television news program, face to face, and Carmichael's speech shows how labor and management are equally guilty of not looking beyond the immediate needs of the moment. He begins ranting and is eventually taken away by the police. He finally realizes that he is not the man to change hundreds of years of things being the way they are, so he decides to chuck it all and go live with his father, Miles Malleson, in a nudist camp. A sharp screenplay and expert farceurs in every role make this one of the great British comedies of the 1950s and 1960s. Many of the "Carry On" gang are here plus Rutherford and her husband, Davis. Even *Punch* editor Muggeridge takes a turn as the moderator of the TV show. It's subtlety and slapstick mixed perfectly in a refreshing glace. British Oscars to Sellers and the screenplay.

p, Roy Boulting; d, John Boulting; w, Frank Harvey, Alan Hackney, John Boulting (based on Hackney's novel *Private Life*); ph, Max Greene; m, Ken Hare, Ron Goodwin; ed, Anthony Harvey; title song sung by Al Saxon.

Comedy **Cas.** **(PR:A MPAA:NR)**

I'M AN EXPLOSIVE** (1933, Brit.) 50m George Smith/FOX bw

Billy Hartnell *(Edward Whimperly)*, Gladys Jennings *(Anne Pannell)*, Eliot Makeham *(Prof. Whimperly)*, D.A. Clarke-Smith *(Lord Ferndale)*, Sybil Grove *(Miss Harriman)*, Harry Terry *(Mould)*, George Dillon *(Shilling)*, Blanche Adele *(French Girl)*.

Contrived, but amusing, story has Hartnell raking in the money when he sues the government after drinking an explosive chemical his brother Makeham had created. In reality, Makeham has done nothing of the sort, but his brother and everyone else thinks he did, so Hartnell takes advantage of the prime situation and uses his large settlement to marry the girl of his dreams.

p, Harry Cohen; d&w, Adrian Brunel (based on the novel by Gordon Phillips); ph, Geoffrey Faithfull.

Comedy **(PR:A MPAA:NR)**

I'M CRAZY ABOUT YOU (SEE: TE QUIERO CON LOCURA, 1935)

I'M DANCING AS FAST AS I CAN** (1982) 106m PAR c

Jill Clayburgh *(Barbara Gordon)*, Nicol Williamson *(Derek Bauer)*, Dianne Wiest *(Julie Addison)*, Joe Pesci *(Roger)*, Geraldine Page *(Jean Martin)*, James Sutorius *(Sam Mulligan)*, Ellen Greene *(Karen Mulligan)*, Cordis Heard *(Fran)*, Richard Masur *(Alan Newman)*, Kasey Connors *(Sound Woman)*, Charles Stavola *(Bartender)*, Roger Etienne *(Waiter)*, Gregory Osborne *(Passerby)*, Eleanor Zee *(Emmy Presenter)*, John Shearin *(Emmy Official)*, David Polk *(Stage Manager)*, Joe Maher *(Dr. Kalman)*, Ann Weldon *(Nurse)*, Angel Ferreira *(Delivery Boy)*, Jeffrey DeMunn *(Dr. Roberts)*, Thomas Hill *(Dr. Morgan)*, Toni Kalem *(Debbie)*, Robert Doqui *(Teddy)*, Daniel Stern *(Jim)*, C. C. H. Pounder *(Anne)*, Anne DeSalvo *(Iris)*, Richard Hamilton *(Joe)*, Dan Hedaya *(Dr. Klein)*, Margaret Ladd *(Lara)*, Ebbe Roe Smith *(Chet)*, Kathleen Widdoes *(Dr. Rawlings)*, Debbie Lynn Foreman *(Cindy)*, Erin Halligan *(Denise)*, Beatrice Lynch *(Patient)*, Eddie Donno, Glenn R. Wilder, Harold Jones *(Orderlies)*, Andrew Winner *(Greg)*, Edward Betz *(Assistant Editor)*, John Lithgow *(Brunner)*, Lara Cody *(Newscaster)*, Wendy Cutler *(Crew Member)*, Malcolm Groome *(Talent Coordinator)*, Devera Marcus *(Therapist)*, Paul Wilson, Gloria Irrizzary *(Patients)*, Andy Goldberg *(Disc Jockey)*, Dennis Lee, Lawrence Sellars, Jordan Derwin *(Doctors)*.

Adapting a novel that gets inside a character's head is never easy, unless the screenwriter uses a voice-over narration. Adapter Rabe (Clayburgh's husband) chooses not to do that and the result is that we see the lead character popping Valium every other minute but we never know the real reasons. Clayburgh is Barbara Gordon (who wrote the true book based on her experiences. They didn't bother to change the name because they wanted to make the point that this is an honest depiction of her addiction), a successful documentarian who works in television. She reaches for the Valium whenever life gets too complex for her. She lives with Williamson, who is as in love with alcohol as she is with her relaxers. They battle verbally, eventually hit each other, and are finally sent off to hospitals for rehabilitation. Wiest is the therapist who takes Clayburgh out of her addiction and back to reality. If you read the book, you know that much of the story was edited for the film and the loss is evident even if you missed the literary work. It's an earnest attempt at baring the horrors of Valium but it fails in the end. Look for John Lithgow in one of his earlier jobs. The best thing about the movie was the controlled cinematography by Dutch master Jan de Bont. The subject matter was much better treated in I'LL CRY TOMORROW, a picture that showed you the heroine, warts and all.

p, Edgar J. Sherick, Scott Rudin; d, Jack Hofsiss; w, David Rabe (based on the novel by Barbara Gordon); ph, Jan de Bont (MovieLab Color); m, Stanley Silverman; ed, Michael Bradsell; prod d, David Jenkins; art d, Fred Kolo; set d, Ken Aichele; cos, Julie Weiss.

Drama **Cas.** **(PR:C-O MPAA:R)**

I'M FROM ARKANSAS* (1944) 68m PRC bw

Slim Summerville, El Brendel, Harry Harvey, Iris Adrian, Bruce Bennett, Maude Eburne, Cliff Nazarro, Al St. John, Carolina Cotton, Danny Jackson, Paul Newlan, Arthur Q. Bryan, John Hamilton, Douglas Wood, Walter Baldwin, Flo Bert, Jimmy Wakely, Pied Pipers, Sunshine Girls, Milo Twins.

Another of Summerville's silly slapstick comedies rests upon the excitement that is generated when a pig gives birth to 10 little piglets. The town of Pitchfork, Arkansas is never the same after hordes of money-grabbers arrive there in search of a new angle.

p, E. H. Klienert, Irving Vershal; d, Lew Landers; w, Marcel Klauber, Joseph Carole (based on the story by Klauber); ph, Robert Pittack; ed, John Link; md, Eddie Paul; art d, F. Paul Sylos.

Comedy **(PR:A MPAA:NR)**

I'M FROM MISSOURI* 1/2 (1939) 77m PAR bw

Bob Burns *(Sweeney Bliss)*, Gladys George *(Julie Bliss)*, Gene Lockhart *(Porgie Rowe)*, Judith Barrett *(Lola Pike)*, William Henry *(Joel Street)*, Patricia Morison *(Mrs. Allison Hamilton Crispin)*, E.E. Clive *(Mr. Arthur)*, Melville Cooper *(Hearne)*, William Collier, Sr. *(Smith)*, Lawrence Grossmith *(Col. Marchbank)*, George P. Huntley *(Capt. Brooks-Bowen)*, Doris Lloyd *(Mrs. Arthur)*, Tom Dugan *(Gen. Starbuck)*, Dennie Moore *(Kitty Hearne)*, James Burke *(Walt Bliss)*, Ethel Griffies *(Miss Wildhack)*, Spencer Charters *(Charley Shook)*, Raymond Hatton *(Darryl Coffee)*, Richard Denning.

There isn't much that can be done with a plot as bad as this one. Burns is a Missouri mule breeder who is determined not to go bankrupt when the mule market collapses. He takes his prize mule to a Kansas livestock show to impress an English army representative. He and his wife then go to England to show off their stock to government mule buyers. And before you know it Burns and George are living high as part of Britain's upper-crust.

p, Paul Jones; d, Theodore Reed; w, John C. Moffitt, Duke Atterberry (based on stories from the book *Sixteen Hands* by Homer Croy and Julian Street); ph, Merritt Gerstad; ed, Archie Marshek.

Drama **(PR:A MPAA:NR)**

I'M FROM THE CITY** (1938) 65m RKO bw

Joe Penner *(Pete)*, Richard Lane *(Ollie)*, Lorraine Krueger *(Rosie)*, Paul Guilfoyle *(Willie)*, Kay Sutton *(Marlene)*, Kathryn Sheldon *(Grandma)*, *Ethan Laidlaw (Jeff)*, Lafe McKee *(Bixby)*, Edmund Cobb *(Red)*, Clyde Kinney *(Butch)*.

Penner is a city boy who is a bareback rider of exceptional talent, but only when hypnotized. As expected, when it's time for the big race Penner must ride without the aid of hypnosis. Overlong at 65 minutes. Two tunes from Hal Raynor include "I'm A Tough Coyote," and "I'm From The City."

p, William Sistrom; d, Ben Holmes; w, Nicholas T. Barrows, Robert St. Clair, John Grey (based on the story by Holmes); ph, Frank Redman; ed, Ted Cheesman; md, Roy Webb; art d, Van Nest Polglase; spec eff, Vernon L. Walker.

Comedy/Western **(PR:A MPAA:NR)**

I'M GOING TO GET YOU . . . ELLIOT BOY zero (1971, Can.) 97m Cinepro/COL c

Ross Stephenson *(Elliot Markson)*, Maureen McGill *(Sherri)*, Richard Gishler *(Benjo)*, Jeremy Hart *(Evans)*.

There isn't anything redeeming in this supposed expose on prison life, nor is there any sign of talent. Stephenson is tossed in jail and encounters a fellow prisoner who has been away from women for too long. After a couple of years of homosexual partners in prison, Stephenson is released and pairs up with his girl friend McGill. She gets greedy and wants the money he was accused of stealing, so he kills her. Bleak, tawdry and a waste of film stock.

p, J.M. Slutker; d, Edward J. Forsyth; w, Joseph E. Duhamel, ph, Peter Reusch; m, Allan Allter; ed, Forsyth; art d, Starcom West, Ltd.

Drama **(PR:O MPAA:NR)**

I'M NO ANGEL**** (1933) 87m PAR bw

Mae West *(Tira)*, Cary Grant *(Jack Clayton)*, Gregory Ratoff *(Benny Pinkowitz)*, Edward Arnold *(Big Bill Barton)*, Ralf Harolde *(Slick Wiley)*, Kent Taylor *(Kirk Lawrence)*, Gertrude Michael *(Alicia Hatton)*, Russell Hopton *(Flea Madigan The Barker)*, Dorothy Peterson *(Thelma)*, William B. Davidson *(Ernest Brown The Chump)*, Gertrude Howard *(Beulah Thorndyke)*, Libby Taylor, Hattie McDaniel *(Maids)*, Nat Pendleton *(Harry A Trapeze Artist)*, Tom London *(Spectator)*, Nigel de Brulier *(Rajah)*, Irving Pichel *(Bob The Attorney)*, Morrie Cohan *(Chauffeur)*, Walter Walker *(Judge)*, George Bruggeman *(Omnes)*, Monte Collins, Ray Cooke *(Sailors)*, Dennis O'Keefe *(Reporter)*, Edward Hearn *(Courtroom Spectator)*.

Even if you don't like Mae West, you'll have to admit that this is one of the funniest films of the 1930s. Strictly a "vehicle" (she was on camera more than 95 percent of the footage), West adapted the screenplay and had total creative control, which was something studios seldom give, but she'd already saved Paramount from bankruptcy with her previous film, SHE DONE HIM WRONG. The only problem with the script is that West gets all the good lines (well, of course she does; she wrote the script and knew which side her bread was buttered on) with very little crusts of wit tossed to the other actors. Arnold manages a one-ring circus in which West works as a side-show attraction. She lives with Harolde but also maintains a place away from the circus where she can take other men to extract some money from them. Davidson comes to her room and is knocked senseless by Harolde, who thinks he's killed the chump. Harolde steals the man's diamond ring and flees. When Davidson awakens from his slight concussion, he notifies the police and Harolde is nabbed by the men in blue. West needs some money to help Harolde so she agrees to put her head in a lion's mouth for the extra cash. The crowd loves it. Enter Taylor, a rich playboy who likes what he sees in West. He brings his cousin, Grant, along. (Grant had co-starred with West in SHE DONE HIM WRONG and did the best with the lines but West took most of the punch out of anyone else's comedy and Grant, no matter how good he is, cannot make people laugh with straight lines.) Taylor soon tires of West and takes up with a socialite, thereby leaving the field open for Grant, whom West likes better anyhow. They woo each other until she decides to sue him for breach of promise. Grant gets even by calling all her ex-lovers into the courtroom. Grant realizes that she really adores him and allows her to win the case by acting as her own attorney. The film ends as the lovebirds are united. West was 12 years older than Grant but it didn't matter as she exuded sex until the day she died and any woman with that much appeal doesn't have to worry about the years. West knew who she was and made no pretence about being anything else. With that healthy attitude, she was able to shape her films the way she wanted them. She knew that audiences liked to see her in 1890s clothes with tight waist and full bottom and she also knew exactly how far she could take her double entendres without losing the Hays Office approval or her audience's affections. The picture was a deserved smash at the box office. Songs include: "I'm No Angel," No One Loves Me Like That Dallas Man Of Mine," "They Call Me Sister Honky Tonk," "I Want You, I Need You," "I've Found A New Way To Go To Town."

p, William LeBaron; d, Wesley Ruggles; w, Mae West, Harlan Thompson (based on "The Lady And The Lions," an unproduced screenplay by Lowell Brentano); ph, Leo Tover; m, Harvey Brooks; ed, Otho Lovering; art d, Hans Dreier, Bernard Herzbrun; m/l, Brooks, Gladys du Bois, Ben Ellison.

Comedy **(PR:C MPAA:NR)**

I'M NOBODY'S SWEETHEART NOW*** (1940) 64m UNIV c

Dennis O'Keefe *(Tod Lowell)*, Constance Moore *(Betty Gilbert)*, Helen Parrish *(Trudie Morgan)*, Lewis Howard *(Andy Manson)*, Berton Churchill *(Sen. Henry Lowell)*, Laura Hope Crews *(Mrs. Lowell)*, Samuel S. Hinds *(George P. Morgan)*, Marjorie Gateson *(Mrs. Morgan)*, Margaret Hamilton *(Mrs. Thriffle)*, Tim Ryan *(Judge Saunders)* Walter Soderling *(Abner Thriffle)*, Walter Baldwin *(Elmer)*, Rex Evans *(Parkins the Butler)*, Gaylord [Steve] Pendleton *(Chuck)*, Hattie Noel *(Bedelia)*, Gene O'Donnell *(Eddie)*, James Craig *(Ray)*, Lee Phelps *(Mac the Guard)*, Max Wagner *(Motorcycle Officer)*, Dorothy Moore *(Elsie)*, Harry Depp *(Judge)*, Harry Strang *(Harry)*, Alphonse Martel *(Headwaiter)*, Clara Blore *(Fat Woman)*, Jose and Antonita de Franco *(The Casinos)*.

A bright B musical which starred O'Keefe and Parrish as the children of politically minded parents. O'Keefe's dad is in the race for governor, while Parrish's is a political boss. Both parents try to pair the kids off, but O'Keefe and Parrish have different ideas. Pretending they like each other, they leave on a date but meet their real loves—O'Keefe with Moore, and Parrish with Howard. It's not long, however, before the politicized pair fall in love, bringing out jealous antics in both Moore and Howard. After Parrish is nearly swept into an overnight marriage with Howard, O'Keefe arranges to marry Parrish. The end has the couple walking up the aisle while the jilted Moore and Howard watch from the church wings. It was Moore as O'Keefe's ex-love who won the audience's hearts, however, as she delivered three tunes, "I'm Nobody's Sweetheart Now" (Gus Kahn, Ernie Erdman, Billy Meyers, Elmer Schoebel), "There Goes My Love," "Got Romance" (Everett Carter, Milton Rosen). There are a number of humorous high points in this pic's consistently funny and well-acted script, which includes this witty interchange as Howard tries to elope with Parrish. It is the middle of the night and the anxious groom awakens the justice-of-the-peace's wife: "Can't you get the justice to marry us?" asks Howard. The woman reluctantly agrees to wake her husband, "But just this once." Margaret Hamilton, cast as the wife, had a year previous appeared as the Witch in THE WIZARD OF OZ. Laura Hope Crews, as the mother of O'Keefe, could be seen in GONE WITH THE WIND as Aunt Pittypat.

p, Joseph G. Sanford; d, Arthur Lubin; w, Scott Darling, Erna Lazarus, Hal Block (based on the story "The Bride Said No" by Darling, Lazarus); ph, Elwood Bredell; ed, Paul Landres; md, Charles Previn; art d, Jack Otterson.

Musical **(PR:A MPAA:NR)**

I'M STILL ALIVE 1/2** (1940) 72m RKO bw

Kent Taylor *(Steve Bonnett)*, Linda Hayes *(Laura Marley)*, Howard da Silva *(Red Garvey)*, Ralph Morgan *(Walter Blake)*, Don Dillaway *(Tommy Briggs)*, Clay Clement, Fred Niblo *(Directors)*.

A quirky little romance about stuntman Taylor and his marriage to screen star Hayes. The relationship is in trouble when a fellow stuntman gets killed, raising objections from the understandably fearful Hayes. They split but are reunited by Taylor's buddies. An enlightening philosophy of stuntmen is spoken in this pic: "Risking your life for a movie isn't as silly as starving to death." Cast as a film director was Fred Niblo, the famed silent film director who brought to the screen such pictures as 1922's awesome BEN HUR. RKO ended up in court over this picture as the subject of a lawsuit by ex-RKO star Helen Twelvetrees. She claimed the story was based on her relationship with ex-husband and stuntman Jack Woody. The suit was settled out of court in 1943 for $1,100.

p, Frederic Ullman, Jr.; d, Irving Reis; w, Edmund North; ph, J. Roy Hunt; m, Roy Webb; ed, Theron Warth; art d, Van Nest Polglase; spec eff, Vernon L. Walker.

Romance **(PR:A MPAA:NR)**

I'VE ALWAYS LOVED YOU** (1946) 117m REP c (GB: CONCERTO)

Philip Dorn *(Leopold Goronoff)*, Catherine McLeod *(Myra Hassman)*, William Carter *(George Sampter)*, Maria Ouspenskaya *(Mme. Goronoff)*, Felix Bressart *(Frederick Hassman)*, Fritz Feld *(Nicholas)*, Elizabeth Patterson *(Mrs. Sampter)*, Vanessa Brown *(Porky at 17)*, Lewis Howard *(Michael Severin)*, Adele Mara *(Senorita Fortaleza)*, Gloria Donovan *(Porky at 5)*, Stephanie Bachelor *(Redhead)*, Cora Witherspoon *(Mrs. Blythe)*.

The British title to this lavish classical event is far more revealing than its American tag. An orchestral conductor, Dorn, engages in a professional but merciless rivalry with a young female pupil, McLeod. He ruins the girl's career while she labors over Rachmaninoff's Concerto No. 2 at Carnegie Hall. The picture's strength lies in its musical virtuosity, showcasing the off-screen talents of pianist Artur Rubenstein as he performs pieces by Chopin, Beethoven, Bach, Mendelssohn, and Wagner. Also included is the title song penned by Aaron Goldmark and Ludwig Flato.

p&d, Frank Borzage; w, Borden Chase; ph, Tony Gaudio (Technicolor); m, Sergei Vassilievich Rachmaninoff, Frederic Chopin, Ludwig van Beethoven, Felix Mendelssohn, Richard Wagner, Johann Sebastian Bach; ed, Richard L. Van Enger; prod d, Ernst Fegte; md, Walter Scharf; spec eff, Howard and Theodore Lydecker; piano recordings by Artur Rubenstein.

Musical **(PR:A MPAA:NR)**

I'VE BEEN AROUND* (1935) 63m UNIV bw

Chester Morris *(Eric Foster)*, Rochelle Hudson *(Drue Waring)*, Isabel Jewell *(Sally Van Loan)*, Gene Lockhart *(Sunny Ames)*, Phyllis Brooks *(Gay Blackstone)*, G.P. Huntley, Jr. *(Franklin De Haven)*, Ralph Morgan *(John Waring)*, Henry Armetta *(Italian)*, William Stack *(Doctor)*, Dorothy Granger, Dorothy Christy, Verna Hillie, Jean Fenwick *(Girls)*, Betty Blythe *(Woman)*, Lorin Raker *(Elevator Man)*.

Hudson is an indecisive society woman who can't stick to one man. After nearly marrying Morris, she admits she doesn't love him, sending the jilted groom to Paris and London, then back to her in New York, where he finds her living it up at a wild party. Angry, he flees. She decides to prove her love for him by swallowing a bottle of iodine in a suicide attempt. She lives, but by this time the story has long since died.

p, B.F. Zeidman; d, Philip Cahn; w, John Meehan, Jr., Zeidman; ph, John Mescall; ed, Raymond Curtis; song, "I've Been Around" (sung by Rochelle Hudson).

Romance **(PR:A MPAA:NR)**

I'VE GOT A HORSE** (1938, Brit.) 77m BL bw

Sandy Powell *(Sandy)*, Norah Howard *(Alice)*, Felix Aylmer *(Lovatt)*, Evelyn Roberts *(Thomas)*, Leo Franklyn *(Joe)*, D.A. Clarke-Smith *(Fowler, Kings Counsel)*, Kathleen Harrison *(Mabel)*, Wilfrid Hyde-White *(Police Constable)*, Frank Atkinson *(Bunker)*, Edward Chapman *(George)*.

Powell becomes the owner of a horse which he enters in a race, only to find out that it is a circus animal as it trots down the homestretch. The horse loses and Powell decides to join a circus instead of living his life at the track. A harmless comedy which is best appreciated by the few existing Powell devotees.

p&d, Herbert Smith; w, Fenn Sherie, Ingram d'Abbes, Sandy Powell; ph, George Stretton.

Comedy **(PR:A MPAA:NR)**

I'VE GOT YOUR NUMBER** (1934) 68m WB bw

Joan Blondell *(Maria Lawson)*, Pat O'Brien *(Terry)*, Glenda Farrell *(Bonnie)*, Allen Jenkins *(John)*, Eugene Pallette *(Flood)*, Gordon Westcott *(Nicky)*, Henry O'Neill *(Mr. Schuyler)*, Hobart Cavanaugh *(Happy Dooley)*, Renee Whitney *(Loretta Kennedy)*, Robert Ellis *(Turk)*, Louise Beavers *(Crystal)*, Milton Kibbee *(Dispatcher)*, Bess Flowers *(Miss Banks)*, Tom Costello *(Ed)*, Selmer Jackson *(Joe)*, Henry Kolker *(Robert Kirkland)*, Charles Wilson *(Welch)*, Douglas Cosgrove *(Turner)*, Wallis Clark *(Madison)*, Cliff Saum *(Operator)*, Lucille Ford *(Sarah)*, Rita LaRoy, Rickey Newell, Lorraine Marshall *(Girls)*, Clay Clement.

Aptly titled, this spicy comedy focuses on the telephone company, and the efforts of two engineers, O'Brien and Jenkins, to clear Blondell's name after she is accused of criminal activities. A moderately funny film which served more of an educational purpose than anything else.

p, Sam Bischoff; d, Ray Enright; w, Warren Duff, Sidney Sutherland (based on a story by William Rankin); ph, Arthur Todd; ed, Clarence Kolster; art d, Esdras Hartley; cos, Orry-Kelly.

Comedy **(PR:A MPAA:NR)**

I'VE GOTTA HORSE**

(1965, Brit.) 92m Windmill/WB-Pathe c (AKA: WONDERFUL DAY)

Billy Fury *(Billy)*, Amanda Barrie *(Jo)*, Michael Medwin *(Hymie Campbell)*, Marjorie Rhodes *(Mrs. Bartholemew)*, Bill Fraser *(Mr. Bartholemew)*, Peter Gilmore *(Jock)*, Jon Pertwee *(Costumer's Assistant)*, Michael Cashman *(Peter)*, The Gamblers, The Bachelors *(Themselves)*, John Kelly *(Donkey Man)*, Fred Emney *(Lord Bentley)*, Pauline Loring *(Lady Bentley)*, Tom Bowman *(Trainer)*, Gareth Robinson *(Jockey)*, Ann Lancaster *(Woman Shopkeeper)*, Sheila O'Neill *(Betty)*, Cal McCord *(Whitney)*, Leslie Dwyer *(Bert)*.

British pop singer Billy Fury is the star of a seaside summer show who pays little attention to rehearsals. Instead, he spends his time playing with the pack of pet dogs he keeps crammed in his dressing room. When he buys a racehorse he goes out to the track to see it compete in the Derby. Being his irresponsible self, he forgets about the show's opening night, returning with no time to spare. Fury does a good job, but his film, like his singing career, has been forgotten.

p, Kenneth Hume, Larry Parnes; d, Hume; w, Ronald Wolfe, Ronald Chesney (based on a story by Hume, Parnes); ph, Ernest Steward (Technicolor); ed, Ernest Hosler; m/l, David Haneker, John Taylor; ch, Ross Taylor.

Musical Comedy **(PR:A MPAA:NR)**

I'VE LIVED BEFORE 1/2** (1956) 82m UNIV bw

Jock Mahoney *(John Bolan)*, Leigh Snowden *(Lois Gordon)*, Ann Harding *(Jane Stone)*, John McIntire *(Dr. Thomas Bryant)*, Raymond Bailey *(Mr. Hackett)*, Jerry Paris *(Russell Smith)*, Simon Scott *(Robert Allen)*, April Kent *(Stewardess)*, Vernon Rich *(Mr. Anderson)*, Phil Harvey *(Dr. Miller)*, Brad Morrow *(Johnny Bolan as a Boy)*, Jane Howard *(Secretary)*, Lorna Thayer *(Mrs. Fred Bolan)*, James Seay *(Fred Bolan)*, Madelon Mitchel *(Maid)*, Mike Dale *(Pilot)*, Ray Quinn *(Intern)*, Bill Anders *(Air Control Officer)*, Marjorie Stapp, Mike Portanova, Charles Conrad, Beatrice

Gray, Earl Hansen *(Spectators)*, Palmer Wray Sherrill, Jimmy Casino, Blanche Taylor *(Bits)*.

Mahoney is a commercial airline pilot who, after seeing passenger Harding, experiences a strange sensation that causes him to reenact an aerial dog fight. The plane begins diving and twisting as if Mahoney himself were the Red Baron. Co-pilot Paris knocks him out and flies the plane to safety before Mahoney loses his imaginary battle. Mahoney awakens in a hospital and explains that, in a past life, he was the husband of Harding and was shot down in a dogfight over France in WW I. This was the first of many films to deal with the subject of reincarnation—a popular notion in the films of 1956, with THE SEARCH FOR BRIDEY MURPHY following suit. Cast as a stewardess was April Kent, daughter of actress June Havoc.

p, Howard Christie; d, Richard Bartlett; w, Norman Jolley, William Talman; ph, Maury Gerstman; m, Herman Stein; ed, Milton Carruth, Fred MacDowell; md, Joseph Gershenson; art d, Alexander Golitzen, Richard H. Riedel, Alfred Sweeney; cos, Bill Thomas.

Drama **(PR:A MPAA:NR)**

ICARUS XB-1

(SEE: VOYAGE TO THE END OF THE UNIVERSE, 1963, Czech.)

ICE zero (1970) 132m Monument bw

Robert Kramer *(Robert)*, Tom Griffin.

A muddled and politically confused film which not surprisingly came out of a period of time known for its muddled and confused politics. A radical left wing group called (take a deep breath) the North American National Committee of International Independent Revolutionary Organizations thrives on terrorist activities, political offensives, and sexual torture. The film is just a means by which this organization tortures an audience.

p, David C. Stone; d&w, Robert Kramer; ph, Robert Machover.

Drama **(PR:O MPAA:NR)**

ICE-CAPADES** (1941) 88m REP bw

James Ellison *(Bob Clemens)*, Jerry Colonna *(Colonna)*, Dorothy Lewis *(Marie)*, Barbara Jo Allen *(Vera Vague)*, Alan Mowbray *(Pete Ellis)*, Phil Silvers *(Larry Herman)*, Gus Schilling *(Dave)*, Tim Ryan *(Jackson)*, Harry Clark *(Reed)*, Renie Riano *(Karen Vadja)*, Carol Adams *(Helen)*, Belita, Lois Dworshak, Megan Taylor, Vera Hruba [Ralston], Red McCarthy, Phil Taylor, Jackson and Lynam, The Benoits, Dench and Stewart *(Ice-Capades Performers)*.

Ellison is a newsreel cameraman who messes up an assignment to cover some Lake Placid ice skaters. He instead fakes it in New York's Central Park with Lewis. When Ice-Capades impresario Silvers sees the woman skate, he makes room for her in his revue. The problem comes when she has to overcome immigration problems. Ellison easily remedies her situation by marrying her. Nearly half of the film is of the skaters which, depending on your tolerance, will either make or break the film. Songs included are "Forever And Ever" (Sol Meyer, George R. Brown, Jule Styne), "Sophisticated Lady" (Duke Ellington).

p, Robert North; d, Joseph Santley; w, Jack Townley, Robert Harari, Olive Cooper, Melville Shavelson, Milt Josefsberg (based on a story by Isabel Dawn, Boyce DeGaw); ph, Jack Marta; ed, Murray Seldeen, Howard O'Neil; md, Cy Feuer; art d, John Victor Mackay; cos, Adele Palmer; skating sequences, Harry Losee.

Drama **(PR:A MPAA:NR)**

ICE-CAPADES REVUE½**

(1942) 79m REP bw (GB: RHYTHM HITS THE ICE)

Ellen Drew *(Ann)*, Richard Denning *(Jeff)*, Jerry Colonna *(Theophilus Twitchell)*, Barbara Jo Allen [Vera Vague] *(Aunt Nellie)*, Harold Huber *(Duke Baldwin)*, Marilyn Hare *(Bubbles)*, Bill Shirley *(Denny)*, Pierre Watkin *(Wiley Stone)*, Si Jenks *(Homer)*, Sam Bernard *(Snake Eyes)*, George Byron *(M.C.)*, Charles Williams *(Menkin)*, William Newell *(Deakin)*, Edward Keane *(Gabby Haskoff)*, Roy Butler, Harrison Greene, Broderick O'Farrell, Cy Ring *(Creditors)*, Jimmy Conlin *(Biddle)*, Mary McCarty *(Miss Trent)*, Betty Farrington *(Mrs. Trent)*, Elmer Jerome *(Mr. Bixby)*, Hal Price, Lee Shumway, Stanley Blystone, George Sherwood *(Cops)*, Dave Willock *(Guide)*, Edwin Stanley *(Otis)*, Frank Jaquet *(Operator)*, Beatrice Maude, Kathryn Sheldon *(The Two Hattie Williamses)*, Emil Van Horn *(Gorilla)*, Jack Norton *(Drunk)*, Irene Shirley *(Mrs. Sawyer)*, Frank Brownlee *(Mr. Sawyer)*, Donna Atwood, Lola Dworshak, Vera Hruba [Ralston], Morgan Taylor, Joe Jackson, Jr., Robin Lee, Rod McCarthy, Phil Taylor, Eric Waite, Jackson and Lynam, The Benoits, Dench and Stewart *(Ice-Capades Skating Stars)*.

Drew is a country girl who inherits an ice show and has to fight an unscrupulous rival producer to stage it. With the help of Denning she puts the skaters on ice outdoors at a New England farm. Colonna is blessed with an entertaining role as a phony millionaire backer who is waiting to strike it rich on a radio call-in show. As with the previous North-produced ice extravaganza, the skaters are the high point of the picture. Czech figureskating champ Vera Hruba is the standout. Musical numbers include "Tequila" (Sol Meyer, George R. Brown, Jule Styne), "The Guy With The Polka-Dotted Tie" (Meyer, Styne), "Song Of The Islands" (Charles E. King), "After All" (Meyer, Walter Scharf), "The Caissons Go Rolling Along" (Edmund L. Gruber), Army Air Corps Song (Robert Crawford).

p, Robert North; d, Bernard Vorhaus; w, Bradford Rogers, Gertrude Purcell (from a story by Robert T. Shannon, Mauri Grashin); ph, John Alton; ed, Thomas Richards; md, Walter Scharf; art d, Russell Kimball; skating sequences, Harry Losee.

Musical **(PR:A MPAA:NR)**

ICE CASTLES** (1978) 113m COL c

Lynn Holly Johnson *(Alexis Winston)*, Robby Benson *(Nick Peterson)*, Colleen Dewhurst *(Beulah Smith)*, Tom Skerritt *(Marcus Winston)*, Jennifer Warren *(Deborah Macland)*, David Huffman *(Brian Dockett)*, Diane Reilly *(Sandy)*, Craig T. McMullen *(Doctor)*, Kelsey Ufford *(Ceciel Monchet)*, Leonard Lilyholm *(Hockey Coach)*, Jean-Claude Bleuze *(French Coach)* Brian Foley *(Choreographer)*, Teresa Willmus *(Annette Brashlout)*, Diana Holden *(X-ray Technician)*, Michelle McLean *(Skater)*, Carol Williams *(TV Producer)* Mary Schuster, Staci Loop *(Special Skating)*, Patti Elder, Jim Nickerson, Dee Ingalls *(Stunts)*.

Johnson is cast as an Olympic hopeful who skates her way into your heart when she is blinded in a freak accident. With the help of Benson, her disgustingly sensitive boy friend, she fights even harder to make it to the top. Dewhurst is superb as the owner of a local skating rink who tries not to live out her failed dreams through Johnson. The film tries far too hard to tug at the tear ducts by making Johnson and Benson wonderfully virginal kids who are struck down by tragedy. Bill Butler's cinematography (THE CONVERSATION, JAWS), as usual, is stunning. Marvin Hamlisch wrote the music, Carole Bayer Sager the lyrics, and Melissa Manchester did the singing.

p, John Kemeny, S. Rodger Olenicoff; d, Donald Wrye; w, Wrye, Gary L. Baim (based on a story by Baim); ph, Bill Butler (Metrocolor); m, Marvin Hamlisch; ed, Michael Kahn, Maury Winetrobe, Melvin Shapiro; prod d, Joel Schiller; cos, Richard Bruno; ch, Brian Foley; m/l, "Ice Castles," Hamlisch, Carole Bayer Sager.

Drama **Cas.** **(PR:A MPA:PG)**

ICE COLD IN ALEX (SEE: DESERT ATTACK, 1960, BRIT.)

ICE FOLLIES OF 1939½** (1939) 81m MGM bw/c

Joan Crawford *(Mary McKay)*, James Stewart *(Larry Hall)*, Lew Ayres *(Eddie Burgess)*, Lewis Stone *(Douglas Tolliver)*, Lionel Stander *(Mort Hodges)*, Truman Bradley *(Paul Rodney)*, Marie Blake *(Effie Lane)*, Bess Ehrhardt *(Kitty Sherman)*, Charles Williams *(Max Norton)*, Eddy Conrad *(Hal Gibbs)*, Arthur Loft *(Director)*, Charles Brown *(Barney)*, Mary Forbes *(Lady Hilda)*, James Flavin *(Doorman)*, Edward Earle *(Man)*, Joe Manz *(Tolliver's Chauffeur)*, Hal K. Dawson *(Publicity Man)*, Louis Aldon *(Dress Designer)*, Charles Judels *(Makeup Man)*, Carl Switzer *(Small Boy)*, Darla Hood *(Sister)*, *Wade Boteler (Cop)*, James McNamara, Eddie Kane *(Politicians)*, Libby Taylor *(Black Maid)*, Harrison Greene *(Agent)*, Adolphe Hebert, Larry Jackson *(Skating Horse)*.

Stewart and Crawford are a husband and wife whose marriage is on thin ice when the latter gets a film contract on the West Coast and her hubby must work on the East. While Stewart is having a tough time finding skating engagements, Crawford is rising fast. To be with her spouse, however, she offers to give up her career. The kind-hearted producer, Stone, does his part to keep the pair together and finds Stewart a job as a film producer. As good as Crawford and Stewart are, they cannot put the lame script on its feet. The film comes to life with a 17-minute Technicolor finale of a Cinderella fantasy performed by the International Ice Follies. In a minor role is Darla Hood of the "Our Gang" comedies. Musical numbers include "Loveland In the Wintertime" (Cliff Friend, Dave Franklin), "Something's Gotta Happen Soon" (Arthur Freed, Nacio Herb Brown), "It's All So New To Me" (Bernice Petkere, Marty Symes), "Cinderella Reel," "Blackbirds" (Roger Edens, Franz Waxman).

p, Harry Rapf; d, Reinhold Schunzel; w, Leonard Praskins, Florence Ryerson, Edgar Allen Woolf (based on the story by Praskins); ph, Joseph Ruttenberg, Oliver T. Marsh; m, Roger Edens; ed, W. Donn Hayes; art d, Cedric Gibbons; cos, Adrian.

Musical **(PR:A MPAA:NR)**

ICE HOUSE, THE**

(1969) 85m C-B Productions/Hollywood Cinemart c (AKA:COLD BLOOD; THE PASSION PITS; LOVE IN COLD BLOOD)

Sabrina *(Venus De Marco)*, Robert Story *(Rick Martin)*, David Story *(Fred Martin)*, Scott Brady *(Lt. Scott)*, Jim Davis *(Jake)*, Kelly Ross *(Kandy Kane)*, Nancy Dow *(Jan Wilson)*.

Robert Story is a psychopathic killer who strangles a stripper and stashes her in the meat freezer. Investigating the crime is his twin brother (played by Robert's real-life twin, David), who hasn't a clue to his brother's murderous ways. Robert goes on killing beauties who give him the cold shoulder, in return giving them a cold torso. When David catches on, he too is murdered. Robert, however, assumes his brother's identity, quits the police force, and returns to his path of ice-cold death. A low-budget horror picture which is even creepier due to its rough edges.

p, Dorrell McGowan; d, Stuart E. McGowan; ph, (Eastmancolor); songs, "The Ice House," "The Scrub" (sung by Ray Peterson).

Horror **(PR:O MPAA:NR)**

ICE PALACE½** (1960) 143m WB c

Richard Burton *(Zeb Kennedy)*, Robert Ryan *(Thor Storm)*, Martha Hyer *(Dorothy Kennedy)*, Jim Backus *(Dave Husack)*, Carolyn Jones *(Bridie Ballantyne)*, Ray Danton *(Bay Husack)*, Diane McBain *(Christine Storm)*, Karl Swenson *(Scotty Ballantyne)*, Shirley Knight *(Grace at 16)*, Barry Kelley *(Einer Wendt)*, Sheridan Comerate *(Ross)*, George Takei *(Wang)*, Steve Harris *(Christopher at 16)*, I. Stanford Jolley *(Mr. Lawson)*, Dorcas Brower *(Thor's Eskimo Wife)*, Sam McDaniel *(Porter)*, Saul Gorss *(White Checkers)*, John Pedrini *(Foreman)*, William Yip *(Chinese Maitre d')*, Helen Seveck *(Old Eskimo Woman)*, Robert Griffin *(Engineer)*, Judd Holdren *(Muriel's Escort)*, Carol Nicholson *(Grace at Age 7)*, Alan Roberts *(Christopher at Age 7)*, Lennie Bremen, Charles Hicks, James Hope *(Doughboys)*,

Serge Mauriet, Carl Ratcliff *(Fishermen-Kazatzka Dancers)*, John Bleifer, David McMahon *(Fishermen)*.

Just as James Michener has explored such vast areas as Hawaii, Poland, Texas, and space, Edna Ferber tried it with great success as she wrote of Alaska in ICE PALACE. But the film version didn't quite have the bite of the book and meandered all over the screen in a vain attempt to pack 40 years of story into 143 minutes. It begins at the end of WW I and goes until Alaska is named a state. Burton, a canner, is a racist and rankles when his daughter runs off with a half-breed. Ryan resents the way Burton is pillaging the country and treating the natives. Burton, who will stop at nothing to gain wealth, marries heiress Hyer. Ryan runs a fishing boat and, at first, he and Burton are friends but when Burton sets eyes on Ryan's bride-to-be, Jones, their friendship ends. Ryan marries an Eskimo woman and it is his son who marries Burton's daughter, thus making their parents in-laws, once removed. When both kids die, their child, McBain, becomes a pawn between the two warring grandfathers. Burton doesn't want statehood because government regulations might put an end to his plundering. Ryan is all for statehood as he realizes the good it will do for everyone in Alaska. At the end, Ryan is trapped on a glacier and Jones convinces Burton to fly his light plane onto the treacherous ice to save Ryan. Both men embrace and peace comes to Alaska. There was little power or scope to what should have been a magnificent saga, but much of the footage looked as though it was shot against studio backdrops. It's a big movie about a big subject, but somehow they've trivialized it and made Alaska feel like Rhode Island. This was Carolyn Jones' best role as she plays the woman who tries to calm the enmities through the years between Burton and Ryan and plays mother confessor to their offspring. Max Steiner's score is very impressive and suits the bigness of the film.

p, Henry Blanke; d, Vincent Sherman; w, Harry Kleiner (based on the novel by Edna Ferber); ph, Joseph Biroc (Technicolor); m, Max Steiner; ed, William Ziegler; cos, Howard Shoup.

Drama **(PR:A-C MPAA:NR)**

ICE STATION ZEBRA** 1/2 (1968) 152m Filmways-MGM c

Rock Hudson *(Cmdr. James Ferraday)*, Ernest Borgnine *(Boris Vaslov)*, Patrick McGoohan *(David Jones)*, Jim Brown *(Capt. Leslie Anders)*, Tony Bill *(Lt. Russell Walker)*, Lloyd Nolan *(Adm. Garvey)*, Alf Kjellin *(Col. Ostrovsky)*, Ted Hartley *(Lt. Jonathan Hansen)*, Ron Masak *(Paul Zabrinczski)*, Murray Rose *(Lt. George Mills)*, Lee Stanley *(Lt. Mitgang)*, Sherwood Price *(Lt. Edgar Hackett)*, Joseph Bernard *(Dr. Jack Benning)*, John Orchard, William O'Connell, Jim Goodwin *(Survivors)*, Michael T. Mikler *(Lt. Courtney Cartwright)*, Jonathan Lippe *(Russian Aide)*, Jim Dixon *(Earl McAuliffe)*, Ted Kristian *(Wassmeyer)*, Boyd Berlind *(Bruce Kentner)*, David Wendel *(Cedric Patterson)*, Ronnie Rondell, Jr. *(Lyle Nichols)*, Craig Shreeve *(Gafferty)*, Michael Grossman *(Kohler)*, Wade Graham *(Parker)*, Michael Rougas *(Fannovich)*, Jed Allan *(Peter Costigan)*, Lloyd Haines *(Webson)*, Buddy Garion *(Edward Rawlins)*, T.J. Escott *(Lt. Carl Mingus)*, Buddy Hart *(Hill)*, Gary Downey *(Lorrison)*, Robert Carlson *(Kelvaney)*, Don Newsome *(Timothy Hirsch)*, Bill Hillman *(Philip Munsey)*, Dennis Alpert *(Gambetta)*, Gerald S. O'Loughlin *(Lt. Cmdr. Bob Raeburn)*.

Intrigue comes in epic proportions in this U.S. versus Russia arctic battle. Hudson is the commander of a super submarine sent on a reconnaissance mission to locate a downed Soviet satellite containing photographs of U.S. and Russian missile sites. En route, the sub is damaged and everyone is suspect—British officer McGoohan, Soviet defector Borgnine, and U.S. captain Brown. When they reach their destination—Ice Station Zebra, a North Pole weather station—Hudson and crew find nothing but fire-gutted buildings and frozen corpses. Borgnine and Brown, both suspicious of each other, sort out their differences with their fists, and when McGoohan sees them fighting he shoots Brown, assuming he is the saboteur. Russian paratroopers descend on the area and Borgnine shows his true character by handing over the satellite to the Reds. McGoohan, to right his earlier wrong, strangles the deceptive Commie. Hudson, however, destroys the capsule and the photographs inside, at least preventing the enemy from getting them. He then makes a pact with the Russian commander, Kjellin, to publicize the incident as a friendly cooperative effort between nations. Photographed in Super Panavision and projected in Cinerama, Daniel L. Fapp's cinematography (much of it brilliantly depicting the arctic environment under ice) went on to receive an Academy Award nomination.

p, Martin Ransohoff, John Calley; d, John Sturges; w, Douglas Heyes (based on the story by Harry Julian Fink from Alistair MacLean's novel); ph, Daniel L. Fapp (Super Panavision, Metrocolor, Cinerama); m, Michael Legrand; ed, Ferris Webster; md, Legrand; art d, George W. Davis, Addison Hehr; set d, Henry Grace, Jack Mills; spec eff, H.E. Millar, Sr., Ralph Swartz, Earl McCoy; additional Arctic ph, John M. Stephens, Nelson Tyler; tech adv, Capt. John M. Connolly, USN.

War Drama **Cas.** **(PR:A MPAA:NR)**

ICELAND** (1942) 79m FOX bw

Sonja Henie *(Katina Jonsdottir)*, John Payne *(Cpl. James Murfin)*, Jack Oakie *(Slip Riggs)*, Felix Bressart *(Papa)*, Osa Massen *(Helga)*, Joan Merrill *(Adele Wynn)*, Fritz Feld *(Tegnar)*, Sammy Kaye and His Orchestra *(Themselves)*, Sterling Holloway *(Sverdrup Svensson)*, Adeline DeWalt Reynolds *(Grandma)*, Ludwig Stossel *(Valtyr's Father)*, Duke Adlon *(Valtyr)*, Ilka Gruning *(Aunt Sophie)*, Eugene Turner *(Skating Partner)*, James Flavin *(Sergeant)*, William Haade *(Sentry)*, James Bush *(Master Sergeant)*, Carol Curtis Brown *(Canteen Girl)*.

Henie does a lot of what she does best—skate—and fills the rest of her screen time up by falling in love with American marine Payne. To put a smile on her parents' faces, she makes up a story that she is going to marry him. This news also pleases her kid sister who must wait until Henie weds before she can marry a herring tycoon. Her little lie eventually comes true and the pair become husband and wife. Tunes include "You Can't Say No To A Soldier," "There Will Never Be Another You," "Lover's Knot," "Let's Bring New Glory To Old Glory," "I Like A Military Tune" (Harry Warren, Mack Gordon).

p, William LeBaron; d, H. Bruce Humberstone; w, Robert Ellis, Helen Logan; ph, Arthur Miller; ed, James B. Clark; md, Emil Newman; art d, Richard Day, Wiard B. Ihnen; skating ensembles, James Gonzales.

Musical **(PR:A MPAA:NR)**

ICEMAN COMETH, THE*** (1973) 239m American Film Theatre c

Lee Marvin *(Hickey)*, Fredric March *(Harry Hope)*, Robert Ryan *(Larry Slade)*, Jeff Bridges *(Don Parritt)*, Bradford Dillman *(Willie Oban)*, Sorrell Booke *(Hugo Kalmar)*, Hildy Brooks *(Margie)*, Nancy Juno Dawson *(Pearl)*, Evans Evans *(Cora)*, Martyn Green *(The Captain/Cecil Lewis)*, Moses Gunn *(Joe Mott)*, Clifton James *(Pat McGloin)*, John McLiam *(Jimmy Tomorrow/James Cameron)*, Stephen Pearlman *(Chuck Morello)*, Tom Pedi *(Rocky Pioggi)*, George Voskovec *(The General/Piet Wetjoen)*, Bart Burns *(Moran)*, Don McGovern *(Lieb)*.

Though this is considered Eugene O'Neill's finest play by some ("Long Day's Journey Into Night" is undoubtedly his best), THE ICEMAN COMETH does not translate well to the screen. No matter what Frankenheimer pulled from his bag of directorial tricks, the work remains stagey and talky on celluloid and even the majestic talent of March cannot turn it around. March runs a saloon peopled by has-beens and drunks. All their lives, including March's, have been lived and lost. Only the memories are there, inside of bitter nostalgia, voiced not in hope but in despair. The only meager salvation for this bevy of forlorn creatures is the expected arrival of Marvin, a hardware salesman who drops by once a year to regale the customers with his forced humor and tired stories about his wife and the iceman. When Marvin does arrive it's a letdown, even though this realistic actor tries hard to walk O'Neill's tightrope between nimble-witted charm and hortatory talk. March is superb and makes up for Marvin's natural deficiencies and Bridges is good as the despairing young man wanting more than promises out of life. Dillman delivers his cynical wisecracks with aplomb and Booke's anarchist role is so crazily rendered that it replaces the intended fear with absurd humor. Ryan, one of filmdom's most underrated actors, does a superlative job as the radical with dark reason and fearful purpose; he makes of the role something almost noble and heroic, a new perspective on a character once thought set in anarchistic stone. Frankenheimer, known for his grimly realistic films (BLACK SUNDAY, SECONDS), shows a heavy hand here and obviously could find no way to tighten up this draggy, overlong film.

p, Ely A. Landau; d, John Frankenheimer; w, Thomas Quinn Curtiss (based on the play by Eugene O'Neill); ph, Ralph Woolsey; ed, Harold Kress; prod d, Jack Martin Smith; set d, Raphael Bretton, cos, Dorothy Jeakins.

Drama **(PR:C MPAA:PG)**

ICHABOD AND MR. TOAD
(SEE: ADVENTURES OF ICHABOD AND MR. TOAD, THE, 1949)

ICHIJOJI NO KETTO (SEE: SAMURAI, PART II, 1967, Jap.)

IDAHO** 1/2 (1943) 70m REP bw

Roy Rogers *(Roy)*, Smiley Burnette *(Frog Millhouse)*, Bob Nolan and the Sons of the Pioneers *(Themselves)*, Virginia Grey *(Terry)*, Harry J. Shannon *(Judge Grey)*, Ona Munson *(Belle Bonner)*, Dick Purcell *(Duke Springer)*, Onslow Stevens *(Chief Ranger)*, Arthur Hohl *(Spike Madagan)*, Hal Taliaferro *(Bud)*, Rex Lease, Tom London, Jack Ingram, James Bush, The Robert Mitchell Boys Choir, Trigger the Horse.

Shannon is cast as a crusading judge who wants to rid his town of gambling and drinking. When saloon owner and gang leader Munson hears of the judge's plans, she tries to blackmail him by revealing his past as an ex-con. Shannon refuses to back off, so Munson's gang robs a bank and frames the judge. Roy and Smiley come along, as usual, and save the day, clearing the judge's name and making the town fit for youngsters to grow up in. Songs included "Lone Buckaroo," "Holy, Holy, Holy," "Idaho." Film marked Republic's first strong effort to launch Rogers into the firmament left vacant when its shining star, Gene Autry, went into the U.S. Army Air Corps.

p&d, Joseph Kane; w, Roy Chanslor, Olive Cooper; ph, Reggie Lanning; ed, Arthur Roberts; md, Morton Scott; art d, Russell Kimball.

Western **Cas.** **(PR:A MPAA:NR)**

IDAHO KID, THE* (1937) 60m Colony bw

Rex Bell *(Idaho)*, Marian Schilling *(Ruth)*, Dave Sharpe *(Kid)*, Earl Dwire *(Hollister)*, Lafe McKee *(Endicott)*, Charles King *(Slagel)*, Phil Dunham *(Tumblebug)*, Lane Chandler *(Peters)*, Dorothy Wood *(Ma Endicott)*, Herman Hack, Edward Cassidy, George Morrell, Jimmy Aubrey, Sherry Tansey, Dick Botiller.

Bell stumbles his way through this story of a son who tries to bring peace to his feuding father, who disowned him, and stepfather, who raised him. They, however, seem more concerned with water rights than with Bell. Another quaint low-budget production from the lower spectrum of the sagebrush studios, which still could not dim the good-natured luster spread by Bell.

p, Arthur Alexander; d, Robert Hill; w, George Plympton (based on the story "Idaho" by Paul Evan Lehman); ph, Robert Cline; ed, Charles Henkel.

Western **(PR:A MPAA:NR)**

IDAHO TRANSFER* (1975) 87m Pando/Cinemation c

Kelley Bohanan *(Karen)*, Kevin Hearst *(Ronald)*, Caroline Hildebrand *(Isa)*, Keith Carradine *(Arthur)*.

A useless piece of drivel about an obnoxious group of teens who get "teleported" into the future, where they are expected to set up a new civilization in Idaho. Slow-moving and more doltish than the worst comic books, IDAHO TRANSFER was Peter Fonda's second directorial attempt.

p, William Hayward; d, Peter Fonda; w, Thomas Matthiesen; ph, Bruce Logan (CFI Color); m, Bruce Langehorne; ed, Chuck McClelland.

Science Fiction **(PR:C MPAA:NR)**

IDEA GIRL** (1946) 60m UNIV bw

Jess Barker *(Larry Brewster)*, Julie Bishop *(Pat O'Rourke)*, George Dolenz *(Wilfred Potts)*, Alan Mowbray *(J.C. Crow)*, Joan [Shawlee] Fulton *(Mabel)*, Laura Deane Dutton *(Cynthia)*, Virginia Christine *(Evelina)*, Lane Chandler *(Plainclothesman)*, Arthur Q. Bryan *(Mayor)*, Tim Ryan *(Max Gifford)*, Norman Leavett *(Mailman)*, Grady Sutton *(Witherspoon)*, Barton Yarborough *(Pete Barlow)*, Maurice Cass *(Coveleski)*, Garry Owen *(Howard)*, Ferris Taylor *(Police Sergeant)*, Matt Willis *(Truck Driver)*, Sarah Padden *(Old Lady No. 1)*, Ruth Lee *(Abigail)*, Sarah Selby *(Esmerilda)*, Billy Nelson *(Taxi Driver)*, Dewey Robinson *(Mug)*, Patricia Alphin *(Messenger Girl)*, Herbert Haywood *(Grumpy Man)*, Roger Neury *(Headwaiter)*, Peter Cusanelli *(Counterman)*, Gabrielle Windsor *(Flower Girl)*, Lucille Vance *(Old Lady No. 2)*, Pietro Sasso *(Latin Professor)*, John Pupillo *(High School Boy)*, John Roche *(Street Guard)*, Audley Anderson *(Violin Player)*, Charlie Barnet and his Orchestra.

Bishop is the girl with ideas who hits on the notion of a song contest in this above average small musical. What she thinks will be great publicity for her song publisher bosses actually produces nothing but headaches. Robinson's mobile camerawork is a pleasant surprise. Songs include: "I Can't Get You Out Of My Mind," "I Don't Care If I Never Dream Again" (Jack Brooks, Edgar Fairchild), "Xango" (George Waggner, Fairchild).

p, Howard Welsch; d, Will Jason; w, Charles R. Marion, Ellwood Ullman (based on a story by Gladys Shelley); ph, George Robinson; ed, Otto Ludwig; md, Frank Skinner; art d, Jack Otterson, Richard H. Riedel.

Musical/Comedy **(PR:A MPAA:NR)**

IDEAL HUSBAND, AN** (1948, Brit.) 96m BL c

Paulette Goddard *(Mrs. Cheveley)*, Michael Wilding *(Viscount Goring)*, Hugh Williams *(Sir Robert Chiltern)*, Diana Wynyard *(Lady Chiltern)*, C. Aubrey Smith *(Earl of Caversham)*, Glynis Johns *(Mabel Chiltern)*, Constance Collier *(Lady Markby)*, Christine Norden *(Mrs. Marchmont)*, Harriette Johns *(Lady Basildon)*, Fred Groves *(Phipps)*, Johns Clifford *(Mr. Mason)*, Michael Ward *(Mr. Trafford)*, Peter Hobbes *(Mr. Montford)*, Michael Anthony *(Vicomte de Nanjac)*, Michael Medwin *(Duke of Nonsuch)*.

Goddard is stunning as a young adventuress who tries to blackmail the politically rising Williams. She discovers that he sold a cabinet secret concerning the Suez Canal in his youth, and threatens to expose him if he doesn't support a phony Argentine canal scheme in Parliament. He initially agrees, but his wife, Wynyard, persuades him to do the opposite. Wilding, his best friend and Goddard's ex-fiance, talks the crafty woman out of the blackmail scheme. Based on an Oscar Wilde play, it comes across very stuffy in its proper 1895 atmosphere. Wilde's wit is no longer that witty, and melodramatics sink the ship of state conflict.

p&d, Alexander Korda; w, Lajos Biro (based on a play by Oscar Wilde); ph, Georges Perinal (Technicolor); m, Arthur Benjamin; ed, Oswald Haffenrichter; md, Hubert Clifford; set d, Vincent Korda; cos, Cecil Beaton; spec eff, W. Percy Day; makeup, Urban P. Hutchinson, Dorrie Hamilton.

Comedy/Drama **(PR:A MPAA:NR)**

IDEAL LODGER, THE*

(1957, Ger.) 98m Wolf Schmidt Film bw (DER IDEALE UNTERMIETER)

Wolf Schmidt, Sibylle Schindler, Lia Woehr, Holger Hagen, Susi Jera.

Intended as a children's film about a youngster who becomes pals with a domestic robot, this German entry is so swamped in the adult themes of conformity and the failure of communication that it goes over the head of anyone it is trying to reach. The hospital shock treatments are definitely not kiddie material. A rather baffling "children's" film.

p,d&w, Wolf Schmidt; ph, Heino Koenig.

Juvenile/Science Fiction **(PR:O MPAA:NR)**

IDENTIFICATION MARKS: NONE½**

(1969, Pol.) 76m Film Polski/New Yorker bw (RYSOPIS)

Jerzy Skolimowski *(Andrzej Leszczyc)*, Elzbieta Czyzewska *(Theresa/Barbara/Housewife)*, Tadeusz Mins *(Mundzek)*, Andrzej Zarnecki *(Raymond)*, Jacek Szczek.

The first feature from Polish director Jerzy Skolimowski (MOONLIGHTING) which he made in 1964 as a graduate thesis for the National Film Academy in Lodz. He starred as a student who studies fish at a university in an attempt to avoid the draft, but he finally gives in and enlists. He is given only a few hours to organize his personal life before going off to basic training. He returns to his apartment without speaking to his wife, finds his dog sick and has it put to sleep, tries to seduce a housewife, and then goes to the store where his wife supposedly works. He then discovers that his wife makes her money in a less respectable way. He heads for the train station and readies himself for two years of military service. A student effort at making an existential statement, and an interesting debut for one of the most significant Polish directors to emerge in the 1960s.

d,w, Jerzy Skolimowski; ph, Witold Mickiewicz; m, Krzysztof Sadowski; art d, Skolimowski.

Drama **(PR:A MPAA:NR)**

IDENTIFICATION OF A WOMAN*** (1983, Ital.) 130m GAU c

Thomas Milian *(Niccolo)*, Daniela Silverio *(Mavi)*, Christine Boisson *(Ida)*, Veronica Lazar *(Carla)*, Sandra Monteleoni, Giampaolo Saccarola, Alessandro Ruspoli, Giada Gerini, Sergio Tardioli, Paola Dominguin, Marcel Bozzuffi, Itaco Nardulli, Enrica Fico, Arianna De Rosa, Maria Stefania D'Amario, Luisa Della Noce, Lara Wendel, Pierfrancesco Aiello, Carlos Valles.

Antonioni's first Italian film in nearly two decades (he did, however, shoot THE MYSTERY AT OBERWALD for video in 1979) and again it deals with his familiar treatment of the relationship between a man and a woman, or, in this case, with two women. Milian is a middle-aged film director (not unlike Antonioni) who gets involved with Silverio, an upper-class woman. He receives anonymous threats to terminate the relationship, which he ignores. Before long, Silverio moves away without telling Milian. He then involves himself with avant-garde stage actress Boisson, but after she informs him that she is pregnant by another man the relationship comes to a halt. Contrary to the standard view of love, Antonioni's characters do not suffer emotionally from their losses. As the director has stated, Milian "doesn't tear his hair out, doesn't despair like one is used to." What one is used to in Antonioni's work is the predominant use of colors and patterns, and again they are in the forefront in this picture.

p, Giorgio Nocella, Antonio Macri; d, Michelangelo Antonioni; w, Antonioni, Tonino Guerra, Gerard Brach; ph, Carlo Di Palma (Technovision, Technicolor); m, John Foxx; ed, Antonioni; md, Andrea Crisanti; art d, Crisanti.

Drama **(PR:C-O MPAA:NR)**

IDENTIKIT (SEE: DRIVER'S SEAT, THE, 1975. Ital.)

IDENTITY PARADE (SEE: LINE-UP, THE, 1934)

IDENTITY UNKNOWN*** (1945) 71m REP bw

Richard Arlen *(Johnny March)*, Cheryl Walker *(Sally MacGregor)*, Roger Pryor *(Rocks Donnelly)*, Bobby Driscoll *(Toddy Loring)*, Lola Lane *(Wanda)*, Ian Keith *(Maj. Williams)*, John Forrest *(Joe Granowski)*, Sarah Padden *(Mrs. Anderson)*, Forrest Taylor *(Mr. Anderson)*, Frank Marlowe *(Frankie)*, Harry Tyler *(Harry)*, Nelson Leigh *(Col. Marlin)*, Charles Williams *(Auctioneer)*, Charles Jordan *(Needles)*, Dick Scott *(Spike)*, Marjorie Manners *(Nurse)*, Eddie Baker *(Motor Cop)*.

An interesting treatment of a soldier's return from WW II and suffering from amnesia. Arlen, cast as the unknown, adopts the tag Johnny March, and march is what he does. To find his real identity, he travels across America visiting a variety of people—a truck driver from Connecticut, an architect in West Virginia, a Chicago mobster, and an Iowa farm couple, and each tells about their personal losses in the war, their feelings on why the war was fought, and how Americans will live after the war's end. Through his searching, Arlen finds himself, especially with the inspiration of his new girl friend, Walker. Arlen's character of Johnny March was a significant and timely symbol for the American soldier returning home, embodying all the fears and joy that this country lived through. A uniquely personal film from director Walter Colmes.

p, Howard Bretherton, Walter Colmes; d, Colmes; w, Richard Weil (based on a story by Robert Newman); ph, Ernest Miller; ed, John Link; md, Jay Chernis.

Drama **(PR:A MPAA:NR)**

IDENTITY UNKNOWN* (1960, Brit.) 66m Danziger/PAR bw

Richard Wyler *(John)*, Pauline Yates *(Jenny)*, Patricia Plunkett *(Betty)*, Beatrice Varley *(Matron)*, Valentine Dyall *(Ambrose)*, Kenneth Edwards *(Reynolds)*, John Gabriel *(Jamieson)*, Nyree Dawn Porter *(Pam)*, Vincent Ball *(Ken)*, Sheldon Lawrence *(Larry)*.

The sorrowful stories of plane crash victims' relatives are told to news reporters in this episodic and poorly constructed picture which offers little in the line of entertainment.

p, Edward J. Danziger, Harry Lee Danziger; d, Frank Marshall; w, Brian Clemens.

Drama **(PR:A MPAA:NR)**

IDIOT, THE ***½

(1948, Fr.) 95m Societe Des Films Sacha Gordine/European Copyrights & Distribution bw (L'IDIOT)

Edwige Feuillere *(Nastasia Philipovna)*, Gerard Philipe *(Prince Muichkine)*, Marguerite Moreno *(General's wife)*, Lucien Coedel *(Rogogine)*, Nathalie Nattier *(Aglae)*, Jean Debucourt *(Totsky)*, Maurice Chambreuil *(Gen. Epantchine)*, Michel Andre *(Gania)*, Felicien Tramel *(Gen. Ivolgin)*, Sylvie *(His Wife)*.

Dostoyevsky's famed Second Coming of Christ fantasy (allegorically, He gets crucified again) is beautifully handled in this somewhat abbreviated version of the novel. The Christ figure (Philipe, in a role which preceded that of his troubled adolescent in DEVIL IN THE FLESH, the film that brought him success as a major star), an innocent aristocrat whose sensitivity to the human condition has brought him to collapse, returns to the society of pre-revolutionary St. Petersburg from a sojourn in a Swiss mental institution. Although isolated from the true turmoil of Mother Russia—the social stratification that was to lead to revolution—his involvements in the venal, petty pursuits of his partrician peers suffice to bring him once again to derangement. Philipe is luminous in his role as Prince Muichkine; Feuillere shines as the strong, self-centered—but ultimately selfless—woman who elects to save him from herself by giving herself to the brutal Coedel, who kills her. Nattier is fine as the child-woman who turns from virgin to virago. All the more pessimistic for its frequent flashes of human kindness even among the lost souls, the film is a gem. Remade by the Soviet Union in 1960 and by Japan's Akira Kurosawa in 1963 in much longer—but not necessarily better—versions. (In French; English subtitles.)

p, Sacha Gordine; d, Georges Lampin; w, Charles Spaak (based on the novel by Feodor Dostoyevsky); ph, Christian Matras; m, Maurice Thiriet; ed, Leonide Azar.

Drama **(PR:A MPAA:NR)**

IDIOT, THE*** (1960, USSR) 122m Mosfilm/FOX c

Yuri Yakovlev *(Prince Myshkin)*, Yulia Borisova *(Nastasia Philippovna)*, Nikita Podgorny *(Ganya Ivolgin)*, Leonid Parkhomenko *(Parfen Rogozhin)*, Raia Maximova *(Aglaya Yepanchina)*, Nikolai Pazhitnov *(Gen. Yepanchin)*, Vera Pashennaya *(His Wife)*, Klavdia Polovikova *(Nina Alexandrovna Ivolgina)*, I. Lyubeznov *(Gen. Ivolgin)*, L. Ivanova *(Varya Ivolgina)*, V. Muraviev *(Ferdishchenko)*, S. Martinson *(Lebedev)*, P. Strelin *(Totsky)*.

The problem in adapting great works of literature into film lies in the differences between the two mediums. Literature is better suited for brooding introspection, whereas film is ill suited for such deep psychological probing without bordering on the pretentious. Such is the problem in this adaptation of Dostoyevsky's classic novel *The Idiot*. The story of Prince Myshkin (Yakovlev) and his love for Nastasia (Borisova) is certainly well played by the cast, with an interesting use of location shooting that captures the flavor of Czarist Russia. But fine though these qualities are, the true feeling of the original is never portrayed, instead giving only a glimpse of a classic.

d&w, Ivan Pyriev (based on the novel by Feodor Dostoyevsky); ph, V. Pavlov (Sovcolor); ed, S. Volkov.

Drama **(PR:O MPAA:NR)**

IDIOT, THE** (1963, Jap.) 165m Shochiku bw (HAKUCHI)

Masayuki Mori *(Kinji Kameda, the Idiot)*, Toshiro Mifune *(Denkichi Akama)*, Setsuko Hara *(Taeko Nasu)*, Takashi Shimura *(Ono, the Father)*, Yoshiko Kuga *(Ayako Ono)*, Chieko Higashiyama *(Satoki Ono, the Mother)*, Minoru Chiaki *(Mutsuo Kayama)*, Chiyoko Fumiya *(Noriko)*, Kokuten Kodo *(Jyunpei)*, Eiko Miyoshi *(Kayama's Mother)*, Notiko Sengoku *(Takako)*, Daisuke Inoue *(Kaoru)*, Eijiro Yanagi *(Tohata)*, Bokuzen Hidari *(Karube)*, Mitsuyo Akashi *(Akama's Mother)*.

A rare failure from Kurosawa, whose devotion to the Feodor Dostoyevski source material (the novel *The Idiot)* spelled doom for this project. By cramming a Russian cultural sensibility unchanged into a Japanese context (the two cultures are diametrically opposed) Kurosawa drains the material of any relevance and confuses its direction and purpose. Mori stars as a soldier who returns to Okinawa from a recent war only to find himself considered mentally ill due to epilepsy. There he meets Mifune, a wealthy man, and they both fall in love with Hara. Seeing the problem, Mori also falls into an affair with another woman, Kuga, who returns his affection. Realizing that he really only loves Hara, he is shattered to find that she has become Mifune's mistress. He offers her money for her love. Touched by his offer, she throws the currency into the fireplace and accepts his love for free. Mifune soon learns of the relationship and the friends quarrel. Enraged that he has lost Hara, Mifune stabs her and both men descend into madness from their grief.

p, Takashi Koide; d, Akira Kurosawa; w, Eijiro Hisaita, Kurosawa (based on the novel by Feodor Mikhailovich Dostoyevsky); ph, Toshio Ubukata, Choichi Nakai; m, Fumio Hayasaka; ed, T. Saito; art d, So Matsuyama.

Drama **(PR:C-O MPAA:NR**

IDIOT'S DELIGHT*** 1/2** (1939) 105m MGM bw

Norma Shearer *(Irene Fellara)*, Clark Gable *(Harry Van)*, Edward Arnold *(Achille Weber)*, Charles Coburn *(Dr. Waldersee)*, Joseph Schildkraut *(Capt. Kirvline)*, Burgess Meredith *(Quillery)*, Laura Hope Crews *(Mme. Zuleika)*, Skeets Gallagher *(Donald Navadel)*, Peter Willes *(Mr. Cherry)*, Pat Patterson *(Mrs. Cherry)*, William Edmunds *(Dumptsy)*, Fritz Feld *(Pittatek)*, Virginia Grey *(Shirley Laughlin)*, Lorraine Krueger *(Bebe)*, Paula Stone *(Beulah Tremeyne)*, Virginia Dale *(Francine)*, Joan Marsh *(Elaine Messiger)*, Bernadene Hayes *(Edna Creesh)*, Edward Raquello *(Chiari)*, Frank Orth *(Benny Zinssar)*, George Sorel *(Major)*, Hobart Cavanaugh *(Frueheim, the Theater Manager)*, Bernard Suss *(Auguste)*, William Irving *(Sandro)*, Harry Strang *(Sergeant)*, Emory Parnell *(Fifth Avenue Cop)*, Bud Geary *(Ambulance Driver)*, Mitchell Lewis *(Indian)*, Joe Yule *(Comic)*, Gertrude Bennett *(Woman with Powders)*, Jim Conlin *(Stagehand)*, Bonita Weber *(Woman with Catsup)*, Rudolf Myzet *(Czech Announcer)*, Adolph Milar *(Fellara)*, Clem Bevans *(Jimmy Barzek)*, Claire McDowell *(Mother)*, Robert Middlemass *(Hospital Commandant)*, Evelyn Knapp *(Nurse)*, Eddie Gribbon *(Cop)*, Buddy Messinger *(Usher)*, Charles Judels *(Greek Restaurant Owner)*, Paul Panzer *(Greek Chef)*, E. Alyn Warren *(Clerk, Grand Hotel)*, Frank Faylen *(Ed)*, Frank M. Thomas *(Bert)*, Gary Owen *(Newsstand Man)*, Lee Phelps *(Train Announcer)*, Francis McDonald *(Flight Captain)*.

The kind of humor displayed in Robert E. Sherwood's Pulitzer Prize-winning play and this film, also written for the screen by Sherwood, is the sophisticated brand of comedy that all but perished after the 1930s: broad, extravagant comedy requiring a perception of the double entrendre and some literary background on the part of the viewer. Gable is a burlesque hoofer who, following WW I, takes a job as an assistant to an alcoholic mind-reader, Crews. He and Crews practice a "code" whereby Gable relates information about the person asking questions in the audience to the blindfolded medium, thus allowing her to render intelligent answers. Crews is so drunk that she confuses the "tips" Gable gives her and mixes up her answers so that she and Gable are booed offstage, especially when ingenue Shearer, waiting in the wings, cues the drunken medium so loudly that the audiencehears it. Shearer apologizes to Gable for ruining the act and he takes her to dinner. She begs Gable to teach her the "code" so that she can become a great medium. Over dinner she fantasizes how her name will be in lights all over the world and that Gable will assist her, of course. She puts on extravagant airs, claiming to be a Russian countess. None of it is true, and Gable knows it, but he tolerates the impersonation; he's all show business and he's used to eccentric behavior. The next day they part. Gable is shown in a montage, performing various routines until, years later, he and his all-girl revue, known as Les Blondes, become a hit in Europe. Traveling to Geneva, his troupe is stopped at the border and sent to an Alpine hotel, the Monte Lodi, until their passports and visas are approved. At the posh resort, Gable meets several interesting characters. One is Meredith, a radical peace worker who loudly condemns the militarists who have taken over Europe and the world war that is certain to come from their insane ambitions. Another is Coburn, a medical scientist who has been experimenting with pet rats to find cures for diseases. A young married couple, Patterson and Willes, are just starting their lives together. Then there is munitions king Arnold who is more responsible than most for the war climate in Europe, and his mistress, a blonde, slinky Russian countess, who is really Shearer, and has been living her fantasy for years. Watching the guests and hotel employees closely is army captain Schildkraut. Among the employees are Feld, a pompous maitre d'; Gallagher, the entertainment director; and Suss, a gentle porter. Gable believes he recognizes Shearer as that fetching and far-fetched ingenue of a decade earlier but he's unsure until he has a drink with her and the young couple, Willes and Patterson. After listening to the blonde vamp recount her life, he recognizes the fantasies of the girl he met in Omaha. Riddling the lengthy conversations are diatribes from Meredith, outbursts so theatrical that few take real note of him. Shearer has grown tired of millionaire Arnold and tells him how disgusted she is with his murderous machinations. He promptly dumps her, leaving her in the lurch when his passport is cleared. In the valley below a huge military airport unleashes waves of bombers which fly off to an unknown target. As the guests flee, including Gable and his troupe, those left behind await the counterstrike which will certainly destroy the mountaintop retreat. Shearer has a drink of champagne with Suss, who is going off to battle, then sits down at the piano in the grand lounge with its bay windows overlooking the valley and begins to play. Gable returns alone for her and she is overjoyed, although she keeps up her impersonation until he compels her to revert to the limelight-hungry American girl he knew so many years earlier. She continues to play the piano as the retaliating bombers destroy the valley below and half the hotel. Somehow Gable and Shearer survive to face the war and life together, after singing "Onward Christian Soldiers" through the bombardment. Unbelievable as the ending is, the film proves quite amusing with many a witty exchange. One of the most charming aspects of the film was Gable and his blonde troupe performing for the hotel guests, singing and dancing to the tune "Puttin' on the Ritz." Brown's direction is speedy but he uses predictable devices to show the passing of time and lets Shearer get way out of hand, even beyond the extravagant character she is playing. Sherwood, who wrote the film script, altered his play considerably, writing an extensive prolog, toning down the anti-war dialog, eliminating any mention of Germany, stressing the romance and providing a happy ending. Gable is fun to watch as he registers a consistently painful expression in response to Shearer's outlandish displays. He also does a commendable singing and dancing job, one which he was reluctant to perform. He rehearsed this sequence (later incorporated into THAT'S ENTERTAINMENT) for six weeks with choreographer George King and also researched his moves by watching early movies of George M. Cohan doing his dance routines. He was still worried about appearing clumsy, and tripping over his own size 11-C shoes. At his insistence studio cops guarded the sound stage to prevent intruders coming onto the set where he was performing his dance numbers. This would be the only time in his career when he would dance before the cameras as an entertainer. To further polish the dance steps, his wife Carole Lombard practiced with him at home. Gable was good-natured about it all. When Brown, directing him in one scene, told him to "hold onto the trapeze with your teeth," Gable responded (with a reference to his false choppers): "What do I hold onto my teeth with?" Gable's reported tightwad habits were inadvertently spoofed when he buys Shearer a seventy-five cent trinket and says: "That's the most expensive present I ever bought a dame."

p, Hunt Stromberg; d, Clarence Brown; w, Robert Sherwood (based on his play); ph, William Daniels; ed, Robert J. Kern; md, Herbert Stothart; art d, Cedric Gibbons, Wade B. Rubottom; set d, Edwin B. Willis; cos, Adrian; ch, George King; m/l, Gus Kahn, Stothart.

Comedy **(PR:A MPAA:NR)**

IDLE ON PARADE (SEE: IDOL ON PARADE, 1959, Brit.)

IDLE RICH, THE** 1/2** (1929) 80m MGM bw

Conrad Nagel *(William Van Luyn)*, Bessie Love *(Helen Thayer)*, Leila Hyams *(Joan Thayer)*, Robert Ober *(Henry)*, Edythe Chapman *(Mrs. Thayer)*, James Neill *(Mr. Thayer)*, Paul Kruger *(Tom Gibney)*, Kenneth Gibson *(Frank Thayer)*.

Hyams is a stenographer from a middle-class background who weds her rich boss, Nagel. When he visits the girl's parents he finds that they feel the need to prove class equality. After being subjected to a long-winded speech on the class system from Hyams' cousin, Nagel decides to move in with the folks, at Hyams' urging. He puts up with endless inconveniences and discomforts in order to prove that love is not a slave to class distinctions. Based on a stage play, this picture contains plenty of laughs along with its fruitful message. Remade in 1938 as RICH MAN, POOR GIRL.

d, William DeMille; w, Clara Beranger (based on the play "White Collars" by Edith Ellis, Franklin Stearns); ph, Leonard Smith; ed, Conrad A. Nervig.

Comedy **(PR:A MPAA:NR)**

IDO ZERO DAISAKUSEN (SEE: LATITUDE ZERO, 1970, U.S./Jap.)

IDOL, THE** (1966, Brit.) 109m EM bw

Jennifer Jones *(Carol)*, Michael Parks *(Marco)*, John Leyton *(Timothy)*, Jennifer Hilary *(Sarah)*, Guy Doleman *(Martin Livesey)*, Natasha Pyne *(Rosalind)*, Caroline Blakiston *(2nd Woman at Party)*, Jeremy Bulloch *(Lewis)*, Fanny Carby *(Barmaid)*, Vernon Dobtcheff *(Man at Party)*, Michael Gordon *(Boy)*, Gordon Gostelow *(Simon)*, Ken Haward *(Policeman)*, Renee Houston *(Woman at Party)*, Priscilla Morgan *(Rosie)*, Edna Morris *(Mrs. Muller)*, Peter Porteous *(Tommy)*, Terry Richards, Derek Ware *(Laborers)*, Jack Watson *(Police Inspector)*, Rita Webb *(Landlady)*, Tina Williams *(Dorothea)*, Philippa Hare.

A twisted movie which has Parks cast as an American art student living in London. He befriends medical student Leyton and soon takes a liking to his girl friend Hilary. She moves into Parks' apartment, much to the chagrin of the jilted Leyton. During a party at Leyton's mother's cottage, Parks and Hilary are discovered in the bedroom by mom Jones. Later, when Parks comes to the aid of Leyton in a pub fight, Jones becomes appreciative and again begins to respect the lad. Parks, however, is still quite a jerk and plans to break up with Hilary as a New Year's present. When Leyton hears of this he rushes off to warn her. Parks goes to pick up Leyton from his house, unaware that he has already left, and encounters Jones instead. The nasty boy proceeds to seduce Leyton's mom, and then staggers drunkenly to the New Year's party. Leyton, upon hearing of his "friend's" deed, pushes the soused Parks into a nearby river, killing him. The police then arrest Leyton for manslaughter. The poor kid has all the luck.

p, Leonard Lightstone; d, Daniel Petrie; w, Millard Lampell (based on a story by Ugo Liberatore); ph, Ken Higgins; m, John Dankworth; ed, Jack Slade; md, Dankworth; art d, George Provis; cos, Yvonne Blake; makeup, Wally Schneiderman.

Drama **(PR:O MPAA:NR)**

IDOL OF PARIS* ½ (1948, Brit.) 106m Premier/WB bw

Michael Rennie *(Hertz)*, Beryl Baxter *(Theresa)*, Christine Norden *(Cora Pearl)*, Miles Malleson *(Offenbach)*, Andrew Osborn *(Antoine)*, Andrew Cruickshank *(Prince Nicholas)*, Kenneth Kent *(Emperor Napoleon)*, Margaretta Scott *(Empress Eugenie)*, Patti Morgan *(Bellanger)*, Genine Graham *(Barucci)*, Henry Oscar *(Lachman)*, Sybilla Binder *(Mrs. Lachman)*, Leslie Perrins *(Count Paiva)*, Campbell Cotts *(George Tremer, Sr.)*, John Penrose *(George Tremer, Jr.)*, April Stride *(Countess de Molney)*, Donald Gray *(Police Inspector)*, June Holden *(Marie)*, Frederick Bradshaw *(Chamberlain)*, Mary Stone *(Theresa's Secretary)*.

Set in Paris and Russia in the 1860s, this trite costume drama follows Baxter's rise from the slums to her reputation as one of the period's most sought-after women. She becomes the toast of Paris, and is powerful enough to give Napoleon the grand kissoff. Everything about it has a suffocating air of stodginess.

p, R.J. Minney; d, Leslie Arliss; w, Norman Lee, Stafford Dickens, Harry Ostrer (based on Alfred Shirokauer's novel *Paiva, Queen of Love*); ph, Jack Cox; m, Mischa Spoliansky; ed, A.S. Bates; art d, Albert Jullion; spec eff, Tom Howard; cos, Honoria Plesch; makeup, Guy Pearce.

Drama **(PR:A MPAA:NR)**

IDOL OF THE CROWDS** ½ (1937) 62m UNIV bw

John Wayne *(Johnny Hanson)*, Sheila Bromley *(Helen Dale)*, Charles Brokaw *(Jack Irwin)*, Billy Burrud *(Bobby)*, Jane Johns *(Peggy)*, Huntley Gordon *(Harvey Castle)*, Frank Otto *(Joe Garber)*, Russell Hopton *(Kelly)*, Virginia Brissac *(Mrs. Dale)*, George Lloyd *(Spike Regan)*, Hal Neiman *(Squat Bates)*, Clem Bevans *(Andy Moore)*, Wayne Castle *(Swifty)*, Lloyd Ford *(Hank)*, Lee Ford *(Elmer)*.

Wayne exudes toughness as a hockey player blessed with integrity. When he and brother Burrud get picked from their Maine chicken farm to play with a big association club, they are confronted with some shady characters. Trying to multiply their profits, Bromley and Brokaw attempt to force the pair into throwing a few games. Bromley, however, falls for the rugged Wayne, as love overshadows greed.

p, Trem Carr, Paul Malvern; d, Arthur Lubin; w, George Waggner, Harold Buckley (based on a story, "Hell on Ice," by Waggner); ph, Harry Neumann; ed, Charles Craft; art d, Charles Clague.

Drama **(PR:A MPAA:NR)**

IDOL ON PARADE** ½ (1959, Brit.) 88m Warwick/COL bw

William Bendix *(Sgt. Lush)*, Anthony Newley *(Jeep Jackson)*, Anne Aubrey *(Caroline)*, Lionel Jeffries *(Bertie)*, Sidney James *(Herbie)*, David Lodge *(Shorty)*, Dilys Laye *(Renee)*, William Kendall *(Commanding Officer)*, Bernie Winters *(Joseph Jackson)*, Harry Fowler *(Ron)*, Norman Atkyns *(Stage Manager)*, Percy Herbert *(Sgt. Herbrides)*, Jane Navello *(Iris)*, Andre Charisse *(Club Manager)*, Rosamund Greenwood *(Spinster)*, Maureen Riscoe, Marigold Russell, Rosemary Davis *(Naafi Girls)*, John Wood *(Jeremy)*, Ian Wilson *(Man in Cinema)*, Rupert Davies *(Sergeant)*, Martin Boddey *(Chucker-out)*, Roderick Cook, Gordon Needham, Tom Bowman, Carl Conway, Michael Bell, Stanley Beard, Lester Nixon, Ian MacNaughtan, John Cowley, Eric Corrie, Sean Kelly.

Newley is a pop singer called up to serve in the British army. Chaotic fan reactions and silly predicaments arise when he dons a pair of army boots. It's all carried off quite well, especially with Bendix as a kind-hearted but loud-mouth boob of a sergeant.

p, Harold Huth; d, John Gilling; w, John Antrobus (based on the novel by William Camp); ph, Ted Moore (CinemaScope); m, Bill Shepherd; ed, Bert Rule; m/l, Gerry Laudan, Len Praverman.

Comedy **(PR:A MPAA:NR)**

IDOLMAKER, THE*** ½ (1980) 107m UA c

Ray Sharkey *(Vincent Vacarri)*, Tovah Feldshuh *(Brenda Roberts)*, Peter Gallagher *(Caesare)*, Paul Land *(Tommy Dee)*, Joe Pantoliano *(Gino Pilato)*, Maureen McCormick *(Ellen Fields)*, John Aprea *(Paul Vacarri)*, Richard Bright *(Uncle Tony)*, Olympia Dukakis *(Mrs. Vacarri)*, Steven Apostlee Peck *(Mr. Vacarri)*, Leonard Gaines *(Luchetti)*, Deney Terrio *(Jerry Martin)*, Charles Guardino *(Jesse)*, Michael Mislove *(Ed Sharp)*, Kenneth O'Brien *(Walt Bennett)*, Michael Perotta *(Carlo)*, Jeffrey Tanner *(Delano)*, Howard Gordon *(Scapio)*, Sweet Inspirations, London Fog.

A first-rate picture about rock and roll with no punches pulled. Bob Marcucci is listed as technical advisor in the credits but anyone who is hip to the music business will know that this is his story and the way he dominated music in the early days of rock and roll when he managed both Frankie Avalon and Fabian as well as many other "Philadelphia-sound" performers. Marcucci is played by Ray Sharkey, who is absolutely splendid in the title role. He truly guides the lives of his charges, Gallagher and Land, and manages everything they do; calling in old favors, laying some money on people, making sure they have the best clothes, the best backup bands, etc. Feldshuh is an editor of a fan magazine who has a fling with Sharkey and uses her media influence to help make Sharkey's boys into stars. All the acting is good but Sharkey is so special in his role that he causes an imbalance by his virtuoso playing. It's all very serious and one would have wished they might have poked just a little fun at themselves. The anachronistic music by Jeff Barry also causes a bit of a problem for anyone who remembers the way the music sounded back then. This was probably done to get some air play for the film's score and to see if they couldn't get a hit or two out of the picture as there have been songs from some movies that have grossed more money than the pictures did. The direction by Hackford (AN OFFICER AND A GENTLEMAN) is excellent and he is a person from whom much will be heard in the future. There have been other films about the grooming of performers (THE ROSE is a lousy example) but this, so far, must rank as the best.

p, Gene Kirkwood, Howard W. Koch, Jr.; d, Taylor Hackford; w, Edward Di Lorenzo; ph, Adam Holender (Technicolor); m, Jeff Barry; ed, Neil Travis; art d, David L. Snyder; set d, Barbara Kreiger; cos, Rita Riggs; ch, Deney Terrio; m/l, Barry; tech advisor, Bob Marcucci.

Drama **Cas.** **(PR:A–C MPAA:PG)**

IDOLS IN THE DUST (SEE: SATURDAY'S HERO, 1951)

IERI, OGGI E DOMANI (SEE: YESTERDAY, TODAY AND TOMORROW, 1964, Fr./Ital.)

IF . . .*** (1968, Brit.) 110m Memorial/PAR bw-c

Malcolm McDowell *(Mick Travers)*, David Wood *(Johnny)*, Richard Warwick *(Wallace)*, Christine Noonan *(The Girl)*, Rupert Webster *(Bobby Philips)*, Robert Swann *(Rowntree)*, Hugh Thomas *(Denson)*, Peter Jeffrey *(Headmaster)*, Mona Washbourne *(Matron)*, Arthur Lowe *(Mr. Kemp, Housemaster)*, Graham Crowden *(History Master)*, Geoffrey Chater *(Chaplain)*, Mary MacLeod *(Mrs. Kemp, Housemaster's Wife)*, Ben Aris *(John Thomas, Undermaster)*, Anthony Nicholls *(Gen. Denson)*, Michael Cadman *(Fortinbras)*, Peter Sproule *(Barnes)*, Charles Lloyd Pack *(Classics Master)*, Tommy Godfrey *(School Porter)*, John Garrie *(Music Master)*, Guy Ross *(Stephans)*, Robin Askwith *(Keating)*, Richard Everett *(Pussy Graves)*, Philip Bagenal *(Peanuts)*, Nicholas Page *(Cox)*, Robert Yetzes *(Fisher)*, David Griffin *(Willens)*, Graham Sharman *(Van Eyssen)*, Richard Tombleson *(Baird)*, Richard Davies *(Machin)*, Brian Pettifer *(Biles)*, Michael Newport *(Brunning)*, Charles Sturridge *(Markland)*, Sean Bury *(Jute)*, Martin Beaumont *(Hunter)*, Ellis Dale *(Motorcycle Salesman)*.

McDowell is a rebellious upperclassman at a strict British boarding school, who, with his friend Wood, refuses to conform. During a rugby match, the pair sneak into town and meet a waitress. Upon their return, McDowell is brutally beaten by the headmaster, sparking revolt in the youngster. Together with his fellow schoolmates, McDowell prepares an attack on the administration. The finale has the gang of youths open fire with an arsenal of weapons during an alumnus speech. From the rooftop of the school, the headmaster is shot in the head by the waitress. IF . . . was seen in the 1960s as a powerful youth statement; today it is less so, due, perhaps, to the timeliness of the subject (which is, perhaps, timeless; this film bears a striking resemblance to Jean Vigo's innovative ZERO DE CONDUITE, 1947). It was originally conceived in 1958 and scripted in 1960 under the title THE CRUSADERS. The film's violence was a subject of great controversy. Its promotional poster depicted a group of youths armed with machineguns and hand grenades asking, "Which side are you on?" The version of IF . . . screened at the Cannes Film Festival (which won the Golden Palm) received an "X" rating, due mainly to a nude shower scene. Only after a few cuts was it granted a rating of "R." The impact the film would have was felt even before production began, with both Universal and CBS turning the project down. With thoughts of a violent REBEL WITHOUT A CAUSE, the picture was even offered to auteur director Nicholas Ray, who suggested it would be best served with a British director.

p, Michael Medwin, Lindsay Anderson, Roy Baird; d, Anderson; w, David Sherwin (based on a script by Sherwin, John Howlett entitled "The Crusaders"); ph, Miroslav Ondricek (Eastmancolor); m, Marc Wilkinson; ed, David Gladwell; md, Wilkinson; prod d, Jocelyn Herbert; art d, Brian Eatwell; makeup, Betty Blattner.

Drama **Cas.** **(PR:O MPAA:R)**

IF A MAN ANSWERS** (1962) 102m Ross Hunter/UNIV c

Sandra Dee *(Chantal Stacey)*, Bobby Darin *(Eugene Wright)*, Micheline Presle *(Maman Stacey)*, John Lund *(John Stacey)*, Cesar Romero *(Robert Swan/Adam*

Wright), Stefanie Powers *(Tina)*, Christopher Knight *(Richard)*, Ted Thorpe *(Florist)*, Roger Bacon *(Messenger)*, John Bleifer *(Tobacconist)*, Pamela Searle *(Model)*, Warrene Ott *(Rita)*, Dani Lynn *(Bunny)*, Charlene Holt *(Lisa)*, Gloria Camacho, Edmay Van Dyke, Rosalee Calvert *(Models)*, Gladys Thornton *(Boston Maid)*.

A featherweight attempt at romantic comedy starring Dee and Darin as newlyweds. When Dee begins to feel that her husband is taking her for granted, she calls on her mother for guidance. Mom tells Dee to treat him like a pet dog, which works until he catches on. Mom then suggests Dee pretend to have a secret lover who hangs up whenever Darin answers. Again Darin catches on and decides to retaliate. He tells Dee that her lover has telephoned and is on his way over. Later an older man appears who is really Darin's father. Everything wraps up nicely when Dee and Darin find out they are going to be parents.

p, Ross Hunter, Edward Muhl; d, Henry Levin; w, Richard Morris (based on the novel by Winifred Wolfe); ph, Russell Metty (Eastmancolor); m, Hans J. Salter; ed, Milton Carruth; art d, Alexander Golitzen; set d, Howard Bristol; cos, Jean Louis; m/l, "If A Man Answers," Bobby Darin (sung by Darin), "Chantal Theme," Darin; makeup, Bud Westmore.

Romantic Comedy (PR:A MPAA:NR)

IF EVER I SEE YOU AGAIN zero (1978) 105m COL c

Joe Brooks *(Bob Morrison)*, Shelley Hack *(Jennifer Corly)*, Jimmy Breslin *(Mario)*, Jerry Keller *(Steve Warner)*, Kenny Karen *(David Miller)*, George Plimpton *(Lawrence)*, Michael Decker *(Young Morrison)*, Julie Ann Gordon *(Young Corly)*, Danielle Brisebois, Branch Emerson *(Morrison Children)*, Shannon Bolin *(Elsa, Housekeeper)*, Caroline Mignini *(Laura Miller)*, Joe Leon *(Sosnick)*, Ed Kovins *(Foster)*, Bob Kaliban *(Supervisor)*, Len Gochman *(Executive)*, Susan Rubenstein *(Copywriter)*, Steve Hiott *(Art Director)*, Gordon Ramsey *(Larry)*, Vinnie Bell, Eric Weisberg *(Guitarists)*, Dan Resin *(Supervisor)*, John Nalpern *(Executive)*, Malcolm Addey *(Engineer)*, Faye Dannick *(Housemother)*, Sal Rapaglia *(Chauffeur)*, Marvin Lichterman *(Doctor)*, Edwin T. Morgan *(Passenger)*, Jimmy Kelly *(Janitor)*, Joy Bond *(Karen)*, Wendy Raebeck *(Carol)*, Sue Jett *(Nurse)*, Bob Lifton *(Pretzel Buyer)*, Howard Weingrow *(Commissioner)*, Robin Siegal *(Renee)*, Simone Schachter, Tom Okon, Liza Moran, Peter Billingsley *(Children)*.

A useless piece of egotistical drivel which is the product of the all-around untalented Joe Brooks, who had a freak hit with YOU LIGHT UP MY LIFE. This time Brooks has cast himself as a composer who sets out to find his old girl friend, Hack. Through flashbacks we see Brooks and Hack as youngsters, hopelessly devoted to one another. Their reunion is so predictable it is not even worth sitting through. Author Breslin is oddly effective as a Madison Avenue executive.

p&d, Joe Brooks; w, Brooks, Martin Davidson; ph, Adam Holender (Technicolor); m, Brooks; ed, Rich Shaine; art d, Don Gilman.

Romance (PR:C MPAA:PG)

IF HE HOLLERS, LET HIM GO* (1968) 106m Forward/Cinerama c

Dana Wynter *(Ellen Whitlock)*, Raymond St. Jacques *(James Lake)*, Kevin McCarthy *(Leslie Whitlock)*, Barbara McNair *(Lily)*, Arthur O'Connell *(Prosecutor)*, John Russell *(Sheriff)*, Ann Prentiss *(Thelma)*, Royal Dano *(Carl Blair)*, Susan Seaforth *(Sally Blair)*, Steve Sandor *(Harry)*, James Craig *(Police Chief)*, Don Newsome *(William Lake)*, Gregg Palmer *(Special Officer)*, James McEachin *(Defense Counsel)*, Don Megowan *(Officer)*, Chet Stratton *(Jackson the Pilot)*, Edward Schaaf *(Henry Wilson)*, Kort Falkenberg *(Gas Station Attendant)*, Jason Johnson *(Truck Driver)*, James H. Drake *(Deputy)*, Pepper Martin *(Prison Guard)*, Frank Gerstle *(Sergeant)*, E.A. Sirianni *(Doctor)*, Todd Martin *(Officer)*, Harold J. Kennedy *(Judge)*, Jon Lormer *(Chaplain)*, Ed Cook *(Officer)*, Mimi Gibson *(Marion)*.

St. Jacques is a black ex-con who escapes from prison after doing time for a murder he didn't commit. He meets McCarthy who offers him cash and safety in exchange for murdering his wealthy wife. St. Jacques declines and instead reminisces about his lost love, McNair. Realizing that he still wants her, he returns to McCarthy for his chance at freedom. He cons McCarthy into taking his wife Wynter to a mountain cottage, safely getting past the police roadblocks. When St. Jacques gets his chance he escapes, taking Wynter with him. They flee to the home of St. Jacques' brother, where he finds that McNair has married him. With her help they set out to find the real murderer and are led to Dano, the dead girl's stepfather. After a bloody shootout McCarthy is killed, Dano is arrested, and St. Jacques is in the clear. Unfortunately, this picture relies on the exploitation of sex and race to bring forth any message it may have.

p,d&w, Charles Martin; ph, William W. Spencer (Eastmancolor); m, Harry Sukman; ed, Richard Brockway; md, Sukman; art d, James W. Sullivan; set d, Dick Pefferle; spec eff, Justus Gibbs; m/l, "A Man Has to Love," "Can't Make It With the Same Man Twice," Sammy Fain, Charles Martin (sung by Barbara McNair), "So Tired," Coleridge-Taylor Perkinson (sung by McNair).

Crime Drama (PR:O MPAA:R)

IF I HAD A MILLION*½** (1932) 88m PAR bw

Gary Cooper *(Gallagher)*, George Raft *(Eddie Jackson)*, Wynne Gibson *(Violet)*, Charles Laughton *(The Clerk)*, Jack Oakie *(Mulligan)*, Frances Dee *(Mary Wallace)*, Charles Ruggles *(Henry Peabody)*. Alison Skipworth *(Emily)*, W. C. Fields *(Rollo)*, Mary Boland *(Mrs. Peabody)*, Roscoe Karns *(O'Brien)*, May Robson *(Mrs. Walker)*, Gene Raymond *(John Wallace)*, Lucien Littlefield *(Zeb)*, Richard Bennett *(John Glidden)*, Grant Mitchell *(The Prison Priest)*, Joyce Compton *(Marie)*, Cecil Cunningham *(Agnes)*, Irving Bacon *(Chinaware Salesman)*, Blanche Frederici *(Head Nurse at Old Ladies' Home)*, Dewey Robinson *(Cook at Old Ladies' Home)*, Gail Patrick *(Secretary)*, Fred Kelsey, Willard Robertson *(Doctors)*, Kent Taylor *(Bank Clerk)*, Jack Pennick *(Sailor)*, Berton Churchill *(Warden)*, James Burtis *(Jailer)*, Edwin Stanley *(Mr. Galloway)*, Gertrude Norman *(Idylwood Resident)*, Ernest Truex *(Mr. Brown)*, Emma Tansey *(Idylwood Resident)*, William V. Mong *(Harry the Fence)*, Margaret Seddon *(Mrs. Small)*, Wallis Clark *(Mr. Monroe)*, Tom Kennedy *(Officer/Joe, Carnival Tough)*, Frank Hagney *(Mike, Carnival Tough)*, Charles McMurphy *(Mike, Bank Guard)*, Henry C. Bradley *(Bank Guard)*, Lew Kelly *(Prison Attendant)*, Samuel S. Hinds *(Attorney)*, Reginald Barlow *(Glidden Employee)*, Clarence Muse *(Prisoner)*, Walter C. Percival *(Carnival Attendant)*, Russ Powell *(Bartender)*, Morgan Wallace *(Mike, a Mobster)*, Hooper Atchley *(Hotel Desk Clerk)*, Margaret Mann *(Idylwood Resident)*, Robert Emmett Homans *(Detective)*, Eddie Baker *(Desk Clerk)*, Joe Winthrop *(Idylwood Resident)*, Larry Steers, John St. Polis, Frederick Santley, Herbert Moulton *(Glidden Employees)*, Marc Lawrence *(Hoodlum)*, James Bush *(Teller)*, Tom Ricketts *(Elderly Man)*, Bess Flowers *(Customer)*, Fred Holmes *(Store Clerk)*, Syd Saylor *(Driver)*, Rolfe Sedan *(Salesman)*, Lester Dorr *(Pedestrian)*, Lydia Knott, Clair Bracy, Bangy Bilby *(Idylwood Residents)*.

This is one of the few episodic films that holds together and by a common and spectacular link—money, lots of it; millions, in fact. Bennett is a multimillionaire who is disgusted with his dollar-clutching relatives. When told by his doctors that he is dying, Bennett decides to pick out total strangers and give them each $1 million, mostly to see what they will do with the money. He draws forth a phone book, closes his eyes, and picks out a name: John D. Rockefeller! Scratching that name, he selects another, Ruggles, a spineless clerk who is forever escaping from shrewish wife Boland by retreating into the washroom and is terrified at work of dropping a piece of china, the cost of which is regularly deducted from his salary. (This segment is entitled "The China Shop" and is directed by James Cruze). With Bennett's check for $1 million in hand, Ruggles the milquetoast turns into Ruggles the lion. He tells off Boland and lays down the law forever. Then, in a moment of divine revenge, he marches into the china shop where, in front of his astonished boss, he smashes every piece of china he can grab. In the next segment, entitled "The Streetwalker," directed by Ernst Lubitsch, the next $1 million goes to Gibson, a prostitute, who immediately abandons her street corner and rents a lavish Park Avenue penthouse apartment. Here she goes into an immense bedroom and slides between silk sheets, determined to sleep alone for a long, long time. Before she nods off, Gibson leaps from her bed and strips from her legs the black stockings and garter belt she has worn as the uniform of her trade, then crawls back between the sheets. Stephen Roberts directs the next segment, "The Forger," which profiles slick Raft who is so notorious that his photo is in every bank where he might cash the check from Bennett. Broke and exhausted after failing to cash the check, the hysterical Raft goes to a flophouse and begs the owner to take the $1 million check for a bed so he can get some sleep. As he dozes off the owner, sneering at what he thinks is another con, lights his cigar with the burning check and then calls the police to come and arrest the wanted forger. The next sequence is entitled "The Auto" or "Rollo and the Road Hogs," directed by Norman Taurog and starring Fields and Skipworth. It is Skipworth who receives the check at her little teashop where she and newly acquired hubby Fields, a worn-out vaudeville juggler, reside, harboring a bone-deep hatred for roadhogs, especially since their new car has just been wrecked by a bevy of these very people. With the $1 million, Fields and Skipworth go to a new car dealership and begin buying one new car after another, taking these onto the streets and ramming into every roadhog they see, destroying *their* cars for a change! Humberstone directs the next segment, "The Condemned Man." Raymond is about to go to the chair when he receives the $1 million and, try as he might, he cannot use the money to save himself. He is dragged to the electric chair hysterically crying and laughing over the ironic twist of fate. "The Clerk," also directed by Lubitsch, who directed the opening sequence, has Laughton as a meek-mannered, much-harassed clerical worker slaving in an office. When he receives his $1 million check he neatly pockets it, stands up quietly and then walks through a series of doors, past startled secretaries and into the resplendent offices of the firm's President. As the man looks up at him angrily, Laughton leans forward and loudly gives the boss the raspberries or the Bronx Cheer, slams the door, and goes into unperturbed retirement. The next $1 million goes to Cooper, a fun-loving Marine who gets his payment on April 1 and thinks it's an April Fools joke, so he uses it as play money in a poker game with his buddies Oakie and Karns. They are all in the brig for fighting and when they get out, they rush to a lunchwagon to see pretty Compton. Knowing lunchwagon cook Littlefield cannot read, Cooper passes off the check for $10 in cash and uses this to take Compton to a carnival that night where he and his buddies get into another fight and wind up behind bars once more. Cooper later looks through the barred window of his cell and sees Littlefield getting into a limousine and now he really has doubts about the check he so cavalierly signed away. This segment, entitled "The Three Marines," was directed by Norman McLeod. "Old Ladies Home" is directed by William A. Seiter and profiles Robson, an inmate at a home for retired old ladies, women who are treated like prison inmates, their every ambition dashed by the overbearing director. The old ladies are not permitted to make food, or even socialize. When Robson's check arrives Robson buys the home and compels the harsh directors to sit back silently and watch all the old ladies pursue their hobbies and enjoy life for a change. Bennett shows up to eat one of Robson's homemade pies and chat with a woman he has grown to like. Most of these stories are well-told, expertly acted, and brilliantly directed as Paramount poured out its best acting and technical talent for this enormous production. For years filmgoers played the game of naming their favorite segment in this memorable film. Most selected either the Fields or Laughton sketches. This film inspired a popular radio and later a TV series, "The Millionaire."

p, Louis D. Lighton; d, Ernst Lubitsch, Norman Taurog, Stephen S. Roberts, Norman McLeod, James Cruze, William A. Seiter, H. Bruce Humberstone, [Lothar Mendes, uncredited]; w, Claude Binyon, Whitney Bolton, Malcolm Stuart Boyland, John Bright, Sidney Buchanan, Lester Cole, Isabel Dawn, Boyce De Gaw, Walter DeLeon, Oliver H. P. Garrett, Harvey Gates, Grover Jones, Lubitsch, Lawton

Mackall, Joseph L. Mankiewicz, William Slavens McNutt, Seton I. Miller, Robert Sparks, Tiffany Thayer (based on the novel *Windfall* by Robert D. Andrews).

Comedy/Drama **(PR:A MPAA:NR)**

IF I HAD MY WAY** (1940) 93m UNIV bw

Bing Crosby *(Buzz Blackwell)*, Gloria Jean *(Patricia Johnson)*, Charles Winninger *(Joe Johnson)*, El Brendel *(Axel Swenson)*, Allyn Joslyn *(Jarvis Johnson)*, Claire Dodd *(Brenda Johnson)*, Moroni Olsen *(Mr. Blair)*, Nana Bryant *(Marian Johnson)*, Donald Woods *(Fred Johnson)*, Kathryn Adams *(Miss Corbett)*, Brandon Hurst *(Hedges)*, Emory Parnell *(Gustav)*, Verna Felton *(Mrs. DeLacey)*, Barnett Parker *(Floorwalker)*, Jo Whitehead *(Si)*, Del Henderson *(Mr. Harris)*, Blanche Ring, Eddie Leonard, Trixie Friganza, Julian Eltinge, Grace LaRue, Paul Gordon, Six Hits and a Miss.

This Bing vehicle doesn't have the charm and wit of his other attempts, especially with him oddly cast as a construction worker. When a fellow worker is killed, Bing becomes the guardian of his 12-year-old daughter, Gloria Jean. Together they set out for New York in search of her vaudevillian uncle. Along with Brendel they find their man. Brendel, however, wastes the trio's money by purchasing a run-down restaurant. Bing saves the day when he turns it into a swinging night spot. Songs include: "I Haven't The Time To Be A Millionaire," "Meet The Sun Halfway," "April Played The Fiddle," "The Pessimistic Character (With The Crab Apple Face)" (Johnny Burke, James V. Monaco); "If I Had My Way" (Lew Klein, James Kendis), "Ida, Sweet As Apple Cider" (Eddie Leonard, Eddie Munson), "Rings On My Fingers" (Maurice Scott, R.P. Western, F.J. Barnes).

p&d, David Butler; w, William Conselman, James V. Kern (based on a story by Butler, Conselman, Kern); ph, George Robinson; ed, Irene Morra; md, Charles Previn; art d, Jack Otterson; set d, Russell A. Gausman.

Musical **(PR:A MPAA:NR)**

IF I WERE BOSS* (1938, Brit.) 72m GS Enterprises/COL bw

Bruce Seton *(Steve)*, Googie Withers *(Pat)*, Ian Fleming *(Mr. Biltmore)*, Zillah Bateman *(Mrs. Biltmore)*, Julie Suedo *(Irma)*, Charles Oliver *(Owen Reeves)*, Paul Sheridan, Michael Ripper.

A nearly unwatchable picture with a thoroughly unlikable main character in Seton, a big-headed clerk at an egg company headed by Fleming. After an inheritance, Seton is put in charge and fails to heed Fleming's know-how and experience, instead taking advice from Oliver, a shady rival. It takes financial ruin and Fleming's ill health before Seton admits his mistake and mends his ways.

p, George Smith; d, Maclean Rogers; w, Basil Mason; ph, Geoffrey Faithfull.

Drama **(PR:A MPAA:NR)**

IF I WERE FREE*½ (1933) 65m RKO bw (GB: BEHOLD WE LIVE)

Irene Dunne *(Sarah Cazenove)*, Clive Brook *(Gordon Evers)*, Nils Asther *(Tono Cazenove)*, Henry Stephenson *(Hector Stribling)*, Vivian Tobin *(Jewel Stribling)*, Tempe Pigott *(Mrs. Gill)*, Lorraine MacLean *(Mrs. Evers)*, Laura Hope Crews *(Dame Evers)*, Halliwell Hobbes *(Evers' Butler)*, Mario Dominici.

An extremely thin plot about a London antique dealer, Dunne, and a lawyer, Brook. With their marriages in shambles the two meet by chance in Paris and fall in love. Brook's wife, however, has no intentions of agreeing to a divorce, and Dunne's missing mate miraculously shows up. Chances are dim, but the wife has a change of heart and Dunne and Brook are free to wed. Hollywood conventions at their most obvious.

p, Kenneth Macgowan, Merian C. Cooper; d, Elliot Nugent; w, Dwight Taylor (based on the play "Behold, We Live" by John Van Druten); ph, Edward Cronjager; ed, Arthur Roberts.

Romance **(PR:A MPAA:NR)**

IF I WERE KING, 1930 (SEE: VAGABOND KING, 1930)

IF I WERE KING*½** (1938) 100m PAR bw

Ronald Colman *(Francois Villon)*, Basil Rathbone *(Louis XI)*, Frances Dee *(Katherine de Vaucelles)*, Ellen Drew *(Huguette)*, C. V. France *(Father Villon)*, Henry Wilcoxon *(Captain of the Watch)*, Heather Thatcher *(Queen)*, Stanley Ridges *(Rene de Montigny)*, Bruce Lester *(Neal le Jolya)*, Walter Kingsford *(Tristan L'Hermite)*, Alma Lloyd *(Colette)*, Sidney Toler *(Robin Turgis)*, Colin Tapley *(Jehan le Loup)*, Ralph Forbes *(Oliver le Dain)*, John Miljan *(Thibaut D'Aussigny)*, William Haade *(Guy Tabarie)*, Adrian Morris *(Colin de Cayculx)*, Montagu Love *(Gen. Dudon)*, Lester Matthews *(Gen. Saliere)*, William Farnum *(Gen. Barbezier)*, Paul Harvey *(Burgundian Herald)*, Barry Macollum *(Watchman)*, May Beatty *(Anna)*, Winter Hull *(Major-Domo)*, Francis McDonald *(Casin Cholet)*, Ann Evers, Jean Fenwick *(Ladies-in-Waiting)*, Russ Powell *(Ruffian)*, Harry Wilson *(Beggar)*, John George *(Dwarf Beggar)*, Stanley King *(Captain of Archers)*, Henry Brandon *(Soldier)*, Ethel Clayton *(Old Woman)*, Judith King, Cheryl Walker *(Girls)*.

No other actor of his day could match Colman in this difficult role and no other actor possessed the mellow and mellifluous voice that could render such lines as: "If I were king—the stars should be your pearls upon a string." Colman is the famous French poet and ne'er-do-well Francois Villon, dweller among the rabble of 15th Century Paris. During a tavern brawl the oppressive Grand Constable of Paris is slain by Colman and the intellectual troublemaker is brought before the cunning King Louis XI, Rathbone. In a shrewd move, Rathbone thinks to satisfy his downtrodden people by elevating their champion to an all-powerful post, one where he can improve conditions he has so loudly condemned. If not, he will be executed for his past transgressions. But he only has a week to perform the miracle. Colman accepts the post, matching wits with the wily monarch while advising him spiritually: "Abolish despair and substitute hope. By knowing the worst in the people, bring out the best." While at court, strutting in his new princely finery, Colman meets and falls in love with noblewoman Dee. He soon wins her heart but he is still about to lose his head. An army of Burgundians advancing on Paris serves as his respite. When the royal army fails to stop the invaders, Colman rallies the peasants of Paris and leads them into battle, routing the would-be conquerors. Grateful Rathbone pardons Colman for his past sins against the crown and sends him into exile instead of to the headsman. As a precious reward he is given Dee's hand in marriage. This opulently produced film, with its thousands of extras and wonderful sets and costuming, is well directed by action helmsman Lloyd. Sturges' screenplay sparkles with penetrating wit and sly badinage, particularly in the mental duels between Colman and Rathbone. Their scenes together are spellbinding, Colman as the upstanding moralist using his wits to survive a monarch's wrath, and Rathbone as a reptilian tyrant attempting to entrap his arrogant victim. Rathbone's makeup is so elaborately designed as to hide his razor sharp features, thoroughly disguising the actor. He renders a hideous, almost heinous portrait that equals anything evil ever brought to the screen. The history of the story is long and eventful. The historical play authored by McCarthy was first filmed in 1920, starring William Farnum (who has a small role in this version), and was made again in a second silent version, THE BELOVED ROGUE, 1927, with John Barrymore flamboyantly essaying the Villon role. Rudolph Friml adapted the play as an operetta which was filmed as THE VAGABOND KING in 1930, starring Dennis King and Jeanette MacDonald, and this was remade in 1955 with Oreste Kirkop and Kathryn Grayson. Writer Sturges always pointed to the script of this film as one of his finest achievements and it truly is a superb screenplay where Sturges lightened the somber, deformed Louis by giving Rathbone deliciously wicked, funny lines. The black humor was never more in evidence than in the macabre response Rathbone has when entering his torture chamber early in the film, crinkling his nose and sniffing the air as would a bloodhound, then quipping: "Nasty smell in here . . . you'd almost think the cook had burned the roast!" Sturges, of course, would go on to write and direct some of the funniest films ever made—THE GREAT McGINTY (1940), THE MIRACLE OF MORGAN'S CREEK (1944), and HAIL THE CONQUERING HERO (1944).

p&d, Frank Lloyd; w, Preston Sturges (based on the play by Justin Huntly McCarthy); ph, Theodore Sparkuhl; m, Richard Hageman; ed, Hugh Bennett; md, Boris Morros; art d, Hans Dreier, John Goodman; set d, A. E. Freudeman; spec eff, Gordon Jennings; cos, Edith Head; makeup, Wally Westmore.

Adventure **(PR:A MPAA:NR)**

IF I WERE RICH** (1936) 58m RKO bw

Jack Melford *(Albert Mott)*, Kay Walsh *(Chrissie de la Mothe)*, Clifford Heatherley *(Gen. de la Mothe)*, Minnie Rayner *(Mrs. Mott)*, Henry Carlisle *(Puttick)*, Frederick Bradshaw *(Jack de la Mothe)*, Ruth Haven *(Nancy)*, Quinton McPherson *(Higginbotham)*, Pat Noonan

A political and social satire in which a Socialist barber amends his political views after discovering he has inherited a royal title. Not that funny overall.

p&d, Randall Faye; w, Brandon Fleming (based on the play "Humpty-Dumpty" by Horace Annesley Vachell); ph, Geoffrey Faithfull.

Comedy **(PR:A MPAA:NR)**

IF I'M LUCKY** (1946) 78m FOX bw

Vivian Blaine *(Linda)*, Perry Como *(Allen Clark)*, Harry James *(Earl Gordon)*, Carmen Miranda *(Michelle O'Toole)*, Phil Silvers *(Wally)*, Edgar Buchanan *(Magonnagle)*, Reed Hadley *(Conklin)*, Harry James' Music Makers *(Themselves)*, Harry Hayden *(Gov. Quilby)*, Harry Cheshire *(Gargan)*, William Halligan *(Bixby)*, Frank Fenton *(Dwyer)*, Lewis Russell *(Gillingwater)*, Charles Tannen *(Secretary)*, Charles Wilson *(Police Captain)*, Frank Ferguson *(Statistician)*, Edward Keane *(Golfer)*, Kay Connors *(Secretary)*, George Davis *(Waiter)*.

Against his wishes, entertainer Como gets pulled into the political ring as a candidate for governor. The usual "common man" speeches are heard throughout the campaign, which is pushed along by his musical colleagues and friends. Some good tunes from Harry James and Carmen Miranda (oddly cast as an Irish lass) drown the inept scripting. Songs include: "If I'm Lucky," "One More Kiss," "Publicity," "Bet Your Bottom Dollar," "Follow The Band," "That American Look" (Josef Myrow, Edgar De Lange). A remake of 1937's THANKS A MILLION.

p, Bryan Foy; d, Lewis Seiler; w, Snag Werris, Robert Ellis, Helen Logan, George Bricker (based on a story by Edward Lanham); ph, Glen MacWilliams; ed, Norman Colbert; md, Emil Newman; ch, Kenny Williams.

Musical **(PR:A MPAA:NR)**

IF IT'S TUESDAY, THIS MUST BE BELGIUM*** (1969) 99m Wolper/UA c

Suzanne Pleshette *(Samantha)*, Ian McShane *(Charlie)*, Mildred Natwick *(Jenny Grant)*, Murray Hamilton *(Fred Ferguson)*, Sandy Baron *(John Marino)*, Michael Constantine *(Jack Harmon)*, Norman Fell *(Harve Blakely)*, Peggy Cass *(Edna Ferguson)*, Marty Ingels (Bert Greenfield), Pamela Britton *(Freda)*, Luke Halpin *(Bo)*, Aubrey Morris *(Harry Dix)*, Reva Rose *(Irma Blakely)*, Hilary Thompson *(Shelly Ferguson)*, Mario Carotenuto *(Giuseppi)*, Patricia Routledge *(Mrs. Featherstone)*, Marina Berti *(Gina)*, Linda Di Felice *(Fiat Driver's Wife)*, Paul Esser *(German Sergeant)*, Jenny White *(Dot)*, Roger Six *(Marcel)*, Frank Lattimore *(George)*, Sonia Doumen *(Miss Belgium)*, Lillian Atterer *(Miss Germany)*, Lucien Krier *(Miss Luxembourg)*, Ben Gazzara, John Cassavetes *(Card Players)*, Vittorio De Sica *(Shoemaker)*, Donovan *(Singer at youth Hostel)*, Anita Ekberg *(Nightclub Performer)*, Catherine Spaak *(Woman Posing for Photographer)*, Robert Vaughn *(Photographer)*, Elsa Martinelli *(Woman on Bridge)*, Joan Collins, Senta Berger, Virna Lisi.

A fast-paced episodic look at whirlwind European tours. With McShane as the tour guide, a group of Americans embark on an 18-day, seven-city bus romp, which is accompanied by hectic and madcap antics. A pleasant spoof which oddly enough paints a pretty accurate portrayal of tourism. Speckled with a number of cameos including directors John Cassavetes and Vittorio De Sica. Inspired by a cartoon which appeared in the "New Yorker" magazine.

p, Stan Margulies; d, Mel Stuart; w, David Shaw; ph, Vilis Lapenieks, Fritz Roland (DeLuxe Color); m, Walter Scharf; ed, David Saxon; art d, Marc Frederix; m/l, "If It's Tuesday, This Must Be Belgium," "Lord of the Reedy River," Donovan (sung by Donovan); makeup, Vittorio Biseo, Ron Berkeley.

Comedy **(PR:A MPAA:G)**

IF PARIS WERE TOLD TO US1/2**
(1956, Fr.) 135m CLM-SNEG-Franco-London/GAU c (SI PARIS NOUS ETAIT CONTE)

Danielle Darrieux *(Agnes Sorel)*, Jean Marais *(Francois I)*, Robert Lamoureaux *(Latude)*, Sacha Guitry *(Louis XI)*, Michelle Morgan *(Gabriel Estree)*, Gerard Philipe *(La Trouvere)*, Francoise Arnoul *(Duchess Bassano)*, Lana Marconi *(Marie Antoinette)*, Gisele Pascal *(Countess de Montebello)*, Jeanne Boitel *(Mme. Geoffrin/Sarah Bernhardt)*, Gilbert Boka *(Louis XVI/Hugues Aubiot)*, Julien Carette *(1st Elegant Man)*, Sophie Desmarets *(Rose Bertin)*, Clement Duhour *(Bruant)*, Odette Joyeux *(Trimming Saleswoman)*, Pierre Larquay *(Pierre Broussel)*, Jean Paredes *(1st Doctor)*, Simone Renant *(Marquis de La Tour Maubourg)*, Renee Saint-Cyr *(Empress)*, Jean Tissier *(Guard at the Carnavalet Museum)*.

An interesting film from a provocative director, Guitry, another of his historical documentations in which he comments on Paris' past in a witty and insightful manner. The film often has the air of spectacle while at the same time being very theatrical (which most of Guitry's work is). Guitry continues to act in his pictures, this time as Louis XI. Nearing the end of his long film career which began in 1930, Guitry had to direct this picture from a wheelchair, retreating to a nearby tent occasionally to relax. IF PARIS WERE TOLD TO US was released a year before his death at age 72.

d&w, Sacha Guitry; ph, Philippe Agostini (Technicolor); m, Jean Francais; ed, Paulette Robert; set d, Rene Renous.

Historical Drama **(PR:A MPAA:NR)**

IF THIS BE SIN** (1950, Brit.) 72m LFP bw (GB: THAT DANGEROUS AGE)

Myrna Loy *(Lady Cathy Brooke)*, Roger Livesey *(Sir Brian Brooke)*, Peggy Cummins *(Monica Brooke)*, Richard Greene *(Michael Barclaigh)*, Elizabeth Allen *Lady Sybil)*, Gerard Heinz *(Dr. Thorvald)*, Jean Cadell *(Nannie)*, G.H. Mulcaster *(Simmons)*, Margaret Withers *(May Drummond)*, Ronald Adam *(Prosecutor)*, Wilfrid Hyde-White *(Mr. Potts)*, Henry Caine *(Mr. Nyburg)*, Patrick Waddington *(Risley)*, Edith Sharpe *(Angela Cane)*, George Curzon *(Selby)*, Robert Atkins *(George Drummond)*, Phyllis Stanley *(Jane)*, Daphne Arthur *(Margot)*, Martin Case *(John)*, Barry Jones *(Arnold Cane)*, Louis Lord *(Ellen)*, Nicholas Bruce *(Charles)*, William Mervyn *(Nicky)*.

Loy, ignored by a husband who devotes more time to his job than to her, innocently begins to make eyes at young Greene. Gossip of their "romance" soon hits the social circle, eventually getting back to husband Livesey and daughter Cummins. When Livesey takes ill, Loy shows her devotion by remaining by his side. Everything wraps up neatly as Greene and Cummins happily pair up. A loving marriage didn't ring so true in Loy's personal life, as she divorced scriptwriter Markey shortly after this picture's release.

p&d, Gregory Ratoff; w, Gene Markey (based on the play "Autumn" by Margaret Kennedy, Ilya Surgutchoff); ph, Georges Perinal, Anchise Bizzi; m, Mischa Spoliansky; ed, G. Turney-Smith; md, Hubert Clifford; art d, Andre Andrejew; set d, Dario Simoni.

Romance **(PR:A MPAA:NR)**

IF WINTER COMES1/2** (1947) 96m MGM bw

Walter Pidgeon *(Mark Sabre)*, Deborah Kerr *(Nona Tybar)*, Angela Lansbury *(Mabel Sabre)*, Binnie Barnes *(Natalie Bagshaw)*, Janet Leigh *(Effie Bright)*, Dame May Whitty *(Mrs. Perch)*, Rene Ray *(Sarah, "Low Jinks")*, Virginia Keiley *(Rebecca, "High Jinks")*, Reginald Owen *(Mr. Fortune)*, John Abbott *(Mr. Twyning)*, Rhys Williams *(Mr. Bright)*, Dennis Hoey *(Tiny Wilson)*, Hugh French *(Lord Tony Tybar)*, Nicholas Joy *(Mr. Pettigrew)*, Halliwell Hobbes *(Coroner)*, Hugh Green *(Freddie Perch)*, James Wethered *(Harold Twyning)*, Owen McGiveney *(Uncle Fonraker)*, Victor Wood *(Mr. Fargus)*, Pat Aherne *(Grimes, the Chauffeur)*, James Fairfax *(George)*, Alex Fraser *(Clint)*, Phyllis Morris *(Mrs. Fargus)*, Joe Strauch *(Fat Youth)*, Ian Wolfe *(Doctor)*, Elspeth Dudgeon *(Mrs. Ward)*, Cyril Smith *(Truck Driver)*, Cyril Thornton *(Jury Foreman)*, Major Sam Harris *(Clerk in Book Shop)*.

Pidgeon is a decent man and a writer of school books living in an English village who befriends a pregnant girl even though he loses his own wife in the process. When the girl dies there is a coroner's hearing to judge whether she committed suicide or Pidgeon poisoned her. His devotion causes him to lose his job and his community standing. He is cleared in the finale and becomes free to pursue his real love, Kerr. A.S.M. Hutchinson's romantic tearjerker with a WW I background, originally made into a film in 1923, here has been updated to WW II. It offers a delightful look at screen newcomer Janet Leigh, at the age of 20, making her second feature film.

p, Pandro S. Berman; d, Victor Saville; w, Marguerite Roberts, Arthur Wimperis (based on the novel by A.S.M. Hutchinson); ph, George Folsey; m, Herbert Stothart; ed, Ferris Webster; art d, Cedric Gibbon, Hans Peters.

Drama **(PR:A MPAA:NR)**

IF YOU COULD ONLY COOK*** (1936) 70m COL bw

Herbert Marshall *(Jim Buchanan)*, Jean Arthur *(Joan Hawthorne)*, Leo Carrillo *(Mike Rossini)*, Lionel Stander *(Flash)*, Alan Edwards *(Bob Reynolds)*, Frieda Inescort *(Evelyn Fletcher)*, Gene Morgan *(Al)*, Ralf Harolde *(Swig)*, Matt McHugh *(Pete)*, Richard Powell *(Chesty)*.

Adorable Jean Arthur is cast as a poor girl who, by chance, meets automotive engineer Marshall and convinces him to pose with her to get a cook-and-butler job in mobster Carrillo's mansion, though neither of them are experienced. The comedy gets progressively screwier as the plot gets more entangled. Carrillo and bodyguard Stander, at one point, kidnap Marshall from a wedding ceremony to a society woman to bring about a reconciliation with Arthur. The pseudo-servant team soon take a liking to each other, causing Arthur to try to sell Marshall's automotive plans to a car company. The finish leaves everybody happy. Arthur is outstanding as she effortlessly slips from a charming comedian to a beautiful romantic.

p, Everett Riskin; d, William Seiter; w, Howard J. Green, Gertrude Purcell (based on the story by F. Hugh Herbert); ph, John Stumar.

Romantic Comedy **(PR:A MPAA:NR)**

IF YOU COULD SEE WHAT I HEAR*1/2
(1982) 102m Cypress Grove/Jensen Farley c

Marc Singer *(Tom Sullivan)*, R.H. Thomson *(Will Sly)*, Sarah Torgov *(Patty Steffen)*, Shari Belafonte Harper *(Heather Johnson)*, Douglas Campbell *(Porky Sullivan)*, Helen Burns *(Mrs. Ruxton)*, Harvey Atkin *(Bert)*, Barbara Gordon *(Molly)*, Sharon Lewis *(Helga)*, Lynda Mason Greene *(Sharon)*, Tony van Bridge *(Dr. Wells)*, Jack Creley *(Dr. Franklin)*, Neil Dainard *(Phil)*, Michael Tate *(Dr. Jamieson)*, David Gardner *(Mr. Steffen)*, Noni Griffin *(Mrs. Steffen)*, Adrienne Pocock *(Blythe)*, Hugh Webster *(Sean)*.

This film's intentions may be right, but the bottom line is lame entertainment. Singer stars in this biography of blind singer-composer Tom Sullivan, who doesn't really warrant having a film made about his life. From his college days to his singing career we see him go through life dealing with his lack of sight. He finds himself involved with the beautiful Harper, but is unaware of a racial difference. Jilted by her, he turns to his profession, getting a musical job in a Cape Cod bar. It is here that he meets Torgov and marries her. A clean and moral movie which tries too hard to fit into the mainstream of today's films. The tune "You're The One" (Michael Lloyd) is performed by Sullivan and Helen Reddy.

p, Eric Till, Stuart Gillard; d, Till; w, Gillard (based on the book by Tom Sullivan, Derek Gill); ph, Harry Makin (Filmhouse Color); ed, Eric Wrate; md, Eric Robertson; art d, Gavin Mitchell; set d, Earle Fiset.

Drama **Cas.** **(PR:A MPAA:PG)**

IF YOU FEEL LIKE SINGING (SEE: SUMMER STOCK, 1950)

IF YOU KNEW SUSIE1/2** (1948) 90m RKO bw

Eddie Cantor *(Sam Parker)*, Joan Davis *(Susie Parker)*, Allyn Joslyn *(Mike Garrett)*, Charles Dingle *(Mr. Whitley)*, Phil Brown *(Joe Collins)*, Sheldon Leonard *(Steve Garland)*, Joe Sawyer *(Zero Zantini)*, Douglas Fowley *(Marty)*, Margaret Kerry *(Marjorie Parker)*, Dick Humphreys *(Handy Clinton)*, Howard Freeman *(Mr. Clinton)*, Mabel Paige *(Grandma)*, Sig Ruman *(Count Alexis)*, Fritz Feld *(Chez Henri)*, Isabel Randolph *(Mrs. Clinton)*, Bobby Driscoll *(Junior)*, Earle Hodgins *(Auctioneer)*, Charles Halton *(Pringle)*, Jason Robards, Sr. *(Ogleby)*, Harry Harvey *(Sedley)*, George Chandler *(Reporter)*, Don Beddoe *(Editor)*, Addison Richards *(Senator)*, Ellen Corby *(Woman)*, Syd Saylor *(Proprietor of Pet Shop)*, Robert Clarke *(Orchestra Leader)*, Tom Keene *(Graham)*, Mary Field *(Telephone Operator)*, J. Farrell MacDonald *(Policeman)*, Donald Kerr *(Window Washer)*, Eddy Hart *(Burly Man)*.

A silly movie which stars Cantor and Davis as a husband and wife vaudeville team. They retire from the stage and settle down in a community where they are snubbed by their neighbors. They then discover a document signed by George Washington regarding the payment of $50,000 to one of their ancestors. They take the note to the government, which tallies up a debt to them of several billion dollars, with interest. The comedian's already-buggy eyes pop out but he patriotically declines to accept. He becomes a national hero and wins community status. A pleasant take-off on GEORGE WASHINGTON SLEPT HERE. Tunes include: "If You Knew Susie" (B.G. DeSylva, Joseph Meyer), "My Brooklyn Love Song" (George Tibbles, Ramez Idriss), "What Do I Want With Money?," "We're Living The Life We Love," "My, How The Time Goes By" (Jimmy McHugh, Harold Adamson).

p, Eddie Cantor; d, Gordon M. Douglas; w, Warren Wilson, Oscar Brodney, Bud Pearson, Lester A. White; ph, Frank Redman; m, Edgar "Cookie" Fairchild; ed, Philip Martin; md, C. Bakaleinikoff; art d, Albert D'Agostino, Ralph Berger.

Musical Comedy **Cas.** **(PR:A MPAA:NR)**

IGOROTA, THE LEGEND OF THE TREE OF LIFE**
(1970, Phil.) 35m Nepomuceno/Fame c

Ric Rodrigo *(Albert)*, Charito Solis *(Princess Maila)*, Fred Galang.

When two lovers from different classes insist on marriage, it causes hard feelings among the families of both bride and groom. The bride is humiliated for years, forcing the couple to move back to her territory. Once there, however, the groom is even less well-received and falls victim to a tribesman's axe. Deeply rooted in Philippine tribal ritual and ceremony.

p,d&w, Luis Nepomuceno; ph, Loreto Isleta; m, Tito Arevalo; ed, Elsa Abutal.

Drama **(PR:O MPAA:NR)**

IKARIE XB 1
(SEE: VOYAGE TO THE END OF THE UNIVERSE, 1963, Czech.)

IKIMONO NO KIROUKU (SEE: I LIVE IN FEAR, 1967, Jap.)

IKIRU*** (1960, Jap.) 140m Toho/Brando bw (AKA: DOOMED, LIVING)

Takashi Shimura *(Kanji Watanabe)*, Nobuo Kaneko *(Mitsuo Watanabe)*, Kyoko Seki *(Kazue Watanabe)*, Miki Odagiri *(Toyo)*, Kamatari Fujiwara *(Ono)*, Makoto Koburi *(Klichi Watanabe)*, Kumeko Urabe *(Tatsu Watanabe)*, Yoshie Minami *(Hayoshi, the Maid)*, Nobuo Nakamura *(Deputy Mayor)*, Minosuke Yamada *(Saito)*, Haruo Tanak *(Sakai)*, Bokuzen Hidari *(Ohara)*, Minoru Chiaki *(Noguchi)*, Shinichi Himori *(Kimura)*, Kazao Abe *(City Assemblyman)*, Masao Shimizu *(Doctor)*, Yunosuke Ito *(Novelist)*, Ko Kimura *(Intern)*, Atsushi Watanabe *(Patient)*, Yatsuko Tanami *(Hostess)*, Seiji Miyaguchi *(Gang-Boss)*, Daisuke Kato *(Gang Member)*, Ichiro Chiba *(Policeman)*, Toranosuke Ogawa *(Park Section Chief)*, Akira Tani *(Old Man in Bar)*.

Kurosawa has created a subtle and moving account of a man faced with finding meaning in the final days of his shallow existence. Shimura is the clerk in a government office who discovers that he has cancer and, at most, only a year to live. Up to this point he has lived strictly according to the book, never allowing for any fluctuations from routine. Now, realizing that he is about to die, with two children who offer him no comfort, Shimura must find something to make him feel that his life has not been a total waste. This comes in the form of a mothers' group who wish to use some abandoned property as the site for a park. His personality changes from gloom to extreme animation as Shimura goes about making sure the mothers are able to have their park—a task that requires him to bypass the red tape that he has rigidly adhered to in the past. The movement of IKIRU is extremely low-key, and the overall emotional impact is quite powerful, with the character of Shimura adequately portraying a metaphor for human individuality in post-war Japan. Though the Japanese culture is Kurosawa's main target, this theme is one that can easily be felt by individuals throughout the world, making IKIRU one of Kurosawa's most universally accepted films. (In Japanese; English subtitles.)

d, Akira Kurosawa; w, Kurosawa, Hideo Oguni, Shinobu Hashimoto; ph, Asakazu Nakai; m, Fumio Hayasaka; art d, So Matsuyama.

Drama **Cas.** **(PR:A MPAA:NR)**

IL BIDONE (SEE: SWINDLE, THE, 1962, Fr./Ital.)

IL BODONE (SEE: SWINDLER, THE, 1955, Ital.)

IL BUONO, IL BRUTTO, IL CATTIVO
(SEE: GOOD, THE BAD, AND THE UGLY, THE, 1967, Ital.)

IL COBRA (SEE: COBRA, THE, 1968)

IL CONFORMIST (SEE: CONFORMIST, THE, 1971, Ital./Fr.)

IL CONTE DI MONTECRISTO
(SEE: STORY OF THE COUNT OF MONTE CRISTO, THE, 1962, Fr./Ital.)

IL DESERTO ROSSO (SEE: RED DESERT, 1964, Fr./Ital.)

IL DESTINO (SEE: DESTINY, 1938)

IL DIABOLICO DR. MABUSE
(SEE: THOUSAND EYES OF DR. MABUSE, 1960, Fr./Ital./Ger.)

IL DISPREZZO (SEE: CONTEMPT, 1963, Ital./Fr.)

IL GATTOPARDO (SEE: LEOPARD, THE, 1963, Ital.)

IL GENERALE DELA-ROVERE
(SEE: GENERALE DELLA-ROVERE, 1960, Ital./Fr.)

IL GIORNO DELLA CIVETTA
(SEE: DAY OF THE OWL, THE, 1968, Fr./Ital.)

IL GIORNO E L'ORA (SEE: DAY AND THE HOUR, THE, 1963, Fr./Ital.)

IL GRIDO** ½**
(1962, U.S./Ital.) 115m SPA Cinematografica-Robert Alexander Prod./Astor Pictures bw (AKA: THE OUTCRY)

Steve Cochran *(Aldo)*, Alida Valli *(Irma)*, Betsy Blair *(Elvia)*, Dorian Gray *(Virginia)*, Lyn Shaw *(Andreina)*, Gabriella Pallotta *(Edera)*, Mirna Girardi *(Rosina)*, Guerrino Campanili *(Virginia's Father)*, Gaetano Matteucci *(Edera's Fiance)*, Pietro Corvelatti *(Old Fisherman)*, Pina Boldrini.

A muddled effort by Antonioni (released in Italy in 1957) which is the only one of his black-and-white films to center on a male character. Cochran is a worker in a Po Valley sugar refinery living in the northern Italian town of Goriano with the married Valli and their daughter, Girardi. When Valli receives word that her husband has died Cochran sees this as his chance to propose marriage. He does but she refuses and takes another lover. Disillusioned in love and life, Cochran takes his daughter and begins to wander through the barren, weather-worn lands. He first meets ex-girlfriend Blair, then service station owner Gray, followed by field worker/prostitute Shaw. In all three instances Cochran finds that he cannot forget Valli. He chooses to return to Goriano and finds Valli living in a different place, taking care of a young child. During an anti-American demonstration at the refinery (the U.S. wants to build an airfield there) Cochran climbs to the top of a tower and jumps (falls?) to his death. Co-produced by an American company, IL GRIDO fails chiefly in its acting. The two Americans in the cast—Cochran and Blair—lack any understanding of the director's methods, delivering the least satisfying performances of any Antonioni film, while Shaw, formerly a British stripper, works wonders with the material she is given. In his next film, L'AVVENTURA (1960) Antonioni would overcome all of IL GRIDO's weaknesses. It is in L'AVVENTURA—a film about forgetting—that Antonioni offers the antithesis to IL GRIDO—a film about not being able to forget.

p, Franco Cancellieri; d, Michelangelo Antonioni; w, Antonioni, Elio Bartolini, Ennio De Concini (based on a story by Antonioni); ph, Gianni Di Veranzo; m, Giovanni Fusco; ed; Eraldo Da Roma; art d, Franco Fontana; cos, Pia Marchesi.

Drama **(PR:C MPAA:NR)**

IL MAESTRO (SEE: TEACHER AND THE MIRACLE, THE, 1961, Ital./Span.)

IL MAESTRO DI DON GIOVANNI (SEE: CROSSED SWORDS, 1954)

IL MAGNIFICO CORNUTO
(SEE: MAGNIFICENT CUCKHOLD, THE, 1965, Fr./Ital.)

IL MITO (SEE: MYTH, THE, 1965, Ital.)

IL NEMICO DI MIA MOGLIE (SEE: MY WIFE'S ENEMY, 1967, Ital.)

IL POZZO DELLE TRE VERITA
(SEE: THREE FACES OF SIN, 1963, Fr./Ital.)

IL RE DEI FAISARI
(SEE: COUNTERFEITERS OF PARIS, THE, 1962, Fr./Ital.)

IL SEGNO DI VENERA (SEE: SIGN OF VENUS, 1955, Ital.)

IL SEME DELL'UOMO (SEE: SEED OF MAN, THE, 1970, Ital.)

IL SEPOLCRO DEI RE (SEE: CLEOPATRA'S DAUGHTER, 1963, Fr./Ital.)

IL SOGNO DI BUTTERFLY
(SEE: DREAM OF THE BUTTERFLY, THE, 1941, Ital.)

IL SUFFIT D'AIMER (SEE: BERNADETTE OF LOURDES, 1962, Fr.)

IL TESORO DI ROMMEL (SEE: ROMMEL'S TREASURE, 1962, Ital.)

IL VANGELO SECONDE MATTEO
(SEE: GOSPEL ACCORDING TO ST. MATTHEW, THE, 1966, Fr./Ital.)

ILL MET BY MOONLIGHT (SEE: NIGHT AMBUSH, 1957, Brit.)

ILLEGAL* ½ (1932, Brit.) 64m WB/Vitagraph bw

Isobel Elsom *(Evelyn Dean)*, D.A. Clarke-Smith *(Franklyn Dean)*, Margot Grahame *(Dorothy Dixon)*, Edgar Norfolk *(Lord Alan Sevingdon)*, Moira Lynd *(Ann Dixon)*, Ivor Barnard, Walter Patch, Margaret Damer, Victor Fairley, Joy Chatwin, Leo Raine, J. Lauriston, C. Glover, Arthur Goulette, H. Heath, Hamilton Keene.

A weak British drama about a mother whose fortune is wasted by her husband, whom she promptly sends packing. With her nestegg gone, she opens a nightclub with a friend. Allowing illegal gambling and liquor sales, she amasses a hefty purse, enabling her two daughters to go to school. Eventually, one of the girls kills the father. Wanting to forget her past and start anew, mom burns the nightclub down to a cinder, and quietly walks away. Not worth discussing even at a tea break.

p, Irving Asher; d, William McGann; w, Roland Pertwee, John Hastings Turner (based on a story by Asher); ph, William Van Enger, C.J. Knowles; art d, J.T. Garside.

Drama **(PR:A MPAA:NR)**

ILLEGAL*** (1955) 88m WB bw

Edward G. Robinson *(Victor Scott)*, Nina Foch *(Ellen Miles)*, Hugh Marlowe *(Ray Borden)*, Robert Ellenstein *(Joe Knight)*, De Forrest Kelley *(Edward Clary)*, Jay Adler *(Joseph Carter)*, James McCallion *(Allen Parker)*, Edward Platt *(Ralph Ford)*, Albert Dekker *(Frank Garland)*, Jan Merlin *(Andy Garth)*, Ellen Corby *(Miss Hinkel)*, Jayne Mansfield *(Angel O'Hara)*, Clark Howatt *(George Graves)*, Henry Kulky *(Taylor)*, Addison Richards *(Steve Harper)*, Howard St. John *(E.A. Smith)*, Lawrence Dobkin *(Al Carol)*, George Ross *(Policeman)*, John McKee, Barry Hudson *(Detectives)*, Kathy Marlowe *(Blonde Girl)*, Ted Stanhope *(Bailiff)*, Charles Evans *(Judge)*, Jonathan Hale *(Doctor)*, Marjorie Stapp *(Night Orderly)*, Fred Coby *(3rd Guard)*, Max Wagner *(Bartender)*, John Cliff *(Barfly)*, Henry Rowland *(Jailer)*, Julie Bennett *(Miss Worth)*, Pauline Drake *(Woman)*, Roxanne Arlen *(Miss Hathaway)*, Archie Twitchell *(Mr. Manning)*, Stewart Nedd *(Phillips)*, Herb Vigran *(1st Policeman)*, Chris Alcaide *(2nd Policeman)*.

The plot is straight out the 1930s Warner Bros. scriptorium but Robinson's dynamic personality lifts this crime melodrama up out of the gutter. He's a district attorney with a conscience and when he learns that he's sent an innocent man to the electric chair, Robinson takes to drink. His married assistants, Foch and Marlowe, urge him to quit prosecuting people and become a criminal defense lawyer. Robinson agrees and takes on Dekker, a nortorious racketeer, as his first client. Slowly, Robinson learns that Dekker has operated high, wide, and handsome for years because he's had inside information from Robinson's own former office leaked to him. He backtracks to discover Marlowe as the highly paid informer and when his investigation gets too close Marlowe tries to kill Foch, who has been helping Robinson uncover the conspiracy. Foch, however, shoots and kills her lethal spouse and Robinson must defend her. This enrages Dekker, who warns Robinson to drop the case. When the intrepid lawyer goes ahead, Dekker has him shot. With typical theatrics that only Robinson could render, he enters the courtroom wounded, dragging in busty, hip-swaying Mansfield, Dekker's former mistress. On the witness stand Mansfield tells all, clearing Foch and ruining Dekker. Scriptwriter Burnett based the story on the play and 1932 film MOUTHPIECE but he also liberally borrowed from THE MAN WHO TALKED TOO MUCH (1940) and his own earlier film, THE ASPHALT JUNGLE (1950), in assembling this absorbing if predictable tale. Mansfield's role is mercifully kept short, although she would linger in Hollywood to appear in another Robinson opus, HELL ON FRISCO BAY, made the same year.

p, Frank P. Rosenberg; d, Lewis Allen; w, W.R. Burnett, James R. Webb (based on the play *The Mouthpiece* by Frank J. Collins); ph, J. Peverell Marley; m, Max Steiner; ed, Thomas Reilly; art d, Stanley Fleischer; cos, Moss Mabry.

Crime Drama **(PR:C MPAA:NR)**

ILLEGAL DIVORCE, THE (SEE: SECOND HAND WIFE, 1933)

ILLEGAL ENTRY**1/2** (1949) 84m UNIV bw

Howard Duff *(Bert Powers)*, Marta Toren *(Anna Duvak)*, George Brent *(Dan Collins)*, Gar Moore *(Lee Sloan)*, Tom Tully *(Nick Gruber)*, Paul Stewart *(Zack Richards)*, Richard Rober *(Dutch Lempo)*, Joseph Vitale *(Joe Bottsy)*, James Nolan *(Benson)*, Clifton Young *(Bill Rafferty)*, David Clarke *(Carl)*, Robert Osterloh *(Crowthers)*, Anthony Caruso *(Teague)*, Donna Martell *(Maria)*, Kenneth Tobey *(Dave)*, Curt Conway *(Thin-Faced Man)*, Waldon Boyle *(Payson)*, Pierce Lyden *(Gunman)*, Vito Scotti *(Mexican Youth)*, Ray Flynn *(Bartender)*, Jack Chefe *(Man)*, Slim Crow *(Immigration Officer)*, Alex Akimoff, Betty Chay *(Aliens)*.

Duff is an undercover federal agent hired to break up a ring smuggling aliens into the U.S. by way of Mexico. He tracks down the gang behind the illegal border crossings and, with the help of Toren, brings them to justice. Better than average performances carry this one.

p, Jules Schermer; d, Frederick de Cordova; w, Joel Malone, Art Cohn (based on a story by Ben Bengal, Herbert Kline, Dan Moore); ph, William Daniels; ed, Edward Curtiss; md, Milton Schwarzwald; art d, Bernard Herzbrun, Richard A. Riedel; set d, Russell A. Gausman, John Austin; cos, Yvonne Wood; spec eff, David S. Horsley; makeup, Bud Westmore.

Crime **(PR:A MPAA:NR)**

ILLEGAL RIGHTS (SEE: HAIL TO THE RANGERS, 1943)

ILLEGAL TRAFFIC**** (1938) 67m PAR bw

J. Carrol Naish *(Lewis Zomar)*, Mary Carlisle *(Carol Butler)*, Robert Preston *(Bent Martin)*, Judith Barrett *(Marie)*, Pierre Watkin *(Jigger)*, Larry "Buster" Crabbe *(Steve)*, George McKay *(Old Man Butler)*, Richard Denning *(Silk Patterson)*, Sheila Darcy *(Mathilde)*, Dolores Casey *(Mamie)*, Richard Stanley *(Cagey Miller)*, John Hart *(Davis)*, Regis Toomey *(Windy)*, William B. Davidson *(Dalton)*, Joseph Crehan *(Chief Daley)*, Monte Blue *(Capt. Moran)*, Archie Twitchell *(Duke)*, Morgan Conway *(State's Attorney Ryan)*, Philip Warren *(Dittmar)*.

Naish is a mobster who is in the business of transporting criminals away from the scene of the crime. G-Man Preston goes undercover and gets inside the ring, putting pressure on Naish. The finale has the agent in the air pursuing Naish's car. After some machinegun blasts and bombings, Preston emerges victorious.

w, William C. Thomas; d, Louis King; w, Robert Yost, Lewis Foster, Stuart Anthony; ph, Henry Sharp; ed, Harvey Johnston; md, Boris Morros; art d, Hans Dreier, John Goodman.

Crime **(PR:A MPAA:NR)**

ILLIAC PASSION, THE zero (1968) 90m Film-Makers' bw

Richard Beauvais *(Prometheus)*, David Beauvis *(His Conscience)*, Robert Alvarez *(Narcissus)*, Taylor Mead *(The Demon or Sprite)*, Sheila Gary *(Echo)*, Peggy Murray *(The Muse)*, Tom Venturi *(Hyacinthus)*, Tally Brown *(Venus)*, Kenneth King *(Adonis)*, Gerard Malanga *(Ganymede)*, Jack Smith *(Orpheus)*, Jan Chippman *(Eurydice)*, Andy Warhol *(Poseidon)*, Phillip Klass *(Daedalus)*, Margot Brier *(Pandora)*, Paul Swan *(Zeus)*, Wayne Weber *(Icarus)*, Carlos Anduze *(Hades)*, Stella Dundas *(The Moon Goddess)*, John Dowd *(Endymion)*, Philip Merker *(Apollo)*, Beverly Grant *(Persephone)*, Clara Hoover *(Io)*, Gregory Battcock *(Phaeton)*, Philip Fagan *(Cupid/Eros)*, Gregory J. Markopoulos *(The Filmmaker/Narrator)*.

A pretentious "underground" 16-mm version of the ancient classic play "Prometheus Bound," which dealt with man's relationship with the gods. Here, taking place entirely in New York City, director Markopoulos comments on his characters' personalities, which are rooted in mythology, urbanism, and homosexuality. Warhol and his cohorts appear but do little to further the theme of man's timelessness with the "all." Bela Bartok's music wins the day.

p,d,w&ph, Gregory J. Markopoulos (based on the play "Prometheus Bound" by Aeschylus); m, Bela Bartok; ed, Markopoulos.

Experimental **(PR:O MPAA:NR)**

ILLICIT**1/2** (1931) 76m WB bw

Barbara Stanwyck *(Anne Vincent)*, James Rennie *(Dick Ives)*, Ricardo Cortez *(Price Baines)*, Natalie Moorhead *(Margie True)*, Charles Butterworth *(Georgie Evans)*, Joan Blondell *(Helen "Duckie" Childers)*, Claude Gillingwater *(Ives Senior)*, Hazel Howell.

A surprisingly risque film for 1931, ILLICIT details the romantic relationship between Rennie, a wealthy young businessman, and Stanwyck, an independent woman who fears that marriage will ruin their love for each other. To solve this dilemma the couple live together on the weekends, much to the dismay of Rennie's father. After months of ardent persuasion, Rennie finally convinces Stanwyck to marry him. Two years go by and Stanwyck's worst fears are realized; they have grown apart and begin seeking excitement elsewhere. Stanwyck hits the town with her zany friends Blondell and Butterworth. Learning that she has the wanderlust, Stanwyck's old flame Cortez zeros in on her. Meanwhile, Rennie has taken up with his old girl friend Moorhead. After much soul-searching and emotional upheaval Rennie and Stanwyck reunite and save their marriage. Though ILLICIT tears down a surprising number of conservative moral conventions by having the Stanwyck character, a *woman*, opposing a wedding in favor of cohabiting without benefit of marriage, its ending embraces traditional attitudes, thus relieving the audience of having to seriously consider questions the film has raised. Unfortunately, this lends one to believe that the whole issue was just being exploited by the filmmakers for some sensational box-office. Social and moral questions aside, ILLICIT fails as interesting drama because the characters are weakly developed and the plot suffers from the usual inane melodramatics that plagued romance films of the 1930s. Warner Bros. exploited the material again two years later in EX-LADY, a virtual remake of ILLICIT starring Bette Davis.

d, Archie Mayo; w, Harvey Thew (based on the play by Edith Fitzgerald, Robert Riskin); ph, Robert Kurrie; ed, Bill Holmes; cos, Earl Luick.

Drama **(PR:C MPAA:NR)**

ILLICIT INTERLUDE*****

(1954, Swed.) 95m Svensk Film Arthur Davis/Gaston Hakim bw (SOMMARLEK; GB: SUMMER INTERLUDE; AKA: SUMMERPLAY)

Maj-Britt Nilsson *(Marie)*, Alf Kjellin *(Nystrom)*, Berger Malsten *(Henrik)*, Georg Funkquist *(Erland)*, Mimi Pollack *(Elizabeth)*, Annalisa Ericson *(Roommate)*, Stig Olin *(Ballet Master)*, Gunnar Olsson, John Botvid *(Karl)*, Douglas Hage *(Nisse)*, Julia Caesar, Carl Strom, The Ballet Theatre of the Stockholm Royal Opera in "Swan Lake."

Britt is an older dancer for a ballet company. After receiving a diary from her old love Malsten, she runs off to a small cabin. While reading the diary the film segues into flashback, showing the courtship and love affair between the two. When the young lovers go to visit an uncle of hers the story flashes back to the present, with Britt thanking the man for sending her the diary. The uncle had recovered it from the hospital where Malsten had died after hurting himself in a diving accident. Britt then turns the diary over to her latest suitor, telling him that he should read it. Now the two can have their first serious talk and Britt has been able to exorcise demons of her past. This is one of Bergman's favorite among his own films, with some fine uses of diffused light during flashback sequences to express mood and ambience. It showed the artistic growth of the director and the promise of things to come.

p, Allan Ekelund; d, Ingmar Bergman; w, Bergman, Herbert Grevenius (story by Bergman); ph, Gunnar Fischer, Bengt Jarnmark; m, Erik Nordgren and excerpts from Tchaikowsky's "Swan Lake"; ed, Oscar Rosander; set d, Nals Svenwall.

Drama **(PR:O MPAA:NR)**

ILLUMINATIONS****

(1976, Aus.) 70m Illumination/Melbourne Filmmakers Cooperative c

Tony Llewellyn-Jones, Gabi Trsek, Tibor Markus.

This beautifully photographed work tries hard to be an Australian version of LAST YEAR AT MARIENBAD but never matches the latter's quality or depth. Jones and Trsek are lovers staying in a country home. Trsek nearly drowns in the bathtub as she daydreams about her father's death, and from there the story takes a headlong plunge into the artistically obscure. The two wander about in medieval dress, confront Trsek's late father, and generally muddle around. It isn't much of a story, though the photography nicely captures the Australian countryside. Markus, the film's producer, makes an appearance as the being who transcends the world of the living and the dead. Ironically he was to die shortly after completion of the film.

p, Tibor Markus; d&w, Paul Cox; ph, Wolfgang Beliharz; m, Norman Kaye, Alex Berry.

Drama **(PR:O MPAA:NR)**

ILLUSION**** (1929) 80m PAR bw

Charles "Buddy" Rogers *(Carlee Thorpe)*, Nancy Carroll *(Claire Jernigan)*, June Collyer *(Hilda Schmittlap)*, Kay Francis *(Zelda Paxton)*, Regis Toomey *(Eric Schmittlap)*, Knute Erikson *(Jacob Schmittlap)*, Maude Turner Gordon *(Queen of Dalmatia)*, Emilie Melville *(Mother Fay)*, William Austin *(Mr. Z)*, Frances Raymond *(Mrs. Y)*, Catherine Wallace *(Mrs. Z)*, J.E. Nash *(Mr. X)*, William McLaughlin *(Mr. Y)*, Eddie Kane *(Gus Bloomberg)*, Michael Visaroff *(Equerry)*, Paul Lukas *(Count Fortuny)*, Richard Cramer *(Magus)*, Bessie Lyle *(Consuelo)*, Col. G.L. McDonell *(Jarman the Butler)*, Lillian Roth *(Singer)*, Harriet Spiker *(Midget)*, Anna Magruder *(Fat Lady)*, Albert Wolffe *(Giant)*, Eugenie Besserer *(Mrs. Jacob Schmittlap)*.

Rogers and Carroll are a circus magic team given a chance to bring their act to vaudeville. Rogers refuses the job, so dejected Carroll teams with another magician. It doesn't last, however, and Rogers and Carroll get back on the right track, realizing their love is more important than their act. A rambling story with some song, as both Carroll and Rogers warble now and then.

p, B.P. Schulberg; d, Lothar Mendes; w, E. Lloyd Sheldon (based on the play by Arthur Chesney Train); ph, Harry Fishbeck; ed, George Nichols, Jr.; m/l, "When the Real Thing Comes Your Way," Larry Spier.

Romance **(PR:A MPAA:NR)**

ILLUSION OF BLOOD**

(1966, Jap.) 107m Toh L/Frank Lee c (YOTSUYA KAIDAN)

Tatsuya Nakadai *(Iuemon Tamiya)*, Mariko Okada *(Oiwa)*, Junko Ikeuchi *(Osode)*, Kanzaburo Nakamura *(Gonbei Naosuke)*, Mayumi Ozora *(Oume)*, Keiko Awaji *(Omaki)*, Yasushi Nagata *(Samon Yotsuya)*, Eitaro Ozawa *(Kihei Ito)*, Masao Mishima *(Takuetsu)*, Kanjiro Taira.

A series of murders occurs after Nakadai commits robbery rather than take a demeaning job. His father-in-law then demands that he divorce his wife so as not to disgrace her any further. Nakadai then murders his father-in-law to keep his marriage together. The finale has the ghosts of the murdered family members returning to haunt their killer as he hides in a Buddhist temple, but there is no escaping the vengeance of ghosts. Fascinating glimpses of sacred Japanese rituals.

p, Ichiro Sato; d, Shiro Toyoda; w, Toshio Yasumi (based on a Kabuki play by Namboku Tsuruya); ph, Hiroshi Murai (Tohoscope, Eastmancolor); m, Toru Takemitsu.

Drama **(PR:O MPAA:NR)**

ILLUSION TRAVELS BY STREETCAR, THE***

(1977, Mex.) 84m Clasa Films Mundiales bw (LA ILLUSION EN TRANVIA)

Lilia Prado *(Lupe)*, Carlos Navarro *(Caireles)*, Domingo Soler, Fernando Soto *(Tarrajas)*, Agustin Isunza *(Pinillos)*, Miguel Manzano, Javier de la Parra, Guillermo Bravo Sosa, Felipe Montojo.

Although made in 1954, THE ILLUSION TRAVELS BY STREETCAR did not have its American premiere until 1977. The film is one of a number from Bunuel's Mexican period, when the director was allowed almost complete control over his material, therefore allowing him to include as many satirical and metaphorical statements against religion and the state as he desired. The story concerns two men who have just discovered that the old streetcar they have painstakingly repaired will no longer be needed for service. Having become quite attached to this product of their labor, they decide to sneak into the garage that night and take the car out for one last run. However, they are forced to keep it out all the next day as well, for they have to wait until night to sneak the car back in. Driving through the streets of the city they pick up a number of passengers, who become suspicious when they discover they do not have to pay. Bunuel's total control over the film does result in a heavy-handed treatment of the characters who load onto the streetcar, but nevertheless, enough surreal and satirical images are provided to keep any serious student of film happy as well as provide audiences with a decent chuckle or two. (In Spanish, English subtitles.)

p, Armando Ozive Alba; d, Luis Bunuel; w, Maurice de la Serna, Jose Revueltas; Juan de la Cabada; ph, Raul Martinez Solares; m, Luis Hernandez Breton; art d, Edward Fitzgerald.

Satirical Drama **(PR:C MPAA:NR)**

ILLUSTRATED MAN, THE** (1969) 103m WB/7 Arts c

Rod Steiger *(Carl)*, Claire Bloom *(Felicia)*, Robert Drivas *(Willie)*, Don Dubbins *(Pickard)*, Jason Evers *(Simmons)*, Tim Weldon *(John)*, Christie Matchett *(Anna)*, Pogo *(Peke, a Dog)*.

This science fiction entry comes from the fertile, ebullient brain of Ray Bradbury, but, like many of his wonderful stories, it does not translate well to the screen; what *reads well* in his florid, adjectival style seems lifeless and unfulfilling in motion pictures. This may or may not have something to do with his lack of verbs in narrative, for verbs mean action and action is necessary for the screen. As Louis B. Mayer, the Casper Houser of filmdom, once said: "Motion pictures *move*!" Steiger gives it all a wonderful effort, assisted by his then-wife Bloom (who overplays her parts and hams it up on the narrative). Steiger is the strange tattooed man and Bloom the futuristic tattoo artist who has covered his entire body with bizarre and wonderful illustrations, each having a story. Drivas, a young vagabond enroute to California in 1933, encounters Steiger and the two tramp along together. When they bed down for the night, even though the shirtless Steiger warns the boy not to stare at the fantastic murals on his torso, Drivas glares at one tattoo and is suddenly swept into a futuristic home where a jungle playground offers live, ferocious beasts concocted by the children of Steiger and Bloom. When the parents grow overbearing the children maliciously entice Steiger and Bloom to their deaths at the hands of their jungle friends. Another tattoo yields an image of a strange planet where astronauts are trapped in incessant rain that slowly drives them crazy, all except Steiger, who makes it safely, at the expense of his comrades, to the sanctuary of a "sun dome." The third tattoo takes Drivas to a mountaintop where Steiger and Bloom decide to kill their children, to save them from the painful death of an impending nuclear holocaust. Bloom, however, believes she has persuaded Steiger to spare their children and is relieved when awakening the next morning to find the world still intact. Her children, however, are not, Steiger having gone ahead and given poison to the children. Drivas' last image bursts from his own imagination. He stares at the only blank spot on the body of the sleeping Steiger and sees himself being strangled by Steiger. He picks up a huge rock and sends this crashing onto Steiger's head. But the Illustrated Man survives, staggers to his feet, and stumbles after Drivas with murderous intent at the fade. The offbeat stories are neither rewarding nor entertaining and they are replete with gratuitous violence. The irony is shallow, the meaning hollow, the message bleak and pessimistic. As the allegorical morality play this film was obviously intended to be, it is pretentious and only Steiger's intense portrayal provides interest.

p, Howard B. Kreitsek, Ted Mann; d, Jack Smight; w, Kreitsek; ph, Philip Lathrop (Panavision, Technicolor); m, Jerry Goldsmith; ed, Archie Marshek; art d, Joel Schiller; set d, Marvin March; cos, Anthea Sylbert; spec eff, Ralph Webb; Steiger's skin illus dsgn, James E. Reynolds; makeup, Gordon Bau; animal trainer, Frank Weatherwax.

Science Fiction **(PR:O MPAA:M)**

IM LAUF DER ZEIT (SEE: KINGS OF THE ROAD, 1976, Ger.)

IM STAHLNETZ DES DR. MABUSE

(SEE: RETURN OF DR. MABUSE, THE, Fr./Ital./Ger.)

IMAGES* (1972, Ireland) 100m Lion's Gate-Hemdale/COL c

Susannah York *(Cathryn)*, Rene Auberjonois *(Hugh)*, Marcel Bozzuffi *(Rene)*, Hugh Millais *(Marcel)*, Cathryn Harrison *(Susannah)*, John Morley *(Old Man)*.

Robert Altman has always fancied himself an auteur and he gets his chance to show how wrong he is in IMAGES, which he wrote and directed. A muddled, though often beautifully shot, movie that is, at its best, pretentious, and, at its worst, incomprehensible. There are many who saw something in this film but twice as many who saw nothing and the response from audiences was apathy. Altman, who made his name with M*A*S*H, should have titled this MISHMASH. York is a schizophrenic housewife who is busy writing a children's book called "In Search Of Unicorns." (All the prose from that fictional book was actually written by York.) She gets a phone call from an anonymous woman whose voice she thinks she knows. The caller says that York's husband, Auberjonois, is having a romantic alliance, and when she gets the address of the trysting place it turns out to be at York's very own apartment building. Auberjonois enters and is suddenly transformed into her late lover, Bozzuffi, who died in a plane accident years ago. Her husband thinks that York is about to step out to lunch (and all other meals) so he hies her away to the place where she was happiest, the lakeside house of her youth. Once there, York sees herself walking around, and when Auberjonois leaves, York again meets Bozzuffi and can't make up her mind whether or not that's her husband. Auberjonois shows up at home with another former York lover, Millais, and York is now rocked when she sees that his daughter is the image of what she was at twelve. In desperation, she gets a gun and shoots the image of Bozzuffi. Then she stops Millais from making advances by fantasizing that she is stabbing him to death. Evidently Altman is trying to show us that York is guilty about her prior lovers, and now that she has mentally dispensed with both of them she drives off to meet her husband. But on the road she sees herself standing and waving at her to stop. She drives right into the image and knocks it off a cliff into a stream. When she gets back to her apartment in the city she looks at herself in the shower and understands how mad she is as she realizes that what she thought was herself on the road was really Auberjonois, her adoring husband. Filmed entirely in Ireland at Loch Bray and Dublin, IMAGES looks lovely and Zsigmond is to be congratulated for his lensing. As a visual experience, IMAGES has merit but Altman seems to love confusing and confounding his audiences. But what else can we expect from the man who gave us BUFFALO BILL AND THE INDIANS, HEALTH, A WEDDING, and QUINTET? How this man keeps getting financial backing for his films may be one of the great mysteries of modern history.

p, Tommy Thompson; d&w, Robert Altman (based on the story "In Search of Unicorns" by Susannah York); ph, Vilmos Zsigmond (Panavision, Technicolor); m, John Williams; ed, Graeme Clifford; prod d, Leon Ericksen; spec eff, Jerry Johnson, makeup, Toni Delaney.

Psychological Drama **(PR:C–O MPAA:R)**

IMAGINARY SWEETHEART (SEE: PROFESSIONAL SWEETHEART, 1933)

IMERES TOU 36 (SEE: DAYS OF 36, 1972, Gr.)

IMITATION GENERAL*** (1958) 88m MGM bw

Glenn Ford *(M/Sgt. Murphy Savage)*, Red Buttons *(Cpl. Chan Derby)*, Taina Elg *(Simone)*, Dean Jones *(Cpl. Terry Sellers)*, Kent Smith *(Brig. Gen. Charles Lane)*, Tige Andrews *(Pvt. Orville Hutchmeyer)*, John Wilder *(Lt. Jeff Clayton)*, Ralph Votrian *(Private First Class)*.

An often funny war spoof has Ford pretending to be a general after the death of his commanding officer, Smith. With morale down and organization suffering, Smith's plan was to stand by his troops, staying with them on the battlefield to raise their hopes. Disregarding consequences, Ford assumes Smith's role and leads the troops to a daring victory. Buttons is outstanding as Ford's comic sidekick.

p, William Hawks; d, George Marshall; w, William Bowers (based on a story by William Chamberlain); ph, George J. Folsey (CinemaScope); ed, Harold F. Kress; art d, William A. Horning, Malcolm Brown.

War/Comedy **(PR:A MPAA:NR)**

IMITATION OF LIFE*½** (1934) 106m UNIV bw

Claudette Colbert *(Beatrice "Bes" Pullman)*, Warren William *(Stephen Archer)*, Ned Sparks *(Elmer)*, Louise Beavers *(Delilah Johnson)*, Juanita Quigley *(Jessie Pullman, Age 3)*, Marilyn Knowlden *(Jessie, Age 8)*, Rochelle Hudson *(Jessie, Age 18)*, Sebie Hendricks *(Peola Johnson, Age 4)*, Dorothy Black *(Peola, Age 9)*, Fredi Washington *(Peola, Age 19)*, Alan Hale *(Martin, Furniture Man)*, Clarence Hummel Wilson *(Landlord)*, Henry Armetta *(Painter)*, Henry Kolker *(Dr. Preston)*, Wyndham Standing *(Butler)*, Alice Ardell *(French Maid)*, Paul Porcasi *(Restaurant Manager)*, William B. Davidson *(Man)*, G.P. Huntley, Jr. *(Man at Party)*, Noel Francis *(Mrs. Eden)*, Walter Walker *(Hugh)*, Franklin Pangborn *(Mr. Carven)*, Tyler Brooke *(Tipsy Man)*, William Austin *(Englishman)*, Alma Tell *(Mrs. Carven)*, Hazel Washington

(Black Maid), Lenita Lane *(Mrs. Dale)*, Barry Norton *(Young Man)*, Joyce Compton *(Woman)*, Reverend Gregg *(Minister)*, Curry Lee *(Chauffeur)*, Claire McDowell *(Teacher)*, Mme. Sul-Te-Wan *(Cook)*, Stuart Johnston *(Undertaker)*, Fred "Snowflake" Toones, Hattie McDaniel *(Bits at Funeral)*, Dennis O'Keefe *(Dance Extra)*, Paulyn Garner *(Mrs. Ramsey)*, Edgar Norton *(Butler)*.

The year 1934 should be designated as Claudette Colbert's "favorite year" because in 12 months she made IT HAPPENED ONE NIGHT, CLEOPATRA, and IMITATION OF LIFE. Although she technically won her Oscar for IT HAPPENED ONE NIGHT, the Academy may have awarded her the statuette for the remarkable accomplishment of having demonstrated such incredible versatility in three diverse roles. In Hurst's smashing novel adaptation, Colbert is a white widow raising her daughter—played by three different actresses at various stages of her life, Juanita Quigley (at 3), Marilyn Knowlden (at 8) and Rochelle Hudson (at 18)—and she ages 15 years in the film, quite believably in each scene. Colbert's maid is Beavers, a wizard with flapjacks, and both women decide to join forces and open a small pancake parlor. Beavers also has a young daughter (played by Hendricks, Black, and Washington at three ages) and the two women are full partners in what becomes a highly successful business. But as their enterprise flourishes, the home front is fraught with emotion. Washington's skin is white enough for her to "pass" but she can't handle it emotionally as she stands in two separate worlds (Lena Horne said publicly that her fair skin also caused her woes in the black community) and she runs away from school and breaks off relations with Beavers in her attempt to stay in the white community. Colbert is shocked to learn that she and Hudson are both in love with Warren William and she has to deal with Hudson's adolescent crush before she can marry the man. Beavers is haunted by her daughter's rejection and eventually dies of a broken heart. She had asked for a slam-bang funeral and Colbert makes certain she gets it with a white hearse drawn by horses, a band of black freemasons, and the adoration of all the many charitable groups supported by Beavers when she was alive. The film ends as Colbert sends William away. It's a bit unresolved but the studio was true to the book and audiences didn't seem to mind the fact that the story lacked a completed ending. Beavers was smashing in her role, with a quiet dignity that belied her youth (she was only 32 at the time; Colbert was 29). There was a great deal of controversy from both blacks and whites over the movie. Southern audiences didn't much cotton to a white woman going into business with her maid, despite the fact that it was Beavers's recipe that made them millionaires. And black critics felt that Beavers should have been shown establishing her own residence rather than staying on with Colbert and continuing to function as sort of a maid. That aside, this is an excellent example of a 1930s tearjerker but made with such good taste that we hardly feel we are being manipulated, which, of course, we are. Baby Jessie grew up to be Juanita Quigley but the other youngsters (except for Hudson) didn't go on to careers of any magnitude after this. Nominated for three Oscars including Best Picture, it was swept aside by the then-unprecedented sweep of IT HAPPENED ONE NIGHT.

p, Carl Laemmle; d, John M. Stahl; w, William Hurlbut (based on the novel by Fannie Hurst); ph, Merritt Gerstad; ed, Phil Cahn.

Drama **(PR:A MPAA:NR)**

IMITATION OF LIFE*** (1959) 125m UNIV c

Lana Turner *(Lora Meredith)*, John Gavin *(Steve Archer)*, Sandra Dee *(Susie, Age 16)*, Dan O'Herlihy *(David Edwards)*, Susan Kohner *(Sarah Jane, Age 18)*, Robert Alda *(Allen Loomis)*, Juanita Moore *(Annie Johnson)*, Mahalia Jackson *(Herself)*, Karen Dicker *(Sarah Jane, Age 8)*, Terry Burnham *(Suzie, Age 6)*, John Vivyan (Young Man), Lee Goodman *(Photographer)* Ann Robinson *(Show Girl)*, Troy Donahue *(Frankie)*, Sandra Gould *(Receptionist)*, David Tomack *(Burly Man)*, Joel Fluellen *(Minister)*, Jack Weston *(Stage Manager)*, Billy House *(Fat Man)*, Maida Severn *(Teacher)*, Than Wyenn *(Romano)*, Peg Shirley *(Fay)*, Cicely Evans *(Louise)*, Bess Flowers *(Geraldine Moore)*, Paul Bradley *(Preston Mitchell)*, Napoleon Whiting *(Kenneth)*, Myrna Fahey *(Actress)*, Eddie Parker *(Policeman)*, George Barrows *(Furniture Mover)*, Forbes Murray, Leota Lorraine, Chuckie Bradley *(Bits)*.

The producers took great liberties with the details of Fannie Hurst's novel but remained true to the central theme in this successful remake of the 1934 picture which starred Claudette Colbert and Louise Beavers. This version was such a winner at the box office that it kept the studio going after Universal had had a series of dim features which failed to attract audiences. Hunter adds his own particular gloss to the production and Turner wears the clothes well and looked as good in 1959 as she had more than a decade earlier. Turner is an aspiring actress raising a daughter, Burnham, on her own. She's at the beach at Coney Island and loses sight of the young girl. Frantically, she searches the beach and finds Burnham in the company of black Moore and her light-skinned daughter, Dicker. The women like each other and Moore goes to work for Turner as a housekeeper. Their two daughters are just as fond of each other as the mothers are, but Turner is more interested in her career than in being a mother. She meets talent agent Alda who helps her get into a play written by O'Herlihy. Her ability catapults her to stardom and she appears in several plays by O'Herlihy, each more successful than the one before. By this time, Dee is the grownup daughter and sorely neglected by Turner, who now has a romantic interest in Gavin, a photographer. Moore is having different kinds of problems with her grown daughter, Kohner, who is white enough to pass and who eventually rejects her mother, preferring to make her way in the white community. This, of course, is heartbreaking to Moore and when Kohner runs away to pursue a career as a cocktail waitress, then a showgirl, Moore grows seriously ill and dies. At the same time, Turner learns that Dee is in love with Gavin, which causes Turner to realize how shallow her life has been. True, she's had fame and fortune, but at the price of losing her relationship with her daughter. Moore has requested an elaborate funeral (a very moving scene highlighted by Mahalia Jackson's singing of "Trouble of the World") and it is there that Kohner returns and asks her dead mother for her blessing. By this time, Gavin has married someone else and all the three women have is each other. The film ends as the trio resolve to stay together. If you've read the account of the 1933 version, you can easily see how the story was altered. Most remakes fail miserably, but this could stand on its own two reels very well. Turner does one of her best acting jobs and even Gavin, who was always somewhat of a stick that the studio was trying to groom into being another Rock Hudson, is effective. Seen in small roles are some actors who went on to much larger parts, such as Jack Weston, John Vivyan, Troy Donahue and the very funny Sandra Gould. Once again, as in the original, the audience is played like a virtuoso on a harpischord. Emotions rise and fall and hankies are evident from start to finish. This was Danish-born Sirk's last film. He moved to Munich afterward and settled down in retirement.

p, Ross Hunter; d, Douglas Sirk; w, Eleanore Griffin, Allan Scott (based on the novel by Fannie Hurst); ph, Russell Metty (Eastmancolor); m, Frank Skinner; ed, Milton Carruth; md, Joseph Gershenson; art d, Alexander Golitzen, Richard H. Riedel; set d, Russell A. Gausman, Julia Heron; cos, Jean Louis, Bill Thomas; spec eff, Clifford Stine; m/l, "Imitation of Life," Sammy Fain, Paul Francis Webster (sung by Earl Grant), "Empty Arms," Arnold Hughes, Frederick Herbert, "Trouble of the World," anon. (sung by Mahalia Jackson).

Drama **(PR:A MPAA:NR)**

IMMEDIATE DISASTER (SEE: STRANGER FROM VENUS, 1954, Brit.)

IMMORAL CHARGE***

(1962, Brit.) 87m Alva/Governor bw (GB: SERIOUS CHARGE; AKA: A TOUCH OF HELL)

Anthony Quayle *(Howard Phillips)*, Sarah Churchill *(Hester Peters)*, Andrew Ray *(Larry Thompson)*, Irene Browne *(Mrs. Phillips)*, Percy Herbert *(Mr. Thompson)*, Noel Howlett *(Mr. Peters)*, Wensley Pithey *(Police Sergeant)*, Leigh Madison *(Mary Williams)*, Judith Furse *(Probation Officer)*, Jean Cadell *(Almshouse Matron)*, Wilfred Brambell *(Verger)*, Olive Sloane *(Mrs. Browning)*, George Roderick *(Fishmonger)*, Cliff Richard *(Curley Thompson)*, Liliane Brousse *(Michelle)*, Wilfred Pickles *(Magistrate)*.

A touchy subject for the time, homosexuality, is handled well in this screen version of Philip King's play "Serious Charge." Quayle, a young, good-looking vicar, arrives in a small town teeming with juvenile delinquency and people bent on gossip. An evil-minded young punk, wanting to ruin the vicar, claims he was a victim of a homosexual attack by Quayle. Churchill, the attractive daughter of the former vicar, is in love with Quayle, but accidentally becomes the star witness against him. He is literally run out of town. A dramatic account of how a man battles slander that ruins his life, the film also shows the destructiveness of small-minded people. Songs include: "No Turning Back," "Living Doll," "Mad" (Lionel Bart; sung by Cliff Richard), "Chinchilla" (Randy Starr, Dick Wolf).

p, Mickey Delamar; d, Terence Young; w, Delamar, Guy Elmes (based on the play "Serious Charge" by Philip King); ph, Georges Perinal; m, Leighton Lucas; ed, Reginald Beck; art d, Allan Harris; set d, Freda Pearson; makeup, Phil Leakey.

Drama **(PR:A MPAA:NR)**

IMMORAL MOMENT, THE**

(1967, Fr.) 105m Films de la Pleiade/Jerand bw (LA DENONCIATION)

Maurice Ronet *(Michel)*, Francoise Brion *(Elsa)*, Nicole Berger *(Eleonore)*, Sacha Pitoeff *(Malferrer)*, Michele Grellier *(Victoire)*, Francois Maistre *(Patrice)*, Laurent Terzieff *(Narrator)*, Florence Loinod, Gisele Hauchecorne, Jacques Santi, Jean-Claude Darval.

Released in Paris in 1962, this crime drama tells the story of Ronet, a former French Resistance fighter who gave out information after being tortured by the Germans. When he witnesses a murder which he is suspected of committing, he is brought in for questioning. The leader of an underground political group is also questioned. He is guilty and fears that Ronet will inform on him the way he had wilted during the Occupation. Ronet remains silent, but is still killed by a member of the underground. A grim look at French secret societies and still more history of WW II.

p, Pierre Braunberger; d&w, Jacques Doniol-Valcroze; ph, Henri Raichi (Franscope); m, Georges Delerue; ed, Bob Wade; art d, Pierre Guffroy.

Crime/Drama **(PR:C MPAA:NR)**

IMMORTAL BACHELOR, THE 1/2** (1980, Ital.) 95m S.J. International c

Giancarlo Giannini *(Gino Benacio)*, Monica Vitti *(Tina Candela)*, Vittorio Gassman *(Andrea Sansoni)*, Claudia Cardinale *(Gabriella Sansoni)*, Renato Pozzetto *(Fulvio)*.

After philandering hubby Giannini is killed by wife Vitti, the cleaning woman must face a jury for the crime. Cardinale is a member of the jury who soon finds the dead man far more appealing than her boring husband (Gassman). Strange and not particularly well-thought-out comedy but the cast makes up for the lackluster script.

p, Elio Scardamaglia; d, Marcello Fondato; w, Fondato, Francesco Scardamaglia; ph, Pasqualino de Santis; m, Guido DeAngelis; art d, Luciano Ricceri; cos, Luca Sabatelli.

Comedy **Cas.** **(PR:O MPAA:NR)**

IMMORTAL BATTALION, THE (SEE: WAY AHEAD, THE, 1944, Brit.)

IMMORTAL GARRISON, THE** (1957, USSR) 90m Mosfilm/Artkino bw

V. Makarov *(Baturin)*, V. Emelyanov *(Kondreyton)*, N. Krychitov *(Kukharkov)*, V. Scrova *(Marie)*.

Fighting between the Nazis and Russian troops is recounted in flashback by Makarov, who was a prisoner of the Germans. The powerful, suspenseful tale is told in a near documentary style incorporating a great deal of stock war footage. It is brilliantly photographed by Edward Tisse (who also directed), the famed Soviet cameraman who shot Sergei Eisenstein's masterpieces (POTEMKIN, OCTOBER, and ALEXANDER NEVSKY) and devised ingenious methods of getting his shots. THE IMMORTAL GARRISON, however, did not display many of the techniques of montage associated with the work of Eisenstein, but concentrated on realistic documentation. (In Russian; English subtitles.)

d, Edward Tisse, Z, Agnanenko; w, Konstantin Simonov; ph, Tisse; m, V. Basner.

Historical/War Drama **(PR:A MPAA:NR)**

IMMORTAL GENTLEMAN**½ (1935, Brit.) 61m Bernard Smith/EPC bw

Basil Gill *(William Shakespeare/Malvolio)*, Rosalinde Fuller *(Ophelia/Juliet/Lady)*, Dennis Hoey *(Soldier/Toby Belch)*, Anne Bolt *(Jane/Maria)*, Edgar Owen *(Ben Jonson/Mercutio)*, J. Hubert Leslie *(Michael Drayton)*, Laidman Browne *(Gambler/Petruchio/Feste)*, Terence de Marney *(Harry Morton/Hamlet/Romeo)*, Derrick de Marney *(James Carter/Tybalt)*, Fred Rains *(Miser)*, Dennis Wyndham *(Voyager)*, Leo Genn *(Merchant/Shylock)*, Roy Byford *(Squire)*, Ivan Berlyn *(Father/Aguecheek)*.

One of the odder renditions of Shakespeare set onto celluloid, this obscure item has Gill portraying the master playwright discussing his work with friends which not too effectively segues into various dramatized scenes from the plays.

p, Bernard Smith; d, Widgey R. Newman; w, John Quin (story by Newman).

Drama **(PR:A MPAA:NR)**

IMMORTAL MONSTER

(SEE: CALTIKI, THE IMMORTAL MONSTER, 1959, Ital.)

IMMORTAL SERGEANT, THE**½ (1943) 90m FOX bw

Henry Fonda *(Colin)*, Maureen O'Hara *(Valentine)*, Thomas Mitchell *(Sgt. Kelly)*, Allyn Joslyn *(Cassity)*, Reginald Gardiner *(Benedict)*, Melville Cooper *(Pilcher)*, Bramwell Fletcher *(Symes)*, Morton Lowry *(Cottrell)*, David Thursby *(Bren Carrier Driver)*, Guy Kingsford *(Lorry Driver)*, Bud Geary *(Driver)*, Peter Lawford, Gordon Clark, John Whitney, John Meredity *(Soldiers)*, Bob Mascagno, Italia DeNubila *(Dance Specialty)*, Donald Stuart *(Post Corporal)*, Eric Wilton *(Headwaiter)*, Anthony Marsh *(Assistant Post Corporal)*, Charles Irwin, James Craven *(Noncommissioned Men)*, Sam Waagenaar *(German)*, John Banner *(Officer)*, Wilson Benge *(Waiter)*, Leslie Vincent *(Runner)*, Hans von Morhart, Henry Guttman, Frederick Giermann *(Soldiers)*.

This was not one of Fonda's favorite films but he was nevertheless effective as a timid citizen-soldier reluctant to lead men into battle and be responsible for the possible loss of their lives. He and his men, commanded by a tough old sergeant Mitchell, are cut off from their lines and face annihilation. During his lonely night vigil, Fonda contemplates a not too bright future, thinking about the men with him lost in the Libyan desert. In flashback through Fonda's thoughts, we see his prewar life as a reporter and would-be novelist and the girl of his heart, O'Hara. He has a strong rival in Gardiner, a polished, self-assertive individual who will apparently win O'Hara's heart because Fonda cannot bring himself to tell her he loves her. The story then creeps toward the present, showing Fonda's enlistment in the British army—he's a Canadian to explain the lack of accent—and how he and the patrol commanded by Mitchell wipe out an Italian armored car, leaving several in the patrol dead and Mitchell severely wounded. Mitchell and Fonda talk as the sergeant lies dying and he delivers an inspiring speech to the young corporal. Knowing he will be a burden to the patrol, Mitchell later shoots himself. Then Fonda, back at the present, leads a desperate attack against a German bastion, destroying the enemy and the supplies stored at the oasis. The burning stores are seen by a British unit which arrives to find only three men left alive, included the wounded Fonda. He recuperates in a Cairo hospital, and then, using the courage he has newly found on the battlefield, sends a wire to O'Hara, proposing. They are married three months later, and Fonda delivers a prayer for Mitchell, the sergeant who inspired him to become a man of action. Basically a propaganda film, THE IMMORTAL SERGEANT had the distinction of being the first American film to portray British troops in action in North Africa. And there's action aplenty in this brisk Trotti-Stahl production. After finishing this film Fonda joined the Navy, preferring not to discuss his patriotic role, but he was commissioned and assigned to Washington, where he asked for active duty. The Navy obliged and he spent the rest of the war in the Central Pacific as an air combat intelligence officer. He received a Bronze Star and a Presidential Citation when he was discharged as a lieutenant senior grade in 1945. Fonda was always ecstatic, however, about his appearance in THE OX-BOW INCIDENT, released about the same time, which showed his true pacifistic nature. The film was shot in Imperial Valley, California, and Fonda dodged talking about it for years, finally and tersely commenting: "It was a silly picture. You want to hear the plot? I won World War II single-handed!"

p, Lamar Trotti; d, John Stahl; w, Trotti (based on the novel by John Brophy); ph, Arthur Miller, Clyde De Vinna; m, David Buttolph; ed, James B. Clark; md, Alfred Newman; art d, Richard Day, Maurice Ransford.

War Drama **(PR:A MPAA:NR)**

IMMORTAL STORY, THE***½ (1969, Fr.) 58m ORTF Albina/Fleetwood-Altura c (UNE HISTOIRE IMMORTELLE)

Orson Welles *(Mr. Clay/Narrator)*, Jeanne Moreau *(Viginie Ducrot)*, Roger Coggio *(Elishama Levinsky, The Bookkeeper)*, Norman Eshley *(Paul, the Sailor)*, Fernando Rey *(Merchant)*.

A small gem of a film, Welles' next-to-last (F FOR FAKE followed; THE DEEP in 1970 and THE OTHER SIDE OF THE WIND in 1972 were never completed), which was produced for French television and eventually released theatrically. The film is set on the isle of Macao in the 19th century and Welles stars as an extremely wealthy, tyrannical merchant who long ago had driven his former partner to bankruptcy and suicide to gain control of the business. Now powerful, but old and impotent, Welles lives alone in a huge mansion attended only by his bookkeeper Coggio who reads his boss the account books at night to lull him to sleep. Welles does not care for fiction, only facts, and when Coggio tries to break the monotony one night by reading the prophesy of Isaiah aloud, the old man interrupts and tells the "true" story of an aging, wealthy merchant who paid a sailor to have sex with his young wife so that she might produce an heir to his fortune. Coggio informs Welles that the story is pure myth and that every sailor in the world has heard it. Disgruntled because the story is not based on fact, Welles decides to make it fact by hiring a woman to pose as his wife and then pay a sailor to have sex with her. Coggio is dispatched to find a woman, while Welles searches for a sailor. As it turns out the woman, Moreau, happens to be the daughter of Welles' dead partner, but she agrees to participate for a large fee. The sailor, Eshley, is a Danish seaman who was shipwrecked and had been living in Macao for a year. Welles brings the young man to his mansion and treats him to a fabulous meal. After dinner he is ushered into the bedroom where Moreau lies naked on the bed awaiting his arrival. During their passionate lovemaking Welles stands outside the door and listens. The next morning a delighted Welles tells the young man that the mythical seafaring story is now truth and he should tell the tale in every port where his roving life takes him. Eshley replies that he has no intention of telling anyone what has happened between him and Moreau, and no one would believe him if he did. The sailor then hands Welles a beautiful seashell and instructs him to give it to Moreau. Profoundly shocked that he has been unable to impose his will on the sailor and turn fiction into fact, Welles drops the shell and dies. THE IMMORTAL STORY is a small, quietly beautiful fable which leaves the viewer with a strange sense of loss and sadness. The film is based on a novel by Isak Dinesen [Karen Blixen], an author Welles had long wanted to bring to the screen. Years before, the great director was conned by a Hungarian man who claimed to be a producer who owned the rights to several of Dinesen's works and wanted the films to be shot in Budapest. Welles and his company went to work on the preproduction in an expensive hotel there, but after a few weeks he realized that the Hungarian had no money and, having run up quite a bill, Welles was forced to slip out of town in the dead of night. Eventually the director's dream was realized when the French state-owned television company ORTF offered to produce. Though certainly no CITIZEN KANE, it is fascinating to compare Mr. Clay of THE IMMORTAL STORY with Charles Foster Kane. Welles gives us two towering figures, both men with amazing potential whose desperate desire for success and power result in lives that end in loneliness and despair. The reason we feel a sense of loss for these frequently cruel men is that their simple need for happiness and satisfaction go tragically unfulfilled—much like the life of their creator.

p, Micheline Rozan; d, Orson Welles; w, Welles, Louise de Vilmorin (based on the novella *Skibsdrengens Fortaeling* by Isak Dinesen [Karen Blixen]); ph, Willy Kurant (Eastmancolor); m, Erik Satie; ed, Yolande Maurette, Marcelle Pluet, Francoise Garnault, Claude Farney; art d, Andre Piltant; cos, Pierre Cardin.

Drama **(PR:C MPAA:NR)**

IMMORTAL VAGABOND**½ (1931, Ger.) 70m UFA/Talking Picture Epics bw (DER UNSTERBLICHE LUMP)

Liane Haid *(Anna)*, Gustav Frolich *(Hans Ritter)*, H.A. Shlettow *(Franz Lechner)*, Karl Gerhardt *(Reisleitner)*, Gavara.

A musician falls in love with a farm girl but her father disapproves. The boy goes to Vienna and makes a name for himself in the opera world. When he returns, he finds his fraulein about to marry a cow breeder. He wanders off in dejection and becomes a vagabond. When a body is found floating in the river, it is assumed to be his and the town erects a monument in his name. He watches the dedication while standing in the shadows. His sweetheart sees him and tells him she still loves him. They walk off and become vagabonds together. In its English version, a quite acceptable little sleeper.

d, Gustav Ucicky; w, Robert Liebmann, Karl Hartl; ph, Carl Hoffman; m, Ralph Benatsky.

Drama **(PR:A MPAA:NR)**

IMPACT*** (1949) 108m UA bw

Brian Donlevy *(Walter Williams)*, Ella Raines *(Marsha Peters)*, Charles Coburn *(Lt. Quincy)*, Helen Walker *(Irene Williams)*, Anna May Wong *(Su Lin)*, Mae Marsh *(Mrs. Peters)*, Tony Barrett *(Jim Torrance)*, William Wright *(District Attorney)*, Robert Warwick *(Capt. Callahan)*, Philip Ahn *(Ah Sing)*, Art Baker *(Eldredge)*, Erskine Sanford *(Dr. Bender)*, Bill Ruhl, Raymond Bond, Linda Johnson, Ruth Robinson, Mike Pat Donovan, Dick Gordon, Arthur Hecht, W.J. O'Brien, Martin Doric, Sammy Finn, Tom Martin, Tom Henry, Frank Pershing, Lucius Cooke, Mary Landa, Tom Greenway, Ben Welden, Hans Herbert, Glenn Vernon, Joel Friedkin, Joe Kirk, Harry Cheshire, Sheilah Graham, Jason Robards.

Donlevy is the target of a murder plot devised by his gold digger wife and her boy friend. Before they can get to him, however, he turns the tables on them and the lover is killed. Mistaken identity then comes to the fore, as the newspapers declare Donlevy dead. His wife is booked and jailed for murder, and Donlevy, while lying low, falls in love with widow Raines. She persuades him to surrender to the police, which he does. Surprising evidence turns up at his trial and he goes free in this decent melodrama that offers a nice mix of music to keep things stirring.

p, Leo C. Popkin; d, Arthur Lubin; w, Dorothy Reid, Jay Dratler; ph, Ernest Lazslo; ed, Arthur Nadel.

Crime **Cas.** **(PR:A MPAA:NR)**

IMPACT** (1963, Brit.) 61m But bw

Conrad Phillips *(Jack Moir)*, George Pastell *(The Duke)*, Ballard Berkeley *(Bill Mackenzie)*, Linda Marlowe *(Diana)*, Richard Klee *(Wally)*, Anita West *(Melanie)*, John Rees *(Charlie)*.

Innocent reporter is wrongly accused after a train is robbed. He seeks out the club owner responsible and proves his innocence. Mediocre programmer breaks no new ground.

p, John I. Phillips; d, Peter Maxwell; w, Maxwell, Conrad Phillips.

Crime (PR:C MPAA:NR)

IMPASSE** 1/2** (1969) 100m Aubrey Schenck/UA c

Burt Reynolds *(Pat Morrison)*, Anne Francis *(Bobby Jones)*, Lyle Bettger *(Hansen)*, Rodolfo Acosta *(Draco)*, Jeff Corey *(Wombat)*, Clarke Gordon *(Trev Jones)*, Miko Mayama *(Mariko Riley)*, Joanne Dalsass *(Penny)*, Vic Diaz *(Jesus J. Riley)*, Dely Atay-Atayan *(Pear Blossom)*, Bruno Punzalan *(Nakajima)*, Lily Campillos *(Maria Bonita)*, Shirley Gorospe *(Sherry)*, Bessie Barredo *(Kiling)*, Robert Wang *(Intern)*, Eddie Nicart *(Kuli)*.

In his pre-sex symbol days Reynolds was a tolerable actor, here cast in an adventurous role as a guy who devises a plan to find $3 million in buried government gold hidden during WW II by a quartet of Army men to keep the Japanese from capturing it. He locates the four men, none of whom are the best of friends. Tension is high as they set out on their excursion. In the meantime, Reynolds has gotten friendly with Francis, the daughter of one of the vets. After a kidnaping and a murder, Reynolds and his now-diminished gang locate the gold. The operation is foiled, however, by a jealous wife of one of the men, who wants Reynolds for herself. The authorities arrive and take Reynolds into custody, without the gold or the ladies.

p, Hal Klein; d, Richard Benedict; w, John C. Higgins; ph, Mars B. Rasca (DeLuxe Color); m, Philip Springer; ed, John F. Schreyer; md, Springer; spec eff, Butler-Glouner, Inc.; m/l, "Dear Sweet Miss Jones," Springer, Irwin Levine; makeup, Totoy Villamin.

Adventure (PR:O MPAA:M)

IMPASSE DES VERTUS (SEE: LOVE AT NIGHT, 1961, Fr.)

IMPASSIVE FOOTMAN, THE (SEE: WOMAN IN BONDAGE, 1932, Brit.)

IMPATIENT MAIDEN** 1/2** (1932) 72m UNIV bw

Lew Ayres *(Dr. Myron Brown)*, Mae Clarke *(Ruth Robbins)*, Una Merkel *(Betty Merrick)*, John Halliday *(Albert Hartman)*, Andy Devine *(Clarence Howe)*, Ethel Griffies *(Nurse Lovett)*, Helen Jerome Eddy *(Mrs. Gilman)*, Bert Roach *(Mr. Gilman)*, Cecil Cunningham *(Mrs. Rosy)*, Berton Churchill *(Dr. Wilcox)*, Monte Montague *(Ambulance Driver)*, Lorin Raker *(Mr. Rosy)*, Arthur Hoyt *(Mr. Thomas)*, Blanche Payson *(Mrs. Thomas)*.

This departure for Whale, the director of FRANKENSTEIN, has Ayres in the operating room as a young surgeon. When girl friend Clarke gets an appendicitis attack she is rushed to the hospital and operated on by Ayres, the only available doctor. There's no horror here, but for fans of Whale (and there is a faithful sect) it is interesting to see his fascination with operating-table closeups, a process which was so important in FRANKENSTEIN.

p, Carl Laemmle, Jr.; d, James Whale; w, Richard Schayer, Winifred Dunn, Donald Henderson Clarke (based on the novel *The Impatient Virgin* by Clarke); ph, Arthur Edeson; ed, Clarence Kolster.

Drama/Romance (PR:C MPAA:NR)

IMPATIENT YEARS, THE** 1/2** (1944) 91m COL bw

Jean Arthur *(Janie Anderson)*, Lee Bowman *(Andy Anderson)*, Charles Coburn *(William Smith)*, Edgar Buchanan *(Judge)*, Charley Grapewin *(Bellboy)*, Phil Brown *(Henry Fairchild)*, Harry Davenport *(Minister)*, Jane Darwell *(Minister's Wife)*, Grant Mitchell *(Hotel Clerk)*, Frank Jenks *(Top Sergeant)*, Frank Orth *(Counterman)*, Charles Arnt *(Marriage Clerk)*, Robert Emmett Keane *(Attorney)*.

Arthur is superb in her role as a young housewife who, when faced with the return of her soldier-husband, is unsure whether she loves him. After an 18-month separation they file for a divorce. At the suggestion of Arthur's father, Coburn, the judge has the couple retrace their original meeting and honeymoon. Their happy reconciliation is topped off by the arrival of a newborn.

p&d, Irving Cummings; w, Virginia Van Upp; ph, Hal Mohr, W. Howard Greene; m, Marlin Skiles; ed, Russell Schoengarth; md, M.W. Stoloff; art d, Lionel Banks, Cary Odell.

Romance (PR:A MPAA:NR)

IMPERFECT LADY, THE, 1935
(SEE: PERFECT GENTLEMAN, THE, 1935)

IMPERFECT LADY, THE** (1947) 97m PAR bw

Ray Milland *(Clive Loring)*, Teresa Wright *(Millicent Hopkins)*, Sir Cedric Hardwicke *(Lord Belmont)*, Virginia Field *(Rose Bridges)*, Anthony Quinn *(Jose Martinez)*, Reginald Owen *(Mr. Hopkins)*, Melville Cooper *(Lord Montglyn)*, Rhys Williams *(Inspector Carston)*, George Zucco *(Mr. Mallam)*, Charles Coleman *(Sam Travers)*, Miles Mander *(Mr. Rogan)*, Gordon Richards *(Gladstone)*, Edmond Breon *(Lord Chief Justice)*, Frederick Worlock *(Henderson)*, Michael Dyne *(Malcolm Gadby)*, Joan Winfield *(Lucy)*, Lilian Fontaine *(Mrs. Gunner)*, Leyland Hodgson *(Bobby)*, Olaf Hytten *(Butler)*, Jack H. Lee, Maj. Sam Harris *(Barristers)*, Doris Lloyd *(Woman in Balcony of Theater)*, Gavin Muir *(Kelvin)*, Crauford Kent *(Headwaiter)*, Hilda Plowright *(Woman Customer)*, Montague Shaw, Boyd Irwin, Stanley Mann *(Men)*, Roberta Daniel *(Suzanne, Rose's Maid)*, Lumsden Hare *(Hardy)*, Winifred Harris, Gwendolyn Logan *(Dowagers)*, Colin Hunter *(Jury Foreman)*, Ted Billings *(Chimney Sweep)*.

A good cast is not used properly in this cliched story of Milland, a charming peer of the realm in Victorian England, who falls hard for Wright, a music hall dancer. Milland's stuffy brother, Hardwicke, tells Wright that if she continues this fling with Milland it just might ruin his standing in the community. She loves him so much that she decides it would be better if she stepped away, so that she does and returns to her own career as a dancer. In one of those ironic twists that only seem to happen in scriptwriters' minds, she leaves the theater one evening and is mistakenly thought to be a prostitute. To avoid being arrested, she manages to get into the apartment of Spanish concert pianist Quinn. Next day, Quinn is arrested (mistakenly again) for having murdered a pawnbroker the night before. Wright is his alibi but he doesn't know her name or how to get in touch with her. The police believe Quinn enough to make an attempt to find Wright. Milland locates Wright and says the heck with his career, he loves her and wants to marry her. As soon as their betrothal is announced, Wright's photograph is published in the newspaper and Quinn tells the cops that she is his alibi. When they question her, Wright denies knowing Quinn or ever having spent a night in his apartment because she fears that kind of scandal might cause the end of her marriage to Milland. Quinn is brought to trial and it looks bad for him until Wright, torn by guilt, shows up in court for the denouement. She tells the court that she did, in fact, stay that night with Quinn. He is freed but the resultant brouhaha causes Milland to resign his position. However, he believes Wright's story and is determined to remain at her side. If there is any justice in this world, we are left with the feeling that her selfless gesture will bear fruit and she and Milland will live happily ever after. A good cast is hampered by a listless script and even more lethargic direction. One side note, Lilian Fontaine is the mother of Olivia de Havilland and Joan Fontaine.

p, Karl Tunberg; d, Lewis Allen; w, Tunberg (based on a story by Ladislas Fodor); ph, John F, Seitz; m, Victor Young; ed, Duncan Mansfield; art d, Hans Dreier, Franz Bachelin; set d, Sam Comer, James M. Walters; spec eff, Farciot Edouart; ch, Billy Daniel, Josephine Earl; m/l, "Picadilly Lily," Jay Livingston, Ray Evans.

Drama (PR:A MPAA:NR)

IMPERIAL VENUS**
(1963, Ital./Fr.) 140m Royal-Cineriz-S.N.E.-Gaumont-France Cinema/Cineriz c (VENERE IMPERIALE)

Gina Lollobrigida *(Paolina)*, Stephen Boyd *(Jules de Canouville)*, Gabrielle Ferzetti *(Freron)*, Raymond Pellegrin *(Napoleon)*, Micheline Presle *(Josephine)*, Massimo Girotti *(Leclerc)*, Giulio Bosetti *(Camillo Borghese)*, Gianni Santuccio *(Canova)*.

A traditional French picture which details the life of Napoleon's nymphomaniac sister Paolina. It's all done in a very grandiose manner, which was meant to please the French and Italian audiences, who had no other choice in films of the 1960s but the New Wave. The picture was made in English, side-by-side with the Franco-Italian version.

d, Jean Delannoy; w, Delannoy, Jean Aurenche, R.M. Arlaud, Leonardo Benvenut, Piero de Bernardi (English dialogue, John Michael Hayes); ph, Gabor Pogany (Technicolor); m, Angelo Lavagnino.

Historical Drama (PR:A MPAA:NR)

IMPERSONATOR, THE** (1962, Brit.) 64m Herald/Continental bw

John Crawford *(Jimmy Bradford)*, Jane Griffiths *(Ann Loring)*, Patricia Burke *(Mrs. Lloyd)*, John Salew *(Harry Walker)*, John Dare *(Tommy Lloyd)*, Yvonne Ball *(Principal Boy)*, John Arnatt *(Police Inspector)*, Edmund Glover.

Crawford is cast as a U.S. airman stationed in England, who becomes the chief suspect in the murders of a number of local women. He tries to disarm suspicion by being hospitable, even inviting a schoolteacher out for an evening. Another murder occurs, however, and the locals become convinced of his guilt. It turns out that the real killer is actually a female impersonator, leaving the road open for romance between Crawford and the teacher. A taut-told mystery that keeps rolling right along to the surprise ending.

p, Anthony Perry; d, Alfred Shaughnessy; w, Shaughnessy, Kenneth Cavender; ph, John Coquillon; m, De Wolfe; ed, John Bloom; art d, Jack Maxsted.

Mystery (PR:C MPAA:NR)

IMPORTANCE OF BEING EARNEST, THE****
(1952, Brit.) 95m Two Cities-Javelin British Film Makers-Asquith/RANK c

Michael Redgrave *(Jack Worthing)*, Michael Denison *(Algernon Moncrieff)*, Edith Evans *(Lady Bracknell)*, Joan Greenwood *(Gwendolen Fairfax)*, Dorothy Tutin *(Cecily Cardew)*, Margaret Rutherford *(Miss Prism)*, Miles Malleson *(Canon Chasuble)*, Richard Wattis *(Seton)*, Aubrey Mather *(Merriman)*, Walter Hudd *(Lane)*, Ivor Barnard.

Oscar Wilde wrote "Ignorance is like a delicate, exotic fruit. Touch it and the bloom is gone." The same could be said for his wittiest play which took 57 years to get to the screen but was well worth the wait. Director-writer Asquith made no pretense of doing anything but photographing a play and begins the film by having a couple enter a stage box and sit down for the curtain's rising. Then it's pell-mell into the frothy story of manners and morals that Wilde wrote in the late 1890s. Stylish, sunny, and as nonsensical as any work can be (at least, on the surface), THE IMPORTANCE OF BEING EARNEST takes great potshots at the pretentious people of the era and cloaks it in badinage containing some of Wilde's very best epigrams and bon mots. Redgrave is a wealthy bachelor and his best friend is Denison, who is poor as a church mouse but lives on credit with Hudd as his long-suffering butler whose main job it seems is convincing the wine merchant that Denison will eventually pay the bill. Redgrave is rather mysterious about where he lives in the country and keeps that from Denison. While in town, he resides at The Albany, a very proper address, but Denison is desperate to know the truth about where Redgrave goes when he's not in London. Redgrave is in love with Denison's cousin, Greenwood. We learn that Redgrave uses the name of Jack when in his country home where his ward, Tutin, lives and is studying under the tutelage of Rutherford, a spinster who specializes in taking care of young people. Rutherford has her bun set on Malleson, the local vicar, but theirs is a Victorian love, fraught with double entendres (of a nonsexual kind). Denison learns of Redgrave's ward, presents himself at the country home as Redgrave's fictitious brother, Earnest. Redgrave employs the guise of having to bail his "brother" out of trouble every time he wants to go to the city. Tutin, having been brought up with wild tales of this fictitious man, falls instantly in love with Denison. Greenwood, who lives in the city, thinks that Redgrave is really named Earnest (a name she dearly loves and would never marry anyone without that name) and Tutin also thinks that Denison's name is Earnest, a name she also admires. Redgrave arrives at his country home dressed in mourning. He thinks it's about time he got rid of the Earnest character and he is appalled to find Denison already at the house masquerading as the young rakehell. When both women think they are engaged to the same man, they play one of the most hysterical scenes in motion pictures as Greenwood and Tutin have tea together and Tutin deliberately puts several sugar cubes into Greenwood's cup and hands her a large slab of cake, just after Greenwood has told her that cake is out and that "the best people only have bread and butter these days." Edith Evans, Greenwood's mother and Denison's aunt, won't hear of Redgrave and Greenwood being together and attempts to put a stop to it in another funny scene where she enquires about Redgrave's qualifications and wealth. "Do you smoke?" she says. "Yes, I do," replies Redgrave. "Good," answers Evans. "A man should have an occupation of some sort." When Evans learns that Denison is enamored by Tutin, she asks that Redgrave give his permission to let her wed the young man. But Redgrave won't do that unless Evans gives *her* permission for him to marry Greenwood. It's a stalemate until Evans recognizes Rutherford as the governess who lost Denison's brother many, many years ago. Rutherford admits that she'd written a book and put it in one bag while she had the child in another and, by mistake, she switched the bags and the child was left at the railway station. Since we discovered earlier that Redgrave had been found in a railway station and adopted by a rich man who provided him with his wealth (as well as the job of supervising Tutin, the late benefactor's niece) we are not surprised when Redgrave shows Rutherford the large handbag and it is identified as the very one the woman was carrying when she made the unfortunate switch. So Denison and Redgrave are actually brothers! Now, the question is. . .what was Denison's Christian name? They look up the name of his father in a book of army officers and discover that his name was Earnest, and so Redgrave, as is the usual custom, had been named after his father. The film ends with Denison and Tutin in each other's arms as well as Redgrave in Greenwood's. Even Rutherford and Malleson are united. The last line of the play is Redgrave's comment that "I now know the vital importance of being earnest." The play was based on a pun and Wilde took it to the limit. Asquith was true to the original and made only the most minor alterations. It's a warhorse of a story and there isn't a theater anywhere that hasn't done it at least once. This film more than does it justice. A delight from start to finish despite not being sure if it's a movie or a filmed play. If they had made a decision to take it all the way cinematically and get some visuality in the picture, this would have been a major screen classic. As it is, THE IMPORTANCE OF BEING EARNEST is as close to flawless as you can get.

p, Teddy Baird; d&w, Anthony Asquith (based on the play by Oscar Wilde); ph, Desmond Dickinson (Technicolor); m, Benjamin Frankel; ed, John D. Guthridge; art d, Carmen Dillon; cos, Beatrice Dawson.

Comedy **(PR:A MPAA:NR)**

IMPORTANT MAN, THE***

(1961, Mex.) 100m Lopert-Azteca/UA bw (ANIMAS TRUJANO)

Toshiro Mifune *(Animas Trujano)*, Columba Dominguez *(His Wife)*, Pepito Romay *(His Son)*, Flor Silvestre *(Catania)*, Antonio Aguilar *(Tadeo)*, Eduardo Fajardo, Guillermina Jimenez, Amado Zumaya, Titina Romay, Luis Aragon, Jose Chavez.

Made interesting by the arresting performance of Japan's internationally recognized hero, Mifune, THE IMPORTANT MAN is a Mexican drama about Mifune's dream to be elected mayor and be respected by the community. However, he is a drunken, vulgar, whore-loving gambler who can't even gain the respect of his family. He manages to buy the election, but is angered and rejected when he finds he has gained no respect at all. He returns to his old ways, finally murdering his favorite prostitute and then confessing to the crime.

p&d, Ismael Rodriguez; w, Rodriguez, Vincent Orona, Jr. (based on the novel *La Mayordomia* by Rogelio Barriga Rivas); ph, Gabriel Figueroa (CinemaScope); m, Raul Lavista; ed, Jorge Bustos, Pedro del Rey; art d, Edward Fitzgerald, Pablo Galvan.

Drama **PR:O MPAA:NR)**

IMPORTANT WITNESS, THE** (1933) 60m Tower bw

Noel Francis, Donald Dillaway, Dorothy Burgess, Noel Madison, Sarah Padden, Franklin Pangborn, Robert Ellis, Ben Hendricks, Jr., Harry Myers, Ethel Wales, Charles Delaney.

A stenographer witnesses a gangland murder and is kidnaped by the killers. The mob boss succumbs to her charms and when she gains his confidence, she escapes. She boards a bus to Los Angeles where she intends to tell all and free her girl friend from suspicion of the murder. The gang is in hot pursuit of the woman, who is forced to drive the bus herself for the last leg of the journey, but she finally makes it. Good minor piece, with Pangborn providing some funny comedy capers.

d, Sam Newfield; w, Douglas Doty, Leslie Simmonds (based on the story by Gordon Morris); ph, Harry Forbes; ed, Al Clark; art d, Ralph De Lacey.

Crime **(PR:A MPAA:NR)**

IMPOSSIBLE LOVER (SEE: HUDDLE, 1932)

IMPOSSIBLE OBJECT***

(1973, Fr.) 110m Franco-London-Euro International/Valoria c (AKA: STORY OF A LOVE STORY)

Alan Bates *(Harry)*, Dominique Sanda *(Nathalie)*, Evans Evans *(Elizabeth)*, Lea Massari *(Woman)*, Michael Auclair *(Georges)*, Laurence De Monaghan *(Cleo)*.

An engaging film made in France by American director Frankenheimer (SECONDS) which is chiefly concerned with the boundaries between the real and the imaginary. Bates is a writer living in a country home with his American wife and children. He meets the sensual Sanda and has an affair with her—or is it a product of his writer's imagination? Wonderful photography and score by Claude Renoir and Michel Legrand, respectively. A gracefully done semi-phantasy tale in English.

d, John Frankenheimer; w, Nicolas Mosley; ph, Claude Renoir (Eastmancolor); m, Michel Legrand; ed, Albert Jurgenson; art d, Alexandre Trauner.

Drama **(PR:C–O MPAA:NR)**

IMPOSSIBLE ON SATURDAY**

(1966, Fr./Israel) 116m Athos-Meroz/Magna bw (PAS QUESTION LE SAMEDI; RAQ LO B'SHABBAT)

Robert Hirsch *(Chaim Silbershatz/Freddie/Frieda/Hans/Carlo/Zvi/Leon/McLeaf)*, Dahlia Friedland *(Debrah, Tulipman's Daughter)*, Misha Asherov *(Yankel Silbershatz)*, Teddy Bilis *(Tulipman, Mayor of Jerusalem)*, Geula Noni *(Aviva)*, Albert Hizkia *(Meier)*, Yona Levi *(Sergeant)*, Rina Ganor, Yael Aviv, Jacob Bodo, Avner Hezkiyahu.

Hirsch is challenged by a number of roles in this interesting French-Israeli coproduction. He plays an orchestra conductor who is near death, his one legitimate son, and his five illegitimate sons (one being a transvestite who goes under two different names). He plans to will his fortune to Jerusalem, but after being visited by the ghost of his father he changes the will. The ghost tells him that the only way he will be redeemed for his sins is to marry his children off to Israeli women before the Sabbath. He calls his sons together and explains to them that they will receive his money if they marry, but one of them refuses and Jerusalem is again made the legal heir.

p, Jacques Steiner; d, Alex Joffe; w, Jean Ferry, Pierre Levy-Corti, Shabatai-Tevet, Joffe (based on a story by Shabatai-Tevet, Jacques Steiner); ph, Jean Bourgoin; m, Sacha Argov; ed, Eric Pluet; md, Jacques Metehen; set d, Joseph Carl; cos, Gina Rosenbach, Maison Repetto; makeup, Serge Groffe.

Fantasy/Comedy **(PR:A MPAA:NR)**

IMPOSSIBLE YEARS, THE*** ½** (1968) 97m Marten/MGM c

David Niven *(Jonathan Kingsley)*, Lola Albright *(Alice Kingsley)*, Chad Everett *(Richard Merrick)*, Ozzie Nelson *(Dr. Herbert Fleischer)*, Cristina Ferrare *(Linda Kingsley)*, Jeff Cooper *(Bartholomew Smuts)*, John Harding *(Dean Harvey Rockwell)*, Rich Chalet *(Freddie Fleischer)*, Mike McGreevey *(Andy McClaine)*, Don Beddoe *(Dr. Elliot Fish)*, Darleen Carr *(Abbey Kingsley)*, Louise Lorimer *(Mrs. Celia Fish)*, Karen Norris *(Mrs. Rockwell)*, Susan French *(Miss Hammer)*, Trudi Ames *(Francine)*, J. Edward McKinley *(Dr. Pepperell)*, Ned Wertimer *(Dr. Bodey)*.

A charming adaptation of the play by Bob Fisher and Arthur Marx (Groucho's son) that ran in 1965 on Broadway. The title refers to those years when a child goes from puberty to adulthood and although we've seen this generation gap story before (and will see it many times in the future) it is well handled by the moviemakers and provides a large chunk of wit, peppered by insights. Niven is a psychiatrist working at a university. His speciality is teenage problems and he is stunned to learn that his teenage daughter, Ferrare, has been arrested for protesting on campus. This is anathema so Niven attempts to straighten Ferrare out. The first thing he does is suggest that she make some new friends. She does this and soon the house is chock-full of kids, all making so much noise that his beloved peace and quiet is jangled and he can't work on his latest research, something that will never do in the academic world of "publish or perish." He needs some time for himself so he lets Ferrare sail to Catalina Island with a group of her friends. Niven and wife Albright are somewhat surprised by the return of Ferrare, who seems to have matured quite a bit over a weekend. Ferrare now admits that she married a man on Catalina. She won't tell them the name of her husband because they are threatening to have it annulled. Niven begins questioning all of her young male friends but they deny being the husband. Ferrare is so embarrassed by this that she runs away, with Niven racing after her on a motorcycle. The chase ends on campus where Niven is dumped off the bike and lands at the feet of the members of the school board, who have just finished appointing him as the chief of the new psychiatric facility. Niven is relieved to learn that Ferrare has not married one of the slack-jawed youths, instead, it was his colleague, Everett. That done, it all seems to be working itself out when the youngest daughter, Carr, enters and announces that she has a new boy friend. Niven and Albright realize then that the impossible years still have some time left to go. It is somewhat dated (hippies and protests, etc.) but the woes of raising teenage daughters have been similar since the Stone Age and this is as good a depiction of those problems as any film you may see. Ferrare left movies to become the wife of auto magnate John De Lorean, by whom she had two children before they divorced. The excellent music was by Don Costa, one of Sinatra's favorite arrangers. For years, Costa lived in New City, New York, on a street called South Mountain, and pop music fans will recognize that name as Costa's publishing firm was called "South Mountain Music." He was a rare arranger in that he did all of his writing and scoring on guitar, rather than keyboards. The title song was written by the singing group The Tokens, and sung by another group, The Cowsills. The Tokens named themselves that because they were one of the early black groups in the business and thought that by dubbing themselves Tokens they were making a wry comment about racism in the music industry.

p, Lawrence Weingarten; d, Michael Gordon; w, George Wells (based on the play by Bob Fisher, Arthur Marx); ph, William H. Daniels (Panavision, Metrocolor); m, Don Costa; ed, James E. Newcom; art d, George W. Davis, Preston Ames; set d, Henry Grace, Hugh Hunt; hairstyles, Sydney Guilaroff; m/l, "The Impossible Years," The Tokens (sung by The Cowsills); makeup, William Tuttle.

Comedy **(PR:A MPAA:G)**

IMPOSTER, THE1/2** (1944) 95m UNIV bw (AKA: STRANGE CONFESSION)

Jean Gabin *(Clement)*, Richard Whorf *(Lt. Varenne)*, Allyn Joslyn *(Bouteau)*, Ellen Drew *(Yvonne)*, Peter Van Eyck *(Hafner)*, *Ralph Morgan (Col. De Bolvan)*, Eddie Quillan *(Cochery)*, John Qualen *(Monge)*, Dennis Moore *(Lafarge)*, Milburn Stone *(Clauzel)*, John Philliber *(Mortourart)*, Charles McGraw *(Menessier)*, Otho Gaines *(Matown)*, John Forrest *(Free French Corporal)*, Fritz Leiber *(Priest)*, Ian Wolfe *(Sergeant Clerk)*, William B. Davidson *(Adjutant)*, Frank Wilcox *(Prosecutor)*, Warren Ashe *(Officer)*, Peter Cookson *(Soldier)*, Leigh Whipper *(Toba)*, Ernest Whitman *(Ekopa)*, Grandon Rhodes *(Captain)*, George Irving *(Prosecutor)*.

After criminal Gabin is saved from the guillotine by a Nazi air raid, he assumes the identity of a dead French soldier and enlists in the French army in WW II. He starts life anew, bravely launching an attack on an Italian desert base. He receives a medal, but under his assumed name. When he finally confesses, he returns to the ranks, later saving his battalion from defeat. Duvivier, even while directing in Hollywood, was able to make Gabin into the same sort of heroic figure that so wonderfully colored his earlier PEPE LE MOKO. A slow-mover but effective which reminds one of UNCERTAIN GLORY.

p&d, Julien Duvivier; w, Duvivier, Marc Connelly, Lynn Starling, Stephen Longstreet; ph, Paul Ivano; m, Dimitri Tiomkin; ed, Paul Landres; md, Tiomkin; art d, John B. Goodman, Eugene Lourie; spec eff, John P. Fulton.

War Drama **(PR:A MPAA:NR)**

IMPOSTORS* (1979) 110m First Run c

Charles Ludlam *(Chuckie)*, Michael Burg *(Mikey)*, Peter Evans *(Peter)*, Lina Todd *(Gina)*, Ellen McElduff *(Tina)*, Randy Danson *(Stephanie)*, Kevin Wade, Shelley Desai, John Brockmeyer, Betty James.

A quirky low-budget picture about a pair of potentially murderous vaudevillians, their lesbian assistant, and a rich young man. Shot in and around New York's SoHo, the film relies on a deadpan style which tries too hard to have camp value.

p,d&w, Mark Rappaport; ph, Fred Murphy; ed, Rappaport, Meri Weingarten; set d, Bob Edmonds.

Comedy **(PR:O MPAA:NR)**

IMPRESSIVE FOOTMAN, THE (SEE: WOMAN IN CHAINS, 1932)

"IMP"PROBABLE MR. WEE GEE, THE* (1966) 75m American Film c

Dick Richards, Hella Grondahl, "Red" Kane, Sonia Silver, Ray Christian, Ines Hallendal, Mary Rooney, Roni Nins, Reuben Guberman *(Wee Gee Voice)*.

This film is as silly as its title. Mr. Wee Gee is a photographer who wants nothing more than to fall in love with a gorgeous woman whom he can control. First he falls in love with a mannequin, then with a ghost; finally, he chases a real woman around Paris. The police follow him to the top of the Eiffel Tower where their pursuit is frozen by the view of a bathing woman and her disrobed neighbors. Keeping in mind the height of the Eiffel Tower, the pursuers must have rather keen vision.

p,d&w, Sherman Price.

Comedy **(PR:A MPAA:NR)**

IMPROPER CHANNELS** (1981, Can.) 92m Paragon/Rank-Crown International c

Alan Arkin *(Jeffrey)*, Mariette Hartley *(Diana)*, Monica Parker *(Gloria)*, Harry Ditson *(Harold)*, Sarah Stevens *(Nancy)*, Danny Higham *(Jack)*, Leslie Yeo *(Fred)*, Richard Farrell *(Fraser)*, Ruth Springford *(Mrs. Wharton)*, Martin Yan *(Hu)*, Tony Rosato *(Dr. Arpenthaler)*, Philip Akin *(Cop)*, Harvey Atkin *(Sergeant)*, Richard Blackburn *(Fraser's Assistant)*, Benjamin Gordon, Kate Lynch, Jane Mallett, Jessica Booker, Ken Camroux, Les Carlson, Eugene Clark, Eric Clavering, Gillie Fenwick, Vanya Frank, Paul Emile Frappier, Angelo Fusco, Joyce Gordon, Luba Goy, Lynda Mason Green, Tim Henry, Alfred Humphreys, Sandy Kovack, Sylvia Llewellyn, David Main, Al Maini, Kate McDonald, Marianne McIsaac, Harry McWilliams, Patrick Patterson, Wayne Robson, Patrick Rose, Stephanie Shouldus, Ted Turner, Linda Very, Mary Charlotte Wilcox, Elias Zarou.

Made in 1979, this generally unfunny picture, co-written by Adam Arkin, stars dad Alan as a frustrated father, who must fight a mistaken computer system that insists he is a child beater. He loses custody of his 5-year-old daughter and has to overcome a silly series of events to get her back.

p, Alfred Pariser, Morrie Ruvinsky; d, Eric Till; w, Ruvinsky, Ian Sutherland, Adam Arkin (based on a story by Ruvinsky); ph, Anthony Richmond (Panavision); m, Micky Erbe, Maribeth Solomon; ed, Thom Noble; art d, Ninkey Dalton, Charles Dunlop.

Comedy **Cas.** **(PR:C MPAA:PG)**

IMPROPER DUCHESS, THE*1/2 (1936, Brit.) 78m City/GFD bw

Yvonne Arnaud *(Duchess of Tann)*, Hugh Wakefield *(King of Poldavia)*, Wilfred Caithness *(Rev. Adam McAdam)*, Arthur Finn *(Sen. Corcoran)*, Gerald Barry *(Baron Kamp)*, Finlay Currie *(Milton Lee)*, James Carew *(Montgomery Curtis)*, Annie Esmond *(Baroness Kamp)*, Ben Welden *(Macabe)*, Andreas Malandrinos *(Mr. Garcia)*, Cynthia Stock *(Gunning)*, Honorine Catto *(Miss Cutting)*, Davis Smith-Dorrien *(Capt. Olven)*, Fleix Aylmer *(Count Seidel)*.

Based on a British play set in Washington D.C., this picture stars Arnaud as a Duchess who is pitted against a group of oil executives in an attempt to get a loan. A few forced laughs, that's all.

p, Maurice Browne; d, Harry Hughes; w, Hughes, Vernon Harris (based on a play by James B. Fagan); ph, Ronald Neame.

Comedy **(PR:A MPAA:NR)**

IMPULSE1/2** (1955, Brit.) 80m Tempean/Eros bw

Arthur Kennedy *(Alan Curtis)*, Constance Smith *(Lila)*, Joy Shelton *(Elizabeth Curtis)*, Jack Allen *(Freddie)*, James Carney *(Jack Forrester)*, Cyril Chamberlain *(Gray)*, Cameron Hall *(Joe)*, Jean St. Clair, Bruce Beeby.

After his wife Shelton goes off on holiday, Kennedy takes the opportunity to have an illicit affair with Smith, a local nightclub songstress. She tells him that her brother is in trouble because of some stolen diamonds but it develops that Smith will say just about anything to obtain the diamonds herself. She fools Kennedy into thinking he killed a man after he buys them both tickets out of the country. Kennedy decides to stay and face the authorities, causing Smith to remain as well so his name can be cleared. This is nothing out of the ordinary as far as thrillers go, though a good sense of suspense is maintained with enough plot twists to hold interest.

p, Robert S. Baker, Monty Berman; d, Charles de la Tour, Cy Endfield; w, Lawrence Huntingdon, Jonathan Roach [Endfield]; ph, Jonah Jones.

Crime/Suspense **(PR:C MPAA:NR)**

IMPULSE zero (1975) 89m Conqueror-Camelot c (AKA: WANT A RIDE, LITTLE GIRL?)

William Shatner, Ruth Roman, Harold Sakata, Kim Nicholas, Jennifer Bishop, James Dobbs, Marcie Knight.

Shatner must have gotten bit by an alien bug up there on the Starship Enterprise. Why else would he appear in this grade Z, no-budget horror film? He plays a maniacal child murderer who is possessed by evil demons. The only thing that could have possessed the makers of this film was the idea of a quick buck.

p, Socrates Ballis; d, William Grefe; w, Tony Crechales; ph, (Technicolor).

Crime **Cas.** **(PR:O MPAA:PG)**

IN (SEE: HIGH, 1969, Can.)

IN A LONELY PLACE***** (1950) 94m Santana/COL bw

Humphrey Bogart *(Dixon Steele)*, Gloria Grahame *(Laurel Gray)*, Frank Lovejoy *(Brub Nicolai)*, Carl Benton Reid *(Capt. Lochner)*, Art Smith *(Mel Lippman)*, Jeff Donnell *(Sylvia Nicolai)*, Martha Stewart *(Mildred Atkinson)*, Robert Warwick *(Charlie Waterman)*, Morris Ankrum *(Lloyd Barnes)*, William Ching *(Ted Barton)*, Steven Geray *(Paul)*, Hadda Brooks *(Singer)*, Alice Talton *(Frances Randolph)*, Jack Reynolds *(Henry Kesler)*, Ruth Warren *(Effie)*, Ruth Gillette *(Martha)*, Guy Beach *(Swan)*, Lewis Howard *(Junior)*, Mike Romanoff *(Himself)*, Arno Frey *(Joe)*, Pat Barton *(2nd Hatcheck Girl)*, Cosmo Sardo *(Bartender)*, Don Hanin *(Young Driver)*, George Davis *(Waiter)*, Billy Gray *(Young Boy)*, Melinda Erickson *(Tough Girl)*, Jack Jahries *(Officer)*, David Bond *(Dr. Richards)*, Myron Healey *(Post Office Clerk)*, Robert Lowell *(Airline Clerk)*, Tony Layng, Robert Davis, Laura K. Brooks, Jack Santoro, Frank Marlowe, Evelyn Underwood, Hazel Boyne, Mike Lally, John Mitchum, Joy Hallward, Allen Pinson, Oliver Cross, June Vincent, Charles Cane.

Superb film noir entry brilliantly directed by the gifted Ray has Bogart as a talented but volatile Hollywood screenwriter. Because of his heavy drinking and truculent nature, Bogart is almost persona non grata with the film studios but his dogged, devoted agent, Smith, manages to get him a writing assignment, adapting a celebrated soap opera novel for the screen. They meet in a Hollywood bar-restaurant (thinly disguised as Chasen's) where Bogart argues with Ankrum, the director of the proposed film, accusing him of making the same film over and over again. His one friend in the bar is a broken down actor, Warwick, and when a strutting, bragging producer, Howard (thinly disguised as Carl Laemmle, Jr.), insults the actor, Bogart knocks Howard about and has to be restrained. A tolerant host, Geray, asks Bogart to calm down and he does, simmering over a drink. Smith urges him to go home and read the novel he must adapt but Bogart knows it's a potboiler and is reluctant. Then the hatcheck girl at the club, Stewart, who has read and loves the novel, offers to tell the tale to Bogart. He takes her home to his bungalow (in a complex that smacks of the famous Garden of Allah, owned and operated by Ali Nazimova, a haven for actors and talented writers such as Robert Benchley and F. Scott Fitzgerald). Watching Bogart and Stewart enter the bungalow is lovely Grahame, a new neighbor. As Stewart rattles on about the story, Bogart slips into his bathrobe, pours himself a drink, and tries to calm Stewart down when she begins enacting scenes from the novel that cause her to go into loud histrionics, which brings Grahame to her upstairs window again to look across the courtyard and see the couple through open windows. Finally, Bogart has had enough. He's tired, he explains. He gives Stewart cab fare and sends her home. Her viciously disfigured body is found the next day and Bogart, thought to be the last person to see her alive, is brought in for questioning before Beverly Hills police captain Reid. With Reid is Lovejoy, an old friend of Bogart's who doesn't for a minute believe that Bogart had anything to do with Stewart's death and says so to Reid. Grahame is also called in and she tells police that the hatcheck girl left Bogart's place alone, providing the screenwriter with a rock-hard alibi. The two are drawn to each other and fall deeply in love. Bogart undertakes to write the script while Grahame types it, encouraging him along with his mother-hen agent Smith, to complete the work. Lovejoy invites Bogart and Grahame to a beach party and there Bogart explodes when he feels his old friend Lovejoy is subtly probing for information on the Stewart killing, implying he might have had something to do with the murder. He jumps in his convertible, Grahame getting in with him, and races along the beach road, driving wildly. A hot rod car almost crashes into Bogart's and when the young driver gets out and calls him a name Bogart goes crazy, punching the youth unconscious. He picks up a rock and is only stopped from bashing in the youth's head when Grahame cries out. Bogart's violence and his jealous nature cause Grahame to become apprehensive. Continuing police queries and remarks about Bogart from her friends create doubts so that Grahame begins to pull away from her lover. Bogart himself does little to dissuade authorities that he wasn't involved in the killing. In one terrifying moment, after dinner with Lovejoy and his wife Donnell, Bogart graphically demonstrates how easily it would have been for an assailant to kill Stewart. Grahame's suspicions about Bogart mount to the point where, on the eve of their impending wedding, she prepares to leave him, flying secretly to New York. He is by now suspicious and takes a phone call for Grahame from the airline, a call to say that her ticket is ready. The betrayal enrages Bogart; he attacks Grahame, choking her. But a killer Bogart is not and he pulls up short, releasing Grahame and going back to his own bungalow. Grahame then gets a call from Reid who tells her that Stewart's boy friend, Ching, has confessed to killing the hatcheck girl. The call has come tragically late. Bogart's display of violence and Grahame's distrust have ruined the relationship. At the film's end, Grahame watches Bogart slowly go back to his lonely place, quoting a line from his manuscript: "I was born when you kissed me. I died when you left me. I lived a few weeks while you loved me." Both Bogart and Grahame are fragile romantics as shown by the perceptive Ray who briefly overcome their jaded views of the world to reveal themselves to each other, but their acquired cynicism eventually destroys the tender moments they have shared. There are priceless scenes in the film, one where Bogart explains to Grahame that true love is exactly what they are doing at the moment, she rubbing sleep from her eyes, he awkwardly trying to cut a grapefruit for their breakfast, another when they quietly talk in a lounge and listen to singer Hadda Brooks aptly sing "I Hadn't Anyone 'Till You." But a tidal wave of events washes it all away, almost as if these moments never existed. Ray's helmsmanship here is superb as he runs the story quickly to a conclusion, dwelling upon loving and frightening scenes with the skilled balance of a master juggler, keeping the viewer doubting and believing in Bogart from scene to scene. Guffey's lensing is also first-rate, a mixture of contrasting shadow and light perfectly fitting the changing moods of the characters. The entire cast is excellent, with Bogart giving an electrifying portrait of a man whose insides bubble like the bowels of a volcano and Grahame, never more beautiful, is captivating as a woman who has been kept too many times and now has one last chance for real love. IN A LONELY PLACE is the epitome of star-crossed lovers incapable of escaping environment and circumstances no matter how hard they try. It is an off-beat film noir entry but one of the most memorable films of the genre, handled intelligently and with precision and care. This is one of Ray's finest efforts, really his film more than Bogart's, following on the heels of KNOCK ON ANY DOOR, where Ray also directed Bogart in a Santana Production, a company owned by Bogart. The one true friend Bogart has in this film, the broken-down actor, Warwick, ironically plays a role that was true to life. When Bogart was struggling with his youthful stage career, Warwick was one of the more successful actors who helped him get parts and encouraged him to keep his hand in when Bogart thought of quitting acting.

p, Robert Lord, Henry S. Kesler; d, Nicholas Ray; w, Andrew Solt (based on a story by Edmund H. North, based on the novel by Dorothy B. Hughes); ph, Burnett Guffey; m, George Antheil; ed, Viola Lawrence; md, Morris W. Stoloff; art d, Robert Peterson; set d, William Kiernan; cos, Jean Louis; makeup, Clay Campbell; tech adv, Rodney Amateau.

Drama **(PR:C MPAA:NR)**

IN A MONASTERY GARDEN** (1935) 72m Twickenham-S&G/AP&D bw

John Stuart *(Michael Ferrier)*, Hugh Williams *(Paul Ferrier)*, Alan Napier *(Count Romano)*, Dino Galvani *(Cesare Bonelli)*, Frank Pettingell *(Bertholdi)*, Humberstone Wright *(The Abbot)*, Gina Malo *(Nina)*, Joan Maude *(Roma Romano)*.

Stuart and Williams are cast as brothers (though they bear no resemblance to one another) who are both enamoured of the same gal. The problem is that she's already engaged to a wealthy count. After a murder that sends one brother to jail, the other gets the girl. He accomplishes this by impressing her with musical compositions he has stolen from the imprisoned brother. The works are considered those of a genius, and, not only does he get the gal, but he gains great fame. The other brother has, in the meantime, joined a monastery and refuses to give up his vows for love or fame.

p, Julius Hagen; d, Maurice Elvey; w, H. Fowler Mear, Michael Barringer (based on a story by Mear); ph, Basil Emmott; ed, Lister Laurence.

Drama **(PR:A MPAA:NR)**

IN A SECRET GARDEN (SEE: OF LOVE AND DESIRE, 1963)

IN A YEAR OF THIRTEEN MOONS**

(1980, Ger.) 129m Tango/New Yorker c (IN EINEM JAHR MIT 13 MONDEN)

Volker Spengler *(Elvira Weishaupt)*, Ingrid Caven *(Red Zora)*, Gottfried John *(Anton Saitz)*, Elisabeth Trissenaar *(Irene)*, Eva Mattes *(Marie-Ann)*, Gunter Kaufmann *(J. Smolik, Chauffeur)*, Lilo Pempeit *(Sister Gudrun)*, Isolde Barth *(Sybille)*, Karl Schedit *(Christoph Hacker)*, Walter Bockmayer *(Seelenfrieda)*, Bob Dorsey *(Man in Street)*, Ursula Lillig *(Cleaning Woman)*, Gunther Holzapfel *(H.H. Brei)*, Janoz Bermez *(Oskar Pleitgen)*, Gerhard Zwerenz *(Burghard Hauer, the Author)*, Peter Kollek *(Drunk)*.

A revealing film about a man (Spengler) who has a sex-change operation in order to please a man he loves. Her world is one of loneliness and a desire to be loved but she is jilted by a live-in male lover, fails to communicate with her wife and daughter, and has no success in winning over the man that she changed for, John. Instead, he prefers to practice his soccer technique, mimic Jerry Lewis dance routines, and sleep with Caven, a prostitute friend of Spengler's. Her rejection grows increasingly for five days until she finally kills herself. The subject no doubt is as bizarre as Fassbinder himself was, cluing us into the darker side of his private life. The film was completed in an intense 25 days with Fassbinder directing, writing, photographing, editing, and working as art director. Only two months before production began, Armin Meier, a lover of Fassbinder's, killed himself (on Fassbinder's birthday) leading some to believe that IN A YEAR OF 13 MOONS is an attempt by the director to absolve himself of his guilt. A provocative film for those already familiar with Fassbinder. The uninitiated, however, will be dealt quite a shock especially during an extremely graphic slaughterhouse scene. (In German; English subtitles.)

d,w&ph, Rainer Werner Fassbinder; m, Peer Raben; ed, Fassbinder; prod d, Franz Vacek; art d, Fassbinder; m/l, "Frankie Teardrop," Suicide, "A Song for Europe," Roxy Music.

Drama **(PR:O MPAA:NR)**

IN CALIENTE 1/2** (1935) 84m FN-WB/WB bw

Dolores Del Rio *(Rita Gomez)*, Pat O'Brien *(Larry MacArthur)*, Leo Carrillo *(Jose Gomez)*, Edward Everett Horton *(Harold Brandon)*, Glenda Farrell *(Clara)*, Phil Regan *(Pat Casey)*, Dorothy Dare *(Baby Blonde)*, Winifred Shaw *(Singer, "Woman in Red")*, Harry Holman *(Biggs)*, Herman Bing *(Mexican Florist)*, William B. Davidson *(Man)*, Luis Alberni *(Magistrate)*, Olive Jones *(Singer)*, John Hyams *(Bob, the Reporter)*, Henry De Silva *(Waiter)*, Milton Kibbee, Sam Appel *(Drivers)*, Chris Pin Martin, C. I. Dafau, Carlos Salazer, L.R. Felix *(Mexican Quartet)*, George Humbert *(Mexican Photographer)*, Soledad Jimenez *(Maid)*, Florence Fair *(Miss G—Larry's Secretary)*, James Donlan *(Swanson)*, Judy, Anne, Zeke and Pete Canova *(Musical Quartet)*, Sally & Tony Marco *(Dance Team)*.

O'Brien is a tough magazine editor who gives a thumbs-down review to Mexican dancer Del Rio, but before long he falls in love with her. Needless to say, the plot is thin. It's the Busby Berkeley dance routines, however, that make the film worthwhile. Musical numbers include "The Lady In Red," "To Call You My Own," "In Caliente" (Mort Dixon, Allie Wrubel), "Muchacha" (Al Dubin, Harry Warren).

d, Lloyd Bacon; w, Jerry Wald, Julius J. Epstein (based on the story "Caliente" by Ralph Block, Warren Duff); ph, Sol Polito, George Barnes; m, Leo F. Forbstein; ed, James Gibbons; ch, Busby Berkeley.

Musical **(PR:A MPAA:NR)**

IN CASE OF ADVERSITY (SEE: LOVE IS MY PROFESSION, 1959, Fr.)

IN CELEBRATION 1/2** (1975, Brit.) 131m American Film Theatre c

Alan Bates *(Andrew Shaw)*, James Bolam *(Colin Shaw)*, Brian Cox *(Steven Shaw)*, Constance Chapman *(Mrs. Shaw)*, Gabrielle Daye *(Mrs. Burnett)*, Bill Owen *(Mr. Shaw)*.

A sombre adaptation of an intense play, IN CELEBRATION was originally staged by Anderson, who came back to direct the picture using the original cast. It all takes place in 24 hours in the lives of a North England family. Coal miner Owen and his wife, Chapman, are celebrating their fortieth anniversary and their three sons, Bates, Bolam, and Cox, have come home for the gala fete. The boys have all been educated above their station in life, with Bates being an attorney, Cox a teacher and Bolam a successful automobile executive. Bates has decided to chuck the law and become an artist. Cox has been writing a book for many years and has just given up the idea. Bolam has embraced the material world and showers his poor parents with gifts. With Bates as the guide, they go back over several incidents in their lives and various revelations are made. They talk of the death of their brother, the first-born son, at the age of seven; of the attempted suicide of their mother; and of the possibility of homosexuality in Bates's life. Powerful and emotional, IN CELEBRATION is the peeling away of facades under Bates's unrelenting scalpel, as one skeleton after another is taken out of the closet, examined, and put back. Somewhat stagey and confined, and surely too long at 131 minutes.

p, Ely Landau; d, Lindsay Anderson; w, David Storey (based on his play); ph, Dick Bush (Cinevision); m, Christopher Gunning; ed, Russell Lloyd; art d, Alan Withy.

Drama **(PR:O MPAA:PG)**

IN COLD BLOOD* (1967) 134m Pax Enterprises/COL bw

Robert Blake *(Perry Smith)*, Scott Wilson *(Dick Hickock)*, John Forsythe *(Alvin Dewey)*, Paul Stewart *(Reporter)*, Gerald S. O'Loughlin *(Harold Nye)*, Jeff Corey *(Hickock's Father)*, John Gallaudet *(Roy Church)*, James Flavin *(Clarence Duntz)*, Charles McGraw *(Smith's Father)*, Jim Lantz *(Officer Rohleder)*, Will Geer *(Prosecuting Attorney)*, John McLiam *(Herbert Clutter)*, Ruth Storey *(Bonnie Clutter)*, Brenda C. Currin *(Nancy Clutter)*, Paul Hough *(Kenyon Clutter)*, Vaughn Taylor *("Good Samaritan")*, Duke Hobbie *(Young Reporter)*, Sheldon Allman *(Rev. Post)*, Sammy Thurman *(Mr. Smith)*, Sadie Truitt *(Herself)*, Myrtle Clare *(Herself)*, Teddy Eccles *(Young Hitchhiker)*, Raymond Hatton *(Elderly Hitchhiker)*, Mary-Linda Rapelye *(Susan Kidwell)*, Ronda Fultz *(Nancy's Friend)*, Al Christy *(Sheriff)*, Don Sollars *(Store Salesman)*, Harriet Levitt *(Mrs. Hartman)*, Stan Levitt *(Insurance Man)*.

This is a brutal filmic exercise which misshapes real events and people and presents a technically well-crafted production with a lie for a story. The mincing Manhattan literary celebrity Capote, whose writing career was in decline, seized upon the real-life mass murder of the Clutter family in Holcomb, Kansas, on November 15, 1959, by two psychopathic killers and turned the grisly tale into a bestseller by championing not the helpless victims but the murderers. Capote's shocking book superficially attempted to show the perpetrators of this senseless crime as mentally misguided, socially rejected, emotionally deprived members of society and, in this way, somehow find a rationale, if not a vindication, for the slaughter. In making the movie, director Brooks went beyond Capote, showing Blake and Wilson, killers of the Clutter family, as the *victims* of society and, subsequently, capital punishment. He first shows vagrants Blake and Wilson desperately fielding about for ways to make an illegal buck, having been cellmates in state prison. Wilson had learned from another inmate that the Clutters reportedly kept $10,000 in their farm home and they invade the home, terrorizing, then savagely slaughtering, the family, leaving with little loot since there was no $10,000 to be found. The killers are shown running to Mexico, then back to the U.S., leaving a trail of bad checks which federal agents follow until they apprehend the killers in Las Vegas. Brooks then spends half of his film displaying Blake and Wilson in the Kansas State Penitentiary at Lansing waiting to be hanged and emphasizing the brutality of the state in taking their lives on the gallows on April 14, 1965, after endless appeals, stays, and agonizing self-searching on the part of the culprits. The entire film is bathed in phony bathos for the criminals and sheds no tears for the murdered Clutters, a great disservice to humanity, justice, and morality. Blake and Wilson are automatons under the manipulative Brooks hand and here the director must take the responsibility of making a thoroughly irresponsible, wholly unacceptable film. It would have been better had he not used a real-life event here, but not much better, given Brooks' inexplicable penchant to champion bestial killers. There is simply no excuse for this film's existence, even as a blatant indulgence in violence for the sake of violence. Children will certainly be traumatized by this movie's excessive, almost glorified violence, and anyone with sensibilities should dismiss it as nothing more than bloody tabloid images transferred to the screen. Blake (real name Michael Gubitosi) was singled out by reviewers at the time of this film's release as a newcomer to the screen which was, of course, in error, since he had first appeared in Our Gang comedies for MGM in the 1930s, and later became a child star, playing Red Ryder's Indian sidekick, Little Beaver, in a popular B-western series produced by Republic. As an adult he concentrated on thug roles, chiefly in REVOLT IN THE BIG HOUSE, 1958, and THE PURPLE GANG, 1960.

p,d&w, Richard Brooks; ph, Conrad Hall (Panavision); m, Quincy Jones; ed, Peter Zinner; art d, Robert Boyle; set d, Jack Ahern; cos, Jack Martell; spec eff, Geza Gaspar; makeup, Gary Morris.

Crime Drama **Cas.** **(PR:O MPAA:R)**

IN DARKNESS WAITING (SEE: STRATEGY OF TERROR, 1969)

IN DER HOLLE IST NOCH PLATZ (SEE: THERE IS STILL ROOM IN HELL, 1963, Ger.)

IN EARLY ARIZONA** (1938) 53m COL bw

"Wild Bill" Elliott *(Gordon)*, Dorothy Gulliver *(Alice)*, Harry Woods *(Bull)*, Jack Ingram *(Marshal)*, Franklin Farnum *(Spike)*, Frank Ellis *(Ben)*, Art Davis *(Art)*, Charles King *(Kaintuck)*, Ed Cassidy *(Weldon)*, Charles "Slim" Whitaker *(Sheriff)*, Al Ferguson, Bud Osborne, Lester Dorr, Tom London, Kit Guard, Jack O'Shea, Frank Ball, Tex Palmer, Sherry Tansey, Dick Dorrell, Oscar Gahan, Jess Cavan, Symona Boniface, Buzz Barton.

A fictionalized account of Wyatt Earp's adventures in Tombstone, with Elliott (playing the Earplike lead) wanting to settle down after his Dodge City escapades. He is given a badge and dispenses with the outlaws in the name of justice.

p, Larry Darmour; d, Joseph Levering; w, Nate Gatzert; ph, James S. Brown, Jr.; ed, Dwight Caldwell.

Western **Cas.** **(PR:A MPAA:NR)**

IN ENEMY COUNTRY** (1968) 108m UNIV c

Tony Franciosa *(Col. Charles Waslow-Carton)*, Anjanette Comer *(Denise Marchois)*, Guy Stockwell *(Lt. Col. Philip Braden)*, Paul Hubschmid *(Baron Frederich von Wittenberg)*, Tom Bell *(Capt. Ian Peyton-Reid)*, Michael Constantine *(Ladislov)*, Harry Townes *(General Marchois)*, John Marley *(Rausch)*, Milton Selzer *(Josef Bartowski)*, Patric Knowles *(Gen. Lloyd Griffis)*, Tige Andrews *(Nicolay)*, Emile Genest *(Gen. Grieux)*, Lee Bergere *(Maj. Maurice Miral)*, Virginia Christine *(Frau Gulden)*, Harry Landers *(Pilot)*, Jim Creech *(Copilot)*, Gerald Michenaud *(Polish Boy)*, Eugene Dynarski *(Capek)*, Ivor Barry *(Air Marshal Evelyn)*, Simon Scott *(General Jomar)*, Paul Busch *(Convoy Commander)*, Norbert Schiller *(Polish Man)*, Murray Matheson.

Second-rate action-adventure film with an uncommonly cliched script from a usually good writer, Anhalt, that stops the flow of activity to wax moralistically on life and war. It's a given fact that we all hate the Nazis, but we must remember one thing: if it weren't for the heinous mob of thugs, we would never have had so many good war movies. This, however, is not one of them. Franciosa is in Paris in 1939. He talks Comer, an intelligence officer in the French government, into marrying Hubschmid, a German Baron, and moving to Germany under the guise of having defected from France. It's now 1943 and Franciosa and fellow officers Stockwell and Bell, learn that the Germans have a new torpedo that is wreaking havoc on Allied shipping. They parachute into Germany and quickly masquerade as POWs in a labor camp near the factory that manufactures the dread torpedo. Constantine is a guard at the factory, but he is, in reality, a Polish agent. With his aid they learn which building houses the machinery. Now Franciosa poses as an electrician and goes to Hubschmid's mansion where he tells Comer the information, which she radios via short wave to London. Bombers are soon overhead and they destroy the factory, but Bell is slain by a German patrol after having escaped the bombs. Franciosa and Stockwell seek shelter at Hubschmid's home, where Comer tells them that some of the Polish partisans have stolen a torpedo so it can be dissected by Allied munitions men. They attempt to escape on a sub but that's stymied, so they have to tote the torpedo through several skirmishes until they get to a small airstrip where a plane is waiting to take them to safety. Once there, Comer announces that she is staying in Germany to continue her undercover job and to stay with her husband, whom she has come to love. A German patrol spots them and opens fire just as the plane flies off to England and the film ends. Coincidence played a large part in the script, and much of it was as hard to swallow as a handful of aspirin. They cut out all of the diatribe for the European release, and it came in at just over 80 minutes, a vast improvement. Dynarksi became a successful Hollywood acting teacher and theatre owner and Landers became one of the busiest dubbing directors around.

p&d, Harry Keller; w, Edward Anhalt (based on a story by Sy Bartlett); ph, Loyal Griggs (Techniscope, Technicolor); m, William Lava; ed, Russell F. Schoengarth; md, Joseph Gershenson; art d, Alexander Golitzen, John Beckman; set d, John McCarthy, Darrell Silvera; cos, Edith Head; stunts, Daivd Sharpe.

War Drama **(PR:A–C MPAA:NR)**

IN FAST COMPANY** (1946) 61m MON bw

Leo Gorcey *(Slip)*, Huntz Hall *(Sach)*, Bobby Jordan *(Bobby)*, Billy Benedict *(Whitey)*, Judy Clark *(Mabel Dumbrowski)*, Jane Randolph *(Marian McCormick)*, David Gorcey *(Chuck)*, Charles D. Brown *(Father Donovan)*, Douglas Fowley *(Steve Trent)*, Paul Harvey *(Patrick McCormick)*, Marjorie Woodworth *(Sally Turner)*, Frank Marlowe *(Mr. Cassidy)*, Dick Wessel *(Pete)*, William Ruhl *(Gus)*, Luis Alberni *(Tony)*, George Eldredge *(Officer)*, Mary Gordon *(Mrs. Cassidy)*, Judy Schenz *(Nora Cassidy)*, Charles Coleman *(Meredith)*, Bernard Gorcey *(Louie)*, Stanley Price *("Blind" Man)*, Marcel de la Brosse *(Chauffeur)*, Walter Soderling *(Old Gentleman)*, Lee Phelps *(O'Hara)*, Jack Cheatham *(Cop)*, Fred Aldrich *(Customer)*, Mike Pat Donovan *(Cop)*, John Indrisano *(Bit)*.

A powerful cab company tries to drive the weaker independent drivers out of business, but Gorcey and the gang come to the aid of the underdogs. (See Bowery Boys series, Index.)

p, Lindsley Parsons, Jan Grippo; d, Del Lord; w, Edmond Seward, Tim Ryan, Victor Hammond, Ray Schrock (based on a story by Martin Mooney); ph, William Sickner; ed, Richard Currier, William Austin; md, Edward Kay.

Comedy/Crime **(PR:A MPAA:NR)**

IN GAY MADRID** (1930) 71m MGM bw

Ramon Novarro *(Ricardo)*, Dorothy Jordan *(Carmina)*, Lottice Howell *(Goyita)*, Claude King *(Marques de Castelar)*, Eugenie Besserer *(Dona Generosa)*, William V. Mong *(Rivas)*, Beryl Mercer *(Dona Concha)*, Nanci Price *(Jacinta)*, Herbert Clark *(Octavio)*, David Scott *(Ernesto)*, George Chandler *(Enrique)*, Bruce Coleman *(Corpulento)*, Nicholas Caruso *(Carlos)*.

Navarro spends too much time watching the girls and not enough time hitting the books, so his father sends him from Madrid to Santiago. He finds that there are senoritas there too, especially Jordan, whom he faithfully woos with his singing. Songs include "Dark Night" (Herbert Stothart, Clifford Grey, Xavier Cugat), "Santiago," "Smile While We May" (Grey, Roy Turk), "Into Your Heart" (Turk, Fred Ahlert).

d, Robert Z. Leonard; w, Bess Meredyth, Salisbury Field, Edwin Justus Mayer (based on the novel *La Casa De La Troya* by Alejandro Perez Luzin); ph, Oliver Marsh; ed, William S. Grey.

Musical **(PR:A MPAA:NR)**

IN GOD WE TRUST zero (1980) 97m UNIV c

Marty Feldman *(Brother Ambrose)*, Peter Boyle *(Dr. Melmoth)*, Louise Lasser *(Mary)*, Richard Pryor *(God)*, Andy Kaufman *(Armageddon T. Thunderbird)*, Wilfrid Hyde-White *(Abbot Thelonius)*, Severn Darden *(Priest)*, Eddie Parkes, Stephanie Ross, Richard A. Roth, Barbara Ann Walters, John J. Koshel, Peter Koshel, Lynda Chase-Chankin, Brayton "Bob" Yerkes, David Bond, Norman Bartold, Len Lawson, Peter Nyberg, Paul Baxley, Larri Thomas, David Burton, Kaisen Chu, Chuck Hicks, Rose Michtom, Sue Angelyn Strain, Terry L. Finch, David Francis Banks.

Feldman, like everyone else in this picture, is pathetically wasted. He is an innocent monk who tries to raise money for his monastery and ends up on Hollywood Boulevard. In a robe and sandals he solicits funds from Kaufman, appropriately cast as a revolting twit of a TV evangelist. Kaufman takes Feldman as a partner in his Church of Divine Profit (funny, isn't it?), but turns against him. Pryor is soberingly unfunny as G.O.D., who receives Feldman's pleas for assistance. Director Feldman proves he has a special (though not entirely unique) talent for bringing together a group of normally comic actors and making them look like bumbling idiots. An infinitely unfunny picture which has the unmitigated nerve to pay homage to Buster Keaton.

p, Howard West, George Shapiro; d, Marty Feldman; w, Feldman, Chris Allen; ph, Charles Correll (Technicolor); m, John Morris; ed, David Blewitt; prod d, Lawrence G. Paull; set d, Peg Cummings; cos, Ruth Myers; ch, Dee Dee Wood; m/l, "Good for God," Harry Nilsson (sung by Nilsson).

Comedy **(PR:C–O MPAA:PG)**

IN HARM'S WAY*** (1965) 165m Sigma Productions/PAR bw

John Wayne *(Capt. Rockwell Torrey)*, Kirk Douglas *(Comdr. Paul Eddington)*, Patricia Neal *(Lt. Maggie Haynes)*, Tom Tryon *(Lt. [jg] William McConnel)*, Paula Prentiss *(Bev McConnel)*, Brandon De Wilde *(Ensign Jeremiah Torrey)*, Jill Haworth *(Ensign Annalee Dorne)*, Dana Andrews *(Adm. Broderick)*, Stanley Holloway *(Clayton Canfil)*, Burgess Meredith *(Comdr. Powell)*, Franchot Tone *(CINCPAC I Admiral)*, Patrick O'Neal *(Comdr. Neal O'Wynn)*, Carroll O'Connor *(Lt. Comdr. Burke)*, Slim Pickens *(CPO Culpepper)*, James Mitchum *(Ensign Griggs)*, George Kennedy *(Col. Gregory)*, Bruce Cabot *(Quartermaster Quoddy)*, Barbara Bouchet *(Liz Eddington)*, Tod Andrews *(Capt. Tuthill)*, Larry Hagman *(Lt. Cline)*, Stewart Moss *(Ensign Balch)*, Richard Le Pore *(Lt. Tom Agar)*, Chet Stratton *(Ship's Doctor)*, Soo Young *(Tearful Woman)*, Dort Clark *(Boston)*, Phil Mattingly *(PT Boat Skipper)*, Henry Fonda *(CINCPAC Admiral)*, Hugh O'Brian *(Air Force Major)*, James Mitchum, George Kennedy, Bruce Cabot, Tod Andrews.

This exciting WW II action film was directed by Preminger with so much care that it seems to lag in an overlong attempt to make it epic. Yet reliable Wayne and intense Douglas pull up the sagging scenes heroically as two U.S. Navy officers who endure through years of sea combat. It begins at Pearl Harbor. Wayne and Douglas are at sea when the Japanese attack the base on December 7, 1941, with a small force of destroyers, Wayne commanding a light cruiser. When advised of the attack, Wayne is sent on a fool's mission to find and destroy the invading Japanese fleet which is long gone. By the time he returns to the wrecked base, he has come up empty handed. Moreover, Douglas finds that his sluttish wife, Bouchet, has been killed during the attack while on an assignation with an air force officer, O'Brien. He becomes embittered, harboring a deep hatred for all females. Wayne's futile errand at sea causes him to be sent to a desk job. He and others in command of surviving vessels are obliquely held responsible for the failure of the Navy to counterattack. Wayne's son De Wilde appears, a Navy ensign who is totally self-serving, smug, and callous, ignoring his father and blatantly trying to further his career through a friendship with conniving fellow officer O'Neal. Subplots involve Wayne with ex-wife Neal, a WAVE officer, newlyweds Prentiss and Tryon, a young Navy officer, and Douglas casting a lecherous eye on fetching Haworth who is in love with De Wilde, all of this swirling about several naval battles conducted by down-scaled warships (each manned by a single technician). Douglas tries to rape Haworth, or does, it's not quite clear, and she commits suicide. Guilt-ridden, Douglas flies off on a suicide mission to spot an enemy fleet to redeem himself and is killed. Wayne and his battleships take on the Japanese fleet. He loses his ship and a leg but wakes up on a hospital ship to discover that he has won a decisive battle, the heart of ex-wife Neal who will nurse him back to health, and the respect of a contrite De Wilde. It's pretty hokey and contrived but the battle scenes are effective, although shot with plenty of fog so as to disguise the models used. Fonda has a small role patterned after Adm. Chester Nimitz but it's hardly worth his effort. Wayne is his usual reliable self in a role he had done many times in the past, playing the indefatigable Navy officer who overcomes all odds in OPERATION PACIFIC, THE FIGHTING SEABEES, THE WINGS OF EAGLES, and THEY WERE EXPENDABLE. Preminger could have cut the film but being a sublime egotist, as well as a superb craftsman, he insisted on telling the story his own methodically slow way. He directed his films in long takes, refusing to insert a lot of cuts in his scenes, believing that repeated cuts interrupt the story line; to sustain viewer interest, Preminger would manipulate his actors and camera, having the actors turn away and then toward the camera, coming up to it for closeups, or slowly dollying the camera in for closeups, a rather static technique from the silent era. Preminger also demanded many takes for this film, especially putting Prentiss through her paces in her last scene of the film (where she learns husband Tryon is missing in action), so frustrating to her that the actress kept kicking herself in the leg. When Preminger finally yelled "cut" Prentiss hobbled off the set and then had to be taken to a hospital with a broken ankle. According to Preminger, the actress was not conscious of her self-inflicted injury during the shooting "because she was concentrating so hard on the scene that she didn't notice it."

p&d, Otto Preminger; w, Wendell Mayes (based on the novel by James Bassett); ph, Loyal Griggs (Panavision); m, Jerry Goldsmith; ed, George Tomasini, Hugh S. Fowler; prod d, Lyle Wheeler; art d, Al Roelofs; set d, Morris Hoffman, Richard Mansfield; cos, Hope Bryce; spec eff, Lawrence W. Butler.

War Drama **(PR:A MPAA:NR)**

IN HIS STEPS** (1936) 78m GN bw

Eric Linden *(Tom Carver)*, Cecilia Parker *(Ruth Brewster)*, Henry Kolker *(Calvin Carver)*, Charles Richman *(Robert Brewster)*, Olive Tell *(Elaine Brewster)*, Harry Beresford *(Davidson)*, Roger Imhof *(Adams)*, Clara Blandick *(Martha Adams)*, Robert Warwick *(Judge Grey)*, Warner Richmond *(Gavin)*, Donald Kirke *(Reynard)*, Stanley Andrews *(Broderick)*.

Two families are pitted against each other when the son from one marries the daughter of the other. Deciding that they have both had enough of their families' pressures, the pair stay away until they are brought to court—the son accused of kidnaping by the daughter's family.

p, B.F. Zeidman; d, Karl Brown; w, Brown, Hinton Smith (based on the novel by Charles M. Sheldon); ph, Harry Jackson; ed, Edward Schroeder, Duncan Mansfield; md, Abe Meyer.

Romance **(PR:A MPAA:NR)**

IN-LAWS, THE*** (1979) 103m WB c

Peter Falk *(Vince Ricardo)*, Alan Arkin *(Sheldon Kornpett)*, Richard Libertini *(Gen. Garcia)*, Nancy Dussault *(Carol Kornpett)*, Penny Peyser *(Barbara Kornpett)*, Arlene Golonka *(Jean Ricardo)*, Michael Lembeck *(Tommy Ricardo)*, Paul Lawrence Smith *(Mo)*, Carmine Caridi *(Angie)*, Ed Begley, Jr. *(Barry Lutz)*, Sammy Smith *(Mr. Hirschorn)*, James Hong *(Bing Wong)*, Barbara Dana *(Bank Teller)*, Rozsika Halmos *(Mrs. Adelman)*, Alvaro Carcano *(Edgardo)*, Jorge Zepeda *(Carlos)*, Sergio Calderon *(Alfonso)*, David Paymer, Kent Williams, John Hancock, John Finnegan, Brass Adams, Eduardo Noriega, Danny Kwan, Maurice Sneed, Rosana Sotto, Jim Goodwin, Mitchell Group, Carmen Dragon, Peter Miller, Hanna King, Dick Wieand, Carlos Montalbo, Tom Degidon, Tony Di Falco, John Day, Art Evans, John Hostetter, Bill Houston.

A likable, very looney comedy starring Falk and Arkin as future father-in-laws who wind up running around in South America for the CIA on the eve of their children's wedding. Falk is the nutty CIA agent who drags the unsuspecting dentist Arkin on a ridiculous trail of mayhem which leads to a banana republic ruled by a crazed dictator (hilariously played by Libertini) who talks to his hand (and the hand talks back). The comedy is strictly from the hit-or-miss school, but director Hiller keeps things moving so fast there isn't time to ponder over the failed bits. The film grossed a small fortune, pulling in nearly $19 million at the box-office.

p, Arthur Hiller, William Sackheim; d, Hiller; w, Andrew Bergman; ph, David M. Walsh (Technicolor); m, John Morris; ed, Robert E. Swink; prod d, Pato Guzman.

Comedy **Cas.** **(PR:A MPAA:PG)**

IN LIKE FLINT*1/2 (1967) 115m FOX c

James Coburn *(Derek Flint)*, Lee J. Cobb *(Cramden)*, Jean Hale *(Lisa)*, Andrew Duggan *(President Trent)*, Anna Lee *(Elisabeth)*, Hanna Landy *(Helena)*, Totty Ames *(Claire)*, Steve Inhat *(Carter)*, Thomas Hasson *(Avery)*, Mary Michael *(Terry)*, Diane Bond *(Jan)*, Jacki Ray *(Denise)*, Herb Edelman *(Russian Premier)*, Yvonne Craig *(Natasha The Ballerina)*, Buzz Henry *(Austin)*, Henry Wills *(Cooper)*, Mary Meade French *(Hilda)*, W.P. Lear, Sr., *(Bill Lear)*, Erin O'Brien, Ginny Gan, Eve Bruce, Inge Jaklyn, Kaye Farrington, Thordis Brandt, Inga Neilsen, Marilyn Hanold *(Amazons)*, Pat Becker, Lyzanne La Due, Nancy Stone *(Salon Clients)*, John Lodge *(Russian Agent)*.

Bad sequel to the James Bond parody OUR MAN FLINT once again sees Coburn (an actor capable of outstanding performances who takes frustratingly long vacations between superior projects to participate in drivel like this) as the title secret agent. In this one he must do battle with a secret society of women villains based in the Virgin Islands (get the joke?), who kidnap American astronauts and replace them with members of their squad to gain access to a space station that controls nuclear missiles, thus gaining control of the planet. In addition to a silly performance from Coburn, Cobb (a space-program official) and Duggan (the President of the U.S.) embarrass themselves respectively. Though the whole thing is done for tongue-in-cheek laughs, the resulting movie comes off lame and stupid.

p, Saul David; d, Gordon Douglas; w, Hal Fimberg; ph, William H. Daniels (CinemaScope, DeLuxe color); m, Jerry Goldsmith; ed, Hugh S. Fowler; art d, Jack Martin Smith, Dale Hennesy; set d, Walter M. Scott, James W. Payne; cos, Ray Aghayan; spec eff, L.B. Abbott, Emil Kosa Jr., Art Cruikshank; ch, Stefan Wenta; m/l, "Your Zowie Face," Goldsmith, Leslie Bricusse.

Comedy/Espionage **(PR:A MPAA:NR)**

IN LOVE AND WAR1/2** (1958) 107m FOX c

Robert Wagner *(Frankie O'Neill)*, Dana Wynter *(Sue Trumbell)*, Jeffrey Hunter *(Nico Kantaylis)*, Hope Lange *(Andrea Lenaine)*, Bradford Dillman *(Alan Newcombe)*, Sheree North *(Lorraine)*, France Nuyen *(Kalai Ducanne)*, Sebastian Cabot *(D. Everett Styles)*, Mort Sahl *(Danny Krieger)*, Steven Gant *(Babe Ricardo)*, Harvey Stephens *(Amory Newcombe)*, Paul Comi *(Father Wallensack)*, Joe di Reda *(Capistron)*, Buck Class *(Derek)*, James Bell *(Sidney Lenaine)*, Edith Barrett *(Mrs. Lenaine)*, Murvyn Vye *(Charlie Scanlon)*, Lili Valenty *(Mrs. Kantaylis)*, Edward "Tap" Canutt *(Lt. D'Allesandro)*, Nelson Leigh *(Lt. Col. Herron)*, Veronica Cartwright *(Allie O'Neill)*, Brian Corcoran *(Bobby O'Neill)*, Mary Patton *(Grace Scanlon)*, Frank Murphy *(Terrence)*.

The story of three young marines, Wagner, Dillman, and Hunter and their experiences with the title subjects. Wagner is a cowardly lad who finds courage in battle, then falls in love with Lange. Hunter is a heroic sergeant who thrives on facing danger. After marrying his pregnant girl friend, he goes off to fight in the South Pacific, where he dies in battle. Dillman, perhaps the most interesting of the trio, is an intellectual whose socialite wife commits suicide, making him turn his affections to Hawaiian nurse Nuyen. He goes through a period of reassessment, questioning both love and war. Actor Edward "Tap" Canutt is the son of Yakima Canutt, a stuntman who pioneered many difficult stunts during his career and was second unit director on many epic films such as BEN HUR (1959), SPARTACUS (1960), EL CID (1961).

p, Jerry Wald; d, Philip Dunne; w, Edward Anhalt (based on the novel *The Big War* by Anton Myrer); ph, Leo Tover (CinemaScope, DeLuxe Color); m, Hugo Friedhofer; ed, William Reynolds; md, Lionel Newman; art d, Lyle R. Wheeler, George W. Davis; set d, Walter M. Scott, Fay Babcock; cos, Adele Palmer.

War/Romance **(PR:A MPAA:NR)**

IN LOVE WITH LIFE** (1934) 66m IN/CHES-FD bw

Lila Lee *(Sharon)*, Dickie Moore *(Boy)*, Onslow Stevens *(Professor)*, Claude Gillingwater *(Morley)*, Rosita Marstini *(Brouquet)*, Betty Kendig, Clarence Geldert, Tom Ricketts, Milla Davenport, William Arnold, James T. Mack.

Gillingwater is perfectly cast as a grouchy old grandfather who adopts his adorable grandson, Moore, but only after disowning his daughter Lee. The stock market crash proves it served some purpose, destroying Gillingwater's fortune, but bringing the three generations together in harmony.

p, Maury Cohen; d, Frank R. Strayer; w, Robert Ellis; ph, M.A. Anderson; ed, Roland Reed.

Drama (PR:A MPAA:NR)

IN MACARTHUR PARK*½ (1977) 75m Western World bw

Adam Silver *(Triam Lee)*, James Espinoza *(Ricky)*, Pete Homer, Sr. *(Triam's Uncle)*, Anna Shorter *(Girl in Bus Station)*, Marcy Eudal *(Ginny)*, Doug Laffoon *(Triam's Son)*, Anita Noble *(Triam's Wife)*.

A moderately interesting social drama about the plight of an American Indian in Los Angeles. Trying to find work, he lives pennilessly with his family in the City of Angels. He, however, resorts to murder "in MacArthur Park," and funnels his energies into returning to his Arizona reservation. The film ends on a disappointingly open note. Originally a 16mm, 15-minute short for public television, this poor quality picture doesn't stand up in its lengthened version.

p,d&w, Bruce R. Schwartz; ph, John Sharaf; m, Rocky Davis; ed, Schwartz, Jerry Kutner; set d, Judith Randall.

Drama (PR:C–O MPAA:NR)

IN NAME ONLY*** (1939) 94m RKO bw

Carole Lombard *(Julie Eden)*, Cary Grant *(Alec Walker)*, Kay Francis *(Maida Walker)*, Charles Coburn *(Mr. Walker)*, Katharine Alexander *(Laura)*, Jonathan Hale *(Dr. Gateson)*, Maurice Moscovich *(Dr. Muller)*, Nella Walker *(Mrs. Walker)*, Peggy Ann Garner *(Ellen)*, Spencer Charters *(Gardener)*, Alan Baxter *(Charley)*, Harriet Mathews, Sandra Morgan *(Women on Boat)*, Harold Miller *(Man on Boat)*, John Dilson, Doug Gordon *(Stewards)*, James Adamson, Tony Merlo *(Waiters)*, Frank Puglia *(Manager)*, Alan Pollard *(Butler)*, Charles Coleman *(Archie Duress)*, Florence Wix, Clive Morgan, Maj. Sam Harris, Kathryn Wilson *(Party Guests)*, Grady Sutten *(Escort)*, Bert Moorhouse *(Colelge Man)*, Byron Foulger *(Owen)*, Arthur Aylsworth *(Farmer on Truck)*, Lloyd Ingraham *(Elevator Operator)*, Gus Glassmire *(Hospital Attendant)*, Mary MacLaren *(Nurse)*, Robert Strange *(Hotel Manager)*, Jack Chapin, Allan Wood, Harold Hoff *(Bellhops)*, George Rosener *(Hotel Doctor)*, Edward Fligle *(Night Clerk)*, John Laing *(Chauffeur)*, Frank Mills *(Bartender)*, Helen Vinson.

Grant is a wealthy, sensitive man who meets and marries Francis. She is everything he isn't—tenacious, scheming, and pathologically possessive. Lombard, a beautiful, lonely widow, takes a summer cottage near Grant's estate and he falls desperately in love with her. A short time later he asks Francis for a divorce but she adamantly refuses. Francis fights viciously to hold on to her man, not out of love, but for his money. Grant keeps pushing her for the divorce and she finally seems to relent, telling him that she will get the decree in Paris, but then she goes to the City of Light with Grant's super wealthy parents, Coburn and Walker, doing everything in her power to ingratiate herself to the old folks in an attempt to obtain the family millions. In Paris, Francis stalls endlessly, putting Grant off through one ruse after another. He and Lombard begin to believe that it's a no-win situation. When Francis finally does return to New York, Grant and Lombard confront her. Francis' true nature emerges in a highly charged scene where she appears like a trapped tigress. She snarls that she will sue Lombard for alienation of affection if Grant files for divorce. After leaving Francis' hotel suite, Grant and Lombard appear hopeless, believing that they will never find happiness together. Grant then catches pneumonia and is on death's door. Physician Moscovich, in a stirring scene, tells the family that only the one Grant truly loves should be at his bedside to pull him through. Lombard is prevented from seeing Grant by Francis, who stands now like some hideous sentinel before the gates of death, spitting out her hatred for Lombard, even admitting that she is clinging to the dying man so she can inherit his fortune. Her remarks are overheard by Coburn and Walker and the old man quickly gets rid of vixen Francis and sends Lombard to her man. Grant recovers and Francis is finally out of the way, forced to agree to the divorce. Lombard and Grant will now find happiness together. IN NAME ONLY is really a four handkerchief film, a tepid potboiler that climbs out of the sudsy bathos through the sheer strength of its leads. Grant is charming and Lombard appealing but lacking her usual zesty flair. Francis discards her sophistication for once and delivers a powerful performance of a woman no man could ever love. Coburn does a solid job and many of the supporting players deliver strong performances, including Baxter, who normally played iceberg gangsters. Here he renders an hilarious bit as a drunken clerk on Christmas Eve. This was the sceen debut of child star Peggy Ann Garner and she comes through somewhat awkward, though she is fetching in her small part. Vinson also scores as an acid-tongued gossip whose wagging tongue is heard by some youths who become frightened at the scandal she drools, another priceless little scene handled so well by the careful Cromwell, a director who could make much more out of the mediocre in well-crafted scenes which he does over and over in this film, even though it smacks of CRAIG'S WIFE and DODSWORTH.

p, George Haight; d, John Cromwell; w, Richard Sherman (based on the novel *Memory of Love* by Bessie Brewer); ph, J. Roy Hunt; m, Roy Webb; ed, William Hamilton; art d, Van Nest Polglase, Perry Ferguson; set d, Darrell Silvera; cos, Irene, Edward Stevenson; spec eff, Vernon L. Walker.

Drama Cas. (PR:A MPAA:NR)

IN OLD AMARILLO½** (1951) 67m REP bw

Roy Rogers *(Himself)*, Estelita Rodriquez *(Pepita)*, Penny Edwards *(Madge Adams)*, Pinky Lee *(Pinky)*, Roy Barcroft *(Clint Burnside)*, Pierre Watkin *(George B. Hills)*, Ken Howell *(Philip Hills)*, Elisabeth Risdon *(Granny Adams)*, William Holmes *(Martin)*, Kermit Maynard, Alan Bridge, The Roy Rogers Riders, Trigger the Horse.

Rogers is called in to aid a group of ranchers who are on the brink of financial ruin due to a damaging drought. When efforts to bring in water are foiled by Barcroft, who sees the possibility of buying cattle cheaply, Rogers stands up for justice. An enjoyable oater.

p, Edward J. White; d, William Witney; w, Sloan Nibley; ph, Jack Marta; m, R. Dale Butts; ed, Tony Martinelli; art d, Frank Hotaling; m/l, "Under The Lone Star Moon," Jack Elliott, Foy Willing (sung by Roy Rogers, Penny Edwards), "Wasteland," Elliott, Willing (sung by Rogers, The Roy Rogers Riders), "If I Ever Fall In Love," Elliott, Willing (sung by Estelita Rodriquez).

Western Cas. (PR:A MPAA:NR)

IN OLD ARIZONA*** (1929) 94m FOX bw

Edmund Lowe *(Sgt. Mickey Dunne)*, Dorothy Burgess *(Tonia Maria)*, Warner Baxter *(The Cisco Kid)*, J. Farrell MacDonald *(Tad)*, Fred Warren *(Piano Player)*, Henry Armetta *(Barber)*, Frank Campeau, Tom Santschi, Pat Hartigan *(Cowpunchers)*, Roy Stewart *(Commandant)*, James Bradbury, Jr., *(Soldier)*, John Dillon *(2nd Soldier)*, Soledad Jiminez *(Cook)*, Frank Nelson, Duke Martin *(Cowboys)*, James Marcus *(Blacksmith)*, Alphonse Ethier *(Sheriff)*, Helen Lynch *(Woman)*, Ivan Linow *(Russian Immigrant)*, Joe Brown *(Bartender)*, Lola Salvi *(Italian Girl)*, Edward Piel, Sr. *(Man)*.

Burgess is the interest of both Baxter, cast as the Cisco Kid, and Lowe, a sergeant in pursuit of Baxter. The crafty gal betrays the dashing Cisco Kid but falls victim to a bullet from Lowe's gun. Famous for being the first major sound western, this picture made progressive use of exterior sound and photography, racking up six major Academy Award nominations. Baxter was the only one, however, to actually receive the prized statuette. The direction was begun by Raoul Walsh who also intended to star as Cisco, but fell victim to an accident which resulted in the loss of an eye—though making way for his trademarked eye patch. Cummings took over the reins and completed the job in a more-than-admirable fashion. (See CISCO KID series, Index)

d, Raoul Walsh, Irving Cummings; w, Tom Barry (based on stories by O. Henry); ph, Arthur Edeson; ed, Louis Loeffler; m/l, "My Tonia," Lew Brown, B.G. DeSylva, Ray Henderson.

Western (PR:A MPAA:NR)

IN OLD CALIENTE** (1939) 55m REP bw

Roy Rogers *(Roy)*, Mary Hart [Lynne Roberts] *(Jean)*, George Hayes *(Gabby)*, Jack LaRue *(Delgado)*, Katherine DeMille *(Rita)*, Frank Puglia *(Don Miguel)*, Harry Woods *(Calkins)*, Paul Marion *(Carlos)*, Ethel Wales *(Felicia)*, Merrill McCormack *(Pedro)*, Trigger the Horse.

Half-breed LaRue makes trouble for Rogers and friends who are settling in California. Not anxious to have new neighbors, LaRue robs Rogers' boss of $40,000 and points a guilty finger at the immigrants. After a fair amount of gunsmoke, the air is cleared for the newcomers.

p&d, Joseph Kane; w, Morman Houston, Gerald Geraghty; ph, William Nobles; ed, Edward Mann; md, Cy Feuer.

Western Cas. (PR:A MPAA:NR)

IN OLD CALIFORNIA*½ (1929) 60m Audible bw

Henry B. Walthall *(Don Pedro DeLeon)*, Helen Ferguson *(Dolores Radanell)*, George Duryea *(Lt. Tony Hopkins)*, Ray Hallor *(Pedro DeLeon)*, Orral Humphrey *(Ike Boone)*, Larry Steers *(Ollie Radanell)*, Richard Carlyle *(Arturo)*, Harry Allen *(Sgt. Washburn)*, Louis Stern *(Ramon De Hermosa)*, Paul Elis *(Jose)*, Carlotta Monta *(Juanita)*, Gertrude Short.

Aboard a stagecoach bound for California, Hallor meets and flirts with Ferguson. Bandits attack the stage and the party is rescued by handsome Duryea, who instantly steals Ferguson's heart. Hallor invites Ferguson, her gambler father (Steers), and Duryea to a fiesta at his father's home. During the evening tensions mount, coming to a head when Hallor's father, Walthall, loses his ranch to Steers in a card game. It is revealed that years ago Steers had gone off with Walthall's wife and young daughter. Hallor is shocked to realize that the woman he is interested in is actually his sister. A gunfight between Hallor and Duryea is the tragic close. Primitive talkie shows most of the limitations of the crude recording techniques of the time. Includes the theme song "Underneath a Spanish Moon." Also released in a silent version that runs slightly shorter.

p, Lon Young; d, Burton King; w, Arthur Hoerl (based on a story by Fred Hart); ph, Charles Boyle; ed, Earl Turner.

Drama (PR:A MPAA:NR)

IN OLD CALIFORNIA** (1942) 88m REP bw

John Wayne *(Tom Craig)*, Binnie Barnes *(Lacey Miller)*, Albert Dekker *(Britt Dawson)*, Helen Parrish *(Ellen Sanford)*, Patsy Kelly *(Helga)*, Edgar Kennedy *(Kegs McKeever)*, Dick Purcell *(Joe Dawson)*, Harry Shannon *(Mr. Carlin)*, Charles Halton *(Mr. Hayes)*, Emmett Lynn *(Whitey)*, Bob McKenzie *(Mr. Bates)*, Milt Kibbee *(Mr. Tompkins)*, Paul Sutton *(Chick)*, Anne O'Neal *(Mrs. Tompkins)*, Minerva Urecal *(Mrs. Carson)*, Robert E. Homans *(Marshal)*, Hooper Atchley, Pearl Early, Ruth Robinson, Frank Jacquet, Jack O'Shea, Jack Kirk, Lynne Carver, James Morton, Horace B. Carpenter, Olin Howlin, Chester Conklin, Ralph Peters, Forrest Taylor, Dick Alexander, Donald Curtis, George Lloyd, Stanley Blystone, Slim Whitaker, Frank Ellis, Frank Hagney, Bud Osborne, Ed Brady, Wade Crosby, Guy Usher, Martin Garralaga, Rex Lease, Karl Hackett, Art Mix, Merrill McCormack, Frank McGlynn.

Set in California after the Gold Rush, this picture has Wayne cast as a pharmacist who meets up with dance-hall queen Barnes and her husband-to-be Dekker. It is soon discovered by Wayne that Dekker is a dishonest gunman who greedily rules the neighboring ranchers. With Wayne posing a threat to his profits, Dekker exchanges some of Wayne's tonic for poison, leading to the death of a local resident. An angry mob nearly lynches Wayne, but not before he is able to prove his innocence and nail Dekker.

p, Robert North; d, William McGann; w, Gertrude Purcell, Frances Hyland (based on a story by J. Robert Bren, Gladys Atwater); ph, Jack Marta; m, David Buttolph; ed, Howard O'Neill, Murray Seldeen; md, Cy Feuer; art d, Russell Kimball.

Western **Cas.** **(PR:A MPAA:NR)**

IN OLD CHEYENNE** (1931) 59m World Wide-Sono Art bw

Rex Lease *(Jim)*, Dorothy Gulliver *(Helen Sutter)*, Jay Hunt *(Frank Sutter)*, Harry Woods *(Winslow)*, Harry Todd *(Ben)*.

Lease stars as a ranch hand out to learn the identity of a horse thief. After a stallion unties the gate's ropes and leads a passel of mares to a secret hideout, Lease begins to put the pieces together, and points the finger at the new ranch owner.

d, Stuart Paton; w, Betty Burbridge (based on the story by Bennet Cohen); ph, William Nobles; ed, Carl Himm.

Western **(PR:A MPAA:NR)**

IN OLD CHEYENNE** (1941) 58m REP bw

Roy Rogers *(Steve Blane)*, George "Gabby" Hayes *(Arapahoe Brown)*, Joan Woodbury *(Dolores Casino)*, J. Farrell MacDonald *(Tim Casey)*, Sally Payne *(Squeak)*, George Rosener, *(Sam Drummond)*, William Haade, *(Davidge)*, Hal Taliaferro *(Pete)*, Jack Kirk *(Rufe)*, Bob Woodward, Jim Corey, Cactus Mack, George Lloyd, Billy Benedict, Jack O'Shea, Edward Piel, Sr., Merrill McCormack, Ted Mapes, Fred Burns, Ben Corbett, Nick Thompson, Trigger the Horse.

When Rogers is sent by his newspaper to cover a story about outlaw activities, he saves Hayes' skin. Originally on Hayes' trail, Rogers—singing at intervals, of course—discovers that he is after the wrong man and points the guilty finger at Rosener.

p&d, Joseph Kane; w, Olive Cooper (based on a story by John Krafft); ph, William Nobles; ed, Charles Craft; md, Cy Feuer.

Western **(PR:A MPAA:NR)**

IN OLD CHICAGO**** (1938) 115m FOX bw

Tyrone Power *(Dion O'Leary)*, Alice Faye *(Belle Fawcett)*, Don Ameche *(Jack O'Leary)*, Alice Brady *(Molly O'Leary)*, Andy Devine *(Pickle Bixby)*, Brian Donlevy *(Gil Warren)*, Phyllis Brooks *(Ann Colby)*, Tom Brown *(Bob O'Leary)*, Sidney Blackmer *(Gen. Phil Sheridan)*, Berton Churchill *(Sen. Colby)*, June Storey *(Gretchen O'Leary)*, Paul Hurst *(Mitch)*, Tyler Brooke *(Specialty Singer)*, J. Anthony Hughes *(Patrick O'Leary)*, Gene Reynolds *(Dion as a Boy)*, Bobs Watson *(Bob as a Boy)*, Billy Watson *(Jack as a Boy)*, Mme. Sul-Te-Wan *(Mattie)*, Spencer Charters *(Beavers)*, Rondo Hatton *(Rondo, Bodyguard)*, Thelma Manning *(Carrie Donahue)*, Ruth Gillette *(Miss Lou)*, Eddie Collins *(Drunk)*, Harry Stubbs *(Fire Commissioner)*, Francis Ford *(Driver)*, Gustav Von Seyffertitz, Russell Hicks *(Men in Jack's Office)*, Charles Hummel Wilson *(Lawyer)*, Frank Dae *(Judge)*, Joe King *(Ship's Captain)*, Robert Murphy, Wade Boteler *(Police Officers)*, Rice and Cady *(Specialty)*, Harry Hayden *(Johnson, Secretary)*, Vera Lewis *(Witness)*, Ed Brady *(Wagon Driver)*, Minerva Urecal *(Frantic Mother)*, Scotty Mattraw *(Beef Baron)*, Charles Lane *(Booking Agent)*.

It's wild and woolly and wonderful, even though it has little to do with the facts. Long a pet project of Fox mogul Zanuck, IN OLD CHICAGO was one of the most expensive productions of its day, its costs zooming beyond $1,800,000. Zanuck had eyed with envy the huge success of MGM's SAN FRANCISCO in 1936 and intended to outdo everyone in the disaster category by presenting once again to the world the great Chicago fire of 1871, a 20-minute sequence that left viewers aghast. Fox thrust its biggest stars at the time, Power, Ameche, and Faye, into this wonderfully set period film which begins where the city of Chicago was spawned, on the open plains of the Midwest as the O'Leary family travels to that toddling town in an open wagon, seeking its fortune. Hughes, the adventurous father, spots a passing train and decides to race it against his wife's (Brady) wishes, his three young sons urging him on. In a frantic dash across rolling hills, the horses break away from the wagon, dragging Hughes along with them, his hands entwined around the reins. He dies in Brady's arms as his sons weep; the family buries him outside of the city that poet Carl Sandburg would later hail as the "hog butcher for the world." Brady and her boys enter the mud-clogged streets of Chicago and she realizes that if there's one thing the citizens desperately need it's clean clothes. She becomes a washerwoman to support her three boys who grow up to be Power, a handsome rake and political schemer, Ameche, an upstanding reformer studying law, and Brown, who has no ambitions other than to marry Storey and have babies. As Power angles his way into owning a grand saloon and Ameche becomes a crusading lawyer, Brown goes on driving his mother's laundry wagon through the clapboard South Side district known as The Patch, a tinder box area jammed with mostly Irish immigrants. Power begins his rise by strolling into a successful emporium, The Hub, owned and operated by shifty Donlevy. He spots beautiful singer Faye and immediately decides to have her, going to her dressing room later and actually wrestling her to the floor, kissing her into seductive submission. He convinces her that she can do much better with him and form an alliance. He opens a posh saloon, The Senate, with Faye as the chief attraction, which eats heavily into Donlevy's business. Donlevy sees the handwriting on the wall and decides to go into politics; he approaches Power with a proposition. He will close his place and leave the saloon business to Power in return for his considerable political support in his race for mayor. Moreover, he offers Power $10,000 for his help. Power takes the deal, but backs his brother Ameche, who wins the mud-slinging race. Now Donlevy is hopping mad and looking for revenge. Power is also getting pressure from his own brother, who has taken over the mayor's office and is rooting out the corrupt elements, including Power. Ameche and Power meet in the mayor's office and Ameche tells Power that he knows all about his crooked ways and that he intends to prove a case against him in court, using Faye, who has told him all about Power's illegal operations. Power gives him his winning smile and then tells Ameche that he can forget it, that he has just married Faye and, as his wife, she cannot testify against him in court. Ameche becomes incensed at Power's underhanded use of sweet Alice and the two get into a head-jarring fistfight, all but destroying Ameche's august chambers. Brady gets word that her two volatile sons are battling and rushes off to intervene, forgetting to put the restraining bar between the legs of the cow she is milking in her barn. The legendary cow kicks over a lantern nearby and this ignites a pile of straw. Soon the barn is ablaze and the fire leaps from rooftop to rooftop, setting the sprawling area, The Patch, on fire, too many fires for the frantic horse-drawn fire wagons to battle. Ameche later calls upon Gen. Sheridan (Blackmer) to help combat the spreading fire and troops quickly plant dynamite charges which will blow up the saloon district and hopefully halt the raging fire which is now threatening to consume the entire city. After the charges are set, Donlevy and his army of goons show up, ready to do battle with Power and Ameche. Power tries to reason with the mob but is shouted down. He then grabs a torch and runs to the buildings to explode the dynamite but he is knocked unconscious by a thrown brick. As he is dragged to safety, Ameche races forth, picks up the torch and sets the fuses. Donlevy shoots the mayor in the back. Power's pal Devine picks up the mortally wounded Ameche and begins to carry him to safety but the dynamite goes off and both are killed. Donlevy and his thugs are sent scurrying by troops and run pell mell before the blaze which has now panicked everyone; thousands flee with their belongings, running ahead of the fire, trying to cross the Chicago River to the North Side of the city. Donlevy is trapped in the stockyards area and when herds of stampeding cows are forced into the streets, he is crushed to death. Brady, Brown, and Storey move with the harried masses to the Lake. Here Power searches for his family and later finds them wading with thousands in the water, his mother in a small boat next to the woman he loves, Faye, who has saved Brady earlier when she was almost trampled to death. Power is penitent for his past sins as he embraces his loved ones and mourns the loss of his heroic brother, Ameche. A panoramic shot shows the city burning to its foundations, totally engulfed by a raging inferno. But all vow that they will rebuild the city into an even greater metropolis, Power stating: "Nothing can lick Chicago!" The film ends with shots depicting the majestic skyscrapers of a modern Chicago (which is the same way MGM ended its epic disaster film SAN FRANCISCO). King's direction is fast and furious like the story and he captures the flavor of the old city from its honky tonk image to its immigrant home life, masterfully engineering vast crowds of extras. King's specialty was spectacle and he makes the most of it here. The film ranks with the great disaster epics of the 1930s, SAN FRANCISCO (1936), THE HURRICANE (1937), and THE RAINS COME (1939), the latter another Fox entry. The studio had originally planned to have Jean Harlow loaned to them by MGM for the role that was later claimed by Faye. They were not disappointed with the buxom blonde Faye; she gave a fine performance as the alluring Belle Fawcett, appearing in one song-and-dance number wearing a scanty costume and a pair of jeweled stockings (worth $1,500) which she had worn in a brief scene in ON THE AVENUE but she had gone unnoticed. She was noticed here as she sang "Carry Me Back to Old Virginny" (James A. Bland), displaying her shapely legs to enthusiastic male viewers who didn't seem to mind that she was slightly knock-kneed (but nowhere near as much as Miriam Hopkins, who appears so knock-kneed in her dancehall numbers in VIRGINIA CITY that one might expect her to fall over herself at any moment). Faye also sang in a pleasing alto voice the following numbers: "In Old Chicago" (Mack Gordon, Harry Revel), "I've Taken a Fancy to You," "Take a Dip in the Sea," and "I'll Never Let You Cry" (Sidney Clare, Lew Pollack). Power is his usual attractive and charming self, and Ameche, though a bit histrionic, provides a more practical balance to his errant brother. Brady, as the struggling and dynamic mother, however, steals the film and is nothing less than superb in her every scene. The 45-year-old actress won an Oscar for her role (in the 1937 awards; some rule bending took place in that the film was actually finished that year but not released until 1938). IN OLD CHICAGO earned five other Oscar nominations but, aside from Brady, the only other winner was Robert Webb, as director of the fabulous disaster sequence. This film showed up in a truncated version, running 45 minutes on TV during the 1956–57 season, retitled CITY IN FLAMES, the 20-minute disaster sequence beefed up with another 25 minutes of reconstructed story, directed by Albert S. Rogell and featuring Kevin McCarthy, Jeff Morrow, Roland Winters, Jack Albertson, Lureen Tuttle, and Anne Jeffreys. This film was Faye's big break and it made her a Hollywood superstar. She had been a Fox contract player until Zanuck spotted her and told her to stop imitating Jean Harlow. He ordered her to redo her hairstyle and adopt a plainer and less exotic look so that American women could more easily relate to her. She complied and he cast her in KING OF BURLESQUE, 1936. She was so well received and so agreeably conformed to Zanuck's image of what she should be that the mogul put her into IN OLD CHICAGO, but only after Jean Harlow, the girl he didn't want Faye to emulate, was no longer available for the role.

p, Darryl F. Zanuck; d, Harry King, Robert Webb (disaster sequence); w, Lamar Trotti, Sonya Levien (based on a story "We the O'Learys" by Niven Busch); ph, Peverell Marley; ed, Barbara McLean; md, Louis Silvers; art d, William Darling, Rudolph Sternad; set d, Thomas Little; cos, Royer; m/l, Mack Gordon, Harry Revel, Sidney Clare, Lew Pollack; spec eff, Fred Sersen, Ralph Hammeras, Louis J. White.

Historical/Epic/Disaster **(PR:A MPAA:NR)**

IN OLD COLORADO** ½** (1941) 67m PAR bw

William Boyd *(Hopalong Cassidy)*, Russell Hayden *(Lucky Jenkins)*, Andy Clyde *(California)*, Margaret Hayes *(Myra Woods)*, Morris Ankrum *(Joe Weller)*, Sarah Padden *(Ma Woods)*, Cliff Nazarro *(Nosey Haskins)*, Stanley Andrews *(George Davidson)*, James Seay *(Hank Merritt)*, Morgan Wallace *(Jack Collins)*, Weldon

Heyburn *(Burton)*, Eddy Waller *(Jim Stark)*, Philip Van Zandt *(Vender)*, Glenn Strange *(Blackie Reed)*, Henry Wills, Curley Dresden.

Ankrum is the blackhat in this film, which canters around a feud over water rights. Sparked by Ankrum's scheming, a pair of ranchers are at odds, while watchfully waiting the bandits hope to swallow up their lands after the two kill each other off. Boyd and his buddies come along and, as expected, deep-drill Ankrum's lawlessness. (See HOPALONG CASSIDY series, Index.)

p, Harry Sherman; d, Howard Bretherton; w, J. Benton Cheney, Norton S. Parker, Russell Hayden (based on the characters created by Clarence E. Mulford); ph, Russell Harlan; ed, Carroll Lewis; art d, Lewis J. Rachmil.

Western **(PR:A MPAA:NR)**

IN OLD KENTUCKY*** (1935) 85m FOX bw

Will Rogers *(Steve Tapley)*, Dorothy Wilson *(Nancy Martingale)*, Russell Hardie *(Lee Andrews)*, Charles Sellon *(Ezra Martingale)*, Louise Henry *(Arlene Shattuck)*, Charles Richman *(Pole Shattuck)*, Alan Dinehart *(Slick Doherty)*, Esther Dale *(Dolly Breckenridge)*, Etienne Girardot *(Pluvius J. Aspinwall, Rainmaker)*, John Ince *(Sheriff)*, Bill Robinson *(Wash Jackson)*, Eddie Tamblyn, Bobby Rose, Fritz Johannet *(Jockeys)*, Everett Sullivan *(Jailer)*, G. Raymond Nye *(Deputy Officer)*, Edward Le Saint *(Steward)*, Dora Clement *(Saleslady)*, Ned Norton *(Bookie)*, Allen Caven, Stanley Andrews *(Stewards)*.

Rogers, with help from tap-dancing Bill "Bojangles" Robinson, carries this much-told story of two opposing clans residing in the hills. Rogers' personality turns the tale into a special pleasure, and he dances with Robinson, as well. This was to be his final film before his death in 1935.

p, Edward Butcher; d, George Marshall; w, Sam Hellman, Gladys Lehman, Henry Johnson (based on a play by Charles T. Dazey); ph, L.W. O'Connell; ed, Jack Murray; md, Arthur Lange; art d, William Darling; cos, William Lambert.

Comedy **(PR:A MPAA:NR)**

IN OLD MEXICO1/2** (1938) 67m PAR bw

William Boyd *(Hopalong Cassidy)*, George Hayes *(Windy Halliday)*, Russell Hayden *(Lucky Jenkins)*, Paul Sutton *(The Fox)*, Betty Amann *(Janet Leeds)*, Al Garcia *(Don Carlos Gonzales)*, Jane Clayton *(Anita Gonzales)*, Glenn Strange *(Burk)*, Trevor Bardette *(Col. Gonzales)*, Anna Demetrio *(Elena)*, Tony Roux *(Pancho)*, Fred Burns, Cliff Parkinson.

Boyd and buddies ride south of the border on a phony summons, only to learn that a good friend has been killed. They solve the mysterious murder with the help of Clayton, the peppy sister of the killer, and a group of concerned horsemen. This picture saw Clayton, the real life wife of Hayden, in her film debut. (See HOPALONG CASSIDY series, Index)

p, Harry Sherman; d, Edward T. Venturini; w, Harrison Jacobs (based on characters created by Clarence E. Mulford); ph, Russell Harlan; ed, Robert Warwick; art d, Lewis J. Rachmil.

Western **(PR:A MPAA:NR)**

IN OLD MISSOURI** (1940) 67m REP bw

Leon Weaver *(Abner)*, Frank Weaver *(Cicero)*, June Weaver *(Elviry)*, June Storey *(Mary)*, Marjorie Gateson *(Mrs. Pittman)*, Thurston Hall *(Mr. Pittman)*, Alan Ladd *(Junior)*, Loretta Weaver *(Violey)*, Andrew Tombes *(Attorney)*, Mildred Shay *(Cheechee)*, Willis Claire *(Robbins)*, Leonard Carey *(Haskins)*, Earle S. Dewey *(McConnell)*, Forbes Murray *(Holt)*, Hall Johnson Choir.

The Weavers are sharecroppers who discover that their millionaire boss is in worse shape than they are. It isn't long before the wealthy fella wants to switch places with the more stable Weavers. Alan Ladd, in an early role, is cast as the landowner's good-for-nothing son.

p, Armand Schaefer; d, Frank McDonald; w, Dorrell McGowan, Stuart McGowan; ph, Ernest Miller; m, Cy Feuer; ed, Ernest Nims.

Drama **(PR:A MPAA:NR)**

IN OLD MONTANA*1/2 (1939) 61m Spectrum bw

Fred Scott, Jean Carmen [Julia Thayer], Harry Harvey, John Merton, Walter McGrail, Wheeler Oakman, Frank LaRue, Allan Cavan, Jane Keckley, Dick Cramer, Buddy Kelly, Gene Howard, Carl Mathews, Cactus Mack.

Routine portrayal of the heroes who had a hand in seeing that Montana became a state. Historical accuracy is sacrificed for heightened action and an attempt to make this drab script dramatic.

p, C.C. Burr; d, Raymond K. Johnson; w, Johnson Parks, Homer King Gordon, Johnson.

Western **Cas.** **(PR:A MPAA:NR)**

IN OLD MONTEREY** (1939) 74m REP bw

Gene Autry *(Gene)*, Smiley Burnette *(Frog)*, June Storey *(Jill)*, George Hayes *(Gabby Whittaker)*, Stuart Hamblen *(Bugler)*, Billy Lee *(Jimmy)*, Jonathan Hale *(Stevenson)*, Robert Warwick *(Maj. Forbes)*, William Hall *(Gilman)*, Eddie Conrad *(Proprietor)*, Hoosier Hot Shots *(Themselves)*, Sarie and Sallie *(Themselves)*, The Ranch Boys *(Themselves)*, Curley Dresden, Victor Cox, Ken Carson, Bob Wilke, Hal Price, Tom Steele, Jack O'Shea, Rex Lease, Edward Earle, James Mason, Fred Burns, Dan White, Frank Ellis, Jim Corey, Champion the Horse.

A routine, though bigger-than-usual-budget, Autry vehicle which pits him against a group of ranchers. Army attache Autry is sent to buy up lands for use in bombing maneuvers. Holding out for a higher purse, an unpatriotic bunch tries to make a buck off of Uncle Sam in a time of need, but are whipped into shape by Autry. The last of the Kane-directed Autry pictures.

p, Armand Schaefer; d, Joseph Kane; w, Gerald Geraghty, Dorell McGowan, Stuart McGowan (based on a story by Geraghty, George Sherman); ph, Ernest Miller; ed, Edward Mann; m/l, Gene Autry, Frank Marvin, Billy Rose, Mabel Wayne, Gus Kahn, Walter Donaldson, Bob Nolan, Fred Rose.

Western **(PR:A MPAA:NR)**

IN OLD NEW MEXICO1/2** (1945) 62m MON bw

Duncan Renaldo *(Cisco Kid)*, Martin Garralaga *(Pancho)*, Gwen Kenyon *(Ellen)*, Norman Willis *(Hastings)*, Donna Day *(Belle)*, Aurora Roche *(Dolores)*, Lee White *(Sheriff)*, Kenneth Terrell *(Cliff)*, John Laurenz *(Brady)*, Richard Gordon *(Doc Wills)*, Pedro de Cordoba *(Padre)*, Harry Depps *(Printer)*, Frank Jacquet, Bud Osborne, Artie Ortego, Edward Earle, John Lawrence, James Farley, The Car-Bert Dancers.

Kenyon is falsely accused of murder, but Renaldo knows she is innocent and kidnaps her from a stagecoach to save her life. With the help of the local sheriff, Renaldo stages a shooting that fools the real killer into confessing. Here Renaldo takes over the role in the CISCO KID series originally played by Warner Baxter. He played the Kid in two more Monogram pictures, and then in a television series. (See CISCO KID series, Index)

p, Philip N. Krasne; d, Phil Rosen; w, Betty Burbridge (based on characters created by O. Henry); ph, Arthur Martinelli; m, David Chudnow; m/l, Hershey Martin and Mayris Chaney

Western **Cas.** **(PR:AA MPAA:NR)**

IN OLD OKLAHOMA**

(1943) 100m REP bw (AKA: WAR OF THE WILDCATS)

John Wayne *(Dan Somers)*, Martha Scott *(Catherine Allen)*, Albert Dekker *(Jim "Hunk" Gardner)*, George "Gabby" Hayes *(Desprit Dan)*, Marjorie Rambeau *(Bessie Baxter)*, Dale Evans *("Cuddles" Walker)*, Grant Withers *(Richardson)*, Sidney Blackmer *(Teddy Roosevelt)*, Paul Fix *(The Cherokee Kid)*, Cecil Cunningham *(Mrs. Ames)*, Irving Bacon *(Ben, Telegraph Operator)*, Byron Foulger *(Wilkins)*, Anne O'Neal *(Mrs. Peabody)*, Richard Graham *(Walter)*, Robert Warwick *(Big Tree)*, Stanley Andrews *(Mason)*, Will Wright *(Doctor)*, Harry Shannon *(Charlie Witherspoon)*, Emmett Vogan *(Pres. Roosevelt's Aide)*, Charles Arnt *(Joe)*, Edward Gargan *(Kelsey, Waiter)*, Harry Woods *(Al Dalton)*, Tom London *(Tom)*, Dick Rich, Charles Whitaker, LeRoy Mason, Lane Chandler, Arthur Loft *(Other Men on the Train)*.

Scott, the local school marm, is hounded out of town because of a "sexy" book she has penned. Aboard her departure train she meets oilman Dekker and good guy cowboy Wayne. Wayne and Dekker take an immediate dislike to each other, and the antagonism intensifies when Dekker tries to drill for oil on Indian land. Wayne allies himself with the locals, getting the oil lease with the provision that he deliver before a deadline. Despite some dirty dealings by Dekker, Wayne makes the deadline and wins Scott's heart in the process. Evans, who sings "Put Your Arms Around Me Honey," would achieve renown as Roy Rogers' gal. Arlene Dahl is said to have made her first screen appearance in this film.

p, Robert North; d, Albert S. Rogell; w, Ethel Hill, Thomson Burtis, Eleanor Griffin (based on the story "War of the Wildcats" by T. Burtis); ph, Jack Marta; m, Walter Scharf; ed, Ernest Nims; art d, Russell Kimball; spec eff, Howard Lydecker, Jr.

Western **(PR:A MPAA:NR)**

IN OLD SACRAMENTO**

(1946) 89m REP bw (AKA: FLAME OF SACRAMENTO)

William Elliott *(Johnny Barrett)*, Constance Moore *(Belle Malone)*, Hank Daniels *(Sam Chase)*, Ruth Donnelly *(Zebby Booker)*, Eugene Pallette *(Jim Wales)*, Lionel Stander *(Eddie Dodge)*, Jack LaRue *(Laramie)*, Grant Withers *(Capt. Marc Slayter)*, Bobby Blake *(Newsboy)*, Charles Judels *(Marchetti)*, Paul Hurst *(Stage Driver)*, Victoria Horne *(Ma Dodge)*, Dick Wessel *(Oscar)*, Hal Taliaferro, Jack O'Shea, H.T. Tsiang, Marshall Reed, Wade Crosby, Eddy Waller, William Haade, Boyd Irwin, Lucien Littlefield, Ethel Wales, Elaine Lange, William B. Davidson, Ellen Corby, Fred Burns.

Elliott graduated from the RED RYDER series to more substantial fare in this film as a gentleman gambler and stagecoach robber who falls for ethically pure saloon girl Moore. She protects her lover from the clutches of the sheriff and local vigilantes, but when a young prospector, who has a crush on Moore, is falsely accused of wrong-doing, Elliott is ever the gentleman and gives himself up. But the law is not nearly as couth, shooting him down and leaving him to die in Moore's arms. Moore sings "Camptown Races" and "Can't Tell Why I Love You." Other ditties are "Speak to Me of Love," "The Man Who Broke the Bank at Monte Carlo," and "My Gal's a High-Born Lady."

p&d, Joseph Kane; w, Frances Lyland, Frank Gruber (based on the story "Diamond Carlisle" by Kane); ph, Jack Marta; ed, Fred Allen; art d, James Sullivan; set d, John McCarthy, Jr., Earl Wooden; spec eff, Howard, Theodore Lydecker; m/l, Jean Lenoir, Bruce Sievier, Fred Gilbert, Will D. Cobb, Gus Edwards.

Western **(PR:C MPAA:NR)**

IN OLD SANTA FE*** (1935) 62m Mascot bw

Ken Maynard *(Himself)*, Evalyn Knapp *(Lila Miller)*, H.B. Warner *(Mr. Miller)*, Kenneth Thomson *(Chandler)*, Wheeler Oakman *(Tracy)*, George Hayes *(Cactus)*, Gene Autry *(Himself)*, Lester "Smiley" Burnette, George Chesebro, George Burton, Jack Rockwell, Jim Corey, Jack Kirk, Edward Hearn, Frank Ellis, Horace B. Carpenter, Tarzan the Horse.

When some gangsters from the city arrive, they set up dude ranch hand Maynard for a frame. He loses his beloved horse Tarzan in a fixed race and gets blamed for a murder. Naturally, everything is righted at the end. This was Maynard's only film done at Mascot, and much more accomplished than any of his serials done at the larger Universal and Columbia studios. It is also famous for the film debut of radio cowpuncher Autry, along with sidekick Burnette. Autry set his pattern early: his songs get in the way of the story line.

p, Nat Levine; d, David Howard; w, Colbert Clark, James Gruen (based on a story by Wallace MacDonald, John Rathmell); ph, Ernest Miller, William Nobles; ed, Thomas Scott.

Western **Cas.** **(PR:A MPAA:NR)**

IN OUR TIME** (1944) 109m WB bw

Ida Lupino *(Jennifer Whittredge)*, Paul Henreid *(Count Stephen Orvid)*, Nancy Coleman *(Janina Orvid)*, Mary Boland *(Mrs. Bromley)*, Victor Francen *(Count Pavel Orvid)*, Nazimova *(Zofya Orvid)*, Michael Chekhov *(Uncle Leopold)*, Marek Windheim *(Antique Dealer)*, Ivan Triesault *(Bujanski)*, John Bleiffer *(Wladek)*, Lotta Palfi *(Wanda)*, Wolfgang Zilzer *(Father Josef)*, Richard Ordynski *(Pyotr)*, Leonid Snegoff *(Conductor)*, Shimen Ruskin *(Bartender)*, Max Willenz *(Headwaiter)*, Mary Landa *(Flower Girl)*, Alex Akimoff *(Wine Seller)*, Frank Reicher *(Count Jarsky)*, Michael Visaroff *(Dr. Kowalik)*, Sylvia Arslan *(Nanetchka)*, Sonia Levkova *(Graffina's Daughter)*, Mici Goty *(Graffina)*.

Well meaning, though ultimately little more than a soap opera, Lupino is an English woman accompanying her friend Boland on a trip to Warsaw. There she meets Polish count Henreid who falls in love with her. Despite the objections of his family, the two marry and settle on Henreid's family farm. But war soon comes and the farm is burned to the ground by the Nazis. Henreid and Lupino know that Poland will one day rise again, however. The screenplay can't make up its mind: Is this a romance or a social statement? The result is an overlong, though well-acted and -photographed, film.

p, Jerry Wald; d, Vincent Sherman; w, Ellis St. Joseph, Howard Koch; ph, Carl Guthrie; m, Franz Waxman; ed, Rudi Fehr; md, Leo F. Forbstein; art d, Hugh Reticker; set d, Casey Roberts.

Drama **(PR:C MPAA:NR)**

IN PERSON** (1935) 90m RKO bw

Ginger Rogers *(Carol Corliss)*, George Brent *(Emory Muir)*, Alan Mowbray *(Jay Holmes)*, Grant Mitchell *(Judge Parks)*, Samuel S. Hinds *(Dr. Aaron Sylvester)*, Joan Breslau *(Minna)*, Louis Mason *(Sheriff Twing)*, Spencer Charters *("Parson" Lunk)*, Lew Kelly *(Mountain Man)*, Bob McKenzie *(Theater Manager)*, Lee Shumway *(Studio Representative)*, William B. Davidson *(Director Bill Sumner)*, Tiny Jones *(Woman in Theater)*, Bud Jamison *(Man in Elevator)*, George Davis *(Cabbie)*.

Rogers, in an early film without regular partner Astaire, is a famous movie star who can't stand to be bothered by her adoring fans. To escape them she dons a black wig, glasses, and false teeth. Average guy Brent finds her on the streets in the midst of an agoraphobic attack. He takes her away to his mountain cabin to help her overcome her fears, and, much to her surprise, he is unimpressed when her true identity is revealed. She gets over her fears and learns a little bit about herself and humility in the process. Rogers tries her best in the film, but without her regular leading man Astaire it doesn't work very well. She does do a few steps though, to some nice tunes by Levant and Fields, including "Don't Mention Love to Me" and "Got a New Lease on Life."

p, Pandro S. Berman; d, William A. Seiter; w, Allan Scott (based on the novel by Samuel Hopkins Adams); ph, Edward Cronjager; ed, Arthur Schmidt; md, Roy Webb; art d, Van Nest Polglase, Carroll Clark; cos, Bernard Newman; ch, Hermes Pan; m/l, Oscar Levant, Dorothy Fields; makeup, Mel Burns.

Musical/Comedy **(PR:A MPAA:NR)**

IN PIENO SOLE (SEE: PURPLE NOON, 1961, Fr./Ital.)

IN PRAISE OF OLDER WOMEN* (1978, Can.) 105m AE c

Tom Berenger *(Andras Vayda)*, Karen Black *(Maya)*, Susan Strasberg *(Bobbie)*, Helen Shaver *(Ann MacDonald)*, Marilyn Lightstone *(Klari)*, Alexandra Stewart *(Paula)*, Marianne McIsaac *(Julika)*, Alberta Watson *(Mitzi)*, Ian Tracey *(Andras Vayda, Jr.)*, Monique LePage *(Countess)*, Mignon Elkins *(Mother Vayda)*, Joan Stuart *(Aunt Alice)*, John Bayliss *(Glen MacDonald)*, Jon Granik *(Tom Horvath)*, Louise Marleau, Jill Frappier, Budd Knapp, Earl Pennington, Michael Kirby, Bronwen Mantel, Wally Martin, Arden Ryshpan, Tibor Polgar, Julie Wildman, Julie Morand, Griffith Brewer, Walter Bolton, Martha Parker, Robert King, Arthur Grosser.

At age twelve, a young Hungarian boy is forced into pimping for a living after World War II. He grows up to be Berenger, a man with a sexual predilection for older women. The film charts seven of his affairs, which range from an anti-Communist musician to a journalist he cures of frigidity. Dull and repetitious (seven times over!) this is a little more than a thinly disguised sex film. The camera work and decor are lush, but can't compensate for a thin and repetitious plot line.

p, Robert Lantos, Claude Heroux; d, George Kaczender; w, Paul Gottlieb (based on the novel by Stephen Vizinczey); ph, Miklos Lente; m, Tibor Polgar; ed, Kaczender, Peter Wintonick; art d, Wolf Kroeger; cos, Olga Dimitrov.

Drama **Cas.** **(PR:O MPAA:R)**

IN ROSIE'S ROOM (SEE: ROSIE, THE RIVETER, 1944)

IN SEARCH OF ANNA*½ (1978, Aus.) 94m Storm Productions c

Richard Moir *(Tony)*, Judy Morris *(Sam)*, Chris Hayward *(Jerry)*, Bill Hunter *(Peter)*, Garry Waddell *(Maxie)*, Ian Nimmo *(Buzz)*, Maurie Fields *(Bert)*, Alex Taifer *(Tony's Father)*, Richard Murphett *(Undertaker)*.

Moir is released from prison after six years. His old comrades return to find out where the stolen money is that he took the rap for. When he doesn't know, they beat him, and then he takes his revenge. After which, he takes off to look for his old girl—but picks up neurotic model Morris along the way. In her 1938 sedan they drive across the Australian countryside, finding each other. The film is sloppily put together and the story is incoherent; the soundtrack is a loud and completely distracting series of bad rock and roll songs; there are unexplained motivations and open endings. Worst of all are the film's arty pretensions via empty montages, and particularly bad editing at the end.

p,d,&w, Esben Storm; ph, Mike Edols; ed, Dusan Werner; prod d, Jane Scott; makeup, Anne Pospischil.

Drama **Cas.** **(PR:O MPAA:NR)**

IN SEARCH OF GREGORY**

(1970, Brit./Ital.) 90m Vic Films-Vera Films/UNIV c (ALLA RICERCA DI GREGORY)

Julie Christie *(Catherine)*, Michael Sarrazin *(Gregory)*, John Hurt *(Daniel)*, Paola Pitagora *(Nicole)*, Adolfo Celi *(Max)*, Roland Culver *(Wardle)*, Tony Selby *(Taxi Driver)*, Jimmy Lynn *(Air Steward)*, Violetta Chiarini *(Paquita)*, Gabriella Giorgelli *(Encarna)*, Luisa De Santis *(Giselle)*, Ernesto Pagno *(Priest)*, Roderick Smith *(Small Boy)*, Gordon Gostelow *(Old Man)*.

Christie is a young woman who goes to her father's wedding on the promise that she will meet a handsome young man named Gregory—who never shows. Instead, Christie fantasizes about him. She imagines him to be the handsome autoball player whose picture she has seen at the airport. She searches for him all over Geneva but her effort are fruitless. She decides to return to Rome, though her brother Hurt, with whom she has had an incestuous affair years before, tries to dissuade her. At the airport she meets the autoball player (Sarrazin) and they take a hotel room for an afternoon of love-making. But he reveals himself to be a dull, German medical student and Christie is crushed. She prepares to leave for Rome once more and calls Hurt from the airport. He tells her that the elusive Gregory has just called and is searching for her. But she decides to leave Geneva, completely unaware that Gregory (whose face is never seen) is in the phone booth next to hers. The film tries to be a Pinter-style psycho-drama but doesn't make it. Co-writer Guerra also contributed to L'AVVENTURA and BLOW UP. This was the last film made by Universal's European production company and the finished product was held for a year before it was released.

p, Joseph Janni, Daniele Senatore; d, Peter Wood; w, Tonino Guerra, Lucile Laks, Ken Levison; ph, Otto Heller, Giorgio Tonti (Technicolor); m, Ron Grainer; ed, John Bloom; art d, Piero Poletto; cos, Gabriella Falk; m/l, "Dreams," Grainer, Don Black (sung by Georgie Fame), "Close," Ken Howard (sung by Fame); makeup, Wally Schneiderman.

Psycho-Drama **(PR:O MPAA:GP)**

IN SEARCH OF HISTORIC JESUS* (1980) 91m Sunn Classics c

John Rubinstein *(Jesus)*, John Anderson *(Caiaphas)*, Nehemiah Persoff *(Herod Antipas)*, Brad Crandall *(Narrator)*, Andrew Bloch *(John)*, Morgan Brittany *(Mary)*, Walter Brooke *(Joseph)*, Annette Charles *(Mary Magdalene)*, Royal Dano *(Prophet)*, Anthony DeLongis *(Peter)*, Lawrence Dobkin *(Pontius Pilate)*, David Opatoshu *(Herod)*, Richard Carlyle *(Astrologer)*, Jeffry Druce, John Hoyt, Stanley Kamel, Al Ruscio, Harvey Solin, Richard Alfieri, Robert Bonvento, Travis DeCastro, Steve DeFrance, John Hansen, James Ingersoll, Richard Jury.

Sunn Classics was famous for taking a popular phenomena like UFOs, Bigfoot, or Noah's Ark sightings and making a quick psuedo-documentary/dramatization "exploring" the topic. The film would receive intense media blitzes and usually turned a nice profit. Here they take the discovery of "the Shroud of Turin," a burial cloth some scientists theorize may have been used to wrap Jesus after his crucifixion. The overly serious narration is done by Crandall in what may be one of the cheapest toupees ever worn in Hollywood. Rubinstein, son of the piano virtuoso, plays the son of a different kind of virtuoso here. Watch him walk on water! Theology is wishy-washy in this film, pandering to its intended religious audience, with just enough tease to bring an atheist or two out to the theater. It's a shame that a talent like Persoff is reduced to working in this sort of material.

p, Charles E. Sellier, Jr., James L. Conway; d, Henning Schellerup; w, Malvin Wald, Jack Jacobs (based on the book by Lee Roddy and Sellier, Jr.); ph, Paul Hipp (Technicolor); m, Bob Summers; ed, Kendall S. Rase; prod d, Paul Staheli; art d, Doug Vandergrift; set d, Randy Staheli; cos, Julie Staheli; spec eff, John Carter.

Historical Drama **Cas.** **(PR:AA MPAA:G)**

IN SEARCH OF THE CASTAWAYS½** (1962, Brit.) 100m BV c

Maurice Chevalier (*Prof. Jacques Paganel*), Hayley Mills (*Mary Grant*), George Sanders (*Thomas Ayerton*), Wilfrid Hyde-White (*Lord Glenarvan*), Michael Anderson Jr. (*John Glenarvan*), Antonio Cifariello (*Thalcave*), Keith Hamshere (*Robert Grant*), Wilfrid Brambell (*Bill Gaye*), Jack Gwillim (*Capt. Grant*), Ronald Fraser (*Guard*), Inia Te Wiata (*Maori Chief*), Norman Bird, Michael Wynne, Milo Sperber, Barry Keegan, George Murcell, Mark Dignam, Roger Delgado, Maxwell Shaw, Andreas Malandrinos, David Spenser.

Chevalier is a professor who finds a message in a bottle. Believing the message to be from the missing Gwillim, he takes the missing man's children Mills and Hamshere off on a search. They persuade Hyde-White, the owner of Gwillim's ship, to finance the expedition. He sails off with them, along with his son Anderson, continually finding leads for the missing captain but never the captain. In South America they have to deal with earthquakes and giant condors. An Indian chief claims to know where the captain is, but this only leads to more natural disaster. From there, it's off to Australia, where they meet Sanders, who claims to know the captain's whereabouts. They are unaware that Sanders had led a mutiny against Gwillim and is responsible for his disappearance. He sets the group up for some trouble from cannibals. By escaping into a cliff, they trigger off a volcanic eruption, but save their lives. Finally, Gwillim is found, Sanders overcome, and everyone lives happily from that moment on. It's a typical Disney live action feature, with simplistic story and characters. Though well below Chevalier's talents, it's always a pleasure to hear him sing. He gets one solo ("Merci Beaucoup") and a few numbers with other cast members. The songs are written by the Sherman brothers, sons of Al Sherman, who wrote many of Chevalier's popular 1930s songs. It's pleasant, if lesser, fare.

p, Walt Disney; d, Robert Stevenson; w, Lowell S. Hawley (based on "Captain Grant's Children" by Jules Verne); ph, Paul Beeson (Technicolor); m, William Alwyn; ed, Gordon Stone; md, Muir Mathieson; art d, Michael Stringer; set d, Vernon Dixon; cos, Margaret Furse; spec eff, Syd Pearson, Peter Ellenshaw; m/l, Richard M. and Robert B. Sherman.

Fantasy/Adventure **Cas.** **(PR:AAA MPAA:NR)**

IN SOCIETY** ½** (1944) 75m UNIV bw

Bud Abbott (*Eddie Harrington*), Lou Costello (*Albert Mansfield*), Marion Hutton (*Elsie Hammerdingle*), Kirby Grant (*Peter Evans*), Ann Gillis (*Gloria Winthrop*), Arthur Treacher (*Pipps the Butler*), Thomas Gomez (*Drexel*), George Dolenz (*Baron Sergei*), Steven Geray (*Count Alexis*), Margaret Irving (*Mrs. Winthrop*), Murray Leonard (*Marlow*), Thurston Hall (*Mr. Van Cleve*), Nella Walker (*Mrs. Van Cleve*), William B. Davidson (*Parker Van Cleve Butler*), Elvia Allman (*Bit Woman*), Milt Bronson (*Bit Man*), Don Barclay (*Drunk in Pool*), Edgar Dearing (*Cop*), Ann Roberts (*Woman*), Ian Wolfe (*2nd Butler*), Charles Sherlock (*Policeman*), Al Thompson (*2nd Bit Man*), Luis Alberni (*Luigi*), Tom Fadden (*Fire Chief*), Charles Coleman (*Van Cleve's Doorman*), Tom Dugan (*Derby Dan*), Dorothy Granger (*Hysterical Woman*), Ralph Dunn (*Cop*), Gladys Blake, Mabel Todd (*Manicurists*), Cyril Ring, Alice Flemming, Rovamel Hilton, Charles Hull, The Three Sisters (*Margie, Bea, Jeri—Specialty*), Will Osborne and his Orchestra.

A&C appear as a pair of plumbers who couldn't get water to run if they were in the middle of the Mississippi. The dimwitted pair do, however, mistakenly get themselves invited to a high society bash. This film is notable for the inclusion of Sid Fields, an old-time burlesque comic who plays the part of a language coach frustrated at Costello's fractured English. One routine has Fields saying: "Did you see that movie with Irene Dunne? Didn't you see what Irene Dunne did?" Costello retorts: "What Irene done did! This guy talks worse than me!" Then Fields asks: "Can you name the consonants?" Replies Costello: "Yes, sir! North America, South America, and Patterson, New Jersey." A similar routine was used by the boys and Fields in MEXICAN HAYRIDE. Abbott and Costello were noted for their kindness to old time burlesque comics they had worked with or knew when they were fledgling comedians trodding the bump-and-grind boards. Whenever an old-timer appeared in Hollywood, the boys would put him up and get him a job in their forthcoming film, talking producers into paying at least $1,000 for the comic's best routine.

p, Edmund L. Hartmann; d, Jean Yarbrough; w, John Grant, Hartmann, Hal Fimberg, Sid Fields (based on a story by Hugh Wedlock, Jr., Howard Snyder); ph, Jerome Ash; ed, Philip Cahn; md, Edgar Fairchild; art d, John B. Goodman, Eugene Lourie; cos, Vera West; spec eff, John P. Fulton; m/l, "My Dreams Are Getting Better All the Time," "No Doubt About It" (Mann Curtis, Vic Muzzy), "What A Change In the Weather" (Kim Cannon, Walter Kent), "Rehearsin'" (Bobby Worth, Stanley Cowan), "Memory Lane" (Larry Spier, Con Conrad, B.G. DeSylva).

Comedy **(PR:AAA MPAA:NR)**

IN SPITE OF DANGER* ½ (1935) 53m COL bw

Wallace Ford (*Bob Crane*), Marian Marsh (*Sally Sullivan*), Arthur Hohl (*Steve Lynch*), Charles B. Middleton (*Mr. Merritt*), Edward Le Saint (*Dr. Daley*), Richard Wessel (*Monk Grady*), Jay Walter Ward (*Tommy Sullivan*).

Ford is an auto race driver recuperating from an accident who meets waitress Marsh and decides to go into the trucking business with her father. They become involved with a rival trucking company that has in its employ the driver who secretly doctored Ford's racing car, causing his accident. Competition between the two companies and the two drivers ensues, but there's very little suspense. Motivations are paper thin, and escapes too hokey to be believed. There are a couple of nifty sequences, including a truck going over a cliff, and another blown up by its dynamite cargo, but production values are otherwise nothing spectacular.

d, Lambert Hillyer; w, Anthony Coldeway; ph, Benjamin Kline; ed, Otto Meyer.

Action/Suspense **(PR:A MPAA:NR)**

IN STRANGE COMPANY (SEE: FIRST AID, 1931)

IN THE COOL OF THE DAY* ½ (1963) 86m MGM c

Jane Fonda (*Christine Bonner*), Peter Finch (*Murray Logan*), Angela Lansbury (*Sibyl Logan*), Arthur Hill (*Sam Bonner*), Constance Cummings (*Mrs. Gellert*), Alexander Knox (*Frederick Bonner*), Nigel Davenport (*Leonard*), John Le Mesurier (*Dr. Arraman*), Alec McCowen (*Dickie Bayliss*), Valerie Taylor (*Lily Kendrick*), Andreas Markos (*Andreas*), George Coulouris.

A sudsy soap opera that features some fine acting. Fonda is not happy in her marriage to Hill, who absolutely dotes on her. She can't stand being confined and so they separate to see if they can be happier apart. In their reconciliation, he promises to allow her to have some "space" and he agrees to let her have a baby. Next, she meets Finch, a publisher pal of Hill's. Finch is trapped in a loveless marriage to Lansbury, who bears the scars of an auto accident that also killed their son. She blames Finch for all her unhappiness and refuses to get on with her life. Fonda and Finch have a mutual attraction, but Finch is too much the gentleman to take advantage. The two couples plan a trip to Greece, but Hill can't make it due to the illness of his father, Knox, so Fonda accompanies Finch and Lansbury. Lansbury decides to stay at the hotel as Finch and Fonda visit the Acropolis and find that they are in love. Meanwhile, Lansbury takes up with another man and, in anger, tells Hill about her husband and his wife. Hill flies to Greece and learns that Fonda is dying of pneumonia. Just before she expires, she makes Finch swear that he'll visit all the places they hoped to see together. How John Houseman, who is usually a producer with exquisite taste, got involved with this claptrap is something we'll never know. A lumbering, almost slumbering film that may have caused more drowsiness than Miltown.

p, John Houseman; d, Robert Stevens; w, Meade Roberts (based on the novel by Susan Ertz); ph, Peter Newbrook (Panavision, Metrocolor); m, Francis Chagrin; ed, Thomas Stanford; prod d, Ken Adam; cos, Orry-Kelly, Pierre Balmain; m/l, "In the Cool of the Day," Manos Hadjidakis, Nikos Gatsos, Liam Sullivan (sung by Nat "King" Cole).

Drama **(PR:C MPAA:NR)**

IN THE COUNTRY** (1967) 65m Blue Van Films bw

William Devane, Catherine Merrill, Jane Kramer, Henry Heifitz, Gerald Long, Thomas Neuman.

A well-scripted picture concerned with the changes people go through when they isolate themselves from their pasts and their surroundings. Devane stars as a political activist who, with his wife, shakes off the roots of his city environment and starts life anew in the country.

p, d&w, Robert Kramer; ph, Robert Machover; ed, Kramer, Machover.

Drama **(PR:A MPAA:NR)**

IN THE DAYS OF THE THUNDERING HERD
(SEE: THUNDERING HERD, THE, 1934)

IN THE DEVIL'S GARDEN (SEE: ASSAULT, 1971, Brit.)

IN THE DOGHOUSE** (1964, Brit.) 84m RANK/Zenith bw

Leslie Phillips (*Jimmy Fox-Upton*), Peggy Cummins (*Sally*), Hattie Jacques (*Primrose Gudgeon*), James Booth (*Bob Skeffington*), Dick Bentley (*Mr. Peddle*), Colin Gordon (*Dean*), Joan Heal (*Mrs. Peddle*), Fenella Fielding (*Miss Fordyce*), Esma Cannon (*Mrs. Raikes*), Richard Goolden (*Ribart*), Joan Hickson (*Miss Gibbs*), Vida Hope (*Mrs. Crabtree*), Harry Locke (*Sid*), Kynaston Reeves (*Colonel*), Peggy Thorpe-Bates (*Mrs. Muswell*), Joan Young (*Middle-Aged Woman*), Judith Furse (*Masseuse*), Philip Ray (*Vicar*), Gerald Andersen (*Johnson*), Freda Bamford (*Miss Ritter*), Jacqueline Jones (*Rita*).

Phillips is a veterinarian who finally passes his exams after 12 years. He sets up shop in a poor neighborhood, working with animals out of genuine love. Booth is his rival, cheating on the exams and then setting up shop in a rich area so he can rake in money. Phillips gets involved with Cummins, an entertainer, after chasing her trained chimpanzee through a ladies' Turkish bath. Unwittingly he becomes involved with Booth in a plan to export horses to France to be butchered. After discovering the nature of the business, he exposes the wrongdoings with the help of Cummins and Jacques, an inspector of the Royal Society for the Prevention of Cruelty to Animals. It's a cute though inconsequential comedy. Phillips is fine in his role of the gentle vet, though his counterpart Booth indulges in too much overacting.

p, Hugh Stewart; d, Darcy Conyers; w, Michael Pertwee (based on the novel *It's a Vet's Life* by Alex Duncan); ph, Alan Hume; m, Philip Green; ed, Roger Cherrill; art d, Maurice Carter; set d, Arthur Taksen; cos, Joan Ellacott, John Hilling; makeup, George Blackler.

Comedy **(PR:A MPAA:NR)**

IN THE FALL OF '55 EDEN CRIED (SEE: EDEN CRIED, 1967)

IN THE FRENCH STYLE***
(1963, U.S./Fr.) 104m Casanna-Orsay/COL bw (A LA FRANCAISE)

Jean Seberg (*Christina James*), Stanley Baker (*Walter Beddoes*), Philippe Forquet (*Guy*), Addison Powell (*Mr. James*), Jack Hedley (*Bill*), Maurice Teynac (*Baron*), James Leo Herlihy (*Dr. John Haislip*), Ann Lewis (*Guy's Fiancee*), Jacques Charon (*Patrini*), Claudine Auger (*Clio*), Barbara Somers (*Madame Piguet*), Moustache (*Bistro Owner*).

Seberg is an American studying painting in Paris. She becomes involved with Forquet, who tells her he is an engineering student. But when they are about to make love in a low-class hotel, he confesses to her that he is only 16 and still in high school. Seberg leaves him and has a series of affairs until she meets Baker, a hard-drinking correspondent. Though he is constantly called away from Paris, she loves him passionately. After he is sent to Tripoli on assignment, Seberg's father, Powell, visits her and tries to convince her to return to Chicago. But she says no, preferring her life with Baker. Finally she comes to the realization that life with Baker is little more than a series of short moments and long separations. She faces reality and meets Herlihy, a doctor from San Francisco. They marry and return to the U.S. with the promise that every three years they will vacation in Paris. Though it's episodic starting off, once Seberg meets Baker the film is on solid ground. Performances are strong, particularly Seberg's. She handles her lead role with the strength and sensitivity necessary. After her success in Godard's BREATHLESS in 1959, she was a favorite with French film goers and she is equally fine here. The camera work is excellent, artistic and well edited without taking anything away from the performers. Herlihy would later write the novel *Midnight Cowboy*, the basis of the excellent 1969 Oscar winner. IN THE FRENCH STYLE is based on two short stories by the American writer Shaw, who served as coproducer and screenwriter.

p, Irwin Shaw, Robert Parrish; d, Parrish; w, Shaw (based on his two short stories "In the French Style" and "A Year to Learn the Language"); ph, Michel Kelber; m, Joseph Kosma; ed, Renee Lichtig; md, Andre Girard, art d, Rino Mondellini; cos, Philippe Venet; makeup, Michele Deruelle.

Romance **(PR:O MPAA:NR)**

IN THE GOOD OLD SUMMERTIME*½** (1949) 102m MGM c

Judy Garland (*Veronica Fisher*), Van Johnson (*Andrew Larkin*), S.Z. Sakall (*Otto Oberkugen*), Spring Byington (*Nellie Burke*), Clinton Sundberg (*Rudy Hansen*), Buster Keaton (*Hickey*), Marcia Van Dyke (*Louise Parkson*), Lillian Bronson (*Aunt Addie*).

Music-filled remake of THE SHOP AROUND THE CORNER has Garland and Johnson working together in a Chicago music store at the turn of century. The change of venue and addition of music to the story were made to better utilize the stars' talents. Working for Sakall, Garland plays piano and sells sheet music, while Johnson sells musical instruments. The two co-workers dislike each other, but coincidentally are also pen pals. The cooler they are to each other, the hotter their letters become. In the end they are united, but not before a predictable mix-up between Sakall's priceless Stradivarius and a more common fiddle, which ends up broken. Sakall also has a long-term relationship with his secretary, Byington. Eighteen-month-old Liza Minelli made her second screen appearance as Johnson and Garland's child at the end of the film following their marriage. (Her first appearance was in EASTER PARADE a year earlier.) Although music dominated the plot, the story was strong enough for a pleasurable film. Music includes: "I Don't Care" (Jean Lenox, Harry Sutton), "Meet Me Tonight In Dreamland" (Beth Slater Whitson, Lee Friedman), "Play That Barbershop Chord" (Ballard MacDonald, William Tracey, Lewis Muir), "In the Good Old Summertime" (George Evans, Ren Shields), "Put Your Arms Around Me Honey" (Junie McCree, Harry von Tilzer), "Merry Christmas" (Janice Torre, Fred Spielman), "Wait Till the Sun Shines Nellie" (Von Tilzer, Andrew B. Sterling), "Chicago" (Fred Fisher).

p, Joe Pasternak; d, Robert Z. Leonard; w, Samson Raphaelson, Francis Goodrich, Ivan Tors, Albert Hackett (based on the play "The Shop Around the Corner" by Miklos Laszlo); ph, Harry Stradling (Technicolor); m, George Stoll; ed, Adrienne Fazan; art d, Cedric Gibbons, Randall Duell; md, Stoll; ch, Robert Alton.

Musical Comedy **(PR:AA MPAA:NR)**

IN THE HEADLINES** (1929) 72m WB bw

Grant Withers (*Nosey Norton*), Marion Nixon (*Anna Lou Anderson*), Clyde Cook (*Flashlight*), Edmund Breese (*Eddy*), Pauline Garon (*Alice Adair*), Frank Campeau (*Detective Robinson*), Vivian Oakland (*Mrs. Kornell*), Hallam Cooley (*Fancy Somerset*), Robert Ober (*Parker*), Ben Hall (*Cub Reporter*), Spec O'Donnell (*Johnny*), Jack Wise (*Levine*).

Newspaper journalist Withers and his assistant Nixon are investigating a strange double murder. Their nosing around gets the pair in hot water but it's all resolved in the end as the crime is solved and the duo ends up at the altar. The plot is full of twists and turns but otherwise it's an average murder mystery.

d, John G. Adolfi; w, Joseph Jackson (based on a story by James A. Starr).

Crime **(PR:A MPAA:NR)**

IN THE HEAT OF THE NIGHT**** (1967) 109m Mirisch Corp/UA c

Sidney Poitier *(Virgil Tibbs)*, Rod Steiger *(Bill Gillespie)*, Warren Oates *(Sam Wood)*, Quentin Dean *(Delores Purdy)*, James Patterson *(Purdy)*, William Schallert *(Webb Schubert)*, Jack Teter *(Philip Colbert)*, Lee Grant *(Mrs. Leslie Colbert)*, Scott Wilson *(Harvey Oberst)*, Matt Clark *(Packy Harrison)*, Anthony James *(Ralph Henshaw)*, Larry Gates *(Eric Endicott)*, Kermit Murdock *(H.E. Henderson)*, Khalil Bezaleel *(Jess)*, Beah Richards *(Mrs. Bellamy [Mama Caleba])*, Peter Whitney *(George Courtney)*, William Watson *(Harold Courtney)*, Timothy Scott *(Shagbag Martin)*, Michael LeGlaire *(Dennis)*, Larry D. Mann *(Watkins)*, Stewart Nisbet *(Shuie)*, Eldon Quick *(Charlie Hawthorne)*, Fred Stewart *(Dr. Stuart)*, Arthur Malet *(Ted Ulam)*, Peter Masterson *(Arnold Fryer)*, Alan Oppenheimer *(Ted Appleton)*, Philip Garris *(Mark Crowell)*, Jester Hairston *(Henry)*, Clegg Hoyt *(Deputy)*, Phil Adams, Nikita Knatz *(Young Toughs)*, David Stinehart *(Baggage Master)*, Buzz Barton *(Conductor)*.

This superb thriller has Steiger in his Oscar-winning role as a simple but shrewd southern sheriff and Poitier as his opposite number—a sensitive, intellectual black detective from the big city—both of them attempting to solve a brutal murder. A wealthy industrialist is found murdered in an alley of Sparta, Mississippi, and deputies begin to comb the city for the killer. Simple-minded Oates arrests a well-dressed black man waiting at the train station, Poitier, who, upon being taken to sheriff Steiger identifies himself as a Philadelphia police detective. Steiger gives Poitier an off-hand apology but the big city cop stays in town, offering Steiger his help, which is grudgingly accepted after Poitier turns up some clues following a postmortem examination of the dead man. When Steiger finds Wilson with the dead man's wallet he accuses him of murdering the industrialist, but Poitier quickly proves that Wilson merely found the body and stole the wallet. Poitier's sophisticated criminology methods fail, however, when he duplicates Steiger's error by wrongly accusing wealthy, bigoted Gates simply because he is a racist. In a telling scene, Gates first welcomes Steiger and Poitier to his mansion and discusses rare plants in his greenhouse, but when Poitier makes a remark as an "uppity nigger," Gates slaps his face. Poitier slaps the white man back which sends Steiger into shock. Gates asks what Steiger intends to do about his being hit by a black man and Steiger slowly replies: "I don't know." After leaving Gates' estate the sheriff tries to "educate" Poitier in the ways of Mississippi society and tries to convince him that black people, even high-minded detectives from the North, don't go around hitting local white power brokers. Poitier is later trapped in a warehouse by a group of thugs obviously sent by Gates and is about to be beaten to a pulp or, worse, killed, but Steiger appears and chases them off. Poitier's welcome has worn out but Steiger finds it difficult to get him out of town, particularly after the victim's wife insists he stay on the case. In one touching moment, Poitier visits Steiger at the sheriff's modest home to witness the lonely existence he endures, but learns that he is really a fair-minded man who wants to do his job properly. Steiger later accuses his own deputy Oates of killing the industrialist. Teenage vamp Dean is dragged into the station by her brother Patterson, enraged at learning from her that Oates has impregnated her; then Poitier goes to an abortionist, Richards. From her he learns that the real culprit is perverse counterman James. When he leaves the abortionist's home, James tries to kill him, as do a mob of white rednecks, but again Steiger appears to save Poitier and James is arrested as the killer. He had simply murdered the industrialist to get money for Dean's abortion. With the case solved, Steiger and Poitier say goodbye at the train station, a reserved and distant farewell but one full of respect for each other. From beginning to end, IN THE HEAT OF THE NIGHT is carefully directed by Jewison who eschews sentimentality and all the racial cliches that could have so easily crept into almost every scene. Steiger's performance is subtle, funny, sad, and completely fascinating, one so compelling that it earned him an Oscar. The film itself shocked many when it beat out BONNIE AND CLYDE and THE GRADUATE for the Academy's Best Picture award. Jones' score is hauntingly memorable and all the technical credits are top notch. Filming was shot in Illinois and Tennessee, the latter representing Mississippi. Poitier would take his character from this film a long way, into THEY CALL ME MR. TIBBS (1970) and THE ORGANIZATION (1971). At first the reserved, polished, and intellectual Tibbs role was impressive and effective but Poitier wore it out and much of his acting reputation with it.

p, Walter Mirisch; d, Norman Jewison; w, Stirling Silliphant (based on the novel by John Ball); ph, Haskell Wexler (DeLuxe Color); m, Quincy Jones; ed, Hal Ashby; art d, Paul Groesse; set d, Robert Priestley; cos, Alan Levine; m/l, Jones, Marilyn Bergman, Alan Bergman; makeup, Del Armstrong.

Crime Drama **(PR:C MPAA:NR)**

IN THE LINE OF DUTY** (1931) 60m MON bw

Sue Carol, Noah Beery, Francis MacDonald, James Murray, Richard Cramer, Frank Selder, Henry Hall.

Beery is a killer who flees his home to begin a new life in the Arctic Circle. He takes his daughter, Carol, and decides to become a hunter. But a mountie is after Beery, and his only clue is the unique way the killer smokes his pipe. There are the usual amounts of fighting and action, including an interesting sequence of a cliff collapsing underneath the officer and his horse. Eventually the officer falls in love with Carol, and Beery and another hunter kill each other. The film closes with the Arctic lovebirds singing the title song. This was a B film, meant for the lower half of double bills. Beery is adequate in his role but, aside from the cliff sequence, there is very little special or different about this film.

d, Bert Glennon; w, G.A. Durlam; ph, Archie Stout; ed, Len Wheeler.

Drama/Romance **(PR:A MPAA:NR)**

IN THE MEANTIME, DARLING** (1944) 74m FOX bw

Jeanne Crain (*Maggie*), Frank Latimore (*Lt. Daniel Ferguson*), Eugene Pallette (*H.B. Preston*), Mary Nash (*Mrs. Preston*), Stanley Prager (*Lt. Red Pianatowski*), Gale Robbins (*Shirley Pianatowski*), Jane Randolph (*Jerry Armstrong*), Doris Merrick (*Mrs. MacAndrews*), Cara Williams (*Ruby Mae Sayre*), Ann Corcoran (*Mrs. Bennett*), Reed Hadley (*Maj. Phillips*), Heather Angel (*Mrs. Nelson*), Bonnie Bannon (*Mrs. Farnum*), William Colby (*Lt. Farnum*), Cliff Clark (*Col. Corkery*), Elisabeth Risdon (*Mrs. Corkery*), Marjorie Masson (*Mrs. Cook*), Lee Bennett (*Lt. Sayre*), Roger Clark (*Lt. Sullivan*), Clarence Muse (*Henry*), Olin Howlin (*Mr. Morehouse*), Mae Marsh (*Emma*), Glenn Langan (*Lt. Larkin*), Paul Harvey (*Gen. Garnett*), Milton Kibbee (*Postman*), Blake Edwards (*Lt. Eley*), Lee March, Ruth Clifford, Frank Wilcox, Mary McCarty, Evelyn Mulhall, Geraldine Wall, Don Hayden, Lillian Bronson, Eddie Acuff, Merrill Rodin, Janet Burston, Marvin Davis, Charles Hayes, Frank McLure, B.S. Pully.

Wartime comedy features Crain as a pampered rich girl who marries army lieutenant Latimore. Army life, with all its traveling and cramped quarters, is more than she can handle. She fights with the other wives in the small hotel she lives in. When Latimore's unit is put on alert, she tries to use her father's influence to get her husband a permanent stateside position. There is a misunderstanding between the couple when he mistakenly believes she is pregnant. In the end, Crain realizes what the war effort is all about and bravely says goodbye as Latimore goes off to war. Crain is amateurish and unbelievable while Latimore, in his film debut, gives a strong, convincing performance. The script constantly goes from point to point, never quite deciding on a main plot line. America was well into WW II at this film's release date, and Hollywood was grinding out countless features supporting the war effort at home and the front. Preminger's direction is nothing special, showing little inkling of what he was really capable of.

p&d, Otto Preminger; w, Arthur Kober, Michael Uris; ph, Joe MacDonald; m, David Buttolph; ed, Louis Loeffler; md, Emil Newman; art d, James Basevi, John Ewing; set d, Thomas Little, Fred J. Rode; cos, Bonnie Cashin; spec eff, Fred Sersen; ch, Geneva Sawyer.

Wartime Comedy **(PR:A MPAA:NR)**

IN THE MONEY* (1934) 66m IN/CHES bw

Skeets Gallagher, Lois Wilson, Warren Hymer, Sally Starr, Arthur Hoyt, Junior Coghlan, Erin La Bissonier, Harold Waldridge, Louise Beavers.

Confusing and muddled mess of a film that tries to be episodic but ends up incomprehensible. Vaudeville comedian Gallagher (of Gallagher and Shean) is the master of ceremonies, introducing each performer and telling exactly what will happen next. This is followed by a black "mammie" who knows each performer by his or her underwear. The "performers" include a strange scientist who writes bad checks and chats with bunnies, a boxer doing a poor imitation of the famed boxer Gene Tunney, and a pouting pansy who lisps in a most repugnant manner. Strange, confusing, and really a waste of time.

d, Frank Strayer; w, Robert Ellis; ph, M.A. Anderson; ed, Roland Reed.

Comedy **(PR:A MPAA:NR)**

IN THE MONEY** 1/2** (1958) 61m AA bw

Huntz Hall (*Horace Debussy "Sach" Jones*), Stanley Clements (*Stanislaus "Duke" Coveleske*), David Gorcey (*Chuck*), Eddie LeRoy (*Blinky*), John Dodsworth (*Mike Cummings*), Patricia Donahue (*Babs DeWitt*), Leonard Penn (*John Clarke*), Paul Cavanagh (*Inspector Herbert Saunders*), Leslie Denison (*Inspector White*), Dick Elliott (*Mike Clancy*), Owen McGiveney (*Dr. Rufus B. Smedley*), Norma Varden (*Dowager*), Ashley Cowan (*Bellboy*), Ralph Gamble (*Randall*), Patrick O'Moore (*Reggie*), Pamela Light (*Girl*), Snub Pollard (*Scotland Yard Valet*), Judy Bamber, Ric Roman, Byron Foulger, Benny Rubin, Ralph Sanford, Joe Devlin, James Flavin, Earle Hodgins, John Mitchum, Jack Mulhall, Fritz Feld, Wilbur Mack, Gloris the Dog.

This final Bowery Boys outing offers a few scenes that are representative of the series' humor but lack the punch of the earlier films. Hall is hired by diamond smugglers to escort their poodle on a trans-Atlantic cruise. Believing they are decent people, Hall defends them from Scotland Yard detectives who have accused them of being crooks. With the entire Bowery gang on board as stowaways, and the smugglers on board to oversee the operation, the search for the diamonds becomes a tangled mess. They eventually discover that a small cache of the gems are hidden on the dog. A disappointing wrap-up for a wonderful era of comedy. (See BOWERY BOYS series, Index).

p, Richard Heermance; d, William Beaudine; w, Jack Townley, Al Martin, Elwood Ullman, Bert Lawrence; ph, Harry Neumann; m, Marlin Skiles; ed, Neil Brunnenkant; art d, David Milton; set d, Joseph Kish; cos, Sidney Mintz; makeup, Emile LaVigne.

Comedy **(PR:AA MPAA:NR)**

IN THE NAME OF LIFE** 1/2** (1947, USSR) 99m Lenfilm/Artkino bw

Victor Kokriakov (*Dr. Vladimir Petrov*), Mikhail Kuznetsov (*Dr. Alexander Kolesov*), Oleg Zhakov (*Dr. Alexei Rodjdestvensky*), Katya Lepanova (*Lena*), Lydia Shaballna (*Vera*), Margarita Gromyko (*Anyushka*), Nikolai Cherkasov (*Attendant*).

Three Soviet soldiers, tired of seeing death, pledge their lives to the medical profession after being discharged. With Kokriakov as the successful leader of the trio, they vow to find a cure for paralysis. A veteran of Moscow's Transport Workers Theater, he does a fine job as the team leader, with good support from Kuznetsov and Zhakov. Unfortunately, the film is marred by realistic, if not actual, sequences of animal vivisection. Unless excellent special effects were employed, a rabbit is vivisected on camera. Standard Soviet propaganda is also edged in, blaming other scientists for stealing Soviet ideas. Edison and Marconi are included in the group, suggesting some wild Stalin-influenced ideas. Nevertheless, the film is well made with some fine camera work and solid, straightforward direction. Don't miss the anti-American message: the Cold War was just beginning around 1947. Cherkasov, who has a minor role in this film, is known to Americans for his work in IVAN THE TERRIBLE and ALEXANDER NEVSKY. (In Russian; English subtitles.)

d, Alexander Zarki, Josef Heifitz; w, Eugene Garbrilovich, Zarki, Heidts; ph, Vladimir Gardanov. (English subtitles: Charles Clement).

Drama **(PR:O MPAA:NR)**

IN THE NAVY** 1/2** (1941) 85m UNIV bw

Bud Abbott (*Smokey Adams*), Lou Costello (*Pomeroy Watson*), Dick Powell (*Tommy Halstead*), Claire Dodd (*Dorothy Roberts*), Andrews Sisters (*Themselves*), Dick Foran (*Dynamite Dugan*), Shemp Howard (*Dizzy*), Billy Lenhart (*Butch*), Kenneth Brown (*Buddy*), Condos Brothers (*Themselves*), William B. Davidson (*Capt. Richards*), Thurston Hall (*Head of Committee*), Robert Emmett Keane (*Travers*), Edward Fielding (*Commander*), Don Terry (*Floor Manager*), Sunnie O'Dea (*Lancer*), Eddie Dunn (*Ticket Taker*), Ralph Dunn (*Traffic Cop*), Dick Alexander (*Big Bruiser*), Lorin Raker (*Small Meek Husband*), Frank Penny (*Bos'n*), Pat Gleason (*Sentry*), Jack Mulhall (*Lt. Scott*), Mickey Simpson (*Tough Civilian*), Lyle Latell (*Marine*), Chuck Morrison (*Truck Driver*), Lee Kass (*Bandleader*), James Sullivan (*Policeman*), Edna Hall (*Fat Woman*), Claire Whitney (*Gushing Mother*), Joe Bautista (*Mess Boy*), Doris Herbert (*Mother*), Charles Sullivan (*Sailor*), Hooper Atchley, Patsy O'Byrne, Richard Crane, Douglas Wood.

After the thundering success of BUCK PRIVATES, Universal sent Abbott and Costello out to sea with a change of clothing. This time they performed some of their classic skits while adjusting to the wavy ocean waters. While Abbott and Costello handle the laughs, Dick Powell handles the story. He's cast as a popular singer who is tired of making all the girls swoon. In an attempt to avoid his ever-present fans he joins the Navy, but soon finds he is pursued by gal reporter Dodd. In one sequence where several sailors spit water into Costello's face, director Lubin began to laugh so hard that the chubby comedian became infected with mirth and broke up; Lubin left the laughing jag in and it proved to be hilarious. The censors of the day reviewing this film ordered Lubin not to show the sailors spitting water directly into Costello's face (labelling this offensive) and it had to be handled with two different takes, such were the ridiculous rules of the day. Some of the boys' ancient routines were resurrected for this one with lines such as (Costello to Powell): "Where do all the little bugs go this time of year?" Powell shrugs and says: "Search me." Costello replies: "No thanks, I was just wondering." Like all Abbott and Costello comedies, IN THE NAVY is one you can laugh at every time. Gene De Paul and Don Raye wrote the songs, which include "Starlight, Starbright" (sung by Dick Powell, reprise by Powell, The Andrews Sisters), "You're Off to See the World," "Hula Ba Lua," "Gimme Some Skin" (sung by the Andrews Sisters), "A Sailor's Life For Me" (sung by Powell, Dick Foran), "We're in the Navy." Instrumentals included were "Anchors Aweigh" and "You're A Lucky Fellow Mr. Smith."

p, Alex Gottlieb; d, Arthur Lubin; w, Arthur T. Horman, John Grant (based on the story "They're in the Navy Now" by Horman); ph, Joseph Valentine; ed, Philip Cahn; spec eff, John P. Fulton; ch, Nick Castle.

Musical Comedy **(PR:AAA MPAA:NR)**

IN THE NEXT ROOM* 1/2 (1930) 68m WB bw

Jane Winton (*The Lady*), Crauford Kent (*The Lover*), Edward Earle (*Husband*), Jack Mulhall (*James Godfrey*), Alice Day (*Lorna*), Robert Emmett O'Connor (*Tim Morel*), John St. Polis (*Philip Vantine*), Claude Allister (*Parks, the Butler*), Aggie Herring (*Mrs. O'Connor*), DeWitt Jennings (*Inspector Grady*), Webster Campbell (*Snitzer*), Lucien Prival (*French Importer*).

A prolog set in 1889 shows Winton being killed by lover Kent. Using newspaper headlines the story is brought up to 1929 and the main plot begins. An odd little antique dealer, his daughter, maid, and butler have moved into the mansion where the original crime took place. The girl's fiance, a reporter, arrives at the mansion and a series of strange murders begins. The film relies on standard characters and plotting. The acting varies from a funny performance by O'Connor to so-so efforts from the rest of the cast. The soundtrack is terrible. By 1930 sound technology had progressed significantly, but this film shows none of its benefits. The direction is all right, though an abundance of plot loopholes leave this an unthrilling thriller.

d, Eddie Cline; w, Harvey Gates, James A. Starr (based on the play by Eleanor Robson Belmont, Harriet Ford, from the book *The Mystery of the Boule Cabinet* by Burton Egbert Stevenson); ph, John Seitz.

Mystery **(PR:A MPAA:NR)**

IN THE NICK** (1960, Brit.) 105m Warwick/COL bw

Anthony Newley (*Dr. Newcombe*), Anne Aubrey (*Doll*), Bernie Winters (*Jinx Shortbottom*), James Booth (*Spider Kelly*), Harry Andrews (*Chief Officer Williams*), Al Mulock (*Dancer*), Derren Nesbitt (*Mick*), Victor Brooks (*Screw Smith*), Ian Hendry (*Ted Ross*), Barry Keegan (*Screw Jenkins*), Niail MacGinnis (*Prison Governor*), Kynaston Reeves (*Judge*).

Four young hoods, led by Booth, are convicted and sent to a progressive prison. There they try to take over and fight with a rival prison gang. Newley is a prison psychologist who tries to understand the new inmates. He attempts to reach them using Booth's girl friend. He succeeds after much effort, and Booth eventually is reformed. Though there are some genuinely funny moments in the film, there is a lot wrong with it. Foremost is the casting of Newley in a serious role. He was a natural comedian and is strained in his part. Though the supporting cast is funny, some of their situations are not. A pantomime show put on by the prisoners just doesn't work, despite the good intentions of the actors. Though straightforward, the plot drops off at the end and meanders into denouement. The editing doesn't work; it's too choppy for the episodic plot structure. Bart, who provided "Must Be" as well as a few other tunes, would go on to write the successful musical "Oliver!" The title is British slang for "in prison."

p, Harold Huth, d&w, Ken Hughes (based on a story by Frank Norman); ph, Ted Moore (CinemaScope); m, Ron Goodwin; ed, Geoffrey Foot; m/l, "Must Be," Lionel Bart.

Comedy **(PR:A MPAA:NR)**

IN THE NIGHT (SEE: GANG'S ALL HERE, THE, 1941)

IN THE SOUP*** (1936, Brit.) 72m Twickenham bw

Ralph Lynn (*Horace*), Judy Gunn (*Kitty*), Morton Selten (*Abernathy Ruppershaw*), Nelson Keys (*Emile Moppert*), Bertha Belmore (*Mme. Moppert*), Michael Shepley (*Paul Hemming*), Olive Melville (*Delphine Moppert*), Morris Harvey (*Bates*), Margaret Yarde (*Mrs. Bates*), Felix Aylmer (*Counsel*), Mervyn Johns (*Meakin*), Olive Sloane (*Defendant*).

After barrister Lynn makes a mess of his first case, he realizes he just might be in the wrong business. To make ends meet he and wife Gunn decide to rent out their apartment to various persons simultaneously. The couple have to impersonate the house servants and throw a dinner party for the residents. Gunn throws a dash of sleeping powder into the soup, and when their guests awake in a variety of embarrassing positions, the couple collects a substantial amount in hush money. Some good fun in this neat and very British farce.

p, Julius Hagen; d, Henry Edwards; w, H. Fowler Mear (based on the play by Ralph Lumley); ph, Sydney Blythe.

Comedy **(PR:A MPAA:NR)**

IN THE WAKE OF A STRANGER** (1960, Brit.) 69m Crescent Film/PAR bw

Tony Wright (*Tom Cassidy*), Shirley Eaton (*Joyce Edwards*), Danny Green (*Barnes*), Willoughby Goddard (*Shafto*), Harry H. Corbett (*McCabe*), Tom Bowman (*Spike*), Alun Owen (*Ferris*), Barbara Archer (*Barmaid*), Vanda Godsell (*Hetty McCabe*), James Ottaway (*Johnson*), Peter Sinclair (*Sea Captain*), Peter Carver (*Lorry Driver*), Frank Pemberton (*Landlord*), Patricia Dean (*Secretary*), David Hemmings (*Schoolboy*), Jemma Hyde (*Schoolgirl*), Vera Lennox (*Housewife*), Betty Anderson (*Stallkeeper*).

Wright is a sailor in trouble. A bookie is found murdered and he is suspected of having committed the crime while drunk. Schoolteacher Eaton helps Wright out and falls for him along the way. The plot is confusing and often illogical. The love story gets in the way of the mystery and is unbelievable. Neither the actors nor director Eady can do much to straighten out the mess they've been given.

p, Jon Penington, Jacques de Lane Lea; d, David Eady; w, John Tully (based on the novel by Ian Stuart Black); ph, Eric Cross; m, Edwin Astley; ed, John Seabourne.

Thriller **(PR:C MPAA:NR)**

IN THE WAKE OF THE BOUNTY* (1933, Aus.) 70m Expeditionary bw

Mayne Lynton (*Capt. Bligh*), Errol Flynn (*Fletcher Christian*), Victor Gourier (*The Blind Fiddler*), John Warwick (*Young*), Patricia Penman (*Isabella*), Arthur Greenaway (*Narrator*).

This little known and poorly made version of the famous "Bounty Mutiny" story features an early performance by Flynn. That's about the only thing worth watching in this unexciting adventure that contains a lot of "travelog" type footage. Flynn, in a cheap blond wig, gives the only decent performance in the film. The story behind the film is far more interesting than the finished product. In 1930 Flynn was captain of a commercial boat in New Guinea. He was persuaded by Dr. Herman F. Erben, (an adventurous scientist with an interest in documentaries) to sail up the Sepik River in order to photograph some head hunters. Two years later this footage was seen by Australian producer-director Chauvel. He was impressed by Flynn's looks and hired him to play Fletcher Christian. "[I was] without the least idea of what I was doing, except I was supposed to be an actor," Flynn later wrote. Flynn went on to a far better career than this debut might hint at. He also wrote a novel in 1946 titled *Showdown* based on the original Sepik River story of Erben's documentary shoot. The "Bounty" story had three remakes with Clark Gable (1935), Marlon Brando (1962), and Mel Gibson (1984) in the Flynn role. MGM used some of the footage from IN THE WAKE OF THE BOUNTY in 1935 for two shorts used in promoting the Gable version.

p,d&w, Charles Chauvel; ph, Tasman Higgins; ed, William Sheperd; md, Lionel Hart.

Adventure **(PR:A MPAA:NR)**

IN THE WHITE CITY*** ½**

(1983, Switz./Portugal) 108m Metro-Filmograph/Grey City c (DANS LA VILLE BLANCHE)

Bruno Ganz (*Paul*), Teresa Madruga (*Rosa*), Julia Vonderlinn, Jose Carvalho, Victor Costa, Francisco Baiao, Jose Wallenstein, Lidia Franco, Pedro Efe, Joana Vicente, Cecilia Guimaraes.

Alain Tanner (JONAH WHO WILL BE 25 IN THE YEAR 2000), who single-handedly brought attention to Swiss cinema, takes his cameras to the streets of Portugal in this revealing portrait of a city and a man who wanders through it. Ganz (THE AMERICAN FRIEND) is a ship's mate who tires of his job and stays behind in Lisbon when his boat returns to sea. He lives in a daze, writing letters to his wife, discovering the city with his super-8mm movie camera, and having an affair with hotel chambermaid Madruga. Almost entirely improvised, IN THE WHITE CITY is as much a discovery for Tanner as it is for Ganz's character, even intercutting the super-8mm footage that Tanner himself shot. What is most engrossing (and often hypnotic) about the film is the identification that the audience feels with Ganz (and Tanner)—being able to discover Lisbon with the same eyes as he.

p, Paulo Branco, Antonio Vaz da Silver, Alain Tanner; d&w, Tanner; ph, Acacio de Almeida; m, Jean-Luc Barbier; ed, Laurent Uhler; art d, Maria Jose Branco.

Drama **(PR:C-O MPAA:NR)**

IN THE WOODS (SEE: RASHOMON, 1951, Jap.)

IN THE YEAR 2889* ½** (1966) 80m Azalea/AIP-TV c (AKA: YEAR 2889)

Paul Petersen (*Steve*), Quinn O'Hara (*Jada*), Charla Doherty (*Joanna*), Neil Fletcher (*Capt. John*), Bill Thurman (*Tim*), Hugh Feagin (*Mickey Brown*), Max Anderson (*Granger*), Byron Lord.

Telepathic cannibal mutants stalk the post-nuclear landscape looking for Petersen and company in this cheesy science fiction opus remade (uncredited) from THE DAY THE WORLD ENDED. Director Buchanan also gave the world the camp classic MARS NEEDS WOMEN. Some fun for the nondiscriminating.

p&d, Larry Buchanan; w, Harold Hoffman (based on a story by Lou Rusoff); ph, Robert C. Jessup; spec eff, Jack Bennett.

Science Fiction **(PR:C MPAA:NR)**

IN THIS CORNER** (1948) 62m EL bw

Scott Brady (*Jimmy Weston*), Anabel Shaw (*Sally Rivers*), Charles D. Brown (*Doc Fuller*), James Millican (*Tug Martin*), Mary Meade (*Birdie Bronson*), Robert Bice (*Comdr. Harris, Navy Medical Officer*), Don Forbes (*TV Announcer*), John Doucette (*Dunkle*), Cy Kendall (*Tiny Reads*), Johnny Indrisano (*Tommy Hart*), Bill Kennedy (*Barton, Announcer*).

Brady is a Navy WW II war veteran who takes up boxing for a living. Crooked manager Millican takes the young palooka under his wing and tries to get him to lose fights to satisfy a pack of gamblers. But Brady will have nothing to do with these schemes. Millican frames him by making it look like his punches have killed a sparring partner, setting off an old memory from the war, when Brady accidentally killed a man with a punch. He loses the next fight and is taking a terrific beating in the following match, when girl friend Shaw rushes in with the supposed dead man and Brady comes back to win the fight. This is an average B feature. The script is a little stiff at moments but the actors are able to overcome this.

p, David L. Stephenson; d, Charles F. Riesner; w, Burk Symon, Fred Niblo Jr.; ph, Guy Roe, Joe LaShelle; ed, Norman Colbert, Alfred DeGaetano; md, Irving Friedman; art d, Edward L. Ilou; m/l, "Out of the Blue."

Sports Drama **(PR:A MPAA:NR)**

IN THIS OUR LIFE** ½** (1942) 97m WB bw

Bette Davis (*Stanley Timberlake*), Olivia de Havilland (*Roy Timberlake*), George Brent (*Craig Fleming*), Dennis Morgan (*Peter Kingsmill*), Charles Coburn (*William Fitzroy*), Frank Craven (*Asa Timberlake*), Billie Burke (*Lavinia Timberlake*), Hattie McDaniel (*Minerva Clay*), Lee Patrick (*Betty Wilmoth*), Mary Servoss (*Charlotte Fitzroy*), Ernest Anderson (*Parry Clay*), William Davidson (*Jim Purdy*), Edward Fielding (*Dr. Buchanan*), John Hamilton (*Inspector*), William Forrest (*Ranger*), Eddie Acuff, Elliott Sullivan, Walter Baldwin, Herbert Heywood, Alan Bridge (*Workers*), George Reed (*Butler*), Dudley Dickerson (*Waiter*), Ruth Ford (*Young Mother*), Walter Huston (*Bartender*), Humphrey Bogart, Mary Astor, Peter Lorre, Sydney Greenstreet, Ward Bond, Barton MacLane, Elisha Cook, Jr. (*Roadhouse Customers*), Ira Buck Wood, Sam McDaniel, Billy Mitchell, Napoleon Simpson, Sunshine Sammy Morrison, Jester Harrison, Freddie Jackson, Fred Kelsey (*Blacks*), Reid Kilpatrick (*Announcer*), Lee Phelps (*Policeman*).

In one of her most overwrought performances, really a self-parody, Davis gesticulates and twitches and stomps across the screen playing one of the worst creatures to crawl across God's earth. Yet even in a role she later condemned, the great actress is utterly absorbing. IN THIS OUR LIFE was adapted from Ellen Glasgow's Pulitzer Prize winning novel and is doggedly directed by Huston, who was later accused of showing favoritism to second lead de Havilland since they were dating at the time. De Havilland is the good sister and Davis the bad, both oddly given masculine names (Davis as Stanley, de Havilland as Roy). Spoiled, selfish Davis is encouraged by her ailing, bedridden mother, Burke, to get everything she can out of life by any means. Burke is constantly deriding her ineffectual, meek husband, Craven, pointing with pride to her brother, Coburn, a ruthless businessman, as the symbol of real masculinity. Davis knows full well what her unmarried uncle is—and that he has been lusting after her for years, a lecherous, incestuous fixation she exploits whenever she wants something from him. Only a week before she is to marry gentle lawyer Brent, Davis inveigles Morgan, her sister's physician-husband, into an affair and they leave together. The self-sacrificing de Havilland agrees to divorce Morgan so he can be with her sister, but Morgan, haunted by guilt, takes his own life first. Davis returns and ingratiates herself with her family. De Havilland forgives her and Davis immediately launches a campaign to take Brent away from her sister, Brent having fallen in love with de Havilland after Davis' departure with Morgan. But Davis' wiles prove ineffective with straightlaced Brent, who spurns her suggestions of having an affair. In a rage, Davis jumps into her car and promptly runs over a mother and child. When the child dies, the police search for Davis' car. They later confront her with the hit-and-run killing but she denies having driven the car, putting the blame on the son (Anderson) of the family's black cook, McDaniel. Police believe McDaniel when she swears that her son never left the house. De Havilland persuades Brent to defend Anderson. The entire family now believes that Davis is guilty but she stubbornly denies her guilt. She turns to Coburn, but even her perverted uncle offers no help. He has learned that he is dying and asks Davis to come and live with him until the end. Davis has nowhere else to turn and no one else to ruin, so she hops in her car again, raging, and drives wildly off, this time crashing the auto and, thankfully, ending her miserable life. This was Huston's second directorial chore and he was reluctant to take it on, but it had been written by Howard Koch, who was later one of the writers of CASABLANCA and one who had been hired at Warner Bros. at Huston's suggestion so he felt obligated to back up Koch's story. Davis simply chewed up Huston, the script, and the entire production; he couldn't control her. Huston later commented: "There is something elemental about Bette—a demon within her which threatens to break out and eat everybody, beginning with their ears . . . I let the demon go." As a gag, the ever-capricious Huston had many in the cast of his first film, the recently completed THE MALTESE FALCON, appear in an unbilled brief scene. At a bar are Humphrey Bogart, Mary Astor, Peter Lorre, Elisha Cook, Jr., Sydney Greenstreet, Ward Bond, and Barton MacLane. The bartender serving them all is Huston's famous actor father, Walter Huston. Davis later claimed that the script by Koch was no good and when she later met the author, Miss Glasgow expressed her "disgust with the outcome. I couldn't have agreed with her more," said Davis, and she apologized for her extravagant performance and doing the St. Vitus dance (or an esoteric Charleston with her lower extremities) through Glasgow's less than inspiring tale.

p, Hal Wallis, David Lewis; d, John Huston; w, Howard Koch, Huston (based on the novel by Ellen Glasgow); ph, Ernest Haller; m, Max Steiner; ed, William Holmes; md, Leo F. Forbstein; art d, Robert Haas; cos, Orry-Kelly; spec eff, Byron Haskin, Robert Burks.

Drama **(PR:C–O MPAA:NR)**

IN TROUBLE WITH EVE* 1/2

(1964, Brit.) 64m Mancunian/Borde bw (AKA: IN WALKED EVE) (GB:TROUBLE WITH EVE)

Robert Urquhart (*Brian Maitland*), Hy Hazell (*Louise Kingston*), Garry Marsh (*Roland Axbridge*), Vera Day (*Daisy*), Sally Smith (*Eve*), Tony Quinn (*Bellchambers*), Denis Shaw (*George*), Brenda Hogan (*Angela*), Grace D. Russell (*Mrs. Mordaunt*), Iris Vandeleur (*Mrs. Biddle*), Bruce Seton (*Mr. Digby Phillpotts*), Kim Shelley (*Mrs. Digby Phillpotts*), Bill Shine (*Artist*), Frank Atkinson (*Taxi Driver*), David Graham (*Car Driver*).

After Hazell converts her cottage into a tearoom, scandal rips through the small British town of Warlock. The local inspector gets caught with his pants down (literally), Hazell's unhappily married daughters raise a fuss, and she winds up marrying the mayor. A barely average British comedy.

p, Tom Blakeley; d, Francis Searle; w, Brock Williams; ph, James Harvey; m, Wilfred Burns; prod d, Charles Leeds; ed, Eric Boyd-Perkins; art d, John Earl; makeup, Jim Hydes.

Comedy **(PR:A MPAA:NR)**

IN WALKED EVE (SEE: IN TROUBLE WITH EVE, 1964, Brit.)

IN WHICH WE SERVE**** (1942, Brit.) 115m Two Cities/BL bw

Noel Coward *(Capt. Kinross)*, John Mills *(Shorty Blake)*, Bernard Miles *(Walter Hardy)*, Celia Johnson *(Alix Kinross)*, Kay Walsh *(Freda Lewis)*, Joyce Carey *(Kath Hardy)*, Michael Wilding *(Flags)*, Penelope Dudley Ward *(Maureen Fenwick)*, Philip Friend *(Torps)*, Derek Elphinstone *(No. One)*, Frederick Piper *(Edgecombe)*, Geoffrey Hibbert *(Joey Mackridge)*, George Carney *(Mr. Blake)*, Kathleen Harrison *(Mrs. Blake)*, Wally Patch *(Uncle Fred)*, James Donald *(Doctor)*, Richard Attenborough *(Young Stoker)*, Walter Fitzgerald *(Col. Lumsden)*, Ann Stephens *(Lavinia Kinross)*, Daniel Massey *(Bobby Kinross)*, Robert Sansom *(Guns)*, Ballard Berkeley *(Engineer Commander)*, Hubert Gregg *(Pilot)*, Kenneth Carten *(Sub-lieutenant)*, Gerald Case *(Capt. Jasper Fry)*, Chimmo Branson *(Snotty)*, Caven Watson *(Brodie)*, Johnnie Schofield *(Coxwain)*, John Boxer *(Hollett)*, Leslie Dwyer *(Parkinson)*, Dora Gregory *(Mrs. Lemmon)*, Lionel Grose *(Reynolds)*, Norma Pierce *(Mrs. Satterthwaite)*, Jill Stephens *(May Blake)*, Eileen Peel *(Mrs. Farrell)*, Barbara Waring *(Mrs. Macadoo)*, Kay Young *(Barmaid)*, Everley Gregg *(Nurse)*, Juliet Mills *(Frieda's Baby)*.

In a series of poignant and revealing vignettes, the story of the British destroyer *Torrin* and its crew presents a stirring WW II drama. Coward, known for his sophisticated comedies, performed brilliantly and unexpectedly here as co-director, writer, score composer, and star. He is the captain of the warship, discarding the foppish and frivolous image of old and assuming the strong role of leader and father-figure to his stalwart men. Constructed like a documentary, IN WHICH WE SERVE is narrated by Coward and recounts this ship's heroic actions. It is first hit by torpedoes but survives, being towed back to England for repairs. The destroyer then serves to evacuate troops from Dunkirk and later participates in naval battles off Crete where it is dive-bombed and sinks. Crew members, including Coward, cling to a raft for hours and, while waiting for rescue, remember their loved ones at home and many touching flashback scenes involving Mills, Johnson, Walsh and others are shown. The men are finally rescued and assigned to another destroyer with Coward in command, ready to go on defending democracy. It's noble and full of understated passion, expertly performed and handled on all levels. Many a future British film star appeared in this film—Mills, Attenborough, Wilding. Coward wisely chose the most distinguished film editor in England at the time, Lean, whose brilliant intercutting of present and flashback scenes told the story without confusion. So impressive was Lean that Coward turned over the direction of the film to him halfway through the $1 million production. This film was unexpectedly and immensely popular in the U.S. and it grossed twice its investment upon initial release, although U.S. censors insisted that words such as "bastard," "damn," "hell," and "God" be eliminated. The reaction was anger in England and the furor over the censorship actually resulted in an uproarious debate in the House of Commons. This high-spirited, patriotic, and moving film undoubtedly inspired the equally impressive American production of ACTION IN THE NORTH ATLANTIC.

p, Noel Coward; d, Coward, David Lean; w, Coward (based on the experiences of Lord Louis Mountbatten); ph, Ronald Neame; m, Coward; ed, Thelma Myers, Lean.

War Drama **(PR:A MPAA:NR)**

INADMISSIBLE EVIDENCE*** (1968, Brit.) 94m Woodfall/PAR bw

Nicol Williamson (*Bill Maitland*), Eleanor Fazan (*Anna Maitland*), Jill Bennett (*Liz*), Peter Sallis (*Hudson*), David Valla (*Jones*), Eileen Atkins (*Shirley*), Ingred Brett (*Jane*), Gillian Hills (*Joy*), Isobel Dean (*Mrs. Garnsey*), Claire Kelly (*Mrs. Anderson*), John Normington (*Maples*), Patsy Huxter (*Hilda Maples*), Hilary Hardiman (*Wendy Watson*), John Savident (*Mr. Watson*), Rufus Dawson (*Scott*), Stephen Martin (*Peter Maitland*), Penny Bird (*Sheila*), Brian Cleaver (*Clerk of Court*), Martin Ryan Grace, Alan Selwyn (*Plainclothesmen*), Joseph Tregonino (*Caretaker*), Lindsay Anderson (*Barrister*), Reg Peters (*Private Agent*), Ron Clarke (*Man Outside Strip Club*), "Lee" (*Striptease Dancer*), Ann Lancaster (*Drinking Club Hostess*), Ellis Dale (*Clergyman*), Debbie Jacobs (*Maples' Daughter*), Ellen Mann (*Hudson's Secretary*), June Brown, Ishaq Bux, Norma Shebbeare, James Ottaway (*Watson's Guests*), Valerie Collier (*Mrs. Anderson's Mother*), Pamela Papworth.

Based on the 1964 play by John Osborne, one of England's "angry young men" of the era, INADMISSIBLE EVIDENCE is a powerful tale of a rotten attorney who bullies, cheats, cajoles, and pays the price. Williamson is the barrister, a Londoner with nothing but contempt for his fellow men and women. His wife, Fazan, is frigid as the Canadian Rockies, his daughter, Brett, barely tolerates his existence, and his son, Martin, is a twit. He takes up with Bennett who becomes his mistress but even that affair doesn't provide him any happiness. His coworkers dislike him for his personal habits, and his secretary, Atkins, is angered that he's broken off their affair and lets him have it with both barrels whenever she can. On one single day, his entire world begins to unravel: Fazan will no longer put up with his running around; Sallis, an attorney who works for him, refuses to take Williamson's offer of a partnership in the firm; Atkins tells Williamson that she is expecting a child and walks out; and, though Williamson has to attend his daughter's birthday party, Bennett won't take that as an excuse for not seeing her. Williamson finds he can no longer function in a professional capacity but he has a number of appointments that day he must keep, including one with Normington, a gay man being harassed by the police, and also one with Dean, a troubled woman seeking a divorce. Unable to take the pressure, Williamson leaves the office and wanders around a seedy section of London, attempting to clear his mind. Somewhat calmer, he returns to his office and is about to consummate lovemaking with his receptionist, Hills, when Fazan catches them in the act. After the birthday party, Williamson returns to his office and smashes the place up. (Oliver Reed did the same thing in I'LL NEVER FORGET WHAT'S 'IS NAME. Evidently, office-smashing was quite popular in England around that time.) He calls his wife and tells her he never wants to see her again, then walks out into the streets of London to seek whatever it is he doesn't have in his shallow life. Dudley Moore did the music for the film. (Yes, *the* Dudley Moore is an accomplished composer and pianist. Songs include: "Gently," "Keep It Up," as well as "Moonlight Becomes You," and "Room 504," a prewar British song. The latter two are sung, fairly well, by Williamson. Many of the scenes had greater effect onstage than onscreen, particularly the confrontation with daughter Brett. The remarkable thing about the film is that Williamson manages to make his boorish and often vicious character into someone to care about and root for. Underneath all that bravado there is probably a decent person and there are enough flashes of that decency for the audience to want him to succeed. But by that time, it's too late and we suspect that the stroll he takes at film's end might be to leap into the Thames.

p, Ronald Kinnoch; d, Anthony Page; w, John Osborne (based on his play); ph, Kenneth Hodges, Anthony Imi; m, Dudley Moore; ed, Derek York; art d, Seamus Flannery; cos, Anne Gainsford.

Drama **(PR:C MPAA:NR)**

INBETWEEN AGE, THE**

(1958, Brit.) 78m But/AA bw (GB:THE GOLDEN DISC)

Lee Patterson (*Harry Blair*), Mary Steele (*Joan Farmer*), Terry Dene (*Terry Dene*), Linda Gray (*Aunt Sarah*), Ronald Adam (*Mr. Dryden*), Peter Dynely (*Mr. Washington*), David Jacobs (*David Jacobs*), David Williams (*Recording Engineer*), Richard Turner (*Morose Man*), Marianne Stone (*Dryden's Secretary*), Olive Milbourn (*Mrs. Simpson*), Dennis Lotis, Nancy Whiskey, Les Hobeaux, Murray Campbell, Sheila Buxton (*Guests*), Phil Seamon Jazz Group, Sonny Stewart's Skiffle Kings, Teddy Kennedy Group, Don Rendell's Six

Patterson and Steele are a plucky young pair who open up a coffee bar and record production company. Their search for a singing sensation takes them to their own handyman (Dene) who shows some vocal talents. He and some of the fledgling company's other singers start making their mark on the charts which leads the record pressing company to attempt a business take over. Things look dark for the kids until an American company merges with them, solving the dilemma handily. Standard formula suffers from some bad acting and fluffy plot line.

p, W. G. Chalmers; d, Don Sharp; w, Sharp, Don Nicholl (based on a story by Gee Nicholl); ph, Geoffrey Faithfull; m, Philip Green; ed, Eily Boland; art d, John Jones; ch, Elizabeth West.

Musical **(PR:A MPAA:NR)**

INBREAKER, THE* 1/2 (1974, Can.) 90m Elliott c

Johnny Crawford (*Chris*), Christopher George (*Roy*), Al Koslik (*Fisherman*), Jonny Yesno (*Muskrat*), Wendy Sparrow (*Carol*), Wally MacSween (*Cannery Manager*), Gordon Robertson (*A Drunk*).

Cliche-ridden, low-budget film from Canada tells the story of Crawford, a university student who goes to see his brother George. George has been financing the younger man's education and now Crawford hopes he'll provide a job as well. But big brother can't use him, so Crawford teams up with Indian fisherman Yesno. Of course George hates Indians, as we discover in a series of barroom brawls, and George shoots Yesno in the end. The photography captures some nice footage of the northwest coast of Canada. But that's the only thing worth looking at in this poorly directed, mean little film.

p, James Margellos; d, George McCowan; w, Jacob Zilber, William Sigurgeirson; ph, Miklos Lente; m, Grant Herrocks; m/l, title song, Michael Palmer.

Drama **(PR:O MPAA:NR)**

INCENDIARY BLONDE*** (1945) 113m PAR bw

Betty Hutton *(Texas Guinan)*, Arturo De Cordova *(Bill Kilgannon)*, Charlie Ruggles *(Cherokee Jim)*, Albert Dekker *(Cadden)*, Barry Fitzgerald *(Mike Guinan)*, Mary Phillips *(Bessie Guinan)*, Bill Goodwin *(Tim Callahan)*, Eduardo Ciannelli *(Nick, The Greek)*, The Maxellos *(Themselves)*, Maurice Rocco *(Himself)*, Ted Mapes *(Waco Smith)*, Charles C. Wilson *(Mr. Ballinger)*, Ann Carter *(Pearl Guinan, Age 7)*, George Nokes *(Tommy Guinan, Age 5)*, Eddie Nichols *(Tommy, Age 15)*, Billy Lechner *(Tommy, Age 19)*, Robert Winkler *(Billie Guinan)*, Patricia Prest *(Texas Guinan, Age 9)*, Billy Curtis *(Baby Joe)*, Edmund MacDonald *(Charley Rinaldo)*, Don Costello *(Gus Rinaldo)*, Erville Alderson, Fred Kelsey, Francis Ford *(Ranch Owners)*, Pat West *(Bartender)*, Matt McHugh *(O'Keefe)*, Russell Simpson *(Jenkins)*, Arthur Loft *(McKee)*, Andrew Tombes *(Hadley)*, Pierre Watkin *(Otto Hammel)*, James Millican *(Hector)*, Edwin Stanley *(Mr. Zweigler)*, Dewey Robinson *(Proprietor of Speakeasy)*, Etta McDaniel *(Maid)*, Frank Faylen *(Hotel Clerk)*, Harry Hayden *(Horace Biggs)*, Jimmie Dundee *(Cadden's Bodyguard)*, Jack Luden

(Man), Ruth Roman *(Woman)*, Emmett Vogan *(Doctor)*, Carlotta Jelm *(Pearl Guinan, Age 17)*, Maxine Fife *(Pearl Guinan, Age 21)*, Ray Walker *(Gus, Stage Manager)*.

Hutton is a hurricane of nonstop action as the frenetic and famous Jazz Age nightclub hostess and personality Texas Guinan, whose "hello suckers!" salutation became a watchword of the Roaring Twenties. Though some liberties were taken with Guinan's background, and nowhere does the film touch upon her numerous brushes with the law when she fronted illegal speakeasies, the film aptly captures the flavor and mood of the eras through which Guinan strutted her stuff. Hutton is shown first in 1909, with her shiftless but lovable father, Fitzgerald, a hopeless dreamer whose schemes always backfire with disastrous financial results. To shore up his latest failure, Hutton enters a rodeo and rides a bucking bronco to win $50. From there her career is given a lift by Goodwin who is briefly married to her and who launches her Broadway career. De Cordova, a bootlegger and gangster, comes into Hutton's life to make here alternately happy and miserable. She escapes his clutches by going to Hollywood and appearing in silent films, including westerns, then heads east during Prohibition to become Queen of the Nightclubs (which was the title of a 1929 Warner Bros. film, the one talkie Guinan did make). Much of the film, ably directed by Marshall, dwells on the wild decade of Guinan's nightclub activities (from 1923 to 1933 when Mary Louise Cecilia Guinan prematurely died at the age of 49). The soundtrack and Hutton's belting delivery may require some earplug use but despite her usual overacting, she provides enormous entertainment. The production numbers are lavish and the period is delightfully profiled in sets and costuming. De Cordova enacts a role loosely based on Guinan's gangster boy friend and Larry Fay, the man who controlled the milk unions in NYC, a millionaire bootlegger who lived a high society life in a Long Island mansion and who was F. Scott Fitzgerald's prototype for *The Great Gatsby*. Songs include: "It Had to Be You" (Gus Kahn, Isham Jones, sung by Hutton), "Ragtime Cowboy Joe" (Maurice Abrahams, Lewis F. Muir, Grant Clarke; sung by Hutton), "Sweet Genevieve" (Henry Tucker, George Cooper; sung by Fitzgerald, chorus), "Oh By Jingo" (Lew Brown, Albert von Tilzer; sung by Hutton, chorus), "Row, Row, Row" (William Jerome, James V. Monaco; sung by Hutton), "Darktown Strutters Ball" (Shelton Brooks, Rocco on the piano), "What Do You Want to Make Those Eyes at Me For" (Howard Johnson, Joseph McCarthy; sung by Hutton), "Ida, Sweet as Apple Cider" (Eddie Leonard, Eddie Munson).

p, Joseph Sistrom; d, George Marshall; w, Claude Binyon, Frank Butler (based on *Life of Texas Guinan* by Thomas and W.D. Guinan); ph, Ray Rennahan; m, Robert Emmett Dolan; ed, Archie Marshek; art d, Hans Dreier, William Flannery; spec eff, Farciot Edouart; ch, Danny Dare; m/l, Maurice Abrahams, Lewis F. Muir, Eddie Leonard, Lew Brown, Albert Von Tilzer, Howard Johnson, Joseph McCarthy, Jimmy Monaco, William Jerome, Shelton Brooks, Gus Kahn, Isham Jones, Henry Tucker, George Cooper.

Musical **(PR:A MPAA:NR)**

INCENSE FOR THE DAMNED**

(1970, Brit.) 87m Lucinda Titan International c (AKA: DOCTORS WEAR SCARLET; THE BLOODSUCKERS)

Patrick Macnee (*Maj. Derek Longbow*), Peter Cushing (*Dr. Goodrich*), Alex Davion (*Tony Seymour*), Johnny Sekka (*Bob Kirby*), Madeline Hinde (*Penelope*), Patrick Mower (*Richard Fountain*), Imogen Hassall (*Chriseis Constandindi*), Edward Woodward (*Holmstrom*), William Mervyn (*Honeydew*), David Lodge (*Colonel*).

Strange, rarely seen horror film finds Macnee playing a retired Greek army major. He lends his assistance to a young lady when her fiance (Mower) comes under the power of a band of devil worshippers. Under their guidance Mower takes to vampirism as an expression of his sexual feelings. Cushing, Britain's leading horror king, shows up in a minor role as a doctor.

p, Peter Newbrook; d, Robert Hartford-Davis; w, Julian More (based on the novel *Doctors Wear Scarlet* by Simon Raven).

Horror **(PR:O MPAA:NR)**

INCHON zero (1981) 140m One Way/MGM-UA c

Laurence Olivier (*Gen. MacArthur*), Jacqueline Bisset (*Barbara Hallsworth*), Ben Gazzara (*Maj. Frank Hallsworth*), Toshiro Mifune (*Saito-San*), Richard Roundtree (*Sgt. August Henderson*), David Janssen (*David Feld*), Nam Goon Won (*Park*), Gabriele Ferzetti (*Turkish Brigadier*), Rex Reed (*Longfellow*), Sabine Sun (*Marguerite*), Dorothy James (*Jean MacArthur*), Karen Kahn (*Lim*), Lydia Lei (*Mila*), James Callahan (*Gen. Almond*), Rion Morgan (*Pipe Journalist*), Anthony Dawson (*Gen. Collins*), Peter Burton (*Adm. Sherman*), John Pochna (*Lt. Alexander Haig*), William Dupree (*Turkish Sergeant*), Grace Chan (*Au Cheu*), Nak Hoon Lee (*Jimmy*), Kwang Nam Yang (*President Rhee*), Il Woong (*North Korean Commissar*), Mickey Knox (*Admiral Doyle*), The Little Angels.

The story of the WW II Inchon landing, as told on the screen, is not much, made up as it is of lots of poorly mismatched shots of action, action, action! The real Gen. Douglas MacArthur was known for his vanity. Here, Olivier exaggerates the general's ego with a cheap wig, latex chin, and a one-pound putty nose. Future secretary of state Alexander Haig told Olivier that MacArthur's speech patterns were similar to W.C. Fields'. So Olivier's interpretation (if one could call it that) comes down to a bad W.C. Fields in drag, all in the midst of explosions, tanks, ships, and troops. That's the movie in a nutshell. This ranks as not only one of the worst films of all time but also as one of the best behind-the-scenes tales as well. The story behind INCHON plays well as comedy-farce, and maybe should be filmed by Mel Brooks. Rev. Sun Myung Moon, leader of the Unification Church (his followers are known as "the Moonies" for the blind faith they show him) got it in his head to produce a movie. He turned to his good friend, loving devotee, and fellow rich guy Mitsuharu Ishii, a Japanese newspaper publisher, and together formed One Way Productions. At first they contemplated doing the life of Jesus, then proposed doing a new picture for Elvis Presley. However Divine Providence stepped in and showed them the light. Ishii, on a visit to Seoul, Korea, found himself overcome with emotion and spent the next six days crying. He finally decided his mood might lighten up by taking in a film. As fate would have it, Ishii wandered into a local theater showing a bad Korean War movie. There Ishii was struck by inspiration. He too would make a bad Korean War film! He felt that MacArthur's surprise landing at Inchon in 1950 would make for an excellent film. To further his point, Ishii called on the general himself. Though the old soldier had long faded away, Ishii consulted psychic Jeanne Dixon to contact the man. After giving her a picture of MacArthur (who Dixon first thought was George Washington), the general's spirit was contacted. Through the astrologist MacArthur claimed to be happy this film was going to be produced and would give his backing for the project 100 percent. (Dixon later chose the film's director as well, Terence Young, who had delivered three of the better James Bond films: DR. NO, FROM RUSSIA WITH LOVE, and THUNDERBALL.) To play MacArthur the producers signed Olivier for a cool figure of $1.25 million. When asked why the former would allow himself to be associated with the project the answer was simple: money. (No word on whether or not MacArthur was pleased with the casting.) Others along for the ride included Gazzara, Bisset, and New York film critic Reed. This was his first film appearance since MYRA BRECKENRIDGE, apparently proving Reed was not just satisfied writing bad movie reviews: he had to be in bad movies as well. INCHON was scripted by Moore, writer of THE FRENCH CONNECTION. He had similar artistic pretensions as Olivier and a special added quirk: he liked to write in the nude. Koenig was also engaged for a rewrite when the final Moore script was apparently as fully dressed as the author. Shooting was on location and, to the surprise of no one, was beset by a myriad of problems. First, political trouble between the Unification Church and the Korean government had to be settled. Movie equipment had to clear customs, which held back production for two months at the tune of $200,000 a day. Weather was constantly changing, and Bisset caught laryngitis which further compounded the trouble. The final sequences, which involved hundreds of ships and troops, proved to be a miniature battle of their own. Olivier, seemingly finished with his role, went home before it was discovered he was needed for one more crucial shot. Rather than return to Seoul, he was summoned to Rome and there recited the Lord's Prayer against a cheap backdrop. Meanwhile, Ishii was taking great delight in bragging about his film being "the most expensive ever made!" People were beginning to grow wary about his infinite source of funds when the truth finally came out: it was Moonie Movie Money! Ishii explained through a press release that, not being a veteran of the war "he turned to Sun Myung Moon as Special Advisor for . . . this project." Moon was prone to giving "artistic suggestions" that were publicly acknowledged as big bucks. Like rats leaving a sinking ship, various production, cast, and crew members (including the U.S. Department of Defense and the 1500 troops provided as extras) fell all over themselves stating they *never* had the slightest knowledge of who was backing the film. Even Dixon felt betrayed. Maybe MacArthur wasn't telling her everything he knew. The problems of production showed clearly in the mismatched shots and nonsensical editing. In one scene Olivier's pants change color twice. Later Roundtree is blown off a bridge in his Jeep, only to reappear minutes later in the same vehicle. Neither man nor machine bore a single scratch. As an epilog to this adventure, One Way Productions announced it was going to make a series of 10 to 15 films based on the Bible, with an optimistic office claiming this project would be funded by the profits from INCHON. (Total costs: $50 million plus; total U.S. and Canadian gross: $1.9 million. Looks like we might have to wait awhile for those Biblical epics.) As for Moon, who received credit as INCHON's "special advisor," he was sentenced to prison (but eventually released) for tax evasion. His followers (many of whom served as extras for this picture) can still be found at your local airport, flower in hand.

p, Mitsuharu Ishii; d, Terence Young; w, Robin Moore, Laird Koenig (based on the story by Moore and Paul Savage); ph, Bruce Surtees; m, Jerry Goldsmith; special advisor on Korean matters, Sun Myung Moon.

War **(PR:O MPAA:NR)**

INCIDENT**** (1948) 66m Master/MON bw

Warren Douglas (*Joe Downey*), Jane Frazee (*Marion*), Robert Osterloh (*Slats*), Joyce Compton (*Joan*), Anthony Caruso (*Nails*), Harry Lauter (*Bill*), Eddie Dunn (*Lt. Madigan*), Meyer Grace (*Knuckles*), Harry Cheshire (*Hartley*), Lynn Millan (*Sally*), Robert Emmett Keane (*Rinsel*), Pierre Watkin (*Sloan*), Ralph Dunn (*Bugs*), John Shay (*Freddie*), Pat Gleason, Patti Brill, William Ruhl, Jimmie Dodd.

Above average Monogram thriller that undoubtedly was one of the reasons Goddard dedicated his classic film BREATHLESS (1959) to this B-picture studio. Douglas, mistaken for another man, is savagely beaten. He sets out to find out why and discovers he's an exact double for a notorious gangster. He stumbles onto both murder and love while exposing a gang of thieves. There's plenty of action along the way, with Monogram's patented gunfights and brawling. Though he ends up bullet ridden and hospitalized, Douglas brings the crooks to justice and wins Frazee's heart. The direction is nicely paced and keeps the lean script moving along nicely. Despite a miniscule budget, the production looks first rate.

p, Harry Lewis, Hall Shelton; d, William Beaudine; w, Fred Niblo, Jr., Samuel Roeca (based on a story by Harry Lewis); ph, Marcel LePicard; ed, Ace Herman; md, Edward J. Kay; art d, Dave Milton.

Crime **(PR:C MPAA:NR)**

INCIDENT, THE½** (1967) 99m Moned/FOX bw

Tony Musante (*Joe Ferrone*), Martin Sheen (*Artie Connors*), Beau Bridges (*PFC Felix Teflinger*), Brock Peters (*Arnold Robinson*), Ruby Dee (*Joan Robinson*), Jack Gilford (*Sam Beckerman*), Thelma Ritter (*Bertha Beckerman*), Ed McMahon (*Bill Wilks*), Diana Van Der Vlis (*Helen Wilks*), Mike Kellin (*Harry Purvis*), Jan Sterling (*Muriel Purvis*), Gary Merrill (*Douglas McCann*), Robert Fields (*Kenneth Otis*),

Robert Bannard (*PFC Phillip Carmatti*), Victor Arnold (*Tony Goya*), Donna Mills (*Alice Keenan*), Kathleen Smith (*Wilks' Daughter*), Henry Proach (*Derelict*), Neal Hynes (*Change Booth Attendant*), Ben Levi (*Man Who Gets Mugged*), Martin Meyers (*Poolhall owner*), Don DeLeo (*Mr. Carmatti*), Nina Hansen (*Mrs. Carmatti*), Ted Lowrie (*Host*), John Servetnik (*Bartender*), Ray Cole (*Young Man No. 1*), Barry Del Rae (*Young Man No. 2*), Nico Hartos (*Policeman*), Maxine McCrey (*Black Woman*).

After mugging an old man, street punks Musante and Sheen wander off to the subway in search of cheap kicks. There they hold hostage a carload of 16 people. The punks intimidate the members of the group one by one, taunting them and exposing each passenger's weakness. Among the characters are a homosexual (Fields); an elderly Jewish couple (Gilford and Ritter); an alcoholic trying to recover (Merrill); and an angry black man (Peters) who enjoys seeing the whites taunted, but proves to be much like his adversaries when Musante and Sheen attack him. Unable to take any more of the torture, Army private Bridges uses the cast on his broken arm to fight back. He is stabbed but manages to beat down the two punks. The train pulls into Grand Central Station and two policemen enter the car to arrest the hoodlums. The passengers exit in an embarrassed and ashamed silence, carefully stepping over the drunk who has slept through the entire episode. Though performances are uniformly excellent and the direction carries the film at a nice pace, the film is hampered by long episodes of character introductions. The camera work is excellent, capturing the frightening claustrophobia of the scene nicely.

p, Monroe Sachson, Edward Meadow; d, Larry Peerce; w, Nicholas E. Baehr (based on his original teleplay "Ride With Terror"); ph, Gerald Hirschfeld; m, Terry Knight; ed, Armand Lebowitz; prod d, Manny Gerard; md, Charles Fox; set d, Robert Drumheller; cos, Muriel Gettinger; makeup, Herman Buchman.

Drama (PR:O MPAA:NR)

INCIDENT AT MIDNIGHT** (1966, Brit.) 57m Merton Park/Schoenfeld bw

Anton Diffring (*Dr. Erik Leichner*), William Sylvester (*Vince Warren*), Justine Lord (*Diane Graydon*), Martin Miller (*Dr. Schroeder*), Tony Garnett (*Brennan*), Philip Locke (*Foster*), Sylva Langova (*Vivienne Leichner*), Warren Mitchell (*Chemist*), Jacqueline Jones (*Vanessa Palmer*), Peter Howell (*Inspector Macready*), Oliver MacGreevy (*Wilkinson*), David Futcher (*Whitehead*), Clifford Earl (*Sergeant*), Geoffrey Palmer (*Dr. Tanfield*).

Miller is a doctor who has lost his medical license due to his addiction to drugs. After a trip to the drug store he spots Diffring, a former Nazi, who turns out to be the head of a local drug ring. The police soon get word of who's heading the ring and break it up, killing Diffring in the process. Miller overcomes his dependence on the pills and is allowed to practice again.

p, Jack Greenwood; d, Norman Harrison; w, Arthur La Bern (based on a story by Edgar Wallace); ph, Bert Mason, James Wilson; m, Bernard Ebbinghouse; ed, Derek Holding; art d, Peter Mullins.

Crime/Mystery (PR:A MPAA:NR)

INCIDENT AT PHANTOM HILL** (1966) 88m UNIV c

Robert Fuller (*Matt Martin*), Jocelyn Lane (*Memphis*), Dan Duryea (*Joe Barlow*), Tom Simcox (*Adam Long*), Linden Chiles (*Dr. Hanneford*), Claude Akins (*Krausman*), Noah Beery, Jr. (*O'Rourke*), Paul Fix (*Gen. Hood*), Denver Pyle (*1st Hunter*), William Phipps (*Trader*), Don Collier (*Drum*), Mickey Finn (*2nd Hunter*).

At the close of the Civil War a group of Confederates, led by Duryea, steals a million dollars in gold from a Union convoy. The gold is hidden in a cave near Phantom Hill, Texas. After being captured, Duryea offers to tell where the gold is in exchange for his freedom. Fuller is the Union soldier who leads the party in the search for the loot. After an attack by Apache warriors, Duryea escapes by plying two of the soldiers with alcohol. He kills the drunken soldiers and runs off leaving Fuller, Long, and Akins, weaponless, to fend for themselves. Duryea gets the gold and Fuller's dance-hall sweetie, Lane. Meanwhile, Fuller survives another Indian attack but loses one of his two companions, Akins, in the process. He and Simcox catch up with Duryea and Lane. The latter throws Fuller a pistol and Duryea is shot. The gold is returned and the happy couple ride off together. Though the possibilities for a good film certainly exist with this plot, it just never quite makes the cut. Despite some nice action sequences, the direction is relatively lackluster and indifferent. Characters really aren't given much motivation and the script never builds up to its promises. The camerawork is fine, and one of the few notable points in the film. Color and scenery are both used nicely.

p, Harry Tatelman; d, Earl Bellamy; w, Frank Nugent, Ken Pettus (based on a story by Tatelman); ph, William Margulies (Techniscope, Technicolor); m, Hans J. Salter; ed, Gene Milford; art d, Alexander Golitzen, Howard E. Johnson; set d, John McCarthy, Ralph Sylos; cos, Helen Colvig; makeup, Bud Westmore.

Western (PR:A MPAA:NR)

INCIDENT IN AN ALLEY** (1962) 83m Harvard/UA bw

Chris Warfield (*Bill Joddy*), Erin O'Donnell (*Jean Joddy*), Harp McGuire (*Frank Frye*), Willis Bouchey (*Capt. Brady*), Nelson Leigh (*Commissioner Bell*), Clancy Cooper (*Sam*), Mike Vandever (*Gussie*), Gary Judis (*Charlie*), James Canino (*Midge*), Bert Michaels (*Preacher*), Renny McEvoy (*McNulty*), Don Keefer (*Swanson*), Brad Trumbull (*Brannan*), Keith Richards (*Peters*), Warren Kemmerling (*Peterson*), Clegg Hoyt (*Manager*), Virginia Christine (*Mrs. Connell*), Jess Kirkpatrick (*Simpkins*), Lia Waggner (*Woman Neighbor*), Charles G. Martin (*Judge*), James Parnell (*Jury Foreman*), Max Mellinger (*Mr. Blake*), Mimi Doyle (*Mrs. Blake*), Frank Leo (*Boo Boo*), Lila Finn (*Charwoman*), Harlan Warde (*District Attorney*), Tom Cound (*Bailiff*), Bobby Fox (*Harvey*).

Based on a story by Rod Serling, this interesting crime melodrama has police officer Warfield called to a music store robbery. As he passes an alley he hears a woman scream and sees a figure running away. After shouting a warning he raises his gun and fires, killing a 14-year-old boy. It turns out that the kid had apparently bumped into the woman and knocked her down. Warfield is brought to trial and acquitted, but is still thought ill of by his fellow officers. Warfield then learns from the dead boy's brother that the kid actually was involved in the robbery, clearing up Warfield's reputation. An interesting Twilight Zone-style thriller.

p, Robert E. Kent; d, Edward L. Cahn; w, Harold Medford, Owen Harris (based on a story by Rod Serling); ph, Gilbert Warrenton; m, Richard La Salle; ed, Robert Carlisle; set d, Harry Reif; cos, Einar Bourman, Barbara Maxwell; makeup, Harry Thomas.

Crime (PR:A MPAA:NR)

INCIDENT IN SHANGHAI* (1937, Brit.) 67m B&D/PAR bw

Margaret Vyner (*Madeleine Linden*), Patrick Barr (*Pat Avon*), Ralph Roberts (*Robert Barlow*), Derek Gorst (*Brian Linden*), John Deverell (*Weepie*), George Courtney (*Mel Purdue*), Lotus Fragrance (*Butterfly Ku*), Rita Davies (*Ada Newell*), Johnnie Schofield (*Ted Higgins*), Lloyd Pearson, Henry Woolston, Douglas Fine.

Plodding romantic drama set in China revolving around the love affair between Vyner, as the bored wife of a doctor working for the Red Cross (Gorst), and pilot Barr. Dramatic high point comes when Barr is wounded and has to go under Gorst's scalpel.

p, Anthony Havelock-Allan; d&w, John Paddy Carstairs (based on the story by A.R. Rawlinson); ph, Francis Carver.

Drama (PR:A MPAA:NR)

INCORRIGIBLE** (1980, Fr.) 93m EDP Films c

Jean-Paul Belmondo (*Victor*), Genevieve Bujold (*Marie-Charlotte*), Julian Guiomar (*Camille*), Charles Gerard (*Raoul*), Daniel Ceccaldi (*Police Prefect*), Capucine (*Helene*), Andrea Ferreol (*The Singer*).

As sweet and charming as ever, an aging Belmondo plays a con artist released from jail who quickly goes about returning to his old habit of selling homes he doesn't own and making gigantic international deals. And all this right under the nose of his parole officer, Bujold, who, despite an innocent-looking exterior, is able to help set this seemingly gutter-minded individual along a straight path. Sickeningly sweet. (In French; English subtitles.)

p, Alexandre Mnouchkine, Georges Dancigers; d, Phillippe de Broca; w, Michel Audiard; ph, Jean Bernard Penzer; m, Georges Delerue.

Comedy (PR:C MPAA:NR)

INCREDIBLE INVASION, THE zero
(1971, Mex./U.S.) 90m Azteca/COL c (INVASION SINIESTRA; LA INVASION SINIESTRO)

Boris Karloff (*Prof. John Meyer*), Enrique Guzman (*Paul*), Christa Linder (*Laura*), Maura Monti (*Isabel*), Yerye Beirute (*Convict*), Tere Valdez, Sango Alemez, Sergio Kleiner, Mariela Flores, Griselda Mejia, Rosangela Balbo, Tito Navarro.

One of four Mexican quickies that the 81-year-old Boris Karloff appeared in before his death in 1969 (two of these, THE FEAR CHAMBER and HOUSE OF EVIL, escaped release). He plays a scientist (who surprisingly is not "mad") who invents a machine which can render useless the destructive powers of enemy weapons. He has positive uses for the machine, but the military and a couple of aliens have other ideas. A flying saucer lands, and alien spirits take over the bodies of a maniacal killer (Beirute), whose murders infuriate the community, and of Karloff. Placing responsibility for the murders on Karloff, the villagers destroy the scientist's laboratory. The evil forces attempt to do in Karloff and his daughter (Linder) but, recovering, he turns the machine on them. He destroys the machine after using it for evil purposes, fearful that other aliens will try to steal it away. An extremely inept picture, which could have been much better. Approached by Mexican director Vergara, Karloff read four scripts, all of which he rejected. After they were rewritten by Hill, Karloff agreed to do them, but on the condition that he would not have to leave Los Angeles (due to his poor health). An agreement was reached and Karloff's scenes were filmed apart from the rest of the picture, which was underway in Mexico. Karloff soon died, however, and Vergara shortly afterwards succumbed to the same fate. The footage, without Hill's knowledge, was re-edited, additional scenes were added, and the story rewritten, bearing no resemblance to the approved projects. A sad way for Karloff to make his exit, but thankfully, he never saw these pictures. Utterly disrespectful.

p, Louis Enrique Vergara; d, Juan Ibanez, Jack Hill; w, Karl Schanzer, Vergara; ph, Austin McKinney, Raul Dominguez (Eastmancolor); m, Alice Uretta; spec eff, Jack Tannenbaum.

Science-Fiction (PR:C-O MPAA:NR)

INCREDIBLE JOURNEY, THE*** (1963) 86m Disney-Cangary/BV c

Emile Genest (*John Longridge*), John Drainie (*Professor Jim Hunter*), Tommy Tweed (*The Hermit*), Sandra Scott (*Mrs. Hunter*), Syme Jago (*Helvi Nurmi*), Marion Finlayson (*Elizabeth Hunter*), Ronald Cohoon (*Peter Hunter*), Robert Christie (*James MacKenzie*), Beth Lockerbie (*Nell MacKenzie*), Jan Rubes (*Carl Nurmi*), Irena Mayeska (*Mrs. Nurmi*), Beth Amos (*Mrs. Oakes*), Eric Clavering (*Bert Oakes*), Rex Allen (*Narrator*), Muffey (*Bodger the Bull Terrier*), Syn Cat (*Tao the Siamese Cat*), Rink (*Luath the Labrador Retriever*).

After their human family goes abroad, Bodger, Tao, and Luath are boarded with family friend Genest, who lives 250 miles from their home. Genest goes on a hunting trip and the furry trio get homesick. They make off for the old abode, encountering various dangers along the way. This includes vicious animal attacks, as well as heartwarming encounters with a little girl and an old hobo. When Drainie and family return from England, they are heartbroken to hear of their beloved pets' disappearance. But there is a happy ending when the two dogs and the cat appear from the woods behind the family home, cheering up immensely an otherwise unhappy birthday. It's a great film for the kids and not too bad for the big people as well. The animals are all highly trained and register emotion with absolutely astonishing believability. The story is episodic and simply told. Though the humans aren't at all bad, it's the animals' show all the way. Some nifty shots of the Canadian high country as well.

p, Walt Disney, James Algar; d, Fletcher Markle; w, Algar (based on the book by Sheila Burnford); ph, Kenneth Peach (Technicolor); m, Oliver Wallace; ed, Norman R. Palmer; art d, Carroll Clark, John B. Mansbridge; set d, Emile Kuri, Charles S. Thompson; cos, Chuck Keehne; makeup, Pat McNalley; animal sup, William R. Koehler, Halleck H. Driscoll, Al Niemela.

Adventure Cas. (PR:AAA MPAA:NR)

INCREDIBLE MELTING MAN, THE**

(1978) 86m Rosenberg-Gelfman/AIP c

Alex Rebar (*The Incredible Melting Man*), Burr DeBenning (*Dr. Ted Nelson*), Myron Healey (*Gen. Perry*), Michael Alldredge (*Sheriff Blake*), Ann Sweeny (*Judy Nelson*), Lisle Wilson (*Dr. Loring*), Rainbeaux Smith (*The Model*), Julie Drazen (*Carol*), Stuart Edmond Rodgers (*Little Boy*), Chris Whitney (*Little Boy*), Edwin Max (*Harold*), Dorothy Love (*Helen*), Janus Blythe (*Nell*), Jonathon Demme (*Matt*).

This film tries to balance horror against morality but ends up shaky at best. Rebar is the only survivor of an ill-fated Saturn expedition. While on his trip he encounters some weird space virus that causes his flesh to melt and his palate to crave human flesh. He is pursued by DeBenning and Alldredge who both want the monster for different reasons. The special effects are all right, but not nearly as gruesome as the film pretends they are. Attempts at humanizing Rebar come in the form of contacts he has with a pair of retired old folks, and a FRANKENSTEIN-inspired encounter with two little boys. When it makes moral statements the film is at its best, though that's not saying a whole lot. The dialog is too simplistic for its own good. Someone should tell the continuity crew that the sun doesn't shine through windows at night. Watch for Demme, an independent director, in a bit part.

p, Samuel W. Gelfman; d&w, William Sachs; ph, Willy Curtis; m, Arlon Ober; art d, Michael Levesque; spec eff, Rick Baker, Harry Woolman; makeup, Rick Baker.

Horror (PR:O MPAA:R)

INCREDIBLE MR. LIMPET, THE 1/2** (1964) 102m WB c

Don Knotts (*Henry Limpet*), Carole Cook (*Bessie Limpet*), Jack Weston (*Lt. George Stickle*), Andrew Duggan (*Adm. Harlock*), Larry Keating (*Adm. Spewter*), Elizabeth MacRae (*Voice of Ladyfish*), Paul Frees (*Voice of Crusty*), Charles Meredith (*Adm. Fourstar*), Oscar Beregi (*Adm. Doemitz*).

Incredible as it sounds, this is an enjoyable film. Knotts is a nervous little Brooklyn bookkeeper who has an overwhelming love for fish. Of course this annoys his wife Cook no end, especially Knotts' desire to actually become a fish. After he is rejected by the Navy for service in WW II, he takes a walk along Coney Island with Cook and his friend Weston, who to make matters worse has just been accepted by the Navy. Knotts slips off the pier and—lo and behold!—through the miracle of animation he is turned into a fish. He meets a snail who shows him the ropes, and falls in love with a lady fish. Knotts finally becomes a war hero by helping the Navy track down German U-Boats. In the end he explains his new life to Cook and swims off to spawn with his finned female love. Sure it's an absurd plot, but it's done well and is fine for the kids. The animated Knotts even comes complete with horned-rimmed glasses. The fantasy works well as a whole, with a nice combination of live action and animation. Producer Rose was a long-time Disney associate and the influence can clearly be seen. The premiere of THE INCREDIBLE MR. LIMPET was appropriately held underwater, in a specially designed glass-enclosed room twenty feet below the water at Weeki Wachee Springs, Florida. Songs: "The Mr. Limpet March (Super Doodle Dandy)," "I Wish I Were a Fish," "Be Careful How You Wish," "Deep Rapture," "Hail To Henry Limpet."

p, John C. Rose; d, Arthur Lubin; w, Rose, Jameson Brewer, Joe DiMona (based on the novel *Mr. Limpet* by Theodore Pratt); ph, Harold Stine (Technicolor); m, Frank Perkins; ed, Donald Tait; art d, LeRoy Deane; set d, William L. Kuehl; cos, Robert Richards, Rose Brawd; spec eff, Vladimir Tytla, Gerry Chiniquy, Hawley Pratt, Robert McKimson, Maurice Noble, Don Peters; m/l, Sammy Fain, Harold Adamson.

Fantasy (PR:AAA MPAA:NR)

INCREDIBLE PETRIFIED WORLD, THE* 1/2

(1959) 70m Governor Films bw

John Carradine (*Dr. Wyman*), Robert Clarke (*Craig Randall*), Phyllis Coates (*Dale Marshall*), Allen Windsor (*Paul Whitmore*), Sheila Noonan (*Lauri Talbot*), George Skaff (*Matheny*), Maurice Bernard (*Ingol*), Joe Maierhouser (*Jim Wyman*), Harry Raven (*Captain*), Lloyd Nelson (*Radioman*), Jack Haffner (*Reporter*).

Carradine is a scientist who develops a submersible device for exploring the ocean bottom. While he waits on the boat, a team of divers man the contraption and take it down. After they bash into underwater mountains and coral reefs, they flee the diving bell and take shelter in a fabulous underwater cave complete with handy air pocket. Before Carradine can rescue the team, volcanic eruptions begin to destroy the cave, and only after one diver is killed by falling rock does Carradine manage to get them to the surface. Low budget science fiction effort slightly redeemed by Carradine's gaunt frame.

p&d, Jerry Warren; w, John W. Sterner; ph, Victor Fisher, Mel Fisher; ed, James Sweeney, Harold McKenzie; md, Josef Zimanich; art d, Marvin Harbert.

Science Fiction (PR:A MPAA:NR)

INCREDIBLE PRAYING MANTIS, THE

(SEE: DEADLY MANTIS, THE, 1957)

INCREDIBLE SARAH, THE* 1/2

(1976, Brit.) 105m Readers Digest Productions c

Glenda Jackson (*Sarah Bernhardt*), Daniel Massey (*Sardou*), Yvonne Mitchell (*Mam'selle*), Douglas Wilmer (*Montigny*), David Langton (*Duc De Morny*), Simon Williams (*Henri De Ligne*), John Castle (*Damala*), Edward Judd (*Jarrett*), Rosemarie Dunham (*Mrs. Bernhardt*), Peter Sallis (*Thierry*), Bridget Armstrong (*Marie*), Margaret Courtenay (*Madame Nathalie*).

In this Reader's Digest interpretation of the immortal Sarah Bernhardt, Jackson is required to play one hysterical crisis after the other, rather than be allowed to portray a well-rounded study of Bernhardt's character. Though the set design and photography are interesting, they are not enough to make this film work. We see Bernhardt up to age thirty-five, well before she had lost her leg, a matter too delicate perhaps for the good people at Reader's Digest. Bernhardt's notorious affairs are also diluted for the PG rating. Ultimately this film has a hard time justifying itself. Everything from directing to music is overdone; and Jackson's role is played too broadly.

p, Helen M. Strauss; d, Richard Fleischer; w, Ruth Wolff; ph, Christopher Challis (Panavision, Technicolor); m, Elmer Bernstein; ed, John Jympson; prod d, Elliot Scott; art d, Norman Reynolds; set d, Peter Howitt; cos, Anthony Mendleson.

Drama/Biography (PR:C MPAA:PG)

INCREDIBLE SHRINKING MAN, THE**** (1957) 81m UNIV bw

Grant Williams (*Scott Carey*), Randy Stuart (*Louise Carey*), April Kent (*Clarice*), Paul Langton (*Charlie Carey*), Raymond Bailey (*Dr. Thomas Silver*), William Schallert (*Dr. Arthur Bramson*), Frank Scannell (*Barker*), Helene Marshall, Diana Darrin (*Nurses*), Billy Curtis (*Midget*).

Without a doubt this ranks as one of the great science fiction pictures of all time. It not only tells a strange tale, it also delivers a fine social commentary. Williams is terrific as the title character. While on a vacation with his wife Stuart (on just an average day, as he tells us in voice-over) Williams is enveloped by a strange cloud. A few days later he begins to shrink. Doctor Bailey theorizes that the cloud was some sort of atomic waste and immediately tries to concoct an antidote. By the time one is manufactured, Williams has already decreased to half his normal size and has run off in a panic to a circus where he falls in love with Kent, an attractive midget. He then misses his injection and continues to shrink with increasing momentum. He is placed in a doll house for protection but is attacked by the family cat. From there he escapes to the basement, but his wife assumes the cat has killed him. While in the cellar Williams battles a spider, finally lancing it with a sewing needle. The film ends with Williams running through his lawn, a forest from his perspective, and it is obvious that he is to go on shrinking to microscopic size. The final shot is of the sky suddenly replaced by footage of molecular structure as Williams' voice is heard shouting "To God, there is no zero!" THE INCREDIBLE SHRINKING MAN is notable for several reasons. The special effects are terrific: Williams' duel with the spider is as harrowing as anything put on film in the late 1950s. More importantly, however, are the film's social, moral, and political implications. Like the classic INVASION OF THE BODY SNATCHERS, THE INCREDIBLE SHRINKING MAN captures well the paranoia that set in during the 1950s. But unlike the former film, this piece has an open ending which is more realistic and all the more chilling. The implication of atomic power was on everyone's mind at the film's release and this too was dealt with competently. Science fiction had an advantage over other genres because it could make political statements without saying the message outright. The genre was seemingly the last bastion for a liberal in 1950s Hollywood, where red-baiting was the order of the day. There's also a fine existential feel to the film, which adds to the horror of the film's protagonist. He knows he is fighting the inevitable and we, fighting it with him, know full well what the outcome will be. Based on his novel, Matheson sold it to the movies only on the condition that he be allowed to write the script. His first novel, *I Am Legend*, had been badly butchered and Matheson had no wish to see that happen again. (Eventually *I Am Legend* was filmed as L'ULTIMO UOMO DELLA TERRA in 1964 from another writer's screenplay.) A remake, THE INCREDIBLE SHRINKING WOMAN (1981), did not come close to the caliber of its predecessor. This is a must-see for anyone interested in 1950s culture and politics.

p, Albert Zugsmith; d, Jack Arnold; w, Richard Matheson (based on his novel *The Shrinking Man*); ph, Ellis W. Carter; m, Fred Carling, E. Lawrence; ed, Al Joseph; md, Joseph Gershenson; art d, Alexander Golitzen, Robert Clatworthy; set d, Russell A. Gausman, Ruby R. Levitt; cos, Jay A. Morely, Jr.; spec eff, Clifford Stine, Roswell A. Hoffmann, Everett H. Broussard.

Science Fiction/Fantasy Cas. (PR:A MPAA:NR)

INCREDIBLE SHRINKING WOMAN, THE** (1981) 88m Lija/UNIV c

Lily Tomlin (*Pat Kramer/Judith Beasley*), Charles Grodin (*Vance Kramer*), Ned Beatty (*Dan Beame*), Henry Gibson (*Dr. Eugene Nortz*), Elizabeth Wilson (*Dr. Ruth Ruth*), Mark Blankfield (*Rob*), Maria Smith (*Concepcion*), Pamela Bellwood (*Sandra Dyson*), John Glover (*Tom Keller*), Nicholas Hormann (*Logan Carver*), James McMullan (*Lyle Parks*), Shelby Balik (*Beth Kramer*), Justin Dana (*Jeff Kramer*), Richard A. "Rick" Baker (*Sidney*).

So-so remake of the original classic, with Tomlin in the lead. She plays two roles, the foremost being a normal housewife who accidentally gets a perfume called "Sexpot" spilled on her. The result: she starts to shrink. The media and consumer manufacturers fall all over themselves trying to exploit the phenomenon, and later Tomlin has to contend with some fiendish crooks who want the formula for their own evil purposes. The problem with the film is that it has no idea what it wants to do: is this a satire or a farce? Attempts are made at a feminist statement, but it's generally weak and ineffectual, as are the overdone "big business and media can be bad" themes. Attempts at camp humor fall flat and it's all over after about an hour. The problem is there's still another 28 minutes to go. Don't miss Hollywood's supreme makeup artist Baker as a gorilla, outfitted in an astonishingly realistic suit of his own design. This film was intended as a project for ANIMAL HOUSE director John Landis but the studio felt his budget was too expensive. Under Shumacher's direction, the film ended up costing about the same amount!

p, Hank Moonjean; d, Joel Schumacher; w, Jane Wagner (based on the novel *The Shrinking Man* by Richard Matheson); ph, Bruce Logan (Technicolor); m, Suzanne Ciani; ed, Jeff Gourson, Anthony Redman; prod d, Raymond A. Brandt; set d, Jennifer Polito; cos, Roberta Weiner; spec eff, Bruce Logan.

Comedy/Science Fiction Cas. (PR:C MPAA:PG)

INCREDIBLE TWO-HEADED TRANSPLANT, THE*
(1971) 87m Mutual General/AIP c

Bruce Dern *(Roger)*, Pat Priest *(Linda)*, Casey Kasem *(Ken)*, Albert Cole *(Cass)*, John Bloom *(Danny)*, Berry Kroeger *(Max)*, Larry Vincent *(Andrew)*, Jack Lester *(Sheriff)*, Jerry Patterson *(Deputy)*, Darlene Duralia *(Miss Pierce)*, Robert Miller *(Station Attendant)*, Leslie Cole *(Young Danny)*, Ray Thorn, Donald Brody, Mary Ellen Clawsen *(Motorcyclists)*, Janice Gelman, Mike Espe, Andrew Schneider, Eva Sorensen *(Teenagers)*, Bill Collins, Jack English *(Patrolmen)*, Laura Lanza, Carolyn Gilbert *(Nurses)*.

Mean little film features Dern as a mad scientist interested in applying an extra head to every living creature imaginable. He's already done snakes, rabbits, and other little creatures and now it's time for some human experimentation. Priest is his long suffering wife, and perennially idiotic disk jockey Kasem is Dern's best friend. The opportunity for Dern's next phase comes in the form of homicidal maniac Cole, who wakes up attached to the body of gentle, mentally handicapped farmhand Bloom. From there on the film degenerates into a sick play on audience emotions, exploiting the amiable retarded man's plight for all it's worth. That Dern ever graduated to A pictures from this is something of a miracle: his performance here equals this inferior fare.

p, John Lawrence; d, Anthony M. Lanza; w, James Gordon White, Lawrence; ph, Jack Steely, Glen Gano, Paul Hipp (DeLuxe Color); m, John Barber; ed, Lanza; md, Barber; art d, Ray Markham; spec eff, Ray Dorn; m/l, title song "It's Incredible," John and Barnabus Hill (sung by Bobbie Boyle); makeup and head design, Barry Noble.

Science Fiction/Horror (PR:O MPAA:PG)

INCREDIBLY STRANGE CREATURES, THE
(SEE: INCREDIBLY STRANGE CREATURES WHO STOPPED LIVING AND BECAME CRAZY MIXED-UP ZOMBIES, THE, 1965)

INCREDIBLY STRANGE CREATURES WHO STOPPED LIVING AND BECAME CRAZY MIXED-UP ZOMBIES, THE 1/2**
(1965) 81m Hollywood Star Pictures c (AKA: TEENAGE PSYCHO MEETS BLOODY MARY; THE INCREDIBLY STRANGE CREATURES)

Cash Flagg *(Jerry)*, Brett O'Hara *(Mme. Estrella)*, Carolyn Brandt *(Marge Neilson)*, Atlas King *(Harold)*, Sharon Walsh *(Angie)*, Madison Clarke *(Madison)*, Erina Enyo *(Carmelita)*, Jack Brady *(Ortega)*, Toni Camel *(Stella)*, Neil Stillman *(Barker)*, Joan Howard *(Angie's Mother)*, James Bowie *(Nightclub Emcee)*, Gene Pollock *(Nightclub Owner)*, Bill Ward *(Dancer)*, Son Hooker *(1st Policeman)*, Steve Clark *(2nd Policeman)*, Don Synder, Carol Kay, Teri Randal *(Singers)*, Titus Moede, Whitey Robinson, Bonnie Berkeley, Denise Lynn, Jill Carson, Patrice Michaels, Cindy Shea, Patti Crandall, Betty Downing, Pat Lynn.

Good cheap thrills about a carnival gypsy who hypnotizes her patrons and disfigures them with acid, thus creating the title characters. Brandt is a carnival singer who tries to stop her, but she is stabbed by a beatnik zombie who just happens to be director Flagg. After Flagg nearly kills his girl friend, the gypsy puts him away once more but the zombies have had enough of her oppressive ways and riot in a well-choreographed dance sequence, merrily killing everyone in sight until the police squelch the proceedings and arrest the gypsy. It's all sadistic fun featuring some great rock and roll pieces like "The Mixed Up Zombie Stomp." Filmed in "Bloody Vision" by master cinematographer Mascelli, who wrote the standard handbook used by the majority of Hollywood cinematographers. He was assisted by future Oscar winner Zsigmond.

p&d, Ray Dennis Steckler [Cash Flagg]; w, Gene Pollock, Robert Silliphant (based on a story by E.M. Kevke); ph, Joseph V. Mascelli, William [Vilmos] Zsigmond (Eastmancolor); m, Henry Price; ed, Don Schneider; art d, Mike Harrington, Pat Kirkwood; ch, Bill Turner, Alan Smith; m/l, Libby Quinn; makeup, Lilly, Tom Scherman.

Horror (PR:O MPAA:NR)

INCUBUS* 1/2 (1966) 78m Daystar bw

William Shatner *(Marc)*, Allyson Ames *(Kia)*, Eloise Hardt *(Amael)*, Robert Fortier *(Olin)*, Ann Alman *(Arndis)*, Milos Milos *(Incubus)*.

Shatner gets involved in the occult in a film that tries hard but doesn't make it. He's a proverbial Good Man, whom the evil spirits are out to destroy. Ames is a witch who falls for him, and Milos is the Incubus set to stop her. According to legend, the Incubus is an evil spirit from hell who seduces women for the devil. The cast speaks all the dialog in "Esperanto," a universal language developed by occultists in 1887. The actors learned the language phonetically, in hopes of giving the film an eerie feeling. However, their efforts were wasted, as the dialog comes off stiff and unnatural. The story is hackneyed and the whole thing is bogged down by its own pretensions.

p, Anthony M. Taylor; d&w, Leslie Stevens; ph, Conrad Hall; m, Dominic Frontiere; ed, Richard K. Brockway.

Horror/Occult (PR:O MPAA:NR)

INCUBUS, THE*
(1982, Can.) 92m Film Ventures International/Artists Releasing c

John Cassavetes *(Dr. Sam Cordell)*, Kerrie Keane *(Laura Kincaid)*, Helen Hughes *(Agatha Galen)*, Erin Flannery *(Jenny Cordell)*, Duncan McIntosh *(Tim)*, John Ireland *(Hank)*, Harvey Atkins *(Joe)*, Dirk McLean *(Incubus)*.

Cassavetes is a doctor with disturbing dreams about some local sex crimes. McIntosh is a local youngster who has similar dreams and fears he is really the rapist, as many of his friends have been victims. Enter reporter Keane, an exact look-alike for Cassavetes' late wife, killed years ago in an auto accident. Lots of random violence, before the denouement: the killer is really a Satanic monster (in a cheap rubber monster suit). This was made under a Canadian tax shelter program by a group of moneywise (and artistically inept) businessmen and looks like the bottom line in horror movies.

p, Marc Boyman, John M. Eckert; d, John Hough; w, George Franklin (based on the novel by Ray Russell); ph, Albert J. Dunk (Medallion Color); m, Stanley Meyers; ed, George Appleby; prod d, Ted Watkins; art d, Hilton Rosemartin; spec eff, Colin Chilvers, Martin Malivoire, Bob Wiggens; stunts, Dwayne McLean; makeup, Maureen Sweeney.

Horror Cas. (PR:O MPAA:R)

IDAGINE SU UN CITTADINO AL DI DOPRA DI OGNI SOSPETTO
(SEE: INVESTIGATION OF A CITIZEN ABOVE SUSPICION, 1970, Ital.)

INDECENT**
(1962, Ger.) 90m Filmaufbau-Cinelux/Constitution bw (SCHWARZE NYLONS-HEISSE NACHTE; AKA: ALL BAD; WAYLAID WOMEN)

Peter Van Eyck *(Alexander)*, Susanne Cramer *(Karen)*, Horst Frank *(Sabri)*, Kai Fischer *(Vera)*, Helga Munster *(Sylvia)*, Eva Schreiber *(Monica)*, Helmut Schmid, Kathe Haack, Karin Maria Ostholt, Eleonore Doodt, Peter Weiss.

Van Eyck is a German reporter investigating the death of a woman nightclub singer. He uncovers not just a murder but a white slave trade operating between Marseilles and Tangiers, and luring unsuspecting girls into their ring. He falls in love with one of the girls, Cramer, and busts the operation wide open before she is forced to demean herself. Released in Germany in 1958. A sometimes inside look at an invidious racket still in operation in the world's waterfronts.

p, Erwin Marno; w, Marno, Hanns Helmut Fischer; ph, Karl Schroeder; m, Fritz Schulz-Reichel; ed, Caspar van den Berg; set d, Hans Luigi, Gerhard Ladner.

Crime (PR:O MPAA:NR)

INDEPENDENCE DAY 1/2** (1976) 87m Independence Day Productions c

Mel Rosier *(Fred)*, Gammy Burdett *(Delores)*, Michelle Davison *(Helen)*, Henry Gayle Sanders *(Charles)*, Charles Branklyn *(Maurice)*, Nikki Sanz *(Kathleen)*, Fred Parker, Jr. *(Glenn)*, Cal Williams *(Felix)*, Robert Rosen *(Rosen)*, Thomas Carter *(Carter)*, Jack Carone *(Jack)*, George Travis *(Travis)*, Kamalo Deen *(Kamalo)*, Martha Charles *(Caroline)*, Tammy Mitchell *(Young Delores)*, Ray Cherry *(Young Fred)*, Herb Schmidt *(Foreman)*.

Interesting independent feature which started as a UCLA student thesis before being expanded to feature length. Rosier and Burdett are a young black couple, newly arrived in Los Angeles from Tennessee. He has just gotten out of prison and can't commit himself to marriage. Burdett gets a job as a domestic, while Rosier becomes a factory worker. He gets involved in a strike at his plant and the two go their separate ways. She enrolls in school, but is laid off from a fairly good job. The film ends with the two meeting once more, both aware how much their lives have changed since their parting. Racial aspects are handled with sensitivity and do not overwhelm the film's plot. Roth handles his actors well, drawing out the story slowly and subtly.

p, Bobby Roth, Neil Rapp; d&w, Roth; ph, Elliot Davis; m, Mauro Bruno; ed, John Carnochan; art d, Jeffrey White.

Drama (PR:C-O MPAA:NR)

INDEPENDENCE DAY** (1983) 110m WB c

Kathleen Quinlan *(Mary Ann Tyler)*, David Keith *(Jack Parker)*, Frances Sternhagen *(Carla Taylor)*, Cliff DeYoung *(Les Morgan)*, Dianne Wiest *(Nancy Morgan)*, Josef Sommer *(Sam Taylor)*, Bert Remsen *(Red Malone)*, Richard Farnsworth *(Evan)*, Brooke Alderson *(Shelly)*, Noble Willingham *(Andy Parker)*, Anne Haney *(Rose Parker)*, Judy Brown *(Janis)*, Jeff Polk *(Billy Morgan)*, Zachary DeLoach *(Joey Morgan)*, Scott and Lane Simpson *(Youngest Morgan Child)*, Cheryl Smith *(Ginny)*, Kenneth E. Reynolds *(Minister)*, Buz Sawyer *(Ticket Taker)*, Donovan R. Sparhawk *(Delivery Man)*, Jacky Martin *(Uncle Sam)*, Bunny Summers, Susan Ruttan *(Nurses)*, David Dunnard *(Orderly)*, Mary Ann Smith *(Linda)*, Lauryl Kays, Lance Gordon, Hurschel G. Dunn, Kenny Studer, Glenn E. Gray, Bruce Flanders, Adrienne Hampton, Don Slatton, Steve Whipple, Mack Jones.

A vivid portrayal of the stifled existence from residing in small town Americana uses Quinlan as the woman who can't get herself to make a final split from comfort and security to go on to bigger and better things. Her major reason for remaining behind is the love she harbors for mechanic Keith, a relationship she values too much to make such a drastic split. The effectiveness of Quinlan's portrayal is somewhat hampered by the uneven direction which can't get straight exactly what it wants to concentrate upon.

p, Daniel H. Blatt, Robert Singer; d, Robert Mandel; w, Alice Hoffman; ph, Charles Rosher; m, Charles Bernstein; ed, Dennis Virkler; prod d, Stewart Campbell; m/l, Jim Messina; cos, Julie Weiss.

Drama Cas. (PR:O MPAA:R)

INDESTRUCTIBLE MAN, THE* (1956) 70m AA bw

Lon Chaney *(The Butcher)*, Marian Carr *(Eva Martin)*, Robert Shayne *(Prof. Bradshaw)*, Ross Elliott *(Paul Lowe)*, Kenneth Terrell *(Joe Marcellia)*, Marvin Ellis *(Squeamy Ellis)*, Stuart Randall *(Police Captain)*, Casey Adams *(Chasen)*.

Strictly routine fare, and not very good at that, with Chaney as the criminal brought back to life after being sent to the gas chamber for a number of murders. He is quickly back to his old ways, seeking revenge against those men responsible for sentencing him to death. Shayne plays the scientist hoping to make a breakthrough with his experiments. It's quite sad to think that Chaney had to depend on many ridiculous roles, such as this, in the latter part of his career.

p&d, Jack Pollexfen; w, Sue Bradford, Vy Russell; ph, John Russell, Jr.; m, Albert Glasser; ed, Fred Feitshans, Jr.; md, Glasser; art d, Ted Holsopple.

Horror Cas. (PR:A MPAA:NR)

INDIAN AGENT*** (1948) 63m RKO bw

Tim Holt *(Dave)*, Noah Beery, Jr. *(Redfox)*, Richard Martin *(Chito)*, Nan Leslie *(Ellen)*, Harry Woods *(Carter)*, Richard Powers *(Hutchins)*, Claudia Drake *(Turquoise)*, Robert Bray *(Nichols)*, Lee "Lasses" White *(Inky)*, Bud Osborne *(Sheriff)*, Iron Eyes Cody *(Wovoka)*.

One of Holt's better pictures features him as the hero of a tribe of Indians. Woods and Powers are trying to divert foodstuffs from the Indian reservations to the more lucrative gold fields. Beery is the chief who wants to go on the warpath, but Holt and sidekick Martin stop the bad guys, averting an Indian war. The action is plenty and nonstop, directed in a straightforward manner. Plot twists in the script keep this from becoming just another B western. Holt, as usual, is fun to watch.

p, Herman Schlom; d, Lesley Selander; w, Norman Houston; ph, J. Roy Hunt; ed, Les Millbrook; art d, Albert D'Agostino.

Western (PR:A MPAA:NR)

INDIAN FIGHTER, THE*** 1/2** (1955) 88m Bryna/UA c

Kirk Douglas *(Johnny Hawks)*, Elsa Martinelli *(Onahti)*, Walter Abel *(Capt. Trask)*, Walter Matthau *(Wes Todd)*, Diana Douglas *(Susan Rogers)*, Lon Chaney *(Chivington)*, Eduard Franz *(Red Cloud)*, Alan Hale, Jr. *(Will Crabtree)*, Elisha Cook *(Briggs)*, Michael Winkelman *(Tommy Rogers)*, Harry Landers *(Grey Wolf)*, William Phipps *(Lt. Blake)*, Buzz Henry *(Lt. Shaeffer)*, Ray Teal *(Morgan)*, Frank Cady *(Trader Joe)*, Hank Worden *(Crazy Bear)*, Lane Chandler *(Head Settler)*.

A surprisingly sympathetic portrayal of the Indian raises this beautifully filmed western above the norm. Douglas is a veteran scout who is hired to guide a wagon train through dangerous Sioux territory as it pushes toward Oregon circa 1870. Seeking to gain permission from the Indians for safe passage, Douglas visits Franz, the Sioux chief. Franz explains the trouble with the Sioux started when unscrupulous white traders tried to steal the Indians' gold by getting them drunk. Douglas promises to clear the matter up with the army and Franz agrees to go to the fort and sign a peace treaty with the soldiers. Despite Franz's cooperation, the potential for disaster exists in the person of Landers, the chief's brother, who harbors deep hatred for the white man. While wandering the Indian encampment Douglas stumbles across the chief's beautiful daughter Martinelli bathing naked in a stream. She realizes the scout has seen her and is mildly irritated at the invasion of her privacy, but she is also intrigued by the handsome white man. Trouble flairs up when an Indian is murdered. Landers captures Matthau and blames him for the crime. Knowing that he will be executed by the Indian, Douglas insists on taking the prisoner to the fort for a legal trial. Landers refuses to give Matthau up, which leads to a knife fight between him and Douglas. The white scout wins the battle, but does not kill the Indian. Franz then agrees to allow Douglas to transport Matthau to the army fort. At the fort Matthau claims that his partner Chaney actually committed the murder and both men are put behind bars. Soon after, Franz arrives at the fort to sign the peace treaty and Douglas finds that a young widow, Diana Douglas (Kirk's ex-wife) and her son have taken a liking to him. Sensing entrapment into marriage, Douglas leaves the fort and continues guiding the wagon train to Oregon. On the trail Douglas becomes lonely and rides back to the Indian encampment to see Martinelli. He is followed by Chaney and Matthau, recently released from jail, who have followed the scout in the hope that he will lead them to a secret Indian gold mine. While Douglas dallies with Martinelli, Chaney and Matthau get an Indian brave drunk and trick him into revealing the location of the gold mine. As the drunken Indian speaks, Landers suddenly appears and a fight breaks out. Landers and several other Indians are killed and the rest of the tribe goes on the rampage. The frightened settlers turn their wagons around and head back for the fort. By the time Douglas catches up with them, the settlers want to hang him for desertion. But when the angry redskins attack, all is forgiven and Douglas leads the defense. The battle lasts until nightfall, whereupon Douglas sneaks out and has Martinelli show him to the gold mine. There, hard at work, are Chaney and Matthau stealing the gold. During the confrontation Matthau sets off an explosion that kills Chaney. The other three escape, leaving Douglas and Martinelli to capture Matthau. They take the evil white man before Franz who is about to launch his final assault on the settlers. After some hurried explanations the Sioux chief calls off the attack and even agrees to let his daughter marry the brave white man. THE INDIAN FIGHTER was the first film to be produced by actor Douglas' production company, Bryna, and the choice was well made. The script by Frank Davis and Ben Hecht gives a fairly realistic and balanced portrait of Indian life. Instead of being faceless marauders, the Sioux are shown to have an intricate society with codes of behavior and honor. The Indians show concern for their families and are decent human beings with an amazing capacity for understanding nature. The Sioux in THE INDIAN FIGHTER are a complex people that are shown to be equal, if not superior in most respects, to the white man. Douglas had "discovered" Italian model Martinelli who, after introducing nudity to the then-contemporary western film, returned to Europe to exploit her new-found fame in a number of Italian productions.

p, William Schorr; d, Andre de Toth; w, Frank Davis, Ben Hecht (based on a story by Ben Kadish); ph, Wilfrid M. Cline (CinemaScope, DeLuxe Color); m, Franz Waxman; ed, Richard Cahoon; art d, Wiard Ihnen; m/l, Irving Gordon.

Western (PR:C MPAA:NR)

INDIAN LOVE CALL (SEE: ROSE MARIE, 1936)

INDIAN PAINT 1/2** (1965) 91m Tejas/Eagle American-Crown International c

Johnny Crawford *(Nishko)*, Jay Silverheels *(Chief Hevatanu)*, Pat Hogan *(Sutamakis)*, Robert Crawford, Jr. *(Wacopi)*, George J. Lewis *(Nopawallo)*, Joan Hollmark *(Amatula)*, Bill Blackwell *(Sutako)*, Robert Crawford, Sr. *(Motopi)*, Al Doney *(Lataso)*, Cinda Siler *(Petala)*, Suzanne Goodman *(Lataso's Widow)*, Marshall Jones *(Comanche Leader)*, Warren L. Dodge *(2nd Comanche)*.

Crawford, a 15-year-old Indian boy, is told in a dream that his future lies with the most prized horse in the tribe. He ends up saving the horse from Indian raiders, names it Mecapo, and Mecapo in turn saves him when he is endangered by a wolf pack. A great friendship develops between them and even though Crawford releases the animal in the wilds, it follows him back to the tribe. A lovely little story about loyalty and a boy's rites of passage.

p, Gene Goree; d&w, Norman Foster; ph, Floyd Crosby (Eastmancolor); m, Marlin Skiles; ed, Robert Crawford, Sr., George White; m/l, "Song of Nishko," Norman Foster (sung by Johnny Crawford).

Adventure (PR:AA MPAA:G)

INDIAN SCOUT (SEE: DAVY CROCKETT, INDIAN SCOUT, 1949)

INDIAN SUMMER (SEE: JUDGE STEPS OUT, THE, 1949)

INDIAN TERRITORY 1/2** (1950) 70m Gene Autry/COL bw

Gene Autry *(Himself)*, Pat Buttram *(Shadrach Jones)*, Gail Davis *(Melody Colton)*, Kirby Grant *(Lt. Randolph Mason)*, James Griffith *(Apache Kid)*, Philip Van Zandt *(Curt Raidler)*, Pat Collins *(Jim Colton)*, Charles Stevens *(Soma)*, Roy Gordon *(Maj. Farrell)*, Robert Carson *(Capt. Wallace)*, Chief Thunder Cloud, Chief Yowlachie, Frank Lackteen, Boyd Stockman, Sandy Sanders, Frank Ellis, Frankie Marvin, John R. McKee, Bert Dodson, Nick Rodman, Wesley Hudman, Robert Hilton, Roy Butler, Kenne Duncan, Chief Thundersky, Champion, Jr. the Horse.

Better than usual Autry picture finds him as an undercover man in the Union army, after switching loyalties from the Confederate cavalry. He is sent to make peace between a group of Indians and white settlers. With the help of Buttram and Grant he exposes Van Zandt, an ex-Austrian officer, along with Collins, as the bad guys behind the Indian uprisings. Along the way Autry gets a couple of numbers including "Chattanooga Shoe Shine Boy." Typical production values, with some action footage taken from the 1940 film ARIZONA.

p, Armand Schaefer; d, John English; w, Norman S. Hall; ph, William Bradford (SepiaTone); m, Mischa Bakaleinikoff; ed, James Sweeney; md, Bakaleinikoff; art d, Charles Clague.

Western (PR:A MPAA:NR)

INDIAN TOMB, THE (SEE: JOURNEY TO THE LOST CITY, 1959, Ger.)

INDIAN UPRISING** (1951) 75m Edward Small/COL c

George Montgomery *(Capt. McCloud)*, Audrey Long *(Norma Clemson)*, Carl Benton Reid *(John Clemson)*, Eugene Iglesias *(Sgt. Ramirez)*, John Baer *(Lt. Whitley)*, Joe Sawyer *(Sgt. Keough)*, Robert Dover *(Tubai)*, Eddy Waller *(Sagebrush)*, Douglas Kennedy *(Cliff Taggert)*, Robert Shayne *(Maj. Nathan Stark)*, Miguel Inclan *(Geronimo)*, Hugh Sanders *(Ben Alsop)*, John Call *(Sgt. Clancy)*, Robert Griffin *(Can Avery)*, Hank Patterson *(Jake Wilson)*, Fay Roope *(Maj. Gen. Crook)*, Peter Thompson *(Lt. Baker)*.

Routine cavalry picture has Montgomery playing a captain trying to keep the peace between famed Indian Geronimo and the local white settlers. The Indian reservation contains rich gold deposits and bad guys Kennedy and Sanders want them. Between their misdeeds and bungling in Washington, D.C. the Indians get hostile and declare war. They attack the cavalry but Montgomery, who had been placed under house arrest for an infraction of army regulations, is freed and saves the day. The usual action and hard riding make this one enjoyable for western film buffs.

p, Bernard Small; d, Ray Nazarro; w, Kenneth Gamet, Richard Schayer (based on a story by Schayer); ph, Ellis Carter (Supercinecolor); m, Rose DiMaggio; ed, Richard Fantl; art d, Walter Holscher.

Western (PR:A MPAA:NR)

INDIANAPOLIS SPEEDWAY**

(1939) 85m WB bw (GB: DEVIL ON WHEELS)

Pat O'Brien *(Joe Greer)*, Ann Sheridan *(Frankie Merrick)*, John Payne *(Eddie Greer)*, Gale Page *(Lee Mason)*, Frank McHugh *(Spud Connors)*, Granville Bates *(Mr. Greer)*, Grace Stafford *(Martha Connors)*, John Ridgeley *(Ted Horn)*, Regis Toomey *(Wilbur Shaw)*, John Harron *(Red)*, William Davidson *(Duncan Martin)*, Ed McWade *(Tom Dugan)*, Irving Bacon *(Fred Haskill)*, Tommy Bupp *(Haskill's Son)*, Robert Middlemass *(Edward Hart)*, Charles Halton *(Mayor)*, Patsy O'Byrne *(Vinegary Female)*, Creighton Hale *(Official)*, Evelyn Mulhall *(Mrs. Martin)*, Georges Renavent *(Headwaiter)*, Billy Wayne *(Stubby)*, Sam Hayes, John Conte, Wendell Niles, Reid Kilpatrick *(Announcers)*, Ed Parker *(Man)*, Monroe Lee *(Baby)*.

Page wants boy friend O'Brien to quit race car driving and settle down with her. Meanwhile, O'Brien is trying to persuade younger brother Payne to stay in school rather than emulate him. But Payne's got the bug and O'Brien gives in. After a fight over Sheridan, Payne and O'Brien face each other in a race. Payne crashes and his friend McHugh is killed. O'Brien takes his brother's place at the Indianapolis 500, winning the race, Page, and his brother's respect. Though the racing scenes are well done, the rest of this film tends to be a snooze. The script is weak, hampered by the fact that this is a remake of the far superior 1932 feature THE CROWD ROARS.

p, Max Siegel; d, Lloyd Bacon; w, Sig Herzig, Wally Klein (based on the story "The Roar of the Crowd" by Howard and William Hawks); ph, Sid Hickox; ed, William Holmes.

Action/Drama **(PR:A MPAA:NR)**

INDISCREET** (1931) 92m UA bw

Gloria Swanson *(Geraldine Trent)*, Ben Lyon *(Tony Blake)*, Monroe Owsley *(Jim Woodward)*, Barbara Kent *(Joan Trent)*, Arthur Lake *(Buster Collins)*, Maude Eburne *(Aunt Kate)*, Henry Kolker *(Mr. Woodward)*, Nella Walker *(Mrs. Woodward)*.

Swanson is a lady with a past. She meets writer Lyon, who refuses to listen to her stories of former affairs. Enter Lyon's sister with her new fiance, who is a former lover of Swanson. Swanson tries to break up the romance and almost succeeds in destroying her new love with Lyon in the process. Swanson had misgivings about this film, and for good reason: the plot and songs are weak. But when Lyon was signed as co-star and McCarey as director (the latter promised his big break with this picture) Swanson agreed to do it. Everyone gave it their best but it doesn't quite make it. Lake is capable in his comic role of the fiance, but the rest of the cast is wasted. Swanson sings a few numbers including "Come to Me"; but her initial fears unfortunately proved right. This was her first film for United Artists, after declining Paramount's offer of a guaranteed $1 million a year.

p, Lew Brown, B.G. DeSylva, Ray Henderson, Joseph M. Schenck; d, Leo McCarey; w, DeSylva, Brown, Henderson (based on the story "Obey That Impulse" by Brown, DeSylva, Henderson); ph, Ray June, Gregg Toland; ed, Hal C. Kern; m/l, DeSylva, Brown, Henderson.

Musical/Romance **Cas.** **(PR:C MPAA:NR)**

INDISCREET*½** (1958) 100m Grandon/WB c

Cary Grant *(Philip Adams)*, Ingrid Bergman *(Anna Kalman)*, Cecil Parker *(Alfred Munson)*, Phyllis Calvert *(Margaret Munson)*, David Kossoff *(Carl Banks)*, Megs Jenkins *(Doris Banks)*, Oliver Johnston *(Mr. Finleigh)*, Michael Anthony *(Oscar)*, Middleton Woods *(Finleigh's Clerk)*, Frank Hawkins, Richard Vernon, Eric Francis, Diane Clare.

INDISCREET is one of those rare movies that is far better than the play from which it was adapted. Based on Norman Krasna's Broadway flop, "Kind Sir," the movie took several giant steps in the screenplay (by Krasna) and emerges as a frothy and often funny film. Bergman, who proved with this movie that she could play comedy with the best of them, is a rich actress living in regal London luxury. Her sister, Calvert, and brother-in-law, Parker, introduce her to Grant, a financial genius who has come to London for a NATO dinner. Grant is a lifelong bachelor who masquerades as a married man to keep his single state secure. (Eleven years later, Bergman appeared opposite Walter Matthau in CACTUS FLOWER. In that, he was a single dentist who asked her to pose as his wife, then fell in love with her.) Grant tells Bergman that he's married and that's all right with her. She has no interest in getting married and no compunctions about having an affair with a man who claims that he's separated and whose wife won't grant him freedom. Grant has to return to the U.S. and wants to fly back to England for her birthday. She has the same idea and plans to see him in America. Now Calvert spills the beans and tells Bergman that Grant is, in fact, single, which occasions the best line in the play and picture as Bergman irately states, "How dare he make love to me when he isn't a married man." She decides to get even with him by making it look as though she's having an affair with a former boy friend, but when he is gurneyed off to a hospital for an emergency appendectomy, she has to impress her chauffeur, Kossoff, into playing the role of her new beau. Grant arrives with the news that his fictional spouse has given him the divorce he's been requesting. Then Kossoff, playing the role to the hilt, enters and Grant is livid that she's cheating on him. He exits fuming and returns later to tell her that he will never marry her. It's then that he discovers what she did and a reconciliation occurs, climaxing with his proposal of matrimony. The play had Charles Boyer and Mary Martin as the stars and as good as they were, Grant and Bergman eclipsed them in the movie. This was a throwback to the Phillip Barry school of drawing room comedy and both Grant and Bergman were up to the challenge of recreating the kind of movie that had been popular 20 years before. (Actually, it wasn't difficult for Grant because he'd been in many of those movies.) Entertaining, glossy, and shallow as a pie pan, INDISCREET is the perfect film to watch when you just want to lean back and smile, knowing full well what the outcome will be. The only surprise in the picture is how deft a comedienne Bergman could be. It was our loss that she didn't make more of these.

p&d, Stanley Donen; w, Norman Krasna (based on his play "Kind Sir"); ph, Frederick A. Young (Technicolor); m, Richard Bennett, Ken Jones; ed, Jack Harris; md, Muir Mathieson; art d, Don Ashton; cos, Quintino; m/l, "Indiscreet," Sammy Cahn, Jimmy Van Heusen; makeup, John O'Gorman.

Romance/Comedy **Cas.** **(PR:A-C MPAA:NR)**

INDISCRETION OF AN AMERICAN WIFE½**
(1954, U.S./Ital.) 63m COL bw (AKA: TERMINAL STATION INDISCRETION)

Jennifer Jones *(Mary Forbes)*, Montgomery Clift *(Giovanni Doria)*, Gino Cervi *(Commissioner)*, Richard Beymer *(Paul, Mary's Nephew)*, Paolo Stoppa *(Baggage Clerk)*, Mando Bruno *(Employee)*, Clelia Matania, Enrico Viarisio, Giuseppe Forelli, Enrico Olorio, Maria Pia Casillo-Ciro.

Jones is a Pennsylvania housewife on holiday in Rome. She bids farewell to her Italian lover, Clift (they get around the lack of an accent by saying that he had an American mother), and makes for the railway station. He follows her there and pleads with her to stay. They sneak into an empty railroad car for one final bout of love-making but their passion is cut short when a worker finds them almost en flagrante delicto and reports them to the authorities. They are taken in to an official and charged with lewd behavior (the original cut showed lots more of their behavior than the final release print). Cervi, the commissioner, changes his mind regarding the charges and sends them off. Jones leaves and Clift looks lovingly at the departing train and that's the whole movie. As is the case with so many movies, the behind-the-scenes activities were far more intriguing than the film. Several writers worked on the script, including Truman Capote, Carson McCullers, Paul Gallico, Alberto Moravia as well as Zavattini, Prosperi, and Chiarini. It didn't help. De Sica couldn't speak English so he wanted to hire an Italian to stand in for Clift and to tell that actor what he wanted. Clift would then ape the actor's movements to get the desired effects. It goes without saying that Clift was adamant. He was also gay and that caused no end of trouble because costar Jones developed an attraction for him and when that wasn't reciprocated, she became understandably depressed. So much so that it is reported she tossed a mink jacket down a toilet in her fury. The original title was "Terminal Station" but David O. Selznick (married to Jones at the time) insisted it be changed. He was not the producer but he stuck his nose in so deeply that there were many arguments between De Sica and his people and Selznick. It was released as a 120-minute film in Europe but pared down to just over an hour for the U.S. market. And at that length, it was still fat. The editing cut out most of the subplots and De Sica's images of the Roman people. It looks choppy and what they must have been trying for was another BRIEF ENCOUNTER (the railway station, the impossible love, etc) but missed by a mile and a half. De Sica was frustrated by the final cut which contained none of the neorealism for which he was famous. Despite all of this, the film made some money, mainly due to the provocative title. It's more of a one-act play than anything else.

p&d, Vittorio De Sica; w, Cesare Zavattini, Luigi Chiarini, Giorgio Prosperi, Truman Capote (based on the story "Terminal Station" by Cesare Zavattini) (Uncredited writers include Alberto Moravia, Carson McCullers, Paul Gallico); ph, G.R. Aldo; m, Alessandro Cicognini; ed, Eraldo da Roma, Jean Barker; md, Franco Ferrara; art d, Virgilio Marchi; cos, Alessandro Antonelli, Christian Dior (for Jones); m/l, "Autumn in Rome," "Indiscretion," Paul Weston, Sammy Cahn (sung by Patti Page).

Drama **Cas.** **(PR:A-C MPAA:NR)**

INDISCRETIONS OF EVE** (1932, Brit.) 63m BIP/Wardour bw

Steffi Duna *(Eve)*, Fred Conyngham *(Sir Peter Martin)*, Lester Matthews *(Ralph)*, Tony Sympson *(Pip)*, Jessica Tandy *(Maid)*, Clifford Heatherley *(Butler)*, Hal Gordon *(Simms)*, Muriel Aked *(Mother)*, Arthur Chesney *(Father)*, George Mozart *(Smart)*, Teddy Brown *(Barman)*, Stella Nelson, Marius B. Winter and His Orchestra.

The love affair between a wealthy aristocrat and a lowly English shop girl is the subject for this light-hearted piece of entertainment. Duna is the girl who makes her living as a model in a shop that makes mannequins, whose charms hit Conyngham so hard he won't stop pestering the girl until she agrees to walk to the altar with him. Actor Arthur Chesney was the brother of Edmund Gwenn. Actress Steffi Duna was married to American actor Dennis O'Keefe. Her most important American film was ANTHONY ADVERSE (1936).

p,d&w, Cecil Lewis; ph, James Wilson, Philip Grindrod.

Musical/Comedy **(PR:A MPAA:NR)**

INFAMOUS (SEE: CHILDREN'S HOUR, THE, 1961)

INFERNAL IDOL (SEE: CRAZE, THE, 1973, Brit.)

INFERNAL MACHINE*½ (1933) 65m FOX bw

Chester Morris *(Robert)*, Genevieve Tobin *(Elinor)*, Victor Jory *(Doreen)*, Elizabeth Patterson *(Elinor's Aunt)*, James Bell *(Spencer)*, Edward Van Sloan *(Prof. Hoffman)*, Arthur Hohl *(Ship's Captain)*, Robert Littlefield *(Rupert)*, J. Carroll Naish *(Bryan)*, Mischa Auer *(Klein)*, Josephine Whittell *(Mme. Albini)*, Leonard Carey *(Hans)*, Harry Shutan, Elise Cavanna, Stanley Blystone.

Messy production values make this a hard film to follow. A Paris-to-New York ocean liner is secretly in danger: the wireless operator intends to blow it up. Meanwhile, stowaway Morris pretends to be high class in order to woo fellow passenger Tobin. The impending doom of their romance is contrasted against the midnight deadline of the "infernal machine" set to blow up the ship. Indifferent direction and the choppy ending make it all incomprehensible.

d, Marcel Varnel; w, Arthur Kober (based on the novel by Carl Sloboda); ph, George Schneiderman.

Drama/Romance **(PR:A MPAA:NR)**

INFERNO*** (1953) 83m FOX c

Robert Ryan *(Carson)*, Rhonda Fleming *(Geraldine Carson)*, William Lundigan *(Joseph Duncan)*, Larry Keating *(Emory)*, Henry Hull *(Sam Elby)*, Carl Betz *(Lt. Mike Platt)*, Robert Burton *(Sheriff)*, Everett Glass *(Detective Mason)*, Adrienne Marden *(Secretary)*, Barbara Pepper *(Waitress)*, Henry Carter *(Fred Parks)*, Robert Adler *(Ken)*, Dan White *(Lee)*.

Ryan is a millionaire playboy who breaks his leg on a desert outing. His sexy wife, Fleming, and business partner, Lundigan, pretend to go off for help but actually leave him to die, as they are lovers. Ryan finally realizes they are not coming back and struggles across the desert for help. He finally confronts Lundigan in a cabin, beating him in a fight and starting a fire. Though too much detail is given, dragging the film in spots, it is overall an interesting piece. This was Fox's first 3-D production and the technique is used effectively. This is one of Ryan's best roles. The details of self-preservation and gutsiness shown by Ryan in overcoming the hazards of nature are gripping.

p, William Bloom; d, Roy Baker; w, Francis Cockrell; ph, Lucien Ballard (Technicolor); m, Paul Sawtell; ed, Robert Simpson; md, Lionel Newman; art d, Lyle Wheeler.

Drama **(PR:O MPAA:NR)**

INFERNO** (1980, Ital.) 107m FOX c

Irene Miracle *(Rose Elliot)*, Leigh McCloskey *(Mark Elliot)*, Eleonora Giorgi *(Sara)*, Daria Nicolodi *(Countess Elise)*, Alida Valli, Sacha Pitoeff, Veronica Lazar.

Miracle and Giorgi are two of three sisters who discover the curse of the "Three Mothers." They try and figure out how their other sister disappeared, and are helped by Nicolodi, an ailing countess archetype so often found in these cheap horror films. Together they discover the source of the curse—a black-gloved assassin. Along the way a disabled bookseller is devoured by rats and Valli falls five floors into a raging fire. Despite the thin plot and bad acting, the film has some sense of style, using Hitchcock-inspired camera angles and red-tinted Technicolor photography.

p, Claudio Argento; d&w, Dario Argento; ph, Romano Albani (Technicolor); m, Keith Emerson; ed, Franco Fraticelli; art d, Giuseppe Bassan; spec eff, Mario Bava.

Horror **(PR:O MPAA:R)**

INFERNO DEI MORTI-VIVENTI
(SEE: ZOMBIE CREEPING FLESH, 1981, Ital./Span.)

INFORMATION KID (SEE: FAST COMPANIONS, 1932)

INFORMATION RECEIVED**
(1962, Brit.) 77m United Co-Production/UNIV bw

Sabina Sesselman *(Sabina Farlow)*, William Sylvester *(Rick Hogan)*, Hermione Baddeley *(Maudie)*, Edward Underdown *(Drake)*, Robert Raglan *(Supt. Jeffcote)*, Frank Hawkins *(Sgt. Jarvie)*, David Courtney *(Mark)*, Peter Allenby *(Patterson)*, Walter Brown *(Vic Farlow)*, Bill Dancy *(Johnny Stevens)*, Don Meadon *(Country Policeman)*, Ted Bushell *(Prison Trustee)*, Tim Brinton *(TV Announcer)*, Johnny Briggs *(Willis)*, David Cargill *(Librarian)*, Larry Taylor *(Darnell)*, Douglas Cameron *(Warder Benham)*, David Ensor *(Judge)*, Tony Shepherd *(Squad Car Policeman)*.

A gang of crooks hires an American safe cracking expert, but he is intercepted by Scotland yard detectives and arrested on an old charge. The gangsters free the safecracker from prison, not knowing the police have let loose a phony in order to infiltrate their gang. Sylvester, the dupe, is taken to the home of Brown and Sesselman. She kills her husband and tries to pin it on Sylvester, but he runs off, hiding out with nice lady Baddeley, from where he contacts the criminal mastermind, Underdown. The safe is finally cracked and secret government plans are stolen. Underdown plans to kill Sylvester and flee with Sesselman, but is apprehended by Scotland Yard and Sylvester tells his real identity. Stylish and witty in parts, the pace just isn't as fast as it should be.

p, John Clein, George Maynard; d, Robert Lynn; w, Paul Ryder (based on a story by Berkely Mather); ph, Nicolas Roeg; m, Martin Slavin; ed, Lee Doig; md, Slavin; art d, William Hutchinson; m/l, "Sabina," Martin Slavin, Abbe Gail (sung by Ronnie Hall); makeup, Jill Carpenter.

Suspense **(PR:C MPAA:NR)**

INFORMER, THE*½ (1929, Brit.) 83m BIP/Wardour bw

Lya de Putti *(Katie Fox)*, Lars Hansen *(Gypo Nolan)*, Warwick Ward *(Dan Gallagher)*, Carl Harbord *(Francis McPhillip)*, Dennis Wyndham *(Murphy)*, Janice Adair *(Bessie)*, Daisy Campbell *(Mrs. McPhillip)*, Craighall Sherry *(Mulholland)*, Ellen Pollock *(Prostitute)*, Johnny Butt *(Publican)*, Raymond Milland *(Bit)*.

Based on the same play that inspired John Ford's masterpiece of 1935 with Victor McLaglen in the role played here by Hansen. Seeing a chance to flee the poverty that surrounds him, the oafish but gentle Hansen decides to turn an IRA comrade into the police. He plans to use the reward money to flee to America with his mistress, only things don't turn out quite as planned, with Hansen haunted by guilt in the form of friends who shared the same Irish Republican ideals. Hansen was not nearly as convincing as McLaglen, nor did Robison possess the skill of Ford. Look for a brief appearance of a young Ray Milland in his second movie role.

d, Arthur Robison; w, Benn W. Levy, Rolfe E. Vanlo (based on the play by Liam O'Flaherty); ph, Werner Brandes, Theodor Sparkuhl, L. Rogers.

Drama **(PR:A MPAA:NR)**

INFORMER, THE***** (1935) 91m RKO bw

Victor McLaglen *(Gypo Nolan)*, Heather Angel *(Mary McPhillip)*, Preston Foster *(Dan Gallagher)*, Margot Grahame *(Katie Madden)*, Wallace Ford *(Frankie McPhillip)*, Una O'Conner *(Mrs. McPhillip)*, J.M. Kerrigan *(Terry)*, Joseph Sawyer *(Bartley Mulholland)*, Neil Fitzgerald *(Tommy Conner)*, Donald Meek *(Pat Mulligan)*, D'Arcy Corrigan *(Blindman)*, Leo McCabe *(Donahue)*, Gaylord Pendelton *(Daley)*, Francis Ford *("Judge" Flynn)*, May Boley *(Mrs. Betty)*, Grizelda Harvey *(An Obedient Girl)*, Dennis O'Dea *(Street Singer)*, Jack Mulhall *(Lookout)*, Robert Parrish *(Soldier)*, Clyde Cook, Barlowe Borland, Frank Moran, Arthur McLaglen.

McLaglen gives the performance of his life as the brutish betrayer, Gypo Nolan, in this telling Ford classic film. This examination of the human soul, or the Irish soul, as it were, was a celluloid experience few viewers were ever to forget. The film gleaned top honors from the Academy, winning Oscars for McLaglen as Best Actor, Nichols for Best Adaptation, Steiner for Best Musical Score, and Ford for Best Director (he also won the New York Critics Best Director award). The film opens with the child-like McLaglen ambling down a Dublin street during the Irish Civil War of 1922. He sees a wanted poster for his best friend, Wallace Ford, and angrily tears it down, tossing it away, but the wind gusts the poster along with McLaglen as he goes down the street and it blows up against his legs and clings to him, signaling his betrayal to come. Through the windows of a pub he sees his friend Wallace Ford, the much-wanted rebel, and the vision of the hated poster offering 20 pounds reward for him appears before him. McLaglen has many visions that night which haunt and nag him. One is his girl Grahame, who is shown standing beneath a lamppost, soft light glowing about her, a portrait of a madonna. Then she is approached by a man and she removes her shawl; the low-key lighting brightens to show her hard features and expose the reality of her streetwalking profession. Goading McLaglen is a window advertisement showing a miniature transatlantic liner and a price tag of 10 pounds for travel to America. The dim-witted giant then gets it into his head that, with a little money, he could escape his troubles by going with Grahame to the new land, America, where all is golden. The thought nags him right to the offices of the Black and Tan, the British paramilitary organization battling the secret Irish Republican Army. Here McLaglen tells the British commanders where they can find the wanted Wallace Ford. They send a small army to his home and Ford shoots it out with them, being killed as he attempts to leap from a second story window. With the twenty pounds reward money in his pocket, McLaglen proceeds to get roaring drunk, carousing through the pubs, buying instant friends with drinks and food. One of these, Kerrigan, a sleazy little con man, dubs McLaglen "King Gypo" and becomes his advance man, touting him through saloons as the finest man in Ireland. IRA members learn of McLaglen's wild spending spree and take the news to their leader, Foster, a gentle, pipe-smoking, trenchcoat-clad captain of the cause. His girl, sweet and considerate Angel, who happens to be Wallace Ford's sister, ironically begs Foster, after Grahame pleads with her, not to execute the suspected traitor McLaglen. But McLaglen is a doomed soul. A "blind man" begging outside the Black and Tan headquarters later tells the IRA leaders that he saw McLaglen leave the place with money, tossing a note into his plate. The rebels begin to add up the traitor's expenditures and it all comes to twenty pounds, the exact blood money offered by authorities for Wallace Ford. By then McLaglen has been steered into a high class drinking club and bordello, populated mostly by British customers. But when McLaglen's money begins to run out, he is asked to leave by the brothel's madam, not before, however, he gives a forlorn female resident enough money to escape her social prison. IRA men burst into the place to take McLaglen to a secret court-martial which is presided over by Foster. Here he is confronted by the "blind man," and others who testify to his whereabouts and spending spree, convincing the court that he is guilty of being a Judas. He is condemned to death and put into a room to await execution. McLaglen escapes and flees to Grahame, but she can do little for him except offer consolation. Sawyer and other IRA men break into her room and McLaglen is shot but escapes once more. In the end, he staggers to a church and there finds Wallace Ford's mother (O'Connor) praying in a pew. He begs her to forgive him for betraying her son. "You didn't know what you were doing," she tells him. Tears stream across McLaglen's broad face as he goes to the altar, looking heavenward and crying out as he collapses in death: "Frankie! Your mother forgives me!" THE INFORMER, made for a paltry $243,000, is undeniably one of Ford's greatest films, technically correct in every detail. August's photography is superbly lit with alternating mood-suggesting shadows and light; the studio sets are perfect reproductions of fog-bound 1920s Dublin, wet cobblestones, sweating walls, gloom and poverty and hopelessness in all the homes, public places, and on the faces of every character actor, framed like painted scenes by Ford. Through this mythic setting Ford moves his characters stoically to their grim fates. This was the first of three films Ford was to do for RKO and it became their most prestigious production for years. Ford came into his own with this film. He had directed many films before THE INFORMER but they were unexceptional except for the silent epic THE IRON HORSE (1924), and THE LOST PATROL (1934). He had approached RKO as early as 1930, asking to film the searing Liam O'Flaherty novel. Studio bosses thought the tale too dark and depressing and its protagonist wholly without sympathy—a drunk, a liar, a man who would betray anyone or do anything despicable to save his own skin. Ford kept pestering the studio, promising to stay to a small budget. He did. Writer Nichols, one of Ford's favorite collaborators, wrote the script in six days, considerably "humanizing" O'Flaherty's repulsive characters. Ford shot the entire film with lightning speed, completing it within another 17 days. His selection of McLaglen, who had starred in his other memorable talkie, THE LOST PATROL, was a masterstroke. McLaglen, barrel-chested, thunderclapping voice, ox-like shoulders, was the perfect hulking, face-scarred Gypo Nolan. Much has been said of McLaglen's lurching, unforgettable performance, that battered face jutting pugnaciously into Ford's cameras (he had once been Heavyweight Champion of Great Britain, having fought Jack Johnson and had had his nose broken for the umpteenth time in a Homeric losing battle). It was later whispered that McLaglen, a great imbiber, was drunk during most of the filming and that Ford engineered this inebriated state as the only means of getting a raw and totally giving performance from the actor. Most of it is gossip, but it is known that before the climactic church scene where Gypo dies, Ford took McLaglen aside and they shared a few nips together before commencing with the scenes. McLaglen would never again reach such heights, although he would appear in 150 films. For Ford, this was the turning point of his majestic career. From here he would go on to make THE HURRICANE (1937), STAGECOACH (1939), THE GRAPES OF WRATH (1940), HOW GREEN WAS MY VALLEY (1941), to name only a few of the masterpieces that made him the greatest sound director of films. This was also a landmark film for composer Steiner, whose marvelous score perfectly fits every scene, from thundering patriotic strokes to lyrical and evocative motifs. THE INFORMER was not an initial success, despite rave reviews from critics at the time, but one day after it was premiered it had the distinction of being shown on the great luxury liner *Normandie* (later sabotaged during WW II in the Brooklyn Navy Yards) on its maiden voyage. When the film was named to the Ten Best Films list compiled at the end of 1935, audiences flocked to see it, making it a box office smash and, over decades of rereleases of the film it earned RKO millions. The O'Flaherty tale was originally filmed by British International as a silent in 1929, a miserable production by comparison to Ford's classic work; in 1968, with an all-black cast under the title UPTIGHT! Jules Dassin directed a remake which was an utter failure.

p, Cliff Reid; d, John Ford; w, Dudley Nichols (based on the novel by Liam O'Flaherty); ph, Joseph H. August; m, Max Steiner; ed, George Hively; art d, Van Nest Polglase, Charles Kirk; set d, Julia Heron; cos, Walter Plunkett.

Drama Cas. (PR:C MPAA:NR)

INFORMERS, THE (SEE: UNDERWORLD INFORMERS, 1965, Brit.)

INFRA-MAN***
(1975, Hong Kong) 92m Shaw Brothers/Joseph Brenner c (AKA: THE SUPER INFRAMAN; THE INFRA SUPERMAN)

Li Hsiu-Hsien *(Raymar/Infra-Man)*, Wang Hsieh *(Prof. Chang)*, Terry Liu *(Princess Demon)*, Lin Wen-wei *(Tu Ming)*, Yuan Man-Tzu *(Chan's Daughter)*.

Without a doubt, this ranks as a classic in the "So Bad It's Good" film genre. INFRA-MAN is a veritable feast for camp fans, with visual design, plot developments, and outrageous dialog which pays little heed to such foolish notions as intelligence or logic. After a Chinese volcano erupts things go haywire. There's a humongous flying lizard and other giant reptiles attacking without mercy; the Earth splits open; and a 20 million-year-old woman, bedecked in snakeskin and skulls, creates havoc. And that's just for openers! Only Infra-man, a sort of solar-powered superhero with beetle-like eyes, can save the world. But first he must fight off additional perils, which this English-dubbed film unashamedly is packed with. The situations and *mise-en-scene* are right out of any good comic book, as is the wonderfully idiotic dialog. The simplest remarks are delivered with the utmost seriousness, making it all the more ridiculous. This production was from the Shaw Brothers, who produced many a cheap exploitation feature in their day.

p, Runme Shaw; d, Hua-Shan; w, Peter Fernandez; ph, (Panavision, Eastmancolor); ed&spec eff, E.H. Glass.

Science Fiction Cas. (PR:C MPAA:PG)

INFRA SUPERMAN, THE (SEE: INFRA-MAN 1975, Hong Kong)

INGAGI* (1931) 75m Congo Pictures/RKO bw

Sir Hubert Winstead, Daniel Swayne *(Themselves)*, Charles Gemora *(Gorilla)*, Louis Nizor *(Narrator)*.

Originally billed as a revelation into some of the exotic wildlife of jungle Africa, and as representing a true life adventure, INGAGI created quite a stir when it was released and could easily be called one of the first great film scams. Supposedly recounting the adventures of two men on an expedition into Africa, some poorly shot jungle footage taken back in 1914 is combined with studio footage of Gemora in gorilla garb attacking native girls. The makers also created their own animals by taking a tortoise and putting an armadillo shell on its back. Several different groups protested against the gross inaccuracies concerning African natural history and a scene in which a "virgin sacrifice" is played topless. In fact, the State of New York would not allow it to be shown for several months. All this publicity only helped to boost consumer interest, as INGAGI was made on a virtual shoestring budget but grossed well over $4,000,000. INGAGI fits more under the heading of circus entertainment than it does film.

p, William Alexander; d, William Campbell; w, Adam Hull Shirk; ph, Harold Williams, George Summerton, Ed Joyce, Fred Webster, L. Gillingham; m, Edward Gage; ed, Grace McKee.

Adventure (PR:C MPAA:NR)

INGLORIOUS BASTARDS
(SEE: COUNTERFEIT COMMANDOS, 1978, Ital.)

INHERIT THE WIND***** (1960) 127m UA bw

Fredric March *(Matthew Harrison Brady)*, Spencer Tracy *(Henry Drummond)*, Gene Kelly *(E. K. Hornbeck)*, Florence Eldridge *(Mrs. Brady)*, Dick York *(Bertram T. Cates)*, Donna Anderson *(Rachel Brown)*, Harry Morgan *(Judge)*, Elliott Reid *(Davenport)*, Philip Coolidge *(Mayor)*, Claude Akins *(Rev. Brown)*, Paul Hartman *(Meeker)*, Jimmy Boyd *(Howard)*, Noah Beery, Jr. *(Stebbins)*, Gordon Polk *(Sillers)*, Ray Teal *(Dunlap)*, Norman Fell *(Radio Announcer)*, Hope Summers *(Mrs. Krebs)*, Renee Godfrey *(Mrs. Stebbins)*.

In the summer of 1925 the sovereign state of Tennessee played host to one of the most spectacular and ludicrous court trials in the history of American jurisprudence. A teacher named John T. Scopes had been arrested for teaching Darwin's theories of evolution in a public school, thus violating a state law backed by rabid fundamentalists. Prosecuting Scopes was the Rock of Ages fundamentalist William Jennings Bryan and defending him was the champion of liberal thinking, Clarence Darrow, truly a battle of the titans. Producer-director Kramer used this high-voltage historical Monkey Trial as the basis of one of his best filmic efforts, having the good fortune to cast acting giants Tracy and March as the legal combatants, and, in another stroke of genius, giving song-and-dance man Kelly the role of the great agnostic journalist, H.L. Mencken, all of them labelled with other names but clearly recognizable in their roles as the real-life participants in the farcical and epic trial. York plays the meek Scopes character, a bow-tie wearing teacher imprisoned for daring to teach sacriligious Darwin in tiny Hillsboro (supplanting the real town, Dayton, Tennessee). His girl friend is the daughter of fundamentalist preacher Akins who goes through many-minded agonies over his daughter's affection for the religious infidel. It is Akins who leads the religious community in sending for March to prosecute the misguided young teacher and win a crowning triumph for fundamentalist beliefs. When March arrives there are bands playing "The Battle Hymn of the Republic" and hordes of right-minded citizens marching him to the courthouse steps to pay homage to the man who ran for the American presidency three times (as did Bryan, losing each time). Hopelessly outnumbered are defense lawyer Tracy and jeering journalist Kelly. After some colorful preliminary skirmishes, with Tracy objecting to the banners festooning the town's buildings which call for York's condemnation and exalting the endless virtues of fundamentalism and March, the trial gets down to its earnest and gutsy telling, scene upon climactic scene where March and Tracy are pitted against each other. Through the intense heat—the participants shedding coats and waging legal battle in shirtsleeves (this in a day without air conditioning)—the York-Anderson love affair is shown in brief scenes, while March takes his after-court bows before an adoring population and leads torch-bearing fundamentalists in prayer during outdoors nighttime services. Tracy spends most of his off hours listening to Kelly sneeringly deride "the rubes" of the town, mocking their religious beliefs. The real battle begins when Tracy engineers March onto the witness stand and then backs him into an untenable fundamentalist position, getting March to state that the earth was literally created in seven days. Tracy pounces, demanding to know if each day of creation was 24 hours and when March says he does not know, Tracy tells him each day of creation could have been as long as thousands of years. "I am more interested in the Rock of Ages than the age of rocks," March quips. But Tracy relentlessly pounds home his Darwinian points and wins almost every round. At one point he corners March, who refuses to concede an evolutionary point, smugly adding: "I don't think about things I don't think about." Retorts Tracy: "Yes, but do you think about the things you do think about?" In the highly prejudicial surroundings, with March's followers packing the courtroom and yelling out fundamentalist slogans, York has no chance at all and neither does his hard-pressed, brilliant lawyer Tracy, even though Tracy has clearly won the case. York is found guilty but judge Morgan realizes that the fundamentalist prosecution has been ridiculous and he fines York a token $100, much to the chagrin of March and his followers. March, who is ignored when he attempts to read a lengthy speech, becomes apoplectic, then topples to the floor with a seizure and dies. Kelly gives Tracy a victory smirk but the valiant lawyer quickly defends his fallen foe by telling the cynical newsman: "A giant once lived in that body!" He is then upbraided by Kelly who watches Tracy pick up two books, Darwin's Theory of Evolution *and* The Bible, holding them tightly together and carrying them off. Kelly calls him a fraud, who really does believe in the Good Book. Tracy tells Kelly he is sorry for him, that he has no beliefs whatsoever and has no friends, that he is a lonely man who needs a friend. INHERIT THE WIND acutely captures the farcical Monkey Trial and offers the awesome talents of two double-Oscar winners Tracy and March in their only film together. In their scenes together they are nothing less than spellbinding, working off each other and holding their own—two of the most forceful images to grace the screen. Though Tracy had the more sympathetic role, that of Darrow (a man more crude and coarse than the actor portrayed him), March made up for his cold character by epitomizing the stunning orator Bryan, duplicating his real-life counterpart by donning a bald pate, adding girth, and employing the very mannerisms and gestures March ardently studied in newsreel footage of Bryan. Tracy never lost a scene to anyone except in this film where March uses every histrionic trick in his acting arsenal to bring the scene to his own presence, his face, hands, and body contorting and moving with every measured line Tracy uttered. "Those two guys really began to feel their oats," Kramer later commented, "and the crew was fascinated." Directing such giants proved a bit of a chore for Kramer. At one point he couldn't hear a line Tracy was delivering and told the actor: "Spence, it's taken me six months to write that line and I couldn't understand what you said." Tracy replied: "It's taken me 25 years to learn how to read a line like that and now you want me to recite it." Kelly is surprisingly good as the sarcastic newsman, hand-picked for the role by Kramer, and so too is Morgan as the thoughtful southern judge. The film contains some of the most witty, literate lines ever put on the screen, kept intact from the successful Broadway play by Lawrence and Lee and first starring Paul Muni and Ed Begley.

p&d, Stanley Kramer; w, Nathan E. Douglas, Harold Jacob Smith (based on theplay by Jerome Lawrence, Robert E. Lee); ph, Ernest Laszlo; m, Ernest Gold; prod d, Rudolph Sternad; ed, Fredric Knudtson; art d, Sternad; cos, Joe King.

Drama Cas. (PR:A MPAA:NR)

INHERITANCE, THE** (1951, Brit.) 103m TC/GFD bw (GB: UNCLE SILAS)

Jean Simmons *(Caroline Ruthyn)*, Katina Paxinou *(Madame de la Rougierre)*, Derrick de Marney *(Uncle Silas)*, Derek Bond *(Lord Richard Ilbury)*, Sophie Stewart *(Lady Monica Waring)*, Manning Whiley *(Dudley Ruthyn)*, Esmond Knight *(Dr. Bryerly)*, Reginald Tate *(Austin Ruthyn)*, Marjorie Rhodes *(Mrs. Rusk)*, John Laurie *(Giles)*, Frederick Burtwell *(Branston)*, George Curzon *(Sleigh)*, Frederick Ranalow *(Rigg)*, Patricia Glyn *(Mary Quince)*, O. B. Clarence *(Vicar)*, Guy Rolfe *(Sepulchre Hawkes)*, Robin Netscher, John Salew.

In 1845 sixteen-year-old Simmons is left to the care of de Marney, her uncle. Accommodations are less than pleasing as Simmons learns de Marney is plotting to do her in, aided by the equally villainous Paxinou. Enter a good doctor who grows to distrust de Marney and, with the juvenile lead, saves Simmons just in the nick of time. De Marney and Paxinou, the latter woefully miscast, ham it up shamelessly in this turgid melodrama. What it lacks in acting and script is slightly made up for by the direction, though this is hardly enough to carry the film.

p, Josef Somlo, Laurence Irving; d, Charles Frank; w, Ben Travers (based on the novel *Uncle Silas* by Sheridan Le Fanu); ph, Robert Krasker, Nigel Huke; m, Alan Rawsthorne; art d, Ralph Brinton.

Drama Cas. (PR:A MPAA:NR)

INHERITANCE, THE** (1964, Jap.) 107m Shochiku bw (KARAMI-AI)

Keiko Kishi *(Yasuko)*, Misako Watanabe *(Senzo)*, So Yamamura *(Clerk)*, Minoru Chiaki *(Marie)*, Tatsuya Nakadai, Yusuke Kawazu, Mari Yoshimura.

A millionaire industrialist is told that he has six months to live, so he has an employee try to locate his three illegitimate children. He then must choose which one will receive his wealth, but none measures up. Much to the dismay of his wife, he takes his secretary on as his mistress and gets her pregnant. On his deathbed he is told that the child will be the beneficiary, but the secretary actually devises a way to get her hands on the money. Another film from director Kobayashi which deals in the mechanics of corruption.

d, Masaki Kobayashi; w, Koichi Inagaki; ph, Ko Kawamata; ed, S. Miyaki.

Drama **(PR:C MPAA:NR)**

INHERITANCE, THE***
(1978, Ital.) 121m FLAG/S.J. International c (EREDITA FERRAMONTI)

Anthony Quinn *(Gregorio Ferramonti)*, Fabio Testi *(Mario Ferramonti)*, Dominique Sanda *(Irene)*, Luigi Proietti *(Pippo Ferramonti)*, Adriana Asti *(Teta Ferramonti)*, Paoloa Bonacelli *(Paolo Furlin)*.

Working-class girl Sanda marries into a wealthy family headed by Quinn. He's the family's aging patriarch, and a lecherous old man to boot. Soon the two are embroiled in a passionate affair in this sex-charged drama. It's full of the things that make soap opera the wonderfully trashy art form it's grown to be: magnificent settings, rich and powerful characters, and of course plenty of sexual encounters. Quinn and Sanda smolder under a competent director who is well acquainted with this sort of material.

p, Gianni Hecht Lucari; d, Mauro Bolognini; w, Ugo Pirro, Sergio Bazzini; ph, Ennio Guarnieri (Eastmancolor); m, Ennio Morricone; ed, Nino Baragli; art d, Luigi Scaccianoce.

Drama **Cas.** **(PR:O MPAA:R)**

INHERITANCE IN PRETORIA* (1936, Ger.) 93m Bavaria-Film-AG bw

Paul Hartmann *(Bernhard Fredersen)*, Charlotte Susa *(Agnes His Wife)*, Paul Henckels *(Petermann, Prokurist)*, Max Weydner *(William Spencer)*, Dr. Philipp Manning *(Adm. Wiethaus, Agnes' Father)*, Gustaf Gruendgens *(Eugen Schliebach)*, Lilo Mueller *(Ines)*, Kurt Vespermann *(Hans Joachim Foerster)*, Richard Revy *(Georg Miller)*, Walter Lantzch *(Capt. Husemann)*, Phillipp Velt *(Gehelmrat Klinger)*, Fita Benkhoff *(Lilly Clausen)*.

Gruendgens is Weydner's private secretary, a wealthy financier. Unbeknownst to his employer, he is also a gentleman bandit. When Spencer dies, Gruendgens goes off with the young woman his late boss had befriended and they have an affair. The film is long winded, making the story confusing and dull. (In German.)

d, Johannes Meyer; w, Walter Wassemann; m, Hans Carate.

Drama **(PR:C MPAA:NR)**

INJUN FENDER** (1973) 100m Duke University Dept. of Foreign Language c

Dennis Campbell *(Fender)*, Nancy Salmon *(Girl)*, Warren Finnerty *(Texan)*.

Campbell plays a native American who doubles as both rock musician and murderer. Played against the backdrop of the late sixties youth culture, Campbell relieves his angers and frustrations through his songs and by killing. The picture is steeped in "meaning" and pseudo-psychology, typical of many minor films of the era. Undoubtedly being produced in accord with Duke University may have had something to do with this. Filmed in 16mm.

p, Robert Cordier, Douglas Cooper; d&w, Cordier; ph, Deidi Von Schaewen; m, M. Tschudin, Magic Tramp Midnight Opera Company.

Drama **(PR:O MPAA:NR)**

INJUSTICE (SEE: ROAD GANG, 1936)

INN FOR TROUBLE** ½ (1960, Brit.) 90m Film Locations/Eros bw

Peggy Mount *(Ada Larkins)*, David Kossoff *(Alf Larkins)*, Leslie Phillips *(John Belcher)*, Glyn Owen *(Lord Bill Osborne)*, Yvonne Monlaur *(Yvette)*, Charles Hawtrey *(Silas)*, A. E. Matthews *(Sir Hector Gore-Blandish)*, Shaun O'Riordan *(Eddie Larkins)*, Ronan O'Casey *(Jeff Rogers)*, Alan Wheatley *(Harold Gaskin)*, Graham Moffatt *(Jumbo Gudge)*, Willoughby Goddard *(Sgt. Saunders)*, Gerald Campion *(George)*, Stanley Unwin *(Farmer)*, Irene Handl *(Lily)*, Fred Robinson *(Fred)*, Arthur Lawrence, Esma Cannon, Frank Williams John Woodnutt, Edward Malin, Barbara Mitchell, Edwin Richfield, Alan Rolfe, Paddy Edwards, Edward Woodward.

Mount and Kossoff are a London couple who inherit a pub in the country. Business is terrible thanks to the scheming of a local brewery, but in the end Mount and Kossoff have the last laugh and better business with the help of a high-proof brew. Based on a British television comedy, this broad farce has some good moments and is amusing in its own way.

p, Norman J. Hyams, Edward Lloyd; d, C. M. Pennington-Richards; w, Fred Robinson (based on his TV series "The Larkins"); ph, Eric Cross.

Comedy **(PR:A MPAA:NR)**

INN OF THE DAMNED** (1974, Aus.) 125m Terryrod/Roadshow c

Judith Anderson *(Caroline Straulle)*, Alex Cord *(Cal Kincaid)*, Michael Craig *(Paul Melford)*, Joseph Furst *(Lazar Straulle)*, Tony Bonner *(Trooper Moore)*, John Meillon *(George Parr)*, Robert Quilter *(Biscayne)*, John Nash, John Morris, Don Barkham, Carla Hoogeveen, Diana Dangerfield, Phil Avalon, Louis Wishart, Graham Corry, Jack Allan, Nat Levison, Lionel Long, Colin Drake, Josie McKay, Linda Broan, Reg Gorman, Graham Ware, Hilary Bamberger, Anna King, Gordon Glenwright.

Anderson and Furst are an old couple who run an out-of-the-way inn. The problem is guests check in but don't check out. Cord is a bounty hunter who comes a-callin'. It is finally revealed that Furst and Anderson's children were killed by an escaped convict years before and they have been driven mad in their bloodthirsty quest for revenge. The dialog is too simplistic for the macabre nature of the story but most of the acting overcomes this. The eerie lighting and cinematography change the 1896 Australian outback into a sort of western gothic horror setting.

p, Terry Bourke, Rod Hay; d&w, Bourke; ph, Brian Probyn (Eastmancolor); m, Bob Young; ed, Hay; prod d, Gary Hansen.

Horror **(PR:O MPAA:NR)**

INN OF THE FRIGHTENED PEOPLE
(SEE: TERROR FROM UNDER THE HOUSE, 1971, Brit.)

INN OF THE SIXTH HAPPINESS, THE*** ½ (1958) 158m FOX c

Ingrid Bergman *(Gladys Aylward)*, Curt Jurgens *(Capt. Lin Nan)*, Robert Donat *(Mandarin)*, Ronald Squire *(Sir Francis Jamison)*, Noel Hood *(Miss Thompson)*, Joan Young *(Cook)*, Moultrie Kelsall *(Dr. Robinson)*, Edith Sharpe *(Secretary)*, Richard Wattis *(Mr. Murfin)*, Athene Seyler *(Mrs. Lawson)*, Peter Chong *(Yang)*, Michael David *(Ho Ka)*, Zed Zakari *(Prison Guard)*, Burt Kwouk *(Li)*, Frank Blaine *(Madman)*, Ronald Kyaing *(Young Lin)*, Tsai Chin *(Sui-Lan)*, Louise Lin *(Mai-Da)*, Michael Wee *(Mandarin's Aide)*, Lian-Shin Yang *(Woman With Baby)*, Ye-Min *(Bai Boa)*, Judith Lai *(Sixpence)*, Frank Goh *(Timothy)*, Andre Mikhelson *(Russian Commissar)*, Stanislaw Mikula *(Russian Conductor)*, Lin Chen *(Innkeeper's Wife)*, Ronald Lee *(Chief Muleteer)*, Christopher Chen *(Tax Collector)*, Aung Min *(Buddhist Priest)*.

The film is set in China, but the Bamboo Curtain had been drawn so tightly by 1958 that the production was shot in Northern Wales to get the proper terrain. Based on the true story of Gladys Aylward, it tells a tale that is at once religious without being dogmatic and without losing any of the entertainment value. Bergman is a domestic servant who works for Squire in London. He is a retired adventurer and a peer of the realm. Squire tells her about Seyler, a British Christian missionary who maintains an inn high in the North China mountains. Seyler provides food and accommodations for travelers and once they are there, she does her best to convert the heathens to the way of the Cross. Bergman likes the thought of doing something important with her life and decides to go to China and help Seyler. Bergman is ill educated, which causes her application for missionary status to be declined. But she is determined and amasses enough to pay for the trek herself aboard the Trans-Siberian railroad. Once at the inn, she meets Seyler and goes to work as her assistant. Bergman is an immediate hit with the people and when Seyler passes away, Bergman takes on the additional employment of "foot inspector." (In China, there had been a custom of binding women's feet and as that custom is outlawed, Bergman's job is to make certain the edict is followed.) She's been assigned the task by Donat, an old Mandarin, and he is so annoyed at her nosiness that he conspires to send her on these inspections as often as he can, if only to keep her out of his pigtail. When she returns from her arduous travels, Donat alters his way of thinking about her as he is most impressed by her abilities. The Japanese are about to attack and Jurgens, a Chinese army officer, is sent to the area to prepare the people for a possible war. Bergman has already demonstrated her power in the area by calming a riot in the local prison so Jurgens asks for her help in notifying the population of the impending invasion. This she does by using some contacts she's made with local Chinese criminals who roam the countryside. Propinquity breeds affection and soon Bergman and Jurgens are in love. When he has to leave to join his unit, he hands her a jade ring and swears that they will eventually be reunited. The Japanese onslaught begins and Bergman heroically leads scores of orphans on a hegira to a safe area. Before doing this, she gets one of her favorite presents from Donat; he agrees to convert to Christianity. The trip is arduous and dangerous and Bergman rallies the youngsters around her as they climb mountains, ford streams, and finally get to a village in the interior where a mission is located. The fact that she made it causes the townspeople to applaud her courage. It is here that she again meets Kelsall, the man who had originally found her ineligible to be a missionary. He is heartened by her incredible feat and welcomes them all, then asks Bergman to stay and help tend the children. She smiles, feels the ring that Jurgens gave her, and says that she must get back to where her work is, to the Inn of the Sixth Happiness. The viewer appreciates her dedication but knows that she's thinking about Jurgens and whether or not she'll ever see him again. The real Aylward was petite so that the casting of Bergman went against reality, but how many people would know that? This was the last film appearance for Donat, which was particularly poignant because his very last line was one of farewell. Heartwarming, sincere, and inspiring, it was almost totally overlooked by the Motion Picture Academy, only managing a nomination for director Robson.

p, Buddy Adler; d, Mark Robson; w, Isobel Lennart (based on the novel *The Small Woman* by Alan Burgess); ph, Frederick A. Young (CinemaScope, DeLuxe Color); m, Malcolm Arnold; ed, Ernest Walter; md, Arnold; art d, John Box, Geoffrey Drake; cos, Margaret Furse.

Drama **Cas.** **(PR:AA MPAA:NR)**

INNER CIRCLE, THE* ½ (1946) 57m REP bw

Adele Mara *(Gerry Travis)*, Warren Douglas *(Johnny Strange)*, William Frawley *(Webb)*, Ricardo Cortez *(Duke York)*, Virginia Christine *(Rhoda Roberts)*, Ken Niles *(Radio Announcer)*, Will Wright *(Henry Boggs)*, Dorothy Adams *(Mrs. Wilson)*, Martha Montgomery *(Anne Travis)*, Edward Gargan, Fred Graham, Eddie Parker, Bob Wilke.

Minor and poorly made mystery has private detective Douglas being framed for murder by his secretary. She's out to protect her baby sister who has been accused of committing the crime. Douglas travels through the usual circles, trying to unravel the mystery. He finally assembles all the suspects in a radio studio and reenacts the crime, revealing the guilty party. But the script is so poorly written that *how* the crime was solved is still a mystery.

p, William J. O'Sullivan; d, Phil Ford; w, Dorrell and Stuart E. McGowan (based on a radio script by Leonard St. Clair, Lawrence Taylor); ph, Reggie Lanning; ed, Tony Martinelli; md, Mort Glickman; art d, Fred A. Ritter.

Mystery **(PR:A MPAA:NR)**

INNER SANCTUM* (1948) 62m FC bw

Charles Russell, Mary Beth Hughes, Lee Patrick, Nana Bryant, Billy House, Dale Belding, Roscoe Ates, Eve Miller, Fritz Lieber, Eddie Parks.

Yet another of the innumerable Landers' low budget specialties that never seem to be able to outshine the limited effort and production facilities. With only the title borrowed from the then-popular radio program, Hughes finds that the train ride she had thought to be a pleasant little jaunt is a real nightmare when Lieber relates a terrifying story.

p, Samuel Rheiner, Walter Shenson; d, Lew Landers; w, Jerome Todd Gollard; ph, Al Ziegler; ed, Fred Feitshans, Jr.; md, Emil Newman.

Mystery **(PR:A MPAA:NR)**

INNERVIEW, THE zero (1974) 90m Richard Beymer bw/c

Joanna Bochco, Richard Beymer, Antranig Mahakian.

Bochco plays the victim of an auto accident; Beymer plays a filmmaker. The film opens with a blank screen and a sound track consisting of heavy breathing, tipping the viewer off to some pseudo-intellectual cinematic fun. Beymer, a real-life Hollywood actor, tries his hand here at avant-garde filmmaking, but misses by a long shot. What he does come up with is a series of shots with distorted angles, banal attempts at pop psychoanalysis, cheap Bergmanesque symbolism, and, ultimately, an incomprehensible mess.

p,d,w,ph,&ed, Richard Beymer.

Drama **(PR:O MPAA:NR)**

INNOCENCE IS BLISS (SEE: MISS GRANT TAKES RICHMOND, 1949)

INNOCENCE UNPROTECTED**** (1971, Yugo.) 75m Avala/Grove Press bw/c (NEVINOST BEZ ZASTITE)

Dragoljub Aleksic *(Acrobat Aleksic)*, Ana Milosavljevic *(Nada The Orphan)*, Vera Jovanovic *(The Wicked Stepmother)*, Bratoljub Gligorijevic *(Mr. Petrovic)*, Ivan Zivkovic *(Aleksic's Brother)*, Pera Milosavljevic *(Servant)*.

In 1942 Aleksic, a Yugoslavian gymnast and stunt man, wrote, produced, directed, and starred in a film titled INNOCENCE UNPROTECTED. Its simple plot concerns an acrobat with a pure heart rescuing young Milosavljevic from the clutches of her evil stepmother, Jovanovic. The final production was subsequently confiscated by the Nazis, fading into cinema obscurity. Aleksic himself was accused (but later exonerated) of collaborating with the enemy. In 1968 Yugoslavian director Dusan Makavejev discovered the long-forgotten movie and reworked it into a film collage, a technique Makavejev further explored in WR: MYSTERIES OF THE ORGANISM. He hand-tinted some of the original footage and edited in newsreels of Nazi-occupied Yugoslavia. To this was added vintage documentary footage of Aleksic performing various stunts and new scenes with surviving members of the original film's cast and crew. The result is a wonderful and highly unusual film experience. Makavejev called it "a montage of attractions," an investigation of what is reality and illusion. The film is often confusing but full of ironies and biting humor, with a youthful exuberance emanating from both the director and Aleksic. A real love for the subject and the art of film radiates throughout the production. (English subtitles.)

d&w, Dusan Makavejev; ph, Branko Perak, Stevan Miskovic (Eastmancolor); m, Vojislav Dostic; ed, Ivanka Vukasovic; m/l, Dostic, Aleksander Popovic.

Drama **(PR:C MPAA:NR)**

INNOCENT, THE*** (1979, Ital.) 112m Analysis Film Releasing Corp. c (L'INNOCENTE)

Giancarlo Giannini *(Tullio Hermil)*, Laura Antonelli *(Guiliana)*, Jennifer O'Neill *(Teresa Raffo)*, Rina Morelli *(Tullio's Mother)*, Massimo Girotti *(Count Stefano Egano)*, Didier Haudepin *(Federico Hermil)*, Marie Dubois *(The Princess)*, Roberta Paladini *(Miss Elviretta)*, Claude Mann *(The Prince)*, Marc Porel *(Filippo d'Arborio, a Writer)*.

The final film by one of the major spokesmen of the Italian Neo-Realist Movement, Luchino Visconti, is a highly stylized work that in technique and structure is a far cry from the grittiness of the films of the early 1950s. Mainly a look into the decadence of the aristocracy of late 19th Century Italy, where the pursuit of hedonistic aims is veiled under a decor of social respectability. Giannini is the wealthy aristocrat married to Antonelli while carrying on a fairly open affair with O'Neill. The wife is tossed to the background and treated as little more than a maid until he discovers her having a passionate affair with a young novelist. In one of the most sensuous and lush scenes of film, Giannini seduces Antonelli with an obsessive intensity while spouting trite philosophy regarding the essence of life. Antonelli turns up pregnant, but the father is the novelist lover, a fact that Giannini is unable to accept, driving him to insanity and eventual suicide. Though given little to do in the form of acting, Antonelli proves an excessively sensuous presence on the screen, mainly because of her innocent looking face. She is used to her maximum strength by Visconti, blending her into the lush backgrounds. Ironically she remains the only likable person in THE INNOCENT, and the only one still possessing a bit of genuine human feeling. Though unequal to his earlier works, THE INNOCENT is still an effective comment on the way bourgeois society stifles human values.

p, Giovanni Bertolucci; d, Luchino Visconti; w, Suso Cecchi D'Amico, Enrico Medioli, Visconti (based on the novel "L'Innocente" by Gabriele d'Annunzio); ph, Pasqualino De Santis (Technovision, Technicolor); m, Franco Mannino; ed, Ruggero Mastroianni; art d, Mario Garbuglai; cos, Piero Tose.

Drama **Cas.** **(PR:O MPAA:R)**

INNOCENT AFFAIR, AN (SEE: DON'T TRUST YOUR HUSBAND, 1948)

INNOCENT AND THE DAMNED (SEE: GIRLS TOWN, 1959)

INNOCENT BYSTANDERS 1/2** (1973, Brit.) 111m Sagittarius/PAR c

Stanley Baker *(John Craig)*, Geraldine Chaplin *(Miriam Loman)*, Donald Pleasence *(Loomis)*, Dana Andrews *(Blake)*, Sue Lloyd *(Joanna Benson)*, Derren Nesbitt *(Andrew Royce)*, Vladek Sheybal *(Aaron Kaplan)*, Warren Mitchell *(Omar)*, Cec Linder *(Mankowitz)*, Howard Goorney *(Zimmer)*, J.C. Devlin *(Waiter)*, Ferdy Mayne *(Marcus Kaplan)*, Clifton Jones *(Hetherton)*, John Collin *(Asimov)*, Aharon Ipale *(Gabrilovitch)*, Yuri Borienko *(Guard)*, Frank Maher *(Daniel)*, Michael Poole *(Zhelkov)*, Cliff Diggins *(Harry Bigelow)*, Tom Bowman *(Guard)*.

Baker is the crack agent of a supersecret British organization. Though he has mishandled cases in the recent past, his superior, Pleasence, gives him one more chance, sending him to find an escaped Russian scientist. Baker engages in the usual James Bond-like spy excitement, along with Chaplin and American agent Andrews. The pace never sags and the resolution matches O. Henry for surprise value. Still, there is a bit too much violence.

p, George H. Brown; d, Peter Collinson; w, James Mitchell (based on his novel under the pseudonym James Munro); ph, Brian Probyn (Eastmancolor); m, John Keating; ed, Alan Pattillo; md, Keating; art d, Maurice Carter; spec eff, Pat Moore; m/l, "What Makes the Man," 'Hurricane Smith' (sung by Smith); stunts, Frank Maher, Les Crawford.

Spy/Action **(PR:O MPAA:PG)**

INNOCENT MEETING 1/2** (1959, Brit.) 62m Danzigers/UA bw

Sean Lynch *(Johnny Brent)*, Beth Rogan *(Connie)*, Raymond Huntley *(Harold)*, Ian Fleming *(Garside)*, Howard Lang *(Macey)*, Arnold Bell *(Fry)*, Colin Tapley *(Stannard)*, Robert Raglan *(Martin)*, Denis Shaw *(Uncle)*, Tony Doonan, Gordon Needham, Robert Raikes, Robert Dorning, Brian Haines, Vernon Smythe, David Coote, Walter Horsbrugh, Hal Osmond, Frank Forsyth, Adrian Cairns, Edwin Richfield, Mark Singleton.

Teenage robber Lynch gets probation and meets Rogan, a well-to-do young lady. She gets him a job in her father's textile business, but when the man's wallet is missing Lynch is blamed. Forced to go on the lam, Lynch holds up a store but is finally tracked down by the police. The wallet is found and Rogan convinces the fugitive to give himself up. Though the characters aren't based heavily in reality, this is an interesting drama with some good performances by the cast.

p, Edward J. Danziger, Harry Lee Danziger; d, Godfrey Grayson; w, Brian Clemens, Eldon Howard; ph, Jimmy Wilson.

Crime/Drama **(PR:C MPAA:NR)**

INNOCENT SINNERS* 1/2 (1958, Brit.) 95m Rank bw

June Archer *(Lovejoy Mason)*, Christopher Hey *(Tip Malone)*, Brian Hammond *(Sparkey)*, Flora Robson *(Olivia Chesney)*, David Kossoff *(Mr. Vincent)*, Barbara Mullen *(Mrs. Vincent)*, Catherine Lacey *(Angela Chesney)*, Susan Beaumont *(Liz)*, Lyndon Brook *(Charles)*, Edward Chapman *(Manley)*, John Rae *(Mr. Isbister)*, Vanda Godsell *(Lovejoy's Mother)*, Hilda Fenemore *(Cassie)*, Pauline Delaney *(Mrs. Malone)*, Andrew Cruickshank *(Doctor)*, Vanda Hudson, Marianne Stone.

Archer plays a young girl ignored by her actress mother Godsell. She finds a packet of cornflower seeds and decides to make something beautiful out of something ugly. In a bombed-out section of London, with the reluctant help of street kids Hey and Hammond, she plants a garden. Of course, the adults don't understand what her project is about. Overall, the film has a half-hearted feel to it. Though the basic plot is interesting enough, the production relies on a too-easy sentimentality.

p, Hugh Stewart; d, Philip Leacock; w, Rumer Godden, Neil Paterson (based on the novel *An Episode of Sparrows* by Godden); ph, Harry Waxman; m, Philip Green; ed, John Guthridge.

Drama **(PR:AAA MPAA:NR)**

INNOCENTS, THE**** (1961, U.S./Brit.) 99m FOX-Achilles/FOX bw

Deborah Kerr *(Miss Giddens)*, Michael Redgrave *(The Uncle)*, Peter Wyngarde *(Peter Quint)*, Megs Jenkins *(Mrs. Grose)*, Martin Stephens *(Miles)*, Pamela Franklin *(Flora)*, Clytie Jessop *(Miss Jessel)*, Isla Cameron *(Anna)*, Eric Woodburn *(Coachman)*.

Certain films benefit from CinemaScope; others are better made with the usual lenses. This is one that would have been more effective if it were smaller. The producers were wise not to use color because that might have also detracted. As it is, THE INNOCENTS is a classic chiller with more goosebumps and sweaty palms than all the HALLOWEEN films could offer. Director Clayton, cinematographer Francis, and the eerie script by Capote and Archibald blend together into one of the most compelling examples of evil incarnate ever seen in films. It's not one of those "shock-a-minute" pictures. Rather, it builds, sometimes almost leisurely, and inextricably weaves the viewer into its vortex until he is on the edge of his seat. In late nineteenth century England, Kerr, a minister's daughter, has been hired to watch over Franklin and Stephens, the niece and nephew of Redgrave, master of a huge country house. The housekeeper, Jenkins, introduces her to Franklin, an angelic little child with a beguiling smile. When Franklin says that her brother is due to arrive (and there is no way to explain her statement other than ESP or some sort of bond between the children), Kerr is surprised but not yet disturbed. A letter is delivered from Stephens' school that says the boy is being expelled for being a bad influence on his fellow students. Kerr doesn't know what to expect, but when Stephens enters and is every bit as innocent and entrancing as his sister, Kerr suspects that the school must have been mistaken; there is no way this adorable child could ever corrupt anyone. The estate is large and cheery and the sounds of the birds and the soft winds are an ominous introduction to what is to come. Kerr thinks she sees a man atop the house but her eyes are temporarily blinded by the sun. When she makes a closer investigation, she finds Stephens feeding the pigeons where she thought the man was. Feeling that her eyes must have played tricks on her, she calms down until she sees the specter of a woman at the window. Then she sees the man again and his face is twisted and ugly. When she describes these apparitions to Jenkins, she is told that the descriptions match those of the estate's former manager and his dead lover, the woman who preceded Kerr as governess. Further information tells her that these two dead lovers had a sadomasochistic relationship and that their influence on the children was palpable. Kerr believes that Stephens and Franklin may have been possessed by the late couple. She makes vain attempts to get the children to own up to what's happening behind those twinkling eyes but the duo will have none of her prying. She tries to frighten Franklin into admitting her possession but the girl becomes hysterical and leaves the house with Jenkins. Kerr believes that her efforts may have helped rid Franklin of the demon so she begins to work on Stephens. She sees the late manager's ghost and forces the boy to say the name of the man she is sure he can see as well as she can. Stephens says "Quint" and falls dead at her feet. She lifts the little figure, kisses his dead lips and begins to pray for his immortal soul as the film ends. Filmed in Sussex at an estate known as Sheffield Park, it is truly a gothic horror story and quite faithful to the Henry James novel on which it is based. The film never appealed to a bloodthirsty public who, at the time of its release, demanded gore and guts. Too bad, because this is a little gem that should not be missed by anyone who appreciates exquisite filmmaking.

p&d, Jack Clayton; w, William Archibald, Truman Capote, John Mortimer (based on the novel *The Turn of the Screw* by Henry James); ph, Freddie Francis (CinemaScope); m, Georges Auric; ed, James Clark; prod d, Wilfred Shingleton; md, Lambert Williamson; art d, Shingleton; set d, Peter James; cos, Sophie Devine, Motley; m/l, "O Willow Waly," Auric, Paul Dehn; makeup, Harold Fletcher.

Horror **(PR:C-O MPAA:NR)**

INNOCENTS IN PARIS** 1/2 (1955, Brit.) 93m Romulus/Tudor bw

Alastair Sim *(Sir Norman Barker)*, Ronald Shiner *(Dicky Bird)*, Claire Bloom *(Susan Robbins)*, Margaret Rutherford *(Gwladys Inglott)*, Claude Dauphin *(Max de Lorne)*, Laurence Harvey *(Francois)*, Jimmy Edwards *(Capt. George Stilton)*, James Copeland *(Andy MacGregor)*, Gaby Bruyere *(Josette)*, Mara Lane *(Gloria Delaney)*, Gregoire Aslan *(Carpet Seller)*, Peter Illing *(Panitov)*, Colin Gordon *(Customs Officer)*, Kenneth Kove *(Bickerstaff)*, Frank Muir *(Hearty Man)*, Peter Jones *(Langton)*, Richard Wattis *(Secretary)*, Reginald Beckwith *(Photographer)*, Monique Gerard *(Raymonde)*, Stringer Davis *(Arbuthnot)*, Georgette Anys *(Mme. Celestin)*, Louis De Funes *(Mons. Celestin)*, Miles Joyce *(Steve Wheeler)*, Alf Goddard *(Sergeant-Major)*, Christopher Lee *(Lt. Whitlock)*, Philip Stainton *(Nobby Clarke)*, Albert Dinan, Joan Winmill, Douglas Ives, Bill Shine, Andrea Malandrinos, John Serret, Frederick Schrecker, Yannick Malloire, Sophie Mallet, Marcelle Fery, Solange Bary, Ludmila Lopato, Charles Deschamps, Max Dalban, Andre Philip, Numes Fils, Sylvain, Joyce Marlowe, Walter Horsbrugh, Roger Fafal, Bouvette, Amato, Jacques Ciron, Moreau, Dita Hands, Lynn Craig, Maurice Baquet, Guy Du Monceau, Kenneth Williams, Joan Benham, Irene DeStrozzi, Hamilton Keene, Peter Rendall, John Brooking, Jack May, Georges Kobakhidze, Vladimir Slastcheff, Polycarpe Pavloff, Vera Gretch, Vladimir Poliakoff, Toke Townley, Ivan Samson, Joseph Bimstone, Evanghelou.

An episodic comedy about seven disparate English people who visit Paris and get into various kinds of scrapes, melees, and pleasantries. It jumps from story to story and takes a little too much time between tales but what's funny is hysterical and what's dull is about as exciting as watching someone get a haircut. Sim is a British peer/diplomat who has to get confirmation of an economic plan from Russian Illing. The Soviet is recalcitrant until he and Sim get together for a night of serious drinking and the man says 'da' instead of 'nyet.' Rutherford is an aged artist who is delighted when she buys a Mona Lisa copy; Edwards goes to gay Paree and spends the entire weekend tippling at a British bar so he may have well stayed in Soho; Bloom is a sweet young thing who is charmed by a Parisian man about town; Shiner is a musician in the Marine band who pub-crawls through the fleshpots of Pigalle; Lane is a lovelorn lass who is stood up at a restaurant and winds up with the waiter; and Copeland is the cliched kilted Scot who woos a local woman. Once again, Rutherford's husband, Davis, does a cameo (it may have been a codicil to all her acting contracts). It was a few years after this that the British Film Industry got their comedy hats on and began to make some of the funniest films ever. This was not one of them but still has enough humor to make it an amusing trifle. Rita Davison is sometimes credited with the script.

p, Anatole de Grunwald; d, Gordon Parry; w, de Grunwald; ph, Gordon Lang; m, Joseph Kosma; ed, Geoffrey Foot; md, Kosma; art d, Tom Goswell; cos, Ann Wemyss.

Comedy **(PR:A MPAA:NR)**

INNOCENTS OF CHICAGO, THE (SEE: WHY SAPS LEAVE HOME, 1932, Brit.)

INNOCENTS OF PARIS** (1929) 78m PAR bw

Maurice Chevalier *(Maurice Marny)*, Sylvia Beecher *(Louise Leval)*, Russell Simpson *(Emile Leval)*, George Fawcett *(Mons. Marny)*, Mrs. George Fawcett *(Mme. Marny)*, John Miljan *(Mons. Renard)*, Margaret Livingston *(Mme. Renard)*, David Durand *(Jo-Jo)*, Johnnie Morris *(Musician)*, Jack Luden *(Jules)*.

Chevalier makes his American debut as a junkman who saves a boy from drowning in the Seine after the child's mother tries suicide/murder. Though unable to save the mother, he rescues the boy and takes him to his grandfather. He meets Beecher, the boy's aunt, and falls in love. The grandfather, however, disapproves. After doing a few of his wonderful songs in the Flea Market, Chevalier is hired by Miljan and Livingston to sing in their theater. Beecher is afraid Chevalier will take a liking to the chorus cuties and begs him to give it all up. But he can't do it for it's his life. Beecher's father finds out about the romance and heads off to kill the amorous singer during a performance. Beecher tricks Chevalier to save his life, having him arrested. But she tells. At the denouement Chevalier sings in the theater at last, but renounces it all for the love of Beecher. Initially Chevalier was against doing the film on the basis of its weak script. But he gave in after Paramount agreed to let him sing some of the songs he had made his name with in France. Thus we get to hear the French version of "Yes We have No Bananas" ("Les Anas"), "Valentine," and "Dites-Moi, Ma Mere." Best of all, Chevalier sang what was to become one of his best loved numbers "Louise." Other than that, the film is a dud. The script is banal and direction is lifeless. Nevertheless, Chevalier's wonderful talents rose above the material and he became an overnight sensation in America. Critics compared him with Chaplin and he went on to become a film archetype of suavity and charm. Songs include "Louise," "Wait Till You See My Cherie," "It's A Habit of Mine," "On Top of the World Alone" (Richard A. Whiting, Leo Robin), "Valentine" (Henri Christine, Herbert Reynolds).

p, Jesse Lasky; d, Richard Wallace; w, Ethel Doherty, Ernest Vajda (based on the story "Flea Market" by Charles E. Andrews); ph, Charles Lang; m, Nathaniel W. Finston; ed, George Arthur; art d, Hans Dreier; ch, Fanchan and Marco, LeRoy Prinz.

Musical/Romance **(PR:A MPAA:NR)**

INNOCENTS WITH DIRTY HANDS (SEE: DIRTY HANDS, 1976, Fr.)

INQUEST** (1931, Brit.) 95m Majestic-New Era/FN bw

Mary Glynne *(Margaret Hamilton)*, Campbell Gullan *(Norman Dennison, King's Counsel)*, Sydney Morgan *(Coroner)*, Haddon Mason *(Richard Hanning)*, G. H. Mulcaster *(Charles Wyatt)*, Lena Halliday *(Mrs. Wyatt)*, Peter Coleman *(Mr. Hamilton)*, Reginald Tippett *(Sir Denton Hume)*, Alex Hunter, Nelson Phillips.

When the corpse of Glynne's late husband is exhumed, the coroner discovers that he died from a bullet wound rather than a heart condition. Glynne is immediately suspect in the man's murder but thanks to the determination of Gullan her innocence is eventually proven. One wonders where the bullet hole could have been located to escape detection in the first place. Remade in 1939.

p, Gordon Craig; d, G.B. Samuelson; w, Michael Barringer (based on the play by Barringer).

Crime **(PR:C MPAA:NR)**

INQUEST** 1/2 (1939, Brit.) 60m Charter/GN bw

Elizabeth Allan *(Margaret Hamilton)*, Herbert Lomas *(Mr. Knight)*, Hay Petrie *(Stephen Neale, Kings Counsel)*, Barbara Everest *(Mrs. Wyatt)*, Olive Sloane *(Lily Prudence)*, Philip Friend *(Richard Neale)*, Harold Anstruther *(Sir Denton Hulme)*, Malcolm Morley *(Dr. MacFarlane)*, Jean Shepherd, Charles Stephenson, Basil Cunard, Richard Coke.

A remake of the 1931 film has Allan suspected of murdering her late husband after a revolver is found in her attic. Coroner Lomas is determined to prove her guilty but thanks to Petrie's clever courtroom work Allan is found innocent. Not bad as courtroom dramas go, this was the first attempt by the Boulting brothers to give higher production values to programmer filmmaking.

p, John Boulting; d, Roy Boulting; w, Francis Miller (based on the play by Michael Barringer); ph, D. P. Cooper.

Crime **(PR:C MPAA:NR)**

INQUISITOR, THE*** (1982, Fr.) 90m Ariane-TF1/Gala c (GARDE A VUE)

Lino Ventura, Michel Serrault, Guy Marchand, Romy Schneider, Didier Agostini, Patrick Depeyrat, Pierre Maguelon, Serge Malik, Jean-Claude Penchenat, Yves Pignot, Mathieu Schiffman, Michel Such, Elsa Lunghini, Mohammed Bekireche.

A gripping psychological police drama which is set almost entirely on the single set of an interrogation room. Being questioned is a suspected child murderer, engaged in a battle of logic for an hour and a half with his interrogator. The drama builds to the point where the suspect accepts the guilt placed upon him, mainly because his life is so uncertain. Bravura performances from Ventura and Serrault, who are given the difficult task of carrying a film that contains almost no camera movement and is shot in near-real time. Fascinating.

p, Georges Dancigers, Alexandre Mnouchkine; d, Claude Miller; w, Miller, Jean Herman, Michel Audiard (based on the novel *Brainwash*, by John Wainwright); ph, Bruno Nuytten (Eastmancolor); m, Georges Delerue; ed, Albert Jurgenson; art d, Eric Moulard.

Crime/Mystery **(PR:C-O MPAA:NR)**

INSECT, THE (SEE: INSECT WOMAN, THE 1964, Jap.)

INSECT WOMAN, THE***
(1964, Jap.) 123m Nikkatsu Corp./Shochiku-Balsam bw (NIPPON KONCHUKI; AKA: THE INSECT)

Sachiko Hidari *(Tome Matsuki)*, Jitsuko Yoshimura *(Nobuko)*, Hiroyuki Nagato *(Matsunami)*, Seizaburo Kawazu *(Karasawa)*, Taiji Tonoyama *(Foreman)*, Shoichi Tsuyuguchi *(Honda)*, Teruko Kishi *(Rin)*, Sumie Sasaki *(En)*, Shoichi Kuwayama *(En's Lover Owagawa)*, Asao Koike *(Sawakichi)*, Emiko Aizawa *(Rui)*, Masumi Harukawa *(Midori)*, Tanie Kitabayashi *(Madam)*, Kazuo Kitamura *(Chuji)*, Daizaburo Hirata *(Kamibayashi)*, Shoichi Ozawa *(Ken)*, Emiko Higashi *(Kane)*.

Forty-five years in the hard life of a Japanese woman are chronicled in this film. Not knowing her parents' identity, Hidari lives with her foster father as his mistress until she is 20. Pregnant and unmarried she goes into the world. She works in a factory, then as a housemaid for the mistress of an American G.I., and finally as a prostitute and madame. Her life comes full circle when she encounters Yoshimura, her grown daughter, pregnant now herself. Yoshimura sleeps with and robs Kawazu, a man her mother once loved. Hidari tracks down her daughter and returns her to Kawazu. This is a powerful film that touches on many issues with a sensitive hand. Hidari is magnificent, aging forty-five years in the space of two hours. The location shooting is effective and gives the film its authentic feel. The wide variety of social issues touched upon is astounding; the exploitation of women, the Westernization of Japan, and the cruelty of human nature are all intricately woven together in this sad, bitter film. It was highly regarded in Japan, where it won 14 major film awards.

d, Shohei Imamura; w, Imamura, Keiji Hasebe; ph, Masahisa Himeda; m, Toshiro Mayuzumi; ed, Mutsuo Tanji; art d, Kimihiko Nakamura.

Drama **(PR:C MPAA:NR)**

INSEL DER AMAZONEN (SEE: SEVEN DARING GIRLS, 1962, Ger.)

INSEMINOID (SEE: HORROR PLANET 1982, Brit.)

INSIDE AMY zero (1975) 100m Dart/Adpix c

Jan Mitchell *(Amy Tishman)*, Eastman Price *(Charlie Tishman)*, Gary Kent *(Jim)*, Marsha Jordan *(Irene)*, Phillip Luther *(Jerry)*, Ann Perry *(Donna)*, Ron Darby *(Bill)*, Rene Bond *(Diane)*, Paul Oberon *(Rod)*, Mickey Nadar *(Marge)*, Ushi Digart *(Lois)*.

Life sure is boring in the suburbs. So Price, a prominent lawyer, talks wife Mitchell into joining a swinging couples' club. At first wife-swapping is appealing to the bar member but gradually he grows jealous of the competition and starts killing off his wife's new lovers. Falling just short of a soft-core pornographic range, this insipid bit of trash features a quality of acting talent one would expect in such material. Perfect for either drive-ins or guitar picks.

p&d, Ron Garcia; w, Helene Arthur; ph, Don Jones (Eastmancolor); m, Jack Preisner; ed, R. Victor Garcia; art d, Ron Foreman.

Drama **(PR:O MPAA:R)**

INSIDE DAISY CLOVER*½ (1965) 128m WB c

Natalie Wood *(Daisy Clover)*, Christopher Plummer *(Raymond Swan)*, Robert Redford *(Wade Lewis)*, Roddy McDowall *(Walter Baines)*, Ruth Gordon *(The Dealer)*, Katharine Bard *(Melora Swan)*, Betty Harford *(Gloria Goslett)*, Paul Hartman *(Dancer)*, John Hale *(Harry Goslett)*, Harold Gould *(Cop)*, Ottola Nesmith *(Old Lady in Hospital)*, Edna Holland *(Cynara)*, Peter Helm *(Milton Hopwood)*.

INSIDE DAISY CLOVER demonstrates that overnight success can also be overnight failure. 15-year-old Wood sends off a recording of herself singing and is summoned to Hollywood. Immediate stardom follows, but it is not all it's cut out to be. Her personal life is a mess: her marriage to movie star Redford goes nowhere (he is a homosexual); her mother, Gordon, is in and out of a sanitarium; even her attempted suicide results only in the destruction of her home. Despite a highly talented cast, this is not a satisfying film. The problem lies in approach: Is it camp fun or serious drama? The producers couldn't make up their minds and ended up with an esoteric and often incomprehensible story. This was one of Redford's first major roles, though he took it hesitantly, advised by his agents that it was against his better interests to play a homosexual. Redford played the Hollywood star as the supreme narcissist, but the producers still wanted to present the character as a homosexual and shot an explanatory scene without Redford's knowledge. Feeling betrayed, he took off a year before working in films again. However, his reviews were excellent and the Hollywood Press Association voted him a Golden Globe award as "Star of the Future."

p, Alan J. Pakula, Robert Mulligan; d, Mulligan; w, Gavin Lambert (based on his own novel); ph, Charles Lang (Panavision, Technicolor); m, Andre Previn; ed, Aaron Stell; prod d, Robert Clatworthy; art d, Dean Tavoularis; set d, George James Hopkins; cos, Bill Thomas, Edith Head; ch, Herbert Ross; m/l, Andre and Dory Previn.

Drama **(PR:O MPAA:NR)**

INSIDE DETROIT** (1955) 80m Clover/COL bw

Dennis O'Keefe *(Blair Vickers)*, Pat O'Brien *(Gus Linden)*, Tina Carver *(Joni Calvin)*, Margaret Field *(Barbara Linden)*, Mark Damon *(Gregg Linden)*, Larry Blake *(Max Harkness)*, Ken Christy *(Ben Macauley)*, Joseph Turkel *(Pete Link)*, Paul Bryar *(Sam Foran)*, Robert E. Griffin *(Hoagy Mitchell)*, Guy Kingsford *(Jenkins)*, Dick Rich *(Toby Gordon)*, Norman Leavitt *(Preacher)*, Katherine Warren *(Ethel Linden)*.

One of a series of "inside story" dramas done by Clover Productions for Columbia. This one takes a look at corruption within the United Auto Workers. Loosely based on the true story of the Reuther brothers, the film opens with an attempted bombing of the union headquarters run by honest union man O'Keefe. His younger brother is killed. O'Brien, a union man about to be released after serving time for racketeering, is the brains behind the bombing, though his troubled son Damon and daughter Field (who was O'Brien's real life daughter) refuse to believe any of it. There's a subplot involving O'Brien's mistress Carver and a model-cum-call girl operation. O'Brien finally discovers he cannot corrupt the union, but not before some more innocents are hurt, including Field. Though strictly a formula piece and woefully naive about the realities of crooked unions, it's a competently produced and acted piece. The pseudo-documentary style fits the film's mood.

p, Sam Katzman; d, Fred F. Sears; w, Robert E. Kent, James B. Gordon; ph, Henry Freulich; ed, Gene Havlick; md, Mischa Bakaleinikoff; art d, Paul Palmentola.

Drama **(PR:O MPAA:NR)**

INSIDE INFORMATION*½ (1934) 60m Stage & Screen bw

Tarzan *(Police Dog)*, Rex Lease, Marion Shilling, Philo McCullough, Charles King, Robert McKenzie, Victor Potel, Jimmy Aubrey, Jean Porter, Henry Hall, Rob Hill, Vance Carrol, Charles Berner, Baby Woods, Henry Roquemore.

It's almost all Tarzan the dog, proving once again that dog is indeed man's best friend, as he is fundamental in bringing a bunch of hoods set on making off with valuable bonds to justice. Another predictable dog story.

d, Robert E. Hill; w, Betty Laidlaw, Bob Lively (based on the story by Bert Ennis, Victor Potel); ph, George Meehan.

Crime **(PR:A MPAA:NR)**

INSIDE INFORMATION** (1939) 61m UNIV bw

June Lang *(Kathleen Burke)*, Dick Foran *(Danny Blake)*, Harry Carey *(Capt. Bill Dugan)*, Mary Carlisle *(Crystal)*, Addison Richards *(Banford)*, Joseph Sawyer *(Grazzi)*, Grant Richards *(Bixby)*, Paul McVey *(Crawford)*, Selmer Jackson *(Huxley)*, Frederick Burton *(Commissioner Fenton)*, John Harmon *(Frenchy)*, Robert E. Homans *(Casey)*.

Carey is a police chief wary of rookie cops. His precinct has been plagued by jewel robberies, so who comes along to solve things but rookie Foran. Foran has fixed a transfer for himself in order to be closer to Carey's niece Lang. Richards is a jeweler, secretly the head of the gang of thieves. When one of his flunkies botches a robbery, Foran traces the crook through a boot mark left at the scene of the crime. He's promoted to undercover work, much to the chagrin of Carey. But he is suspended when the clue leads nowhere. Continuing the investigation anyway, Foran is about to break the case when Carey puts him in a cell for breaking suspension. But while incarcerated Foran makes a clay model of Richards, based on police alias records, and proves to Carey who the real culprit is. Nicely acted and directed despite the cliched plot line.

p, Irving Starr; d, Charles Lamont; w, Alex Gottlieb (based on a story by Martin Mooney, Burnet Hershey); ph, Arthur Martinelli; ed, Harry Keller.

Mystery/Crime **(PR:A MPAA:NR)**

INSIDE INFORMATION (SEE: LONE PRAIRIE, THE, 1945)

INSIDE JOB*½ (1946) 65m UNIV bw

Preston Foster *(Bart Madden)*, Alan Curtis *(Eddie Norton)*, Ann Rutherford *(Claire Gray)*, Joe Sawyer *(Capt. Thomas)*, Joan [Shawlee] Fulton *(Ruth)*, Milburn Stone *(District Attorney Sutton)*, Jimmie Moss *(Skipper)*, Samuel S. Hinds *(Judge Kinkaid)*, Howard Freeman *(Mr. Wickle)*, *John Berkes (Freddie)*, Harry Brown *(Pop Hurley)*, Joe Kirk *(Fenway)*, Oliver Prickett *(Man)*, Ruby Dandridge.

Curtis and Rutherford are a pair of former crooks trying to go straight. But their honest life is nearly destroyed by Foster, a gangster who knows all about their past. He blackmails them into burglarizing the department store where they work. They go along with him, but not before making a few plans of their own. Foster ends up being killed by a cop, and the two unwilling accomplices turn themselves in. The script is pure hokum and the direction appears to have been phoned in. A time waster.

p, Ben Pivar, Jean Yarbrough; d, Yarbrough; w, George Bricker, Jerry Warner (based on a story by Tod Browning, Garrett Fort); ph, Maury Gertsman; ed, Otto Ludwig; art d, Jack Otterson, Abraham Grossman.

Crime Drama **(PR:A MPAA:NR)**

INSIDE LOOKING OUT** (1977, Aus.) 90m Illumination c

Briony Behets *(Elizabeth)*, Tony Llewellyn-Jones *(Robert)*, Danni Eddy *(Danni)*, Juliet Bacskai *(Juliet)*, Norman Kaye *(Alex)*, Elke Neidhart *(Marianne)*.

An ambitious independent feature which focuses on the routine marriage of Behets and Llewellyn-Jones, a young couple who stay together only for the sake of their daughter. When the child disappears, however, they are brought together. A character study which holds attention, thanks to a number of fine, motivated performances.

p&d, Paul Cox; w, Cox, Susan Holly Jones; ph, Cox, Peter Tammer, Bryan Gracey; m, Norman Kaye; ed, Cox, Russell Hurley; art d, Alan Stubenrauch.

Drama **(PR:C MPAA:NR)**

INSIDE MOVES½** (1980) 113m Goodmark/Associated c

John Savage *(Roary)*, David Morse *(Jerry)*, Diana Scarwid *(Louise)*, Amy Wright *(Ann)*, Tony Burton *(Lucius Porter)*, Bill Henderson *(Blue Lewis)*, Steve Kahan *(Burt)*, Jack O'Leary *(Max)*, Bert Remsen *(Stinky)*, Harold Russell *(Wings)*, Pepe Serna *(Herrada)*, Harold Sylvester *(Alvin Martin)*, Arnold Williams *(Benny)*, The Golden State Warriors.

Savage attempts suicide but fails. Instead he ends up partly paralyzed, confined to a wheelchair. He frequents a bar where other patrons are handicapped and befriends Morse, who is recovering from knee surgery. Savage falls in love with waitress Scarwid but his romantic intentions are hampered by his disability. Burton is a mean pimp who steals the volatile Morse's girl friend. Morse recovers from surgery and begins a fantastic basketball career, ignoring his old friends, and they are hurt. Savage eventually comes to terms with himself and his disability. This is a well-meaning film though it tends to cliches and stereotypes. The plot is familiar and the ending predictable. The film's redeeming factor is the cast. Russell as a card-playing bar regular makes his first film appearance since his portrayal of a paraplegic in THE BEST YEARS OF OUR LIVES. This film is director Donner's interesting followup to the much ballyhooed SUPERMAN.

p, Mark M. Tanz, R.W. Goodwin; d, Richard Donner; w, Valerie Curtin, Barry Levinson (based on the novel by Todd Walton); ph, Laszlo Kovacs (Panavision/Technicolor); m, John Barry; ed, Frank Morriss; prod d, Charles Rosen; set d, Dick Goddard; cos, Ron Talsky.

Drama **Cas.** **(PR:C MPAA:PG)**

INSIDE OUT (SEE: LIFE UPSIDE DOWN, 1964, Fr.)

INSIDE OUT** ½**

(1975, Brit.) 97m Kettledrum/WB c (AKA: HITLER'S GOLD; THE GOLDEN HEIST)

Telly Savalas *(Harry Morgan)*, Robert Culp *(Sly Wells)*, James Mason *(Ernst Furben)*, Aldo Ray *(Sgt. Prior)*, Guenter Meisner *(Schmidt)*, Adrian Hoven *(Dr. Maar)*, Wolfgang Lukschy *(Reinhold Holtz)*, Charles Korvin *(Peter Dohlberg)*, Constantin De Goguel *(Col. Kosnikov)*, Richard Warner *(Wilhelm Schlager)*, Don Fellows *(U.S. Colonel)*, Lorna Dallas *(Meredith Morgan)*, Sigrid Hanack *(Siggi)*, Peter Schlesinger *(Udo Blimperman)*.

Savalas is an ex-American WW II POW who returns to Germany 30 years after the war. He teams up with Mason, the former commander of his prison camp. Together they spring a Nazi war criminal (Lukschy) from jail. Seems he's the only one left who knows where a secret wartime cache of gold is hidden. The trio go through a series of mishaps in their quest for the loot. It's an entirely unbelievable film but with a good sense of breakneck silly fun, and a dash of suspense thrown in for good measure. Savalas gets his first top-billing in the movies with this film, probably on the basis of his popular "Kojak" television series of the time.

p, Judd Bernard; d, Peter Duffell; w, Bernard, Stephen Schneck; ph, John Coquillon (Technicolor); m, Konrad Elfers; ed, Thom Nobel; art d, Peter Lamont, Jan Schlubach.

Comedy **Cas.** **(PR:C MPAA:NR)**

INSIDE STORY** ½**

(1939) 61m FOX bw

Michael Whalen *(Barney Callahan)*, Jean Rogers *(June White)*, Chick Chandler *(Snapper Doolan)*, Douglas Fowley *(Gus Brawley)*, John King *(Paul Randall)*, Jane Darwell *(Aunt Mary Perkins)*, June Gale *(Eunice)*, Spencer Charters *(Uncle Ben Perkins)*, Theodore Von Eltz *(Whitey)*, Cliff Clark *(Collins)*, Charles D. Brown *(J.B. Douglas)*, Charles Lane (District Attorney), Jan Duggan *(Flora)*, Louise Carter *(Dora)*, Bert Roach *(Hopkins)*.

Whalen is a reporter with a heart. He wants to find the loneliest woman in New York and show her an old-fashioned Christmas on a farm. He meets Rogers, whom he believes to be a stenographer. Actually she's a tough nightclub owner, but her toughness wears down with the Christmas spirit and she learns to enjoy the simpler things life offers. There is a subplot involving a murder Whalen is investigating, for which Rogers helps him compile evidence. Too sentimental but a nice film. This is tall, dark, and handsome Cortez's first directorial effort after 16 years as an actor. A good debut.

p, Howard J. Green; d, Ricardo Cortez; w, Jerry Cady (based on a short story "A Very Practical Joke" by Ben Ames Williams); ph, Virgil Miller; ed, Jack Murray, Norman Colbert; md, Samuel Kaylin; art d, Bernard Herzbrun, Albert Hogsett.

Drama/Crime **(PR:A MPAA:NR)**

INSIDE STORY, THE****

(1948) 87m REP bw

Marsha Hunt *(Francine Taylor)*, William Lundigan *(Waldo Williams)*, Charles Winninger *(Uncle Ed)*, Gail Patrick *(Audrey O'Connor)*, Florence Bates *(Geraldine Atherton)*, Gene Lockhart *(Horace Taylor)*, Hobart Cavanaugh *(Mason)*, Allen Jenkins *(Eddy Hale)*, Roscoe Karns *(Eustace Peabody)*, Robert Shayne *(Tom O'Connor)*, Will Wright *(Jay Jay Johnson)*, William Haade *(Rocky)*, Frank Ferguson *(Eph)*, Tom Fadden *(Ab Follansbee)*.

Homespun humor about a small Vermont town and $1,000. The film starts with a flashback to 1933 when a New York hotel guest puts his money in the house safe. Taken illegally from the safe to pay off a debt, the money circulates all over town until it is returned to its original spot, in the nick of time. Dwann's direction is sharp and keeps the film from dipping too far into hokum. Winniger, Lockhart, Jenkins, and Karns carry the film's broad humor with just the right amount of spunk.

d, Allan Dwan; w, Mary Loos, Richard Sale (based on a story by Ernest Lehman, Geza Herczeg); ph, Reggie Lanning; ed, Arthur Roberts; md, Morton Scott; art d, Frank Arrigo.

Comedy **(PR:A MPAA:NR)**

INSIDE STRAIGHT****

(1951) 87m MGM bw

David Brian *(Rip MacCool)*, Arlene Dahl *(Lily Douvane)*, Barry Sullivan, *(Johnny Sanderson)*, Mercedes McCambridge *(Ada Stritch)*, Paula Raymond *(Zoe Carnot)*, Claude Jarman, Jr. *(Rip MacCool, Age 16)*, Lon Chaney, Jr. *(Shocker)*, Monica Lewis *(Cafe Singer)*, John Hoyt *(Flutey Johnson)*, Roland Winters *(Alexander Tomson)*, Barbara Billingsley *(Miss Meadson)*, Richard Hale *(Undertaker)*, Hayden Rorke *(Carlson)*, Jerry Hartleben *(John MacCool, Age 3)*, Dale Hartleben *(John MacCool, Age 8)*, Lou Nova *(Connegan)*.

McCambridge owns a bank in 1870 San Francisco. A run on the bank is threatened and rich man Brian is called to help stem the spread of panic throughout the town. He and McCambridge meet in her home to play cards with the bank as the stakes. During the game, Brian tells his life story to her. His story shows him as a ruthless man more interested in money than people. Dahl is his first wife, who cheats him out of some money and runs off. Raymond, his second wife, dies in childbirth. The film ends with Brian leaving McCambridge's home without revealing his hand to her or to the audience. Brian turns in a fine performance despite the overwritten script and lagging direction. McCambridge puts in a solid performance and absolutely seethes in her hatred for Brian.

p, Richard Goldstone; d, Gerald Mayer; w, Guy Trosper; ph, Ray June; m, Lennie Hayton; ed, Newell P. Kimlin; art d, Cedric Gibbons, Daniel B. Cathcart.

Western **(PR:O MPAA:NR)**

INSIDE THE LAW****

(1942) 65m PRC bw

Wallace Ford, Frank Sully, Harry Holman, Luanna Walters, Lafayette McKee, Barton Hepburn, Danny Duncan, Earl Hodgins, Rose Plumer.

When the town bank falls into the hands of a gang of crooks the temptation becomes almost too great, but they manage to overcome natural inclination to remain "inside the law." A different type of theme allows for plenty of comic situations here.

p, Dixon R. Harwin; d, Hamilton MacFadden; w, Jack Natteford; ph, Arthur Martinelli; ed, Cal Pierson; md, David Chudnow.

Comedy **(PR:A MPAA:NR)**

INSIDE THE LINES* ½**

(1930) 72m RKO bw

Betty Compson *(Jane Gershon)*, Ralph Forbes *(Eric Woodhouse)*, Montagu Love *(Governor of Gibraltar)*, Mischa Auer *(Amahdti)*, Ivan Simpson *(Capper)*, Betty Carter *(Lady Crandall)*, Evan Thomas *(Maj. Bishop)*, Reginald Sharland *(Archie)*, William Von Brincken *(Spy School Chief)*.

Compson and Forbes are spies during WW I. They fall in love, despite the fact that both think the other is a German spy. Eventually they find out they're on the same side and unite to keep Auer from bombing a British position. The film is based on a 1915 Broadway flop that didn't improve with age or translation to film. The direction is indifferent, and the acting is superficial. Though it starts off well, the film quickly slips into tedium.

p, William LeBaron; d, Roy J. Pomeroy; w, Ewart Adamson, John Farrow (based on the play by Earl Derr Biggers); ph, Nick Musuraca; art d, Max Ree.

Spy Drama **(PR:A MPAA:NR)**

INSIDE THE MAFIA** ½**

(1959) 75m UA bw

Cameron Mitchell *(Tony Ledo)*, Elaine Edwards *(Anne Balcom)*, Robert Strauss *(Sam Galey)*, Jim L. Brown *(Doug Blair)*, Ted De Corsia *(Augie Martello)*, Grant Richards *(Johnny Lucero)*, Richard Karlan *(Chins Dayton)*, Frank Gerstle *(Julie Otranto)*, Sid Clute *(Beery)*, Louis Jean Heydt *(Rod Balcom)*, Steve Roberts *(Raycheck)*, Hal Torey *(Molina)*, Carl Milletaire *(Dave Alto)*, Carol Nugent *(Sandy Balcom)*, Edward Platt *(Dan Regent)*, Michael Monroe *(Buzz)*, Jack Daley *(Joe the Barber)*, Jim Bannon *(Corino)*, Raymond Guth *(Morgan)*, Anthony Carbone *(Kronis)*, Jack Kenney *(Vince DeMao)*, House Peters, Jr. *(Marty Raven)*, Sheldon Allman *(Dyer)*, Tony [Anthony] Warde *(Bob Kalen)*, Donna Dale *(Manicurist)*, John Hart *(Police Sergeant)*.

Some nasty business, based loosely on a true Mafia case in the late 1950s. In an upstate New York airport, a pack of Mafiosos await the arrival of exiled mob boss Richards. Though deported 10 years previously, he is secretly returning in order to solve the internal struggle within the upper echelons of the Mafia. Mitchell is an aide to another gang boss, who was nearly killed in an assassination attempt. Mitchell wants to kill Richards, paving the way for his boss to gain leadership. But the airport manager gets in the way and Mitchell is forced to take the man, his two daughters, and several others hostage in a nearby house. This is a dark and violent film, with strong acting by the cast. The direction is fast paced. The brutality may be a little rough by 1950s standards. It's interesting that this film could be called INSIDE THE MAFIA, when one considers that the Italian Anti-Defamation League's protests 12 years later banned the use of the word "Mafia" from the classic mobster film THE GODFATHER.

p, Robert E. Kent; d, Edward L. Cahn; w, Orville H. Hampton; ph, Maury Gertsman; ed, Grant Whytock; art d, Bill Glasgow; set d, Morris Hoffman; cos, Einar Bourman.

Crime **(PR:O MPAA:NR)**

INSIDE THE ROOM** ½**

(1935, Brit.) 66m Twickenham/UNIV bw

Austin Trevor *(Pierre Santos)*, Dorothy Boyd *(Dorothy Ayres)*, Garry Marsh *(Geoffrey Lucas)*, George Hayes *(Henry Otisse)*, Brian Buchel *(Adam Steele)*, Robert Horton *(Sir George Frame)*, Frederick Burtwell *(Inspector Grant)*, Marjorie Chard *(Lady Groombridge)*, Vera Bogetti *(Agnes Judd)*, Dorothy Minto *(Lilian Hope)*, Claude Horton, Kenji Takase.

After a noted actress passes away a strange series of murders takes place at a house party. Trevor, playing a Hercule Poirot-styled detective, goes off to investigate and finds the dead woman's daughter, a singer, is behind the crimes. Typical for the genre.

p, Julius Hagen; d, Leslie Hiscott; w, H. Fowler Mear (based on the play by Marten Cumberland); ph, William Luff.

Crime **(PR:C MPAA:NR)**

INSIDE THE WALLS OF FOLSOM PRISON ***

(1951) 87m WB bw

Steve Cochran *(Chuck Daniels)*, David Brian *(Mark Benson)*, Philip Carey *(Red Pardue)*, Ted De Corsia *(Warden Rickey)*, Scott Forbes *(Frazier)*, Lawrence Tolan *(Leo Daly)*, Dick Wesson *(Tinker)*, Paul Picerni *(Jeff Riordan)*, William Campbell *(Ferretti)*, 07321 *(Murder)*, 08438 *(Arson)*, 04327 *(Forgery)*, 06752 *(Kidnaper)*, Ed Norris, Dorothy Hart, Matt Willis.

Though it's loaded with the usual prison yarn cliches and stereotype guards and cons, this incarceration tale is above average because of a superb cast and plenty of action. Set in the 1920s and actually filmed in California's tough Folsom Prison, Cochran is the toughest con in the joint and his diehard followers are dedicated to Cochran's escape plans. Goading them on is sadistic warden De Corsia and a bevy of brutal guards that could qualify as Nazi concentration camp guards. The prisoners under De Corsia's vicious gaze are indiscriminately beaten and tortured, their lives made into hellish nightmares. Then humane Brian enters the system as guards captain and immediately begins to institute reforms, defying the warden and making life a little easier for the inmates, causing the tension to ease and the violence to subside. Brian's rehabilitating measures are against De Corsia's wishes and repeated clashes with him cause Brian to be fired. Cochran and company can no longer tolerate conditions, especially now that benefactor Brian has been removed, and they make their bloody break for freedom, all being gunned down in a bloodbath which De Corsia obviously relishes. The public outcry, however, is long and loud and causes the warden to be removed and Brian brought back to run the battered institution. Brian is forceful and convincing as the fair-minded reformer and De Corsia is so effective as the brutal warden that he falls all over himself in a successful effort to be hated. Cochran of the dark look and slick black hair has enough good points to have the viewer rooting for him at times, even though he's a crook through and through. The film is well directed by action helmsman Wilbur and DuPar's photography is grimly realistic and properly stark.

p, Bryan Foy; d&w, Crane Wilbur (based on the story "Folsom Story" by Wilbur); ph, Edwin DuPar; m, William Lava; ed, Owen Marks; ard d, Douglas Bacon.

Prison Drama **(PR:C MPAA:NR)**

INSIDIOUS DR. FU MANCHU, THE (SEE: MYSTERIOUS DR. FU MANCHU, 1929)

INSPECTOR, THE (SEE: LISA, 1961, Brit.)

INSPECTOR CALLS, AN*** (1954, Brit.) 79m Watergate/BL bw

Alastair Sim *(Inspector Poole)*, Arthur Young *(Arthur Birling)*, Olga Lindo *(Sybil Birling)*, Eileen Moore *(Sheila Birling)*, Bryan Forbes *(Eric Birling)*, Brian Worth *(Gerald Croft)*, Jane Wenham *(Eva Smith)*, Pat Neal *(1st Maid)*, Norman Bird *(Foreman)*, John Welsh *(Shopwalker)*, Barbara Everest *(Committee Member)*, Jenny Jones *(Girl)*, Amy Green *(2nd Maid)*, Catherine Willmer *(Senior Factory Woman)*, Olwen Brookes *(Miss Francis)*, Bill Raymond, Walter Cross, George Hirste, Brenda Duncan, Helen Cleverley, Winnie Wiblin, Mabel Etherington, Charles Saynor, Vi Endean, George Woodbridge.

Sim is a police inspector who has gathered the family of a dead girl together. Through flashback the story of events leading to her death is told. Young is the father of the girl (Wenham) who has fired his daughter from his factory for causing trouble. It seems she led a group of workers in asking for a raise. Her sister, Moore, did a similar task after Wenham gets a job in a local shop. Moore's fiance helps Wenham get an apartment on her own. But she fails at this and has to take charity after her mother (Lindo) refuses to help. Forbes plays a brother turned to crime after he impregnates his sister. Sim's summation concludes that each person is in some way responsible for Wenham's suicide. Though it's a little slow going in parts, this is really a well-told tale.

p, A.D. Peters; d, Guy Hamilton; w, Desmond Davis (based on the play by J.B. Priestley); ph, Ted Scaife; m, Francis Chagrin; ed, Alan Osbiston.

Drama **(PR:O MPAA:NR)**

INSPECTOR CLOUSEAU*** (1968, Brit.) 96m Mirisch/UA c

Alan Arkin *(Inspector Jacques Clouseau)*, Delia Boccardo *(Lisa Morrel)*, Frank Finlay *(Superintendent Weaver)*, Patrick Cargill *(Sir Charles Braithwaite)*, Beryl Reid *(Mrs. Weaver)*, Barry Foster *(Addison Steele)*, Clive Francis *(Clyde Hargreaves)*, John Bindon *(Bull Parker)*, Michael Ripper *(Frey)*, Tutte Lemkow *(Frenchy LeBec)*, Anthony Ainley *(Bomber LeBec)*, Wallas Eaton *(Hoeffler)*, David Bauer *(Geffrion)*, Richard Pearson *(Shockley)*, George Pravda *(Wulf)*, Eric Pohlmann *(Bergesch)*, Geoffrey Bayldon *(Gutch)*, Arthur Lovegrove *(Innkeeper)*, Kathya Wyeth *(Meg)*, Tracey Crisp *(Julie)*, Marjie Lawrence *(Peggy)*, Craig Booth *(David)*, Julie Croft *(Nicole)*, Robert Russell *(Stockton)*, Susan Engel *(Policewoman Carmichael)*, Will Stampe *(Fishmonger)*, Barbara Dana *(Nun)*.

This was the third film using the Blake Edwards and Maurice Richlin character and one of the weakest in the series, mainly because Edwards was replaced by director Yorkin and Arkin took over the acting chores from Sellers. Cargill is a Scotland Yard knight who uncovers the news that the plunder gleaned from the famous Great Train Robbery is now being employed to underwrite another robbery. He suspects that an associate may be in cahoots with the malfeasants so he calls for Arkin, the famed shamus from Paris. The first place Arkin goes in search of information is the barber shop at Wormwood Scrubs prison where Foster, an incarcerated member of the famed gang, is busy cutting the locks of Francis, the very gay son of the warden. Foster (who was so good in Hitchcock's FRENZY) subdues Arkin and escapes jail. Arkin outfits himself with the latest crime-fighting gear and calls on policeman Finlay and his sexy wife, Reid. The trio go to a small fair where Arkin is tailed by one of the gang members who has been assigned to kill him. Inadvertently, Arkin kills the gangster. Next night, Arkin tails Finlay's maid, Boccardo, to a small hotel but he is again overcome by two women who make a cast of his face. He recovers consciousness and chases the women. In doing so, he clutzily kills yet another crook when a bed collapses on the man. He returns to France and meets Boccardo again, only to learn that she is an INTERPOL agent who has been assigned to the same case. While he is off chasing crooks, the gang has made several masks of Arkin's face and has now robbed more than a dozen banks wearing the disguises. They put all the loot in candy wrappers and load the stash aboard a barge going down the Rhine. Arkin and Boccardo get onto the barge where he manages to, again inadvertently kill Finlay (who is the snake in the Scotland Yard grass). They are captured and learn that Francis, the lisping lad, is the leader of the pack. Francis offers Arkin money to get off the case but the Frenchman won't hear of it and manages to sink the barge by putting a hole in the hull with his James Bond-type laser beam lighter. Cops arrive and nab the gang, then Arkin is given an award for his bravery. Arkin gets on a plane to see Boccardo in Paris and finds himself seated next to Reid, who is just as amorous as ever. Arkin escapes her clutches by parachuting from the airliner as the film fades out. Arkin is one of those actors who can play many different kinds of roles. He is excellent when he creates the part, such as the mute in THE HEART IS A LONELY HUNTER or the killer in WAIT UNTIL DARK. But when he has to follow in the shambling footsteps of Sellers, a comparison must be made and Arkin must be the loser. Dana is Arkin's wife (and sometime screenwriter) and does a small bit. Lemkow is a well-known British actor and dancer who has never received his due although he did play the title role in FIDDLER ON THE ROOF (not Tevya, Lemkow was the Fiddler). If we'd never seen the genius of Sellers and the prior scripts by Edwards, this might have been funnier. Even on its own, it's a lot better than many of the alleged comedies made in the 1980s. DePatie-Freleng did the title art as they have on all the Pink Panther films. What most people don't recall is that the Pink Panther (now a famous cartoon character) was really the name of the jewel stolen in the first film and it had nothing to do with the character of Clouseau, just as THE THIN MAN was not William Powell at all. Rather, it was the designation given to the murder victim in the first of that long-running series. Yorkin has always been a good journeyman director. He hit gold when he and his partner, Norman Lear, sold their company for countless millions of dollars. Lear was the power behind the company and Yorkin was quite content to direct, rather than build an empire. Nevertheless, he benefited by Lear's television work and is now one of the wealthiest men in show business. Filmed in France and England.

p, Lewis Rachmil; d, Bud Yorkin; w, Tom and Frank Waldman (based on a character created by Blake Edwards and Maurice Richlin); ph, Arthur Ibbetson (Panavision, DeLuxe Color); m, Ken Thorne; ed, John Victor Smith; prod d, Michael Stringer; art d, Norman Dorme; set d, Terence Morgan III; cos, Ivy Baker, Dinah Greet; makeup, Ernest Kelly, Wally Schneiderman.

Comedy **(PR:A MPAA:G)**

INSPECTOR GENERAL, THE*** (1937, Czech.) 71m Meissner/Garrison bw

Vlasia Burian *(Inspector General)*, T. Tregl *(Josef)*, J. Marvan *(Mayor)*, Z. Baldova *(His Wife)*, T. Grosslichtova *(Their Daughter)*, J. Rovensky *(Postmaster)*, Fr. Hlavaty *(School Inspector)*, Fr. Czerny *(Innkeeper)*, Jose Vosalik *(Bobsinsky)*, A. Dvorsky *(Dobsinsky)*.

Based on the Gogol play, this is the story of a small Russian town run by corrupt officials. They hear an inspector general of the Czar is coming for a visit. The foolish politicians immediately set about sprucing up the town, along with their already pumped up egos. Enter a con man, innocent of what is going on. He is simply passing through but in their haste the politicians think he is the Inspector General. He plays along, taking the suckers for every last ruble he can. The film ends with the sharpy splitting as the real Inspector General arrives. This is one of the few Czechoslovakian films that was seen in America during the 1930s. Gogol's farce holds up nicely in its translation to film, with Burian playing his role for as many laughs as he can. A lesser musical version of the story was made in America in 1949 with Danny Kaye.

d, Mac Fric; w, V. Solin, V. Menger, Prof. Mathesius (based on the play by Nikolai Gogol); ph, Jan Stallich.

Comedy **(PR:A MPAA:NR)**

INSPECTOR GENERAL, THE*** (1949) 102m WB c (AKA: HAPPY TIMES)

Danny Kaye *(Georgi)*, Walter Slezak *(Yakov)*, Barbara Bates *(Leza)*, Elsa Lanchester *(Maria)*, Gene Lockhart *(The Mayor)*, Alan Hale *(Kovatch)*, Walter Catlett *(Col. Castine)*, Rhys Williams *(Inspector General)*, Benny Baker *(Telecki)*, Norman Leavitt *(Laszlo)*, Sam Hearn *(Gizzick)*, Lew Hearn *(Izzick)*, Byron Foulger *(Burbis)*, Lennie Bremen *(Lieutenant)*, Nestor Paiva *(Gregor)*.

A loose adaptation of the famous Gogol play turns into a showcase for Kaye's many talents. Mistaken as an emissary for the Czar, a group of corrupt small-town Russian officials treat illiterate medicine show helper Kaye with all the respect due a royal inspector. It's Kaye's show from there on out as he sings, dances, and mugs his way through the film. "The Gypsy Drinking Song" is a wonderful comic piece for Kaye, co-written by his wife Fine, along with Mercer. Overall it's not a bad film, though the end results, funny as they are, have little resemblance to the play. Songs include "Onward Onward," "The Medicine Show," "The Inspector General," "Lonely Heart," "Gypsy Drinking Song," "Soliloquy For Three Heads," "Happy Times," "Brodny."

p, Jerry Wald; d, Henry Koster; w, Philip Rapp, Harry Kurnitz (based on the play by Nikolai Gogol); ph, Elwood Bredell; m, Johnny Green; ed, Rudi Fehr; md, Green; art d, Robert Haas; m/l, Johnny Mercer, Sylvia Fine.

Musical/Comedy **Cas.** **(PR:AAA MPAA:NR)**

INSPECTOR HORNLEIGH** 1/2** (1939, Brit.) 76m FOX bw

Gordon Harker *(Inspector Hornleigh)*, Alastair Sim *(Sgt. Bingham)*, Miki Hood *(Ann Gordon)*, Wally Patch *(Sam Holt)*, Steve Geray *(Kavanos)*, Edward Underdown *(Peter Dench)*, Hugh Williams *(Bill Gordon)*, Gibb McLaughlin *(Alfred Cooper)*, Ronald Adam *(Wittens)*, Eliot Makeham *(Leather Worker)*.

When the Chancellor of the Exchequer's bags are stolen Harker, along with bumbling sidekick Sim, is assigned to recover the stolen goods. Harker suspects a foreign millionaire of taking the bags for the budget plans they held. Though well-plotted and acted (Sim is hilarious) the thick English and Scottish accents were often incomprehensible to American audiences. Aside from that, the suspense is nicely built towards a good denouement. This is the first of three films based on the British radio series of the time "Monday Night At Eight."

p, Robert T. Kane; d, Eugene Forde; w, Bryan Wallace, Gerald Elliott, Richard Llewellyn (based on British radio characters created by Hans Wolfgang Priwin); ph, Philip Tannura, Derek Williams; ed, James B. Clark.

Crime/Comedy **(PR:A MPAA:NR)**

INSPECTOR HORNLEIGH GOES TO IT (SEE: MAIL TRAIN, 1940, Brit.)

INSPECTOR HORNLEIGH ON HOLIDAY*** (1939, Brit.) 90m FOX bw

Gordon Harker *(Inspector Hornleigh)*, Alastair Sim *(Sgt. Bingham)*, Linden Travers *(Miss Meadows)*, Wally Patch *(Police Sergeant)*, Edward Chapman *(Capt. Fraser)*, Philip Leaver *(Bradfield)*, Kynaston Reeves *(Dr. Manners)*, John Turnbull *(Chief Constable)*, Wyndham Goldie *(Sir George Winbeck)*, Cyril Conway, Eileen Bell.

Last of the INSPECTOR HORNLEIGH series finds Harker, along with erstwhile sidekick Sim, taking a holiday on the English seaside. Their two-week vacation is just about over when a fellow boarding house guest goes over a cliff in his auto and is burned to death. The local police regard it as an accident, but Harker thinks there's more than meets the eye in this case. His investigation reveals that a group of gangsters have used another corpse in order to cash in on an insurance policy. The script and acting are excellent, and so is the view of the British coastline. Sim as always, is great fun.

p, Edward Black; d, Walter Forde; w, Sidney Gilliat, Frank Launder, J.O.C. Orton (based on British radio characters created by Hans Wolfgang Priwin and the novel *Stolen Death* by Leo Grex); ph, John J. Cox.

Crime/Comedy **(PR:A MPAA:NR)**

INSPECTOR MAIGRET (SEE: MAIGRET LAYS A TRAP, 1958, Fr.)

INSPIRATION** (1931) 73m MGM bw

Greta Garbo *(Yvonne)*, Robert Montgomery *(Andre Martel)*, Lewis Stone *(Delval)*, Marjorie Rambeau *(Lulu)*, Judith Vosselli *(Odette)*, Beryl Mercer *(Marthe)*, John Miljan *(Coutant)*, Edwin Maxwell *(Julian Montell)*, Oscar Apfel *(Vignaud)*, Joan Marsh *(Madeleine)*, Zelda Sears *(Pauline)*, Karen Morley *(Liane)*, Gwen Lee *(Gaby)*, Paul McAllister *(Jouvet)*, Arthur Hoyt *(Gavarni)*, Richard Tucker *(Garland)*.

Garbo is radiant but her star doesn't shine brightly enough to overcome the dim script of this movie that cost more than $400,000 to produce, and that was back when money went a lot further. There were several legal problems caused by the movie, based on a story by James Forbes taken from a novel by Alphonse Daudet, *Sappho*. The difficulty came about because European copyright laws are different than those in the U.S. and while the story was in the public domain in the U.S., it was still protected in many countries across the pond. Pathe successfully sued MGM for infringement and the film was shelved until an agreement was reached. It was all a tempest in a thepot (just a little French pun there. Hope you don't mind) because the film sank faster than the *Titanic*. Garbo is a Parisian model who serves as inspiration to an artist, a writer, a composer, and a sculptor. She falls in love with Montgomery, a conservative lad who is studying for work in the French consul service. When he learns that she has had many men before him, he leaves her. Her life spirals downward and she is broke. Montgomery again encounters Garbo and buys her a home in the suburbs. But that's all he'll do for her as he is about to marry another woman. Garbo's pal, Morley, jumps out a window when her boy friend, Stone (as an old lech) leaves her. Now Montgomery decides that his career in the service is piffle compared to his love for Garbo so he comes to the house and discovers her with another former lover who is asking that she return with him to Paris. Undaunted by this, Montgomery will still be happy to take her back into his arms. Montgomery falls asleep and Garbo, who senses that she'll never change, does a "tis a far, far better thing I do now" and writes Montgomery a "Dear Robert" letter before she goes back to Paris and her dissolute life. A tiresome picture that is only highlighted by Garbo's face, for whom the camera must have been invented.

p&d, Clarence Brown; w, Gene Markey (based on a treatment by James Forbes [uncredited], from *Sappho* by Alphonse Daudet [also uncredited]; ph, William Daniels; ed, Conrad A. Nervig.

Drama **(PR:C MPAA:NR)**

INSULT** ½ (1932, Brit.) 79m PAR Brit. bw

Elizabeth Allan *(Pola Dubois)*, John Gielgud *(Henri Dubois)*, Hugh Williams *(Captain Ramon Nadir)*, Sam Livesey *(Major Dubois)*, Sydney Fairbrother *(Arabella)*, Abraham Sofaer *(Ali Ben Achmed)*, Edgar Norfolk *(Captain Jean Conte)*, Hal Gordon *(Sergeant)*, Dinah Gilly *(Singer)*.

Williams is a half-Arab member of the Foreign Legion who has previously been court-martialed for insubordination. His commander (Livesey) distrusts the man and finally has him locked up. Livesey then sends his own son (Gielgud, in an early screen role) into battle against native troops. Williams escapes from his cell and manages to save Gielgud's life, though losing his own in the process. Turgid and somewhat violent affair.

p, S.E. Fitzgibbon; d, Harry Lachman; w, Basil Mason (based on a play by Jean Fabricus).

Adventure **(PR:C MPAA:NR)**

INSURANCE INVESTIGATOR** (1951) 60m REP bw

Richard Denning *(Tom Davison)*, Audrey Long *(Nancy Sullivan)*, John Eldredge *(John Hammond)*, Hillary Brooke *(Addie Wilson)*, Reed Hadley *(Chuck Malone)*, Jonathan Hale *(Russell James)*, Roy Barcroft *(Duke Wallace)*, Wilson Wood *(Jimmy Marshall)*, William Tannen *(1st Hood)*, Phillip Pine *(2nd Hood)*, Crane Whitley *(Chief Meyers)*, Ruth Lee *(Miss Pringle)*, Patricia Knox *(Hat Check Girl)*, M'Liss McClure *(Cigarette Girl)*, Maurice Samuels *(Tony)*.

Denning investigates the death of a real estate operator before his firm pays out a whopping double indemnity claim. The death appears to be an accident but Denning is convinced it's murder. Long is the victim's daughter, who gets Denning a job in the real estate firm as a front for the investigation. He soon finds out that the dead man's partner Eldredge owed Hadley huge gambling debts. This leads to the discovery of Hadley's "accidental" death racket to cash in on insurance policies. Denning is captured by the gang but the police save him in a climactic ending. Good pacing by the director and capable acting, this is a simple straightforward piece that entertains within its formula constraints.

p, William Lackey; d, George Blair; w, Gertrude Walker (based on a story by Walker, Beth Brown); ph, John MacBurnie; m, Stanley Wilson; ed, Harold Minter; art d, Frank Hotaling.

Crime **(PR:C MPAA:NR)**

INTELLIGENCE MEN, THE (SEE: SPYLARKS, 1965, Brit.)

INTENT TO KILL*** (1958, Brit.) 89m Zonic/FOX bw

Richard Todd *(Dr. Bob McLaurin)*, Betsy Drake *(Dr. Nancy Ferguson)*, Herbert Lom *(Juan Menda)*, Warren Stevens *(Finch)*, Carlo Justini *(Francisco Flores)*, Paul Carpenter *(O'Brien)*, Alexander Knox *(Dr. McNeil)*, Lisa Gastoni *(Carla Menda)*, Peter Arne *(Kral)*, Catherine Boyle *(Margaret McLaurin)*, John Crawford *(Boyd)*, Kay Callard *(Carol's Friend)*, Jackie Collins *(Carol Freeman)*, John McLaren *(Anaesthetist)*, Maggie McGrath *(Night Nurse)*, Brenda Dunrich *(Day Nurse)*, John Carson, Stella Bonheur, Natalie Lynn, Kathryn Sadler, Nancy Lewis, Ann Stephens, Hedger Wallace, Mark Baker, William Sherwood, Diana Hammond, Edouard Assaly, Michelle Aslanoff.

Todd is a doctor in Montreal with numerous problems. His shrewish wife, Boyle, wants him to leave for a more fashionable London position. Meanwhile, he's falling in love with his colleague, Drake. Things get out of his control when a South American leader (Lom) arrives for delicate brain surgery. He's the target of an assassination plot by his wife, Gastoni, in league with Justini, a crooked ambassador. It builds to a dramatic and action-filled climax with Todd and detective Carpenter saving the leader's life. Once the thriller element is added, the excitement never stops. Shot on location in Montreal.

p, Adrian D. Worker; d, Jack Cardiff; w, Jimmy Sangster (based on the novel by Michael Bryan); ph, Desmond Dickinson (CinemaScope); m, Kenneth V. Jones; ed, Tom Simpson; md, Muir Mathieson; art d, Allan Harris.

Drama/Thriller **(PR:A MPAA:NR)**

INTERFERENCE** (1928) 90m PAR bw

Evelyn Brent *(Deborah Kane)*, William Powell *(Philip Voaze)*, Clive Brook *(Sir John Marlay)*, Brandon Hurst *(Inspector Haynes)*, Louis Payne *(Childers)*, Wilfred Noy *(Dr. Gray)*, Donald Stuart *(Freddie)*, Raymond Lawrence *(Reporter)*, Doris Kenyon *(Faith Marlay)*.

Long, dull, and too much dialog but that really doesn't matter considering this film's historical significance. It is Paramount's first all-dialog picture, originally shot as silent, but redone to cash in on the new addition to film technology. Brent is a blackmailer working on Kenyon. She thinks she can prove bigamy against the Grande Dame. The acting is nothing special and the film is padded out beyond a reasonable length. Still, it's a good item for film historians to take a peek at. Powell, in an early role, is a standout.

d, Roy J. Pomeroy; w, Hope Loring, Ernest Pascal (based on a silent version directed by Lothar Mendes from a stage play by Roland Pertwee and Harold Dearden); ph, J. Roy Hunt; ed, George Nichols, Jr.

Crime **(PR:A MPAA:NR)**

INTERIORS**** (1978) 93m UA c

Kristin Griffith *(Flyn)*, Marybeth Hurt *(Joey)*, Richard Jordan *(Frederick)*, Diane Keaton *(Renata)*, E.G. Marshall *(Arthur)*, Geraldine Page *(Eve)*, Maureen Stapleton *(Pearl)*, Sam Waterston *(Mike)*, Henderson Forsythe *(Judge Bartel)*.

Woody Allen fans didn't like this Bergmanesque examination of love, life, and death because they kept expecting it suddenly to turn humorous. It never did. But it is one of his best pictures on every level and proves that Allen is capable of anything he cares to do. It's a direct homage to Allen's love for Bergman and he makes no attempt to mask that as he photographs the principals against blank walls, has them speak directly into the camera, and uses many of the techniques developed by the Swedish director. The story is ripe for satire (Allen did it funnily in one segment of EVERYTHING YOU EVER WANTED TO KNOW ABOUT SEX, etc.) but Allen keeps a tight rein on his usual wit and plays the picture seriously. Marshall and Page are the parents of three Chekovian sisters, Keaton, Griffith, and Hurt. Marshall is rich and Page is mentally disturbed. He announces one day that he is leaving her and the news causes her to disintegrate. He plans to marry Stapleton (in one of her best roles) and the daughters rush to their mother's side to help her through the crisis, even though they are having problems of their own. Keaton is a poet married to Jordan, a hack novelist. Hurt is the most talented of the trio but as unfocused as a $3 camera. Griffith works as a TV actress and is self-centered. How they work out this late-in-life difficulty forms the center of INTERIORS which is, at 93 minutes, longer than most of Allen's movies, some of which have come in under 75 minutes. Much of the film was made on Long Island, near the Atlantic, and so resembles Bergman's films which were made near the sea. Allen likes to throw his audiences curve balls and they often respond by striking out. Just as Neil Simon has continued to expand his interests past the glib one-liners, Allen does the same with such attempts at breaking new ground as in this, ZELIG, and THE PURPLE ROSE OF CAIRO. Though it failed to earn much money, Allen is to be congratulated for having the guts to break the mold he'd been placed in by his fans. The costumer, Schumacher, went on to become a writer-director with CARWASH. Nominated for Oscars in the category of Best Script, Best Direction, Page as Best Actress, and Stapleton as Best Supporting Actress.

p, Charles H. Joffe; d&w, Woody Allen; ph, Gordon Willis (Technicolor); ed, Ralph Rosenblum; prod d, Mel Bourne; cos, Joel Schumacher.

Drama **Cas.** **(PR:C-O MPAA:PG)**

INTERLUDE (SEE: INTERMEZZO, 1937, Swed.)

INTERLUDE* ½ (1957) 90m UNIV c

June Allyson *(Helen Banning)*, Rossano Brazzi *(Tonio Fischer)*, Marianne Cook *(Reni Fischer)*, Francoise Rosay *(Countess Reinhart)*, Keith Andes *(Dr. Morley Dwyer)*, Frances Bergen *(Gertrude Kirk)*, Jane Wyatt *(Prue Stubbins)*, Lisa Helwig *(Housekeeper)*, Herman Schwedt *(Henig)*, Anthony Tripoli *(Dr. Smith)*, John Stein *(Dr. Stein)*.

Bad remake of the 1939 film WHEN TOMORROW COMES. Allyson is an American in Munich for a vacation. She meets Brazzi, a conductor. The two go on a picnic, get caught in a thunderstorm, and are thunderstruck with each other as well. She doesn't know he's concealing a shrewish wife. Meanwhile, the love-struck Andes is pursuing her across Europe. Brazzi finally attempts suicide and Allyson leaves for America with Andes. The characters are stock types and the film ventures headlong into cliches. The scenery is nice. This film was remade again in 1968 with the same title.

p, Ross Hunter; d, Douglas Sirk; w, Daniel Fuchs, Franklin Coen, Inez Cocke (based on a screenplay WHEN TOMORROW COMES by Dwight Taylor from the novel "Serenade" by James M. Cain); ph, William Daniels (CinemaScope, Technicolor); m, Frank Skinner, Joseph Gershenson; ed, Russell F. Schoengarth; art d, Alexander Golitzen, Robert E. Smith; set d, Russell A. Gausman; cos, Jay A. Morley, Jr.; m/l "Interlude," Paul Francis Webster, Frank Skinner (sung by the McGuire Sisters); themes from Ludwig van Beethoven, Wolfgang Amadeus Mozart, Richard Wagner, Johannes Brahms, Franz Liszt, Robert Schumann.

Romance **(PR:A MPAA:NR)**

INTERLUDE** 1/2 (1968, Brit.) 113m COL c

Oskar Werner *(Stefan Zelter)*, Barbara Ferris *(Sally)*, Virginia Maskell *(Antonia)*, Donald Sutherland *(Lawrence)*, Nora Swinburne *(Mary)*, Alan Webb *(Andrew)*, Bernard Kay *(George Selworth)*, Geraldine Sherman *(Natalie)*, Gino Mulvazzi *(Mario)*, Muguette De Braie *(Mario's Wife)*, Robert Lang *(Humphrey Turnbull)*, Roslyn DeWinter *(Humphrey's Secretary)*, Janet Davies *(Nanny)*, Sarah Jane Stratton *(Sarah Jane)*, Simon Davis *(Simon)*, Stephan Plytas *(Frederico)*, Gay Cameron *(Andrew's Girl Friend)*, Derek Jacobi *(Paul)*, Richard Pescud *(Ernest)*, Humphrey Burton *(T.V. Director)*, Ernest Fleischmann *(Orchestra Manager)*, John Cleese *(TV Publicist)*, Rosalie Westwater *(Hotel Receptionist)*, Anjula Harman *(Lawrence's Pupil)*.

Werner is a middle-aged, temperamental orchestra conductor who newspaper reporter Ferris is interviewing. The story is told in flashback: the paper prints a libelous remark Werner makes and he is sued. Blacklisted temporarily, he goes off on a holiday and finds himself in love with Ferris. Werner's wife, Maskell, unselfishly tells him that he can love the girl but he must never give up music. But the film ends with Ferris giving up the romance: though she has great feelings for Werner, she is already married. The film falls somewhere between INTERMEZZO and BRIEF ENCOUNTER but never quite captures the level of these two films. However, Werner and Ferris do have a nice chemistry and make the story work. Billington made his film debut here after much BBC television work.

p, David Deutsch; d, Kevin Billington; w, Lee Langley, Hugh Leonard; ph, Gerry Fisher (Technicolor); m, Georges Delerue; ed, Bert Bates; prod d, Tony Woollard; set d, Peter Young; cos, Jocelyn Richards; Music: "Symphony No. 5" (Ludwig van Beethoven), "Symphony No. 1" (Petr Ilich Tchaikovsky), "Adagio in C Minor" (Wolfgang Amadeus Mozart), "Glass Harmonica" (Bruno Hoffmann), "Carnival Overture" (Anton Dvorak), "Symphony No. 3" (Johannes Brahms), "Symphony No. 2" (Sergei Rachmaninoff), "Adagio for Organ and Strings" (Tommaso Albinoni), all played by the British Royal Philharmonic Orchestra; makeup, W.T. Partleton.

Drama **(PR:C MPAA:PG)**

INTERMEZZO** 1/2 (1937, Ger.) 80m Majestic/American Tobis bw

Tresi Rudolph *(Adrienne Madelon)*, Albrecht Schoenhals *(Trent)*, Franz Weber *(Jean Cukler)*, Erich Fiedler *(Pierre Cukler)*, Rudolph Schindler *(Radio Announcer)*, Ernest Legal *(Ballon)*, S.O. Schoenig *(Martinetti)*, Kurt Seifert *(Don Ramiro)*, Henry Lorenzen *(Billie)*, Hilde Sezak *(Blanche)*, Rudolph Klein-Rogge *(Ponbiquet)*, Hansi Arnstead *(Jean Cukler's Wife)*.

A noted opera singer is about to marry the fabulously wealthy Fiedler in gay Paris. But the two quarrel before the ceremony, and would-be bride Rudolph manages to leap from the car before arriving at the church. Soon she is without money, having only her voice for collateral. She loses the rights to her abilities in a bet with Schoenhals, who secretly is a noted composer. He uses Rudolph for his own means but, of course, the film ends on a happy note. The story is enjoyable, told with a good sense of humor that makes the unlikely premise work.

d, Joseph von Baky; w, Karl Peter Gillman; m, Theo Mackeben.

Comedy **(PR:A MPAA:NR)**

INTERMEZZO**

(1937, Swed.) 88m A.B. Svensk/Scandinavian Talking Pictures bw (AKA: INTERLUDE)

Gosta Ekman *(Holger Brandt)*, Inga Tidblad *(Margit Brandt)*, Hans Ekman *(Ake)*, Britt Hagman *(Ann- Marie)*, Erik Berglund *(Charles Moller)*, Ingrid Bergman *(Anita Hoffman)*, Hugo Bjorne *(Thomas Stenborg)*, Emma Meissner *(Greta)*, Anders Henrikson, Millan Bolander, George Fant, Folke Helleberg, Margit Orth, Carl Strom.

Fine Swedish film, later remade (also with Bergman) by David O. Selznick in 1939. Gosta Ekman is the successful musician who comes to teach Hagman piano. Through her he meets Bergman and what starts as mutual admiration grows into love. Ekman forsakes his wife and children to tour with Bergman: he on violin, she on piano. But the love of his wife and children is too much and Bergman comes to realize this love will not last. She leaves him, yet he is too frightened to return home. But the urge to see his daughter is overpowering and he leaves for his village. When his daughter sees him she runs towards her father but is hit by a truck. The family is reunited in the hospital as the girl recovers and the father realizes where his true love really lies. The film is one of great beauty and care. (In Swedish; English subtitles.)

d, Gustaf Molander; w, Gosta Stevens, Molander, (based on a story by Molander); ph, Ake Dahlquist; m, Heinz Provost; song, "Intermezzo," Provost.

Drama **(PR:A MPAA:NR)**

INTERMEZZO: A LOVE STORY*****

(1939) 70m SELZ/UA bw (AKA: INTERMEZZO)

Leslie Howard *(Holger Brandt)*, Ingrid Bergman *(Anita Hoffman)*, Edna Best *(Margit Brandt)*, John Halliday *(Thomas Stenborg)*, Cecil Kellaway *(Charles Moler)*, Enid Bennett *(Greta Stenborg)*, Ann Todd *(Ann Marie Brandt)*, Douglas Scott *(Eric Brandt)*, Eleanor Wesselhoeft *(Emma)*, Marie Flynn *(Marianne)*.

Bergman made her American debut in this wonderfully touching and tender romance and became an overnight sensation and star of the first magnitude, as they used to say at MGM. She had appeared in a Swedish production of the same story in 1937 but it lacked the tasteful and rich production values Selznick and Howard (who coproduced and starred) infused into this mellow film. Howard is a brilliant, aging violinst, a bit weary of his international fame. After a smashing tour, he returns to his home in Sweden and to the arms of his wife, Best, adoring daughter, Todd, and son Scott. He finds a deep attraction toward the fresh-faced, bright-eyed Bergman, the childrens' piano teacher, and when she gives an impromptu recital before the family he picks up his violin and joins her. She is a pupil of Halliday's, who is Howard's accompanist. Some days later the two meet by accident and go to a cafe and talk. They both realize that they are emotionally drawn to each other and, meeting by planned meeting, they fall in love so deeply that Howard asks for his freedom from Best. His wife still loves him, however, and asks him to take his time, to reconsider. Howard goes abroad with Bergman and she becomes his accompanist. Both perform brilliantly and enjoy one triumph after another, and, for a while, their love for each other flourishes, but Bergman notices how Howard dotes on other people's children and realizes how desperately he misses his own. Halliday visits the couple at a Mediterranean resort and sees through their somewhat forced gaiety. He tells Bergman, "I wonder if happiness was ever built upon the unhappiness of others." The thought haunts her until she leaves Howard to go on a tour of her own, writing him a farewell note and undergoing great emotional stress. Howard returns home but his daughter, Todd, overjoyed to see him, crosses a street in front of her school without looking and is struck by a car. Howard stays by her bedside until the crisis passes and reaffirms the love of his young son, Scott, who has been deeply hurt by his desertion of the family. Feeling that he has failed his family, Howard prepares to leave as Best watches him go out the door. She calls to him and he turns about, going back into her arms and heart, closing the door behind him. INTERMEZZO is one of those European romance tales that discards realism but is so delicately performed and lovingly directed by Ratoff that it succeeds on every level. No small credit to the beautifully photographed tale by Toland is the effervescent Bergman, who electrified the critics and public alike. Her deep talent showed in every frame, her vivacious and insoucient personality charmed viewers. Here was an actress destined for superstardom from her first American film, a different kind of actress without predictable mannerisms. There was nothing precise about her, all was refreshingly spontaneous, arrestingly vital. She was warm, beautiful, without the aloofness of her fellow Swede, Greta Garbo, who retired from the screen two years after INTERMEZZO was released. Howard is also superb as the world-weary artist who momentarily walks backward hand-in-hand with Bergman to a youthful romance, only to realize that his emotional roots are more important. Best as the wife and Halliday as the confidante to both Bergman and Howard, are outstanding in their small but essential roles, as are the children, Todd and Scott. The memorable theme music, "Intermezzo" (composed by Heinz Provost) became a tremendously popular hit; the piece was employed in both Swedish and American versions. Producer Selznick took great pains to make sure that his hand-picked star Bergman would be properly photographed and he took Harry Stradling off the cinemagraphic chore just after shooting began and replaced him with Toland, believing that Toland's inventive angles, lighting, and setups would show her in the best light. Typical of Bergman, when the actress learned that Stradling was to be replaced she broke into tears, telling Selznick that she would rather look less beautiful than have this cameraman hurt in any way. William Wyler was originally signed to direct INTERMEZZO but the shooting script took so long that he had to honor a previous commitment to Samuel Goldwyn and Ratoff was given the directorial assignment. Bombastic and thick-accented, the Russian-born Ratoff would bellow so loudly on sets that he reportedly gave many an actor and actress instant nervous breakdowns. But he treated Bergman with kid gloves. Ratoff, however, at one point, asked the actress to repeat a line he read. She repeated it exactly as Ratoff had spoken it, including the thick Russian accent, which sent her language coach, Ruth Roberts, into a panic. "Never repeat what he says," she cautioned the actress. "Use the accent we rehearsed." Selznick, true to his obsessive habit, constantly interrupted Ratoff's direction and insisted upon endless retakes, particularly the opening scene of the film when Bergman first meets Howard. The actress was later to state: ". . .we'd finished the movie and we were still doing retakes of that first scene." Following the film's completion, she was leaving on the train from Los Angeles, going to New York and then by boat back to Sweden, when the producer caught her and actually had her do one more retake of that first all-important scene. "I had to race out of that studio," she would recall, "still wearing the clothes I wore on the set, shouting goodbye to the crew, and throw myself into the car to catch the train by seconds...that's David Selznick for you."

p, David O. Selznick; d, Gregory Ratoff; w, George O'Neil (based on a story by Gosta Stevens, Gustav Molander); ph, Gregg Toland; ed, Hal C. Kern, Francis D. Lyon; md, Lou Forbes; ard d, Lyle Wheeler; cos, Irene, Travis Banton; spec eff, Jack Cosgrove.

Romance **Cas.** **(PR:A MPAA:NR)**

INTERNATIONAL CRIME** 1/2 (1938) 64m GN bw

Rod La Rocque *(Lamont Cranston/The Shadow)*, Astrid Allwyn *(Phoebe Lane)*, Thomas Jackson *(Commissioner Weston)*, Oscar O'Shea *(Heath)*, William Von Brinken *(Flotow)*, William Pawley *(Honest John)*, Walter Bonn *(Stefan)*, William

Moore *(Burke)*, Lew Hearn *(Moe Shrevnitz)*, Tenen Holtz, John St. Polis, Lloyd Whitlock, Jack Baxley.

Based on a comic book story (which subsequently became a popular radio series) the film stars La Rocque as a crime reporter for newspaper and radio. He also plays detective himself and solves the murder mystery of a wealthy financier. The dialog is so-so and the bumbling efforts of the police are unbelieveable. Still, it's an entertaining little piece.

p, Max and Arthur Alexander; d, Charles Lamont; w, Jack Natteford (based on a short story "The Fox Hound" by Maxwell Grant); ph, Marcel Le Picard; ed, Charles Henkel; md, Dr. Edward Kileyni; art d, Ralph Berger.

Mystery **Cas.** **(PR:A MPAA:NR)**

INTERNATIONAL HOUSE**** (1933) 70m PAR bw

Peggy Hopkins Joyce *(Herself)*, W.C. Fields *(Prof. Quail)*, Stuart Erwin *(Tommy Nash)*, Sari Maritza *(Carol Fortescue)*, George Burns *(Dr. Burns)*, Gracie Allen *(Nurse Allen)*, Bela Lugosi *(Gen. Petronovich)*, Edmund Breese *(Dr. Wong)*, Lumsden Hare *(Sir Mortimer Fortescue)*, Franklin Pangborn *(Hotel Manager)*, Harrison Greene *(Herr von Baden)*, Henry Sedley *(Serge Borsky)*, James Wong *(Inspector Sun)*, Sterling Holloway *(Entertain/Sailor)*, Rudy Vallee *(Himself)*, Col. Stoopnagle and Budd *(Themselves)*, Cab Calloway and his Orchestra *(Themselves)*, Baby Rose Marie *(Herself)*, Ernest Wood *(Newsreel Reporter)*, Edwin Stanley *(Mr. Rollins)*, Clem Beauchamp/Jerry Drew *(Cameraman)*, Norman Ainslee *(Ticket Manager)*, Louis Vincenot *(Hotel Clerk)*, Bo-Ling *(Chinese Girl at Cigar Counter)*, Etta Lee *(Peggy's Maid)*, Bo-Ching *(Bellhop)*, Lona Andre *(Chorus Queen)*, Andre Cheron *(Guest)*.

A manic and almost maniacal comedy, INTERNATIONAL HOUSE offers a bevy of funny people whose antics border on the lunatic but provide loads of laughter from a script that could have been written in a padded cell. Breese is an eccentric inventor (are there any other kind?) who intends to exhibit his marvelous radioscope, an early-day version of television, before a group of international buyers. Foremost of these is Russian general Lugosi, who arrives at the hotel to be greeted by his ex-wife, Joyce, a blonde vamp who's looking for pockets to loot. Arriving later is Fields, who lands on the hotel roof with an autogryo, half airplane, half helicopter. He has flown from Mexico dropping beer bottles en route and injuring countless victims below, according to reports read by Burns and Allen, the doctor and his addle-brained nurse who are on the staff of the hotel, The International House in the mythical land of Wuhu, China. Meanwhile, American envoy Erwin is busy trying to woo Maritza, while Joyce attempts to seduce him. Fields creates utter confusion when he arrives. When he is told he is in the land of Wuhu, Fields shouts: "Then what is Wuhu doing where Kansas City ought to be?" "Maybe you're lost," manager Pangborn volunteers. "Kansas City is lost!" replies Fields. "I am here!" The great comedian dominates the film from that point on, filling the screen with double entendres, sight gags, slapstick and his own peculiar brand of mayhem. When his top hat is crushed over his eyes, temporarily blinding him, Joyce yanks it away and says: "Now can you see anything?" Over dinner later old smoothie Fields tells Joyce: "Well, sweet buttercup, now that I'm here and see what's to be had, I shall dally in the valley, and believe me, I can dally." He gets entangled in myriad telephone lines of the switchboard and screams he has been attacked by a "Chinese noodle swamp." Finally all the players gather to view Breese's new invention. A fleet of battle ships is shown on the television set and Fields pulls out a pistol, shooting the leading warship which promptly sinks, a gag he had been trying to get into films from his earliest silent movies. After some more frantic escapades, Erwin finally winds up buying Breese's new invention, mostly to escape the hotel which has been quarantined when Erwin came down with the measles. During the last demonstrations Breeze fails to pick up the six day bicycle races from Madison Square Garden as promised but does manage to show Baby Rose Marie warbling out a torch song, then tunes in Cab Calloway singing a song called "Reefer Man" which later became a camp classic; the song's lyrics commending the wonders of marijuana and blatantly suggesting that the use of the drug by jazz musicians and blacks brings them to their creative zenith. (This number is invariably cut from the prints shown on today's TV.) Before the cast escapes the madhouse, there are several big musical production numbers that are on a Busby Berkeley scale. Erwin winds up with Maritza and Fields, for the only time in his movie career, winds up with the girl, Joyce. Fields had first appeared with Joyce in the 1917 Ziegfeld Follies but she had gone on to a successful Hollywood career where Fields' silent film attempts had failed miserably, a fate which Fields blamed on his then director Sutherland, saying that the director in those days had refused to let him perform sure-fire vaudeville bits of his own invention. In INTERNATIONAL HOUSE, Sutherland let Fields do practically what he wanted, inserting gags and routines that somehow caught the public's fancy and made him a comic star overnight. The great comedian received $12,000 for his four-week performance in the film which was so well received that he parlayed a new contract at Paramount into a $100,000-a-year, three-pictures-a-year deal for three years. Pangborn, Burns and Allen, even Lugosi as a comic heavy, are all hilarious but the film belongs to master funnyman Fields. One rare excerpt of this film occurred during a mild California earthquake while Fields was preparing to go on the set. The camera was rolling when the chandelier on the set began to sway and pictures began to fall from walls. The cameraman panicked and dashed for the soundstage door but Fields is shown calmly telling everyone not to panic as the camera kept recording this fascinating real-life drama for some 20 or 30 seconds.

d, Edward Sutherland; w, Francis Martin, Walter DeLeon (based on a story by Lou Heifetz, Neil Brant); ph, Ernest Haller; cos, Travis Banton; m/l, Ralph Rainger, Leo Robin.

Comedy **(PR:A MPAA:NR)**

INTERNATIONAL LADY 1/2** (1941) 100m UA bw

George Brent *(Tim Hanley)*, Ilona Massey *(Carla Nillson)*, Basil Rathbone *(Reggie Oliver)*, Gene Lockhart *(Sidney Grenner)*, George Zucco *(Webster)*, Francis Pierlot *(Dr. Rowan)*, Martin Kosleck *(Bruner)*, Charles D. Brown *(Tetlow)*, Marjorie Gateson *(Mrs. Grenner)*, Leyland Hodgson *(Moulton)*, Clayton Moore *(Sewell)*, Gordon DeMain *(Denby)*, Frederic Worlock *(Sir Henry)*, Jack Mulhall *(Desk Clerk)*, Ralph Dunn *(Don)*, Robert Fiske *(Headwaiter)*, Selmer Jackson *(Colonel)*, John Dilson *(Decoding Expert)*, William Forrest *(Frank Cromwell, American Consul)*, Martin Garralaga *(Lisbon Cab Man)*, Charles McAvoy *(New York Airport Guard)*, Marten Lamont *(Lt. Fenwick)*, Trevor Bardette *(Krell the Chemist)*, Otto Reichow *(German Radio Operator)*, Harold Goodwin *(Decoder On Piano)*.

The complicated plot has Massey broadcasting arias over German radio to U-Boat captains. Brent is an American agent who knows she's sending out a code. Rathbone is a Scotland Yard inspector (not unlike his regular Sherlock Holmes character) who is also trying to crack the case. It's easy to get lost in the plot by not paying attention, but there are some nice comic bits along the way. The camera treats Massey in a flattering manner for her first straight role. Don't miss the pre-LONE RANGER appearance by Moore.

p, Edward Small; d, Tim Whelan; w, Howard Estabrook (based on a story by E. Lloyd Sheldon, Jack DeWitt); ph, Hal Mohr; m, Lucien Moraweck; ed, Grant Whytock, William Claxton; md, Lud Gluskin; art d, John DuCasse Schulze; cos, Gwen Wakeling.

Drama/Suspense **(PR:A MPAA:NR)**

INTERNATIONAL POLICE (SEE: PICK-UP ALLEY, 1957, Brit.)

INTERNATIONAL SETTLEMENT 1/2** (1938) 75m FOX bw

Dolores Del Rio *(Lenore Dixon)*, George Sanders *(Del Forbes)*, June Lang *(Joyce Parker)*, Dick Baldwin *(Wally Burton)*, Ruth Terry *(Specialty Song)*, John Carradine *(Murdock)*, Keye Luke *(Dr. Wong)*, Harold Huber *(Joseph Lang)*, Leon Ames *(Monte Silvers)*, Pedro de Cordoba *(Maurice Zabello)*, Bruce Wong *(Bellboy)*, Walter Miller, Jeffrey Sayre *(Gangsters)*, Creighton Hale *(Clerk)*, James B. Leong, Russ Clark *(Officers)*, Edwin Stanley *(Doctor)*, Nora Cecil *(English Woman)*, Rosina Galli *(Italian Woman)*, Al Kikume *(Doorman)*, James C. Morton *(Bartender)*, Hal K. Dawson *(Master of Ceremonies)*, Bert Roach *(Lord Fauntleroy)*, Forbes Murray *(Man)*.

Sanders is a gunrunner in China who gets involved in a plot to deliver custom certificates but his contact has died and no one knows where the money is. He is running from the pursuing smugglers when Japanese bombs are dropped on Shanghai. Caught in the firestorm, he is saved by French singer Del Rio. They fall in love and leave together on a refugee ship. It's a kinetic plot interspersed with stock footage of Shanghai under siege. The studio shots and stock shots are nicely matched, giving the film a highly realistic feeling.

p, Sol M. Wurtzel; d, Eugene Forde; w, Lou Breslow, John Patrick (based on a story by Lynn Root and Frank Fenton), ph, Lucien Andriot; ed, Nick De Maggio; md, Samuel Kaylin; art d, Bernard Herzbrun, Albert Hogsett; m/l, "You Made Me That Way," Sidney Clare, Harry Akst, Harold Spina (sung by Del Rio).

Adventure/Romance **(PR:A MPAA:NR)**

INTERNATIONAL SQUADRON*** (1941) 85m WB bw

Ronald Reagan *(Jimmy Grant)*, James Stephenson *(Charles Wyatt)*, Olympe Bradna *(Jeanette)*, William Lundigan *(Lt. Reg Wilkins)*, Joan Perry *(Connie)*, Julie Bishop *(Mary)*, Tod Andrews *(Michele Edme)*, Cliff Edwards *(Omaha McGrath)*, John Ridgely *(Bill Torrence)*, Selmer Jackson *(Saunders)*, Addison Richards *(Chief)*, Holmes Herbert *(Sir Basil Wryxton)*, Eddy Conrad *(Greek Waiter)*, Crauford Kent *(Maj. Fresney)*, Richard Travis, William Hopper *(Radio Operators)*, Frank Faylen *(Process Server)*, Marjorie Whatley, Shirley Coates *(Girls)*, Jean Ames *(Blonde)*, Ann Edmonds *(French Girl)*, Gerald Gavin, Marten Lamont, Tom Stevenson, Tom Skinner *(Officers)*, Helmut Dantine, Ernest Lenart, John Meredith, Knud Kreuger, Ivan Molnar *(Flyers)*, Doris Lloyd *(Mother)*, Brenda Henderson *(Child)*, Frank Baker, Leyland Hodgson *(Wardens)*, Ottola Nesmith *(Mrs. Harris)*, Harry Lewis *(Pilot)*, Leslie Denison *(Ground Chief)*, Frederick Giermann, Henry Rowland *(Germans)*, Pat O'Hara, David Thursby, Cyril Thornton, Hugh Huntley *(Instructors)*.

Reagan plays a stunt pilot who is delivering a bomber to the RAF. Upon his arrival, he meets his old commander, Stephenson, and old flying buddy, Lundigan. They've joined the RAF and try to persuade Reagan to do the same. He refuses as he's too much of a playboy. But that night when the Nazis bomb London in an air raid, Reagan sees a child killed. The brutality of the youth's death causes a change in the flyer and he decides to fight the Nazis. Still unable to control his cavalier ways, he flirts with Bradna, causing him to miss a patrol mission in which a substitute pilot is killed. Stunned by the death, Reagan sees the error of his ways and decides to atone for his friend's death by bumping a buddy from a dangerous bombing mission. Reagan takes on a group of German fighter planes, shooting them down but dying in a fiery death. The war film is loosely based on CEILING ZERO, a 1935 Cagney film that was far superior to the Reagan version. Warner, like other studios during the WW II era, had full cooperation of airplane manufacturers for their flying epics. The Lockheed plant was located only two miles from the Warner lot and their Hudson bomber was used often in this and other war pictures. But there was little access to foreign planes and stock footage had to be relied upon. The plane Reagan flies in INTERNATIONAL SQUADRON was a Ryan monoplane, made to look like the British Spitfire. The film drew laughs in London houses because of the many obvious differences between the two craft.

p, Edmund Grainger; d, Lothar Mendes; w, Barry Trivers, Kenneth Gamet (based on the play "Ceiling Zero" by Frank Wead); ph, James Van Trees, Ted McCord; ed, Frank McGee; spec eff, Robert Burks.

War/Aviation Drama **(PR:A MPAA:NR)**

INTERNATIONAL VELVET**½ (1978, Brit.) 125m MGM/UA c

Tatum O'Neal *(Sarah Brown)*, Christopher Plummer *(John Seaton)*, Anthony Hopkins *(Capt. Johnson)*, Nanette Newman *(Velvet Brown)*, Peter Barkworth *(Pilot)*, Dinsdale Landen *(Mr. Curtis)*, Sarah Bullen *(Beth)*, Jeffrey Byron *(Scott Saunders)*, Richard Warwick *(Tim)*, Daniel Abineri *(Wilson)*, Jason White *(Roger)*, Martin Neil *(Mike)*, Douglas Reith *(Howard)*.

Fair sequel to the 1944 Elizabeth Taylor film NATIONAL VELVET. O'Neal plays the niece of Newman (Taylor's role in the first film) who resides with her aunt and live-in boy friend, writer Plummer. Newman is training O'Neal to follow in her footsteps and become an Olympic equestrian. Hopkins is the team trainer who also helps the protege. Byron, an American opponent, is O'Neal's romantic interest. Though Taylor was considered for the role (ultimately declining), Newman gives a fine performance as the grown-up Velvet. However, the film runs a little long and tends to lose its focus occasionally. The photography and production design are classy though, and kids should enjoy it. Actress Nanette Newman is married to the producer, director, and writer of this film, Bryan Forbes. The interplay and relationships between main stars O'Neal, Plummer, and Newman are very well handled and create a feeling of warmth that is rare in modern film. Plummer particularly impresses one in his handling of his role.

p,d&w, Bryan Forbes (based on the novel *National Velvet* by Enid Bagnold) ph, Tony Imi (Metrocolor); m, Francis Lai; ed, Timothy Gee; prod d, Keith Wilson; set d, Ian Whittaker; cos, John Furness, Dorothy Edwards, John Hilling; stunts, Richard Graydon.

Drama **Cas.** **(PR:AAA MPAA:PG)**

INTERNECINE PROJECT, THE**
(1974, Brit.) 89m Lion International-Hemisphere/AA c

James Coburn *(Robert Elliot)*, Lee Grant *(Jean Robertson)*, Harry Andrews *(Albert Parsons)*, Ian Hendry *(Alex Hellman)*, Michael Jayston *(David Baker)*, Keenan Wynn *(E.J. Farnsworth)*, Christiane Kruger *(Christina)*, Terence Alexander *(Tycoon)*, Philip Anthony *(Elliot's Secretary)*, David Swift *(Chester Drake)*, Julian Glover *(Arnold Pryce Jones)*, Ray Callaghan *(Producer)*, Geoffrey Burridge *(Floor Manager)*, Robert Tayman *(Mixer)*, Judy Robinson *(Production Assistant)*, Kevin Scott *(Maxwell)*, John Savident *(German)*, Richard Cornish *(1st Officer)*, Carrie Kirstein *(Air Stewardess)*, Richard Marner *(German Delegate)*, Ralph Ball *(Executive Type)*, Brian Tully, Michael Knightingale *(Executives)*, Ewan Roberts *(Senior Lab Technician)*, Susan Magolier *(Laboratory Assistant)*, Mary Larkin *(Jean's Secretary)*.

Coburn is on his way to becoming a key advisor to the president of the U.S. but four individuals who know about his shady deals could ruin everything so they must be "removed." He arranges things so the four (Andrews, Kruger, Jayston, and Hendry) appear to have killed one another. It's a nice thriller plot line, though less than perfect in execution. It takes the first two-thirds of the film to set up the murders and then gets a little too clever. The ending is a letdown, and Grant's talents are wasted.

p, Barry Levinson, d, Ken Hughes; w, Levinson, Jonathan Lynn (based on the novel *Internecine* by Mort W. Elkind); ph, Geoffrey Unsworth (Eastmancolor); m, Roy Budd; ed, John Shirley; prod d, Geoffrey Drake; art d, David Minty.

Thriller **(PR:O MPAA:PG)**

INTERNES CAN'T TAKE MONEY**½
(1937) 77m PAR bw (GB: YOU CAN'T TAKE MONEY)

Barbara Stanwyck *(Janet Haley)*, Joel McCrea *(Jimmie Kildare)*, Lloyd Nolan *(Hanlon)*, Stanley Ridges *(Innes)*, Gaylord Pendleton *(Interne Jones)*, Lee Bowman *(Interne Weeks)*, Irving Bacon *(Jeff)*, Barry Macollum *("Stooly" Martin)*, Pierre Watkin *(Dr. Fearson)*, Charles [Levison] Lane *(Grote)*, James Bush *(Haines)*, Nick Lukats *(Interne)*, Anthony Nace *(Dr. Riley)*, Fay Holden *(Sister Superior)*, Frank Bruno *(Eddie)*, Jack Mulhall *(1st Mug)*, Lillian Harmer *(Mrs. Mooney)*, May Wallace *(Mother Superior)*, John "Skins" Miller *(Weaselpuss)*, Elmer Jerome *(Wipey)*, George Lynn *(Joe)*, Lee Phelps *(Bus Announcer)*, Lillian West *(Admittance Clerk)*, Gertrude Simpson *(Stout Woman)*, Helen Brown, Frances Morris, Priscilla Lawson *(Nurses)*, Harvey Clark *(Cashier)*, Agostino Borgato *(Popcorn Vendor)*, Jack Raymond *(Taxi Driver)*, Eddie Dunn *(Ambulance Driver)*, May Carlson *(Ora)*, Jean Peterson *(Frances)*, Pat Church *(Chloe)*, Yvonne Dunkerley, Donna Staley *(Girls)*, Charles Sherlock *(Man in Bookie's Office)*, Charles Moore *(Elevator Boy)*, Alexander Schonberg *(Violinist)*, Ellen Drew [Terry Ray] *(Bit)*.

McCrea is a young doctor who helps ex-convict Stanwyck find her missing three-year-old daughter. Nolan is a gangster with a heart whose life is saved by a crude operation performed by McCrea with the implements at hand in a barroom. True to the film's title, McCrea will not accept payment for exercising his surgical skills. Ridges, a not-so-nice gangster, is holding the daughter for both money and for Stanwyck herself. When Ridges is shot before he can reveal the whereabouts of the daughter, McCrea must once again operate to save his life. The operation is a success, of course, and mother and daughter are reunited. This was the first film based on cowboy classic writer Brand's DOCTOR KILDARE characters (see Index), which MGM picked up as a series featuring Lew Ayres and Laraine Day.

p, Benjamin Glazer; d, Alfred Santell; w, Rian James, Theodore Reeves (based on a magazine story by Max Brand); ph, Theodor Sparkuhl; m, Gregory Stone; ed, Doane Harrison; md, Boris Morros; art d, Hans Dreier, Roland Anderson; cos, Travis Banton.

Medical/Crime **(PR:A MPAA:NR)**

INTERNS, THE**½ (1962) 130m COL bw

Michael Callan *(Dr. Considine)*, Cliff Robertson *(Dr. John Paul Otis)*, James MacArthur *(Dr. Lew Worship)*, Nick Adams *(Dr. Sid Lackland)*, Suzy Parker *(Lisa Cardigan)*, Haya Harareet *(Mado)*, Anne Helm *(Mildred)*, Stefanie Powers *(Gloria)*, Buddy Ebsen *(Dr. Sidney Wohl)*, Telly Savalas *(Dr. Riccio)*, Katharine Bard *(Nurse Flynn)*, Kay Stevens *(Didi Loomis)*, Gregory Morton *(Dr. Hugo Granchard)*, Angela Clarke *(Mrs. Auer)*, Connie Gilchrist *(Nurse Connie Dean)*, Ellen Davalos *(Loara)*, Charles Robinson *(Dr. Dave Simon)*, Carroll Harrison *(Olga)*, John Banner *(Dr. Duane)*, Mari Lynn *(Samantha)*, Brian G. Hutton *(Dr. Joe Parelli)*, J. Edward McKinley *(Dr. Bonny)*, Bobo Lewis *(Gwen)*, Bill Gunn *(Rosco)*, William O. Douglas *(Dr. Apschult)*, Don Edmonds *(Dr. Petchek)*, Mavis Neal *(Mrs. Lawrence)*, Brent Sargent *(Dr. Baker)*, Mark Kantor *(Samantha's Son)*, Peter Brocco *(Auer)*, Roger Bronte *(1st Intern)*, Michael Fox *(Dr. Greenberg)*, Baruch Lumet *(Byrd)*, Harry Hines *(Slattery)*, Jackie Stoloff *(Betay-Model)*, Ira Barmak, Jud Taylor.

Love, romance, intrigue, dirty dealings, back stabbing, death, life, abortion, feminism, and all the other wonderful things that one finds in a hospital soaper are present here. This follows a group of four interns during their first year of practice at a big hospital. Little attention is paid to their medical practices; after all, romance is more fun. Robertson, the standout here, is a serious-minded med student whose world changes when he meets a New York model (Parker) who wants an illegal abortion. MacArthur falls for nurse Powers but she doesn't want to marry a doctor; Callan is a two-timer, carrying on with socialite Helm while using Nurse Bard both sexually and career-wise. Finally, there's Adams in the token role of the doctor who falls for a dying patient. It's all good trashy fun with an interesting feminist element, 10 years before it was fashionable. Savalas (who would become TV's "Kojak") is an older doctor who believes it's a waste of time to educate women, but he learns a trick or two from Harareet. This film spawned a sequel, called THE NEW INTERNS, as well as a television series. Turk Murphy and His Jazz Orchestra perform "Bye and Bye."

p, Robert Cohn; d, David Swift; w, Walter Newman, Swift (based on the novel by Richard Frede); ph, Russell Metty; m, Leith Stevens; ed, Al Clark, Jerome Thoms; art d, Don Ament; set d, Richard Mansfield; makeup, Ben Lane.

Drama/Romance **(PR:O MPAA:NR)**

INTERPOL (SEE: PICK-UP ALLEY, 1957, Brit.)

INTERRUPTED HONEYMOON, THE*** (1936, Brit.) 72m BL bw

Claude Hulbert *(Victor)*, Francis L. Sullivan *(Alphonse)*, Hugh Wakefield *(Uncle John)*, Jane Carr *(Greta)*, Glennis Lorimer *(Edith Hobson)*, Robb Wilton *(Henry Briggs)*, Jack Hobbs *(George)*, David Horne *(Colonel Craddock)*, Martita Hunt *(Nora Briggs)*, Wally Patch *(Police Constable)*, Helen Haye *(Aunt Harriet)*, Hal Walters *(Valet)*.

When Hulbert and his new wife go off on their honeymoon a friend takes over his apartment, bringing along his mistress to liven things up. Meanwhile, Hulbert finds himself in deep trouble in Paris after he inadvertently kisses the wife of a jealous hotel man. Returning from the honeymoon sooner than expected and fighting with his wife, Hulbert is surprised by what is waiting at home. Some good moments in an extremely lively comedy.

p, Herbert Smith; d, Leslie Hiscott; w, Michael Barringer, Wyndham Brown, Neil Tyfield (based on the play by Ernst Bach, Franz Arnold).

Comedy **(PR:A MPAA:NR)**

INTERRUPTED HONEYMOON, AN, 1948
(SEE: HOMICIDE FOR THREE, 1948)

INTERRUPTED JOURNEY, THE** (1949, Brit.) 80m Valiant/Lopert bw

Valerie Hobson *(Carol North)*, Richard Todd *(John North)*, Christine Norden *(Susan Wilding)*, Tom Walls *(Mr. Clayton)*, Ralph Truman *(Inspector Waterson)*, Vida Hope *(Miss Marchmont)*, Alexander Gauge *(Jerves Wilding)*, Dora Bryan *(Waitress)*, Arnold Ridley *(Saunders)*, Cyril Smith *(Publican)*, Dora Sevening, Elsie Wagstaffe, Nigel Neilson, Arthur Lane, Vincent Ball, Jack Vyvyan, Gwyneth Vaughan.

A minor league thriller with a cliche ending. The acting is all excellent and much of the dialog crackles, but the final result is not worth the wait. Todd is a married author who is running off with Norden, the wife of Gauge, his publisher. He is married to Hobson but he and Norden leave on a train to find a new life with each other. When Todd thinks he may have made a mistake, he pulls the overhead emergency cord to stop the train and leaps off. Now the train is involved in an accident and Norden is killed. We then learn that her death was not caused by the accident. She was shot in the back and there is an investigation by Walls and Truman. The killer is discovered to be Gauge, the publisher-husband, but we are told that the whole thing was (are you ready?) a dream. Yechh. It's fast-moving and has lots of action, which is about all we can say for it, though Todd's and Hobson's performances are excellent. Hobson was married to the producer at the time.

p, Anthony Havelock-Allan; d, Daniel Birt; w, Michael Pertwee; ph, Erwin Hillier, Eric Besche; ed, Danny Chorlton.

Crime Drama **(PR:A-C MPAA:NR)**

INTERRUPTED MELODY***½ (1955) 105m MGM c

Glenn Ford *(Dr. Thomas King)*, Eleanor Parker *(Marjorie Lawrence)*, Roger Moore *(Cyril Lawrence)*, Cecil Kellaway *(Bill Lawrence)*, Peter Leeds *(Dr. Ed Ryson)*, Evelyn Ellis *(Clara)*, Walter Baldwin *(Jim Owens)*, Ann Codee *(Mme. Gilly)*, Leopold Sachse *(Himself)*, Stephen Bekassy *(Comte Claude des Vigneux)*, Charles R. Keane *(Ted Lawrence)*, Fiona Hale *(Eileen Lawrence)*, Doris Lloyd *(Volunteer Worker)*, Alex Frazer *(Adjudicator)*, Penny Santon *(Gilly Secretary)*, Phyllis Altivo *(Louise)*, Gabor Curtiz *(Tenor's Manager)*, Claude Stroud *(Tenor)*, Andre Charlot

(Mon. Bertrand), Paul McGuire *(Metropolitan Cashier)*, Doris Merrick *(Nurse)*, Sandra Descher *(Suzie)*, Jack Raine *(Mr. Norson)*, Freda Stoll *(Accompanist)*, Gloria Rhods *(Mrs. Schultz)*, Stuart Whitman *(Man On Beach)*, Eileen Farrell *(Vocal Student)*.

Superlative screen biography of Marjorie Lawrence, the opera singer struck by polio who regained her strength to once more appear at the Metropolitan Opera. Parker, who was nominated for an Oscar, gives an excellent portrayal of the woman dealt the damaging blow at the height of her career. Ford is the doctor who helps with her rehabilitation and becomes her husband. The two share the film's most moving scene: despite her pleas Ford puts on a record of her singing and Parker drags herself across the floor to turn off the machine. It is a well-crafted and sensitively handled moment and the story's turning point. The finale at the Met, where Parker performs in a special showing of "Tristan and Isolde" is magnificent. With her singing voice dubbed by Eileen Farrell, Parker's miming fits perfectly. She does eight arias including "Musetta's Waltz" from Giacomo Puccini's "La Boheme" and "Habanera" from Georges Bizet's "Carmen." The classic song "Over the Rainbow" from THE WIZARD OF OZ (Harold Arlen, E.Y. Harburg) is also heard. A must for opera fans. Winner of the "Best Adapted Screenplay" Oscar. Other songs and operatic excerpts: Brunnhilde's Immolation from Richard Wagner's "Gotterdammerung," "Seguidilla," from "Carmen," Finale to Act One of 'Il Trovatore" (Giuseppe Verdi), "One Fine Day" from "Madame Butterfly" (Giacomo Puccini), "Waltzing Matilda" (A.B. Paterson, Marie Cowan).

p, Jack Cummings; d, Curtis Bernhardt; w, William Ludwig, Sonya Levien (based on the book by Marjorie Lawrence); ph, Joseph Ruttenberg, Paul C. Vogel (CinemaScope, Eastmancolor); m, Adolph Deutsch; ed, John Dunning; md, Deutsch, Saul Chaplin, Walter Du Cloux, Vladimir Rosing, Harold Gelman; art d, Cedric Gibbons, Daniel B. Cathcart; cos, Helen Rose.

Drama **(PR:A MPAA:NR)**

INTERVAL** (1973, Mex./U.S.) 84m Euro-American, Churubusco/AE c

Merle Oberon *(Serena Moore)*, Robert Wolders *(Chris)*, Claudio Brook *(Armando Vertiz)*, Russ Conway *(Fraser)*, Charles Bateman *(Husband)*, Britt Leach *(Leonard)*, Peter Von Zerneck *(Broch)*, Fernando Soler, Jr. *(Waiter)*, Gloria Mestre *(Rosalia)*, Christina Moreno *(Jody)*, Betty Lyon *(Ellie)*, Anel *(Jackie)*, Barbara Ranson *(Susan)*.

While vacationing in Mexico the middle-aged Oberon meets Wolders, a painter about 20 years her junior. They carry on a heated romance, adding zest to the life of the lonely Oberon. Through flashbacks, we learn that she spent some time in an institution after killing a lover in an auto accident. Better suited for soap opera viewers than avid fans of the big screen. Oberon was 62 when she acted in and produced this, her final picture. She also would soon become Mrs. Wolders, marrying her younger jet-setting companion.

p, Merle Oberon; d, Daniel Mann; w, Gavin Lambert; ph, Gabriel Figueroa; m, Armando Manzanero, Ruben Fuentes; ed, Howard S. Deane; cos, Luis Estevez.

Romance **(PR:C MPAA:PG)**

INTIMACY** (1966) 87m Goldstone bw (AKA: THE DECEIVERS)

Jack Ging *(Jim Hawley)*, Joan Blackman *(Barbara Nicholson)*, Nancy Malone *(Virginia Hawley)*, Barry Sullivan *(Walter Nicholson)*, Jackie DeShannon *(Carrie Lane)*.

Sullivan, determined to get a government contract, blackmails Washington official Ging by placing a concealed camera in his hotel room. He then sends in hooker DeShannon to turn on the heat. When Sullivan gets the film back he gleefully watches until his own wife appears as one of Ging's lovers. Sullivan drops to the floor suffering a fatal heart attack, never knowing that he had been awarded the contract. His wife arrives at his office and finds the film still running. The scene she is treated to is Ging and his estranged wife clearing up the marital problems. A plethora of ironies add up to "contrived."

p, David Heilwell; d, Victor Stoloff; w, Harvey Flaxman, Eva Wolas (based on an idea by Stanley Z. Cherry); ph, Ted and Vincent Saizis; m, Geordie Hormel.

Drama **(PR:O MPAA:NR)**

INTIMATE LIGHTING*** ½

(1969, Czech.) 71m Barandov/Altura-Fleetwood bw (INTIMNI OSVETLENI)

Vera Kresadlova *(Stepa)*, Zdenek Bezusek *(Peter)*, Jan Vostrcil *(Grandfather)*, Vlastimila Vlkova *(Grandmother)*, Karel Blazek *(Bambas)*, Jaroslava Stedra *(Marie)*, Karel Uhlik *(Pharmacist)*, Miroslav Cvrk *(Kaja)*, Dagmar Redinova *(Young Marie)*.

A genuinely engaging tale of two old friends from music college who are scheduled to give a concert in a small Czech town. Bezusek arrives in the town with his selfish girl friend. They go to a funeral and then dinner with Blazek, who lives with his grandparents, wife, and children. The two friends get drunk that evening and decide to leave their lives behind. After a short time they return home, sober up, and accept their situations. Passer, a director of exceptional talent but little output, would later come to the U.S. and direct the excellent CUTTER'S WAY. Released in Czechoslovakia in 1966.

d, Ivan Passer; w, Passer, Jaroslav Papousek, Vaclav Sasek; ph, Miroslav Ondricek, Josef Strecha; m, Oldrich Korte, Josef Hart; prod d, Frantisek Sandr; ed, Jirina Lukesova; art d, Karel Cerny.

Drama **(PR:A MPAA:NR)**

INTIMATE RELATIONS** (1937, Brit.) 66m Tudor/ABF bw

June Clyde *(Molly Morrell)*, Garry Marsh *(George Gommery)*, Jack Hobbs *(Freddie Hall)*, Vera Bogetti *(Jane Gommery)*, Cynthia Stock *(Maggie)*, Moore Marriott *(Toomley)*, Arthur Finn *(Goldfish)*, Bruce Winston *(Stetson)*, Oliver Gordon, Lew Stone and His Band.

A weak programmer has Marsh and Bogetti playing a married couple who want to expand their marriage. Clyde, a film actress, and Hobbs, an old pal, are enlisted for respective affairs with the couple but they ruin the whole plan by falling in love with each other instead. Dumb and overlong comedy.

p, Herbert Wynne; d, Clayton Hutton; w, Frank Atkinson (based on a play by Stafford Dickens); ph, John Stumar.

Comedy **(PR:A MPAA:NR)**

INTIMATE RELATIONS, 1948
(SEE: LES PARENTS TERRIBLES, 1948, Fr.)

INTIMATE RELATIONS, 1953 (SEE: DISOBEDIENT, 1953, Brit.)

INTIMATE STRANGER, THE (SEE: FINGER OF GUILT, 1956, Brit.)

INTIMNI OSVETLENI (SEE: INTIMATE LIGHTING, 1969, Czech.)

INTO THE BLUE (SEE: MAN IN THE DINGHY, THE, 1950, Brit.)

INTO THE STRAIGHT** (1950, Aus.) 80m EM/UNIV bw

Charles Tingwell *(Sam Curzon)*, Muriel Steinbeck *(Laura Curzon)*, George Randall *(W.J. Curzon)*, Nonnie Piefer *(June Curzon)*, James Workman *(Hugh Duncan)*, Margot Lee *(Zra Marlow)*, Alan White *(Paul Duncan)*, Charles Zoli *(Paddy)*.

This Australian import deals with life in and around a racetrack. Various intrigues are played out involving the spicy ladies who prove to be a temptation to the horsemen. Not much, but well made for what it is.

p&d, Tom O. McCreadle; w, Zelma Roberts.

Drama **(PR:C MPAA:NR)**

INTRAMUROS (SEE: WALLS OF HELL, THE, 1964, US/Phil.)

INTRIGUE* ½ (1947) 90m Star/UA bw

George Raft *(Brad Dunham)*, June Havoc *(Tamara Baranoff)*, Helena Carter *(Linda Arnold)*, Tom Tully *(Marc Andrews)*, Marvin Miller *(Ramon)*, Dan Seymour *(Karidian)*,Philip Ahn *(Lui Chan)*, Marc Krah *(Nicco)*, Jay C. Flippen *(Bartender)*, Charles Lane *(Hotel Clerk)*, Phil Taylor *(Eddie Lane)*, Edna Holland *(Miss Carr)*, David Leonard *(Headwaiter)*, Gordon Clark *(Cigar Clerk)*, Peter Chong *(Editor)*, Michael Visaroff *(Capt. Masters)*, Nan Wynn *(Cafe Singer)*, Maria San Marco *(Ling)*, Michael Ansara *(Radio Operator)*, Wei F. Hsueh *(Chinese Doctor)*, Reginald Billado, Ralph Winters *(Pilots)*, Victor Sen Yung *(Cable Clerk)*, Paul Fierra *(Warehouseman)*, Philson Ahn *(Chinese Official)*, Stan Ross *(Assistant Warehouseman)*, Jean Wong *(Nurse)*, Rod Red Wing *(Manuscript Thief)*, Leon Lontoc *(Mechanic)*, Hassan Ezzat, Robert Gilbert, Alex Montoya, Hassan Khayyan, Al Rhein *(Karidian's Henchman)*, Nancy Hsueh *(Little Chinese Girl)*, Richard Wong, Kenneth Chuck, Ronald Louie, William Louie, Hayward Soo Hoo *(Little Chinese Boys)*.

INTRIGUE is anything but intriguing. It looks like a comic strip and has just about every cliche associated with stories about the Orient. Raft is an ex-Army pilot who has been discharged for flying smuggled goods during WW II. It's a false charge but he can't prove it. He arrives in Shanghai and doesn't realize that he is now involved with the very crooks who framed him, led by Havoc in an Occidental Dragon Lady role. Tully is a newsman pal who tries to talk Raft out of black marketeering with Havoc. Tully is doing undercover work on a story that will lay bare the truth about Havoc. She has him killed for his troubles and Raft finally realizes that Havoc is behind it all. The crooks have a heavily guarded warehouse which Raft opens to the starving Shanghai-nese. Havoc is accidentally killed and Raft seeks solace in the arms of Carter, a local social worker who had been dropping into the film from time to time. Jay C. Flippen, Marvin Miller, and Dan Seymour do small bits and the assistant warehouseman is played by Stan Ross, who later made a living as Milton Berle's foil (and later Jackie Gleason's) on TV. Also seen briefly are Wynn (who sings the title song) and Ansara, a TV star in the 1960s and one-time husband of Barbara Eden.

p, Samuel Bischoff; d, Edwin L. Marin; w, Barry Trivers, George Slavin (based on a story by Slavin); ph, Lucien Andriot; m, Louis Forbes; ed, George Arthur; art d, Arthur Lonergan; set d, Robert Priestley; m/l, "Intrigue," Harry Akst, Samuel Lerner (sung by Nan Wynn).

Adventure **(PR:A MPAA:NR)**

INTRIGUE IN PARIS (SEE: MISS V FROM MOSCOW, 1943)

INTRUDER, THE* ½ (1932) 66m Allied Pictures bw

Monte Blue *(John Brandt)*, Lila Lee *(Connie Wayne)*, Gwen Lee *(Daisy)*, Arthur Housman *(Reggie Wayne)*, Sidney Bracy *(Valet)*, Mischa Auer *(Wild Man)*, Harry Cording *(Cramer)*, William B. Davidson *(Samson)*, Wilfred Lucas *(Mr. Wayne)*, Lynton Brent *(Purser)*, Jack Beek *(Hanson)*, Allen Cavan *(Captain)*.

Murder on board ship, wrecked on a desert island, a second murder, flight from a wild man—hero Blue has his work cut out for him. The beautiful Lee is charming and even able to say, "I slept with a skeleton last night," twice in this unintentionally funny film. With a shaky script, there is no real suspense, and some really laughable miniatures pretending to be ships. Housman performs one of the many drunk routines of his career.

p, M.H. Hoffman, Jr.; d, Alfred Ray; w, Frances Hyland; ph, Harry Neumann, Tom Galligan; ed, Mildred Johnston, Leete R. Brown; md, Abe Meyer; art d, Gene Hornbostel.

Drama **(PR:A MPAA:NR)**

INTRUDER, THE** ½** (1955, Brit.) 84m BL bw

Jack Hawkins *(Wolf Merton)*, Hugh Williams *(Tim Ross)*, Michael Medwin *(Ginger Edwards)*, George Cole *(John Summers)*, Dennis Price *(Leonard Perry)*, Duncan Lamont *(Donald Cope)*, Arthur Howard *(Bertram Slake)*, Marc Sheldon *(Astley)*, George Baker *(Adjutant)*, Nicholas Phipps *(Capt. Fetherstonhaugh)*, Sydney Linton *(Tank Driver)*, Richard Wattis *(School Master)*, Dora Bryan *(Dora Bee)*, Gene Anderson *(June Maple)*, David Horne *(General)*, Patrick Barr *(Inspector Williams)*, Edward Chapman *(Walter Lowden)*, Susan Shaw *(Tina)*, Harold Lang, Bette Vivian, Frances Gowens, Eric Berry, Bruce Beeby, Michael Ripper, Campbell Singer, Charles Lamb, Leonard Sharpe, Peter Martyn, Robert Adair, Elizabeth Digby-Smith, Rowena Gregory, Norman Hargood, Michael McGuire, Graham Tunbridge, Richard Morris.

Hawkins is an ex-soldier who is surprised when a burglar he catches is none other than Medwin, a former member of his regiment. Medwin thinks Hawkins is calling the police and he flees. Hawkins begins a cross-country search for the other regiment members to find out what happened to Medwin. The film varies then, between real time and flashback, as it is discovered what happened to the old corps. Well acted, and the flashbacks between wartime and peacetime are nicely integrated. However, the film tends to get tedious after a while and once the message of the post-war troubles of veterans is made clear, there's little left to say.

p, Ivan Foxwell; d, Guy Hamilton; w, Robin Maugham, John Hunter, Anthony Squire (based on the novel *Line on Ginger* by Maugham); ph, Ted Scaife; m, Francis Chagrin; ed, Alan Osbiston; art d, Joseph Bato; cos, John McCorry.

Drama **(PR:C MPAA:NR)**

INTRUDER, THE* ½**

(1962) 84m Pathe-America bw (AKA: I HATE YOUR GUTS; SHAME; GB: THE STRANGER)

William Shatner *(Adam Cramer)*, Frank Maxwell *(Tom McDaniel)*, Beverly Lunsford *(Ella McDaniel)*, Robert Emhardt *(Verne Shipman)*, Jeanne Cooper *(Vi)*, Leo Gordon *(Sam Griffin)*, Charles Barnes *(Joey Green)*, Charles Beaumont *(Mr. Paton)*, Katherine Smith *(Ruth McDaniel)*, George Clayton Johnson *(Phil West)*, William Nolan *(Bart Carey)*, Phoebe Rowe *(Mrs. Lambert)*, Bo Dodd *(Sheriff)*, Walter Kurtz *(Gramps)*, Ocee Ritch *(Jack Allardyce)*.

Fine portrayal of racism in the southern U.S. Shatner plays a member of the "Patrick Henry Society" who goes to a small southern town to instigate a hate campaign against integration. He charms his way into the hearts of local whites, getting them to harass black students newly enrolled at the high school. Maxwell is the voice of reason, a newspaper publisher who will not go along. Shatner seduces Cooper, whose husband is out of town as a traveling salesman. When the town's anger increases a black minister is killed by a bomb tossed into his congregation. Maxwell tries to lead the black students into the high school and loses an eye as a result. Shatner confronts Lunsford and threatens to kill her father unless she says that Barnes raped her. Scared by the threat, she agrees and Barnes is lashed by a lynch mob to a school yard swing. But Lunsford confesses her lie and the crowd becomes angry with Shatner. They leave and Shatner stands alone. Shatner is fine as the bigot, a mean hate-filled man. The film was shot on location in Charleston, Missouri, using local people as extras. In addition, screenwriter Beaumont plays a small role. The film is a frighteningly honest portrayal of America in the late 1950s, early 1960s.

p&d, Roger Corman; w, Charles Beaumont (based on a novel by Beaumont); ph, Taylor Byars; m, Herman Stein; ed, Ronald Sinclair.

Drama **(PR:C MPAA:NR)**

INTRUDER IN THE DUST**** (1949) 87m MGM bw

David Brian *(John Gavin Stevens)*, Claude Jarman, Jr. *(Chick Mallison)*, Juano Hernandez *(Lucas Beauchamp)*, Porter Hall *(Nub Gowrie)*, Elizabeth Patterson *(Miss Habersham)*, Charles Kemper *(Crawford Gowrie)*, Will Geer *(Sheriff Hampton)*, David Clarke *(Vinson Gowrie)*, Elzie Emanuel *(Aleck)*, Lela Bliss *(Mrs. Mallison)*, Harry Hayden *(Mr. Mallison)*, Harry Antrim *(Mr. Tubbs)*, Dan White *(Will Legate)*, Alberta Dismon *(Paralee)*, R.X. Williams *(Mr. Lilley)*, Edmund Lowe, Ephraim Lowe *(The Gowrie Twins)*, Julia S. Marshbanks *(Molly Beauchamp)*, Jack Odom *(Truck Driver)*, John Morgan, James Kirkwood *(Black Convicts)*, Ben Hilbun *(Attendant)*, Ann Hartsfield *(Girl)*.

There were no stars to speak of but that didn't stop this from being one of the most powerful movies about racial prejudice ever made. The year 1949 was the one when Hollywood woke up to the fact that blacks were being exploited so three films were made in addition to this one, PINKY, LOST BOUNDARIES, and HOME OF THE BRAVE, all of which dealt with the black-white conflict. William Faulkner lived around Oxford, Mississippi, and Brown took his camera and crew there to lend authenticity to the novel upon which Maddow's screenplay is based. More than 500 people appeared in the movie and only a dozen or so were pro actors, the others having been culled from the local population. Hernandez is an old black man who owns his own property, something the local folks resent. The police arrest him for the murder of a townsman because he was discovered near the body and the revolver he carried had just been fired. He's being taken to jail when he sees Jarman, a young white lad with whom he has had some friendly conversations. He asks Jarman to get Brian, Jarman's attorney uncle, to come to the jail. Brian resists the idea of defending Hernandez because anyone who takes on the task of defense attorney will surely suffer a loss of business in the small town. Jarman pleads with Brian who agrees to talk with Hernandez with no promises of taking the case. Kemper, brother of the dead man, spreads the word and Brian is quickly made a pariah as Kemper is rousing the rabble to lynch Hernandez. In jail Hernandez tells Brian that he had been beaten by the victim because lumber had been stolen from the man's cache and the dead man felt that Hernandez had either done it or knew who did it. When Brian asks if Hernandez knows the identity of the wood-thief, Hernandez won't disclose it and Brian exits the jail. Jarman asks Hernandez what it was that Brian refused to do. Hernandez says that the only way to prove his innocence is to disinter the body of the slain man to prove that the bullet didn't come from his gun. Jarman, Patterson and one of Jarman's black friends dig up the coffin and it's empty. Brian and Geer, who has always believed Hernandez, search for the corpse with the aid of Hall, the dead man's father, and find it deep in the quicksand of the creek. The bullet is not from Hernandez's gun and Geer tells the people of Oxford that he is about to free the old black farmer but it's a ruse. Hernandez stays safely in jail while Geer waits in the old man's cabin for the real killer. Geer arrests the dead man's brother, Kemper, tells the crowd the truth, and the mob, which had been eagerly awaiting a lynching, leaves quietly. The most chilling scene in the movie is a lengthy sequence of several cuts; the people of Oxford gleefully assemble (not unlike the crowd to see the man trapped below ground in ACE IN THE HOLE) at the jail to see what they hope will be a lynching; music is played; kids are eating ice cream; everyone is in a jolly mood in direct contrast to the grisly plans they have for the prisoner. This is not a pretty story and it doesn't feature the people of Mississippi in anything but a redneck light (except for the protagonists). Brown must have had a silver tongue to convince so many locals to play in the film, when one considers how they are portrayed. After many years of seeing stereotyped blacks like Mantan Moreland and Willie Best, Hernandez's role was a revelation as he stood up to the charges with the dignity of innocence. It received no Oscars or nominations from the Academy who honored such films as A LETTER TO THREE WIVES, BATTLEGROUND, SHE WORE A YELLOW RIBBON, ADVENTURES OF DON JUAN, and MIGHTY JOE YOUNG, that year.

p&d, Clarence Brown; w, Ben Maddow (based on the novel by William Faulkner); ph, Robert Surtees; m, Adolph Deutsch; ed, Robert J. Kern; art d, Cedric Gibbons, Randall Duell; set d, Edwin B. Willis, Ralph S. Hurst; makeup, Jack Dawn.

Drama **(PR:C-O MPAA:NR)**

INVADER, THE (SEE: OLD SPANISH CUSTOM, AN, 1935, Brit.)

INVADERS, THE,*****

(1941) 105m GFD/ORTUS/COL bw (GB: 49TH PARALLEL)

Leslie Howard *(Philip Armstrong Scott)*, Raymond Massey *(Andy Brock)*, Laurence Olivier *(Johnnie)*, Anton Walbrook *(Peter)*, Eric Portman *(Lt. Hirth)*, Glynis Johns *(Anna)*, Niall MacGinnis *(Vogel)*, Finlay Currie *(Factor)*, Raymond Lovell *(Lt. Kuhnecke)*, John Chandos *(Lohrmann)*, Basil Appleby *(Jahner)*, Eric Clavering *(Art)*, Charles Victor *(Andreas)*, Ley On *(Nick the Eskimo)*, Richard George *(Bernsdorff)*, Peter Moore *(Kranz)*, Frederick Piper *(David)*, Tawera Moanna *(George, an Indian)*, Charles Rolfe *(Bob)*, O.W. Fonger, Theodore Salt *(U.S. Customs Officers)*.

Made in Montreal and at Denham, England, with second units providing awesome footage of the vast Canadian landscape, this war drama is one of the few episodic films to prove highly effective. This tense WW II drama unfolds when the U-37, a German submarine, surfaces in the Gulf of St. Lawrence. One of its officers, Portman, leads six crew members ashore to search for supplies and, from a hilltop, they witness two RCAF bombers attack the submarine and sink it. The stranded men then march to a trading outpost on Hudson's Bay which is run by Currie. Here they make a visiting French-Canadian trapper, Olivier, prisoner along with Currie. Olivier taunts them jocularly, telling the Germans that his father and others beat them in WW I and the same will happen again. A ham operator in the U.S. keeps calling the station to play his regular long distance chess game with Currie, and Portman and Lovell decide that the two must play chess or the U.S. operator might become suspicious. During the tense game, Olivier makes a break for the radio and tries to get out a message for which he is shot. He lies dying as the Germans attack and kill two company officers who arrive by seaplane the next day. Currie, bound in a chair, asks one of the young German seamen, MacGinnis, to give the dying Olivier his rosary and, after making sure he is not seen by the other Germans, the kind-hearted seaman presses the rosary into Olivier's hands, then goes to a wall and slashes the sign of the German swastika with his bayonet before leaving. The six Germans climb into the small seaplane and begin to take off. One of them hanging on the outside of the plane is shot by an Eskimo and falls dead into the water, thus allowing the overweight plane to take off. The plane runs out of gas, however, and crash lands in a lake, killing the inept pilot, Lovell. Portman and his three followers doggedly trek on, crossing vast stretches of Canada until coming to a German Hutterite encampment in Manitoba, a religious, peaceful farming community. Here a young girl, Johns, befriends them and takes them to the leader of the commune, Walbrook. Playing upon the German bloodlines of the group, Portman delivers a hortatory lecture to them about joining the Third Reich and its ambitions of global domination. The quiet, reserved Walbrook responds by telling Portman that "our Germany is dead . . . Our children grow up against new backgrounds, new horizons. And they are free! Free to grow up as children, free to run and to laugh without being forced into uniforms, without being forced to march up and down the streets singing battle songs! You talk about a new order in Europe! A new order . . . You and your Hitler are like the microbes of some filthy disease, filled with a longing to multiply yourselves until you destroy everything healthy in the world. No, we are not your brothers." When Portman later believes that Johns might tell authorities beyond the community about them, he orders her killed, but MacGinnis disobeys him and escorts the girl to her home. When the thoroughly rejected Nazis leave the farming settlement, Portman has MacGinnis, the only decent man in the lot, executed. The Nazis, now numbering three, come across a businessman changing a tire on his car and offer to help him. They kill him and take his clothes and car instead. Next they appear in Banff, Alberta, during the Indian celebrations. Here authorities make public announcements describing the wanted Nazis and one of them is grabbed. Portman and Chandos proceed on foot to a beautiful lake in the Three Sisters Mountain range and find successful writer Howard leisurely enjoying a fishing vacation while working on a book about Indian history and customs. Howard extends great hospitality to the two Nazis whom he thinks have wandered away from a nearby resort. In his tent he proudly displays his Picasso painting and rare books, including his precious Indian manuscript. They later destroy the painting, the manuscript, and tie up their host as they escape once more. Howard's men, however, free him and he tracks Chandos to a cave, advancing against the man who empties his gun at him, wounding him. Yet Howard enters the cave and knocks the Nazi cold, then emerges, surprised at his own bold actions, remarking to himself: "One armed superman against one unarmed decadent Democrat. I wonder how Dr. Goebbels will explain that?" Meanwhile, Portman, alone, tries to make it to the American border while German propagandists applaud his ability to escape capture, heralding him as a great Nazi superior to the Canadian forces tracking him. In southern Ontario, Portman stows away on board a train going into the U.S. Also in the freight car where he is hiding is Massey, a Canadian soldier gone AWOL who is trying to return to his post. Massey engages Portman in friendly conversation, telling him about his background, grousing about the military and how he hasn't been sent across the Atlantic to fight the Germans. He complains about military food and regulations and Portman immediately interprets this as a sign of political discontent. Massey is quick to tell him otherwise and Portman knocks him out and puts on his uniform. When the train comes to Niagara Falls, Portman holds a gun on Massey and both are sent across the border into the U.S., a country not then at war with Germany and one where Portman knows he will find political sanctuary until returned to the Fatherland. As the train crosses the border, Portman gloats about his victory, proclaiming himself to be a Nazi and how Germany will win the war against such weaklings as Massey. But at the border, Portman turns over his gun and demands that two American customs officials take him to the German Embassy. Massey explains that Portman is an escaping Nazi but the officials tell him that it's a job for immigration. Then Massey says that Portman is not on the shipping manifest and the enlightened officials return the car to Canada. As the train chugs back into Canada, Massey, wearing a big grin, advances upon the terrified Portman, and demands Portman return his uniform. "I'm not asking for those pants," Massey says. "I'm just taking them!" With that he cold-cocks the Nazi. THE INVADERS is expertly crafted and tautly directed by Powell, taking 18 months to complete, its meager $100,000 budget supplied by England's Ministry of Information. All the members of the outstanding cast worked on half salary as part of the war effort and, even though they are seen briefly, Olivier, Walbrook, and Howard, along with Portman, are electrifying. The script by Pressburger and Ackland is bright and intelligent and eschews overt patriotic antics. The Nazis are portrayed as insidious, divisive creatures who will ruthlessly destroy anyone in their path and without the slightest traces of humanity, except for MacGinnis. Sixty-nine-year-old Ralph Vaughn Williams was persuaded to compose the score, his first for films, which was brief but stirring, chiefly played with the opening credits which are shown over a slow pan of the Canadian Rockies. Two thirds of the film was shot in Canada and the crew and many cast members had to travel great distances to get the footage, all of which was impressive. Though the Canadian government assisted the production greatly, lending servicemen and policemen whenever necessary for shooting, it refused to lend the film company one of its few submarines for the opening shots. The tiny submarine force was then fully committed to patrolling Canadian waters. The U-37 shown in the opening scenes was an ingenious replica exclusively constructed for the movie in the Halifax, Nova Scotia, shipyards. The film was a great success, earning back its investment within three months of initial release, with American viewers, wholly sympathetic to the Allied war effort, universally endorsing the film and its powerful message. This story was probably inspired by the sensational escape of a German air force officer, Lt. Franz von Werra, from a Canadian prison camp. The fine German actress Elizabeth Bergner signed with Powell to play the Hutterite girl. She left England just as Hitler's armies were massing across the Channel to invade the home isles, but once in Canada and after a few weeks shooting, she defected from the film company and crossed into the U.S., obviously using her acting assignment as a pretext to reach a safe U.S. haven, an act for which she was later criticized severely. She was replaced by the talented British actress Johns, but Bergner can still be seen in long shots. The original running time for this film when released in England was 123 minutes, but several scenes, mostly those of a travelog nature, were cut from the film before its American release.

p, Michael Powell, John Sutro; d, Powell; w, Rodney Ackland, Emeric Pressburger (based on a story by Pressburger); ph, Frederick Young; m, Ralph Vaughn Williams; ed, David Lean; md, Muir Mathieson; art d, David Rawnsley; Canadian advisor, Nugent M. Cloucher.

War Drama **(PR:A MPAA:NR)**

INVADERS FROM MARS*** (1953) 73m FOX c

Jimmy Hunt *(David MacLean)*, Helena Carter *(Dr. Patricia Blake)*, Arthur Franz *(Dr. Stuart Kelston)*, Morris Ankrum *(Col. Fielding)*, Leif Erickson *(George MacLean)*, Hillary Brooke *(Mary MacLean)*, Max Wagner *(Sgt. Rinaldi)*, Milburn Stone *(Capt. Roth)*, Walter Sande *(Sgt. Finley)*, Janine Perreau *(Kathy Wilson)*, John Eldredge *(Mr. Turner)*, Robert Shayne *(Dr. Wilson)*, Luce Potter *(Martian Leader)*, Lock Martin, Max Palmer *(Mutants)*, Bill Phipps.

Nifty, atmospheric science fiction film. Hunt is a young boy who wakes in the middle of the night after hearing strange noises outside the house. He sees a spaceship land and burrow itself into the earth. Erickson, his father, goes out to investigate but returns with a strange air about him. Soon his mother is the same way, and Hunt discovers radios buried in their necks. When a neighbor girl disappears into the ground, he calls the police but to no avail. More people are controlled by the Martians until psychologist Carter and astronomer Franz come to help. Hunt and Carter are kidnaped by the creatures but saved in the nick of time by Ankrum, an army colonel who sends his troops in to destroy the Martian ship. The film ends with Hunter waking up; he has dreamed it all. But as he realizes it's all a dream the same noise he heard at the beginning happens once more. This is an unusual and well thought out film. Originally to be shot in 3-D, this was abandoned but it was the first film of its type to be shot in color. A longer European version ends differently: the story remains the same, though the nightmare ending is removed and an additional scene in an observatory is added.

p, Edward L. Alperson; d, William Cameron Menzies; w, Richard Blake, John Tucker Battle, Menzies (based on a story by Battle); ph, John F. Seitz (Cinecolor); m, Raoul Kraushaar; ed, Arthur Roberts; prod d, Menzies; art d, Boris Leven; cos, Norma; spec eff, Jack Cosgrove, Jack Rabin, Irving Block, Howard Lydecker; makeup, Gene Hibbs, Anatole Robbins.

Science Fiction **Cas.** **(PR:A MPAA:NR)**

INVASION 1/2** (1965, Brit.) 82m Merton Park bw

Edward Judd *(Dr. Vernon)*, Yoko Tani *(Lystrian Leader)*, Valerie Gearon *(Dr. Claire Harlan)*, Lyndon Brook *(Brian Carter)*, Tsai Chin *(Nurse Lim)*, Eric Young *(Lystrian Man)*, Barrie Ingham *(Maj. Muncaster)*, Glyn Houston *(Sgt. Draycott)*, Anthony Sharp *(Lawrence Blackburn)*, Jean Lodge *(Barbara Gough)*, Peter Sinclair *(Old Joe)*.

A low-budget science fiction picture which, instead of portraying a mass invasion of the world, concentrates on a small-scale invasion by a band of aliens who want a prisoner returned. After they crash their spaceship near an English hospital, Vernon takes it upon himself to harbor the alien criminal. The visitors surround the hospital but the doctor outwits them. Highly atmospheric.

p, Jack Greenwood; d, Alan Bridges; w, Roger Marshall (based on a story by Robert Holmes); ph, James Wilson; spec eff, Ronnie Whitehouse, Jack Kline, Stan Shields.

Science Fiction **(PR:A MPAA:NR)**

INVASION EARTH 2150 A.D.
(SEE: DALEKS—INVASION EARTH 2150 A.D., 1966, Brit.)

INVASION FORCE (SEE; HANGAR 18, 1980)

INVASION FROM THE MOON (SEE: MUTINY IN OUTER SPACE, 1965)

INVASION OF ASTRO-MONSTERS (SEE: MONSTER ZERO, 1970, Jap.)

INVASION OF THE ANIMAL PEOPLE* 1/2
(1962, U.S./Swed.) 55m Gustav Unger-Fortuna/ADP bw (RYMDINVASION I LAPPLAND; AKA: TERROR IN THE MIDNIGHT SUN; SPACE INVASION FROM LAPLAND; SPACE INVASION OF LAPLAND; HORROR IN THE MIDNIGHT SUN)

John Carradine *(Dr. Frederick Wilson/Narrator)*, Barbara Wilson *(Diane Wilson)*, Robert Burton *(Eric Engstrom)*, Bengt Blomgren *(Col. Robert Bottiger)*, Ake Gronberg *(Dr. Henrik)*, Brita Borg *(Singer)*, Stan Gester, Jack Haffner.

The Swedes and their U.S. cohorts took a lesson from the Japanese on this rampaging-monster movie, selectively cutting and adding new scenes for the English-language release. Star power was added in the form of Carradine—the Japanese more often used Raymond Burr—as the good investigative scientist, the part originally played by Burton, who was downgraded to Carradine's assistant. Mysteriously traumatized Wilson is sent to northern Sweden to recuperate with her geologist father, Carradine, who is exploring a strange meteor which recently fell to earth on a mountain in Lapland. The "meteor" proves to be a spaceship lodged in the snow, with enormous footprints leading from it. Wilson is captured by a hairy critter, but Carradine and Burton precipitate an avalanche, which frightens the furry fiend to the point where it packs up and takes off for home.

p, Bertil Jernberg, Jerry Warren; d, Virgil W. Vogel, Warren; w, Arthur C. Pierce; ph, Hilding Bladh, Warren; m, Allan Johannson, Harry Arnold, Pierce; art d, Nils Nilsson.

Science Fiction **(PR:A MPAA:NR)**

INVASION OF THE ASTROS (SEE: MONSTER ZERO, 1970, Jap.)

INVASION OF THE BEE GIRLS***
(1973) 85m Centaur c (AKA: GRAVEYARD TRAMPS)

William Smith *(Neil Agar)*, Anitra Ford *(Dr. Susan Harris)*, Victoria Vetri *(Julie Zorn)*, Cliff Osmund *(Capt. Peters)*, Wright King *(Dr. Henry Murger)*, Ben Hammer *(Herb Kline)*, Anna Aries *(Nora Kline)*, Andre Phillippe *(Aldo Ferrara)*, Sid Kaiser *(Stan Williams)*, Latie A. Saylor *(Gretchen Grubowsky)*, Beverly Powers *(Harriet Williams)*, Tom Pittman *(Harv)*, William Keller *(Joe)*.

A bizarre and perverse science fiction comedy about a genuine race of *femme fatales*. Federal agent Smith comes across the unbelievable report that a number of women have been transformed into "bee girls," who seduce men and kill them during love-making. He succeeds in dispatching the nymphomaniacs but in the end succumbs to one himself. Classy looking women help move this unlikely story to its ironic conclusion. Writer Meyer also wrote the novel *The Seven Per Cent Solution*, wrote the screenplay for the same, wrote and directed TIME AFTER TIME (1979), and directed STAR TREK: THE WRATH OF KHAN (1982).

d, Denis Sanders; w, Nicholas Meyer; ph, Gary Graver (CFI Color); m, Chuck Bernstein; ed, B. and R. Travis.

Science Fiction/Comedy **Cas.** **(PR:O MPAA:R)**

INVASION OF THE BLOOD FARMERS* (1972) 84m NMO c

Cynthia Fleming *(Onhorrid)*, Norman Kelly *(Roy)*, Tanna Hunter *(Jenny)*, Bruce Detrick *(Don)*, Frank Iovieno *(Chief)*.

A disappointingly bad horror quickie which can only boast a good title and a finale that is tinted red, with everything in between a crop gone rotten. The local townsfolk are being terrorized by a group of killers who drain people's blood to nourish their coffin-confined Queen.

p&d, Ed Adlum; w, Adlum, Ed Kelleher.

Horror **Cas.** **(PR:O MPAA:PG)**

INVASION OF THE BODY SNATCHERS**** (1956) 80m AA bw

Kevin McCarthy *(Miles Bennel)*, Dana Wynter *(Becky Driscoll)*, Larry Gates *(Dr. Dan Kauffmann)*, King Donovan *(Jack)*, Carolyn Jones *(Theodora)*, Jean Willes *(Sally)*, Ralph Dumke *(Nick Grivett)*, Virginia Christine *(Wilma Lentz)*, Tom Fadden *(Uncle Ira Lentz)*, Kenneth Patterson *(Driscoll)*, Guy Way *(Sam Janzek)*, Eileen Stevens *(Mrs. Grimaldi)*, Beatrice Maude *(Grandma)*, Jean Andren *(Aunt Eleda Lentz)*, Bobby Clark *(Jimmy)*, Everett Glass *(Pursey)*, Dabbs Greer *(Mac)*, Pat O'Malley *(Man Carrying Baggage)*, Guy Rennie *(Proprietor)*, Marie Selland *(Martha)*, Whit Bissell *(Dr. Hall)*, Sam Peckinpah *(Charlie Buckholtz)*, Richard Deacon *(Dr. Harvey Bassett)*, Harry J. Vejar *(with Man Carrying Baggage)*

This low-budget science fiction tale is a superbly crafted film by innovative director Siegel and later became one of the great cult classics of the genre. McCarthy, a doctor from the small town of Santa Mira, arrives in San Francisco in an hysterical condition; he raves to physician Bissell that his community has been invaded by aliens who have literally taken over the bodies of his friends and relatives. He's a candidate for the lunatic asylum, most agree, but Bissell hears him out and we see the story unfold in flashback. McCarthy returns from a medical convention to Santa Mira to find a great number of people jamming his office to complain that their loved ones are acting so strangely that it is doubted they are the same people, let alone human. McCarthy is sidetracked from following up his curiosity by stunning beauty Wynter, an old girlfriend who has returned home after being divorced. The next day McCarthy's suspicions are aroused even more when those who had been swamping his office with complaints the day earlier tell him that there's nothing to worry about, that they were merely being silly. Later that night McCarthy and Wynter have dinner with friends Donovan and Jones and, to their horror, they find enormous pods growing in Donovan's greenhouse, and these are slowly transforming into the exact physical reproductions of Donovan, Jones, Wynter, and McCarthy. McCarthy and Wynter run for their lives with half the population turned into an alien force. The police have been taken over and even the once friendly gas station owner refuses to sell McCarthy enough gas to get out of town, saying his pumps are empty. The phone system is also under the alien grip; when McCarthy tries to call federal authorities he is told by operators that all the lines to Washington, D.C., are tied up. He and Wynter take refuge in his office, sleeping there over night. At dawn they see trucks from many farms arrive in the local square with townspeople dumbly removing pods from the trucks and taking them to cars, these pods to be taken to neighboring towns where the pods will transform themselves into other human forms. Town psychiatrist Gates arrives with others and brings along a couple of pods which are placed in the next room. Gates explains that all Wynter and McCarthy have to do is go to sleep and they will awake as one of the new creatures and will never again know pain, no hate, no worry, no problems. But, McCarthy adds, there will also be no joy nor love, and this he and Wynter reject. They overpower Gates and guards and flee, running out of the town to hide in a cave. Later Wynter goes to sleep and is transformed into an alien, a fact easily learned by McCarthy when kissing her. She cries out for the aliens to come and get McCarthy and he flees, followed closely by the aliens. McCarthy manages to outdistance his pursuers and make it to the freeway leading into San Francisco. There he shouts and waves at passing cars, warning them of the coming aliens; it's a nightmare scene as hundreds of motorists simply ignore him, thinking him drunk or crazy. He is finally taken to Bissell for examination. He is about to be judged unbalanced when Bissell learns that a truck from Santa Mira has overturned and that strange pods have fallen from the vehicle. Bissell quickly believes McCarthy's wild story and alerts the local police and the FBI to seal off Santa Mira; the world is finally waking up to the alien invasion, it seems. This film was originally intended by producer Wanger as a good B-programmer but Siegel made much more of it, with writers Mainwaring and (uncredited) Peckinpah (a future director of bloody action films) injecting it with subtle humor and no little horror. It's a quick paced chiller that captivates the viewer with every tension-filled scene. Much has been read into this story, some claiming it was a subtle attack on McCarthyism and political witchhunts of the era, others claiming it was strongly anti-Communist, indicting the Big Brother system. Wanger, upon viewing the film, had much of Peckinpah's black humor lines taken out and several scenes were cut. The McCarthy prolog and epilog with Bissell were added to lessen the feeling of hopelessness. The film was remade in 1978 with an enormous budget and lavish production values but it came nowhere near to being as frightening and effective as the original.

p, Walter Wanger; d, Don Siegel; w, Daniel Mainwaring, (uncredited) Sam Peckinpah (based on the novel *The Body Snatchers* by Jack Finney); ed, Robert S. Eisen; prod d, Joseph Kish; ph, Ellsworth Fredericks; m, Carmen Dragon; art d, Edward Haworth; spec eff, Milt Rice.

Science Fiction **Cas.** **(PR:A MPAA:NR)**

INVASION OF THE BODY SNATCHERS ½** (1978) 115m UA c

Donald Sutherland *(Matthew Bennell)*, Brooke Adams *(Elizabeth Driscoll)*, Leonard Nimoy *(Dr. David Kibner)*, Veronica Cartwright *(Nancy Bellicec)*, Art Hindle *(Geoffrey)*, Lelia Goldoni *(Katherine)*, Kevin McCarthy *(Running Man)*, Jeff Goldblum *(Jack Bellicec)*, Don Siegel *(Cab Driver)*.

This is a colorful and expensive remake of the 1956 sci-fi classic, and it's pretty good through the first half of the film, with mopey, sleepy-eyed Sutherland playing the part originated by Kevin McCarthy as a health inspector giving a hard time to San Francisco restaurant owners when finding rat droppings in their kitchens. Instead of a little town in California, as was the setting in the original film, the whole sprawling city of San Francisco is now under alien attack by the mysterious pods, with Nimoy as the psychiatrist advocating the takeover. The film collapses midway through unsure and sloppy direction, splintered story continuity, and overacting on the part of Adams, Cartwright, and others. The battle between Sutherland and the aliens in the "pod factory" at the end is simply absurd and sophomoric. As a nod to the earlier classic, McCarthy appears at the beginning of the film, shouting hysterical warnings to motorists until he is struck and killed by a car. A great number of shots show the Transamerica pyramid building in downtown San Francisco, a subtle self-plug for the movie since its distributor has its corporate offices in this building.

p, Robert H. Solo; d, Philip Kaufman; w, W. D. Richter (based on the novel by Jack Finney); ph, Michael Chapman (Technicolor); m, Denny Zeitlin; ed, Douglas Stewart; prod d, Charles Rosen; spec eff, Dell Rheaume, Russ Hessey.

Science Fiction **Cas.** **(PR:C-O MPAA:PG)**

INVASION OF THE BODY STEALERS

(SEE: BODY STEALERS, THE, 1969, Brit.)

INVASION OF THE FLYING SAUCERS

(SEE: EARTH VERSUS THE FLYING SAUCERS, 1956)

INVASION OF THE HELL CREATURES

(SEE: INVASION OF THE SAUCER MEN, 1957)

INVASION OF THE SAUCER MEN* ½

(1957) 69m AIP bw (AKA: INVASION OF THE HELL CREATURES; THE HELL CREATURES; SPACEMEN SATURDAY NIGHT)

Steve Terrell *(Johnny)*, Gloria Castillo *(Joan)*, Frank Gorshin *(Joe)*, Raymond Hatton *(Larkin)*, Lyn Osborn *(Art)*, Russ Bender *(Doctor)*, Douglas Henderson *(Lt. Wilkins)*, Sam Buffington *(Colonel)*, Jason Johnson *(Detective)*, Don Shelton *(Mr. Hayden)*, Scott Peters *(1st Soldier)*, Jan Englund *(Waitress)*, Kelly Thordsen *(Sgt. Bruce)*, Bob Einer *(Soda Jerk)*, Patti Lawler *(Irene)*, Calvin Booth *(Paul)*, Ed Nelson, Jim Bridges *(Boys)*, Roy Darmour *(Sgt. Gordon)*, Audrey Conti, Joan Dupuis *(Girls)*, Jimmy Pickford, Orv Mohler *(Boys in Soda Shop)*, Buddy Mason *(Policeman)*, Angelo Rossito, Floyd Dixon, Dean Neville, Edward Peter Gibbons.

A science fiction picture which is intentionally funny. Terrell and Castillo are newlyweds who accidentally run over a Martian. The vengeful little green men plot to get back at the lovers by turning them into alcoholics. This is accomplished by drunk-inducing injections from the Martians' needle-like fingertips. The couple, however, discover that the Martians evaporate when hit with car headlight beams. Comedian and impressionist Gorshin spends his time trying to hide an alien in his refrigerator. Paul Blaisdell's creatures were a bunch of midgets with oversized, brain-exposed heads. Remade in 1965 as THE EYE CREATURES.

p, James H. Nicholson, Robert J. Gurney, Jr.; d, Edward L. Cahn; w, Gurney, Jr., Al Martin (based on a story by Paul Fairman); ph, Frederick E. West; m, Ronald Stein; ed, Ronald Sinclair, Charles Gross, Jr.; art d, Don Ament; spec eff, Paul Blaisdell, Howard A. Anderson.

Science Fiction/Comedy **(PR:C MPAA:NR)**

INVASION OF THE STAR CREATURES* (1962) 70m AIP bw

Robert Ball *(Philbrick)*, Frankie Ray *(Penn)*, Gloria Victor *(Dr. Tanga)*, Dolores Reed *(Professor Puna)*, Mark Ferris *(Colonel Rank)*, Slick Slavin, Mark Thompson, Sid Kane, Mike Del Piano, Lenore Bond, Anton Van Stralen, James Almanzar, Allen Dailey, Joseph Martin.

A moronic low-budget science fiction comedy with an Abbott and Costello-type team of soldiers (Ball and Ray), who wander away from the ranks. They discover some poorly costumed star creatures and follow them into a cave, where they find, instead of the creatures, two sexy alien scientists who control the others. They have come to earth to conquer it, but the two bungling soldiers save the day by winning over the woman invaders and giving them their first kisses.

p, Berj Hagopian; d, Bruno Ve Sota; w, Jonathan Haze; ph, Basil Bradbury; m, Jack Cookerly, Elliott Fisher; prod d, Amos Powell; ed, Lewis J. Guinn; art d, Mike McCloskey; cos, Dell Adams; makeup, Joseph Kinder.

Science Fiction/Comedy **(PR:A MPAA:NR)**

INVASION OF THE VAMPIRES, THE*

(1961, Mex.) 92m Tele-Talia/Trans-International bw (LA INVASION DE LOS VAMPIROS)

Carlos Agosti *(Count Frankenhausen)*, Rafael Etienne, Bertha Moss, Tito Junco, Erna Martha Bauman, Fernando Soto, Enrique Garcia Alvarez, David Reynoso, Rafael del Rio.

A low-budget Mexican horror picture that shows off some nicely atmospheric 16th century sets, but has a story which is all too familiar. A vampire expert is out to convince a young lady that her father, a count, is a bloodsucking killer. He realizes his pleas are falling on the deaf ears of the daughter, who is under her father's spell. After vampires descend on the village, the usual bat transformations occur and the count is killed by an acid injection. The vampires return to their graves and the town is saved. No surprises here.

p, Rafael Perez Grovas; d&w, Miguel Morayta; ph, Raul Martinez Solares; m, Luis Hernandez; ed, Gloria Schoemann; art d, Manuel Fontanals.

Horror **(PR:O MPAA:NR)**

INVASION OF THE ZOMBIES

(SEE: HORROR OF PARTY BEACH, THE, 1964)

INVASION QUARTET** (1961, Brit.) 87m MGM bw

Bill Travers *(Maj. Freddie Oppenheimer)*, Spike Milligan *(Lt. Godfrey Pringle)*, John LeMesurier *(Colonel)*, Gregoire Aslan *(Maj. Pierre Debrie)*, Maurice Denham *(Dr. Barker)*, Millicent Martin *(Sister Kay Manning)*, Thorley Walters *(Lt. Cmdr. Cummings)*, Thelma Ruby *(Matron)*, Cyril Luckham *(Col. Harbottle)*, John Wood *(Duty Officer)*, Bernard Hunter *(Coding Officer)*, Alexander Archdale *(Brigadier)*, David Lander *(Maquis Leader)*, William Mervyn *(Naval Officer)*, Peter Swanwick *(German

Gun Commander), Ernst Ulman *(German Sergeant)*, Eric Sykes *(German Band Conductor)*, Ian Ainsley *(German Officer)*, Gerald Case, John Dunbar *(Medical Board Officers)*, Charles Brodie *(Maquis Deputy Leader)*, John Crocker *(The Storeman)*.

A group of injured officers escapes from a military hospital and devises a plan to shell a Nazi cannon. They proceed across the English Channel in a stolen boat, sneak into France, and dismantle the weapon. They try to bicycle back to safety disguised as Germans, but are captured by members of the French Resistance, who naturally mistake them for the enemy. They are released finally, hailed as heroes, and sent on another mission by British intelligence. A comedy that works in spots, especially in its slapstick routines.

p, Ronald Kinnoch; d, Jay Lewis; w, Jack Trevor Story, John Briley (based on a story by Norman Collins); ph, Geoffrey Faithfull, Gerald Moss; m, Ron Goodwin; ed, Ernest Walter; art d, Elliot Scott; makeup, Jim Hydes.

War/Comedy **(PR:A MPAA:NR)**

INVASION 1700* 1/2

(1965, Fr./Ital./Yugo.) 112m Europa-Comptoir-Kosutnjak/Medallion c (COL FERRO E COL FUOCO; AKA: WITH FIRE AND SWORD; DAGGERS OF BLOOD)

Jeanne Crain *(Elena)*, John Drew Barrymore *(Bohun)*, Pierre Brice *(Col. Jan Ketusky)*, Akim Tamiroff *(Baron Zagloba)*, Elena Zareschi *(Princess Kinzevich)*, Gordon Mitchell *(Ulrich)*, Raoul Grassilli *(Basilio)*, Bruno Nessi *(Longhin)*, Eleonora Vargas *(Horpina)*, Gabriella Andreini *(Anussia)*, Nerio Bernardi *(Geremia)*, Giacomo Rossi Stuart, Ornella Vanoni, Nando Angelini, Alberto Stefanini, Milena Vukotic, Marcello Selmi, Alberto Mareschalchi, Alberto Archetti.

A 17th Century costumer about a Polish colonel, Brice, who falls in love with princess Crain, who is already betrothed to Ukraine commander Barrymore. The charming Brice convinces the princess to break off her engagement and leave with him. Barrymore, however, retaliates by setting Crain's palace afire and killing all inside. He kidnaps the princess and engineers an attack on Brice's unit. The Poles stand their ground, Barrymore is killed, and Crain and Brice are reunited. Filled with the usual bland ingredients that accompany so many of these pasta imports.

d, Fernando Cerchio; w, Henry Sienkiewickz (based on his novel *The Elite of the Crowd)*; ph, Pier Ludovico Pavoni (Euroscope, Eastmancolor); m, Giovanni Fusco, Francesco De Masi; prod d, Gianpaolo Bigazzi, Jean Maumy; ed, Antonietta Zita; art d, Arrigo Equini; cos, Giancarlo Bartolini Salimbeni.

War Drama **(PR:C MPAA:NR)**

INVASION U.S.A.** (1952) 73m AM/COL bw

Gerald Mohr *(Vince)*, Peggie Castle *(Carla)*, Dan O'Herlihy *(Mr. Ohman)*, Robert Bice *(George Sylvester)*, Tom Kennedy *(Bartender)*, Wade Crosby *(Congressman)*, Erik Blythe *(Ed Mulvory)*, Phyllis Coates *(Mrs. Mulvory)*, Aram Katcher *(5th Column Leader)*, Edward G. Robinson, Jr., Noel Neill.

An interesting piece about the threat of communism and nuclear war. O'Herlihy is a stranger who pays a visit to a New York bar and convinces people inside that the H-bomb has been unleashed on America. They react accordingly, some taking their own lives, until they realize that they have been hypnotized by O'Herlihy. It is full of propaganda, stock footage, and overacting, but it still relays a provocative message about this country's ignorance of nuclear obliteration.

p, Albert Zugsmith, Robert Smith; d, Alfred E. Green; w, Smith (based on a story by Smith, Franz Spencer); ph, John L. Russell; m, Albert Glasser; ed, W. Donn Hayes; art d, James Sullivan; set d, John Sturtevant.

Drama **(PR:A MPAA:NR)**

INVESTIGATION OF A CITIZEN ABOVE SUSPICION* 1/2**

(1970, Ital.) 112m Vera/COL c (INDAGINE SU UN CITTADINO AL DI SOPRA DI OGNI SOSPETTO)

Gian Maria Volonte *(Police Inspector)*, Florinda Bolkan *(Augusta Terzi)*, Salvo Randone *(Plumber)*, Gianni Santuccio *(Police Commissioner)*, Arturo Dominici *(Mangani)*, Orazio Orlando *(Biglia)*, Sergio Tramonti *(Antonio Pace)*, Massimo Foschi *(Augusta's Husband)*, Aldo Rendine *(Homicide Functionary)*, Aleka Paizi, Vittorio Duse, Pino Patti, Giuseppe Licastro, Filippo Degara, Fulvio Gramaldi, Ugo Adinolfi, Giacomo Bellini, Giuseppe Terranova, Vincenzo Falanga, Roberto Bonanni, Guido Buzzelli, Gino Usai, Franco Marletta.

The winner of 1970's foreign film Oscar, this Italian picture tells the story of a recently promoted police inspector (Volonte) who, one Sunday afternoon, slits his mistress' throat. He then plants phony evidence and makes an anonymous call to report the crime. The police unearth some clues that point to Volonte, but ignore them due to the suspect's standing. The killer eventually writes a confession and awaits his capture, while planning to receive an acquittal. A superb look into the mind of a killer, as well as a pointed satire of investigative techniques in fascist Italy, as seen by Communist Petri. (In Italian: English subtitles.)

p, Daniele Senatore; d, Elio Petri; w, Ugo Pirro, Petri; ph, Luigi Kuveiller (Technicolor); m, Ennio Morricone; ed, Ruggero Mastroianni; prod d, Romano Cardarelli, md, Bruno Nicolai; cos, Angela Sammaciccia, Mayer; makeup, Franco Corridoni; English subtitles, Sonya Mays Friedman.

Crime **(PR:O MPAA:R)**

INVESTIGATION OF MURDER, AN

(SEE: LAUGHING POLICEMAN, THE, 1973)

INVINCIBLE GLADIATOR, THE* 1/2

(1963, c.u. Ital./Span.) 96m Film Columbus-Variety-Atenea/SevenArts c (IL GLADIATORE INVINCIBLE; EL GLADIADOR INVENCIBLE)

Richard Harrison *(Rezius)*, Isabelle Corey *(Sira)*, Livio Lorenzon *(Itus)*, Leo Anchoriz *(Rabirius)*, Jose Marco Davo *(Vibius)*, Ricardo Canales, Antonio Molino, Edoardo Nevola, Jole Mauro, Giorgio Ubaldi.

Gladiator Harrison is given command of an army after saving the life of Anchoriz, an evil ruler who governs in the name of a 10 year old king. When Anchoriz tries to take everything for himself and kill both Harrison and the youngster, the heroic gladiator fights back, killing the greedy ruler.

p, Cleto Fontini, Italo Zingarelli, Alberto De Martino; d, Frank Gregory; w, Francesco De Feo, Francesco Thellung, Fontini; ph, Eloy Mella (Techniscope, Technicolor); m, Carlo Franci; art d, Santiago Ontanon.

Adventure **(PR:C MPAA:NR)**

INVINCIBLE SIX, THE zero

(1970, U.S./Iran) 96m Moulin Rouge/Continental c

Stuart Whitman *(Tex)*, Elke Sommer *(Zari)*, Curt Jurgens *(The Baron)*, Ian Ogilvy *(Ronald)*, Behrooz Vosugi *(Jahan)*, Lon Sutton *(Mike)*, Isarco Ravaioli *(Giorgio)*, James Mitchum *(Nazar)*, Anoush Artin *(Capt. Baruk)*, Warrene Ott *(Shirine)*, Shai Nazemi *(Crown Jewels Guide)*, Manoocher Naderi *(Mayor)*, Homayoon Bahadoran *(Fake Officer)*, Amir Jafari *(Darab)*, Poori Banai *(Jahan's Wife)*, Iran Dafteri *(Malik's Mother)*, Susan Ghasemi *(Village Girl)*.

A U.S.-Iran co-production tells the tale of a gang of thieves who, after failing to steal the crown jewels of Tehran, flee in the direction of another adventure. They roll into a village that is constantly raided by bandits and badly in need of protection. They offer their protection to the townspeople and inhabitant Sommer, who is determined to get her hands on a hidden treasure. One gang member is kidnaped during a raid and the thieves retaliate by burning the bandit village to the ground. In the midst of all this destruction, Sommer's treasure map is destroyed, prompting her to join the thieves on yet another adventure. Rudolf Nureyev (yes, the dancer) served as choreographer.

p, Mostafa Akavan; d, Jean Negulesco; w, Guy Elmes, Chester Erskine (based on the novel *The Heroes of Yucca* by Michael Barrett); ph, Piero Portalupi (Movielab Color); m, Manos Hadjidakis; ed, Derek York; prod d, Hushang Shafti; art d, Ivan Girard; set d, Pak Nejad; cos, Shai Nazemi; makeup, Giannetto De Rossi, Fabrizio Sforza; ch, Rudolf Nureyev; spec eff, Benasseti Pasquino.

Adventure **Cas.** **(PR:A MPAA:NR)**

INVISIBLE AGENT 1/2** (1942) 79m UNIV bw

Ilona Massey *(Maria Sorenson)*, Jon Hall *(Frank Raymond)*, Peter Lorre *(Baron Ikito)*, Sir Cedric Hardwicke *(Conrad Stauffer)*, J. Edward Bromberg *(Karl Heiser)*, Albert Basserman *(Arnold Schmidt)*, John Litel *(John Gardner)*, Holmes Herbert *(Sir Alfred Spencer)*, Keye Luke *(Surgeon)*, Philip Van Zandt *(Nazi SS Man)*, Matt Willis *(Nazi Assassin)*, Mabel Colcord *(Maid)*, John Holland *(Spencer's Secretary)*, Marty Faust *(Killer)*, Alberto Morin *(Free Frenchman)*, Henry Guttman *(Storm Trooper)*, Wolfgang Zilzer *(Von Porten)*, Ferdinand Munier *(Bartender)*, Eddie Dunn, Hans Schumm *(SS Men)*, John Burton *(RAF Flier)*, Lee Tung-Foo *(Gen. Chin Lee)*, Milburn Stone *(German Sergeant)*, Michael Visaroff *(Verichen)*, Walter Tetley *(Newsboy)*, Pat West *(German Taxi Driver)*, Leslie Denison *(British Radio Operator)*, William Ruhl, Otto Reichow *(Gestapo Agents)*, Bobby Hale, Wally Scott *(English Tommies)*, Mabel Conrad *(Housekeeper)*, Charles Flynn, Phil Warren, Paul Bryar, John Merton *(German Soldiers)*, Lee Shumway *(Brigadier General)*, Henry Zynder *(Col. Kelenski)*, Ferdinand Schumann-Heink *(German Telephone Operator)*, Victor Zimmerman, Bill Pagan *(Storm Troopers)*, Lane Chandler, Duke York, Donald Curtis *(German Sentries)*, Charles Regan *(Ordnance Car Driver)*, Sven Hugo-Borg *(German Captain)*, James Craven *(Ship's Radio Man)*, Pat McVey *(German)*.

The third sequel to 1933's THE INVISIBLE MAN, which now has the secret formula being used to defeat the Nazis. In the lead role, Hall takes the drug and succeeds in baffling the Germans as he goes around gathering important information—such as the plans for an aerial attack on New York—for the Allies. Lorre is cast in a variation on his Mr. Moto character as a malevolent Japanese officer who resorts to committing hara-kiri. Siodmak's script delivers a number of intentional laughs, plus a fair amount of unintentional ones.

p, Frank Lloyd; d, Edwin L. Marin; w, Curtis Siodmak (based on characters suggested in H.G. Wells's *The Invisible Man)*; ph, Lester White; m, H.J. Salter; ed, Edward Curtiss; art d, Jack Otterson; spec eff; John P. Fulton.

Spy/Fantasy **(PR:A MPAA:NR)**

INVISIBLE AVENGER, THE 1/2**

(1958) 60m REP bw (AKA: BOURBON ST. SHADOWS)

Richard Derr *(Lamont Cranston/The Shadow)*, Mark Daniels *(Jogendra)*, Helen Westcott *(Tara)*, Jeanne Neher *(Felicia Ramirez)*, Dan Mullin *(Pablo Ramirez)*, Lee Edwards *(Colonel)*, Jack Doner *(Billy)*, Steve Dano *(Tony Alcalde)*, Leo Bruno *(Rocco)*, Sam Page *(Charlie)*.

Derr is super detective "The Shadow," who can make himself invisible in this suspense picture based on the exploits of the famed radio character. While looking into the murder of a New Orleans jazzman Derr finds the mystery takes a few unusual twists, leading him all the way to an exiled Latin American dictator. In 1962 the film was re-released as BOURBON ST. SHADOWS with additional footage tacked on, under the direction of Parker. The film's original director Howe was a noted cinematographer in the 1940s and 1950s.

p, Eric Sayers, Emanuel Demby; d, James Wong Howe, John Sledge, Ben Parker;

w, George Bellak, Betty Jeffries; ph, Willis Winford, Joseph Wheeler; ed, John Hemel; md, Edward Dutreil.

Mystery **(PAR: MPAA:NR)**

INVISIBLE BOY, THE*** (1957) 90m Pan/MGM bw

Richard Eyer *(Timmie Merrinoe)*, Philip Abbott *(Dr. Merrinoe)*, Diane Brewster *(Mary Merrinoe)*, Harold J. Stone *(Gen. Swayne)*, Robert H. Harris *(Prof. Allerton)*, Dennis McCarthy *(Col. Macklin)*, Alexander Lockwood *(Arthur Kelvaney)*, John O'Malley *(Dr. Baine)*, Gage Clark, Than Wyenn, Jefferson Dudley Searles, Alfred Linder, Ralph Votrian, Michael Miller.

An underrated science-fiction film about a young boy, Eyer, and his relationship with Robby the Robot (a refugee from FORBIDDEN PLANET). Eyer's dad is a genius who invents a supercomputer that soon begins to act on its own, taking over the "conscience" of Robby. Eyer puts an end to the chaos by smashing his father's machine, a deed the father can't bear to do. The picture's strong point comes from its viewpoint—that of the child. Everything that occurs favors Eyer and the sympathetic robot, making the adults in the picture appear as insensitive as the machines. It is the robot that becomes a surrogate father to Eyer, in much the same way as the alien in Steven Spielberg's E.T.

p, Nicholas Nayfack; d, Herman Hoffman; w, Cyril Hume (based on a story by Edmund Cooper); ph, Harold Wellman; m, Les Baxter; ed, John Faure; art d, Merrill Pye; spec eff Jack Rabin, Irving Block, Louis DeWitt.

Science Fiction **(PR:AA MPAA:NR)**

INVISIBLE CREATURE, THE

(SEE: HOUSE IN MARSH ROAD, THE, 1959, Brit.)

INVISIBLE DR. MABUSE, THE***

(1965, Ger.) 89m CCC/Thunder bw (DIE UNSICHTBAREN KRALLEN DES DR. MABUSE; AKA: THE INVISIBLE HORROR)

Lex Barker *(Joe Como)*, Karin Dor *(Liane Martin)*, Siegfried Lowitz *(Inspector Brahm)*, Wolfgang Preiss *(Dr. Mabuse)*, Rudolf Fernau *(Professor Erasmus)*, Kurd Pieritz *(Dr. Bardorf)*, Walo Luond *(Detective Hase)*, Heinrich Gies *(Optician)*, Hans Schwarz *(Max)*, Werner Peters, Martin Droste, Bobo the Clown, Carl de Voigt *(Floor Walker)*.

Priess plays the villainous Dr. Mabuse (as he did in Fritz Lang's THE THOUSAND EYES OF DR. MABUSE) in this addition to the German series. This time Priess wants to get his hands on a potion known as "Operation X," which makes people invisible. Invented by the badly disfigured Fernau to keep his girlfriend (Dor) from seeing his face, it ends up in the evil Mabuse's hands when Dor is kidnaped. New York detective Barker arrives on the scene and prevents an invisible Mabuse army from taking over the world.

p, Arthur Brauner; d, Harold Reinl; w, Ladislas Fodor; ph, Ernst W. Kalinke; m, Peter Sandloff; ed, Hermann Haller; prod d, Heinz Gotze; art d, Gabriel Pellon, Oskar Pietsch; cos, Irms Pauli; spec eff, Karl-Ludwig Ruppel; makeup, Heinz Stamm.

Horror **(PR:C MPAA:NR)**

INVISIBLE ENEMY* ½ (1938) 66m REP bw

Alan Marshal *(Jeffrey Clavering)*, Tala Birell *(Sandra)*, Mady Correll *(Stephanie)*, C. Henry Gordon *(Kamarov)*, Herbert Mundin *(Higgs)*, Gerald Oliver Smith *(Bassett)*, Ivan Simpson *(Michael)*, Elsa Buchanan *(Sophia)*, Dwight Frye *(Alex)*, Leonard Willey *(Donbridge)*, Ian Maclaren *(Sir Joshua)*, Egon Brecher *(Kirman)*.

Marshal plays the investigator for a large British oil company, whose heroics know no bounds as he uses his ingenuity to divert disaster from his oil company, not to mention the rest of the world. Gordon is brilliant as the chief menace in Marshal's path, though his personality lurks beneath a preposterous plot which is nearly impossible to weave through.

d, John H. Auer; w, Albert J. Cohen, Alex Gottlieb, Norman Burnstine (based on the story by Cohen, Robert T. Shannon); ph, Jack Marta; ed, William Morgan.

Crime/Mystery **(PR:A MPAA:NR)**

INVISIBLE GHOST, THE* (1941) 66m BAN/MONO bw

Bela Lugosi *(Dr. Charles Kessler)*, Polly Ann Young *(Virginia)*, John McGuire *(Ralph)*, Clarence Muse *(Evans)*, Terry Walker *(Cecile)*, Betty Compson *(Mrs. Kessler)*, Ernie Adams *(Jules)*, George Pembroke *(Williams)*, Fred Kelsey *(Ryan)*, Jack Mulhall *(Tim)*.

Not one of Lugosi's choice roles, this film was the first he made in a three-picture deal for Monogram. The story has Lugosi as a sweet and kindly old doctor who thinks his lovely wife, Compson, is dead. She is alive, but has amnesia. When Lugosi sees her alive, he goes into a spell of homicidal insanity, causing him to try to strangle anyone within choking distance.

p, Sam Katzman; d, Joseph H. Lewis; w, Helen Martin, Al Martin; ph, Marcel Le Picard; ed, Robert Golden.

Horror **Cas.** **(PR:C MPAA:NR)**

INVISIBLE HORROR, THE

(SEE: INVISIBLE DR. MABUSE, THE, 1965, Ger.)

INVISIBLE INFORMER* ½ (1946) 57m REP bw

Linda Stirling *(Eve Rogers)*, William Henry *(Mike Reagan)*, Adele Mara *(Marie Ravelle)*, Gerald Mohr *(Eric Baylor)*, Peggy Stewart *(Rosalind Baylor)*, Donia Bussey *(Grandma Shroud)*, Claire DuBray *(Martha Baylor)*, Tristam Coffin *(David Baylor)*, Tom London *(Eph Shroud)*, Charles Lane *(Nick Steele)*, Cy Kendall *(Sheriff Ladeau)*, Francis McDonald *(Jules Ravelle)*.

A pair of private eyes with the usual romantic interests try to track down a missing necklace insured for $100,000. A trail of bodies which have either been strangled or torn apart by police dogs leads the snooping duo to the culprit. Actress Linda Stirling was better known for starring in serials before retiring in 1947, and attending college; since 1965 she has been an associate professor of English and drama at Glendale College in California.

p, William J. O'Sullivan; d, Philip Ford; w, Sherman L. Lowe (based on a story by Gerald Drayson Adams); ph, William Bradford; ed, Richard L. Van Enger; art d, James Sullivan.

Mystery **(PR:A MPAA:NR)**

INVISIBLE INVADERS* ½ (1959) 67m Premium/UA bw

John Agar *(Maj. Bruce Jay)*, Jean Byron *(Phyllis Penner)*, Robert Hutton *(Dr. John LaMont)*, John Carradine *(Dr. Karol Noymann)*, Philip Tonge *(Dr. Adam Penner)*, Hal Torey *(The Farmer)*, Eden Hartford *(WAAF Secretary)*, Jack Kenney *(Cab Driver)*, Paul Langton *(Gen. Stone)*, Don Kennedy *(Pilot)*, Chuck Niles *(Hockey Game Announcer)*.

In the days before it was common knowledge that moon monsters didn't exist, this sort of picture ran rampant. Again those dastardly moonmen try to take over planet Earth. This time, however, they have a compelling plot. In a precursor to NIGHT OF THE LIVING DEAD, the aliens take over the bodies of dead earthlings and nearly conquer the world before Agar saves the day. He comes up with a machine that emits high-frequency sounds to drive the aliens back to their own turf. Carradine has a small role as a dead scientist who leads the zombie forces out of their graves.

p, Robert E. Kent; d, Edward L. Cahn; w, Samuel Newman; ph, Maury Gertsman; ed, Grant Whytock; art d, William Glasgow; spec eff, Roger George; makeup, Phil Scheer.

Science Fiction **(PR:C MPAA:NR)**

INVISIBLE KILLER, THE* ½ (1940) 61m PRC bw

Grace Bradley *(Sue)*, Roland Drew *(Jerry)*, William Newell *(Pat)*, Alex Callam *(Ensler)*, Frank Coletti *(Vani)*, Sydney Grayler *(Lefty)*, Clem Wilenchick *(Sutton)*, Boyd Irwin *(Cunningham)*, Jeanne Kelly *(Gloria)*.

A hokey plot about poison fumes traveling through telephone lines that probably wouldn't work even if Alfred Hitchcock had directed. Reporter Bradley gets some help from cop Drew to capture the mysterious killer caller.

p, Sigmund Neufeld; d, Sherman Scott [Sam Newfield]; w, Joseph O'Donnell (based on a story by Carter Wayne); ph, Jack Greenhalgh; ed, Holbrook N. Todd.

Mystery **Cas.** **(PR:A MPAA:NR)**

INVISIBLE MAN, THE* ½** (1933) 71m UNIV bw

Claude Rains *(Jack Griffin, The Invisible One)*, Gloria Stuart *(Flora Cranley)*, William Harrigan *(Doctor Kemp)*, Henry Travers *(Dr. Cranley)*, Una O'Connor *(Mrs. Jenny Hall)*, Forrester Harvey *(Mr. Herbert Hall)*, Holmes Herbert *(Chief of Police)*, E. E. Clive *(Jaffers)*, Dudley Digges *(Chief of Detectives)*, Harry Stubbs *(Inspector Bird)*, Donald Stuart *(Inspector Lane)*, Merle Tottenham *(Milly)*, Walter Brennan *(Man With Bike)*, Dwight Frye *(Reporter)*, Jameson Thomas *(Doctor)*, John Carradine *(Informer)*, John Merivale *(Boy)*

Rains, or a brief glimpse of him, made his American debut in this macabre horror/comedy as the title character. He is a scientist who has been experimenting with a drug of his own concoction, something he calls monocaine, and he finds that it has turned his entire body invisible. He goes to the small village of Ipping, England wrapped in bandages and wearing dark glasses. He takes a room in the local inn and his meals are served to him there. He never steps from his room and subsequently arouses the curiosity of the local residents. While Rains continues experimenting, his megalomania, a side-effect of the strange brew he creates and swills, begins to dominate his personality, not unlike DR. JEKYLL AND MR. HYDE. When the proprietor of the inn inadvertently discovers her guest walking about in his room without a visible head she gets hysterical and police are summoned. Havoc ensues as Rains toys with the police and populace. First he plays pranks, then robs a bank for the sheer caprice of it, throwing the money he has taken through the streets to see people greedily grab for it. The drug takes its insidious effect, turning Rains into a maniac; he commits murders which soon have half the police in England after him. He is tracked to a barn and then driven out, followed by police ringing the place, their arms locked. They follow his footsteps—clearly marked in the snow—and he is shot and captured, his naked body wrapped in a blanket and taken to a hospital where his one-time girl friend, Stuart, comforts him as he dies. At the finish, the drug wears off and Rains' face becomes visible. The film is directed with style and snap by stellar helmsman Whale, who had earlier directed FRANKENSTEIN and would go on to direct THE BRIDE OF FRANKENSTEIN. The dialog by R. C. Sheriff (who had authored "Journey's End") and Philip Wylie (uncredited) is witty and often humorous in a dark way, and the special effects were wondrous to behold in 1933. The invisibility was achieved by dressing a stuntman in black velvet and then removing the bandages and clothes against a black velvet background; Rains' appearance at the end, his head seeming to come out of nowhere as he lies dying, was accomplished through elaborate stop motion. Universal would milk this film and its subsequent sequel, THE INVISIBLE MAN RETURNS, 1940, with a low-budget series of invisible man films, culminating with a just-average clown vehicle, ABBOTT AND COSTELLO MEET THE INVISIBLE MAN, 1951.

p, Carl Laemmle, Jr.; d, James Whale; w, R. C. Sheriff (uncredited, Philip Wylie) (based on the novel by H. G. Wells); ph, Arthur Edeson; m, W. Frank Harling; art d, Charles D. Hall; spec eff, John P. Fulton, John Mescall; makeup, Jack Pierce.

Horror/Mystery **(PR:C MPAA:NR)**

INVISIBLE MAN, THE* 1/2
(1958, Mex.) 95m Cinematografica Calderon bw (EL HOMBRE QUE LOGRO SER INVISIBLE; EL HOMBRE INVISIBLE)

Arturo de Cordova, Ana Luisa Peluffo, Raul Meraz, Augusto Benedico, Nestor Barbosa, Jorge Mondragon, Roberto G. Rivera, Roy Fletcher.

Freely adapting the H.G. Wells novel, this Mexican version of THE INVISIBLE MAN stars de Cordova as the title character. While in prison, he receives the drug from his brother, who invented the formula. De Cordova begins to suffer illusions of grandeur but his reign at the top is cut short by a policeman's bullet. This is a typical Mexican horror-fantasy picture.

p, Guillermo Calderon; d, Alfredo B. Crevenna; w, Alfredo Salazar, Julio Alejandro (based on a novel by H.G. Wells); ph, Raul Martinez Solares.

Science Fiction **(PR:A MPAA:NR)**

INVISIBLE MAN, THE** (1963, Ger.) 94m Aero bw (DER UNSICHTBARE)

Ivan Desny, Ellen Schwiers, Charles Regnier, Ilse Steppat, Hannes Schmidhauser, Hans von Borsody, Herbert Stass, Harry Fuss, Christiane Nielsen, Joachim Hansen.

An amalgam of the classic H.G. Wells novel *The Invisible Man* and the Dr. Mabuse series (see THE INVISIBLE DR. MABUSE), this thriller concerns the search of Regnier and Schwiers, who set out to find Prof. von Borsody, who has disappeared.

p&d, Raphael Nussbaum; w, Vladimir Semitjof, Nussbaum; ph, Michael Marszalek.

Science Fiction/Crime **(PR:A MPAA:NR)**

INVISIBLE MAN RETURNS, THE*** (1940) 81m UNIV bw

Sir Cedric Hardwicke *(Richard Cobb)*, Vincent Price *(Geoffrey Radcliffe)*, Nan Grey *(Helen Manson)*, John Sutton *(Dr. Frank Griffin)*, Cecil Kellaway *(Inspector Sampson)*, Alan Napier *(Willie Spears)*, Forrester Harvey *(Ben Jenkins)*, Frances Robinson *(Nurse)*, Ivan Simpson *(Cotton)*, Edward Fielding *(Governor)*, Harry Stubbs *(Constable Dukesbury)*, Mary Field *(Woman)*, Harry Cording *(Shopworker)*, Edmund MacDonald *(Mineworker)*, Matthew Boulton *(Policeman)*, Bruce Lester *(Chaplain)*, Paul England *(Detective)*, Mary Gordon *(Cook)*, Eric Wilton *(Fingerprint Man)*, Leyland Hodgson *(Chauffeur)*, Dave Thursby *(Bob, a Warden)*, Jimmy Aubrey *(Plainclothesman)*, Louise Brien *(Griffin's Secretary)*, Ernie Adams *(Man)*, Frank Hagney *(Bill, a Policeman)*, Frank O'Connor *(Policeman at Colliery)*, Frank Hill *(Policeman attending Cobb)*, Ellis Irving, Dennis Tankard, George Lloyd, George Kirby, George Hyde *(Miners)*.

In his first starring role, Price is cast in this sequel to THE INVISIBLE MAN as the brother of the original film's lead character. Wrongly accused of murder, Price has scientist Sutton inject him with a serum to make him invisible. The standard effects are used to their fullest, with Price accidentally reappearing at the wrong times, and the proverbial floating gun that takes the guilty party by surprise. Hardwicke is fine as the evil nemesis. Claude Rains, the star of the original THE INVISIBLE MAN, does appear in a photograph.

p, Ken Goldsmith, d, Joe May; w, Curt Siodmak, Lester Cole, Cecil Belfrage (based on a story by Siodmak, May); ph, Milton Krasner; m, H.J. Salter, Frank Skinner; ed, Frank Gross; md, Charles Previn; cos, Vera West; spec eff, John P. Fulton.

Crime/Fantasy **(PR:A MPAA:NR)**

INVISIBLE MAN'S REVENGE** (1944) 78m UNIV bw

Jon Hall *(Robert Griffin)*, Alan Curtis *(Mark Foster)*, Evelyn Ankers *(Julie Herrick)*, Leon Errol *(Herbert Higgens)*, John Carradine *(Dr. Peter Drury)*, Doris Lloyd *(Maud)*, Himself *(Gray Shadow)*, Gale Sondergaard *(Lady Irene Herrick)*, Lester Matthews *(Sir Jasper Herrick)*, Halliwell Hobbes *(Cleghorn)*, Leyland Hodgson *(Sir Frederick Travers)*, Billy Bevan *(Sergeant)*, Ian Wolfe *(Jim Feeny)*, Skelton Knaggs *(Al Parry)*.

This was the fifth film in the INVISIBLE MAN series. Hall, who starred in THE INVISIBLE AGENT (1942), is a criminal who, with the aid of scientist Carradine, becomes invisible. He then stalks an English couple, Sondergaard and Matthews, until they give him their fortune and daughter, Ankers. The English couple had left Hall for dead during a safari five years earlier. Journalist Curtis puts an end to the Invisible Man as he tries to stop his invisibility from fading. The only outstanding item of this film is John P. Fulton's special effects.

p&d, Ford Beebe; w, Bertram Millhauser (based on the novel *The Invisible Man* by H.G. Wells); ph, Milton Krasner; m, H.J. Salter; ed, Saul Goodkind; spec eff, John P. Fulton.

Science Fiction/Horror **(PR:A MPAA:NR)**

INVISIBLE MENACE, THE** (1938) 54m WB bw

Boris Karloff *(Jevries)*, Marie Wilson *(Sally)*, Eddie Craven *(Eddie Pratt)*, Eddie Acuff *(Cpl. Sanger)*, Regis Toomey *(Lt. Matthews)*, Henry Kolker *(Col. Hackett)*, Cy Kendall *(Col. Rogers)*, Charles Trowbridge *(Dr. Brooks)*, Frank Faylen *(Private of the Guard)*, William Haade *(Pvt. Ferris)*, Harland Tucker *(Reilly)*, Phyllis Barry *(Aline Dolman)*, John Ridgely *(Pvt. Innes)*, Jack Mower *(Sgt. Peterson)*, Anderson Lawlor *(Pvt. Abbott)*, John Harron *(Pvt. Murphy)*.

An undistinguished B murder mystery with Karloff as a civilian employee of a military post who's accused of murdering an Army officer. Craven is a private at the base who smuggles in his new bride, Wilson, and hides her in an empty building. A sentry finds her and at the same time, the body of an officer pinned to the wall with a bayonet. Then a bomb is found in Kolker's office. Kolker calls in Kendall of military intelligence, who suspects Karloff because he had arrested him for embezzling 10 years before. With all the evidence pointing to Karloff, the investigation is to be closed when Wilson accidentally discovers the real killer. Of course it's the least likely suspect.

p, Bryan Foy; d, John Farrow; w, Crane Wibur (based on the play "Without Warning" by Ralph Spencer Zink); ph, L. William O'Connell; ed, Harold McLernon.

Mystery **(PR:A MPAA:NR)**

INVISIBLE MESSAGE, THE (SEE: GUN PLAY, 1935)

INVISIBLE OPPONENT**
(1933, Ger.) 87m Pan-Film/Markische bw (UNSICHTBARE GEGNER)

Gerda Maurus *(Sybil Herford)*, Paul Hartmann *(Peter Ugron)*, Oskar Homolka *(James Godfrey)*, Peter Lorre *(Henry Pless)*, Paul Kemp *(Hans Mertens)*, Raoul Aslan *(J. Delmonte)*, Leonard Steckel *(Santos)*, H. Kyser *(Sir Thomas)*, Eva Schmidt-Kaiser *(Eva Ugron)*.

An early Lorre film that casts him as a henchman for Steckel, who is interested in buying Aslan's financially ailing oil company. Steckel's men kill Aslan and replace him with one of their own agents, who is sent to a meeting with Europa Oil, the other prospective buyer. Lorre and his thugs also try to kill Hartmann, an engineer for Aslan. He evades them, however, and is aided by Maurus in getting a photo of the real Aslan. The phony Aslan makes the deal with Europa Oil, but when he and his men try to cash the check they are hauled in by the police, thanks to Hartmann's efforts. Also filmed with a French cast (of which Lorre also is a part) as LES REQUINS DU PETROLE, or THE OIL SHARKS.

p, Sam Spiegel; d, Rudolf Katscher; w, Lothar Mayring, Heinrich Oberlander, Richard Steinbicker (based on an idea by Ludwig von Wohl); ph, Eugen Schufftan, Georg Bruckbauer; m, Rudolph Schwarz; ed, Rudolf Schaad, Phillis Fehr; art d, Erwin Scharf.

Crime **(PR:A MPAA:NR)**

INVISIBLE POWER (SEE: WASHINGTON MERRY-GO- ROUND, 1932)

THE INVISIBLE RAY 1/2** (1936) 82m UNIV bw

Boris Karloff *(Dr. Janos Rukh)*, Bela Lugosi *(Dr. Felix Benet)*, Frances Drake *(Diane Rukh)*, Frank Lawton *(Ronald Drake)*, Walter Kingsford *(Sir Francis Stevens)*, Beulah Bondi *(Lady Arabella Stevens)*, Violet Kemble Cooper *(Mother Rukh)*, Nydia Westman *(Briggs)*, Georges Renavent *(Chief of Surete)*, Frank Reicher *(Prof. Meikeljohn)*, Paul Wegel *(Prof. Noyer)*, Adele St. Maur *(Mme. Noyer)*, Lawrence Stewart *(No. 1 Boy)*, Etta McDaniel *(Zulu)*, Daniel Haines *(Headsman)*, Inez Seabury *(Celeste)*, Winter Hall *(Minister)*.

Scientist Karloff, with the help of his time and space travel machine, is able to pinpoint a meteor that landed in Africa. With the help of fellow scientist Lugosi, Karloff puts together an expedition to retrieve the meteor, which contains "Radium X," a substance more powerful than radium. Upon finding the meteor, Karloff is contaminated by the radioactive substance and discovers that he kills whatever he touches. Lugosi comes up with a short-term antidote, but the radiation is making Karloff go mad. Thinking that Lugosi and others from the expedition have cheated him out of the limelight by presenting the meteor to the Scientific Congress, Karloff kills them and almost kills his wife, Drake. Karloff's mother, Cooper, destroys his antidote. The scientist bursts into flames and jumps through a window to his death. John P. Fulton's special effects are a standout (he did the special effects for the INVISIBLE MAN series). Director Hillyer did mostly westerns and made only one other horror film, DRACULA'S DAUGHTER.

p, Edmund Grainger; d, Lambert Hillyer; w, John Colton (based on a story by Howard Higgin and Douglas Hodges); ph, George Robinson; m, Franz Waxman; ed, Bernard Burton; art d, Albert S. D'Agostino; spec eff, John P. Fulton; makeup, Jack P. Pierce.

Science Fiction/Horror **(PR:C MPAA:NR)**

INVISIBLE STRIPES*** (1940) 82m FN/WB bw

George Raft *(Cliff Taylor)*, Jane Bryan *(Peggy)*, William Holden *(Tim Taylor)*, Humphrey Bogart *(Chuck Martin)*, Flora Robson *(Mrs. Taylor)*, Paul Kelly *(Ed Kruger)*, Lee Patrick *(Molly Daniels)*, Henry O'Neill *(Parole Officer Masters)*, Frankie Thomas *(Tommy McNeil)*, Moroni Olsen *(Warden)*, Margot Stevenson *(Sue)*, Marc Lawrence *(Lefty Sloane)*, Joseph Downing *(Johnny Hudson)*, Leo Gorcey *(Jimmy)*, William Haade *(Shrank)*, Tully Marshall *(Old Peter)*, Chester Clute *(Mr. Butler)*, Jack Mower *(Guard in Charge)*, Frank Mayo *(Guard at Gate)*, George Taylor *(Paully, a Prisoner)*, Frank Bruno *(Smitty, a Prisoner)*, John Irwin *(Prisoner)*, G. Pat Collins *(Alec, a Prisoner)*, Mack Gray, Joe Devlin, Mike Lally, Al Hill *(Henchmen)*, Bert Hanlon *(Shorty)*, Joseph Crehan *(Mr. Chasen, the Garage Manager)*, John Ridgely *(Employment Clerk)*, Victor Kilian *(Foreman)*, Pat Flaherty *(Worker)*, William Davidson *(Chief Foreman)*, Irving Bacon *(Personnel Director)*, Dorothea Wolbert *(Flower Woman)*, J. Anthony Hughes, Max Hoffman, Jr. *(Chauffeurs)*, William Hopper *(Young Man)*, Walter James, Harry Wilson *(Workers)*, Harry Strang *(Bartender at Party)*, Jane Gilbert *(Young Lady)*, Ralph Dunn *(Doorman)*, Al Hill, Jr., Richard Clayton *(Boys)*, Stan Meyers *(Orchestra Leader)*, Maude Allen *(Woman)*, Charles Wilson, Robert Elliott, Lane Chandler *(Detectives)*, Claude Wisberg *(Older Boy)*, Lew Harvey *(Man)*, Selmer Jackson, Pat O'Malley *(Lieutenants)*, Frank Faylen *(Steve the Henchman)*, Emory Parnell, Wade Boteler, Cliff Clark *(Policemen)*, Ray Cooke *(Pinky)*, Eddy Chandler *(Police Driver)*, Ethan Laidlaw *(Cop Outside Station House)*, Sammy Finn *(Spotter)*, John Hamilton *(Capt. Johnson)*, Bruce Bennett *(Rich Man)*

Raft and Bogart are recently released convicts with two goals in mind. Raft turns his back on crime and opts for a straight life while Bogart, a hard-hearted, unrehabilitated criminal, goes right back to his crooked ways. Raft tries hard to get a job but can't; when his kid brother Holden gets him a position, Raft is fired after the manager finds out he's served time. Holden wants to get married but he has no money. Raft learns Holden has rolled a drunk to buy gifts for girl friend Bryan. To get his brother enough money to marry, Raft joins Bogart's gang, goes on a few capers, and then finances Holden in a new garage. Holden gets married and Raft later quits Bogart when he has enough money in the bank. Then Bogart shows up wounded, having been shot by rival gangsters Kelly and Lawrence. He hides out in Holden's garage, convincing Holden that brother Raft is still with his mob. Holden is later arrested for harboring Bogart. Raft visits Holden in jail and tells him he's clean; he finds out that Bogart has taken refuge in Bryan's apartment. Raft tells the police to keep Holden under protective custody and then goes to the apartment. He finds Bogart but so do Kelly and Lawrence and both Raft and Bogart are mortally wounded. The police then arrive to arrest killers Kelly and Lawrence. Just before they die, Raft and Bogart console themselves with the thought that they won't see the inside of another cell. Director Bacon handles the hot-and-heavy action well and Raft delivers a solid performance with Bogart playing the stereotyped crooked pal and the 21-year-old Holden the predictable kid brother verging on the wayward. It's a mostly routine story but nevertheless absorbing. An inside joke of the film shows Raft seeing Bogart and the girl friend Patrick leave a movie; Raft looks up at the theater marquee to see the title YOU CAN'T GET AWAY WITH MURDER, a Bogart film. In a touching scene with his mother (played by the woefully miscast Robson, an excellent British actress) Raft jitterbugs to the strains of "Sweet Georgia Brown" (Ben Bernie, Maceo Pinkard, Kenneth Casey) and then slow-dances with his mom to "The Japanese Sandman" (Richard A. Whiting, Raymond B. Egan).

p, Louis F. Edelman; d, Lloyd Bacon; w, Warren Duff, Jonathan Finn (based on the book by Warden Lewis E. Lawes); ph, Ernest Haller; m, Heinz Roemheld; ed, James Gibbon; art d, Max Parker; cos, Milo Anderson; spec eff, Byron Haskin; Makeup, Perc Westmore.

Crime Drama **(PR:A MPAA:NR)**

INVISIBLE WALL, THE* 1/2 (1947) 72m FOX bw

Don Castle *(Harry Lane)*, Virginia Christine *(Mildred Elsworth)*, Richard Gaines *(Richard Elsworth)*, Arthur Space *(Hanford)*, Edward Keane *(Marty Floyd)*, Jeff Chandler *(Al Conway)*, Harry Cheshire *(Hamilton)*, Mary Gordon *(Mrs. Bledsoe)*, Harry Shannon *(Detective Captain)*, Rita Duncan *(Alice Jamison)*.

A confusing tale told in flashback about an ex-GI who returns from WW II and resumes his position as a bookie. His penchant for gambling leads him to Las Vegas, where he squanders $10,000 of his boss bookmaker's cash and is accused of a murder he didn't commit. By the time he is cleared of the crime, however, no one actually cares whether or not he is guilty.

p, Sol M. Wurtzel; d, Eugene Forde; w, Arnold Belgard (based on a story by Howard J. Green, Paul Frank); ph, Benjamin Kline; m, Dale Butts; ed, William Claxton; md, Morton Scott; art d, Walter Koessler.

Crime **(PR:A MPAA:NR)**

INVISIBLE WOMAN, THE 1/2** (1941) 70m UNIV bw

Virginia Bruce *(Kitty Carroll)*, John Barrymore *(Prof. Gibbs)*, John Howard *(Richard Russell)*, Charlie Ruggles *(George)*, Oscar Homolka *(Blackie Cole)*, Edward Brophy *(Bill)*, Donald MacBride *(Foghorn)*, Margaret Hamilton *(Mrs. Jackson)*, Shemp Howard *(Frankie)*, Anne Nagel *(Jean)*, Kathryn Adams *(Peggy)*, Maria Montez *(Marie)*, Kay Leslie *(Model)*, Charles Lane *(Growley)*, Mary Gordon *(Mrs. Bates)*, Thurston Hall *(John Hudson)*, Eddie Conrad *(Hernandez)*, Kay Linaker, Sarah Edwards *(Buyers)*, Kitty O'Neil *(Mrs. Patten)*, Harry C. Bradley *(Want Ad Man)*, Kernan Cripps *(Postman)*.

In the continuation of Universal's "Invisible" series, Barrymore stars as a crazy professor who discovers the secret of invisibility. Bruce plays the model who becomes the subject of his scientific experiment and soon finds herself transparent. She gets involved with a wacky group of bandits who try to steal the machine for their own illegal use. Bruce sets out on her own, with attempts at romance with the inventor's son, John Howard, and evening the score with her former employer. The typical "invisible" special effects are employed, though this time with a little more humor. Based on a story by Siodmak and May, the same team that wrote THE INVISIBLE MAN RETURNS.

p, Burt Kelly; d, A. Edward Sutherland; w, Robert Lees, Fred Rinaldo, Gertrude Purcell (based on a story by Curt Siodmak, Joe May); ph, Elwood Bredell; ed, Frank Gross; art d, Jack Otterson; cos, Vera West; spec eff, John P. Fulton.

Comedy/Fantasy **(PR:A MPAA:NR)**

INVITATION* ** (1952) 84m MGM bw

Van Johnson *(Dan Pierce)*, Dorothy McGuire *(Ellen Pierce)*, Ruth Roman *(Maud Redwick)*, Louis Calhern *(Simon Bowker)*, Ray Collins *(Dr. Warren Pritchard)*, Michael Chekhov *(Dr. Fromm)*, Lisa Golm *(Agnes)*, Diane Cassidy *(Molly)*, Stapleton Kent *(Gardener)*, Barbara Ruick *(Sarah)*, Norman Field *(Arthur)*, Matt Moore *(Paul)*, Patrick Conway *(Bill)*, Alex Gerry *(Mr. Redwick)*, Lucile Curtis *(Mrs. Redwick)*.

This somewhat emotionally contrived film centers on McGuire as a young lady who is dying of a heart condition, and Calhern as her wealthy, indulgent father who decides to give his daughter the ultimate gift of marriage. He pays Johnson to wed the girl, only to have her find out about the scheme as she nears her untimely death. Johnson, however, has genuinely fallen in love with her, which gives her the needed strength to submit to an operation that will extend her life. The film leaves the audience with the hope of a happy marriage and long life for McGuire.

p, Lawrence Weingarten; d, Gottfried Reinhardt; w, Paul Osborn (based on a story by Jerome Weidman); ph, Ray June; m, Bronislau Kaper; ed, George Boemler; art d, Cedric Gibbons, Urie McCleary.

Romance **(PR:A MPAA:NR)**

INVITATION, THE* 1/2**

(1975, Fr./Switz.) 100m Citel-Group 5-Swiss TV-Planfilm/Janus c

Jean-Luc Bideau *(Maurice)*, Francois Simon *(Emile)*, Jean Champion *(Alfred)*, Corinne Coderey *(Simone)*, Michel Robin *(Remy)*, Cecile Vassort *(Aline)*, Rosine Rochette *(Helene)*, Jacques Rispal *(Rene)*, Neige Dolsky *(Emma)*, Pierre Collet *(Pierre)*, Lucie Aveney *(Mme. Placet)*, Roger Jendely *(Thief)*.

One of the most impressive works to come out of Switzerland (along with the films of Alain Tanner) THE INVITATION was nominated for an Academy Award for Best Foreign Film. It is a subtle, naturalistic picture which takes place during an office party. As with all parties of this sort, the workers get out of hand and reveal facets of themselves that they usually keep hidden from 9 to 5. The party, thrown by meek dullard Robin, comes to life when office stud Bideau begins his conquest of women. It is up to Simon, a cultured, patient butler, to keep things in order—a seemingly futile task. A thoroughly watchable film which is blessed with acting and dialog that seems completely effortless. (In French, English subtitles).

d, Claude Goretta; w, Goretta, Michel Viala; ph, Jean Zeller; m, Patrick Moraz; ed, Joelle van Effenterre.

Comedy/Drama **(PR:C-O MPAA:NR)**

INVITATION TO A GUNFIGHTER*** (1964) 91m Kramer/UA c

Yul Brynner *(Jules Gaspard D'Estaing)*, Janice Rule *(Ruth Adams)*, Brad Dexter *(Kenarsie)*, Alfred Ryder *(Doc Barker)*, Mike Kellin *(Tom)*, George Segal *(Matt Weaver)*, Clifford David *(Crane Adams)*, Pat Hingle *(Sam Brewster)*, Bert Freed *(Sheriff)*, Curt Conway *(McKeever)*, Clifton James *(Tuttle)*, Clarke Gordon *(Hickman)*, Arthur Peterson *(Schoop)*, Strother Martin *(Fiddler)*, Gertrude Flynn *(Widow Guthrie)*, John Alonzo *(Manuel)*, William Hickey *(Jo-Jo)*, Gerald Hiken *(Gully)*, Dal Jenkins *(Dancer)*.

An interesting, offbeat, and sometimes confusing western, starring Brynner as an educated half-black, half-Creole gunfighter named Jules Gaspard D'Estaing. He is hired by Hingle to kill Confederate veteran Segal, who has returned to his hometown after the war only to find that his property has been sold by Hingle, his former fiancee, Ruth, has married a Union soldier, and his neighbors are Union sympathizers, aligned against him. After Segal kills the new owner of his property, he barricades himself inside. Enter Brynner, who has a penchant for killing white folks but only after they correct their pronunciation of his name. However, Brynner becomes uncontrollable and, in a weird twist of script, Hingle hires Segal to kill the hired gunman. The story ends with Brynner killed by the man who he was out to kill.

p&d, Richard Wilson; w, Wilson, Elizabeth Wilson, Alvin Sapinsley (based on the story by Hal Goodman, Larry Klein); ph, Joe McDonald (DeLuxe Color); m, David Raksin; ed, Robert C. Jones; art d, Robert Clatworthy.

Western Cas. **(PR:C MPAA:NR)**

INVITATION TO A HANGING (SEE: LAW OF THE LAWLESS, 1964)

INVITATION TO HAPPINESS*** (1939) 97m PAR bw

Irene Dunne *(Eleanor Wayne)*, Fred MacMurray *(Albert "King" Cole)*, Billy Cook *(Albert Cole, Jr.)*, Charlie Ruggles *(Pop Hardy)*, William Collier, Sr. *(Mr. Wayne)*, Marion Martin *(Lola)*, Oscar O'Shea *(Divorce Judge)*, Burr Caruth *(Butler)*, Eddie Hogan *(The Champ)*, Gordon Jones *(Dutch Arnold)*, Allen Wood, Don Laterre *(Youths)*, Mack Gray *(Usher)*, Bob Evans *(Galliette)*, Charles Randolph, Russ Clark *(Referees)*, Jack Roper *(Scat)*, Billy Newell *(Waiter)*, Heinie Conklin *(Cook)*, Franklin Parker, Wheaton Chambers, Joseph Franz, Jack Gargan, Jack Knoche, Harry Hayden, Robert Stevenson, Jerry Fletcher *(Reporters)*, Joe Caits *(Man In Office)*, Guy Usher *(Spectator)*, Joe Cunningham *(Announcer)*, Hank Hankison *(Fighter)*, Emerson Treacy *(Photographer)*, Bill Knudsen *(Attendant)*, Lee Moore *(Headwaiter)*, Doodles Weaver *(Band Leader)*, Myra Marsh *(Maternity Nurse)*, Virginia Brissac *(Eleanor's Nurse)*, William Orr *(Bellboy)*.

MacMurray is a boxer who spends too much time in the ring and not enough around the dinner table. As a young fighter, he marries Dunne after her father, Collier, purchases a half interest in his contract, and she reluctantly submits to the considerable amount of time he must spend on the road and in training. He is out of town fighting when Dunne has their first child. He continues, however, to live for the sport in the hopes of getting a crack at the championship. But after nearly 10 years of MacMurray's lifestyle, his son is a virtual stranger to him. His attempts at getting close to the boy fail, and soon after Dunne files for divorce. Her action neatly coincides with her husband's chance to become world champ. His son comes to the fight and when dad gets knocked to the mat, the sight of junior gives him the strength to get back up. MacMurray puts up a good fight but is defeated. He is, however, at least able to win back the love and respect of his family. A fine attempt at showing the strains life in the spotlight can have on a family.

p&d, Wesley Ruggles; w, Claude Binyon (based on a story by Mark Jerome); ph, Leo Tover; m, Frederick Hollander; ed, Alma Macrorie; art d, Hans Dreier, Ernst Fegte.

Drama **(PR:A MPAA:NR)**

INVITATION TO MURDER** (1962, Brit.) 65m Atlantic bw

Robert Beatty *(Private Investigator)*, Lisa Daniely, Catherine Feller *(Granddaughters)*, Douglas Wilmer *(Police Inspector)*, Ernest Thesiger *(Millionaire)*, Bud Knapp *(Attorney)*, Denis Shaw *(Millionaire's Assistant)*, Guy Kingsley Poynter *(Secretary)*, Olga Dickie *(Nurse)*, Joan Howlett, Keith Pyott.

A British crime drama set on the French Riviera has a reclusive, dying millionaire willing his estate to the survivor among his potential beneficiaries. After a series of murders is discovered by detective Beatty, the detective learns that the killer has been hired by one of the granddaughters. She is arrested shortly after, thereby leaving the innocent granddaughter with all the money. The story ends with the new heiress leaving town with the detective, pledging to give the entire fortune to charity.

p, Harry Alan Towers; d, Robert Lynn; w, Joel Murdock.

Mystery **(PR:C MPAA:NR)**

INVITATION TO THE DANCE* 1/2** (1956) 93m MGM c

"Circus": Igor Youskevitch *(The Lover)*, Claire Sombert *(The Loved)*, Gene Kelly *(The Clown)*; "Sinbad the Sailor": Carol Haney *(Scheherazade)*, David Kasday *(The Genie)*, Kelly *(Sinbad)*; "Ring Around the Rosy": David Paltenghi, *(The Husband)*, Youskevitch *(The Artist)*, Daphne Dale *(The Wife)*, Claude Bessy *(The Model)*, Tommy Rall *(Flashy Boyfriend)*, Belita *(Debutante)*, Irving Davies *(The Crooner)*, Diana Adams *(Hat Check Girl)*, Kelly *(The Marine)*, Tamara Toumanova *(The Street Walker)*.

INVITATION TO THE DANCE was four years in the making and by the time it was released, its day had come and gone. By then, audiences were accustomed to seeing dancing on TV and the resultant box office receipts were nowhere near what had been expected. It's all dancing, with no singing or dialog, and was originally conceived as a four part film, with no thread holding the numbers together. The segment cut was "Dance Me A Song" because Kelly couldn't make up his mind about whether or not he approved of the material. The nabobs of MGM were totally against the project, but Kelly was persuasive and had made so much money for the studio over the years that they finally agreed, with the proviso that he shoot it in England where they had a great deal of money and couldn't bring it out. (This is not uncommon and for years millions of rupees languished in India with the same thing happening in several countries.) The picture was mostly filmed at Elstree studios and shooting began in October, 1952. In "Circus," Kelly is a Pagliacci working in the eighteenth century with a small Italian circus. He loves Sombert, the circus star, but she is in love with Youskevitch, the high wire performer. They arrive at a small village where the circus people juggle, do acrobatics, and mime for the townsfolk. Later, Kelly watches Sombert and Youskevitch as they dance. He is sad to see how happy they are with each other and now picks up a cloak and begins to dance with it as though it were a woman. Sombert sees this and Kelly notices her watching. Now he begins to cavort and prance in order to keep her from moving away. Eventually, he climbs up on the wire and attempts to continue delighting her. The result is tragic as he falls to his death. Sombert and Youskevitch look at the sad clown on the ground and embrace. They now realize how short life can be and they will love each other for as long as life allows. The music by Jacques Ibert was not memorable but served the purpose. Sombert was a classical ballet student Kelly discovered and Youskevitch at the time was acknowledged as one of the best dancers of the era. In the second segment, "Ring Around The Rosy," Kelly has appropriated Schnitzler's LA RONDE plot with a major change. In that play, several people passed around a venereal disease. Here, a bracelet is passed by a man to his wife to an artist to his model to a thief to a debutante to a nightclub singer to a hat-check dolly to a sailor to a hooker and, you guessed it, back to the husband who began it all. The most fascinating part of this was that the original music was by British composer Malcolm Arnold, but the studio didn't like his work so Kelly was told to scrap the score and hire someone else. Yet, they were unwilling to re-shoot so Kelly had to locate some genius who could write music to an already-existing dance film! That he did in Andre Previn and the result is so good that one would never know that that is the way it was done. The excellence of MGM's Hanna-Barbera team is what caused them to call the film back to the U.S. to shoot the final section, "Sinbad The Sailor," which featured Kelly and animated figures. Almost 40 artists were used and more than 250,000 sketches were made to synchronize Kelly's dancing with the animated figures. Using music by Nikolai Rimski-Korsakov (adapted by Roger Edens), Kelly is an American sailor on furlough in Baghdad. He buys a lamp and the genie that appears is not the Rex Ingram-type of ogre; instead, it's Kasday, a young lad. Kelly prevails on Kasday to transform himself into a sailor and the two dance a thousand and one steps as they cross a valley of diamonds, avoid snakes, and get to the castle of a sultan where they escape his fierce guards and steal his fiance. Carol Haney is seen briefly as Scheherazade (which is the title of R-K's music). Haney had a brief career and an early death. It was her broken ankle in the Broadway show "Pajama Game" that gave Shirley MacLaine the chance to fill in and be seen by Hal B. Wallis who happened to be there that night. Kelly was more an acrobatic dancer than a classical one and was out of his league in the "Circus" routine. The animation for "Sinbad" was good but not nearly as fantastic as what was done for ANCHORS AWEIGH. Kelly has always been a champion of dancing and thought this picture would introduce that lively art to huge audiences. It didn't and the result was a box-office blah.

p, Arthur Freed; d&w, Gene Kelly; ph, Freddie Young, Joseph Ruttenberg (Technicolor); m, Jacques Ibert, Andre Previn, Roger Edens (based on music by Nikolai Andreevich Rimski-Korsakov); ed, Raymond Poulton, Adrienne Fazan, Robert Watts; md, John Hollingsworth, Johnny Green, Previn; art d, Alfred Junge, Cedric Gibbons, Randall Duell; spec eff, Tom Howard; cartoon eff., Irving Reis; cartoon sequence, Fred Quimby, Joe Barbera, William Hanna; cos, Rolf Gerard, Elizabeth Haffenden; ch, Kelly.

Dance Musical **Cas.** **(PR:A MPAA:NR)**

INVITATION TO THE WALTZ* 1/2 (1935, Brit.) 80m BIP bw

Lilian Harvey *(Jenny Peachey)*, Wendy Toye *(Signora Picci)*, Carl Esmond *(Carl)*, Harold Warrender *(Duke of Wurtemberg)*, Richard Bird *(Weber)*, Esme Percy *(Napoleon Bonaparte)*, Eric Stanley *(Sir Francis, British Ambassador)*, Alexander Field *(George Peachey)*, Anton Dolin *(Chief Dancer)*, Hay Petrie *(Periteau)*, Charles Carson *(Lombardi)*, Hal Gordon *(Sergeant)*, Gus McNaughton *(Valet)*.

An unsuccessful attempt at mixing music, romance, and history has Harvey playing an English ballerina at Drury Lane. Set in the early 1800s, Harvey becomes the mistress of Warrender, Duke of Wurtemberg, and tricks him into signing a treaty with England against Napoleon. Carl Esmond is the young officer who loves her, but fears she is the Duke's mistress. Typically continental in direction, this film does succeed in keeping with the period story.

p, Walter C. Mycroft; d, Paul Merzbach; w, Merzbach, Clifford Grey, Roger Burford (based on a radio play by Holt Marvell, Eric Maschwitz, George Posford); ph, Ronald Neame, Claude Friese-Greene; m, Weber, Beethoven, Mozart, George Posford.

Musical **(PR:A MPAA:NR)**

IO . . . TU . . . Y . . . ELLA* 1/2 (1933) 73m FOX bw

Gilbert Roland *(Husband)*, Catalina Barcena *(Wife)*, Mona Maris *(Ella)*, Rosita Moreno *(Bride)*.

Spanish language romance ("I...Thou...and...She") filmed in the U.S. and intended for Latin American distribution as well as the domestic Spanish-speaking audience. Set in Paris, Venice, and Madrid, the film stars Roland as the philandering husband of Barcena, who eventually forgives him for his infidelities. Little more than a historical curiosity. (In Spanish.)

d, John Reinhardt; w, (based on the novel *Mujer* by Martinez Sierra).

Drama **(PR:A MPAA:NR)**

IOLANTA (SEE: YOLANTA, 1964, USSR)

IPCRESS FILE, THE* 1/2** (1965, Brit.) 109m Lowndes-Steven/UNIV c

Michael Caine *(Harry Palmer)*, Nigel Green *(Dalby)*, Guy Doleman *(Maj. Ross)*, Sue Lloyd *(Jean)*, Gordon Jackson *(Jock Carswell)*, Aubrey Richards *(Radcliffe)*, Frank Gatliff *(Bluejay)*, Thomas Baptiste *(Barney)*, Oliver MacGreevy *(Housemartin)*, Freda Bamford *(Alice)*, Pauline Winter *(Charlady)*, Anthony Blackshaw *(Edwards)*, Barry Raymond *(Gray)*, David Glover *(Chilcott-Oakes)*, Stanley Meadows *(Inspector Keightley)*, Peter Ashmore *(Sir Robert)*, Michael Murray *(Raid Inspector)*, Anthony Baird *(Raid Sergeant)*, Tony Caunter *(O.N.I. Man)*, Charles Rea *(Taylor)*, Ric Hutton *(Records Officer)*, Douglas Blackwell *(Murray)*, Richard Burrell *(Operator)*, Glynn Edwards *(Police Station Sergeant)*, Zsolt Vadaszffy *(Prison Doctor)*, Joseph Behrmann, Max Faulkner, Paul S. Chapman *(Prison Guards)*.

Harry Saltzman, the Canadian who went to Europe to coproduce so many James Bond films, acquired the rights to Deighton's anti-hero novel and hired fellow Canadian Furie to direct it. This was the first and the best of the Deighton novels about myopic, flabby Harry Palmer (played by Caine). The sequels were FUNERAL IN BERLIN and BILLION DOLLAR BRAIN and neither came close in content or style. In the case of THE IPCRESS FILE, perhaps there was too much style, as Furie was so in love with his camera that he might have been arrested for cinemasturbation. The picture has so many lensing gimmicks that it detracts from a superb cast and makes us realize that someone is actually directing this movie, something the great ones like Lubitsch and Wilder never did. Caine is transferred from Green's civil intelligence staff to Doleman's military investigations department where he is assigned to find out whatever happened to Richards, a doctor who has evidently been kidnaped and whose bodyguard has been slain. There have been several scientists kidnaped lately and their return has been marked by a singular drain on their brains. Richards has an important file in his possession and it's imperative that he be rescued before that information gets into the wrong hands. Caine visits Gatliff, a broker in illegal defense information, but that lead doesn't pan out. He eventually gets to a deserted manufacturing facility and finds some recording tape with the word "Ipcress" on it. Green makes a deal with Gatliff to get Richards back. Now Jackson, a Green aide, is mysteriously murdered just when it seems he's broken the case. Caine is taken to the factory to have his brain washed in a frightening sequence. He manages to survive that and confronts Green and Doleman. He has a gun on them and doesn't know which is the villain. Finally, Green is perceived as the traitor and Caine shoots him. The best part of the movie is Caine's characterization. He is anything but the super-hero. Rather, he is sort of an ordinary chap who is tossed into a maelstrom in much the same way Hitchcock used to place his people into situations beyond their scope and then let them triumph over what seemed to be unbeatable odds. Executive producer Charles Kasher, an old pal of Saltzman's, is the same man who made millions in the 1950s with his Charles Antell line of hair products ("made with lanolin" if you recall). If Furie wouldn't have insisted on weird angles, shooting under arms and between drum cymbals, this would have been much better, as the script had lots of wit and moved like a Ferrari at high speed.

p, Harry Saltzman; d, Sidney J. Furie; w, Bill Canaway, James Doran (based on the novel by Len Deighton); ph, Otto Heller (Techniscope, Technicolor); m, John Barry; ed, Peter Hunt; md, Barry; prod d, Ken Adam; art d, Peter Murton; set d, Michael White; makeup, Phil Leakey.

Spy Drama **(PR:A-C MPAA:NR)**

IPHIGENIA 1/2** (1977, Gr.) 130m Greek Film Center/Cinema 5 c

Irene Papas *(Clytemnestra)*, Costa Kazakos *(Agamemnon)*, Costa Carras *(Menelaus)*, Tatiana Papamoskou *(Iphigenia)*, Christos Tsangas *(Ulysses)*, Panos Michalopoulos *(Achilles)*, Angelos Yannoulis *(Servant)*, Dimitri Aronis *(Calchas)*, Georges Vourvahakis *(Orestes)*, Irene Koumarianou *(Nurse)*, Georges Economou *(Messenger)*.

A Greek tragedy based on a play written in 407 B.C. which tells the story of Kazakos, the leader of the Greek army, and the attempted sacrifice of his daughter Iphigenia, played by Papamoskou. His planned sacrifice is met with the approval of the gods, but Papas is less pleased, begging Kazakos to reconsider. Cacoyannis, one of Greece's finest directors, seems fully suited to adapt ancient Greek drama but the result is not especially thrilling in cinematic terms. (In Greek, English subtitles).

d&w, Michael Cacoyannis (based on the play "Iphigenia In Aulis" by Euripides); ph, Georges Arvantis; m, Mikis Theodorakis; ed, Cacoyannis, Takis Yannopoulos.

Drama **Cas.** **(PR:A MPAA:NR)**

IPNOSI (SEE: HYPNOSIS, 1966, Ital./Span./Ger.)

IRELAND'S BORDER LINE**

(1939, Ireland) 62m O.D. Productions/William Alexander bw (GB: BLARNEY)

Jimmy O'Dea *(Billy Brannigan)*, Myrette Morven *(Annie Burke)*, J.H. Edwin *(Michael O'Connor)*, Hazel Hughes *(Maura)*, Ronald Malcomson *(Sgt. MacAleer)*, Noel Purcell *(Sgt. Hogan)*, Julie Suedo *(Sadie Tyler)*, Jimmy Wildman *(Scutty Whelan)*, Tom Dunne *(Bullock Byrne)*, Kenneth Warrington *(Albert Tyler)*.

A comedy set in Ireland which plays up the rivalry between the free state and Ulster. O'Dea is a handyman who gets involved with a couple of crooks after doing some repair work on their car. His bag becomes mixed with theirs containing stolen jewels. The basic plot involves the crooks trying to get their bag back from O'Dea, who has no idea of the switch. Once he gets wise to the contents, however, he realizes that they are neighbors in disguise and employs the help of a local cop. The title of the film reflects a side story that has cops in both the north and the south trying to crack the case and the daughter of the pub owner where O'Dea becomes employed in love with a man from one side, while her father attempts to marry her off to someone from the other side. In the end the local cop cracks the case and also wins the favors of the lovely lass.

p&d, Harry O'Donovan; w, O'Donovan, Jimmy O'Dea.

Comedy **(PR:A MPAA:NR)**

IRENE*** (1940) 101m RKO bw-c

Anna Neagle *(Irene O'Dare)*, Ray Milland *(Don Marshall)*, Roland Young *(Mr. Smith)*, Alan Marshal *(Bob Vincent)*, May Robson *(Granny O'Dare)*, Billie Burke *(Mrs. Herman Vincent)*, Arthur Treacher *(Betherton)*, Marsha Hunt *(Eleanor Worth)*, Isabel Jewell *(Jane McGee)*, Doris Nolan *(Lillian)*, Stuart Robertson *(Freddie)*, Ethel Griffies *(Princess Minetti)*, Tommy Kelly *(Michael O'Dare)*, Juliette Compton *(Emily Newlands Grey)*, Roxanne Barkley *(Helen)*, Johnny Long and His Orchestra *(Themselves)*, Martha Tilton *(Susie Smith)*, The Dandridge Sisters *(Singers)*, Hattie Noel *(Mama)*, Louis Jean Heydt *(Biffy Webster, the Columnist)*, Rod Bacon *(Usher)*, Cyril Ring, Tom Quinn, Rosemary La Planche *(Dance Extras)*, Larry Steers, Major Sam Harris *(Guests)*, Nella Walker *(Mrs. Marshall)*, Alex D'Arcy *(Dumont, the Couturier)*, Syd Saylor *(Gardener)*.

The logical choices for this remake of the 1926 picture which was based on a 1919 musical would have been Astaire and Rogers. Neither wanted to make the film so the star chores were turned over to Milland and Neagle, who had just finished playing Queen Victoria and Nurse Edith Cavell. Neagle, an English actress, plays an Irish girl who moves from the slums to become a Cinderella and play with the rich folks on the north shore of Long Island. Milland and Marshal both fall for her and battle it out over her affections. Roland Young isn't given much to do as the man who manages the fashionable couturier shop where Neagle works. Marsha Hunt is the girl who would like to marry Marshal, but he turns her aside in favor of Neagle. Neagle is so Irish that we can barely understand her accent, and her grandmother, Robson, is even more Gaelic. Milland owns the business and is known as Mme. Lucy (in the 1926 version, George Arthur played the part as a gay). Lots of pleasant music, enough to warrant doing it again as a play many years later with Debbie Reynolds and Patsy Kelly. It was a hit once more and can probably still be attended somewhere almost every week in some small theater. There is a grand ball sequence shot in Technicolor, and Neagle's hair is seen to be bright red, something you might never know from the black and white shots. Songs include: "Irene," "Castle of Dreams," "You've Got Me Out On A Limb," "Alice Blue Gown," "Worthy Of You," "There's Something In the Air," "Sweet Vermosa Brown."

p&d, Herbert Wilcox; w, Alice Duer Miller (based on the musical comedy by James H. Montgomery), ph, Russell Metty; ed, Elmo Williams; md, Anthony Collins; art d, L.P. Williams; spec eff, Vernon Walker; ch, Alda Broadbent; m/l, Harry Tierney and Joseph McCarthy.

Musical/Comedy **(PR:A MPAA:NR)**

IRISH AND PROUD OF IT* 1/2 (1938, Ireland) 78m Crusade/Guaranteed bw

Richard Hayward *(Donogh O'Connor)*, Dinah Sheridan *(Moira Flaherty)*, Gwenilian Gill *(Mary Johnson)*, George Pembroke *(Mike Finnegan)*, Liam Gaffney *(Sean Casey)*, Herbert Thorpe *(Benito Colombo)*, Jimmy Mageen *(Old Flaherty)*, Jack Clifford, Shaun Desmond, J. Miles Merwyn, Wolf Curran, Charles Fagan.

Irish tenor Hayward is cast as an Irish businessman in London whose biggest blunder is admitting that he misses his homeland. Some of his mates "kidnap" him and drop him in the fields near his birthplace. A romance buds with farm gal Sheridan and he gets mixed up with some Chicago mobsters and their bootlegging operation. All ends well when he overcomes the gangsters and ends up striking a deal to sing radio spots in the U.S. for a food line he's developed.

p, Victor M. Greene; d, Donovan Pedelty; w, David Evans, Pedelty (based on the story by Dorothea Donn Byrne); ph, Geoffrey Faithfull.

Comedy **(PR:A MPAA:NR)**

IRISH EYES ARE SMILING*** (1944) 90m FOX c

Monty Woolley *(Edgar Brawley)*, June Haver *(Mary "Irish" O'Brien)*, Dick Haymes *(Ernest R. Ball)*, Anthony Quinn *(Al Jackson)*, Beverly Whitney *(Lucille Lacey)*, Maxie Rosenbloom *(Stanley Ketchel)*, Veda Ann Borg *(Belle La Tour)*, Clarence Kolb *(Betz)*, Chick Chandler *(Stage Manager)*, Kenny Williams *(Dancer)*, Michael Dalmatoff *(Headwaiter)*, Marian Martin *(Prima Donna)*, Charles Williams *(Song Plugger)*, Art Foster *(Sparring Partner)*, George Chandler *(Electrician)*, Mary Gordon *(Irish Woman)*, Emmett Vogan *(Purser)*, Pat O'Malley *(Steward)*, Minerva Urecal *(Militant Wife)*, Arthur Hohl *(Barker)*, J. Farrell MacDonald *(Doorman)*, Eddie Acuff *(Harry)*, Leonard Warren, Blanche Thebom *(Metropolitan Opera Singers)*, William "Billy" Newill *(Ticket Clerk)*, Robert E. Homans *(Cop)*, Charles E. Wilson *(Detective)*, John Sheehan *(Referee/Stage Manager)*, Marietta Canty *(Phoebe the Maid)*, Sam Wren *(Piano Player)*, Leo Mostovoy *(Pawnbroker)*, Maurice Cass *(Dr. Medford)*, Harry Seymour *(Pianist)*, Mary Adams Hayes, Ray Spiker *(Acrobats)*, Frank Marlowe, Ray Walker *(Hoofers)*, Joey Ray *(2nd Electrician)*, Max Smith, Martin Sperzel, John Rarig, Gurney Bell *(Sportsmen's Quartette)*.

A fictitious biography of songwriter Ernest R. Ball who, after getting kicked out of the Cleveland Conservatory of Music, tries his luck selling his tunes to a burlesque house. It is here that he sees Haver and, mistaking her for the show's star, falls for her. She gets fired and he follows her to New York. He tries to get work and ends up in a small nightclub. He sings a couple of his own melodies and impresses Whitney, a local celebrity. She takes his songs to the stage and turns him into an overnight sensation. Tunes include: "When Irish Eyes Are Smiling" (Ernest R. Ball, Chauncey Olcott, George Graff; sung by Dick Haymes), "Mother Machree" (Ball, Olcott, Rida Johnson Young), "Dear Little Boy Of Mine" (Ball, J. Keirn Brennan), "Let The Rest Of The World Go By" (Ball, Brennan), "A Little Bit Of Heaven" (Ball, Brennan), "Strut Miss Lizzie" (Henry Creamer, Turner Layton), "I'll Forget You" (Ball, Annalu Burns), "Love Me And The World Is Mine" (Ball, Dave Reed, Jr.), "I Don't Want A Million Dollars," " Bessie In A Bustle" (Mack Gordon, James V. Monaco), "Be My Little Baby Bumble Bee" (Stanley Murphy, Henry I. Marshall).

p, Damon Runyon; d, Gregory Ratoff; w, Earl Baldwin, John Tucker Battle (based on a story by E.A. Ellington); ph, Harry Jackson (Technicolor); ed, Harmon Jones; md, Alfred Newman, Charles Henderson; art d, Lyle Wheeler, Joseph C. Wright; spec eff, Fred Sersen; ch, Hermes Pan.

Musical **(PR:A MPAA:NR)**

IRISH FOR LUCK* 1/2 (1936, Brit.) 68m WB/FN-WB bw

Athene Seyler *(Duchess)*, Margaret Lockwood *(Ellen O'Hare)*, Patric Knowles *(Terry O'Ryan)*, Gibb McLaughlin *(Thady)*, Edward Rigby *(Hon. Denis Maguire)*, Eugene Leahy *(O'Callaghan)*, George Dillon *(Mooney)*, Terry Conlin *(Costello)*.

Seyler plays a penniless Irish duchess whose orphan niece, Lockwood, travels to England to seek fame as a singer and meets up with street guitarist Knowles. The two return, unsuccessful, to Ireland and find Seyler is now wealthy.

p, Irving Asher; d, Arthur Woods; w, Woods, Brock Williams (based on the novel by L.A.G. Strong).

Comedy **(PR:A MPAA:NR)**

IRISH HEARTS (SEE: NORAH O'NEALE, 1935, Brit.)

IRISH IN US, THE*** (1935) 84m FN/WB bw

James Cagney *(Danny O'Hara)*, Pat O'Brien *(Pat O'Hara)*, Olivia de Havilland *(Lucille Jackson)*, Frank McHugh *(Mike O'Hara)*, Allen Jenkins *(Car-Barn McCarthy)*, Mary Gordon *(Mrs. O'Hara)*, J. Farrell MacDonald *(Capt. Jackson)*, Thomas Jackson *(Doc Mullins)*, Harvey Perry *(Joe Delaney)*, Mabel Colcord *(Neighbor)*, Edward Keane *(Doctor)*, Herb Heywood *(Cook)*, Lucille Collins *(Girl)*, Bess Flowers *(Lady in Ring)*, Jack McHugh *(Messenger Boy)*, Mushy Callahan *(Referee)*, Emmett Vogan, Edward Gargan, Huntley Gordon, Will Stanton *(Men)*, Sailor Vincent *(Chick)*, Harry Seymour *(Announcer)*.

Gordon is a thick-brogued mother of three lovable Irish sons, Cagney, a sometimes fight manager, O'Brien, a tough cop, and McHugh, a daffy fireman. O'Brien tumbles for de Havilland who is the police captain's daughter, but she's head over heels in love with Cagney, which causes a rift between the brothers. Cagney then becomes obsessed with promoting fighter Jenkins into a champ, a hopeless cause. On the eve of the big fight, Jenkins dives into a bottle and gets stinko, forcing Cagney to put on the gloves and climb into the ring to save his face and win de Havilland's heart, as well as the respect of brother O'Brien. This is routine but fast-paced comedy with Cagney and O'Brien interplaying beautifully. The story is all Irish blarney but, as such, is charming, with McHugh and Jenkins providing plenty of laughs. This kind of film, Cagney later stated, was called a "cuff opera," since he, O'Brien, and others added dialog to the script off-the-cuff.

p, Samuel Bischoff; d, Lloyd Bacon; w, Earl Baldwin (based on the story by Frank Orsatti); ph, George Barnes; ed, James Gibbon; md, Leo F. Forbstein; art d, Esdras Hartley; cos, Orry-Kelly; makeup, Perc Westmore.

Comedy **(PR:A MPAA:NR)**

IRISH LUCK** (1939) 58m MON bw

Frankie Darro *(Buzzy O'Brien)*, Dick Purcell *(Lanahan)*, Lillian Elliott *(Mrs. O'Brien)*, Sheila Darcy *(Kitty Monahan)*, James Flavin *(Fluger)*, Dennis Moore *(Jim)*, Mantan Moreland *(Jefferson)*, Howard Mitchell *(Hotel Manager)*.

Darro is a bellhop-turned-sleuth who tries to uncover the mysterious goings-on in the hotel where he works. Darcy is a pretty young lass who is suspected of murder, but is cleared, thanks to Darro's skill and the "luck o' the Irish."

p, Scott R. Dunlap, Grant Withers; d, Howard Bretherton; w, Mary C. McCarthy (based on the story "Death Hops The Bells" by Charles Molyneaux Brown); ph, Harry Neumann; ed, Russell Schoengarth.

Mystery/Comedy **(PR:A MPAA:NR)**

IRISH WHISKEY REBELLION** (1973) 93m GSF-Cinerama c

William Devane, Anne Meara, Richard Mulligan, David Groh, Stephen Joyce, Judie Rolin, William Challee.

A surface probe of an Irish rum running operation in 1927 while America was in the midst of prohibition. The profits were then sent back home to help the IRA's cause. Devane's performance is up to his usual high standard and the period atmosphere is believable, but that's still not enough to raise the film above mediocrity. Actress Anne Meara has toured with husband Jerry Stiller in a comedy act and with him has also done humorous TV commercials. She also starred in and wrote a TV movie "The Other Woman." Actor Richard Mulligan starred on the TV series "Soap" and received an Emmy for same in 1980.

d, J.C. Works [Chester Erskine].

Drama **(PR:C MPAA:PG)**

IRISHMAN, THE*** (1978, Aus.) 108m Forest Home/Greater Union c

Michael Craig *(Paddy Doolan)*, Simon Burke *(Michael Doolan)*, Robin Nevin *(Jenny Doolan)*, Lou Brown *(Will Doolan)*, Tui Lorraine Bow *(Granny Doolan)*, Andrew Maguire *(Grandpa Doolan)*, Tony Barry *(Robert Dalgliesh)*, Marcella Burgoyne *(Mrs. Dalgliesh)*, Vincent Ball *(Bailey Clark)*, Roberta Grant *(Mrs. Clark)*, Gerard Kennedy *(Chad Logan)*, Bryan Brown *(Eric Haywood)*, Roger Ward *(Kevin Quilty)*, Babette Stevens *(Hotel Missus)*.

Craig is an Irish immigrant teamster in 1920s Australia who doesn't take kindly to progress. He reacts stubbornly to the advent of the internal combustion engine when he realizes it will put an end to his team of 20 Clydesdale horses. What develops is a powerful struggle between members of his family and his own self-esteem. While sentimental in some parts, it is effective in its portrayal of human emotions and individuality.

p, Anthony Buckley; d, Donald Crombie; w, Crombie (based on a novel by Elizabeth O'Conner); ph, Peter James (Agfacolor); m, Charles Marawood; ed, Tim Wellburn; prod d, Owen Williams; art d, Graham Walker; cos, Judith Dorsman.

Drama **Cas.** **(PR:A MPAA:NR)**

IRMA LA DOUCE*** (1963) 147m Mirisch-Phalanx-Alperson/UA c

Jack Lemmon *(Nestor)*, Shirley MacLaine *(Irma La Douce)*, Lou Jacobi *(Moustache)*, Bruce Yarnell *(Hippolyte)*, Herschel Bernardi *(Inspector LeFevre)*, Hope Holiday *(Lolita)*, Joan Shawlee *(Amazon Annie)*, Grace Lee Whitney *(Kiki the Cossack)*, Tura Satana *(Suzette Wong)*, Harriette Young *(Mimi the MauMau)*, Paul Dubov *(Andre)*, Howard McNear *(Concierge)*, Cliff Osmond *(Police Sergeant)*, Diki Lerner *(Jojo)*, Herb Jones *(Casablanca Charlie)*, Jane Earl, Ruth Earl *(Zebra Twins)*, James Brown *(Texan Customer)*, Bill Bixby *(Tattooed Sailor)*, Sheryl Deauville *(Carmen)*, Lou Krugman, John Alvin *(Customers)*, Susan Woods *(Poule With the Balcony)*, Billy Beck *(Officer DuPont)*, Jack Sahakian *(Jack)*, Don Diamond *(Man With Samples)*, Edgar Barrier *(General Lafayette)*, Richard Peel *(Englishman)*, Joe Palma *(Prison Guard)*, Shorty *(Coquette, a Dog)*.

IRMA LA DOUCE has had a curious history; a French musical in 1956, an American adaptation (with British actors) in 1960, then this music-less film. At 147 minutes, it was far too long to be a light-hearted farcical romp, and the dull spots outnumber the high spots, but MacLaine and Lemmon manage to overcome the fat Diamond/Wilder script and Wilder's often lethargic direction. Wilder had long been the master of this type of film and was the logical choice to adapt it with his collaborator, Diamond, but it just missed. MacLaine is a streetwalker near the Les Halles area of Paris who gives all of her money to handsome Yarnell, her pimp. Into the street comes Lemmon, a cop who is the forerunner of Clouseau in his bumbling ineptitude, but sincere attitude. Lemmon cannot believe all the women plying their trade and seeks to reform the area so he personally raids a local bistro run by Jacobi. In the raid, Bernardi, the chief police inspector, is arrested and Lemmon is rewarded by being sacked from his job. Lemmon and MacLaine become an item and she fires Yarnell and takes Lemmon on as her "protector." The one thing a pimp must be above is falling in love with his charges, but Lemmon has never done this kind of work before and is soon enamored of MacLaine and increasingly jealous of her professional work. Lemmon gets Jacobi to help him pose as a titled, aged Englishman, who wants to rent MacLaine and pay her well for one visit per week. Furthermore, Lemmon (as the old man) claims he is unable to perform sexually and just wants to talk to her. He figures that if she makes enough money from this fictitious old man, she won't have to do the things she's been used to doing. But that requires more money than he has, so Lemmon must go to work at a Les Halles produce market. He toils all night and gets home too weak to make love to her. Believing he may be seeing another woman, *she* becomes jealous, and asks Lemmon (as the old man) to take her to England. On that trip, she brings his impotence to a halt. Lemmon thinks it is about time to get rid of the old man so he dumps the clothes into the Seine. Yarnell has been following Lemmon and, upon seeing the floating clothes, turns Lemmon in as the killer of the old Englishman. The irony is that Lemmon won't reveal the truth, lest he lose MacLaine. In jail, he learns that MacLaine is pregnant and that inspires him to escape. The only way to clear himself of the murder of a man who didn't ever exist is to come back as that man, so Lemmon again dons the mustache and white hair and convinces everyone that he was never dead. Lemmon and MacLaine get married and at the end of the ceremony, she gives birth in the church. Lemmon gets his old policeman's job back and he and MacLaine are presumed to live happily ever after. Previn won an Oscar and MacLaine and La Shelle were nominated, but this was a far from satisfying critical success. Elizabeth Taylor was once considered for the lead and Charles Laughton's death kept him from playing the Jacobi role. Although it grossed almost $13 million in its first go-around, IRMA LA DOUCE should have had music to sing and dances to dance. Jacobi was wonderful as the bistro owner. He always does a good job in whatever role he takes, from the addled waiter in TV's "Coffee, Tea Or Me," to the rest home owner in OFF YOUR ROCKER (two of his more obscure jobs). The set was constructed in a 360-degree fashion so shooting could be done in any direction. For this role, MacLaine won the Golden Globe as well as the Best Actress award from *Film Daily*, a motion picture trade paper. But the feeling lingers about what might have been with either a half hour cut out or 12 good songs by Strouse and Adams, or Coleman and Leigh.

p&d, Billy Wilder; w, Wilder, I.A.L. Diamond (based on the play by Alexandre Breffort); ph, Joseph La Shelle (Panavision, Technicolor); m, Andre Previn (based on a score by Marguerite Monnot); ed, Daniel Mandell; art d, Alexander Trauner; set d, Edward G. Boyle, Maurice Barnathan; cos, Orry-Kelly; spec eff, Milton Rice; ch, Wally Green; makeup, Emile Lavigne, Harry Ray, Frank Westmore.

Comedy **Cas.** **(PR:C-O MPAA:NR)**

IRO (SEE: SPOILS OF THE NIGHT, 1969, Jap.)

IRON ANGEL*½ (1964) 84m Ken Kennedy Prod. bw

Jim Davis *(Sergeant Walsh)*, Margo Woode *(Nurse Fleming)*, Donald Barry, R. Wayland Williams, L.Q. Jones, Dave Barker, Joe Jenckes, John S. Hirohata.

A half-dozen soldiers are on a mission to locate North Korean guns which serve as an obstacle to their "Crazy Fox" convoy. They are held back more by personal problems than by enemy fire, especially with Walsh suffering a pair of breakdowns. Regulation-enforcing nurse Woode shows up in her "Iron Angel" ambulance, and slows the operation even further, but they are eventually successful in putting the guns out of commission.

p, Daniel P. Foley; d&w, Ken Kennedy.

War **(PR:A MPAA:NR)**

IRON COLLAR, THE (SEE: SHOWDOWN, 1963)

IRON CURTAIN, THE***

(1948) 87m FOX bw (AKA: BEHIND THE IRON CURTAIN)

Dana Andrews *(Igor Gouzenko)*, Gene Tierney *(Anna Gouzenko)*, June Havoc *(Karanova)*, Berry Kroeger *(Grubb)*, Edna Best *(Mrs. Foster)*, Stefan Schnabel *(Ranev)*, Nicholas Joy *(Dr. Norman)*, Eduard Franz *(Maj. Kulin)*, Frederic Tozere *(Col. Trigorin)*, Noel Cravat *(Bushkin)*, Christopher Robin Olsen *(Andrei)*, Peter Whitney *(Winikov)*, Leslie Barrie *(Editor)*, Mauritz Hugo *(Leonard Loetz)*, John Shay *(Sergeyev)*, Victor Wood *(Capt. Class)*, Anne Curson *(Helen Tweedy)*, Helena Dare *(Mrs. Kulin)*, Eula Morgan *(Mrs. Trigorin)*, Reed Hadley *(Commentator)*, John Ridgeley *(Policeman Murphy)*, Michael J. Dugan *(Policeman)*, John Davidson *(Secretary)*, Joe Whitehead *(William Hollis)*, Harry Carter *(Fairfield)*, Robert Adler *(Wilson)*, Arthur E. Gould-Porter *(Mr. Foster)*, Matthew Boulton *(Inspector Burns)*.

Based on the actual case of a defecting Soviet spy, Andrews plays Gouzenko, a code clerk who leaves his embassy in Ottawa and asks Canadian authorities for asylum. Andrews informs the Allies of Soviet espionage activities and the Russians demand that he be returned to them. Many attempts are made on Andrews' life but he manages to survive the machinations of the Russian killers. He has undertaken to help the Western countries at the urging of his wife Tierney so that his newly born child will grow up in a free country. Wellman directed this film with his usual fine skill and both Tierney and Andrews are exceptional but the plot is hackneyed and the script a bit predictable. Shot on location in Canada.

p, Sol C. Siegel; d, William A. Wellman; w, Milton Krims (based on the memoirs of Igor Gouzenko); ph, Charles C. Clark; m, Dmitri Shostakovich, Serge Prokofieff, Aram Khachaturian, Nicholas Miaskovsky; ed, Louis Loeffler; md, Alfred Newman; art d, Lyle Wheeler, Mark Lee Kirk; set d, Thomas Little; cos, Bonnie Cashin; spec eff, Fred Sersen; makeup, Ben Nye, Dick Smith.

Spy Drama **(PR:A MPAA:NR)**

IRON DUKE, THE½** (1935, Brit.) 80m GAU bw

George Arliss *(Duke of Wellington)*, Gladys Cooper *(Duchess of Angouleme)*, Emlyn Williams *(Bates)*, Ellaline Terriss *(Duchess Kitty)*, A. E. Matthews *(Lord Hill)*, Allan Aynesworth *(Louis XVIII)*, Lesley Wareing *(Lady Frances Webster)*, Edmund Willard *(Marshal Ney)*, Franklin Dyall *(Blucher)*, Felix Aylmer *(Lord Uxbridge)*, Gibb McLaughlin *(Talleyrand)*, Peter Gawthorne *(Duke of Richmond)*, Norma Varden *(Duchess of Richmond)*, Walter Sondes *(Wedderburn Webster)*, Campbell Gullan *(D'Artois)*, Gyles Isham *(Castlereagh)*, Frederick Leister *(King of Prussia)*, Gerald Lawrence *(Czar)* Edmund Willard, Farren Souter, Paddie Naismith.

Famed thespian George Arliss made a career of playing historical figures important in the development of Western Civilization (Voltaire, Disraeli, Richelieu, Rothschild, Alexander Hamilton) on stage and screen. In THE IRON DUKE Arliss adds another to his resume with his portrayal of Britain's Duke of Wellington. The film only details the events in Wellington's life from 1815 to 1816, but this year was packed with enough conflict and intrigue to last a lifetime. After defeating Napoleon at the Battle of Waterloo, Arliss discovers that he must contend with a political hornet's nest that has been stirred up by his decision not to impose severe sanctions on the French. The British House of Lords decries the decision, wanting to take territory and goods from the defeated French, but Arliss refuses because the whole of Europe would be shattered. Meanwhile Cooper, the daughter of Marie Antoinette, schemes to ruin Arliss by revealing his affair with a married woman to the press. Eventually Arliss redeems himself with the House of Lords and the public, securing his place in history. For all its pretensions of epic historical grandeur, THE IRON DUKE is a very episodic, claustrophobic film that fails to convey the scope of Wellington's life and times. The Battle of Waterloo is staged with such a sparse number of extras that the scene never really opens up to show the panoramic sweep of this important military event. The manner in which the battle is introduced and presented makes it seem casual and unimportant and thus the film fails to impart just how vital the events afterward were to the fate of Europe. Not only is the pace and direction of THE IRON DUKE uninspired and haphazard, but the script is rife with historical inaccuracies, the glossing over of less flattering events, and definite misrepresentation in the case of Marshal Ney's (Willard) execution. THE IRON DUKE came at the end of a cycle of European historical dramas and the genre had just about run its course by then, leaving the critics and the public cold.

p, Michael Balcon; d, Victor Saville; w, Bess Meredyth (based on incidents in the life of the Duke of Wellington); ph, Curt Courant.

Historical Biography **(PR:A MPAA:NR)**

IRON FIST (SEE: AWAKENING OF JIM BURKE, 1935)

IRON GLOVE, THE½** (1954) 77m COL c

Robert Stack *(Charles Wogan)*, Ursula Thiess *(Ann Brett)*, Richard Stapley *(James Stuart)*, Charles Irwin *(James O'Toole)*, Alan Hale, Jr. *(Patrick Gaydon)*, Leslie Bradley *(Duke of Somerfield)*, Paul Cavanagh *(Cavenly)*, Otto Waldis *(King George)*, Rica Owen *(Princess Clementina)*, Eric Feldary *(Austrian Lieutenant)*,

David Bruce *(Austrian Sergeant)*, Shirley Whitney *(Anny)*, Ingard Dawson *(Gretzel)*, Louis D. Merrill *(Count DuLusac)*.

Stack is a swashbuckling Irish swordsman who, with Scottish prince Stapley, tries to seize the throne of King George I. His bravery allows him to rescue Stapley's bride-to-be and to win the affections of Thiess, a spy who succumbs to Stack's charms. The drama and romance are average, though Castle's direction of the swordplay is calculated for maximum excitement.

p, Sam Katzman; d, William Castle; w, Jesse L. Lasky, Jr., DeVallon Scott, Douglas Heyes (based on a story by Robert E. Kent, Samuel J. Jacoby); ph, Henry Freulich (Technicolor); m, Mischa Bakaleinikoff; ed, Gene Havlick.

Action/Romance **(PR:A MPAA:NR)**

IRON KISS, THE (SEE: NAKED KISS, THE, 1964)

IRON MAIDEN, THE (SEE: SWINGING MAIDEN, THE, 1962, Brit.)

IRON MAJOR, THE*** (1943) 85m RKO bw

Pat O'Brien *(Frank Cavanaugh)*, Ruth Warrick *(Florence "Mike" Ayres Cavanaugh)*, Robert Ryan *(Father Tim Donovan)*, Leon Ames *(Robert Stewart)*, Russell Wade *(Pvt. Manning)*, Bruce Edwards *(Lt. Jones)*, Richard Martin *(Davis Cavanaugh)*, Robert Bice *(Coach)*, Virginia Brissac *(Mrs. Ayres)*, Lew Harvey *(Lieutenant)*, Bud Geary *(Sergeant)*, Walter Brooke *(Lt. Stone)*, Louis Jean Heydt *(Recruiting Sergeant)*, Frank Puglia *(Nurse)*, Pierre Watkin *(Col. White)*, Walter Fenner *(Doctor)*, Louis Borell *(French Officer)*, Billy Roy *(Bob as a Boy)*, Robert Winkler *(Frank as a Boy)*, Joel Davis *(Davie as a Boy)*, Cy Ring *(Ross)*, Henry Roquemore *(Evans)*, Barbara Hale *(Sarah Cavanaugh)*, Kirk Alyn *(John Cavanaugh)*, James Jordan *(Philip Cavanaugh)*, Dean Benton *(William Cavanaugh)*, Margaret L. Landry *(Sis Cavanaugh)*, Myron Healey *(Paul Cavanaugh)*, Wheaton Chambers *(Army Doctor)*, Pat O'Malley *(Charlie)*, Arnold Stanford, Bob Thom *(Soldiers)*, Harry Tyler, Eddie Woods *(Friends)*, Gloria Duran, Ramon Ros *(Dancers)*, Bonnie Braunger *(Baby)*, Sada Simmons, Mary Currier *(Nurses)*, Joseph Crehan *(Judge)*, Joe King *(Defense Attorney)*, Eddie Hart *(Bailiff)*, Milton Kibbee *(Watkins)*, Paul Le Pere *(Court Clerk)*, Joe O'Connor *(2nd Defense Attorney)*, Victor Kilian *(Francis Cavanaugh)*, Ian Wolfe *(Prof. Runnymead)*, Harold Landon, James Courtney, Buddy Varus, Mel Schubert, Greg McClure *(Boston College Players)*, Charles D. Brown, William Forrest *(Officials)*, Sam McDaniel *(Pete)*, John Miljan *(Oregon Coach)*, Larry Lund, Robert Benton, Steve Barclay *(Football Players)*, Walt Robbins, Sid Jordan *(Drivers of 2- Up)*, James Flavin, Russ Clark *(Umpires)*, Brooks Benedict, Brandon Beach *(Alumni)*, John B. Williams *(Pullman Porter)*, Florence Hansen *(Bob's Girl Friend)*, Fred Kohler, Jr. *(Boston College Captain)*, John Dilson *(Doctor)*, James Magill, Steve Winston, Gordon Clark *(Students)*, Dorothy Vaughn *(Ma Cavanaugh)*, Frank Shannon *(Pa Cavanaugh)*, Paul McVey *(Athletic Coach)*, Chuck Hamilton *(Fordham Player)*, Richard Davies *(Chuck)*, Roland DuPree, Michael Miller, Bobby Larson, Richard Dillon *(Boys)*, Robert Anderson, Mike Lally, Lee Phelps, Craig Flanagan, Michael Road.

Pat O'Brien returns to the gridiron after his 1940 portrayal of Knute Rockne, this time as legendary coach Frank Cavanaugh of Dartmouth, Boston College, and Fordham. Raising a family of 10 children and coming home from WW I a major, Cavanaugh believed in three things—"love of God, love of country, and love of family." With his wife Warrick (who was also cast as Charlie Kane's wife in CITIZEN KANE) at his side, O'Brien consistently took his teams to victory. Even with his eyesight nearly gone, the great coach took his team to the top after winning the famed 1932 Fordham-Oregon State game. O'Brien's energetic and charismatic performance truly captures the spirit of Cavanaugh. Ryan turns in a fine job of acting as O'Brien's priest and former teammate. Based on a story by Cavanaugh's wife, and edited by Robert Wise.

p, Robert Fellows; d, Ray Enright; w, Aben Kandel, Warren Duff (based on a story by Florence Cavanaugh), ph, Robert de Grasse; m, Roy Webb; ed, Robert Wise, Philip Martin, Jr.; md, C. Bakaleinikoff; art d, Albert S. D'Agostino, Carroll Clark; set d, Darrell Silvera, Al Fields.

Drama/Biography **(PR:A MPAA:NR)**

IRON MAN, THE*** (1931) 73m UNIV bw

Lew Ayres *(Kid Mason)*, Robert Armstrong *(George Regan)*, Jean Harlow *(Rose Mason)*, John Miljan *(Paul H. Lewis)*, Eddie Dillon *(Jeff)*, Mike Donlin *(McNeil)*, Morrie Cohan *(Rattler O'Keefe)*, Mary Doran *(The Show Girl—Rose's Pal)*, Mildred Van Dorn *(Gladys DeVere)*, Ned Sparks *(Riley)*, Sam Blum *(Mandel)*, Sammy Gervon *(Trainer)*, Tom Kennedy *(Bartender)*, Bob Perry *(Referee)*, Wade Boteler *(Reporter)*, Claire Whitney *(Louise Lewis)*.

Armstrong, a fight manager, becomes increasingly worried when his best prospect, Ayres, demonstrates an alarming lack of sound judgment regarding his scheming wife Harlow. The lovesick boxer is totally dominated by the woman, and it is obvious to Armstrong that she's only in it for the money. When Ayres loses a big fight, Harlow leaves him and goes to Hollywood in search of fame and fortune in the movies. Armstrong seizes the opportunity and submerges the depressed Ayres into an intensive training program. The hard work and concentration pay off, shooting Ayres on his way to the championship. When Harlow hears of her husband's new success, she abandons her dead-end film career and returns to him to reap the profits. Disgusted that she has returned, Armstrong tells Ayres what he thinks of Harlow. The boxer angrily socks his manager, forcing Armstrong to tear up their contract. This of course delights Harlow, who then cons her husband into hiring her secret lover, Miljan, as his new manager. Miljan is more interested in Harlow than in managing Ayres and by the time of the big fight, the boxer is badly out of shape. On the night of the fight, Armstrong visits Ayres and discovers a letter from Miljan's wife which states she is naming Harlow as the third party in a divorce suit. Finally awakened to his wife's true nature, Ayres throws both Harlow and Miljan out. Ayres enters the ring with a clear head, and though he loses the fight, he has learned his lesson. Known mainly for his horror films (LONDON AFTER MIDNIGHT, DRACULA, FREAKS, MARK OF THE VAMPIRE), director Browning also had years of experience directing melodramas in the silent era. In THE IRON MAN, Browning returned to the form and did some competent, if unremarkable, work from a script based on a W. R. Burnett novel. Though the featured stars were Ayres and Harlow, the film really belongs to Armstrong, who grabs the picture away from them with his rapid-fire delivery and hard-boiled mannerisms. Harlow, who was being given high exposure since the release of HELL'S ANGELS (1930), gives a weak performance here. This was her one and only leading role at Universal, and the only time she worked with Ayres. The "blonde bombshell" had trouble with serious histrionics and she really wouldn't hit big onscreen until she left Universal for MGM and was allowed to bring her comedic talents to the fore in such pictures as RED-HEADED WOMAN, RED DUST, and DINNER AT EIGHT. THE IRON MAN was remade in 1937 as SOME BLONDES ARE DANGEROUS and again in 1951 under its original title.

p, Carl Laemmle, Jr.; d, Tod Browning; w, Francis Edward Faragoh (based on the novel by W. R. Burnett); ph, Percy Hilburn; ed, Maurice Pivar, Milton Carruth.

Drama **(PR:A MPAA:NR)**

IRON MAN, THE1/2** (1951) 81m UNIV bw

Jeff Chandler *(Coke Mason)*, Evelyn Keyes *(Rose Warren)*, Stephen McNally *(George Mason)*, Joyce Holden *(Tiny)*, Rock Hudson *(Speed O'Keefe)*, Jim Backus *(Max Watkins)*, Jim Arness *(Alex)*, Paul Javor *(Pete)*, Steve Martin *(Joe Savella)*, Eddie Simms *(Jackie Bowden)*, George Baxter *(Herb Riley)*, Raymond Gray *(Jo Jo Meyers)*, Walter "Whitey" Ekwart *(Whitey)*, John Maxwell *(Dr. Rowan)*, Larry J. Blake *(Ralph Crowley)*, Ken Patterson *(Herb Daly)*, Herbert Vigran *(Melio)*, Peter Scott *(Nick Noraworski)*, Gene Wesson *(Sports Writer)*, Johnny Call *(Mike Durant)*, Steve Roberts *(Brad Morris)*, Bob Evans *(Loomis)*, Frank Marlowe *(Trainer)*, Charles Sullivan *(Referee of Championship Fight)*, Stu Wilson *(Man)*, James Lennon *(Announcer)*, Barbara Ann Knudson *(Girl)*, Gregg Sherwood *(Gwendolyn)*, Cy Ring *(Headwaiter)*, Ethan Laidlaw *(Miner)*, John Indrisano *(Referee at Chicago Arena)*, Mushy Callahan *(Referee at Allentown Arena)*, Frank Moran *(Handler)*, John Carpenter *(Spectator)*, John Nikcovich *(Bit)*.

The third screen version of W.R. Burnett's boxing novel, this time starring Chandler as a poor coal miner who is desperate to marry his girl friend Keyes and get out of the mines. The ambitious young man has his eye on a small radio store for sale and, knowing that it would take years for him to save the money from his mining salary, he decides to become a prizefighter. Managed by his older brother, McNally, Chandler soon makes it big on the boxing circuit. Unfortunately, the good-hearted miner turns vicious in the ring, especially after being hurt. Chandler soon falls out of favor with the public due to his savage punching, and he takes severe beatings himself despite the fact that he wins his fights. Worried that he will be consumed by the violence, Keyes and McNally try to get him thrown out of boxing. Chandler uncovers the plot before they can set it into motion and disowns them both. Pushing on with new managers, Chandler becomes the champion. Refusing to give up, Keyes and McNally arrange for Chandler's best friend, Hudson, to fight him. When confronted with the reality of having to savage his closest friend, Chandler drops his killer instincts and boxes in a more civilized manner. The move reinstates the public's faith in him and patches things up between him and his loved ones. Director Pevney keeps things moving along at a rapid clip and is greatly aided by a strong cast of supporting players, especially Hudson as the friend and Backus as a sportswriter.

p, Aaron Rosenberg; d, Joseph Pevney; w, George Zuckerman, Borden Chase (based on the story by William R. Burnett); ph, Carl Guthrie; ed, Russell Schoengarth; md, Joseph Gershenson; art d, Bernard Herzbrun, Robert Boyle; cos, Bill Thomas.

Drama **(PR:C MPAA:NR)**

IRON MASK, THE*** (1929) 95m UA bw

Douglas Fairbanks *(D'Artagnan)*, Belle Bennett *(The Queen Mother)*, Marguerite de la Motte *(Constance)*, Dorothy Revier *(Milady De Winter)*, Vera Lewis *(Mme. Peronee)*, Rolfe Sedan *(Louis XIII)*, William Bakewell *(Louis XIV/Louis XIV's Twin)*, Gordon Thorpe *(The Young Prince/The Young Prince's Twin)*, Nigel de Brulier *(Cardinal Richelieu)*, Ullrich Haupt *(Rochefort)*, Lon Poff *(Father Joseph)*, Charles Stevens *(Planchet, D'Artagnan's Servant)*, Henry Otto *(The King's Valet)*, Leon Bary *(Athos)*, Stanley J. Sandford *(Porthos)*, Gino Corrado *(Aramis)*.

The last of Douglas Fairbanks' true swashbuckling adventures, THE IRON MASK is something of a sequel to his phenomenally popular THE THREE MUSKETEERS and reunites many of the original cast members (de Brulier, Poff, de la Motte, and Bary). The film opens as the wife of King Louis XIII gives birth to twins. Cardinal Richelieu (de Brulier) learns of the two births, seizes one of the infants, and takes it to Spain in order to safeguard the throne. The evil Haupt, who has designs on the kingdom, kidnaps de la Motte, a seamstress who witnessed the births, and holds her captive lest she reveal what she has seen. Haupt's plot is interrupted by Fairbanks as D'Artagnan, the lover of de la Motte, and he rides to the rescue. Tragically, de la Motte is killed in the rescue attempt, leaving an angry and embittered Fairbanks lusting for revenge against Haupt. Upon his return, Fairbanks is told by his superiors to guard the young prince. Meanwhile, Haupt has kidnaped the second twin and raises the boy to be the rightful heir to the throne. Years later, when the boys have grown into young men and the rule of France has shifted to the first twin, Haupt surfaces and sets his plan into action. The villain kidnaps Louis XIV and imprisons him in a faraway cell. He then installs his protege, the second twin, as king. Fairbanks learns of the plot, and, together with his companions Athos (Bary), Porthos (Sandford), and Aramis (Corrado), he rides to the true king's rescue. In the ensuing battle all the musketeers are killed, with Fairbanks dying last at the hands of the young impostor. The musketeers did not die in vain, however, because the real Louis XIV is saved and the impostor condemned to spend the rest of his life in an iron mask. The film ends as the spirits of Sandford, Corrado, and Bary beckon for Fairbanks to join them in the netherworld. His spirit rises and the four brave comrades walk off into the distance arm-in-arm. THE IRON MASK is basically a silent film with sparse passages of dialog spliced in for added box office appeal. Veteran helmsman Dwan, who directed Fairbanks in ROBIN HOOD (1922), simply added a spoken prologue and epilog to appease the studio. The first sound sequence opens with Fairbanks asking the audience to join him in those swashbuckling days of yesteryear and the second vocal is similar to the first. The rest of the film is silent, with music and sound effects synchronized with the visuals. Unfortunately, this would be the last time audiences were treated to Fairbanks' athletic derring-do. His subsequent films (THE TAMING OF THE SHREW, REACHING FOR THE MOON, AROUND THE WORLD IN 80 MINUTES, MR. ROBINSON CRUSOE, and THE PRIVATE LIFE OF DON JUAN) required little in the way of physical prowess and their stories lacked the excitement of his best work. Remade as THE MAN IN THE IRON MASK.

d, Allan Dwan; w, Elton Thomas (based on the novels *The Three Musketeers* and *The Viscount of Bragelonne* by Alexandre Dumas pere); ph, Henry Sharpe, Warren Lynch; m, Hugo Riesenfeld; prod d, Maurice Leloir; ed, William Nolan; art d, Burgess Beall; cos, Maurice Leloir, Gilbert Clark; spec eff, Walter Pallman; m/l, "One for All, All for One," Ray Klages, Louis Alter; makeup, Fred C. Ryle.

Adventure **Cas.** **(PR:A MPAA:NR)**

IRON MASTER, THE** (1933) 65m Hoffman/AA bw

Reginald Denny *(Steve Mason)*, Lila Lee *(Janet Stillman)*, J. Farrell MacDonald *(J.C. Stillman)*, Esther Howard *(Mrs. Stillman)*, William Janney *(David Stillman)*, Virginia Sale *(Miss Smith)*, Richard Tucker *(Paul Rankin)*, Astrid Allwyn *(Flo Lancert)*, Tom London *(Turner)*, Nola Luxford *(Diana)*, Otto Hoffman *(Grange)*, Freddie Frederick *(Little Billy)*, Ronnie Cosbey *(Little Billy)*.

Denny is a young, intelligent mill worker who is left to manage his dead boss's estate, much to the chagrin of the surviving family members. He has the boss's son and daughter go to work for him in the factory against their will. To get back at Denny they begin to give trade secrets to a rival company until the daughter falls in love and thereby cleans up her act.

d, Chester M. Franklin; w, Adele Buffington (based on the stage play "Le Maitre Des Forges" by Georges Ohnet); ph, Harry Neumann, Tom Galligan; ed, Mildred Johnston; art d, Gene Hornbostel.

Drama **(PR:A MPAA:NR)**

IRON MISTRESS, THE** 1/2 (1952) 110m WB c

Alan Ladd *(Jim Bowie)*, Virginia Mayo *(Judalon de Bornay)*, Joseph Calleia *(Juan Moreno)*, Phyllis Kirk *(Ursula de Veramendi)*, Alf Kjellin *(Philippe de Cabanal)*, Douglas Dick *(Narcisse de Bornay)*, Tony Caruso *("Bloody Jack" Sturdevant)*, Ned Young *(Henri Contrecourt)*, George Voskovec *(James Audubon)*, Richard Carlyle *(Rezin Bowie)*, Robert Emhardt *(Gen. Cuny)*, Donald Beddoe *(Dr. Cuny)*, Harold Gordon *(Andrew Marschalk)*, Gordon Nelson *(Dr. Maddox)*, Jay Novello *(Judge Crain)*, Nick Dennis *(Nez Coupe)*, Sarah Selby *(Mrs. Bowie)*, Dick Paxton *(John Bowie)*, George Lewis *(Col. Wells)*, Edward Colmans *(Don Juan de Veramendi)*, Daria Massey *(Teresa de Veramendi)*, Ramsey Hill *(Mulot)*, Eugene Borden *(Cocquelon)*, Jean Del Val *(St. Sylvain)*, Amanda Randolph *(Maria)*, Reed Howes, Dick Cogan *(Players)*, Salvador Baguez *(Mexican Artist)*, Madge Blake *(Mrs. Cuny)*, David Wolfe *(James Black)*, Richard Crane.

This was Ladd's first film for Warner Bros. after leaving Paramount where he had been one of that studio's great stars for more than a decade. Warner Bros. lavished a big production on his first time out for them. Here he plays the flamboyant frontiersman and adventurer Jim Bowie, gambler, real estate entrepreneur, knife-fighting duellist and lover of beautiful Southern belles. Ladd arrives in New Orleans to sell his family's lumber, hewn out of the remote bayou lands. Voskovec (as the famed naturalist and painter James Audubon) befriends him and introduces him to high Southern society, including the beauteous but totally self-centered Mayo, whose whole life has been lived in luxury and with the flattering attention of adoring males. Ladd, the naive country boy, falls hard for Mayo but must contend with a number of beaus pitching wild woo at her—Calleia, a ruthless politician; Young, a rich and sinister duelist; and playboy Kjellin. In no time at all Ladd has sold his lumber and his family's mill, gambled with the shrewdest cardsharps of New Orleans to win more money, and bought a sprawling plantation, all to win the mercenary heart of Mayo. His close, newly-acquired friend Dick, Mayo's brother, is killed in a duel, and still Ladd hasn't won Mayo's hand. He needs more money, so he teams up with bayou killer Caruso to enter a horse in the Duncan Cup Race, beating Calleia's prize horse and incurring Calleia's wrath ever after. With his racetrack winnings, Ladd is now wealthy and he goes to Mayo to ask her to marry him, but discovers that she's married Kjellin, who instantly threatens Ladd. The latter goes to a blacksmith and a double-edged knife is forged allegedly from a meteorite, which, the smith tells Ladd, "has a bit of heaven in it or a bit of hell." Calleia then tries to kill Ladd but Ladd uses the famed knife to dispatch his mortal enemy. Mayo next comes to Ladd, begging him to save her errant husband from the clutches of gambler Caruso, promising to leave Kjellin if Ladd rescues him. Without hesitation, Ladd attacks Caruso and is severely wounded in a wild knife fight, nursed back to health by Kirk, who is the daughter of the vice-governor of Texas and who finds him bleeding to death alongside a road. Later, on board a riverboat, Ladd meets Mayo and Kjellin and also Caruso. In a series of battles, Kjellin and Caruso are killed and Mayo tries to worm her way into Ladd's arms. He rejects her now, realizing that although a great beauty, she's shallow and worthless. He rides off toward Texas to marry Kirk. THE IRON MISTRESS is jammed with action, much of it exceedingly violent and bloody, and the Ladd-Mayo relationship is perplexing. Ladd is his usual strong, resilient self but Mayo overacts flagrantly. There is little of the real Jim Bowie here. Born in 1799, Bowie was bred in Georgia and was a shady character most of his life. He gambled, smuggled slaves, looted ships with pirate Jean Laffite, and killed many a man in gun and knife duels. Moreover, he operated a land swindle with his brother but did ship lumber to New Orleans for a brief legitimate period of his life. All of these dark deeds were redeemed by the courageous Bowie when he died with 186 other incredible heroes at the Alamo in 1836. The action in THE IRON MISTRESS is well-handled by director Douglas, who specialized in robust sagas. Seitz's color photography is lavish and impressive. Douglas would go on to direct Ladd in THE BIG LAND, SANTIAGO, and CONNELL STORY. Although married to Michael O'Shea at the time, Mayo later admitted that she fell in love with Ladd during the production. The two-fisted Ladd insisted upon doing his own stunts as usual. While performing some of Douglas' typically ferocious action scenes, Ladd injured his knee and, while missing a thrown punch, slammed his right fist onto a concrete floor and broke a bone, requiring a cast which was cleverly camouflaged shortly before the completion of the film.

p, Henry Blanke; d, Gordon Douglas; w, James R. Webb (based on a story by Paul I. Wellman); ph, John Seitz; m, Max Steiner; ed, Alan Crosland, Jr.; art d, John Beckman; set d, George James Hopkins.

Biography **(PR:C MPAA:NR)**

IRON MOUNTAIN TRAIL** (1953) 53m REP bw

Rex Allen *(Rex)*, Slim Pickens *(Slim)*, Grant Withers *(Roger McCall)*, Nan Leslie *(Nancy Sawyer)*, Roy Barcroft *(Mate Orrin)*, Forrest Taylor *(Sam Sawyer)*, Alan Bridge *(Marshall)*, John Hamilton *(Circuit Judge)*, George H. Lloyd *(John Brockway)*, Koko the Miracle Horse.

Allen is a postal inspector sent to California to find out why mail delivery is taking so long. It turns out that black hats Withers and Barcroft are behind the wrongdoings. The plot turns to a race between Allen on Koko the Miracle Horse on land, with Withers and Barcroft traveling via ship. The object is to see which method delivers the mail most efficiently. Allen and his wonder ninny also save an innocent man from being hanged with not a moment to spare. With all this in less than an hour, you can get tired just thinking about it.

p, Edward J. White; d, William Witney; w, Gerald Geraghty (based on a story by William Lively); ph, Bud Thackery; m, Stanley Wilson; ed, Tony Martinelli; art d, Frank Arrigo.

Western **(PR:A MPAA:NR)**

IRON PETTICOAT, THE* 1/2 (1956, Brit.) 96m Remus Setafilm/MGM c

Bob Hope *(Chuck Lockwood)*, Katharine Hepburn *(Vinka Kovelenko)*, James Robertson Justice *(Col. Sklarnoff)*, Robert Helpmann *(Ivan Kropotkin)*, David Kossoff *(Dr. Dubratz)*, Alan Gifford *(Col. Newton Tarbell)*, Paul Carpenter *(Maj. Lewis)*, Noelle Middleton *(Connie)*, Nicholas Phipps *(Tony Mallard)*, Sidney James *(Paul)*, Alexander Gauge *(Sen. Holly)*, Doris Goddard *(Maria)*, Tutte Lemkow *(Sutsiyawa)*, Sandra Dorne *(Tityana)*, Richard Wattis *(Lingerie Clerk)*, Maria Antippas *(Sklarnoff's Secretary)*, Martin Boddey *(Grisha)*.

A grim, humorless attempt at recreating NINOTCHKA that gets a resounding "nyet" on every level. Based on a story by Harry Saltzman (producer of the James Bond films as well as countless others), Ben Hecht's script falls far short of his usual quality. Even the addition of numerous one-liners by the Hope staff writers, who were always brought in to pepper his scripts with bon mots, is no help. Hepburn and Hope were imported to England to make this picture and how two such veterans could have been hoodwinked into appearing in such a turkey is a marvel of money. (It had to be that. Why else would they have agreed to do this after reading the script?) Hepburn is a Russian pilot who gets angry at her bosses and flies to the American section of Berlin. There she is introduced to Hope, a major in the Army whose job it is to convert her to western ways. At the same time she tries to convert him to the joys of Communism. She is not against her country's government policy, just the people who run it. They travel to London where Hope shows her what capitalism can do. It's not long before Hepburn doffs her bulky uniform, dons some frou-frou clothes, quaffs a bit of the bubbly, and falls hard for Hope. The Russians don't like it a bit so Hepburn is kidnaped and taken back to Moscow where they plan to do her in. Hope tries to rescue her off the plane but both are taken to Russia for execution. Then there's a change of mind; they get married; East and West are united, and their twains do meet happily. Good work from the British contingent of Justice, James, Lemkow, Kossoff, and Helpmann helps but it's basically a bore. Hepburn's attempt at a Russian accent is too ludicrous to describe. Hecht asked for his name to be removed from the credits. It was granted.

p, Betty E. Box; d, Ralph Thomas; w, Ben Hecht [uncredited] (based on a story by Harry Saltzman); ph, Ernest Steward (VistaVision, Technicolor); m, Benjamin Frankel; ed, Frederick Wilson; md, Frankel; art d, Carmen Dillon; set d, Vernon Dixon; cos, Yvonne Caffin; makeup, W.T. Partleton.

Comedy **(PR:A MPAA:NR)**

IRON ROAD, THE (SEE: BUCKSKIN FRONTIER, 1943)

IRON SHERIFF, THE** 1/2 (1957) 73m Grand/UA bw

Sterling Hayden *(Sheriff Galt)*, Constance Ford *(Claire)*, John Dehner *(Pollock)*, Kent Taylor *(Quincy)*, Darryl Hickman *(Benjie)*, Walter Sande *(Ellison)*, Frank Ferguson *(Holloway)*, King Donovan *(Leveret)*, Mort Mills *(Sutherland)*, Peter Miller *(Jackson)*, Kathy Nolan *(Kathi)*, I. Stanford Jolley *(Walden)*, Will Wright *(Judge)*, Ray Walker *(Bilson)*, Bob Williams *(Tilyou)*.

An interesting western has sheriff Hayden's court evidence convict his own son of murder. However, Hayden is convinced of the boy's innocence. The sheriff tells of a deathbed confession which points the guilty finger. He is able to disprove the accusations, and finally track down the real culprit. While in pursuit, one is never quite sure whether the sheriff is going to kill the murderer in cold blood as he threatens, or bring him in peacefully to stand trial. Upholding a moral balance, the murderer is judged under the eyes of the law.

p, Jerome C. Robinson; d, Sidney Salkow; w, Seeleg Lester; ph, Kenneth Peach; m, Emil Newman; ed, Grant Whytock; md, Newman; art d, William Ross.

Western **(PR:A MPAA:NR)**

IRON STAIR, THE* (1933, Brit.) 51m REA/RKO bw

Henry Kendall *(Geoffrey/George Gale), Dorothy Boyd (Eva Marshall)*, Michael Hogan *(Pat Derringham)*, Michael Sherbrooke *(Benjamin Marks)*, Steffi Duna *(Elsa Damond)*, A. Bromley Davenport *(Sir Andrew Gale)*, S. Victor Stanley *(Ben)*, Charles Groves *(Sam)*, Charles Paton *(Sloan)*, John Turnbull *(Major Gordon)*.

Kendall plays the dual role of two brothers. One frames the second in order to get his hands on their father's vast fortune. The good son escapes from prison, only to learn his evil brother has been killed in an accident. He does clear his name with the help of Duna, his brother's mistress, who was also implicated in the crime. A swift direction speeds through the complicated plot line.

p, Julius Hagen; d, Leslie Hiscott; w, H. Fowler Mear (based on his novel *Rita)*.

Crime **(PR:A MPAA:NR)**

IROQUOIS TRAIL, THE**

(1950) 85m UA bw (AKA: THE TOMAHAWK TRAIL)

George Montgomery *(Hawkeye)*, Brenda Marshall *(Marion Thorne)*, Glenn Langan *(Capt. West)*, Reginald Denny *(Capt. Brownell)*, Monte Blue *(Sagamore)*, Sheldon Leonard *(Ogane)*, Paul Cavanagh *(Col. Thorne)*, Dan O'Herlihy *(Lt. Blakely)*, Don Gerner *(Tom Cutler)*, Marcel Gourmet *(Gen. Montcalm)*, Arthur Little, Jr. *(Adjutant Dickson)*, Esther Somers *(Ma Cutler)*, John Doucette *(Sam Girty)*, Holmes Herbert *(Gen. Johnson)*.

Set against the backdrop of the French and Indian War, this film has Montgomery aiding the British in battles against the French for control of the St. Lawrence and Hudson River regions. There's an abundance of redcoats and Indians involved in double-crossing but the script never moves beyond the surface.

p, Bernard Small; d, Phil Karlson; w, Richard Schayer (based on "The Leatherstocking Tales" by James Fenimore Cooper); ph, Henry Freulich; ed, Kenneth Crane; art d, Edward Ilou.

Western **(PR:A MPAA:NR)**

IS EVERYBODY HAPPY?* (1929) 110m WB bw

Ted Lewis *(Tod Todd)*, Alice Day *(Gail Wilson)*, Ann Pennington *(Lena Schmidtt)*, Lawrence Grant *(Victor Molnar)*, Julia Swayne Gordon *(Mrs. Molnar)*, Otto Hoffman *(Landlord)*, Purnell B. Pratt *(Stage Manager)*.

Lewis is cast as a violinist who comes to America with his Hungarian mom and pop. They have dreams of him becoming a concert musician but the evil grip of jazz takes hold. Lewis is soon blowing on a sax and clarinet. Dad stupidly believes his son is playing with the New York Symphony and attends one of their performances. He and his wife are distressed to learn that Lewis is nowhere to be seen. After the show they take in a meal, only to find their son jamming away on stage. Pop goes nuts, vows he never wants to see his son again, and disappears. When Lewis finally does make it to Carnegie Hall he is playing in a benefit performance. In the wings is an old janitor gleefully watching. It's pop, who now is infinitely happy. Everybody, including Lewis's band, shows up for a nice Hungarian Christmas dinner. The title question is better off unanswered. Tunes include: "Wouldn't It Be Wonderful?," "I'm The Medicine Man For The Blues," "Samoa," "New Orleans" (Grant Clarke, Harry Akst), "In The Land Of Jazz," "Start Up The Band" (Ted Lewis), "St. Louis Blues" (W.C. Handy), "Tiger Rag" (Jelly Roll Morton, Nick La Rocca), "Is Everybody Happy Now?" (Maurice Rubens, Jack Osterman, Lewis). A weak rip-off of the Al Jolson hits, THE JAZZ SINGER (1927) and THE SINGING FOOL (1928).

d, Archie Mayo; w, Joseph Jackson, James A. Starr; ph, Ben Reynolds; ed, Desmond O'Brien; ch, Larry Ceballos.

Musical **(PR:A MPAA:NR)**

IS EVERYBODY HAPPY?** (1943) 73m COL bw

Ted Lewis *(Ted Lewis)*, Michael Duane *(Tom)*, Nan Wynn *(Kitty)*, Larry Parks *(Jerry)*, Lynn Merrick *(Ann)*, Bob Haymes *(Artie)*, Dick Winslow *(Joe)*, Harry Barris *(Bob)*, Frank Stanford *(Frank)*, Fern Emmett *(Mrs. Broadbelt)*, Eddie Kane *(Salbin)*, Ray Walker *(Lou Merwin)*, Anthony Marlowe *(Carl Muller)*, George Reed *(Missouri)*, Perc Launders *(Rod)*, Paul Bryant *(Snowball)*, Herbert Heyes *(Colonel)*, Madeline Grey *(Colonel's Wife)*, Broderick O'Farrell *(Justice of the Peace)*, Billy Bletcher *(Waiter)*, Charles D. Wilson *(Mr. Smaltz)*, Donald Kerr *(Bouncer)*, George McKay *(Cop)*, Tom Kennedy *(Desk Sergeant)*, Phyllis Kennedy *(Daley)*, Dick Rush *(Jailer)*, Clinton Rosemond *(Doorman)*, Jesse Graves *(Doctor)*, Vi Athens *(Girl)*, John Tyrrell *(Caller Bit)*, Eddie Laughton *(Clerk Bit)*, Eddie Bruce *(Proprietor)*, Kirk Alyn *(Thew)*, Muni Seroff *(Maitre D')*, Jack Salling *(Newsboy)*, William Sloan *(Boy)*.

Lewis, playing his music in San Francisco, runs into the son of an old friend. The lad (Parks) isn't sure if he should wed the gal he loves. Parks fears that he'll return from the war an invalid. Worse yet, he may not return at all, leaving his girl a widow. Lewis tells him a story, in flashback, of a WW I vet who, it turns out, is the soldier's father. After seeing the parallel, the soldier decides to take the walk down the aisle. This corny tale is saved by a barrage of fine tunes. Included are "It Had to Be You" (Gus Kahn, Isham Jones), "More Than Anyone Else in the World" (Charles Kenny, Ruth Lowe), "This Old Hat of Mine" (Ted Lewis), "Cuddle Up a Little Closer" (Otto Harbach, Karl Hoschna), "I'm Just Wild About Harry" (Eubie Blake, Noble Sissle), "Way Down Yonder in New Orleans" (Henry Creamer, Turner Layton), "On the Sunny Side of the Street" (Dorothy Fields, Jimmy McHugh), "St. Louis Blues" (W. C. Handy), "Pretty Baby" (Kahn, Tony Jackson, Egbert Van Alstyne), "Am I Blue?" (Grant Clarke, H. Akst).

p, Irving Briskin; d, Charles Barton; w, Monte Brice; ph, L. William O'Connell; ed, James Sweeney; md, M. W. Stoloff; art d, Lionel Banks.

Musical **(PR:A MPAA:NR)**

IS MY FACE RED? 1/2** (1932) 67m RKO bw

Helen Twelvetrees *(Peggy Bannon)*, Ricardo Cortez *(William Poster)*, Jill Esmond *(Mildred Huntington)*, Robert Armstrong *(Ed Maloney)*, Arline Judge *(Bee)*, ZaSu Pitts *(Telephone Operator)*, Sidney Toler *(Tony Mugatti)*, Clarence Muse *(Horace)*, Fletcher Norton *(Angelo Spinello)*.

Cortez is a tough Walter Winchell-esque journalist who keeps a good eye out for dirt, and revels in printing it. The portrait director Seiter creates is one which is generally realistic. He doesn't think twice about hitting the journalistic profession where it counts, but at the same time raises it to a romantic level. After Cortez receives his due, old flame Twelvetrees is there to ease the fall. Pitts has a comic, but uninspired, routine as the "Gazette" telephone operator.

p, Harry Joe Brown; d, William Seiter; w, Bartlett Cormack, Ben Markson, Casey Robinson (based on a play by Markson, Allen Rivkin); ph, Leo Tover; ed, Joseph Kane.

Drama **(PR:A MPAA:NR)**

IS PARIS BURNING?* 1/2**

(1966, U.S./Fr.) 173m Transcontinental-Marianne/PAR bw/c (PARIS BRULE-T-IL?)

Jean-Paul Belmondo *(Morandat)*, Charles Boyer *(Monod)*, Leslie Caron *(Françoise Labe)*, Jean-Pierre Cassel *(Lt. Henri Karcher)*, George Chakiris *(G.I. in Tank)*, Claude Dauphin *(Lebel)*, Alain Delon *(Jacques Chaban-Delmas)*, Kirk Douglas *(Gen. George Patton)*, Glenn Ford *(Gen. Omar Bradley)*, Gert Fröbe *(Gen. Dietrich von Choltitz)*, Daniel Gélin *(Yves Bayet)*, E. G. Marshall *(Intelligence Officer Powell)*, Yves Montand *(Marcel Bizien)*, Anthony Perkins *(Sgt. Warren)*, Claude Rich *(Gen. Jacques Leclerc)*, Simone Signoret *(Cafe Proprietress)*, Robert Stack *(Gen. Edwin Sibert)*, Jean-Louis Trintignant *(Serge)*, Pierre Vaneck *(Maj. Roger Gallois)*, Marie Versini *(Claire)*, Skip Ward *(G.I. with Warren)*, Orson Welles *(Consul Raoul Nordling)*, Bruno Crémer *(Col. Rol)*, Suzy Delair *(A Parisienne)*, Pierre Dux *(Parodi)*, Billy Frick *(Hitler)*, Harry Meyen *(von Arnim)*, Hannes Messemer *(Jodl)*, Michel Piccoli *(Pisani)*, Sacha Pitoeff *(Joliot-Curie)*, Wolfgang Preiss *(Ebernach)*, Michel Berger *(Chief of Explosives)*, Gehrard Borman *(von Choltitz's Secretary)*, Georges Claisse *(Intern with Monod)*, Germaine de France *(Old Woman)*, Doc Ericson *(Jeep Driver)*, Michel Etcheverry *(Luizet)*, Pascal Fardoulis *(Gilet)*, Bernard Fresson *(Liaison Agent)*, Ernst Fritz Furbringer *(von Boineburg)*, Clara Gansard *(Wife of Col. Rol)*, Rol Gauffin *(Consul Nordling's Secretary)*, Georges Géret *(Comm. George)*, Michel Gonzales *(Jacques)*, Konrad Georg *(von Model)*, Claus Holm *(Huhm)*, Jean-Pierre Honoré *(Alain Perpezat)*, Peter Jacob *(Gen. Burgdorf)*, Catherine Kamenka *(Diane)*, Billy Kearns *(Patton Aide)*, Joëlle Latour *(Young Girl with Warren)*, Michel Lonsdale *(Debû-Bridel)*, Roger Lumont *("Jade Amicol")*, Maria Machado *(Stella)*, Aimé de March *(Roland Pré)*, Félix Marten *(Landrieu)*, Paloma Matta *(The Bride)*, Pierre Mirat *(Cafe Proprietor)*, Harald Momm *(Col. Jay)*, Georges Montant *(Doctor)*, Russ Moro *(Lieutenant with Warren)*, Del Negro *(Officer with Chaban-Delmas)*, Jean Negroni *(Villon)*, Alain Pommier *(Franjoux)*, Georges Poujouly *(Landrieux)*, Michel Puterflam *(Laffont)*, Christian Rode *(Blache)*, Serge Rousseau *(Col. Fabien)*, Michel Sales *(Gallois' friend)*, Wolfgang Saure *(Hegel)*, Georges Staquet *(Capt. Dronne)*, Otto Stern *(Wagenknecht)*, Henia Suchar *(Prefecture Switchboard Operator)*, Toni Taffin *(Bernard Labe)*, Pierre Tamin *(Mauranes)*, Jean Valmont *(Bazooka)*, Jo Warfield *(Major with Chaban-Delmas)*, Joachim Westhoss *(German Officer with Claire)*, Jean-Pierre Zola *(Cpl. Mayer)*, Karl Otto Alberty, Albert Remy, Joachim Hansen, Gunter Meisner, Helmut Schneider.

The WW II liberation of Paris in 1944 became the focal point of this mammoth, almost overwhelming production so loaded with star talent that the war seems secondary. As such, the film is topheavy with talent and this wobbles an already unwieldy story with cross-cutting between the Allies and Germans that is often confusing. IS PARIS BURNING? is nevertheless an enjoyable, action-crammed opus that is worthy of attention for the many memorable scenes it does offer. The German commander, Frobe, is summoned by Hitler. Hitler states that if the Allies, having landed in Normandy, appear to be able to take Paris, the city is to be reduced to rubble, all of its national monuments, shrines, museums, art institutions, the image and soul of the great city, all of it, is to be blown up, such is the insane Fuhrer's rancor (if he can't possess the City of Light, no one can). Delon, who commands the Free French forces under the leadership of General De Gaulle, a force which has already taken over most the city, argues with the communist factions not be begin overt insurrection until help from the Allied armies is assured. He fears the city will be the center of a bloodbath, as was Warsaw. Welles, the Swedish consul, is asked to persuade the Germans to free an important political prisoner, but—with Caron, the prisoner's wife at his side—he fails to get the man released; the prisoner is shot on orders of a fanatical Nazi officer as prisoners are about to be shipped to concentration camps from the train depot. Meanwhile, Belmondo and a female aide take over police headquarters while resistance breaks out in the streets and French and Germans openly battle along the deserted boulevards and across the rooftops of Paris. Frobe reluctantly orders demolition squads to begin planting explosives under all the bridges and in all the national monuments. The resistance fighters then learn that the Allies, to save Paris from destruction, have decided to push to the Rhine and bypass the city entirely. The Free French quickly dispatch one of their officers, Vanek, to make contact with the Allied command and get the Americans, British, and French to come to the aid of Paris. Frobe, meanwhile, is subtly persuaded to stall Hitler's demands to destroy the city—that the German cause is lost and, by saving Paris, he will save centuries of history. Frobe stalls Hitler and his generals, who keep calling to ask: "Is Paris Burning?" Vanek, after some harrowing experiences, makes it through the German lines outside Paris and meets with generals Stack (Sibert), Douglas (Patton), Ford (Bradley), and Rich (Leclerc), persuading this high command to come to the aid of the resistance. Rich with his all-French unit is dispatched to take Paris accompanied by American tank units. Many short vignettes are shown as French soldiers such as Montand—returning to Paris and his family—and Perkins—a G.I. enamored of the thought of seeing Paris for the first time—fight their way along the boulevards and are tragically killed. When the city is liberated Frobe is relieved to be taken prisoner. None of the explosives has been set off and the city is saved. Producer Graetz underwent innumerable headaches in assembling vintage WW II trucks, tanks, jeeps, cars, and uniforms for the thousands of extras employed in the film, and the script, which kept getting larger and larger to incorporate additional star talent got out of hand. Only a few weeks after the film was finished the 65-year-old Graetz died of a heart attack. Clement's direction incorporates much documentary footage and this is cleverly meshed with live footage, so that it's hard to tell the difference between 1944 and 1965 shots. But the script is a disaster, despite the convincing cameo parts played by all. Scenes flit from the French to the Americans to the Germans almost willy-nilly and keeping the story together is a full-time job for any viewer. Typical of the film's lack of continuity is the opening scene where Frobe and another German general are en route to see Hitler (Frick) at his headquarters in East Prussia. They speak English until they are in Hitler's presence when the dialog reverts to German with subtitles. Clement was a director who often used the semi-documentary approach, but much more successfully in his BATTLE OF THE RAILS, 1949. The public did not respond well to the film, which obviously came a little too late to interest a new generation with its eyes on Vietnam, not the liberation of Paris in a war won long ago.

p, Paul Graetz; d, Rene Clement; w, Gore Vidal, Francis Ford Coppola, Jean Aurenche, Pierre Bost, Claude Brule, Marcel Moussy, Beate von Molo; ph, Marcel Grignon; m, Maurice Jarre; ed, Robert Lawrence; art d, Willy Holt; set d, Roger Volper; cos, Jean Zay, Pierre Nourry; spec eff, Robert MacDonald, Paul Pollard; makeup, Michel Deruelle, Aida Carange.

War Drama **(PR:A MPAA:NR)**

IS THERE JUSTICE?*½ (1931) 60m Sono Art-World Wide bw

Rex Lease, Blanche Mehaffey, Henry B. Walthall, Robert Ellis, Joseph Girard.

A district attorney, Walthall, becomes the target of gang violence when he imprisons a crook and his innocent wife, who later dies while behind bars. The gangsters retaliate by blackmailing Walthall's daughter after obtaining a photograph of her dressed in shorts (such a scandal!). Lease, a helpful news reporter, gets caught in the middle of the affair and winds up taking the rap for a gangster's murder. He's innocent, of course, and Mehaffey steps forth to prove it. To answer the title question, yes.

d, Stuart Paton; w, Betty Burbridge.

Crime **(PR:A MPAA:NR)**

IS THIS TRIP REALLY NECESSARY? zero
(1970) 84m Dorn-Thor/Hollywood Star c (AKA: TRIP TO TERROR; BLOOD OF THE IRON MAIDEN)

Marvin Miller, Carole Kane, John Carradine, Peter Duryea, Barbara Mallory, Patti Heider, Darrin Daniels, Benes Mardon, Tod Spence.

Carradine stars as a maniacal director shooting an epic sex film with a couple of young lovelies who trip-out on LSD. A heroic young man tries to save the girls but before he is successful two are killed, one meeting a gruesome end in an iron maiden. An early screen appearance by an 18-year-old Kane is the only reason to watch.

p&d, Ben Benoit; w, Lee Kalcheim; ph, Austin McKinney; m, Paul Norman, Ron Blackmer, Bob Page; ed, Fred Brown; art d, Ray Markham; spec eff, Robert Beck; makeup, Dodie Warren.

Horror **(PR:O MPAA:M)**

IS YOUR HONEYMOON REALLY NECESSARY?**
(1953, Brit.) 80m Advance/Adelphi bw

David Tomlinson *(Frank Betterton)*, Diana Dors *(Candy Markham)*, Bonar Colleano *(Cmdr. Laurie Vining)*, Diana Decker *(Gillian Vining)*, Sidney James *(Hank Hanlon)*, Audrey Freeman *(Lucy, the maid)*, Hubert Woodward *(Hicks)*, McDonald Parke *(Adm. Fields)*, Lou Jacobi *(Capt. Noakes)*, Warren Stanhope *(Young Lt.)*, C. Denier Warren *(Tony)*.

This standard bedroom comedy has Colleano on a honeymoon in London with his second wife Decker. Their big night is hampered by the arrival of first wife Dors from California. She claims their separation isn't valid. Friend and legal aide Tomlinson is brought in to clear the mess up, but finds himself posing as Dors' husband.

p, David Dent; d, Maurice Elvey; w, Talbot Rothwell (based on the play by E.V. Tidmarsh); ph, Phil Grindrod; m, William Trytel; ed, Lilo Caruthers.

Comedy **(PR:A MPAA:NR)**

ISABEL½** (1968, Can.) 108m Quest/PAR c

Genevieve Bujold *(Isabel)*, Mark Strange *(Jason)*, Gerard Parkes *(Uncle Matthew)*, Therese Cadorette *(Sister Estelle)*, Elton Hayes *(Eb)*, Ede Kerr *(Viola)*, Albert Waxman *(Herb)*, Ratch Wallace, Lynden Bechervaise *(His Friends)*, Eric Clavering *(Postmaster)*, Rob Hayes *(Fisherman)*, J. Donald Dow *(Storekeeper)*, the Citizens of Shigawake, Quebec, Canada.

The infinitely adorable Bujold stars in this odd psychological drama about a girl who returns to her country home as her mother is dying. Bujold is emotionally haunted by her parent's subsequent death, as well as the deaths of her father and brother. She stays in the village to take care of a senile uncle, is attacked by a group of drunkards, and befriended by a fisherman. He has a fondness for Bujold, and with his help she is able to overcome the traumas of the past. A fine actress in the hands of more skilled directors, Alain Resnais and Philippe De Broca (LA GUERRE EST FINIE and KING OF HEARTS, respectively), Bujold suffers somewhat from the overly psychiatric script penned by husband Almond.

p,d&w, Paul Almond; ph, Georges Dufaux (Technicolor); m, Harry Freedman; ed, George R. Appleby; cos, Roger Palmer; m/l, Marc Strange.

Drama **(PR:O MPAA:NR)**

ISADORA* (1968, Brit.) 128m UNIV c (AKA: THE LOVES OF ISADORA)

Vanessa Redgrave *(Isadora Duncan)*, James Fox *(Gordon Craig)*, Jason Robards *(Paris Singer)*, Ivan Tchenko *(Sergei Essenin)*, John Fraser *(Roger)*, Bessie Love *(Mrs. Duncan)*, Cynthia Harris *(Mary Desti)*, Libby Glenn *(Elizabeth Duncan)*, Tony Vogel *(Raymond Duncan)*, Wallas Eaton *(Archer)*, John Quentin *(Pim)*, Nicholas Pennell *(Bedford)*, Ronnie Gilbert *(Miss Chase)*, Christian Duvaleix *(Armand)*, Margaret Countenay *(Raucous Woman)*, Arthur White *(Hearty Husband)*, Iza Teller *(Alicia)*, Vladimir Leskovar *(Bugatti)*, John Warner *(Mr. Sterling)*, Ina De La Haye *(Russian Teacher)*, John Brandon *(Gospel Billy)*, Lucinda Chambers *(Deirdre)*, Simon Lutton Davies *(Patrick)*, Alan Gifford *(Tour Manager)*, David Healy *(Chicago Theater Manager)*, Zuleika Robson Noel Davies, Arnold Diamond, Anthony Gardner, Sally Travers, Mark Dignam, Robin Lloyd, Constantine Iranski, Lucy Saroyan, Jan Conrad, Hall Galilli, Roy Stephens, Cal McCord, Richard Marner, Stefan Gryss.

This bloated pseudo-biography (originally 177 minutes, later cut to 128 minutes) offers an expensive production and a nitwit story that would have offended the worst producer of B films at Monogram or Mascot. Wholly miscast is Redgrave as Isadora Duncan, the celebrated interpretive dancer, sexual vamp, and all-around eccentric. The film opens with Redgrave at age 49 dictating her unreliable memoirs, recounting her adolescent awe of ancient Greek tribal dancing, her music hall period as "Peppy Dora," her tempestuous love affairs with artist Gordon Craig (Fox), marriage to sewing machine magnate, Paris Singer (Robards), and marriage to lunatic Russian poet Sergei Essenin (Tchenko), along with the tragic death of her two small children (Singer's boy and girl drowned when the family chauffeur got out of the limousine to check something and the car rolled into a river). In flashback we painfully see Redgrave trying to enact the role of a teenage Isadora and a youthful Isadora and a ravishing Isadora bedding and wedding men willy-nilly, looking haggard, drawn, and old throughout, until she dies herself in a freak accident on the Riviera (her long silk scarf entwining around the wheel of a sportscar which roared away and snapped her neck in two). Redgrave and her supporting players, including the normally reliable Robards, are simply awful. She overreaches for the elusive character she is playing in every scene and her dewy-eyed closeups are embarrassing. When Redgrave does her dance numbers (she reportedly trained for six months to imitate Duncan's style), her 6-foot frame lumbers and thunders about like an elephant with the gout. Here she is simply awkward, graceless, and completely unattractive, particularly when doing her seven (or one) veiled dance before Russian troops, showing thighs that should have been displayed in the Chicago stockyards. But this side of beef is wholly unappetizing and oddly repulsive in every frame. In her frenetic attempt to capture the free-thinking Isadora, Redgrave does nothing but make a fool of herself, an unconvincing fool at that. This film was momentarily popular in the 1960s when women's libbers thought Redgrave and Isadora were one in the same, little realizing that neither cared a hoot about their cause. In one sense there is an acute similarity; both were shamefully self-indulgent and had about as much talent as an empty tube of lipstick.

p, Robert Hakim, Raymond Hakim; d, Karel Reisz; w, Melvyn Bragg, Clive Exton, Margaret Drabble (based on the book *My Life* by Isadora Duncan, "Isadora Duncan, An Intimate Portrait" by Sewell Stokes); ph, Larry Pizer (Technicolor); m, Maurice Jarre; ed, Tom Priestley; prod d, Jocelyn Herbert; art d, Michael Seymour; set d, Bryan Graves, Harry Cordwell; cos, Herbert; ch, Litz Pisk, m prod, Impromptu in B Flat, opus 142, Franz Peter Schubert, "Washington Post March," John Philip Sousa, Waltz in A Flat, opus 42, Frederic Francois Chopin, Symphony No. 7 in A, Ludwig van Beethoven, "Rejouissance" from Suite No. 4 in D, Johann Sebastian Bach, Poeme opus 32 No. 1, Aleksandr Nikolaevich Scriabin, Symphony No. 2 in B Minor, Aleksandr Porfiryevich Borodin, "March Slav," Petr Ilich Tchaikovsky.

Drama **(PR:O MPAA:M)**

ISLAND, THE½**
(1962, Jap.) 96m Kindai Eiga Kyokai/Zenith bw (HADAKA NO SHIMA; AKA: NAKED ISLAND)

Nobuko Otowa *(Toyo)*, Taiji Tonoyama *(Senta)*, Shinji Tanaka *(Taro)*, Masanori Horimoto *(Jiro)*.

This somber piece from Japan deals with a family that lives on an isolated island. Their days are filled by rigorous routine, much of which consists of hauling water up a rocky surface to sustain their crops. Despite the many hardships, the parents and two boys are content with their lot. What happiness they do have is abruptly halted when the oldest son dies. His mother breaks down after the burial and destroys some of the crops before finally accepting the tragedy, and returning with her patient husband to the never-ending routine.

p, Kaneto Shindo, Eisaku Matsura; d&w, Shindo; ph, Kiyoshi Kuroda; m, Hikaru Hayashi; ed, Toshio Enoki.

Drama **Cas.** **(PR:C MPAA:NR)**

ISLAND, THE zero (1980) 114m UNIV c

Michael Caine *(Maynard)*, David Warner *(Nau)*, Angela Punch McGregor *(Beth)*, Frank Middlemass *(Windsor)*, Don Henderson *(Rollo)*, Dudley Sutton *(Dr. Brazil)*,

Colin Jeavons *(Hizzoner)*, Zakes Mokae *(Wescott)*, Brad Sullivan *(Stark)*, Jeffrey Frank *(Justin)*, John O'Leary, Bruce McLaughlin, Jimmy Casino *(Doctors)*, Suzanne Astor *(Mrs. Burgess)*, Reg Evans *(Jack the Bat)*, Susan Bredhoff *(Kate)*, Cary Hoffman *(Mr. Burgess)*, William Schilling *(Baxter)*, Stewart Steinberg *(Hiller)*, Bob Westmoreland *(Charter Boat Captain)*.

Caine stars as a British journalist who investigates the disappearance of a ship in the Bermuda Triangle. He is forced to crash land on a remote island. With son Frank, they discover the place is inhabited by a gang of pirates who, for the last 300 years, have been looting and killing anyone who nears their territory. The pair are taken prisoner with the intention of preparing Frank to be the gang's new leader. They brainwash the lad and sadistically torture Caine. The waterlogged script from the repulsive pen of Peter Benchley proves that his past success (providing the original material for JAWS) was a pure fluke. This picture offers nothing but a seemingly endless barrage of graphic violence: Frank has his eyes stretched with pegs; Caine is stung by jellyfish and bled by leeches; a dope smuggler is offed by a grappling hook; and a cat is skinned alive. Of course they didn't leave out the sex angle—Caine is seduced/raped in a stupid subplot about the pirates' poor fertility rate. This was a $22 million investment which the producers deserved to lose—and did. The only thing to surface above this cinematic cesspool is the score by Ennio Morricone.

p, Richard D. Zanuck, David Brown; d, Michael Ritchie; w, Peter Benchley (based on his novel); ph, Henri Decae (Panavision, Technicolor); m, Ennio Morricone; ed, Richard A. Harris; prod d, Dale Hennesy; set d, Robert de Vestel; cos, Ann Roth; spec eff, Albert Whitlock.

Adventure Cas. (PR:O MPAA:R)

ISLAND AT THE TOP OF THE WORLD, THE*** (1974) 95m Disney/BV c

David Hartman *(Prof. Ivarsson)*, Donald Sinden *(Sir Anthony Ross)*, Jacques Marin *(Capt. Brieux)*, Mako *(Oomiak)*, David Gwillim *(Donald Ross)*, Agneta Eckemyr *(Freyja)*, Gunnar Ohlund *(The Godi)*, Lasse Kolstad *(Erik)*, Erik Silju *(Torvald)*, Rolf Soder *(Lawspeaker)*, Torsten Wahlund *(Sven)*, Sverre Ousdal *(Gunnar)*, Niels Hinrichsen *(Sigurd)*, Denny Miller *(Town Guard)*, Brendan Dillon *(The Factor)*, James Almanzar *(French Engineer)*, Ivor Barry *(The Butler)*, Lee Paul *(Chief of Boat Archers)*.

Reminiscent of Jules Verne fantasies this Disney pic sends a team of Arctic explorers into an uncharted area at the turn of the century. Sinden, a wealthy Englishman, organizes the team in an attempt to locate his missing son. With Hartman, a professor of Nordic history accompanying him, they venture into a mysterious valley that borders on a massive volcano. They soon find a settlement of Vikings which makes their search even more dangerous. Stunningly photographed scenery and authentic looking visual effects make this film one of Disney's more believable attempts. Fun for the kids.

p, Winston Hibler; d, Robert Stevenson; w, John Whedon (based on the novel *The Lost Ones* by Ian Cameron); ph, Frank Phillips (Technicolor); m, Maurice Jarre; ed, Robert Stafford; prod d, Peter Ellenshaw; art d, John B. Mansbridge, Walter Tyler, Al Roelofs; cos, Bill Thomas; spec eff, Art Cruikshank, Danny Lee.

Adventure Cas. (PR:AAA MPAA:G)

ISLAND CAPTIVES zero (1937) 53m Falcon/Principal bw

Eddie Nugent *(Tom Willoughby)*, Joan Barclay *(Helen Carsons)*, Henry Brandon *(Dick Bannister)*, Charles King *(Kelly)*, Forrest Taylor *(Hudson)*, Carmen LaRoux *(Taino)*, Frederick Palmer *(Graham)*, John Beck *(Carsons)*, John Sheean *(Police Captain)*.

The South Sea Islands are the backdrop for this trite tale. A lusty beach-comber is in pursuit of a frightened local gal, only to find smugglers, killers, and a shipwreck.

d, Glenn Kershner, w, Al Martin; ph, Dan Milner.

Adventure (PR:A MPAA:NR)

ISLAND CLAWS zero

(1981) 82m CBS/Island Claws c (AKA: THE NIGHT OF THE CLAW)

Robert Lansing, Steve Hanks, Nita Talbot, Jo McDonnell, Barry Nelson, Luke Halpin.

A ridiculous killer crab picture about a marine experiment that goes awry in Florida resulting in 8-foot land crabs. Not only do these shelled terrors kill everything in their paths, but they also roar while they're doing it. Originally intended for theatrical release, ISLAND CLAWS was so bad that it was sent to TV as THE NIGHT OF THE CLAW and now only pops up on video under its original title.

d, Hernan Cardenas; w, Jack Cowden, Ricou Browning (based on a story by Hernan Cardenas, Colby Cardenas); ph, James Pergola; m, Bill Justis; art d, Don Ivey; spec eff, Glenn Robinson, Ray Scott, Don Chandler.

Science Fiction Cas. (PR:O MPAA:NR)

ISLAND IN THE SKY** (1938) 62m FOX bw

Gloria Stuart *(Julie Hayes)*, Michael Whalen *(Michael Fraser)*, Paul Kelly *(Doyle)*, Robert Kellard *(Peter Vincent)*, June Storey *(Lucy Rhodes)*, Paul Hurst *(Happy)*, Leon Ames *(Marty Butler)*, Willard Robertson *(Walter Rhodes)*, George Humbert *(Trompas)*, Aggie Herring *(Mrs. O'Shea)*, Charles D. Brown *(Inspector Whitehead)*.

Stuart, about to marry the district attorney, postpones the big day and sets out to prove a recently condemned man's innocence. With the help of ex-mobster Kelly, she digs up the necessary evidence and saves the accused killer's life. Pretty standard.

p, Sol M. Wurtzel; d, Herbert I. Leeds; w, Frances Hyland, Albert Ray (based on a story by Jerry Cady); ph, Edward Cronjager; ed, Harry Reynolds; md, Samuel Kaylin; art d, Bernard Herzbrun, Chester Gore.

Crime (PR:A MPAA:NR)

ISLAND IN THE SKY*** (1953) 108m Wayne-Fellows/WB bw

John Wayne *(Capt. Dooley)*, Lloyd Nolan *(Stutz)*, Walter Abel *(Col. Fuller)*, James Arness *(McMullen)*, Andy Devine *(Moon)*, Allyn Joslyn *(J.H. Handy)*, James Lydon *(Murray the Navigator)*, Harry Carey, Jr. *(Hunt)*, Hal Baylor *(Stankowski the Engineer)*, Sean McClory *(Frank Lovatt the Copilot)*, Wally Cassell *(D'Annunzia the Radioman)*, Gordon Jones *(Walrus)*, Frank Fenton *(Capt. Turner)*, Robert Keys *(Maj. Ditson)*, Sumner Getchell *(Lt. Cord)*, Regis Toomey *(Sgt. Harper)*, Paul Fix *(Miller)*, Jim Dugan *(Gidley)*, George Chandler *(Rene)*, Louis Jean Heydt *(Fitch)*, Bob Steele *(Wilson)*, Darryl Hickman *(Swanson)*, Touch [Michael] Connors *(Gainer)*, Carl Switzer *(Hopper)*, Cass Gidley *(Stannish)*, Guy Anderson *(Breezy)*, Tony DeMario *(Ogden)*, Ann Doran *(Moon's Wife)*, Dawn Bender *(Murray's Wife)*, Phyllis Winger *(Girl in Flashback)*, Tim Wellman, Mike Wellman, Tom Irish, Richard Walsh, Gene Coogan, Johnny Indrisano.

Wayne, a veteran flyer for the Army Transport Command, is forced to crash land in uncharted Labrador after ice weighs down the wings of his plane. He and a crew of four find themselves trapped in a snowy, below-freezing environment with little hope of being found. A rescue mission made up of Wayne's buddies sets out and nearly locates the wreck, flying directly over them but not noticing. On the ground Wayne tries to keep the crew's morale up while fighting the elements. After refueling, the rescue mission sets out again and this time is more successful. While sometimes talky, the script does a fine job of showing men battling nature. Exceptional performances, especially from the rescue team, are a plus. Coproduced by Wayne.

p, Robert Fellows; d, William A. Wellman; w, Ernest K. Gann (based on his novel); ph, Archie Stout (aerial ph, William H. Clothier); m, Emil Newman; ed, Ralph Dawson; art d, James Basevi.

Adventure (PR:A MPAA:NR)

ISLAND IN THE SUN* 1/2 (1957) 120m FOX c

James Mason *(Maxwell Fleury)*, Joan Fontaine *(Mavis Norman)*, Dorothy Dandridge *(Margot Seaton)*, Joan Collins *(Jocelyn Fleury)*, Michael Rennie *(Hilary Carson)*, Diana Wynyard *(Mrs. Fleury)*, John Williams *(Col. Whittingham)*, Stephen Boyd *(Euan Templeton)*, Patricia Owens *(Sylvia Fleury)*, Basil Sydney *(Julian Fleury)*, John Justin *(Denis Archer)*, Ronald Squire *(The Governor)*, Hartley Power *(Bradshaw)*, Harry Belafonte *(David Boyeur)*.

Five stories move simultaneously through this yawning picture that marked Darryl Zanuck's return to independent production after spending so much time running Fox studios. The background of the Caribbean is just gorgeous but the actors make the mistake of walking and talking in front of the scenery and therein lies the difficulty. Mason is the rich son of a wealthy family that lives on the small island. He wants to run for political office against Belafonte, a popular union leader. When stories begin appearing that purport to prove Mason's mixed-blood heritage, the man is delighted, believing that will rally some of the on-the-fence voters to elect him. Meanwhile, Belafonte is having a fling with white woman Fontaine. At the same time, Justin is affairing with Dandridge, a black woman and Belafonte's one-time amour. Mason's younger sister, Collins, wants to marry Boyd, the governor's son. To entrap him, she becomes pregnant. Mason suspects Rennie, a snobbish drifter, of sleeping with his wife, Owens, and murders the man. Mason is defeated in the election. He then gives himself up for Rennie's slaying to policeman Williams who has been doggedly pursuing him. Collins learns that she is not really Mason's sister or Sydney's daughter and has no black blood in her. She marries Boyd and leaves the island on the same plane as Justin and Dandridge. Belafonte walks away from Fontaine as he fears that an open affair with her will harm his political ambitions. Williams and Boyd's father, Squire, end the film by ruminating about what will happen to Mason when his trial comes up. Belafonte sings a bit but it doesn't help. Songs include: "Island In The Sun," "Lead Man Holler." A great-looking picture that makes one want to visit the Caribbean but such a disjointed story that the viewer struggles with the plot until finally giving up.

p, Darryl F. Zanuck; d, Robert Rossen; w, Alfred Hayes (based on the novel by Alec Waugh); ph, Frederick A. Young (CinemaScope, DeLuxe Color); m, Malcolm Arnold; ed, Reginald Beck; art d, William C. Andrews; cos, David Ffolkes; m/l, Belafonte, Irving "Lord" Burgess.

Drama (PR:C MPAA:NR)

ISLAND MAN (SEE: MEN OF IRELAND, 1938, Irish)

ISLAND OF ALLAH* (1956) 78m Studio Alliance/Joseph Brenner c

Isa Sabbagh *(Khalid)*, Nasir Ibn Mubarak *(Hamad)*, Fatima Bint Ali *(Fatima)*, James C. Stewart *(Max)*, Albert Clements *(Al)*, Ira Constad *(Benson)*, John R. Jones *(Ibn Saud, the Warrior)*, Said Shawa *(Ajlan)*, Zafir Hussaini *(Ibn Jilui)*, Princess Yasmina *(Dancing Girl)*, Fredric March *(Narrator)*.

Nothing more than a tasteless combination of travelog, historical drama, and documentary about the Arab world. It does little more than recreate some of the more prominent moments in Arab history as it rambles across the desert. Fredric March serves as a sort of commentator during part of the sojourn.

p&d, Richard Lyford.

Historical Drama (PR:A MPAA:NR)

ISLAND OF DESIRE, 1930 (SEE: LOVE TRADER, THE, 1930)

ISLAND OF DESIRE***

(1952, Brit.) 102m Coronado Productions/RKO c (GB: SATURDAY ISLAND)

Linda Darnell *(Elizabeth Smythe)*, Tab Hunter *(Michael J. "Chicken" Dugan)*, Donald Gray *(William Peck)*, John Lourie *(Grimshaw)*, Sheila Chong *(Tukua)*, Russell Waters *(Dr. Snyder)*, Hilda Fenemore *(Ollie)*, Brenda Hogan *(Jane)*, Diana Decker *(Mike)*, Peggy Hassard *(Maggie)*, Michael Newell *(Eddie)*, Lloyd Lamble

(Officer of the Watch), Peter Butterworth *(Wounded Marine)*, Harold Ayer *(Marine Sergeant)*, MacDonald Parke *(Ship's Captain)*.

A sensuous, steamy story of nurse Darnell and Marine Hunter marooned on an island together for a year after their ship is torpedoed during WW II. The two begin as friendly enemies, bickering and badgering with each other but they eventually fall in love. An RAF pilot, Gray, crash-lands on the island and is seriously injured. Darnell is now able to practice her medical knowledge and amputate's Gray's arm to save his life. A *menage a trois* then develops with Darnell loving both men but unable to make up her mind which one to choose. She decides on Gray after they are rescued. Most of the film is puerile and flabby in story and dialog, but Darnell, wandering about in scanty rags, presents a sultry image of alluring pulchritude and the photography presents lush color. Hunter offers little talent but Gray provides some interest. Filmed on location in Jamaica.

p, David E. Rose; d, Stuart Heisler; w, Stephanie Nordli (based on the novel *Saturday Island* by Hugh Brooke); ph, Arthur Ibbetson; m, William Allwyn; ed, Russell Lloyd; art d, John Howell.

Romance (PR:C MPAA:NR)

ISLAND OF DR. MOREAU, THE* (1977) 98m Wetherly-Cinema 77/AIP c

Burt Lancaster *(Dr. Moreau)*, Michael York *(Andrew Braddock)*, Nigel Davenport *(Montgomery)*, Barbara Carrera *(Maria)*, Richard Basehart *(Sayer of the Law)*, Nick Cravat *(M'Ling)*, The Great John "L." *(Boarman)*, Bob Ozman *(Bullman)*, Fumio Demura *(Hyenaman)*, Gary Baxley *(Lionman)*, John Gillespie *(Tigerman)*, David Cass *(Bearman)*.

A monumental waste of 6 million of their dollars and 98 minutes of our time, THE ISLAND OF DR. MOREAU is an inferior remake of the picture, THE ISLAND OF LOST SOULS, one of the best horror films ever made. Shot in color (a mistake) and starring Lancaster (another mistake), this picture should stand as yet another example of attempting to remake a picture that was already a classic. It's 1911 and York and his shipmate are adrift on the sea after their ship has sunk. They land on a small island in an uncharted area of the South Pacific and York's buddy is immediately captured and pulled into the foliage by a band of odd-looking, hirsute natives. York runs after them, is knocked out, and wakes up days later at the home of Lancaster, the mad scientist who owns the island. Davenport, Lancaster's man Friday, is the one who saved York and tells him that his pal is dead of exhaustion, a story York foolishly accepts. Enter Carrera, Lancaster's "ward," a mysterious young woman with a predilection for felines. Lancaster explains that he is on the island working on what he believes will be a momentous discovery: the isolation of the chromosome in humans which determines how they grow and why they look different from each other. A series of events happen which cause York to look at his situation in a new light. He sees Cravat (Lancaster's longtime pal in real life who was so good in THE CRIMSON PIRATE), the boss' Asian assistant, on his hands and knees drinking from a water hole. Then he hears all sorts of yowls and growls coming from the locked lab. York goes to repair his small boat and is pursued by the same crew who took his pal. They are closing in on him but when Lancaster arrives on the scene, these inhuman creatures run. Later, York is in the experiment room and cringes as Lancaster injects a potion into a half-man, half-bear monster. Lancaster explains that he is working on a drug that will effectively alter animals into humans. York is repelled and escapes the building only to fall into the hands of several creatures who have already suffered under Lancaster's work. These beasts want to kill York, but again Lancaster arrives and saves York's bacon. Basehart is half-man, half-wolf, and the leader of the submissive pack who must state aloud Lancaster's tenet which is to walk on two legs, to avoid hunting humans, and to cause no blood to be spilled. York is now in love with Carrera and wants to get off the island with her before he becomes one of Lancaster's charges. He's repaired the boat and is ready to exit when Lancaster injects him with a drug that reverses the usual procedure and turns a man into an animal. Davenport has had it with Lancaster and attempts to stop the procedure but is killed. Lancaster keeps giving York the drug and York, by sheer force of will, is resisting the genetic alteration. The creatures find Davenport's corpse and realize that Lancaster has broken his own rules about killing. They burn down the house and surrounding out-building, kill Lancaster, and begin to hunt York and Carrera in a MOST DANGEROUS GAME sequence in the jungle. York and Carrera get into the boat and the drugs begin to wear off York as he slowly returns to his human form. But Carrera, now that she is free of the serum, starts to transform into what she was before, a large tigress-type animal. A rescue boat is approaching them at sea at the fadeout. The makeup was the star of this film. It was created by the same team of geniuses who did the PLANET OF THE APES. Made in the Virgin Islands and photographed well by Fisher, it looks much better than it really is. Lancaster is overplaying his hand as the insane doctor and the whole thing is so self-conscious about its genetic experiments that it verges on being satire. Had they gone one step further and made it a funny horror movie, it might have made some sense and money. As it is, reports are that it did not recoup its cost. The director is the same Taylor who acted in so many MGM films.

p, Skip Steloff, John Temple-Smith; d, Don Taylor; w, John Herman Shaner, Al Ramrus (based on the novel by H. G. Wells); ph, Gerry Fisher (Movielab Color); m, Laurence Rosenthal; ed, Marion Rothman; prod d, Philip Jeffries; set d, James Berkey; cos, Richard La Motte, Emma Porteous, Rita Woods; spec eff, Cliff Wenger; stunts, Eric Cord, Tony Epper; makeup, John Chambers, Dan Striepeke, Tom Burman.

Horror Cas. (PR:C MPAA:PG)

ISLAND OF DOOM½** (1933, USSR) 60m Rosfilm/Artkino bw

Calina Kravchenko *(Actress)*, Peter Solobevski *(Sailor)*, Vladimir Kruegar *(Spy)*.

An interesting Soviet picture which makes little attempt to bring the usual political messages into the forefront. The story concerns a spy and his girl friend who are boating and stop on a nearby island. The island has been booby-trapped with a bomb by the spy's cohorts, a fact the spy unfortunately forgot. He tries to get away but finds his boat is out of gas. A sailor, abandoned on the island, attempts to flee with the pair but the spy, who is trying frantically to make some oars, flatly refuses and is promptly hit on the head with a brick. The sailor takes the girl and makes his getaway, but she swims back to her lover. In the nick of time the pair locate and dismantle the explosives. The attempt at dialog hardly seems necessary, for this film seems to stand on its keen visuals.

d&w, Semen Timoshenko; ph, Yuri Utekin; m, Gavril Popov; set d, Nikolai Surorov.

Drama (PR:A MPAA:NR)

ISLAND OF DOOMED MEN½** (1940) 68m COL bw

Peter Lorre *(Steve Danel)*, Rochelle Hudson *(Lorraine Danel)*, Robert Wilcox *(Mark Sheldon)*, Don Beddoe *(Brand)*, George E. Stone *(Siggy)*, Kenneth McDonald *(Doctor)*, Charles Middleton *(Capt. Cort)*, Stanley Brown *(Eddie)*, Earl Gunn *(Mitchell)*, Don Douglas *(Official)*, Bruce Bennett *(Hazen, Guard)*, Sam Ash *(Ames)*, Eddie Laughton *(Borgo)*, John Tyrrell *(Durkin)*, Richard Fiske *(Hale)*, Al Hill *(Clinton)*, Trevor Bardette *(District Attorney)*, Howard Hickman *(Judge)*, Addison Richards *(Jackson)*, Ray Bailey *(Mystery Man)*, Lee Prather *(Warden)*, Forbes Murray *(Parole Board Chairman)*, George McKay *(Bookkeeper)*, Bernie Breakston *(Townsend)*, Walter Miller *(Detective)*, Harry Strang, Charles "Chuck" Hamilton *(Cops)*.

Lorre is the owner of Dead Man's Isle, a place where paroled prisoners are sent, then forced to mine for diamonds. After killing an investigating agent from the Department of Justice, Lorre is pitted against agent Wilcox, who organizes a revolt among the workers. It is Lorre's servant, however, who deals the death blow, getting revenge for the shooting of his pet monkey. Lorre's character is described in press kits as being a "fastidious connoisseur of human suffering who cannot bear the sight or sound of physical torture." This simply means he plays Chopin's "Nocturnes" loudly to avoid hearing the enslaved men being flogged.

p, Wallace MacDonald; d, Charles Barton; w, Robert D. Andrews; ph, Benjamin Kline; ed, James Sweeney; md, M. W. Stoloff; art d, Lionel Banks; cos, Robert Kalloch.

Drama (PR:C MPAA:NR)

ISLAND OF LOST MEN** (1939) 63m PAR bw

Anna May Wong *(Kim Ling)*, J. Carrol Naish *(Gregory Prin)*, Anthony Quinn *(Chang Tai)*, Eric Blore *(Herbert)*, Broderick Crawford *(Tex Ballister)*, Ernest Truex *(Frobenius)*, Rudolf Forster *(Prof. Sen)*, William Haade *(Hambly)*, Richard Loo *(Gen. Ahn Ling)*, Philip Ahn *(Sam Ring)*, Torben Meyer *(Cafe Manager)*, Lal Chand Mehra *(Hindu)*, George Kirby *(Waiter)*, Vivien Oakland *(Blonde)*, Jack Parry *(Blonde's Escort)*, Ruth Rickaby *(1st Tourist)*, Ethyl May Halls *(2nd Tourist)*, Bruce Mitchell *(Ship's Officer)*.

Wong is the daughter of a Chinese official who has skipped town with $300,000 of the government's money. She decides that she will leave town herself and try to clear her father's name. After snooping around for clues, she makes her way to the villainous Naish's jungle labor camp. With Quinn acting undercover as one of Naish's henchmen, Wong locates the money and a number of fugitives from the law. American cheat Crawford shows up, blows Quinn's identity, and tries to blackmail Naish. The typical native uprisings follow and Wong, reunited with her father, is able to make a getaway with Quinn, who is unconvincingly Oriental in this dull remake of WHITE WOMAN.

p, Eugene Zukor; d, Kurt Neumann; w, William R. Lipman, Horace McCoy (based on the play "Hangman's Whip" by Norman Reilly Raine, Frank Butler); ph, Karl Struss; ed, Ellsworth Hoagland; md, Boris Morros; art d, Hans Dreier, Frank Bachelin.

Drama (PR:A MPAA:NR)

ISLAND OF LOST SOULS**** (1933) 67m PAR bw

Charles Laughton *(Dr. Moreau)*, Bela Lugosi *(Sayer of the Law)*, Richard Arlen *(Edward Parker)*, Leila Hyams *(Ruth Walker)*, Kathleen Burke *(Lota, the Panther Woman)*, Arthur Hohl *(Montgomery)*, Stanley Fields *(Capt. Davies)*, Robert Kortman *(Hogan)*, Tetsu Komai *(M'Ling)*, Hans Steinke *(Ouran)*, Harry Ekezian *(Gola)*, Rosemary Grimes *(Samoan Girl)*, Paul Hurst *(Donahue)*, George Irving *(American Consul)*, Alan Ladd, Joe Bonomo, Randolph Scott, John George, Larry "Buster" Crabbe, Duke York *(Ape Men)*, Constantine Romanoff, Jack Burdette, Robert Milasch, Bob Kerr, Evangelus Berbas, Jack Walters.

There's not a wasted frame of film in this chilling horror film that was banned in England when released. Wells, from whose novel the screenplay was written, hated the picture from start to finish because he felt that the makers missed his point about a man playing God and opted for the easy way out. It reeks of atmosphere and foreboding, and much of the terror was hinted at, rather than graphically shown, thus using the audience's imagination. Laughton is a smiling, almost benign, man (all the more frightening when we learn what he's up to) who greets shipwrecked Arlen on his own private island. Arlen will wait until the next freighter goes by so he can hitch a ride home. While he waits, Arlen learns that the natives who serve Laughton are really animals who have been transformed into humans by the doctor's experiments in an area known as "The House of Pain." They all shrink away whenever they hear the words spoken. Laughton's singular distaff creature is Burke (she was a 19 year old contestant in a nationwide publicity search for a woman to play in the film whose "feline" look got her the part) and she and Arlen are instantly attracted to each other (in a 67 minute film, there's no time for long engagements). Laughton hopes to mate them, thereby making the first human-animal child (Burke is really a large feline that has been transformed). Then Hyams, Arlen's fiancee, arrives. She has been brought there at her own expense by the captain of a ship. They'd been looking for Arlen and had a vague idea of where he might be. Hyams and Burke vie for Arlen's affections, then Burke orders one of the creatures to attack Hyams. Meanwhile, Laughton has the captain, Fields, killed. Once having seen blood shed, the creatures rise up against Laughton, who threatens them all with sessions in "The House of Pain." Meanwhile, Arlen and Hyams are trying to escape via the boat that brought her. Leader of the rebels is Lugosi (in a small, but very effective, role) who drags Laughton to "The House of Pain" where the creatures delightedly begin to perform surgery on him. Fire breaks out and the island burns as Hyams and Arlen escape by sea. The footage with the boats was shot at Catalina Island and they were lucky to get fog sweeping in, thereby giving it an eerie instead of cheery effect. Studio publicists launched an early promotion for the picture in the shape of a "Panther Woman" contest, inviting catlike contestants nationwide to try out for the part of Lota. A number of the losers were signed by the studio, including Gail Patrick and Lona Andre; thus did the majors replenish their stock of starlets. Burke had been a dental aide in Chicago before beating more than 60,000 young women for the role. Hyams had been in another well-known horror film, FREAKS, and was being typecast until she broke away and returned to comedy with THE POOR RICH, RUGGLES OF RED GAP, PEOPLE WILL TALK, and many more. The same set was used later for WHITE WOMAN, which also starred Laughton. Viewers with sharp eyes will be able to spot actors Scott, Ladd, Crabbe, and strongman Bonomo (who later made millions selling his salt water taffy at beach resorts on the East Coast) in the cast. So many countries (as well as many midwestern states) banned the movie that it took a while to recoup the cost but it remains, to this day, an eminently scarifying movie. The remake, THE ISLAND OF DR. MOREAU, with Lancaster in Laughton's role, and Michael York in Arlen's part, was abysmal. Remade in 1959 as TERROR IS A MAN.

d, Erle C. Kenton; w, Philip Wylie, Waldemar Young (based on the novel *The Island of Dr. Moreau* by H.G. Wells); ph, Karl Struss; spec eff, Gordon Jennings; makeup, Wally Westmore.

Horror **(PR:C MPAA:NR)**

ISLAND OF LOST WOMEN*½ (1959) 66m Jaguar/WB bw

Jeff Richards *(Mark Bradley)*, Venetia Stevenson *(Venus)*, John Smith *(Joe Walker)*, Diane Jergens *(Urana)*, June Blair *(Mercuria)*, Alan Napier *(Dr. Lujan)*, Gavin Muir *(McBain)*, George Brand *(Garland)*.

An unconvincing story about a pilot and a radio commentator who crash-land on an island near Australia. What they find is mad scientist Napier and his three daughters, tagged Venus, Urana, and Mercuria, who've never seen men before (that doesn't say too much for dad). When commentator Richards threatens to expose Napier and his atomic experiments, the angry scientist destroys their airplane, thus stranding them. However, with the help of the daughters, Richards builds a raft. Before it is completed, the scientist causes a violent explosion, bringing an investigation from Australia and an eventual rescue.

p, Albert J. Cohen; d, Frank W. Tuttle; w, Ray Buffum (based on a story by Prescott Chaplin); ph, John Seitz; m, Raoul Kraushaar; ed, Roland Gross; art d, Jack Collins; cos, Howard Shoup.

Adventure **(PR:A MPAA:NR)**

ISLAND OF LOVE½**

(1963) 101m Belgrave/WB c (AKA: NOT ON YOUR LIFE)

Robert Preston *(Steve Blair), Tony Randall (Paul Ferris)*, Georgia Moll *(Elena Harakas)*, Walter Matthau *(Tony Dallas)*, Betty Bruce *(Cha Cha Miller)*, Vassili Lambrinos *(Prof. Pappas)*, Michael Constantine *(Andy)*, Titos Vandis *(Father Anaxagoras)*, Miranda Murat (Mama Harakas), Lewis Charles *(Louie)*, Peter Mamakos *(Nick)*, Nick Dimitri, Tony Rollins, Vic Lundin, Greg Benedict *(Hoods)*, Lillian Miniati *(Miranda)*, Cozette Hutner, Diane Simpson, Larri Thomas, Barbara Hines, Charlene Holt, Kathy Bennett, Don Easton, Norma Varden, Maj. Sam Harris, Kirk Elliott, Pat Olson, Ken Raymond, Stacy Keach, Jan Arvan, Andreas Zambikies, Michael Apostoulou, Lou Krugman, Lois Roberts, Henry Corden, Marianne Gaba, Costas Baladinas, Stavros Farnakis, Andreas Filippidis, Theoderos Kamenidis, Mitsos Lygizos, Effie Mela, Rita Moussouri, Nikis Neoyennis, Yanik de Pardos, Cosmos Panayotidis, Nicos Paschalidis, Theodore Roumbanis, Dimos Starenios, Yovanna, Priamus Mitromaras.

Preston and Randall con millionaire gangster Matthau into fronting $2 million for the production of a lusty film about Adam and Eve, starring the mobster's stripper girl friend. The film, like so many others, is a disaster, forcing the pair to flee to Greece. The enterprising Preston comes up with another lame-brained idea, this time promoting a sagging tourist trap as a lover's paradise. He eventually falls in love with Matthau's niece, which saves him from seemingly unavoidable doom. Matthau is the one who carries the film with his likable gangster portrayal.

p&d, Morton DaCosta; w, David R. Schwartz (based on a story by Leo Katcher); ph, Harry Stradling, Sr. (Panavision, Technicolor); m, George Duning; ed, William Ziegler; art d, Edward Carrere; set d, George James Hopkins; cos, Don Feld; m/l, Sammy Fain, Harold Adamson.

Comedy **(PR:A MPAA:NR)**

ISLAND OF MONTE CRISTO (SEE: SWORD OF VENUS, 1952)

ISLAND OF PROCIDA, THE*** (1952, Ital.) 90m Casolaro bw

Claudio Gora *(Paul)*, Carlo Ninchi *(Mania)*, Vera Carmi *(Elena)*, Franca Marzi *(Lucy)*, Giulio Donnini *(Father Elia)*, Mario Gallina *(Director)*, Agostino Salviette *(Ombra)*, Annibale Beltrone *(Doctor)*, Checco Durante *(Faina)*, Fausto Guerzoni *(Marciano)*, Pio Campa *(Morabito)*, Paolo Reale *(Giacomo)*, Angelo Dessy *(Rogni)*, Giovanni Petti *(Michele)*, Armando Guernieri *(Esposito)*, Janella Montis *(Giulietta)*.

Gora realistically portrays a top surgeon who is imprisoned for 20 years after being convicted of murdering his adulterous wife. With little hope, Gora struggles through the meager existence of a life behind bars. After performing an emergency operation on a small child, he falls in love with her older sister and finds a new reason to live. Their affair strengthens, and at the culmination of his sentence, the pair wed. (In Italian; English subtitles.)

p, Luciano Dorio; d, Mario Cequi; w, L. Giacosi; ph, Tonino Delli Colli; m, Ezio Carabella.

Drama **(PR:C MPAA:NR)**

ISLAND OF TERROR½**

(1967, Brit.) 90m Protelco-Planet/UNIV c (AKA: NIGHT OF THE SILICATES; THE CREEPERS).

Peter Cushing *(Dr. Stanley)*, Edward Judd *(Dr. David West)*, Carole Gray *(Toni Merrill), Eddie Byrne (Dr. Landers)*, Sam Kydd *(Constable Harris)*, Niall MacGinnis *(Mr. Campbell)*, James Caffrey *(Argyle)*, Liam Gaffney *(Bellows)*, Roger Heathcote *(Dunley)*, Peter Forbes-Robertson *(Dr. Phillips)*, Richard Bidlake *(Carson)*, Joyce Hemson *(Mrs. Bellows)*, Edward Ogden *(Helicopter Pilot)*, Keith Bell *(Halsey)*, Shay Gorman *(Morton)*.

Cushing is a scientist brought to an Irish island to study some newly discovered boneless corpses. The bodies turn out to be those of a doctor and his assistants who have been working on a cancer cure. What they develop instead is a bizarre silicon-based life form which feeds on calcium and cannot be harmed even by dynamite. The creatures, which multiply every six hours, kill practically everyone on the island. Once a dangerous isotope is injected into the island's cattle, however, the creatures die off of poisoning. A rather shaky plot is boosted by Cushing's ever effective performance and Fisher's tight direction. Fisher also helmed a number of Hammer horror films including, THE CURSE OF FRANKENSTEIN and HORROR OF DRACULA.

p, Tom Blakeley; d, Terence Fisher; w, Edward Andrew Mann, Allan Ramsen; ph, Reg Wyer (Eastmancolor); m, Malcolm Lockyer; ed, Thelma Connell; md, Lockyer; art d, John St. John Earl; spec eff, Earl, Michael Albrechtson, Barry Gray.

Horror **Cas.** **(PR:C MPAA:NR)**

ISLAND OF THE BLUE DOLPHINS½** (1964) 93m UNIV c

Celia Kaye *(Karana)*, Larry Domasin *(Ramo)*, Ann Daniel *(Tutok)*, George Kennedy *(Aleut Captain)*, Carlos Romero *(Chowig)*, Hal Jon Norman *(Kimki)*, Martin Garralaga *(The Priest)*, Alex Montoya *(Spanish Captain)*, Julie Payne *(Lurai)*, Jon Alvar *(Tainer)*, Junior *(Rontu, the Dog)*, Manchester Tribe of the Poma Nation, Kashia Tribe of the Poma Nation.

Set in the remote Aleutian Islands, Kaye plays a young native girl during the early 1800s who is forced to flee her island home with the rest of her tribe when white hunters threaten. Realizing her young brother has been left behind, she jumps ship and swims back. The two remain on the island and endure solitude for nearly 20 years. She learns to hunt and fish, make a home, and domesticate a wild dog. Her brother, however, is not so resourceful and falls victim to a pack of wild animals. Distrustful, she passes up a chance at rescue when another group of white hunters arrive on the island. Years later, after her trusty canine companion has died, she gets a second chance to be saved. She goes with the hunters, bringing her collection of pets along for the ride. Taken from a novel based on an actual incident. (Note: the part of Lurai is played by Payne, daughter of John Payne and Anne Shirley.)

p, Robert B. Radnitz, Edward Mull; d, James B. Clark; w, Ted Sherdeman, Jane Klove (based on the novel by Scott O'Dell, adapted by Radnitz); ph, Leo Tover (Eastmancolor); m, Paul Sawtell; ed, Ted J. Kent; md, Joseph Gershenson; art d, Alexander Golitzen, George Webb; set d, Oliver Emert; cos, Rosemary Odell; makeup, Bud Westmore, Jack Freeman.

Drama **Cas.** **(PR:AAA MPAA:NR)**

ISLAND OF THE BURNING DAMNED**

(1971, Brit.) 94m Planet/Maron c (GB: NIGHT OF THE BIG HEAT; AKA; ISLAND OF THE BURNING DOOMED)

Christopher Lee *(Hanson)*, Peter Cushing *(Dr. Stone)*, Patrick Allen *(Jeff Callum)*, Sarah Lawson *(Frankie Callum)*, Jane Merrow *(Angela Roberts)*, William Lucas *(Ken Stanley)*, Kenneth Cope *(Tinker Mason)*, Jack Bligh *(Ben Siddle)*, Thomas Heathcote *(Bob Hayward)*, Sidney Bromley *(Old Tramp)*, Percy Herbert *(Gerald Foster)*, Anna Turner *(Stella Haywood)*, Barry Halliday *(Radar Operator)*.

Vaguely interesting science fiction film involving an alien protoplasm that invades a British isle and causes a massive heat wave that burns most of the residents to death. Lee is the scientist who figures out what's happening but is unable to do anything to help. Eventually a thunderstorm melts the extraterrestrial threat.

p, Tom Blakeley; d, Terence Fisher; w, Ronald Liles, Pip Baker, Jane Baker (based on the novel *Night Of The Big Heat* by John Lymington); ph, Reg Wyer (Eastmancolor); m, Malcolm Lockyer; ed, Rod Keys; md, Lockyer; art d, Alex Vetchinsky.

Science Fiction **(PR:C MPAA:GP)**

ISLAND OF THE BURNING DOOMED

(SEE: ISLAND OF THE BURNING DAMNED, 1971, Brit.)

ISLAND OF THE DAMNED*½

(1976, Span.) 100m AIP c (QUIEN PUEDE MATAR A UN NINO; AKA: WHO CAN KILL A CHILD?; WHO WOULD KILL A CHILD?)

Lewis Fiander *(Tom)*, Prunella Ransome *(Evelyn)*, Antonio Iranzo, Miguel Naros, Marisa Porcel, Maria Luisa Arias.

Better than average as Spanish horror films go, ISLAND OF THE DAMNED tells us the horrific tale of a married couple who travel to a resort island only to discover that it has been overrun by murderous children. The kiddies have killed all the adults in sight and are planning to do the same to the newlyweds. More suspense and intelligence than most of its kind.

p, Manuel Perez; d, Narciso Ibanez Serrador; w, Luis Penafiel (based on the novel "El Juego" by J.J. Plans); ph, Jose Luis Alcaine (Movielab Color); m, Waldo De Los Rios.

Horror **(PR:O MPAA:R)**

ISLAND OF THE DOOMED* 1/2
(1968, Span./Ger.) 88m Orbita-Tefi/AA c (LA ISLA DE LA MUERTE; DAS GEHEIMNIS DER TODESINSEL; AKA: MAN EATER OF HYDRA)

Cameron Mitchell *(Baron von Weser)*, Elisa Montes *(Beth Christiansen)*, George Martin *(David Moss)*, Kai Fischer *(Cora Robinson)*, Rolf von Naukoff *(James Robinson)*, Herman Nelsen *(Professor Julius Demerist)*, Matilde Sampedro-Munoz *(Myrtle Callahan)*, Ricardo Valle *(Alfredo)*, Mike Brendel *(Baldi)*.

Mitchell is a deranged botanist who cultivates a man-eating, blood-sucking tree which systematically kills off a group of tourists. The suspicious Martin puts down his camera and begins to do some snooping, finding Mitchell's servant dumping one of the bodies. He tries to destroy the killer tree, battling the angry scientist in the process. The finale of this English dubbed film has Mitchell devoured by his own creation. Director Welles appeared in Roger Corman's similar THE LITTLE SHOP OF HORRORS.

p, George Ferrer; d, Mel Welles; w, Stephen Schmidt (based on the story by Ira Meltcher, Ernst Ritter Von Theumer); ph, Cecilio Paniagua (Techniscope, Technicolor); m, Anton Garcia Abril; ed, Antonio Canovas; art d, Francisco Canet.

Horror **(PR:C MPAA:NR)**

ISLAND OF THE FISHMEN, THE (SEE: SCREAMERS, 1978, Ital.)

ISLAND RESCUE 1/2**
(1952, Brit.) 89m British Film Makers/UNIV bw (GB: APPOINTMENT WITH VENUS)

David Niven *(Maj. Valentine Morland)*, Glynis Johns *(Nicola Fallaize)*, George Coulouris *(Capt. Weiss)*, Barry Jones *(Provost)*, Kenneth More *(Lionel Fallaize)*, Noel Purcell *(Trawler Langley)*, Bernard Lee *(Brigadier)*, Jeremy Spenser *(Georges)*, Patric Doonan *(Sgt. Forbes)*, Martin Boddey *(Sgt. Vogel)*, John Horsley *(Kent)*, Michael Evans *(2nd Officer)*, David Horne *(Magistrate)*, Geoffrey Sumner *(Major)*, Peter Butterworth *(Rating)*, Anton Diffring *(German)*, George Benson *(Senior Clerk)*, Richard Wattis *(Higher Executive)*, Raymond Young, Richard Marner, Herbert C. Walton, Malcolm Farquhar, Charles Cullum, Stanley Rose, John Stratton, Peter Martyn, Neil Wilson, Geoffrey Denton, Michael Ward, Pat Nye, Marianne Stone, Betty Cooper, Noel Johnson, Jeanne Pali, Oscar Nation, Helen Goss, Philip Stainton, Derek Blomfield, Harold Goodwin, Basil Dignam, Olwen Brookes, Charles Lamb, Michael Ritterman, Henrik Jacobsen, Fritz Krenn, Johnnie Schofield, Terence Longden.

Set during WW II, Niven and Johns are assigned the mission of retrieving from a Nazi-occupied island the prized "Venus." However, this is not the Venus of Milo fame, but rather a cow named Venus—of Milk fame. Smuggling a cow through occupied territory isn't easy and results in a wacky chain of events for the rescuers.

p, Betty E. Box; d, Ralph Thomas; w, Nicholas Phipps (based on a story and adaptation by Jerrard Tickell from his novel *Transit of Venus*); ph, Ernest Steward; m, Benjamin Frankel; ed, Gerald Thomas; art d, George Provis.

Comedy **(PR:A MPAA:NR)**

11459A

ISLAND WOMAN (SEE: ISLAND WOMEN, 1958)

ISLAND WOMEN* (1958) 72m Security/UA bw (AKA: ISLAND WOMAN)

Marie Windsor *(Elizabeth)*, Vince Edwards *(Mike)*, Marilee Earle *(Jan)*, Leslie Scott *(Eban)*, Irene Williams *(Iron Woman)*, Kay Barnes *(Mary Ann)*, Paul White *(Constable)*, Maurine Duvalier *(Calypso Mama)*, The Bahamian Calypso Entertainers, George Symonette, "Blind Blake" Higgs, "Peanuts" Taylor, Vincent Martin, "Chipple" Chipman, Johnny Kemp, Harold McNair, Becky Chipman, Naomi, Sweet Richard, David Kemp.

A brainless calypso drama which has sea captain Edwards and Caribbean tourist Earle falling in love with each other. Earle's aunt (Windsor) wants Edwards for herself, however, and does her best to break up the relationship but to no avail.

p&d, William Berke; w, Philip Yordan (based on a story by Andrew Alexander); ph, Arthur Feindel; ed, Everett Sutherland; md, Boyd Raeburn; art d, Frank Perry; cos, Susan Burke; m/l, Alice D. Simms, Charles Lofthouse.

Drama **(PR:A MPAA:NR)**

ISLANDS IN THE STREAM*** (1977) 105m PAR c

George C. Scott *(Thomas Hudson)*, David Hemmings *(Eddy)*, Gilbert Roland *(Capt. Ralph)*, Susan Tyrrell *(Lil)*, Richard Evans *(Willy)*, Claire Bloom *(Audrey)*, Julius Harris *(Joseph)*, Hart Bochner *(Tom)*, Brad Savage *(Andrew)*, Michael-James Wixted *(David)*, Charles Lampkin *(Constable)*, Hildy Brooks *(Helga Ziegner)*, Jessica Rains *(Andrea)*, Walter Friedel *(Herr Ziegner)*.

Scott is the best thing about this touch-and-go Hemingway-based film, taken from his posthumously published novel of 1970, a book Hemingway did not release in his lifetime but his widow Mary did, and that, too, was a mistake. The story is basically a rehash of an earlier, better-told, less self-indulgent tale, *To Have and Have Not*. Scott is a distinguished artist living on Bimini in the Bahamas. He is well-to-do and can afford a retinue of servants and friends to whom he supplies booze, stories, and his radiant personality. He drinks, he fishes, he fantasizes. Hemmings, his drunken sailor pal, and Harris, his black servant, are on hand to make sure he doesn't fall out of the boat. Tyrell is the local good-natured prostitute and Bloom is Scott's wealthy ex-wife, by whom he has had one son (a close-shave portrait of Hemingway's first wife, Hadley Richardson). His three sons, the youngest two from another marriage (Hemingway's second wife, Pauline Pfeiffer), come to visit Scott and they share some joys and pains fishing and talking. Wixted is at war with his father over painful arguments he remembers his parents having years earlier. Bochner, the oldest son, swims out too far one day and is almost eaten by a shark but rummy Hemmings grabs a machinegun and kills the shark first. Bochner later joins the RAF to fight the Germans (this before the U.S. was in the war), and his mother, Bloom, later visits Scott to tell him that she is remarrying and that their son has been killed in action. Scott now becomes a man of action, almost as if having nothing more to live for, and rescues a group of Jewish refugees, smuggling them ashore while his boat and crew are shot to pieces by gunboats (national origin not known). He tries to evade capture by setting fire to the inland water channels with gasoline but is mortally wounded and dies, saying at the last, while having hallucinations of Bloom and his sons returning to him: "I now know there is no one thing that is true. It is all true." *Islands In The Stream* is pretentious and the only captivating moments are those willed into being by Scott's magnetic personality. But the Hemingway credo of masculine survival by sword and fire rings false in a world that had long discarded such one dimensional notions. The philosophy, such as it is, is only hopeful that someone, anyone, might come along and fill in its implications with some permanent intellectuality. The reader used to do that for Hemingway when dealing with his oft-times magical words, but it's an impossibility in film where all is naked and the unbelievable and the unsaid must somehow find reality and voice. Perhaps the failure of the film is because ***Islands in the Stream* was unfinished and never ready to go when its author put a shotgun to his head. And it was all said and done by then, lived and done and dead.**

p, Peter Bart, Max Palevsky; d, Franklin J. Schaffner; w, Denne Bart Petitclerc (based on the novel by Ernest Hemingway); ph, Fred J. Koenekamp (Panavision, Metrocolor); m, Jerry Goldsmith; ed. Robert Swink; prod d, William J. Greber; set d, Raphael Bretton; cos, Tony Scarano; spec eff, Alex Weldon; makeup, Del Acevedo, Rich Sharp.

Drama/Adventure **Cas.** **(PR:C MPAA:PG)**

ISLE OF DESTINY* 1/2 (1940) 83m RKO c

William Gargan *("Stripes" Thornton)*, Wallace Ford *("Milly" Barnes)*, June Lang *(Virginia Allerton)*, Gilbert Roland *(Barton)*, Etienne Girardot *("Doc" Spriggs)*, Katherine DeMille *(Inda)*, Grant Richards *(Lt. Allerton)*, Tom Dugan *(Sgt. Reikker)*, Ted Osborne *(Max)*, Harry Woods *(Capt. Lawson)*.

Society gal aviator Lang is kidnaped by gunrunner Roland after flying her amphibious airplane into the wrong part of a South Seas jungle. But quick to come to her rescue are the never-too-tough Gargan and Ford. The best thing about this mindless script is DeMille's main character—the wild jungle woman who prowls about with her murderous blow gun. Includes the tune "Moonlight Magic" (Irving Bibo, Eddie Cherkose).

p, Franklyn Warner; d, Elmer Clifton; w, Arthur Hoerl, M. Coates Webster, Robert Lively (based on a story by Allan Vaughn Elston); ph, Edward Linden (Cosmocolor); ed, John Rawlins, Robert Crandall; md, Constantin Bakaleinikoff; art d, Fred Preble.

Adventure **(PR:A MPAA:NR)**

ISLE OF ESCAPE* 1/2 (1930) 60m WB bw

Monte Blue *(David Wade)*, Myrna Loy *(Moira)*, Betty Compson *(Stella Blackney)*, Noah Beery *(Tom Shane)*, Ivan Simpson *(Judge)*, Jack Ackroyd *(Hank)*, Nina Quartero *(Loru)*, Duke Kahanamoku *(Manua)*, Rose Dione *(Ma Blackney)*, Adolph Milar *(Dutch Planter)*, Nick De Ruiz *(Dalobe)*.

The unhappily married Compson leaves despotic hubby Beery and ends up kidnaped by a group of dancing, ritualistic, head-hunting natives. Beery and Compson's true love, Blue, try to rescue her from danger's grip and encounter the alluring Loy. Overdressed in an unnaturally long sarong, Loy devises numerous ways to hook nice guy Blue, who rejects her. Beery obligingly dies in the rescue attempt. A pretty generic look to the "exotic" South Seas. Actor Duke Kahanamoku was a full-blooded Hawaiian and an Olympic swimming champion.

d, Howard Bretherton; w, Lucien Hubbard, J. Grubb Alexander (based on a story by Jack McLaren from a play by G.C. Dixon); m/l, "My Kalua Rose," Ed Ward, Al Bryan.

Adventure **(PR:C MPAA:NR)**

ISLE OF FORGOTTEN SINS** (1943) 82m PRC bw

John Carradine *(Clancy)*, Gale Sondergaard *(Marge)*, Sidney Toler *(Krogan)*, Frank Fenton *(Burke)*, Rita Quigley *(Diane)*, Veda Ann Borg *(Luana)*, Rick Vallin *(Johnny Pacific)*, Betty Amann *(Olga)*, Tala Birell *(Christine)*, Patti McCarty *(Bobbie)*, Marian Colby *(Mimi)*, William Edmonds *(Native Chief)*.

Carradine and Fenton are a couple of divers who search the South Pacific waters for a $3 million treasure in gold. When they find the purse the two are nabbed by the rotten ship captain, who swipes the gold for himself. A killer monsoon floods the island, washing the entire cast into the seas. The good guys wash back to shore, but without any gold. A jumpy and only partly engaging picture which seems to have been rearranged thanks to the Hays Code, this film had one of the best casts ever put together by poverty-row PRC.

p, Peter R. Van Duinen; d, Edgar G. Ulmer; w, Raymond L. Schrock (based on a story by Ulmer); ph, Ira Morgan; m, Leo Erdody; ed, Charles Henkel, Jr.; art d, Fred Preble; spec eff, Gene Stone.

Drama **(PR:A MPAA:NR)**

ISLE OF FURY** (1936) 60m WB bw (AKA: THREE IN EDEN)

Humphrey Bogart *(Val Stevens)*, Margaret Lindsay *(Lucille Gordon)*, Donald Woods *(Eric Blake)*, Paul Graetz *(Capt. Deever)*, Gordon Hart *(Anderson)*, E.E. Clive *(Dr. Hardy)*, George Regas *(Otar)*, Sidney Bracy *(Sam)*, Tetsu Komai *(Kim Lee)*, Miki Morita *(Oh Kay)*, Houseley Stevenson, Sr. *(Rector)*, Frank Lackteen *(Old Native)*.

Bogie is a crook-gone-straight in this island film based on a W. Somerset Maugham novel. Shortly after wedding Lindsay, Bogart is called on to rescue Woods and Graetz from a sinking ship. It turns out that Woods is a detective assigned to hunt down a fugitive, who happens to be Bogart. After saving Bogart's life and having a near-affair with Lindsay, Woods sees that Bogart's not such a bad guy after all and leaves the island, and his lover behind. Tolerable only for Bogie's presence, even though he would never confess to being in this uneventful and poorly conceived picture. It does, however, include an underwater battle with an octopus.

p, Bryan Foy; d, Frank McDonald; w, Robert Andrews, William Jacobs (based on the novel *The Narrow Corner* by W. Somerset Maugham); ph, Frank Good; m, Howard Jackson; ed, Warren Low; art d, Esdras Hartley; spec eff, Fred Jackman, Willard Van Enger, H.F. Koenekamp.

Adventure (PR:A MPAA:NR)

ISLE OF LOST SHIPS** ½ (1929) 84m FN bw

Jason Robards, Sr. *(Frank Howard)*, Virginia Valli *(Dorothy Renwick)*, Clarissa Selwynne *(Aunt Emma)*, Noah Beery, Sr. *(Capt. Forbes)*, Robert Emmett O'Connor *(Jackson)*, Margaret Fielding *(Mrs. Gallagher)*, Harry Cording *(Gallagher)*, Katherine Ward *(Mother Burke)*, Robert E. Homans *(Mr. Burke)*, Jack Ackroyd *(Harry)*, Sam Baker *(Himself)*.

Robards heads a cast of motley passengers aboard a steamer that drifts into the Sargasso Sea. They eerily drift by a floating graveyard of abandoned and wrecked ships, eventually ending up stranded on a remote island. The direction is often atmospheric, though it struggles a bit with plausibility. At one point Robards is fired out of a submarine's torpedo tube and surfaces safely without much of a problem. A remake of a 1923 silent. Includes the song "Ship Of My Dreams."

d, Irving Willat; w, Fred Myton, Paul Perez (based on the novel *The Isle of Dead Ships* by Crittenden Marriott); ph, Sol Polito; ed, John Rawlins.

Adventure (PR:A MPAA:NR)

ISLE OF LOST WRANGLERS (SEE: 99 WOUNDS, 1931)

ISLE OF MISSING MEN* ½ (1942) 67m MON bw

John Howard, Helen Gilbert, Gilbert Roland, Alan Mowbray, Bradley Page, George Chandler, Geraldine Gray, Egon Brecher, Kitty O'Neill, Dewey Robinson, Charles Williams, Ernie Adams, Kenneth Duncan, Alex Havier.

Fairly exciting adventure tale in which the members of a prison island attempt to escape. Gilbert is the woman who follows her man to the ends of the earth just to be near him, despite his being kept behind bars.

p&d, Richard Oswald; w, Robert Chapin (based on the story "White Lady" by Gina Kaus, Ladislas Fodor); ph, Paul Ivano; ed, Jack Dennis; md, Edward Kay; art d, Paul P. Sylos.

Adventure/Drama (PR:A MPAA:NR)

ISLE OF SIN* ½

(1963, Ger.) 74m Rapid/Manson bw (FLITTERWOCHEN IN DER HOLLE)

Christiane Nielsen *(Martine Duval)*, Erwin Strahl *(Michael Damon)*, Jan Hendriks *(Mario Bertelli)*, Georg Thomas *(Peter Lorenz)*, Slavo Schwaiger *(Bert Frank)*, Dorothee Glocklen *(Ellen Frank)*, Otto Storr *(Neils Larson)*, Walter Faber *(Henry Boone)*, Demeter Bitenc *(Jose Antonio Garcia)*, Mladen Kozina, Beate Norden, Danilo Bezlay.

A film about the way people revert to their animal impulses when all means of social restraints are removed. The cast is a cross section of humanity, all passengers on a flight from Mexico to Venezuela which makes an unscheduled landing on an uncharted island. The good virtues of man are represented in a priest, and his evil counterpart comes in the form of a convict, both of whom try to influence the surviving passengers. Much murder and mayhem occurs as the ties of civilization are thrown off. The end sees good triumphing over evil as the survivors are rescued and the convict is killed.

p, Wolfgang Hartwig; d&w, Johannes Kai; ph, Georg Krause; m, Karl Bette.

Drama (PR:C-O MPAA:NR)

ISLE OF THE DEAD*** (1945) 72m RKO bw

Boris Karloff *(Gen. Nikolas Pherides)*, Ellen Drew *(Thea)*, Marc Cramer *(Oliver Davis)*, Katherine Emery *(Mrs. St. Aubyn)*, Helene Thimig *(Kyra)*, Alan Napier *(Mr. St. Aubyn)*, Jason Robards, Sr. *(Albrecht)*, Skelton Knaggs *(Henry Robbins)*, Sherry Hall *(Colonel)*, Ernst Dorian *(Dr. Drossos)*, Erick Hanson *(Officer)*.

Karloff is a Greek general who, after leading his troops in a victorious Balkan War battle, travels to a nearby island to visit the grave of his wife. He finds that the coffin has been exhumed, and, along with American reporter Cramer, begins a search for the remains. The two are taken in by Robards, who explains that some locals have taken to grave robbing. Karloff decides to go after the culprits and dismisses fellow houseguest Thimig's story about the "vrykolakas," which are Greek vampires. Members of Robards' household come down with the plague and begin dying off. To avoid spreading the disease, Karloff decides to remain on the isle. Thimig continues to press on with her theory, telling Karloff that Drew is one of the undead. When Emery goes into a trance, the others believe her dead and prepare the body for burial. She wakes up in a tomb and escapes while poor Karloff, driven mad by illness and Thimig, decides to kill Drew. In her daze, Emery kills Thimig but saves Drew before Karloff does her in. She kills the general and falls to her own death from atop a cliff. A frightening film which has the usual atmospheric flair of producer Lewton, though it is likely to be viewed as one of his lesser efforts. Karloff, like his film character, was physically stricken during the production, though not with the plague. While on the set he was aggravated by an old back injury and rushed to the hospital for an emergency spinal operation. Emery was a replacement for actress Rose Hobart.

p, Val Lewton; d, Mark Robson; w, Ardel Wray, Josef Mischel, Lewton (suggested by a painting by Arnold Boecklin); ph, Jack Mackenzie; m, Leigh Harline; ed, Lyle Boyer; md, Constantin Bakaleinikoff; art d, Albert S. D'Agostino, Walter Keller; set d, Darrell Silvera, Al Greenwood; cos, Edward Stevenson.

Horror Cas. (PR:C MPAA:NR)

ISLE OF THE SNAKE PEOPLE (SEE: SNAKE PEOPLE, 1968, Mex./U.S.)

ISN'T IT ROMANTIC?* ½ (1948) 87m PAR bw

Veronica Lake *(Candy)*, Mona Freeman *(Susie)*, Mary Hatcher *(Rose)*, Billy De Wolfe *(Horace Frazier)*, Roland Culver *(Maj. Euclid Cameron)*, Patric Knowles *(Richard Brannon)*, Richard Webb *(Benjamin Logan)*, Kathryn Givney *(Clarisse Thayer)*, Larry Olsen *(Hannibal)*, Pearl Bailey *(Addie)*, Charles Evans *(Judge Thomas Logan)*, Jeff York *(Burly Gent)*, Eddie Johnson *(Jerry, the Piano Player)*, Johnny Garrett *(Jasper)*, Dick Keene *(Mr. Hagerty)*, Olin Howlin *(Hotel Clerk)*, Bill Meader *(Assistant Clerk)*, Perle Kincaid, Julia Otho, Mattie Kennedy, Mabel Hart, Sally Hale, Ethel Getty, Ivanetta Gardner, Rose DeHaven, Mabel Butterworth *(Corinthian Circle Members)*, Syd Saylor *(Bartender)*, Hal Bartlett *(Carter Dixon)*, Chester Conklin, Snub Pollard, Duke York, Bobby Barber *(Men)*, Sarah Edwards (Bird-Like Woman).

"Romantic" isn't quite the right word; dull is more like it. Culver is a batty old Hoosier who lives with his three daughters. He's still fighting the Civil War, though it ended a few years earlier. Culver comes to the conclusion he is broke and then falls for an unconvincing oil scheme. Lake can't do much with the half-baked script, though Pearl Bailey, as a housemaid, shows her talent. Tunes include: "I Shouda Quit While I Was Ahead," "Wondering When," "Indiana Dinner" (Jay Livingston, Ray Evans), "Isn't It Romantic" (Richard Rogers, Lorenz Hart).

p, Daniel Dare; d, Norman Z. McLeod; w, Theodore Strauss, Joseph Mischel, Richard L. Breen (based on a story by Jeanette C. Nolan); ph, Lionel Linden; ed, LeRoy Stone; md, Joseph J. Lilley; art d, Hans Dreier, Robert Clatworthy.

Musical (PR:A MPAA:NR)

ISN'T LIFE A BITCH? (SEE: LA CHIENNE, 1975, Fr.)

ISN'T LIFE WONDERFUL!** ½ (1953, Brit.) 83m ABF/Pathe c

Cecil Parker *(Father)*, Eileen Herlie *(Mother)*, Donald Wolfit *(Uncle Willie)*, Peter Asher *(Charles)*, Eleanor Summerfield *(Aunt Kate)*, Dianne Foster *(Virginia van Stuyden)*, Robert Urquhart *(Frank)*, Russell Waters *(Green)*, Cecil Trouncer *(Dr. Barsmith)*, Philip Stainton *(Dr. Mason)*, Edwin Styles *(Bamboula)*, Arthur Young *(Sir George Probus)*, Fabia Drake *(Lady Probus)*, George Woodbridge *(Cockie)*, Viola Lyel *(Aunt Jane)*, Wensley Pithey, Alec Finter, Cecily Paget-Bowman, Basil Cunard, John Welsh, Margot Lister, Henry Hewitt.

Wolfit is the black sheep of a British family. He's set up in a bicycle repair shop to impress a visiting American fiancee. Wolfit has no desire to work with bikes and would rather spend his time tipping a bottle of ale, but the shop begins to prosper. A pleasant little charmer set at the turn of the century.

p, Patrick Ward; d, Harold French; w, Brock Williams (based on his novel *Uncle Willie and the Bicycle Shop*); ph, Edwin Hillier (Technicolor); m, Philip Green; ed, E. B. Jarvis; song, Phil Park.

Comedy (PR:A MPAA:NR)

ISTANBUL** (1957) 84m UNIV c

Errol Flynn *(Jim Brennan)*, Cornell Borchers *(Stephanie Bauer/Karen Fielding)*, John Bentley *(Inspector Nural)*, Torin Thatcher *(Douglas Fielding)*, Leif Erickson *(Charlie Boyle)*, Peggy Knudson *(Marge Boyle)*, Martin Benson *(Mr. Darius)*, Nat "King" Cole *(Danny Rice)*, Werner Klemperer *(Paul Renkov)*, Jan Arvan *(Kazim)*, Nico Minardos *(Ali)*, Ted Hecht *(Lt. Sarac)*, David Bond *(Dr. Sarica)*, Roland Varno *(Mr. Florian)*, Hillevi Rombin *(Air Hostess)*, Frederic Melchior *(Said)*, Vladimir Sokoloff *(Aziz Rakim)*, Didi Ramati *(Sabiya)*, Otto Reichow, Michael Dale *(Thugs)*, Peri Hatman *(Turkish Travel Agent)*, Michael Raffetto *(Priest)*, Albert Carrier *(Mauret)*, Edward Colmans *(Hotel Clerk)*, Paul Thierry *(Middle-Aged Man)*, Franco Corsaro *(Butler)*, Peter Norman *(Clerk)*, Bobker Ben Ali *(Customs Man)*, Manuel Paris *(Waiter)*, George Calliga *(Headwaiter)*.

For his first Hollywood film in five years (the previous outing being AGAINST ALL FLAGS), Flynn was cast in this remake of 1947's SINGAPORE. The change in title locations has Flynn in Turkey's capital city discovering a bracelet containing 13 (apparently his unlucky number) valuable jewels. He is soon the subject of pursuing smugglers who want the gems themselves, but he is deported by Turkish customs officials. Flynn returns five years later to rescue the stones from their hotel hiding place and again is chased by the persistent gang and the greedy customs people. If this isn't enough there's also a sub-plot about Flynn's presumed-dead-wife, Borchers. She was thought to have been burned to death on their wedding night. However, the woman lives, an amnesiac who has since remarried. Notably present is singer Nat "King" Cole who croons "I Was A Little Too Lonely" (Jay Livingston and Ray Evans) and "When I Fall In Love" (Victor Young and Edward Heyman). Klemperer, later Col. Klink of television's "Hogan's Heroes," also makes an appearance.

p, Albert J. Cohen; d, Joseph Pevney; w, Seton I. Miller, Barbara Gray, Richard Alan Simmons (based on the story by Miller); ph, William Daniels (CinemaScope,

Technicolor); ed, Sherman Todd; md, Joseph Gershenson; art d, Alexander Golitzen, Eric Orbom; set d, Russell A. Gausman, Julia Heron; cos, William Thomas; makeup, Bud Westmore.

Drama **(PR:A MPAA:NR)**

IT!* (1967, Brit.) 96m Gold Star/WB c (AKA; CURSE OF THE GOLEM)

Roddy McDowall *(Arthur Pimm)*, Jill Haworth *(Ellen Grove)*, Paul Maxwell *(Jim Perkins)*, Aubrey Richards *(Prof. Weal)*, Ernest Clark *(Harold Grove)*, Oliver Johnston *(Trimingham)*, Noel Trevarthen *(Inspector White)*, Ian McCulloch *(Wayne)*, Richard Goolden *(Old Man)*, Dorothy Frere *(Miss Swanson)*, Tom Chatto *(Capt.)*, Steve Kirby *(Ellis)*, Russell Napier *(Boss)*, Frank Sieman *(Workman)*, Brian Haines *(Joe Hill)*, Mark Burns, Raymond Adamson *(Officers)*, Lindsay Campbell *(Policeman)*, John Baker *(Guard)*, Alan Sellers *(The Golem)*.

McDowall is a Norman Bates-type character (from PSYCHO) who lives with his mother's remains. When the man he assists at a museum is killed in a fire, McDowall takes charge of a mysterious statue. By reading an inscription the unbalanced man learns the piece is really the famed Golem of Czechoslovakia. McDowall learns how to control the Golem (Sellers) telepathically, then uses the creature for his own mad desires. After he kills several people and destroys London Bridge, officials decide the only way to stop the creature is by that ever-popular bad movie device: an atomic bomb. The bomb gets McDowall handily (to say the least) but the statue escapes by walking off into the sea. This poor re-hash of Yiddish Golem legends and the noted 1920 German film DER GOLEM is too leaden to be good camp. Direction and screenplay move too slowly, though McDowall gives one of his patented psychotic performances. It was originally released on a double bill with director Leder's much better effort THE FROZEN DEAD.

p,d&w, Herbert J. Leder (based on his story "Curse of the Golem"); ph, Davis Boulton (Eastmancolor); m, Carlo Martelli; ed, Tom Simpson; md, Philip Martell; art d, Scott MacGregor; cos, Mary Gibson; makeup, Eric Carter.

Horror **(PR:O MPAA:NR)**

IT AIN'T EASY* 1/2 (1972) 90m Dandelion c

Lance Henriksen *(Randy)*, Barra Grant *(Ann)*, Bill Moor *(Gimma)*, Granville Van Dusen *(Paul)*, Joseph Maher *(Charlie)*, Pierrino Mascarino *("T")*, Penelope Allen *(Jenny)*, William Schoppert *(Merle)*.

Snowmobiling is the big thing for this uneventful picture photographed in chilly Minnesota. Henriksen is a rather Nordic trapper who returns to his home town to find there's no market for pelts. He does the next logical thing: becomes a snowmobile racer. Before the big race comes along his girl friend is inexplicably bludgeoned to death and a local heroin dealer is shot and killed. Henriksen, for some shaky reasons, is suspected and taken into custody. A typical early 1970s film with a familiar look, acting "technique," rock music score (with vocal by Blue Batch), and not to forget, that all-important picturesque outdoor photography.

p, Richard A. Diercks; d, Maury Hurley; w, Mary Olson; ph, Ron Eveslage, Jan d'Alquen; m, Dale Menten; ed, Lyle McIntyre.

Drama **(PR:C-O MPAA:PG)**

IT AIN'T HAY 1/2** (1943) 79m UNIV bw (GB: MONEY FOR JAM)

Bud Abbott *(Grover Mockridge)*, Lou Costello *(Wilbur Hoolihan)*, Grace McDonald *(Kitty McGloin)*, Eugene Pallette *(Gregory Warner)*, Leighton Noble *(Pvt. Joe Collins)*, Cecil Kellaway *(King O'Hara)*, Patsy O'Connor *(Princess O'Hara)*, Shemp Howard *(Umbrella Sam)*, Eddie Quillan *(Harry the Horse)*, David Hacker *(Chauncey the Eye)*, Richard Lane *(Slicker)*, Samuel S. Hinds *(Col. Brainard)*, Harold De Garro *(Stilt-Walker)*, The Vagabonds *(Musical Specialty)*, Andrew Tombes *(Bighearted Charlie)*, Pierre Watkin *(Maj. Harper)*, William Forrest *(Banker)*, Ralph Peters *(Man at Mike)*, Wade Boteler *(Reilly)*, Bobby Watson *(Clerk)*, James Flavin *(Cop)*, Jack Norton *(Drunk)*, Tom Hanlon *(Radio Announcer)*, Harry Harvey *(Shorty)*, Herbert Vigran *(Man In Mike Room)*, Ed Foster *(Grafter)*, Harry Strang *(Policeman)*, Mike Mazurki, Sammy Stein *(Bouncers)*, Herbert Hayes *(Manager)*, Barry Macollum *(Hack Driver)*, Eddie Bruce *(Good Humor Man)*, Paul Dubov *(Tout)*, Charles Bennett *(S.P.C.A. Driver)*, Rod Rogers *(Jockey)*, Janet Ann Gallow *(Little Girl)*, Kate Drain Lawson *(Matron)*, Frank Penny *(Ticket Seller)*, Fred Cordova *(Attendant)*, Spec O'Donnell *(Newsboy)*, Stephen Gottlieb *(Child)*, The Step Brothers *(Themselves)*, Selmer Jackson *(Grant)*, The Hollywood Blondes, Leighton Noble and His Orchestra, Finnegan the Horse, Charles Coleman, Robert E. Homans, Matt Willis, Kit Guard.

Bud and Lou attempt to replace Kellaway's horse which was accidentally fed candy and ended up dead. They find one at a race track and take it with them, not knowing it's a champion racer named "Tea Biscuit." The usual antics occur, culminating with Lou's feeble jockeying of the animal. Based on a Damon Runyon story, this was a remake of the 1935 film PRINCESS O'HARA. Includes the tunes: "The Sunbeam Serenade," "Hang Your Troubles On A Rainbow," "Glory Be," "Old Timer" (Paul Francis Webster, Harry Revel). (See ABBOTT AND COSTELLO series, Index)

p, Alex Gottlieb; d, Erle C. Kenton; w, Allen Boretz, John Grant (based on the story "Princess O'Hara" by Damon Runyon); ph, Charles Van Enger; ed, Frank Gross; md, Charles Previn; art d, John B. Goodman.

Comedy **(PR:AAA MPAA:NR)**

IT ALL CAME TRUE** (1940) 95m WB bw

Ann Sheridan *(Sarah Jane Ryan)*, Jeffrey Lynn *(Tommy Taylor)*, Humphrey Bogart *(Grasselli/Chips Maguire)*, ZaSu Pitts *(Miss Flint)*, Una O'Connor *(Maggie Ryan)*, Jessie Busley *(Mrs. Nora Taylor)*, John Litel *(Mr. Roberts)*, Grant Mitchell *(Rene Salmon)*, Felix Bressart *(The Great Boldini)*, Charles Judels *(Henri Pepi de Bordeaux/Leantopopulos)*, Brandon Tynan *(Mr. Van Diver)*, Howard Hickman *(Mr. Prendergast)*, Herbert Vigran *(Monks)*, Tommy Reilly, The Elderbloom Chorus, Bender and Daum, White and Stanley, The Lady Killer's Quartet.

Every year, TV networks are besieged by people who think they have new ideas. One of the treatments that comes across their desks regularly is the one about "the theatrical boarding house where anything can happen, and usually does." It's become a joke among the executives but the truth is that someone actually made that story and it was called IT ALL CAME TRUE. A feeble attempt at comedy in the Damon Runyon mold (although based on a Louis Bromfield opus), this is a hit-and-miss affair with some offbeat casting. Sheridan and Lynn are, respectively, a singer and a songwriter. Their mothers, O'Connor and Busley, run the aforementioned boarding house. The two youngsters return to the house, with Lynn bringing Bogart in tow. It seems that Bogie killed a cop but did it with Lynn's revolver. Lynn, to protect himself, is going to hide Bogart at the boarding house until the heat is off. He tells everyone that Bogart is a nervous type who has to stay in his room because he's suffering from a phobia. Sheridan spies Bogart and recognizes him as a former nightclub owner for whom she'd once sung. Bogart hides out for a few days but succumbs to the ministrations of O'Connor and Busley who want to help out the man. Getting a little stir-crazy, Bogart comes down into the parlor to stretch his legs and sees that the boarding house is full of talent. They put on a show for each other. Bogart suggests converting the place into a night club and charging admission. The place is in trouble as they are in arrears on their taxes so the plan is agreed to. On opening night Pitts, the housekeeper, finks to the cops and they arrive to arrest Bogart. But instead of fighting it out, Bogart has become a sentimental softie and gives up without a shot. Lynn is cleared so he and Sheridan can get married and raise a bunch of tap- dancers. The show is a huge success and the house is saved. Not too many funny lines but the songs are plentiful. They include "Angel in Disguise" (Kim Gannon, Stephen Weiss, Paul Mann), "The Gaucho Serenade" (James Cavanaugh, John Redmond, Nat Simon), "Pretty Baby", "Memories" (Gus Kahn and Egbert van Alstyne), "Ain't We Got Fun" (Richard Whiting), "Put On Your Old Grey Bonnet" (Stanley Murphy and Percy Wenrich), "When Irish Eyes Are Smiling" (Chauncey Olcott and George Graff, Jr.).

p, Mark Hellinger; d, Lewis Seiler; w, Michael Fessier, Lawrence Kimble (based on the novel *Better Than Life* by Louis Bromfield); ph, Ernest Haller; m, Heinz Roemheld; ed, Thomas Richards; art d, Max Parker; spec eff, Byron Haskin, Edwin B. DuPar; ch, Dave Gould.

Comedy/Crime/Musical **(PR:A-C MPAA:NR)**

IT ALWAYS RAINS ON SUNDAY** (1949, Brit.) 92m RANK/EL bw

Googie Withers *(Rose Sandigate)*, Edward Chapman *(George Sandigate)*, Susan Shaw *(Vi Sandigate)*, Patricia Plunkett *(Doris Sandigate)*, David Lines *(Alfie Sandigate)*, Sydney Tafler *(Morry Hyams)*, Betty Ann Davies *(Sadie Hyams)*, John Slater *(Lou Hyams, Morry's Brother)*, Jane Hylton *(Bessie Hyams, Morry's Sister)*, Meier Tzelniker *(Solly, Morry's Father)*, John McCallum *(Tommy Swann)*, John Carol *(Freddie Price)*, Jack Warner *(Detective Sgt. Fothergill)*, Frederick Piper *(Detective Sgt. Leech)*, Hermione Baddeley *(Mrs. Spry, Doss-House Keeper)*, John Salew *(Caleb Neesley)*, Gladys Henson *(Mrs. Neesley)*, Michael Howard *(Slopey Collins)*, Jimmy Hanley *(Whitey)*, Alfie Bass *(Dicey)*, Edie Martin *(Mrs. Watson)*, Betty Baskcomb *(Barmaid of the "Two Compasses")*, Gilbert Davis *(Pub Owner Of The "Two Compasses")*, Al Millen *(Bill Hawkins)*, Vida Hope *(Mrs. Wallis)*, Arthur Hambling *(Yardmaster)*, Grace Arnold *(Ted's Landlady)*, John Vere *(Rev. Black)*, Patrick Jones *(Chuck Evans)*, Joe E. Carr *(Joe)*, Fred Griffiths *(Sam)*, Francis O'Rawe *(Bertie Potts)*, David Knox *(Newspaper Boy)*.

In films rain almost always is synonymous with depression, and this picture is no exception. The residents of London's dreary East End become upset when they get word that former neighbor McCallum has escaped from prison. He comes back to town and pays a visit to his former girl, now married and the mother of grown children. She harbors the criminal until he is found by the police. The tone gets even darker when the girl attempts suicide. As grim as the subject may be, the picture offers a thoughtful portrayal of the fugitive, and relations between neighbors.

p, Henry Cornelius; d, Robert Hamer; w, Hamer, Angus McPhail, Cornelius (based on the novel by Arthur La Bern); ph, Douglas Slocombe; m, Georges Auric, Stanley Black, E. O. Pogson; ed, Michael Truman; md, Ernest Irving; art d, Duncan Sutherland; cos, Anthony Mendleson, Horrockses Fashions; spec eff, Cliff Richardson, R. Dendy; m/l, "Theme Without Words," Mischa Spoliansky; makeup, Ernest Taylor.

Crime/Drama **(PR:C MPAA:NR)**

IT CAME FROM BENEATH THE SEA 1/2** (1955) 79m Clover/COL bw

Kenneth Tobey *(Pete Mathews)*, Faith Domergue *(Lesley Joyce)*, Ian Keith *(Adm. Burns)*, Donald Curtis *(John Carter)*, Dean Maddox, Jr. *(Adam Norman)*, Lt. C. Griffiths *(Griff)*, Harry Lauter *(Bill Nash)*, Captain R. Peterson *(Capt. Stacy)*, Del Courtney *(Robert Chase)*, Tol Avery *(Navy Intern)*, Ray Storey *(Reporter)*, Rudy Puteska *(Hall)*, Ed Fisher *(McLoed)*, Jack Littlefield *(Aston)*, Jules Irving *(King)*.

The first of the Schneer-produced Harryhausen films which, as expected, features special effects animation. Naval submarine captain Tobey spots a mutant killer octopus in the mid-Pacific and tries to blow it to smithereens. Before he has any success, the feisty monster sojourns in San Francisco, where it destroys the Golden Gate Bridge and the Market Street Tower before taking to the city's streets. A nuclear torpedo finally defeats the creature. Look real close at the octopus, and count the tentacles. That's right, only five! Domergue, at one time the subject of a massive publicity build-up by a smitten Howard Hughes, is the only name player in the entire cast.

p, Charles H. Schneer; d, Robert Gordon; w, George Worthing Yates, Hal Smith (based on a story by Yates); ph, Henry Freulich; ed, Jerome Thoms; md, Mischa Bakaleinikoff; art d, Paul Palmentola; spec eff, Ray Harryhausen, Jack Erickson.

Science- fiction **Cas.** **(PR:A MPAA:NR)**

IT CAME FROM OUTER SPACE*½** (1953) 80m UNIV bw/3d

Richard Carlson *(John Putnam)*, Barbara Rush *(Ellen Fields)*, Charles Drake *(Sheriff Matt Warren)*, Russell Johnson *(George)*, Kathleen Hughes *(Jane)*, Joseph Sawyer *(Frank Daylon)*, Dave Willock *(Pete Davis)*, Alan Dexter *(Dave Loring)*, George Eldredge *(Dr. Snell)*, Brad Jackson *(Snell's Assistant)*, Warren MacGregor *(Toby)*, George Selk *(Tom)*, Edgar Dearing *(Sam)*, Morey Amsterdam.

One of the better science-fiction films to come out of that over-seen genre of the 1950s. Carlson is an astronomer who sees an alien spacecraft, in the form of a meteor, crash land on Earth. The creatures are invisible and replace the locals with alien doubles, which makes it tough for Carlson to prove they exist. He tells the townspeople but no one wants to believe his tale. He soon learns that they are Xenomorphs who merely want to repair their downed craft and need humans to help them. The locals begin to accept Carlson's theories and try to destroy the creatures. Carlson, however, shows his morality to the others and fights for the aliens' safety. They fix their ship, fly away, and honorably return the missing locals. Based on a Ray Bradbury story, this film had the added bonus of being photographed in 3-D which, if one could stand the annoying glasses, was quite worth the experience. Johnson, as one of the first people to be replaced, later gained fame as the Professor on TV's "Gilligan's Island." Producer Alland, a protege of Orson Welles at Mercury, was the reporter in CITIZEN KANE. This was director Arnold's first science fiction work, a genre in which he was to make quite a mark.

p, William Alland; d, Jack Arnold; w, Harry Essex (based on the story "The Meteor" by Ray Bradbury); ph, Clifford Stine (3-D); m, Herman Stein; ed, Paul Weatherwax; md, Joseph Gershenson; art d, Bernard Herzbrun, Robert Boyle; spec eff, David S. Horsley; makeup, Bud Westmore.

Science Fiction **Cas.** **(PR:A MPAA:NR)**

IT CAME WITHOUT WARNING (SEE: WITHOUT WARNING, 1980)

IT CAN BE DONE** (1929) 60m UNIV bw

Glenn Tryon *(Jerry Willard)*, Sue Carol *(Anne Rogers)*, Richard Carlyle *(Rogers)*, Richard Carle *(Watson)*, Jack Egan *(Ben Smith)*, Tom O'Brien *(Detective)*.

Tryon stars in this entertaining part-talkie as a clerk suffering from a severe case of inferiority, after being fired from his job. When he is mistaken for the boss by author's daughter Rogers he gladly accepts her father's new manuscript. Continuing his charade as the boss, the clerk addresses a publishing convention and gives a heavy pitch in favor of the book. The response is overwhelming and Tryon wins back his job, as well as the girl. It's not quite the real world, but it's fun all the same.

d, Fred Newmeyer; w, Joseph Poland, Albert De Mond, Earle Snell, Nan Cochrane (based on a story by Mann Page, Edward J. Montagne); ph, Ross Fisher; ed, Ted Kent.

Comedy **(PR:A MPAA:NR)**

IT CAN'T LAST FOREVER*½ (1937) 68m COL bw

Ralph Bellamy *(Russ Mathews)*, Betty Furness *(Carol Wilson)*, Robert Armstrong *(Al Tinker)*, Raymond Walburn *(Dr. Fothergill)*, Thurston Hall *(Fulton)*, Ed Pawley *(Cronin)*, Wade Boteler *(Capt. Rorty)*, Charles Judels *(Mr. Appadelius)*, Barbara Burbank *(Prima Donna)*, Armando and Lita *(Adagio Dancers)*, The Blenders.

Bellamy is cast as a theatrical agent who, with news girl Furness, gets mixed up with a gang of racketeers, gains fame doubling as a radio act, and "prophetically" locates a missing pearl for police. It's improbable, complicated, and not worth the trouble.

p, Harry L. Decker; d, Hamilton MacFadden; w, Lee Loeb, Harold Buchman; ph, Allen G. Siegler; ed, Gene Milford; m/l, Ben Oakland, Herb Magidson.

Comedy/Crime **(PR:A MPAA:NR)**

IT COMES UP LOVE½** (1943) 64m UNIV bw

Gloria Jean *(Victoria Peabody)*, Ian Hunter *(Tom Peabody)*, Donald O'Connor *(Ricky)*, Frieda Inescort *(Portia Winthrop)*, Louise Allbritton *(Edo Ives)*, Mary Lou Harrington *(Constance Peabody)*, Raymond Roe *(Carlton Winthrop)*, Charles Coleman *(Tilton)*, Leon Belasco *(Orchestra Leader)*, Beatrice Roberts *(Bernice)*.

A fun little picture which exploits the youthful exuberance of stars Jean and O'Connor. Hunter is a debonaire executive whose secretary falls for him. He's also trying to convince his two daughters to live with him in the big city. A goodly amount of snappy dialog, bright performances, and help tunes from Jean as the eldest daughter. Her three numbers are "Love's Old Sweet Song," "What the Rose Said," and "Say, Si Si-."

p, Ken Goldsmith; d, Charles Lamont; w, Dorothy Bennett, Charles Kenyon (based on a story by Aleen Leslie, Jay Dratler); ph, George Robinson; m, Leo Edwards, J.L. Malloy, Ernest Lecuono, Rubin Guevara; ed, Paul Landres; md, Charles Previn; art d, Jack Otterson.

Musical **(PR:A MPAA:NR)**

IT COMES UP MURDER (SEE; HONEY POT, THE, 1967)

IT CONQUERED THE WORLD½** (1956) 68m Sunset/AIP bw

Peter Graves *(Paul Nelson)*, Beverly Garland *(Claire Anderson)*, Lee Van Cleef *(Tom Anderson)*, Sally Fraser *(Joan Nelson)*, Charles B. Griffith *(Pete Shelton)*, Russ Bender *(Gen. Patrick)*, Jonathan Haze *(Pvt. Manuel Ortiz)*, Richard Miller *(Sgt. Neil)*, Karen Kadler *(Ellen Peters)*, Paul Blaisdell *(Visitor From Venus)*.

Van Cleef is an idealistic scientist who communicates with Venus on his ham radio until one of the Venusians ends up outside his window. The misled scientist believes these cone-shaped aliens with arms and obnoxious overbites will bring peace to Earth. Instead they begin a plan to transform mankind. With the aid of "bat-mites" the Venusians attempt to turn everyone into zombie-like slaves. Van Cleef's wife (Garland) is killed and, in angry retaliation, the scientist takes a blow-torch to the critter. Graves turns out to be the picture's ultimate hero, fending off the invasion. Produced and directed by Corman, the film displayed his belief that "in science-fiction films the monster should always be bigger than the leading lady." The monster, played by the film's special effects man, Blaisdell, is undoubtedly larger than Garland. This better-than-average flying saucer film was followed in 1966 with the inferior remake ZONTAR, THE THING FROM VENUS.

p&d, Roger Corman; w, Lou Rusoff; ph, Frederick West; m, Ronald Stein; ed, Charles Gross; spec eff, Paul Blaisdell.

Science-fiction **(PR:A MPAA:NR)**

IT COULD HAPPEN TO YOU*½ (1937) 71m REP bw

Alan Baxter *(Bob Ames)*, Andrea Leeds *(Laura)*, Owen Davis, Jr. *(Fred Barrett)*, Astrid Allwyn *(Angela)*, Walter Kingsford *(Prof. Schwab)*, Al Shean *(Pa Barrett)*, Christian Rub *(Clavish)*, Elsa Janssen *(Mrs. Clavish)*, Edward Colebrook *(Pogano)*, Stanley King *(Detective)*, Nina Campana *(Italian Woman)*, Frank Yaconelli *(Greek)*, John Hamilton *(Judge)*, Paul Stanton *(District Attorney)*.

A hackneyed tale of two near-siblings, one the natural and the other the adopted son of a kindly old immigrant. The adoptee, Baxter, is a bad non-seed who, when caught in a petty theft, accidentally kills his discoverer. Defended against the resulting murder charge by his goody-goody attorney almost-brother Davis, Jr., the misbegotten young man is acquitted. Seared by remorse about his misdeeds, Baxter pronounces himself guilty and serves as his own executioner, leaving the upstanding Davis, Jr. to marry Leeds, the girl they both loved. It could happen that nobody much cares.

p, Leonard Fields; d, Phil Rosen; w, Samuel Ornitz, Nathanael West (based on a story by West); ph, Jack Marta; m, Alberto Colombo; ed, Murray Seldeen, Ernest Nims.

Drama **(PR:A MPAA:NR)**

IT COULD HAPPEN TO YOU½** (1939) 71m FOX bw

Stuart Erwin *(Mackinley Winslow)*, Gloria Stuart *(Doris Winslow)*, Raymond Walburn *(J. Hadden Quigley)*, Douglas Fowley *(Freddie Barlow)*, June Gale *(Agnes Barlow)*, Clarence Kolb *(Alfred Wiman)*, Paul Hurst *(Sandy)*, Richard Lane *(District Attorney)*, Robert Greig *(Pedley)*.

Erwin is a dunderhead ad man who freely tells his ideas to other workers. They are then promptly stolen. While his friends rise up the ladder of success, the boss doesn't even know Erwin exists. Before long Erwin is accused of murder when a body is found in the trunk of his car. Wife Stuart begins sleuthing to clear her obviously innocent puppy of a spouse. She learns that the killer placed the stiff in Erwin's car by accident, mistaking it for his own identical car. A pleasurable balance of comedy and mystery.

p, David Hempstead; d, Alfred Werker; w, Allen Rivkin, Lou Breslow (based on a story by Charles Hoffman); ph, Ernest Palmer; ed, Nick De Maggio; md, Samuel Kaylin.

Comedy/Mystery **(PR:A MPAA:NR)**

IT COULDN'T HAVE HAPPENED
(SEE: IT COULDN'T HAVE HAPPENED—BUT IT DID, 1936)

IT COULDN'T HAVE HAPPENED—BUT IT DID*
(1936) 70m IN bw (AKA: IT COULDN'T HAVE HAPPENED)

Reginald Denny *(Greg)*, Evelyn Brent *(Beverly)*, Jack LaRue *(Smiley)*, Inez Courtney *(Linda)*, John Marlowe *(Forrest)*, Claude King *(Holden)*, Bryant Washburn *(Carter)*, Robert E. Homans *(O'Neill)*, Crauford Kent *(Bennett)*, Robert Frazer *(Schaefer)*, Miki Morita *(Hashi)*, Henry Herbert *(Sherwood)*, Lynton Brent *(Landsdale)*, Broderick O'Farrell *(Johnson)*, Dian Manners *(Louise)*, Emily LaRue *(Ingenue)*.

Confused, talky, and overly-stagy mystery concerning a muddled murder that goes on backstage at a play. Everyone involved is weighed down by the plot. The package includes a gangster who wants his moll to get a part, a frustrated playwright, and two murdered producers. Denny falls short as the playwright, as does Brent in the role of producer's wife. Only Courtney is able to rise above the sludge, as the stenographer who wants to identify the killers.

p, Maury M. Cohen; d, Phil Rosen; w, Arthur T. Horman (based on his story); ph, M.A. Andersen; ed, Roland D. Reed; art d, Edward C. Jewell.

Mystery **(PR:A MPAA:NR)**

IT FELL FROM THE SKY* (1980) 87m Firebird c (AKA: ALIEN DEAD)

Mike Bonavia *(Miller Haze)*, John Leirier *(Paisley)*, Rich Vogan *(Krelboin)*, Buster Crabbe *(Sheriff Kowalski)*, Raymond Roberts, Linda Lewis.

A low-budget horror entry about an alien force which attacks the inhabitants of a Florida houseboat and transforms them into ghastly creatures. Buster Crabbe, at age 72, appears as the local sheriff. The names of the characters are taken from various AIP features like LITTLE SHOP OF HORRORS.

p&d, Fred Olen Ray; w, Ray, Allan Nicholas.

Horror **(PR:C MPAA:NR)**

IT GROWS ON TREES½** (1952) 84m UNIV bw

Irene Dunne *(Polly Baxter)*, Dean Jagger *(Phil Baxter)*, Joan Evans *(Diane Baxter)*, Richard Crenna *(Ralph Bowen)*, Edith Meiser *(Mrs. Pryor)*, Sandy Descher *(Midge Baxter)*, Dee Pollock *(Flip Baxter)*, Les Tremayne *(Finlay Murchison)*, Malcolm Lee Beggs *(Henry Carollman)*, Forrest Lewis *(Dr. Harold Burrows)*, Frank Ferguson *(John Letherby)*, Bob Sweeney *(McGuire)*, Emile Avery *(TV Man)*, John Damler *(Cleanshave)*, Clark Howat *(Mustache)*, Elmer Peterson *(Commentator)*, Dee J. Thompson *(Miss Reid)*, Thurston Hall *(Sleamish)*, Cliff Clark *(Sergeant)*, Madge

Blake *(Woman)*, Hal K. Dawson *(Tutt)*, Jimmy Dodd *(Treeburger Proprietor)*, Anthony Radecki, Charles Gibb, Perc Launders, Charles McAvoy *(Policemen)*, Mary Benoit, Vera Burnett *(Assistants)*, William O'Leary *(Gonnigle)*, Bob Carney *(Bus Driver)*, Burman Bodil *(Badge Vendor)*, Ralph Montgomery *(Umbrella Vendor)*, Jack Reynolds *(Reporter)*, Bob Edgecomb *(Interviewer)*, Jeanne Blackford *(Lady)*, Frank Howard, Robert Strong *(Ad Lib Cameramen)*, Walter Clinton *(Delivery Man)*, Chuck Courtney *(Paper Man)*.

The plot is about as far-fetched as they come. Dunne is a daffy housewife who one day finds that two trees in her backyard are sprouting 5 and 10 dollar bills. Husband Jagger isn't eager to believe her unlikely story and neither is the Treasury Department. They do, however, eventually recognize the cash as legitimate. Dunne treats herself like royalty, going on lavish spending sprees until she finds that the bills, like leaves, crumble up and disintegrate. A pleasant and whimsical moral tale which was Dunne's final film.

p, Leonard Goldstein; d, Arthur Lubin; w, Leonard Praskins, Barney Slater; ph, Maury Gertsman; m, Frank Skinner; ed, Milton Carruth; art d, Bernard Herzbrun, Alexander Golitzen; set d, Russell A. Gausman, Julia Heron.

Fantasy/Comedy **(PR:A MPAA:NR)**

IT HAD TO BE YOU** (1947) 98m COL bw

Ginger Rogers *(Victoria Stafford)*, Cornel Wilde *("George"/Johnny Blaine)*, Percy Waram *(Mr. Stafford)*, Spring Byington *(Mrs. Stafford)*, Ron Randell *(Oliver H.P. Harrington)*, Thurston Hall *(Mr. Harrington)*, Charles Evans *(Dr. Parkinson)*, William Bevan *(Evans)*, Frank Orth *(Conductor Brown)*, Harry Hays Morgan *(George Benson)*, Douglas Wood *(Mr. Kimberly)*, Mary Forbes *(Mrs. Kimberly)*, Nancy Saunders *(Model)*, Douglas D. Coppin *(Boy Friend)*, Virginia Hunter *(Maid of Honor)*, Michael Towne *(Fireman)*, Fred Sears *(Tillerman, Fireman)*, Jerry Hunt *(Indian Boy)*, Carol Nugent *(Victoria, Age 6)*, Judy Nugent *(Victoria, Age 5))*, Mary Patterson *(Victoria, Age 3)*, Paul Campbell *(Radio Announcer)*, Ralph Peters, Garry Owen, Allen Wood *(Cab Drivers)*, Dudley Dickerson *(Porter)*, Harlan Warde *(Atherton)*, Myron Healey *(Standish)*, Jack Rice *(Floorwalker)*, Anna Q. Nilsson *(Saleslady)*, George Chandler *(Man)*, Vernon Dent *(Man in Drug Store)*, Vera Lewis *(Mrs. Brown)*, Oscar O'Shea *(Irish Neighborhood Watchman)*, Maurice Prince, Joe Gray *(Prize Fighters)*, Gerald Fielding *(Peabody)*, Edward Harvey *(Dr. Thompson)*, Cliff Clark *(Fire Chief)*, Victor Travers *(Drug Store Manager)*.

A mostly silly comedy that is only saved by Rogers. Wilde, in one of his early attempts at doffing the doublet and hose, should have stuck to buckling his swash because his comedy timing was virtually nil. Not that Panama and Frank gave him much to work with. Rogers is a socialite who has been married thrice. She is about to make the same mistake with Randell but decides to toss him over. Rogers had a dream lover (Wilde) since she was a tot. When she meets him in the flesh, Rogers falls for him. Wilde is a fireman in real life and quite unlike the others she'd known. The usual predictable mix-ups occur (and there is some humor) with an overlay of psychological theories (she did it better in LADY IN THE DARK) and everyone winds up happy. The attempt at fantasy-comedy genre falls a bit flat because the people behind it weren't Howard Hawks or Ben Hecht. Good-looking sets including the famous staircase from HOLIDAY.

p, Don Hartman; d, Hartman, Rudolph Mate; w, Norman Panama, Melvin Frank (based on a story by Allen Boretz, Hartman); ph, Vincent Farrar, Mate; m. Heinz Roemheld; ed, Gene Havlick; md, Morris W. Stoloff; art d, Stephen Goosson, Rudolph Sternad; set d, Wilbur Menefee, William Kiernan; cos, Jean Louis; makeup, Clay Campbell.

Comedy **(PR:A MPAA:NR)**

IT HAD TO HAPPEN*** (1936) 79m FOX bw

George Raft *(Enrico Scaffa)*, Leo Carillo *(Giuseppe Badjagaloupe)*, Rosalind Russell *(Beatrice Newnes)*, Alan Dinehart *(Rodman Drake)*, Arthur Hohl *(Honest John Pelkey)*, Arline Judge *(Miss Sullivan)*, Andrew Tombes *(Dooley)*, James Burke *(Foreman)*, John Sheehan *(Pelkey's Secretary)*, Torben Meyer *(Sign Painter)*, Thomas Jackson *(Mayor's Secretary)*, Robert Emmett O'Connor *(Policeman)*, Selmer Jackson, Wallis Clark *(Immigration Officers)*, Matt McHugh *(Elevator Man)*, Michael Romano *(Santora)*, Inez Palange *(Italian Mother)*, George Bookasta *(Italian Boy)*, Tommy Bupp *(Shine Boy)*, Raymond Turner *(Zeke)*, Frank Moran, John Kelly *(Moving Men)*, George Irving *(Jury Foreman)*, Ben Taggart *(New York Cop)*, Harry Stubbs *(Bailiff)*, John Dilson *(Juror)*, Charles Levison Lane *(State Examiner)*, Lloyd Whitlock, John Hyams *(Men in Cafe)*, Gladden James, Bud Geary, Frank De Voe, Lew Kelly *(Chauffeurs)*, Jack Hatfield, J. Anthony Hughes, Sam Ash, Cully Richards, Emmett Vogan, Franklyn Ardell *(Reporters)*, Frank Meredith *(Motor Cop)*, Loo Loy *(Chinese)*, Ben Hendricks, Jack Curtis, James Dundee, Harry Woods, Paul Hurst, G. Pat Collins *(Workmen)*, Maxine Reiner *(Bit)*, Pauline Garon *(French Maid)*, Edward Keane *(Politician)*, James C. Morton *(Bartender)*, Herbert Heywood *(Trainer)*, Pierre Watkin *(District Attorney)*, Paul Stanton *(Mayor of New York)*.

Sometimes interesting crime comedy-drama with Raft in one of his best roles. He's asked to act in this one, not just flip coins or look tough or dance and, under Del Ruth's direction, turns in a good performance. Raft and Carrillo are Italian immigrants who come to the U.S. in search of their destinies. Raft gets a job digging ditches and does well. He's taken off the manual labor and moved up to being the man who waves down the cars to stop them at construction sites. He does this with aplomb and waves down the car of New York's mayor, Stanton, who sees that Raft is not an ordinary lout but a man who has some pride in what he does, no matter how low the task. Stanton helps Raft get a job with the city and Raft responds by moving up quickly through the bureaucracy until he is a powerful force. But he does it with sincerity and honesty, rather than the usual back-stabbing associated with moving higher in the civil-service ranks. He must be a sharp guy because he loses his thick Italian accent instantly while Carrillo retains his. Four years earlier, when the two men came across in steerage, Russell had been traveling first class. Raft now makes a beeline for her since he is a man of "respect" with the city and feels he can talk to her on a new level. The woman now is married to banker Dinehart, who is in big trouble for misappropriating funds. To get on Russell's good side, Raft helps Dinehart out of the pickle by arranging for the man to return the money in order to avoid prosecution. Now Raft is accused of using his position to unduly influence and his career is in jeopardy. Meanwhile, he has been trying to woo Russell, but she is just stringing him along in order to get Dinehart out of hot water. Russell is very cool toward him and admits to drinking a great deal in order to pretend she liked Raft. In the end, Raft beats the grand jury rap and winds up with Russell (could one doubt that for a moment?). It wasn't a comedy and not quite a drama, just one of those films that fell somewhere in between. A combination of a Horatio Alger tale and CINDERFELLA, this didn't satisfy either one's funny bone or one's tear ducts.

p, Darryl F. Zanuck; d, Roy Del Ruth; w, Howard Ellis Smith, Kathryn Scola (based on a story by Rupert Hughes); ph, J. Peverell Marley; ed, Allen McNeil; md, Arthur Lange.

Comedy **(PR:A MPAA:NR)**

IT HAPPENED AT THE INN*½** (1945, Fr.) 96m Minerva/MGM bw (GOUPI MAINS ROUGE)

Fernand Ledoux *(Red Hands)*, Maurice Schutz *(The Emperor)*, Georges Rollin *(M'sieu)*, Blanchette Brunoy *(Primrose)*, Arthur Devere *(Pinchpenny)*, Guy Favieres *(The Law)*, Germaine Kerjean *(Ten Drops)*, Rene Genin *(Ditto)*, Lino Noro *(Marie)*, Albert Remy *(Jean)*, Marcelle Hainia *(Chatterbox)*, Marcel Peres *(Brigadier Jerome)*, Pierre Labry *(Maurice, the Carpenter)*.

A wonderful study of a group of peasants operating a country tavern in the French countryside. The illustriously nicknamed inhabitants are shaken when Schutz, "The Emperor," suddenly takes ill, even though he is 106 years old. They are also jolted by a robbery, the murder of Kerjean, "Ten Drops," and a romance between Rollin and Brunoy. Second only to Renoir in his realistic portrayal of humanity, Becker was respected in his native country by the enthusiastic New Wave, who offered him great praise. While many criticized his work (his masterpiece CASQUE D'OR was a failure in France), director Francois Truffaut became one of his loudest proponents, writing in 1960: "Essentially he wanted to achieve an exactitude of tone, refining it more and more until it became evident, clear. . . . Since he was on guard against the exceptional, he constantly imagined himself in the place of his characters, and quite naturally, he began to trace his own portrait from film to film." This picture contains some of the earliest sketches of Becker's "portrait." (In French; English subtitles.)

d, Jacques Becker; w, Pierre Very; ph, Pierre Montazel.

Drama **(PR:A MPAA:NR)**

IT HAPPENED AT THE WORLD'S FAIR½** (1963) 105m MGM c

Elvis Presley *(Mike Edwards)*, Joan O'Brien *(Diane Warren)*, Gary Lockwood *(Danny Burke)*, Vicky Tiu *(Sue-Lin)*, H.M. Wynant *(Vince Bradley)*, Edith Atwater *(Miss Steuben)*, Guy Raymond *(Barney Thatcher)*, Dorothy Green *(Miss Ettinger)*, Kam Tong *(Walter Ling)*, Yvonne Craig *(Dorothy Johnson)*.

Not much plot is necessary to please the die-hard Elvis fans, just lots of songs and the King himself. And that's what this picture offers. Bush pilot Elvis goes to the 1962 Seattle World's Fair and finds himself falling in love with nurse O'Brien while taking care of adorable tot Tiu. Sidekick Lockwood informs the welfare authorities of the adorable oriental's whereabouts in order to get Presley back in the piloting business so the two can redeem their debt-impounded airplane. The flyer the flyers undertake proves to be an illegal smuggling deal. Tot Tiu, terrified of the prospect of life in an orphanage, runs off, but Presley retrieves her on the fairgrounds and takes her to the waiting smuggling aircraft. Suspicious of supposed savior Wynant, Presley questions his cargo. A struggle ensues; the bad folks are thwarted. Presley gets O'Brien and Tiu rejoins her misplaced uncle, Tong. Elvis sings "I'm Falling In Love Tonight," "They Remind Me Too Much Of You" (Don Robertson); "Take Me To The Fair," "Relax" (Sid Tepper, Roy C. Bennett); "How Would You Like To Be" (Ben Raleigh, Mark Barkan); "Beyond The Bend" (Ben Weisman, Fred Wise, Dolores Fuller); "One Broken Heart For Sale" (Otis Blackwell, Winfield Scott); "Cotton Candy Land" (Ruth Batchelor, Bob Roberts); "A World Of Our Own" (Bill Giant, Bernie Baum, Florence Kaye); "Happy Ending" (Sid Wayne, Weisman).

p, Ted Richmond; d, Norman Taurog; w, Si Rose, Seaman Jacobs; ph, Joseph Ruttenberg (Panavision, Metrocolor); m, Leith Stevens; ed, Fredric Steinkamp; art d, George W. Davis, Preston Ames; set d, Henry Grace, Hugh Hunt.

Musical **Cas.** **(PR:A MPAA:NR)**

IT HAPPENED HERE*½** (1966, Brit.) 99m Rath/Lopert bw

Pauline Murray *(Pauline)*, Sebastian Shaw *(Dr. Richard Fletcher)*, Fiona Leland *(Helen Fletcher)*, Honor Fehrson *(Honor Hutton)*, Col. Percy Binns *(Immediate Action commandant)*, Frank Bennett *(IA Political Leader)*, Bill Thomas *(IA Group Leader)*, Reginald Marsh *(IA Medical Officer)*, Rex Collett *(IA NCO)*, Nicolette Bernard *(IA Woman Commandant)*, Nicholas Moore *(IA Group Leader Moorfield)*, Peter Urbe, Graham Adam *(SS Officers)*, Brewster Cross *(American Officer)*, Col. Pickering *(British Partisan Officer)*, Jeremy Dacon *(British Medical Officer)*, Bart Allison *(Skipworth)*, Ralph Wilson *(Dr. Walton)*, John Herrington *(Dr. Westerman)*, Bertha Russell *(Matron)*, Stella Kemball *(Nurse Drayton)*, Claire Allan, Carol James *(IA Girls)*, Miles Halliwell *(IA Political Lecturer)*, Werner Mallé, Peter Dineley, Alfred Ziemen *(German Officers)*, John Snagge, Alvar Liddell, Frank Phillips, Michael Mellinger *(Announcers)*, Frank Gardner, Pat Kearney, Derek Milburn, Michael Passmore, Barrie Pattison, Ronald Phillips, Christopher Slaughter, Pat Sullivan, Peter Elkins, Hans Joachim Schmiedel, Klaus Umjo, Christopher Bell, Norbert Dingeldein, Bob Parker, George Parker, Tony Oliver, Jim Joslyn, Rose Paddon, H.G. White, Rae Wills, Andrew Mollo, Peter Watkins, Richard Golding.

With a title redolent of Sinclair Lewis' terrifying novel of 1935, *It Can't Happen Here*, an intensely interesting film from historians Kevin Brownlow and Andrew

Mollo (both in their mid-twenties) about what could have happened in WWII England had the Germans successfully invaded. Murray is a British nurse employed by the Fascist government. She is shocked to learn that Russian and Polish hospital patients are being killed. She raises loud protests, is taken into custody and eventually joins the resistance. Made on a miniscule budget of only $20,000, this production—partly filmed in 16mm—took 10 years to complete.

p,d&w, Kevin Brownlow, Andrew Mollo (based on an idea by Brownlow); ph, Peter Suschitsky, Brownlow; m, Jack Beaver, Anton Bruckner; ed, Brownlow; art d, Mollo, Jim Nicolson.

Drama **(PR:C MPAA:NR)**

IT HAPPENED IN ATHENS* (1962) 100m FOX c

Jayne Mansfield *(Eleni Costa)*, Maria Xenia *(Christina Gratsos)*, Trax Colton *(Spiridon Loues)*, Nico Minardos *(Volakos)*, Bob Mathias *(Coach Graham)*, Lili Valenty *(Mama Loues)*, Ivan Triesault *(Grandpa Loues)*, Bill Browne *(Drake)*, Brad Harris *(Garrett)*, Paris Alexander *(Nico Loues)*, Marion Siva *(Maria Loues)*, Charles Fawcett *(Ambassador Gaylord)*, Titos Vandis *(Father Loues)*, Todd Windsor *(Burke)*, Jean Murat *(Decoubertin)*, Gustavo De Nardo *(George)*, Roger Fradet *(Dubois)*, Paul Muller *(Priest)*, Denton De Gray *(O'Toole)*, John Karlsen *(King of Greece)*, Ben Bennett *(Connolley)*, George Stefan *(Fat Man)*, George Graham *(Announcer)*, Alan Caillou *(Narrator)*.

Mansfield is cast as a Greek actress who announces she'll marry the winner of the 26-mile marathon. It is Athens during the 1896 Olympic Games, the first competition in 2,672 years. Thinking that her lover Minardos will emerge victorious, she is unconcerned with the outcome. A poor shepherd, Colton, is the first to cross the finish line. Everything wraps up neatly, however, as Colton decides to marry Xenia, his true love. Although based on a true incident, the film falls short. Bob Mathias is appropriately cast as an American coach. Actual Olympic Games footage was used in the film which was shot on location in Greece.

p, James S. Elliott; d, Andrew Marton; w, Laslo Vadnay; ph, Curtis Courant (CinemaScope, Deluxe Color); m, Manos Hadjidakis; ed, Jodie Copelan; art d, Marilena Aravantinou; set d, Aurelio Crugnola; cos, Adele Parmenter.

Drama/Comedy **(PR:A MPAA:NR)**

IT HAPPENED IN BROAD DAYLIGHT*½

(1960, Ger./Switz.) 97m Prasens Film-CCC Film-Charmatin, S.A./Continental bw (ES GESHAH AM HELLICHTEN TAG)

Heinz Ruhmann *(Inspector Matthai)*, Michel Simon *(Jacquier)*, Roger Livesey *(Dr. Manz)*, Gert Frobe *(Schrott)*, Berta Drews *(Mrs. Schrott)*, Anita Van Ow *(Anne Marie Heller)*, Maria Rosa Salgado *(Mrs. Heller)*, Sigfrit Steiner *(Detective Feller)*, Siegfried Lowitz *(Inspector Henzi)*, Hans Gaugler *(Mr. Moser)*, Magrit Winter *(Mrs. Moser)*, Heinrich Gretler *(Chief of Police)*, Anneliese Betschart *(School Teacher)*, Barbara Haller *(Ursula)*, Ettore Cella *(Garage Owner)*.

A poorly conceived murder mystery gets in the way of some terrific views of the Swiss Alps. Ruhmann plays the man behind the investigation of the murder of a young girl in the mountains. Most evidence seems to point to Simon, the poor peddler who happened upon the girl, who eventually is driven to suicide because of the harassment he receives. But Ruhmann is persistent in pursuing the real culprit, a feat he accomplishes without evoking the least amount of interest. A nearly light-hearted mood is in direct conflict with the story.

p, Lazar Wechsler; d, Ladislao Vajda; w, Vajda, Friedrich Duerrenmatt, Hans Jacoby (based on the story "The Pledge" by Duerrenmatt); m, Bruno Canfora.

Crime **(PR:A MPAA:NR)**

IT HAPPENED IN BROOKLYN*** (1947) 104m MGM bw

Frank Sinatra *(Danny Webson Miller)*, Kathryn Grayson *(Anne Fielding)*, Peter Lawford *(Jamie Shellgrove)*, Jimmy Durante *(Nick Lombardi)*, Gloria Grahame *(Nurse)*, Marcy McGuire *(Rae Jakobi)*, Aubrey Mather *(Digby John)*, Tamara Shayne *(Mrs. Kardos)*, Billy Roy *(Leo Kardos)*, Bobby Long *(Johnny O'Brien)*, William Haade *(Police Sergeant)*, Lumsden Hare *(Canon Green)*, Wilson Wood *(Fodderwing)*, Raymond Largay *(Mr. Dobson)*, William Tannen *(Captain)*, Al Hill *(Driver)*, Dick Wessel *(Cop)*, Lennie Bremen *(Corporal)*, Bruce Cowling *(Soldier)*, Mitchell Lewis *(Printer)*.

A charming small musical, filmed in black and white which makes it difficult to see on TV these days, as most stations prefer their movies in color. Sinatra is a returning GI without a family who moves in with Durante, the janitor at New Utrecht High School in Brooklyn. Grayson is a teacher at the school and a singer. Neither have had success pounding the Manhattan pavement. While overseas, Sinatra had met Lawford, a priggish son of a wealthy British family. Lawford arrives in Brooklyn with a song he has written. Lawford's grandfather wanted him to go to Brooklyn to lose some of his stuffiness. With Sinatra and Grayson to help, the song is done at the school. Lawford likes Grayson and it seems that might be a problem as Sinatra also has some feeling for her. Any real danger is averted when Sinatra falls for Grahame, an army nurse he met while in the service. The film ends with the two couples happily united. Very likely, nothing will cause you to think for an instant in this film. The songs are good and Sinatra delivers his lines well. New Utrecht High School really does exist and it was the spawning place for such talents as Phil Foster, Vic Damone, Jack Carter, Harvey Lembeck, and many more. One of your authors attended New Utrecht briefly and claims none of the female teachers looked one bit like Grayson. The prettier ones were more like Durante. Besides the good songs, the background music was done by a diminutive 17 year old Andre Previn, who had just taken a job at the studio. Songs include: "Time After Time," "I Believe," "Brooklyn Bridge," "Whose Baby Are You?" "It's the Same Old Dream," "The Song's Gotta Come From the Heart" (Jule Styne, Sammy Cahn); "La Ci Darem La Mano" (from "Don Giovanni," Wolfgang Amadeus Mozart); "The Bell Song" (from "Lakme," Leo Delibes); "Otchichornya" (traditional).

p, Jack Cummings; d, Richard Whorf; w, Isobel Lennart (based on a story by John McGowan); ph, Robert Planck; m, Johnny Green; ed, Blanche Sewell; md, Jack Donohue; art d, Cedric Gibbons, Leonard Vasian; set d, Edwin B. Willis, Alfred E. Spencer; ch, Donohue.

Musical Comedy **(PR:A MPAA:NR)**

IT HAPPENED IN CANADA** (1962, Can.) 95m Temple bw

Gisela Zdunek *(Rita)*, Nello Zordan *(Andrea)*, Dedena Morello *(Maria)*, Pino Ubaldo *(Carlo)*, Alfredo Gerard, Frank Benevenuto, Joe Maniscola, Adelino Barbati, Renee Walters, Renata Di Faveri, Antonietta Martino, Frank Picchioni, Italia Bacovich.

A sincere film about Zdunek, a Roman girl who travels to Canada to wed Zordan, a man she has never met. Instead of a Prince Charming, however, she finds an aging worker who is haunted by thoughts of his dead wife. She soon falls in love with Ubaldo, the nephew of Zordan, but feels guilty that she jilted Zordan. When Ubaldo dies in a construction accident, she takes care of his child and starts anew with Zordan. An interesting tale of immigrants' melancholy lives, it was filmed in Toronto's Italian Quarter. (In Italian; English subtitles.)

p,d,w&ph, Luigi Petrucci; m, Carmine Rizzo; ed, Petrucci.

Drama **(PR:A MPAA:NR)**

IT HAPPENED IN FLATBUSH½** (1942) 80m FOX bw

Lloyd Nolan *(Frank Maguire)*, Carole Landis *(Kathryn Baker)*, Sara Allgood *(Mrs. McAvoy)*, William Frawley *(Sam Sloan)*, Robert Armstrong *(Danny Mitchell)*, Jane Darwell *(Mrs. Maguire)*, George Holmes *(Roy Anderson)*, Scotty Beckett *(Squint)*, Joseph Allen, Jr. *(Walter Rogers)*, James Burke *(Shaunnessy)*, Roger Imhof *(Maguire)*, Matt McHugh *(O'Doul)*, LeRoy Mason *(Scott)*, Pat Flaherty *(O'Hara)*, Dale Van Sickel *(Stevenson)*, John Burger *(Harding)*, Jed Prouty *(Judge)*, Robert E. Homans *(Collins)*, Mary Gordon *(Mrs. Collins)*.

Nolan is a former baseball player with a past who is given a second chance in the big leagues, this time as a manager. He takes the helm of the Brooklyn club, and when the team's owner dies, he has to boost the club's morale in their playoff drive. Under Nolan, the team improves, while his relationship with team heiress Landis heats up. The team gets into the playoffs but cracks under the pressure, signing a petition to have Nolan removed. He refuses to go, whipping the club back into shape. A fine baseball picture, but like most others of this sort you have to like the game to like the movie.

p, Walter Morosco; d, Ray McCarey; w, Lee Loeb, Harold Buchman; ph, Charles Clarke; ed, J. Watson Webb; md, Emil Newman, art d, Richard Day, Lewis Creber.

Sports Drama **(PR:A MPAA:NR)**

IT HAPPENED IN GIBRALTAR***

(1943, Fr.) 85m Gibraltar/Vigor bw (AKA: GIBRALTAR)

Vivianne Romance *(Mercedes)*, Roger Duchesne *(Robert Jackson)*, Jean Perrier *(General)*, Erich von Stroheim *(Marson)*, Yvette Lebon *(Maud Wilcox)*, Georges Flament *(Maori)*, Abel Jacquin *(Frank Lloyd)*, Andre Roanne *(Gen. Wilcox)*, Madeleine Suffel *(Manicurist)*, Talazac *(Dresser)*.

The perpetually stoical Erich von Stroheim heads a spy ring and enlists the aid of dancer Romance, the mistress of a British officer. She persuades the officer to steal some secret plans, but he is careless and gets caught. During a prison stint, he escapes and joins up with von Stroheim. Loyalty looks the officer in the eye, however, and he exposes the spy ring. He is the only one of the three to escape death. Thinking that Romance has talked, von Stroheim kills her, only to be downed by the gun of the officer. Released in France in 1939, this is a well-made thriller which was co-penned by Jacques Companeez (THE LOWER DEPTHS, CASQUE D'OR). (In French; English subtitles.)

d, Fedor Ozep; w, Jean Stelli, Jacques Companeez, Ernest Neuville, S. Gantillon; ph, Ted Pahle; m, P. Simon, Paul Dessau; English subtitles, Herman G. Weinberg.

War/Drama **(PR:A MPAA:NR)**

IT HAPPENED IN HOLLYWOOD (SEE: ANOTHER FACE, 1935)

IT HAPPENED IN HOLLYWOOD** (1937) 67m COL bw

Richard Dix *(Tim Bart)*, Fay Wray *(Gloria Gay)*, Victor Kilian *(Slim)*, Franklin Pangborn *(Mr. Forsythe)*, Charlie Arnt *(Jed Reed)*, Granville Bates *(Sam Bennett)*, William B. Davidson *(Al Howard)*, Arthur Loft *(Pete)*, Edgar Dearing *(Stevens)*, James Donlan *(Shorty)*, Billy Burrud *(Billy)*, Zeffie Tilbury *(Miss Gordon)*, Harold Goodwin *(Buck)*, Charles Brinley *(Pappy)*.

Dix and Wray are a couple of fading western stars trying to make the transition to sound. Wray is considerably more successful than Dix, whose voice doesn't appeal to talkies. He is without a job but decides to stay in Hollywood anyway, and soon goes broke, refusing to take roles in gangster movies because of his squeaky-clean image. When he meets Burrud, a crippled child who idolizes the old cowboy, he is rejoined by Wray. She quits the silver screen, feeling that she cannot perform well without Dix at her side. Of course the money-minded producers don't want to lose Wray so they find a role for Dix. Even though this was a decidedly B-film effort, critics unfairly compared it with another Hollywood film released that year, a blockbuster entitled A STAR IS BORN, slamming IT HAPPENED IN HOLLYWOOD for not measuring up to the Janet Gaynor film. The Dix film does have a startling scene which depicts a lavish Hollywood party replete with major celebrities, including James Cagney, Charlie Chaplin, W.C. Fields, Clark Gable, Bing Crosby, Fred Astaire, Mae West and Ginger Rogers, except that these stars are not really present, their cameo appearances made by their doubles. Victor McLaglen is even substituted by his brother, Arthur.

d, Harry Lachman; w, Sam Fuller, Ethel Hill, Harvey Fergusson (based on a story by Myles Connolly); ph, Joseph Walker; ed, Al Clark.

Drama **(PR:A MPAA:NR)**

IT HAPPENED IN NEW YORK** (1935) 65m UNIV bw

Lyle Talbot *(Charley Barnes)*, Gertrude Michael *(Vania Nardi)*, Heather Angel *(Chris Edwards)*, Hugh O'Connell *(Haywood)*, Robert Gleckler *(Venetti)*, Rafael Storm *(The Prince)*, Adrienne D'Ambricourt *(Fleurette)*, Huntley Gordon *(Hotel Manager)*, Wallis Clark *(Joe Blake)*, Dick Elliott *(Publicity Man)*, Bess Stafford *(Landlady)*, Phil Tead *(Radio Announcer)*, Guy Usher, Herman Bing, King Baggot, Phyllis Ludwig.

A taxi driver who needs extra money is paid to go to a film premier with the movie's star when she decides she doesn't want to go with her date, a prince. When the cabbie's girlfriend shows up, she becomes upset, but is silenced with a paid proposition to attend the opening with the prince. A jewel robbery occurs and the finale reveals that it was all part of a publicity stunt. Thin but entertaining.

p, Edmund Grainger; d, Alan Crosland; w, Rian James, Seton I. Miller (based on the story "Bagdad on the Hudson" by Ward Morehouse, Jean Dalrymple); ph, George Robinson; ed, Murray Selden.

Comedy **(PR:A MPAA:NR)**

IT HAPPENED IN PARIS*½ (1935, Brit.) 68m Wyndham/ABF bw

John Loder *(Paul)*, Nancy Burne *(Jacqueline)*, Edward H. Robbins *(Knight)*, Esme Percy *(Pommier)*, Lawrence Grossmith *(Bernard)*, Dorothy Boyd *(Patricia)*, Jean Gillie *(Musette)*, Bernard Ansell *(Simon)*, Paul Sheridan *(Baptiste)*, Warren Jenkins *(Raymond)*, Kyrle Bellew *(Ernestine)*, Margaret Yarde *(Marthe)*, Minnie Raynor, Billy Shine, Dennys Val Norton, Nancy Pawley, Eve Chipman, Roy Emerton, Bela Mila.

This initial directorial effort for Carol Reed (in partnership with Robert Wyler) was hardly an indication of things to come. Weak tale centers on the efforts of the wealthy Loder to romance Burne, with the blockhead denying his great wealth in order to impress the girl.

p, Bray Wyndham; d, Robert Wyler, Carol Reed; w, John Huston, H.F. Maltby (based on the play "L'Arpete" by Yves Mirande).

Comedy **(PR:A MPAA:NR)**

IT HAPPENED IN PARIS, 1938
(SEE: DESPERATE ADVENTURE, A, 1938)

IT HAPPENED IN PARIS, 1940 (SEE: LADY IN QUESTION, THE, 1940)

IT HAPPENED IN PARIS**

(1953, Fr.) 90m Le Monde En Images/AGDC bw (C'EST ARRIVE A PARIS)

Evelyn Keyes *(Pat)*, Henri Vidal *(Vlad)*, Frederic O'Brady *(Otto)*, Jean Wall *(Hugo)*, Paul Faivre *(Uncle)*.

Standard story has Keyes as an American heiress in Paris bored with her uncle's insistence on sightseeing. She meets a Russian prince who is really a con man trying to win her over. Two versions of this film were made, one in English and one in French.

d, Henri Lavorel; w, S. B. Levenson; ph, Jean Bourgoin; ed, Marcel Cadiz.

Comedy **(PR:A MPAA:NR)**

IT HAPPENED IN ROME** (1959, Ital.) 95m Athena/Rank/Lopert bw

June Laverick *(Margaret)*, Isabelle Corey *(Josette)*, Ingeborg Schoener *(Hilde)*, Vittorio de Sica *(The Count)*, Isabel Jeans *(Cynthia)*, Massimo Girotti *(Ugo Parenti)*, Alberto Sordi *(Sergio)*, Antonio Cifariello *(Gino)*, Gabriele Ferzetti *(Lawyer Cortini)*, Mario Carotenuto *(The Hunter)*, Umberto Aquilino *(Police officer)*, Caryl Gunn *(Hostess)*, Rafaello Gambino *(Franco)*, Anna Sanmartin *(Gino's sister)*, Elvira Tonelli *(Keeper's Mother)*, Francesco Mule *(Lawyer Mazzoni)*, Margherita Autori *(Lady Professor)*, Franca Mazzone *(Lady Professor)*.

Mainly a travelogue of some of the hot Italian spots of Venice, Florence, and Rome, with a thin plot about three girls, with various backgrounds and temperaments searching for excitement and love. Offers some light and enjoyable moments, as well as stunning photography of the varied landscapes and architecture.

p, Ermanno Donati, Luigi Carpentieri; d, Antonio Pietrangeli; w, Age, Scarpelli, Dario Fo, Pietrangeli; ph, Aldo Tonti, Carlo Carlini (Technirama, Technicolor); m, Lelio Luttazzi.

Comedy **(PR:A MPAA:NR)**

IT HAPPENED IN SOHO* (1948, Brit.) 55m FC Films/ABF bw

Richard Murdoch *(Bill Scott)*, Patricia Raine *(Susan Marsh)*, John Bailey *(Paul Sayers)*, Henry Oscar *(Inspector Carp)*.

Another strangler is on the loose and terrorizing the female population of London's Soho District, sending reporter Murdoch into a flurry of sleuthing as he sacrifices all to get the scoop, which almost includes his girl friend. About as intriguing as the ride home from work.

p&d, Frank Chisnell; w, Terry Sanford; ph, Ronnie Pilgrim.

Crime **(PR:C MPAA:NR)**

IT HAPPENED ON 5TH AVENUE** (1947) 116m AA/MON bw

Don DeFore *(Jim Bullock)*, Ann Harding *(Mary O'Connor)*, Charlie Ruggles *(Michael O'Connor)*, Victor Moore *(Aloysius T. McKeever)*, Gale Storm *(Trudy O'Connor)*, Grant Mitchell *(Farrow)*, Edward Brophy *(Felton)*, Cathy Carter *(Alice)*, Edward Ryan, Jr. *(Hank)*, Dorothea Kent *(Margie)*, Arthur Hohl *(Brady)*, Anthony Sydes *(Jackie Temple)*, Linda Lee Solomon *(Baby)*, Alan Hale, Jr. *(Whitey)*, Garry Owen *(Detective)*, George Lloyd *(Foreman)*, George Meader *(Music Store Manager)*, John Hamilton *(Harper The Superintendent)*, John Arthur *(Apartment Manager)*, Chester Clute *(Phillips)*, Howard Mitchell, Rowland McCracken, William Kline, Al Fenney, Al Winters, Bert Howard, Jack George, Major Kieffer, Lt. George Blagoi, Carl Leviness, Adolph Faylauer, William O'Brien, Vic Travers, David Martell *(Executives)*, Florence Auer *(Miss Parker)*, Charles Lane *(Landlord)*, James Cardwell *(Young Man in Barracks)*, James Flavin, Ed Gargan *(Cops)*, Max Willenz, Leon Belasco *(Musicians)*, Pat Goldin *(Waiter)*, Eddie Marr *(Spieler)*, Dudley Dickerson *(Chauffeur)*, Abe Reynolds *(Finklehoffe)*, Joan Andren *(Secretary)*, The Kings Men.

Ruggles is a millionaire who allows Moore, a local vagabond, to live in his Fifth Avenue mansion every winter while vacationing in South Carolina. Leading a life of luxury, Moore befriends DeFore, an ex-GI, and takes him in. Before long he has a houseful of visitors, including the millionaire and his daughter, both in disguise. Fun at times, but somewhat long. Songs include: "Speak My Heart," "That's What Christmas Means to Me," "It's A Wonderful, Wonderful Feeling" (Harry Revel), "You're Everywhere" (Revel, Paul Webster).

p&d, Roy Del Ruth; w, Everett Freeman, Vick Knight (based on a story by Herbert Clyde Lewis, Frederick Stephani); ph, Henry Sharp; m, Edward Ward; ed, Richard Heermance; art d, Lewis Creber; set d, Ray Baltz, Jr.

Comedy/Musical **(PR:A MPAA:NR)**

IT HAPPENED ONE NIGHT***** (1934) 105m COL bw

Claudette Colbert *(Ellie Andrews)*, Clark Gable *(Peter Warne)*, Roscoe Karns *(Oscar Shapeley)*, Henry Wadsworth *(Drunk Boy)*, Claire McDowell *(Mother)*, Walter Connolly *(Alexander Andrews)*, Alan Hale *(Danker)*, Arthur Hoyt *(Zeke)*, Blanche Frederici *(Zeke's Wife)*, Jameson Thomas *(King Westley)*, Wallis Clark *(Lovington)*, Hal Price *(Reporter)*, Ward Bond, Eddy Chandler *(Bus Drivers)*, Ky Robinson, Frank Holliday, James Burke, Joseph Crehan *(Detectives)*, Milton Kibbee *(Drunk)*, Matty Roubpert *(Newsboy)*, Sherry Hall *(Reporter)*, Mickey Daniels *(Vender)*, Charles C. Wilson *(Joe Gordon)*, George Breakston *(Boy)*, Earl M. Pingree, Harry Hume *(Policemen)*, Oliver Eckhardt *(Dykes)*, Bess Flowers *(Secretary)*, Fred Walton *(Butler)*, Ethel Sykes *(Maid of Honor)*, Edmund Burns *(Best Man)*, Father Dodds *(Minister)*, Eva Dennison *(Society Woman)*, Eddie Kane *(Radio Announcer)*, Harry Holman *(Manager Auto Camp)*, Tom Ricketts *(Prissy Old Man)*, Maidel Turner *(Manager's Wife)*, Irving Bacon *(Station Attendant)*, Frank Yaconelli *(Tony)*, Harry C. Bradley *(Henderson)*, Harry Todd *(Flag Man)*, Bert Starkey, Rita Ross, Ernie Adams, Billy Engle, Allen Fox, Marvin Loback, Dave Wengren, Kit Guard, *(Bus Passengers)*.

This was the great sleeper of 1934, an enormous blockbuster of a movie produced by little Columbia Pictures and directed by one of the great filmic geniuses of the 1930s, Frank Capra. No one expected IT HAPPENED ONE NIGHT to be a hit, even its stars. No expensive advertising campaign, no publicity gimmicks heralded this film. It appeared suddenly and utterly captured the affection of the American public. This was the film that launched the genre of the screwball comedy-romance and it did it better than most of those that tried to imitate its magic. Millionaire Connolly is feuding with his spoiled daughter, Colbert. She has married a fortune-hunter, Thomas, whom her father despises, and the cigar-chomping tycoon tries to save Colbert from the errors of her ways by having private detectives kidnap her and bring her to his yacht where Connolly lectures her about Thomas. She won't hear a word of criticism about the man she claims she loves. Strong-willed, spoiled down to her high heels, Colbert sasses Connelly to the point where he loses control and slaps her, instantly regretting it. Colbert bides her time and, when the yacht anchors off Miami, she dives overboard. She next buys a bus ticket for New York, trying to evade her father's phalanxes of detectives. In the bus station is Gable, a hard-drinking, two-fisted newspaper reporter; he is standing in a phone booth telling off his editor for firing him for drinking on an assignment; "When you fired me you fired the best newshound your filthy scandal sheet ever had . . . You gashouse palooka!" On the bus Gable and Colbert find themselves jammed together in a small seat and when the bus lurches wildly, she bumps him, causing the caustic Gable to remark: "Next time you drop in, bring your folks!" She leans the other way and falls asleep, embarrassed when she wakes up to find herself sleeping on his protective shoulder. The two argue and bicker until Colbert changes her seat, sitting down next to slippery salesman Karns who instantly tries to seduce Colbert. She is soon back with Gable who recognizes Colbert; he knows that her father has put out a $10,000 reward for her recovery. He's interested in staying close to her for only one reason, to get the scoop, and get back his newspaper job. Later, Karns also identifies Colbert as the missing heiress and intends to cash in on the reward, but Gable takes him aside and tells him he's a gangster and that his mob has kidnaped Colbert, that he expects trouble in New York and has "a couple of machine guns in my suitcase . . . I'll let you have one . . . Have to shoot it out with the cops." Karns is so frightened that he takes off running when the bus is stopped. Gable and Colbert by then have made a truce and when the bus stops at an auto court they take a cabin together as man and wife to save money. Gable strings a line between the two beds and drapes a blanket over it, saying: "Behold the walls of Jericho. Maybe not as thick as the one Joshua blew down with his trumpet, but a lot safer. You see I have no trumpet." When Colbert seems undecided about the arrangement, Gable tosses her a pair of his pajamas, then begins to take off his clothes, explaining that no two men undress alike, taking off his socks and shoes, then his shirt. (When Gable removed his shirt he revealed a bare chest and the fact that he was wearing no undershirt sent female viewers swooning, and set a trend for decades to come. This little scene was a disaster for men's haberdashers when millions of men followed his lead. Later Gable would say: "That's just the way I lived. I hadn't worn an undershirt since I stared school.") When Gable makes a move for his belt buckle, Colbert dashes to her side of the blanket. In the morning Gable brings Colbert a doughnut for breakfast and proceeds to teach her the art of dunking same. Minutes later two detectives arrive at the cabin door and, to put them off, Gable and Colbert pretend to be a long-time married couple, in the middle of a typical argument. "You don't have to lose your temper," she shouts at him, as the gumshoes enter, brushing her hair over her face. "That's what you said the other night at the Elks Dance," he roars back, "when that big Swede made a pass at you . . . Kept pawin' you all over the dance floor!" "He didn't," she retorts, "you were drunk." "Aww, nuts," he tells her, "you're just like your old man. Once a plumber's daughter, always a plumber's daughter." The embarrassed detectives apologize and back out. Gable and Colbert laugh at their little triumph, having accomplished something together for the first time. They decide it's no longer safe on the bus so they take to the road, hitchhiking. They sleep outdoors the next night, Gable making a bed for Colbert at the side of haystack. When she dozes off and then abruptly wakes up, Colbert panics to find Gable missing. He quickly returns when she shouts hysterically for him, complaining about her anxiety, explaining that he went off to get her some food. He hands her a carrot. The next day, on the road, Gable attempts to show Colbert "the power of the thumb" and proceeds to display the many ways one hitches a ride, but none of them work. Colbert tells him that she'll stop a car and quick. He laughs at her but she steps to the road and, at the first sign of an approaching car, pulls up her skirt to adjust her stocking, revealing a shapely leg. The driver, Hale, jams on the brakes and the couple are soon sitting in the back of Hale's car. When they stop for food, Hale drives off with Gable's suitcase, Gable running after him. He shows up some time later driving Hale's car, telling Colbert he gave the luggage thief a sound beating and borrowed his car. The couple spend another night at a motel again separated by a blanket stretched between their beds. The two lie in bed and Colbert, who by then has fallen for Gable, asks him what kind of girl he's seeking. He stares up at the ceiling and says: "I've even been a sucker enough to make plans. You know, I saw an island in the Pacific once. Never been able to forget it That's where I'd like to take her. But she'd have to be the sort of girl who . . . well . . . who would jump in the surf with me, and love it as much as I did. You know, nights when you and the moon and the water all become one and and you feel that you're a part of something big and marvelous. That's the only place to live. Where the stars are so close over your head you feel you could reach up and stir them around. Certainly, I've been thinking about it. Boy, if I could ever find a girl who's hungry for those things . . . " The camera has stayed mostly on Colbert during this lyrical speech and he wins her heart. She is beside his bed, saying she could be that girl for Gable. He sends her back to her bed but thinks about it. Before she awakes, Gable rushes to New York and collects $1,000 from his editor to write the scoop, then drives back to the cabin, intending to marry the heiress. But Colbert has awakened and, finding Gable gone, believes he's deserted her. She calls her father and his fast limousine passes Gable's beat-up jalopy and he sees Colbert going the other way within minutes. He believes she was lying to him. Gable returns the scoop money and then sends Connolly a note demanding cash. Colbert learns of this and believes Gable is nothing more than another fortune hunter. She makes plans to wed Thomas in a lavish, formal ceremony, while Connolly still tries to talk her out of it. The wedding party is enormous and Thomas lands on Connolly's estate in his autogyro, an early-day helicopter (a facsimile of this weird flying machine was also used by W.C. Fields in INTERNATIONAL HOUSE). Only hours before the nuptials, Gabel shows up to demand that he receive no more than $36.60, exactly what he spent on Colbert during their adventures. Connolly is glad to pay, realizing Gable is a decent man, then asks the reporter if he loves his daughter. Before departing Gable shouts: "Yes, but don't hold that against me—I'm nuts!" As Connolly walks Colbert down the aisle toward the waiting Thomas, a man she really does not love, he whispers to her: "You're a sucker to go through with this." He explains that Gable came to collect only the money he spent on her, that "he loves you. If you change your mind, your car's waiting at the gate." At the last moment, Colbert refuses to say "I do," picks up her long wedding gown skirts and dashes across the lawn to her car, escaping the pursuing, astonished guests and the jilted Thomas. Connolly later pays off Thomas for an annulment and then gets a cable from Gable reading, "What's holding up the annulment? The walls of Jericho are toppling." Connelly wires back: "Let 'em topple." The last scene shows an auto camp manager and his wife looking at the cabin they've just rented to Gable and Colbert. The wife asks why the young couple requested a blanket and a rope. The manager replies: "Blamed if I know. I just brung him a trumpet, one of them toy things. They sent me to a store to get it. "What in the world do they want a trumpet for?" asks the wife. "Dunno," replies the manager. The camera shows the cabin light go out as the trumpet is tooted. The walls of Jericho have crashed. IT HAPPENED ONE NIGHT at first saw nothing but small and indifferent reviews and a short and poor box office showing. Columbia brought it back a short time later and it suddenly exploded into an overnight smash hit, millions pouring into theaters to see the down-to-earth, realistic love story, a reverse Cinderella tale where the rich girl accepted middle-class values and got the poor boy. Critics with smart and sophisticated pretensions labeled the style of the film and others like it made out of "Capra-corn," but it's a thoroughly entertaining film with a sharp, witty script and direction that takes advantage of every delightful scene. Louis B. Mayer, head of MGM, was given first right of refusal of the story by Samuel Hopkins Adams but he summarily turned it down as a film possibility; always the staunch Republican, Mayer felt that the tycoon father was shown as a buffoon and such captains of industry must be seen in a better light. When Columbia took over the property, Robert Montgomery and Myrna Loy were selected to play the lead roles but they had commitments elsewhere—at MGM. Mayer actually agreed to lend Montgomery and Loy but both stars read the script and refused to go to Columbia. About Loy's rejection of the part, Mayer shrugged and lied: "I never ask one of my little girls to play a part she don't want." Columbia head Harry Cohn and his top director, Capra, kept trying. Miriam Hopkins, Constance Bennett, and Margaret Sullavan also turned down the female lead. Cohn then asked Mayer if he could have Gable on loan, telling him MGM could later use the rare talents of Capra. Mayer thought Gable had been goldbricking, checking himself into a hospital just to relax. He was sent over the Columbia as punishment. Gable hated the idea, as he later complained, of being sent "to a little independent on Poverty Row—Siberia for me." According to one report, Mayer's decision to loan out Gable to rinky-dink Columbia was purely monetary. "I got an actor here who's being a bad boy," Mayer told Cohn. "Wants more money. And I'd like to spank him. You can have Clark Gable." Replied Cohn: "Louie, suppose he don't like the script?" Mayer snorted: Herschel [Harry Cohn's real first name], this is Louis Mayer talking. I'm *telling* you to take Gable!" Capra was not happy to get Gable but Cohn told him that if he wanted to make IT HAPPENED ONE NIGHT he would have to take Gable or no picture. Capra realized that Cohn had to make the film, now, to please Mayer. "Whenever Mayer sneezed," Capra later stated, "Cohn took aspirin." Gable showed up in Capra's office stone drunk, telling the then relatively unknown director that his office smelled and he didn't care what Capra did with his script. He reeled in and out of the tiny Columbia studio shouting at extras: "Hey, if this is Siberia, how come you guys aren't wearing parkas?" Cohn then suggested Capra get Colbert for the female lead. The French-born actress was a Paramount star and had four weeks free. Capra went to her house, was promptly bitten so hard by her French poodle that he dripped blood all over Colbert's white carpet, and he offered her the part. She told him that she received $25,000 per film at Paramount. To act at Columbia she would have to have $50,000 for the film and Capra had to finish it in four weeks so she could join friends for Christmas in Sun Valley. He got Cohn to pay the money and did, indeed, finish the film in that time frame all on a $325,000 budget. Colbert gave Capra a hard time, argued with him over his casual way of setting up shots and holding impromptu rehearsals, and really balked at taking off any clothes to reveal her gorgeous body (which she did with alacrity for Cecil B. DeMille in SIGN OF THE CROSS and CLEOPATRA). Instead, Capra merely had her toss her undergarments on top of the blanket while standing unseen, fully clothed, on the other side of it. Then came the famous skirt-raising scene where Colbert proves her leg is more powerful than Gable's thumb. She refused to show her leg, which dismayed Capra no end. He later stated: "There are no more lucious gams in the world than Colbert's, not even Marlene's [Dietrich]." Capra called in a chorus girl with sensational legs and intended to substitute in closeup the leg of the chorine for Colbert's. But when the actress saw the girl posing, she angrily stepped forth and shouted: "Get her out of here! I'll do it. That's not *my* leg!" When she finished shooting, Colbert dashed out of the studio and went to Sun Valley, telling her friends upon arrival: "Am I glad to be here. I've just finished the worst picture in the world!" Capra and Gable, despite a rough start, became friends and the director allowed Gable to act his normal boyish, roughhouse, good-natured self. The real Clark Gable came through for the first time on the screen. "He was playing himself." Capra would comment later, "and maybe for the only time in his career." The simple clothes Gable wore in the film, a Norfolk jacket, a V-neck sweater, a snap-brim hat he adjusted to fit his moods during certain scenes, and a trenchcoat, became the fad following the film's huge success. Ever after Gable wore a trenchcoat in most of his film's, considering the style his "lucky" coat. Colbert and Gable were a magical match in the film, both playing themselves, she the spoiled, nose-in-air actress, Gable the man of the people who sees through her phony sophistication and makes a real woman of her. The film not only captured the affection of the public but it swept the five top Academy Awards to make Harry Cohn's Columbia Studio a contender. It received Oscars for Best Picture, Best Director for Capra, Best Screenplay for Riskin, Best Actor for Gable and Best Actress for Colbert. Up to the end, Colbert thought the film and she had no chance. She was about to get on a train to go to New York when Academy officials caught her at Los Angeles' Union Station and took her off the Super Chief, whisking her by police escort to the Biltmore Hotel for the Awards. She was wearing her brown traveling suit when she was announced the winning actress. Stunned, Colbert took the Oscar from Irvin S. Cobb, said nothing, and began to leave the stage ("gold statuette in hand like a kewpie doll she won in a carnival" Capra recalled). Then she turned and ran back to the microphone to say with emphasis: "I owe Frank Capra for this!" Remade as EVE KNEW HER APPLES and YOU CAN'T RUN AWAY FROM IT.

p, Harry Cohn; d, Frank Capra; w, Robert Riskin (based on the story "Night Bus" by Samuel Hopkins Adams); ph, Joseph Walker; ed, Gene Havlick; md, Louis Silvers; art d, Stephen Gooson; cos, Robert Kallock.

Comedy **Cas.** **(PR:A MPAA:NR)**

IT HAPPENED ONE SUMMER (SEE: STATE FAIR, 1945)

IT HAPPENED ONE SUNDAY* (1944, Brit.) 97m ABF/Pathe bw

Robert Beatty *(Tom Stevens)*, Barbara White *(Moya Malone)*, Marjorie Rhodes *(Mrs. Buckland)*, Ernest Butcher *(Mr. Buckland)*, Judy Kelly *(Violet)*, Irene Vanbrugh *(Mrs. Bellamy)*, Kathleen Harrison *(Mrs. Purkiss)*, George Moore Marriott *(Porter)*, C.V. France *(Magistrate)*, Marie Ault *(Madame)*, Brefni O'Rorke *(Engineer)*, Charles Victor *(Frisco Joe)*, Paul Demel *(Cassio)*, Robert Adams, Frederick Piper, Philip Godfrey, Kathryn Beaumont, Arthur Hambling, David Keir, Vic Wise, Patric Curwen, Hal Gordon, Tonie Edgar Bruce.

White is an Irish lass living in Liverpool who rises above her maid status when she falls for a Canadian seaman. After a bout with a gang of crooks everything wraps up neatly.

p, Victor Skutezky; d, Karel Lamac; w, Skutezky, Stephen Black, Frederick Gottfurt, Paul Vincent Carroll, Frank Harvey (based on the play "She Met Him One Sunday" by Skutezky); ph, Basil Emmott.

Romance **(PR:A MPAA:NR)**

IT HAPPENED OUT WEST** (1937) 56m FOX bw

Paul Kelly *(Dick Howe)*, Judith Allen *(Anne Martin)*, Johnny Arthur *(Thaddeus Cruikshank)*, Leroy Mason *(Burt Travis)*, Steve Clemente *(Pedro)*, Nina Campana *(Maria)*, Frank La Rue *(Sheriff)*, Reginald Barlow *(Middleton)*.

Kelly is sent from a New York bank to advise Arizona rancher Allen on the sale of her milk farm and learns that a local foreman and his banker friend are trying to get the silver-laden land for themselves. He foils their plans and wins Allen.

p, Sol Lesser; d, Howard Bretherton; w, Earle Snell, Harry Chandler, John Roberts (based on a novel by Harold Bell Wright); ph, Harry Neumann; ed, Olive Hofman.

Western **(PR:A MPAA:NR)**

IT HAPPENED TO JANE** 1/2
(1959) 100m Arwin/COL c (AKA: TWINKLE AND SHINE)

Doris Day *(Jane Osgood)*, Jack Lemmon *(George Denham)*, Ernie Kovacs *(Harry Foster Malone)*, Steve Forrest *(Larry Hall)*, Teddy Rooney *(Billy Osgood)*, Russ Brown *(Uncle Otis)*, Walter Greaza *(Crawford Sloan)*, Parker Fennelly *(Homer Bean)*, Philip Coolidge *(Wilbur Peterson)*, Mary Wickes *(Matilda Runyon)*, Casey Adams *(Selwyn Harris)*, John Cecil Holm *(Aaron Caldwell)*, Gina Gillespie *(Betty Osgood)*, Dick Crockett *(Clarence Runyon)*, Napoleon Whiting *(Porter)*, Bob Paige, Dave Garroway, Garry Moore, Bill Cullen, Jayne Meadows, Henry Morgan, Betsy Palmer, Steve McCormick, Gene Raeburn, Bess Myerson.

A Capra-esque comedy which has Day running a New England lobstery and finding herself up against railroad tycoon Kovacs. When a shipment of expired lobsters arrives, Day decides to take the cigar-chomping big city capitalist to court. With good friend Lemmon, she hires a lawyer, and in the spirit of small-town America, emerges victorious. Day sings three songs: "It Happened to Jane" (Joe Lubin, I.J. Roth), "Be Prepared" (Fred Karger, Richard Quine), and "Twinkle and Shine" (Dunham).

p&d, Richard Quine; w, Norman Katkov (based on a story by Max Wilk, Katkov); ph, Charles Lawton, Jr. (CinemaScope, Eastmancolor); m, George Duning; ed, Charles Nelson; md, M.W. Stoloff; art d, Cary Odell; set d, Louis Diage.

Comedy **(PR:A MPAA:NR)**

IT HAPPENED TO ONE MAN**
(1941, Brit.) 81m British Eagle/RKO bw (GB: GENTLEMAN OF VENTURE)

Wilfrid Lawson *(Felton Quair)*, Nora Swinburne *(Alice Quair)*, Marta Labarr *(Rita)*, Ivan Brandt *(Leonard Drayton)*, Reginald Tate *(Ackroyd)*, Brian Worth *(Jack Quair)*, Edmond Breon *(Adm. Drayton)*, Patricia Roc *(Betty Quair)*, Thorley Walters *(Ronnie)*, Athole Stewart *(Lord Kenley)*, Ruth Maitland *(Lady Rapscombe)*, Ian Fleming *(Sir Francis Hay)*.

Lawson is a financier and manipulator who is exposed by his ruthless partner Tate and ends up serving time in prison. His family life in disarray, he sets out to find the hiding Tate, and in an unlikely showing of British action, exchanges gunfire. The end has Lawson's once impatient wife returning her love. The film was made in Britain by RKO during WW II with "frozen funds." Because of wartime restrictions, these funds could not leave the country.

p, Victor Hanbury; d, Paul Stein; w, Paul Merzbach, Nina Jarvis (based on a play by Roland Pertwee, John Hastings Turner); ph, Walter Harvey.

Drama **(PR:A MPAA:NR)**

IT HAPPENED TOMORROW*** 1/2 (1944) 84m UA bw

Dick Powell *(Larry Stevens)*, Linda Darnell *(Sylvia)*, Jack Oakie *(Cigolini)*, Edgar Kennedy *(Inspector Mulrooney)*, John Philliber *(Pop Benson)*, Edward Brophy *(Jake Schomberg)*, George Cleveland *(Mr. Gordon)*, Sig Rumann *(Mr. Beckstein)*, Paul Guilfoyle *(Shep)*, Eddie Acuff *(Jim)*, George Chandler *(Bob)*, Marion Martin *(Nurse)*, Jack Gardner *(Reporter)*, Eddie Coke *(Sweeney)*, Robert E. Homans *(Mulcahey)*, Emma Dunn *(Mrs. Keever)*.

Powell is a novice newsman who miraculously foretells the news one day in advance. Befriended by the newspaper's recently deceased librarian, Powell is given the next day's events in the form of a newspaper. The first day, he reads of a holdup and conveniently shows up on the scene. On the second day, he turns to the horse racing page and decides which picks to put his money on. The third day, however, has him reading his own obituary. He tries to avoid the hotel lobby where he is slated to die, but inevitably winds up there. A second twist of fate has him live through the day, followed by a lengthy marriage to lovely spiritualist Darnell who keeps him winning at the track. Directed by the acclaimed French Director Clair.

p, Arnold Pressburger; d, Rene Clair; w, Clair, Dudley Nichols, Helene Fraenkel (based on the story by Lord Dunsany, Hugh Wedlock, Howard Snyder and ideas of Lewis R. Foster); ph, Archie Stout; ed, Fred Pressburger; prod d, Erno Metzer; md, Robert Stolz.

Fantasy **(PR:A MPAA:NR)**

IT HAPPENS EVERY SPRING**** (1949) 87m FOX bw

Ray Milland *(Vernon Simpson)*, Jean Peters *(Deborah Greenleaf)*, Paul Douglas *(Monk Lanigan)*, Ed Begley *(Stone)*, Ted de Corsia *(Dolan)*, Ray Collins *(Prof. Greenleaf)*, Jessie Royce Landis *(Mrs. Greenleaf)*, Alan Hale, Jr. *(Schmidt)*, Bill Murphy *(Isbell)*, William E. Green *(Prof. Forsythe)*, Edward Keane *(Bell)*, Gene Evans *(Mueller)*, Al Eben *(Parker)*, Ruth Lee *(Miss Collins)*, John Butler *(Fan)*, Jane Van Duser *(Miss Mengalstein)*, Ray Teal *(Mac)*, Don Hicks *(Assistant to Announcer)*, Mickey Simpson *(Policeman)*, Johnny Calkins *(Boy)*, Harry Cheshire *(Doctor)*, Ward Brant, John McKee *(Baseball Players)*, Debra Paget *(Alice)*, Mae Marsh *(Maid)*, Tom Hanlon *(St. Louis Broadcaster)*, Sam Hayes *(New York Announcer)*, Douglas Spencer *(Conductor)*, Pat Combs *(Messenger Boy)*, Robert Patten *(Cab Driver)*.

That superb actor Milland, at home with drama or comedy, shines as a professorial scientist-turned-baseball-wizard in a side-splitting comedy that has since become a minor classic. Davies, who wrote the marvelous script for MIRACLE ON 34TH STREET, came up with another winner here. Milland is a mild-mannered chemistry professor in love with Peters but he has not popped the question because his meager salary won't support two. While developing a bug repellant for trees, he invents a solution that repels any kind of wood that comes in contact with it. He's already a baseball fan of the first order so he soon concocts a clever scheme to earn additional money. He'll join a major league team as a pitcher and secretly use his solution to rub on baseballs which will avoid the wooden bats of hitters. He goes to a major league team (obviously the Cardinals) and tries out. Naturally, the rookies scoff at the middle-aged man on the mound, but he miraculously strikes out every man he faces, his "screwball" hopping, bouncing, jerking, and flitting around the mightily swung bats. He is signed as a starting pitcher and, using his secret solution, manages to win 38 games that season and almost single-handedly win the World Series for the Cardinals. There are many hilarious moments in IT HAPPENS EVERY SPRING, not the least of which occurs when Douglas, Milland's catcher roommate, finds the bottle of solution and, thinking it's hair tonic, sprinkles it on his head. When trying to brush it with a wooden brush, Douglas watches in shock as his hair does a St. Vitus Dance. Milland is very funny as the furtive scientist-pitcher and Peters is attractive, even though little used. Begley as the baseball club owner and de Corsia as the club manager, are fine. The most uproarious scenes take place on the baseball fields where Milland's doctored ball sends players and fans into hysterics. The baseball footage itself is a marvel as director Bacon manages to reproduce an atmosphere that appears completely authentic.

p, William Perlberg; d, Lloyd Bacon; w, Valentine Davies (based on a story by Davies, Shirley W. Smith); ph, Joe MacDonald; m, Leigh Harline; ed, Bruce Pierce; md, Lionel Newman; art d, Lyle Wheeler, J. Russell Spencer; set d, Thomas Little, Stuart Reiss; cos, Bonnie Cashin; m/l, Mack Gordon, Joseph Myrow.

Comedy **(PR:AAA MPAA:NR)**

IT HAPPENS EVERY THURSDAY*** (1953) 80m UNIV bw

Loretta Young *(Jane MacAvoy)*, John Forsythe *(Bob MacAvoy)*, Frank McHugh *(Fred Hawley)*, Edgar Buchanan *(Jake)*, Palmer Lee [Gregg Palmer] *(Chet Dunne)*, Harvey Grant *(Steve McAvoy)*, Jimmy Conlin *(Matthew)*, Jane Darwell *(Mrs. Spatch)*, Gladys George *(Mrs. Holmes)*, Regis Toomey *(Mayor Hull)*, Willard Waterman *(Myron Trout)*, Edith Evanson *(Mrs. Peterson)*, Edward Clark *(Homer)*, Kathryn Card *(Mrs. Dow)*, Eddy Waller *(Bartlett)*, Laureen Perreau *(Baby McAvoy)*, Francis Pierlot *(Loomis)*, Edward Earle *(Van Fleet)*, Dennis Weaver *(President, Chamber of Commerce)*, Madge Blake *(Clubwoman)*, Sylvia Sims *(Woman)*, Francis Ford *(Old Gentleman)*, *Richard Eyer (Stan)*, Walter Lawrence *(Clerk)*, Rudee Lee *(Cub Scout)*, George Ramsey *(Vendor)*.

Forsythe, a big-city newsman, and his wife, Young, purchase a small California newspaper and try to make it a successful operation. With a couple of old-time typesetters, they do their best with the town's meager news, putting various births, including their own daughter's, on page one. To boost circulation, they print contests and eventually try to bring rain to the drought-stricken community. When the rains do come, Forsythe is given all the credit for what is actually only a coincidence. He also gets all the blame when the showers become floodwaters. The couple, accepting the blame, prepares to move. But a weather expert saves the day by showing up and explaining that the storm had nothing to do with their efforts. Young is excellent in her final screen appearance.

p, Anton Leader, Leonard Goldstein, d, Joseph Pevney; w, Dane Lussier, Leonard Praskins, Barney Slater (based on the novel by Jane S. McIlvaine); ph, Russell Metty; ed, Frank Gross; art d, Bernard Herzbrun, Robert Clathworthy.

Drama/Comedy **(PR:A MPAA:NR)**

IT HAPPENS IN ROME (SEE: IT HAPPENED IN ROME, 1959, Ital.)

IT HURTS ONLY WHEN I LAUGH (SEE: ONLY WHEN I LAUGH, 1981)

IT ISN'T DONE** (1937, Aus.) 90m Cinesound/British Empire bw

Cecil Kellaway *(Hubert Blaydon)*, Shirley Ann Richards *(Patricia Blaydon)*, Frank Harvey *(Lord Denvee)*, John Longden *(Peter Ashton)*, Harvey Adams *(Jarms)*, Campbell Copelin *(Ronald Dudley)*, Sylvia Kellaway *(Veronica Blaydon)*, Nellie Ferguson *(Mrs. Blaydon)*, Douglass Channel *(Harry Blaydon)*, Frank Dunn *(Mr. King))*, Leslie Victor *(Mr. Potter)*, Harold Meade *(Lord Addersley)*, Rita Pauncefort *(Mrs. Dudley)*, Hildra Dorrington *(Mrs. Ashton)*, Bobbie Hunt *(Lady Denvee)*, Ron Whelan *(Perroni)*.

A stagy comedy from down-under which is saved by its charm. Kellaway is an Australian rancher who receives word that he is of royal blood. He brings his family to Britain to meet the members of the nobility, but before long is referring to their "snobility." British Lord, Harvey, makes his dislike of Kellaway quite obvious, constantly reprimanding and telling him that certain things just aren't done. Their differences are settled when they meet, by chance, at the grave of a relative. Richards, as Kellaway's daughter, does well in her first film role as the love interest of a British author.

d, Ken G. Hall; w, Frank Harvey (based on a story by Cecil Kellaway); ph, George Heath.

Comedy **(PR:A MPAA:NR)**

IT LIVES AGAIN*** (1978) 91m Larco/WB c (AKA: IT'S ALIVE II)

Frederic Forrest *(Eugene Scott)*, Kathleen Lloyd *(Jody Scott)*, John P. Ryan *(Frank Davis)*, John Marley *(Mallory)*, Andrew Duggan *(Dr. Perry)*, Eddie Constantine *(Dr. Forrest)*, James Dixon *(Detective Perkins)*.

In this superior sequel to Cohen's amazingly successful horror film IT'S ALIVE, he combines a well-written, insightful script, with polished direction and aided substantially by a good cast. IT LIVES AGAIN picks up where IT'S ALIVE left off. The film opens as a young couple, Forrest and Lloyd, celebrate the upcoming birth of their first child with a baby shower attended by friends and family. In the living room, among the guests, is a mysterious stranger (Ryan, the father of the first monster baby in IT'S ALIVE) that no one seems to know. After all the guests have left, the couple is surprised to see Ryan still sitting in their house. Ryan tells the couple who he is and that he has come to ensure the protection of their baby from the authorities who have formed a task-force to abort all suspected monster-baby pregnancies (this is determined by whether or not the mother had taken the defective drug). Forrest resents the implication that they are about to have one of the "freak" kids and tries to kick Ryan out of his house, but the man's obvious sincerity strikes Lloyd and she eventually convinces her husband to trust the stranger. Ryan is convinced that the children have a superior intelligence that may be on the cutting edge of a new human evolution and that they respond to affection that only their parents can give them. Ryan takes the couple to a secret institute run by a group of scientists that want to nurture and study the babies (they have developed their own task-force that tries to get to the parents of the monster children before the government does). The opposition is led by Marley, a parent of a monster child himself, who has sworn to stamp out all of the killer babies after his child murdered his wife. Upon the birth of their child Forrest is disgusted and repulsed, and Lloyd maternal, but wary. The parents go through a complex series of acceptance and rejection of what they have wrought, which eventually leads to the only true "family reunion" when Forrest saves his marriage by shooting the mutant child. IT LIVES AGAIN is a more complex and insightful film that delves into its thematics more clearly and skillfully than the original film and is directed with a confidence and style only stabbed at in IT'S ALIVE. Bernard Herrmann (who wrote the music for CITIZEN KANE, MAGNIFICENT AMBERSONS and several Alfred Hitchcock films) had died before this film was made and Laurie Johnson (writer of the score for TV's "The Avengers") reworked some of his leftover themes from IT'S ALIVE. Not for all tastes.

p,d,&w, Larry Cohen; ph, Fenton Hamilton (Technicolor); m, Bernard Herrmann, Laurie Johnson; ed, Curt Burch, Louis Friedman, Carol O'Blath.

Horror **Cas.** **(PR:O MPAA:R)**

IT LIVES BY NIGHT (SEE: BAT PEOPLE, THE, 1947)

IT ONLY HAPPENS TO OTHERS 1/2**

(1971, Fr./Ital.) 90m Films 13-Marianne-Mars/GSF c (CA N'ARRIVE QU'AUX AUTRES)

Marcello Mastroianni *(Marcello)*, Catherine Deneuve *(Catherine)*, Serge Marquand *(Xavier, Marcello's Brother)*, Dominique Labourier *(Marguerite)*, Catherine Allegret *(Young Girl in Park)*, Daniele Lebrun *(Sophie, Marcello's Mother)*, Marc Eyraud, Rosa Chira Magrini, Benoit Ferreux, Marie Trintignant, Edouard Niermans, Michel Gudin, Andree Damant.

Mastroianni and Deneuve head a fine cast as the parents of an 18-month old girl who dies tragically. They withdraw themselves from normal social activity, staying in their apartment for weeks with the curtains drawn. Finally Mastroianni attempts to break from the ennui by leaving the apartment with Deneuve. Primarily a study of the characters, it is based on a real life incident which happened to the director and her husband, actor Jean-Louis Trintignant (A MAN AND A WOMAN, THE CONFORMIST). (In French; English subtitles.)

p, Claude Lelouch; d&w, Nadine Trintignant; ph, Willy Lubtchansky (Eastmancolor); ed, Nicole Lubtchansky, Carol Marquand; art d&cos, Gitt Magrini; m/l, "Rainbow in Curved Air," Michel Polnareff, Jean Loup Dabadie (sung by Molnareff); English subtitles, Sonya Friedman.

Drama **(PR:C MPAA:GP)**

IT ONLY TAKES 5 MINUTES (SEE: ROTTEN APPLE, THE, 1963)

IT PAYS TO ADVERTISE 1/2** (1931) 66m PAR bw

Norman Foster *(Rodney Martin)*, Carole Lombard *(Mary Grayson)*, Skeets Gallagher *(Ambrose Peale)*, Eugene Pallette *(Cyrus Martin)*, Lucien Littlefield *(Adams)*, Helen Johnson *(Comtesse de Beaurien)*, Louise Brooks *(Thelma Temple)*, Morgan Wallace *(Donald McChesney)*, Tom Kennedy *(Perkins)*, Junior Coghlan *(Office Boy)*, John Howell *(Johnson)*, John Sinclair *(Window Cleaner)*, Marcia Manners *(Miss Burke)*, Judith Woods *(Countess)*.

Foster, the son of soap manufacturer Pallette, decides to rival his father and enter the business. With the help of beautiful secretary Lombard and ad man Gallagher, Foster comes up with the phenomenally popular slogan for his "Thirteen" brand of soap: "Thirteen—unlucky for dirt." Unfortunately for Foster he cannot produce enough soap to keep up with the demand. Pallette steps forward and purchases the trademark for a nifty sum, while Foster and Lombard have fallen in love. An amusing comedy which featured silent star Louise Brooks, one of the cinema's great beauties, in a role which is almost completely forgotten.

d, Frank Tuttle; w, Arthur Kober, Ethel Doherty (based on the play by Roi Cooper Megrue, Walter Hackett); ph, Archie J. Stout.

Comedy **(PR:A MPAA:NR)**

IT SEEMED LIKE A GOOD IDEA AT THE TIME zero

(1975, Can.) 106m Quadrant/Ambassador c

Anthony Newley *(Sweeney)*, Stefanie Powers *(Georgina)*, Isaac Hayes *(Moriarity)*, Lloyd Bochner *(Burton)*, Yvonne DeCarlo *(Julia)*, Henry Ramer *(Prince)*, Lawrence Dane *(Broom)*, John Candy *(Kopek)*, Moya Fenwick *(Mrs. Chorley)*.

A horridly cast Canadian film about a husband who sleeps with his ex-wife once a week. She also finds time to get herself into a predicament with a rising politician. Once-popular singer Isaac Hayes has a role as a sculptor, though he seems to have gotten lost on the way to the recording studio. Newley's performance is the best joke in the picture, unless the shot of his bare bottom is included. Second City television star John Candy makes an early appearance (and one which shows his promised talent) as a stupid policeman.

p, David Perlmutter; d, John Trent; w, David Main, Trent (based on a story by Claude Harz); ph, Harry Makin; m, William McCauley; ed, Tony Lower; art d, Claude Bonniere; anim, Manola Corvera.

Comedy **(PR:0 MPAA:PG)**

IT SHOULD HAPPEN TO YOU**** (1954) 86m COL bw

Judy Holliday *(Gladys Glover)*, Jack Lemmon *(Pete Sheppard)*, Peter Lawford *(Evan Adams III)*, Michael O'Shea *(Brod Clinton)*, Connie Gilchrist *(Mrs. Riker)*, Vaughn Taylor *(Entrikin)*, Heywood Hale Broun *(Sour Man in Central Park)*, Rex Evans *(Con Cooley)*, Arthur Gilmore *(Don Toddman)*, Whit Bissell *(Robert Grau)*, Walter Klavun *(Bert Piazza)*, Melville Cooper, Constance Bennett, Ilka Chase, Wendy Barrie *(Guests on TV Panel Show)*, Ralph Dumke *(Beckhard, Salesman)*, Lennie Bremen *(Allie)*, Chick Chandler *(Engineer)*, Frank Nelson *(Salesman)*, Mary Young *(Old Lady Customer)*, Cora Witherspoon *(Saleslady)*, James Nusser, Edwin Chandler, Stan Malotte, Robert Berger, Earl Keen, George Becwar, Tom Hennesy, Leo Curley *(Board Members)*, Ted Thorpe, Tom Cound *(Assistant Photographers)*, Sandra Lee, Stephany Hampson *(Teenagers)*, Harold J. Kennedy, Don Richards *(Photographers)*, James Hyland *(Bartender)*, Margaret McWade *(Elderly Lady)*, George Kitchel *(Lieutenant)*, Jack Kruschen *(Joe)*, Stanley Orr *(Makeup Man)*, Herbert Lytton *(Sound Man)*, John Saxon *(Boy Watching Argument in Park)*.

Charming, funny, satirical, and engaging are just some of the words that can be used to describe this film. Lemmon's debut allowed him to start at the top in a co-starring role that delighted everyone. Matched with the flawless Holiday, Lemmon more than held his own. The original working title of the movie was "A Name For Herself" and that might have been a better title when one considers the story. Holliday is a poor model from Binghampton who has come to New York to seek whatever it is she can. She is one of the little people who walk the streets of the Big Apple thinking if they can make it there, they will make it anywhere. She's observed by film documentarian Lemmon who is roaming Central Park with his camera. Suddenly, Holliday looks up and sees an empty billboard and promptly uses all of her money to have her name printed in huge letters on the space: G-L-A-D-Y-S G-L-O-V-E-R. Suddenly, all of New York is wondering who she is and why she's done this. Lawford is an executive for a huge soap company and he wants that billboard for his products so he makes a deal with Holliday and gives her several billboards in return for the big one. Lemmon and Holliday are now lovers but he doesn't like what is transpiring. He thinks Holliday is cheapening herself by becoming a media puppet, and he wishes she would stop the campaign and settle in with him. But fame follows her and she becomes a celebrity, appearing on talk shows, doing commercials (like Zsa Zsa Gabor, who is famous for being famous) and becoming well-known. Lemmon disgustedly leaves her. But that is just a stage until they get back together for the customary happy ending. Before the fadeout, we've been treated to some wonderful *farceurs* operating in a witty Kanin script. Cukor's direction was a little slow and only the clothing dates it. The advertising and television barbs are just as funny and fresh today as they were then, perhaps because nothing much seems to have changed in those commercial ventures. Mike O'Shea does well as a huckster-agent and the panelists (Copper, Barrie, Bennett, and Chase) spoof the inanities of TV talk shows perfectly. Lemmon and Holliday also get a chance to sing with "Let's Fall In Love" by Harold Arlen and Ted Koehler, which had been written almost 20 years earlier. In a tiny role, John Saxon is the young man watching the argument in the park.

p, Fred Kohlmar; d, George Cukor; w, Garson Kanin; ph, Charles Lang; m, Frederick Hollander; ed, Charles Nelson; md, Morris Stoloff; art d, John Meehan; set d, William Kiernan; cos, Jean Louis; m/l, Harold Arlen, Ted Koehler; makeup, Clay Campbell.

Comedy **Cas.** **(PR:A MPAA:NR)**

IT SHOULDN'T HAPPEN TO A DOG 1/2** (1946) 70m FOX bw

Carole Landis *(Julia Andrews)*, Allyn Joslyn *(Henry Barton)*, Margo Woode *(Olive Stone)*, Henry Morgan *(Gus Rivers)*, Reed Hadley *(Mike Valentine)*, Jean Wallace *(Bess Williams)*, Roy Roberts *(Mitchell)*, John Ireland *(Bennie Smith)*, Charles Tannen *(Glass)*, John Alexander *(Joe Parelli)*, Kathryn Card *(Mrs. James)*, Ralph Sanford *(Nick)*, Jeff Corey *(Sam Black)*, Charles Cane *(Madigan)*, Clancy Cooper *(House Detective)*, James Flavin *(Police Lieutenant)*, Lee Tung Foo *(Chinese Laundry Man)*, Tom Dugan *(Cab Driver)*, Pat Flaherty *(Policeman)*, Whitner [Whit] Bissell *(Chester Frye)*.

A humorous mystery which has Landis cast as a detective with a snooping Doberman pinscher at her side. She and the dog allegedly have robbed a local tavern owner and newsman Joslyn, already in trouble with his editor, takes to reporting the incident. Together with Landis, he ends up on the trail of a black market operation. Landis and Joslyn are fine, but the dog steals the show, proving the old show biz adage about animals and children.

p, William Girard; d, Herbert I. Leeds; w, Eugene Ling, Frank Gabrielson (based on the story by Edwin Lanham); ph, Glen MacWilliams; m, David Buttolph; ed, Fred J. Rode; md, Emil Newman; art d, James Basevi, Chester Gore; spec eff, Fred Sersen.

Comedy/Crime **(PR:A MPAA:NR)**

IT SHOULDN'T HAPPEN TO A VET

(SEE: ALL THINGS BRIGHT AND BEAUTIFUL, 1979, Brit.)

IT STALKED THE OCEAN FLOOR

(SEE: MONSTER FROM THE OCEAN FLOOR, THE, 1954)

IT STARTED AT MIDNIGHT

(SEE: SCHWEIK'S NEW ADVENTURES, 1943, Brit.)

IT STARTED IN NAPLES** (1960) 100m PAR c

Clark Gable *(Mike Hamilton)*, Sophia Loren *(Lucia Curcio)*, Marietto *(Nando)*, Vittorio De Sica *(Mario Vitale)*, Paolo Carlini *(Renzo)*, Claudio Ermelli *(Luigi)*, Giovanni Filidoro *(Gennariello)*.

There's not much to this story other than some colorful Neopolitan lensing by Surtees. Gable is a wealthy Philadelphia lawyer who arrives in Naples to clean up his brother's estate. He learns how his brother and his brother's Italian girl friend died and that he has a 10-year-old errant nephew from that common-law marriage. The boy, Marietto, lives with his sultry, voluptuous aunt, Loren, a nightclub stripper, on the island of Capri. Gable and Loren clash, especially after Gable finds that the boy is shilling for Loren's club, is a small-fry thief, and smokes cigarettes. The arguments culminate in a court suit where Gable's lawyer goes slavishly crazy over the full-bodied Loren and practically hands her the case. Loren, however, thinks it over and concludes that the boy will be better off in America where Gable wants to take him. She makes the devoted Marietto go to Gable by pretending to dislike him. Gable is about to leave Naples with his nephew when he decides to take some lucious pasta with him to the U.S. He goes to Loren and she rushes into his arms. Gable is still his reliable self here but shows his age. Loren is smoky and alluring but her acting is on a par with any high school production. She does a couple of dances as a stripper which lack style and grace, lumbering about on the stage kicking, loudly singing, presenting her own unique version of a Beef Trust on the hoof.

p, Jack Rose; d, Melville Shavelson; w, Shavelson, Rose, Suso Cecchi d'Amico (based on a story by Michael Pertwee, Jack Davies.); ph, Robert L. Surtees (VistaVision, Technicolor); m, Alessandro Cicognini, Carlo Savino; ed, Frank Bracht; art d, Hal Pereira, Roland Anderson

Romance (PR:C MPAA:NR)

IT STARTED IN PARADISE** (1952, Brit.) 94m GFD bw

Martita Hunt *(Mme. Alice)*, Jane Hylton *(Martha Watkins)*, Muriel Pavlow *(Alison)*, Ian Hunter *(Arthur Turner)*, Brian Worth *(Michael)*, Terence Morgan *(Edouard)*, Ronald Squire *("Mary Jane")*, Joyce Barbour *(Lady Burridge)*, Kay Kendall *(Lady Caroline)*, Dagmar [Dana] Wynter, Barbara Allen, Naomi Chance, Audrey White *(Models)*, Mara Lane *(Popsie)*, Harold Lang *(Louis)*, Jack Allen *(Lord Chandos)*, *(Crystal Leroy)*, Lucienne Hill, Margaret Withers, Frank Tickle, Helen Forrest, Venora McIndoe, Diana Salisbury, Arthur Lane, Alan Gifford, Dorinda Stevens, Conrad Phillips, Bill Travers, Avis Scott, Douglas Muir, Basil Hoskins, June Brown, Teresa Dunnien, Naomi Chance.

Hunt is a fashion designer in London's West End who is behind the times, catering to the tastes of her older customers. Hylton comes along with modern styles and a shrewd business mind, and nudges Hunt out of the market. History repeats and Hylton, after a spotted career and involvement in the WW II blackmarket, is bumped out by a younger and fresher Pavlow. Lots of fashion, lots of ambitious women, not much else. Note Dana Wynter (INVASION OF THE BODY SNATCHERS, D DAY SIXTH OF JUNE, SINK THE BISMARCK) and Bill Travers (WEE GEORDIE, RING OF BRIGHT WATER, BORN FREE) in small roles.

p, Sergei Nolbandov, Leslie Parkyn; d, Compton Bennett; w, Marghanita Laski, Hugh Hastings (based on a story by Laski); ph, Jack Cardiff; m, Malcolm Arnold; ed, Alan Osbiston.

Drama (PR:A MPAA:NR)

IT STARTED IN THE ALPS* 1/2
(1966, Jap.) 94m Toho c (ARUPUSU NO WAKADAISHO)

Yuzo Kayama *(Yuichi Tanuma)*, Yuriko Hoshi *(Sumiko)*, Kinuyo Tanaka *(Shinjiro)*, Ichiro Arishima *(Yuichi's Father)*, Choko Iida *(Yuichi's Grandmother)*, Edith Hanson *(Lucienne)*, Akiko Wakabayashi, Tatsuyoshi Ebara, Machiko Naka.

Collegiate skier Kayama makes a trip with his professor to the Swiss Alps and falls in love with a stewardess. The budding romance takes a quick run down a short slope when Kayama's French girl friend makes a surprise visit. A Japanese cast and director influenced by Western ways, resulting in a picture that is of questionable market value to either culture.

p, Sanezumi Fujimoto; d, Kengo Furusawa; ph, Tadashi Iimura (Tohoscope).

Romance/Comedy (PR:A MPAA:NR)

IT STARTED WITH A KISS 1/2** (1959) 103m Arcola/MGM c

Glenn Ford *(Sgt. Joe Fitzpatrick)*, Debbie Reynolds *(Maggie)*, Eva Gabor *(Marquesa de la Rey)*, Gustavo Rojo *(Antonio Soriano)*, Fred Clark *(Gen. O'Connell)*, Edgar Buchanan *(Congressman Tappe)*, Robert Warwick *(Congressman Muir)*, Henry [Harry] Morgan *(Charles Meriden)*, Francis Bavier *(Mrs. Tappe)*, Netta Packer *(Mrs. Muir)*, Robert Cunningham *(The Major)*, Alice Backes *(Sally Meriden)*, Carmen Phillips *(Belvah)*.

Reynolds is a showgirl with her heart set on wedding a millionaire, but when she kisses Ford she gives up those illusions and gets married. Ford is a U.S. Air Force sergeant without much in his pocket who, luckily, wins a car worth $40,000. After a few hours, the newlyweds pack up and head for Spain where Reynolds puts her mate through a test. To find out if he married her for purely physical reasons, she declares her body off limits for a 30-day period. Ford, shocked by her absurdity, succeeds in convincing her otherwise. An amusing bedroom farce.

p, Aaron Rosenberg; d, George Marshall; w, Charles Lederer (based on a story by Valentine Davies); ph, Robert Bronner (CinemaScope, Metrocolor); m, Jeff Alexander; ed, John McSweeney, Jr.; md, Alexander; art d, Hans Peters, Urie McCleary; cos, Helen Rose; m/l, "It Started with a Kiss," Rudy Render, Charles Lederer (sung by Debbie Reynolds).

Comedy (PR:C MPAA:NR)

IT STARTED WITH EVE 1/2** (1941) 90m UNIV bw

Deanna Durbin *(Anne Terry)*, Charles Laughton *(Jonathon Reynolds)*, Robert Cummings *(Jonathon Reynolds, Jr.)*, Guy Kibbee *(Bishop)*, Margaret Tallichet *(Gloria Pennington)*, Catharine Doucet *(Mrs. Pennington)*, Walter Catlett *(Dr. Harvey)*, Charles Coleman *(Roberts)*, Leonard Elliott *(Reverend Stebbins)*, Irving Bacon and Gus Schilling *(Ravens)*, Wade Boteler *(Newspaper Editor)*, Dorothea Kent *(Jackie)*, Clara Blandick *(Nurse)*, Sig Arno, Marie McDonald.

Durbin goes from a lowly hatcheck girl to the fiancee of a multimillionaire in the flash of an eye when called upon to act as a substitute for the bride-to-be of Cummings because Cummings' pop (Laughton) hasn't much time left to live, and his last desire is to meet the girl his son has just brought back from Mexico and is about to marry. This girl not being available, Cummings settles for the next best thing, which just happens to be Durbin. But Laughton somehow manages to put off his final demise, becoming quite healthy with a number of years left to live. He has also become attached to the charms of Durbin, making for a sticky situation for Cummings and the woman he's supposed to marry. Laughton once again proved his abilities as an actor, giving a delightful and well-timed performance as a cranky millionaire who succumbs to the feminine charms of Durbin. Songs include: "Clavelitos" (Valverde), "Going Home" (Dvorak). Remade in 1964 as I'D RATHER BE RICH.

p, Joe Pasternak, Henry Koster; d, Koster; w, Norman Krasna, Leo Townsend (based on the story "Almost An Angel" by Hans Kraly); ph, Rudolph Mate; m, Hans J. Salter; ed, Bernard W. Burton; md, Charles Previn; art d, Jack Otterson.

Musical/Comedy (PR:A MPAA:NR)

IT TAKES A THIEF**
(1960, Brit.) 93m Alliance-Alexandra/Valiant bw (AKA: THE CHALLENGE)

Jayne Mansfield *(Billy Lacrosse)*, Anthony Quayle *(Jim Maxton)*, Carl Mohner *(Kristy)*, Peter Reynolds *(Buddy)*, John Bennett *(Spider)*, Barbara Mullen *(Ma Piper)*, Peter Pike *(Joey)*, Robert Brown *(Bob Crowther)*, Dermot Walsh *(Inspector Willis)*, Edward Judd *(Detective Sgt. Gittens)*, John Stratton *(Rick)*, Patrick Holt *(Max)*, Lorraine Clewes *(Mrs. Rick)*, Percy Herbert *(Shop Steward)*, Liane Marelli *(Stripteaser)*, Bill McGuffie *(Nightclub Pianist)*, Lloyd Lamble *(Dr. Westerly)*, John Wood *(School Inspector)*, Arthur Brough *(Landlord)*, Wally Patch *(Ticket Collector)*, Bryan Pringle *(Sergeant)*, Marigold Russell *(Hostess)*, Victor Brooks *(Foreman)*, Bill Shine *(Farm Laborer)*, Richard Shaw *(Lorry Driver)*, David Davenport *(Policeman)*.

Mansfield plays a ruthless black-wigged gang leader who shifts her affections away from a recently jailed gang member. Upon his release, he digs up the stashed cash from the heist for which he served time. Mansfield's old gang kidnaps his son in an effort to recoup the loot. Stiff performances, except for Quayle's, hamper the film as a whole.

p, John Temple-Smith; d&w, John Gilling (based on a story by Gilling); ph, Gordon Dines; m, Bill McGuffie; ed, Alan Osbiston, John Victor Smith; art d, Tom Morahan, Jim Morahan; m/l, "The Challenge," McGuffie, Robert Halfin (sung by Jayne Mansfield).

Crime (PR:C MPAA:NR)

IT TAKES ALL KINDS** (1969, U.S./Aus.) 97m Goldsworthy-COM/COM c

Robert Lansing *(Tony Gunther)*, Vera Miles *(Laura Ring)*, Barry Sullivan *(Orville Benton)*, Sid Melton *(Benji)*, Penny Sugg *(J.P. Duncan)*, Chris Christensen, Ted Hepple, Allen Bickford, Reg Gorman, Dennis Miller, Barry Spicer.

Lansing is a seaman who leaves his ship in Sydney, Australia after he gets into a fight with another sailor. Lansing is knocked unconscious and awakens to find himself in the apartment of Miles, a secretary for a shipping company. She tells him that he killed the other sailor and that the police are looking for him. A call from a detective confirms this. Miles makes a deal with Lansing: she will hide him if he helps her steal a silver chalice from a museum. He agrees, and it turns out that there isn't a chalice and what Miles wants is a stained-glass window of the museum. After Lansing removes the window to get in the building, Miles disappears. Miles hooks up with Sullivan, a crooked art dealer, and Lansing chases after them. He meets Sugg, an insurance investigator, and with her help is able to retrieve the window. Miles is killed in a shower of wheat in a granary and Lansing and Sugg get married to make for a happy ending.

p&d, Eddie Davis; w, Davis, Charles E. Savage (based on the story "A Girl Like Cathy" by Edward D. Hoch); ph, Mick Bornemann; m, Bob Young.

Crime Drama (PR:C MPAA:NR)

IT! THE TERROR FROM BEYOND SPACE 1/2**
(1958) 68m Vogue/UA bw (AKA: IT! THE VAMPIRE FROM BEYOND SPACE)

Marshall Thompson *(Col. Carruthers)*, Shawn Smith *(Ann Anderson)*, Kim Spalding *(Col. Van Heusen)*, Ann Doran *(Mary Royce)*, Dabbs Greer *(Eric Royce)*, Paul Langton *(Calder)*, Robert Bice *(Purdue)*, Richard Benedict *(Bob Finelli)*, Richard Hervey *(Gino Finelli)*, Thom Carney *(Kienholz)*, Ray "Crash" Corrigan *("It")*.

A good low-budget space thriller, the basic plot of which was re-used by Ridley Scott for his ALIEN (1979). Thompson, stranded on Mars, is the lone survivor of a space probe who is rescued by a ship commanded by Spalding. The latter suspects Thompson of having murdered his colleagues in order to ensure sufficient provender for his own survival, and takes off for Earth with Thompson a prisoner. The space shipmates are killed off one-by-one by alien stowaway "It," played by Corrigan in a rubber suit. They isolate the bloodsucking beast in a cargo compartment, but "It" claws "Its" way through a bulkhead. The surviving crew members attempt to destroy the monster by every means at their disposal, using bullets, bombs, and bait, but all to no avail until Thompson, his tale verified, hits on the idea of having the survivors don space suits and then evacuates the air from the space ship. "It" obligingly suffocates. Back on Earth, the brave band is bemedalled.

p, Robert E. Kent; d, Edward L. Cahn; w, Jerome Bixby; ph, Kenneth Peach, Sr.; m, Paul Sawtell, Bert Shefter; ed, Grant Whytock; art d, William Glasgow; set d, Herman Schoenbrun; cos, Paul Blaisdell.

Science-fiction (PR:C MPAA:NR)

IT! THE VAMPIRE FROM BEYOND SPACE
(SEE: IT! THE TERROR FROM BEYOND SPACE, 1958)

IT WON'T RUB OFF, BABY! (SEE: SWEET LOVE, BITTER, 1967)

IT'S A BET** ½ (1935, Brit.) 69m BIP/Wardour bw

Gene Gerrard *(Rollo Briggs)*, Helen Chandler *(Clare)*, Judy Kelly *(Anne)*, Allen Vincent *(Norman)*, Dudley Rolph *(Harry)*, Nadine March *(Miss Parsons)*, Polly Ward *(Maudie)*, Alf Goddard *(Joe)*, Jimmy Godden *(Mayor)*, Frank Stanmore *(Tramp)*, Ronald Shiner *(Fair Man)*, Ellen Pollock *(Mrs. Joe)*, Violet Farebrother *(Lady Allway)*, George Zucco *(Convict))*, Raymond Raikes, Charlotte Parry.

Gerrard is a reporter who gets fired when he writes a story about the police department's inefficiency in finding missing people. He takes a bet from a rival reporter that he can't stay in hiding for a month. The stakes are a new job at the rival paper if he wins or turn over his sweepstakes ticket if he's the loser. On his trek his car is stolen and used in a holdup. His picture is in every newspaper. He bounces from village to village, works for a carnival, and meets Chandler, who helps him win his bet. Gerrard gets the job at the newspaper, his sweepstakes ticket wins him $150,000, and he marries Chandler.

p, Walter C. Mycroft; d, Alexander Esway; w, L. DuGarde Peach, Frank Miller, Kurt Siodmak (adapted from the novel *Hide And I'll Find You* by Marcus McGill).

Comedy **(PR:A MPAA:NR)**

IT'S A BIG COUNTRY** (1951) 88m MGM bw

Ethel Barrymore *(Mrs. Brian Patrick Riordan)*, Keefe Brasselle *(Sgt. Maxie Klein)*, Gary Cooper *(Texas)*, Nancy Davis *(Miss Coleman)*, Van Johnson *(Adam Burch)*, Gene Kelly *(Icarus Xenophon)*, Janet Leigh *(Rosa Szabo)*, Marjorie Main *(Mrs. Wrenley)*, Fredric March *(Papa Esposito)*, George Murphy *(Mr. Callaghan)*, William Powell *(Professor)*, S.Z. Sakall *(Stefan Szabo)*, Lewis Stone *(Sexton)*, James Whitmore *(Mr. Stacey)*, Keenan Wynn *(Michael Fisher)*, Leon Ames *(Secret Service Man)*, Angela Clarke *(Mama Esposito)*, Bobby Hyatt *(Joseph Esposito)*, Sharon McManus *(Sam Szabo)*, Elisabeth Risdon *(Woman)*, Bill Baldwin *(Austin)*, Mickey Martin *(Copy Boy)*, Ned Glass *(Receptionist)*, William H. Welsh, Sherry Hall, Fred Santley, Henry Sylvester, Roger Moore, Roger Cole, Harry Stanton *(Officials)*, June Hedin *(Kati)*, Luana Mehlberg *(Lenka)*, Jeralyn Alton *(Yolande)*, Jacqueline Kenley *(Margit)*, Tony Taylor *(Baby Sitter)*, Benny Burt *(Soda Jerk)*, George Economides *(Theodore)*, Hal Hatfield, George Conrad, Richard Grindle, Anthony Lappas, Tom Nickols, David Alpert, Costas Morfis *(Greek Athletes)*, A. Cameron Grant *(Proprietor of Inn)*, Don Fields *(George)*, Jerry Hunter *(Frank Grillo)*, Donald Gordon *(Mervin)*, Lucile Curtis *(Miss Bloomburg)*, Dolly Arriaga *(Concetta Esposito)*, Elena Savanarola *(Amelia Esposito)*, Carol Nugent *(Girl)*, George McDonald, Charles Myers, David Wyatt, Mickey Little *(Boys)*, Tiny Francone *(Girl in Classroom)*, Rhea Mitchell *(School Teacher)*.

IT'S A BIG COUNTRY was a big yawn. Eight separate episodes done by some of the best writers and directors in the MGM stable, with some of the best actors in front of the camera, but it was too much and not enough at the same time. Openly made as a propaganda film, with no attempt to mask that, it begins with William Powell lecturing Whitmore on America. Powell is a university professor and his lecture segues into the vignettes. In Boston, Barrymore is annoyed by the national census takers for being overlooked. Wynn and Murphy also appear. Next is a brief montage about the accomplishments of black Americans. Then Kelly plays a Greek who takes the hand of Leigh, despite arguments by her Hungarian father, Sakall. Next, Brasselle delivers a letter from Korea to a gold-star mother played by Main. After that, Cooper delivers a semi-humorous tribute to Texas. Van Johnson, in the seventh segment, is a minister who gets to meet the President. Finally, March is an Italian-American who resists buying a set of glasses for his son, Hyatt. The stories are slim and unrelated so there is no sustained interest. The credits list reads like "who's who" in the movie business, but someone didn't know "what's what," so the picture sank quickly. At 88 minutes, you can gather how short each segment is. No one has enough time to stand out, so what goes by is a panoply rather than anything we can sink our teeth into. Roger Moore is seen briefly (as is just about everyone else).

p, Robert Sisk; d, Richard Thorpe (Powell and Whitmore segment); John Sturges (Barrymore, Wynn, Murphy); Charles Vidor (Kelly, Leigh, Sakall): Don Weis (Main, Brasselle); Clarence Brown (Cooper); William Wellman (Johnson, Stone); Don Hartman (March, Hyatt, Davis, Clarke); w, Dore Schary, William Ludwig, Helen Deutsch, George Wells, Allen Rivkin, Dorothy Kingsley, Isobel Lennart (based on stories by Edgar Brooke, Ray Chordes, Joseph Petracca, Lucille Schlossberg, Claudia Cranston, John McNulty from an idea by Dore Schary); ph, John Alton, Ray June, William Mellor, Joseph Ruttenberg; m, Bronislau Kaper, Rudolph G. Kopp, David Raksin, David Rose, Charles Wolcott, Lennie Hayton, Alberto Colombo, Adolph Deutsch; ed, Ben Lewis, Frederick Y. Smith; md, Johnny Green; art d, Cedric Gibbons, Malcolm Brown, William Ferrari, Eddie Imazu, Arthur Lonergan, Gabriel Scognamillo.

Drama **(PR:AA MPAA:NR)**

IT'S A BIKINI WORLD* ½ (1967) 86m Trans American c

Deborah Walley *(Delilah Dawes)*, Tommy Kirk *(Mike Samson/Herbert Samson)*, Robert Pickett *(Woody)*, Suzie Kaye *(Pebbles)*, Jack Bernardi *(Harvey Pulp)*, William O'Connell *(McSnigg)*, Sid Haig *(Daddy)*, Jim Begg *(Boy)*, Lori Williams *(Girl)*, Pat McGee *(Cindy)*, The Animals, The Castaways, The Toys, The Gentrys.

Not one of the better films in the "Beach Party" genre, this film stars Kirk as a beach jock who is bugged that the girl of his dreams, Walley, thinks that he is a big zero. In order to win her love, he pretends to be his bookworm twin. She, of course, is bowled over by the twerp, but the charade doesn't last long. The only redeeming value of this film is the great 1960s bands, The Gentrys, The Toys, The Animals, and The Castaways.

p, Charles S. Swartz; d, Stephanie Rothman; w, Swartz, Rothman; ph, Alan Stensvold (Colorscope, Technicolor); m, Mike Curb, Bob Summers; ed, Leo Shreve; set d, Harry Reif; m/l, "Liar, Liar" (performed by the Castaways).

Comedy/Musical **(PR:A MPAA:NR)**

IT'S A BOY** ½ (1934, Brit.) 74m Gainsborough/GAU bw

Leslie Henson *(James Skippett)*, Edward Everett Horton *(Dudley Leake)*, Heather Thatcher *(Anita Gunn)*, Alfred Drayton *(Eustace Bogle)*, Albert Burdon *(Joe Piper)*, Robertson Hare *(Allister)*, Joyce Kirby *(Lillian)*, Wendy Barrie *(Mary Bogle)*, Helen Haye *(Mrs. Bogle)*, J.H. Roberts *(Registrar)*.

IT'S A BOY was adapted from a German stage play and was translated to become a very successful play in England. Horton is about to get married when a man shows up claiming to be his son. Best man Henson helps to prove the impostor to be a bastard figuratively, if not literally, as is the blackmailing blackguard's claim.

p, Michael Balcon; d, Tim Whelan; w, Austin Melford, Leslie Howard Gordon, John Paddy Carstairs (based on a play by Franz Arnold, Ernst Bach, Melford); ph, Mutz Greenbaum [Max Greene].

Comedy **(PR:A MPAA:NR)**

IT'S A COP* (1934, Brit.) 86m B&D/UA bw

Sydney Howard *(Constable Robert Spry)*, Dorothy "Chili" Bouchier *(Babette)*, Donald Calthrop *(Charles Murray)*, Garry Marsh *(James Risden)*, Annie Esmond *(Mrs. Spry)*, Cyril Smith *(Lewis)*, John Turnbull *(Inspector Gray)*, Ronald Simpson *(Bates)*.

Lackluster programmer centers on the efforts of dimwit cop Howard to regain his lost honor, as well as his job, after messing up in the simple duty of watching over a house. To do so he attempts to capture the responsible gang, which includes Bouchier as the woman who diverted his attention while the heist was under way.

p, Herbert Wilcox; d, Maclean Rogers; w, R.P. Weston, Bert Lee, Jack Marks, John Paddy Carstairs, Robert Cullen (based on the sketch "Parker PC" by Charles Austin.

Comedy **(PR:A MPAA:NR)**

IT'S A DATE** (1940) 103m UNIV bw

Deanna Durbin *(Pamela Drake)*, Kay Francis *(Georgia Drake)*, Walter Pidgeon *(John Arlen)*, Samuel S. Hinds *(Sidney Simpson)*, S.Z. Sakall *(Carl Ober)*, Lewis Howard *(Freddie Miller)*, Cecilia Loftus *(Sarah Frankenstein)*, Henry Stephenson *(Capt. Andrews)*, Eugene Pallette *(Governor)*, Joe King *(First Mate)*, Fritz Feld *(Headwaiter)*, Charles Lane *(Horner)*, John Arledge *(Newcomer)*, Romaine Callender *(Evans)*, Virginia Brissac *(Holden)*, Leon Belasco *(Captain)*, Anna Demetrio *(Cook)*, Mary Kelley *(Governor's Wife)*, Eddie Acuff *(Ship's Steward)*, Johnny Day *(Sleepy-Eyed Blonde)*, Fay McKenzie, Linda Deane, Phyllis Ruth, Virginia Engels *(Young Girls)*, Eddie Polo *(Quartermaster)*, Mary Shannon *(Wardrobe Mistress)*, Mark Anthony *(Officer)*, Harry Owens and His Royal Hawaiians.

Durbin is the daughter of a famous actress, Francis, and she would like to follow in her mother's footsteps. Durbin attends a summer-stock school while her mother is in Honolulu. She's picked for the lead in the fall show, a role originally assigned to her mother. Durbin goes to Hawaii to be coached by her mother. She meets millionaire Pidgeon and begins chasing him. He falls in love with her mother, Francis, who retires from the stage for marriage, making it possible for Durbin to become a famous stage actress. This was S. Z. "Cuddles" Sakall's Hollywood film debut. Songs include "Musetta's Waltz" from the opera *La Boheme* by Giacomo Puccini; "Ave Maria" (Franz Schubert); "Loch Lomond" (traditional ballad); "Love Is All" (Pinky Tomlin, Harry Tobias); "It Happened in Kaloha" (Ralph Freed, Frank Skinner); "Rhythm of the Islands" (Eddie Cherkose, Leon Belasco, Jacques Press); "Hawaiian War Chant" (Ralph Freed, Johnny Noble, Prince Leleiohaku of Hawaii).

p, Joseph Pasternak; d, William A. Seiter; w, Norman Krasna (based on a story by Jane Hall, Fredrick Kohner, Ralph Block); ph, Joseph Valentine; m, Charles Previn; ed, Bernard Burton.

Musical Comedy **(PR:A MPAA:NR)**

IT'S A DEAL*** (1930) 72m Majestic bw

Helen Vinson *(Betty)*, Philip Reed *(Charles)*, Claire Dodd *(Ruth)*, Amanda Duff *(Louise)*, Glenn Tryon *(Happy)*, Bob McKenzie *(Mark)*, Ed Lewis *(Marvin)*, Dina Kay *(Jane)*.

A tight-fast-moving gem of a comedy with a light-hearted script and well-paced direction. Vinson and Reed are a Florida husband and wife who put all their money into a real estate fraud run by Lewis, a sharp salesman who specializes in lots that can only be seen at low tide because they disappear when the Atlantic rolls in. Vinson works as a secretary and Reed as a gas station jockey and they learn that Lewis has also bilked Dodd and Duff and Tryon (a brother and two sisters) in the same manner. Once the deed is discovered, the five of them join forces to chase after Lewis and get their money back. But Lewis has fled to Key West and is hiding out in his girlfriend's home. Kay is the amour, a rich nudist widow who has no idea that Lewis is up to no good. Lewis is a charmer and could sell aspirin to Christian Scientists and he has invested all of his ill-gotten gains in another real-estate scam run by McKenzie, who is an even bigger thief than Lewis is (thus proving the old adage that the easiest person to sell anything to is a salesman). But McKenzie, who thought his land was worthless, has actually sold off several hundred acres that the government wants to build a base upon. Now McKenzie has to buy it all back at inflated prices, thus giving Lewis enough money to repay the quintet who have been stalking him all over the state. Everyone winds up with enough money to cover everything and, in the course of the action, the film uses almost every inch of Florida real estate for laughs. There's a chase in the swamps, a scene where Lewis falls into the water and has to wrestle an alligator, an hysterical foray into a nudist camp by Reed and Tryon where they meet Kay, the woman who runs the place, and they have to take off all their clothes in order to gain entry. This results in a sunburn that is so painful you can almost see the red skin on the black and white film. The story is loosely based on the actual real estate flim-flams that were run in the Palm Beach area.

p&d, Thomas Bentley; w, J. G. Alexander (from an unpublished story by Wilson Mizner); ph, William Rees; m, Arnold Goldner; ed, Larry Lipson; art d, Arlene Barco; set d, Marvin Kidas.

Comedy **(PR:A-C MPAA:NR)**

IT'S A DOG'S LIFE (SEE: BAR SINISTER, THE, 1955)

IT'S A GIFT***** (1934) 73m PAR bw

W. C. Fields *(Harold Bissonette, Proprietor)*, Jean Rouverol *(Mildred Bissonette, Lovesick Daughter)*, Julian Madison *(John Durston, Salesman)*, Kathleen Howard *(Amelia Bissonette)*, Tom Bupp *(Norman Bissonette, Skate-Wearing Son)*, Tammany Young *(Everett Ricks, Clerk)*, Baby LeRoy *(Baby Ellwood Dunk)*, Morgan Wallace *(Jasper Fitchmueller, Kumquats Customer)*, Charles Sellon *(Mr. Muckle/Blind Man/ House Detective)*, Josephine Whittell *(Mrs. Dunk)*, Diana Lewis *(Miss Dunk)*, T. Roy Barnes *(Insurance Salesman)*, Spencer Charters *(Gate Guard)*, Guy Usher *(Harry Payne Bosterly, Promoter)*, Jerry Mandy *(Vegetable Man)*, Patsy O'Byrne *(Mrs. Frobisher, Doing Her Wash)*, Edith Kingdom *(Old Woman in Limousine)*, James Burke *(Iceman)*, William Tooker *(Old Man in Limousine)*, Billy Engle *(Bit)*, Jack Mulhall *(Butler)*, Bud Fine *(Driver)*, Eddie Baker *(Yard Attendant)*, Chill Wills and the Avalon Boys *(Campfire Rustics/Singers)*, Jane Withers *(Hopscotch Girl)*, Buster the Dog.

This is not only the finest, funniest movie W.C. Fields ever made, it's one of the greatest comedies ever put on the screen, thanks to the solo performance of the great comedic genius Fields. This is a grand, side-splitting, rollicking spoof of middle-class marriage and mainstream ambitions. Fields is a henpecked, harrassed small town shopowner with children and a nagging wife whose last name should have been Borgia. Right from the opening scene the viewer easily realizes that Fields is a man without hope. His daughter Rouverol barges into the bathroom while Fields is shaving and opens and closes the cabinet mirror so many times he must improvise with another tiny mirror which she also usurps. He gives up and goes to a breakfast that could have been served to him in the death house. He arrives like a kite, stepping on a skate belonging to his young son, Bupp, and falling the full flight of stairs, sailing into the living room, and landing flat on his behind. He jauntily jumps up and sits at the table, apparently unperturbed, yet he removes a carnation from his buttonhole, jams this in his mouth and sticks his cigar into a water glass. The family, oblivious to his pratfalls and plight, continues to discuss the demise of an uncle and how much the family will receive from his estate. Bupp, though sworn to secrecy by Fields, immediately blurts his father's plans to buy a California orange grove with the inheritance money. While the wife, Howard, and Rouverol eat all of the breakfast food, leaving Fields with only a sugarless cup of coffee, they launch into weeping tirades against him for planning to ruin their lives with his ridiculous orange grove scheme. Rising from the table, Fields roars: "Listen, you all got to realize one thing!" Then in a lower voice: "I am the master of this household." He then beats a hasty retreat to his small grocery store where he finds a customer demanding 10 pounds of kumquats. He begins to write down the order when he spots the house detective at the Grand Hotel, Mr. Muckle, Sellon, who is blind and wildly wielding his cane about. Fields shouts to his assistant, Young, to "Open the door for Mr. Muckle. Open the door for Mr. Muckle the blind man!" Of course, it's too late. Sellon jabs the glass on the front door and smashes it to shards, then enters, annoyed, saying to Fields: "You got that door closed again." Fields calms him down, then seats him on a chair and begs him to not move around. Directly across from the blind detective is an enormous pile of light bulbs which Fields gives a sideways glance, then saying to Sellon: "Please, Mr. Muckle, please, dear." The customer demanding the kumquats is getting nasty, shouting for his order to be filled. Fields hurries behind the counter only to look back at Sellon who is up, swinging his cane, toppling a light bulb from the pile. It pops on the floor, then another, as Field dashes for the blind man. But the entire pile of bulbs collapses into tiny pieces under Sellon's swinging cane. Fields then asks the detective what he wants and Sellon tells him a pack of chewing gum. Fields asks for five cents. The indignant blind man snorts: "I'm not going to lug that with me. Send it!" Fields wraps the pack of gum and takes down a delivery address, one on a distant rural route. Sellon then heads for the door and smashes the glass in the other front door. Fields escorts him to the street, then lets Sellon go across the heavily trafficked street alone, wincing as one car after another just misses the man. The customer demanding the kumquats is becoming incensed while Fields is interrupted by his wife, who storms into the store and tells Fields loudly: "If you don't have any kumquats why don't you tell him?" The customer leaves the store about to explode. Madison, who is engaged to Rouverol, arrives to tell Fields that the land he bought out West is nothing but barren desert, that nothing will ever grow on it, particularly oranges, and he wants to give Fields back his money, asking for the return of the deed. Fields thinks he is being hornswoggled, that his future son-in-law is trying to get back the land because he sold it too cheaply, and he runs Madison out of his store. Whittell and her young son, Baby LeRoy enter the store and, while Fields is distracted by the mother, LeRoy opens the spigot of the molasses keg and begins walking around in the infernal gluey mess accumulating on the floor. Fields begins yelling at assistant Young and Young says defensively: "I told him [LeRoy] I wouldn't do it if I was him." Fields makes a face at his simpleminded helper, then says: "I hate you!" Fields next locks up the store and hangs up a sign stating CLOSED ON ACCOUNT OF MOLASSES. Fields returns home where Howard starts in on him about his crazy orange grove scheme, a nonstop harangue that goes on until the wee hours of the morning. Sleepless and exhausted, he takes a phone call and explains to her that it was someone calling the maternity hospital, a wrong number. Howard looks suspiciously at Fields and says: "Funny thing the maternity hospital should be calling you at this hour." Fields rolls over in bed to tell her that "they weren't calling me, dear. They wanted to know if this was the maternity hospital." Howard snorts: "Now you change it. Don't make it any worse. How do you expect anyone to get any sleep around here with you hopping in and out of bed all night, tinkering around the house, waiting up for telephone calls. I have to get up in the morning, make breakfast for you and the children. I have no maid, you know, probably never shall have one . . . " On she goes, on and on and on. The fatigued Fields takes a blanket and staggers in his pajamas out to the back porch where he tries to make himself comfortable in a porch swing. He is on the second level of a three-tier back porch structure which opens to the back yard. He tests the strength of the chains holding the swing, then lies down and one of the chains breaks and sends him crashing to the floor. He props up the swing with a chair and again tries to get some sleep. Just as he closes his eyes, the milkman arrives, carting a metal container full of glass milk bottles all the way up to the third floor to make a delivery to Whittell's apartment. The bottles clink and clank in exaggerated noises to the groggy Fields who begs the milkman: "A special favor—please stop playing with those sleigh bells." The milkman ignores Fields and leaves a bottle of milk and a coconut at Whittell's door. As he leaves his bottles clank even louder. Then the coconut rolls forward and down the stairs, thundering downward to Fields' ears, a roar as loud as a lightning storm, bouncing down each stair, precariously balancing for moments, then proceeding, as Fields waits with great angst for the next bounce, until the orb, with an apparent mind of its own, starts up again, crashes down the stairs, and smashes with a roar into some garbage cans. Fields stands up, deciding that he might as well fix the swing. As he tries to adjust the chain, a nattily dressed insurance salesman, Barnes, arrives in the back yard. He shouts up to Fields who has his back to him: "Is this Prill Avenue?" Fields doesn't bother to turn around. "No, it is not," he tells the salesman. "Is there a Prill Avenue in the neighborhood," persists the salesman loudly. "I don't know," replies Fields wearily. Then the salesman booms loudly, as if delivering a speech to an outdoor meeting of a million members of the Elks Club: "Do you know a Carl LaFong? Capital 'L,' small 'a,' capital 'F,' small 'o,'small 'n,' small 'g.'" And now salesman Barnes is roaring in a stentorian voice: "LaFong, Carl LaFong!" Fields finishes attaching the chain and walks to the back porch railing to face his bombastic tormentor. He looks down with a sneer at the dapper visitor and answers with slow contempt: "No, I don't know a Carl LaFong, capital 'L,' small 'a,' capital 'F,' small 'o,' small 'n,' small 'g'. And if I did know a Carl LaFong I wouldn't admit it!" Fields goes back to the swing, lies down, and covers his head with the blanket. But the salesman hangs on like a terrier. He shouts up to Fields: "He's a railroad man and he leaves very early in the morning!" "He's a chump," grumbles Fields. "I hear he's interested in an annuity policy," continues Barnes. "Isn't that wonderful," mumbles Fields. Barnes is out for a sale this dawn, no matter what. He bounds up the stairs and confronts Fields, saying: "Yes, it is! The public's buying them like hotcakes. Maybe you'd be interested in such a policy." "No, I would not," the dog-tired Fields responds. Barnes will never take no for an answer and begins to make out a policy. "What's your age?" "None of your business,"Fields tells him. Barnes checks his guidebook, studies Fields' sprawling body and says: "I'd say you're a man of about fifty." "You would say that," Fields retorts. Barnes rummages through the guidebook pages, talking loudly to himself. "Fifty, fifty, fifty . . . ah, here we are. If you buy a policy now you could retire when you're ninety on a comfortable income." The back door opens and there stands wife Howard with a vicious look on her face. She snaps at Fields: "If you and your friend wish to exchange ribald stories, please take him downstairs." Fields has had enough. He bolts upright. "My friend! I never want to see him again!" Says Howard: "Then why did you invite him up here?" Explodes Fields: "I? Invite him?" He dashes inside the apartment and returns with a menacing meat cleaver, chasing the terrified salesman to the stairs. As Barnes runs for his life, Fields shouts after him: "And I suppose if I live to be two hundred I'll get a velocipede!" Howard returns to her bed and Fields tries once more to get some sleep on the swing, finally dozing off. Above him is Baby LeRoy who is now playing on the porch dropping grapes through a knothole, striking Fields on his considerable nose, then one into his open mouth as he sleeps. He coughs, spits out the grape, and, after dozing off again, LeRoy drops an icepick which narrowly misses Fields, alarming him so that he grabs the lethal icepick and begins to stalk LeRoy, murmuring: "Even a worm will turn." Whittell then steps out on her porch and accuses Fields of giving her child the colic by feeding him grapes. She grabs the child and takes him inside before Fields can take his revenge. Her daughter, Lewis, next bounds down the stairs noisily as Fields still desperately tries to get some sleep. From the back yard, Whittell and Lewis conduct a loud conversation about what to purchase at the store, and what store to go to. Very quietly, Fields says: "I'd like to tell you both where to go." Roars Whittell to her daughter from the porch above Fields: "It's no use. I can't hear a word you're saying. Somebody's shouting on the floor below." Fields goes back into his apartment, lies down in the now vacant bedroom, and is soon confronted with his irate wife, who is as accusatory as Torquemada of the Spanish Inquisition: "Who were those women you were talking to?" In a torpor, Fields replies: "Mrs. Dunk upstairs." She sneers: "It seems you're getting pretty familiar with Mrs. Dunk *upstairs*!" Just when Fields is finally about to slip into slumber a vegetable man shows up screaming his wares. When the man goes into the apartment downstairs, Fields bursts from the back door of his apartment to stand on the porch. He holds a shotgun and calls out sweetly: "Oh, vegetable man . . . vegetable gentleman." He grows tired of waiting and sits down on the swing, and the gun goes off accidentally, blowing away the other chain which sends the swing crashing down with Fields. He is thoroughly exhausted, a physical wreck, sitting on the porch floor in his pajamas. He spots a fly which lands nearby and grabs a swatter, bringing it down quickly to kill the insect, the only object to which he can apply his limitless wrath. (This back porch segment, delivered with Fields' precise timing and paced with a bagful of his acting tricks, is probably the funniest sequence ever made in any comedy at any time.) The following day Fields packs his family and belongings into the four-door convertible Ford and heads West for the promised land. At one point, he fails to see a "No Trespassing" sign and pulls into a broad estate with manicured lawns and exquisite statuary, believing it to be a public park. He and his family picnic on the lawn, littering it with all manner of debris, before the irate owner arrives with his caretaker to drive out Fields and family. The family finds its way to California; they are driving through an area with resplendent houses and rich orange groves. Fields' property, however, is nothing more than a ramshackle building about to fall down at any moment and land that looks like it was transported en masse from the middle of the Gobi Desert. After one look, Howard calls her husband an "old fool" and leaves Fields stranded, heading for home with the children. Fields is finished. He sits down on the broken porch of a house about to topple over and is joined by the only living creature still loyal (or who ever was) to him, the family dog. Just then a neighbor named Abernathy (Henderson) races up to tell him that the contractors building a nearby racetrack have miscalculated the slant of the afternoon sun and must now have his property upon which to build a grandstand. "Don't let them kid you," cautions the neighbor. "Hold out for any price." Fields pulls out a flask and takes a belt of fortification. Moments later a dapper looking gentleman and his associates roar onto the property and the entrepreneur tells Fields that he wants to build a gas station on the property and offers him $5,000 for his piece of worthless land. Howard and the children have returned to see what all the fuss is about. She screams for Fields to accept the offer. He merely takes another long pull on the flask and says nothing. The entrepreneur offers $10,000. Another swig and still silence while Howard is beside herself yelling for him to accept. He says no, a swig, and another no at $15,000. Howard is on the verge of an apoplectic attack, but Fields asserts himself, telling her to stay out of it, that "this is a private argument." The entrepreneur snarls at Fields: "You're drunk!" Fields stands up to him and shouts: "Yeah, and you're crazy. I'll be sober tomorrow, and you'll be crazy for the rest of your life!" The man is exasperated with Fields but he hangs on to the conversation, asking Fields what he wants. Fields holds up a pamphlet showing a picture of a beautiful orange grove and says: "This orange grove and $40,000—no, $44,000. Mr. Abernathy needs his commission." The entrepreneur and his associates huddle, then accept the deal. Howard faints dead away and is revived with a swig from Fields' flask. When she comes to, she manages a weak smile and says: "You're an idiot but I can't help but love you." The last scene (shot at Fields' newly purchased seven-acre estate at Encino, California) shows Fields sitting on a handsome porch waving goodbye to his family who drive off in a limousine to a social engagement. He prefers to stay at home, however, and, as soon as they are out of sight, Fields pours an enormous glass of gin. He plucks an orange from the branch of a nearby tree and squeezes only a few drops of juice into his glass, smiling in ecstasy as he lifts the glass to his lips. IT'S A GIFT is nonstop humor, loaded with Fields' hoarded sight gags, slapstick, and routines, and packaged in a way where, although Fields is the butt of awful fate and oppressive situations, he triumphs. Much of the material Fields resurrected from other sources, such as his silent film IT'S THE OLD ARMY GAME and the 1925 play, "The Comic Supplement." the latter providing the grist for the back porch and picnic scenes. Fields ran the film, really, with director McLeod's blessings, and his wonderful, caustic humor came through on every frame. He picked his own cast, including Baby LeRoy. Though most later thought Fields hated the child actor for stealing his scenes, he learned that LeRoy was not being given parts any longer because he was too old—at two-and-a-half! Fields insisted upon using the child and got him. It was during this film that Fields pulled his infamous prank on the youngster. LeRoy was acting up on the set, crying and screaming and, no matter what director McLeod said or did, he could not placate the child, nor could his nurse. The production was held up as Baby LeRoy's nurse fed him his bottle. Unnerved at the delay, Fields asked the nurse to get him a racing form, volunteering to feed the child. While she was gone he dropped some gin into the baby's milk bottle. When shooting resumed, Baby LeRoy unsteadily toddled across the set wobbly-legged, then sat down and keeled over. He was out cold and it took hours to revive him. As nurses and aides fussed over the child, Fields stomped around chewing on a cigar and moaning: "Walk him around, walk him around—I told you the kid was no trouper!" In addition to the scenes Fields lifted from his earlier work and writing the story for IT'S A GIFT under the fictitious name of Charles Bogle, he took bits and pieces of his own life and inserted them into this priceless film. The grocery store customer going berserk over the exotic kumquats is a ploy Fields drew from his youth in Philadelphia; he would vex his father, a pushcart vendor, by running a block ahead of the cart, not to herald what the senior Fields was really selling but to shriek out the availability of "pomegranates, artichokes, coconuts!" Though cheaply produced and hurriedly made, this film remains one of the truly great American film comedies.

p, William LeBaron; d, Norman Z. McLeod; w, Jack Cunningham (uncredited) W.C. Fields (based on "The Comic Supplement" by J.P. McEvoy, [uncredited] W.C. Fields, and a story by Charles Bogle [W.C. Fields]); ph, Henry Sharp; art d, Hans Dreier, John B. Goodman.

Comedy **(PR:AAA MPAA:NR)**

IT'S A GRAND LIFE*

(1953, Brit.) 102m Film Studios Manchester/Mancunian bw

Frank Randle *(Pvt. Randle)*, Diana Dors *(Cpl. Paula Clements)*, Dan Young *(Pvt. Young)*, Michael Brennan *(Sgt.-Maj. O'Reilly)*, Jennifer Jayne *(Pvt. Desmond)*, John Blythe *(Pvt. Philip Green)*, Anthony Hulme *(Capt. Saunders)*, Charles Peters *(Pvt. Rubenstein)*, Arthur White *(Pvt. Prendergast)*, Ian Fleming *(Mr. Clements)*, Ruth Taylor *(Mrs. Clements)*, Winifred Attwell, Jack Pye.

Poorly constructed plot that depends too heavily on overused slapstick routines in an attempt to force a chuckle or two, with Randle playing the misfit soldier proving he has some value when he saves corporal Dors from an amorous sergeant-major and introduces her to the private who loves her from afar.

p&d, John E. Blakely; w, H.F. Maltby, Frank Randle (based on the story by Maltby); ph, Ernest Palmer.

Comedy **(PR:A MPAA:NR)**

IT'S A GRAND OLD WORLD ½** (1937, Brit.) 71m BL bw

Sandy Powell *(Sandy)*, Gina Malo *(Joan)*, Cyril Ritchard *(Brian)*, Frank Pettingell *(Bull)*, Garry Marsh *(Stage-Manager)*, Ralph Truman *(Banks)*, Fewlass Llewellyn *(Father)*, John Turnbull *(Auctioneer)*, Iris Charles.

Though Powell doesn't take to working for a living very well, he really isn't all that bad a fellow, which he proves when he gives his winnings from a football pool to Malo after she is threatened with foreclosure on her much loved home. A little bit of charm, but not enough to sustain an entire film.

p, Tom Arnold; d, Herbert Smith; w, Arnold, Sandy Powell.

Comedy **(PR:A MPAA:NR)**

IT'S A GREAT DAY* 1/12 (1956, Brit. 71m Grove/But bw

Ruth Dunning *(Gladys Grove)*, Edward Evans *(Bob Grove)*, Sidney James *(Harry Mason)*, Vera Day *(Blondie)*, Sheila Sweet *(Pat Grove)*, Peter Bryant *(Jack Grove)*, Nancy Roberts *(Gran)*, Margaret Downs *(Daphne Grove)*, Christopher Beeny *(Lennie Grove)*, Victor Maddern *(Charlie Mead)*, John Stuart *(Inspector)*, Henry Oscar *(Surveyor)*, Marjorie Rhodes *(Landlady)*, Michael Balfour, Nan Braunton, Spencer Hale, Donald Finlay, Patrick Jordan, Ian Whittaker, Peggyann Clifford, Jack May, Stanley Rose, Vi Stevens.

A mishmash of a film with a lot of running around to little or no effect. Evans is a builder who gets himself into hot water over some stolen property which he innocently receives. This only compounds the aggravation surrounding his attempts to get a housing estate completed in time for a visit from a princess. Pace is exhaustingly fast.

p, Victor Lyndon; d, John Warrington; w, Roland and Michael Pertwee (based on their TV series "The Groves"); ph, Cedric Williams.

Comedy **(PR:A MPAA:NR)**

IT'S A GREAT FEELING*** (1949) 85m WB c

Dennis Morgan *(Himself)*, Doris Day *(Judy Adams)*, Jack Carson *(Himself)*, Bill Goodwin *(Arthur Trent)*, Irving Bacon *(Information Clerk)*, Claire Carleton *(Grace)*, Harlan Warde *(Publicity Man)*, Jacqueline De Wit *(Trent's Secretary)*, The Mazzone-Abbott Dancers *(Themselves)*, Wilfred Lucas *(Mr. Adams)*, Pat Flaherty *(Gate Guard)*, Wendy Lee *(Manicurist)*, Sue Casey, Nita Talbot, Eve Whitney, Carol Brewster, Joan Vohs *(Models)*, Lois Austin *(Saleslady)*, Tom Dugan *(Wrestling Fan in Bar)*, James Holden *(Soda Jerk)*, Jean Andren *(Headwaitress)*, Dudley Dickerson *(Porter)*, Sandra Gould *(Train Passenger in Upper Berth)*, Shirley Ballard *(Beautiful Girl on Bike)*, Errol Flynn *(Jeffrey Bushfinkle, the Groom)*, Gary Cooper, Joan Crawford, Sydney Greenstreet, Danny Kaye, Patricia Neal, Eleanor Parker, Ronald Reagan, Edward G. Robinson, Jane Wyman, David Butler, Michael Curtiz, King Vidor, Raoul Walsh *(Themselves)*.

A silly but genuinely funny comedy that provides an invaluable (although distorted) look at the activity on the Warner Bros. lot in the late 1940s. Dennis Morgan and Jack Carson (playing themselves) are slated to star in a new picture. Unfortunately, every director on the lot refuses to work with the egotistical Carson (among them are Michael Curtiz, Raoul Walsh, and King Vidor) leaving producer Goodwin with no choice other than to ask Carson to direct himself. Carson accepts the assignment willingly, but an outraged Morgan declares he'll drop out of the project. Desperate to get his picture off the ground, Carson begs a young studio waitress, Day, to pose as his pregnant wife and lay it on thick with Morgan how she and Carson need the money to feed their family. In return, Carson will get Day started as an actress. She agrees and soon a guilt-riddled Morgan signs his contract to do the picture. Casting begins, but there's no part for Day. The disappointed would-be starlet confesses to Morgan and decides to move back to Wisconsin and marry her high-school sweetheart. Meanwhile, nearly every actress on the lot has refused to work with Carson, including Jane Wyman, who faints when asked. Morgan suggests that they convince Goodwin that Day is the girl for the part. The duo then launch into a series of ridiculous schemes to get Goodwin to notice Day, but none of them pan out. Depressed and dejected, Day packs her bags and heads for the train. Before she makes it to the station she is suddenly "discovered" by Goodwin who has just heard her sing and he offers her the lead in his film. Fed up with Hollywood, Day refuses and catches her train. Not to be denied, Goodwin demands Carson and Morgan follow Day to Wisconsin and bring her back. The pair arrive in town just in time to hear Day exchange wedding vows with her local boy friend. The duo's disappointment then turns to shock when the newly married couple turn around and the groom looks exactly like Errol Flynn (played by Flynn himself, of course). Though not exactly high comedy, IT'S A GREAT FEELING is a very likable movie which contains several priceless moments for fans of the old Hollywood system. The cameos of Edward G. Robinson, Sydney Greenstreet, Danny Kaye, Joan Crawford, Gary Cooper, and especially Ronald Reagan (whose face is covered with a hot towel while sitting in a barber's chair through most of the scene) are unexpected and done with a refreshing nonchalance. Also the chance to see great directors like Vidor, Curtiz, and Walsh having a bit of fun before the cameras is reason enough to see IT'S A GREAT FEELING. Songs include "It's a Great Feeling," "At the Cafe Rendezvous," "There's Nothing Rougher than Love," "That Was a Big Fat Lie," "Give Me a Song With a Beautiful Melody," " Blame My Absent-Minded Heart," and "Fiddle-dee-dee" (Jule Styne, Sammy Cahn).

p, Alex Gottlieb; d, David Butler; w, Jack Rose, Melville Shavelson (based on a story by I.A.L. Diamond); ph, Wilfrid M. Cline (Technicolor); ed, Irene Morra; md, Ray Heindorf; art d, Stanley Fleischer; set d, Lyle B. Reifsnider; cos, Milo Anderson; spec eff, William McGann, H.F. Koenekamp; ch, LeRoy Prinz; makeup, Perc Westmore.

Comedy **(PR:A MPAA:NR)**

IT'S A GREAT LIFE* (1930) 94m MGM bw/c

Rosetta Duncan *(Casey Hogan)*, Vivian Duncan *(Babe Hogan)*, Lawrence Gray *(Jimmy Dean)*, Jed Prouty *(David Parker)*, Benny Rubin *(Benny Friedman)*.

The Duncan Sisters, well-known stage entertainers of the time, play two sisters working in the sheet-music section of a large department store. They get fired and become vaudeville performers. Each goes her own way when Vivian falls in love with piano-playing Gray. In the end, they get back together on the stage, and as friends. The film bombed at the box-office. Songs include "Let a Smile Be Your Umbrella On a Rainy Day" (Irving Kahal, Francis Wheeler, Sammy Fain); "Smile, Smile, Smile," "Lady Love," "I'm the Son of a—," "I'm Following You," "It Must Be an Old Spanish Custom," "Hoosier Hop," "I'm Sailing On a Sunbeam" (Dave Dreyer, Ballard MacDonald).

p&d, Sam Wood; w, Willard Mack, Al Boasberg (based on a story by Byron Morgan Alfred Block); ph, J. Peverell Marley (Technicolor); ed, Frank Sullivan; art d, Cedric Gibbons.

Musical Drama **(PR:A MPAA:NR)**

IT'S A GREAT LIFE* (1936) 63m PAR bw

Joe Morrison *(Johnny Barclay)*, Paul Kelly *(Rockie Johnson)*, Charles "Chic" Sale *(Grandpa Barclay)*, Rosalind Keith *(Mary)*, Baby LeRoy *(Buddy)*, Dean Jagger *(Arnold)*, William Frawley *(Lt. McNulty)*, David Holt *(Ruddy)*, Gloria Ann White *(Elizabeth)*, Florence Nash *(Ma)*, Oscar Polk *(Lazy Bones)*, Jack Murphy *(Stevens)*, Allan Cavan *(Doctor)*, Irving Bacon, Duke York, Oscar Rudolph.

An unentertaining film drama about the government's Civilian Conservation Corps project during the Depression. Morrison joins the CCC and becomes friends with a hobo. His girl friend falls in love with the hobo but most of the film centers around Morrison and friends putting out fires and saving dams.

p, Harold Hurley; d, Edward F. Cline; w, Paul Gerard Smith, Harlan Thompson (based on a story by Arthur Lake and Sherman Rogers); ph, Ben Reynolds; ed, Paul Weatherwax; m/l, Leo Robin, Lewis E. Gensler, Frederick Hollander.

Drama **(PR:A MPAA:NR)**

IT'S A GREAT LIFE** (1943) 68m COL bw

Penny Singleton *(Blondie)*, Arthur Lake *(Dagwood)*, Larry Simms *(Alexander)*, Hugh Herbert *(Timothy Brewster)*, Jonathan Hale *(J.C. Dithers)*, Danny Mummert *(Alvin Fuddle)*, Alan Dinehart *(Collender Martin)*, Douglas Leavitt *(Bromley)*, Irving Bacon *(Mailman)*, Marjorie Ann Mutchie *(Cookie)*, Si Jenks *(Piano Tuner)*, Ray Walker *(Salesman)*, Dickie Dillon *(Bit Boy)*, Daisy the Dog, Reggie the Horse.

A typical Blondie film with comedy that is appealing to children and the childlike. Slapstick action centers on Dagwood buying a horse when he should be buying a house. As always, his stupidity is the center of most of the gags. Of course, Blondie saves the day, the family, and Dagwood, but not the movie. (See BLONDIE series, Index.)

p&d, Frank R. Strayer; w, Connie Lee, Karen De Wolf; ph, L.W. O'Connell; m, M.W. Stoloff; ed, Al Clark; art d, Lionel Banks.

Comedy **(PR:AA MPAA:NR)**

IT'S A JOKE, SON!* 1/2 (1947) 63m EL bw

Kenny Delmar *(Sen. Claghorn)*, Una Merkel *(Magnolia Claghorn)*, June Lockhart *(Mary Lou)*, Kenneth Farrell *(Jeff Davis)*, Douglas Dumbrille *(Dan Healey)*, Jimmy Conlin *(Sen. Leeds)*, Matt Willis *(Ace)*, Ralph Sanford *(Knifey)*, Vera Lewis *(Hortense)*, Margaret McWade, Ida Moore *(Whipple Sisters)*.

Delmar is a southern aristocrat still living the glory of the pre-Civil War days. His only income is from his mint bed. His bossy wife, Merkel, is chosen by the Daughters of Dixie to be their candidate for state senator. Political bosses convince Delmar to run against his wife to split the vote so that their candidate will win. After a bungled kidnaping, Delmar wins the election, squares away the relationship between his daughter and her boy friend, and shows his wife who the real boss is. Although successfully funny as "Senator Claghorn" of the old Fred Allen radio show, on film Delmar's character isn't humorous enough to carry this 63-minute film. Kenny Delmar had a small part in David Wark Griffith's classic silent film ORPHANS OF THE STORM (which starred Lillian and Dorothy Gish).

p, Aubrey Schenck; d, Ben Stoloff; w, Robert Kent, Paul Gerard Smith; ph, Clyde de Vinna; m, Alvin Levin; ed, Norman Colbert; md, Irving Friedman; art d, Edward C. Jewell.

Comedy **(PR:A MPAA:NR)**

IT'S A KING* (1933, Brit.) 70m British and Dominions/GAU-W&F bw

Sydney Howard *(Albert King/King Albert)*, Joan Maude *(Princess Yasma)*, Cecil Humphreys *(Count Yenoff)*, George de Warfaz *(Col. Brandt)*, Arthur Goullet *(Leader)*, Franklyn Bellamy *(Salvatore)*, Lew Stone and the Monseigneur Orchestra, Bela Berkes and his Gypsy Orchestra.

A slow British comedy that follows the age-worn plot of a man who is discovered to be the exact double of a king. Taking place in mythical Ruritania, Howard portrays an insurance agent who not only looks like the king of Helgia, but has his name in reverse. The insurance man enjoys romance with a princess and saves his royal double from a group of anarchists who are trying to kill the real king.

p, Herbert Wilcox; d, Jack Raymond; w, R.P. Weston, Bert Lee, Jack Marks (based on a story by Claude Hulbert, Paul England); ph, F.A. Young.

Comedy **(PR:A MPAA:NR)**

IT'S A MAD, MAD, MAD, MAD WORLD**** (1963) 192m Casey/UA c

Spencer Tracy *(Capt. C.G. Culpeper)*, Milton Berle *(J. Russell Finch)*, Sid Caesar *(Melville Crump)*, Buddy Hackett *(Benjy; Benjamin)*, Ethel Merman *(Mrs. Marcus)*, Mickey Rooney *(Ding Bell)*, Dick Shawn *(Sylvester Marcus)*, Phil Silvers *(Otto Meyer)*, Terry-Thomas *(J. Algernon Hawthorne)*, Jonathan Winters *(Lennie Pike)*, Edie Adams *(Monica Crump)*, Dorothy Provine *(Emmeline Finch)*, Eddie "Rochester" Anderson *(1st Cab Driver)*, Jim Backus *(Tyler Fitzgerald)*, Ben Blue *(Airplane Pilot)*, Alan Carney *(Police Sergeant)*, Barrie Chase *(Mrs. Haliburton)*, William Demarest *(Chief of Police)*, Peter Falk *(2nd Cab Driver)*, Paul Ford *(Col. Wilberforce)*, Leo Gorcey *(3rd Cab Driver)*, Edward Everett Horton *(Dinckler)*, Buster Keaton *(Jimmy the Crook)*, Don Knotts *(Nervous Man)*, Carl Reiner *(Tower Control)*, The Three Stooges *(Firemen)*, Joe E. Brown *(Union Official)*, Andy Devine *(Sheriff Mason)*, Sterling Holloway *(Fire Chief)*, Marvin Kaplan *(Irwin, Gas Station Attendant)*, Arnold Stang *(Ray, Gas Station Attendant)*, Charles Lane *(Airport Manager)*, Howard Da Silva *(Airport Officer)*, Charles McGraw *(Lieutenant)*, ZaSu Pitts *(Switchboard Operator)*, Madlyn Rhue *(Police Secretary)*, Jesse White *(Radio Tower Operator)*, Lloyd Corrigan *(Mayor)*, Selma Diamond *(Voice of Culpeper's Wife)*, Stan Freberg *(Deputy Sheriff)*, Louise Glenn *(Voice of Billie Sue)*, Ben Lessy *(George, the Steward)*, Bobo Lewis *(Pilot's Wife)*, Mike Mazurki *(Miner)*, Nick Stuart *(Truck Driver)*, Sammee Tong *(Chinese Laundryman)*, Stanley Clements, Norman Fell, Nicholas Georgiade *(Detectives)*, Jimmy Durante *(Smiler Grogan)*, Allen Jenkins *(Police Officer)*, Harry Lauter *(Radio Operator)*, Doodles Weaver *(Salesman)*, Tom Kennedy *(Traffic Cop)*, Eddie Ryder *(Tower Radioman)*, Don Harvey *(Helicopter Observer)*, Roy Engel, Paul Birch *(Patrolmen)*, Don Van Sickel *(Stuntman)*, Jack Benny *(Man on Road)*, Jerry Lewis *(Mad Driver)*, Chick Chandler, Barbara Pepper, Cliff Norton, Roy Roberts.

This is the movie that proves that the whole world is crazy and everybody in it, but some people are definitely crazier than others. The people in this movie are the craziest and they provide non-stop laughs in their devious, ruthless, maniacal, insidious, crackpot, and dimwitted race for a pot of gold or, in this case, buried gangster loot. It all starts out tamely enough until an ancient thief—Durante, as Smiler Grogan, recently released from the jug—pushes his car a little too fast and too far over a cliff, sailing down an embankment and crashing. The passengers of several cars and a truck brake to a stop, horrified, and rush down to aid the stricken Durante. With his dying gasp, Durante whispers his biggest secret—$350,000 of stolen money can be found buried beneath the "Big W." He dies, literally kicking an old bucket near his twitching foot. The assembled people stare in disbelief. They are Berle, his wife Provine, his mother-in-law Merman, Caesar and his wife Adams, Hackett and buddy Rooney, and big dumb truckdriver Winters. The motorists get back into their cars and begin discussing the possibility that Durante was telling the truth. They quickly conclude that he was and the drivers, trying to avoid appearing anxious to each other gradually increase their speeds until they are all zooming along the mountain road. Winters, following at the end of the line of cars, sees the cars sprint forward and squints, saying: "Trying to lose the big boy, huh?" From that moment forward, these normally decent human beings turn into crazed, greedy creatures who will stop at nothing to make the pot of gold theirs as they head for their destination, Santa Rosita State Park. Berle and Provine, harassed all the way by loud-mouthed mother-in-law Merman, have a breakdown and wind up hitching a ride with Terry Thomas. Rooney and Hackett get drunken millionaire Backus to fly them crazily about, even smashing through a billboard. Caesar and wife Adams get trapped in the basement of a hardware store and ignite explosives to free themselves, wrecking the place. Winters takes Silvers into his confidence and the salesman leaves the truckdriver in the lurch. Incensed, Winters later goes berserk when two gas station attendants who have just opened a garage in the middle of nowhere, Stang and Kaplan, attempt to tie him up; Silvers has told them that Winters is an escaped lunatic. Winters attacks not only them but the station itself, utterly destroying the brand-new structure, leaving it flat and Stang and Kaplan running for their lives. Monitoring all these crazy antics is Tracy, a veteran cop who charts the courses of the money searchers, believing they will lead him to the stolen loot. They do, all of them meeting in the state park with shovels, spades, hoes and rakes. He stands by as they finally discover the "Big W," two crossed palm trees. The arguing group, joined by cabdrivers Anderson and Falk and beatnik Shawn find the money but Tracy steps forth and appropriates the loot in the name of the law. He does not return to the station, however. His long life has been made miserable by police problems and a wife whose nagging hasn't stopped for decades (Diamond, heard only over the phone). Instead, Tracy makes a break for the Mexican border but the money searchers get wise to him and pursue Tracy to a condemned building where all the men wind up on a fire escape struggling for the suitcase containing the money. A massive crowd assembles as the fire escape begins to give way. Firemen arrive and attempt to take the men off the wobbling fire escape, but all of the men on the fire escape try to get on the long extended ladder which causes it to go out of control, flipping back and forth and shooting the men off like wads of paper shot from a rubber band. They all wind up in the hospital in casts from head to foot. When Merman walks into their hospital ward screaming and carrying on, she falls on a banana peel and the whole lot of them explode into gales of laughter. And laughter is what this revisit to the Keystone Kops is all about, a wonderful and mirthful pageant of slapstick. The stunts are spectacular; Kramer spared no expense using 39 stunt men, half of the members of the Stuntmen's Association, paying them $252,000 for some of the most incredible feats on film. This was one of Tracy's last films and he was ill during the shooting, weak and drinking only one glass of beer a night. He loved the cast and they adored him but he would not drink with them off camera, except to take a glass of milk with an ice cube in it. Kramer demanded little of Tracy and shortened his work to six hours a day. His performance did not register well, but the frantic energy of the madcap actors racing about him made up for Tracy's inert posture. The film was designed to be the biggest, most lavish comedy ever made and it almost made it, earning back considerable profits beyond its $7 million price tag. Other great clowns appearing in cameo roles include Jerry Lewis, Buster Keaton, Joe E. Brown, Leo Gorcey, Stan Freberg, Don Knotts, ZaSu Pitts, Carl Reiner, Edward Everett Horton, Ben Blue, and The Three Stooges. Music is performed by the Los Angeles Philharmonic Orchestra. Songs, in addition to the title song, are "Thirty One Flavors," " You Satisfy My Soul" (all by Ernest Gold, Mack David). A dance sequence is sung by The Shirelles and played by The Four Mods.

p&d, Stanley Kramer; w, William and Tania Rose; ph, Ernest Laszlo (UltraPanavision, Technicolor); m, Ernest Gold; ed, Frederic Knudtson, Robert C. Jones, Gene Fowler, Jr.; prod d, Rudolph Sternad; art d, Gordon Gurnell; set d,

Joseph Kish; cos, Bill Thomas; spec eff, Danny Lee, Linwood G. Dunn; m/l, Gold, Mack David; makeup, George Lane, Lynn Reynolds; stunts, Carey Loftin.

Comedy **Cas.** **(PR:AAA MPAA:NR)**

IT'S A PLEASURE** (1945) 89m International Pictures/RKO c

Sonja Henie *(Chris Linden)*, Michael O'Shea *(Don Martin)*, Bill Johnson *(Buzz Fletcher)*, Marie McDonald *(Mrs. Buzz Fletcher)*, Gus Schilling *(Bill Evans)*, Iris Adrian *(Wilma)*, Cheryl Walker *(Loni)*, Peggy O'Neill *(Cricket)*, Arthur Loft *(Jack Weimar)*, Alyce Fleming *(Maid)*, George Brown *(Hockey Referee)*, Jack Chefe *(Canadian Hockey Star)*, Don Loper *(Dancing Partner)*, Tom Hanlon *(Announcer)*, Lane Watson *(Photographer)*, Edward Earle *(Manager of Jewelry Store)*, Nelson Leigh *(Waiter)*, Jimmy Conlin *(Messenger)*, Kenneth Scott *(Card Sharp)*, Donald Kerr *(Hoofer)*.

One-time ice skating star Henie plays the wife of hockey player O'Shea. Her husband has been barred from the game because of his frequent fighting. He tries to make a comeback as an ice-show performer, but his drinking causes him to fail. Henie, on the other hand, becomes a star skater. The two split, but hook up again in the end when O'Shea turns over a new leaf. Henie was a wonderful skater, but she had limited acting ability. The skating numbers are entertaining, but the story line is weak.

p, David Lewis; d, William A. Seiter; w, Lynn Starling, Elliot Paul; ph, Ray Rennahan (Technicolor); m, Arthur Lange; ed, Ernest Nims; md, Lange; art d, Wiard B.Ihnen; ch, Don Loper; m/l, "Romance," Edgar Leslie, Walter Donaldson.

Drama **(PR:A MPAA:NR)**

IT'S A SMALL WORLD* 1/2 (1935) 67m FOX bw

Spencer Tracy *(Bill Shevlin)*, Wendy Barrie *(Jane Dale)*, Raymond Walburn *(Judge Julius B. Clummerhorn)*, Virginia Sale *(Lizzie)*, Astrid Allwyn *(Nancy Naylor)*, Irving Bacon *(Cal)*, Charles Sellon *(Cyclone)*, Nick [Dick] Foran *(Motor Cop)*, Belle Daube *(Mrs. Dale)*, Frank McGlynn, Sr. *(Snake Brown, Jr.)*, Frank McGlynn, Jr. *(Snake Brown III)*, Bill Gillis *(Snake Brown, Sr)*, Ed Brady *(Buck Bogardus)*, Harold Minjir *(Freddie Thompson)*, Charles R. Moore *(Doorman)*, Frank Austin, Bob McKinsey, Sam Adams, Lew King, F.W. Watson, W.H. Davis *(Bits)*.

Barrie, a socialite, and Tracy, a young lawyer smash their cars in a small Louisianna town. Walburn is the town's judge and garage owner who decides to hold a trial to find out who was at fault in the accident. Tracy falls in love with Barrie, but she keeps her distance until the final moments. A far-fetched comedy that never hits the funny bone.

p, Edward Butcher; d, Irving Cummings; w, Samuel Hellman, Gladys Lehman (based on the novel *Highway Robbery* by Albert Treynor); ph, Arthur Miller; m, Arthur Lange; art d, William Darling.

Romance/Comedy **(PR:A MPAA:NR)**

IT'S A SMALL WORLD** (1950) 74m EL bw

Paul Dale *(Harry Musk)*, Lorraine Miller *(Buttons)*, Will Geer *(Father Musk)*, Nina Koshetz *(Rose Ferris)*, Steve Brodie *(Charlie)*, Anne Sholter *(Dolly Burke)*, Todd Karns *(Sam)*, Margaret Field *(Janie at 16 Years)*, Shirley O. Mills *(Susie at 16 Years)*, Tom Browne Henry *(Jackson)*, Harry Harvey *(Dr. Brown)*, Paul E. Burns *(Farmer)*, Jacqui Snyder *(Susie at 8 Years)*, Lora Lee Michel *(Janie at 8 Years)*.

An off-beat exploitative film about midgets. Dale is the hero who goes through childhood being the butt of practical jokes and cruel comments. As a young man he meets a woman who tries to steer him into a life of crime. He dumps her and joins the Cole Bros. circus. A seldom shown film that attempts to take a serious look at the problems confronting midgets.

p, Peter Scully; d, William Castle; w, Otto Schreiber, Castle; ph, Karl Struss; m, Karl Hajos; ed, Peter Sullivan; m/l, "It's a Small World," Hajos, Charles Newman.

Drama **(PR:A MPAA:NR)**

IT'S A 2'6" ABOVE THE GROUND WORLD*

(1972, Brit.) 96m Welbeck/BL c (AKA: THE LOVE BAN)

Nanette Newman, Hywel Bennett, Russell Lewis, Simon Henderson, Milo O'Shea.

Foul-mouthed sex comedy taken from the stage has a Catholic couple risking their souls by using the pill. Neither provocative nor funny.

p, Betty E. Box, Ralph Thomas; d, Thomas; w, Kevin Laffan (based on the play by Laffan); ph, Tony Imi (Eastmancolor); m, Stanley Myers.

Comedy **(PR:O MPAA:NR)**

IT'S A WISE CHILD** (1931) 73m MGM bw

Marion Davies *(Joyce)*, Sidney Blackmer *(Steve)*, James Gleason *(Cool Kelly)*, Polly Moran *(Bertha)*, Lester Vail *(Roger)*, Marie Prevost *(Annie)*, Clara Blandick *(Mrs. Stanton)*, Robert McWade *(G.A. Appleby)*, Johnny Arthur *(Otho)*, Hilda Vaughn *(Alice)*, Ben Alexander *(Bill)*, Emily Fitzroy *(Jane Appleby)*.

A comedy about a sedate family that believes a daughter is pregnant. The story centers around the family's search for the father, whom they believe could be one of three men: the girl's ex-fiance, her present fiance, or her lawyer-guardian. As a sideline to the tale, the son, while drunk, secretly marries the family maid, who is also with child. The story ends with the daughter admitting she made up her pregnancy to protect the maid, the son annulling his marriage, and the maid marrying her first love, the ice man.

d, Robert Z. Leonard; w, Laurence E. Johnson (based on his play); ph, Oliver T. Marsh; ed, Margaret Booth.

Comedy **(PR:A MPAA:NR)**

IT'S A WONDERFUL DAY* 1/2

(1949, Brit.) 50m Knightsbridge/Equity British bw

John Blythe, Dorothee Baroone, Eva Benyon, Jack Hodges, Lew Sherman, Yvonne Griffiths, The Seven Imeson Brothers, George Mitchell and His Swing Orchestra.

Weak plot works as an excuse to spin some unmemorable musical numbers and light moments. Blythe is the musician who wanders about the countryside in the hopes of getting rest, but finds the local talent too tantalizing to let pass. A sweet country lass is also keeping him busy by stealing his heart away. Too brief and slight to make much impression.

p,d&w, Hal Wilson; ph, Brooks-Carrington, Stanley Clinton.

Musical **(PR:A MPAA:NR)**

IT'S A WONDERFUL LIFE***** (1946) 129m Liberty Films/RKO bw

James Stewart *(George Bailey)*, Donna Reed *(Mary Hatch)*, Lionel Barrymore *(Mr. Potter)*, Thomas Mitchell *(Uncle Billy)*, Henry Travers *(Clarence)*, Beulah Bondi *(Mrs. Bailey)*, Frank Faylen *(Ernie)*, Ward Bond *(Bert)*, Gloria Grahame *(Violet Bick)*, H.B. Warner *(Mr. Gower)*, Frank Albertson *(Sam Wainwright)*, Samuel S. Hinds *(Pa Bailey)*, Todd Karns *(Harry Bailey)*, Mary Treen *(Cousin Tilly)*, Virginia Patton *(Ruth Dakin)*, Charles Williams *(Cousin Eustace)*, Sarah Edwards *(Mrs. Hatch)*, Bill Edmunds *(Mr. Martini)*, Lillian Randolph *(Annie)*, Argentina Brunetti *(Mrs. Martini)*, Bobby Anderson *(Little George)*, Ronnie Ralph *(Little Sam)*, Jean Gale *(Little Mary)*, Jeanine Anne Roose *(Little Violet)*, Danny Mummert *(Little Marty Hatch)*, George Nokes *(Little Harry Bailey)*, Sheldon Leonard *(Nick)*, Frank Hagney *(Potter's Bodyguard)*, Ray Walker *(Joe at Luggage Shop)*, Charlie Lane *(Real Estate Salesman)*, Edward Keane *(Tom)*, Carol Coomes *(Janie Bailey)*, Karolyn Grimes *(Zuzu Bailey)*, Jimmy Hawkins *(Tommy Bailey)*, Larry Simms *(Pete Bailey)*, Carl "Alfalfa" Switzer *(Freddie)*, Hal Landon *(Marty Hatch)*, Harry Holman *(High School Principal)*, Bobby Scott *(Mickey)*, Harry Cheshire *(Dr. Campbell)*, Charles Halton *(Bank Examiner)*, Ed Featherstone *(Bank Teller)*, Stanley Andrews *(Mr. Welch)*, J. Farrell MacDonald *(House Owner)*, Marion Carr *(Mrs. Wainwright)*, Gary Owen *(Bill Poster)*, Lane Chandler, Ellen Corby, Almira Sessions, Lee Frederick, Bert Moorehouse.

Capra and Stewart teamed up for this majestic, heartwarming classic film (it remained the favorite of each) which has gone on to become one of the most popular movies ever made, and for so many good reasons it's hard to chronicle all of them. This wonderful fantasy begins in the heavens with angels talking about a small-town young man, George Bailey—Stewart—and how his problems have overwhelmed him to the point where he is contemplating suicide. In flashback we see Stewart's life from boyhood: how he saved the life of his younger brother, how he worked at the local drugstore owned by Warner and met his childhood sweetheart who grows up to be Reed. As a child, George Bailey discovers that druggist Warner, who has been drinking due to a family tragedy, has mistakenly mixed a prescription containing poison; the boy stops him from sending it to a patient. Angrily, before the boy can tell him of the mistake, Warner boxes the boy's ears. When he realizes his error, Warner breaks down and begs the boy for forgiveness. By the time the boy grows up to be Stewart, he can't wait to get out of tiny Bedford Falls and away from his father's building and loan association. He has sacrificed his college savings so that his younger brother, Karns, could go to college instead. Stewart stayed behind and now his brother, graduated, is returning home to take his place. Stewart is exuberant; he's going to travel around the world and see all the wonderful places he's dreamed about visiting. He even buys a new suitcase and has it packed, but when Karns shows up he introduces one and all to his new wife; he reluctantly agrees to take Stewart's place at the loan company but Stewart lets him go off to make a life of his own, especially after his father, Hinds, dies and it appears that the most miserable man in town, banker Barrymore, will take over the loan company. Stewart makes a speech to the board of directors, defending his father's high-minded principles, and the board later tells him that they won't let Barrymore gut the company if he, Stewart, will stay on and run the company. He does. Stewart is not a happy young man, even with Reed to keep him occupied. They have always been deeply in love but Stewart has not wanted to admit it. In one of their many enchanting scenes together, they do a Charleston at a high school dance, thinking to win the prize. One of the wise-guy students hits a switch which activates the hydraulic system that slowly pulls back the gymnasium floor which has a pool beneath it. Everyone sees this happening but Stewart and Reed who keep dancing ever closer to the opening, the spotlight engulfing them, the crowd waiting expectantly, oohing and ahhing as the couple dance ever closer to the opening. "We must be pretty good," Stewart beams to Reed just before they topple into the pool, causing others to join them. They walk home together that night, she in a long bathrobe, he in an ill-fitting football uniform. He tells her he'll get her the moon but all Reed wants is a deserted old house, that and Stewart and a future family to go inside it. He throws a few rocks through the house's windows for luck but she stops him. Before they can embrace, Stewart gets the news that his father has suffered an attack; he races off leaving Reed hiding in a bush because she has lost her robe. Stewart is now stuck with the struggling company and he is miserable, realizing that he may never get the chance to travel to all those exotic places. He wanders past Reed's home and steps inside just when she gets a call from Albertson, one of her old beaus; Reed carries on conversations with both Stewart and Albertson, until Stewart, protesting his ambition to get married, takes Reed in his arms and kisses her, still telling her he wants to see the world, not marry and get stuck forever in Bedford Falls. Stewart and Reed marry and are about to leave on a worldwide honeymoon. Just as their favorite cab driver, Faylen, is about to take them to the train station, they pass the bank owned by mean-minded skinflint banker Barrymore where crowds of anxious people are waiting for the bank to open, a bank whose doors appear to be locked. There's not only a run on the bank during this Depression year but crowds begin to assemble outside the savings and loan. Stewart has Faylen stop the cab and he rushes back to his company. There he tries to calm the crowds, but his depositors are adamant. There is a run on the bank and they can't get their money from Barrymore, who has locked his doors. They want their money from the tiny savings and loan company and they want it now. Stewart explains that there isn't any money on hand, that the deposits are in houses they built and small businesses they financed, those owned by the depositors themselves. No, they insist, the money, and now. Reed arrives with the nest egg she and Stewart were going to use on their honeymoon, offering it to her husband. Stewart uses this money to give to his depositors, most of whom take only enough to live on until the bank reopens. At the end of the day, Stewart is still in business with only $2 left. He gets a call from his brand-new wife Reed who tells him to come home, giving him the address of the old house she has always liked. Stewart arrives escorted by friends Faylen and Bond, the local cop, to find his wife waiting for him in the patched-up mansion, decorated with travel posters advertising exotic places Stewart will obviously never see. Stewart settles down and he and Reed have four children. WW II comes and he is rejected for being deaf in the one ear that Warner so furiously boxed when Stewart was a child, but he becomes an air raid warden and does his bit. His brother Karns, however, becomes a navy pilot and winds up shooting down an enemy bomber about to sink a U.S. troopship, saving all on board and winning the Congressional Medal of Honor. Stewart, friends, and relatives, including the imbibing uncle, Mitchell, celebrate Karns' fame, shown boldly on the front page of the Bedford Falls newspaper. So enthusiastic is Mitchell that he absent-mindedly wraps an $8,000 deposit he is about to make in Barrymore's bank in the newspaper carrying the story about Stewart's brother. When Barrymore appears in the bank, Mitchell proudly hands the miserable banker the newspaper so he can read about Karns. Once in his office, Barrymore unwraps the paper to discover the deposit but he doesn't tell Mitchell about it, knowing that if he conceals the money, the savings and loan company—which he has always sought to either control or destroy—will be finished. When Mitchell returns to the office in a panic, he tells Stewart that the money is missing. The bank inspector, Halton, is on hand and should he discover the error, the company will be closed. Stewart also panics and goes to Barrymore, attempting to borrow the money to put his books in order. Barrymore takes perverse delight in Stewart's plight, telling him with a sneer: "You used to be so cocky. You were going to go out and conquer the world. You once called me a 'warped, frustrated old man.' What are you but a warped, frustrated young man, a miserable little clerk crawling in here on your hands and knees and begging for help, no securities, no stocks, no bonds, nothing but a miserable little $500 equity in a life insurance policy. You're worth more dead than alive. Why don't you go to the riff-raff you love so much and ask them to let you have your $8,000? You know why, because they'd run you out of town on a rail. But I'll tell you what I'm going to do for you, George. Since the state examiner is still here, as a stockholder of the Building and Loan, I am going to swear out a warrant for your arrest, misappropriation of funds, manipulation, malfeasance . . . " Stewart gets up and starts to leave. "Go ahead, George, you can't hide in a little town like this." But Stewart does attempt to hide, running home to his wife and four children, annoyed at the preparations they make for Christmas. When he learns that his youngest child, Grimes, is sick in bed with a cold, he unjustly accuses the child's teacher, blasting her on the phone when she calls to inquire about her health, and threatening to punch the teacher's husband when he gets on the phone to protest. Stewart visits Grimes in his room, putting a few petals from her flower into his pocket. He then goes out, looking for help, but winding up in a small bar run by Edmunds, one of his depositors, a man whose restaurant-bar and home came into being, like so many others in Bedford Falls, because of the savings-and-loan company Stewart has struggled for some years to keep alive. Here he meets the husband of his child's teacher, who punches him in the nose for his abusive phone conversation. In his cups, Stewart staggers to a nearby bridge, looking down despairingly at the dark waters below. He concludes that Barrymore is right; he is worth more dead than alive, and he is about to jump to his own watery death when suddenly another body hurtles into the water, an elderly gentleman, Travers, who begins to flounder and call for help. Stewart leaps into the water and yanks the old man to safety. They later dry out in the bridgetender's house. Here Travers casually talks with Stewart about his life and Stewart asks him how he came to jump in the river. Travers shrugs and simply says that he's Stewart's guardian angel, "Clarence Oddbody, angel second class," and he jumped in the river so Stewart would save him instead of taking his own life. He adds that he still must earn his wings. With this news, the bridgetender falls out of his chair and runs outside, thinking he's dealing with lunatics. Stewart says that the old man is crazy, then adds that it would have been better had he never been born. Travers thinks about this, looks skyward for approval, then brings the notion to reality. Stewart can suddenly hear out of an ear that has been deaf since childhood. He checks his pockets and finds that the petals from his daughter's flower have disappeared. Now Travers quickly takes Stewart through a nightmare of his own making, his worst nightmare. He goes to his mother's house to find Bondi. But his own mother does not recognize him, saying that she has no son named George. She is a distrustful and lonely widow, her home turned into a boarding house. Through the town Stewart runs, confused, frightened. He goes to Martini's place to find bartender Leonard has taken over and turned the place into a hellhole. He and Travers have a drink but Leonard throws them out for "being a couple of pixies" and because Travers has stated that he is an angel "second class" who is trying to earn his wings. Stewart and Travers are tossed out into the snow, and Leonard repeatedly hits the no sale button of his cash register, causing the bell to ring and saying: "Hey, get me, I'm handing out wings!" Stewart sees that the main street has been converted into a miniature Babylon. It bulges with burlesque houses, peep shows, bucket-of-blood bars, pawn shops. Drunks and prostitutes roam the streets. Police are raiding one brothel, dragging women to a paddy wagon. One of these is Grahame, a girl Stewart had earlier known and liked. The town has completely changed from a quiet, decent community to a dark den of sin, crime, and corruption. Even the name is no more; Bedford Falls is now called Pottersville, named after the cruel tyrant Barrymore, who has taken it over. Stewart races to the area where his savings-and-loan company had established a subdivision of inexpensive but attractive homes. It doesn't exist; in its place is the old cemetery and there Stewart finds the grave of his younger brother. He turns to Travers to tell him that this grave cannot exist, that it's a lie, his brother did not die in childhood, that he grew up to save a troopship full of men and win the Congressional Medal of Honor. Travers replies that all of what Stewart has seen has happened because he had never been born, and he has left "an awful hole." His mother was forced to run a boarding house, his uncle died in an insane asylum, his brother died when he fell through the ice as a child because he, Stewart, was not there to save him, and all the men died on the troopship because his brother was not there to save them. Stewart begins to see that he was important to his fellow man, in fact, vital to many of them. He demands that Travers now tell him what happened to his wife Reed. Travers refuses but Stewart shakes it out of him; she's the old-maid librarian. Stewart rushes to the library and catches Reed just as she is locking up the library. He holds her in his arms shouting for her to recognize him, but she only pulls away, screaming, as if being attacked by a madman. Bond, the cop, appears. He and Faylen had earlier seen Stewart on the street and not recognized him when he took them to the old, deserted house that he called his home and then disappeared. Now Bond tries to arrest Stewart who knocks the cop down and runs wildly through the street. Bond pulls his gun and fires at the fleeing, terrified man. Stewart makes his way back to the bridge, grabbing the rail and looking down at the inky water, begging for Travers "to get me back, get me back . . . I want to live again." He begins to weep, begging to rejoin the living. A cop car turns onto the bridge and Bond rushes forward, addressing Stewart in a friendly manner. Stewart prepares to fight him until he realizes that Bond knows him. He finds the petals from his daughter's flower in his pocket. With great joy he embraces Bond, realizing he is not dead nor a soul in limbo, but is very much part of life. Stewart races home, running through the town as he had known it (where the local movie house is playing THE BELLS OF ST. MARY'S), shouting "Merry Christmas" to one and all, bursting with happiness. He even bangs on the bank window to wish a scowling Barrymore a loud "Merry Christmas!" Barrymore shouts after him: "And a happy New Year's . . . in jail!" Stewart bursts through the door of his house to blissfully embrace his children. In the parlor waits the dour bank examiner, Halton, and the local sheriff. Stewart greets them with a wide smile, saying: "Isn't it wonderful—I'm going to jail!" But Stewart does not go to jail. Reed runs into the house and into his arms. Behind her, flooding into his home, are all his depositors, friends, relatives, brought there by Reed when she learned that her husband was in trouble. They begin to empty their pockets into a large basket, thousands of dollars, in gratitude for what Stewart and his company have done in enriching their lives. A wire arrives in which Albertson, now a millionaire manufacturer, states that he has made $25,000 available to Stewart if he needs it. The sheriff tears up his warrant and even Halton contributes. The hero brother Karns arrives and drinks are passed out. Karns toasts Stewart: "To my big brother George—the richest man in town." All burst into "Old Lang Syne." Someone or something brushes the Christmas tree next to Stewart, Reed and their children, and the bells on the branches tinkle. Grimes, held in Stewart's arms, says: "Look, daddy, teacher says that every time a bell rings, an angel gets his wings." Stewart grins broadly and says: "That's right, that's right." He looks upward and gives a wink, saying: "Attaboy, Clarence." Everything about this film gets the blood pumping and in the right direction, straight to the heart. It is true that IT'S A WONDERFUL LIFE deals with middle-class values and around the edges of every problem and joy is Capra's personal stamp of sentimentality, or perhaps American sentimentality. Was there ever a more American director than the great Frank Capra? For years the cute academic critics condemned any film out of hand if it showed the slightest bit of sentiment, opting for sterile, clammy dramas where issues and "statements" inadequately replaced human beings. But here is sentiment wonderfully and carefully crafted by master filmmaker Capra. It is honest, it is fresh, it was as true then as it is today. And in drama, comedy, or any genre, nothing is greater than an examination of the human heart, a display of true human emotions. "The heart has its reasons which reason does not know," wrote Blaise Pascal and here Capra etched those reasons upon the screens of America and in the open hearts of viewers everywhere. Stewart, quite simply, is everyman, and he is, as we all are, vitally important in the world because he belongs to mankind. IT'S A WONDERFUL LIFE really recaps John Donne's memorable lines about "each man's death diminishes me because I am involved in mankind and therefore never send to know for whom the bell tolls; it tolls for thee." In this case it's tiny Christmas bells tolling, not for death, but for life and love. This film was always Stewart's favorite film and he is nothing less than stirring as the small town dreamer who sacrifices his life for his fellow man. He's no saint; he gripes and complains like everyone else, but he is a great leader of men because his brave, impetuous heart will not—can not—be ruled by the subtle, conniving minds of others. Stewart, as he proved time and again in the enlightening and enriching film, shows his vulnerability, his weaknesses, his dogged yet distant hopes in a character who refuses to quit the burden of community. Early on, he declares otherwise when telling Reed: "Mary, I know what I'm going to do tomorrow, and the next day, and next year, and the year after that. I'm shaking the dust of this crummy little town off my feet and I'm gonna see the world, Italy, Greece, the Parthenon, the Coliseum, and then I'm coming back here and go to college and see what they know, and then I'm gonna build things. I'm gonna build airfields, skyscrapers a hundred stories high. I'm gonna build bridges a mile long." Stewart builds other things: a strong community of independent, secure citizens with a future much brighter than banker Barrymore would ever paint had he, instead of Stewart, stroked the canvas of the town's future with his own brush. The young Stewart can do anything, achieve anything. "I'll give you the moon," he tells Reed when they stroll along a street in their youth. "I'll take it," she tells him, and somehow he does give her what she wants—a family, affection, a home. Reed, borrowed from MGM—as were Grahame and Barrymore—is excellent as the loyal, trusting wife who knew since childhood she would be Mrs. George Bailey. Barrymore, the only man Capra would settle for as the vicious old skinflint, embodies scheming evil where Stewart is bright-hope good. The rest of the cast is simply terrific, a casting director's dream come true of matchless character players Mitchell, Warner, Bond, Bondi, Hinds, Faylen, Albertson and that softspoken, venerable Travers. Capra felt that this film surpassed any movie he ever made, stating in his autobiography, *The Name Above the Title*: "I thought it was the greatest film I ever made. Better yet, I thought it was the greatest film *anybody* ever made. It wasn't made for the oh-so-bored critics or the oh-so-jaded literati. It was my kind of film for my kind of people." The script is bright and full of humor, fashioned expertly by Goodrich and Hackett, with additional dialog by Swerling. The idea for the story came about in a unique way. Author Philip Van Doren Stern wrote the story, entitled "The Greatest Gift," and sent it out to his friends as a Christmas card. So well did they receive it that Stern published the tale and RKO immediately bought it for the screen. The studio assigned the script to a variety of writers—Dalton Trumbo, Clifford Odets, Marc Connelly—but none of them could develop the right approach. Then Capra took it over, and made it into a classic. This was his first film in several years, and Stewart's first film for Capra in six years, both of them recently getting out of the service. IT'S A WONDERFUL LIFE struggled at the box office when first released, competing with an another blockbuster of the time, THE BEST YEARS OF OUR LIVES. (The latter film was helmed by William Wyler, one of Capra's collaborators—along with George Stevens and Sam Briskin—in the new independent production company, Liberty Films, formed by the four after WW II with the idea of giving good directors the full artistic control that Capra had previously enjoyed on his pictures. Wyler's classic was *not* a product of the new company, though.) The first time around, the film actually lost money, $525,000. But it's been in constant rerelease since then and uncounted millions have seen and loved it in the past forty years. It undoubtedly ranks among the ten most popular movies ever made, and it is one of the best ever made.

p&d, Frank Capra; w, Frances Goodrich, Albert Hackett, Capra, Jo Swerling (based on the story "The Greatest Gift" by Philip Van Doren Stern); ph, Joseph Walker, Joseph Biroc; m, Dmitri Tiomkin; ed, William Hornbeck; md, Tiomkin; art d, Jack Okey; set d, Emile Kuri; cos, Edward Stevenson; spec eff, Russell A. Cully.

Romance/Comedy/Fantasy Cas. (PR:AAA MPAA:NR)

IT'S A WONDERFUL WORLD*½** (1939) 86m MGM bw

Claudette Colbert *(Edwina Corday)*, James Stewart *(Guy Johnson)*, Guy Kibbee *(Capt. Streeter)*, Nat Pendleton *(Sgt. Koretz)*, Frances Drake *(Vivian Tarbel)*, Edgar Kennedy *(Lt. Meller)*, Ernest Truex *(Willie Heyward)*, Richard Carle *(Maj. Willoughby)*, Cecilia Callejo *(Dolores Gonzales)*, Sidney Blackmer *(Al Mallon)*, Andy Clyde *(Gimpy)*, Cliff Clark *(Capt. Haggerty)*, Cecil Cunningham *(Mme. Chambers)*, Leonard Kibrick *(Herman Plotka)*, Hans Conried *(Stage Manager)*, Grady Sutton *(Bupton Peabody)*.

This one is played for slapstick but Colbert and Stewart, under Van Dyke's smooth direction, make it a bright and often hilarious screwball comedy. Truex is an irresponsible millionaire and Stewart is hired to keep an eye on him; this is one of his first cases and he's as green a private detective as ever slipped on a gumshoe. Tycoon Truex gets involved in a murder and the bumbling Stewart is also framed for the same crime. He is sent to prison with Truex but escapes on the train taking them to the pen and resolves to dig up the evidence that will exonerate himself and his client. He stops Colbert, a lady poet, and more or less holds her captive until he can piece the clues together. The couple get involved in a series of wild adventures and Stewart must impersonate an actor, a chauffeur, and a Boy Scout leader. He replaces goofy Sutton as the leader of a group of Boy Scouts, donning Sutton's short-pants uniform and wearing glasses so thick they look like telescopes and render Stewart almost blind. Some of the exchanges between Colbert and Stewart as they fumble about in the woods are side-splitting. It all works out well, with Colbert falling in love with her gentle kidnaper and saving him repeatedly from pitfalls and dangers, until he can pinpoint the culprit. Colbert and Stewart interplay beautifully in this Ben Hecht comedy but it smacks too closely of IT HAPPENED ONE NIGHT, the kind of screwball comedy the public once loved but, by the time of this film's release, was growing a bit predictable. The supporting cast is outstanding, loaded with comic veterans Sutton, Pendleton, Kennedy, Truex, Clyde, and Conried.

p, Frank Davis; d, W.S. Van Dyke II; w, Ben Hecht (based on a story by Hecht, Herman J. Mankiewicz); ph, Oliver Marsh; ed, Harold F. Kress; art d, Cedric Gibbons; cos, Adrian.

Comedy (PR:A MPAA:NR)

IT'S A WONDERFUL WORLD** (1956, Brit.) 89m George Minter/REN c

Terence Morgan *(Ray Thompson)*, George Cole *(Ken Miller)*, Kathleen Harrison *(Miss Gilly)*, Mylene Nicole [Demongeot] *(Georgie Dubois)*, James Hayter *(Bert Fielding)*, Harold Lang *(Mervyn Wade)*, Maurice Kaufman *(Paul Taylor)*, Richard Wattis *(Harold)*, Reginald Beckwith *(Manager)*, Derek Blomfield *(Arranger)*, Maya Koumani *(Henrietta)*, Walter Crisham *(American)*, Ted Heath *(Himself)*, Dennis Lotis *(Himself)*, Charles Clay *(Sir Thomas van Broughton)*, Jock McKay, Hal Osmond, Sam Kydd, George Moon, Douglas Blackwell, Keith Sawbridge, Angela Braemar, Stan Thomason, Charles Brodie, Brian Sunners, Leslie Weston, Patricia Ryan, Avril Sadler, Jeanette Pearce, Howard Williams, Shirley Ann Field, Colin Crofk, Roger Snowden, Douglas Bradley-Smith, Bernard Rebel, Francesco Russe, Lellah Sabarathy.

Morgan and Cole are poor struggling British composers who aren't having any luck with their music, which has gone out of style. Morgan gets a job at a publishing house to pay the bills. Cole gets a brainstorm idea to reverse a popular song and say it came from a famous foreign composer who is now in seclusion. The sham works well, the song is played at Albert Hall, and it causes the critics to rave. Nicole brings fame to them legitimately when she performs one of their songs at the Royal Command Performance. Songs include: "When You Came Along," "Rosanne," "Girls! Girls! Girls!" (Ted Heath, Moira Heath), "A Few Kisses Ago" (Robert Farnon, Val Guest), "The Hawaiian War Chant" (Ted Heath).

p, Denis O'Dell; d&w, Val Guest; ph, Wilkie Cooper (SpectaScope, Technicolor); m, Ted Heath, Robert Farnon; ed, John Pomeroy.

Musical/Comedy (PR:A MPAA:NR)

IT'S ALIVE*½ (1968) 80m Azalea bw

Tommy Kirk, Shirley Bonne, Billy Thurman, Corveth Osterhouse, Annabelle Macadams.

Nonsensical sci-fi film starring Osterhouse as a slightly crazed farmer who discovers a prehistoric monster on his land and kidnaps three people (Kirk, Bonne, and Thurman) to feed to his "pet." The three scheme about ways to escape, until finally Kirk is successful. Buchanan's other works include ZONTAR and THE THING FROM VENUS.

p,d&w, Larry Buchanan (based on the novel *Being* by Richard Matheson); ph, Robert Alcott; spec eff, Jack Bennett.

Science Fiction (PR:C MPAA:NR)

IT'S ALIVE** (1974) 90m Larco/WB c

John Ryan *(Frank Davies)*, Sharon Farrell *(Lenore Davies)*, Andrew Duggan *(The Professor)*, Guy Stockwell *(Clayton)*, James Dixon *(Lt. Perkins)*, Michael Ansara *(The Captain)*, Robert Emhardt *(The Executive)*, William Wellman, Jr. *(Charlie)*, Daniel Holzman *(Chris Davies)*, Shamus Locke *(Doctor)*, Mary Nancy Burnett *(Nurse)*, Diana Hale *(Secretary)*, Patrick MacAllister, Gerald York, Jerry Taft, Gwil Richards, W. Allen York *(Expectant Fathers)*.

Larry Cohen (THE PRIVATE FILES OF J. EDGAR HOOVER, IT LIVES AGAIN, and "Q") has always been a fascinating genre screenwriter of intelligence, insight, and social perceptiveness and his films *read* well, but his directing style (probably due to the miniuscule budgets he is forced to work with) leaves much to be desired. IT'S ALIVE, his most famous film, contains brilliant and horrifying ideas about the American family and its support of potentially harmful, uncaring institutions such as the drug industry, the police, and even doctors and hospitals. The film opens as proud and excited parents, Ryan and Farrell, go to the hospital to deliver their new child. Suddenly all hell breaks loose in the delivery room when Farrell gives birth to a monstrous child that kills several hospital personnel before scurrying off into the night. The reason for the mutated birth is explained by Farrell's intake of a new fertility drug that was obviously defective, produced by a major (and powerful) drug corporation. Ryan and Farrell's marriage is ripped asunder as both try to deal with what they have brought into the world. Farrell feels strong maternal instincts for the child, while Ryan wishes to kill it. Ryan aids the police in their search for his monster child, but as the hunt gets closer, he, too, begins to feel parental concern for the baby, and attempts to save it (the child is killed when Ryan is forced to throw it at the evil drug corporation executive). In the end, it is announced that another monster child has been born in a different part of the country. Though the film is well-written and fascinating thematically with small touches of comedy, at times the film is shoddy technically. Nevertheless, IT'S ALIVE went on to make more than $7 million at the boxoffice, putting it among the top low-budget money makers.

p,d&w, Larry Cohen; ph, Fenton Hamilton (Panavision, Technicolor); m, Bernard Herrmann; ed, Peter Honess; spec eff, Rick Baker; makeup, Baker.

Horror Cas. (PR:O MPAA:PG)

IT'S ALIVE II (SEE: IT LIVES AGAIN, 1978)

IT'S ALL HAPPENING (SEE: DREAM MAKER, THE, 1964, Brit.)

IT'S ALL OVER TOWN** (1963, Brit.) 55m Delmore/BL c

Lance Percival *(Richard Abel)*, William Rushton *(Fat Friend)*, Frankie Vaughan, Mr. Acker Bilk and the Paramount Jazz Band, The Springfields, The Bachelors, The Hollies, April Olrich, Jan & Kelly, Caroline Maudling, Cloda Rogers, Ingrid Anthofer, Ivor Cutler, Paul Raymond Bunnies, Wayne Gibson.

Mainly an excuse to show off some of the popular British groups of the time, of which only The Hollies have retained much prominence. Percival is the stage worker kept from his job through his daydreaming of the various bands he would rather be seeing. Slight but of some passing interest.

p, Ben Nisbet, Jacques De Lane Lea; d, Douglas Hickox; w, Stewart Farrar, Lance Percival (based on a story by Farrar); ph, (Eastmancolor).

Musical (PR:A MPAA:NR)

IT'S ALL YOURS** (1937) 80m COL bw

Madeleine Carroll *(Linda Gray)*, Francis Lederer *(Jimmy Barnes)*, Mischa Auer *(Baron Rene de Montigny)*, Grace Bradley *(Constance Marlowe)*, Victor Kilian *(City Clerk)*, George McKay *(License Clerk)*, J.C. Nugent *(E.J. Barnes)*, Richard Carle *(Judge Reynolds)*, Arthur Hoyt *(Dabney)*, Charles Waldron *(Alexander Duncan)*, Connie Boswell.

Carroll plays an attractive secretary who has recently come into money. She soon meets rich playboy Lederer, disguised as a male secretary. He takes it upon himself to protect her from Auer, playing the bad-guy Baron who is out to steal Carroll's money. Lederer loses a fist-fight with Auer, but in the end wins Carroll.

p, William Perlberg; d, Elliott Nugent; w, Mary C. McCall, Jr. (based on the story by Adelaide Heilbron); ph, Henry Freulich; ed, Gene Havlick; md, Morris W. Stoloff; art d, Stephen Goosson; cos, Kalloch; m/l, Ben Oakland, Milton Drake.

Comedy (PR:A MPAA:NR)

IT'S ALWAYS FAIR WEATHER**** (1955) 102m MGM c

Gene Kelly *(Ted Riley)*, Dan Dailey *(Doug Hallerton)*, Cyd Charisse *(Jackie Leighton)*, Dolores Gray *(Madeline Bradville)*, Michael Kidd *(Angie Valentine)*, David Burns *(Tim)*, Jay C. Flippen *(Charles Z. Culloran)*, Steve Mitchell *(Kid Mariacchi)*, Hal March *(Rocky Lazar)*, Paul Maxey *(Mr. Fielding)*, Peter Leeds *(Mr. Trasker)*, Alex Gerry *(Mr. Stamper)*, Madge Blake *(Mrs. Stamper)*, Wilson Wood

(Roy, TV Director), Richard Simmons *(Mr. Grigman)*, Almira Sessions *(Lady)*, Eugene Borden *(Chef)*.

A scathing satire of the advertising world is only part of this hard-bitten and often cynical musical that masks the seriousness of the theme with many excellent song and dance numbers. The same team that made the landmark SINGIN' IN THE RAIN got together to do this one. It had originally been conceived as sort of a sequel to ON THE TOWN, but after Sinatra took an Oscar for FROM HERE TO ETERNITY, he decided he was a thespian and not a song-and-dance man so the whole thing had to be re-thought. Sailors became soldiers and Dailey and Kidd were cast. Kelly, Dailey, and Kidd come home from WW II, dance in the streets (in the celebrated trash-can cover number), drink their ways across New York, and decide to meet exactly 10 years later. It's 1945 and the world is their oyster. But 10 years later, after a montage of news headlines and such to indicate time passing, that oyster is now spoiled. The trio come back to the same bar and all believe they will be the only one to arrive. But they all come back and learn a lot about each other and themselves. Kelly, who had dreams of being a wheeler-dealer, is now a fight promoter handling second-rate boxers. Dailey, who wanted to be a great artist, has sold out and is now an executive at an advertising agency. Kidd, who believed he had the talent to be a great chef, instead runs a small diner. The men, who were once so close and united under the banner of fighting for their country, see they have little in common and the evening disintegrates into nostalgia. Then Kelly meets Charisse, who isn't that taken by him until he mentions his feelings about his reunion. She works for a local TV station and needs guests for the talk show hosted by Gray who usually takes one small section of her egocentric program to meet "the little people who make up little ol' New York." Charisse thinks the story of these three men would be good for that segment and selfishly maneuvers the men to share their thoughts on the show. Once there, the three men's sad story is turned into a phony human interest piece, that's shoe-horned in between a biting look at Gray's TV show which features all the worst things about television, like lousy commercials, giveaways, audience participation and terrible singing (nothing's changed!). Each man comes to grips with his life and Kelly quits the fight game after knocking out his own fighter to avoid him taking a dive. Then Kelly has to get away from the bad guys on roller skates and he eventually winds up with Charisse. There are a few moments when the bad guys chase Kelly into the TV station and are whipped by Kelly, Kidd, and Dailey, and that battle is what brings the men back together with a new sense of purpose. Directors Kelly and Donen made some of the best use of the wide CinemaScope screen by splitting it to achieve a heretofore unattainable intimacy. The songs have almost nothing to do with the plot and perhaps it is that lack of organic material that caused this picture to not do the business it deserved. Some of the songs in this very ambitious and pioneering film are "Stillman's Gym," "March, March," "Why Are We Here (Blue Danube)?," "Music is Better Than Words," "Once Upon A Time," "The Time For Parting," "I Like Myself," "Baby You Knock Me Out," "Thanks A Lot But No Thanks" (Andre Previn, Betty Comden, Adolph Green), "Situation Wise," "Sleeper Phones" (Previn), "The Binge," and "Ten Year Montage" (Previn).

p, Arthur Freed; d, Stanley Donen, Gene Kelly; w, Betty Comden, Adolph Green; ph, Robert Bronnen (CinemaScope, Eastmancolor); ed, Adrienne Fazan; md, Andre Previn; art d, Cedric Gibbons, Arthur Lonergan; set d, Edwin B. Willis, Hugh Hunt; cos, Helen Rose; spec eff, Irving G. Reis, Warren Newcombe; ch, Donen, Kelly; makeup, William Tuttle.

Musical/Comedy **(PR:A MPAA:NR)**

IT'S GREAT TO BE ALIVE 1/2** (1933) 69m FOX bw

Raul Roulien *(Carlos Martin)*, Gloria Stuart *(Dorothy Wilton)*, Edna May Oliver *(Dr. Prodwell)*, Herbert Mundin *(Brooks)*, Joan Marsh *(Toots)*, Dorothy Burgess *(Al Moran)*, Emma Dunn *(Mrs. Wilton)*, Edward Van Sloan *(Dr. Wilton)*, Robert Greig *(Perkins)*.

Brazilian tenor Roulien portrays a playboy type who decides to fly the Pacific after an argument with his fiancee, Stuart. He crash-lands his plane on a remote island and is spared from deadly disease, "masuclitis," that kills off the entire world male population. After five years on the island, Roulien is discovered and is brought into the female world to be auctioned off to the highest bidder. Gangster Burgess is the one behind the auction. Roulien is rescued by the police and the international congress headed by Oliver. It's her plan to pass him around to all the women of the world, but Roulien wants no part of it. He wants to get back with Stuart, which he does. A remake of THE LAST MAN ON EARTH (1924), IT'S GREAT TO BE ALIVE bombed at the box-office possibly because of the unknown cast and strange storyline. Roulien was a big draw in the Spanish cinema and a Spanish language version of this film was made simultaneously. Songs include: "Goodbye Ladies," "I'll Build a Nest," "Women," "It's Great To Be The Only Man Alive" (William Kernell).

d, Alfred Werker; w, Paul Perez, Arthur Kober (based on a story by John D. Swain); ph, Robert Planck; ed, Barney Wolf; ch, Sammy Lee.

Science Fiction/Musical **(PR:A MPAA:NR)**

IT'S GREAT TO BE YOUNG* 1/2 (1946) 69m COL bw

Leslie Brooks *(Terry)*, Jimmy Lloyd *(Ricky Malone)*, Jeff Donnell *(Georgia Johnson)*, Robert Stanton *("Spud" Winters)*, Jack Williams *("Ivory" Timothy)*, Jack Fina *(Jack)*, Frank Orth *(Franklin Johnson)*, Ann Codee *(Mrs. Johnson)*, Pat Yankee *(Anita)*, Frank Sully *(Burkett)*, Grady Sutton *(Ambrose Kenton)*, Vernon Dent *(Pop)*, Milton DeLugg and His Swing Wing.

A group of ex-GIs decide that show biz is their lives and try to make it to the big time. They have the cliche setbacks and heartbreaks, then stage a show at a summer resort where a Broadway producer is vacationing. This lands them on Broadway. No surprise and no entertainment. Songs include, "It's Great To Be Young," "A Thousand And One Sweet Dreams," "Five Of The Best," "That Went Out With High Button Shoes," "Frankie Boogie" (Doris Fisher, Allan Roberts), "Bumble Boogie"—based on Nikolai Rimsky-Korsakov's "Flight Of The Bumble Bee" (Jack Fina).

p, Ted Richmond; d, Del Lord; w, Jack Henley (based on a story by Karen DeWolf); ph, Henry Freulich; ed, Aaron Stell; md, Saul Chaplin; art d, Sturges Carne; m/l, Allan Roberts, Doris Fisher, Jack Finn.

Musical **(PR:A MPAA:NR)**

IT'S GREAT TO BE YOUNG***

(1956, Brit.) 94m Marble Arch/Associated British-Pathe c

John Mills *(Dingle)*, Cecil Parker *(Frome)*, John Salew *(Routledge)*, Elizabeth Kentish *(Mrs. Castle)*, Mona Washbourne *(Miss Morrow)*, Mary Merrall *(Miss Wyvern)*, Derek Blomfield *(Paterson)*, Jeremy Spenser *(Nicky)*, Dorothy Bromiley *(Paulette)*, Brian Smith *(Ginger)*, Wilfred Downing *(Browning)*, Robert Dickens *(Morris)*, Dawson France *(Crowther)*, Carole Shelley *(Peggy)*, Richard O'Sullivan *(Lawson)*, Norman Pierce *(Publican)*, Eleanor Summerfield *(Barmaid)*, Bryan Forbes *(Organ Salesman)*, Marjorie Rhodes *(Landlady)*, Eddie Byrne *(Morris)*, Russell Waters *(School Inspector)*, Ruby Murray, Humphrey Lyttelton, Edna Savage.

The co-eds at a British grammar school revolt when their favorite teacher is fired. Mills is sacked by the new headmaster, Parker, because he bought musical instruments and was rehearsing the students for a national music festival. A fresh comedy with Mills at top form.

p, Victor Skutezky; d, Cyril Frankel; w, Ted Willis; ph, Gilbert Taylor (Technicolor); m, Ray Martin; ed, Max Benedict; md, Louis Levy; art d, Robert Jones.

Musical Comedy **(PR:A MPAA:NR)**

IT'S HARD TO BE GOOD**

(1950, Brit.) 93m Two Cities-RANK/Pentagon GFD bw

Jimmy Hanley *(Capt. James Gladstone Wedge VC)*, Anne Crawford *(Mary)*, Raymond Huntley *(Williams)*, Geoffrey Keen *(Sgt. Todd)*, Elwyn Brook-Jones *(Budibent)*, David Horne *(Edward Beckett)*, Joyce Carey *(Alice Beckett)*, Muriel Aked *(Ellen Beckett)*, Lana Morris *(Daphne)*, Edward Rigby *(Parkinson)*, Cyril Smith, Leslie Weston.

An ex-army officer and war hero, Hanley, has some lofty ideas and goals when he gets out of the service. He believes the problem with the world is there's not enough good-will and goes around testing his theory. The results are slightly comical, adhering more to slapstick comedy than social commentary. Crawford is the love interest who attempts to tone down Hanley's saintly outlook.

p, John Gossage; d&w, Jeffrey Dell; ph, Laurie Friedman; m, Anthony Hopkins; ed, Helga Cranston.

Comedy **(PR:A MPAA:NR)**

IT'S HOT IN HELL (SEE: MONKEY IN WINTER, A, 1962, Fr.)

IT'S HOT IN PARADISE zero

(1962, Ger./Yugo.) 86m Rapid-Intercontinental/Pacemaker bw (EIN TOTER HING IM NETZ; AKA: BODY IN THE WEB; THE SPIDER'S WEB; GIRLS OF SPIDER ISLAND; HORRORS OF SPIDER ISLAND; HOT IN PARADISE)

Alex D'Arcy *(Gary)*, Barbara Valentin, Harald Maresch, Helga Neuner, Helga Franck, Rainer Brandt, Dorothee Glocklen, Eva Schauland, Gerry Sammer.

An incredibly bad horror film made by Germans and set on a desert island where eight beautiful showgirls and their manager have been stranded. Too bad for the scantily clad (and frequently unclad) gals that their trusted manager has been bitten by a ridiculous spider-monster and has himself turned into an equally ridiculous spider-monster. Basically just an excuse to have eight voluptuous women running around on a desert island buck naked, the film can't even claim that dubious success due to the ineptness of its execution.

p, Gaston Hakim; d, Fritz Bottger [Jamie Nolan]; ph, Georg Krause; m, Karl Bette, Willy Mattes.

Horror **(PR:C MPAA:NR)**

IT'S IN THE AIR* 1/2 (1935) 80m MGM bw

Jack Benny *(Calvin Churchill)*, Ted Healy *("Clip" McGurk)*, Una Merkel *(Alice Churchill)*, Nat Pendleton *(Henry Potke)*, Mary Carlisle *(Grace Gridley)*, Grant Mitchell *(W. R. Gridley)*, Harvey Stephens *(Sidney Kendall)*, Charles Trowbridge, Johnny Arthur, Al Shean, Purnell B. Pratt, William Tannen, Phillips Smalley, Howard Hickman, Larry Wheat, Dick Dipling, Jim Toney, Maude Allen.

This weak Benny comedy understandably flopped at the box-office. He plays a gambler who's in debt and being chased by the I.R.S. His wife Merkel leaves, but Benny sets out to win her back. He gives the slip to revenue agents, then cons advertisers to put up money for a hot-air balloon in order to fly to Merkel in Palm Springs. Benny gets Healy to go with him. They safely crash-land; Benny gets his wife back; and the tax men get off his back. At the time, Benny was the top radio comedian in the U.S., but MGM's powers-that-be failed to capitalize on the popularity of the man's beloved skinflint persona.

p, E. J. Mannix; d, Charles F. Riesner; w, Bryon Morgan, Lou Lipton; ph, Charles Schoenbaum; ed, William S. Gray.

Comedy **(PR:A MPAA:NR)**

IT'S IN THE AIR*

(1940, Brit.) 74m B.S.B. bw (AKA: GEORGE TAKES THE AIR)

George Formby *(George Brown)*, Polly Ward *(Peggy)*, Garry Marsh *(Commanding Officer)*, Julien Mitchell *(Sergeant-Major)*, Jack Hobbs *(Cpl. Craig)*, C. Denier Warren *(Sir Philip Bargrave)*, Michael Shepley *(Adjutant)*, Hal Gordon *(Nobby*

Clark), Ilena Sylvia *(Anne Brown)*, Frank Leighton *(Bob Bullock)*, Jack Melford *(Pilot)*, Elliot Makeham *(Gardener)*, Joe Cunningham *(Sergeant)*, O. B. Clarence, Esma Cannon, Scruffy the Dog.

A British wartime comedy with Formby being mistaken for an RAF pilot. This creates some worn slapstick situations and a familiar stunt flying scene. An uninspired comedy that forgot to be funny.

p, Basil Dean; d&w, Anthony Kimmins; ph, Ronald Neame, Gordon Dines; m/l, George Formby, Harry Girrard, Fred E. Cliffe, Harry Parr-Davis.

Comedy **(PR:A MPAA:NR)**

IT'S IN THE BAG* (1936, Brit.) 80m WB-FN/WB bw

Jimmy Nervo *(Jimmy)*, Teddy Knox *(Teddy)*, Jack Barty *(Bert)*, George Carney *(Blumfield)*, Rene Hunter *(Ethel)*, Ursula Hirst *(Vi)*, Aubrey Dexter *(Peters)*, Hal Gordon *(Boss)*, Ernest Sefton *(Jerry Gee)*, C. Denier Warren *(Emery)*, Glen Alyn *(Fifi)*, Gaston & Andree, Charles B. Cochran's Young Ladies, Cora Beaucaire, Frederick Burtwell.

Though fired from their porter jobs, Nervo and Knox are on the up-and-up as they open a nightclub made possible by the discovery of a bunch of five pound notes. The money turns out to be counterfeit, though, putting an end to their short lived glory. The comic antics of Nervo and Knox were given little to hang plot from here. "One Shot" Beaudine did a typically hack job in the director's chair.

p, Irving Asher; d, William Beaudine; w, Brock Williams (based on a story by Russell Medcraft); ph, Basil Emmott.

Comedy **(PR:A MPAA:NR)**

IT'S IN THE BAG** (1943, Brit.) 80m But bw

Elsie Waters *(Gert)*, Doris Waters *(Daisy)*, Ernest Butcher *(Sam Braithwaite)*, Lesley Osmond *(April Vaughan)*, Gordon Edwards *(Alan West)*, Reginald Purdell *(Joe)*, Irene Handl *(Mrs. Beam)*, Anthony Holles *(Costumier)*, Tony Quinn *(Prendergast)*, Vera Bogetti *(Rose Trelawney)*, Megs Jenkins *(Peach St. Clair)*, Margaret Yarde, Edie Martin, Esma Cannon, Benita Lydell, Jonathon Field, Richard Molinas, Jack Vyvyan, Terry Conlin, Noel Dainton, Hugh Stewart.

A mad romp is spurred on by the Water's Sisters chase after a dress they have recently sold before discovering it had 20,000 pounds hidden in its creases. Their pursuit is made even more intense when Purdell discovers the secret and begins his own search. An exploding bomb finally allows the girls to grab the loot when it destroys a theater.

p, F.W. Baker; d, Herbert Mason; w, Con West.

Comedy **(PR:A MPAA:NR)**

IT'S IN THE BAG½** (1945) 87m UA bw (GB: THE FIFTH CHAIR)

Fred Allen *(Fred Floogle)*, Jack Benny *(Himself)*, William Bendix *(Himself)*, Binnie Barnes *(Eve Floogle)*, Robert Benchley *(Parker)*, Jerry Colonna *(Dr. Greengrass, Psychiatrist)*, John Carradine *(Pike)*, Gloria Pope *(Marion)*, William Terry *(Perry)*, Minerva Pious *(Mrs. Nussbaum)*, Dickie Tyler *(Homer)*, Sidney Toler *(Detective Sully)*, George Cleveland *(Hotel Manager)*, John Miljan *(Arnold)*, Ben Welden *(Monte)*, Emory Parnell *(Mr. Buddoo)*, Don Ameche, Victor Moore, Rudy Vallee *(Guest Stars)*.

Radio personality Allen plays a flea-circus operator who discovers that he's inherited $12 million from a grand uncle. He also learns that the money is missing and that most of it is stuffed in a chair. The movie revolves around Allen's frantic search for his inheritance. Allen meets Benny, who lampoons his own stingy radio character. Bendix plays a racketeer who can't abide guns being fired and runs a gang inherited from his mother. A small but lively comedy. Screenwriter Alma Reville was the wife of Alfred Hitchcock and cooperated with him on many of his early pictures including THE 39 STEPS and THE LADY VANISHES.

p, Jack H. Skirball; d, Richard Wallace; w, Lewis R. Foster, Fred Allen, Jay Dratler, Alma Reville (based on a story by Morrie Ryskind); ph, Russell Metty; m, Werner Heymann; ed, William M. Morgan; md, Charles Previn; art d, Lionel Banks.

Comedy **Cas.** **(PR:A MPAA:NR)**

IT'S IN THE BLOOD*** (1938, Brit.) 56m WB/FN-WB bw

Claude Hulbert *(Edwin Povey)*, Lesley Brook *(Jill Borden)*, James Stephenson *(Milky Joe)*, Max Leeds *(James Renton)*, Clem Lawrence *(Dave Grimmett)*, Glen Alyn *(Celestin)*, Percy Walsh *(Jules Barres)*, George Galleon *(Gendarme)*.

Milquetoast movie fan Hulbert goes off on a trip to Boulogne and finds himself caught up in an adventure beyond his imagination. First he's robbed by a group of British thieves. After returning home on an onion boat Hulbert and girl friend Brook go after the gang, who turn out to be jewel thieves. The pair are trapped in the house where the group keeps their booty and danger is imminent, but fortunately the cops arrive at the last minute to save the day. Small, but good fun in this light programmer comedy. Actor James Stephenson who had a beautiful speaking voice appeared in this film shortly before going to Hollywood to appear in such films as BEAU GESTE, THE SEA HAWK and THE LETTER. He died in 1941 of a heart attack.

p, Irving Asher; d, Gene Gerrard; w, Reginald Purdell, John Dighton, J. O. C. Orton, Brock Williams, Basil Dillon (based on the novel *The Big Picture* by David Whitelaw); ph, Basil Emmott.

Comedy **(PR:A MPAA:NR)**

IT'S LOVE AGAIN½** (1936, Brit.) 82m GAU bw

Jessie Matthews *(Elaine Bradford)*, Robert Young *(Peter Carlton)*, Sonnie Hale *(Freddie Rathbone)*, Ernest Milton *(Archibald Raymond)*, Robb Wilton *(Boy)*, Sara Allgood *(Mrs. Hopkins)*, Cyril Wells *(Gigolo)*, Warren Jenkins *(Geoffrey Woolf)*, David Horne *(Durland)*, Athene Seyler *(Mrs. Durland)*, Glennis Lorimer *(Montague's Typist)*, Robert Hale *(Col. Egerton)*, Cyril Raymond *(Montague)*, Terry-Thomas *(Extra)*.

Young is a journalist who makes up stories for his paper in order to compete with femme rival Matthews. When he makes up a person named "Mrs. Smythe-Smythe," an alleged tiger hunter from India, Matthews decides to impersonate the fictional person. She gets herself tangled up in a mess, however, when she is forced into a shooting contest. There she gives an embarrassing display of ineptitude. She finally gives up the game and weds Young. A better-than-average musical entry from Britain which includes the tunes "It's Love Again," and "Heaven In Your Arms" (Sam Coslow, Harry Woods).

p, Michael Balcon; d, Victor Saville; w, Marion Dix, Lesser Samuels, Austin Melford; ph, Glen MacWilliams; ed, Al Barnes; ch, Buddy Bradley.

Musical **(PR:A MPAA:NR)**

IT'S LOVE I'M AFTER***** (1937) 90m WB–FN bw

Leslie Howard *(Basil Underwood)*, Bette Davis *(Joyce Arden)*, Olivia de Havilland *(Marcia West)*, Eric Blore *(Digges)*, Patric Knowles *(Henry Grant)*, George Barbier *(William West)*, Spring Byington *(Aunt Ella Paisley)*, Bonita Granville *(Gracie Kane)*, E.E. Clive *(Butler)*, Veda Ann Borg *(Elsie)*, Valerie Bergere *(Joyce's Maid)*, Georgia Caine *(Mrs. Kane)*, Sarah Edwards *(Mrs. Hinkle)*, Grace Field *(Mrs. Babson)*, Harvey Clark *(Mr. Babson)*, Thomas Pogue *(Mr. Hinkle)*, Ed Mortimer *(Mr. Kane)*, Thomas R. Mills *(Butler)*, Lionel Belmore *(Friar Lawrence)*, Ellen Clancy [Janet Shaw], Patricia Walthall, Rosella Towne, Helen Valkis *(Autograph Hunters)*, Herbert Ashley *(Doorman)*, Paul Irving *(House Manager)*, Jack Mower *(Hotel Clerk)*, Irving Bacon *(Elevator Man)*, Georgie Cooper *(Woman Guest)*.

A warm, witty, wacky and wonderful romp that starts with some huge laughs and keeps on going. Howard and Davis had appeared with each other twice before, both times in heavy stories (OF HUMAN BONDAGE and THE PETRIFIED FOREST), so when they were handed the opportunity to exercise their funny sides, they jumped at the chance. It's a screwball comedy in every sense of the word, and the sharp lines are just as funny today. Howard is an egocentric matinee idol engaged to Davis, an equally famous star. They have called off their marriage 11 times because as loving as they are on stage, they constantly bicker off stage. Howard revels in the adoration of his stage-door Janies, which Davis can't stand. The most blatant swooner is de Havilland who comes to every performance and sits there starry-eyed and almost salivating. Though engaged to Knowles, that doesn't stop her from visiting the backstage dressing room and declaring her love to Howard. Later, Knowles confronts Howard and pleads with him to turn de Havilland away so he can marry the girl. Howard sees this as a chance to help Knowles and have some fun. With the help of his valet, Blore, he arrives at de Havilland's mansion and acts like the ultimate boor. Her parents are shocked, as are the relatives and servants, but as unmannerly as Howard gets, de Havilland continues to forgive him. It's a hysterical scene because there doesn't seem to be anything he can do to turn her off. One night, Howard decides to go all the way and becomes a total cad, forcing his attentions on her. Instead of being insulted, she is thrilled and the next morning tells everyone that her marriage to Knowles is cancelled. Howard is desperate to get this moon-eyed girl out of his life so he asks Davis to pose as his wife. She agrees, but has some fun on her own. She tells de Havilland to go for Howard and then informs Knowles what's happened. Eventually, de Havilland is sure she can get Howard and tells everyone that she intends to marry the man as soon as he can be free of Davis. It's then that Davis thinks enough is enough and shows de Havilland phony photos of two adorable children and tells the girl that these are hers by Howard. Davis says she has no recourse but to sue for desertion if de Havilland runs off with Howard, and name her as correspondent. Upon hearing this, de Havilland is finally doused and tells Howard she will have nothing more to do with him and is going back to Knowles. Relieved, Howard and Davis return to the stage, and she makes plans to get him to the altar before he changes his mind. There is not one satirical point that's missed in Robinson's screenplay. It's diverting and bright, and Mayo's direction of the two stars is noteworthy in that he keeps them both in hand. It looks as though they've been playing this comedy for five years onstage before taking it to the screen. Each scene is a diamond on its own, and put together, a tiara. Davis never thought much of this movie but stars are not often the best judges of their own work. This is a prime example. It's the best comedy she ever made and one of the best to come out of Warner Brothers. Another great one from Wallis who ranks on top with Goldwyn, Zanuck, Selznick and Griffith.

p, Hal B. Wallis; d, Archie Mayo; w, Casey Robinson (based on the story "Gentleman After Midnight" by Maurice Hanline); ph, James Van Trees; m, Heinz Roemheld; ed, Owen Marks, Tony Martinelli; md, Leo F. Forbstein; art d, Carl Jules Weyl; cos, Orry-Kelly.

Comedy **PR:A MPAA:NR)**

IT'S MAGIC (SEE: ROMANCE ON THE HIGH SEAS, 1948)

IT'S MY LIFE (SEE: MY LIFE TO LIVE, 1963, Fr.)

IT'S MY TURN*** (1980) 91m Rastar-Martin Elfand/COL c

Jill Clayburgh *(Kate Gunzinger)*, Michael Douglas *(Ben Lewin)*, Charles Grodin *(Homer)*, Beverly Garland *(Emma)*, Steven Hill *(Jacob)*, Teresa Baxter *(Maryanne)*, Joan Copeland *(Rita)*, John Gabriel *(Hunter)*, Charles Kimbrough *(Jerome)*, Roger Robinson *(Flicker)*, Jennifer Salt *(Maisie)*, Daniel Stern *(Cooperman)*, Dianne Wiest *(Gail)*, Robert Ackerman *(Good Will Man)*, Ralph Mauro *(Jerry Lanz Man)*, Noah Hathaway *(Homer's Son)*, Marlyn Gates *(Homer's Daughter)*, Raymond Singer *(Rabbi)*, Ronald C. Frazier, Edwin J. McDonough, Toshi Toda *(Professors)*.

Clayburgh stars in this well-acted but typical, romantic comedy, as a spirited mathematics professor who is perfectly content in her relationship with Chicago building developer Grodin. She is soon surprised to find herself falling in love with

Douglas, the son of her father's bride-to-be. Douglas pursues Clayburgh, but when she responds to his advances he is shocked at her forwardness and backs down.

p, Martin Elfand; d, Claudia Weill; w, Eleanor Bergstein; ph, Bill Butler (Metrocolor); m, Patrick Williams; ed, Byron "Buzz" Brandt, Marjorie Fowler, James Coblenz; prod d, Jack DeGovia; set d, Geoff Hubbard; cos, Ruth Myers; m/l, "It's My Turn" (sung by Diana Ross).

Romance/Comedy **Cas.** **(PR:C MPAA:R)**

IT'S NEVER TOO LATE** (1958, Brit.) 95m Park Lane/ABF-Pathe c

Phyllis Calvert *(Laura Hammond)*, Patrick Barr *(Charles Hammond)*, Susan Stephen *(Tessa Hammond)*, Guy Rolfe *(Stephen Hodgson)*, Jean Taylor Smith *(Grannie)*, Sarah Lawson *(Anne)*, Delphi Lawrence *(Mrs. Dixon)*, Peter Hammond *(Tony)*, Richard Leech *(John)*, Robert Ayres *(Crane)*, Peter Illing *(Guggenheimer)*, Stanley Maxted *(Lee Sax)*, Irene Handl *(New Neighbor)*, Barbara Cavan *(Nurse)*, John Fernald *(Producer)*, Shirley Ann Field.

Calvert is a housewife who is the calm eye of the family hurricane. Her husband Barr is a loafer; Smith is her grumbling mother, Stephen, her daughter with a different emotional crisis for every hour of the day, and another daughter is constantly fighting with her husband. When Calvert's sideline of writing gets her noticed by a film producer, she's off to Hollywood to work on a script. However, compared to her family the wild ways of California are much too sedate and Calvert must return to the turmoil of her family to get the job done. Some clever moments but the film suffers from a staginess that makes this a mildly amusing comedy at best.

p, George Pitcher; d, Michael McCarthy; w, Edward Dryhurst (based on the play by Felicity Douglas); ph, C. Pennington-Richards (Eastmancolor); m, Wally Stott.

Comedy **(PR:A MPAA:NR)**

IT'S NEVER TOO LATE TO MEND ** 1/2** (1937, Brit.) 67m George King/MGM bw

Tod Slaughter *(Squire Meadows)*, Marjorie Taylor *(Susan Merton)*, Jack Livesey *(Tom Robinson)*, Ian Colin *(George Fielding)*, Lawrence Hanray *(Lawyer Crawley)*, D. J. Williams *(Farmer Merton)*, Roy Russell *(Reverend Eden)*, Johnny Singer *(Joseph)*.

Great fun in the old cloak-and-dagger melodrama style. Slaughter is a heavy breathing nasty out to marry Taylor against the young maiden's will. He sends her fiance, Livesey, off to jail but is thwarted in the end as the young lovers are reunited. Played in an exaggerated, bigger-than-life manner, this nineteenth-century-based melodrama is a good enough outing, particularly for fans of camp.

p, George King; d, David Macdonald; w, H. F. Maltby (based on the play by Charles Reade, Arthur Shirley).

Drama **(PR:A MPAA:NR)**

IT'S NOT CRICKET ** 1/2** (1937, Brit.) 63m WB/FN-WB bw

Claude Hulbert *(Willie)*, Henry Kendall *(Henry)*, Betty Lynne *(Yvonne)*, Sylvia Marriott *(Jane)*, Clifford Heatherley *(Sir George Harlow)*, Violet Farebrother *(Lady Harlow)*, Frederick Burtwell *(Morton)*.

When Lynne is all but lost by her husband because of his cricket matches, she decides to get even. Incorporating her husband's mousey pal Hulbert, Lynne stages a ruse that the couple have run off to Paris in the throes of love. The scheme works as Lynne gets back her husband and Hulbert becomes engaged to his girlfriend, Marriott. An enjoyable enough romp with some good moments.

p, Irving Asher; d, Ralph Ince; w, Henry Kendall; ph, Basil Emmott.

Comedy **(PR:A MPAA:NR)**

IT'S NOT CRICKET ** 1/2** (1949, Brit.) 77m Gainsborough/GFD bw

Basil Radford *(Maj. Bright)*, Naunton Wayne *(Capt. Early)*, Susan Shaw *(Primrose Brown)*, Maurice Denham *(Otto Fisch)*, Alan Wheatley *(Felix)*, Nigel Buchanan *(Gerald Lawson)*, Jane Carr *(Virginia Briscoe)*, Leslie Dwyer *(Batman)*, Patrick Waddington *(Valentine Christmas)*, Edward Lexy *(Brig. Falcon)*, Frederick Piper *(Yokel)*, Diana Dors *(Blonde)*, Mary Hinton *(Lady Lawson)*, Margaret Withers, Brian Oulton, Cyril Chamberlain, Charles Cullum, John Mann, Hal Osmond, Sheila Huntington, John Warren, Viola Lyel, Arthur Hambling, Hamilton Keene, Meinhart Maur, John Boxer.

After Radford and Wayne accidentally let Nazi Denham escape from their guard, the pair are drummed out of the army. They open up a private detective agency but are still given trouble by Denham, who follows the team along on every case. In a crazed climax, the three get involved in a wild game of cricket where a stolen diamond is concealed inside the ball. Some good belly laughs and at times uproarious, though occasionally the comedy gets carried away with itself.

p, Betty Box; d, Alfred Roome, Roy Rich; w, Bernard McNab, Gerard Bryant, Lyn Lockwood; ph, Gordon Lang.

Comedy **(PR:A MPAA:NR)**

IT'S NOT THE SIZE THAT COUNTS* 1/2

(1979, Brit.) 90m Betty E. Box-Ralph Thomas/Joseph Brenner c (AKA: PERCY'S PROGRESS)

Leigh Lawson *(Percy)*, Elke Sommer *(Clarissa)*, Denholm Elliott *(Emmanuel Whitebread)*, Judy Geeson *(Dr. Fairweather)*, Milo O'Shea *(Dr. Klein)*, Vincent Price *(Stavos Mammonian)*, Julie Ege *(Miss Hanson)*, George Coulouris *(Professor)*, Harry H. Corbett, Adrienne Posta.

A tame sequel to the British comedy PERCY, the infamous tale of the first man to receive a below-the-belt transplant. This time the entire population of the world is contaminated by a chemical in the drinking water, leaving only Lawson unaffected. The result is Lawson being the only man left who has not become impotent. Like its predecessor, this film has a promising premise which never delivers.

p, Betty E. Box; d, Ralph Thomas; w, Sid Colin, Ian LaFrenais (based on a story by Harry Corbett); ph, Tony Imi (Eastmancolor); m, Tony Macaulay; ed, Ray Watts.

Comedy **(PR:O MPAA:R)**

IT'S ONLY MONEY, 1951 (SEE: DOUBLE DYNAMITE, 1951)

IT'S ONLY MONEY*** (1962) 84m York Pictures-Jerry Lewis/PAR bw

Jerry Lewis *(Lester March)*, Zachary Scott *(Gregory DeWitt)*, Joan O'Brien *(Wanda Paxton)*, Mae Questel *(Cecilia Albright)*, Jesse White *(Pete Flint)*, Jack Weston *(Leopold)*, Ted De Corsia *(Policeman)*, Pat Dahl, Francine York *(Sexy Girls)*, Barbara Pepper *(Fishing Woman)*, Mike Ross *(Policeman)*, Dick Whittinghill *(TV Speaker)*, Francesca Bellini *(Model on Beach)*, Gary Lewis *(Lester as a Boy)*, Alberto Morin, Milton Frome, Del Moore.

This Jerry Lewis vehicle sees him making a return to the kind of slapstick and craziness that won him such popularity in his earlier films. He plays an aspiring private eye who, with his friend, White, watches a TV newscast where spinster, Questel, offers a reward to locate her missing nephew, who also happens to be heir to a billion dollar electronics empire. Lewis, hoping to play detective, goes to Questel's mansion and is identified as the missing nephew by Questel's money-grabbing attorney, Scott. He tries to kill Lewis in a multitude of slapstick ways, but Lewis seems to bounce back from these attempts in a typically zany manner. Family nurse, O'Brien, recognizes that Lewis is the heir, and informs the confused dope. Scott beefs up his murder attempts, nearly succeeding when they release a threatening barrage of lawn mowers. However, a happy ending is had as the crooks are apprehended, leaving Lewis with his fortune and loving nurse, O'Brien.

p, Paul Jones; d, Frank Tashlin; w, John Fenton Murray; ph, W. Wallace Kelley; m, Walter Scharf; ed, Arthur P. Schmidt; art d, Hal Pereira, Tambi Larsen; cos, Edith Head; spec eff, John P. Fulton, Farciot Edouart; ch, Bobby Van.

Comedy **(PR:A MPAA:NR)**

IT'S SAM SMALL AGAIN (SEE: SAM SMALL LEAVES HOME, 1937, Brit.)

IT'S THAT MAN AGAIN** (1943, Brit.) 84m Gainsborough/GFD bw

Tommy Handley *(Mayor Handley)*, Greta Gynt *(Stella Ferris)*, Jack Train *(Lefty/Funf)*, Sidney Keith *(Sam Scram)*, Horace Percival *(Ali Oop/Cecil)*, Dorothy Summers *(Mrs. Mop)*, Dino Galvani *(Signor Soso)*, Clarence Wright *(Clarence)*, Leonard Sharp *(Claude)*, Claude Bailey *(C.B. Cato)*, Vera Frances *(Daisy)*, Jean Kent *(Kitty)*, Richard George, Raymond Glendenning, Peter Noble, Franklin Bennett.

In order to save the war ravaged Olympic Theater, Handley, the Mayor of Foaming-at-the Mouth, will go to any length. After begging, borrowing, and outright stealing funds he appropriates the rights to a new play by an alcoholic writer. He stages the show, all the while fleeing creditors. He can't escape the students of a dramatic academy though, as they come to ruin the show after Handley has cheated them. This war-time comedy has some genuinely funny moments but never rises to the fevered pitch that would really give this the needed craziness. It's taken from a delightfully loopy British radio show but the translation to screen just doesn't work.

p, Edward Black; d, Walter Forde; w, Howard Irving Young, Ted Kavanagh (based on the radio series by Kavanagh).

Comedy **(PR:A MPAA:NR)**

IT'S TOUGH TO BE FAMOUS** (1932) 80m FN-WB bw

Douglas Fairbanks, Jr. *(Scotty McClenahan)*, Mary Brian *(Janet)*, Oscar Apfel *(Boynton)*, Emma Dunn *(Moms)*, Walter Catlett *(Chapin)*, J. Carroll Naish *(Lt. Blake)*, David Landau *(Steve)*, Claire MacDowell *(Mrs. Porter)*, Louise Beavers *(Ada)*, Ivan Linow *(Ole Olafson)*, Harold Minjir *(Sutter)*, Lillian Bond, Terrence Ray.

Fairbanks, Jr. plays a hero that doesn't want to be one. The story was based on a novel that wasn't even in the bookstores before the film was out. He is a young submarine officer, whose sub has sunk. To save the men, he sends them out on the torpedo tubes, sacrificing himself in the process, but Navy divers get to him just in time. He receives a big welcome back in New York, complete with ticker-tape parade and all types of offers from media-hungry firms. To escape, he marries his long-time girlfriend, Brian, but the continued barrage of publicity nearly drives them apart. A good early film that shows our obsession with heroes and how we sometimes smother them in the process.

d, Alfred E. Green; w, Robert Lord (based on the story "The Goldfish Bowl" by Mary McCall); ph, Sol Polito, Byron Haskin; ed, Jack Killifer; m/l, "Scotty Boy" (sung by Clarence Nordstrom).

Drama **(PR:A MPAA:NR)**

IT'S TRAD, DAD! (SEE: RING-A-DING RHYTHM, 1962, Brit.)

IT'S TURNED OUT NICE AGAIN (SEE: TURNED OUT NICE AGAIN, 1941, Brit.)

IT'S WHAT'S HAPPENING (SEE: HAPPENING, THE, 1967)

IT'S YOU I WANT** (1936, Brit.) 73m BL bw

Seymour Hicks *(Victor Delaney)*, Marie Lohr *(Constance Gilbert)*, Hugh Wakefield *(Otto Gilbert)*, Jane Carr *(Melisande)*, Lesley Wareing *(Anne Vernon)*, H.G. Stoker *(Braille)*, Gerald Barry *(Maj. Entwhistle)*, Ronald Waters *(Jimmy Watts)*, Dorothy Hammond *(Lady Maureen)*.

Essentially a filmed stage play, this dry British comedy is set mainly in the flat of Hicks, a 50-year-old playboy, who is shocked to discover his place being runover by flirtatious women, married friends, their mistresses, and a madcap selection of comic results. The single location adds to the claustrophobic confines of the stage in this moderately funny film.

p, Herbert Smith; d, Ralph Ince; w, Cyril Campion (based on the play by Maurice Braddell); ph, George Stretton, Harry Rose.

Comedy (PR:A MPAA:NR)

ITALIAN CONNECTION, THE**

(1973, U.S./Ital./Ger.) 87m Cineproduzioni Daunia 70-Hermes Synchron/AIP c (LA MALA ORDINA; AKA: MANHUNT)

Mario Adorf *(Luca Canali)*, Henry Silva *(Dave)*, Woody Strode *(Frank)*, Adolfo Celi *(Don Vito)*, Luciana Paluzzi *(Eva)*, Sylva Koscina *(Lucia)*, Cyril Cusack *(Corso)*, Franco Fabrizi *(Enrico)*, Femi Benussi *(Nana)*, Gianni Macchia *(Nicolo)*, Francesca Romana Coluzzi *(Triney)*.

On the coat-tails of THE FRENCH CONNECTION, this partly-dubbed picture tells the story of a Milano pimp, Adorf, who is framed in a major heroin bust. With no idea of what is going on, Adorf suddenly finds himself with a contract on his head. His wife, Koscina, is murdered by the hoods, but Adorf is able to finally kill off hitmen Strode and Silva.

d, Fernando Di Leo; w, Di Leo, Augusto Finocchi, Ingo Hermann (based on a story by Di Leo); ph, Franco Villa (Eastmancolor); m, Armando Trovaioli; ed, Amedeo Giomini; set d, Francesco Cuppini.

Crime/Action (PR:O MPAA:R)

ITALIAN JOB, THE 1/2** (1969, Brit.) 100m Oakhurst/PAR c

Michael Caine *(Charlie Croker)*, Noel Coward *(Mr. Bridger)*, Benny Hill *(Professor Simon Peach)*, Raf Vallone *(Altabani)*, Tony Beckley *(Freddie)*, Rossano Brazzi *(Beckerman)*, Maggie Blye *(Lorna)*, Irene Handl *(Miss Peach)*, John Le Mesurier *(Governor)*, Fred Emney *(Birkenshaw)*, Graham Payn *(Keats)*, Michael Standing *(Arthur)*, Harry Baird *(Big William)*, Robert Rietty *(Police Chief)*, Simon Dee *(Shirtmaker)*, Lelia Goldoni *(Mme. Beckerman)*, George Innes *(Bill Bailey)*, Robert Powell *(Yellow)*, John Forgeham *(Frank)*, Derek Ware *(Rozzer)*, Frank Jarvis *(Roger)*, Stanley Caine *(Coco)*, John Clive *(Garage Manager)*, Barry Cox *(Chris)*, David Salamone *(Dominic)*, Richard Essame *(Tony)*, Mario Volgoi *(Manzo)*, Renato Romano *(Cosca)*, Timothy Bateson *(Dentist)*, Arnold Diamond *(Senior Computer Room Official)*, Alistair Hunter *(Warder in Prison Cinema)*, Louis Mansi *(Computer Room Official)*, Franco Novelli *(Altabani's Driver)*, Henry McGee *(Tailor)*, Valerie Leon, Dave Kelly, Lana Gatto, John Morris.

Caine is a small-time crook who, with British patriot Coward, carries out a planned robbery of a gold shipment. Their scheme involves causing a major traffic jam in the middle of Turin, Italy, where they steal the ingots from an armored car. The gold is then stashed in a bus, and the predictable chase ensues. The fleet of cars travels around and about the winding Swiss mountains, with the crooks' bus nearly going over the edge. They teeter on the brink of disaster for a few moments before they all make it to safety. Hill plays an insane computer wiz who joins up with Caine and Coward.

p, Michael Deeley; d, Peter Collinson; w, Troy Kennedy Martin; ph, Douglas Slocombe (Panavision, Eastmancolor); m, Quincy Jones; ed, John Trumper; prod d, Disley Jones; art d, Michael Knight; cos, Dinah Greet; spec eff, Pat Moore, Ken Morris; m/l, "On Days Like These" Jones, Don Black (sung by Matt Monro), "Getta Bloomin' Move On!" Jones, Black (sung by The Italian Job); stunts, L'Equipe Remy Julienne; makeup, Freddie Williamson.

Crime/Action (PR:A MPAA:G)

ITALIAN MOUSE, THE

(SEE: MAGIC WORLD OF TOPO GIGIO, THE, 1961, Ital.)

ITALIAN SECRET SERVICE** (1968, Ital.) 105m Cineriz c

Nino Manfredi *(Natalino)*, Francoise Prevost *(Elvira)*, Clive Revill *(Charles)*, Jean Sobiewski *(Edward)*, Giampiero Albertini *(Ottone)*, Georgia Moll *(Secret Agent)*, Gastone Moschin *(Avvocato)*, Alvero Piccardi *(Giro)*, Enzo Andronico *(Femore)*.

Manfredi is a former hero of the Italian Resistance who, as a normal civilian, is a total failure. He is hired by U.S. agents to eliminate Sobiewski, a neo-Nazi spy who is trying to get his soft drink formula to the Communists. Manfredi's payment is $100,000, but his wife, Prevost, finds a killer who will do the job for half the price. He, in turn, hires another one and each one in turn another, until a hit-squad of five are on the loose. Expectedly, the assassination is botched. The end sees Sobiewski confessing and then committing suicide. An occasionally fresh satire on the perils of secret agents.

p, Angelo Rizzoli; d, Luigi Comencini; w, Leo Benvenuti, Piero De Bernardi, Massimo Patrizi, Comencini; ph, Armando Nannuzzi (Eastmancolor); m, Fiorenzo Carpi; art d, Carlo Egidi.

Comedy (PR:C MPAA:NR)

ITALIANI BRAVA GENTE

(SEE: ITALIANO BRAVA GENTE, 1965, Ital./USSR)

ITALIANO BRAVA GENTE**

(1965, Ital./USSR) 156m Galatea-Coronet-Mosfilm/EM bw (ITALIANI BRAVA GENTE; ONI SHLI NA VOSTOK; AKA: ATTACK AND RETREAT)

Arthur Kennedy *(Ferro Maria Ferri)*, Zhanna Prokhorenko *(Katya)*, Raffaele Pisu *(Gabrielli)*, Tatyana Samoylova *(Sonya)*, Andre Checchi *(Sermonti)*, Riccardo Cucciolla *(Sanna)*, Valeriy Somov *(Giuliani)*, Peter Falk *(Medic Captain)*, Nino Vingelli *(Amalfitano)*, Lev Prygunov *(Bazzocchi)*, Grigoriy Mikhaylov *(Russian Partisan)*, Gino Pernice *(Collidi)*, Boris Kozhukhov *(A Major)*, Vincenzo Polizzi *(A Sicilian)*, S. Lukyanov *(Partisan Commander)*, I. Paramonov *(German Deserter)*, Yuriy Nazarov *(Russian Prisoner)*, E. Knausmyuller *(German General)*, Otar Koberidze *(Wounded Italian)*, Ya. Yanakiyev, A. Sakhnovskiy, E. Lezhdey, D. Stolyarskaya, L. Masokha, V. Golovnenko, N. Nikitina, L. Ulyanenko, V. Berezko.

An international cast of Italians, Russians, and Americans brings to life this WW II tale about the savage ways of the German troops. After a small act of kindness, an Italian squadron bands together with Russian prisoners who are brutally treated by their German captors. Much of the malicious treatment comes from Fascist leader Kennedy, who pushes the Italians too far and pays for it with his life. This interesting war picture about loyalty and the bonds between soldiers was excellently photographed on location in the Ukraine.

p, Lionello Santi; d, Giuseppe DeSantis; w, DeSantis, Ennio de Concini, Sergey Smirnov, Augusto Frassinetti, Giandomentico Giagni (based on a story by de Concini, DeSantis); ph, Antonio Secchi, V. Khovanskaya; m, Armando Trovajoli; ed, Mario Serandrei; art d, David Vinitskiy; set d, Ermanno Manco; spec eff, Boris Travkin, A. Rudachenko.

War (PR:A MPAA:NR)

IVAN GROZNYI

(SEE: IVAN THE TERRIBLE, PARTS I & II, 1947, 1958, USSR)

IVAN THE TERRIBLE****

(Part I, 1947, USSR) 96m Central Cinema/Artkino bw (Part II, 1959, USSR) 87m Central Cinema-Alma Ata-Sovexportfilm/Janus bw/c (IVAN GROZNYI)

Nikolai Cherkassov *(Tsar Ivan IV)*, Serafima Birman *(The Boyarina Efrosinia Staritskaya, Tsar's Aunt)*, Pavel Kadochnikov *(Vladimir Andreyevich Staritsky)*, Mikhail Zharov *(Malyuta Skuratov)*, Andrei Abrikosov *(Boyar Fyodor Kolychev)*, Alexander Mgebrov *(Archbishop Pimen)*, Nikolai Nazvanov *(Prince Andrei Kurbsky)*, Alexei Buchma *(Alexei Basmanov)*, Mikhail Kuznetsov *(Fyodor Basmanov)*, Vladimir Balashov *(Pyotr Volynets)*, Pavel Massalsky *(King Sigismund Augustus of Poland)*, Ludmila Tselikovskaya *(Anastasia, the Tsarina)*, Vsevolod Pudovkin *(Nikola, a Beggar Simpleton)*, Maxim Mikhailov *(Archdeacon)*, Erik Pyriev *(Tsar Ivan as a Child)*, Ada Voitsik *(Yelena Glinskaya)*.

As you can see, the first part was released in 1947 and 12 years passed until the second film came out. There are several reasons for the wait, including Eisenstein's fall from Soviet favor (especially Stalin's), and the second half was held back until three years after the leader's death. The picture was actually completed many years before (the director died in 1948), but politics not only makes strange bedfellows, it makes for strange censorship. This film has been wrongfully called "a classic" but what most people are remembering is Eisenstein's body of work, not IVAN THE TERRIBLE specifically. He shot it without a script, just notes and a notion, and that lack of preparation is evident immediately and gets audiences infuriated—as it did when the film was shown in Paris and the audience was alternately laughing and booing. Cherkassov is young Ivan, the new Czar. The coronation scene goes on for eons and Eisenstein cuts from face to face in the crowd, with each actor mugging more than the one before. For some unknown reason, Cherkassov is next seen dying and he wills all to his infant son in front of several witnesses who gather for his demise. But he fools them all and pulls through. Nazvanov, the ambitious commander of the army, wants to see the Czar dead because he has eyes for Tselikovskaya, the empress. Birman, the wicked aunt of the Czar, puts some poison in a goblet and his wife drinks it and dies. In part two, the final sequence of which is in color, Birman wants to put her own dim-witted son in office. The Czar dresses his retarded nephew in the official clothing and the boy is mistakenly killed by an assassin. Birman falls apart at the news but Cherkassov can now continue his work as Czar. Eisenstein wanted to make three films but he died before he could. This was a terrible way for such a monumental talent to go out but he had become so egotistical that one wonders if De Palma, Cimino and Altman take him as their inspiration. In the end, no one could tell him anything. It's a big story and no expense was spared (what the heck, slave laborers as extras are easy to come by in the USSR). He tried to do a Russian version of Shakespearean tragedy and fell several steppes short. In the end, very few people cared about the Czar, Czarina, or even all the little Czardines that never were born. It was choppy, poorly edited, hammily acted, and yet it survives for its scope and the fact that it is but one of a few films done by an acknowledged master. He should have stopped with ALEXANDER NEVSKY. (In Russian; English subtitles.)

p,d&w, Sergei Eisenstein; ph, Edward Tisse, Andrei Moskvin; m, Sergei Prokofiev; art d, Isaac Shpinel; cos, Isaac Shpinel; subtitles, Charles Clement.

Historical Drama Cas. (PR:A MPAA:NR)

IVAN'S CHILDHOOD (SEE: MY NAME IS IVAN, 1963, USSR)

IVANHOE**** (1952, Brit.) 106m MGM c

Robert Taylor *(Ivanhoe)*, Elizabeth Taylor *(Rebecca)*, Joan Fontaine *(Rowena)*, George Sanders *(De Bois-Guilbert)*, Emlyn Williams *(Wamba)*, Robert Douglas *(Sir Hugh De Bracy)*, Finlay Currie *(Cedric)*, Felix Aylmer *(Isaac)*, Francis De Wolff *(Font De Boeuf)*, Guy Rolfe *(Prince John)*, Norman Wooland *(King Richard)*, Basil Sydney *(Waldemar Fitzurse)*, Harold Warrender *(Locksley)*, Patrick Holt *(Philip De Malvoisin)*, Roderick Lovell *(Ralph de Vipont)*, Sebastian Cabot *(Clerk of Copmanhurst)*, John Ruddock *(Hundebert)*, Michael Brennan *(Baldwin)*, Megs Jenkins *(Servant to Isaac)*, Valentine Dyall *(Norman Guard)*, Lionel Harris *(Roger of Bermondsley)*, Carl Jaffe *(Austrian Monk)*.

Next to QUO VADIS, also starring the inimitable Robert Taylor, IVANHOE was one of the biggest, most lavish color films of the early 1950s, a box office smash and a superbly crafted production on every level. This full-blown epic contains wonderful pageantry, intrigue, romance, and absorbing action, as well as an anti-Semitic subplot intelligently treated. The film was exceptionally loyal to the celebrated Sir Walter Scott novel published in 1819, where fact, fiction, and legend are excitingly blended. It is 1190 and Robert Taylor, as the brave knight Sir Wilfred of Ivanhoe, returns secretly to England, from the Crusades. He has served England's King Richard the Lionhearted well in the Third Crusade, but the king has been captured and held for ransom in Austria. It is Taylor's job to raise the enormous sum to free

Richard (Wooland). Taylor is a Saxon knight, son of Saxon lord Currie, who more or less disowned his son when he went to fight with Richard, a Norman king. Taylor encounters on his route home three Norman knights—Sanders, Douglas and DeWolff—all in league with Prince John (Rolfe), who intends to usurp his missing brother, Richard. Taylor tells the knights that Currie's castle is nearby if they should wish to seek shelter for the night, and he escorts them to his father's estates. Watching this encounter is Warrender, playing Locksley (Robin Hood), and his woodsmen who were about to drive arrows into the hated Norman knights. But, seeing Taylor with the Normans, Warrender holds his men back, telling them he will wait to see what Taylor is up to. The Norman knights are given a cool reception by Currie but they are nevertheless extended the hospitality of the day. At dinner these knights meet Currie's ward, the beautiful Fontaine, whom Douglas immediately covets. Sitting at the end of the table is Taylor, Fontaine's true love, who is recognized by his father when he toasts King Richard but Currie refuses to immediately talk to his errant son. He later communicates with Taylor through his servant-fool Williams. After Taylor leaves the castle, with Williams as his newly appointed squire, he rescues a rich Jew, Aylmer, from anti-Semitic Normans and is later given jewels by Aylmer's grateful daughter, Elizabeth Taylor, so he can buy horse and armor to enter the jousting tournament at Ashby and win more money to ransom Richard. Before he leaves Aylmer, the patriarch promises Robert Taylor that he will help raise a great deal of money from his people to be put toward the ransom. It is also clear that Elizabeth loves the heroic and noble Robert from the first moment she sees him and that he loves her but they also know that their stations in life make it virtually impossible for them to ever wed. Robert Taylor enters the lists as Ashby, where all the Normans are successful until his appearance, disguised in all-black armor, riding a magnificent black horse. He challenges all five Norman champions by riding past their tents and striking their shields with his lance, vexing Prince John (Rolfe). One by one, Taylor unseats the Norman knights, including DeWolff, Douglas, and even Sanders, but is himself critically wounded. Before meeting the enemy he dedicates his upcoming battle to Elizabeth Taylor, causing the assembled crowds to gossip over his selection of a Jewess. This does not go unnoticed by Sanders who spies the beautiful girl and vows to make her his own. After Taylor wins three jousts, Rolfe reluctantly gives him the tiara to be worn by the queen of the tournament and the knight offers it to Saxon princess Fontaine, which brings forth cheers from Warrender and his men. After the fifth and final joust with Sanders, where both men are carried from the field wounded, Taylor is visited in his tent by Elizabeth Taylor and by Fontaine, who is sent by Currie to aid his son. Elizabeth insists upon treating the serious wounds of the champion and Fontaine yields to her medical expertise. He is nursed back to health by Elizabeth and the two fall even deeper in love. Rolfe now learns that Robert Taylor and Currie are behind the movement to pay the ransom for his brother, which he seeks to quash, intending to let Richard rot in the Austrian prison and put himself upon the throne of England. He orders Sanders and his knights to crush the movement. Sanders kidnaps Currie, Fontaine, Aylmer, and Elizabeth Taylor, taking them to the great fortress of Torquilstone Castle which is commanded by DeWolff. Here Douglas tells Fontaine he intends to have her as his own and Sanders makes his lecherous moves on Elizabeth Taylor. As soon as Robert Taylor hears of the kidnaping, he rides alone to the castle and offers to give himself up to the Norman knights if they free their prisoners. Sanders gives his word as a knight that this will be done but as soon as Taylor is inside the castle, that word is broken and Taylor is brought to the dungeon where Currie, Aylmer, and Williams are being held captive. Then Warrender appears with a huge army of Saxon bowmen and demands the release of the prisoners. DeWolff's answer is to bring Robert Taylor to the highest battlement and threaten to have his throat cut if the Saxons attack. A well-aimed arrow kills the executioner holding Taylor and the knight battles his way to the dungeon while the Saxons besiege the castle. Robert Taylor frees his father Currie, Williams, and Aylmer and they battle through in the now burning castle. DeWolff drives Williams into a burning corridor and the valiant squire is killed when the roof and floor collapse in flames. Taylor then hacks DeWolff to death. Taylor is able to save Fontaine after subduing Douglas but the wily Sanders escapes the Saxon-conquered castle with Elizabeth Taylor. She is put on trial and condemned as a witch before Rolfe but Robert Taylor appears and demands that he be able to defend her under the knightly code of "trial by combat." Sanders is ordered to represent the crown (he is now a villain in a no-win situation, having to fight for the right to execute the woman he wishes to save). Robert Taylor and Sanders meet in a to-the-death combat, unhorsing each other and then going at each other with ax and mace, hammering their shields to pulps. Taylor finally gets in a blow with the ax that mortally wounds Sanders. As he dies, he vows his eternal and posthumous love for Elizabeth Taylor. Just then Richard appears, having been freed with the ransom money Robert Taylor has provided. He banishes Rolfe from England, along with his evil followers, and asks that Norman and Saxon live as one people. Robert Taylor then swears his love to the woman he intends to marry, Fontaine. IVANHOE is correct in almost every detail and on a grand scale, with majestic and historically accurate sets brilliantly reconstructed by Junge. The costuming is also precise to the 12th Century, painstakingly created by Furse. MGM spared no expense in making IVANHOE, and this became the costliest epic ever produced in England. The truth is that the studio had no choice. MGM had accumulated millions of dollars in British banks but was restrained from taking this money out of the country; the studio had to spend it in England and it was spent on IVANHOE. Almost every square foot of Boreham Wood Studios, outside of London, a sprawling 120 acres, was employed in shooting the film. The enormous Torquilstone Castle was built on a full-scale level, an exact replica of a 12th Century fortress with experts from the London Museum on hand to make sure each stone was authentic looking. A moat 20 feet wide and 10 feet deep was cut around the castle (a set later used in the filming of THE WARRIORS with Errol Flynn in 1955) which took two years to assemble. More than 1,000 extras were used in the battle scenes depicting the siege of the castle, which runs more than 30 minutes, expertly directed by action helmsman Thorpe and cleverly edited by Clarke, quick intercutting that kept the pace charging along to sustain viewer interest. Managing the enormous crowds, particularly the battling knights and bowmen, required military training by a bevy of army experts. Scores of stuntmen were employed and their feats recorded on film are spectacular, many falling from the high battlements into the moat during the siege. Colonel Linden White, one of the military advisers for the film, later commented: "How any old-time knight fought for years without injury is a mystery. The chain mail armor of Ivanhoe's time was like the mesh rings in a modern woman's purse. A pointed barb could go through. The 12- and 15-foot lances were lethal weapons. We made them as replicas, but with hollow centers and rubber ends. We had to design special saddles so that a falling rider wouldn't be trampled by a horse, and we had one of the hardest jobs teaching players how to charge at full speed with a 40-to-60 pound suit of armor. We had some accidents, but luckily nothing too serious." Robert Taylor is a standout as the title character, forceful and confident in his role of chivalric hero. He read the script of Dore Shary's pet project and then told MGM that he preferred to do westerns, but he was in England preparing for the role of IVANHOE the next week all the same. The heavy armor and weighty swords wore Taylor out and he later wrote to a friend: "I'm getting mighty tired of those iron jockstraps!" What enticed the actor into the role, he later admitted, was that it would also star Elizabeth Taylor. He considered Elizabeth Taylor the most beautiful woman he had ever acted with, or met, including the great Greta Garbo whom he had appeared with in CAMILLE. Said Taylor: "When I was told to do IVANHOE much against my wishes, it wasn't as boring as I had expected. I had Elizabeth Taylor in that one, and when I knew she was going to be my leading lady I kind of hoped this time I might get 'somewhere' with her. She was in full bloom then, but to my disappointment she was head over heels in love with Michael Wilding, and if it hadn't been for that, I would have tried my luck with her." Robert Taylor had appeared with luscious Elizabeth Taylor in one earlier movie, THE CONSPIRATOR, 1950, and he wasn't the only person deeply in love with this stunning actress. Actually, Elizabeth Taylor had been ordered by MGM to go to England to appear in IVANHOE in order that her affair with director Stanley Donen be broken up; the then all-powerful studio had decided that such love interests would interfere with her movie career. She was even threatened with replacement and possible suspension if she did not accept the assignment. MGM, not getting a response from Elizabeth, announced Deborah Kerr for the role of Rebecca and Margaret Leighton to play Rowena. But Taylor agreed to play the role at the last minute and Fontaine was then substituted for Leighton. Miserable at being manipulated and having to play an unimportant female lead, or at least a part far less important than Robert Taylor's, Elizabeth Taylor was depressed and unhappy when arriving in England. Her first night there, however, was brightened by the appearance of British actor Michael Wilding who took her to dinner and won her heart. Although Elizabeth Taylor always considered the film "just a big medieval western," IVANHOE is one of the most superbly crafted epics ever produced, earning more than $6 million in its initial release; it was Oscar nominated as Best Picture of 1952 but lost to THE GREATEST SHOW ON EARTH. Miklos Rosza's lush and stirring score for this film is a minor masterpiece and was deeply researched by the composer who spent months studying 12th century compositions so that his music would fit the historical images projected on the screen. IVANHOE had been filmed twice as a silent, both British and American versions, shot in England, appearing in 1913; the American production starred King Baggott and Leah Baird, the British film offering Lauderdale Maitland and Edith Bracewell in the leads. Producer Walter Wanger announced in 1935 that he would make IVANHOE with Gary Cooper, Sylvia Sidney, and Madeleine Carroll but the film never went beyond the preliminary planning stage. Roger Moore would star in a short-lived TV series "Ivanhoe" in 1957.

p, Pandro S. Berman; d, Richard Thorpe; w, Noel Langley (based on the novel by Sir Walter Scott); ph, Freddie A. Young (Technicolor); m, Miklos Rosza; ed, Frank Clarke; art d, Alfred Junge; cos, Roger Furse; spec eff, Tom Howard.

Historical Epic **Cas.** **(PR:A MPAA:NR)**

IVANOVO DETSTVO (SEE: MY NAME IS IVAN, 1963, USSR)

IVAN'S CHILDHOOD (SEE: MY NAME IS IVAN, 1963, USSR)

IVORY-HANDLED GUN** (1935) 59m UNIV bw

Buck Jones *(Buck Ward)*, Charlotte Wynters *(Paddy Moore)*, Walter Miller *(Wolverine Kid)*, Carl Stockdale *(Bill Ward)*, Frank Rice *(Pike)*, Joseph Girard *(Pat Moore)*, Robert Kortman, Stanley Blystone, Lafe McKee, Lee Shumway, Charles King, Ben Corbett, Eddie Phillips, Niles Welch, "Silver".

Feuding sheepmen are at the center of this unusually intelligent oater as Jones and Miller carry on the battles that raged between their fathers. The outcome of the sons' feuds (fought, of course, with ivory-handled guns) is identical to that of their fathers', with Jones ending up a cripple. An interesting extension of the standard oater plots.

p, Buck Jones; d, Ray Taylor; w, Jack Neville (based on a story by Charles E. Barnes); ph, Allen Thomspon, Herbert Kirkpatrick; ed, Bernard Loftus.

Western **(PR:A MPAA:NR)**

IVORY HUNTER** ½

(1952, Brit.) 97m EAL/UNIV c (GB: WHERE NO VULTURES FLY; AKA: THE IVORY HUNTERS)

Anthony Steel *(Robert Payton)*, Dinah Sheridan *(Mary Payton)*, Harold Warrender *(Mannering)*, Meredith Edwards *(Gwil Davies)*, William Simons *(Tim Payton)*, Orlando Martins *(M'Kwongwi)*, Phillip Birkinshaw *(District Commissioner)*, Jack Arundel Mallett *(Chief Game Warden)*, Kenneth Augustus Jeremy *(Watson)*, Wallace Needham-Clark *(Chief Veterinary Officer)*, Edmund Stewart *(1st Hunter)*, John Lawrence *(2nd Hunter)*, Paul N'Gei *(Ondego)*, David Osieli *(Kali)*, Johanna Kitau *(Kimolo)*, Jafeth Ananda *(Scarface)*, Bartholomew Sketch *(Scarface's Brother)*, Andrew Cruickshank.

Fed up with the senseless slaughter of native African wildlife, game warden Steel decides to establish a national safari park. With his wife, Sheridan, Steel fends off a group of poachers headed by Warrender. The latter is finally killed as he runs from the law while Steel goes on to establish Africa's Mt. Kilimanjaro National Park and Animal Sanctuary. Good enough for a family adventure film though it took a critical bashing upon release. The public paid little heed to the critics and the film became England's biggest hit of 1952.

p, Michael Balcon; d, Harry Watt; w, Ralph Smart, W.P. Lipscomb (based on a story by Leslie Norman Watt); ph, Geoffrey Unsworth, Paul Beeson (Technicolor); m, Alan Rawsthorne; ed, Jack Harris; md, Ernest Irving.

Adventure/Family Film **(PR:A MPAA:NR)**

IVORY HUNTERS, THE (SEE: IVORY HUNTER, 1952, Brit.)

IVY 1/2** (1947) 98m Wood's Interwood/UNIV-International bw

Joan Fontaine *(Ivy)*, Patric Knowles *(Dr. Roger Gretorex)*, Herbert Marshall *(Miles Rushworth)*, Richard Ney *(Jervis Lexton)*, Sir Cedric Hardwicke *(Inspector Orpington)*, Lucile Watson *(Mrs. Gretorex)*, Sara Allgood *(Martha Huntley)*, Henry Stephenson *(Judge)*, Rosalind Ivan *(Emily)*, Lillian Fontaine *(Lady Flora)*, Molly Lamont *(Bella Crail)*, Una O'Connor *(Mrs. Thrawn)*, Isobel Elsom *(Misa Chattle)*, Alan Napier *(Sir Jonathan Wright)*, Paul Cavanagh *(Dr. Herwick)*, Sir Charles Mendl *(Sir Charles Gage)*, Gavin Muir *(Sergeant)*, Mary Forbes *(Lady Crail)*, Norma Varden *(Joan Rodney)*, Lumsden Hare *(Dr. Lancaster)*, Matthew Boulton *(Tom Lumford)*, Lydia Bilbrook *(Mary Hampton)*, Alan Edmiston *(Jenks)*, Harry Hays Morgan *(Lord Ventner)*, Holmes Herbert *(Mulloy)*, C. Montague Shaw *(Stevens)*,Claire Du Brey *(Shopkeeper)*, Gerald Hamer *(Man From Paris Office)*, Colin Campbell *(Chaplain)*, Leon Lenoir *(Dock-Worker)*, Alan Edmiston *(Man, Fortune Teller Scene)*, David Cavendish, Jean Fenwick, David Ralston, Ella Ethridge, Renee Evans, Judith Woodbury *(Guests)*, Dave Thursby *(Groves)*, Art Foster *(Constable)*, Lois Austin *(English Lady)*, Herbert Clifton *(Bates)*, James Lagan *(Aviator)*, Eric Wilton *(Steward)*, Charles Knight *(Solicitor)*, Herbert Evans *(Deck Official)*, Manuel Paris *(Cook's Tour Guide)*, Wyndham Standing *(Assistant Chief Justice)*, Clive Morgan *(Assistant King's Council)*, Elsa Peterson *(Yacht Guest)*, Bess Flowers *(Set Rehearsal)*, James Fairfax *(English Newsvendor)*.

Fontaine is cast as a full-fledged femme fatale in this strongly-scripted drama. She is surrounded by a trio of men—her husband, Ney, her lover, Knowles, and Marshall, an English fellow she has her sights on. In order to assure that she gets Marshall, she poisons her husband and then frames the lover for the murder. She doesn't get away with it, however, and is forced to admit her guilt. Look for the part of Lady Flora, portrayed by Fontaine's mother.

p, William Cameron Menzies; d, Sam Wood; w, Charles Bennett (based on novel *The Story of Ivy* by Marie Belloc Lowndes); ph, Russell Metty; m, Daniele Amfitheatrof; ed, Ralph Dawson; art d, Richard H. Riedel; set d, Russell A. Gausman, T.F. Offenbecker; m/l, Hoagy Carmichael.

Drama **(PR:A MPAA:NR)**

J

J.D.'S REVENGE** ½** (1976) 95m AIP c

Glynn Turman *(Ike)*, Joan Pringle *(Christella)*, Lou Gossett, Jr. *(Rev. Bliss)*, Carl Crudup *(Tony)*, James Louis Watkins *(Carl)*, Alice Jubert *(Roberta/Betty Jo)*, Stephanie Faulkner *(Phyllis)*, Fred Pinkard *(Theotis)*, Fuddle Bagley *(Enoch)*, Jo Anne Meredith *(Sarah)*, David McKnight *(J.D. Walker)*.

This film, with an all-black cast, is a cut above most black exploitation films of its time, though it still revels in blood and gore. The story opens with the murder of gangster McKnight on Bourbon St. in 1942, then flashes forward to 1976 in New Orleans where law student Turman is slowly being possessed by the gangster's spirit. Gossett plays a minister who was involved in the murder plot and becomes the object of the possessed Turman's attempt to get revenge. Pop superstar Prince, a relative unknown in 1976, did the music and sang "I Will Never Let You Go."

p&d, Arthur Marks; w, Jaison Starkes; ph, Harry May (Movielab Color); m, Robert Prince; ed, George Folsey, Jr.; m/l, "I Will Never Let You Go," Prince, Joseph A. Greene.

Horror **(PR:O MPAA:R)**

J.R. (SEE: WHO'S THAT KNOCKING AT MY DOOR!, 1968)

J.W. COOP*** (1971) 112m COL c

Cliff Robertson *(J.W. Coop)*, Geraldine Page *(Mama)*, Christina Ferrare *(Bean)*, R.G. Armstrong *(Jim Sawyer)*, R.L. Armstrong *(Tooter Watson)*, John Crawford *(Rancher)*, Wade Crosby *(Billy Sol Gibbs)*, Marjorie Durant Dye *(Big Marge)*, Paul Harper *(Warden Morgan)*, Son Hooker *(Motorcycle Cop)*, Richard Kennedy *(Sheriff)*, Bruce Kirby *(Diesel Driver)*, Mary Robin Redd *(Bonnie May)*, Claude Stroud *(Rodeo Manager)*, Wayne Taylor *(Gas Station Attendant)*, Augie Vallejo *(Hector)*, Dennis Reiners *(Billy Hawkins)*, Myrtis Dightman *(Myrtis)*, Frank Hobbs *(Deacon)*, Billy Hogue *(Hogue)*, Billy Martinelli *(Eddie)*, Clyde W. Maye *(Cisco)*, Larry Clayman *(Finals Clown)*, Larry Mahan *(Himself)*, John Ashby *(Johnny)*, Robert Christensen *(Bobby)*, Velma Cooper *(Maylene)*, Jim Madland *(Himself)*, Beverly Powers *(Dora Mae)*, Sharron Rae *(Herself)*, Quail Dobbs *(Woodlake Clown)*, Kathy Beaudine *(Young Fan)*, Sandy Dempsey *(Cabaret Dancer)*, Judy Farrell *(Barmaid)*, Charles W. Knapp *(Bar Owner)*, Jay MacIntosh *(Housewife)*, Gus Peters *(Deputy)*, Lex Connelly, Johnnie Jackson, Mel Lambert, Clem McSpadden *(Announcers)*, Gary Leffew, John Wilson *(Rodeo Riders)*.

Robertson produced, directed, co-wrote and starred in this film about a rodeo rider's attempt to adjust to a new way of life after spending ten years in prison. Society in general, and the rodeo in specific, have changed dramatically during Robertson's imprisonment and he struggles to adapt to both, going after a national championship in the process. The cast features members of the Rodeo Cowboys Association, and much of the action footage was shot during actual rodeo events. He tries to rebuild his career in the vastly changed rodeo, as well as carry on a relationship with Ferrare, finding that women's attitudes have changed as much as those of rodeo riders.

p&d, Cliff Robertson; w, Robertson, Gary Cartwright, Bud Shrake; ph, Frank Stanley, Adam Hollander, Ross Lowell, Fred Waugh (Eastmancolor); m, Louie Shelton, Don Randi; ed, Alex Beaton; spec eff, Tim Smyth; additional music, Nashville Marimba Band.

Drama **(PR:A MPAA:PG)**

J-MEN FOREVER** ½** (1980) 80m International Harmony bw

Phil Proctor, Peter Bergman.

In the manner of Woody Allen's WHAT'S UP TIGER LILY? Proctor and Bergman of the comedy troupe Firesign Theatre have assembled cuts from a number of old adventure films and added their own bizarrely comical narration. They also intercut footage of themselves, as well as popular rock and roll from The Tubes, Billy Preston, and Head East. The main idea behind this collage is that the superhero J-Men form a group called MUSAC (Military Underground Sugared Airwaves Command) to fend off the attempts of an evil villain to destroy the world by popularizing rock music. It's funny at times, but Firesign Theatre's record albums ("The Adventures of Nick Danger" for example) deal with similar themes on a much funnier level.

p, William Howard; w, Phil Proctor, Peter Bergman; m, Billy Preston, The Tubes, Badazz, Budgie, Head East, Richard Thiess.

Comedy **(PR:C MPAA:PG)**

JABBERWOCKY** (1977, Brit.) 100m Umbrella/Cinema 5 c

Michael Palin *(Dennis Cooper)*, Max Wall *(King Bruno the Questionable)*, Deborah Fallender *(Princess)*, John Le Mesurier *(Chamberlain)*, Annette Badland *(Griselda Fishfinger)*, Warren Mitchell *(Mr. Fishfinger)*, Brenda Cowling *(Mrs. Fishfinger)*, Harry H. Corbett *(Squire)*, Rodney Bewes *(Other Squire)*, Bernard Bresslaw *(Landlord)*, Alexandra Dane *(Betsy)*, Derek Francis *(Bishop)*, Peter Cellier *(First Merchant)*, Frank Williams *(Second Merchant)*, Anthony Carrick *(Third Merchant)*, John Bird *(First Herald)*, Neil Innes *(Second Herald & Drummer)*, Paul Curran *(Mr. Cooper Senior)*, Graham Crowden *(Fanatics' leader)*, Gordon Rollings *(King's Taster)*, Glenn Williams *(First Gate Guard)*, Bryan Pringle *(Second Gate Guard)*, Terry Jones *(Poacher)*, Brian Glover *(Armorer)*, John Gorman *(First Peasant)*, Julian Hough *(Second Peasant)*, Dave Prowse *(Red Herring Knight/Black Knight)*, Harold Goodwin *(Third Peasant)*, Tony Sympson *(Fourth Peasant)*, Simon Williams *(Prince)*, Jerrold Wells *(Wat Dabney)*, Gordon Kaye *(Sister Jessica)*.

Terry Gilliam, animator for British television's "Monty Python's Flying Circus," directed and coscripted this silly medieval fantasy inspired by the Lewis Carroll poem of the same name. A feisty creature, the Jabberwocky is ripping apart poor wanderers in the woods of King Bruno the Questionable, played by Wall. Palin, another member of the Python troupe, is a meek country dweller who travels into the king's domain and gets mixed up in an endless string of wild situations. Wall has called all his knights to the city and orders them to duel to the death, with the winner getting the hand of Fallender and the chance to slay the Jabberwocky. After a few bloodbaths, Wall opts for a nice game of hide-and-seek instead. Unfortunately for Palin, he wins. Fortunately, he kills the monster. Even more fortunately, he wins the hand of Fallender. Unfortunately for the audience it is all very predictable and below the Python troupe's usual level of humor.

p, Sandy Lieberson; d, Terry Gilliam; w, Gilliam, Charles Alverson (based on a poem by Lewis Carroll); ph, Terry Bedford (Technicolor); m, De Wolfe; prod d, Roy Smith; ed, Michael Bradsell; art d, Millie Burns; spec eff, John F. Brown; cos, Hazel Pethig, Charles Knode.

Fantasy/Comedy **Cas.** **(PR:O MPAA:PG)**

J'ACCUSE*** ½**

(1939, Fr.) 95m Forrester-Parant bw (AKA: I ACCUSE; THAT THEY MAY LIVE)

Victor Francen *(Jean Diaz)*, Jean Max *(Henri Chimay)*, Delaitre *(Francois Laurin)*, Renee Devillers *(Helene)*, Line Noro *(Edith)*, Marie Lou *(Flo)*, Georges Saillard *(Giles Tenant)*, Paul Amiot *(Captain)*, Andre Nox *(Leotard)*, Rollin *(Pierre Fonds)*.

An excellent antiwar film, J'ACCUSE is all the more poignant considering it was produced and released in France shortly before the Occupation. Francen invents a device he believes will stop war forever, only to see it used by his government as a defense measure against the enemy. Driven mad by this exploitation, Francen decides only the war dead marching through the streets will stop the people's thirst for an upcoming war. In his delusion bodies rise from their graves and march through the streets. The sight of war's actual horrors so terrifies the patriotic countrymen that all thoughts of war are abandoned. Gance's plot is a simple one, but told with enormous power and passion for the theme. The ravaged faces of the dead are a disturbing, powerful image that is not soon forgotten. The antiwar message is told clearly, without preaching, and with a sensitivity toward pacifism. Like so many films of this nature, its peaceful message was considered unsuitable by Nazi Germany and the film was banned in that country. (French; English subtitles)

p&d, Abel Gance; w, Gance, Steve Passeur; ph, Roger Hubert; m, Henry Verdun; (English subtitles by Pierre Van Paassen).

Drama **(PR:C-O MPAA:NR)**

JACK AHOY!* ½ (1935, Brit.) 70m GAU bw

Jack Hulbert *(Jack Ponsonby)*, Nancy O'Neil *(Patricia Fraser)*, Alfred Drayton *(Admiral Fraser)*, Tamara Desni *(Conchita)*, Henry Peterson *(Larios)*, Sam Wilkinson *(Dodger)*.

A British farce about a likable sailor, Hulbert, who becomes enamored of his admiral's daughter, O'Neil. When the latter is kidnaped by a Chinese gang, Hulbert goes into action, turns the whole Chinese navy upside down, and rescues her in his submarine. Remade in 1954 as UP TO HIS NECK.

p, Michael Balcon; d, Walter Forde; w, Jack Hulbert, Leslie Arliss, Gerard Fairlie, Austin Melford (based on a story by Sidney Gilliat, J.O.C. Orton); ph, Bernard Knowles; m/l, "My Hat's On the Side of My Head," Harry Woods, Claude Hulbert.

Comedy **(PR:A MPAA:NR)**

JACK AND THE BEANSTALK** ½** (1952) 78m Exclusive/WB bw/c

Bud Abbott *(Dinklepuss)*, Lou Costello *(Jack)*, Buddy Baer *(Sgt. Riley/Giant)*, Dorothy Ford *(Polly)*, Barbara Brown *(Mother)*, David Stollery *(Donald)*, William Farnum *(The King)*, Shaye Cogan *(Eloise Larkin/Princess)*, James Alexander *(Arthur Royal/Prince)*, Joe Kirk *(Villager)*, Johnny Conrad and Dancers, Patrick, the Harp.

Abbott and Costello are unleashed in fairy-tale land when Costello sells the family cow to Abbott, a crooked butcher, for five magic beans. Costello plants the beans and overnight a giant beanstalk climbs to the clouds where an evil giant—one-time prizefighter Baer—lives, along with a talking harp and a hen that lays golden eggs. Climbing to the giant's elevated domain, Abbott and Costello try to rescue a prince and princess, Cogan and Alexander, from his evil clutches. Slapstick chases ensue which are among the comedy duo's best. Songs include "I Fear Nothing," "He Never Looked Better in His Life," "Darlene," and "Dreamers Cloth," all by Lester Lee and Bob Russell.

p, Alex Gottlieb; d, Jean Yarbrough; w, Nat Curtis (based on a story by Pat Costello, Felix Adler, from the fairy tales); ph, George Robinson (SuperCinecolor); m, Heinz Roemheld; ed, Otho Lovering; art d, McClure Capps.

Juvenile/Comedy **Cas.** **(PR:AAA MPAA:NR)**

JACK AND THE BEANSTALK* (1970) 62m Cinetron/R&S c

Dorothy Stokes, Mitchell Poulos, Chris Brooks, Renato Boracherro, John Loomis, Sami Sims, George Wadsworth.

Inane adaptation of the classic fairy tale might appeal to pre-schoolers, but to no one else. Producer-director-writer Mahon made dozens of cheap skin flicks including BUNNY YEAGER'S NUDE LAS VEGAS, FANNY HILL MEETS DR. EROTICO, and A GOOD TIME WITH A BAD GIRL before devoting himself to more wholesome efforts like this. Unfortunately the quality of the films did not improve with the change in subject.

p,d&w, Barry Mahon; ph, Bill Tobin; m, Eugene Ventresca; ed, Steve Cuiffo; set d, Thelma Raniero; cos, Peggy Praigg; m/l, George Linsenmann, Ralph Falco; makeup, Tom Brumberger.

Children **(PR:AA MPAA:G)**

JACK FROST*** (1966, USSR) 79m Gorky/EM c (MOROZKO)

Aleksandr Khvylya *(Jack Frost)*, Natasha Sedykh *(Nastenka)*, Eduard Izotov *(Ivan)*, Inna Churikova *(Marfushka)*, Pavel Pavlenko *(Father)*, Vera Altayskaya *(Stepmother)*, Georgiy Millyar *(Witch)*, M. Yanshin, G. Borisova *(Old Mushrooms)*, Anatoliy Kubatskiy *(Bandit Chieftain)*, Valentin Bryleyev *(Eligible Bachelor)*, T. Pelttser *(Eligible Bachelor's Mother)*, T. Barysheva *(Matchmaker)*, V. Popova *(Old Woman)*, Z. Vorkul *(Ivan's Mother)*, A. Zuyeva *(Storyteller, Russian Version)*, D. Bakhtin, V. Zhukovskiy, N. Zorina, K. Kozlenkova, M. Korabelnikova, A. Mukhin, V. Petrova, O. Peshkov, L. Potyomkin, A. Stapran, K. Starostin, A. Timontayev, T. Kharchenko, Yu. Chekulayev, A. Chumina, M. Shcherbakov, Olya Yukina, Tanya Yukina.

An enchanting children's film from Russia, which is filled with an interesting assortment of characters and enough visual excitement to keep any pair of wandering eyes on the screen. Essentially it is a Cinderella-type tale about an emotionally battered young girl who is forced to work by her wicked stepmother, while her sister gets to enjoy life. The girl falls in love with a handsome village boy, who gets his head turned into that of a bear by a gremlin, Father Mushroom. He must prove his worth by performing a good deed, and only then will he be returned to his normal state. An endless string of adventures makes this fantasy a joy for both young and old.

d, Aleksandr Rou; w, Mikhail Volpin, Nikolay Erdman (based on the fairy tale "Morozko"); ph, Dmitriy Surenskiy; m, Nikolay Budashkin; art d, Arseniy Klopotovskiy; m/l, Budashkin, Volpin; animal trainer, G. Alekseyev, M. Simonov.

Fantasy/Juvenile **(PR:AAA MPAA:NR)**

JACK LONDON1/2** (1943) 94m UA bw

Michael O'Shea *(Jack London)*, Susan Hayward *(Charmain Kittredge)*, Osa Massen *(Freda Maloof)*, Harry Davenport *(Prof. Hilliard)*, Frank Craven *(Old Tom)*, Virginia Mayo *(Mamie)*, Ralph Morgan *(George Brett)*, Louise Beavers *(Mammy Jenny)*, Johnathan Hale *(Kerwin Maxwell)*, Leonard Strong *(Capt. Tanaka)*, Paul Hurst *("Lucky Luke" Lannigan)*, Regis Toomey *(Scratch Nelson)*, Hobart Cavanaugh *(Mike)*, Olin Howlin *(Mailman)*, Albert Van Antwerp *(French Frank)*, Ernie Adams *(Whiskey Bob)*, John Kelly *(Red John)*, Robert Homans *(Capt. Allen)*, Morgan Conway *(Richard Harding Davis)*, Edward Earle *(James Hare)*, Arthur Loft *(Fred Palmer)*, Lumsden Hare *(English Correspondent)*, Brooks Benedict *(American Correspondent)*, Mei Lee Foo *(Geisha Dancer)*, Robert Katcher *(Hiroshi)*, Pierre Watkin *(American Consul)*, Paul Fung *(Japanese General)*, Charlie Lung *(Interpreter)*, Bruce Wong *(Japanese Official)*, Eddie Lee *(Japanese Sergeant)*, John Fisher *(Spider)*, Jack Roper *(Victor)*, Sven Hugo Borg *(Axel)*, Sid Dalbrook *(Pete)*, Davison Clark *(Commissioner)*, Harold Minjir, Roy Gordon, Torben Mayer *(Literary Guests)*, Charlene Newman *(Bit Child)*, Edmond Cobb *(Bit Father)*, Wallis Clark *(Theodore Roosevelt)*, Charles Miller *(William Loeb)*, Richard Loo *(Japanese Ambassador)*, Dick Curtis *(Cannery Foreman)*, Sarah Padden *(Cannery Woman)*, Evelyn Finley *(Indian Maid)*, Rose Plummer *(Chairman's Secretary)*.

An action-packed but somewhat fanciful screen adaptation of the life of famed American adventurer and author Jack London, based on the biography written by his wife Charmian. Beginning during London's (O'Shea) early adult life, the film details the series of odd jobs he held while living in the Pacific Northwest. After a failed romance with Mayo, and the death of his friend Toomey, O'Shea sets out for Yukon gold territory in search of more adventure. In the Yukon, O'Shea begins to mature and gain insight into his lifestyle which he decides to write about. His books prove extremely popular with the public and he soon finds himself something of a celebrity. One day the beautiful Hayward walks into O'Shea's life, she having fallen in love with him from reading his books. The two grow close and decide to marry, but when the Boer War breaks out O'Shea deserts her in favor of adventure. Leaving his publisher, Morgan, to watch over his bride-to-be, O'Shea travels to London on the first leg of his journey to Africa. Upon his arrival in London, O'Shea is disappointed to learn that the Boer War has ended. Returning home, O'Shea and Hayward begin to make wedding plans, but he is snatched away once again when he goes off to cover the Russo-Japanese War. O'Shea arrives in Japan accompanied by two other reporters, Earle and Conway, but they soon learn that the Japanese will not allow American reporters on the front. Not one to be stopped by bureaucracy, O'Shea manages to make his way to the front and cover the fighting under the watchful eye of Japanese captain Strong. There he witnesses horrible atrocities committed by the Japanese army and he is arrested for taking pictures of the carnage. It appears as if O'Shea will be left in prison to rot, but U.S. President Theodore Roosevelt (Clark) arranges to have him released and deported back to the States. Imbued with a new sense of commitment, O'Shea returns to his country with a passionate plea to beware the Japanese military, for the future of the world may depend on it. Though JACK LONDON makes the usual concessions to hero worship and myth-making while ignoring the facts regarding the subject's life that are not entirely flattering (London was an alcoholic, addicted to morphine, and he had a distinct self-destructive bent), it succeeds as an interesting adventure picture. Unfortunately, the vehemently anti-Japanese segments in which the filmmakers were able to slip in some timely WW II propaganda date the film badly and seem incongruous with the rest of the plot when viewed today. The other problem with the film is the casting of O'Shea as London. The role was originally slated for John Garfield, but when he proved to be unavailable the studio went with O'Shea. Although he was up to the physical demands of the role, O'Shea lacked the personality and emotional depths needed for a truly engrossing portrayal. Hayward makes the most of a fairly thankless role in which she is supposed to be deeply in love while waiting for her man to return on short visits. Her character could easily have slipped into that of the mindless, infinitely patient hero-worshiping spouse, but Hayward does manage to bring some intelligence and dignity to the part. A romantic footnote: star O'Shea and featured player Mayo met on the set and were married soon after shooting was completed.

p, Samuel Bronston; d, Alfred Santell; w, Ernest Pascal (based on the book *The Book of Jack London*) by Charmian London), ph, John W. Boyle; ed, William Ziegler; md, Fred Rich; art d, Bernard Herzbrun; set d, Earl Wooden; cos, Maria Donovan, Arnold McDonald; spec eff, Harry Redmond.

Biography/Adventure **Cas.** **(PR:A MPAA:NR)**

JACK LONDON'S KLONDIKE FEVER (SEE: KLONDIKE FEVER, 1980)

JACK MCCALL, DESPERADO** (1953) 76m COL c

George Montgomery *(Jack McCall)*, Angela Stevens *(Rose Griffith)*, Douglas Kennedy *("Wild" Bill Hickok)*, James Seay *(Bat McCall)*, Eugene Iglesias *(Grey Eagle)*, William Tannen *(Spargo)*, Jay Silverheels *(Red Cloud)*, John Hamilton *(Col. Cornish)*, Selmer Jackson *(Col. Braud)*, Stanley Blystone *(Judge)*, Gene Roth *(Attorney)*, Alva Lacy *(Hisega)*, Joe McGuinn *(U.S. Marshal)*.

An average western with some gripping action sequences, starring Montgomery as a Southerner in the Union Army. Framed and sentenced to death, he escapes and is pursued by Seay and Kennedy. They murder Montgomery's parents and when the war ends he seeks revenge, getting it when he kills both men. He's tried for murder, but acquitted, and also cleared of the original charges.

p, Sam Katzman; d, Sidney Salkow; w, John O'Dea (based on a story by David Chandler); ph, Henry Freulich (Technicolor); ed, Aaron Stell; md, Mischa Bakaleinikoff; art d, Paul Palmentola.

Western **(PR:A MPAA:NR)**

JACK OF ALL TRADES (SEE: TWO OF US, THE, 1936, Brit.)

JACK OF DIAMONDS, THE** (1949, Brit.) 73m VS/Exclusive bw

Nigel Patrick *(Alan Butler)*, Cyril Raymond *(Roger Keen)*, Joan Carol *(Joan Keen)*, Darcy Conyers *(Colin Campbell)*, Vernon Sewell *(Engineer)*.

Patrick plays a conniving treasure seeker with a plot to make off with a chest of diamonds that belongs to someone else. Raymond and Carol are the owners of the boat Patrick leases and also major elements in halting his criminal plan. Well paced effort that takes full advantage of characterizations and the ocean background.

p, Walter d'Eyncourt; d, Vernon Sewell; w, Nigel Patrick, Cyril Raymond; ph, Moray Grant.

Adventure **(PR:A MPAA:NR)**

JACK OF DIAMONDS*1/2

(1967, U.S./Ger.) 107m Harris Associates-Bavaria Atelier/MGM c

George Hamilton *(Jeff Hill)*, Joseph Cotten *(Ace of Diamonds)*, Marie Laforet *(Olga)*, Maurice Evans *(Nicolai)*, Wolfgang Preiss *(Von Schenk)*, Karl Lieffen *(Helmut)*, Alexander Hegarth *(Brugger)*, Eduard Linkers *(Geisling)*, Carroll Baker, Zsa Zsa Gabor, Lilli Palmer *(Themselves)*, Charles Hickman, Al Hoosman, Bob Cheslock.

A lifeless cat-burglar thriller which has Hamilton taking over as top jewel thief from his mentor, Cotten, the Ace of Diamonds. Ignoring Cotten's warnings to stop before he is caught, Hamilton teams up with Laforet and master thief Evans to pull off a heist of the priceless Zaharoff diamonds. An alarm is triggered during the caper and Cotten appears, letting himself get nabbed by the police so that Hamilton and Laforet can escape. Hamilton will not watch Cotten do time for a crime he has committed and makes a deal to give up the stolen gems in return for Cotten's release.

p, Sandy Howard, Helmut Jedele; d, Don Taylor; w, Jack DeWitt, Robert L. Joseph, Howard; ph, Ernst Wild (Panavision, Metrocolor); m, Peter Thomas, Bob Harris; ed, Hans Nikel; md, Thomas; art d, Rolf Zehetbauer; cos, Nicola Holtz; makeup, Jonas Muller, Heidi Moser.

Crime **(PR:A MPAA:NR)**

JACK SLADE*1/2 (1953) 89m AA bw (GB: SLADE)

Mark Stevens *(Jack Slade)*, Dorothy Malone *(Virginia Dale)*, Barton MacLane *(Jules Reni)*, John Litel *(Judge)*, Paul Langton *(Dan Traver)*, Harry Shannon *(Tom Carter)*, John Harmon *(Hollis)*, Jim Bannon *(Farnsworth)*, Lee Van Cleef *(Toby Mackay)*, Sammy Ogg *(Joey Slade)*, Nelson Leigh *(Alf Slade)*, Ron Hargrave *(Ned Prentice)*, David May *(Tump)*, John Halloran, Richard Reeves, Dorothy Kennedy, Duane Thorsen, Harry Landers, Ann Navarro.

The completely fictional saga of Jack Slade, a rather interesting man in real life, begins with his first murder at age 13 and continues through his days as a gunslinger aiding the law in battling stagecoach bandits. He gradually deteriorates, becoming nothing more than a hard-drinking, cold-blooded killer who is mercifully shot down by a friend.

p, Lindsley Parsons; d, Harold Schuster; w, Warren Douglas; ph, William Sickner; m, Paul Dunlap; ed, Leonard W. Herman; md, Dunlap; art d, David Milton; m/l, Britt Wood, Ed Bloodworth.

Western **(PR:C MPAA:NR)**

JACK THE GIANT KILLER*** (1962) 94m Zenith/UA c

Kerwin Mathews *(Jack)*, Judi Meredith *(Princess Elaine)*, Torin Thatcher *(Pendragon)*, Walter Burke *(Garna)*, Roger Mobley *(Peter)*, Barry Kelley *(Sigurd)*, Don Beddoe *(Imp in Bottle)*, Dayton Lummis *(King Mark)*, Anna Lee *(Lady Constance)*, Helen Wallace *(Jack's Mother)*, Tudor Owen *(Chancellor)*, Robert Gist *(Capt. McFadden)*, Ken Mayer *(Boatswain)*.

Nearly a carbon-copy of THE SEVENTH VOYAGE OF SINBAD, this medieval fantasy concerns an evil wizard (Thatcher) who attempts to regain lost magical powers by abducting princess Meredith. The hardy Mathews, a farmer's son, rescues her by killing Thatcher's giant flunky and is thus asked to escort the damsel to safety at a faraway convent. Over the course of the trip Mathews battles an assortment of witches, dragons, sea monsters, and the like. He's helped along by a magic leprechaun, a dog, and even a chimpanzee. Nasty old Thatcher tries to stop the crew one last time by turning himself into a dragon but is promptly slain for a happy ending. The live animation was created by Danforth, who had earlier worked on the popular "Gumby" shorts with Art Clokey. Despite the ripped off plot line, this carries its own share of thrills, making for a generally fun outing. Undoubtedly the kids will love it.

p, Edward Small; d, Nathan Juran; w, Orville H. Hampton, Juran (based on story by Hampton); ph, David S. Horsley (Fantascope, Technicolor); m, Paul Sawtell, Bert Shefter; ed, Grant Whytock; art d, Fernando Carrere, Frank McCoy; set d, Edward G. Boyle; cos, David Berman; spec eff, Howard A. Anderson, Jim Danforth, David Pal; ch, Jon Gregory; makeup, Charles Gemora.

Fantasy **(PR:AA MPAA:NR)**

JACK THE RIPPER* 1/2 (1959, Brit.) 84m Mid-Century/PAR bw/c

Lee Patterson *(Sam Lowry)*, Eddie Byrne *(Inspector O'Neill)*, Betty McDowall *(Anne Ford)*, Ewen Solon *(Sir David Rogers)*, John Le Mesurier *(Dr. Tranter)*, George Rose *(Clarke)*, Philip Leaver *(Music Hall Manager)*, Barbara Burke (Kitty Knowles), Anne Sharpe *(Helen)*, Denis Shaw *(Simes)*, Endre Muller *(Louis Benz)*, Esma Cannon *(Nelly)*, George Woodbridge (Blake), Bill Shine *(Lord Sopwith)*, Marianne Stone *(Drunken Woman)*, Garard Green *(Dr. Urquhart)*, Jack Allen *(Assistant Commissioner)*, Jane Taylor *(Hazel)*, Dorinda Stevens *(Margaret)*, Hal Osmond *(Snakey)*, George Street *(Station Sgt.)*, Olwen Brooks *(Mrs. Bolton)*, The Montparnasse Ballet *(Dancing Troupe)*, Helena Digby *(1st Victim)*.

Fairly gruesome re-telling of the "Jack the Ripper" legend has American detective Patterson joining up with Scotland Yard man Byrne in an attempt to track down the man brutally murdering Victorian London prostitutes. Patterson falls in love with McDowall during the course of investigation. It's proved her uncle Le Mesurier, a surgeon, is the man behind the slaughter. The guilty man meets a gruesome end of his own when he's crushed in an elevator shaft. This closing sequence is the only one in color and is not for the squeamish, as the murderer's end is given a somewhat graphic portrait. Though there are occasional atmospheric moments, this is largely a bloody, exploitive exercise in filmmaking.

p, Robert S. Baker, Monty Berman; d, Baker; w, Jimmy Sangster (based on an original story by Peter Hammond, Colin Craig); ph, Berman; m, Stanley Black; ed, Peter Benzencenet.

Crime Drama **(PR:O MPAA:NR)**

JACKALS, THE** (1967, South Africa) 93m FOX c

Vincent Price, Dana Ivarson, Robert Gunner, Bob Courtney, Patrick Mynhardt, Bill Brewer, Johnny Whitney.

An unusual role for Price has him down in South Africa searching for gold. His long efforts, which have soured his personality, are nearly wasted when a gang of robbers attempts to make off with his gleanings. Basically a remake of YELLOW SKY (1948), but lacking the directorial skill of a William Wellman.

p&d, Robert D. Webb; w, Lamar Trotti, Austin Medord (based on a story by W. R. Burnett).

Adventure **(PR:A MPAA:NR)**

JACKASS MAIL 1/2** (1942) 80m MGM bw

Wallace Beery *(Marmaduke "Just" Baggott)*, Marjorie Main *(Clementine "Tiny" Tucker)*, J. Carroll Naish *(Signor O'Sullivan)*, Darryl Hickman *(Tommie Gargan)*, William Haade *("Red" Gargan)*, Hobart Cavanaugh *("Gospel" Jones)*, Dick Curtis *(Jim Swade)*, Joe Yule *(Barky)*, Harry Fleischmann *(Carp)*, Louis Mason *(Slim)*, George Carleton *(Pastor)*, Bobby Larson *(Boy)*, Mary Currier *(Mother)*, Harry Woods *(Ranch Owner)*, Paul "Tiny" Newlan *(Rancher)*, Murdock MacQuarrie *(Hickory Jake)*, Duke York *(Rancher)*, Esther Howard, Babe London *(Dance Hall Girls)*, Wade Boteler *(Doctor)*, Ruth Warren *(Doctor's Wife)*, LeRoy Mason *(Vigilante)*, Bobb Barker *(Storekeeper)*, Robert Emmett O'Conner *(Peter Lawson)*, Eddie Hart, Al Ferguson, Art Belasco, Robert E. Perry *(Miners)*, Frank Darien *(Postmaster)*, Malcolm Waite *(Cocky)*.

This harmless western casts Beery as a horse thief and mail robber. He cares for the son of a fellow Beery had shot in self-defense. The boy (Hickman) isn't aware, however, that Beery killed his outlaw dad, and now idolizes the man. It doesn't take long for Hickman to discover the truth, and he turns on Beery. Eventually the lad comes to understand why his father was killed for a happy ending. There are some good comic moments and Beery gives a neat performance. Main is involved in a romantic sub-plot which detracts from the central story.

p, John W. Considine, Jr.; d, Norman Z. McLeod; w, Lawrence Hazard (based on a story by C. Gardner Sullivan); ph, Clyde De Vinna; m, David Snell, Earl Brent; ed, Gene Ruggiero; art d, Cedric Gibbons, Leonid Vasian; set d, Edwin B. Willis; cos, Howard Shoup, Gile Steele; ch, Sammy Lee.

Western **(PR:A MPAA:NR)**

JACKIE ROBINSON STORY, THE** (1950) 76m EL bw

Jackie Robinson *(Jackie Robinson)*, Ruby Dee *(Rae Robinson)*, Minor Watson *(Branch Rickey)*, Louise Beavers *(Jackie's Mother)*, Richard Lane *(Hopper)*, Harry Shannon *(Charlie)*, Ben Lessy *(Shorty)*, Bill Spaulding *(Bill Spaulding)*, Billy Wayne *(Clyde Sukeforth)*, Joel Fluellen *(Mack Robinson)*, Bernie Hamilton *(Ernie)*, Kenny Washington *(Tigers' Manager)*, Pat Flaherty *(Karpen)*, Larry McGrath *(Umpire)*, Emmett Smith *(Catcher)*, Howard Louis MacNeely *(Jackie as a Boy)*, George Dockstader *(Bill)*

Jackie Robinson took some time out after leading the Dodgers to their 1949 pennant to make the story of his life. He was a better infielder than he was an actor but anyone who knows baseball will be intrigued by the story of this UCLA star who broke the color barrier in the previously lily-white major leagues. It's a straightforward account of his trials and tribulations as he came from the Dodger farm club in Montreal and faced some difficult moments at the hands and taunts of various redneck players who were determined to keep blacks out of baseball. Robinson's voice was always slightly nasal and fell hard on the ear but who better to play him than him? Ruby Dee is believable as his wife, as is Beavers as his mother. They couldn't really use the language that was thrown at Robinson on the field because that would never have passed the censor. He was the victim of more abuse than any athlete who had ever stepped on a field and he held his normally hot temper in check as a promise to Dodger boss Branch Rickey (played by Watson), a true gentleman of sports. Once Robinson had made his mark (and he was one of the most exciting players who ever donned a pair of spiked shoes), the gates opened for black players and he was joined on the Dodgers by pitcher Dan Bankhead (who holds the rare distinction of being one of the few players to ever hit a home run on their first at-bat in the majors) and the beloved Roy Campanella. Some license was taken by the screenwriters, but not enough to warrant any serious pokes at their authenticity.

p, Mort Briskin; d, Alfred E. Green; w, Lawrence Taylor, Arthur Mann (based on a story by Louis Pollock); ph, Ernest Laszlo; m, David Chudnow; ed, Maurie M. Suess, Arthur H. Nadel.

Biography **(PR:AA MPAA:NR)**

JACKPOT, THE*** (1950) 85m FOX bw

James Stewart *(Bill Lawrence)*, Barbara Hale *(Amy Lawrence)*, James Gleason *(Harry Summers)*, Fred Clark *(Mr. Woodruff)*, Alan Mowbray *(Leslie)*, Patricia Medina *(Hilda Jones)*, Natalie Wood *(Phyllis Lawrence)*, Tommy Rettig *(Tommy Lawrence)*, Robert Gist *(Pete Spooner)*, Lyle Talbot *(Fred Burns)*, Charles Tannen *(Al Vogel)*, Bigelow Sayre *(Capt. Sullivan)*, Dick Cogan *(Mr. Brown)*, Jewel Rose *(Mrs. Brown)*, Eddie Firestone *(Mr. McDougall)*, Estelle Etterre *(Mrs. McDougall)*, Claude Stroud *(Herman Wertheim)*, Caryl Lincoln *(Susan Wertheim)*, Valerie Mark *(Mary Vogel)*, Joan Miller *(Mabel Spooner)*, Walter Baldwin *(Watch Buyer)*, Syd Saylor *(Ernie the Mailman)*, John Qualen *(Mr. Ferguson)*, Fritz Feld *(Long-Haired Pianist)*, Kathryn Sheldon *(Mrs. Simpkins)*, Robert Dudley *(Mr. Simpkins)*, Billy Wayne *(Photographer)*, Minerva Urecal *(Strange Woman)*, Milton Parsons *(Piano Player)*, Kim Spalding *(Mr. Dexter)*, Dulce Daye *(Mrs. Dexter)*, Andrew Tombes *(Pritchett)*, Marjorie Holliday, Carol Savage *(Telephone Operators)*, June Evans *(Washerwoman)*, Harry Hines *(Elevator Man)*, Ann Doran *(Miss Bowen)*, Jerry Hausner *(Al Stern)*, Billy Lechner *(Johnny the Office Boy)*, Sam Edwards, George Conrad *(Parking Lot Attendants)*, Jay Barney, Jack Mather *(Detectives)*, Harry Carter, Colin Ward, Ken Christy *(Men)*, Peggy O'Connor *(Salesgirl)*, Jack Roper, Dick Curtis, Guy Way *(Moving Men)*, Elizabeth Flournoy *(Woman)*, Franklin "Pinky" Parker *(Poker Player)*, Robert Bice, Tudor Owen, John Roy *(Policemen)*, John Bleifer *(Bald Man)*, Bill Nelson *(Truck Driver)*, Philip Van Zandt *(Flick Morgan)*, Frances Budd *(Saleslady)*.

THE JACKPOT is one of the overlooked films of the early 1950s and is just as funny today as when it was first released. All one need do is substitute a TV show for a radio show and the story plays perfectly. Stewart is a nice, ordinary guy who works in a department store in Smalltown, USA. He's married to Hale and they have two adorable kids, Wood and Rettig. Their tranquil lives are tossed into turmoil when Stewart gets a phone call from a radio show and is able to supply the correct answer to the question: "Who Is The Mystery Husband?" (At that time one of the more popular shows was doing a phone segment where they played the sound of someone walking, gave a few clues, and called listeners. The winner received lots of prizes.) His house is filled with people who congratulate him on his good luck (he'd had some help from newspaperman Gleason) but it turns sour when he is besieged by thousands of dollars worth of soup, a live pony, a dozen timepieces, several thousand dollars worth of plants, a movable swimming pool, and a host of other things that he doesn't need. Their small house has no room for all of the bounty and his favorite furniture is moved to the garage. Now the IRS wants their cut. He had no idea he'd have to pay income tax on the loot. Hale gets annoyed because one of his prizes is a portrait that will be painted by Medina, a knockout artist. Mowbray arrives as a weird interior decorator who attempts to alter Stewart's favorite place, his living room. Stewart's boss at the store, Clark, can't take all the notoriety and plans to fire him right away. To raise money to pay his taxes, Stewart attempts to sell one of the wristwatches to a bookie just as the cops raid the betting parlor and he has to spend a night in jail, triggering his loss of job. Stewart learns that the maxim "there can be too much of a good thing" rings true. In the end, his formerly dull life is restored and he is content to return to what he'd thought was a bore but now welcomes. Stewart proves an admirable farceur here, as do Hale and Gleason. Mowbray, who usually played butlers, gets a welcome respite from that and is very funny. Rettig and Wood are little more than window dressing. THE JACKPOT is a delightful satire that everyone in the family will enjoy.

p, Samuel G. Engel; d, Walter Lang; w, Phoebe and Henry Ephron (based on a *New Yorker* article by John McNulty); ph, Joseph La Shelle; m, Lionel Newman; ed, J. Watson Webb, Jr.; art d, Joseph C. Wright, Lyle Wheeler.

Comedy **(PR:A MPAA:NR)**

JACKPOT* 1/2 (1960, Brit.) 71m Eternal/GN bw

William Hartnell *(Supt. Frawley)*, Betty McDowell *(Kay Stock)*, Eddie Byrne *(Sam Hare)*, George Mikell *(Carl Stock)*, Michael Ripper *(Lenny Lane)*, Victor Brooks *(Sgt. Jacks)*, Tim Turner *(Peter)*.

Minor crime drama revolving around a convict's desire to go straight after his release from jail. The dream to lead a normal life is quickly destroyed when his wife is not willing to share his goals, or flat, or anything else for that matter, so he looks up an old pal and returns to old habits, becoming involved in a nightclub heist.

p, Maurice J. Wilson; d, Montgomery Tully; w, Wilson, Tully (based on a story by John Sherman).

Crime **(PR:A MPAA:NR)**

JACK'S WIFE (SEE: HUNGRY WIVES, 1973)

JACKSON COUNTY JAIL ** 1/2 (1976) 89m New World c

Yvette Mimieux *(Dinah Hunter)*, Tommy Lee Jones *(Coley Blake)*, Robert Carradine *(Bobby Ray)*, Frederic Cook *(Hobie)*, Severn Darden *(Sheriff Dempsey)*, Nan Martin *(Allison)*, Mary Woronov *(Pearl)*, Howard Hesseman *(David)*, John Lawlor *(Deputy Burt)*, Britt Leach *(Dan Oldum)*, Betty Thomas *(Waitress)*, Patrice Rohmer *(Cassie Anne)*, Nancy Noble, Lisa Copeland, Clifford Emmich, Michael Ashe, Edward Marshall, Marcie Drake, Ken Lawrence, Arthur Wong, Marci Barkin, Michael Hilkene, Roy David Hagle, William Molloy, Ira Miller, Jackie Robin, Gus Peters, Amparo Mimieux, Richard Lockmiller, Jack O'Leary, Duffy Hambleton, Mark Carlton, Don Hinz, James Arnett, Norma Moye, Hal Needham.

This average chase/exploitation feature was surprisingly praised by critics upon release and developed somewhat of a cult following. Mimieux is a career woman who heads off to New York on a lark. She starts a long drive across the country, picking up some hitchhikers en route. Mimieux is subsequently beaten up and the car is stolen. She's thrown into a small town jail on false charges, and raped there by Darden's psychotic deputy. Mimieux manages to kill her attacker and flees the jail with Jones, another inmate. A destructive car chase follows and Jones is killed during a wild (and unintentionally funny) shootout amidst a bicentennial parade. The direction takes the story at a rapid pace, bombarding the viewer with sudden and violent images. However a lack of plausibility or dramatic honesty result in an occasionally interesting "almost but not quite" effort. Director Miller later remade this as a television film entitled OUTSIDE CHANCE.

p, Jeff Begun; d, Michael Miller; w, Donald Stewart; ph, Bruce Logan (Metrocolor); m, Loren Newkirk; ed, Caroline Ferriol; art d, Michael McCloskey; cos, Cornelia McNamara; stunts, James Arnett.

Drama **Cas.** **(PR:O MPAA:R)**

JACKTOWN ** (1962) 62m Pictorial International Prod bw

Patty McCormack *(Warden's Daughter)*, Richard Meade *(Thief)*, Douglas Rutherford *(Warden)*, Mike Tancredi, Johanna Douglas, John Anthony, Gordon Grant, Alice Gordon, Harry Newman, George F. Taylor, Russ Paquette.

Meade is a young hood caught in the back seat of his car with a fifteen year old girl. He's arrested for statutory rape and sent to Southern Michigan Prison. There Meade is taken under warden Rutherford's care and allowed to tend the compassionate man's garden. The situation between the two takes a sour twist when Rutherford's daughter McCormack falls in love with Meade. Meade manages to escape during a prison riot and takes refuge with his love. Eventually the escapee returns on his own volition, with McCormack's promise to wait for Meade's release date. Filmed on location, JACKTOWN also incorporates newsreel footage of the institution's 1952 riots for some added realism. Editor Rosenblum went on to such films as A THOUSAND CLOWNS, THE PAWNBROKER, and some of Woody Allen's early pictures.

p,d&w, William Martin; ph, Arthur J. Ornitz; m, Aldo Provenzano; ed, Ralph Rosenblum; md, Provenzano; art d, Jerry Kay.

Drama **(PR:A MPAA:NR)**

JACOB TWO-TWO MEETS THE HOODED FANG ** 1/2 (1979, Can.) 80m Gulkin/Cinema Shares International c

Stephen Rosenberg *(Jacob Two-Two)*, Alex Karras *(The Hooded Fang)*, Guy L'Ecuyer *(Master Fish)*, Joy Coghill *(Mistress Fowl)*, Earl Pennington *(Mr. Cooper/Judge)*, Claude Gai *(Mr. Fox)*, Marfa Richler *(Emma/Shapiro)*, Thor Bishopric *(Noah/O'Toole)*, Victor Desy *(Louis Loser)*.

This funny and delightful children's film is the tale of a boy who fantasizes he's been arrested after insulting some adults. The lad is sentenced for two years, two months, two weeks, two days, two hours, and two minutes in the most foreboding dungeon around. The place is guarded by the Hooded Fang, played by former Detroit Lions defensive tackle Karras. He turns in an enjoyable performance as a kid-hater who is nasty because youngsters find the man cute. Though undoubtedly little ones will eat this up, it unfortunately lacks the slickness deserved. Based on a novel by Canadian Mordecai Richler (author of THE APPRENTICESHIP OF DUDDY KRAVITZ), this fantasy is highly reminiscent of THE 5000 FINGERS OF DR. T., but Flicker's original film was reedited from his original intent.

p, Harry Gulkin; d&w, Theodore J. Flicker (based on the novel by Mordecai Richler); ph, Francois Protat; m, Lewis Furey; ed, Stan Cole; art d, Seamus Flannery; cos, Francois Barbeau; m/l, Furey.

Juvenile/Fantasy **Cas.** **(PR:AAA MPAA:G)**

JACQUELINE ** 1/2 (1956, Brit.) 93m RANK bw

John Gregson *(Mike McNeil)*, Kathleen Ryan *(Elizabeth McNeil)*, Jacqueline Ryan *(Jacqueline McNeil)*, Noel Purcell *(Mr. Owen)*, Cyril Cusack *(Mr. Flannagan)*, Maureen Swanson *(Maggie)*, Tony Wright *(Jack McBride)*, Liam Redmond *(Mr. Lord)*, Maureen Delaney *(Mrs. McBride)*, Marie Kean *(Mrs. Flannagan)*, Richard O'Sullivan *(Michael)*, Rita Begley *(Sara Flannagan)*, Josephine Fitzgerald *(Mrs. McMullen)*, Barry Keegan *(Bob Quinton)*, James Devlin *(Mr. Lord's Servant)*, Harold Goldblatt *(Schoolmaster)*, Jack McGowran *(Campbell)*, Sam Kydd *(Foreman)*, Christopher Steele *(Mr. Pike)*.

Working man Gregson loses his job when vertigo attacks affect his performance at the shipyards. His drinking goes from an occasional tiff to out-and-out drunkenness, which doesn't help the situation. Fortunately for the man, his young daughter (Ryan) is a stock plucky type. She inspires her father after being picked to solo at a church festival, and eventually helps Gregson get a job with businessman Redmond. The emotional manipulation within the drama does its job effectively, though every trick shines through without shame. The performers' sincerity helps out, rising above the largely unbelievable script.

p, George H. Brown; d, Roy Barker; w, Patrick Kirwan, Liam O'Flaherty, Patrick Campbell, Catherine Cookson; ph, Geoffrey Unsworth; m, Cedric Thorpe Davie; ed, John D. Guthridge; md, Muir Mathieson; art d, Jack Maxted.

Drama **(PR:A MPAA:NR)**

JACQUELINE SUSANN'S ONCE IS NOT ENOUGH
(SEE: ONCE IS NOT ENOUGH, 1975)

JACQUES BREL IS ALIVE AND WELL AND LIVING IN PARIS **
(1975) 98m American Film Theater c

Elly Stone *(Lady With Shopping Bag)*, Mort Shuman *(Taxi Driver)*, Joe Masiell *(Marine)*, Jacques Brel.

Once again the American Film Theatre adapts a stage play (or in this case a musical) for the screen and comes up with a fairly tedious end product that saps the life out of the work it was supposed to document. This is a revue of the words and music of Jacques Brel, the internationally known Belgian singer/songwriter/actor. The off-Broadway production on which this was based had over 1,800 performances at New York's Village Gate Theater. The show (and the film) contains 26 Brel songs as performed by three singer/actors who take turns relating the various aspects of the composer's works. Brel's songs spanned the emotional realm from sweetly sentimental to disarmingly cynical. Unfortunately the visual, literal translation of the material breaks down the basic, simple appeal of the work by destroying the subtlety that makes Brel's work so vital. Songs include: "Carousel," "Old Folks," "Marathon," and Brel himself sings "Ne Me Quittes Pas."

p, Paul Marshall; d, Denis Heroux; w, Eric Blau (based on the stage production by Blau and Mort Shuman); ph, Rene Verzier; m, Jacques Brel; ed, Yves Longlois; md, Francois Rauber; art d, Jean Andre; cos, Jeannine Vergne; ch, Moni Yakim.

Musical **(PR:A MPAA:PG)**

JADA, GOSCIE, JADA (SEE: GUESTS ARE COMING, 1965, Pol.)

JADE MASK, THE ** (1945) 69m MON bw

Sidney Toler *(Charlie Chan)*, Mantan Moreland *(Birmingham Brown)*, Edwin Luke *(Tommy)*, Janet Warren *(Jean)*, Edith Evanson *(Lousie)*, Hardie Albright *(Meeker)*, Frank Reicher *(Harper)*, Cyril Delevanti *(Roth)*, Alan Bridge *(Mack)*, Dorothy Granger *(Stella)*, Joe Whitehead *(Peabody)*, Ralph Lewis *(Kimball)*, Jack Ingram *(Archer)*, Lester Dorr *(Michael)*, Henry Hall *(Godfrey)*.

One among many in the CHARLIE CHAN series, this one has Toler promoted to inspector for the government. He uncovers a sick murderer and his wife. The pair try to make it appear as if their victims are still alive using masks and human puppetry. Edwin Luke, Keye Luke's brother, takes on the role of Toler's son Eddie. (See CHARLIE CHAN Series, Index)

p, James S. Burkett; d, Phil Rosen; w, George Callahan; ph, Harry Neumann; ed, Dick Currier; art d, Dave Milton.

Mystery **(PR:A MPAA:NR)**

JAGA WA HASHITTA (SEE: CREATURE CALLED MAN, THE, 1970, Jap.)

JAGUAR ** (1956) 66m REP bw

Sabu *(Juano)*, Chiquita *(Rita)*, Barton MacLane *(Steve Bailey)*, Jonathan Hale *(Dr. Powell)*, Touch (Mike) Connors *(Marty Lang)*, Jay Novello *(Tupi)*, Fortunio Bonanova *(Francisco Servente)*, Nacho Galindo *(Garcia Solimos)*, Redwing *(1st Porter)*, Pepe Hern *(Jorge)*, Raymond Rosas *(Motilon Boy)*.

Mickey Rooney's production company put up the money for this routine jungle outing. Sabu is a primitive boy taken from his rain forest home in South America by British doctor Hale, and raised as British. Later in life, while on an expedition for oil, Sabu fears he may be reverting back to his savage state when the party suspects him of a rather nasty murder. Sabu isn't sure of his innocence as he may have been under the influence of powerful drugs when the murder took place. After being kidnapped by his old tribe, Sabu learns the truth and is relieved that he is not the killer. The story is riddled with cliches and stock characterizations, all of which add up to little.

p, Mickey Rooney, Maurice Duke; d, George Blair; w, John Fenton Murray, Benedict Freedman; ph, Bud Thackery; m, Van Alexander; ed, Cliff Bell; md, Alexander; art d, Al Goodman; cos, Adele Palmer.

Mystery/Adventure **(PR:A MPAA:NR)**

JAGUAR *** (1980, Phil.) 90m Atienza c

Phillip Salvador *(Poldo)*, Amy Austria *(Cristy)*, Menggie Cobarrubias *(Sonny)*, Anita Linda *(Mother)*, Johnny Delgado *(Direk)*, Tonio Gutierrez *(Jing)*.

A surprisingly good film from the Philippines, a sort of *film noir*, which stars Salvador as a poor man struggling to better his life by taking a job as a security guard in a swanky apartment house. Salvador, supporting his mother and two sisters, suddenly finds himself involved in a dangerous situation when he comes to the aid of one of the residents, who is being attacked by a sleazy nightclub owner and his "goons." The man is so grateful, he offers Salvador a job as his bodyguard. However, his benefactor is not much better than the nightclub owner; he is a publisher of pornographic magazines. Later, it's revealed that the conflict between these two men arose over a woman, and Salvador is given the task of baby-sitting her. The two are attracted to each other and Salvador, against his better judgment, makes love to her. Soon after, the gang war escalates and there is a fight in which Salvador kills a man. Trapped, the magazine publisher offers to save Salvador and his family if he will keep quiet. Angry at the man for luring him into a life of crime, Salvador flies into a violent fury that puts him in prison. JAGUAR has a real *noir* sensibility which sees its main character trapped in an amoral world with no escape. This is one of the very few Filipino films ever to show at the Cannes Film Festival.

d, Lino Brocka; w, Jose Lacaba, Richardo Lee; ph, Conrado Balthazar; m, Max Jocson; ed, Rene Tala.

Drama/Crime **(PR:C MPAA:NR)**

JAGUAR LIVES zero (1979) 90m AIP c

Joe Lewis *(Jonathan Cross/Jaguar)*, Christopher Lee *(Caine)*, Donald Pleasence *(Gen. Villanova)*, Barbara Bach *(Anna)*, Capucine *(Zina)*, Joseph Wiseman *(Ben Ashir)*, Woody Strode *(Sensei)*, John Huston *(Ralph Richards)*, Gabriel Melgar *(Ahmed)*, Anthony DeLongis *(Brett)*, Sally Faulkner *(Terry)*, Gail Grainger *(Consuela)*, Anthony Heaton *(Coblintz)*, Luis Prendes *(Habish)*, Simon Andreu *(Petrie)*, James Smilie *(Reardon)*, Oscar James *(Collins)*, Ray Jewers *(Jessup)*, Ralph Brown *(Logan)*.

Beware of all-star casts participating in runaway productions (shooting all over the world because it's cheaper than paying American union crews); these films are usually unsatisfactory and JAGUAR LIVES is no exception. Heavyweight karate champ Joe Lewis (no, not the boxer) hacks his way around the world in an effort to end the reign of terror perpetrated by an international drug cartel. The cameos by Pleasence (as a South American dictator, no less, which is almost as bad as casting him as the President of the United States in ESCAPE FROM NEW YORK), Lee, and Huston are embarrassing. Unfortunately, Woody Strode, a fine actor who deserved more than he got from Hollywood in the 1970s, is totally wasted.

p, Derek Gibson; d, Ernest Pintoff; w, Yabo Yablonsky; ph, John Cabrera (Movielab Color); m, Robert O. Ragland; ed, Angelo Ross; art d, Adolfo Cofino; cos, Ron Talsky; ch, Joe Lewis.

Martial Arts **(PR:C MPAA:PG)**

JAIL BAIT* (1954) 70m Howco bw (AKA: HIDDEN FACE)

Dolores Fuller, Lyle Talbot, Herbert Rawlinson, Steve Reeves, Clancy Malone, Tim Farrell, Theodora Thurman, Cotton Watts, Chick.

For low-budget filmmaker Edward D. Wood, Jr. (the man who made such terrible films as PLAN NINE FROM OUTER SPACE, and GLEN OR GLENDA) this movie is no exception. The story has the good son of plastic surgeon Rawlinson turning to crime under the influence of Farrell, a juvenile delinquent. After Rawlinson's son kills a night watchman during a theater holdup, he is, in turn, "bumped off" by Farrell when, stricken with guilt, he wishes to confess. But Farrell and Rawlinson's son were identified during the robbery, so Farrell goes to Rawlinson. He tells him he has hidden his son, and unless he performs plastic surgery to disguise his looks from the police, Rawlinson will never see his son alive. Rawlinson agrees to Farrell's demands, but just before the operation he discovers his dead son's body. Rawlinson performs the operation anyway, and when the bandages are removed two weeks later, Farrell is shocked to discover the face of Rawlinson's murdered son replacing his own. Minutes later he is killed while trying to escape from the police who are still searching for the holdup man, Rawlinson's son. Reeves, in his first speaking role, and Talbot are hysterical as a couple of detectives. This was Rawlinson's last film, he died the day following the film's completion. The minstrel show production number was borrowed from a 1951 movie, YES SIR MR. BONES; the score was lifted directly from MESA OF LOST WOMEN.

p&d, Edward D. Wood, Jr.; w, Wood, Jr., Alex Gordon; ph, Bill Thompson; m Hoyt Xurtin; ed, Charles Clement, Igor Kantor.

Crime **Cas.** **(PR:C MPAA:NR)**

JAIL BAIT***
(1977, Ger.) 99m Intertel/New Yorker c (WILDWECHSEL; AKA: WILD GAME; GAME PASS)

Eva Mattes *(Hanni Schneider)*, Harry Baer *(Franz Bermeier)*, Jorg von Liebenfels *(Erwin Schneider, Hanni's father)*, Ruth Drexel *(Hilda Schneider, Hanni's Mother)*, El Hedi Ben Salem, Rudolph Waldemar Brem *(Franz's Friends)*, Kurt Raab *(Factory Boss)*, Hanna Schygulla *(Gynecologist)*, Karl Scheydt, Klaus Lowitsch *(Policemen)*, Irm Hermann, Marquard Bohm *(Police Officials)*.

Though originally made in 1972, JAIL BAIT was not released in the U.S. until five years later when the popularity of Fassbinder had grown. A literal translation of the German title reads "Wild Game" a much more appropriate description of the fourteen year-old Mattes' attitude toward the events in which she becomes involved. Looking and dressing like someone five years her senior, she is picked up by the older Baer. Serving a jail sentence for his sexual liaison with the girl, he is released to start up where he had left off with the nymphet. This time Mattes turns up pregnant, forcing her into a bind which has her persuading Baer to murder her father. When originally released on German TV quite a stir was made by the excessive manner in which teenage sexuality was treated. The young Mattes has a matter-of-fact attitude toward sex treating it as little more than a game. The killing of her father is just a continuation of the scenario she has created with Baer, an event for which she feels no remorse. Both Mattes and Baer are perfect characterizations with which to explore the empty alienation of post World War II Germany, where ideals are rapidly becoming an extinct phenomenon. After its release the original author of the play (Kroetz) strongly indicated that he wanted absolutely no connection with this controversial film. (In German; English titles)

d&w, Rainer Werner Fassbinder (based on the play by Franz-Xaver Kroetz); ph, Dietrich Lohmann; m, Peer Raben, Ludwig von Beethoven; ed, Thea Eymesz; art d, Kurt Raab; makeup, Freddy Arnold; m/l, "You Are My Destiny," Paul Anka (sung by Anka).

Drama **(PR:O MPAA:NR)**

JAIL BUSTERS 1/2** (1955) 61m AA bw

Leo Gorcey *(Terrence Aloysius "Slip" Mahoney/41326)*, Huntz Hall *(Horace Debussy "Sach" Jones/41328)*, Bennie Bartlett *(Butch Williams/41327)*, David Condon *(Charles "Chuck" Anderson)*, Bernard Gorcey *(Louie Dumbrowski)*, Percy Helton *(Warden B. W. Oswald)*, Barton MacLane *(Guard Jenkins)*, Anthony Caruso *(Ed Lannigan)*, Murray Alper *(Gus)*, Michael Ross *(Big Greenie)*, Fritz Feld *(Dr. Fernando F. Fordyce)*, Lyle Talbot *(Cy Bowman)*, Henry Kulky *(Marty)*, Emil Sitka *(Mug Photographer)*, John Harmon *(Tomcyk)*, Henry Tyler *(Hank/12784)*.

A later film in the long-running BOWERY BOYS series. This one has Gorcey and Hall helping a reporter friend who was beaten while investigating an undercover story about a local prison. Condon's editor, Talbot, is only too happy to help them stage a bogus jewel robbery so Hall and Gorcey can be put in prison. Once behind bars, however, the boys discover that Talbot has kept the stolen jewels, and their stay is now indefinite. Although Gorcey and Hall get themselves into all sorts of predicaments and humorous situations once inside the prison, they also manage to expose a scam (involving certain inmates paying prison guards for the easy jobs), clear their names, and follow up on Condon's original story. (See BOWERY BOYS series, Index)

p, Ben Schwalb; d, William Beaudine; w, Edward Bernds, Elwood Ullman; ph, Carl Guthrie; ed, Lester A. Sansom, William Austin; md, Marlin Skiles; art d, David Milton; set d, Joseph Kish; cos, Bert Henrickson; makeup, Emile LaVigne.

Comedy **(PR:AA MPAA:NR)**

JAIL HOUSE BLUES** (1942) 62m UNIV bw

Nat Pendleton *(Sonny McGann)*, Anne Gwynne *(Doris Daniels)*, Robert Paige *(Cliff Bailey)*, Horace MacMahon *(Swifty)*, Elisabeth Risdon *(Mrs. McGann)*, Warren Hymer *(Big Foot Louie)*, Samuel S. Hinds *(Mr. Daniels)*, Cliff Clark *(Warden)*, John Kelly *(Snork)*, Reed Hadley *(Boston)*, Paul Fix *(Danny)*, Dewey Robinson *(Liverlip)*.

Pendleton plays a convict transformed into an obsessive stage producer when given the job for the prison show. His preparation is temporarily interrupted when his jail sentence ends, but this gives him the chance to round up some new talent as well as reclaim the escapee who had been assigned the duties of feminine lead. All Pendleton's efforts prove to be worthwhile as Broadway looks like the first stop after prison. Entertaining mindlessness.

p, Ken Goldsmith; d, Albert S. Rogell; w, Paul Gerard Smith, Harold Tarshis (based on the story "Rhapsody in Stripes" by Tarshis); ph, Elwood Bredell; ed, Frank Gross.

Comedy **(PR:A MPAA:NR)**

JAILBIRDS, 1931 (SEE: PARDON US, 1931)

JAILBIRDS 1/2** (1939, Brit.) 73m But bw

Albert Burdon *(Bill Smith)*, Shaun Glenville *(Col. Pepper)*, Charles Farrell *(Spike Nelson)*, Charles Hawtrey *(Nick)*, Lorraine Clewes *(Mary Smith)*, Sylvia Coleridge *(Mrs. Smith)*, Harry Terry *(Narky)*, Cyril Chamberlain *(Bob)* Nat Mills and Bobbie *(Mr. & Mrs. Popodopulous)*.

Burdon and Hawtrey are a pair of convicts who escape by dressing in drag. They take jobs at a bakery, where a fellow escapee gives them some stolen gems to hide. When the loaf of bread they hid the loot in gets sold to a detective, the inept crooks break back into jail and pretend they've been there all along. Funnier than most British comedies of the time.

p, F. W. Baker; d, Oswald Mitchell; w, Con West (based on a sketch by Fred Karno); ph, Geoffrey Faithfull.

Comedy **(PR:A MPAA:NR)**

JAILBREAK* (1936) 60m WB bw (GB: MURDER IN THE BIG HOUSE)

June Travis *(Jane Rogers)*, Craig Reynolds *(Ken Williams)*, Barton MacLane *(Detective Capt. Rourke)*, Richard Purcell *(Ed Slayden)*, Addison Richards *(Dan Varner)*, George E. Stone *(Weeper)*, Eddie Acuff *(Sig Patton)*, Joseph King *(Big Mike Egan)*, Joseph Crehan *(Warden)*, Mary Treen *(Gladys Joy)*, Henry Hall *(Pop Anderson)*, Charles Middleton *(Dan Stone)*, Robert Emmett Keane *(City Editor)*.

Just one more of many prison films from Warner Bros., this one with a cast of relative unknowns and a trite plot. Purcell does a respectable James Cagney imitation as a convict housed in a cell in close proximity to his gangland arch-rival, King. A third prison inmate murders the latter in order to partake of the small fortune King has concealed outside the prison walls. Suspicion naturally falls on Purcell, but he is cleared with the aid of the kind offices of reporter Reynolds who, in this implausible story, is given the run of the prison. Detective MacLane bumblingly follows false trails while big-house employee Travis ambles on-screen from time to time, supplying Reynolds with the mandatory love interest. Remade in 1939 with Ronald Reagan as SMASHING THE MONEY RING.

p, Bryan Foy; d, Nick Grinde; w, Robert D. Andrews, Joseph Hoffman (based on a story "Murder in Sing Sing" by Jonathan Finn); ph, Arthur Todd; ed, Harold McLernon.

Crime **(PR:A MPAA:NR)**

JAILBREAKERS, THE zero (1960) 63m AIP bw

Robert Hutton *(Tom)*, Mary Castle *(June)*, Michael O'Connell *(Lake)*, Gabe Delutri *(Joe)*, Anton Van Stralen *(Stearn)*, Toby Hill *(Karen)*, Carlos Chavez *(Bushman)*.

Three convicts search for stolen loot in a ghost town, while taking husband Hutton and wife Castle hostage. But there is fighting among the thieves which leads to their demise. Far from exciting.

p,d&w, Alex Grasshoff; m, Andre Brummer.

Crime (PR:A MPAA:NR)

JAILHOUSE ROCK 1/2** (1957) 96m MGM bw

Elvis Presley *(Vince Everett)*, Judy Tyler *(Peggy Van Alden)*, Mickey Shaughnessy *(Hunk Houghton)*, Jennifer Holden *(Sherry Wilson)*, Dean Jones *(Teddy Talbot)*, Anne Neyland *(Laury Jackson)*, Hugh Sanders *(Warden)*, Vaughn Taylor *(Mr. Shores)*, Mike Stoller *(Pianist)*, Grandon Rhodes *(Prof. August Van Alden)*, Katherine Warren *(Mrs. Van Alden)*, Don Burnett *(Mickey Alba)*, George Cisar *(Jake the Bartender)*, Glenn Strange *(Simpson, Convict)*, John Indrisano *(Convict)*, Robert Bice *(Bardeman, TV Studio Manager)*, Percy Helton *(Sam Brewster)*, Peter Adams *(Jack Lease)*, William Forrest *(Studio Head)*, Dan White *(Paymaster)*, Robin Raymond *(Dotty)*, John Day *(Ken)*, S. John Launer *(Judge)*, Dick Rich *(Guard)*, Elizabeth Slifer *(Cleaning Woman)*, Gloria Pall *(Stripteaser)*, Fred Coby *(Bartender)*, Walter Johnson *(Shorty)*, Frank Kreig *(Drunk)*, William Tannen *(Record Distributor)*, Wilson Wood *(Record Engineer)*, Tom McKee *(TV Director)*, Donald Kerr *(Photographer)*, Carl Milletaire *(Drummond)*, Francis DeSales *(Surgeon)*, Harry Hines *(Hotel Clerk)*, Dorothy Abbott *(Woman in Cafe)*, The Jordanaires *(Musicians)*.

This was Elvis' third film after LOVE ME TENDER and LOVING YOU and it set the "standard" (if such a thing could be standardized) for the next several movies. It was filmed in black-and-white, which is the reason why it isn't seen all that often on TV in these days when station managers would rather program a turkey in color. Elvis is a good ol' boy who saves a woman and kills the man who was harassing her in a bar. This heroism gets him sent to the local clink for manslaughter. While in prison Elvis gets to know Shaughnessy, another felon, who convinces Elvis to perform in the slammer's convict show. After he is freed, he meets Tyler and they start their own record company. In less time than it takes to say "You Ain't Nothin' But A Houn' Dog," Elvis is a national star and on his way to Hollywood. Tyler sees him changing, becoming an egomaniac only interested in himself (there are those who claim that life imitated art and that's exactly what Elvis became in the end), and she can't stand it. (Note. The same situation was explored by Budd Schulberg in his brilliant A FACE IN THE CROWD). Elvis falls hard for his leading lady, Holden, and Tyler is distraught as he plans to sell the record company and leave her. Shaughnessy shows up, whacks the King around, and hits him in the throat, thereby causing a temporary loss of voice. Tyler and Shaughnessy stick by Elvis while others flee and he realizes that she really does love him and will forever. All ends happily as Elvis plans to marry Tyler. This was Tyler's second film after starring on Broadway in Rodgers and Hammerstein's "Pipe Dream," a musical based on the works of John Steinbeck. She died in a car crash soon afterward and just about everyone connected with that play found that it was their swan song. The songs were mostly by Lieber and Stoller, who became millionaires before they were thirty, but proved they had staying power in pop music by writing "(I'm Going To) Kansas City" and "Is That All There Is?" among their scores of hits. Stoller, who is married to jazz pianist and harpist Corky Hale, can be seen as the pianist in the "Jailhouse Rock" sequence. Other tunes include; "Treat Me Nice," "Baby, I Don't Care," "Young And Beautiful," "Don't Leave Me Now," "I Wanna Be Free," and "One More Day." Assistant director Robert Relyea grew up to be a film producer. Screenwriter Trosper wrote many excellent movies including BIRDMAN OF ALCATRAZ, his last. The title song sold 2 million records within two weeks and served to hype the picture which grossed several million, of which Elvis received fifty percent of the profits.

p, Pandro S. Berman; d, Richard Thorpe; w, Guy Trosper (based on a story by Ned Young); ph, Robert Bronner (CinemaScope); ed, Ralph E. Winters; md, Jeff Alexander; art d, William A. Horning, Randell Duell; spec eff, A. Arnold Gillespie; m/l, Mike Stoller, Jerry Lieber, Roy C. Bennett, Abner Silver, Ben Weisman, Aaron Schroeder, Sid Tepper; makeup, William Tuttle.

Musical Drama Cas. (PR:A MPAA:NR)

JAK BYC KOCHANA (SEE: HOW TO BE LOVED, 1965, Pol.)

JALNA** (1935) 75m RKO bw

Kay Johnson *(Alayne)*, Ian Hunter *(Renny)*, C. Aubrey Smith *(Nicholas)*, Nigel Bruce *(Maurice)*, David Manners *(Eden)*, Peggy Wood *(Meg)*, Jessie Ralph *(Gran)*, Molly Lamont *(Pheasant)*, Theodore Newton *(Piers)*, Halliwell Hobbes *(Ernest)*, Forrester Harvey *(Rags)*, George Offerman, Jr. *(Finch)*, Clifford Severn *(Wakefield)*.

A decent adaptation of Mazo de la Roche's novel concerning the lives and loves of the eccentric Whiteoak family who live on their palatial estate, Jalna, located in beautiful southern Ontario. Manners plays a young novelist who meets and marries Johnson while on a trip to New York. He brings his shy bride back to Canada where she is soon bombarded with the problems of his entire family. After sorting out the rather maudlin developments that transpired in his absence (this brother married that illegitimate daughter of that neighbor, etc.), Manners begins some extramarital adventures that focus on Lamont, the "sexy dame" who turned up on the family's porch one day. Unfortunately for him, before he has a chance to revel in these lustful desires, he is killed by a nasty fall. The now-widowed Johnson realizes it's Hunter whom she loves, and they marry. Seventy-five minutes is perhaps not enough for a film crowded with so many intrigues.

p, Kenneth Macgowan; d, John Cromwell; w, Anthony Veiller, Garrett Fort, Larry Bachman (based on the novel by Mazo de la Roche); ph, Edward Cronjager; m, Al Colombo; ed, William Morgan; art d, Van Nest Polglase, Charles Kirk.

Drama (PR:A MPAA:NR)

JALOPY*** (1953) 62m AA bw

Leo Gorcey *(Terrence Aloysius "Slip" Mahoney)*, Huntz Hall *(Horace Debussy "Sach" Jones)*, David Condon *(Chuck)*, Bennie Bartlett *(Butch)*, Bernard Gorcey *(Louie Dumbrowski)*, Robert Lowery *(Skid Wilson)*, Jane Easton *(Bobbie Lane)*, Leon Belasco *(Prof. Bosgood Elrod)*, Richard Benedict *(Tony Lango)*, Murray Alper *(Red Baker)*, Tom Hanlon *(Race Announcer)*, Mona Knox *("Invented" Girl)*, Conrad Brooks *(Party Guest)*, Robert Rose, George Dockstader, George Barrows, Fred Lamont, Teddy Mangean, Bud Wolfe, Carey Loftin, Louis Tomei, Dude Criswell, Dick Crockett, Pete Kellett, Carl Saxe *(Jalopy Drivers)*.

By 1953 the BOWERY BOYS series was beginning to drag. Stars Gorcey and Hall, who had been with the many-named series since DEAD END in 1937, were rapidly approaching middle-age and felt foolish pretending to still be the same juvenile delinquents they had portrayed in the first film. Seeking a change of format, Gorcey and Hall pushed for a new producer, Ben Schwalb, and a new director, William Beaudine (affectionately dubbed "One Shot" because it was rumored that he never allowed a second take). These men convinced the cast that the BOWERY BOYS should "grow-up" and play adults: the slapstick, befuddled parodies of adults to which children (the largest audience for the films) could still relate. This new approach revitalized the series and it ran another five years. JALOPY sees the boys desperate for a way to bail their pal Bernard Gorcey out of his financial troubles. Leo Gorcey enters his junky jalopy in a race to win some quick cash, but he finishes dead last. Luckily, Hall who had recently been experimenting with some chemicals, discovers a super-fuel that will transform any normal vehicle into an unbelievable speed machine. The formula works, and Gorcey's car whips around the track in just over ten seconds. Meanwhile, crooked gambler Lowery gets wind of the new fuel and tries to snatch it for himself, but the boys manage to keep it out of his hands. On the day of the big race, Hall accidentally mixes up a worthless batch and Gorcey is forced to begin the race without the benefit of super-fuel. Halfway through the race, Hall perfects his formula and fills Gorcey's car. But this time the super-fuel only works in reverse, so Gorcey turns the car around and zooms through the pack backwards, winning the race and saving Louie's store. In another interesting deviation from the conventions of the series, Hall's elixir is made to seem to have the further mystical power of causing beautiful young women to appear from nowhere, a circumstance that quite literally added body to the film. (See BOWERY BOYS series, Index)

p, Ben Schwalb; d, William Beaudine; w, Tim Ryan, Jack Crutcher, Edmond Seward, Jr., Bert Lawrence (based on a story by Ryan, Crutcher); ph, Harry Neumann; m, Martin Skiles; ed, William Austin; art d, David Milton; set d, Robert Priestley; cos, Frank Beetson.

Comedy (PR:AA MPAA:NR)

JALSAGHAR (SEE: MUSIC ROOM, THE, 1963, India)

JAM SESSION 1/2** (1944) 78m COL bw

Ann Miller *(Terry Baxter)*, Jess Barker *(George Carter Haven)*, Charles D. Brown *(Raymond Stuart)*, Eddie Kane *(Lloyd Marley)*, George Eldredge *(Berkley Bell)*, Renie Riano *(Miss Tobin)*, Clarence Muse *(Henry)*, Pauline Drake *(Evelyn)*, Charles La Torre *(Coletti)*, Anne Loos *(Neva Cavendish)*, Ray Walker *(Fred Wylie)*, Marguerite Campbell *(Girl Jitterbug)*, George McKay *(Policeman)*, Robert Williams *(Taxi Driver)*, Vernon Dent *(Butler)*, John Dilson *(Man)*, Ethan Laidlaw *(Jackson)*, Victor Travers *(Actor)*, Charles Haefell *(Rostler)*, Allen Fox *(Cutter)*, Eddie Hall *(Smart Young Man)*, Eddie Bruce *(Guide)*, Bill Shawn *(Dancer)*, Ted Mapes *(Guard)*, Hank Bell *(Driver)*, John Tyrrell *(Director)*, Terry Frost *(Asst. Director)*, Paul Zeremba *(Rip)*, Marilyn Johnson *(Stenographer)*, Constance Worth *(Miss Dooley)*, Nelson Leigh *(Blake)*, Joanne Frank *(Girl)*, Jay Eaton *(Designer)*, George Carleton *(Cop)*, Margaret Fealy *(Old Lady)*, Ben Taggart *(Willie)*, Eddie Laughton *(2nd Asst. Director)*, Thomas Kingston *(Sound Engineer)*, J. Reilly Thompson *(Boy Jitterbug)*, and featuring the orchestras of Louis Armstrong, Charlie Barnet, Jan Garber, Teddy Powell, Alvino Rey, Glen Gray and his Casa Loma Orchestra, The Pied Pipers and Nan Wynn.

The facile plot in this one is just an excuse to allow some swing bands a chance to play. Miller stars as a country girl who comes out on top in a dance contest and wins a round-trip ticket to Hollywood. She goes there seeking fame and fortune and finds herself in love with screenwriter Barker. After rolling through a number of swing tunes, Miller nearly destroys Barker's career through the usual set of contrived misunderstandings; but it really doesn't matter because it's the music that counts. Songs include: "Cherokee" (Ray Noble), "I Can't Give You Anything But Love" (Dorothy Fields, Jimmy McHugh), "Murder He Says" (Frank Loesser, McHugh), "I Lost My Sugar in Salt Lake City" (Leon Rene, Johnny Lange), "Brazil" (S.K. Russell, Ary Barroso), "It Started All Over Again" (Bill Carey, Carl Fisher), "Victory Polka" (Sammy Cahn, Jule Styne), "No Name Jive" (Glen Gray).

p, Irving Briskin; d, Charles Barton; w, Manny Seff (based on a story by Harlan Ware, Patterson McNutt); ph, L.W. O'Connell; ed, Richard Fantl; md, M.W. Stoloff; art d, Lionel Banks, Paul Murphy; set d, William Kiernan.

Musical (PR:A MPAA:NR)

JAMAICA INN** (1939, Brit.) 99m Mayflower/PAR bw

Charles Laughton *(Sir Humphrey Pengallan)*, Maureen O'Hara *(Mary Yelland)*, Leslie Banks *(Joss Merlyn)*, Emlyn Williams *(Harry the Peddler)*, Robert Newton *(Jem Trehearne)*, Wylie Watson *(Salvation Watkins)*, Marie Ney *(Patience Merlyn)*, Morland Graham *(Sea-Lawyer Sydney)*, Stephen Haggard *(Boy)*, Mervyn Johns *(Thomas)*, Edwin Greenwood *(Dandy)*, Horace Hodges *(Chadwick, the Butler)*, Jeanne de Casalis, Basil Radford, George Curzon *(Guests)*, John Longden *(Capt. Johnson)*, Hay Petrie *(Groom)*, Frederick Piper *(Agent)*, William Devlin, Herbert Lomas, Clare Greet *(Tenants)*, A. Bromley Davenport *(Another Guest)*, Mabel Terry Lewis, Aubrey Mather, Marie Ault, O. B. Clarence, Mary Jerold, Archibald

Harradine, Harry Lane, William Fazan, Alan Lewis, Peter Scott, Philip Ray, George Smith, Robert Adair, Sam Lee, Roy Frumkes.

JAMAICA INN had many interesting incidents associated with it. Unfortunately, very little of that interest reached the screen. Laughton had opened his own production company, Mayflower, and this, the third and final film, finally sank the ship. Prior to it they had made THE BEACHCOMBER and SIDEWALKS OF LONDON and they hoped that the addition of Hitchcock, who had just finished his successful THE LADY VANISHES, would help the feeble script. Not even the great Alfred could make this one fly. Laughton and Hitch had some knockdown battles on the set, but as Laughton was also the co-producer, Hitchcock couldn't make the man understand and the result was a hammier performance than any performed by Porky Pig. This was to be Hitchcock's last film in pre-war England before coming to the USA and beginning his memorable work. Laughton is an oily squire in Cornwall on the coast of England. He leads a pack of cutthroats who lure boats to the area with false lights, then allow them to be dashed on the rocks in the rough seas. Once that's done, Laughton and his brigands kill the passengers and loot the boats. Jamaica Inn is a local hostelry and O'Hara (just eighteen and breathtakingly beautiful in her first major role) has arrived to stay with her aunt and uncle, Ney and Banks. It isn't long before she realizes that the inn is the headquarters of the killers. Newton is from Lloyds of London and is working undercover to see if he can learn why it is that so many ships meet their fate in this particular area. When his identity is discovered, the pirates mean to lynch him but O'Hara saves his life. In the end Laughton goes mad, climbs to the crow's nest of a ship, screams at anyone who'll listen, then jumps and goes right through the deck. The picture opened to big business but word of mouth travels faster than the speed of light and JAMAICA INN soon closed forever. Creaky, old hat, and forgettable. Hitchcock had worked with co-producer Pommer once before when he toiled as a writer and art director on the silent film THE BLACKGUARD in 1924. He should have waited another fifteen years before being talked into this job.

p, Erich Pommer, Charles Laughton; d, Alfred Hitchcock; w, Sidney Gilliat, Joan Harrison, J.B. Priestley, Alma Reville (based on the novel by Daphne du Maurier); ph, Harry Stradling, Bernard Knowles; m, Eric Fenby; ed, Robert Hamer; md, Frederic Lewis; set d, Tom N. Moraham; cos, Molly McArthur; spec eff, Harry Watts.

Historical Drama Cas. (PR:C MPAA:NR)

JAMAICA RUN** (1953) 92m Clarion/PAR c

Ray Milland *(Patrick Fairlie)*, Arlene Dahl *(Ena Dacey)*, Wendell Corey *(Todd Dacey)*, Patric Knowles *(William Montague)*, Laura Elliot *(Janice Clayton)*, Carroll McComas *(Mrs. Dacey)*, William Walker *(Human)*, Murray Matheson *(Inspector Mole)*, Clarence Muse *(Mose)*, Michael Moore *(Robert Clayton)*, *Rex Evans (Judge Henry)*, Robert Warwick *(Court Judge)*, Lester Matthews *(Judge)*, Robert A. Davis *(Rob)*.

Seafaring programmer starring Milland as the no-nonsense captain of a schooner that sails off the Jamaica coast. He soon comes to the aid of Dahl, who is struggling to keep the family mansion from the evil clutches of Knowles, who claims she doesn't really own it. Dahl is forced to go to Milland for help because her mother, McComas, and brother, Corey, are too drunk to care. As it turns out, the proof of ownership is buried beneath the sea in a sunken ship, and it's up to Milland to find it before Knowles does. In the end it doesn't matter because the mansion goes up in flames.

p, William H. Pine, William C. Thomas; d, Lewis R. Foster; w, Foster (based on the novel *The Neat Little Corpse* by Max Murray); ph, Lionel Lindon (Technicolor); m, Lucien Cailliet; ed, Howard Smith; art d, Hal Pereira, Earl Hedrick.

Action (PR:A MPAA:NR)

JAMBOREE (SEE: ROOKIES ON PARADE, 1941)

JAMBOREE** (1944) 71m REP bw

Ruth Terry *(Ruth Cartwright)*, George Byron *(Joe Mason)*, Paul Harvey *(P.J. Jarvis)*, Edwin Stanley *(Sam Smith)*, Freddie Fisher and His Schnickelfritz Band, The Music Maids, Ernest Tubb and His Texas Troubadors, Don Wilson, Isabel Randolph, Rufe Davis, Shirley Mitchell, George "Shug" Fisher.

A pretty dim hillbilly musical in which struggling country-band Freddie Fisher and his Schnickelfritz Band are "dumped on" by their manager, Byron, when they can't land a job. Once in the big city, however, Byron learns that a rich radio sponsor is willing to sponsor Ernest Tubbs and His Texas Troubadors. Seeking to get Fisher and his ensemble into the studio before Tubbs, Byron dashes back to the farm to grab them and they land the job. But trouble arises on the big day when their farm boss, Terry, won't let them walk out on her. This leaves the door open for Tubbs and his boys, who replace Fisher. In the end, everything works out for the best. Songs include: "Jamboree" (Fisher), and "Maggie Went to Auggie" (Charles Henderson). Mainly an effort to showcase some radio talent of the time.

p, Armand Schaefer; d, Joseph Santley; w, Jack Townley (based on the original by Townley and Taylor Caven); ph, William Bradford; ed, Richard Van Enger; md, Morton Scott; art d, Russell Kimball.

Musical (PR:A MPAA:NR)

JAMBOREE** 1/2 (1957) 85m WB bw (GB: DISC JOCKEY JAMBOREE)

Kay Medford *(Grace Shaw)*, Bob Pastine *(Lew Arthur)*, Paul Carr *(Pete Porter)*, Freda Holloway *(Honey Wynn)*, Dave King-Wood *(Warren Sykes)*, Jean Martin *(Cindy Styles)*, Tony Travis *(Stage Manager)*, Leonard Schneider *(Assistant Stage Manager)*, Aaron Schroeder *(Songwriter)*, Fats Domino, Jerry Lee Lewis, Jimmy Bowen, Buddy Knox, Charlie Gracie, Count Basie Orchestra, Joe Williams, Jodie Sands, The Four Coins, Frankie Avalon, Lewis Lymon Teenchords, Slim Whitman, Andy Martin, Carl Perkins, Ron Coby, Rocco & His Saints, Connie Francis, Joe Smith, Joe Finan, Keith Sandy, Zenas Sears, Milt Grant, Dick Clark, Barry Kaye, Sandy Singer, Ray Perkins, Gerry Myers, Jocko Henderson, Ed Bonner, Robin Seymour, Dick Whittinghill, Howard Miller, Werner Goetze, Chris Howland, Jack Payne, Jack Jackson, Tony Travis, Leonard Schneider, Jean Martin.

With 17 great recording stars, 21 hit tunes, and 21 popular disc jockeys, JAMBOREE is a potpourri of early rock' n' roll, rockabilly, and swing. The slapdash plot concerns two young singing stars, Medford and Pastine, who fall in love but are dragged apart by their agents, who are divorced. That's not important. What is important is a chance to see Jerry Lee Lewis belt out on screen for the first time "Great Balls of Fire." Other songs include "Jamboree," "Record Hop Tonight," "For Children Of All Ages," "Glad All Over," "Who Are We To Say," "Teacher's Pet," "Siempre," "Cool Baby," "Sayonara," "Toreador," "Your Last Chance," "If Not For You," "Unchain My Heart," "A Broken Promise," "One O'clock Jump," "I Don't Like You No More," "Cross Over," "Hula Love," "Wait and See," and "Twenty-four Hours A Day."

p, Max J. Rosenberg, Milton Subotsky; d, Roy Lockwood; w, Leonard Kantor; ph, Jack Etra; m, Neil Hefti, Otis Blackwell; ed, Robert Broekman, Anita Posner; art d, Paul Barnes.

Musical (PR:A MPAA:NR)

JAMES BROTHERS, THE
(SEE: TRUE STORY OF JESSE JAMES, THE, 1957)

JANE AUSTEN IN MANHATTAN** (1980) 108m Contemporary c

Anne Baxter *(Lilianna)*, Robert Powell *(Pierre)*, Michael Wager *(George Midash)*, Tim Choate *(Jamie)*, John Guerrasio *(Gregory)*, Katrina Hodiak *(Katya)*, Kurt Johnson *(Victor)*, Philip Lenkowsky *(Fritz)*, Nancy New *(Jenny)*, Charles McCaughan *(Billy)*, Sean Young *(Ariadne)*, Bernard Barrow *(Poison)*, Lee Doyle *(Jarvis)*, Bella Jarett *(Miss Klein)*, Naomi Riordan *(Mrs. Poison)*.

A weak effort from Merchant and Ivory that concerns two teachers—Powell and rival Baxter—who battle over the right to bring an unproduced Jane Austen play, written when she was 12 years old, to the stage. Baxter wants it performed as an operetta, while Powell plans on staging it as an avant garde piece, performed on a stage of foam rubber. Both interpretations befuddle and do not bedazzle and it is hard to work up sympathy or involvement for the story or the cast.

p, Ismail Merchant; d, James Ivory; w, Ruth Prawer Jhabvala (based on the libretto of "Sir Charles Grandison," by Jane Austen and Samuel Richardson); ph, Ernst Vincze; m, Richard Robbins; ed, David E. McKenna; set d, Michael Yeargan; cos, Jenny Beavan.

Comedy (PR:A MPAA:NR)

JANE EYRE* (1935) 62m MON/FD bw

Virginia Bruce *(Jane Eyre)*, Colin Clive *(Edward Rochester)*, Beryl Mercer *(Mrs. Fairfax)*, Jameson Thomas *(Charles Craig)*, Aileen Pringle *(Blanche Ingram)*, David Torrence *(Brocklehurst)*, Lionel Belmore *(Lord Ingram)*, Joan Standing *(Daisy)*, Edith Fellowes *(Adele Rochester)*, Desmond Roberts *(Dr. Rivers)*, John Rogers *(Sam Poole)*, Clarissa Selwynne *(Mrs. Reed)*, Hylda Tyson *(Bessie)*, Gretta Gould *(Miss Temple)*, Claire duBrey *(Bertha Rochester)*, Ethel Griffies *(Grace Poole)*, Edith Kingston *(Lady Ingram)*, William Wagner *(Halliburton)*, Olaf Hytten *(Jeweler)*, William Burress *(Minister)*, Gail Kaye *(Mary Lane)*, Jean Darling *(Young Jane)*, Richard Quine *(John Reed)*, Anne Howard *(Georgianna Reed)*.

A stiff adaptation of Bronte's gothic romance, which stars Bruce in the title role, following her from her distressing childhood to a job as governess for Clive. There she falls under the spell of love and makes plans to marry Clive. But the plans are foiled when she discovers that Clive has an insane wife locked in the house. Bruce flees and finds shelter with Roberts, whom she now intends marrying. Fortunately word reaches her that Clive's house has burned down (his insane wife consumed by the flames and he going blind) just in time for her to cancel the marriage with Roberts and reunite with her true love. Remade in 1944 and 1970 under the same title.

p, Ben Verschleiser; d, Christy Cabanne; w, Adele Comandini (based on the novel by Charlotte Bronte); ph, Robert Planck; ed, Carl Pierson; md, Abe Meyer.

Romance/Drama (PR:A MPAA:NR)

JANE EYRE**** (1944) 97m FOX bw

Orson Welles *(Edward Rochester)*, Joan Fontaine *(Jane Eyre)*, Margaret O'Brien *(Adele)*, Peggy Ann Garner *(Jane as a Child)*, John Sutton *(Dr. Rivers)*, Sara Allgood *(Bessie)*, Henry Daniell *(Brockelhurst)*, Agnes Moorehead *(Mrs. Reed)*, Aubrey Mather *(Col. Dent)*, Edith Barrett *(Mrs. Fairfax)*, Barbara Everest *(Lady Ingraham)*, Hillary Brooke *(Blanche)*, Ethel Griffies *(Grace Poole)*, Eily Malyon *(Mrs. Sketcher)*, Ivan Simpson *(Mr. Woods)*, Erskine Sanford *(Mr. Braggs)*, John Abbott *(Mason)*, Elizabeth Taylor *(Helen Burns)*, Mae Marsh *(Leah)*, Mary Forbes *(Mrs. Eshton)*, Thomas Louden *(Sir George Lynn)*, Gerald Oliver Smith *(Footman at Gateshead)*, Adele Jergens, Ruthe Brady, Billie Seward *(Girls at Party)*, Colin Campbell *(Proprietor)*, Tempe Pigott *(Fortune Teller)*, Billy Bevan *(Bookie)*, Brandon Hurst, Barry Macollum *(Trustees)*, Charles Coleman, Harry Allen, David Clyde *(Guards)*, Yorke Sherwood *(Beadle)*, Ronald Harris *(John)*, Charles Irwin *(Auctioneer)*, Gwendolen Logan, Moyna Macgill *(Dowagers)*, Jean Fenwick, Bud Lawler, John Meredith, Leslie Vincent, Roseanne Murray, Marion Rosamond, Dan Wallace, *(Guests)*, Eustace Wyatt *(Dr. Carter)*, Alec Craig *(Footman)*, Frederick Worlock *(Waiter)*, George Kirby *(Old Gentleman)*, Arthur Gould-Porter *(Young Man)*, Alan Edmiston *(Dealer)*, Nancy June Robinson *(Girl)*.

This was the fifth time around for the doughty British lady. In 1913 Irving Cummings and Ethel Grand did it. In 1915 it was Alan Hale and Louise Vale. Mabel Ballin and Norman Trevor tried again in 1921; then Virginia Bruce and Colin Clive made the first talkie version in 1934. Later, in 1957, it was done with Patrick Macnee and Joan Elan and then again in 1971 with George C. Scott and Susannah York, both of those versions made for television. Although shot on the West Los Angeles sound stages of Twentieth Century Fox, Barnes' eerie cinematography was truly evocative of the bleakness of the novel and set a mood for the actors to strut their stuff. Fontaine is an orphan girl who has been tossed about by fate and managed to survive a Dickensian upbringing. (In the early scenes Fontaine's role is essayed by the charming Peggy Ann Garner.) Fontaine takes a job as governess to Yorkshireman Welles' ward, O'Brien. They live on the Yorkshire moors in a huge house called Thornfield Hall. Fontaine appears as though she'll remain a spinster for the rest of her days but there is an attraction growing between her and Welles. He is a troubled man, brooding and enigmatic, and we can't fathom why. Fontaine has come to love him and a wedding is planned but it fails to take place when Jane learns that Welles is already married and his wife, a raving lunatic, is imprisoned in the top floor attic of the manse. Fontaine leaves and goes through a series of deprivations but she feels what must be an ESP call to return to Thornfield. Once there, she discovers a blinded Welles walking through the ruins of the estate and trying to find his way through the timbers. His wife had set fire to the place and was consumed by the flames. If you think the story is simple, be aware that the literate screenplay by three writers examines much more than the surface treatment of the plot. There are those who regard it as an exercise in Victorian Romance Novels, but the fact that JANE EYRE has survived for so long and in so many versions is a tribute to Bronte's ability to capture the depth of love in her writing. The sets are pure Gothic, the music, by longtime Welles associate Bernard Herrmann, is rich and emotional, and every actor is painstakingly cast. In one of the early orphanage scenes, you'll have to watch closely to see a very young Elizabeth Taylor in her third role. In the original book Jane was the protagonist and Rochester was more of a large supporting part. To accommodate Welles, who was emerging as one of the country's most popular actors, the male role was made larger and he received billing above Fontaine. Composer Herrmann must have liked the Bronte sisters because he later based an opera on Charlotte's sister Emily's *Wuthering Heights*. It was interesting to watch the bombastic Welles acting opposite the dainty and demure Fontaine, a mixture of styles that worked to the advantage of the picture under Stevenson's sure direction. Some would carp that this was just so much overly sentimental hogwash but they are cynics who must be left in the cold. JANE EYRE is an eternal love story that combines romance, terror, madness, and every bit of emotion that can be wrung from the human psyche. Co-author Huxley was, of course, the noted novelist who gave us *Brave New World* and Houseman can still be found, well into his 80s, working on the cable TV show "The Paper Chase" and extolling the virtues of hamburgers and an investment firm. Peggy Ann Garner was simply magnificent as the young Jane and won a special Oscar as the "outstanding child performer of 1945" for her work in A TREE GROWS IN BROOKLYN. Watching her and O'Brien in the same film was a treat, as they were the best in the business at the time, and may have been the best pre-teen actresses ever, if one discounts Shirley Temple.

p, William Goetz; d, Robert Stevenson; w, Aldous Huxley, Stevenson, John Houseman (based on the book by Charlotte Bronte); ph, George Barnes; m, Bernard Herrmann; ed, Walter Thompson; art d, James Basevi, Wiard B. Ihnen; set d, Thomas Little, Ross Dowd; spec eff, Fred Sersen; cos, Rene Hubert.

Drama **(PR:A MPAA:NR)**

JANE EYRE** (1971, Brit.) 110m Omnibus-Sagittarius/BL c

George C. Scott *(Rochester)*, Susannah York *(Jane Eyre)*, Ian Bannen *(Rev. St. John Rivers)*, Jack Hawkins *(Mr. Brocklehurst)*, Nyree Dawn Porter *(Blanche Ingram)*, Rachel Kempson *(Mrs. Fairfax)*, Constance Cummings *(Mrs. Reed)*, Kenneth Griffith *(Mason)*, Peter Copley *(John)*, Michele Dotrice *(Mary Rivers)*, Kara Wilson *(Diana Rivers)*, Sarah Gibson *(Young Jane)*, Jean Marsh *(Mrs. Rochester)*, Rosalyn Landor *(Helen Burns)*, Sharon Rose *(Adele)*, Clive Morton *(Mr. Eshton)*, Hugh Latimer *(Col. Dent)*, Nan Munro *(Lady Ingram)*, Peter Blythe *(Frederick Lynn)*.

An embarrassingly miscast version of Charlotte Bronte's novel with York (too pretty) and Scott (too tough). The direction focuses attention towards story episodes, veering away from the characters. This consequently reduces the classic tale to soap opera. Some atmospheric photography helps and the film is fine as pleasant entertainment, but it's far from faithful to Bronte.

p, Frederick Brogger; d, Delbert Mann; w, Jack Pulman (based on the novel *Jane Eyre* by Charlotte Bronte); ph, Paul Beeson (Eastmancolor); m, John Williams; ed, Peter Boita; art d, Vetchinsky; cos, Anthony Mendelson; spec eff, Cliff Culley.

Romance/Drama **(PR:A MPAA:G)**

JANE STEPS OUT** (1938, Brit.) 70m ABF bw

Jean Muir *(Beatrice Wilton)*, Diana Churchill *(Jane Wilton)*, Peter Murray Hill *(Basil Gilbert)*, Fred Emney *(Gen. Wilton)*, Judy Kelly *(Margot Kent)*, Athene Seyler *(Grandma)*, Iris Hoey *(Mrs. Wilton)*.

A variation on the Cinderella theme, this film is the story of two sisters in love with the same man. The bad sister (Muir) is engaged to Hill, but the good one (Churchill) manages to steal him away with the help of grandma Seyler. Some cute moments but easily forgettable.

p, Walter C. Mycroft; d, Paul L. Stein; w, Dudley Leslie, William Freshman (based on the play by Kenneth Horne); ph, Claude Friese-Greene.

Comedy **(PR:A MPAA:NR)**

JANIE 1/2** (1944) 106m WB bw

Robert Hutton *(Pvt. Dick Lawrence)*, Edward Arnold *(Charles Conway)*, Ann Harding *(Lucille Conway)*, Robert Benchley *(John van Brunt)*, Alan Hale *(Reardon)*, Clare Foley *(Elsbeth Conway)*, Barbara Brown *(Mrs. Thelma Lawrence)*, Hattie McDaniel *(April)*, Dick Erdman *(Wilber "Scooper" Nolan)*, Jackie Moran *(Mickey)*, Ann Gillis *(Paula Rainey)*, Ruth Tobey *(Bernadine Dodd)*, Virginia Patton *(Carrie Lou Trivett)*, Colleen Townsend *(Hortense Bennett)*, William Frambes *("Dead Pan" Hackett)*, George Lee Settle *(Susan Wiley)*, Russell Hicks *(Col. Lucas)*, Joyce Reynolds *(Janie Conway)*, Peter Stackpole, John Alvin *(Photographers)*, Sunset Carson [Michael Harrison] *(Sgt. Carl)*, Virginia Noe, Ladell Buchanan, Karole Lee, Tanis Chandler, *(High School Girls)*, Jim Menzies, Sandy Shaw, Johnny Fleming, Terry Grafton, Roger McGee, Douglas Cooper, Norman Salling, Frank Wierick, Truman Van Dyke, Corky Geil *(High School Boys)*, William Benedict, Joe Gilbert *(Soda Jerks)*, George-Ellen Ferguson *(Reardon's Secretary)*, Jimmy Dodd *(Pvt. Frank Parker)*, Eddie Bruce *(Bus Driver)*, Williams Brothers *(Quartette)*, John Nelson, Danny Jackson, John Forrest, Warren Burr, Keefe Brasselle, Arnold Stanford, Dick Balkney, Michael Carter, Milton Douglas, Martin Lord *(Soldiers)*, Lane Chandler, Monte Blue *(Policemen)*, Virginia Sale *(Neighbor)*, Bill Hunter *(M.P. Sergeant)*, Kirk Barron *(M.P.)*, Harry Leavitt, Bob McGurk, Ricki Tanzi, Jordan Shelly, Jack Robbins, Douglas Pierce, Charles Schrader, Brent Gaylor, Clay Martin *(Bits)*.

Reynolds plays a precocious teenager who takes full advantage of the fact that an Army base has been built in their small town by running off in search of romance with a soldier. Arnold, her father, an outraged newspaper editor, has tried to stop the installation of the base, fearing the repercussions scores of young, cooped-up men will have on the young cooped-up females in town. Reynolds falls in love with young soldier Hutton and arranges a private party for him in her home when her folks are away. Jealous local ex-boyfriend Erdman busts up the romantic evening by inviting all of Hutton's army buddies over as well. Of course, the folks come home early, just ahead of the M.P.'s, and everybody manages to come out with a minimum of heartache.

p, Alex Gottlieb; d, Michael Curtiz; w, Agnes Christine Johnston, Charles Hoffman (based on a play by Josephine Bentham, Herschel V. Williams, Jr.); ph, Carl Guthrie; m, Heinz Roemheld; ed, Owen Marks; md, Leo F. Forbstein; art d, Robert Haas; spec eff, Lawrence Butler, William Lynch; m/l, "Keep Your Powder Dry," Jule Styne, Sammy Cahn, "Janie," Lee David.

Comedy **(PR:AA MPAA:NR)**

JANIE GETS MARRIED* 1/2 (1946) 89m WB bw

Joan Leslie *(Janie Conway)*, Robert Hutton *(Dick Lawrence)*, Edward Arnold *(Charles Conway)*, Ann Harding *(Lucille Conway)*, Robert Benchley *(John Van Brunt)*, Dorothy Malone *(Sgt. Spud Lee)*, Dick Erdman *(Lt. "Scooper" Nolan)*, Clare Foley *(Elsbeth Conway)*, Donald Meek *(Harley P. Stowers)*, Hattie McDaniel *(April)*, Barbara Brown *(Thelma Van Brunt)*, Margaret Hamilton *(Mrs. Angles)*, Ann Gillis *(Paula Rainey)*, Ruth Tobey *(Bernadine Dodd)*, William Frambes *("Dead Pan" Hackett)*, Theo Washington *(Rose)*, Rudy Wissler *(Copy Boy)*, Geraldine Wall, Philo McCullough *(Reporters)*, Jack Mower *(Benson)*, John O'Connor, Monte Blue *(Drapery Men)*, Charles Jordan *(Clarke, the City Editor)*, Mel Torme, John Sheridan, John Miles, Art Kassel *(Dick's Buddies)*, Lynne Baggett *(Hostess)*, Forbes Murray *(Businessman)*.

Pretty silly trivialities abound in this humorous portrayal of the troubles a pair of newlyweds encounter in their first year of marriage. Leslie and Hutton, the latter just out of the army, are the pair that soon discover that marriage is no bed of roses. Though it isn't problems between these two that cause all the trouble as much as the continual interference from outside forces on their domestic happiness. Despite a good performance here and there, these constant bickerings begin to get nauseatingly cute and the humor rapidly wears thin. This sequel to JANIE had Leslie, unfittingly so, replacing Joyce Reynolds in the role of the energetic and hard headed young woman who wouldn't give up until she had her way.

p, Alex Gottlieb; d, Vincent Sherman; w, Agnes Christine Johnston (based on characters in the stage play "Janie" by Josephine Bentham and Herschel V. Williams, Jr.); ph, Carl Guthrie; m, Frederick Hollander; ed, Christian Nyby; md, Leo F. Forbstein; art d, Robert M. Hass; m/l, Ted Koehler, M. K. Jerome.

Comedy **(PR:A MPAA:NR)**

JANITOR, THE (SEE: EYEWITNESS, 1981)

JAPANESE WAR BRIDE*** (1952) 91m FOX bw

Shirley Yamaguchi *(Tae Shimizu)*, Don Taylor *(Jim Sterling)*, Cameron Mitchell *(Art Sterling)*, Marie Windsor *(Fran Sterling)*, James Bell *(Ed Sterling)*, Louise Lorimer *(Harriet Sterling)*, Philip Ahn *(Eitaro Shimizu)*, Sybil Merritt *(Emily Shafer)*, Lane Nakano *(Shiro Hasagawa)*, Kathleen Mulqueen *(Mrs. Milly Shafer)*, Orley Lindgren *(Ted Sterling)*, George Wallace *(Woody Blacker)*, May Takasugi *(Emma Hasagawa)*, William Yokota *(Mr. Hasagawa)*, Susie Matsumoto *(Tae's Mother)*, Weaver Levy *(Kioto)*, Jerry Fujikawa *(Man at Fish Market)*, Chieko Sato, Tetsu Komai *(Japanese Servants)*, Hisa Chiba *(Old Japanese Woman)*, David March *(Man at Plant)*.

Korean War vet Taylor falls in love with his Japanese nurse, Yamaguchi, and brings her back to his California home as his wife. His neighboring farmers still harbor anti-Japanese sentiment from WWII and try to break up the marriage, but to no avail.

p, Joseph Bernhard; d, King Vidor; w, Catherine Turney (based on a story by Anson Bond); ph, Lionel Lindon; m, Emil Newman, Arthur Lange; ed, Terry Morse; art d, Danny Hall.

Drama **(PR:A MPAA:NR)**

JASON AND THE ARGONAUTS****

(1963, Brit.) 104m COL c (AKA: JASON AND THE GOLDEN FLEECE)

Todd Armstrong *(Jason)*, Nancy Kovack *(Medea)*, Gary Raymond *(Acastus)*, Laurence Naismith *(Argus)*, Niall MacGinnis *(Zeus)*, Michael Gwynn *(Hermes)*, Douglas Wilmer *(Pelias)*, Jack Gwillim *(King Aeetes)*, Honor Blackman *(Hera)*, John Cairney *(Hylas)*, Patrick Troughton *(Phineas)*, Andrew Faulds *(Phalerus)*, Nigel

Green *(Hercules)*, Gernando Poggi *(Castor)*, John Crawford *(Polydeuces)*, Douglas Robinson *(Euphemus)*.

This film and THE SEVENTH VOYAGE OF SINBAD are special effects master Ray Harryhausen's finest efforts. JASON AND THE ARGONAUTS brings the viewer into the mythological world of dragons, living statues, harpies, and Gods. Pelias murders Aristo, the king of Thessaly, and steals his rightful throne. Aristo's baby son, Jason (Armstrong), survives due to the intervention of the goddess Hera (Blackman). Twenty years later Armstrong searches for the Golden Fleece, which, in his possession, will install him on his rightful throne. Armstrong assembles a crew of brave men (including Hercules, played quite humanly by Green in a bravura performance) and they set out on a glorious adventure in search of the Golden Fleece, aided from Olympus by Blackman. When the ship stops to take on fresh water and food, the crew is menaced by a giant, living statue named Talos, who tries to wreck the ship and kill Armstrong's men (the scene when the previously immobile statue turns its head and stares at Hercules is absolutely terrifying). Luckily, with Blackman's help, Armstrong spots a screw on Talos' foot, which he opens, draining the molten life-fluid out of the metal monster, causing it to become stiff and brittle. Soon the dying statue collapses and breaks into a dozen pieces. After fixing the damage to the ship, Armstrong and his crew discover the blind prophet Phineas (Troughton) being tortured by two Harpies (some of Harryhausen's most impressive motion-work). Armstrong and his men subdue the creatures and put them in a cage. The grateful Troughton thanks the men by telling them how to get through the "clashing rocks" to their destination and presents them with a medallion of Neptune for protection. As the ship attempts to sail through the dangerous pass (the floating rocks threaten to crush the ship to splinters), Armstrong throws the medallion into the water, summoning the giant Neptune (a man, not stop-motion effects, but well-done, nevertheless) to push the rocks apart so that the ship may sail through. After finding Armstrong's love interest Kovack stranded on an empty ship, the crew finally make their way to the fleece, which is guarded by the terrifying seven-headed hydra. After killing the hydra and taking the fleece, Armstrong and his men are halted once again by the evil king Gwillim, who spreads the teeth of the hydra on the ground, which grow into seven armed, living skeletons that attack the few brave sailors left. In an absolutely stunning display of technical wizardry, Armstrong and his remaining men fight the seven grinning skeletons (which Harryhausen somehow imbues with distinct personalities) to the death. Eventually this threat, too, is defeated and Armstrong (along with Kovack) sails off with the fleece to regain his throne. In JASON AND THE ARGONAUTS, Harryhausen is at his most creative and brilliant. The stop-motion models of the monsters are sculpted with fine detail, and the rendering of their motion is outstanding in every scene. The technical ambition and brilliance of the final sword fight with the skeletons (seven stop-motion figures interacting with three "real" actors, quite often in the same frame) is absolutely amazing (Harryhausen has yet to equal this sequence). The film is surprisingly well-directed and acted (Harryhausen's films are notoriously bad in these departments), and the photography of the beautiful Mediterranean is wonderful. Herrmann's musical score is one of his best and adds greatly to the final effect. A great film for kids, with enough "adult" elements to please even the most discriminating viewer. A must-see.

p, Charles H. Schneer; d, Don Chaffey; w, Jan Reed, Beverly Cross; ph, Wilkie Cooper (Dynamation 90, Eastmancolor); m, Bernard Herrmann; ed, Maurice Rootes; prod d, Geoffrey Drake; md, Mario Nascimbene, Hermann; art d, Herbert Smith, Jack Maxsted, Toni Sarzi-Braga, spec eff, Ray Harryhausen.

Fantasy/Adventure **Cas.** **(PR:AA MPAA:NR)**

JASSY1/2** (1948, Brit.) 96m Gainsborough/UNIV c

Margaret Lockwood *(Jassy Woodroffe)*, Patricia Roc *(Dilys Helmar)*, Dennis Price *(Christopher Hatton)*, Dermot Walsh *(Barney Hatton)*, Basil Sydney *(Nick Helmar)*, Nora Swinburne *(Mrs. Hatton)*, Linden Travers *(Mrs. Helmar)*, Grace Arnold *(Housemaid)*, Ernest Thesiger *(Sir Edward Follesmark)*, Cathleen Nesbitt *(Elizabeth Twisdale)*, Jean Cadell *(Meggie)*, John Laurie *(Woodroffe)*, Grey Blake *(Stephen Fennell)*, Clive Morton *(Sir William Fennell)*, Torin Thatcher *(Bob Wicks)*, Beatrice Varley *(Mrs. Wicks)*, Maurice Denham *(Jim Stoner)*, Alan Wheatley *(Sir Edward Walker)*, Esma Cannon *(Lindy)*, Bryan Coleman *(Sedley)*, Joan Haythorne *(Kathleen Hamilton)*, Hugh Pryse *(Sir John Penty)*, Stewart Rome, Susan Shaw, Dennis Harkin, Constance Smith.

A long, overplotted drama about a young man, Walsh, who befriends a gypsy girl, Lockwood, who has psychic powers. They are separated, but she manages to avenge the misfortunes of Walsh's father, getting back the country home that he lost in a card game by marrying the man who won it. When she is accused of murder, Walsh comes to her aid, clears her name, and the pair are forever united. A bit implausible, but still entertaining.

p, Sydney Box; d, Bernard Knowles; w, Dorothy and Campbell Christie, Geoffrey Kerr (based on the novel by Norah Lofts); ph, Geoffrey Unsworth (Technicolor); m, Henry Geehl; ed, Charles Knott; md, Louis Levy; art d, George Provis; cos, Elizabeth Haffenden; makeup, W.T. Partleton.

Drama **(PR:A MPAA:NR)**

JAVA HEAD*1/2 (1935, Brit.) 70m ATP/FN-WB bw

Anna May Wong *(Taou Yen)*, Elizabeth Allan *(Nettie Vollar)*, John Loder *(Gerrit Ammidon)*, Edmund Gwenn *(Jeremy Ammidon)*, Ralph Richardson *(William Ammidon)*, Herbert Lomas *(Barzil Dunsack)*, George Curzon *(Edward Dunsack)*, Roy Emerton *(Broadrick)*, John Marriner *(John Stone)*, Grey Blake *(Roger Brevard)*, Amy Brandon Thomas *(Rhoda)*, Frances Carson *(Kate)*.

In the mid-1800s English ship builder Loder marries a Chinese girl, Wong, and brings her back to a small English port. When she discovers that her husband loves a British woman, Wong kills herself as a sacrifice, so Loder may marry his new love.

p, Basil Dean; d, J. Walter Ruben; w, Martin Brown, Gordon Wellesley (based on the novel by Joseph Hergesheimer); ph, Robert G. Martin; m, Ernest Irving.

Romance **(PR:C MPAA:NR)**

JAVA SEAS (SEE: EAST OF JAVA, 1935)

J'AVAIS SEPT FILLES (SEE: MY SEVEN LITTLE SINS, 1956, Fr./Ital.)

JAWS**** (1975) 124m UNIV c

Roy Scheider *(Police Chief Martin Brody)*, Robert Shaw *(Quint)*, Richard Dreyfuss *(Matt Hooper)*, Lorraine Gary *(Ellen Brody)*, Murray Hamilton *(Mayor Larry Vaughn)*, Carl Gottlieb *(Meadows)*, Jeffrey C. Kramer *(Deputy Hendricks)*, Susan Backlinie *(Chrissie Watkins)*, Jonathan Filley *(Cassidy)*, Ted Grossman *(Estuary Victim)*, Chris Rebello *(Michael Brody)*, Jay Mello *(Sean Brody)*, Lee Fierro *(Mrs. Kintner)*, Jeffrey Voorhees *(Alex Kintner)*, Craig Kingsbury *(Ben Gardner)*, Dr. Robert Nevin *(Medical Examiner)*, Peter Benchley *(Interviewer)*, Jonathan Filley *(Cassidy)*, Robert Chambers *(Charlie)*, Edward Chalmers, Jr. *(Denherder)*, Cyprien P. R. Dube *(Posner)*, Robert Carroll *(Polk)*, Donald Poole *(Harbor Master)*, Alfred Wilde *(Iteisel/Mr. Wiseman)*.

The one, the only, the original JAWS grossed more than a half billion dollars at the box-office and was the number one movie of all time until STAR WARS took the nod two years later. It had been a best-selling book by Peter Benchley (Nathaniel's son and Robert's grandson, so there *is* some truth about genes when it comes to creativity) and he co-authored the script with former improvisational comedian Carl Gottlieb, who also played a small role as "Meadows." It was a smash the instant it came out and stands as one of the best films of its kind; i.e. sci-fi/horror. It also established Spielberg as a filmmaker, after he had done the mildly successful SUGARLAND EXPRESS. From this he went on to do one hit after another with a brief time out for some mistakes, 1941, and I WANNA HOLD YOUR HAND. JAWS was a mixture of terror and humor that ignited the 1975 public that summer and caused as many people to stay out of the water as Hitchcock did with his PSYCHO shower scene. A huge promotional budget, sensational poster art, and carefully planned advertising by Universal's ad department all contributed to preparing a panting public for the event. We're on Amity Island, a place not unlike New York's Fire Island, when there is a plague of shark attacks and several innocents are slain. Mayor Hamilton is one of those people who doesn't believe in rocking the boat (or ruining the business during the short summer season) so he tries to keep the news quiet and tells the local fishermen that he would appreciate it if they can take some time out from clamming and lobster traps to hunt down whatever it is out there. A good-sized shark is captured and killed and Hamilton happily assures tourists and newsmen that the danger has passed, it's now safe to go back in the water again. The more fool he. Dreyfuss, a charming expert on undersea creatures, arrives to look deeper into the dead shark and quickly becomes convinced that this creature could not possibly be the same one that did all the bloody work. He tells Police Chief Scheider that there is no way this piddling fish could have been responsible. No, sir, this has to have been the work of . . . A Great White Shark! Scheider thinks Dreyfuss is wrong but is soon convinced when there's yet another attack. Dreyfuss and Scheider bring this to the attention of everyone at a town meeting, over the objections of Hamilton, who still wants to keep everything under wraps. The fishermen, upon hearing that the culprit is a Great White, decide that their lives are too valuable to risk in stalking such a beast. Shaw is a sea man with a penchant for foul language and a loner attitude. He steps forward and says he can kill the gargantuan fish if they come up with some serious money. The town council hems and haws and finally agrees and the trio of Shaw, Dreyfuss, and Scheider join forces on Shaw's boat for the hunt. It now becomes MOBY DICK as Shaw trails the shark the way Ahab did. There's a bit of time out for some funny dialog between the disparate men but then the action begins in earnest. They spot the shark and Shaw harpoons it several times but it's like pinpricks to the 28-foot shark and he toys with them. With John Williams' haunting theme playing underneath, the shark starts to counterattack and tows the boat further out to sea. Now the shark gets annoyed by these infidels who've come to *his* neck of the ocean and decides to go after *them*. The final sequences are one shock after another as the shark capsizes the boat, swallows Shaw whole, and, in the end, Scheider saves himself and Dreyfuss by wedging an air tank in the mouth of the shark and exploding it. Spielberg showed great restraint in his handling of the menace. The shark wasn't seen, except for bits and pieces and shadows underwater, for an hour and twenty minutes into the movie. So the first time it lurches above the water, grown men screamed and those of faint heart reached for their nitroglycerine pills. Everyone connected with the picture had their fortunes soar. Dreyfuss went on to make some superb movies, one of which earned him an Oscar (THE GOODBYE GIRL), Scheider became a major star, Shaw did the same (and died not long after). The shark, designed by Joe Alves (who later directed JAWS 3-D), cost almost a quarter million dollars and can be seen as part of Universal's Movie Tour. The second shark, built for JAWS II, was larger but less effective. Benchley does a small role as a newsman and should stick to his typewriter. There were several production problems at the Martha's Vineyard location and some worry that the film would never be completed. The wait was worth it. Williams took an Oscar for his music but the film was oddly overlooked by the Film Academy except for a nomination as Best Picture. But that was the year when ONE FLEW OVER THE CUCKOO'S NEST took most of the kudos, if not most of the money, and Spielberg had to be content with millions of dollars instead of the statuette. Although many of the actors had appeared in films before, none was an accredited "bankable" star. This should prove to any and all producers who scream that they have to have a "name" that it matters not. The story and the execution are far more important than watching Burt Reynolds (who has made more bombs than the average terrorist) or Clint Eastwood (who seems to flop in any role other than the no-named cowboy or Dirty Harry) or any number of stars who demand huge fees. All production credits are terrific and the casting was perfect. The movie occasioned a series of ripoffs, including ORCA, but none could hold a fishing pole to JAWS.

p, Richard D. Zanuck, David Brown; d, Steven Spielberg; w, Peter Benchley, Carl Gottlieb (Howard Sackler-uncredited) (based on a novel by Peter Benchley); ph, Bill Butler (Panavision, Technicolor); m, John Williams; ed, Verna Fields; prod d, Joseph Alves, Jr.; set d, John M. Dwyer; spec eff, Robert A. Mattey; underwater ph, Rexford Metz; shark footage, Ron and Valerie Taylor.

Drama/Horror Cas. (PR:C-O MPAA:PG)

JAWS OF DEATH, THE (SEE: MAKO: THE JAWS OF DEATH, 1976)

JAWS OF JUSTICE** (1933) 58m Principal bw

Richard Terry [Jack Perrin] *(Kinkaid)*, Ruth Sullivan *(Judy Dean)*, Gene Toller *(Kickabout)*, Lafe McKee *(Seeker Dean)*, Robert Walker *(Boone)*, Kazan, the Dog, Teddy *(Kazan's Friend)*.

Kazan the wonder dog comes to the rescue when Sullivan discovers that her prospector father (McKee) has been murdered by Walker, a man they had accepted as their close friend. The story starts with Walker driving McKee to a hidden mine, but returning with the excuse that McKee has gotten a ride from someone else. A full year passes without any message from McKee, and only Kazan acts in a manner distrustful of Walker, proving that a dog's instincts far outweigh man's analytical ability. When a young deaf boy is finally able to fit together the puzzle of the location of the mine, Walker attempts to flee, but falls victim to the jaws of Kazan. The story is paced to take full advantage of mounting tension and action sequences. Acting honors go to Kazan, who switches his persona from loving dog to viciousness with an unusual air of believability.

p, Sol Lesser; d, Spencer Gordon Bennet; w, Joseph Anthony Roach (based on the story "The Gold Bug" by Edgar Allan Poe).

Western (PR:A MPAA:NR)

JAWS OF SATAN* (1980) 92m UA c (AKA: KING COBRA)

Fritz Weaver *(Father Farrow)*, Gretchen Corbett *(Dr. Sheridan)*, Jon Korkes *(Paul)*, Norman Lloyd *(Monsignore)*, Diana Douglas *(Evelyn)*, Bob Hannah *(Matt)*, Nancy Priddy *(Elizabeth)*, Christina Applegate *(Kim)*, John McCurry *(Sheriff)*, Jack Gordan *(Mayor)*.

A snake—actually the devil in disguise—makes life miserable for poor Weaver, and allows an innumerable amount of slimy creatures to crawl across the stage and make people curl up in their seats.

p, Bill Wilson; d, Bob Claver; w, Gerry Holland (based on the story by James Callaway); ph, Dean Cundey (Technicolor); m, Roger Kellaway; ed, Len Miller; art d, Robert Topol; spec eff, Eoin Sprott.

Horror (PR:O MPAA:R)

JAWS OF THE JUNGLE**

(1936) 60m Jay Dee Kay Productions bw (AKA: JUNGLE VIRGIN)

Teeto *(The Boy)*, Minta *(The Girl)*, Gukar *(The Rejected Suitor)*, Walla *(The Ape)*, Agena *(The Honey Bear)*.

Jungle adventure from the wilds of Ceylon follows the troubles of village members besieged by vampire bats and other dangers of the jungle as the tribesmen attempt to find safety after journeying across the jungle to seek blessing for a wedding. Teeto and Minta are the two villagers who desire to marry, but find that they must overcome a number of obstacles before their wish can be fulfilled. Among the problems they encounter is the jealous suitor of Minta driven to attacks on Teeto when he can't have the girl of his dreams. With the realistic jungle footage spliced together with studio stuff, and the exotic yet universally human tale, JAWS OF THE JUNGLE was able to maintain an air of authenticity, as well as provide thrills and chills.

p, J.D. Kendis; w, Eddy Graneman; ed, Holbrook N. Todd.

Adventure (PR:C MPAA:NR)

JAWS 3-D** (1983) 97m Landsburg/UNIV c 3-D

Dennis Quaid *(Mike Brody)*, Bess Armstrong *(Kathryn Morgan)*, Simon MacCorkindale *(Philip FitzRoyce)*, Louis Gossett, Jr. *(Calvin Bouchard)*, John Putch *(Sean Brody)*, Lea Thompson *(Kelly Ann Bukowski)*, P.H. Moriarty *(Jack Tate)*, Dan Blasko *(Dan)*, Liz Morris *(Liz)*, Lisa Maurer *(Ethel)*, Harry Grant *(Shelby)*, Andy Hansen *(Silver Bullet)*, P.T. Horn *(Guide)*, John Edson, Jr. *(Bob)*, Kaye Stevens *(Mrs. Kallender)*, Archie Valliere *(Leonard)*, Alonzo Ward *(Fred)*, Cathy Cervenka *(Sherrie)*, Steve Mellor *(Announcer)*, Ray Meunich *(Paramedic)*, Les Alford, Gary Anstaett *(Reporters)*, Muffett Baker *(Guide)*, William Bramley, Scott Christoffel, Debbie Connoyer, Mary David Duncan, Barbara Eden, John Floren, John Gaffey, Joe Gilbert, Will Knickerbocker, Jackie Kuntarich, Edward Laurie, Holly Lisker, M. J. Lloyd, Carl Mazzocone, Brendan Murray, Kim Nordstrom, Ken Olson, Ronnie Parks, Al Pipkin.

The third time was *not* the charm in the case of the JAWS series. This time, the action moves from Amity Island to Florida's Sea World with a new cast (except for the fact that Roy Scheider's two sons are now old enough to be played by Quaid and Putch). Gottlieb again co-authored the screenplay but he would have been wise to have bypassed this job. Gossett runs the theme park and Armstrong is a marine biologist who works at the place and lives with Quaid. A baby great white is caught after some divers disappear. They think they have a great attraction in "the only great white in captivity." But they haven't reckoned on a mother's love for her offspring so when Big Mama comes to call, things get out of hand and she wrecks the place. This one is 35 feet long and if this were the first JAWS, it might have had some impact, but the film submerged immediately for any number of reasons; we'd seen it before, the effects weren't startling, the blood-count was low, the acting was ordinary, the 3-D photography wasn't unique, and there were hardly any characterization. Consequently, when various actors were chewed, we didn't care at all. It cost almost $15 million to make and may not have recovered that in rentals. Putting it on TV, sans the 3-D process, only pointed up the flaws even more and it became funny, sort of like the 3-D satires the Second City troupe did on their late night TV shows from Canada in the early 1980s. Would that this were as enjoyable. Gossett, a graduate of Coney Island's Lincoln High School, spent his early life at the beach near the ocean. He should have recognized the smell of old fish when he accepted this assignment after his stirring job in AN OFFICER AND A GENTLEMAN. In a small role, look for chanteuse Kaye Stevens, who was a Las Vegas sensation in the 1960s when she brought her own redheaded madness to the nightclub stage. She has since decided to become a legitimate actress and that's a loss to saloon patrons who never failed to give her a standing ovation for her boite work. Director Alves had been production designer on the first two JAWS features and was rewarded for his efforts by the assignment to handle the lensing for this.

p, Rupert Hitzig; d, Joe Alves; w, Richard Matheson, Carl Gottlieb (based on a story by Guerdon Trueblood suggested by the novel *Jaws* by Peter Benchley); ph, James A. Contner (ArriVision 3-D, Stereovision, Technicolor); m, Alan Parker (shark theme, John Williams); ed, Randy Roberts; prod d, Woods Mackintosh; art d, Chris Horner; Paul Eads; cos, Dresden Urquhart; spec. eff., Praxis; underwater operator, Jeff Simon; visual creative cons, Roy Arbogast; visual design cons, Philip Abramson.

Drama/Horror Cas. (PR:C-O MPAA:PG)

JAWS II*** (1978) 117m UNIV c

Roy Scheider *(Police Chief Martin Brody)*, Lorraine Gary *(Ellen Brody)*, Murray Hamilton *(Mayor Larry Vaughan)*, Joseph Mascolo *(Len Peterson)*, Jeffrey Kramer *(Deputy Jeff Hendricks)*, Collin Wilcox *(Dr. Lureen Elkins)*, Ann Dusenberry *(Tina Wilcox, Miss Amity)*, Mark Gruner *(Mike Brody)*, Barry Coe *(Andrews)*, Susan French *(Old Lady)*, Gary Springer *(Andy)*, Donna Wilkes *(Jackie)*, Gary Dubin *(Ed)*, John Dukakis *(Polo)*, G. Thomas Dunlop *(Timmy)*, David Elliott *(Larry Vaughan, Jr.)*, Marc Gilpin *(Sean Brody)*, Keith Gordon *(Doug)*, Cynthia Grover *(Lucy)*, Ben Marley *(Patrick)*, Martha Swatek *(Marge)*, Billy Van Zandt *(Bob Burnside)*, Gigi Vorgan *(Brooke Peters)*, Jerry M. Baxter *(Helicopter Pilot)*, Jean Coulter *(Ski Boat Driver)*, Daphne Dibble, David Tintle *(Swimmers)*, Christine Freeman *(Water Skier)*, April Gilpin *(Renee)*, William Griffith *(Lifeguard)*, Frank Sparks, Greg Harris *(Divers)*, Coll Red McLean *(Red)*, Susan O. McMillan, David Owsley *(Denise & Donnie, Sailors)*, Allan L. Paddack *(Crosby)*, Oneida Rollins *(Ambulance Driver)*, Kathy Wilson *(Mrs. Bryant)*, Jim Wilson *(Swimmer With Child)*, Thomas A. Stewart *(Asst. Dive Master)*, Herb Muller *(Phil Fogarty)*, William "Bill" Green *(Irate Man)*.

JAWS II is a fairly good sequel to JAWS but most of the suspense is gone because we've already seen the behemoth wreak so much havoc in the first film. Missing here is the humor in the original, despite being co-authored by the funnyman-writer Gottlieb (who can also be seen in many roles as an actor. He appeared as "Meadows" in the first film which he also co-wrote with originator Benchley). Most of the old Amity Island crowd has returned to face the threat of the shark and they don't seem to have learned much from the first onslaught. A few years have passed and the island is now again busy with scads of tourists. Two divers and a water skier turn up missing and that sets Police Chief Scheider's antenna tingling. Could it be? An underwater camera that belonged to one of the missing divers is found and the processed film indicates what appears to be a large shark fin. Naturally, the wimp mayor, Hamilton, wants to keep this quiet because he recalls how this hurt business on the island a few years before. Scheider climbs the observation tower and watches the water. When he sees a dark shadow cutting through the waves, he panics and orders all the swimmers out of the sea. Later investigation proves his fear to be unfounded as the shadow came from a school of benign fish. Scheider gets fired for his efforts and his wife, Gary, stands by his side—as all good wives must do in times of stress. Dusenberry and Dubin are two youngsters who sail their small boat to a quiet area where they are attacked by the shark. Dubin is swallowed and Dusenberry watches in horror. Scheider locates Dusenberry and his worst dreams have been corroborated; another great white shark has arrived to dine on the community. Scheider's two sons, Gruner and Gilpin, have gone on a small fishing trip with a couple of pals and he is frightened for their safety. A helicopter is sent to look for them and just as the pilot is about to save the lads, the shark rears its head and drags the chopper into the water in the most spectacular sequence of the film. Scheider doesn't hear from the ill-fated copter pilot so he takes a cabin cruiser and goes out searching for the kids on his own. All this time, the shark is toying with the kids and eyeing them like canapes. Scheider gets there in the nick of time and recalls that sharks are attracted to clanging noises (this theory was used in 1985 in real life when a hump-backed whale swam up the wrong stream in Northern California and was helped out to sea by several boat owners who banged on pipes and drove the whale back to his, or her, natural habitat) so he hits a metal cable that supplies power. The shark rushes toward the sound and Scheider is saved when the huge teeth bite through the metal and the shark electrocutes itself. JAWS II began with John Hancock as director but a dispute erupted when he and producers Zanuck and Brown didn't see eye to eye, so Szwarc, a TV director, was hired to take over the direction. Despite the flaws of being a sequel, it had enough "legs" to earn more than two hundred million dollars. Not bad for a sequel, and a lesser one at that. Lorraine Gary is an underused actress but she prefers it that way and has now decided to spend most of her time as the wife of Universal Studios chief Sid Sheinberg. Barry Coe will be recognized as one of the bright young men seen in many Fox films of the 1950s and 1960s. JAWS II is an escapist movie that did well enough to, unfortunately, give birth to JAWS 3-D.

p, Richard D. Zanuck, David Brown; d, Jeannot Szwarc; w, Carl Gottlieb, Howard Sackler (Dorothy Tristan—Uncredited) (based on characters created by Peter Benchley); ph, Michael Butler (Panavision, Technicolor); m, John Williams; ed, Neal Travis, Steve Potter, Arthur Schmidt, Freeman Davies, Jr., Michael T. Elias, Robert Hernandez, Sherrie Sanet Jacobson; prod d, Joe Alves; art d, Gene Johnson, Stu

Campbell; set d, Philip Abramson; cos, Bill Jobe; makeup, Ron Snyder, Dick Sharp, Bob Jiras; spec eff, Robert A. Mattey; Roy Arbogast, stunts, Ted Grossman.

Drama Horror Cas. (PR:A—C MPAA:PG)

JAYHAWKERS, THE** (1959) 100m PAR c

Jeff Chandler *(Luke Darcy)*, Fess Parker *(Cam Bleeker)*, Nicole Maurey *(Jeanne Dubois)*, Henry Silva *(Lordan)*, Herbert Rudley *(Gov. William Clayton)*, Frank DeKova *(Evans)*, Don Megowan *(China)*, Leo Gordon *(Jake)*, Shari Lee Bernath *(Marthe)*, Jimmy Carter *(Paul)*.

Pre-Civil War Kansas is the backdrop of this tale about the top Jayhawker, Chandler, and his attempts to reign supreme over his plains empire. He is brought down, however, by Parker, who avenges the death of his family at Chandler's hands. There are a number of references comparing Chandler's character to Napoleon, a novel idea that still makes for nothing more than a lavishly mounted, hollow spectacle.

p, Norman Panama, Melvin Frank; d, Frank; w, Frank, A.I. Bezzerides, Frank Fenton, Joseph Petracca; ph, Loyal Griggs (VistaVision, Technicolor); m, Jerome Moross; ed, Everett Douglas; art d, Roland Anderson; cos, Edith Head.

Western (PR:A MPAA:NR)

JAZZ AGE, THE ** 1/2** (1929) 62m RKO bw

Douglas Fairbanks, Jr. *(Steve Maxwell)*, Marceline Day *(Sue Randall)*, Henry B. Walthall *(Mr. Maxwell)*, Myrtle Steadman *(Mrs. Maxwell)*, Gertrude Messinger *(Marjorie)*, Joel McCrea *(Todd Sayles)*, William Bechtel *(Mr. Sayles)*, E.J. Ratcliffe *(Mr. Randall)*, Ione Holmes *(Ellen McBride)*, Edgar Dearing *(Motor Cop)*.

With only a few lines of dialog, this mostly silent film centers on Fairbanks, Jr., the protective brother of younger sister who falls in with a bad group of people. He falls for the jazz-loving Day, whose dishonest father is an enemy of Fairbanks' father. A race between Fairbanks, in an auto, and McCrea, in a trolly car, is the picture's big event, sending both to jail.

d, Lynn Shores; w, Paul Gangelin, Randolph Bartlett; ph, Ted Pahle; m, Joseph Zuro; ed, Ann McKnight.

JAZZ BABIES ** 1/2** (1932) 81m PEERLESS bw

Madge Evans *(Clarissa)*, Elizabeth Patterson *(Babs)*, Marjorie Gateson *(Ellie)*, Harvey Stephens *(Bentley Collingford)*, Hobart Bosworth *(Wilson Tuttle)*, Lucien Littlefield *(Barney)*, Maude Eburne *(Lola)*, Monroe Owsley *(Mr. Finchley)*, Catherine Phipps *(Mrs. Finchley)*, Otto Lederer *(Hans)*, Jim & Jack Black *(The Morgan Brothers)*, Hap Johnson *(Danny)*, The Leo Lyons Orchestra.

A rollicking musical comedy about three young women, Evans, Patterson, and Gateson, who work as dancer-singers at The Dew Drop Inn, a Chicago nightspot frequented by all the lowlifes. The club is owned by Littlefield and is in danger of being closed down by bluenose Owsley who just bought the property and believes that what goes on inside the building is not fit for general amusement, and he's right. It's a Texas Guinan-type club where the girls wear very little and you could cut the smoke with a chain saw. To convince him that he's wrong, the girls, with the help of Lederer, the doorman with a literary bent, decide to stage a show just for Owsley with a room full of friends there to make it seem legit. They are doing a musical version of "Midsummer Night's Dream" and all of the roles are played by the vaudevillians who appear in the regular stage presentation. So Johnson, the ventriloquist who does questionable material, is asked to play Ariel and the two black tap dancers play sprites. Meanwhile, Evans and Patterson are being courted by two Illinois grain traders, Stephens and Bosworth, who wish they would give it all up and marry them and move to Evanston. The girls really love the men but they won't leave their pals in the lurch until they straighten out the problem with Owsley. Eburne, however, has other plans. She's the spurned girl friend of Bosworth and she knows what's going on and is going to spill the beans to Owsley. Gateson kidnaps Eburne in a hearse and keeps her under wraps until the show is over and Owsley has agreed to allow the club to stay there, prior to his one-year voyage around the world with his new wife, Phipps, who is even more prudish than he is. Now, a problem arises. Owsley and Phipps love the show so much that they decide to produce it for Broadway, rather than take their extended honeymoon. The entire cast takes this haphazard adaptation to New York, where the Big Apple critics are lying in wait for any show that comes from anywhere but Manhattan. The show closes in one night but Owsley and Phipps are not disturbed by it all (he has scads of money) and go off on their honeymoon thinking that they tried to bring some culture to Sodom By The Narrows but it just didn't work. The girls marry their guys in a funny sequence at the grain exchange. No tunes stepped out to be big hits but the serviceable score included; "How Do I Love Thee?" "Dream On," "Jazz Babies," "Corn-Fed Cutie," "Jump For Joy," "Seek And Ye Shall Find," "Small Time," "We Like Chicago," "Rush Street Blues," "Tell Me A Story," "Summertime Tap" (instrumental only), and "The Night Was Made For Jazz." Jim and Jack Black, the tap dancers, were both tragically killed in a car accident on Highway 101 in California shortly after the film was completed. Leo Lyons played himself and was featured on saxophone in the nightclub sequences.

d, Alexander Hall; w, Jack Cunningham (based on a story by Lance Barger); ph, Ray June; md, James Lewis; ed, Bill Cameron; art d, Seymour Fuller; set d, P.F. Fleischer; m/l, Jack Reinach, Lou Krasny.

Musical Comedy (PR:A MPAA:NR)

JAZZBAND FIVE, THE *** 1/2** (1932, Ger,) 88m UFA bw (FUNF VON DER JAZZBAND)

Jenny Jugo *(Jessie)*, Rolf von Goth *(Jim)*, Fritz Klippel *(Moritz)*, Karl Stepanek *(Jean)*, Gunther Vogdt *(Bill)*, Theo Shall *(Martin)*, Werner Pledath *(Director)*, Arthur Mainzer *(Sasse)*, Heinrich Gretler *(Judge)*, Walter Steinbeck *(Spinner)*, E. Helmke-Dassel *(Erika)*, Fritz Melchior *(Stage Manager)*, Vera Spohr *(Chambermaid)*, Frida *(Chambermaid)*, Peter Lorre *(Thief)*.

A mishap lands Jugo a job with a group of musical acrobats, though she has little talent to warrant her hiring. After her first rehearsal, this is soon realized by the entire group. A flustered Jugo then goes to a local pub to drown her sorrows, where she meets and takes a liking to Shall. Her new love affair is almost ruined when she is wrongly named by Lorre as an accomplice in the theft of Shall's auto, thus keeping suspicion from the real culprits. This confusion makes her late for a performance with the acrobats, but everything turns out all right when a quick replacement proves much better than Jugo, and Shall realizes she had no involvement in the theft of his car. Good acting, solid production values, and a strong directorial hand make this simple story into quite a little gem. Writer Hermann Kosterlitz later came to America after directing a few German films, anglicized his name to Henry Koster, went to Universal where he turned Deanna Durbin into a gold mine for them in such pictures as THREE SMART GIRLS (1936), ONE HUNDRED MEN AND A GIRL (1937), IT STARTED WITH EVE (1941), and later went to Fox where he directed some of their CinemaScope pictures including the first one, THE ROBE (1953).

d, Erich Engel; w, Hermann Kosterlitz [Henry Koster], Curt Alexander; ph, Reimer Kuntze; m, Theo Mackeben.

Drama (PR:A MPAA:NR)

JAZZ BOAT** (1960, Brit.) 96m Warwick/COL bw (GB: JAZZBOAT)

Anthony Newley *(Bert Harris)*, Anne Aubrey *(The Doll)*, Lionel Jeffries *(Sgt. Thompson)*, David Lodge *(Holy Mike)*, Bernie Winters *(The Jinx)*, James Booth *(Spider Kelly)*, Al Mulock *(The Dancer)*, Joyce Blair *(Rene)*, Leo McKern *(Inspector)*, Jean Philippe *(Jean)*, Liam Gaffney *(Spider's Father)*, Henry Webb *(Barman)*, Ted Heath and His Orchestra.

While imitating American gangster films, this simple picture also provides a look at the British "Teddy Boy" subculture. Electrician Newley brags that he is a cat burglar. When he is conned into a jewel heist by a gang of rookie crooks, he gets into some amusing situations, though none are particularly memorable.

p, Harold Huth; d, Ken Hughes; w, Hughes, John Antrobus (based on a story by Rex Rienits); ph, Ted Morre, Nicolas Roeg (CinemaScope); m, Kenneth V. Jones; ed, Geoffrey Foot; art d, Ray Simm; m/l, Joe Henderson, Hughes, Anthony Newley, Huburg Giraud, Michael Julien.

Crime Musical (PR:A MPAA:NR)

JAZZ CINDERELLA * 1/2** (1930) 66m Chesterfield/State Right bw

Myrna Loy *(Mildred Vane)*, Jason Robards, Sr. *(Herbert Carter)*, Nancy Welford *(Patricia Murray)*, Dorothy Phillips *(Mrs. Consuelo Carter)*, David Durand *(Danny Murray)*, Freddie Burke Frederick *(Junior Carter)*, Frank McGlynn, Sr. *(Henry Murray)*, James Burtis *(Ollie)*, George Cowl *(Darrow)*, Murray Smith *(Epstein)*, William Strauss *(Fireman)*, June Gittleson *(Sylvia de Sprout)*.

Robards' love life is run by his mother, who tries to steer him into a marriage with society girl Loy, though he loves a poor model, Welford. Helplessly, he becomes engaged to Loy, but breaks it off in favor of his true love.

p, George R. Batcheller; d, Scott Pembroke; w, Pemborke, Arthur Howell, Adrian Johnson (based on a story by Edwin Johns, Oliver Jones); ph, M.A. Anderson; ed, Donn Hayes; m/l, "You're Too Good to Be True," "Hot and Bothered Baby," "True Love," Jesse Greer, Ray Klages.

Romance (PR:A MPAA:NR)

JAZZ HEAVEN ** 1/2** (1929) 80m RKO bw

John Mack Brown *(Barry Holmes)*, Clyde Cook *(Max Langley)*, Blanche Frederici *(Mrs. Langley)*, Sally O'Neil *(Ruth Morgan)*, Joseph Cawthorn *(Herman Kemple)*, Albert Conti *(Walter Klucke)*, Henry Armetta *(Tony)*, Ole M. Ness *(Prof. Rowland)*, J. Barney Sherry *(John Parker)*, Adele Watson *(Miss Dunn)*.

Spiffy little tale of a poor songwriter, Brown, who comes from the South to Tin Pan Alley with just his piano and a melody to play on it. He moves into a boarding house and falls in love with O'Neil, but they are thrown out when caught in the same room by the landlady. She keeps Brown's piano for his back rent, and when her husband tries to sneak away with it, he drops it down the stairs, smashing it into a million pieces. Luckily, O'Neil works for a couple wacky music publishers, Cawthorn and Conti, who make the pair rich and famous by selling Brown's hit songs—stealing the film with their comedy in the process.

p, William Le Baron; d, Melville Brown; w, Cyrus Wood, J. Walter Ruben (based on a story by Dudley Murphy, Pauline Forney); ph, Jack MacKenzie; ed, Ann McKnight, George Marsh; m, Oscar Levant, Sidney Clare; m/l, "Someone," Levant, Clare.

Comedy Drama (PR:A MPAA:NR)

JAZZ SINGER, THE*** (1927) 88m WB bw

Al Jolson *(Jakie Rabinowitz/Jack Robin)*, May McAvoy *(Mary Dale)*, Warner Oland *(Cantor Rabinowitz)*, Eugenie Besserer *(Sara Rabinowitz)*, Bobby Gordon *(Jakie at Thirteen)*, Otto Lederer *(Moishe Yudelson)*, Cantor Josef Rosenblatt *(Himself)*, Richard Tucker *(Harry Lee)*, Nat Carr *(Levi)*, William Demarest *(Buster Billings)*, Anders Randolf *(Dillings)*, Will Walling *(Doctor)*, Roscoe Karns *(The Agent)*, Myrna Loy, Audrey Ferris *(Chorus Girls)*, Jane Arden, Violet Bird, Ernest Clauson, Marie Stapleton, Edna Gregory, Margaret Oliver *(Extras in Coffee Dan's Sequence)*.

The story is corny, even by 1927 standards, the dialog could have been written by any high school student *but* it was spoken dialog. This was the film that revolutionized the motion picture industry, cast out hundreds of leading players who could not or would not speak in films, and made stars out of unknowns dying to give voice to films. With THE JAZZ SINGER the movies finally, and forever, talked! The film was not all-talking, far from it. There is only a smattering of dialog, when Jolson talks to his mother, Besserer, once at a piano and another time while she sits in an audience watching him perform. But Jolson sings "Mammy" (Sam Lewis, Joe Young, Walter Davidson) and other songs that would always be exclusively his own, and the singing and dancing he performs is a wonder to behold. As the Warner Bros. ads read: "Jolson 'Out-Jolsons' Jolson" and from this, his first film appearance, millions learned why Al Jolson was considered the world's greatest entertainer. (Jolson's numbers, six in total, only average two to three minutes each, but when they were first heard audiences gaped in wonder.) The story, such as it is, concerns Jolson as Jakie Robinowitz who longs to have a Broadway career as a jazz singer, but his father, Oland, insists that he eventually take over his position in his synagog as leading cantor. This leads to conflict between father and son with mother Besserer playing referee. Jolson breaks with his father completely, taking the gentile name of Jack Robin, and going into a Broadway show, encouraged by his girl friend McAvoy, a glamorous showgirl. Jolson gets his big break and is about to appear in a Broadway show. Hearing that his father has suddenly become very ill, Jolson hurries home to find him dying and to sing the "Kol Nidre," which delays the opening of the show. But he does open on Broadway to become the great jazz singer, his mother rooting him on in the audience. Movie-goers around the world flocked to see this innovative film and were electrified by the few words spoken by Jolson, 281 words in all to be exact, words that surrounded some of Jolson's songs and were largely Jolson's idea; he simply ad-libbed his way into immortality, uttering these first words to his mother: "Wait a minute, wait a minute, you ain't heard nothin' yet! Wait a minute, I tell you. You ain't heard nothin' yet. Do you want to hear 'Toot, Toot, Tootsie?'." Actually, the first voice heard in the film is that of Bobby Gordon, playing Jolson as a child, singing in a saloon during the opening sequence. The film, by today's standards, is mawkish, crudely filmed, and full of *schmaltz*, but fascinating also since director Crosland took his cameras on location into the New York Jewish ghetto around Hester and Orchard Streets, and then along the Great White Way of Broadway to show the colorful, divergent aspects of immigrant and show business life. Of course, the idea of sound was not new with THE JAZZ SINGER. Lee de Forrest made some primitive sound shorts in 1923 and Warner Bros. pioneered sound with the release (on August 6, 1926) of DON JUAN, starring John Barrymore, employing the Vitaphone sound-on-disc system. Despite the success of DON JUAN, Warners was almost bankrupt by 1927. The four brothers, Sam, Jack, Harry, and Albert, desperately needed a blockbuster to turn around their fortunes. They decided—or rather Sam convinced the other three—to pool all their funds into making THE JAZZ SINGER. The Raphaelson story, supposedly based on Jolson's own life, was turned into a popular stage play, starring George Jessel, one on Jolson's many imitators. Jessel, who had already appeared in a Warner movie, PRIVATE IZZY MURPHY (1926), was slated to appear in the revolutionary film. When Jessel was told that songs would be in the film he insisted that he be paid considerably more. Warners said no and went to Eddie Cantor. The bug-eyed comedian backed away from the project, fearing that, if the experiment failed, his career would take a nose dive. The brothers Warner refused to go back to Jessel, who was upping his price every time somebody even mentioned the movie. Sam Warner then decided that he might as well go after the greatest entertainer of them all, Al Jolson, a singing and dancing dynamo who had owned Broadway since 1911. He was the King of Broadway and all who ever saw him perform went away convinced that this energetic, indefatigable man in black face, combining jazz and minstrel styles in his own inimitable routines, was a matchless human being. The 41-year-old Jolson was always ready for anything new; he accepted a $75,000 fee for the film, a third of this amount to be paid in cash, the balance paid in weekly increments of $6,250, and part of this weekly salary was to be reinvested in the film in which Jolson would share in the profits. Jolson arrived in Hollywood to begin shooting and was feted and honored by Charlie Chaplin, John Barrymore, Douglas Fairbanks, Sr., all the luminaries of Tinsel Town, but he was unimpressed. He didn't think THE JAZZ SINGER had a chance. "I thought the picture would be a terrible flop," he later admitted in *Jolson*, by Michael Freedland, "because everything was new and strange to me." Crosland, who had helmed DON JUAN for Warners, relentlessly demanded that the temperamental star redo scenes over and over again. "I would do a scene five times with tears in my eyes," Jolson would remember, "and then Alan Crosland would say, 'Do it again, and put some feeling into it!" I wanted to go away and hide." Upon the film's completion, the studio went all out to premiere the movie at the Warner Brothers Theater in Manhattan. They insisted that Jolson be there in person. The "Mammy" singer recalled how "the Warner brothers got me by the collar, threw me on a train, and packed me off to New York for the opening, which went over with a bang and made me very happy." It also made Jolson richer by $4 million when his percentages from the film were finally tallied. After all its expenses were paid, $500,000, THE JAZZ SINGER netted $3,500,000, an enormous sum for that day. Warner Bros. was suddenly no longer a struggling studio but, overnight, one of the three biggest filmmaking organizations in the U.S. Shot on location in New York, the studio also built Manhattan street sets and a marvelous full-scale replica of the synagog on Orchard Street in New York. The film was the most sensational event in motion picture history, causing all the studios to panic and order sound to be installed in every theater. RKO came into being just to make talking films. Where sound was not available, THE JAZZ SINGER was shown as a silent and still did well. The explosive novelty became the standard and the industry suddenly found a voice. Many of the voices of great silent stars, however, remained mute, and many others failed to make the transition, even some of Warner's own stars, such as Colleen Moore, Billie Dove, and Corinne Griffith. Oddly, the man who brought it all about, Sam Warner, died at the premature age of 41, one day before the New York premiere of THE JAZZ SINGER on August 6, 1927. (Warner died of a sinus infection; he had suffered a broken nose years earlier and had an operation to correct the problem, then five more when complications developed.) Only Jolson was present at the premiere, the surviving Warner brothers, Harry, Albert, and Jack immediately going to Los Angeles to attend Sam's funeral on August 9. Of the cast in THE JAZZ SINGER, Jolson would go on to make a string of successful musicals for Warner Bros. in the 1930s, Oland would become a memorable Charlie Chan in the popular series, and Demarest, who had made his film debut a year earlier in Warners FINGERPRINTS, would go on to become one of the finest character actors in the business. He was always Jolson's favorite thespian, and, when THE JOLSON STORY was made in 1946 by Columbia, Jolson insisted that Demarest, with whom he had shared scenes in THE JAZZ SINGER two decades earlier, be given the role of the vaudevillian who gets him started in show business. THE JAZZ SINGER, with all its technical inadequacies, was the result of scientific experiments by Western Electric and Bell Telephone Laboratories. Sam Warner went to see a demonstration of the new Vitaphone system and enthusiastically endorsed it, telling his brother Harry: "It's far from perfect, but it's farther along now than films were when they first swept the country. It can be improved rapidly, and it will sweep the world." (As quoted from *The History of the American Film Industry* by Benjamin B. Hampton.) Warners went all out for sound after THE JAZZ SINGER, producing in 1927 OLD SAN FRANCISCO, from a Darryl F. Zanuck story, the first film to offer sound effects, men and women screaming and shouting as walls tumbled and streets gaped open. Myrna Loy, who appeared in THE JAZZ SINGER as a chorine, would appear in an early part-talkie, STATE STREET SADIE (1929). In 1928, Warners offered TENDERLOIN, directed by Michael Curtiz and starring Dolores Costello and Conrad Nagel, which had about fifteen minutes of dialog in its 85-minutes-long story. Warners abandoned the old silent technique of title cards altogether with a mystery thriller THE TERROR, in 1928, which was also part-talking, offering Edward Everett Horton in his first speaking role. In 1929 the studio created more "firsts," offering THE DESERT SONG, the first musical romance, and ON WITH THE SHOW, the first all-color musical sound production. Only months after THE JAZZ SINGER stunned the world, Warners released the first all-talking film, LIGHTS OF NEW YORK, 1928, a crime melodrama. It was advertised as "100 percent all-taking picture," but the dialog stemming from the 57-minute film was a string of cliches. They were nevertheless startling, as audiences heard for the first time such gangland terms as "take him for a ride!" Yet, no one who was present at the Warner Theater in New York on August 6, 1927, would ever forget the incredible premiere of THE JAZZ SINGER, nor the songs so vibrantly belted out by Jolson. These include: "Toot, Toot, Tootsie Goodbye" (Gus Kahn, Ernie Erdman, Dan Russo), "Blue Skies" (Irving Berlin), "My Gal Sal" (Paul Dresser), "Waiting for the Robert E. Lee" (Wolfe Gilbert, Lewis E. Muir), "Dirty Hands, Dirty Face" (Edgar Leslie, Grant Clarke, Jolson, James V. Monaco), "Mother, I Still Have You" (Jolson, Louis Silvers). Remade in 1953 by Warners, starring Danny Thomas and again in 1980 with Neil Diamond and Laurence Olivier, neither of these remakes having anywhere the impact of the original. The film was given a special Academy Award for its innovative achievement.

d, Alan Crosland; w, Alred A. Cohn (titles), Jack Jarmuth (based on the play "Day of Atonement" by Samson Raphaelson); ph, Hal Mohr; m, Louis Silvers; ed, Harold McCord.

Musical **Cas.** **(PR:A MPAA:NR)**

JAZZ SINGER, THE** 1/2 (1953) 107m WB c

Danny Thomas *(Jerry Golding)*, Peggy Lee *(Judy Lane)*, Mildred Dunnock *(Mrs. Golding)*, Eduard Franz *(Cantor Golding)*, Tom Tully *(McGurney)*, Alex Gerry *(Uncle Louie)*, Allyn Joslyn *(George Miller)*, Harold Gordon *(Rabbi Roth)*, Hal Ross *(Joseph)*, Justin Smith *(Phil Stevens)*, Anitra Stevens *(Yvonne)*.

The sentimental, tear-jerking story which had blockbusted the talkies in 1927 was revamped and brought back in living color with Thomas in the role of the jazz singing cantor's son. Thomas returns from the Korean War to his family in Philadelphia. Here he longs for the bright lights of Broadway and argues with father Franz who wants him to take over the role of cantor in their synagog. Broadway wins out and Thomas goes on to warble some pleasant tunes with girl friend Lee. Curtiz could do nothing with the mawkish material and just let the sloppy sentiment ooze. The show numbers are exceptional, as are all the technical credits. The film was edited by Alan Crosland, Jr., the son of the man who directed the original film in 1927. Songs include: "Lover" (Richard Rodgers, Lorenz Hart), "If I Could Be You" (Henry Creamer, Jimmy Johnson), "Breezin' Along with the Breeze" (Richard A. Whiting, Seymour Simons, Haven Gillespie), "I'll String Along with You" (Al Dubin, Harry Warren), "Living the Life I Love," "What Are New Yorkers Made Of," "Hush-A-Bye," "Oh Moon," "I Hear the Music Now" (Sammy Fain, Jerry Seelen), "Birth of the Blues" (B.G. DeSylva, Lew Brown, Ray Henderson), "Just One of Those Things" (Cole Porter), "This Is A Very Special Day" (Peggy Lee).

p, Louis F. Edelman; d, Michael Curtiz; w, Frank Davis, Leonard Stern, Lewis Meltzer (based on the play by Samson Raphaelson); ph, Carl Guthrie (Technicolor); ed, Alan Crosland Jr.; ch, LeRoy Prinz.; cos, Howard Shoup.

Musical **(PR:A MPAA:NR)**

JAZZ SINGER, THE* (1980) 115m Associated Film c

Neil Diamond *(Jess Robin)*, Laurence Olivier *(Cantor Rabinovitch)*, Lucie Arnaz *(Molly Bell)*, Catlin Adams *(Rivka Rabinovitch)*, Franklyn Ajaye *(Bubba)*, Paul Nicholas *(Keith Lennox)*, Sully Boyar *(Eddie Gibbs)*, Mike Bellin *(Leo)*, James Booth *(Paul Rossini)*, Luther Waters *(Teddy)*, Rod Gist *(Timmy)*, Oren Waters *(Mel)*, Walter Janowitz *(Rabbi Birnbaum)*, Janet Brandt *(Aunt Tillie)*, John Witherspoon *(M.C. Cinderella Club)*, Dale Robinette *(Tommy)*, Judy Gibson *(Peg)*, Hank Garrett *(Police Sergeant)*, James Karen *(Barney Callahan)*, Jill Jaress *(Cowgirl)*, Victor Paul *(Irate Driver)*.

The third and final (hopefully) remake of THE JAZZ SINGER is the least interesting of the lot and its music is forgettable. Diamond, even reverting to Jolson's immortal black face for one sequence, is wholly unbelievable as the cantor's son who forsakes the synagog for the bright lights of a pop singer. This $15 million bomb failed to generate much interest and Olivier didn't help much by overplaying his role as the cantor in the same histrionic style as Warner Oland employed six decades earlier, replete with eye-rolling, chest-thumping, and hand-wringing. Olivier made no bones about taking this role, saying jocularly: "I always wanted to play a rabbi." He told others that he wanted "to make as much money as I can for my children." Songs include: "America," "You Baby Baby," "Jerusalem," "Love on the Rocks," "Summer Love," "On the Robert E. Lee," "Louise," "Songs of Life," "Hello Again," "Amazed and Confused."

p, Jerry Leider; d, Richard Fleischer; w, Herbert Baker, Stephen H. Foreman (based on the play by Samson Raphaelson); ph, Isidore Mankofsky (DeLuxe Color); m, Neil Diamond; ed, Frank J. Urioste, Maury Weintrobe; prod d, Harry Horner; art d, Spencer Deverill; set d, Christopher Horner, Mark Poll, Ruby Levitt, Robert de Vestel; cos, Albert Wolsky; ch, Don McKayle; m/l, Neil Diamond.

Musical **Cas.** **(PR:C MPAA:PG)**

JAZZBOAT (SEE; JAZZ BOAT, 1960, Brit.)

JE T'AIME*

(1974, Can.) 90m Tele-Capitale-Ltee-Les/Mutuels bw (AKA: I LOVE YOU)

Jeanne Moreau *(Elisa Boussac)*, Roseline Hoffman *(Martine Boussac)*, Lionel Villeneuve *(Marcellin)*, Jean Duceppe *(Arthur Tremblay)*, Jean-Rene Ouellet *(Jerome Demers)*.

Leaving behind France and the famly she detests, Moreau makes a new home in rural Quebec. Hoffman, her pregnant daughter, shows up on her doorstep. Ouellet, the baby's father, follows and falls in love with Moreau. Store owner Duceppe and Villeneuve, Moreau's hired man, also bid for her hand. Too heavy to carry anywhere.

p, Claude Heroux; d, Pierre Duceppe; w, Duceppe, Jean Salvy, Alex Pelletier; ph, Rene Verzier; m, Frank Dervieux.

Drama **(PR:C MPAA:NR)**

JE T'AIME, JE T'AIME***

(1972, Fr./Swed.) 91m Parc-Fox Europa/New Yorker c

Claude Rich *(Claude Ridder)*, Olga Georges-Picot *(Catrine)*, Amouk Ferjac *(Wiana Lust)*, Marie-Blanche Vergne *(Young Woman)*, Dominique Rozan *(Dr. Haesserts)*, Van Doude *(Jan Rouffer)*, Annie Fargue *(Agnes de Smet)*, Bernard Fresson *(Bernard Hannecart)*, Yvette Etievant *(Germaine Coster)*, Irene Tunc *(Marcelle Hannecart)*, Yves Kerboul, Ray Verhaege, Pierre Barbaud, Alain MacMoy, Vania Vilers, Georges Jamin, Carla Marlier, Claire Duhamel, Annie Bertin, Helene Callot, Bernard Valdeneige, Jean Martin, Georges Walter, Alan Adair, Ian MacGregor, Jean-Louis Richard, M. Floquet, Pierre Motte, Rene Bazart, Jean Perre, Michele Blondel, Jean Michaud, Ben Danou, Catherine Robbe-Grillet, Alain Robbe-Grillet, Jacques Doniol-Valcroze, Sylvain Dhomme, Francois Regis-Bastide, Francis Lacassin, Jean-Claude Romer, Gerard Lorin, Guilene Pean, Alain Tercinet, Michel Choquet, Jorge Semprun, Billy Fasbender.

Resnais continues exploring the relation of time and memory to individual perceptions and feelings, the pervasive theme in his work since HIROSHIMA MON AMOUR. This time he gives himself a science fiction-like environment to do his investigations in. Rich plays a man recovering from a suicide attempt, who is able to go back into time and become involved once more in the love affair that led to his attempted suicide. Though eventually released to normal time structures, Rich is still trapped inside his mind with past events. A tight collaboration between Resnais and screenwriter Sternberg has woven complex thematic content into a film more accessible than any of Resnais' earlier works. (In French; English subtitles).

p, Mag Bodard; d, Alain Resnais; w, Resnais, Jacques Sternberg; ph, Jean Boffety (Eastmancolor); m, Krystof Penderecki, Jean-Claude Pelletier, Jean Dandeny; ed, Albert Jurgenson, Colette Leloup; art d, Jacques Dugied, Auguste Pace.

Drama/Science Fiction **(PR:C MPAA:NR)**

JE VOUS SALUE, MAFIA (SEE: HAIL MAFIA, 1965)

JEALOUSY* (1929) 66m PAR bw

Jeanne Eagels *(Yvonne)*, Fredric March *(Pierre)*, Halliwell Hobbes *(Rigaud)*, Blanche Le Clair *(Renee)*, Henry Daniell *(Clement)*, Hilda Moore *(Charlotte)*, Carlotta Coerr *(Louise)*, Granville Bates *(Lawyer)*, Virginia Chauvernet *(Maid)*.

Adapted from the Broadway play by Louis Verneuil, this film, set in France, was fraught with difficulties. The leading lady was Eagels, an actress with a big following at the time; the original leading man was Anthony Bushell. But after shooting a version with him, Eagels was dissatisfied, and demanded that another version be shot with March opposite her. Eagels was seriously ill while shooting the second version, (she died later that year) and she barely managed to finish it. Even the addition of March fails to save this lackluster tale of jealousy. Young artist March is concerned about his wife Eagels' relationship with Hobbes, an older man she had been involved with before her marriage. Hobbes, meanwhile, poses as her guardian. When Eagels is in financial straits, she borrows money from Hobbes and is discovered in his apartment, after she has lied to March about her whereabouts. March kills Hobbes and an innocent man is accused. In the end, however, March confesses.

d, Jean De Limur; w, Garret Fort, Eugene Walter, John D. Williams (based on the play by Louis Verneuil and the translation and stage adaptation by Walter); ph, Alfred Gilks; art d, William N. Sauter; set d, Charles Kirk; cos, H.M.K. Smith.

Drama **(PR:C MPAA:NR)**

JEALOUSY* 1/2 (1931, Brit.) 56m Majestic/New Era bw

Mary Newland *(Joyce Newcombe)*, Malcolm Keen *(Henry Garwood)*, Harold French *(Bernard Wingate)*, Gibb McLaughlin *(Littleton Pardmore)*, Sam Livesey *(Inspector Thompson)*, Henrietta Watson *(Mrs. Delahunt)*, Henry Carlisle *(Clayton)*, Frank Pettingell *(Prof. Macguire)*, Dino Galvani, Frederick Atwell.

Tired melodrama revolving around the attempts of Newland to pursue a romance despite the efforts of her guardian (Keen) to do everything possible to make sure the affair doesn't come off.

p, Gordon Craig; d&w, G.B. Samuelson (based on the play "The Green Eye" by John McNally).

Drama **(PR:A MPAA:NR)**

JEALOUSY* 1/2 (1934) 66m COL bw

Nancy Carroll *(Jo Douglas)*, George Murphy *(Larry O'Roark)*, Donald Cook *(Mark Lambert)*, Raymond Walburn *(Phil)*, Arthur Hohl *(Mike Callahan)*, Inez Courtney *(Penny)*, Josephine Whittell *(Laura)*, Arthur Vinton *(Tony)*, Ray Mayer *(Hook)*, Ray Cooke *(Line)*, Huey White *(Sinker)*, The Nicholas Brothers *(Themselves)*, Lee Ramage *(Fighter)*, James Burtis *(Brownie)*, Niles Welch *(Police Doctor)*, Selmer Jackson *(Radio Announcer)*, James J. Jeffries *(Capt. Scott)*, Charles Keppen *(Announcer)*, Edwin Stanley *(Editor)*, Harry Holman *(Man with Dog)*, Edward Keane *(District Attorney)*, Montague Shaw *(Judge)*, Kathrin Clare Ward *(Jury Woman)*, Phil Dunham *(Jury Man)*, Abe Roth *(Referee)*, K.S. Hubley *(Ramage's Manager)*, Freddy Welsh *(Russ)*, Robert Graves *(Headwaiter)*, Broderick O'Farrell *(Minister)*, Gladden James *(Court Clerk)*, James Farley *(Bailiff)*, Pietro Sosso *(Chaplain)*, Emmett Vogan, Sherry Hall, James Bradbury, Jr., Jack Kenney, Jack La Barba, Mike Schwartz, Jack Mack, James Quinn, Billy West, Sammy Blum, Charles Marsh *(Reporters)*, William Irving, Stanley Mack, Ernest Young *(Photographers)*, Tom London, Charles King, Bobbie Dale, Theodore Lorch, Sidney D'Albrook, Billy Engle, John Beck, Dutch Hendrian, Max Asher, William Ryno *(Men)*, Dulcie Day *(Nurse)*, Edward Le Saint *(Hospital Doctor)*, Ethan Laidlaw *(Taxicab Driver)*, Alice Dahl, Jean Dudley, Patricia Royale, Irene Coleman, Ann Hughes, Jean Eddy, Pat O'Neill, Elinor Fields *(Women)*, Lucille Ball *(Girl)*, Matty Roubert *(Newsboy)*, Jack Cheatham *(Guard)*, Charles McAvoy, Ky Robinson *(Detectives)*, Amelia Batchelor *(Stand-In for Nancy Carroll)*, Chuck Colean *(Stand-In for George Murphy)*, Clara Blandick, Arthur Hoyt.

JEALOUSY stars Murphy as a boxer whose fiancee (Carroll) won't marry him unless he stops acting so jealously. When Murphy finds his wife (he has accepted her conditions and they have married) and her boss, Cook, in a hotel room, he goes berserk and kills Cook. Carroll goes to trial for the crime and just as the verdict is to be read, Murphy confesses, getting sentenced to the electric chair. While waiting to die, Murphy asks the priest to give him a 10-count. By the time the priest gets to 9, we hear a referee's voice and realize that it was all a dream, which occured while the boxer was on the canvas: a horrible end to an otherwise interesting picture.

d, Roy William Neill; w, Joseph Moncure, Kubec Glasmon (based on a story by Argyle Campbell); ph, John Stumar; ed, Roy Snyder.

Drama **(PR:C MPAA:NR)**

JEALOUSY** (1945) 71m REP bw

John Loder *(Dr. David Brent)*, Jane Randolph *(Janet Urban)*, Karen Morley *(Dr. Monica Anderson)*, Nils Asther *(Peter Urban)*, Hugo Haas *(Hugo Kral)*, Holmes Herbert *(Melvyn Russell)*, Michael Mark *(Shop Owner)*, Mauritz Hugo *(Bob)*, Peggy Leon *(Secretary)*, Mary Arden *(Nurse)*, Noble "Kid" Chissell *(Expressman)*.

In this familiar, weak whodunit, Asther, a famous refugee novelist, finds it difficult to adjust to ordinary work. He becomes jealous of his wife, Randolph, who tries to take up the financial slack by becoming a taxi driver. She picks up Loder and they become friends. When Asther is found murdered, Loder is naturally accused, and must prove his innocence.

p&d, Gustav Machaty; w, Arnold Phillips, Machaty (based on a story by Dalton Trumbo); ph, Henry Sharp; m, Hanns Eisler; ed, John Link; art d, Frank Sylos; m/l, "Jealousy," Rudolf Friml.

Mystery **(PR:A MPAA:NR)**

JEALOUSY (SEE: EMERGENCY WEDDING, 1950)

JEAN MARC OR CONJUGAL LIFE

(SEE: ANATOMY OF A MARRIAGE, 1964, Fr.)

JEANNE EAGELS 1/2** (1957) 109m COL bw

Kim Novak *(Jeanne Eagels)*, Jeff Chandler *(Sal Satori)*, Agnes Moorehead *(Mme. Neilson)*, Charles Drake *(John Donahue)*, Larry Gates *(Al Brooks)*, Virginia Grey *(Elsie Desmond)*, Gene Lockhart *(Equity Board President)*, Joe de Santis *(Frank Satori)*, Murray Hamilton *(Chick O'Hara)*, Will Wright *(Marshal)*, Sheridan Comerate *(Actor-Confederate Officer)*, Lowell Gilmore *(Rev. Dr. Davidson)*, Juney Ellis *(Mrs. Davidson)*, Beulah Archuletta *(Mrs. Horn)*, Jules Davis *(Mr. Horn)*, Florence MacAfee *(Mrs. McPhail)*, Snub Pollard *(Quartermaster Bates)*, Joseph Novak *(Patron)*, Johnny Tarangelo *(Pvt. Griggs)*, Bert Spencer *(Dr. McPhail)*, Richard Harrison *(Cpl. Hodgson)*, Ward Wood *(Stage Manager)*, Myrtle Anderson *(Jeanne's Maid)*, Michael Dante *(Sgt. O'Hara)*, Joseph Turkel *(Eddie)*, George Neise *(Jerry the Traveling Salesman)*, Charles Couch, William Couch, Sammy Finn, Wallace Ross, Walter Ridge *(Barkers)*, Richard Gaines *(Judge)*, Patricia Mowry *(Hefty Bathing Beauty)*, Junius Matthews *(Court Clerk)*, George de Normand *(Police Sergeant)*, Tom McKee *(Police Lieutenant)*, Eleanor Audley *(Sob Sister)*, Bill Suiter *(Sailor)*, Myna Cunard *(Neilson Maid)*, Bob Hopkins *(Reporter)*, Judd Holdren *(Actor)*, John Celentano, Tommy Nolan *(Satori's Sons)*, Raymond Greenleaf *(Elderly Lawyer)*, Doris Lloyd *(Mrs. Corliss)*, Carlyle Mitchell *(Equity Spokesman)*, James Gonzales *(Equity Man)*, Joe Mell *(Kevin)*, Jennie Lea *(Young Ingenue at Equity Trial)*, Helen Marr Van Tuyl *(Great Lady on Equity Board)*, Bradford Jackson *(Young Man on Equity Board)*, Lillian Culver *(Equity Board Woman)*, Alyn Lockwood *(Rosalie Satori)*, Deon Robb, Rebecca Godinez *(Satori's Daughters)*, Irving Mitchell *(Lawyer)*, George J. Lewis *(Foreman)*, Frances Driver *(Maid)*, Joan Harding, Reita Green, Myrna Fahey, Joy Stoner *(Girls)*, Hal Le Sueur *(Disgruntled Man)*, Leon Tyler *(Bellhop)*, Ted Marcuse *(Dr. Richards)*, Giselle D'Arc *(French Maid)*, Lee Trent

(Leading Man on Equity Board), Kenneth Gibson *(Middle-Aged Man)*, Jean Vachon *(Middle-Aged Woman)*, Whitey Haupt, Paul De Rolf, Larry Larson, Gary Pagett *(Wise Teenagers)*, Nanette Fabares, Brenda Lomas *(Teenage Girls)*, Eugene Jackson *(Piccaninny)*, Jimmy Murphy *(Assistant Director)*, Cosmo Sardo, Larry Blake, Walter Conrad, Eugene Sherman *(Reporters)*, William "Tex" Carr *(Specialty Fire Eater)*, Frank Borzage *(Director)*, Lou Borzage *(Assistant Director)*, Jack Ano *(Soldier)*.

Good production values and interesting performances from Chandler and Novak give this unusual film biography more value than the hackneyed script originally provided. The story, reportedly based on the ill-starred Broadway actress Jeanne Eagels, opens with a contradictory statement: " . . . all events in this photoplay are based on fact and fiction." For the rest of the film, the producers couldn't seem to make up their minds which way to take the script. And Novak, as Eagels, seems to go both ways, too, sometimes confused at her split personality character. She begins scantily clad as a sensuous cooch dancer shimmying and shaking for carnival owner Chandler, who is perfectly happy with what he's got and goes out of his way to persuade Novak from pursuing a Broadway career. She persists however, and, after several encounters with male promoters, winds up starring in Somerset Maugham's "Rain," for which the real Jeanne Eagels became famous, then a slow decline into booze and, implied, prostitution. Chandler remains the lover who has affection for her but cannot bring himself to help Novak in her time of need. That he's just plain jealous of her success is also evident, and when she dies tragically, all Chandler can do is go to a theater to see his now dead girl friend in a movie singing "I'll Take Romance" (dubbed by Eileen Wilson). Novak's passive performance is at odds with her desperate desire to become a star, using her acting coach Moorehead and double-crossing an aging actress, Grey, to land the part in "Rain." Lovely to look at but lightweight in the acting department, Novak became incensed when she learned that Chandler was getting $20,000 for his role and she only $13,000. After finishing the picture, Novak fired her agent and the William Morris office took over her career. When Novak refused to report to her next film, Columbia's Harry Cohn suspended her, then gave a rare press interview complaining about stars getting out of control. Novak stayed out on suspension, supported by her agency which continued to pay her salary until Cohn finally capitulated and signed a new, hefty contract with the star. Columbia had other problems with JEANNE EAGELS; Elaine Eagels Nicklas sued the studio for $950,000 claiming that its film about her relative showed her as a "dissolute and immoral person." The suit was later settled out of court. Novak was one of the few people who liked JEANNE EAGELS, remarking later: "I think I got what I saw in the character."

p&d, George Sidney; w, Daniels Fuchs, Sonya Levien, John Fante (based on a story by Fuchs); ph, Robert Planck; m, George Duning; ed, Viola Lawrence, Jerome Thoms; art d, Ross Bellah; md, Morris Stoloff; cos, Jean Louis.

Biography (PR:C MPAA:NR)

JEANNIE (SEE: GIRL IN DISTRESS, 1941, Brit.)

JEDDA, THE UNCIVILIZED** (1956, Aus.) 88m Distributors Corp. of America c

Narla Kunogh *(Jedda)*, Robert Tudewali *(Marbuck)*, Betty Suttor *(Sarah McMann)*, Paul Reynall *(Joe)*, George Simpsom-Little *(Douglas McMann)*, Tas Fitzer of the Northern Territory Mounted Police, Wason Byers, Willie Farrar, Aborigines of the Pitjantara Tribe, Aranda, Pintudi, Yungman, Djauan, Waugite and Tiwi Tribes of North and Central Australia.

Brought up in the warm and happy surroundings of a white couple's farm, the aborigine Kunogh runs off into the wilds when she falls in love with a tribesman who has been wandering across those reaches. The picture does a good job of detailing the initial finding of the girl and the manner in which she fits into the white family, but interest quickly falls apart when an attempt at adding fiery drama is included. Said to be the first color feature from Australia, the scenic wonders of this film help when the story starts to slacken.

p&d, Charles Chauvel; w, Elsa and Charles Chauvel; ph, Carl Kayser (Eastmancolor); m, Isador Goodman; ed, Alec Ezard, Jack Gardiner, Pam Bosworth; md, Goodman; art d, Ronald McDonald.

Drama (PR:A MPAA:NR)

JEDER FUR SICH UND GOTT GEGEN ALLE (SEE: EVERY MAN FOR HIMSELF AND GOD AGAINST ALL, 1975, Ger.)

JEEPERS CREEPERS** (1939) 69m REP bw

Leon Weaver *(Abner)*, Frank Weaver *(Cicero)*, Elviry [June Weaver] *(Elviry)*, Roy Rogers *(Roy)*, Maris Wrixon *(Connie)*, Billy Lee *(Skeeter)*, Lucien Littlefield *(Grandpa)*, Thurston Hall *(M.K. Durant)*, Loretta Weaver *(Violey)*, John Arthur *(Peabody)*.

A harmless Weaver Brothers picture in which Hall is sentenced to dig with a pick for a day as punishment for nearly causing a fire. While digging, he discovers coal on the Weaver's property and proceeds to sneakily acquire their land. Before long the carelessness of Hall's hirelings results in a major forest fire, and the Weavers are called on to help Hall out of the mess. (See WEAVER FAMILY series, Index)

p, Armand Schaefer; d, Frank McDonald; w, Dorrell and Stuart McGowan; ph, Ernest Miller; ed, Ernest Nims; md, Cy Feuer.

Western (PR:A MPAA:NR)

JEKYLL AND HYDE . . . TOGETHER AGAIN* 1/2 (1982) 87m PAR c

Mark Blankfield *(Jekyll/Hyde)*, Bess Armstrong *(Mary)*, Krista Errickson *(Ivy)*, Tim Thomerson *(Dr. Lanyon)*, Michael McGuire *(Dr. Carew)*, Neil Hunt *(Queen)*, Cassandra Peterson *(Busty Nurse)*, Jessica Nelson *(Barbara)*, Peter Brocco *(Hubert)*, Michael Klingher, Noelle North, David Murphy *(Students)*, Mary McCusker *(Patient)*, Liz Sheridan *(Mrs. Larson)*, Alison Hong *(Asian Girl)*, Walter Janowitz *(Elderly Man)*, Belita Moreno *(Nurse Gonzales)*, Leland Sun *(Wong)*, George Wendy *(Injured Man)*, Glen Chin *(Sushi Chef)*, Dan Barrows *(Customer)*, Virginia Wing *(Mme. WooWoo)*, Jesse Goins *(Dutch)*, Jack Collins *(Baron)*, Michael Ensign *(Announcer)*, John Dennis Johnston *(Macho Kid)*, David Ruprecht *(Brigham)*, Clarke Coleman *(Box Boy)*, Sam Whipple *(Produce Man)*, Nancy Lenehan *(Mother)*, Barret Oliver *(Child)*, Tony Cox, Selwyn Emerson Miller *(Lawn Jockeys)*, Art LaFleur *(Clockman)*, Bernadette Birkett *(Mrs. Simpson)*, Lin Shaye *(Nurse)*, Madelyn Cates *(Helen)*, George Chakiris *(Himself)*, Sheila Rogers, Gerald Saunderson Peters, Bud Davis, Jose Borcia, Maher Bouros, Kate Fitzmaurice, Howard George.

This version of Robert Louis Stevenson's classic tale would most likely send the author spinning relentlessly in his grave. The modernized tale stars the comically talented Blankfield as a surgeon-researcher who one day snorts cocaine accidentally, turning him into his hip alter ego. As Hyde he rejects his square fiancee, Armstrong, and gravitates toward a punk rock singer, Errickson. Unfortunately, Belson's first directorial effort is short on laughs and inventiveness.

p, Lawrence Gordon; d, Jerry Belson; w, Monica Johnson, Harvey Miller, Belson, Michael Lesson (based on the novel *The Strange Case of Dr. Jekyll and Mr. Hyde* by Robert Louis Stevenson); ph, Philip Lathrop (Metrocolor); m, Barry DeVorzon; ed, Billy Weber; prod d, Peter Wooley; cos, Marilyn Kay Vance; spec eff, Michael Boddicker, D.G. Grigg; makeup, John M. Elliott, Jr, Mark Bussan.

Comedy Cas. (PR:O MPAA:R)

JEKYLL'S INFERNO (SEE: HOUSE OF FRIGHT, 1961)

JENIFER HALE** (1937, Brit.) 66m FOX bw

Rene Ray *(Jenifer Hale)*, Ballard Berkeley *(Richard)*, John Longden *(Inspector Merton)*, Paul Blake *(Ives)*, Frank Birch *(Sharman)*, Richard Parry *(Jim Watson)*, Ernest Sefton *(Sgt. Owen)*, Kay Seely *(Mr. Joyce)*, Philip Thomas, Jo Monkhouse, Raymond Ellis, Dominick Sterlini.

Fairly intriguing crime drama in which Ray plays a chorus girl running from a murder rap by taking off to Birmingham. Her brief period of peace is soon interrupted when the partner of the producer she is believed to have killed tails her to the architect with whom she has since fallen in love. Predictable ending has Ray getting off the hook by producing some last-minute evidence. Ray gives quite a good performance, but not enough to gain her much recognition, though anything lacking is more the fault of the uneven direction.

p, John Findlay; d, Bernard Mainwaring; w, Ralph Stock, Mainwaring, Edward Dryhurst (based on the novel by Rod Eden); ph, Stanley Grant.

Crime (PR:A MPAA:NR)

JENNIE* 1/2 (1941) 75m FOX bw

Virginia Gilmore *(Jennie)*, William Henry *(George Schermer)*, George Montgomery *(Franz)*, Ludwig Stossel *(Fritz Schermer)*, Dorris Bowdon *(Lottie)*, Rand Brooks *(Karl)*, Joan Valerie *(Clara)*, Rita Quigley *(Amelia)*, Hermine Sterler *(Mother Schermer)*, Harlan Briggs *(Mr. Veitch)*, Irving Bacon *(Real Estate Broker)*, Almira Sessions *(Mrs. Willoughby)*, Aldrich Bowker *(Dr. Hildebrand)*.

A contrived drama, starring Stossel as a tough shoe store owner who refuses to change with the times. When Gilmore marries into the family, she organizes a household strike. The entire clan leaves the house and the old man, but comes back when he fakes a heart attack and admits that he pushes them too hard.

p, Sol M. Wurtzel; d, David Burton; w, Harold Buchman, Maurice Rapf (based on a story by Jane Eberle); ph, Virgil Miller; m, Emil Newman; ed, Al De Gaetano.

Drama (PR:A MPAA:NR)

JENNIE (SEE: PORTRAIT OF JENNIE, 1948)

JENNIE GERHARDT*** (1933) 85m PAR bw

Sylvia Sidney *(Jennie Gerhardt)*, Donald Cook *(Lester Kane)*, Mary Astor *(Letty Pace)*, Edward Arnold *(Sen. Brander)*, H.B. Warner *(William Gerhardt)*, Theodore von Eltz *(Robert Kane)*, Dorothy Libaire *(Louise Kane)*, Gilda Storm *(Vesta, Age 17)*, Greta Meyer *(Ada)*, David O'Brien *(Bass Gerhardt)*, Morgan Wallace *(O'Brien)*, Ernest Wood *(Will Whitney)*, Frank Reicher *(Old Weaver)*, Gene Morgan *(Hotel Clerk)*, Rose Coghlan *(Old Weaver's Granddaughter)*, Jane Darwell *(Boarding House Keeper)*, Lillian Harmer *(Midwife)*, Louise Carter *(Mrs. Gerhardt)*, Cora Sue Collins *(Vesta, Age 6)*, Walter Walker *(Archibald Kane)*, David Durand *(Willie Gerhardt)*, Betty Ann Hisle *(Veronica Gerhardt)*.

Sidney is the heroine of this Dreiser tale, a woman beset by a series of tragedies, including the deaths of two lovers and her daughter and estrangement from her family. Gering and a competent cast make the most of the story's melodramatics. This was the second time Sidney starred as one of Dreiser's doomed characters, the first time being in AN AMERICAN TRAGEDY (1931).

p, B. P. Schulberg; d, Marion Gering; w, Josephine Lovett, Joseph Moncure March, S. K. Lauren, Frank Portos (based on the novel by Theodore Dreiser); ph, Leon Shamroy.

Drama (PR:A MPAA:NR)

JENNIE LESS HA UNA NUOVA PISTOLA (SEE: GUNMEN OF THE RIO GRANDE, 1965, Fr./Ital./Span.)

JENNIFER* 1/2 (1953) 73m AA bw

Ida Lupino *(Agnes)*, Howard Duff *(Jim)*, Robert Nichols *(Orin)*, Mary Shipp *(Lorna)*, Matt Dennis *(Himself)*, Ned Glass *(Grocery Clerk)*, Kitty McHugh *(Landlady)*, Russ Conway *(Gardener)*, Lorna Thayer *(Grocery Clerk)*.

Lupino's new job as the caretaker for a large estate gives her more than she had bargained for when a mysterious murderer crosses her path. Lots of gloomy and foreboding atmosphere is provided by the big old house and its abundant grounds, but so much so that any possibilities for the story to develop are almost totally buried.

p, Berman Swartz; d, Joel Newton; w, Virginia Myers; ph, James Wong Howe; m, Ernest Gold; ed, Everett Douglas.

Crime Drama **(PR:A MPAA:NR)**

JENNIFER zero

(1978) 90m AIP c (AKA: JENNIFER (THE SNAKE GODDESS))

Lisa Pelikan *(Jennifer Baylor)*, Bert Convy *(Jeff Reed)*, Nina Foch *(Mrs. Calley)*, Amy Johnston *(Sandra Tremayne)*, John Gavin *(Sen. Tremayne)*, Jeff Corey *(Luke Baylor)*, Louise Hoven *(Jane Delano)*, Ray Underwood *(Dayton Powell)*, Wesley Eure *(Pit Lassiter)*, Florida Friebus *(Miss Tooker)*, Georganne La Piere *(Deedee Martin)*.

A blatant CARRIE ripoff which took the mindless aspects of Brian DePalma's picture and stretched them into 90 minutes. Pelikan is the outcast student who gets sweet revenge on her classmates, especially a snooty blonde of the sort that everyone would like to banish to hell. She also has a religious nut for a father, a la Piper Laurie's role in CARRIE. Taking up where BEN and WILLARD left off, Pelikan gets snakes to do her dirty work.

p, Steve Krantz; d, Brice Mack; w, Kay Cousins Johnson (based on a story by Krantz); ph, Irv Goodnoff (CFI Color); ed, Duane Hartzell; m/l, "Jennifer," Porter Jordan (sung by Jordan).

Horror **(PR:C-O MPAA:PG)**

JENNIFER ON MY MIND zero (1971) 90m UA c

Michael Brandon *(Marcus)*, Tippy Walker *(Jenny)*, Lou Gilbert *(Max)*, Steve Vinovich *(Ornstein)*, Peter Bonerz *(Sergei)*, Renee Taylor *(Selma)*, Chuck McCann *(Sam)*, Bruce Kornbluth *(Dolci)*, Barry Bostwick *(Nanki)*, Jeff Conaway *(Hanki)*, John Frederick *(George)*, Nick Lapadula *(Motorcycle Cop)*, Joseph George *(Toll Booth Cop)*, Jack Hollander *(State Trooper)*, Mike McClanathan, Allan Nicholls, Ralph J. Pinto *(Hells Angels)*, Lieb Lansky *(Cantor)*, Victor Rendina *(Old Man)*, Erich Segal *(Gondolier)*, Robert De Niro *(Gypsy Cab Driver)*.

A collaboration between Black (PRETTY POISON) and Segal (LOVE STORY), this was a film that confounded critics who were unable to determine if it was a black comedy or a straight drama. They did agree, however, that it was very bad. The story opens in Venice where Brandon meets and falls in love with Walker. He follows her back to New York and continues to pursue her as she becomes a heavy drug user. She eventually dies from a heroin overdose and Brandon returns to Venice. Reportedly, the film was extensively edited in an effort to save it, with a part played by Kim Hunter, originally one of the movie's stars, being completely removed. It didn't help. Note Robert De Niro in an early small part as well as writer Erich Segal in a bit part. Actor Barry Bostwick appeared on Broadway in "Grease" and appeared in the TV mini-series "George Washington" and "Scruples."

p, Bernard Schwartz; d, Noel Black; w, Erich Segal (based on the novel *Heir* by Roger L. Simon); ph, Andy Laszlo (DeLuxe Color); m, Stephen J. Lawrence; prod d, Adeline Leonard; ed, Jack Wheeler; art d, Ben Edwards; cos, Joseph Aulisi; spec eff, Ira Anderson.

Comedy **(PR:O MPAA:R)**

JENNIFER (THE SNAKE GODDESS) (SEE: JENNIFER, 1978)

JENNY*

(1969) 86m ABC-Palomar/Cinerama c (AKA: AND JENNY MAKES THREE)

Marlo Thomas *(Jenny Marsh)*, Alan Alda *(Delano)*, Marian Hailey *(Kay)*, Elizabeth Wilson *(Mrs. Marsh)*, Vincent Gardenia *(Mr. Marsh)*, Stephen Strimpell *(Peter)*, Fay Bernardi *(Woman in Bus)*, Charlotte Rae *(Bella Star)*, Phil Bruns *(Fred)*, Estelle Winwood, Fred Willard, Michael Mislove.

Alda, a draft-evading filmmaker, suggests to film buff Thomas that they marry for convenience sake—he wants to avoid the draft, she needs a father for her soon-to-be-born baby. They wed, but keep separate bedrooms, each continuing with their normal affairs. Eventually Alda falls in love with Thomas, the baby is born and the draft board rejects the deferment. Marred by a typically late-1960s mentality with its politically brash youth and tell-it-like-it-is philosophy. Includes a clip from A PLACE IN THE SUN.

p, Edgar J. Scherick; d, George Bloomfield; w, Martin Luvat, Bloomfield (based on a story by Diana Gould); ph, David Quaid (DeLuxe Color); m, Michael Small; ed, Kent McKinney; art d, Trevor Williams; set d, John Alan Hicks; cos, Ann Roth; makeup, Tom Case, John Alese; m/l, "Waiting," Nilsson (sung by Nilsson), "Queen of Feeling," Michael Small, Michael Benedikt (sung by Joe Butler).

Drama **Cas.** **(PR:A MPAA:GP)**

JENNY LAMOUR***

(1948, Fr.) 102m Majestic/Vog bw (QUAI DES ORFEVRES)

Simone Renant *(Dora)*, Suzy Delair *(Jenny Lamour)*, Bernard Blier *(Maurice Martineau)*, Charles Dullin *(Brignon the Industrialist)*, Louis Jouvet *(Inspector Antoine)*, Rene Blancard *(Police Commissioner)*, Pierre Larquey *(Taxi Driver)*, Claudine Dupuis *(Manon)*, Robert Dalban *(Paulo, a Vagrant)*, Jean Durand *(Picard)*.

A gripping mystery from Clouzot, the French master of suspense, his second feature. A pair of unhappy lovers, Blier and Delair, unwittingly get involved in the murder of a sleazy film producer. Delair pays a visit to his house in hopes of finding work, but when he makes advances she hits him on the head with a champagne bottle. Meanwhile, Blier has rushed into the house in hopes of doing the producer in, but finds that he's too late. When the police investigate, Blier is suspected. However, his alibi is proven valid when Delair confesses. It turns out that neither is guilty when an underworld mobster is charged with the crime. While the story is thin, Clouzot uses his unmeasurable skills to raise the picture above the standard for the genre. (In French; English subtitles.)

d, Henri-Georges Clouzot; w, Clouzot, Jean Ferry (based on the novel *Legitimate Defense* by Stanislas-Andre Steeman); ph, Armand Thirard; ed, Charles Clement; set d, Max Douy; cos, Jacques Fath; m/l, Francis Lopez, A. Hornez; English titles, Noel Meadows, Harry L. Ober.

Mystery **(PR:A MPAA:NR)**

JENNY LIND (SEE: LADY'S MORALS, A, 1930)

JENSEITS DES RHIENS

(SEE: TOMORROW IS MY TURN, 1962, Fr./Ital./Ger.)

JEOPARDY ½** (1953) 68m MGM bw

Barbara Stanwyck *(Helen Stilwin)*, Barry Sullivan *(Doug Stilwin)*, Ralph Meeker *(Lawson)*, Lee Aaker *(Bobby Stilwin)*, Bud Wolfe *(Lieutenant's Driver)*, Saul Gorss *(Captain's Driver)*, Bob Castro *(Machine Gunner)*, Paul Fierro *(Mexican Lieutenant)*, Juan Torena *(Mexican Police Chief)*, Felipe Turich *(Mexican Border Official)*, Natividad Vacio *(Vendor)*, George Derrick *(Gas Station Attendant)*, Rico Alaniz *(Mexican Officer)*, Salvador Baguez *(2nd Officer)*, Charles Stevens *(Mexican Father)*, Margarita Martin *(Mexican Mother)*, Alex Montoya *(Walkie-Talkie Officer)*, Louis Tomei, Ken Terrell *(Barricade Officers)*, George Navarro, Carlos Conde *(Vendors)*.

Based on a radio play by Maurice Zimm, this was expanded by three times to make a tight little thriller by Mel Dinelli that is a good example of how to make a melodrama without wasting one frame of film. Stanwyck is married to Sullivan. Their son is Aaker and the three are off on a short holiday down the California coast and into Baja, part of Mexico. They arrive and discover a charming but empty fishing village next to the sea and decide to camp overnight. Aaker is a bold little lad and goes out on a decrepit pier. Sullivan seeks to rescue him and gets caught in the rotting timbers and there doesn't seem to be a way for him to get out of the wooden entanglement. This happens at low tide and Stanwyck realizes that she must get him out before the water rises and drowns Sullivan. Since she has no equipment of any sort, Stanwyck gets into the family sedan to find help or a strong enough rope to pull Sullivan free. On the road, she meets Meeker, a criminal fleeing Mexican police. He takes over the car and intends using it to escape but she uses her wiles to convince him that she finds him attractive and just might favor him with her affections if he agrees to help. She hints that she'll accompany him on his flight if he first saves Sullivan. Meeker, a cruel and sadistic killer, has his heart cockles warmed enough to aid and abet the rescue and leaves soon after when he sees that Stanwyck and Sullivan are truly a committed couple. Short, tense and effective, JEOPARDY made money for the studio and was a "sleeper" that year that many flocked to see. It's wonderful to realize how much story and emotion can be packed into under 70 minutes when placed in the right hands.

p, Sol Baer Fielding; d, John Sturges; w, Mel Dinelli (based on the radio play "A Question of Time" by Maurice Zimm); ph, Victor Milner; ed, Newell P. Kimlin; md, Dimitri Tiomkin; art d, Cedric Gibbons, William Ferrari; set d, Edwin B. Willis, Fred McLean; cos, Helen Rose, Frank Delmar.

Drama **(PR:A MPAA:NR)**

JEREMIAH JOHNSON* ½** (1972) 108m WB c

Robert Redford *(Jeremiah Johnson)*, Will Geer *(Bear Claw)*, Stefan Gierasch *(Del Gue)*, Allyn Ann McLerie *(Crazy Woman)*, Charles Tyner *(Robidoux)*, Josh Albee *(Caleb)*, Joaquin Martinez *(Paints His Shirt Red)*, Paul Benedict *(Reverend)*, Matt Clark *(Qualen)*, Richard Angarola *(Lebeaux)*, Jack Colvin *(Lt. Mulvey)*, Delle Bolton *(Swan)*.

Redford is a lone wolf who dislikes civilization. He moves into the Rocky Mountains in the 1830s but he can barely manage to stay alive until old trapper Geer meets him and takes him under his wing. For a year, Redford learns all the basic knowledge and skills it takes to survive in the wilderness and then he's off on his own. Redford comes upon a settlement that has been wiped out by marauding Indians who have left only a woman and a boy alive. He buries the dead and adopts the boy. Later, he finds another rugged trapper, bald-headed Gierasch (who shaves his head so the Indians will not attempt to scalp him), left buried up to his neck. They rescue him and later Gierasch and Redford raid an Indian camp and Gierasch scalps several of his victims. When they are again on the trail, Gierasch spots advancing Indians and puts the scalps into Redford's pack. They are not hostile, however, but friendly and when they discover the scalps of their enemy in Redford's possession, he is hailed as a great warrior. These Flathead Indians also insist that the chief's virginal daughter, Bolton, be taken as a wife by Redford. At the risk of insulting them and losing his own scalp, the young trapper takes the Indian woman with him. He, the boy, Albee, and Bolton grow to have deep affection for each other as they carve out a cabin and clearing in the wilderness. All is tranquil until a U.S. Calvary unit arrives and asks Redford to guide the troopers through the mountains to a stranded wagon train of settlers. He does, reluctantly leading the soldiers through the sacred burial grounds of the Crow Indians. By the time Redford returns to his cabin, the Crows have taken their revenge, burning down his cabin and slaughtering his commonlaw wife and adopted son. Redford is consumed with hatred for the Crows and embarks on a one-man war against the entire Crow nation. He lives only to hunt down Crow warriors, ambushing them singly and in groups, killing them and taking their scalps. They, too, begin to hunt him over the years, sending one after another of their best warriors after him, all of whom die in the attempt. In the end, when Redford has had enough and is en route to Canada to begin a new life, he meets the Crow chief. But instead of attacking him, the chief merely waves a salute in recognition of Redford being a great warrior. Redford waves back and continues on. Beautifully photographed in the wilds of Utah, the film is superbly directed and handsomely acted by Redford and the scant supporting cast. This story is based on a purportedly real trapper known as "Liver Eatin' Johnson," so called because of how he disposed of his victims. Director Pollack had to argue Warner Brothers into letting him shoot this fine film on location and he was told that he could go ahead but that he could not spend one dime more than what the film would cost to shoot on the studio lot. Much of the film was shot in the Utah mountains at elevations of 12,000 feet, causing severe hardships to cast and crew. Not until the very end of the shooting did Pollack decide how Redford would meet his fate. "Pollack wanted me to freeze to death," Redford was later quoted, "but I preferred to leave Johnson's fate up to the audience's imagination by having him disappear into the mountains." That, of course, is exactly what did happen to the real Johnson and it is the same ambiguous fate that ovetakes Redford. JEREMIAH JOHNSON was an enormous hit, no small credit going to the immensely popular Redford, the film grossing more than $22 million. The picture had been completed before the Redford vehicle THE CANDIDATE, but was held back in release until the later film was distributed to take advantage of its election-year theme.

p, Joe Wizan; d, Sydney Pollack; w, John Milius, Edward Anhalt (based on the novel *Mountain Man* by Vardis Fisher, and the story "Crow Killer" by Raymond W. Thorp and Robert Bunker); ph, Andrew (Duke) Callaghan (Panavision, Technicolor); m, John Rubenstein, Tim McIntire; ed, Thomas Stanford; art d, Ted Haworth; set d, Raymond Molyneaux; makeup, Gary Liddiard, Ken Chase; animal supervision, Kenneth Lee.

Adventure **Cas.** **(PR:C-O MPAA:PG)**

JEREMY** (1973) 90m Kenasset/UA c

Robby Benson *(Jeremy Jones)*, Glynnis O'Connor *(Susan Rollins)*, Len Bari *(Ralph Manzoni)*, Leonardo Cimino *(Cello Teacher)*, Ned Wilson *(Susan's Father)*, Chris Bohn *(Jeremy's Father)*, Pat Wheel *(Jeremy's Mother)*, Ted Sorel *(Music Class Teacher)*, Bruce Friedman *(Candy Store Owner)*, Eunice Anderson *(Susan's Aunt)*.

A sensitive and touching, yet too sweet, love story between two sensitive and touching, yet too sweet, teenagers. Benson is a cello-playing horse-lover who falls in love with dance student O'Connor. They wander blissfully through the film in their own little world, with nothing but the love they have for each other, that is, until O'Connor's father drops a bomb on their romance and decides to move the family away.

p, George Pappas; d,w, Arthur Barron; ph, Paul Goldsmith; m, Lee Holdridge, Joseph Brook; ed, Zina Voynow, Nina Feinberg; art d, Peter Bocour; m/l, title song, Holdridge, Dorothea Joyce (sung by Glynnis O'Connor).

Romance **(PR:A MPAA:PG)**

JERICHO (SEE: DARK SANDS, 1937, Brit.)

JERK, THE** (1979) 104m UNIV c

Steve Martin *(Navin Johnson)*, Bernadette Peters *(Marie)*, Catlin Adams *(Patty Bernstein)*, Mabel King *(Mother)*, Richard Ward *(Father)*, Dick Anthony Williams *(Taj)*, Carl Reiner *(Himself)*, Bill Macy *(Stan Fox)*, M. Emmet Walsh *(Madman)*, Dick O'Neill *(Frosty)*, Maurice Evans *(Hobart)*, Helena Carroll *(Hester)*, Ren Wood *(Elvira)*, Pepe Serna *(Punk No. 1)*, Sonny Terry, Brownie McGee *(Blues Singers)*, Jackie Mason *(Harry Hartounian)*, David Landsberg *(Bank Manager)*, Domingo Ambriz *(Father De Cordoba)*, Richard Foronjy, Lenny Montana *(Con Men)*, Carl Gottlieb *(Iron Balls McGinty)*, Clete Roberts *(Announcer)*.

Martin's film debut, released at the height of the comedian's short-lived popularity. He is cast as a poor "black" boy, raised in the South by a black family, only to discover one day that he is really white. After struggling for a time he decides to hitchhike to fame and fortune. Acting like the ultimate jerk (the title truly lives up to the character), Martin finds unlimited luxury when an invention of his—glasses that won't slip off the nose—brings in oodles of cash. His tragic downslide occurs when it is medically proven that the glasses cause wearers' eyes to cross.

p, David V. Picker, William E. McEuen; d, Carl Reiner; w, Steve Martin, Carl Gottlieb, Michael Elias (based on a story by Martin, Gottlieb); ph, Victor J. Kemper (Technicolor); m, Jack Elliott; ed, Bud Molin; prod d, Jack T. Collins; set d, Joe Hubbard, Richard Goddard; cos, Theodora Van Runkle.

Comedy **Cas.** **(PR:O MPAA:R)**

JERRICO, THE WONDER CLOWN (SEE: THREE RING CIRCUS, 1954)

JERUSALEM FILE, THE* ½ (1972, U.S./Israel) 96m Sparta-Leisure/MGM c

Bruce Davison *(David Armstrong)*, Nicol Williamson *(Prof. Lang)*, Daria Halprin *(Nurit)*, Donald Pleasence *(Maj. Samuels)*, Ian Hendry *(Gen. Mayers)*, Koya Yair Rubin *(Barak)*, Zeev Revan *(Raschid)*, David Smader *(Herzen)*, Jack Cohen *(Altouli)*, Isaac Neeman *(Yussof)*, Ori Levy *(Capt. Ori)*, Arie Elias *(Informer)*, Itzik Weiss *(Barak's Brother)*, Yona Elian *(Raschel)*, Yossi Werzanski *(Alex)*, Johnnie Phillips *(Lieutenant)*, Gabi Eldor *(Hospital Receptionist)*, Yael Duryanoff *(Prof. Lang's Secretary)*, Moshe Yanai *(Officer)*, Pink Wigoder *(Student)*, Ali Mohammad Hasan *(Fuad)*, Samib Mohammad Najib *(Achmed)*, Salah Darwish *(Security Officer)*.

A confusing film that tries to make a political statement that is lost in the confusion. Taking place at Jerusalem University following the decisive Six Day War of 1967, the plot stirs Israeli and Arab students as well as a group of terrorists into a mixture of ambiguosity that even the authentic location shots fail to alleviate.

p, Ram Ben Efraim; d, John Flynn; w, Troy Kennedy Martin; ph, Raoul Coutard, Brian Probyn (Metrocolor); m, John Scott; ed, Norman Wanstall; art d, Peter Williams; spec eff, Jacob "Jackie" Neumann.

Drama **(PR:C MPAA:PG)**

JESSE AND LESTER, TWO BROTHERS IN A PLACE CALLED TRINITY**

(1972, Ital.) 97m H.P. International Film Productions c (DUE FRATELLI IN UN POSTO CHIAMATO TRINITA)

Richard Harrison, Donald O'Brien, Anna Zinneman, George Wong, Gino Maturano.

Farcical spaghetti western about two antagonistic brothers pursuing opposite desires, one leading to a whorehouse, the other to a Mormon church, in a town filled with villains. Written and directed in a routine manner, but given some light through the characters of the villains.

p, Richard Harrison, Fernando Piazza; d, James London; w, Renzo Genta; ph, Antonio Modica.

Western **(PR:A MPAA:NR)**

JESSE JAMES**** (1939) 105m FOX c

Tyrone Power *(Jesse James)*, Henry Fonda *(Frank James)*, Nancy Kelly *(Zee)*, Randolph Scott *(Will Wright)*, Henry Hull *(Major Rufus Cobb)*, Brian Donlevy *(Barshee)*, John Carradine *(Bob Ford)*, Jane Darwell *(Mrs. Samuels)*, Donald Meek *(McCoy)*, Slim Summerville *(Jailer)*, J. Edward Bromberg *(George Runyon)*, Charles Middleton *(Doctor)*, George Breakston *(Farmer's Boy)*, Lon Chaney, Jr. *(Outlaw)*, John Russell *(Jesse James, Jr.)*, George Chandler *(Roy)*, Charles Tannen *(Charles Ford)*, Claire Du Brey *(Mrs. Ford)*, Willard Robertson *(Clark)*, Paul Sutton *(Lynch)*, Harold Goodwin *(Bill)*, Spencer Charters *(Preacher)*, Ernest Whitman *(Pinky)*, Eddy Waller *(Deputy)*, Paul Burns *(Hank)*, Arthur Aylesworth *(Tom)*, Charles Halton *(Heywood)*, Virginia Brissac *(Farmer's Wife)*, Harry Tyler *(Farmer)*, Edward Le Saint *(Judge Rankin)*, Erville Alderson *(Old Marshal)*, John Elliott *(Judge Mathews)*, Leonard Kibrick *(Boy)*, George O'Hara *(Tiller)*, Don Douglas *(Infantry Captain)*, Wylie Grant, Ethan Laidlaw *(Barshee's Cohorts)*, Tom London *(Soldier)*, James Flavin *(Calvary Captain)*.

For sheer gusto, excitement, and action, it's hard to beat this classic western which unfolds the legendary saga of the notorious James boys, notably Jesse Woodson James (1847–1882). Johnson's script absorbs all the saga and colorful tales attributed to the bad man from Missouri and does not include facts that get in the way of the story line. Director King infused his special brand of zest to produce this blockbuster, one that still best captures the image and era of that infamous outlaw, if not the reality of his character. Power is a sympathetic, dashing, and utterly charming Jesse who lives on his mother's farm with his brother Frank—slow, deliberate, dependable Fonda. Through their Missouri landscape, moving like a locust, is Donlevy, a representative of the hated, land-grabbing St. Louis Midland Railroad, buying up land in and around the area through which the railroad will be built. If his dirt-cheap offers are not accepted, Donlevy and his thugs merely beat sellers into submission. When Donlevy and company arrive at the James farm, the shifty-eyed Donlevy tries to browbeat Darwell (Mother James) into selling her farm. She tells him she won't sign any papers until her lawyer looks at them. Donlevy tries to force her to sign and suddenly Fonda appears, telling Donlevy to go away, that if his mother won't sign, she won't sign. Donlevy offers his hand, trying his usual trick of yanking a victim toward him and then coldcocking him. This time it backfires and it's Fonda who knocks Donlevy down. The railroad thug and his fellow goons advance upon Fonda when a shot rings out. Power stands smiling nearby with a smoking pistol in his hands. "You ain't all gonna jump on him, are you?" While Power holds the others at bay with his six-gun, Fonda gives Donlevy a beating, then both Fonda and Power run the men off. Hull, the local newspaper editor and friend of the James family, along with other neighbors, assemble outside the James farmhouse when Donlevy and his goons return with the local lawmen. The boys have ridden away, Hull tells Donlevy. When Donlevy sees a light go out in the farmhouse, he shouts for Power and Fonda to come out, then quickly throws a bomb through the window which kills Darwell. Donlevy later looks down on her dead body and Hull looks up and says: "I'm mighty sorry." "I'm sorry, too," replies a nervous Donlevy. "Oh, I ain't sorry for her," Hull tells Donlevy, "she's gone. It's you I'm sorry for." Power's fiancee, Kelly, rides into the hills and tells Power and Fonda what happened. It's decided that Power will take revenge upon the killer of their mother. He next appears in town just as Donlevy is about to lift a drink in a saloon. Power tells the bartender to count three and duck. Donlevy, hands quivering, begs Power not to go for his gun, but Power begins counting and by the count of three Donlevy is dead. Power and Fonda then embark on a series of raids against the St. Louis Midland Railroad, robbing the trains and passengers and telling their victims to sue the railroad. In these early days, most in the state of Missouri support the outlaw brothers, not the least among whom are Hull and Kelly. Even Scott, the U.S. Marshal, empathizes with the boys, but it's his duty to hunt them down. Meek, head of the railroad, offers Power amnesty if he'll turn himself in but when he does—escorted to jail by Scott—Meek reneges and promises to hang Power. Scott protests but is ignored. Then two deputies bring Fonda in, but they turn out to be members of the James gang and they and Fonda break Power out of jail. The gang expands its activities now, robbing banks as well as trains. Scott plays cat-and-mouse with Power, even meeting him one night in Kelly's kitchen but letting him go for Kelly's sake since he's in love with her. Kelly and Power marry and the gang later heads for the bank in distant Northfield, Minnesota. But Carradine, playing the traitorous Bob Ford, alerts Pinkerton detective Bromberg and the whole town is waiting for the James gang. When the outlaws arrive they are sprayed with lead, only Power and Fonda escaping back to Missouri. Here Power decides he will go straight and take his little family to California and a new life. Carradine and Tannen, the Ford brothers—now in the secret employ of the Pinkertons—meet with Power in his St. Joseph, Missouri home. While he leaves his wife and child in an upstairs bedroom, Power takes his fellow outlaws into the parlor and there stands upon a chair to fix a picture on the wall. With quavering hand holding a pistol, Carradine shoots Power in the back, and he and Tannen run from the home. Power dies in Kelly's arms. Hull later unveils a graveyard memorial and says that "the times produced him . . . . He was the gol-darndest buckeroo that ever lived!" The camera closes up on the plaque over the grave which reads: "In loving remembrance, Jesse W. James, died April 3, 1882, aged 34 years, 6 months, 28 days, murdered by a traitor and coward whose name is not worthy to appear here." The picture finishes with hard fact, these words being the actual ones found to this day on Jesse's tombstone. Up to this film the 24-year-old Power had been an attractive matinee idol but here he proved that he could act convincingly and capture the good and evil in one of America's most enigmatic men. Though Fonda has fewer scenes, he renders a stalwart, prosaic performance, one so effective that Fox cast him in the successful sequel, THE RETURN OF FRANK JAMES, 1940. JESSE JAMES was the film that made Fonda a star. Both King and Johnson had been eager to do a film on the legendary outlaw, a full-blown epic. Johnson researched Jesse James in Missouri, drawing most of his historic notions from the Sedalia *Gazette*, a strongly pro-James paper which promoted the idea that the James boys came into existence because of railroad and Union Army persecution following the Civil War. (In the beginning this was mostly true but even Missouri residents grew tired of this excuse as the James-Younger gang went on looting for almost two decades; in fact Jesse James was at large for eighteen years before being gunned down by Bob Ford on April 3, 1882. Frank James was acquitted after a sensational trial and lived until February 18, 1915.) Scripter Johnson opted for nostalgia and legend and left much of the outlaw's grim career alone. Jo Frances James, granddaughter of Jesse James, was hired as a consultant on the film but she was later disappointed with it, commenting: "I don't know what happened to the history part of it. It seemed to me the story was fiction from beginning to end. About the only connection it had with fact was that there once was a man named James and he did ride a horse." Some of the stunt work for the film, however, was as real as could be. In one scene Power and Fonda, to escape the crossfire at Northfield, crash their horses through the window of a shop and ride through it to escape out the back door. In another they plunge their horses off a high cliff into a lake to escape a posse. In one of these falls, the horse was killed and the stuntman almost smashed to pieces. King shot much of the film around Pineville, Missouri, a town that was much the same as those in the James era, with wooden sidewalks and dirt streets. Many local residents were hired as extras and even two elderly men claimed they had ridden with the James and Younger boys (the Younger brothers are oddly not even mentioned in the film). All the cast members were taken to Pineville and spent many weeks there on location. Claire Du Brey was flown in from Los Angeles for only one scene, playing Bob Ford's wife, outside his weathered farm house. A number of accidents occurred during the shooting. A runaway team of horses almost trampled a group of extras, but Donlevy jumped up and grabbed the reins, halting them. Nancy Kelly was thrown onto a barbed wire fence when her horse bolted but her heavy dress and two petticoats prevented her from being seriously hurt. Veteran actor Lon Chaney, Jr. took a fall from a horse and sprained an ankle. When he couldn't or wouldn't get on a horse the next day, director King accused him of drinking too much during off hours and sent him back to California. Even Power and Fonda weren't immune. Power gashed his foot while swimming and Fonda accidentally shot himself in the leg with a blank cartridge and required medical attention. The old Technicolor process has never been more richly reproduced than in JESSE JAMES which offers spellbinding hues of deep green, brown, and gold, giving the countryside portrayed the soft appearance of mellow history. There have been many films dealing with America's most celebrated outlaw but this is the best in terms of production values. Jesse James would be played many times—Reed Hadley would play the outlaw in I SHOT JESSE JAMES, 1948, Audie Murphy would reenact the part in KANSAS RAIDERS, 1950, MacDonald Carey would play the outlaw in THE GREAT MISSOURI RAID, 1951. Fox would officially remake the Power-Fonda classic in 1957 with lightweights Robert Wagner as Jesse and Jeffrey Hunter as Frank in THE TRUE STORY OF JESSE JAMES. Others playing the outlaw include Lawrence Tierney in BADMAN'S TERRITORY, 1946, Willard Parker in THE GREAT JESSE JAMES RAID, 1953, Dale Robertson in FIGHTING MAN OF THE PLAINS, 1959, Wendell Corey in ALIAS JESSE JAMES, 1959, Ray Stricklyn in YOUNG JESSE JAMES, 1960, Robert Duvall in THE GREAT NORTHFIELD MINNESOTA RAID, 1972, and James Keach in THE LONG RIDERS, 1980, the latter being one of the most realistic portrayals of the bandit to date.

p, Darryl F. Zanuck, Nunnally Johnson; d, Henry King; w, Johnson (based on historical data assembled by Rosaline Schaeffer, Jo Frances James); ph, W. Howard Greene, George Barnes (Technicolor); m, Louis Silvers; ed, Barbara McLean; md, Silvers; art d, William Darling, George Dudley.

Western **(PR:A MPAA:NR)**

JESSE JAMES AT BAY 1/2** (1941) 56m REP bw

Roy Rogers *(Jesse James/Clint Burns)*, George "Gabby" Hayes *(Sheriff)*, Sally Payne *(Polly Morgan)*, Pierre Watkin *(Krager)*, Ivan Miller *(Judge Rutherford)*, Hal Taliaferro *(Sloane)*, Gale Storm *(Jane Fillmore)*, Roy Barcroft *(Vern Stone)*, Jack Kirk *(Rufe Balder)*, Billy Benedict, Jack O'Shea, Rex Lease, Edward Piel, Sr., Jack Rockwell, Kit Guard, Curley Dresden, Hank Bell, Bill Wolfe, Lloyd Ingraham, Karl Hackett, Budd Buster, Fred Burns, Ray Jones, Fern Emmett, Bob Woodward, Chuck Morrison, Trigger the Horse.

Casting clean-cut Rogers as the bank-robbing Jesse James results in this film taking a Robin Hood approach to the James legend. Rogers comes back to Missouri to find that a crook with the railroad company, Barcroft, has been trying to cheat local homesteaders out of their residences to make a profit selling their land to the railroad. Rogers begins to rob the trains, giving the loot to the poor homesteaders so they can hold onto their land. Thrown into the plot for confusion is a man who is Rogers' exact double. Mountains in the background make the Missouri setting hard to believe.

p&d, Joseph Kane; w, James R. Webb (based on a story by Harrison Jacobs); ph, William Nobles; ed, Tony Martinelli.

Western **Cas.** **(PR:A MPAA:NR)**

JESSE JAMES, JR.* (1942) 55m REP bw

Don "Red" Barry *(Johnny Barrett)*, Lynn Merrick *(Joan Perry)*, Al St. John *(Pop Sawyer)*, Douglas Walton *(Archie McDonald)*, Karl Hackett *(Amos Martin)*, Lee Shumway *(Tom Perry)*, Stanley Blystone *(Sam Carson)*, Jack Kirk *(Sheriff)*, Bob Kortman, George Chesebro, Frank Brownlee, Forbes Murray, Jim Corey, Kermit Maynard, Ken Cooper, Tommy Coats.

An inferior oater which takes place in a town lacking both a marshal and a telegraph office. The townsfolk try to get a telegraph brought in, but an outlaw gang interferes. When Barry is called on to administer justice, the locals rest assured that the lawbreakers will be caught.

p&d, George Sherman; w, Richard Murphy, Doris Schoeder, Taylor Caven (based on a story by Murphy); ph, John MacBurnie; m, Cy Feuer; ed, William Thompson.

Western **(PR:A MPAA:NR)**

JESSE JAMES MEETS FRANKENSTEIN'S DAUGHTER* 1/2 (1966) 82m Circle/EM c

John Lupton *(Jesse James)*, Cal Bolder *(Hank Tracy/Igor)*, Narda Onyx *(Maria Frankenstein)*, Steven Geray *(Rudolph Frankenstein)*, Felipe Turich *(Manuel)*, Rosa Turich *(Nina)*, Estelita *(Juanita)*, Jim Davis *(Marshal McFee)*, Raymond Barnes *(Lonny)*, William Fawcett *(Jensen the Pharmacist)*, Page Slattery, Nestor Paiva, Dan White, Roger Creed, Fred Stromsoe, Mark Norton.

Lupton is the famed outlaw who, with a gang member, Bolder, escapes from a posse and seeks the help of a young Mexican woman, Estelita. She takes them to some ruins run by Onyx, the granddaughter of Baron Frankenstein (the title wrongly calls her his daughter). In the family tradition, Onyx transplants the brain from her grandfather's monster into Bolder, turning him into a mindless killer outlaw named Igor. The marshal soon comes on the scene and kills both Onyx and Bolder, bringing Lupton to jail. After more than 150 feature films this was William "One Shot" Beaudine's last, and it is a weak swan song.

p, Carroll Case; d, William Beaudine; w, Carl K. Hittleman; ph, Lothrop Worth (Pathe Color); m, Raoul Kraushaar; ed, Roy Livingston; art d, Paul Sylos; set d, Harry Reif; makeup, Ted Coodley.

Western/Horror **(PR:A MPAA:NR)**

JESSE JAMES VERSUS THE DALTONS* 1/2 (1954) 65m COL c

Brett King *(Joe Branch)*, Barbara Lawrence *(Kate Manning)*, *James Griffith (Bob Dalton)*, Bill Phipps *(Bill Dalton)*, *John Cliff (Grat Dalton)*, Rory Mallinson *(Bob Ford)*, William Tannen *(Emmett Dalton)*, Richard Garland *(Gilkie)*, Nelson Leigh *(Father Kerrigan)*, Raymond Largay *(Corey Bayless)*.

Having nothing to do with the title, since James never makes an appearance, this quickie has King living as an outcast because of a rumor that he is the son of Jesse. To check the rumor's validity, he joins the Dalton gang, thinking that his supposed father is still alive. After a shootout the Daltons are history, while King survives to learn that he is not Jesse's son. Originally shown in 3-D; even that did not lift it to a worthwhile dimension.

p, Sam Katzman; d, William Castle; w, Robert E. Kent, Samuel Newman (based on a story by Edwin Westrate); ph, Lester H. White (3D, Technicolor); m, Mischa Bakaleinikoff; ed, Viola Lawrence; art d, Paul Palmentola; set d, Sidney Clifford.

Western **PR:A MPAA:NR)**

JESSE JAMES' WOMEN* (1954) 83m Panorama/UA c

Don Barry *(Jesse James)*, Jack Beutel *(Frank James)*, Peggie Castle *(Waco Gans)*, Lita Baron *(Delta)*, Joyce Rhed *(Caprice Clark)*, Betty Brueck *(Cattle Kate Kennedy)*, Laura Lee *(Angel Botts)*, Sam Keller *(Cole Younger)*.

The only directorial effort of Don "Red" Barry, this poorly made western has the romanticized title character taking refuge in a small Mississippi town where he romances all the women in the cast before returning to Missouri. Beutel had the leading role in Howard Hughes' THE OUTLAW, a film in which he proved that he was one of the world's worst actors. This film, made a decade later in Beutel's long slide to the bottom, reaffirms that woeful lack of talent.

p, Lloyd Royal, T.V. Garraway; d, Don Barry; w, D.D. Beauchamp; ph, Ken Peach (Eastmancolor); m, Walter Greene; ed, Burton E. Hayes; ch, Jess Saunders, Ann Royal, m/l, "Careless Lover," George Antheil (sung by Lita Baron); "In the Shadows of My Heart," Stan Jones (sung by Baron).

Western **(PR:A MPAA:NR)**

JESSICA* 1/2 (1962, U.S./Ital./Fr.) 105m Arts and Artists/UA c

Angie Dickinson *(Jessica)*, Maurice Chevalier *(Father Antonio)*, Noel Noel *(Old Crupi)*, Gabriele Ferzetti *(Edmondo Raumo)*, Sylva Koscina *(Nunzia Tuffi)*, Agnes Moorehead *(Maria Lombardo)*, Marcel Dalio *(Luigi Tuffi)*, Danielle DeMetz *(Nicolina Lombardo)*, Antonio Cifariello *(Gianni Crupi)*, Kerima *(Virginia Toriello)*, Carlo Croccolo *(Beppi Toriello)*, Georgette Anys *(Mamma Parigi)*, Rossana Rory *(Rosa Masudino)*, Alberto Rabagliati *(Pietro Masudino)*, Angelo Galassi *(Antonio Risino)*, Marina Berti *(Filippella Risino)*, Manuela Rinaldi *(Lucia Casabranca)*, Gianni Glori Musy *(Filippo Casabranca)*, Joe Pollini *(Rosario)*.

Dickinson is an endearing midwife (who rides around on a motor scooter) living and working in a Sicilian village where she is constantly hounded by the town's lecherous married men. When their wives decide they've had enough, they unite and put a ban on sexual relations. They figure if they bear no children, then Dickinson's services will no longer be needed, forcing her to leave. Chevalier, the village priest, informs Dickinson of the situation and urges her to marry. She weds Ferzetti, a widower who lives in a castle, thereby easing the marital tensions in the village. It turns out, however, that none of the women kept their no-sex pledge when they all announce they are pregnant.

p, Jean Negulesco; d, Negulesco, Oreste Palella; w, Edith Sommers, Ennio DeConcini (based on the novel *The Midwife of Pont Clery* by Flora Sandstrom); ph, Piero Portalupi (Panavision, Technicolor); m, Mario Nascimbene; prod d, Nate H. Edwards; ed, Renzo Lucidi, Marie-Sophie Dubus; art d, Giulio Bongini; cos, Dusty Negulesco, Annalisa Nasalli-Rocca; m/l, "It Is Better to Love," "Will You Remember," "Jessica," Dusty Negulesco, Marguerite Monnot (sung by Maurice Chevalier), "The Vespa Song," Dusty Negulesco, Nascimbene (sung by Chevalier).

Drama **(PR:C MPAA:NR)**

JESSICA, 1970 (SEE: MISS JESSICA IS PREGNANT, 1970)

JESSIE'S GIRLS*

(1976) 86m Manson Productions c (AKA: WANTED WOMEN)

Sondra Currie, Geoffrey Land, Ben Frank, Regina Carrol, Jennifer Bishop, Ellen Stern, Joe Cortese, Jon Shank, Biff Yeager, Gavin Murrell, Rigg Kennedy, William Hammer, Hugh Warden, Joe Arrowsmith, John Durren, Rod Cameron.

Dull presentation about three female prisoners rescued by Currie from jail, who in return for the favor help her stalk the man who killed her husband and raped her. Plodding presentation of a terror-filled story.

p, Michael F. Goldman, Al Adamson; d, Adamson; w, Budd Donnelly; ph, Gary Graver.

Western **Cas.** **(PR:O MPAA:R)**

JEST OF GOD, A (SEE: RACHEL, RACHEL, 1968)

JESUS zero (1979) 117m WB c

Brian Deacon *(Jesus)*, Rivka Noiman *(Mary)*, Yossef Shiloah *(Joseph)*, Niko Nitai *(Simon Peter)*, Gadi Rol *(Andrew)*, Itzhak Ne'eman *(James)*, Shmuel Tal *(John)*, Kobi Assaf *(Philip)*, Michael Varshaviak *(Bartholomew)*, Mosko Alkalai *(Matthew)*, Nisim Gerama *(Thomas)*, Leonid Weinstein *(James, Son of Alphaeus)*, Rafi Milo *(Simon Zelotes)*, David Goldberg *(Judas, Son of James)*, Eli Danker *(Judas Iscariot)*, Eli Cohen *(John The Baptist)*, Talia Shapira *(Mary Magdalene)*, Richard Peterson *(Herod)*, Miki Mfir *(Simon the Pharisee)*, Peter Frye *(Pontius Pilate)*, Alexander Scourby *(Narrator)*.

An incredibly uninspired tale of Jesus Christ adapted from The Gospel According to St. Luke, shot on location in Israel with a largely Israeli cast. Narrated by Alexander Scourby, the voice behind the Living Bible, this film has all the dimension of an animated cartoon and the action of a grade school religious film strip.

p, John Heyman; d, Peter Sykes, John Kirsh; w, Barnet Fishbein (based on the Gospel according to St. Luke); cos, Rochelle Zaltzman.

Religious Biography **Cas.** **(PR:A MPAA:G)**

JESUS CHRIST, SUPERSTAR** (1973) 107m UNIV c

Ted Neeley *(Jesus Christ)*, Carl Anderson *(Judas Iscariot)*, Yvonne Elliman *(Mary Magdalene)*, Barry Dennen *(Pontius Pilate)*, Bob Bingham *(Caiaphas)*, Larry T. Marshall *(Simon Zealotes)*, Joshua Mostel *(King Herod)*, Kurt Yahgjian *(Annas)*, Philip Toubus *(Peter)*, Pi Douglass, Jonathan Wynne, Richard Molinare, Jeffrey Hyslop, Robert LuPone, Thommie Walsh, David Devir, Richard Orbach, Shooki Wagner *(Apostles)*, Darcel Wynne, Sally Neal, Vera Biloshisky, Wendy Maltby, Baayork Lee, Susan Allanson, Ellen Hoffman, Judith Daby, Adaya Pilo, Marcia McBroom, Leeyan Granger, Kathryn Wright, Denise Pence, Wyetta Turner, Tamar Zafria, Riki Oren, Lea Kestin *(Women)*, Zvulun Cohen, Meir Israel, Itzhak Sidranski, David Rfjwan, Amity Razi, Avi Ben-Haim, Haim Bashi, David Duack *(Priests)*, Steve Boockvor, Peter Luria, David Barkan, Danny Basevitch, Cliff Michaelevski, Tom Guest, Stephen Denenberg, Didi Liekov *(Roman Soldiers)*, Doron Gaash, Noam Cohen, Zvi Lehat, Moshe Uziel *(Temple Guards)*.

It began as an album, then went to the stage where it attracted huge crowds in London and New York, and now this picture proves that you *can* screw up The Greatest Story Ever Told. Once again, Protestant Jewison has been tapped to tell what is essentially a very Jewish story. (He'd already darkened FIDDLER ON THE ROOF, another Jewish story, and made one of the most successful musicals of all time into a so-so picture.) Although Jewison shares credit for the screenplay, one wonders what he and Bragg did as the story is told entirely in Webber's and Rice's music and lyrics. Filmed beautifully in Israel by Douglas Slocombe, it's a show within a show. A group of young tourists re-enact Jesus's last seven days amid the modern-day war machines that are Israel today. Lots of gorgeous visual images but no motivation at all is given for much of it. They manage to trivialize the well-known tale with campy performances like Mostel's (as Herod) and erratic choices of locales. The songs are the key to the film's success (it grossed nearly $20 million) although the receipts were nothing near what was anticipated. There was virtually not one line of dialog and that was okay as the songs carry the story along just splendidly. They include: "Jesus Christ, Superstar," "I Don't Know How To Love Him," "What's the Buzz?" "Herod's Song," "Heaven On Their Minds," "Strange Thing, Mystifying," "Then We Are Decided," "Everything's Alright," "This Jesus Must Die," "Simon Zealotes," "Poor Jerusalem," "Pilate's Dream," "The Temple," "Damned For All Time," "Could We Start Again, Please?" "John 1941," "Crucifixion," "Judas's Death," "The Arrest," "Peter's Denial," "Pilate And Christ," "Blood Money," "The Last Supper," "Gethsemane," "Trial Before Pilate," and "Hosanna." Yvonne Elliman was electrifying as Mary Magdalene and Carl Anderson couldn't have been better as Judas, but Teddy Neeley just couldn't cut the role as Jesus and appeared more whiney than heroic. Andre Previn got the only Oscar nomination for his musical direction. Webber went on to write the music for a succession of hits with and without Rice. They include: "Cats," "Evita," "Song And Dance," "Starlight Express," and "Joseph And His Amazing Technicolor Dream Coat." His stage royalties from all these productions have been calculated at more than $100,000 per week, but when he heard that Spielberg earned $1 million in the first 10 days of E.T.'s release, he is purported to have said: "A million dollars in 10 days! Boy, am I in the wrong business." Robert Stigwood, who co-produced, was also the producer of "Evita" as well as such films as SATURDAY NIGHT FEVER and GREASE. An ignoble effort, saved only by the score and the cinematography.

p, Norman Jewison, Robert Stigwood; d, Jewison; w, Jewison, Melvyn Bragg (based on the rock opera with book and lyrics by Tim Rice, music by Andrew Lloyd Webber); ph, Douglas Slocombe (Technicolor); ed, Anthony Gibbs; md, Andre Previn; prod d, Richard Macdonald; art d, John Clark; cos, Yvonne Blake; ch, Rob Iscove.

Biblical Musical **Cas.** **(PR:A MPAA:G)**

JESUS TRIP, THE* (1971) 84m Emco c

Elizabeth "Tippy" Walker *(Sister Anna)*, Robert Porter *(Waco)*, Billy "Green" Bush *(Clay Tarboro, Cop)*, Diana Ivarson, Virgil Frye, Carmen Argenziano, Wally Strauss, Bebe Louie, Jenny Hecht *(Gang Members)*, Hanna Hertalanda *(Older Nun)*, Frank Orsati, Robert Tessier, Allan Gibbs *(Vigilantes)*.

A low-budget biker picture which casts an actress named "Tippy" as a crusading nun! Porter's gang hides out in a desert convent when the police discover that their copters are concealing heroin. Highway patrolman Bush hunts down the gang after they kidnap Walker and flee the convent. In the end, Walker falls in love with biker Porter, leaves religious life behind her, and lives on the back of a Harley Davidson. Offbeat, occasionally brutal, sometimes blasphemous, but very well done.

p, Joseph Feury; d, Russ Mayberry; w, Dick Poston; ph, Flemming Olsen (DeLuxe Color); m, Bernardo Segall; ed, David Berlackie; art d, James Eric.

Action Crime **(PR:C MPAA:GP)**

JET ATTACK zero (1958) 68m AIP bw (AKA: JET SQUAD)

John Agar *(Tom Arnett)*, Audrey Totter *(Tanya)*, Gregory Walcott *(Bill)*, James Dobson *(Sandy)*, Leonard Strong *(Maj. Wan)*, Nicky Blair *(Chick)*, Victor Sen Yung *(Chon)*, Joe Hamilton *(Olmstead)*, Guy Prescott *(Maj. Garver)*, George Cisar *(Col. Catlett)*, Stella Lynn *(Muju)*, Robert Carricart *(Col. Kuban)*, Weaver Levy *(Orderly)*, Paul Power *(Phillips)*, Hal Bogart *(AP Sergeant)*, Madeline Foy *(WAAC Corporal)*, Bob Gilbreath *(Signalman)*.

One of the worst films ever made about war. The story is about a jet scientist who gets shot down over Korea, his plane crashing in a fire ball, but he miraculously survives. Agar leads a squad of soldiers on a rescue mission, killing Koreans wholesale. When it looks as if they've "had it," they are saved by guerrillas, who give them refuge in a cave. Enter a lovely Russian aide, Totter, who joins the team and leads Agar to a hospital where the scientist is being brainwashed. Agar and his boys adopt Totter's comical Russian accent, toss on some white clothes, and pretend to be doctors. The scientist is saved, Totter is killed, and half of the rescue team dies in a collision with a Korean jet. As with any movie this bad (Edward L. Cahn again stooping to a new low), it is often funny, especially when the Air Force is reduced to this description by the patriotic Blair: "With wings you swing, without a pair you're nowhere." Words to live by.

p, Alex Gordon, Israel M. Berman; d, Edward L. Cahn; w, Orville H. Hampton (based on a story by Mark Hanna); ph, Frederick E. West; m, Ronald Stein; ed, Robert S. Eisen; md, Stein; art d, Don Ament.

War Drama **(PR:A MPAA:NR)**

JET JOB*½ (1952) 63m MON bw

Stanley Clements *(Joe Kovak)*, Elena Verdugo *(Marge Stevenes)*, John Litel *(Sam Bentley)*, Bob Nichols *(Dynamo Jackson)*, Tom Powers *(Oscar Collins)*, Dorothy Adams *(Mrs. Kovak)*, Todd Karns *(Peter Arlen)*, Paul Stanton *(Chairman)*, Dave Willock *(Ripple)*, John Kellogg *(Alvin Fanchon)*, Russ Conway *(Stanley Reid)*, Steve Roberts *(Jack Bradford)*, Arthur Space *(Davison)*, William Forrest *(Gen. Mason)*, William Tannen *(Col. Jamison)*.

Clements is a test pilot who works for jet manufacturer Litel, and who pushes his luck too far by not following orders while testing a new plane. Litel has had enough of his attitude and fires him. Clements retaliates by working for Litel's rival, Powers. After a crash, Clements is grounded but he determinedly steals Litel's new test plane and successfully demonstrates it for the Army, putting him back in the good graces of his boss. Still, this one barely gets off the ground.

p, Ben Schwalb; d, William Beaudine; w, Charles R. Marion; ph, Marcel LePicard; m, Edward J. Kay; ed, Walter Hannemann; md, Kay; art d, Martin Obzina.

Aviation Drama **(PR:A MPAA:NR)**

JET MEN OF THE AIR (SEE: AIR CADET, 1951)

JET OVER THE ATLANTIC** (1960) 95m Inter Continent bw

Guy Madison *(Brett Matoon)*, Virginia Mayo *(Jean Gruney)*, George Raft *(Stafford)*, Ilona Massey *(Mme. Galli-Cazetti)*, George Macready *(Lord Robert Leverett)*, Anna Lee *(Ursula Leverett)*, Margaret Lindsay *(Mrs. Lanvard)*, Venetia Stevenson *(June Elliott)*, Mary Anderson *(Maria)*, Brett Halsey *(Dr. Vanderbird)*, Argentina Brunetti *(Miss Hooten)*, Frederic Worlock *(Dean Halltree)*, Tudor Owen *(Mr. Priestwood)*, Cindy Lee *(Laura Lanvard)*, Hilda Moreno *(Mrs. Priestwood)*, Tito Junco *(Gen. Ramirez)*, Rebecca Iturbide *(Stewardess)*, Carlos Muzquiz *(Purser)*, Cesar Agarte *(Copilot)*, Armando Saenz *(Pilot)*, John Kelly *(Garbotz)*, Jose Espinoza *(Carson)*, Rafael Alcarde, Breck Martin, Selene Walters, Fanny Schiller *(Passengers)*.

Madison plays a convicted murderer being returned to the U.S. by FBI agent Raft, when a psychotic places a fume bomb on the plane and kills the crew. As a former pilot, Madison must guide the plane to a safe landing in New York, which he does, where another man confesses to his crime and Madison goes free. Standard disabled airplane fare.

p, Benedict E. Bogeaus; d, Byron Haskin; w, Irving H. Cooper; ph, George Stahl; m, Lou Forbes; ed, James Leicester; art d, John Mansbridge, Ramon Rodriguez Granada; m/l, Forbes and Jack Hoffman.

Aviation Drama **(PR:A MPAA:NR)**

JET PILOT** (1957) 112m RKO/UNIV c

John Wayne *(Col. Shannon)*, Janet Leigh *(Anna)*, Jay C. Flippen *(Maj. Gen. Black)*, Paul Fix *(Maj. Rexford)*, Richard Rober *(George Rivers)*, Roland Winters *(Col. Sokolov)*, Hans Conried *(Col. Matoff)*, Ivan Triesault *(Gen. Langrad)*, John Bishop *(Maj. Lester Sinclair)*, Perdita Chandler *(Georgia Rexford)*, Joyce Compton *(Mrs. Simpson)*, Denver Pyle *(Mr. Simpson)*, Elizabeth Flournoy *(WAF Captain)*, Jack Overman, Ken Tobey, Harry Lauter *(Sergeants)*, Vince Gironda, Armand Tanny *(Muscle Men)*, Ruthelma Stevens, Lois Austin *(Saleswomen)*, Ruth Lee *(Mother)*, Alan Dinehart III *(Fresh Kid)*, Phil Arnold *(Bellboy)*, Tom Daly *(Hotel Clerk)*, Keith McConnell *(Bartender)*, Herbert Lytton, Nelson Leigh *(FBI Men)*, Al Murphy, Mike Lally, Theodore Rand, Joey Ray *(Waiters)*, Smoke Whitfield *(Henry)*, Jane Easton, Dorothy Abbott, Janice Hood *(Girls)*, Allen Matthews *(Headwaiter)*, Darrell Huntley *(Officer)*, Billy Vernon *(Drunk)*, Gene Roth *(Sokolov's Batman)*, Jimmy Dime, Paul Bakanas *(Russian Security Men)*, Michael Mark *(Russian General)*, Greg Barton, Jack Shea *(MPs)*, Gene Evans *(Airfield Sergeant)*, Bill Erwin *(Sergeant-GAC)*, Richard Norris, Dave Ormond *(Russian Interrogators)*, Mamie Van Doren, Barbara Freking *(WAAFs)*, Wendell Niles *(Major)*, Bill Yaeger *(Captain)*, John Morgan *(Lieutenant)*, Joan Jordan, Joan Whitney *(WAC Sergeants)*, Sylvia Lewis *(WAC Corporal)*, Paul Frees *(Lt. Tiompkin)*, Jack Overman, Don Haggerty, Carleton Young.

Only some startlingly good aerial shots and overall good production values bring this impossible story to the acceptable level. Wayne does his macho best as an American Air Force colonel in charge of an Alaskan Air Force base. He is suddenly confronted by a defecting Russian pilot unlike any he might expect, a beautiful bosomy blonde, Leigh. They fly to Washington, D.C. and there Wayne learns to love this truculent but beauteous cold war enemy. They marry but Wayne comes to believe Leigh is a spy planted in the U.S. to get top secrets. He agrees to pretend to defect to Russia to learn what he can but it's Leigh who learns that her side is tyrannical and she and Wayne fly back to the U.S. in a stolen Soviet jet. They settle down in Palm Springs, California, eating enormous steaks, Leigh wiping away a streak of gravy from her face so Wayne can plant a final kiss on her pouting lips. The dialog is so corny that it wouldn't play in Iowa and the plot is absolutely ludicrous. Producer Hughes decided to make JET PILOT a modern HELL'S ANGELS and his constant tinkering and doctoring of an already poor script caused the film to be delayed eight years before being released. He tried to convert innocent-looking Leigh into another sex symbol a la Jean Harlow or Jane Russell, parading her about in skimpy negligees. In one scene an embarrassed Wayne tries to search the well-endowed Leigh and in another the actress bounces about in only a towel after a shower. Director von Sternberg, noted for his sensitive Marlene Dietrich films of the 1930s, was brought in to direct but soon ran afoul of Hughes who couldn't keep his hands off the production. Nicholas Ray was then brought in to shoot more scenes and the Furthman script was diluted even more. Then Hughes kept trying to update the film with the latest jets and aerial footage that became hopelessly dated as he tried to edit 150,000 feet of film (about 25 hours) and wound up with a lifeless mess. The whole mistake cost Hughes $4 million and did nothing for its stars who looked incongruously young in 1957 (their scenes first shot in 1949).

p, Jules Furthman; d, Josef von Sternberg; w, Furthman; ph, Winton C. Hoch (Technicolor); m, Bronislau Kaper; ed, James Wilkinson, Michael R. McAdam, Harry Marker, William M. Moore; md, C. Bakaleinikoff; art d, Albert S. D'Agostino, Feild Gray; set d, Darrell Silvera, Harley Miller; cos, Michael Woulfe; aerial cam, Philip G. Cochran, Winton C. Hoch.

Aviation Drama **(PR:C MPAA:NR)**

JET SQUAD (SEE: JET ATTACK, 1958)

JET STORM**
(1961, Brit.) 90m Pendennis/Britannia-BL bw (AKA: KILLING URGE, JETSTREAM)

Richard Attenborough *(Ernest Tilley)*, Stanley Baker *(Captain Bardow)*, Hermione Baddeley *(Mrs. Satterly)*, Bernard Braden *(Otis Randolf)*, Diane Cilento *(Angelica Como)*, Barbara Kelly *(Edwina Randolf)*, David Kossoff *(Dr. Bergstein)*, Virginia Maskell *(Pam Leyton)*, Harry Secombe *(Binky Meadows)*, Elizabeth Sellars *(Inez Barrington)*, Sybil Thorndike *(Emma Morgan)*, Mai Zetterling *(Carol Tilley)*, Marty Wilde *(Billy Forrester)*, Patrick Allen *(Mulliner)*, Paul Carpenter *(George Towers)*, Megs Jenkins *(Rose Brock)*, Jackie Lane *(Clara Forrester)*, Cec Linder *(Colonel Coe)*, Neil McCallum *("Gil" Gilbert)*, Lana Morris *(Jane Tracer)*, George Rose *(James Brock)*, Peter Bayliss *(Bentley)*, John Crewdson *(Whitman)*, Paul Eddington *(Victor Tracer)*, Glyn Houston *(Michaels)*, Peter Illing *(Gelderen)*, Jeremy Judge *(Jeremy Tracer)*, George Murcell *(Saunders)*, Alun Owen *(Green)*, Irene Prador *(Sophia Gelderen)*.

Thanks to an outstanding cast, this air disaster film manages to limp to a landing with its "thriller" status intact. Attenborough, a once brilliant scientist, has booby-trapped a transatlantic jetliner because ever since his daughter was killed in a plane crash he has been possessed by thoughts of revenge. He accuses fellow passenger Rose of being the man responsible for his daughter's death, and panic ensues when Allen tries to kill Rose to pacify Attenborough. A fight breaks out and windows shatter, sucking Allen out into the wild blue. It is not until Attenborough notices a child on board, which reminds him of his daughter, that he abandons his mad plan to crash the plane.

p, Steven Pallos; d&w, Cy Raker Endfield; w, Sigmund Miller, Cy Raker Endfield (based on a story by Miller); ph, Jack Hildyard; m, Thomas Rajna; ed, Oswald Hafenrichter; md, Rajna; art d, Scott MacGregor; cos, May Walding; m/l, Marty Wilde.

Aviation Drama **(PR:A MPAA:NR)**

JETLAG** (1981, U.S./Span.) 104m Wieland Schulz-Keil-Figaro c

Jeanine Mestre *(Elena)*, Norman Brisky *(David)*, Pep Munne *(Javier)*, Robert Fields *(Tom)*, Marvin Cohen *(Jogger)*, Norris Church *(Susan)*, Jay Ginger *(Tom's Friend)*, Nicholas Wyman *(Foundation Officer)*, Mariane Ray *(Jane)*, Jesus Tovar *(David's Son)*, Althea Lewis *(Waitress)*.

A slow-paced, moderately interesting film about a Spanish woman's obsessive search for her former lover in New York City. Mestre travels from her Barcelona home to New York with the sole purpose of locating her love, Brisky, who left years earlier. When her search turns successful, she learns that he wants nothing to do with her. She spends the rest of her time in New York spying on Brisky's apartment from a bar across the street. It doesn't seem to help her much, and she returns home alone to Barcelona.

p, Bob Bordiga; d&w, Gonzalo Herralde; w, Herralde, Aldo Vigliarolo; ph, Al Ruban (Duart Film Labs Color); m, Carlos Santos; ed, Teresa Alcocer; art d, Maria Pallais, Miteira Riera.

Drama **(PR:C MPAA:NR)**

JETSTREAM (SEE: JET STORM, 1961, Brit.)

JEU DE MASSACRE (SEE: KILLING GAME, THE, 1968, Fr.)

JEUNE FILLE, UN SEUL AMOUR, UNE (SEE: MAGNIFICENT SINNER, 1963, Fr.)

JEUNES FILLES EN UNIFORME (SEE: MAEDCHEN IN UNIFORM, 1965, Fr./Ger.)

JEUX D'ADULTES (SEE: HEAD OF THE FAMILY, 1970, Fr./Ital.)

JEUX PRECOCES (SEE: LIPSTICK, 1965, Fr./Ital.)

JEW SUSS (SEE: POWER, 1934, Brit.)

JEWEL, THE* (1933, Brit.) 67m Venture/PAR bw

Hugh Williams *(Frank Hallam)*, Frances Dean *(Jenny Day/Lady Joan)*, Jack Hawkins *(Peter Roberts)*, Mary Newland *(Lady Maude Carleigh)*, Eric Cowley *(Maj. Brook)*, Annie Esmond *(Mme. Vanheim)*, Geoffrey Goodheart *(Mr. Day)*, Clare Harris *(Mrs. Day)*, Vincent Holman.

The far-fetched efforts of Williams to keep his aunt's expensive jewel secure turn out to be a total waste due to the aunt's shrewd forethought. As with Williams' struggles, this film also proves a waste of effort.

p, Hugh Percival; d, Reginald Denham; w, Basil Mason (based on a novel by Edgar Wallace).

Crime **(PR:A MPAA:NR)**

JEWEL ROBBERY*** (1932) 63m WB bw

William Powell *(The Robber)*, Kay Francis *(Baroness Teri von Horhenfels)*, Hardie Albright *(Paul)*, Andre Luguet *(Count Andre)*, Henry Kolker *(Baron Franz von Horhenfels)*, Spencer Charters *(Johann Christian Lenz)*, Alan Mowbray *(Fritz)*, Helen Vinson *(Marianne)*, Lawrence Grant *(Prof. Bauman)*, Jacques Vanaire *(Manager)*, Harold Minjur *(Clark)*, Ivan Linow *(Chauffeur)*, Charles Coleman *(Charles the Butler)*, Ruth Donnelly *(Berta the Maid)*, Clarence Wilson *(The Commissioner)*, Leo White *(Assistant Robber)*, Donald Brodie, Eddie Kane *(Robbers)*, Gordon "Bill" Elliott *(Girl-Chasing Gendarme)*, Lee Kohlmar *(Hollander)*, *C. Henry Gordon (Fritz)*, Robert Greig *(Henri)*, Harold Waldridge *(Leopold)*, Herman Bing *(Alpine Tourist)*.

Dieterle's direction gives this film a break neck comic pace as Powell plays a debonair master thief who charms his victims while his henchmen steal the jewels. Francis is the bored wife of a banker who prefers the company of Powell over that of her stuffy spouse. Powell is sparkling as usual and it's all very posh and roguish.

d, William Dieterle; w, Erwin Gelsey (based on the play by Ladislaus Fodor); ph, Robert Kurrle; ed, Ralph Dawson.

Crime/Comedy **(PR:A MPAA:NR)**

JEWELS OF BRANDENBURG* 1/2 (1947) 64m FOX bw

Richard Travis *(Johnny Vickers)*, Micheline Cheirel *(Claudette Grandet)*, Leonard Strong *(Marcel Grandet)*, Carol Thurston *(Carmelita Mendoza)*, Lewis Russell *(Roger Hamilton)*, Louis Mercier *(Pierre)*, Fernando Alvarado *(Pablo)*, Eugene Borden *(Miguel Solomon)*, Ralf Harolde *(Koslic)*, Otto Reichow *(Paul Rosholt)*, Harro Meller *(Frillman)*, Emmett Vogan, William Gould, Joel Friedkin.

Travis, a U.S. agent, is sent to recover a stash of stolen jewels which ended up in double-agent Strong's hands at the close of WW II. Posing as a jewel smuggler, Travis tries to work his way into Strong's confidence, eventually discovering where the jewels are hidden and recovering them.

p, Sol M. Wurtzel; d, Eugene Forde; w, Irving Cummings, Jr., Robert G. North, Irving Elman (based on a story by Cummings, Jr. and North); ph, Benjamin Kline; m, Darrell Calker; ed, William Claxton, Frank Baldridge; md, David Chudnow; art d, Robert Peterson.

Spy Drama **(PR:A MPAA:NR)**

JEZEBEL**** (1938) 104m WB bw

Bette Davis *(Julie Morrison)*, Henry Fonda *(Preston Dillard)*, George Brent *(Buck Cantrell)*, Margaret Lindsay *(Amy Bradford Dillard)*, Fay Bainter *(Aunt Belle Massey)*, Richard Cromwell *(Ted Dillard)*, Donald Crisp *(Dr. Livingstone)*, Henry

O'Neill *(Gen. Theopholus Bogardus)*, John Litel *(Jean LeCour)*, Gordon Oliver *(Dick Allen)*, Janet Shaw *(Molly Allen)*, Spring Byington *(Mrs. Kendrick)*, Georgia Caine *(Mrs. Petion)*, Irving Pichel *(Huger)*, Georges Renavent *(De Lautrec)*, Fred Lawrence *(Bob)*, Ann Codee *(Mme. Poulard the Dressmaker)*, Lew Payton *(Uncle Cato)*, Eddie Anderson *(Gros Bat)*, Theresa Harris *(Zette)*, Stymie Beard *(Ti Bat)*, Sam McDaniel *(Driver)*, Charles Wagenheim *(Customer)*, Jacques Vanaire *(Durette)*, Daisy Bufford *(Black Flower Girl)*, Jesse A. Graves *(Black Servant)*, Frederick Burton, Edward McWade *(Bank Directors)*, Frank Darien *(Bank Bookkeeper)*, Suzanne Dulier *(Midinette)*, John Harron *(Jenkins)*, Phillip "Lucky" Hurlic *(Erronens)*, Dolores Hurlic *(Errata)*, Davison Clark *(Deputy Sheriff)*, Trevor Bardette *(Sheriff at Plantation)*, George Guhl *(Fugitive Planter)*, Maurice Brierre, Tony Paton, Jack Norton *(Drunks)*, Louis Mercier *(Bar Companion)*, Alan Bridge *(New Orleans Sheriff)*, Margaret Early *(Stephanie Kendrick)*, Jac George *(Orchestra Leader)*, Charles Middleton *(Officer)*.

Nominated for Oscars as Best Picture, for Best Scoring, and Best Cinematography, it managed to win Davis her second Academy Award as Best Actress and Bainter her first as Best Supporting Actress. JEZEBEL was released many months before GONE WITH THE WIND and set a high standard for Southern epics but was soon eclipsed by GWTW. It was a good movie, though not as good when one looks at it today. Davis took the Oscar but there are those who felt she should have won it for OF HUMAN BONDAGE and that this was a consolation prize. No such thing for Bainter, though. She was magnificent in her role and richly merited her statuette. Davis claims she named the award "Oscar" because it reminded her of the posterior of her then-husband, Harmon Oscar Nelson, a big band leader of the 1930s. She claimed that the idol's rear looked just like Nelson's (whose nickname was "Ham" in later years when he became a Los Angeles ad executive and then a talent agent before his death) and she still gets a charge when others refer to the Award as the Oscar. But enough sidelights, let's learn about JEZEBEL. It had been a slight success on Broadway with Miriam Hopkins in the lead, who was rankled because she was bypassed for the role. The same went for Tallulah Bankhead who felt that no one but a dyed-in-the-wool Southerner should play the part. Nevertheless, Davis was tapped and gave one of the best performances of her life. It could have been pride in her work or it might have been that she had been overlooked by Selznick in the search for Scarlett O'Hara, a role she desperately wanted to play. Warner was willing to lend her to Selznick but insisted that David O. also take Errol Flynn as Rhett. Davis thought Flynn was wrong for the role and she wouldn't agree to it. Warner then rushed JEZEBEL into the works to take advantage of the national interest in GONE WITH THE WIND and the fact that Davis almost had the coveted role. New Orleans, 1852—Davis is the egocentric lah-dee-dah lady who pouts when she doesn't get her way. She is engaged to Fonda, an equally self-centered banker who won't let her get away with anything. They are to attend an all-white ball and she decides to dress in red, a shocking color when the tradition is that all unmarried ladies wear white. Fonda tries to talk her out of it but she's adamant. They go to the ball and she is stared at by all of polite New Orleans society. When she feels embarrassed and wants to leave, Fonda shows his strength by insisting that they continue dancing. Everyone else leaves the floor and Fonda keeps whirling Davis around the floor to a magnificent Max Steiner waltz. Fonda is secretly happy that Davis has made a spectacle of herself. She is abjectly humiliated and turns to Brent, a long-time admirer, for solace. He escorts her home, much to Fonda's consternation. This causes Fonda to break off their engagement and leave Louisiana to work at his family's branch bank in Philadelphia. Davis cannot believe that he has left and won't come back. She becomes a recluse for the next three years and seldom ventures out. Then she receives word from her guardian, O'Neill, that Fonda is returning to New Orleans to help out at the bank. An outbreak of Yellow Jack (similar to the dread Yellow Fever) has decimated the staff at the bank. Davis is thrilled, the bloom is back in her cheeks, and she is smiling ear-to-ear, planning a welcome home party at her family estate, Halcyon. She is shocked when Fonda arrives with Lindsay, the woman he married up north. Davis is enraged at that news and tells Brent that her honor has been besmirched by Fonda. Brent challenges Fonda to a duel but Fonda has to get back to the city where the fever is taking its toll. Fonda's younger brother, Cromwell, takes his place on the field of honor and kills Brent. The epidemic is now raging and Fonda is stricken by it. Martial law has been declared and people are dying by the second. Anyone still alive is to be evacuated from the city and sent to a nearby island for quarantine. Fonda is ready to go and Davis asks that she accompany the mortally ill Fonda instead of Lindsay. She promises to personally nurse him, like a Dixie Nightingale, and if he lives, she will send him back to Lindsay so they can resume their marriage. Lindsay is finally convinced and the picture ends with Davis going to the island with Fonda on the long shot that he will survive the fever. It's all implausible and the fact that this Jezebel should have such an abrupt change of heart in the last reel falls heavily on one's logic department. Still, Davis' acting (under Wyler's firm but benevolent hand) is so persuasive that we are taken in by the artifice and hope Fonda and Davis will eventually get together. Fonda had made a deal with the studio that his work had to be done by early December so he could fly back to New York where his wife was awaiting their first child (born on December 21st, named Jane). Although they tried to rush things, Wyler's slow pace put the film behind schedule and Davis had to do their closeups and inserts without him around. Davis didn't mind Wyler's painstaking ways and made THE LETTER and THE LITTLE FOXES with him a few years later. Two songs were featured: "Jezebel" and "Raise a Ruckus." It cost slightly over $1 million but made lots of money for everyone involved and got the country in an antebellum mood that was fully realized with the release of Selznick's greatest work. Bainter's small role as Belle was truly a "supporting actress" as opposed to so many actresses today who take major roles but let themselves receive supporting billing thinking that might garner them an Oscar. It sometimes works as in the case of Streep in KRAMER VERSUS KRAMER, Steenburgen in MELVIN AND HOWARD, and, the most blatant case of all, Redgrave as Julia in JULIA.

p, Hal B. Wallis, Henry Blanke; d, William Wyler; w, Clements Ripley, Abem Finkel, John Huston, Robert Bruckner (based on the play by Owen Davis, Sr.); ph, Ernest Haller; m, Max Steiner; ed, Warren Low; md, Leo F. Forbstein; art d, Robert Haas; cos, Orry-Kelly; m/l, "Jezebel," Harry Warren, Johnny Mercer, "Raise a Ruckus," Al Dubin, Warren.

Period Drama **Cas.** **(PR:A MPAA:NR)**

JEZEBELS, THE (SEE: SWITCHBLADE SISTERS, 1975)

JIG SAW 1/2** (1965, Brit.) 97m BL/Beverly bw

Jack Warner *(Detective-Inspector Fellows)*, Ronald Lewis *(Detective-Sgt. Wilks)*, Yolande Donlan *(Jean Sherman)*, Michael Goodliffe *(Clyde Burchard)*, John Le Mesurier *(Mr. Simpson)*, Moira Redmond *(Joan Simpson)*, Christine Bocca *(Mrs. Simpson)*, Brian Oulton *(Frank Restlin)*, Ray Barrett *(Sgt. Gorman)*, Geoffrey Frederick *(Sgt. Unwin)*, Norman Chappell *(Andy Roach)*, John Barron *(Ray Tenby)*, Joan Newell *(Mrs. Banks)*, Peter Ashmore *(Mr. Bunnell)*, Reginald Marsh *(Hilders)*, Graham Payn *(Mr. Blake)*, Robert Raglan *(Chief Constable)*, John Horsley *(Superintendent Ramsey)*, Gerald Campion *(Glazier)*, Robert Moore *(Dr. MacFarlane)*, Charles Houston *(Garage Foreman)*, Timothy Bateson *(Porter)*, Harry Brunning *(Luggage Clerk)*.

Brighton police inspector Warner and his assistant Lewis investigate a burglary where the thieves got away with property leases from a real estate office. They learn of the theft from the realtor's assistant and follow his clues. The inspectors find the body of a disfigured woman whom they mistakenly believe to be an old spinster. Their trail of clues, however, leads them back to the real estate office, where, with the help of the very much alive spinster, Donlan, they discover that the assistant is the culprit.

p,d&w, Val Guest (based on the novel *Sleep Long, My Love* by Hillary Waugh); ph, Arthur Grant; ed, Bill Lenny; art d, Geoffrey Tozer; cos, Molly Arbuthnot; makeup, Tony Sforzini.

Crime/Mystery **(PR:A MPAA:NR)**

JIGGS AND MAGGIE IN SOCIETY* 1/2 (1948) 65m MON bw

Joe Yule *(Jiggs)*, Renie Riano *(Maggie)*, Dale Carnegie *(Himself)*, Arthur Murray *(Himself)*, Sheilah Graham *(Herself)*, Tim Ryan *(Dinty Moore)*, Wanda McKay *(Millicent)*, Lee Bonnell *(Van De Graft), Pat Goldin (Dugan)*, Herbert Evans *(Jenkins)*, June Harrison *(Nora)*, Scott Taylor *(Tommy)*, Jimmy Aubrey *(McGurk)*, Thayer Roberts *(Pete)*, Richard Irving *(Al)*, William Cabanne *(George)*, Dick Ryan *(Grogan)*, Constance Purdy *(Mrs. Blackwell)*, Edith Leslie *(Mary)*, Helena Dare *(Aggie)*, Leslie Farley *(Miami)*, Betty Blythe *(Mrs. Vacuum)*, Marcelle Imhof *(Mrs. Heavydoe)*.

The cartoon characters Maggie and Jiggs are brought to the screen in the form of Riano and Yule. Their slapstick antics are in evidence as they climb up the social ladder and on the way, find themselves mingling with a gang of jewel thieves. Trying to appear more socially acceptable, Riano follows the dance steps of Arthur Murray, and Yule takes etiquette lessons from Dale Carnegie. This was the second of a string of films based on the popular comic strip "Bringing Up Father" starring Yule, Mickey Rooney's father in real life, as the irascible, henpecked *nouveau riche* Irish emigre. (See JIGGS AND MAGGIE series, Index)

p, Barney Gerard; d, Eddie Cline; w, Cline, Gerard (based on cartoon characters created by George McManus); ph, L.W. O'Connell; ed, Ace Herman; md, Edward J. Kay; art d, Dave Milton.

Comedy **(PR:AA MPAA:NR)**

JIGGS AND MAGGIE OUT WEST* 1/2 (1950) 66m MON bw

Joe Yule *(Jiggs)*, Renie Riano *(Maggie)*, George McManus *(Himself)*, Tim Ryan *(Dinty Moore)*, Jim Bannon *(Snake Bite)*, Riley Hill *(Bob Carter)*, Pat Goldin *(Dugan)*, June Harrison *(Nora)*, Henry [Kulky] Kulkovich *(Bomber)*, Terry McGinnis *(Cyclone)*, Billy Griffith *(Lawyer Blakely)*.

Cartoon characters Jiggs (Yule) and Maggie (Riano) venture to the wild west when Riano inherits a gold mine from her uncle. They tangle with a bandit (Bannon) who wants the mine for himself, but eventually Yule and Riano emerge on top. McManus, the creator of the cartoon strip, appears as himself and explains that the entire tale is just a product of his imagination. Another in the series that started with BRINGING UP FATHER (1946), itself a remake of a silent made in 1928, with J. Farrell MacDonald and Marie Dressler. (See JIGGS AND MAGGIE series, Index)

p, Barney Gerard; d, William Beaudine, Sr.; w, Gerard, Adele Buffington (based on a story by Gerard and Eddie Cline, and George McManus' cartoon strip, "Bringing Up Father"); ph, L.W. O'Connell; ed, Roy V. Livingston; md, Edward Kay; art d, Dave Milton.

Comedy **(PR:AA MPAA:NR)**

JIGOKUHEN (SEE: PORTRAIT OF HELL, 1969, Jap.)

JIGOKUMEN (SEE: GATE OF HELL, 1953, Jap.)

JIGSAW 1/2** (1949) 70m UA bw (AKA: GUN MOLL)

Franchot Tone *(Howard Malloy)*, Jean Wallace *(Barbara Whitfield)*, Myron McCormick *(Charles Riggs)*, Marc Lawrence *(Angelo Agostini)*, Winifrid Lenihan *(Mrs. Hartley)*, Betty Harper *(Caroline Riggs)*, Hedley Rainnie *(Sigmund Kosterich)*, Walter Vaughn *(District Attorney Walker)*, George Breen *(Knuckles)*, Robert Gist *(Tommy Quigley)*, Hester Sondergaard *(Mrs. Borg)*, Luella Gear *(Pet Shop Owner)*, Alexander Campbell *(Pemberton)*, Robert Noe *(Waldron)*, Alexander Lockwood *(Nichols)*, Ken Smith *(Wylie)*, Alan Macateer *(Museum Guard)*, Manuel Aparico *(Warehouse Guard)*, Brainard Duffield *(Butler)*, Marlene Dietrich, Fletcher Markle *(Nightclub Patrons)*, Henry Fonda *(Nightclub Waiter)*, John Garfield *(Street Loi-*

terer), Marsha Hunt *(Secretary-Receptionist)*, Leonard Lyons *(Newspaper Columnist)*, Burgess Meredith *(Bartender)*, Everett Sloane.

An odd little crime film which was financed by its star, Tone, and his producers, the Danziger brothers, for a sum of $400,000. Tone plays a crusading New York assistant district attorney determined to expose and smash a vile "hate group" made up of supposedly patriotic Americans after they have murdered his buddy, McCormick, a newspaper columnist. The group however, is prepared for Tone and sends a female operative, Wallace, to seduce the crime fighter. Wallace isn't all bad of course, and just as she is about to confess the truth to Tone, she is murdered by the gang. Now totally enraged, Tone pushes even harder against the evildoers and eventually discovers that the ringleader happens to be one of the most respected and powerful women in New York. All the loose ends are tied up in the climax, which takes place in a modern art museum. JIGSAW is a competent, albeit uninspired crime drama peppered with cameo appearances by Tone's Hollywood friends. Dietrich shows up as the patron of the Blue Angel nightclub (something of a joke?), Fonda has a bit as a waiter, Meredith is a bartender, and Garfield even makes a brief appearance.

p, Edward J. Danziger, Harry Lee Danziger; d, Fletcher Markle; w, Markle, Vincent McConnor (based on a story by John Roeburt); ph, Don Malkames; m, Robert W. Stringer; ed, Robert Matthews; spec eff, William L. Nemeth; makeup, Fred Ryle.

Crime **(PR:A MPAA:NR)**

JIGSAW, 1965 (SEE: JIG SAW, 1965)

JIGSAW* 1/2 (1968) 97m UNIV c

Harry Guardino *(Arthur Belding)*, Bradford Dillman *(Jonathan Fields)*, Hope Lange *(Helen Atterbury)*, Pat Hingle *(Lew Haley)*, Diana Hyland *(Sarah)*, Victor Jory *(Dr. Edward Arkroyd)*, Paul Stewart *(Dr. Simon Joshua)*, Susan Saint James *(Ida)*, Michael J. Pollard *(Dill)*, Susanne Benton *(Arlene)*, James Doohan *(Building Superintendent)*, Donald Mitchell *(Peter)*, Roy Jenson *(Arnie)*, Ralph Maurer, Jim Creech, Kent McCord, Joan Bradley.

This drug-related mystery has Dillman finding himself in someone else's apartment with a dead woman submerged in the bathtub. Discovering dried blood on his hand, he wonders if he was responsible for her death during an accidental LSD-induced blackout the night before. He hires Guardino to find out what really happened. Under Guardino's supervision he takes a dose of the drug, attempting to recall the previous night's events. They discover Dillman's co-worker Hingle had slipped LSD into his coffee as part of an intricate blackmail scheme. In order to get Dillman's girlfriend and his job in a government think tank, Hingle set him up. Amidst many special camera techniques which try to approximate the drug's effects, it turns out that Dillman's superior, Jory, had been involved with the dead woman. She had been blackmailed as a result, and when she threatened to go to the police, Hingle killed her, and Jory as well. In a confrontation with Dillman, Hingle gets his, plummeting to the pavement from a high-up window of their think-tank office building. Three of the people in the cast are better known for their TV work, Susan Saint James for "McMillan and Wife" (with Rock Hudson), James Doohan for "Star Trek" and Kent McCord for "Adam 12".

p, Ranald MacDougall; d, James Goldstone; w, Quentin Werty, (based on the screenplay MIRAGE by Peter Stone based on the novel *Fallen Angel*, by Howard Fast); ph, John L. Russell (Technicolor); m, Quincy Jones; ed, Edward A. Biery; md, Stanley Wilson; art d, Howard E. Johnson; set d, John McCarthy, Hal Overell; cos, Grady Hunt; makeup, Bud Westmore; m/l, "Jigsaw," "Bullets La Verne," Jones, performed by Dr. West's Medicine Show and Junk Band.

Mystery **(PR:O MPAA:NR)**

JIM HANVEY, DETECTIVE* 1/2 (1937) 71m REP bw

Guy Kibbee *(Jim Hanvey)*, Tom Brown *(Terry)*, Lucie Kaye *(Joan)*, Catharine Doucet *(Mrs. Frost)*, Edward Brophy *(Romo)*, Edward Gargan *(Smith)*, Helen Jerome Eddy *(Mrs. Ellis)*, Theodore von Eltz *(Dunn)*, Kenneth Thomson *(Elwood)*, Howard Hickman *(Frost)*, Oscar Apfel *(Lambert)*, Charles Williams *(Brackett)*, Wade Boteler *(Davis)*, Robert Emmett Keane *(Editor)*, Harry Tyler, Frank Darien, Robert E. Homans.

A limp detective yarn with Kibbee as an ace detective called in by an insurance company after the theft of an emerald. The gem is supposed to have been stolen from Kaye, the daughter of a wealthy man. It is soon revealed that the theft is a ruse by Kaye's boy friend Brown, a budding novelist researching material for a book he wants to write. Problems start when the emerald is stolen for real. Working on the case, Kibbee discovers the crook is an insurance company official. During the 1930s and 1940s, "The Saturday Evening Post," with its Norman Rockwell covers and its down-home flavor, was among America's favorite reading matter. Actor Kibbee tended to gravitate toward films made from the magazine's series stories, such as this one, EARTHWORM TRACTORS (1936), and SCATTERGOOD BAINES (1941).

p, Albert E. Levoy; d, Phil Rosen; w, Joseph Krumgold, Olive Cooper (based on a story by Octavus Roy Cohen); ph, Jack Marta; ed, William Morgan.

Mystery **(PR:A MPAA:NR)**

JIM, THE WORLD'S GREATEST**

(1976) 94m New Breeds/UNIV c (AKA: STORY OF A TEENAGER)

Gregory Harrison *(Jim Nolan)*, Robbie Wolcott *(Kelly Nolan)*, Rory Guy *(Jim's Father)*, Marla Pennington *(Jan)*, Karen McLain *(Lisa)*, David Lloyd *(Brian)*, Larry Gabriel *(Counselor)*, Tony Lucatorto *(Quarterback)*, Ralph Richmond *(Head Coach)*, Tim Simmons *(Kid)*, Reggie Bannister *(O.D. Silengsly)*, Larry Southwick *(Southwick)*, David Pollock *(Young Jim)*, Larry Pollock *(Principal)*, Shirley Coscarelli *(Receptionist)*, Ernie Morrison *(Teacher)*, Charlotte Mitchell *(School Secretary)*, George M. Singer, Jr. *(Rowdy)*, Walter Inman *(Terry)*, Mark Annerl *(Guy)*, Steve Goldman *(Guy Wanting Bathroom)*, Cyndie Coscarelli *(Student Body President)*, Keith Mitchell *(Drunk)*, D.A. Coscarelli, J.D. Sarver *(Asst. Coaches)*, Richard Byers *(Job Applicant)*.

Written by a pair of 17-year olds whose parents acted as executive producers, this ambitious picture about teen life was finally released when the writers (who also edited, photographed and directed) were at the ripe old age of 22. It stars Harrison as a struggling teen who lives with his alcoholic father, Guy, and physically abused younger brother, Wolcott. When not protecting his brother, he engages in the usual teen practices of football, parties, and juggling girl friends, Pennington and McLain. Produced for about $250,000 (half of which came before Universal's involvement). It is a commendable first feature, but barely average in comparison to the rest of the market.

p, Don Coscarelli; d&w, Coscarelli, Craig Mitchell; ph, Rex Metz, Coscarelli, Mitchell (Technicolor); m, Fred Myrow; ed, J. Terry Williams, Coscarelli, Mitchell; art d, Phil Barber, Phil Neel, E.G. Culman, James Catti; m/l, "Story of a Teenager," America, "It's Life," Dan Peek, "Thursday's Child," The Strawbs.

Drama **(PR:A MPAA:PG)**

JIM THORPE—ALL AMERICAN****

(1951) 107m WB bw (GB: MAN OF BRONZE)

Burt Lancaster *(Jim Thorpe)*, Charles Bickford *(Glenn S. "Pop" Warner)*, Steve Cochran *(Peter Allendine)*, Phyllis Thaxter *(Margaret Miller)*, Dick Wesson *(Ed Guyac)*, Jack Big Head *(Little Boy)*, Suni Warcloud *(Wally Denny)*, Al Mejia *(Louis Tewanema)*, Hubie Kerns *(Tom Ashenbrunner)*, Nestor Paiva *(Hiram Thorpe)*, Jimmy Moss *(Jim Thorpe, Jr.)*, Billy Gray *(Young Jim Thorpe)*, Ed Max *(Football Manager)*.

Lancaster is terrific as America's greatest athlete, the wondrous Jim Thorpe, a Sac and Fox Indian who captured gold medals for most of the major events of the 1912 Olympics only to have those medals taken away. The story opens at a dinner where the leading citizens of Oklahoma are gathered to honor Thorpe. Bickford, in a dynamic performance of coach "Pop" Warner, addresses the crowd and begins to recount the life and times of the incredible athlete. In flashback Billy Gray, as the young Jim Thorpe, is shown being taken to school by his father, Paiva, and running to his home on the reservation, a distance of 12 miles, beating his father back home. Paiva does not take a whip to his son, but instead explains to him that all he will ever have on the reservation is a boy's world of hunting and fishing, and that the world awaits him but he must go to school to realize his fortunes. "Be whatever you want to be," Paiva tells Gray. "It's all in the books and the books are in the schools." He adds: "If anybody wants something from you he ain't gonna get it by whipping you." Later, the boy grows up to be Lancaster and he attends the all Indian college at Carlisle, Pennsylvania. There he slowly withdraws from his cocoon and eases his tensions with studies by joining the track team under the guidance and encouragement of Bickford. He begins to win one track event after another, earning his letter which he takes to a sewing class. Here Thaxter sews his letter on his sweater and he is smitten with her. He spots her walking with cocky Cochran, an upperclassman and football star. To get Thaxter's attention he joins the football squad and slowly becomes the greatest back the team ever had. Still reticent and withdrawn, Lancaster blurts his love for Thaxter as he strolls with her on campus, then walks away. He learns that Thaxter is not an Indian and that she has left school but he continues to see her when she returns as a nurse to the school. They are later married. Lancaster is wholly absorbed with sports and wants to become a coach like his mentor, Bickford. He battles his way through four years of gridiron wars, thundering over the opposition, described by Bickford as "a twisting, hard-running flash of fire." A battle of the titans takes place in Lancaster's senior year. He is up for a coaching job if his team wins the big game against Penn. He is by then an All-American but Penn also has an All-American, Tom Ashenbrunner (Kerns), who is also up for the same job. The two fullbacks battle all afternoon against each other in a Homeric 13-13 tie. The job goes to Kerns, not to Lancaster. The stunned and embittered athlete decides to make a real name for himself, an image no one in the world can ignore. He tells Bickford that he will go to the 1912 Olympics in Stockholm. There Lancaster performs miraculous feats, winning more gold medals than any single competitor. The King of Sweden places a victor's wreath on Lancaster's head and states: "Sir, you are the greatest athlete in the world." Still, Lancaster cannot get a coaching job. Moreover, all his medals and trophies are taken from him by an obviously prejudiced Olympic Committee when it learns that Lancaster played semipro ball during one summer at Carlisle. (This was substantially true but Thorpe played merely for room and board and had no idea that he was breaking any amateur rules.) Stripped of his medals, Lancaster becomes a professional baseball and football player, but he slowly sinks into bitterness and takes to drink. When his small boy dies of illness, the blow kills Lancaster's spirit, and he becomes a drunk, turning on Thaxter, who finally leaves him. Lancaster is later visited by Bickford while the athlete performs as an Indian in a sideshow. He offers him a ticket to the 1932 Olympics being held in Los Angeles. Lancaster rejects the offer as pity, tearing up the ticket, but he later tapes it together and joins Bickford in the stands to hear the opening address by the Vice President of the U.S., Charles Curtis, an Indian. Bickford points out the fact that Curtis, an Indian like Lancaster, has overcome impossible odds to become one of the highest elected officials in America. Lancaster is later shown teaching boys how to play football. Flash forward to the dinner at Oklahoma with Bickford finally introducing the guest of honor, a wiser Thorpe. The film is directed with great zest by action expert Curtiz, and Steiner's score is stirring. Lancaster performed most of his own feats and is more than convincing as the great athlete. The supporting cast is excellent and the script is intelligent and thought-provoking. JIM THORPE—ALL AMERICAN establishes the image of a great athlete, although it does not compensate for the dastardly act committed by a prejudiced Olympic Committee which took Thorpe's medals from him, medals and records that were reinstated in recent years, along with a commemorative stamp issued by the U.S. Post Office, one showing the proud face of America's greatest athlete. The wrongs were righted, posthumously, of course.

p, Everett Freeman; d, Michael Curtiz; w, Douglas Morrow, Frank Davis, Everett Freeman (based on the story "Bright Path" by Morrow, Vincent X. Flaherty, based on the biography by Russell J. Birdwell and James Thorpe); ph, Ernest Haller; m, Max Steiner; ed, Folmar Blangsted; art d, Edward Carrere; set d, William Wallace; cos, Milo Anderson; tech adv, James Thorpe.

Sports Drama **(PR:A MPAA:NR)**

JIMMY AND SALLY* 1/2 (1933) 65m FOX bw

James Dunn *(Jimmy O'Connor)*, Claire Trevor *(Sally Johnson)*, Harvey Stephens *(Ralph Andrews)*, Lya Lys *(Pola Wenski)*, Jed Prouty *(E.W. Marlowe)*, Gloria Roy *(Shirley)*, Alma Lloyd *(Mary)*, John Arledge *(Joe)*.

Dunn is the Jimmy of the title, a ripe young publicity man mixed up with a gang of mobsters after working with cabaret singer Lys. Trevor finally pulls him out of trouble when she helps with his publicity work. An innocent comedy has Trevor getting Dunn's romantic interest but no credit for her professional advice. Sally Eilers was originally supposed to be opposite Dunn, hence the title. Songs include "You're My Thrill," "Eat Marlowe's Meat," and "It's the Irish in Me" (Sidney Clare, Jay Gorney).

d, James Tinling; w, Paul Schofield, Marguerite Roberts, William Conselman; ph, Joseph Valentine; m, Jay Gorney; m/l, Sidney Clare, Gorney.

Comedy **(PR:A MPAA:NR)**

JIMMY BOY* (1935, Brit.) 71m Baxter & Barter/UNIV bw

Jimmy O'Dea *(Jimmy)*, Guy Middleton *(The Count)*, Vera Sherburne *(Nora)*, Enid Stamp-Taylor *(The Star)*, Elizabeth Jenns *(The Princess)*, Harold Williams *(The Prince)*, Edgar Driver *(The Liftman)*, Harry O'Donovan *(O'Brien)*, Peggy Novak *(The Maid)*, Kathleen Drago, Johnnie Schofield, Elizabeth Vaughan, J.H. Edwin, Stanley Kirby, Syd Crossley, Noel Purcell, Sherman Fisher Girls, The Mackay Twins, Reginald Forsyth and His Band.

A film that attempted to do something with the comic talents of tiny O'Dea, here playing an elevator boy in a posh hotel. His involvement in the plot to keep a group of foreign spies from completing their plan to blow up London, knowledge he receives because of his lowly position. Makes for a pretty uninteresting movie.

p, John Barter; d, John Baxter; w, Con West, Harry O'Donovan; ph, George Dudgeon Stretton.

Comedy **(PR:A MPAA:NR)**

JIMMY ORPHEUS* 1/2 (1966, Ger.) 52m Atlas bw

Klaus Schichan *(Jimmy Orpheus)*, Orthrud Beginnen *(Girl)*.

Unfortunately the best thing about this short debut feature from Germany's Klick is the witty title. After that the picture falls into a series of cliches centering on the title character. A dock worker who gets locked out of his asylum/shelter spends the midnight hours wandering around Hamburg. He meets a young woman in the shabby part of town and wants to have an affair, but it never materializes. Nicely photographed by Robert van Ackeren who has slowly moved to the forefront of the commercial German cinema.

p, Hanns Eckeikamp, Ernst Liesenhoff; d&w, Roland Klick; ph, Robert van Ackeren; m&ed, Klick.

Drama **(PR:C MPAA:NR)**

JIMMY THE GENT 1/2** (1934) 67m WB bw

James Cagney *(Jimmy Corrigan)*, Bette Davis *(Joan Martin)*, Alice White *(Mabel)*, Allen Jenkins *(Louie)*, Arthur Hohl *(Joe Rector [Monty Barton])*, Alan Dinehart *(James J. Wallingham)*, Philip Reed *(Ronnie Gatson)*, Hobart Cavanaugh *(The Imposter)*, Mayo Methot *(Gladys Farrell)*, Ralf Harolde *(Hendrickson)*, Joseph Sawyer *(Mike)*, Philip Faversham *(Blair)*, Nora Lane *(Posy Barton)*, Joseph Crehan *(Judge)*, Robert Warwick *(Civil Judge)*, Merna Kennedy *(Jitters)*, Renee Whitney *(Bessie)*, Monica Bannister *(Tea Assistant)*, Don Douglas *(Man Drinking Tea)*, Bud Flanagan [Dennis O'Keefe] *(Chester Coote)*, Leonard Mudie *(Man in Flower Shop)*, Harry Holman *(Justice of the Peace)*, Camille Rovelle *(File Clerk)*, Stanley Mack *(Pete)*, Tom Costello *(Grant)*, Ben Hendricks *(Ferris)*, Billy West *(Halley)*, Eddie Shubert *(Tim)*, Lee Moran *(Stew)*, Harry Wallace *(Eddie)*, Robert Homans *(Irish Cop)*, Milton Kibbee *(Ambulance Driver)*, Howard Hickman *(Doctor)*, Eula Guy *(Nurse)*, Juliet Ware *(Viola)*, Rickey Newell *(Blonde)*, Lorena Layson *(Brunette)*, Dick French *(2nd Young Man)*, Jay Eaton *(3rd Young Man)*, Harold Entwistle *(Rev. Amiel Bottsford)*, Charles Hickman *(Bailiff)*, Olaf Hytten *(Steward)*, Vesey O'Davoren *(2nd Steward)*, Lester Dorr *(Chalmers)*, Pat Wing *(Secretary)*.

Being tough and ruthless is what the early cinematic days of Cagney were all about and this film is no exception. He is a scheming, apparently conscienceless estate hunter. Cagney, with his assistant Davis at his side, tracks down heirs to sizable unclaimed estates and takes a hefty slice after putting the missing heirs in touch with their money. Davis is repelled at Cagney's reprehensible ways for, often as not, he provides phony heirs to estates. When Davis sees the suave, cultured Dinehart, who is in the same business, she compares him with uncouth Cagney and leaves her roughneck employer, going to work for Dinehart. Cagney tries to convince her that Dinehart, despite his polished ways and fancy office, is a bigger crook than he is, but to no avail. Then Cagney decides to beat them by joining them. He clutches culture with both fists, redoing his offices, taking diction and speech instruction, serving tea to this thug staffers, and donning formal wear. He meanwhile exposes Dinehart as a thief in an elaborate scheme. Next, when Dinehart realizes his business is being ruined by Cagney he offers his competitor a partnership, which Cagney promptly rejects. Then Dinehart proposes to Davis and she gives him the thumbs down. She returns to Cagney, realizing he's got a good heart even though his larceny streak is a bit thick. He promises to reform, but the viewer is left with only a "maybe" in the mind. Curtiz takes this film through its paces at his usual fast clip. Although less antisocial and violent than his other crime capers on film, Cagney presents plenty of colorful moxie as a con man with a sense of humor. The film is also played for laughs by Davis and the rest of the cast, even Methot, who later became Humphrey Bogart's wife. Neither Cagney nor Davis wanted to do this film. As a protest, Cagney appeared on the set with his head almost shorn so that his dome resembled a pineapple. Studio chief Wallis thought he had done this as a personal insult to him, and director Curtiz, helming his first Cagney picture, almost passed out at the sight of the actor. In one of the first scenes Cagney turned his head away from the camera and Curtiz spotted several ugly scars on the back of his star's head, scars that would have normally been covered up with hair. He yelled "cut!" and complained loudly until Cagney admitted it was just a stunt, that he had asked a pal in the makeup department to put the scars there. The fake scars were removed and the shooting went on, but Davis, who was also battling with Jack Warner at the time, would have nothing to do with Cagney, refusing to take publicity stills with him. Davis was about to appear in her first major film, OF HUMAN BONDAGE, but Warners wanted to use her quickly while she waited to go into that production. So she was hustled into doing JIMMY THE GENT and resented it, also disdaining Cagney for his scar-on-the-back-of-the-head routine. She would appear with him again seven years later in THE BRIDE CAME C.O.D., and that film didn't work too well, either.

p, Robert Lord; d, Michael Curtiz; w, Bertram Milhauser (based on the story "Heir Chaser" by Laird Doyle, Ray Nazarro); ph, Ira Morgan; ed, Tommy Richards; art d, Esdras Hartley; cos, Orry-Kelly; makeup, Perc Westmore.

Comedy/Crime **(PR:A MPAA:NR)**

JIMMY THE KID* (1982) 85m Zephyr Films/New World c

Gary Coleman *(Jimmy)*, Paul LeMat *(John)*, Dee Wallace *(May)*, Don Adams *(Harry)*, Walter Olkewicz *(Andrew)*, Ruth Gordon *(Bernice)*, Cleavon Little *(Herb)*, Fay Hauser *(Nina)*, Avery Schreiber *(Dr. Stevens)*, Pat Morita *(Maurice)*.

Another of the nauseating film efforts for little tot Coleman, starring as the kidnap victim of a couple of crooks who don't even know how to tie their shoelaces properly. Coleman's little adventure is the best thing that ever happened to him as it gives him a taste of the little things in life his upper class parents could never provide for him, being more concerned with the development of his talents. Though the basic idea for this film is good, the presence of Coleman in the lead quickly diminishes any form of sincerity, not to mention how sad it is to see some talented actors having to center their abilities around this obnoxious ball of energy.

p, Ronald Jacobs; d, Gary Nelson; w, Sam Bobrick (based on the novel by Donald E. Westlake); m, John Cameron.

Comedy **Cas.** **(PR:A MPAA:PG)**

JIMMY VALENTINE (SEE: ALIAS JIMMY VALENTINE, 1928)

JINCHOGE (SEE: DAPHNE, THE, 1967, Jap.)

JINX MONEY 1/2** (1948) 68m MON bw

Leo Gorcey *(Terrence Aloysius "Slip" Mahoney)*, Huntz Hall *(Horace Debussy "Sach" Jones)*, Billy Benedict *(Whitey)*, David Gorcey *(Chuck)*, Bennie Bartlett *(Butch)*, Sheldon Leonard *(Lippy Harris)*, Gabriel Dell *(Gabe the Reporter)*, Donald MacBride *(Capt. James Q. Broaderik)*, Betty Caldwell *(Candy McGill)*, John Eldredge *(Lullaby Kane)*, Ben Welden *(Benny the Meatball)*, Lucien Littlefield *(Tipper)*, Bernard Gorcey *(Louie Dumbrowski)*, Benny Baker *(Augie Pollack)*, Ralph Dunn *(Jack "Cold Deck" Shapiro)*, Wanda McKay *(Virginia)*, Tom Kennedy *(Officer Rooney)*, William Ruhl *(Sgt. Ryan)*, Stanley Andrews *(Bank President)*, George Eldredge *(Tax Man)*, William H. Vedder *(Meek Man)*, Mike Pat Donovan *(Bank Guard)*.

The Bowery Boys have their hands full when Gorcey and Hall discover $50,000 left in the street by a murdered gangster. They manage to give most of it to charity while hiding out from mobsters and a killer who are hot on their trail for the loot. Five more murders are committed before the actual culprit is brought to justice with the help of "the boys." (See BOWERY BOYS series, Index).

p, Jan Grippo; d, William Beaudine; w, Edmond Seward, Tim Ryan, Gerald Schnitzer (based on a story by Jerome T. Gollard); ph, Marcel Le Picard; ed, William Austin; md, Edward J. Kay; art d, David Milton; set d, Raymond Boltz, Jr.; cos, Richard Bachler.

Crime/Comedy **(PR:A MPAA:NR)**

JINXED!* (1982) 103m MGM-UA c

Bette Midler *(Bonita)*, Ken Wahl *(Willie)*, Rip Torn *(Harold)*, Val Avery *(Milt)*, Jack Elam *(Otto)*, Benson Fong *(Dr. Wing)*.

Torn portrays a gambler whose scheming girlfriend, Midler, concocts a plan with casino dealer, Wahl, to do in her lover and collect an inheritance. Unfortunately, Torn, probably the funniest character in the film, is dead after the first hour, leaving this weak script dragging. This picture really lived up to its name. Reportedly, there was bitter rivalry off-screen between Midler and Wahl over "creative differences." That may be why their relationship on-screen is not very believable. Midler does manage to fit in a couple of songs.

p, Herb Jaffe; d, Don Siegel; w, David Newman, Bert Blessing (based on a story by Blessing); ph, Vilmos Zsigmond (Technicolor); m, Bruce Roberts, Miles Goodman; ed, Doug Steward; prod d, Ted Haworth; set d, Robert Benton, Wally Graham, Julie Harmount; cos, Bob De Mora.

Comedy **Cas.** **(PR:O MPAA:R)**

J'IRAI CRACHER SUR VOS TOMBES
(SEE: I SPIT ON YOUR GRAVE, 1962, Fr.)

JITTERBUGS** (1943) 74m FOX bw

Stan Laurel *(Himself)*, Oliver Hardy *(Himself)*, Vivian Blaine *(Susan Cowan)*, Bob Bailey *(Chester Wright)*, Douglas Fowley *(Malcolm Bennett)*, Noel Madison *(Tony Queen)*, Lee Patrick *(Dorcas)*, Robert Emmett Keane *(Henry Corcoran)*, Charles Halton *(Cass)*, Francis Ford *(Old-timer/Shill in League with Con Man Bailey)*.

Laurel and Hardy find themselves stranded on a desert road after their car has run out of gas. Along comes swindler Bailey (a nice guy at heart), rescuing the pair and enlisting their help in his carnival con game—selling pills that supposedly turn water into gasoline. Performing as a two-man jitterbug band, the boys draw potential customers, including love interest Blaine. Her mother has been cheated in a land deal and Bailey and the guys agree to help out, traveling with her to New Orleans in hope of catching the crooks. Blaine gets a gig singing on a showboat owned by one of the real estate swindlers, Laurel disguises himself as Blaine's Boston aunt, and Hardy adopts the guise of a charming southern millionaire. They manage to retrieve the money, but the crooks soon catch on. Bailey saves the day, arriving with the police, as Laurel and Hardy tumble into the river. Though short on their brand of slapstick and nowhere near the quality of their marvelous short films, JITTERBUGS is the best of Laurel and Hardy's later features. Yet, the film really belongs to Blaine. The studio was using it as a showcase for the newly discovered talent, giving her three songs during the riverboat nightclub sequences. Kudos to Basevi for his art direction.

p, Sol M. Wurtzel; d, Malcolm St. Clair; w, Scott Darling; ph, Lucien Andriot; ed, Norman Colbert; md, Emil Newman; art d, James Basevi, Chester Gore; set d, Thomas Little, Al Orenbach; cos, N'Was McKenzie; spec eff, Fred Sersen; ch, Geneva Sawyer; m/l, "The Moon Kissed The Mississippi," "If The Shoe Fits, Wear It," "I've Got To See For Myself," Charles Newman, Lew Pollack (sung by Vivian Blaine).

Comedy (PR:AAA MPAA:NR)

JIVARO** ½ (1954) 93m PAR c (GB: LOST TREASURE OF THE AMAZON)

Fernando Lamas *(Rio)*, Rhonda Fleming *(Alice Parker)*, Brian Keith *(Tony)*, Lon Chaney, Jr. *(Pedro)*, Richard Denning *(Jerry Russell)*, Rita Moreno *(Maroa)*, Marvin Miller *(Kovanti)*, Morgan Farley *(Vinny)*, Pascual Pena *(Sylvester)*, Nestor Paiva *(Jacque)*, Charles Lung *(Padre)*, Gregg Barton *(Edwards)*, Kay Johnson *(Umari)*, Rosa Turich *(Native Woman)*, Marian Mosick *(Sylvester's Wife)*, Richard Bartell *(Locket Native)*, Eugenia Paul *(Indian Girl)*.

Fleming arrives at the Amazon-jungle outpost run by Lamas. She's come from California to marry the fiance she hasn't seen for two years. Unable to convince Fleming that her true love (Denning) has degenerated into a drunken dreamer intent on finding gold, Lamas takes the lass into the jungle, falling for her along the way. They hear that Denning has been killed by Jivaros, the vicious Indian headhunters that live along the Amazon. Fleming is also attacked by the scoundrels but Lamas saves the day. The best thing going for this otherwise average film is the wonderful Technicolor photography. Rather than use stock shots, the producers sent a camera crew to the Amazon jungle and were rewarded with some beautiful background footage. Keith shines in an early role.

p, William H. Pine, William C. Thomas; d, Edward Ludwig; w, Winston Miller (based on a story by David Duncan); ph, Lionel Lindon (Technicolor); m, Gregory Stone; ed, Howard Smith; art d, Hal Pereira, Earl Hedrick.

Adventure/Romance (PR:A MPAA:NR)

JIVE JUNCTION** (1944) 62m PRC bw

Dickie Moore *(Peter)*, Tina Thayer *(Claire)*, Gerra Young *(Gerra)*, Johnny Michaels *(Jimmy)*, Jack Wagner *(Grant)*, Jan Wiley *(Miss Forbes)*, Beverly Boyd *(Cubby)*, Bill Halligan *(Maglodian)*, Johnny Duncan *(Frank)*, Johnny Clark *(Chick)*, Fredrick Feher *(Feher)*, Odessa Laurin *(Girl)*, Bob McKenzie *(Sheriff)*, Carol Ashley *(Mary)*.

Moore plays a classically trained teenage musician who switches to jazzier tunes to gain acceptance at his new high school. Overwhelmed with grief at the death of his aviator father in WW II, he organizes a show for local servicemen, winning the heart of Thayer. In the end Moore leads his school band to victory in a nationwide competition. Though it has its light moments, the film is too serious for its own good. Moore gives a mildly appealing performance as he graduates to serious teenage movies after achieving fame as a child star. This film is typical of most made to support the war effort. Screenwriter Wallace would later gain prominence as a novelist. The songs included "The Bell Song" (from "Lamke," Leo Delibes—sung by Gerra Young), "We're Just in Between."

p, Leon Fromkess; d, Edgar G. Ulmer; w, Irving Wallace, Walter Doniger, Malvin Wald (based on a story by Wald, Doniger); ph, Ira Morgan; m, Leo Erdody; ed, Robert Crandall; art d, Frank Sylos; ch, Don Gallaher.

Musical Cas. (PR:A MPAA:NR)

JOAN AT THE STAKE*
(1954, Ital./Fr.) 80m Produzione Cinematografiche-Franco-London c (GIOVANNA D'ARCO AL ROGO)

Ingrid Bergman *(Giovanna)*, Tullio Carminati *(Fra Domenico)*, Giacinto Prantelli, Augusto Romani, Plinio Clabassi, Saturno Meletti, Agnese Dubbini, Pietro de Palma, Aldo Tenossi, Silvio Santanelli, Gerardo Gaudioso, Anna Tarallo, Luigi Paolillo; Voices of: Pina Esca, Marcella Pillo, Giovanni Acolati, Miriam Pirazzini.

Bergman plays the famous saint in this adaptation of Claudel and Honegger's opera. Initial response to this film was so poor that it was almost impossible for it to be booked in any theaters.

p, Giorgio Criscuolo, Franco Francese; d&w, Roberto Rossellini (based on the story by Paul Claudel and the oratorio by Claudel, Arthur Honegger); ph, Gabor Pogany (Gevacolor); ed, Jolanda Benvenuti.

Opera (PR:A MPAA:NR)

JOAN BEDFORD IS MISSING (SEE: HOUSE OF HORRORS, 1946)

JOAN OF ARC*** ½ (1948) 145m RKO c

Ingrid Bergman *(Jeanne d'Arc)*, Jose Ferrer *(The Dauphin, Charles VII)*, Francis L. Sullivan *(Pierre Cauchon)*, J. Carroll Naish *(Count John of Luxembourg)*, Ward Bond *(La Hire)*, Shepperd Strudwick *(Father Jean Massieu)*, Gene Lockhart *(Georges la Tremouille)*, Leif Erickson *(Jean Dunois)*, Cecil Kellaway *(Jean Le Maistre)*, Selena Royle *(Isabelle d'Arc)*, Robert Barrat *(Jacques d'Arc)*, James Lydon *(Pierre d'Arc)*, Rand Brooks *(Jean d'Arc)*, Roman Bohnen *(Durand Laxart)*, Irene Rich *(Catherine LeRover)*, Nestor Paiva *(Henri le Royer)*, Richard Derr *(Jean De Metz)*, Ray Teal *(Bertrand de Poulengy)*, David Bond *(Jean Fournier)*, George Zucco *(Constable of Clervaux)*, George Coulouris *(Sir Robert D. Baudricort)*, John Emery *(Duke of Alencon)*, Nicholas Joy *(Archbishop of Thiems)*, Richard Ney *(Duke of Claremont)*, Vincent Donahue *(Alain Chartier)*, John Ireland *(St. Severe)*, Henry Brandon *(Giles de Raiz)*, Morris Ankrum *(Poton De Xantrailles)*, Tom Brown Henry *(Raoul de Gaucourt)*, Gregg Barton *(Adm. de Culan)*, Ethan Laidlaw *(Jean d'Aulon)*, Hurd Hatfield *(Father Pasquerel)*, Frederic Worlock *(Duke of Bedford)*, Dennis Hoey *(William Glasdale)*, Colin Keith-Johnston *(Duke of Burgundy)*, Mary Currier *(Jeanne, Countess of Luxembourg)*, Roy Roberts *(Wandamme, a Captain)*, Taylor Holmes *(Bishop of Avranches)*, Alan Napier *(Earl of Warwick)*, Philip Bourneuf *(Jean d'Estivet)*, Aubrey Mather *(La Fontaine)*, Stephen Roberts *(Thomas de Courcelle)*, Herbert Rudley *(Isombard de La Pierre)*, Frank Puglia *(Nicholas de Houppeville)*, William Conrad *(Guillaume Erard)*, John Parrish *(Jean Beaupere, a Judge)*, Victor Wood *(Nicholas Midi)*, Houseley Stevenson *(Winchester)*, Jeff Corey *(Prison Guard)*, Bill Kennedy *(Thirache the Executioner)*, James Kirkwood *(Judge Mortemer)*, Herbert Rawlinson *(Judge Marguerie)*, Matt Moore *(Judge Courneille)*, Frank Elliott *(Dr. Tiphane)*, Barbara Woodell *(Woman with Baby)*, Arthur Space *(Luxembourg Guard)*, Eve March *(Peasant Woman)*, Greta Granstedt, Marjorie Wood, Julia Faye *(Townswomen)*, James Fallet *(Louis de Conte)*, Lee Miller *(Colet de Vienne/Townsman/French Soldier)*, Leo McMahon *(Richard the Archer/French Soldier)*, Henry Wills *(Julian)*, Chuck Hamilton *(Jean de Honeycourt/French Soldier)*, Kate Lawson *(Marguerite)*, James Logan *(Beaudricourt's Clerk)*, Charles Wagenheim *(Calot, Taxpayer)*, Robert Bice *(Dying English Archer)*, Jean Ahlin *(Hauviette)*, Victor Travers *(Bishop of Therouanne)*, Robert E. Burns *(Bishop of Norwich)*, Mike Donovan *(Bishop of Noyon)*, Joseph Grandby *(Giles de Fecamp)*, Patrick O'Conner *(Guillaume Manchon)*, Lon Poff *(Guillaume Colles)*, Ed Biby *(Nicholas Taquel)*, Alex Harford *(Lyonnel)*, Alvin Hammer *(Court Jester)*, Jack Lindquist *(Beaudricourt's Page)*, James Garner, Walter Cook, Raymond Saunders, Russell Saunders, George Suzanne *(Tumblers)*, June Lavere, William Wagner, Symona Boniface, June le Pre, Lester Dorr, Beatrice Gray, Hazel Keener *(Peasants)*, Phyllis Hill, Sally Cooper, Jean La Vell, Dorothy Tuttle, June Harris *(Court Ladies)*, Eve Whitney, Beverly Loyd *(Court Ladies/Camp Followers)*, Carl Knowles *(Guard)*, Babe London, Lorna Jordan, June Harris, Gloria Grafton, June Benhow *(Camp Followers)*, Clancy Cooper *(1st Soldier)*, Lee Phelps *(2nd Soldier)*, Frank Hagney *(3rd Soldier)*, Herschel Graham *(Constable)*, John Epper *(Demetz)*, Art Dupuis *(1st Peasant)*, George Dee *(2nd Peasant)*, Jack Gargan *(3rd Peasant)*, Bob Whitney, John Perdrini *(Deacons)*, Gregory Marshall *(Boy)*, Mary Field *(Boy's Mother)*, Vernon Steele *(Boy's Father)*, Wally Cassell *(French Soldier)*, Harry Hays Morgan *(Guard)*, Art Foster *(Marksman)*, Burt Stevens, Jim Drum, George Magrill, John Moss, Allen Pinson *(English Knights)*, George Backus *(English Knight/English Man at Arms)*, Minerva Urecal *(Old Woman)*, Raymond Bond *(Hauviette's Father)*, Russell Simpson *(Old Man with Pipe)*, Robert Anderson *(Soldier at the Inn)*, Leo Borden *(Pot Boy)*, Benjamin Litrenta *(2nd Pot Boy)*, George Davis *(Farmer)*, Jack George *(Merchant)*, Frances Morris, Eula Guy *(Women at the Inn)*, Jean Ransome, Maurice Brierre, Al Winters, Stella Le Saint, Stan Jolley *(Domremy Peasants)*, Pete Sosso *(Domremy Peasant/Townsman)*, Manuel Paris *(Judge Chatillon)*, Peter Seal *(Judge Albane)*, Vincent Neptune *(Judge Alespee)*, Tom Leffingwell *(Judge Grouchet)*, Charles Meakin *(Judge Barbier)*, Stuart Holmes *(Judge Benoit)*, Allen Schute *(Judge Etienne)*, Scott Seaton *(Judge Edmond)*, Curt Furberg *(Judge Jerome)*, Albert Godderis *(Judge Tobie)*, Louis Payne *(Judge Thibault)*, John Bohn *(Judge Gustinel)*, Phillip Keiffer *(Judge Haiton)*, Frank Marlowe, Michael Cirillo *(Guards)*, Everette Glass *(Judge Anselene)*, Percival Vivien *(Judge Laurent)*, Pat Lane *(Luxembourg Guard)*, Bob Thom, Bob McLean *(Burgundian Guard)*, Bob Bentley *(English Man at Arms)*, George Robotham *(English Knight)*, Leland Hodgson *(English Guard at 1st Trial/English Soldier)*, Jerry Elliott, Gretchen Gailing, Maria Tavares, Frances Sanford, Kiki Kellet *(Townspeople)*, Dave Dunbar, Clive Morgan, Sanders Clark *(English Soldiers)*, Dick Alexander *(Man on Boulevard)*, Herbert Evans *(Bailiff)*, Julius Aicardi, Sam Calprice, Jim Cooley, Erno Kiraly, William Wagner, Ford Raymond *(Priests in Cauchon's Box)*, Henry Hebert *(Winchester's Secretary)*, Charles Quirk *(Townsman/French Soldier)*, Fred Zendar *(Townsman/French Soldier)*, Bill Cody, J.W. Cody *(English Guards)*, John Roy, George Barrows, Philip Ahlm, Shephard Houghton, Roger Creed, Bob Crosby, Byron Poindexter, Harry Raven, Eric Alden, Victor Romito *(French Soldiers)*, Ann Roberts *(Riding Double)*, Jerry Elliott *(Running Double)*, Peggy O'Neil, Gail Goodson *(Armor Doubles)*, Patricial Marlowe *(Stand-In)*.

Bergman is compelling and often spellbinding as the 15th Century French peasant girl who led her people in battle against an invading British horde, became a national hero and, after her capture, torture, and execution by the British, a Catholic saint. Bergman is a young girl living in Domremy in the province of Lorraine when she hears voices from nowhere instructing her to go to the aid of France and drive out the English interlopers. Sponsored by Coulouris, she is sent to the court of the Dauphin Charles VII (Ferrer), whom she intends to crown king, despite the efforts of the English to the contrary. The ironist Ferrer, a clever and worldly creature, discounts the stories of this saintly maid and quickly devises a scheme to show her up. He has one of his posturing courtiers, Ney, pretend to be the Dauphin, but when Bergman is introduced to him, she turns away and picks Ferrer out of the crowd in court, going to him and identifying him, speaking to him in such earnest and loyal terms that he, of all people, is moved and suddenly believes that she has been sent by heavenly forces. He encourages her to gather an army, giving her funds and his best generals, Ireland, Bond, and Emery. With standard in hand, she and her armored soldiers lift the siege of Orleans and march on to one stunning victory after another. The French people adore the maid as her battle standards are raised in many great triumphs, and the army is inspired by her great spirit and its military leaders startled by her eloquence and command of tactics. Bergman's greatest achievement in her eyes, one she claims she was commanded to perform from on high, is seeing Ferrer crowned king at Rheims. But Ferrer fears Bergman's incredible influence and he discards her to make money and land deals to enrich his personal coffers. Depressed and mostly deserted, Bergman is taken captive by the English and put through an ecclesiastical trial, then tried again in a civil court. Her persecutor is Sullivan, playing the vile, unscrupulous Cauchon, the judge who railroads her into a death sentence. The English, making a martyr out of a simple peasant girl, burn Bergman at the stake. Bergman, although surrounded by a great array of superlative supporting players, must carry this very long but lavishly mounted film alone and she almost turns it into a solo masterpiece. She is genuinely effulgent, exuding a goodness that bespeaks sainthood, and many of her scenes are nothing less than inspired, as was the original Joan of Arc. Her battle scenes and, particularly, her death scene at the stake with her head shorn and her face registering every kind of agony (not unlike the almost all-closeup film silent classic, THE PASSION OF JOAN OF ARC) is absolutely riveting. No one in the modern era of sound film ever approached Bergman's interpretation of the maid from Lorraine, although Alida Valli does give a smashing cameo performance of St. Joan in MIRACLE OF THE BELLS. Bergman later stated that one of her lifelong goals was to play the part of Joan of Arc and that she and her director, Fleming, put everything into it, yet it failed because it was too big, too long. For years, wherever she went around the world, she would be met by moviegoers who remembered her as the crop-headed saintly leader. For 15 years, whenever Bergman returned to France, customs officials would greet her with the same line: "Ah, Jeanne d'Arc—welcome home." The script by Anderson and Solt, based on Anderson's hit play, "Joan of Lorraine," is beautifully written, full of solid and often stirring dialog, but Anderson, in an attempt to make his own religious points, often dipped into the hortatory and came up with tedium, particularly in the long, drawn-out trial sequences. Ferrer is excellent as the devious Dauphin, and Bond, Emery, and Ireland are simply great as military men who follow Bergman through fire and smoke. Fleming's direction is superb, particularly the battle and crowd scenes; he was a master of handling massive mobs of people as he had proved so effectively in THE WIZARD OF OZ and GONE WITH THE WIND.

p, Walter Wanger; d, Victor Fleming; w, Maxwell Anderson, Andrew Solt (based on the play "Joan of Lorraine" by Anderson); ph, Joseph Valentine (Technicolor); m, Hugo Friedhofer; ed, Frank Sullivan; md, Emil Newman; art d, Richard Day; set d, Edwin Roberts, Joseph Kish; cos, Karinska, Dorothy Jeakins; spec eff, Jack Cosgrove, John Fulton; makeup, Jack Pierce.

Historical Epic **Cas.** **(PR:A MPAA:NR)**

JOAN OF OZARK** 1/2 (1942) 80m REP bw (GB: QUEEN OF SPIES)

Judy Canova *(Judy Hull)*, Joe E. Brown *(Cliff Little)*, Eddie Foy Jr. *(Eddie McCabe)*, Jerome Cowan *(Philip Munson)*, Wolfgang Zilzer *(Kurt)*, Alexander Granach *(Guido)*, Anne Jeffreys *(Marie Lamont)*, Otto Reichow *(Otto)*, Hans Van Twardowski *(Hans)*, William Dean *(Karl)*, Paul Fung *(Yamatako)*, Donald Curtis *(Jones)*, George Eldredge *(Chandler)*, Olin Howlin *(Game Warden)*, Ralph Peters *(Window Cleaner)*, Chester Clute *(Salesman)*, Emmett Lynn *(Hillbilly Driver)*, Kam Tong *(Japanese Commander)*, Cyril Ring, Eric Alden, Ralph McCullough *(Reporters)*, Lloyd Whitlock *(Col. Ashley)*, Horace B. Carpenter *(Mountaineer)*, Bobby Stone *(Newsboy)*, Bud Jamison *(Cop)*, Tyler Gibson *(Zeke)*, William Sundholm *(Si)*, William Worth *(Clem)*, Robert Cherry *(Young Hillbilly)*, William Nestell *(Joe)*, William Vaughn *(German Radio Operator)*, Harry Hayden *(Mayor Fadden)*, Gladys Gale *(Mrs. Fadden)*, Charles Miller *(Mr. Graham)*, Laura Treadwell *(Mrs. Graham)*, Nora Lane *(Mrs Ashley)*, Bob Stevenson *(Hillbilly)*, Peppy Walters, Peanuts Walters *(Specialty Dancers)*, Jason Robards, Sr., Ernest Hilliard, Dick Keene *(Theatrical Agents)*, Bert Moorhouse *(Drunk)*, Fred Santley, Pat Gleason, Charles Williams *(Representatives)*, Joan Tours, Sally Cairns, Eleanor Bayley, Billie Lane, Jane Allen, Ruby Morie, Kay Gordon, Aileen Morris, Jean O'Connell, June Earle, Patsy Bedell, Pearl Tolson, Jeanette Dickson, Helen Seamon, Barbara Clark, Mary Jo Ellis, Midgie Dare, Audreno Brier, Maxine Ardell *(Dancers)*.

Silly little film has Canova bagging a pigeon one day while quail hunting in the Ozarks. It turns out her find is a Nazi carrier pigeon and she turns it over to the FBI. Canova is declared "No. 1 Patriot," incurring the wrath of Nazi spy head Cowan, who runs a New York nightclub as a front. Enter Brown as a theatrical agent. He wants to bring Canova to New York to sing at a nightclub (guess who owns it?) But she won't go until Brown claims to be an FBI agent, drafting her into government service. He brings her to Cowan's club and the expected mayhem results. The film runs a little long, trying to decide if it wants to be a satire. In one of the better moments Brown has some fun parodying Hitler. "The Lady From Lockheed" (Mort Greene, Harry Revel) is an excellent showcase for Canova's singing. Other songs include "Backwoods Barbecue" (Greene, Revel—sung by Judy Canova), and "Wabash Blues" (Dave Ringle, Fred Meinken—sung by Canova).

p, Harriet Parsons; d, Joseph Santley; w, Robert Harari, Eve Greene, Jack Townley, Monte Brice, Bradford Ropes; ph, Ernest Miller; ed, Charles Craft; md, Cy Feuer; art d, Russell Kimball; ch, Nick Castle.

Musical/Comedy **(PR:A MPAA:NR)**

JOAN OF PARIS*** (1942) 93m RKO bw

Paul Henreid *(Paul Lavallier)*, Michele Morgan *(Joan)*, Thomas Mitchell *(Father Antoine)*, Laird Cregar *(Herr Funk)*, May Robson *(Mlle. Rosay)*, Alan Ladd *(Baby)*, Jimmy Monks *(Splinter)*, Jack Briggs *(Robin)*, Richard Fraser *(Geoffrey)*, Alexander Granach *(Gestapo Agent)*, Paul Weigel (Janitor), John Abbott *(English Spy)*, George Cleveland, Robert Mitchell Boy Choir.

JOAN OF PARIS was a good little war movie that had several interesting sidelights attached to it. Henreid and Morgan made their American debuts in the film and Ladd and Cregar were both tabbed for greater things after their work was seen. Although made before America's involvement in the war, it was held in the can until after Pearl Harbor and did big business because it was as current as that morning's headlines when it finally came out in January, 1942. Morgan is a French barmaid whose patron saint is, you guessed it, Joan of Arc. Five flyers land in France behind Nazi lines and meet later in a Paris church where the priest, Mitchell, helps them. Henreid, a Free French operative, is in love with Morgan, who is being tracked by the dread Gestapo officer, Granach, who reports to his boss, Cregar. The Frenchmen have to get these men out of the country and Morgan bravely leads the Nazis a merry chase away from the flyers until the Ratzis get wise and put her in front of a firing squad for her efforts. It's a factual account of the French underground and was one of the earliest films to come out that publicized the plight of the Europeans under Hitler's yoke. Ladd is excellent as the baby-faced member of the group who is wounded and dies before he can get back to England. The film is filled with patriotic speeches and lots of pathos (almost verging on bathos) but never goes over the top, and, consequently, captured large audiences. Ladd had been in films since his first in 1932, ONCE IN A LIFETIME, but this role was the one that brought him to the notice of the studio chiefs at RKO. His wife, Sue, was his agent and she wisely declined the RKO offer of $500 per week for Ladd as she had already been submitted a script for his approval by Paramount. He took that job and shot to the top of the motion picture world with his role in THIS GUN FOR HIRE. Cregar was only 24 years old when he played the Gestapo boss. He was also in THIS GUN FOR HIRE with Ladd and died at 28 after he attempted a crash diet that damaged his heart. Cregar's five year career consisted of many excellent roles in some fine films, the best of which was his portrayal of Jack the Ripper in HANGOVER SQUARE. In later years the role of the huge villain was assumed by burly Victor Buono whose girth also shortened his life considerably.

p, David Hempstead; d, Robert Stevenson; w, Charles Bennett, Ellis St. Joseph (based on a story by Jacques Thery, Georges Kessel); ph, Russell Metty; m, Roy Webb; ed, Sherman Todd; md, Constantin Bakaleinikoff; art d, Albert S. D'Agostino, Carroll Clark.

War Drama **(PR:A MPAA:NR)**

JOAN OF THE ANGELS** 1/2

(1962, Pol.) 101m Film Polski/Telepix bw (MATKA JOANNA OD ANIOLOW; AKA: MOTHER JOAN OF THE ANGELS)

Lucyna Winnicka *(Mother Joan)*, Mieczyslaw Voit *(Father Jozef Suryn/The Rabbi)*, Anna Ciepielewska *(Sister Margaret)*, Maria Chwalibog *(Awdosia)*, Kazimierz Fabisiak *(Father Brym)*, Stanislaw Jasiukiewicz *(Squire Chrzaszczewski)*, Zygmunt Zintel *(Wolodkowicz The Inkeeper)*, Franciszek Pieczka *(Odryl)*, Jerzy Kaczmarek *(Kaziuk)*, Jaroslaw Kuszewski *(Juarj)*, Lech Wojciechowski, Marian Nosek, Jerzy Walden, Marian Nowak, Zygmunt Malawski, Stanislaw Szymczyk.

In 17th Century Poland Winnicka is the Mother Superior for a convent of Ursuline nuns. She becomes possessed by Satanic forces and efforts are made to end this horror. Two priests are burned at the stake for fathering children by her, while four other priests try in vain to exorcise the evil spirits. The other nuns, with the exception of Ciepielewska, follow Winnicka's lead, letting evil spirits enter their own bodies. Voit is a devout priest who comes to try an exorcism. Using all of his powers and knowledge, including prayer and self-flagellation, he tries his best but cannot overcome the Satanic possession. In fear, he seeks the advice of an old rabbi (Voit again, in an unusual dual role). The Rabbi suggests that the so-called spirits may simply be human nature. Voit finds himself becoming possessed by Winnicka, drawn to her by his own emotional and physical needs. In desperation he kills two innocent stable grooms in order to offer his soul to the forces holding Winnicka. He meets Ciepielewska after she has spent the night with a nobleman who subsequently kicked her out. Voit tells the emotionally wrought sister to return to the convent to tell Winnicka of his deed. This film takes on added dimension when one stops to consider modern Poland's unique position in the world (its Communist government and its strong Catholic traditions).

d, Jerzy Kawalerowicz; w, Kawalerowicz, Tadeusz Konwicki (based on the story "Matka Joanna od Aniolow" by Jaroslav Iwaszkiewcz); ph, Jerzy Wojcik; m, Adam Walacinski; ed, Wieslawa Otocka, Felicja Ragowska; art d, Roman Mann, Tadeusz Borowczyk.

Religious Drama **(PR:O MPAA:NR)**

JOANNA** 1/2 (1968, Brit.) 107m Laughlin/FOX c

Genevieve Waite *(Joanna)*, Christian Doermer *(Hendrik Casson)*, Calvin Lockhart *(Gordon)*, Donald Sutherland *(Lord Peter Sanderson)*, Glenna Forster-Jones *(Beryl)*, David Scheuer *(Dominic Endersley)*, Marda Vanne *(Granny)*, Geoffrey Morris *(Father)*, Michele Cooke *(Margot)*, Manning Wilson *(Inspector)*, Clifton Jones *(Black Detective)*, Dan Caulfield *(White Detective)*, Michael Chow *(Lefty)*, Anthony Ainley *(Bruce)*, Jane Bradbury *(Angela)*, Fiona Lewis *(Miranda De Hyde)*, Jayne Sofiano *(Teacher)*, Elizabeth MacLennan *(Nurse)*, Richard Hurndall *(Butler)*, Annette Robertson *(Maid)*, Jenny Hanley *(Married Woman)*, John Gulliver *(Art Dealer)*, Brenda Kempner *(Bespectacled Woman)*, Peter Porteous *(Taxi Driver)*, David Collings *(Critic)*, Sibylla Kay *(Critic's Wife)*.

Waite is a naive young woman who has come to London to study art. She has an affair with her teacher Doermer and takes up with Forster-Jones, a black woman living off of rich men and welfare. She introduces Waite into an entirely different world. Waite has another affair, this time with Scheuer, while Forster-Jones takes up with wealthy lord Sutherland. The four go off to Sutherland's home in Morocco where he confides to Waite that he is dying of leukemia. He explains that his slow death has taught him to live life to the fullest by committing himself to others. He sponsors a show of Doermer's paintings and then dies. After the funeral Waite takes up with Forster-Jones' brother Lockhart, a nightclub owner, who gets mixed up with gangsters and ends up in the slammer. Waite, now pregnant, returns to her father's home to have the child. Slightly surreal, with sunshine-and-roses songs by poet McKuen, the film is most notable for its attempt at dealing openly and honestly with miscegenation. However, the rest of the film falters, particularly from the confusion between what is real and what is imagined. Sutherland steals the film as the dying man. Sexual liaisons are only hinted at: lots of necking but relatively little activity. (Sarne may have been trying to make up for this when he made MYRA BRECKENRIDGE). The American release was cut down from the version screened at Cannes and the English release.

p, Michael S. Laughlin; d&w, Michael Sarne; ph, Walter Lassally, David Muir (Panavision, DeLuxe Color); m, Rod McKuen; ed, Norman Wanstall; prod d, Michael Wield; md, Arthur Greenslade; art d, Wield; cos, Sue West, Virginia Hamilton-Kearse; m/l, "Joanna," "All Catch the Sun," McKuen, "When Joanna Loved Me," Robert Wells, Jack Segal (sung by Scott Walker); makeup, Gordon Kay.

Drama/Musical **(PR:O MPAA:R)**

JOAQUIN MARRIETA (SEE: MURIETA, 1965, Span.)

JOCK PETERSEN (SEE: PETERSEN, 1975, Aus.)

JOE*** (1970) 107m Cannon c

Peter Boyle *(Joe Curran)*, Susan Sarandon *(Melissa Compton)*, Patrick McDermott *(Frank Russo)*, Tim Lewis *(Kid in Soda Shop)*, Estelle Omens *(Woman in Bargain Store)*, Bob O'Connell *(Man in Bargain Store)*, Dennis Patrick *(Bill Compton)*, Audrey Caire *(Joan Compton)*, Marlene Warfield *(Bellevue Nurse)*, Mary Case, Jenny Paine *(Teeny Boppers)*, Reid Cruickshanks *(American Bartender)*, Rudy Churney *(Man in Bar)*, K. Callan *(Mary Lou Curran)*, Robert Emerick *(TV Newscaster)*, Gloria Hoye *(Janine)*, Bo Enivel *(Sam)*, Frank Moon *(Gil Richards)*, Jeanne M. Lange *(Phyllis)*, Perry Gerwitz *(Hippie on Street)*, Morty Schloss *(Waiter in Guitar Joint)*, Frank Vitale *(Hippie in Group)*, Al Sentesy *(Poster Shop Proprietor)*, Patti Caton *(Nancy)*, Gary Weber *(George)*, Claude Robert Simon *(Bob)*, Francine Middleton *(Gail)*, Max Couper *(Ronnie)*, Patrick O'Neal *(Bartender at Ginger Man)*.

A huge success that put Cannon Films on the map, JOE cost less to make than the director, Avildsen, now gets as his fee (he went on to helm ROCKY and THE KARATE KID). This is a funny, vicious, and often startling film that occasioned a great deal of controversy when released and can barely be shown on TV due to the foul language and the violence. McDermott is a drug addict who gets his girl friend, Sarandon to try some heavy stuff. She's sent to the hospital after overdosing and when her father, straitlaced advertising account man Patrick, comes to her meager apartment to get her things, McDermott pokes fun at the man and Patrick flies into a fit of rage and beats the youth to death. After the murder Patrick is shaken and wanders into a tough bar where Boyle, a bigot who hates anyone who isn't white or Christian, is downing a few brews. Patrick is desperate to talk and tells Boyle what he did but Boyle doesn't believe him. The picture of this Madison Avenue man taking the life of one of those hippies is too much for Boyle to fathom. Later, when Boyle is with his wife, Callan, he sees the television news report on the dead hippie and phones Patrick with his congratulations. It isn't long before these two very different men are drinking buddies and find that, despite the rift in their classes, they are cut from the same cloth. Their friendship deepens and Patrick feels that his secret is safe with Boyle. Sarandon learns that her father killed McDermott and she leaves home, taking refuge somewhere in Greenwich Village. The two men go out searching for her and wind up at a marijuana party and "org-gy" (as Boyle pronounces it). While at the party they have their wallets stolen and then force the youths to divulge the location of the thieves. Boyle and Patrick get shotguns and drive to a rural area outside the city where several young people have set up a commune. The snow is deep around the house and the two men stealthily sneak up to the residence and begin to shoot the inhabitants. Once Boyle starts shooting, Patrick realizes that he, too, must participate and they have to kill everyone there in order to escape without being traced. At the conclusion Patrick sadly realizes that in the bloodbath he has shot his own daughter, Sarandon. Screenwriter Wexler received an Oscar nomination for the film, although if one were to cut all the swear words, the script would probably lose thirty pages. He also wrote SATURDAY NIGHT FEVER and co-wrote SERPICO with Waldo Salt. Avildsen still does his own cinematography and prides himself on that ability. He later took an Oscar for ROCKY but he has odd taste in his choice of work and occasionally gets involved with sex-oriented pictures (such as FOREPLAY and GUESS WHAT WE LEARNED IN SCHOOL TODAY?) in between doing such mainstream films as SAVE THE TIGER and SLOW DANCING IN THE BIG CITY. In a small role, look for Patrick O'Neal as the bartender at "The Ginger Man," a boite he owns in real life. Boyle burst on the movie scene with JOE (after some small roles) and later played the monster in YOUNG FRANKENSTEIN, as well as the campaign manager in THE CANDIDATE, but his career has not nearly been as large as had been expected after getting involved with some huge turkeys like F.I.S.T., SWASHBUCKLER, and THE BRINK'S JOB. JOE was originally called "The Gap" and that may have been a more prophetic title. Shot in mid-winter in New York City and Rockland County, it is very authentic and true to the theme. It was shortly after this that Cannon Films was acquired by schlockmeisters Golan and Globus, who parlayed the world's lack of taste into a fortune. Although Wexler was venting his spleen against bigotry with his delineation of JOE, there were theaters where the killing of the hippies (and Boyle's bigoted references) were cheered by the crew cut audience.

p, David Gil; d, John G. Avildsen; w, Norman Wexler; ph, Avildsen (DeLuxe Color); m, Bobby Scott; ed, George T. Norris; md, Scott; cos, Andrew Kay; spec eff, Louis Antzes; m/l, "Hey Joe," Scott, Danny Meehan (sung by Dean Michaels), "You Don't Know What's Going On," Exuma (sung by Exuma), "Where Are You Going?" "You Can Fly," Scott (sung by Jerry Butler).

Drama **Cas.** **(PR:O MPAA:R)**

JOE AND ETHEL TURP CALL ON THE PRESIDENT*** (1939) 70m MGM bw

Ann Sothern *(Ethel Turp)*, Lewis Stone *(The President)*, Walter Brennan *(Jim)*, William Gargan *(Joe Turp)*, Marsha Hunt *(Kitty Crusper)*, Tom Neal *(Johnny Crusper)*, James Bush *(Henry Crusper)*, Don Costello *(Fred)*, Muriel Hutchinson *(Francine La Vaughn)*, Jack Norton *(Parker)*, Aldrich Bowker *(Mike O'Brien)*, Frederick Burton *(Bishop Bannon)*, Al Shean *(Father Reicher)*, Robert Emmett O'Connor *(Pat Donegan)*, Cliff Clark *(Garage Owner)*, Russell Hicks *(Mr. Graves)*, Paul Everton *(Senator)*, Charles Trowbridge *(Cabinet Member)*, Louis Jean Heydt *(Dr. Standish)*, Ann Teeman *(Mrs. Standish)*, Mary Gordon *(Mrs. O'Leary)*.

The title tells the tale of this quirky little film based on a Damon Runyon story. When a local postman is suspended for destroying a letter to shield his childhood sweetheart from some unhappiness, the local Flatbush neighborhood is up in arms. Not satisfied with the actions taken, Gargan and Sothern take their case to fatherly Chief of State Stone. The story is told in flashback and Stone reinstates the postman. The couple's bickering in the Oval Office (and Stone's reactions), as well as the flashback storytelling, makes this an enjoyable and amusing little film. Watch for Shean, famed vaudevillian and uncle to the Marx Brothers, in a minor role.

p, Edgar Selwyn; d, Robert B. Sinclair; w, Melville Baker (based on the story "A Call on the President" by Damon Runyon); ph, Leonard Smith; ed, Gene Ruggiero.

Comedy **(PR:A MPAA:NR)**

JOE BUTTERFLY** (1957) 90m UNIV c

Audie Murphy *(Pvt. John Woodley)*, George Nader *(Sgt. Ed Kennedy)*, Keenan Wynn *(Henry Hathaway)*, Burgess Meredith *(Joe Butterfly)*, Kieko Shima *(Cheiko)*, Fred Clark *(Col. E.E. Fuller)*, Charles McGraw *(Sgt. Jim McNulty)*, Shinpei Shimazaki *(Little Boy)*, Reiko Higa *(False Tokyo Rose)*, Tatsuo Saito *(Father)*, Chizu Shimazaki *(Mother)*, Herbert Anderson *(Maj. Ferguson)*, Eddie Firestone *(Sgt. Oscar Hulick)*, Frank Chase *(Chief Yeoman Saul Bernheim)*, Harold Goodwin *(Col. Hopper)*, Willard Willingham *(Soldier)*, John Agar *(Sgt. Dick Mason)*.

Murphy is the leader of a journalistic bunch trying to publish a magazine for the occupying American forces in postwar Japan. He leads his group through Army red tape with the help of wily Japanese native Meredith. This film is similar to THE TEAHOUSE OF THE AUGUST MOON, released the year earlier, but not nearly as clever or original. The military high jinks seem contrived but Meredith, in his first film after a long absence, steals the show with his clever and often hilarious characterization. Director Jesse Hibbs directed 5 films that starred Audie Murphy in the 1950s including TO HELL AND BACK (1955, based on Murphy's autobiography). Filmed in Japan.

p, Aaron Rosenberg; d, Jesse Hibbs; w, Sy Gomberg, Jack Sher, Marion Hargrove (based on a play by Evan Wylie, Jack Ruge); ph, Irving Glassberg (CinemaScope, Technicolor); ed, Milton Carruth; md, Joseph Gershenson; art d, Alexander Golitzen, Alfred Sweeney.

Comedy **(PR:A MPAA:NR)**

JOE DAKOTA** (1957) 79m UNIV c

Jock Mahoney *(The Stranger)*, Luana Patten *(Jody Weaver)*, Charles McGraw *(Cal Moore)*, Barbara Lawrence *(Myrna Weaver)*, Claude Akins *(Aaron Grant)*, Lee Van Cleef *(Adam Grant)*, Anthony Caruso *(Marcus Vizzini)*, Paul Birch *(Frank Weaver)*, George Dunn *(Jim Baldwin)*, Steve Darrell *(Sam Cook)*, Rita Lynn *(Rosa Vizzini)*, Gregg Barton *(Tom Jensen)*, Anthony Jochim *(Claude Henderson)*, Jeane Wood *(Bertha Jensen)*, Juney Ellis *(Ethel Cook)*.

Mahoney arrives in a small California oil town in search of an Indian who once served him as a scout. But when he discovers his old companion missing and the man's land now used for oil drilling, Mahoney starts asking questions. Told that the Indian had been hanged for attacking a local woman, the incredulous Mahoney investigates the disappearance for himself. Working with Patten, the woman who supposedly was attacked, he discovers that evil oil man McGraw framed the dead man in order to get to the oil deposits on his land. Slow-moving, the film is similar to BAD DAY AT BLACK ROCK, though not nearly as well done. The direction meanders, receiving no help from the weak script. Key suspense points, such as Mahoney's relationship with the Indian, are revealed much too early in the film. The film carries the distinction of being one of the few westerns where there is not a single bullet fired. Actor Jock Mahoney was a stuntman for many years before becoming a hero in B Movies, played Tarzan in one film, and is the stepfather of Sally Field, Oscar winning actress. Co-writer William Talman was also an actor and is better known for being bested by Raymond Burr in court battles for the "Perry Mason" TV series.

p, Howard Christie; d, Richard Bartlett; w, William Talman, Norman Jolley; ph, George Robinson (Eastmancolor); m, Joseph Gershenson; ed, Fred MacDowell; md, Gershenson; art d, Alexander Golitzen, Bill Newberry; set d, Russell A. Gausman, Ray Jeffers; cos, Marilyn Sotto; m/l, "The Flower of San Antone", Mack David, Ray Joseph.

Western **(PR:C MPAA:NR)**

JOE, EL IMPLACABLE (SEE: NAVAJO JOE, 1967, Ital./Span.)

JOE HILL½** (1971, Swed./U.S.) 114m Film-Sagittarius/PAR c

Thommy Berggren *(Joe Hill)*, Anja Schmidt *(Lucia)*, Kelvin Malave *(Fox)*, Evert Anderson *(Blackie)*, Cathy Smith *(Cathy)*, Hasse Persson *(Paul)*, David Moritz *(David)*, Wendy Geier *(Elizabeth)*, Franco Molinari *(Tenor)*, Richard Weber

(Richard), Joel Miller *(Ed Rowan)*, George Faeder *(George)*, Liska March *(Charity Woman)*.

Somewhat fictionalized film-bio of the famed labor leader as played by Berggren. After immigrating to America from Sweden, the title character tramps around the U.S. until getting involved with the Industrial Workers of the World (the famed Wobblies). He quickly learns his way around the union and the strike-breaking police, takes his ever-present banjo, and begins writing labor songs for the people. After achieving some success and power within the Wobblies he goes to Utah where he takes the fall for a murder to protect a girl he loves. He eventually, in an emotionally frightening sequence, is arrested, tried, and executed. Politically the film only touches on issues and that in a simplistic manner. It approaches the topic from the time it was made (1971) rather than in the actual period the events occurred in from the 1930s, imposing a somewhat sentimental and patronizing feel on the story rather than letting events speak for themselves.

p&d, Bo Widerberg; w, Widerberg, Richard Weber, Steve Hopkins; ph, Petter Davidsson, Jorgen Persson (Eastmancolor); m, Stefan Grossman; ed, Widerberg; art d, Ulf Axen; m/l, "I Dreamed I Saw Joe Hill Last Night," Earl Robinson, Alfred Hayes (sung by Joan Baez).

Biography **(PR:C MPAA:GP)**

JOE KIDD** (1972) 87m Malpaso/UNIV c

Clint Eastwood *(Joe Kidd)*, Robert Duvall *(Frank Harlan)*, John Saxon *(Luis Chama)*, Don Stroud *(Lamarr)*, Stella Garcia *(Helen Sanchez)*, James Wainwright *(Mingo)*, Paul Koslo *(Roy)*, Gregory Walcott *(Sheriff Mitchell)*, Dick Van Patten *(Hotel Manager)*, Lynne Marta *(Elma)*, John Carter *(Judge)*, Pepe Hern *(Priest)*, Joaquin Martinez *(Manolo)*, Ron Soble *(Ramon)*, Pepe Callahan *(Naco)*, Clint Ritchie *(Calvin)*, Gil Barreto *(Emilio)*, Ed Deemer *(Bartender)*, Maria Val *(Vita)*, Chuck Hayward *(Eljay)*, Michael R. Horst *(Deputy)*.

Some extraordinary talents assembled to make a very ordinary film with JOE KIDD. Considering Eastwood had just been named NATO "Male Star Of The Year" and Sturges was the same man who gave us THE GREAT ESCAPE and BAD DAY AT BLACK ROCK and the screenwriter, Leonard, has since become a cover story for *Time* magazine, it's amazing that they could put out such a routine, sluggish film. Eastwood is, for the umpteenth time, the Mysterious Stranger. He comes to the New Mexican town of Sinola in 1900 where the local Mexican-Americans are led by Saxon, who is protesting the illegal acquisition of their land by monied interests. The land had been part of the Spanish grants and the poor folks are being driven off it through a tangle of legalities. Eastwood is in jail after a drunken spree and watches as Saxon's crowd, enraged by the judge (Carter) who refuses to listen to their woes, steals the forged land grants from the courthouse and sets them on fire. The Saxon bunch is about to kidnap the judge but he's saved by Eastwood. A posse is formed and Eastwood is invited to be part of it but refuses. Now Duvall, a mean land owner with a thirst for blood, offers Eastwood $500 to join the posse and Eastwood declines again. Later he learns that his own small ranch has been raided and a hand has been injured by Saxon's men. Duvall ups the offer to $1,000 and Eastwood goes along. The posse, which includes Stroud, a sadistic sharpshooter, captures Garcia, one of Saxon's people. They then take more Mexican-Americans hostage and let Saxon know they will kill five of them unless he surrenders. Meanwhile, Eastwood and Garcia are falling for each other and he feels that Duvall's tactics are cruel. Duvall senses Eastwood can be a problem so he has him tossed into jail. Eastwood escapes the clink with a weapon supplied by Hern, the local padre. Eastwood arranges Stroud's death, saves the hostages, takes Garcia to Saxon's hideaway and is chagrined to see that Saxon is quite willing to allow the hostages to be killed rather than allow his own imprisonment. Eastwood captures Saxon and will take him back to town to stand trial but Duvall wants the man dead before that. In a scene not unlike his later film THE GAUNTLET, Eastwood delivers Saxon to the cowardly sheriff, Walcott, by riding a locomotive into town, off the tracks, and into the saloon. Duvall and Eastwood have a shoot-out, Eastwood hands Saxon to Walcott, and rides back to what's left of his ranch with Garcia. The story sounds better than it played. It was "presented by" long-time Universal studio executive Jennings Lang and holds the dubious distinction of being one of the lowest grossers ever made by Eastwood. Bad editing, leisurely direction, and a script that teetered precariously on the verge of being a John Wayne parody all combined to make JOE KIDD just a plodding shoot-em-up, nothing more. They had a real opportunity to strike a blow for the downtrodden Mexican-Americans but missed by miles.

p, Sidney Beckerman; d, John Sturges; w, Elmore Leonard; ph, Bruce Surtees (Panavision, Technicolor); m, Lalo Schifrin; ed, Ferris Webster; art d, Alexander Golitzen, Henry Bumstead; set d, Charles S. Thompson; stunts, Buddy Van Horn.

Western **Cas.** **(PR:C MPAA:PG)**

JOE LOUIS STORY, THE*½** (1953) 88m UA bw

Coley Wallace *(Joe Louis)*, Paul Stewart *(Tad McGeehan)*, Hilda Simms *(Marva Louis)*, James Edwards *(Chappie Blackburn)*, John Marley *(Mannie Seamon)*, Dotts Johnson *(Julian Black)*, Evelyn Ellis *(Mrs. Barrow)*, Carl Rocky Latimer *(Arthur Pine)*, John Marriott *(Sam Langford)*, P. Jay Sidney *(Handler)*, Isaac Jones *(Johnny Kingston)*, Royal Beal *(Mike Jacobs)*, Buddy Thorpe *(Max Schmeling)*, Ruby Goldstein *(Himself)*, Ralph Stantley, Anita Ellis, Ellis Larkins Trio, Herb Ratner, David Kurlan, Norman Rose, Josef Draper, Ossie Davis.

An excellent film biography that displays a rare quality within the genre: honesty. The film shows Louis as a man, not as a god and is all the better for it. Wallace, in the title role, is an uncanny look-alike for the champ. The story begins with him as a pug fighter, slowly working his way to the top. The two bouts with the German fighter Schmeling (Thorpe) are portrayed, as well as the disastrous attempt to come out of retirement in 1951, resulting in a pummeling by Marciano. Louis' failed marriage is sensitively dealt with. The story is told in flashback, with real-life fight footage edited in. Coley's portrayal is the role of a lifetime. His work in the ring looks real and the champ's confusion with his celebrity status is nicely handled. Direction is excellent, keeping a high level throughout. THE JOE LOUIS STORY was one of the first films with a nearly all-black cast to show the black people in an honest, unpatronizing manner—hardly a hint of stereotyping. A fine, humanistic film.

p, Stirling Silliphant; d, Robert Gordon; w, Robert Sylvester; ph, Joseph Brun; m, George Bassman; ed, David Kummins.

Sports Drama/Biography **Cas.** **(PR:A MPAA:NR)**

JOE MACBETH½** (1955) 90m COL bw

Paul Douglas *(Joe MacBeth)*, Ruth Roman *(Lily MacBeth)*, Bonar Colleano *(Lennie)*, Gregoire Aslan *(Duca)*, Sidney James *(Banky)*, Nicholas Stuart *(Duffy)*, Robert Arden *(Ross)*, Minerva Pious *(Rosie)*, Harry Green *(Big Dutch)*, Bill Nagy *(Marty)*, Kay Callard *(Ruth)*, Walter Crisham *(Angus)*, Mark Baker *(Benny)*, Alfred Mulock *(1st Assassin)*, George Margo *(2nd Assassin)*, Philip Vickers *(Tommy)*, Teresa Thorne *(Ruth)*, Beresford Egan, Victor Baring, Robert O'Neill, Johnny Ross, Launce Maraschal, Shirley Douglas, Louise Grant, Sheila Woods.

This is an interesting, though flawed, updating of Shakespeare's "Macbeth" updated as a gangster story. Roman is the wife of Douglas, a right-hand man of a powerful gangster. Roman wants it all and pushes her husband into becoming a top crime figure himself. But Douglas has his downfall at the hands of Colleano, a mob member whose father and wife are killed by Douglas. Though the literary allusions don't always work, the updating of the story is a clever idea. The film has a nice look and feel to it, with an excellent cast and fast-paced directional style that never lets go of the mounting tension.

p, Mike Frankovich; d, Ken Hughes; w, Phillip Yordan (based on the play "Macbeth" by William Shakespeare); ph, Basil Emmott; m, Richard Taylor; ed, Peter Rolfe Johnson; md, Taylor; art d, Alan Harris.

Crime **(PR:C MPAA:NR)**

JOE NAVIDAD (SEE: CHRISTMAS KID, THE, 1968, Span.)

JOE PALOOKA (SEE: PALOOKA, 1934)

JOE PALOOKA, CHAMP½** (1946) 70m MON bw

Leon Errol *(Knobby Walsh)*, Elyse Knox *(Anne)*, Joe Kirkwood, Jr. *(Joe Palooka)*, Eduardo Ciannelli *(Florini)*, Joe Sawyer *(Lefty)*, Elisha Cook, Jr. *(Eugene)*, Sam McDaniel *(Smoky)*, Robert Kent *(Brewster)*, Sarah Padden *(Mom Palooka)*, Michael Mark *(Pop Palooka)*, Lou Nova *(Al Costa)*, Russ Vincent *(Curly)*, Alexander Laszlo *(Aladar)*, Carole Dunne *(Mrs. Oberlander)*, Carol Hughes *(Mrs. Van Praag)*, Betty Blythe *(Mrs. Stafford)*, Philip Van Zandt *(Freddie Wells)*, Jimmy McLarnin *(Referee)*, Joe Louis, Manuel Ortiz, Ceferino Garcia, Henry Armstrong, Jack Roper *(themselves)*.

Ham Fisher's comic strip is once more adapted for the screen, after originally being filmed in 1934. It's the old fight story of a talented youngster being discovered by a fight manager and trained for the big fight. There are gangsters out to stop him and a society girl who falls for the big lug despite the differences in their social classes. This was the first of Monogram's films based on the comic strip and it doesn't do much except string together the stock cliches. The fight sequences are a standout, however. Errol is okay as the gruff manager and Kirkwood is a good character in the title role. Nova and McLarnin, real life fighters, are given cameos as the champ and a referee. Don't miss brief cameos by boxing greats Louis, Ortiz, Garcia, and Armstrong. (See JOE PALOOKA series, Index)

p, Hal E. Chester; d, Reginald Le Borg; w, Cyril Endfield, Albert DePina (based on a story by Chester from the comic strip by Ham Fisher); ph, Benjamin Kline; ed, Bernard W. Burton; md, Edward J. Kay; art d, Edward C. Jewell.

Boxing **(PR:AA MPAA:NR)**

JOE PALOOKA IN FIGHTING MAD (SEE: FIGHTING MAD, 1948)

JOE PALOOKA IN HUMPHREY TAKES A CHANCE*

(SEE: HUMPHREY TAKES A CHANCE)

JOE PALOOKA IN THE BIG FIGHT½** (1949) 66m MON bw

Leon Errol *(Knobby Walsh)*, Joe Kirkwood Jr. *(Joe Palooka)*, Lina Romay *(Maxine)*, David Bruce *(Tom Conway)*, George O'Hanlon *(Louie)*, Virginia Welles *(Anne Howe)*, Greg McClure *(Grady)*, Taylor Holmes *(Dr. Benson)*, Ian MacDonald *(Mike)*, Lou Lubin *(Talmadge)*, Bert Conway *(Pee Wee)*, Lyle Talbot *(Lt. Muldoon)*, Benny Baker *(Flight Secretary)*, Eddie Gribbon *(Canvas)*, Jack Roper *(Scranton)*, Frances Osborne *(Wardrobe Woman)*, Harry Hayden *(Commissioner Harris)*, Frank Fenton *(Detective)*, George Fisher *(Contest Announcer)*, John Indrisano, Ted Pavelec.

Better than average JOE PALOOKA film finds our hero once more tangled up with gangsters. Kirkwood is framed on a drunk charge and then a murder rap by gangsters who want their own man in a big fight. Kirkwood conducts his own investigation to prove his innocence. The story has a number of plot lines that are ably held by the direction. It moves at a nice pace and the script has realistic dialog. Surprisingly, there is not too much boxing footage. (See JOE PALOOKA series, Index).

p, Hal E. Chester; d, Cyril Endfield; w, Stanley Prager, Endfield (based on the comic strip by Ham Fisher); ph, Mack Stengler; ed, Fred Maguire; md, Edward Kay; art d, Dave Milton; set d, Raymond Boltz, Jr.; fight sequences staged by John Indrisano.

Boxing/Gangster **(PR:AA MPAA:NR)**

JOE PALOOKA IN THE COUNTERPUNCH½** (1949) 74m MON bw

Leon Errol *(Knobby Walsh)*, Joe Kirkwood, Jr. *(Joe Palooka)*, Elyse Knox *(Anne Howe)*, Marcel Journet *(Anton Kindel)*, Sheila Ryan *(Myra)*, Harry Lewis *(Chick Bennett)*, Frank Sully *(Looie)*, Ian Wolfe *(Prof. Lilliquist)*, Sam Hayes *(Fight

Announcer), Walter Sande *(Austin)*, Douglas Dumbrille *(Capt. Lance)*, Douglas Fowley *(Thurston)*, Eddie Gribbon *(Canvasback)*, Suni Chorre *(Cardona)*, Ralph Graves *(Dr. Colman)*, Martin Garralaga *(Announcer)*, Roland Dupree *(Bell Boy)*, Gertrude Messinger *(Nurse)*, John Hart *(Pedro)*, Robert Conway *(Steward)*, John Indrisano, Joe Herrera *(Referees)*.

Based on the old comic strip series, this picture has Kirkwood and Errol off to South America to meet the Latino fighting champ. But aboard their ship, they get mixed up with some counterfeiters. Kirkwood joins up with the Feds and helps solve the crime in time to meet the Latin American fighter. Love scenario includes kiss-and-make-up scenes between Kirkwood and his girl friend, Knox. Despite its typical fight plot, plus the stereotyping of the South American champ as a hothead, slapstick comedy combined with suspense make this one of the more enjoyable films in the Palooka series. (See JOE PALOOKA series, Index).

p, Hal E. Chester; d, Reginald Le Borg; w, Henry Blankfort, Cyril Endfield (based on the comic strip by Ham Fisher); ph, William Sickner; m, Edward J. Kay; ed, Warren Adams; md, Kay; art d, David Milton; set d, Raymond Boltz, Jr.

Comedy/Mystery **(PR:AAA MPAA:NR)**

JOE PALOOKA IN THE SQUARED CIRCLE 1/2** (1950) 63m MON bw

Joe Kirkwood, Jr. *(Joe Palooka)*, James Gleason *(Knobby Walsh)*, Lois Hall *(Anne Howe)*, Edgar Barrier *(Brogden)*, Myrna Dell *(Sandra)*, Robert Coogan *(Humphrey Pennyworth)*, Dan Seymour *(Crawford)*, Charles Halton *(Merkle)*, Frank Jenks *(Looie)*, Greg McClure *(Pete)*, Eddie Gribbon *(Canvas)*, Robert Griffin *(Kebo)*, John Harmon *(Phillips)*, Jack Roper *(Gunsel)*, Sue Carlton *(Felice)*, William Haade *(Bubbles)*, Stanley Prager *(TV Announcer)*, Mervin Williams *(2nd Reporter)*, Hal Feiberling *(Pinky Thompson)*, John Merrick *(Tiny)*, Paul Bryar *(Roderick)*.

Kirkwood witnesses a mob killing and vows to bring the killers to justice. But since the body is missing, the cops can't help him. He brings his story to the papers and names names. Two of the killers Kirkwood fingers come after him, but they are caught and sent to jail. The suspenseful fight sequence features Kirkwood unknowingly doped up, valiantly trying to hold his crown. Gleason, in the meantime (replacing Leon Errol in the role of Kirkwood's manager), is held by gangsters. While captive he and a gangster watch the fight on television. The mobster comments on what a terrific medium TV is for boxing, which seems prophetic considering that boxing and wrestling were two of early television's prime shows. Hall is upgraded from girl friend to wife for this film, and the production values are standard for the genre. (See JOE PALOOKA series, Index).

p, Hal E. Chester; d, Reginald Le Borg; w, Jan Jeffrey (based on the story by B.F. Melzer from the comic strip by Ham Fisher); ph, Marcel Le Picard.

Boxing/Gangster **(PR:A MPAA:NR)**

JOE PALOOKA IN TRIPLE CROSS** (1951) 60m MON bw

Joe Kirkwood, Jr. *(Joe Palooka)*, James Gleason *(Knobby Walsh)*, Cathy Downs *(Anne)*, John Emery *(The Professor)*, Steve Brodie *(Dutch)*, Don Harvey *(Chuck)*, Rufe Davis *(Kenny Smith)*, Jimmy Wallington *(Himself)*, Mary Young *(Mrs. Reed)*, Eddie Gribbon *(Canvas)*, Sid Tomack *(Looie)*, Dickie Leroy *(Bub)*, Jimmy Lloyd *(Bill)*, Cliff Clark *(Sheriff Malin)*, Hank Worden *(Farmer)*.

Kirkwood, his wife Downs, and manager Gleason are on a fishing trip when they run into some escaped convicts. The crooks kidnap the trio as a cover to dodge the cops. Emery, as one of the baddies, decides to do away with his partners in crime and make Kirkwood throw a fight so that he can win some big bucks. At the big fight, Emery comes disguised as Downs' aunt. All is going according to plan until Kirkwood gets himself knocked out of the ring long enough to beat up Emery and stop the caper—but in enough time to get back in the ring to beat his sparring partner before the countdown. This picture was the last in the JOE PALOOKA series by Monogram. (See JOE PALOOKA series, Index).

p, Hal E. Chester; d, Reginald Le Borg; w, Jan Jeffrey (based on the story by Harold Bancroft from the comic strip by Ham Fisher); ph, William Sickner; m, Darrell Calker; art d, Martin Obzina.

Boxing/Gangster **(PR:AA MPAA:NR)**

JOE PALOOKA IN WINNER TAKE ALL 1/2** (1948) 64m MON bw

Joe Kirkwood, Jr. *(Joe Palooka)*, Elyse Knox *(Anne Howe)*, William Frawley *(Knobby Walsh)*, Stanley Clements *(Tommy)*, John Shelton *(Greg Tanner)*, Mary Beth Hughes *(Millie)*, Sheldon Leonard *(Herman)*, Frank Jenks *(Louie)*, Lyle Talbot *(Henderson)*, Jack Roper *(Waldo)*, Eddie Gribbon *(Canvas)*, Wally Vernon *(Taxi Driver)*, Ralph Sanford *(Lt. Steve Mulford)*, Bill Martin *(Sportscaster)*, "Big" Ben Moroz *(Bobo Walker)*, Hal Fieberling *(Sammy Talbot)*, William Ruhl *(Talbot's Manager)*, Chester Clute *(Doniger)*, Douglas Fowley, Stanley Prager *(Reporters)*, Hugh Charles, Forrest Matthews *(Instructors)*, Gertrude Astor *(Mrs. Howard)*, Hal Gerard *(Television Announcer)*.

Kirkwood is in the big fight once more, with Frawley taking the role of the manager. This PALOOKA film differs from most of the others in the series in that less attention is given to dialog, with more fight sequences. The direction has a nice building pace and Kirkwood physically fulfills Fisher's pen-and-ink rendition of the hero. (See JOE PALOOKA series, Index).

p, Hal E. Chester; d, Reginald Le Borg; w, Stanley Rubin, Monte V. Collins (based on the comic strip by Ham Fisher); ph, William Sickner; m, Edward J. Kay; ed, Otho Lovering; art d, Dave Milton.

Comedy/Boxing **(PR:AA MPAA:NR)**

JOE PALOOKA MEETS HUMPHREY 1/2** (1950) 65m MON bw

Leon Errol *(Knobby/Lord Cecil Poole)*, Joe Kirkwood, Jr. *(Joe Palooka)*, Robert Coogan *(Humphrey)*, Jerome Cowan *(Belden)*, Joe Besser *(Carlton)*, Don McGuire *(Mitchell)*, Pamela Blake *(Anne Howe)*, Donald MacBride *(Mayor)*, Curt Bois *(Pierre)*, Clem Bevans *(Mr. Edwards)*, Frank Sully *(Looie)*, Eddie Gribbon *(Canvas)*, Meyer Grace *(Referee)*, Lillian Bronson *(Prunella)*, Sam Balter *(Announcer)*, Frosty Royce, Russ Kaplan, Sandra Gould, Bert Conway, Ray Walker, Knox Manning.

Kirkwood and bride Blake are off on their honeymoon, while manager Errol gets Kirkwood booked into a charity fight. Then Errol doubles as fight manager in an attempt to foul up the works. Coogan is introduced into the series as Kirkwood's dumb and brawny, though nice guy opponent. He gives a good comic performance, as does Errol in his dual role. Overall, it could have been funnier than it is, but not a bad entry for the JOE PALOOKA films. (See JOE PALOOKA series, Index).

p, Hal E. Chester; d, Jean Yarbrough; w, Henry Blankfort (based on the comic strip by Ham Fisher); ph, William Sickner; m, Edward J. Kay; ed, Otho Lovering, art d, Dave Milton.

Boxing/Comedy **(PR:AA MPAA:NR)**

JOE PANTHER 1/2** (1976) 110m Artists Creation c

Brian Keith *(Capt. Harper)*, Ricardo Montalban *(Turtle George)*, Alan Feinstein *(Rocky)*, Cliff Osmond *(Rance)*, A. Martinez *(Billy Tiger)*, Ray Tracey *(Joe Panther)*, Robert W. Hoffman *(George Harper)*, Gem Thorpe Osceola *(Tommy Panther)*, Lois Red Elk *(Joe's Mother)*, Monika Ramirez *(Jenny Rainbow)*.

Tracey is in the title role as a young Seminole Indian who has mixed emotions about the white world in which he lives. He finally achieves satisfaction and some recognition as a professional alligator wrestler. Tracey's performance is sensitive, likable, and thoroughly believable, but his fine acting ability is far outweighed by the negative aspects of this film. The real issue of white treatment of native Americans is treated simplistically in manner, dividing the white world into "the good guys" and "the bad guys." Montalban is laughable as an old Indian chief dispensing contradictory advice to the young men on how to deal with whites. The alligator sequence, though nicely put together, is backed with a score that unashamedly rips off the music of JAWS.

p, Stewart H. Beveridge; d, Paul Krasny; w, Dale Eunson (based on the novel by Zachary Ball); ph, Robert L. Morrison, Jordon Klein (CFI Color); m, Fred Karlin; ed, Mike Vejar, Millie Moore; m/l, "The Time Has Come," Norman Gimbel, Karlin (sung by England Dan and John Ford Coley); stunts, Courtney Brown.

Family Drama **(PR:AAA MPAA:G)**

JOE SMITH, AMERICAN* 1/2**

(1942) 63m MGM bw (GB: HIGHWAY TO FREEDOM)

Robert Young *(Joe Smith)*, Marsha Hunt *(Mary Smith)*, Harvey Stephens *(Freddie Dunhill)*, Darryl Hickman *(Johnny Smith)*, Jonathan Hale *(Blake McKettrick)*, Noel Madison *(Schricker)*, Don Costello *(Mead)*, Joseph Anthony *(Conway)*, William Forrest *(Gus)*, Russell Hicks *(Mr. Edgerton)*, Mark Daniels *(Pete)*, William Tannen *(Eddie)*, Frank Faylen *(Expectant Father)*, Edgar Sherrod *(Minister)*, Ava Gardner *(Girl)*, Selmer Jackson.

The title should tell you that this was a flag-waver and in the dark days of 1942, America needed to see Old Glory wafting in the breeze. However, such good taste and restraint are used in the movie that the audience never realized they were being manipulated into the "war mode" and the result was a box-office hit and a good and proud feeling on the part of everyone who saw it. It's about "the little guy"—one of the scores of people who are behind every fighting man on the battle lines—and the character is not unlike the person played by Robert Cummings in Hitchcock's SABOTEUR. Young is a happily married factory worker, an average Joe with an average wife, Hunt, and an average son, Hickman. He has the blueprints for a secret new bombsight (like the famed Norden bombsight that turned the war around and permitted high-level bombing). He is kidnaped and tortured by Nazi thugs who attempt to get him to reveal his knowledge. In order to keep his wits about him, Young flashes back to all the happiness of his life: his wooing of Hunt, the birth of Hickman, etc. He finally escapes their clutches and leads the FBI operatives to the hideout. The film sought to show that anyone, even the most ordinary guy, could be a hero in his own way. Executive Producer Dore Schary had started a low-budget division at MGM but refused to make them into exploitation films, feeling that important themes could be brought to the screen at a reasonable cost. Since Schary was a writer before becoming a producer, he realized that the play, rather than the deal, was the thing and he had some crackerjack screenplays written for him before leaving the studio to join David O. Selznick. This was Hickman's eighth film and he was only 11 years old. In later years, he became an executive producer of soap operas at CBS and works there today in the current programming department at Television City in Hollywood. Hickman's younger brother, Dwayne, also appeared in many movies and starred as "Dobie Gillis" on TV. Producer Jack Chertok went on to great TV success with many TV series in the 1960s, including "The Addams Family" and "My Favorite Martian." Remade in 1959 as THE BIG OPERATOR with Mickey Rooney.

p, Jack Chertok; d, Richard Thorpe; w, Allen Rivkin (based on a story by Paul Gallico); ph, Charles Lawton; ed, Elmo Veron; art d, Cedric Gibbons.

Spy Drama **(PR:A MPAA:NR)**

JOEY BOY* 1/2 (1965, Brit.) 91m Temgrange/BL bw

Harry H. Corbett *(Joey Boy Thompson)*, Stanley Baxter *(Benny "The Kid" Lindowski)*, Bill Fraser *(Sgt. Dobbs)*, Percy Herbert *(Mad George Long)*, Lance Percival *(Clarence Doubleday)*, Reg Varney *(Rabbit Malone)*, John Arnatt *(Brig. Chapman)*, Yvonne Ball *(Rabbit's 2nd Girl)*, Basil Dignam *(General)*, Stephanie Beaumont *(Anna)*, John Harvey *(Signals Officer)*, Lloyd Lamble *(Sir John Averycorn)*, Moira Lister *(Lady Thameridge)*, Sean Lynch *(Clancy)*, Nora Nicholson *(Middle Aged Lady)*, Derek Nimmo *(Lt. Hope)*, Toni Palmer *(Angie)*, Eric Pohlmann *(Italian Farmer)*, John Phillips *(Inspector Morgan)*, Norman Rossington *(R.A. Corporal)*, Bill Shine *(Ticket Collector)*, Veronica Strong *(Bella)*, Ernest

Walder *(Lt. Walther)*, Thorley Walters *(Colonel)*, Edward Chapman *(Tom Hobson)*, RSM Brittain *(Sergeant)*.

Faced with a choice between jail or the army, a group of sharpies choose the latter. They make the services the base of operations for a gambling and liquor club, doing quite well in their business. Overseas, the operations change but the results are similar. Asked to start a social club for troop morale, the group opens up a facility that falls short of being a brothel. They try to keep this a secret from visiting members of parliament, but the peers discover what their fighting men are really doing. What could have been a great farce is reduced to a bunch of stock situations and highly stereotyped characters.

p, Sidney Gilliat, Leslie Gilliat, Frank Launder; d, Launder; w, Launder, Mike Watts (based on the novel by Eddie Chapman); ph, Arthur Lavis; m, Philip Green; ed, John Shirley.

Comedy **(PR:O MPAA:NR)**

JOHANSSON GETS SCOLDED*½
(1945, Swed.) 101m Scandia Films bw (VAR HERR LUGGAR JOHANSSON)

Sigurd Wallen *(Johansson)*, Dagmar Ebbesen *(His Wife)*, Anders Ek *(Olle)*, Bogan Westin *(Lena)*, Hans Lindgren *(Ake)*.

Boring import from Sweden about domestic problems with an ordinary family. Wallen is a small manufacturer who starts expanding the business. His wife wants to keep up with the neighbors and spends beyond the family means, and his son is arrested for robbery. The grandmother, who knows everything and will gladly expound without invitation, moves in to cause further havoc. The script is cliched and tedious, though the actors do their best with the material. (In Swedish; English subtitles.)

d, Sigurd Wallen; w, Erik Lundegard; m, Erik Baumann, Nathan Gorling.

Domestic Situations **(PR:A MPAA:NR)**

JOHN AND JULIE* ** (1957, Brit.) 83m Group 3/BL c

Colin Gibson *(John Pritchett)*, Lesley Dudley *(Julie)*, Noelle Middleton *(Miss Stokes)*, Moira Lister *(Dora)*, Wilfrid Hyde-White *(Sir James)*, Sidney James *(Mr. Pritchett)*, Megs Jenkins *(Mrs. Pritchett)*, Constance Cummings *(Mrs. Davidson)*, Joseph Tomelty *(Mr. Davidson)*, Patric Doonan *(Jim Webber)*, Andrew Cruickshank *(Uncle Ben)*, Colin Gordon *(Mr. Swayne)*, Winifred Shotter *(Mrs. Swayne)*, Peter Jones *(Jeremy)*, Peter Sellers *(Police Constable Diamond)*, Vincent Ball *(Digger)*, Peter Coke *(Captain)*, Richard Dimbleby, Wynford Vaughan Thomas, Mona Washbourne.

Gibson and Dudley are two children who decide to travel 150 miles to London to see the coronation of Elizabeth II in Westminster Abbey. They travel via foot, bicycle, train, and automobile and meet a good number of characters along the way, including an early appearance by Sellers. They make it to London in time to see the coronation. This is a charming little film and great for the kids. There is some nice stock footage of the actual coronation blended in.

p, Herbert Mason; d&w, William Fairchild; ph, Arthur Grant (Eastmancolor); m, Philip Green; ed, Bernard Gribble; md, Green.

Comedy/Family **Cas.** **(PR:AAA MPAA:NR)**

JOHN AND MARY*½** (1969) 92m Debrod/FOX c

Dustin Hoffman *(John)*, Mia Farrow *(Mary)*, Michael Tolan *(James)*, Sunny Griffin *(Ruth)*, Stanley Beck *(Ernest)*, Tyne Daly *(Hilary)*, Alix Elias *(Jane)*, Julie Garfield *(Fran)*, Marvin Lichterman *(Dean)*, Marian Mercer *(Mags Elliot)*, Susan Taylor *(Minnie)*, Olympia Dukakis *(John's Mother)*, Carl Parker *(Tennis Player)*, Richard Clarke *(Charlie)*, Cleavon Little *(Film Director)*, Marilyn Chris *(His Wife)*, Alexander Cort *(Imaginary Film Director)*, Kristoffer Tabori *(Boy Scout)*.

They took some large chances with this slim story by making it as adult as they could—something unique for 1969. There are no tricks to the movie, just a careful examination and dissection of the social mores of the period but done with such wit and good humor that it leaves the audience feeling wonderful at the conclusion. Hoffman is a furniture designer out at Maxwell's Plum, a well-known East Side Manhattan singles bar, when he meets Farrow, an assistant in an art gallery. With hardly any warning, they are soon in his apartment making love. Afterwards, she awakens and wants to see if she can learn anything about him through his possessions, so she examines his books, music, and pictures of his former lover, Griffin, a model. Farrow enters the bathroom to shower and Hoffman now peruses her purse to see what he can learn about her. They share breakfast and we can see how wary both of them are, due to so many past affairs that wounded their psyches. In a series of flashbacks, they reveal the sources of their hurt. Griffin had once arrived at Hoffman's apartment with all her gear and announced that she was moving in with him; Farrow had an abortive affair with Tolan, a married politico. Their conversation is lively but non-committal. Farrow leaves, then returns when she realizes she's left her keys at Hoffman's apartment. He prepares lunch for her, then she naps in his bed and the spectre of Tolan appears in her dream. By the time she awakens, Hoffman has noted a similarity between her and his mother which disturbs him enough to ask her to leave. Before she does, she writes her phone number on a mirror. Hoffman wipes that off and attends a noisy party thrown by Griffin but keeps thinking about Farrow. He taxis to her neighborhood and searches for her in vain, then returns to his apartment where she is cooking dinner for him. They climb into bed again and finally give each other their names, something that was studiously (and conveniently) avoided in the previous 91 minutes. And what was a casual sex date now begins to develop into a legitimate relationship. That's about the entire plot but it rings so true that we are enmeshed in their stories and quietly root for them to find happiness with each other. Written with great depth by British playwright/attorney Mortimer, JOHN AND MARY is, on the surface, deceptively simple. However, watching it closely, one revels in the insights. A lovely film on all levels.

p, Ben Kadish; d, Peter Yates; w, John Mortimer (based on a novel by Mervyn Jones); ph, Gayne Rescher (Panavision, DeLuxe Color) m, Quincy Jones; ed, Frank P. Keller; prod d, John Robert Lloyd; art d, Robert Wightman; set d, Philip Smith; cos, Anthea Sylbert; spec eff, L.B. Abbott, Art Cruickshank; m/l, "Maybe Tomorrow," Jones, Alan and Marilyn Bergman; makeup, Irving Buchman.

Drama **(PR:O MPAA:R)**

JOHN GOLDFARB, PLEASE COME HOME**
(1964) 95m Parker-Orchard/FOX c

Shirley MacLaine *(Jenny Ericson)*, Peter Ustinov *(King Fawz)*, Richard Crenna *(John Goldfarb)*, Jim Backus *(Miles Whitepaper)*, Scott Brady *(Sakalakis)*, Fred Clark *(Heinous Overreach)*, Wilfrid Hyde-White *(Mustafa Guz)*, Harry Morgan *(Deems Sarajevo)*, Patrick Adiarte *(Prince Ammud)*, Richard Deacon *(Maginot)*, Jerome Cowan *(Brinkley)*, Leon Askin *(Samir)*, David Lewis *(Cronkite)*, Milton Frome *(Air Force General)*, Charles Lane *(Editor of "Strife")*, Jerry Orbach *(Pinkerton)*, Jackie Coogan *(Father Ryan)*, Telly Savalas *(Harem Recruiter)*, Angela Douglas *(Mandy)*, Richard Wilson *(Frobish)*, Nai Bonet, Sultana *(Specialty Dancers)*, Barbara Bouchet *(Astrid Porche)*, Ann Morell *(Floating Harem Girl)*, Shelby Grant, Eve Bruce, Gari Hardy, Irene Tsu, Jane Wald, Linda Foster *(Harem Girls)*, Stanley Ralph Ross *(Muezzin)*.

A mostly silly, sometimes amusing but, in general, flat attempt at an international comedy that would have lost a fortune were it not for the fact that Notre Dame University sued the studio and many people flocked to the theaters to see the reason why. CIA boss Clark dispatches Crenna on a U-2 flight over the USSR, despite the objections of Deacon, U.S. Secretary of Defense. (Some readers will recall this did actually happen and President Eisenhower denied it vehemently, despite the fact that the pilot was shot down and captured by the Russians). Crenna, known as "Wrong Way" Goldfarb because he once ran a touchdown in the wrong direction for his team and also took his team to the state of Washington when they were supposed to play in Florida, crash-lands in the mythical Arabian country of Fawzia. At the same time, MacLaine, an American magazine journalist is insinuating herself into the king's harem so she can write an exposé. Ustinov is the bumbling king of the desert land and currently livid because his son, Adiarte, has been sent home from Notre Dame after being cut from the football squad. Ustinov has a football field built for Adiarte and, in a fit of pique, calls off relations with the U.S. This upsets Washington as they'd hoped to build a base in Fawzia, which is quite close to Russia. When Crenna lands, Ustinov, a football fan, recognizes him and demands that he either coach the Fawzia University football team or be turned over to Russia as a spy. Crenna takes the job, but his charges are such klutzes that he gets depressed. Ustinov then offers him his choice of the harem and MacLaine pleads that he choose her. This he does and they soon fall in love. Ustinov informs Cowan, the envoy, that the U.S. may build their facility on the condition that Notre Dame send their squad to play against Fawzia. The team arrives with instructions to throw the game, but coach Brady won't hear of it. In the end, MacLaine is given the ball to carry and the collegians are too kind to tackle her so she crosses the line with the winning touchdown. MacLaine looked boyish alongside the harem dwellers, and Ustinov was hammier than the Smithfield packing house. It was produced by MacLaine's husband, Parker, and cost more than $4 million. Notre Dame, which objected to a scene where the collegians were entertained by the harem girls, lost the case on appeal at the New York State Court at Albany.

p, Steve Parker; d, J. Lee Thompson; w, William Peter Blatty; ph, Leon Shamroy (CinemaScope, DeLuxe Color); ed, William B. Murphy; m, Johnny Williams; art d, Jack Martin Smith, Dale Hennesy; set d, Walter M. Scott, Stuart A. Reiss; cos, Edith Head, Adele Balkan; spec eff, L.B. Abbott, Emil Kosa, Jr.; ch, Paul Godkin; m/l, "John Goldfarb, Please Come Home," Williams, Don Wolf (sung by Jaye P. Morgan); makeup, Ben Nye, Frank Westmore.

Comedy **(PR:A-C MPAA:NR)**

JOHN HALIFAX—GENTLEMAN* (1938, Brit.) 69m MGM bw

John Warwick *(John Halifax)*, Nancy Burne *(Ursula March)*, Ralph Michael *(Phineas Fletcher)*, D.J. Williams *(Abel Fletcher)*, Brian Buchel *(Lord Luxmore)*, Billy Bray *(Tully)*, Elsie Wagstaffe *(Jael)*, W.E. Holloway, Hugh Bickett, Roddy McDowall.

Highpoint of this listless melodrama is a glimpse of Roddy McDowall prior to his wartime evacuation to the U.S. and HOW GREEN WAS MY VALLEY, though his role here is extremely minor. Not much overall value in this costume drama, set in the late Eighteenth Century as Warwick plays the man with beginnings as a mere vagrant, who, through hard work, a compassionate nature, and the desire to see that justice is maintained, rises to be wealthy and much loved. As acted and directed here, such a depiction of admirable characteristics does not make for a very good film.

p&d, George King; w, A.R. Rawlinson (based on the novel by Mrs. Craik); ph, Hone Glendinning.

Drama **(PR:A MPAA:NR)**

JOHN LOVES MARY½** (1949) 96m WB bw

Ronald Reagan *(John Lawrence)*, Jack Carson *(Fred Taylor)*, Patricia Neal *(Mary McKinley)*, Wayne Morris *(Lt. O'Leary)*, Edward Arnold *(Sen. McKinley)*, Virginia Field *(Lilly Herbish)*, Katherine Alexander *(Phyllis McKinley)*, Paul Harvey *(Gen. Biddle)*, Ernest Cossart *(Oscar Dugan)*, Irving Bacon *(Beachwood)*, George B. Hickman *(Soldier)*, Larry Rio *(Cab Driver)*, Nino Pepitone *(Raoul, the Headwaiter)*, Rodney Bell, Creighton Hale *(Waiters)*, Rudy Friml *(Orchestra Leader)*, Ray Montgomery *(Elevator Man)*, Jack Mower *(Bartender)*, Russell Arms *(Corporal)*, Douglas Kennedy *(Colonel)*, Philo McCullough *(Desk Clerk)*.

Reagan plays a soldier stationed in England who owes his buddy Carson a big favor for saving his life. Carson's girl friend, Field, wants to go the U.S. to marry her beau, but can't travel as a single girl. Reagan agrees to marry her on condition that they divorce after arrival. Word gets back to Reagan's fiancee, Neal, about the marriage and she tells her father, Arnold, the senator. Reagan discovers that Carson has already married someone else and is an expectant father. His life is seemingly ruined until it is discovered that army lieutenant Morris had secretly married Field in England, and then had himself reported killed in order to escape the marriage. All is righted and Reagan marries the senator's daughter. When the idea for this film was proposed, Reagan protested, saying that stories about returning soldiers were growing stale. However, the Broadway version was a big hit and Reagan's protests were ignored. The film is an amusing little comedy, though nothing special. Reagan gives his usual nice guy performance. This film was to have been the screen debut of Neal, but the studio wisely held it back until after the release of the much more impressive THE FOUNTAINHEAD.

p, Jerry Wald; d, David Butler; w, Phoebe Ephron, Henry Ephron (based on the play by Norman Krasna); ph, J. Peverell Marley; m, David Buttolph; ed, Irene Morra; art d, Robert Haas; set d, William Kuehl; cos, Milo Anderson; spec eff, William McGann, Robert Burks; makeup, Perc Westmore, Bill Crosley.

Comedy **(PR:A MPAA:NR)**

JOHN MEADE'S WOMAN** (1937) 81m PAR bw

Edward Arnold *(John Meade)*, Francine Larrimore *(Teddy Connor)*, Gail Patrick *(Caroline Haig)*, George Bancroft *(Tim Mathews)*, John Trent *(Mike)*, Sidney Blackmer *(Rodney)*, Jonathan Hale *(Melton)*, Stanley Andrews *(Westley)*, Harry Hayden *(Gallatin)*, Robert Strange *(Blaney)*, Aileen Pringle *(Mrs. Melton)*, Willard Robertson.

Arnold, a timber magnate, meets Larrimore, a country girl who marries him on the rebound. When her new husband starts to cheat farmers out of their land, she takes the side of the underdog and unites them in a revolt against Arnold. This was Larrimore's screen debut and she deserved far better fare. The film's message comes through loud and clear—you'd have to be sleeping to miss it, and there's a good chance you may be.

p, B.P. Schulberg; d, Richard Wallace; w, Vincent Lawrence, Herman J. Mankiewicz (based on an original story by John Bright, Robert Tasker); ph, Harry Fischbeck; m, Frederick Hollander; ed, Robert Bischoff.

Drama **(PR:C MPAA:NR)**

JOHN OF THE FAIR** 1/2 (1962, Brit.) 63m Merton Park/Continental bw

John Charlesworth *(John Claydon)*, Arthur Young *("Doc" Claydon)*, Richard George *(William Samuels)*, Michael Mulcaster *(Jasper Sly)*, Hilda Barry *(Ma Miggs)*, Carol Wolveridge *(Jill)*, Sidney Bland *(Gilroy)*, David Garth *(Sir Thomas Renton)*, Fanny Wright *(Sarah Wilmott)*, Tom Clegg *(Valdar)*.

Charlesworth is a 14-year-old boy who assists Young at his carnival medicine booth. He assumes the man is his father but is kidnaped by evil uncle Garth and discovers he has inherited an important title. Actually Garth wants the title for himself and, after the boy manages to escape, starts a fire that kills Young. Led by Clegg, the carnival strongman, a fight ensues between the good and bad forces. Charlesworth is brought to trial but parish records prove his true background and he inherits his title. Nice little story, circa 18th century England. Though released in Britain in 1952, American audiences didn't see it until 10 years later.

p, Frank A. Hoare; d&w, Michael McCarthy (based on "John Of The Fair" by Arthur William Groom); ph, Joe Ambor; m, Max Saunders; ed, Eric Hodges; art d, George Haslam.

Children's Adventure **(PR:AAA MPAA:NR)**

JOHN PAUL JONES*** (1959) 126m WB c

Robert Stack *(John Paul Jones)*, Bette Davis *(Catherine the Great)*, Marisa Pavan *(Aimee de Tellison)*, Charles Coburn *(Benjamin Franklin)*, Erin O'Brien *(Dorothea Danders)*, Macdonald Carey *(Patrick Henry)*, Jean Pierre Aumont *(King Louis XVI)*, David Farrar *(John Wilkes)*, Peter Cushing *(Capt. Pearson)*, Susana Canales *(Marie Antoinette)*, Jorge Riviere *(Russian Chamberlain)*, Tom Brannum *(Peter Wooley)*, Bruce Cabot *(Gunner Lowrie)*, Basil Sydney *(Sir William Young)*, John Crawford *(George Washington)*, Felix de Pomes *(French Chamberlain)*, Thomas Gomez *(Esek Hopkins)*, Judson Laure, Bob Cunningham, John Charles Farrow *(John Paul)*, Eric Pohlmann, Pepe Nieto, Patrick Villiers, Frank Latimore *(Lt. Richard Dale)*, Ford Rainey *(Lt. Simpson)*, Bruce Seton, Paul Curran, George Rigaud, Rupert Davies, Nicholas Brady, Robert Ayres, Christopher Rhodes, Macdonald Parke *(Arthur Lee)*, John Phillips, David Phethean, Mitchell Kowal, Reed de Rouen, Charles Wise, Archie Lyall, Al Brown, Randolph McKenzie, Phil Brown, Archie Duncan.

It's big, expensive, and sometimes tedious, in the style producer Bronston made acceptable if not famous, with Stack in the most important role of his on-and-off career. Stack is America's greatest naval hero, John Paul Jones, who begs a tiny command out of the impoverished Continental Congress during the Revolutionary War. He wins great battles but is seldom recognized and he even delivers the famous line: "I have not yet begun to fight!" during the heroic battle between the American warship *Bon Homme Richard* and the British *Serapis*. Following the conclusion of the war, Jones urges the Congress to maintain a strong Navy but is ignored. To get the pesky seaman out of the way, he is sent to Russia to help out Catherine the Great. He meets Catherine—Davis in a startling 60-second cameo—then goes on to win more sea battles in the Black Sea. Ill, Stack returns to France, long his home, where he dies in the arms of Pavan, a royal lady who has spurned him in the past, as has another, O'Brien, because of his low-born station in life. Stack is believable if not energetic in this somewhat wooden biopic, which comes alive especially during the battle scenes. Farrow's direction flags between the action scenes and the overlong film grows boring in spots. Carey, as the patriotic Patrick Henry, and Coburn, as the crusty but wise Benjamin Franklin, are well cast, but Pavan is a disaster; she cannot act and worse, she appears unattractive and even ill.

p, Samuel Bronston; d, John Farrow; w, Farrow, Jesse Lasky, Jr. (based on the story "Nor'wester" by Clements Ripley); ph, Michel Kelber (Technirama, Technicolor); m, Max Steiner; ed, Eda Warren; art d, Franz Bachelin; cos, Phyllis Dalton; ch, Hector Zaraspe; spec eff, Roscoe S. Cline; makeup, Neville Smallwood.

Biography **(PR:A MPAA:NR)**

JOHN WESLEY***

(1954, Brit.) 77m Radio & Film Commission of Methodist Church c

Leonard Sachs *(John Wesley)*, Gerald Loham *(Wesley as a Child)*, Neil Heayes *(Wesley as a Student)*, Keith Pyott *(Rev. Samuel Wesley)*, Curigwen Lewis *(Susannah Wesley)*, John Witty *(Peter Bohler, a Moravian)*, Derek Aylward *(Charles Wesley)*, Patrick Barton *(George Whitefield)*, John Slater *(Condemned Man)*, Philip Lever *(Beau Nash)*, Joss Ambler, Col. Oglethorpe, Andrew Cruickshank, Horace Sequiera, Sidney Monckton, Erik Chitty, George Bishop, Milton Rosmer *(Trustees for Georgia)*, Henry Hewitt *(Bishop of Bristol)*, Patrick Holt *(Thomas Maxfield)*, Arthur Young *(King George II)*, Vincent Holman *(Beaumont, a Quaker)*, Edward Jewesbury *(James Hutton)*, Julian Mitchell *(Tom Dekkar)*, Harry Towb *(Michael O'Rory)*, Neil Arden *(William Holland)*, F.B.J. Sharp *(Vicar)*, Roger Maxwell *(Gen. Holt)*, Rodney Hughes *(Mr. Bligh)*.

This handsomely mounted biography of the great Methodist leader was originally conceived as a short black and white film. It was expanded, however, to include more of Wesley's life and work. It was financed by J. Arthur Rank, an important Methodist layman, and produced through their church. The film's plot is short, showing the young Wesley through his studies and the development of his principles. The production values are excellent and Sachs' portrayal is superb. The initial release of the film went to some 500 churches who all contributed to the $200,000 budget in return for first rights on viewing.

d, Norman Walker; w, Lawrence Barrett; ph, Hone Glendenning, Stanley Grant (Eastmancolor); m, Henry Reed; ed, Dave Powell.

Religious Biography **(PR:AAA MPAA:NR)**

JOHNNY ALLEGRO** (1949) 80m COL bw (GB: HOUNDED)

George Raft *(Johnny Allegro)*, Nina Foch *(Glenda Chapman)*, George Macready *(Morgan Vallin)*, Will Geer *(Schultzy)*, Gloria Henry *(Addie)*, Ivan Triesault *(Pelham Vetch)*, Harry Antrim *(Pudgy)*, William "Bill" Phillips *(Roy)*, Walter Rode *(Grote)*, Thomas Browne Henry *(Detective)*, Paul E. Burns *(Gray)*, Matilda Caldwell *(Servant)*, Joe Palma, Charles Hamilton, Brick Sullivan *(Guards)*, George Offerman *(Elevator Boy)*, Fred Sears *(Desk Clerk)*, Eddie Acuff *(Maintenance Man)*, Saul Gorss *(Jeffrey)*, Cosmo Sardo *(Waiter)*, Larry Thompson *(Operator)*, Frank Dae *(Dr. Jaynes)*, Mary Bear *(Nurse)*, Gaylord "Steve" Pendleton *(Young Man)*, Harlan Warde *(Coast Guard Officer)*.

JOHNNY ALLEGRO has a little bit of several movies, including THE MOST DANGEROUS GAME, in its heritage. Raft is an ex-gangster who is tapped by the Treasury Department to do some investigative work on their behalf. Macready is a villain flooding the U.S. with counterfeit money. He heads a plot of right-wingers who want to overthrow the U.S. government from his private island in the Caribbean. Raft poses as a fugitive and is taken in by Macready, an effete, classical-music lover in the villainous mold of so many who came later in the James Bond films. Once on the island, Raft learns that Macready likes to hunt his guests down with silver-tipped arrows. Raft has enlisted Foch to be part of his plot, and the two of them are in danger of being killed when the Feds, led by Geer, arrive in the nick of time to save them. Raft had a lot of physical work to do in this film, including several fights, lots of running, and enough to get a 54-year-old (his age at the time) quite winded. His acting was, as usual, almost devoid of any emotion, but there was a coterie of Raft fans who liked him that way. Macready was always believable in his many black roles and showed himself off to be one of the best there was at that job. He was born to play the heavy and always looked much older than he was. Matter of fact, he was only 40 at the time of this film. In later years, Macready teamed with Vincent Price in an art gallery and made many voice-over commercials, including a stint as the spokesman for Hunt Foods. The scar on his cheek that caused his face to be permanently malevolent was the result of a car accident, not a duel at Heidelberg, as many once thought. Despite being little more than a potboiler, JOHNNY ALLEGRO had enough originality in the plot to keep it moving, and one can recognize many of the twists and turns in subsequent spy films. This was Raft's second "Johnny" picture, the first being JOHNNY ANGEL, four years earlier.

p, Irving Starr; d, Ted Tetzlaff; w, Karen DeWolf, Guy Endore (based on a story by James Edward Grant); ph, Joseph Biroc; m, George Duning; ed, Jerome Thoms; md, Morris Stoloff; art d, Perry Smith; set d, Frank Tuttle; cos, Jean Louis; makeup, Irving Berns.

Crime Drama **(PR:A-C MPAA:NR)**

JOHNNY ANGEL** (1945) 79m RKO bw

George Raft *(Johnny Angel)*, Claire Trevor *(Lilah)*, Signe Hasso *(Paulette)*, Lowell Gilmore *(Sam Jewell)*, Hoagy Carmichael *(Celestial O'Brien)*, Marvin Miller *(Gustafson)*, Margaret Wycherly *(Miss Drumm)*, J. Farrell MacDonald *(Capt. Angel)*, Mack Gray *(Bartender)*, Jason Robards, Sr., Marc Cramer *(Officers)*, Bill Williams *(Big Sailor)*, Robert Anderson, Bryant Washburn, Russell Hopton, Carl Kent *(Reporters)*, Chili Williams *(Redhead)*, Rusty Farrell *(Blond)*, Virginia Belmont *(Cigarette Girl)*, Rosemary LaPlanche *(Hatcheck Girl)*, Ann Codee *(Charwoman)*, Wade Crosby *(Watchman)*, O.M. Steiger *(Frenchman)*, Eddy Hart *(Seedy Sailor)*, Johnny Indrisano *(Al)*, Jack Overman *(Biggsy)*, Bert Holm *(Isherwood)*, Eddie Lewis *(Black Boy)*, Aina Constant *(Secretary)*, Ed Dearing, Philip Morris *(Cops)*, Louis Mercier *(Cigar Maker)*, Theodore Rand *(Headwaiter)*, James Flavin *(Mate)*, Don Brodie *(Clerk on Putnam)*, Kernan Cripps, Perc Launders *(Officials)*, John Hamilton *(Ship Captain)*, Marcel De La Bross *(French Civilian)*, Al Rhein *(Checker)*, Joe Ray *(3rd Mate)*, Leland Hodgson *(Paul Jewell)*, Alf Haugan, Charles Sullivan,

Jimmy O'Gatty *(Sailors)*, Ernie Adams *(Leslie)*, Al Murphy *(Lookout)*, George Magrill *(Man)*.

JOHNNY ANGEL did better at the box office than it deserved. It's complex, filled with klutzy flashbacks, and much of the acting is ordinary. Fortunately, Marin's direction may have saved the day as it is moody and reeks of the film noir genre. MacDonald, captain of the "Quincy," is bringing $5 million worth of Free French bullion back from Casablanca to New Orleans, his home port. When he and his men are found dead on the vessel, Raft, his son, vows to find his father's murderers. Raft is also a ship's captain and uses his contacts in his search. One of his pals is Carmichael, a cab driver with a penchant for bon mots. Miller, who owned the ship, evinces a strange lack of interest in the murders. He's an odd sort who has been raised by Wycherly, his nurse, since childhood and she is now his secretary. Raft and Carmichael nose around until they locate Hasso, who saw the crime. Carmichael puts her on ice until she spills the truth: Miller killed MacDonald and the others and escaped with the gold. Raft goes after Miller and works on him until he admits the killings, claiming that it was his wife, Trevor, who put him up to it. Miller is about to kill Raft when Wycherly enters and kills Miller. Raft cedes Trevor over to the cops and is now satisfied that his job is done. New Orleans is the backdrop and the photography is excellent. Miller is good as a child in a man's body who is manipulated by his money-hungry wife and the mother figure who eventually takes his life. Too much talk and not enough action are what mars this film most of all. Pereira, better known for his special effects work on Cecil B. DeMille's REAP THE WILD WIND, for which he won an Oscar, makes his debut here as a producer.

p, William L. Pereira; d, Edwin L. Marin; w, Steve Fisher, Frank Gruber (based on the novel *Mr. Angel Comes Aboard* by Charles Gordon Booth); ph, Harry J. Wild; m, Leigh Harline; ed, Les Millbrook; md, Constantin Bakaleinikoff; art d, Albert S. D'Agostino, Jack Okey; set d, Darrell Silvera, William Stevens; cos, Rennie; spec eff, Vernon L. Walker; m/l, "Memphis in June," Hoagy Carmichael, Paul Francis Webster.

Crime Drama **Cas.** **(PR:A MPAA:NR)**

JOHNNY APOLLO* 1/2** (1940) 93m FOX bw

Tyrone Power *(Bob Cain [Johnny Apollo])*, Dorothy Lamour *(Mabel "Lucky" DuBarry)*, Lloyd Nolan *(Mickey Dwyer)*, Edward Arnold *(Robert Cain, Sr.)*, Charley Grapewin *(Judge Emmett T. Brennan)*, Lionel Atwill *(Jim McLaughlin)*, Marc Lawrence *(John Bates)*, Jonathan Hale *(Dr. Brown)*, Russell Hicks *(District Attorney)*, Fuzzy Knight *(Cellmate)*, Charles Lane *(Assistant District Attorney)*, Selmer Jackson *(Warden)*, Charles Trowbridge *(Judge Penrose)*, George Irving *(Mr. Ives)*, Eddie Marr *(Harry the Henchman)*, Anthony Caruso *(Joe the Henchman)*, Harry Rosenthal *(Piano Player)*, Eric Wilton *(Butler)*, Harry Tyler *(Trusty)*, Stanley Andrews *(Welfare Secretary)*, Wally Albright *(Office Boy)*, Charles Tannen, Milburn Stone *(Reporters)*, Tom Dugan *(Tom the Prisoner)*, James Flavin *(Guard)*, Walter Miller *(Guard in Solitary)*, Robert Shaw *(Clerk)*, Ed Gargan *(Detective)*, Gary Breckner *(Announcer)*, Bess Flowers *(Secretary)*, Geneva Sawyer *("La Conga" Dancer)*, William Pawley *(Paul)*, Charles Williams *(Photographer)*, Phil Tead *(Reporter)*, Jim Pierce, William Haade, Louis Jean Heydt, Stanley Blystone, Don Rowan, James Blain *(Guards)*, Emmett Vogan *(Guard-Announcer)*, Charles D. Brown *(Detective)*.

A taut, well-acted gangster melodrama, JOHNNY APOLLO stars the handsome Power, then the biggest star at Fox, wonderfully supported by Arnold as his father, Lamour as his paramour, and Nolan as his bad guy pal. Power is the son of a wealthy broker, Arnold, and hasn't a worry in the world. He attends an Ivy League school and is a model student and a devoted son. Arnold is suddenly accused of embezzling and is sent to jail. Power is so disgusted with his father that he changes his name, thinking no one will hire him if he uses his father's name. Oddly, he is fired from a white collar job by an employer who learns Power's real name, telling Power that *his* father made a mistake once and he kept his name and worked hard to make it good again. Power finally comes to his senses and decides to get enough money to get Arnold out of prison. He goes to a drunken lawyer, Grapewin, a known fixer, who tells Power that he must get a lot of money to set Arnold free. To that end, Power gets a job with mobster Nolan who takes a liking to Power's charm and educated style. So too does Lamour, Nolan's girl. Power takes another alias, Johnny Apollo, and becomes infamous under that sobriquet. When Grapewin gets religion and decides to present enough evidence to the authorities that will imprison Nolan, the mobster has him killed. Nolan and Power are later sent to prison together where Arnold refuses to recognize his son, hating him for becoming a gangster. Nolan attempts a break but Arnold, who has been warned by Lamour who wants to help Power rehabilitate himself, steps forward, trying to stop Nolan. The vicious gangster drops his nice guy pose and shoots Arnold, which enrages Power. Power and Nolan struggle for the gun and Nolan is killed. Power is about to be tried as Nolan's killer but Arnold regains consciousness and clears his son by telling the warden that Power helped him stop the break. Both father and son are later released to make new lives for themselves, Lamour at Power's side. Though somewhat predictable, the tale of big city crime moves along swiftly under Hathaway's expert direction. Power is convincing as the errant son and Arnold is a standout as the noble father who made one big mistake and willingly pays for it by slaving away in the prison boiler shop. Grapewin has some good moments as the mostly stewed barrister and Nolan is a nice guy on the outside and rotten to the core inside, a patented posture. Lamour as the song-and-dance girl in Nolan's nightclub is only fair. She strains her voice and shows a lot of leg but she's merely a cute prop for the boys to fondle. This was the first of five films Power would make with Hathaway.

p, Darryl F. Zanuck; d, Henry Hathaway; w, Philip Dunne, Rowland Brown (based on a story by Samuel G. Engel, Hal Long); ph, Arthur Miller; m, Frank Loesser, Lionel Newman, Alfred Newman, Mack Gordon; ed, Robert Bischoff; md, Cyril J. Mockridge; art d, Richard Day, Wiard B. Ihnen; set d, Thomas Little; cos, Gwen Wakeling; m/l, "Dancing for Nickels and Dimes," "Your Kiss," Alfred Newman, Frank Loesser, "This is the Beginning of the End," Mack Gordon.

Crime Drama **(PR:A MPAA:NR)**

JOHNNY BANCO* 1/2

(1969, Fr./Ital./Ger.) 95m Norddeutsche-Chrysaor-Le Film d'Art Variety/Ben Barry c (JOHNNY BANCO—GELIEBTER TAUGENICHTS)

Horst Buchholz *(Johnny Banco)*, Sylva Koscina *(Laureen Moore)*, Michel de Re *(Orso Sebastiani)*, Jean Paredes *(Anchois)*, Fee Calderon *(Mignon de Brandie)*, Elisabeth Wiener *(Nati)*, Luciana Vincenzi *(Mary)*, Friedrich Joloff *(Aristopoulos)*, Romain Bouteille *(Eveillee)*, Walter Giller *(Commissioner Jakubowski)*, Mario Pisu.

Buchholz is the owner of a gambling casino in Barcelona who steals 100 million francs from de Re, a reputed gangster and dealer of bogus antiques. Chased by de Re's bloodthirsty henchmen, Buchholz heads to Monte Carlo, pretending to be a millionaire, and marries rich American widow Koscina. When de Re hears of the marriage, he and Buchholz's former mistress, Wiener, go to Monte Carlo and win back his fortune. This forces Buchholz to consider murdering his bride to collect her wealth but de Re beats him to the task, and has Buchholz accused of the crime. Rambling and ultimately boring, the film is further hampered by Buchholz's weak performance as he tries to play it for laughs while lacking the necessary comic talents.

p, Gottfried Wegeleben, Paul Temps; d, Yves Allegret; w, Jean Vermorel, Allegret, James Garter, Michel Audiard; ph, Michel Kelber (Eastmancolor); m, Michel Magne, Luigi Russelli; ed, Henri Rust; art d, Jean d'Eaubonne.

Action/Drama **(PR:O MPAA:NR)**

JOHNNY BELINDA***** (1948) 102m WB bw

Jane Wyman *(Belinda McDonald)*, Lew Ayres *(Dr. Robert Richardson)*, Charles Bickford *(Black McDonald)*, Agnes Moorehead *(Aggie McDonald)*, Stephen McNally *(Locky McCormick)*, Jan Sterling *(Stella McGuire)*, Rosalind Ivan *(Mrs. Peggety)*, Dan Seymour *(Pacquet)*, Mabel Paige *(Mrs. Lutz)*, Ida Moore *(Mrs. McKee)*, Alan Napier *(Defense Attorney)*, Monte Blue *(Ben)*, Douglas Kennedy *(Mountie)*, James Craven *(Interpreter)*, Richard Taylor *(Floyd McQuiggen)*, Richard Walsh *(Fergus McQuiggen)*, Joan Winfield *(Mrs. Tim Moore)*, Ian Wolfe *(Rector)*, Holmes Herbert *(Judge)*, Jonathan Hale *(Dr. Gray)*, Ray Montgomery *(Tim Moore)*, Creighton Hale *(Bailiff)*, Fred Worlock *(Prosecutor)*, Barbara Bates *(Gracie Anderson)*, Blayney Lewis *(Dan'l)*, Charles Horvath *(Churchgoer)*, Snub Pollard, Franklyn Farnum *(Jurymen)*.

After 15 years of hoofing her way through Warner Bros. films as a chorus girl and second fiddle friend of lady leads, Wyman finally got her dream part as the sensitive deaf-mute in JOHNNY BELINDA. She not only made the most of a compelling and utterly fascinating role, she drew from wellsprings of creativity a performance no one in Hollywood ever believed possible. Wyman, as the forlorn Belinda, is the unwanted daughter of Bickford, a stoic, iron-willed New England farmer who has never forgiven his child for the death of a wife who died giving her birth. Ayres is a kindly doctor practicing in the nearby town who befriends Wyman and teaches her sign language, chastising all in the community who cruelly refer to her as "The Dummy." Slowly, Wyman's true nature, one that is sweet and loving, emerges which attracts the attention of brutish McNally, the local bully. Drunk, he attacks and rapes Wyman one night. She delivers a child which everyone believes has been fathered by Ayres, a situation which later forces him to leave the community in disgrace. At first Bickford, too, believes Ayres is the father of little Johnny Belinda but he learns that McNally is the guilty party and confronts the thug. McNally kills Bickford and tosses his body over a cliff to make the murder appear like an accident. Bickford's death is accepted as misadventure but McNally undoes himself when he suddenly decides that he wants his child. He goes to Wyman and raves on, wrongly convincing her that he intends to harm the infant. Wyman grabs a gun and kills her tormentor and is later put on trial for murder. All seems hopeless as the prosecution appears to offer an airtight case against the hapless deaf-mute, but Sterling, McNally's wife, courageously steps forward and tells the court that her sleazy husband was the real father of Johnny Belinda and it is soon accepted that Wyman acted in self-defense. She is freed and the enlightened citizens not only see the cruel errors of their ways in dealing with Wyman but they open their hearts to her. At the finish, patient and loving Ayres is waiting for Wyman and her child. This fragile theme could have been completely destroyed by less competent hands than director Negulesco and scripters von Cube and Vincent. The story, based on the smash play by Harris, was almost filmed word for word from the original, so well did it lend itself to lensing. Wyman, of course, renders a role that was unequalled as she miraculously drew forth an incandescent portrait of beauty and innocence. Much to his credit, producer Wald decided to spare no expense in making the film. He hired Bickford, who had scored heavily in THE FARMER'S DAUGHTER for which many felt he would receive an Oscar nomination, paying this splendid character actor a substantial $5,000 a week. Ayres was signed as the doctor, then a normal choice since he had just finished playing a physician with great results in THE DARK MIRROR with Olivia de Havilland. Rory Calhoun was tested for the rapist role, but McNally, who had appeared in the original stage play as the doctor, and who had been very effective as a villain in recent movies, won the part. The role of the rapist's unhappy wife almost went to Janis Paige but Jan Sterling, a newly arrived actress, was given it after an impressive screen test. Ayres was unhappy when he was told that his own selection for the deaf-mute part, Teresa Wright, was not available, and he showed more displeasure when he was told that Wyman had been assigned the role. "It's all in the breaks," Wyman later said. "I have to thank Jerry Wald for JOHNNY BELINDA. When he was casting the picture, he insisted I do the part. I wasn't so sure, but he won out and I'm really grateful." A sign language expert, Elizabeth Gessner, was hired at $35-a-day to help Wyman with the deaf mute part. Moreover, the actress studied the behavior of real deaf-mutes as she underwent the most difficult role of her career. She labored for weeks to capture what she called an "anticipation light," one, she observed, is uniquely expressed by deaf people who have a look of eager curiosity to learn and understand. Still Wyman felt an element was absent in her performance: "But even after weeks of tests, my tests, something was missing. Suddenly I realized what was wrong. I could hear. I could act deaf but it lacked a realistic feeling and that showed on my face." She huddled with director Negulesco who suggested that she stuff her ears with wax, which she did, sealing off every noise, except the sound of loud percussions. This created some confusion for her when trying to pick up cue lines from other actors but it was this faltering and groping appearance Wyman projected that made her all the more convincing in her near-impossible role. Making it more difficult were the marital difficulties between Wyman and her husband-actor, Ronald Reagan. He would visit the set with their children regularly but most of his time during this period he was consumed by his absorbing interest in politics, a subject that bored Wyman to tears. Since the story was originally set on the dank and forbidding New England coast, Negulesco, cast and crew, traveled to the rough, jagged coastal area near Mendocino, about 200 miles north of San Francisco. Here cinematographer McCord beautifully captured the deep fog, heavy rain, and driving winds, all of which further dramatized an already dynamic story. None of the special handling of this film impressed the usually thick-witted Jack Warner, head of the studio. When getting the on-location bills for the movie, Warner shouted: "They're up there shooting fog and a bunch of damned seagulls! Who wants to see a picture where the leading lady doesn't say a word?" But the world did want to see this film and Wyman in it; audiences marveled at a performance that cried out to be given an Oscar. Few actresses ever deserved the award more than Wyman. She had been exceptional in THE LOST WEEKEND, but in JOHNNY BELINDA she was spectacular, joining the ranks of the world's greatest actresses. And she did win an Academy Award for her magnificent portrayal, accepting the Oscar and saying: "I accept this award very gratefully—for keeping my mouth shut. I think I'll do it again."

p, Jerry Wald; d, Jean Negulesco; w, Irmgard von Cube, Allen Vincent (based on the play by Elmer Harris); ph, Ted McCord; m, Max Steiner; ed, David Weisbart; md, Mel Dellar; art d, Robert Haas; set d, William Wallace; cos, Milo Anderson; spec eff, William McGann, Edwin DuPar; makeup, Perc Westmore; tech adv, Elizabeth Gessner.

Drama Cas. (PR:C—O MPAA:NR)

JOHNNY COME LATELY**

(1943) 97m UA bw (GB: JOHNNY VAGABOND)

James Cagney *(Tom Richards)*, Grace George *(Vinnie McLeod)*, Marjorie Main *(Gashouse Mary)*, Marjorie Lord *(Jane)*, Hattie McDaniel *(Aida)*, Edward McNamara *(W.W. Dougherty)*, Bill Henry *(Pete Dougherty)*, Robert Barrat *(Bill Swain)*, George Cleveland *(Willie Ferguson)*, Margaret Hamilton *(Myrtle Ferguson)*, Norman Willis *(Dudley Hirsh)*, Lucien Littlefield *(Blaker)*, Edwin Stanley *(Winterbottom)*, Irving Bacon *(Chief of Police)*, Tom Dugan *(1st Cop)*, Charles Irwin *(2nd Cop)*, John Sheehan *(3rd Cop)*, Clarence Muse *(Dougherty's Butler)*, John Miller *(1st Tramp)*, Arthur Hunnicutt *(2nd Tramp)*, Victor Kilian *(Tramp in Box Car)*, Wee Willie Davis *(Bouncer)*, Henry Hall *(Old Timer)*, Joseph Crehan *(Judge Flynn)*, Alec Craig *(Court Bailiff)*.

George had been a stage star for many years before deciding to do a film. This feeble comedy-drama was the only one she ever made, and it did not show off her great stage presence to good advantage. Cagney's brother produced it and that nepotism may have had something to do with the fact that no one noticed it was a lame script. In this, Cagney is an itinerant journalist who is jailed as a vagrant in a tiny town, then paroled to George, the publisher of the local paper. He learns that the city is in the hands of some powerful and corrupt men, and he is determined to toss them out of their influential positions. McNamara, the leader of the bad guys, gets very angry at Cagney's actions. Main runs a dance hall with a no-nonsense attitude and knows where all the town's bodies are buried but won't give Cagney any help. When an election is held, the local honest leaders are dragged off to jail by McNamara's band. Finally, Main acquiesces and tells Cagney of an embezzlement plot that she's uncovered. The crooks are using money collected for an orphanage to maintain their positions. Once he knows this, Cagney publishes the truth in the local paper and the town rises up against the villains. Cagney wastes his talents on this film and has little opportunity to demonstrate his rat-a-tat style. The music by Harline was good enough to get an Oscar nomination but lost out to Alfred Newman for THE SONG OF BERNADETTE in 1943. The best part of the picture was the casting of several superior character people, especially Hamilton, McDaniel, Cleveland and Hunnicutt. It's pleasant enough, and the 1900's sets and costumes are quite authentic, but it never catches fire. The film was made between YANKEE DOODLE DANDY and BLOOD ON THE SUN, two of Cagney's finest. Producer Cagney also oversaw BLOOD ON THE SUN, so it is presumed that he learned a great deal from JOHNNY COME LATELY, his first production.

p, William Cagney; d, William K. Howard; w, John Van Druten (based on the novel *McLeod's Folly* by Louis Bromfield); ph, Theodore Sparkuhl; ed, George Arthur; md, Leigh Harline; art d, Jack Okey; set d, Julia Heron.

Comedy-Drama (PR:A MPAA:NR)

JOHNNY COMES FLYING HOME** (1946) 65m FOX bw

Richard Crane *(Johnny Martin)*, Faye Marlowe *(Sally)*, Martha Stewart *(Ann Cummings)*, Charles Russell *(Miles Carey)*, Roy Roberts *(J.P. Hartley)*, Henry [Harry] Morgan *(Joe Patillo)*, Charles Tannen *(Harry)*, Elaine Langan *(Peggy-Lou)*, Marietta Canty *(Jennie)*, Anthony Sydes *(Butch)*, Selmer Jackson *(Dr. Gunderson)*, John Hamilton *(Metters)*, Harry Tyler *(Grigsby)*, Frank Meredith *(Motorcycle Officer)*, Tom Dugan *(Watchman)*, Grayce Hampton *(Mrs. Bixler)*, Hugh Beaumont *(Engineer)*, Bernie Sell *(Technician)*, Walter Baldwin *(Henry)*, Will Wright *(Foreman)*.

Crane, Russell, and Morgan are three pilots home after WW II, who decide to use their combined knowledge and finances to start their own air freight business. Russell takes on a hazardous test pilot assignment in order to raise additional capital, despite the fact that his wife is about to have a baby. But Crane tricks him out of the job and does the dangerous testing himself, even though he suffers from a mysterious nerve ailment that grounded him during the war. The film is tedious and highly predictable, with less-than-exciting direction. The stock footage of test planes looks good, but that's about it for the visuals. Morgan went on to serve in the Korean War with the highly successful television series M.A.S.H.

p, Aubrey Schenck; d, Ben Stoloff; w, Jack Andrews, George Bricker (based on a story by Andrews); ph, Harry Jackson; m, David Buttolph; ed, John McCafferty; md, Emil Newman; art d, James Basevi, Chester Gore; spec eff, Fred Sersen.

Aviation Drama (PR:A MPAA:NR)

JOHNNY CONCHO* 1/2 (1956) 84m Kent/UA bw

Frank Sinatra *(Johnny Concho)*, Keenan Wynn *(Barney Clark)*, William Conrad *(Tallman)*, Phyllis Kirk *(Mary Dark)*, Wallace Ford *(Albert Dark)*, Christopher Dark *(Walker)*, Howard Petrie *(Helgeson)*, Harry Bartell *(Sam Geen)*, Dan Russ *(Judge Tyler)*, Willis Bouchey *(Sheriff Henderson)*, Robert Osterloh *(Duke Lang)*, Leo Gordon *(Mason)*, Dorothy Adams *(Sarah Dark)*, Jean Byron *(Pearl Lang)*, Claude Akins *(Lem)*, John Qualen *(Jake)*, Wilfred Knapp *(Pearson)*, Ben Wright *(Benson)*, Joe Bassett *(Bartender)*.

One wonders "who would be dumb enough to star New Jersey-born Sinatra in a western?" Then one notes the name of the co-producer is the same as that of the star and the question is answered. Sinatra plays the younger brother of a gunman who had been the fastest gun in Cripple Creek, Arizona, in 1875, until he drew a little slower than the competition, Conrad and Dark. Now the small burg looks to Sinatra to get rid of the killers who have established themselves as the bosses of the town. But Sinatra is a bully and coward and flees the confrontation. He meets Kirk and preacher Wynn, a gun-carrying man of the cloth. They both convince Sinatra that he has to return to Cripple Creek to avenge his brother's murder and to come to grips with his own fears. He goes back to the town and rouses the people to stand up and fight against the villains. There's the customary show-down and Sinatra is wounded, then aided by the townspeople in ridding the village of the criminals. In the end, Sinatra is hailed by the burghers as being his own man and no longer standing in the footsteps of his late brother. It's light on the action and heavy on the dialog, which one might expect from McGuire, a former actor turned novelist and screenwriter. McGuire co-wrote TOOTSIE, as well as MEET DANNY WILSON, and many others. He can be a very funny writer, as witnessed by his novel *1600 Floogle Street*, but you couldn't tell by the screenplay for this one. Conrad went on to become a producer at Warners, as well as the star of his own TV series "Cannon." Gordon was yet another double-duty person in the cast, having written the screenplay for TOBRUK as well as many others, in between being one of the best villains around.

p, Frank Sinatra, Hank Sanicola, d, Don McGuire; w, David P. Harmon, McGuire (based on the story "The Man Who Owned the Town" by Harmon); ph, William Mellor; m, Nelson Riddle; ed, Eda Warren; md, Riddle; art d, Nicolai Remisoff; set d, Gustav Bernsten; cos, Gwen Wakeling, makeup, Bernard Ponedel, Ernest J. Park.

Western (PR:A MPAA:NR)

JOHNNY COOL* (1963) 103m Chrislaw/UA bw

Henry Silva *(Johnny Cool/Giordano)*, Elizabeth Montgomery *(Dare Guiness)*, Richard Anderson *(Correspondent)*, Jim Backus *(Louis Murphy)*, Joey Bishop *(Used Car Salesman)*, Brad Dexter *(Lennart Crandall)*, Wanda Hendrix *(Miss Connolly)*, Hank Henry *(Bus Driver)*, Marc Lawrence *(Johnny Colini)*, John McGiver *(Oby Hinds)*, Gregory Morton *(Jerry March)*, Mort Sahl *(Ben Morro)*, Telly Savalas *(Mr. Santangelo)*, Joan Staley *(Suzy)*, Sammy Davis, Jr. *("Educated")*, Katherine Bard *(Mrs. Crandall)*, Steve Peck *(Kromlein)*, Frank Albertson *(Bill)*, Elisha Cook, Jr. *(Undertaker)*, John Dierkes *("Cripple")*, Douglas Henderson *(FBI Man)*, Mary Scott *(Margaret Huntington)*, Robert Armstrong, Douglas Dumbrille *(Gang Members)*, Joseph Calleia *(Tourist)*, George Neise.

JOHNNY COOL is a bloodbath that never seems to stop. In order to take some of the onus off the non-stop violence, executive producer Peter Lawford called on some of his old pals to make cameo appearances so everyone would know that this wasn't for real. Consequently, the talents of many gifted people are squandered, including Davis, Sahl, Backus, Savalas, and even such old-timers as Dumbrille, Armstrong and Calleia make token appearances. Lawrence is a deported Mafia leader in Sicily (like Lucky Luciano) who has a vendetta against several people who were instrumental in getting him shipped back. He saves the life of Sicilian thug Silva, then grooms him to return to the U.S. to exact vengeance. Silva goes on a killing spree, eliminating many of Lawrence's enemies and in the course of these inhuman events, meets Montgomery (who was married to the producer-director at the time), a rich divorcee. She joins him in his blood-letting and is severely beaten by some surviving hoodlums as a warning to Silva to cease and desist. The FBI soon takes notice and gets on Silva's trail. Dexter, a Hollywood gangster, is next on Silva's list. His house is bombed and the police get a make on Montgomery's car. She now realizes that his thirst for blood doesn't seem to ever be slaked so she finks on him to the gang members, then turns herself in to the authorities. Silva is later murdered in a bloody conclusion. JOHNNY COOL seems to have been made for one reason only, to get a bunch of pals together for a good time. *They* may have had a good time, but anyone watching this picture will be appalled by the gratuitous violence and the "stunt" casting of so many familiar faces. If there was any chance that we could believe the goings-on, it is washed aside with scenes that include Bishop, Hendrix, and Cook in tiny roles. Sammy Davis sings "The Ballad Of Johnny Cool" (Sammy Cahn, Jimmy Van Heusen), and if anyone bought a copy of that record, they must have been deaf.

p&d, William Asher; w, Joseph Landon (based on the book "The Kingdom of Johnny Cool" by John McPartland); ph, Sam Leavitt; m, Billy May; ed, Otto Ludwig; art d, Frank T. Smith; set d, Budd S. Friend; cos, Bob Wolfe; makeup, Frank La Rue.

Crime Drama (PR:O MPAA:NR)

JOHNNY DARK** ½ (1954) 85m UNIV c

Tony Curtis *(Johnny Dark)*, Piper Laurie *(Liz Fielding)*, Don Taylor *(Duke Benson)*, Paul Kelly *(Jim "Scotty" Scott)*, Ilka Chase *(Abbie Binns)*, Sidney Blackmer *(James Fielding)*, Ruth Hampton *(Miss Border-to-Border)*, Russell Johnson *(Emory)*, Joseph Sawyer *(Svenson)*, Robert Nichols *(Smitty)*, Pierre Watkin *(E.J. Winston)*, Ralph Montgomery *(Morgan)*, William Leslie *(Phil Clark)*, Brett Halsey *(Co-driver)*, Scatman Crothers *(Himself)*, Vernon Rich *(Ross)*, Robert Bice *(Guard)*, Byron Kane *(Reno Radio Announcer)*, Emily Belser *(Waitress)*, Don Mitchell *(Announcer)*, Rick Burgess *(Elevator Operator)*, John McKee *(Patrolman)*.

Curtis, an employee for an independent automobile manufacturer, designs and builds a race car for the company but discovers that he is being used by owner Blackmer as a pawn in a company battle against stockholder Watkin. Angered, Curtis steals the car and enters a Canada-to-Mexico cross-country race. His main competition is ex-buddy Taylor, with whom Curtis has fallen out. Of course you know who's going to win the big race, but there's still some exciting action footage along the way, as well as watching Laurie win Curtis' heart. Despite a thin plot, the direction keeps things interesting and the final sequences are good as far as racing films go. Supporting actor Johnson later achieved renown of sorts as one of the castaways on television's "Gilligan's Island." JOHNNY DARK was remade as THE LIVELY SET in 1964.

p, William Alland; d, George Sherman; w, Franklin Coen; ph, Carl Guthrie (Technicolor); m, Joseph Gershenson; ed, Edward Curtiss; art d, Bernard Herzbrun, Robert Boyle.

Action/Racing Drama (PR:A MPAA:NR)

JOHNNY DOESN'T LIVE HERE ANY MORE** ½

(1944) 77m King Brothers/MON bw (AKA: AND SO THEY WERE MARRIED)

Simone Simon *(Kathie Aumont)*, James Ellison *(Mike O'Brien)*, William Terry *(Johnny Moore)*, Minna Gombell *(Mrs. Collins)*, Chick Chandler *(Jack)*, Alan Dinehart *(Judge)*, Gladys Blake *(Sally)*, Robert Mitchum *(CPO Jeff Daniels)*, Dorothy Granger *(Irene)*, Grady Sutton *(George)*, Chester Clute *(Mr. Collins)*, Fern Emmett *(Shrew)*, Jerry Maren *(Gremlin)*, Janet Shaw *(Gladys)*, Charles Williams *(Court Recorder)*, Douglas Fowley *(Rudy)*, Harry Depp *(David, a Neighbor)*, Duke York *(Cab Driver)*, Emmett Lynn, Pat Gleason *(Cab Passengers)*, Milton Kibbee *(Conductor)*, Sid Melton *(Recruit)*, George Chandler *(Charlie Miller, Silk Stocking Salesman)*, Dick Rich *(Marine Sergeant)*, Frank Scannell *(Chauffeur)*, Rondo Hatton *(B. Graves, Undertaker)*, Mike Vallon *(Florist)*, Mary Field *(Subscription Lady)*, George Humbert *(Grocer)*.

Amusing little farce that opens with Terry being inducted into the Army. When his friend Simon needs a place to stay, he gives her the keys to his apartment, forgetting one minor detail: a set of keys belongs to almost every one of his male friends, who use his apartment for their own amusements. Nice-guy Ellison is one of the key-holders and Simon falls in love with him along the way. Good performances, a creative script, and a jaunty directional style make this a fun little comedy. Don't miss an early appearance by Mitchum. This film was reissued several years later and renamed AND SO THEY WERE MARRIED (not to be confused with the 1936 film of the same title), due to Mitchum's quick success. Also his name was moved up to an above-the-title billing, alongside Simon, even though he only appears in the final reel.

p, Maurice King; d, Joe May; w, Philip Yordan, John H. Kafka (based on a story by Alice Means Reeve); ph, Ira Morgan; m, Frank W. Harling; ed, Martin G. Cohn; md, Harling; art d, Paul Palmentola, George Moskov; spec eff, Ray Mercer.

Comedy (PR:A MPAA:NR)

JOHNNY DOUGHBOY** (1943) 64m REP bw

Jane Withers *(Ann Winters/Penelope Ryan)*, Henry Wilcoxon *(Oliver Lawrence)*, Patrick Brook *(Johnny Kelly)*, William Demarest *(Harry Fabian)*, Ruth Donnelly *("Biggy" Bigsworth)*, Etta McDaniel *(Mammy)*, Joline Westbrook *(Jennifer)*, Bobby Breen, Baby Sandy, "Alfalfa" Switzer, "Spanky" McFarland, Butch and Buddy, Cora Sue Collins, Robert Coogan, Grace Costello, The Falkner Orchestra, Karl Kiffe *(Members of the 20 Minus Club)*.

Withers, a 16-year-old movie star tired of playing kid roles, tries a romance with "older man" Wilcoxon, a middle-aged playwright. After much disappointment she finally comes upon happiness (as well as an opportunity to show off some new tap dancing skills) when she joins the "Junior Victory Caravan," a young people's version of the "Hollywood Caravan," touring army camps to give the fighting men a boost of morale. This was intended as a vehicle to elevate Withers to glamor girl status but the results fall far short of that goal. Instead it becomes one of the many Hollywood WW II era films, designed to support the war effort. "Our Gang" comedy youngsters Switzer and McFarland are featured in the "20 Minus Club," as well as former child singing star Breen who was given no songs here as his voice had changed considerably with adolescence. Tunes include: "Baby's A Big Girl Now," "All Done All Through," "It Takes A Guy Like I," "Victory Caravan" (Sammy Cahn, Jule Styne), "All My Life" (Sidney Mitchell, Sammy Stept), "Johnny Doughboy Found A Rose In Ireland," "Better Not Roll Those Big Blue Eyes At Somebody Else" (Kay Twomey, Al Goodhart).

p&d, John H. Auer; w, Lawrence Kimble (based on an original story by Frederick Kohner); ph, John Alton, ed, Wallace Grissell; md, Walter Scharf; art d, Russell Kimball; ch, Nick Castle.

Musical (PR:AA MPAA:NR)

JOHNNY EAGER*** ½ (1942) 107m MGM bw

Robert Taylor *(Johnny Eager)*, Lana Turner *(Lisbeth Bard)*, Edward Arnold *(John Benson Farrell)*, Van Heflin *(Jeff Hartnett)*, Robert Sterling *(Jimmy Lanthrop)*, Patricia Dane *(Garnet)*, Glenda Farrell *(Mae Blythe)*, Barry Nelson *(Lew Rankin)*, Henry O'Neil *(A.J. Verne)*, Charles Dingle *(A. Frazier Marco)*, Cy Kendall *(Bill Halligan)*, Don Costello *(Billiken)*, Paul Stewart *(Julio)*, Diana Lewis *(Judy Sanford)*, Lou Lubin *(Benjy)*, Connie Gilchrist *(Peg Fowler)*, Robin Raymond *(Matilda Fowler)*, Cliff Danielson *(Floyd Markham)*, Leona Maricle *(Miss Mines)*, Joseph Downing *(Ryan)*, Byron Shores *(Joe Agridowski, Officer 711)*, Nestor Paiva *(Tony)*, Douglas Newland *(Cop)*, Gladys Blake, Janet Shaw *(Girls in Verne's Office)*, Alonzo Price, Edward Earle, Hooper Atchley, Stanley Price *(Men)*, Beryl Wallace *(Mabel)*, Georgia Cooper *(Wife)*, Richard Kipling *(Husband)*, Sheldon Bennett *(Headwaiter)*, Joyce Bryant *(Woman)*, Anthony Warde *(Guard)*, Elliott Sullivan *(Ed)*, Pat West *(Hanger-on)*, Jack Carr *(Cupid)*, Art Miles *(Lt. Allen)*, Mike Pat Donovan *(Switchman)*, Gohr Van Vleck *(Frenchman)*, Joe Whitehead *(Ruffing)*, Alice Keating *(Maid)*, John Dilson *(Pawnbroker)*, Charles Thomas *(Bus Conductor)*, Art Belasco, Larry Clifford, Harrison Greene, James C. Morton *(Card Players)*, Alex Pollard *(Butler)*, Alonzo Price *(Man)*, Emory Parnell *(Traffic Cop)*.

Here is crime wrapped in ermine and expensive leather, an underworld that sinks into deep armchairs and drinks imported Scotch, courtesy of MGM's richly mounted JOHNNY EAGER. The suave, excruciatingly handsome Taylor is the title character, as shifty a malefactor as ever bribed a high official or gunned down a rival hoodlum. But at the opening Taylor misleads viewers and his parole officer. He wears a cab driver's hat and coat and reports to his kindly old parole officer, O'Neil, explaining how diligently he drives his hack, and stays on the straight and narrow path. O'Neil introduces the slick Taylor to two earnest, pretty sociology students, Turner and Lewis, but Turner thinks he's anything but what he pretends to be. Her instincts are right, even though her heart takes her in another direction, one where she will irresponsibly love Taylor, even die for him, an essentially worthless, self-serving cad. Taylor dutifully gets into his cab after meeting with O'Neil and charming Lewis and Turner, then drives to an unopened dog track and reports to the front desk, but goes into the inner offices without seeking approval, then into an even posher living quarters where he discards his cab driver's outfit and dons expensive tie and suitcoat. He begins giving orders to his ugly minions, and it is apparent that Taylor is not only back in the rackets but that he's running them, all of them, a Mr. Big who owns the city's crime monopoly. He dispatches orders to nightclub owner Nelson and partner Dingle, then is visited by his closest friend and admirer, enigmatic, Shakespeare-quoting, alcoholic Heflin. Later that night, Taylor exposes his real nature and station in life when he confronts Nelson in his nightclub, threatening him unless he does his bidding. This is witnessed by Turner whom he escorts home to father Arnold, the same prosecuting attorney who had sent him to prison. Arnold explodes when seeing Taylor with Turner, threatening to return him to prison if he ever sees his daughter again. Taylor backs off but hatches a plan to take revenge on Arnold, seduce Turner, and guarantee his ability to open his dog track without interference from the authorities. He inveigles Turner to his lavish apartment where he is attacked by a vicious hoodlum, Stewart, who is really acting out a staged scene. Stewart is about to kill Taylor, it seems to Turner, and she grabs a convenient gun and ostensibly kills Stewart. Taylor hustles the traumatized Turner home. Later he sends the very much alive Stewart out of town and begins to blackmail Arnold; either Arnold uses his influence to allow him to open his dog track or he will reveal how his daughter murdered Stewart. Arnold complies and Turner is bedridden, ill from guilt but longing for lover boy Taylor, who cruelly ignores her. Heflin has tried throughout to probe for Taylor's soft spot, a way to a heart apparently ringed with iron. He works on the mob boss to relent and make things right with Turner, "the poor kid" he has set up and used. Heflin knows Taylor really loves her and tells him so, incurring Taylor's wrath. Sterling, Turner's earlier boy friend, begs Taylor to go back to Turner, to marry her, to snap her out of her sick-to-death love for Taylor. The pressure finally gets to Taylor and he admits his love for Turner by going to her and begging her to get well, confessing that Stewart was not killed by her, that it was a set up so that he could blackmail her father. Turner comes to life while Taylor confronts some of his arch rivals in a shootout. He dispatches his enemies but is sorely wounded, and, as he staggers down the street, a cop stops him. He aims a gun at the cop and the cop shoots and fatally wounds him. Taylor dies in Heflin's arms as the intellectual sidekick weeps over him. Ironically, the cop who has killed Taylor is one whom Taylor had transferred earlier as a favor so that the cop would be in a decent district. JOHNNY EAGER is an offbeat but absorbing film in which Taylor wholly abandons his good guy image and becomes a believable bad guy whose sliver of human kindness causes his death. It is one of his finest roles. The luscious 21-year-old Turner totally captivated Taylor and he later unabashedly related how he was drawn romantically to her. At the time, Turner reciprocated Taylor's advances; she was then suing bandleader Artie Shaw for divorce and was known as "The Sweater Girl." MGM's publicity campaign made the most of the torrid on and off-screen romance between Taylor and Turner, taking out one ad which read: "TNT—Taylor 'n' Turner—Together They're Terrific!" Although there is a synthetic element to JOHNNY EAGER, the glossy crime melodrama is so well handled by LeRoy that it is wholly fascinating. Heflin was the presence that gave depth to the film as the drunken conscience of cold-hearted Taylor. He won an Oscar as Supporting Actor in this film. Yet MGM had no idea of what to do with this sensitive, introspective actor. They put him in such above-average B-films as KID GLOVE KILLER and GRAND CENTRAL MURDER. He was given the star treatment for TENNESSEE JOHNSON, which was an utter failure, and then Heflin went into the service during WW II, serving as a combat photographer. When he returned to MGM following the war, he was again used in supporting roles in such films as GREEN DOLPHIN STREET, THE THREE MUSKETEERS, both starring Turner, and MADAME BOVARY, before saying goodbye to MGM. Taylor and Turner would make only this single film together, and this was the first film in which LeRoy would direct Turner; the director was responsible for bringing the sex film goddess to MGM in 1938.

p, John W. Considine, Jr.; d, Mervyn LeRoy; w, John Lee Mahin, James Edward Grant (based on a story by Grant); ph, Harold Rosson; m, Bronislau Kaper; ed, Albert Akst; art d, Cedric Gibbons, Stan Rogers; set d, Edwin B. Willis; cos, Robert Kalloch.

Crime Drama PR:C MPAA:NR)

JOHNNY FRENCHMAN** (1946, Brit.) 104m EAL/UNIV-Prestige bw

Francoise Rosay *(Lanec Florrie)*, Tom Walls *(Nat Pomeroy)*, Patricia Roc *(Sue Pomeroy)*, Ralph Michael *(Bob Tremayne)*, Paul Dupuis *(Yan Kervarec)*, Frederick Piper *(Zacky Penrose)*, Arthur Hambling *(Steve Matthews)*, Judith Furse *(Jane Matthews)*, James Harcourt *(Joe Pender)*, Paul Bonifas *(Jerome)*, Marcel Poncin *(Theo)*, Pierre Richard *(Mayor of Lanec)*, Richard George *(Charlie West)*, Bill Blewitt *(Dick Trewhiddle)*, Beatrice Varley *(Mrs. Tremayne)*, Drusilla Wills *(Miss Bennett)*, Grace Arnold *(Mrs. Matthews)*, Stan Paskin *(Tim Bassett)*, James Knight, George Hirste, Franklin Bennett, Leslie Harcourt, Bernard Fishwick, Herbert Thomas, Denver Hall, Vincent Holman, Henri Bollinger, Jean-Marie Balcon, Louise Gournay, Charles Jezequel, Jean-Marie Nacry, Joseph Menou, Carroll O'Connor *(Mr. Harper)*, Alfie Bass *(Corporal)*.

War breaks out between rival fishermen as the men of Cornwall take on a band of "Froggies." Walls is a Cornwall harbor master who has to deal with a French poacher, the wily Rosay. Complications come in the form of across-the-water romances and everything is resolved in the end. The cast includes real fishermen and villagers from Cornwall, along with members of the Free French resistance movement.

p, Michael Balcon; d, Charles Frend; w, T.E.B. Clarke; ph, Roy Kellino; m, Clifton Parker; ed, Michael Truman; art d, Duncan Sutherland.

Drama (PR:A MPAA:NR)

JOHNNY GOT HIS GUN** (1971) 111m Cinemation c

Timothy Bottoms *(Joe Bonham)*, Kathy Fields *(Kareen)*, Marsha Hunt *(Joe's Mother)*, Jason Robards *(Joe's Father)*, Donald Sutherland *("Christ")*, Diane Varsi *(4th Nurse)*, Sandy Brown Wyeth *(Lucky)*, Donald Barry *(Jody Simmons)*, Peter Brocco *(Ancient Prelate)*, Kendell Clarke *(Hospital Official)*, Eric Christmas *(Cpl. Timlon)*, Eduard Franz *(Col./Gen. Tillery)*, Craig Bovia *(Little Guy)*, Judy Howard Chaikin *(Bakery Girl)*, Robert Cole *(Orator)*, Maurice Dallimore *(British Colonel)*, Robert Easton *(3rd Doctor)*, Larry Fleischman *(Russ)*, Tony Geary *(Redhead)*, Edmund Gilbert *(Priest)*, Ben Hammer *(2nd Doctor)*, Milton Barnes *(1st Reader)*, Wayne Heffley *(Captain)*, Lynn Hanratty *(Elizabeth at 6)*, Ernestine Johnston *(Farm Woman)*, Joseph Kaufman *(Rudy)*, Mike Lee *(Bill)*, Kerry MacLane *(Joe at 10)*, Charles McGraw *(Mike)*, William Mims *(Gentleman)*, Byron Morrow *(Brigadier General)*, Alice Nunn, Marge Redmond, Jodean Russo *(Nurses)*, David Soul *(Swede)*, Etienne Veazie *(Black Boy)*, Peter Virgo, Jr. *(Attendant)*, Gigi Vorgan *(Catherine at 13)*, Jeff Walker *(5th Guy)*, Bruce Watson *(Technician)*, Cynthia Wilson *(Catherine at 7)*, Sandy Brownwyeth *(Lucky)*.

A pretentious and almost sanctimonious film, JOHNNY GOT HIS GUN is the ultimate victim movie enacted in thought passage—voice-over by victim Bottoms—in relationship to images of the mind. He has been hit by a bomb during a WW I battle and has been rendered deaf, dumb, and blind and all of his limbs have been amputated. He survives in the hospital only by fantasizing, moralizing, and endlessly probing the causes of war, an exercise that goes round and round, designed to prevent him from going mad. He figures out how to communicate by tapping out a Morse code and tells his doctors that he wishes to be put on display so as to prevent more wars, a request that goes unanswered. Certainly a strong antiwar movie, the endless sermonizing and virtuous mental diatribes will tire any viewer not seeking a sharp cathartic experience or, at least, the strong urge for a mental enema. Trumbo wrote and directed this failure, which was based on his startling novel. The trouble is that Trumbo, one of the most gifted screenwriters in the business, brought too much Trumbo to the screen. As early as 1965, Luis Bunuel planned to make the film but nothing materialized. Warner Bros. got as far as allocating $2 million for a budget to cover production but that, too, evaporated. Trumbo and producer Bruce Campbell then raised $750,000 from private investors and shot the film in 42 days in 1970. Trumbo admitted that the film, as the novel, stemmed from his own life, at least that part related to the victim's boyhood. He went on to state that he got the idea in 1933 when reading about a British officer who died that year and who had been so horribly disfigured in WW I that authorities lied to his family, saying he had been killed during the war, when he lived for another 15 years as a human vegetable.

p, Bruce Campbell; d&w, Dalton Trumbo (based on his novel), ph, Jules Brenner (Eastmancolor); m, Jerry Fielding; ed, William P. Dornisch; prod d, Harold Michelson; cos, Theodora Van Runkle.

Drama Cas. (PR:O MPAA:GP)

JOHNNY GUITAR*** (1954) 110m REP c

Joan Crawford *(Vienna)*, Sterling Hayden *(Johnny Guitar)*, Mercedes McCambridge *(Emma Small)*, Scott Brady *(Dancin' Kid)*, Ward Bond *(John McIvers)*, Ben Cooper *(Turkey Ralston)*, Ernest Borgnine *(Bart Lonergan)*, John Carradine *(Old Tom)*, Royal Dano *(Corey)*, Frank Ferguson *(Marshal Williams)*, Paul Fix *(Eddie)*, Rhys Williams *(Mr. Andrews)*, Ian MacDonald *(Pete)*, Will Wright *(Ned)*, John Maxwell *(Jake)*, Robert Osterloh *(Sam)*, Trevor Bardette *(Jenks)*, Sumner Williams, Sheb Wooley, Denver Pyle, Clem Harvey *(Posse)*, Frank Marlow *(Frank)*.

Lurid, garish in fuzzy Trucolor, this flamboyant, giddy, and often absurd western—which attempts to prove Crawford a pioneer women's liberationist—has become a minor cult film, particularly with French directors and aesthetes whose notion of the American West is certainly camp if not crude. Crawford is a tough ex-dancehall lady who kicks off her high heels, rolls down her hose and slips on breeches, boots and a six-gun. She dresses in black, the garb of the traditional bad guy, and to her newly opened saloon she draws a host of neurotic characters including Hayden, a gunfighter who is weary of battle and longs to settle down. As the saloon prospers, neighboring Arizona citizens rankle at Crawford's success. Hating her openly is McCambridge who feels that Crawford's current outlaw lover, Brady, is responsible for her brother's death. McCambridge badgers the local sheriff to order Crawford and her outlaw brood out of the territory as undesirable elements. Crawford's staff deserts her but Hayden stays on, he being her ex-lover. McCambridge then rounds up a mob and the saloon is burned down around an irate Crawford. She and her persecutor, McCambridge, then square off in a ridiculous gun duel and, after the smoke clears, Crawford is alive and McCambridge stiff. Crawford and Hayden wind up in each other's arms if not in the hearts of the viewers. Directed by Nicholas Ray, mostly an on-target genius helmsman, this film inexplicably suffers under stodgy, shuffling direction that neither develops character nor expands plot. The story is fragile, the performances are lame, even that of the normally dynamic Crawford. Everyone looks like they're lost and wondering exactly what part of the West they're occupying. The set for Crawford's saloon was built at Ray's instructions, following a design by architect Frank Lloyd Wright whom the director admired and which embodied the philosophy that "a house should not be *on* a hill, but *of* a hill." Some have said that this film spoofs Fritz Lang's offbeat western RANCHO NOTORIOUS, or that it is a Freudian exercise, using western locales as strange sex symbols—tunnels, mineshafts, caves, and Crawford's fear that the railroad will *penetrate* her land. Others have held that it's a McCarthy-era allegory, with McCambridge and her minions representing the House Un-American Affairs Committee and Crawford's cohorts representing the persecuted players. It's none of the above, only a mess. Crawford reportedly hated McCambridge's bursting histrionics—which matched her own—especially when the crew applauded one of McCambridge's scenes. Ray prudently shot McCambridge's scenes early in the morning but when Crawford found out about this special treatment she raced into McCambridge's dressing room and slashed all her costumes to pieces. Then, according to McCambridge, she had the actress blacklisted for more than two years.

p, Herbert J. Yates; d, Nicholas Ray; w, Philip Yordan (based on the novel by Roy Chanslor); ph, Harry Stradling, Jr. (TruColor); ed, Richard L. Van Enger; m, Victor Young; prod d, John McCarthy, Jr., Edward G. Boyle; art d, James Sullivan; cos, Sheila O'Brien; spec eff, Howard and Theodore Lydecker; m/l, "Johnny Guitar," Young, Peggy Lee (sung by Lee).

Western Cas. (PR:C MPAA:NR)

JOHNNY HAMLET* 1/2

(1972, Ital.) 91m Daiano-Leone/Transvue c (QUELLA SPORCA STORIA DEL WEST)

Chip Corman [Andrea Giordana] *(Johnny/Hamlet)*, Gilbert Roland *(Horace/Horatio)*, Horst Frank *(Claude/Claudius)*, Pedro Sanchez [Ignazio Spalla] *(Gil/Guildenstern)*, Enio Girolami *(Ross/Rosencrantz)*, Gabriella Grimaldi *(Ophelia)*, Francoise Prevost *(Gertrude)*, Stefania Careddu *(Player Queen)*, Giorgio Sanmartin *(Polonio)*, Franco Latini, Manuel Serrano, John Bartha, Franco Leo, Fabio Patella.

Poor, violent attempt to turn Shakespeare's classic play into a "spaghetti western." The story follows the "Hamlet" plot, though the language has changed considerably. Just try to find some iambic pentameter in this dialog. The ending is somewhat different in that this Hamlet does not die—he rides off into the sunset. Released in Italy in 1968, it was not shown in the U.S. until 1972. (In English.)

p, Ugo Guerra, Elio Scardamaglia; d, Enzo G. Castellari [Enzo Girolami]; w, Castellari, Tito Carpi, Francesco Scardamaglia (based on a story by Sergio Corbucci adapted from the play "Hamlet" by William Shakespeare); ph, Angelo Filippini (Techniscope, Technicolor); m, Franceso de Masi; ed, Tatiana Casini; art d, Enzo Bulgarelli; spec eff, Gino Vagniluca.

Western (PR:O MPAA:PG)

JOHNNY HOLIDAY*** (1949) 94m UA bw

William Bendix *(Sgt. Walker)*, Allen Martin, Jr. *(Johnny Holiday)*, Stanley Clements *(Eddie Duggan)*, Jack Hagen *(Jackson)*, Herbert Newcomb *(Dr. Piper)*, Donald Gallagher *(Supt. Lang)*, Greta Granstedt *(Mrs. Holiday)*, George Cisar *(Barney Duggan)*, Leo Cleary *(Trimble)*, Leo Curlay *(Spencer)*, Alma Platt *(Miss Kelly)*, Jeanne Juvelier *(Mrs. Bellini)*, Gov. Henry F. Schricker *(Himself)*, Hoagy Carmichael *(Himself)*, Buddy Cole *(Himself)*, The Staff and Boys of the Indiana Boys School.

This interesting and sensitive study of juvenile delinquents is loosely based on the early life of its producer, Alcorn. Martin is a good kid who falls under the influence of local hood Clements. Caught in a robbery, Martin is sent to the Indiana Boys School, a home for wayward youths, where he is befriended by guard Bendix. Clements, who is picked up on a different charge, is also sent to the home. Once more they team up, but Martin discovers new interests and in one of the film's best scenes, is forced to kill a horse he loves so its foal may live. Cameo appearances include Carmichael singing "My Christmas Song for You" at a school celebration. Indiana governor Schricker makes an appearance, delivering a speech at the school. The film was shot on location with the school inmates playing extras. This lends a certain air of realism to the film. The direction is tight, with a semi-documentary style pre-dating the similar French classic, THE 400 BLOWS.

p, R.W. Alcorn; d, Willis Goldbeck; w, Jack Andrews, Frederick Stephani, and Goldbeck (based on a story by Alcorn); ph, Hal Mohr; m, Franz Waxman; ed, Richard Fritch.

Drama (PR:A MPAA:NR)

JOHNNY IN THE CLOUDS* 1/2**

(1945, Brit.) 87m TC/UA bw (GB: THE WAY TO THE STARS)

Michael Redgrave *(David Archdale)*, John Mills *(Peter Penrose)*, Rosamund John *(Miss Toddy Todd)*, Douglass Montgomery *(Johnny Hollis)*, Renee Asherson *(Iris Winterton)*, Stanley Holloway *(Palmer)*, Basil Radford *(Tiny Williams)*, Felix Aylmer *(Rev. Charles Moss)*, Bonar Colleano, Jr. *(Joe Friselli)*, Trevor Howard *(Squadron Leader Carter)*, Joyce Carey *(Miss Winterton)*, Bill Owen [Rowbotham] *(Nobby Clarke)*, Jean Simmons *(Singer)*, Nicholas Stuart *(Wally Becker)*, David Tomlinson *(Pilot Officer Prune Parsons)*, Johnnie Schofield *(Jones)*, Charles Victor *(Fitter)*, Hartley Power *(Col. Page)*, Vida Hope *(Elsie, Waitress)*, Peter Cotes *(Aircraftsman)*,

Anthony Dawson *(Bertie Steen)*, Hugh Dempster *(Tinker Bell)*, Alf Goddard *(Sergeant)*, Tryon Nichol *(American Airman)*, Grant Miller *(Wally)*, Murray Matheson, John McLaren, Charles Farrell, Bill Logan, John Howard, Jacqueline Clarke, Caven Watson, Sydney Benson, Ian Warner McGilvray, Ann Wilton, Alan Sedgewick, O. B. Clarence.

A superior war film that has virtually no footage of actual battle. The presence of the war is continually felt, however, through the film's atmosphere and in the subtle and effective performances. The picture concentrates on the effects of war upon soldiers' romances. Mills is the young pilot unwilling to make a commitment to the girl he has fallen in love with, because the influence of Redgrave's death has left him with the impression that it isn't right for a soldier to marry in the midst of a war. Even when an American soldier tries to make off with Winterton, Mills refuses to go where his heart leads until John, the widow of Redgrave, convinces him that marriage is the right thing to do. This is just one of several sagas that are effectively interwoven to create a well-rounded picture of airmen on the ground. A prominent theme is the introduction of American forces onto the British base. The film details how the uneasiness caused by this new presence eventually develops into camaraderie and friendship, the Americans having to contend with the same emotional problems as the British. A tremendously successful film at the time of its release, JOHNNY IN THE CLOUDS captured a certain patriotic spirit that had been lurking in British hearts. Director Asquith had the perceptiveness to recognize the flow of feeling in Britain, and to bring it to the forefront without becoming bogged down in sentimentalism. In performances, techniques, scripting, and all other facets, a very fine achievement.

p, Anatole de Grunwald; d, Anthony Asquith; w, Terence Rattigan, de Grunwald (based on the story by Rattigan, Richard Sherman); ph, Derek Williams; m, Nicholas Brodzsky; ed, Fergus McDonnell; art d, Paul Sheriff, Carmen Dillon.

War Drama **(PR:A MPAA:NR)**

JOHNNY NOBODY** (1965, Brit.) 88m Viceroy/Medallion bw

Nigel Patrick *(Father Carey)*, Yvonne Mitchell *(Miss Floyd)*, Aldo Ray *(Johnny)*, William Bendix *(Mulcahy)*, Cyril Cusack *(Prosecuting Counsel)*, Niall MacGinnis *(Defending Counsel)*, Bernie Winters *(Photographer)*, Noel Purcell *(Brother Timothy)*, Eddie Byrne *(Landlord)*, Jimmy O'Dea *(Postman)*, John Welsh *(Judge)*, Joe Lynch *(Tinker/Ballad Singer)*, Michael Brennan *(Supt. Lynch)*, J.G. Devlin *(Caretaker)*, Christopher Casson *(Father Bernard)*, Norman Rodway *(Father Healey)*, May Craig *(Tinker's Mother)*, Michael O'Duffy, Dominic Behan *(Ballad Singers)*.

Bendix is an alcoholic Irish writer who defies God to strike him dead. Ray, claiming to be guided by a heavenly force, shoots Bendix. He is arrested and dubbed "Johnny Nobody" by the townspeople when he claims to have no memory of anything prior to the incident. Patrick, the local priest, becomes involved when Ray's lawyer asks him to support the claim that Ray's act was really an act of God. Patrick pursues his own investigation which reveals that Ray, in cahoots with his wife, reporter Mitchell, conspired to kill the writer for stealing material from Ray's unpublished book. Before this evidence can be presented in court, Ray blasphemes during a passionate courtroom argument and dies of a heart attack. Though the initial premise is provocative, interest drops off considerably when the mystery-suspense elements are added. What's more, the ending is unbelievable. This was the second directorial effort for Patrick. It was released in England in 1961, but didn't arrive in the U.S. until 1965, nearly a year after Bendix had died.

p, John R. Sloan; d, Nigel Patrick; w, Patrick Kirwan (based on a story by Albert Z. Carr); ph, Ted Moore; m, Ron Goodwin; ed, Geoffrey Foot; art d, Tony Inglis; m/l, (songs sung by Joe Lynch, Paddy MacGowen, Delia Murphy).

Drama/Mystery **Cas.** **(PR:O MPAA:NR)**

JOHNNY NORTH (SEE: KILLERS, THE, 1964)

JOHNNY O'CLOCK*** 1/2 (1947) 95m J.E.M. Productions/COL bw

Dick Powell *(Johnny O'Clock)*, Evelyn Keyes *(Nancy Hobbs)*, Lee J. Cobb *(Inspector Koch)*, Ellen Drew *(Nelle Marchettis)*, Nina Foch *(Harriet Hobbs)*, Thomas Gomez *(Pete Marchettis)*, John Kellog *(Charlie)*, Jim Bannon *(Chuck Blayden)*, Mabel Paige *(Slatternly Woman)*, Phil Brown *(Hotel Clerk)*, Jeff Chandler *(Turk)*, Kit Guard *(Punchy)*, Charles Mueller, Allen Mathews *(Bodyguards)*, Virginia Farmer *(Mrs. Wilson)*, Pat Lane *(Onlooker)*, Robert Ryan *(Policeman)*, Jerry Franks *(Man)*, Jesse Graves *(Redcap)*, Matty Fain *(Fleming)*, Cy Malis, Bob Perry, Cy Schindell, Charles Perry, Sam Shack, Charles St. George, Gene Delmont, Ralph Volkie *(Dealers)*, Brooks Benedict, Bill Wallace, Jeffrey Sayre, Paul Bradley, Richard H. Gordon *(Card Players)*, Jack Smith, Fred Beecher, Ralph Freedman, Thomas H. O'Neil, Joe Helper, Bill Stubbs, John Terrano, Edward Margolis, George Zouzaniles, George Alesko *(Practical Dealers)*, Raoul Freeman, Carle Saxe *(Detectives)*, Shimen Ruskin *(Storekeeper)*, Robin Raymond *(Hatcheck Girl)*, John P. Barrett *(Floorman)*, Charles Wexler *(Bartender)*, Victoria Faust *(Marion)*, John Berkes *(Waiter)*, Al Hill, George Lloyd *(Workmen)*, Ken MacDonald *(Customer)*, Charles Marsh *(Businessman)*.

This was Rossen's first directorial assignment and it's a good mixture of crime melodrama and black humor, personified in the tough-guy personality of Powell who had drastically changed his screen image from flyweight crooner to two-fisted gumshoe in MURDER, MY SWEET three years earlier. JOHNNY O'CLOCK is Powell, who has a shaky gambling casino partnership with Gomez. Crooked cop Bannon tries to move in on the operation, ingratiating himself with Gomez and attempting to replace Powell. Foch, Bannon's girl friend, is found dead in her apartment an apparent suicide, but suspicion of murder lingers, particularly when Bannon vanishes. Powell is befriended by Keyes, Foch's sister, who believes her sibling was murdered and she asks Powell to investigate. He plays fast and loose with her; his life is already crammed with females, including Gomez's sultry wife, Drew, who has just given him an expensive watch, one identical to the one she has given her husband. Detective Cobb suspects both Gomez and Powell of murder, especially after Bannon's body is found floating in a nearby river and poison is discovered in Foch's body. Gomez learns about Powell's watch and, in a jealous rage, gives orders for his partner to be killed, but Powell is too fast for him, escaping and then later confronting Gomez, dissolving their business partnership. Gomez won't listen to reason; he pulls a gun and shoots Powell, who returns fire and kills Gomez. Drew comes racing in to claim the spoils—Powell. But when he rejects her, Drew goes berserk, calls the police, and tells them Powell has cold-bloodedly murdered her husband. Powell takes Cobb hostage and prepares to shoot it out with the cops surrounding his place but when he learns that Keyes is outside he admits he loves her, and gives himself up. By then Cobb has figured out the rather obvious fact that Powell is innocent and the killings were performed by others. The wiseguy gambler appears headed for happiness with Keyes. Rossen's direction is slick and telling, and Powell and supporting cast do much to keep interest high. The dialog is genuinely witty and full of offbeat humor. All of this is to Rossen's credit; he pounded out the superb script. Charles Vidor was originally slated to direct the film but when he refused to work for Columbia's Harry Cohn, the mogul bravely gave Rossen his first opportunity to direct this expensive film (which cost more than $1 million). Before JOHNNY O'CLOCK was released, word spread that it would be a winner, and it was. Charles Einfeld, who had just formed Enterprise Pictures, was considering Rossen as the director of a powerful boxing film, BODY AND SOUL, to star John Garfield. He called Cohn and asked to see the yet-to-be released JOHNNY O'CLOCK so he could decide about Rossen. Snorted the cantankerous Cohn: "I never saw any film by Rossen! I took a chance on him! Why shouldn't you?" Einfeld did and Rossen produced one of the greatest films on boxing ever made, and he would go on to make another masterpiece, ALL THE KING'S MEN (1949).

p, Edward G. Nealis; d, Robert Rossen; w, Rossen (based on a story by Milton Holmes); ph, Burnett Guffey; m, George Duning; ed, Warren Low, Al Clark; md, Morris Stoloff; art d, Stephen Goosson, Cary Odell; set d, James Crowe; cos, Jean Louis.

Crime Drama **(PR:A MPAA:NR)**

JOHNNY ON THE RUN***

(1953, Brit.) 68m International Realist-Children's Film Foundation/ABF bw

Eugeniusz Chylek *(Johnny)*, Sydney Tafler *(Harry)*, Michael Balfour *(Fingers)*, Jean Anderson *(Mrs. MacIntyre)*, Moultrie Kelsall *(Mr. MacIntyre)*, Mona Washbourne *(Mrs. MacGregor)*, Margaret McCourt *(Janet MacGregor)*, Edna Wynn, David Coote, Cleopatra Sylvestre, Louis Alexander, Elizabeth Saunders, Keith Faulkner, John Levitt.

Chylek plays an orphaned child with dreams of returning to his native Poland, a feat which he attempts to accomplish, but which only gets him into a great deal of hot water. A group of jewel thieves decide they can easily put Chylek to use as an aid in several robberies, something the lad doesn't catch onto until it is almost too late. Luckily he happens upon a small village filled with people from all over the world; they take him in, give him their trust and friendship, and help protect him against the evil forces that are after him. Well-paced effort that is given added strength through a realistic treatment of children as people quite capable of individual thought.

p, Victor Lyndon; d, Lewis Gilbert, Vernon Harris; w, Patricia Latham; ph, Gerald Gibbs.

Adventure **(PR:AAA MPAA:NR)**

JOHNNY ON THE SPOT* (1954, Brit.) 72m E.J. Fancey/New Realm bw

Hugh McDermott *(Johnny Breakes)*, Elspet Gray *(Joan Ingram)*, Paul Carpenter *(Paul Carrington)*, Jean Lodge *(Sally Erskine)*, Ronald Adam *(Inspector Beveridge)*, Valentine Dyall *(Tyneley)*, Adrienne Scott, Graham Stark, Pauline Olsen.

Haphazardly scripted film has a man returning home from prison in order to clear his name of the murder he was sentenced for. This premise serves as the springboard for a number of disjointed events, ranging from murder to kidnaping and a few other incidents that have no relation to the rest of the picture. Lack of consistent plot development makes this picture almost impossible to watch.

p, E.J. Fancey; d&w, Maclean Rogers (based on the novel *Paid in Full* by Michael Cronin); ph, Geoffrey Faithfull.

Crime **(PR:A MPAA:NR)**

JOHNNY ONE-EYE** 1/2 (1950) 77m UA bw

Pat O'Brien *(Martin Martin)*, Wayne Morris *(Dane Cory)*, Dolores Moran *(Lily White)*, Gayle Reed *(Elsie)*, Lawrence Cregar *(Ambrose)*, Jack Overman *(Lippy)*, Raymond Largay *(Lawbooks)*, Donald Woods *(Vet)*, Harry Bronson *(Freddy)*.

O'Brien and Morris are two former partners-in-crime. Morris turns O'Brien in on a five-year-old murder charge during a police crackdown. O'Brien goes on the run, trying to find his ex-comrade and make him change his story. He hides in an abandoned house, along with Reed and her dog, Johnny One-Eye. Eventually the two partners meet and have it out in a gun battle. Based on a Damon Runyon story with all of his standard characters and situations in tow, the film starts out well but drops off rapidly. Florey's pace is too slow, but there is some good location shooting in New York, and the acting is fine.

p, Benedict Bogeaus; d, Robert Florey; w, Richard Landau (based on a story by Damon Runyon); ph, Lucien Andriot; ed, Frank Sullivan; md, Louis Forbes.

Crime **(PR:A MPAA:NR)**

JOHNNY ORO (SEE: RINGO AND HIS GOLDEN PISTOL, 1966, Ital.)

JOHNNY RENO** 1/2 (1966) 83m A.C. Lyles/PAR c

Dana Andrews *(Johnny Reno)*, Jane Russell *(Nona Williams)*, Lon Chaney, Jr. *(Sheriff Hodges)*, John Agar *(Ed Tomkins)*, Lyle Bettger *(Jess Yates)*, Tom Drake *(Joe Connors)*, Richard Arlen *(Ned Duggan)*, Robert Lowery *(Jake Reed)*, Tracy

Olsen *(Maria Yates)*, Reg Parton *(Bartender)*, Rodd Redwing *(Indian)*, Charles Horvath *(Wooster)*, Dale Van Sickle *(Ab Connors)*, Paul Daniel *(Chief Little Bear)*, Chuck Hicks *(Bellows)*, Edmund Cobb *(Townsman)*.

Andrews is a U.S. Marshal riding to his new assignment in Stone Junction, Kansas. Van Sickle and Drake mistakenly believe the marshal is after them and they engage in a gun battle. Van Sickle is killed, while Drake is brought to town for trial. Andrews arrives to discover that a lynch-mob mentality reigns in mayor Bettger's town. Russell provides the love interest as the saloon keeper and Drake's ex-fiancee. The townspeople decide to lynch both Andrews and Drake, but an Indian attack gives Andrews a chance to escape with Russell. There are quite a few plot twists, nicely handled by the director. The final sequence is particularly well done as the warring Indians tear apart Stone Junction. Performances are fine and there's a good use of color.

p, A.C. Lyles; d, R. G. Springsteen; w, Steve Fisher (based on a story by Fisher, Lyles, Andrew Craddock); ph, Hal Stine (Techniscope, Technicolor); m, Jimmie Haskell; ed, Bernard Matis; art d, Hal Pereira, Malcolm Brown; set d, Jerry Welch, Robert R. Benton; cos, John A. Anderson, Thalia Phillips; m/l, "Johnny Reno," By Dunham (sung by Jerry Wallace); makeup, Wally Westmore, Lou Haszillo.

Western **(PR:O MPAA:NR)**

JOHNNY ROCCO** (1958) 84m AA bw

Richard Eyer *(Johnny)*, Stephen McNally *(Rocco)*, Coleen Gray *(Lois)*, Russ Conway *(Inspector Garron)*, Leslie Bradley *(Father Regen)*, James Flavin *(Mooney)*, M.G. [Matty] Fain *(Dino)*, John Mitchum *(Stakeout Officer)*, Bob Mitchel *(Choir Leader)*, Frank Wilcox *(Lane)*, Harry Loftin *(Motorcycle Cop)*, The Mitchell Boy's Choir.

Eyer is the son of McNally, an important crime figure. He is so shocked by Dad's dirty dealings that he starts to stutter. Gray, the boy's teacher, takes an interest in the child but finds more than she bargained for when the boy becomes a mob target. He has information that could hurt the organization, and the film becomes a chase between cops and mobsters. The idea is an interesting twist on old themes, but is hampered by a heavy dose of cliches. Eyer is not bad as the kid and McNally handles his difficult, if slightly unbelievable, role nicely.

p, Scott R. Dunlap; d, Paul Landres; w, James O'Hanlon, Samuel F. Rocca (based on a story by Richard Carlson); ph, William Margulies; m, Edward J. Kay; ed, George White; md, Kay; art d, David Milton.

Crime **(PR:A MPAA:NR)**

JOHNNY STEALS EUROPE***

(1932, Ger.) 86m Ariel/Deutsche Universal bw (JONNY STIEHLT EUROPA)

Harry Piel, Alfred Abel, Darry Holm, Margarete Sachse, Walter Steinbeck, Hermann Blass, Carl Ballhaus, Charly Berger, Kurt Lilien, Wolfgang V. Schwind, Gerhard Damann, Hans Wallner, Fritz Spira, Bruno Ziener.

"Europe" is a horse owned by Piel. The film concerns the comic difficulties he must overcome to enter the horse in the Grand Prix at Nice and win the prize money he needs to pay off his numerous creditors. Piel, known as "the German Douglas Fairbanks," wrote and directed the film, and it has a nice rollicking pace along with a fine supporting cast. Enjoyable, and a rare example of pre-Hitler German cinema of the early 1930s.

p, Joe Pasternak; d&w, Harry Piel (based on a novel by Werner Scheff); ph, Ewald Daub; m, Fritz Wenneis; set d, Gustav A. Knauer.

Comedy **(PR:A MPAA:NR)**

JOHNNY STOOL PIGEON** ½ (1949) 76m UNIV bw

Howard Duff *(George Morton)*, Shelley Winters *(Terry)*, Dan Duryea *(Johnny Evans)*, Anthony [Tony] Curtis *(Joey Hyatt)*, John McIntire *(Avery)*, Gar Moore *(Sam Harrison)*, Leif Erickson *(Pringle)*, Barry Kelley *(McCandles)*, Hugh Reilly *(Charlie)*, Wally Maher *(Benson)*, Nacho Galindo *(Martinez)*, Gregg Barton *(Treasury Man)*, Robert Foulk *(Pete)*, Duke York *(Body Guard)*, Pat Shade *(Bell Boy)*, Patricia Alphin *(McCandles' Secretary)*, Charles Drake *(Hotel Clerk)*, Ken Patterson *(Dallas)*, Leslie Dennison *(Canadian Undercover Man)*, Edwin Max *(Carter)*, Grace Lenard *(Woman Informer)*, Al Ferguson, Colin Kenny *(Porters)*, Robert Kimball *(Bartender)*, Robert O'Neil *(Informer)*, Harry H. Evans *(Federal Judge)*.

Duff is a Federal Narcotics Agent who springs Duryea from Alcatraz for help in smashing a ring of dope dealers. The trail takes them to San Francisco, Vancouver, Tucson, and Mexico, before the finale back in Tuscon. Winters is the girl friend of smuggler Kelley, who jilts her guy for Duff. Gang member Curtis is killed by Duryea when he attempts to knock off Duff. Winters tips off the duo about a big deal and the agents swoop in at the climax. It's a standard police drama, though there are some exciting moments. Castle's direction keeps things moving briskly.

p, Aaron Rosenberg; d, William Castle; w, Robert L. Richards (based on a story by Henry Jordan); ph, Maury Gertsman; m, Milton Schwarzwald; ed, Ted J. Kent; md, Schwartzwald; art d, Bernard Herzbrun, Emrich Nicholson; set d, Russell A. Gausman, John Austin; cos, Orry-Kelly; spec eff, David S. Horsley; makeup, Bud Westmore.

Crime **(PR:C MPAA:NR)**

JOHNNY THE GIANT KILLER** (1953, Fr.) 60m Jean Image/Lippert c

An early feature-length cartoon from France, with a story loosely based on the fairy tale. Plot involves an attempt by Johnny and his pals to slay the giant, which leads to their being captured and reduced to miniature size. An escape and a series of adventures with birds, spiders, bees, and wasps follow, before Johnny finally rescues his friends and they all regain their normal size. Some quality animation and good background music, but the slow-moving story limits the appeal to the younger set.

p, Jean Image; d, Image, Charles Frank; w, Frank, Paul Collins, Nesta MacDonald (based on an idea by Eraine); ph, Kostia Tchikine (Technicolor); m, Rene Cloerec; animation, Albert Champeaux, Denis Boutin, O'Klein, Marcel Breuil.

Animated Fantasy **Cas.** **(PR:AA MPAA:NR)**

JOHNNY TIGER** ½ (1966) 102m Nova-Hugh/UNIV c

Robert Taylor *(George Dean)*, Geraldine Brooks *(Doc Leslie Frost)*, Chad Everett *(Johnny Tiger)*, Brenda Scott *(Barbara Dean)*, Marc Lawrence *(William Billie)*, Ford Rainey *(Sam Tiger)*, Carol Seflinger *(Wendy Dean)*, Steven Wheeler *(Randy Dean)*, Pamela Melendez *(Shalonee)*, Deanna Lund *(Louise)*.

Restless college professor Taylor takes his three children (Scott, Seflinger and Wheeler) to the Florida Everglades where he intends to teach Seminole Indians. Shocked by the backward conditions on the Indian reservation, Taylor protests to local health official Brooks, but to no avail. Everett enters the story as a halfbreed who saves Scott from a herd of stampeding buffalo. Noting that Everett has the respect of the other Indian children, Taylor enlists his help in getting the children to attend school. He is rebuked until Everett falls for Scott and begins attending school himself. Rainey, as the old chief who is Everett's grandfather, is upset by Everett's actions, and demands that he reject white society. When Everett and Scott elope, tensions build between Taylor and Rainey until a brush fire nearly claims the life of Taylor's son Wheeler. The boy is saved by Rainey, who suffers fatal burns himself in the fire, and the two adversaries reconcile before the chief dies. Though the film is plagued by wavering attitudes toward racism and cultural assimilation, it has a sincerity that's largely attributable to Taylor's faith in the project. Believing the film would provide him with a new image, he gave a strong performance in a demanding role, and went to great lengths to promote the film. Universal studio heads were less enthusiastic about the property, and eventually released it as part of an unlikely double bill with MUNSTER GO HOME.

p, R. John Hugh; d, Paul Wendkos; w, Paul Crabtree, Thomas Blackburn, Philip Wylie, Hugh (based on a story "Tiger on the Outside" by Hugh); ph, Charles Straumer (Technicolor); m, John Green; ed, Harry Coswick; md, Green; art d, Dick Williams; spec eff, Williams; makeup, Guy Del Russo; wildlife supervisor, Hal Granberry.

Drama **Cas.** **(PR:A MPAA:NR)**

JOHNNY TREMAIN*** ½ (1957) 80m BV c

Hal Stalmaster *(Johnny Tremain)*, Luana Patten *(Cilla Lapham)*, Jeff York *(James Otis)*, Sebastian Cabot *(Jonathan Lyte)*, Dick [Richard] Beymer *(Rab Silsbee)*, Walter Sande *(Paul Revere)*, Rusty Lane *(Samuel Adams)*, Whit Bissell *(Josiah Quincy)*, Will Wright *(Ephraim Lapham)*, Virginia Christine *(Mrs. Lapham)*, Walter Coy *(Dr. Joseph Warren)*, Geoffrey Toone *(Maj. Pitcairn)*, Ralph Clanton *(Gen. Gage)*, Gavin Gordon *(Col. Smith)*, Lumsden Hare *(Adm. Montagu)*, Anthony Ghazlo Jr. *(Jehu)*, Charles Smith *(Horse Tender)*.

This fine adaptation of Esther Forbes's novel opens in 1773 when Stalmaster is a silversmith's apprentice. He severely burns his hand in molten silver, rendering it useless. Unable to find employment, he becomes involved with revolutionary colonists, though he is uncommitted to their cause. His views change when he takes a silver cup embellished with his family crest to nobleman Cabot, claiming the crest proves they are related. The cup was a gift from Stalmaster's late mother, but Cabot accuses him of theft and has him arrested. Though he is found innocent at his trial, the incident leaves him more receptive to the revolutionary cause and he follows the advice of Sande as Paul Revere, who encourages him to become an active participant in the struggle. He joins the Sons of Liberty and takes part in the Boston Tea Party, which is followed by a torchlight parade through the town as the rebels sing "The Liberty Tree." Then it's 1775 when Clanton as the British general in charge of the colonies warns the colonists they must cooperate, and promises fair treatment if they do. The patriots reject his plea and the stage is set for a confrontation with British troops, under the command of Gordon, at Lexington Green. Though both sides have been ordered not to fire, a shot rings out from an unknown source and the American Revolution begins. In the film's final scene rebels are gathered around a bonfire, symbolizing the burning revolution that is overtaking the land. The film was originally meant to be a two-part television drama, but escalating production costs dictated its release as a feature. However, the two-part structure was maintained. A great film for children, JOHNNY TREMAIN makes history come alive. Stalmaster is very believable as an average young man caught up in tumultuous times. The film offers a balanced portrayal of both sides of the conflict, and the characters are presented as human beings first, historical figures second. This was the first Disney picture directed by Stevenson (ironically a British native) who went on to direct most of the studios live action films of the 1960s. Also includes the title tune "Johnny Tremain."

p, Walt Disney; d, Robert Stevenson; w, Tom Blackburn (based on the novel by Esther Forbes); ph, Charles P. Boyle (Technicolor); m, George Bruns; ed, Stanley Johnson; prod d, Peter Ellenshaw; art d, Carroll Clark; set d, Emile Kuri, Fred MacLean; cos, Chuck Keehne, Gertrude Casey; m/l, Bruns, Blackburn; makeup, David Newell.

Historical Drama **Cas.** **(PR:AAA MPAA:NR)**

JOHNNY TROUBLE*** (1957) 80m Clarion/WB bw

Ethel Barrymore *(Mrs. Chandler)*, Cecil Kellaway *(Tom McKay, Chandler chauffeur)*, Carolyn Jones *(Julie)*, Jesse White *(Parsons)*, Rand Harper *(Phil)*, Paul Wallace *(Paul)*, Edward [Edd] Byrnes *(Elliott)*, Edward Castagna *(Tex)*, Nino Tempo *(Charlie)*, Jim Bridges *(Ike)*, Paul Lukather *(Bill)*, James Bell *(Rev. Harrington)*, Samuel Colt *(Mr. Reichow)*, Kip King *(Boy)*, Gavin Muir *(Madden)*, Stuart Whitman *(Johnny)*, Jack Larson *(Eddie)*.

Barrymore, in her last film, plays a wealthy widowed invalid who refuses to leave her apartment after the building is sold to a local university and converted into a dormitory. She continues to hope that her son, who was expelled from the college and disappeared 27 years earlier, will return. She is adopted as the house "Nana" by the students and when ex-Marine Whitman moves in, Barrymore is convinced that he is her grandson because he has the same name as her son. She helps Whitman with romantic problems and during a conflict with school authorities. Shortly before Whitman's father is due to arrive, Barrymore dies, never realizing that Whitman is not really her grandson. What could have easily turned into soap opera is instead a sensitive drama thanks to Barrymore's dignified performance. She handles herself well, creating a sympathetic character. Whitman is fine in support.

p&d, John H. Auer; w, Charles O'Neil, David Lord (based on the story "Prodigal's Mother" by Ben Ames Williams); ph, J. Peverell Marley; m, Frank De Vol; ed, Tony Martinelli; md, De Vol; art d, James W. Sullivan; m/l, Peggy Lee (sung by Eddie Robertson).

Drama **(PR:A MPAA:NR)**

JOHNNY VAGABOND (SEE: JOHNNY COME LATELY, 1943)

JOHNNY VIK ** 1/2** (1973) 90m Nauman c

Warren Hammack *(Johnny Vik)*, Kathy Amerman *(Girl)*, Gina McCormick *(Rita)*.

Hammack is an Indian half-breed who is arrested and jailed for 30 days for urinating in public. He escapes and hides out in the woods, hallucinating about his problems and the clash between his two heritages. Eventually he is befriended by a young girl, who takes him to a cabin hide out. Here he finds happiness until a posse tracks him down and shoots him. Though well meaning, the film is hampered by self-conscious "arty" techniques. There is a preponderance of symbolism and the transitions between reality and hallucination do not always work. However Hammack carries the film nicely giving his unhappy character a sense of dignity.

p,d&w, Charles Nauman; ph, Marcel Shain (Eastmancolor); m, Bill Marx.

Drama **(PR:C MPAA:G)**

JOHNNY, YOU'RE WANTED**

(1956, Brit.) 71m Merton Park/Anglo-Amalgamated bw

John Slater *(Johnny)*, Alfred Marks *(Marks)*, Garry Marsh *(Balsamo)*, Chris Halward *(Julie)*, Joan Rhodes *(Herself)*, Jack Stewart *(Inspector Bennett)*, John Stuart *(Surgeon)*, Thelma Ruby *(PCW/Smuggler)*, Ann Lynn *(Chorus Girl)*, Frank Thornton, Peter Burton, Eric Corrie, Jimmy Vyvyan, Thelma Ruby, John Helier, Joan Carol.

Well-conceived thriller in which Slater plays a truck driver who suddenly finds himself in the midst of murder and intrigue. This comes when drug smugglers murder the girl he gave a lift to, putting the innocent Slater right in the middle of things and providing the impetus for him to attend to a bit of undercover operations of his own. The situations and performances are a bit forced, but otherwise interest is easily maintained.

p, George Maynard; d, Vernon Sewell; w, Michael Leighton, Frank Driscoll (based on the TV series by Maurice McLoughlin); ph, Basil Emmott.

Crime **(PR:A MPAA:NR)**

JOHNNY YUMA* 1/2 (1967, Ital.) 99m West Tiger/Clover c

Mark Damon *(Johnny Yuma)*, Lawrence Dobkin *(L.J. Carradine)*, Rosalba Neri *(Samantha Felton)*, Louis Vanner [Luigi Vannucchi] *(Pedro)*, Fidel Gonzales *(Sanchez)*, Gus Harper [Gustave D'Arpe] *(Henchman)*, Leslie Daniel *(Thomas Felton)*, Gianni Solaro, Dada Gallotti, Nando Poggi, Frank Liston [Franco Lauteri], Mirella Pamphili.

Spaghetti western with a plot that's little more than an excuse for some sadistic sequences. Neri has her wealthy husband killed, then must contend with his nephew, Damon, named as the sole heir in her husband's will. She enlists the aid of former lover Dobkin, but her attempts at a doublecross result in Damon and Dobkin joining forces, killing off Neri's henchmen in a gun battle. Dobkin is killed, but before he dies he sabotages the water supply Neri has packed for her escape across the desert. Film ends with Damon finding her body in the desert. The production values are negligible with poor camera setups and badly edited sequences. Acting is just about what you'd expect and the music is an imitation of the genre classic A FISTFUL OF DOLLARS.

p, Italo Zingarelli; d, Romolo Guerrieri; w, Sauro Scavolini, George Simonelli, Fernando Di Leo, Guerrieri (based on story by Scavolini); ph, Mario Capriotti (Eastmancolor); m, Nora Orlandi; ed, Sidney Klaber; m/l, "Johnny Yuma," Paul Orlandi, Nora Orlandi (sung by The Wilder Brothers).

Western **(PR:O MPAA:NR)**

JOI-UCHI (SEE: REBELLION, 1967, Jap.)

JOIN THE MARINES*** (1937) 70m REP bw

Paul Kelly *(Phil Donlan)*, June Travis *(Paula Denbrough)*, Purnell Pratt *(Col. Denbrough)*, Reginald Denny *(Steve)*, Warren Hymer *(Holman)*, Irving Pichel *(Col. Leonard)*, Sterling Holloway *(Steward)*, Ray Corrigan *(Lt. Hodge)*, John Holland *(Lieutenant)*, Carleton Young *(Corporal)*, John Sheehan *(O'Day)*, Arthur Hoyt *(Capt. James)*, Richard Beach *(Marine)*, Howard Hickman *(Pruitt)*, Val Duran *(Chinese Bartender)*, Landers Stevens *(McCullough)*.

In this likeable comedy Kelly is a New York City cop wrongly accused of drunkenness and dismissed from the Olympic team where he was to have been a boxer. Travis is the woman accidentally responsible for the misunderstanding and she falls for him. His problems mount as he is kicked off the force. To make a good impression with Travis's father, Pratt, he joins the Marines. By working hard, he swiftly rises through the ranks, winning both a commission and Pratt's blessing on the marriage. The dialog is fresh, the pace is quick and there are some nice plot twists within the simple framework. Kelly and Travis have a good chemistry going in this thoroughly enjoyable film.

p, Nat Levine; d, Ralph Staub; w, Joseph Krumgold, Olive Cooper (based on a story by Karl Brown); ph, Ernest Miller; md, Harry Gray, ed, Ernest Nims, Lester Orlebeck.

Comedy **(PR:A MPAA:NR)**

JOKER, THE ** 1/2** (1961, Fr.) 86m AJYM/Lopert bw (LE FARCEUR)

Anouk Aimee *(Helene Laroche)*, Jean-Pierre Cassel *(Edouard Berlon)*, Genevieve Cluny *(Pilou)*, Anne Tonietti *(Olga)*, Pierre Palau *(Uncle Theodose)*, Georges Wilson *(Guillaume Berlon)*, Francois Maistre *(Andre Laroche)*, Jean-Pierre Rambal, Liliane Patrick, Irene Chabrier.

Cassel is a young Parisian who finds joy in everything and everyone he meets—especially the numerous young ladies with whom he falls madly in love. He lives with Paulau, his ever-encouraging uncle, as well as his brother, Wilson, and his wife, Cluny, who once was Cassel's lover. The home also is shared by Tonietti the maid, four massive dogs, and Cassel's two beloved illegitimate children. When Cassel meets Aimee, the wife of a rich industrialist, he once more falls in love, but she spurns him and Cassel responds by playing a mournful tune on a bassoon and waiting for death. Aimee is charmed by this odd behavior and the two run off together. Cassel's happiness is short-lived as Aimee proves to be a complainer and frigid to boot. C'est la vie! At film's end, Cassel heads off once more, this time with a young waitress. A nice light story, just right for the hopelessly romantic.

p, Roland Nonin; d, Philippe de Broca; w, de Broca, Daniel Boulanger; ph, Jean Penzer; m, Georges Delerue; ed, Laurence Mery; art d, Jacques Saulnier.

Comedy **(PR:O MPAA:NR)**

JOKER IS WILD, THE* 1/2** (1957) 126m PAR bw (AKA: ALL THE WAY)

Frank Sinatra *(Joe E. Lewis)*, Mitzi Gaynor *(Martha Stewart)*, Jeanne Crain *(Letty Page)*, Eddie Albert *(Austin Mack)*, Beverly Garland *(Cassie Mack)*, Jackie Coogan *(Swifty Morgan)*, Barry Kelley *(Capt. Hugh McCarthy)*, Ted de Corsia *(Georgie Parker)*, Leonard Graves *(Tim Coogan)*, Valerie Allen *(Flora)*, Hank Henry *(Burlesque Comedian)*, Harold Huber *(Harry Bliss)*, Ned Glass *(Johnson)*, Ned Wever *(Dr. Pierson)*, Walter Woolf King *(Mr. Page)*, John Harding *(Allen)*, Sid Melton *(Runner)*, Wally Brown, Don Beddoe, Mary Treen *(Hecklers)*, Sophie Tucker *(Herself)*, Maurice Hart *(Squawk Box Voice)*, Paul Gary, Billy Snyder, Joseph Dante, Ralph Montgomery *(Men in Hotel Suite)*, Bill Hickman, Paul T. Salata *(Mugs)*, Frank Mills *(Florist Truck Driver)*, Eric Alden *(Doorman at Copacabana)*, Eric Wilton *(Butler)*, Ruby Fleming *(Girl)*, Mabel Rea *(Chorus Girl)*, Dick Elliott *(Man Shaving)*, Lucy Knoch *(Girl)*, William Pullen *(Letty's Husband)*, Oliver McGowan *(Judge)*, James J. Cavanaugh *(Straight Man)*, Harriette Tarler, Paula Hill *(Burlesque Girls)*, George Offerman *(Elevator Starter)*, James Cross *(Jack)*, Eric Wilton *(Butler)*, Kit Guard *(Doorman of the Valencia)*, John D. Benson *(Mug)*, Dennis McMullen, John Benson, David Seigel, Robert Asquith, Larry Knight, Arturo Petterino, Paul Bryar, Billie Bird, Ned LeFevre, Bill Baldwin, Leon Martin, Russell Bender, Arthur Lewis.

Sinatra is Joe E. Lewis in this taut and compelling biography which chronicles the nightclub era and one of its highest paid entertainers. It's Chicago during the Roaring Twenties and one of its roaringest singers is Sinatra. He's so successful that he packs the nightclub where he works and draws the attention of gangsters who own a competing club. They invite him to quit his job and go to work for them but Sinatra not so politely declines. Mobsters later visit him and cut his throat, almost from ear to ear. With his vocal cords nearly severed, Sinatra's singing days are over. He sinks into deep depression, then begins to use his caustic wit to establish a new career as a comedian. The great Sophie Tucker helps Sinatra reestablish himself on the burlesque circuit. Meanwhile, two women, socialite Crain and sassy chorus girl Gaynor, fall in love with Sinatra, with leggy Gaynor walking to the altar with him, even though he goes on loving Crain. With accompanist Albert at his side, Sinatra wows them with his humor until he's in demand everywhere. But he's unhappy and starts to belt down a lot of booze to go with the off-color jokes, making his nightclub toast to audiences famous: "It's post time!" Alcohol is Sinatra's undoing. He is more of a celebrated drunk than entertainer near the finish, insulting and intolerable, so that the long-suffering Gaynor walks out on him and even his patient friend Albert leaves him, too. Realizing his self-destructive ways, Sinatra reforms and at the finale appears to be making a comeback with friends and loved ones. It's a bleak story, often grim but handled with great style by Vidor and Sinatra's self-indulgent performance is somehow appealing. Much of the film is based on true incidents in the life of Lewis, who was attacked by goons working for Machine-Gun Jack McGurn (a Capone lieutenant) and slashed when he wouldn't go to work in a Capone saloon. Sinatra sings one smashing song, "All the Way" (James Van Heusen, Sammy Cahn) which won the Academy Award for Best Song. Other songs include: "Out of Nowhere" (John Green, new lyrics by Harry Harris), "At Sundown" (Walter Donaldson), "If I Could Be with You" (Jimmy Johnson, Henry Creamer), "I Cried for You" (Arthur Freed, Gus Arnheim, Abe Lyman), "Mimi" (Richard Rodgers, Lorenz Hart), "June in January" (Leo Robin, Ralph Rainger), "Chicago" (Fred Fisher), "Swinging On A Star" (Van Heusen, new lyrics by Harris), "I Love My Baby" (Bud Green, Harry Warren), "Naturally" (from Flotow's "Martha," new lyrics by Harris).

p, Samuel J. Briskin; d, Charles Vidor; w, Oscar Saul (based on the book *Life of Joe E. Lewis* by Art Cohn); ph, Daniel L. Fapp (Vista Vision); m, Walter Scharf; ed, Everett Douglas; md, Scharf; art d, Hal Pereira, Roland Anderson; set d, Sam Comer, Grace Gregory; cos, Edith Head; ch, Josephine Earl; spec eff, John P. Fulton.

Biography **(PR:C MPAA:NR)**

JOKERS, THE* 1/2** (1967, Brit.) 94m Gildor-Scimitar-Adastra/UNIV c

Michael Crawford *(Michael Tremayne)*, Oliver Reed *(David Tremayne)*, Harry Andrews *(Inspector Marryatt)*, James Donald *(Col. Gurney-Simms)*, Daniel Massey

(Riggs), Michael Hordern *(Sir Matthew)*, Gabriella Licudi *(Eve)*, Lotte Tarp *(Inge)*, Frank Finlay *(Harassed Man)*, Warren Mitchell *(Lennie)*, Rachel Kempson *(Mrs. Tremayne)*, Peter Graves *(Mr. Tremayne)*, Ingrid Brett *(Sarah)*, Brian Wilde *(Sgt. Catchpole)*, Edward Fox *(Lt. Sprague)*, Michael Goodliffe *(Lt. Col. Paling)*, William Devlin *(Brigadier)*, William Mervyn *(Uncle Edward)*, William Kendall *(Maj. Gen. Jeffcock)*, Kenneth Colley *(De Winter, the Chauffeur)*, Charlotte Curzon *(Camilla)*, Mark Burns *(Capt. Browning)*, Brook Williams *(Capt. Green)*, Freda Jackson *(Mrs. Pervis)*, Nan Munro *(Mrs. Jeffcock)*, Brian Peck *(Policeman)*, Basil Dignam *(Bank Manager)*, John Kidd *(Solicitor)*, Nicky Henson, Eric Thompson, Peter Gilmore, Julian Holloway.

THE JOKERS is long on style and short on content, but has enough wit and anarchistic joy to merit a look-see. Reed and Crawford are nihilistic brothers; Reed is an architect and Crawford has just been tossed out of military school. They plan to steal the British Crown Jewels as a lark, then return them after a week, just to prove it can be done. After a campaign of bomb scares to see how the Bomb Disposal Unit and Scotland Yard handle the crises, they hide a bomb in the Tower Of London's Jewel Room, then call the authorities. Next, they don clothing that allows them to slip into the heavily-guarded room with the official Bomb Disposal Unit. As soon as they are inside, they drug the men in the unit, steal the jewels, drench themselves in prop "blood," and race to an ambulance where they knock the drivers out and escape. It's the "crime of the century" and the whole country is perplexed. Before the robbery, both brothers had written pre-dated letters explaining the criminal plans and were supposed to send them. Reed sent his to the authorities, but Crawford did not. Reed is arrested and Crawford denies having had anything to do with the crime. Eventually Crawford puts the jewels on the scales of the statue of "Justice" which stands majestically some 200 feet above the famed courthouse of Old Bailey. Both brothers are now in jail and the film ends as they plan their escape. It's not much more than an elongated prank, but the derring-do is so much fun that it doesn't feel as though it's taken too long to reveal. All of the actors are excellent and the humor flies thick and fast. Many of the secondary players have gone on to great success in other films and TV series. You'll recognize a large cadre of some of the finest British farceurs ever assembled, but the question remains: why did they make this film other than as an exercise? If you can put logic aside, you'll thoroughly enjoy THE JOKERS. Anyone interested in seeing what life was like in London during the legendary "swinging 60s" will do well to see this picture. It's a most accurate depiction of the times. Raymond Massey's son, Daniel, is first-rate as a photographer, but don't confuse this cast's Peter Graves with the one from "Mission Impossible" fame who is James Arness's brother. The character here is a British actor. Excellent photography by Hodges is a highlight.

p, Maurice Foster, Ben Arbeid,; d, Michael Winner; w, Dick Clement, Ian La Frenais (based on a story by Winner); ph, Kenneth Hodges (Technicolor); m, Johnny Pearson; ed, Bernard Gribble; art d, John Blezard; cos, Tony Armstrong; makeup, Jim Hydes.

Comedy **(PR:A-C MPAA:NR)**

JOLLY BAD FELLOW, A1/2**

(1964, Brit.) 94m Tower-Pax-BL/CD bw (AKA: THEY ALL DIED LAUGHING)

Leo McKern *(Prof. Bowles-Ottery)*, Janet Munro *(Delia Brooks)*, Maxine Audley *(Clarinda Bowles-Ottery)*, Duncan Macrae *(Dr. Brass)*, Dennis Price *(Prof. Hughes)*, Miles Malleson *(Dr. Woolley)*, Leonard Rossiter *(Dr. Fisher)*, Alan Wheatley *(Epicene)*, Patricia Jessel *(Mrs. Pugh-Smith)*, Dinsdale Landen *(Fred)*, George Benson *(Inspector Butts)*, Mark Dignam *(The Master)*, Jerome Willis *(Armstrong)*, Ralph Michael *(Supt. Kastleigh)*, Mervyn Johns *(Willie Pugh-Smith)*, Raymond Ray *(The Waiter)*, Joyce Carey *(Hotel Receptionist)*, Cliff Michelmore *(Himself, a TV Commentator)*, Wally Patch *(Landlord)*.

Goofy British black comedy stars McKern as a nutty-but-evil professor who discovers a poison that drives victims into hysterics and then kills them, leaving no trace in the body behind. Originally intending to use the poison for the good of mankind, McKern's mind snaps when university politics threaten his experiments and he begins to bump off his enemies with the poison. Not only does this kill his victims, but the hysterical aspect of the drug forces them to humiliate themselves before they die. Eventually McKern's well-endowed girl friend and lab assistant, Munro, begins to suspect that she's next on his list and threatens to expose him unless he divorces his wife and marries her. Calmly he offers her a cigarette and she accepts, realizing as she begins to giggle uncontrollably that the smoke has been poisoned. Before she dies Munro calls the police. McKern laughs at her attempt to have him arrested because the poison leaves no trace, and defiantly lights up a cigarette to wait for the cops to come. Unfortunately, he, too, realizes too late that he's just smoked a poisoned cigarette and he goes insane, jumps into his car, and drives it into a steamroller, which, as steamrollers do, flattens him. A poised and sophisticated comedy written by one of the most stylish screenwriters and directors in the Ealing stable, Robert Hamer, just before he died, and directed by Don Chaffey, noted for his saucy comedies and adults-only pictures. JOLLY BAD FELLOW also offers audiences a glimpse of a modern hero in the person of Price, Prof. Hughes in the story, who was seriously wounded in WW II but survived that tragedy to become a top character and comedy actor.

p, Donald Taylor; d, Don Chaffey; w, Robert Hamer, Taylor (based on the novel *Don Among the Dead Men* by C.E. Vulliamy); ph, Gerald Gibbs; m, John Barry; ed, Peter Tanner; art d, George Provis.

Comedy **(PR:C MPAA:NR)**

JOLLY OLD HIGGINS (SEE: EARL OF PUDDLESTONE, 1940)

JOLSON SINGS AGAIN*1/2** (1949) 96m COL c

Larry Parks *(Al Jolson)*, Barbara Hale *(Ellen Clark)*, William Demarest *(Steve Martin)*, Ludwig Donath *(Cantor Yoelson)*, Bill Goodwin *(Tom Baron)*, Myron McCormick *(Ralph Bryant)*, Tamara Shayne *(Mama Yoelson)*, Eric Wilton *(Henry)*, Robert Emmett Keane *(Charlie)*, Larry Parks *(Himself)*, Frank McLure, Jock Mahoney *(Men)*, Betty Hill *(Woman)*, Margie Stapp *(Nurse)*, Nelson Leigh *(Theater Manager)*, Virginia Mullen *(Mrs. Bryant)*, Philip Faulkner, Jr. *(Sound Mixer)*, Morris Stoloff *(Orchestra Leader)*, Helen Mowery *(Script Girl)*, Michael Cisney, Ben Erway *(Writers)*, Martin Garralaga *(Mr. Estrada)*, Dick Cogan *(Soldier)*, Peter Brocco *(Captain of Waiters)*, Charles Regan, Charles Perry, Richard Gordon, David Newell, Joe Gilbert, David Horsley, Wanda Perry, Louise Illington, Gertrude Astor, Steve Benton, Eleanor Marvak *(Bits)*.

Sequels are seldom as good as the original, but this one came as close as any of them do. Once THE JOLSON STORY was released to such sensational business, the studio realized that they'd better rush another one into production, although it took almost three years for the second to be done. Once again, the music is the entire reason for seeing the film, as it is a wall-to-wall tune-a-thon with many of the same songs as heard in the original. Parks, as Jolson, was excellent, and most of the actors reprised the roles they played in the Sidney Skolsky production in 1946. This film begins with Parks doing a nightclub performance and his long-suffering wife responding by strolling out on him. Next comes the war and a series of shows for the "boys in uniform" with the result being that Parks contracts a lung ailment in Africa. In the hospital, he meets Hale, a nurse; they fall in love and the rest of the picture is what leads up to the making of the first picture; i.e. hiring Larry Parks (who plays both himself and Jolson in a double-exposure sequence.) The film also reveals how Parks learned Jolson's moves and did all of the "looping" sequences to Jolson's voice. In any musical film, the songs are pre-recorded, and the same actor who recorded them then mouths the lyrics. That's been going on since the dawn of sound movies. What usually happens is the stage is set, the playback takes place, and the actor-singer will truly sing the tune (although there is no open microphone) so that all the vocal mannerisms can be exact, the neck can be seen to strain on the high notes, etc. It's much more difficult when one mimes to another person's voice and Parks, with the help of Jolson, does it wonderfully. As in the opener, they gloss over Jolson's persona in favor of his talents, although they do show his financial extravagances and his sadness at being left behind by the up-and-coming stars after a lifetime of top billing. They never acknowledge Skolsky's involvement beyond a line saying that "a certain Hollywood columnist" was responsible for the idea for THE JOLSON STORY. Donath and Shayne play Jolson's parents once again, and Goodwin (who spent so many years as a radio announcer before an untimely death in Palm Springs) replays his role as Jolson's pal. Hale doesn't have much to do as Jolson's second wife because there isn't much time to develop any new characterizations with that much music pouring off the screen at such a breakneck pace. Hale's character is based on Erle Chennault Galbraith (a relative of the Flying Tiger's Gen. Chennault) of Little Rock, Arkansas, and this was her first major role after having appeared in many small parts since 1943. She is married to actor Bill Williams and, in between co-starring as Della Street for many years on the "Perry Mason" TV series, she managed to raise a son, William Katt, who went on to have his own series, "The Great American Hero." The multitude of songs sung by Jolson includes: "After You've Gone" (Harry Creamer, Turner Layton), "Chinatown, My Chinatown" (Joe Young, Sam Lewis, Jean Schwartz), "Give My Regards to Broadway" (George M. Cohan), "I Only Have Eyes for You" (Al Dubin, Harry Warren), "I'm Just Wild About Harry" (Noble Sissle, Eubie Blake), "You Made Me Love You" (Joseph McCarthy, James V. Monaco), "I'm Looking Over a Four Leaf Clover" (Mort Dixon, Harry Woods), "Is It True What They Say About Dixie?" (Sammy Lerner, Irving Caesar, Gerald Marks), "Ma Blushin' Rose" (Edgar Smith, John Stromberg), "Let Me Sing and I'm Happy" (Irving Berlin), "Baby Face" (Benny Davis, Harry Akst), "Sonny Boy" (Buddy De Sylva, Lew Brown, Ray Henderson), "About a Quarter to Nine" (Al Dubin, Harry Warren), "Anniversary Song" (Saul Chaplin, Al Jolson, J. Ivanovici), "For Me and My Gal" (Edgar Leslie, E. Ray Goetz), "California Here I Come" (De Sylva, Jolson, Joseph Meyer), "Rockabye Your Baby" (Lewis, Young, Schwartz), "Carolina in the Morning" (Gus Kahn, Walter Donaldson), "Toot Toot Tootsie Goodbye" (Kahn, Ernie Erdman, Dan Russo), "April Showers" (De Sylva, Louis Silvers), "Swanee" (George Gershwin, Caesar), "My Mammy" (Lewis, Young, Donaldson). Also included were "I'll Take Romance" (Oscar Hammerstein II, Ben Oakland), "It's A Blue World" (Bob Wright, Chet Forrest), "Learn to Croon" (Sam Coslow, Arthur Johnston, sung by Bing Crosby), "Back in Your Own Backyard" (Jolson, Billy Rose, Dave Dreyer), "When the Red Red Robin Comes Bob, Bob, Bobbin' Along" (Woods).

p&w, Sidney Buchman; d, Henry Levin; ph, William Snyder (Technicolor); m, George Duning; ed, William Lyon; md, Morris Stoloff; art d, Walter Holscher; set d, William Kiernan; cos, Jean Louis.

Musical/Biography **(PR:A MPAA:NR)**

JOLSON STORY, THE*1/2** (1946) 128m COL c

Larry Parks *(Al Jolson)*, Evelyn Keyes *(Julie Benson)*, William Demarest *(Steve Martin)*, Bill Goodwin *(Tom Baron)*, Ludwig Donath *(Cantor Yoelson)*, Tamara Shayne *(Mrs. Yoelson)*, John Alexander *(Lew Dockstader)*, Jo-Carroll Dennison *(Ann Murray)*, Ernest Cossart *(Father McGee)*, Scotty Beckett *(Jolson as a Boy)*, William Forrest *(Dick Glenn)*, Ann E. Todd *(Ann as a Girl)*, Edwin Maxwell *(Oscar Hammerstein)*, Emmett Vogan *(Jonsey)*, Eddie Kane *(Ziegfeld)*, Jimmy Lloyd *(Roy Anderson)*, Coulter Irwin *(Young Priest)*, Adele Roberts *(Ingenue)*, Bob Stevens *(Henry)*, Harry Shannon *(Riley, Policeman)*, Bud Gorman *(Call Boy)*, Charles Jordan *(Asst. Stage Manager)*, Pierre Watkin *(Architect)*, Lillian Bond *(Woman)*, Eugene Borden *(Headwaiter)*, Eddie Rio *(M. C.)*, Will Wright *(Sourpuss Movie Patron)*, Arthur Loft *(Stage Manager)*, Edward Keane *(Director)*, Eddie Fetherston *(Asst. Stage Manager)*, Bill Brandt *(Orchestra Leader)*, Pat Lane *(Cameraman)*, Mike Lally *(Lab Manager)*, George Magrill *(Gaffer)*, Helen O'Hara *(Dancer-Actress)*, Jessie Arnold *(Wardrobe Woman)*, Donna Dax *(Girl Publicist)*, Fred Sears *(Cutter)*, Eric Wilton *(Harry, Butler)*, Franklyn Farnum *(Man in Audience)*, The Robert Mitchell Boy Choir *(Choir)*, Major Sam Harris *(Nightclubber)*.

THE JOLSON STORY was a smash at the box office, despite the fact that it utilized just about every show business cliche ever devised. It also played a bit with the truth because Jolson is remembered by everyone who knew him as one of the most difficult men who ever trod the boards. This was Parks' first big role after five years of strictly small-time work, and he took advantage of the opportunity. Jolson's real story was a mixture of joy, anger, bitterness and big-time success. He'd starred in the first sound movie, THE JAZZ SINGER, but, by the time they decided to do his story, his day had come and gone. Nevertheless, older audiences who recalled his abilities, flocked to the theaters, and young people who had been brought up on the "cool" style of Crosby, Sinatra, and Como were electrified by the energy pouring off the screen. Jolson, who wanted to play himself, was in his 60s and Harry Cohn convinced him that was a bad idea. The parts that were omitted could have made a movie on their own. Jolson paid little attention to his son and fought so hard with his wife, Ruby Keeler, that she refused to let them use her name in the film and so her character is named Julie Benson. The mixture of fact and fiction showed Jolson's young life (played well by Beckett); how his voice broke, his parents' desire that he follow another career, and his eventual rise to the top. Jolson's mannerisms are perfectly captured by Parks (who was coached by Jolson): the whistling, the deliberate interruptions in the middle of a show to stop and banter with the audience. Jolson was a lot of things and none of them was beloved. They totally avoid his flaws and concentrate on the music. Not a bad idea when your star has feet of clay. A literal sing-a-long with one exception, and no one seems to know why "Sonny Boy" was not included. So, if you like music, you'll love THE JOLSON STORY, but don't expect any new insights into the man's character. When the subject of a film biography is still alive and has been hired to work on the film (besides coaching Parks, Jolson was seen in a long shot), you are not going to get anything unvarnished. Long-time Hollywood columnist Skolsky was the brains behind the film. Until his death, he could be found seated daily on the same stool at Schwab's Drug Store on Sunset Boulevard and his stories are still told with fondness by the old-timers (who've taken their business to Theodore's Restaurant in West Hollywood) since Schwab's closed its doors in 1984. Songs include "Swanee" (Irving Caesar, George Gershwin), "You Made Me Love You" (Joseph McCarthy, James V. Monaco), "By the Light of the Silvery Moon" (Edward Madden, Gus Edwards), "I'm Sitting On Top of the World" (Sam Lewis, Joe Young, Ray Henderson), "There's a Rainbow Round My Shoulder" (Al Jolson, Billy Rose, Dave Dreyer), "My Mammy" (Lewis, Young, Walter Donaldson), "Rock-A-Bye Your Baby With a Dixie Melody" (Lewis, Young, Jean Schwartz), "Liza" (Gus Kahn, George and Ira Gershwin), "Waiting For the Robert E. Lee" (L. Wolfe Gilbert, Lewis F. Muir), "April Showers" (Buddy De Sylva, Louis Silvers), "About a Quarter to Nine" (Al Dubin, Harry Warren), "I Want a Girl Just Like the Girl That Married Dear Old Dad" (Will Dillon, Harry von Tilzer), "The Anniversary Song" (Jolson, Saul Chaplin, J. Ivanovici), "The Spaniard Who Blighted My Life" (Billy Merson), "Let Me Sing and I'm Happy" (Irving Berlin), "When You Were Sweet Sixteen" (James Thornton), "Toot Toot Tootsie Goodbye" (Gus Kahn, Ernie Erdman, Dan Russo), "Eli Eli" (traditional), "On the Banks of the Wabash" (Paul Dresser), "Ma Blushin' Rosie" (Edgar Smith, John Stromberg), "Ave Maria" (Franz Schubert), "After the Ball" (Charles K. Harris), "Blue Bell" (Edward Madden, Theodore F. Morse), "Every Little Movement Has a Meaning Of its Own" (Otto Harbach, Karl Hoschna), "Avalon" (Jolson, Vincent Rose), and a medley of songs including "Lullabye of Broadway," "42nd Street, " "She's a Latin From Manhattan," "We're In the Money" (Al Dubin, Harry Warren).

p, Sidney Skolsky; d, Alfred E. Green; w, Stephen Longstreet, Harry Chandlee, Andrew Solt; ph, Joseph Walker (Technicolor); ed, William Lyon; md, Morris Stoloff; art d, Stephen Goosson, Walter Holscher; set d, William Kiernan, Louis Diage; cos, Jean Louis; ch, Jack Cole, Joseph H. Lewis; makeup, Clay Campbell.

Musical/Biography **(PR:A MPAA:NR)**

JONAH—WHO WILL BE 25 IN THE YEAR 2000* 1/2**

(1976, Switz.) 116m Action-Citel-Societe Francaise de Production-SSR Swiss Television/New Yorker c (JONAS—QUI AURA 25 ANS EN L'AN 2000)

Jean-Luc Bideau *(Max Stigny)*, Myriam Boyer *(Mathilde Vernier)*, Myriam Mziere *(Madeleine)*, Jacques Denis *(Marco Perly)*, Roger Jendly *(Marcel Certoux)*, Dominique Labourier *(Marguerite)*, Miou-Miou *(Marie)*, Raymond Bussieres *(Old Charles)*, Rufus *(Mathieu Vernier)*, Jonas *(Himself)*, Pierre Holdener, Maurice Aufair, Jean Schlegel, Gilbert Costa, Christine Wipf, Guillaume Cheneviere, Robert Schmid, Daniel Stuffel, Francis Reusser, Michel Fidanza, Nicole Die, Domingo Semedo, Mady Deluz, Jiairo Daghini, Albino Palumbo, Cecile, Coralie, Nathalie, David, Lionel, Nicholas, Sten, Calvin College Theater Group.

Unlike most films that seem to dwell on the lost ideals of the children of the 1960s, JONAH is an extremely exhilarating film with characters that are filled with life and who refuse to become trapped in endless dreams that can never come true. Though each of these people is kept from achieving some desire, that failure doesn't result in a state of personal decay or self-pity. Perhaps this is a function of the beliefs they fought for in the 1960s: goals which were never quite reached, but which left them with the satisfaction of knowing they had tried. Whatever the case, all these characters are extremely likable, filling the screen with an uplifting energy that is easily transmitted to the viewer. Prime among them are Miou-Miou, a grocery clerk who steals food for a retired engineer (Bussieres), and Denis, a teacher who can't keep a steady job. But it would be blasphemous to limit the credit to just these two; every one of the characters is a total joy. Tanner weaves them together in a subtle fashion and knows when to turn off their exhilaration to allow his own themes to take over. (In French; English subtitles).

p, Yves Gasser, Yves Peyrot; d, Alain Tanner; w, John Berger, Tanner; ph, Renato Berta (Eastmancolor); m, Jean-Marie Senia; ed, Brigitte Sousselier, Marc Blavet.

Comedy **(PR:C MPAA:NR)**

JONAS: QUI AURA 25 ANS EN L'AN 2000

(SEE: JONAH: WHO WILL BE 25 IN THE YEAR 2000 1976, Switz.)

JONATHAN***

(1973, Ger.) 103m Iduna/New Yorker c (JONATHAN, VAMPIRE STERBEN NICHT)

Jurgen Jung *(Jonathan)*, Hans Dieter Jendreyko *(Josef)*, Paul Albert Krumm *(Count)*, Thomas Astan *(Thomas)*, Ilse Kunkele *(Lena's Mother)*, Eleonore Schminke *(Lena)*, Oskar Von Schab *(Professor)*, Ilone Grubel *(Eleonore)*.

Superior vampire piece has Jung preying on the local peasants, in an allegory comparing vampirism to fascism. Extra scenes of sex and violence were added after the film's initial release to improve its marketability.

d&w, Hans W. Geissendorfer (based on the novel *Dracula* by Bram Stoker); ph, Robby Muller (Eastmancolor); m, Roland Kovacs; ed, Wolfgang Hedinger; art d, Hans Gailling; cos, Ute Wilhelm.

Horror **(PR:O MPAA:NR)**

JONATHAN LIVINGSTON SEAGULL* (1973) 114m PAR c

James Franciscus *(Jonathan's Voice)*, Juliet Mills *(Girl's Voice)*, Hal Holbrook *(Elder's Voice)*, Philip Ahn *(Chang's Voice)*, David Ladd *(Fletcher's Voice)*, Kelly Harmon *(Kimmy's Voice)*, Dorothy McGuire *(Mother's Voice)*, Richard Crenna *(Father's Voice)*.

Truly one of the most boring pictures ever done but with enough attractive photography to merit your brief attention. The book was a runaway success as it preached a philosophy of self-involvement. It did not translate to the screen where most of the dialog seemed unbearably pretentious and Diamond's monotonous music didn't help a bit. The moralizing is nitwit in conception, but the actors do a fine job mouthing the words and will probably manage to convince people who are running their engines a quart low. It's a cartoon technique but with live cinematography that would have been far more effective if less words were spoken. Seagulls in the harbor are battling for fish heads and their dialog establishes who they are and their feelings about the lives they lead. One of them (Franciscus) hates eating garbage and longs to fly away and see what the world is like on the other side of the horizon. He is a rebellious seagull and is cashiered out of the flock by Holbrook for his anarchistic views. He then flies around the world, dies, and goes to bird heaven where he encounters a female gull (Mills) and a high priest (Ahn) who show him that seagulls are not limited to scavenging. They teach him how to fly like the Red Baron. He returns from the dead to tell the others of his regular flock that there's lots more to do than fight over refuse. Ladd plays Fletcher, a gull with a problem whom Franciscus shows how to loop-the-loop, barrel roll and do several dangerous moves. Ladd crashes and dies and Franciscus brings him back to life (do you draw the parallel with Lazarus?) and Franciscus is acknowledged by the others as being "the son of the great gull." They now want him to stay and teach them everything he knows, but he decides that there are other gulls who need the benefit of his teachings and so he goes flying off to spread the word. Hallelujah. It was around this time that America fell in love with EST and a few other self-help programs, but those had to be experienced in order to derive any benefits. In this film, we never do feel anything more than revulsion at the endless posturing of the dialog and the crude attempts to find Jesus in a Seagull. Several lawsuits were filed after the film's release. Ovady Julber claimed that many of the scenes were direct steals from his LA MER. Diamond sued because his music was cut and replaced in a few scenes. Bach sued because he never approved the screenplay and felt they'd cut it too deeply and that his book was not followed. Millions were spent developing all the ancillary products they thought would reap a fortune. Everything from Jonathan Livingston Seagull games to napery, to T-shirts, patches, pins, shoes, and so on and so forth. When the picture laid an egg, so did the products. Jonathan Livingston Seagull was no Donald Duck.

p&d, Hall Bartlett; w, Richard Bach, Bartlett (based on the novel by Bach); ph, Jack Couffer (Panavision, DeLuxe Color); m, Neil Diamond, Lee Holdridge; ed, Frank Keller; prod d, Boris Leven.

Drama **Cas.** **(PR:A MPAA:G)**

JONES FAMILY IN HOLLYWOOD, THE** (1939) 60m FOX bw

Jed Prouty, Spring Byington, Ken Howell, George Ernest, June Carlson, Florence Roberts, Billy Mahan, William Tracy, June Gale, Marvin Stephens, Hamilton MacFadden, Matt McHugh.

In this entry in the Jones family series, Prouty goes to Hollywood for an American Legion meeting, taking the entire family with him. Carlson is picked up by Tracy, who manages to get her a disastrous screen test. There are some very funny moments as the family members create havoc in a movie studio. The great silent comedian Buster Keaton wrote this story at breakneck speed in the darkest days of his vanishing career; he needed money badly and churned this one out overnight. It shows. (See JONES FAMILY series, Index).

p, John Stone; d, Malcolm St. Clair; w, Harold Tarshis (based on a story by Joseph Hoffman and Buster Keaton and characters created by Katherine Kavanaugh); ph, Edward Snyder; md, Samuel Kaylin.

Comedy **(PR:A MPAA:NR)**

JONI 1/2** (1980) 108m World Wide Pictures c

Joni Eareckson *(Joni Eareckson)*, Bert Remsen *(Mr. Eareckson)*, Katherine De Hetre *(Jay)*, Cooper Huckabee *(Dick)*, John Milford *(Doctor)*, Michael Mancini *(Don)*, Richard Lineback *(Steve)*, Jay W. MacIntosh, Louise Hoven, Cloyce Morrow, Sarah Rush, Jeff Austin, Cheryl Harvey, Ernie Hudson, Barbara Mallory, Jane Ralston, Betsy Jones-Moreland, Stephen Parr.

Eareckson plays herself in this story of a woman who becomes a quadriplegic after breaking her spine in a diving accident. Operations prove futile, and, filled with her despair, she returns to her parents' ranch in Maryland. She starts sketching and painting, holding the brushes in her mouth, and slowly begins to adjust to her confinement. The film attempts to deal realistically with the problems of the handicapped, particularly with respect to how they are perceived by others.

Eventually, Eareckson finds solace in religion, and the film shows her speaking to church crowds about her new-found faith. Eareckson, who has the difficult task of reliving her life for the movie screen, does a fine job and is a natural actress. Be sure to watch for evangelist Billy Graham in the crowd during one of Eareckson's speeches—he was one of the film's financial backers.

p, Frank R. Hacobson; d&w, James F. Collier (based on the book by Joni Eareckson); ph, Frank Raymond (Metrocolor); m, Ralph Carmichael; ed, Duane Hartzell; art d, Bill Ross.

Biography **(PR:A MPAA:G)**

JONIKO (SEE: JONIKO AND THE KUSH TA KA, 1969)

JONIKO AND THE KUSH TA KA** ½**
(1969) 94m Alaska Pictures/ANE c (AKA: JONIKO; ALASKA BOY; FRONTIER ALASKA)

Tony Tucker Williams *(Joniko)*, Jimmy Cane *(Grandfather)*, Richard Stitt *(Father)*, Teresa Stitt *(Mother)*, Charlie Paddock, Jesse Paddock *(Twins)*, Penton James, Chuck Nowlin *(Seal Hunters)*, Sheldon Allman *(Narrator)*

Williams is a 12-year-old Alaskan descended from the Tlingit Eskimos. He finds a geologist and guides him through the country until the man falls and breaks his leg. Williams takes his canoe and sets off to find his father, Stitt, who has left for the northern seal grounds. Along the way Williams sees native animals, including grizzly bears and sperm whales. He enters a huge sea of ice and becomes afraid of evil spirits, but he overcomes Kush Ta Ka, the spirit of fear, finds his father, and saves the geologist. Some nice scenery, but strictly for the kids.

p, Chuck D. Keen; d, Ford Beebe; w&ph, Keen; m, Hoyt Curtain, William Loose; ed, Leoncid Ortiz-Gil.

Adventure **(PR:AAA MPAA:G)**

JORY* (1972) 97m Minsky-Kirschner-Cinematografice Marco Polo/AE c

John Marley *(Roy)*, B. J. Thomas *(Jocko)*, Robby Benson *(Jory)*, Brad Dexter *(Jack)*, Claudio Brook *(Ethan)*, Patricia Aspillaga *(Carmelita)*, Todd Martin *(Barron)*, Ben Baker *(Jordan)*, Carlos Cortes *(Logan)*, Linda Purl *(Amy)*, Anne Lockhart *(Dora)*, Betty Sheridan *(Mrs. Jordan)*, Ted Markland *(Evans)*, Quintin Bulnes *(Walker)*, John Kelly *(Thatcher)*, Eduardo Lopez Rojas *(Cookie)*.

Benson is the young gunslinger who, due to the influence of wizened Marley and the experiences of a cattle drive, forsakes a career as a gunslinger for that of a rancher. Uneven script further damaged by plodding direction. Filmed in Mexico.

p, Howard Minsky; d, Jorge Fons; w, Gerald Herman, Robert Irving (based on a novel by Milton R. Bass); ph, George Stahl; m, Al DeLory; ed, Fred Chulak, Sergio Ortega; prod d, Earl Hedrick.

Western **(PR:A MPAA:PG)**

JOSEPH AND HIS BRETHREN
(SEE: STORY OF JOSEPH AND HIS BRETHREN, 1962)

JOSEPH ANDREWS** (1977, Brit.) 103m WF/PAR c

Ann-Margret *(Lady Booby)*, Peter Firth *(Joseph Andrews)*, Michael Hordern *(Parson Adamis)*, Beryl Reid *(Mrs. Slipslop)*, Jim Dale *(Peddler)*, Natalie Ogle *(Fanny Goodwill)*, Peter Bull *(Sir Thomas Booby)*, Kenneth Cranham *(Wicked Squire)*, Karen Dotrice *(Pamela)*, James Villiers *(Mr. Booby)*, John Gielgud, Peggy Ashcroft, Hugh Griffith.

Firth is a young servant in 18th century England who was switched at birth. He goes through various adventures, including an affair with the mysterious Ann-Margret. It's a long and tedious film that desperately tries to capture the feeling of Richardson's wild and wonderful TOM JONES. Richardson's direction just doesn't match up to his previous effort though, which also was based on another Fielding novel. Gielgud, Ashcroft, and Griffith make brief cameos, but to no avail. The one saving grace is the attention to detail. The film has the look and feel of 18th Century England. Pity it has no plot.

p, Neil Hartley; d, Tony Richardson; w, Allan Scott, Chris Bryant (based on a story by Richardson and the novel by Henry Fielding); ph, David Watkin (Movielab Color); m, John Addison; ed, Thom Noble; prod d, Michael Annals; art d, Bill Brosie; set d, Ian Whittaker, cos, Annals, Arthur Davey, Jean Hunnisett, Patrick Wheatley; m/l, Jim Dale, Bob Stewart; stunts, William Hobbs.

Comedy **Cas.** **(PR:O MPAA:R)**

JOSEPH SOLD BY HIS BROTHERS
(SEE: STORY OF JOSEPH AND HIS BRETHREN, THE, 1962, Ital.)

JOSEPHINE AND MEN** (1955, Brit.) 98m Charter Film-Boulting/BL c

Glynis Johns *(Josephine Luton)*, Jack Buchanan *(Uncle Charles Luton)*, Donald Sinden *(Alan Hartley)*, Peter Finch *(David Hewer)*, Heather Thatcher *(Aunt May Luton)*, Ronald Squire *(Frederick Luton)*, William Hartnell *(Inspector Parsons)*, Gerald Sim *(Detective)*, Hugh Moxey *(Police Inspector)*, Sam Kydd *(Police Sergeant)*, Tonie McMillan *(Mrs. McFee)*, Wally Patch *(Landlord "Five Bells")*, Peggy Ann Clifford *(Landlady)*, Victor Maddern *(Henry)*, Thorley Walters *(Salesman)*, Laurence Naismith *(Porter)*, John le Mesurier *(Registrar)*, Lisa Gastoni *(Girl)*, Leo Ciceri, Pauline David.

Buchanan is the lady-chasing bachelor-uncle of Johns. Through flashbacks he tells her story. She is a constant fighter for the underdog, abandoning her wealthy fiance the night before the wedding to marry his starving playwright friend, Finch. Soon he becomes a success, when who should turn up but Sinden, the jilted fiance. Now he's the one in trouble, on the lam from the cops. Once more Johns' affections switch, but when Sinden is cleared, she comes to her senses. Unfortunately, this film never reaches its humorous potential, perhaps due to its passive direction and the fact that there are too many minor details clogging up the script.

p, John Boulting; d, Roy Boulting; w, Nigel Balchin, Frank Harvey, R. Boulting (based on a story by Balchin); ph, Gilbert Taylor (Eastmancolor); m, John Addison; ed, Maxwell Benedict.

Comedy **(PR:A MPAA:NR)**

JOSETTE** ½** (1938) 70m FOX bw

Don Ameche *(David Brossard, Jr.)*, Simone Simon *(Renee Le Blanc)*, Robert Young *(Pierre Brossard)*, Bert Lahr *(Barney Barnaby)*, Joan Davis *(May Morris)*, Paul Hurst *(A. Adolphus Heyman)*, William Collier, Sr. *(David Brossard, Sr.)*, Tala Birell *(Mlle. Josette)*, Lynn Bari *(Mrs. Elaine Dupree)*, William Demarest *(Bill)*, Ruth Gillette *(Belle, Bill's Wife)*, Armand Kaliz *(Thomas, Headwaiter)*, Maurice Cass *(Ed Furrier)*, George H. Reed *(Mose the Butler)*, Paul McVey *(Hotel Manager)*, Fred Kelsey *(Hotel Detective)*, Robert Kellard *(Kearney, Reporter)*, Robert Lowery *(Officer)*, Lon Chaney, Jr. *(Boatman)*, Slim Martin *(Orchestra Leader)*, June Gale *(Cafe Girl)*, Mary Healy *(Ringsider)*, Ferdinand Gottschalk *(Papa Le Blanc)*, Lillian Porter *(Toinette)*, Eddie Collins *(Custom Inspector)*, Ruth Peterson *(Switchboard Operator)*, Jayne Regan, Zeffie Tilbury, Harry Holman, Raymond Turner.

Collier is a wealthy man who marries gold digger Birell. His two sons, Ameche and Young, hear about their father's folly and try to stop him. They meet Simon, a young cabaret singer, convinced that she's the seductress. But it turns out she isn't nor is she a nightclub singer. She's faking it in order to help Lahr save his nightclub. Despite their best efforts, Young and Ameche find themselves falling in love with Simon and vie for her affections. Her true identity is finally revealed and she ends up with Ameche. Amusing though very slight comedy. The direction works with the lightweight script, using actors and locale to their fullest.

p, Gene Markey; d, Allan Dwan; w, James Edward Grant (based on the play by Paul Frank, George Fraser from the story by Ladislaus Vadnai); ph, John Mescall; ed, Robert Simpson; md, David Buttolph; art d, Bernard Herzbrun, David Hall; set d, Thomas Little; ch, Nick Castle, Geneva Sawyer; m/l, "May I Drop a Petal in Your Glass of Wine?" "Where in the World," "In Any Language," Mack Gordon, Harry Revel.

Comedy **(PR:A MPAA:NR)**

JOSHUA* (1976) 80m Po'boy/Lone Star c

Fred Williamson, Isela Vega, Calvin Bartlett, Brenda Venus.

Williamson runs around eating cigars, chasing bad guys, fighting, and making love in this incomprehensible mess that takes place shortly after the Civil War. The script was written by Williamson, but he hasn't gone to too much trouble; there's barely enough dialog to justify a script. This is a perfect example of the dubious 1970s genre known as "blaxploitation films." Made cheaply with little quality in production or acting, the films were generally released in theaters catering to black audiences.

p&d, Larry Spangler; w, Fred Williamson.

Drama **(PR:O MPAA:R)**

JOSSER IN THE ARMY** (1932, Brit.) 79m BIP/Wardour bw

Ernie Lotinga *(Jimmy Josser)*, Betty Norton *(Joan)*, Jack Hobbs *(Paul Langdon)*, Hal Gordon *(Parker)*, Jack Frost *(Ginger)*, Arnold Bell *(Becker)*, Harold Wilkinson *(Seeley)*.

Lotinga is up to his mischievous antics again, this time during WW I. The Germans become victims of his madcap heroics, when he serves as a prisoner of war and later impersonates a German officer. The picture achieves its goal of getting a belly laugh or two. (See JOSSER series, Index)

p, John Maxwell; d, Norman Lee; w, Frank Launder (based on a story by Con West, Herbert Sargent).

Comedy **(PR:A MPAA:NR)**

JOSSER JOINS THE NAVY** (1932, Brit.) 69m BIP/Wardour bw

Ernie Lotinga *(Jimmy Josser)*, Cyril McLaglen *(Langford)*, Jack Hobbs *(Lt. Comdr. Cole)*, Lesley Wareing *(Lesley Beauchamp)*, Renee Gadd *(Polly)*, Jack Frost *(Spud)*, H. Saxon-Snell *(Ling Foo)*, Charles Paton *(Prof. Black)*, Florence Vie *(Mrs. Black)*, Leslie Stiles *(Admiral)*.

A vehicle designed specifically to portray the whimsical talents of Lotinga as Josser, a hapless character he would portray in several other films. Here Lotinga quits his porter job to join the Navy and retrieve a top-secret formula. Not very believable or to be taken seriously for a moment, this film, like those of THE THREE STOOGES, has a certain appeal which leaves some fans rolling in the aisles. (See JOSSER series, Index)

p&d, Norman Lee; w, Con West, Herbert Sargent.

Comedy **(PR:A MPAA:NR)**

JOSSER ON THE FARM* ½** (1934, Brit.) 63m FOX bw

Ernie Lotinga *(Jimmy Josser)*, Betty Astell *(Betty)*, Garry Marsh *(Granby)*, Muriel Aked *(Mrs. Savage)*, John Gattrell *(Dennis)*, Hope Davy *(June)*, [Wilfrid] Hyde-White *(Brooks)*, Edwin Ellis *(Spud)*, H.F. Maltby *(Luke)*, James Craig, Franklyn Kelsey, Johnnie Schofield.

One of the lesser Lotinga vehicles has him working on a farm which he saves from the hands of a greedy entrepreneur. A deed which leads to his election as a magistrate and eventually to marriage with the girl of his dreams. Strictly for Lotinga fans. (See JOSSER series, Index)

p&d, T. Hayes Hunter; w, Con West, Herbert Sargent, Lotinga.

Comedy **(PR:A MPAA:NR)**

JOSSER ON THE RIVER*
(1932, Brit.) 75m BIP-British Instructional/Wardour bw

Ernie Lotinga *(Jimmy Josser)*, Molly Lamont *(Julia Kaye)*, Charles Hickman *(Eddie Kaye)*, Reginald Gardiner *(Donald)*, Wallace Lupino *(Uncle Abel)*, Joan Wyndham *(A Little Lady)*, Arty Ash *(Hank)*.

Lotinga takes to blackmailing in order to try and make a few bucks, hooking up with Ash to take photographs of individuals caught in seedy situations. Their efforts only succeed in landing them jobs on the houseboat owned by two of the people they were trying to blackmail. Hard, even for fans of Lotinga, to find much to chuckle over here. (See JOSSER series, Index)

p&d, Norman Lee; w, Lee, Leslie Arliss.

Comedy **(PR:A MPAA:NR)**

JOTAI (SEE: VIXEN, 1970, Jap.)

JOUR DE FETE****
(1952, Fr.) 90m Francinex-Cady/Meyer-Kingsley bw (AKA: HOLIDAY)

Jacques Tati *(Francois, the Postman)*, Guy Decombie *(Roger, the Circus Owner)*, Paul Frankeur *(Marcel, Roger's Circus Partner)*, Santa Relli *(Roger's Wife)*, Maine Vallee *(Jeanette, the Young Girl)*, Roger Rafal *(Barber)*, Beauvais *(Cafe Proprietor)*, Delcassan *(Gossipy Old Cinema Operator)*, the Inhabitants of St. Severe-Sur-Indre.

The first feature film by Jacques Tati was actually a lengthened version of his short L'ECOLE DES FACTEURS, and helped to give Tati somewhat of an international reputation as one of the best, if not the very best, film comics to come out of France. Also starring in JOUR DE FETE, Tati plays the postman of a small sleepy village who becomes obsessed with applying the methods of the American postal system, as seen in a short educational film, to his job. This simple premise provides an abundance of opportunities for the lengthy and buffoonish-looking Tati to engage in some spectacular jokes. The emphasis of Tati's style was always aimed at the visual, music and dialog being used only to enhance what was being seen. The results were quite successful in producing laughter from cinema patrons in almost every country, and had a large impact upon the editing techniques later to be used by Jean-Luc Goddard and Francois Truffaut. (In French; English subtitles)

p, Fred Orain; d, Jacques Tati; w, Tati, Rene Wheeler, Henri Marquet; ph, Jean Mercanton; m, Jean Yatove; ed, Marcel Morreau; art d, Rene Moullaert.

Comedy **(PR:A MPAA:NR)**

JOURNAL OF A CRIME** (1934) 64m FN/WB bw

Ruth Chatterton *(Francoise Moliet)*, Adolphe Menjou *(Paul Moliet)*, Claire Dodd *(Odette Florey)*, George Barbier *(Chautard)*, Douglas Dumbrille *(Germaine Cartier, Attorney General)*, Noel Madison *(Costelli)*, Philip Reed *(Young Man)*, Henry Kolker *(Henri Marcher, Lawyer)*, Henry O'Neill *(Doctor)*, Edward McWade *(Rigaud, Doorman)*, Frank Reicher *(Winterstein)*, Clay Clement *(Inspector)*, Olaf Hytten *(Victor, Butler)*, Walter Pidgeon *(Florestan, Baritone)*, Jane Darwell *(Guest)*, Edward Peil, Sr. *(Jailer)*, Claire McDowell *(Sister)*, Larry Steers *(Celebrant)*, Sidney D'Albrook, Paul Panzer *(Truck Drivers)*, Ann Hovey, Marjorie Lytell *(Girls)*, Frank Darien *(Stage Manager)*, Elsa Janssen *(Frau Winterstein)*, Leila Bennett.

This compact, fast-moving film stars Chatterton as the wife of the unfaithful Menjou. In a fit of jealous rage, she goes backstage at the theater where his actress mistress, Dodd, is in a play. The scorned femme shoots Dodd and escapes, and the blame for the crime falls on the shoulders of a fugitive who is hiding in the theater from another crime. Her crime of "passion" wins her nothing, however, as Menjou grows to hate her for her deed. Guilt finally consumes Chatterton, and she decides to go to the police and confess. En route to the station she is hit by a car and loses her memory of the murder. Menjou softens in his feelings, and the movie ends with his love for his wife restored. Though the plot is somewhat weak in parts, this picture is unusual in the fact that most movies of this time period contained the inviolate rule that all crime must be paid for.

p, Henry Blanke; d, William Keighley; w, F. Hugh Herbert, Charles Kenyon (based on a play by Jacques Deval); ph, Ernest Haller; ed, William Clemens; art d, John Hughes; cos, Orry-Kelly.

Crime **(PR:C MPAA:NR)**

JOURNEY, THE½** (1959, U.S./Aust.) 122m Alby/MGM c

Deborah Kerr *(Lady Diana Ashmore)*, Yul Brynner *(Maj. Surov)*, Robert Morley *(Hugh Deverill)*, Jason Robards, Jr. *(Paul Kedes/Fleming)*, E.G. Marshall *(Harold Rhinelander)*, Anne Jackson *(Mrs. Margie Rhinelander)*, Ronny Howard *(Billy Rhinelander)*, Flip Mark *(Flip Rhinelander)*, Kurt Kasznar *(Czepege)*, David Kossoff *(Simon Avron)*, Gerard Oury *(Teklel Hafouli)*, Marie Daems *(Francoise Hafouli)*, Anouk Aimee *(Eva)*, Barbara Von Nady *(Borbala)*, Maurice Sarfati *(Jacques Fabbry)*, Fred Roby *(Rosso)*, Siegfried Schurenberg *(Von Rachlitz)*, Maria Urban *(Gisela)*, Jerry Fujikawa *(Mitsu)*, Erica Vaal, Dimitry Fedotoff, Leonid Pylajew, Wolf Neuber, Michael Szekely, Charles Regnier, Ivan Petrovich, Ernst Konstantin.

The journey referred to in the title was actually just a trip and even more like a short hop. It only lasted 100 miles but that was enough to unwind this complicated story in the DINNER AT EIGHT and GRAND HOTEL tradition, with several characters of diverse backgrounds coming together for one intense moment. Set against the abortive Hungarian revolution of 1956, THE JOURNEY was shot in Austria, with many scenes in Vienna and in that territory near the Hungarian border. A group of travelers are caught by the Russian invasion as they attempt to escape at the Budapest airport. There are 16 people (two children) and they are bused across Hungary to the Austrian border and what they pray will be safety. Kerr is a British Lady trapped by the political unrest. Robards carries a British identity card but he is not what he seems and appears to be wounded and in pain. Near the border, the bus is stopped by the Russians, under the command of Brynner, a major in the Soviet army. Brynner likes Kerr and keeps everyone stalled while he ostensibly checks on her passport's validity. Kerr, however, has fallen for Robards who is, in truth, a Hungarian Freedom Fighter. His presence is endangering everyone else and they conspire to turn him in so they can get on with their journey. Kerr and Robards are about to escape together when they are betrayed by a local woman. Kerr now agrees to sleep with Brynner if he will allow them safe passage. Brynner is so moved by her willingness to do what he perceives is a repugnant act to her that he personally escorts them all the the border and is then killed by patriots. The acting is all excellent but the film is far too long in telling the tale. Brynner is particularly good in a noncliched role as the Russian. Kerr does her usual understated job. We've all seen this multi-character story of many people in a forced environment. It's been a staple of dramatists for years. With better handling, this could have been as good as IDIOT'S DELIGHT but Litvak and Tabori missed the boat by having a few too many stories going simultaneously, thus lessening the impact of the Kerr-Brynner-Robards problem. In the end, it was much too predictable to merit serious consideration as little more than an expensive programmer. Look for TV star E.G. Marshall in a small role as a U.S. businessman that is refreshingly true-to-life, rather than satirical. Actor-Director Ronny Howard makes his film debut as a 5 year old.

p&d, Anatole Litvak; w, George Tabori; ph, Jack Hildyard (Metrocolor); m, Georges Auric, Michel Michelet; ed, Dorothy Spencer; art d, Werner and Isabella Schlichting; cos, Rene Hubert.

Drama **(PR:A-C MPAA:NR)**

JOURNEY* (1977, Can.) 87m Quest/EPOH c

Genevieve Bujold *(Saguenay)*, John Vernon *(Boulder Allin)*, George Sperdakos *(Vid)*, Elton Hayes *(Piers)*, Luke Gibson *(Luke)*.

Bujold plays a girl rescued from drowning by Vernon. He brings her to the commune he has established in the mountains of Quebec. Although she remains silent at first, Bujold watches the activities of the residents and falls in love with Vernon. She finally starts talking and cements her membership in the group by helping in the birthing of a calf. In an unclear deja vu revelation, she decides she's been there before and that by staying, she is a bad omen. So she has Vernon return her to the river where he found her. Despite some really beautiful scenic settings, this film is confusing, long, and tedious, overdosing on unclear symbolism that is never quite resolved in its meaning.

p,d&w, Paul Almond; ph, Jean Boffety; m, Luke Gibson; ed, Almond, Honor Griffith; art d, Glenn Gibson; set d, Ann Pritchard.

Drama **Cas.** **(PR:O MPAA:PG)**

JOURNEY AHEAD** (1947, Brit.) 62m Random/Independent Film Renters bw

Ruth Haven *(Anne Franklin)*, John Stevens *(Mike Baxter)*, Nora Gordon *(Mrs. Deacon)*, Howard Douglas *(Adam Baxter)*.

In an attempt to cope with the loss of her husband during the war, Haven seeks a retreat along the coast. Hardly having much of a chance to rest and relieve her ailing psyche, she finds herself involved in another love affair, which appears to have a short life span when she discovers this new man is a smuggler. Her worries turn out to be for naught, as this new love is an undercover cop trying to get the goods on the actual smugglers. A decent rendition of a woman attempting to cope with psychological turmoil.

p&d, Peter Mills; w, Warren Tute.

Drama **(PR:A MPAA:NR)**

JOURNEY AMONG WOMEN**
(1977, Aus.) 93m Ko-An/Greater Union Organization c

Lillian Crombie *(Kameragul)*, June Pritchard *(Elizabeth Harrington)*, Martin Phelan *(Capt. McEwan)*, Rose Lilley *(Emily)*, Diane Fuller *(Bess)*, Nell Campbell *(Meg)*, Lisa Peers *(Charlotte)*, Jude Kuring *(Grace)*, Kay Self *(Sheila)*, Robyn Moase *(Moira)*, Michelle Johnson *(Biddie)*, Kenneth Laird *(Judge)*, Tim Elliot *(Dr. Hargreaves)*, Ralph Cotterell *(Corporal Porteous)*.

Poor period feminist piece features a group of women convicts in Australia. They kill a guard and disappear into the outback, taking Pritchard, the daughter of a local judge. The cons learn to survive in the wilderness, but are soon found by soldiers sent to capture them. The climactic battle is violent and savage. This film was one of the many that came to the U.S. from Australia in the late 1970s, though it is clearly one of the lesser ones. The few problems within the script are covered by fast paced direction and some very artistic camera work. The background music is haunting, nicely complementing the visuals. Not for everyone, but well worth a look for the serious film student.

p, John Weiley; d, Tom Cowan; w, Weiley, Cowan, Dorothy Hewett (based on a story by Cowan); ph, Cowan (Eastmancolor); m, Roy Ritchie; ed, John Scott; set d, Sally Campbell; stunts, Heath Harris.

Historical Drama **(PR:O MPAA:NR)**

JOURNEY BACK TO OZ** (1974) 90m Filmation c

Voices: Milton Berle, Herschel Bernardi, Paul Ford, Margaret Hamilton, Jackie Leonard, Paul Lynde, Ethel Merman, Liza Minnelli, Mickey Rooney, Rise Stevens, Danny Thomas, Mel Blanc, Dallas McKennon, Larry Storch.

This animated feature was originally made in 1964, but for some reason was not released until nearly 10 years later. Dorothy (with the voice of Liza Minnelli, keeping things in the family) voyages back to the "land over the rainbow" to discover that evil forces have not totally disappeared since her previous visit. This evil mainly being due to the presence of the Wicked Witch of the West's sister, who has green elephants instead of flying monkeys to do her dirty work. This film lacks the intrigue and story inventiveness found in the original, but is worth a glimpse for old time's sake at least.

p, Norm Prescott, Lou Scheimer; d, Hal Sutherland; w, Fred Ladd, Prescott; m/l, James Van Heusen, Sammy Cahn.

Animated Feature Cas. (PR:AAA MPAA:G)

JOURNEY BENEATH THE DESERT**

(1967, Fr./Ital.) 105m CCM-Fides/EM c (ANTINEA, L'AMANTE DELLA CITTA SEPOLTA; L'ATLANTIDE)

Haya Harareet *(Antinea)*, Jean-Louis Trintignant *(Pierre)*, Rad Fulton *(Robert)*, Amedeo Nazzari *(Tamal)*, Georges Riviere *(John)*, Giulia Rubini *(Zinah)*, Gabriele Tinti *(Max)*, Gian Maria Volonte *(Tarath)*, Ignazio Dolce.

Trintignant, Fulton, and Riviere are mining engineers whose helicopter is forced down in the Sahara by a storm. They land near a nuclear test site and save local sheik Nazzari's life. He leads them to a secret cave which is the entrance to the lost city of Atlantis. Harareet, the queen of Atlantis, takes a cruel liking to her unexpected guests. When Riviere tries to escape, she turns him into a golden statue. Fulton also tries to get away, and is killed by Trintignant, who has come under Harareet's power. A slave girl, (Rubini) falls in love with Trintignant, and helps him escape before a nuclear bomb destroys the city. The film moves slowly and is quite dull. The American release has the additional handicap of poor dubbing. The film suffers from a clear lack of direction. The project initially started with Borzage, but he was soon replaced by Ulmer (who also served as production designer) and Masini. Though Ulmer had a good reputation for science fiction films, he could not save this mess. There are still some nice visual effects, particularly in the tunnel of the secret cave. Released in Rome in 1961, the film was not shown in the U.S. until 1967. The story had been filmed at least three times before: L'ATLANTIDE, by the French in 1921, DIE HERREN VON ATLANTIS, by the Germans in 1932, and in the U.S., SIREN OF ATLANTIS in 1948.

p, Luigi Nannerini; d, Edgar G. Ulmer, Giuseppe Masini, Frank Borzage; w, Andre Tabet, Ugo Liberatore, Remigio Del Grosso, Amedeo Nazzari (based on the story "L'Atlantide" by Pierre Benoit); ph, Enzo Serafin (Technirama, Eastmancolor); m, Carlo Rustichelli; ed, Renato Cinquini; prod d, Ulmer; md, Franco Ferrara; art d, Piero Filippone; cos, Vittorio Rossi; spec eff, Giovanni Ventimiglia.

Fantasy/Science Fiction (PR:A MPAA:NR)

JOURNEY FOR MARGARET*1/2**

(1942) 81m MGM bw

Robert Young *(John Davis)*, Laraine Day *(Nora Davis)*, Fay Bainter *(Trudy Strauss)*, Signe Hasso *(Anya)*, Margaret O'Brien *(Margaret)*, Nigel Bruce *(Herbert V. Allison)*, William Severn *(Peter Humphreys)*, G. P. Huntley, Jr. *(Rugged)*, Doris Lloyd *(Mrs. Barrie)*, Halliwell Hobbes *(Mr. Barrie)*, Jill Esmond *(Susan Fleming)*, Charles Irwin *(Fairoaks)*, Elisabeth Risdon *(Mrs. Bailey)*, Lisa Golm *(Frau Weber)*, Herbert Evans *(Man)*, Clare Sandars *(Child)*, Leyland Hodgson *(Censor)*, Anita Bolster *(Woman)*, Matthew Boulton *(Warden)*, Lilyan Irene *(Nurse)*, Olaf Hytten *(Manager)*, Ottola Nesmith *(Nurse)*, John Burton *(Surgeon)*, Colin Kenny *(Steward)*, Jimmy Aubrey *(Porter)*, Heather Thatcher *(Mrs. Harris)*, Joan Kemp *(Isabel)*, Norbert Muller *(Hans)*, Al Ferguson *(Policeman)*, Bea Nigro *(Nora's Mother)*, Cyril Delavanti *(Stage Manager)*, Jody Gilbert *(Mme. Bornholm)*, Crauford Kent *(Everton)*, Keye Luke *(Japanese Statesman)*, David Thursby *(Air Raid Warden)*, Henry Guttman *(Polish Captain)*, Doris Stone *(Mother)*, Eric Snowden *(Porter)*, Clive Morgan *(Father)*, Hal Welling *(Tailor)*, Gay Bennes *(Screaming Girl)*, Elisabeth Williams, Stephanie Insall, Gil Perkins, Major Douglas Francis, Allan Schute, Sybil Bacon, Lotus Thompson *(Subway Bits)*.

An unabashed three-hanky movie that went directly for the heartstrings and tear ducts and didn't stop until the eyes had been cried dry. This was director Van Dyke's final film after a long and distinguished career. He died at 53 soon afterwards. O'Brien was one of the most remarkable child actresses since Shirley Temple and had the ability to cry on cue and give the audience anything from tears on the lids to huge gobs of lachryma down the cheeks. Her real name was Angela Maxine O'Brien but, like so many other actors, she took her name from the character she played and stuck with it. (The same held true for L.Q. Jones and Gig Young). Her parents had been circus people and she'd missed getting a large role at the age of four in BABES ON BROADWAY, but that didn't daunt the plucky tyke. She came back for this film and won the audition. Based on a novel by William L. White, it's the story of Young and Day, two Americans in London during the Blitz. Day is awaiting her first child while Young plies his trade as a journalist covering the war, before the U.S. officially enters the fracas. Young is in the midst of an air raid when he meets Severn and takes him to a home for orphan waifs. Day is hurt in the air raid and loses their unborn child and must be taken to hospital. Day returns to the U.S. and Young remains in London to finish his work, promising her that he will return as soon as he can. Young visits Severn and meets O'Brien, his sister, a child who seems to be afraid of everything. Young takes the two children under his wing and begins to act as their surrogate father. Later, he contacts Day and says that he wants to bring the two children back to the States with him and adopt them both. Day is all for it and the trip is joyfully planned. On the brink of leaving England, Young learns that he is forbidden to take both children on the plane as space and weight are at a premium and he must jettison 40 pounds of baggage. It all works out when another passenger takes one of the children with her and they arrive in the U.S. where Day is waiting to welcome them with open arms. Young was particularly believable in the role, a part that was mostly based on White's experiences. Many years later, while shooting his television program, "Marcus Welby," Young and O'Brien were united again in one of the segments. The movie was a large success and served to reveal the personal side of the tragedy of war through the eyes of its most innocent victims, the children. O'Brien showed her talents several times during the 1940s, including the charming THE CANTERVILLE GHOST which again teamed her with Young. But, like Temple and so many other tykes, her career began to wane as she neared puberty. She won a special Oscar as "Outstanding Child Actress" in 1944 but her life in American films was virtually over by the time she made HELLER IN PINK TIGHTS in 1960. A decade later she made two Peruvian films that are better left forgotten. For the record, they were DIABOLIC WEDDING and ANNABELLE LEE. It's a shame that she couldn't have stayed at 10 years of age because O'Brien is acknowledged by many to be one of the best, if not the greatest, child actress to ever come across the screen. Bainter does a wonderful role as the director of the home for orphans and all other roles are equally well cast. Day doesn't have enough to do (because of the nature of the story) but what she does is excellent.

p, B. P. Fineman; d, W. S. Van Dyke II; w, David Hertz, William Ludwig (based on the book by William L. White); ph, Ray June; m, Franz Waxman; ed, George White; art d, Cedric Gibbons, Wade B. Rubottom; set d, Edwin B. Willis, Dick Pefferle; cos, Robert Kalloch.

War Drama (PR:AA MPAA:NR)

JOURNEY INTO DARKNESS**

(1968, Brit.) 107m Hammer c

Robert Reed, Jennifer Hilary, Michael Tolan, Nanette Newman, Jill Collins.

Two episodes of a popular British television show were edited together in order to create this feature for theatrical consumption, though the two stories remain markedly separate. (This approach differs quite a bit from THE KARATE KILLERS, in which episodes from "The Man From U.N.C.L.E." TV series were edited to create a single story.) The first episode has a very wealthy man creating a bizarre game in which he appoints himself as a divine judge of life and death. And all of this is done just to relieve the unending tedium of his life (the result of too much money and too much time on his hands). The second story centers on the attempts of one in a group of quadruplets to control his brothers through extrasensory powers—getting them to do some very nasty stuff.

p, Joan Harrison; d, Peter Sasdy, James Hill; w, Oscar Millard, John Gould.

Horror (PR:A MPAA:NR)

JOURNEY INTO FEAR****

(1942) 71m Mercury/RKO bw

Joseph Cotten *(Graham)*, Dolores Del Rio *(Josette)*, Ruth Warrick *(Stephanie)*, Agnes Moorehead *(Mme. Mathews)*, Jack Durant *(Gogo)*, Everett Sloane *(Kopeikin)*, Eustace Wyatt *(Haller)*, Frank Readick *(Mathews)*, Edgar Barrier *(Kuvetli)*, Jack Moss *(Banat)*, Stefan Schnabel *(Purser)*, Hans Conried *(Oo Lang Sang the Magician)*, Robert Meltzer *(Steward)*, Richard Bennett *(Ship's Captain)*, Orson Welles *(Col. Haki)*, Shifra Haran *(Mrs. Haklet)*, Herbert Drake, Bill Roberts *(Men)*.

This is a strange, obsessive, and often brilliant film offering thrills, suspense, and a terrific performance by Cotten. He's an engineer of newly developed American naval guns and is to return to the U.S. with his beautiful wife Warrick after a business conference in Istanbul. Sloane, a Turkish representative for Cotten's firm, takes him away from his hotel and wife Warrick for a business meeting which occurs in a walk-down nightclub where exotic singers are awkwardly trying to sing American swing tunes, and Del Rio does an exotic dance with Durant. Meanwhile, Sloane tries to carry on a conversation with Cotten who can hardly hear a word the little man is saying. Into the place steps Moss, a vile and repulsive Nazi executioner. During a magic act conducted by Conried, one in which Cotten is put into a box from which he will supposedly and magically be transferred to a trunk offstage, a shot rings out. The box is opened and out falls magician Conried, quite dead. Cotten, who has already been transferred, opens the trunk to find out that it was he, not Conried, who was the intended victim. Sloane hustles Cotten to secret police headquarters where he meets intelligence chief Welles, who tells Cotten that Nazi agents are trying to kill him and that the best way he can stay alive is to take a freighter out of the country, not the train, as planned. Welles tells Cotten that he will escort his wife by train to safety and they will meet in the next town down the coast. Reluctantly, the confused Cotten allows himself to be put on board a foul-smelling freighter which is carrying a few passengers, a polyglot group. Del Rio makes a play for Cotten, who isn't interested. Also on board is the man who tried to kill Cotten in the nightclub, Moss. Cotten tests the waters with the small group of passengers and finds that only Barrier is an ally and he turns out to be one of Welles' agents, put on board to protect Cotten. Wyatt, a friendly doctor, however, turns out to be a Nazi spymaster and he and Moss kill Barrier. When Cotten learns their identities, knowing they intend to kidnap him just as he leaves the ship when it docks, he turns to other passengers but they prove to be of no help. He is abducted when the ship comes into port and taken away in a car. The car has a flat tire in the middle of a crowded bazaar and Cotten makes his move, using a pen knife, the only "weapon" he could scare up from the passengers, to jam into the car's horn. This disturbance brings authorities and, in the confusion, Cotten escapes. He goes to his hotel but Wyatt and Moss follow him, taking him out of his suite where he and his wife are talking. Again, Cotten escapes, stepping onto the ledge of the hotel during a fierce rainstorm. Moss follows him, inching after him on the ledge, firing at him. Suddenly Welles appears and begins to fire at Moss, wounding him, but he himself is wounded and he crashes through a window, falling into one of the hotel rooms. Cotten continues to flee the wounded Moss along the ledge but the killer is blinded by the rain coating his thick glasses and Cotten, using Welles' gun, shoots the murderer, who topples to his death. In a final scene where Welles extolls the beauty and charm of Warrick, the meek-mannered Cotten finally spews indignation and anger, and tells off the haughty official. JOURNEY INTO FEAR is a wonderfully murky study of espionage, realistically portrayed in all its mayhem and confusion, one spy not really knowing what the other spy is up to, but operating on instinct to get results. Cotten's quiet, unassuming part is so well played that the viewer gets frustrated at his inability to either act or even think clearly. Welles, in his brief appearances, is all bluster and bravado but when he does appear on screen, electricity crackles. Then there are the familiar faces of his great Mercury Players—Sloane, Warrick and Moorehead—doing well with their small roles. Moss, an obese, truly ugly character actor, is the embodiment of evil here; everything about him is foul, a genuinely scary character. Though Foster is given credit for direction, the film bears the unmistakable stamp of

Welles in almost every frame and it is known that he really helmed this superlative film. Struss' photography superbly captures the shadowy mood and the dark world the story chronicles. Robson turns in a marvelous editing job here; he worked for over a year to tighten up a film that was fairly jumbled when Welles put it into the can, and a few scenes were added to increase the film's 69 minutes to 71 minutes by release time. This was the last film made through the Mercury-RKO alliance, a shaky one at best following the expensive productions CITIZEN KANE and THE MAGNIFICENT AMBERSONS which were completed under that partnership. JOURNEY INTO FEAR was remade in 1976 as a Canadian production which was a hopeless failure.

p, Orson Welles; d, Norman Foster; w, Welles, Joseph Cotten (based on a novel by Eric Ambler); ph, Karl Struss; m, Roy Webb; ed, Mark Robson; md, Constantin Bakaleinikoff; art d, Albert S. D'Agostino, Mark-Lee Kirk; set d, Darrell Silvera, Ross Dowd; cos, Edward Stevenson; spec eff, Vernon L. Walker; m/l, "C'est Mon Coeur" ["Chagrin d'Amour"], "Three Little Words," Harry Ruby, Bert Kalmar.

Spy Drama **Cas.** **(PR:A MPAA:NR)**

JOURNEY INTO FEAR** (1976, Can) 97m Sterling Gold c (AKA: BURN OUT)

Sam Waterston *(Graham)*, Zero Mostel *(Kopeikin)*, Yvette Mimieux *(Josette)*, Scott Marlowe *(Jose)*, Ian McShane *(Banat)*, Joseph Wiseman *(Col Haki)*, Shelley Winters *(Mrs. Mathews)*, Stanley Holloway *(Mathews)*, Donald Pleasence *(Kuvetli)*, Vincent Price *(Dervos)*, Alicia Amman *(Old Lady)*.

Waterston is a research scientist caught up in a web of international intrigue in this remake of the Eric Ambler novel which was better adapted by Orson Welles. This version was shot all over Europe with well-known guest artists who ought to have known better, and directed by Mann who has done much better.

p, Trevor Wallace; d, Daniel Mann; w, Wallace (based on the novel by Eric Ambler); ph, Harry Waxman (Technicolor); m, Alex North; m/l, North, Hal David.

Spy Drama **(PR:O MPAA:NR)**

JOURNEY INTO LIGHT 1/2** (1951) 87m FOX bw

Sterling Hayden *(John Burrows)*, Viveca Lindfors *(Christine Thorssen)*, Thomas Mitchell *(Gandy)*, Ludwig Donath *("Doc" Thorssen)*, H.B. Warner *(Wiz, Wino)*, Jane Darwell *(Mack)*, John Berkes *(Racky)*, Peggy Webber *(Jane Burrows)*, Paul Guilfoyle *(Fanatic)*, Charles Evans *(Bishop Logan)*, Marian Martin *(Diana)*, Everett Glass *(Deacon Adams)*, Raymond Bond *(Deacon Edwards)*, Billie Bird *(Gertie)*, O.Z. Whitehead *(Lippy)*, Myron Healey *(Jerry)*, Byron Keith *(Policeman)*, Kathleen Mulqueen, Leslie Turner *(Church Women)*, Fritz Feld *(Clothing Salesman)*, Lorin Raker *(Interviewer)*, Emmett Lynn, Paul Brinegar, David Marsh *(Bums)*, Bernard Gorcey *(Flophouse Clerk)*, Lynn Whitney *(Handbill Woman)*, Helene Huntington *(Nurse)*, Kate Drain Lawson *(Woman In Fight)*, Fred Aldrich *(Foreman)*, Ed Hinton *(Police Sergeant)*, Smoki Whitfield *(Truck Driver)*.

Hayden is a New England minister who loses his faith and leaves his church when his alcoholic wife commits suicide. Wandering out west he ends up on skid row, where he meets Donath, a preacher, who, with blind daughter Lindfors, runs a mission for down and outers. Without revealing his past, Hayden takes a janitorial job in the mission and helps bring some of the skid row denizens into church services. When Lindfors is hurt in an accident, Hayden has a spiritual rebirth, returning to the pulpit. Finding a new purpose in life, he stays with the mission and marries Lindfors. The film is hampered by a verbose script and a tendency to preach to the audience. But the cast is good with some excellent support by the skid row ensemble. Direction is good and the other production values are up to par.

p, Joseph Bernhard, Anson Bond; d, Stuart Heisler; w, Stephen Nordi, Irving Shulman (based on a story by Bond); ph, Elwood Bredell; m, Emil Newman, Paul Dunlap; ed, Terry Morse.

Drama **(PR:C MPAA:NR)**

JOURNEY INTO MIDNIGHT** (1968, Brit.) 100m Hammer/FOX c

Chad Everett, Julie Harris, Edward Fox, Tom Adams.

Two portions of the Hammer television series JOURNEY TO THE UNKNOWN were brought to the big screen to allow a few more chills and thrills to be enjoyed by an audience that never seemed to reach satisfaction. The opening episode has an unsuspecting man dealing with more than he had bargained for when he goes to a costume party and is given a quick (and pretty depressing) look into days gone by. The second stars the popular actress Harris as a woman who is easy prey for a wolf who wants to romance her for her money. Luckily for the unsuspecting woman, an Indian spirit makes sure that this worthless gent is not allowed to carry out his plans.

p, Joan Harrison; d, Roy Ward Baker, Alan Gibson; w, Robert Bloch, Jeremy Paul.

Horror **(PR:A MPAA:NR)**

JOURNEY INTO NOWHERE 1/2**

(1963, Brit.) 75m Avon/Planet-Globe-President bw (AKA: MURDER BY AGREEMENT)

Sonja Ziemann *(Maria)*, Tony Wright *(Ricky)*, Helmut Schmid *(Joe)*.

Wright is a gambler deep in debt. He has 48 hours to come up with some money or he's in big trouble with the syndicate. He meets Ziemann, an artist contemplating suicide as she is going blind. The two decide to take out a joint insurance policy. In order to receive the money one of the pair must kill the other, but their plans are hampered when they fall in love. Ziemann is killed by a railroad car that has been uncoupled by a third party, Schmid. He is an old acquaintance of Wright's and a syndicate member who knows all about the policy. Wracked with grief, Wright collects the money and pays off his debt. An interesting *film noir*, with a new twist on the "double indemnity" theme so popular in movies. Filmed on location in South Africa, the British cut ran 8 minutes shorter than the American version.

p, Bruce Yorke; d, Denis Scully; ph, Vaclav Vich.

Crime **(PR:O MPAA:NR)**

JOURNEY THROUGH ROSEBUD** (1972) 93m GSF c

Robert Forster *(Frank)*, Kristoffer Tabori *(Danny)*, Victoria Racimo *(Shirley)*, Eddie Little Sky *(Stanley Pike)*, Roy Jenson *(Park Ranger)*, Wright King *(Indian Agent)*, Larry Pennell *(Sheriff)*, Robert Cornthwaite *(Hearing Officer)*, Steve Shemayne *(John)*, Beau Little Sky *(Stu)*, Lynn Burnette *(Raymond)*, Dianne Running *(Mrs. Blackwing)*, Olive McCloskey *(Mrs. Graham)*, Pat Iyotte *(Police Officer)*, Nancy White Horse, Robert Wagner, the People of the Rosebud Sioux Indian Reservation.

Tabori, a draft dodger, finds himself on the Rosebud Reservation, where he meets Forster, the cynical Viet Nam veteran and unofficial leader of the reservation. Racimo is Forster's ex-wife, an idealistic yet practical person who still has much control over Forster. The film rambles as a three person character study, never going anywhere until Forster is killed in an auto crash, causing a rift between Tabori and Racimo. Nothing is explained well, although there is a nice portrayal of reservation life. That was not enough to justify the film, and audiences learned quickly. This was a box office bomb.

p, David Gil; d, Tom Gries; w, Albert Ruben; ph, Minervino Rojas (Panavision, Movielabcolor); m, Johnny Mandel; ed, Patricia Finn Lewis; makeup, Byrd Holland.

Drama **(PR:O MPAA:PG)**

JOURNEY TO FREEDOM** (1957) 60m REP bw

Jacques Scott, Genevieve Aumont, George Graham, Morgan Lane, Jean Ann Lewis, Peter E. Besbas, Don McArt, Dan O'Dowd, Barry O'Hara, Fred Kohler, Jr., Tor Johnson, Don Marlowe, Miles Shepard.

Scott is an activist for "Voice of Freedom," chased from Bulgaria to the U.S. by Soviet agents. Aumont plays the nurse who falls in love with him as he regains his health after being injured in an accident. The relationship is tested by the pursuing Russian agents.

p, Stephen C. Apostolof; d, Robert C. Dertano; w, Herbert F. Niccolls (based on a story by Niccolls and Apostolof); ph, William C. Thompson; m, Josef Zimanich; ed, Dertano.

Spy Drama **(PR:A MPAA:NR)**

JOURNEY TO ITALY (SEE: STRANGERS, 1955, Ital.)

JOURNEY TO LOVE** (1953, Ital.) 95m Bomba Film/IFE bw

Umberto Spadaro *(Torquato Merumi)*, Vera Carmi *(Teresa, his Wife)*, Enzo Stajola *(Cesar, his Child)*, Anna Di Leo *(Caterina, the Grandmother)*, Nando Bruno *(Saletti)*, Edoardo Passarelli *(Punugli)*, Sonia Lo Guidice *(Woman on the Train)*.

Spadaro, a popular Italian screen comic, is an accountant rewarded with money for his honesty. He takes it and goes on vacation from his nagging family. Along the way he flirts with Lo Guidice, a thief who claims to be a countess, who steals his wallet. He arrives in Rome broke, wearing painfully tight shoes. Unable to find a place to stay, and in great discomfort, he joins a pilgrimage visiting St. Peter's Square during Holy Year, wanders around the city, and finally takes employment as a gardener in a monastery. Upon hearing his son is ill, he returns home. Although Spadaro is funny in his role, too much of the script pretends to be a Chaplin-style pathos/comedy, never quite making it. His wanderings around Rome may look like a travelog to American viewers, with some nice footage of the Pope cut into the action. Lo Guidice is interesting in her minor role.

d, Giorgio Pastina; w, Vitaliano Brancati (based on a story by Fabrizio Saranzani); ph, Augusto Tiezzi.

Comedy **(PR:A MPAA:NR)**

JOURNEY TO SHILOH*** (1968) 101m UNIV c

James Caan *(Buck Burnett)*, Michael Sarrazin *(Miller Nalls)*, Brenda Scott *(Gabrielle DuPrey)*, Don Stroud *(Todo McLean)*, Paul Peterson *(J.C. Sutton)*, Michael Burns *(Eubie Bell)*, Michael Vincent *(Little Bit Lucket)*, Harrison Ford *(Willie Bill Bearden)*, John Doucette *(Gen. Braxton Bragg)*, Noah Beery, Jr. *(Sgt. Mercer Barnes)*, Tisha Sterling *(Airybelle Sumner)*, James Gammon *(Tellis Yeager)*, Brian Avery *(Carter Claiborne)*, Clarke Gordon *(Col. Mirabeau Cooney)*, Robert Pine *(Collins)*, Sean Kennedy *(Custis Claiborne)*, Wesley Lau *(Col. Boykin)*, Chet Stratton *(Mr. Claiborne)*, Bing Russell *(Greybeard)*, Lane Bradford *(Case Pettibone)*, Rex Ingram *(Jacob)*, Charles Lampkin *(Edward)*, Myron Healey *(Sheriff Briggs)*, Eileen Wesson *(Ella Newsome)*, Albert Popwell *(Samuel)*.

Caan and six other young volunteers from West Texas set out to join the Confederate army during the middle of the Civil War, riding hundreds of miles to get to the Rebel ranks before the battle of Shiloh in Tennessee ensues. The group calls itself the Concho County Comanches and, one by one, the adventure-seeking, noble-hearted volunteers meet separate fates. They encounter class prejudice and perils all the way. Caan is wounded during the battle of Shiloh and he wakes up to find his arm amputated. He hears that the only other survivor of his little group, Sarrazin, has deserted and is being hunted. He finds his friend in a barn, dying. Caan then tells the story of the group to sympathetic Confederal Gen. Bragg (Doucette) and is told to go home to Texas, which he does. The dialog flows too thickly in this film in its attempt to find a parallel with the then raging Vietnam War, and much of what the enthusiastic boys blather is banal which is, of course, part of an accurate portrayal of these naive cowboy youths. Hale's direction is loose but the few action scenes he does permit are snappy and scary. It's an overall good adventure tale that accurately, if briefly, depicts the horrors of war.

p, Howard Christie; d, William Hale; w, Gene L. Coon (based on a novel by Will Henry); ph, Enzo A. Martinelli (Techniscope, Technicolor); m, David Gates; ed, Edward W. Williams; md, Joseph Gershenson; art d, Alexander Golitzen, George Patrick; set d, John McCarthy, James M. Walters; cos, Edward Armand, Tack

Takeuchi, Leslie Hall; spec eff, Roland Skeete; stunts, Paul Baxley; makeup, Bud Westmore, Dick Blair, Jack Freeman.

Adventure/War (PR:C MPAA:NR)

JOURNEY TO THE BEGINNING OF TIME 1/2**
(1966, Czech) 87m Gottwaldov Film Studio-Ceskoslovensky Film/New Trend Associates-Childhood Productions bw(CESTA DO PRAVEKU AKA;VOYAGE TO PREHISTORY)

Vladimir Bejval *(Jirka)*, Peter Hermann *(Tonik)*, Zdenek Hustak *(Jenda)*, Josef Lukas *(Petr)*, James Lucas *(Doc)*, Victor Betral *(Joe/Jo-Jo)*, Charles Goldsmith *(Ben)*.

After a visit to the dinosaur exhibit at the New York City Museum of Natural History, four boys row out onto Central Park Lake. They paddle through a secret cave and into a mysterious world inhabited by the same creatures they had just seen in the museum. As the boys go farther they arrive in the ice age. After falling asleep in the boat, they awaken in the museum to discover their adventures were all in their dreams. It is a great film for children and the odd dinosaur fan. Though an American cast is listed, most of the footage was taken from a Czechoslovakian film. New scenes were shot with American youngsters for U.S. audiences. It was also condensed into serial form for television.

p, William Cayton; d, Karel Zeman; w, Zeman, J.A. Novotny, Cayton, Fred Ladd; ph, Vaclav Pazdernik, Antonin Horak, Anthony Huston); m, E.F. Burian, Frantisek Strangmuller; ed, Zdenek Stehlik; art d, Zeman, Zdenek Rozkopal, Ivo Mrazek.

Fantasy (PR:AAA MPAA:NR)

JOURNEY TO THE CENTER OF THE EARTH* 1/2** (1959) 132m FOX c

Pat Boone *(Alec McEwen)*, James Mason *(Prof. Oliver Lindenbrook)*, Arlene Dahl *(Carla)*, Diane Baker *(Jenny)*, Thayer David *(Count Saknussemm)*, Peter Ronson *(Hans)*, Robert Adler *(Groom)*, Alan Napier *(Dean)*, Alex Finlayson *(Prof. Bayle)*, Ben Wright *(Paisley)*, Mary Brady *(Kirsty)*, Frederick Halliday *(Chancellor)*, Alan Caillou *(Rector)*.

Half camp, half serious, and all fun, this is an excellent combination of witty scripting and fine acting. Mason plays a geology professor in Edinburgh who travels with student Boone to Iceland and a planned journey to the center of the earth through a volcano. In Iceland, they meet the recently widowed Dahl whose late husband had planned a similar excursion. She talks Mason into letting her join his expedition, and Ronson, a local duck tender, and his duck Gertrude round out the group. They begin the descent, encountering prehistoric beasts, perilous rock slides and the evil David. David is the murderer of Dahl's husband and he is determined to be the first to reach the earth's core. Threatening the group at gunpoint, he attempts to force them to abandon their quest, but is overpowered and allowed to join Mason's forces. The trek continues, but David is killed in a fall before the others reach the lost city of Atlantis and a subterranean ocean. They appear to be trapped, but an explosion propels them back to the earth's surface, leaving them in the ocean near Italy where they are rescued. A well-photographed film, with location footage shot in Carlsbad Caverns, featuring great special effects and a Herrmann score that heightens the excitement. Script writers Reisch and Brackett were former Billy Wilder collaborators. Mason is charming and debonair, and the whole thing is captivating, silly fun, especially for children.

p, Charles Brackett; d, Henry Levin; w, Brackett, Walter Reisch (based on the novel *Voyage au Centre de la Terre* by Jules Verne); ph, Leo Tover (CinemaScope, DeLuxe Color); m, Bernard Herrmann; ed, Stuart Gilmore, Jack W. Holmes; md, Lionel Newman; art d, Lyle R. Wheeler, Franz Bachelin, Herman A. Blumenthal; set d, Walter M. Scott, Joseph Kish; cos, David Ffolkes; spec eff, L. B. Abbott, James B Gordon, Emil Kosa, Jr.; m/l, "My Love is Like a Red, Red Rose," James Van Heusen, Robert Burns; "Twice as Tall," "The Faithful Heart," Sammy Cahn, Van Heusen; sung by Boone

Science Fiction/Fantasy Cas. (PR:AAA MPAA:G)

JOURNEY TO THE CENTER OF TIME**
(1967) 82m Borealis Enterprises-Dorad/American General Pictures-Western International c

Scott Brady *(Stanton Jr.)*, Anthony Eisley *(Mark Manning)*, Gigi Perreau *(Karen White)*, Abraham Sofaer *(Dr. von Steiner)*, Austin Green *(Mr. Denning)*, Poupee Gamin *(Vina)*, Tracy Olsen *(Susan)*, Andy Davis *(Dave)*, Lyle Waggoner, Larry Evans, Jody Millhouse.

This low budget film is unintentionally humorous; an example of the "so bad it's good" genre. Sofaer, and assistants Eisley and Perreau, show off their time capsule to Brady, the heir and future owner of their research center. Complications start when the crew find themselves transported to the year 6968. They are greeted by evil aliens attacking Earth. Their escape from the future takes a wrong turn, landing them in one million B.C. They survive several vicious attacks from dinosaurs and other creatures, but the capsule's power supply, a ruby, is destroyed. Luckily, a nearby cave contains the same precious stones needed to replace the gem. Sofaer is killed by a puddle of lava, but Brady is able to bring back the needed gems. He is killed attempting to take off in the capsule alone. The capsule reappears and Eisley and Perreau are able to leave. Arriving at the research center a day before the adventure began, they have to reboard and try to come back on the correct plane of time and space. The story is silly, but the production values are worse. Many repeated stock shots are used for locales, and continuity is poor. This film seems to be nearly a remake of Hewitt's equally low budgeted THE TIME TRAVELERS.

p, David L. Hewitt, Ray Dorn; d, Hewitt; w, David Prentiss; ph, Robert Caramico (Pathe Color); ed, William Wellburn; art d, Edward D. Engoron; spec eff, Modern Film Effects.

Science Fiction Cas. (PR:A MPAA:NR)

JOURNEY TO THE FAR SIDE OF THE SUN**
(1969, Brit.) 94m Century 21/UNIV c (GB: DOPPELGANGER)

Ian Hendry *(John Kane)*, Roy Thinnes *(Col. Glenn Ross)*, Patrick Wymark *(Jason Webb)*, Lynn Loring *(Sharon Ross)*, Loni von Friedl *(Lise)*, Herbert Lom *(Dr. Hassler)*, George Sewell *(Mark Neuman)*, Franco Derosa *(Paulo Landi)*, Edward Bishop *(David Poulson)*, Philip Madoc, Vladek Sheybal, George Mikell.

This strange little piece features Thinnes as an astronaut of the 21st Century assigned to an unusual mission. Wymark has discovered a new planet on the far side of the sun. He sends Thinnes, along with Hendry, in a space ship and puts the two into a state of suspended animation. Three weeks later the ship crashes and Hendry is seriously hurt. An unknown ship rescues them and takes them back to Wymark, where Hendry dies as Thinnes tries to explain things to Wymark. But his boss doesn't understand and when Thinnes sees a newspaper with reverse writing, he realizes that he is on the newly discovered planet and that it is a mirrored image of earth. He talks the other world Wymark into financing a mission back to Earth, but this ship also crashes. Wymark is killed and Thinnes is taken away to an insane asylum, as his story is too strange for the inhabitants of this world to believe. This interesting premise is severely hampered by an overwritten script and an unnecessary subplot involving espionage. However, the special effects are first rate. This was produced by the Andersons, a British couple who created the puppet TV shows SUPERCAR and THUNDERBIRDS, as well as the live action UFO and SPACE 1999.

p, Gerry Anderson, Sylvia Anderson; d, Robert Parrish; w, Gerry, Sylvia Anderson, Donald James (based on a story by Gerry, Sylvia Anderson); ph, John Read (Technicolor); m, Barry Gray; ed, Len Walter; md, Gray; art d, Bob Bell; spec eff, Harry Oakes.

Science Fiction (PR:A MPAA:G)

JOURNEY TO THE LOST CITY*
(1960, Ger./Fr./Ital.) 95m Rizzoli-Regina and Criterion/AIP c (DER TIGER VON ESCHNAPUR; DAS INDISCHE GRABMAL; GB: TIGER OF BENGAL)

Debra Paget *(Seta)*, Paul Christian (Hubschmid) *(Harald Berger)*, Walter Reyer *(Prince Chandra, the Maharajah of Eschnapur)*, Claus Holm *(Dr. Walter Rhode)*, Sabine Bethmann *(Irene, his Wife)*, Valery Inkijinoff *(Yama, High Priest)*, Rene Deltgen *(Prince Ramigani)*, Jochen Brockmann *(Padhu)*, Jochen Blume *(Asagana)*, Luciana Paoluzzi *(Bahrani)*, Guido Celano *(Gen. Dagh)*, *Richard Lauffen (Bhowana)*, Helmut Hildebrand *(Ramigani's Servant)*, Panos Papadopoulos *(Messenger)*, Victor Francen.

DER TIGER VON ESCHNAPUR and DAS INDISCHE GRABMAL, based on two films made in 1919 and directed by Joe May. The two films were re-edited as a single feature and released to American audiences. The result is a poorly cut and incoherently dubbed serial-style film, undeserving of Lang's name. Christian is an architect in India, who comes upon a lost city that is divided by the Prince, Reyer, and his rival brother, Deltgen. There he finds snakes, lepers, a man-eating tiger and the beautiful dancer, Paget. Paget is loved by Reyer, but when he realizes that she and Christian are in love, he gives them his blessing. The best parts about this dubbed film are the scenic views, which occasionally give a feel for what the film could have been. Songs include "Tiger," "Grabmal."

p, Louise de Masure, Eberhard Meischner; d, Fritz Lang; w, Lang, Werner Jorg Luddecke, Thea von Harbou (based on the novel by von Harbou); ph, Richard Angst (Colorscope); m, Michel Michelet, Gerhard Becker; ed, Walter Wischniewsky; art d, Willy Schatz, Helmut Nentwig; cos, Gunter Brosda, Claudia Herberg; ch, Robby Gay, Billy Daniel.

Adventure (PR:A MPAA:NR)

JOURNEY TO THE SEVENTH PLANET**
(1962, U.S./Swed.) 80m Cinemagic Alta Vista/AIP c

John Agar *(Don)*, Greta Thyssen *(Greta)*, Ann Smyrner *(Ingrid)*, Mimi Heinrich *(Ursula)*, Carl Ottosen *(Eric)*, Ove Sprogoe *(Barry)*, Louis Miehe Renard *(Svend)*, Peter Monch *(Karl)*, Annie Birgit Garde *(Ellen)*, Ulla Moritz *(Lise)*, Bente Juel *(Colleen)*.

In the year 2001, Agar leads a UN exploration team on an expedition to Uranus. There they find that the planet is controlled by an evil Being that feeds on their past unconscious fears and desires. For example, they all meet ex-girl friends and one homesick crew member sees his old home town. Another is afraid of rodents and is attacked by a giant rat. The men finally hunt down the Being and destroy it by freezing it to death, thus escaping from their past and returning to their present. A space odyssey with a predictable plot. Nearly the entire cast and crew went on to make REPTILICUS in 1962.

p&d, Sidney Pink; w, Ib Melchior, Pink (based on the story by Pink); ph, Aage Wiltrup (Techniscope, Eastmancolor); m, Ib Glindemann; ed, Tove Palsbo, Thok Sondergaard; md, Glindemann; art d, Otto Lund; set d, Helge Hansen; spec eff, Brent Barfod Film; makeup, Calma; m/l, "Journey to the Seventh Planet," Jerry Capehart, Mitchell Tableporter (sung by Otto Brandenburg).

Science Fiction/Adventure (PR:C MPAA:NR)

JOURNEY TOGETHER* 1/2** (1946, Brit.) 95m RAF Film Unit/EFI bw

Sgt. Richard Attenborough *(David Wilton)*, Aircraftsman Jack Watling *(John Aynesworth)*, Flying Officer David Tomlinson *(Smith)*, Warrant Officer Sid Rider *(A Fitter)*, Squadron Leader Hugh Wakefield *(An Acting Lieutenant)*, Squadron Leader Stuart Latham *(A Flight Sergeant Fitter)*, Leading Aircraftsman Bromley Challenor *(A.C. 2 Jay)*, Flying Officer Z. Peromowski *(An Anson Pilot)*, Edward G. Robinson *(Dean McWilliams)*, Patrick Waddinton *(Flight Lt. Mander)*, Flight Lt. Sebastian Shaw *(Squadron Leader Marshall)*, Wing Commander Ronald Adam *(The Commanding Officer)*, Bessie Love *(Mary McWilliams)*, Sgt. Norvell Crutcher *(A Driver)*, Rex Harrison, John Justin, George Cole, Miles Malleson, Ronald Squire,

Leslie Nixon, Arthur Bolton, Fletcher Markle, Jack Baker, Stuart Dick, Peter Naylis, Nick Stuart, Tommy Tomlinson, Michael McNeile, Jerry Fitzgerald, Eric Worth, Hamish Nichol, Murray Matheson, the Personnel of the Royal Air Force, Royal Canadian Air Force, and the United States Army.

Shot mainly with a military film crew and cast, this was a strong picture made to support the allied war effort. Attenborough, a cockney, and Watling, a college graduate, wish to become pilots in the Royal Air Force. They begin training in England and are later sent to Arizona for additional instruction with Robinson, in a brief cameo as a tough but understanding instructor. Walting is a team player and tries to get Attenborough to follow his example, but to no avail. Eventually the cockney is sent to Canada for navigational classes, while Watling receives his pilot wings. Though disappointed with his status as navigator, Attenborough quickly learns that he too is crucial to the war effort. The two youths are later reunited on a flying mission to Berlin. On their return home the plane is hit and they are forced to abandon it in the North Sea. When they are rescued, each acknowledges his partner's role in the mission. The film serves as an excuse for a documentary showing the British Air Force—but no matter. The military crew (many of whom were in the film business as civilians) do a professional job with the production. The crash of the bomber into the North Sea was shot from inside the plane and looks frighteningly real. Robinson's part is little more than a cameo, though he's excellent in the role. Sgt. Attenborough was later knighted Sir Richard, winning an Oscar for his direction of the film GHANDI.

d&w, John Boulting (based on the story by Terence Rattigan), ph, Harry Waxman; m, Gordon Jacob; prod d, John Howell; spec eff, Ray Morse.

War **(PR:A MPAA:NR)**

JOURNEY'S END*** (1930) 130m Gainsborough/TIF bw

Colin Clive *(Capt. Denis Stanhope)*, Ian Maclaren *(Lt. Osborne)*, David Manners *(2nd Lt. James Raleigh)*, Billy Bevan *(2nd Lt. Trotter)*, Anthony Bushell *(2nd Lt. Hibbert)*, Robert Adair *(Capt. Hardy)*, Charles Gerrard *(Pvt. Mason)*, Tom Whiteley *(Sgt. Major)*, Jack Pitcairn *(Colonel)*, Warner Klinger *(German Prisoner)*.

Long before this poignant and powerful antiwar story reached the screen, it became a British institution as a long-running play. Set during WW I, most of the action takes place in an underground bunker set in the trenches of the Western Front. Clive is a commander of troops who merely waits for orders to take a few feet of ground and then sees his men die in a stalemated war, a hopeless, thankless fate where all is doom. He cannot bear to give orders that will take more lives so he takes to drinking heavily. He begins to argue with his second-in-command, Maclaren, who is losing faith in him, and he works over Manners, who is the brother of the girl he loves. In one scene Bushell, who is about to crack under the strain of battle, pretends he is ill and insists upon going on sick call to escape the next attack. Clive sees through this act and confronts the young soldier with his cowardice so that he turns Bushell around. Clive then sends him into combat, which further aggravates his sense of guilt. In another scene Clive intercepts a letter Manners has written his sister, one in which he believes Manners has vilified him. But the captain learns that Manners has nothing but respect for him and, in his letter, relates how Clive is the best loved commander at the front. Bevan and Gerrard are the comic clowns of the company but they can infuse little humor in a film that is by its nature depressing and even morose. Yet Clive's incredible performance and Whale's tight direction lift this histrionic tale above the average. It's a cliche now, but the story and its early talkie rendering still remains a historic work that should be studied merely for the early-day techniques it offers. Whale would go on to make such monster classics as FRANKENSTEIN (1931), which starred Clive, THE OLD DARK HOUSE (1932), and BRIDE OF FRANKENSTEIN (1935). Remade as ACES HIGH in 1976.

p, George Pearson; d, James Whale; w, Joseph Moncure March, V. Gareth Tundrey (based on the play by R.C. Sheriff); ph, Benjamin Kline; ed, Claude Berkeley; art d, Harvey Libbert.

War Drama **(PR:C MPAA:NR)**

JOURNEYS FROM BERLIN—1971 ½** (1980) 125m Center For Public Cinema bw/c

Annette Michelson, Ilona Halberstadt, Gabor Vernon, Chad Wollen, Amy Taubin, Vitto Acconci, Lena Hyun, Yvonne Rainer, Ruth Rainero, Leo Rainer, Cynthia Beatt, Antonio Skarmeta.

A surrealistic independent film that mixes psychoanalysis, modern German terrorism, Bolshevik Russia, and a myriad of hallucinatory images. Michelson is on her psychiatrist's couch, revealing a stream-of-consciousness which unfolds into scenes of terrorism, sex, and suicide. It's not as morose as it sounds: there's a particularly funny bit involving an obscene phone call by none other than a heavy-breathing Leon Trotsky. Definitely for the literate-minded audience. Shot in 16mm.

d, Yvonne Rainer; ph, Carl Teitelbaum, Michael Steinke, Wolfgang Senn, Jon Else, Shinichi Tajiri; ed, Rainer.

Surreal Drama **(PR:O MPAA:NR)**

JOVITA ½** (1970, Pol.) 95m Syrena-Film Polski/Altura bw (JOWITA)

Barbara Lass [Kwiatkowska] *(Agnes/Jovita)*, Daniel Olbrychski *(Marc Arens)*, Zbigniew Cybulski *(Edouard)*, Kalina Jedrusik *(Helene)*, Anna Halcewicz-Pleskaczewska *(Dorota)*, Ignacy Gogolewski *(Michal)*, Iga Cembrzynska *(Lola)*, Anna Ciepiela *(Alina)*, Ryszard Filipski *(Policeman)*, Aleksander Fogiel *(President)*, L. Pilarska, M. Cebulski, L. Nowak, C. Kasznia.

Olbrychski is an architect and runner who, while attending a concert, recollects a lost love. In a flashback he is seen at a costume ball, where he encounters a beautiful woman (Lass) dressed as an houri. He pursues her but she rebuffs his advances. Meanwhile, an artist friend of Lass falls in love with Olbrychski, unbeknownst to him. He has affairs with other women, but he cannot forget Lass. Frustrated, he gets into a fight and is jailed. There he again meets the artist and hears she is about to marry. He also discovers that she is the woman he has been pursuing all along.

p, Jerzy Nitecki; d, Janusz Morgenstern; w, Tadeusz Konwicki (based on the novel *Disneyland* by Stanislaw Dygat); ph, Jan Laskowski; m, Aram Khachaturyan; ed, Wieslawa Otocka; set d, Zdzislaw Kielanowski; cos, Mario Karmolinska; makeup, Mieczyslaw Posmiechowicz.

Drama **(PR:O MPAA:NR)**

JOY zero (1983, Fr./Can.) 100m ATC 3000-RSL FILMS/UGC c

Claudia Udy *(Joy)*, Gerard Antoine Huart *(Marc)*, Agnes Torrent *(Margo)*, Elisabeth Mortensen *(Joelle)*, Jeffrey Kime *(Helmut)*, Manuel Gelin *(Alain)*, Kenneth Le Gallos *(Bruce)*, Claire Nadeau, Septimu Sever, John Stocker, Jerome Tiberghien, Danielle Godet, Michel Caron, Remy Azzolini, Geoffrey Cary, Fabrice Guinard, Corrine Corson, Jean-Jacques Rousselet, Claudine Raffali, Christianna Dousnard, Lisa Braconnier, Eric Franquelin, Helena Canneli, Marianna Lors, Jacqueline Jolivet, Ingrid Rossi, Florence Frezza, Jean-Marie Vauclin, Nancy Cser, James Rae, Jean-Louis D'Amour, Joanne McKay.

A sexual bore that just stops short of actual pornography. Based on what is purported to be a thinly veiled autobiography, JOY is no joy. Udy plays the title role, a fun-loving, very attractive model who is in love with her father and that permeates her existence. Her dad left long ago when she caught him making love and this is the driving force behind her desire to find an older man who will take care of her. Naturally, her quest becomes the entire *raison d'etre* for the film and a series of sexual adventures follow. They have attempted to meld Freud, the Electra complex, and sex, wrap it up in glossy cinematography, and sell it to an unsuspecting audience. Whereas in EMMANUELLE and some of the better soft-core films, there is, at least, some leavening humor to take the sting out of the heavy breathing, here there is virtually none of that and the picture is a succession of *cinematus interruptus* sequences that only punctuates what little ersatz psychological balderdash they serve. The director, Bergon, comes from the world of commercials and his eye is good but he must learn that the play, not the lens, is the thing.

p, Benjamin Simon; d, Serge Bergon; w, Marie-Francoise Hans, Robert Geoffrion, Christian Charriere, Bergon (based on the novel by Joy Laurey); ph, Rene Verzier, Richard Ciupka (Fujicolor); m, Alain Wisniak; ed, Michel Lewin; art d, Eric Moulard, Csaba Kertesz; cos, Claire Fraisse; m/l, Francoise Valery; makeup, Aida Thivat-Carange.

Drama **(PR:O MPAA:NR)**

JOY HOUSE**

(1964, Fr.) 98m Cipra-Cite Films/MGM bw (LES FELINS; AKA: THE LOVE CAGE)

Alain Delon *(Marc)*, Jane Fonda *(Melinda)*, Lola Albright *(Barbara)*, Sorrell Booke *(Harry)*, Carl Studer *(Loftus)*, Andre Oumansky *(Vincent)*, Arthur Howard *(Rev. Nielson)*, Nick Del Negro *(Mick)*, Jacques Bezard *("Napoleon")*, Berett Arcaya *(Diana)*, Douking *(Tramp)*, Jean-Pierre Honore *(Tailor)*, Marc Mazza *(Corsican)*, Annette Poivre *(Employee)*, George Gaynes.

This French production features Delon as a man on the run. He has had an affair with the wife of a top New York mobster and must flee for his life. Albright finds him hiding in a mission for the poor and hires him as her chauffeur. While at the chateau, he meets Albright's niece, Fonda, and discovers Oumansky, Albright's lover. (Oumansky having murdered Albright's husband must now hide in the chateau.) At this point Albright and Oumansky plot to kill Delon to get his passport thus enabling Oumansky to escape to South America. But Delon and Albright have an affair, and when Oumansky discovers this he kills Albright instead. Subsequently Oumansky is killed by the gangsters who mistake him for Delon. Fonda and Delon are hiding the bodies when she learns he plans to leave without her. She therefore dupes the police into believing Delon is guilty of the murders and he must now hide in the chateau (like Oumansky before him). The confusing plot, unfolding in an uneven mix of American- and French-style filmmaking, just doesn't work, and the film quickly becomes incomprehensible and dull. Fonda is all wrong for the part, and the talents of Delon and Albright are completely wasted. Famed director Costa-Gavras served as an assistant director.

p, Jacques Bar; d, Rene Clement; w, Clement, Pascal Jardin, Charles Williams (based on the novel by Day Keene); ph, Henri Decae (Franscope); m, Lalo Schifrin; ed, Fedora Zincone; art d, Jean Andre; cos, Pierre Balmain; makeup, Aida Carange.

Crime/Romance **Cas.** **(PR:O MPAA:NR)**

JOY IN THE MORNING** (1965) 101m MGM c

Richard Chamberlain *(Carl Brown)*, Yvette Mimieux *(Annie McGairy)*, Arthur Kennedy *(Patrick Brown)*, Oscar Homolka *(Stan Pulaski)*, Donald Davis *(Anthony Byrd)*, Joan Tetzel *(Beverly Karter)*, Sidney Blackmer *(Dean James Darwent)*, Virginia Gregg *(Mrs. Lorgan)*, Chris Noel *(Mary Ellen Kincaid)*, Bartlett Robinson *(Prof. Victor Newcole)*, Ellen Atterbury *(Clerk)*, Harvey Stephens *(Dr. Marson)*, Ira Barmak *(Dr. Kirkson)*, Valerie Szabo.

Chamberlain, a law student in the late 1920s, marries girl-next-door type Mimieux, despite their parents' objections. His wealthy father, Kennedy, tries to break up the marriage by withdrawing financial support. Chamberlain then tries to make ends meet by taking a job as a night watchman, and Mimieux works as a babysitter for Tetzel, who is having an affair with married man Homolka. She also consorts with some of the other small town's outcasts, including Davis, a gay florist. When she later finds out she is pregnant, she leaves Chamberlain to save him from future worries. Kennedy, seeing how unhappy his son is, brings them back together. The film is a bit melodramatic, and the direction is uneven. Chamberlain's performance is average, and Mimieux isn't too bad. The film is based on the novel by Betty Smith, who also wrote *A Tree Grows in Brooklyn*.

p, Henry T. Weinstein; d, Alex Segal; w, Sally Benson, Alfred Hayes, Norman Lessing (based on the novel by Betty Smith); ph, Ellsworth Fredricks (Panavision, Metrocolor); m, Bernard Herrmann; ed, Thomas J. McCarthy; art d, George W. Davis, Carl Anderson; set d, Henry Grace, George R. Nelson; cos, Don Feld; spec eff, J. McMillan Johnson; m/l, Sammy Fain, Paul Francis Webster (sung by Chamberlain); makeup, William Tuttle.

Drama **(PR:O MPAA:GP)**

JOY OF LEARNING, THE (SEE: LE GAI SAVOIR, 1968, Fr.)

JOY OF LIVING* 1/2 (1938) 90m RKO bw

Irene Dunne *(Margaret "Maggie" Garret)*, Douglas Fairbanks, Jr. *(Dan Webster)*, Alice Brady *(Minerva)*, Guy Kibbee *(Dennis)*, Jean Dixon *(Harrison)*, Eric Blore *(Potter)*, Lucille Ball *(Salina)*, Warren Hymer *(Mike)*, Billy Gilbert *(Cafe Owner)*, Frank Milan *(Bert Pine)*, Dorothy Steiner *(Dotsy Pine)*, Estelle Steiner *(Betsy Pine)*, Phyllis Kennedy *(Marie)*, Franklin Pangborn *(Radio Broadcast Orchestra Leader)*, James Burke *(Mac)*, John Qualen *(Oswego)*, Spencer Charters *(Magistrate)*, George Chandler *(Taxi Driver)*, Grady Sutton *(Florist)*, Charles Lane *(Dress Extra)*, Pat Flaherty *(Autograph Hound)*, Harry Woods *(Cop-Autograph Hound)*, Bert Roach *(German Waiter)*, Charles Williams *(Sideshow Barker)*, Fuzzy Knight *(Sideshow Piano Player)*, Frank Moran *(Cop with Gravel Voice)*, Dennis O'Keefe *(Man in Building Lobby)*, Frank M. Thomas.

JOY OF LIVING was not a joy to watch. With several tunes by Jerome Kern, one might have expected something special but this film labored from the first frame and what little humor there was was forced. Dunne is a very successful star with a radio show that pays her more than a half million per year. Her family is a bunch of pilot-fish who suck at her, her spending is enormous, and her income tax problems would thwart a battalion of accountants. Fairbanks is a ship owner from Boston who saves her from a mob of adoring fans but his actions are misconstrued and he is arrested as a masher. Now, see if you can swallow the next twist; Dunne is appointed as Fairbanks' parole officer and he must report to her twice weekly. That enforced propinquity takes them around the watering holes, gets them drunk, has them roller skate, and, you guessed it, they fall in love. The picture was expensive to shoot and it shows. What doesn't show is all the money it lost. Even the comedic talents of Pangborn, Blore, Gilbert, Kibbee, and Lucille Ball, in a very short bit, fail to raise the level of the slapstick. The songs include: "You Couldn't Be Cuter," "A Heavenly Party," "What's Good About Goodnight?" "Just Let Me Look At You." All in all, it's a good way to fall asleep on one of those nights when you're fighting with your pillow.

p, Felix Young; d, Tay Garnett; w, Gene Towne, Graham Baker, Allan Scott (based on a story by Dorothy Fields, Herbert Fields); ph, Joseph Walker; m, Jerome Kern, Dorothy Fields; ed, Jack Hively; art d, Van Nest Polglase, Carroll Clark; md, Frank Tours; spec eff, Vernon L. Walker; m/l, Kern, Dorothy Fields.

Musical Comedy **(PR:A MPAA:NR)**

JOY PARADE, THE (SEE: LIFE BEGINS IN COLLEGE, 1937)

JOY RIDE* 1/2 (1935, Brit.) 78m City/ABF bw

Gene Gerrard *(Bill Shepherd)*, Zelma O'Neal *(Virgy Maxwell)*, Betty [Anne] Davies *(Anne Maxwell)*, Paul Blake *(Dippy)*, Gus McNaughton *(String)*, Violet Vanbrugh *(Duchess)*, Cynthia Stock *(Selina Prune)*, Charles Sewell *(Sir Aubrey Mutch-Twistleton)*, Amy Veness *(Lady Clara)*, W.G. Saunders *(Bishop)*, Vernon Harris, Bryan Farley, Molly Hamley Clifford, Robert Maclachlan, Ian Wilson, Jeanne d'Arcy, Buddy Bradley Rhythm Girls.

Two chorus girls and their worthless male pals try and take advantage of their elderly uncle, basically blackmailing him to put up with their shenanigans by bringing up some past incidents which are a black spot on his career as an admiral. Things end in a fashion that keeps both sides happy in this forced comedy that relies too heavily upon far-fetched situations.

p, Basil Humphreys; d, Harry Hughes; w, Vernon Harris; ph, Ronald Neame.

Comedy **(PR:A MPAA:NR)**

JOY RIDE** (1958) 65m AA bw

Rad Fulton *(Paul)*, Ann Doran *(Grace)*, Regis Toomey *(Miles)*, Nicholas King *(Arnie)*, Robert Levin *(Vince)*, Jim Bridges *(Dirk)*, Roy Engel *(Barrett)*, Robert Colbert *(Taverner)*, Robert Anderson *(Ellensten)*.

When Fulton, King, Bridges, and Levin—a teenage gang of hoodlums—spy Toomey's sports car, they ask to ride in it. Toomey is hesitant but kind, and the young men, mistaking this for fear, launch a campaign of terror. Eventually they break into Toomey's home and succeed in giving Toomey's wife (Doran) a heart attack. The four youths are imprisoned, but Toomey remains tolerant as ever and pleads that their charges be reduced. (Maybe he saw BOYS TOWN once too often.) The film is simplistic though there are some fine directorial moments and the cast is excellent. It's based on an *Ellery Queen Mystery Magazine* story.

p, Ben Schwalb; d, Edward Bernds; w, Christopher Knopf (based on a story by C.B. Gilford); ph, Carl Guthrie; m, Marlin Skiles; ed, William Austin; art d, David Milton.

Crime Drama **(PR:C MPAA:NR)**

JOYRIDE** (1977) 92m AIP c

Desi Arnaz, Jr. *(Scott)*, Robert Carradine *(John)*, Melanie Griffith *(Susie)*, Anne Lockhart *(Cindy)*, Tom Ligon *(Sanders)*, Cliff Lenz *(Henderson)*, Robert Loper *(Simon)*, Diana Grayf *(Rhonda)*, Diane O'Mack *(Debbie)*, Susan Ludlow *(Personnel Lady)*, Ted D'Arms *(Site Manager)*, Gail Rosella *(Cashier)*, Richard Mazzola *(Car Salesman)*, Michael O'Neill *(Henderson's Assistant)*, Duncan Maclean *(Diner Owner)*, Richard Riehle *(Bartender)*, Richard Tietjen *(Sam)*, Paul Fleming *(Big Ed)*.

Arnaz, Carradine, and Griffith are bored Californians who head to the Alaskan pipeline in search of adventure. They soon turn to robbery and take the consenting Lockhart hostage. Although the film shows shades of gravity, it can't escape its exploitative nature, ultimately compromising any serious intentions. The cast is an odd mix of second-generation Hollywood: Arnaz is the son of Desi and Lucy; Carradine the son of John; Lockhart the daughter of June; and Griffith the daughter of Tippi Hedren. Unfortunately not many of their parents' talents were inherited. Scripted by "Mademoiselle" magazine's film critic Rainer, along with Ruben (director of JOYRIDE and the earlier THE POM POM GIRLS), this is certainly one of the odder writing teams in film history.

p, Bruce Cohn Curtis; d, Joseph Ruben; w, Ruben, Peter Rainer; ph, Stephen M. Katz (DeLuxe Color); m, Jimmie Haskell; ed, Bill Butler; cos, Cheryl Beasley; m/l, Electric Light Orchestra, Jeff Lynne, Barry Mann, Cynthia Weil; stunts, Thomas Huff.

Action/Crime **(PR:O MPAA:R)**

JOYSTICKS* (1983) 88m Jensen Farley c (AKA: VIDEO MADNESS)

Joe Don Baker *(Mr. Rutter)*, Leif Green *(Eugene Groebe)*, Jim Greenleaf *(Jonathan Andrew McDorfus)*, Scott McGinnis *(Jefferson Bailey)* Jonathan Gries *(King Vidiot)*, Corinne Bohrer *(Patsy Rutter)*, John Diehl *(Arnie)*, John Voldstad *(Max)*, Reid Cruickshanks *(Coach)*, Morgan Lofting *(Mrs. Rutter)*, Kym Malin *(Lola)*, Kim G. Michel *(Alva)*, Jacqulin Cole *(Alexis)*, Logan Ramsey *(Mayor)*, Hugo Stanger.

Baker's an angry parent who is determined to shut down the video game parlor of River City. Of course the kids fight back with the usual escapades and hijinks found in this sort of movie. And guess who wins? Lots of scatological jokes, cheap sex, flat humor and bad pop music. Clark, the film's director, had previously worked on blaxploitation films TOM, and BLACK SHAMPOO. Is this achieving racial equality? Those having speaking roles are all white.

p&d, Greydon Clark; w, Al Gomez, Mickey Epps, Curtis Burch; ph, Nicholas von Sternberg (Movielab Color); m, John Caper, Jr.; ed, Larry Bock; art d, Donn Greer; m/l, Ray Khenetsky, Bill Scott.

Comedy **Cas.** **(PR:O MPAA:R)**

JUAREZ***** (1939) 132m WB bw

Paul Muni *(Benito Pablo Juarez)*, Bette Davis *(Empress Carlotta von Habsburg)*, Brian Aherne *(Maximilian von Habsburg)*, Claude Rains *(Louis Napoleon)*, John Garfield *(Porfirio Diaz)*, Donald Crisp *(Marechal Bazaine)*, Gale Sondergaard *(Empress Eugenie)*, Joseph Calleia *(Alejandro Uradi)*, Gilbert Roland *(Col. Miguel Lopez)*, Henry O'Neill *(Miguel Miramon)*, Pedro de Cordoba *(Riva Palacio)*, Montagu Love *(Jose de Montares)*, Harry Davenport *(Dr. Samuel Basch)*, Walter Fenner *(Achille Fould)*, Alex Leftwich *(Drouyn de Lhuys)*, Robert Warwick *(Maj. DuPont)*, John Miljan *(Mariano Escobedo)*, Irving Pichel *(Carbajal)*, Walter Kingsford *(Prince Metternich)*, Monte Blue *(Lerdo de Tejada)*, Louis Calhern *(LeMarc)*, Vladimir Sokoloff *(Camilo)*, Georgia Caine *(Countess Battenberg)*, Gennaro Curci *(Senor de Leon)*, Bill Wilkerson *(Tomas Mejia)*, Hugh Sothern *(John Bigelow)*, Fred Malatesta *(Senor Salas)*, Carlos de Valdez *(Tailor)*, Frank Lackteen *(Coachman)*, Walter O. Stahl *(Senator del Valle)*, Frank Reicher *(Duc de Morny)*, Holmes Herbert *(Marshall Randon)*, Egon Brecher *(Baron von Magnus)*, Manuel Diaz *(Pepe)*, Mickey Kuhn *(Augustin Iturbide)*, Lillian Nicholson *(Josefa Iturbide)*, Noble Johnson *(Regules)*, Grant Mitchell *(Mr. Harris)*, Charles Halton *(Mr. Roberts)*, Martin Garralaga *(Negroni)*, William Edmunds, Gilbert Emory.

Mexico has had many saviors, some bad, some good, a few great ones, the greatest being Benito Pablo Juarez who was to that downtrodden, woebegone country what Abraham Lincoln was to the United States. In fact, both of them lived at the same time and Juarez was profoundly influenced by the North American president; he even took to wearing a stovepipe hat and long black Prince Albert coat to emulate his idol Lincoln. And Juarez, like Lincoln, was physically homely, stoical, yet full of wisdom and spiritual handsomeness that were irresistible to his people. Playing him to the hilt in this classic film biography is the great Muni. The film opens with Rains, playing the calculating, evil Napoleon III, appointing Aherne (Archduke Maximilian von Habsburg of Austria) emperor of Mexico. Through his agents in Mexico, Rains has set up a fake election by which Aherne has been chosen the monarch of a people he has never seen. Aherne and wife Davis (Carlotta) journey to Mexico, escorted by an army commanded by Crisp. Meeting the royal couple are thousands of jubilant peasants in Mexico City, but the royal couple is again deceived by the insidious French who have staged the reception. The duly elected president of Mexico, Muni, however, leads his people in revolt against the monarchs imposed upon Mexico by Rains. To mollify the people Aherne offers Muni the powerful position of Secretary of State but this is rejected. Aherne still proves himself to be a benevolent monarch by refusing to sign edicts that would return the land to rich patrons, estates given to peons during the rise of Juarez. Further, he refuses to sign other harsh edicts such as shooting those out of hand who are found to have weapons. He believes that he can unite the Mexican people by adopting a native prince and he and his wife formally make the little boy their own in an elaborate ceremony. Yet, when they take their new son to the balcony of their palace to show to their ostensibly adoring subjects, a tremendous explosion rocks the area. Juaristas have just blown up a huge ammunition dump of the French army. So enraged by this "slap" is Aherne that he signs the shoot-to-kill order for those found with weapons. Wholesale executions ensue, and soon even those who have paid homage to Aherne and Davis turn against the monarchy. A full-scale revolution breaks out with the U.S. ordering the French army to leave Mexico under the Monroe Doctrine. Not wishing to risk war with the U.S., Rains orders his commander, Crisp, to quit Mexico. Aherne and Davis make plans to leave with their French protectors, abdicating their fragile monarchy (known historically as "The Cactus Throne"). Meanwhile, Muni has problems of his own. When Aherne's generals score some minor victories, Calleia, a local don, takes over the town of

Matamores, stating that Muni is no longer President; that, because of the prolonged war with the French, no new elections have been held and he is no longer officially in office. Calleia refuses to yield to Muni's authority and openly states that if Muni has the audacity to come to Matamores he will have him shot. Hearing this, Muni, alone, goes into the armed town, marching stoically through threatening crowds that soon change their opinion of the liberator, impressed by the courage he displays. He marches up to the government house and Calleia, seeing him coming, orders his men to shoot Muni. None does, fearing that the now partisan crowd shouting for Calleia to come out will tear them to pieces. Calleia himself finally steps to the porch and draws a gun to shoot Muni but a peon in the crowd fires first and kills the usurper. Muni now stands supreme as the leader of the Mexican people. He orders a full attack along all fronts against Aherne's French forces which slowly crumble. Davis, fearing for her husband's life, returns to Europe to beg Rains to reinforce the French divisions. He manages to avoid giving her an audience. At the end of her tether, Davis finally barges in on the emperor and empress (Sondergaard), hysterically imploring Rains to save her husband, a man he, Rains, manipulated into taking a crown Mexico did not wish to bestow. When Rains tells her nothing can be done, that he's ordered all his troops back to Europe, Davis goes haywire, loudly accusing Rains of purposely setting up this catastrophe and murdering her husband. She completely loses her mind (as did the real Carlotta) and must be institutionalized; not even her closest friends and relatives can penetrate the hazy fog that engulfs her reason. With the French forces gone, Aherne tries vainly to hold onto his evaporating empire with Mexican troops loyal to his cause—and these were few—led by Roland, O'Neill, and Wilkerson. His army is finally surrounded and Roland turns traitor, leading the enemy under the command of Miljan into the fortress under cover of darkness. Aherne and his entire staff are captured. Roland, however, has made a deal with the Mexican commander, who orders that Aherne be released. "You are free to go," Miljan tells Aherne, refusing to recognize him. Aherne, resplendent in white uniform and gold braid and sash, insists upon identifying himself but still Miljan tells him to go in peace, that he recognizes no emperor in the group of prisoners. The noble Aherne demands that he be taken prisoner with his men and insists that Miljan accept his sword as an official token of surrender. Reluctantly, Miljan takes his sword and Aherne is put into a cell to await trial. Garfield, playing the mercurial Diaz—the ablest Juarista general, and who has met Aherne and is convinced that he is a decent man, one who was hoodwinked into taking a throne that did not exist—pleads with his mentor Muni not to take Aherne's life. Yet Muni, who does not act out of vengeance, tells Garfield that Aherne is a symbol and as long as he is alive the monarchist forces can rally to his support. In the end, Aherne is condemned. He and his two loyal generals, Wilkerson and O'Neill, are taken to a little hill. Aherne has requested that his wife's favorite song, "La Paloma" ("The Song of the Dove"), be sung at his execution. A woman sweetly sings the lyrical song while the star-crossed emperor hands out little sacks of gold and requests that the firing squad aim "straight at my heart." He, O'Neill, and Wilkerson are then shot to death. At that moment, in a dark room in Europe, Davis, moving as if in a stupor, walks to the French windows, throws them open, and steps through a huge shaft of light to the terrace, calling out her husband's name. Aherne is later displayed in death inside a huge cathedral in Mexico City. Alone, Muni goes to see him in his coffin, looking down and whispering, "I'm sorry." He then turns and walks stoically from the church at the fadeout. Prior to shooting JUAREZ, Muni, always painstaking in his research of any biographical role he was to enact, went to Mexico with director Dieterle, and spent six weeks visiting the areas in which Benito Juarez lived, worked, and administered his infant republic. The actor studied hundreds of books, documents, and photographs of his subject, absorbing every detail about the man he was to play. The part of Juarez was wholly manufactured for the film insofar as the play by Franz Werfel, which served as one source of the film, concentrated only upon Maximilian and Carlotta. Actually, the film was unique in that it was shot as two films—first the Aherne-Davis story, then the Juarez portion—both stories then edited together. Muni only meets Aherne when viewing his corpse, and even this scene is spliced together. Muni had the benefit of viewing the edited first portion of the film before going in front of the cameras to play Juarez and, to offset the Davis histrionics, he underplayed his role almost down to a whisper. Muni was afforded the privilege since he was then the most important actor on the Warner Bros. lot. The actor also kept foremost in his mind that he was playing a stoic native-born Mexican Indian who was naturally reserved and reticent. Yet he is commanding and inspiring in his part. Garfield, on the other hand, appears in only a few scenes and is little more than a cipher rather than a character, mouthing Muni's philosophy, as Porfirio Diaz. (Diaz would have made a grand subject for a film himself, first a dedicated patriot fighting for the cause of the common people, then a disillusioned champion of the people slowly corrupted by power until he openly defied Juarez and contributed to the great leader's death in 1872 when he rebelled and then took over Mexico, running it as a despot for 40 years until he ran into a couple of men just like his youthful self—Emiliano Zapata and Pancho Villa.) Aherne really dominates the film as the kind, gentle, and well-intentioned Emperor Maximilian, one of the most tragic characters of history, and his performance is nothing less than inspiring. Davis has only a small role but it was one she coveted when the project was first begun in 1937, that of the unbalanced Carlotta. She knew she would have one fantastic scene, where Carlotta goes mad after confronting the scheming Napoleon III (Rains) and she played it to the hilt, the viewer treated (or mistreated as the case may be) to visual dementia descending over the mind of a crazed empress. Muni, such was his stature at the studio, was actually consulted about having the great actress in the film; he was never called anything except "Mr. Muni" at the studio. One memo from Warner Bros. producer Hall Wallis to Muni indicates the power the actor wielded: "Mike Levee has informed us of your willingness to permit us to costar Bette Davis with you in JUAREZ. I want you to know that we appreciate very much your graciousness in acceding to this request." Yet the celebrated Davis temperament flared often and she was instrumental in shutting down the production several times. When she entered Aherne's study just two weeks into the film she froze and could not speak her lines, announcing that she was, for the first time in her life, unprepared. She promptly changed her costume and drove home. In another scene, while adorned in full 19th-Century skirts Davis sat down right in the middle of the set while the cameras were rolling, shouting to director Dieterle: "This costume was made for a stunt woman, not an actress!" Davis had never cared for Dieterle, believing him to be pompous and aloof, more of a man's director than one who understood the nuances of female role interpretations, such as the gentle William Wyler, or Edmund Goulding, her favorites. Some of her scenes were cut by Muni to make room for the Juarez part, which did not endear the actor to Davis, yet her mad scene is one of the most spectacular on record and worth the viewing of the entire film—which is in and of itself a great document and a flawless production. The makeup and costuming for this historical epic typified the care the studio lavished on the production. Makeup genius Westmore adorned Davis in a black wig which was specially made by his own wigmaker, but with the part of Juarez, Westmore really rebuilt Muni's face. Westmore was later quoted as saying: "We started by taking photographs of Muni, then painting the likeness of the Indian Juarez over them. We took plaster casts of his face. We had to accentuate his bone structure, make his jaws appear wider, square his forehead, and give him an Indian nose. He had to be darker than anyone else in the picture, so we used a dark reddish-brown makeup, highlighted with yellow. We wrote down every step of the process so it could be repeated." A film test was then done just for makeup, as was the procedure for any important film, and shown to Jack Warner, studio boss. Snorted the mogul: "You mean we're paying Muni all this dough and we can't even recognize him?" Muni was a perfectionist and drove the makeup people to their chore; he also insisted that the studio find someone who actually knew Juarez, no little chore since Juarez had been dead for 64 years. Incredibly, a 116-year-old Mexican who had served with Juarez was unearthed in Mexico and was flown to Hollywood, where Muni grilled the old man for hours on end concerning Juarez's appearance, habits, speech patterns, physical movements, and mannerisms. Costumer and gown designer Orry-Kelly went through the same painstaking research before clothing the actors (more than 1,000 extras) in this most accurate historical film. He also employed what he termed "visual psychology" in showing Davis' decline into insanity, clothing her first in white gowns, then grey, then all black from her first to last scenes. Veteran cinematographer Gaudio adopted the same technique, employing sharp, contrasting scenes at the opening of the film, then, particularly for Davis' scenes, lengthening the shadows down into darkness, with only shafts of hazy light to illuminate the subject. Gaudio dispensed with standard floodlighting techniques and opted for spotlights with dimmers affixed to the lamp rails above the sets. He could thus control single beams of light which could accent any object or person. In this way, when Davis sees Rains, the calculating Napoleon who has sent her husband to certain death, she realizes his evil visually; Rains is first shown in normal light, then all darkens about him, with only a shaft of light accenting the most sinister facets of a face that is nothing less than demonic. Art director Grot and his helpers exhausted their energies on this film, drawing more than 3,600 sketches and taking 7,360 blueprints from these before constructing 54 mammoth sets, including 12 villages, four cities, and various castles and palaces, the crowning achievement being the Chapultapec Palace in Mexico City where Maximilian and Carlotta briefly reigned. Maximilian's throne room was constructed with a 250-foot long and 50-foot high backdrop which showed the old Mexico City and in the background the towering Popocatapetl Mountain. The musical score was as lavish and well-researched as all other production elements. Its composer, Korngold, noted for his rich scores, created more than 3,000 bars of music for the film. He later told *Film Guide:* "In writing the score I discovered that the music composed in Mexico during the period from 1864 to 1870 was not Mexican music at all! But unmistakably Viennese. Some of the castanets also tapped out the rhythms of Chopin and Schubert. The European influence was so strong at the time that the composers abandoned their native music. Fandangos and native polkas of the period are actually Swiss waltzes and marches. Only the instrumentation was changed. Instead of violins and cellos the Mexican players undoubtedly used their native guitars and mandolins; thus, the people of the country failed to note the really subtle change. But imagine what would have happened had I not recognized Strauss and used instead the music of those historic years?" Nothing was left to chance in making this film which was ultimately received as being a masterpiece of filmmaking but one which did not suit the public's fancy and lost money. Dieterle could not be blamed, for it is one of his finest achievements and he did all in his power to make it so, even calling upon powers not of this earth. He went so far as to consult his astrological chart and then began shooting early one morning in October, 1938, ordering the principal actors and Gaudio on the set for the first shots, since that day, he was convinced, placed the stars most favorably in his personal destiny!

p, Hal B. Wallis; d, William Dieterle; w, John Huston, Wolfgang Reinhardt, Aeneas MacKenzie (based on the novel *The Phantom Crown* by Bertita Harding and the play *Juarez & Maximillian* by Franz Werfel); ph, Tony Gaudio; m, Erich Wolfgang Korngold; ed, Warren low; md, Leo F. Forbstein; art d, Anton Grot; cos, Orry-Kelly.

Biography/Historical Epic Cas. (PR:A MPAA:NR)

JUAREZ AND MAXIMILLIAN (SEE: MAD EMPRESS, THE, 1939)

JUBAL* 1/2** (1956) 100m COL c

Glenn Ford *(Jubal Troop)*, Ernest Borgnine *(Shep Horgan)*, Rod Steiger *(Pinky)*, Valerie French *(Mae Horgan)*, Felicia Farr *(Naomi Hoktor)*, Basil Ruysdael *(Shem Hoktor)*, Noah Beery, Jr. *(Sam)*, Charles Bronson *(Reb Haislipp)*, John Dierkes *(Carson)*, Robert Burton *(Dr. Grant)*, Juney Ellis *(Charity Hoktor)*, Don C. Harvey *(Jim Tolliver)*, Guy Wilkerson *(Cookie)*, Larry Hudson *(Bayne)*, Mike Lawrence, Robert "Buzz" Henry *(Tolliver Boys)*, William Rhinehart *(Matt)*, Bob Cason *(Cowboy)*, John Cason *(Rancher)*, Ann Kunde *(Girl)*, Jack Elam *(McCoy)*.

A first-rate "adult" western that's packed with action, sex, surprises, and some humor. Shot among the magnificent Grand Teton mountains of Wyoming, JUBAL is the name of Ford, a drifter who arrives in the area and takes a job at the ranch owned by Borgnine. When Borgnine's sensuous wife, French, comes on to Ford very strongly, Steiger, her ex-lover, gets rankled and means to get rid of Ford. French admits to Borgnine that she has the warms for Ford and Borgnine attacks Ford and is killed in self-defense. Despite knowing that, Steiger rabble-rouses a posse to lynch Ford. Steiger is still enraged at French for having given him up so he rapes and beats her. With her dying words, she gets Ford off the hook and he winds up with Farr, a sweet, lovely girl whom he'd met earlier. Steiger is so mean as Ford's rival that you'll hate him for the next three movies after seeing this. The role is not unlike Judd in OKLAHOMA or any of several villains Steiger has played. The battle lines are drawn early and the suspense mounts as we wait for the inevitable conclusion between Ford and Steiger. There's no question as to who will win but the way they get to it is the enjoyable part. Instead of concentrating on the scenery and the vistas (the way Kasdan did in his imitative SILVERADO), Daves elects to examine the humanity instead of the sagebrush and the result is an unusually good story that could fit in almost any milieu. Bronson is one of the ranch hands and gives no indication of his coming stardom. Also seen are Elam (who can be one of the funniest actors on any screen when given the right role) and Buzz Henry, who became a stunt director for several movies before his untimely death in an auto accident. Henry had been a child star known as "Buzzy" Henry and appeared in many low-budget films. Farr gave up her career in the 1970s to concentrate on her marriage to Jack Lemmon.

p, William Fadiman; d, Delmer Daves; w, Russell S. Hughes, Daves (based on the novel *Jubal Troop* by Paul I. Wellman); ph, Charles Lawton, Jr., (CinemaScope, Technicolor); m, David Raksin; ed, Al Clark; md, Morris W. Stoloff; art d, Carl Anderson; set d, Louis Diage; cos, Jean Louis; makeup, Clay Campbell.

Western (PR:C MPAA:NR)

JUBILEE* 1/2** (1978, Brit.) 103m Megalovision/Cinegate c

Jenny Runacre *(Queen Elizabeth I)*, Jordan *(Amyl Nitrite)*, Little Nell *(Crabs)*, Linda Spurrier *(Viv)*, Hermine Demoriane *(Chaos)*, Toyah Willcox *(Mad)*, Richard O'Brien *(John Dee)*, Adam Ant *(Kid)*, Ian Charleson *(Angel)*, Karl Johnson *(Sphinx)*, Neil Kennedy *(Max)*, Orlando *(Borgia Ginz)*, Lindsay Kemp and Troupe *(Cabaret)*, Gene October.

Neat and quirky, this is undoubtedly one of the freshest black comedies around. Runacre is the famed British monarch of 1578 who is magically transported into the London of the future; namely, the late 1970s punk movement. Presently she finds herself with a woman's collective featuring every kind of social pariah, and they take her on a whirlwind tour of the "New London." This frenzied film delivers interesting social commentary and the fast-paced editing does a terrific job to enhance this. Occasionally the film gets out of control but not enough to hinder it noticeably. The performances are energetic and Runacre is satisfactory in her unusual role. Featured in the cast are Little Nell and O'Brien of THE ROCKY HORROR PICTURE SHOW fame. The music is by some of London's best punkers, including Adam Ant in a featured role. It deserves to be a cult classic.

p, Howard Malin, James Whaley; d&w, Derek Jarman, Christopher Hobbs; ph, Peter Middleton; m, Suzi Pinns, Brian Eno, Adam and the Ants, Siouxsie and the Banshees, Chelsea, Wayne County, Electric Chairs, Maneaters, Amilcar; ed, Tom Priestley, Nick Barnard; prod d, Christopher Hobbs.

Black Comedy Cas. (PR:O MPAA:NR)

JUBILEE TRAIL 1/2** (1954) 103m REP c

Vera Ralston *(Florinda Grove/Julie Latour)*, Joan Leslie *(Garnet Hale)*, Forrest Tucker *(John Ives)*, John Russell *(Oliver Hale)*, Ray Middleton *(Charles Hale)*, Pat O'Brien *(Ernest "Texas" Conway)*, Buddy Baer *(Nicolai Gregorovitch Karakozeff)*, Jim Davis *(Silky)*, Barton MacLane *(Deacon Bartlett)*, Richard Webb *(Capt. Brown)*, James Millican *(Rinardi)*, Nina Varela *(Dona Manuela)*, Martin Garralaga *(Don Rafael Velasco)*, Charles Stevens *(Pablo, a Peon)*, Nacho Galindo *(Rico, Bartender)*, Don Beddoe *(Mr. Maury, Hotel Manager)*, John Holland *(Mr. Drake)*, William Haade *(Jake the Sailor)*, Alan Bridge *(Mr. Turner)*, John Halloran, Sayre Dearing *(Turner's Men)*, Stephen Chase *(Mr. Forbes, an Admirer)*, Daniel M. White *(Henry)*, Eugene Borden *(Kimball, a Detective)*, Morris Buchanan *(Waiter)*, Rodolfo Hoyos, Jr., Rico Alansiz *(Spaniards)*, Bud Wolfe *(Blandy)*, Paul Stader *(Barbour)*, Don Haggerty *(Detective)*, Maurice Jara *(Vaquero)*, Rosa Turich *(Senora Silva)*, Manuel Lopez *(Senor Silva)*, Frances Dominguez *(Woman)*, Richard Dodge *(Sentry)*, Perry Lopez *(Silva's Son)*, Claire Carleton *(Estelle, the Madame)*, Peter Ortiz *(Horseman)*, Victor Sen Yung *(Mickey, the Chinese Man)*, Edward Colmans, George Navarro *(Orosco Guests)*, John Mooney *(Dan)*, Grant Withers *(Maj. Lynden)*, Alma Beltran *(Servant Girl)*, Anna Navarro *(Conchita)*, Frank Puglia *(Don Orosco)*, Pepe Hern *(Ranch Hand)*, Glenn Strange *(Tom Branders)*, Joe Dominguez *(Ernesto)*, Felipe Turich *(Pedro)*, Gloria Varela *(Dolores)*, Linda Danceil *(Rosita)*, Emil Sitka *(Chair Bit)*, Brett Houston *(Man at Bar)*, Bill Chandler *(Handsome Man at Table)*, Norman Kent *(Drunk at Table)*, Emmett Lynn *(Drunk Man with Little Hat)*, Joe Ploski *(Pace Holding Bit)*, Tex Terry *(Penrose)*, Rocky Shahan *(Mexican Rider)*, Chuck Hayward, Bob Burrows *(Velasco Riders)*, Pilar Del Rey *(Carmelita Velasco)*, James Lilburn *(Sgt. Aherne)*, Jack O'Shea *(Corporal)*, Jack Elam *(Sergeant)*, Tina Menard *(Isabel)*, Raymond Johnson *(Corporal)*, Manuel Paris *(Mexican)*, Charles Sullivan *(Card Player)*, Ralph Brooks *(Bartender)*, Robert "Buzz" Henry, Ted Smile *(Velasco's Sons)*.

This is one of Republic studios' biggest films. But even its terrific cast and enormous budget cannot conceal the overgrown B western lurking beneath. It takes place along a wagon train from New Orleans to California, and the myriad characters are restricted to a few intertwining stories. Leslie marries Russel, much to the chagrin of his older brother Middleton. After settling in Los Angeles, Leslie has a baby, and, when her husband is killed, Middleton tries to steal the baby but is finally killed by the drunken doctor, O'Brien. Tucker and Webb are Leslie's new suitors, and Ralston is a dance-hall girl who shows naive Leslie a few things. In addition, Ralston gets a couple of songs including "Clap Your Hands," "A Man is a Man," "Saying No," and the title song, done as a duet with Baer. Ralston was the wife of Republic's owner, Herbert J. Yates, and one can't help but wonder if this had anything to do with the inflated budget. It's really not a bad film, just overdone and longer than necessary. The acting is satisfactory and the directorial/photographic team of Kane and Marta handle the epic-sized task with proficiency.

p, Herbert J. Yates; d, Joseph Inman Kane; w, Bruce Manning (based on the novel by Gwen Bristow); ph, Jack Marta (Trucolor); m, Victor Young; ed, Richard L. Van Enger; md, Young; art d, Frank Arrigo; set d, John McCarthy, Jr., George Milo; cos, Adele Palmer; ch, Bob Mark; m/l, Young, Sidney Clare.

Western (PR:A MPAA:NR)

JUBILEE WINDOW* (1935, Brit.) 61m British and Dominions/PAR bw

Sebastian Shaw *(Peter Ward)*, Ralph Truman *(Dan Stevens)*, Olive Melville *(Margery Holroyd)*, Frank Birch *(Ambrose Holroyd)*, Margaret Yarde *(Mrs. Holroyd)*, Michael Shepley *(Dacres)*, Winifred Oughton *(Mrs. Tribbets)*, Robert Horton *(Sir Edward Musgrove)*, Dorothy Hammond *(Lady Musgrove)*, Mark Daly *(Dave)*, Walter Amner, Frank Bertram, Doris Hare.

This poor excuse for a comedy centers on the efforts of a gang of jewel thieves to use the excitement of a giant celebration for their own advantage, making off with a costly diamond. The silly and forced slapstick humor just isn't funny.

p, Anthony Havelock-Allan; d, George Pearson; w, Gerald Elliott, Pearson (based on a story by Elliott).

Comedy (PR:A MPAA:NR)

JUD* (1971) 80m Duque Films/Maron Films c

Joseph Kaufmann *(Jud Carney)*, Robert Deman *(Bill Arness)*, Alix Wyeth *(Shirley Simon)*, Norman Burton *(Uncle Hornkel)*, Claudia Jennings *(Sunny)*, Maurice Sherbanee *(Salvadore Javelli)*, Victor Dunlap *(Vincent Barber)*, Bonnie Bittner *(Kathy)*, Jo Levitt Cato *(Ben)*, Ken Schnell, Denise Lynn, Paul Heslin, Leigh Hemingway, Lee James, Roger Lane, Bill Collins, John Cardos, Janice Dryer, Valerie Fitzgerald, Gloria Hill, Harry Wowchuk, Phil Presly, Lisa Deborah Kantor, Gene Jesso.

A trite and utterly dishonest portrayal of a returning Vietnam veteran, Kaufmann, and the adjustments he must make. When Kaufmann discovers his fiancee has left him, he moves into a boarding house peopled with stock-movie oddballs. Flashback memories of the war and the suicide of fellow house resident Deman, reduce Kaufmann to a broken and bitter man. The plot has potential but never goes anywhere with the provided script. Sample dialog: "Jud, if you don't want to be crucified, don't stay around crosses." The production values are poor, which is a major disappointment considering that the producer is former Columbia editor Kantor. Jennings, a Playboy Playmate of the Year, displays the impoverished talent most of Hefner's would-be actresses possess.

p, Igo Kantor; d&w, Gunther Collins; ph, Isidore Mankofsky (Movielab Color); m, Stu Phillips; m/l, "One Too Many Mornings," Bob Dylan (sung by John Hartford).

Drama Cas. (PR:O MPAA:GP)

JUDAS CITY (SEE: SATAN'S BED, 1965)

JUDAS WAS A WOMAN (SEE: LA BETE HUMAINE, 1938, Fr.)

JUDEX* 1/2**

(1966, Fr./Ital.) 96m Comptoir Francais du Film-Filmes Cinematografica/Continental bw

Channing Pollock *(Judex/Vallieres)*, Francine Berge *(Diana Monti/Marie Verdier)*, Edith Scob *(Jacqueline Favraux)*, Michel Vitold *(Favraux)*, Jacques Jouanneau *(Cocantin)*, Sylva Koscina *(Daisy)*, Theo Sarapo *(Morales)*, Benjamin Boda *(Reglisse)*, Philippe Mareuil *(Amaury de la Rochefontaine)*, Rene Genin *(Pierre Kerjean)*, Jean Degrave *(Notary)*, Luigi Cortese *(Pierrot)*, Roger Fradet *(Leon)*, Ketty France *(Jeanne-Marie Bontemps)*, Suzanne Gossen *(Landlady)*, Andre Melies *(Doctor)*.

Excellent. Pollock (in civilian life an American magician) is the son of a man driven to suicide by banker Vitold. For revenge he kidnaps Vitold at a masked ball and (while disguised) tells the banker's daughter, Scob, of her father's immoral dealings. She promptly reacts by denying her inheritance. Berge is a governess in love with Vitold but having an affair with Sarapo. Eventually she kills her lover then herself, and Vitold commits suicide, leaving Pollock and Scob to marry. Though it sounds gruesome and complicated it's really quite well done. There are lots of masks and disguises as well as a circus aerialist. This is based on a 12-part 1917 serial of the same name by Louis Feuillade (who created the original FANTOMAS). This version was directed by Franju, known for THE HORROR CHAMBER OF DR. FAUSTUS. It was released in France and Italy in 1964, with the American preview two years later.

p, Robert de Nesle; d, Georges Franju; w, Francis Lacassin, Jacques Champreux, Louis Feuillade, Arthur Bernede; ph, Marcel Fradetal; m, Maurice Jarre; ed, Gilbert Natot; art d, Robert Giordani; cos, Christiane Courcelles; makeup, Maguy Vernadet; English titles, Herman G. Weinberg.

Mystery/Adventure Cas. (PR:C MPAA:NR)

JUDGE, THE** (1949) 69m Emerald/F bw

Milburn Stone *(Martin Strang)*, Katherine deMille *(Lucille Strang)*, Paul Guilfoyle *(William Jackson)*, Stanley Waxman *(Dr. James Anderson)*, Norman Budd *(James Tilton)*, John Hamilton *(Lt. Edwards)*, Jonathan Hale *(The Judge)*, Joe Forte *(District Attorney)*, Jesse Kirkpatrick *(Patrick Riley)*, Herb Vigran, Barney Philips,

Charles Williams *(Reporters)*, Tom Holland *(Court Photographer)*, Bob Jellison *(Clerk)*.

Thin and tenuous thriller about infidelity, murder and courtroom intrigue. Stone is a lawyer who finds out that wife deMille is cheating on him. He gets Guilfoyle off on a murder charge and uses the man for his own nefarious purposes. He arranges for deMille and her lover Waxman to be killed, but the plan backfires with Stone ending up the corpse. The two lovers look guilty and Waxman kills himself, leaving deMille destitute. Unable to live with the guilt, the real killer confesses to the crime. Though it has its moments, THE JUDGE is hampered by pursuing too many tangents. At times it runs too long making potentially suspenseful scenes dull and tedious. The acting is all right but nothing out of the ordinary for B crime films.

p, Anson Bond; d, Elmer Clifton; w, Samuel Newman, Clifton, Bond (based on the story by Bond and Julius Long); ph, Ben Kline, Ray Foster; m, Gene Lanham; ed, Fred Maguire.

Crime **(PR:O MPAA:NR)**

JUDGE AND THE ASSASSIN, THE*** (1979, Fr.) 130m Libra c (LE JUGE ET L'ASSASSIN)

Philippe Noiret *(Judge Rousseau)*, Michel Galabru *(Sgt. Joseph Bouvier)*, Isabelle Huppert *(Rose)*, Jean-Claude Brialy *(Villedieu, Attorney)*, Renee Faure *(Mme. Rousseau)*, Cecile Vassort *(Louise Lesueur)*, Yves Robert *(Prof. Degueldre)*, Jean-Roger Caussimon *(Street Singer)*, Jean Bretonniere *(Deputy)*, Monique Chaumette *(Louise's Mother)*, Francois Dyreck *(Freed Tramp)*, Liza Braconnier *(Hospital Nun)*, Arlette Bonnard *(Farm Girl With Soup)*, Jean Amos *(Caretaker)*, Gilbert Bahon, Rene Morard, Henry Vart *(Travelers)*, Jean-Claude de Gorros *(Dr. Dufour)*, Yvon Lech *(Chief Marista)*, Eddy Ross *(1st Priest)*, Aude Landry *(Suzanne)*, Jean-Pierre Leroux *(Radeuf)*, Michel Fortin *(Surgeon at Dole Hospital)*, Bob Dorel *(Red Donkey)*, Maurice Jacquemont *(Priest Saint-Robert)*, Catherine Verlor *(Francine)*, Jean-Pierre Sentier *(1st Journalist)*, Jean-Marie Galley *(2nd Journalist)*, Gerard Jugnot *(Photographer)*, Gilles Dyreck *(Victor)*, Daniel Russo *(Guardian)*, Antoine Baud *(Mounted Policeman)*, Marcel Azzola *(Accordion Player)*, Philippe Sarde *(Pianist)*, Jean-Francois Gondre *(NCO)*, Richard Hendry *(Trade Unionist)*, Christine Pascal, Didier Haudepin.

This film takes place at the end of the 19th Century, during a period of relative political upheaval in France; Noiret plays a judge given the difficult task of determining whether or not a seemingly psychotic killer of children is actually insane. The concentration is mainly on detailing the developing relationship between Noiret and Galabru, the killer, showing how the former is able to see beyond the challenge offered by the case and to gain a more humane understanding of a person he would normally despise. The killer eventually gives in to Noiret, telling him of the things which have helped to mold his emotionally disturbed persona. But Galabru is declared insane despite Noiret's efforts. This was an impressive directorial effort for Tavernier, as he created an intriguing film out of a simple plot. Noiret was quite good as the judge, looking like a bigot faced with having his shallow ideals threatened. (French, English subtitles.)

p, Raymond Danon; d, Bertrand Tavernier; w, Tavernier, Jean Aurenche, Pierre Bost; ph, Pierre William Glenn (Panavision, Eastmancolor); m, Philippe Sarde; ed, Armand Psenny; art d, Antoine Roman; cos, Jacqueline Moreau; m/l, Jean-Roger Causimon, Philippe Sarde.

Drama **(PR:C MPAA:NR)**

JUDGE AND THE SINNER, THE 1/2** (1964, Ger.) 84m Casino bw (DER JUGENDRICHTER)

Heinz Ruehmann *(Judge Ferdinand Bluhme)*, Karin Baal *(Inge Schumann)*, Lola Muthel *(Elisabeth Winkler)*, Hans Nielsen *(District Court President)*, Rainer Brandt *(Kurt)*, Michael Verhoeven *(Fred)*, Peter Thom *(Bill)*, Lore Schulz *(Paula Burg)*, Monika John *(Maria, Maid)*, Hans Epskamp *(Senate President)*, Erich Fiedler *(Vogel, Salesman)*, Gerd Frickhoffer *(Businessman)*, Harry Engel *(The "Black Case" Peters)*, Willi Rose *(Patrol Officer)*, Kathe Alving, Kunibert Gensichen, Knut Hartwig, Jan Hendriks, Hilla Hofer, Friedrich Maurer, Friedrich Siemers.

Ruehmann is a judge who believes in reforming juveniles rather than sentencing them. When Baal is convicted of blackmail, Ruehmann tests his beliefs. But first he sentences Baal to prison for eight months, so he can distance her from the baleful influence of boy friend Brandt. She, however, threatens suicide and the judge is forced to release her. He secures her a job waiting tables at the boarding house where he lives, though Muthel, the owner, dislikes housing criminals. Then Brandt suddenly reappears and coerces Baal to steal from another boarder. The judge covers up for her thefts, and she finds herself falling in love with him. Brandt interprets this affection as an opportunity to blackmail Ruehmann by exposing the judge and Baal as lovers. Ruehmann, ever the stoic figure, goes to Brandt's gang and speaks a sermon about reform. It's a well-intentioned film, sort of a German version of BOYS TOWN. Ruehmann certainly has all the sincerity of a Father Flanagan. The film was released in Germany in 1960.

p, Kurt Ulrich; d, Paul Verhoeven; w, Hans Jacoby, Istvan Bekeffi; ph, Erich Claunick; m, Raimund Rosenberger; ed, Hermann Haller; set d, Rolf Zehetbauer; cos, Manon Hahn; makeup, Josef Coesfeld, Freddy Arnold, Herta Schwarz.

Drama **(PR:C MPAA:NR)**

JUDGE HARDY AND SON*** (1939) 88m MGM bw

Lewis Stone *(Judge Hardy)*, Mickey Rooney *(Andy Hardy)*, Cecilia Parker *(Marian Hardy)*, Ann Rutherford *(Polly Benedict)*, Fay Holden *(Mrs. Hardy)*, Sara Haden *(Aunt Milly)*, Maria Ouspenskaya *(Mrs. Volduzzi)*, June Preisser *(Euphrasia Clark)*, Martha O'Driscoll *(Elvie Norton)*, Leona Maricle *(Mrs. Norton)*, Margaret Early *(Clarabelle Lee)*, Egon Brecher *(Mr. Volduzzi)*, Edna Holland *(Nurse Trowbridge)*, Jack Mulhall *(Interne)*, Henry Hull *(Dr. Jones)*, George Breakston *("Beezy")*, Marie Blake *(Augusta)*, Joe Yule.

This is the eighth film in MGM's profitable and entertaining ANDY HARDY series. This time Rooney gets in trouble with girls and money when he tries to manipulate winning a cash prize for an essay contest. Wise father Stone (who sadly was to die of a heart attack chasing some punks who had thrown rocks at his home) comes in to give the mixed-up though well-meaning young man some sage advice. The family is also drawn closer when Holden is struck ill with pneumonia. Rutherford is back as Rooney's girl pal, though she gets some competition from Preisser (Rooney's co-star from BABES IN ARMS). Yule, Rooney's real-life father, has a bit part. MGM mogul Louis B. Mayer took special interest in the popular Andy Hardy series. In fact, the brash youth with the heart of gold was his pet and the mogul watched with a careful eye each production twist in every one of these lucrative B-films. While writer Wilson labored on the script of JUDGE HARDY AND SON, Mayer burst into Wilson's office. He had just read the pages where Andy offers up a windy and weepy prayer for his mother who is hovering near death in a sickbed. "You see, you're now a Hollywood character," stormed Mayer at Wilson. "You've forgotten your simple, honest boyhood. You don't remember how a real boy would pray. This is how a boy would do it." With that the mogul dropped to his knees at Wilson's desk, lifted pressed hands upward and followed the direction with upturned eyes, saying fervently: "Dear God, please don't let my mom die, because she's the best mom in the world. Thank you, God." Mayer shot upright and glared downward at Wilson: "Let me see you beat that for a prayer!" The prayer went into the film verbatim and became the standard offering to Heaven in all the studio's subsequent films. With this film Seitz goes back to directing the HARDY series, after a brief lapse with a previous film, ANDY HARDY GETS SPRING FEVER. The results are excellent and this is a fine addition to the series. For some reason Ostrow produced this film anonymously. (See ANDY HARDY series, Index.)

p, Lou Ostrow; d, George B. Seitz; w, Carey Wilson (based on characters created by Aurania Rouverol); ph, Lester White; m, David Snell; ed, Ben Lewis; art d, Cedric Gibbons.

Family Drama **(PR:AAA MPAA:NR.)**

JUDGE HARDY'S CHILDREN* 1/2** (1938) 78m MGM bw

Lewis Stone *(Judge Hardy)*, Mickey Rooney *(Andy Hardy)*, Cecilia Parker *(Marian Hardy)*, Fay Holden *(Mrs. Hardy)*, Ann Rutherford *(Polly Benedict)*, Betsy Ross Clarke *(Aunt Milly)*, Robert Whitney *(Wayne Trenton)*, Ruth Hussey *(Margaret Bee)*, Leonard Penn *(Steve Prentiss)*, Jacqueline Laurent *(Suzanne Cortot)*, Janet Beecher *(Miss Budge)*, Boyd Crawford *(Radio Announcer)*, Don Douglas *(J.O. Harper)*, Edward Earle *(Peniwill)*.

Rooney captured the ANDY HARDY series with this film and never let go. In the third film of the series, the Hardy family travels to Washington, D.C. with Stone, who has to sit in on important utilities hearings. This meshed well with the current headlines in 1938; involving the Tennessee Valley Authority, as well as Supreme Court rulings on utility companies. But it's certainly not all politics. Rooney, as usual, has girl troubles, and, at one point, teaches a marvelously energetic dance—"the Big Apple"—to Laurent, the daughter of a French ambassador. Clarke plays Rooney's aunt for this film, temporarily replacing Sara Haden. It's good innocent fun and Rooney's a delight to watch. (See ANDY HARDY series, Index.)

d, George B. Seitz; w, Kay Van Riper (based on characters created by Aurania Rouverol); ph, Lester White; m, David Snell; ed, Ben Lewis.

Family Drama **(PR:AAA MPAA:NR)**

JUDGE PRIEST 1/2** (1934) 79m FOX bw

Will Rogers *(Judge William "Billy" Priest)*, Henry B. Walthall *(Reverend Ashby Brand)*, Tom Brown *(Jerome Priest)*, Anita Louise *(Ellie May Gillespie)*, Rochelle Hudson *(Virginia Maydew)*, David Landau *(Bob Gillis)*, Berton Churchill *(Senator Horace K. Maydew)*, Brenda Fowler *(Mrs. Caroline Priest)*, Hattie McDaniel *(Aunt Dilsey)*, Stepin Fetchit *(Jeff Poindexter)*, Frank Melton *(Flem Tally)*, Roger Imhof *(Billy Gaynor)*, Charley Grapewin *(Sgt. Jimmy Bagby)*, Francis Ford *(Juror No. 12)*, Paul McAllister *(Doc Lake)*, Matt McHugh *(Gabby Rives)*, Hyman Meyer *(Herman Feldsburg)*, Louis Mason *(Sheriff Birdsong)*, Grace Goodall *(Mrs. Maydew)*, Ernest Shields *(Milan)*, Paul McVey *(Trimble)*, Vester Pegg *(Herringer)*, Winter Hall *(Judge Fairleigh)*, Duke Lee *(Deputy)*, Mary Rousseau *(Guitar Player)*, Margaret Mann *(Governess)*, George H. Reed *(Colored Servant)*, Harry Tenbrook, Pat Hartigan, Harry Wilson, Frank Moran, Constantine Romanoff *(Townsmen in Saloon)*, Gladys Wells, Beulah Hall Jones, Melba Brown, Thelma Brown, Vera Brown *(Colored Singers)*, Robert Parrish.

The insubstantial plot of this film is no more than a vehicle for Rogers, but it serves him very well. In the role of Judge Priest, Rogers is presiding over Landau's trial. The latter, who fought with the man who insulted "orphan girl" Louise (secretly Landau's daughter), is later involved in a knife fight with the same man. Lawyer Brown, Rogers' nephew and Louise's fiance, agrees to defend Landau. When the opposition gets wind of this, they voice their disapproval, claiming that Rogers and Brown are family. Presently it is revealed that Landau is the girl's true father, which excuses his actions and sets him free. Furthermore, Brown and Louise can now marry without regard to family status. The picture is not very believable, but Rogers is so wonderful it doesn't matter. The one sour note in the film is the racist portrayal of blacks by Fetchit and by McDaniel in the highly caricatured "white Hollywood" vision of how "negroes" behave. It looked bad then, and horrible today. Remade in 1953 by John Ford as THE SUN SHINES BRIGHT.

p, Sol M. Wurtzel; d, John Ford; w, Dudley Nichols, Lamar Trotti (based on the character from the stories of Irvin S. Cobb); ph, George Schneiderman; m, Cyril J. Mockridge; md, Samuel Kaylin; art d, William Darling; m/l, Mockridge, Nichols, Trotti.

Comedy **Cas.** **(PR:AAA MPAA:NR)**

JUDGE STEPS OUT, THE** ½**

(1949) 91m RKO bw (GB:INDIAN SUMMER)

Alexander Knox *(Judge Bailey)*, Ann Sothern *(Peggy)*, George Tobias *(Mike)*, Sharyn Moffett *(Nan)*, Florence Bates *(Chita)*, Frieda Inescort *(Evelyn Bailey)*, Myrna Dell *(Mrs. Winthrop)*, Ian Wolfe *(Hector Brown)*, H.B. Warner *(Chief Justice Haynes)*, Martha Hyer *(Catherine Bailey)*, James Warren *(John Struthers III)*, Whitford Kane *(Dr. Boyd)*, Harry Hayden *(Judge Davis)*, Anita Bolster *(Martha)*.

Knox has a "mid-life crisis" before the term was even in vogue. He plays a judge who's weary of his nagging wife (Inescort) and daughter (Hyer). Finally he escapes home to journey to California, where he finds a job as a cook. Sothern, the restaurant's owner, lends the judge a sympathetic ear before he resolves to return to his Boston home. It's a nice, if simple, comedy; well-played though too long. The script is by Knox and director Ingster. Both Knox and Sothern were on loan to RKO for the film, he from Columbia and she from MGM. Completed in 1947, the studio held onto the finished work until two years later.

p, Michel Kraike; d, Boris Ingster; w, Ingster, Alexander Knox (based on a story by Ingster); ph, Robert de Grasse; m, Leigh Harline; ed, Les Millbrook; md, C. Bakaleinikoff; art d, Albert S. D'Agostino, Feild Gray.

Comedy **(PR:A MPAA:NR)**

JUDGMENT AT NUREMBERG* ½** (1961) 190m Roxlom/UA bw

Spencer Tracy *(Judge Dan Haywood)*, Burt Lancaster *(Ernst Janning)*, Richard Widmark *(Col. Tad Lawson)*, Marlene Dietrich *(Mme. Bertholt)*, Maximilian Schell *(Hans Rolfe)*, Judy Garland *(Irene Hoffman)*, Montgomery Clift *(Rudolph Petersen)*, William Shatner *(Capt. Harrison Byers)*, Edward Binns *(Sen. Burkette)*, Kenneth MacKenna *(Judge Kenneth Norris)*, Werner Klemperer *(Emil Hahn)*, Alan Baxter *(Gen. Merrin)*, Torben Meyer *(Werner Lammpe)*, Ray Teal *(Judge Curtiss Ives)*, Martin Brandt *(Frieidrich Hofstetter)*, Virginia Christine *(Mrs. Halbestadt)*, Joseph Bernard *(Maj. Abe Radnitz)*, Ben Wright *(Halbestadt)*, John Wengraf *(Dr. Wieck)*, Karl Swenson *(Dr. Geuter)*, Howard Caine *(Wallner)*, Otto Waldis *(Pohl)*, Olga Fabian *(Mrs. Lindnow)*, Sheila Bromley *(Mrs. Ives)*, Bernard Kates *(Perkins)*, Jana Taylor *(Elsa Scheffler)*, Paul Busch *(Schmidt)*, Joseph Crahan *(Spectator)*.

As with most courtroom dramas, JUDGMENT AT NUREMBERG is overlong and static but, when released in its day, it was sensational as the first film to deal seriously with judging Nazi war criminals. Even more provocative was the fact that it dealt with the Nazi judges who sent countless victims either to their deaths or, sometimes worse, to medical experimentation that left the victims sterile or mindless. Tracy plays the chief Allied judge, sent to Germany after failing to be reelected to his New England post in America, a political payoff that does not go unnoticed by his adversaries. Widmark, the prosecuting attorney—an Army colonel—opens the film with a seething indictment of the several German judges on trial who abandoned law in order to enforce Hitler's mad mandates. Schell, in a powerful performance—the film's best—roars back that his clients were merely upholding Hitler's laws and to place them on trial is to judge all of Germany. In his off-the-bench hours Tracy wanders about the ancient city of Nuremberg trying to understand what went wrong with a whole people and a great culture. He meets and is fascinated by the enigmatic Dietrich, widow of a German general who was executed for ordering the slaughter of captured American soldiers at Malmedy. She presents herself and her aristocratic class as "junkers," Prussian old guard that existed long before Hitler and were merely the victims of his new order. They had nothing really to do with the extermination of six million racial, political, and religious victims. At one point, Widmark, slightly inebriated, overhears this talk and tells Tracy that, to hear it told in Germany, nobody was responsible for the mass killings; "it was the Eskimos" he sarcastically adds. A number of pathetic witnesses are put on the stand to testify against the German judges, especially chief judge Lancaster. One of these is Clift, who presents a spastic portrait of a dim-witted victim of sterilization. Another is Garland who states that an elderly Jewish friend was executed during the Hitler years and she was branded a pollutor of the Aryan race, accused of having sex with her friend. Schell mercilessly goes after her, accusing her of lying, driving her hysterical on the witness stand until Lancaster erupts from the prisoner's box to shout at his own defense counsel to stop: "Are we going to do this all over again?" he inquires with disgust, later admitting his guilt to a shocked court, confessing that he either rationalized or condoned Hitler's racial decrees for the ultimate good of Germany. With the Soviets now blockading Berlin, pressure is brought against Tracy to be lenient with the German judges, that Germans and Germany will be necessary to the West in maintaining world order, particularly as a buffer state between the free West and the Soviet bloc. Tracy will not yield, however, and states that he will uphold "justice, truth, and the value of a single human being." He sentences the defendants to life imprisonment, even though the sneering Schell declares that they will be free in five years. The audience is given a grim reminder of Schell's prediction when the following words rolled up at the finale: ". . . of the 99 men sentenced to prison by the time the Nuremberg trials ended on July 14, 1949, not one of the guilty is still serving a sentence." The film is absorbing but bleak from beginning to end offering a standout performance from the frenetic Schell as a defender of the old order, a man confused in his zeal to defend both the past and his present clients. Tracy is rather stoic but this actor never gave a bad performance and he does what he can with a role that calls for judicious temperament. Tracy reported that the story for the film was "the best script I've read in years," and went on to laud producer-director Kramer as a man trying to make good films and not driven by acquiring money. However, he almost didn't make the film. Tracy was upset when he learned that Laurence Olivier, who was to play the chief German judge, had dropped out of the film and that Lancaster would replace him. The film, shot on location in Berlin, required Tracy to fly to Germany. He was escorted to Idlewild Airport by UA executives and the ever-present Katharine Hepburn. He got on the plane, then, before takeoff, unbuckled his seat belt and quickly left the plane, causing studio officials to panic. Hepburn took Tracy aside and talked to him quietly, kissing him on the cheek. He turned about without a word and got back on the plane. Tracy was ill at the time and told reporters that he would be doing no more films after JUDGMENT AT NUREMBERG, unless it was a Stanley Kramer film. (His last film was a Kramer production, GUESS WHO'S COMING TO DINNER.) Another Kramer selection, Clift, was also ill, having turned into a stone alcoholic who could or would not dry out. Kramer offered the actor a seven-minute part as one of the witnesses, a man who had been castrated by the Nazis as part of their sterilization program. Clift's agents, MCA, demanded he be paid what he received for THE MISFITS, $200,000. Kramer offered $50,000 and this was rejected. Then Kramer went directly to Clift, who said he would perform the role for expenses only which he did, without ever having read the script. He was a physical disaster when he appeared in the courtroom scene. (The courtroom was a magnificent set, all on wheels so the camera would have full fluidity, built in the Hollywood Revue studios.) Clift couldn't remember a line from his long monolog. His hands shook terribly, his face twitched, and his eyes almost rolled uncontrollably. He went to Kramer and said: "I don't think I can do this thing." Kramer soothed him with: "What you're doing is all right until you find out how to do it better." Still Clift kept breaking down. Tracy watched him with considerable agony, a compassionate man who had struggled with his own alcoholism for decades. Tracy went to Clift and put his arms around him and said: "Just look into my eyes and do it. You're a great actor and you understand this guy. Stanley doesn't care if you throw aside the precise lines. Just do it. Do it into my eyes and you'll be magnificent." Clift followed Tracy's instructions and was so compelling that he received his fourth Oscar nomination for the cameo role, this time as Best Supporting Actor. Clift did not renew his rivalry with Lancaster in this film but heatedly argued with Schell, who was compelled to badger him as the defense counsel. Ironically, it was Schell who would walk away with an Oscar for Best Actor for his relentless role in JUDGMENT AT NUREMBERG, beating out Tracy, who was also nominated for the same film. Clift formed a deep friendship with Garland during the production; she also played a cameo part as a victim of Nazi oppression. Garland had been paid $50,000 by Kramer to make her first appearance since A STAR IS BORN and she rendered one of the best dramatic roles of her career. Clift watched her do her scene on the set, crying as Garland related how she was labelled a polluted German woman because she had befriended an elderly Jew. Gerold Frank, writing in his *Judy*, the biography of the actress, described Clift as "a strange little ape, so pathetic, huddled up, holding his knees, the tears rolling down his face." Yet, apparently moved by Garland's delivery, Clift, according to Robert LaGuardia in *Monty*, nevertheless went to Kramer, the tears still wet on his cheeks and inexplicably told the director: "You know, she did that scene all wrong." Clift, however, was living his life all wrong. Immediately after JUDGMENT AT NUREMBERG, he signed to do the worst film of his life, FREUD, directed by John Huston, the last film released during his painful lifetime (his last, released posthumously in 1966 was THE DEFECTOR). Garland, when signing to do her small role, immediately went on a diet and began to make herself beautiful, all of which upset Kramer, who told her: "If you want to go to some spa and drop a few pounds, you want to look pretty, O.K., but it's not right for this." She agreed and played it plain and was terrific. Kramer decided that JUDGMENT AT NUREMBERG should be premiered in Berlin and scheduled the event for December 1961, asking his entire cast to appear. Notable for their absence from the much-touted premiere were Lancaster and Dietrich. Lancaster, who played the role of the German judge with restrained efficiency, claimed he had pressing matters to attend to; this fine actor, wrongly criticized for not attending the premiere (which, no one doubted, was being made into a political statement), had earlier promoted Kramer and the film, telling members of the Golden Globe Foreign Press Awards: ". . . if you want to see some real honest-to-goodness acting, you should come to our set of JUDGMENT AT NUREMBERG and watch Spencer Tracy and Miss Judy Garland do some real emoting for you." Dietrich was another matter. The exotic German star had openly declared her sentiments about Germany and the German people during the Hitler years, refusing to stay in the country or even visit her native land while that monster was in power. During WW II she had made countless broadcasts condemning the Nazi regime and its madman leader. Many years earlier, just as Hitler was coming to power, she told reporters: "Ever since I lost my country and my language, ever since I left Germany in 1930, I've been a traveler without any roots." She took the role of the widow of the German general to point out the stubborn idea in the German people that no one was really at fault, except Hitler and his hierarchy of lunatics, that the military caste that had always ruled Germany were victims of the war too. As the widow, Dietrich tells Tracy that her husband was denied his honor, stating: "He was entitled to a soldier's death. He asked for that. I tried to get that for him . . . just that he be permitted the dignity of a firing squad. You know what happened. He was hanged with the others." Dietrich also knew what to expect from her former countrymen. In 1960, a year before making JUDGMENT AT NUREMBERG, she had visited Germany on a singing tour, her first return to her native land since 1930, and the first time she had sung to audiences in her native tongue since that date. She was told that she should expect an angry reception by some Germans, even violence (and there were a few reports that someone might shoot at her during a performance), that she might be showered by rotten food. At the time, she quipped: "It's not the tomatoes I fear, but the eggs; their stains never wash out." She would later subtly narrate an indicting documentary, THE BLACK FOX, which chronicled Hitler's nefarious and insidious rise and rule. (THE BLACK FOX would win an Oscar for the best feature-length documentary in 1962.) No, Marlene Dietrich did not attend the Berlin premiere of JUDGMENT AT NUREMBERG and had good reason not to be present. Kramer, nevertheless, made the premiere into a world event, flying more than 300 newsmen to West Berlin from twenty-six countries (from New York alone there were 120 columnists, critics, and political scribes). It became one of the most expensive press junkets of all time, costing Kramer more than $150,000. The enormous Congress Hall where the film was being shown was packed to the rafters, and it was no commercial coincidence, critics later pointed out, that this event took place on December 14, 1961, shortly after the Russians erected the infamous wall dividing East and West Berlin and one day before Adolf Eichmann was to be sentenced for his war crimes in Israel. Willy Brandt, then mayor of West Berlin, was prevailed upon to make a political statement regarding the film (more as a precaution against open violence, perhaps, than as an endorsement of the philosophy set down in the movie). Before the film the courageous Brandt stood upon the stage and stated: "We cannot deny the fact, and we do not want to deny it, that the roots of the present position of our people, our country and our city lie in this fact—that we did not prevent right from being trampled underfoot during the time of the Nazi power. Anyone who remains blind to this fact can also not properly understand the rights which are today still being withheld from our people. It will probably be difficult for us to watch and hear this film. But we will not shut our eyes to it. If this film serves justice, we welcome it. We will still welcome it, even if we have to feel shame at many of its aspects. Anything that helps the cause of right helps Berlin, and anyone who wants to help the cause of right can also depend on the help of Berliners. The film JUDGMENT AT NUREMBERG, which will raise a great many questions, is insuring by its world premiere in Berlin that its own importance as well as that of Berlin as a center of spiritual conflict are heavily underlined . . . I hope that world-wide discussion will be aroused by both this film and this city, and that this will contribute to the strengthening of right and justice." Following the showing of the film, the German audience remained stunned into silence. Only the members of the foreign press applauded the film. The German reporters loudly condemned Kramer for disinterring the German past, for stirring up old hatreds, for pricking the nerve of a hypersensitive subject. Kramer stood up to them all, saying that truth and justice must be shown and he encouraged German filmmakers to make movies about Hitler's Third Reich, but that day would be a long time coming from a generation of German filmmakers who were born free of the Nazi cancer. Cruelly, German press members loudly called Tracy a coward for leaving the Congress Hall before the film was over, statements that angered a normally unperturbable Kramer who patiently explained that Tracy was very ill, which he was, and had to leave with an upset stomach. Tracy was still ill when returning to the U.S. a week later. JUDGMENT AT NUREMBERG, despite the controversy it caused in Germany, was an astounding success, gleaning $5,500,000 in rentals the first time around. It remains a fascinating if not entertaining document to this day. This powerful drama was originally offered on TV as a Playhouse 90 production in 1959, directed by George Roy Hill and starring Claude Rains as Haywood, Paul Lukas as Janning, and Maximilian Schell as the lawyer, the role which he repeated in the film.

p&d, Stanley Kramer; w, Abby Mann; ph, Ernest Laszlo; m, Ernest Gold; ed, Frederic Knudtson; prod d, Rudolph Sternad; md, Art Dunham; set d, George Milo; cos, Joe King; m/l, "Lili Marlene," Norbert Schultze, Hans Liep, Thomas Conner; "Liebeslied," Gold, Alfred Perry; makeup, Robert J. Schiffer.

Drama **Cas.** **(PR:C MPAA:NR)**

JUDGMENT DEFERRED**½ (1952, Brit.) 88m Group 3/ABF bw

Hugh Sinclair *(David Kennedy)*, Helen Shingler *(Kay Kennedy)*, Abraham Sofaer *(Chancellor)*, Leslie Dwyer *(Flowers)*, Joan Collins *(Lil Carter)*, Harry Locke *(Bert)*, Elwyn Brook-Jones *(Coxon)*, Marcel Poncin *(Stranger)*, Martin Benson *(Pierre Desportes)*, Bransby Williams *(Dad)*, Michael Martin-Harvey *(Martin)*, Harry Welchman *(Doc)*, Wilfrid Walter *(Judge)*, Maire O'Neill *(Mrs. O'Halloran)*, Mary Merrall *(Lady Musterby)*, Edgar Driver *(Blackie)*, Billy Russell *(Ginger)*, Bud Flanagan, June Elvin, Harold Goodwin, Fred Griffiths, Ann Lancaster, Cyril Smith, Freddie Watts, John Wynn, Herbert C. Walton, Michael Hogarth, Edmundo Ros and His Orchestra.

Reporter Sinclair becomes involved in an effort to help an innocent man framed in a drug trafficking case. The victim's innocence is brought to Sinclair's interest by the accused's down-and-out-pals, who are doing everything their meager capabilities will allow to get their buddy out of jail. Luckily the reporter sides with them, using his influence to see that justice is done, and that the actual operators of the drug ring get their just rewards. This remake of DOSS HOUSE (1933), also by Baxter, is captivating mainly because of the novelty of the story and the many strange characters that are introduced.

p, John Baxter, John Grierson; d, Baxter; w, Geoffrey Orme, Barbara K. Emary, Walter Meade (based on the story by Herbert Ayres); ph, Arthur Grant.

Crime **(PR:A MPAA:NR)**

JUDGMENT IN THE SUN (SEE: OUTRAGE, THE, 1964)

JUDITH* (1965) 109m Cumulus-Command/PAR c

Sophia Loren *(Judith)*, Peter Finch *(Aaron Stein)*, Jack Hawkins *(Maj. Lawton)*, Hans Verner *(Gustav Schiller)*, Zharira Charifai *(Dr. Rachel)*, Shraga Friedman *(Nathan)*, Joseph Gross *(Yaneck)*, Zipora Peled *(Hannah)*, Terence Alexander *(Carstairs)*, Gilad Konstantiner *(Dubin)*, Alexander Yahalomi *(Zvi)*, Frank Wolff *(Eli)*, Andre Morrel *(Chaim)*, Aldo Foa *(Interrogator)*, Rober Beaumont *(Zeer)*, Daniel Ocko *(Arab Guide)*, Roland Bartrop *(Aba)*, Peter Burton *(Conklin)*, John Stacey *(Researcher)*.

We are asked to believe the impossible here (which is nothing new for almost any Loren film), that this towering, voluptuous, sensuous, swarthy, sex-oozing female is a Jewish victim of Nazi oppression, seeking noble retribution from her missing Nazi husband in Israel. It's the troubled year of 1947 and Palestine is about to erupt into race war but is still a British protectorate. Finch, a leader of the Jewish underground paramilitary organization, Haganah, learns that Verner, a Nazi war criminal, is training an Arab legion to attack the newly formed Jewish state. Finch smuggles Loren into the country, she being Verner's ex-wife and full of hate for her husband. He had denounced her as a Jewess during the war and had her thrown into a concentration camp with their young son. The boy is still missing and Loren is desperate to find him. Finch is just as desperate to locate Verner but doesn't quite know where he is; he does know that the British commander, Hawkins, has a file and address on Verner so he ruthlessly uses Loren, or rather her Amazonian body, to entice the information out of Hawkins. But when Loren vamps the address out of Hawkins, following an assignation Finch has set up, she keeps it to herself, tracking Verner to Damascus, Finch and his Haganah minions right behind her. Loren locates Verner and promptly puts a bullet into him, but Finch saves him for interrogation and he's lugged back to Palestine. There he clams up, refusing to tell the Israelis when the Arab attack will begin. When the British evacuate, the Arabs unleash their murderous onslaught. Loren, still seething with hate for her ex-husband, vamps her way past guards and confronts Verner once more. He's terrified of her and blurts the Arab plan of attack which helps the Israelis counterattack successfully; moreover, Verner tells Loren that her son is still alive. He tells her that he will only reveal where her son is if he is assured that he will be released. Loren promises, but the Arab attack bombarding the compound where they are located blows up several buildings, including the one housing Verner. He is killed before he can tell Loren how to find her son. Finch, at the fadeout, promises Loren he will locate the boy for her. This film is nothing more than a showcase for Loren and does little for the Israeli cause, much less than did EXODUS and CAST A GIANT SHADOW. The Italian actress, her accent mangling the English as usual, appears as anything but the person she's playing. She parades about in hot pants to show off her long, fleshy legs and wears a shirt so tight that little is left to imagine the proportions of her magic mammaries. Her hair is always coiffeured as if a hairdresser followed her about through communes and battles. Everything about Loren, her expansive peasant gestures so indigenously Italian, her exaggerated walk, forward-tilt, and various shimmies, shakes, and slithers, embody anything but a concentration camp victim. Her performance is simply dreadful and Finch and the rest of the cast aren't much better. The story is implausible and perversely uses the real plight of the Israelis as a ploy to exhibit Loren's physical wares. The much-read Durrell story suffers drastically under the slipshod directorial hands of Mann. Only the expert lensing by Wilcox keeps this one from being a total disaster.

p, Kurt Unger; d, Daniel Mann; w, John Michael Hayes (based on a story by Lawrence Durrell); ph, John Wilcox (Panavision, Technicolor); m, Sol Kaplan; ed, Peter Taylor; prod d, Wilfrid Shingleton; art d, Tony Woollard, Tony Rimmington; set d, Peter Russell; cos, Yvonne Blake, spec eff, Cliff Richardson, Roy Whybrow.

War Drama **(PR:C-O MPAA:NR)**

JUDO SAGA**½ (1965, Jap.) 159m Takarazuka-Kurosawa Films/Toho International bw

Yuzo Kayama *(Sugata Sanshiro)*, Toshiro Mifune *(Shogoro Yano)*, Eiji Okada, Tatsuo Yamazaki, Yumiko Kokonoe, Yunosuke Ito, Daisuke Kato.

A simplistic karate movie that is helped by the screenplay of noted director Kurosawa. Kayama is a judo student, taking up the sport to gain the respect of his peers. Along the way he learns about the spiritual side of the art from Mifune, his judo master. He refuses to accept this lesson until he fights the father of his girl friend, thus learning the true nature of judo. This film is a remake of the 1943 and 1945 two-part Japanese film SUGATA SANSHIRO.

d, Seiichiro Uchikawa; w, Akira Kurosawa.

Martial Arts **(PR:C MPAA:NR)**

JUDO SHOWDOWN**½ (1966, Jap.) 87m Shochiku c (YAWARA SEMPU DOTO NO TAIKETSU)

Toshiya Wazaki *(Sanshiro Sugata)*, Ryohei Uchida *(Daizaburo Himon)*, Shoichi Hirai *(Shogoro Yano)*, Seizaburo Kawazu *(Okakura)*, Maki Katsura *(Kaori, His Daughter)*, Sanae Nakahara *(Tone)*, Shinsuke Mikimoto *(Gondo)*, Keiko Sajita, Yoko Matsuyama, Keiji Yano, Shintaro Kuraoka.

Wazaki is a student of the Kodokan judo methods who saves Katsura from a dynamite explosion and discovers she is the daughter of Kawazu, chief martial arts advisor to the Tokyo police. Wazaki shows instructor Hirai his new throw, but the master disapproves of it, saying the throw could be dangerous and lethal. The budding romance between Katsura and Wazaki is threatened by Uchida, a leading jujitsu expert who also wants Kawazu's job. He kills the next in line to the job but problems occur when Hirai is then appointed next in line. The film ends with Wazaki and Uchida fighting a duel, a symbolic clash between two schools of martial arts. Wazaki wins both the combat and Katsura.

d, Masateru Nishiyama; w, Daisei Motoyama, Narahiro Matsumura (based on a series of novels by Tsuneo Tomita); ph, Shozo Honda (Grandscope/Eastmancolor); m, Eiichi Yamada.

Martial Arts **(PR:C MPAA:NR)**

JUDY GOES TO TOWN (SEE: PUDDIN' HEAD, 1941)

JUDY'S LITTLE NO-NO*½ (1969) 84m Schooner Bay c (AKA: LET'S DO IT)

Elisa Ingram, John Lodge, Joe E. Ross, Zorita, Marlene.

Minor nonsense involving everything from jewel robberies to Cuban intrigue. After saving a stripper flung from a passing boat, a skin diver helps her get her clothing and a paycheck from the nightclub she works at in Miami. Arriving at her apartment they discover her roommate bound and gagged and the place ransacked. Seems some Castroites were looking for a package given to the stripper by her murdered Cuban refugee boy friend. The pair return to the Bahamas where they had met. They are followed by murderers but manage to escape. Back at the nightclub, the missing package is found; it contains a jewel which belly dancer Marlene puts in her navel. When thieves try to steal it, she throws it to the young couple, who give it to an anti-Castroite. The stripper is kidnaped but saved in a shootout. Complicated and dull.

p, Edward Jacobs; d&w, Sherman Price.

Crime **(PR:O MPAA:R)**

JUGGERNAUT** (1937, Brit.) 64m Twickenham/GN bw

Boris Karloff *(Dr. Sartorius)*, Joan Wyndham *(Eve Rowe)*, Arthur Margetson *(Roger Clifford)*, Mona Goya *(Lady Yvonne Clifford)*, Anthony Ireland *(Capt. Arthur Halliday)*, Morton Selten *(Sir Charles Clifford)*, Nina Boucicault *(Mary Clifford)*, Gibb McLaughlin *(Jacques)*, J.H. Roberts *(Chalmers)*, Victor Rietti *(Dr. Bousquet)*.

Karloff is a doctor whose research into paralysis has left him penniless. He meets Goya, the wife of elderly cotton tycoon Selten. She wants Selten's money and Karloff agrees to kill the old man in exchange for half his estate. Karloff is hired on as the family physician, and Selten's health declines. Selten begins to smell the plot and transfers his estate to a son by a previous marriage (Margetson). Goya has Karloff administer a lethal injection to Selten, and together they start planning a way to kill Margetson. Wyndham, Karloff's nurse, has fallen in love with the new heir and suspects Karloff's plan. Karloff kidnaps her, but she escapes to save her lover from a lethal injection. In the end, Karloff gives the deadly injection to himself. Karloff, sans FRANKENSTEIN makeup, is adequately sinister in his role, but the rest of the film has trouble matching him.

p, Julius Hagen; d, Henry Edwards; w, Cyril Campion, H. Fowler Mear, Heinrich Fraenkel (based on the novel by Alice Campbell); ph, Sydney Blythe, William Luff; m, W.L. Trytel; ed, Michael Chorlton; art d, James Carter.

Suspense Cas. (PR:O MPAA:NR)

JUGGERNAUT*** (1974, Brit.) 109m UA c

Richard Harris *(Fallon)*, Omar Sharif *(Capt. Brunel)*, David Hemmings *(Charlie Braddock)*, Anthony Hopkins *(Supt. John McCleod)*, Shirley Knight *(Barbara Banister)*, Ian Holm *(Nicholas Porter)*, Clifton James *(Mr. Corrigan)*, Roy Kinnear *(Social Director Curain)*, Caroline Mortimer *(Susan McCleod)*, Mark Burns *(1st Officer Hollingsworth)*, John Stride *(Hughes)*, Freddie Jones *(Mr. Buckland)*, Julian Glover *(Cmdr. Marder)*, Jack Watson *(Chief Engineer Mallicent)*, Roshan Seth *(Azad)*, Kenneth Colley *(Det. Brown)*, Andrew Bradford *(3rd Officer Hardy)*.

Fairly tight thriller that bore no resemblance to any of Irwin Allen's boat-disaster films. Sharif is captain of an ocean liner upon which several bombs have been planted by Jones, a demolition expert who demands a ransom or he will blow up the ship and all of the people at sea. Knight, James, and Kinnear are on board, as is Mortimer, wife of Hopkins, a detective. Harris, Hemmings, and some others are dispatched by helicopter to the ship to attempt to defuse the bombs and the rest of the film is a tense battle between the bomb experts and Jones, who stays on a telephone and taunts them with his plot. Lester, who had mainly been known for his comedies (HARD DAY'S NIGHT, etc.) does a good job in keeping the palms sweating and the behind on the edge of the seat. The fact that they did not have the explosion with all the attendant cliches (floating debris, heroism, moans, and groans) was to their credit but that lack of denouement is what caused the picture to sink out of sight. Anyone who has ever been on a cruise will recognize Kinnear's cheery social director character as having been drawn directly from life. The romantic subplot between Sharif and Knight is little more than punctuation to the derring do of Harris and Hemmings. Two other directors had been penciled in for the job (Bryan Forbes and Don Medford) but departed for various reasons. The title does not refer to the ship, rather it is Jones' *nom de guerre*. In the end, Harris must decide which wire to clip on the final bomb and he can't fathom the answer until he psychologically tricks Jones (who has been patched in via radio-telephone) and wins the war of wits. A very good-looking film but too many words and not enough action to take it out of the slightly-better-than-ordinary. Mortimer is the daughter of writers John and Penelope Mortimer and the one-time amour of veteran British comedian Leslie Phillips. Her father, John, was a Queen's Counsel in the Old Bailey and used that experience as a barrister to write his TV series "Rumpole of the Bailey" starring Leo McKern. Does life imitate art? In 1985, terrorists claimed they planted bombs on the liner *Achille Lauro* but that was later found to be a ruse.

p, Richard DeKoker; d, Richard Lester; w, DeKoker, Alan Plater; ph, Gerry Fisher (DeLuxe Color); m, Ken Thorne; ed, Tony Gibbs; prod d, Terence Marsh; art d, Alan Tomkins; spec eff, John Richardson; aerial ph, Peter Allwork.

Sea Drama Cas. (PR:A-C MPAA:PG)

JUGGLER, THE**** (1953) 84m COL bw

Kirk Douglas *(Hans Muller)*, Milly Vitale *(Ya'El)*, Paul Stewart *(Detective Karni)*, Joey Walsh *(Yehoshua Bresler)*, Alf Kjellin *(Daniel)*, Beverly Washburn *(Susy)*, Charles Lane *(Rosenberg)*, John Banner *(Emile Halevy)*, Richard Benedict *(Kogan)*, Oscar Karlweis *(Willy Schmidt)*, John Bleifer *(Mordecai)*, Greta Granstedt *(Carah)*, Jay Adler *(Papa Sander)*, Shep Menken *(Dr. Traube)*, Gabriel Curtiz *(Dr. Sklar)*.

A superb "little" film that never did find enough of an audience. Douglas is a German Jew who survived the Nazi concentration camps but lost his wife and children. He was a famous juggler before the war and now finds himself with thousands of other displaced persons in Israel. He arrives in a temporary camp and his actions are odd enough to merit notice by the camp psychiatrist. He runs away on his first night and is followed by Benedict, an Israeli cop, who finally stops Douglas and wants to see his papers. Douglas is instantly sent back in his memory to when a Nazi asked the same thing and knocks Benedict out, then flees. His actions are seen by Banner, a newsman. He escapes Haifa and makes his way to Mount Carmel where he spends the night. In the morning he is discovered by several children whom he tells he is an American tourist. Walsh, one of the young boys, is traveling to a kibbutz near Syria and Douglas joins him. Douglas wants to get to Egypt where he has some friends who he feels will help him. Stewart is a detective assigned to track Douglas down and a chase begins that takes them through most of Israel, including Jerusalem, Nazareth, bombed-out villages and high-rise housing developments, and the Sea of Galilee. The relationship between Douglas and Walsh deepens as they make their way across the country, with Douglas delighting the young man by teaching him how to juggle. Once near their destination, Walsh steps on a land mine and is hurt badly. Douglas accompanies him to the hospital and is given a place to sleep by Vitale, an Israeli woman whose husband was killed by the Arabs. Their love develops in a series of brief scenes and finally Douglas can no longer keep the secret; he admits that he is not an American and that he has murdered a police officer. Vitale loves Douglas and will not betray him. Douglas gives a juggling performance to the children at the kibbutz and is interrupted by the appearance of Stewart, who has been doggedly trailing him. Douglas gets a gun and is about to fight for his life when Stewart explains that Benedict is not dead and the worst thing that can happen to Douglas is a trial for assault. Considering the circumstances and Douglas' mental health at the time of arrival, Stewart is certain that charge will be dropped. Stewart explains that he is also a refugee, as are so many in Israel, and that Douglas need not fear those around him as they are all in the same boat. Douglas finally understands that he has a new home. A terrific movie in many ways, THE JUGGLER did not ignite much interest in mass markets but remains a gem. Benedict later became a TV director and Walsh grew up to be a writer-producer (CALIFORNIA SPLIT, etc). Paul Stewart was one of the original Mercury Players on radio and came West with Welles for CITIZEN KANE, in which he played the butler. Stewart, one of the best character men in the business, continued working well into his 70s. Writer Blankfort, a former president of the Writers Guild, died when he fell in his driveway in a freak accident. Jay Adler was Luther and Stella's brother.

p, Stanley Kramer; d, Edward Dmytryk; w, Michael Blankfort (based on his novel); ph, Roy Hunt; m, George Antheil; ed, Aaron Stell; md, Morris Stoloff; art d, Robert Peterson.

Drama (PR:C-O MPAA:NR)

JUKE BOX JENNY** 1/2** (1942) 65m UNIV bw

Ken Murray *(Malcolm Hammond)*, Harriet Hilliard *(Genevieve Horton)*, Don Douglas *(Roger Wadsworth)*, Iris Adrian *(Jinx Corey)*, Marjorie Gateson *(Mrs. Horton)*, Sig Arno *(Randini)*, Joe Brown, Jr. *(Tommy)*, Reed Hadley *(Brother Wicks)*, Jack Arnold *(Brother Childs)*, Charles Halton *(Judge)*, William Ruhl *(Jinx's Lawyer)*, Don Dillaway *(Graves)*, Claire DuBrey *(Miss Carruthers)*, James Flavin *(First Customs Officer)*, LaRiana *(Dancer)*, Charles Barnet and His Orchestra, Wingy Manone and His Orchestra, The Milt Herth Trio, The King's Men, The Eddie Beal Trio.

The plot line is thin, but the film's main objective was to showcase popular music and performers of the era, so nobody seemed to mind. Murray plays a fast-talking sales manager for a record company whose boss, Douglas, is engaged to Hilliard. Douglas ends up marrying Adrian following a drunken binge, and that leads to romance between Murray and Hilliard. Cleverly doctoring her recordings, Murray turns her into a singing star, the title character. Musical numbers abound, and are nicely arranged and performed.

p, Joseph G. Sanford; d, Harold Young; w, Robert Lees, Fred Rinaldo, Arthur V. Jones, Dorcas Cochran; ph, John W. Boyle; ed, Paul Landers; md, Charles Previn; m/l, "Swing It Mother Goose," "Give Out," "Macumba," Everett Carter, Milton Rosen, "Fifty Million Nickels," Charles Barnet; "Sweet Genevieve," George Cooper, Henry Tucker; "Then You'll Remember Me," Alfred Bunn, Michael Balfe.

Musical (PR:AA MPAA:NR)

JUKE BOX RACKET* 1/2 (1960) 62m Brenner bw

Steve Karmon *(Bob)*, Arlene Corwin *(Judy)*, Peter Clune *(Mario)*, William DePrato *(Pop)*, Beverly Nazarow *(Ginger)*, Seymour Cassel *(Seymour)*, Dalene Young *(Betty)*, Lou Anne Lee *(Lulu Belle)*, Emy Boselli *(Mom)*, Ray Singer *(Morty)*, Peter Szabo *(Himself)*.

One of the six "assembly line" made films Mahon made in 1960 aimed at the teen market. A group of teens fight to keep a mob-owned juke box out of their neighborhood hangout, where elderly store owner DePrato has one already to their liking. Mahon also directed Errol Flynn's last picture, CUBAN REBEL GIRLS, 1959. Songs include: "Free Passes To The Movies," "Picnic Day," "Drip, Drip," "Lost" (Steve Karmen), "Suzie Rock" (Peter Szabo).

p, Jim Geallis, George Barrie; d, Barry Mahon.

Drama (PR:A MPAA:NR)

JUKE BOX RHYTHM 1/2** (1959) 82m COL bw

Jo Morrow *(Princess Ann)*, Jack Jones *(Riff Manton)*, Brian Donlevy *(George Manton)*, George Jessel *(Himself)*, Hans Conried *(Balenko)*, Karin Booth *(Leslie Anders)*, Marjorie Reynolds *(Martha Manton)*, Freida Inescort *(Aunt Margaret)*, Edgar Barrier *(Ambassador Truex)*, Fritz Feld *(Ambrose)*, Hortense Petra *(Redhead)*, Earl Grant Trio, The Nitwits, Johnny Otis, The Treniers *(Themselves)*.

Cute, but silly, rock and roll story features Morrow as a princess coming to the Big Apple to buy her coronation robe. Jones, who soon became a big star in far better material, falls for the princess. He tries to get her to change from her wardrobe stylist to his junkman buddy, Conried. Donlevy is Jones' father who tries to use the princess as a publicity stunt to help his Broadway show "Juke Box Jamboree." In between is a lot of good old rock and roll, with star appearances by Earl Grant Trio, The Nitwits, Johnny Otis, and The Treniers. Songs, all by Richard Quine, Fred Karger, and Stanley Styne, include: "Let's Fall in Love" (sung by Morrow), "The Freeze," "Make Room For the Joy," (sung by Jones), "I Feel It Right Here," "Last Night" (sung by Earl Grant Trio), "Get Out of the Car" (sung by The Treniers), "Willie and the Hand Jive" (sung by Johnny Otis), Juke Box Rhythm," "Spring is the Time For Remembering."

p, Sam Katzman; d, Arthur Dreifuss; w, Mary C. McCall, Jr., Earl Baldwin (based on the story by Lou Morheim); ph, Fred Jackman; m, Richard Quine, Fred Karger, Stanley Styne; ed, Saul A. Goodkind; art d, Paul Palmentola; ch, Hal Belfer.

Musical (PR:A MPAA:NR)

JUKE GIRL** (1942) 90m WB bw

Ann Sheridan *(Lola Mears)*, Ronald Reagan *(Steve Talbot)*, Richard Whorf *(Danny Frazier)*, George Tobias *(Nick Garcos)*, Gene Lockhart *(Henry Madden)*, Alan Hale *("Yippee")*, Betty Brewer *(Skeeter)*, Donald MacBride *("Muckeye" John)*, Howard da Silva *(Cully)*, Willard Robertson *(Mister Just)*, Faye Emerson *(Violet Murphy)*, Willie Best *(Jo-Mo)*, Fuzzy Knight *(Ike Harper)*, Spencer Charters *(Keene)*, William B. Davidson *(Paley)*, Frank Wilcox *(Truck Driver)*, William Haade *(Watchman)*, Eddy Waller *(Man in Car)*, Alan Bridge, Jack Gardner, Fred Kelsey, Frank Pharr, Ray Teal, Bill Phillips, Guy Wilkerson, Milton Kibbee, Ed Peil, Sr., Glenn Strange, Victor Zimmerman *(Men)*, Paul Burns *(Ed)*, Frank Darien *(Elderly Farmer)*, William Edmunds *(Travitti)*, Dewey Robinson, Kenneth Harlan *(Dealers)*, Joan Fitzgerald *(Juke Girl)*, Sol Gorss, William Gould *(Deputies)*, William Hopper *(Clerk)*, Frank Mayo *(Detective)*, Pat Flaherty *(Mike)*, Forrest Taylor, Clancy Cooper, Pat McVey *(Farmers)*.

Reagan and Sheridan had just come off the superb KINGS ROW and went from the sublime to the ridiculous with this one. Lots of action and a terrific acting job by Sheridan who almost, but not quite, takes this turkey out of the oven. Reagan and Whorf (who was so good as Sam Harris in YANKEE DOODLE DANDY before becoming an excellent film and TV director) are Florida drifters who toil in the tomato fields. Lockhart owns the packing plant and is embroiled in a battle with Tobias who owns a small farm. Reagan sides with the growers, Whorf takes up the cudgel of the packers, and their friendship falls apart at the seams. Sheridan is the hostess in a juke joint. She loves Reagan and aids him but gets fired for her efforts. Reagan and Sheridan help Tobias sell his crop for better money to another buyer, and when Tobias is murdered, they are framed for the killing (which was actually done by Lockhart). Just before Reagan and Sheridan are about to be the guests of honor at a necktie party, Whorf saves the day by getting Lockhart to come clean and the film ends happily. It was shot, of course, in California and the nights were freezing so all the actors had to rub glycerine and other goop on their faces to simulate perspiration. The air was so frigid that the actors were all asked to smoke cigarettes in order to justify the vapor that came from their mouths. Who knows how many ex-smokers got the habit again from working in this film? There is one huge fight scene with management scabs wrecking tons of tomatoes owned by independent farmers who had them waiting to be shipped to waiting markets. The tomatoes were smashed and reused often as the crew went for the long shots and the various close-ups. By the end of the scene, the smell of tomatoes was darn near permanently soaked in everyone's skin. It's the Florida version of GRAPES OF WRATH but nowhere near as good as that film. Alan Hale and Howard da Silva have small but telling roles. The title is a misnomer and many in the audience thought they were coming to see a musical and not a melodrama. Jerry Wald and Jack Saper were the associate producers, which means, in essence, they did the "line" producing. Wallis was usually busy with more important 1942 films like CASABLANCA, AIR FORCE, and WATCH ON THE RHINE.

p, Hal B. Wallis; d, Curtis Bernhardt; w, A.I. Bezzerides, Kenneth Gamet (based on the story "Jook Girl" by Theodore Pratt); ph, Bert Glennon; m, Adolph Deutsch; ed, Warren Low; art d, Robert Haas.

Crime Drama (PR:A MPAA:NR)

JULES AND JIM*****

(1962, Fr.) 110m Films du Carosse/JANUS bw (JULES ET JIM)

Jeanne Moreau *(Catherine)*, Oskar Werner *(Jules)*, Henri Serre *(Jim)*, Marie Dubois *(Therese)*, Vanna Urbino *(Gilberte)*, Sabine Haudepin *(Sabine)*, Boris Bassiak *(Albert)*, Kate Noelle *(Birgitta)* Anny Nelsen *(Lucie)*, Christiane Wagner *(Helga)*, Jean-Louis Richard *(1st Customer in Cafe)*, Michel Varesano *(2nd Customer in Cafe)*, Pierre Fabre *(Drunkard in Cafe)*, Danielle Bassiak *(Albert's Friend)*, Bernard Largemains *(Merlin)*, Elen Bober *(Mathilde)*, Dominique Lacarriere *(Woman)*, Michel Subor *(Narrator)*.

Based on an obscure semi-autobiographical novel by a one-time Parisian playboy who became an art dealer, JULES AND JIM was a triumph for everyone concerned. Truffaut convinced author Roche that he was the man to adapt the novel. Roche agreed but died in 1959, before the film was made. The book covered the years from 1907 through 1927, although Truffaut and his co-screenwriter, Gruault, moved it to 1912–1933 to include the Nazi book burnings which took place at the time. Werner is a shy German Jew who becomes best friends with his personality opposite, Serre, a life-loving Frenchman. They have many of the same interests though they pursue them quite differently. On a trip to an island off Greece, they see a statue with a unique smile and when they return to Paris they meet Moreau, who looks like the sculpture. The three Bohemians team up, and have many warm moments together as they ride their bikes, roam the meadows, frolic on the beach. While the world trembles around them, they are determined to have a marvelous time and live for the moment. Werner falls in love with Moreau and pleads with Serre to allow him to woo her and to not interfere. Serre steps back and the trio go to the South of France where they have an exquisite vacation. Werner proposes and Moreau accepts. Back in Paris, the inseparable trio visit the theater and see an avant-garde Scandinavian play about a modern-day Nora (from A DOLL'S HOUSE). Werner doesn't think much of the play and begins to chauvinistically comment on women as they stroll along the river Seine. Moreau reacts to Werner by leaping into the Seine, thus shocking Werner but endearing herself to Serre. Moreau and Werner go back to Germany just as WW I erupts. The two friends battle in opposite camps and, after the November 11 Armistice, Werner contacts Serre and asks him to come visit their home, a chalet in the Rhineland area. Werner and Moreau now have a young daughter, Haudepin, a 5 year old. Serre can see at once that the marriage is in trouble. She lists all of her lovers for Serre in a memorable scene in a cafe, but Werner means to keep her at all costs, even in spite of an affair with Bassiak, another friend. Now Werner decides that if he can't have Moreau, his best friend should and he gives his approval to them to have a liaison. Werner will divorce Moreau so Serre and she can marry. All Werner wants is the ability to just see her now and again. Serre must go back to Paris for some business and takes up again with Urbino, his long-time mistress who wishes they would marry and makes no bones about her desires. Moreau runs away with Bassiak and when she comes back, she rationalizes it by saying that if Serre can have Urbino, she can have Bassiak. Serre and Moreau get back together and spend their next weeks in an attempt to conceive, believing that a pregnancy would indicate that they are right for each other. Serre returns to Paris and learns, from a letter by Werner, that Moreau miscarried their love child and no longer wants to communicate with Serre. Sometime later, Werner and Serre meet once more in France. Werner and Moreau have decided to live in France again and when Serre and Moreau meet at the Werner house, she becomes kittenish and attempts to seduce Serre. He will have none of it, though, and clearly indicates the reasons why. There is no way that they can make a go of it because she is far too mercurial and they are of totally different thoughts about how to maintain a relationship. Besides, Serre intends to give up his bachelor life, marry Urbino, and raise a family. Enraged by the rejection, Moreau attempts to shoot Serre but fails. Still later, the three meet again and decide to have dinner, for old time's sake, in a country cafe. They use Moreau's car for the drive. At the cafe, Moreau tells her long-suffering husband that he should watch closely; she wants to take Serre for a brief ride. While Werner observes, she drives a few hundred yards down the road, turns sharply onto a washed-out bridge, flashes her enigmatic smile at Serre, and sends the car directly into the water, thus drowning herself and Serre. A bewildered Werner has their bodies cremated and leaves the cemetery at the end, a widower with a young child. Many people wondered what all of this meant and read all sorts of social significance into it. Truffaut was content with attempting to show the deep affection between two men and the impossibility of a *menage a trois*, no matter how much three people loved each other. Although a period film, there is nothing dated about the material as human nature is one of the most constant things in the universe. Truffaut establishes the period by using various silent film techniques in a mixed trove of cinematic tricks that he appropriated as well as invented. Many of the same devices were later utilized by Lelouch in his AND NOW MY LOVE. There is no reason for us to root for any of the three as they don't seem to be doing much of anything beyond exploring each other. Their lives are a dream which they live in reality and, in the end, they pay for their pleasures tragically. Individual scenes are gems, such as the one where Serre exults about the excellence of German beer and Moreau counters by naming several great French wines. In another scene, Moreau is burning love letters and her dress bursts into flame. It's a film that will enthrall some, anger others, and must take its place in the Academe of Great French Cinema (if such an organization exists). People took sides with the men when they saw the film and one of the capsule comments that could not have been more apropos was: "Loved him, hated him." And you can take your choice as to which was which. The song, written by Bassiak and sung by Moreau, is called "The Whirlwind" and speaks of lovers, how they meet, fall apart, and begin again. Filmed in Paris, Venice, and Alsace—that part of France that once was Germany and still maintains a distinctly Teutonic flavor despite having been ceded to France as part of the surrender in WW I. Truffaut set himself a difficult task; how to make Moreau's character sympathetic in spite of all the curious and quirky and destructive things she does. He succeeded far beyond his hopes and JULES AND JIM remains as captivating to modern audiences as it did when first released.

p, Marcel Berbert; d, Francois Truffaut; w, Truffaut, Jean Gruault (based on the novel by Henri-Pierre Roche); ph, Raoul Coutard (Franscope); m, Georges Delerue; ed, Claudine Bouche; cos, Fred Capel; m/l, "Le Tourbillon," Boris Bassiak.

Period Drama Cas. (PR:C-O MPAA:NR)

JULES VERNE'S ROCKET TO THE MOON

(SEE: THOSE FANTASTIC FLYING FOOLS, 1967, Brit.)

JULIA**** (1977) 116m FOX c

Jane Fonda *(Lillian Hellman)*, Vanessa Redgrave *(Julia)*, Jason Robards *(Dashiell Hammett)*, Maximilian Schell *(Johann)*, Hal Holbrook *(Alan Campbell)*, Rosemary Murphy *(Dorothy Parker)*, Meryl Streep *(Anne Marie)*, Dora Doll, Elisabeth Mortensen *(Train Passengers)*, John Glover *(Sammy)*, Lisa Pelikan *(Young Julia)*, Susan Jones *(Young Lillian)*, Cathleen Nesbitt *(Grandmother)*, Maurice Denham *(Undertaker)*, Gerard Buhr *(Passport Officer)*, Stefan Gryft *("Hamlet")*, Phillip Siegel *(Little Boy)*, Molly Urquhart *(Woman)*, Antony Carrick *(Butler)*, Ann Queensberry *(Woman in Berlin Station)*, Edmond Bernard *(Man in Berlin Station)*, Jacques David *(Fat Man)*, Jacqueline Staup *(Woman in Green Hat)*, Hans Verner *(Vienna Concierge)*, Christian de Tiliere *(Paris Concierge)*, Mark Metcalf *(Pratt)*, Shane Rimmer *(Customs Officer, New York Port Authority)*, Don Koll *(First-Nighter at Sardi's)*, *Jim Kane (Sardi)*, Dick Marr *(Sardi Customer)*, Vincent Sardi, Jr. *(Extra)*.

Nominated for nine Oscars (Best Picture, Best Director, Best Cinematography, Best Music, Best Actress, Best Supporting Actor (twice), Best Supporting Actress), it won three for the script, Redgrave, and Robards. Any other year it might have done better but 1977 was reserved for ANNIE HALL, CLOSE ENCOUNTERS OF THE THIRD KIND, and STAR WARS. Based on Lillian Hellman's memoirs *(Pentimento)*, JULIA takes place in the 1930s as Fonda, playing the authoress, lives with Robards, as Hammett, in a beach house. She's actively writing her first play and turns to famed writer Robards for his helpful (and sometimes cruel) criticism. When it's done and produced successfully, Fonda now can take a rest and decides to visit a childhood friend, Redgrave, with whom she shared some wonderful moments in their youth (shown in flashbacks with Pelikan and Jones as the girls). Redgrave moved to Austria to study medicine with Freud and became a crusader in social matters, joining the anti-fascists. She was injured in a battle with the Hitler Youth and is now in a hospital in Vienna. Fonda visits Redgrave as she is recovering. Later, on a trip to Moscow, Fonda is asked by Schell, a pal of Redgrave's, if she will smuggle a large sum of money from Russia to Germany where it will be used to aid the effort against the Nazis. Fonda takes the money and delivers it to Redgrave and when she returns to America she learns that Redgrave has been killed by the

Fascists, almost immediately after they saw each other for the last time. It was a short story, little more than an incident in Hellman's rich life, but Zinnemann and Sargent invested it with suspense, color, and a highly complex relationship between the two women. Too much time was spent discussing issues and old times but no one could fault the believability of the actors. Particularly notable was Murphy as Dorothy Parker. Murphy is a much underrated actress whose background includes having been raised in Europe where her father was a U.S. Envoy. JULIA is essentially a character study rather than a heavily plotted film, but the friendship of these two disparate women is often inspiring and, as an exercise in film-making, it should be studied by cinema students for years to come. Highly literary in execution, it nevertheless attracted a large general audience and was one of Fox's hits for that year. Streep made her feature debut in JULIA and showed the radiance that has taken her to the top of her craft.

p, Richard Roth; d, Fred Zinnemann; w, Alvin Sargent (based on the story in the book *Pentimento* by Lillian Hellman; ph, Douglas Slocombe (Technicolor); m, Georges Delerue; ed, Walter Murch, Marcel Durham; md, Delerue; prod d, Willy Holt, Gene Callahan, Carmen Dillon; set d, Tessa Davies, Pierre Charron; cos, Anthea Sylbert, Joan Bridge, Annalisa Nasalli Rocca, John Apperson, Colette Baudot; makeup, George Frost, Bernadine Anderson.

Drama **Cas.** **(PR:A-C MPAA:PG)**

JULIA, DU BIST ZAUBER-HAFT (SEE: ADORABLE JULIA, 1964, Fr.)

JULIA MISBEHAVES*½** (1948) 99m MGM bw

Greer Garson *(Julia Packett)*, Walter Pidgeon *(William Sylvester Packett)*, Peter Lawford *(Ritchie Lorgan)*, Cesar Romero *(Fred Gennochio)*, Elizabeth Taylor *(Susan Packett)*, Lucile Watson *(Mrs. Packett)*, Nigel Bruce *(Col. Willowbrook)*, Mary Boland *(Mrs. Gennochio)*, Reginald Owen *(Bennie Hawkins)*, Ian Wolfe *(Hobson)*, Phyllis Morris *(Daisy)*, Edmond Breon *(Jamie)*, Fritz Feld *(Pepito)*, Marcelle Corday *(Gabby)*, Veda Ann Borg *(Louise)*, Aubrey Mather *(Vicar)*, Henry Stephenson *(Lord Pennystone)*, Winifred Harris *(Lady Pennystone)*, Elspeth Dudgeon *(Woman in Pawn Shop)*, Stanley Fraser *(Pawn Shop Clerk)*, Victor Wood *(Postman)*, Herbert Wyndham *(Piano Player in Pub)*, Sid D'Albrook *(Waiter in Pub)*, Jimmy Aubrey *(Drunk)*, Roland Dupre *(French Messenger)*, Alex Goudavich *(Bellhop)*, Andre Charlot *(Stage Doorman)*, Joanee Wayne *(The Head)*, Mitchell Lewis *(Train Official)*, Joi Lansing, Lola Albright, Gail Langford, Patricia Walker, Shirley Ballard, Elaine Sterling, Ruth Hall, Marjorie Jackson *(Mannequins)*, Art Foster, George Goldsmith, Dave Thursby *(English Sailors)*, Alphonse Martell *(Frenchman in Theater)*, Torben Meyer *(Commissar)*, James Logan *(Moving Man)*, Ted DeWayne, Henry Monzello, William Snyder, Ray Saunders, Michael Kent *(Acrobatic Troupe)*, Connie Leon, Almira Sessions *(Women in Street)*, Jimmy Fairfax, Harry Allen, Cyril Thornton, Jim Finlayson *(Bill Collectors)*, Jean Del Val *(Croupier)*, Albert Pallot *(Bartender)*, Ottola Nesmith, Nan Boardman *(Salesladies)*, George Volck *(Urchin)*, Kay Norton, Fern Eggen, Susan Perry *(Girls in Hotel Lobby)*, Berta Feducha *(Woman in Theater)*.

A charming comedy that shows off Garson's flair for light-heartedness in an unaccustomed role. This time, she's a vaudevillian in England who is always on the brink of bankruptcy. With her innate charm, she gets her various friends to ease her debts but she is always one step ahead of her creditors. Garson was once married to Pidgeon but hasn't seen him or her daughter, Taylor, for almost 20 years. An invitation to Taylor's wedding arrives. Taylor and Pidgeon currently live in France with his tyrannical matriarch, Watson. Garson gets the necessary money for the channel crossing from Owen, a long-time crony. On the boat, she encounters Boland and her quintet of acrobatic sons, a circus act visiting Paris for an engagement. When Boland takes ill, Garson replaces her in the act and does some singing and an hysterical attempt at physicality. Romero, one of the circus people, falls for her, but she bids him farewell in order to get to the wedding at Watson's huge chateau. Watson is all ice but Pidgeon and Taylor are thrilled to see her. Needing money to buy a wedding gift, Garson returns to Paris, toys with British nabob Bruce, buys the gift, and races back to the chateau where she learns that Taylor is really in love with Lawford, not her intended. Garson encourages Taylor as Pidgeon finds himself falling in love with Garson again. Romero arrives and rankles as he sees Garson and Pidgeon getting closer. Bruce arrives and it turns out he's a friend of Watson's. Garson attempts to explain what she did in Paris with Bruce when Taylor and Lawford elope. Pidgeon and Garson chase the youngsters and wind up stranded in a chalet in the mountains where they reaffirm their love for each other. A knockabout farce with several wonderful slapstick scenes and an opportunity for Garson to let her usually coiffed red hair down. Lola Albright and Joi Lansing are briefly seen in bits. Don't miss this one.

p, Everett Riskin; d, Jack Conway; w, William Ludwig, Harry Ruskin, Arthur Wimperis, Gina Kaus, Monckton Hoffe (based on the novel *The Nutmeg Tree* by Margery Sharp); ph, Joseph Ruttenberg; m, Adolph Deutsch; ed, John Dunning; art d, Cedric Gibbons, Daniel B. Cathcart; set d, Edwin B. Willis, Jack D. Moore; cos, Irene; spec eff, Warren Newcombe; m/l, "When You're Playing with Fire," Jerry Seelen, Hal Borne; makeup, Jack Dawn.

Comedy **(PR:A MPAA:NR)**

JULIE** (1956) 109m MGM bw

Doris Day *(Julie Benton)*, Louis Jourdan *(Lyle Benton)*, Barry Sullivan *(Cliff Henderson)*, Frank Lovejoy *(Detective Capt. Pringle)*, John Gallaudet *(Detective Cole)*, Harlan Warde *(Detective Pope)*, Jack Kruschen *(Detective Mace)*, Aline Towne *(Denice Martin)*, Ann Robinson *(Valerie)*, Ed Hinton *(Pilot)*, Jack Kelly *(Co-Pilot)*, Barney Phillips *(Doctor)*, Carleton Young *(Field Man)*, Pamela Duncan *(Peggy)*, Mae Marsh *(Hysterical Passenger)*, Edward Marsh *(Company Official)*, Hank Patterson *(Ellis)*.

Unimaginative suspenser has Day worried that her second husband Jourdan is trying to kill her. After discovering that he offed her first spouse, Day realizes that husband number two would rather do the same to her than lose his wife to someone else. The anti-climactic finish has Day working as a stewardess on a plane which Jourdan boards. In flight, he kills the pilot and wounds the co-pilot before he himself is killed. Of course it's all up to Day to safely land the winged beast. It's fast and furious, but suffers from an overstuffed plot.

p, Martin Melcher; d&w, Andrew L. Stone; ph, Fred Jackson, Jr.; m, Leith Stevens, Tom Adair; piano composition "Midnight On The Cliffs," Leonard Pennario; ed, Virginia Stone; m/l, "Julie," Stevens, Adair.

Drama/Suspense **(PR:A MPAA:NR)**

JULIE DARLING* (1982, Can./Ger.) 100m TAT-Cinequity c

Anthony Franciosa *(Harold Wilding)*, Isabelle Mejias *(Julie Wilding)*, Sybil Danning *(Susan)*, Cindy Gurling *(Irene)*, Paul Hubbard *(Sam Weston)*, Benjamin Schmoll *(Dennis)*.

A poorly dubbed "thriller" about a malevolent gal (Mejias) who hates her mother, sees the woman raped and killed by a delivery man, then tries to kill her stepmom. Pacing is too slow for tension to be maintained effectively. Freudians, however, might have a field day with the subject.

p, Ernt Van Theumer, Maurice Smith; d, Paul Nicolas; w, Nicolas, Smith; ph, Miklos Lente; m, Joachim van Ludwig; ed, Fred Srp; art d, Lindsay Goddard.

Drama/Suspense **(PR:O MPAA:NR)**

JULIE THE REDHEAD½** (1963, Fr.) 100m Les Films Matignon-Films Metzger et Woog/Shawn, Ellis bw (JULIE LA ROUSSE)

Daniel Gelin *(Edouard Lavigne/Jean Lavigne)*, *Pascale Petit (Julie)*, Rene-Louis Lafforgue *(Max Piccalo)*, Margo Lion *(Mme. Lavigne)*, Lilian Patrick *(Tamira)*, Jocelyne Darche *(Violette)*, Gabrielle Fontan *(Concierge)*, Jean Ozenne *(Uncle Roger)*, Frederic O'Brady *(Hamib)*, Jacques Dufilho *(Waiter)*, Pierre Doris *(Hotel Manager)*, Rene Blancard *(Mons. Lavigne)*, Michel Etcheverry *(Notary)*, Michel Thomas, C. Conti, Aime de March, L. Vivet, Alvarez et Confortes, Jean Guyon.

An engaging comedy which has the two leads (Gelin and Petit) playing two generations of characters. As artist Edouard Lavigne, Gelin falls in love with his red-headed model, Julie (Petit) and wants to marry her. His father, however, wants him to carry on in the family nail business. He agrees, though always wishing he had pursued the artistic goal. After a number of years Edouard dies, leaving behind a son Jean and two-thirds of the estates' inheritance to "Julie the Redhead." Jean goes on a search for this Julie in order to buy out a control portion, but learns that the woman has died. She has left the inheritance to her daughter, who soon is courted by the greedy Jean. In order to acquire her riches, Jean marries Julie. On the wedding night he is told that his wife is not really the redhead's daughter, but a shrewd niece, who is also trying to deceptively make some cash. This well-scripted and humorous film originally was released in Paris in 1959.

p, Georges Glass; d, Claude Boissol; w, Paul Andreota, Beatrice Rubinstein, Boissol; ph, Roger Fellous; m, Rene-Louis Lafforgue; ed, Louis Devaivre; art d, Robert Guisgand; ch, Georges Reich.

Comedy **(PR:A MPAA:NR)**

JULIET OF THE SPIRITS**** (1965, Fr./Ital./W.Ger.) 148m Federiz-Francoriz-Rizzoli-Eichberg/Rizzoli c (GIULIETTA DEGLI SPIRITI; JULIETTE DES ESPRITS; JULIA UND DIE GEISTER)

Giulietta Masina *(Juliet)*, Alba Cancellieri *(Juliet as a Child)*, Mario Pisu *(Giorgio)*, Caterina Boratto *(Juliet's Mother)*, Luisa Della Noce *(Adele)*, Sylva Koscina *(Sylva)*, Sabrina Gigli, Rosella di Sepio *(Granddaughters)*, Lou Gilbert *(Grandfather)*, Valentina Cortese *(Valentina)*, Silvana Jachino *(Dolores)*, Elena Fondra *(Elena)*, Jose-Luis de Vilallonga, Cesarino Miceli Picardi *(Friends of Giorgio)*, Milena Vucotich, Elisabetta Gray *(Juliet's Maids)*, Sandra Milo *(Susy/Iris/Fanny)*, Irina Alexeieva *(Susy's Grandmother)*, Alessandra Mannoukine *(Susy's Mother)*, Gilberto Galvan *(Susy's Chauffeur)*, Yvonne Casadei, Hildegarde Golez, Dina de Santis *(Susy's Maids)*, Seyna Seyn *(Masseuse)*, Edoardo Torricella *(Russian Teacher)*, Dany Paris *(Desperate Friend)*, Raffaele Guida *(Oriental Lover)*, Fred Williams *(Arabian Prince)*, Alberto Plebani *(Lynx-Eyes)*, Federico Valli, Remo Risaliti, Grillo Rufino *(Lynx Eyes' Agents)*, Waleska Gert *(Bhisma)*, Asoka Rubener, Sujata Rubener, Walter Harrison *(Bhisma's Helpers)*, Felice Fulchignoni *(Don Raffaele)*, Anne Francine *(Psychoanalyst)*, Mario Conocchia *(Family Lawyer)*, Friedrich Ledebur *(Headmaster)*, Genius *(Medium)*, Massimo Sarchielli *(Valentina's Lover)*, Giorgio Ardisson, Bob Edwards, Nadir Moretti *(Dolores' Models)*.

There were several cuts of this superb film. In Italy, it ran two hours, in France it was 150 minutes, in Germany it ran 145 minutes and in the U.S. it came in at 148 minutes and 137 minutes. But whatever the length, there is no disputing the genius behind the scenes. Masina (Fellini's wife for more than 40 years) is married to Pisu. She's in her middle thirties, not attractive and more or less resigned to a dull life with a dull husband who pays her little attention. She thinks it's just the pressures of business that cause him to be so diffident but soon she begins to wonder if he may have someone else. Their life near Fregene is uneventful and she is chastised by her mother, Boratto, and gorgeous sisters, Koscina and Della Noce, for allowing herself to be content with such boredom. One night, Pisu and some friends hold a seance and Masina discovers that she can conjure up the spirits of her grandfather and various others. These wraiths begin to say that she deserves to have some enjoyment in her life and that she should give herself a treat. Cortese takes her to meet Gert, a mystic who tells her to listen to the spirits. Now she decides to see if her intuition is correct and she hires a sleuth who corroborates her worst fears about Pisu having affairs. She is distraught, then makes friends with Milo, a sensualist who lives for the moment and whose friends are as wild and fun-loving as Masina is conservative. Pisu is going off to a spa with his latest mistress when Masina almost commits suicide. It is that brush with the Hereafter that convinces her she can live without Pisu and, with that, she exorcises herself of the spirits haunting her. It's sort of the female version of 8 1/2, with memories and bits and pieces of the past sewn into what is happening now. Nothing is what it seems except for the indomitable fortitude of a woman on the brink of decision. Not for people who enjoy literal movies, JULIET OF THE SPIRITS will invade your recollections for years.

p, Angelo Rizzoli; d, Federico Fellini; w, Fellini, Tullio Pinelli, Ennio Flaiano, Brunello Rondi (based on a story by Fellini, Pinelli); ph, Gianni De Venanzo (Technicolor); m, Nino Rota; ed, Ruggero Mastroianni; art d, Piero Gherardi; set d, Luciano Ricceri, E. Benazzi Taglietti, Giantito Burchiellaro; cos, Gherardi; makeup, Otello Fava, Emilio Trani.

Drama **Cas.** **(PR:A-C MPAA:NR)**

JULIETTA*1/2 (1957, Fr.) 96m Indusfilms/Kingsley International bw

Jean Marais *(Andre Landecourt)*, Dany Robin *(Julietta)*, Jeanne Moreau *(Rosie Facibey)*, Denise Grey *(Mme. Valendor)*, Bernard Lancret *(Le Prince d'Alpen)*, Nicole Berger *(Martine)*, Georges Chamarat *(Arthur)*, Francois Joux *(Le Commissaire)*.

A light-hearted, whimsical, French romantic farce that doesn't have much of anything beyond the good cast to recommend it. Except for Robin, the members of the cast even look sorely out of place. Marais plays the handsome young man with trouble on his hands: he must keep the girl who has unexpectedly paid him a visit secret from his fiancee. Robin is the unwanted guest who ousts Moreau from the romance with Marais. Nothing to create much of a stir.

d, Marc Allegret; w, Francoise Giroud (based on the novel by Louise De Vilmorin); ph, Henri Alekan.

Comedy **(PR:A MPAA:NR)**

JULIUS CAESAR** (1952) Avon/Brandon bw

Harold Tasker *(Julius Caesar)*, Robert Holt *(Octavius Caesar)*, Charlton Heston *(Marcus Antonius)*, Theodore Cloak *(Emil Lepidus)*, David Bradley *(Brutus)*, Grosvenor Glenn *(Cassius)*, William Russell *(Casca)*, Frederick Roscoe *(Decius)*, Arthur Sus *(Cinna)*, Cornelius Peeples *(Popilius)*, Alfred Edyvean *(Flavius)*, John O'Leary *(Marullus)*, Homer Dietmeier *(Artemidorus)*, Don Walker *(Soothsayer)*, Russell Gruebner *(Cinna The Poet)*, George Gilbert *(Strato)*, George Hinners *(Lucius)*, Sam Needham *(Pindarus)*, Helen Ross *(Calpurnia)*, Mary Darr *(Portia)*.

One of the two "unofficial" films (the other being PEER GYNT) Heston appeared in before his 1950 "debut" film DARK CITY. Independently produced in and around the Chicago area, it tells the familiar tale of Caesar, with Heston cast as Marc Antony, a role he would again tackle in 1970's JULIUS CAESAR. With a budget of less than $15,000, director Bradley was forced to rely on ingenuity; for example, shooting Caesar's funeral on the steps of Chicago's Museum of Science and Industry—a building modeled after early Roman architecture. Interesting more as a novelty than anything else, though it is a more than capable piece of filmmaking.

p&d, David Bradley (based on the play by William Shakespeare); m, John Becker.

Historical Biography **(PR:A MPAA:NR)**

11977A

JULIUS CAESAR*** (1953) 120m MGM bw

James Mason *(Brutus)*, Marlon Brando *(Marc Antony)*, Louis Calhern *(Julius Caesar)*, John Gielgud *(Cassius)*, Edmond O'Brien *(Casca)*, Greer Garson *(Calpurnia)*, Deborah Kerr *(Portia)*, George Macready *(Marullus)*, Michael Pate *(Flavius)*, Richard Hale *(Sooothsayer)*, Alan Napier *(Cicero)*, William Cottrell *(Cinna)*, John Hardy *(Lucius)*, John Hoyt *(Decius Brutus)*, Tom Powers *(Metellus Cimber)*, Jack Raine *(Trebonius)*, Ian Wolfe *(Ligarius)*, Lumsden Hare *(Publius)*, Morgan Farley *(Artemidorus)*, Victor Perry *(Popilius Lena)*, Douglas Watson *(Octavius Caesar)*, Douglas Dumbrille *(Lepidus)*, Rhys Williams *(Lucilius)*, Michael Ansara *(Pindarus)*, Dayton Lummis *(Messala)*, John Lupton *(Varro)*, Preston Hanson *(Claudius)*, John Parrish *(Titinius)*, Joe Waring *(Clitus)*, Stephen Roberts *(Dardanius)*, Thomas Browne Henry *(Volumnius)*, Edmund Purdon *(Strato)*, John Doucette *(Carpenter)*, Chester Stratton *(Servant to Caesar)*, Bill Phipps *(Servant to Antony)*, Paul Guilfoyle, Lawrence Dobkin, David Bond, Jo Gilbert, Ann Tyrell, John O'Malley, Oliver Blake, Alvin Hurwitz, Donald Elson *(Citizens of Rome)*.

When Houseman and Mankiewicz, brother of Herman, decided to film Shakespeare's "Julius Caesar," they picked an elegant and distinguished cast—Mason, Gielgud, Calhern, O'Brien—but they also shocked the industry and not too few literary scholars by selecting Brando to play Marc Antony. He was then still known as "The Mumbler" and "The Slob," as per his brutish performance as Stanley Kowalski in A STREETCAR NAMED DESIRE. But Brando turned that opinion about in a startling performance. Calhern as Caesar has by 44 B.C. become virtual dictator of the Roman Empire, with power that is staggering, so much so that Gielgud (Cassius), O'Brien (Casca), and others plan to assassinate him. The plotters convince Mason (Brutus), one of the most influential Romans alive, to join their conspiracy. Though a moralist and full of conscience, as well as being one of Calhern's best friends, Mason believes, like the others, that the only way to stave off Calhern's tyranny is to kill him. Calhern's superstitious wife, Garson (Calpurnia), has a dream in which she sees her husband slain at the hands of friends and she warns him not to attend the Senate the next day, the Ides of March. Calhern laughs off the nightmare and proceeds to the Senate. Farley (Artemidorus) warns Calhern as he approaches the Senate of his impending bloody fate, but Calhern ignores him. At the foot of Pompey's statue Calhern is approached by the conspirators who insist he reply to their question about accepting full power from the Senate. Before Calhern can give an adequate reply, O'Brien steps forward with a dagger, shouting: "Speak hands, for me!" He plunges the dagger into Calhern as do Gielgud and others. Calhern reels, mortally wounded, to his close friend Mason, who also raises his dagger. Dying, Calhern delivers the immortal line: "Et tu, Brute?" ("You, too, Brutus?") He falls dead while the conspirators disperse. Brando (Marc Antony) races to the Senate to behold Calhern's bloody corpse, pretending to sympathize with the conspirators but secretly plotting with Watson (Octavius Caesar) to avenge the murder by slaying the conspirators. Mason addresses a huge throng, explaining the actions of the killers, stating that this was done to prevent a monarchy from being established by Calhern. He is loudly cheered but when Brando passionately, eloquently speaks to the mob he turns them against the conspirators with his "Friends, Romans, countrymen, lend me your ears" speech. Mason, Gielgud, and the other conspirators flee Rome, raising an army to combat the legions quickly formed by Brando and Watson. The two armies clash at Philippi and the battle is soon won by the forces of Brando and Watson. Upon hearing of the defeat, Gielgud orders his slave to stab him to death. The news is taken to the conscience-stricken Mason who has been in agony through the night, haunted by the ghost of Calhern, and he, too, kills himself. Brando, coming upon the corpse of Mason, pays homage to his honorable enemy, saying: "This was the noblest Roman of them all." JULIUS CAESAR was the brainchild of Houseman and Mankiewicz, the producer having worked with Orson Welles and the Mercury Players on the 1937 version of "Caesar." Houseman, who had been lobbying to make the film for years, heard that the property was seriously being considered and contacted studio boss Dore Schary, saying that if he were not named the producer he would leave MGM. He was reluctantly given the chore and a small budget ($2,070,000) which forced such cost-saving devices as portraying the battle of Philippi (for no more than $150,000) as a small ambush in the mountains shown in montage, although Houseman later claimed that at least 900 extras were used, shot in a few days in Bronson Canyon, a stone quarry near the Hollywood Bowl. Mankiewicz made the whole thing believable by portraying the cast in quickly-paced scenes as middle-class people audiences could identify with, excepting the aloof intellectuals Mason and Gielgud, who identified only with themselves. Calhern is effective as Caesar if not as glib as the suave, crooked lawyer he essayed in THE ASPHALT JUNGLE. The sets were spare, crammed with bric-a-brac to fill out space, and Caesar's apartments were made up of sets cannibalized from the QUO VADIS sets in Rome which were shipped to the MGM lot. Although Gibbons and Carfagno won Oscars for art direction and set decoration, there was a plywood look to the film with steps going into the Senate that show no wear at all. Italian director Vittorio De Sica visited the set of JULIUS CAESAR and exclaimed: "Ah, what realism! It looks exactly like modern-day Ferrara." MGM did not expect much from this production. Films based on the works of the Immortal Bard had been box office poison at best, even the prestigious ROMEO AND JULIET, produced by MGM in 1936 starring Leslie Howard and Norma Shearer, a pet project of then production chief Irving Thalberg. But this film surprisingly turned in a considerable profit and much of this was due to the astounding performance of Brando as Marc Antony, a role first intended for Paul Scofield, then Leo Genn or Charlton Heston. Brando was approached by Mankiewicz with the idea of playing the role and he almost passed out, stating: "Oh, my God!" He said nothing for a month while he studied records of John Barrymore, his idol, and Laurence Olivier, doing works of Shakespeare. Then Brando did his own renditions and played the tapes for Mankiewicz who responded with: "You sound exactly like June Allyson." But he worked feverishly on the part and sought out Gielgud's help. The accomplished British thespian helped Brando with his timing and delivery, working with him on his speech patterns particularly so that when he delivered the "Friends, Romans and countrymen" speech, he was a cultured and eloquent leader of men, anything but "The Slob." It was an amazing performance, aided mightily by Mankiewicz, who kept cutting to the crowd to get reaction to Brando's speech and then back to Brando to reinforce his effectiveness. Gielgud was so much impressed with Brando that he invited him to London to perform with him and other accomplished Shakespearean actors in some of the great playwright's works. Brando respectfully declined, saying that he had to go scuba diving in the Bahamas. Brando was nominated for Best Actor but lost the Oscar to William Holden for STALAG 17. The production is superb on every level and is undoubtedly the best JULIUS CAESAR ever put on film. One British critic went even further, confessing: "It is maddening to be forced to admit it, but it has been left to Hollywood to make the finest film version of Shakespeare yet to be seen on our screens." Mason gives a subdued, almost emotionless performance, one that won him kudos, except from himself (he was always his own worst critic). Said Mason of his Brutus: "My vote was with the anti-Masons. It seemed to me that the only faultless performance was that of Eddie O'Brien as Casca." His modesty aside, Mason was undoubtedly the best Brutus to ever grace the screen. It is nevertheless Mankiewicz's film, expertly crafted from every angle, with the mob and murder scenes adroitly fixed. (Mankiewicz's handling of crowds in this production was wholly unlike the unwieldy mess he made of the hordes of extras he flooded into CLEOPATRA a decade later, when he almost bankrupted Fox Studios.) Much of the film's effectiveness was due, according to Mankiewicz, to its being shot in black and white when the studio pushed for color. In this way, the director later stated, he could simulate an almost newsreel approach to the historic events. The director later stated: "It's not in color because I've never seen a good, serious, dramatic movie in color, except maybe GONE WITH THE WIND. You can't get drama and make people real in color. This is a picture of mood, of violence, of real people—their ambitions, their dreams. People dream in black and white. They don't dream in Technicolor." For the New York premiere, MGM leased a legitimate theater, The Booth, to create the aura of a first-class stage production. But studio bosses still tinkered with this classic, blowing up the 35mm print for a wide-screen showing. Mankiewicz exploded as seeing "an opening night disaster, with Edmond O'Brien's head completely cut off the screen, at one point, as well as the heads and feet of anyone going up the steps of the Senate." He raced into the offices of Nick Schenck, who was president of Loew's and financial head of MGM, and got into a "screaming fight" over the blown-up print. Schenck ordered Mankiewicz out of his office, with the oft-yelled threat of: "you'll never work in this business again." The musical score, or the absence of it, later became a source of great controversy for Hollywood insiders. Houseman and Mankiewicz wanted the brilliant Bernard Hermann to compose the score but MGM's then musical director, Johnny Green, screamed that Hermann would cost too much and that Miklos Rosza, who was under contract at $1,500 a week, would do nicely. Mankiewicz said he did not want a Rosza score, that it would be all wrong for his film. Nevertheless, Rosza did the score, creating an entire overture to be used in the credits. Then Green insisted that another overture, playing Tchaikovsky's "Capriccio Italien," be substituted. Both were scratched to keep peace, although one piece Rosza did compose, a tune sung by a boy in a tent, can be heard in the final print. Rosza's overture was later made available in an LP record.

p, John Houseman; d&w, Joseph L. Mankiewicz (based on the play by William Shakespeare); ph, Joseph Ruttenberg; m, Miklos Rosza; ed, John Dunning; art d, Cedric Gibbons, Edward Carfagno, Edwin B. Willis, Hugh Hunt; cos, Hershel McCoy; spec eff, Warren Newcombe; makeup, William Tuttle.

Drama **(PR:C MPAA:NR)**

JULIUS CAESAR** (1970, Brit.) 117m COM/AIP c

Charlton Heston *(Mark Antony)*, John Gielgud *(Julius Caesar)*, Jason Robards *(Brutus)*, Richard Johnson *(Cassius)*, Robert Vaughn *(Casca)*, Richard Chamberlain *(Octavius Caesar)*, Diana Rigg *(Portia)*, Jill Bennett *(Calpurnia)*, Christopher Lee *(Artemidorus)*, Alan Browning *(Marullus)*, Norman Bowler *(Titinius)*, Andrew Crawford *(Volumnius)*, David Dodimead *(Lepidus)*, Peter Eyre *(Cinna the Poet)*, Edwin Finn *(Publius)*, Derek Godfrey *(Decius Brutus)*, Michael Gough *(Metellus Cimber)*, Paul Hardwick *(Messala)*, Laurence Harrington *(Carpenter)*, Thomas Heathcote *(Flavius)*, Ewan Hooper *(Strato)*, Robert Keegan *(Lucilius)*, Andre Morell *(Cicero)*, David Neal *(Cinna the Conspirator)*, Preston Lockwood *(Trebonius)*, John Moffatt *(Popilius Lena)*, Steven Pacey *(Lucius)*, Ron Pember *(Cobbler)*, John Tate *(Clitus)*, Damien Thomas *(Pindarus)*, Liz Geghardt *(Calpurnia's Maid)*, Ken Hutchinson *(1st Plebian)*, Michael Keating *(2nd Plebian)*, Derek Hardwicke *(3rd Plebian)*, Michael Wynne *(4th Plebian)*, David Leland *(5th Plebian)*, Ronald McGill, Linbert Spencer, Trevor Adams *(Caesar's Servants)*, Robin Chadwick *(Servant to Octavius)*, Christopher Cazenove *(Servant to Antony)*, Roy Stewart *(Lepidus's Slave)*.

This version of Shakespeare's classic drama is a workmanlike production that ill-combines the staginess of theater with the visual medium of cinema. Heston is fine in his portrayal of Marc Antony (though not up to the standards set by Marlon Brando in the 1953 version), but the remainder of the cast is uninspired. Most simply deliver their lines without any feel for motivation. Robards gives an unusually bad performance, one of the worst of his career. *Miseenscene* fluctuates between grandiose and gaudy, with lavish, sometimes poorly photographed sets. Gielgud, a veteran of the 1953 version, returned once more, taking the title role this time. Though not a great film, box office response was enough to warrant the sequel, ANTONY AND CLEOPATRA, with Heston repeating his role.

p, Peter Snell; d, Stuart Burge; w, Robert Furnival (based on the play by William Shakespeare); ph, Ken Higgins (Panavision, Technicolor); m, Michael Lewis; ed, Eric Boyd Perkins; prod d, Julia Trevelyan Oman; art d, Maurice Pelling; cos, Robin Archer; makeup, Cliff Sharpe.

Historical Drama **(PR:A MPAA:G)**

JULY PORK BELLIES (SEE: FOR PETE'S SAKE, 1977)

JUMBO** (1962) 123m Euterpe-Arwin/MGM c (AKA: BILLY ROSE'S JUMBO)

Doris Day *(Kitty Wonder)*, Stephen Boyd *(Sam Rawlins)*, Jimmy Durante *(Pop Wonder)*, Martha Raye *(Lulu)*, Dean Jagger *(John Noble)*, Joseph Waring *(Harry)*, Lynn Wood *(Tina)*, Charles Watts *(Ellis)*, James Chandler *(Parsons)*, Robert Burton *(Madison)*, Wilson Wood *(Hank)*, Norman Leavitt *(Eddie)*, Grady Sutton *(Driver)*, Sydney, the Elephant *(Jumbo)*, John Hart *(Marshal)*, Roy Engel, Jack Boyle *(Reporters)*, Robert Williams *(Deputy)*, Sue Casey *(Dottie)*, Fred Cob *(Andy)*, William Hines *(Roustabout)*, Michael Kostrick *(Michaels)*, Ralph Lee *(Perry)*, Paul Wexler *(Sharpie)*, Otto Reichow *(Hans)*, Billy Barty *(Joey)*, Chuck Haren *(Lennie)*, J. Lewis Smith *(Dick)*, Ron Henon, The Carlisles, The Pedrolas, The Wazzans, The Hannefords, Corky Cristians, Victor Julian, Richard Berg, Joe Monahan, Miss Lani, Adolph Dubsky, Pat Anthony, Janos Prohaska, The Barbettes.

A great film in terms of size but not in artistic quality, and ultimately box office receipts. The original Hecht-MacArthur script was based on entrepreneur Billy Rose's 1935 circus-musical extravaganza held at New York City's appropriately named Hippodrome. Transference to the screen was much less spectacular, a pale ghost compared to DeMille's THE GREATEST SHOW ON EARTH some 10 years previous. Underneath all the glitz was a standard plot involving Day and her father (Durante) attempting to salvage their tiny circus. Durante's gambling doesn't help any but things look better when jack-of-all-trades Boyd is hired to help out. Unbeknownst to Durante, Boyd is the son of rival circus owner Jagger. The man is determined to wipe out the competition and wants his son's help. Budding romance between Day and Boyd quells the nefarious plans and the tiny Wonder Circus once more is a success. The story was typical for an MGM musical. This was intended to revive the glory days of the studio's grandiose, colorful extravaganzas. Enthusiasm is there but that alone can't cover the weaknesses. Credited as Second Unit Director and organizing the circus-act sequences was the elderly Busby Berkeley, failing to recapture his old magic. The Rogers and Hart tunes are "Over and Over Again," "Circus on Parade," "Why Can't I," "This Can't Be Love," "The Most Beautiful Girl in the World," "My Romance," "Little Girl Blue," "What is a Circus," "Sawdust, Spangles and Dreams."

p, Joe Pasternak, Martin Melcher; d, Charles Walters; w, Sidney Sheldon (based on the musical play by Ben Hecht, Charles MacArthur); ph, William H. Daniels (Panavision, Metrocolor); ed, Richard W. Farrell; art d, George W. Davis, Preston Ames; set d, Henry Grace, Hugh Hunt; cos, Morton Haack; spec eff, A. Arnold Gillespie, Robert R. Hoag, J. McMillan Johnson; makeup, William Tuttle, Jack Wilson.

Musical **(PR:AA MPAA:NR)**

JUMP* 1/2 (1971) 97m Cannon c

Tom Ligon *(Chester Jump)*, Logan Ramsey *(Babe Duggers)*, Collin Wilcox-Horne *(April May)*, Sudie Bond *(Ernestine)*, Conrad Bain *(Lester)*, Norman Rose *(Dutchman)*, Lada Edmund, Jr. *(Enid)*, Bette Craig *(Beulah)*, Vicky Lynn *(Mercy)*, Jack Nance *(Ace)*, Ron St. Germaine *(Billy Rae)*, Johnny Hicks *(Starter)*, James Tallent *(Young Boy)*, Kentucky Mountain Boys *(Themselves)*.

A picture about stock car racing with Ligon cast as a gutsy, naturally talented driver who makes it to the top. He meets the usual complications of temptations and family troubles but ultimately loses his status thanks to a self-serving race impresario. Despite the thin plot and numerous cliches, Ligon manages to stand out with a fine performance. He's backed with good support from the ensemble and occasional moments of flair within the direction. JUMP never reaches its potential but works nicely on a simple level.

p, Christopher C. Dewey; d, Joe Manduke; w, Richard Wheelwright; ph, Greg Sandor (DeLuxe Color); ed, George T. Norris.

Sports Drama **(PR:A MPAA:GP)**

JUMP FOR GLORY (SEE: WHEN THIEF MEETS THIEF, 1937, Brit.)

JUMP INTO HELL* 1/2 (1955) 92m WB bw

Jack [Jacques] Sernas *(Capt. Guy Bertrand)*, Kurt Kasznar *(Capt. Jean Callaux)*, Arnold Moss *(The General)*, Peter Van Eyck *(Lt. Heinrich Heldman)*, Marcel Dalio *(Sgt. Taite)*, Norman Dupont *(Lt. Andre Maupin)*, Lawrence Dobkin *(Maj. Maurice Bonet)*, Pat Blake *(Gizele Bonet)*, Irene Montwill *(Jacqueline)*, Alberto Morin *(Maj. Riviere)*, Maurice Marsac *(Capt. LeRoy)*, Louise Mercier *(Capt. Darbley)*, Peter Bourne *(Lt. Robert)*, Roger Valmy *(Lamoreaux)*, Lisa Montell *(Jacqueline)*, George Chan *(Thai)*, Jack Scott *(Dejean)*, Harold Dyrenforth *(Plandrin)*, Leon Lontoc *(Pham)*.

Even the inclusion of newsreel footage failed to make this picture about France's dramatic stand at Dien Bien Phu in Indochina look realistic. A group of four volunteers from France are called upon to parachute into hell (Indochina), to help defeat the enemy. Of course each man has his own reason for volunteering, but the overlong film fails to deliver much in excitement or honesty.

p, David Weisbart; d, David Butler; w, Irving Wallace; ph, J. Peverell Marley; m, David Buttolph; ed, Irene Morra; md, Buttolph; art d, Stanley Fleischer.

War **(PR:A MPAA:NR)**

JUMPING FOR JOY** (1956, Brit.) 88m RANK bw

Frankie Howerd *(Willie Joy)*, Stanley Holloway *("Captain" Jack Montague)*, A.E. Matthews *(Lord Cranfield)*, Tony Wright *(Vincent)*, Alfie Bass *(Blagg)*, Joan Hickson *(Lady Cranfield)*, Lionel Jeffries *(Bert Benton)*, Susan Beaumont *(Susan)*, Terence Longdon *(John Wyndham)*, Colin Gordon *(Max)*, Richard Wattis *(Carruthers)*, Danny Green *(Plug Ugly)*, Barbara Archer *(Marlene)*, William Kendall *(Blenkinsop)*, Ewen Solon *(Haines)*, Reginald Beckwith *(Smithers)*, Bill Fraser, Michael Ward, Beatrice Varley, Tom Gill, Charles Hawtrey, David Hannaford, A. J. "Man Mountain " Dean, Jack Lambert, John Warren.

Sporadically funny comedy about a lad (Howerd) fired from a greyhound track after he's suspect in a doping scandal. After nursing a sick canine back to health, Howerd wins a big race and proves his innocence. He's helped out by the zany trio of Holloway, Matthews, and Hickson. Despite some slick direction, the story never rises above its relative simplicity.

p, Raymond Stross; d, John Paddy Carstairs; w, Jack Davies, Henry E. Blythe; ph, Jack Cox; m, Larry Adler; ed, John D. Guthridge.

Comedy **(PR:A MPAA:NR)**

JUMPING JACKS** (1952) 96m PAR bw

Dean Martin *(Chick Allen)*, Jerry Lewis *(Hap Smith)*, Mona Freeman *(Betty Carter)*, Don DeFore *(Kelsey)*, Robert Strauss *(Sgt. McCluskey)*, Ray Teal *(Gen. Timmons)*, Marcy McGuire *(Julia Loring)*, Danny Arnold *(Evans)*, Richard Erdman *(Dogface Dolan)*, Edwin Max *(Sam Gilmore)*, Alex Gerry *(Earl White)*, Charles Evans *(Gen. Bond)*.

Martin and Lewis succeed in bringing out the laughs as a couple of vaudevillians who perform for Army troops. The shows are close to being cancelled when Lewis is brought on the scene, disguised as a GI by singer-turned-soldier Martin. After the usual turn of events, the moronic Lewis ends up in maneuvers preparing to parachute into enemy territory. In top zany form, he pulls it off and accidentally captures an enemy general. Songs include: "Keep A Little Dream Handy," "Do The Parachute Jump," "I Can't Resist A Boy In A Uniform," "What Have You Done For Me Lately?," "I Know A Dream When I See One," "Big Blue Sky."

p, Hal B. Wallis; d, Norman Taurog; w, Robert Lees, Fred Rinaldo, Herbert Baker, James Allardice, Richard Weil (based on a story by Brian Marlow); ph, Daniel L. Fapp; ed, Stanley Johnson; art d, Hal Pereira, Henry Bumstead; m/l, Jerry Livingston, Mack David.

Comedy **(PR:A MPAA:NR)**

JUNCTION CITY* (1952) 54m COL bw

Charles Starrett *(Steve Rollins/Durango Kid)*, Lester "Smiley" Burnette *(Himself)*, Jack [Jock] Mahoney *(Himself)*, Kathleen Case *(Penny)*, John Dehner *(Emmett Sanderson)*, Steve Darrell *(Black Murphy)*, George Chesebro *(Sheriff Jeff Clinton)*, Anita Castle *(Penelope Clinton)*, Mary Newton *(Ella Sanderson)*, Robert Bice

(Bleaker), Hal Price *(Sheriff)*, Hal Taliaferro *(Sandy Clinton)*, Cris Alcaide *(Jarvis)*, Bob Woodward *(Keely)*, Frank Ellis, The Sunshine Boys.

A poor oater in which the hand of the screenwriter comes through clearly and is told unconvincingly in flashbacks. The tale involves a young beauty saved by the Durango Kid from the hands of wicked relatives trying to take over a gold mine. (See DURANGO KID series, Index).

p, Colbert Clark; d, Ray Nazarro; w, Barry Shipman; ph, Henry Freulich; ed, Paul Borofsky; md, Mischa Bakaleinikoff; art d, Charles Clague; set d, Frank Tuttle.

Western **(PR:A MPAA:NR)**

JUNE BRIDE*** (1948) 97m WB bw

Bette Davis *(Linda Gilman)*, Robert Montgomery *(Carey Jackson)*, Fay Bainter *(Paula Winthrop)*, Betty Lynn *(Boo Brinker)*, Tom Tully *(Mr. Brinker)*, Barbara Bates *(Jeanne Brinker)*, Jerome Cowan *(Carleton Towne)*, Mary Wickes *(Rosemary McNally)*, James Burke *(Luke Potter)*, Raymond Roe *(Bud Mitchell)*, Marjorie Bennett *(Mrs. Brinker)*, Ray Montgomery *(Jim Mitchell)*, George O'Hanlon *(Scott Davis)*, Sandra Gould *(Miss Rubens)*, Esther Howard *(Mrs. Mitchell)*, Jessie Adams *(Mrs. Lace)*, John Vosper *(Stafford)*, Jack Mower *(Varga)*, Lottie Williams *(Woody)*, Mary Stuart *(Plane Hostess)*, Ann Kimbell, Barbara Wittlinger *(Girls on Sleigh Ride)*, Raymond Bond *(Minister)*, Patricia Northrop, Alice Kelley, Debbie Reynolds *(Boo's Girl Friends)* .

Davis shed her usual histrionics to prove that she could play comedy with the best of them in this entertaining and satirical tale. She is one of those female editors at a slick women's magazine that features all the usual cliched articles. Montgomery is a foreign correspondent who returns from Europe and is given the job of working with Davis by publisher Cowan. A long time ago, Davis and Montgomery had been unofficially engaged and now he is employed as her aide, a position that nettles him. She thinks he's a chauvinist and reckons he won't last long at the job if she makes it tough on him so he is assigned to accompany her to Indiana where the magazine is doing a feature on a typical middle-America marriage, truly a boring task. Montgomery does his best to keep his sharp tongue in check as Davis' assistants, Bainter and Wickes, proceed to re-do the Indiana household into what they think will appeal to their readers. The lovely house is taken apart and put back together in a ghastly fashion, as is the mother of the bride, Bennett, who is transformed into a creature that bears no resemblance to the woman we first meet. Now trouble rears in Paradise. Lynn, the younger daughter of the family, loves the prospective bridegroom, Roe. At the same time, Bennett's older daughter, bride-to-be Bates, is really ga-ga over Roe's brother, Ray Montgomery. Once Robert Montgomery becomes aware of the potential mismatch, he talks Bates into running off with Ray Montgomery and goads Lynn into catching Roe. Davis is infuriated by his Yenta-like matching and orders him sacked because she now has no story for her June issue. However, she has second thoughts and realizes that this is an even better story. Davis returns to New York where Robert Montgomery is about to go abroad. She knows he'll have nothing to do with her if she stays at her job and she loves him dearly so she gives her resignation to Cowan and tells Montgomery that she wants to accompany him to Europe. He doesn't think she's sincere but she proves her point by picking up his suitcases and acting like a dutiful "little woman." This is a fast-moving comedy with some hilarious scenes. All of the actors snap off their lines with aplomb and now, decades later, the movie is undated in its dispute between feminism and chauvinism, although if made today, Montgomery would quit his job and stay home while she worked. Look for Debbie Reynolds in a tiny role as one of Lynn's girl friends.

p, Henry Blanke; d, Bretaigne Windust; w, Ranald MacDougall (based on the play "Feature for June" by Eileen Tighe, Graeme Lorimer); ph, Ted McCord; m, David Buttolph; ed, Owen Marks; md, Buttolph; art d, Anton Grot; set d, William Wallace; cos, Edith Head; spec eff, William McGann, H.D. Koenekamp; makeup, Perc Westmore.

Comedy **(PR:A MPAA:NR)**

JUNE MOON* (1931) 73m PAR bw

Jack Oakie *(Frederick Martin Stevens)*, Frances Dee *(Edna Baker)*, June MacCloy *(Eileen Fletcher)*, Ernest Wood *(Paul Sears)*, Harry Akst *(Maxie Schwartz)*, Sam Hardy *(Sam Hart)*, Wynne Gibson *(Lucille Sears)*, Ethel Sutherland *(Goldie)*, Frank Darien *(Window Cleaner)*, Harold Waldridge *(Young Goebel)*, Jean Bary *(Miss Rixey)* .

Oakie is a dumb oaf with ambitions of becoming a Tin Pan Alley lyricist. He meets the usual pitfalls along the way, but girl friend Dee helps her man out. The screenplay unwisely shifted this Kaufman-Lardner comedy from satire to romance and the result is disappointing. There's a few good laughs but the story is largely unrealistic. Oakie and his pals are unconvincing as street characters and direction misses more often than it hits. Besides the title tune, there's also the song "Montana Moon." Remade in 1937 as BLONDE TROUBLE.

d, A. Edward Sutherland; w, Keene Thompson, Joseph L. Mankiewicz, Vincent Lawrence (based on the play by Ring Lardner, George S. Kaufman); ph, Allan Siegler.

Comedy **(PR:A MPAA:NR)**

JUNGE LORD, DER (SEE: YOUNG LORD, THE, 1970)

JUNGE SCHRIE MORD, EIN (SEE: BOY CRIED MURDER, THE 1966)

JUNGE TORLESS, DER (SEE: YOUNG TORLESS, 1968)

JUNGLE, THE zero (1952) 74m Lippert bw

Rod Cameron *(Steve Bentley)*, Cesar Romero *(Rama Singh)*, Marie Windsor *(Princess Mari)*, Sulochana *(The Aunt)*, M.N. Nambiar *(Mahaji)*, David Abraham *(Prime Minister)*, Ramakrishna *(Young Boy)*, Chitra Devi *(The Dancer)*.

Cameron and gang make a trip to India where a local princess doesn't take kindly to their intentions of an elephant hunt. All hell breaks loose when it is discovered the jungle is full of woolly mammoths. They toss a few hand grenades and defeat the prehistoric Dumbos, but not before Cameron is killed saving Her Highness. The filmmakers would have been better off saving their money from the flight to India where this was filmed. Locale may look like the real thing, but the mammoths are merely elephants with some hair glued on. The film is awkwardly tinted in a sepia tone.

p&d, William Berke; w, Carroll Young, Orville Hampton; ph, Clyde De Vinna; m, Dakshinamoorthy, G. Ramanathan; ed, L. Balu; art d, A.J. Dominic, P.B. Krishnan; ch, Hiralai.

Adventure **(PR:AA MPAA:NR)**

JUNGLE ATTACK (SEE: CROSSWINDS, 1951)

JUNGLE BOOK****

(1942) 108m UA c (AKA: RUDYARD KIPLING'S JUNGLE BOOK)

Sabu *(Mowgli)*, Joseph Calleia *(Buldeo)*, John Qualen *(The Barber)*, Frank Puglia *(The Pundit)*, Rosemary De Camp *(Messua)*, Patricia O'Rourke *(Mahala)*, Ralph Byrd *(Durga)*, John Mather *(Rao)*, Faith Brook *(English Girl)*, Noble Johnson *(Sikh)*.

Rudyard Kipling wrote two Jungle Books while living in Vermont, where he had married an American woman. There were few writers who could excite young people's imaginations at the time and Kipling may have been the best of the lot. The loose adaptation by Stallings utilizes several incidents from both books and stars the diminutive Sabu as a young man who'd wandered away from his native village and been raised by a pack of wolves in a Romulus and Remus style (this was later used as the plot for THE WILD CHILD by Truffaut) until he returns to the home and meets his mother, DeCamp. Sabu has no idea of human language or customs. His father has been killed by a tiger, Shere Kahn, who terrorizes the area. Calleia is the narrator of the film, an aged villain, and his daughter, O'Rourke, is captivated by Sabu who quickly learns to speak and regales her with tales of the jungle and all of his animal pals. (Some similarities with TARZAN can also be drawn.) Sabu wants to find the tiger and wreak vengeance on the beast for having slain his father. He and O'Rourke trek into the jungle and discover the last vestiges of a lost civilization. The old ruins are filled with treasures and when O'Rourke returns to the village with a gold coin she's found, Calleia's villainy rears up and he wants Sabu to divulge the location of the treasure trove. Sabu refuses and thinks that the town should remain pristine and sacrosanct. Calleia convinces the other townspeople that Sabu is an infidel with ties to the Devil and the young lad is sentenced to be burned at the nearest convenient stake. But he escapes and is pursued into the jungle by a pack of gold-feverish rowdies. All of them die for their troubles, except Calleia, who lives on to tell us the tale. The photography by Garmes was dazzling and the animals seen are almost human. It was shot at Lake Sherwood, just outside Los Angeles, with much of the interiors done at General Service Studios (the same one that was later bought and lost by Francis Ford Coppola). Rozsa's score was brilliant and he even devised individual themes for each of the animals on screen. An enchanting film for viewers of all ages, JUNGLE BOOK received Oscar nominations for Garmes and Rozsa but failed to get any awards. It was later remade as a cartoon by Disney but it wasn't the same as the real live jungle denizens. The three Korda brothers were true professionals who had a no-nonsense attitude toward their work and turned out several gems before they retired. The sound track of JUNGLE BOOK was made as a record album (the first time that was ever done) with narration by Sabu. It was later re-recorded with Leo Genn narrating, but if you can get your ears on the original, it is a treat in the same genre as the Peter Ustinov "Peter And The Wolf" album. Sabu was a real elephant boy in Mysore, India, before being discovered by Robert Flaherty.

p, Alexander Korda; d, Zoltan Korda; w, Laurence Stallings (based on the books by Rudyard Kipling); ph, Lee Garmes (Technicolor); m, Miklos Rozsa; ed, William Hornbeck; prod d, Vincent Korda; spec eff, Lawrence Butler; set d, Jack Okey, J. MacMillan Johnson, Julia Heron.

Adventure **Cas.** **(PR:AAA MPAA:NR)**

JUNGLE BOOK, THE* ½** (1967) 78m Disney/BV c

Voices of: Phil Harris *(Baloo the Bear)*, Sebastian Cabot *(Bagheera the Panther)*, Louis Prima *(King Louie of the Apes)*, George Sanders *(Shere Khan the Tiger)*, Sterling Holloway *(Kaa the Snake)*, J. Pat O'Malley *(Col. Hathi the Elephant)*, Bruce Reitherman *(Mowgli the Man Cub)*, Verna Felton, Clint Howard *(Elephants)*, Chad Stuart Lord, Tim Hudson *(Vultures)*, John Abbott, Ben Wright *(Wolves)*, Darleen Carr *(The Girl)*.

A fine animated feature from the Disney camp based on the famous Rudyard Kipling story. Abandoned as a child Mowgli spends his youth raised by wolves, but is befriended by a panther who wants to return him to civilization. He takes the unenthusiastic Mowgli along for a while until realizing that the wolf-boy doesn't want to leave the jungle. Mowgli's happy-go-lucky trail leads to a meeting with a lazy bear; kidnapping by monkeys and their leader; and an encounter with a fire-fearing tiger. The finale has Mowgli notice a beautiful young girl near the edge of the forest. They fall in love and he forsakes his animal ways to be with her. The last animated film to be directly overseen by Walt Disney himself, it contained some of the studio's most vividly cinematic animation techniques. It also, for the first time, employed the voices of well-known personalities: Harris, Cabot, Prima, Sanders—a notion which disturbed adults far more than children. The film, however, went on to be one of Disney's most successful pictures. As the eighth largest grossing picture of 1968 ($11.5 million), it was nominated for Best Song Oscar ("The Bare Necessities" by Terry Gilkyson) and received positive critical acclaim from nearly all critics. Richard Schickel from *Life* magazine called it "the best thing of its kind since DUMBO." THE JUNGLE BOOK was released exactly 39 years after Disney's debut animated feature SNOW WHITE AND THE SEVEN DWARVES, and 10 months after the death of Disney. *Time* magazine said it was "the happiest possible way to remember Walt Disney." Also includes the tunes: "Trust In Me," "Colonel Hathi's March," "That's What Friends Are For," "My Own Home," "I Wanna Be Like You," "Kaa's Song" (Richard B. Sherman, Robert M. Sherman).

p, Walt Disney; d, Wolfgang Reitherman; w, Larry Clemmons, Ralph Wright, Ken Anderson, Vance Gerry (based on the "*Mowgli*" stories and *The Jungle Book* by Rudyard Kipling); m, George Bruns; ed, Tom Acosta, Norman Carlisle; anim d, Milt Kahl, Franklin Thomas, Oliver Johnson, Jr., John Lounsbery; layout d, Don Griffith; background d, Al Dempster.

Animated Feature (PR:AAA MPAA:NGR)

JUNGLE BRIDE* (1933) 53m MON bw

Anita Page *(Doris Evans)*, Charles Starrett *(Gordon Wayne)*, Kenneth Thomson *(John Franklin)*, Eddie Borden *(Eddie Stevens)*, Clarence Geldert *(Capt. Andersen)*, Gertrude Simpson, Jay Emmett.

Starrett is on the run after falsely being accused of murder. A newspaper man, with special legal credentials, is sent after the accused. The reporter brings his fiancee, Page, on board the ship Starrett's using in his flight. Normally a singing cowpoke, the hero gets in some guitar work before the ship is wrecked, and the trio must slug it out with jungle lions. Finally Page's jailed brother is proven the real murderer. The ending matches the film's confusing starting point as Starrett and Page marry, while the reporter is left by himself. Poorly written, with some unintentionally funny moments.

p, Arthur F. Beck; d, Harry O. Hoyt, Albert Kelly; w, Leah Baird; ph, Harry Jackson; m, Harry Stoddard, Marcy Klauber.

Crime/Adventure Cas. (PR:A MPAA:NR)

JUNGLE CAPTIVE** (1945) 63m UNIV bw (AKA: WILD JUNGLE CAPTIVE)

Otto Kruger *(Dr. Stendahl)*, Amelita Ward *(Ann Forrester)*, Phil Brown *(Don Young)*, Jerome Cowan *(Harrigan)*, Eddie Acuff *(Bill)*, Ernie Adams *(Jim)*, Charles Wagenheim *(Fred)*, Eddy Chandler *(Motorcycle Cop)*, Jack Overman *(Detective)*, Vicky Lane *(Paula the Ape Woman)*, Rondo Hatton *(Moloch)* .

This second sequel to CAPTIVE WILD WOMAN has Kruger performing mad scientist-type experiments on Ape Woman Lane in an attempt to revive her. Why? She's mean, hairy, and kills people. This simple motivation leads to standard murder and sadistic-science plot developments until Kruger's demise at the hands of the ape lady. Though cast had changed from the predecessors CAPTIVE WILD WOMAN and JUNGLE WOMAN, the plot held few variations. Good camp fun, with direction that tries its best in spite of material limitations.

p, Morgan B. Cox; d, Harold Young; w, M. Coates Webster, Dwight V. Babcock; ph, Maury Gertsman; ed, Fred R. Freitshans, Jr.; md, Paul Sawtell; art d, John B. Goodman, Robert Clatworthy.

Horror (PR:A MPAA:NR)

JUNGLE FIGHTERS

(SEE: LONG, AND THE SHORT, AND THE TALL, THE, 1962)

JUNGLE FLIGHT** (1947) 67m PAR bw

Robert Lowery *(Kelly Jordan)*, Ann Savage *(Laurey Roberts)*, Barton MacLane *(Case Hagin)*, Douglas Blackley *(Andy Melton)*, Douglas Fowley *(Tom Hammond)*, Curt Bois *(Tony)*, Duncan Renaldo *(Police Captain)*.

Lowery and Blackley are pilots who fly back and forth between Latin-American countries for a mining company. They get greedy and fill the plane to its gills, crash landing en route to the States. Blackley dies, but Lowery makes it back to the mine, taking Savage, the mine's cook, with him. When her rotten husband comes to take Savage back, Lowery fights the brute off, and keeps the girl. The story is helped along by its fast pace, and some good aerial photography.

p, William Pine, William Thomas; d, Peter Stewart; w, Whitman Chambers (based on a story by David Lang); ph, Jack Greenhalgh (aerial photography by Fred Jackman, Jr.); ed, Howard Smith; art d, E. Paul Sylos.

Adventure/Romance (PR:A MPAA:NR)

JUNGLE GENTS* ½ (1954) 64m AA bw

Leo Gorcey *(Terence Aloysius "Slip" Mahoney)*, Huntz Hall *(Horace Debussy "Sach" Jones)*, David Condon *(Chuck)*, Bennie Bartlett *(Butch)*, Bernard Gorcey *(Louie Dumbrowski)*, Patrick O'Moore *(Grimshaw)*, Rudolph Anders *(Dr. Goebel)*, Harry Cording *(Dan Shanks)*, Woody Strode *(Malaka)*, Laurette Luez *(Anatta)*, Jett Norman [Clint Walker] *(Tarzan)*, Joel Fluellen *(Rangori the Witch Doctor)*, Eric Snowden *(Trader Holmes)*, Murray Alper *(Fats Lomax)*, Emory Parnell *(Capt. Daly)*, Emil Sitka *(Painter on Boat)*, Roy Glenn, Sr. *(Omotowa)*, John Harmon *(Harmes)*, Pat Flaherty *(Officer Cady)*.

One of the least interesting Bowery Boys pictures has Gorcey and Hall traveling around in Africa. Hall thinks he is blessed after discovering the ability to smell diamonds. The boys believe they're going to strike it rich, when a group of natives also find a use for Hall's proboscis. Oddly, this episode has Hall, quite out of character, try to commit suicide—a rather unlikely and morbid action for the usually freewheeling buffoon. Director Bernds, along with screenwriter Ullman, went on to gain some cult fame as the men behind THE THREE STOOGES MEET HERCULES and THE THREE STOOGES IN ORBIT. (See BOWERY BOYS series, Index.)

p, Ben Schwalb; d, Edward Bernds; w, Elwood Ullman, Bernds; ph, Harry Neumann; ed, Sam Fields; md, Marlin Skiles; art d, David Milton; spec eff, Augie Lohman.

Comedy/Adventure (PR:AA MPAA:NR)

JUNGLE GODDESS* ½ (1948) 62m Lippert/Screen Guild bw

George Reeves *(Mike Patton)*, Wanda McKay *(Greta Vanderhorn)*, Armida *(Wanama)*, Ralph Byrd *(Bob Simpson)*, Smoki Whitfield *(Oolonga the Witch Doctor)*, Dolores Castle *(Yvonne)*, Rudy Robles *(Nugara)*, Linda Johnson *(Helen)*, Helena Grant *(Mrs. Fitzhugh)*, Fred Coby *(Pilot)*, Onest Conley *(Drummer)*, Zach Williams *(Chief M'Benga)*, Jack Carroll *(Accompanist)*.

A laughable work has Reeves and Byrd searching African jungles for a lost heiress. They find their woman, McKay, dressed in a leopardskin outfit employed as a native tribe's chief executioner. Byrd bites the dust, but Reeves and McKay manage to make it back to civilization. Byrd had just finished a stint as Dick Tracy in DICK TRACY'S DILEMMA and DICK TRACY MEETS GRUESOME. Reeves was readying himself to appear as TV's "Superman." Good for a chuckle or two with a sappy story and poor production values.

p, William Stephens; d, Lewis D. Collins; w, Joseph Pagnano; ph, Carl Berger; ed, Norman Cerf.

Adventure (PR:A MPAA:NR)

JUNGLE HEAT* (1957) 75m Bel-Air/UA bw

Lex Barker *(Dr. Jim Ransom)*, Mari Blanchard *(Ann McRae)*, Glenn Langan *(Roger McRae)*, James Westerfield *(Harvey Mathews)*, Rhodes Reason *(Maj. Richard Grey)*, Miyoko Sasaki *(Kimi-San Grey)*, Glenn Dixon *(Felix Agung)*, Bob Okazaki *(Kuji)*, Jerry Frank *(Corporal)*, Daniel Wong *(Kaem)*, Andrew Gross *(Folger)*, Yun Kui Chang *(Jules)*, Kunio Fudimura *(Freight Agent Attendant)*, Leo Ezell *(Expectant Mother)*.

Just before the attack on Pearl Harbor, troubleshooter Langan and Blanchard pay a visit to Kauai Island, Hawaii. He is sent to solve some problems among the sugar plantations and ends up wiping out the Japanese Fifth Column. It's been said that cliches are used so much because they work. Director Koch has succeeded in filling this picture with impotent cliches.

p, Aubrey Schenck; d, Howard W. Koch; w, Jameson Brewer; ph, William Margulies; m, Les Baxter; ed, John A. Bushelman.

Adventure Cas. (PR:A MPAA:NR)

JUNGLE ISLAND (SEE: WOLVES OF THE SEA, 1938)

JUNGLE JIM** (1948) 71m COL bw

Johnny Weissmuller *(Jungle Jim)*, Virginia Grey *(Hilary Parker)*, George Reeves *(Bruce Edwards)*, Lita Baron *(Zia)*, Rick Vallin *(Kolu)*, Holmes Herbert *(Commissioner Marsden)*, Tex Mooney *(Chief Devil Doctor)*.

Weissmuller found himself another niche as "Jungle Jim," after his parting with the more familiar Tarzan series, or, as one reviewer put it, he became "Tarzan in clothes." Based on a comic book character, this picture was the first of a string of successful Saturday matinee films. Weissmuller fights wild animals, sea serpents, and a witch doctor in an effort to get a special potion which can be used to fight infantile paralysis. Tarzan with a social conscience. (See JUNGLE JIM series, Index.)

p, Sam Katzman; d, William Berke; w, Carroll Young (based on the cartoon strip "Jungle Jim" created by A. Raymond); ph, Lester White; ed, Aaron Stell; md, Mischa Bakaleinikoff; art d, Paul Palmentola; set d, Sidney Clifford.

Adventure (PR:AAA MPAA:NR)

JUNGLE JIM IN THE FORBIDDEN LAND** (1952) 64m COL bw

Johnny Weissmuller *(Jungle Jim)*, Angela Greene *(Linda Roberts)*, Jean Willes *(Denise)*, Lester Matthews *(Commissioner Kingston)*, William Tannen *(Doc Edwards)*, George Eldredge *(Fred Lewis)*, Frederic Berest *(Zulu)*, Clem Erickson *(Giant Man)*, Irmgard H.H. Raschke *(Giant Woman)*, William Fawcett *(Old One)*, Frank Jacquet *(Quigley)*, Zamba the Chimp.

Anthropologist Greene and territory commissioner Matthews try to get Weissmuller to lead them to the land of the giant people. Weissmuller refuses but is eventually forced into the expedition where he and Zamba the talented chimp must tackle a hippo, a panther, and some angry giants. The film's jungle sequences are in Sepia toning.(See JUNGLE JIM Series, Index.)

p, Sam Katzman; d, Lew Landers; w, Samuel Newman (based on the comic strip "Jungle Jim" created by A. Raymond); ph, Fayte M. Brown; ed, Henry Batista; md, Mischa Bakaleinikoff; art d, Paul Palmentola.

Adventure (PR:AAA MPAA:NR)

JUNGLE MAN* (1941) 63m PRC bw

Buster Crabbe, Sheila Darcy, Charles Middleton, Vince Barnett, Weldon Heyburn, Robert Carson, Paul Scott, Hal Price, Floyd Shackleforth.

Crabbe braves the dangers of the jungle while perfecting a serum to fight a killer fever. Before the cure can reach the afflicted, however, the ship that is carrying it is sunk by a German U-Boat. It's up to Crabbe to dive down to the wreckage and resurface with the serum, saving the villagers and girl friend Darcy, who also has contracted the fever.

p, T.H. Richmond; d, Henry Fraser; w, Rita Douglas; ph, Mervyn Freeman; ed, Holbrook N. Todd.

Adventure (PR:A MPAA:NR)

JUNGLE MAN-EATERS** (1954) 67m COL bw

Johnny Weissmuller *(Jungle Jim)*, Karin Booth *(Bonnie)*, Richard Stapley *(Bernard)*, Bernard Hamilton *(Zuwaba)*, Lester Matthews *(Commissioner Kingston)*, Paul Thompson *(Zulu)*, Vince M. Townsend, Jr. *(Chief Boganda)*, Louise Franklin *(N'Gala)*, Gregory Gay *(Latour)*, Tamba the Chimp.

Jungle Jim heads into treacherous territory again to round up a gang of smugglers. When a diamond workers' strike is organized in the jungles, the world gem market teeters near disaster. Weissmuller and chimp Tamba this time find themselves battling lions, bulls, and a crocodile. Unlike other series entries, the natives here are more realistically portrayed by black actors rather than the series' usual Polynesians. (See JUNGLE JIM series, Index.)

p, Sam Katzman; d, Lee Sholem; w, Samuel Newman; (based on the "Jungle Jim" comic strip created by Alex Raymond); ph, Harry Freulich; ed, Gene Havlick; md, Mischa Bakaleinikoff; art d, Paul Palmentola.

Adventure **(PR:AAA MPAA:NR)**

JUNGLE MANHUNT** (1951) 66m COL bw

Johnny Weissmuller *(Jungle Jim)*, Bob Waterfield *(Bob Miller)*, Sheila Ryan *(Ann Lawrence)*, Rick Vallin *(Bono)*, Lyle Talbot *(Dr. Mitchell Heller)*, William P. Wilkerson *(Maklee Chief)*, Tamba the Chimp.

A Los Angeles photographer sets out to find football star Waterfield (a real-life pigskinner of the time) in the wilds of Africa. She finds Jungle Jim instead, who, amazingly, comes across the footballer with almost no effort (and no map). A plot involving synthetic diamonds (if that sounds familiar, see JUNGLE MAN-EATERS) adds a bit more intrigue as Weissmuller and the girl rescue Waterfield, who has a quarterback's knack for tossing grenades. Some pretty hokey dinosaurs give Jim and Tamba some tough times. (See JUNGLE JIM series, Index.)

p, Sam Katzman; d, Lew Landers; w, Samuel Newman (based on the comic strip "Jungle Jim" created by A. Raymond); ph, William Whitney; ed, Henry Batista; md, Mischa Bakaleinikoff; art d, Paul Palmentola.

Adventure **(PR:AAA MPAA:NR)**

JUNGLE MOON MEN** (1955) 69m COL bw

Johnny Weissmuller *(Himself)*, Jean Byron *(Ellen Marston)*, Helen Stanton *(Oma)*, Bill Henry *(Bob Prentice)*, Myron Healey *(Mark Santo)*, Billy Curtis *(Damu)*, Michael Granger *(Nolimo)*, Frank Sully *(Max)*, Benjamin F. Chapman, Jr. *(Marro)*, Kenneth L. Smith *(Link)*, Ed Hinton *(Regan)*.

High priestess Stanton succeeds where Ponce de Leon failed, living eternally while ruling over a tribe of moon-worshipping pygmies. Weissmuller (having decided to go with his own name instead of Jungle Jim) and a female writer pay a visit to Stanton's temple and find a kidnapped man serving as her high priest. (See JUNGLE JIM series, Index.)

p, Sam Katzman; d, Charles S. Gould; w, Dwight V. Babcock, Jo Pagano (based on a story by Pagano from a character in the "Jungle Jim" comic series created by A. Raymond); ph, Henry Freulich; ed, Henry Batista; md, Mischa Bakaleinikoff; art d, Paul Palmentola.

Adventure **(PR:AAA MPAA:NR)**

JUNGLE OF CHANG*
(1951) 67m Svensk Filmindustri/RKO bw (AKA: HANDFUL OF RICE)

Leonard Bucknall Eyre *(Commentator)*, Po Chai, Me Ying, Chang the Elephant.

Originally released in 1940 in Sweden as HANDFUL OF RICE, this docudrama about a pair of newlywed youngsters from Siam was repackaged by RKO for reasons that could only have amounted to the proverbial "quick buck." Its story of Po Chai and his wife trying to fend for themselves in the jungles, working as rice farmers, and taming elephants has little or no entertainment value, but on an anthropological level it is somewhat informative.

d, Paul Fejos, Gunnar Skoglund; ph, Gustaf Boge; m, Jules Sylvain, Gunnar Jonason.

Drama **(PR:A MPAA:NR)**

JUNGLE PATROL** 1/2 (1948) 71m FOX bw

Kristine Miller *(Jean)*, Arthur Franz *(Mace)*, Ross Ford *(Skipper)*, Tom Noonan *(Ham)*, Gene Reynolds *(Minor)*, Richard Jaeckel *(Dick)*, Mickey Knox *(Louie)*, Harry Lauter *(Derby)*, Bill Murphy *(Johnny)*, G. Pat Collins (Sgt. Hanley).

A gripping war story dealing with eight fliers stationed at a temporary airfield. Their mission is to hold Japanese forces until a permanent air base can be constructed. Between them they down nearly 100 enemy planes without suffering a loss. They begin to fear the thought of who will be the first to go. Visiting USO entertainer Miller finds the time to entertain the troops with the tune "Forever And Always" (Al Rinker).

p, Frank N. Seltzer; d, Joe Newman; w, Francis Swan (based on the play by William Bowers); ph, Mack Stengler; m, Emil Newman, Arthur Lange; ed, Bert Jordan; art d, Jerome Pycha, Jr.

War **(PR:A MPAA:NR)**

JUNGLE PRINCESS, THE** 1/2 (1936) 82m PAR bw

Dorothy Lamour *(Ulah)*, Ray Milland *(Christopher Powell)*, Akim Tamiroff *(Karen Neg)*, Lynne Overman *(Frank)*, Molly Lamont *(Ava)*, Ray Mala *(Melan)*, Hugh Buckler *(Col. Neville Lane)*, Sally Martin *(Ulah, as a Child)*, Robert Law *(Lin)*, Erville Alderson *(Priest)*, Bernard Siegel *(Ulah's Grandfather)*, Richard Terry *(Maley Hunter)*, Nick Shaid *(Headman of Tribe)*, Dan Crimmins *(Head Tribesman)*, John George, Bhogwan Singh, Eddie Sturges, James P. Spencer, Al Kikume, Kim Maki, Mickey Phillips, Inez Gomez, Mural Sharada, Emilia Diaz, Ray Roubert *(Natives)*, Limau the Tiger, Bogo the Chimp.

Lamour's film debut has her growing up in the jungle, a la Tarzan, along with a baby tiger. Time passes and she has become quite the wild woman, eventually falling in love with adventurer Milland. He spends time with Lamour in her jungle home, teaching the woman English and a little song as well. After some months Milland is rescued, though he has a fiancee to contend with on his return. Lamour delivers the tune "Moonlight And Shadows" (Frederick Hollander, Leo Robin).

p, E. Lloyd Sheldon; d, William Thiele; w, Cyril Hume, Gerald Geraghty, Gouverneur Morris (based on a story by Max Marcin); ph, Harry Fischbeck; ed, Ellsworth Hoagland; md, Boris Morros.

Adventure/Romance **(PR:A MPAA:NR)**

JUNGLE RAMPAGE (SEE: RAMPAGE, 1963)

JUNGLE SIREN** (1942) 68m PRC bw

Ann Corio, Buster Crabbe, Evelyn Wahl, Milton Kibbee, Paul Bryar, Arno Frey, Jess Brooks, Manart Kippen, James Adamson.

Evil Nazis are trying to goad jungle natives into revolting against the white population. Enter Crabbe and a companion, two Americans working with the French underground to combat the Germans and jungle denizens. The duo's quest is made all the easier thanks to the aid of Corio, a white woman who has been raised in the jungle. A simple-minded programmer with a bottom-of-the-barrel, anti-Nazi plot.

p, Sigmund Neufeld; d, Sam Newfield; w, George W. Sayre, Sam Robins (based on a story by Sayre, Milton Raison); ph, Jack Greenhalgh; ed, Holbrook N. Todd; m/l, Johnny Lang, Lew Porter.

Adventure **Cas.** **(PR:A MPAA:NR)**

JUNGLE STREET (SEE: JUNGLE STREET GIRLS, 1963, Brit).

JUNGLE STREET GIRLS* 1/2
(1963, Brit.) 89m Theatrecraft/Ajay-Manhattan bw (GB: JUNGLE STREET)

David McCallum *(Terry Collins)*, Kenneth Cope *(Johnny)*, Jill Ireland *(Sue)*, Brian Weske *(Joe Lucas)*, Vanda Hudson *(Lucy Bell)*, Edna Dore *(Mrs. Collins)*, Thomas Gallagher *(Collins)*, Howard Pays *(Sgt. Pelling)*, Joy Webster *(Rene)*, Martin Sterndale *(Inspector Bowden)*, John Chandos *(Jacko Fielding)*, Meier Tzelniker *(Mr. Rose)*, Larry Burns *(Barman)*, Fred Griffiths *(Dealer)*, Julie Shearing *(Cashier)*, Faye Craig *(Native Dancer)*, Anne Scott *(Margot)*, Gillian Watt *(Dancing Girl)*, Alfred Farrell *(Mr. Burns)*, Jacqueline Jones *(Dolly)*, William Wilde *(Sid Porter)*, Howard Douglas *(Old Bill)*, Richard McNeff *(Policeman)*, Marion Collins *(Announcer)*.

McCallum mugs an old man who subsequently dies. Weske finds out about the deed and blackmails McCallum, threatening to turn him in to the police. Cope agrees to help McCallum rob the safe at a night club, but McCallum doublecrosses him, taking off with the money and Cope's girl friend. As the police close in on McCallum, he kills a tailor, and then is nabbed as he attempts to flee.

p, Guido Coen; d, Charles Saunders; w, Alexander Dore (based on a story by Coen); ph, James Harvey; m, Harold Geller; ed, Peter Bezencenet; md, Geller; art d, Duncan Sutherland; m/l, "I'm Only A Girl," Geller, Perry Ford.

Crime **(PR:A MPAA:NR)**

JUNGLE TERROR (SEE: FIREBALL JUNGLE, 1968)

JUNGLE VIRGIN (SEE: JAWS OF THE JUNGLE, 1936)

JUNGLE WOMAN* (1944) 60m UNIV bw

Acquanetta *(Paula Dupree)*, Evelyn Ankers *(Beth Mason)*, J. Carroll Naish *(Dr. Carl Fletcher)*, Samuel S. Hinds *(Coroner)*, Lois Collier *(Joan Fletcher)*, Milburn Stone *(Fred Mason)*, Douglas Dumbrille *(District Attorney)*, Richard Davies *(Bob Whitney)*, Nana Bryant *(Miss Gray, Dr. Fletcher's Nurse)*, Pierre Watkin *(Dr. Meredith)*, Christian Rub *(George)*, Alec Craig *(Morgue Attendant)*, Edward M. Hyans, Jr. *(Willie)*, Richard Powers *(Joe, Fingerprint Man)*, John Carradine *(Dr. Walters—in Flashback)*.

Acquanetta stars as the alluring jungle woman who runs about in the wilds, sometimes in human form and on other occasions as an ape. When scientist Naish discovers her, he drugs her and carts the ape-lady back to his research center. While performing some tests, however, he administers an overdose and kills her. Naish is brought to trial for her death but is acquitted when the body appears as an ape's. The film is told in flashback as Naish gives his story to a jury. Footage from CAPTIVE WILD WOMAN, this story's predecessor, is incorporated, including some scenes with Carradine. A third film, JUNGLE CAPTIVE, followed.

p, Will Cowan; d, Reginald Le Borg; w, Henry Sucher, Bernard Schubert, Edward Dein (based on a story by Sucher); ph, Jack MacKenzie; ed, Ray Snyder; art d, John B. Goodman, Abraham Grossman.

Fantasy/Adventure/Crime **(PR:A MPAA:NR)**

JUNGLE WOMAN (SEE: NABONGA, 1944)

JUNIOR ARMY* 1/2 (1943) 70m COL bw

Freddie Bartholomew *(Freddie Hewlett)*, Billy Halop *(Jimmie Fletcher)*, Bobby Jordan *(Cowboy)*, Huntz Hall *(Bushy Thomas)*, Boyd Davis *(Maj. Carter)*, William Blees *(Cadet Capt. Rogers)*, Richard Noyes *(Cadet Sgt. Sable)*, Joseph Crehan *(Mr. Ferguson)*, Don Beddoe *(Saginaw Jake)*, Charles Lind *(Cadet Pell)*, Billy Lechner *(Cadet Baker)*, Peter Lawford *(Cadet Wilbur)*, Robert O. Davis *(Horner)*.

A thin and uninspired picture which has British kid Bartholomew playing his standard role. Bartholomew is living on his uncle's ranch trying to keep from getting dirty, when he saves the life of ex-Dead End Kid, Halop. Bartholomew's uncle wants to help. The boy rises to the ranks of the respectable, and is sent to the same military academy as young Freddie. Halop has trouble finding his niche but eventually fits in. Halop and his Dead End mates Hall and Jordan were all veteran juvenile delinquents from ANGELS WITH DIRTY FACES.

p, Colbert Clark; d, Lew Landers; w, Paul Gangelin (based on a story by Albert Bein); ph, Charles Schoenbaum; ed, Mel Thorsen.

Drama **(PR:AA MPAA:NR)**

JUNIOR BONNER*** (1972) 100m ABC/CINERAMA c

Steve McQueen *(Junior Bonner)*, Robert 'reston *(Ace Bonner)*, Ida Lupino *(Elvira Bonner)*, Ben Johnson *(Buck Roan)*, Joe Ion Baker *(Curly Bonner)*, Barbara Leigh *(Charmagne)*, Mary Murphy *(Ruth Bonne*, Bill McKinney *(Red Terwiliger)*, Sandra Deel *(Nurse Arlis)*, Donald "Red" Barr *(Homer Rutledge)*, Dub Taylor *(Del, Bartender)*, Charles Gray *(Burt)*, Matthw Peckinpah *(Tim Bonner)*, Sundown Spencer *(Nick Bonner)*, Rita Garrison *(Flhie Girl in Bar)*, Casey Tibbs, Rod Hart.

Peckinpah eschewed his usual violence in vor of a deeper story and the result was a critical success that didn't have the sae sort of box office receipts as his, or McQueen's, prior films. McQueen is a rod rider who returns to his small town and learns that nothing stays the same. His pants, Lupino and Preston, have split and Preston is currently dallying with nurse Dl. McQueen's brother, Baker, is a real estate developer married to Murphy ande two are not close as McQueen is his own man and Baker is a phony businessn, the type who shakes your hand and grabs your elbow at the same time. McKiry is one of McQueen's rivals and Leigh is the girl friend of sharpie Gray. McQueand Leigh have a brief encounter that winds up going nowhere. McQueen is saned to see that his home is now being developed by Baker into a real estate syntion. In between all the brief subplots, there's a barroom brawl, some fine rodeotage, and a few winning characterizations, such as Ben Johnson as the man wsupplies the livestock for the rodeo as well as Dub Taylor as the owner of the. There's much to recommend here, especially McQueen's performance as thowboy who realizes that he can't go home on the range again. The director's Matthew Peckinpah, is seen briefly as one of Baker's offspring. There are simies between this film and Peckinpah's RIDE THE HIGH COUNTRY (10 years er) and THE ELECTRIC HORSEMAN (seven years later) in that they all deal whe fish out of water, the anachronism of a man out of his time and searching foues that have since disappeared. The associate producer was Wizan's long-tiride, Mickey Boroksky, who accompanied Wizan through a series of studio jhat sometimes wound up with Wizan resigning, after having made too many flThis may have been that producer's best film. All production credits were excand Fielding's music was particularly suited to the action. In a small role, Donaed" Barry is outstanding. He'd been making westerns since 1936 and died t own hand in 1980, a great loss to anyone who enjoyed horse operas. Thend unit direction by Frank Kowalski was superb.

p, Joe Wizan; d, Sam Peckinpah; w, Jeb rook; ph, Lucien Ballard (Todd-AO, Movielab Color); m, Jerry Fielding; ed, RWolf; art d, Edward S. Haworth; set d, Angelo Graham, Jerry Wunderlich; ml Hart.

Rodeo Drama **C** **(PR:A-C MPAA:PG)**

JUNIOR MISS*** (1945) 94m FOX bw

Peggy Ann Garner *(Judy Graves)*, Allyn *(Harry Graves)*, Michael Dunne *(Uncle Willis)*, Faye Marlowe *(Ellen Cu*Mona Freeman *(Lois)*, Sylvia Field *(Grace Graves)*, Barbara Whiting *(Fuff*ley Prager *(Joe)*, John Alexander *(J.B. Curtis)*, Connie Gilchrist *(Hilda)*, Sckett *(Haskell Cummings, Jr.)*, Alan Edwards *(Haskell Cummings, Sr.)*, DoChristy *(Mrs. Cummings)*, William Frambes *(Merrill Feuerbach)*, Ray Kling*ald Parker)*, Mickey Titus *(Tommy Arbuckle)*, Mel Torme *(Sterling Brown*, Hudson *(Albert Kunody)*, Lillian Bronson *(Maid)*, Tommy Mack *(Sign Pa*illiam Henderson *(Barlow Adams)*, Howard Negley *(Doctor)*, Ruth Rickaby*idy)*, Ruby Dandridge *(Rheba)*.

Garner continues the clean-cut imagertrayed in A TREE GROWS IN BROOKLYN as a bubbly teenager who er family on their toes. The picture successfully captures what it was like grc in the 1940s. Garner humorously displays her naive excitement when sher first fur-collared coat and high heels, as well as when she marries off hto the daughter of her dad's boss. Silly but entertaining fare.

p, William Perlberg; d, George Seaton;on (based on the play by Jerome Chodorov, Joseph Fields from the storie Benson); ph, Charles Clarke; m, David Buttolph; ed, Robert Simpson; l Newman; art d, Lyle Wheeler, Mark-Lee Kirk; spec eff, Fred Sersen.

Comedy **(PR:AAA MPAA:NR)**

JUNIOR PROM** (1946) 69m MON bw

Freddie Stewart *(Freddie)*, June Preiss, Judy Clark *(Addie)*, Noel Neill *(Betty)*, Jackie Moran *(Jimmy)*, Franki*Roy)*, Warren Mills *(Lee)*, Murray Davis *(Tiny)*, Mira McKinney *(Mrs. R*oe Mitchell *(Miss Hinklefink)*, Milt Kibbee *(Professor Townley)*, Sam Flint*t)*, Charles Evans *(Uncle Daniel)*, Hank Henry *(Tony)*, Abe Lyman OrcheHeywood Orchestra, Harry "The Hipster" Gibson, The Airliners.

A group of teenagers is presented ackdrop of class elections in this mediocre effort to capture the effervesc1940s high school set. The junior class candidacy has a spoiled rich boy the post against some youngsters who just love to sing. It's all just an excur some more tunes. Included are: "Keep The Beat," "Teen Canteen" (STrimball For President" (Stanley Cowan), "My Heart Sings" (Jamblan Kld Rome), "Loch Lomond" and "It's Me Oh Lawd."

p, Sam Katzman; d, Arthur Dreifuss; wrus, Hal Collins; ph, Ira Morgan; ed, William Austin; md, Abe Lyman; ollins.

Musical **(PR:AA MPAA:NR)**

JUNKET 89** (1970, Brit.ur/Children's Film Foundation c

Stephen Brassett *(Junket)*, John Blun, Linda Robson *(Daisy)*, Mario Renzullo *(Boofles)*, Freddy Foote *(Burns)*, John Barrow *(Boston)*, Fanny Carby *(Mrs. Trowser-Legge)*, Gary Sobers *(Himself)*, Richard Wilson.

Children's adventure tale has Brassett as a schoolboy who transports himself to different lands by sticking chewing gum onto an invention of his teachers. Written and directed for a child's point of view, without slipping into sentimentality.

p, Carole K. Smith; d, Peter Plummer; w, David Ash; ph, Tony Imi (Eastmancolor).

Fantasy **(PR:AAA MPAA:NR)**

JUNKMAN, THE* (1982) 96m Halicki c

H.B. Halicki, Christopher Stone, Hoyt Axton, Susan Shaw, Lang Jeffries, George Barris, Lynda Day George, Freddy Cannon, The Belmonts.

This not-so-great orgy of auto crashes includes an array of banging, smashing, screeching and exploding vehicles. The interesting cast includes Barris, the man who supplies the stars with their cars. Don't strain yourself with the storyline.

p,d&w, H.B. Halicki; ph, Tony Syslo (DeLuxe Color); ed, Warner E. Leighton; prod d, Halicki; stunts, Tony Ostermeier.

Action **Cas.** **(PR:C-O MPAA:PG)**

JUNO AND THE PAYCOCK 1/2** (1930, Brit.) 99m BIP/Waldour bw (AKA: THE SHAME OF MARY BOYLE)

Sara Allgood *(Juno Boyle)*, Edward Chapman *(Capt. John "Paycock" Boyle)*, Sydney Morgan *(Joxer Daly)*, John Longden *(Chris Bentham)*, Kathleen O'Regan *(Mary Boyle)*, John Laurie *(Johnny Boyle)*, Donald Calthrop *(Needle Nugent)*, Maire O'Neill *(Maisie Madigan)*, Dave Morris *(Jerry Devine)*, Fred Schwartz *(Kelly)*, Dennis Wyndham *(Mobilizer)*, Barry Fitzgerald *(Orator)*.

A smash success as a stage play, JUNO AND THE PAYCOCK did not translate well to film, even under the sure hand of master filmmaker, Hitchcock. This was Hitchcock's second sound film, after MURDER (1930), but he could do little with it other than film the stage play by the venerable O'Casey. It's a poignant story about a lower class family that expects to inherit what is for them a great fortune. Some of the family members lose their heads completely in blue-skying a fortune that never comes and others remain level-headed and fatalistic. And there's much tragedy here, more than happiness or mirth. The daughter is about to give birth to an illegitimate child and the son is shot as an informer during the Dublin uprising. Allgood does a commendable if stoic job as the resolute mother, but Chapman is much too flamboyant as the Paycock, mugging his way through a role that requires as much introspection as exaggeration. Though well photographed, the action is incredibly slow for Hitchcock. He does make the most of that novelty of the era, sound, adding, whenever possible, squeaking floorboards, stomping feet, the noises of Irish tenement life which he captures well. Hitchcock was always uncomfortable with any theatrical productions not created by himself and his own hand-picked writers and this film was no exception, although he would later experiment with theatrical techniques in such films as UNDER CAPRICORN and ROPE. Hitchcock later stated that he used O'Casey as a role model for the man in the cafe who announces the end of the world in his terrifying film THE BIRDS.

p, John Maxwell; d, Alfred Hitchcock; w, Hitchcock, Alma Reville (based on the play by Sean O'Casey); ph, Jack Cox; ed, Emile de Ruelle; art d, Norman Arnold.

Drama **(PR:A MPAA:NR)**

JUPITER** (1952, Fr.) 90m Sirius bw

Georges Marchal *(Jupiter)*, Dany Robin *(Yvette)*, Jean Tissier *(Benjamin)*, Huguette Duflos *(Clemeance)*, Francois Guerin *(Gilbert)*.

An occasionally charming picture, suffering from too much talkiness, about a slightly daffy old man who spends all his free time digging for Roman ruins and one day finds a statue of Jupiter. This fact, coupled with an even wackier lunatic asylum escapee, makes for a few chuckles.

p, Raoul Ploquin; d, Gilles Grangien; w, Rene Wheeler (based on a play by Robert Boisey); ph, Marc Fossard; m, Georges Van Parys; ed, Madeleine Gug.

Comedy/Drama **(PR:A MPAA:NR)**

JUPITER'S DARLING* 1/2 (1955) 95m MGM c

Esther Williams *(Amytis)*, Howard Keel *(Hannibal)*, Marge Champion *(Meta)*, Gower Champion *(Varius)*, George Sanders *(Fabius Maximus)* Richard Haydn *(Horatio)*, William Demarest *(Mago)*, Norma Varden *(Fabia)*, Douglas Dumbrille *(Scipio)*, Henry Corden *(Carthalo)*, Michael Ansara *(Maharbal)*, Martha Wentworth *(Widow Titus)*, John Olszewski *(Principal Swimming Statue)*, Cris Alcaide *(Ballo)*, Tom Monroe *(Outrider)*, Bruno VeSota *(Bystander)*, Paul Maxey *(Lucullus)*, William Tannen *(Roman Courier)*, Alberto Morin *(Arrow Maker)*, Richard Hale *(Auctioneer)*, Frank Jacquet *(Senator)*, Paul Newlan *(Roman Captain)*, Jack Shea *(Drunken Guard)*, Mitchell Kowal *(Sentry)*, Frank Radcliffe *(Specialty)*, Mort Mills, Gene Roth, Michael Dugan *(Guards)*, The Swimming Cherubs.

An old melange of ingredients went into this adaptation of Robert Sherwood's play "Road To Rome." As you can see by the cast list, it concerns that matinee idol, Hannibal, and the various people who surrounded him on his trip over the Alps. It's a spoof of the famous trek (elephants included) with Williams taking to the water, the Champions taking to their dance shoes, and a few tunes tossed in for good measure. It was such a turkey that Williams, Sidney, and the Champions were all released from their MGM contracts after the picture sank. In essence, Williams has the job of turning Keel away from the Eternal City before he sacks it. Satire always requires the audience to understand exactly what is being satirized to make it funny. When one's frame of reference does not include the details of such an esoteric saga as Hannibal crossing the Alps, all humor is lost. It's as though someone wanted to spoof Bosch's "Garden Of Earthly Delights." If you had no idea who Bosch was, the humor would be lost. Songs included: "I Have A Dream," "If This Be Slav'ry," "I Never Trust A

Woman," "Hannibal's Victory March," "Don't Let This Night Get Away," "The Life Of An Elephant," (Music, Burton Lane; Lyrics, Harold Adamson), "Horatio's Narration" (Music, Saul Chaplin; Lyrics, George Wells, Adamson, Chaplin—sung by Richard Haydn). Good underwater photography and mucho money spent on production. Keel's voice is glorious and Williams swims like Mark Spitz, but the combination of a classic saga, comedy, fantasy, music, and swimming just doesn't hold water. It took almost 30 years for the play to go from the stage to the movies. They should have waited another 30 years. Good second barbarians in the cast (Demarest, Haydn, Corden, Dumbrille, et al) although they were hampered by the lame script and the even lamer conceit that this story would gather an audience. The Champions choregraphed the painted elephants to good advantage but there just wasn't enough content to sustain the brief 95-minute running time.

p, George Wells; d, George Sidney; w, Dorothy Kingsley (based on the play "Road to Rome" by Robert Sherwood); ph, Paul C. Vogel (CinemaScope, Eastmancolor); m, David Rose; ed, Ralph E. Winters; md, Saul Chaplin; cos, Helen Rose, Walter Plunkett; ch, Hermes Pan.

Musical/Comedy **(PR:A MPAA:NR)**

JURY OF ONE (SEE: VERDICT, THE, 1974, Fr./Ital.)

JURY OF THE JUNGLE (SEE: FURY OF THE JUNGLE, 1934)

JURY'S EVIDENCE*½ (1936, Brit.) 71m BL bw

Hartley Power *(Edgar Trent)*, Margaret Lockwood *(Betty Stanton)*, Nora Swinburne *(Mary Trent)*, Sebastian Shaw *(Philip)*, Jane Millican *(Agatha)*, Patrick Ludlow *(Cyril)*, Charles Paton *(Crowther)*, Eve Gray *(Ruby)*, Tracey Holmes *(John Stanton)*, W.E. Holloway *(The Judge)*, Dick Francis *(Hodson)*, Philip Strange *(Geoffrey)*, Aubrey Fitzgerald *(Murphy)*.

An interesting idea which suffers from some stilted performances and a hokey treatment. After viewing the evidence against a man on trial, a hung jury tries to convince the only holdout, Power, that the defendant is guilty. He won't give in and asks the jury to reconstruct the crime with him which finally uncovers the identity of the real murderer.

p, Herbert Smith; d, Ralph Ince; w, Ian Dalrymple (based on the play by Jack de Leon, Jack Celestin); ph, George Stretton, Harry Rose.

Crime Drama **(PR:A MPAA:NR)**

JURY'S SECRET, THE** (1938) 64m UNIV bw

Kent Taylor *(Walter Russell)*, Fay Wray *(Linda Ware)*, Larry Blake *(Bill Sheldon)*, Nan Grey *(Mary Norris)*, Samuel S. Hinds *(Brandon Williams)*, Halliwell Hobbes *(John the Butler)*, Granville Bates *(Judge Pendergast)*, Leonard Mudie *(District Attorney)*, Ted Osborne *(Reporter Thompson)*, Billy Wayne *(Reporter Baker)*, Robert Spencer *(Reporter Smith)*, Harry C. Bradley *(Jury Foreman)*, Edward Broadley *(William's Butler)*, Bert Roach *(Juror Hackenmier)*, Virginia Sale *(Miss Montague)*, John Miller *(Juror Simms)*, Lillian Elliott *(Mrs. Muller)*, Drew Demarest *(4th Reporter)*, Ferris Taylor *(Attorney Appleby)*, Dick Rush *(Bailiff)*, William B. Davidson *(Page)*, Jane Darwell, Fritz Leiber.

An interesting but highly implausible idea which has Taylor, a ghostwriter, serving on the jury for the murder trial of book publisher Hinds. It is Taylor, however, who is guilty of the crime committed. His conscience gets the better of him, and Taylor confesses to the crime.

p, Edmund Grainger; d, Ted Sloman [Edward Sloman]; w, Lester Cole, Newman A. Levy (based on the story by Cole); ph, Milton Krasner; ed, Phillip Cahn.

Crime **(PR:A MPAA:NR)**

JUST A BIG, SIMPLE GIRL*

(1949, Fr.) 100m Famous/UA bw (UNE GRANDE FILLE TONTE SIMPLE)

Madeleine Sologne *(Stepha)*, Jean Desailly *(Michel)*, Raymond Roulean *(Simon)*, Andree Clement *(Esther)*, Jacques Francois *(Mick)*, Gabrielle Dorziat *(Aunt Edmee)*.

A flat picture about romance among various actors in a stage play. Once the leads start carrying on, things get complicated, especially when another woman enters the scene, literally. Hard to follow and short on humor. (In French; English subtitles.)

d, Jacques Manuel; w, Andre Roussin; ph, M. Kruger; m, P. Capdevielle.

Comedy **(PR:A MPAA:NR)**

JUST A GIGOLO* (1931) 71m MGM bw

William Haines *(Lord Robert Brummell)*, Irene Purcell *(Roxana Hartley)*, C. Aubrey Smith *(Lord George Hampton)*, Charlotte Granville *(Lady Jane Hartley)*, Lilian Bond *(Lady Agatha Carol)*, Maria Alba *(Claudette, a French Wife)*, Albert Conti *(A French Husband)*, Raymond Milland *(Freddie)*, Lenore Bushman *(Gwenny)*, Gerald Fielding *(Tony)*, Yola d'Avril *(Pauline the Maid)*, George Davis *(Waiter)*, Henry Armetta *(Hotel Manager)*, Rolfe Sedan *(Headwaiter)*, Ann Dvorak *(Dance Extra)*, Leni Stengel.

Haines is a rich kid whose uncle is trying to arrange his marriage to keep him out of trouble with the femmes. He passes himself off as a gigolo just to keep all the gals from going after him for his cash. Purcell, however, is on to his game and, of course, she is the one he falls for. Confusing film, fraught with technical deficiencies. Haines doubled as the film's art director.

p&d, Jack Conway; w, Hans Kraly, Claudine West, Richard Schayer (based on the stage play "Dancing Partner" by Alexander Engel, Alfred Grunwald); ph, Oliver T. Marsh; ed, Frank Sullivan; art d, William Haines.

Comedy **(PR:A MPAA:NR)**

JUST A GIGOLO*** (1979, Ger.) 98m Leguan/UA c

David Bowie *(Paul)*, Sydne Rome *(Cilly)*, Kim Novak *(Helga)*, David Hemmings *(Capt. Kraft)*, Marlene Dietrich *(Baroness von Semering)*, Maria Schell *(Mutti)*, Curt Jurgens *(Prince)*, Erika Pluhar *(Eva)*, Rudolf Schundler *(Gustav)*, Hilde Weissner *(Aunt Hilda)*, Werner Pochath *(Otto)*, Bela Erny *(Von Lipzig)*, Friedhelm Lehmann *(Von Muller)*, Rainer Hunold *(Lothar)*, Evelyn Kunneke *(Frau Aeckerle)*, Karin Hardt *(Frau Uexkull)*, Gudrun Genest *(Frau von Putzdorf)*, Ursula Heyer *(Greta)*, Christiane Maybach *(Gilda)*, Martin Hirthe *(Director)*, Rene Kolidehoff *(Agent)*, Gunter Meisner *(Drunken Worker)*, Peter Schlesinger *(First Man in Bath)*.

Interesting, if only for its cast, is this tale of a Prussian WW I veteran who wanders around Berlin, eventually becoming a gigolo. David Bowie again proves that his talents are not limited to rock music in startling performance as the male whore. Rome is the luscious woman whose sexual prowess (of the same erotic sort as Polanski's WHAT!) is shot down by Bowie. David Hemmings, who also directed, manages to look even less photogenic this time out. If that is not enough, the cast also includes Marlene Dietrich and Kim Novak. Dietrich, a mere 53 years after her first film, appears briefly as a grande dame, and also sings the title tune. This entrancing and exciting moment alo[illegible] is worth struggling through hundreds of horrible films to discover. Novak turns a commanding portrayal of a lusty widow. But great casts do not a film make. Try hold out for the more coherent 147 minute version and take a pass on the limpi[illegible]98 minute one.

p, Rolf Thiele; d, David Hemmings; Joshua Sinclair, Ennio de Concini; ph, Charly Steinberger; m, Gunther Fischer[illegible]ed, Susan Jaeger, Fred Srp, Maxine Julius; art d, Peter Rothe; cos, Ingrid Zore; Herbert F. Schubert.

Drama **(PR:O MPAA:R)**

JUST ACROSS THE STREET*[illegible] (1952) 78m UNIV bw

Ann Sheridan *(Henrietta Smith)*, [illegible] Lund *(Fred Newcombe)*, Robert Keith *(Walter Medford)*, Cecil Kellaway [illegible]*p Smith)*, Harvey Lembeck *(Al)*, Alan Mowbray *(Davis)*, Natalie Schafer [illegible]*rtrude Medford)*, George Eldredge *(John Ballanger)*, Burt Mustin *(Ed Timens*[illegible]*llie Bird (Pearl)*, Jack Kruchen *(Character)*, Lou Lubin *(Man in Trouble)*, Herb[illegible]gran *(Liquor Salesman)*, Steve Roberts *(C. L.)*, Fritzi Dugan *(Woman in Hous*[illegible]eorge "Shorty" Chirello *(Flower Vendor)*, Miles Shepard, Wally Walker *(Cab*[illegible]*ers)*.

Slight romantic comedy has Sher[illegible] needing a job to support herself and her father. Plumber Lund hires her, mi[illegible]nly believing she is the daughter of the town banker, a misconception she e[illegible]ages. Everyday he drives her "home," dropping her off at the banker's h[illegible] though she lives across the street. A series of complications arise from the [illegible]otion, but eventually all is set straight as Sheridan and Lund fall in love. S[illegible]ipt yields few laughs.

p, Leonard Goldstein; d, Joseph[illegible]ey; w, Roswell Rogers, Joel Malone; ph, Maury Gertsman; ed, Virgil V[illegible]nd, Joseph Gershenson; art d, Bernard Herzbrun, Emrich Nicholson.

Comedy/Romance **(PR:A MPAA:NR)**

JUST AROUND THE CORN[illegible] (1938) 70m FOX bw

Shirley Temple *(Penny Hale)*, [illegible]es Farrell *(Jeff Hale)*, Joan Davis *(Kitty)*, Amanda Duff *(Lola)*, Bill Rob[illegible]*(Corp. Jones)*, Bert Lahr *(Gus)*, Franklin Pangborn *(Waters)*, Cora Withe[illegible] *(Aunt Julia Ramsby)*, Claude Gillingwater, Sr. *(Samuel G. Henshaw)*, B[illegible]artlett *(Milton Ramsby)*, Hal K. Dawson *(Reporter)*, Charles Williams *(Cameraman)*, Eddie Conrad *(French Tutor)*, Tony Hughes, Orville Cald[illegible]*venshaw's Assistants)*, Marilyn Knowlden *(Gwendolyn)*.

The first Temple film that was [illegible]ajor box office hit, this one has ten-year-old Shirley cast as the daughter o[illegible]ct Farrell. Wiped out by the depression, he goes from the penthouse to th[illegible]ent, figuratively and literally, as his financial troubles force him to move ou[illegible]osh top-floor apartment to take over as the building's maintenance man. [illegible]millionaire Gillingwater leases the vacant apartment and by film's end [illegible]has charmed him into coming up with the money to give Dad a second c[illegible]he plot line is even weaker than usual for a Temple vehicle, but sprightly [illegible]umbers keep things rolling. Davis and Lahr join Temple on "This Is a Ha[illegible] Ditty," and she also sings "I'm Not Myself Today," "I'll Be Lucky With Y[illegible] the title tune. She teams up with Robinson for a song and dance on "I Lo[illegible]k in the Rain," and he does a solo on "Brass Buttons and Epaulets." Songs [illegible]alter Bullock and Harold Spina. Good VCR fare—just fast forward to the[illegible]d skip the inane plotting.

p, Darryl F. Zanuck; d, Irving[illegible]gs; w, Ethel Hill, J. P. McEvoy, Darrell Ware (based on the novel *The Luc*[illegible]by Paul Gerard Smith); ph, Arthur Miller; m, Walter Bullock, Harold Spi[illegible]arvey Johnson; md, Louis Silvers; art d, Bernard Herzbrun, Boris Le[illegible]

Musical **(PR:AAA MPAA:NR)**

JUST BEFORE DAWN*[illegible] (1946) 65m COL bw

Warner Baxter *(Dr. Robert* [illegible]delle Roberts *(Claire Foster)*, Martin Kosleck *(Karl Ganss)*, Mona Barrie [illegible]*ravers)*, Marian Miller *(Casper)*, Charles D. Brown *(Inspector Burns)*, [illegible]nolds *(Jack Swain)*, Robert Barrat *(Clyde Travers)*, Milton Graff *(Alex*[illegible]*rd)*, Charles Lane *(Dr. Steiner)*, Charles Arnt *(Allan S. Tobin)*, Ted Hecht[illegible]*orcei)*, Peggy Converse *(Connie Day)*, Irene Tedrow *(Florence White)*, [illegible]kson *(Walter Cummings)*.

The seventh of 10 CRIME D[illegible]ms, JUST BEFORE DAWN had Baxter again on the trail of a murderous[illegible]ing him through the night, the doctor wraps up the mystery with his u[illegible]ing himself, his reputation as a psychiatrist, and the endangered Robe[illegible]IME DOCTOR series, Index).

p, Rudolph C. Flothow; [illegible]astle; w, Eric Taylor, Aubrey Wisberg; ph, Philip Tannura, Henry Fre[illegible]ight Caldwell; md, Mischa Bakaleinikoff; art d, Hans Radon.

Crime/Mystery **(PR:A MPAA:NR)**

JUST BEFORE DAWN* 1/2 (1980) 90m Juniper-Picturemedia/Oakland c

Chris Lemmon, Gregg Henry, Deborah Benson, George Kennedy, Mike Kellin, Ralph Seymour, John Hunsaker, Jamie Rose.

A group of teenagers ignore the wise words of forest ranger Kennedy and venture into the woods after dark—just as they weren't supposed to do. Their disobedience results in an encounter with a pair of mutant twins who stalk their victims and slice them with machetes. It's not as bad as it sounds, though the film offers nothing to differentiate it from a horde of others. Actor Chris Lemmon is the son of Jack Lemmon; George Kennedy and Jamie Rose have had their own TV series ("Blue Knight" & "Lady Blue", respectively), coincidentally, both cop shows.

p, David Sheldon, Doro Vlado Hreljanovic; d, Jeff Lieberman; w, Mark L. Arywitz, Gregg Irving (based on a story by Joseph Middleton); ph, J. King, D. King (Panavision); m, Brad Fiedel; art d, Craig Stearns, Randy Moore; spec makeup eff, Matthew Mungle, John Morello.

Horror **Cas.** **(PR:O MPAA:R)**

JUST BEFORE NIGHTFALL**

(1975, Fr./Ital.) 100m Boetie-COL-Cinegai/Libra c (JUSTE AVANT LA NUIT)

Stephane Audran *(Helen)*, Michel Bouquet *(Charles)*, Francois Perier *(Francois)*, Jean Carmet *(Jeannot)*, Dominique Zardi *(Prince)*, Henri Attal *(Cavanna)*, Paul Temps *(Bardin)*, Marina Ninchi *(Ginette)*, Clelia Matania *(Mme. Masson)*, Anna Douking *(Laura)*, Daniel Lecourtois *(Dorfmann)*, Celia *(Jacqueline)*, Pascal Gillot *(Auguste)*, Brigitte Perin *(Josephine)*, Marcel Gassouk *(Barman)*.

A surburban crime melodrama from French New Wave director Chabrol which opens as Parisian advertising man Bouquet strangles his mistress, the wife of his best friend, Perier. His guilt goes undetected by the police but he cannot live with his crime. He pitifully tells his wife, Audran, of his affair and the subsequent murder. She accepts the news with surprising calm, talking him out of turning himself in. He then confesses to Perier, who also accepts the news as if he were just told a weather report. Bouquet reveals that his relationship with Perier's wife was a sado-masochistic one, with his act of punishment being carried a bit too far. It is now his turn to be punished, but his confessions only bring solace. One evening (the nightfall of the title representing death) Bouquet quietly meets his death after taking an overdose of sleeping medicine that his wife has prepared. As interesting as the plot may seem, JUST BEFORE NIGHTFALL is more concerned with its poke at the middle class than with the characters or pacing. The result is an incredibly slow-moving picture, which is as ugly visually (the modernized, split-level, glassy house they live in is colored with putrid oranges and greens) as the film's psychological themes are. One wishes that Bouquet had strangled Perier, who designed the house, instead of his wife. (In French; English subtitles.)

p, Andre Genoves; d&w, Claude Chabrol (based on the novel *The Thin Line* by Edouard Atiyah); ph, Jean Rabier (Eastmancolor); m, Pierre Jansen; ed, Jacques Gaillard; art d, Guy Littaye.

Crime/Drama **(PR:A-C MPAA:PG)**

JUST FOR A SONG* 1/2

(1930, Brit.) 94m Gainsborough-Ideal/Sono-Art-World Wide bw/c

Lillian Davis *(Norma Wentworth)*, Roy Royston *(Jack)*, Constance Carpenter *(Jill)*, Cyril Ritchard *(Craddock)*, Nick Adams *(Agent)*, Syd Crossley *(Stage Manager)*, Dick Henderson, [Albert] Rebla, Mangan Tillerettes, Syd Seymour's Mad Hatters.

A minor musical about a boy-girl music hall team whose act nearly gets split in half by a jealous booking agent who wants the girl for himself. Photographed in black-and-white with a color sequence.

p, Michael Balcon; d&w, V. Gareth Gundrey (based on a story by Desmond Carter).

Musical **(PR:A MPAA:NR)**

JUST FOR FUN* (1963, Brit.) 84m COL bw

Mark Wynter *(Mark)*, Cherry Roland *(Cherry)*, Richard Vernon *(Prime Minister)*, Reginald Beckwith *(Opposition Leader)*, John Wood *(Official)*, Jeremy Lloyd *(Prime Minister's Son)*, Harry Fowler *(Interviewer)*, Edwin Richfield *(Man With Badge)*, Alan Freeman, David Jacobs, Jimmy Savile *(Disc Jockeys)*, Irene Handl *(Housewife)*, Hugh Lloyd *(Plumber)*, Dick Emery *(Jury Panel)*, Mario Fabrizi *(Diner)*, Ken Parry, Gary Hope, Douglas Ives, Ian Gray, John Martin, Jack Bentley, Frank Williams, Gordon Rollings, Bobby Vee, The Crickets, Freddy Cannon, Johnny Tillotson, Ketty Lester, Joe Brown and the Breakaways, Karl Denver, Kenny Lynch, Jet Harris, Tony Meehan, Cloda Rodgers, Louise Cordet, Lyn Cornell, The Tornados, The Springfields, The Spotnicks, Jimmy Powell, Brian Poole and the Tremeloes, Sounds Incorporated, The Vernon Girls.

Teens in England win the right to vote, so the two major political parties try hard to win this new voting block to their side. However, teens Wynter and Roland have other plans, and form their own party. They throw the election in their favor with the help of popular recording artists. Pre-Beatle movie that was one of the last in the teen-musical era. Songs and performers include: "Vote for Me" (Mark Wynter), "Sweet Boy" (Cloda Rodgers), "Let Her Go" (Joe Brown and the Breakaways), "All on a Warm Summer Day" (Ketty Lester), "I Gotta Get Up Early in the Morning" (Freddy Cannon), "Touch Me" (Bobby Vee), "Crazy Crazes" (Kenny Lynch), "Kisses Can Lie" (Lyn Cornell), "Keep On Dancin'" (Brian Poole and the Tremeloes), "Lyin' to You" (Karl Denver), "Which Way the Wind Blows" (Louise Cordet), "What's the Name of the Game" (Joe Brown and the Breakaways), "I'm Happy With You" (Wynter), "Sailing on a Little Boat" (The Springfields), "Monument" (Lynch), "Just Another Girl" (The Vernon Girls), "Doing the Hully Gully" (Tony Meehan, Jet Harris), "My Bonnie Lies Over the Ocean" (The Spotnicks), "Ups and Downs of Love" (Cannon), "Judy" (Johnny Tillotson), "The Night Has a Thousand Eyes" (Vee), "My Little Girl" (The Crickets), "Just for Fun" (Wynter, Roland).

p, Milton Subotsky; d, Gordon Flemyng; w, Subotsky; ph, Nicholas Roeg; ed, Raymond Poulton; md, Franklyn Boyd; art d, William Constable; cos, John Stevens; spec eff, Key Sinclair.

Musical **(PR:AA MPAA:NR)**

JUST FOR THE HELL OF IT zero (1968) 85m Argent/Unusual c

Rodney Bedell *(Doug)*, Ray Sager *(Dexter)*, Nancy Lee Noble *(Bitsy)*, Agi Gyenes *(Jeanne)*, Steve White *(Denny)*, Ralph Mullin *(Lummox)*, Larry Williams *(Cransy)*, A.V. Dreeson *(Lt. Sanders)*, A.V. Dreeson Sr. *(Police Chief)*, Geraldine Young, Toni Newsholme, Julia Ames, Andrea Barr *(Teenyboppers)*, John Shackleford, John Chaffin *(Policemen)*.

More mindless action from the king of sleazy filmmakers, Herschell Gordon Lewis. Sager, Noble, White, and Mullin are a gang that goes around starting trouble "just for the hell of it." When an old woman sees the hoodlums terrorizing a bunch of baseball-playing kids, she calls the police, but mistakenly identifies innocent bystander Bedell as the instigator. Bedell is locked up while the gang begins terrorizing his girl friend, Gyenes. Eventually the police sort the matter out, and White and Noble are killed while fleeing on a motorcycle. Nothing worthwhile here.

p&d, Herschell Gordon Lewis; ph, Roy Collodi (Eastmancolor); m, Larry Wellington; ed, Richard Brinkman; set d, Robert Enrietto; m/l, "Destruction Inc!," Robert Lewis, Sheldon Seymour (sung by Tary Rebenar).

Crime **(PR:O MPAA:NR)**

JUST FOR YOU 1/2** (1952) 95m PAR c

Bing Crosby *(Jordan Blake)*, Jane Wyman *(Carolina Hill)*, Ethel Barrymore *(Allida de Bronkhart)*, Robert Arthur *(Jerry Blake)*, Natalie Wood *(Barbara Blake)*, Cora Witherspoon *(Mrs. Angevine)*, Ben Lessy *(Georgie Polansky)*, Art Smith *(Leo)*, Regis Toomey *(Hodges)*, Leon Tyler *(David McKenzie)*, Willis Bouchey *(Hank Ross)*, Herbert Vigran *(George)*, Nancy Hale *(Guest)*, Franklyn Farnum *(Cook)*, Brick Sullivan *(Policeman)*, Buck Harrington *(Police Sergeant)*, Jack Mulhall *(Major)*, Max Keith *(Stage Manager)*, Robert S. Scott *(Lieutenant)*, Irene Martin *(Member of USO Troupe)*, Daniel Nagrin, Miriam Pandor, Florence Lessing *(Specialty Dancers)*, Bess Flowers, Mary Bayless *(Women)*.

Teaming up again after HERE COMES THE GROOM, a widower, Crosby, and Wyman play an engaged couple, the former a successful Broadway producer. Crosby spends too much time at rehearsals and not enough time with his kids, 18-year old Arthur and a 14-year old Wood. He takes them to a resort for a few days, but has trouble talking to them. In comes Wyman to save the day by explaining their father's devotion to the stage. Arthur, however, develops a crush for Wyman and writes her a love song, which is good enough for Bing to publish. Despondent over the unrequited love, Arthur joins the Air Force and Wood leaves the resort, too, to attend a posh finishing school. Crosby becomes concerned about his son's welfare and so joins a USO tour in the hopes of finding and being reunited with his son. All ends well when he locates his son, who has forgotten his adolescent crush on Wyman. Includes the songs: "Zing A Little Zong," "He's Just Crazy For Me," "The Live Oak Tree," "A Flight Of Fancy," "I'll Si-Si Ya In Bahia," "On The 10:10 (From Ten-Ten-Tennessee)," "Just for You" (Harry Warren, Leo Robin).

p, Pat Duggan; d, Elliott Nugent; w, Robert Carson (based on the work, "Famous" by Stephen Vincent Benet); ph, George Barnes (Technicolor); m, Harry Warren; ed, Doane Harrison; md, Emil Newman; art d, Hal Pereira, Roland Anderson; set d, Sam Comer, Rad Moyer; cos, Edith Head; ch, Helen Tamiris.

Musical/Comedy **(PR:A MPAA:NR)**

JUST GREAT (SEE: TOUT VA BIEN, 1973, Fr.)

JUST IMAGINE 1/2** (1930) 104m FOX bw

El Brendel *(Single O)*, Maureen O'Sullivan *(LN-18)*, John Garrick *(J-21)*, Marjorie White *(D-6)*, Frank Albertson *(RT-42)*, Hobart Bosworth *(Z-4)*, Kenneth Thomson *(MT-3)*, Wilfred Lucas *(X 10)*, Mischa Auer *(B-36)*, Sidney De Gray *(AK-44)*, Joseph Girard *(Commander)*, Joyzelle *(Loo Loo/Boo Boo)*, Ivan Linow *(Loko/Boko)*, Mary Lansing, Helen Mann, Mary Carr, Margaret La Marr, Janet De Vine, Kay Gordon, Marbeth Wright, Charles Alexander, Robert Keith, Clarence Simmons, Ed Rockwell, Don Prosser, Clarence Smith, J. Harold Reeves *(Chorus)*.

There's not much here in terms of story, but what this picture does have is worth the price of admission. Set in the future world of 1980 (!) it concerns government-approved marriages and Brendel's attempt to show that he is worthy enough to take the 19-year-old O'Sullivan as his wife. To prove his derring-do, he hops in a rocket and takes off for Mars, where everybody has a twin. The futuristic sets of Manhattan aren't so far off base, nor are the videophones, automatic doors, or test-tube babies. All the characters' names are numbers, and the costumes are so bizarre they would probably sell in some chic boutique. Add to all this an array of very bad songs and there is the potential for cult movie status. The songs include: "The Drinking Song," "The Romance of Elmer Stremmingway," "Never Never Wed," "There's Something About an Old-Fashioned Girl," "Mothers Ought to Tell Their Daughters," "I Am The Words, You Are The Melody," "Dance Of Victory," "Never Swat A Fly" (cut from the original 113m version).

p, Ray Henderson, B.G. De Sylva, Lew Brown; d, David Butler; ph, Ernest Palmer; w, Henderson, Butler, De Sylva, Brown; ph, Ernest Palmer; ed, Irene Morra; md, Arthur Kay; art d, Stephen Goosson, Ralph Hammeras; set d, Goosson, Hammeras; cos, Sophie Wachner, Dorothy Tree, Alice O'Neil; ch, Seymour Felix, m/l, De Sylva, Brown, Henderson.

Science Fiction/Musical **(PR:A MPAA:NR)**

JUST JOE* (1960, Brit.) 73m Parkside/Archway bw

Leslie Randall *(Joe)*, Joan Reynolds *(Sybil)*, Michael Shepley *(Fowler)*, Anna May Wong *(Peach Blossom)*, Jon Pertwee *(Prendergast)*, Howard Pays *(Rodney)*, Martin Wyldeck *(Bill)*, Bruce Seton *(Charlie)*, Betty Huntley Wright *(Miss Appleby)*.

An obscure British comedy which has a supposedly heroic chap fighting a blackmailer who wants the secret formula to a new detergent. One of Wong's final pictures (the more respectable PORTRAIT IN BLACK was released the same year) before her death in 1961.

p, Roger Proudlock; d, Maclean Rogers; w, Donald Bull; w, Raymond Drewe (based on a story by Donald Bull).

Comedy **(PR:A MPAA:NR)**

JUST LIKE A WOMAN** (1939, Brit.) 71m Alliance bw

Gertrude Michael *(Ann Heston)*, John Lodge *(Tony Walsh)*, David Burns *(Pedro)*, Jeanne de Casalis *(Poppy Mayne)*, Hartley Power *(Al)*, Arthur Wontner *(Escubar)*, Felix Aylmer *(Sir Robert Hummel)*, Henry Hewitt *(Simpson)*, Ralph Truman *(Maharajah)*, Fred Emney *(Sir Charles Devoir)*, Anthony Ireland *(Roderique)*.

Lodge is in pursuit of Michael, who has gotten her hands on a valuable string of black pearls. He rescues her from a gang of crooks, only to find out that she is the daughter of his jeweler boss.

p, Walter C. Mycroft; d, Paul Stein; w, Alec Coppel (based on the story by Paul Hervey Fox); ph, Claude Friese-Greene; ed, Flora Newton.

Comedy **(PR:A MPAA:NR)**

JUST LIKE A WOMAN** (1967, Brit.) 89m Dormar/Monarch c

Wendy Craig *(Scilla Alexander)*, Francis Matthews *(Lewis McKenzie)*, John Wood *(John Martin)*, Dennis Price *(Bathroom Salesman)*, Miriam Karlin *(Ellen Newman)*, Peter Jones *(Saul Alexander)*, Clive Dunn *(Graff Von Fischer)*, Ray Barrett *(Australian)*, Sheila Steafel *(Isolde)*, Aubrey Woods *(TV Floor Manager)*, Barry Fantoni *(Elijah Stark)*, Juliet Harmer *(Lewis's Girl Friend)*, Mark Murphy *(Singer)*, Michael Brennan *(Commissionaire)*, Angela Browne *(Scilla's Friend)*.

A vocalist for a weekly TV show run by her husband quits and walks off with another man. She moves in with the chap, who is really just a friend, and tries to begin life anew. She also attempts to derail any of her husband's plans to find a replacement singer for the show. After a party, which ends up in an orgy, and an attack by a drunken Australian who is fended off by her husband, they reunite.

p, Robert Kellett; d&w, Robert Fuest; ph, Billy Williams (Eastmancolor); m, Ken Napper, Kevin Sutton; ed, Jack Slade; art d, Brian Eatwell; cos, Caroline Mott.

Comedy **(PR:C MPAA:NR)**

JUST LIKE HEAVEN* (1930) 65m TIF bw

Anita Louise, David Newell, Yola D'Avril, Gaston Glass, Thomas Jefferson, Mathilde Comont, Albert Roccardi, Torben Meyer, Emil Chautard.

A romance between a Parisian balloon vendor and a ballet dancer with a traveling dog circus is the central idea in this incredibly boring picture. A duplicate of the silent film SEVENTH HEAVEN, this one could only be helped if it, too, were silent.

d, R. William Neill; w, Adele Buffington (based on her story); ph, Max DuPont; ed, Charles Hunt.

Comedy **(PR:A MPAA:NR)**

JUST ME*1/2 (1950, Fr.) 90m DIF bw (MA POMME; AKA: MY APPLE)

Maurice Chevalier *(Ma Pomme)*, Jean Wall *(M. Peuchat)*, Sophie Desmarets *(Mme. Peuchat)*, Jane Marken *(Mme. Deply)*, Vera Norman *(Claire)*, Jacques Baumer *(Dubuisson)*, Raymond Bussieres *(Fricotard)*, Felix Paquet *(Valentin)*, Dynam *(Jaques Turpin)*, Jean Hebey *(Le Patron)*.

Chevalier plays a happy-go-lucky hobo who inherits a large sum of money, which changes his life from rags to riches. But he learns that he must also become executor of the estate, a role he disdains. Unfortunately, the other two co-heirs, Wall and Marken, cannot claim their part of the inheritance unless Chevalier claims his. They set about changing his mind and, in the process, a fourth heir is discovered. She is Norman, who is greatly in need of the money. The film ends with Chevalier, disgusted at what he views as the wasted lives of the rich, setting up a rest camp for hoboes and returning to life on the road. Though Chevalier manages to convey some charm, he is ill at ease in his role as the bum. Clumsy direction and a poor script mar any hopes of this being a convincing farce.

p, Michel Safra, Andre Paulve; d&w, Marc-Gilbert Sauvajon; ph, Henri Alekan; ed, Roger Dwyre; set d, Jean D'Eaubonne; m/l, "Ma Pomme—The Hobo's Serenade," Jean Marion (sung by Chevalier).

Comedy **(PR:A MPAA:NR)**

JUST MY LUCK** (1933, Brit.) 77m British & Dominions/W&F bw

Ralph Lynn *(David Blake)*, Winifred Shotter *(Peggy Croft)*, Davy Burnaby *(Sir Charles Croft)*, Robertson Hare *(Trigg)*, Vera Pearce *(Lady Croft)*, Frederick Burtwell *(Stromboli)*, Phyllis Clare *(Babs)*.

Lynn is a middle-aged music teacher who tries to overcome his shyness by taking a "How To Succeed" course. Hotel owner Burnaby who also happens to be the father of his girl friend, Shotter, puts him in charge of the hotel. When the books do not seem to add up suspicion is cast upon Lynn, but he clears his name by catching his accountant in the act.

p, Herbert Wilcox; d, Jack Raymond; w, Ben Travers (based on the play "Fifty-Fifty" by H.F. Maltby); ph, F.A. Young.

Comedy **(PR:A MPAA:NR)**

JUST MY LUCK** (1957, Brit.) 86m RANK bw

Norman Wisdom *(Norman)*, Jill Dixon *(Anne)*, Leslie Phillips *(Hon. Richard Lumb)*, Delphi Lawrence *(Miss Daviot)*, Margaret Rutherford *(Mrs. Dooley)*, Edward Chapman *(Mr. Stoneway)*, Marjorie Rhodes *(Mrs. Hackett)*, Joan Sims *(Phoebe)*, Peter Copley *(Weaver)*, Michael Ward *(Cranley)*, Felix Felton *(Man In Cinema)*, Bill Fraser *(Powell)*, Sam Kydd *(Roberts)*, Beth Rogan, Marigold Russell *(Nurses)*, Campbell Cotts *(Lord Beale)*, Robin Bailey *(Sir George)*, Michael Brennan *(Masseur)*, Eddie Leslie *(Man In Hole)*, Ian Wilson *(2nd Man In Hole)*, Ballard Barkeley *(Starter At Goodwood)*, Vic Wise *(Eddie Diamond)*, Sabrina *(Herself)*, Frank Atkinson *(Green)*, James Bree *(Ford)*, Lynne Cole *(Usherette)*, Joan Ingram *(Theater Sister)*, John Warwick *(1st Ambulance Man)*, Leslie Davenport *(2nd Ambulance Man)*, Sylvia Childs *(Kathie)*, Eddie Dillon *(Teddy Boy)*, Stringer Davis *(Attendant)*, Marianne Stone *(Tea Bar Girl)*, Jill Clifford, Tom Naylor.

An entertaining British slapstick which features once-popular comedian Norman Wisdom, a dopey sort of chap you readily feel sorry for. When he tries to impress the girl of his meager dreams, he places a $2.80 bet on a six-race parlay, miraculously winning.

p, Hugh Stewart; d, John Paddy Carstairs; w, Alfred Shaughnessy, Peter Blackmore; ph, Jack Cox; m, Philip Green; ed, Roger Cherrill.

Comedy **(PR:A MPAA:NR)**

JUST OFF BROADWAY1/2** (1942) 66m FOX bw

Lloyd Nolan *(Michael Shayne)*, Marjorie Weaver *(Judy Taylor)*, Phil Silvers *(Roy Higgins)*, Janis Carter *(Lillian Hubbard)*, Richard Derr *(John Logan)*, Joan Valerie *(Rita Darling)*, Don Costello *(George Dolphin)*, Chester Clute *(Sperry)*, Francis Pierlot *(Arno)*, George Carleton *(Judge)*, Grant Richards *(District Attorney)*, Alexander Lockwood *(Count Telmachio)*, William Haade *(Watchman)*, Leyland Hodgson *(Butler)*, Oscar O'Shea *(Stage Doorman)*.

Private eye Nolan goes AWOL from jury duty when he discovers some discrepancies in the murder suspect's alibi. He and reporter-girl friend Weaver do some sleuthing and dig up two more murders to pin on the defendant, Derr. Nolan does 60 days in jail for his maneuver.

p, Sol M. Wurtzel; d, Herbert I. Leeds; w, Arnaud D'Usseau (based on an idea by Joe Elsinger from the character created by Brett Halliday); ph, Lucien Androit; ed, Louis Loeffler; md, Emil Newman; art d, Richard Day, Chester Gore.

Crime **(PR:A MPAA:NR)**

JUST ONCE MORE** (1963, Swed.) 78m Svensk/Janus bw (CHANS; AKA: JUST ONE MORE)

Lillevi Bergman *(Mari)*, Gosta Ekman, Jr. *(Stefan)*, Bertil Anderberg *(Natan)*, Eivor Landstrom *(Mari's Mother)*, Sture Ericson *(Mari's Father)*, Ake Fridell *(Uncle)*, Ake Lagergren *(The Poet)*, Torsten Wahlund *(Martin)*, Hans Wigren *(Money)*, Betty Tuven *(Female Supervisor)*, Nils Fritz *(Manager)*, Gudrun Brost *(Store Owner)*, Kotti Chave *(Policeman)*, Marianne Karlbeck *(Policewoman)*.

Bergman is a teenager who, after getting paroled from reform school, is sent to the country to work. Instead she returns to her native Stockholm to hang out with her gang member friends. After being rejected by her former boy friend, Wigren, she has numerous affairs and then starts seeing a drug dealer who is under police surveillance. When she returns to his place drunk one evening, the cops pick her up and return her to reform school for violating parole.

p, Gosta Ekman, Jr., David Norberg; d, Gunnar Hellstrom; w, Birgitta Stenberg; ph, Martin Bodin; m, Torbjorn Lundquist; set d, P.A. Lundgren.

Drama **(PR:O MPAA:NR)**

JUST ONE MORE (SEE: JUST ONCE MORE, 1963, Swed.)

JUST OUT OF REACH*1/2 (1979, Aus.) 62m Australian Film Commision c

Lorna Lesley *(Cath)*, Sam Neill *(Mike)*, Martin Vaughan *(Cath's Father)*, Judi Farr *(Cath's Mother)*, Ian Gilmour *(Steve)*, Jackie Dalton *(Cath's Sister)*, Lou Brown *(John)*.

Highly personal film about a teenage girl's (Lesley) struggle to move past a suicide attempt. Told frequently in flashbacks, the story shows events that lead up to the attempt, including an overbearing father, plus conflicts with her mother, sister, and boy friend, culminating in an impulse-marriage to Neill, an aspiring poet. Lesley becomes what she had hoped to escape, an echo of her loud and overbearing father, and the audience is left to wonder whether her problems are really environmental or self-inflicted. Perhaps a bit of both.

p, Ross Matthews; d&w, Linda Blagg; ph, Russell Boyd, Nixon Binney (Eastmancolor); m, Bill Motzig; ed, Ted Otton; art d, Grace Walker; spec eff, Bob McCarron.

Drama **(PR:C MPAA:NR)**

JUST SMITH (SEE: LEAVE IT TO SMITH, 1934)

JUST TELL ME WHAT YOU WANT** (1980) 112m WB c

Ali McGraw *(Bones Burton)*, Alan King *(Max Herschel)*, Myrna Loy *(Stella Liberti)*, Keenan Wynn *(Seymour Berger)*, Tony Roberts *(Mike Berger)*, Peter Weller *(Steven Routledge)*, Sara Truslow *(Cathy)*, Judy Kaye *(Baby)*, Dina Merrill *(Connie Herschel)*, Joseph Maher *(Dr. Coleson)*, John Walter Davis *(Stan)*, Annabel Lukins *(New Baby)*, Jeffrey Anderson-Gunter *(Teddy)*, Michael Gross *(Lothar)*, Joseph Leon *(Julie Raskin)*, Raymond Thorne *(Dr. Jowdy)*, Tom Batten *(Dr. Kierstein)*, Leslie Easterbrook *(Hospital Nurse)*, Paul E. Guskin *(Mark Gosse)*, Stanley Greene *(Bones' Lester)*, Lee H. Doyle *(Party Major Domo)*, Mike Howard *(Dr. Benecek)*, Paddy Croft, Margie Swearingen, Lacey Neuhaus, Phil Leto, Tony Munafo, David Rasche, John Gabriel, Ruth Holden, Paul Farentino, Bill Masi, Ron Millkie.

A good example of second-rate trash raised to the highest levels. Whatever possessed such luminaries as Lumet and Allen to spend their time on this is a mystery. King is a tycoon married to Merrill but he maintains relationships on the side, mostly with McGraw, a TV producer with whom he has dallied for a long time. Merrill is a lush and McGraw has a lover of her own besides King, Weller, a Sam Shepard-type playwright. Loy is King's long-time secretary and privy to all his business and personal complications. We've all met women like Loy's character, totally devoted to their bosses and the keeper of the keys when it comes to getting into the executive's sanctum. King is excellent as the rich and ruthless magnate who fears he is losing McGraw to Weller. There are several subplots including one concerning King's business enemy, Wynn, whose son, Roberts, is a gay executive at a film studio in California. This is essentially a New York story and anyone who is familiar with the New York mentality will have more fun with the film than those in hinterlands. The dialog is "adult" (read "racy") and that's what garners the "R" rating. Some funny scenes but most of it is one long and dizzy complaint on everyone's part. They should have called this 'The Daze of Whine and Roses." Loy is terrific, a veteran who makes the others seem to labor while she effortlessly tosses off whatever good lines came her way. Nurse Easterbrook is a musical comedy actress who didn't get an opportunity to show her stuff. A very funny comedienne with the right material. But the whole thing winds up to be one of those movies where audiences ask, "Why did they spend good money making this?" Still, it doesn't advertise itself as being anything else but what it is—bubble gum for the mind.

p, Jay Presson Allen, Sidney Lumet; d, Lumet; w, Allen (based on her novel); ph, Oswald Morris (Technicolor); m, Charles Strouse; ed, John J. Fitzstephens; prod d, Tony Walton; art d, John Jay Moore; cos, Walton, Gloria Gresham.

Comedy **Cas.** **(PR:C MPAA:R)**

JUST THIS ONCE½** (1952) 90m MGM bw

Janet Leigh *(Lucy Duncan)*, Peter Lawford *(Mark MacLene)*, Lewis Stone *(Judge Samuel Coulter)*, Marilyn Erskine *(Gertrude Crome)*, Richard Anderson *(Tom Winters)*, Douglas Fowley *(Frank Pirosh)*, Hanley Stafford *(Mr. Blackwell)*, Henry Slate *(Jeff Parma)*, Jerry Hausner *(Stanley Worth)*, Benny Rubin *(Herbert Engel)*, Charles Watts *(Adam Backwith)*.

Leigh is a lawyer who is hired to keep a watchful eye on the fortune of spendthrift millionaire Lawford, who has a penchant for extravagance. She soon tames him by canceling his charge accounts, putting him on a meager weekly allowance, and having him move in with her. This causes friction with her fiance, Anderson. Brightly and energetically directed by Weis.

p, Henry Berman; d, Don Weis; w, Sidney Sheldon (based on a story by Max Trell); ph, Ray June; m, David Rose; ed, Frederick Y. Smith; art d, Cedric Gibbons, James Basevi.

Comedy **(PR:A MPAA:NR)**

JUST TO BE LOVED (SEE: NEW LIFE STYLE, THE, 1970)

JUST WILLIAM** (1939, Brit.) 72m Associated British-Pathe bw

Dicky Lupino *(William Brown)*, Fred Emney *(Mr. Brown)*, Basil Radford *(Mr. Sidway)*, Amy Veness *(Mrs. Bott)*, Iris Hoey *(Mrs. Brown)*, Roddy McDowell *(Ginger)*, Norman Robinson *(Douglas)*, Peter Miles *(Henry)*, David Tree *(Marmaduke Bott)*, Jenny Laird *(Ethel Brown)*, Simon Lack *(Robert Brown)*, Aubrey Mather *(Fletcher)*, Eric Searle.

Lupino is the "William" of the title, a young ragamuffin who organizes his pals in an attempt to help his father get elected to the city council. The kids get themselves into trouble when they inadvertently help a couple of jewel thieves escape. They redeem themselves as they uncover an illegal plot by the opposing candidate and clinch the office for Lupino's dad. An 11-year-old McDowell makes one of his earliest appearances as one of the mischief-makers.

p, Walter C. Mycroft; d, Graham Cutts; w, Doreen Montgomery, Ireland Wood (based on the stories by Richmal Crompton); ph, Walter Harvey.

Comedy **(PR:AA MPAA:NR)**

JUST WILLIAM'S LUCK* (1948, Brit.) 91m Alliance/UA bw

William Graham *(William Brown)*, Garry Marsh *(Mr. Brown)*, Jane Welsh *(Mrs. Brown)*, Hugh Cross *(Robert Brown)*, Kathleen Stuart *(Ethel Brown)*, Leslie Bradley *(The Boss)*, A. E. Matthews *(The Tramp)*, Muriel Aked *(Emily, the Brown's Maid)*, Brian Roper *(Ginger)*, James Crabbe *(Douglas)*, Brian Weske *(Henry)*, Audrey Manning *(Violet Elizabeth)*, Hy Hazell *(Gloria Gail)*, Patricia Cutts *(Gloria's Secretary)*, Ivan Hyde *(Hubert Lane)*, Michael Balfour *(Jenks)*, John Powe *(Glazier)*, Joan Hickson *(Hubert's Mother)*, Anna Marie *(Masseur)*, Leslie Hazell, Peter Davis, John O'Hara *(Hubert's Gang)*, Michael Medwin, John Martel, Ivan Craig *(The Boss' Gang)*, Jumble *(Dog)*.

Graham plays a mischievous leader of a boys' gang, who pulls such pranks as stealing his sister's lipstick, breaking windows, and exchanging the shoe polish for shaving cream. In the final episode of the film, he regains his parents' approval when he aids police in capturing a band of thieves that inhabit a haunted house. "William" books were extremely popular in 1940s England.

p, David Coplan, James Carter; d&w, Val Guest (based on the stories by Richmal Crompton); ph, Leslie Rowson; m, Robert Farnon, ed, Ann Barker; art d, Andrew Mazzei, Harry Moore.

Comedy **(PR:A MPAA:NR)**

JUST YOU AND ME, KID* (1979) 93m COL c

George Burns *(Bill)*, Brooke Shields *(Kate)*, Burl Ives *(Max)*, Lorraine Gary *(Shirl)*, Nicolas Coster *(Harris)*, Keye Luke *(Dr. Device)*, Carl Ballantine *(Reinhoff the Remarkable)*, Leon Ames *(Manduke the Magnificent)*, Ray Bolger *(Tom)*, John Schuck *(Stan)*, Andrea Howard *(Sue)*, Christopher Knight *(Roy)*, William Russ *(Demesta)*, Robert Doran *(Box Boy)*.

An 83-year-old George Burns turns in another funny performance as an ex-vaudevillian who finds a naked Brooke Shields in the trunk of his car. It's then up to Burns to keep Shields, a runaway, hidden from the police and a dope pusher who's after her for burning him of $20,000. Gary plays his bitter daughter who is continually trying to have him committed for his generous allegiance to his old show business pals. Burns is as funny as ever. Unfortunately, the laughs are few and far between and Shields is awful, one of those who vie with Ali McGraw for the title of "world's worst actress."

p, Irving Fein, Jerome M. Zeitman; d, Leonard Stern; w, Oliver Hailey, Stern (based on a story by Tom Lazarus); ph, David Walsh; m, Jack Elliott; ed, John W. Holmes; prod d, Ron Hobbs; art d, Sig Tinglof; set d, Rick Simpson.

Comedy **(PR:C MPAA:PG)**

JUSTE AVANT LA NUIT (SEE: JUST BEFORE NIGHTFALL, 1975, Fr./Ital.)

JUSTICE CAIN (SEE: CAIN'S WAY, 1970)

JUSTICE FOR SALE (SEE: NIGHT COURT, 1932)

JUSTICE OF THE RANGE** (1935) 58m COL bw

Tim McCoy *(Tim Condon)*, Billie Seward *(Janet McLean)*, Ward Bond *(Bob Brennan)*, Guy Usher *(Hadley Graves)*, Edward LeSaint *(John McLean)*, Alan Sears, Jack Rockwell, Jack Rutherford, George Hayes, Bill Patton, Stanley Blystone, Earl Dwire, Dick Rush, J. Frank Glendon, Frank Ellis, Tom London, Bud Osborne, Dick Botiller.

McCoy is a cattle detective who gets hired by both sides in a feuding range war. He soon is accused of killing the ranch foreman, but is able to prove himself innocent. Some nice suspense and gunplay won't disappoint. Strong supporting performances include "Gabby" Hayes and Bond.

p, Irving Briskin; d, David Selman; w, Ford Beebe; ph, George Meehan; ed, Albert Clark.

Western **(PR:A MPAA:NR)**

JUSTICE TAKES A HOLIDAY* (1933) 63m Weeks/Mayfair bw

H.B. Warner, Huntley Gordon, Syd Saylor, Matty Kemp, Audrey Ferris, Robert Frazer, Patricia O'Brien.

A far-far-fetched tale about an adopted girl whose father is a convict, though there's evidence that proves him innocent. At the trial the old judge tells the man that he'd be glad to adopt the child while he's in prison. The con agrees and the girl grows up nicely in the judge's home. It comes out, however, that the judge is ignoring overwhelming evidence of the man's innocence, just to hang onto the girl. When dad breaks out he seeks revenge at the judge's place only to return to jail when he finds out how happy his daughter is. There's more sap in this 63 minutes of celluloid than a giant sequoia.

d, Spencer Gordon Bennett; w, John Thomas Neville (based on a story by Walter Anthony Merrill); ph, Jules Cronjager; ed, Byron Robinson.

Crime/Drama **(PR:A MPAA:NR)**

JUSTINE** (1969) 117m FOX c

Anouk Aimee *(Justine)*, Dirk Bogarde *(Pursewarden)*, Robert Forster *(Narouz)*, Anna Karina *(Melissa)*, Philippe Noiret *(Pombal)*, Michael York *(Darley)*, John Vernon *(Nessim)*, Jack Albertson *(Cohen)*, Cliff Gorman *(Toto)*, George Baker *(Mountolive)*, Elaine Church *(Liza)*, Michael Constantine *(Memlik Pasha)*, Marcel Dalio *(French Consul General)*, Michael Dunn *(Mnemjian)*, Barry Morse *(Maskelyne)*, Severn Darden *(Balthazar)*, Amapola Del Vando *(Mrs. Scrapamoun)*, Abraham Sofaer *(Proprietor)*, Peter Mamakos *(Kawwass)*, Stanley Waxman *(Serapamoun)*, DeAnn Mears *(Woman at Ball)*, Tutte Lemkow *(Prisoner)*.

Even if one had read Lawrence Durrell's *Alexandria Quartet*, which consisted of *Justine*, *Balthazar*, *Mountolive*, and *Clea*, this film would be difficult slogging. Screenwriter Marcus has attempted to meld them all into one cohesive story and it's marred by not enough motivation, sloppy writing and heavy direction from Cukor (who replaced Joe Strick just as the film began). Told in flashback with York as the narrator, JUSTINE is the story of Aimee, an Alexandrian Jewess, and her husband, a Christian millionaire played by Vernon. They are planning to send arms to Palestine so the Jews there can overcome the Moslems and thereby help the various Christian Arabs who fear the wrath of the Islamics. Interspersed are Aimee's various pals; Bogarde, a British official who has an incestuous affair with his sister, Church, who is blind; Forster, her obsessive brother-in-law; York, a schoolmaster from Ireland, and Gorman as a homosexual (something he also did in THE BOYS IN THE BAND before breaking out to do the stage play "Lenny"). York gets to Alexandria and takes up with Karina, a consumptive belly dancer from Greece who is the mistress of Albertson, a Jewish furrier who is a pal of Aimee's. Aimee has all of her friends involved in the cabal and she is worried that Karina may have told the truth to York so, to involve him, she gets York to be her lover. Karina is angered by Aimee's snatching away of York so she tells Bogarde of the arms deal. Bogarde is bowled over by the plot, tells his superior, Baker, then commits suicide. Aimee and her husband are immediately arrested but she captivates the head of security, Constantine, and it is presumed that she and Vernon will be spared. That's the basic story but there are many memorable scenes, including a brothel with preteen prostitutes and a fabulous carnival fete. Shot on location in Tunis, JUSTINE suffers from an attempt at too much crammed into the 116 minutes. It probably would have made a fine six-hour TV mini-series that could have explored all of the rich characters in Durrell's four books. As it stands, it's a stew that has been cooked so long and so densely that it's difficult to tell the meat from the potatoes.

p, Pandro S. Berman; d, George Cukor; w, Lawrence B. Marcus (based on the novels in "The Alexandria Quartet" by Lawrence Durrell); ph, Leon Shamroy (Panavision, DeLuxe Color); m, Jerry Goldsmith; ed, Rita Roland; art d, Jack Martin Smith, William Creber; set d, Walter M. Scott, Raphael Bretton; cos, Irene Sharaff; ch, Gemze de Lappe; makeup, Dan Striepeke, Ed Butterworth; tech adv, Aaron Haddad.

Drama **PR:C MPAA:R)**

JUSTINE**

(1969, Ital./Span.) 89m AIP c (AKA: MARQUIS DE SADE: JUSTINE)

Klaus Kinski *(The Marquis de Sade)*, Jack Palance, Mercedes McCambridge, Sylva Koscina, Maria Rohm, Akim Tamiroff.

One of the Marquis de Sade's most notorious works finally graces the screen. The story is stripped to its basics, with Palance using nude women for his macabre combinations of sex, black magic, and the Marquis' inspired practices of sadism. Kinski turns in a fairly good performance as the Marquis himself, but the film is mostly exploitive garbage. It's a shame no filmmaker looked at the Marquis' social, theistic, and political philosophies: De Sade's revolutionary ideas would almost certainly be more interesting (and less lurid) than his outrageous sexual descriptions.

d, Jesse Franco; w, Arpad De Riso, Erich Krohnke (based on the novel *Justine* by the Marquis de Sade).

Drama **(PR:O MPAA:NR)**

JUVENILE COURT** (1938) 60m COL bw

Paul Kelly *(Gary Franklin)*, Rita Hayworth *(Marcia Adams)*, Frankie Darro *(Stubby Adams)*, Hally Chester *(Lefty)*, Don Latorre *(Mickey)*, David Gorcey *(Pighead)*, Dick Selzer *(Ears)*, Allan Ramsey *(Davy)*, Charles Hart *(Squarehead)*, Howard Hickman *(Gov. Stanley)*, Joseph DeStefani *(Judge)*, John Tyrell *(Dutch Adams)*, Dick Curtis *(Detective)*, Kane Richmond *(Bradley)*, James Blaine, Lee Shumway, Edmund Cobb, Tom London, Harry Strang, George Chesebro, Eddie Hearn, *(Cops)*, Edward LeSaint *(Mr. Lambert)*, Lee Prather *(Mr. Allen)*, Gloria Blondell *(Gary's Secretary)*, Stanley Andrews *(Mayor)*, Harry Bailey, Steve Clark, Stanley Mack, Dan Wolheim *(Men)*, Cleo Ridgely, Dorothy Vernon, Eva McKenzie *(Women)*, Kernan Cripps, Charles Hamilton, Ethan Laidlaw *(Radio Cops)*, Al Herman *(Postman)*, Bud Osborne *(Driver)*, Lester Dorr *(Druggist)*, Harry Bernard *(Hick)*, Vernon Dent *(Schultz)*, Tina Marshall *(Davey's Mother)*, Jack Long *(Truck Driver)*, Buster Slaven *(Joe)*, George Billings *(Kid)*, Cy Schindell *(Referee)*, Helen Dixon *(Matron)*, Reggie Streeter, John Fitzgerald *(Boys)*, Bob Perry *(Bartender)*, Nick Copeland *(Drunk)*, Reginald Simpson, Sam Ash, Don Reed *(Reporters)*, Eddie Brian *(Box Office Boy)*, Ed Cecil *(Butler)*.

A conscientious public defender organizes a Police Athletic League which gives the street punks and guttersnipes an honest way to spend their days. When a couple of tough kids decide to stage a holdup, their senses take hold and they head back to the baseball diamond instead. A standard j.d. picture which was done much better by the Dead End Kids. Not to be confused with the 1932 Bette Davis and Pat O'Brien vehicle JUVENILE COURT, which also played as HELL'S HOUSE.

p, Ralph Cohn; d, D. Ross Lederman; w, Michael L. Simmons, Robert E. Kent, Henry Taylor; ph, Benjamin Kline; ed, Byron Robinson; md, Morris Stoloff; art d, Stephen Goosson.

Drama **(PR:A MPAA:NR)**

JUVENILE JUNGLE* 1/2 (1958) 69m Coronado/REP bw

Corey Allen *(Hal McQueen)*, Rebecca Welles *(Glory)*, Richard Bakalyan *(Tick Tack)*, Anne Whitfield *(Carolyn Elliot)*, Joe Di Reda *(Monte)*, Walter Coy *(John Elliot)*, Taggart Casey *(Lt. Milford)*, Hugh Lawrence *(Officer Ellis)*, Leon Tyler *(Usher)*, Harvey Grant *(Pete)*, Louise Arthur *(Mrs. Elliot)*.

Allen is a hip teen whose big ideas overshadow those of his average delinquent buddies. He concocts a plan to kidnap the daughter of a wealthy merchant and collect a $40,000 ransom. The problem is that he falls in love with the too-sexy-for-her-own-good Welles. When his cohorts realize what's happened, and they're not going to get the big bucks, they shoot poor Allen in the belly. Don't fret though, he'll live through it.

p, Sidney Picker; d, William Witney; w, Arthur T. Horman; ph, (Naturama); m, Gerald Roberts; ed, Joseph Harrison; art d, Ralph Oberg.

Crime/Drama **(PR:A MPAA:NR)**

JUVENTUD A LA IMTEMPERIE (SEE: UNSATISFIED, THE, 1964)

KADOYNG*** (1974, Brit.) 60m Shand-Children's Film Foundation

Teresa Codling, Adrian Hall, David Williams, Stephen Bone, Leo Maguire *(Alien)*, Bill Owen.

This light science fiction film has Maguire as an alien who befriends a group of children. Accepted as one of them, he helps in preventing a new highway from being built.

p, Roy Simpson; d, Ian Shand; w, Leo Maguire; ph, Mark McDonald.

Fantasy/Children (PR:AAA MPAA:NR)

KAGEMUSHA****

(1980, Jap.) 179m Toho-Kurosawa/FOX c (AKA: THE DOUBLE; THE SHADOW WARRIOR)

Tatsuya Nakadai *(Takeda Kagemusha)*, Tsutomu Yamazaki *(Katsuyori)*, Kenichi Hagiwara *(Son)*, Kota Yui *(Takemaru)*, Hideji Otaki *(Yamagata)*, Hideo Murata *(Baba)*, Daisuke Ryu *(Oda)*, Kaori Momoi *(Otsuyanokata)*.

For Akira Kurosawa's first film after a long period of inactivity, he returned to a samurai theme, a genre of which he was the unequivocal master. A warlord who likes to use doubles for himself on the battlefield is killed, leaving his current lookalike, a petty thief, to take over. Nakadai, in a powerful dual role, is prepared by assistants so the people's morale will not die. After an accident with a horse, Nakadai is exposed as a fake by a concubine and subsequently banished. But as a climactic battle takes place, Nakadai is unable to restrain himself, grabbing a flag and rushing into the thick of battle. He is shot, and stumbles to the lake where his predecessor has been laid to rest. He falls dead into the waters to silently float off. Kurosawa's epic is alive with color, and filled with some thought-provoking themes. The ideas of loyalties and roles are well explored, played out against a tapestry of political intrigue and war. Kurosawa's battle scenes rank with the best of his work, using color, light, and shadow amidst the enormous cast with great style. The film was co-winner of the Golden Palm at the Cannes Film Festival and opened the New York Film Festival in 1980. It was presented in America by George Lucas and Francis Ford Coppola. When asked what his favorite film between these two directors was, Kurosawa thought for a moment, then replied "STAR WARS." (In Japanese; English subtitles.)

p, Akira Kurosawa, Masato Ide; d, Kurosawa; w, Kurosawa, Ide; ph, Takao Saito, Shoji Ueda, Kazuo Miyagawa, Asaichi Nakai (Panavision, Eastmancolor); m, Shinichiro Ikebe; art d, Yoshiro Muraki.

Drama Cas. (PR:C MPAA:PG)

KAGI (SEE: ODD OBSESSION, 1961)

KAIDAN (SEE: KWAIDAN, 1965, Jap.)

KAIJU DAISENSO (SEE: MONSTER ZERO, 1970, Jap.)

KAIJU SOSHINGEKI (SEE: DESTROY ALL MONSTERS, 1969, Jap.)

KAITEI GUNKA (SEE: ATRAGON, THE FLYING SUPERSUB, 1965, Jap.)

KAJA, UBIT CU TE (SEE: KAYA I'LL KILL YOU, 1969, Jap.)

KAJIKKO (SEE: ANGRY ISLAND, 1960, Jap.)

KALEIDOSCOPE** (1966, Brit.) 102m Winkast/WB c

Warren Beatty *(Barney Lincoln)*, Susannah York *(Angel McGinnis)*, Clive Revill *(Inspector "Manny" McGinnis)*, Eric Porter *(Harry Dominion)*, Murray Melvin *(Aimes)*, George Sewell *(Billy)*, Stanley Meadows *(Dominion Captain)*, John Junkin *(Dominion Porter)*, Larry Taylor *(Dominion Chauffeur)*, Yootha Joyce *(Museum Receptionist)*, Jane Birkin *(Exquisite Thing)*, George Murcell *(Johnny)*, Anthony Newlands *(Leeds)*, Peter Blythe, Sean Lynch, John Bennett, Michael Balfour, Jose Sukhum Boonlive.

An entertaining bit of flummery with the standard caper mentality, some witty lines, and lots of gorgeous photography. Beatty is not one of the best when it comes to delivering punch lines and his role is weak because of that. Putting him and York in the company of such accomplished farceurs as Revill and Porter only points up their lack of ability in that light comedy department. Beatty plays a character not unlike the real-life image he gives off—a playboy with lots of money who goes from thrill to thrill, just for the sheer enjoyment of it. He has a fling with York, a Mary Quant-type designer of mod clothes for the swinging 1960s Carnaby Street crowd. Next, he flies to Geneva where he breaks into the pasteboard factory and secretly marks all the cards that will be used at Europe's top gambling dens. Then he makes the rounds of the casinos and wins a fortune playing with the cards he's altered. York suspects something is awry and tattles to her dad, Revill, a Scotland Yard man (just one of many bits of coincidence that mar the film). Revill won't arrest Beatty if he agrees to help nab Porter, a notorious drug dealer. Porter is angry, nabs York, and uses her to get Beatty out to his estate where he wants to recover all the money he's lost. The couple attempt to flee, are almost done in by Porter and his thugs, but are saved when Revill and his Yardmen arrive. The picture was long on plot and short on characterization. Nice to look at but not to listen to, KALEIDOSCOPE was one of several flops Beatty made before having his phenomenal success with BONNIE AND CLYDE. Until that time, he'd been associated with more turkeys than a poultry farmer. The associate producer was Peter Medak who later directed THE RULING CLASS with Peter O'Toole.

p, Elliott Kastner, Jerry Gershwin; d, Jack Smight; w, Robert Carrington, Jane-Howard Carrington; ph, Christopher Challis (Technicolor); m, Stanley Myers; ed, John Jympson; md, Myers; art d, Maurice Carter; set d, David Ffolkes; cos, Sally Tuffin, Marion Foale; makeup, W.T. Partleton, Bob Lawrence.

Crime/Comedy (PR:A-C MPAA:NR)

KAMIGAMI NO FUKAKI YOKUBO

(SEE: KURAGEJIMA—LEGENDS FROM A SOUTHERN ISLAND, 1970, Jap.)

KAMIKAZE '89** (1983, Ger.) 106m Trio-Oase c

Rainer Werner Fassbinder *(Police Lieutenant Jansen)*, Gunther Kaufmann *(Anton)*, Boy Gobert *(Blue Panther)*, Arnold Marquis *(Police Chief)*, Richy Muller *(Nephew)*, Nicole Heesters *(Barbara)*, Brigitte Mira *(Personnel Director)*, Jorg Holm *(Vice President)*, Hans Wyprachtiger *(Zerling)*, Petra Jokisch *(Elena Farr)*, Ute Fitz-Koska *(Police Doctor)*, Frank Ripploh *(Gangster)*, Hans-Eckardt Eckardt *(Policeman)*, Christoph Baumann *(Plainclothesman)*, Juliane Lorenz *(Nurse)*, Christel Harthaus *(Policewoman)*, Franco Nero *(Weiss)*.

Futurist intrigue with Fassbinder as a police lieutenant searching for a bomb in a high-tech world. The mishmash of styles in the film detracts from its overall effectiveness, though the settings and music by Tangerine Dream create a cold atmosphere. The last screen appearance of Fassbinder before his death.

p, Regina Ziegler; d, Wolf Gremm; w, Robert Katz, Gremm (based on the novel *Murder on the 31st Floor* by Per Wahloo and Maj Sowall); ph, Xaver Schwarzenberger; m, Edgar Froese; ed, Thorsten Nater; set d, Furcht, Mabille; cos & makeup, Barbara Naujok, Ursula Sonntag.

Fantasy/Drama Cas. (PR:O MPAA:NR)

KAMOURASKA 1/2**

(1973, Can./Fr.) 120m France Film-Carle-Lamy-Parc-SDICC/New Line c

Genevieve Bujold *(Elisabeth)*, Richard Jordan *(Nelson)*, Philippe Leotard *(Antoine)*, Marcel Cuvilier *(Jerome)*, Suzie Baillargeon *(Aurelie)*, Huguette Oligny *(Mme. d'Aulinieres)*, Janine Sutto *(Aunt Adelaide)*, Olivette Thibault *(Aunt Gertrude)*, Marie Fresnieres *(Aunt Angelique)*, Camille Bernard *(Mme. Rassy)*, Colette Courtois *(Florida)*, Gigi Duckett *(Anne-Marie)*, Len Watt *(Governor)*, Andre Cailloux *(Ernest)*.

An interesting but not entirely successful story which revels in the juxtaposition of time through flashbacks and flashforwards (as well as a combination of the two). The coquettish Bujold is the one doing the reminiscing as a 45-year old dame (what a sin it is to cover that face with makeup) sitting bedside with her dying hubby. She thinks about her first husband, whom she plotted to kill with her new, more passionate love (the dying second husband). The title comes from the small village where their chance meeting occurred, followed by their treacherous plotting. (In French; English subtitles.)

d, Claude Jutra; w, Anne Herbert, Jutra (based on the novel by Herbert); ph, Michel Brault (Eastmancolor); m, Maurice LeRoux; ed, Renee Lichtig, Francois London, Madeline Guerin, Suzan Kay; art d, Francois Barbeau.

Drama (PR:O MPAA:R)

KANAL* 1/2**

(1961, Pol.) 96m Film Polski/M.J.P.-Kingsley-International bw (AKA: THEY LOVED LIFE)

Teresa Izewska *(Daisy Stokrotka)*, Tadeusz Janczar *(Cpl. Korab)*, Wienczyslaw Glinski *(Lt. Zadra)*, Tadeusz Gwiazdowski *(Sgt. Kula)*, Stanislaw Mikulski *(The Slim [Smukly])*, Wladyslaw Sheybal *(Composer)*, Emil Karewicz *(The Wise [Madry])*, Teresa Berezowska *(Halinka)*, Adam Pawlikowski *(German Officer)*, Zofia Lindorf, Students of the Lodz Film School.

During the Nazi invasion of Poland, a group of patriots is forced to hide in the shelter of a bombed-out hotel. Eventually the group is led into the sewers, where the members must split off on separate paths, each to meet a tragic end.

p, Stanislaw Adler; d, Andrej Wajda; w, Jerzy Stefan Stawinski (based on his short story), ph, Jerzy Lipman; m, Jan Krenz; ed, Halina Nawrocka; art d, Roman Mann; cos, Jerzy Szeski.

War Drama (PR:C MPAA:NR)

KANCHENJUNGHA*** (1966, India) 102m N.C.A./Harrison c

Chhabi Biswas *(Indranath Choudhuri)*, Karuni Bannerjee *(Labanya)*, Anil Chatterjee *(Anil)*, Nilima Roy Chowdhury *(Monisha)*, Anubhe Gupta *(Anima)*, Subrata Sen Sharma *(Shankar)*, Arun Mukherjee *(Ashoke)*, N. Viswanathan *(Bannerjee)*, Pahari Sanyal *(Jagadish)*, Indrani Singh *(Tuklu)*, Vidya Singh *(Shibsankar Roy)*.

Wealthy industrialist Biswas and his family vacation in Darjeeling. The family problems are brought into the open, with an attempt made at solving them. Evident throughout is the conflict between the old and the young, ancient customs and modern life.

p,d&w, Satyajit Ray; ph, Subrata Mitra (Eastmancolor); ed, Dulal Dutta; m, Ray; art d, Bansi Chandragupta.

Drama (PR:A MPAA:NR)

KANGAROO 1/2** (1952) 84m FOX c

Maureen O'Hara *(Dell McGuire)*, Peter Lawford *(Richard Connor)*, Finlay Currie *(Michael McGuire)*, Richard Boone *(Gamble)*, Chips Rafferty *(Trooper Leonard)*, Letty Craydon *(Kathleen)*, Charles Tingwell *(Matt)*, Ron Whelan *(Fenner)*, John Fegan *(Burke)*, Guy Doleman *(Pleader)*, Reg Collins *(Ship's Officer)*, Clyde Combo

(Aborigine Stockman), Henry Murdock *(Black Tracker)*, Sid Chambers, Joe Tomal, Archie Hull, James Doogue, Bill Bray, Ossie Wenban, Alex Cann, Kleber Claux *(Sailors)*, Larry Crowhurst *(Cockatoo at Door)*, Dennis Glenny *(Well-Dressed Cockatoo)*, Stan Tolhurst *(Policeman)*, John Clark *(Ferret Face)*, Frank Catchlove *(Publican)*, Eve Abdullah *(Woman Servant)*, Frank Ransom *(Burton-Station Foreman)*, Douglas Ramsey *(Kelly-Station Foreman)*, Alan Bardsley *(Cook on Cattle Drive)*.

Gorgeous Technicolor photography of stunning Australian locations can't hide the shortcomings of this unusual western which stars Lawford and Boone as two desperate crooks trying to swindle cattle rancher Currie out of some cash. After a botched robbery in Sydney, the pair happen upon Currie's ranch and the evil Boone decides to convince the old man and his daughter O'Hara that the good-hearted Lawford is in fact the rancher's long lost son. To be even more convincing, Boone and Lawford help the father and daughter on a cattle drive from the outback to the watering hole. Many challenges are met (brush fire, stampede, dust storms), but finally a mounted policeman, Rafferty, catches up with the would-be robbers and the jig is up. In a gunfight with the law, Boone is killed and Lawford is wounded, but the authorities promise O'Hara they'll go easy on the younger bandit because he gave up and confessed. Aside from the Australian locations the script is fairly standard western fare that has been done to death in countless B oaters. O'Hara is as beautiful as Boone is delightfully evil, but fans of director Milestone are bound to be a bit disappointed.

p, Robert Bassler; d, Lewis Milestone; w, Harry Kleiner (based on a story by Martin Berkeley); ph, Charles G. Clarke (Technicolor); m, Sol Kaplan; ed, Nick De Maggio; md, Alfred Newman; art d, Lyle Wheeler, Jack-Lee Kirk.

Western **(PR:A MPAA:NR)**

KANGAROO KID, THE** (1950, Aus./U.S.) 72m Allied Australian bw

Jock O'Mahoney *(Tex Kinnane)*, Veda Ann Borg *(Stella Grey)*, Douglas Dumbrille *(Vincent Moller)*, Martha Hyer *(Mary Corbert)*, Alec Kellaway *(Baldy Muldoon)*, Guy Doleman *(Sgt. Jim Penrose)*, Alan Gifford *(Steve Corbett)*, Grant Taylor *(Phil Romero)*, Haydee Seldon *(Ma Muldoon)*, Frank Ransome *(Robey)*, Clarrie Woodlands *(Black Tracker)*.

For the most part this is a mindless action picture in which O'Mahoney is sent to Australia, where he finds rampant lawlessness. He gets caught up in it all as he tries to bring crooked lawyer Dumbrille back to the States. It does, however, manage to thoroughly exploit the scenery Down Under.

p, Howard C. Brown; d, Lesley Selander; w, Sherman Lowe (based on a story by Anthony Scott Veitch); ph, Russell Harlan.

Western **(PR:A MPAA:NR)**

KANOJO (SEE: SHE AND HE, 1967, Jap.)

KANSAN, THE** (1943) 79m UA bw

Richard Dix *(John Bonniwell)*, Jane Wyatt *(Eleanor Sager)*, Albert Dekker *(Steve Barat)*, Eugene Pallette *(Tom Waggoner)*, Victor Jory *(Jeff Barat)*, Robert Armstrong *(Malachy)*, Beryl Wallace *(Soubret)*, Clem Bevans *(Bridge Tender)*, Hobart Cavanaugh *(Mayor Josh Hudkins)*, Francis McDonald *(Gil Hatton)*, Willie Best *(Bones)*, Douglas Fowley *(Ben Nash)*, Rod Cameron *(Kelso)*, Eddy Waller *(Ed Gilbert)*, Raphael [Ray] Bennett *(Messenger)*, Sam Flint, Glenn Strange, Jack Norton, Merrill McCormack, Byron Foulger.

With Oregon as his destination, Dix makes a pit stop in a Kansas town, foils a raid by the James gang and winds up as town marshal. He's soon pitted against Dekker, a wealthy banker who wants control of the town. Wyatt suffices as the gal who leaves one man for the love of Dix. The old standard "When Johnny Comes Marching Home," and "Lullaby Of The Herd" (Foster Karling, Phil Ohman) are a couple of the tunes heard on the range. This marked the first of three "A" budget films producer Sherman worked on for United Artists.

p, Harry Sherman; d, George Archainbaud; w, Harold Shumate (based on a novel by Frank Gruber); ph, Russell Harlan; ed, Carroll Lewis.

Western **Cas.** **(PR:A MPAA:NR)**

KANSAS CITY BOMBER*

(1972) 99m Artists Entertainment Complex/MGM c

Raquel Welch *(Diane "K.C." Carr)*, Kevin McCarthy *(Burt Henry)*, Helena Kallianiotes *(Jackie Burdette)*, Norman Alden *(Horrible Hank Hopkins)*, Jeanne Cooper *(Vivien)*, Mary Kay Pass *(Lovey)*, Martine Bartlett *(Mrs. Carr)*, Cornelia Sharpe *(Tammy O'Brien)*, William Gray Espie *(Randy)*, Dick Lane *(Len)*, Russ Marin *(Dick Wicks)*, Stephen Manley *(Walt)*, Jodie Foster *(Rita)*, Georgia Schmidt *(Old Woman)*, Shelly Novack, Jim Nickerson *(Fans)*, Patti "Moo-Moo" Calvin *(Big Bertha Bogliani)*.

Welch stars as a Kansas City roller derby queen manipulated by McCarthy, an unscrupulous team owner and promoter of the pseudo-sport. The loosely connected story follows Welch, a divorced mother of two, as she enters into an affair with McCarthy and the effect this romance has on her career. Other skaters, particularly Kallianiotes, resent Welch's status with McCarthy. Alden, who secretly loves Welch, comes to her aid during a nasty brawl. Because of his feelings for Welch, McCarthy has the bruising skater transferred to another team. When Welch is ordered to throw a grudge match against Kallianiotes, she ignores the order. Though it won't help her career by winning, Welch has grown tired of her lover's manipulations and wants to show some independence. Like a roller derby match, this is loud, violent, and shows occasional moments of interest. The characterizations range from well drawn (Kallianiotes) to obnoxious. Welch gave this film her all (which isn't much), doing her own skating and delaying production for six weeks after breaking her wrist in a fall. She was one of the film's cosponsors as well, working through the Artists Entertainment Complex. The script was based on a master's thesis in screenwriting by a UCLA student. To no one's surprise, KANSAS CITY BOMBER did its best box office in cities where the roller derby was popular entertainment.

p, Marty Elfand; d, Jerrold Freedman; w, Thomas Rickman, Calvin Clements (based on a story by Barry Sandler); ph, Fred Koenekamp (Panavision, Metrocolor); m, Don Ellis; ed, David Berlatsky; art d, Joseph R. Jennings; cos, Ronald Talsky; makeup, Bruce Hutchinson, Richard Cobos; m/l, "Rounds and Spheres," Don Ellis, Maria Eckstein, "Your Way Ain't My Way," Ellis, Howard Liebling, Jeff Thomas, "All Night Market," Ellis, Liebling.

Sports Drama **(PR:O MPAA:PG)**

KANSAS CITY CONFIDENTIAL***

(1952) 98m UA bw (GB: THE SECRET FOUR)

John Payne *(Joe Rolfe)*, Coleen Gray *(Helen)*, Preston Foster *(Timothy Foster)*, Dona Drake *(Teresa)*, Jack Elam *(Harris)*, Neville Brand *(Kane)*, Lee Van Cleef *(Tony)*, Mario Seletti *(Timaso)*, Howard Negley *(Andrews)*, Ted Ryan *(Morelli)*, George Wallace *(Olson)*, Vivi Janiss *(Mr. Rogers)*, Helen Keeb *(Mrs. Crane)*, Archie Twitchell, House Peters, Jr., George Dockstader, Don House, Brick Sullivan, Jack Shea, Tom Dillon, Tom Greenway, Paul Fierro *(Police)*, Kay Wiley *(Woman)*, Harry Hines *(News Vendor)*, Don Orlando *(Diaz)*, Al Hill, Mike Lally *(Shooters)*, Charles Sherlock, Frank Scannell *(Stickmen)*, Charles Sullivan, Carlos Rivero, Sam Scar, Barry Brooks, Eddie Foster *(Players)*, Joe Ray *(Houseman)*, Paul Hogan *(Bouncer)*, Paul Dubov *(Eddie)*, Ric Roman *(Brother)*, Sam Pierce *(Workman)*, Eduardo Coch *(Airline Clerk)*, William Haade *(Detective Barney)*, Charles Cane *(Detective Mullins)*, Ray Bennett *(Prisoner)*, Orlando Beltran *(Porter)*, Carleton Young *(Assistant District Atty. Martin)*, Phil Tead *(Collins)*, Lee Phelps *(Jailer)*.

A brutal crime dossier which punches and kicks its way into the audience's unsuspecting laps. Foster is an embittered former Kansas City policeman who retreats into the criminal life and sets into motion a delicately engineered armored car robbery. Foster employs a trio of felons—Brand, Van Cleef, and Elam—to assist him by blackmailing them with incriminating evidence. To assure that the robbery will be "perfect," Foster has the three wear masks in order to keep their identities secret even from each other. The heist goes off as planned, as far as Foster is aware. Police, however, pick up a suspect, Payne, an embittered ex-con who happened to be driving a van similar to the one used in the getaway. Payne is riled by his near frameup and leaves Kansas City in search of the real crooks. After combing the *noir* underworld for clues, Payne finds himself south of the border on the trail of one of the secret criminals. He persuasively pounds some answers out of his victim, leaving him to be killed by the town police. Payne, seizing a golden opportunity, assumes the dead man's identity. He soon finds himself falling for Gray, the alluring and lonely daughter of Foster. Payne manages to squeeze his way into a meeting with the secret gang members, where the truth behind Foster's shady ways finally surfaces—he plans to rat on his accomplices and then collect the reward money being offered by the insurance company. Payne intervenes and bursts of gunfire are exchanged. When the smoke clears, the mysterious accomplices lie dead, as does the snaky Foster. The police arrive on the scene with Gray in tow. To save face for Gray, Payne falsifies his story and credits Foster with helping him round up the gang. Gray, of course, is duly impressed and gives herself to the heroic Payne. KANSAS CITY CONFIDENTIAL is noteworthy chiefly for the gritty and violent underworld vision of director Karlson, the immediacy of the semi-documentary cinematography, and the complexity of its characters. In the tradition of *film noir*, both hero Payne and antihero Foster have a dark side to their personalities. Payne is a refugee of underworld life who, by the finale, has surfaced on the side of the law (though only partly; he still is sympathetic about Foster's involvement). Foster, on the other hand, has begun as a policeman and in his attempt to embarrass the Kansas City police has taken a fatal step into the underworld. A stark crime expose which is well worth a viewing.

p, Edward Small; d, Phil Karlson; w, George Bruce, Harry Essex (based on a story by Harold R. Greene, Rowland Brown); ph, George E. Diskant; m, Paul Sawtell; ed, Buddy Small; art d, Edward L. Ilou.

Crime **(PR:C-O MPAA:NR)**

KANSAS CITY KITTY 1/2** (1944) 72m COL bw

Joan Davis *(Polly Jasper)*, Bob Crosby *(Jimmy)*, Jane Frazee *(Eileen Hasbrook)*, Erik Rolf *(Dr. Henry Talbot)*, Tim Ryan *(Dave Clark)*, Robert Emmett Keane *(Joe Lathim)*, Matt Willis *(Oscar Lee)*, John Bond *(Chaps Wiliker)*, Charles Wilson *(Mr. Hugo)*, Lee Gotch *(Ali Ben Ali)*, Charles Williams *(George W. Pivet)*, William Newell *(Gas Man)*, The Williams Brothers *(Specialty)*, Edward Earle *(Mr. Burgess)*, Vivian Mason *(Check Room Girl)*, Doodles Weaver *(Joe)*, Vic Potel *(Painter)*, Ed Allen *(Cop)*.

Davis plays a recent purchaser of a music publishing house who finds herself in the middle of a lawsuit concerning the song from which this film received its title. Songs include: "Kansas City Kitty," (Walter Donaldson, Edgar Leslie), "Tico Tico," (Zequinha Abreu, Ervin Drake), "Nothing Boogie From Nowhere," (Saul Chaplin), "Pretty Kitty Blue Eyes," (Mann Curtis, Vic Mizzy).

p, Ted Richmond; d, Del Lord; w, Manny Self; ph, Burnett Guffey; ed, Gene Havlick; md, Marlin Skiles; art d, Lionel Banks.

Musical **(PR:A MPAA:NR)**

KANSAS CITY PRINCESS** (1934) 64m WB bw

Joan Blondell *(Rosy)*, Glenda Farrell *(Marie)*, Robert Armstrong *(Dynamite)*, Hugh Herbert *(Junior Ashcraft)*, Osgood Perkins *(Marcel Duryea)*, Hobart Cavanaugh *(Sam Waller)*, Gordon Westcott *(Jimmy, the Dude)*, Ivan Lebedeff *(Dr. Sascha Pilnikoff)*, T. Roy Barnes *(Jim Cameron)*, Renee Whitney *(Mrs. Ashcraft)*, Arthur Hoyt *(Greenway)*, Eddie Shubert *(Shooting Gallery Proprietor)*, Arthur Housman *(Salesman)*, Harry Seymour *(Waiter)*, Edward Keane *(Captain)*, Lorena Layson

(Cashier), Jack Wise *(Soda Clerk)*, Lillian Harmer *(Scout Mistress)*, Maxine Doyle *(Dumb Girl)*, Henry Otho *(Policeman)*, Jack Richardson *(Porter)*, Leo White, Andre Cheron *(French Stewards)*, Alphonse Martell *(Officer)*, Edith Baker *(Saleslady)*, John Binnet *(French Clerk)*, Vince Barnett *(Quincy)*.

Blondell and Farrell are a pair of adventurous women who split from their home town and head East, stopping first in New York, then in Paris. They pay the rent by conning unsuspecting men out of their cash. A bad comedy that plays like a light piece, when it should have been directed as a farce.

p, Lou Edelman; d, William Keighley; w, Manuel Seff, Sy Bartlett (based on a story by Bartlett); ph, George Barnes; ed, William B. Clemens; art d, John Hughes.

Comedy **(PR:A MPAA:NR)**

KANSAS CYCLONE** ½ (1941) 57m REP bw

Don "Red" Barry *(Jim Randall)*, Lynn Merrick *(Martha)*, William Haade *(Sheriff Ed King)*, Milt Kibbee *(Cal Chambers)*, Harry Worth *(Jud Parker)*, Dorothy Sebastian *(Helen King)*, Jack Kirk *(Jim Turner)*, Forrest Taylor *(Ben Brown)*, Charles Moore *(T-Bone)*, Eddie Dean, Reed Howes, Guy Usher, Edward Piel, Sr., Yakima Canutt, Cactus Mack, Bob Woodward, Tex Terry, George J. Lewis, Angie Gomez, Buddy Roosevelt, William Kellogg.

A fine oater has Barry going undercover as a geologist to break up a gang that has been knocking off Wells Fargo coaches. The robbers are caught, and a posse rounds them up. Kibbee does a commendable job as a Fargo employee, but it's gorgeous Merrick who steals the show by oozing sexuality—a rare departure from the usual dusty barmaids.

p&d, George Sherman; w, Oliver Drake, Doris Schroeder (based on a story by Louis Sarecky); ph, William Nobles; ed, Charles Craft; md, Cy Feuer.

Western **(PR:A MPAA:NR)**

KANSAS PACIFIC** (1953) 73m AA c

Sterling Hayden *(John Nelson)*, Eve Miller *(Barbara Bruce)*, Barton MacLane *(Calvin Bruce)*, Harry Shannon *(Smokestack)*, Tom Fadden *(Gustavson)*, Reed Hadley *(Quantrill)*, Douglas Fowley *(Janus)*, Bob Keys *(Lt. Stanton)*, Irving Bacon *(Casey)*, Myron Healey *(Morey)*, James Griffith *(Farley)*, Clayton Moore *(Stone)*, Jonathan Hale *(Gen. Scott)*.

Hayden is an Army engineer sent by the government to oversee the construction of the Kansas Pacific railroad line. In the period before the outbreak of the Civil War, the laying of the tracks is hampered by Southern sympathizers who don't want the railway to stretch to the West Coast. There are an equal number of Northerners doing all they can to keep it moving. Photographed in color by Neumann and directed by Nazarro, this essentially is just a big budgeted B western.

p, Walter Wanger; d, Ray Nazarro; w, Dan Ullman; ph, Harry Neumann (Cinecolor); m, Albert Sendrey; ed, William Austin, Walter Hannemann; art d, David Milton.

Western **Cas.** **(PR:A MPAA:NR)**

KANSAS RAIDERS** ½ (1950) 80m UNIV c

Audie Murphy *(Jesse James)*, Brian Donlevy *(Quantrill)*, Marguerite Chapman *(Kate Clarke)*, Scott Brady *(Bill Anderson)*, Tony Curtis *(Kit Dalton)*, Richard Arlen *(Union Captain)*, Richard Long *(Frank James)*, James Best *(Cole Younger)*, John Kellogg *(Red Leg Leader)*, Dewey Martin *(James Younger)*, George Chandler *(Willie)*, Charles Delaney *(Pell)*, Richard Egan *(1st Lieutenant)*, Dave Wolfe *(Tate)*, Mira McKinney *(Woman)*, Sam Flint *(Bank President)*, Buddy Roosevelt *(Another Red Leg)*, Larry McGrath *(Man in Crowd)*, Ed Peil, Sr. *(Bank Teller)*.

Despite a good cast (including Curtis in one of his earliest roles), this film suffers from a gutless portrayal of the subject. Murphy is the famed western outlaw who idolizes Donlevy. The two take on Curtis, along with Best and Martin, to school them in outlaw ways. There's no attempt at character sketching. Instead, the famous names are bandied about between a series of raids and hard riding. Murphy begins questioning his blind loyalty towards his mentor, and finally goes out on his own after Donlevy is gunned down. Action fans will be pleased but a fine potential was completely wasted.

p, Ted Richmond; d, Ray Enright; w, Robert L. Richards (based on his story); ph, Irving Glassberg (Technicolor); m, Joseph Gershenson; ed, Milton Carruth; art d, Bernard Herzbrun, Emrich Nicholson.

Western **(PR:A MPAA:NR)**

KANSAS TERRITORY** ½ (1952) 64m MON bw

Wild Bill Elliott *(Joe Daniels)*, House Peters, Jr. *(Carruthers)*, Peggy Stewart *(Kay Collins)*, Lane Bradford *(Fred Jethro)*, I. Stanford Jolley *(Slater)*, Fuzzy Knight *(Fuzzy)*, Stanley Andrews *(Governor)*, Lyle Talbot *(Collins)*, Marshall Reed *(Bob Jethro)*, John Hart *(Marshal)*, William Fawcett *(Weatherbee)*, Lee Roberts *(Larkin)*, Pierce Lyden *(Johnson)*, Ted Adams *(Hank)*, Terry Frost *(Stark)*.

A top-notch B Western which has Elliott heading back to Kansas in order to avenge the death of his brother. Elliott remembers his brother as a decent, honest youngster, but soon learns that he was actually a ruthless card cheat, outlaw, and killer. He then realizes the kid had it coming, and accepts the fact. Nice photography, if you can stand the sepia tint.

p, Vincent M. Fennelly; d, Lewis Collins; w, Dan Ullman (based on his story); ph, Ernest Miller; m, Raoul Kraushaar; ed, Richard Heermance; art d, David Milton.

Western **(PR:A MPAA:NR)**

KANSAS TERRORS, THE** (1939) 57m REP bw

Robert Livingston *(Stoney Brooke)*, Raymond Hatton *(Rusty Joslin)*, Duncan Renaldo *(Renaldo)*, Jacqueline Wells [Julie Bishop] *(Maria)*, Howard Hickman *(Governor General)*, George Douglas *(Commandante)*, Frank Lackteen *(Capt. Gonzales)*, Myra Marsh *(Duenna)*, Yakima Canutt *(Sergeant)*, Ruth Robinson *(Juanita)*, Richard Alexander *(Miguel)*, Merrill McCormack, Artie Ortego, Curly Dresden, Al Haskell.

Livingston once again assumes the lead in this fourth season of the "Three Mesquiteers" film series, replacing John Wayne who had appeared previously. It is also the first film of the series to feature Renaldo as one of the trio, and to have Grey as producer (taking up where William Berke left off). Livingston and Hatton head for a remote Caribbean island to deliver a herd of horses, and end up aiding a gang of rebel fighters (led by Renaldo) in their battle against the island's unjust leader. Livingston occasionally seems to be in the wrong film, donning the mask and riding the white horse that he made famous in serials such as "The Lone Ranger." (See "THREE MESQUITEERS" series, Index).

p, Harry Grey; d, George Sherman; w, Jack Natteford, Betty Burbridge (from the story by Luci Ward, based on the characters created by William Colt MacDonald); ph, Ernest Miller; m, William Lava; ed, Tony Martinelli.

Western **(PR:A MPAA:NR)**

KAPHETZOU (SEE: FORTUNE TELLER, THE, 1961)

KAPITANLEUTENANT PRIEN—DER STIER VON SCAPA FLOW (SEE: U-47 LT. COMMANDER PRIEN, 1967)

KAPO***

(1964, Ital./Fr./Yugo.) 116m Vides-Zebra-Cineriz-Francinex-Lovcen/Lionex-Promenade bw

Susan Strasberg *(Edith/Nicole)*, Laurent Terzieff *(Sascha)*, Emmanuelle Riva *(Terese)*, Didi Perego *(Sofia)*, Gianni Garko *(German Soldier)*, Annabella Besi, Graziella Galvani, Mira Dinulovic, Dragomir Felba.

An Academy Award nominee for Best Foreign film in 1960 (losing out to Bergman's THE VIRGIN SPRING), this concentration camp story didn't make it to the U.S. until 4 years later. It tells the story of an impressionable 14-year-old Jewish girl (Strasberg) who, with her family, is captured by the Nazis. She is able to change identities with the help of a camp doctor and works her way up to the rank of "kapo," or camp guard. Strasberg becomes more and more obsessed with her power, and eventually falls in love with a Russian prisoner (Terzieff). When her friend Riva commits suicide, Strasberg is shaken back into reality. She reveals her true identity to the Russian, and suggests a mass breakout. To save the lives of the others Strasberg sacrifices her own. Riva gives a riveting performance as Strasberg's closest friend. There is also a less captivating 90-minute version.

p, Morris Ergas; d, Gillo Pontecorvo; w, Pontecorvo, Franco Solinas; ph, Goffredo Bellisario, Alexander Sekulovic; m, Carlo Rustichelli; ed, Roberto Cinquini; art d, Piero Gherardi.

War Drama **(PR:O MPAA:NR)**

KARAMAZOV** ½

(1931, Ger.) 100m Terra/Tobis bw (DER MORDER DIMITRI KARAMASOFF; AKA: THE MURDERER DMITRI KARAMAZOV; THE BROTHERS KARAMAZOV)

Fritz Kortner *(Dmitri Karamazov)*, Anna Sten *(Grushenka)*, Fritz Rasp *(Smerdyakov)*, Bernard Minetti *(Ivan Karamazov)*, Dr. Max Pohl *(Fyodor Karamazov)*, Hanna Waag *(Katya)*, Liese Neuman *(Fenya)*, Fritz Alberti *(Judge)*, Werner Hollmann *(Grushenka's Lover)*.

A loose adaptation of Dostoyevsky's classic novel which, while directed by a Soviet, owes more to silent German Expressionist films than to the Russian style of filmmaking. The massive volume has been severely cut, and the action centers around Kortner as Dmitri. He gives up a fine living and a devoted fiancee after becoming enamored of Sten, a prostitute who had also entranced Kortner's father Minetti. When Minetti is found murdered, Kortner is convicted of patricide. He's sent to Siberia, with Sten at his side, accompanying the man she loves. This early sound film is clearly rooted in the artistic movements that began in Germany's silent era. Emotional moods are represented by inanimate objects, and a symbolic *mise-en-scene*. Though undoubtedly the performances were excellent for their time, they unfortunately reflect a style far better suited for stage work than cinema. KARAMAZOV was one of many German films of the period to deal with rebellion, a theme that was soon to disappear with Hitler's rise to power. Actress Sten, playing Grushenka, was widely compared to Dietrich in this role. The Russian-born player was brought to Hollywood following her succession of German films, sponsored by Samuel Goldwyn. Her U.S. films were not notably successful; she earned the industry-wide sobriquet "Goldwyn's Folly." Remade in 1957 as THE BROTHERS KARAMAZOV with Yul Brynner.

p, Eugen Tuscherer; d, Fyodor Ozep; w, Leonhard Frank, Ozep, Victor Trivas, Erich Engel (based on the novel *The Brothers Karamazov* by Fyodor Dostoyevsky); ph, Fridl Behn-Grund; m, Karol Rathaus; set d, Heinrich Richter, Trivas.

Drama **(PR:C MPAA:NR)**

KARAMI-AI (SEE: INHERITANCE, THE, 1964)

KARATE KILLERS, THE** (1967) 92m MGM c

Robert Vaughn *(Napoleon Solo)*, David McCallum *(Illya Kuryakin)*, Curt Jurgens *(Carl von Kesser)*, Joan Crawford *(Amanda True)*, Herbert Lom *(Randolph)*, Telly Savalas *(Count de Franzini)*, Terry-Thomas *(Constable)*, Kim Darby *(Sandy True)*, Diane McBain *(Margo True)*, Jill Ireland *(Imogen True)*, Leo G. Carroll *(Alexander Waverly)*, Danielle De Metz *(Yvonne True)*, Irene Tsu *(Reikko)*, Jim Boles *(Dr. True)*, Philip Ahn *(Sazami Kyushu)*, Arthur Gould-Porter *(Magistrate)*, Rob Okazaki *(Police Inspector)*, Maria Lennard *(Show Girl)*, Lindsay Workman *(Leading Scientist)*, Rick Traeger *(Hotel Clerk)*, Frank Arno *(Chief Fireman)*, Julie Ann Johnson, Sharon Hillyer *(U.N.C.L.E. Girls)*, William Burnside *(Bartender)*, Gloria Neil *(Stewardess)*, William Bryant *(Technician)*, Jason Wingreen, Grant Woods *(Engin-*

eers), Dick Crockett, Paul Bailey, Jerry Summers, Fred Stromsor *(The Karate Killers)*.

This is simply a few episodes of the popular "Man from U.N.C.L.E." television series spliced together for theatrical release. The bad spies over at T.H.R.U.S.H. are after a professor and his formula for changing sea water into gold. It's an enjoyable and exciting romp, though it clearly belongs on the smaller screen. Watching the stars of the film is good fun and Crawford, in a small role, gives it her all. Surprisingly, this proved to be a much needed boost for her career, stopping its steady downslide.

p, Boris Ingster; d, Barry Shear; w, Norman Hudis (based on a story by Ingster); ph, Fred Koenekamp; m, Gerald Fried, Jerry Goldsmith; ed, William B. Gulick, Ray Williford; art d, George W. Davis, James W. Sullivan; set d, Henry Grace, Dick Pefferle, Don Greenwood, Jr.; m/l, title theme, Jerry Goldsmith.

Spy Drama (PR:A MPAA:NR)

KARATE, THE HAND OF DEATH** (1961) 80m Joseph Brenner-AA bw

Joel Holt *(Matt Carver)*, Frank Blaine *(Ivan Mayberry)*, Akira Shiga *(Akira Harakawa)*, Joe Hirakawa *(Kosaka Harakawa)*, Reiko Okada *(Reiko Harakawa)*, Ken Noyle *(Rohmer)*, Fujio Ito *(Lt. Okada)*, Mayana *(Dancer)*, Bob Markworth *(Hantaro)*, Maurice Gruel *(Maurice)*, Rie Sugiura *(Nurse)*, Tony Sugahara *(Waiter)*, Naboro Kudisahi *(Plumber)*, Kanji Hayashi *(Coin Dealer)*, Tom Moore *(Herr Blucher)*, Akiko Seo *(Flower Girl)*, Takao Minami *(Little Boy)*, Tadashi Yamaki *(1st Thief)*, Akio Watanabe *(Pickpocket)*, Shigayaoshi Kawai *(Radio Shop Clerk)*, Yoichi Wada, Jipp Endo *(Gangsters)*, Kasuo Ushida *(Taxi Driver)*, Taro Yamashita, Jiro Kodama, Sho Onoda *(Soldiers)*, Kinji Inoue *(Rag Picker)*, Men of the Japan Karate Association *(Karate Players)*.

Holt plays a karate expert who takes possession of a coin that is the alleged key to a supply of platinum smuggled out of Germany. He enlists the help of his friend Blaine, who later double-crosses him. Further investigation finally leads Holt to Shiga, the brain behind the smuggling operation. The two clash head on in grand karate style, and naturally, the better man (Holt) emerges victorious. Holds some interest because of location scenes filmed in Japan.

p&d, Joel Holt; w, David Hill (based on his story); ph, Tatsuo Namikawa; m, Minoru Miki; ed, Ken Tanaka; md, Miki; cos, Andrew Pallack; ch, Hidetako Nishiyama.

Martial Arts (PR:C MPAA:NR)

KARE JOHN (SEE: DEAR JOHN, 1964)

KAREN, THE LOVEMAKER*

(1970) 95m International Film/Manson c (AKA:AFRICA EROTICA; HAPPENING IN AFRICA)

Darr Poran *(Robert)*, Carrie Rochelle *(Karen)*, Alice Marie.

Photographer Poran takes Rochelle to Africa to model nude in the jungle. An adolescent trauma has made her fearful of sex, but the two gradually draw closer. While driving his amphibious car down the Nile, Poran recounts an unhappy love affair he had in Hong Kong years before. He is so caught up in his reveries that he does not see the deadly rapids ahead. Rochelle screams and they barely escape with their lives, now firmly in love. A stupefyingly inane movie whose only saving feature is the silliness of seeing an amphibious car drive down the Nile. A film not likely to be revived.

p&d, Zygmunt Sulistrowski; w, Jordan Arthur Deutsch (based on a story by Sulistrowski); ph, Herbert Theis, Celeste Sebastiano (Eastmancolor); m, Moacir Santos, Sulistrowski, Enrico Simonetti; ed, Sulistrowski.

Adventure (PR:O MPAA:R)

KARMA** (1933, Brit./India) 68m Indian and British Film bw

Devika Rani *(Maharani)*, Himansu Rai *(Prince)*, Abraham Sofaer *(Holy Man)*.

The "Romeo and Juliet" theme with an Indian setting here as poor little rich princess Rani falls in love with Rai, the prince next door. Of course her father strongly objects, but who can fight true love?

p, Himansu Rai; d, J. L. Freer-Hunt; w, Rai.

Drama (PR:A MPAA:NR)

KATE PLUS TEN** (1938, Brit.) 81m Wainwright/GFD bw

Jack Hulbert *(Inspector Mike Pemberton)*, Genevieve Tobin *(Kate Westhanger)*, Noel Madison *(Gregori)*, Francis L. Sullivan *(Lord Flamborough)*, Arthur Wontner *(Col. Westhanger)*, Frank Cellier *(Sir Ralph Sapson)*. Peter Haddon *(Boltover)*, Googie Withers *(Lady Moya)*, Edward Lexy *(Sergeant)*, Felix Aylmer *(Bishop)*, Leo Genn *(Dr. Gurdon)*, Queenie Leonard, Walter Sondes, James Harcourt, Albert Whelan, Arthur Brander, Geoffrey Clark, Vincent Holman, Paul Sheridan, Oliver Johnston, Ronald Adam, Philip Leaver.

Police inspector Hulbert tracks Tobin, a Lord's secretary, when the Lord's bank is emptied of its gold bullion. Since she's recognized as the leader of a notorious gang, she is the first suspected. Her 10 cohorts, however, take the gold for themselves, and a chase ensues with Hulbert and Tobin on board a train trying to cut off the gang's getaway cars.

p, Richard Wainwright; d, Reginald Denham; w, Jack Hulbert, Jeffrey Dell (based on a novel by Edgar Wallace); ph, Roy Kellino.

Crime (PR:A MPAA:NR)

KATERINA IZMAILOVA*** ½ (1969, USSR) 118m Lenfilm/Artkino c

Galina Vishnevskaya *(Katerina Lvovna Izmailova)*, Artyom Inozemstsev *(Sergey)*, Nikolay Boyarskiy *(Zinoviy Borisovich)*, Aleksandr Sokolov *(Boris Timofeyevich)*, R. Tkachuk *(Village Drunk)*, Tatyana Gavrilova *(Sonetka)*, V. Titova, L. Malinovskaya, K. Adashevskiy, I. Bogolyubov, K. Tyagunov, V. Lyubimova, A. Zhila, G. Krasulya, V. Gerasimchuk, M. Reshetin; Voices: V. Tretyakov *(Sergey)*, V. Radziyevskiy *(Zinoviy Borisovich)*, A. Vedernikov *(Boris Timofeyevich)*, S. Strezhnev *(Village Drunk)*, V. Reka *(Sonetka)*, Shevchenko Opera and Ballet Theatre Chorus.

Nineteenth-century period piece uses an operatic structure to emphasize its melodramatic points. Vishnevskaya is the bored wife of the merchant class who falls in love with the farm laborer Inozemstsev. When her father-in-law Sokolov learns of the affair he beats the laborer. Vishnevskaya poisons Sokolov as an act of revenge and later plots the murder of her husband Boyarskiy. The post-Revolutionary overtones are obvious. Film is notable for its operatic score composed by Shostakovich.

d, Mikhail Shapiro; w, Dmitriy Dmitriyevich Shostakovich (based on a novel, *Ledi Makbet Mtsenskogo Uyezda*, by Nikolai Leskov); ph, Rostislav Davydov, Vladimir Ponomaryov (Sovcolor); m, Shostakovich; md, Konstantin Simeonov conducting the Shevchenko Opera and Ballet Theatre Orchestra; art d, Yevgeniy Yeney.

Opera/Drama (PR:A MPAA:NR)

KATHLEEN** ½

(1938, Ireland) 70m Hoffberg bw (KATHLEEN MAVOURNEEN)

Sally O'Neil *(Kathleen O'Moore)*, Tom Burke *(Michael Rooney)*, Jack Daly *(Dennis O'Dwyer)*, Sara Allgood *(Mary Ellen O'Dwyer)*, Jeanne Stuart *(Barbara Fitzpatrick)*, Ethel Griffies *(Hannah O'Dwyer)*, Pat Noonan *(Sean O'Dwyer)*, Baby Brenda *(Sheila O'Moore)*, John Forbes-Robertson *(Pat O'Moore)*, Denis O'Neil *(Mat Cooney)*, Fred Duprez *(Walter Bryant)*, Talbot O'Farrell *(Dan Milligan)*, J. A. O'Rourke *(Tim Maloney)*, Mark Stone *(Dock Worker)*, Terry Conlin *(Stage Announcer)*, Fred Withers *(Joe O'Flanagan)*, Frank Crawshaw *(Brian Slattery)*, Jeanne Stuart *(Barbara Fitzpatrick)*, Patrick O'Moore, Rory O'Connor, Sean Dempsey, Frank Lee's Tara Ceilidh Band, Arthur Lucan, Kitty McShane, Guy Jones, Tara Irish Dancers.

A simple Irish love story has O'Neil playing a waitress in a cafe where she meets Burke, a singing waiter who aspires to a great musical career. She's courted by him, as well as by a wealthy, older man, but it's the tenor she really wants. Burke's romantic intentions are nearly thwarted, however, when his rich aunt refuses to admit a common waitress into the family. Pleasant little musical which features some good Irish specialty acts and good performances by the leads. It marked a growth in the Irish film industry as one of the first films of that country to take advantage of the advancing film technology.

p, John Argyle; d, Norman Lee; w, Marjorie Deans, John Glen (based on the novel by Clara Mulholland); ph, Bryan Langley; md, Guy Jones.

Romance/Musical (PR:A MPAA:NR)

KATHLEEN** (1941) 88m MGM bw

Shirley Temple *(Kathleen Davis)*, Herbert Marshall *(John Davis)*, Laraine Day *(Dr. Angela Martha Kent)*, Gail Patrick *(Lorraine Bennett)*, Felix Bressart *(Mr. Schoner)*, Lloyd Corrigan *(Dr. Montague Foster)*, Nella Walker *(Mrs. Farrell)*, Guy Bellis *(Jarvis)*, Wade Boteler *(Policeman)*, Charles Judels *(Manager)*, Else Argal *(Maid)*, Margaret Bert *(Margaret)*, Joe Yule *(Sign Poster)*, James Flavin, Monty Collins *(Moving Men)*.

If this picture wasn't a Temple vehicle, it would have been forgotten a lot sooner. She certainly lays on the charm as a young girl upset with her father's lack of attention, his unfriendly lady friend, and a bossy nursemaid. A new nurse comes into the picture, however, and Temple takes a liking to her—and so does her father. Louis B. Mayer had tried for some time to get Temple's name up on the MGM marquee, and he finally succeeded. KATHLEEN didn't do much box office though, despite the fact the popular child star had been off the screen for a year. KATHLEEN thus ended up being her only film for the studio. She still had all the charm she ever had, but the novel cuteness had started to wear off, making way for a budding (just barely) sexuality which blossomed in THE BACHELOR AND THE BOBBY SOXER. Only one tune is featured, "Around the Corner" (Roger Edens, Earl Brent). Look for a small appearance by Yule, father of another MGM child star, Mickey Rooney.

p, George Haight; d, Harold S. Bacquet; w, Mary C. McCall, Jr. (based on a story by Kay Van Riper); ph, Sidney Wagner; m, Franz Waxman; ed, Conrad A. Nervig; art d, Cedric Gibbons.

Comedy/Drama (PR:AAA MPAA:NR)

KATHLEEN MAVOURNEEN** (1930) 57m TIF bw

Sally O'Neil *(Kathleen)*, Charles Delaney *(Terry)*, Robert Elliott *(Dan Moriarity)*, Aggie Herring *(Aunt Nora Shannon)*, Walter Perry *(Uncle Mike Shannon)*, Francis Ford *(Butler)*.

O'Neil arrives from Ireland to marry plumber Delaney, but is wooed by political boss Elliott. Despite Delaney's objections, they decide to marry, but on the day of the wedding, a man turns up who accuses Elliott of having a man killed. In front of O'Neil, Elliott pulls out a gun and shoots the man in the back. Realizing the magnitude of her mistake, O'Neil gives back her engagement ring and returns to Delaney. Routine melodrama that has not held up over the years.

d, Albert Ray; w, Frances Hyland (based on the play by Dion Boucicault); ph, Harry Jackson.

Drama (PR:A MPAA:NR)

KATHLEEN MAVOUREEN, 1938 (SEE: KATHLEEN, 1938, Ireland)

KATHY O'*** ½ (1958) 99m UNIV c

Dan Duryea *(Harry Johnson)*, Jan Sterling *(Celeste Saunders)*, Patty McCormack *(Kathy O'Rourke)*, Mary Fickett *(Helen Johnson)*, Sam Levene *(Ben Melnick)*, Mary Jane Croft *(Harriet Burton)*, Rickey Kelman *(Robert "Bo" Johnson)*, Ainslie Pryor *(Lt. Chavez)*, Barney Phillips *(Matt Williams)*, Mel Leonard *(Sid)*, Casey Walters

(Billy Blair), Walter Woolf King *(Donald C. Faber)*, Alexander Campbell *(Bixby)*, Joseph Sargent *(Mike)*, Mary Carver *(Marge)*, Terry Kelman *(Tommy Johnson)*.

McCormack appeared two years earlier in Mervyn LeRoy's THE BAD SEED, as a rotten vermin of a child. In KATHY O' she plays a similar role as an insolent child star "loved by millions, yet loved by no one." When she refuses to be bossed around by studio publicist, Duryea, he nearly has to bribe her to do an interview with his ex-wife, columnist Sterling. McCormack takes kindly to the lady, however, and eventually runs away from home to be with her. Complications arise and Duryea gets arrested for kidnapping, but everybody's happy at the end as McCormack turns over a new leaf. A warm-hearted well-handled effort.

p, Sy Gomberg; d, Jack Sher; w, Gomberg, Sher (based on a *Saturday Evening Post* story "Memo on Kathy O'Rourke" by Sher); ph, Arthur E. Arling (CinemaScope, Eastmancolor); m, Frank Skinner; ed, George Gittens; md, Joseph Gershenson; art d, Alexander Golitzen, Bill Newberry; cos, Bill Thomas; m/l, Charles Tobias, Ray Joseph, Sher (sung by The Diamonds).

Comedy **(PR:A MPAA:NR)**

KATHY'S LOVE AFFAIR (SEE: COURTNEY AFFAIR, 1947, Brit.)

KATIA (SEE: MAGNIFI-SINNER, 1960, Fr.)

KATIE DID IT** (1951) 81m UNIV bw

Ann Blyth *(Katherine Standish)*, Mark Stevens *(Peter Van Arden)*, Cecil Kellaway *(Nathaniel B. Wakely VI)*, Jesse White *(Jim Dilloway)*, Harold Vermilyea *(Merill T. Grumby)*, Craig Stevens *(Stuart Grumby)*, William Lynn *(Clarence Spivvens)*, Elizabeth Patterson *(Aunt Priscilla)*, Jimmy Hunt *(Steven)*, Irving Bacon *(Conductor)*, Raymond Largay *(Rev. Turner)*, Peter Leeds *("Odds" Burton)*, Ethyl May Halls *(Abigail)*.

Blyth is a country lass who heads for the Big Apple in hopes of selling her uncle's song to a publisher. She intends to give the profits to the boozing uncle so he can pay off his gambling debts. There are no buyers for the song, but Blyth does make some change by posing—scantily clad—for painter Mark Stevens. Before you can say "pin-up girl," her curvaceous body is plastered up on billboards across America. In retaliation, she plans to wed Craig Stevens, a banker's son, but Mark intervenes at the final moment. Though cliches abound, it's all handled with a light touch that gives this some occasional charm.

p, Leonard Goldstein; d, Frederick de Cordova; w, Jack Henley, Oscar Brodney; ph, Russell Metty; m, Frank Skinner; ed, Frank Gross; art d, Bernard Herzburn, Robert Clatworthy; m/l, Lester Lee, Dan Shapiro.

Comedy **(PR:A MPAA:NR)**

KATINA (SEE: ICELAND, 1942)

KATOK I SKRIPKA (SEE: VIOLIN AND ROLLER, 1962, USSR)

KAWAITA MIZUUMI (SEE: YOUTH IN FURY, 1961)

KAYA, I'LL KILL YOU½**
(1969, Yugo./Fr.) 80m Jadran-Cineaste-Mosaic/Fleetwood-Altura c (KAJA, UBIT CU TE)

Zaim Muzaferija *(Kaya)*, Ugljesa Kojadinovic *(Piero)*, Antun Nalis *(Tonko)*, Jolanda Dacic *(Mare Karantanova)*, Izet Hajdarhodzic *(Ugo Bala)*, Husein Cokic *(Nikica)*.

A small town on the Dalmatian coast which has been free of crime for nearly 300 years is suddenly infested with Italian troops during WW II. One resident, Kojadinovic, a cripple and Fascist convert, sets out to kill his elderly neighbor, Muzaferija. Meanwhile, the other residents indulge in a host of cruelties such as killing birds and harassing the village idiot, and so do nothing to stop the murder of the old man. The disastrous psychological effects of war and occupation are obvious—and are graphically presented in a relentlessly depressing manner.

p, Branko Lustig; d, Vatroslav Mimica; w, Mimica, Kruno Quien (based on a story by Quien); ph, Frano Vodopivec (Eastmancolor); m, Lidija Jojic; ed, Joja Remenar; art d & cos, Vladimir Tadej.

War/Drama **(PR:A MPAA:NR)**

KAZABLAN*** (1974, Israel) 110m MGM-UA c

Yehoram Gaon, Arie Elias, Efrat Lavie, Yehudah Efroni, Joseph Graber, Esther Grotes, Aliza Azikri, Misha Asherov, Moshe Hilel, Abraham Ronai, Geta Luka.

When a neighborhood is about to go down under the wrecker's ball, street smart war hero Gaon rallies everyone to fight back. The neighborhood is saved in good fashion, with plenty of singing and dancing along the way. Gaon repeated his role from the popular Israeli musical, giving this entertaining film some fine spirit. It was shot on location in Old Jaffa and Jerusalem in an English language production.

p&d, Menahem Golan; w, Golan, Haim Hefer, David Paulsen; (based on the musical by Yigal Mossinson, Yoel Silberg); ph, David Gurfinkel; m, Dov Seltzer; ed, Dov Hoenig; ch, Shimon Bruan; m/l, Seltzer, Hefer, Dan Almagor, Amos Ettinger, David Paulsen.

Musical **(PR:A MPAA:PG)**

KAZAN* (1949) 65m COL bw

Stephen Dunne *(Thomas Weyman)*, Lois Maxwell *(Louise Maitlin)*, Joe Sawyer *(Sandy Jepson)*, Roman Bohnen *(Maitlin)*, George Cleveland *(Trapper)*, John Dehner *(Henri LeClerc)*, Ray Teal *(McCready)*, Loren Gage *(Bartender)*.

Some brutal Canadian woodsmen find a white dog roaming wild and decide to turn him into a vicious pit bull. Of course, sadists never win for long in simplistic movies such as this, so it's not long before hero Dunne enters the scene. He retrains the pup, making him as docile as a lamb. With its near absence of motivations, coupled with a deadly sluggish tempo, KAZAN is one dog movie that may live up to its name.

p, Robert Cohn; d, Will Jason; w, Arthur A. Ross (based on the novel by James Oliver Curwood); ph, Henry Freulich; ed, Richard Fantl; md, Mischa Bakaleinikoff; art d, Paul Palmentola.

Adventure **(PR:AA MPAA:NR)**

KEELER AFFAIR, THE (SEE: CHRISTINE KEELER AFFAIR, THE, 1964)

KEEP, THE** (1983) 96m Capital/PAR c

Scott Glenn *(Glaeken Trismegestus)*, Alberta Watson *(Eva)*, Jurgen Prochnow *(Woermann)*, Robert Prosky *(Father Fonescu)*, Gabriel Byrne *(Kempffer)*, Ian McKellen *(Dr. Cuza)*, Morgan Sheppard *(Alexandru)*, Royston Tickner *(Tomescu)*, Michael Carter *(Radu)*, Phillip Joseph *(Oster)*, John Vine *(Lutz)*, Jona Jones *(Otto)*, Wolf Kahler *(S.S. Adjutant)*, Rosalie Crutchley *(Josefa)*, Frederick Warder, Bruce Payne *(Border Guards)*, David Cardy *(Alexandru's Son)*, Philip Bloomfield *(Josefa's Son)*, Yashar Adem *(Carlos)*.

A minor disaster. Director Mann (whose great crime film THIEF was virtually ignored by critics until the success of his NBC television show "Miami Vice") wrought upon the public this fantastic-*looking* movie, filled with great production values, and lush cinematography. Unfortunately, these are combined with a totally incoherent narrative punctuated by incredibly inept performances from usually fine actors (Prosky who was so good in THIEF is an embarrassment here, as is McKellen). Set in Eastern Europe during WW II, just what is going on here is hard to say. The plot has something to do with a castle in the Carpathian Mountains that possesses a powerful, evil force which sucks up every Nazi it comes across and spits out their bloody entrails. Called by psychic impulses (or something like that), a mysterious traveler (Glenn) arrives to do battle with the evil force. One of the most visually interesting and haunting films in recent years, THE KEEP's narrative weaknesses are all the more frustrating.

p, Gene Kirkwood, Howard W. Koch, Jr.; d&w, Michael Mann (based on a novel by F. Paul Wilson); ph, Alex Thomson (Metrocolor); m, Tangerine Dream; ed, Dov Hoenig; prod d, John Box; art d, Herbert Westbrook, Alan Tomkins; cos, Anthony Mendleson; spec eff, Wally Veevers, Robin Browne, Roger Simons; makeup, Nick Allder, Graham Freeborn.

Horror **Cas.** **(PR:O MPAA:R)**

KEEP 'EM FLYING** (1941) 86m UNIV bw

Bud Abbott *(Blackie Benson)*, Lou Costello *(Heathcliffe)*, Martha Raye *(Barbara Phelps/Gloria Phelps)*, Carol Bruce *(Linda Joyce)*, William Gargan *(Craig Morrison)*, Dick Foran *(Jinx Roberts)*, Truman Bradley *(Butch)*, Charles Lang *(Jim Joyce)*, William B. Davidson *(McGonigal)*, Frank Penny *(Spealer)*, Loring Smith *(Maj. Barstow)*, Stanley Smith, James Horne, Jr., Charles King, Jr., Scotty Groves, Regis Parton *(Cadets)*, Dorothy Darrell, Elaine Morey, Marcia Ralston *(USO Girls)*, Doris Lloyd *(Lady With Lipstick)*, Emil Van Horn *(Man In Gorilla Suit)*, James Seay *(Lieutenant)*, William Forrest *(Captain)*, Earle Hodgins *(Attendant)*, Harry Strang *(Truck Driver)*, Carleton Young *(Orchestra Leader)*, Harold Daniels *(Announcer)*, Dick Crane *(Cadet Stevens)*, Paul Scott *(Doctor)*, Virginia Engels *(Hat Check Girl)*, Dorothy L. Jones *(Brunette)*, Gene O'Donnell *(Radio Control Operator)*, Mickey Simpson *(Deputy)*, Phil Warren *(Pilot)*, Princess Luana *(Herself)*, The Six Hits.

Abbott and Costello appear again as a couple of dim-witted guys in this, their third service comedy, and fourth film in a 10-month span. The boys spend some time at Cal-Aero Academy for fliers, but evidently not enough. Foran is a stunt pilot who provides the duo with some typical hair-raising thrills, while Raye, playing twin sisters, serves as Costello's romantic interest—and disinterest. Tunes include "Pig Foot Pete," "Together," "I'm Looking For the Boy with the Wistful Eyes," "Let's Keep 'Em Flying" (Don Raye, Gene de Paul), "I'm Getting Sentimental Over You" (Ned Washington, George Bassman). (See ABBOTT & COSTELLO series, Index.)

p, Glenn Tryon; d, Arthur Lubin; w, True Boardman, Nat Perrin, John Grant (based on a story by Edmund L. Hartmann); ph, Joseph Valentine, Elmer Dyer; ed, Philip Cahn, Arthur Hilton; spec eff, John Fulton.

Comedy/Musical **(PR:AAA MPAA:NR)**

KEEP 'EM ROLLING*½ (1934) 65m RKO bw

Walter Huston, Frances Dee, Minna Gombell, Frank Conroy, G. Pat Collins, Robert Shayne, Ralph Remley, Army Personnel of 16th Field Artillery.

A horse named Rodney saves Huston's life in WW I, and naturally the soldier grows enamored of the equine. However, when Huston and the critter are separated by an insensitive officer, the angered man goes AWOL. He nearly faces a court martial, but everything wraps up nicely when the president retires Rodney and makes Huston his caretaker. Slowed down by a high sap-per-frame ratio. Shot at Fort Myers, Va., with the 16th Field Artillery. First Lt. E. L. Gruber provided "The Caisson Song."

p, William Sistrom; d, George Archainbaud; w, Albert Shelby LeVino, F. McGrew Willis (based on the story "Rodney" by Leonard Nason); ph, Harold Wenstrom; ed, William Hamilton.

Comedy/Drama **(PR:A MPAA:NR)**

KEEP 'EM SLUGGING** (1943) 60m UNIV bw

Bobby Jordan *(Tommy)*, Huntz Hall *(Pig)*, Gabriel Dell *(String)*, Norman Abbott *(Ape)*, Evelyn Ankers *(Sheila)*, Elyse Knox *(Suzanne)*, Frank Albertson *(Frank)*, Don Porter *(Jerry)*, Shemp Howard *(Binky)*, Samuel S. Hinds *(Mr. Carruthers)*, Joan Marsh *(Lola)*, Milburn Stone *(Duke Rodman)*, Joseph Crehan *(Detective-Sergeant)*, Wade Boteler *(Police-Sergeant)*, Paul McVey *(Mr. Meecham)*, Joe King *(Scott)*, Minerva Urecal *(Miss Billings)*, Arthur Hoyt *(Mr. Quink)*, Cliff Clark *(Macklin)*, Alice Fleming *(Matron)*, Dorothy Vaughan *(Mrs. Meegan)*, Mary Gordon *(Mrs. Banning)*, William Gould *(1st Detective)*, Mira McKinney *(Customer)*, Janet Shaw *(Young Girl)*, Dave Durand *(Bingo)*, Jimmy Dodd *(Shorty)*, Dick Chandlee *(Sammy)*, Ernie

Adams *(Dugan)*, Milton Kibbee *(McGann)*, Fern Emmett *(Lady In "Poiple")*, Harry Holman *(Fat Man)*, Johnny Walsh *(1st Student)*, Budge Patty *(2nd Student)*, Lew Kelly *(Jailer)*, Ben Erway *(Sharkey)*, Anthony Warde, Joey Ray *(Thugs)*, Peter Michael *(Young Lover)*, Harryette Vine *(His Girl)*, Frank O'Connor *(2nd Detective)*, Caroline Cooke *(Languid Customer)*, Rex Lease, Bob Hill, Howard Mitchell *(Personnel Managers)*, Bob Spencer *(Mike)*, Jack C. Smith *(Policeman)*, Roy Brent *(Waiter)*, Jane Frazee, Robert Paige *(Stars in Moviehouse Film)*.

Jordan (in Billy Halop's usual role) talks his buddies into giving up crime for the summer and getting a job to free draft-age men for military service. When he lands a department store position he gets mixed up in a hijacking plot. He stays straight, however, and finds himself framed. One of the more responsible of the Bowery Boys series, successfully combining melodrama with the standard wise-cracking. (See BOWERY BOYS series, Index).

d, Christy Cabanne; w, Brenda Weisberg (based on a story by Edward Handler, Robert Gordon); ph, William Sickner; ed, Ray Snyder; md, Hans J. Salter; art d, John B. Goodman; cos, Vera West.

Comedy/Drama **(PR:AA MPAA:NR)**

KEEP FIT** (1937, Brit.) 82m Associated Talking Pictures/ABF bw

George Formby *(George Green)*, Kay Walsh *(Joan Allen)*, Guy Middleton *(Hector Kent)*, Gus McNaughton *(Publicity Man)*, Edmund Breon *(Sir Augustus Marks)*, George Benson *(Ernie Gill)*, Evelyn Roberts *(Barker)*, C. Denier Warren *(Editor)*, Hal Walters, Leo Franklyn *(Racing Toughs)*, Hal Gordon *(Reporter)*, Aubrey Mallalieu *(Magistrate)*, D.J. Williams, Bob Gregory.

A breezy comedy which pits weakling barber Formby against muscular Middleton in a contest to win over manicurist Walsh. Things look gloomy for Formby, but he manages to expose the athletic chap as a crook and then takes his show of strength into the boxing ring. Of course he's the one who ends up with Walsh in his arms.

p, Basil Dean; d, Anthony Kimmins; w, Kimmins, Austin Melford; ph, Ronald Neame, Gordon Dines.

Comedy **(PR:A MPAA:NR)**

KEEP HIM ALIVE (SEE: GREAT PLANE ROBBERY, THE, 1940)

KEEP IT CLEAN* 1/2 (1956, Brit.) 75m Marksman/Eros bw

Ronald Shiner *(Bert Lane)*, James Hayter *(Mr. Bouncenboy)*, Ursula Howells *(Pat Anstey)*, Diane Hart *(Kitty)*, Jean Cadell *(Mrs. Anstey)*, Tonia Bern *(Colette Dare)*, Colin Gordon *(Peter)*, Benny Lee *(Tarbottom)*, Joan Sims *(Vi Tarbottom)*, Gerald Campion *(Rasher)*, Albert Whelan *(Gregson)*, Denis Shaw, Mark Daly, Arthur Goullet, Norman Rossington, Violet Gould, Bert Brownhill, Tony Sympson, Pauline Winter, Lillemor Knudsen, Henry Longhurst, Roger Maxwell.

This nonsensical comedy sees Shiner as an advertising agent who is trying to market his brother-in-law's new cleaning machine. He gets financial assistance from Howells, a Purity Leaguer, and after a number of unfunny situations manages to get the product to the public. Writer R. F. Delderfield is better known for his novels of various aspects of English life *(A Horseman Riding By, To Serve Them All My Days* —these two have been made into British TV mini-series).

p, Maxwell Setton, John R. Sloan; d, David Paltenghi; w, R. F. Delderfield, Carl Nystrom (based on a story by Delderfield).

Comedy **(PR:A MPAA:NR)**

KEEP IT COOL (SEE: LET'S ROCK, 1958)

KEEP IT QUIET* 1/2 (1934, Brit.) 64m BL/MGM bw

Frank Pettingell *(Joe Puddlefoot)*, Jane Carr *(Nancy)*, Davy Burnaby *(Sir Charles Good)*, Cyril Raymond *(Jack)*, D. A. Clarke-Smith *(Vendervell)*, Bertha Belmore *(Mrs. Puddlefoot)*.

A group of jewel thieves wants to remove some hot rocks from a young man's house. In order to gain access to the place, the boy's uncle (Pettingell) is blackmailed by the gang to pose as his nephew's butler. A minor British comedy programmer.

p, Herbert Smith; d, Leslie Hiscott; w, Michael Barringer.

Comedy **(PR:A MPAA:NR)**

KEEP MY GRAVE OPEN* (1980) 78m Wells/Jefferson & Century c

Camilla Carr *(Lesley Fontaine)*, Gene Ross, Stephen Tobolowsky, Ann Stafford, Annabelle Weenick, Chelsea Ross, Sharon Bunn, Bill Thurman.

Carr imagines herself as her long-missing brother, as well as imagining having an incestuous relationship with him. Occasionally she kills stray men who make a pass at her, believing that she is her brother defending her. The victims are killed with a sword then stashed in the backseat of an old car. A drug overdose finally does in the seriously disturbed young lady, just as the long-lost brother returns home. Director Brownrigg has some interesting ideas, but never seems to pull a decent movie out of them. For hardcore gore fans only.

p&d, S.F. Brownrigg; w, F. Amos Powell; ph, John Valtenburgs; m, Robert Farrar; makeup, Jackie Barnes.

Horror **Cas.** **(PR:O MPAA:R)**

KEEP SMILING** (1938) 77m FOX bw

Jane Withers *(Jane Rand)*, Gloria Stuart *(Carol Walters)*, Henry Wilcoxon *(Jonathan Rand)*, Helen Westley *(Mrs. Willoughby)*, Jed Prouty *(Jerome Lawson)*, Douglas Fowley *(Cedric Hunt)*, Robert Allen *(Stanley Harper)*, Pedro de Cordoba *(J. Howard Travers)*, Claudia Coleman *(Mrs. Bowman)*, Paula Rae Wright *(Bettina Bowman)*, Etta McDaniel *(Violet)*, Carmencita Johnson *(Brutus)*, Mary McCarthy *(Froggy)*, Hal K. Dawson *(Casting Director)*, The Three Nelsons *(Themselves)*.

Youngster Withers has her hopes set on breaking into Hollywood as an actress on the silver screen, but runs into some not-too-shining realities. She tries to enlist the aid of her uncle, a film director, and finds him a washed-up, bottle-tipping has-been with no future. Her charisma and unrelenting energy work wonders and Withers becomes a sensation, while Wilcoxon's career is reborn. A cute comedy that takes some nasty looks at the movie business and child stars.

p, John Stone; d, Herbert I. Leeds; w, Frances Hyland, Albert Ray (based on a story by Frank Fenton, Lynn Root); ph, Edward Cronjager; ed, Harry Reynolds; md, Samuel Kaylin.

Drama **(PR:A MPAA:NR)**

KEEP SMILING, 1938 (SEE: SMILING ALONG, 1938)

KEEP YOUR POWDER DRY** (1945) 93m MGM bw

Lana Turner *(Valerie Parks)*, Laraine Day *(Leigh Rand)*, Susan Peters *(Ann Darrison)*, Agnes Moorehead *(Lt. Col. Spottiswoode)*, Bill Johnson *(Capt. Bill Barclay)*, Natalie Schafer *(Harriet Corwin)*, Lee Patrick *(Gladys Hopkins)*, Marta Linden *(Capt. Sanders)*, June Lockhart *(Sarah Swanson)*, Edith Leach *(Mary Carter)*, Jess Barker *(Junior Vanderheusen)*, Michael Kirby *(Capt. John Darrison)*, Henry O'Neill *(Brig. Gen. Rand)*, Tim Murdock *(Capt. Mannering)*, Sondra Rodgers *(WAC Hodgekins)*, Marjorie Davies *(WAC Polhemus)*, Rex Evans *(Marco Cummings)*, Pierre Watkin *(Mr. Lorrison)*, Shirley Patterson *(WAC Brooks)*, Barbara Sears [Bobo Rockefeller] *(WAC McBride)*, George Peters *(Lieutenant)*, Marie Blake, Claire Rochelle *(WAC Corporals)*, Elizabeth Russell *(WAC Sergeant)*, Dorothy Ackers, Claire Whitney *(Fitters)*, Ruth Lee *(Instructor)*, Ray Teal *(Army Captain)*, Early Cantrell *(WAC Company Commander)*, Charlotte Hunter, Margaret Kays, Jetsy Parker, Jane Ray, Beth Renner, Melba Snowden, Bobbie Woods, Judi Blacque, Marilyn Christine, Rita Dunn, Jeanne Frances, Jean French *(WACS)*, Geraldine Wall *(Judo Instructor)*.

Just as so many films had appealed to the patriotic hearts of young men, this is the film that excited young women and caused a slight run on the WAC recruitment headquarters around the country. Turner, Peters, and Day are the Three Musketettes who join the Women's Army Corps for different reasons. Turner is a New York City deb who is in line for a family fortune, but she's spent so much time being a playgirl that the bankers who tend her legacy are loath to award it to her. She joins the WACs to engender their good wishes and to prove that she has more depth than what appears on the surface. But that's a sham and she plans to wash out of the service as soon as she gets her money and then return to visiting the watering spots of cafe society. Day is an Army "brat," so it's logical for her to join. Peters is married to Kirby, who's already in the service, so she signs up in order to be near him. Turner and Day are rivals, with Day, due to her military background and knowledge, constantly twitting Turner, a softie. (One wonders if the authors of PRIVATE BENJAMIN saw this film because there are enough similarities between Turner and Goldie Hawn to draw that conclusion.) Day and Turner zing each other, with Peters acting as a referee. Day is named cadet commander and continues to make Turner's life difficult. Turner holds her tongue and temper in check until Day reads her off in front of the other recruits on the drill field and Turner responds (to the delight of the audience who were wondering "how much more of this will she take?") by slapping Day. Naturally, an inquiry is held, and Turner is vindicated when it is learned that Day has been abusing her rank and is not considered good officer material. Meanwhile, Kirby is killed in action, but Peters keeps that news to herself and spends most of her time attempting to sew up the tear in the fabric of Turner's and Day's relationship. When they learn of Peters' loss, the two women unite and help Peters over the tragedy. In the end, Turner decides that she likes the service and her pals, and will remain in the WACs. This was a fairly authentic look at the corps, although it must be admitted that MGM ladled the glamour on when it came to make-up and off-duty clothes. Bobo Rockefeller has a tiny role here before her marriage to Nelson.

p, George Haight; d, Edward Buzzell; w, Mary C. McCall, Jr., George Bruce; ph, Ray June; m, David Snell; ed, Frank E. Hull; art d, Cedric Gibbons, Leonid Vasian; set d, Edwin B. Willis, Ralph S. Hurst; cos, Irene, Marion Keyes.

War Drama **(PR:A MPAA:NR)**

KEEP YOUR SEATS PLEASE 1/2**
(1936, Brit.) 82m Associated Talking Pictures/ABF bw

George Formby *(George)*, Florence Desmond *(Flo)*, Gus McNaughton *(Max)*, Alastair Sim *(Drayton)*, Harry Tate *(Auctioneer)*, Fiona Stuart *(Bimkie)*, Hal Gordon *(Sailor)*, Fred Culpitt *(Magician)*, Margaret Moffatt *(Landlady)*, Maud Gill *(Spinster)*, Mike Johnson *(Landlord)*, Ethel Coleridge, Tom Payne, Beatrix Fielden-Kaye.

A young man finds out about some gems and, with his shady attorney, sets out to claim the inheritance. There's just one catch: the gems are sewn into the lining of one of six missing antique chairs. This entertaining romp was adapted from a popular Russian play. The story was the subject of many film treatments, most notably Mel Brooks' THE TWELVE CHAIRS. Songs include the title tune and "When I'm Cleaning Windows."

p, Basil Dean; d, Monty Banks; w, Tom Geraghty, Anthony Kimmins, Ian Hay (based on the play "Twelve Chairs" by Elie Ilf, Eugene Petrov); ph, John W. Boyle.

Comedy **(PR:A MPAA:NR)**

KEEPER, THE* (1976, Can.) 88m Lions Gate c

Christopher Lee *(The Keeper)*, Tell Schrieber *(Dick Driver)*, Sally Gray *(Mae B. Jones)*, Ross Vezarian *(Inspector Clarke)*, Ian Tracey *(The Kid)*, Jack Leavy, Leo Leavy *(Messrs. Big)*, Bing Jensen *(Danny)*.

Lee is cast as a crippled administrator of Underwood Asylum, though he could easily be a patient himself, in this tolerable spoof on the genre. It does have a monstrous keyboard machine which, at the touch of a button, administers punishments to the inmates, and two seven-foot-tall twins who contribute to the mad cripple's downfall.

p, Donald Wilson; d&w, Tom Drake (based on a story by David Curnick, Wilson); ph, Doug McKay; m, Eric Hoyt; ed, Sally Patterson, George Johnson; art d, Keith Pepper.

Horror/Satire **Cas.** **(PR:A MPAA:NR)**

KEEPER OF THE BEES*½ (1935) 76m MON bw

Neil Hamilton *(Jamie)*, Betty Furness *(Molly)*, Emma Dunn *(Margaret)*, Edith Fellowes *(Scout)*, Hobart Bosworth *(Bee Master)*, Helen Jerome Eddy *(Shorty)*, Marion Shilling *(Louise)*, James Burtis *(Red)*, Barbara Bedford *(Nurse)*, Lafe McKee *(Dr. Grayson)*, George Cleveland *(Judge)*, William Worthington *(Colonel)*.

This confusing tale involves the story of a faith healer and a woman in charge of her daughter and niece. The two young girls protect one another, but the rest of the plot is difficult to decipher. The story meanders off into a variety of tangents but never really goes anywhere. Hamilton, a fine actor in numerous B films (and later Commissioner Gordon of TV's "Batman") gives this his usual best, which is much better than what the role called for.

p, Trem Carr; d, Christy Cabanne; w, Adele Buffington, George Waggner (based on the novel by Gene Stratton Porter); ph, Harry Neumann; ed, Carl Pierson.

Drama **(PR:A MPAA:NR)**

KEEPER OF THE BEES* (1947) 68m COL bw

Michael Duane, Jo Ann Marlowe, J. Farrell MacDonald, Will Wright, Frances Robinson, George Meader, Gloria Henry, Harry Davenport, Jane Darwell.

Artist Duane has his faith in humanity restored when he meets a bookkeeper, a young girl, and an attractive woman. A thoroughly second-rate programmer. First made in 1935 under the same title.

p, John Haggot; d, John Sturges; w, Lawrence E. Watkin, Malcolm Stuart Boylan (based on a story by Gene Stratton Porter); ph, Henry Freulich; m, Paul Sawtell; ed, James Sweeney; art d, Harold MacArthur.

Drama **(PR:A MPAA:NR)**

KEEPER OF THE FLAME*** (1942) 100m MGM bw

Spencer Tracy *(Steven O'Malley)*, Katharine Hepburn *(Christine Forrest)*, Richard Whorf *(Clive Kerndon)*, Margaret Wycherly *(Mrs. Forrest)*, Donald Meek *(Mr. Arbuthnot)*, Stephen McNally *(Freddie Ridges)*, Audrey Christie *(Jane Harding)*, Frank Craven *(Dr. Fielding)*, Forrest Tucker *(Geoffrey Midford)*, Percy Kilbride *(Orion)*, Howard da Silva *(Jason Richards)*, Darryl Hickman *(Jeb Richards)*, William Newell *(Piggot)*, Rex Evans *(John)*, Blanche Yurka *(Anna)*, Mary McLeod *(Janet)*, Clifford Brooke *(William)*, Crauford Kent *(Ambassador)*, Mickey Martin *(Messenger Boy)*, Manart Kippen, Donald Gallaher, Cliff Danielson *(Reporters)*, Jay Ward *(Pete)*, Rita Quigley *(Susan)*, Maj. Sam Harris, Art Howard, Harold Miller *(Men)*, Dick Elliott *(Auctioneer)*, Edward McWade *(Lawyer)*, Irvin Lee *(Boy Reporter)*, Diana Douglas, Gloria Tucker *(Girls)*, Robert Pittard *(Tim)*, Louis Mason *(Gardener)*, Dr. Charles Frederick Lindsley *(Minister's Voice)*.

This is an offbeat gothic mystery that would be nothing more than a muddled mire if not for the compelling presence of Tracy and Hepburn. Tracy is a war correspondent who is assigned to write the life story of Robert V. Forrest (never seen), a super American patriot who has died tragically in an accident, driving his car through an open bridge. The widow, Hepburn, has shut herself up in a great house, becoming a recluse, yet Tracy is able to penetrate her mourning state and gets her to talk about her hero husband. She agrees to help Tracy reconstruct her husband's life. Tracy begins to feel that all is not right when he overhears Hepburn carrying on a conversation with Hickman that makes him suspect that she had a hand in her husband's death. Slowly, working on Hepburn, he unravels the true nature of the greatly admired deceased man. He was no hero at all and this is evident when Tracy follows Hepburn to a private retreat on the estate, one which reveals the dead man's love for fascism, not democracy. Here Hepburn admits the real insidious nature of her husband. Tracy accuses her of murdering her spouse, which she denies. But she does admit that she knew that the bridge was out and purposely failed to warn him, preferring to have him die than to go on living and attempting to build a neo-fascist organization. She wishes to preserve the good name of her dead husband and so she sets fire to the retreat, dying in the flames while Tracy survives to write the true story. Both Hepburn and Tracy complained to MGM's front office during the production of this film that writer Stewart was reshaping the script as anti-fascist propaganda; they were certainly anti-facist but they did not want the film to be turned into a blatant propaganda piece. Given the success of WOMAN OF THE YEAR, where Tracy and Hepburn were first teamed together, MGM felt they could put this couple into any vehicle and it would work. KEEPER OF THE FLAME did work but not as well as other films in which the duo appeared. Even the accomplished Cukor could do little more than give the film an impressive buildup in the first half for the slow letdown at the end. He later admitted that the film had a "certain wax-works" feel about it. This was the first film Tracy did with Cukor, known as a "ladies' director," one who fussed over details and ordered endless takes, habits contrary to the impatient Tracy. Yet the film was geared to Tracy so both men got along well. Cukor was one of Hepburn's favorite directors since he let her have free reign in interpreting her role, but she sometimes tried to take over the film completely. At one point she instructed Cukor how to set the fire in the retreat house and the urbane, intellectual director glared at her, sighed, then said: "It must be wonderful to know all about acting and all about fires." This caused Tracy to laugh uproariously. When it came to billing it was no laughing matter with Tracy. His name always came first before Hepburn's (a policy the actress contested less and less until, at the end, she sacrificed much more than top billing). Writer Garson Kanin, who was a close friend to both Tracy and Hepburn, once asked the actor why he insisted upon first billing above Hepburn. "Why not?" asked Tracy. "Well," reasoned Kanin, "she's the lady, you're the man. Ladies first?" Snorted Tracy: "This is a movie, chowderhead, not a lifeboat!"

p, Victor Saville; d, George Cukor; w, Donald Ogden Stewart (based on the novel by I.A.R. Wylie); ph, William Daniels; m, Bronislau Kaper; ed, James E. Newcom; art d, Cedric Gibbons, Lyle Wheeler; set d, Edwin B. Willis, Jack Moore; cos, Adrian; spec eff, Warren Newcombe; makeup, Jack Dawn.

Drama **(PR:A MPAA:NR)**

KEEPERS OF YOUTH** (1931, Brit.) 70m BIP/Wardour bw

Garry Marsh *(Knox)*, Ann Todd *(Millicent)*, Robin Irvine *(David Lake)*, John Turnbull *(Gordon Duff)*, O. B. Clarence *(Slade)*, Herbert Ross *(Sullivan)*, Mary Clare *(Mrs. Venner)*, John Hunt *(Henry Venner)*, Ethel Warwick *(Matron)*, Rene Ray *(Kitty Williams)*, Vaughan Powell, Matthew Boulton.

Trouble accompanies the arrival of Marsh, the new sports instructor at a British public school. He uses his forceful personality to influence his colleagues and the headmaster, and then attempts to force himself on the assistant matron, Todd. Irvine comes to her rescue, and he and Todd put the ugly incident behind them, leaving Blighty to start over in Canada.

p, John Maxwell; d, Thomas Bentley; w, Bentley, Frank Launder, Walter C. Mycroft (based on a play by Arnold Ridley); ph, James Wilson, Bert Ford.

Drama **(PR:A MPAA:NR)**

KEEPING COMPANY*½ (1941) 79m MGM bw

Frank Morgan *(Harry C. Thomas)*, Ann Rutherford *(Mary Thomas)*, John Shelton *(Ted Foster)*, Irene Rich *(Mrs. Thomas)*, Gene Lockhart *(Mr. Hellman)*, Virginia Weidler *(Harriet Thomas)*, Virginia Grey *(Anastasia Atherton)*, Dan Dailey, Jr. *(Jim Reynolds)*, Gloria De Haven *(Evelyn Thomas)*, Sara Haden *(Mrs. Foster)*, Henry O'Neill.

The madcap and zany domestic adventures of dad Morgan and his three frolicking daughters. 79 minutes of typical family antics which weren't funny enough to keep this premier episode of an intended series around for a sequel.

p, Samuel Marx; d, S. Sylvan Simon; w, Harry Ruskin, James H. Hill, Adrian Scott (based on a story by Herman J. Mankiewicz); ph, Karl Freund; ed, Elmo Veron.

Comedy **(PR:A MPAA:NR)**

KEK BALVANY (SEE: BLUE IDOL, THE, 1931, Hung.)

KELLY AND ME** (1957) 86m UNIV c

Van Johnson *(Len Carmody)*, Piper Laurie *(Mina Van Runkel)*, Martha Hyer *(Lucy Castle)*, Onslow Stevens *(Walter Van Runkel)*, Herbert Anderson *(Ben Collins)*, Gregory Gay *(Milo)*, Dan Riss *(Stu Baker)*, Maurice Manson *(Mr. Johnson)*, Douglas Fowley *(Dave Gans)*, Frank Wilcox *(George Halderman)*, Yvonne Peattie *(Miss Boyle)*, Elizabeth Flournoy *(Miss Wilk)*, Lyle Latell *(Joe Webb)*, Kelly the Dog.

Kelly is a talented German shepherd and "me" is a down-on-his-luck vaudevillian, Johnson; they team up and start a successful act. Realizing everyone is coming to see the dog, Johnson has some second thoughts and nearly loses Kelly to its rightful owner. Kelly doesn't forget who made him a star, however, and stays by his side.

p, Robert Arthur; d, Robert Z. Leonard; w, Everett Freeman; ph, Maury Gertsman, Clifford Stine (CinemaScope, Technicolor); ed, Ted J. Kent; md, Joseph Gershenson; art d, Alexander Golitzen, William Newberry; cos, Rosemary Odell; ch, Kenny Williams.

Comedy/Musical **(PR:AA MPAA:NR)**

KELLY OF THE SECRET SERVICE** (1936) 69m Victory/Principal bw

Lloyd Hughes *(Ted Kelly)*, Sheila Manors [Sheila Manners, Sheila Bromley] *(Sally Flint)*, Fuzzy Knight *(Lefty Hogan)*, Syd Saylor *(Red)*, Jack Mulhall *(George Lesserman)*, Forrest Taylor *(Dr. Marston)*, John Elliott *(Dr. Walsh)*, Miki Morita *(Ylon)*, Jack Cowell *(Chief Wilson)*.

Agent Hughes is assigned to find out who stole the plans for a guided missile designed by Taylor. He eventually discovers that Taylor stole the invention from Elliott and claimed it for himself. Hughes confronts Taylor, who tries to hypnotize him. Hughes pretends to be under Taylor's control until he sees his chance to subdue the villain. Despite plot holes big enough to drive a missile through, this is a quite entertaining second feature, fast-paced and relatively well acted. The production values are higher than almost any of Victory's other programmers showing some care in lighting and camera work. Mindless entertainment of the best kind.

p, Sam Katzman; d, Robert Hill; w, Al Martin (based on the story "On Irish Hill' by Peter B. Kyne); ph, William Hyer; ed, Daniel Milner; set d, Fred Preble.

Crime **(PR:A MPAA:NR)**

KELLY OF THE U.S.A. (SEE: KING KELLY OF THE USA, 1934)

KELLY THE SECOND*½ (1936) 70m MGM bw

Patsy Kelly *(Molly Kelly)*, Guinn "Big Boy" Williams *(Cecil Callahan)*, Pert Kelton *(Gloria)*, Charley Chase *(Dr. J. Willoughby Klum)*, Edward Brophy *(Ike Arnold)*, Harold Huber *(Spike)*, Maxie Rosenbloom *(Butch Flynn)*, DeWitt C. Jennings *(Judge)*, Billy Gilbert *(Fur Trader)*, Syd Saylor *(Dan)*.

A slow-mover from producer Hal Roach with Kelly as the trainer of a punch-drunk fighter played by Williams. With the help of manager Chase, the Kid becomes a champ. Billy Gilbert, the great comic character actor who played the governor's messenger in HIS GIRL FRIDAY, is again on target as a fur trader.

p, Hal Roach; d, Gus Meins; w, Jack Jevne, Gordon Douglas, Tom Bell, Arthur V. Jones, Jeff Moffitt, William Terhune; ph, Art Lloyd; ed, Jack Ogilvie.

Comedy **(PR:A MPAA:NR)**

KELLY'S HEROES** 1/2** (1970, U.S./Yugo.) 148m Katzka-Loeb/MGM c

Clint Eastwood *(Kelly)*, Telly Savalas *(Big Joe)*, Don Rickles *(Crapgame)*, Donald Sutherland *(Oddball)*, Carroll O'Connor *(Gen. Colt)*, Gavin McLeod *(Moriarty)*, Hal Buckley *(Maitland)*, Stuart Margolin *(Little Joe)*, Jeff Morris *(Cowboy)*, Richard Davalos *(Gutowski)*, Perry Lopez *(Petuko)*, Tom Troupe *(Job)*, [Harry] Dean Stanton *(Willard)*, Dick Balduzzi *(Fisher)*, Gene Collins *(Babra)*, Len Lesser *(Bellamy)*, David Hurst *(Col. Dankhopf)*, Fred Pearlman *(Mitchell)*, Michael Clark *(Grace)*, George Fargo *(Penn)*, George Savalas *(Mulligan)*, Dee Pollock *(Jonesy)*, John G. Heller *(German Lieutenant)*, Shepherd Sanders *(Turk)*, Karl Otto Alberty *(German Tank Commander)*, Ross Elliott *(Booker)*, Hugo De Vernier *(French Mayor)*, Harry Goines *(Supply Sergeant)*, David Gross *(German Captain)*, James McHale *(Guest)*, Robert McNamara *(Roach)*, Read Morgan *(U.S. Lieutenant)*, Tom Signorelli *(Bonsor)*, Donald Waugh *(Roamer)*, Vincent Maracecchi *(Old Man in Town)*, Sandy Kevin, Frank J. Garlotta, Phil Adams *(Tank Commanders)*.

While technically a war picture, it is perhaps more accurately described as a bank robbery film set against the backdrop of WW II. Filmed in Yugoslavia, Eastwood is an atypical U.S. Army lieutenant who, while boozing with a captured German general, finds out about $16 million dollars worth of gold bars behind enemy lines. With a wonderfully colorful cast of characters, Eastwood stages the heist, blazing a trail of destruction en route. Sutherland is exceptionally weird, proving his diversity as an actor (look at DON'T LOOK NOW or EYE OF THE NEEDLE), as the driver of a stolen Sherman tank. Some light-hearted moments help the movie work. A version of "I've Been Working On The Railroad" as they destroy a train station; a hysterical spoof on the Spaghetti Western musical scores of Ennio Morricone as Kelly and his cohorts prepare for a showdown with a German tank. Unfortunately it has almost no pace to speak of, and not much of a script . . . but it is sure to deliver some laughs. Eastwood, unhappy with the fact that director Hutton didn't get the final cut, begged for it to return to the editing room, even offering his own services as editor.

p, Gabriel Katza, Sidney Beckerman; d, Brian G. Hutton; w, Troy Kennedy Martin; ph, Gabriel Figueroa (Panavision, Metrocolor); m, Lalo Schifrin; ed, John Jympson; prod d, Jonathan Barry; art d, Barry; set d, Mike Ford; cos, Anna Maria Fea; spec eff, Karli Bumgartner; m/l, "Burning Bridges," Schifrin, Mike Curb (sung by Mike Curb Congregation), "Si tu me dis," Schifrin, Gene Lees (sung by Monique Aldebert); "Sunshine" (sung by Hank Williams, Jr.); makeup, Trevor Crole-Rees; stunts, Alf Joint; tech adv, Alexander Gerry.

War/Comedy **Cas.** **(PR:C-O MPAA:GP)**

KEMPO SAMURAI (SEE: SAMURAI FROM NOWHERE, 1964)

KENNEL MURDER CASE, THE*** 1/2** (1933) 73m WB bw

William Powell *(Philo Vance)*, Mary Astor *(Hilda Lake)*, Eugene Pallette *(Sgt. Heath)*, Ralph Morgan *(Raymond Wrede)*, Jack LaRue *(Eduardo Grassi)*, Helen Vinson *(Doris Delafield)*, Paul Cavanagh *(Sir Bruce MacDonald)*, Robert Barrat *(Archer Coe)*, Arthur Hohl *(Gamble)*, Robert McWade *(District Attorney John F. X. Markham)*, Henry O'Neill *(Dubois)*, Frank Conroy *(Brisbane Coe)*, Etienne Girardot *(Dr. Doremus)*, Spencer Charters *(Snitkin)*, Charles Wilson *(Hennessey)*, James Lee *(Liang)*, Harry Allen *(Sandy, the Dog Trainer)*, George Chandler *(Reporter)*, Milton Kibbee *(Charlie Adler, Reporter)*, Wade Boteler *(Sergeant)*, Leo White *(Desk Clerk)*, Don Brodie *(Photographer)*, James Burke *(Cop)*, Monte Vandegrift *(Detective)*.

Probably the best of the Philo Vance series which, for the fourth time, starred the inimitable William Powell as the debonaire detective. This time the mystery takes place in a Long Island kennel club and Philo, with the assistance of his Doberman, solves a double murder. Michael Curtiz skillfully helmed this film based on a novel by S.S. Van Dine [Willard Wright]. Powell's earlier Philo Vance films had been produced at Paramount; this was his first for Warner Bros., and the studio moguls apparently felt that his price was too high, despite the picture's success. The next one in the series, THE DRAGON MURDER CASE, starred a lower-priced but still quite effective Warren William. Remade in 1940 as CALLING PHILO VANCE. (See PHILO VANCE series, Index).

p, Robert Presnell; d, Michael Curtiz; w, Robert N. Lee, Peter Milne, Presnell (based on the novel *The Return of Philo Vance* by S.S. Van Dine); ph, William Reese; ed, Ed N. McLarnin; art d, Jack Okey; cos, Orry-Kelly.

Mystery **Cas.** **(PR:A MPAA:NR)**

KENNER 1/2** (1969) 90m M&M/MGM c (AKA: YEAR OF THE CRICKET)

Jim Brown *(Kenner)*, Madlyn Rhue *(Anasuya)*, Robert Coote *(Henderson)*, Ricky Cordell *(Saji)*, Charles Horvath *(Tom Jordan)*, Prem Nath *(Sandy)*, Kuljit Singh *(Young Sikh)*, Sulochana *(Mother Superior)*, Ursula Prince *(Sister Katherine)*, Tony North *(American Friend)*, G.S. Aasie *(Shoe Merchant)*, Mahendra Jhaveri *(Young Hindu)*, Nitin Sethi *(Customs Officer)*, R.P. Wright *(Gym Owner)*, Ming Hung *(Ring Referee)*, Ravi Kaant *(Bald Disciple)*, Hercules, Khalil Amir *(Robed Men)*.

An elementary film made in Bombay casting Brown as an American seaman searching for his friend's killer. He encounters a nine-year-old native boy (Cordell) who is searching for his American father. The boy does not know that he and his mother were abandoned before a marriage could have taken place. Brown chases down the drug-smuggling killer, Horvath, but not before Horvath's evil henchmen can get their hands on him. They drug Brown and attempt to kill him, but the boy creates a distraction and with his help, Brown is able to escape. Brown becomes close to the boy and his mother, with Cordell looking at Brown as a father-figure. Later on when Brown chases Horvath through a railroad yard, an oncoming locomotive flattens the boy's mother. Both the boy and Horvath are fans of cricket fighting. Brown uses Cordell to get into Horvath's hideout during a contest held there. During the cricket fight Brown fights his man and decides to return to the U.S. with the boy who has no family left, but a great love for the old halfback.

p, Mary Phillips Murray; d, Steve Sekely; w, Harold Clemins, John R. Loring (based on a story by Murray); ph, Dieter Liphardt (Metrocolor); m, Piero Piccioni, Prem Dhawan; ed, Richard Heermance; art d, Ram Yedekar; cos, Janice Bond; spec eff, Don Courtney; ch, Sudarshan Kumar; makeup, Rudiger Von Sperle.

Adventure/Crime **(PR:C MPAA:G)**

KENNY AND CO.** 1/2** (1976) 90m FOX c

Dan McCann *(Kenny)*, Mike Baldwin *(Doug)*, Jeff Roth *(Sherman)*, Ralph Richmond *(Big Doug)*, Reggie Bannister *(Mr. Donovan)*, Clay Foster *(Mr. Brink)*, Ken Jones *(Mr. Soupy)*, Willy Masterson *(Johnny Hoffman)*, David Newton *(Pudwell)*, James E. dePriest *(Dad)*, S.T. Coscarelli *(Mom)*, Terri Kalbus *(Marcie)*.

Depending on your judgment all the praise, or blame, goes to young Don Coscarelli who produced, directed, wrote, and shot this film, his second (JIM, THE WORLD'S GREATEST was his debut). There isn't much of a story, just a series of incidents seen from preteen McCann's point of view. A nice homage to kids, which can be seen on a much more brilliant and poetic level in Francois Truffaut's SMALL CHANGE.

p,d,w&ph, Don Coscarelli; m, Fred Myrow; ed, Coscarelli; art d, S.T. Coscarelli; cos, Cyndie Coscarelli.

Drama **(PR:C MPAA:PG)**

KENTUCKIAN, THE** 1/2** (1955) 103m Hecht-Lancaster/UA c

Burt Lancaster *(Big Eli)*, Dianne Foster *(Hannah)*, Diana Lynn *(Susie)*, John McIntire *(Zack)*, Una Merkel *(Sophie)*, Walter Matthau *(Bodine)*, John Carradine *(Fletcher)*, Donald MacDonald *(Little Eli)*, John Litel *(Babson)*, Rhys Williams *(Constable)*, Edward Norris *(Gambler)*, Lee Erickson *(Luke)*, Clem Bevans *(Pilot)*, Lisa Ferraday *(Woman Gambler)*, Douglas Spencer, Paul Wexler *(Fromes Brothers)*, Whip Wilson.

An occasionally brutal, but generally plodding western from Lancaster (his first and only as director) who fails to pump much life into an anemic script which does not give the cast much to do. Directing himself, Lancaster journeys off for a better life in Texas with his son MacDonald, but gets involved with a pair of feuding families. The best scene has an unarmed Lancaster pitted against a leathery Walter Matthau (in his first role), who viciously beats him with a bullwhip. A superb score, as we have come to expect, from Bernard Herrmann.

p, Harold Hecht; d, Burt Lancaster; w, A.B. Guthrie, Jr. (based on the novel *The Gabriel Horn* by Felix Holt); ph, Ernest Laszlo (CinemaScope, Technicolor); m, Bernard Herrmann; ed, William B. Murphy; md, Roy Webb; prod d, Edward S. Haworth; m/l, Irving Gordon; cos, Norma.

Western **Cas.** **(PR:A MPAA:NR)**

KENTUCKY*** 1/2** (1938) 95m FOX c

Loretta Young *(Sally Goodwin)*, Richard Greene *(Jack Dillon)*, Walter Brennan *(Peter Goodwin)*, Douglas Dumbrille *(John Dillon, 1861)*, Karen Morley *(Mrs. Goodwin, 1861)*, Moroni Olsen *(John Dillon, II 1937)*, Russell Hicks *(Thad Goodwin, Sr., 1861)*, Willard Robertson *(Bob Slocum)*, Charles Waldron *(Thad Goodwin, 1937)*, George Reed *(Ben)*, Bobs Watson *(Peter Goodwin, 1861)*, Delmar Watson *(Thad Goodwin, Jr., 1861)*, Leona Roberts *(Grace Goodwin)*, Charles Lane *(Auctioneer)*, Charles Middleton *(Southerner)*, Harry Hayden *(Racing Secretary)*, Robert Middlemass *(Track Official)*, Billy McClain *(Zeke)*, Madame Sul-Te-Wan *(Lily)*, Cliff Clark *(Melish)*, Meredith Howard *(Susie May)*, Charles Trowbridge *(Doctor)*, Eddie Anderson *(Groom)*, Stanley Andrews *(Presiding Judge)*, Fred Burton *(Presiding Officer)*, John Nesbitt *(Commentator)*, Joan Valerie *(Lucy Pemberton)*, Chick Chandler *(Clerk)*, Thaddeus Jones *(Zeb)*, Walter Miller *(Cavalry Sergeant)*, Lee Shumway *(Sergeant)*, John Elliott *(Purchaser)*, Stymie Beard *(Boy)*, Edward Earle *(Man)*, Margaret Irving *(Woman)*, Lee Murray *(Palisades' Jockey)*, Willie Saunders *(Postman's Jockey)*, Bobbie Thomson *(Blue Grass' Jockey)*, Robert Lowery *(Dance Partner at Ball)*, Douglas Wood *(Race Track Patron)*.

An entertaining and bright showcase of Kentucky, whose picturesque blue grass shines, thanks to Technicolor. Akin to "Romeo and Juliet at the Derby," the film has Greene and Young as two lovers hampered by the feud between their families. The feud began when Greene's family took over the girl's grandfather's horse stables during the Civil War in 1861. Brennan, the girl's uncle and one of the original feuders, still keeps the fire alive. Greene works for his father in the family bank until he refuses to grant a loan to Young's family. Already a horse trainer by hobby, Greene goes off and begins training Young's horse. The feud had prevented him from admitting his true identity. But in the midst of their growing love affair before the Kentucky Derby, Young discovers his identity, and orders him out of the stable. When race day arrives, it is a two-horse race between the two families' horses. Young's horse wins, but Brennan dies before he can get much of a taste of the very sweet victory. At his funeral, it is a member of Greene's family who eulogizes him and the feud is forgotten. Brennan won his second Oscar for best supporting actor in as many years for his strong performance here. He went on to win a third two years later (1936, COME AND GET IT; 1938, KENTUCKY; 1940, THE WESTERNER).

p, Darryl F. Zanuck, Gene Markey; d, David Butler; w, Lamar Trotti, John Taintor Foote (based on the book *The Look of Eagles* by Foote); ph, Ernest Palmer, Ray Rennahan (Technicolor); ed, Irene Morra; md, Louis Silvers; art d, Bernard Herzbrun.

Drama/Romance **(PR:AA MPAA:NR)**

KENTUCKY BLUE STREAK* 1/2 (1935) 60m Puritan bw

Eddie Nugent, Patricia Scott, Junior Coghlan, Margaret Mann, Cornelius Keefe, Roy D'Arcy, Roy Watson, Joseph W. Girard.

A jockey imprisoned for a crime he did not commit breaks out to ride the title horse in the big race. He wins the race and his innocence is proved. Worthless little programmer, all but forgotten today.

p, C.C. Burr; d, Raymond K. Johnson; w, Homer King Gordon (based on a story by C. B. Carrington); ph, I.W. Akers.

Drama **Cas.** **(PR:A MPAA:NR)**

KENTUCKY FRIED MOVIE, THE**
(1977) 90m Kentucky Fried Theatre/United Film bw/c

Marilyn Joi *(Cleopatra)*, Saul Kahan *(Schwartz)*, Marcy Goldman *(Housewife)*, Joe Medalis *(Paul)*, Barry Dennem *(Claude)*, Rich Gates *(Boy)*, Tara Strohmeir *(Girl)*, Neil Thompson *(Newscaster)*, George Lazenby *(Architect)*, Henry Gibson, Bill Bixby *(Themselves)*, Donald Sutherland *(Clumsy)*, Evan Kim *(Loo)*, Derek Murcott *(Pennington)*, Master Bong Soo Han *(Dr. Klahn)*, Tony Dow, Richard A. Baker, David Zucker, Jerry Zucker, Jim Abrahams.

A routine drive-in or college party movie which is made up of a series of comedy sketches from a fresh young group formed at the University of Wisconsin in the early 1970s. Depending on the mood, or level of sobriety, it can be a hysterical picture and the worthy recipient of a playfully tossed empty beer can. The top episode is a lengthy (30 minutes) Kung-Fu parody which casts two actual martial arts experts in a surprisingly lavish—and safe—environment. John Landis, who is getting logarithmically more objectionable, would have been better off (and so would many others) had he stopped making movies after this one. Writers Zucker, Zucker, and Abrahams went on to make the absurd AIRPLANE.

p, Robert K. Weiss; d, John Landis; w, David Zucker, Jerry Zucker, Jim Abrahams; ph, Stephen M. Katz (part DeLuxe Color); ed, George Folsey, Jr; md, Igo Kantor; art d, Rich Harvel; cos, Deborah Nadoolman, Joyce Unruh.

Comedy **Cas.** **(PR:O MPAA:R)**

KENTUCKY JUBILEE** (1951) 72m Lippert bw

Jerry Colonna *(Jerry Harris)*, Jean Porter *(Sally Shannon)*, James Ellison *(Jeff Benson)*, Raymond Hatton *(Ben White)*, Fritz Feld *(Rudolph Jouvet)*, Vince Barnett *(Mugsy)*, Chester Clute *(Mayor Tilbury)*, Michael Whalen *(Touhy)*, Archie Twitchell *(Barney Malone)*, Russell Hicks *(T.J. Hoarsely)*, Margia Dean *(Cashier)*, Si Jenks *(Constable)*, Ralph Sanford *(Steve Frome)*, Jack Reitzen *(Fatso)*, Cliff Taylor *(Hotel Clerk)*, Charlie Williams *(Yes Man)*, George Chesebro, Bob Carney, George Sanders, Tom Plank *(Barkers)*, Phil Arnold *(Emcee)*, Mickey Simpson *(Hood)*, Glen Story *(Square Dance Caller)*, Marvel Andre *(Woman)*, McQuaig Twins, Les "Carrot Top" Anderson, Fred Kirby, Chris Randall, Penny McGuiggan, Donna Kaye, Broome Brothers, Bobby Clark, Y-Knot Twirlers, Claude Casey, Slim Andrews, Frankie Vincent, John Braislin, Buck & Chickie Eddy, Edna and Gracia Dreon.

A group of city folk venture into the state of the title and, after initial cultural shock, become accustomed and even enjoy the area. Colonna is cast as the graduate of an entertainers' correspondence school who handles the emcee duties for a grand blue grass jubilee. Don't stay up too late to watch this one.

p&d, Ron Ormond; w, Maurice Tombragel, Ormond; ph, Jack Greenhalgh; ed, Hugh Winn; md, Walter Greene; art d, F. Paul Sylos.

Musical/Comedy **(PR:A MPAA:NR)**

KENTUCKY KERNELS** (1935) 74m RKO bw (GB: TRIPLE TROUBLE)

Bert Wheeler *(Willie)*, Robert Woolsey *(Elmer)*, Mary Carlisle *(Gloria)*, "Spanky" McFarland *(Spanky)*, Noah Beery, Sr. *(Col. Wakefield)*, Lucille LaVerne *(Hannah Milford)*, Sleep 'n' Eat [Willie Best] *(Buckshot)*, William Pawley *(John Wakefield)*, Louis Mason *(Col. Ezra Milford)*, Frank McGlynn, Jr. *(Jess Wakefield)*, Richard Alexander *(Hank Wakefield)*, Paul Page *(Jerry Bronson)*, Margaret Dumont.

Comedy duo Wheeler and Woolsey are a pair of out-of-work magicians, who adopt McFarland ("Spanky" from the Our Gang comedies). It turns out the kid is a missing heir, so it's off to Kentucky for the happy trio, to cash in on the loot. Instead they find themselves in the middle of a family feud and all the Southern stereotyped humor the filmmakers can muster. McFarland steals the show as only movie brats can. Despite the talent behind the writing (Kalmar and Ruby did some of the best material for the Marx Brothers), there's really not much to this comedy. The direction is fast paced though, covering the plot holes and giving the illusion that something funny actually is taking place. The film's two Kalmar and Ruby songs are "One Little Kiss" and "Supper Song."

p, H. N. Swanson; d, George Stevens; w, Bert Kalmar, Harry Ruby, Fred Guiol (based on a story by Kalmar, Ruby); ph, Edward Cronjager; ed, James Morley.

Comedy **(PR:A MPAA:NR)**

KENTUCKY MINSTRELS* (1934, Brit.) 84m REA/UNIV bw

Scott & Whaley *(Mott & Bayley)*, C. Denier Warren *(Danny Goldman)*, April Vivian *(Maggie)*, Wilson Coleman *(Ben)*, Madge Brindley *(Landlady)*, Roddy Hughes *(Town Clerk)*, Norman Green *(Massa Johnson)*, Nina Mae McKinney, Terence Casey, Leslie Hatton, Polly Ward, Eight Black Streaks, Harry S. Pepper and His White Coons, Debroy Somers and His Band, Edgar Driver, Jack Gerrard, Leo Sheffield.

A weak programmer about a pair of minstrel showmen (Scott & Whaley) who do their best to continue making a living as entertainers. They have to resort to real work before finally getting their second chance and hitting it big with an all new, modern revue.

p, Julius Hagen; d, John Baxter; w, Harry S. Pepper, C. Denier Warren (based on the radio series by Pepper).

Musical **(PR:A MPAA:NR)**

KENTUCKY MOONSHINE 1/2**
(1938) 87m FOX bw (GB: THREE MEN AND A GIRL)

The Ritz Brothers *(Themselves)*, Tony Martin *(Jerry Wade)*, Marjorie Weaver *(Caroline)*, Slim Summerville *(Hank Hatfield)*, John Carradine *(Reef Hatfield)*, Wally Vernon *(Gus Bryce)*, Berton Churchill *(J.B.)*, Eddie Collins *("Spats" Swanson)*, Cecil Cunningham *(Landlady)*, Paul Stanton *(Mortimer Hilton)*, Mary Treen *("Sugar" Hatfield)*, Francis Ford *(Grandpa Hatfield)*, Brian Sisters *(Specialty)*, Clarence Hummel Wilson *(Attorney)*, Claude Allister *(Lord Boffingwell)*, Frank McGlynn, Jr. *(Clem Hatfield)*, Jan Duggan *(Nurse)*, Si Jenks *(Buckboard Driver)*, Joe Twerp *(Clerk)*, Irving Bacon *(Hotel Clerk)*, Olin Howland *(Tom Slack)*, John Heistand, Carroll Nye, Tom Hanlon *(Radio Announcers)*.

This probably rates as the zany Ritzes' best flick. After hearing that a major radio show is looking for a hillbilly act they take Weaver along and head for the hills. Along comes city slicker Martin, the radio talent scount. He's fooled by the boys' act and takes them off to New York. But the Ritzes have unfortunately taken on the guise of the Hatfield family, upsetting members of the real feudin' clan. The farce plays well and there are some really good laughs here. Songs: "Moonshine Over Kentucky," "Reuben, Reuben," "I've Been Swingin'," "Sing a Song of Harvest," "Isn't It Wonderful, Isn't It Swell?" (Lew Pollock, Sidney D. Mitchell), "Kentucky Opera" (Jule Styne), Sidney Clare. Additional comedy skits and songs by Sid Kuller and Ray Golden.

p, Darryl F. Zanuck; d, David Butler; w, Art Arthur, M.M. Musselman (based on a story by Musselman and Jack Lait, Jr.); ph, Robert Planck; ed, Irene Morra; md, Louis Silvers; art d, Bernard Herzbrun, Lewis Creher.

Musical Comedy **(PR:AAA MPAA:NR)**

KENTUCKY RIFLE** (1956) 82m Howco c

Chill Wills, Lance Fuller, Cathy Downs, Jess Barker Jeanne Cagney, Sterling Holloway, Henry Hull, John Alvin, Rory Mallinson, John Pickard, George Keymas, Clyde Houck, Alice Rolph, I. Stanford Jolley.

The members of a wagon left behind by a western bound wagon train attempt to make their way through tough Indian country by any means they have available, including money. When word gets out that the wagon contains rifles, the group is in greater danger of Indian attack. Handled in a fashion to prolong the mounting tensions.

p&d, Carl K. Hittleman; w, Hittleman, Lee J. Hewitt.

Western **Cas.** **(PR:A MPAA:NR)**

KEPT HUSBANDS** (1931) 76m RKO bw

Dorothy Mackaill *(Dot)*, Joel McCrea *(Dick)*, Robert McWade *(Parker)*, Florence Roberts *(Mrs. Parker)*, Clara Kimball Young *(Mrs. Post)*, Mary Carr *(Mrs. Brunton)*, Lita Chevret *(Gwen)*, Ned Sparks *(Hughie)*, Bryant Washburn *(Bates)*, Freeman Wood *(Mr. Post)*.

Working class steel worker McCrea marries rich girl Mackaill. He has saved two people in a factory accident, so the boss invites him for dinner. The boss' daughter is impressed and decides she'll land him in a month's time. After the marriage McCrea becomes the man of the title as his wife's extravagances easily eat away at his salary and his ego. But he wins back his self-esteem and her respect by the end as they agree to live on his salary alone. Somewhat dull and rather witless, this film relfects the typical chauvinism of the era.

p, William LeBaron; d, Lloyd Bacon; w, Alfred Jackson, Forrest Halsey (based on a story by Louis Sarecky); ph, Jack MacKenzie.

Drama **(PR:C MPAA:NR)**

KES 1/2** (1970, Brit.) 112m WF-Kestrel/UA c

David Bradley *(Billy Casper)*, Colin Welland *(Mr. Farthing)*, Lynne Perrie *(Mrs. Casper)*, Freddie Fletcher *(Jud)*, Brian Glover *(Mr. Sugden)*, Bob Bowes *(Mr. Gryce)*, Trevor Hasketh *(Mr. Crossley)*, Eric Bolderson *(Farmer)*, Geoffrey Banks *(Mathematics Teacher)*, Zoe Sunderland *(Librarian)*, Joe Miller *(Mrs. Casper's Friend)*, Joey Kaye *(Comedian at Pub)*, Bernard Atha *(Youth Employment Officer)*, Robert Naylor *(MacDowell)*, David Glover *(Tibbutt)*, Douggie Brown *(Milkman)*, Stephen Crossland, George Speed, Frank Norton *(Billy's Friends)*, Martin Harley *(Younger Boy)*, Billy Dean *(Fish and Chip Shop Man)*.

Bradley is the product of a broken home and the victim of school bullies. He takes refuge in his comic books and shoplifting. One day he finds a baby kestrel (a small falcon) and determines to raise the bird. He names it "Kes" and promptly steals a book on falconry. He becomes quite adept at his newfound skills and catches the eye of his teacher Welland. But when his brother Fletcher asks him to put some money on a horse, Bradley spends it on food for Kes. The horse turns out to be a big winner and Fletcher is furious at not getting his expected winnings. He kills Kes in revenge and the film ends with Bradley sadly burying his beloved falcon. Though it's a sensitive and well-handled film, the Yorkshire accents of the actors are nearly impossible to understand, thus limiting the film's real potential. It was filmed on location on the English moors.

p, Tony Garnett; d, Kenneth Loach; w, Loach, Garnett, Barry Hines (based on the novel *A Kestrel for a Knave* by Hines); ph, Chris Menges (DeLuxe Color); m, John Cameron; ed, Roy Watts; md, Cameron; art d, William McCrow.

Children's Drama **(PR:C MPAA:GP)**

KETTLE CREEK (SEE: MOUNTAIN JUSTICE, 1930)

KETTLES IN THE OZARKS, THE 1/2** (1956) 81m UNIV bw

Marjorie Main *(Ma Kettle)*, Arthur Hunnicutt *(Sedge Kettle)*, Ted de Corsia *(Professor)*, Una Merkel *(Miss Bedelia Baines)*, Richard Eyer *(Billy Kettle)*, David O'Brien *(Conductor)*, Joe Sawyer *(Bancroft Baines)*, Richard Deacon *(Cod Head)*, Sid Tomack *(Benny)*, Pat Goldin *(Small Fry)*, Harry Hines *(Joe)*, Jim Hayward *(Jack*

Dexter), Olive Sturgess *(Nancy Kettle)*, George Arglen *(Freddie)*, Eddie Pagett *(Sammy)*, Cheryl Callaway *(Susie)*, Pat Morrow *(Sally)*, Bonnie Franklin *(Betty)*, Louis DaPron *(Mountaineer)*, Sarah Padden *(Miz Tinware)*, Roscoe Ates *(Man)*, Kathryn Sheldon *(Old Woman)*, Stuart Holmes *(Bald-Headed Man)*, Elvia Allman *(Meek Man's Wife)*, Paul Wexler *(Reverend Martin)*, Robert Easton *(Lafe)*.

Percy Kilbride was no longer around as Pa Kettle but Main continued to play her role for this eighth film in Universal's KETTLE series. Hunnicutt is brought in as "Uncle Sedge," a character cut from the same folksy cloth as Pa Kettle. The "plot" has Main and the kids traveling to the Ozarks to visit their uncle. There's some trouble with some bootleggers and a sub-plot involving Hunnicutt's twenty-year "fence-sitting romance" with Merkel. This is a slight film, even by previous KETTLE film standards. The jokes and gags have seen better days. (See MA AND PA KETTLE series, Index.)

p, Richard Wilson; d, Charles Lamont; w, Kay Lenard (based on her original story); ph, George Robinson; ed, Edward Curtiss; md, Joseph Gershenson; art d, Alexander Golitzen, Alfred Sweeney; cos, Jay Morley, Jr.

Comedy **(PR:AAA MPAA:NR)**

KETTLES ON OLD MACDONALD'S FARM, THE 1/2** (1957) 79m UNIV bw

Marjorie Main *(Ma Kettle)*, Parker Fennelly *(Pa Kettle)*, Gloria Talbott *(Sally Flemming)*, John Smith *(Brad Johnson)*, George Dunn *(George)*, Claude Akins *(Pete Logan)*, Roy Barcroft *(J.P. Flemming)*, Pat Morrow *(Bertha)*, George Arglen *(Henry)*, Ricky Kelman *(Elmer)*, Donald Baker *(Abner)*, Polly Burson *(Agnes Logan)*, Hallene Hill *(Granny)*, Sara Taft *(Clarabelle)*, Harvey B. Dunn *(Judge)*, Don Clark, Boyd Red Morgan, Glenn Thompson *(Shivaree Men)*, Edna Smith, Verna Korman *(Shivaree Women)*, Roger Creed, Frank Hagney, Henry Wills, Clem Fuller *(Townsmen)*, Carl Saxe, George Barrows *(Hunters)*, Eva Novak, Chuck Hamilton, George Hickman *(Ad Libs)*.

Last of Universal's KETTLE films as well as Main's final screen appearance. This time Fennelly has the role of Pa Kettle, replacing Percy Kilbride. The couple plays matchmaker for Smith, an honest, though poor, lumberman. Talbott is the spoiled rich girl who Main coaches in the ways of the backwoods so she'll make a suitable wife for Smith. There's also a comical chase involving a bear named "Three Toes." Simplistic and about as interesting as it sounds. (See MA AND PA KETTLE series, Index.)

p, Howard Christie; d, Virgil Vogel; w, William Raynor, Herbert Margolis; ph, Alfred E. Arling; ed, Edward Curtiss; md, Joseph Gershenson; art d, Alexander Golitzen, Philip Barber; cos, Marilyn Sotto.

Comedy **(PR:AAA MPAA:NR)**

KETTO GENRYU JIMA (SEE: SAMURAI III, 1967, Jap.)

KEY, THE*** (1934) 82m WB bw

William Powell *(Capt. Tennant)*, Edna Best *(Norah Kerr)*, Colin Clive *(Andre Kerr)*, Halliwell Hobbes *(General)*, Hobart Cavanaugh *(Homer)*, Henry O'Neill *(Dan)*, J.M. Kerrigan *(O'Duffy)*, Donald Crisp *(Conlan)*, Arthur Treacher *(Lt. Merriman)*, Maxine Doyle *(Pauline O'Connor)*, Arthur Aylesworth *(Kirby)*, Lew Kelly *(Angular Man)*, Dixie Loftin *(Irish Woman)*, Olaf Hytten, Desmond Roberts, David Thursby *(Regulars)*, Robert E. Homans, Ralph Remley *(Bartenders)*, Luke Cosgrave *(Man)*, John Elliott *(Padre)*, James May *(Driver)*, Douglas Gordon *(Operator)*, Mary McLaren *(Street Walker)*, Pat Somerset *(Laramour)*, Wyndham Standing *(Officer)*, Aggie Herring, Kathrin Clare Ward *(Flower Women)*, Dawn O'Day [Anne Shirley] *(Flower Girl)*, Gertrude Short *(Barmaid)*, Charles Irwin *(M.C.)*, Lewin Cross *(Dispatch Rider)*, Edward Cooper *(Lloyd)*.

Though it has not aged well with time, this is an interesting drama about the conflict between the Black and Tans and the Irish Revolutionaries in the 1920s struggle for Irish independence. At the heart of the drama is Powell, an officer decorated three times, once for bravery and twice for "indiscretions." Clive, in an excellent portrayal, is a British intelligence officer whose wife (Best in her American film debut) is having an affair with Powell. The crowd scenes, particularly the one involving a mother and child in prayer before prison gates, are nicely handled. Unfortunately, some street fighting and sniper scenes look like studio shots. Curtiz would later deal more successfully with freedom fighters in the timeless film CASABLANCA.

p, Robert Presnell; d, Michael Curtiz; w, Laird Doyle (based on a play by R. Gore Browne, J.L. Hardy); ph, Ernest Haller; ed, William Clemens, Thomas Richards; art d, Robert Haas; m/l "There's a Cottage in Killarney," Mort Dixon, Allie Wrubel.

Political/Romantic Drama **(PR:A MPAA:NR)**

KEY, THE 1/2** (1958, Brit.) 125m Open Road COL bw

William Holden *(David Ross)*, Sophia Loren *(Stella)*, Trevor Howard *(Chris Ford)*, Oscar Homolka *(Capt. Van Dam)*, Kieron Moore *(Kane)*, Bernard Lee *(Wadlow)*, Beatrix Lehmann *(Housekeeper)*, Noel Purcell *(Hotel Porter)*, Bryan Forbes *(Weaver)*, Russell Waters *(Sparks)*, James Hayter *(Locksmith)*, Irene Handl *(Clerk)*, John Crawford *(U.S. Captain)*, Jameson Clark *(English Captain)*, Sidney Vivian *(Grogan)*, Rupert Davies *(Baker)*.

A gloomy but sometimes thought-compelling film, THE KEY centers about the key to a small apartment occupied by Swiss-Italian immigrant Loren. Canadian tugboat captain Holden arrives in Plymouth, England to perform convoy rescue duty during WW II, going to the aid of vessels damaged by Nazi planes and subs. He meets his old friend Howard who takes him to the small flat to meet Loren. She has always been at the apartment, it seems, and is passed from tugboat captain to tugboat captain as they sense their impending death, passing the key to a friend along with Loren as a hand-to-hand lover. The key passes hands when each tugboat captain feels that his number's up. Before Howard is killed, he gives Holden the key, and, upon his death, Holden moves in with Loren. She accepts these new men like a shell-shocked victim, with an almost bored attitude, implying but hardly justifying her actions as the plight of the eternal refugee. Holden and Loren fall in love, an emotion the apartment tramp has never before experienced, we are asked to believe. This time it's worthwhile, permanent, and she says that he, Holden, will be the last man to whom she will give herself. (She's not much of a prize, what with the unknown numbers of men before him, but it's wartime and rooms are scarce.) Holden, who has been daring at sea when rescuing vessels, begins to pull back, afraid of taking chances, especially when his tug, inadequately armed, is dogged by the same German U-boat. Soon, he believes he will be killed and, in a moment of panic, gives the key to the apartment to another tugboat captain, hulking Moore, who has cast a lecherous eye on Amazonian Loren from the beginning. Holden, however, survives the next voyage and races to the apartment. Loren is gone and Moore gives him back the key, telling Holden that Loren rejected him and left for London. Holden frantically races to the station but just misses the train Loren has taken. He vows he will go to London and find her and make amends. The whole story is far-fetched, master filmaker Reed failing to develop a love story between the excellent at-sea scenes. Loren is nothing special as actress or as a character, exuding neither charm nor grace, and her appeal to Holden is never developed beyond her being his hefty bedwarmer. The film is bleakly photographed and, except for Holden's top-level performance and Howard's almost cameo role, there is little more to recommend. Loren took the role in this less than enviable Foreman opus against the wishes of her husband, film producer Carlo Ponti, wanting to attain status by working with such stellar talents as Reed, Howard, and Holden. Ponti's distrust of the situation consisted of his providing male chaperones for his voluptuous wife whose "raw sensuality" apparently attracted both Holden and Reed. Bob Thomas, writing in *Golden Boy, The Untold Story of William Holden*, stated: "He [Holden] was determined to get her to bed. So was Carol Reed. Both failed because of the bodyguards provided by Miss Loren's husband, Carlo Ponti." During the production actor Bryan Forbes visited the set and showed Holden a scandal magazine which had published photos of Loren from her earlier, cheapie Italian movies in which she bared her enormous breasts. According to Donald Zec, writing in *Sophia*, Holden got so upset he drew Loren's attention. "What is it?" she asked him. Holden handed her the magazine opened to the photos of her and said: "This—isn't it dreadful?" Loren looked appreciatively at the photos, then replied: "I don't think *they're* dreadful. *They* look pretty good to me." The remark was typical of a woman who had peddled her body photographically into major films, a place where she never belonged, but a position she occupied due to the self-indulgence and perhaps wistful hopes of producers, directors, and actors ogling her through one dreary film after another. In one of her films, director Jean Negulesco stripped Loren of her sexual sheath, calling her vain to her face, which completely quashed her fierce posture as an actress. Would that others might have found the courage to do the same; they might have spared viewers the tedium and low acting standards Loren established for too many years.

p, Aubrey Baring; d, Carol Reed; w, Carl Foreman (based on the novel *Stella* by Jan De Hartog); ph, Oswald Morris (CinemaScope); m, Malcolm Arnold; ed, Bert Bates; md, Arnold; prod d, Wilfred Shingleton; art d, Geoffrey Drake; cos, Valerie Leslie; spec eff, Arthur Ibbetson; makeup, Peter Handford, W. Milner.

Drama **(PR:O MPAA:NR)**

KEY LARGO***** (1948) 101m WB bw

Humphrey Bogart *(Frank McCloud)*, Edward G. Robinson *(Johnny Rocco)*, Lauren Bacall *(Nora Temple)*, Lionel Barrymore *(James Temple)*, Claire Trevor *(Gaye Dawn)*, Thomas Gomez *(Curley)*, Harry Lewis *(Toots)*, John Rodney *(Deputy Clyde Sawyer)*, Marc Lawrence *(Ziggy)*, Dan Seymour *(Angel Garcia)*, Monte Blue *(Sheriff Ben Wade)*, Jay Silverheels *(John Osceola)*, Rodric Redwing *(Tom Osceola)*, William Haade *(Ralph Feeney)*, Joe P. Smith *(Bus Driver)*, Alberto Morin *(Skipper)*, Pat Flaherty, Jerry Jerome, John Phillips, Lute Crockett *(Ziggy's Henchmen)*, Felipa Gomez *(Old Indian Woman)*.

The casting could not have been better, the script more apt and biting, and the direction more taut than what was brought together for this nostalgic and suspenseful look backward to a faded gangster era. Bogart is a disillusioned WW II veteran who travels to Key Largo, Florida, going to a broken-down hotel operated by the invalid Barrymore and Bacall, the widow of Bogart's best Army friend, who was killed in battle. When he enters the hotel he's told by several tough-looking characters that the place is closed. Bogart steps into the bar where an inebriated Trevor is rooting for a horse in a race being described on the radio. Trevor's conversation with Bogart is interrupted when she is summoned upstairs. Gomez tells Bogart again that the hotel is closed. When he asks what he and the others are doing there, Gomez tells him: "We're here by special arrangement." Bogart steps outside to meet the owner, Barrymore and his daughter-in-law, Bacall. The sheriff, Blue, and his deputy, Rodney, appear, looking for two Indian brothers who have broken out of jail, but they find no sign of them around the hotel and leave. Upstairs, Gomez escorts a screaming Trevor to her room, creating a commotion. Gomez explains to Bacall and Bogart that Trevor "is a lush, the lady . . . after she bends the elbow a few times, she begins to see things—rats, roaches, snakes, bats, you know . . . a sock in the kisser is the only thing that will bring her out of it." Bacall then tells Bogart that Robinson and his friends have arrived in a bog boat anchored offshore and that Barrymore has allowed them to stay for a while because of his need for money. Bogart next shares his memories of Barrymore's son, describing him as a hero: ". . . It's a wonder he lasted until Cassino." Bogart describes where Barrymore's son is buried in Italy. A gust of wind comes up and Bacall reminds Barrymore that there has been a storm warning. When Bogart and Bacall stroll along the pier, he tells her that he'd like to get a job on a fishing boat, that "life on land has become too complicated for my taste." Bogart helps Bacall anchor the hotel boat and exhibits a fair knowledge of seamanship before the observing Gomez and Haade. Several small boats with Seminole Indians arrive, seeking shelter from the approaching storm, including the wanted Silverheels and Redwing, the Osceola Brothers. Silverheels tells Bacall that they are there to give themselves up. It begins to rain and thunder and the windows of the hotel are quickly boarded up. The strange men inside the hotel fan hats, walk about in their shirtsleeves. The storm causes them to talk about hurricanes which frequent the area. Fans grind slowly overhead. It is clammy and claustrophobic. Haade is really nervous, saying: "I hear that a hurricane blows off roofs, uproots trees, puts the snatch on people and they all go flying around in the sky trogether. That right?" The phone rings and Gomez answers it, telling the caller that Barrymore and Bacall are not available, refusing to turn over the phone to the startled Bacall. Upstairs, in a bathtub, sits Robinson, smoking a cigar, drinking some booze, his heavyset body cooled by a whirring fan. Gomez comes in to tell Robinson that they had to get tough with Barrymore, Bacall, and Bogart, showing them their guns to keep them in control. Later Barrymore asks if they are thieves and Lewis quips: "That's right, pop, we're gonna steal all your towels!" Barrymore vilifies the group, calling Lewis "scum." Robinson tells him to shut up. He then tells them that Barrymore, Bacall, and Bogart are *his* guests for a while. A groan is heard and then Rodney, the deputy, is seen staggering out of a bedroom. He had been waylaid by the gang after returning to investigate, recognizing one of its members. "You won't get away with it, Rocco," he says. Bogart recognizes Robinson but Barrymore fails to identify him. "Johnny Rocco the gangster," Bogart sneers, "the one and only Rocco." Says Barrymore to Robinson: "But they threw you out of the country." "Yeah," snorts Robinson, "that's right . . . after living in the U.S.A. for more than 30 years they called me an undesirable alien, me, Johnny Rocco! Like I was a dirty Red or something!" Barrymore glares at him and says: "You're right, you shouldn't have been deported, you should have been exterminated!" When Robinson makes a move toward the wheelchair-bound old man, Bogart intervenes, saying "I must apologize for Mr. Temple . . . He doesn't know what he's talking about or who to . . . Johnny Rocco was more than a king; he was an emperor. His rule extended over booze, slot machines, the numbers racket, and a dozen other forbidden enterprises. He was a master of the fix. Whom he couldn't corrupt he terrified; whom he couldn't terrify, he murdered." Barrymore calls Robinson a few more names but Bogart says sarcastically that he's old-fashioned and still living in a time "when America thought it could get along without the Johnny Roccos." Then to Robinson: "Welcome back, Rocco. It was all a mistake. America is sorry for what it did to you." Even Robinson's men are astounded to hear that he was once that powerful. "Yeah," that's me," Robinson says, reveling in his notoriety. "Sure, I was all of those things and more! When Rocco talked everybody shut up and listened. What Rocco said went! Nobody was as big as Rocco. It'll be like that again, only more so! I'll be back up there one of these days and then you're gonna really see something!" Barrymore tells Robinson he won't ever get power back. Then Robinson asks if Bogart was a hero during the war and he denies it. "Why'd you stick your neck out?" the mobster asks him. "No good reason," says the cynical Bogart. He adds that he fought because he believed in some words, and quotes from a speech by President Roosevelt. Barrymore is inspired by the patriotic words and tries to get at the gangsters but falls down helplessly. Bacall tries to claw Robinson but he pins her hands. He is distracted when Haade tells him that the Indians outside want shelter and the mobster tells Haade to keep them outside. Robinson then takes a call from a Miami gangster who tells him he's on the way to their rendezvous. The captain of the boat that brought the gang to Key Largo arrives to tell Robinson that he must move the boat or the hurricane will destroy it. Robinson tells him that if he moves the boat he'll kill him. Robinson goes back into the room where Rodney and the others are being held and sits down while Seymour gives him a shave. He lectures all of them about his importance, calling them "hicks," and complaining about the politicians he put into office, especially the mayor of the city he once controlled (a reference to Big Bill Thompson, no doubt, since Robinson is the absolute prototype of Al Capone.) He then talks about Trevor and how she was once good-looking and a fine singer. Robinson goes to Bacall and whispers some obscenities, until she spits in his face. Shocked, the gangster glares at her. Says Barrymore: "Look at him—the great Johnny Rocco, with Nora's spittle hanging from his face! . . . Come over here—I'd like to spit on you!" Enraged, Robinson asks for a gun. Robinson holds a gun on them, talking about killing all of them, but Bogart talks him out of it, saying he'd have to kill everyone, including his own men, to get rid of the witnesses. The storm grows louder and Robinson walks sullenly into another bedroom. Trevor comes into the room and vainly attempts some cheerful conversation. She asks for a drink but the gangsters tell her no, that Robinson said she could not have any more booze. When Robinson comes back, Trevor makes up to him but he brushes her away. He has dressed, discarding his bathrobe. The fierce wind blows open a window and Robinson takes alarm. Then he tests Bogart by giving him a gun and telling him to shoot him if he's got the courage. Bogart throws the gun on a chair but Rodney makes a dive for it and then holds the gun on Robinson, moving toward the door. He opens it and Robinson shoots him. Rodney squeezes the trigger of the gun but it doesn't fire; it's empty. Barrymore still trying to believe in Bogart, tells him: "You knew the gun was empty by the weight, didn't you?" Bogart tells him no, he had no idea. He admits that he was afraid and he doesn't care if Robinson lives or dies. "Let him come back to America," he says. "Let him be President." Bacall loses all respect for Bogart, calling him a coward. All make their way down to the bar area where Trevor tries to get a drink but Robinson stops her. Outside, the Indians call for Barrymore to let them in, but he can do nothing for them. Robinson looks disapprovingly at Trevor and says: "If there's one thing I can't stand it's a dame who's drunk. They turn my stomach; they're no good to themselves or anybody else. She's got the shakes, see, so she has a drink to get rid of them. It tastes so good she has another one and the first thing you know, she's stinko again!" Trevor replies defensively: "You gave me my first drink, Johnny." "Oh, so it's all my fault now? Everybody has their first drink, don't they? But everybody ain't a lush!" Trevor says: "If I'd known you were gonna act like this I wouldn't come here." Robinson sneers: "If I had known what you were like you wouldn't been asked." Robinson then cruelly demands she sing one of her old songs, telling her if she sings a song she can have a drink. Trevor is terrified; her face twitches and she wrings her hands, then resolves to go through with it, describing how her act used to be: "My gowns were gorgeous, very decollete . . . I wore hardly any makeup, just some lipstick, that's all. No lights, just a baby spot. I wouldn't have any entrance—they'd play the intro in the dark, the spot would come on, and there I'd be." Robinson applauds and tells her to sing. Trevor struggles agonizingly through a terrible rendition of "Moanin' Low," her voice cracking, off-pitch, flat, and wholly unappealing, drawing embarrassed looks from Bacall and Bogart. Finishing, she makes a dive for the bar, saying: "Give me that drink now, Johnny." Says Robinson: "No!" "But you promised," she says in shock. "But you were rotten," he sneers. The woman is near collapse. Silently, Bogart stands up, goes behind the bar, and pours a drink, handing it to Trevor, who gratefully gulps it down. Robinson, irate at being upstaged and overruled, slaps Bogart's face. Bogart takes it and then sits down. The storm begins to howl and Robinson grows increasingly nervous, asking Barrymore how bad can the storm get. Barrymore tells him a horror story (based on real fact) about how a hurricane in 1935 washed overt Matecumbe Key and swept all the inhabitants out to sea. Bacall then tells Bogart that she knows, because of what he's done for Trevor, that he's really brave and decent. Robinson paces back and forth like a jittery tiger as glass breaks and the wind whistles through the old hotel. He notices the chandeliers swaying and his fear is recognized by all. He orders his men to make conversation and Gomez nervously launches into an inane monolog about how Prohibition will certainly come back. Robinson calls Barrymore a liar, saying that nobody would live in the area after such a disaster as he has described. Barrymore, to goad the gangster, elaborates how the 1935 hurricane blew an entire train off its tracks and out to sea. Bogart smiles and says: "You don't like it, Rocco, the storm. Show it your gun, why don't you? If it doesn't stop, shoot it." The mob boss becomes enraged when he catches Barrymore praying for a big wave to come crashing down on all of them so that Robinson will be destroyed. Just then a tree crashes through the window and the lights go out. The full fury of the hurricane lashes against the hotel and almost sweeps over the entire key. Outside, huddled on the porch, the hapless Indians cower under the fierce winds and waves, cursing Barrymore for not allowing them inside. The storm abates and Bacall and Barrymore ask Bogart to stay on with them, to consider them his family. Lewis comes in shouting to Robinson that the boat they came in has gone. Robinson looks outside, then returns, saying: "He did it. I told him I'd kill him, but he did it just the same." "Maybe he'll come back," volunteers Gomez. "No," says Robinson. "Why not?" demands Gomez. "Because he believed me when I told him I'd kill him." Robinson is unperturbed. He tells his men that they'll use the hotel boat to return to Cuba and that Bogart will skipper the ship. Robinson tells him that if he doesn't comply, Lewis will work him over. Blue shows up and Robinson orders everyone to act normally. Blue asks if anyone has seen his deputy, the murdered Rodney. All deny seeing him. Blue later finds Rodney's body outside and mistakenly shoots and kills the Osceola Brothers, thinking they were the killers of his deputy. Then Lawrence and his mob arrive. As the rival gangsters eye each other, Robinson and Lawrence speak in mock friendship, then get down to business. Lawrence has his expert inspect a shipment of counterfeit money which Robinson has brought from Cuba and it is pronounced good merchandise. Lawrence leaves a small case of money as payment and departs with his gang. Bogart is forced to take Robinson and gang to Cuba but Trevor smuggles him a gun just before he leaves and, during the trip, he manages to kill all the gangsters, including Robinson, though he is wounded. He calls Bacall on the ship-to-shore radio, telling her he is coming back to her. In the final scene Bogart is shown at the wheel of the launch, guiding it surely through the fog, back to Key Largo. The film was revamped in setting and time from the 1939 Anderson verse play (which ran for 105 performances on Broadway), where Paul Muni played the lead role, a fatalistic ex-member of the Loyalist Army who has returned from the Spanish Civil War. Huston and Brooks, in writing the film script, changed Bogart's role to that of a WW II veteran who had served in the Italian campaign. The writers emphasized the ideals of the early Roosevelt years and how, through public apathy, those ideals were eroding as the gangster element began to once more come to the forefront. Robinson was never better than as the one-time crime czar Rocco, even though he, by this time, resented the gangster image he had so well entrenched in the public mind with such films as LITTLE CAESAR and BROTHER ORCHID, yet he was the epitome of the snarling, sadistic, lascivious, antiromantic, misogynist who would rather put a bullet into someone than say hello. He was perfectly cast here and no one doubted that he was essaying the worst crime monster of them all, Al Capone, who retired to Florida and died there of paresis of the brain (brought on by advanced syphillis) a year before this film was made. Writer Brooks later stated that in his research he also incorporated into the Rocco character the background of Charles "Lucky" Luciano, who had been deported and had gone to Cuba, most believing that he would sneak into the U.S. for one nefarious caper or another. His impact in the film was staggering and even Huston remembered Robinson as the strongest image produced in the movie, stating: "I think KEY LARGO is best remembered by most people for the introductory scene, with Eddie in the bathtub, cigar in mouth. He looked like a crustacean with its shell off." Robinson, however, is an anachronism. He and his gang, except for Lewis, are all out-of-step with the times, living in the Prohibition past, ancient artifacts of a machinegun era long gone. Robinson is magnificent in his portrayal of consummate evil, adroitly playing off Bogart's reluctant hero; the timing of these two faultless actors and their interaction has seldom been matched on film. Offscreen, they had nothing but respect for each other. Ironically, Robinson (in his first film for Warners in six years) makes reference to being treated like "a dirty Red or something," and this was just after he had had a brush with the Hollywood blacklist for his liberal political views. After signing to do the film, Robinson's agent called the actor and told him that he would not get star billing, that his name would come beneath Bogart's. In *All My Yesterdays*, Robinson commented: "The journey down. No suspense to this. I didn't even argue. Why not second billing? At fifty-three I was lucky to get any billing at all." But Bogart treated Robinson with great deference during the production. "On that set *he* gave it all to me," recalled Robinson.

"Second billing or no, I got the star treatment because he insisted upon it—not in words but in action. When asked to come on the set, he would ask: 'Is Mr. Robinson ready?' He'd come to my trailer dressing room to get me. Lionel Barrymore was in the picture and we both gave *him* the deference he deserved." Barrymore also was stupendous, operating out of his wheelchair. He had been invalided for a long period but the 70-year-old actor never missed a cue. When the cameras stopped rolling, Barrymore would entertain the cast by telling funny stories about his theater days and then bursting into Irish songs, particularly "Molly Malone" while employing a Yiddish accent. In *Lauren Bacall By Myself*, the actress recalled a scene where Barrymore "had to draw himself out of his chair defending Franklin Roosevelt. As it happened in real life he hated Roosevelt. John [Huston] told us to watch how he gritted his teeth when he had to praise him—John loved stuff like that." Huston nevertheless admitted in his memoirs, *An Open Book*, that he "especially liked working with Lionel," and that Barrymore confided to Huston that the undoing of his tragic brother John Barrymore was all due to John's appropriation of a sacred Eskimo totem pole while on an Alaskan fishing vacation, how he planted the totem pole in his garden, and that the Great Profile's luck went sour thereafter. "Lionel attributed this entirely to the totem pole. John had handled this holy object casually and thereby angered some Eskimo god." Trevor, whom all admired, would walk away with an Oscar for Best Supporting Actress, playing the alcoholic, faded gangster's moll, her only ambition being to swill down another drink to blot out the sight of the criminal world that had consumed her. Her part, too, according to Huston (quoted in *Inside Warner Brothers, 1935–1951* by Rudy Behlmer) was based on a real life gun moll; " . . . Luciano's mistress, Gay Orlova, an American showgirl I met in London in the early 1930s . . . From time to time I saw her name in the newspapers—when she made the statement she would follow Luciano out of the country if he were deported, the occasional alcoholic difficulties she encountered, etc. The last item I recall was that she had been sentenced to be executed by a German or French firing squad . . . " Everything about the film is superb, including the meticulous sets by MacLean (contrary to popular belief there was no hotel in Key Largo used in the film, the entire building, surrounding area, plus the beach area facing a studio tank, was constructed on the Warner Bros. lot), and Steiner's marvelous score, forceful, yet lyrical and nostalgic. The exterior shots of the hurricane were taken from stock footage used in another Warner film, NIGHT UNTO NIGHT, made before KEY LARGO but not released until 1949. Though there is a similarity to THE PETRIFIED FOREST (1936), the Huston film is singularly unique, presenting the old criminal world of America pitted against post-WW II optimism and a new world that had been made safe for democracy and free of the tyrannies practiced by "the Johnny Roccos of the world." It's really a confrontation of ideologies and psychologies, expertly drawn on a common level of understanding, packed with tension and suspense. The climactic gun battle on board the boat where Bogart outwits the entire gang while Robinson pleads for his life while holding out a gun to shoot his unseen nemesis Bogart is full of action and alleviates the claustrophobic scenes in the hotel which was the setting for the Anderson play. In the end the viewer will be forced to conclude that Huston was right; Robinson walks away with the picture. He is a swaggering electric charge zapping everything and everyone in sight, epitomized in lines of dialog when asked by Barrymore what he wants out of life. "More," he says, "yeah, more." "Ever get enough?" Bogart asks him. "Never have, guess I never will." Witty, basic, touching all the deep human emotions and nevertheless providing riveting entertainment, KEY LARGO stands as a masterpiece of *film noir*, a production against which most crime films can be judged and few can match.

p, Jerry Wald; d, John Huston; w, Richard Brooks (based on the play by Maxwell Anderson); ph, Karl Freund; m, Max Steiner; ed, Rudi Fehr; art d, Leo K. Kuter; set d, Fred M. MacLean; cos, Leah Rhodes; spec eff, William McGann, Robert Burke; m/l, Ralph Rainger, Howard Dietz; makeup, Perc Westmore.

Crime Drama **Cas.** **(PR:C MPAA:NR)**

KEY MAN, THE* 1/2
(1957, Brit.) 63m Insignia/Anglo-Amalgamated bw (AKA: LIFE AT STAKE)

Lee Patterson *(Lionel Hulme)*, Hy Hazell *(Gaby/Eva)*, Colin Gordon *(Larry Parr)*, Philip Leaver *(Smithers)*, Paula Byrne *(Pauline)*, Henry Vidon *(Hallow)*, Harold Kasket *(Dimitriadi)*, Maudie Edwards *(Mrs. Glass)*, George Margo *(Jeff, Photographer)*, Ian Wilson *(Process Server)*, Billy Milton *(French Waiter)*, Dennis Castle *(Inspector)*, Dave Rhodes *(2nd Barber)*, James McLaughlin *(Customer)*, Rex Rashley *(Custodian)*.

Radio crime show host Patterson recreates a murder on the air and soon finds himself mixed up with some real gangsters. He is sent on a search for a safe-deposit box loaded with a fortune, but his ingenuity and cunning leads to the capture of the criminals. He also learns a thing or two about messing with crime.

p, Alex C. Snowden; d, Montgomery Tully; w, J. McLaren Ross (based on his play); ph, Philip Grindrod.

Crime **(PR:A MPAA:NR)**

KEY TO HARMONY* (1935, Brit.) 68m British and Dominions/PAR bw

Belle Chrystal *(Mary Meynell)*, Fred Conyngham *(Victor Barnett)*, Reginald Purdell *(Tom Kirkwood)*, Olive Sloane *(Nonia Sande)*, Ernest Butcher *(Mr. Meynell)*, Muriel George *(Mrs. Meynell)*, D. A. Clarke-Smith *(Rupert Golder)*, Cyril Smith *(Fred)*, Joan Harben, Jack Knight.

A struggling music composer (Conyngham) marries an actress (Chrystal) and then begins achieving some deserved recognition. However, success makes him a mite heady and the thought of leaving his wife for greener pastures is more than tempting.

p, Anthony Havelock-Allan; d, Norman Walker; w, Basil Mason (based on the novel *Suburban Retreat* by John B. Wilson).

Drama **(PR:A MPAA:NR)**

KEY TO THE CITY 1/2** (1950) 99m MGM bw

Clark Gable *(Steve Fisk)*, Loretta Young *(Clarissa Standish)*, Frank Morgan *(Fire Chief Duggan)*, Marilyn Maxwell *(Sheila)*, Raymond Burr *(Les Taggart)*, James Gleason *(Sgt. Hogan)*, Lewis Stone *(Judge Silas Standish)*, Raymond Walburn *(Mayor Billy Butler)*, Pamela Britton *(Miss Unconscious)*, Zamah Cunningham *(Mrs. Butler)*, Clinton Sundberg *(Clerk)*, Marion Martin *(Emmy)*, Bert Freed *(Emmy's Husband)*, Emory Parnell *(Council Chairman)*, Clara Blandick *(Liza)*, Richard Gaines *(Speaker)*, Roger Moore *(Assistant Clerk)*, Dorothy Ford *(Miss Construction)*, Pierre Watkin *(Mayor Cabot)*, Nana Bryant *(Mrs. Cabot)*, Victor Sen Yung *(Chinese MC)*, Marvin Kaplan *(Francis)*, Byron Foulger *(Custodian)*, Edward Earle, Jack Elam, Frank Ferguson, Alex Gerry, James Harrison, Frank Wilcox *(Councilmen)*, Shirley Lew *(Elevator Operator)*, Bill Cartledge *(Page Boy)*, Helen Brown *(Woman)*, Dick Wessel *(Washer)*, Harry Harvey, Sr. *(Waiter)*, James Flavin *(Cop)*, Charles Smith *(Bellboy)*.

A pleasant comedy with some sharp lines, a bit of satire, and an unfortunate choice of roles to mark Morgan's last film, as he died, at 59, shortly after the film's completion. There's a mayors' convention in Baghdad by The Bay, San Francisco. Young is the spinsterish mayor of a tiny town in Maine, and Gable an ex-stevedore who now runs a Northern California city. Although cut from very different cloths, they are both seriously honest about their work. The convention gets a bit rowdy and both are pushed into each other's arms through a series of circumstances. Several funny complications ensue and both achieve enough notoriety in the local press to get them almost thrown out of their offices. They are close to going to jail (where Gleason is excellent as the booking sergeant) when they find that they love each other in a romantic scene amid fog banks on Telegraph Hill and wind up in a clinch. When Gable takes her back to his small town, they unite to defeat Burr, a crooked politician with aspirations for the mayor's job. Early in the film, they get a flower-laden key to the city, a huge souvenir. As the picture unfolds, the flowers fall off and they are left with a skinny piece of metal that looks very ugly. Morgan is Gable's fire chief, a man with pyromaniacal tendencies, and Walburn is a noisy Texas mayor, not unlike Kenny Delmar's radio character of Sen. Claghorn on the Fred Allen show of the 1940s. Maxwell is "The Other Woman," a bubble dancer who would like to take Gable away until Young, using some judo, shows Maxwell that she means to keep her man. Many of MGM's stable of excellent character actors were used, including Blandick (who will forever be known as "Auntie Em" in WIZARD OF OZ), Sundberg, Freed, Foulger, Stone, and a very young Elam. Gable and Young deliver their comedy lines with the same conviction they always applied to their dramatic roles, so even the most feeble joke has a ring of believability. They've taken the usual convention story and added the element of puncturing pomposity to it by making the revelers mayors instead of Moose or Elks or Lions, or any of the others in the menagerie of men's service organizations. Some slapstick, some romance, a few bon mots, and excellent situations all add up to an amusing trifle.

p, Z. Wayne Griffin; d, George Sidney; w, Robert Riley Crutcher (based on the story by Albert Beich); ph, Harold Rosson; m, Bronislau Kaper; ed, James E. Newcom; art d, Cedric Gibbons, Hans Peters.

Comedy **(PR:A MPAA:NR)**

KEY WITNESS* (1947) 67m COL bw

John Beal *(Milton Higby)*, Trudy Marshall *(Marge Andrews)*, Jimmy Lloyd *(Larry Summers)*, Helen Mowery *(Sally Guthrie)*, Wilton Graff *(Albert Loring)*, Barbara Reed *(Martha Higby)*, Charles Trowbridge *(John Ballin)*, Harry Hayden *(Custer Bidwell)*, William Newell *(Smiley)*, Selmer Jackson *(Edward Clemmons)*, Robert Williams *(Officer Johnson)*, Victoria Horne *(Nurse Sibley)*.

A very insubstantial B film involving the adventures of Beal as an inventor accidentally caught up in the murder of his girl friend. He tries to change his identity by disguising himself as a hobo, but only succeeds in getting himself into further trouble. The continuity is incomprehensible and the acting is unbelievable. This is an excellent lesson in how not to make a movie.

p, Rudolph C. Flothow; d, D. Ross Lederman; w, Edward Bock, Raymond L. Schrock (based on a story by J. Donald Wilson); ph, Philip Tannura; ed, Dwight Caldwell; md, Mischa Bakaleinikoff; art d, Harold MacArthur.

Crime Drama **(PR:C MPAA:NR)**

KEY WITNESS 1/2** (1960) 81m Avon/MGM bw

Jeffrey Hunter *(Fred Morrow)*, Pat Crowley *(Ann Morrow)*, Dennis Hopper *("Cowboy")*, Joby Baker *("Muggles")*, Susan Harrison *(Ruby)*, Johnny Nash *("Apple")*, Corey Allen *("Magician")*, Frank Silvera *(Detective Rafael Tomo)*, Bruce Gordon *(Arthur Robbins)*, Terry Burnham *(Gloria Morrow)*, Dennis Holmes *(Phil Morrow)*.

Hunter and Crowley are a nice suburban couple. While using a pay-phone in the Los Angeles slums, Hunter sees a street gang (led by a young Hopper) knife another youth. He comes forward to the cops and the gang terrorizes him. Though well-played, the film is a little too sadistic for its own good. Some nice performances though, and the direction builds tension effectively. The ending resolves things just a little too neatly and glosses over some racial prejudice. Pandro Berman was the original producer of this film but apparently was displeased with the results and had his name struck from the credits, thus giving associate producer Kathryn Hereford the producer's billing.

p, Kathryn Hereford; d, Phil Karlson; w, Alfred Brenner, Sidney Michaels (based on the novel by Frank Kane); ph, Harold E. Wellman (CinemaScope); m, Charles Wolcott; ed, Ferris Webster; art d, George W. Davis, Malcolm Brown; cos, Kitty Mager.

Crime/Drama **(PR:O MPAA:NR)**

KEYHOLE, THE** (1933) 70m WB bw

Kay Francis *(Anne Valee Brooks)*, George Brent *(Neil Davis)*, Glenda Farrell *(Dot)*, Allen Jenkins *(Hank Wales)*, Monroe Owsley *(Maurice Le Brun)*, Helen Ware *(Portia Brooks)*, Henry Kolker *(Schuyler Brooks)*, Ferdinand Gottschalk *(Brooks' Lawyer)*, Irving Bacon *(Grover The Chauffeur)*, Clarence Wilson *(Weems, Head of the Detective Agency)*, George Chandler *(Joe The Desk Clerk)*, Heinie Conklin *(Departing Guest)*, Renee Whitney *(Cheating Wife)*, John Sheehan *(Bartender)*, Gordon "Bill" Elliott *(Dancing Extra)*, George Humbert, Gino Corrado *(Waiters)*, Maurice Black *(Salesman)*, Leo White *(Porter)*.

Francis is married to millionaire Kolker but discovers that her supposed ex-husband Owsley never got the divorce he said he would. Now he wants $50,000 to keep the whole affair under wraps. She confesses to her sister-in-law Ware and heads down to Havana to get a quickie divorce. But Kolker has been suspicious of his wife and hires private detective Brent to follow her, not explaining their relationship. Brent becomes friendly with Francis and they spend a good deal of time together. Owsley follows Francis to Havana, as she hoped. He is not an American citizen and she is hoping her wealthy sister-in-law can pull some strings to deny him re-entry. But Ware hears about Kolker's dealings and tells him the whole story. He flies off to Cuba and sends Brent a telegram notifying him of his impending arrival. Meanwhile, Francis tells Brent her story and he levels with her— also revealing that in the course of his work he has fallen in love with her. Owsley arrives but Brent succeeds in getting rid of him. But in Owsley's haste to flee, he falls to his death off a hotel balcony. Kolker arrives at last but Francis tells him off, saying she is through with him. Besides, they aren't legally wed. The film ends with her and Brent beginning a life together. Though advertised as "the only picture . . . that keeps abreast of 1933's changing moral standards!" the film is little more than soap opera with some fine acting. Francis had achieved enormous success in TROUBLE IN PARADISE and CYNARA while on loan to other studios (as well as some excellent teamings with William Powell including ONE WAY PASSAGE for Warners), but the executives at Warners overlooked her natural comedic gifts and stuck her in low-quality films like this. Her basic duty is to go through the motions and serve as a clothes horse, but Francis is too good an actress to allow herself to be reduced to such triffle. She gives a fine performance, overcoming the weak script and limited support from Brent.

p, Hal Wallis; d, Michael Curtiz; w, Robert Presnell (based on the story "Adventuress" by Alice D.G. Miller;) ph, Barney McGill; ed, Ray Curtiss; md, Leo F. Forbstein; art d, Anton Grot; cos, Orry-Kelly.

Drama **(PR:A MPAA:NR)**

KEYS OF THE KINGDOM, THE*** (1944) 137m FOX bw

Gregory Peck *(Father Francis Chisholm)*, Thomas Mitchell *(Dr. Willie Tullock)*, Vincent Price *(Rev. Angus Mealy)*, Rose Stradner *(Mother Maria Veronica)*, Roddy McDowall *(Francis, as a Boy)*, Edmund Gwenn *(Rev. Hamish MacNabb)*, Sir Cedric Hardwicke *(Monsignor Sleeth)*, Peggy Ann Garner *(Nora, as a Child)*, Jane Ball *(Nora)*, James Gleason *(Dr. Wilbur Fiske)*, Anne Revere *(Agnes Fiske)*, Ruth Nelson *(Lisbeth Chisholm)*, Benson Fong *(Joseph)*, Leonard Strong *(Mr. Chia)*, Edith Barrett *(Aunt Polly)*, Philip Ahn *(Mr. Pao)*, Sara Allgood *(Sister Martha)*, Arthur Shields *(Father Tarrant)*, Richard Loo *(Lt. Shon)*, Ruth Ford *(Sister Clotilde)*, Kevin O'Shea *(Father Craig)*, H.T. Tsiang *(Hosannah Wong)*, Si-Len Chen *(Philomena Wang)*, Eunice Soo Hoo *(Anna)*, Dennis Hoey *(Alex Chisholm)*, Abner Biberman *(Bandit Captain)*, J. Anthony Hughes *(Ned Bannon)*, George Nokes *(Andrew)*, Hayward Soo Hoo *(Chia-Yu)*, Joseph Kim, Richard Wang *(Chinese Servants)*, James Leong *(Taoist Priest)*, Moy Ming *(Chinese Physician)*, Frank Eng *(Father Chou)*, Oie Chan *(Grandmother)*, Clarence Lung *(She Wing Soo Hoo, Orderly)*, Ruth Clifford *(Sister Mercy Mary)*, Ethel Griffies *(Mrs. Glennie)*, Lumsden Hare *(Daniel Glennie)*, Terry Kilburn *(Malcom Glennie)*, Beal Wong *(Chinese Captain)*, Eugene Louie *(Joshua, Chinese Orphan)*.

Fox had a smash religious picture the year before with THE SONG OF BERNADETTE and someone must have figured that there was gold in that mine so they bought Cronin's best-seller and put it into production. It was Peck's second film and made him a star. Although only in his late 20s, Peck played an aging Catholic priest who is about to be retired to a home for old missionaries in Scotland. Hardwicke has been chosen to determine if Peck should be farmed out to a green pasture. As he reviews Peck's career, he realizes that this humble, self-effacing man had done some wonderful things for the church. Told in several flashbacks, we see the young man (played by McDowall) view his father murdered solely on the grounds of being a Catholic. Peck takes over the acting chores and goes to China where he assembles a large following from the villagers of Tai Pan. Interwoven is a battle of wits between Peck and haughty Mother Superior Stradner, a German aristocrat who learns the meaning of humility from him. Price is a boyhood pal of Peck's, but he has become a snob and makes the local peasants carry him around. Gleason is a Methodist missionary toiling in the same area. Gwenn is another Scotsman and mentor; Mitchell is a doctor friend. There really isn't much of a story beyond the character study of Peck and all of those whose lives he touches with his devout faith. At 137 minutes, it was a fat film, which was odd when one considers the two screenwriters, Mankiewicz and Johnson. Mankiewicz would be more guilty of thick scripts in his later years, but Johnson seldom wrote anything longer than 110 pages in his entire career (producers use the rule of thumb that one script page equals one minute on screen). Even at that length, it moved at a medium pace and managed to make its points without moralizing or propagandizing Christianity. It was a huge success in 1944 and managed to glean Oscar nominations for Peck, cinematographer Miller, and composer Newman. There were many excellent set-piece scenes, including Peck's life-saving of a local Mandarin's son when the boy's arm is blood-poisoned. Peck was excellent as the priest, as he has been in several other movies in which he was thoughtfully cast. But when he is miscast, such as in MOBY DICK, it's not a pretty picture. Lots of good work from several character people, including the luminous Garner, Revere, Ahn, and Loo. Editor Clark later gave up the scissors and became a director in television where he had success with many of his projects, including a stint with "Batman." Seeing Gleason as a missionary was unusual as he mostly made his mark in films playing the Irish fight manager, a cop, or a reporter. Gleason was also a playwright with many credits and received screenwriter credit on several films, including BROADWAY MELODY.

p, Joseph L. Mankiewicz; d, John M. Stahl; w, Mankiewicz, Nunnally Johnson (based on the novel by A. J. Cronin); ph, Arthur Miller; m, Alfred Newman; ed, James B. Clark; art d, James Basevi, William Darling; set d, Thomas Little, Frank E. Hughes; spec eff, Fred Sersen.

Drama **(PR:A MPAA:NR)**

KHARTOUM**** (1966, Brit.) 134m UA c

Charlton Heston *(Gen. Charles Gordon)*, Laurence Olivier *(The Mahdi)*, Richard Johnson *(Col. J.D.H. Stewart)*, Ralph Richardson *(Mr. Gladstone)*, Alexander Knox *(Sir Evelyn Baring)*, Johnny Sekka *(Khaleel)*, Michael Hordern *(Lord Granville)*, Zia Mohyeddin *(Zobeir Pasha)*, Marne Maitland *(Sheikh Osman)*, Nigel Green *(Gen. Wolseley)*, Hugh Williams *(Lord Hartington)*, Douglas Wilmer *(The Khalifa Abdullah)*, Edward Underdown *(Col. Hicks)*, Alec Mango *(Bordeini Bey)*, George Pastell *(Giriagis Bey)*, Peter Arne *(Maj. Kitchener)*, Alan Tilvern *(Awaan)*, Michael Anthony *(Herbin)*, Jerome Willis *(Frank Power)*, Leila *(The Dancer)*, Ronald Leigh-Hunt *(Lord Northbrook)*, Ralph Michael *(Sir Charles Dilke)*, Leo Genn *(Narrator)*.

This is a richly photographed historical epic, a great spectacle that, in spite of its enormity and scope, is well-written and acted, and provides suspense and entertainment decidedly on the dark side. Heston is more impressive in this thickly colored pageant than in most of his other epics, playing with incisive authority that mystical British general, Sir Charles "Chinese" Gordon, martyr of Khartoum, killed on January 26, 1885 by fanatical Sudanese tribesmen under the leadership of a religious zealot known as "The Mahdi" (the chosen one) after they overran Khartoum following a 317-day siege. It was of Gordon that the British poet Alfred, Lord Tennyson was moved to write: "This earth hath never born a nobler man." Gordon, a paradoxical creature, was both realist and idealist, and Heston somehow manages to capture the elusive enigma in his superb characterization. Underdown (Col. Billy Hicks), commanding 8,000 untrained Egyptian troops, is lured from the El Dueim river and into the desert 100 miles beyond Khartoum, the destination of this relief force. The British-led troops are ambushed by 80,000 fierce Sudanese warriors commanded by the Mahdi and massacred. Richardson, playing British Prime Minister Gladstone, learns of the massacre and that Olivier, The Mahdi, is fighting a holy war, a Jihad, intent upon getting rid of all infidels in the Sudan and taking the great city of Khartoum to prove his power and divine mission. Heston is sent to try to make peace with the zealot and also to discover a way of evacuating the Egyptian army defending the city and protecting the inhabitants. He journeys toward Khartoum and learns that he is no longer respected as a great leader of men, that the natives have shifted their allegiance to Olivier. But when he arrives in Khartoum, the terrified populace receives him as a savior. Heston soon goes into the desert and meets with Olivier whom he addresses as "Mohammed Ahmed." Olivier corrects him: "Mohammed el Mahdi," then adds, "I do not often meet with a Christian, Gordon Pasha. Is it because you are a Christian that I feel myself in the presence of evil?" Heston responds unperturbed: "I think not for I smell the same evil on your own person, and you are not a Christian. So it cannot be that, can it?" Angry at the sharp retort, Olivier tells Heston that he must leave, that he does not wish to take his life. He goes on to describe how he has a holy mission, instructed from on high to "pray not only in the mosque of Khartoum but in the mosques of Cairo and Mecca and Baghdad, and Constantinople." He has declared his plan for world domination, or, at least an empire of all the Arab nations. He insists that the Egyptian army remain in Khartoum to be destroyed by his hordes: "The Egyptians must remain in Khartoum, for I shall take it in blood and the streets must flow with blood; the Nile must taste of blood for a thousand miles downstream so that the whole of Islam will learn that my miracle is a great and terrible thing, and no man will stand against me." Heston returns to Khartoum and dispatches his aide Johnson to England with a strong plea that a British army be sent, explaining to Richardson that there will be no reasoning with a madman like Olivier. Johnson's boat is attacked while Heston prepares to defend the walled city, ordering that a moat be created about the city so that the Nile floods it and offers a natural barrier. Heston leads a raid into the desert, stealing a great herd of cattle from Olivier's camps, but food is still in short supply. The Nile recedes and soon the city will again be vulnerable to attack. Heston then receives word that a British relief force is approaching the city. Then Olivier summons him to another meeting in the desert. There, in his tent, the zealot shows Heston the heads of foreigners who were captured on the escape boat—and the severed hand of Johnson, his aide—adding that there is no British relief column, that he had sent the message to build false hope. He asks that Heston leave Khartoum, promising that he will not be molested. Heston realizes that by staying—even alone, and to be killed—he can become a more deadly foe, a martyred symbol around which Britain and her allies can build their own crusade which will overcome Olivier in the end. "I will not leave Khartoum," he tells Olivier, "for I, too, perform miracles. And you shall witness one. While I may die for your miracle, you will certianly die of mine." At dawn the Sudanese swarm over the ancient walls of the city, slaughter the populace, and Heston is speared to death, his head severed and brought to Olivier's tent, impaled on a pole. Olivier realizes the error of this important death instantly, shrieking: "I forbade it! I forbade it!" Plague spreads from rats eating the corpses in the devastated city and decimates Olivier's armies in five months and he, too, is dead within that time and with him his dreams of a holy war. Everything about this film, from costumes to armaments, is historically correct, producer Blaustein being a stickler for authenticity. He even sent the literate script to the grandson of the Mahdi who returned it with a note reading: "It's an extremely fine script." He added that to his knowledge Gordon and his grandfather never met. Blaustein expressed his regret that the script showed them meeting but the present Mahdi replied: "Ah, but

Mr. Blaustein, they should have!" Heston would later remark about the historical character he so admirably portrayed, saying: "Gordon was a fantastic man. A little mad, I think, but fascinating. He had a serenity of nature, along with a somewhat irrational temper. He was something of a martinet as well, and a lot of other complicated things. But he did not have that curious neuroticism that, say, Lawrence [of Arabia] had, though they both had a sort of soldier mysticism." KHARTOUM's photography is outstanding and the color brilliant. Olivier is fascinating but a few critics accused him of appearing as a black-faced minstrel; such critics were obviously unaware of the true hue of the Sudanese, although there is no doubt that Olivier, who was always a technical mimic, borrowed Rex Harrison's physical look from KING RICHARD AND THE CRUSADERS, just as he had borrowed character actor Albert Basserman's voice for his role in THE BOYS FROM BRAZIL. Olivier had just finished playing Othello in a British production and was undoubtedly still under the influence of the dark-faced moor. He is, nevertheless, stunning and frightening in his barbaric role. Richardson renders his usual expert performance as Gladstone, infusing the part with cynical amusement. Also outstanding is Johnson as Heston's loyal-unto-death aide and Sekka as Heston's fearless servant who dies with him in the doomed city of Khartoum. The action sequences in KHARTOUM are visually awesome and the credit for them should go to Yakima Canutt who directed them. A four-minute prolog depicting the Nile valley and narrated by Eliot Elisofon, a photographic treasure, was cut from the film after its release.

p, Julian Blaustein; d, Basil Dearden; w, Robert Ardrey, ph, Edward Scaife (Ultra-Panavision, Technicolor); m, Frank Cordell; ed, Fergus McDonell; md, Cordell; art d, John Howell; set d, Pamela Cornell, John Bodimeade; cos, John McCorry; spec eff, Richard Parker.

Historical Epic/Biography **(PR:C MPAA:NR)**

KHYBER PATROL1/2** (1954) 71m World/UA c

Richard Egan *(Cameron)*, Dawn Addams *(Diana)*, Raymond Burr *(Ahmed)*, Patric Knowles *(Lt. Kennerly)*, Paul Cavanagh *(Melville)*, Donald Randolph *(Ishak Khan)*, Philip Tonge *(Col. Rivington)*, Patrick O'Moore *(Brusard)*, Laura Mason *(Krushia)*.

Egan is the leader of the British Lancers, a group of soldiers stationed along the Khyber pass. His team is fighting off the Russian-backed border tribesmen. He's also trying to romance Addams, the commander's daughter. This film is standard fare, with nothing special in its production. The cast, however, is excellent despite its hum-drum approach. The uncredited producer was Edward Small.

p, Edward Small [uncredited]; d, Seymour Friedman; w, Jack DeWitt (based on a story by Richard Schayer); ph, Charles Van Enger (Color Corporation of America); m, Irving Gertz.

Action/Drama **(PR:A MPAA:NR)**

KIBITZER, THE** (1929) 77m PAR bw (GB: THE BUSYBODY)

Harry Green *(Ike Lazarus, The Kibitzer)*, Mary Brian *(Josie Lazarus)*, Neil Hamilton *(Eddie Brown)*, David Newell *(Bert Livingston)*, Lee Kohlmar *(Yankel)*, Henry Fink *(Kikapoupolos)*, Tenen Holtz *(Meyer)*, Guy Oliver *(McGinty)*, Albert Gran *(James Livingston)*, Eddie Kane *(Phillips)*, E. H. Calvert *(Westcott)*, Thomas Curran *(Briggs)*, Henry A. Barrows *(Hanson)*, Paddy O'Flynn *(Reporter)*, Dick Rush *(Mullins)*, Eugene Pallette *(Klaus)*.

Story about a Yiddish man who insists on giving everyone advice. Through a mistake he is given untold riches in stocks, which he is free to spend as he pleases. Meanwhile, his daughter (Brian) has fallen in love with Hamilton (Commissioner Gordon of TV's BATMAN thirty-five years later), a poor boy with a good heart. Following Green's advice, Hamilton bets on a horse that doesn't stand a chance of winning. Of course, the nag comes in on the money and Hamilton is now well off. The story climaxes as Green has seemingly lost everything when his stock suddenly bottoms out, but it turns out he has been saved by his brother. The only English that the brother knows is "Yes, sure, certainly," which was his response to a phone call asking whether they wanted to sell the stock. What could have been a charming little film is hampered by too much straying away from the plot and poor directorial decisions. Too much atmosphere is injected and some odd glitches in the continuity hurt the film's structure. But former vaudevillian Green gives a wonderful comic performance that is definitely worth a look.

d, Edward Sloman; w, Sam Mintz, Viola Brothers Shore (based on the play by Jo Swerling, Edwin G. Robinson); ph, Alfred Gilks; ed, Eda Warren.

Comedy **(PR:A MPAA:NR)**

KICK IN*1/2 (1931) 75m PAR bw

Clara Bow *(Molly Hewes)*, Regis Toomey *(Chick Hewes)*, Wynne Gibson *(Myrtle Sylvester)*, Juliette Compton *(Piccadilly Bessie)*, Leslie Fenton *(Charles)*, James Murray *(Benny LaMarr)*, Donald Crisp *(Garvey)*, Paul Hurst *(Whip Fogarty)*, Wade Boteler *(Diggs)*, J. Carrol Naish, Donald MacKenzie, Ben Taggart.

Bow's heyday was just about over in the early 1930s and she was given relatively little to do in this clunker. She's the wife of Toomey, a gangster who is now walking on the straight and narrow. The pair accidentally get involved in another robbery through some circumstantial evidence. The real culprit is Bow's younger brother, Fenton, a dope fiend. Crisp is the cop investigating the case along with dumb sidekick Hurst. Though its production values are fine, the film's story, based on a popular 1914 play, is pretty dull.

d, Richard Wallace; w, Bartlett Cormack (based on the play by Willard Mack); ph, Victor Milner.

Crime/Drama **(PR:C MPAA:NR)**

KICKING THE MOON AROUND (SEE: PLAYBOY, THE, 1938)

KID BLUE*** (1973) 100m FOX c

Dennis Hopper *(Bickford Waner)*, Warren Oates *(Reese Ford)*, Peter Boyle *(Preacher Bob)*, Ben Johnson *(Sheriff "Mean John" Simpson)*, Lee Purcell *(Molly Ford)*, Janice Rule *(Janet Conforto)*, Ralph Waite *(Drummer)*, Clifton James *(Mr. Hendricks)*, Jose Torvay *(Old Coyote)*, Mary Jackson *(Mrs. Evans)*, Jay Varela *(Mendoza)*, Claude Ennis Starrett Jr. *(Tough Guy)*, Warren Finnerty *(Wills)*, Howard Hesseman *(Confectionery Man)*, M. Emmet Walsh *(Barber)*, Henry Smith *(Joe Cloudmaker)*, Bobby Hall *(Bartender)*, Melvin Stewart *(Blackman)*, Eddy Donno *(Huey)*, Owen Orr, Richard Rust *(Train Robbers)*.

Hopper is an outlaw at the turn of the century. After a botched train robbery, he decides it is time to go straight and settles down in Dime Box, Texas. He takes a series of menial jobs, but is constantly under the more than slightly jaundiced eye of Johnson, cast against his normal type as the local sheriff. Hopper just can't cut the straight life though, and steals the Christmas payroll of a local factory, making a successful getaway with some Indian friends. The film is a nice little satire about many things: the American work ethic, the end of the cowboy era, and a little bit of a self-parody as well. The supporting cast is excellent. Frawley's direction is even-handed, keeping the comedy at a good pace and letting the characters tell the story. The film was completed in 1971 and titled DIME BOX, but was held for two years before release with a new name.

p, Marvin Schwartz; d, James Frawley; w, Edwin Shrake; ph, Billy Williams (Panavision, DeLuxe Color); m, Tim McIntire, John Rubinstein; ed, Stefan Arnsten; prod d, Joel Schiller; cos, Theodora Van Runkle.

Comedy/Western **(PR:C MPAA:PG)**

KID COLOSSUS, THE (SEE: ROOGIE'S BUMP, 1954)

KID COMES BACK, THE1/2** (1937) 61m WB bw

Wayne Morris *(Rush Conway)*, Barton MacLane *(Gunner Malone)*, June Travis *(Mary)*, Dickie Jones *(Bobby Doyle)*, Maxie Rosenbloom *(Stan Wilson)*, James Robbins *(Ken Rockwell)*, Joseph Crehan *(Danny Lockridge)*, Frank Otto *(Joey Meade)*, David Carlyle [Robert Paige] *(Radio Announcer)*, Herbert Rawlinson *(Redmann)*, Robert E. Homans *(Mike Dougherty)*, Ken Niles *(Radio Announcer)*.

When boxer MacLane sees youngster Morris duke it out in a street brawl, he discovers a raw talent worth developing. He takes the fledgling pugster under his wing and trains the kid to be a champ. Travis, Morris' sister, soon enters into a romance with her brother's benefactor. Morris becomes a top fighter but then finds he must face off against MacLane for a big fight. He can't bring himself to go up against his mentor and would-be brother-in-law, but MacLane, with the help of a sportswriter, tricks the kid into taking on this all-important match. The elder fighter knocks out the kid, but the two remain close when Morris and Travis marry. A standard fight story with every cliche intact, but it's a good package. MacLane gives a fine performance that rises nicely above the material, giving it a much needed touch of originality. Look for an appearance by ex-fighter-turned-movie actor Rosenbloom.

p, Bryan Foy; d, B. Reeves Eason; w, George Bricker (based on the story "Trial Horse" by E. J. Flanagan); ph, Arthur Edeson; ed, Warren Low.

Sports Drama **(PR:A MPAA:NR)**

KID COURAGEOUS*1/2 (1935) 58m Supreme/William Steiner bw

Bob Steele, Renee Borden, Kit Guard, Arthur Loft, Jack Powell, Lafe McKee, Dave Calvert, Barry Senry, Perry Murdock, John Elrod.

Typical western hero Steele plays the agent trying to track down the thieves of an ore shipment. In addition to bringing the crooks to justice, Steele rescues a lady in distress, one who is in an unhappy marriage.

p, A.W. Hackel; d&w, Robert N. Bradbury; ph, William Hyer; ed, S. Roy Luby.

Western **Cas.** **(PR:A MPAA:NR)**

KID DYNAMITE*

(1943) 73m BAN/MON bw (AKA: QUEEN OF BROADWAY)

Leo Gorcey *(Ethelbert "Muggs" McGinnis)*, Bobby Jordan *(Danny Lyons)*, Huntz Hall *(Glimpy McGleavey)*, "Sunshine Sammy" Morrison *(Scruno)*, Bobby Stone *(Harry "Stony" Stone)*, Bennie Bartlett *(Beanie Miller)*, Dave Durand *(Joe "Skinny" Collins)*, Pamela Blake *(Ivy McGinnis)*, Gabriel Dell *(Harry Wyckoff)*, Henry Hall *(Louis Gendick)*, Charles Judels *(Nick)*, Vince Barnett *(Klinkhammer)*, Wheeler Oakman *(Tony)*, Daphne Pollard *(Mrs. McGinnis)*, Margaret Padula *(Mrs. Lyons)*, Dudley Dickerson *(Scruno's Dad)*, Kay Marvis [Mrs. Leo] Gorcey *(Kay, Muggs' Dancing Partner)*, Minerva Urecal *(Judge)*, Marion Miller *(Band Singer)*, Snub Pollard *(Dance Official)*, Ray Miller *(Thug)*, Jack Mulhall *(Man)*, Mike Riley's Orchestra.

Another so-called comedy from the East Side Kids series. This time Gorcey's a boxer, kidnaped by gamblers to keep him out of a big fight. His brother, Jordan, is substituted, instigating a feud between the two. Gorcey's first of five wives (who later became the second Mrs. Groucho Marx) plays his dance partner. There's also an appearance by silent film comic Snub Pollard, reduced to this fare, as a dance official. (See BOWERY BOYS series, Index.)

p, Sam Katzman, Jack Dietz; d, Wallace Fox; w, Gerald J. Schnitzer, Morey Amsterdam (based on the short story "The Old Gang" by Paul Ernst); ph, Mack Stengler; ed, Carl Pierson; md, Edward Kay; art d, David Milton.

Comedy **(PR:AA MPAA:NR)**

KID FOR TWO FARTHINGS, A****

(1956, Brit.) 91m LFP-Big Ben/IF-Lopert c

Celia Johnson *(Joanne)*, Diana Dors *(Sonia)*, David Kossoff *(Kandinsky)*, Joe Robinson *(Sam)*, Jonathan Ashmore *(Joe)*, Brenda de Banzie *("Lady" Ruby)*, Vera Day *(Mimi)*, Primo Carnera *(Python Macklin)*, Sydney Tafler *(Mme. Rita)*, Sidney James *(Ince Berg)*, Daphne Anderson *(Dora)*, Lou Jacobi *(Blackie Isaacs)*, Harold

Berens *(Oliver)*, Danny Green *(Bason)*, Irene Handl *(Mrs. Abramowitz)*, Alfie Bass *(Alf, the Bird Man)*, Eddie Byrne *(Sylvester, Photographer)*, Joseph Tomelty *(Vagrant)*, Rosalind Boxall *(Mrs. Alf)*, Harry Purvis *(Champ)*, Harry Baird *(Jamaica)*, Lily Kann *(Mrs. Kramm)*, Arthur Lovegrove *(Postman)*, Madge Brindley *(Mrs. Quinn)*, Harold Goodwin *(Chick Man)*, George Hurst, Eddie Malin, Peter Taylor *(Dog Men)*, Derek Sydney *(Fortune Teller)*, Asher Day *(Indian Girl)*, Norah Gordon, Max Denne *(Customers)*, James Lomas *(Sandwich Board Man)*, Bart Allison *(Auctioneer)*, Arthur Skinner, Norman Mitchell *(Stallholders)*, Marigold Russell *(3rd Customer)*, Judith Nelmes *(Alf's Customer)*, Meier Leibovitch *(Mendel)*, Locarno *(Pigeon Man)*, Mollie Palmer, Barbara Denney, Barbara Archer, Ann Chaplin, Anita Arley *(Workroom Girls)*, Raymond Rollett *(Breakaway China Stallholder)*, Bruce Beeby *(Policeman)*, Lew Marao *(Referee)*, Frank Blake *(M.C.)*, Ray Hunter, Charlie Green *(Wrestlers)*, Sam Kydd, Charles Saynor.

An absolutely delightful and charming comedy-fantasy set against the Jewish tradesmen's life in London's Petticoat Lane. Based on the novel by Mankowitz (who also wrote the screenplay), it's the story of a young boy, Ashmore, who has been told stories about a unicorn by tailor Kossoff. When the boy buys a goat with only one horn, he is convinced that he has purchased a unicorn because "magical" things begin to happen to the denizens of the area. Kossoff has but one great desire in his life—to own his own steam press—and he gets it. Dors is a buxom blonde who has been waiting (not unlike Adelaide in GUYS AND DOLLS) for many years to marry muscular Robinson. She gets her wish when he enters the ring and wins a bout and enough money to make her romantic dream come true. Robinson has to wrestle Primo Carnera, the behemoth Italian heavyweight boxer. Johnson plays Ashmore's mother, but doesn't have enough to do to merit her casting. Tafler, a terrific comic actor who was so funny in MAKE MINE MINK, is again shown to good advantage as a local storekeeper, and Canadian, Lou Jacobi, makes one of his earliest appearances as the wrestling promoter. Charm just pours off the screen in every frame, and Reed, working for the first time in color, shows how well he deals with children. He used this ability before in THE FALLEN IDOL and later with the musical version of OLIVER! for which he took an Oscar. Naturally, all of the miracles are logically explained but, to the boy, it's the unicorn that has brought all the happiness to Petticoat Lane. When the animal dies Ashmore is destroyed, but they buy him a new pet and the people who inhabit this most colorful and bustling area have all been changed by the presence of the kid that only cost two farthings. Many of the best British-Jewish actors (Handl, Bass, James, et al) played small roles. It's a small picture that is ripe for a remake and would serve well as the book for a musical. To see it is to love it.

p&d, Carol Reed; w, Wolf Mankowitz (based on his novel); ph, Ted Scaife (Eastmancolor); m, Benjamin Frankel; ed, A. S. Bates; art d, Wilfred Shingleton; cos, Anne Duse.

Comedy/Fantasy **(PR:A MPAA:NR)**

KID FROM AMARILLO, THE zero (1951) 56m COL bw

Charles Starrett *(The Durango Kid)*, Smiley Burnette *(Himself)*, Harry Lauter *(Tom Mallory)*, Fred F. Sears *(Jonathan Cole)*, Don Megowan *(Rakim)*, Scott Lee *(Snead)*, Guy Teague *(Dirk)*, Charles Evans *(Jason Summerville)*, George Lewis *(Don Jose Figaroa)*, Henry Kulky *(Zeno)*, George Chesebro *(El Loco)*, Jerry Scroggins *(Leader)*, The Cass County Boys.

Probably one of the worst of Starrett's Durango Kid films. This time the Kid is out to stop some silver smugglers along the U.S.-Mexican border. The normally funny sidekick Burnette gives barely a hint of his real talent and Starrett has the wrong physique for a cowboy role. The Cass County Boys interrupt with a few songs here and there. There's no love interest, which could have helped. (See DURANGO KID series, Index).

p, Colbert Clark; d, Ray Nazarro; w, Barry Shipman; ph, Fayte Browne; ed, Paul Borofsky; md, Mischa Bakaleinikoff; art d, Charles Clague.

Western **(PR:A MPAA:NR)**

KID FROM ARIZONA, THE* (1931) 56m Cosmos/States Rights bw

Jack Perrin, Josephine Hill, Robert Walker, Henry Rocquemore, George Chesebro, Ben Corbett.

Perrin is a marshal out to stop some renegade Indians. But the local judge's horses are stolen and one, a racing entry, has been maimed. Perrin takes the fall for both but redeems himself when he proves that the so-called Indians are really white smugglers. The thin plot is just an excuse for some ridin', ropin', and roughhousin'.

p&d, Robert J. Horner; w, Robert Walker (based on a story by Horner); ph, Jules Cronjager.

Western **(PR:A MPAA:NR)**

KID FROM BROKEN GUN, THE* (1952) 55m COL bw

Charles Starrett *(Steve Reynolds/The Durango Kid)*, Smiley Burnette *(Himself)*, Jack [Jock] Mahoney *(Himself)*, Angela Stevens *(Gail Kingston)*, Tristram Coffin *(Martin Donohugh)*, Myron Healey *(Kiefer)*, Helen Mowery *(Dixie King)*, Mauritz Hugo *(Sheriff)*, Edgar Dearing *(Judge Halloway)*, Chris Alcaide *(Matt Fallon)*, Pat O'Malley *(Doc Handy)*, John Cason *(Chuck)*, Eddie Parker.

Last of the seven-year-long Durango Kid series and a very weak ending at that. Using stock footage from other Durango Kid films, the story is told in flashback. Mahoney is charged with murder and Starrett proves his lawyer Stevens is really the guilty party. Making the woman a lawyer (a murderous one at that) is a novel move for the time and genre. That's about the only item of interest here. (See DURANGO KID Series, Index.)

p, Colbert Clark; d, Fred F. Sears; w, Ed Earl Repp, Barry Shipman; ph, Fayte Browne; ed, Paul Borofsky; md, Mischa Bakaleinikoff; art d, Charles Clague.

Western **(PR:A MPAA:NR)**

KID FROM BOOKLYN, THE*** (1946) 114m Goldwyn/RKO c

Danny Kaye *(Burleigh Sullivan)*, Virginia Mayo *(Polly Pringle)*, Vera-Ellen *(Susie Sullivan)*, Walter Abel *(Gabby Sloan)*, Eve Arden *(Ann Westley)*, Steve Cochran *(Speed MacFarlane)*, Lionel Stander *(Spider Schultz)*, Fay Bainter *(Mrs. E. Winthrop LeMoyne)*, Clarence Kolb *(Wilbur Austin)*, Victor Cutler *(Photographer)*, Charles Cane *(Willard)*, Jerome Cowan *(Fight Ring Announcer)*, Don Wilson, Knox Manning *(Radio Announcers)*, Kay Thompson *(Matron)*, Johnny Downs *(M.C.)*, Pierre Watkin *(Mr. LeMoyne)*, Frank Riggi *(Killer Kelly)*, Karen X. Gaylord, Ruth Valmy, Shirley Ballard, Virginia Belmont, Betty Cargyle, Jean Cronin, Vonne Lester, Diana Mumby, Mary Simpson, Virginia Thorpe, Tyra Vaughn, Kismi Stefan, Betty Alexander, Martha Montgomery, Joyce MacKenzie, Helen Kimball, Jan Bryant, Donna Hamilton *(The Goldwyn Girls)*, Frank Moran *(Fight Manager)*, John Indrisano *(Boxing Instructor)*, Almeda Fowler *(Bystander)*, Snub Pollard *(Man Who Reacts to Lion)*, Robert Wade Chatterton *(Man Who Lifts Up Susie)*, Torben Meyer, William Forrest, Jack Norton *(Guests)*, Billy Nelson, Ralph Dunn *(Seconds)*, Billy Wayne, George Chandler *(Reporters)*, Betty Blythe, James Carlisle *(Mrs. LeMoyne's Friends)*, Robert Strong, William "Billy" Newell, Tom Quinn *(Photographers)*, Billy Bletcher, George Sherwood, Donald Kerr, Jack Roper, Steve Taylor, Al Hill, Jay Eaton, Syd Saylor, Eddie Hart, Eric Wilton, Alexander Pollard, Billy Benedict, Mary Forbes, Hal K. Dawson, Dulce Day, Jack Gargan, Lester Dorr, Jack Cheatham *(Bits)*, Gil Dennis, Bob Gompers, Tony Conde, Danny Drake, Rudolph Andrean, Michael Collins, Rudolph Silva, Kenneth McAndish, Alfred Burke, Robert Forrest, Jimmy Kelly, Eddie Cutler, Harvey Karels, Al Ruiz *(Dancers)*, Jody Black, Mabel Boehlke, Betty Yeaton, Dorothy Clarke, Gertrude Gault, Shirley Sharon *(Acrobatic Dancers)*, Virginia Mayo singing dubbed by Dorothy Ellers, Vera-Ellen singing dubbed by Betty Russell.

Goldwyn came up with a gold mine when he discovered Kaye and put him into movies. This was the third duet between the men after UP IN ARMS and WONDER MAN and grossed more money than the previous two. It cost more than $2 million and every penny is up there on the screen. Based on the 1936 Harold Lloyd film, THE MILKY WAY (which was, in turn, based on a play by Root and Clork that never clicked on Broadway), THE KID FROM BROOKLYN is an unlikely story that is overcome by the tunes and the style, and the result is a happy amalgam of nonsense and laughter. Kaye is a wimpy milkman who loves his horse almost as much as he loves his girl friend, the comely Mayo, a nightclub singer. Vera-Ellen is Kaye's sister and when he visits the club where she and Mayo work, he finds her being annoyed by Cochran and Stander, who are at least eight sheets to the wind. A brawl ensues and Stander inadvertently knocks out Cochran, but Kaye is given credit for the blow. This wouldn't be big news except that Cochran is the middleweight boxing champion of the world! Cochran's manager, Abel, is thrown for a loop as Cochran's reputation is destroyed. Vera-Ellen tells Kaye that he must apologize for what he did, so he hies to Cochran's apartment where an accidental punch lands on the boxer's jaw just as several gentlemen of the press enter the residence. Abel realizes that he is going to lose a lot of money if he doesn't do something fast, so he decides to make mild-mannered Kaye into a boxer and take over his management. His plan is to set up a "grudge match" between Kaye and Cochran that will rake in the sheckels. Kaye is against it until Abel explains that he can make enough money to marry Mayo. A training sequence begins and Abel's girl friend, Arden, teaches him how to move to a Viennese waltz. With each round, Kaye gains confidence in himself. Soon he starts to think that he really is a boxer and Abel arranges several fights in which the other fighters take better dives than Greg Louganis. As his faith in himself enlarges, Kaye gets a swelled head and loses the affections of Mayo, as well as the support of Vera-Ellen, who has now become Cochran's girl friend. Kolb, the owner of the dairy where Kaye worked, buys his contract from Abel and will donate his share of winnings to Bainter, a wealthy woman who is in charge of a milk fund for underprivileged children. The stage is set for the fight and Stander, now in Kaye's corner, is to give Kaye knock-out drops to insure Cochran's win. Stander, who played the same role in the Lloyd version, gives Cochran the drops by mistake and Kaye wins the fight—and the hand of Mayo. This allows him to retire, become a partner in the dairy, and see his sister marry Cochran. Stander and Abel leave the fight business and take jobs as milkmen in the dairy belonging to Kaye and Kolb. As you can see, there was as much reality to this story as ALICE IN WONDERLAND, but it was done with such an amiable and good-natured overview that one doesn't mind the incredulity at all. The songs were done by everyone but Kaye, save for the special piece written by Liebman and Kaye's wife, Sylvia Fine, a satire on ballet called "Pavlova." The other Cahn and Styne tunes were: "Sunflower Song," "Hey, What's Your Name?" "You're The Cause Of It All," "Welcome, Burleigh," "I Love An Old-Fashioned Song," and "Josie." In the Broadway play, Brian Donlevy played the Abel role, Hugh O'Connell was the milkman and Gladys George essayed the Arden part. It only lasted less than 50 performances, but the story lives on in this movie. The Goldwyn Girls were shown to good advantage, but none of this crop went on to greater glory as happened with Lucille Ball and many others. There was solid second banana work from Cowan, Thompson, Wilson, and Cutler. The picture earned more than $5 million first time around and can still be seen from time to time on television. Kaye, born David Kaminski, really came from Brooklyn but never finished high school and dropped out to become a "toomler" in the Catskill Mountains. "Toomle" is the Yiddish word for ruckus and many of the resort hotels employed bright, young men to just stir things up, entertain, and keep the customers happy. Kaye has kept millions happy since then.

p, Samuel Goldwyn; d, Norman Z. McLeod; w, Don Hartman, Melville Shavelson (based on the screenplay by Grover Jones, Frank Butler, Richard Connell from the play "The Milky Way" by Lynn Root, Harry Clork); ph, Gregg Toland (Technicolor); m, Carmen Dragon; ed, Daniel Mandell; art d, Perry Ferguson, Stewart Chaney; ch, Bernard Pearce; m/l, Jule Styne, Sammy Cahn, Sylvia Fine, Max Liebman.

Musical Comedy **Cas.** **(PR:AA MPAA:NR)**

KID FROM CANADA, THE**
(1957, Brit.) 57m Anvil-Children's Film Foundation/BL bw

Christopher Braden *(Andy Cameron)*, Bernard Braden *(Joe)*, Bobby Stevenson *(Neil)*, Eleanor Laing *(Margaret)*, Pamela Stirling *(Jean)*, David Caldwell *(Ian)*, Alex Mackenzie *(Macfarlane)*, Peter Macdonell, Katherine Page.

Braden, a 10-year-old Canadian living in Scotland, is constantly bragging about his horse show accomplishments impressing the locals not one iota. However, when a shepherd is endangered, the braggart proves himself and stages a heroic rescue. Strictly for the kids.

p, Ralph May; d, Kay Mander; w, John Eldridge; ph, Paddy Carey.

Children's Film **(PR:AA MPAA:NR)**

KID FROM CLEVELAND, THE** (1949) 89m REP bw

George Brent *(Mike Jackson)*, Lynn Bari *(Katherine Jackson)*, Rusty Tamblyn *(Johnny Barrows)*, Tommy Cook *(Dan Hudson)*, Louis Jean Heydt *(Carl Novak)*, Ann Doran *(Emily Novak)*, K. Elmo Lowe *(Dave Joyce)*, Johnny Berardino *(Mac)*, Bill Veeck, Lou Boudreau, Tris Speaker, Hank Greenberg, Bob Feller, Gene Bearden, Satchel Paige, Bob Lemon, Steve Gromek, Joe Gordon, Mickey Vernon, Ken Keltner, Ray Boone, Dale Mitchell, Larry Doby, Bob Kennedy, Jim Hegan *(Cleveland Indians)*, Franklin Lewis, Gordon Cobbledock, Ed MacAuley *(Sportswriters)*, Bill Summers, Bill Grieve *(Umpires)*.

Tamblyn is a juvenile delinquent abandoned by his stepfather. Sports announcer Brent takes the lad under his wing and introduces him to the Cleveland Indians baseball team, and the kid straightens out. A parallel story, showing the team pull together and go on to win the World Series, is nicely handled. The real treat is a chance to see some great baseball names in action, with actual footage of the 1948 World Series included in the film. Then Indians' owner Veeck gives a terrific performance, though this should come as no surprise to anyone familiar with this baseball legend. Actor, dancer, and Academy Award winner Russ Tamblyn's second credited film. He was then 15 years of age.

p, Walter Colmes; d, Herbert Kline; w, John Bright (based on a story by Kline, Bright); ph, Jack Marta; m, Nathan Scott; ed, Jason H. Bernie; spec eff, Consolidated Film Industries; makeup, Bob Mark, Louis Hipple.

Sports/Juvenile Drama **(PR:A MPAA:NR)**

KID FROM GOWER GULCH, THE*½ (1949) 56m Friedgen/Astor bw

Spade Cooley, Bob Gilbert, Wanda Cantlon, Billy Dix, Jack Baxley, Joe Hiser, William Val.

Cooley makes the rounds as a warbling cowboy and manages to get himself entered into a rodeo competition. The catch is he doesn't know the first thing about rodeo riding—but he learns quickly. An entertaining minor oater which was shot in 1947 and held back for a couple of years.

p, Raymond Friedgen; d, Oliver Drake; w, Elmer S. Pond [Elmer Clifton].

Western **(PR:A MPAA:NR)**

KID FROM KANSAS, THE*½ (1941) 61m UNIV bw

Dick Foran *(Kansas)*, Leo Carrillo *(Pancho)*, Andy Devine *(Andy)*, Ann Doran *(Smitty)*, Francis McDonald *(Cesar)*, James Seay *(Walker)*, Marcia Ralston *(Linda)*, Nestor Paiva *(Jamaica)*, Antonio Moreno *(Chief of Police)*, Leyland Hodgson *(York)*, Wade Boteler *(Russell)*, Guy Usher *(Maloney)*.

Carrillo is a South American planter. He and the other farmers have trouble when someone starts destroying their equipment and they are forced to sell their crops at ridiculously cheap levels. Devine, Carrillo's foreman, hires drifter Foran. Foran is framed for murder but escapes from jail and exposes the evil trio of McDonald, Ralston, and Boteler who are trying to take over the planter's land. The film is far too talky and lacks action. Foran is okay in the title role, though his two songs are just padding.

p, Ben Pivar; d, William Nigh; w, Griffin Jay, David Silverstein (based on a story by Jay); ph, John W. Boyle; ed, Arthur Hilton.

Action/Drama **Cas.** **(PR:C MPAA:NR)**

KID FROM KOKOMO, THE**
(1939) 92m WB bw (GB: ORPHAN OF THE RING)

Pat O'Brien *(Bill Murphy)*, Wayne Morris *(Homer Baston)*, Joan Blondell *(Doris Harvey)*, Jane Wyman *(Marian Bronson)*, May Robson *(Ma "Maggie" Martin)*, Maxie Rosenbloom *(Curly Bender)*, Ed Brophy *(Eddie Black)*, Stanley Fields *(Muscles)*, Sidney Toler *(Judge Bronson)*, Winifred Harris *(Mrs. Bronson)*, Morgan Conway *(Louie)*, John Ridgely *(Sam)*, Frank Mayo *(Durb)*, Al Hill *(Lippy)*, Clem Bevans *(Jim)*, Ward Bond *(Klewicke)*, Olin Howland *(Stan)*, Paul Hurst, Tom Wilson, Frank Hagney, Bob Perry *(Old Men)*, Reid Kilpatrick, John Harron *(Radio Announcers)*, Cliff Saum *(Boy)*, Frederick Clark *(Black Butler)*, Nat Carr *(Court Clerk)*, Jack Mower *(Hotel Clerk)*, Dick Wessel *(Mug)*, Emmett Vogan *(Fight Announcer)*, Charles Randolph *(Referee)*, Herbert Evans *(Bronson's Butler)*, Loia Cheaney *(Bronson's Maid)*, Robert E. Homans *(Old Cop)*, Ned Crawford *(Young Cop)*.

Poor comedy boxing film stars O'Brien as fight manager for Morris, a brainless pugster who believes his mother is also the lady in the famed picture by Whistler. Robson is a drunken kleptomaniac who is brought in to pose as the mother, and she brings her buddy Fields to play father. The direction is competent, keeping the film running at a nice pace, but that can't save the insipid plot. The story, surprisingly, was by Dalton Trumbo.

p, Sam Bischoff; d, Lewis Seiler; w, Jerry Wald, Richard Macauley (based on the story "Broadway Cavalier" by Dalton Trumbo); ph, Sid Hickox; ed, Jack Killifer.

Comedy **(PR:A MPAA:NR)**

KID FROM LEFT FIELD, THE½** (1953) 80m FOX bw

Dan Dailey *(Larry "Pop" Cooper)*, Anne Bancroft *(Marian)*, Billy Chapin *(Christy)*, Lloyd Bridges *(Pete Haines)*, Ray Collins *(Whacker)*, Richard Egan *(Billy Lorant)*, Bob Hopkins *(Bobo Noonan)*, Alex Gerry *(J.R. Johnson)*, Walter Sande *(Barnes)*, Fess Parker *(McDougal)*, George Phelps *(Tony)*, John Gallaudet *(Hyams)*, Paul Salata *(Larson)*, John Berardino *(Hank Dreiser)*, Gene Thompson *(Jim Cary)*, Malcolm Cassell *(Jimmy)*, Ike Jones *(John Grant)*, Ron Hargrave *(Craig)*, John Goddard *(Riordan)*, John McKee *(Hunchy Harrison)*, Claude Olin Wurman *(Bermudez)*, Sammy Ogg *(Herman)*, Robert Winans *(Skeets)*, Jonathan Hole *(Truant Officer)*, John Call *(Ticket Taker)*, Al Green *(Spectator)*, George Garner, Rush Williams *(Yankee Players)*, Leo Cleary *(Yankee Manager)*, John "Beans" Reardon *(Umpire)*, James Griffith *(Proprietor)*, James F. Stone *(Mack)*, Richard Shackelton *(Newsboy)*, Larry Thor, Robert Kelly, Mark Scott *(Announcers)*, Ruth Warren *(Welfare Worker)*, Camillo Guercio *(Principal)*, King Donovan *(Bartender)*, Katherine Givney *(Judge)*, Ken Christy, Charles Tannen, Anthony De Mario *(Fans)*.

Cute baseball story features Dailey as an ex-big leaguer now reduced to hawking peanuts in the stands. Chapin is his nine-year-old son, the team's bat boy. The team is in a slump and dad gives his boy some tips to pass onto manager Bridges. The team starts to improve and when owner Collins discovers the reason he promotes the kid to the manager's position, not knowing Dailey was calling the plays. When the truth comes out, Dailey is appointed manager. A little hard to swallow but the warm, believable performances make it pleasant fare. Re-made in 1979 as a far less charming made-for-television movie with Gary Coleman. Note Fess Parker in a small part, one year before he donned a coonskin cap and made it big in TV's "Davy Crockett" and then continued on into "Daniel Boone".

p, Leonard Goldstein; d, Harmon Jones; w, Jack Sher; ph, Harry Jackson; m, Lionel Newman; ed, William Reynolds; art d, Lyle Wheeler, Addison Hehr.

Comedy **Cas.** **(PR:AAA MPAA:NR)**

KID FROM SANTA FE, THE*½ (1940) 57m MON bw

Jack Randall *(Santa Fe)*, Clarene Curtis *(Anne Holt)*, Forrest Taylor *(Sheriff Holt)*, Claire Rochelle *(Millie Logan)*, Tom London *(Bill Stewart)*, George Chesebro *(Kent)*, Dave O'Brien *(Chester)*, Jimmy Aubrey *(Henry Lupton)*, Kenne Duncan *(Joe Lavida)*, Carl Mathews *(George)*, Steve Clark *(Herman)*, Buzz Barton, Tex Palmer.

An economy Western if ever one was made. Taylor calls on Randall for assistance in catching some smugglers led by London. Randall does the job in record time and gets the sheriff's daughter (Curtis) as well. The economy shows in the production. Bad guys put up fights that make one wonder how they got into the outlaw business, but they are so tough they don't bleed after being shot!

p, Harry S. Webb; d, Raymond K. Johnson; w, Carl Krusada (based on a story by Joseph P. Murphy); ph, Edward A. Kull, William Hyer; ed, Robert Golden.

Western **(PR:AA MPAA:NR)**

KID FROM SPAIN, THE*½** (1932) 118m Goldwyn/UA bw

Eddie Cantor *(Eddie Williams)*, Lyda Roberti *(Rosalie)*, Robert Young *(Ricardo)*, Ruth Hall *(Anita Gomez)*, John Miljan *(Pancho)*, Noah Beery *(Alonzo Gomez)*, J. Carrol Naish *(Pedro)*, Robert Emmett O'Connor *(Detective Crawford)*, Stanley Fields *(Jose)*, Paul Porcasi *(Gonzales, Border Guard)*, Sidney Franklin *(American Matador)*, Julian Rivero *(Dalmores)*, Theresa Maxwell Conover *(Martha Oliver)*, Walter Walker *(The Dean)*, Ben Hendricks, Jr. *(Red)*, Grace Poggi *(Specialty Dancer)*, Edgar Connor *(Black Bull Handler)*, Leo Willis *(Thief)*, Harry Gribbon *(Traffic Cop)*, Eddie Foster *(Patron)*, Harry C. Bradley *(Man on Line at Border)*, Jean Allen, Loretta Andrews, Consuelo Baker, Betty Bassett, Lynn Browning, Maxie Cantway, Hazel Craven, Dorothy Rae Coonan, Shirley Chambers, Patricia Farnum, Sarah Jane Fulks, [Jane Wyman], Betty Grable, Paulette Goddard, Jeannie Gray, Ruth Hale, Pat Harper, Margaret La Marr, Adele Lacey, Bernice Lorimer, Nancy Lynn, Vivian Mathison, Nancy Nash, Edith Roark, Marian Sayers, Renee Whitney, Diana Winslow, Toby Wing *(The 1932 Goldwyn Girls)*.

Goldwyn wanted to become the Flo Ziegfeld of movies by producing opulent, entertaining musicals that he could charge a fortune for. He succeeded far beyond his dreams with THE KID FROM SPAIN which asked for, and got, more than $2 a ticket in an era when 75 cents was the top price for a first-run movie. It was the depths of the Depression and musicals weren't drawing flies until this picture made a breakthrough and the flood gates opened. Cantor and Young are college roommates who are tossed out of school after being caught in the girls' dorm. The opening number, led by Grable and staged by Berkeley, sets the tone for the nonsense to come. Young, a Mexican lad, invites Cantor to join him south-of-the-border. Before they leave, Young stops at his local bank to take out his money while Cantor waits outside. Just then the bank gets robbed, and Cantor is mistaken by the robbers as their getaway driver. Cantor flees to Mexico to escape the crooks as he is the only person who can identify them and fears they will knock him off for having that knowledge. When he gets to the U.S.-Mexican border, the guard won't let him through until Cantor convinces the man that he is a Mexican. On the other side of the border, he is again mistaken for someone he isn't—the toreador offspring of the legendary bullfighter, Don Sebastian. Cantor does not deny the claim, knowing he is being tracked down by American cop O'Connor, who wants Cantor to blow the whistle on the crooks. Cantor arrives at Young's home and finds him romantically enmeshed with Hall, whose father would prefer that she take bullfighter Miljan as her husband. Meanwhile, Cantor gets involved with Hall's friend, Roberti, and the two fall in love, even though Miljan's tough pal, Naish, also has his eye on her. Between avoiding Naish and O'Connor, Cantor has to keep his banjo eyes open wide. When Sunday comes, Cantor is shamed into performing in the bull ring. Young promises to get Cantor a tame animal but Naish switches the docile beast for an angry one. Young has told Cantor that the tame bull will stop short the moment anyone says the name of Mexico's famous volcano, Popocatepetl, a word Cantor immediately forgets. The bullfight is hilarious as Cantor wears the animal down by running faster than it can. In the end he overcomes the bull with chloroform, gets the hand of Roberti and straightens out the amor of Young and Hall. The picture is chock-full of laughs, some fine songs, and an excellent performance by Polish-born Roberti (daughter of the famous clown, Roberti), who had her promising career cut short when she died of a heart attack at the age of 32. Franklin, "the bullfighter from Brooklyn," should not be confused with the actor and the director, both of whom had the same name but were not related. Among the Goldwyn Girls, look for Grable, Wyman, Bruce, Goddard, and Wing. Director McCarey did a wonderful job that sent him from this film to The Marx Brothers for DUCK SOUP. The tunes, mostly by Kalmar and Ruby (who also co-wrote the screenplay), include: "The College Song," "Look What You've Done," "In The Moonlight," "What A Perfect Combination," and an untitled dance number by Poggi. Berkeley was not yet at the top of the form (that came later at MGM), but he showed enough inventiveness in THE KID FROM SPAIN to show everyone that he was a comer.

p, Samuel Goldwyn; d, Leo McCarey; w, William Anthony McGuire, Bert Kalmar, Harry Ruby; ph, Gregg Toland; ed, Stuart Heisler; md, Alfred Newman; art d, Richard Day; cos, Milo Anderson; ch, Busby Berkeley; m/l, Kalmar, Ruby, Irving Caesar, Harry Akst, Grace Poggi.

Musical Comedy **(PR:AA MPAA:NR)**

KID FROM TEXAS, THE** (1939) 70m MGM bw

Dennis O'Keefe *(William Quincy Malone)*, Florence Rice *(Margo Thomas)*, Anthony Allan *(Bertie Thomas)*, Jessie Ralph *(Aunt Minetta)*, Buddy Ebsen *("Snifty")*, Virginia Dale *("Okay" Kinney)*, Robert Wilcox *("Duke" Hastings)*, Jack Carson *(Stanley Brown)*, Helen Lynd *(Mabel)*, J.M. Kerrigan *(Farr)*, Tully Marshall *(Adam Lambert)*.

This is certainly a different B Western. O'Keefe is a cowhand who dreams of being a polo player. He falls in love with polo-loving heiress Rice but makes a fool of himself during a big match. He runs off to join a Wild West show but continues his love of polo by organizing a cowboys and Indians polo match! Rice ends up with him at the end, beating out Dale in a match of their own. A funny idea, badly executed. The first half is clever and fresh but then it all becomes predictable and more than a little stupid. O'Keefe does his best and is fun to watch.

p, Edgar Selwyn; d, S. Sylvan Simon; w, Florence Ryerson, Edgar Allan Woolf, Albert Mannheimer (based on a story by Milton Merlin, Byron Morgan); ph, Sidney Wagner; m, Dr. William Axt; ed, Frederick Y. Smith; m/l, Ormand Ruthven, Merlin, Mannheimer.

Comedy Western **(PR:AAA MPAA:NR)**

KID FROM TEXAS, THE* 1/2 (1950) 78m UNIV c

Audie Murphy *(Billy the Kid)*, Gale Storm *(Irene Kain)*, Albert Dekker *(Alexander Kain)*, Shepperd Strudwick *(Jameson)*, Will Geer *(O'Fallon)*, William Talman *(Minniger)*, Martin Garralaga *(Morales)*, Robert H. Barrat *(General Lew Wallace)*, Walter Sande *(Crowe)*, Frank Wilcox *(Sheriff Pat Garrett)*, Dennis Hoey *(Maj. Harper)*, Ray Teal *(Sheriff Rand)*, Don Haggerty *(Morgan)*, Paul Ford *(Copeland)*, John Phillips *(Sid Curtis)*, Harold Goodwin *(Matt Curtis)*, Zon Murray *(Lucas)*, Rosa Turich *(Marita)*, Dorita Pallais *(Lupita)*, Pilar Del Rey *(Margarita)*, Tom Trout *(Denby)*.

Slow-moving recounting of the life of western anti-hero Billy the Kid. Murphy, in his first western, plays the kid as a sympathetic young man who turns to violence after the rancher who was helping him reform is murdered. He goes off on a string of murders before he is gunned down by Wilcox. The filmmakers mean well, but the story drags. The photography is magnificent as Technicolor beautifully captures the landscapes of New Mexico where the film was shot.

p, Paul Short; d, Kurt Neumann; w, Robert Hardy Andrews, Karl Kamb (based on a story by Andrews); ph, Charles Van Enger (Technicolor); m, Milton Schwarzwald; ed, Frank Gross, md, Schwarzwald; art d, Bernard Herzbrun, Emrich Nicholson.

Western **(PR:C MPAA:NR)**

KID GALAHAD* 1/2** (1937) 101m WB bw (AKA: THE BATTLING BELLHOP)

Edward G. Robinson *(Nick Donati)*, Bette Davis *(Louise "Fluff" Phillips)*, Humphrey Bogart *(Turkey Morgan)*, Wayne Morris *(Kid Galahad/Ward Guisenberry)*, Jane Bryan *(Marie Donati)*, Harry Carey *(Silver Jackson)*, William Haade *(Chuck McGraw)*, Soledad Jiminez *(Mrs. Donati)*, Joe Cunningham *(Joe Taylor)*, Ben Welden *(Buzz Stevens)*, Joseph Crehan *(Editor Brady)*, Veda Ann Borg *(Redhead at Party)*, Frank Faylen *(Barney)*, Harland Tucker *(Gunman)*, Bob Evans *(Sam McGraw)*, Hank Hankinson *(Jim Burke)*, Bob Nestell *(Tim O'Brien)*, Jack Kranz *(Denbaugh)*, George Blake *(Referee)*, Charlie Sullivan *(Second)*, Joyce Compton *(Drunken Girl on Phone)*, Eddie Foster *(Louie, Pianist)*, George Humbert *(Barber)*, Emmett Vogan *(Ring Announcer)*, I. Stanford Jolley *(Ringsider)*, Harry Harvey, Horace MacMahon, John Shelton, Max Hoffman, Edward Price, Billy Arnold, Philip Waldron, Eddie Featherstone, Don Brodie, Milton Kibbee *(Reporters)*, Ralph Dunn *(Reporter at Dinner)*, Mary Doran *(Operator)*, Mary Sunde *(Blonde)*, Billy Wayne *(Bell Captain)*, Virginia Dabney *(Girl at Party)*, Carlyle Moore, Jr. *(Bellhop)*, John Ridgely *(Photographer)*, Curtis Benton *(Announcer)*, Eddie Chandler *(Title Fight Announcer)*, Lane Chandler *(Timekeeper)*, Don DeFore *(Ringsider)*.

Pictures about prize fighters have always been a staple and this is one of the better ones. It was remade as THE WAGONS ROLL AT NIGHT with the story switched to a circus, then made again with Elvis Presley, with the milieu being taken back to the ring. To keep from confusing it with the Presley movie, they've changed the name of it for television to THE BATTLING BELLHOP. Robinson is an honest fight manager who has lost all of his case money on a bout that was fixed by Bogart, his rival in the business. He tosses a party in his hotel suite and smiles through his disappointment as he and his girl friend, Davis, attempt to make merry. Morris is a bellhop who's been assigned to the party to help serve the drinks. Haade is Bogart's star attraction, a heavyweight. When Haade puts a move on Davis and sullies her honor, Morris springs to her defense and knocks out Haade. Davis thinks Morris is a regular Sir Galahad so she christens him "Kid Galahad" and she and Robinson take him upstate to train at Robinson's farm with old-time fight man, Carey. There, Morris falls for Davis's younger sister, Bryan. Robinson gets jealous of Morris because he feels that Davis, as well as her sister, has a yearning for the young choir-boy lad. In order to get revenge, Robinson arranges a fight between Haade and Morris and believes that the young man will be woefully outclassed and get knocked onto "queer street" by Haade's punches. Morris fights a succession of bouts, knocks everyone out, including Haade's brother. Robinson, who doesn't think Morris has a chance, tells Bogart that the fix is in and that even he is betting on Haade. He doesn't tell this to Morris, though, because he knows the boy would never deliberately throw a fight. Instead, he knows that Morris is a boxer and Haade is a slugger so he gives Morris the worst possible ring instructions and tells the boy to get in there and slug it out. Bogart warns Robinson that if this is a double-cross, he will pay for it with his life. Robinson assures him that it's in the bag. For seven rounds, Morris is beaten to a Tex Cobb pulp (Cobb's loss at the hands of Larry Holmes is what caused Howard Cosell to quit calling boxing matches) but somehow stays on his feet. Davis and Bryan want Robinson to throw in the towel. Robinson sees the error of his ways and, despite having bet against him, tells Morris to box, not slug. The tide of the fight changes and Morris knocks Haade out in the 11th round. Bogart has also lost a fortune and comes gunning for Robinson after the bout. Cops have taken Morris and Robinson to the dressing room but Bogart gets past them and pulls a gun on Robinson, Morris, and Carey in the dressing room. Robinson also carries a gun and both men fire at each other. Bogart is killed and Robinson lies mortally wounded. With his final breath, Robinson gives his okay to Morris and Bryan for them to wed and he dies, happy in knowledge that he has bred a champion. Morris decides to retire as a champion and quits the fight business. Davis wishes them well and walks out to find a new life for herself. A solid story with good characterizations and sensational prizefight footage that is as authentic as Robert Wise's THE SET-UP. In small roles, look hard to see Horace MacMahon as a reporter and Don DeFore, while he was still Don DeFoe, as a ringside spectator. Bogart and Robinson make admirable enemies and both die in the final reel, something they did quite often during their Warner Bros. days.

p, Hal B. Wallis; d, Michael Curtiz; w, Seton I. Miller (based on the novel by Francis Wallace); ph, Tony Gaudio; m, Heinz Roemheld, Max Steiner; ed, George Amy; md, Leo F. Forbstein; art d, Carl Jules Weyl; cos, Orry-Kelly; spec eff, James Gibbons, Edwin B. DuPar; m/l, "The Moon is in Tears Tonight," M.K. Jerome, Jack Scholl.

Sports Drama **(PR:A-C MPAA:NR)**

KID GALAHAD** (1962) 95m Mirisch/UA c

Elvis Presley *(Walter Gulick)*, Gig Young *(Willy Grogan)*, Lola Albright *(Dolly Fletcher)*, Joan Blackman *(Rose Grogan)*, Charles Bronson *(Lew Nyack)*, Ned Glass *(Lieberman)*, Robert Emhardt *(Maynard)*, David Lewis *(Otto Danzig)*, Michael Dante *(Joie Shakes)*, Judson Pratt *(Zimmerman)*, George Mitchell *(Sperling)*, Richard Devon *(Marvin)*, Jeffrey Morris *(Ralphie)*, Liam Redmond *(Father Higgins)*.

They took the 1937 picture starring Edward G. Robinson and Humphrey Bogart, added several songs, and came in six minutes shorter so you know that lots of story content had to have been removed to make that happen. This was the third version of the story as it had already been recirculated with a circus background in THE WAGONS ROLL AT NIGHT. This time around, Presley has just been mustered out of the Army and is working as a sparring partner at an upstate New York training camp operated by Young and his girl friend, Albright. Young sees some boxing ability in Presley (though he was considerably overweight when he made this film; a portent of avoirdupois to come) and convinces him to become a professional, over and above Albright's objections. When Presley saves Albright from the clutches of some gangsters, she dubs him "Kid Galahad." He wins a number of bouts and falls in love with Albright's younger sister, Blackman, then decides to quit the game after his next, and final, bout. Young still owes money to hoodlum Lewis and decides that the only way to repay the debt is to arrange a fight Presley can't possibly win against a much more experienced fighter. Albright is disgusted at Young for doing that and leaves him. Lewis offers Presley's trainer, Bronson, a bribe to allow one of the hoods to work the corner to assure that any cuts Presley sustains will not be repaired. Bronson refuses and his hands are broken by the toughs. Presley gets hurt during the fight but comes back to win. Albright returns to Young and Presley stays true to his word, he quits fighting and will open his own garage and marry Blackman. Presley, of course, sings a number of songs, including: "King Of The Whole Wide World," "This Is Living," "I Got Lucky," "A Whistling Tune," "Home Is Where The Heart Is," "Riding The Rainbow," and "Love Is For Lovers." The role didn't test Elvis's abilities beyond just being the nice, soft-spoken lad he really was in those days. It was shot in Idyllwild, California, to look like the Catskills and only lovers of eastern flora will be able to tell the difference. Bronson is excellent as the trainer and delivers his lines with the underplaying that became his trademark in later years. Director Karlson, who helmed such excellent action films as THE PHENIX CITY STORY and WALKING TALL, does the best with what he has but how much can one do with the story of a singer boxer?

p, David Weisbart; d, Phil Karlson; w, William Fay (based on the novel by Francis Wallace); ph, Burnett Guffey (DeLuxe Color); m, Jeff Alexander; ed, Stuart Gilmore; art d, Cary Odell; set d, Edward G. Boyle; spec eff, Milt Rice; m/l, Ruth Batchelor, Bob Roberts, Ben Weisman, Fred Wise, Sherman Edwards, Hal David, Dee Fuller, Sharon Silbert; makeup, Lynn Reynolds.

Musical/Boxing Drama **(PR:A MPAA:NR)**

KID GLOVE KILLER*** (1942) 74m MGM bw

Van Heflin *(Gordon McKay)*, Marsha Hunt *(Jane Mitchell)*, Lee Bowman *(Gerald I. Ladimer)*, Samuel S. Hinds *(Mayor Daniels)*, Cliff Clark *(Capt. Lynch)*, Eddie Quillan *(Eddie Wright)*, John Litel *(Matty)*, Catherine Lewis *(Bessie Wright)*, Nella Walker *(Mrs. Daniels)*, Ava Gardner *(Car Hop)*, James Flavin.

A terrific debut film for both Van Heflin and for Fred Zinnemann in the director's chair. Heflin is a police criminologist on the trail of the local mayor's killer. The trail leads him to lawyer Litel. The acting is terrific and Zinnemann's direction is taut and suspenseful. After directing many of the "Crime Does Not Pay" short features (including the Oscar-winning THAT MOTHERS MIGHT LIVE), the studio felt Zinnemann was ready for more substantial work. Here he used the documentary techniques learned creating the shorts and the results are terrific. Producer Chertok also worked on the "Crime" series.

p, Jack Chertok; d, Fred Zinnemann; w, Allen Rivkin, John C. Higgins (based on a story by Higgins); ph, Paul Vogel; m, David Snell; ed, Ralph Winters; art d, Cedric Gibbons.

Crime/Mystery **(PR:C MPAA:NR)**

KID GLOVES** (1929) 69m WB bw

Conrad Nagel *(Kid Gloves)*, Lois Wilson *(Ruth)*, Edward Earle *(Penny)*, Edna Murphy *(Lou)*, Maude Turner Gordon *(Aunt)*, Richard Cramer *(Butch)*, Tommy Dugan *(Duffy)*, John Davidson *(Stone)*.

Wilson is a socialite who accidentally gets caught in the gunfire of a gang war. Nagel, a hijacker, takes her to safety. They are found by Davidson, Wilson's fiance who also dabbles in bootlegging himself. He blackmails the duo into marriage, though they never consummate the marriage. Davidson comes to realize the truth behind Wilson and Nagel's original meeting and decides to kill Nagel. But in order to save the man's life, Wilson decides to leave her husband to marry Davidson, rather than see more senseless crime. When Davidson is involved in a murder, he must go on the lam, leaving Wilson and Nagel to develop a new-found love for one another. Both silent and sound versions of this gangster picture were released in 1929, accommodating theatres incapable of handling the new sound technology.

d, Ray Enright; w, Robert Lord (based on a story by Fred Myton); ph, Ben Reynolds; ed, George Marks.

Crime **(PR:C MPAA:NR)**

KID MILLIONS 1/2** (1934) 90m UA bw/c

Eddie Cantor *(Eddie Wilson, Jr.)*, Ann Sothern *(Joan Larrabee)*, Ethel Merman *(Dot Clark)*, George Murphy *(Jerry Lane)*, Jesse Block *(Ben Ali)*, Eve Sully *(Fanya)*, Berton Churchill *(Col. Larrabee)*, Warren Hymer *(Louie the Lug)*, Paul Harvey *(Sheik Mulhulla)*, Otto Hoffman *(Khoot)*, Doris Davenport *(Toots)*, Edgar Kennedy *(Herman)*, Stanley Fields *(Oscar)*, Jack Kennedy *(Pop)*, John Kelly *(Adolph)*, Guy Usher *(William Slade)*, Nicholas Brothers *(Specialty Number)*, Mathew Beard *(Stymie)*, Henry Kolker *(Attorney)*, Tommy Bond *(Tommy)*, Leonard Kibrick *(Leonard)*, William Arnold *(Steward)*, Harry C. Bradley *(Bartender)*, Edward Peil, Sr. *(Assistant Bartender)*, Harry Ernest *(Page Boy)*, Eddie Arden *(Busboy)*, Ed Mortimer *(Ship's Officer)*, Zack Williams, Everett Brown *(Slaves)*, Fred Warren, Harrison Greene *(Spielers)*, George Regas, Noble Johnson *(Attendants)*, Lon Poff *(Recorder)*, Constantine Romanoff, Tor Johnson *(Torturers)*, Ivan Linow, Lalo Encinas, Bud Fine, Leo Willis, Larry Fisher *(Warriors)*, Sam Hayes *(Eddie's Announcer)*, Malcolm Waite, Bob Reeves *(Trumpeteers)*, Clarence Muse *(Col. Witherspoon)*, Steve Clemento, Art Mix, Silver Harr, M. Rourie, Bob Kortman, Robert Ellis *(Desert Riders)*, Louise Carver *(Native Woman)*, Theodore Lorch *(Native Fakir)*, Bobbie LaManche *(Native Boy)* Bobby Jordan *(Tourist)*, J. Macher, John Dowd, Charles Hall *(Natives)*, Mickey Rentschler, Jacqueline Taylor, Carmencita Johnson, Patricia Ann Rambeau, Ada Mae Bender, Billy Seay, John Collum, Wally Albright *(Children on Tug)*, Lucille Ball, Irene Bentley, Dudone Blumier, Mary Jane Carey, Lynne Carver, Mary Lou Dix, Bonnie Bannon, Helen Ferguson, Gail Goodson, Jane Hamilton, Betty-Joy Howard, Vivian Keiffer, Caryl Lincoln, Mary Lange, Janice Jarratt, Ruth Moody, Barbara Pepper, Wanda Perry, Charlotte Russell, Virginia Reed, Gwen Seager, Helen Wood *(The 1934 Goldwyn Girls)*.

A simplistic script about Cantor inheriting $77 million from his archaeologist father is just an excuse for some gags and wonderful musical numbers. Merman is terrific and nearly steals the picture from Cantor. Sothern and Murphy are fine as the romantic couple, singing the Adamson-Lane tune "Your Head on My Shoulder." The final number, "Ice Cream Fantasy," was filmed in Technicolor. Be sure to watch for Lucille Ball as one of the Goldwyn Girls during this dance number set in a Brooklyn ice cream factory. Songs include "An Earful of Music," "When My Ship Comes In," "Okay Toots," "Ice Cream Fantasy," (Gus Kahn, Walter Donaldson); "Your Head on My Shoulder," "I Want to Be a Minstrel Man," (Harold Adamson, Burton Lane); "Mandy" (Irving Berlin).

p, Samuel Goldwyn; d, Roy del Ruth (b&w), Willy Pogany (Technicolor); w, Arthur Sheekman, Nat Perrin, Nunnally Johnson; ph, Ray June (b&w), Ray Rennahan (Technicolor); ed, Stuart Heisler; md, Alfred Newman; art d, Richard Day; cos, Omar Kiam; ch, Seymour Felix.

Musical Comedy **(PR:AAA MPAA:NR)**

KID MONK BARONI** (1952) 80m REA bw

Richard Rober *(Father Callahan)*, Bruce Cabot *(Mr. Hellman)*, Allene Roberts *(Emily Brooks)*, Mona Knox *(June Travers)*, Leonard Nimoy *(Paul "Monk" Baroni)*, Jack Larson *(Angelo)*, Budd Jaxon *(Knuckles)*, Archer MacDonald *(Pete)*, Kathleen Freeman *(Maria Baroni)*, Joseph Mell *(Gino Baroni)*, Paul Maxey *(Mr. Petry)*, Stuart Randall *(Mr. Moore)*, Chad Mallory *(Joey)*, Maurice Cass *(Pawnbroker)*, Bill Cabanne *(Seattle Wildcat)*.

On the Bowery, parish priest Rober tries to reform street punk Nimoy by teaching him how to box and involving him in church activities. Nimoy's face is disfigured (the pointed ears would come later in STAR TREK) and the locals have nicknamed him "Monk." All goes well until a gang fight. Nimoy hits the priest and gets out of town. Cabot takes the younger fighter and transforms him into a pro. After plastic surgery, Nimoy is a new man, with an ego to match. He takes up with Knox, and she uses him until his earnings dry up. Nimoy soon flops in the ring in his efforts to protect his new face. Eventually he gives it up and returns to his old neighborhood, becoming the church's athletic director. Script and direction are mundane and uninspiring.

p, Jack Broder; d, Harold Schuster; w, Aben Kandel; ph, Charles Van Enger; m, Herschel Burke Gilbert; ed, Jason Bernie; art d, James Sullivan.

Drama/Boxing **(PR:C MPAA:NR)**

KID NIGHTINGALE 1/2** (1939) 57m WB bw

John Payne *(Steve Nelson)*, Jane Wyman *(Judy Craig)*, Walter Catlett *(Skip Davis)*, Ed Brophy *(Mike Jordan)*, Charles D. Brown *(Charles Paxton)*, Max Hoffman, Jr. *(Fitts)*, John Ridgely *(Whitey)*, Harry Burns *(Strangler Colombo/Rudolfo Terrassi)*, William Haade *(Rocky)*, Helen Troy *(Marge)*, Winifred Harris *(Mrs. Reynolds)*, Lee Phelps *(Announcer)*, Frankie Van *(Trainer)*, Steve Mason *(Fighter)*, Claude Wisberg *(Messenger)*, Creighton Hale *(Boxing Commission Official)*, Pat Flaherty *(Soxey)*, Jerry Mandy *(Orchestra Leader)*, Constantine Romanoff, Mike Tellegen *(Wrestlers)*, Nat Carr, Frank Mayo *(Men)*.

Payne is a singing waiter who agrees to box in fixed fights. A band plays just as Payne knocks out an opponent, after which he warbles a tune. This, promoters believe, will attract a female market to watch the fights. Payne's only condition is that he be provided with a vocal coach. Burns (in a dual role), who in reality is a wrestler, is assigned to the task. Wyman discovers the deception and finds him a real teacher (Burns again), getting him out of the ring for instruction just as he and the champ knock each other out in the big battle. It's pretty funny once one accepts the zany premise. The direction, script, and Payne's singing are more than passable. Songs are mostly standard stuff, with the exception of one original, "Who Told You I Cared?" a ballad duet sung by Payne and Wyman.

p, Bryan Foy; d, George Amy; w, Charles Belden, Raymond Schrock (based on the story "Singing Swinger" by Lee Katz); ph, Arthur Edeson; ed, Frederick Richards; m/l, George Whiting, Bert Reisfeld.

Comedy/Musical/Sports Drama **(PR:A MPAA:NR)**

KID RANGER, THE* 1/2 (1936) 57m Supreme/William Steiner bw

Bob Steele, William Farnum, Joan Barclay, Earl Dwire, Charles King, Lafe McKee, Frank Ball, Reetsy Adams, Paul and Paulina, Buck Moulton.

Steele gets himself in a jam when he shoots a man he wrongly believes to be a member of an outlaw gang. He puts everything in order, however, when he fingers the real culprit and brings justice upon him.

p, A.W. Hackel; d&w, Robert N. Bradbury.

Western **Cas.** **(PR:A MPAA:NR)**

KID RIDES AGAIN, THE* 1/2 (1943) 55m PRC bw

Buster Crabbe *(Billy the Kid)*, Al St. John *(Fuzzy Jones)*, Iris Meredith *(Joan)*, Glenn Strange *(Tom)*, Charles King *(Vic)*, I. Stanford Jolley *(Mort)*, Edward Piel *(Ainsley)*, Ted Adams *(Sheriff)*, Slim Whitaker *(Texas Sheriff)*, Karl Hackett, Kenne Duncan, Curley Dresden, Snub Pollard, John Merton.

Crabbe, well past his FLASH GORDON heyday, plays the famous outlaw in Producers Releasing Corp.'s film series BILLY THE KID. Here he is more handsome than anything else. Falsely arrested for train robbery, Crabbe breaks out of jail to find the real outlaw and clear his name. In the process he uncovers a group of bad guys masquerading as ranchers. He recovers the stolen money and all is made right. The film is historically inaccurate and nothing more than a formula action piece. Look for old silent film comics St. John and Pollard.

p, Bert Sternbach, Sigmund Neufeld; d, Sherman Scott [Sam Newfield]; w, Fred Myton; ph, Jack Greenhalgh; ed, Holbrook N. Todd.

Western **(PR:A MPAA:NR)**

KID RODELO* (1966, U.S./Span.) 91m Trident-Fenix/PAR bw

Don Murray *(Kid Rodelo)*, Janet Leigh *(Nora)*, Broderick Crawford *(Joe Harbin)*, Richard Carlson *(Link)*, Jose Nieto *(Thomas Reese)*, Julio Pena *(Balsas)*, Miguel Del Castillo *(Chavas)*, Jose Villa Sante *(Cavalry Hat)*, Alfonso San Felix *(Gopher)*, Emilio Rodriguez *(Warden)*, Fernando Hilbeck *(Perryman)*, Roberto Rubenstein *(Doctor)*, Bill Christmas *(Guard)*, Alvaro de Luna, Guillermo Mendez, Mike Brendel, Juan Olaguibel.

Murray is fresh out of prison and is chasing his former partners Crawford and Carlson (the latter also being the film's director) in a race for gold. They team up, although Murray doesn't know he's about to be double-crossed. However, the audience should have no problem figuring that out. Along the way Leigh and some Indians enter the picture, leading toward a bloody climax. The rambling script is filled with cliches and is completely predictable. The actors (especially Crawford and Leigh) are wasted and don't seem to care about what they're doing. Murray starts off having a Texas drawl, which disappears by the film's end. Most disturbing is that this fairly violent picture was made with a child audience in mind. Shot on location in Spain.

p, Jack O. Lamont, James J. Storrow, Jr.; d, Richard Carlson; w, Jack Natteford (based on a story by Louis L'Amour); ph, Manuel Merino; m, Johnny Douglas; ed, Allan Morrison; art d, Jaime Perez Cubero, Jose Luis Galicia; cos, Peris; m/l, "Love Is Trouble" Tom Glazer; makeup, Fernando Martinez.

Western **(PR:C MPAA:NR)**

KID SISTER, THE½** (1945) 56m PRC bw

Roger Pryor *(J. Waldo Barnes)*, Judy Clark *(Joan Hollingsworth)*, Constance Worth *(Ethel Hollingsworth)*, Frank Jenks *(Burglar)*, Tom Dugan *(Michael the Cop)*, Richard Byron *(Tommy)*, Minerva Urecal *(Mrs. Wiggins)*, Ruth Robinson *(Mrs. Hollingsworth)*, Peggy Wynne *(Martha)*.

Clark is the title character, the younger sibling of Worth. According to the psychology book she's been reading, Clark is officially "grown up" and she immediately starts chasing Worth's fiance. She's locked in her room for a party in Pryor's honor, but escapes and poses as a maid for the affair. She meets a burglar (Jenks) and he mistakes her for a moll. The two end up in Pryor's home, and the film ends with Clark winning the heart of her sister's beau. A delightful comedy.

p, Sigmund Neufeld; d, Sam Newfield; w, Fred Myton; ph, James Brown; ed, Holbrook N. Todd; md, David Chudnow; art d, Paul Palmentola.

Romance/Comedy Cas. (PR:A MPAA:NR)

KID VENGEANCE* (1977) 94m Golan-Globus-Irwin Yablans c

Jim Brown, Lee Van Cleef, John Marley, Glynnis O'Connor, Matt Clark, Timothy Scott, Leif Garrett.

Garrett plays a young man seeking vengeance for the murder of his parents. He joins forces with Brown, whose gold was stolen by Van Cleef, the outlaw who killed Garrett's parents.

p, Menahem Golan, Alex Hacohen; d, Joe Manduke; w, Budd Robbins, Jay Telfer (based on a story by Kenneth Globus); ph, David Gurfinkel.

Western Cas. (PR:C MPAA:PG)

KIDNAP OF MARY LOU, THE (SEE: ALMOST HUMAN, 1974)

KIDNAPPED, 1934 (SEE: MISS FANE'S BABY IS STOLEN, 1934)

KIDNAPPED*** (1938) 93m FOX bw

Warner Baxter *(Alan Breck)*, Freddie Bartholomew *(David Balfour)*, Arleen Whelan *(Jean MacDonald)*, C. Aubrey Smith *(Duke of Argyle)*, Reginald Owen *(Capt. Hoseason)*, John Carradine *(Gordon)*, Nigel Bruce *(Neil MacDonald)*, Miles Mander *(Ebenezer Balfour)*, Ralph Forbes *(James)*, H. B. Warner *(Rankeiller)*, Arthur Hohl *(Riach)*, E. E. Clive *(Minister MacDougall)*, Halliwell Hobbes *(Dominie Campbell)*, Montagu Love *(English Officer)*, Donald Haines *(Ransome)*, Moroni Olsen *(Douglas)*, Leonard Mudie *(Red Fox)*, Mary Gordon *(Mrs. MacDonald)*, Forrester Harvey *(Innkeeper)*, Clyde Cook *(Cook)*, Russell Hicks *(Bailiff)*, Billy Watson *(Bobby MacDonald)*, Eily Malyon *(Mrs. Campbell)*, Kenneth Hunter *(Capt. Frazer)*, Charles Irwin *(Sgt. Ellis)*, John Burton *(Lt. Stone)*, David Clyde *(Blacksmith)*, Holmes Herbert *(Judge)*, Brandon Hurst *(Donnelly)*, Vernon Steele *(Captain)*, C. Montague Shaw *(Scotch Statesman)*, R. T. Noble *(Warden)*,.

Robert Louis Stevenson might turn over, nay, *spin*, in his grave if he'd seen the liberties taken with his classic novel, but his efforts would have been for naught as this is one of those rare times when the adaptation did the original some justice. Just about every British actor living and unemployed in Hollywood was used in the picture and their presence lent credulity to the story. Bartholomew is the young heir to a fortune in the 18th Century, the time of the war between Scotland and England. His evil uncle arranges for the lad to be kidnaped and sent to sea. However, Bartholomew meets Baxter, a fugitive from the British authorities and one of the rebels against the crown. The older man, in between buckling and unbuckling his swash, joins forces with the youth and a series of incidents takes place, at the end of which the lad is restored to his true position. Baxter and Whelan, one of Zanuck's "discoveries," wind up with each other at the end. The story is so convoluted and filled with derring-do that it is reminiscent of the relationship between the young Prince and Errol Flynn's Miles in THE PRINCE AND THE PAUPER, but nowhere near as exciting or humorous. Good work for Owen as a heinous captain and Smith as the Duke of Argyle. Smith's film career began in 1915 and he remained a working actor until his death in 1948 at the age of 85. His last film was LITTLE WOMEN. Carradine was only 34 when KIDNAPPED was made and was already appearing in his 29th film in a career that includes more than 500 movies. Though totally shot in California, the studio's art directors managed to successfully evoke the feeling of Scotland, right down to the heather and the fog.

p, Darryl F. Zanuck [Kenneth MacGowan]; d, Alfred Werker; w, Sonya Levien, Eleanor Harris, Ernest Pascal, Edwin Blum (based on the novel by Robert Louis Stevenson); ph, Gregg Toland; m, Arthur Lange; ed, Allen McNeil; md, Lange.

Period Adventure (PR:AAA MPAA:NR)

KIDNAPPED** (1948) 80m MON bw

Roddy McDowall *(David Balfour)*, Sue England *(Aileen Fairlie)*, Dan O'Herlihy *(Alan Breck)*, Roland Winters *(Capt. Hoseason)*, Jeff Corey *(Shuan)*, Houseley Stevenson *(Ebenezer)*, Erskine Sanford *(Rankeillor)*, Alex Frazer *(Fairlie)*, Winefried McDowall *(Innkeeper's Wife)*, Bobby Anderson *(Ransome)*, Janet Murdoch *(Janet Clouston)*, Olaf Hytten *(The Red Fox)*, Erville Alderson *(Mungo)*.

A lesser adaptation of the Robert Louis Stevenson novel from Monogram Studios, which was better known for gangster films and westerns. McDowall comes to claim an inheritance from his uncle, only to be nabbed and sold off into slavery. He is saved by adventurer O'Herlihy, and both take up with England, making their way across the Scottish countryside to claim McDowall's rightful dues. The film is too slow-paced for what should be exciting material. However, the photography is excellent, giving the film a highly polished look.

p, Lindsley Parsons; d, William Beaudine; w, W. Scott Darling (based on the novel *Kidnapped* by Robert Louis Stevenson); ph, William Sickner; m, Edward J. Kay; ed, Leonard W. Herman; md, Kay; art d, Dave Milton.

Adventure (PR:AAA MPAA:NR)

KIDNAPPED** (1960) 97m BV c

Peter Finch *(Alan Breck Stewart)*, James MacArthur *(David Balfour)*, Bernard Lee *(Capt. Hoseason)*, Niall MacGinnis *(Shuan)*, John Laurie *(Uncle Ebenezer Balfour)*, Finlay Currie *(Cluny MacPherson)*, Peter O'Toole *(Robin Oig MacGregor)*, Miles Malleson *(Mr. Rankeillor)*, Oliver Johnston *(Mr. Campbell)*, Duncan MacRae *(The Highlander)*, John Pike *(Cabin Boy)*, Andrew Cruickshank *(Colin Roy Campbell)*, Abe Barker *(Donald Dhu MacLaren)* Eileen Way *(Jennet Clouston)*, Alex MacKenzie *(The Ferryman)*, Norman MacOwan *(Tinker)*, Jack Stewart, Edie Martin.

A completely faithful—and surprisingly dull—adaptation of the famed novel. MacArthur is the young lad who is cheated out of his inheritance and sold into slavery by Laurie, his uncle. Put on a ship as the cabin boy, he meets Finch, a Scottish loyalist who has asked the captain (Lee) to take him to Scotland. After MacArthur finds out Lee plans to kill Finch, the two join forces to take over the ship. After the ship runs aground and MacArthur is washed ashore, he meets up with Cruickshank, who is shot. Finch is placed near the scene of the crime, but claims innocence. MacArthur eventually makes it back to the estate and claims his rightful inheritance. Finch sets sail once more, and the two say their farewells, knowing they may meet again one day. This is a handsome-looking production, with an excellent cast. But the script's attention to detail ultimately bogs down the story's pace. The film was not very successful and Disney ended up televising it on "Wonderful World of Disney" a few years after theatrical release. The studio claimed that the director, Robert Stevenson, was a distant relative of Robert Louis Stevenson. However, the director later denied this claim. This was Disney's first British-based production since THE SWORD AND THE ROSE. Stevenson, a Briton by birth, made his name in California.

p, Walt Disney; d&w, Robert Stevenson (based on the novel *Kidnapped* by Robert Louis Stevenson); ph, Paul Beeson (Technicolor); m, Cedric Thorpe Davie; ed, Gordon Stone; prod d, Frank Ernst; md, Muir Mathieson; art d, Carmen Dillon; set d, Vernon Dixon; cos, Margaret Furse; spec eff, Peter Ellenshaw; makeup, Stewart Freeborn.

Adventure Cas. (PR:AAA MPAA:NR)

KIDNAPPED*½** (1971, Brit.) 100m Omnibus/AIP c

Michael Caine *(Alan Breck)*, Trevor Howard *(Lord Advocate Grant)*, Jack Hawkins *(Capt. Hoseason)*, Donald Pleasence *(Ebenezer Balfour)*, Gordon Jackson *(Charles Stewart)*, Vivien Heilbron *(Catriona Stewart)*, Lawrence Douglas *(David Balfour)*, Freddie Jones *(Cluny Macpherson)*, Andrew McCulloch *(Andrew)*, Eric Woodburn *(Doctor)*, Roger Booth *(Duke of Cumberland)*, Russell Waters *(Lord Advocate's Secretary)*, John Hughes *(Simon Campbell)*, Claire Nielson *(Barbara Grant)*, Geoffrey Whitehead *(Lt. Duncansby)*, Peter Jeffrey *(Riach)*, Terry Richards *(Mungo Campbell)*, Jack Watson *(James Stewart)*.

A very interesting distinction must be accorded this fourth version of Robert Louis Stevenson's novel: it's better than the others in almost every way. Made originally in 1937 and released in 1938 with Warner Baxter and Freddie Bartholomew in the leads, it was re-made in 1948 by Monogram with Roddy McDowall and Dan O'Herlihy, then again with James MacArthur and Peter Finch (and a young actor named Peter O'Toole in a small role) in 1960. That film was directed by, of all people, Robert Stevenson, and there are those ill-educated people who actually thought that the same man wrote the novel and lensed the movie! In this version, the screenplay has taken the best of the novel and added material from the sequel, *Catriona*, and combined the two under the deft handiwork of scenarist Pulman, who also wrote the TV mini-series, "I, Claudius." It's the final years of the 18th Century and the British are cruelly ravaging the Scottish forces of the Jacobite Rebellion. Douglas is an orphan boy who comes to the home of his wicked uncle, Pleasence. Douglas doesn't know that he is the rightful heir of the family fortune and Pleasence is not about to tell him. Pleasence hires Hawkins, a ruthless sea captain, to impress the boy into sea service and sell him into slavery in the New World. The ship is on its way to the Carolinas and rams into a small boat, sinking it and drowning every hand aboard save Caine, a rebel on his way to France to raise some money to continue the war against the Crown. Caine and Douglas hit it off immediately and join forces to battle Hawkins's cutthroat crew. A storm hits and the ship is wrecked. Caine and Douglas make their way to shore and then to Caine's cousin's home where Watson hopes that Caine will give up the battle and make a truce with the British. Caine is happy to see Watson's daughter, Heilbron, a young woman now and grown to comely maturity. The home is raided by Richards, a Scot turncoat to the cause, who leads a band of British to capture Caine. There is a battle and Richards is killed, Watson is wounded and taken by the British, and Caine, Heilbron, and Douglas escape. They get to Edinburgh where Caine finds yet another cousin, Jackson, who is a lawyer. Caine asks for Jackson's aid in getting him to France. Once Jackson meets Douglas, he realizes that the boy is the true heir to Pleasence's fortune so they get the needed money from Pleasence, as well as an admission of his duplicity. Now, Caine learns that cousin Watson is on trial for having slain Richards and is in danger of execution. Douglas asks the British advocate, Howard, to drop the charge and Howard agrees if Douglas will testify. But that will put his life in danger. Undaunted by this danger, Douglas will speak at the trial. Heilbron, upon hearing this, goes to Caine, who is in hiding, awaiting the next boat to France. Caine is touched by her appeal and realizes that the rebellion will never succeed so he goes to Howard and admits that *he* killed Richards. Watson is freed and Douglas plans to marry Heilbron. He is now a rich young man with everything to live and love for. This time, they went to England and Scotland to capture the proper backgrounds and the photography is splendid and serves well against the familiar story. After a decade of "Beach Party" films, AIP decided to remake classics and foisted some dreadful ones upon the public, WUTHERING HEIGHTS and JULIUS CAESAR among them. Happily, this is the best of the lot although it packs so much plot into the story that it may be difficult for "G" audiences to follow and that's the very crowd of tots they'd hoped would flock to the theaters. Caine, a city boy who can never seem to lose his Bow Bells accent, shows his costume mettle in this role, which was a welcome change from the spies and cads he'd played until making KIDNAPPED. A little too much talk and not enough action but still enjoyable. One song, "For All My Days" (Budd, Jack Fishman) was sung by Mary Hopkin. This was the fourth remake of the classic Stevenson novel.

p, Frederick H. Brogger; d, Delbert Mann; w, Jack Pulman (based on the novels *Kidnapped* and *Catriona* by Robert Louis Stevenson); ph, Paul Beeson (Panavision, Movielab Color); m, Roy Budd; ed, Peter Boita; md, Budd; art d, Alex Vetchinsky; set d, Arthur Taksen; cos, Olga Lehmann; spec eff, Cliff Cully; m/l, Roy Budd, Jack Fishman; stunts, Bob Anderson; makeup, Roy Ashton, W.T. Partleton.

Adventure **(PR:AA MPAA:G)**

KIDNAPPERS, THE, 1953 (SEE: THE LITTLE KIDNAPPERS, 1953)

KIDNAPPERS, THE**

(1964, U.S./Phil.) 78m Halcyon-Cirio H. Santiago/Manson bw

Burgess Meredith *(Louis Halliburton)*, Olivia Cenizal *(Christine Halliburton)*, William Phipps *(Jay)*, Paul Harber, Carol Varga, Armando Cortez, Zaldy Zshornack, Johnny Monteiro.

Meredith is cast as an American living in the Philippines whose son has been kidnaped, forcing him to enlist the aid of his wife's former fiance (Phipps), a former FBI agent. Phipps attempts to double-cross Meredith by keeping the ransom money for himself. The plot is foiled when his girl friend finds out and tries to stop him.

d, Eddie Romero; w, Harry Harber; ph, Felipe Sacdalan; m, Ariston Avelino; ed, Joven Calub.

Drama **(PR:A MPAA:NR)**

KIDNAPPING OF THE PRESIDENT, THE 1/2**

(1980, Can.) 113m Sefel Pictures International/Crown International c

William Shatner *(Jerry O'Connor)*, Hal Holbrook *(President Adam Scott)*, Van Johnson *(Vice President Ethan Richards)*, Ava Gardner *(Beth Richards)*, Miguel Fernandes *(Roberto Assanti)*, Cindy Girling *(Linda Steiner)*, Michael J. Reynolds *(MacKenzie)*, Elizabeth Shepherd *(Joan Scott)*, Gary Reineke *(Deitrich)*, Maury Chaykin *(Harvey Cannon)*, Murray Westgate *(Archie)*, Michael Kane *(Herb)*, Jackie Burroughs, Aubert Pallascio, Virginia Podesser, Elias Zarov, Larry Duran, Patrick Brymar, Gershon Resnik, John Stocker, Chappelle Jaffe, John Romaine.

Fernandes is a Third World terrorist who handcuffs himself to U.S. President Holbrook and claims to be wired with explosives, which will be detonated unless his group's demands are met. Shatner is the Secret Service man who is trying to free his boss unharmed. A subplot involving Johnson as the vice president involved in a potentially damaging scandal is nicely integrated. Johnson and Gardner, as his wife, are teamed for the first time since THREE MEN IN WHITE in 1944. The film runs a little longer than necessary which hurts some of the suspense but the denouement is well-handled and exciting. The film was a box office disaster, however, and quickly sank without a trace.

p, George Mendeluk, John Ryan; d, Mendeluk; w, Richard Murphy (based on the novel by Charles Templeton); ph, Michael Molloy (Panavision, DeLuxe Color); m, Paul J. Zaza; ed, Michael McLaverty; art d, Douglas Higgins; spec eff, Peter Hutchinson, Richard Albain.

Thriller/Political **(PR:O MPAA:R)**

KID'S LAST FIGHT, THE (SEE: LIFE OF JIMMY DOLAN, THE, 1933)

KID'S LAST RIDE, THE* 1/2 (1941) 55m MON bw

Ray Corrigan *(Crash)*, John King *(Dusty)*, Max Terhune *(Alibi)*, Luana Walters *(Sally)*, Edwin Brian *(Jimmy)*, Al Bridge *(Harmon)*, Glenn Strange *(Bart)*, Frank Ellis *(Wash)*, John Elliott *(Disher)*, George Havens *(Johnny)*, Tex Palmer, Carl Mathews, George Morrell.

Poor entry in the RANGE BUSTERS series produced by Monogram. Corrigan, King, and Terhune enter a rough town to settle a feud with outlaw brothers Strange and Bridge united against Brian and Walters. Seems Brian's dad was a judge who sentenced the younger brother of the outlaw pair to hang. Brian is killed, but the Range Busters fix everything in the end. The photography is bad. Lots of violence and not much else in this time waster.

p, George W. Weeks; d, S. Roy Luby; w, Earle Snell; ph, Robert Cline; ed, Roy Claire; m/l, "Call of the Wild," Harry Tobias, Jean George, "It's All Part of the Game," Tobias, Roy Ingraham.

Western **Cas.** **(PR:A MPAA:NR)**

KIEV COMEDY, A***

(1963, USSR) 76m Dovshenko Film Studio/Artkino c (ZA DVUNMYA ZAYTSAMI; AKA: CHASING TWO HARES)

Albert Borisov *(Golokhvostyy)*, Margarita Krinitsyna *(Pronya)*, Nikolai Yakovchenko *(Serko)*, A. Kushnirenko *(Serchikha)*, N. Koperzhinskaya *(Sekleta)*, Natalia Naum *(Galva), A. Yurchenko (Stepan)*, K. Yershov *(Plyashka)*, T. Litvinenko *(Khimka)*, O. Vikland *(Ninon)*, L. Alfimova, N. Antonova, A. Bykov, V. Grudynin, S. Karamash, V. Kostyrenko, N. Talyura, R. Shablovskaya, V. Shiryayev, V. Koretskiy, F. Ivanova, N. Lapshina.

A barber loses his shop in a game of cards. To remedy his problems he attempts to marry into a wealthy family. When the marriage is almost set he falls in love with a poor girl and must choose between his heart and his wallet. The fortune hunter finally is disgraced and flees the scene after a sound beating.

d&w, Victor Ivanov (based on a play by Mikhaylo Petrovich Staritskiy); ph, V. Ilyenko; m, V. Gomolyaka; ed, V. Bondina; art d, I. Yutsevich; cos, L. Baykova; spec eff, I. Tregubova, V. Deminskiy; m/l, Ye. Kravchenko.

Comedy **(PR:C MPAA:NR)**

KIGEKI DAI SHOGEKI (SEE: HOT-SPRINGS HOLIDAY, 1970, Jap.)

KIKI* (1931) 84m UA bw

Mary Pickford *(Kiki)*, Reginald Denny *(Victor Randall)*, Joseph Cawthorn *(Alfred Rapp)*, Margaret Livingston *(Paulette Vaile)*, Phil Tead *(Eddie)*, Fred Walton *(Bunson)*, Edwin Maxwell *(Dr. Smiley)*, Betty Grable *(Girl)*, Fred Warren.

Denny is a divorced musical producer being pursued by Pickford. Despite his sourpuss personality and his tirades, she continues until she has him by film's end. An unfunny film far beneath the talents of the woman who was known as "America's Sweetheart" in the 1920s. Fifteen year old Betty Grable already was showing her great complexion and wonderful legs in this, her second year in movies.

p, Joseph M. Schenck; d&w, Sam Taylor (based on the play by David Belasco from the French of Andre Picard); ph, Karl Struss; ed, Allen McNeil.

Comedy **(PR:A MPAA:NR)**

KIL 1 (SEE: SKIN GAME, THE, 1965)

KILL 1/2** (1968, Jap.) 115m Toho/Frank Lee International bw (AKA: KIRU)

Tatsuya Nakadai *(Genta)*, Etsushi Takahashi *(Hanijiro)*, Shigeru Koyama *(Ayuzawa)*, Eijiro Tono *(Moriuchi)*, Yuriko Hoshi *(Chino)*, Yoshio Tsuchiya *(Matsuo)*, Tadao Nakamaru *(Shoda)*, Hideo Amamoto, Nami Tamura, Ko Hashimoto, Akira Kubo.

A one-time samurai comes out of retirement to assist a band of samurai rebelling against a tyrannical overseer, who has double-crossed the group. This adventure also serves as a lesson to a young friend of the aging samurai, about the nature of good and evil.

d, Kihachi Okamoto; w, Akira Murao, Okamoto (based on a story by Shugoro Yamamoto); ph, Rokuro Nishigaki (Tohoscope); m, Masaru Sato; ed, Okamoto, Yoshitami Kuroiwa; art d, Iwao Akune.

Martial Arts **(PR:C MPAA:NR)**

KILL, THE ** (1968) 70m Canyon c

Antoinette Maynard, Tony Brooks, Walt Phillips, Sharon Wells, Natasha, Nancy McGavin, Tod Badker, Pam English, John Lee, Harry Stone, Gail Lavon, Larry Vincente, April O'Connor, Shari Stevens, Bonnie Walker.

Low-budget thriller has private detective hired by a girl to find her missing brother, a member of a heroin smuggling gang. His attempts force the gang to harass him for his nosiness. A violent showdown ends this seamy tale.

p, Ed DePriest; d&w, Gary Graver; ph, Graver; m, Ernest Alexander; md, Alexander.

Crime **(PR:O MPAA:NR)**

KILL (SEE: KILL! KILL! KILL!, 1972, Fr./Span./Ital./Ger.)

KILL A DRAGON* 1/2 (1967) 91m UA c

Jack Palance *(Rick)*, Fernando Lamas *(Patrai)*, Aldo Ray *(Vigo)*, Alizia Gur *(Tisa)*, Kam Tong *(Win Lim)*, Don Knight *(Ian)*, Hans William Lee *(Jimmie)*, Judy Dan *(Chunhyang)*.

Complicated plot centers around nitroglycerin and a lot of karate action. A dangerous load of the chemical lands on a beach where the islanders claim it as their own. But its owner, Lamas, wants it back and threatens to blow up the island. Tong slips out to Hong Kong and appeals to Palance, a man for hire. He agrees in exchange for gold and also in sympathy for the islanders. Assisted by two karate experts, Palance overcomes Lamas in a violent conclusion. The film is riddled with cliches and little more than a series of fights and action scenes strung together. Palance and Ray do give it their best in a failing cause.

p, Hal Klein; d, Michael Moore; w, George Schenck, William Marks; ph, Emmanuel Rojas (DeLuxe Color); m, Philip Springer, Buddy Kaye; ed, John F. Schreyer; spec eff, Roger George.

Action/Martial Arts **(PR:O MPAA:NR)**

KILL AND GO HIDE (SEE: CHILD, THE, 1977)

KILL AND KILL AGAIN** (1981) 100m Film Ventures International c

James Ryan *(Steve Chase)*, Anneline Kriel *(Kandy Kane)*, Ken Gampu *(Gorilla)*, Norman Robinson *(Gypsy Billy)*, Stan Schmidt *(The Fly)*, Bill Flynn *(Hotdog)*, Michael Mayer *(Marduk)*, Marloe Scott-Wilson *(Minerva)*, John Ramsbottom *(Dr. Horatio Kane)*, Eddie Dorie *(Optimus)*, Mervyn Johns *(President)*.

Silly plot has Ryan out to rescue a kidnaped scientist. Seems the man has discovered a way to convert potatoes into a high-level energy fuel source and inadvertently created a mind-controling drug as well. Evil scientist (the type that abounds in this sort of adventure) Mayer wants the drug to create his state of "New Babylonia." This leads to numerous karate fights, helicopter explosions, and assorted mayhem, all directed with tongue firmly planted in cheek. Not bad for the genre. This is a sequel to the highly successful KILL OR BE KILLED from the year before.

p, Igo Kantor; d, Ivan Hall; w, John Crowther; ph, Tai Krige (DeLuxe Color); ed, Peter Thornton, Robert Leighton; ch, Norman Robinson, Stan Schmidt.

Martial Arts **Cas.** **(PR:O MPAA:PG)**

KILL BABY KILL***

(1966, Ital.) 83m F.U.L./Europix Consolidated c (OPERAZIONE PAURA; AKA: CURSE OF THE LIVING DEAD)

Erika Blanc *(Monica Schuftan)*, Giacomo Rossi Stuart *(Dr. Paul Eswai)*, Fabienne Dali *(Ruth the Sorceress)*, Giana Vivaldi *(Baroness Graps)*, Piero Lulli *(Police Commissioner Kroger)*, Max Lawrence *(Kerl)*, Micaela Esdra, Giuseppe Addobbati, Mariella Panfili, Franca Dominici, Valerio Valeri.

A chilling horror film made by the often unseen director (BLACK SABBATH) Mario Bava. In the small Transylvanian town of Karmingan, the population is plagued with a series of mysterious deaths. Lulli receives a letter from a young girl requesting his help. He arrives too late, however, for she is dead. When the autopsy reveals a coin embedded in the girl's heart, the police pay a visit to Dali, a local witch. Dali explains the coin was her doing, in order to protect the girl's ghost from Vivaldi, a local baroness. It appears that when the baroness' young daughter had been killed a few years back, her pleas had gone unnoticed by the villagers. This event whetted the baroness' appetite for revenge. They then discover that Blanc, the dead girl's younger sister, is the next intended victim. To stop Vivaldi, the sorceress must kill her, thus saving the girl and the town. The film is well-crafted, with an atmospheric lighting that helps set the mood. The different lines of the plot are woven together deftly, keeping the audience constantly on edge. Released in America with a dubbed soundtrack as part of an "Orgy of the Living Dead" triple feature.

p, Nando Pisani, Luciano Catenacci; d, Mario Bava; w, Bava, Romano Migliorini, Roberto Natale, John Hart; ph, Antonio Rinaldi (Eastmancolor); m, Carlo Rustichelli; ed, Romana Fortini; art d, Sandro Dell 'Orco.

Horror **(PR:O MPAA:NR)**

KILL CASTRO (SEE: CUBA CROSSING, 1980)

KILL HER GENTLY* ½ (1958, Brit.) 75m COL bw

Marc Lawrence *(William Connors)*, George Mikell *(Lars Svenson)*, Griffith Jones *(Jeff Martin)*, John Gayford *(Truck Driver)*, Roger Avon *(Constable Brown)*, Maureen Connell *(Kay Martin)*, Shay Gorman *(Dr. Landers)*, Marianne Brauns *(Raina)*, Frank Hawkins *(Inspector Raglan)*, Patrick Connor *(Detective Sgt. Thompson)*, Jonathan Meddings *(Bank Clerk)*, Peter Stephens *(Bank Manager)*, Susan Neil *(Barmaid)*, David Lawton *(Slade)*, Elaine Wells *(Mrs. Douglas)*.

After being placed in a mental institution, Jones decides that his wife is responsible and therefore must die. He meets two escaped cons, Lawrence and Mikell, and promises to help aid in their escape if they will murder Connell. They agree but plans are bungled and the film ends with the three killed or caught in the process. The story is old hat with no freshness in the telling.

p, Guido Coen; d, Charles Saunders; w, Paul Erickson; ph, Walter J. Harvey; m, Edwin Astley; ed, Margery Saunders; md, Astley; art d, Harry White.

Suspense **(PR:O MPAA:NR)**

KILL! KILL! KILL!**

(1972, Fr./Ger./Ital./Span.) 102m Cocinor c (AKA: KILL!)

Jean Seberg *(Emily)*, James Mason *(Alan)*, Stephen Boyd *(Killian)*, Curt Jurgens *(Chief)*, Daniel Emilfork *(Inspector)*, Henri Garcin *(Lawyer)*.

Mason is an Interpol agent off to Italy to squelch an international heroin smuggling ring. Seberg is his bored wife, who longs for the adventure she finds in the form of Boyd, an unorthodox vigilante who believes brute force is the only method to use with drug dealers. Seberg falls for him and also becomes involved in the investigation after finding corpses in her automobile. The film ends with a shootout between smugglers and the less than righteous drug agents. The film, written and directed by Seberg's husband, is a mixed bag, with a script full of cliches. Often the violence is lurid and shown merely for the sake of violence. (In English.)

p, Alexandre and Ilya Salkind; d&w, Romain Gary; ph, Edmond Rechad (Eastmancolor); m, Berto Pisano, Jacques Charmont; ed, Robert Dwyre.

Crime/Action/Suspense **(PR:O MPAA:NR)**

KILL ME TOMORROW** (1958, Brit.) 80m Delta/REN-Tudor bw

Pat O'Brien *(Bart Crosbie)*, Lois Maxwell *(Jill Brook)*, George Coulouris *(Heinz Webber)*, Wensley Pithey *(Inspector Lane)*, Freddie Mills *(Waxy)*, Ronald Adam *(Brook)*, Robert Brown *(Steve)*, April Olrich *(Bella Braganza)*, Tommy Steele *(Himself)*, Richard Pasco *(Dr. Fisher)*, George Eugeniou *(Nico)*, Al Mulock *(Rod)*, Stuart Nichol *(Sgt. Bellamy)*, Vic Wise *(Lou)*, Claude Kingston *(Jimmy Crosbie)*, Peter Swanwick *(Harrison)*.

O'Brien stars as a hard-drinking reporter who has hit upon some tough times. First his wife is killed in an auto accident, then he loses his newspaper job, and later discovers that his son needs a $5,000 eye operation in Switzerland. He decides to ask his former boss for his job back, but when he enters the office he finds the man dead. Coulouris, a diamond smuggler, is the murderer and he offers O'Brien the needed sum if he'll take the blame for the crime. O'Brien feels he has no other choice but to accept. When he confesses to Scotland Yard authorities, however, they do not believe his story. Coulouris, thinking that O'Brien has not kept his part of the bargain, tries to prevent the boy's plane from leaving for Switzerland. Maxwell, the dead editor's niece, goes into action, sees to it that the plane takes off, and rounds up Coulouris and his gang. It's overplayed and melodramatic, but has enough intrigue to make it watchable.

p, Francis Searle; d, Terence Fisher; w, Robert Falconer, Manning O'Brine; ph, Geoffrey Faithfull; m, Temple Abady; ed, Ann Chetwidden; m/l, "Rebel Rock," Tommy Steele.

Crime Drama **(PR:C MPAA:NR)**

KILL OR BE KILLED** (1950) 67m EL bw

Lawrence Tierney *(Robert Warren)*, George Coulouris *(Victor Sloma)*, Marissa O'Brien *(Maria Marek)*, Rudolph Anders *(Gregory Marek)*, Lopes da Silva *(Huerta)*, Veloso Pires *(Damiae)*, Leonor Maia, Joao Amaro, Licinio Sena, Helga Line, Mira Lobo.

Tierney is framed for murder and heads into the South American jungle to hide from the law. He meets O'Brien, and discovers her husband (Anders) set him up. Helping him in his flight, she falls in love with the fugitive. Eventually Anders and his partner Coulouris end up dead and Tierney is cleared. The drama runs at a good pace, keeping things coming fast and furious. Some nice jungle footage.

p, Walter Jurmann; d, Max Nosseck; w, Arnold Phillips, Nosseck, Lawrence Goldman; ph, J. Roy Hunt; m, Karl Hajos; ed, Douglas Bagier; art d, Erwin Scharf.

Adventure/Mystery **(PR:C MPAA:NR)**

KILL OR BE KILLED**

(1967, Ital.) 92m Regal/Rizzoli, Cinemation (UCCIDI O MUORI)

Robert Mark *(Johnny Ringo/Gerry)*, Elina De Witt *(Lisa Drummond)*, Gordon Mitchell *(Hired Gunman)*, Andrea Bosic, Men Fury, Tony Rogers, Fabrizio Moroni, Albert Farley, Benjamin May, Mary Land.

Spaghetti western has Mark as a gunslinger who, traveling incognito, wanders into a feud between two families. Forced into a showdown, he kills a member of one of the families. Discovered by the sheriff, pursued by a revengeful family, he escapes with the aid of an old man, and continues to kill the remaining members of the family with whom he had the showdown. In the end he rides off with a daughter from the rival family, leaving the town in renewed peace.

p, Luigi Rovere; d, Amerigo Anton; w, Mario Amendola (based on a story by Amendola); ph, Aldo Giordani; m, Carlo Rustichelli; ed, Cleofe Conversi; art d, Saverio D'Eugenio; cos, Giorgio Desideri.

Western **(PR:C MPAA:NR)**

KILL OR BE KILLED** (1980) 90m Film Ventures International c

James Ryan, Norman Combes, Charlotte Michelle, Daniel DuPlessis.

Nasty ex-Nazi general cum karate coach is out to get even with the Japanese coach who defeated his team during WW II. The deal is, if the Germans win this time, the Japanese coach must give a public apology. This thoroughly ridiculous plot is merely an excuse for lots of karate fighting—some quite good. Made on a minuscule budget, the public ate it up like movie popcorn (it earned well over $6 million in domestic receipts) and inspired a sequel, KILL AND KILL AGAIN, in 1981.

p, Ben Volk; d, Ivan Hall; w, C.F. Beyers-Boshoff; ph, Mane Eotha; ed, Brian Varaday; karate ch, Norman Robinson.

Martial Arts **Cas.** **(PR:C MPAA:PG)**

KILL OR CURE** (1962, Brit.) 88m MGM bw

Terry-Thomas *(J. Barker-Rynde)*, Eric Sykes *(Rumbelow)*, Dennis Price *(Dr. Crossley)*, Lionel Jeffries *(Inspector Hook)*, Moira Redmond *(Frances Reitman)*, Katya Douglas *(Rita Fallows)*, David Lodge *(Richards)*, Ronnie Barker *(Burton)*, Hazel Terry *(Mrs. Crossley)*, Derren Nesbitt *(Roger)*, Harry Locke *(Higgins)*, Arthur Howard *(Clerk)*, Tristram Jellinek *(Assistant Clerk)*, Peter Butterworth *(Barman)*, Patricia Hayes *(Waitress)*, Anna Russell *(Margaret Clifford)*, Sidney Vivian, Julian Orchard, Junia the Dog.

Terry-Thomas is called by Russell to a posh health club where some strange goings-on have upset the lady. But on the detective's arrival she has been murdered and secretary Redmond nearly dead herself from poison. Posing as a health club patron Terry-Thomas joins forces with the club's instructor Sykes. They investigate every possible lead abetted by Jeffries and Price, until it is discovered that Redmond herself is responsible. Russell's will is read, with the bulk of the estate going to her beloved pooch. The film, despite an excellent cast, is about as unfunny as they come.

p, George H. Brown; d, George Pollock; w, David Pursall, Jack Seddon; ph, Geoffrey Faithfull; m, Ron Goodwin; ed, Bert Rule; md, Goodwin; art d, Harry White; set d, A. Thatcher; cos, Elizabeth Haffenden; spec eff, Tom Howard; makeup, Basil Newal; dog trainer, John Holmes, Barbara Woodhouse.

Comedy/Mystery **(PR:C MPAA:NR)**

KILL SQUAD zero (1982) 83m KS Services/Summa Vista c

Cameron Mitchell *(Dutch)*, Jean Glaude, Jeff Risk, Jerry Johnson, Bill Cambra, Francisco Ramirez, Marc Sabin, Gary Fung, Alan Marcus.

Low-budget martial arts feature has six former Vietnam veterans rounded up to save their former squad commander from a culprit, Mitchell, who is trying to take over his electronics business. The film features a lot of action and physical prowess, but little "acting".

p, Michael D. Lee, Patrick G. Donahue; d&w, Donahue; ph, Christopher W. Strattan; m, Joseph Conlan; ed, Rick Yacco; stunts, Mike Donahue; makeup, Andy Moore.

Martial Arts **Cas.** **(PR:O MPAA:R)**

KILL THE UMPIRE ½** (1950) 77m COL bw

William Bendix *(Bill Johnson)*, Una Merkel *(Betty Johnson)*, Ray Collins *(Jonah Evans)*, Gloria Henry *(Lucy)*, Richard Taylor *(Bob Landon)*, Connie Marshall *(Susan)*, William Frawley *(Jimmy O'Brien)*, Tom D'Andrea *(Roscoe Snooker)*, Luther Crockett *(Sam Austin)*, Jeff York *(Panhandle Jones)*, Glenn Thompson *(Lanky)*, Bob Wilke *(Cactus)*, Jim Bannon *(Dusty)*, Alan Hale, Jr. *(Harry Shay)*.

Fun little film, especially for baseball fans. Bendix is the ultimate baseball fan who can't hold on to a job as long as his favorite sport is in season. He finally agrees to go to umpire school so his wife (Merkel) won't walk out on him. An added advantage is that he can watch his favorite game and get paid for it. He gets a job in the Texas leagues, and gives a controversial call that results in the home team forfeiting the game. The film has a wild chase as the crowd tries to get Bendix for the call. All is seemingly solved when the catcher says that Bendix is right. But as the film ends Bendix calls one against the home team that incites the crowd to shout out the film's title. It's nice light fare, aptly played by Bendix and the supporting cast.

p, John Beck; d, Lloyd Bacon; w, Frank Tashlin; ph, Charles Lawton Jr.; ed, Charles Nelson; md, Morris Stoloff; art d, Perry Smith.

Sports Comedy (PR:AA MPAA:NR)

KILL THEM ALL AND COME BACK ALONE 1/2**
(1970, Ital./Span.) 97m Fida-Centauro/Fanfare c (AKA: AMMAZZALI TUTTI E TORNA SOLO; MATALOS Y VUELVE)

Chuck Connors *(Clyde)*, Frank Wolff *(Captain Lynch)*, Franco Citti *(Hoagy)*, Leo Anchoriz *(Deker)*, Ken Wood *(Kid)*, Hercules Cortes *(Bogard)*, Alberto Dell'Acqua *(Blade)*, John Bartha, Furio Meniconi, Antonio Molino, Rojo, Alfonso Rojas, Ugo Adinolfi.

Spaghetti western has Connors as head of an outlaw gang which successfully steals gold from a Union fort and hides it before Connors is captured by the Union army. One of the Army officers, Wolff, is a trader who originally induced Connors to commit the robbery, and who tortures him to find the whereabouts of the gold. Fast-paced direction helps gloss over problems in the script.

p, Edmondo Amati; d, Enzo G. Castellari; w, Tito Carpi, Castellari, Scardamaglia, Joaquin Romero Hernandez (based on a story by Carpi and Castellari); ph, Alejandro Ulloa (Techniscope, Technicolor); m, Francesco De Masi; ed, Tatiana Morigi Casini, Maria Luisa Soriano; art d, Enzo Bulgarelli; set d, Jaime Perez Cubero.

Western (PR:O MPAA:R)

KILLER, THE (SEE: MYSTERY RANCH, 1932)

KILLER, THE
(SEE: SACRED KNIVES OF VENGEANCE, THE, 1974, Hong Kong)

KILLER APE** (1953) 68m COL bw

Johnny Weissmuller *(Jungle Jim)*, Carol Thurston *(Shari)*, Max Palmer *(Man-Ape)*, Burt Wenland *(Ramada)*, Nestor Paiva *(Andrews)*, Paul Marion *(Mahara)*, Eddie Foster *(Achmed)*, Rory Mallinson *(Perry)*, Ray Corrigan *(Norley)*, Nick Stuart *(Maron)*, Tamba the Chimp.

One of Weissmuller's "Jungle Jim" films which is indistinguishable from the others in the series. This time he's out to stop bad guy scientist Paiva who has invented a drug that stops animals cold. But Paiva is killed by real-life giant Palmer who has taken natives Thurston and Marion hostage and it's up to Weissmuller to save the day. It's a cliche *tour-de-force* replete with bad acting and apathetic direction. Forget Weissmuller and company and watch the far more accomplished actor, Tamba the chimp. (See JUNGLE JIM series, Index).

p, Sam Katzman; d, Spencer Gordon Bennet; w, Carroll Young, Arthur Hoerl (based on a story by Young from the comic strip by Alex Raymond); ph, William Whitley; ed, Gene Havlick; md, Mischa Bakaleinikoff; art d, Paul Palmentola.

Adventure (PR:AA MPAA:NR)

KILLER AT LARGE* 1/2 (1936) 54m COL bw

Mary Brian *(Linda Allen)*, Russell Hardie *(Tommy Braddock)*, Betty Compson *(Kate)*, George McKay *(Kelly)*, Thurston Hall *(Inspector O'Hara)*, Henry Brandon *(Mr. Zero)*, Harry Hayden *(Bentley)*, Boyd Irwin *(Whitley)*.

Confusing and illogical murder mystery with Brian as a store detective who gets involved chasing a murderer. The film tries to be mysterious but fails in the long run because the killer, Brandon, has not been set up enough to be a real figure of terror, perhaps as a result of Hayes office censorship. Stalking sequences in a cemetery and in a wax room are not the terrifying bits of suspense they pretend to be.

d, David Selman; w, Harold Shumate (based on a story by Carl Clausen); ph, Allen G. Seigler.

Crime/Suspense (PR:O MPAA:NR)

KILLER AT LARGE 1/2** (1947) 61m PRC bw

Robert Lowery *(Paul Kimberly)*, Anabel Shaw *(Anne Arnold)*, Charles Evans *(Vincent Arnold)*, Frank Ferguson *(Edward Denton)*, George Lynn *(Rand)*, Dick Rich *(Bull Callahan)*, Ann Stanton *(Margo)*, Leonard Penn *(Brent Maddux)*, Eddie Parks *(Clerk)*, Stanley Blystone *(Capt. McManus)*, Howard Mitchell *(Whiteman)*, Jack Cheatham *(Brandon)*, Hazel Kerner *(Miss Riley)*, Hildegard Ackerman *(Hatcheck Girl)*, Charles King *(Bartender)*, Brooks Benedict *(Croupier)*, Phil Arnold *(Taxi Driver)*.

Lowery is a newspaperman on the trail of a hot story. Someone is giving refuge to lonely soldiers on leave and murdering them. It's his job to find out who. A nifty little thriller, well directed within "B" constraints and only marginally hampered by an unnecessary love story.

p, Buck Gottlieb; d, William Beaudine; w, Fenton Earnshaw, Tom Blackburn; ph, James Brown; m, Alvin Levin; ed, Harry Reynolds; art d, Glen Thompson.

Thriller/Suspense (PR:O MPAA:NR)

KILLER BATS (SEE: DEVIL BAT, THE, 1941)

KILLER BEHIND THE MASK, THE (SEE: SAVAGE WEEKEND, 1983)

KILLER DILL* (1947) 71m Screen Guild bw

Stuart Erwin *(Johnny Dill)*, Anne Gwynne *(Judy)*, Frank Albertson *(Allen)*, Mike Mazurki *(Little Joe)*, Milburn Stone *(Maboose)*, Dorothy Granger *(Millie)*, Anthony Warde *(Louie)*, Ben Welden *(Moroni)*, Will Orlean *(Gangster in Movie)*, Shirley Hunter *(Gloria)*, Charles Knight *(Jack)*, Stanley Andrews *(Mr. Jones)*, Julie Mitchum *(Secretary)*, Stanley Ross *(Mushnose)*.

Erwin is an unassuming, mild-mannered salesman. He finds himself in deep trouble when he is mistaken for a killer who has bumped off a rival gangster. Though he's good in the role, the film is ultimately a dud thanks to a preponderance of plot holes and weak directorial style.

p, Max M. King; d, Lewis D. Collins; w, John O'Dea (based on a story by Alan Friedman); ph, William Sickner; ed, Marty Cohn; art d, Frank Sylos.

Crime/Thriller (PR:C MPAA:NR)

KILLER DINO (SEE: DINO, 1957)

KILLER ELITE, THE** (1975) 122m Exeter-Persky-Bright/UA c

James Caan *(Mike Locken)*, Robert Duvall *(George Hansen)*, Arthur Hill *(Cap Collis)*, Gig Young *(Laurence Weyburn)*, Mako *(Yuen Chung)*, Bo Hopkins *(Jerome Miller)*, Burt Young *(Mac)*, Tom Clancy *(O'Leary)*, Tiana *(Tommie Chung)*, Kate Heflin *(Amy)*, James Wing Woo *(Tao Yi)*, George Kee Cheung *(Bruce)*, Simon Tam *(Jimmy Fung)*, Rick Alemany *(Ben Otake)*, Hank Hamilton *(Hank)*, Walter Kelley *(Walter)*, Billy J. Scott *(Eddie)*, Johnnie Burrell *(Donnie)*, Matthew Peckinpah *(Kid)*, Sondra Blake *(Josephine)*, Helmut Dantine *(Vorodny)*.

Caan is an ex-CIA hit man who's brought out of injury-induced retirement to protect Mako, an Asian political leader. There's a contract out on the man's life and the number-one killer assigned to the job is none other than Caan's former comrade Duvall, the man responsible for Caan's debilitating wounds. The thin plot is padded out with plenty of action, chases and shoot-outs, that are certainly well handled. But this is definitely a lesser film than it should be when one considers what Sam Peckinpah was capable of accomplishing. The neat combination of story and violence in THE WILD BUNCH is sorely missed here. The film's executive producer, actor Dantine, is killed early on by the double-crossing Duvall, which may strike the audience as no more than justice. Some of the chase scenes occur amidst the mothballed hulls of de-activated naval vessels.

p, Martin Baum, Arthur Lewis; d, Sam Peckinpah; w, Marc Norman, Stirling Silliphant (based on the novel by Robert Rostand); ph, Phil Lathrop (DeLuxe Color); m, Jerry Fielding; ed, Garth Craven, Tony De Zarraga, Monte Hellman; prod d, Ted Haworth; set d, Rick Gentz; stunts, Whitey Hughes.

Action/Thriller Cas. (PR:O MPAA:PG)

KILLER FISH zero
(1979, Ital./Braz.) Carlo Ponti-Filmar Do Brasil-Fawcett-Majors/Associated Films c (AKA: TREASURE OF THE PIRANHA; DEADLY TREASURE OF THE PIRANAH)

Lee Majors *(Robert Lasky)*, Karen Black *(Kate Neville)*, James Franciscus *(Paul Diller)*, Margaux Hemingway *(Gabrielle)*, Marisa Berenson *(Ann)*, Gary Collins *(Tom)*, Roy Brocksmith *(Ollie)*, Dan Pastorini *(Hans)*, Frank Pesce *(Warren Bailey)*, Charlie Guardino (Lloyd Bailey), Anthony Steffen *(Max, Ship Captain)*, Fabio Sabag *(Quintin)*, George Cherques *(Inspector)*, Chico Arago *(Ben)*, Sonia Citicica *(Nurse)*, Celso Faria *(Airline Passenger)*.

JAWS rip-off co-produced by a company jointly owned by Majors and his then-wife, the immortally blond Farrah Fawcett-Majors. All the roles are well-played, as this film ranks as one of the best stereotype casting jobs in film history. The story has evil-guy Franciscus hiding some diamonds in a lake full of man-eating piranhas. Other gang members go after the rocks, but are eaten in the expected gory fashion, that gets more disgusting with each new victim. The story is compounded by appropriate romantic interludes as the luxury resort hotel at which the criminals are staying suffers the additional indignity of an invasion by some glamorous fashion models and a photographic crew. The already skeletal Hemingway and Berenson appear to offer little nourishment for the ferocious fish. Though well directed and acted (considering the talents displayed) this is a disgusting film. Directed by the same man who gave us CANNIBALS IN THE STREET.

p, Alex Ponti; d, Anthony M. Dawson [Antonio Margheriti] (underwater sequences, Herbert V. Theiss); w, Michael Rogers; ph, Alberto Spagnoli; m, Guido and Maurizio De Angelis; ed, Roberto Sterbini; art d, Francesco Bronzi; cos, Adriana Berselli, Salvatore Russo.

Adventure/Thriller (PR:O MPAA:PG)

KILLER FORCE**
(1975, Switz./Ireland) 100m AIP (AKA: DIAMOND MERCENARIES, THE)

Telly Savalas *(Harry Webb)*, Peter Fonda *(Mike Bradley)*, Hugh O'Brian *(Lewis)*, O. J. Simpson *("Bopper" Alexander)*, Maud Adams *(Clare Chambers)*, Christopher Lee *(Chilton)*, Ian Yule *(Legrand Woods)*, Michael Mayer *(Adams)*, Victor Melleney *(Ian Nelson)*, Richard Loring *(Roberts)*, Stuart Brown *(George Chambers)*, Marina Christelis *(Danielle)*, Frank Shelley *(Keller)*, Peter Van Dissell *(Rick)*, Cocky Thlothlalemaje *(Franklyn)*, Ian Hamilton *(Doctor)*, Dale Cutts *(Plotter), Don McCorkindale (Radio Operator)*, Marigold Russell *(Salesgirl)*, Frank Douglas *(Barman)*, Erica Rogers *(Lady Doctor)*, Kevin Basel *(Guardhouse Sergeant)*, David Anderson *(Gate Guard)*, Anthony Fridjhon *(Pilot—SM 4)*, Clive Scott *(Pilot—Webb)*, Giles Ridley *(Young Security Guard)*.

Savalas is the chief of security at a South African diamond mine. When some thefts are discovered, he teams up with local deputy Fonda to solve the crime. Little does he know that Fonda is the mastermind behind it all. It's a standard story with plenty of action and violence, some of it a little farfetched. O'Brian, Simpson, and Lee are Fonda's henchmen; Adams is his girl. It's competently put together but you won't remember it the next day. The high point of the film is the security-system busting break-in at the vaults, followed by the attendant break-out and chase. Pre-release publicity suggested that Jack Palance had originally signed on for the role actually played by O'Brian.

p, Nat and Patrick Wachsberger; d, Val Guest; w, Guest, Michael Winder, Gerald Sanford; ph, David Millin, Vincent Cox, Ken Eddy (Movielab Color); m, Georges Garvarentz; ed, Bill Butler; art d, Peter Church, John Stodel; cos, John Lambon; spec eff, Josh Du Toit; stunts, Reo Ruiters.

Thriller/Action Cas. (PR:O MPAA:R)

KILLER GRIZZLY (SEE: GRIZZLY, 1976)

KILLER INSIDE ME, THE 1/2** (1976) 99m Devi/WB c

Stacy Keach *(Lou Ford)*, Susan Tyrrell *(Joyce Lakeland)*, Tisha Sterling *(Amy Stanton)*, Keenan Wynn *(Chester Conway)*, Charles McGraw *(Howard Hendricks)*, John Dehner *(Bob Maples)*, Pepe Serna *(Johnny Lopez)*, Royal Dano *(Father)*, Julie Adams *(Mother)*, John Carradine *(Dr. Smith)*, Don Stroud *(Elmer)*.

A seemingly rambling film that apparently suffers from some poor post-production studio editing is definitely worth a look for the fine performance Keach gives. He plays a psychotic deputy sheriff who has fits of a brutally violent nature during childhood flashbacks. The photography gives the film a modern *film noir* look. However the only-average script and some weak supporting roles ultimately hamper the film. Director Kennedy also directed the somewhat similarly styled WELCOME TO HARD TIMES. Actress Tisha Sterling is the daughter of actor Robert Sterling and actress Anne Jeffreys. Music writers Tim McIntire and John Rubinstein (both also actors) are the sons of John McIntire and pianist Artur Rubinstein.

p, Michael W. Leighton; d, Burt Kennedy; w, Edward Mann, Robert Chamblee (based on the novel by Jim Thompson); ph, William A. Fraker (Metrocolor); m, Tim McIntire, John Rubinstein; ed, Danford B. Greene, Aaron Stell.

Crime Drama **(PR:O MPAA:R)**

KILLER IS LOOSE, THE 1/2** (1956) 73m Crown/UA bw

Joseph Cotten *(Sam Wagner)*, Rhonda Fleming *(Lila Wagner)*, Wendell Corey *(Leon "Foggy" Poole)*, Alan Hale, Jr. *(Denny)*, Michael Pate *(Chris Gillespie)*, Virginia Christine *(Mary Gillespie)*, John Larch *(Otto Flanders)*, John Beradino *(Mac)*, Paul Bryar *(Greg)*, Dee J. Thompson *(Grace Flanders)*.

Corey is a bank clerk nicknamed "Foggy" because of his thick glasses. He's the inside man for a group of bank robbers, but their plan is thwarted. During his arrest, his wife is accidently shot and killed. Corey blames arresting officer Cotten; it is revealed at his trial that Corey wants to even the score by killing Cotten's wife, Fleming. Corey is convicted but becomes a model prisoner. He is sent to a minimum security prison farm and soon escapes. Prison life has changed the man for he is now a raging psychotic, taking several hostages. Cotten tries to get the police to protect Fleming, but she is used as bait to lure Corey into a trap. He stalks and almosts kills her, but is shot down in the nick of time. It's not a great film, but is not bad by fifties gangster standards. The direction is undistinguished but effective and the art direction gives the film a nice look. Corey is fine in his role as the man driven over the edge. Boetticher directed THE RISE AND FALL OF LEGS DIAMOND as well as several Randolph Scott westerns.

p, Robert L. Jacks; d, Budd Boetticher; w, Harold Medford (based on a short story by John and Ward Hawkins); ph, Lucien Ballard; m, Lionel Newman; ed, George Gittens; art d, Leslie Thomas.

Crime Drama/Suspense **(PR:O MPAA:NR)**

KILLER LEOPARD** (1954) 70m AA bw

Johnny Sheffield *(Bomba)*, Russ Conway *(Maitland)*, Bill Walker *(Jonas)*, Milton Wood *(Conji)*, Barry Bernard *(Charlie Pulham)*, Donald Murphy *(Fred Winters)*, Beverly Garland *(Linda Winters)*, Smoki Whitfield *(Eli)*, Rory Mallinson *(Deevers)*, Leonard Mudie *(Commissioner Barnes)*, Harry Cording *(Saunders)*, Guy Kingsford *(Policeman)*, Roy Glenn *(Daniel)*, Charles Stevens *(Gonzales)*.

Sheffield dons his loincloth once again in the African jungles as he aids movie actress Garland in her search for her missing husband. Along the way, they have to battle the titled menace who has a penchant for ripping human limbs from their torsos. This would be one of Sheffield's final appearances as the jungle "boy," since he was by now 23 years old. (See BOMBA, THE JUNGLE BOY series, Index.)

p, Ford Beebe; d, Beebe, Edward Morey, Jr.; w, Beebe; ph, Harry Neumann; art d, David Milton.

Adventure **(PR:A MPAA:NR)**

KILLER McCOY 1/2** (1947) 104m MGM bw

Mickey Rooney *(Tommy McCoy)*, Brian Donlevy *(Jim Caighn)*, Ann Blyth *(Sheila Carrson)*, James Dunn *(Brian McCoy)*, Tom Tully *(Cecil Y. Walsh)*, Sam Levene *(Happy)*, Walter Sande *(Bill Thorne)*, Mickey Knox *(Johnny Martin)*, James Bell *(Father Ryan)*, Gloria Holden *(Mrs. McCoy)*, Eve March *(Mrs. Martin)*, June Storey *(Waitress)*, Douglas Croft *(Danny Burns)*, Bob Steele *(Sailor Graves)*, David Clarke *(Pete Mariola)*.

A film of many firsts, KILLER McCOY marked 25-year-old Rooney's first crack at portraying a man of his actual age and it also marked young starlet Blyth's MGM debut. Basically a remake of the 1938 MGM-Robert Taylor film THE CROWD ROARS, Rooney stars as a young hoofer who tours the dives with his alcoholic father, Dunn, providing song-and-dance numbers for a show starring lightweight boxing champion Knox. During the tour Knox and Rooney become friends with the boxer soon encouraging the dancer to enter the ring. Rooney finds the fight game more exciting than dancing with his drunken father and before long he is set to fight Knox for the championship. It is a brutal bout, and in the end Rooney kills his friend. Badly shaken by the fight, Rooney drifts into the company of a reprehensible gambler, Donlevy, who uses the young champ to further his own financial interests. Luckily Donlevy's daughter, Blyth, sees what her father is doing to the confused young boxer and rescues him from a bad fate. The pair fall in love and after one final bout Rooney tosses in the towel on his boxing career. Though a bit heavy on the melodramatics, KILLER McCOY contains some fine performances from Rooney, Donlevy, and Dunn. Oater fans should watch for diminutive cowboy star Bob Steele in a rare nonwestern role as a boxer.

p, Sam Zimbalist; d, Roy Rowland; w, Frederick Hazlitt Brennan (based on story and screenplay by Thomas Lennon, George Bruce, George Oppenheimer); ph, Joseph Ruttenberg; m, David Snell; ed, Ralph E. Winters; art d, Cedric Gibbons, Eddie Imazu; m/l, "Swanee River," Stanley Donen.

Boxing Drama **(PR:A MPAA:NR)**

KILLER ON A HORSE (SEE: WELCOME TO HARD TIMES, 1967)

KILLER SHARK* 1/2 (1950) 76m MON bw

Roddy McDowall *(Ted)*, Laurette Luez *(Maria)*, Roland Winters *(White)*, Edward Norris *(Ramon)*, Rick Vallin *(Agapito)*, Douglas Fowley *(Bracado)*, Nacho Galindo *(Maestro)*, Ralf Harolde *(Slattery)*, Dick Moore *(Jonesy)*, Ted Hecht *(Gano)*, Charles Lang *(McCann)*, Robert Espinoza *(Pinon)*, Julio Sebastian *(Tony)*, Julian Rivero *(Doctor)*, Frank Sully *(Pat)*, George Slocum *(Capt. Hansen)*.

McDowall is a college boy off to visit his fisherman father (Winters) on a trip to Florida. He joins the old man on a shark hunting expedition. He's nothing like his father, though, and his ineptitude and clumsiness cause his father and a crewman to be bitten by sharks. However, all is righted at the end, when a suddenly manly McDowall recovers a stolen catch for his father. About the only thing exciting here is the film's title. McDowall is deadly dull and Winters isn't much better. The direction is too slowly paced to give this one any real interest. The miscast McDowall served as co-executive producer.

p, Lindsley Parsons; d, Oscar [Budd] Boetticher; w, Charles Lang; ph, William Sickner; ed, Leonard Herman; md, Edward J. Kay; art d, Dave Milton.

Adventure **(PR:A MPAA:NR)**

KILLER SHREWS, THE* 1/2
(1959) 69m Hollywood/McLendon Radio Pictures bw

James Best *(Thorne Sherman)*, Ingrid Goude *(Ann Craigis)*, Baruch Lumet *(Dr. Craigis)*, Ken Curtis *(Jerry Lacer)*, Gordon McLendon *(Radford Baines)*, Alfredo DeSoto *(Mario)*, J.H. *("Judge")*, Dupree *(Rook)*.

KING KONG featured a giant gorilla, GODZILLA had an enormous lizard, so the only terrifying animal left for Ken Curtis to make a film about was that evil little creature, the *shrew*! Curtis served as both producer and supporting player in this so-bad-it's-good feature. Lumet—real-life father of director Sidney—is an evil scientist who creates a formula that makes the tiny shrew resemble something like a collie with a shrew-mask. During a storm the little devils get loose and go after Best and his girl friend Goude, who was Miss Universe of 1957. Good dumb fun, it was paired in production and released on a double feature with THE GIANT GILA MONSTER, another little-to-big animal adventure by the same crew. Curtis, who had served as a B-Western singing cowboy, returned to his old genre soon after this film, playing Festus on TV's "Gunsmoke." Director Kellogg had previously done second-unit work with John Ford and Howard Hawks before turning to direction himself. In this piece of amiable idiocy, the taming of the shrews is accomplished by means of a tank-like vehicle crafted by the brilliant Best from old storage barrels.

p, Ken Curtis; d, Ray Kellogg, w, Jay Simms; ph, Wilfred Cline; m, Harry Bluestone, Emil Cadkin; ed, Aaron Steel.

Science Fiction/Horror **Cas.** **(PR:C MPAA:NR)**

KILLER THAT STALKED NEW YORK, THE 1/2** (1950) 79m COL bw

Evelyn Keyes *(Sheila Bennet)*, Charles Korvin *(Matt Krane)*, William Bishop *(Dr. Ben Wood)*, Dorothy Malone *(Alice Lorie)*, Lola Albright *(Francie Bennet)*, Barry Kelley *(Johnson)*, Carl Benton Reid *(Commissioner Ellis)*, Ludwig Donath *(Dr. Cooper)*, Art Smith *(Moss)*, Roy Roberts *(Mayor)*, Whit Bissell *(Sid Bennet)*, Connie Gilchrist *(Belle)*, Dan Riss *(Skrip)*, Harry Shannon *(Officer Houlihan)*, Beverly Washburn *(Welda Kowalski)*, Celia Lovsky *(Mrs. Kowalski)*, Richard Egan *(Owney)*, Walter Burke *(Danny)*, Peter Virgo *(Joe Dominic)*, Arthur Space *(Dr. Penner)*, Don Kohler *(Ted James)*, Jim Backus *(Willie Dennis)*, Peter Brocco *(Tom)*, Tommy Ivo *(Jerry)*, Angela Clarke *(Mrs. Dominic)*.

Keyes, along with husband Korvin, is smuggling stolen diamonds into New York. Little does she know she is carrying smallpox as well as stones. Korvin is having an affair with Albright, Keyes' sister, and tells his wife—who's being followed by a Treasury agent—to remain at her hotel. But she's feeling ill and sneaks out to the office of doctor Bishop, losing the T-man in the process. Her symptoms are treated as a cold, but when a little girl who was also at the office dies of smallpox, the truth is realized. Bishop and the agents try to locate her and ultimately trace her path of destruction to a cheap hotel owned by her brother. Meanwhile, Keyes discovers her husband's infidelity—he means to depart with the diamonds and Albright—and tries to kill him. She fails, but he dies in a fall from a building. Keyes turns herself in and gives the police a list of people with whom she has come in contact. The film ends with her death from smallpox. Some nice documentary-style shooting gives this film a realistic look. The diamond-smuggling story gets in the way of the film's true interest. This film was based on a magazine story about a real smallpox epidemic in New York City. Keyes is fine in her role and the support isn't too bad. This film was similar to Twentieth Century Fox's film PANIC IN THE STREETS which was released a few weeks before Columbia finished production. Consequently, it was shelved and released later than anticipated.

p, Robert Cohn, d, Earl McEvoy; w, Harry Essex (based on a magazine article by Milton Lehman); ph, Joseph Biroc; m, Hans J. Salter; ed, Jerome Thoms; md, Morris Stoloff; art d, Walter Holscher; set d, Louis Diage; makeup, Bob Schiffer.

Drama **(PR:O MPAA:NR)**

KILLER WALKS, A* (1952, Brit.) 57m Leontine Entertainments/GN bw

Laurence Harvey *(Ned)*, Trader Faulkner *(Frankie)*, Susan Shaw *(Joan Gray)*, Laurence Naismith *(Doctor)*, Sheila Shand Gibbs *(Brenda)*, Ethel Edwards *(Gran)*.

An unsatisfying murder story which limps along through its troublesome script as a couple of brothers, Harvey and Faulkner, live on the grandmother's farm. Harvey, the wicked black sheep, kills the old woman in order to get her money and give it to his city slicker girl friend Shaw. Faulkner, the spineless sibling, gets framed for the crime, but it doesn't take much police work to prove that Harvey is the guilty one.

p, d&w, Ronald Drake (based on the play "Gathering Storm" by Gordon Glennon and the novel *Envy My Simplicity* by Rayner Barton); ph, Jack Asher, Phil Grindrod.

Crime (PR:A MPAA:NR)

KILLER WITH A LABEL (SEE: ONE TOO MANY, 1950)

KILLERS, THE**** (1946) 102m UNIV bw

Edmond O'Brien *(Jim Reardon)*, Ava Gardner *(Kitty Collins)*, Albert Dekker *(Big Jim Colfax)*, Sam Levine *(Lt. Sam Lubinsky)*, Virginia Christine *(Lilly Lubinsky)*, John Miljan *(Jake)*, Vince Barnett *(Charleston)*, Burt Lancaster *(Swede)*, Charles D. Brown *(Packy Robinson)*, Donald MacBride *(Kenyon)*, Phil Brown *(Nick Adams)*, Charles McGraw *(Al)*, William Conrad *(Max)*, Queenie Smith *(Queenie)*, Garry Owen *(Joe)*, Harry Hayden *(George)*, Bill Walker *(Sam)*, Jack Lambert *(Dum Dum)*, Jeff Corey *(Blinky)*, Wally Scott *(Charlie)*, Gabrielle Windsor *(Ginny)*, Rex Dale *(Man)*, Harry Brown *(Paymaster)*, Beatrice Roberts *(Nurse)*, Howard Freeman *(Police Chief)*, John Berkes *(Plinther)*, John Sheehan *(Doctor)*, Charles Middleton *(Farmer Brown)*, Al Hill *(Customer)*, Noel Cravet *(Lou Tringle)*, Rev. Neal Dodd *(Minister)*, George Anderson *(Doctor)*, Vera Lewis *(Mrs. Hirsch)*, Ann Staunton *(Stella)*, William Ruhl *(Motorman)*, Therese Lyon *(Housekeeper)*, Perc Launders, Geoffrey Ingraham, Howard Negley *(Policemen)*, Ernie Adams *(Gimp)*, Jack Cheatham *(Police Driver)*, Ethan Laidlaw *(Conductor)*, Michael Hale *(Pet)*, Wally Rose *(Bartender)*, Audley Anderson *(Assistant Paymaster)*, Mike Donovan *(Timekeeper)*, Nolan Leary, John Trebach, Milton Wallace *(Waiters)*.

This was the first Universal production supervised by one-time reporter turned film producer Hellinger, and is as powerful as his earlier crime movies, THE ROARING TWENTIES and HIGH SIERRA. This classic *film noir* entry with its now famous musical score (later used in the Dragnet TV series) by Rosza, saw Lancaster's film debut and brought a powerful new talent to the screen. The superb crime director Siodmak uses the bare bones of Hemingway's terse story upon which to build a taut and fascinating tale of murder, robbery, and a scheming Jezebel who leads the hero to his death. It opens with Hemingway's killers, McGraw and Conrad, entering the diner, looking for Lancaster, "The Swede," with a murder contract to fulfill. They ask about him, but the owner tells them little, only that he should be coming in for dinner soon. Brown, playing the Hemingway character of Nick Adams, only a small role, overhears the intent of the killers and runs to a boarding house to warn Lancaster. He hears of the threat but continues to indifferently lie on his bed, merely telling Brown that he got "into some trouble once," and, as Adams leaves, he goes on waiting for his murderers. They soon burst into his room and shoot him to death. Enter the energetic O'Brien, an insurance investigator who has to pay off on Lancaster's death. He begins to reconstruct Lancaster's turbulent life and we see him as a young boxer who is thrust into a posh and corrupt world of crime, overlorded by boss Dekker. He becomes enamored of sexy Gardner, Dekker's woman, who promises him that she will leave the boss for him if he helps in an elaborate robbery of an armored car, that they will then take the loot, doublecross Dekker, and flee to a life of their own. Lancaster goes through with it, but in the end, O'Brien learns, Gardner betrays Lancaster for Dekker and the crime boss assigns McGraw and Conrad to kill the duped young man. O'Brien purposely sets himself up as a decoy and the killers come looking for him but before they can kill O'Brien, police step in and arrest them. Then Dekker and Gardner are trapped in the boss' lavish home by police and are killed in a shootout. The cast is excellent and Siodmak's direction is tight as a drum. Lancaster's personality overawed viewers seeing him for the first time and he would soon reach star status with BRUTE FORCE, I WALK ALONE, ALL MY SONS, and other heavyweight films. Lancaster, a former circus acrobat, began his career here at age 32 but looked much younger. He exuded a dark masculinity seldom captured on the screen, a reserved but forceful presence that has never really been equalled. Harold Hecht, with whom Lancaster would later produce films, was a starving agent at the time and Lancaster was one of his first actor clients (they had been introduced by Sam Levene, who also appears in THE KILLERS). Hecht managed to get Lancaster a screen test in January, 1946, and this led to Hellinger selecting him for the Swede role in THE KILLERS, even though he had originally thought to cast Wayne Morris in the role but didn't want to pay Warner Bros. the $75,000 the studio demanded for a loan-out. Hellinger also considered Sonny Tufts for the part but didn't think he measured up after viewing some tests. Hellinger met with Lancaster, who convinced him he could handle the part. The actor later stated (in *Burt Lancaster* by Minty Clinch): "I'd always been a Hemingway *aficionado*. I'd read everything he'd ever written. I remember Mark Hellinger asking me what I thought about the script and I said, 'Well, the first 16 pages are Hemingway verbatim, and after that you have a rather interesting whodunit film . . . " Remarked Hellinger: " . . . you're not really a dumb Swede after all." Oddly, Hellinger had thought to have Don Siegel direct this film but opted for Siodmak; Siegel would direct the remake in 1964 which proved much less effective. Gardner, as the raven-haired vixen of THE KILLERS, is breathtaking. She was loaned out to Hellinger from MGM to play the sultry, two-timing gun moll whose only interest is acquiring money and jewels. This was her first important dramatic role and she never forgot Hellinger for casting her in the part: "Mark saw me as an actress, not as a sexpot. He trusted me from the beginning, and I trusted him. I knew he was a genius. He gave me a feeling of the responsibility of being a movie star which I had never for a moment felt before." Hemingway himself worked briefly on the script for this film, advising Huston on some points and he and the writer-director formed a lasting friendship during the production. Hemingway also admired Gardner's essaying of the eternal vixen and they, too, became lifelong friends. She would appear in other Hemingway vehicles, notably THE SNOWS OF KILIMANJARO and THE SUN ALSO RISES. Pay close attention to the musical score used on the TV series Dragnet.

p, Mark Hellinger; d, Robert Siodmak; w, Anthony Veiller, John Huston (based on the story by Ernest Hemingway); ph, Woody Bredell; m, Miklos Rosza; ed, Arthur Hilton; art d, Jack Otterson, Martin Obzina; set d, Russell A. Gausman, E.R. Robinson; cos, Vera West; spec eff, D.S. Horsley; m/l "The More I Know of Love," Miklos Rosza, Jack Brooks; makeup, Jack P. Pierce.

Crime Drama Cas. (PR:C MPAA:NR)

KILLERS, THE***

(1964) 93m Revue/UNIV c (AKA: ERNEST HEMINGWAY'S THE KILLERS)

Lee Marvin *(Charlie)*, Angie Dickinson *(Sheila Farr)*, John Cassavetes *(Johnny North)*, Ronald Reagan *(Browning)*, Clu Gulager *(Lee)*, Claude Akins *(Earl Sylvester)*, Norman Fell *(Mickey)*, Virginia Christine *(Miss Watson)*, Don Haggerty *(Mail Truck Driver)*, Robert Phillips *(George)*, Kathleen O'Malley *(Receptionist)*, Ted Jacques *(Gym Assistant)*, Irvin Mosley *(Mail Truck Guard)*, Jimmy Joyce *(Salesman)*, Davis Roberts *(Maitre d')*, Hal Brock *(Race Marshal)*, Burt Mustin *(Elderly Man)*, Peter Hobbs *(Instructor)*, John Copage *(Porter)*, Tyler McVey *(Steward)*, Seymour Cassel *(Postal Clerk)*, Scott Hale *(Hotel Clerk)*.

Hit men Marvin and Gulager are ordered to go to a school for the blind and kill Cassavetes, one of the teachers there, who puts up no resistance. They wonder why he accepted his death so passively and who ordered him killed. The killers connect him to an armored car heist several years before from which the money was never recovered. They learn that Cassavetes was a race car driver in love with Dickinson, the mistress of crime czar Reagan. She persuaded him to drive the getaway car in the armored car job and they planned to double cross Reagan. Instead, Cassavetes is betrayed as he learns that Dickinson has married Reagan. Marvin and Gulager track down Reagan and confront him, but he kills Gulagher and wounds Marvin. Dying, Marvin kills Reagan. Dickinson pleads for her life, saying Reagan forced her to betray Cassavetes. Marvin says, "Lady, I haven't got the time," then shoots her. With a suitcase full of the money from the robbery, he leaves the house, but dies on the front lawn. Reagan's last film, and the only one where he's the villain, the film was originally produced for TV by NBC, but censors determined it was too violent for that medium so it was released in theaters. Reagan was reluctant to play the heavy, but the head of Universal at the time was Reagan's former agent and he talked him into accepting the part, a decision Reagan still regrets. Though the film does not stand up to the 1946 version with Burt Lancaster, it has its own pleasures, including Marvin's rather likable role of an assassin, the exciting robbery sequence, and of course, the villainous Reagan getting his just desserts. Two years later he was elected governor of California.

p&d, Donald Siegel; w, Gene L. Coon (based on the story by Ernest Hemingway); ph, Richard L. Rawlings (Eastmancolor); m, Johnny Williams; ed, Richard Belding; md, Stanley Wilson; art d, Frank Arrigo, George Chan, George O'Connell; set d, John McCarthy, James S. Redd; cos, Helen Colvig; m/l, "Too Little Time," Henry Mancini, Don Raye, sung by Nancy Wilson; makup, Bud Westmore.

Crime (PR:C-O MPAA:NR)

KILLERS ARE CHALLENGED (SEE: SECRET AGENT FIREBALL, 1966)

KILLER'S CAGE (SEE: CODE OF SILENCE, 1960)

KILLERS FROM KILIMANJARO

(SEE: KILLERS OF KILIMANJARO, 1960, Brit.)

KILLERS FROM SPACE* (1954) 71m Planet Filmplays/RKO bw

Peter Graves, James Seay, Frank Gerstle, Steve Pendleton, John Merrick, Barbara Bestar, Shep Menken, Jack Daly, Ron Kennedy, Ben Welden, Burt Wenland, Lester Dorr, Robert Roark, Ruth Bennett, Mark Scott *(Narrator)*.

Graves is a scientist aboard a plane that crashes during an atomic bomb experiment in Nevada. Dead, he is revived by some aliens from Astron Delta and brainwashed by the creatures, who want some top-secret information. He agrees, but his wife Bestar and assistant Gerstle notice a change in the man—he is committing espionage. After a shot of sodium pentathol reveals the truth, they decide he's insane. But the brainwashing soon wears off and Graves returns to the aliens' cave, shutting off their power source and destroying them in a nuclear explosion. Cheap and idiotic, but with some motifs that might suggest allusions to 1950s politics had there been more intelligent minds behind this film. As it is, it contains bad stock footage, bad costuming for the aliens, and bad acting from everyone involved. The producer-director is the brother of famed director Billy Wilder.

p&d, W. Lee Wilder; w, Bill Raynor (based on a story by Myles Wilder); ph, William H. Clothier; m, Manuel Compinsky; ed, William Faris; makeup, Harry Thomas.

Science Fiction Cas. (PR:A MPAA:NR)

KILLER'S KISS 1/2** (1955) 67m Minotaur/UA bw

Frank Silvera *(Vincent Rapallo)*, Jamie Smith *(Davy Gordon)*, Irene Kane *(Gloria Price)*, Jerry Jarret *(Albert, the Fight Manager)*, Mike Dana, Felice Orlandi, Ralph Roberts, Phil Stevenson *(Gangsters)*, Julius Adelman *(Owner of the Mannequin Factory)*, David Vaughan, Alec Rubin *(Conventioneers)*, Ruth Sobotka *(Iris, the dancer)*.

Smith is a second-rate prizefighter who gets involved with Kane, a young dancer who lives across the courtyard in his apartment building. After returning from losing a fight he sees Silvera, owner of the nightclub she dances in, trying to rape her. He rescues her and they decide to leave for his uncle's home in Seattle. But first he has to collect some money from Jarret, his manager. Kane tells Silvera she is leaving town with the fighter. Silvera tells his men to kill Smith, but they accidentally kill Jarret. Kane is held prisoner by Silvera in a mannequin warehouse. In a rooftop fight, Smith kills Silvera and flees to Grand Central Station. He is convinced he has lost Kane, but she turns up at the end and they leave together. This was Kubrick's second film, financed for $75,000 by various friends and relatives. He served not only as a director and producer, but also filmed and edited the project. Though the story is little more than cliche (and gives no hint of what Kubrick was capable of as a writer) his direction takes some interesting chances. His flashbacks and surrealistic nightmare sequences are well handled. The nightmares are shown on negative film stock, an interesting and effective choice. Kubrick ran out of money during post-production and was forced to do the sound editing himself. Interesting Kubrick touches are the contrapuntal use of a bloody boxing match on a television screen while an equally violent near-rape occurs between the couch-sitting nominal viewers, and the employment of the dismembered limbs of female mannequins as weapons during a brutal fight sequence. All in all, it's hardly Kubrick's best work but is a nice look at a visual style that would improve with age in such films as 2001: A SPACE ODYSSEY (1968). This film was also the inspiration for Matthew Chapman's 1984 film STRANGERS KISS.

p, Stanley Kubrick, Morris Bousel; d, Kubrick; w, Kubrick, Howard O. Sackler (based on a story by Kubrick); ph, Kubrick; m, Gerald Fried; ed, Kubrick; ch, David Vaughan.

Drama (PR:C MPAA:NR)

KILLERS OF KILIMANJARO** (1960, Brit.) 91m Warwick/COL c

Robert Taylor *(Robert Adamson)*, Anthony Newley *(Hooky Hook)*, Anne Aubrey *(Jane Carlton)*, Gregoire Aslan *(Ben Ahmed)*, Allan Cuthbertson *(Saxton)*, Martin Benson *(Ali)*, Orlando Martins *(Chief)*, Donald Pleasence *(Captain)*, John Dimech *(Pasha)*, Martin Boddey *(Gunther)*, Earl Cameron *(Witch Doctor)*, Harry Baird *(Boraga)*, Anthony Jacobs *(Mustaph)*, Joyce Blair, Barbara Joyce, Christine Pockett.

KING SOLOMON'S MINES redux with a tired, lined Taylor tritely trying the Great White Hunter role essayed so well by Stewart Granger ten years earlier, and with Aubrey the fiance-seeking, flame-tressed pest who insists on accompanying him across the African veldt, a characterization perfectly performed by Deborah Kerr in the earlier film. Taylor is an uncivil civil engineer assigned to survey the Kenyan bush and forest for a prospective railroad line, a task previously attempted unsuccessfully by Aubrey's missing father and fiance. Recruiting his safari bearers from a group of convicts—the only natives willing to brave the unspeakable evils of the interior, their freedom being payment— and joined by Aubrey and comic-relief sidekick Newley, Taylor's surveying safari snakes its way through a bevy of beasts, a veritable Noah's Ark of stock shots, many of them badly color- and exposure-matched to the actor-reaction takes. Taylor's gruff rebuffs to the frequently frightened but persistent Aubrey, and his rifle-shooting rescues of Newley, who at one point, holding a surveyor's leveling rod, backs into a pride of lions, form much of the substance of the film. Taylor picks up a secondary sidekick, young Dimech, whose father, Aslan, is the chief villain of the piece. Slave-trader Aslan wants to use the proposed railroad himself to ship his living cargo, and needs to have the tracks follow a route different from the one that Taylor plans. Son Dimech opposes his father's evil intentions. The hackneyed plot has the frightened bearers deserting the party, Taylor gaining the respect of a once-threatening native chief, and a traitorous guide in the pay of Aslan. The latter, with his minions, trails Taylor's tenderfeet and launches an all-out attack. The mandatory last-cartridge, last-minute rescue occurs. The mortally wounded Aslan, who tried to halt the assault upon learning of son Dimech's presence in the assailed party, makes peace with the boy and expires. Aubrey's fiance is found, now an irredeemable alcoholic, and the engagement is broken so that she and Taylor may enjoy an implicit amour on their return journey.

p, John R. Sloan; d, Richard Thorpe; w, John Gilling, Earl Felton, Richard Maibaum, Cyril Hume (based on the book *African Bush Adventures* by J.A. Hunter and Dan P. Mannix); ph, Ted Moore (CinemaScope, Eastmancolor); m, William Alwyn; ed, Geoffrey Foot; md, Muir Mathieson; art d, Ray Sim; cos, Elsa Fennell; spec eff, Cliff Richardson; makeup, Paul Rabiger.

Adventure (PR:A MPAA:NR)

KILLERS OF THE PRAIRIE (SEE: KING OF THE SIERRAS, 1938)

KILLERS OF THE WILD* 1/2
(1940) 58m Times bw (AKA: CHILDREN OF THE WILD)

Joan Valerie *(Margaret Weston)*, James Bush *(Jim Turner)*, LeRoy Mason *(Pete Taylor)*, Ruth Coleman *(Laura Morton)*, Jill L'Estrange *(Jill Morton)*, Trevor Bardette *(Joe Morton)*, Fred Santley *(Chuck Foster)*, Lyons Wickland *(The Coroner)*, Goldie *(The Eagle)*, Silver Wolf *(The Dog)*.

A Rin-Tin-Tin-like story about a police dog that is wrongly blamed for someone's death. When a child is—improbably—carried off to an eagles' nest, Silver Wolf runs off and saves the day. He fights Goldie and rescues the child with everything ending happily. The kids undoubtedly will love this action piece. The humans aren't nearly as good in this film as the animals are, but that really doesn't matter. Both the dog and eagle were well trained for their exciting climactic fight. There are a number of other good action sequences, including a forest fire. Mason is outstanding as the animal-hating murderer who has alibied his crime by throwing suspicion on the dog, and L'Estrange is a capable child actress, despite being the producer's daughter.

p, Dick L'Estrange; d, Vin Moore, Charles Hutchinson; w, Arthur Hoerl, Hilda May Young (based on a story by Charles Diltz); ph, Robert Doran; m, Edward Kilenyi.

Adventure (PR:AAA MPAA:NR)

KILLERS THREE* (1968) 88m AIP c

Robert Walker, Jr. *(Johnny Ward)*, Diane Varsi *(Carol Ward)*, Dick Clark *(Roger)*, Norman Alden *(Guthrie)*, Maureen Arthur *(Elvira Sweeney)*, Tony York *(J.J. Ward)*, Merle Haggard *(Charlie)*, Bonnie Owens *(Singer)*, John Cardos *(Bates)*, Beach Dickerson *(Scotty)*, Jerry Petty *(R.C.)*, Clint Stringer *(Sheriff Homer Brown)*, Fairy Sykes *(Mrs. Harmon)*, William Alspaugh *(Lester Meed)*, Douglas Barger *(Felix)*, The Strangers *(Singing Group)*.

Very bad rip-off of BONNIE AND CLYDE features Walker and Clark (of American Bandstand fame!) as two backwoods North Carolinians who unsuccessfully attempt to rob a bootlegger of $250,000. They kill a federal agent while escaping and, with Walker's wife Varsi and his five-year-old son York, the crooks head for California. Varsi's brother, a highway patrolman, stops them at a diner. Rather than turn in his sister, he gives them ten minutes to escape. But Clark has been in the men's room during this discussion and, unaware of the situation, kills the man. They're off once more and Clark is killed in a police ambush. Varsi and Walker escape in the car but she is wounded and dies as they return to their home. Clark served as producer in addition to his acting chores and can't seem to tell the difference between the movies and his TV shows. Here he inserts unnecessary song footage of country star Haggard, which bogs down the already bad film. His performance itself has about as much depth as his television appearances and it's almost funny to watch him as an explosives expert. Clark went from producing bad movies in the 1960s to producing bad television shows in the 1970s and 1980s. Songs include "Mama Tried" and "Killers Three."

p, Dick Clark; d, Bruce Kessler; w, Michael Fisher (based on a story by Fisher, Clark); ph, J. Burgi Contner (Perfect Color); m, Sidewalk Productions, Mike Curb, Harley Hatcher, Jerry Styner; ed, Renn Reynolds; makeup, Ted Coodley; cos, Richard Bruno; m/l, Merle Haggard.

Crime (PR:O MPAA:M)

KILLING, THE**** (1956) 83m UA bw

Sterling Hayden *(Johnny Clay)*, Coleen Gray *(Fay)*, Vince Edwards *(Val Cannon)*, Jay C. Flippen *(Marvin Unger)*, Marie Windsor *(Sherry Peatty)*, Ted De Corsia *(Randy Kennan)*, Elisha Cook, Jr. *(George Peatty)*, Joe Sawyer *(Mike O'Reilly)*, Tim Carey *(Nikki Arane)*, Jay Adler *(Leo)*, Joseph Turkel *(Tiny)*, Maurice Oboukhoff *(Kola Kwarian)*, James Edwards *(Black Man)*, William "Billy" Benedict *(Airline Clerk)*, Tito Vuolo.

This Kubrick *film noir* production has become a cult film, a methodical, cleanly directed movie that ruthlessly chronicles the robbery of a racetrack, not dissimilar in mood and structure to THE ASPHALT JUNGLE. Hayden is an ex-con who tells his childhood sweetheart Gray that he and a few others are going to make a big score and it will be his last caper. Hayden, Flippen, a retired friend, De Corsia, a cop who owes the syndicate money, Sawyer, a bartender at the racetrack who needs money for his sick wife, and Cook, a cashier at the track with a money-grubbing wife (Windsor) all meet to plan the robbery. Kubrick inspects the lives of each before the caper, depicting them as little people with problems that are getting too big for them to handle, forcing them into risky business. Windsor actually compels her meek-mannered husband Cook to go through with the theft even when he wants to back out, so she can live in luxury. During the seventh race, the gang plans to loot the money room where the betting take is kept and Carey, a brutal killer, is to shoot one of the horses on the far turn to create a diversion. The men break into the money room during the race and quickly loot the stacks of bills, stuffing these into sacks and tossing them out of a window where De Corsia picks them up and puts them into his patrol car, driving off. Carey kills the intended horse but is himself killed by a suspicious black whom Carey had earlier insulted by calling him a "nigger." Following the robbery the gang members wait for Hayden to bring the money to them for the split-up, but Edwards, Windsor's secret lover, shoots them all and is himself killed in the gun battle. Only Cook survives to stagger home to Windsor, realizing that she had set them all up so Edwards could take the loot and flee with his wife. Cook shoots Windsor, then falls dead over her corpse. Hayden goes to a motel room he has earlier rented and picks up the money which De Corsia has placed there. Knowing of the shootout, Hayden packs the money in a suitcase and he and Gray go the airport. There a bumbling porter drops the suitcase which bursts open and the money goes flying across the runway while Hayden and Gray stand in shock watching their fortune vanish. "What's the difference," shrugs the fatalistic Hayden. He mutely stands there and allows the approaching police to arrest him. This was Kubrick's third film, the first two being FEAR AND DESIRE, 1953, and KILLER'S KISS, 1955, both miserable little films shot on miniature budgets (for about $40,000 each). THE KILLING is where Kubrick came to the attention of the industry as a major directorial talent even though this film, too, was produced with a small budget, $320,000, and it shows. The sets are like cardboard but Kubrick emphasizes the fact, panning his camera from one room to another, showing partitions, the camera being the "fourth wall" so to speak, devising every conceivable angle from which to shoot so that the space in which his actors move appears as it really is, confining, cramped, claustrophobic and extending this visual image to the attitudes of his characters. Kubrick admitted later that he was influenced by French director Max Ophuls, and it's obvious in his fluid camera work; the story is a visual treat, unraveled in truck, dolly, and pan shots, mostly medium set-ups to include most of the main characters and reinforce the image of the gang. There is a documentary feel to the movie, which is superbly edited by Steinberg (undoubtedly with Kubrick standing over her shoulder since he feels that editing is one of the most vital responsibilities in filmmaking, a correct assumption). Hayden is stoical but top drawer as the nominal leader of this unprofessional gang of thieves and Cook gives one of the best performances of his life as the henpecked little man who suffers an avalanche of insults from his wretched wife Windsor before giving her a well-aimed (if not deserved) bullet. Spectacular in her evil is Windsor herself, amply giving reason to the words "woman hater."

p, James B. Harris; d, Stanley Kubrick; w, Kubrick, Jim Thompson (based on the novel *Clean Break* by Lionel White); ph, Lucien Ballard; m, Gerald Fried; ed, Betty Steinberg; art d, Ruth Sobotka Kubrick; cos, Rudy Harrington.

Crime Drama (PR:C MPAA:NR)

KILLING GAME, THE 1/2**
(1968, Fr.) 94m A.J. Films-Coficitel-Les Films Modernes-Francinor/Regional c (JEU DE MASSACRE; AKA: ALL WEEKEND LOVERS)

Jean-Pierre Cassel *(Pierre Meyrand)*, Claudine Auger *(Jaqueline Meyrand)*, Michel

Duchaussoy *(Bob Neuman)*, Eleonore Hirt *(Madame Neuman)*, Anna Gaylor *(Lisbeth)*, Guy Saint-Jean *(Ado)*, Nancy Holloway *(Nancy)*, Regine, Oyo, Nora, Ysmane My, Roger Curel, Jean Dewever.

Cassel and Auger are a husband-and-wife cartoonist team. They meet a wealthy playboy who has lived out the fantasies presented in their comic strip. Duchaussoy, the playboy, takes the couple to his chalet, where they create another strip about a killer. Duchaussoy starts to act out this comic strip as well, attempting to murder Auger, but is stopped in the nick of time by Cassel. Duchaussoy attempts suicide, but is saved by the police, who send him to a sanitarium. Upon his release, he rejoins the cartoonists and a new, non-criminally oriented comic strip is produced by the group.

p, Rene Thevenet; d&w, Alain Jessua; ph, Jacques Robin, Bandes Dessinees, Guy Peellaert (Eastmancolor); m, Jacques Loussier; ed, Nicole Marko; art d, Claire Forestier; m/l, The Alan Brown Group.

Drama/Comedy **(PR:C MPAA:NR)**

KILLING HOUR, THE* (1982) 90m Lansbury-Berun c

Perry King, Norman Parker, Kenneth McMillan, Elisabeth Kemp.

Another of the too numerous "mad slasher" gore movies. This one deals with an art student with troubling dreams. The dreams turn out to be premonitions of murders to be committed. An easily forgettable piece of garbage.

d, Armand Mastroianni.

Horror **Cas.** **(PR:O MPAA:NR)**

KILLING KIND, THE 1/2** (1973) 95m Media Trend c

Ann Sothern *(Thelma)*, John Savage *(Terry)*, Ruth Roman *(Rhea)*, Luana Anders *(Librarian)*, Cindy Williams *(Roomer)*, Sue Bernard *(Raped Girl)*.

Savage is a young man just released from prison on a trumped-up rape charge. Ten years inside have hardened him; all he can think about is revenge on Roman, the lawyer whose ineptitude got him incarcerated, and Bernard, his accuser. He settles in his mother Sothern's boarding house where the roomers include Williams of TV's "Laverne and Shirley." He manages to get Roman drunk and sets her house on fire. Sothern suspects her son's up to no good, but when he kills Williams, she helps him dispose of the body. It's a weird little film, definitely not for everyone. Savage's portrait of the psychotic young man is riveting, and Sothern is good in her role, as well. Though the film gets predictable towards the end, the director handles the subject well.

p, George Edwards; d, Curtis Harrington; w, Lony Crechales, Edwards; ph, Mario Losi; m, Andrew Belling.

Suspense/Psycho-Drama **Cas.** **(PR:O MPAA:R)**

KILLING OF A CHINESE BOOKIE, THE* 1/2 (1976) 135m Faces c

Ben Gazzara *(Cosmo Vitelli)*, Timothy Agoglia Carey *(Flo)*, Zizi Johari *(Rachel)*, Meade Roberts *(Mr. Sophistication)*, Seymour Cassel *(Mort Weil)*, Alice Friedland *(Sherry)*, Donna Gordon *(Margo)*, Robert Phillips *(Phil)*, Morgan Woodward *(John the Boss)*, Virginia Carrington *(Betty the Mother)*, John Red Kullers *(Eddie-Red)*, Al Ruban *(Marty Reitz)*, Soto Joe Hugh *(The Chinese Bookie)*, Haji *(Haji)*, Carol Warren *(Carol)*, Derna Wong Davis *(Derna)*, Kathalina Veniero *(Annie)*, Yvette Morris *(Yvette)*, Jack Ackerman *(Musical Director)*, David Rowlands *(Lamarr)*, Trisha Pelham, Arlene Allison *(Waitresses)*, Eddie Ike Shaw, John Finnegan *(Cabbies)*, Salvatore Aprile *(Sonny)*, Gene Darcy *(Commodore)*, Benny Marino *(Bartender)*, Vince Barbi *(Vince)*, Val Avery *(Blair Benoit)*, Elizabeth Deering *(Lavinia)*, Catherine Wong *(The Bookie's Girl)*, Miles Ciletti *(Mickey)*, Mike Skloot *(Scooper)*, Frank Buchanan *(Flo's Friend)*, Jason Kincaid *(Parking Lot Attendant)*, Frank Thomas, Jack Krupnick *(Poker Players)*.

John Cassavetes can be boring, annoying, and enigmatic with his films but they are usually creative and interesting. Not so with this one. Gazzara proudly runs a two-bit Sunset Strip night spot and is in hock to the local loan sharks. It's an odd club in that it features pageants rather than floor shows with the usual singer, ventriloquist, dancers, et al. Gazzara writes and directs the shows, which include things like "The Gun Fight At The O.K. Corral." His girl friend is Johari, one of the performers in the Crazy Horse West, an attempt at duplicating the Parisian landmark. Gazzara makes his last payment to Ruban, the former owner of the club (and the producer of the picture), then goes off to gamble at a private club run by Cassel, where he loses more than $20,000 he doesn't have. When he can't come up with the money, they make him an offer: the loss will be forgotten if Gazzara agrees to kill a Chinese bookie, Soto Joe Hugh, who is causing them some woes. Gazzara agrees to murder the guy because he can't stand the thought of re-mortgaging the club. What he doesn't know is that Hugh is not just your average Asian bookmaker. He is actually a heavyweight mob boss. Gazzara is driving to the hit when his tire goes flat and he has to get a cab. He murders Hugh as well as the tough bodyguards but botches it somewhat and the newspapers and TV are filled with the case. Cassel is angered at the brouhaha and sends two hoods, Carey and Phillips, to kill Gazzara. They attempt to murder him but only succeed in wounding him. Bleeding badly, he lurches around trying to find someone to help but he is spurned by everyone, including Johari's mother. He eventually returns to the only place where he feels safe, his club. He walks in, introduces one of the acts, then walks outside to bleed to death or to be finally dispatched by the criminals, we're not certain. This picture seems to go on forever and only has a few scenes worth watching—the totally improbable nightclub, the scene between the bookie and his girl friend as they frolic in the swimming pool before the shooting, and the brief stop for hamburgers to feed Hugh's vicious dogs. Carey, who was so wonderful in Kubrick's PATHS OF GLORY, is allowed to roll his eyes and overplay the villain to the point where it is laughable. We're never sure where the script ends and the improvisation begins and the result is a flat, endless series of scenes with no "buttons" on them. Points are made, remade, and made again. Cassavetes seems to be taking boredom lessons from Robert Altman. In a small role look for Kathalina Veniero, who later starred in BIGFOOT and TO KILL THE GOLDEN GOOSE. Hollywood denizens will recognize her for quite another reason, though. She and her husband, Red, run one of the town's brightest jazz clubs and restaurants on trendy Melrose Avenue, "The Nucleus Nuance." It's hard to believe Cassavetes is so spotty in his work. This, after all, is the same man who made GLORIA and A WOMAN UNDER THE INFLUENCE. Then, again, he also made HUSBANDS and FACES. Just about everyone in Hollywood was pressed into the "extra" ranks if they happened to be wherever Cassavetes had his cameras at the time. Included in that was the renowned painter-author, Donato Rico, whose work is in the Metropolitan Museum of Art in New York and whose 60 novels were often filched by producers who ripped off his original stories. If you know Hollywood people, you'll have a laugh at the other famous faces that can be seen for snippets of time in the various backgrounds.

p, Al Ruban; d&w, John Cassavetes; ph, Mike Ferris, Michael Stringer (MGM Color); m, Bo Harwood; ed, Tom Cornwell; prod d, Sam Shaw; art d, Phedon Papamichael; cos, Mary Herne.

Crime **(PR:C MPAA:R)**

KILLING OF ANGEL STREET, THE 1/2** (1983, Aus.) 101m Satori c

Liz Alexander *(Jessica)*, John Hargreaves *(Elliot)*, Alexander Archdale *(B.C.)*, Reg Lye *(Riley)*, Gordon McDougall *(Sir Arthur)*, David Downer *(Alan)*, Ric Herbert *(Ben)*, Brendon Lunney *(Scott)*, Allen Bickford *(Collins)*, John Stone *(Benson)*.

Yet another Australian picture which borrows a plot line from the American western. Here the heroes—geologist Alexander and communist Hargreaves—battle malicious realtors who are putting pressure on homeowners in an effort to get them to sell cheap. It's well-executed but predictable.

p, Anthony Buckley; d, Donald Crombie; w, Evan Jones, Michael Craig, Cecil Holmes (based on a story by Craig); ph, Peter James; m, Brian May; ed, Tim Wellburn; art d, Lindsay Hewson.

Drama **Cas.** **(PR:A MPAA:PG)**

KILLING URGE (SEE: JET STORM, 1959)

KILROY ON DECK (SEE: FRENCH LEAVE, 1948)

KILROY WAS HERE** (1947) 68m MON bw

Jackie Cooper *(John J. Kilroy)*, Jackie Coogan *(Pappy Collins)*, Wanda McKay *(Connie Harcourt)*, Frank Jenks *(Butch Miller)*, Norman Phillips *(Elmer Hatch)*, Rand Brooks *(Rodney Meadows)*, Barton Yarborough *(Professor Shepherd)*, Frank Scannell *(First Cab Driver)*, Patti Brill *(Marge Connors)*, Robert Coogan *(First Soldier)*, Joe Forte *(Registrar)*, Allen Mathews *(Second Cab Driver)*, Sidney Melton *(Third Cab Driver)*, Pat Goldin *(Waiter)*.

Two former child stars are paired together as college chums in what may be the first movie ever inspired by a slogan. Cooper is a college student who just happens to be *the* Kilroy of "Kilroy Was Here" fame. He's in college on the G.I. bill, though the deans don't want him in their school due to his wartime infamy and lack of school credits. However, members of a snobbish fraternity want him for themselves until they discover he has lower-class friends. Coogan is Cooper's buddy, somehow managing to get his friend in and out of trouble. It's a little dated, and some of the situations are pretty silly. However, the two Jackies are a nice combination, with good working chemistry between them.

p, Dick Irving Hyland, Sidney Luft; d, Phil Karlson; w, Hyland, Louis Quinn (based on a story by Hyland, Lee Wainer); ph, William Sickner; ed, Jodie Caplan; md, Edward J. Kay.

Comedy **(PR:AA MPAA:NR)**

KIM*** (1950) 113m MGM c

Errol Flynn *(Mahbub Ali, the Red Beard)*, Dean Stockwell *(Kim)*, Paul Lukas *(Lama)*, Robert Douglas *(Col. Creighton)*, Thomas Gomez *(Emissary)*, Cecil Kellaway *(Hurree Chunder)*, Arnold Moss *(Lurgan Sahib)*, Reginald Owen *(Father Victor)*, Laurette Luez *(Laluli)*, Richard Hale *(Hassan Bey)*, Roman Toporow, Ivan Triesault *(Russians)*, Hayden Rorke *(Maj. Ainsley)*, Walter Kingsford *(Dr. Bronson)*, Henry Mirelez *(Wanna)*, Frank Lackteen *(Shadow)*, Frank Richards *(Abul)*, Henry Corden, Peter Mamakos *(Conspirators)*, Donna Martell *(Haikun)*, Jeanette Nolan *(Foster Mother)*, Rod Redwing *(Servant)*, Michael Ansara *(Guard)*, Stanley Price *(Water Carrier)*, Movita Castenada *(Woman with Baby)*, Edgar Lansbury *(Young Officer)*, Francis McDonald *(Letter Writer)*, Adeline DeWalt Reynolds *(Old Maharanee)*, Mike Tellegan *(Policeman)*, Richard Lupino *(Sentry)*, Olaf Hytten *(Mr. Fairlee)*, George Khoury *(Little Man)*.

An adaptation of the classic Rudyard Kipling novel with bright-eyed youngster Stockwell in the title role as the adventure-seeking rebel son of an English envoy living in India in the 1880s. Stockwell does his darndest to avoid the rigid rules of schooling and instead assumes the role of a turbaned peasant boy wandering through the Indian marketplace. He is befriended by Lukas, a philosophizing lama who treats him with a fatherly warmth and offers him invaluable advice. Lukas, however, is contrasted by the flamboyant Flynn, a horse thief who doubles as an agent with British intelligence. From Flynn, Stockwell learns the finer points of espionage, or as Flynn calls it—"that great game." The fun and adventure continue as the three get involved with an explosive political situation in India as the Russians prepare an invasion of the Khyber Pass. Luxuriously photographed in Technicolor, KIM offers countless panoramic views of India, views which are only enhanced if they are seen on a big screen. Interestingly, however, a large portion of KIM was filmed in California and the film's 13-year-old star, Stockwell, never set foot in India. Flynn and Lukas did manage to film some of their scenes in India. At their initial meeting in that country's airport, Flynn, in another of his "wicked, wicked ways," decided to play a practical joke on the normally well-composed Lukas. Before Lukas' arrival, Flynn conned the Chief Inspector of Customs into letting him borrow his uniform for a half hour. He then added a turban, some dark makeup, a beard, and a rifle. To heighten the effect Flynn coached a voluptuous local girl to act as the president of the Paul Lukas Fan Club of India—which, needless to say, never existed. When Lukas appeared at the gate he was met by a stern and inquisitive Flynn, whom he didn't recognize. Flynn fired off an inexorable string of questions which only pressed Lukas' waning patience. In the meantime, the girl was throwing herself at Lukas and pleading for him to take her home. As Flynn wrote in his biography *My Wicked, Wicked Ways:* "Lukas was floundering fast. His tension was almost visible like marks breaking out on the chart of a radar screen, and I felt he'd had enough . . . I allowed my turban to fall to the floor and took my beard off at the same time. Paul gaped, speechless. Rage replaced any possible Academy Award performance he could have put on at that time. He screamed like a wounded panther and to everyone's astonishment grabbed his hat, dashed it on the floor and began jumping up and down on it like a yo-yo." Flynn undoubtedly enjoyed his stay in India, receiving a royal treatment from the Maharajah and discovering a love of hunting. He could have been spending his time in Africa, however. Initially he was slated for the lead in the superior KING SOLOMON'S MINES (1950), but opted for what amounted to little more than a supporting role in this film. Stewart Granger then went on to Africa for KING SOLOMON'S MINES. KIM had been kicked around MGM for some time before it finally went into production. Freddie Bartholomew and Robert Taylor had first crack at KIM in 1938, but WW II halted the production. The Kipling tale resurfaced again in 1942 with Mickey Rooney, Conrad Veidt, and Basil Rathbone cast. The touchy situation of India's fight against British Imperialism led to another shutdown. With India's independence in 1948, MGM finally thought it safe to begin, and was granted permission to bring a camera crew into India. Although it's a bit long and stodgy for some viewers, KIM is still a fine family picture which allows younger viewers to identify with Stockwell's adventurous character.

p, Leon Gordon; d, Victor Saville; w, Gordon, Helen Deutsch, Richard Schayer (based on the novel by Rudyard Kipling); ph, William V. Skall (Technicolor); m, Andre Previn; ed, George Boemler; art d, Cedric Gibbons, Hans Peters; set d, Edwin B. Willis, Arthur Krams, Hugh Hunt; cos, Valles; spec eff, A. Arnold Gillespie, Warren Newcombe; makeup, William Tuttle, Ben Lane.

Adventure (PR:AA MPAA:G)

KIMBERLEY JIM** (1965, South Africa) 81m Emil Nofal-Jamie Uys/EM c

Jim Reeves *(Jim Madison)*, Madeleine Usher *(Julie Patterson)*, Clive Parnell *(Gerry Bates)*, Arthur Swemmer *(Bert Patterson)*, Tromp Terre'Blanche *(Ben Vorster)*, Vonk De Ridder *(Danny Pretorious)*, Mike Holt *(Punchy)*, Dawid Van Der Walt *(Jan le Roux)*, June Neethling *(Elize)*, George Moore *(Fred Parker)*, Freddie Prozesky *(Neels le Roux)*, Don Leonard *(Rube)*, Morris Blake *(Max Bloom)*, The Blue Boys, Eddie Domingo, Webster Booth, Johan Du Plooy, Olive King, June Hern, Marie-Louise Otten, Deborah Frances, Charmain Peker, Pieter Hauptfleisch, Dick O'Shaughnessy, Ralph Loubser, Dale Swanepoel, George Lane, Billy Pretorious.

Set in South Africa's Kimberley diamond mines around 1910, famed country singer Reeves (in a rare screen appearance) and Parnell are two Americans who sell snake oil and hustle at cards with the diamond miners in order to make a living. After winning Swemmer's unproductive mine in a bet, and meeting his daughter Usher, they take up partnership with him to help him meet the debts he owes. But wicked bar owner Terre'Blanche raises the water rates and the trio find themselves desperate for some cash. The Americans put on a musical show and raise the money, but lose it all on a boxing match. Suddenly, fortunately, the mine starts producing untold wealth. However, Reeves and Parnell have had it with the diamond business and head on, leaving the rocks to Swemmer and his daughter Usher. The story is only so-so; the real treat is for the country music fans. Reeves sings his tunes which are fitted nicely into the story. The supporting cast is fine and production credits are standard.

p,d&w, Emil Nofal; ph, Judex C. Viljoen (Scanoscope, Agfacolor); m, Billy Walker; ed, Harry Hughes; art d, Ian MacLeod; cos, Anna Richter-Visser; ch, Sheila Wartski.

Musical/Comedy (PR:A MPAA:NR)

KIN FOLK (SEE: KINFOLK, 1970)

KIND HEARTS AND CORONETS**** (1949, Brit.) 105m EAL/GFD bw

Dennis Price *(Louis Mazzini)*, Valerie Hobson *(Edith D'Ascoyne)*, Joan Greenwood *(Sibella)*, Alec Guinness *(The Duke/The Banker/The Parson/The General/The Admiral/Young Ascoyne D'Ascoyne/Young Henry/Lady Agatha)*, Audrey Fildes *(Mama)*, Miles Malleson *(The Hangman)*, Clive Morton *(Prison Governor)*, John Penrose *(Lionel)*, Cecil Ramage *(Crown Counsel)*, Hugh Griffith *(Lord High Steward)*, John Salew *(Mr. Perkins)*, Eric Messiter *(Burgoyne)*, Lyn Evans *(The Farmer)*, Barbara Leake *(The Schoolmistress)*, Peggy Ann Clifford *(Maud)*, Anne Valery *(The Girl in the Punt)*, Arthur Lowe *(The Reporter)*.

This was Alec Guinness's third film after GREAT EXPECTATIONS and OLIVER and served to make him an international star. Although Price had the largest role in the picture, Guinness took the lion's share of the reviews with a tour de force performance that had him playing eight roles, all members of the same family. Guinness had been offered four of the parts but he felt he could handle them all and asked for and was granted the opportunity. The theme of the story is that mass murder *can* be funny. And if you find that hard to swallow, then you haven't seen KIND HEARTS AND CORONETS, one of the funniest movies ever made in England and surely one of the most memorable and notorious. It's 1900 or so and Price is a duke, several times removed. He is an amusing cad who finds that the only way he can assume the mantle he feels is rightfully his is by removing all the stumbling blocks standing in his way. The fact that those stumbling blocks are human beings who must be murdered seems to not matter a trifle. Price sets about dispatching the family, all of whom bear more than a passing resemblance to each other as they are the roles played by Guinness. Greenwood, who was to play opposite Guinness in the equally delightful THE MAN IN THE WHITE SUIT, is Price's long-time lover before he marries and while he's married. Valerie Hobson plays the wife of one of the victims. Price begins knocking off the relatives in various ways; his uncle is blown up, his aunt is sent to Kingdom Come when she boards a balloon, etc. Six of the relatives are murdered and two others die by chance and, suddenly, Price is the duke. Then he's arrested for a crime he did *not* commit, when Greenwood's husband takes his own life. Just as he is to be executed for his murder, he is reprieved and freed and is walking out to choose between Hobson and Greenwood, both of whom are outside the prison walls waiting for him in separate carriages. It seems that a "suicide note" has been conveniently found and Price can now go about his business. However, he's been spending his spare time writing his memoirs and telling the whole truth and nothing but the truth in the memoirs because he felt he had nothing to lose and was so proud of his accomplishments that he wanted the world to share them. As he exits the prison, a publisher approaches him for the right to print his story and Price realizes that he's left the memoirs in his cell and, even as the two men speak, they are being read. Price is eventually taken to the scaffold by the redoubtable Miles Malleson, who usually played vicars, as in THE IMPORTANCE OF BEING EARNEST. This time, the cherubic Malleson is the hangman. This film is one of the few movies that knows how to use the flashback technique without ever making us feel there is unnecessary exposition. The dialog is worthy of Oscar at his Wildest with many quotable quotes, such as "Revenge is the dish which people of taste prefer to eat cold!" and, after dispatching old lady Agatha in her balloon, he tersely remarks: "I shot an arrow in the air . . . she fell to earth in Berkeley Square." Unfortunately, these bon mots take up the bulk of the screen time, to the exclusion of cinematic unfolding, so it feels as much like a play as it does a movie. The story is loosely based on Roy Horniman's turn of the century novel *Israel Rank.* Hamer and Dighton used the core of the novel and dispensed with many of the details to write their own screenplay, which was totally overlooked by all of those award-givers but much beloved by the public. There is talk these days of doing a remake of the film but, save for the late Peter Sellers, who is around to repeat the feat of Guinness? In lieu of that, the producers will probably get eight actors to play the eight roles and that will miss the point completely. KIND HEARTS AND CORONETS is one of those films that can be seen annually, like CITIZEN KANE or CASABLANCA or GONE WITH THE WIND, and one can always find something new that one didn't see before. If one could only see one British comedy as an example of how movies were made on that tight little island, see this. As a combination of satire, rollicking humor and enormous pokes at many Jolly Olde Types, nothing else comes close.

p, Michael Balcon; d, Robert Hamer; w, Hamer, John Dighton (based on a novel by Roy Horniman); ph, Douglas Slocombe; m, Wolfgang Amadeus Mozart ("Don Giovanni"); ed, Peter Tanner; art d, William Kellner.

Comedy Cas. (PR:A-C MPAA:NR)

KIND LADY* (1935) 76m MGM bw (AKA: HOUSE OF MENACE)

Aline MacMahon *(Mary Herries)*, Basil Rathbone *(Henry Abbott)*, Mary Carlisle *(Phyllis)*, Frank Albertson *(Peter)*, Dudley Digges *(Mr. Edwards)*, Doris Lloyd *(Lucy Weston)*, Nola Luxford *(Rose)*, Murray Kinnell *(Doctor)*, Eily Malyon *(Mrs. Edwards)*, Justine Chase *(Ada)*, Barbara Shields *(Aggie)*, Donald Meek *(Foster)*, Frank Reicher *(Roubet)*.

MacMahon is an Englishwoman, disappointed in love and life, who lets charming stranger Rathbone and his family into her home. He proves to be up to no good. Rathbone begins doping up the lady with drugs to keep her quiet, then blackmailing her. She is finally rescued and Rathbone is arrested. The whole thing, though well acted, is completely unbelievable and rather tedious to watch. It was remade in 1951 with Ethel Barrymore and Maurice Evans.

p, Lucien Hubbard; d, George B. Seitz; w, Bernard Schubert (based on the play by Edward Chodorov from "The Silver Casket" by Hugh Walpole); ph, George Folsey; m, Edward Ward; ed, Hugh Wynn.

Mystery/Crime (PR:A MPAA:NR)

KIND LADY*** (1951) 77m MGM bw

Ethel Barrymore *(Mary Herries)*, Maurice Evans *(Henry Springer Elcott)*, Angela Lansbury *(Mrs. Edwards)*, Keenan Wynn *(Edwards)*, Betsy Blair *(Ada Elcott)*, John Williams *(Mr. Foster)*, Doris Lloyd *(Rose)*, John O'Malley *(Antique Dealer)*, Henri Letondal *(Monsieur Malaquaise)*, Moyna Macgill *(Mrs. Harkley)*, Barry Bernard *(Mr. Harkley)*, Sally Cooper *(Lucy Weston)*, Arthur Gould-Porter *(Chauffeur)*, Sherlee Collier *(Aggie Edwards)*, Phyllis Morris *(Dora)*, Patrick O'Moore *(Constable Orkin)*, Keith McConnell *(Jones)*, Leonard Carey *(Postman)*, Victor Wood *(Doc)*.

Far superior to the 1935 version, MGM re-made this story with a better feel for suspense that overcomes some story implausibilities. Barrymore is an elderly woman with an interest in art. Evans is an artist who tricks her into taking him, along with wife Blair and sinister couple Lansbury and Wynn, into her home. They hold her prisoner in her own home while they proceed to remove her valuable collection of art. Eventually she is able to escape and the villains are captured. Though it starts off a little too slowly, once the film gets going the suspense is maintained. The acting is excellent, both major and supporting players doing a good job. The photography is also good, nicely capturing the English countryside. Doris Lloyd appears in both the 1935 version and this one.

p, Armand Deutsch; d, John Sturges; w, Jerry Davis, Edward Chodorov, Charles Bennett (based on the play by Chodorov from the story "The Silver Casket" by Hugh Walpole); ph, Joseph Ruttenberg; m, David Raksin; ed, Ferris Webster; art d, Cedric Gibbons, William Ferrari.

Suspense (PR:O MPAA:NR)

KIND OF LOVING, A*½** (1962, Brit.) 112m Vic-Waterhall/Governor bw

Alan Bates *(Vic Brown)*, June Ritchie *(Ingrid Rothwell)*, Thora Hird *(Mrs. Rothwell)*,

Bert Palmer *(Mr. Brown)*, Gwen Nelson *(Mrs. Brown)*, Malcolm Patton *(Jim Brown)*, Pat Keen *(Christine)*, David Mahlowe *(David)*, Jack Smethurst *(Conroy)*, James Bolam *(Jeff)*, Michael Deacon *(Les)*, John Ronane, David Cook *(Draughtsmen)*, Norman Heyes *(Laisterdyke)*, Leonard Rossiter *(Whymper)*, Fred Ferris *(Mr. Althorpe)*, Patsy Rowlands *(Dorothy)*, Annette Robertson *(Phoebe)*, Ruth Porcher *(Mrs. Keen)*, Henry Markham *(Railwayman)*, Peter Madden *(Registrar)*, Katherine Staff *(Mrs. Oliphant)*, Edna Ridgway *(Pub Pianist)*, Graham Rigby *(Pub Politician)*, Bud Ralston *(Pub Comedian)*, Bryan Mosley, Joe Gladwin *(Bus Conductors)*, Jerry Desmonde *(Television Compere)*, Reginald Green *(Television Competitor)*, Douglas Livingstone *(Window Cleaner)*.

This was John Schlesinger's first feature after a successful sojourn in commercials and marked an auspicious beginning for a career that later included DARLING, YANKS and THE FALCON AND THE SNOWMAN. It was not a hit until it took the Best Picture award at the Berlin Film Festival. Even then, it just barely eked out a profit despite being an excellent movie of the "kitchen sink" type of workingman's drama, which included Wesker's THE KITCHEN and Delaney's A TASTE OF HONEY. Bates works as a draftsman in a factory somewhere in Lancashire. Ritchie is a typist in the factory and the two are soon attracted to each other. They have several dates and he eventually sleeps over one night when Ritchie's widowed mother, Hird, is out of town. Ritchie is mad for Bates, but after he has been with her, he is no longer interested and seeks other romances. Ritchie, however, is pregnant. Once Bates learns of that, he reluctantly offers to marry her. They honeymoon at a beach resort, then move in with Hird, a domineering snob who feels that her daughter has married beneath her station. Ritchie has a miscarriage and Bates is now annoyed that he took the plunge. Ritchie goes off sex and Bates finds himself drinking more and more, until he gets drunk one night and has a confrontation with Hird. He leaves the house and attempts to find some sort of sympathy from others, including his sister, but he eventually returns to Ritchie and they realize that the only way they can make a go of their relationship is to flee the clutches of her possessive mother and establish their own home. If that can be done, they might be able to achieve "a kind of loving." It's not much of a story when told in a synopsis, but the script and direction elevate this film far beyond the norm. It's shot in an almost-documentary style that adds to the feeling that we are watching real people in real situations. Other than Bates, most of the actors were newcomers with little or no film experience. That also helps in establishing the realistic feel, much in the same manner as Milos Forman did in THE FIREMAN'S BALL, a comedy where no one was recognizable. Sometimes the casting of a star works against the intent of the picture, and here is a good example of how to get good performances out of tyros and cause the audience to believe everything they see on screen—the suspension of disbelief. There's nary a false moment in the entire picture and it merits your attention and perusal. Best of all, despite the grimy surroundings and the downbeat theme, there is enough humor to leaven it and give you a total experience. Not surprising when you realize that Waterhouse and Hall also wrote BILLY LIAR and many other funny films.

p, Joseph Janni; d, John Schlesinger; w, Willis Hall, Keith Waterhouse (based on the novel by Stan Barstow); ph, Denys Coop; m, Ron Grainer; ed, Roger Cherrill; md, Grainer; art d, Ray Simm; set d, Maurice Fowler; cos, Laura Nightingale.

Drama **(PR:A-C MPAA:NR)**

KIND STEPMOTHER* 1/2
(1936, Hung.) 95m Hermes/Danubia bw (EDES MOSTOSHA; AKA: SWEET STEPMOTHER)

Antal Pager *(Baron Andrew Hartigay)*, Maria Tasnady-Fekete *(Maria)*, Gizy Pecsy *(Erzsike)*, Julius Gozon *(Gardner)*, Piroska Vaszary *(Ibolya)*, Mici Erdelyi.

Made as a showcase for Pecsy, the six-year-old Hungarian Shirley Temple clone whose dimples and dances can charm your socks off, the film was sufficiently appealing that the story was purchased by Hollywood as a possible vehicle for Temple. Tasnady, who later acted in German films using the name von Tasnady, is excellent as the love-smitten miss who befriends the tot as a means to win the affection of her widower father, the handsome, wealthy baron, Pager. Heartaches alternate with chuckles throughout the well-directed film as its makes its inexorable progress to a happy ending for the principal players. (In Hungarian; English subtitles.)

d, Bela Balogh; w, Arthur Lakner; m, Sandor Szlatloay.

Children's Film **(PR:AAA MPAA:NR)**

KINFOLK zero
(1970) 84m Clover c (AKA: KIN FOLK; THE CLOSEST OF KIN; ALL THE LOVIN' KINFOLK)

Jay Scott *(Zeb)*, Mady Maguire *(Cindy)*, Ann Ryan *(Tricia)*, Janice Douglas *(Mrs. Pruitt)*, Donna Young *(Sue)*, William Guhl *(Luke)*, Ruth Stanley *(Babs)*, Marland Proctor *(Cpl. Simpson)*, Lynn York *(Rose)*, John Dennis *(Bartender)*, Buck Stahl *(Mr. Wilson)*, Richard Gentry *(Randy)*.

Maguire and cousin Scott leave their home in the mountains for life in town. They meet with a series of disappointments and Maguire eventually becomes a prostitute, seducing her cousin when she discovers that he is having an affair with the daughter of his boss. A stupid redneck melodrama with great dollops of sex intended mainly for the Southern drive-in circuit.

p, Daniel Cady, John Hayes; d&w, Hayes; ph, Paul Hipp (Eastmancolor); m, Mario Toscana; cos, Logan Costume; m/l, "Leavin' These Mountains," Ellen Bender, Toscana (sung by Larry Adair).

Drama **(PR:O MPAA:NR)**

KING, THE (SEE: ROYAL AFFAIR, A, 1950, Fr.)

KING AND COUNTRY**** (1964, Brit.) 86m BHE/AA bw

Dirk Bogarde *(Capt. Hargreaves)*, Tom Courtenay *(Pvt. Arthur Hamp)*, Leo McKern *(Capt. O'Sullivan)*, Barry Foster *(Lt. Webb)*, James Villiers *(Capt. Midgley)*, Peter Copley *(Colonel)*, Barry Justice *(Lt. Prescott)*, Vivian Matalon *(Padre)*, Jeremy Spenser *(Pvt. Sparrow)*, James Hunter *(Pvt. Sykes)*, David Cook *(Pvt. Wilson)*, Larry Taylor *(Sergeant-Major)*, Jonah Seymour *(Corp. Hamilton, M.P.)*, Keith Buckley *(Corporal of the Guard)*, Richard Arthure *(Guard "Charlie")*, Derek Partridge *(Captain at Court Martial)*, Brian Tipping *(Lieutenant at Court Martial)*, Raymond Brody, Dan Cornwall, Terry Palmer *(Soldiers in Hamp's Platoon)*.

Deserving a place among such classic WW I films as ALL QUIET ON THE WESTERN FRONT (1930) and PATHS OF GLORY (1957), this brutally frank, thoughtful, and deeply moving war film contains no battle scenes and little gunfire. Bogarde is a British captain assigned to defend a slow-witted soldier, Courtenay, who has been accused of desertion. Being highly educated and a strict military disciplinarian, Bogarde approaches his mission with distaste. Feeling the whole thing a waste of valuable time, Bogarde accepts his superior's suggestion that he ignore Courtenay's shell-shocked state and push for a quick conviction. Under questioning, Bogarde learns that Courtenay had enlisted in the army on a dare from friends. Three years later the uneducated soldier is well on his way to shell-shock after learning that his wife has been unfaithful and his having been the sole survivor of his unit. Fed up and tired, Courtenay simply wanted to "go for a walk" and left. He was picked up after a day of wandering and put into custody. During the testimony Bogarde begins to feel sympathy for the obviously sincere and somewhat confused Courtenay. For the first time in his military career, Bogarde begins to question the army's methods and attitudes toward its men. Bogarde's new-found support for his client leads to an impassioned plea for leniency at the trial, but an unsympathetic and impatient court finds Courtenay guilty and sentences him to death. On the eve of Courtenay's execution, his fellow soldiers pilfer some rum from the officers and visit the condemned man in his cell. The men become so drunk that the next morning they bungle the execution when their first volley of shots fails to kill Courtenay. Horrified, Bogarde steps up and shoots Courtenay once in the head, killing him. Later that day a letter is dispatched to Courtenay's family stating that he has been killed in action. KING AND COUNTRY is a grim indictment of the arrogant, simple-minded mentality of the men who send their fellow citizens off to war. A good army is driven by discipline and a devotion to duty, but director Losey shows us that things are not that simple. Bogarde's character is a cold, unblinking automaton, and therefore, quite successful in the military. His interviews with Courtenay change all that. Bogarde is forced to open up and think clearly about the war and its purpose. Courtenay's simple honesty stuns Bogarde into reassessing the military mentality he has been so devoted to. Perhaps the upper echelon understood quite clearly the effect that a freed Courtenay would have on their carefully controlled discipline, making it absolutely necessary that his life be snuffed out. KING AND COUNTRY is an extremely claustrophobic film that takes place in dark, dirty, rat-infested interiors. Some critics of the film decried this stage-like quality, saying that the material had originally been written for the stage, but the argument is irrelevant. The film is a study of men entrapped in the machinery of war and we need not see the battles, just the effect. Losey shows us that we are all responsible for the senseless slaughter. Courtenay's ignorant complacency is just as reprehensible as the military's willingness to send him off to a pointless death. No one comes out cleansed of culpability in KING AND COUNTRY; we all share the responsibility for the horror of war.

p, Joseph Losey, Norman Priggen; d, Losey; w, Evan Jones (based on the play "Hamp" by John Wilson from a story by James Lansdale); ph, Denys Coop; m, Larry Adler; ed, Reginald Mills; prod d, Richard MacDonald; art d, Peter Mullins; cos, Roy Ponting.

War **(PR:C MPAA:NR)**

KING AND FOUR QUEENS, THE** (1956) 83m Russ-Field-Gabco/UA c

Clark Gable *(Dan Kehoe)*, Eleanor Parker *(Sabina)*, Jo Van Fleet *(Ma McDade)*, Jean Willes *(Ruby)*, Barbara Nichols *(Birdie)*, Sara Shane *(Oralie)*, Roy Roberts *(Sheriff Larrabee)*, Arthur Shields *(Padre)*, Jay C. Flippen *(Bartender)*.

Gable was known as "the King" in the movie business but this picture could have deposed him forever. Not that it's bad, it just isn't good enough to merit the kind of attention given to it by the actors or the creators. Gable is a cowboy-on-the-run who arrives at the semi-abandoned town of Wagon Mound. Van Fleet, a pistol-packing Mama, lives there with her four daughters-in-law, Willes, Nichols, Shane, and Parker, who isn't one of the daughters-in-law at all. Rather, she is masquerading as one because she knows that Van Fleet's sons have secreted $100,000 in gold somewhere in the town—the loot taken from a stagecoach holdup. Three of the boys are dead, but no one knows which three, so all the wives hope that the surviving man is her husband. Gable puts a move on each of the young women and thinks that he can wind up with the money if he plays his cards right. Parker and Gable find the money and are racing away with it when they are stopped by the posse that has captured the last surviving brother. The sheriff, Roberts, takes the gold but gives Gable and Parker a $5,000 reward for finding it. Sadder, but wiser, and somewhat richer, Gable and Parker ride off together in the sunset, two connivers in search of a way to make a fast buck. It's a cynical film and pokes fun at the Old West and itself, as was often the case in Walsh's later films. There's not enough humor in it to make the film an out-and-out comedy and there's not enough reality to take it seriously. This one falls somewhere in the middle and that's no place to be when you have such high-priced and high-powered talent strutting and fretting across the screen. Gable is so charming as the confidence man that he almost succeeds in pulling the picture together, but, in the end, it's an empty exercise, as meaningless as a politician's handshake. Van Fleet is the other standout as the mother of the dead crooks. One would have to look hard in her resume to find a bad performance. The executive producer was former footballer (and first husband of Jane Russell) Bob Waterfield.

p, David Hempstead; d, Raoul Walsh; w, Margaret Fitts, Richard Alan Simmons (based on a story by Fitts); ph, Lucien Ballard (CinemaScope, DeLuxe Color); m, Alex North; ed, Louis Loeffler, David Brotherton; md, North; art d, Wiard Ihnen; cos, Renie, Oscar Rodriguez, Marjorie Henderson.

Comedy/Drama/Western (PR:A MPAA:NR)

KING AND I, THE***** (1956) 133m FOX c

Deborah Kerr *(Anna Leonowens)*, Yul Brynner *(The King)*, Rita Moreno *(Tuptim)*, Martin Benson *(Kralahome)*, Terry Saunders *(Lady Thiang)*, Rex Thompson *(Louis Leonowens)*, Carlos Rivas *(Lun Tha)*, Patrick Adiarte *(Prince Chulalongkorn)*, Alan Mowbray *(British Ambassador)*, Geoffrey Toone *(Ramsay)*, Yuriko *(Eliza)*, Marion Jim *(Simon Legree)*, Robert Banas *(Keeper of the Dogs)*, Dusty Worrall *(Uncle Thomas)*, Gemze de Lappe *(Specialty Dancer)*, Thomas and Dennis Bonilla *(Twins)*, Michiko Iseri *(Angel in Ballet)*, Charles Irwin *(Ship's Captain)*, Leonard Strong *(Interpreter)*, Irene James *(Siamese Girl)*, Jadin and Jean Wong *(Amazons)*, Fuji, Weaver Levy *(Whipping Guards)*, William Yip *(High Priest)*, Eddie Luke *(Messenger)*, Josephine Smith *(Guest at Palace)*, Jocelyn New *(Princess Ying Yoowalak)*.

How many times have you heard this? "Yes, the movie was okay, but you should have seen the play. Now *that* was something!" Well, the reverse is true of THE KING AND I. This film more than eclipses the play in emotion, opulence, and in most of the performances. Based on the novel by Margaret Landon, which was then made into a movie starring Rex Harrison as the king and Irene Dunne as the British schoolteacher, THE KING AND I features Yul Brynner in the role he was born to play. By the time of his death in 1985, he had been the King for more than 4000 performances, and he breathed new life into the role every night. Kerr is a schoolteacher who has been engaged to teach the King's many children. She arrives in Siam with her son, Thompson, and the polarization of two people and the difference in their cultures is what forms the basis for the story. Brynner has several wives, including Moreno, and one of the stories concerns Kerr convincing Brynner that he must not keep Moreno there because she loves someone else, Rivas. Brynner's portrayal of a man clinging to the old ways but realizing that he must come forward in time to accept new customs is a marvel to behold. As the picture unspools, the chauvinistic Brynner becomes more appreciative of this mere "woman" who has come to upset his Mee Krob bowl. His personality is more complex than most of the musical heroes of the stage and we are privy to several glimpses of the man beneath the bluster as he seeks and strives to overcome a lifetime of arrogance and to become a man of today. The two principals spar and jockey with each other until a grudging love emerges between them that is never consummated, but the subtlety of their final scene, as Brynner lays dying, is enough to let us know that they dearly do care for each other. The story, without the music, has laughs, tears, and just about every emotion that excellent writing can elicit. But the music, that glorious score by Rodgers and Hammerstein, makes this nonpareil. So many of the songs have gone into the musical lexicon that one hardly knows where to begin. The original play had even more and three of the tunes were jettisoned, with no loss to the film, because it was already an embarrassment of tuneful riches. Those songs were "My Lord And Master," "Western People Funny," and "Shall I Tell You What I Think Of You?" Kerr's voice was looped by the most ubiquitous of all film loopers, Marni Nixon (wife of film composer Ernest Gold). The songs which survived were "Shall We Dance?" "Getting To Know You," "Hello, Young Lovers," "We Kiss In A Shadow," "I Whistle A Happy Tune," "March Of The Siamese Children," "I Have Dreamed," "A Puzzlement," "Something Wonderful," "Song of The King." One of the great set-pieces was Jerome Robbins' staging of "The Little House Of Uncle Thomas," the Siamese version of "Uncle Tom's Cabin," which was presented by the children of the castle to visitors to prove that they were not barbarians. It is at once hilarious and touching. The screenplay by Ernest Lehman, who went on to write the adaptation for Rodgers and Hammerstein's THE SOUND OF MUSIC, was true to the play and improved on the original. The movie cost a paltry $6.5 million (by today's standards) and made a fortune. It was nominated as Best Picture, for Best Actress, Best Cinematography, and Best Direction and didn't win any of those. It did, however, get Oscars for Brynner, Newman, and Ken Darby. The 133 minutes went by like a flash of lightning. This was a monumentally successful stage musical that ran as long as Brynner was alive. In years to come there will be others who will attempt the role, but just as Brando will always be Stanley Kowalski, and Leigh will always be Scarlett O'Hara, Brynner will always be the King. On the stage, the late Gertrude Lawrence, a fine singer, was Anna. She died four years before the film, but anyone who saw her on stage was blessed. It was her life that Julie Andrews essayed in the disastrous STAR.

p, Charles Brackett; d, Walter Lang; w, Ernest Lehman (based on the musical by Oscar Hammerstein II, Richard Rodgers, from the book *Anna and The King of Siam* by Margaret Landon); ph, Leon Shamroy (CinemaScope, DeLuxe Color); m, Richard Rodgers; ed, Robert Simpson; md, Alfred Newman; art d, Lyle R. Wheeler, John de Cuir; set d, Walter M. Scott, Paul S. Fox; cos, Irene Sharaff; ch, Jerome Robbins; m/l, Rodgers, Hammerstein.

Musical Cas. (PR:AAA MPAA:G)

KING AND THE CHORUS GIRL, THE½** (1937) 95m WB bw (GB: ROMANCE IS SACRED)

Fernand Gravet [Gravey] *(Alfred)*, Joan Blondell *(Dorothy)*, Edward Everett Horton *(Count Humbert)*, Alan Mowbray *(Donald)*, Jane Wyman *(Babette)*, Mary Nash *(Duchess Anna)*, Shaw and Lee *(Folies Bergere Entertainers)*, Kenny Baker *(Soloist)*, Luis Alberni *(Gaston)*, Ben Welden *(Waiter)*, Lionel Pape *(Professor Kornish)*, Leonard Mudie *(Footman)*, Adrian Rosley *(Concierge)*, Ferdinand Schumann-Heink *(Chauffeur)*, Torben Meyer *(Eric)*, Armand Kaliz *(Theatre Manager)*, Velma Wayne *(Bolero Dancer)*, Georgette Rhodes *(Hatcheck Girl)*, George Sorel, Alphonse Martel *(Servants)*, Sam Ash, Lee Kohlmar *(Violinists)*, Carlos San Martin *(Policeman)*, Gaston Glass *(Junior Officer)*, Jacques Lory *(Waiter)*, Robert Graves *(Captain of the Ocean Liner)*, Adele St. Maur *(Stewardess)*, Georges Renavent *(Yacht Captain)*.

Belgian actor Gravet, long-tenured in French films, makes his American film debut in this tale as a deposed former monarch who falls in love with Blondell, a chorus girl at the Folies Bergere. Horton is the monarch's long-suffering factotum and is as droll as can be. The film maintains a good level of farce, with some nice musical numbers including "For You" and "On the Rue de la Paix." Things drop off toward the end, but it's still good fun to watch. The usually brassy Blondell performed her role in an uncharacteristically restrained and sympathetic manner. Wyman, later a wife of a president-to-be, is seen here in one of her first featured parts. Prolific director LeRoy made his debut as producer here; the following year he defied the Hollywood conventions of nepotism—his wife was the daughter of a studio mogul—and switched his allegiance from Warner Bros. to MGM. The film did well at the box office. It was most timely; three months prior to its release, King Edward VIII of Great Britain abdicated his throne to wed a commoner, divorcee Wallis Warfield Simpson.

p&d, Mervyn LeRoy; w, Norman Krasna, Groucho Marx (based on their story "Grand Passion"); ph, Tony Gaudio; ed, Thomas Richards; md, Leo F. Forbstein; art d, Robert Haas; cos, Orry-Kelly; ch, Bobby Connolly; m/l, Werner Richard Heymann, Ted Koehler.

Comedy (PR:AA MPAA:NR)

KING ARTHUR WAS A GENTLEMAN** (1942, Brit.) 99m Gainsborough/GFD bw

Arthur Askey *(Arthur King)*, Evelyn Dall *(Susan Ashley)*, Anne Shelton *(Gwen Duncannon)*, Max Bacon *(Maxie)*, Jack Train *(Jack)*, Peter Graves *(Lance)*, Vera Frances *(Vera)*, Al Burnett *(Slim)*, Brefni O'Rorke *(Col. Duncannon)*, Ronald Shiner *(Sergeant)*, Freddie Crump, Ernie [Victor] Feldman, John Wynn, Veronica Turleigh, Elizabeth Flateau, Margot Hunter, Sonia Somers, Virginia Keiley, Cameron Hall, Vincent Holman, Clifford Cobbe, Clifford Buckton, Bryan Herbert.

Askey is a British soldier in Africa whose brilliant swordplay turns him into a hero. It is really his belief that he possesses King Arthur's sword, "Excalibur," that gives Askey his courage. When he learns that his weapon is not really the famed sword, he feels a bit of a dope but still manages to rescue his friends from the enemy. A promising premise which never quite delivers.

p, Edward Black; d, Marcel Varnel; w, Val Guest, Marriott Edgar; ph, Arthur Crabtree.

Comedy (PR:A MPAA:NR)

KING BLANK* (1983) 71m King Blank/Metafilms Inc. bw

Rosemary Hochschild *(Queenie Blank)*, Ron Vawter *(King Blank)*, Will Patton *(Bar Customer)*, Pete Richardson *(Bouncer)*.

Vawter is an Army vet who, along with his wife Hochschild, has holed up in a cheap motel near a New York City airport. Their relationship is quickly ending as they carry their arguments back and forth between their room and the motel's bar. The latter is frequented by various sleazy people: drunks, prostitutes, and perverts. Shot in 16mm, this is a crude and technically incompetent exercise in filmmaking. The story has little merit, though Hochschild gives her performance a good deal of energy. This marked the debut of Oblowitz as a director. Born in South Africa, he settled in America to make films.

p&d, Michael Oblowitz; w, Oblowitz, Rosemary Hochschild; ph, Oblowitz; m, Anton Fig; ed, Susanne Rostack.

Drama (PR:O MPAA:NR)

KING COBRA (SEE: JAWS OF SATAN, 1980)

KING CREOLE*** (1958) 116m PAR bw

Elvis Presley *(Danny Fisher)*, Carolyn Jones *(Ronnie)*, Dolores Hart *(Nellie)*, Dean Jagger *(Mr. Fisher)*, Liliane Montevecchi *("Forty" Nina)*, Walter Matthau *(Maxie Fields)*, Jan Shepard *(Mimi Fisher)*, Paul Stewart *(Charlie LeGrand)*, Vic Morrow *(Shark)*, Brian Hutton *(Sal)*, Jack Grinnage *(Dummy)*, Dick Winslow *(Eddie Burton)*, Raymond Bailey *(Mr. Evans)*, Ziva Rodann, Franklyn Farnum, Hazel "Sonny" Boyne, Minta Durfee Arbuckle.

KING CREOLE was, perhaps, the best acting job Presley ever did. Whether this was due to the rough tactics of Michael Curtiz, who had directed Cagney, Bogart, Garfield, Flynn and who will always be revered for CASABLANCA; or the script by Herbert Baker and Michael Gazzo (author of A HATFUL OF RAIN and an actor whose assignments included THE GODFATHER, PART TWO); or the fact that the story was based on a novel Harold Robbins wrote before he became a cottage industry—who knows? Still, it will be remembered for the many facets of Elvis that emerged. Presley is a singing busboy at a sleazy Bourbon Street night spot. One night, during a drunken party, he rescues Jones from a drunk who is pawing at her. (So far this sounds like the start of another Presley picture, KID GALAHAD.) Jones is the girl friend of local hood Matthau and she'd like to leave him but fears for her safety. Presley is going to school and when Jones gives him a kiss goodbye, he is razzed by his fellow students and rebels by tossing a few punches. When that skirmish is witnessed by the school's principal Presley is told that he will not be allowed to graduate. Later he is jumped by a gang of toughs led by Morrow, brother of the boy he bloodied earlier. He is outnumbered but acquits himself well and is invited to join the gang but declines. Presley's father, Jagger, has a new job at a drug store. He pleads with Elvis to go back to school, but Presley thinks his father is a weak-willed wimp and decides to join Morrow and his crew of thieves who rob the drug store while Elvis sings and acts as a decoy. Presley meets Hart, a lovely young thing who works at the store, and makes a date with her. Elvis is working at the Bourbon Street Club when Jones enters with Matthau. Elvis innocently greets Jones and is surprised when she doesn't seem to recognize him and tells Matthau that she only heard him sing once before. Matthau is mightily impressed by Elvis' singing and so is Stewart, another club owner who happens to be there. Stewart offers Presley a job at his club, the King Creole. Presley takes the job and soon the customers are packing the place. He begins seeing Hart, who would like him to give up this wastrel life and marry her. Simultaneously he and Jones are developing a mutual attraction, but she lives in fear of the cruel Matthau and won't let the relationship go beyond a primary stage. Matthau wants Presley to leave Stewart's club and come work for him so he uses Jones to help convince Elvis. Jones, however, double-crosses Matthau and warns Elvis to stay away from the man, as he is bad news indeed. Matthau is irked; he calls upon Morrow to help blackmail Elvis into quitting Stewart. Elvis is implicated in a holdup (all phony, of course) and Jagger reacts by having to be hospitalized. Presley, upon learning who is behind this turn of events, beats up Matthau and becomes a marked man with every New Orleans thug gunning for him. Next, Elvis whips Morrow but is hurt in the process. Jones takes Presley to a place in the country and helps him back to health. Matthau finds them, pulls a gun and kills Jones; then he is killed by one of his own thugs. Elvis and Hart are reunited at the fade-out. This was a heavy plot for a musical but they managed to cram it all in, plus several songs from many different writers. The tunes were "King Creole," "Banana," "New Orleans," "Turtles, Berries and Gumbo," "Crawfish," "Don't Ask Me Why," "As Long As I Have You," "Trouble," "Hard-Headed Woman," "Lover Doll," "Dixieland Rock," "Young Dreams" and "Steadfast, Loyal and True." Morrow had played a similar role in THE BLACKBOARD JUNGLE, and, before his death, emerged as one of the better actors around Hollywood. Jones was marvelous in her small but effective part. She also died young and will be missed. This was Elvis' last film before being drafted into the Army and he never again reached these acting heights. Co-writer Baker, the son of vaudevillian Belle Baker, was acknowledged as one of the best special material writers in the business and wrote the Writers Guild opening number for many years. One of his last parodies was of "A Chorus Line's" "I Can Do That," in which he wrote the reasons why he became a writer, saying: "Read Shakespeare, really dug that cat. I said I Can Write That, I Can Write That." And he could. In a tiny role, silent-screen actress Minta Durfee Arbuckle is seen. She was the widow of the legendary Fatty Arbuckle.

p, Hal B. Wallis; d, Michael Curtiz; w, Herbert Baker, Michael Vincente Gazzo (based on the novel *A Stone for Danny Fisher* by Harold Robbins); ph, Russell Harlan (VistaVision); m, Walter Scharf; ed, Warren Low; art d, Hal Pereira, Joseph MacMillan Johnson; cos, Edith Head; spec eff, John P. Fulton; ch, Charles O'Curran; m/l, Jerry Lieber, Mike Stoller, Claude Demetrius, Aaron Schroeder, Fred Wise, Ben Weisman, Sid Tepper, Abner Silver, Roy C. Bennett, Sid Wayne, Martin Kalmanoff, Rachel Frank, Al Wood, Kay Twomey; makeup, Wally Westmore.

Musical Cas. (PR:A MPAA:NR)

KING DINOSAUR* (1955) 59m Zimgor/Lippert bw

Bill Bryant *(Dr. Ralph Martin)*, Wanda Curtis *(Dr. Patricia Bennett)*, Douglas Henderson *(Richard Gordon)*, Patti Gallagher *(Nora Pierce)*, Marvin Miller *(Narrator)*.

Four scientists blast off to the planet Nova. There they encounter stock footage from the 1940 film ONE MILLION B.C., and rear-projection shots of gila monsters and armadillos. They spend a lot of time running, being scared, and having other standard reactions, but the boy-girl, boy-girl casting does allow for a little smooching here and there. They save themselves with another stock shot, this being a 1950s A-Bomb. The film was shot in just over a weekend, and it shows. Miller, of the old "The Millionaire" television series, serves as narrator.

p, Bert I. Gordon, Al Zimbalist; d, Gordon; w, Tom Gries (based on a story by Gordon, Zimbalist); ph, Gordon Avil; m, Mischa Terr; ed, John Bushelman, Jack Cornwall; spec. eff., Howard A. Anderson Company.

Science Fiction/Horror Cas. (PR:AA MPAA:NR)

KING FOR A NIGHT½** (1933) 78m UNIV bw

Chester Morris *(Bud Williams)*, Helen Twelvetrees *(Lillian Williams)*, Alice White *(Evelyn)*, John Miljan *(Walter Douglas)*, Grant Mitchell *(Rev. John Williams)*, George E. Stone *(Hymie)*, George Meeker *(John Williams)*, Frank Albertson *(Dick)*, Warren Hymer *(Goofy)*, John Sheehan *(Manny)*, Maxie Rosenblum *(Heavyweight)*, Harlan Tucker, Harry Galfund, Clarence Wilson, Dorothy Granger, George Billings, Wade Boteler.

A dichotomous boxing-*cum*-murder film, with the initial half detailing the pains and pleasures of a budding prizefighter who becomes a champion for a day, and the latter half a Dostoevskian drama of crime and sacrifice. Morris gives a sterling performance as the small-town slugger whose paralyzed pacifistic minister father, Mitchell, bemoans his penchant for pugilism. Battling his way to New York City and big-time boxing, moving toward the middleweight title with the help of promoter Miljan, he finds fame, fortune, and floozies galore. Unbeknownst to him, his loving sister, Twelvetrees, has been the source of his rise: she has accorded her sexual favors to Miljan to advance her brother's dream. When he discovers his sister's sacrifice, Morris seeks out Miljan with murder on his mind. Twelvetrees reaches the perfidious promoter before he does, and she kills the rotter. Morris makes a reciprocal sacrifice, rearranging the evidence so that it points to him, and then contributing to his conviction for murder by a jury of his peers. Mitchell recovers from his paralysis to walk the last mile with his death-sentenced son; we know not whether Mitchell and his family know of the sacrifices of the siblings.

d, Kurt Neumann, w, William Anthony McGuire, Jack O'Donnell, Scott Pembroke (based on a story by McGuire); ph, Charles Stumar; ed, Phil Cahn.

Crime/Drama (PR:C MPAA:NR)

KING IN NEW YORK, A½** (1957, Brit.) 105m Attica/Archway bw

Charles Chaplin *(King Shadhov)*, Dawn Addams *(Ann Kay)*, Oliver Johnston *(The Ambassador)*, Maxine Audley *(Queen Irene)*, Harry Green *(Lawyer Green)*, Phil Brown *(Headmaster)*, John McLaren *(Macabee Senior)*, Allan Gifford *(School Superintendent)*, Shani Wallace, Jay Nichols *(Night Club Vocalists)*, Michael Chaplin *(Rupert Macabee)*, John Ingram *(Mr. Cromwell)*, Sidney James *(Mr. Johnson)*, Jerry Desmonde *(Prime Minister)*, Robert Arden *(Lift Boy)*, Lauri Lupina-Lane, George Truzzi *(Comedy Act)*.

This little satire which, as usual, was an all-Chaplin production, just barely comes off and is really Chaplin's answer to those who were accusing him of being a Communist. He is a king who has lost his tiny kingdom of Estrovia after a peasant revolt. He and wife Audley move to New York where, though penniless, they are swarmed over by status-seeking title-lovers who become instant benefactors. Addams, an advertising executive, pays Chaplin a lot of money to endorse her terrible food products but the deal goes flat when he chokes on one of the items while before a TV camera. He is persuaded to have his face lifted but then goes through agony in a nightclub when trying to suppress laughter as a performing comedian so his stitches won't burst. Everywhere Chaplin goes he is assaulted by the modern world of the 1950s—rock 'n' roll, TV, and, worst of all, rampant, witchhunting McCarthyism. He befriends a little runaway boy whose parents have been accused by the House Un-American Activities Committee (the same group that had earlier denounced Chaplin as a Communist sympathizer) as being unpatriotic in their refusal to testify. Chaplin helps the boy out and also the parents who later admit that they refused to testify so they could remain private. Only the master comedian's brilliant little touches, his great timing, and that special perspective of his that saw humor in everything, even the humorless, keeps this one from sinking altogether. The film was not well-received, lost money, and caused Chaplin, like the hero of this film, to beat a hasty retreat back to Europe and permanent exile.

p,d&w, Charles Chaplin; ph, Georges Perinal; m, Chaplin; ed, Spencer Reeves.

Comedy/Drama Cas. (PR:A MPAA:NR)

KING IN SHADOW***

(1961, Ger.) 78m Bavaria Filmkunst/Exclusive International Films c (HERRSCHER OHNE KRONE)

O. W. Fischer *(Friedrich Struensee)*, Horst Buchholz *(King Christian)*, Odile Versois *(Queen Mathilde)*, Gunther Hadank *(State Minister)*, Fritz Tillmann *(Count Rantzau)*, Elisabeth Flickenschildt *(Queen Juliane)*, Siegfried Lowitz *(Chamberlain Goldberg)*, Ingeborg Schoner *(Gertrud von Eyben)*, Wilfried-Jan Heyn *(Baron Enevied Brandt)*, Helmut Lohner *(Count Holck, Chamberlain)*, Gerhard Ritter *(Dr. Berger)*, Peter Esser *(Court Chaplain Muenter)*, Horst Gnekow *(Gen. Reventlau)*.

Yet another tale of a melancholy Dane, the 19-year-old king, Buchholz, whom queenly stepmother Flickenschildt hopes to depose and replace with her natural son. In a plot resembling that of SUDDENLY, LAST SUMMER, released two years previously, the wicked queen mother enlists the aid of brain specialist Fischer, relying on him to diagnose the young king's depression as debilitating, rendering the latter unfit to swing a sceptre. Fischer, unswayed by the rewards implicit in her importunities, remains true to the ethic of his calling: his harried highness is sane. Fischer brings to the young king's regime a new regimen, that of psychotherapy, and the much-maligned monarch casts off his cloak of melancholy and reaches reconciliation with his alienated English wife, Versois. Fischer finds fortune in the royal transformation, being rewarded with the appointment of Prime Minister, chief confidant to his princely patient. Alas, the once-humble healer, now powerful beyond his wildest pre-Freudian dreams, is smitten with the Briton, and she with him. Unable to conceal their concupiscience within the crowded confines of the castle, their love affair is soon discovered, becoming common knowledge to the courtiers and attendants. Reluctantly, Buchholz condemns the lovers to death, at the urging of those who once sought to depose him. Fischer, protesting her innocence, dissembles to save his sweetheart Versois. She is exiled to England; the good doctor goes to his doom. As the bells knell his passing, Buchholz breaks up, slipping into madness. A somber psychological story, set in the late 18th century, based on historical occurrences. Well acted and directed, with fine color filming and excellent interiors.

p, Georg Richter; d, Harald Braun; w, Odo Krohmann, Gerhard Menzel, Braun (English version, Nina Maguire, William De Lane Lea, based on the novel *Der Favorit der Konigen* by Robert Neumann); ph, Goran Strindberg (Agfacolor); m, Werner Eisbrenner; ed, Hilwa von Boro; art d, Walter Haag.

History/Drama (PR:A MPAA:NR)

KING KELLY OF THE U.S.A* (1934) 64m MON bw

Guy Robertson *(Kelly)*, Irene Ware *(Tania)*, Edgar Kennedy *(Happy)*, Franklin Pangborn *(Brockton)*, Joyce Compton *(Maxine)*, Ferdinand Gottschalk *(King)*, William Von Brincken *(Stranger)*, Otis Harlan *(Minister)*.

A tired, static semi-musical which could only come up with a couple of negligible tunes. The plot is equally throwaway, with Robertson on board a transatlantic liner and in love with a princess. Nothing to write home about.

p, Trem Carr, George Bertholon; d, Leonard Fields; w, Fields, David Silverstein (based on a story by Bertholon, Howard Higgins); ph, Robert Planck; ed, Jack Ogilvie; m/l, Bernie Grossman, Joe Sanders.

Romance (PR:A MPAA:NR)

KING KONG***** (1933) 100m RKO bw

Fay Wray *(Ann Darrow)*, Robert Armstrong *(Carl Denham)*, Bruce Cabot *(John Driscoll)*, Frank Reicher *(Capt. Englehorn)*, Sam Hardy *(Charles Weston)*, Noble Johnson *(Native Chief)*, Steve Clemento *(Witch King)*, James Flavin *(2nd Mate Briggs)*, Victor Wong *(Charley)*, Paul Porcasi *(Socrates)*, Russ Powell *(Dock Watchman)*, Ethan Laidlaw, Blackie Whiteford, Dick Curtis, Charles Sullivan, Harry Tenbrook, Gil Perkins *(Sailors)*, Vera Lewis, Leroy Mason *(Theatre Patrons)*, Frank

Mills, Lynton Brent *(Reporters)*, Jim Thorpe *(Native Dancer)*, George MacQuarrie *(Police Captain)*, Madame Sul-te-wan *(Handmaiden)*, Etta MacDaniel *(Native Woman)*, Ray Turner *(Native)*, Dorothy Gulliver *(Girl)*, Carlotta Monti *(Girl)*, Barney Capehart, Bob Galloway, Eric Wood, Dusty Mitchell, Russ Rogers *(Pilots)*, Reginald Barlow *(Engineer)*, Merian C. Cooper *(Flight Commander)*, Ernest B. Schoedsack *(Chief Observer)*.

One of the greatest adventure films ever made, KING KONG has been one of a handful of films that have become an enduring icon of American popular culture and justly praised as a true motion picture classic. The film's lasting popularity is staggering. Since its initial release in 1933, KING KONG has seen major re-release in 1938, 1942, 1946, 1952, 1956 and continues to be a world-wide favorite today on television and revival movie house showings. Its influence cannot be overstated, for the film has inspired dozens of imitators, the Japanese giant-monster craze, and a ridiculously overblown remake in 1976. Its story is simple, yet pure genius. Though tampered with by RKO studios upon its re-release in 1938 (scenes were cut), the following synopsis will detail the original, uncut version which has been thankfully restored to revival theaters and video tape. The film opens with a shot of Manhattan from the Hoboken Docks. It is 1932. Hardy, a well-attired show biz agent, approaches a huge ship named the "Venture." He meets the night watchman and asks, "Is this the moving picture ship?" The response is affirmative and Hardy is led aboard by Cabot, the ship's first mate. Inside Capt. Reicher's cabin we meet Armstrong, a fast-talking Hollywood showman who is known far and wide for his stunning nature films which have been shot in exotic locations throughout the world under the most harrowing of circumstances. Armstrong has brought along large amounts of ammunition and a case of gas grenades for his latest adventure. When Hardy enters the scene, the anxious Armstrong immediately asks if the agent has found an actress for his new movie. Hardy hasn't and explains to Armstrong that no self-respecting actress would commit herself to a long sea voyage on a ship full of roughnecks without knowing where she was going or what she was to do when she got there. Armstrong appreciates this dilemma, but insists that the destination must remain a secret. Frustrated, Armstrong heads off to find a woman for his movie himself. In Manhattan, the movie producer searches the Depression-era bread lines and women's flophouses for the "right" face. Pausing at a street vendor's grocery, Armstrong spots a young woman, Wray, about to be dragged off by the proprietor for filching an apple. Feeling sorry for the obviously starving waif, Armstrong pays a dollar for the apple. Upset and malnourished, Wray swoons, but is caught by Armstrong before she can fall. For the first time Armstrong can see her face and it immediately hits him that this is the girl he's been looking for. Armstrong takes Wray to a coffee shop and after feeding her, explains who he is and what he wants. After assuring her there's to be no "funny stuff," Armstrong convinces Wray to agree to go on the voyage. The next morning the "Venture" is under way. Armstrong has given only the vaguest instructions to Capt. Reicher and the crew as to their destination, promising to reveal all when they arrive at a specific location. Wray's presence on board causes a bit of a stir, especially for Cabot, who thinks women on long voyages are bad luck. However, as the voyage progresses, Wray and Cabot begin to warm to each other. At length the ship steams to a point in the middle of the Indian Ocean. Armstrong then produces a map drawn by a Norwegian skipper that shows the location of Skull Island. Though Reicher protests that there are no islands in these waters, Armstrong explains that the tiny island is populated by natives that have built a huge wall around their encampment. The wall keeps out something they fear and worship known only as "Kong" and, if it exists, he intends to photograph it. Soon after, Armstrong shoots a screen test with Wray while Cabot and Reicher watch from the bridge. With Wray dressed in a flowing white gown, the movie producer asks his star to pretend she sees something huge, something horrible. "It's horrible but you can't look away . . . You're helpless . . . If only you could scream . . . Cover your eyes and scream, Ann, scream for your life!" Wray lets out a frightful scream that sends chills down Cabot's spine. "What does he think she's really gonna see?" he asks warily. The next day the "Venture" approaches Skull Island through an eerie fog. The low rumble of tribal drums can be heard, as the ship anchors and Armstrong takes a small party ashore accompanied by Wray and his camera. As they approach the native village the crew can hear the word "Kong" being chanted. Hiding in the brush, the adventurers witness an elaborate native ceremony wherein a young girl adorned with flowers is put on an altar while half a dozen dancers dressed in ape skins parade around her. Standing at the top of a long flight of ancient stone stairs that lead to two huge doors is Johnson, the tribal chief. Armstrong drags his camera into the open and tries to get a shot of the bizarre scene, but Johnson spots the curious white men and halts the ceremony. The chief walks slowly down the stone steps and, followed by his whole tribe, confronts the strangers. Capt. Reicher is able to speak their language and explains that they have come in peace. Clemento, the witch doctor, insists that the whites must be killed for interrupting the ceremony, but Johnson is fascinated by the blonde Wray and offers to buy her. Armstrong refuses and the crew slowly backs up to the beach and returns to the ship. That night, a shy Cabot confesses that he has fallen in love with Wray, and she reciprocates his feelings. Cabot is called to the bridge for a meeting with the captain, and while he is gone the witch doctor and his men silently board the ship and kidnap Wray. During the struggle one of the natives loses a bracelet and its discovery by the ship's cook, Wong, sounds the alarm. Armstrong and the crew arm themselves and take off back to the island to rescue Wray. By the time they arrive on the island, the natives have opened the magnificent gate that leads to the jungle and have strapped Wray to a stone altar. The natives then quickly close the gate and push the huge wooden bolt closed. The tribe then gathers at the top of the wall, with the chief standing before a giant gong in the center. The chanting natives are told to be silent and the gong is rung several times. From a distance the sounds of trees being snapped and a loud growl is heard. As Wray struggles to free herself, Kong, a giant ape, emerges from the jungle and stands before the altar. The huge ape's face looks with approval upon this new offering and he grabs the screaming Wray from the altar and carries her off into the jungle. The ship's crew arrives just as Kong wanders away, with Cabot getting one horrified eyeful of the giant gorilla. Ignoring the natives, Armstrong and the brave crew of the "Venture" open the gates and race after Kong and his "bride." Following Kong's huge footprints, the men slowly make their way through the jungle. Coming upon a clearing, the men are amazed to spy a giant prehistoric dinosaur in the distance. The stegosaurus (a huge dinosaur with a small head and heavy bony plates and sharp spines on its backbone) sees the men and charges. The huge beast is met with a volley of rifle fire and a gas bomb. The weapons seem to do the trick and the monster falls over on its side. The men are overconfident, however, and as they approach the prone beast it suddenly bolts upright and begins lashing its deadly spiked tail at them. Armstrong remains calm and fires one final bullet into the beast's brain, killing it. The men then follow Kong to the edge of a swamp. The gorilla easily wades through the water, but the men are forced to build rafts to traverse its expanse. While crossing the foggy swamp, the head and neck of another colossal dinosaur rises out of the water unseen by the crew. The beast disappears under the water only to rise again before the rafts. The men panic and scream at the sight, the beast once again disappears beneath the swamp. Suddenly the rafts are overturned by the monster and as the terrified men splash to shore, several of their number are devoured by the beast. The survivors run onto shore and through the jungle in a desperate effort to escape the monster. The dinosaur, too, comes ashore, revealing itself to be a brontosaurus (a long, slender neck, a small head, and a thick, tapering tail). One unfortunate crew member is left behind and climbs a tree to hide. The brontosaurus easily plucks the man from the tree with his teeth and devours him. Meanwhile, Kong crosses a log bridge that stretches over a deep chasm. Noticing his pursuers, Kong places Wray high in the crook of a dead tree and goes back to the bridge to do battle. Cabot manages to cross the bridge and take cover in a small cave on the side of the cliff. Armstrong never makes it across the bridge, for Kong lifts the huge log and begins shaking it free of the remaining sailors. The men lose their grip on the log and plunge headlong to their deaths below. Only one man remains on the log and Kong drops the bridge into the ravine, killing him as well. Having seen Cabot escape, Kong reaches over the side to grab him but is met with the sharp sting of a knife. The giant gorilla quickly brings his pricked hand up and examines it curiously. While Kong looks at his wound, a giant lizard begins climbing toward the cave up a vine, but Cabot spots the creature and cuts the vine letting the creature drop into the chasm. Kong tries once again to grab at Cabot, but is met with the same sharp sting. This deadly game of hide and seek is interrupted by the scream of Wray. Kong immediately abandons Cabot and rushes off to see what the trouble is. Into the jungle has wandered a vicious Tyrannosaurus Rex (the king of the dinosaurs), even larger than Kong. The two huge creatures enter into a titanic battle. During the fight, the dead tree Wray was placed in is knocked over, sending the terrified woman falling to the ground. Pinned beneath the felled tree, Wray sits and helplessly watches the creatures fight for their lives. Kong finally manages to pull the giant lizard's jaws apart, kiilling it. He then frees Wray and continues on his journey. Back at the gorge, Armstrong calls to Cabot on the other side. Cabot decides to push on, while Armstrong goes back to the ship for reinforcements. Kong makes it to his lair, a cave atop Skull Mountain, the highest peak on the island. Even the giant beast's home is fraught with danger, as he is forced to do battle with a huge snake-like reptile which tries to eat Wray. Wrapping its long body around Kong's neck, the creature nearly strangles the gorilla, but Kong disengages himself and whips the monster against the rocks, killing it. The exhausted Wray faints during the episode, and Kong brings the girl to the ledge of Skull Mountain. There the giant ape sits down with his blonde sacrifice and examines her beauty. Curious, Kong pulls off the girl's dress and inspects the items. The gorilla strokes the tiny woman with his finger and sniffs her scent. Meanwhile, Cabot has caught up to the beast and accidently knocks over a boulder. Kong leaves Wray to investigate the loud crash and while he's gone a giant winged Pterodactyl spies Wray and tries to snatch her. Wray screams in horror and Kong comes to her rescue, killing the prehistoric reptile. During the battle, Cabot manages to reach Wray and they attempt to climb down off the cliff on a vine. After dispatching the Pterodactyl over the side, Kong notices the escape and begins pulling on the vine, bringing the couple back up the mountain. Seeing no choice, Cabot and Wray let go of the vine and fall hundreds of feet into the lake below. The pair survive and run through the dangerous jungle, back to the native encampment. It is nightfall when they return and the exhausted couple are incredulous when they hear that Armstrong is determined to capture Kong. Before anyone can dissuade him from this insane idea, an angry Kong arrives at the gate. Assisted by the natives, the men try to hold the huge gate closed, but Kong breaks through and destroys the native village while searching for Wray. The crew runs to the beach with Kong in hot pursuit, and though it seems they are trapped by the giant gorilla, Armstrong throws one of his powerful gas bombs at the beast. The noxious fumes knock Kong out and he collapses, helpless for the first time in his life. An inspired Armstrong orders the men to build a huge raft to float the animal back to civilization. "He's always been king of his world . . . ," declares Armstrong, " . . . but we'll teach him fear. Why, the whole world will pay to see this! . . . In a few months it'll be up in lights: 'Kong, the Eighth Wonder of the World!" Fulfilling Armstrong's prophecy we see a neon sign with the exact phrase stationed over the biggest theater in New York. An excited and curious opening night crowd pushes their way to their seats inside the huge auditorium. One man makes a crack about the steep $20 ticket price and declares that the show better be good. Backstage, a nervous Wray and Cabot, who are to be married the next day, stand and wait for their entrance. Armstrong walks on stage and introduces Kong. The curtains rise to reveal the huge gorilla chained to a giant steel platform. The normally blase New York audience is awestruck at the sight of the beast. Armstrong then introduces Cabot and Wray, explaining their part in the adventure. He then invites the members of the press to take pictures of the couple. The unusually docile Kong suddenly springs to life, scared by the pops and blinding glare of the flashbulbs. "Stop! . . . " Armstrong yells to the reporters, . . . "He thinks you're harming the girl!" The scoop-crazy press ignores the warning and Kong retaliates by easily freeing himself. The audience panics and races for the exits, trampling anyone unfortunate enough to tarry. Armstrong, Cabot, and Wray manage to escape into the alley as Kong breaks down the wall and spots them entering a hotel. After killing a few passersby, the giant ape climbs up the side of the hotel, peering into rooms in search of Wray. Kong spies a young woman asleep on a bed. He smashes the window and grabs the woman, only to discover it isn't Wray. Irritated, Kong simply drops the woman to her death and continues his search. At last Kong finds Wray in one of the rooms and recaptures her. Cabot and Armstrong give chase as Kong attacks an elevated train, tearing up a section of tracks. The trainman is shocked to see the head and arm of the giant ape emerge from the middle of the tracks. The train is derailed and Kong smashes the cars with his mighty fists. Kong then arrives at the base of the Empire State Building, the world's tallest man-made structure. Possibly because it reminds him of his lair on Skull Mountain, Kong scales the building with Wray in hand. By morning Kong has reached the dirigible mooring mast on the top of the Empire State Building and roars in defiance of the puny humans below. By this time, however, the humans have dispatched a squadron of Navy biplanes armed with machine guns to shoot the huge beast down. Sensing the danger, Kong places Wray safely on the ledge and swats at the noisy planes that spit round after round of lead into his huge body. Wave after wave of aircraft spray Kong with bullets. The giant beast manages to send one plane spinning into the side of the building where it explodes and crashes to the ground below. Dying, Kong picks up Wray for one last time and looks at her sadly. He places her back on the ledge and touches her gently. Another plane dives at Kong and fires a final burst into the animal's throat (the death blow was dealt by none other than producer-directors Cooper and Schoedsack, who played the pilots in the plane). Kong grasps at the wound and his fingers slowly let go of the mooring mast. The giant ape falls from his perch and tumbles thousands of feet to the street below. Cabot rushes to the roof and embraces the terrified Wray. Below, the police have cordoned off the area around the dead ape's huge body. Armstrong pushes through the crowd and looks sadly at the fallen monster. A police captain observes that it was the planes that finally got the ape. Armstrong shakes his head and states "Oh, no. It wasn't the airplanes. It was Beauty killed the Beast." The story of the making of KING KONG is almost as amazing as the film itself. While the inspiration and driving force behind the creation can be laid at the doorstep of co-producer-director Merian C. Cooper, the film is a testament to the Hollywood studio system and could not have been made without the creative participation of dozens of skilled craftsmen. Cooper and his partner, Ernest B. Schoedsack, had made quite a reputation for themselves with their exciting nature documentaries GRASS and CHANG, which were shot on location in Africa and Southeast Asia. While on location in Africa shooting wild animal footage for their first dramatic film, THE FOUR FEATHERS, Cooper became fascinated by wild gorillas. Letting his imagination run rampant, Cooper envisioned a tale which told of a giant, super-intelligent gorilla fighting to the death with a huge Komodo lizard. Taking his idea a step further, he wondered what such a beast would do if placed in modern-day Manhattan. For the climax the gorilla could climb the newly built Empire State Building where it would be shot down by a squadron of airplanes. Cooper originally saw the film made with live gorillas and Komodo lizards which would then be made to look like giants through trick photography. Meanwhile, special effects genius Willis O'Brien was hard at work trying to top his 1925 silent dinosaurs epic, THE LOST WORLD. His idea, entitled "Creation," was optioned by RKO-Radio and complex preproduction was begun. Surprisingly similar to Cooper's giant gorilla idea, "Creation" saw a group of modern-day explorers finding a lost land of dinosaurs hidden in the jungles of South America. Unfortunately, the project required expensive and time consuming tests and the budget-strapped executives at RKO pulled the plug on O'Brien's epic. In 1931, Paramount's boy-wonder, David O. Selznick, was made vice-president of production at RKO. Being a friend of Cooper's, Selznick convinced the rugged producer to join him at the helm. Cooper came to New York, and among the projects-in-production screened was test footage of "Creation." While agreeing that the project had become too expensive, Cooper immediately knew that O'Brien and his assistants could make his giant gorilla story a reality. Cooper obtained permission from Selznick to shoot a test reel and the giant ape project was now known as Production 601. After deciding on a suitable design for the ape, O'Brien and his monster-maker, Marcel Delgado, went to work. Delgado built a fully articulated 18-inch skeleton, called an armature, from aluminum alloy. He then built muscles on the skeleton by using a combination of rubber and sponge. This was covered with skillfully fitted rabbit's fur and King Kong was born. The other beasts were built in a similar fashion. Cooper then turned his attention to the script and snared famed British mystery author Edgar Wallace, who had just arrived in Hollywood after accepting a lucrative contract from RKO. After a visit to O'Brien's workshop to see what exactly Cooper had in mind, Wallace prepared to begin work on what was now known as "The Beast." Soon after, on February 10, 1932, Wallace died of pneunomia. According to Cooper, he hadn't written a word, but would receive screen credit anyway. The job of scriptwriting was given to James Creelman and Schoedsack's wife, Ruth Rose, who made the Carl Denham character in the image of her husband and his partner. Now dubbed "The Eighth Wonder," studio executives were treated to test footage of the effects. O'Brien employed a variety of tricks for KING KONG. He brought the animals to life with stop-motion animation. Simply stated, stop-motion entails moving the armature slightly, exposing one frame of film, then moving the armature again, exposing another frame of film and so on, until a motion is completed. The process takes great skill and patience, for sound film is projected at 24 frames per second, so an afternoon of tedious and complicated work (several animated figures moving at the same time) could yield *one second* of magic on screen. The 18-inch models are made to appear huge by combining live-action actors into the frame at the proper scale. This is achieved a variety of ways. In some cases (Armstrong and his men walking past the dead stegosaurus) the animation is filmed ahead of time and then rear-projected onto a highly reflective screen that the actors stand in front of. The animation is then rephotographed, losing little image quality, and the actors can react to what they see on their side of the screen which is opposite the projector. Having combined the elements to the proper scale, the scene is then photographed by a camera on the actor's side of the rear-projection screen. This method can be used successfully for medium shots and sequences that require little interaction between man and beast. For the more complicated scenes, stationary and traveling mattes have to be used. For these scenes O'Brien shot his animated creatures with an area of the frame matted off. This means that a portion of the frame is covered and kept from being exposed on film. Then another unit films the live-action actors reacting to what the director tells them to with the animated portion of the frame matted off. Then the two separate pieces of film are fitted together exactly in an optical printer and rephotographed as one (Skull Mountain and other large, stationary objects were also made in miniature or painted on glass and matted into a larger frame). To enhance the effect, tiny human armatures made to scale replace the live actor and are animated when the creatures reach down to actually grab a victim. The log-bridge scene and Kong's battle with the Tyrannosaurus were screened for those RKO executives assembled and the film met with an enthusiastic response. Cooper's giant gorilla project was given the full go-ahead. Meanwhile, Schoedsack had started production of an adventure film based on Richard Connell's popular short story, THE MOST DANGEROUS GAME at an adjoining sound stage. His film starred Joel McCrea as the hero, British actor Leslie Banks as the villain, Fay Wray as the heroine, with Robert Armstrong and Noble Johnson in supporting roles. Cooper took a liking to Wray, Armstrong and Johnson, and decided he wanted them for his film as well. Armstrong was cast as Denham, Wray as Ann, and Johnson as the Native Chief. Both THE MOST DANGEROUS GAME and what was soon to be called KING KONG were shot at the same time on the same massive jungle sets. Even the log bridge appears in both films. Cooper would lie on the sidelines waiting for a break in production of THE MOST DANGEROUS GAME and then snatch Wray, Armstrong, and Johnson away from Schoedsack. The actors were more than a bit confused, with both Cooper and Schoedsack pulling them away, changing their costumes and barking orders as they ran through the jungle. The script for KING KONG had yet to be completed, but Cooper knew that he wanted specific scenes and filmed them as the pages trickled in. Soon romantic lead Cabot was signed after having to prove his physical prowess to Cooper by climbing down a rope connected to the log bridge—it was his first feature film. After weeks of difficult and haphazard shooting, the scriptwriters filled in all the plot holes and principal photography was completed. Now the success of the film was left to the genius of Willis O'Brien. While O'Brien was hard at work on the special effects, THE MOST DANGEROUS GAME was released by RKO. The film opened a full year before KING KONG, because KONG's special effects were so time-consuming. In addition to the 18-inch models and the special stop-motion animation effects, O'Brien and Delgado decided to make full-scale, actual size portions of Kong's body. A massive mechanical head-and-shoulders bust of Kong was made to be used in closeups where the gorilla is seen chewing on helpless humans. Three men could sit inside the giant head and manipulate Kong's eyes, lips, nose, brows, and mouth by using a variety of levers and compressed air devices. Also made in full scale were one giant hand and one giant foot. The hand is seen frequently in closeups of Wray being held by Kong. The foot was used in only one scene when Kong squashes a native into the dirt. When O'Brien and his team finished the special effects photography, the film was turned over to RKO's sound department where Murray Spivak created a chilling variety of roars, growls, chirps, and screeches for O'Brien's creatures by recording actual animal sounds at various speeds and then playing them backwards. These were only a small portion of the sound effects created, for everything from waterfalls to gunshots were skillfully timed with the visuals for optimum dramatic effect. After sound effects, it was musical composer Max Steiner's turn to work his special brand of magic. KING KONG was one of the very first films to have a completely original musical score specifically written for the screen. Before KING KONG most film scores were derived from classical works that had been re-orchestrated to suit whatever film they were to be used in. For KING KONG, Steiner created a wholly original score and synchronized his music to the action on screen. One of the most memorable music and visual moments comes when the Native Chief walks slowly down the long flight of stone steps, accompanied by Steiner's music—a note for each step the man takes. Steiner's score was enormously influential throughout the film community and its value to the overall effect of KING KONG cannot be overstated. In the end, KING KONG cost RKO $672,000, nearly $300,000 over its original budget. MGM offered to buy the film from the financially ailing RKO for $400,000 over the cost, but the studio heads wisely refused and released KING KONG themselves. Following a massive publicity campaign, Cooper and Schoedsack's masterpiece opened in New York in 1933. The only film ever to play both Radio City Music Hall and the RKO Roxy theaters simultaneously, KING KONG was met with tremendous critical and popular response. Audiences were amazed by O'Brien's masterful effects and thrilled to Creelman and Rose's well-paced, tightly constructed screenplay that knew how to build suspense and deliver action. Most patrons and critics were dumbfounded as to how the amazing events on screen were executed. A *Variety* reviewer apparently thought Kong was a man in suit and wrote, "The errors arrive when mechanical figures are obviously used in place of the *ape impersonator*." Though several former stuntmen and even an article published by *Screen Book* magazine claimed that most of the effects were done by a man in an ape suit, no such cheap trickery *was ever used*. Audiences could not have warmed up to a man in a hairy suit (as Dino De Laurentiis discovered in his rank 1976 remake) playing Kong. Only O'Brien's skillfull animating could have brought such a response. O'Brien endowed his creation with a distinct, expressive personality wholly its own. Of course Kong was a fearful monster who killed and could destroy entire cities if given a chance, but he had desires, a temper, needs, fears, and could feel emotions that audiences to this day identify with. No man in an ape suit could convey such a complex variety of emotions—only a fine actor, or a master in the art of stop-motion animation. On its initial release, at the height of the Great Depression, KING KONG grossed $1,761,000 and single handedly saved the studio that produced it from bankruptcy. Unfortunately, RKO had little respect for its savior. In 1938, the studio decided to rerelease its classic, but took several steps to tone it down. Cut were the scenes of Kong chewing and crushing human beings. Gone was the scene where a curious Kong strips Fay Wray of her clothing. In fact, RKO made the new release prints several shades darker in an effort to tone down the incredible detail of O'Brien's work (dying dinosaurs bleeding, etc.) that made everything seem so realistic. This travesty practically obliterated the steps O'Brien took to ensure his creations would *live* on screen. Generations of movie-goers and television watchers were denied the true, uncut brilliance of Cooper, Schoedsack, and O'Brien's vision until the late 1960s when restored prints of KING KONG began to circulate once again. Since its release in 1933, KING KONG has become totally assimilated into American popular culture. Kong has become a beloved American institution and is a very real figure to children and adults alike throughout the world. People visit the Empire State Building not to marvel at its amazing architecture, but to see where King Kong took his love and met his doom. The gift shop at the Empire State Building is full of King Kong souvenirs, as if the fabled incident actually occurred. In 1983, the 50th birthday of KING KONG, New York City attempted to place a life-sized inflatable Kong on the top of the Empire State Building for all the world to see. It was an ambitious, expensive, and amazing project that unfortunately ended in defeat due to high-winds, bad weather, and technical problems. Kong remained perched atop his tower only partly inflated. Perhaps only Willis O'Brien could make Kong come back to New York. KING KONG was followed by a sequel, SON OF KONG (1934). It was a low-budget, hurried effort that no one, especially O'Brien, was pleased with. In 1947 Cooper, Schoedsack, and O'Brien tried again with MIGHTY JOE YOUNG, a much more successful effort and quite entertaining, though obviously aimed at younger audiences. A young Ray Harryhausen did most of the animation under O'Brien's supervision and he would soon take the master's place as the preeminent genius of the special effects medium with such films as THE SEVENTH VOYAGE OF SINBAD (1958) and JASON AND THE ARGONAUTS (1963). The Japanese created their own giant monster in the King Kong mold by introducing GODZILLA (1956) to an unsuspecting public. The success of the Japanese giant-monster series is legendary and even included a few manifestations of Kong himself in KING KONG VS. GODZILLA (1963) and KING KONG ESCAPES (1968) (he was, of course, played by a man in a suit). In 1976, Italian super-producer Dino De Laurentiis spent $20 million on his disastrous version of KING KONG which combined brief shots of a ridiculous looking full-scale mechanical monster with Rick Baker's fairly amazing gorilla suit. Few, if any, of these post-Kong films came close to approaching the epic magnitude of their inspiration. The original KING KONG remains an outstanding achievement in motion picture history and a moving, lasting testament to the human imagination that will endure as long as there is an audience to thrill to its unparalleled mastery of the medium.

p&d, Merian C. Cooper, Ernest B. Schoedsack; w, James Creelman, Ruth Rose (based on a story by Cooper and Edgar Wallace); ph, Edward Linden, Vernon L. Walker, J.O. Taylor; m, Max Steiner; ed, Ted Cheeseman; art d, Carroll Clark, Al Herman, Van Nest Polglase; set d, Thomas Little; spec eff, Willis O'Brien, E.B. Gibson, Marcel Delgado, Fred Reefe, Orville Goldner, Carroll Shepphird, Mario Larrinaga, Byron L. Crabbe.

Adventure/Fantasy **Cas.** **(PR:A-C MPAA:NR)**

KING KONG* 1/2 (1976) 134m PAR c

Jeff Bridges *(Jack Prescott)*, Charles Grodin *(Fred Wilson)*, Jessica Lange *(Dwan)*, John Randolph *(Capt. Ross)*, Rene Auberjonois *(Bagley)*, Julius Harris *(Boan)*, Jack O'Halloran *(Joe Perko)*, Dennis Fimple *(Sunfish)*, Ed Lauter *(Carnahan)*, John Agar *(City Official)*, Jorge Moreno *(Garcia)*, Mario Gallo *(Timmons)*, John Lone *(Chinese Cook)*, Garry Halberg *(Army General)*, Keny Long *(Ape Masked Man in Dance)*, Sid Conrad *(Petrox Chairman)*, George Whiteman *(Army Helicopter Pilot)*, Wayne Heffley *(Air Force Colonel)*, Rick Baker *(King Kong)*.

Without a doubt, Dino De Laurentiis' remake of Merian C. Cooper and Ernest B. Schoedsack's classic is the biggest con job ever pulled on the unsuspecting American public. Having spent somewhere in the vicinity of $24 million on his epic, De Laurentiis told the world that his Kong was a fabulously expensive and technically amazing, full-sized mechanical ape that stood 40 feet tall, when in reality the majority of Kong's scenes were played by a man in a monkey suit! The Italian producer fought hard to bring his version of the 1933 classic to the screen and was even forced to give Universal's rival production, "The Legend of King Kong," a percentage of his profits to persuade them to abandon their version which was being produced simultaneously. The updated script was fairly clever and De Laurentiis managed to assemble a tolerable cast of performers. Grodin, an official of Petrox oil, discovers an unknown island in the Pacific that is rumored to be brimming with oil. Seeking to secure the island's wealth of crude for his company, Grodin assembles a crew and sets sail. While out at sea the crew discovers Bridges, a fairly hip paleontologist who has stowed away. When confronted, Bridges informs Grodin that his expedition is actually headed for the legendary "Skull Island," a land where time has stopped and prehistoric monsters still roam. Grodin scoffs at the idea, but when Bridges tells of the tribe of vicious natives who worship a giant beast called "Kong," he begins to pay attention. Soon after, the crew spots a beautiful blonde woman in the water clinging to some debris (Lang, in her first screen appearance—a role she's still trying to live down). The girl is an aspiring actress and was shipwrecked when the yacht she was on sunk. A flirtatious relationship between Lange and Bridges begins. The ship arrives at Skull Island and the crew, accompanied by Bridges and Lange, go exploring. They stumble across a tribal ritual where a native girl is sacrificed to Kong. The native chief sees the blonde woman and insists she be used as the next sacrifice. Lange is taken back to the ship in a hurry. That night, Lange is kidnapped by the natives and spirited back to the island. The crew discovers she is missing and gives chase, but they arrive too late, for Lange has been taken away by a huge gorilla (played by special makeup genius Rick Baker—despite what De Laurentiis claims). The crew follows the monster into the dense jungle. After the obligatory homage to the log bridge scene of the 1933 film, most of the crew are killed, leaving it up to the clever Bridges to figure out a way to subdue the beast. Meanwhile, Lange and Kong have developed an odd relationship. After her initial fear and anger (she actually calls him a "male chauvinist pig ape"), Lange warms to the beast and begins to feel protective of him. After several idyllic scenes of tiny woman and big ape enjoying each other's company (Kong playfully strips Lange revealing her breasts for the audience; he also holds her under a waterfall so she can wash the jungle mud off herself), Bridges finally manages to distract the huge simian and make off with Lange. An angry Kong chases the pair and runs into a trap that had been set on the beach. Having subdued the monster, Grodin decides to bring him to New York as part of Petrox Oil's new commercial campaign. Kong is placed (somehow) inside a giant oil tanker and shipped back to the Big Apple. During the voyage, Lange grows more and more upset over the ape's treatment. In New York a massive outdoor rally is held to present Kong to the public. A giant gas pump is wheeled into the auditorium and is slowly lifted up to reveal the huge ape trapped in a strange metal contraption with a crown on his head (this is the *only* time in the film that De Laurentiis' stiff, unrealistic, 40-foot robot and the contrast between it and Baker's amazing monkey suit is embarrassing). Lange, in a stunning evening gown, has reluctantly agreed to participate in the show. The photographer's frenzy of flashbulbs sets Kong off and he breaks out of his cage and goes wild (once again played by Baker). Grodin is killed during the rampage, leaving Lange and Bridges to high tail it out of there. After wrecking much of lower Manhattan, Kong catches up with Lange and takes her up to the World Trade Center for a lovely view of Battery Park and the Statue of Liberty. New York mayor Agar (king of several classic, cheap sci-fi films of the 1950s) orders the beast to be shot off the tower. Assault helicopters are called in and Kong's bullet-riddled body goes splat on the sidewalk below. Pushing her way through thousand's of curious New Yorkers (supposedly 45,000 showed up on the night of shooting), Lange stands next to the corpse of her big friend and screams with rage at the injustice of it all. Believe it or not, De Laurentiis' debacle garnered amazingly favorable reviews from incredibly short-sighted critics who seemed anxious to denigrate the 1933 version and praise the modernness and technical advances of the remake. Considering that throughout 99 percent of the film Kong was a man in an ape costume (albeit a very good costume), the special effects are simple and not particularly well executed. The only impressive advancements technically are the fully articulated hydraulic giant ape hands and arms that were used when Lange was being held by Kong. The 40-foot robot Kong was a failure that never worked properly, looked ridiculous, and is downright laughable. De Laurentiis, however, claimed that the robot was used during the entire film and Baker was only around for closeups of Kong's face. This blatant lie was fostered in a paperback book about the making of the film which made it seem as though Baker was some nominally talented young actor who was chosen to play Kong on the basis of his height! Though some mention of Baker's special makeup experience is mentioned in passing (he had built monsters for such low-budget films as SCHLOCK, OCTAMAN, and IT'S ALIVE, and would soon go on to do the marvelous effects for AN AMERICAN WEREWOLF IN LONDON) his participation in the creation of Kong was almost totally ignored. Baker, who actually *played* Kong in the vast majority of scenes, giving the ape a personality and life, was not even given screen credit for his work. When KING KONG won a special Oscar for its special effects, stop-motion animator-special effects master Jim Danforth disgustedly resigned from the Motion Picture Academy in protest. Technical arguments notwithstanding, De Laurentiis was determined to make his film a hit so he saturated every newspaper, TV station, magazine, billboard, and toy store with his Kong's image in a desperate effort to spur interest in his massive expenditure (he even had a candy bar and alcoholic drink named after Kong). The film opened in 2,200 theaters across America and was Paramount's major Christmas release. Incredibly, the film was a hit and turned a slim profit. De Laurentiis announced a sequel entitled "King Kong Goes to Africa." Luckily it has yet to be made.

p, Dino De Laurentiis; d, John Guillermin; w, Lorenzo Semple, Jr. (based on a screenplay by James Creelman, Ruth Rose, from a concept by Merian C. Cooper, Edgar Wallace); ph, Richard H. Kline (Panavision, Metrocolor); m, John Barry; ed, Ralph E. Winters; prod d, Mario Chiari, Dale Hennesy; art d, Archie J. Bacon, David A. Constable, Robert Gundlach; set d, John Franco, Jr.; cos, Moss Mabry, Anthea Sylbert, Arny Lipin, Fern Weber; spec eff, Frank Van Der Meer, Barry Nolan, Harold E. Wellman; stunts, Bill Couch; mechanical Kong crew, Carlo Rambaldi, Glen Robinson, Don Chandler, John True, Eddie Surkin; Kong costume, Rick Baker, Carlo Rambaldi.

Adventure/Fantasy **Cas.** **(PR:C-O MPAA:PG)**

KING KONG ESCAPES* 1/2

(1968, Jap.) Rankin-Bass-Toho/UNIV 98m c (KING KONG NO GYAKUSHU; KINGU KONGO NO GYAKUSHU; AKA: THE REVENGE OF KING KONG; KING KONG'S COUNTERATTACK)

Rhodes Reason *(Cmdr. Nelson)*, Mie Hama *(Madame Piranha)*, Linda Miller *(Susan)*, Akira Takarada *(Lt. Jiro Nomura)*, Eisei Amamoto *(Dr. Who)*.

Reason is leading an expedition in the deep jungle when he and his comrades are suddenly attacked by a giant dinosaur. Who should come along to save the day but King Kong! (Actually, it's an actor in a gorilla suit, but any port in a storm.) The mighty ape falls in love with expedition member Miller but the inter-species romance is busted by Amamoto as a mad scientist about to take over the world. He must have gotten an "A" in "Taking Over the World 101" at mad scientist college, for he has all the right tools to do it. Unable to get the real Kong, he creates the robotic Mechni-Kong. When this breaks down, he kidnaps the real Kong and the expedition crew as well. Kong gets to fight Gorosaurus (Godzilla may have been working on another film) and eventually has it out with his metallic clone high atop the Tokyo Tower. It's all as campy as can be and a great time waster if you've already trimmed your toenails. Rankin, Jr. (the film's American-version producer, who made a name for himself with American Saturday morning television cartoons) directed additional footage with the American actors that was tacked on for U.S. distribution. The original director was Inoshiro Honda, the man who created GODZILLA.

p, Tomoyuki Tanaka, Arthur Rankin, Jr.; d, Inoshiro Honda, Rankin, Jr.; w, William J. Keenan, Kaoru Mabuchi; ph, Hajime Koizumi (Tohoscope, Eastmancolor); m, Akira Ifukube; art d, Takeo Kita; spec eff, Eiji Tsuburaya.

Science Fiction/Horror **(PR:C MPAA:G)**

KING KONG VERSUS GODZILLA* 1/2

(1963, Jap.) 91m Toho/UNIV c (KING KONG TAI GODZILLA; KING KONG TAI GOJIRA)

Michael Keith *(Eric Carter)*, James Yagi *(Yataka Omura)*, Tadao Takashima *(O. Sakurai)*, Mie Hama *(Fumiko Sakurai)*, Kenji Sahara *(Kazuo Fujita)*, Yu Fujiki *(Kinzaburo Furue)*, Ichiro Arishima *(Mr. Tako)*, Harry Holcombe *(Dr. Arnold Johnson)*, Tatsuo Matsumura *(Dr. Markino)*, Akihiko Hirata *(Premier Shigezawa)*, Eiko Wakabayshi *(Tamiye)*, Senkichi Omura *(Konno)*.

The two giants of the screen finally have a chance to meet, and you can bet it's not for tea. This film started in Hollywood with the idea of giving Kong a new playmate. The first choice was Frankenstein's monster, then a creature called the "Ginko." Someone got the bright idea of teaming the giant ape with Prometheus and the treatment was bounced around some more. Eventually it bounced all the way to Japan, where famed GODZILLA filmmaker Inoshiro Honda fixed up his own creation with the American simian. The plot is nothing less than great camp. Kong has to fight off a giant octopus and befriends some fishermen. Enter Godzilla. He comes out of an iceberg, makes nasty with a nuclear submarine, and takes off for Japan. The two outsize critters fight it out over Mount Fuji, and their battle sets off an earthquake. The pair are tossed into the sea, with Kong the only one to emerge. Godzilla remained undersea until his next film, GODZILLA MEETS MOTHRA, in 1963. There's some semblance of a human story as well, with Kong being kidnapped from the fishermen who worship him as a deity. The American release had additional English-language footage edited into the film. Amazingly enough, this film inspired a re-make in 1976.

p, Tomoyuki Tanaka, John Beck; d, Inoshiro Honda, Thomas Montgomery; w, Shinichi Sekizawa, Paul Mason, Bruce Howard (based on a story by Willis O'Brien); ph, Hajime Koizimi (Tohoscope, Eastmancolor); m, Akira Ifukube; ed, Peter Zinner; md, Zinner; sp eff, Eiji Tsuburaya.

Science Fiction/Horror **(PR:C MPAA:NR)**

KING KONG'S COUNTERATTACK

(SEE: KING KONG ESCAPES, 1968, Jap.)

KING LEAR*** (1971, Brit./Den.) 137m Filmways-Athena-Laterna/Altura bw

Paul Scofield *(King Lear)*, Irene Worth *(Goneril)*, Jack MacGowran *(Fool)*, Alan Webb *(Duke of Gloucester)*, Cyril Cusack *(Duke of Albany)*, Patrick Magee *(Duke of Cornwall)*, Robert Lloyd *(Edgar)*, Tom Fleming *(Earl of Kent)*, Susan Engel *(Regan)*, Annelise Gabold *(Cordelia)*, Ian Hogg *(Edmund)*, Barry Stanton *(Oswald)*, Soren Elung Jensen *(Duke of Burgundy)*.

Placing all the arguments aside on whether or not Shakespeare's "King Lear" is adaptable, this picture is a superbly acted, exceptionally photographed, emotionally tragic powerhouse. To condemn it solely because a play is not meant to be filmed is to overlook Scofield's gripping performance as the title king, a man who offers his kingdom to his three daughters—Worth, Engel, and Gabold. Worth and Engel butter up to their father, deceiving him with their affection, while Gabold refuses to take part in their insincerity. She is promptly cast away by Scofield who doesn't realize until it is too late that he drove the wedge in the wrong place. He soon realizes how rotten his other two daughters really are and attempts to find his only faithful daughter. A battle ensues between the two sides of the family, and in the tragic end all are killed—Engel is murdered by Worth, Worth smashes her head on a rock, Gabold is hung—and Scofield's heart gives way. Surprisingly, this is the first sound version of "King Lear" to be adapted for the screen, although a CBS "Omnibus" version had Orson Welles as Lear. Other versions include a 1909 one-reeler, a 1916 silent version, and 1985's RAN, an ambitious epic undertaking by the 75-year-old Japanese director, Akira Kurosawa.

p, Michael Birkett; d&w, Peter Brook (based on William Shakespeare's play "King Lear"); ph, Henning Kristiansen; ed, Kasper Schyberg; prod d, Georges Wakhevitch; cos, Adele Angard; makeup, Ken Lintott, Ruth Mahler.

Drama **(PR:C MPAA:GP)**

KING MURDER, THE** (1932) 67m CHES bw

Conway Tearle, Natalie Moorhead, Marceline Day, Dorothy Revier, Don Alvarado, Huntley Gordon, Robert Frazer, Maurice Black, Rose Dione.

High-society sleuth Tearle is called on to help solve the mystery of the demise of a dangerous damsel—a gorgeous extortionist—which may be murder, although no weapon has been found. Confusion is compounded when a corpse-watching cop also quits his earthly abode, again without an apparent instrument of elimination. When the truth dawns on Tearle that the death-dealing device is a poisoned needle, his ever-helpful friend—the murdering blackmail victim—attempts to palm the poisoned pricker. Himself punctured in the process, he is taken by the toxin and expires, hoist with his own petard. Low-budget lensing apparently based on an actual murder case.

d, Richard Thorpe; w, Charles Reed Jones; ph, M. A. Anderson.

Murder Mystery **(PR:0 MPAA:NR)**

KING, MURRAY**

(1969) 86m Amram Nowak-Leeam Lowin/EYR-Iconographic bw/c

Murray Ramsey King *(King, Murray)*, Laura Kaye *(1st Girl on Trip)*, Jackie Morris *(2nd Girl on Trip)*, Gloria Riegger *(Socialite)*, Addie Pezzotta *(Girl in Shower)*, George Koski *(Masseur)*, Barbara Linden, Nora Lord *(Other Girls)*, Amram Nowak, David Hoffman, Jonathan Gordon *(Themselves)*.

Strange piece features real-life insurance salesman King taking real-life filmmaker Nowak along on a weekend to Las Vegas. It's billed as a "fictional documentary" but it's impossible to figure out what's real and what's not. King is a foul-mouthed, obnoxious lout, but also a terrific salesman. He's fascinating in his repulsiveness. In one sequence he takes a shower with a buxom young lady, a scene he argues that the filmmakers should let him do. He also describes an orgy he attended, then claims to have made up the whole thing. The film ends with a dream sequence involving a big-busted woman on a beach. The technical qualities are poor, with switches back and forth from color to black-and-white film stock. The dream sequence was shot in Super 8, with the rest of the film done in 16mm, all blown up to 35mm. Bizarre stuff, but Brechtians might want to take a look.

p, Amram Nowak; d, Jonathan Gordon, David Hoffman; ph, Hoffman.

Fictionalized Documentary **(PR:O MPAA:NR)**

KING OEDIPUS (SEE: OEDIPUS REX, 1957, Can.)

KING OF AFRICA (SEE: ONE STEP TO HELL, 1969)

KING OF ALCATRAZ* 1/2** (1938) 55m PAR bw

Gail Patrick *(Dale Borden)*, Lloyd Nolan *(Raymond Grayson)*, Harry Carey *(Captain Glennan)*, J. Carrol Naish *(Steve Murkil)*, Robert Preston *(Robert MacArthur)*, Anthony Quinn *(Lou Gedney)*, Richard Stanley [Dennis Morgan] *(First Mate Rogers)*, Virginia Dabney *(Bonnie Larkin)*, Nora Cecil *(Nora Kane)*, Emory Parnell *(Olaf)*, Dorothy Howe *(Dixie)*, John Hart *(First Radio Operator)*, Phillip Warren *(Second Radio Operator)*, Porter Hall *(Mathew Talbot)*, Richard Denning *(Harry Vay)*, Tom Tyler *(Gus Banshek)*, Konstantin Shayne *(Murok)*, Harry Worth *(Pietr Mozda)*, Edward [Eddie] Marr *(Dave Carter)*, Clay Clement *(Fred Cateny)*, Monte Blue *(Officer)*, Gustav von Seyffertitz *(Bill Lustig)*, Paul Fix *("Nails" Miller)*, John Harmon *(Silver)*, Jack Knoche *(Ed Vierick)*, Jack Norton *(First Officer)*, Stanley Blystone *(Second Officer)*, George Anderson *(Third Officer)*, Eddie Acuff *(Steward)*, Pierre Watkin *(Ship Doctor)*, Buddy Roosevelt *(Purser)*, Charles McAvoy *(Quartermaster)*, Ruth Rogers *(Girl)*.

This nifty little film has been given a misleading title, for it has nothing to do with the famed prison at all. It starts off as a light comedy and takes a dramatic turn that really takes the audience for a ride. Nolan and Preston (in his screen debut) are two radio operators aboard different ships, both owned by Hall. They are continually trying to outdo each other until Hall gets tired of their games and puts them on the same boat. Patrick is a nurse on board the luxury liner, who formerly dated the two but won't have a thing to do with them now. The three discover that a group of gangsters is aboard ship and the "kindly old lady" who recently boarded is none other than gang leader Naish, a recent escapee from Alcatraz. The mobsters hijack the ship and order its captain, Carey, to head for Central America. Nolan is shot and wounded while trying to stop the gang and Patrick is allowed to receive radio instructions on how to remove the bullet. The crew stops the mobsters during the delicate operation but not before Preston is killed. Patrick completes the task and ends up with Nolan. The tricky switch from comedy to tense drama is masterfully done by Robert Florey's direction, changing the tone dramatically but without the slightest hint of unbelievability. Running slightly less than an hour, the film maintains a nice pace and the acting is terrific. Nolan and Preston are great as a team.

p, William C. Thomas; d, Robert Florey; w, Irving Reis, ph, Harry Fischbeck; m, Boris Morros; ed, Eda Warren; art d, Hans Dreier, Earl Hedrick.

Comedy/Drama **(PR:C MPAA:NR)**

KING OF BURLESQUE*** (1936) 85m FOX bw

Warner Baxter *(Kerry Bolton)*, Alice Faye *(Pat Doran)*, Jack Oakie *(Joe Cooney)*, Arline Judge *(Connie)*, Mona Barrie *(Rosalind Cleve)*, Gregory Ratoff *(Kolpolpeck)*, Dixie Dunbar *(Marie)*, Fats Waller *(Ben)*, Kenny Baker *(Arthur)*, Charles Quigley *(Stanley Drake)*, Keye Luke *(Wong)*, Gareth Joplin *(The Bootblack)*, Paxton Sisters *(Specialty Dancers)*, Andrew Tombes *(Slattery)*, Shirley Deane *(Phyllis Sears)*, Herbert Ashley *(Jake)*, Harry "Zoop" Welch *(Spud La Rue)*, Claudia Coleman *(Belle Weaver)*, Maurice Cass *(Men's Tailor)*, Torben Meyer *(Valet)*, Ellen E. Lowe *(Miss Meredith)*, Jerry Mandy *(Frankie)*, Shaw and Lee *(Henkle and Keefe)*, Herbert Mundin *(English Impresario)*, Nick Long, Jr. *(Anthony Lamb)*, Sarah Jane Fulks [Jane Wyman] *(Girl)*.

Yet another backstage musical but with a bright script and some nice tunes, KING OF BURLESQUE is about Baxter, the Ziegfield of the G-string, who wants to get into Broadway-type shows because he feels he's ready to step up in class. Faye is his dance director and number one singer and Oakie is Baxter's sidekick. Both of them think Baxter should stick with what he knows. Faye is in love with Baxter, but he regards her as an employee. The three of them, together with Judge, Oakie's girl friend, go to a furnishings auction at the Mansion of Barrie, a formerly rich woman who has fallen upon hard times. Baxter is bombastic toward Barrie and she refuses to sell him the item (a ship's model) that he craves. When Barrie needs money, she goes to Baxter's office and relents, offering to sell him the model. Baxter becomes interested in her, they have a courtship that lasts about a minute, and get married. Faye is thunderstruck and leaves Baxter to go to London where she soon becomes a smashing success. Baxter and Barrie honeymoon in Europe and, upon their return, she asks Baxter to hire Quigley for his new show, as he has been her long-time "protege." Baxter presents a classy and first-rate show, but it doesn't have the raucousness that made Baxter's burlesque shows into hits and fails almost immediately. Now that he's down at the heels, Barrie divorces Baxter and he finds consolation making the rounds of the tackier watering holes of the city. Faye returns with a lot of money and she and Oakie engage Ratoff to pose as a millionaire eager to back Baxter's latest efforts. Faye knows that Baxter would never knowingly take money from her so she has to use that ploy. It is successful and Baxter opens a Billy

Rose's Diamond Horseshoe-type theatre-restaurant. Faye agrees to star in the new show and Waller, the elevator man, also joins the cast, as do Dunbar, Long, and Baker, formerly the telephone operator, office boy and a failed Hollywood dancer, in that order. Need we add that the show is a hit? Baxter is, once again, in business and he realizes that Faye is the cause of it all. They are happily united at the fade as Oakie and Judge, already an item, look on and smile. It was remade in 1943 as HELLO, FRISCO, HELLO with John Payne in the Baxter role and Faye and Oakie reprising. Baxter had already played this producer (or one just like him) in 42ND STREET, so he had no trouble in the part. Fats Waller does one of his rare feature appearances but sings none of his own songs, more's the pity. Songs include: "I'm Shooting High," "Whose Big Baby Are You?" "I've Got My Fingers Crossed," "Spreading Rhythm Around" (Jimmy McHugh, Ted Koehler—sung by Alice Faye), "Lovely Lady" (McHugh, Koehler), "I Love To Ride The Horses" (Jack Yellen, Lew Pollack).

p, Darryl F. Zanuck; d, Sidney Lanfield; w, Gene Markey, Harry Tugend, James Seymour (based on a story by Vina Delmar); ph, Peverell Marley; ed, Ralph Dietrich; md, Victor Baravalle; art d, Hans Peter; set d, Thomas Little; cos, Gwen Wakeling; ch, Sammy Lee.

Musical Comedy **(PR:A MPAA:NR)**

KING OF CHINATOWN 1/2** (1939) 56m Stuart Walker/PAR bw

Anna May Wong *(Dr. Mary Ling)*, Akim Tamiroff *(Frank Baturin)*, J. Carrol Naish *(The Professor)*, Sidney Toler *(Dr. Chang Ling)*, Phillip Ahn *(Robert "Bob" Li)*, Anthony Quinn *(Mike Gordon)*, Bernadene Hayes *(Dolly Warren)*, Roscoe Karns *(Rep. Harrigan)*, Ray Mayer *(Potatoes)*, Richard Denning *(Interne)*, Archie Twitchell [Michael Branden] *(Second Interne)*, Edward [Eddie] Marr *(Bert)*, George Anderson *(Detective)*, Charles B. Wood *(1st Gangster)*, George Magrill *(2nd Gangster)*, Charles Trowbridge *(Dr. Jones)*, Lily King *(Chinese Woman)*, Wong Chong *(Chinese Man)*, Chester Gan *(Mr. Foo)*, Pat West *(Fight Announcer)*, Guy Usher *(Investigator)*, Pierre Watkin *(District Attorney Phillips)*, Sam Ash *(Barber)*, Jimmy Vaughn *(Slugger Grady)*, Alex Pollard *(Heath)*.

A quintessential gangster film for Paramount featuring their three biggest bad men on the lot: Naish, Tamiroff, and Quinn. Tamiroff is a mob boss in Chinatown. He's convinced henchman Quinn has doublecrossed him by having one of his fighters lose a heavily bet on match. He sends Naish to show Quinn a proper response, but instead Quinn talks Gordon into conspiring to kill Tamiroff and then splitting his territories fifty-fifty. They wound the boss and he is nursed back to health by doctor Wong. She is the daughter of Tamiroff's old rival Tolex, but discovers that her father really wasn't murdered by this gangster, as she had thought for so long. Meanwhile, the two confederates wage a bloody battle in dividing the spoils and then hear that their former employer is still alive. They decide to see him off properly this time during his recovery at home. Tamiroff has fallen in love with Wong and proposes to her, but she tells him she wants to do relief work for the raging war in China. He is grateful for her care and gives her $50,000 for the cause. Enter would-be killer Naish. He exclaims that he and Quinn are the killers of Wong's father and are now going to be rid of Tamiroff as well. He dies, but not as expected, for he succumbs to a heart attack as Naish points the gun. Neat and quick, the film moves at a nice pace in its not-quite-hour run. Despite some bad editing early in the film, this is an interesting thriller, with a great cast.

p, Harold Hurley; d, Nick Grinde; w, Lillie Hayward, Irving Reis (based on a story by Herbert Biberman); ph, Leo Tover; ed, Eda Warren; md, Boris Morros; art d, Hans Dreier, Robert Odell.

Gangster **(PR:O MPAA:NR)**

KING OF COMEDY, THE**** (1983) 108m FOX c

Robert De Niro *(Rupert Pupkin)*, Jerry Lewis *(Jerry Langford)*, Diahnne Abbott *(Rita)*, Sandra Bernhard *(Masha)*, Ed Herlihy *(Himself)*, Lou Brown *(Band Leader)*, Whitey Ryan *(Stage Door Guard)*, Doc Lawless *(Chauffeur)*, Marta Heflin *(Young Girl)*, Katherine Wallach, Charle Kaleina *(Autograph Seekers)*, Richard Baratz *(Caricaturist)*, Catherine Scorsese *(Rupert's mom)*, Cathy Scorsese *(Dolores)*, Chuck L. Low *(Man in Chinese Restaurant)*, Liza Minnelli *(Herself)*, Leslie Levinson *(Roberta Posner)*, Margo Winkler *(Receptionist)*, Tony Boschetti *(Mr. Gangemi)*, Shelley Hack *(Cathy Long)*, Matt Russo *(Cabbie)*, Thelma Lee *(Woman in Phone Booth)*, Dr. Joyce Brothers *(Herself)*, George Kapp *(Mystery Guest)*, Victor Borge *(Himself)*, Ralph Monaco *(Raymond Wirtz)*, Rob-Jamere Wess *(Security Guard No. 1)*, Kim Chan *(Jonno)*, Audrey Dummett *(Cook)*, June Prud'Homme *(Audrey)*, Fred De Cordova *(Bert Thomas)*, Martin Scorsese *(TV Director)*, Tony Randall *(Himself)*, Loretta Tupper, Peter Potulski, Vinnie Gonzales *(Fans)*, Alan Potashnick, Michael Kolba, Robert Colston, Ramon Rodrigues, Chuck Coop, Sel Vitella *(Men at Telephone)*, Mick Jones, Joe Strummer, Paul Simmion, Kosmo Vynil, Ellen Foley, Pearl Harbour, Gaby Salter, Jerry Baxter-Worman, Dom Letts *(Street Scum)*, Edgar J. Scherick *(Wilson Crockett)*, Thomas M. Tolan *(Gerrity)*, Ray Dittrich *(Giardello)*, Richard Dioguardi *(Capt. Burk)*, Jay Julien *(Langford's Lawyer)*, Harry Ufland *(Agent)*, Scotty Block *(Crockett's Secretary)*, Jim Lyness *(Ticket Taker)*, Jeff David *(Announcer)*, Bill Minkin *(McCabe)*, Diane Rachell *(Mrs. McCabe)*, Jimmy Raitt *(Stage Manager)*, Charles Scorsese, Mardik Martin *(Men at Bar))*, Matt Russo *(Cabbie)*, Dennis Mulligan, Tony Devon, Peter Fain, Michael F. Stodden, Jerry Murphy *(Plainclothesmen)*, William Jorgensen, Marvin Scott, Chuck Stevens, William Littauer *(Voice of Newsmen)*, Jeff David *(Announcer)*.

De Niro, one of America's greatest actors, is compelling, funny, tragic, idiotic, clever, and clumsy as a no-talent street *wunderkind* who creates a national TV career through sheer persistence and a scheme that the Lavender Hill Mob would dismiss as assinine. As Rupert Pupkin, a Times Square hangabout, he dogs celebrities for autographs but imagines himself the greatest comic in the world, patterning himself after funnyman talk show host Lewis (who leaves no doubt that he is doing Johnny Carson). It is De Niro's blinding ambition to appear on Lewis' show and become an overnight sensation. He ingratiates himself to Lewis by fending off autograph seekers so that Lewis can get into his car, jumping in with him. He tells Lewis he is a comedian who has worked out a terrific routine and Lewis tells him to bring some of his material to his office. He does, but a stuffy blonde producer turns down De Niro, telling him to get some club dates and build up the act first. De Niro won't take no for an answer, sitting in the network waiting room until realizing Lewis won't see him. He later invades the offices and is physically thrown out. Still, he deludes himself into believing that he and Lewis are good friends and he takes his black girl friend, Abbott, to see Lewis at his country estate where Lewis insults him and kicks him out. De Niro now resorts to drastic measures. He and another groupie, Bernhard, an ugly, obnoxious status-seeker with money, abduct Lewis and hold him for a strange ransom—De Niro must be allowed to do his show before he is released. He goes on TV, does the show, then, under police escort, goes to the bar where Abbott is working and they watch the show before De Niro is led away to jail. When released, however, De Niro has become the international star he always imagined himself to be, authoring his best-selling autobiography and having his own network TV talk show. De Niro carries the entire film and does it beautifully, becoming the strange offbeat character most normal people see coming down the street and instantly avoid. More than a comedy, this is a tragedy about talentless, lonely people whose ambitions are as pedestrian and vacuous as the people they admire.

p, Arnon Milchan; d, Martin Scorsese; w, Paul D. Zimmerman; ph, Fred Schuler (DeLuxe Color); m, Robbie Robertson; ed, Thelma Schoonmaker; md, Robertson; prod d, Boris Leven; art d, Edward Pisoni, Lawrence Miller; set d, George DeJitta, Sr., Daniel Robert; cos, Richard Bruno.

Comedy/Drama **Cas.** **(PR:C MPAA:PG)**

KING OF DODGE CITY** (1941) 63m COL bw

Bill Elliott *(Wild Bill Hickok)*, Tex Ritter *(Tex Rawlings)*, Judith Linden *(Janice Blair)*, Dub Taylor *(Cannonball)*, Guy Usher *(Morgan King)*, Rick Anderson *(Judge Lynch)*, Kenneth Harlan *(Jeff Carruthers)*, Pierce Lyden *(Reynolds)*, Francis Walker *(Carney)*, Harrison Greene *(Stephen Kimball)*, Jack Rockwell *(Martin)*, Edmund Cobb, George Chesebro, Steve Clark, Tris Coffin, Jack Ingram, Tex Cooper, Russ Powell, Frosty Royce, Ed Coxen, Lee Prather, Jay Lawrence, Ned Glass.

The first of eight films that co-starred Elliott and Ritter has the two of them working separately to clean up a post-Civil-War Kansas town. Elliott is the famed cowboy Hickok while Ritter is the new sheriff in town. Eventually their paths cross and they unite to fight off some bad guys in a standard gun-fightin' finish. Along the way Ritter sings three songs. This film operates under what the B-western producers called "the Drake formula." It was named after Oliver Drake, who wrote many of the THREE MESQUITEERS films and always involved the multiple heroes uniting to solve a problem they'd been working on separately. It's simplistic but made for many a glorious Saturday afternoon in the 1940s. This was the last of ten films that comic sidekick Taylor was to make with Elliott.

p, Leon Barsha; d, Lambert Hillyer; w, Gerald Geraghty; ph, Benjamin Kline; ed, Jerome Thoms.

Western **(PR:A MPAA:NR)**

KING OF GAMBLERS**

(1937) 77m PAR bw (AKA: CZAR OF THE SLOT MACHINES)

Claire Trevor *(Dixie)*, Lloyd Nolan *(Jim)*, Akim Tamiroff *(Steve Kalkas)*, Larry "Buster" Crabbe *(Eddie)*, Helen Burgess *(Jackie Nolan)*, Porter Hall *(George Kramer)*, Harvey Stephens *(J. G. Temple)*, Barlowe Borland *(Mr. Parker)*, Purnell Pratt *(Strohm)*, Colin Tapley *(Joe)*, Paul Fix *(Charlie)*, Cecil Cunningham *(Big Edna)*, Robert Gleckler *(Ed Murkil)*, Nick Lukats *(Taxi Driver)*, Fay Holden *(Nurse)*, John Patterson *(Freddie)*, Evelyn Brent *(Cora)*, Estelle Etterre *(Laura)*, Priscilla Lawson *(Grace)*, Louise Brooks *(Joyce Beaton)*, Harry Worth *(Chris)*, Connie Tom *(Tika)*, Richard Terry *(Solly)*, Alphonse Martell *(Headwaiter)*, Natalie Moorhead *(Woman at Table)*, Ethel Clayton, Gloria Williams *(Women)*, Gertrude Messinger *(Telephone Operator)*, Frank Puglia *(Barber)*, Russell Hicks *(Man at Temple's Table)*.

Nightclub singer Trevor gets involved with the sinister slot machine "czar" Tamiroff who is guilty of killing off her roommate Burgess. Newsman Nolan can't be fooled, however, and he follows the clues which point to Tamiroff as the murderer. Director Florey does all he can with the feeble script but comes up with nothing more than mediocrity. Buried in the hefty cast is silent screen beauty Louise Brooks (PANDORA'S BOX, 1929) who had to endure just one more Poverty Row western before retiring from films in 1938. She kept a low profile in New York until her death in 1985.

d, Robert Florey; w, Doris Anderson (based on a story by Tiffany Thayer); ph, Harry Fischbeck; ed, Harvey Johnstone; md, Boris Morros; art d, Hans Dreier, Robert Odell; m/l, "Hate To Talk About Myself," "I'm Feeling High," Ralph Rainger, Richard A. Whiting, Leo Robin, Burton Lane, Ralph Freed (sung by Trevor).

Crime **(PR:A MPAA:NR)**

KING OF HEARTS** (1936, Brit.) 82m BUT bw (AKA: LITTLE GEL)

Will Fyffe *(Bill Saunders)*, Gwenllian Gill *(May Saunders)*, Richard Dolman *(Jack Ponsonby)*, Amy Veness *(Mrs. Ponsonby)*, O.B. Clarence *(Mr. Ponsonby)*, Jock McKay *(George)*, Googie Withers *(Elaine)*, Margaret Davidge *(Mrs. Saunders)*, Ronald Shiner *(Tomkins)*, Patrick Ludlow *(Reggie)*, Paul Neville, Sybil Grove, Trevor Watkins, Frakson, Java's Tzigane Band, Constance, Lilyan and Malo, Horace Sheldon's Orchestra.

When a well-to-do young man falls in love with a waitress, his mother does everything in her power to bust up the blooming romance. She arranges for the girl to be fired from her job, then attempts to bribe her father in order to get him into her plans. But the lowly dock worker is unimpressed by the woman's riches, and helps the young people finally make their way to the altar. This is routine, predictable class comedy, with a few songs tossed in for good measure. However, Fyffe, as the dockworker father, gives this some needed life with his good comic touches.

p,d&w, Oswald Mitchell, Walter Tennyson (based on the play "The Corduroy Diplomat" by Matthew Boulton); ph, Desmond Dickinson.

Musical **(PR:AA MPAA:NR)**

KING OF HEARTS1/2**

(1967, Fr./Ital.) 100m Artistes Associes-Cinematografica Montoro-Fildebroc/Lopert-UA c (LE ROI DE COEUR; TUTTI PAZZIO MENO LO).

Alan Bates *(Pvt. Charles Plumpick)*, Pierre Brasseur *(Gen. Geranium)*, Jean-Claude Brialy *(The Duke—Le Duc de Trefle)*, Genevieve Bujold *(Coquelicot)*, Adolfo Celi *(Col. Alexander MacBibenbrook)*, Micheline Presle *(Mme. Eglantine)*, Francoise Christophe *(The Duchess)*, Julien Guiomar *(Bishop Daisy—Monseigneur Marguerite)*, Michel Serrault *(The Crazy Barber)*, Marc Dudicourt *(Lt. Hamburger)*, Daniel Boulanger *(Col. Helmut von Krack)*, Jacques Balutin *(Mac Fish)*, Pierre Palau *(Alberic)*, Madeleine Clervanne *(Brunehaut)*, Jean Sylvain *(Beadle)*, Jacky Blanchot *(Sailor)*, Louis Jojot *(Gontrand)*, Pier Paolo Capponi.

A wildly popular cult film among college students both in the U.S. and abroad, KING OF HEARTS is remembered affectionately by anyone who saw it then, in the midst of the Viet Nam war, but it is sadly dated and uses a cudgel to make its points where a feather would do just as well. Based on a supposedly true story, KING OF HEARTS takes place in the waning days of the WWI. The Huns are retreating from Marville, a French town they'd occupied, and a bomb has been planted that will explode at the witching hour. One of the townspeople finds out about it and alerts the populace, who immediately flee. Celi, the British colonel, is advancing on the town with his men and selects Bates, a gentle French-speaking Scotsman given to poetry, to enter and defuse the bomb, if he can find it. A few Huns remain in Marville and chase after Bates until he hides himself behind the walls of the local insane asylum, where the mental cases become convinced that he is "The King of Hearts." The Germans leave and Bates has an accident that knocks him briefly unconscious. When he awakens, the inmates have left the asylum and returned to what they did before being committed, so the town looks as though it's functioning. Bates' assignment is to find the bomb, but the loonies aren't interested in anything beyond crowning him king. The little village is an odd sight, with wild animals, people in strange clothes, etc. . . And when some Germans return, the townspeople steal their tanks and gear, and send the Krauts packing. Now the Scots arrive and are equally shocked by the goings-on; they race back to Celi where they breathlessly tell him what they've seen. Bates, the king, has begun to care about these simple-minded citizens and knows that a bomb is due to blow, so he attempts to lead them, Pied-Piper-style, out of town, but their mental conditions are such that they are almost all paranoid and won't depart. In short order, Bates has fallen in love with Bujold, a virgin who has been assigned to be his mistress by Presle, the madam of the local brothel. Bates uses his brains to figure that the bomb is in the clock tower, so he scales it and defuses the bomb just before it's due to ka-boom. The inmates thank Bates and decide to celebrate his feat for the next three years. Bates and Bujold are about to get to some serious love-making when Celi arrives with his troops. Celi has no idea that he is being welcomed by a few hundred nuts so he joins in the party and soon is fascinated by Presle. The party goes on all night, and in the morning Bujold is sad to see that Bates must leave, so she and some of her compatriots gag him and tie him up. They all watch from a balcony as the Germans return to the town and the Scots engage them in combat. All of the soldiers on both sides are killed. The regular Marville-ites come back and the inmates walk back into the asylum. Bates is torn between doing his duty as a soldier and the love and affection he'd felt from the patients, so he strips off all his clothes and stands outside the asylum gates until they allow him in. The picture was made in Senlis, France, with a French- speaking cast. The theme that "war is hell" has been seen many times and the secondary theme of "who is really crazy?" is also a hoary one. Many wonderful comic opportunities are missed and the inmates all seem to be the same type of mental case with the only difference being what they wear and what they did before going inside. The picture suffers from being too cute for its own good and what might have been a three-dimensional story is made flat by the dialogue and De Broca's self-conscious direction. Still, with all of that, the outrageousness of the situation is enough to carry the film to a semi-satisfying conclusion and to light a spark in collegians wherever it was shown.

p&d, Philippe de Broca; w, Daniel Boulanger (based on an idea by Maurice Bessy); ph, Pierre L'Homme (Techniscope, DeLuxe Color); m, Georges Delerue; ed, Francoise Javet; art d, Francois de Lamothe; set d, Robert Christides; cos, Jacques Fonteray.

Comedy/Drama **Cas.** **(PR:C MPAA:NR)**

KING OF HOCKEY* (1936) 57m WB bw (GB: KING OF THE ICE RINK)

Dick Purcell *(Gabby Dugan)*, Anna Nagel *(Kathleen O'Rourke)*, Marie Wilson *(Elsie)*, Wayne Morris *(Jumbo Mullins)*, George E. Stone *(Nick Torga)*, Joseph Crehan *(Mike Trotter)*, Gordon Hart *(Dr. Noble)*, Ann Gillis *(Peggy O'Rourke)*, Dora Clement *(Mrs. O'Rourke)*, Guy Usher *(Mr. O'Rourke)*, Garry Owen *(Jitters McCarthy)*, Max Hoffmann, Jr. *(Torchy Myers)*, Andre Beranger *(Evans)*, Frank Faylen *(Swede)*, Frank Bruno *(Loogan)*, Harry Davenport *(Tom McKenna)*.

This brief sports film has Purcell a hockey star who goes blind after being injured by teammate Morris. He has to leave the sport and ends up alone and feeling miserable. But his girl friend, Nagel, and her terminally cute kid sister Gillis manage to get him the money for an operation to restore his sight. In the end, he leads his team to the championship. The hockey footage is fairly good, but you can probably see better on the TV. Stage actor Purcell does well in a most unsympathetic role for his feature film debut. Morris, in the sidekick spot, was working for Warner Bros. for the first time. The buxom blonde Wilson, as Morris' girl friend, does well with the comic relief. The dialog—as is often the case with films of the period—is fast and snappy, outshining the plot.

p, Bryan Foy; d, Noel Smith; w, George Bricker (based on his story "The Shrinking Violet"); ph, L. W. O'Connell; ed, Harold McLernon.

Sports/Drama **(PR:AA MPAA:NR)**

KING OF KINGS*1/2** (1961) 168m MGM c

Jeffrey Hunter *(Jesus Christ)*, Siobhan McKenna *(Mary)*, Hurd Hatfield *(Pontius Pilate)*, Ron Randell *(Lucius, The Centurion)*, Viveca Lindfors *(Claudia)*, Rita Gam *(Herodias)*, Carmen Sevilla *(Mary Magdalene)*, Brigid Bazlen *(Salome)*, Harry Guardino *(Barabbas)*, Rip Torn *(Judas)*, Frank Thring *(Herod Antipas)*, Guy Rolfe *(Caiphas)*, Maurice Marsac *(Nicodemus)*, Gregoire Aslan *(King Herod)*, Royal Dano *(Peter)*, Edric Connor *(Balthazar)*, Robert Ryan *(John The Baptist)*, George Coulouris *(Camel Driver)*, Conrado San Martin *(Gen. Pompey)*, Gerard Tichy *(Joseph)*, Jose Antonio *(Young John)*, Luis Prendes *(Good Thief)*, David Davies *(Burly Man)*, Jose Nieto *(Caspar)*, Ruben Rojo *(Matthew)*, Fernando Sancho *(Madman)*, Michael Wager *(Thomas)*, Felix de Pomes *(Joseph of Arimathea)*, Adriano Rimoldi *(Melchior)*, Barry Keegan *(Bad Thief)*, Rafael Luis Calvo *(Simon of Cyrene)*, Tino Barrero *(Andrew)*, Francisco Moran *(Blind Man)*, Orson Welles *(Narrator)*.

Jeffrey Hunter was a radiant Jesus, all the smaller roles were well cast, the picture was made with the proper reverence, and still it was dull. But so much love and care was put into it that we must set that dullness aside because the filmmakers are hindered, as the whole world knows the story and how it ends. One cannot change the past and so we can only see a depiction based on the familiar writings in the New Testament. BEN HUR and THE TEN COMMANDMENTS and THE SIGN OF THE CROSS and countless other films have been made from the Bible but seldom better than this one. It covers the 33 years from His birth in Bethlehem through the relationship with John and his murder; the 40 days in the desert; the choosing of the Apostles; The Sermon On The Mount, Judas' betrayal at the Passover Seder that was Jesus' Last Supper; the Passion; The Crucifixion; The Resurrection and the Ascension. The spirituality is evident in every scene, although some of the acting was a bit on the emoting side. This was expected to be a huge road show success but it fell far short of the projections. It was filmed in Spain by the Bronston unit that was there during the 1950s and 1960s. Although Ray Bradbury is not noted in the credits, the narration by Orson Welles was supposedly written by him. Ryan was superb as John, but Hatfield, who made his mark in THE PICTURE OF DORIAN GRAY, goes a bit over the top as Pilate. Other outstanding acting work from Dano, Guardino, Lindfors, and Torn. It's an epic, filled with vistas and scope, yet there are enough intimate moments for the audience to realize that these were real people, not just the creations of the scribes who wrote the Bible.

p, Samuel Bronston; d, Nicholas Ray; w, Philip Yordan; ph, Franz F. Planer, Milton Krasner, Manuel Berenguer (Technirama 70, Technicolor); m, Miklos Rozsa; ed, Harold F. Kress, Renee Lichtig; set d&cos, Georges Wakhevitch; spec eff, Alex Weldon, Lee LeBlanc; ch, Betty Utey; makeup, Mario Van Riel, Charles Parker.

Biblical Epic **Cas.** **(PR:AA MPAA:NR)**

KING OF MARVIN GARDENS, THE1/2** (1972) 103m BBS/COL c

Jack Nicholson *(David Staebler)*, Bruce Dern *(Jason Staebler)*, Ellen Burstyn *(Sally)*, Julia Anne Robinson *(Jessica)*, Benjamin "Scatman" Crothers *(Lewis)*, Charles Lavine *(Grandfather)*, Arnold Williams *(Rosko)*, John Ryan *(Surtees)*, Sully Boyar *(Lebowitz)*, Josh Mostel *(Frank)*, William Pabst *(Bidlack)*, Gary Goodrow *(Nervous Man)*, Imogene Bliss *(Magda)*, Ann Thomas *(Bambi)*, Tom Overton *(Spot Operator)*, Maxwell "Sonny" Goldberg *(Sonny)*, Van Kirksey, Tony King *(Messengers)*, Jerry Fujikawa *(Agura)*, Conrad Yama *(Fujito)*, Scott Howard, Henry Foehl *(Auctioneers)*, Frank Hatchett, Wyetta Turner *(Dancers)*.

Alternately dreary and fascinating, THE KING OF MARVIN GARDENS is half of a terrific film, but director Rafelson didn't know which half. After the success of FIVE EASY PIECES, Rafelson (who made his mark and his money producing the TV series "The Monkees") attempted to be as different as he could but his quest for uniqueness is what did him in. Nicholson is a long-winded FM talk jockey on a Philadelphia radio station. Instead of playing records, he waxes on about his brother, Dern, and the things they did as children. He dubs Dern "The King Of Marvin Gardens," which veteran Monopoly players will recall is a yellow box on the board and an actual place in Atlantic City. The character of Nicholson appears to have been drawn from the real-life Jean Shepherd, a midwest radio man and author who worked in New York at WOR and talked every night for five hours, reminiscing about his Indiana life and seldom accepting phone calls or guests or playing records. Nicholson goes back to Atlantic City for a visit. Dern now works for Crothers, who heads a black crime syndicate. This film was shot before the new construction in Atlantic City and the once-proud city is a shambles, rotting away in the depths of winter. Dern is in jail on a "grand theft auto" charge and is released on bail. Nicholson and Dern have a happy reunion and Dern introduces his baby brother to Burstyn, a one-time beauty queen who is fading like the city in which they live, and her stepdaughter, Robinson. Dern has big plans and wants to buy his own island, a small atoll called Tiki near Hawaii, where he can build his own resort, so the two brothers can live in warmth and riches forever. Nicholson easily sees that it's a pipe dream and he can't convince Dern that it's impossible. Nevertheless, he humors him, and the foursome decide to stage an elaborate spoof of the Miss America pageant at the convention center. The quartet dine with some Japanese land salesmen and Nicholson is shocked when he finds out that Dern means to use Crothers' money to buy the island. Realizing that can lead to a dangerous situation, Nicholson visits Crothers, who admits that he framed Dern on the car theft charge and that if Dern doesn't stop representing himself as Crothers' man, he's going to have Dern put away. Crothers knows about Dern's harebrained Hawaiian scheme and means to put a stop to it. Nicholson goes to Dern's residence and cannot dissuade him from leaving for Hawaii. Dern truly believes that he can make the resort plan fly without Crothers. Burstyn is there and has become increasingly annoyed at Dern's neglect of her and what she perceives as his untoward interest in Robinson. Her rage increases until it becomes hysteria. She gets Dern's revolver and shoots him dead! Later, Nicholson brings Dern's body back to Philadelphia and returns to the radio and his interminable memories. Still later, he goes to the home of his grandfather, Lavine, and sees the old man watching home movies of Dern and Nicholson when they were little boys frolicking on the Jersey beach, building sand castles and totally unaware of how their lives would go. It's a touching moment that will affect anyone. Much of the film has been deliberately confused (or so it seems) by Rafelson and Brackman in order to flatten the crease between fantasy and reality. For all its faults, THE KING OF MARVIN GARDENS has some merit and many of the individual scenes linger in the memory. It appeared to be a melange of the 1960s mentality of FIVE EASY PIECES with a 1940s-type plot of irony and surprise. Rafelson decided to go back to that latter era for his remake of THE POSTMAN ALWAYS RINGS TWICE. The weakest part of the film was the repetitious and indulgent dialog credited to Brackman, but one wonders how much of that was in the script and how much Rafelson and his actors improvised. It was a daring attempt at originality but forgot some of the basics of dramaturgy, the most important of which is "if you're going to care about the movie, you have to care about the people." We were not allowed that pleasure.

p&d, Bob Rafelson; w, Jacob Brackman (based on a story by Brackman, Rafelson); ph, Laszlo Kovacs, (Eastmancolor); ed, John F. Link II; art d, Toby Carr Rafelson; cos, Tony Scarano.

Drama **(PR:C-O MPAA:R)**

KING OF PARIS, THE** (1934, Brit.) 75m British and Dominions/UA bw

Cedric Hardwicke *(Max Till)*, Marie Glory *(Maika Tamara)*, Ralph Richardson *(Paul Lebrun)*, Phyllis Monkman *(Gismonde)*, John Deverell *(Bertrand)*, Lydia Sherwood *(Juliette Till)*, Jean Stuart *(Yvonne)*, Joan Maude *(Lea Rossignol)*, O. B. Clarence *(Mayor)*.

Hardwicke stars as a dedicated theatrical impresario, playwright, and actor who lives and breathes theater, priding himself on his talent at turning ordinary women into fine actresses. He falls for Glory, a Russian girl, and cons her into marrying him. She soon falls in love with his friend Richardson, however, and runs out on the marriage. Supposedly based on the career of French playwright Sacha Guitry who had written well over 100 plays and, by the time this film was made, was on his way to a fulfilling film career.

p, Herbert Wilcox; d, Jack Raymond; w, John Drinkwater, W. P. Lipscomb, Paul Gangelin (based on the play "La Voie Lactee" by Alfred Savoir, John Van Druten).

Drama/Romance **(PR:A MPAA:NR)**

KING OF THE ALCATRAZ (SEE: KING OF ALCATRAZ, 1938)

KING OF THE ARENA** (1933) 61m UNIV bw

Ken Maynard *(Firebrand Kenton)*, Lucile Browne *(Mary Hiller)*, John St. Polis *(Governor)*, Bob Kortman *(Bargoff)*, Michael Visaroff *(Baron Petroff)*, James Marcus *(Colonel Hiller)*, Jack Rockwell *(Saunders)*, Frank Rice, Fred MacKaye, Blue Washington, William Steele, Ed Coxen, Robert Walker, Jack Mower, Bobby Nelson, Steve Clemente, Robert Burns, Merrill McCormick, Artie Ortego, Chief Big Tree, Buck Bucko, Jack Kirk, Horace B. Carpenter, Pascale Perry, Bud McClure, Helen Gibson, Lafe McKee, Iron Eyes Cody, "Tarzan" (Horse).

Maynard is a Texas Ranger chasing a bad guy known as "Black Death" because the chemical bullets he shoots turn his victims black. Maynard joins a wild west show that the crook appears to be trailing—a show in which Maynard coincidentally used to perform. He catches up with the crook and chases him into Mexico, but gets him in the end. There are a few neat plot twists away from the normal Maynard western which nearly throw the film into the science-fiction genre. The standard amounts of action, suspense, and gunplay are firmly locked into place. Maynard served as producer.

p, Ken Maynard; d, Alan James; w, James (based on a story by Hal Berger and Ray Bouk); ph, Ted McCord.

Western **(PR:A MPAA:NR)**

KING OF THE BANDITS 1/2** (1948) 65m MON bw

Gilbert Roland *(Cisco Kid)*, Angela Greene *(Alice Mason)*, Chris-Pin Martin *(Pancho)*, Anthony Warde *(Smoke Kirby)*, Laura Treadwell *(Mrs. Mason)*, William Bakewell *(Capt. Mason)*, Rory Mallinson *(Burl)*, Pat Goldin *(Pedro)*, Cathy Carter *(Connie)*, Boyd Irwin *(Col. Wayne)*, Antonio Filauri *(Padre)*, Jasper Palmer *(U.S. Marshal)*, Bill Cabanne *(Orderly)*, Jack O'Shea.

This was Roland's last time as the Kid, but Martin returned after an absence as his sidekick. This time the Mexican Robin Hood is blamed for some stagecoach robberies that have really been the work of Warde disguised as the Cisco Kid. Roland is imprisoned by U.S. Marshals but escapes to capture Wade and clear his own name. It's a standard entry for Monogram's CISCO KID series, but still good fun. Greene holds up nicely as the romantic interest and Roland and Martin are great together. Roland helped with the screenplay. (See CISCO KID series, Index).

p, Jeffrey Bernerd; d, Christy Cabanne; w, Bennett R. Cohen, Gilbert Roland (based on an original story by Cabanne, from characters created by O. Henry); ph, William Sickner; ed, Roy Livingston; md, Edward J. Kay.

Western **(PR:A MPAA:NR)**

KING OF THE BULLWHIP** (1950) 59m Western Adventure/REA bw

Lash LaRue *(Lash LaRue)*, Al St. John *(Fuzzy Q. Jones)*, Jack Holt *(James Kerrigan)*, Tom Neal *(Benson)*, Anne Gwynne *(Jane Kerrigan)*, George J. Lewis *(Rio)*, Michael Whalen *(Henchman)*, Dennis Moore *(Joe Chester)*, Tex Cooper *(Buffalo Bill)*, Hugh Hooker, Jimmie Martin, Roy Butler, Cliff Taylor, Frank Jacquet, Willis Houck.

A routine western, though there are some interesting touches that make this a bit different from most. The film's climactic whip fight between LaRue and Moore is played over the opening credits. LaRue and former Mack Sennett clown St. John are a pair of marshals out to stop an outlaw. Seeing how he uses Lash's favorite weapon, our hero goes undercover, pretending to be the bad guy. He discovers Moore, a corrupt bank clerk, to be the villain stealing gold bullion. This leads to the climactic fight first seen at the film's beginning. Exciting in parts, and less gunplay, as pistols have been traded for leather. Producer Ormond went on to use film climaxes in credits for several films after this.

p&d, Ron Ormond; w, Jack Lewis, Ira Webb; ph, Ernest Miller; ed, Hugh Winn.

Western **Cas.** **(PR:C MPAA:NR)**

KING OF THE CASTLE* 1/2 (1936, Brit.) 69m City/GFD bw

June Clyde *(Marilyn Bean)*, Claude Dampier *(Pullen)*, Billy Milton *(Monty King)*, Cynthia Stock *(Elsie)*, Wally Patch *(Trout)*, Arthur Finn *(Henry Bean)*, Paul Blake *(Sir Percival Trellis)*, H. F. Maltby *(Mr. Crow)*, Mavis Villiers *(Billie)*, Jimmy Godden *(Bailiff)*, Hiram Martin, Quinton McPherson, Cecil Bevan, Johnny Singer.

A lively butler, Dampier, undertakes the comic chore of locating a missing heir. Milton turns out to be the person he is looking for and, with Dampier's help, the chap gets his inheritance. He's as lucky in love as in money, winning the affections of Clyde, his endearing heartthrob.

p, Basil Humphrys; d, Redd Davis; w, George Dewhurst (based on a story by Frank Atkinson).

Comedy **(PR:A MPAA:NR)**

KING OF THE CORAL SEA*
(1956, Aus.) 74m Southern International/AA bw

Chips Rafferty *(Ted King)*, Charles Tingwell *(Peter Merriman)*, Ilma Adey *(Rusty King)*, Rod Taylor *(Jack Janiero)*, Lloyd Berrell *(Yusep)*, Frances Chin Soon *(Serena)*, Reginald Lye *(Grundy)*, Salapata Sagigi.

Smugglers try to bring illegal Asian migrants into Australia via Thursday Island, the main pearling area of Down Under. An unimaginative and unexciting plot doesn't help this film at all, though there is some nice underwater footage. Rafferty, who co-wrote and produced the film, was known to American audiences for his role in DESERT RATS. This was one of Australian stage actor Taylor's two films made in Koalaland before he went to Hollywood and became a major star. The film was released in its native country in 1954.

p, Chips Rafferty; d, Lee Robinson (undersea d, Noel Monkman); w, Rafferty, Robinson; ph, Ross Wood, Keith Loone; m, Wilbur Sampson; ed, Alex Ezard; md, Sampson.

Adventure/Crime **(PR:C MPAA:NR)**

KING OF THE COWBOYS*** (1943) 67m REP bw

Roy Rogers *(Roy)*, Smiley Burnette *(Frog Millhouse)*, Peggy Moran *(Judy Mason)*, Bob Nolan and The Sons of the Pioneers *(Themselves)*, Gerald Mohr *(Maurice)*, Dorothea Kent *(Ruby Smith)*, Lloyd Corrigan *(William Kraly)*, James Bush *(Dave Mason)*, Russell Hicks *(Governor Shuville)*, Irving Bacon *(Deputy Alf Cluckus)*, Stuart Hamblen *(Duke Wilson)*, Emmet Vogan *(Saboteur)*, Eddie Dean *(Tex)*, Forrest Taylor *(Cowhand)*, Dick Wessell *(Hershel)*, Jack Kirk *(Bartender)*, Edward Barle *(Manufacturer)*, Yakima Canutt, Charles King, Jack O'Shea *(Henchmen)*, "Trigger".

Rogers is a rodeo performer-*cum*-government agent who is appointed by Hicks to discover who has been blasting military warehouses filled with the goods needed to win the battle against the Axis powers in WW II. The sabotage appears to be propinquitous with the presence of a traveling tent show. Rogers joins the show and discovers that the saboteurs receive their cryptic instructions through messages coded by the show's spiritualist, transmitted during performances. Mohr, chief aide to governor Hicks, is discovered to be the mastermind behind the Nazi villainy. Star Rogers had recently been the subject of a cover story in the enormously popular *Life* magazine, which accorded him the appelation "King of the Cowboys." Consequently, studio chiefs upped production budgets for Rogers' features following this aptly titled film. The tent-show setting affords ample opportunities for musical numbers from both the star and the Sons of the Pioneers. After crooning a few, Rogers decodes the evil plan and proceeds to the next targeted warehouse. Wounded, he defuses a bomb as his cronies shoot it out with the saboteurs. All ends well, and the Allies win the war. Rogers and the Sons of the Pioneers manage to add a few enjoyable tunes: "I'm An Old Cowhand," "Gay Ranchero," "Roll Along Prairie Moon," and "Red River Valley."

p, Harry Grey; d, Joseph Kane; w, Olive Cooper, J. Benton Cheney (based on an original story by Hal Long); ph, Reggie Lanning; ed, Harry Keller; md, Morton Scott.

Western **Cas.** **(PR:AAA MPAA:NR)**

KING OF THE DAMNED* 1/2 (1936, Brit.) 81m GAU bw

Conrad Veidt *(Convict 83)*, Helen Vinson *(Anna Courvin)*, Noah Beery, Sr. *(Mooche)*, Cecil Ramage *(Ramon Montez)*, Percy Walsh *(Capt. Perez)*, Peter Croft *("Boy" Convict)*, C. M. Hallard *(Commandant Courvin)*, Raymond Lovell *(Captain Torres)*, Gibson Gowland *(Priest)*, Edmund Willard *(The Greek)*, Percy Parsons *(Lumberjack)*, Allan Jeayes *(Dr. Prada)*.

Convicts on an island prison revolt against the cruel administration run by Hallard. Veidt is the convicts' leader and brings the revolt to a successful conclusion. Hallard is killed and Veidt falls in love with Vinson. Hallard secretly managed to get a message out before he died and a warship begins shelling the island. But Vinson pleads for the men and they are given a fair trial. So-so drama is hampered by some confusing miscasting. The characters' names are, for the most part, Spanish, yet Veidt has a German accent and Beery is all-American. Vinson is inept in her role as the love interest, while Veidt, miscast as he is, does a fair job with the material. The battle scenes are handled well.

p, Michael Balcon; d, Walter Forde; w, Charles Bennett, Sidney Gilliat, A. R. Rawlinson (based on a play by John Chancellor); ph, Bernard Knowles; ed, Otto Ludwig.

Adventure/Crime **(PR:C MPAA:NR)**

KING OF THE GAMBLERS* 1/2 (1948) 60m REP bw

Janet Martin *(Jean Lacey)*, William Wright *(Dave Fowler)*, Thurston Hall *("Pop" Morton)*, Stephanie Bachelor *(Elsie Pringle)*, George Meeker *(Bernie Dupal)*, Wally Vernon *(Mike Burns)*, William Henry *(Jerry Muller)*, James Cardwell *("Speed" Lacey)*, Jonathan Hale *(Sam Hyland)*, Selmer Jackson *(Judge)*, Howard J. Negley *(Jordon)*, John Holland *(Symonds)*, George Anderson *(O'Brien)*, Ralph Dunn *(Cassidy)*, John Albright *(Bartender)*.

When a football player threatens to expose a fixed game operation run by a gambler and sports magazine publisher, he is killed and another player is framed for the murder. A crusading D.A., who is also the publisher's stepson, defends the accused man in court and exposes the crooked scheme. Standard stuff with some plot twists that don't ring true. Acting is fair and the direction is spotty, giving some excitement one moment and dull the next.

p, Stephen Auer; d, George Blair; w, Albert DeMond, Bradbury Foote; ph, John MacBurnie; ed, Robert Leeds; art d, Morton Scott.

Sports Drama/Crime **(PR:A MPAA:NR)**

KING OF THE GRIZZLIES** (1970) 93m Disney-Robert Lawrence/BV c

John Yesno *(Moki)*, Chris Wiggins *(Col. Pierson)*, Hugh Webster *(Shorty)*, Jack Van Evera *(Slim)*, Winston Hibler *(Narrator)*, "Big Ted" *(Wahb, the Grizzly Bear)*.

While a child, Yesno adopts an orphaned grizzly cub and nurtures him until he is ready to go off on his own. Years later, while Yesno is working as a ranch hand for Wiggins, the bear returns and frightens some people and he is ordered to capture it. But he cannot take his old friend and the bear goes free. When Yesno and the bear encounter each other in the woods after several years, the grizzly doesn't harm him and Yesno is convinced their destinies are linked. Later the bear reappears at the ranch, causing a stampede. Wiggins tries to kill it, despite Yesno's warnings. When the bear tries to attack the white man the Indian makes a friendship sign and his old friend retreats. Before he leaves, he scratches a mark onto a tree, a sign that he will not return. It's the thinnest of plots tacked onto some really nice nature photography. The story is too corny, even for the worst of the live action Disney films. Hibler, who also produced the film, provides the weak narration. The bear, however, is not bad at all. The kids will probably enjoy it.

p, Winston Hibler; d, Ron Kelly; w, Jack Speirs, Rod Peterson, Norman Wright (based on the book *The Biography of a Grizzly* by Ernest Thompson Seton); ph, Reginald Morris (Technicolor); m, Buddy Baker; ed, Gregg McLaughlin; set d, Wilf Culley; m/l, "The Campfire Is Home," Speirs.

Nature/Adventure Drama **(PR:AAA MPAA:G)**

KING OF THE GYPSIES* 1/2** (1978) 112m DD/PAR c

Sterling Hayden *(King Zharko Stepanowicz)*, Shelley Winters *(Queen Rachel)*, Susan Sarandon *(Rose)*, Brooke Shields *(Tita Stepanowicz)*, Annette O'Toole *(Sharon)*, Eric Roberts *(Dave Stepanowicz)*, Judd Hirsch *(Groffo)*, Annie Potts *(Persa)*, Michael V. Gazzo *(Spiro Georgio)*, Antonia Rey *(Danitza Georgio)*, Stephen Mendillo *(Adolf Mikel)*, Joe Zaloom *(Rui Ilanovitch)*, Lou Cevetillo *(Pete Stepanowicz)*, Zvee Scooler *(Phuro)*, David Rounds *(Mr. Kessler)*, Michael Higgins *(Judge)*, Mary Louise Wilson *(Willie)*, Daniel Spira *(Zio Miller)*, Robert Gerringer, Tom Quinn, Fred Coffin, Paul Sparer, William Duell, Harris Laskaway, Sam Coppola, Cory Einbinder, Matthew Laborteaux, Bliss Verdon, Danielle Brisebois, Tiffany Bogart, Marc Vahanian, Stephane Grappelli, Roy Brocksmith, Rebecca Darke, Glen Gianfrancisco, Patti LuPone, David Little, Joe Maruzzo, Robert Garcia, Linda Manz, C. A. R. Smith, James Shannon, MacIntyre Dixon, Mark Victor, Kathi Moss, Mary Wynn, Julie Garfield, Chris Manor, Jon Oppenheim, Bernie McInerney, Tom Mason, Jamil Zakkai, Ed Wagner, Leonard Jackson, William Thomas, Jr., Franklyn Scott, Jay Norman, Black-Eyed Susan, Kate Manheim, Sands Hall, Cecile Santos, Randy Danson, Richard Valladeres, John Del Ragno, Joe Ramezani.

Though it has some miscastings—especially Shields, whose performance is disappointing—this is an often fascinating look at gypsy culture in America. Roberts gives an impressive performance, in his screen debut, as the unwilling heir to the gypsy throne. He tries to break away from a culture he finds outmoded and archaic to modern times, and yet is always drawn back. The sequences involving gypsy scams are fascinating and often humorous in their simplicity. Real-life gypsies served as extras and were often caught trying to scam the producers out of more money for themselves. It stands a reasonable chance they were more often *not* caught at their games.

p, Federico De Laurentiis; d&w, Frank Pierson (based on the book by Peter Maas); ph, Sven Nykvist (Technicolor); m, David Grisman; ed, Paul Hirsch; prod d, Gene Callahan; art d, Jay Moore; set d, Robert Drumheller, John Godfrey; cos, Anna Hill Johnstone; ch, Julie Arenal.

Biographical Drama **Cas.** **(PR:O MPAA:R)**

KING OF THE ICE RINK (SEE: KING OF HOCKEY, 1936)

KING OF THE JUNGLE** (1933) 65m PAR bw

Buster Crabbe *(Kaspa, the Lion Man)*, Frances Dee *(Anne Rogers)*, Douglas Dumbrille *(Ed Peters)*, Robert Adair *(John C. Knolls)*, Florence Britton *(Mrs. Knolls)*, Ronnie Cosby *(Kaspa at age 3)*, Robert Barrat *(Joe Nolan)*, Sam Baker *(Gwana)*, Patricia Farley *(Kitty)*, Sidney Toler *(Neil Forbes)*, Nydia Westman *(Sue)*, Irving Pichel *(Corey)*, Warner Richmond *(Gus)*.

Crabbe follows the lead of fellow Olympic swimmer Johny Weissmuller and plays a human raised by jungle beasts in darkest Africa. Instead of apes, Crabbe is raised by lions after the death of his photographer parents. The campy plot doesn't give any of the basics such as how Crabbe was raised by the overgrown kitties, but that doesn't matter. This is good old escapism with lots of beefcake for the female audience. When Crabbe is caught with his lion friends by some circus people, he's brought back to the States by boat (he's listed as "What Is It" on the passenger list) but jumps ship and shows off his swimming prowess. Crabbe finally arrives in New York, runs around in his leopard skin loin cloth, learns English with amazing ease from love interest Dee and, of course, lives happily ever after. The spectacular climax where wild animals escape during a fire and roam the panic-stricken streets of New York, with elephants turning over buses and the clawing of a woman by a striped cat, provided Cecil B. de Mille with part of the magnificent train wreck scene in THE GREATEST SHOW ON EARTH. Crabbe had screen tested for MGM's TARZAN THE APE MAN but settled for this instead. He later achieved plenty of fame in the great serial FLASH GORDON. Cheerfully dumb, with some great animal footage, this film is fun for both kids and camp connoisseurs.

d, H. Bruce Humberstone, Max Marcin; w, Philip Wylie, Fred Niblo, Jr., Marcin (based on "The Lion's Way" by Charles Thurley Stoneham); ph, Ernest Haller.

Adventure **(PR:A MPAA:NR)**

KING OF THE JUNGLELAND (SEE:DARKEST AFRICA, 1936)

KING OF THE KHYBER RIFLES, 1929

(SEE: BLACK WATCH, THE, 1929)

KING OF THE KHYBER RIFLES* 1/2** (1953) 100m FOX c

Tyrone Power *(Capt. Alan King)*, Terry Moore *(Susan Maitland)*, Michael Rennie *(Brig. Gen. Maitland)*, John Justin *(Lt. Heath)*, Guy Rolfe *(Karram Khan)*, Richard Stapley *(Lt. Baird)*, Murray Matheson *(Maj. MacAllister)*, Frank DeKova *(Ali Nur)*, Argentina Brunetti *(Lali)*, Sujata *(Native Dancer)*, Frank Lackteen *(Ahmed)*, Gilchrist Stuart *(Officer of the Week)*, Karam Dhaliwal *(Pal-Singh)*, Aly Wassil *(Raschild)*, John Farrow *(Cpl. Stuart)*, Richard Peel *(Sgt. Fowler)*, Alberto Morin *(Rahim Bey)*, Alan Lee *(Ishmael)*, Aram Katcher *(Napur)*, Gavin Muir *(Maj. Lee)*, Tom Cound *(Capt. Rogers)*, Patrick Whyte *(Lt. White)*, Ramsey Hill *(Cavalry Officer)*, Maurice Colbourne *(Hamid Bahri)*, David Cota *(Singer)*, Naji Cabbay, Mohinder Bedi *(Servants)*, Hassan Khayyam *(Mullah)*, Harry Carter, William Wilkerson, George Khoury, George Keymas *(Akridi Horsemen)*, Lal Chand Mehra, Eghishe Harout, Joe Sawaya *(Tribal Chieftains)*.

This rousing adventure film, a remake of John Ford's 1929 THE BLACK WATCH, was given the full treatment by Fox who made this early CinemaScope epic their major Christmas release. Power stars as a half-caste captain who leads a supply column to the British outpost at Peshawar, India. On the trail his unit is ambushed by rebellious Afridi tribesmen led by Rolfe, a former childhood friend of Power's. The soldiers fend off the attack and make it to Peshawar where they are greeted by the garrison commander, Rennie, and his beautiful daughter, Moore. Power and Moore immediately take a liking to each other, which leads to a romantic rivalry between the half-caste captain and his roommate, Justin. In an effort to ruin Power, Justin spreads the word among the officers that his roommate is a half-caste. The full-blooded British make their distrust of Power felt, but Rennie is unfazed by the news and treats the soldier on the basis of his flawless military record. Rennie puts Power in charge of the Khyber Riflemen, a company of native soldiers. Power launches into his new assignment with enthusiasm and soon turns the undisciplined natives into a crack fighting unit. Despite his trust of Power in military matters, Rennie is dismayed at his daughter's burgeoning romance with the half-caste and forbids her from seeing him. Soon after, Moore is kidnaped by Rolfe's rebels and Power manages to rescue her. Stranded in the desert, the pair are rescued by a search party only to learn that Rolfe has captured another group of soldiers helping in the search. Rolfe decrees that the unit will be killed unless the British hand over a new shipment of high-powered rifles. Power volunteers to infiltrate Rolfe's headquarters and kill his boyhood friend, but Rennie refuses to give permission. Undaunted, Power goes off on his own and makes his way to Rolfe's encampment. There, he manages to convince the rebel leader that he has grown tired of British prejudice over his ethnic heritage and he has deserted in favor of his people. When the opportunity to kill Rolfe comes, Power hesitates for a moment and is caught. Rolfe executes several of his captives, but then lets Power free with a warning that he will not be so generous again. Power returns to the British and is promptly arrested for disobeying orders. Meanwhile, Rolfe has started uprisings throughout India and Power is freed to lead his riflemen against the rebels. A rumor spreads that the new rifles have been smeared with lard, and the religious Indian riflemen refuse to touch their guns. Power tells them to use their swords instead and his unit attacks Rolfe's encampment. During the battle Power is wounded by Rolfe, but the villainous rebel leader hesitates before finishing him off. The wait proves fatal when one of Power's men throws a knife and kills Rolfe. The rebels are soon defeated and the amazing victory wins Power the respect of the British and the hand of Moore. KING OF THE KHYBER RIFLES is a marvelously entertaining adventure yarn directed with flair by King. Though the majority of the film was shot on the backlot in California's Lone Pine area, the illusion of India is supported by some second-unit location footage of the Himalayas.

p, Frank P. Rosenberg; d, Henry King; w, Ivan Goff, Ben Roberts (based on the novel by Talbot Mundy); ph, Leon Shamroy (CinemaScope, Technicolor); m, Bernard Herrmann; ed, Barbara McLean; art d, Lyle Wheeler, Maurice Ransford; set d, Walter M. Scott, Fred J. Rode, Paul S. Fox; cos, Travilla; ch, Osoka.

Adventure **(PR:A MPAA:NR)**

KING OF THE LUMBERJACKS*½ (1940) 58m WB bw

John Payne *(Slim)*, Gloria Dickson *(Tina)*, Stanley Fields *(Dominic)*, Joe Sawyer *(Jigger)*, Victor Kilian *(Joe)*, Earl Dwire *(Dr. Vance)*, Herbert Haywood *(Laramie)*, G. Pat Collins *(Gregg)*, John Sheehan *(Bartender)*, Pat West *(Waiter)*, Nat Carr *(Waiter)*, Jack Mower *(Truck Driver)*, John "Skins" Miller *(Cooky)*.

Trite film about a love triangle in a lumber camp. Fields is a lumberjack who marries former nightclub singer Dickson. Who should be at the same camp but her former sweetie Payne. They realize they're still in love but don't want to hurt the kindhearted Fields. He sees them in an embrace and tries putting them on a runaway train, but he just can't do it and unhitches their car right before the rest of the train is turned into toothpicks at the bottom of a gorge. There's also some two-fisted barroom brawling along the way and some stock footage of lumberjacking. Routine production values, average acting, and a wholly laughable script.

p&d, William Clemens; w, Crane Wilbur (based on the story "Timber" by Robert E. Kent); ph, Sid Hickox; ed, Doug Gould; art d, Esdras Hartley.

Romance **(PR:A MPAA:NR)**

KING OF THE MOUNTAIN, 1964 (SEE: BEDTIME STORY, 1964)

KING OF THE MOUNTAIN** (1981) 90m Polygram/UNIV c

Harry Hamlin *(Steve)*, Joseph Bottoms *(Buddy)*, Deborah Van Valkenburgh *(Tina)*, Richard Cox *(Roger)*, Dennis Hopper *(Cal)*, Dan Haggerty *(Rick)*, Seymour Cassel *(Barry Tanner)*, Jon Sloan *(Billy T.)*, Steve Jones *(Policeman)*, Ashley Cox *(Elaine)*, Lillian Muller *(Jamie Winter)*, Cassandra Peterson *(Neighbor)*, Buddy Joe Hooker *(Fast Joe Otis)*, Ron Trice *(Keyboard Player)*, Curt Ayers *(Fatburger)*, Larry Beezer *(Dean)*, Bill Forsythe *(Big Tom)*, Joey Camen *(Suds)*, Douglas Dirkson *(Davey)*, Jay May *(Guitar Player)*, Susan McDonald *(Buddy's Girl)*, Amy Gibson *(Roger's Girl)*, Gary Hudson *(Gang Leader)*, Dennis Hull, Vincent Guastaferro, Anthony DeLongis *(Gang Members)*, Preston Sparks *(Parking Lot Attendant)*, Tara Fellner *(Iris)*, Howard Alk *(Party Guest)*, Tony Lettieri, Sonny LaRocca *(Friends)*, Steve Davison *(Van Man)*, R. P. Cohen *(Cashier)*, Owen Orr *(Bartender)*, Lisa Friedman *(Spandex Girl)*, Hamilton McRae *(Guest)*, Chuck Tamburro *(Cop Driver)*, Hank Bill Hooker *(Cop)*, Ted Markland *(Limo Driver)*, Jay Meyer *(Agent)*, Tony Berg, Jeff Eyrich, Art Woods, Ronald Raison, *(Themselves)*, John Dukakis *(Duke)*, Kathy McCullen *(Duke's Girl)*, Juliette Marshall *(Big Tom's Girl)*, Russell Forte *(Joel)*, Steve Halladay, Debbie Dirkson.

Cliched film features Hamlin as a garage mechanic in his mid-20s trying to figure out what direction he wants to take with his life. He is the "king" of Mulholland Drive, a Los Angeles road, popular among fast drivers. His buddies include songwriter Bottoms and Cox, an obnoxious record producer. The story follows their lives but between all the stereotypes, cliches, and endless tire-screeching footage it's hard to care much about what goes on here. Hopper has a cameo as Hamlin's co-worker, the inevitable burned out former "king" of Mulholland Drive.

p, Jack Frost Sanders; d, Noel Nosseck; w, H. R. Christian (based on the magazine article by David Barry called "Thunder Road"); ph, Donald Peterman (Technicolor); m, Michael Melvion; ed, William Steinkamp; prod d, James H. Spencer; set d, Gary Moreno; cos, Susan Becker; stunts, David Ellis.

Psychological Drama/Racing **Cas.** **(PR:O MPAA:PG)**

KING OF THE NEWSBOYS** (1938) 65m REP bw

Lew Ayres *(Jerry Flynn)*, Helen Mack *(Mary Ellen Stephens)*, Alison Skipworth *(Nora)*, Victor Varconi *(Wire Arno)*, Sheila Bromley *(Connie Madison)*, Alice White *(Dolly)*, Horace MacMahon *(Lockjaw)*, William Benedict *(Squimpy)*, Victor Ray Cooke *(Pussy)*, Jack Pennick *(Lefty)*, Mary Kornman *(Peggy)*, Gloria Rich *(Maizie)*, Oscar O'Shea *(Mr. Stephens)*, Marjorie Main *(Mrs. Stephens)*, Tony [Anthony] Warde *(Henchman)*, Ralph Dunn *(Guard)*, Byron Foulger *(Gazette Owner)*, Emmett Vogan *(Newsman)*, Ferris Taylor *(John Sampson)*, Ethan Laidlaw *(Hood)*, Dale Van Sickel *(Escort)*, Howard Hickman *(Judge)*, John Baird *(Henchman)*, Inez Palange *(Neighbor)*, Allan Cavan *(Mr. Madison)*, Alphonse Martel *(Head Waiter)*, Horace Carpenter *(Fisherman)*, Ben Taggart *(Lawyer)*, Paul Stanton *(Jeweler)*, Joe Cunningham *(Gazette Managing Editor)*, Harry Semels *(Grocer)*, Frances Morris *(Mabel)*, Jack Chefe *(Waiter)*, Harry Wilson *(Coachman)*, Charlie Sullivan *(Bookie)*, Bob Livingston *(Passerby)*.

Ayres is a small-time guy with big dreams. Mack is his girl who listens to him but can only take so much and eventually dumps him for the more lucrative Varconi, a mobster. Ayres decides to show her who's big time and becomes successful in the newspaper trucking business. He gets himself a Park Avenue penthouse and tries once more for his lost love. Meanwhile, Mack has grown disillusioned with Varconi. In the end, Ayres winds up losing his penthouse but regaining the heart of his true love. The story is nothing new, but the acting does give it some freshness. The direction keeps things moving along so you won't mind the cliches too much. Unfortunately, the New York City atmosphere, so wonderfully captured in many of Republic's B films, is completely missing here.

p&d, Bernard Vorhaus; w, Louis Weitzenkorn, Peggy Thompson (based on a story by Samuel Ornitz, Horace McCoy); ph, Jack Marta; m, Alberto Columbo; ed, Ernest Nims.

Drama/Romance **(PR:A MPAA:NR)**

KING OF THE PECOS*** (1936) 54m REP bw

John Wayne *(John Clayborn)*, Muriel Evans *(Belle)*, Cy Kendall *(Stiles)*, Jack Clifford *(Ash)*, J. Frank Glendon *(Brewster)*, Herbert Heywood *(Josh)*, Arthur Aylesworth *(Hank)*, John Beck *(Clayborn, Sr.)*, Mary McLaren *(Mrs. Clayborn)*, Bradley Metcalfe, Jr. *(Little John)*, Yakima Canutt *(Smith)*, Edward Hearn, Earl Dwire, Tex Palmer, Jack Kirk.

Wayne is a law student who returns home to avenge the murder of his parents by the local cattle baron. He first attempts to do so legally, but his efforts are thwarted and he resorts to taking the law in his own hands. The end sees Wayne killing the cattle baron, Kendall, in a final shootout. Well-paced direction and superior photography.

p, Paul Malvern; d, Joseph Kane; w, Bernard McConville, Dorrell McGowan, Stuart McGowan (based on a story by McConville); ph, Jack Marta; ed, Joseph H. Lewis, Lester Orlebeck.

Western **(PR:A MPAA:NR)**

KING OF THE RITZ*½ (1933, Brit.) 81m Gainsborough-BL/GAU bw

Stanley Lupino *(Claude King)*, Betty Stockfeld *(Mrs. Cooper)*, Hugh Wakefield *(King of Blitz)*, Henry Kendall *(Teddy Smith)*, Gina Malo *(Victoria)*, Gibb McLaughlin *(Baron Popov)*, Harry Milton *(Alonso)*, Johnny Singer *(Pageboy)*.

Lupino is the well-liked head porter of Paris' Ritz Hotel whose life takes a comic turn when he falls for Stockfeld, a rich widow staying at the hotel. He saves her jewels and is rewarded with the title of Duke, as well as given an ancestral home to live in. He and Stockfeld plan a life together, much to the chagrin of Malo, the hotel maid who swoons over Lupino. When the home turns out to be worthless Lupino returns to his hotel kingdom and the love of Malo.

p&d, Carmine Gallone; w, Clifford Grey, Ivor Montagu (based on the play "Le Roi Des Palaces" by Henri Kistemaeckers).

Musical Comedy **(PR:A MPAA:NR)**

KING OF THE ROARING TWENTIES—THE STORY OF ARNOLD ROTHSTEIN½** (1961) 106m AA bw (GB: THE BIG BANKROLL)

David Janssen *(Arnold Rothstein)*, Dianne Foster *(Carolyn Green)*, Mickey Rooney *(Johnny Burke)*, Jack Carson *("Big Tim" O'Brien)*, Diana Dors *(Madge)*, Dan O'Herlihy *(Phil Butler)*, Mickey Shaughnessy *(Jim Kelly)*, Keenan Wynn *(Tom Fowler)*, Joseph Schildkraut *(Abraham Rothstein)*, William Demarest *(Hecht)*, Murvyn Vye *(Williams)*, Regis Toomey *(Bill Baird)*, Robert Ellenstein *(Lenny)*, Teri Janssen *(Joanie)*, Jim Baird *(Arnold, as a Boy)*, Tim Rooney.

The true story of Arnold Rothstein has yet to be made as a movie, but this will have to suffice until that day dawns. Based on Leo Katcher's *The Big Bankroll*, this movie bites off more than it can chew, in that there was so much to Rothstein's life that one movie couldn't do it justice (or injustice, so to speak). Janssen is the son of devout Jewish parents and he has been blessed with a mind like a computer and cursed with the ambition of a Borgia. He is a gambler by nature and soon emerges as a top dog in the New York gambling community when he is set up in business by Carson, a criminal politician. Janssen and Shaughnessy open their own establishment but Janssen soon gets rid of his partner by bilking him. Next, Janssen marries Foster, a Broadway actress, but he gives her very little of himself and spends most of his nights out with his pals. Janssen hates O'Herlihy, a childhood enemy, who is now with the police department and on the take. He wants to get even with O'Herlihy on several counts and persuades Rooney, another old friend, to reveal O'Herlihy's history of taking bribes to a local newspaper. Rooney is killed for his efforts and Janssen senses that O'Herlihy was behind that murder, so he enlists attorney Wynn to help investigate the case and O'Herlihy is tried, convicted, and fries in the hot seat. Janssen's star rises but his domestic life crumbles as Foster leaves him. He will stop at nothing to get his way and is eventually murdered while playing poker in a hotel room. All his life, the gambler had never been dealt a royal flush but that's his final hand when the professional killers gun him down. Whether or not that really happened is a matter of conjecture. What's missing from the movie is Rothstein's alleged involvement in the Black Sox scandal of 1919, as well as several other of his most famous scams. There's no question that Rothstein was a villain and the character that Runyon based Sky Masterson upon, in part. But he was a fascinating villain, one-of-a-kind and, although they do an "A" job for a "B" movie, one wishes there might have been greater depth in the portrayal. That shallowness was not Janssen's fault, as the actor can only do as well as the words he or she is given. Screenwriter Swerling knew his way around Runyon, having co-written the book for "Guys and Dolls" many years before. Rooney does the standout performance in a small but effective role.

p, Samuel Bischoff, David Diamond; d, Joseph M. Newman; w, Jo Swerling (based on the book *The Big Bankroll* by Leo Katcher); ph, Carl Guthrie; m, Franz Waxman; ed, George White; md Waxman; art d, David Milton; set d, Joseph Kish; cos, Roger J. Weinberg, spec eff, Milt Olsen; makeup, Allan Synder.

Crime Drama **(PR:C MPAA:NR)**

KING OF THE ROYAL MOUNTED½** (1936) 61m FOX bw

Robert Kent *(Sergeant King)*, Rosalind Keith *(Helen Lawton)*, Alan Dinehart *(Becker)*, Frank McGlynn, Sr. *(Dundas)*, Arthur Loft *(Sneed)*, Grady Sutton *(Slim Blandon)*, Jack Luden *(Smith)*, Artie Ortego *(Indian Joe)*.

Kent is a handsome member of the famed Royal Canadian Mounted Police. He falls in love with Keith, but their romance suffers a setback when she is charged with murdering her father. McGlynn is the bad guy, a lawyer who's framing the young lady so he can have her father's mine for himself. Of course the dashing Kent saves the day and the film ends happily. Well paced and good, wholesome fun, with nice performances by the leads. The film was inspired by the popular newspaper comic strip of the day, which itself was spawned from a Zane Grey story. Two serials from Republic studios based on the famed Mountie were released in 1940 and 1942.

p, Sol Lesser; d, Howard Bretherton; w, Earl Snell (based on a comic strip and a story by Zane Grey); ph, Hermann Neumann; ed, Robert Crandell.

Adventure/Mystery/Romance **(PR:A MPAA:NR)**

KING OF THE SIERRAS** (1938) 53m GN bw

Hobart Bosworth *(Uncle Hank)*, Harry Harvey, Jr. *(Tom)*, Frank Campeau *(Jim)*,

Harry Harvey, Sr. *(Pete)*, Jack Lindell *(Trainer)*, The Horses: Sheik *(Whitey)*, Rex *(El Diablo)*.

A different, though awkwardly told western, involves a story between two horses. Bosworth is an old uncle telling his 4-year-old nephew (Harvey, Jr.) the story of a white horse that protects his mares from a black stallion. The horse footage is integrated into the old man's story but really doesn't work well. This film is at its best when the humans shut up and the horses are left to their own devices. The animals actually aren't too bad, despite the cliched plot they're stuck in. However, they don't seem to mind and make this an enjoyable fable for the kiddies.

p, George A. Hirliman; d, Samuel Diege; w, W. Scott Darling (based on a story by Frank Gay); ph, Jack Greenhalgh, Jr., Tom Galligan; ed, Carl Pierson.

Western **(PR:A MPAA:NR)**

KING OF THE STALLIONS*½ (1942) 63m MON bw

Chief Thundercloud, Princess Bluebird, Chief Yowlachie, Rick Vallin, Dave O'Brien, Barbara Felker, Sally Cairns, Ted Adams, Gordon DeMain [G. D. Woods], Forrest Taylor, Joe Cody, Bill Wilkerson, Chief Many Treaties, George Sky Eagle, Charles Brunner, Iron Eyes Cody, Willow Bird, Nakoma the Wonder Horse, Paint the Killer Stallion.

Chief Thundercloud heads this wilderness western along with a largely Indian cast. A killer stallion threatens the rest of the herd, as well as local cowboys and Indians, and it's up to Thundercloud to tame the animal. Iron Eyes Cody, who made himself a national figure in anti-litter commercials, also appears.

p&d, Edward Finney; w, Arthur St. Claire, Sherman Lowe (based on a story by Roger Merton); ph, Marcel LePicard; m, Frank Aanucci; ed, Fred Bain; md, Aanucci.

Western **(PR:A MPAA:NR)**

KING OF THE TURF*** (1939) 88m UA bw

Adolphe Menjou *(Jim Mason)*, Roger Daniel *(Goldie)*, Dolores Costello *(Mrs. Barnes)*, Walter Abel *(Mr. Barnes)*, Alan Dinehart *(Grimes)*, William Demarest *(Arnold)*, Harold Huber *(Santelli)*, George McKay *(Murphy)*, Lee M. Moore *(Carr)*, Oscar O'Shea *(Bartender)*, Cliff Nazarro *(1st Tout)*, George Chandler *(2nd Tout)*, Milburn Stone *(Taylor)*, Charles McAvoy *(Policeman)*, William Bakewell *(Intern)*, Harry Semels, Donald Kerr, Tommy Quinn, Barlow Borland, Charles Sherlock.

Menjou is a down-and-out horseman who's lost everything he had as a stable owner and has nothing to live for except alcohol. Then he meets Daniel, a young boy who loves racing and has run away from home to become a stable boy. He lets Menjou ride in a stable car that he's responsible for and listens to the man's story. During the ride he persuades Menjou to quit the bottle and try once more to become a top man in the racing world. The pair are able to purchase an auctioned horse for only $2 and Menjou becomes the trainer with Daniel the jockey. Just when the two become a famous team and inseparable friends, along comes the boy's mother, Costello, and Menjou discovers that Daniel is the son he abandoned many years before. Not wanting Daniel to know the truth, he tells the boy to lose a big race, hoping he will then go back to his mother and Menjou can keep his secret. Daniel goes on to win the race anyway and things are resolved by the film's end. Despite some hard to swallow plot points, this is really a nice film and Menjou and Daniel are terrific together.

p, Edward Small; d, Alfred E. Green; w, George Bruce; ph, Robert Planck; ed, Grant Whytock.

Sports/Drama **(PR:A MPAA:NR)**

KING OF THE UNDERWORLD½** (1939) 69m WB bw

Humphrey Bogart *(Joe Gurney)*, Kay Francis *(Carole Nelson)*, James Stephenson *(Bill Forrest)*, John Eldredge *(Niles Nelson)*, Jessie Busley *(Aunt Margaret)*, Arthur Aylesworth *(Dr. Sanders)*, Raymond Brown *(Sheriff)*, Harland Tucker *(Mr. Ames)*, Ralph Remley *(Mr. Robert)*, Murray Alper *(Butch)*, Charles Foy *(Eddie)*, Joe Devlin *(Porky)*, Elliott Sullivan *(Mugsy)*, Alan Davis *(Slick)*, John Harmon *(Slats)*, John Ridgely *(Jerry)*, Richard Bond *(Intern)*, Paul MacWilliams *(Anesthetist)*, Richard Quine *(Student)*, Stuart Holmes *(Doorman)*, Vera Lewis *(Woman)*, William Gould *(Chief of Police)*, Clem Bevans, Carl Stockdale, Nat Carr *(Villagers)*, Jack Mower, John Harron *(G-Men)*, Sherwood Bailey *(Boy)*, Jimmy O'Gatty, Frank Bruno, Paul Panzer, Cliff Saum, Doc Stone *(Gangsters)*, Sidney Bracy, Lottie Williams *(Farmer Couple)*, Tom Wilson, Glen Cavender *(Deputies)*, Pierre Watkin *(District Attorney)*, Charles Trowbridge *(Dr. Ryan)*, Edwin Stanley *(Dr. Jacobs)*.

A remake of 1935's DR. SOCRATES which tries a different angle and changes the sex of the lead character by casting Kay Francis in Paul Muni's role. Francis and her husband, Eldredge, are both celebrated surgeons at County Hospital. Eldredge, however, has a weakness for gambling and accepts a high-paying offer from gangster Bogart to act as his gang's doctor. Francis is kept in the dark about her husband's underworld involvement and, one night, follows him to Bogart's hideout where he has been called to patch up one of the henchman's wounds. The police arrive and Bogart, thinking that he's been squealed on, kills Eldredge. Francis witnesses the bloodletting and is arrested, while Bogart and his boys make a fast getaway. Although Francis is acquitted, her future at County Hospital is ruined and she nearly loses her license to practice. Francis, however, is a woman determined. She begins her search for the men who killed her husband and winds up in a small town where two of the gang members are jailed. She opens a small practice and meets novelist Forrest, who has been hired by Bogart, in a moment of Napoleonic weakness, to pen his biography. She convinces Forrest that he will be killed by Bogart as soon as the book is completed. Forrest heeds Francis' warning and agrees to help bring about the gang's demise. Meantime, Bogart engineers the jailbreak of his two men and is wounded, necessitating Francis' medical assistance. She ingeniously infects Bogart's wound and then proceeds to blind him and his entire gang with an eyedrop solution, under the guise that she is preventing infection. In the film's finest sequence, the blinded Bogart wakes up to the ruse and stumbles helplessly through a number of rooms in the hopes of killing Francis and Forrest. The police burst onto the scene and fell Bogart in a flurry of bullets. Originally conceived as a vehicle for the waning Francis, KING OF THE UNDERWORLD soon began falling apart at the seams. The film was not, as the ad-mats promised, "The Scorching Story of Gangdom's Last Stand!" Seiler's direction lacked intensity and the project was temporarily shelved. Additional scenes were added and the film was finally released, but with Bogart top-billed and Francis demoted. Seizing yet another opportunity to kick Francis while she was down, Warner Bros. placed her name below the title and at half the size of Bogart's. While the film is entertaining, it lacks the verve of Bogart's better vehicles. After viewing the film, Noel Coward confronted Bogart with the pointed question: "Have you and Jack Warner no shame?" Bogart retorted, "None."

d, Lewis Seiler; w, Vincent Sherman, George Bricker, Vincent Sherman (based on the story "Dr. Socrates" by W. R. Burnett); ph, Sid Hickox; m, Heinz Roemheld; ed, Frank Dewar; md, Leo Forbstein; art d, Charles Novi; cos, Orry-Kelly.

Crime **(PR:A-C MPAA:NR)**

KING OF THE UNDERWORLD*½ (1952, Brit.) 82m BUS/Ambassador bw

Tod Slaughter *(Terence Riley)*, Patrick Barr *(Inspector Morley)*, Tucker McGuire *(Eileen Trotter)*, Ingeborg Wells *(Marie)*, Frank Hawkins *(Inspector Cranshaw)*, Len Sharp *(Mullins)*, Ann Valery *(Susan)*, Larry Burns.

Scotland Yard inspector Barr is on an endless chase after the amiable but ruthless criminal, Slaughter, who has stolen some costly jewels, a secret formula, and is involved in a blackmail scheme. Somehow, Slaughter always manages to keep one step ahead of the persistent detective.

p, Gilbert Church; d, Victor M. Gover; w, John Gilling; ph, S. D. Onions.

Crime **(PR:A MPAA:NR)**

KING OF THE WILD (SEE: KING OF THE WILD HORSE, THE, 1934)

KING OF THE WILD HORSES, THE*

(1934) 60m COL bw (AKA: KING OF THE WILD; KING OF WILD HORSES)

"Rex" *(Rex, the Hero)*, "Lady" *(Lady, the Heroine)*, "Marquis" *(Marquis, the Villain)*, William Janney *(Red Wolf)*, Dorothy Appleby *(Wanima)*, Wallace MacDonald *(Clint Bolling)*, Harry Semels *(Big Man)*, Ford West *(Davidson)*, Art Mix *(Cowboy)*.

The equestrian trio share top billing in this story. Rex is the good horse, Lady his steady mare, and Marquis plays the four- legged heavy. In between, there are too many unnecessary (and completely unrealistic) scenes of Navajo ceremonies and a poor Ed Wynn impersonator. The photography, direction, and script lack any artistic value. For horse lovers only.

d, Earl Haley; w, Fred Myton (based on a story by Haley); ph, Ben Kline; ed, Clarence Kolster.

Western **(PR:A MPAA:NR)**

KING OF THE WILD HORSES** (1947) 79m COL bw

Preston Foster, Gail Patrick, Bill Sheffield, Guinn "Big Boy" Williams, Buzz Henry, Charles Kemper, Patti Brady, John Kellogg, Ruth Warren, Louis Faust.

Another boy and his pet story, though in this case the animal is not so tame, but rather a wild horse whose captivating rescues of the boy make for quite a bit of exciting adventure. Picture tugs at the heart in its portrayal of the bond that exists between boy and horse, but these are woven in well with an abundance of action.

p, Ted Richmond; d, George Archainbaud; w, Brenda Weisberg (based on the story by Ted Thomas); ph, George B. Meehan, Philip Tannura; ed, Henry Batista; md, Mischa Bakaleinikoff; art d, Hans Radon.

Adventure **(PR:A MPAA:NR)**

KING OF THE WILD STALLIONS½** (1959) 76m AA c

George Montgomery *(Randy)*, Diane Brewster *(Martha)*, Edgar Buchanan *(Idaho)*, Emile Meyer *(Matt)*, Jerry Hartleben *(Bucky)*, Byron Foulger *(Orcutt)*, Denver Pyle *(Doc)*, Dan Sheridan *(Woody)*, Rory Mallinson *(Sheriff)*.

Brewster owns a ranch but needs $500 to pay off Meyer, a cattle baron. Coincidentally, that is just the amount of the reward he's offering for the capture of the title beast. Brewster's son Hartleben catches the animal but wants to keep it himself. Enter Montgomery as the ranch foreman (and Brewster's suitor) to settle everything. It's a nice story, told well by director Springsteen. Though the theme is an old one, he doesn't resort to much cliche. There's also some nice footage of wild horses edited in. The film was written by veteran western serial director Beebe. The innocence of the film was a refreshing change from the many psychopathic westerns that were cropping up in the late 1950s.

p, Ben Schwalb; d, R.G. Springsteen; w, Ford Beebe; ph, Carl Guthrie (CinemaScopes/DeLuxe Color); m, Marlin Skiles; ed, George White; art d, David Milton.

Western **(PR:AAA MPAA:NR)**

KING OF THE ZOMBIES* (1941) 67m MON bw

Dick Purcell, Joan Woodbury, Mantan Moreland, Henry Victor, John Archer, Patricia Stacey, Guy Usher, Marguerite Whitten, Leigh Whipper, Madame Sul-Te-Wan, Jimmy Davis, Lawrence Criner.

With the war in mind, Victor decides to give his Axis countries a boost in numbers and fighting power by creating an army of Zombies. But Purcell is able to make things safe for democracy and protect poor maidens from becoming victims of evil forces. Directed with Yarbrough's usual flair for slackness and disregard for the cinematic medium. Only the comic antics of Moreland rise above the poor handling and breathe some life into a picture as dead as the beings which are its subject.

p, Lindsley Parsons; d, Jean Yarbrough; w, Edmund Kelso; ph, Mack Stengler; ed, Richard Currier; md, Edward Kay; art d, Charles Clague.

Horror **Cas.** **(PR:C MPAA:NR)**

KING, QUEEN, KNAVE** (1972, Ger./U.S.) 92m David Wolper-Maran/AE c (HERZBUBE)

Gina Lollobrigida *(Martha Dreyer)*, David Niven *(Charles Dreyer)*, John Moulder-Brown *(Frank Dreyer)*, Mario Adorf *(Prof. Ritter)*, Carl Fox-Duering *(Enricht)*, Barbara Valentin *(Optician)*, Sonia Hofmann *(Sonia)*, Erica Beer *(Frieda)*, Elma Karlowa *(Hanna)*, Mogens von Gadow *(Piffke)*, Felicitas Peters *(Ida)*, Christopher Sandford *(Hofmann)*, Christine Schubert *(Isolda)*.

Brown is invited by his uncle, Niven, to come and visit him in Germany. Niven is an Englishman who has made a fortune in postwar Germany and married a sensual Italian woman, Lollobrigida. Upon his arrival the young lad finds himself being seduced by his aunt who wants him to kill Niven so she can have his fortune for herself. Based on a novel by Nabokov (the author of *Lolita*), this film is highly visual with some nice touches. Characters, however, are not drawn carefully enough, and the film is spotty at best. Lollobrigida does have some moments trying to seduce the boy, but the film never settles on whether it's satire or slapstick. Co-produced by West Germany and the U.S. with English actors, an Italian actress, and a Polish director (based on a book by a Russian born author as well), this truly is an international film. (In English.)

p, Lutz Hengst, David Wolper; d, Jerzy Skolimowski; w, David Seltzer, David Shaw (based on the novel by Vladimir Nabokov); ph, Charly Steinberger (Eastmancolor); m, Stanley Meyers (electronic music by Francis Monkman); ed, Melvin Shapiro; art d, Rolf Zehetbauer.

Comedy **Cas.** **(PR:O MPAA:R)**

KING RAT **$^{1/2}$** (1965) 134m Coleytown/COL bw

George Segal *(Cpl. King)*, Patrick O'Neal *(Max)*, Todd Armstrong *(Tex)*, Sammy Reese *(Kurt)*, Joseph Turkel *(Dino)*, Michael Stroka *(Miller)*, William Fawcett *(Steinmetz)*, Dick Johnson *(Pop)*, James Fox *(Flight Lt. Marlowe)*, Denholm Elliott *(Lt. Col. Denholm Larkin)*, Leonard Rossiter *(Maj. McCoy)*, John Standing *(Capt. Daven)*, Hamilton Dyce *(Chaplain Drinkwater)*, Wright King *(Brough)*, John Ronane *(Capt. Hawkins)*, Geoffrey Bayldon *(Squadron Leader Vexley)*, John Levingston *(Myner)*, John Barclay *(Spence)*, David Frankham *(Cox)*, Tom Courtenay *(Lt. Grey)*, David Haviland *(Masters)*, Roy Dean *(Peterson)*, John Mills *(Col. Smedley-Taylor)*, Gerald Sim *(Col. Jones)*, Alan Webb *(Col. Brant)*, John Merivale *(Foster)*, John Warburton *(Commandant)*, James Donald *(Dr. Kennedy)*, Hedley Mattingly *(Dr. Prodhomme)*, Michael Lees *(Stephens)*, Reg Lye *(Tinkerbell)*, John Orchard *(Pvt. Gurble)*, Laurence Conroy *(Townsend)*, Arthur Malet, *(Blakely)*, Edward Ashley *(Prouty)*, Richard Dawson *(Weaver)*, Dale Ishimoto *(Yoshima)*, Teru Shimada *(Japanese General)*, Louis Neervort *(Torusumi)*, George Pelling *(Maj. Barry)*, Anthony Faramus.

Interesting, if overlong, adaptation of Clavell's novel about a Japanese POW camp during WW II. Segal heads a black market operation inside the camp confines with his principal product being the rats he raises for the prisoners to supplement their meager food rations. He becomes aligned with Fox, a British officer who can speak the language of their captors, thus helping Segal expand his operation. When Fox becomes ill, Segal manages to bargain some antibiotics from their captors and saves his friend's life. Though filmed in California, the mise en scene looks and feels like a prison camp in Japan. Absolute attention to detail is maintained throughout and gives the film its realistic look. Segal is excellent as the black marketeer and the supporting roles are equally as good. Author Clavell, by the way, was actually a POW in the same location as the story.

p, James Woolf; d&w, Bryan Forbes (based on the novel by James Clavell); ph, Burnett Guffey; m, John Barry; ed, Walter Thompson; md, Barry; art d, Robert Smith; set d, Frank Tuttle; cos, Ed Ware; spec eff, John Burke; makeup, Ben Lane, Joe Dibella.

War Drama **Cas.** **(PR:O MPAA:NR)**

KING RICHARD AND THE CRUSADERS** (1954) 113m WB c

Rex Harrison *(Emir Ilderim)*, Virginia Mayo *(Lady Edith)*, George Sanders *(King Richard III)*, Laurence Harvey *(Sir Kenneth)*, Robert Douglas *(Sir Giles Amaury)*, Michael Pate *(Montferrat)*, Paula Raymond *(Queen Berengaria)*, Lester Matthews *(Archbishop of Tyre)*, Antony Eustrel *(Baron De Vaux)*, Henry Corden *(King Philip of France)*, Wilton Graff *(Duke Leopold of Austria)*, Nick Cravat *(Nectobanus)*, Leslie Bradley *(Castelain Captain)*, Nejla Ates *(Moorish Dancing Girl)*, Larry Chance *(Castelain Bowman)*, Robin Hughes *(King's Guard)*, Leonard Penn, Lumsden Hare, Leonard Mudie, Gavin Moore *(Physicians)*, Erik Blythe *(Drill Master)*, John Alderson *(Mob Leader)*, Harry Cording *(Castelain Spokesman)*, Paul Marion *(Arab Falconer)*, Abdullah Abbas *(Arab)*, Mark Hanna *(Courier)*, John Epper *(Wounded Castelain)*, Bruce Lester, Mark Dana, Peter Ortiz *(Castelains)*, Herbert Dean *(Captain of Royal Guard)*, Otto Reichow, Rudolph Anders *(German Knights)*, John Alderson *(Mob Leader)*.

Silly costume epic has Sanders as King Richard the Lionhearted surviving an assassination attempt by disloyal nobles during the Third Crusade. Harvey steps forward as the only knight to be trusted and he tries to gather evidence against the conspirators while trying to woo Sander's cousin, Mayo. Harrison, the chief of the Arabs, rides into camp posing as a doctor and works to save Sanders' life so he will have an honorable opponent in the war. He, too, falls for Mayo. Harvey weeds out the traitors, fights some duels, jousts a bit, and generally proves himself worthy of Mayo's hand. he and Mayo return to Scotland over Sanders' protest that he needs Harvey for a new campaign. An extraordinarily bad script is the chief culprit in this misfired epic, poorly structured and leaving Harrison (looking ridiculous with his face painted brown) with nothing but platitudes to speak and an awful song to sing. The battle scenes, usually the best thing about films like this, are boring, and almost all the acting is downright bad. Filmed at a cost of $3 million, it still had not recouped its investment more than 30 years later.

p, Henry Blanke; d, David Butler; w, John Twist (based on the novel *The Talisman* by Sir Walter Scott); ph, J. Peverell Marley (CinemaScope, Warner Color); m, Max Steiner; ed, Irene Morra; art d, Bertram Tuttle; m/l, "Dream, Dream," Twist, Ray Heindorf, sung by Rex Harrison.

Historical Epic **(PR:A MPAA:NR)**

KING SOLOMON OF BROADWAY** (1935) 75m UNIV bw

Edmund Lowe *(King Solomon)*, Dorothy Page *(Sheba)*, Pinky Tomlin *(Himself)*, Louise Henry *(Nikki Bradbury)*, Edward Pawley *("Ice" Larson)*, Charles Grapewin *(Uncle Winchester)*, Bradley Page *(Roth)*, Arthur Vinton *(Murray)*, Clyde Dilson *(Schultz)*.

Lowe is the nightclub owner with a yen for gambling. This has gotten him into trouble with kingpin Pawley, whose release from jail causes Lowe to break out of his calm facade. Lowe's efforts to keep Pawley off his back have him resorting to a scheme—with the assistance of gangsters antagonistic to Pawley—that takes advantage of the latter's shaky parole stance. They kidnap a wealthy woman, then make all the evidence point toward Pawley, thus getting him off Lowe's back. Lots of nightclub sequences help provide the appropriate atmosphere, but the film never quite leaves the ranks of a common gangster yarn. Songs include: "That's What You Think" (Tomlin), "Flower in My Lapel" (Conrad, Magidson), and "Moaning in the Moonlight."

p, Julius Bernheim; d, Alan Crosland; w, Albert J. Cohen, Robert T. Shannon, Harry Clork, Doris Malloy (based on the story by Cohen, Shannon); ph, George S. Robinson; ed, Daniel Mandell; md, David Klatzkin; m/l, Pinky Tomlin, Klatzkin, Herb Magidson, Con Conrad.

Crime **(PR:A MPAA:NR)**

KING SOLOMON'S MINES*** (1937, Brit.) 80m GAU bw

Paul Robeson *(Umbopa)*, Cedric Hardwicke *(Allan Quartermaine)*, Roland Young *(Comdr. Good)*, John Loder *(Henry Curtis)*, Anna Lee *(Kathy O'Brien)*, Sydney Fairbrother *(Gagool)*, Majabalo Hiubi *(Kapsie)*, Ecce Homo Toto *(Infadoos)*, Robert Adams *(Twala)*, Frederick Leister *(Wholesaler)*, Alf Goddard *(Red)*, Arthur Sinclair *(O'Brien)*, Arthur Goullett *(Sylvestra)*.

Memorable version of H. Rider Haggard's oft-filmed novel which boasts superior production values and a magnificent performance from Robeson. The adventure begins as a spunky Irish girl, Lee, becomes determined to search for her father who has disappeared deep in the African jungles while searching for the fabled diamond cache known as King Solomon's Mines. Lee is accompanied by explorers Hardwicke, Young, and Loder and is guided through the treacherous territory by dignified African native Robeson. After hacking their way through desert and jungle, the small party finally arrives at an encampment of natives who look to the white explorers as gods. The tribe is run by an evil king who had stolen the throne from Robeson years ago with the help of an ancient witch, Fairbrother. Seeing that the presence of the white men and Robeson are a definite threat to his reign, the king and Fairbrother plot to kill them. The explorers sense their peril and decide to defend themselves by capitalizing on a soon-to-arrive solar eclipse to prove that their magic is more powerful than Fairbrother's. The warriors are won over by Robeson and the whites, thus deposing the bogus king and his witch doctor. Refusing to give up, the deposed king counters with an attack by rival warrior tribes. The battle is heated, but the evildoer is killed in the attack and his supporters give up the fight and return home. Meanwhile, the white men have discovered the location of King Solomon's Mines and move in to fill their coffers, but a gigantic volcano erupts and seals the massive diamond mine forever. Luckily, Robeson helps the explorers escape with their lives and they return to England empty handed, but filled with stories of adventure. While Robeson (who does manage to find the time to sing), Hardwicke, Fairbrother, and Young are standouts in KING SOLOMON'S MINES, the romantic leads suffer from uneven scripting and acting. Lee and Loder are dull performers at best and their interludes tend to put a damper on the film between action scenes. KING SOLOMON'S MINES was remade in 1952 and 1985. The 1985 version had little interest in the original source material and was basically an effort to exploit the success of the Indiana Jones films.

d, Robert Stevenson; w, A. R. Rawlinson, Charles Bennett, Ralph Spence (based on the novel by H. Rider Haggard); ph, Bernard Knowles.

Adventure **Cas.** **(PR:A MPAA:NR)**

KING SOLOMON'S MINES**** (1950) 102m MGM c

Deborah Kerr *(Elizabeth Curtis)*, Stewart Granger *(Allan Quartermain)*, Richard Carlson *(John Goode)*, Hugo Haas *(Van Brun)*, Lowell Gilmore *(Eric Masters)*, Kimursi *(Khiva)*, Siriaque *(Umbopa)*, Sekaryongo *(Chief Gagool)*, Baziga *(King Twala)*, Cpl. Munto Anampio *(Chief Bilu)*, Gutare *(Kafa, Double for Umbopa)*, Ivargwema *(Blue Star)*, Benempinga *(Black Circle)*, John Banner *(Austin)*, Henry Rowland *(Traum)*.

For those who love thrilling, big-scale adventure films loaded with action and exotic scenery KING SOLOMON'S MINES is a must. MGM spent a fortune (for those days), $3,500,000, in producing this wonderful movie which has something for everyone (except for those, who, like Woody Allen in ANNIE HALL, are addicted only to documentaries such as THE SORROW AND THE PITY). Granger is a great white hunter who has had 15 years of bloodthirsty clients abusing nature and he's sick of it, planning to give up the safari business and return to the peace and quiet of England. Entering his life is beautiful Kerr and her impetuous but idealistic brother, Carlson. They are in search of the fabled King Solomon's diamond mines, they tell Granger, but, emphasizes the aloof Kerr, she is really looking for her husband who has vanished while seeking the great treasure. The great hunter laughs at them, telling them they are pipe-dreaming, that the story about the mines is only an old legend, that there are no mines. Kerr turns his doubt around a bit when offering him 5,000 pounds to lead them into the uncharted lands where the mines are reported to be. He accepts, planning to use this fee for his retirement to England. The safari proves arduous and full of hazards and soon the very proper Kerr must change her formal clothing to more casual traveling garb. She and Carlson soon learn to follow Granger's instructions, especially after they come close to being attacked by wild animals or drowning in treacherous rapids. On and on they go, through swamps, forests, over mountains, and across deserts. A brush fire causes a thundering stampede of animals which they barely survive. When they come to a small village they meet sleazy Haas, a white renegade who admits that Kerr's husband passed through his village a year earlier. By his questionable actions and probing queries, Haas is suspected by Granger to be dangerous; he concludes that Haas intends to unleash his blood-thirsty warriors upon the group and so Granger takes him hostage, holding a gun on him until Haas guides them beyond the village. Haas later attacks Granger, who shoots him. Only Granger, Kerr, and Carlson are now left, their bearers having deserted in fear of the unknown dangers ahead., Suddenly a towering, dignified native appears and tells them he is making a journey in the same direction and offers to be their bearer. The four proceed to the beautiful rolling hills of the Watusi and it turns out that their silent bearer is the king of the Watusi who has returned to claim a throne taken from him by a usurper. The imposter king gives the whites a cool reception, then his medicine man makes a move toward the trio and Granger shoots him. This cows the tribe and the pretender to the throne who assigns several of his warriors to escort the whites to the legendary mines. Once inside the huge cavern, however, the entrance is sealed by the warriors and they are trapped. Inside, the trio finds the incredible wealth of King Solomon, huge chests and barrels packed with diamonds. They also find the skeletal remains of Kerr's missing husband. Granger notices a downdraft and the three find a narrow passage through the rocks which they follow to freedom. They make their way back to the village where they witness a confrontation between their friend, the real king, and the pretender. Both men duel with spears and shields while the tribe encircles them, waiting to proclaim the victor king. The real king manages to kill the pretender and take his rightful throne. He and his tribe are now friendly toward the visitors, and the king provides bearers and supplies so the whites can return to civilization. By this time the animosity between Kerr and Granger has changed to deep affection and it is obvious they will marry. KING SOLOMON'S MINES is one of the most majestically filmed adventure yarns ever put on celluloid, thanks to the superlative efforts of cinematographer Robert Surtees who won an Oscar for his photographic achievement (another Oscar went to Winters and Nervig for editing but the film lost out as Best Picture to ALL ABOUT EVE). Twenty years earlier MGM had sent a cast and crew to trek through the wilds of Africa to make its then spectacular TRADER HORN, taking all of six weeks just to get to the Dark Continent, and when the group did arrive it underwent countless horrors and illness. The KING SOLOMON'S MINES crew went prepared, going first to Nairobi and then, by specially built trucks and airplanes, to Kenya, Tanganyika, and the Belgian Congo, covering more than 14,000 miles and all the while contending with temperatures soaring between 140 and 152 degrees. Decimating their ranks were all manner of exotic diseases—amoebic dysentery, malaria, fever. They were plagued by swarms of snakes and tsetse flies. The elements even worked hardships on the natives, hundreds of them working as extras for about 30 cents a day. Director Bennett was utterly exhausted after the five-month shooting schedule so that Marton finished off the film, although producer Zimbalist later claimed that Marton easily directed half the film and was responsible for most of the miles and miles of incredible footage captured by Surtees' cameras. There was so much excess footage of great quality that MGM kept using it up in many movies, including WATUSI (1959), TARZAN THE APE MAN (1959), DRUMS OF AFRICA (1963), TRADER HORN (1973), and even the 1977 remake of KING SOLOMON'S MINES, the third sound version, the first being a British production in 1937 with Cedric Hardwicke. In the entire cast and crew of rugged he-men, Kerr surprisingly turned out to be the most sturdy of the lot. Cinematographer Surtees later remembered: "Sure it was tough. Many of us became ill—at one time we had just four members of the crew left behind the cameras, and 500 natives in front of it. All of us must have been homesick many times. But there was always Deborah, ready for whatever was next, with never a complaint of any sort. A man just couldn't gripe." Carlson would recall how Kerr's "good nature always astonished crew and cast alike. We were all convinced that no other girl in the picture business would have taken the beating she had to take on this African safari." A sample of the exhausting work during the shooting was described by codirector Bennett concerning the shooting at the top of towering Murchison Falls: "We had our camp at the foot of the falls. Every morning we spent nearly two hours crawling up to the top—a distance of some 500 feet. Then we'd work on a love scene between Deborah and Stewart Granger in 140-degree heat. We were using Technicolor film, so the reflectors had to be just twice as close to the principals. This threw more light and heat into their faces. It's a wonder they are not both blind." There were other dangers. At one point the chiefs of the Masai lifted the ban on the ancient dances so that the film company could see how they performed their old war rituals. More than 500 warriors chanted, writhed, jumped, and screamed for two days, accompanied by incessant drumming, until, in mass hysteria, the warriors began to hurl their spears at the whites, until calmer leaders stopped dozens of them by sitting on their heads. Seven spears were plucked out of the camera case and Kerr was found high in a tree where she had climbed when the spears began to fly. To entertain the natives, the company showed a film, PERFECT STRANGERS (VACATION FROM MARRIAGE) (1945), starring Kerr. Before the end of reel one, Kerr's own porter stood up and began to walk away. He said to an interpreter: "Can't be. She's up there [on the screen], she's here [in the camp], can't be!" Kerr, of course, gives one of her impeccable performances while Carlson is good in support and Granger is excellent as the all-knowing white hunter. Granger was making his first star-billed appearance in an American film here and it put him into superstar status. He was 37 years old at the time and the makeup people even added white to his temples to give him deeper maturity as the great white hunter. After signing a six-year contract with MGM, Granger gave an interview which largely discounted his considerable British film career: "I made all those pictures for [J. Arthur] Rank at a time when we were trying to make too many, and there aren't many of them that I am proud of. Except in a few localities like New York, nobody knows me in America, and actually, I can start all over again." Granger, however, almost didn't appear in KING SOLOMON'S MINES. Errol Flynn had been the first choice for the daring white hunter role but he became involved in another major production, KIM, and so the part went to Granger. The British actor clashed with codirector Bennett who later stated that Granger was hard to work with, but Marton felt that the actor had "guts in proportion to his ego." Carlson added that "everything about him is on a huge scale—his physique, his voice, his laugh, his enthusiasm, his frustrations, his temperament, and his generosity. I often had the feeling he would have been happier as an Elizabethan." Kerr gave him reserved admiration: "Women sense that there's a bit of the brute in him. A woman's intuition tells her that being a gentleman hasn't watered down his virility, and that he would as soon thwack her on the rear as not." He was nevertheless perfect as the hero invented by Sir Henry Rider Haggard (1856–1925), a gentleman explorer-hunter who spent many years in Africa, recording its wonders and perils and creating his finest hero in 1885 with the publication of *King Solomon's Mines.* Some criticism was leveled at scriptwriter Deutsch (and it's ironic that such a he-man film was so well-written by a woman); she was accused of scaling down the novel drastically to allow more room for the love story but she left action and adventure aplenty.

p, Sam Zimbalist; d, Compton Bennett, Andrew Marton; w, Helen Deutsch (based on the novel by Sir Henry Rider Haggard); ph, Robert Surtees (Technicolor); ed, Ralph E. Winters, Conrad A. Nervig; art d, Cedrick Gibbons, Nervig; set d, Edwin B. Willis, Keogh Gleason; cos, Walter Plunkett; m/l, Eric Maschwitz, Mischa Spoliansky.

Adventure **(PR:A MPAA:NR)**

KING SOLOMON'S TREASURE* (1978, Can.) 88m Gold Key-TV/Canafox-Towers c

David McCallum, John Colicos, Patrick Macnee, Britt Ekland, Wilfrid Hyde-White, Hugh Rose, Ken Gampu, Yvon Dufour.

A group of intrepid explorers goes off in search of the secret lost Phoenician city in the heart of darkest Africa. Being a low-class Canadian production, Canadian locations are used in place of the real thing. Some bargain basement special effects dinosaurs also provide a limiting menace with a cast of seasoned veterans (McCallum, Macnee, Ekland) providing embarrassingly bad performances. Surprisingly the photography is not bad at all.

d, Alvin Rakoff; w, Colin Turner, Allan Prior (based on the novel *Allan Quartermain* by H. Rider Haggard); ph, Paul van der Linden; m, Lew Lehman; art d, Gauthier, Wetherup; makeup, M. A. Protat.

Adventure **(PR:A MPAA:NR)**

KING STEPS OUT, THE*** (1936) 85m COL bw

Grace Moore *(Cissy)*, Franchot Tone *(Franz Josef)*, Walter Connolly *(Maximilian)*, Raymond Walburn *(von Kempen)*, Victor Jory *(Palfi)*, Nana Bryant *(Louise)*, Elizabeth Risdon *(Sofia)*, Frieda Inescort *(Helena)*, Thurston Hall *(Major)*, Herman Bing *(Pretzelberger)*, George Hassell *(Herlicka)*, John Arthur *(Chief of the Secret Police)*.

Though this was not von Sternberg's usual type of film, THE KING STEPS OUT is a well-made production. Based on the operetta "Cissy" and loosely depicting the life of Elizabeth of Austria, Inescort is a young princess and the object of Emperor Tone's affections. Moore, the poor girl's sister, saves her from an unwanted marriage by pretending to be a common dressmaker and winning the royal man's heart herself. Moore is given some marvelous closeups during her songs, which evoke the fairy tale feel of the film. Songs include "The Old Refrain," "Learn How to Lose," "Stars in My Eyes," "Madly in Love," "Soldier's March," "What Shall Remain?" "Call to Arms" (Kreisler, Dorothy Fields). A light and gay film, von Sternberg was ultimately displeased with his foray into opera and later asked that this not be included in a retrospective of his films.

p, William Perlberg; d, Josef von Sternberg; w, Sidney Buchman (based on the play "Cissy" by Gustav Hohn, Ernest Decsey and the operetta by Hubert and Ernst Marischka); ph, Lucien Ballard; m, Fritz Kreisler; ed, Viola Lawrence; art d & set d, Stephen Goosson; cos, Ernest Dryden; ch, Albertina Rasch.

Musical **(PR:A MPAA:NR)**

KINGDOM OF THE SPIDERS*** (1977) 94m Arachnid/Dimension c

William Shatner *(Rack Hansen)*, Tiffany Bolling *(Diane Ashley)*, Woody Strode *(Walter Colby)*, Lieux Dressler *(Emma Washburn)*, Altovise Davis *(Birch Colby)*, David McLean *(Sheriff Smith)*, Natasha Ryan *(Linda Hansen)*, Marcy Rafferty *(Terry Hansen)*, Joe Ross *(Vern Johnson)*, Adele Malis *(Betty Johnson)*, Roy Engel *(Mayor Connors)*.

Chemical insecticides kill off the food supply of some deadly desert tarantulas sending them swarming into the town of Verde, Arizona. Though the story itself is predictable, this is far better than you might think. The script is witty and doesn't rely on shock effects or giant creatures. The terror here slowly mounts with a sly sense of wit to it, as well. Shatner is fine as the veterinarian investigating the phenomenon, giving a slightly tongue-in-cheek performance. Rafferty, his real-life wife, is also seen here. The visual effects are marvelous (over 5,000 live tarantulas were used). Bolling's scene in the shower is definitely worth a few good screams. A slightly eerie ending is reminiscent of Hitchcock's 1963 thriller, THE BIRDS.

p, Igo Kanter, Jeffrey Sneller; d, John "Bud" Cardos; w, Richard Robinson, Alan Caillou; ph, John Morrill (Eastmancolor); m, Dorsey Burnette; ed, Steve Zaillian, Kantor; set d, Rusty Rosene; spec eff, Greg Auer.

Horror **Cas.** **(PR:C MPAA:PG)**

KINGFISH CAPER, THE* 1/2
(1976, South Africa) 90m Cavalier Film/Cinema Shares International c (AKA: THE KINGFISHER CAPER)

David McCallum *(Benedict)*, Hayley Mills *(Tracy)*, Jon Cypher *(Johnny)*.

The backlands of South Africa serve as the setting for this rather routine drama centering around the attempts of two power-hungry brothers to outmaneuver each other in order to claim the family empire. Everything from romance to mystery is thrown into the plot, but it still fails to look much different from a slick Dallas.

p, Ben Vlok; d, Dirk DeVilliers; w, Roy Boulting (based on the novel by Wilbur Smith).

Drama **Cas.** **(PR:A MPAA:PG)**

KINGFISHER CAPER, THE
(SEE: KINGFISH CAPER, THE, 1976, South Africa)

KING'S CUP, THE* 1/2
(1933, Brit.) 76m British and Dominions/Wolfe and Freedman bw

Dorothy Bouchier *(Betty Conway)*, Harry Milton *(Dick Carter)*, William Kendall *(Capt. Richards)*, Rene Ray *(Peggy)*, Tom Helmore *(Ronnie Helmore)*, Lewis Shaw *(Peter)*, Sydney King *(Crasher)*, Leila Page *(Lena)*, Syd Crossley *(Crossley)*, Anna Lee, Lew Stone and His Band.

Bouchier and Milton play a husband and wife flying team whose aeronautical feats become severely limited after Milton allows a crash to keep him from going up in the air again. He gets his chance to prove his flying abilities once more when Bouchier is unable to fly during a big race, forcing Milton to take her place in the pilot's seat. The novelty of four directors did nothing out of the ordinary in terms of what appears on the screen.

p, Herbert Wilcox; d, Wilcox, Robert J. Cullen, Sir Alan Cobham, Donald Macardle; w, Cobham; ph, F. A. Young.

Adventure/Drama **(PR:A MPAA:NR)**

KINGS GO FORTH*** (1958) 109m Frank Ross-Eton/UA bw

Frank Sinatra *(Lt. Sam Loggins)*, Tony Curtis *(Sgt. Britt Harris)*, Natalie Wood *(Monique Blair)*, Leora Dana *(Mrs. Blair)*, Karl Swenson *(Colonel)*, Ann Codee *(Mme. Brieux)*, Edward Ryder *(Cpl. Lindsay)*, Jackie Berthe *(Jean Francoise)*, Marie Isnard *(Old Woman with Wine)*, Jazz Combo: Pete Candoli *(Trumpet)*, Red Norvo *(Vibraphone)*, Mel Lewis *(Drums)*, Richie Kamuca *(Tenor Sax)*, Red Wooten *(Bass)*, Jimmy Weible *(Guitar)*.

Frank Sinatra never served in the Army during WW II but his portrayals of men in uniform have been excellent. Among them are ANCHORS AWEIGH, FROM HERE TO ETERNITY, VON RYAN'S EXPRESS, and this, one of his best acting efforts. This time, it's 1944 and Sinatra and Curtis are in France, battling the Nazis with the Seventh Army. On a brief furlough from the fray, Sinatra meets Wood, a gorgeous American living in Nice with her mother, Dana, a widow. The two of them fall in love but when he asks for her hand, she refuses. He can't understand why, and she finally explains that she is the result of a mixed marriage and that her father was black. Sinatra doesn't see that as a deterrent, but what does matter is that Wood is apparently in love with Curtis. Sinatra tells Curtis about Wood's parentage but that doesn't bother Curtis at all. They are about to return to the war and a particularly deadly mission when Curtis, a cad, admits that he had no intention of marrying Wood. When she learns that, she is crushed. Sinatra is so angered that he intends to kill Curtis while on the assignment, but the Nazis do it first. In the battle Sinatra loses an arm. When the war ends, Sinatra returns to Nice and learns that Dana has died and Wood has converted the Cote D'Azur mansion into a school for orphans of the war. The issue of miscegenation may have been a hot topic when Brown wrote the book but it had little impact in the film. Much of the movie was spent with long dialogue sequences, and, although it's set against the war, there's very little feeling that anything momentous is going on beyond the mission Sinatra and Curtis take, which has something to do with directing the artillery fire onto a German munitions depot. Frank and Richard Ross are brothers and have produced or co-produced many films through the years. Some good jazz is provided by Candoli, Norvo, Lewis, Kamuca, Wooten, Weible.

p, Frank Ross; Richard Ross; d, Delmer Daves; w, Merle Miller (based on the novel by Joe David Brown); ph, Daniel L. Fapp; m, Elmer Bernstein; ed, William B. Murphy; md, Bernstein; art d, Fernando Carrere; set d, Darrell Silvera; cos, Leah Rhodes; makeup, Bernard Ponedel.

War Drama **(PR:A MPAA:NR)**

KING'S JESTER, THE* 1/2** (1947, Ital.) 95m Scalera/Superfilm bw

Michel Simon *(Rigoletto)*, Rossano Brazzi *(Francesco I)*, Maria Mercader *(Gilda)*, Paola Barbara *(Marchesa di Cosse)*, Doris Duranti *(Margot)*, Elli Parvo *(Gypsy)*, Carlo Ninchi *(Count St. Vallier)*, Juan De Lando *(Sparafucile)*.

Excellent adaptation of Verdi's famed opera "Rigoletto," with the score used as incidental music. Simon is the poor hunchback reduced to a royal fool because of his condition. His job is to bring women to the young king (Brazzi) who uses them for his own lusty purposes. Simon has one secret: he has a beautiful daughter whom he wants to keep away from the king. But he is tricked and the king has his way with her, as well. The hunchback swears revenge and hires Duranti, a gypsy girl, to seduce the king and kill him. But she, too, is wooed by the man's charms. When Simon returns to collect the body, he is handed a sack with a corpse. He is about to dump it into the river when he hears the king singing and discovers, to his horror, that the dead body he is carrying is his daughter. Passionate and moving, Simon gives a tour-de-force performance running an emotional gamut within a highly controlled performance. The supporting players are equally good. As the drama unfolds the viewer is swept up by a myriad of circumstances, all well handled and delicately expressed in the screenplay. The camera work is second to none, with an excellent lighting pattern that accentuates the drama. It's hard to believe that a film this opulent, with such incredible set decor as well, could have come out of war-torn Italy, when most other films of that country were depicting the tragedy of the modern-day man in bleak surroundings. (In Italian; English subtitles.)

d, Mario Bonnard; w, (based on Giuseppe Verdi's opera "Rigoletto"); ph, Ubaldo Arata; subtitles, Armando V. Macaluso.

Drama **(PR:O MPAA:NR)**

KINGS OF THE ROAD* 1/2**
(1976, Ger.) 176m Filmverlag der Autoren bw (IM LAUF DER ZEIT)

Rudiger Vogler *(Bruno)*, Hanns Zischler *(Robert)*, Lisa Kreuzer *(Cashier)*, Rudolf Schuendler *(Robert's Father)*, Marquard Bohm *(Man Who Lost His Wife)*.

Although director Wenders is better known for THE AMERICAN FRIEND, there is no doubt that KINGS OF THE ROAD is his best film. Beautifully photographed in black and white by Robbie Mueller, the film traces the adventures of two men as they wander along the back roads of Germany, going from one small town to another. Vogler is a motion picture projector repairman; he lives in his van and must travel to the various towns to fix the projectors in the dilapidated theaters. One day, as he wakes up and shaves, looking in the mirror of his van, he notices a Volkswagen plunge off a dock and into the water. Out of the water comes Zischler (one of Germany's foremost film critics), a linguist whose wife has left him and who has failed at this suicide attempt. Zischler takes a ride with Vogler as he works on his route, their friendship developing as they embark upon one experience after another. Eventually Zischler decides that he can no longer keep up with this life of a nomad and returns to the modern world as represented by the city. In the manner to which Vogler has become accustomed in his travels, one which does not allow him to betray his loneliness, he gives a brief nod to the parting friend. Although the story is simple, and yet takes a long time to unwind, KINGS OF THE ROAD is filled with countless wonders. Whether it be in the expressive images captured by Mueller or the gestures of the actors, this film leaves much for the viewer to ponder. Beneath it all Wenders seems to be saying that individuals are becoming more and more separated from each other as the modern world of mass media has greater and greater impact on individuality. A metaphor can even be drawn about the death of the cinema in the manner in which many of the theaters that Vogler visits are forced to shut their doors, or even worse show pornographic films or other forms of popular Hollywood trash.

p,d&w, Wim Wenders; ph, Robbie Mueller, Martin Schafer, Peter Przygodda; m, Axel Linstadt.

Drama **(PR:C MPAA:NR)**

KINGS OF THE SUN** (1963) 108m Mirisch/UA c

Yul Brynner *(Black Eagle)*, George Chakiris *(Balam)*, Shirley Anne Field *(Ixchel)*, Richard Basehart *(Ah Min)*, Brad Dexter *(Ah Haleb)*, Barry Morse *(Ah Zok)*, Armando Silvestre *(Isatai)*, Leo Gordon *(Hunac Ceel)*, Victoria Vettri *(Ixzubin)*, Rudy Solari *(Pitz)*, Ford Rainey *(The Chief)*, Angel Di Steffano *(Balam, the Elder)*, Jose Moreno *(The Youth)*.

Chakiris is chosen king of the Mayans after his father is killed in a war. His tribe leaves Mexico and resettles on the coast where Brynner, the chief of a local Indian tribe, leads an attack on the newcomers. He is wounded in the battle but nursed back to health by Field, Chakiris' fiancee. The two leaders decide to live in harmony but Gordon, Chakiris' old enemy, is intent on destroying the Mayans. When he leads his warriors on an attack, Brynner and Chakiris unite to defeat him, but the Indian chief is killed saving his new friend's life. Despite the realistic setting—having been filmed in the Mexican outlands and mountains—the story itself is superficial. Motivations are simplistic, and the script gives the actors plenty of "solemn" moments. The battle sequences are nicely put together, but the rest of the drama lags.

p, Lewis J. Rachmil; d, J. Lee Thompson; w, Elliott Arnold, James R. Webb (based on a story by Arnold); ph, Joseph MacDonald (Panavision, DeLuxe Color); m, Elmer Bernstein; ed, William Reynolds; art d, Alfred Ybarra; cos, Norma Koch; spec eff, Roscoe Cline; makeup, Emile La Vigne.

Historical Drama **(PR:O MPAA:NR)**

KING'S PIRATE** (1967) 100m UNIV c

Doug McClure *(Lt. Brian Fleming)*, Jill St. John *(Jessica Stephens)*, Guy Stockwell *(John Avery)*, Mary Ann Mobley *(Princess Patma)*, Kurt Kasznar *(Zucco)*, Richard Deacon *(Swaine)*, Torin Thatcher *(Capt. Cullen)*, Diana Chesney *(Molvina MacGregor)*, Ivor Barry *(Cloudsly)*, Bill Glover *(Capt. Hornsby)*, Woodrow Parfrey *(Gow)*, Sean McClory *(Sparkes)*, Michael St. Clair *(Collins)*, Emile Genest *(Capt. Misson)*, Ted De Corsia *(Capt. McTigue)*, Alex Montoya *(Caraccioli)*, Tanya Lemani, Aime Luce, Robert Terhune, Chuck Couch, Bill Couch, Loren Janes, Hank Monzello, William Snyder, Rodney Hoeltzel, Danny Rees *(Zucco's Troupe)*.

The year is 1700 and McClure plays a courageous British naval officer who heads to Madagascar to help rid it of pirates. He goes undercover, landing a job as a navigator under Stockwell, and the two vie for the affections of St. John. McClure's true identity is revealed as British war vessels roll into the harbor. (Remake of AGAINST ALL FLAGS, 1952.) Fast-paced direction helps hide any weaknesses in the script. Performances are adequate.

p, Robert Arthur; d, Don Weis; w, Paul Wayne, Aeneas MacKenzie, Joseph Hoffman (based on story by MacKenzie); ph, Clifford Stine (Technicolor); m, Ralph Ferraro; ed, Russell F. Schoengarth; art d, Alexander Golitzen, George C. Webb; set d, John McCarthy, John Austin; cos, Vittorio Nino Novarese; stunts, Ronnie Rondell; makeup, Bud Westmore.

Adventure **(PR:A MPAA:NR)**

KING'S RHAPSODY** 1/2 (1955, Brit.) 93m Everest/UA c

Anna Neagle *(Marta Karillos)*, Errol Flynn *(King Richard of Laurentia)*, Patrice Wymore *(Princess Christiane)*, Martita Hunt *(Queen Mother)*, Finlay Currie *(King Paul)*, Francis de Wolff *(Prime Minister)*, Joan Benham *(Countess Astrid)*, Reginald Tate *(King Peter)*, Miles Malleson *(Jules)*, Edmund Hockridge *(Singer's Voice)*, Lionel Blair, Jon Gregory, Terence Theobald.

In one of his final roles Flynn plays an heir who chooses to abdicate in order to be with Neagle, the woman he loves. But when his father dies, he returns to accept the throne and the hand of Wymore (Flynn's third wife at the time of filming), whom he eventually learns to love. Flynn unenthusiastically performs this role, while the rest of the cast is adequate. The photography, most of which is in Barcelona, Spain, is uneven, but the sets and costumes are realistic. Interesting use of flashbacks to portray Flynn's exile.

p&d, Herbert Wilcox; w, Pamela Bower, Christopher Hassall, A. P. Herbert (based on the play by Ivor Novello); ph, Max Greene (CinemaScope, Eastmancolor); m, Novello; ed, Reginald Beck; md, Robert Farnon; art d, William C. Andrews; cos, Anthony Holland; ch, Jon Gregory; m/l, Novello, Hassall.

Romance/Drama **(PR:A MPAA:NR)**

KING'S ROW**** (1942) 127m WB bw

Ann Sheridan *(Randy Monoghan)*, Robert Cummings *(Parris Mitchell)*, Ronald Reagan *(Drake McHugh)*, Betty Field *(Cassandra Tower)*, Charles Coburn *(Dr. Henry Gordon)*, Claude Rains *(Dr. Alexander Tower)*, Judith Anderson *(Mrs. Harriet Gordon)*, Nancy Coleman *(Louise Gordon)*, Kaaren Verne *(Elise Sandor)*, Maria Ouspenskaya *(Mme. Von Eln)*, Harry Davenport *(Col. Skeffington)*, Ernest Cossart *(Pa Monoghan)*, Pat Moriarity *(Tom Monoghan)*, Ilka Gruning *(Ann the Maid)*, Minor Watson *(Sam Winters)*, Ludwig Stossel *(Dr. Berdoff)*, Erwin Kalser *(Mr. Sandor)*, Egon Brecher *(Dr. Candell)*, Ann Todd *(Randy as a Child)*, Douglas Wheat *(Drake as a Child)*, Scotty Beckett *(Parris as a Child)*, Mary Thomas *(Cassandra as a Child)*, Joan Duval *(Louise as a Child)*, Danny Jackson *(Benny Singer)*, Henry Blair *(Willie)*, Leah Baird *(Aunt Mamie)*, Eden Gray *(Mrs. Tower)*, Julie Warren *(Poppy Ross)*, Mary Scott *(Ginny Ross)*, Bertha Powell *(Esther)*, Walter Baldwin *(Deputy Constable)*, Jack Mower *(Freight Conductor)*, Frank Mayo *(Conductor)*, Thomas W. Ross *(Patterson Lewes)*, Frank Milan *(Teller)*, Hank Mann *(Livery Stable Keeper)*, Fred Kelsey *(Bill Hockinson)*, Herbert Heywood *(Arnold Kelly)*, Emory Parnell *(Harley Davis)*, Elizabeth Valentine *(Nurse)*, Ludwig Hardt *(Porter)*, Hattie Noel *(Gordon's Maid)*, Hermine Sterler *(Secretary)*.

This is a startling film, at least for its day, in that it portrayed a small town in America not with the poignancy and little joys seen in Thorton Wilder's OUR TOWN but in grim and almost unrelenting tragedy where, behind the Victorian houses and across the broad, mowed lawns lurked sadism, incest, suicide, homosexuality, and murder. It was the PEYTON PLACE of its day but drawn on more literate and compassionate levels, and it offered the finest peformances ever given by Ann Sheridan and Ronald Reagan. No light-hearted film this, but drama, clouded with mystery and fatalism that barely offered hope, unlike the bleak novel upon which the film is based. The town of King's Row is shown at the turn-of-the-century, seen through the eyes of children, especially five children and what they grow up to be. The central character is a boy named Parris, played by Beckett as a child, whose best friend is Cassandra, Thomas as a child. They play and go swimming together but she is a lonely, strange little girl. Beckett's best friends are Drake, played by Wheat as a child, tomboy Randy, played by Todd as a child, and snobbish Louise, played by Duval as a child. Beckett returns home one day to find that he has two party invitations, one from Duval and one from Thomas and he tells his wise old grandmother, Ouspenskaya, that he will attend the Thomas party because not many children will attend. Later Thomas comes to Beckett and tells him tearfully that she won't be seeing much of him since her father, Rains, a psychiatrist, is taking her out of school to be tutored privately at home. The children grow up to be Cummings as Parris, Reagan as Drake, Sheridan as Randy, Field as Cassandra, and Coleman as Louise. Cummings is a brilliant medical student who studies with Rains and still sees his daughter occasionally but Field is strangely aloof and distant. Sheridan, still the aggressive young lady, loves Cummings and Reagan while Coleman is kept from socializing by her strict parents, Coburn and Anderson. Sheridan falls in love with Reagan who lives like a playboy from a large inheritance, and when they go together Coleman becomes distraught, believing Sheridan is taking her man. Cummings announces that he's going to Vienna to further his studies and Field desperately begs to go with him but something tells him not to respond. A short time later Cummings' wonderful grandmother, Ouspenskaya, dies of cancer and he is doubly shocked to learn that Field is dead, murdered by her father, Rains, who then took his own life. Cummings first learns that Rains thought his daughter hopelessly insane and that is why he shot her to death, but even later he learns that Field was pregnant at the time of her death. He goes off to Vienna while Reagan's fortunes plummet. He takes a job working on the railroad, continuing to see Sheridan. He has an accident and Coburn, a doctor, is called. The vicious old man hates Reagan for his playboy ways and for ignoring his daughter Coleman (who has since become a complete neurotic, expressing her hatred for her father and mother at every turn for ruining her life with their repressive ways). Coburn inspects Reagan's damaged legs and decides they must be amputated. Coburn's action prove to be one of the most vindictive acts ever recorded on film. When Reagan awakes he looks down to see his legs gone. He cries out for Sheridan who runs into his room to hold on to him to counter the shock. Reagan cries out: "Where's the rest of me?" Cummings then returns from his European studies and finds another doctor, Kalser, and his lovely daughter, Verne, occupying his former home. He falls in love with Verne and they find happiness together. Cummings meets once more with the legless Reagan and tells him he must be brave enough to face the truth, then tells him that his legs were amputated by the warped Coburn as an evil act of punishment and vengeance. Instead of collapsing into despair, Reagan vows that Coburn, since dead, will not destroy his spirit as he undoubtedly planned to do, that he will go on with his plans for the future with Sheridan at his side. All in this superb cast are outstanding, though Cummings was acting beyond his usual capacity. (Warner Bros. originally wanted Fox to loan out Tyrone Power for the role but that studio refused to part with its top star.) Field is a bit old for her part here but she does a fine job as the unbalanced Cassandra. Wood's direction is a careful balance of drama and occasional light-heartedness; he never allows the film to sink into bathos or sloppy sentiment. Korngold's rich score is haunting and the meticulous sets by Menzies are stunning and perfectly constructed to the story. The brilliant cinematographer Howe gave all the credit to Menzies for the superlative production values the film offered, stating (in *Hollywood Cameramen* by Charles Higham): "William Cameron Menzies designed the sets and did the sketches for the shots; he'd tell you how high the camera should be. He'd even specify the kind of lens he wanted for a particular shot; the set was designed for one specific shot only, and if you varied your angle by an inch you'd shoot over the top. Everything, even the apple orchard, was done in the studio. The orchard was such a low set that it was very, very hard not to show the banks of lights. I had to hang shreds of imitation skys over it, blending one with another to hide all that equipment. Menzies created the whole look of the film. I simply followed orders. Sam Wood just directed the actors; he knew nothing about visuals." Robinson's script is both lyrical and sensitive, although the scriptwriter did tone down the more macabre features of the novel, ignoring how Parris reportedly slew his grandmother in a mercy killing, and how Drake died of cancer at the end. Though this proved to be Reagan's most memorable part, he almost didn't get it. Warners went down an impressive list of actors before coming to his name. The studio first considered Dennis Morgan, Jack Carson, Jeffrey Lynn, Eddie Albert, Franchot Tone, and Robert Preston. Reagan, once cast, worked harder on this part than any other of his career, he later admitted. Before shooting the scene where he discovers that the evil Coburn has sliced off his limbs, he spent endless hours without sleep, worrying about the scene. He later stated: "Gradually the affair began to terrify me. In some weird way, I felt something horrible had happened to my body. Then gradually I became aware that the crew had quietly assembled, the camera was in position, and the set all lighted. Sam Wood, the director, stood beside me, watching me sweat . . . There were cries of 'Lights!' and 'Quiet, please!' I lay back and closed my eyes, as tense as a fiddlestring. I heard Sam's low voice call 'Action!' There was the sharp clack which signaled the beginning of the scene. I opened my eyes dazedly, looked around, slowly let my gaze travel downward. I can't describe even now my feelings as I tried to reach for where my legs should be. 'Randy!' I screamed. Ann Sheridan (bless her), burst through the door. She wasn't in the shot, and normally wouldn't have been on hand until we turned the camera around to get her entrance, but she knew it was one of those scenes where a fellow actor needed all the help he could get and at that moment in my mind, she was Randy answering my call. I asked the question—the words that had been haunting me for so many weeks—'Where's the rest of me?' There was no retake. It was a good scene and it came out that way in the picture. Perhaps I never did quite as well again in a single shot."

p, Hal B. Wallis; d, Sam Wood; w, Casey Robinson (based on the novel by Henry Bellamann; ph, James Wong Howe; m, Erich Wolfgang Korngold; ed, Ralph Dawson; art d, Carl Jules Weyl; prod d, William Cameron Menzies.

Drama **Cas.** **(PR:C-O MPAA:NR)**

KING'S THIEF, THE** 1/2 (1955) 78m MGM c

Ann Blyth *(Lady Mary)*, Edmund Purdom *(Michael Dermott)*, David Niven *(Duke of Brampton)*, George Sanders *(Charles II)*, Roger Moore *(Jack)*, John Dehner *(Capt. Herrick)*, Sean McClory *(Sheldon)*, Tudor Owen *(Simon)*, Melville Cooper *(Henry Wynch)*, Alan Mowbray *(Sir Gilbert Talbot)*, Rhys Williams *(Turnkey)*, Joan Elan *(Charity Fell)*, Ashley Cowan *(Skene)*, Ian Wolfe *(Fell)*, Paul Cavanagh *(Sir Edward Scott)*, Lillian Kemble Cooper *(Mrs. Fell)*, Isobel Elsom *(Mrs. Bennett)*, Milton Parsons *(Adam Urich)*, Lord Layton *(Jacob Hall)*, Queenie Leonard *(Apothecary's Wife)*, Owen McGiveney *(Hoskins)*, Bob Dix, Michael Dugan *(Huskies)*, James Logan *(Guard)*, Matt Moore *(Gentleman)*.

Costumed swashbuckler with Niven as an evil duke, who uses his influence with the king, Sanders, for his own self-gain. Purdom attempts to steal the crown jewels and is thus given an audience with Sanders, enabling him to expose the corrupt Niven. Inventive scripts keep the action moving, aided by competent performances. Other facets of the production are all adequate.

p, Edwin H. Knopf; d, Robert Z. Leonard; w, Christopher Knopf (based on a story by Robert Hardy Andrews); ph, Robert Planck (CinemaScope, Eastmancolor); m, Miklos Rozsa; ed, John McSweeney, Jr.; md, Rozsa; art d, Cedric Gibbons, Malcolm Brown; cos, Walter Plunkett.

Adventure **(PR:A MPAA:NR)**

KING'S VACATION, THE** 1/2 (1933) 60m WB bw

George Arliss *(Philip)*, Florence Arliss *(Queen Wilhelmina)*, Marjorie Gateson *(Helen)*, Dudley Digges *(Lord Chamberlain)*, Dick Powell *(John Kent)*, Patricia Ellis *(Millicent)*, O. P. Heggie *(Joe Thorpe)*, Douglas Gerrard *(Count Gouvain)*, James Bell *(Anderson)*, Charles Evans *(Page)*, Helena Phillips *(Comtesse)*, Maude Leslie *(Amelia)*, Alan Birmingham *(Baron Munsle)*, Harold Minjur *(Fred Neerhoff)*, Vernon Steele *(Barstowe)*, Desmond Roberts *(Sgt. Footman)*.

In the midst of a revolution, a king (George Arliss) desires to return to the simpler life he had with the wife he forsook upon taking the throne. His present wife, the queen (Florence Arliss), grants him leave, hinting at her own possible suitor. He meets his former wife, Gateson, only to discover her surrounded by the grotesque splendor he wanted to escape. The king returns to his queen to find her alone in a humble cottage, where the two presumably live out their lives. Though Arliss delivers a commendable performance with given material, the script remains lacking and plodding.

p, Lucien Hubbard; d, John Adolfi; w, Ernest Pascal, Maude T. Howell (based on a story by Pascal); ph, James Van Trees; ed, Owen Marks; art d, Anton Groff.

Romance **(PR:A MPAA:NR)**

KIPPS (SEE: REMARKABLE MR. KIPPS, THE, 1941)

KIRI NI MUSEBU YORU (SEE: HARBOR LIGHT YOKOHAMA, 1970, Jap.)

KIRLIAN WITNESS, THE***

(1978) 91m Sampson and Cranor c (AKA: THE PLANTS ARE WATCHING)

Nancy Snyder *(Rilla)*, Ted Laplat *(Dusty)*, Joel Colodner *(Robert)*, Nancy Boykin *(Laurie)*, Lawrence Tierney *(Detective)*, Maia Danziger *(Claire)*.

Snyder is able to communicate telepathically with a plant which indirectly causes her to become witness to a murder. Well-paced direction is aided by atmospheric photography, creating an intriguing picture. Actual Kirlian photography is used to create auras around images. This was a first feature by director Sarno, who once did production work for pornographic director Gerard Damiano of DEEP THROAT fame.

p&d, Jonathan Sarno; w, Sarno, Lamar Sanders (based on a story by Sarno); ph, Joao Fernandes (Technicolor); m, Harry Mandredini; ed, Len Dell'Amico, Edward Salier.

Mystery **(PR:O MPAA:PG)**

KIRU (SEE: KILL, 1968, Jap.)

KISENGA, MAN OF AFRICA**

(1952, Brit.) 90m TC/International Releasing c (GB: MEN OF TWO WORLDS)

Robert Adams *(Kisenga)*, Eric Portman *(District Commissioner Randall)*, Orlando Martins *(Magole)*, Phyllis Calvert *(Dr. Caroline Munro)*, Arnold Marle *(Prof. Gollner)*, Cathleen Nesbitt *(Mrs. Upjohn)*, David Horne *(Concert Agent)*, Cyril Raymond *(Education Officer)*, Sam Blake *(Chief Raki)*, Uriel Porter *(Saidi)*, George Cooper *(Orchestra Conductor)*, Viola Thompson *(Kisenga's Mother)*, Napoleon Florent *(Kisenga's Father)*, Eseka Makumbi *(Saburi)*, Tunji Williams *(Ali)*, Rudolph Evans *(Abram)*, Cicely Dale, Brenda Davies.

Adams is an African-born composer who becomes a big splash in Europe. However, when his home tribe comes under the spells of a witch doctor (Martins), Adams returns home to help Portman stop the man. Martins throws a curse on Adams, claiming he will die under the next full moon. This frightens the composer, despite all he has learned abroad. It is only with the support of his friends that Adams is able to realize that the curse is utter nonsense. This film means well, trying valiantly to tell a sincere story. However, there is a lack of any hard conviction, which ultimately reduces the story to silly voodoo magic.

p, John Sutro; d, Thorold Dickinson; w, Dickinson, Herbert W. Victor (based on a story by E. Arnot Robertson, Joyce Cary); ph, Desmond Dickinson (Technicolor); m, Muir Mathieson, Arthur Bliss.

Drama **(PR:C MPAA:NR)**

KISMET*** (1930) 90m FN-WB bw

Otis Skinner *(Haji)*, Loretta Young *(Marsinah)*, David Manners *(Caliph Abdallah)*, Mary Duncan *(Zeleekha)*, Sidney Blackmer *(Wazir Mansur)*, Ford Sterling *(Amru)*, Edmund Breese *(Jawan)*, Blanche Frederici *(Narjis)*, Montagu Love *(The Jailer)*, Richard Carlyle *(The Muezzin)*, John St. Polis *(Iman Mahmud)*, Otto Hoffman *(Azaf)*, John Sheehan *(Kazim)*, Theodore von Eltz *(Nazir the Guide)*, Charles Clary, Noble Johnson, Carol Wines, Sidney Jarvis, Lorris Baker, Olin Francis, Will Walling.

Costly costume production with Skinner (at age 72, portraying a character half his age) as a rogue who will do anything for gold. Within the course of 12 hours, he kills two enemies, arranges his daughter's wedding, and goes from rags to riches and back again. Skinner played this part superbly, but Young and Duncan—though captivating—do little acting. Good production with solid direction.

p, Robert North; d, John Francis Dillon; w, Howard Estabrook (based on the play by Edward Knoblock); ph, John B. Seitz (Vitascope); ed, Al Hall.

Drama **(PR:A MPAA:NR)**

KISMET*** (1944) 100m MGM c (AKA: ORIENTAL DREAM)

Ronald Colman *(Hafiz)*, Marlene Dietrich *(Jamilla)*, James Craig *(Caliph)*, Edward Arnold *(Mansur the Grand Vizier)*, Hugh Herbert *(Feisal)*, Joy Ann Page *(Marsinah)*, Florence Bates *(Karsha)*, Harry Davenport *(Agha)*, Hobart Cavanaugh *(Moolah)*, Robert Warwick *(Alfife)*, Beatrice Kraft, Evelyne Kraft *(Court Dancers)*, Barry Macollum *(Amu)*, Victor Killian *(Jehan)*, Charles Middleton *(The Miser)*, Harry Humphrey *(Gardener)*, Nestor Paiva *(Captain of Police)*, Eve Whitney *(Cafe Girl)*, Minerva Urecal *(Retainer)*, Cy Kendall *(Herald)*, Dan Seymour *(Fat Turk)*, Dale Van Sickel *(Assassin)*, Pedro De Cordoba *(Meuzin)*, Roque Ybarra *(Miser's Son)*, Joe Yule *(Attendant)*, Morgan Wallace *(Merchant)*, John Maxwell *(Guard)*, Walter De Palma *(Detective)*, Jimmy Ames *(Major Domo)*, Charles La Torre *(Alwah)*, Noble Blake *(Nubian Slave)*, Anna Demetrio *(Proprietress of Cafe)*, Mitchell Lewis *(Sheik)*, Phiroz Nair, Asit Ghosh *(Nabout Fighters)*, Carmen D'Antonio *(Specialty Dancer)*, Jessie Tai Sing, Zedra Conde, Barbara Glenz, Frances Ramsden *(Cafe Girls)*, Charles Judels *(Rich Merchant)*, Harry Cording, Joseph Granby *(Policemen)*, Frank Penny, Peter Cusanelli *(Merchants)*, Zack Williams *(Executioner)*, Gabriel Gonzales *(Monkey Man)*, John Merton, Eddie Abdo, Dick Botiller, Jack "Tiny" Lipson *(Mansur's Aides)*, Lynne Arlen, Leslie Anthony, Rosalyn Lee, Sonia Carr, Carla Boehm, Yvonne De Carlo, Eileen Herric, Shelby Payne *(Queen's Retinue)*, Paul Singh *(Caliph's Valet)*, Eddie Abdo *(Voice—Prayer in Arabic)*, Paul Bradley *(Magician)*, Louis Manley *(Fire-Eater)*, Sammy Stein *(Policeman)*, John Schaller, Ramiro Rivas, William Rivas *(Juggling Trio)*.

It's all hokum surrounded by lavish sets, a fable brushed with rich color but Dietrich's extraordinary performance and her Salome-like dance with her legs painted thickly with gold paint, along with Colman's satiric performance, makes KISMET good entertainment. Colman is the beggar-magician Hafiz, a quick-witted rascal who tries to pass his daughter, Page, off as a princess so she can wed royalty. Page isn't interested since she and Craig, a gardener's son, are deeply in love. But Craig isn't really a gardener's son after all; he is the all-powerful Caliph of Baghdad, who is in disguise so he can spy on Arnold, the local Grand Vizier who has been taxing Craig's subjects mercilessly. Moreover, Colman, who calls himself the "Prince of Hassir," has been seeing Dietrich, the sexy, snaked-hipped wife of Arnold and queen of the castle. Colman just about has Arnold persuaded to toss Dietrich aside (so Colman can have her to himself) and take Colman's daughter as his wife and new queen when disaster strikes. The resplendent clothes Colman wears are stolen, it is revealed, and his charade is exposed. Mean-streaked Arnold orders that Colman, now reduced to the status of ordinary thief, have his hands chopped off. Colman offers a counter-proposal; he will murder Arnold's arch enemy, the young Caliph, if Arnold will free him *and* take his daughter as his wife. Arnold agrees and Colman goes to the Caliph's palace as a wizard to perform magical feats. As he is performing, Colman tries to stab Craig but misses and then must run for his life, going back to Arnold's palace to retrieve his daughter. But Arnold is on to him and his guards attack Colman, who kills a number of them, including Arnold himself. Craig's guards then capture Colman and drag him back before the Caliph. When Craig learns that Colman is Page's father, he pardons him and makes him a prince, ordering him to leave the city forever. Colman happily departs with his true love Dietrich, while Craig and Page find happiness together. This film, though heavy-handed and offering an impossible plot, is marvelously photographed by Rosher, and the art direction by Gibbons and Cathcat, and the stupendous sets by Willis and Pefferle (all of whom received Oscar nominations) makes this an extravaganza that must be seen to be appreciated. MGM spared no expense in this war-time production, pumping more than $3 million into the film, and it shows in every frame. The play and earlier movies were always synonymous with the flamboyant actor Otis Skinner, who first starred in this most durable vehicle on Broadway in 1911 and, for years, in a touring show, and went on to film it twice, in 1920 which also featured his daughter, Cornelia Otis Skinner, and again for First National in 1930 as an early-day and somewhat creaky talkie. It would be filmed again, after the Colman-Dietrich romp, as a lavish musical, also by MGM, in 1955, with Howard Keel and Ann Blyth. Colman plays the role of the shifty magician with all the elan Skinner ever produced but adds his own brand of camp which makes it all the more amusing. Dietrich is used sparingly, appearing in only five sequences, most notably to do her famous dance. The studio had the Hays Office, the official Hollywood censor at the time, crawling over Dietrich's dance sequence like bees in a hive. Her skimpy costume was examined in detail and censors decreed that the bangles covering her arms and breasts had to be backed up with sheer skin-toned material. Dietrich's navel could not be shown and had to be covered with chiffon but censors insisted that her panty line be seen by viewers lest they think she was naked beneath the spangles encircling her lower parts. In addition, the makeup department created a towering Dietrich (standing more than six feet) by placing her on high heels and adorning her head with a four-inch topknot hairpiece. Her fingernails were painted carmine and four coats of gold paint were brushed onto her luscious legs, perhaps the most famous legs in the world. This was the first time in films that Dietrich actually did a full dance on those legs and it was termed a "novelty" number, sort of a variation of Garbo's slinky dance in MATA HARI. Actually, Dietrich more or less poses through the dance in seductive positions, prone, bending back, forward, with cutaway shots to give the impression of more movement that was actually performed, a dance that was really created in the editing room. She did have some strenuous movements to perform, according to dance instructor Jack Cole, and suffered some bruises from falls so that this number was postponed a number of times before completion. Dietrich's brief dance was what the studio promoted, showing stills of her and, in Times Square, on a huge billboard, as she slithered around pillars and reclined sensuously on divans. The censors were not pleased with the advertising campaign but were able to forbid MGM from using the word "harem" in their production and subsequent publicity, a minor victory for Mrs. Grundy.

p, Everett Riskin; d, William Dieterle; w, John Meehan (based on the play by Edward Knoblock); ph, Charles Rosher (Technicolor); m, Herbert Stothart; ed, Ben Lewis; art d, Cedric Gibbons, Daniel B. Cathcart; set d, Edwin B. Willis, Richard Pefferle; cos, Irene; spec eff, A. Arnold Gillespie, Warren Newcombe; m/l, "Willow in the Wind," "Tell Me, Tell Me, Evening Star," Harold Arlen, E. Y. Harburg.

Fantasy **(PR:A MPAA:NR)**

KISMET** 1/2** (1955) 113m MGM c

Howard Keel *(The Poet)*, Ann Blyth *(Marsinah)*, Dolores Gray *(Lalume)*, Vic Damone *(Caliph)*, Monty Woolley *(Omar)*, Sebastian Cabot *(Wazir)*, Jay C. Flippen *(Jawan)*, Mike Mazurki *(Chief Policeman)*, Jack Elam *(Hassan-Ben)*, Ted De Corsia *(Police Subaltern)*, Patricia Dunn, Reiko Sato, Wonci Lui *(Princesses of A Ba Bu)*, Julie Robinson *(Zubbediya)*.

Dizzying Baghdadian luxury pours from the screen in this opulently colored, CinemaScope presentation of the popular stage musical. Filmed silently in 1920, then in 1930, and again in 1944 with Marlene Dietrich and Ronald Colman, this version features the talents of Keel and Blyth. Keel takes the role of Haaj, the poet-beggar, who goes along with a scheme engineered by the power-hungry wazir, Cabot. Keel is forced into using his supposed magical powers in a scheme to marry Cabot's son, Damone, off to a princess. Keel, however, is in a bind because his daughter, Blyth, is in love with Damone. The fun-loving Keel goes along with Cabot's folly and finds himself figuring out a way to get Blyth and Damone together.

Fate, or kismet, takes its course and the picture steamrolls to an exuberant end. A fluffy piece of entertainment, KISMET never really captures the electricity that the stage show generated. This is, perhaps, because Minnelli was roped into directing this film in order to get LUST FOR LIFE, a project he desperately wanted. "The cast tried hard," Minnelli remarked. "The whole enterprise sank. The experience taught me never again to accept an assignment when I lacked enthusiasm for it." Although the cast did a commendable job, the real draw of the film is the splendid art direction and the thoroughly hummable tunes penned by Wright and Forrest, including "And This Is My Beloved," "Night Of My Nights," "Stranger In Paradise," "Baubles, Bangles, And Beads," "Not Since Ninevah," "Bored," "Fate," "Gesticulate," "The Olive Tree," "The Sands Of Time," "Rahadlakum," "Rhymes Have I," and "Dance Of The 3 Princesses Of ABaBu."

p, Arthur Freed; d, Vincente Minnelli; w, Charles Lederer, Luther Davis (based on the play by Edward Knoblock); ph, Joseph Ruttenberg (CinemaScope, Eastmancolor); ed, Adrienne Fazan; md, Andre Previn, Jeff Alexander; art d, Cedric Gibbons, Preston Ames; ch, Jack Cole; m/l, Robert Wright, George Forrest (based on musical themes of Alexander Borodin); cos, Tony Duquette.

Fantasy **Cas.** **(PR:A MPAA:NR)**

KISS AND KILL (SEE: BLOOD OF FU MANCHU, THE, 1968, Brit.)

KISS AND MAKE UP** (1934) 78m PAR bw

Cary Grant *(Dr. Maurice Lamar)*, Helen Mack *(Anne)*, Genevieve Tobin *(Eve Caron)*, Lucien Littlefield *(Max Pascal)*, Mona Maris *(Countess Rita)*, Edward Everett Horton *(Marcel Caron)*, Kay Williams *(Vilma)*, Lucille Lund *(Magda)*, Rafael Storm *(Rolondo)*, Mme. Bonita Weber *(Mme. Severac)*, Doris Lloyd *(Mme. Durand)*, Milton Wallace *(Maharajah of Baroona)*, Sam Ash *(Plumber)*, Helena Phillips *(Landlady)*, Toby Wing *(Consuelo of Claghorne)*, Henry Armetta *(Chairman of Banquet)*, George Andre Beranger *(Jean, the Valet)*, Clara Lou [Ann] Sheridan *(Beauty Operator)*, Dorothy Christy *(Greta)*, Rita Gould *(Mme. Dupont)*, Ann Hovey *(Lady Rummond-Dray)*, GiGi Parrish *(Radio Listener)*, Helene Cohan *(Radio Announcer)*, Jean Carmen *(Maharajah's Wife)*, Dorothy Drake *(Bit)*, Chick Collins, John Sinclair *(Taxi Drivers)*, Betty Bryson, Jacqueline Wells [Julie Bishop] *(Beauty Clinic Patients)*, Judith Arlen, Jean Gale, Hazel Hayes, Lu Ann Meredith *(Beauty Clinic Nurses)*, the Wampas Baby Stars of 1934.

More gags than story in this comedy about a beauty doctor, Grant, who falls for one of his own creations, Tobin, only to discover that there is little behind her make-up. He attempts to go back to his ever-faithful secretary, Mack, but she is about to marry Tobin's ex-husband. In the end both couples manage to get back together.

p, B. P. Schulberg; d, Harlan Thompson; w, Thompson, George Marion, Jr., Jane Hinton (based on a play by Stephen Bekeffi); ph, Leon Shamroy; m, Ralph Rainger; art d, Hans Dreier, Ernst Fegte; m/l, Rainger, Leo Robin.

Romance/Comedy **(PR:A MPAA:NR)**

KISS AND TELL** ½ (1945) 90m Abbott/COL bw

Shirley Temple *(Corliss Archer)*, Jerome Courtland *(Dexter Franklin)*, Walter Abel *(Mr. Archer)*, Katharine Alexander *(Mrs. Archer)*, Robert Benchley *(Uncle George)*, Porter Hall *(Mr. Franklin)*, Edna Holland *(Mrs. Franklin)*, Virginia Welles *(Mildred Pringle)*, Tom Tully *(Mr. Pringle)*, Darryl Hickman *(Raymond Pringle)*, Scott McKay *(Pvt. Jimmy Earhart)*, Scott Elliott *(Lenny Archer)*, Kathryn Card *(Louise)*, Mary Philips *(Mrs. Dorothy Pringle)*, Darren McGavin *(Technical Sergeant)*, Jessie Arnold *(Mrs. Waldo)*, Frank Darien *(Elmer K. Waldo)*, Isabel Withers *(Nora Wilcox)*.

Light-hearted farce with Temple as a teenager who must keep the secret of her brother's marriage to his neighborhood sweetheart. Problems arise while the brother is away in the military, and it is learned that his young wife is pregnant. To protect the couple Temple pretends that she is pregnant, hoping to divert attention from her secret sister-in-law. Temple is unable to emit the same charm she did as a child star, but the rest of the cast is quite competent. Well-paced direction and a plausible script help make this a worthy production.

p, Sol C. Siegel; d, Richard Wallace; w, F. Hugh Herbert (based on the play by Herbert); ph, Charles Lawton, Jr.; m, Werner R. Heymann; ed, Charles Nelson; md, M. W. Stoloff; art d, Stephen Goosson, Van Nest Polglase; set d, Joseph Kish; cos, Jean Louis.

Comedy/Romance **(PR:A MPAA:NR)**

KISS BEFORE DYING, A*** (1956) 94m UA c

Robert Wagner *(Bud Corliss)*, Jeffrey Hunter *(Gordon Grant)*, Virginia Leith *(Ellen Kingship)*, Joanne Woodward *(Dorothy Kingship)*, Mary Astor *(Mrs. Corliss)*, George Macready *(Leo Kingship)*, Robert Quarry *(Dwight Powell)*, Howard Petrie *(Chesser)*, Bill Walker *(Butler)*, Molly McCart *(Annabelle)*, Marlene Felton *(Medical Student)*.

Wagner plays a money-hungry youth, who kills his girl friend, Woodward, when her pregnancy threatens his chances of being accepted by her wealthy family. Woodward's sister, Leith, refuses to believe the police report that the death was a suicide, and does some investigating on her own. She runs into Wagner, ignorant of his relation with her sister, and a romance between the two begins. When Leith discovers Wagner's relation to Woodward, he attempts to kill her, but is thwarted, falling to his own death. An excellent script, subtle direction, and good photography help gloss over any weaknesses in the performances.

p, Robert Jacks; d, Gerd Oswald; w, Lawrence Roman (based on the novel by Ira Levin); ph, Lucien Ballard (CinemaScope, DeLuxe Color); m, Lionel Newman; ed, George A. Gittens; art d, Addison Hehr; cos, Henry Helfman, Evelyn Carruth; m/l, "A Kiss Before Dying," Newman, Carroll Coates (sung by Dolores Hawkins).

Mystery/Drama **(PR:A MPAA:NR)**

KISS BEFORE THE MIRROR, THE** (1933) 67m UNIV bw

Nancy Carroll *(Maria Held)*, Frank Morgan *(Dr. Paul Held)*, Paul Lukas *(Dr. Walter Bernsdorf)*, Gloria Stuart *(Frau Lucie Bernsdorf)*, Jean Dixon *(Hilda Frey)*, Walter Pidgeon *(Bachelor)*, Donald Cook *(Maria's Lover)*, Allen Connor *(Hilda's Lover)*, Charles Grapewin *(Mr. Schultz)*, Wallis Clark *(Prosecutor)*, Reginald Mason *(Judge)*, Robert Adair *(Court Officer)*, May Boley, Christian Rub, John Ince, Walter Brennan, Carolyn Rankin.

This murder yarn has Morgan as a criminal lawyer defending a man for killing his wife during a fit of jealousy. In the meantime Morgan discovers that his own wife, Carroll, is unfaithful. Script and direction are effective despite the unacceptable story line and a modest budget of $260,192. Performances are generally flat and underplayed. Remade as WIVES UNDER SUSPICION (1938).

p, Carl Laemmle, Jr.; d, James Whale; w, William Anthony McGuire (based on the play by Ladislaus Fodor); ph, Karl Freund; ed, Ted J. Kent.

Drama **(PR:A MPAA:NR)**

KISS FOR CORLISS, A* ½

(1949) 88m Enterprise Studios/UA bw (AKA: ALMOST A BRIDE)

Shirley Temple *(Corliss Archer)*, *David Niven (Kenneth Marquis)*, Tom Tully *(Harry Archer)*, Darryl Hickman *(Dexter Franklin)*, Virginia Welles *(Mildred)*, Robert Ellis *(Raymond Archer)*, Richard Gaines *(Taylor)*, Kathryn Card *(Louise)*, Gloria Holden *(Mrs. Archer)*, Roy Roberts *(Uncle George)*.

In this disappointing vehicle for the teenage Temple, she plays a young girl who gets involved without getting involved with playboy Niven. Niven goes along with the story Temple concocts until Tully, as the protective father, blows his top. The weak, plodding script is further marred by the miscasting of Temple and Niven. Sequel to KISS AND TELL.

p, Colin Miller; d, Richard Wallace; w, Howard Dimsdale (based on characters created by F. Hugh Herbert); ph, Robert de Grasse; m, Werner R. Heymann; ed, Frank Doyle; md, Rudolph Polk; art d, Rudolph Sternad; set d, Edward G. Boyle; cos, Eloise Jenssen.

Comedy **(PR:A MPAA:AA)**

KISS FROM EDDIE, A (SEE: AROUSERS, THE, 1970)

KISS IN THE DARK, A** ½ (1949) 88m WB bw

David Niven *(Eric Phillips)*, Jane Wyman *(Polly Haines)*, Victor Moore *(Horace Willoughby)*, Wayne Morris *(Bruce Arnold)*, Broderick Crawford *(Mr. Botts)*, Joseph Buloff *(Peter Danilo)*, Maria Ouspenskaya *(Mme. Karina)*, Curt Bois *(Schloss)*, Percival Vivian *(Benton)*, Raymond Greenleaf *(Martin Soames)*, Frank Dae *(Hiram Knabe)*, Joe Devlin *(Electrician)*, Grayce Hampton *(Mrs. Stuybedan)*, Claire Meade *(Anna the Cook)*, Betty Hill *(Mrs. Beal)*, Jack Mower *(Chris the Chauffeur)*, Phyllis Coates *(Mrs. Hale)*, Jimmy Dodd *(Stuffy Nelson)*, Stuart Holmes *(Stage Manager)*, Larry Rio *(Cab Driver)*, Parker Eggleston *(Willie)*, Norman Ollestad *(Freddie)*, Creighton Hale, Bess Myers, Paulette Evans, Paul Panzer, Jack Wise, Fred Marlow *(Tenants)*.

Niven plays a promising concert pianist, whose manager buys for him an apartment building filled with an assortment of characters, including the stunningly photographed Wyman. Although at first annoyed with the upset to his routine, Niven develops an appreciation for his neighbors and some of the less refined things in life. Spotty script is made up for by a strong performance from Niven and fine portrayals from the other players.

p, Harry Kurnitz; d, Delmer Daves; w, Kurnitz (based on the story "Cleopatra Arms" by Everett and Devery Freeman); ph, Robert Burks; m, Max Steiner; ed, David Weisbart; art d, Stanley Fleischer; m/l, "A Kiss in the Dark," Victor Herbert.

Comedy/Romance **(PR:A MPAA:NR)**

KISS ME (SEE: LOVE KISS, THE, 1930)

KISS ME AGAIN** (1931) 76m FN-WB c (GB: TOAST OF THE LEGION)

Bernice Claire *(Mlle. Fifi)*, Walter Pidgeon *(Paul de St. Cyr)*, Edward Everett Horton *(Rene)*, Claude Gillingwater *(Count de St. Cyr)*, Frank McHugh *(Francois)*, Judith Vosselli *(Mme. Cecile)*, June Collyer *(Marie)*, Albert Gran *(Gen. de Villafranc)*, Sisters "G" *(Specialty Dancers)*.

Shopgirl Claire leaves her lover because of his parents' opposition, managing to create a career as a famous opera star. In the end she is finally able to wed her original love. The famous operetta on which this film is based doesn't transfer readily to the screen, giving this picture a certain awkwardness. Other than Claire's performance the acting is unexceptional. Songs include: "Kiss Me Again," "The Mascot Of The Troop," "The Time, the Place and the Girl," "When the Cat's Away," "I Want What I Want When I Want It," and "Love Me, Love My Dog" (Victor Herbert, Henry Blossom).

d, William A. Seiter; w, Julian Josephson, Paul Perez (based on the operetta "Mademoiselle Modiste" by Victor Herbert, Henry Blossom); ph, Al Gilkes, Lee Garmes (Technicolor); ed, Peter Frinch.

Musical **(PR:A MPAA:NR)**

KISS ME DEADLY**** (1955) 105m Parklane/UA bw

Ralph Meeker *(Mike Hammer)*, Albert Dekker *(Dr. Soberin)*, Paul Stewart *(Carl Evello)*, Maxine Cooper *(Velda)*, Gaby Rodgers *(Gabrielle/Lily Carver)*, Wesley Addy *(Pat Chambers)*, Juano Hernandez *(Eddie Yeager)*, Nick Dennis *(Nick)*, Cloris Leachman *(Christina Bailey/Berga Torn)*, Marian Carr *(Friday)*, Jack Lambert *(Sugar Smallhouse)*, Jack Elam *(Charlie Max)*, Jerry Zinneman *(Sammy)*, Percy Helton *(Morgue Doctor)*, Fortunio Bonanova *(Carmen Trivago)*, Silvio Minciotti *(Mover)*, Leigh Snowden *(Girl at Pool)*, Madi Comfort *(Singer)*, James Seay *(FBI Man)*, Mara McAfee *(Nurse)*, Robert Cornthwaite *(FBI Man)*, James McCallian *(Super)*, Jesslyn Fax *(Mrs. Super)*, Mort Marshall *(Piker)*, Strother Martin *(Harvey*

Wallace, Truck Driver), Marjorie Bennett *(Manager)*, Art Loggins *(Bartender)*, Bob Sherman *(Gas Station Man)*, Keith McConnell *(Athletic Club Clerk)*, Paul Richards *(Attacker)*, Eddie Beal *(Sideman)*.

Private eye Meeker is driving his convertible on a dark highway when in his headlights he sees barefoot Leachman running down the middle of the road. He picks her up and shortly afterward the car is forced off the road. Meeker is knocked unconscious while Leachman (her legs, jerking, her only visible entities) is tortured to death with a pair of pliers. Both she and Meeker are put back in Meeker's car, which is then pushed off a cliff. Meeker survives and begins to investigate, his curiosity aroused by an FBI warning to stay away. He learns where Leachman lives and there finds a book of poetry that gives him a clue. He also learns where Rodgers, Leachman's roommate, is hiding out. Meeker goes to see gangster Stewart but quickly learns that while Stewart is nominally running the show, someone is pulling his strings. Meeker's mechanic friend Dennis is killed when a car is dropped on him and the detective's secretary, Cooper, is kidnaped. Meeker is kidnaped too, and tortured, but he escapes and kills his tormentors. Meeker figures out that Leachman swallowed a key that will lead to whatever everyone is after and he convinces a morgue attendant to give it to him by slamming the man's fingers in a drawer. He goes to a health club and slams around the attendant until he shows Meeker the locker the key opens. Inside is a box, but when Meeker tries to open it, it glows eerily and burns his hand. He locks it up again and learns soon after that the box contains nuclear material. Rodgers, who is not what she seems, manages to get the box and take it to Dekker, the chief villain. Meeker traces them to a beachhouse and goes there looking for Cooper. Rodgers wants to see what's in the box but Dekker tells her that it's too dangerous. She shoots him dead, then wounds Meeker as he enters. She opens the box and lets out a scream as she bursts into flame. Meeker finds Cooper and they flee the house just as it blows up. One of the most brutal detective films ever made, KISS ME DEADLY enjoys a huge cult following. There's not a single completely likable character to be found; everyone wants something, and down these mean streets stalks the neanderthal Meeker, who barely gives people a chance to say no to him before he starts beating on them. Aldrich's direction heightens the misanthropy of the script, shooting with extreme close-ups and disorienting angles. When the car is dropped on Dennis, the camera swoops in on his screaming face as we hear the hiss of the hydraulic jacks. No less than six times do scenes end with Meeker knocked out, each following scene beginning with him waking up and rubbing his head. When the film was released Aldrich was so concerned about possible negative reactions to all the violence that he wrote a defense of the film that appeared in the New York Herald-Tribune. An important film that takes a number of *film noir* elements to their most extreme conclusions, leaving us in the horrible, violent, atomically threatened world we find ourselves in when we leave the theater.

p&d, Robert Aldrich; w, A. I. Bezzerides (based on the novel by Mickey Spillane); ph, Ernest Laszlo; m, Frank DeVol; ed, Michael Luciano; art d, William Glasgow; m/l, "Rather Have the Blues," DeVol, sung by Nat "King" Cole.

Crime **(PR:O MPAA:NR)**

KISS ME GOODBYE**

(1935, Brit.) 79m Windsor/STER-Celebrity bw (GB: GOING GAY)

Arthur Riscoe *(Jack)*, Naunton Wayne *(Jim)*, Magda Schneider *(Grete)*, Grete Natzler *(Conductor's Daughter)*, Joe Hayman *(Impresario)*, Wilfred Noy *(Conductor)*, Ruth Maitland *(Mother)*, Bertha Belmore *(Masculine Lady)*, Brenda Senton, Victor Fairley, Richard Wydler.

Light and whimsical tale about two devoted friends (Riscoe and Wayne) who turn into cross-eyed lovers when they encounter the tempting Schneider. The two become vicious rivals in their efforts to court the girl, each promising her stardom and then attempting to pave a path for the talented girl's road to success. Actress Magda Schneider is the mother of Romy Schneider who appeared in THE VICTORS (1962) and THE CARDINAL (1963).

p, Frank A. Richardson; d, Carmine Gallone; w, Selwyn Jepson, Jack Marks, K.R.G. Browne (based on the story by Jepson); ph, W. Goldberger.

Musical/Comedy **(PR:A MPAA:NR)**

KISS ME GOODBYE* 1/2

(1982) 101m Boardwalk-Burt Sugarman-Keith Baris/FOX c

Sally Field *(Kay Villano)*, James Caan *(Jolly Villano)*, Jeff Bridges *(Rupert Baines)*, Paul Dooley *(Kendall)*, Claire Trevor *(Charlotte Banning)*, Mildred Natwick *(Mrs. Reilly)*, Dorothy Fielding *(Emily)*, William Prince *(Rev. Hollis)*, Maryedith Burrell *(Mrs. Newman)*, Alan Haufrect *(Mr. Newman)*, Stephen Elliott *(Edgar)*, Michael Ensign *(Billy)*, Edith Fields *(Waitress)*, Lee Weaver *(Mr. King)*, Gene Castle *(Guest)*, Lyla Graham *(Miss Wells)*, Christopher Graver *(Little Boy)*, Robert Miano *(Michael)*, Wolf Muser *(Mark)*, Norman Alexander Gibbs *(Roland)*, Adam Wade *(Roscoe)*, Abraham Gordon *(Workman)*, Vincent J. Isaac *(Messenger)*, Jeffrey Lampert, Jude Farese *(Movers)*, Bernadette Birkett *(Mother)*, Barret Oliver *(Little Boy)*.

Widowed Field is about to remarry when the ghost of her husband reenters her life. She goes through with marriage to Bridges anyway, creating a rather bizarre triangle. This goes on until the ghost (Caan) decides he is just getting in the way. Although technically competent, the film is performed with little enthusiasm. Remake of the Brazilian film DONA FLOR AND HER TWO HUSBANDS (1978).

p&d, Robert Mulligan; w, Charlie Peters (based on material by Jorge Amado, Bruno Barreto); ph, Donald Peterman (DeLuxe Color); m, Ralph Burns; ed, Sheldon Kahn; prod d, Philip M. Jefferies; art d, John V. Cartwright; set d, Beverli Eagan, Donald Woodriff, Jim Berkey; ch, Gene Castle; m/l, Peter Allen.

Comedy **Cas.** **(PR:C MPAA:PG)**

KISS ME KATE****

(1953) 109m MGM c

Kathryn Grayson *(Lilli Vanessi/Katherine)*, Howard Keel *(Fred Graham/Petruchio)*, Ann Miller *(Lois Lane/Bianca)*, Tommy Rall *(Bill Calhoun/Lucentio)*, Bobby Van *(Gremio)*, Keenan Wynn *(Lippy)*, James Whitmore *(Slug)*, Kurt Kasznar *(Baptista)*, Bob Fosse *(Hortensio)*, Ron Randell *(Cole Porter)*, Willard Parker *(Tex Callaway)*, Dave O'Brien *(Ralph)*, Claud Allister *(Paul)*, Ann Codee *(Suzanne)*, Carol Haney, Jeanne Coyne *(Specialty Dancers)*, Hermes Pan *(Specialty Sailor Dance)*, Ted Eckelberry *(Nathaniel)*, Mitchell Lewis *(Stage Doorman)*.

KISS ME KATE is an almost, but not quite, satisfying cinemusical version of the Broadway hit. The fact that they filmed it in 3-D is what does it in, and so many effects are used (such as Miller kicking up those magnificent legs to the camera) that detract from the wonderful score that it is ultimately less than rewarding. It's a parallel story of the musical mounting of Shakespeare's "The Taming Of The Shrew" and what is happening simultaneously in the lives of the actors. It is well-plotted and surely has one of the most interesting and intelligent musical books ever. Keel is an actor-director and Randell portrays Cole Porter. They are planning to musicalize the bard's comedy and both feel there is only one woman to play the role, Keel's ex-wife, Grayson. Grayson listens to the score at Keel's apartment with mild interest. Miller, Keel's current amour, enters and says that she is going to be the younger sister in the show. Grayson won't hear of playing someone older than Miller and she announces that she can't do it as she's about to be married. Then Miller shrugs, says that she'll do the lead in that case. Grayson suddenly changes her mind and accepts. Rehearsals commence and are fraught with problems. Keel enjoys needling his ex; Rall, who is Miller's dancing partner, arrives late and we learn that he is a compulsive gambler and has signed Keel's name on an I.O.U. for a couple of thousand dollars. Wynn and Whitmore are two gangsters who arrive opening night to collect the debt but Keel denies he signed it. Allister, Keel's valet, gives Grayson's maid, Codee, a bouquet of flowers from Keel; but he has erred, in that the flowers were to go to Miller. Keel learns of Allister's mistake and tries to get the love note back from Grayson (who hasn't read it yet). She put it in her copious cleavage as the show's curtain rises. Now the musical begins (Miller's three beaus, Rall, Fosse, and Van, cannot really woo her until her older sister, Grayson, has wed, an old tradition. Since no one will marry the shrew, all seems lost. Then Keel, playing a pal of Rall's, arrives and makes a deal with Kasznar, Grayson and Miller's father, to take the hoyden off his hands. Grayson, on a brief break, reads the note and sees that it was meant for Miller, so as the play on stage progresses, she begins to deviate from the rehearsed material and exacts vengeance on Keel. Act One ends as Keel takes her over his knee and spanks her. Grayson is infuriated and announces that she is leaving the show and will marry her suitor, Parker, immediately. Simultaneously Miller convinces Rall to confess that he signed the I.O.U. to the gamblers. Wynn and Whitmore, who have been hanging around during the show, hear that Grayson is quitting. That means that the show will close and the money owed will never be repaid, so they force Grayson to stay for Act two. Parker arrives at the theatre and Miller recognizes him as a one-time Texas lover of hers. Wynn calls his boss to say that everything is going okay, but as the conversation takes place, shots are heard on the other end of the line and Wynn's boss has been killed. With no employer, Wynn and Whitmore have no reason to stay any longer so they exit. Grayson is about to depart with Parker but Keel admits that he has carried the torch for her ever since their divorce. Further, she is a woman of the theater and will never be happy as the mistress of a ranch in Texas. As the finale is being performed, Keel informs Kasznar that the understudy will be replacing Grayson. Suddenly, Grayson realizes that everything Keel has said is correct, so she comes back to finish the show and to rekindle the flame that once lit Keel's and her heart. The play, presented by Lemuel Ayers and Arnold St. Subber, gave more than 1000 performances on Broadway and starred Alfred Drake, Patricia Morison, Harold Lang, and Lisa Kirk. Fosse had a small role, then decided that performing was not for him so he became a Renaissance Man by writing, producing, and directing such diverse projects as LENNY, ALL THAT JAZZ, and STAR 80 in between his Broadway chores. In a small chorus role, you might spot Carol Haney, who skyrocketed to fame the following year in "The Pajama Game" on Broadway. It was her ankle injury that caused a young understudy to go on for her and, in a moment right out of 42ND STREET, that young woman was spotted by a producer and offered a film contract. Her name? Shirley MacLaine. Wynn and Whitmore, both looking very young, do a wonderful job as the Runyonesque hoods singing "Brush Up Your Shakespeare" which contains some of Porter's wittiest lyrics. Despite the choice tunes and the sensational dancing, KISS ME KATE remains just a notch below classic stature in movies due to the way it was shot. The score was one of Porter's best and if that wasn't enough, they also borrowed a tune from his earlier play "Out Of This World" and folded in "From This Moment On." "Wunderbar" (sung by Kathryn Grayson, Howard Keel), which was supposed to be a satire of every schmaltzy Viennese song, took off as a hit on its own merits. The other Porter-written songs include: "So In Love" (sung by Grayson, Keel), "I Hate Men" (sung by Grayson), "Were Thine That Special Face," "I've Come To Wive It Wealthily In Padua," "Where Is The Life That Late I Led?" (sung by Keel), "Always True To You Darling In My Fashion," "Why Can't You Behave" (sung by Ann Miller, Tommy Rall), "Kiss Me Kate" (sung by Grayson, Keel, chorus), "Tom, Dick or Harry," and "We Open in Venice" (sung by Grayson, Keel, Miller, Rall), "Too Darn Hot" (tap dance, Ann Miller).

p, Jack Cummings; d, George Sidney; w, Dorothy Kingsley (based on the play by Cole Porter, Samuel Spewack, Bella Spewack from the play "The Taming of the Shrew," by William Shakespeare); ph, Charles Rosher (3-D, Ansco Color); ed, Ralph E. Winters; md, Andre Previn, Saul Chaplin; art d, Cedric Gibbins, Urie McCleary; set d, Edwin B. Willis, Richard Pefferle; cos, Walter Plunkett; spec eff, Warren Newcombe; ch, Hermes Pan.

Musical/Comedy **(PR:AA MPAA:NR)**

KISS ME, SERGEANT*

(1930, Brit.) 56m BIP/Wardour bw

Leslie Fuller *(Bill Biggles)*, Gladys Cruickshank *(Kitty)*, Gladys Frazin *(Burahami)*, Syd Courtenay *(Lieutenant)*, Mamie Holland *(Fanny Adams)*, Frank Melroyd

(Colonel), Lola Harvey *(Colonel's Wife)*, Roy Travers *(Sergeant)*, Olivette, Marika Rokk, Gotham Quartette.

Far-fetched comedy with Fuller as a British soldier in India, where he makes a shamble of the locals' religious idol. His antics prove to be a saving grace for the village when Fuller's impersonation of the statue uncovers a plot to steal a priceless jewel. Comedy routines rarely overcome the level of forced slapstick here.

p, John Maxwell; d, Monty Banks; w, Val Valentine (based on the play "The Idol Of Moolah" by Syd Courtenay, Lola Harvey).

Comedy **(PR:A MPAA:NR)**

KISS ME, STUPID*½ (1964) 126m Mirisch-Phalanx-Claude/Lopert bw

Dean Martin *(Dino)*, Kim Novak *(Polly the Pistol)*, Ray Walston *(Orville J. Spooner)*, Felicia Farr *(Zelda Spooner)*, Cliff Osmond *(Barney Millsap)*, Barbara Pepper *(Big Bertha)*, Doro Merande *(Mrs. Pettibone)*, Howard McNear *(Mr. Pettibone)*, Henry Gibson *(Smith)*, Alan Dexter *(Wesson)*, Tommy Nolan *(Johnnie Mulligan)*, Alice Pearce *(Mrs. Mulligan)*, John Fiedler *(Rev. Carruthers)*, Arlen Stuart *(Rosalie Schultz)*, Cliff Norton *(Mack Gray)*, James Ward *(Milkman)*, Mel Blanc *(Dr. Sheldrake)*, Bobo Lewis *(Waitress)*, Bern Hoffman *(Bartender)*, Susan Wedell *(1st Showgirl)*, Eileen O'Neill *(2nd Showgirl)*, Gene Darfler *(Nevada State Trooper)*, Henry Beckman *(Truck Driver)*, Laurie Fontaine, Mary Jane Saunders, Kathy Garber, Sam the Parakeet.

Despite the presence of some vaunted talents, this is a mess from start to finish. Martin plays a nightclub crooner renowned for heavy tippling and ogling. He finishes a stint in Las Vegas and is driving back to Los Angeles when he is forced to detour into the little burg of Climax, Nevada. (Just the title of the town should give you an inkling of the comedy level.) Once there, he meets Osmond, a gas station worker; and Walston, the local music teacher who is married to Farr, the most attractive woman in the area. Osmond and Walston are amateur songwriters and they want to sell him some of their work, so they do some dirty work on his fancy Italian sports car and tell him that they have sent to Milan for the needed replacement parts in order to keep him there. Walston offers his home to Martin, but is soon concerned about wife Farr's sexuality when he hears Martin complain that he gets terrible headaches on any day when he doesn't make love. Walston doesn't want Farr to sleep with Martin so he starts an argument with her and she leaves. Now Walston arranges for Novak, a local hooker, to come by and pose as his wife, whom Martin still hasn't met. It seems to be working out well until Walston forgets that Novak isn't his wife at all and throws the singer out. Martin goes to the local roadhouse where Novak does secondary work as a waitress, and Walston and Novak stay the night with each other. Farr is at the roadhouse, drunk as Jack Norton, and the owner lets her stay in Novak's trailer. Martin wanders into the trailer and thinks that Farr is the hooker-waitress. Martin is able to make love to Farr, as she is his biggest fan. Several weeks later, Farr and Walston are watching TV and hear Martin sing one of his and Osmond's songs. He can't figure out how that happened but Farr knows and she smiles an enigmatic grin as the film mercifully ends. It's just a long sex joke, and not a very good one at that. Wilder let the actors get out of hand, even the most minor parts, and scenery was chewed with abandon. KISS ME, STUPID was filmed in the California desert near 29 Palms, in Las Vegas, and at the Moulin Rouge nightclub on Sunset Boulevard in Hollywood. It was sad to see Wilder at the bottom of his form.

p&d, Billy Wilder; w, Wilder, I.A.L. Diamond (based on the play "L'Ora Della Fantasia" by Anna Bonacci); ph, Joseph LaShelle (Panavision); m, Andre Previn; ed, Daniel Mandell; prod d, Alexander Trauner; art d, Robert Luthardt; set d, Edward G. Boyle; cos, Bill Thomas; spec eff, Milton Rice; ch, Wally Green; m/l, "Sophia," "I'm a Poached Egg," "All the Livelong Day," George Gershwin, Ira Gershwin; makeup, Emile LaVigne, Loren Cosand.

Comedy **(PR:C MPAA:GP)**

KISS MY BUTTERFLY (SEE: I LOVE YOU, ALICE B. TOKLAS, 1968)

KISS OF DEATH****** (1947) 98m FOX bw

Victor Mature *(Nick Bianco)*, Brian Donlevy *(D'Angelo)*, Coleen Gray *(Nettie)*, Richard Widmark *(Tom Udo)*, Karl Malden *(Sgt. William Cullen)*, Taylor Holmes *(Earl Howser)*, Howard Smith *(Warden)*, Anthony Ross *(Williams)*, Mildred Dunnock *(Ma Rizzo)*, Millard Mitchell *(Max Schulte)*, Temple Texas *(Blondie)*, J. Scott Smart *(Skeets)*, Wendell Phillips *(Pep Magone)*, Lew Herbert, Harry Kadison, Lawrence Tiernan, Bernard C. Sell, Jack Rutherford, Arthur Holland, George Smith, Pat Malone, Bill O'Leary *(Policemen)*, John Kullers *(Prisoner)*, Victor Thorley, Rollin Bauer, Arthur Foran, Jr., James Doody, William Zuckert *(Sing Sing Guards)*, Paul Lilly, Herbert Holcombe *(City Jail Guards)*, Steve Roberts, Dennis Bohan, Greg Martell, Richard Midgley *(Guards)*, Iris Man *(Congetta)*, Marilee Grassini *(Rosaria)*, Norman McKay *(Capt. Dolan)*, Harry Cooke, Richard Taber, Jesse White *(Taxi Drivers)*, Robert Karnes *(Hoodlum)*, Harry Carter, Robert Adler, Charles McClelland *(Detectives)*, Yvonne Rob, Carl Milletaire *(Customers)*, Gloria O'Connor, Consuela O'Connor *(Girls)*, Harold Crane *(Mr. Moremann)*, Mel Ruick *(Moremann's Assistant)*, John Marley *(Al)*, Lee Sanford *(Chips Cooney)*, John Stearns *(Harris)*, Eda Heinemann *(Mrs. Keller)*, Eva Condon, Irene Shirley *(Nuns)*, Mary Morrison *(Mother Superior)*, Alexander Campbell *(Train Conductor)*, George Shelton, David Fresco *(Waiters)*, Harold Gary *(Doorman)*, Dort Clark *(Man in Car)*, Arthur Kramer *(Mr. Sulla)*, Perc Launders *(Lieutenant)*, Olga Borget *(Cashier)*, Don Giovanni *(Gangster)*, Tito Vuolo *(Luigi)*.

A hard hitting, often frightening crime drama from the Hecht-Lederer typewriter, KISS OF DEATH has the look and feel of a real police lineup, mostly because expert helmsman Hathaway insisted upon shooting the film totally in New York. It pulls no punches and shows exactly what it's like on the seamy side of the street, as well as introducing an electric personality to the screen, Richard Widmark, in a role no viewer would ever forget. Narrating the film is Gray, who is Mature's girl friend and wife-to-be, someone who has loved him from adolescence and recounts his tough street life. She describes how Mature, while the rest of the world was busy buying presents at Christmastime, plans and executes a robbery of a jewelry shop. He and others enter a skyscraper and take an elevator to the shop many floors above. They loot the place but, as they are leaving, one of the employees manages to free his bound hands and press an alarm button which brings swarms of police to the building. Just as the crooks reach the lobby, the police arrive and close the entrances, sealing off those inside. Mature tries to escape by going through a side door into a shop facing the street and then out on to the street but police shoot and wound him, taking him prisoner. He goes to prison without implicating other members of the gang, assured by the gang's crooked lawyer, Holmes, that his family will be taken care of, a lie. While in prison Mature learns that his wife has committed suicide because of lack of funds and that his two little girls have been placed in an orphanage. In a rage, he asks to see district attorney Donlevy, believing he has been betrayed by the mob; he now betrays the gang, offering to inform on them. He and Donlevy make a deal. He is paroled and must go on informing on gang members. Donlevy is particularly interested in getting evidence that will send sadistic killer and gang boss Widmark to prison. Mature ingratiates himself to the perverted murderer, drinking with him, listening to his braggadocio talk, going with him to bordellos. Meanwhile, Mature falls in love with Gray and they marry, living in a small house with Mature's two little girls. Though he's living under an assumed name, it's only a matter of time before Mature's cover is blown. Donlevy compels him to testify against Widmark and he becomes a marked man. He knows that the psychopathic Widmark will kill him and-or his entire family as soon as police surveillance lifts. The kind of heartless killer Widmark really is was graphically demonstrated earlier. Widmark had been looking for a small-time hoodlum and found only his invalided mother in an apartment. Incensed, and to show the wanted man he meant business, Widmark tied a cord around the old lady and rolled her wheelchair to the top of a steep flight of stairs, then pushed her down to her death while mercilessly laughing in a high-pitched voice. At night, Mature finds it impossible to sleep. Every little sound outside alerts him to imagined dangers and he prowls the house, checking the doors and windows, peering into the street. Finally, he sees a suspicious-looking car and grabs a gun, waiting for Widmark and gang to break into his house for the final shootout. But it's Donlevy who comes through the door, checking to see if he's all right. Mature finds the situation unbearable and, before Donlevy can lock him up for safekeeping, escapes and decides to confront his nemesis, Widmark. He goes to the gangster's favorite Italian restaurant and waits. Soon Widmark comes out of the back room and tells him that he'll take care of him in his own time. Mature responds by saying he knows Widmark has no gun, that he wouldn't dare break the law while under surveillance. He next calls him "a squirt," and tells him that he'll kill him if he goes anywhere near his family. He insults the gangster to the point where Widmark steps outside and waits for him with his henchmen in a car parked in front of the restaurant. Mature has now engineered the gangster into an untenable position. He calls Donlevy and tells him where he's at, and to arrive in five minutes with the police, that he'll find Widmark with a gun in his hand. He waits a few minutes, then steps to the street. One of Widmark's gunsels is about to shoot him when Mature challenges Widmark: "What's the matter, big man," he sneers. "Afraid to do it yourself?" Widmark grabs the gun and pumps some bullets into Mature who collapses to the sidewalk, but just then the police arrive with sirens screaming. Widmark's car takes off, but is blocked by patrol cars. Widmark jumps out of the car and tries to escape, firing at several advancing cops. He is shot to death and his gang captured. An ambulance is called and Mature, still alive, is taken to the hospital, wounded, but alive; he will return to Gray and his daughters to face a better day. The fact that Hathaway insisted upon shooting all the locales in New York gave great authenticity to KISS OF DEATH and it is reminiscent of other crime films employing a documentary approach, including CALL NORTHSIDE 777, THE NAKED CITY, even the spy drama, THE HOUSE ON 92ND STREET. Mature is exceptional in the film as the reluctant squealer and Donlevy is solid as the crusading district attorney, but it is Widmark, with his maniacal eyes, falsetto baby talk, and hyena-like laughter, that captured the public's imagination (if not its nightmares). He was an overnight sensation and was quickly signed to a long-term contract by Fox. The Hecht-Lederer script is taut and clever, even literate for a gangster film, with well-developed characters and a starkly believable plot line. The story itself would be used for the horror cult film, THE FIEND WHO WALKED THE WEST (1958).

p, Fred Kohlmar; d, Henry Hathaway; w, Ben Hecht, Charles Lederer (based on a story by Eleazar Lipsky); ph, Norbert Brodine; m, David Buttolph; ed, J. Watson Webb, Jr.; md, Lionel Newman; art d, Lyle Wheeler, Leland Fuller; set d, Thomas Little; cos, Charles LeMaire; spec eff, Fred Sersen; makeup, Ben Nye.

Crime Drama **(PR:C-O MPAA:NR)**

KISS OF EVIL***

(1963, Brit.) 88m Hammer/UNIV c (GB: KISS OF THE VAMPIRE, THE)

Clifford Evans *(Prof. Zimmer)*, Noel Willman *(Dr. Ravna)*, Edward De Souza *(Gerald Harcourt)*, Jennifer Daniel *(Marianne Harcourt)*, Barry Warren *(Carl Ravna)*, Jacqueline Wallis *(Sabena Ravna)*, Isobel Black *(Tania)*, Peter Madden *(Bruno)*, Vera Cook *(Anna)*, Brian Oulton *(1st Disciple)*, Noel Howlett *(Father Xavier)*, John Harvey *(Police Sergeant)*, Stan Simmons *(Servant)*, Olga Dickie *(Woman at Graveyard)*, Margaret Read *(1st Girl Disciple)*, Elizabeth Valentine *(2nd Girl Disciple)*.

In this suspenseful chiller a newlywed couple is stranded at an inn near a villa inhabited by a cult of vampires. De Souza and his bride, Daniel, are invited to dinner by the mysterious host of the villa, Willman. After a pleasant meal they are invited back the next evening for a masquerade ball. At the ball De Souza is drugged, while Daniel is put into a trance, paving the way for the vampires. Waking up, De Souza is able to enlist the help of Evans, who rescues Daniel and sprinkles the castle with garlic, unleashing a horde of bats onto the vampires. This well-paced drama is aided by strong characterizations, as well as designs and photography which create the proper mood.

p, Anthony Hinds; d, Don Sharp; w, John Elder [Hinds]; ph, Alan Hume (Eastmancolor); m, James Bernard; ed, James Need; prod d, Bernard Robinson; art d, Don Mingaye; cos, Molly Arbuthnot; spec eff, Les Bowie; makeup, Roy Ashton.

Horror **(PR:C MPAA:NR)**

KISS OF FIRE, THE***

(1940, Fr.) 83m Paris/Juno bw (UNE BAISER DE FEU)

Viviane Romance *(Lolita)*, Tino Rossi *(Mario)*, Michel Simon *(Michel)*, Mireille Balin *(Assunta)*, Dalio *(The Photographer)*, Jeanne *(Aunt Theresa)*.

A pleasant French satire about femme fatale Romance entrapping any man she comes in contact with. Simon picks her up at church, innocently bringing her back to his apartment. He quickly falls in love with her, as does his roommate Rossi, who forsakes his intended marriage for Romance. The two eventually get wise to Romance, tossing her out, and returning to their normal lives. Exceptional performances overshadow incompetent technical work. (In French; English subtitles.)

d, Augusto Genina; w, Auguste Bailley; ph, LeFevre; m, Vincent Scotto.

Romance/Comedy **(PR:A MPAA:NR)**

KISS OF FIRE** (1955) 87m UNIV c

Jack Palance *(El Tigre)*, Barbara Rush *(Princess Lucia)*, Rex Reason *(Duke of Montera)*, Martha Hyer *(Felicia)*, Leslie Bradley *(Vega)*, Alan Reed *(Diego)*, Lawrence Dobkin *(Padre Domingo)*, Joseph Waring *(Victor)*, Pat Hogan *(Pahvant)*, Karen Kadler *(Shining Moon)*, Steven Geray *(Ship Captain)*, Henry Rowland *(Acosta)*, Bernie Gozier.

This period piece follows heiress Rush as she travels from Sante Fe, New Mexico, to Spain in order to claim the throne. Along the way she falls in love with her escort Palance, deciding to relinquish the throne for her new love. Capable direction and production do not help the plodding script. Performances are adequate, though Palance is miscast as a statuesque nobleman.

p, Samuel Marx; d, Joseph M. Newman; w, Franklin Coen, Richard Collins (based on the novel *The Rose and The Flame*, by Jonreed Lauritzen); ph, Carl Guthrie (Technicolor); ed, Arthur H. Nadel; md, Joseph Gershenson; art d, Alexander Golitzen, Robert Boyle; cos, Jay A. Morley, Jr.

Romance **(PR:A MPAA:NR)**

KISS OF THE TARANTULA* (1975) 85m Cinema-Vu/Omni c

Eric Mason, Suzanne Ling, Herman Wallner, Patricia Landon, Beverly Eddins, Jay Scott, Rita French, Rebecca Eddins, Linda Spatz.

Tormented high schooler Ling unleashes her pet tarantulas on her enemies, gaining her due revenge.

p, Daniel B. Cady; d, Chris Munger; w, Warren Hamilton, Jr. (based on a story by Cady); ph, Henning Schellerup (Eastmancolor); m, Phillan Bishop.

Horror **Cas.** **(PR:O MPAA:R)**

KISS OF THE VAMPIRE, THE , (SEE: KISS OF EVIL, 1963, Brit.)

KISS THE BLOOD OFF MY HANDS***

(1948) 79m Harold Hecht-Norma/UNIV bw (GB: BLOOD ON MY HANDS)

Joan Fontaine *(Jane Wharton)*, Burt Lancaster *(Bill Saunders)*, Robert Newton *(Harry Carter)*, Lewis L. Russell *(Tom Widgery)*, Aminta Dyne *(Landlady)*, Grizelda Hervey *(Mrs. Paton)*, Jay Novello *(Sea Captain)*, Colin Keith-Johnston *(Judge)*, Reginald Sheffield *(Superintendent)*, Campbell Copelin *(Publican)*, Leland Hodgson *(Tipster)*, Peter Hobbes *(Young Father)*, Thomas P. Dillon *(Welshman)*, Joseph Granby *(Theater Manager)*, Robin Hughes, Harry Cording, Art Foster, Don MacCracken *(Policemen)*, Harry Allen *(Drunk)*, Valerie Cardew *(Change Girl)*, Ben H. Wright *(Cockney Tout)*, Wally Scott *(Hanger-On)*, Harold Goodwin *(Whipper)*, Keith Hitchcock *(Official)*, Alec Harford *(Doctor)*, Lora Lee Michel *(Little Girl)*, Jimmy Aubrey *(Taxi Driver)*, Leslie Denison *(Constable)*, Arthur Gould-Porter, Kenneth Harvey, Tommy Hughes, Tom Pilkington *(Bookies)*, Charles McNaughton *(Telescope Man)*, Filippa Rock *(Woman)*, Timothy Bruce, Anne Whitfield, Suzanne Kerr, Patty King *(Children)*, Colin Kenny *(Proprietor)*, Ola Lorraine *(Donald's Mother)*, Frank Hagney, James Logan, David McMahon *(Seamen)*, Al Ferguson *(Marker)*, David Dunbar *(Large Man)*, Richard Glynn *(Donald)*, Marilyn Williams *(Barmaid)*, Jack Stoney *(Man)*, Mildred Hale *(Woman)*, James Fowler, Robert Hale, Fred Fox, Jack Carol *(Tipsters)*, George Bunny *(Bookie)*, Harry Wilson *(Man in Pub)*, Duke Green, Wesley Hopper *(Men)*.

Though the story is somewhat trite, Foster's direction and Metty's contrasty photography, as well as top emoting from Lancaster, Fontaine, and Newton, make this production absorbing *film noir*. Lancaster is a WW II veteran scarred by memories of battle who has little regard for human life. He gets into an argument with the owner of a pub in England and the pubkeeper is killed. Lancaster flees from the police and hides in Fontaine's room. The faint-hearted nurse believes his story about the death being an accident and takes him in. Newton, however—a jack-of-all-criminal-trades—recognizes Lancaster and tries to rope him into a caper, but Lancaster avoids him. Next Lancaster gets into an imbroglio with a cop and knocks him about; he is given six months in prison and a whipping which further deepens Lancaster's hatred for society. Fontaine gets him a job as a truck driver for her clinic when he is released. Newton tries to blackmail Lancaster into stealing a load of drugs which he plans to sell on the black market, but Fontaine unexpectedly gets into Lancaster's truck on the day it will be hijacked and Lancaster decides against going through with the plan, taking another route. Later, Fontaine is approached by the menacing Newton in her apartment, as the blackmailer tries to rearrange the hijacking, telling her he knows all about Lancaster's killing of the pub-owner and will reveal this information to police unless she and Lancaster go through with the hijacking. She refuses and Newton's anger boils to the surface; when he approaches Fontaine in a threatening manner, the nurse kills him. Lancaster arrives and decides to come clean with the police, admitting the whole mess, the killing of the pub owner, the plan with Newton, all of his criminal machinations, knowing that although he will go to prison Fontaine will be free on grounds of justifiable homicide. Lancaster and Fontaine are solid as the star-crossed lovers but this film is dominated by the incredible Newton who made a specialty of playing oily, detestable creatures, an image he brings to towering proportions here. Foster directs with a sure hand and moves the story along at a dizzying pace, in much the same vein as his JOURNEY INTO FEAR, which was directorially nudged by Orson Welles. Set in London—where it was shot on location—this film has the same feeling of alienation as other *film noir* entries of the late 1940s, chiefly NIGHT AND THE CITY with Richard Widmark. There is a stark brutality to the film, one where a pervasive feeling of hopelessness overshadows everything.

p, Richard Vernon; d, Norman Foster; w, Leonardo Bercovici, Walter Bernstein, Hugh Gray, Ben Maddow (based on the novel by Gerald Butler); ph, Russell Metty; m, Miklos Rozsa; ed, Milton Carruth; art d, Bernard Herzbrun, Nathan Juran; set d, Russell A. Gausman, Ruby R. Levitt; spec eff, David S. Horsley; makeup, Bud Westmore.

Crime Drama **(PR:C-O MPAA:NR)**

KISS THE BOYS GOODBYE ½** (1941) 83m PAR bw

Mary Martin *(Cindy Lou Bethany)*, Don Ameche *(Lloyd Lloyd)*, Oscar Levant *(Dick Rayburn)*, Virginia Dale *(Gwen Abbott)*, Barbara Jo Allen [Vera Vague] *(Myra Stanhope)*, Raymond Walburn *(Top Rumson)*, Elizabeth Patterson *(Aunt Lilly Lou)*, Jerome Cowan *(Bert Fisher)*, Connee Boswell *(Polly)*, Eddie "Rochester" Anderson *(George)*, John Scott Trotter *(Himself)*, Minor Watson *(Uncle Jeff)*, Harry Barris *(Fisher's Publicity Agent)*, George Reed *(House Servant)*, Thelma Long *(Cleo)*, Emory Parnell, Tom Fadden.

Searching for a southern beauty to play the lead in a Broadway musical, Ameche and Levant are forced to listen to an audition by Martin. They agree to give her the role, but she is soon sent packing. Ameche follows her to pursue his own romantic interests. Strong performances by entire cast, with a special display of talent by Martin. Songs include: "Find Yourself a Melody", "I'll Never Let a Day Go Past", "Kiss the Boys Goodbye" (Schertzinger, Frank Loesser), "That's How I Got My Start" (Schertzinger, Loesser, sung by Mary Martin), "Sand in My Shoes" (Schertzinger, Loesser, sung by Connee Boswell).

p, William LeBaron; d, Victor Schertzinger; w, Harry Tugend, Dwight Taylor (based on a play by Clare Boothe); ph, Ted Tetzlaff; ed, Paul Weatherwax; md, Victor Young.

Musical/Romance **(PR:A MPAA:NR)**

KISS THE BRIDE GOODBYE** (1944, Brit.) 89m But bw

Patricia Medina *(Joan Dodd)*, Jimmy Hanley *(Jack Fowler)*, Frederick Leister *(Capt. Blood)*, Marie Lohr *(Emma Blood)*, Claud Allister *(Adolphus Pickering)*, Ellen Pollock *(Gladys Dodd)*, Wylie Watson *(David Dodd)*, Jean Simmons *(Molly Dodd)*, Muriel George *(Mrs. Fowler)*, Irene Handl *(Mrs. Victory)*, Aubrey Mallalieu *(Rev. Glory)*, Hay Petrie *(Fraser)*, C. Denier Warren *(Reporter)*, Julie Suedo *(Part-time Worker)*, Ben Williams, Hal Gordon, Noel Dainton, Vi Kaley, Beatrice Marsden, Ann Kennington, Frank Atkinson, Ethel Beal, Eve Llewellyn.

Medina plays a young lass whose romantic affairs turn into a mess when her anxious mother persuades her to accept a marriage proposal from her boss. Medina's true love then returns from the war only to leave town in a rage when he finds out what's going on. There are the usual number of misadventures before the two finally settle down to a happy ending. The appeal of this comedy rests upon the capable performances, adding charm where the humor starts to lag.

p&d, Paul Stein; w, Jack Whittingham (based on the story by Stein); ph, Geoffrey Faithfull.

Comedy **(PR:A MPAA:NR)**

KISS THE GIRLS AND MAKE THEM DIE*

(1967, U.S./Ital.) 105m DD/COL c (SE TUTTE LE DONNE DEL MONDO; OPERAZIONE PARADISO)

Michael Connors *(Kelly)*, Dorothy Provine *(Susan Fleming)*, Raf Vallone *(Mr. Ardonian)*, Terry-Thomas *(Lord Aldric/James)*, Margaret Lee *(Grace)*, Nicoletta Machiavelli *(Sylvia)*, Beverly Adams *(Karin)*, Marilu Tolo *(Gioia)*, Seyna Seyn *(Wilma Soong)*, Oliver MacGreevy *(Ringo)*, Sandro Dori *(Omar)*, Jack Gwillim *(British Ambassador)*, Andy Ho *(Ling)*, Hans Thorner *(Kruger)*, Nerio Bernardi *(Papal Envoy)*, Michael Audley *(Maj. Davis)*, Edith Peters *(Maria)*, K. Wang *(Kasai)*, Renato Terra, George Leech, Roland Bartrop.

There is little to recommend in this secret agent spoof. Vallone is a power crazy industrialist who attempts to take over the world from his Brazilian headquarters. His plan is to sterilize mankind through ultrasonic waves. Connors and Provine are the undercover agents whose duty it is to thwart Vallone. Everything from the sloppy special effects to the irritating music radiates an uncanny cheapness. Dubbed in English.

p, Dino De Laurentiis; d, Henry Levin, Dino Maiuri; w, Jack Pulman, Maiuri (based on a story by Maiuri); ph, Aldo Tonti (Technicolor); m, Mario Nascimbene; ed, Ralph Kemplen, Alberto Gallitti; md, Robert Pregadio; art d, Mario Garbuglia; set d, Emilio D'Andria; cos, Maria De Matteis, Piero Gherardi; spec eff, Augie Lohman; m/l, title song, Nascimbene, Howard Greenfield (sung by Lydia MacDonald).

Spy Drama **(PR:O MPAA:NR)**

KISS THE OTHER SHEIK*

(1968, Fr./Ital.) 85m CHAM-CON/MGM c (AKA: THE BLONDE WIFE)

Marcello Mastroianni *(Michele)*, Pamela Tiffin *(Pepita)*, Virna Lisi *(Dorothea)*,

Luciano Salce *(Arturo Rossi)*, Raimondo Vianello, Lina Valonghi, Lelio Luttazzi, Ennio Balbo, Luciano Bonanni.

An attempt by Carlo Ponti to salvage a picture or two after Embassy refused to release his original PARANOIA in the U.S. He shot more footage and attempted to release two separate features from the original film. The result in this one is nearly slapstick comedy. Mastroianni and Tiffin are husband and wife involved in excessive marital strife, eventually leading each to sell the other to a sheik. Although performances are adequate, the film is badly marred by its awkward editing. (The other picture made by Ponti from PARANOIA was THE MAN WITH THE BALLOONS.)

p, Carlo Ponti; d, Luciano Salce, Eduardo De Filippo; w, Goffredo Parise, Renato Castellani, Pipolo, Salce, De Filippo, Isabella Quarantotti; ph, Mario Montuori, Gianni Di Venanzo (Panavision, Metrocolor); m, Luis Enriquez Bacalav, Nino Rota; ed, Adrianni Novelli, Marcello Malvestiti; art d, Luigi Scaccianoce, Ferdinando Scarfiotti.

Comedy **(PR:C MPAA:PG)**

KISS THEM FOR ME** (1957) 103m FOX c

Cary Grant *(Crewson)*, Jayne Mansfield *(Alice)*, Suzy Parker *(Gwenneth)*, Leif Erickson *(Eddie Turnbill)*, Ray Walston *(Lt. "Mac" McCann)*, Larry Blyden *(Mississip)*, Nathaniel Frey *(C.P.O. Ruddle)*, Werner Klemperer *(Cmdr. Wallace)*, Jack Mullaney *(Ens. Lewis)*, Ben Wright *(RAF Pilot)*, Michael Ross *(Gunner)*, Harry Carey, Jr. *(Roundtree)*, Frank Nelson *(Neilson)*, Ann McCrea *(Lucille)*, Caprice Yordan *(Debbie)*, John Doucette *(Shore Patrol Lieutenant)*, Kip King *(Marine)*, Bob St. Angelo *(Hotel Porter)*, Barbara Gould *(WAC Corporal)*, Mike Mahoney *(Marine)*, Sue Collier *(Girl at Party)*, Jan Reeves *(Blonde)*, Jack Mather *(Man)*, Peter Leeds *(Reporter)*, Jonathan Hale *(Nightclub Manager)*, Hal Baylor *(Big Marine)*, Jane Burgess *(Girl)*, William Phipps *(Lt. Hendricks)*, Ray Montgomery *(Lt. j.g.)*, Larry Lo Verde *(C.P.O., Submarine)*, Michael Fox, Robert Sherman, Harry Carter, Richard Shannon *(War Correspondents)*, Kathleen Freeman *(Nurse Wilinski)*, Nancy Kulp *(Wave at Switchboard)*, Richard Deacon *(Hotchkiss)*, Maudie Prickett *(Chief Nurse)*, Linc Foster *(Co-Pilot)*, Rachel Stephens *(Wave)*, B. Suiter, James Stone *(Bellhops)*.

First a novel by Frederic Wakeman, then a play by Luther Davis, finally a screenplay by Julius Epstein, KISS THEM FOR ME is a pleasant trifle with some wit, some sentimentality, and a touch of Grant's class to round it out. It's WW II and three navy flyers, Grant, Blyden, and Walston, take a much needed holiday in San Francisco. They're heroes and Walston is even running for federal office in his home state. Klemperer is the Public Relations officer assigned to look after the men. They rent a hotel suite, despite the shortage of rooms in San Fran, and decide to toss the party to end all parties. It's there that they meet Mansfield and Parker, two very different types. Parker is a Nob Hill sophisticate who falls for Grant and Mansfield is a pneumatic blonde who feels that her job in life is to "make the boys feel at home." War profiteer Erickson, a shipbuilder, attempts to get the heroes to appear in his yards, but Grant sees that the man is insincere and nixes it. Erickson and Parker are an item, but Parker finds Grant attractive. Erickson and Grant have a fight and Grant knocks him down. Then Parker tells Erickson that the wedding is off. Parker would like to nail Grant but he is as elusive as mercury in her palm. Walston hears that he's been elected in absentia and that means that, as a congressman, he is out of the Navy immediately. The party gets increasingly noisy and the Shore Patrol takes them away briefly. Once out, they plan to go back to their carrier, then learn the ship has been bombed. In the end, Grant and Parker make plans for the rest of their lives. The book had been a cynical look at the way war manufacturers use America's heroes. Then the play took a mildly comedic turn and the film attempted to make it a flat-out farce. Epstein was a co-writer on CASABLANCA, Wakeman also wrote THE HUCKSTERS, and Davis wrote the screenplay for that film as well as many other projects, including the book for "Kismet" as well as "Timbuctoo." In later years, he became a stage producer.

p, Jerry Wald; d, Stanley Donen; w, Julius Epstein (based on the play "Kiss Them for Me" by Luther Davis, from the novel *Shore Leave* by Frederic Wakeman); ph, Milton Krasner (CinemaScope, DeLuxe Color); m, Lionel Newman; ed, Robert Simpson; art d, Lyle R. Wheeler, Maurice Ransford; set d, Walter M. Scott, Stuart A. Reiss; cos, Charles LeMaire; spec eff, L. B. Abbott; m/l, "Kiss Them For Me," Newman, Carroll Coates (sung by The McGuire Sisters); makeup, Ben Nye.

Comedy/Drama **(PR:A MPAA:NR)**

KISS TOMORROW GOODBYE*** (1950) 102m WB bw

James Cagney *(Ralph Cotter)*, Barbara Payton *(Holiday Carleton)*, Helena Carter *(Margaret Dobson)*, Ward Bond *(Inspector Weber)*, Luther Adler *(Cherokee Mandon)*, Barton MacLane *(Reece)*, Steve Brodie *(Jinx Raynor)*, Rhys Williams *(Vic Mason)*, Herbert Heyes *(Ezra Dobson)*, John Litel *(Chief of Police Tolgate)*, William Frawley *(Byers)*, Robert Karnes *(Gray)*, Kenneth Tobey *(Fowler)*, Dan Riss *(District Attorney)*, Frank Reicher *(Doc Green)*, John Halloran *(Cobbett)*, Neville Brand *(Carleton)*, George Spaulding *(Judge)*, Mark Strong *(Bailiff)*, Jack Gargan *(Clerk of Court)*, Frank Marlowe *(Joe, the Milkman)*, Mack Williams *(Hartford)*, Ann Tyrrell *(Miss Staines)*, Clark Howatt *(Intern)*, John Day, William Murphy *(Motorcycle Policemen)*, Dan Ferniel *(Highness)*, Matt McHugh *(Satterfield)*, Georgia Caine *(Julia)*, Charles Meredith *(Mr. Golightly)*, King Donovan *(Driver)*, Dick Rich, Ric Roman *(Collectors)*, Gordon Richards *(Butler)*, Fred Revelala *(Rafael)*, Frank Wilcox *(Doctor)*, Thomas Dillon *(Apperson)*, William Cagney *(Ralph's Brother)*.

This is a particularly brutal Cagney film and the great star reverts to the ruthless character he established in PUBLIC ENEMY, but here it's not grapefruits in the face his peers receive but bullets, bribery, and blackmail. Cagney and partner Brodie escape from a prison farm and take refuge in a small town where corrupt elements control the police force. Learning this while staying with Brodie's sister, Payton, Cagney proceeds to set up a market robbery while paying off crooked cops Bond and MacLane to look the other way. While not busy planning the robbery, Cagney dallies with luscious blonde Payton, a trampy sort who is drawn to his evil personality like the moth to the flame. To possess her, Cagney kills Brand, his ex-partner and Payton's husband. When Payton later expresses hatred for him, Cagney mercilessly beats her up. Bond and MacLane (who teamed as the cops dogging Humphrey Bogart in THE MALTESE FALCON) try to extort more money from Cagney but he tape-records their demands and uses this to blackmail *them* into submission. Cagney also blackmails a local politician after setting up his daughter in a compromising position. With payoff money in his pocket, Cagney plans to leave town with another woman but Payton takes her revenge by killing him. The local cops are exposed and justice—way out in left field in this film—triumphs in the end. The script is poor and production values are at a minimum; only the always fascinating Cagney lifts this mediocre crime melodrama from the dust. Payton would later fall far from grace, ending her days in police courts for prostitution and writing bad checks. KISS TOMORROW GOODBYE made money, despite its failings. Cagney fondly remembered Adler in the film, one of the actors he most admired, and one who taught him a little trick he always remembered and used later: "Luther's really chilling moment in the picture came as he was sitting at a desk, just about to look up at me. Instead of lifting his face and looking at me at the same time, he lifted his face only, his eyes remaining hooded, looking down. *Then*, after his head was fully raised, he lifted his eyelids and stared slowly at me with infinite menace. Such a little thing but such a powerful thing. I had never seen an actor do that in my life and I had been around a bit. Later I suggested that particular bit of business for Dana Wynter to use in the Irish picture we did, SHAKE HANDS WITH THE DEVIL. And when she whipped those big brown eyes from the ground at me it was a decided jolt."

p, William Cagney; d, Gordon Douglas; w, Harry Brown (based on the novel by Horace McCoy); ph, Peverell Marley; m, Carmen Dragon; ed, Truman K. Wood, Walter Hannemann; prod d, Wiard Ihnen; art d, Ihnen; set d, Joe Kish; cos, Adele Parmenter; spec eff, Paul Eagler; makup, Otis Malcolm.

Crime Drama **(PR:C-O MPAA:NR)**

KISSES FOR BREAKFAST** (1941) 81m WB bw

Dennis Morgan *(Rodney Trask)*, Jane Wyatt *(Laura Anders)*, Shirley Ross *(Juliet Marsden)*, Lee Patrick *(Betty Trent)*, Jerome Cowan *(Lucius Lorimer)*, Una O'Connor *(Ellie)*, Romaine Callender *(Dr. Burroughs)*, Barnett Parker *(Phillips)*, Lucia Carroll *(Clara Raymond)*, Cornel Wilde *(Chet Oakley)*, Willie Best *(Arnold)*, Louise Beavers *(Clotilda)*, Clarence Muse *(Old Jeff)*, Leon Belasco *(Accompanist)*, Frank Orth *(T.C. Barett the Hobo)*, John Sheehan *(Police Captain)*, Edgar Dearing *(Motorcycle Cop)*, Fred Graham *(Double for Cornel Wilde)*.

Newlywed Morgan suffers amnesia after a knock on the head during a fight. The only information he has on him is the address of his bride's cousin. He makes his way to the cousin, Wyatt, helping to rescue her plantation from debt and eventually marrying her. The newlyweds decide to visit Wyatt's cousin, Morgan's first wife, arriving just after she's been told her husband is dead and is about to remarry. What started as a first-rate comedy turns into nothing but slapstick, losing the story line in the process. A remake of THE MATRIMONIAL BED, 1930.

p, Harlan Thompson; d, Lewis Seiler; w, Kenneth Gamet (based on a play by Yves Mirande and Andre Mouezy-Eon and a play adaptation by Seymour Hicks); ph, Arthur Edeson; ed, James Gibson.

Comedy **(PR:A MPAA:NR)**

KISSES FOR MY PRESIDENT 1/2**
(1964) 113m Pearlayn/WB bw (AKA: KISSES FOR THE PRESIDENT)

Fred MacMurray *(Thad McCloud)*, Polly Bergen *(Leslie McCloud)*, Arlene Dahl *(Doris Reid)*, Edward Andrews *(Senator Walsh)*, Eli Wallach *(Valdez)*, Donald May *(John O'Connor)*, Bill Richards *(Harry Holcombe)*, Anna Capri *(Gloria McCloud)*, Ronnie Dapo *(Peter McCloud)*, Richard St. John *(Jackson)*, Bill Walker *(Joseph)*, Adrienne Marden *(Miss Higgins)*.

Bergen plays the first woman to be elected President, with MacMurray as the spouse who must adapt to his role as "First Man." Their family begins to dissolve, and Bergen is faced with South American dictator Wallach, and other problems, but then— fortunately—has to resign because of pregnancy. Other than its initial novelty, the story has little to hold it together. Given the material, direction and performances are competent, though Bergen is miscast.

p&d, Curtis Bernhardt; w, Claude Binyon, Robert G. Kane; ph, Robert Surtees; m, Bronislau Kaper; ed, Sam O'Steen; art d, Herman Blumenthal; set d, John P. Austin; cos, Howard Shoup; makeup, Gordon Bau.

Comedy **(PR:A MPAA:NR)**

KISSES FOR THE PRESIDENT

(SEE: KISSES FOR MY PRESIDENT, 1964)

KISSIN' COUSINS** (1964) 96m MGM c

Elvis Presley *(Josh Morgan* and *Jodie Tatum)*, Arthur O'Connell *(Pappy Tatum)*, Glenda Farrell *(Ma Tatum)*, Jack Albertson *(Capt. Robert Salbo)*, Pam Austin *(Selena Tatum)*, Cynthia Pepper *(Midge)*, Yvonne Craig *(Azalea Tatum)*, Donald Woods *(Gen. Alvin Donford)*, Tommy Farrell *(M. Sgt. William Bailey)*, Beverly Powers *(Trudy)*, Hortense Petra *(Dixie)*, Robert Stone *(General's Aide)*.

Presley is a member of the Air Force sent to a rural area to talk the local inhabitants into selling their land for a base. O'Connell does not want to sell for fear that his moonshining business may be upset. Several romantic liaisons develop: between Presley and his distant cousins, between Presley (in a dual role as O'Connell's nephew) and a WAC, Pepper, and others. Everything works out for the best in the end; the Air Force gets its land and both Presleys get the girl. Two "Elvises" make this already very thin plot even less believable than otherwise. Oddly, or maybe not so oddly, the story seems to stop at any point just to allow Presley to sing. Songs, all sung by Elvis, include: "Kissin' Cousins," "There's Gold in the Mountains," "One Boy, Two Little Girls," "Catchin' on Fast," "Tender Feeling" (Bill Giant, Bernie Baum, Florence Kaye); "Smokey Mountain Boy" (Lenore Rosenblatt, Victor Millrose); "Anyone Could Fall in Love With You" (Bennie Benjamin, Sol Marcus, Louis A. DeJesus); "One is Enough" (Sid Tepper, Roy C. Bennett); "Barefoot Ballad" (Dolores Fuller, Lee Morris); Echoes of Love" (Bob Roberts, Paddy McMains); "It's a Long Lonely Highway" (Doc Pomus, Mort Shuman).

p, Sam Katzman; d, Gene Nelson; w, Gerald Drayson Adams, Nelson (based on a story by Adams); ph, Ellis W. Carter (Panavision, Metrocolor); ed, Ben Lewis; md, Fred Krager; art d, George W. Davis, Eddie Imazu; set d, Henry Grace, Budd S. Friend; ch, Hal Belfer; makeup, William Tuttle.

Musical **(PR:A MPAA:NR)**

KISSING BANDIT, THE* (1948) 102m MGM c

Frank Sinatra *(Ricardo)*, Kathryn Grayson *(Teresa)*, J. Carroll Naish *(Chico)*, Mildred Natwick *(Isabella)*, Mikhail Rasumny *(Don Jose)*, Billy Gilbert *(General Torro)*, Sono Osato *(Bianca)*, Clinton Sundberg *(Col. Gomez)*, Edna Skinner *(Juanita)*, Vincente Gomez *(Mexican Guitarist)*, Carlton Young *(Count Belmonte)*, Henry Mirelez *(Pepito)*, Nick Thompson *(Pablo)*, Jose Dominguez *(Francisco)*, Alberto Morin *(Lotso)*, Pedro Regas *(Esteban)*, Julian Rivero *(Postman)*, Mitchell Lewis *(Fernando)*, Byron Foulger *(Grandee)*, Ricardo Montalban, Ann Miller, Cyd Charisse *(Fiesta Dancers)*.

Sinatra comes back to California to take over his father's innkeeping business. He learns that his father was actually a bandit who would leave all his victims a kiss, and the old members of the gang encourage Sinatra to resume his father's role, which he does. Except for an exciting dance by Montalban, Miller, and Charisse, "Dance of Fury," this film has nothing exceptional to offer. Songs include "Love Is Where You Find It" and "Tomorrow Means Romance," sung by Grayson; "What's Wrong With Me" and "Senorita," sung by Grayson and Sinatra; "If I Steal a Kiss" and "Siesta," sung by Sinatra; and "I Like You," sung by Sono Osato.

p, Joe Pasternak; d, Laslo Benedek; w, Isobel Lennart, John Briard Harding; ph, Robert Surtees (Technicolor); m, George Stoll, Albert Sendrey, Scott Bradley, Andre Previn; ed, Adrienne Fazan; md, Stoll; art d, Cedric Gibbons, Randall Duell; set d, Edwin B. Willis, Jack D. Moore; cos, Walter Plunkett; spec eff, A. Arnold Gillespie; ch, Stanley Donen; m/l, Nacio Herb Brown, Earl Brent, Edward Heyman; makeup, Jack Dawn.

Musical **(PR:A MPAA:NR)**

KISSING CUP'S RACE* 1/2 (1930, Brit.) 75m But bw

Stewart Rome *(Lord Rattlington)*, Madeleine Carroll *(Lady Mollie Adair)*, John Stuart *(Lord Jimmy Hilhoxton)*, Richard Cooper *(Rollo Adair)*, Chili Bouchier *(Gabrielle)*, Moore Marriott *(Joe Tricker)*, J. Fisher White *(Marquis of Hilhoxton)*, James Knight *(Detective)*, Gladys Hamer *(Maid)*, Wally Patch *(Bookie)*, Charles Wade.

Tepid drama in which Stuart plays a down-and-out lord and horse lover. Unwilling to part with his beloved animals, he retains one young colt out of the herd he must sell for some quick cash. Stuart soon finds himself back on his feet after it takes first place in the big race in this predictable racetrack tale.

p&d, Castleton Knight; w, Knight, Blanche Metcalfe, J. Bertram Brown, Benedict James (based on the poem by Campbell Rae Brown).

Drama **(PR:A MPAA:NR)**

KIT CARSON* 1/2** (1940) 97m UA bw

Jon Hall *(Kit Carson)*, Lynn Bari *(Dolores Murphy)*, Dana Andrews *(Capt. John C. Fremont)*, Harold Huber *(Lopez)*, Ward Bond *(Ape)*, Renie Riano *(Miss Genevieve Pilchard)*, Clayton Moore *(Paul Terry)*, Rowena Cook *(Alice Terry)*, Raymond Hatton *(Jim Bridger)*, Harry Strang *(Sgt. Clanahan)*, C. Henry Gordon *(Gen. Castro)*, Lew Merrill *(Gen. Vallejo)*, Stanley Andrews *(Larkin)*, Edwin Maxwell *(John Sutter)*, Peter Lynn *(James King)*, Charles Stevens *(Ruiz)*, William Farnum *(Don Miguel Murphy)*, Iron Eyes Cody *(Indian)*.

An excellent action film with marvelous cinematography that captures the splendor of the Old West, KIT CARSON mixes fact and legend and comes up with a stirring tale. Hall is the fabled scout, perhaps the greatest who ever lived, guiding Andrews (as John C. Fremont) and his troops—plus a caravan of prairie schooners—across the plains and mountains to the promised land of California. They encounter storms, Indian attacks, and a love triangle between Hall, Andrews, and Bari that is genteel and full of understanding. Once in California a new menace arrives in the form of Mexican general Gordon and his soldiers, intent upon making the state a province of Mexico. Hall and his two erstwhile pioneer pals, Bond and Huber, defend a walled hacienda against the invading Mexicans while Fremont gathers his forces. After a titanic battle, the Mexicans rush the hacienda and kill Bond and Huber. Hall is saved with the arrival of Andrews and the U.S. troops who rout Gordon and save the day. Bari winds up with Hall, much to the tongue-tied scout's surprise, with Andrews gallantly stepping out of the picture. Producer Small spared no expense in mounting this fine western. Where the script is weak, the action and lensing are strong, with credit going to helmsman Seitz. Hatton appears in some memorable scenes as the legendary trailblazer Jim Bridger and silent film star Farnum, once the western idol of the two-reelers, performs as the owner of the hacienda. Bari is lovely, Hall and Andrews dashing, and the whole film is pure enjoyment. The great scout, Christopher "Kit" Carson (1809–1868) has been profiled in films many times. Fred Thomson played the scout in a 1928 silent. Johnny Mack Brown played him in FIGHTING WITH KIT CARSON, 1933, Sammy McKim essayed the man in THE PAINTED STALLION, 1938, and Wild Bill Elliott played him again in OVERLAND WITH KIT CARSON, 1939. Rip Torn would later play the intrepid scout in a 1986 TV mini-series featuring Richard Chamberlain as John C. Fremont. Along with Buffalo Bill Cody (who named his one and only son after Carson, Kit Carson Cody, a boy who died of illness in infancy), Daniel Boone and Jim Bridger, Carson was the stuff of legend, an image this film captures with a wonderful flair.

p, Edward Small; d, George B. Seitz; w, George Bruce; ph, John Mescall, Robert Pittack; m, Edward Ward; ed, Fred Feitshans, Jr., William Claxton; md, Ward; art d, John DuCasse Schulze; spec eff, Jack Cosgrove, Howard A. Anderson.

Western **(PR:A MPAA:NR)**

KITCHEN, THE*** (1961, Brit.) 76m A.C.T. Films/Kingsley International bw

Carl Mohner *(Peter)*, Mary Yeomans *(Monica)*, Brian Phelan *(Kevin)*, Tom Bell *(Paul)*, Howard Greene *(Raymond)*, Eric Pohlmann *(Mr. Marango)*, James Bolam *(Michael)*, Scot Finch *(Hans)*, Gertan Klauber *(Gaston)*, Martin Boddey *(Max)*, Sean Lynch *(Dimitri)*, Joseph Behrman *(Magi)*, George Eugeniou *(Nick)*, Frank Pettitt *(Frank)*, Charles Lloyd Pack *(Chef)*, Frank Atkinson *(Alfred)*, Andreas Markos *(Mangolis)*, Jeanne Hepple *(Hattie)*, Patricia Greene *(Anne)*, Jessie Robins *(Bertha)*, Fanny Carby *(Winnie)*, Patricia Clapton *(1st Jiving Waitress)*, Lynn Barton *(2nd Jiving Waitress)*, Claire Isbister *(5th Waitress)*, Veronica Wells *(6th Waitress)*, Gwen Nelson *(8th Waitress)*, Jennifer Wallace *(9th Waitress)*, Joan Geary *(14th Waitress)*, Rosalind Knight *(17th Waitress)*, Susan Field *(20th Waitress)*, Ida Goldapple *(19th Waitress)*, Nilo Christian *(21st Waitress)*, Madeline Leon *(23rd Waitress)*, Ruth Meyers *(34th Waitress)*, Andreas Constantine *(2nd Porter)*, Andreas Lysandrou *(1st Dishwasher)*.

The kitchen of a busy London restaurant is the setting for this witty look at a diversified working-class world. Mohner plays the cook who tells his fellow workers to dream of a better life, but himself goes into a fury when he realizes his own plans of marrying the waitress Yeomans cannot be fulfilled. The underlying message of the kitchen as a microcosm of the world is never fully developed, but this is easily overlooked because of the fast-paced direction and rich characterizations. Song: "Something's Cooking" (Les Vandyke), sung by Adam Faith.

p&w, Sidney Cole; d, James Hill; ph, Reginald Wyer; m, David Lee; ed, Gerry Hambling; art d, William Kellner.

Drama/Comedy **(PR:A MPAA:NR)**

KITTEN WITH A WHIP zero (1964) 82m UNIV bw

Ann-Margret *(Jody Dvorak)*, John Forsythe *(David Patton)*, Peter Brown *(Ron)*, Patricia Barry *(Vera)*, Richard Anderson *(Grant)*, James Ward *(Buck)*, Diane Sayer *(Midge)*, Ann Doran *(Mavis Varden)*, Patrick Whyte *(Philip Varden)*, Audrey Dalton *(Virginia)*, Leo Gordon *(Enders)*, Patricia Tiara *(Striptease Dancer)*, Nora Marlowe *(Matron)*, Frances Robinson *(Martha)*, Maxine Stuart *(Peggy)*, Mildred Von Hollen *(Saleslady)*, Jerry Dunphy *(Newscaster)*, Doodles Weaver *(Salty Sam)*, Hal Hopper *(Chauffeur)*, Gary Lockwood.

The only reason to give this film any mention at all is the always-dependable work of John Forsythe and the lensing by veteran Joe Biroc. Otherwise, it would merit only your disdain. Ann Margret is a vicious escapee from a girls' juvenile home who has stabbed one of the matrons and set fire to the dorm. Next, she breaks into Forsythe's house. He is planning to run for office and must overcome the stigma of being separated from his wife. He comes home after a social engagement and finds Ann-Margret there. He wants to call the cops but she uses threats and cajolery to keep him from doing that. Eager to get rid of her, Forsythe hands her some cash to buy new clothes and a bus ticket to Los Angeles. She leaves, then returns and says she'll ruin his political aspirations unless he agrees to allow her and some of her lowlife pals to stay. Forsythe is helpless and a wild party begins. During the drinking bout, Brown, another teenage delinquent, is slashed by Ward, an overage surfer. Forsythe is forced to drive Brown to a doctor in Baja, California, as any U.S. physician would be forced to report the razor injury. Brown is dropped off and Ward is tossed out of the car, then Ann-Margret makes Forsythe rent a room at a fleabag motel so she can hide from Ward and Brown. While there, Forsythe meets some friends from Northern California but manages to bring off his presence without a hitch. Forsythe is about to leave the motel when the two thugs arrive and Ward thrashes Forsythe, leaving him comatose. Ann-Margret feels terrible about what she's gotten the gentle Forsythe into and puts him into the car for the drive north. Ward and Brown chase the first car, there's a crash, and the autos explode and burn. Only Forsythe is saved and, while lying in the hospital, he learns that Ann-Margret got him off any hook with her last words before expiring. A thoroughly hideous and unpleasant movie, this may have been one of the films that cost Universal Production Chief Ed Muhl his job. Los Angeles newscaster Jerry Dunphy plays himself, and what little humor comes from Spike Jones' comic Doodles Weaver, whose brother, Sylvester "Pat" Weaver is acknowledged to have been one of the giants of the television industry, having invented "The Today Show" and "The Tonight Show," as well as several other innovations in broadcasting. Would that the programming wizard had read this script.

p, Harry Keller; d&w, Douglas Heyes (based on the book by Wade Miller); ph, Joseph Biroc; ed, Russell F. Schoengarth; art d, Alexander Golitzen, Malcolm Brown; set d, John McCarthy, John P. Austin, Oliver Emert; cos, Burton Miller; spec eff, Charles Spurgeon; makeup, Frank McCoy, Dorothy Parkinson.

Drama **(PR:C-O MPAA:NR)**

KITTY* (1929, Brit.) 92m BIF-Burlington/Wardour bw

Estelle Brody *(Kitty Greenwood)*, John Stuart *(Alex St. George)*, Dorothy Cumming *(Mrs. St. George)*, Marie Ault *(Sarah Greenwood)*, Winter Hall *(John Furnival)*, Olaf Hytten *(Leaper)*, Charles O'Shaughnessy *(Reuben)*, E.F. Bostwick *(Dr. Dazely)*, Jerrold Robertshaw *(The Artist)*, Rex Maurice *(Dr. Drake)*, Gibb McLaughlin *(The Electrician)*, Moore Marriott, Charles Ashton, Charles Levey.

Stuart is a young pilot who marries Brody, then is quickly packed off to war. His jealous mother, Cumming, writes to tell him that his wife has been seeing other men, at which point Stuart's plane crashes and he comes home a cripple. The rest of the film centers around his trying to walk again, and whether or not the two newlyweds will get around Cumming and meet again. Sound is not introduced into the picture until the last 25 minutes, making the already haphazard production even more ridiculous.

p&d, Victor Saville; w, Violet Powell, Benn W. Levy (based on a novel by Warwick Deeping); ph, Karl Puth.

Drama **(PR:A MPAA:NR)**

KITTY*** (1945) 103m PAR bw

Paulette Goddard *(Kitty)*, Ray Milland *(Sir Hugh Marcy)*, Patric Knowles *(Brett Hardwood, the Earl of Carstairs)*, Reginald Owen *(Duke of Malmunster)*, Cecil Kellaway *(Thomas Gainsborough)*, Constance Collier *(Lady Susan Dewitt)*, Dennis Hoey *(Jonathan Selby)*, Sara Allgood *(Old Meg)*, Eric Blore *(Dobson)*, Gordon Richards *(Sir Joshua Reynolds)*, Michael Dyne *(The Prince of Wales)*, Edgar Norton *(Earl of Campton)*, Patricia Cameron *(Elaine Carlisle)*, Mary Gordon *(Nancy)*, Anita Bolster *(Mullens)*, Heather Wilde *(Lil)*, Charles Coleman *(Majordomo)*, Mae Clarke *(Molly)*, Ann Codee *(Mme. Aurelia)*, Douglas Walton *(Philip)*, Alec Craig *(McNab)*, Edward Cooper *(Sir Herbert Harbord)*, Anne Curson *(Duchess of Gloucester)*, Tempe Pigott *(Woman in Window)*, John Rice *(Cockney Cart Driver)*, Doris Lloyd *(Woman Fish Hawker)*, Sybil Burton *(Magic Lantern Woman)*, Snub Pollard *(Hugh's Rental Coachman)*, Ruth St. Denis *(Duchess)*, Mary McLeod *(Mrs. Sheridan)*, Dodo Bernard *(Taffy Tarts Peddler)*, Gibson Gowland *(Prison Guard)*, Cyril Delevanti *("All Hot" Hawker)*, Byron Poindexter *(Col. St. Leger)*, Percival Vivian *(Dr. Holt)*, Crauford Kent, Colin Kenny, Hilda Plowright, Charles Irwin, Jean Ransome, Mary MacLaren.

Based on a hit "romance novel" (long before that phrase was invented), KITTY is an opulent and very authentic look at 18th-century England, and Goddard is at the top of her beauty and form. It's yet another version of the "Pygmalion" story with Goddard as the poor Cockney girl who rises to become a duchess. She is first noticed by Kellaway, as the famous artist Gainsborough, who adores her looks and paints her portrait. Now she is taken under the wing of the calculating Milland, a foppish nobleman, and his drunken dowager aunt, Collier. They plan to use her beauty to their advantage and begin to educate her, cause her to lose her accent, and teach her the manners of a lady. Next, a marriage is arranged between Goddard and elderly Hoey, an ironmonger. Hoey dies shortly thereafter but Owen, a duke, is waiting in the wings. However, Goddard is expecting the baby of her late husband. She manages to convince Owen that the child is his and when it finally arrives, Owen is so thrilled that he topples over from a heart attack. Goddard is now a duchess and can finally marry the man she's loved all along, the scheming Milland. The picture is a visual delight and Leisen, after attempting to actually borrow some of Gainsborough's more famous works and being rebuffed, had some copies painted. The sets and costumes are lovely and the acting is more than competent. Despite having seen this story a few times before, the creative team brings it off well and it was a large winner for Paramount. They used to call this kind of movie "a woman's picture," but the truth is that anyone can appreciate the care that went into it. Character actor Reginald Owen was one of the top-notch Britishers in Hollywood and as the Duke of Malmunster, he really shined, using a cute little trot through the hallways and up the stairs of the duke's palace.

p, Karl Tunberg; d, Mitchell Leisen; w, Darrell Ware, Tunberg (based on the novel by Rosamund Marshall); ph, Daniel L. Fapp; m, Victor Young; ed, Alma Macrorie; art d, Hans Dreier, Walter Tyler; set d&cos, Raoul Pene DuBois; ch, Billy Daniels; spec eff, Gordon Jennings.

Period Drama **(PR:A MPAA:NR)**

KITTY AND THE BAGMAN** (1983, Aus.) 95m Quartet c

Liddy Clark *(Kitty O'Rourke)*, Val Lehman *(Lil)*, John Stanton *(Bagman)*, Gerard McGuire *(Cyril)*, Collette Mann *(Doris)*, Reg Evans *(Chicka)*, Kylie Foster *(Sarah)*, Ted Hepple *(Sam)*, David Adcock *(Thomas)*, David Bradshaw *(Larry)*, Anthony Hawkins *(Simon)*, Paul Chubb *(Slugger)*, John Ewart *(Train Driver)*.

Set in 1920s Sydney, Clark plays the young woman who, with the help of a crooked cop, manages to work her way up the ladder to become head of the underworld. The setting and atmosphere accurately portray the times, but impact of the entire film is rather negligible.

p, Anthony Buckley; d, Donald Crombie; w, John Burney, Phillip Cornford; ph, Dean Semmler.

Comedy/Drama **Cas.** **(PR:O MPAA:R)**

KITTY FOYLE 1/2** (1940) 105m RKO bw

Ginger Rogers *(Kitty Foyle)*, Dennis Morgan *(Wyn Strafford)*, James Craig *(Mark)*, Eduardo Ciannelli *(Giono)*, Ernest Cossart *(Pop)*, Gladys Cooper *(Mrs. Strafford)*, Odette Myrtil *(Delphine Detaille)*, Mary Treen *(Pat)*, Katharine [K.T.] Stevens *(Molly)*, Walter Kingsford *(Mr. Kennett)*, Cecil Cunningham *(Grandmother)*, Nella Walker *(Aunt Jessica)*, Edward Fielding *(Uncle Edgar)*, Kay Linaker *(Wyn's Wife)*, Richard Nichols *(Wyn's Boy)*, Florence Bates *(Customer)*, Heather Angel *(Girl in Prologue)*, Tyler Brooke *(Boy in Prologue)*, Hattie Noel *(Black Woman)*, Frank Milan *(Parry)*, Charles Quigley *(Bill)*, Harriette Brandon *(Miss Bala)*, Howard Entwistle *(Butler)*, Billy Elmer *(Neway)*, Walter Sande *(Trumpeter)*, Ray Teal *(Saxophonist)*, Joey Ray *(Drummer)*, Mel Ruick *(Violinist-Leader)*, Doodles Weaver *(Pianist)*, Theodore Von Eltz *(Hotel Clerk)*, Max Davidson *(Flower Man)*, Charles Miller *(Doctor)*, Mary Gordon *(Charwoman)*, Fay Helm *(Prim Girl)*, Helen Lynd *(Girl in Elevator)*, Dorothy Vaughan *(Charwoman)*, Mimi Doyle *(Jane)*, Hilda Plowright *(Nurse)*, Spencer Charters *(Father)*, Gino Corrado *(Guest)*, Frank Mills *(Taxi Driver)*, Joe Bernard, Tom Herbert *(Waiters)*, Julie Carter, Jane Patten, Renee Haal, Mary Currier, Patricia Maier, Brooks Benedict, Tom Quinn.

Ginger Rogers won the Oscar for her portrayal of KITTY FOYLE though we haven't yet figured out how she beat Hepburn (THE PHILADELPHIA STORY), Fontaine (REBECCA), Martha Scott (OUR TOWN), and Bette Davis (THE LETTER). Perhaps it was because Rogers was doing her first starring dramatic role after a few smaller straight parts. This was her fortieth movie and she'd already established herself as a musical star so the Academy may have just awarded her the statuette because they were surprised that she emoted as well as she tapped. The film was also nominated as Best Picture, for Best Direction, Best Sound, and Best Screenplay, but lost out on those counts. Rogers is the hard-working daughter of hard-working Cossart. She has Cinderella dreams of marrying someone in the upper crust. She is betrothed to young doctor Craig but disposes him when old flame Morgan comes back into her life. Morgan is the weakling son of a Philadelphia Main Line family and she decides to marry him over the objections of his snobbish family. Soon enough she sees that he is as shallow as a baby pool and she leaves him, not knowing that she's pregnant. She gives birth to a stillborn child and never tells him. After a while, Craig steps back into her life and she realizes that he's the man for her. You could barely see the screen for all the suds. Director Wood used a stream-of-consciousness narration, with Rogers talking to herself in the mirror and the mirror answering back. Sentimental, often mushy, and with some dialogue that Trumbo wishes he could have back, KITTY FOYLE is an okay film but not worthy of being included with the big ones of 1940. Nevertheless, it retained a tidy profit for RKO and convinced Rogers that she didn't have to sing and dance to make movies. The book concentrated on the differences in the social classes and made some satiric points, but the screenplay tossed most of that aside and focused on the character's humanity, her hopes and desires, and her response to the two men. Actress Katharine Stevens (formerly married to Hugh Marlowe who appeared in THE DAY THE EARTH STOOD STILL, 1951) is the daughter of director Sam Wood and was billed as K. T. in later films.

p, David Hempstead; d, Sam Wood; w, Dalton Trumbo, Donald Ogden Stewart (based on the novel by Christopher Morley); ph, Robert de Grasse; m, Roy Webb; ed, Henry Berman; art d, Van Nest Polglase, Mark-Lee Kirk; set d, Darrell Silvera; cos, Renie; spec eff, Vernon L. Walker; makeup, Mel Burns.

Drama **Cas.** **(PR:A-C MPAA:NR)**

KLANSMAN, THE* (1974) 112m PAR c

Lee Marvin *(Sheriff Bascomb)*, Richard Burton *(Breck Stancill)*, Cameron Mitchell *(Deputy Butt Cut Bates)*, Lola Falana *(Loretta Sykes)*, Luciana Paluzzi *(Trixie)*, David Huddleston *(Mayor Hardy)*, Linda Evans *(Nancy Poteet)*, O. J. Simpson *(Garth)*, Spence Wil-Dee *(Willy Washington)*, Hoke Howell *(Bobby Poteet)*, Eve Christopher *(Mrs. Martha Shaneyfelt)*, Ed Call *(Mr. Shaneyfelt, Martha's Husband)*, Morgan Upton *(N. Y. Times Reporter)*, Charles Briggs *(Associated Press Reporter)*, Robert Porter *(Rev. Josh Franklin, Demonstrator)*, Gary Catus *(Charles Peck, Demonstrator)*, Larry Williams *(Lightning Rod)*, Bert Williams *(Doctor)*, Wendell Wellman *(Alan Bascomb, Sheriff's Son)*, Susan Brown *(Maybelle Bascomb, Sheriff's Wife)*, John Alderson *(Vernon Hodo)*, John Pearce *(Taggart)*, David Ladd *(Flagg)*, Vic Perrin *(Hector)*, Virgil Fry *(Johnson)*, Jeannie Bell *(Mary Anne)*, Jo Ann Cowell *(Annie)*, Scott E. Lane *(Jim Hodo)*.

Marvin plays a sheriff in a small southern town that is a hotbed of KKK activity. Emotions flare when Evans is raped, with the Klan, headed by town mayor Huddleston, harassing an innocent black youth. There is further unfair harassment of Falana, a visitor to town accused of being an outside agitator. Directed and performed with little belief in the project.

p, William Alexander; d, Terence Young; w, Millard Kaufman, Samuel Fuller (based on a novel by William Bradford Huie); ph, Lloyd Ahern (Technicolor); m, Dale O. Warren, Stu Gardner; ed, Gene Milford; prod d, John S. Poplin; set d, Raymond Molyneaux; m/l, Mack Rice, Bettye Crutcher.

Drama **(PR:C MPAA:R)**

KLAUN FERDINAND A RAKETA

(SEE: ROCKET TO NOWHERE, 1962, Czech.)

KLEINES ZELT UND GROSSE LIEBE

(SEE: TWO IN A SLEEPING BAG, 1964, Ger.)

KLONDIKE** (1932) 68m MON bw

Lyle Talbot *(Dr. Cromwell)*, Capt. Frank Hawks *(Donald Evans)*, Thelma Todd *(Klondike)*, Henry B. Walthall *(Mark Armstrong)*, Jason Robards, Sr. *(Jim Armstrong)*, Ethel Wales *(Sadie Jones)*, Tully Marshall *(Editor Hinman)*, Pat O'Malley *(Burke)*, Priscilla Dean *(Miss Porter)*, Myrtle Stedman *(Miss Fielding)*, George ["Gabby"] Hayes *(Tom Ross)*, Lafe McKee *(Seth)*.

Talbot plays a doctor who crashes while in a plane trip over the Klondike. The pilot is killed, but Talbot is saved by the members of a nearby trading post. A love triangle develops between Talbot, Todd, and Robards, a young man who suffers from a disease Talbot failed at properly treating in London. This time he safely performs the operation, leaving Todd to Robards. The direction is jerky and ill-timed, with the only commendable performances by Robards and Hawks, an actual pilot.

p, William T. Lackey; d, Phil Rosen; w, Tristam Tupper.

Drama **(PR:A MPAA:NR)**

KLONDIKE ANNIE 1/2** (1936) 78m PAR bw

Mae West *(The Frisco Doll Rose Carlton)*, Victor McLaglen *(Capt. Bull Brackett)*, Phillip Reed *(Inspector Jack Forrest)*, Helen Jerome Eddy *(Sister Annie Alden)*, Harry Beresford *(Brother Bowser)*, Harold Huber *(Chan Lo)*, Conway Tearle *(Vance Palmer)*, Lucille Webster Gleason *(Big Tess)*, Esther Howard *(Fanny Radler)*, Soo Yong *(Fah Wong)*, Ted Oliver *(Grigsby)*, John Rogers *(Buddie)*, Tetsu Komai *(Lan Fang)*, James Burke *(Bartender)*, George Walsh *(Quartermaster)* Chester Gan *(Ship's Cook)*, Jack Daley *(2nd Mate)*, Jack Wallace *(3rd Mate)*,

D'Arcy Corrigan, Arthur Turner Foster, Nell Craig, Nella Walker *(Missionaries)*, Philip Ahn *(Wing)*, Mrs. Wong Wing *(Ah Toy)*, Guy D. Ennery *(Alvaredos)*, Maidel Turner *(Lydia Bowley)*, Huntley Gordon *(Clinton Reynolds)*, Paul Kruger, Edwin Brady, John Lester Johnson *(Sailors)*, Jack Mulhall *(Officer)*, Gene Austin *(Organist)*, Russ Hall *(Candy)*, Otto Heimel *(Cocoa)*, Gladys Gale, Edna Bennett, Pearl Eaton, Kathleen Key, Ilean Hume, Marie Wells *(Dance Hall Girls)*, Mrs. Chan Lee *(Blind Woman)*, Dick Allen *(Miner)*, Jackson Snyder *(Little Boy)*, Lawrence Grant *(Sir Gilbert)*, Vladimir Bykoff *(Marinoff)*, Philo McCullough *(Extra)*.

The censor was yapping at West's feet by the time she made this, and so many cuts were taken from the film that it appears choppy and much of the motivation is gone for what she does. Despite that, the Legion Of Decency found it morally objectionable. Worst of all, audiences were not in love with the structure, the attempt at drama, or the whole theme of a murderess who finds God and goes straight. West is a Barbary Coast mistress to Chinese man Huber. She was a street woman whom Huber found and adorned with the finest frippery. But there's a price to be paid and that's Huber's jealousy. West wants to leave Huber and go to Alaska. Her maid, Yong, will go with her and Tearle is setting up the escape. When Huber learns of this, he tries to stop her. (In the original print, we actually see West kill Huber in self-defense, but that was edited in the final cut.) Next thing you know, she's aboard the ship bound for the "frozen north" and ship's captain McLaglen is after her. Most of the trip is spent attempting to fend him off. They dock at Seattle and Yong departs. It's here that McLaglen learns West is a killer and he uses the information to blackmail her into sleeping with him. They move up to Vancouver, and Eddy, a soul-saver, comes aboard and shares the cabin with West. Soon, Eddy gets sick and dies and when the cops come on board in Nome West has assumed the identity of the late zealot. On land, West keeps up the sham and everyone thinks she's a missionary doll. McLaglen would like to take her to a warmer climate like Tahiti but West feels she must stay in Alaska and do what the late Eddy would have done—save a few sinners from Hell. There is a small mission in Nome and it is in desperate need of funds to tend to the poor and starving types who come there for solace and soup. Her methods are quite a bit different from what Eddy would have used but her results are evident. She enlists the local dancers to help, gives sermons in no-nonsense language, redoes the words to hymns and sets them to pop music, and musters an army of one-armed men to work as her ushers for collections. Reed arrives. He's a Northwest Mounted Policeman and he and West hit it off right away, which angers McLaglen. McLaglen confronts West in her hotel room and Reed hears it all, but assures West that her background doesn't mean anything to him. He loves West and will do anything for her. West won't hear of his self-sacrifice. She doffs her dowdy garb and puts on her old San Fran clothing, which shocks the town, especially Beresford, one of the officials at the mission. The place is on its feet now and they don't need her anymore, as she'd raised lots of money, but she asks that they change the name of the mission to Sister Annie Alden's Settlement House, after the late Eddy. She climbs aboard McLaglen's ship intent on returning to San Francisco and clearing her name of the murder charge. And that's where it ends. This was a more serious West than anyone had ever seen and the result was similar to what happened when other deeply-ingrained screen personas tried something completely different—apathy. Clint Eastwood tried it with BRONCO BILLY and flopped. Burt Reynolds did THE END and it was. West tried to meld her wisecracks with some dramatic structure and a meaningful story but audiences weren't ready for it. Songs include: "Little Bar Butterfly," "Mr. Deep Blue Sea," "I'm An Occidental Woman In An Oriental Mood For Love," "Open Up Your Heart And Let The Sunshine In," "Cheer Up, Little Sister," "I Hear You Knockin' But You Can't Come In," "It's Never Too Late To Say No," "This May Not Be Love But It's Wonderful," and "It's Better To Give Than Receive," (Gene Austin, James Johnson), "My Medicine Man" (Sam Coslow).

p, William LeBaron; d, Raoul Walsh; w, Mae West (based on the play "Frisco Kate" by West, the unpublished story "Halleluyah I'm A Saint" by Marion Morgan, George B. Dowell, and the short story "Lulu Was A Lady" by Frank Mitchell Dazey); ph, George Clemens; ed; Stuart Heisler; art d, Hans Dreier, Bernard Herzgrup; set d, A. E. Freudeman.

Musical Comedy/Drama (PR:A-C MPAA:NR)

KLONDIKE FEVER* ½
(1980) 60m CFI Investments c (AKA: JACK LONDON'S KLONDIKE FEVER)

Jeff East *(Jack London)*, Rod Steiger *(Soapy Smith)*, Angie Dickinson *(Belinda McNair)*, Lorne Greene *(Sam Steele)*, Barry Morse *(John Thornton)*, Michael Hogan *(Will Ryan)*, Merritt Sloper *(Robin Gammell)*, Lisa Langlois *(Gertie)*, Sherry Lewis *(Louise)*.

East plays the young novelist Jack London in his encounter with the great northern wilderness, the inspiration for many of his stories. Unused to the rugged ways of the north, East gets into several misadventures because of his naivete, one being a run-in with Steiger, a priest gone bad, due to Steiger's mistreatment of a dog. The film fails to capture the enthusiasm London must have felt for this rugged landscape.

p, Gilbert W. Taylor; d, Peter Carter; w, Charles E. Israel, Martin Lager; ph, Bert Dunk; m, Hagood Hardy; ed, Stan Cole; prod d, Seamus Flannery; spec eff, John Thomas.

Drama (PR:A MPAA:NR)

KLONDIKE FURY** (1942) 68m MON bw

Edmund Lowe *(Dr. John Mandre)*, Lucille Fairbanks *(Peg)*, Bill Henry *(Jim Armstrong)*, Ralph Morgan *(Dr. Brady)*, Mary Forbes *(Mrs. Langton)*, Jean Brooks *(Ray Langton)*, Vince Barnett *(Alaska)*, Clyde Cook *(Yukon)*, Robert Middlemass *(Sam Armstrong)*, John Roche *(Brad Rogers)*, Monte Blue, Kenneth Harlan *(Flight Dispatchers)*, Marjorie Wood.

Lowe is a surgeon who takes up flying to keep his mind off a failed operation. Caught in a storm in the Klondike, he crashes and is nursed back to health by Fairbanks at a northern trading post. The son of the trading post owner requires the same operation at which Lowe initially failed. This time he successfully performs the operation, regaining his self-esteem. He returns to the east—but leaves behind the girl he loves.

p, Maurice King; d, William K. Howard; w, Henry Blankfort (based on a story by Tristam Tupper); ph, L. William O'Connell; ed, Jack Dennis; md, Edward Kay; art d, E. R. Hickson.

Drama (PR:A MPAA:NR)

KLONDIKE KATE* ½ (1944) 64m Irving Briskin/COL bw

Ann Savage *(Kathleen O'Day)*, Tom Neal *(Jefferson Braddock)*, Glenda Farrell *(Molly)*, Constance Worth *(Lita)*, Sheldon Leonard *(Sometime Smith)*, Lester Allen *(Duster Dan)*, George Cleveland *(Judge Crossit)*, George McKay *(Bartender)*, Dan Seymour *(Piano Player)*.

A large hotel in the Klondike burns down, settling the disagreement over its rightful ownership by three people: a businessman, a gambler, and the girl who claims it as her inheritance. Illogical script is not saved by production or performances.

p, Irving Briskin; d, William Castle; w, M. Coates Webster (based on a story by Webster, Houston Branch); ph, John Stumar; ed, Mel Thorsen; md, M. W. Stoloff; art d, Lionel Banks; ch, Mary Carroll; m/l, Harry Revel, Paul Francis Webster.

Western (PR:A MPAA:NR)

KLUTE** (1971) 114m WB c

Jane Fonda *(Bree Daniels)*, Donald Sutherland *(John Klute)*, Charles Cioffi *(Peter Cable)*, Roy R. Scheider *(Frank Ligourin)*, Dorothy Tristan *(Arlyn Page)*, Rita Gam *(Trina)*, Vivian Nathan *(Psychiatrist)*, Nathan George *(Lt. Trask)*, Morris Strassberg *(Mr. Goldfarb)*, Jean Stapleton *(Goldfarb's Secretary)*, Barry Snider *(Berger)*, Anthony Holland *(Actor's Agent)*, Richard Shull *(Sugarman)*, Betty Murray *(Holly Gruneman)*, Fred Burrell *(Man in Chicago Hotel)*, Robert Milli *(Tom Gruneman)*, Jane White *(Janie Dale)*, Shirley Stoler *(Mama Reese)*, Margaret Linn *(Evie)*, Rosalind Cash *(Pat)*, Lee Wallace *(Nate Goldfarb)*, Robert Ronan *(Off-Broadway Director)*, Richard Ramos *(Off-Broadway Stage Manager)*, Antonia Rey *(Mrs. Vanek, Landlady)*, Mary Louise Wilson *(Ad Agency Secretary)*, Jan Fielding *(Psychiatrist's Secretary)*, Joe Silver *(Dr. Spangler)*, Jerome Collamore *(Custodian)*, Tony Major *(Bill Azure)*.

A routine crime melodrama with a lot of weird lensing passed off as innovative, KLUTE did well at the box office (more than $6 million the first time out), but it fails to satisfy upon second viewing. Fonda is an expensive prostitute approached by detective Sutherland who is looking for a missing research scientist, Milli, and suspects her of servicing him. After tailing her about as she makes her house calls, Sutherland confronts the whore and asks for her cooperation. She tells him that Milli has written her one obscene love letter but she doesn't know his real name and he may be the brutal sadist who repeatedly calls her with threats. Fonda puts Sutherland on to one of her girl friends, Tristan, another prostitute, who was also physically abused by the caller one night. Sutherland and Fonda meanwhile fall in love but she's so sexually worn out that she derives no pleasure from their lovemaking; in fact Fonda cannot even express love for Sutherland, despite the fact that she feels affection for him. Another letter arrives addressed to Fonda but it's not from the scientist. After analyzing the letter, Sutherland realizes it has been written by Cioffi, a friend of Milli's, and he soon learns that Coiffi killed Milli when the latter learned of his sexual perversions. Fonda is so upset by all the threats that she goes to a psychiatrist but his office is empty and there she finds Cioffi lurking in a corner. He's been tracking her, knowing she is working with Sutherland to expose him. Cioffi tries to kill Fonda but Sutherland and the cops arrive and Cioffi goes out a window to his death in the struggle. Sutherland persuades Fonda to give up prostitution and service only him for the rest of their haphazard lives. The script is predictable, the direction by Pakula spotty and often confusing, and the leads play their parts as if improvising while waiting for a real movie to come along. Small's score is genuinely scary and the atmospherics of the film are above average but that's about it. Playing a prostitute has somehow become a must for any accomplished actress; some play them with hearts of gold, some with mercenary streaks, but here Fonda plays the whore with psychological problems which is ironic if not outright moronic when applied to her headless profession. KLUTE is sordid, sadistic, and not for children or any viewer looking for literacy or entertainment. Sutherland reportedly had an affair with his costar during the production of KLUTE and became even more of a political radical under Fonda's influence, ironic in that Sutherland's wife Shirly was the person who allegedly introduced Fonda to political radicalism.

p, Alan J. Pakula, David Lang; d, Pakula; w, Andy, Dave Lewis; ph, Gordon Willis (Panavision, Technicolor); m, Michael Small; ed, Carl Lerner; art d, George Jenkins; set d, John Mortensen; cos, Ann Roth; makeup, Irving Buckman.

Crime Drama Cas. (PR:O MPAA:R)

KNACK, THE (SEE: KNACK . . . AND HOW TO GET IT, THE, 1965, Brit.)

KNACK . . . AND HOW TO GET IT, THE****
(1965, Brit.) 84m Woodfall/Lopert bw (AKA: THE KNACK)

Rita Tushingham *(Nancy Jones)*, Ray Brooks *(Tolen)*, Michael Crawford *(Colin)*, Donal Donnelly *(Tom)*, William Dexter *(Dress Shop Owner)*, Charles Dyer *(Man in Photo Booth)*, Margot Thomas *(Female Teacher)*, John Bluthal *(Father)*, Wensley Pithey *(Teacher)*, Helen Lennox *(Blonde in Photo Booth)*, Peter Copley *(Picture Owner)*, Dandy Nichols *(Landlady)*, Timothy Bateson *(Junkman)*, George Chisholm *(Porter)*, Frank Sieman *(Surveyor)*, Bruce Lacey *(Surveyor's Assistant)*, Edgar Wreford *(Man in Phone Booth)*, Wanda Ventham *(Gym Mistress)*, Gerald Toomey *(Boy in Classroom)*, Katherine Page *(Woman in House)*, Rose Hillier *(Unsuitable Customer)*, Charles Wood *(Soldier)*, Walter Horsbrugh *(Old Man)*,

Julian Holloway, Vincent Harding, Kenneth Farrington, John Porter Davison *(Guardsmen)*, Charlotte Rampling, Lucy Bartlett *(Water Skiers)*, Jacqueline Bisset.

Director Lester continued with the style that seemed to break all forms of filmic convention in the film he made with the Beatles, A HARD DAY'S NIGHT, in this, his next feature. The style was extremely fast paced, with characters who were nonstop talkers and moved about incessantly. Essentially created in the cutting room, his films relied upon techniques which had been common throughout commercial film history, but never combined in as flamboyant a manner. The plot for THE KNACK revolves around the somewhat thin theme of a young swinger type, Brooks, whose extreme luck with girls baffles his landlord, school-teacher Crawford. So Brooks decides to help Crawford along by giving him lessons. One of the first things he decides Crawford needs is a new brass bed. So they set off across London to find one, which they then roll back through the streets, causing traffic jams and general hysteria. Along the way they meet wandering Tushingham, a girl new to London trying to find her way to a place to stay. She accompanies the two on their trek home, with Crawford getting a yen for her. But back at the boarding house Brooks takes control of Tushingham, running off with her on his motorbike. Crawford follows in hot pursuit, only to find the couple in the park where Tushingham is loudly accusing Brooks of rape, forcing Brooks to lose his patience with the girl and allowing Crawford his chance. The characters are cardboard types. They talk all the time, but never say much of anything. They do, however, manage to portray quite a bit of personality, which can be attributed to Lester's techniques in not over-dramatizing any situations and his reliance upon semi-improvisational material.

p, Oscar Lewenstein; d, Richard Lester; w, Charles Wood (from the play by Ann Jellicoe); ph, David Watkins; m, John Barry; ed, Anthony Gibbs; art d, Assheton Gorton; cos, Jocelyn Rickards; m/l, Alan Haven.

Comedy (PR:C MPAA:NR)

KNAVE OF HEARTS (SEE: LOVERS HAPPY LOVERS, 1954)

KNICKERBOCKER HOLIDAY** (1944) 85m PCA/UA bw

Nelson Eddy *(Brom Broeck)*, Charles Coburn *(Pieter Stuyvesant)*, Constance Dowling *(Tina Tienhoven)*, Ernest Cossart *(Tienhoven)*, Johnnie "Scat" Davis *(Ten Pin)*, Richard Hale *(Tammany)*, Shelley Winter [Winters] *(Ulda Tienhoven)*, Glenn Strange *(Big Muscle)*, Fritz Feld *(Poffenburgh)*, Otto Kruger *(Roosevelt)*, Percival Vivian *(De Vries)*, Charles Judels *(Renssaler)*, Ferdinand Munier *(De Pyster)*, Percy Kilbride *(Schermerhorn the Jailer)*, Chester Conklin *(Town Crier)*, Richard Baldwin *(1st Pal)*, Lang Page *(2nd Pal)*, Connie Conrad, Freda Stoll, Veta Lehman, May Cloy, Harriet Dean *(Councilmen's Wives)*, Herbert Corthell *(Captain)*, Phil Green *(Sailor)*, Gerald Oliver Smith *(English Colonist)*, John Sheehan *(Irish Colonist)*, Sven Hugo Borg *(Swedish Colonist)*, Dorothy Granger *(Barmaid)*, Patti Sheldon, Ruth Tobey *(Giggling Girls)*, Fern Emmett *(Critical Woman)*, Bruce Cameron, Irving Fulton, Walter Pietela, Paul Allen Spears, Tony Shaller *(Tumblers)*, Harold De Garro *(Stilt Walker)*, Harry Johnson, Fred Johnson, Johnny Johnson *(Jugglers)*, Lou Manley *(Punch and Judy Show)*, Casey MacGregor *(Fire Eater)*, Harry Bayfield, Buster Brody, Bobbie Hale *(Clowns)*, The Carmen Amaya Troupe *(Gypsy Dancers)*, Sabicas *(Guitarist)*, Irving Bacon *(Peter Van Stoon)*. Cut from release print: Ralph Dunn *(Guard)*, Edward Earle *(Barker)*, Harry C. Bradley, George Bunny *(Old Men)*.

The original play lasted about six months on Broadway and never captured the audience's imagination, despite the smash hit "September Song" sung by Walter Huston on the stage and Coburn in the film. It's 1650s Nieuw Amsterdam (New York) and Chester Conklin, the town crier, announces the arrival of Coburn (Stuyvesant), the new governor, who is reputed to be a tough old bird. With valet Feld, Coburn lands and immediately establishes his iron will by suggesting they celebrate his arrival with a hanging. Nominated as chief guest for the necktie party is Eddy, a newspaper publisher who campaigns against the grafting politicians that rule the city. They attempt to find some reason to hang Eddy but none of his crimes are hangable, so they just put him in the stocks. Eddy has a romance with Dowling, the daughter of councilman Cossart and sister of a gorgeous Shelley Winter, who is palling around with Eddy's buddy, Davis. Coburn is making everyone unhappy with his stern rule and Eddy keeps writing fierce editorials about it so he is jailed. Once Eddy is out of the way, Coburn makes a move for Dowling. Coburn, eventually prevailed upon to release Eddy, sends him into the hinterlands to unite various factions among the colonists. Coburn intends to get all of the graft money and put it into his own pocket, but Eddy shows him the folly of his ways and makes him realize that he is missing an opportunity to be a much-beloved member of history if he will straighten out his ambitions. Coburn does just that and Eddy and Dowling are in a clinch at the finale. There's a great deal of flag-waving and nods to patriotism and The American Way, and many in the audience thought they were attending a musical history lesson. Although Brown gets credit for production and direction, it was Eddy who was behind the film, having invested in the 1938 production of the play. Coburn, who had the lead role, though he took second billing, was a marvelous actor but not right for this film. Even though Walter Huston was an older man when he played that role on stage, one could still believe he had a twinkle when he sang "September Song." Coburn was too stocky and pompous to ever get us to believe that he had something lurking beneath those pantaloons. Only three songs from the original musical totally survived. They were "There's Nowhere To Go But Up" (Kurt Weill, Maxwell Anderson—sung by Nelson Eddy, male chorus), "The One Indispensable Man" (Weill, Anderson—sung by Charles Coburn, Ernest Cossart), "September Song" (Weill, Anderson—sung by Coburn). "It Never Was You," from the stage play, was only heard as background music and the "Jail Song" had the Anderson lyrics replaced by words from Eddy and Furman Brown. The other tunes were all by other writers, including Werner Heymann, who won the Oscar for his background score. The remaining songs were "Hear Ye" (Jule Styne, Sammy Cahn—sung by Chester Conklin, chorus), "Holiday" (Theodore Paxton, Nelson Eddy—sung by Johnnie "Scat" Davis, chorus), "Let's Make Tomorrow Today" (Heymann, Brown—sung by Eddy, chorus), "Sing Out" (Franz Steininger, Brown—sung by Eddy, chorus), "One More Smile" (Styne, Cahn—sung by Eddy, Constance Dowling—possibly dubbed by Sally Sweetland), "Love Has Made This Such a Lovely Day" (Styne, Cahn—sung by Eddy, Dowling, Shelley Winter), "Zuyder Zee" (Styne, Cahn—sung by Male Quartet), "Dutch March" (Heymann), and a Spanish Dance (traditional—performed by Carmen Amaya and her troupe).

p&d, Harry Joe Brown; w, David Boehm, Roland Leigh, Harold Goldman, Thomas Lennon (based on the musical by Kurt Weill, Maxwell Anderson); ph, Philip Tannura; m, Werner R. Heymann, ed, John F. Link; md, Jacques Samossoud; m/l, Weill, Anderson, Heymann, Sammy Cahn, Jule Styne, Theodore Paxton, Furman Brown, Franz Steininger, Nelson Eddy.

Musical/Comedy/Drama Cas. (PR:A MPAA:NR)

KNIFE IN THE BODY, THE (SEE: MURDER CLINIC, THE, 1967, Ital./Fr.)

KNIFE IN THE WATER****

(1963, Pol.) 94m Film Polski/Kanawha Films bw (NOZ W WODZIE)

Leon Niemczyk *(Andrez)*, Jolanta Umecka *(Christine)*, Zygmunt Malanowicz *(The Young Man)*.

Polanski's first feature, KNIFE IN THE WATER, became a top winner at the Venice Film Festival and a nominee for an Academy Award for the Best Foreign Film. This early film showed a fascination with human cruelty and violence, as well as an intense interest in exploring the complex tensions involved in close relations, themes which were to recur throughout Polanski's career. Niemczyk is a successful sportswriter who, while on a trip with his wife, Umecka, picks up a young hitchhiker, Malanowicz. They ask the boy to join them on their short boating excursion. Jealous of the boy's youth and attractiveness, Niemczyk boasts of his physical prowess, chiding the boy for his inabilities in sailing and swimming. The continual presence of violence is suggested by the pocket knife the boy carries around with him, the knife eventually leading to a skirmish between Niemczyk and Malanowicz, in which the later falls into the water. Since the boy can't swim, Niemczyk jumps into the water to search for him. Meanwhile, the boy comes back to the boat, where Umecka comforts him, then makes love with him. She drops the boy ashore and tells her husband what has transpired. The end.

p, Stanislaw Zylewicz; d, Roman Polanski; w, Polanski, Jerzy Skolimowski, Jakub Goldberg; ph, Jerzy Lipman; m, Kryzystof Komeda.

Drama Cas. (PR:O MPAA:NR)

KNIGHT IN LONDON, A**

(1930, Brit./Ger.) 75m WB bw (EINE NACHT IN LONDON)

Lilian Harvey *(Aline Morland)*, Ivy Duke *(Lady Morland)*, Robin Irvine *(Harry Erskine)*, Bernard Nedell *(Prince Zalnoff)*, Robert English *(Mr. McComber)*, Zena Dare, Hon. Angela Brett.

When Harvey accidentally enters the wrong hotel room, she finds herself in the middle of a romantic battle between two men from opposite sides of the social strata. As the aristocrat in the affair, Nedell proves willing to resort to tactics far below his station in order to attain his desires. Made in Germany as a silent with the sound added a year after production.

p, Ludwig Blattner; d, Lupu Pick; w, Charles Lincoln (based on a story by Mrs. Horace Tremlett); ph, Karl Freund.

Drama (PR:A MPAA:NR)

KNIGHT OF THE PLAINS** (1939) 57m Spectrum bw

Fred Scott, Al St. John, Marion Weldon, Richard Cramer, John Merton, Frank LaRue, Lafe McKee, Emma Tansey, Steve Clark, Budd Buster, Carl Mathews, Jimmy Aubrey, Sherry Tansey, George Morell, Cactus Mack, Olin Francis, Bob Burns.

Merton sells phony land grants to easterners, prompting a feud between the existing landowners and the new arrivals. Scott manages to settle the problem before violence ensues. Scott, a former opera singer, sings, and Weldon, a sweater girl, appears in a sweater.

p, Stan Laurel, Jed Buell; d, Sam Newfield; w, Fred Myton; ph, Mack Stengler; ed, Robert Jahns; m/l, Lew Porter, L. Wolfe Gilbert, Harry Tobias.

Western (PR:A MPAA:NR)

KNIGHT WITHOUT ARMOR*****

(1937, Brit.) 107m Korda-London Film/UA bw (AKA: KNIGHT WITHOUT ARMOUR)

Marlene Dietrich *(Alexandra Vladinoff)*, Robert Donat *(Ainsley Fothergill)*, Irene Vanbrugh *(Duchess of Zorin)*, Herbert Lomas *(Gen. Gregor Vladinoff)*, Austin Trevor *(Col. Adraxine)*, Basil Gill *(Axelstein)*, John Clements *(Poushkoff)*, Miles Malleson *(Drunken Soldier)*, Hay Petrie *(Station Master)*, David Tree *(Alexis Maronin)*, Lyn Harding *(Bargee)*, Frederick Culley *(Stanfield)*, Lawrence Hanray *(Forrester)*, Lisa d'Esterre *(Czarina)*, Franklin Kelsey *(Tomsky)*, Allan Jeayes, Raymond Huntley *(White Officers)*, Lawrence Baskcomb *(Commissar)*, Dorice Fordred *(Maid)*, Paul O'Brien, Peter Evan Thomas *(Gen. Andreyevitch)*, Torin Thatcher *(Passport Official)*, Peter Bull *(Commissar)*.

This is a smashing adventure yarn, full of mystery, suspense, and thrills, superbly acted by Donat and Dietrich and directed with vitality and insight by Feyder. As is the case with most Korda films, the entire production is meticulously correct in sets and lavish in cast, thousands, indeed, herein storming through that great calamity of the 20th Century—the Russian Revolution. The film opens with Dietrich attending the derby in England, a Russian countess in exquisite finery who, with her father (a noble who is in the Czar's cabinet), draws as much attention from the crowd as do the thoroughbreds in the race. Another scene shows Donat, a British interpreter who speaks and writes fluent Russian, applying for a passport to Russia where he will translate books. Donat goes to St. Petersburg and is later brought before authorities who are offended by an article he has written, saying that it attacks the Imperial way of life. Though Donat protests, he is ordered to leave Russia within 48 hours. That night Donat dines with Culley, a friend from England, and is surprised to learn that he is a British secret agent. Culley tells him that if he's willing to perform espionage for England, he will find a way for him to stay in Russia. The prospect appeals to Donat's strong sense of patriotic duty and he agrees. His assignment is to monitor the nefarious activities of the revolutionary groups working to unseat the Czar. His first contacts are made through a bookstore owner, Gill, and he is soon thought by the radicals to be a kindred spirit. One of Donat's new-found friends, a young revolutionary, becomes involved in an assassination plot to kill Dietrich's father, Lomas, the Minister of the Interior. He throws a bomb at several carriages, one of which is carrying Dietrich to her wedding with Trevor. Horses and guards are killed but she is safe, as is her father, who escorts Dietrich in a magnificent wedding dress from a wrecked carriage to another, her white train trailing over snow and the blood of the slain to stain the gown. Wounded by guards, the young revolutionary staggers to Donat's apartment and dies in his arms. Police then arrest Donat and his sponsor, Gill, sending them to a Siberian prison camp. They languish there for years, learning little about events in the outside world, a snow-bound wasteland that drives many a prisoner mad. Tidbits of information leak into the camp concerning WW I which has been raging for years. Then, in 1917, Donat and Gill learn that there has been a revolution. The revolutionaries overcome the Czar's palace in St. Petersburg and Dietrich's husband is killed. She retreats to her palatial summer home in Khalinsk. One morning she awakens and finds no servants answering her call. In a flowing white negligee she frantically searches for the household maids and butlers. All gone. Running outside to the river, she spies one servant washing clothes but the woman flees when Dietrich calls her name. Turning, Dietrich sees hordes of armed men and women appear over the rise of a hill, advancing upon her. Proudly, *she* advances upon them and they halt in their tracks. Terrified of her commanding presence, the revolutionaries are petrified until a woman in their ranks yells out: "What's the matter with you—she's only a woman!" They rush Dietrich and make her their prisoner. Hordes of revolutionaries spill into the white palace, hacking priceless paintings to pieces, smashing rare sculpture, venting a national spleen upon a dynasty that has oppressed its people for centuries. Dietrich is locked in her chambers, an armed guard placed outside, while a revolutionary committee decides what to do with her. Released from captivity, Donat and Gill enter Khalinsk as heroes of the revolution. Gill is instantly made chief commissar and proceeds with Donat, now his righthand man, to Dietrich's estate, ordering the revolutionaries to stop destroying property of the new regime. One of the local commissars demands that Dietrich be shot, along with many of her servants, some of which, loyal to the Czar, having been lined up and executed. Dietrich sits upstairs in her rooms listening to the firing squads do their dirty work and going slightly insane. Dietrich is to be taken to Petrograd (changed from St. Petersburg) for a public trial, decrees Gill, and he orders Donat to escort the countess to that city. Donat enters Dietrich's rooms to see her sitting in a daze, looking at her own disheveled image in a huge mirror. "Stand up," he orders. She does, turning around to spit insults. He tells her she must accompany him to Petrograd to face trial. She screams that she wants to be shot. He calms her down and then spirits her through the mobs of revolutionaries with two guards to a nearby train depot where they await the train that will take them away. Donat orders the two guards to return to the Dietrich estate but one of them believes that Donat "wants the woman for himself." As they wait for the train alone in the small depot, Donat tells Dietrich that he's British and recites some English poetry for her. She recites a little Russian poem for him. His poem is full of optimism, hers full of doom. Just then the two guards return and a struggle ensues, Donat knocking one guard out and wrestling the other to the floor, his gun falling free. Dietrich picks up the pistol and, just before the guard can knock out Donat, fires, killing the guard. The other guard comes to, kicks out a window, and escapes. Then Donat hears the station master, Petrie, calling out the arrival of a train bound for Petrograd. Donat goes outside but sees no train. When he asks Petrie about it, he finds that the man has gone daft. Says Petrie to Donat in a whisper: "Trains that are seen are being blown up." Donat returns to Dietrich not knowing what to do. Then scores of peasants appear outside and Donat and Dietrich join the crowd. When Donat questions one of the peasants, he is told that the White Army of Cossacks fighting for restoration of the Czar is nearby. Donat escorts Dietrich to the White Army camp and leaves her, knowing she will be safe. Dietrich, once recognized by the Russian commander, is coddled once more as a countess; the commander orders that new gowns be brought to Dietrich who then takes a much needed bath in a tub. Changing into her new finery, Dietrich presides over a resplendent dinner with White officers. Then the city is bombarded. Meanwhile, Donat encounters a huge army of Reds which is about to storm the city. He watches helplessly as Dietrich is once more made a prisoner of the Reds when the city surrenders. He later falls in with a drunken commissar, Malleson, from whom he steals a signed order, making him commissar of prisons. He thus releases Dietrich and they escape dressed like Cossacks. While massive search parties hunt them in the dense forests, Donat has Dietrich hide in a thicket, covering her with leaves, while he joins the searchers, getting one soldier drunk from his flask when the man draws too near Dietrich's hiding place. He later returns for her and she runs into his arms. "What are you thinking?" he asks her, "that I wouldn't come back?" He kisses her and she realizes that she, too, is in love with him. They spend a few idyllic days in the forest where Dietrich takes another bath in a brook, then dresses in peasant clothes Donat has stolen from a nearby village, along with food and wine. They later go to a railroad siding where hundreds of peasants are gathered; the crowd stops an approaching train by blocking the tracks with their bodies and all clamber aboard, including Donat and Dietrich, traveling in a boxcar as brother and sister. When the train reaches Kazan, their hands are inspected and, when no callouses are found, they are taken aside, thought to be members of the aristocracy. Brought before Clements and another commissar, Donat tells the suspicious Reds that he has not been in the army because of having to take care of his sister, who is ill. The other commissar believes he recognizes Dietrich as the wanted countess but Clements rebuffs the identification, saying he will fetch a gardener who worked on Dietrich's estate and he will solve the question. Clements returns with the old man who denies that Dietrich is the countess, saying he is willing to swear "in front of the altar, comrade." The disbelieving commissar is further persuaded to let Dietrich and Donat go when Clements states he will escort them to Samara, where he must make a report. On the train trip Clements, obviously entranced by Dietrich, admits he did recognize her and even made sure that the gardener lied. Donat and Dietrich share their food with Clements and he breaks down later and weeps, finding real friends for the first time. When they reach their destination, Clements points out the way to the border, then leaves them. He shoots himself rather than turn them in and Donat and Dietrich flee, escaping by barge down the Volga. They are later waylaid at a border train station where Donat is being held for questioning but Dietrich, treated for exhaustion, is put on board an American Red Cross train, going out of Red territory and to safety. Donat learns about her departure and breaks away from a firing squad, racing after the train, and climbing aboard, shouting Dietrich's name. She hears him, leans out of a window and Donat works his way to her, embracing her as the train speeds them to safety. KNIGHT WITHOUT ARMOR offers superlative production in grand period sets by Meerson. Rosza's score is properly thunderous and majestic in captioning the stirring and cataclysmic events depicted. Dietrich was never more beautiful nor Donat more dashing. His severe asthmatic condition, however, delayed the filming for many weeks. Dietrich expressed no annoyance at the delay, but actually nursed her costar on the set. She even had a hand in directing some scenes, arranging "several angles for a scene between Mr. Donat and myself so that we would appear in the same shot simultaneously." She carried about a strip of 35mm film from a scene she had directed, proudly displaying this to one and all. When the great Alexander Korda came on to the set he, too, was shown the strip of film by the beaming star. Said Korda: "You can direct here any time you want."

p, Alexander Korda; d, Jacques Feyder; w, Lajos Biro, Arthur Wimperis, Frances Marion (based on the novel *Without Armour* by James Hilton); ph, Harry Stradling, Bernard Browne, Jack Cardiff; m, Miklos Rosza; ed, William Hornbeck, A.W. Watkins; md, Muir Matheson; set d, Lazare Meerson; cos, George Benda; spec eff, Ned Mann; tech adv, Roman Goul, Col. Zinovieff.

Adventure/Romance (PR:A MPAA:NR)

KNIGHTRIDERS*** (1981) 145m Laurel/United Film Distribution c

Ed Harris *(Billy)*, Gary Lahti *(Alan)*, Tom Savini *(Morgan)*, Amy Ingersoll *(Linet)*, Patricia Tallman *(Julie)*, Christine Forrest *(Angie)*, Warner Shook *(Pippin)*, Brother Blue *(Merlin)*, Cynthia Adler *(Rocky)*, John Amplas *(Whiteface)*, Ken Hixon *(Steve)*, John Hostetter *(Tuck)*, Albert Amerson *(Indian)*, Don Berry *(Bagman)*, Amanda Davies *(Sheila)*, Martin Ferrero *(Bontempi)*, Ken Foree *(Little John)*, Harold Wayne Jones *(Bors)*, Randy Kovitz *(Punch)*, Michael Moran *(Cook)*, Scott Reiniger *(Marhalt)*, Maureen Sadusk *(Judy)*, Ronald Carrier *(Hector)*, Tom Dileo *(Corncook)*, David Early *(Bleoboris)*, John Harrison *(Pellinore)*, Steven King.

Horror director Romero departed from his usual territory to direct this original, fun, romantic and vastly underrated elegy to rugged individualism and idealism. The film stars Harris (an outstanding actor who played John Glenn in THE RIGHT STUFF) as the leader of a troupe of motorcyclists who fancy themselves the inheritors of Camelot and make a living traveling to various towns and setting up a fair where they sell items made by the skilled craftsmen who ride with them. The group lives in a societal structure based on the Arthurian legend, with Harris as the king who is surrounded by his loyal knights. There is also an evil, ambitious adversary, Savini (Romero's bloody special effects genius, who also acts), who also has men loyal to him. The motorcyclists ride their big, noisy machines, instead of horses, into jousts and battles, trussed up in complete Medieval regalia, much to the delight of fun-seeking tourists who pay to watch. Trouble begins for the financially-ailing nomads when their ranks are split by an ambitious promoter who wants to make Savini a star in his own right. Savini sees this as his opportunity, finally, to make some money, and though he is torn between his loyalty to the troupe and his own ambition, he decides to leave. In a confrontation with Harris, who refuses to yield his honor or dignity for mere money, Savini tells him it is time to grow up and face reality. Harris refuses and stoically sticks to his idealistic vision of Camelot. The film is overlong and at times fairly undramatic, but if the viewer sticks with it and accepts the premise, there is much of interest to be found in KNIGHTRIDERS.

p, Richard P. Rubenstein; d&w, George A. Romero; ph, Michael Gornick (Technicolor); m, Donald Rubinstein; ed, Romero, Pasquale Buba; prod d, Cletus Anderson; stunts, Gary Davis.

Drama Cas. (PR:C MPAA:R)

KNIGHTS FOR A DAY* 1/2 (1937, Brit.) 69m Pearl/Pathe bw

Nelson Keys *(Bert Wrigley)*, John Garrick *(Prince Nicholas of Datria)*, Nancy Burne *(Sally Wrigley)*, Frank Atkinson *(Timothy Trout)*, Cathleen Nesbitt *(Lady Agatha)*, Billy Bray *(Brandt)*, Fred Duprez *(Custer)*, Gerald Barry *(Krampf)*, Wyn Weaver *(Lord Croke)*, Percy Walsh *(Lord Southdown)*, Charles Bray, Raymond Ellis, Harry Clifford, D.J. Williams, Lawrence Hanray, Miriam Leighton, The Three Diamond Brothers.

Forced comedy taking place in that mythical land (known only in filmdom), Ruritania. Keys is the visiting barber who suddenly finds himself in the midst of a revolution which ends on a happy note when the prince marries his niece.

p, Aveling Ginever; d, Norman Lee, Ginever; w, Ginever, Frank Atkinson, Charles Bray.

Comedy (PR:A MPAA:NR)

KNIGHTS OF THE BLACK CROSS

(SEE: KNIGHTS OF THE TEUTONIC ORDER, 1960, Pol.)

KNIGHTS OF THE RANGE** ½** (1940) 70m PAR bw

Russell Hayden *(Renn Frayne)*, Victor Jory *(Malcolm Lascalles)*, Jean Parker *(Holly Ripple)*, Morris Ankrum *(Gamecock)*, Britt Wood *(Laigs)*, J. Farrell MacDonald *(Cappy)*, Ethel Wales *(Myra Ripple)*, Rad Robinson *(Brazos)*, Raphael [Ray] Bennett *(Bill Heaver)*, Edward Cassidy, Eddie Dean, The King's Men.

Hayden is a member of a gang of cattle rustlers who changes sides when he falls for the rancher's daughter, Parker. Ankrum a rustler, and Jory, a crooked lawyer, try to swindle Parker out of the ranch, but are thwarted by Hayden. Competent direction smooths over script's unevenness.

p, Harry Sherman; d, Lesley Selander; w, Norman Houston (based on a story by Zane Grey); ph, Russell Harlan; m, Victor Young, John M. Leopold; ed, Carroll Lewis.

Western **(PR:A MPAA:NR)**

KNIGHTS OF THE ROUND TABLE*** (1953) 115m MGM c

Robert Taylor *(Sir Lancelot of the Lake)*, Ava Gardner *(Queen Guinevere)*, Mel Ferrer *(King Arthur)*, Anne Crawford *(Morgan Le Fay)*, Stanley Baker *(Sir Modred)*, Felix Aylmer *(Merlin)*, Maureen Swanson *(Elaine)*, Gabriel Woolf *(Percival)*, Anthony Forwood *(Gareth)*, Robert Urquhart *(Sir Gawaine)*, Niall MacGinnis *(Green Knight)*, Ann Hanslip *(Nan)*, Jill Clifford *(Bronwyn)*, Stephen Vercoe *(Agravaine)*, Howard Marion Crawford *(Simon)*, John Brooking *(Bedivere)*, Peter Gawthorne *(Bishop)*, Alan Tilvern *(Steward)*, John Sherman *(Lambert)*, Dagmar Wunter [Dana Wynter] *(Vivien)*, Mary Germaine *(Brigid)*, Martin Wyldeck *(John)*, Barry MacKay *(Green Knight's 1st Squire)*, Derek Tansley *(Green Knight's 2nd Squire)*, Roy Russell *(Leogrance)*, Gwendoline Evans *(Enid)*, Michel De Lutry *(Dancer)*.

Taylor plays the legendary sixth-century knight who bravely battles for his king, and Gardner is the queen who falls for him. Extensive attention to detail of sets and costumes, superior photography, and standout performances by Taylor, Ferrer, and Woolf put this a cut above other Arthurian legend films.

p, Pandro S. Berman; d, Richard Thorpe; w, Talbot Jennings, Jan Lustig, Noel Langley (based on the 15th Century prose collection *Le Mort D'Arthur* by Sir Thomas Malory); ph, F. A. Young, Stephen Dade (CinemaScope, Technicolor); m, Miklos Rozsa; ed, Frank Clarke; art d, Alfred Junge, Hans Peters.

Drama **Cas.** **(PR:A MPAA:NR)**

KNIGHTS OF THE TEUTONIC ORDER, THE***

(1962, Pol.) 180m Film Polski/Amerpol Enterprise c (KRZYZACY; AKA: KNIGHTS OF THE BLACK CROSS)

Urszula Modrzynska *(Jagienka)*, Grazyna Staniszewska *(Danusia)*, Andrzej Szalawski *(Jurand)*, Henryk Borowski *(Siegfried de Lowe)*, Aleksander Fogiel *(Macko)*, Mieczyslaw Kalenik *(Zbyszko)*, Emil Karewicz *(King Jagiello)*, Tadeusz Bialoszczynski *(Duke of Mazovia)*, Tadeusz Kosudarski *(Brother Rotgier)*, Lucyna Winnicka *(Duchess of Mazovia)*, Mieczyslaw Voit *(Kuno von Lichtenstein)*, Janusz Strachocki *(Grand Master Konrad)*, Stanislow Jasiukiewicz *(Grand Master Ulrich)*, Leon Niemczyk *(Fulko de Lorche)*, Zbiginiew Skowronski *(Tolime)*, Mieczyslaw Stoor *(Hlawa)*, Wlodzimierz Skoczylas *(Sanderus)*, Seweryn Butrym *(Count Wende)*.

During the Teutonic invasion of Poland in the 15th Century, Szalawski's wife is put to death because of her husband's brave fighting against the victors. Years later his daughter, Staniszewska, visits the court of Mazovia and falls in love with Kalenik, who swears to avenge the mother's death. He is caught attacking a Teutonic emissary, and is sentenced to death. Staniszewska saves him by placing her veil over his head, and the two become engaged. But the Teutonic knights capture Staniszewska and her father, torturing the latter. When a new king takes over Teutonic rule, he declares war on Poland, and is defeated at The Battle of Grunewald. Kalenik continues his search for Staniszewska, but when he finds her she is insane. When she dies, he returns home to his childhood girl friend.

d, Aleksander Ford; w, Jerzy Stefan Stawinski, Ford, Leon Kruczkowski; ph, Mieczyslaw Jahoda (Dyaliscope, Eastmancolor); m, Kazimierz Serocki; ed, Miroslawa Garlicka, Alina Fafik; md, Jan Krenz; art d, Roman Mann.

History/Drama **(PR:A MPAA:NR)**

KNIVES OF THE AVENGER***

(1967, Ital.) 86m Sider/World Entertainment c (I COLTELLI DEL VENDICATORE) (AKA: RAFFICA DI COLTELLI)

Cameron Mitchell *(Rurik)*, Fausto Tozzi *(Aghen)*, Luciano Polletin *(Moki)*, Elisa Mitchell [Elissa Picelli] *(Karen)*, Jack Stewart [Giacomo Rossi] *(Harald)*, Mike Moore, Renato Terra, Sergio Cortona.

Viking tale has Cameron Mitchell as a "stranger" who saves the wife, Elisa Mitchell, of a chieftain, Stewart, who is away on a journey for several years. Thinking that a marriage to Elisa Mitchell will make him the legitimate sovereign, exiled warrior Tozzi attempts to abduct her but is thwarted by Cameron Mitchell who has a long-standing grudge against Tozzi for beheading his wife and child. Stewart returns to find his wife with Cameron Mitchell, a former enemy. Battle ensues, but when it is discovered that Tozzi has abducted Stewart's son, the two men unite to save the child. Cameron Mitchell slays Tozzi to gain complete vengeance. Strong direction pays particular attention to the camerawork, picking up on details of color and action in this excellent action story from Italy dubbed unevenly into English.

p, P. Tagliaferri; d, John Hold [Mario Bava]; w, Alberto Liberati, George Simonelli, Mario Bava; ph, Antonio Rinaldi (Techniscope, Technicolor); m, Marcello Giombini; ed, Othello [Otello Colangeli].

Action/Drama **(PR:A MPAA:NR)**

KNOCK* ½ (1955, Fr.) 95m Sirius bw (AKA: DR. KNOCK)

Louis Jouvet *(Dr. Knock)*, Jean Brochard *(Dr. Parpalaid)*, Yves Deniaud *(Tambour, the Town Crier)*, Pierre Bertin *(the Professor)*, Pierre Renoir *(the Druggist)*, Jane Marken *(Mme. Parpalaid)*, Bernadette Lange *(Mariette)*, Genevieve Morel *(Peasant Woman)*, Marguerite Pierry *(Rich Woman)*, Mireille Perrey *(Mme. Remy)*, Jean Carmet, A. Dalibert *(Workers)*.

Jouvet plays a corrupt doctor who takes over a small town practice, using his position to gain control over the town by convincing everyone that they are sick. Jouvet is the only bright spot in this poorly written, unevenly directed attempt at satire. Jouvet performed in an earlier version of this play in 1936.

p, Jacques Roltfield; d, Guy LeFranc; w, LeFranc, Jules Romains, George Neveux (based on a play by Romains); ph, Claude Renoir; ed, Louisette Hautecoeur.

Drama **(PR:A MPAA:NR)**

KNOCK ON ANY DOOR* ½** (1949) 100m Santana/COL bw

Humphrey Bogart *(Andrew Morton)*, John Derek *(Nick Romano)*, George Macready *(District Attorney Kerman)*, Allene Roberts *(Emma)*, Susan Perry *(Adele)*, Mickey Knox *(Vito)*, Barry Kelley *(Judge Drake)*, Dooley Wilson *(Piano Player)*, Cara Williams *(Nelly)*, Jimmy Conlin *(Kid Fingers)*, Sumner Williams *(Jimmy)*, Sid Melton *(Squint)*, Pepe Hern *(Juan)*, Dewey Martin *(Butch)*, Robert A. Davis *(Sunshine)*, Houseley Stevenson *(Junior)*, Vince Barnett *(Bartender)*, Thomas Sully *(Officer Hawkins)*, Florence Auer *(Aunt Lena)*, Pierre Watkin *(Purcell)*, Gordon Nelson *(Corey)*, Argentina Brunetti *(Ma Romano)*, Dick Sinatra *(Julian Romano)*, Carol Coombs *(Ang Romano)*, Joan Baxter *(Maria Romano)*, Evelyn Underwood, Mary Emery, Franz Roehn, Betty Hall, Jack Jahries, Rose Plumer, Mabel Smaney, Joy Hallward, John Mitchum, Sidney Dubin, Homer Dickinson, Netta Packer *(Jury Members)*, Ann Duncan, Lorraine Comerford *(Teenagers)*, Chuck Hamilton, Ralph Volkie, Frank Marlo *(Bailiffs)*, Joe Palma, Dick Bartell, Eddie Randolph, Eda Reiss Merin, Joan Danton *(Reporters)*, Donald Kerr *(Court Clerk)*, Myron Healey *(Assistant District Attorney)*, Jane Lee, Dorothy Vernon *(Women)*, John Indrisano, Blackie Whiteford, Charles Sullivan, Ray Johnson, Jack Perry, Joe Brockman, Franklin Farnum, Dudley Dickerson, Tex Swan, Harry Wilson, Joe Dougherty, George Hickman, Eddie Borden, Cliff Heard, Jeff York, Paul Kreibich, Charles Camp, Charles Colean *(Men)*, Connie Conrad, Ann Cornwall, Beulah Parkington, Betty Taylor, Hazel Boyne, Roberta Haynes *(Women)*, Jack Clisby, Glen Thompson, Paul Baxley, Lee Phelps *(Policemen)*, Gary Owen *(Larry)*, Chester Conklin *(Barber)*, George Chandler *(Cashier)*, Theda Barr *(Girl)*, Wesley Hopper *(Boss)*, Sid Tomack *(Duke)*, Frank Hagney, Peter Virgo *(Suspects)*, George Hickman, Saul Gorss, Al Hill, Phillip Morris *(Detectives)*, Helen Mowery *(Miss Holiday)*, Jody Gilbert *(Gussie)*, Curt Conway *(Elkins)*, Edwin Parker, Al Ferguson *(Guards)*.

This is a hard-hitting crime melodrama with exceptional direction from Ray, and an outstanding performance from Bogart as the crusading attorney who tries to save from the electric chair an embittered slum youth, Derek, who has been charged with killing a policeman. Bogart, who has known the youth and been a product of the slums himself, begins to piece the boy's life together in mustering a defense. He recalls in flashback how he and his wife, Perry—at her insistence—tried earlier to help Derek, taking him on a fishing trip where the youth stole from them. Derek's life seems to change, however, after he marries Roberts. He takes a job, then several more, never seeming to hold onto permanent employment. When Roberts tells him that she's pregnant, right after he has thrown all his money away on gambling, Derek goes to pieces. He had tried to win money to buy his young wife some jewelry and now he must worry about another mouth to feed. Derek abandons the straight life and returns to thieving, expressing his new motto: "Live fast, die young, and have a good-looking corpse." After committing several robberies Derek returns home to find his wife dead, a suicide. She has taken the life of her unborn baby as well as her own rather than continue living with a dedicated criminal. Derek goes berserk and, while attempting another robbery, is confronted by a cop, Sully, into whom he maliciously fires every bullet from his gun. When captured, he adroitly and convincingly lies to Bogart, who comes to believe he is innocent and takes his case. Derek is a hardened product of the gutter and knows how to lie to survive. He uses his boyish appearance of innocence and does not deviate from his manufactured story. Even dogged district attorney Macready can't shake Derek's story until he asks Derek how his wife has died. He sees the youth's once-impenetrable composure begin to crack and pounces on him, hitting him with rapid-fire questions. Derek finally collapses and admits killing the officer. Bogart, stunned by the confession, nevertheless goes before the jury with an impassioned last appeal, saying that Derek was also guilty of growing up fatherless, guilty of watching his friends be brutalized in a sadistic reform school, guilty of living in one of the worst slums in the world. Bogart tells the jurors to "knock on any door," and they will find someone like Derek. His powerful argument does not affect the jury's verdict: Derek is sentenced to death in the electric chair. Bogart later stays with the youth and watches him go to his death. This is a relentlessly grim film in every sense and Ray makes us feel the oppressive filth and poverty of slum life, conjuring sympathetic sentiment for Derek. This was Derek's debut and he is only acceptable, his pretty face and near-monotone delivery making him appear a novice actor (which he was). Bogart's long summation speech in KNOCK ON ANY DOOR was too much of a chore for him. He told director Ray: "I've never delivered a speech that long in my life. It's impossible." Ray calmed Bogie down and told him: "Look, we'll rehearse it a few times and then try it one more time for the cameras and if it doesn't work, we'll try something else." Ray purposely withheld the fact that one of the cameras was rolling during the first rehearsal and Bogart delivered the speech flawlessly in the one take. And that was the take used in the film. This was the first film financed by Bogart's independent film company, Santana Productions, named after his much-sailed yacht, and it did well. It is now considered to be a minor *film noir* classic, as is IN A LONELY PLACE, also directed by Ray and produced under the Santana banner. TOKYO JOE and SIROCCO, also produced by the same company were less effective (all were distributed by Columbia). For the most part, Bogart's independently produced films are not up to the quality of the classics made at Warner

Bros.—THE MALTESE FALCON, CASABLANCA, THE BIG SLEEP, THE TREASURE OF THE SIERRA MADRE. Yet KNOCK ON ANY DOOR has enough powerful moments to make it worthwhile viewing. Sequel: LET NO MAN WRITE MY EPITAPH.

p, Robert Lord; d, Nicholas Ray; w, Daniel Taradash, John Monks, Jr. (based on the novel by Willard Motley); ph, Burnett Guffey; m, George Antheil; ed, Viola Lawrence; md, Morris W. Stoloff; art d, Robert Peterson; set d, William Kiernan; cos, Jean Louis; makeup, Clay Campbell.

Crime Drama **Cas.** **(PR:C MPAA:NR)**

KNOCK ON WOOD*** (1954) 103m Dena/PAR c

Danny Kaye *(Jerry)*, Mai Zetterling *(Ilse Nordstrom)*, Torin Thatcher *(Langston)*, David Burns *(Marty Brown)*, Leon Askin *(Gromeck)*, Abner Biberman *(Papinek)*, Gavin Gordon *(Car Salesman)*, Otto Waldis *(Brodnik)*, Steven Geray *(Dr. Kreuger)*, Diana Adams *(Princess)*, Patricia Denise *(Mama Morgan)*, Virginia Huston *(Audrey)*, Paul England *(Chief Inspector Wilton)*, Johnstone White *(Langston's Secretary)*, Henry Brandon *(2nd Trenchcoat Man)*, Lewis Martin *(Inspector Cranford)*, Philip Van Zandt *(Brutchik)*, Winifred Harris *(English Woman)*, Kenneth Hunter *(Old Man)*, Carl Milletaire *(1st Trenchcoat Man)*, Noel Drayton *(Little Man)*, Phil Tully *(Irishman)*, Rex Evans *(Customer)*, Donald Lawton *(French Stage Manager)*.

Kaye is a ventriloquist with a dummy that talks when he doesn't want him to and insults the customers. His manager, Burns, suggests he see psychiatrist Zetterling. Meanwhile, the plans for a new weapon have been stolen and two rival groups are after them. The blueprints are placed in, you guessed it, the dummy. The spies begin chasing Kaye all over the place and that's where most of the comedy happens. It's all a raison d'etre to get Kaye into several funny situations, including his dancing with a Russian ballet troupe to avoid being found by the spies. (Something similar to this was done by Alfred Hitchcock in THE 39 STEPS when Robert Donat steps in front of a political rally and masquerades as a speaker while the espionage criminals look on.) The chase also leads Kaye into a convention of Irishmen, where he sings "The Drastic, Livid History of Monahan O'Han," a special material song by Kaye's wife and long-time writer, Sylvia Fine. Kaye gets the chance to wear several disguises, to sing a few tunes (including a nice ballad "All About You"), and, in general, to do what Danny Kaye does best. At the end of the film, Kaye has cured his doctor of her mental problems and the two are wed. If Hitchcock had worked with Kaye, this is similar to what he might have produced, because it has all the classic elements of the master's early movies: an innocent man is accused of a crime he didn't commit, is chased, has a female who doesn't believe him, etc. Kaye never won an Oscar in the Academy voting but this one must have impressed them as they awarded him a special statuette that year "for his unique talents, his service to the Academy, the motion picture industry and the American People." And if they left someone out, we can't figure who that might have been.

p,d&w, Norman Panama, Melvin Frank; ph, Daniel Fapp (Technicolor); ed, Alma Macrorie; md, Victor Young; ch, Michael Kidd; m/l, "All About You" (sung by Danny Kaye), "Knock On Wood," Sylvia Fine.

Comedy **(PR:A MPAA:NR)**

KNOCKOUT 1/2** (1941) 71m FN-WB bw

Arthur Kennedy *(Johnny Rocket)*, Olympe Bradna *(Angela Grinnelli)*, Virginia Field *(Gloria Van Ness)*, Anthony Quinn *(Trego)*, Cliff Edwards *(Pinky)*, Cornel Wilde *(Tom Rossi)*, William Edmunds *(Louis Grinnelli)*, Richard Ainley *(Allison)*, John Ridgely *(Pat Martin)*, Frank Wilcox *(Denning)*, Ben Welden *(Pelky)*, Vera Lewis *(Mrs. Turner)*, Charles Wilson *(Monigan)*, Edwin Stanley *(Doctor)*, DeWolf [William] Hopper, Herbert Anderson, Creighton Hale *(Reporters)*, Grace Hayle *(Mrs. Smithers)*, Frank Faylen, Paul Phillips, Jack Merrick *(Fighters)*, Frank Mayo *(Doctor)*, Frank Moran, Elliott Sullivan, David Kerwin, Jimmy O'Gatty *(Pugs)*, Frank Riggi *(Hanson)*, Pat O'Malley *(Announcer)*, Al Seymour *(Referee)*, John Kellogg *(Murphy)*, Bill Phillips *(Kovacs)*, David Clarke *(Peters)*, Gaylord Pendleton *(Stanley)*, Kid Chissell *(Hawkins)*, Joe Grey *(Kent)*, Lee Phelps *(Announcer)*.

Kennedy plays a young and promising fighter who gives up the ring to open a health farm with his new bride, Bradna. Manager Quinn, seeing the marketing potential of the young boxer, talks Kennedy back into fighting. After several successful fights and a growing popularity, socialite Field attaches herself to Kennedy, forcing his marriage to disintegrate. For a chance to win big money, Quinn bets against Kennedy and puts a drug in his mouthpiece. Kennedy loses both the fight and Field, suffering a brain concussion in the process. Unable to fight, Kennedy wanders aimlessly until Bradna takes him back in, and they open the originally planned health farm. Smooth script yields consistent direction and standard performances. Ring scenes add a sense of realism.

p, Edmund Grainger; d, William Clemens; w, M. Coates Webster (based on a story by Michael Fessier); ph, Ted McCord; m, Heinz Roemheld; ed, Doug Gould.

Drama **(PR:A MPAA:NR)**

KNOWING MEN** (1930, Brit.) 95m UA bw

Carl Brisson *(George Vere)*, Elissa Landi *(Korah Harley)*, Jeanne de Casalis *(Delphine)*, C.M. Hallard *(Marquis de Jarnais)*, Henry Mollison *(Frank Bramber)*, Thomas Weguelin *(Michelet)*, Marjorie Loring *(Blanche)*, Helen Haye *(Marquise de Jarnais)*.

Landi plays a society girl who sneaks away from boarding school to learn about the man, Brisson, her aunt, Haye, has arranged for her to marry. Brisson has been carrying on with Casalis, and is discovered when he tries to retrieve the love letters he has written her. Excellent photography and settings are marred by uneven performances.

p&d, Elinor Glyn; w, Glyn, Edward Knoblock (based on a novel by Glyn); ph, Charles Rosher.

Romance/Comedy **(PR:A MPAA:NR)**

KNUTE ROCKNE—ALL AMERICAN****
(1940) 98m WB bw (GB: A MODERN HERO)

Pat O'Brien *(Knute Rockne)*, Gale Page *(Bonnie Skilles Rockne)*, Ronald Reagan *(George Gipp)*, Donald Crisp *(Father Callahan)*, Albert Basserman *(Father Julius Nieuwland)*, John Litel *(Chairman of Committee of Educators)*, Henry O'Neill *(Doctor)*, Owen Davis, Jr. *(Gus Dorais)*, John Qualen *(Lars Knutson Rockne)*, Dorothy Tree *(Martha Rockne)*, John Sheffield *(Knute Rockne as a boy)*, Nick Lukats *(Harry Stuhldreher)*, Kane Richmond *(Elmer Laydon)*, William Marshall *(Don Miller)*, William Byrne *(James Crowley)*, John Ridgely *(Reporter)*, George Reeves *(Player)*, Dutch Hendrian *(Hunk Anderson)*, Gaylord [Steve] Pendleton *(Player)*, Richard Clayton *(Student)*, Howard Jones, Glenn "Pop" Warner, Alonzo Stagg, Bill Spaulding *(Themselves)*, Robert O. Davis [Rudolph Anders], Egon Brecher, Fred Vogeding *(Elders)*, Phil Thorpe *(Boy Center)*, Dickie Jones *(Boy Captain)*, George Billings *(Boy Quarterback)*, Cliff Clark *(Post Office Paymaster)*, William Haade, Eddy Chandler, Pat Flaherty *(Workers)*, Creighton Hale *(Secretary)*, Lee Phelps *(Army Coach)*, Peter Ashley, Carlyle Moore, Jr., Michael Harvey *(Players)*, Charles Wilson *(Gambler)*, William Hopper, David Bruce, Frank Mayo *(Reporters)*, Peter B. Good *(Bill Rockne at age 2)*, Bunky Fleischman *(Bill Rockne at age 5)*, David Dickson *(Bill Rockne at age 10)*, Jack Grant, Jr. *(Bill Rockne at age 14)*, David Wade *(Knute Rockne, Jr. at age 7)*, Billy Dawson *(Knute Rockne, Jr. at age 12)*, Bill Gratton *(Jackie Rockne at age 4)*, Patricia Hayos *(Joanne Rockne at age 10)*, Charles Trowbridge *(Notre Dame Professor)*, Harry Hayden *(Professor)*, Frank Coghlan, Jr. *(Messenger)*, Bill Sheffield *(Knute Rockne at age 4)*, James Flavin *(Coach)*, George Haywood, George Irving, Edgar Dearing, the Moreau Choir of Notre Dame.

This is one of the best remembered pictures of its era but not as good as you might recall if you saw it then. No question that the football scenes were excellent and O'Brien's stirring portrayal of the Norwegian legend was flawless, yet it was a fairly standard biographical picture that wouldn't have occasioned that much notice were it not for the fact that the central character died so tragically at the top of his career. Qualen and Tree are a Norwegian couple who emigrate to the U.S. with their sons in tow. The young boy who was to grow up as "America's coach" is played, at various stages of his life, by Scheffield, Dawson, Wade, and O'Brien. He works at the Chicago Post Office, then saves up enough to pay for an education at Notre Dame in South Bend, Indiana, where he is torn between studying chemistry and playing football. They recreate the famous pass tossed by Dorais (Davis, Jr.) to Rockne that defeated the seemingly awesome Army squad; a brief romantic interlude is shown to indicate his courtship and marriage to Page and, upon graduation, O'Brien stays on at the school as an assistant coach and part-time chemistry instructor. With Crisp, the priest who runs the school, as his supporter, Rockne becomes coach and tosses aside a career in chemistry. The middle of the film concerns his creative coaching abilities, the emergence of the passing game, the tactical shift, his work with the Four Horsemen (played by Marshall, Lukats, Richmond, Byrne), and, of course, his well-known situation with George Gipp (Reagan), the brilliant player who died of pneumonia at an early age and exhorted his team to "win one for the Gipper!" (one of the most famous lines in movies and surely the most memorable line Reagan ever spoke, short of his inauguration speech). Seen in the film are four of Rockne's contemporaries as themselves: Amos Alonzo Stagg, the grandfather of all coaches; Howard Jones of USC; William Spaulding; and the man after whom the peewee football leagues are named, "Pop" Warner. The picture should have ended with the plane crash that took Rockne's life, but they added a scene at his funeral to extract every last tear from the audience's eyes. Much of the football coverage was taken from actual newsreel coverage of the games and was edited in to add to the action. Although Warner and Wallis were listed as producers (this was before the day when "executive producer" became a credit on screen), much of the work on the film was supervised by Robert Fellows, who is listed as Associate Producer. The role of George Gipp was Reagan's favorite part and he went after it with determination. Several other actors wanted the role but it was only after Reagan showed the producers photographs of himself in uniform and let them know that he attended college only because of his football abilities, that they allowed him to test. Reagan went to the studio for the screen test and expected to find a flunky reading his cue lines. Not so. O'Brien himself arrived, fully made up, and worked opposite Reagan in the test. To this day, Reagan considers O'Brien one of the greats because of that gesture.

p, Jack Warner, Hal B. Wallis; d, Lloyd Bacon; w, Robert Buckner (based on the private papers of Mrs. Knute Rockne); ph, Tony Gaudio; m, Ray Heindorf; ed, Ralph Dawson; md, Leo F. Forbstein; art d, Robert Haas; spec eff, Byron Haskin, Rex Wimpy; tech adv, Nick Lukats, J.A. Haley.

Biography **Cas** **(PR:AA MPAA:NR)**

KOENIGSMARK*** (1935, Fr.) 114m Capitol bw

Elissa Landi *(Princess Aurore)*, John Lodge *(Grand Duke Frederick)*, Pierre Fresnay *Raoul Vignerte)*, Frank Vosper *(Major Baron de Boise)*, Marcelle Rogez *(Countesse Melusine)*, Allan Jeayes *(Grand Duke Rodolphe)*, Romilly Lunge *(Lt. de Hagen)*, Cecil Humphreys *(de Marcais)*.

Period piece has Fresnay solving the royal murder of Landi's husband. Technical flaws and a spotty script are glossed over by the expensive sets. Performances are acceptable. Landi, Lodge, and Fresnay played their parts in both the French and English versions, a remarkable linguistic feat. (English version.)

p, Roger Richebe; d, Maurice Tourneur; w, (uncredited, based on the novel by Pierre Benoit).

Drama/Romance **(PR:A MPAA:NR)**

KOGDA DEREVYA BYLI BOLSHIMI
(SEE: WHEN THE TREES WERE TALL, 1965)

KOHAYAGAWA-KE NO AKI (SEE: EARLY AUTUMN, 1962, Jap.)

KOJIRO***
(1967, Jap.) 152m Toho c (SASAKI KOJIRO)

Kikunosuke Onoe *(Kojiro Sasaki)*, Yoko Tsukasa *(Okinawa Princess)*, Mayumi Ozora *(Geisha Girl)*, Tatsuya Nakadai *(Musashi Miyamoto)*, Kenjiro Ishiyama *(Lord Tomita)*, Jotaro Togami *(Pirate Nachimaru)*, Keiko Sawai *(Kabuki Dancer)*, Tatsuya Mihashi *(Jubei Minamiya)*, Yuriko Hoshi *(Tone)*, Isamu Nagato *(Shimabei)*, Yoshio Tsuchiya *(Kojiro's Ancient Enemy)*.

Samurai saga about a peasant boy, Onoe, who overcomes feudal traditions to become a famous warrior. His reputation established, he is honored with riches and beautiful women. The only feat left for him to conquer is to face the legendary Miyamoto (Nakadai), where Onoe meets his tragic end.

p, Ken-ichiro Tsunoda; d, Hiroshi Inagaki; w, Yoshio Shirasaka, Kenro Matsuura, Inagaki (based on a story by Genzo Murakami); ph, Takao Saito (Tohoscope, Eastmancolor); m, Goichi Sakaide; art d, Hiroshi Ueda.

Samurai **(PR:A MPAA:NR)**

KOKKINA PHANARIA (SEE: RED LANTERNS, THE, 1965, Greece)

KOKOSEI BANCHO (SEE: WAY OUT, WAY IN, 1970, Jap.)

KOL MAMZER MELECH (SEE: EVERY BASTARD A KING, 1970, Israel)

KOLBERG*
(1945, Ger.) 84m UFA c (AKA: BURNING HEARTS)

Kristina Soderbaum *(Maria)*, Heinrich George *(Nettelbeck)*, Horst Caspar *(Gen. Gneisenau)*, Paul Wegener *(Col. von Loucadou)*, Gustav Diessl *(Maj. Schill)*.

Joseph Goebbels attempt to outdo GONE WITH THE WIND, reportedly the most expensive German film ever, with over 90 hours of footage, and film stock designed by Nazi chemists specifically for this picture. This propaganda story is fittingly about the heroic attempts of a Prussian town, Kolberg, to ward off the advancing French troops during the Napoleonic wars. George (who was to die in a Russian prison camp in 1946) is the town mayor who organizes civilians to fight advancing troops, with Soderbaum (the director's wife) as a farmer's daughter who convinces her brothers and boy friend to die for the glory of Prussia. After a year in production, the film premiered at La Rochelle, with the advancing Allies just miles away, and future showings being extremely limited due to the war. When released as a historical document in 1966, screenings were met with protests and pickets. Copies of KOLBERG made their way to Argentina, providing entertainment for the Nazi criminals in hiding. Although not credited, Goebbels was a major contributor to the script. A total of 187,000 Wehrmacht extras were reassigned from the various besieged war fronts to lend authenticity to the movie that Nazi chieftains had begun to believe was more important than a great military victory. As if that were not enough, where citizens were going hungry because the railroads had a hard time shipping food to the cities, 100 boxcars were diverted to the KOLBERG set filled with salt to "create" snow for a Christmas scene, and munitions factories were ordered to produce thousands of blank bullets for the film.

d, Veit Harlan; w, Alfred Braun, Thea von Harbou; m, Norbert Schultze.

War/History **(PR:O MPAA:NR)**

KOLYBELNAYA (SEE: LULLABY, 1961, USSR)

KOMMANDO SINAI (SEE: SINAI COMMANDOS, 1968, Israel/Ger.)

KONA COAST**
(1968) 93m WB c

Richard Boone *(Capt. Sam Moran)*, Vera Miles *(Melissa Hyde)*, Joan Blondell *(Kittibelle Lightfoot)*, Steve Ihnat *(Kryder)*, Chips Rafferty *(Charlie Lightfoot)*, Kent Smith *(Akamai)*, Sam Kapu, Jr. *(Kimo)*, Gina Villines *(Mim Lowry)*, Duane Eddy *(Tiger Cat)*, Scott Thomas *(Tate Packer)*, Erwin Neal *(Junior Packer)*, Doris Erikson *(Doris Erickson)*, Gloria Nakea *(Dee)*, Lucky Luck *(Kunewa)*, Kaai Hayes *(Butler)*, Dr. Mark Thomas *(Macklin)*, Red Kanuha *(Bartender)*, Sue Paishon *(Sue)*, Dina Kunewa *(Dino)*, Earl Perry *(Earl)*, Pocho Kanuha *(Pocho)*, Willie Erikson *(Willie)*.

Boone sets out for revenge when he finds his daughter, Nakea, dead on the beach. His main target is Ihnat, the playboy who introduced narcotics to the girl. In the process, Ihnat has Boone beaten and his boat burned, injuring his good friend Rafferty, who tries to save the boat. Stable performances by Boone and Blondell, aided by fast-paced direction. Color photography of Hawaii gives an exotic atmosphere.

p&d, Lamont Johnson; w, Gil Ralston (based on the story "Bimini Gall" by John D. MacDonald); ph, Joseph LaShelle (Technicolor); m, Jack Marshall; ed, Alec McCombie; stunts, Erwin Neal.

Drama **(PR:C MPAA:NR)**

KONEC SPRNA V HOTELU OZON
(SEE: END OF AUGUST AT THE HOTEL OZONE, THE, 1967, Czech.)

KONGA, 1939 (SEE: KONGA, THE WILD STALLION, 1939)

KONGA**
(1961, Brit.) 90m AIP c

Michael Gough *(Dr. Charles Decker)*, Margo Johns *(Margaret)*, Jess Conrad *(Bob Kenton)*, Claire Gordon *(Sandra Banks)*, Austin Trevor *(Dean Foster)*, Jack Watson *(Supt. Brown)*, George Pastell *(Prof. Tagore)*, Vanda Godsell *(Bob's Mother)*, Stanley Morgan *(Inspector Lawson)*, Grace Arnold *(Miss Barnesdell)*, Leonard Sachs *(Bob's Father)*, Nicholas Bennett *(Daniel)*, Kim Tracy *(Mary)*, Rupert Osborne *(Eric)*, Waveney Lee *(Janet)*, John Welsh *(Commissioner Garland)*, Sam Sylvano *(Konga the Chimpanzee)*.

Gough is a botany professor who returns to London, after a year in the jungle, with a serum extracted from a carnivorous plant. Injected into a chimpanzee, the animal grows to the size of a gorilla. Maddened by his new power, Gough hypnotizes the gorilla and has it kill his enemies, one of these being the boy friend of Gordon, with whom he has fallen in love. When Johns, Gough's assistant and girl friend, learns of his feelings toward Gordon, she injects Konga with a big dose of the serum. The ape grows to monstrous proportions, going on a rampage throughout London with Gough in his hand until the army stops it with rockets and machine guns. Performances are stale but this is made up for by a fine technical staff. American actors are given British accents and a process called SpectaMation is credited for the spectacular special effects.

p, Herman Cohen; d, John Lemont; w, Cohen, Aben Kandel; ph, Desmond Dickinson (SpectaMation, Eastmancolor); m, Gerard Schurmann; ed, Jack Slade; md, Muir Mathieson; spec eff, Derek Holding; makeup, Jack Craig.

Horror/Drama **(PR:C MPAA:NR)**

KONGA, THE WILD STALLION***
(1939) 62m COL bw

Fred Stone *(Calhoun)*, Rochelle Hudson *(Judith Hadley)*, Richard Fiske *(Steve Calhoun)*, Eddy Waller *(Gloomy)*, Robert Warwick *(Hadley)*, Don Beddoe *(Martin)*, Carl Stockdale *(Mason)*, George Cleveland *(Tabor)*, Burr Caruth *(Breckenridge)*.

Stone plays an aging rancher whose love for horses is threatened by invading civilization and the change of grassland into farmland. A feud develops between Stone and his farmer neighbor, Warwick, when horses knock down fences and trample wheat fields. Warwick shoots several horses, including Stone's pet stallion, Konga, forcing Stone to retaliate by shooting Warwick. Chances of a peaceful future are hinted at as a love affair develops between Fiske, Stone's son, and Hudson, Warwick's daughter. Good performances in this competently made film.

p, Wallace MacDonald; d, Sam Nelson; w, Harold Shumate; ph, Benjamin Kline; ed, Charles Nelson.

Western/Drama **(PR:AA MPAA:NR)**

KONGI'S HARVEST**
(1971, U.S./Nigeria) 85m Calpenny Nigerian Films-Herald Productions c

Wole Soyinka *(Kongi)*, Rashidi Onikoyi *(King Oba Daniola)*, Femi Johnson *(Organizing Secretary)*, Nina Baden-Semper *(Segi)*, Orlando Martins *(Dr. Gbenga)*, Dapo Adelugba *(Daodu)*.

American actor Ossie Davis embarked upon his mission to help bring prominence to Third World art. Here he took a successful play by one of Africa's foremost writers (Soyinka, who also stars), and attempted to bring it to the screen. Soyinka plays the dictator who has recently ousted the king and must now try and find a means whereby he can bring his country into the 20th century, even though many of his subjects are from diverse tribes and still adhere to their own customs. The politics this new ruler relies on are not always the most honest, and frequently has him trying to attain the aid of the recently deposed king (Onikoyi). He also makes a somewhat silly attempt to retain African cultural identity by having government officials wear traditional African clothing. The things that were easily emphasized in the play do not always make it to the screen, instead coming off as overly wordy monologs. Soyinka shows absolutely no ability as an actor, his character remaining incredibly shallow.

d, Ossie Davis; w, Wole Soyinka (based on the play by Soyinka); ph, Ake Lindqvist.

Drama **(PR:A MPAA:NR)**

KONGO***
(1932) 86m MGM bw

Walter Huston *(Flint)*, Lupe Velez *(Tula)*, Conrad Nagel *(Dr. Kingsland)*, Virginia Bruce *(Ann)*, C. Henry Gordon *(Gregg)*, Mitchell Lewis *(Hogan)*, Forrester Harvey *(Cookie)*, Curtis Nero *(Fuzzy)*.

That great character actor Huston never gave a more brutal and shocking performance than he did in KONGO. Huston is a white renegade who has been crippled in a confrontation with arch enemy Gordon years earlier. He cannot walk and drags himself about his ramshackled tropical house with powerful arms. He controls the local tribesmen of the Congo through voodoo and threats of death from his magical instruments, guns. Moreover, he abuses every white person he meets, including Bruce, whom he believes is the daughter of his nemesis Gordon. For sport he drives others mad and hooks young doctor Nagel on drugs. He degrades Bruce slowly, agonizingly, until she is reduced to a quivering mass of slavish flesh, laughing sadistically at her plight. Meanwhile, Velez hangs about to pick up any scrap of attention that monster Huston cares to toss her way. But the inhuman Huston gets his comeuppance. Gordon visits him and they struggle. Before Gordon dies, he tells Huston that Bruce is Huston's daughter, not his own. Now Huston goes through agony and his Boris Karloff-like makeup seems to soften as he tries to make amends, sending Bruce and Nagel out of the hellhole where he lives to safety as the natives, finally wise to their bogus voodoo master, close in for the horrible kill. This gruesome film is really a horror show that is both frightening and disturbing. Although Huston is superb as the evil renegade living for revenge, the bizarre story is so offbeat that few will be able to identify with the antihero's plight. Remake of WEST OF ZANZIBAR.

d, William Cowen; w, Leon Gordon (based on the play by Chester DeVonde and Kilbourn Gordon); ph, Harry Rosson; ed, Conrad A. Nervig; art d, Cedric Gibbons.

Horror **(PR:O MPAA:NR)**

KONSKA OPERA (SEE: LEMONADE JOE, 1966, Czech.)

KOREA PATROL**
(1951) 59m EL bw

Richard Emory *(Lt. Craig)*, Al Eben *(Sgt. Abrams)*, Benson Fong *(Kim)*, Li Sun *(Ching)*, Teri Duna *(The Girl)*, Danny Davenport *(Cpl. Dykes)*, Wong Artarne *(Murphy)*, Harold Fong *(Lee)*, John V. Close *(Capt. Green)*, Richard Barron *(Maj. Wald)*.

A quickie made to exploit American entry into the Korean conflict. Emory is in charge of a six-man patrol ordered to blow up a bridge that is important to the North Koreans. Though three men are killed along the way, the remaining patrol members finish the assignment. The acting and direction are good for what this is, though the spliced-in war footage is often mismatched to the story.

p, Walter Shenson; d, Max Nosseck; w, Kenneth G. Brown, Shenson; ph, Elmer Dyer; m, Alexander Gerens; ed, Norman Cerf; art d, Fred Preble.

War Drama **(PR:C MPAA:NR)**

KORT AR SOMMAREN (SEE: SHORT IS THE SUMMER, 1968, Swed.)

KOSHOKU ICHIDAI ONNA (SEE: LIFE OF OHARU, 1964, Jap.)

KOTCH***
(1971) 113m Kotch-ABC/Cinerama c

Walther Matthau *(Joseph P. Kotcher)*, Deborah Winters *(Erica Herzenstiel)*, Felicia

Farr *(Wilma Kotcher)*, Charles Aidman *(Gerald Kotcher)*, Ellen Geer *(Vera Kotcher)*, Darrell Larson *(Vincent Perrin)*, Paul Picerni *(Dr. Gaudillo)*, Lucy Saroyan *(Sissy)*, Jane Connell *(Miss Roberts)*, Jessica Rains *(Dr. McKernan)*, James E. Brodhead *(Weaver)*, Lawrence Linville *(Peter Herzenstiel)*, Donald and Dean Kowalski *(Duncan Kotcher)*, Biff Elliot *(Motel Manager)*, Dee Carroll *(Dorothy Ballinger)*, Arlen Stuart *(Mrs. Fisher)*, Janya Brannt *(Mrs. Pugh)*, Penny Santon *(Mrs. Segura)*, Jack Lemmon *(Stranger on Bus)*.

Matthau and the Hamlisch-Mercer tune took Oscar nominations in this, the only picture ever directed (so far) by Jack Lemmon. Unfortunately, there was too much nepotism involved to make this work, as Lemmon used his wife, Farr, to play Matthau's daughter-in-law; his press agent was the producer; and the daughters of four well-knowns all had small roles: Will Geer's Ellen, William Saroyan's Lucy, Claude Rains' Jessica and Winters, the daughter of actress Penny Edwards. Lemmon also gave himself a bit as a sleeping passenger on a bus. Matthau is a crotchety 72-year-old living with son Aidman, daughter-in-law Farr, and their tiny son (played by twins Donald and Dean Kowalski). Matthau is totally alert, perhaps too alert for Farr, who wishes he'd move into a retirement home as his presence is invasive to her. He's happy as the babysitter for his grandson but becomes irked when Farr hires Winters, a teenager, to take over those chores. Matthau catches Winters making out with her boy friend in the house and lets Farr know about it. Winters is dismissed but Farr is annoyed that her rule of the house is being questioned by Matthau, so she prevails on Aidman to find Matthau quarters in a retirement home. Matthau and Aidman inspect one such place, but the old fellow will have none of it and decides to smooth things over by taking a long bus trip to northern California, hoping that by the time he comes back, Farr's feathers will no longer be as ruffled. He's about to leave but feels some guilt toward Winters for getting her sacked, so he goes to her high school to apologize, and she admits that she's pregnant and will stay with relatives until the baby is born. Matthau presses some money on her and says it's only a loan. Later, Matthau gets a postcard from Winters saying goodbye. Matthau searches for Winters and finds her in Palm Springs. He rents a house and asks her to stay with him until she gives birth. Time passes and the two form a symbiotic relationship, each caring more for the other than they might like to admit. Winters decides to offer the baby to a barren couple, then leaves the desert house to stay in a mountain cabin until she gives birth. Matthau again traces her to her new abode and is present when the labor pains start. They race to a hospital but don't make it in time and Matthau helps deliver the baby in a filling station's restroom. A few days later, Winters surreptitiously leaves with the baby and Matthau finds a note saying that she's changed her mind and will keep the child. Aidman and Farr ask Matthau to come back to them, but he's found that he enjoys the desert and living alone and declines, still hurt about what happened before. In the final scene, he finds a letter that Winters had written to her then-unborn child (when she was still planning to give the baby up) to the effect that "Kotch didn't have all his marbles but he would have been one helluva grandfather." Matthau smiles and the film ends. Lemmon attempted to examine the plight of being old in a society where youth is treasured. He missed the boat by attempting to be too cute. Old people are wise, cantankerous, abrasive, and proud; but they are seldom, if ever, cute. What is most surprising is that Lemmon never directed anything else after this, as he had a good eye, worked well with the actors, and came out with a movie that had more plusses than minuses. The song was "Life Is What You Make It" and it was, at best, a minor effort from Hamlisch and Mercer.

p, Richard Carter; d, Jack Lemmon; w, John Paxton (based on the novel by Katharine Topkins); ph, Richard Kline (Metrocolor); m, Marvin Hamlisch; ed, Ralph E. Winters; art d, Jack Poplin; set d, William Kiernan; cos, John Anderson; spec eff, Jack Erickson; makeup, Harry Ray; hairstyles, Jean Austin.

Comedy/Drama **Cas.** **(PR:A-C MPAA:GP)**

KOTO (SEE: TWIN SISTERS OF KYOTO, 1964, Jap.)

KOTO NO TAIYO (SEE: NO GREATER LOVE THAN THIS, 1969, Jap.)

KRADETSUT NA PRASKOVI (SEE: PEACH THIEF, THE, 1969)

KRAKATIT** 1/2** (1948, Czech.) 106m CFD bw

Karel Hoeger *(Prokop)*, Florence Marly *(Wilhelmina)*, Frantisek Smolik *(Dr. Tomes)*, Edward Linkers *(Carson)*, Vkasta Fabianova *(Veiled Girl)*, Natasa Tanska *(Anne)*, Miroslav Homolka *(Tomes)*, Bedrich Vrbsky *(Baron Rohn)*, Jiri Platcy, Jaroslav Prucha, Karel Dostal.

Interesting though talky film features Hoeger as a scientist working with explosives. He comes up with a new device called Krakatit, which is equivalent to a nuclear device. The difference is that this is easier to control and thus could theoretically eliminate nuclear warfare. An interesting moral question is played with here: what is the role of the scientist when he creates something of immense and overwhelming power? Made as the Soviets were beginning to control Eastern Europe and only three years after Hiroshima. Vavra was a noted lecturer and experimental filmmaker in his later days. He remade this story as CERNE SLUNCE in 1979.

d, Otakar Vavra; w, Vavra, Frantisek Milic (based on a story by Karel Capek); ph, Vaclav Hanus.

Science Fiction/Satire **(PR:C MPAA:NR)**

KRAKATOA, EAST OF JAVA** 1/2**
(1969) 148m Security/Cinerama c (AKA: VOLCANO)

Maximilian Schell *(Capt. Chris Hanson)*, Diane Baker *(Laura Travis)*, Brian Keith *(Connerly)*, Barbara Werle *(Charley)*, John Leyton *(Douglas Rigby)*, Rossano Brazzi *(Giovanni Borghese)*, Sal Mineo *(Leoncavallo Borghese)*, J.D. Cannon *(Danzig)*, Jacqui Chan *(Toshi)*, Marc Lawrence *(Jacobs)*, Geoffrey Holder *(Bazooki Man)*, Sumi Hari, Victoria Young, Midorri Arimoto *(Japanese Divers)*, Niall MacGinnis *(Henley)*, Alan Hoskins *(Jan)*, Robert Hall *(Guard)*, Peter Kowalski *(Peter)*, Joseph Hann *(Kuan)*.

Despite all of the spectacular effects and technical expertise, this film was almost as much of a disaster as the actual disaster it depicted. Aimed for the youngsters (the G rating indicates that), it's a fairly simple-minded story about one of the most devastating natural events that ever took place. It's 1883 at Singapore. Schell's ship leaves for Krakatoa to find another ship, laden with pearls, that has been sunk along the volcanic island. Using the GRAND HOTEL and SHIP OF FOOLS formula, there are various types aboard. Baker is the widow of the downed ship's captain. Keith is a diver, Brazzi and Mineo are balloonists, Leyton is a diving bell pilot with claustrophobia (how he got into that business, we'll never know), Chan leads a crew of Japanese women who can dive deeply to recover items such as the aforementioned baubles, and Cannon is a criminal who is allowed to roam the deck. He is one of three score of brigands who are to be incarcerated. The ship nears Krakatoa and several incidents mar the voyage: accidents, natural and unnatural weather problems, etc. Soon enough, the convicts mutiny and take command of the vessel. Schell, captain of the ship, kills Cannon and sets the crooks to sea in life boats. Meanwhile, Krakatoa is rumbling all the while like an unfed stomach. The girls and Leyton recover the sunken ship's safe, but it's empty except for the log. Baker really didn't care much for her late husband, but the man had taken their son and placed him somewhere and that's what she's after. The staff of the Krakatoa Catholic mission is fleeing from the island and drifting at sea. Schell's boat picks them up and Baker is united with her son, who also happens to have the pearls with him. Baker divides the booty as the island erupts and huge tidal waves begin. The passengers lash themselves to the ship and attempt to ride it out as the picture ends. The locations were in Spain and the island of Majorca, and the film is visually attractive but the acting is mostly wooden. The only person missing from this picture is Charlton Heston, but he was busy that year making his own disaster movie, NUMBER ONE. (Not that it was meant to be a disaster movie, it just turned out that way.) Good miniatures and special effects but the generally lackluster story sinks it.

p, William R. Forman; d, Bernard L. Kowalski; w, Clifford Newton Gould, Bernard Gordon; ph, Manuel Berenguer (Cinerama, Technicolor); m, Frank De Vol; ed, Maurice Rootes, Warren Low, Walter Hannemann; prod d, Eugene Lourie; art d, Julio Molina, Luis Perez Espinosa; set d, Antonio Mateos; cos, Laure de Zarate, spec eff, Alex Welden; m/l, "A Nice Old-Fashioned Girl," "East of Java," Mack David; makeup, Julian Ruiz.

Disaster **(PR:A MPAA:G)**

KRALJ PETROLEJA
(SEE: RAMPAGE AT APACHE WELLS, 1966, Ger./Yugo.)

KRAMER VS. KRAMER****** (1979) 105m COL c

Dustin Hoffman *(Ted Kramer)*, Meryl Streep *(Joanna Kramer)*, Jane Alexander *(Margaret Phelps)*, Justin Henry *(Billy Kramer)*, Howard Duff *(John Shaunessy)*, George Coe *(Jim O'Connor)*, JoBeth Williams *(Phyllis Bernard)*, Bill Moor *(Gressen)*, Howland Chamberlain *(Judge Atkins)*, Jack Ramage *(Spencer)*, Jess Osuna *(Ackerman)*, Nicholas Hormann *(Interviewer)*, Ellen Parker *(Teacher)*, Shelby Brammer *(Ted's Secretary)*, Carol Nadell *(Mrs. Kline)*, Judith Calder *(Receptionist)*, Peter Lownds *(Norman)*, Kathleen Keller *(Waitress)*, Dan Tyra *(Court Clerk)*, David Golden *(Grocer)*, Petra King *(Petie Phelps)*, Melissa Morell *(Kim Phelps)*, Donald Gantry *(Surgeon)*, Ingeborg Sorenson, Iris Alhanti, Richard Barris, Evelyn Hope Bunn, Joann Friedman, Quentin J. Hruska, Joe Seneca, Frederic W. Hand, Scott Kuney.

Winner of several awards, including Oscars for Hoffman (Best Actor), Benton (Best Director and Best Screenplay—adaptation), Streep (Best Supporting Actress), and Best Picture, KRAMER VS. KRAMER was, essentially, a television movie that was raised into the feature category by the excellence of the execution. With Robert Reed in the Hoffman role and Suzanne Pleshette as his wife, it would have been a typical CBS entry. Based on a novel by Avery Corman, the story takes place in New York City and shows Streep, an independent woman, leaving husband Hoffman, an art director in an ad agency, for no other reason than that she wants to "find herself." (All she had to do is look in the mirror and there she is!) Hoffman is left to care for their young son, Henry. The extra strain of having to be both father and mother to Henry causes Hoffman to make some mistakes at work and lose a major account. That causes him to be fired. On top of that, Streep surfaces and is suing for custody of the child she'd abandoned. Streep has an excellent job and can afford day care for Henry so she wants him back. Hoffman hires Duff, a high-powered attorney, and learns that he must get a job if he expects to keep Henry. Hoffman takes a job with a tiny agency, just to show that he has employment. Despite Streep's behavior, she is awarded custody at the hearing. In a scene reminiscent of THE CHAMP, Hoffman tells Henry that they won't be living together any longer, and when Streep sees that, she decides to allow the two of them to stay together. It's as soapy as a washer full of Tide but so well done that we can overlook Benton's manipulations of our emotions and let our feelings flow. Movies about divorce and the wrenching apart of families have been part of the motion picture scene since the silents. However, they will always work if the writing is honest and if the acting is sincere. KRAMER VS. KRAMER is as sincere as an ad-man's necktie and although we know we are being maneuvered, Benton does it so well that we sit still for it for 105 minutes, in much the same way as we did for James Brooks with TERMS OF ENDEARMENT. Not a great movie and surely not as good as 1979's BEING THERE, THE TIN DRUM, or ALL THAT JAZZ, it nevertheless touched the hearts of the Academy and swept the major awards. Nominations also went to Almendros and Greenberg. Benton also took the Writers Guild award. The picture grossed almost $70 million and is still making money on TV.

p, Stanley R. Jaffe; d&w, Robert Benton (based on the novel by Avery Corman); ph, Nestor Almendros (Panavision, Technicolor); m, Henry Purcell, Antonio Vivaldi; ed, Jerry Greenberg; prod d, Paul Sylbert; set d, Alan Hicks; cos, Ruth Morley; makeup, Alan Weisinger.

Drama **Cas** **(PR:A MPAA:PG)**

KRASNAYA PALATKA (SEE: RED TENT, THE, 1971, Ital./USSR)

KREMLIN LETTER, THE***** (1970) 118m FOX c

Bibi Andersson *(Erika Boeck)*, Richard Boone *(Ward)*, Nigel Green *(Janis, "The Whore")*, Dean Jagger *(The Highwayman)*, Lila Kedrova *(Mme. Sophie)*, Michael MacLiammoir *(Sweet Alice)*, Patrick O'Neal *(Lt. Comdr. Charles Rone)*, Barbara Parkins *(B.A.)*, Ronald Radd *(Potkin)*, George Sanders *(The Warlock)*, Raf Vallone *(Puppet Maker)*, Max von Sydow *(Col. Vladimir Kosnov)*, Orson Welles *(Aleksei Bresnavitch)*, Sandor Eles *(Grodin)*, Niall MacGinnis *(Erector Set)*, Anthony Chinn

(Kitai), Guy Deghy *(Professor)*, John Huston *(Admiral)*, Fulvia Ketoff *(Sonia)*, Vonetta McGee *(Negress)*, Marc Lawrence *(Priest)*, Cyril Shaps *(Police Doctor)*, Christopher Sandford *(Rudolph)*, HanaMaria Pravda *(Mrs. Kazar)*, George Pravda *(Kazar)*, Ludmilla Dudarova *(Mrs. Potkin)*, Dimitri Tamarov *(Ilya)*, Pehr-Olof Siren *(Receptionist)*, Daniel Smid *(Waiter)*, Victor Beaumont *(Dentist)*, Stephen Zacharias *(Dittomachine)*, Laura Forin *(Elena)*, Saara Rannon *(Mikhail's Mother)*, Rune Sandlunds *(Mikhail)*, Sacha Carafa *(Mrs. Grodin)*.

Beautifully photographed in Finland, Italy, Mexico, and New York, THE KREMLIN LETTER is a hopelessly convoluted spy drama with so many intricate interweavings that one truly needs a scorecard to keep track of the plotters. Everybody has a code name plus their own, and a double-cross is the most minor twist. An American official signs an agreement with the USSR that both will attack China. Once the top dogs at the U.S. find out about this unauthorized "Kremlin Letter" they want it back and gather a cadre of agents to secure the document. Jagger is the leader and his crew includes: O'Neal, a one-time Naval officer; Parkins, whose safecracker father was supposed to go on the assignment, but his illness forced her to go in his stead; Green, the sleazy pimp in a south-of-the-border whorehouse; Sanders, a transvestite who hangs out at a San Francisco gay bar; and Boone, right-hand man to Jagger. They begin by getting a lesbian to sleep with the daughter of Radd, a Russian spy, in order to be able to use his Moscow flat as a base for their plot to recover the letter. Once there, they arrange a surveillance on the apartment of von Sydow, whose wife is Andersson, already the widow of another spy. Von Sydow and Welles, a politician, are enemies and grappling for power in the Soviet hierarchy. Parkins and O'Neal become lovers, then she is captured by Welles. Boone leaves Russia on a trumped-up reason. But Welles is a traitor to Russia and O'Neal finds that out, as well as the fact that the letter has already been delivered to the bosses in China. Now we learn that American Boone is a double-agent working for Welles. Boone returns to Russia, murders Andersson (who had figured out a way to secret O'Neal back to the West), then kills von Sydow. O'Neal has had it with spying, then he learns that Parkins is being held by Boone and will only be freed if O'Neal takes another assignment—to return to the U.S. and kill Radd's wife, Dudarova, and their daughter. This was more like a TV mini-series than a film, but it was so densely packed that one needed a shovel to clear away the debris. Boone is a standout as the double agent, but it was sad to see the elegant Sanders, in his next to last picture, doing such a wimpy role. Huston takes credit for the direction, half the blame for the script, and does a cameo to boot.

p, Carter De Haven, III, Sam Wiesenthal; d, John Huston; w, Huston, Gladys Hill (based on the novel by Noel Behn); ph, Ted Scaife (Panavision, DeLuxe Color); m, Robert Drasnin, Tashiro Mayuzumi; ed, Russell Lloyd; prod d, Ted Haworth; md, Drasnin, Mayuzumi; art d, Elven Webb; set d, Dario Simone; cos, John Furness; spec eff, Augie Lohman; makeup, George Frost, Amato Barbini.

Spy Drama **(PR:C-O MPAA:GP)**

KRUEZER EMDEN (SEE: CRUISER EMDEN, 1932, Ger.)

KRIEGSGERICHT (SEE: COURT MARTIAL, 1962, Ger.)

KRIVI PUT (SEE: CROOKED ROAD, THE, 1965, Brit./Yugo.)

KRONOS*** (1957) 78m FOX bw

Jeff Morrow *(Dr. Leslie Gaskell)*, Barbara Lawrence *(Vera Hunter)*, John Emery *(Dr. Eliot)*, George O'Hanlon *(Dr. Arnie Culver)*, Morris Ankrum *(Dr. Albert R. Stern)*, Kenneth Alton *(McCrary)*, John Parrish *(Gen. Perry)*, Jose Gonzales-Gonzales *(Manuel)*, Richard Harrison *(Pilot)*, Marjorie Stapp *(Nurse)*, Robert Shayne *(General)*, Donald Eitner *(Weather Operator)*, Gordon Mills *(Sergeant)*, John Halloran *(Guard)*.

A fun science fiction film with a different kind of monster. Kronos is a 100-foot-tall metal alien who arrives on the California coast. He heads east, soaking up energy from his surroundings. His energy field eventually takes over the mind of scientist Emery, much to the dismay of his colleague, Morrow. As Kronos takes in more energy, he grows larger. Morrow finally devises a way to short-circuit the monster. It ends up sapping its own energy and eventually disappears. Despite a low budget, this isn't a bad film. The special effects, though not top-notch, are rather good.

p, Kurt Neumann, Jack Rabin, Irving Block, Louis DeWitt; d, Neumann; w, Lawrence Louis Goldman (based on a story by Block); ph, Kurt Struss (Regalscope); m, Paul Sawtell, Bert Shefter; ed, Jodie Copelan; prod d, Theobald Holsopple; art d, Holsopple; set d, Walter M. Scott, Chester Bayhi; spec eff, Rabin, Block, DeWitt, Menrad von Mulldorfer, William Rheinhold, Gene Warren.

Science Fiction **Cas.** **(PR:A MPAA:NR)**

KRONOS, 1974 (SEE: CAPTAIN KRONOS: VAMPIRE HUNTER, 1974)

KRULL*½ (1983) 117m COL c

Ken Marshall *(Colwyn)*, Lysette Anthony *(Lyssa)*, Freddie Jones *(Ynyr)*, Francesca Annis *(Widow of the Web)*, Alun Armstrong *(Torquil)*, David Battley *(Ergo)*, Bernard Bresslaw *(Cyclops)*, Liam Neeson *(Kegan)*, John Welsh *(Seer)*, Graham McGrath *(Titch)*, Tony Church *(Turold)*, Bernard Archard *(Eirig)*, Belinda Mayne *(Vella)*, Dicken Ashworth *(Bardolph)*, Todd Carty *(Oswyn)*, Robbie Coltrane *(Rhun)*, Clare McIntyre *(Merith)*, Bronco McLoughlin *(Nennog)*, Andy Bradford *(Darro)*, Gerard Naprous *(Quain)*, Bill Weston *(Menno)*.

Borrow a handful of ideas from other movies in the genre, and make a gentle little nothing called KRULL. Marshall is a mythical leader of a sword and sorcery group which is after "the Beast" that has kidnaped his fiance, Anthony. On that slim line, bits of STAR WARS, THE WIZARD OF OZ, ROBIN HOOD, and RAIDERS OF THE LOST ARK creep in and make a hodgepodge of what was meant to be a whimsical tale with a few engaging characters.

p, Ron Silverman; d, Peter Yates; w, Stanford Sherman; ph, Peter Suschitzky (Panavision, Metrocolor); m, James Horner; ed, Ray Lovejoy; prod d, Stephen Grimes; art d, Tony Reading, Colin Grimes, Norman Dorme, Tony Curtis, Francesco Chianese; set d, Herbert Westbrook; cos, Anthony Bermans and Nathans Ltd.; spec eff, Derek Meddings, John Evans, Mark Meddings; makeup, Nick Maley.

Fantasy **Cas.** **(PR:A MPAA:PG)**

KUMONOSUJO (SEE: THRONE OF BLOOD, 1957, Jap.)

KUNGSLEDEN (SEE: OBSESSION, 1968, Swed.)

KUNISADA CHUJI (SEE: GAMBLING SAMURAI, THE, 1966, Jap.)

KURAGEJIMA—LEGENDS FROM A SOUTHERN ISLAND½**

(1970, Jap.) 150m Toho c (KAMIGAMI NO FUKAKI YOKUBO; AKA: DEEP DESIRE OF GODS)

Rentaro Mikuni *(Brother)*, Hideko Okiyama *(Retarded Sister)*, Kanjuro Arashi *(Patriarch)*, Yasuko Matsui *(Sister)*, Kazuo Kitamura *(Engineer)*, Jun Hamamura, Yoshi Kato, Choichiro Kawarazaki, Hosei Lomatsu, Taiji Tonoyama, Chikako Hosokawa, Chikage Ogi.

After being alone on a small island a family develops some unusual ideas for procreation. Arashi is the family patriarch who sees incest as an acceptable life style for the ruling family of the island. He is both father and grandfather to Mikuni, who is having an affair with his sister, Matsui. Okiyama is a retarded sister who is a nymphomaniac. When Kitamura comes to the island to map out plans for a sugar refinery, he is seduced by Okiyama and finds himself seduced by this strange world as well. But in the end Mikuni and Matsui are condemned for their affair and Mikuni must dig a huge pit to bury a large boulder a tidal wave has washed ashore. Strange and unusual visualization of sexual mores, to say the least.

p, Masanori Yamanoi; d, Shohei Imamura; w, Imamura, Keiji Hasebe (based on a story by Imamura); ph, Masao Tochizawa; m, Toshiro Mayuzumi.

Drama **(PR:O MPAA:GP)**

KUREIZI OGON SAKUSEN (SEE: LAS VEGAS FREE-FOR-ALL, 1968, Jap.)

KUROBE NO TAIYO (SEE: TUNNEL TO THE SUN, 1968, Jap.)

KUROENKO**

(1968, Jap) 99m Toho bw (YABU NO NAKA NO KURONEKO; AKA: THE BLACK CAT)

Kichiemon Nakamura *(Gintoki)*, Nobuko Otowa *(Mother)*, Kiwako Taichi *(Daughter-in-Law)*, Kei Sato *(Raiko)*, Taiji Tonoyama *(A Farmer)*, Rokko Toura *(A Samurai)*, Hideo Kanze *(Mikado)*.

Two women in 12th Century Japan are murdered by a band of samurai and thereafter haunt their killers in the guise of ghosts. The leader of the samurai returns to the scene of the crime and sees a woman who resembles one of those his men killed and she seduces, then murders him. A warrior selected to destroy the samurai's killer is, by chance, the husband of one of the slain woman and the son of the other. The outcome is, as can be imagined, butchery, and the whole thing is excitingly macabre.

p, Nichiei Shinsha; d&w, Kaneto Shindo; ph, Kiyomi Kuroda (Tohoscope); m, Hikaru Hayashi; ed, Hisao Enoki; art d, Takashi Marumo; makeup, Shigeo Kobayashi.

Horror **(PR:O MPAA:NR)**

KVARTERET KORPEN (SEE: RAVEN'S END, 1970)

KVINNORS VANTAN (SEE: SECRETS OF WOMEN, 1961)

KWAIDAN**** (1965, Jap.) 125m Toho/CD c (KAIDAN)

Rentaro Mikuni *(Samurai)*, Michiyo Aratama *(1st Wife)*, Misako Watanabe *(2nd Wife)*, Katsuo Nakamura *(Hoichi)*, Ganjiro Nakamura *(Head Priest)*, Takashi Shimura *(Priest)*, Joichi Hayashi *(Yoshitsune)*, Ganemon Nakamura *(Kannai)*, Noboru Nakay *(Heinai)*, Tetsuro Tamba.

Three short stories on ghostly themes, based on the tales of Hearn, an American who settled in Japan in 1890. The first is called "Black Hair." Mikuni is a samurai who leaves his devoted wife to marry Watanabe. But she is a selfish woman and after many years he decides to return to Aratama, his first wife. They spend the night and when Mikuni wakes the next morning he goes mad as he discovers Aratama is a corpse. "Hoichi, the Earless" features Katsuo Nakamura as a blind musician. He works at a temple and is well known for his ballad of the Heike clan, which was defeated in a battle at sea in 1185. One night a samurai ghost asks him to sing for a dead infant lord. He does and the high priests assume Nakamura is possessed. They paint his body with holy scenes but neglect to paint his ears. The samurai spirit returns and cuts off the unpainted ears! After recovering from the trauma, Nakamura makes a fortune telling people his strange story. "In a Cup of Tea" Ganemon Nakamura sits drinking his afternoon tea. He sees the face of another samurai but ignores it. When the face appears in a second cup he destroys the face by drinking the tea. That night the same figure attacks him but he fights him off. When three samurai arrive the next night to avenge the wounded man, Nakamura fights them off as well. Often eerie and always fascinating. A fourth story, "The Woman of the Snow" ("Yuki-onna") featuring Keiko Kishi, Tatsuya Nakadai, Mariko Okada, was left out of the American edition of this film. This story told the tale of two woodcutters trapped in a lonely cabin by a blizzard. Kishi arrives from nowhere and strange goings on ensue. She kills one of the woodsmen, allowing the other to live providing he never reveal what happened. Years later when he is married, he tells his wife the story. She replies by telling him that she is the snow witch.

p, Shigeru Wakatsuki; d, Masaki Kobayashi; w, Yoko Mizuki (based on the stories of Lafcadio Hearn); ph, Yoshio Miyajima (Tohoscope, Eastmancolor); m, Toru Takemitsu; art d, Shigemasa Toda.

Horror/Fanatasy **Cas.** **(PR:O MPAA:NR)**

KYOMO WARE OZORANI ARI (SEE: TIGER FLIGHT, 1965, Jap.)

KYONETSU NO KISETSU (SEE: WEIRD LOVE MAKERS, THE, 1963)

KYUBI NO KITSUNE TO TOBIMARU

(SEE: FOX WITH NINE TAILS, THE, 1969)